Flying the
Colors

ACKNOWLEDGEMENTS

FLYING THE COLORS: TEXAS RECOGNIZES GRATEFULLY THE FOLLOW-
ING FOR THEIR COOPERATION IN MAKING THIS BOOK POSSIBLE.

UNITED STATES

Department of Agriculture, Economic Research Service and Soil Conservation
Service. Congress, Congressional Budget Office. Department of Commerce,
Bureau of Census, Bureau of Economic Analysis, Economic Development
Administration, Environmental Sciences Administration, International Trade
Administration and National Oceanic and Atmospheric Administration. Depart-
ment of Defense, Army Corps of Engineers. Equal Employment Opportunity
Commission. Department of Energy, Energy Information Administration.
Environmental Protection Agency. Federal Communications Commission. Federal
Home Loan Bank Board. Federal Reserve Bank of Dallas. Department of Health
and Human Services, Bureau of Vital Statistics. Department of Interior, Bureau
of Land Management, Bureau of Mines, Land and Water Resources and
Geological Survey. Interstate Commerce Commission. Department of Labor,
Bureau of Labor Statistics, Employment Standards Adminstration, Employment
and Training Administration and Management and Services Administration.
National Aeronautics and Space Administration. Nuclear Regulatory Commission. Department of Transportation, Federal Aviation Administration and Urban
Mass Transportation Administration. U.S. Postal Service. Veterans Administration.

STATE OF TEXAS

Adjutant General's Department. Aeronautics Commission. Governor's Committee
on Aging. Department of Agriculture. Governor's Task Force on Agricultural
Development. The Texas Agricultural Experiment Station of the Agricultural
Extension Service at Texas A & M Unversity. Air Control Board. Alcoholic
Beverage Commission. Commission on the Arts. Governor's Task Force on State
Aviation Policy. State Bar of Texas. East Texas Chamber of Commerce. College
and University System Coordinating Board. Comptroller of Public Accounts.
Department of Corrections. V.G. Young Institute of County Government. Credit
Union Department of Texas. Economic Development Commission. Bureau of
Economic Geology. Texas Education Agency. Texas Employment Commission.
Energy and Natural Resources Advisory Council. Fireman's Pension Commis-
sioner. Commission on Fire Protection Personnel and Education. The Fire Pro-
tection Training Division of the Engineering Extension Service at Texas A & M
University. Governor's Task Force on Foreign Investments in Texas. Texas Forest
Service. Office of the Governor, Criminal Justice Division and Texas State Data
Center. Department of Health, Emergency Medical Services Division, Bureau
of State Health Planning and Resource Development, Manpower Special Reports,
Quality Standards Division and Bureau of Vital Statistics. Governor's Task Force
on Higher Education. State Department of Highways and Public Transporta-
tion, Motor Vehicle Division, Transportation Planning Division and Travel and
Information Division. The Texas State Historical Association. Texas Historical
Commission. Department of Human Resources. Industrial Commission. State
Board of Insurance. Advisory Commission on Intergovernmental Relations. Com-
mission on Jail Standards, Judicial Council, Office of Court Administration.
Commission on Law Enforcement Officers Standards-Education. Legislative
Budget Board. Texas State Library, Library Development Division. Department
of Mental Health and Mental Retardation. Parks and Wildlife Department. State
Property Tax Board. Select Committee on Public Education. Department of Public
Safety, Uniform Crime Reporting Bureau. Railroad Commission of Texas. Real
Estate Research Center. Savings and Loan Department of Texas. Secretary of
State, Election Division. State Soil and Waste Conservation Board. Tourist
Development Board. Governor's Task Force on Traffic Safety. Texas Turnpike
Authority. The University Interscholastic League. Veterans Affairs Commission.
Low Level Radioactive Waste Disposal Authority. Department of Water Resources.

Flying the Colors

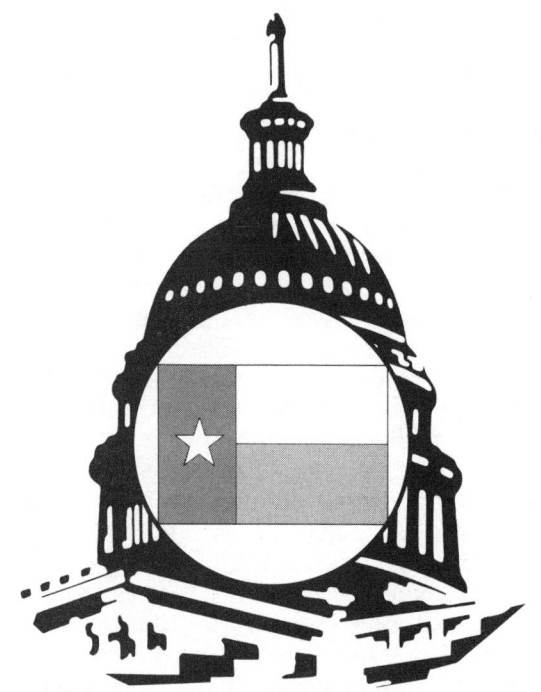

TEXAS

by
JOHN CLEMENTS

PUBLISHED BY
CLEMENTS RESEARCH, INC.
A SUBSIDIARY OF POLITICAL RESEARCH, INC.
DALLAS, TEXAS

A WORD OF EXPLANATION

All data is the most current available at the time of publication. All the facts are from federal, state and local governments. Data on less than five individuals or families has been withheld from publication to avoid disclosure of information concerning individuals. The County Charts have an asterisk (*) to denote figures withheld to avoid disclosure of information concerning individuals, or individual business operations. Totals may not add due to information withheld, or due to rounding. **AGRICULTURE** The total number of acres planted includes acres replanted. If adverse weather has caused large amounts of replanting, the figure for acres planted will be inflated, according to the Texas Department of Agriculture. Although melons and tomatoes are fruits, the Texas Department of Agriculture reports their production data under vegetables. **ALCOHOLIC BEVERAGES** Local option elections are constantly changing the status of alcoholic beverage sales. As a result, the Texas Alcoholic Beverage Commission only reports that "sales of mixed beverages are legal in all or part of the county" and does not specify whether it is legal in part of the county or all of the county. **BUREAU OF CENSUS** The U.S. Bureau of Census figures for the changes in urban and rural population in counties with few or no incorporated places may be inaccurate due to the method used to compute those figures. Therefore, those figures which appear on the County Population Chart as reported by the Bureau of Census should be used with caution. **HUNTING/ FISHING** The seasons and species change frequently. Please contact the proper authority for the current regulations at the time you wish to hunt or fish in Texas. **JUDICIAL SYSTEM** The courts and prisons listed in this publication are those in the Texas judicial system. Federal courts and prisons are not included. Therefore, when the term district court is used, it refers to a state district court. **POPULATED PLACES** The list of Populated Places includes incorporated places, unincorporated areas and railroad stations (RRS). **POPULATION** The 1982 estimated population figures in the county descriptions are from the U.S. Bureau of Census, released June, 1984. The 1982 population estimates on the County Population Chart are state figures used in the calculation of vital statistics. Both sets have been included due to significant variations in some areas. **SAVINGS AND LOAN ASSOCIATIONS** The dollar figures are reported only by association and not by branch. Therefore, in a county with only savings and loan association branches, no dollar figure is available. **SOIL CONSERVATION SERVICE** The Soil Conservation Service uses the term "improper grassland management" instead of overgrazing.

TABLE OF CONTENTS

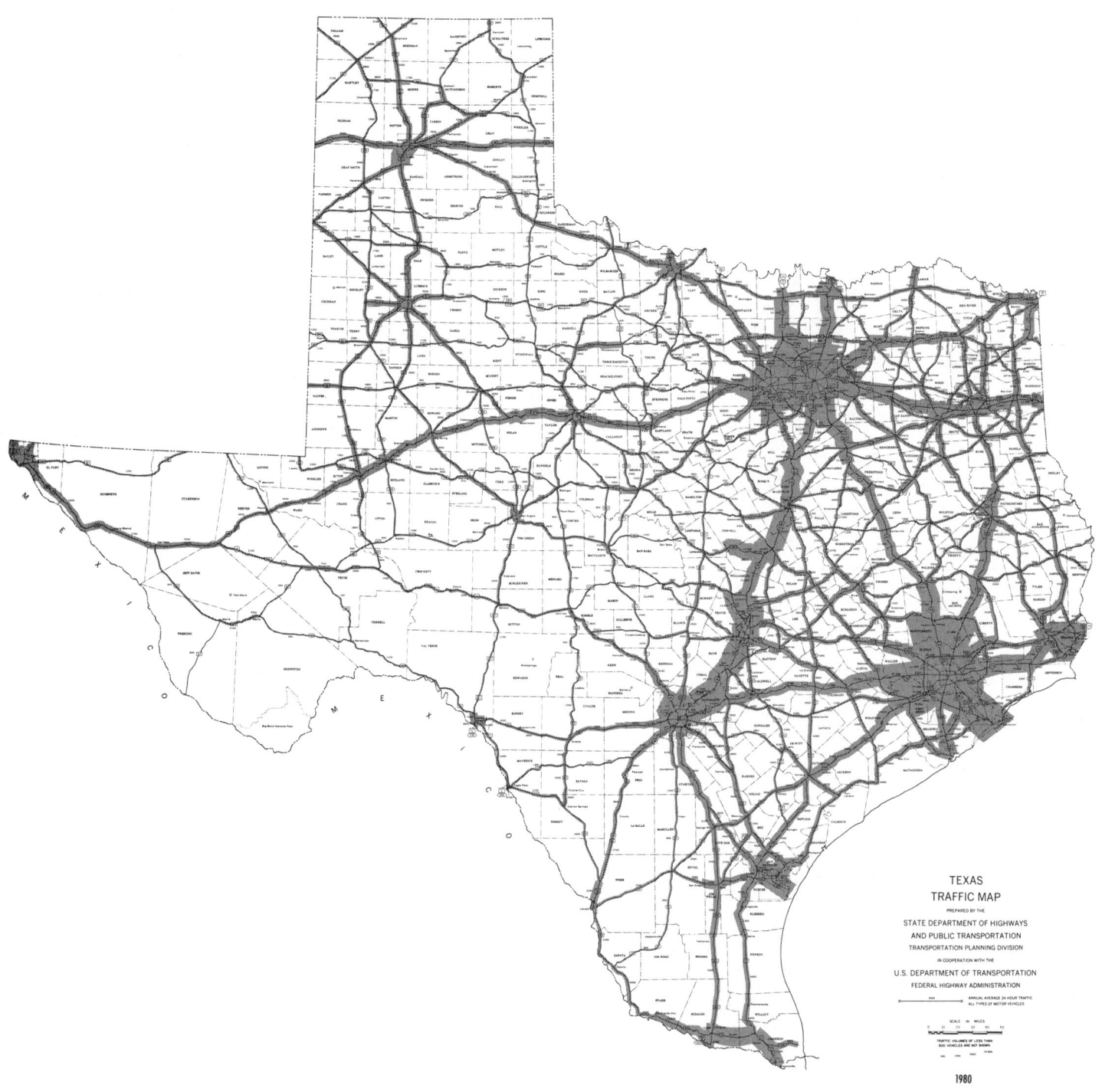

TEXAS
TRAFFIC MAP

PREPARED BY THE

STATE DEPARTMENT OF HIGHWAYS
AND PUBLIC TRANSPORTATION

TRANSPORTATION PLANNING DIVISION

IN COOPERATION WITH THE

U.S. DEPARTMENT OF TRANSPORTATION

FEDERAL HIGHWAY ADMINISTRATION

ANNUAL AVERAGE 24 HOUR TRAFFIC
ALL TYPES OF MOTOR VEHICLES

SCALE   IN   MILES

TRAFFIC VOLUMES OF LESS THAN
500 VEHICLES ARE NOT SHOWN

1980

TEXAS TODAY From the Great Plains in the north to Mexico, between the desert Southwest, the Rocky Mountains and the deep South, Texas offers a variety of natural scenic attractions. Few realize that Texas has more acres of inland water (over three million) than any other state except Alaska and Minnesota. Rivers and lakes provide unlimited recreational opportunities, from a lazy sail to an action-packed raft ride, and a sunny climate makes water sports a year round possibility. Tranquility to some means a bass breaking the surface in the morning mist rising off a lake in deep East Texas with the stillness broken only by an occasional heron's cry. Over 23 million acres of lake-studded forests blanket the eastern part of Texas. To others, getting away from it all means the spray of Gulf Coast saltwater and the whine of the reel as a 100 pound marlin takes the bait and runs. The Gulf Coast of Texas has 624 miles of sunny, inviting beaches. In the Central Texas Hill Country, the lakes are springfed and the rivers run cool and clear. Limestone caves in an infinitely varied landscape invite exploration. Oceans of grain are part of the panoramic vistas of the High and Rolling Plains where the sky is an all-encompassing canopy and the sunsets a dramatic conclusion. Majestic peaks soar over West Texas in rugged mountain ranges with 90 peaks towering over one mile above sea level. The romance of a soft tropical night amid the bougainvillea and Spanish architecture in the Rio Grande Valley is part of a year round playground at the southern tip of Texas. Tucked away in every corner of Texas are carefully preserved towns with Victorian facades echoing a frontier past. Texans are proud of their history and historical monuments, such as the Spanish Missions, reminders of the influences which helped to shape the state. Old frontiers and new frontiers, Texas encompasses them both. Sleek, glass and metal buildings crowd the skylines in the major cities. Shopping in Texas means glamorous specialty stores with international buyers, county flea markets and Mexican bazaars along the border. At night outstanding beef and seafood can make a meal in a Texas restaurant a memorable experience. Texas cities have become major cultural centers with museums displaying noted collections of contemporary, classical and western art, ballet and opera companies, and an astonishing array of theaters and music. Music has always been a part of Texas with ethnic and regional styles, resident orchestras and classical music festivals. Sports are an important part of the Texas way of life, from the glamour and pageantry of a professional football game to the exuberance of a game in a community park. Texas is now the nation's third most populous state, a melting pot of cultures. Almost one-fourth of all Texans speak a language other than English at home. Texas emerged as an economic pacesetter during the 1970s and now exceeds the national average in several economic measurements. Over one-fourth of all the energy produced in the nation is produced in Texas and more new manufacturing jobs were added in Texas than in any other state during the 1970s. A leader in the development of high technology, in little more than one generation Texas has been transformed from a largely rural state into one with a predominantly urban character. **THE LAND** Texas covers 266,807 square miles including 4,790 square miles of inland water. The elevation range extends from sea level to the 8,749 foot Guadalupe Peak. The boundaries are 801 miles apart north to south and 773 miles apart east to west. The Coastal Prairies and Marshes extend along the Gulf of Mexico from the Sabine River to Corpus Christi. The sandy soils and marshes along the coast change to savannahs a few miles inland with stands of timber and saltgrasses. The East Texas forestlands extend northward along the Louisiana border with generous rainfall and abundant plant and animal life. Just north of Beaumont the Big Thicket Preserve contains one of the state's last areas of near wilderness. West of the Pineywoods are the Central Prairies with rolling grasslands punctuated with some trees, usually oaks and mesquite. The Hill Country to the west of Austin is dotted with cedar and juniper. To the south the Rio Grande Valley is the fruit and vegetable area of Texas. The Edwards Plateau spreads across the lower west central area of the state at the foot of the mountains and basins of the Trans-Pecos in far west Texas, which is true mountain and desert country. The High Plains are separated from the land to the south by the Cap Rock Escarpment. The demand for land and land use has changed recently. The amount of cropland has declined from 41.5 million acres in 1958 to 33.5 million in 1982, while urban areas grew from 4.3 million acres in 1958 to 7.7 million in 1982. Forest lands capable of commercial production declined to 9.2 million acres in 1982, and over 111 million acres are now pasture and rangelands. Federal and state agencies have administrative control over 3.2 million acres primarily for outdoor recreation. Texas has seven national parks and ten national wildlife refuges. State, county and municipal parks and wildlife management areas cover over one million acres. **CLIMATE** Tuesday March 27, 1984 was a typical spring day in Texas. In midafternoon it was snowing in Dalhart and Amarillo, it was cloudy with 106 °F. in Brownsville and Harlingen, thunderstorms in north central and northeast Texas spawned a tornado which touched down in White Rock, heavy rain and hail covered the Dallas-Fort Worth area, scattered brush fires fueled by strong winds and dry grass burned out of control in the Hill Country, Corpus Christi steamed with 96 °F. under partly cloudy skies and winds of 69mph were recorded at the Midland Regional Airport. One of the worst seasons for wind damage to land since records began 49 years ago, between November 1, 1983 and May 31, 1984 an estimated 5,691,800 acres were damaged in Texas, almost half the damage reported in the entire U.S. Great Plains Region. During the same period in 1982-83 only 1,805,900 acres in Texas were damaged. The below normal precipitation, inadequate crop residue and lack of plant cover were cited as the cause of such extensive damage. In April, a west Texas duststorm shrouded most of the Panhandle and North Central Texas including the Dallas-Fort Worth area, reducing visibility to less than one and one-half miles. Climate is the history of weather for any given location over a long period of time. Texas, due to its location and size, experiences a variety of different weather conditions, frequently at the same time. Imagine our atmosphere as an ocean 50 to 60 miles deep. In this ocean of air surrounding the earth, one-half of the density of the atmosphere is below 20,000 feet and it is within this layer that much of our "weather" originates. This lower portion of air, known as the troposphere, varies in height from a winter low near 25,000 feet when associated with an Arctic airmass to a high near 50,000 feet when associated with a Tropical airmass. Uneven heating of the earth's surface and its rotation induces circulation patterns and a conflict between warm and cold air masses. Boundaries between these large bodies of air are known as frontal zones, or simply as "fronts". Although fronts are depicted on weather maps and charts as two dimensional, they are in fact three dimensional extending to much higher levels in the troposphere than first suspected. They are the cause of much of the clear air turbulence experienced by turbo-jet aircraft flying above "the weather". **CLOUDS** Dust and other particulate matter in the atmosphere play an important role in the formation of clouds and precipitation as they act as nuclei upon which moisture collects to form tiny droplets. These droplets can become either fog or clouds. There are four basic types of clouds: stratus, nimbus, cumulus and cirrus. Stratus is the very low cloud type usually seen during early morning. Cirrus is the wispy high clouds seen on an otherwise clear day, but sometimes completely covering the sky. Nimbus is the rain cloud and cumulus is the billowy white cloud seen on warm, humid days. We may also see combinations of cloud types such as the strato-cumulus or cumulo-nimbus. The energy necessary to bring our atmosphere to life is of course our sun: heat energy absorbed by the earth's surface is transferred back into the atmosphere, or from one area of the atmosphere to another, by convection, conduction or radiation. All of these processes are important weather regulators, but the most important one is convection since it plays such an important role in the precipitation process. Texas, due to its geographic location, receives a generous amount. **WINDS** How is all this energy distributed? It is to a large extent involved with the perennial question, "Which way does the wind blow?" The answer to that has a profound effect upon the weather in Texas. Air moves across the state from literally all directions, but mainly from the south to southeast bringing Maritime Tropical air over much of the state. Air moving across the state from the southwest will bring Continental Tropical air, a hot, dry wind from the steppes of Mexico in summer which is associated with July and August heat waves and drought conditions. When the wind blows from the west, Maritime Pacific air moves through the state and is quite clear, mild and dry, having been lifted over the mountains to the west and losing much of its moisture. When the north wind blows, it means only one thing to most Texans, cooler weather and welcome relief from summer heat. In winter it brings Continental Polar or in extreme cases Continental Arctic into the state. Sudden temperature changes associated with these airmasses are responsible for what is known to Texans as a "blue norther". The characteristic features of this event are a warm, sunny day, a noticeable dark blue color to the northern skies which is a cloud line caused by the sudden change in temperature associated with the very cold north wind and the mercury dropping 15 to 20 degrees in slightly over an hour. An east wind means rain to most Texans. This is frequently true in winter whenever weak low centers are forming along old stationary frontal systems, usually along the Texas coast line. **ENVIRONMENT** The Conservation Foundation released a study in December, 1983 which ranked the environmental efforts of each state. Texas ranked 39th among the 50 states with the worst performance rating among the larger states. One of the environmental problems facing Texas is hazardous waste. Texas is one of the leaders in the production of hazardous waste, generating an estimated 25.2 million tons in 1982. Industry is the primary source of those toxic materials, although municipal services and agriculture create a part. The petrochemical and refining industries generate at least 70 to 80% of the hazardous waste, with metals, machinery, paper and electronic industries contributing. Hazardous waste can cause fire, explosions, illnesses and death; the pollution of Georgetown's drinking water supply caused some 8,000 illnesses. Texas leads the nation in the number of hazardous waste disposal facilities; however, land

fills and underground injections have been used to dispose of 95% of the hazardous waste. Land disposal is cheaper, but often causes problems. There are 426 hazardous waste disposal sites in Gulf Coast counties, 218 in the Metroplex counties, 151 in the Plains counties, 105 in the Central Corridor counties and 48 sites in the Border counties. The U.S. Environmental Protection Agency (EPA) identified 1,044 potentially hazardous waste sites in Texas, announced that Texas had 11 of the country's worst uncontrolled sites and classified nine sites eligible for Superfund money with another six sites under consideration. The hazardous waste dump in Galveston County, which has been compared to Love Canal, is one of the federally designated Superfund sites and cleanup costs are estimated at $150 to $200 million. Because hazardous wastes can contaminate groundwater, soil and surface waters, the health, quality of life and the economy of Texas are at risk. Texas is nearing the nuclear age with four nuclear reactors close to completion; therefore, nuclear wastes will soon be added to the problem of hazardous wastes in Texas. The Texas Low-Level Radioactive Waste Disposal Authority has projected that the waste volume from those plants will be 105,000 cubic feet per year. Including nuclear wastes from other sites, the Authority estimates that 139,000 cubic feet of nuclear waste will be generated each year in Texas between 1990 and 2030. The U.S. Department of Energy has proposed sites in Deaf Smith and Swisher Counties in Texas for nuclear waste disposal under consideration. The owners of the South Texas Nuclear Project power plant have commissioned a study to determine if the nuclear plant could be converted to a coal burning facility. Acid rain is precipitation which contains pollutants, primarily oxides of sulfur and nitrogen, which result from the burning of fossil fuels (coal and petroleum) and are emitted into the atmosphere by automobiles, coal and oil fired power plants and industries. The Texas Energy and Natural Resources Advisory Council released a report on acid rain in Texas in August, 1983. The report, the result of a two year study, states that rain in Texas has become consistently more acidic at the same time that emissions of sulfur and nitrogen oxides from fossil fuel combustion have increased. Normal rainfall has a pH of 5.6 and over, with each number lower than 5.6 ten times more acidic. For example, pH 4.6 is ten times more acidic than pH 5.6. The study reported the most acidic rain (pH 2.9) was found in Dallas. The majority of pH readings in Texas ranged from pH 3.5 to pH 7.1. The utilization of coal in Texas is expected to increase from 14 million tons in 1975 to 195 million tons in 2000, a 1,300% increase. As a result, sulfur emissions will increase from 1.1 million tons to 6.7 million tons, a 510% increase. Nitrogen oxide emissions will increase from 2.1 million tons in 1975 to 3.8 million tons in 2000, an 18% increase. In addition, solid waste generation from coal utilization in Texas is expected to increase from 3 million tons in 1975 to 77 million tons in 2000, a 2,467% increase. In 1970 most of the electricity in Texas was generated by natural gas, which is one of the cleaner fuels. By 1982 there were 14 power plants burning lignite coal with seven operating without emission controls. Acid rain has damaged crops, killed trees and fish, corroded metal and stone and caused untold damage in the United States and Europe. East Texas, with its acidic soils, forests and lakes is a prime candidate for acid rain damage. The U.S. Clean Air Act is before Congress for revision and renewal and the U.S. Environmental Protection Agency (EPA) and the Texas Air Control Board have been working with several areas in Texas on air quality control. Various proposals have been made such as annual inspections of the emission control equipment on motor vehicles and requiring various industries to install devices for monitoring and controlling emissions. In 1982 a total of $478.9 million was spent on air pollution abatement in Texas.

THE PEOPLE Texas ranked fourth in the nation in population increase between 1980 and 1983 with a 1983 estimated population of 15,724,000, a 10.6% gain since 1980. The state's population growth since 1970 has been unprecedented in Texas history. Between 1970 and 1980 the population of Texas grew from 11,200,000 to 14,200,000, making it the second fastest growing of the ten most populous states. This growth trend began in the 1960s and by the mid 1970s Texas had moved from sixth to third in total population. The population growth rate rose from 17% between 1960 and 1970 to 27% between 1970 and 1980. According to federal estimates, over half of the state's growth in the Seventies came from a net migration into Texas of more than a million Americans from other states. In the 1950s, 6% of the state's growth was due to migration; 13% in the 1960s and 58% in the 1970s. Between 1975 and 1980 Texas ranked second with a net population gain from migration of 574,000 immigrants. Of the 1,400,000 people who moved to Texas, 521,000 were from other Southern states, 372,000 from the North Central states, 348,000 from the West and 195,000 from the Northeast. Prior to 1950 Texas had a lower proportion of residents living in urban areas than the national average. By 1980, however, 80% of its residents lived in urban areas and Texas ranked 11th among all states in proportion of urban population, well above the national average of 74%. In July 1981, four out of five Texans lived in cities. By 1982 Houston moved from the fifth to fourth largest U.S. city with an 8% increase since 1980, Dallas remained 7th with a 4% increase and San Antonio moved from 11th to 10th with a 4% increase. The population of most other American cities grew slowly, or declined. Population in the metropolitan areas of Texas grew at an estimated 29% from 1970 to 1980, more than double the rate for all U.S. metropolitan areas. Of the nation's 25 fastest growing urban areas, five were in Texas: Austin, Bryan-College Station, Brownsville-Harlingen-San Benito, Houston and McAllen-Pharr-Edinburg. In percentage of population gain between 1980 and 1982 Bryan-College Station had the highest increase in the state with a 25% gain. Midland was second at 18% and Odessa third with a 16% gain. Both the urban and rural areas increased by 27% between 1970 and 1980. Following 30 years of population losses the rural areas in Texas gained 630,000 people. In 1980 Texas ranked third in the nation in size of rural population with 2,896,174 rural residents. Rural population in Texas exceeds the total population of 23 states. The rural farm population totaled 268,893 and 442,603 persons lived in rural communities of 1,000 to 2,500 persons. In 1980 half of Texas' counties had more rural than urban residents with the entire population of 52 Texas counties classified as rural. In 1980 population densities varied from 1,769 persons per square mile in Dallas County to 0.1 in Loving County. The most densely populated area in the state is East Texas. While changes in age, sex and racial compositions in Texas are similar to national trends, differences exist. Although the median age of Texans rose about two years during the 1970s, the 1982 median age in the state was 28.2, about two years lower than the national average. While the total U.S. population under 20 years of age declined by 6% between 1970 and 1980, Texas had a 10% gain. Persons over age 64 comprised 11% of the U.S. population in 1980 as compared with 9.6% in Texas. Five Texas counties have unusually young populations with median ages of under 23 with residents of Maverick County having the lowest at 22.3 years. Other counties were Coryell, Hays, Starr and Brazos. On the other hand four Texas counties have populations with median ages of over 45 with residents in Llano County having the highest at 55.4 years. Other counties were Hamilton, Loving and Mills. The number of elderly Americans rose sharply from 1970 to 1980 with Texas as one of the top five favorite destinations. According to the Census Bureau, Texas' population 65 and over since 1960 has nearly doubled with a 191% increase. The state has the fifth largest 60-plus population in the United States. It is projected that this age group will increase 18% between 1980 and 2000. The state ranks second in highest percentage of persons of Hispanic origin which rose from 16% in 1970 to 21%, or 2,895,824 persons, in 1980. Texas ranks 17th in the Black population with 12% of its residents, or 1,710,175 persons, within that category. There are 40,074 American Indians living in Texas. In 1980 3,083,333 Texans were of English descent, 2,420,367 were of Irish descent and 2,168,947 were of German descent. Persons of French descent totaled 673,765, those of Italian descent numbered 189,799 and those of Polish descent were 167,465. Texas ranks 11th in the nation in highest percent of foreign born residents with 6% of its population within that category. In addition state and federal officials offer estimates ranging from 186,000 to 3,000,000 in the current number of undocumented workers in Texas. It is projected that Texas will continue to grow faster than the nation as a whole throughout the 1980s reaching 17,498,200 by 1990. Projections for the state population by the year 2000 vary from 20 million to 27 million thus suggesting that the population may double in the next 20 years with the most rapid growth occurring in the Houston-Galveston area which has a predicted growth of 25 to 32% between 1980 and 1990. Forecasts for other major metropolitan areas include a 17% increase in Dallas–Fort Worth area residents and a 16% population gain for the San Antonio area. When population grows so largely from migration, projections into the future seem especially hazardous because changes in conditions in the states of origin may be as significant as conditions in Texas. Secondly, growth from migration may produce a different age profile of the population as compared with growth due to natural increase. Between 1970 and 1980 the most rapid growth in Texas' population was in ages 20 to 39 which had a 58% increase. A 38% gain occurred among persons over age 64. With the greatest population gain among those in the family formation years, it is now anticipated that the 1980s will see another surge of school age children in Texas. The "echo" of the baby boom of two decades ago will be compounded by immigration. **VOTER PARTICIPATION** In the 1982 general election 3,190,853 of the 6,414,988 registered voters in Texas voted in the governor's race, 50% of the state's registered voters. This represents a 34% increase in the actual number of participating voters compared to the 1978 gubernatorial election when 2,369,764 of the 5,069,267 registered voters in Texas or some 47% of the registered voters went to the polls. Turnout in the 1983 gubernatorial race ranged from a low of 28% in Sutton County to a high of 74% in King County. In the primary election of May 1, 1982 nearly every major statewide office appeared on the ballot, including seven statewide executive posts, three Supreme Court seats, three Court of Criminal Appeals seats, 27 Congressional seats and one U.S. Senate seat, 150 Texas House seats and 31 Texas Senate seats. As a reuslt of the recent population growth and the redistricting process, Texas gained three new Congressional offices in 1982 and these offices appeared on the ballot along with numerous other new precinct offices. All in all, more than 8,200 candidates filed for races on the May 1 primary election ballot. The voter turnout in the May 1 election was 24% of the state's registered voters marking it the lowest turnout in recent Texas history—1,583,535 out of 6,629,092 registered voteres participated in the primary election. In the Democratic primary 20% or 1,300,000 voted and 4% or 265,000 voted in the Republican primary. On November 4, 1980 there were 6,639,661 registered voters. The presidential general election of that year had a 68% voter turnout, compared to a 64% turnout in the 1976 presidential election. In the 1980 election 55% voted Republican and 51% voted Democratic.

TEXAS TODAY

THE ECONOMY In the past decade, while other regional economies bowed to the effects of inflation, recession and rising prices, the Texas economy out-performed them all. Texas has become the nation's strongest regional economy, a title earned in the Seventies and retained on into the Eighties. As one of the nation's leaders in production of cattle, oil and cotton, Texas has also become prominent in food processing and in the production of apparel and machinery. A leading producer of computer software, Texas is also the nation's second largest electonics manufacturer. The population boom of the Seventies has sharply increased the number of Texans working and looking for work. In the last decade, the labor force grew over 35 percent. The national increase was about 24 percent. Much of the Texas increase came as new Texas residents entered the work force. In spite of the enlarged labor force, the Texas unemployment rate has remained substantially below the national average and consistently below rates in other large states. Among all 50 states Texas' unemployment was tenth lowest in 1980. Per capita personal income has also shown remarkable growth. In 1970 Texans' personal income amounted to $3,507 per capita, 90% of the national average. By 1979 the Texas figure was $8,778 per capita, just over the national average. Texans' adjusted per capita income, accounting for variations in living costs around the country, is substantially above the U.S. average, ranking seventh among all 50 states. Virtually every other economic indicator reflects phenomenal growth in Texas. At the start of the 1980s, new building permits and contract awards totaled more than $13,000,000,000, ranking Texas second in total construction. Growth in Texas retail sales has consistently outpaced the U.S. average in recent years. Between 1978 and 1979, for example, Texas retail sales grew almost 16 percent, while the U.S. average rose only about 11 percent. The value of farm and ranch receipts more than doubled during the decade from an estimated $3,800,000,000 in 1970 to more than $10,000,000,000 in 1980. Texas ranked third in the 1982 cash value of agricultural commodities, and was second in the nation in the value of cattle sales and fourth in cotton, wool and grain sorghum production. Low taxes, a growing market and the availability of energy resources—particularly crude oil and natural gas—have been other significant factors contributing to the state's economic attractiveness. **EMPLOYMENT** In recent years the Texas labor force has experienced significant changes in the distribution of workers among occupations. A rapid decrease in the number of workers employed in the agricultural sector has made manpower available for large increases in manufacturing and construction. In addition, the service sector of the Texas economy now accounts for at least two-thirds of the work force. Also noteworthy is the high percentage of white-collar employment in this fast-growing sector. Rapid growth in the labor force and low unemployment add up to a tremendous increase in the number of Texas wage earners. Nonfarm employment in the last decade grew by almost 2,000,000 persons, and increase of over 54%—more than twice the national growth rate. Even as the U.S. employment declined in the mid-1970 recession, Texas employment increased 2.4%. Leading Texas' industrial growth between 1970 and 1979 was mining with 96,000 employees—a 92.7% increase—triggered by dramatic hikes in world oil prices in the mid-1970s. Employees in construction increased 76% with 181,000 workers, far outdistancing the 29% increase recorded nationally. Gains in Texas construction reflected a huge demand for new factories, offices and housing created by a booming Texas economy. Employees in finance, insurance and real estate increased 66% with 125,000 workers. Employees in services increased 64% with 376,000 workers. Employees in wholesale and retail trade increased 61% with 519,000 workers. The Texas manufacturing sector gained almost 288,000 jobs—more than any other state. Durable goods manufacturing—furniture, machinery, etc.—grew at a much faster pace than nondurable manufacturing—food, textiles, chemicals, etc. Between 1973 and 1983 the Texas unemployment rate remained between four and six percent until 1982 when the rate hit unprecedented heights with a high of 8% in September, as the effects of the nationwide recession and the excess of oil and gas brought employment growth in many sectors to a standstill. The 1982 annual average among those unemployed included 6% of the white civilian labor force, 12.7% of the Black civilian labor force and 10.4% of the Hispanic civilian labor force. Unemployment in 1983 was 8.0%, the highest annual average since 1970. However, numerous factors including diversification and growth in several sectors caused a gradual lowering until by June, 1984 Texas unemployment had fallen to 4.8%, reaching its lowest level in more than three years. In April, 1984 Austin had the lowest unemployment rate in the state at 3.7%. Dallas-Fort Worth and Bryan-College Station tied for second at 3.9%. The winter freeze of 1984 affected citrus and vegetable growers in the Rio Grande Valley. Unemployment in Laredo in April, 1984 reached 20.8% and 23% in McAllen. By 1982 the number of Texas women in the labor force increased from 1,605,770 in 1970 to 3,047,000 in 1982, an increase of 190% during the twelve-year period. **INCOME** Texas showed remarkable growth in the Seventies in another important economic barometer, per capita personal income. Texas ranked 18th in personal income among the 50 states in 1980; this was a significant increase over the ranking of 31st in 1970 and 29th in 1975. This reflects that per capita personal income for Texans increased 170% from 1970 to 1980 compared with 141% for the U.S. per capita income. Average weekly wages for workers in employment covered by the Texas Unemployment Compensation Act for second quarter 1983 ranged from $451.63 in Somervell County to $169.64 in Starr County. The state average was $338.54 as compared with $266.00 in 1979. In August, 1983 the average Texas employee in manufacturing earned $8.88 per hour as compared with $8.60 a year prior. Average weekly hours in August, 1984 were 40.7 as compared with 39.6 a year prior. The average manufacturing production worker was earning $9.03 per hour in January, 1984 for an average work week of 41.8 hours and averaging $377.45 per week. Per capita income in Texas increased by 2.4% in 1983 as compared with a rise of 5.2% in the nation. The state ranked 17th in the nation and was $11,702 in 1983, up from $11,423 the year prior. The national average increased to $11,675 from $11,100 in 1982. The cost of living during the same time period increased 3.9%. **UNIONS** Texas has statutes prohibiting union security contracts. Important Texas statutes in the industrial relations field contain these provisions with appropriate penalties and judicial recourse for enforcement. All Texans have the right to earn an honest living at the work of their own choice and no one has the right to coerce or intimidate them to keep them from working at the job of their choice. The closed shop, the union shop and maintenance of membership provisions in labor contracts are illegal. The Texas checkoff law provides that the employer can make no deduction for labor unions dues or assessments without the written authorization of the employee. Strikes or picketing for recognition or bargaining are prohibited unless the union in fact represents a majority of the employees in the particular establishment. The use of coercion in a labor dispute is a felony. Mass picketing, secondary boycotts, secondary strikes and secondary picketing are illegal. Labor organizations are responsible for damages resulting from strikes or picketing in breach of contract and are liable to Texas' anti-trust laws. They must hold annual elections and file reports with the Secretary of State. In November, 1980 there were 669,000 union members in Texas out of 5,868,000 nonagricultural employees or 11.4% of the labor force. Total union membership in the Southwest-including Arkansas, Louisiana, New Mexico, Oklahoma and Texas—totaled 1,307,000 or 13.4% of the total employed.

AGRICULTURE Historically growth and development in Texas have been closely associated with a progressive and productive agricultural industry. The production of agricultural products expands economic activity in Texas far beyond the farm gate. Suppliers, processors, distributors—all agribusiness—benefit from agricultural production; one dollar of farm sales stimulates over $3.40 in activity within the Texas economy. In 1981, $10 billion of farm and ranch sales generated nearly $34 billion in the state economy—about 18% of the gross state product. The value of farm and ranch assets, $84 billion, equals about three-fourths of the total capital assets of the state and national banks in Texas not including the vast assets in agribusiness activities. In 1982 Texas ranked first in the United States in the production of cattle, calves, sheep and goats. In field crops it ranked first in production of hay other than alfalfa, first in grain sorghum, second in the production of cotton and third in winter wheat. In vegetables the state ranked second in broccoli, carrots, honeydew melons and onions. In fruit it ranked second in grapefruit, third in oranges and fourth in pecans. In 1982, 42.6% of all cash receipts to farmers and ranchers in Texas were for cattle and calves, 13.8% were for cotton (lint and seed), 6.0% from wheat, 5.9% from sorghum grain, 5.7% from milk (wholesale and retail) and 3.1% from corn. Cash receipts in Texas in 1982 from farm marketings in total crops, livestock and payments were $10,323,263,000 with $4,248,953,000 from crops, $5,430,712,000 from livestock and livestock products and $643,598,000 from government payments. Total cash receipts were less in 1982 than in 1979 which had the highest receipts of any year from 1978 through 1982 at $10,358,144,000. Gross farm income rose steadily in Texas from $10,121,200,000 in 1980 to $11,361,900,000 in 1982. Net farm income totaled $1,149,400,000 in 1980 and $1,170,600,000,000 in 1982, a decrease from $1,195,300,000 in 1981. The value of farm real estate—land and buildings—totaled $82,071,000,000 in 1983, an increase from $79,718,000,000 in 1982. However, farmland values have tumbled nationwide with the United States recording three straight yearly declines in the value of farmland in many states. The decline, caused by shrinking farm profits, was offset in Texas by the spread of residential and industrial development causing farmland values in the state to have increased 31.3% over the past three years, the highest increase in the nation. Several significant events impacted Texas agriculture the past two years. The Payment-in-Kind (PIK) program was instituted by the federal government in January, 1983 as a means to support farm income and to reduce surplus commodities by cutting production. Income statistics were calculated using statewide yields for the return on PIK acres, current prices as of November, 1983 and the number of acres idled under PIK. The results show that corn and sorghum farmers will receive around $206 million or $156 per acre. Wheat producers will receive $155 million, about $83 an acre. Rice farmers will receive only $48 million in in-kind payments but this is almost $300 per acre or $24,000 per farm. Cotton growers will get over $225 million or nearly $110 per acre. In total, Texas farmers will share around $637 million in in-kind payments. This compares to $9,700,000,000 in cash receipts from farm marketings in 1982. A second event began on December 23, 1983 when the temperature in extreme South Texas dropped below 32°F. and stayed there for 48 hours. Hidalgo, Cameron, Starr and Willacy were among the counties declared disaster areas by President Reagan. Preliminary estimates were made that food processing output would decline by $200 million. The value to farmers of crops destroyed by the freeze is estimated at $99 million. At the time of the freeze about 70% of the crops were unharvested. Only 15% of the vegetables were harvested. One hundred percent of the Valencia oranges were still on the trees, while 21.5% of the grapefruit and 45% of the early oranges were harvested. Approximately 30% of the farmers in Cameron.

County lost at least 40% of their crops. The third event was a drought which devastated ranchers and farmers for the past two years in West Texas and the Panhandle. Loss to the region has been estimated at $70 million in cotton, wheat, sorghum and other crops. The drought also caused ranchers to sell livestock at low prices leaving them with cattle of low quality and an estimated livestock loss of $46 million. In June, 1984, 82 West Texas counties were eligible for federal disaster loans. The Farmers Home Administration reported more than half of in loans granted to Texas farmers and ranches—worth about $609,000,000—were overdue. United States Agriculture Secretary John Block has declared 166 Texas counties—about two-thirds of the state—eligible for federal aid because of drought. The state's rapid population growth will present critical problems in agriculture but it also offers a great potential for new markets and new products. The diverse geographical regions in Texas provide a unique diversity of commodities and perspectives and offer a stable commodity mix. Texas enjoys a superior strategic location for fostering national international trade. However, the current cost-price squeeze, primarily based on increased cost of inputs, along with low prices for commodities and severe weather, has created an unprecedented income and liquidity crisis for Texas farmers. Improved productivity and profitability is crucial to the success of agriculture in Texas. Yet, much of existing agricultural technology is based on the assumption of continued abundant land, water and other resources used coupled to availability of inexpensive energy. The disparity between this and the present situation in Texas clearly underscores the need for rapid technology development. Continuing the experience of the 1970s, Texas agriculture in the future will have to struggle to maintain even productivity and output. To remain competitive in the market for agricultural products Texas must keep up with productivity increases in the United States and overseas. Increasing agricultural productivity means more output per acre. However, from 1969 onward, Texas agricultural productivity has not followed the U.S. productivity growth but rather has moved erratically up and down with no clear trend. With lagging productivity Texas agriculture is threatened with the possibility of becoming a high-cost producer relative to other agricultural exporters, unable to retain customers in very competitive agricultural markets. The Governor's Task Force on Agriculture Development stated in its December, 1982 report that the need for increased state funding for agricultural research and education was a critical issue for Texas agriculture in order to maintain a competitive position in production agriculture and combat the high cost of production. In 1982 the State of Texas provided nearly $40 million for agricultural research out of a budget of over $12 billion or less than 0.4%. The task force also recommended the development of financing for water conservation equipment, the development and funding of a continuing and comprehensive water research and education program for Texas and the expansion of local water districts to assist development of efficient groundwater management. Rapidly growing population converts prime farmland to urban and suburban use, putting heavy demands on the existing water supplies. Over 70% of the water used for irrigation in Texas comes from underground supplies. Statewide 12 million acre feet of water is being drained from under ground annually while only seven million trickles back into the aquifers. Irrigated land is Texas' most productive acreage. Although just 25% of the state's cropland is irrigated, that land provides farmers with 50% of their net revenues. Without irrigation Texas farmers would lose 40% of their earnings. With higher energy costs and depletion of water stocks, water from subsurface sources is becoming increasingly uneconomic. Energy costs have escalated over recent years. In 1973 the average cost of natural gas used in pumping water to an acre of sorghum was about $0.25; today the cost is $3.50.

TEXAS TODAY

INDUSTRY Texas has been a consistent leader in industrial expansion. Over the past five years 14% of all new manufacturing in the United States has located in Texas. Value added by manufacture totaled $51,000,000,000 in 1983 placing Texas third in the nation as compared with seventh in 1977 at $33,150,000,000. During 1983 the Texas manufacturing sector added 10,200 employees increasing employment in this area to 1,016,100 over the previous year. The greatest increase was in durable goods with an additional 4,500 employees in the production of stone, clay and glass products. Of that number 2,400 were employed in industries manufacturing concrete, gypsum and plaster products. The second largest employment increase between December, 1982 and December, 1983 in the category of durable goods was in the electric and electronic equipment industry, an area long noted to be a key economic factor in Texas. Employees increased 4,400 rising from 99,100 in December, 1982 to 103,500 in December, 1983. Transportation equipment employees rose from 75,000 to 78,100. The greatest decrease occurred in the nonelectrical machinery industry which dropped from 149,100 employees in December, 1982 to 141,500 in December, 1983. Within that category employees in the oil field machinery industry alone fell from 50,800 in December, 1982 to 45,200 in December, 1983. In the manufacture of nondurable goods employment growth was greatest in the apparel and textile products industry with 2,700 employees added by the end of the year thereby raising the total to 66,300. The printing and publishing industry, a major employer in the nondurable goods area, had an increase of 1,800 employees, rising from 67,300 in December, 1982 to 69,100 in December, 1983. The greatest employment decline among producers of nondurable goods occurrerd in the chemical and allied products industry dropping from 81,400 employees in December, 1982 to 79,300 in December, 1983. One of the most significant economic forces in Texas is the petroleum industry which had a total employment of 255,000 in March, 1984, an increase of 1,100 employees from the previous month but still lower than its labor force in January, 1983 of 263,700. In 1983 Texas produced 849.1 million barrels of crude oil—a 2.6% drop from 1982 production. Pecos County was the leading producer with 50.25 million barrels. Other counties in the top 10, in order of production were Ector, Yoakum, Gaines, Hockley, Andrews, Gregg, Scurry, Crane and Refugio. Total number of operating oil and gas rigs in Texas was 977 during the week ending December 23, 1983 as well as during the week ending December 24, 1982. Natural gas production also decreased from 16,474,000,000 cubic feet during August, 1982 to 15,678,000,000 cubic feet during August, 1983. However, Texas rig count increased in early 1984 and offshore drilling has been particularly strong. Inventories of oil field machinery and tubular goods have declined. These developments may signal an end to the energy-related employment declines of the past two years. In other nonmanufacturing areas the greatest employment change occurred in the construction industry which dropped 30,600 employees from 409,100 in December, 1982 to 378,500 in December, 1983. The greatest increase occurred in retail trade which increased 22,300 employees from 1,123,900 in December, 1982 to 1,146,200 in December, 1983. The second greatest increase was in the services sector with an increase of 15,900 employees rising from 1,161,500 to 1,177,400. Earnings by place of work was highest in manufacturing which reached $25,147,375,000 in 1981 as compared with $21,493,389 in 1980. Durable goods was the area of greatest growth with an increase from $12,866,836,000 in 1980 to $15,351,833,000 in 1981. The second largest sector by total earnings was services which reached $19,468,909,000 in 1981 as compared with $16,613,280,000 in 1980. **BUSINESS** The state of Texas was a leader in many areas of wholesale trade in 1982. Texas led all states in petroleum bulk station and terminal sales with a total of $18,800,000,000. Sales per establishment average $12,400,000.

Dollar volume of Texas service establishment equipment and supplies wholesale trade placed the state third in the nation at $507,000,000. Texas also led all states in sales by general-line grocery wholesalers with 1982 sales of $5,600,000,000. Measured in dollar volume of sales, Texas led all states in the industrial supply wholesale trade with 1982 sales of $4,100,000,000. Texas retail sales for 1982 totaled $82,732,000,000 as compared with $45,816,000,000 in 1976 making the state rank second in the nation. During this five year period the greatest increase in retail sales was in food stores which rose from $9,737,000,000 in 1977 to $19,261,000,000 in 1982. Automotive dealers increased sales significantly from $11,259,000,000 in 1977 to $16,821,000,000 in 1982. Retail sales in December, 1983 totaled $9,316,000,000, an 11.7% increase from December, 1982 which totaled $8,340,000,000. January through May, 1984 retail sales were higher than in the same 1983 period as reflected by the 17% increase in city sales tax collected throughout the state. Each of the 20 biggest sales tax cities were ahead of last year's totals. The largest increase occurred in Austin with a 31% rise followed by Dallas and Fort Worth, each with a 24% gain. Local sales tax collected in San Antonio and Houston reflected lower growth at 19% and 12% respectively. In spite of the Christmas freeze that wrecked the citrus industry and the 1983 retail slump that followed devaluation of the Mexican peso, sales tax revenues were up 14% in Brownsville and 19% in McAllen. One of the fastest-growing businesses in Texas is restaurants. The state's 39,445 restaurants grossed sales of $7,700,000,000 in 1982. Gross sales for restaurants increased $757,900,000 between 1981 and 1982 with the number of restaurants increasing by 4,843 over 1981. Regionally the Gulf Coast led with gross sales of $2,590,000,000. The Dallas-Fort Worth area was second with $2,000,000,000. A significant factor in Texas business is the underground or off-the-books economy which may generate as much as $38,000,000,000 per year. This activity includes unreported moonlighting, pocketing unreported tips, dealing in cash and duplicate bookkeeping. Nationwide the underground economy has been estimated at $500,000,000,000 annually and is reported to be growing faster than the gross national product. One of the components of the Texas underground economy is the 2,000 mile border with Mexico which accounts for a major portion of the $20,000,000,000 generated off the books each year by illegal immigrants. The steady growth of the business community is apparent by studying the business stock from 1981 through 1983. Filings for new corporate charters increased by 9% with 11,181 charters filed. Filings of new limited partnerships increased by about 13% to 1,141 filings. The rate of filings of incorporations was up 17% over comparable filings in 1982. There was an increase in the rate of corporate dissolutions of about 10% over the year before. The total number of incorporations in Texas metropolitan areas increased in the second quarter of 1983 when compared to the first quarter data. There were 10,436 incorporations in April, May and June, amounting to an increase of about 6%. This improvement was still 3% less than the high in the fourth quarter of 1982. The major metropolitan areas of Houston and Dallas-Fort Worth still accounted for a large share of total incorporations. With 3,505 Houston accounted for 33.6% of incorporations in metropolitan areas while the 3,575 incorporations in the Dallas-Fort Worth area accounted for 34.3%. Several economic factors predict a period of steady growth over the next few years in Texas. Oil prices have remained relatively stable and drilling activity is increasing. Although oil well completions and gas production declined in 1983 total wildcat wells drilled increased from 4,455 in 1982 to 5,004 in 1983. Increased defense spending will continue to spur economic activity, especially in the Dallas-Fort Worth, Austin and San Antonio areas. Manufacturing activity continues to increase chiefly due to strong growth in high-technology industries.

CONSTRUCTION/HOUSING In 1980 Texas ranked 29th in the nation in housing value with values averaging $47,000. It also ranked 39th in owner-occupied housing with 64.3% of its households living in owner-occupied homes. The median monthly cost for owner-occupied housing was $348. There were 1,759,755 renter-occupied housing units with a median gross rent of $245. Personal income in Texas by earnings in construction rose from $4,959,301,000 in 1976 to $9,630,980,000 in 1981 with only a slight increase occurring between 1979 and 1980 followed by a sharp rise in 1981. The last quarter of 1982 through the first three quarters of 1983 was a record period for building activity in Texas with the real value of construction authorized in the state up 27% over a strong early 1982 performance with new construction having a total value of $13,394,000,000. Approximately 7,749,000,000 new dwelling units were authorized, a 58% increase over the previous 12 months. The upsurge in construction activity that began in late 1982 grew to more than $4,300,000,000 of permits authorized in the second quarter of 1983 but began to level off in the third quarter. Home sales grew steadily from the fourth quarter 1982 through the third quarter 1983. During 1982 and 1983 residential construction led the economic downturn as well as the recovery. In the fourth quarter of 1982 residential construction activity began to gain strength. The dollar volume of residential construction permits continued steady growth in all types through the second quarter of 1983, subsequently declining about 15% in the third quarter. The strength of nonresidential construction permit activity depends on type of intended use. Generally, healthy growth occurred in lodging, retail and public construction from the third quarter of 1982 through the next three quarters. Texas industrial and office construction permit activity was weak during this period. The other types of nonresidential construction permit activity followed the same patterns as total nonresidential construction permit activity since the third quarter 1982. Fluctuations in nonresidential construction was significantly greater than residential construction. The total dollar volume of construction permit was essentially constant in the first three quarters of 1983. The 1983 year to date dollar volume in each quarter; however, was more than 20% greater than the comparable year to date dollar volume in 1982. The quarterly dollar volume of the additions, alterations and repair category over the first three quarters of 1983 was about 10% greater than that during 1982. Quarterly nonresidential construction permit dollar volume in the first three quarters of 1983 was roughly equal to the 1982 quarterly average. The total dollar volume of nonresidential permits was relatively constant for the fourth quarter 1982 through third quarter 1983. For each of these quarters the year to date dollar volume of permits issued for lodging facilities was ahead of the previous 12 months' comparable figures. From the fourth quarter 1982 through the third quarter 1983 industrial construction permit volume ranged between $95 million and $110 million. This was down as much as one-third from the volume one year before. Except for a $125 million drop in the first quarter 1983, retail construction permit volume was steady in the $350 to $390 million range in each quarter from the fourth quarter 1982 through the third quarter 1983. Although office construction was fairly constant in a range of about $500 to $550 million per quarter since the end of 1982, 1983 year to date volume for each of the first three quarters was roughly 20 to 40% less than comparable 1982 year to date periods. Following the energy slump and devaluation of the Mexican peso in 1983, Houston became vastly overbuilt as the demand for office space dropped considerably. Dallas office space was in high demand during the first quarter of 1984 largely due to the city's active economy and large number of companies moving into the area. While office construction activity was the

poorest performer, public construction made the best gains in nonresidential construction permit activity during the first three quarters of 1983. Public construction 1983 year to date dollar volume for each of the first three quarters was from 25% to more than 50% greater than the comparable 1982 year to date volume. Quarterly residential construction permit dollar volume the first three quarters of 1983 was roughly twice the quarterly amount of nonresidential volume. The indicated value per one-family residential unit of new construction increased steadily from $58,300 in the fourth quarter of 1982 to $62,700 in the third quarter of 1983. This was approximately an 11% increase in construction costs for the average home. The cost per unit of two to four family and apartment construction did not increase during this period. The per unit cost of apartment units was relatively constant between $21,000 and $22,000 from the fourth quarter of 1982 through the third quarter of 1983. The number of home sales during this period gained strength rapidly. In each of the first three quarters of 1983 existing home sales 1983 year to date dollar volume was more than 30% greater than that in comparable 1982 year to date periods. The quarterly sales dollar volume grew steadily from $1.2 billion in the fourth quarter of 1982 to $2.25 billion in the third quarter of 1983. This was nearly a 90% increase. The average sales price of an existing home increased steadily from about $73,000 in the fourth quarter of 1982 to about $87,000 in the third quarter of 1983, a 19% increase. Median resale prices of existing single-family homes in the Dallas-Fort Worth area was $81,300 in the first quarter of 1984, an 11% increase from the previous year and $78,400 in Houston, a 2% increase from the previous year. There was steady growth in construction lending between the fourth quarter of 1982 and the second quarter of 1983. Although the third quarter of 1983 construction lending was more than twice the level of the third quarter of 1982, it dropped from the second quarter of 1983. Most of this drop occurred in Houston. Dallas-Fort Worth also had a substantial decrease between the second and the third quarters of 1983. Austin and San Antonio, however, recorded major increases during the same time period. Residential lending constituted about 25% of total savings and loan lending from the fourth quarter of 1982 through the third quarter of 1983. Residential loans closed statewide in the second quarter of 1982 were $641 million, increasing to $1.39 billion in the third quarter of 1983. Although nonresidential lending grew from $93 million in the second quarter of 1982 to $340 million in the third quarter of 1983, growth during this period fluctuated. Examples of these wide variations were Austin with $5 million in the third quarter of 1982 to $144 million the following quarter to $6 million the first quarter of 1983 and Dallas with $9 million in the fourth quarter of 1982 to $77 million in the first quarter of 1983 to $44 million the following quarter. Refinancing activity by Texas savings and loan associations was relatively stable from the fourth quarter of 1982 through the third quarter of 1983 at a quarterly volume of about $185 million. **FOREIGN INVESTMENT** Total assets and employment, two of the broadest measures of foreign business activity in the United States, increased sharply in 1981. Foreign business assets in the United States increased 35% to $395 billion and employment increased 15% to 2,343,000 in 1981. Texas was the most popular state in the United States for foreign investments where the petroleum industry attracted most of the business. Foreign investment value in Texas rose from nearly $14 billion in 1980 to over $21 billion in 1981 with approximately 175,000 jobs created in 1981, an increase of 50,000 from 1980. In June, 1984 the Dallas-Fort Worth area has 536 foreign-owned companies and 10 foreign banks with offices in the city. Houston has 500 foreign-owned companies and 55 foreign banks with offices in the city.

IMPORTS AND EXPORTS Texas ports account for much of the State's flow of imported and exported goods. For exporting to foreign markets the dominant cargos leaving Texas ports are agricultural products with chemical and allied products a distant second. For imports, 85% of the volume is crude oil with metal mining ore a distant second at 6%. In 1982, 290 million tons of cargo moved through Texas ports. While the United States did $30 billion worth of trade with countries of Latin America in 1982, about $4 billion worth moved through Texas. In fact, about 13% of all U.S. exports passed through Texas. In 1981 Texas had 300,000 export related manufacturing jobs. Only two other states had more manufacturing jobs related to exporting. In 1981 17% of U.S. exports went to Latin America but Texas exported 53% of its foreign bound goods to that area. Texas has realized the importance of foreign trade. In 1980 the state spent $739,794 on export promotion which was seventh highest in the nation. Texas even maintains a foreign trade office in Mexico. **FINANCIAL INSTITUTIONS** Financial institutions in Texas have experienced a number of changes over the past several years. Institutions are now using different techniques to attract funds. Commercial banks, savings and loan associations and credit unions have all been affected by new banking technology, strategies and the Garn-St. Germain Depository Institution Act of 1982. Financial institutions are prohibited from branching nationwide, but with the expanding use of electronic banking and the establishment of nonbank institutions, some banks are overcoming many of the barriers to interstate banking. Since Texas has become a financial center, some of these banking characteristics can be seen in the state. For instance, automated teller machines have become widespread in recent years. They allow customers to do some of their banking at various times and locations. The use of these machines by banks and the consolidation of networks so customers can use the machines to make deposits and withdrawals from their hometown bank while they are in various locations around the United States have helped set the basis for possible national interstate banking legislation. On March 23, 1984, the Board of Governors of the Federal Reserve System approved the application of U.S. Trust Corp. of New York to convert its Florida subsidiary from a nondepository trust company to an institution that accepts demand deposits and makes consumer loans. The Bank Holding Company Act defines a bank as an institution that both accepts demand deposits and makes commercial loans. Because the Florida subsidiary does not make commercial loans it is not technically a bank. This has motivated other financial institutions to apply for approval to provide similar services across the country. Twenty eight financial institutions, as of April 26, 1984, had applied to establish 165 institutions nationwide. Texas banks had applied for 17 institutions to be set up around the country. Eleven banking organizations had applied for permission to open nonbanks in Texas. Several Texas banks have bought into banks in other states in anticipation of changing laws regarding interstate banking. National banks have been prohibited from acquiring banks across state lines since the passage of the McFadden Act in 1927. Bank holding companies, also, have been limited in this way since the Douglas Amendment to the Bank Holding Company Act of 1956. The advent of new technology and anticipated change in banking laws are major considerations in the way Texas financial institutions conduct certain aspects of their operations. Texas, as of June 30, 1983, had 1,679 commercial banks. These banks had $135.6 billion in domestic deposits and $158.9 billion in domestic assets. Some financial institutions experienced difficulties in 1982 as seven banks failed. In 1983, three banks in Texas failed. Problems with energy-related loans were blamed for the failures. There were 284 savings and loan associations in Texas, June, 1983, with 231 state-chartered. The state associations control about 80% of the assets held by Texas savings and loan associations, and they can participate directly in all areas of real estate development, including the taking of equity positions in projects they finance. In 1974 state-chartered savings and loan associations were given the authority to make commercial, consumer, inventory, agricultural, and oil and gas loans, but real estate remains the primary area of investment. In 1983 they started becoming more involved in construction financing. For the first three months in 1983, one-half of the volume of loans closed by savings and loan associations in Texas financed construction. As of December 31, 1981, Texas had 498 state-chartered credit unions with 1,343,458 members. Banks, savings and loan associations and credit unions have all developed some common strategies such as checking accounts that pay interest, and all are making an increasing number of loans whose rates vary automatically with changes in market conditions. Between 1970 and 1982 Texas financial institutions were influenced by a combination of rising and variable interest rates as well as a rapidly growing state economy. Banks and savings and loan associations increased their loan total at a rate considerably above the national average. For banks the increase was due to the strength of business and real estate loans. For savings and loan associations it was due to the strong housing market in the state. Banks with assets over $750 million increased from five in 1970 to 21 by 1982. Since 1970, there has been a major shift from noninterest bearing demand accounts and fixed-rate passbook savings accounts toward sources of funds whose yields respond quickly to changes in market interest rates. During the period, Texas had growth rates in population, employment and personal income that outgained the national average. Oil price increases in 1973 and again in 1979, the removal of federal controls on crude oil prices between 1979 and 1981 and the revision of natural gas prices in 1978 all helped Texas employment and income grow at rates well above the national average. So more money became available for Texas financial institutions. Throughout the period, high interest rates caused a decline in deposit growth at banks and savings and loan associations. Credit unions, whose interest rate ceilings were higher than other institutions, were generally unaffected by the rates and their deposit growth continued. As interest rate ceilings have been lifted, the difference between the institutions has lessened, thus negating the advantage credit unions once had. Generally, Texas financial institutions registered major increases in construction lending in 1982. Thus, the period between 1970 and 1982 brought various changes to the financial institutions of Texas. **NATURAL RESOURCES** Texas has an abundance of natural resources from coal, oil, gas and minerals to hardwood and pine forests. Petroleum is the most valuable resource, however. In 1984, the oil and gas industry in Texas is an estimated $37 billion enterprise employing 400,000 people. In 1983 alone, oil and gas companies spent an estimated $8.5 billion drilling for energy resources and there are 85,000 miles of pipeline criss-crossing the state. In 1981, total wellhead value of crude petroleum was $33.6 billion and ranked highest in the nation. It also accounted for 33% of the U.S. total. Texas has been the leader in oil production for many years and today it holds about 27% of the nation's proven oil reserves. Yet, the bulk of oil in Texas has been discovered and is being or has been produced. It is estimated that 88% of all oil in the state has been discovered. About 156 billion barrels of oil have been found in Texas with approximately 46 billion barrels produced and eight billion in proven reserves. This leaves about 100 billion barrels of oil unrecoverable by present techniques. So the future rate of oil production depends, to a degree, on the ability to extract oil from fields where it is not recoverable by conventional methods today. Even though the state's petroleum production has been declining over the past 20 years, rapidly rising prices led to dramatic gains in the value of production. That is, until recent declines in crude oil prices. Even with the production declines,

Texas accounts for approximately one-third of all oil and gas produced nationally. Within the state, four counties accounted for approximately 20% of total oil production in 1983. They were Pecos, Ector, Yoakum and Gaines Counties. In 1982, oil production totaled 836.8 million barrels, down 4.7% from 1981. Since decontrol of oil prices in 1981, declines in production have slowed somewhat. The effects of decontrol are evident when oil pricing information is analyzed. From 1979 to 1981 the price of Texas crude oil rose dramatically as it adjusted to worldwide market conditions. However, by 1982, the world price fell as supply exceeded demand. Thus, the price of Texas crude oil fell for the first time in recent years. The decline continued through 1983 causing further declines in the value and production of Texas oil. The production of natural gas has also been declining; in 1983, it declined 7.7%. However, like oil, price increases for natural gas have kept the value of production rising. Natural gas is still regulated, but complete decontrol is expected by 1985. Gas production has tended to be more erratic than oil. Sharp drops in production have occurred periodically, followed by slow declines or increases. Natural gas production tends to respond more rapidly to other fuels rather than seasonal or climatic changes in energy demand. Production is also related to natural gas prices and, since Texas natural gas is still under federal price controls, both prices and production are expected to increase when decontrol of a large portion of the State's natural gas occurs in 1985. In 1982 natural gas production fell sharply, due in large part to a national recession that lessened business demand, a mild winter which lessened consumer demand and higher gas prices relative to other fuels caused some utilities to switch to cheaper fuels such as coal. Production in 1983 declined 7.7% to 5.6 trillion cubic feet. Even though production declined, Texas still ranked first in natural gas production. Twenty-six counties produced 50% of the natural gas in Texas. Pecos, Kleberg, Crane and Waller Counties were the major natural gas producers. The total revenue from sale of natural gas amounted to approximately $8.3 billion in 1982. The estimated proven reserves of natural gas in Texas in 1981 were 53,688 billion cubic feet, 25.6% of the U.S. total, and first in the nation. Although Texas' economy is closely linked to oil and gas, other resources are being developed. Coal is the most notable. Even though coal production decreased in most coal producing states in 1983, Texas increased its production by 4.2 million short tons which was a 12% increase. All coal production in 1981 was from surface mines, and virtually all was lignite. Texas was the nation's leader in lignite production in 1981, with 64% of the total. Reliance on a dwindling oil and gas supply has prompted Texas to look for alternative sources of energy. With its own oil and gas reserves and production declining, Texas has looked to new technology to squeeze more oil out of the ground. However, with the state's abundant supply of heavy oil, tar sands and lignite, it may develop a sythetic oil and gas industry that would provide high economic benefits for the state. Synfuels are defined by federal law as fuels obtained from domestic sources of coal (including lignite and peat, oil shale, tar sands and heavy oil). To qualify as a synthetic fuel, a substance must be a substitute for natural gas, petroleum or petrochemical feedstocks. The relative expense of currently developing the synthetic fuels as compared to the current price of oil and gas make most synthetic fuels too costly. Though economic conditions are not presently supportive of a major synthetic fuel industry in Texas, there is definitely future potential given the state's natural resources. Not all of Texas' natural resources are pumped from a well. Texas has about 23.3 million acres of forest land. In 1981, Texas produced 475.4 million cubic feet of wood. Pine made up about 398 million cubic feet and hardwood was 77 million cubic feet. In addition to wood, Texas produces minerals such as aluminum. In 1981 Texas ranked fourth in primary aluminum production, recovered from

alumina in bauxite. Production dropped almost 25% due in large part to the increased cost of natural gas for energy. The aluminum industry has been trying to reduce its costs by boosting its production efficiency. In 1981 traces of gold and silver mineralization reportedly were found in the Lower Cretaceous marine sediments of the Comanchean Series in north-central Texas. The areas of primary interest were Erath and Comanche Counties. Another discovery was reported southeast of Fort Worth in Tarrant County. In 1981, as demand for steel products fell, iron ore output in Texas dropped almost 31%. Yet, value per long ton of ore was up 26%. Cass and Morris Counties produced limonite and siderite ores from open pit mines. The ores were used mainly to produce pig iron. Production of magnesium compound in Texas declined about 6% in 1981; however, the value per short ton rose about 10%. Because of a depressed silver price, silver exploration and development in the state have been curtailed. Throughout Texas there are many refineries that produce metals from raw ores that are imported from other parts of the country or other nations. Nonmetals have major importance in Texas as well. Asphalt is found in asphalt-impregnated limestone. In 1981 it was mined chiefly in Uvalde County and used mainly for road surfacing. Texas, in 1981, produced 90% of the nation's total of asphalt. Texas does not produce borite, but does have grinding mills and imports the borite. Total cement shipments increased 7.5%, in 1981, with energy-related, commercial and industrial demands remaining high. Portland cement comprised 98% of the total output. Ready-mix companies used about 60% of the cement produced by the 22 cement plants in Texas, in 1981. Most of the clay produced in the state is used in the oil and gas drilling industry. In 1981 clay production from the state's 88 mines, in 39 counties, was up 11%. In 1981, Texas led the nation in crude gypsum mined and continued as second in calcined gypsum production. Seven companies mined the gypsum in six counties and provided 15% of the nation's total. Separation and recovery of crude helium from natural gas declined in 1981, but high-purity helium increased from 35 million cubic feet to 238 million cubic feet. Lime production declined but unit value rose about $4 a ton. Though Texas no longer mines perlite, it processes imported quantities. The state ranked fourth in production of expanded perlite, in 1981. Texas ranked second in output of salt in 1981, fourth in industrial sand, third in sand and gravel and Texas continued to lead the nation in crushed stone and total stone output. Four companies in five counties produced frasch sulfur in 1981. Texas ranked second in the nation for talc production with 25% of the tonnage and about 13% of the value. Other minerals and rocks are found in Texas. Collectors can find a variety of rocks and minerals in any part of the state. Some interesting specimens found are topaz, the Texas State Gem, from colorless to the blue variety. Many successful finds have been made in Mason County. A variety of agates are found in abundance around Alpine, Marfa, Sierra Blanca, Hovey Flats west of Fort Stockton and along much of the Rio Grande. Granite is found in huge domes in Central Texas. The red and pink granite is used for buildings and monuments. The Texas State Capitol is made of Texas Pink Granite. Petrified palm wood is found in abundance and is the Texas State Stone. Amethyst is a prized purple or violet gemstone often found with perfect six-sided prisms. They can be found around Alpine and the Sierra Blanca and Quitmand Mountains near Sierra Blanca. Cinnabar, a red, heavy, soft mercury ore, is found west of the Big Bend National Park. Tektites are found in Texas. They are spheres of dark natural glass that show characteristics of objects that have passed through the atmosphere at extreme speed.

TEXAS TODAY

TOURISM: Texas sights, services and hospitality drew over 34.8 million persons to visit Texas in 1982. Texas' 200,000 hotel rooms generated $40.4 million in revenue for the state from the hotel occupancy tax. The average room rental was $45.20 in 1983 and the total amount of room revenue from vacationers amounted to $1.5 billion. Visitors to Texas in 1983 can be broken down into 10.7 million persons for business purposes and 24.1 million persons for pleasure travel. Also 31.7 million were from the United States and 3.1 million from foreign countries of which 1.2 million were from Mexico. This is a sizeable drop from the estimated four million Mexican visitors in 1981 and it is attributable to the fall in the value of the peso. The number of travel generated jobs in 1982 for the whole state of Texas was 283,917 (with Harris and Dallas Counties heading the list). Total travel expenditures by visitors amounted to $13.7 billion and this compares to $2.1 billion in 1973. There are 156 representative Texas visitor attractions as determined by the Texas Tourist Development Agency. State parks led the list of checkpoints with 1,787,876 visitors for the January to February, 1984 period. Other checkpoints for this same time period were: U.S. Corps of Engineers lakes (1,541,755), Museums (837,886), Private Attractions (such as one major one: Grand Prairie's Traders Village) (608,916), U.S. Department of Interior sites (397,866), State Tourist Bureaus (394,716), National Forests (128,119) and City Visitor Centers (81,021). Texas currently invests $4.3 million for travel development (ranking thirteenth in the nation) and the Texas Tourist Development Agency has a budget of $1.7 million. Media advertising cost $1.1 million. There are nearly 1,000 events that visitors can attend while enjoying Texas. For the first time in Texas history the Texas Capitol will not be open to the public on a 24-hour basis because of security precautions. One of the major tourist attractions in Texas is the Lyndon B. Johnson Space Center in Houston where over one million visitors arrive each year. On display is a docking module used for training astronauts and visitors may see the control room where U.S. missions are monitored. Also there is a full-scale mockup of the Space Shuttle. Tourist visits have increased for Texas' two national parks—Big Bend and Gaudalupe Mountains—both of which are somewhat isolated in far west Texas. **GAMBLING** Texas (unlike 17 states and the District of Columbia) does not have a state lottery. Texas law defines a bet as "an agreement that, dependent on chance even though accompanied by some skill, one stands to win or lose something of value." In this respect a person commits an offense (Class C misdemeanor) when betting on the partial or final result of a game or contest or performance of a participant in a game or contest or performance of a participant in a game or contest. Also it is illegal to bet on the result of a political nomination, appointment or election or to place bets in games played with cards, dice or balls. Exceptions to this law are when a person is in a private place, no one receives any economic benefit other than personal winnings and where the risks of losing and the chances of winning are the same for all participants. It is a felony of the third degree to be a professional gambler operating in a gambling place, receiving, recording or forwarding bets and promoting or selling any chances or lottery. The same offense applies to anyone who knowingly uses or permits someone to keep a gambling place. Nevertheless, the Texas Bingo Enabling Act of 1981 permits qualified organizations to operate legal bingo games to raise money for charitable, educational, religious and civic (such as medical, research, veterans and firefighting) causes. There can be a local tax on the proceeds of bingo games and the Comptroller of Public Accounts collects such taxes and returns them to communities where local voters have legalized bingo and where local governments have decided to levy the tax. A county, city or justice of peace precinct may permit or prohibit bingo games by resorting to an election. An organization that qualifies to conduct bingo games must get a license and pay an annual license fee based on annual gross receipts. Bingo games may not be held by a licensed organization more than three days per calendar week and for no more than four hours in any 24-hour period. No prize can exceed $500 in a single game and the total value of all prizes cannot be more than $25,000 on one occasion. Players under 18 years of age must be accompanied by a parent or guardian and no one can be denied admission to a game because of race, color, creed, religion, national origin, sex or handicap. There has been interest in Texas to revive legal gambling. Pro-gambling groups see it as a way to improve local and state revenue and draw tourists, but anti-gambling groups think it would increase crime and is the wrong kind of industry to attract to the state of Texas. **ALCOHOL** State laws govern the drinking age (presently 19) and the hours of sale and consumption of liqour. The degree to which a county or parts of a county are "wet" or "dry" is determined by local option. The Texas Alcoholic Beverage Commission is responsible for enforcing regulations dealing with the manufacture, importation, exportation, storage, distribution and sale of all alcoholic beverages. Licenses and permits to businesses selling liqour are issued by the Alcoholic Beverages Commission; beer and wine permits are issued by county judges. Texas raised the drinking age from 18 to 19 in 1981. It may be anticipated, however, that the drinking age will be raised to 21 on or before October 1, 1986. Under a federal law passed in July, 1984 states that have not enacted a drinking age of 21 will lose 5% of the federal funds allocated to highway construction during the fiscal year 1987 and 10% in fiscal year 1988. This is estimated at a $33.2 million loss for Texas in 1987 and a loss of $66.4 million in 1988. Currently 23 states have a drinking age of 21; four require a minimum age of 20; 11, including Texas, set it at 19; three at 18; and in nine states the minimum age varies between 18 and 21 depending upon the type of beverage. HOURS OF SALE AND CONSUMPTION. No person may sell, offer for sale, or deliver any liqour to the public on Christmas Day, any Sunday or before 10 A.M. or after 9 P.M. on any other day. A wholesaler may sell or deliver liqour to a retailer between 7 A.M. and 9 P.M. except on Sundays and Christmas Day. Mixed beverages may be sold between 7 A.M. and midnight on any day except Sunday. On Sunday mixed beverages may be sold between midnight and 1:00 A.M. and between noon and midnight. Hours may be extended in counties with a population larger·than 300,000 or by county or municipal ordinance. WET AND DRY COUNTIES. As of August 31, 1983 there were 171 counties in which the sale of distilled spirits is legal. The sale of mixed beverages was legal in all or parts of 87 of these counties; 36 were totally wet for distilled spirits; 75 counties were dry in part. In 12 counties only 4% beer is legal. In two counties beer and wines with a content up to 14% are legal. Sixty-nine counties are wholly dry. In the year ending August 31, 1983 there were 44 local option elections which changed the status in 19 counties with 25 counties electing to retain the status quo. REVENUES FROM ALCOHOL. During fiscal year 1983 the Texas Alcoholic Beverage Commission collected $287,108,056.91 in revenues from permits, taxes and confiscated sales. Permit and License Fees produced $12,186,756.25; beer, liqour, malt liqour and wine excise taxes, direct taxes, gross receipts taxes, service fees and cigarette taxes produced $273,597,425.13; confiscated sales produced $16,429.44. A miscellaneous category produced another $1,307,446.00 in revenue. Tax collection stations are maintained at 18 international crossings along the Texas-Mexico border. The Ports of Entry inspectors at these sites are responsible for collecting state tax on all alcoholic beverages imported by individuals into the State of Texas. Revenue derived from tax collections at Ports of Entry in fiscal year 1983 totaled $1,812,314.78. For reasons such as unlawful size, excessive amounts, intoxicated persons transporting liquor, refusal to pay tax, smuggling and possession by persons under 19 years, 8,374 containers of alcoholic beverages were destroyed. Ports of Entry are located at Amistad, Brownsville (2), Del Rio, Eagle Pass, El Paso (2), Fabens, Falcon, Hidalgo, Laredo (2), Los Ebanos, Presidio, Progreso, Rio Grande City, Roma and Ysleta. PERMITS AND LICENSES. During fiscal year 1983 the Alcoholic Beverages Commission issued 35,160 liqour permits and 55,182 beer licenses and wine and beer retailer's permits. ENFORCEMENT. In fiscal year 1983 local fines for violations of the Alcoholic Beverages Code amounted to $886,355.97. There were 25,532 criminal complaints filed and 15,052 convictions obtained which included 554 jail sentences. Dismissals numbered 2,139 and acquittals 58. There were 3,008 cases resulting in hearings for cancellation or suspension of permits or licenses in which no criminal complaint was filed. Three stills were seized; 110 gallons of mash and 16 gallons of moonshine liqour were destroyed at still sites. **DEFENSE** In peacetime the Texas Army and Air National Guard have a dual mission. They function as the organized state militia under the command of the Governor; they can be ordered to state active duty to provide trained and equipped units to assist civil authorities in the protection of life and property and the preservation of peace, order and public safety in the State of Texas. They are also the first line reserve components of the U.S. Army and the U.S. Air Force. In that role they can be ordered into active service by the President of the United States to provide trained and equipped units for war or national emergencies, or at such times as national security may require the augmentation of the United States Armed Forces. The Texas Air National Guard also has the peacetime mission of supporting the U.S. Air Force requirements worldwide on a day-to-day basis. The size and structure of the National Guard is determined by Congress. The composition and organization is determined by the Secretary of the Army and the Secretary of the Air Force. Allocations are made to the various states by the National Guard Bureau, as approved by the state governors. The Texas State Guard is a state reserve force subject to active duty in the service of the state, in time of emergency, to provide trained and equipped units to supplement the Texas National Guard and to replace the National Guard when that force is called into federal service. The size and structure of the Texas State Guard is determined by the Governor, through the Adjutant General of Texas. The authorized strength of the National Guard and State Guards of Texas is 25,438 (18,786 Army Guard; 3,663 Air Force Guard; and 2,989 State Guard). The actual strength is 18,109, Army Guard (including 743 women); 3,402 Air Force Guard (including 72 women); and 1,882 State Guard. Federal expenditures totaled $166,014,360 in 1983 ($107,872,00 Army; $58,142,360 Air Force). State expenditures totaled $7,035,852 ($5,252,448 Army; $128,012 Air Force; $230,815 Texas State Guard; $1,414,577 Department Administration). The state military forces are under the control and administration of the Adjutant General's Department of Texas, which is headquartered at Camp Mabry. **FEDERAL** During fiscal year 1983 the United States Department of Defense maintained 46 military installations in Texas. The ten army installations covered 425,054 acres and had an authorized fulltime assigned personnel (AFTA) of 90,091 (68,508 military; 21,583 civilian). A total of 112,449 persons were assigned to these army installations during 1983. The largest army installation in Texas is Fort Hood at Killeen, which covers 216,946 acres and has a total AFTA of 43,826 (38,970 military; 4,856 civilian) comprising the 1st Cavalry Division and the 2nd Armored Division. The 11 navy installations covered 29,461 acres and had an AFTA of 13,923 (7,553 military; 6,370 civilian). A total of 16,999 persons were assigned to navy installations in 1983. The largest naval installations are at Corpus Christi (2,718 acres; 7,059 AFTA) and Kingsville (3,986 acres; 2,379 AFTA). In both the major military-activity is flight training. The 25 air force installations covered 51,336 acres and

had an AFTA of 70,541 (39,100 military; 31,441 civilian). A total of 95,296 persons were assigned to air force installations in 1983. The largest air force installations are at San Antonio (Kelly Air Force Base: 4,721 acres; 18,252 AFTA; an air logistics center and Lackland Air Force Base: 6,784 acres; 8,212 AFTA; USAF Basic Military School). In total, military installations covered 505,851 acres in Texas and have a total AFTA of 174,556, including 115,161 miitary and 59,394 civilians, with 224,744 persons assigned to Texas military installations during 1983. Military spending by the United States Defense Department in Texas during the fiscal year ending September 30, 1983 totaled $13.6 billion (per capita spending $862). Texas ranks third behind California and Virginia in U.S. military expenditure. Included in this amount is $6,995,633,000 in defense contracts awarded to Texas firms. **NATIONAL AERONAUTICS AND SPACE ADMINISTRATION** The Lyndon B. Johnson Space Center is located on NASA Road 1, adjacent to Clear Lake, two miles east of the town of Webster and about 20 miles southeast of downtown Houston. Additional Johnson Space Center facilities are located at nearby Ellington Air Force Base. The Lyndon B. Johnson Space Center was established in September, 1961 as NASA's primary center for design development and manufacture of manned spacecraft, selection and training of space flight crews, for ground control of manned flights and many of the medical, engineering and scientific experiments carried aboard the flights. The Mission Control Center from which the manned flights, starting with Gemini IV, through the Apollo and Skylab series to the continuing Space Shuttle missions are monitored. The Space Center covers 1,620 acres and employs around 3,600 engineers, scientists, technicians and managers, while a further 6,100 aerospace industry employees work at the Center or in the surrounding business community. **VETERANS** The Veterans' Affairs Commission was created in 1927 as the Veterans State Service Office and renamed in 1947. Prior to 1927 the state provided direct benefits to the veterans of the Texas War of Independence and the Civil War, while federal benefits were provided directly to the veterans of the Indian Wars, the Spanish American War, Mexican border actions and World War I. The purpose of the Veterans' Affairs Commission is to ensure that the veteran and his or her dependents and survivors receive all the benefits to which they are entitled. Texas ranks fourth in veteran population and in 1982 ranked third among the states in the receipt of veterans' benefit expenditures. According to the Veterans Affairs Commission, as of March 31, 1982 there were 1,658,000 veterans in Texas, including 21,000 from World War I, 662,000 from World War II, 235,000 from the Korean conflict; 168,000 from service between Korea and the Vietnam War; 497,000 from the Vietnam War and 75,000 from the post Vietnam War period. In 1982 Veterans' Benefit Expenditures totaled $1,604,337,972, which included $138,538,064 in readjustment benefits; $367,177 in direct loans; $942,924,084 in compensation and pensions; $68,486,585 in insurance and indemnities; $446,708,594 in medical services and administrative costs; and $7,313,468 in hospital and domiciliary construction. There are ten Veterans Administration Medical Centers (hospital care components). In 1982 average operating beds totalled 4,846 and 84,612 patients were treated. In addition 1,786 veterans were admitted into and treated at seven non-V.A. hospitals. There are five national cemeteries in Texas at Fort Bliss, Fort Sam Houston, Houston, Kerrville and San Antonio. In 1982 there were 3,782 interments at these cemeteries. In addition to the veterans, there are 135,000 active duty military personnel who cite Texas as their home of record and there are more than 100,000 military retirees in Texas. Texas ranks second in both categories among the states, exceeded only by California.

TEXAS TODAY

TAXES Texas does not have a state income tax, yet its total state revenue for fiscal 1983 (September, 1982–August, 1983) was $14.62 billion. When trust and suspense funds are excluded revenues were $13.58 billion, a 1% increase over 1982 and the smallest increase in five years. Of the $13.58 billion 83.6% came from state taxes and federal funds. Tax collections decreased 1.8% in 1983. This was the first decrease in over 20 years. Federal funds made up 21% of the total receipts in 1983, up 17% over 1982. Taxes are the major source of revenue for the state government. Since 1979, tax collections averaged annual increases of 14.5% until the decline in 1983. The major source of state taxes was the sales tax. Sales tax receipts of $3.3 billion constituted 38.9% of total tax collections and about one quarter of total state revenue. The state sales tax in fiscal 1983 declined 4.5%, or $156,500,000 from 1982. The preceding year tax receipts had grown by 16%. Retail sales accounted for 61% of collections from this tax in fiscal 1983. The other 39% came from taxable sales and purchases in a wide range of other industries, including manufacturing, wholesaling, construction and mining. From the first three months of 1983 taxable sales from the retail part of tax fell by 2.3%. However, taxable sales in nonretail industries lowered 16.6%, because of a decline in business investment in the state. In the preceding two years, taxable purchases by business—of machinery, equipment and so on—grew at rapid rates. After the middle of 1982, however, these purchases dropped dramatically. Taxable purchases for exploration and production related to the oil and gas industry were down 43.5% between the first three months of 1983, a by-product of the oil and gas drilling slump which began to be felt in Texas in mid-1982 affecting construction, manufacturing and even retail sales. About 11% of sales tax receipts comes directly from various phases of the oil and gas industry, including exploration and production, refining, field services and retail marketing. An additional 19% is indirectly linked to the industry, so almost a third of the tax statewide is influenced by oil and gas activity, directly or indirectly. Sales tax receipts are forecast to grow 10.8% in 1984 and 9.9% in 1985. Oil production and regulation taxes, the second largest source of tax dollars in 1983, also felt the effects of the over supply of world oil. Tax is levied at a rate of 4.6% of the value of production. Oil tax receipts of $1.19 billion was a 9.6% drop from 1982. The natural gas production tax managed a bare increase in collections of 0.4 percent. Total severance taxes on oil and natural gas decreased $123 million due to the sharp decline in the oil production and regulation taxes. Total severance taxes represented 26.5% of all taxes in 1983, compared to 27.4% in 1982. The motor fuels taxes declined 1.2% to $490.4 million. Motor vehicle sales and rental taxes increased $9 million or 1.6% from 1982. However, these receipts had increased by almost 13% the year before. Corporate franchise tax receipts increased 15.4% to $555.3 million. These revenues increased in spite of a national recession due to a healthy Texas economy and the influx of new corporations to the state. Cigarette and tobacco taxes increased 2.6% to $355 million. Like license and fall revenues these taxes are levied at flat rates. Alcoholic beverage taxes increased 1.6% to $271.9 million. Beer and liquor, both levied at flat rates, brought in the most revenue. Occupation taxes on insurance companies increased 11.8% to $233.7 million in 1982. Increased premiums and the population growth aided the increase. Utility taxes reached $224.5 million in fiscal 1983. This was an increase of 19.3% over 1982, and a 41% increase over the past two years. Inheritance tax collections were down 18% to $88.4 million in 1983. The decrease was due in large measure to a change in the inheritance tax structure. Other tax sources include the telephone tax and the hotel and motel occupancy tax, as well as a number of smaller levies. Telephone tax receipts were $84.9 million in 1983. The hotel and motel tax totaled 40.6 million. The rest of the tax categories brought in $22.9 million,

a drop of 23.1%. At the present time the state legislature has passed, in a special session, a tax increase package that has been signed by the Governor. It raises the sales tax to 4.125 cents on the dollar, doubles gasoline tax from five cents to ten cents, raises auto taxes from 3 to 4% on sales and rentals, increases auto license fees, cigarette, liquor and hotel taxes as well as increasing corporate franchise taxes from $4.25 to $5.25 per $1,000 of property or capital stock and expanding the types of items covered by sales tax. These taxes have been changed mainly to increase expenditures on state highways and education. In 1983 then, per capita tax collections were $542.81, a 4.1% decrease from 1982. The proportion of taxes to income was an estimated 4.73% of personal income. State taxes are deposited in major state funds such as the General Revenue Fund which acts as the state "purse" even though much of the money must be spent on specific purposes according to the state constitution or state statutes. The State Highway Fund gets funds allocated to it for the purpose of constructing and maintaining highways. The Highway Motor Fuel Tax Fund holds funds that are allocated to various expenditures. One other major fund is the Mixed Drinks Tax Clearance Fund, which receives mixed drinks gross receipts tax revenue. On a quarterly basis 15% of these receipts are allocated to counties where the tax collection originates. Another 15% goes to cities on the same basis. The remainder is transferred to the General Revenue Fund. Federal funds are important sources of revenue for the state government. In 1983 Texas received $2.85 billion with about 83% coming for welfare, education and highways/transportation. The state administers federal grants and provides grants of its own to cities and counties. In 1983 it provided $71.6 million in grants, down 19.2% from 1982. State funds made up 69.1% of the total with the rest coming from federal grants administered by the state. Cities received 55.1% of the grants and counties received 44.9%. In addition to the funds received from state grants, cities have the option to impose a 1% sales tax. In 1983, 982 cities imposed the 1% sales tax to be collected with the state sales tax. About $897.9 million was returned to the cities in 1983. In addition metropolitan transit authorities (MTA) are authorized to impose up to an additional 1% sales tax. Currently Dallas, Fort Worth, Houston and San Antonio impose some portion of the 1% tax for their MTAs. The collected taxes provide the state with funds in order to operate and carry out its objectives. In 1983, Texas spent a total of $13.64 billion from all of its accounts combined. $13.54 billion was spent from all accounts except trust and suspense accounts. The greatest single category of state expenditure in 1983 was education. It accounted for 51.1% of the total expenditures with 46.5% going to support state and local education and 4.6% for the teacher retirement fund. Payments for welfare totaled 15.8% of all funds and 11.2% was spent on maintenance and contruction. Mental health, state homes and corrections spent 5.9% of the state expenditures. The rest of the funds were spent in a variety of areas from payment on a public debt to administrative expenditures. The federal government also had significant expenditures in the state. It had direct expenditures or obligations of about $37.6 billion in the state during fiscal year 1983, including $12.3 billion by the U.S. Department of Defense. In addition, the federal government provided $4.7 billion in grant awards, paid $6.4 billion in salaries and wages, made direct payments to individuals of $17.4 billion including $12.5 billion in retirement and disability payments, awarded $8.2 billion in procurement contracts and spent $962 million in other expenditures and obligations. The federal government also provided $1.2 billion in direct loans and $22 billion in guaranteed loans and insurance. **COMMUNICATION** The greatest change in communications has occurred in the telephone industry. Deregulation and the break-up of American Telephone and Telegraph has changed the nature of the industry. Texans now can choose their telephone equipment and long distance service from a variety of sources. In 1970, 87% of Texas households had telephones and by 1980, 95% had telephones. With the rapid population growth in many parts of Texas, the industry has been faced with the challenge of maintaining and expanding its services. For instance, Southwestern Bell Telephone Company, had to change the dialing procedure for people in the 214 area code making long distance calls within the 214 area itself. They will no longer dial just a one or zero plus the number. As of June 3, 1984 they now must dial one or zero plus their area code (214) and the rest of the number. This procedure was implemented because of the rapid population growth in the area. **TRANSPORTATION** Texas had 1.1 million more registered vehicles in 1983 than it did in 1982 giving it a total of 13.5 million registered vehicles. In 1983 there were 71,853 miles of roads in cities and 200,589 miles of roads outside of cities. Thus, there is about one car registered for every 100 feet of Texas roadway. Traffic congestion can be especially troublesome in the metropolitan areas. The Gulf Coast area of Texas had the most vehicle registrations per mile of roadway in 1983 with 88.1 vehicles per mile. The Dallas-Fort Worth Metroplex followed with 86.6 vehicles per mile. Comparatively, the Plains Region in western Texas had only 22.1 vehicles registered per mile. Construction and maintenance of the State's highways is a pressing problem for Texas. The State has built one of the finest highway systems in the country, but it is aging and construction costs are rising. The average lifespan of a road is 20 years, and presently Texas roads average 17.8 years old. Farm to Market roads are the oldest with an average age of 19.7. The Texas Legislature addressed this problem during a special session in the summer of 1984. It passed a nickel-a-gallon gasoline tax increase and greater motor vehicle charges which would help finance road contruction. In 1983 there were 3,823 reported traffic deaths which were down from the 4,271 reported in 1982. In 1983 deaths were counted as traffic related only if the injured died within 30 days of the accident. In addition, there were 208,157 reported traffic injuries in 1983. Traffic violations often lead to accidents. The most common violation reported in 1983 was driving at speeds under the limit. This violation contributed to 112,526 accidents with 558 deaths. Speeding over the limit contributed to 20,400 accidents, but 763 deaths were caused from this violation. Of violations reported, driving under the influence of liquor or drugs contributed to 934 traffic deaths in 1983, the most of any single violation. With the swelling of auto population on Texas roads, especially in metropolitan areas, the cost and type of mass transportation has become a much debated issue across the State. The most common form of urban public transportation in Texas is the bus. The size of transportation systems varies from a system that has one bus and two 15-passenger vans to a large metropolitan bus fleet of over 800 buses. Texas cities have never developed rapid transit such as rail; however, Dallas voters approved a metropolitan transit authority in July, 1983 that was empowered to expand the city's bus service and build a 160-mile rail system. Rapid public transportation is an issue that will be before Texas citizens for some time to come. There are two categories for municipal transit systems. A "regular" system in Texas is a system with five or more vehicles in scheduled, fixed route, intracity service. In August, 1982 there were 18 regular municipal transit systems in Texas. All of them were publicly owned. All other systems which perform some limited or special municipal transit service are classified as "special" systems. Texas transit systems have become generally unprofitable and government assistance has increased substantially. Farebox receipts covered only 28.5% of the operating expenses in 1982 with 17.2% of the operating revenue coming from federal assistance and over 50% from local government. Transit ridership in Texas' 18 municipal transit systems increased 1.1% between 1981 and 1982. The greatest increase was in Houston where it went up almost

2%. Over 90% of transit users are located in Texas' six largest cities. To supplement other sources of revenue and provide adequate funds for Texas' fastest growing metropolitan areas, seven cities are permitted to levy up to 1% sales tax for mass transit funds if approved by voters. The eligible cities are Houston, Dallas, San Antonio, Fort Worth, Austin, El Paso and Corpus Christi. Currently, Houston (1%), San Antonio (1/2%), Dallas (1%) and Fort Worth (1/4%) have approved a sales tax increase to fund mass transit. These funds are collected by the Comptroller of Public Accounts along with city and state sales tax. Each month the Comptroller sends the individual Metropolitan Transit Authority its share of the sales tax. Taxicab companies perform a vital transportation function in Texas. In many of the small urban and rural areas they are the only available form of public transportation. At least 339 taxicab companies were identified in 1981. Human Services Transportation Systems within Texas have evolved out of the need to transport clients of different agencies to needed goods and services. Many of the people using these services require specially-equipped vehicles and personal attention in order to travel. In some cases, local taxicab companies have contracted with the Human Services Agency to provide transportation for their clients. Texas has a vanpool program which has been successful, especially in the Houston area. In fact, 17% of all vanpools in the United States are in Texas giving it the most of any state. As of January 1, 1982, an estimated 2,700 vanpools were in operation on Texas roads. Intercity bus transportation is a very important form of transportation in Texas. In 1982 Texas had 119 certified motor bus carriers operating in Texas with intercity bus service available to approximately 1,000 cities. This was a slight decline in cities served, due partially to the drop in passengers travelling short distances between intermediate stops. Besides passenger transportation, buses also carry significant amounts of package express. As of September 30, 1982, the Texas Railroad Commission registered approximately 6,662 certified motor carriers. Usually, the motor freight lines can offer overnight service to the major population centers of the Southwest. Many carriers have interchange agreements with other motor freight lines which provide for their trailers loaded in Texas to go direct without transfer of cargo to most large metropolitan areas of the nation and to some areas of Canada and Mexico. Railroads play an important role in the state. In 1981 Texas was served by eight Class I railroad companies and 23 Class II and III companies. An average of 9.7 million gross ton-miles per mile of track moved over Texas lines in 1981. The average length of a haul in Texas by a Class I railroad was 540 miles in 1981. The most tonnage in 1981 of commodities carried on Texas lines were farm products with chemicals and allied products second, followed closely by non-metallic minerals and coal. Passengers are carried on two routes through the state. The Eagle, an Amtrak passenger train, runs north to south from Texarkana to San Antonio covering 529 miles. The second route is the Sunset Limited, also an Amtrak passenger train. It runs east to west from Orange County to El Paso covering about 900 miles. Because of the vastness of Texas and its varied economy, Texas has become more dependent upon aviation than any other state, except Alaska. As a result, there have been growing numbers of business and private aircraft in Texas. Transportation is by water as well as air. Texas has 604 miles of coastline with 35 ports, 12 of which are considered major deepwater ports. The Gulf Intercoastal Waterway runs in Texas from the Sabine River to Brownsville on the Mexican border. Crude petroleum and its related products are the main cargos through the ports with agricultural products also very important. The Intercoastal Waterway links the Texas ports with 9,812 miles of navigable waterways of the Mississippi and its tributaries as well as 2,500 miles of waterways in the Gulf South. In 1980 the Texas portion of the Intercoastal Waterway carried 65,607,467 tons of cargo.

TEXAS TODAY

EDUCATION Texas ranks 37th nationwide in median years of education of adults with 12.4 years of education per adult in 1982 compared with a 40th ranking in 1972 with 11.6 years. In 1970 less than half the adults in Texas had graduated from high school. Ten years later, over 60% had completed high school and almost 17% had earned college degrees. Among Texas cities, El Lago located near NASA in Harris County, had the highest percentage of adult high school graduates in 1980. Ninety-seven percent of the town's 3,000 residents had diplomas. Among the ten largest Texas cities, Arlington led the state in both census years. Over two-thirds of the city's adults were high school graduates in 1970. In 1980, 83.3% had diplomas. The city of Austin had the largest proportion of adults with four or more years of college—20.7% in 1970 and 30.6% in 1980. Fall enrollment data shows an increase of 7.3% in the total numbers of students in the 1,100 public school districts active in Texas within the past ten year period with an average annual growth rate of 79%. Total student enrollment in 1982-83 was 2,985,659. Over 55% of the 1982-83 student population was White, over 29% Hispanic, 15% Black, 1% Asian and .1% American Indian. Over 8% of the student population is handicapped. Texas ranked fifth nationwide in 1982 in percentage of minority enrollment as compared with a sixth place ranking in 1972. Total minority student enrollment increased from 39% in 1973-74 to 44.9% in 1982-83. From 1972 to 1982 minority enrollment increased by 255,787 while the number of white students decreased by 52,279. The net total increase from 1973-74 to 1982-83 was 203,508 students. Hispanic increases alone accounted for more than eight out of ten minority students added during this period with a 33% increase within this category. Asian student membership increased 629%, the greatest percentage increase during this ten year period. Texas, like other states, is seeking to improve schools and creating stronger educational policies. The Texas effort has been centered in the Select Committee on Public Education—a special panel of citizens and lawmakers created by the Texas Legislature in May, 1983. Common concerns included illiteracy, Scholastic Aptitude Test scores which fell 53% between 1972 and 1982 and lack of quality teaching. Texas with 2.8 million school children in 1983 and a projected school population of 3.8 million by the year 2000 faces a bigger challenge than states where school populations are dropping. Momentum to make comprehensive, fundamental changes to correct these problems has grown over the last year. While no final solutions have been adopted at this writing, recommendations for Texas, as in other states, have been concentrated in several areas such as attracting and keeping top quality teachers, improving courses and instruction time, providing adequate and fair financial support and streamlining the organization and management of the school system. Nationwide enrollment in colleges of education have been declining and those who chose the profession often come from the lower half of college classes. Inadequacies of Texas teachers were demonstrated when 62% of Houston teachers failed the reading portion of a professional skills test given in the spring of 1983. Forty-six percent failed the math portion and 26% failed the writing section of the exam. Low initial pay combined with little hope for advancement to a professional wage have been the most frequently cited reasons for the inability to attract top teachers. Nationally teacher salaries for the 1982-83 school year ranged from $14,000 to $34,000. Texas teachers averaged $19,500, 24th among the 50 states. Teacher pay increases have occurred in many states based on various reforms such as incentive pay plans providing more pay for outstanding teachers, master teacher program, increased minimum of average pay, professional improvement bonuses, bonuses to senior teachers or financial aid to retrain teachers in shortage subjects. Reforms proposed in Texas are similar to actions taken in other states. One proposal would raise a starting teacher's guaranteed base salary from $11,000 to $15,000 per year. The proposal would also add incentives through a career ladder program. The career ladder proposal would allow an outstanding teacher to advance to a professional wage while remaining in the classroom. Advancement would be based on classroom performance, additional academic training and added responsibilities. Other proposals which have gotten close attention include tightening course requirements in schools of education and allowing teachers to come directly from other undergraduate degree programs provided they apprentice under more experienced teachers. Other suggested changes include requiring all teachers to pass a basic skills competency test and strengthening accreditation standards. The quality of academic programs is another major concern. Suggestions for upgrading Texas programs have focused on how school time is used and what is taught. The Texas average Scholastic Aptitude Test score decreased from 921 in 1972 to 868 in 1982. The U.S. average was 937 in 1972 and 893 in 1982. The high school graduation percentage in Texas decreased to 68.2 in 1982 from 70.2 in 1972. Texas ranked 25th in graduation percentage and the national average was 72.8%. Texas reported an average 18.4 pupils per teacher in 1982 as compared with 22 per teacher a decade earlier. The national average for 1982 was 18.9 and Texas ranked 25th within this category. Texas is considering the extension of time spent on instruction during the school day, possibly increasing the school year from 175 days to 185 days. Some proposals provide for 220 days in the school year. Many Texas districts have already put in place an "exit" test requirement before granting a diploma. In addition, the Texas State Board of Education has considered a statewide two-track sequence of high school courses. Both programs would require more math and English and would add computer training to the school curriculum. Math and Enlish would also be emphasized in early grades. No less than two hours of daily instruction of English and one hour a day in math would be required in the first three years of elementary school. Major recommendations call for restricting class size through fourth grade to 15 students and making kindergarten mandatory at age five. Other suggested changes include required tutorial courses for failing grammar school students, creating an optional preschool program and tightening requirements for participation in extra-curricular activities. However, finding a way to pay for these changes has become one of the tougher issues of education reform. The state ranked 14th in percentage of federal funds received in 1982, up from 21st in 1972. In expenditures per pupil per capita income, Texas ranked 50th in 1982 and 49th in 1972. In percent of student population in poverty, Texas reported 18.4% of students between ages five and 17 living in poverty as compared with 21.5% in 1972. The exact costs of changes proposed for Texas schools are unknown. Estimates have ranged from an additional $100 million to over $3 billion extra each year, depending on which changes are adopted. Currently, Texas spends a total of $2,300 per student each year, 42nd among the 50 states. The estimated costs of suggested reform could increase spending per student by as little as two percent or as much as 47%. The Texas Comptroller of Public Accounts presented a proposal for simplification of state funding formulas and a more equitable distribution of state resources to the children of Texas, based more accurately on the taxable property values of each school district. Under this program, the state will continue to pay the biggest share of public school operating costs. Last year the state paid $3.5 billion to local schools through the Foundation School Program, a quarter of the total state budget and 52% of public school operating costs. Texas proposals would abolish the elected 27-member state board of education and replace it with a nine-member board appointed by the governor. Also proposed are giving the state board authority to set statewide education standards and strengthening school district accreditation requirements.

14

HIGHER EDUCATION A follow-up study that was conducted in the summer of 1982 revealed that 58.8% of May graduates of Texas colleges and universities had entered the job market and 39.6% of them had found work within three months of graduation. Some 90% of the graduates remained in Texas to work; 62.2% in the Houston and Dallas/Fort Worth areas. The study surveyed close to 10,000 graduates of 13 Texas public and independent universities. In Texas there are 47 community/junior colleges which are public, two-year institutions of higher education. Each of these colleges is controlled by a locally elected governing board. They are open-door institutions available to all persons and are sensitive to the educational needs of their communities. The colleges offer over 149 different technical/vocational programs and provide more than 90% of the postsecondary technical and vocational training in Texas. University parallel programs are offered for students who will transfer to senior (four year) institutions. Total appropriations to the public community/junior colleges for the 1982-83 biennium was $700,189,276, a 42% increase over the 1980-81 biennium appropriation of $491,908,162. The Texas legislature included funds for new campus startups including the establishment of the Southwest Collegiate Institute for the Deaf at Harvard County Community College. Funding for the various programs offered by the colleges is from five primary sources. Public community colleges receive an appropriation from the state, based on a contract hour of instruction rate for approved vocational/technical programs, through the Central Education Agency and for approved academic courses through the Coordinating Board. With this assistance the colleges use local tax revenues, tuitions, fees, gifts and grants to finance their operations. For fiscal year 1980, the state appropriation provided 64% of the total cost of operations. The Coordinating Board, Texas College and University System, is responsible for higher educational planning and coordination. In addition to those duties, it also distributes trustee funds for numerous public and private entities and activities ranging from Baylor College of Medicine to Tuition Equalization Grants. Appropriations for the state's 33 senior colleges and universities for the 1982-83 biennium totaled $1,996,100,000. The total appropriations represent an increase of nearly 24% over the appropriations in the previous biennium. The major appropriation increases were in the areas of staff benefits, faculty salaries, library and building maintenance. Enrollments in Texas colleges and universities grew 6.28% in the fall of 1982, the largest increase in six years. Growth was concentrated in public universities and community colleges where close to 42,000 additional students enrolled. In 1982 all Texas public universities, including community/junior colleges, had a fall 1982 enrollment of 645,072, a seven percent increase from the previous year. Independent institutions had a total enrollment of 80,465, a 0.34% increase from the previous year. While continuing to stress efficient use of existing facilities and academic resources, the Coordinating Board authorized 32 new degree programs and $127 million in campus construction and repair projects to accommodate the growing student population. A proposed constitutional amendment would provide a permanent source of building funds for public universities outside the University of Texas and Texas A & M University Systems and would allow all University of Texas and Texas A & M schools to participate in the Permanent University Fund. New state programs are underway to increase equal educational opportunity. The state has pledged to upgrade Prairie View A & M University and Texas Southern University by implementing a state of high-demand degree programs and launching capital improvement plans totaling close to $250 million. Other higher education concerns in Texas are the need to reduce costly remedial education among entering college students, to increase state financial support of organized research in public colleges and universities and to improve recruitment efforts and career opportunities for nurses to avert future shortages. Although higher education reaped a 22.7% increase in appropriations for the 1984-85 biennium, a recurrent drop in available state revenues during the 68th legislative session underscored the need for effective use of limited resources. Higher education appropriations totalled $5.8 billion granted for an increase in funding for departmental operating expenses to replace obsolete teaching equipment. A 23% funding increase was approved for fiscal 1984, with an additional 2.4% funding increase allotted for 1985. Appropriations were also raised for utilities. Less than $9 million was earmarked for organized research at public colleges and universities in 1984, about $330,000 more than 1983 appropriations. Some $9.2 million was allocated for 1985. Advocates of additional funding for research cite the economic benefits reaped by the state from such projects. One example is the success of the cotton module project at Texas A & M University which has contributed to improved cotton production in the state. Researchers estimate that the $410,000 invested in the project has generated a return of $229 million per year. State appropriations for medical education in fiscal 1984 included $5.7 million for family practice residency training programs and $3 million for training resident physicians. The family practice training program is part of the state's attempt to provide medical services to rural and other underserved areas of the state. For the first time state funds will be provided for compensation of resident physicians at seven Texas medical schools with a total of $3 million to be administered in 1984. The average salary for faculty members of all ranks at Texas public colleges and universities rose above the national average in 1982-83. The average Texas salary was $29,200, compared with $29,100 nationwide. In the area of academic programs emphasis is being placed on academic quality rather than academic growth. Proposed new rules will make it more difficult for colleges and universities to create new institutions, departments or doctoral programs which could dilute available resources for other needs. In 1983 a total of 32 new degree programs for 21 public universities were approved, including five doctoral programs, 15 master's programs and 12 baccalaureate programs. New doctoral programs approved include a Ph.D. in physical therapy to be offered on the Houston campus of Texas Woman's University. The first of its kind in Texas and one of the few offered nationwide, the program will educate specialists in physical therapy research and teaching. By the year 1990 Texas institutions of higher education are projected to have combined enrollment of more than 850,000. The annual average growth rate of approximately one percent is considerably lower than the six percent growth rate during the 1970s and early 1980s. Yet the steady gain for most Texas colleges and universities places them in a more favorable situation than institutions nationwide which are expected to maintain relatively level enrollments thoughout the 1980s. Public junior and community colleges are predicted to grow at a slightly faster rate than the public universities between 1983 and 1990. During this period the universities are projected to enroll about 26,000 additional students. Anticipated changes in the state's demographic structure and the age distribution of the students are likely to strongly influence the growth patterns of all institutions of higher education as the pool of traditional college-aged students diminishes.

TEXAS TODAY

LIBRARIES Most Texans had access to a local public library. The State has a Legislative Reference Library which is an independent agency of the Legislature to perform functions and duties that had been performed by the Texas State Library. Operation is under the control of and administered by the Legislative Library Board, composed of the Lieutenant Governor, Speaker of the House of Representatives, Chairman of the House Appropriations Committee and one member each of the Senate and the House, appointed by the Lieutenant Governor and the Speaker of the House, respectively. The library contains reference material consisting of checklists and catalogues of current legislation of Texas and other states, bills and resolutions presented in both houses of the Legislature, all reports issued by departments, agencies, boards and commissions of the State and digests of public laws of Texas and other states as available. Materials include approximately 22,000 volumes; 1,500 bound journals, primarily in the fields of public affairs, law and current events and 2,500 rolls of microfilm. The Texas State Library and Archives Commission is the governing body for the Texas State Library. The commission has the responsibility for administering regional library systems in the State and encouraging public library development. It maintains and makes available for researchers the historical archives of Texas and administers the Regional Historical Resource Depository program. The agency also provides library service to state agencies, serves as a depository for U.S. government publications and administers the state documents program. The library serves directly the blind and physically handicapped citizens of Texas with recorded material, Braille and large print books. The agency maintains a records center, which stores and references semi-active records of state agencies and operates a microfilm laboratory. The Texas State Library and Archives Commission sets criteria and certifies Texas public libraries for membership in the Texas Library System. Public libraries must meet minimum requirements regarding expenditures, collection size, hours of service, staffing and service policies. County librarians must be certified by the State Library. Requirements vary according to the population of the county. A master's degree in library science is required for librarians in counties with more than 25,000 persons. **CHILD CARE** In 1983, Texas had 22,822 licensed day care facilities and 3,665 licensed 24-hour facilities. The Department of Human Resources (DHR) pays for child day care to help low-income families while parents are working, training for jobs or looking for employment. Single parents made up 84% of the families receiving this help. The services are furnished through contracts with churches, schools, commercial facilities and others. They offer children opportunities to develop physical coordination, self-esteem, good health habits, self-expression, social skills and communication skills. Victims of child abuse or neglect also are served in day care facilities when requested by child protective services workers. DHR contracted for $32.2 million in services for approximately 13,907 children per day at nearly 800 facilities. In 1983, the DHR spent $62.3 million for child protective services. The money provided a wide range of services to 165,664 clients from all socio-economic groups. When protection was required, the staff attempted to work with the child and family in the home, relying on the family's and community's resources. Sometimes, a court order was needed to remove a child from the home temporarily. The department would use a variety of resources to care for children removed from their homes. These included emergency shelters, foster families, group homes, foster treatment homes, institutions and residential treatment centers. In 1983, an average of 2,364 children per month received Aid to Families with Dependent Children (AFDC) foster care at a cost of $10.2 million in federal and state funds. An average of 1,525 children per month received foster care at a cost of $6.6 million paid entirely with state funds. From 1977 to 1983, the number of child care facilities under DHR regulation increased by 106%. **CHURCHES** In 1980, Texas had 16,111 churches with an estimated membership of 4,311,259 communicant confirmed, full members. There were a total of 7,781,967 religious adherents. It was estimated in 1983 that the U.S. Roman Catholic Church had the most members in Texas, with 2.8 million and the Southern Baptist General Convention of Texas was second, with 2.3 million members. **HEALTH CARE** Medical care is a vital aspect of the quality of life in Texas. The state has approximately 26,000 physicians and dentists, over 37,000 registered nurses and about 560 hospitals. It had 993 ambulance services as of December, 1983. These services included 240 private/commercial, 32 private/commercial receiving subsidies, 60 funeral home, four funeral home receiving subsidies, 93 fire department, 16 police department, 58 municipal, two government, 51 county department, 134 volunteer, 129 volunteer fire department, 61 hospital-based, 64 industrial, 11 air and 38 other ambulance services. In 1983 the Texas Department of Mental Health and Mental Retardation served more than 193,000 people from infants to the elderly. A governor-appointed board of nine members determines goals and policies and appoints a commissioner to administer programs. The department tries to provide treatment and services, when appropriate, in the community, so those with mental impairments can remain close to their families and friends. For the most severely disabled who require residential care, the department maintains a system of state schools for the mentally retarded, psychiatric hospitals and state centers. Because more people are being helped locally the number of people receiving care at residential centers declined slightly in 1983. However, many of those served at the centers tend to require longer-term, more intense care. These residential facilities never close. They offer complete care from bed, board, education and health care to recreation. Charges for service are based on financial ability to pay. State mental hospital are located in Austin, Big Spring, Kerrville, Rusk, San Antonio, Terrell, Vernon and Wichita Falls. Each state school operates as an independent school district. The restorative, rehabilitative and educational programs aid in the development of the physical, personal, social and economic resources of the mentally impaired. State schools for the mentally retarded are located in Abilene, Austin (with two schools), Brenham, Corpus Christi, Denton, Fort Worth, Lubbock, Lufkin, Mexia, Richmond, San Angelo and San Antonio. A facility at Waco is for emotionally disturbed youths, aged 10 to 17. State centers, located in Amarillo, Beaumont, El Paso, Harlingen and Laredo, offer special education, day care, respite and residential services for the mentally impaired. The Texas Research Institute of Mental Sciences, Houston, a nationally recognized research and professional training facility, also provides client services for many Harris County residents. A recreation center at Leander, north of Austin, is a rural setting for therapeutic programs involving camping, swimming, boating, fishing and outdoor activities for all persons who need the department's services. Many local services are offered by a statewide network of 31 community mental health and mental retardation centers. The centers help avoid unnecessary admissions to psychiatric hospitals and residential facilities for the mentally retarded, and they assist discharged clients as they readjust to life in the community. The number of people served at the community centers rose from 122,000 in 1982 to 135,370 in 1983. Volunteers are very important to the system. In 1983, active volunteers at 28 facilities gave 868,171 hours of service, which is equivalent to 489 full-time paid employee hours. An average of 11,290 volunteers each month aided department clients. Another area of care involves those people who require long-term care, such as the elderly. The fastest growing segment of the Texas population is the group 75 and older. This group increased by 38% between 1970 and 1980 and is expected to increase by 145% from 1980 to 2000. This group and the younger disabled are the most likely to have chronic illnesses or health conditions that limit their ability for self care and require social or medical assistance for an extended time. The Texas Department of Human Resources provides services for the aged and disabled. During the fiscal year of 1983, services were provided to an average of 42,400 aged and disabled individuals per month at an annual cost of $95.2 million. Community care services are provided to persons who meet the financial and medical-functional criteria for the services. These services include family care, that is furnished to aged and disabled adults who are functionally limited in daily activities. Services, for up to 20 hours per week, include assistance with personal care, housekeeping, meal preparation and escort services. These are provided through contracts with licensed health agencies. Primary home care is provided to eligible medical and certain other individuals whose chronic health problems cause them to be functionally limited in daily living. This home care is nontechnical and is prescribed by a physician and supervised by a registered nurse. Special services are provided to the handicapped such as counseling, personal care and help with the development of skills needed for independent living in the community. An Emergency Response System consists of full-time electronic monitoring for functionally impaired elderly or disabled persons who live alone or who are isolated in the community. Pressing a call button in an emergency activates a telephone and brings a response from the appropriate person or service agency. During the fiscal year of 1983, about 700 persons per month were able to live alone, with assurance of emergency response. Home delivered meals or meals served in a central dining area, provided hot, nutritious food for those elderly or impaired who needed it. Day activity and health services are delivered by licensed facilities and are available at least 10 hours per day, Monday through Friday. The services they offer include nursing and personal care services, physical and rehabilitative services, nutrition services, transportation services and other supportive services. Supervised living was available to eligible adults who required access to services on a 24-hour basis, but who did not require daily nursing care. Adult foster care has been provided by families serving up to three clients in their homes by preparing special diets, helping with daily living activities and by furnishing remedial speech, reading exercises or reality orientation, as well as other special services. Emergency care was provided in adult foster care homes or supervised living facilities or other facilities for up to 15 days with up to two 15-day extensions, if necessary. Adult protective services are provided without regard to income. This service provides protective services for individuals unable to protect themselves against abuse, neglect or exploitation. The department investigated 4,019 cases in 1983. Institutional care is provided by approximately 950 licensed facilities. These facilities provided care to about 57,000 patients per month. **SOCIAL SERVICES** The Department of Human Resources administers a variety of aids and benefits to help the needy. For low-income families with children, temporary financial assistance from Aid to Families with Dependent Children (AFDC) is a basic source for food, clothing and shelter. Case assistance usually consists of a monthly AFDC payment, supplemented by food stamps and energy assistance for eligible households. Cash assistance was furnished to an average of 303,000 children and their parents or caretakers per month in fiscal year 1983. That is up from the 286,850 persons served in the previous year. Total AFDC payments rose to $163.6 million in fiscal 1983, from $140.9 million in 1982. Payments averaged approximately $34 a month per person or about $1.13 a day. The Federal Food Stamp program is administered by the state Department of Human Resources. In 1983, food stamp applications increased by almost 20%. Total food stamp distribution to all the counties in the state in fiscal 1983 was $680,255,062 with

an average of 1,357,739 participants each month. There are several other areas of need that the Department of Human Resources (DHR) tends to and they do not always concern the economically disadvantaged. One problem that transcends categories is family violence. Family violence can occur in any home or family. The problem is serious enough in the United States for the Surgeon General to declare it a serious health problem. The Texas Department of Human Resources did a survey and found that 440,000 or 8.5% of the women in Texas were abused by their husband or live-in partner during the past 12 month period and 29.7% or 1.5 million women in Texas have been abused during their lifetimes. They also found that medical treatment was required for 30% of the abused women and less than 1% of the Texas women abused in their lifetime ever made use of a family violence shelter center. The Department of Human Resources supports community-based shelter centers for individuals during a family violence emergency. The shelter centers include temporary room and board, a 24-hour hotline telephone, information and referral, counseling, emergency medical care, emergency transportation, employment services, legal service or referral, community education and educational arrangements for children. Another area of family support is helping couples decide if and when to have children. Federal law required, in 1983, that the Department of Human Resources furnish planning services to Aid to Families with Dependent Children recipients who request them and to all qualified adults and minors at risk of births out of wedlock. Services include physical examinations, laboratory services, birth control prescriptions, devices and supplies, as well as counseling and education. In some cases, sterilization is furnished. According to a report by the Texas House Select Committee on teen-age pregnancy, more than 50% of all teen-age mothers were unwed and 80% never finished high school. It was also reported that 18% of sexually active women in Texas were teen-agers, who accounted for 46% of births out of wedlock. Health screening is another service provided to qualified persons in Texas. The Early and Periodic Screening, Diagnosis and Treatment program furnished periodic medical and dental checkups and follow-up treatment for individuals under the age of 21, who are eligible for Medicaid. During fiscal 1983 nearly 66,000 individuals received medical screening, while 74,000 received dental services. The cost was $12.9 million. In addition to health care assistance, energy assistance was provided to help low-income families cope with rising heating and cooling costs. The Home Energy Assistance program, for instance, furnished more than $35 million in benefits to more than 285,000 households, in fiscal 1983. The average household received about $121. The Energy Crisis Intervention program prevented energy cutoffs for low-income households. Direct payments of up to $90 per household were made to utility providers to prevent termination of service. In fiscal 1983, Department of Human Resources assisted about 6,800 low-income families, primarily the elderly and handicapped, with home energy conservation measures. Through contracts with community action agencies and other public service organizations, the Department of Human Resources furnished up to $1,000 per household for insulation, storm-windows, caulking and weatherstripping. Other areas of assistance were provided to needy Texans. Many of the assistance programs are funded by the federal government. For instance, in addition to food stamps the state administers other programs funded by the United States Department of Agriculture such as the National School Lunch program, which served $61 million in donated foods during the year to an average of 1.5 million children per day. Thus, the State of Texas provides and administers a variety of benefit programs to aid needy citizens throughout the state. In fact, state benefits for fiscal year 1983 came to a total of $1,926,445,313.

TEXAS TODAY

FIRE PROTECTION One of the finest examples of voluntary citizen participation is the volunteer firefighter. Fire destroys more property and takes more lives each year than any other natural disaster. According to the State Firemen and Fire Marshals' Association, there are some 1,550 fire departments and approximatley 50,000 firefighters in the State of Texas. Of these, only 15,495 firefighters are fulltime, paid professional firefighters; the vast majority of firefighters in Texas are volunteers. While fire protection is basically a local responsibility, some services, as well as assistance and training, are provided at the state level. Texas Forest Service conducts training programs to assist rural communities to fulfill their fire protection needs. In 1980 a new system was set up by the Texas Forest Service using "Contact Trainers" in ten different areas of the State. Basic courses in wildland fire behavior and tactics are provided for some 5,000 paid and voulunteer rural firefighters each year. The training is conducted in the towns and at the convenience of the fire departments. A new system, introduced in 1982, is known as "Train the Trainer". Since 1982 some 1,645 individuals have benefited from this program and returned to pass on that training in their home areas. Texas Forest Service is responsible for forest fire protection to 22.4 million acres of land in East Texas. Of the 450 employees of the TFS, around 300 can be made available for forest fire fighting. The TFS contracts outside of the service for fire-spotting planes and pilots as needed. In very dry periods, 15 to 18 planes and pilots may be in the air above East Texas forests at any given time. The Texas Forest Service operates a Rural Community Fire Protection program to provide firefighting equipment and training programs to eligible communities all over the State. As part of this program 609 firetrucks have been provided to communities in 172 counties. The RCFP program, which is funded at the federal and state level, was established following a 1978 study which showed there to be 1,427 towns with populations of less than 5,000 which had no organized fire department and no trained firefighters. FIRE-FIGHTERS' TRAINING The Texas Engineering Extension Service of the Texas A & M University System has a Fire Protection Training Division that offers a broad range of courses to firefighters each year. Between July 1, 1982 and June 30, 1983 the Division offered 303 different programs which were attended by 17,537 firefighters. Among these were: Basic Firefighting: 41 classes attended by 1,009 firefighters; Advanced Firefighting (14: 278); Volunteer Fire Service Management (7: 133); Marine Firefighting (14: 264); Industrial Fire Training (53: 3,113); Weekend Firefighting (19: 823); Nuclear Plant Fire Control (1: 11); and Fire Cause Investigation (4: 83). Three classes of the Firemen's Training School attracted 3,544 firefighters. In addition 5,517 persons attended area conferences and 580 attended workshops conducted by the Fire Protection Training Division. The Texas Engineering Extension Service Also has an Oil and Hazardous Material Control Training Division which offers a variety of related courses such as oil spill control training, a tank truck rollover training course and a hazardous material control course. Thses are conducted at the Brayton Firemen Training Field at College Station. FIRES Information about fire incidents maintained by the State Fire Marshall are compiled from 17% of the fire departments serving 45% of the population in the State. In 1983 there were 66,754 fires of which 17,274 or 26% involved buildings, 14,933 or 22% involved vehicles and 34,547 or 52% were outside fires (trash, brush and natural cover). The losses from these fires was estimated at $188,966,000, while Statewide losses from fire were estimated at $500,000,000 in 1983. Fire-related deaths reported to the State Fire Marshal in 1983: 165 civilians (several firefighters also died in fires). Fire-related injuries: 869 civilians: 668 firefighters. A statewide projection of rural fire incidents (5 year average: 1978-1982) made by the Rural Community Fire Protection Division of the Texas Forest Service anticipates an annual average of 55,452 rural fires, of which 65% occur outside a city and 35% inside a city. Of these fires, 9,470 or 17% involved residences; 7,484 or 13% involve vehicles and 28,373 or 51% are natural cover fires. In 1983 the Texas Forest Service reported 1,132 forest fires in East Texas, burning 12,055 acres of forestland. This represented a 42% decrease in number of fires and a 48% decrease in acreage over the previous year. However in the first six months of 1984 the TFS has reported 1,626 fires, burning 28,000 acres. Causes of forest fires in 1983 were debris burning: 54%; incendiary: 24%; careless smokers: 4%; campfires: 3%; miscellaneous (railroads, equipment etc.): 14%; lightning: less than one percent. **LAW ENFORCEMENT** In Texas law enforcement is considered primarily a local responsibility. The State contribution is coordinated by the Department of Public Safety (DPS) which has three divisions: Traffic Law Enforcement Division; Criminal Law Enforcement Division; and Support Division. The Traffic Law Enforcement Division is primarily responsible for the police traffic supervision program and a range of support programs serving local law enforcement agencies and other divisions of the department. Highway patrol functions are the responsibility of the Highway Patrol Service, which in 1984 has an authorized strength of 1,534 commissioned officers. The Highway Patrol also assists local authorities in the handling of major crimes, civil disturbances and natural disasters such as hurricanes, tornados and floods. The Driver License System operates with an authorized complement of 397 commisssioned officers supported by around 350 clerks. This unit issues original licenses to more than 1,000 new applicants daily and renews over 2.5 million licenses a year. The License and Weight Service supervises commercial vehicle traffic operating on Texas highways. Primary duties include the enforcement of laws regulating weight, lease requirements, motor carrier regulations for-hire transportation of property and regulations applicable to the transportation of hazardous materials. Secondary responsibilities include limited traffic and general law enforcement on rural highways and providing assistance to local authorities during emergencies such as natural disasters or civil disobedience. This service has an authorized complement of 196 commissioned officers. The Motor Vehicle Inspection Service supervises more than 8,500 licensed vehicle inspection stations, conducts training schools and checks testing equipment. The service employs 118 troopers and supervisors who oversee approximately 16,500 certified inspectors. The 36 officers assigned to the Safety Education Service conduct a comprehensive program for the education of citizens of the state on matters of public safety and crime prevention and detection. The Criminal Law Enforcement Division coordinates statewide efforts against crime and lawlessness in all forms by providing specialized assistance to county and city law enforcement agencies and cooperating closely with federal law enforcement officers. The Texas Ranger Service is now a part of the CLE Division, having an authorized strength of 94 commissioned officers. The Texas Ranger Force is the oldest law enforcement agency with statewide jurisdiction in the United States. It was established in 1823 by Stephen F. Austin, who called for volunteers to "range" across wide areas to provide protection for the early settlers. The force was formally organized in October, 1835, just prior to the Texas War of Independence and remained as a (Texas) nationwide law enforcement agency. The experience and expertise of the Texas Rangers in the protection of the frontier and the Mexican border remained in demand after annexation. The modern Texas Rangers are responsible for the investigation of major felony crimes, the suppression of riots and civil disturbances and the apprehension of fugitives. The Narcotics Service, which had a strength of 169 commissioned officers in 1983, conducts narcotics investigations and apprehends individuals and organizations involved in trafficking and abuse of controlled substances. It exchanges information and maintains close liaison and reciprocal cooperation with local, other state and federal law enforcement agencies. The Motor Vehicle Theft Service with an authorized strength of 30 commissioned officers, coordinates investigations into motor vehicle theft among other law enforcement agencies in the state. The Criminal Intelligence Service conducts a broad range of specialized investigations involving organized crime and criminal matters of a general nature. The 50 officers assigned to this service work closely with local officers and coordinate active criminal intelligence activities. The Support Division is responsible for executive administration and administrative support functions. This division also includes units responsible for the Driver and Vehicle Record; Identification and Criminal Records; and Emergency Management. **CRIME** The Texas Crime Clock shows that in 1983 one major crime was committed every 34 seconds. One violent crime (murder, rape, robbery and aggravated assault) was committed every 6 minutes and 30 seconds and one property crime (burglary, theft and motor vehicle theft) was committed every 37 seconds. The overall crime rate in Texas showed a 6.2% decrease over the 1982 rate, with 8% fewer violent crimes and 3% fewer property crimes. The value of property stolen in 1983 has been estimated at $1,014,000,000 compared with $927,052,176 in 1982. In 1983 approximately $243,000,000 in stolen property was recovered by the police. In 1983, 7486 arson cases were reported compared to 8,201 cases in 1982 (an 8.9% decrease) with property damage amounting to $92,000,000. VIOLENT CRIME In 1983 there were 2,238 murders (compared with 2,463 in 1982), 6,334 rapes (6,814 in 1982), 29,769 robberies (33,603 in 1982) and 42,195 cases of aggravated assault (45,221 in 1982). PROPERTY CRIMES In 1983 there were 262,214 burglaries (285,757 in 1982), 503,555 thefts (501,312 in 1982) and 82,522 cases of motor vehicle theft (87,090 in 1982). STATEWIDE CLEARANCE PERCENTAGES Murder: 75%; Rape 58%; Robbery: 32%; Aggravated Assault: 63%; Burglary: 17%; Theft: 20%; Motor Vehicle Theft: 19%; and Arson: 23%. Almost 14% of the crimes were committed by persons under 18 years of age. The total number of arrests increased slightly in 1983 (913,888 compared with 908,858 in 1982). However arrests for DWI showed a 33% increase (149,621 in 1983 compared to 112,409 in 1982) and drug arrests (50,744) represented a 2.6% increase over 1982. Arrests for drunkenness (267,855) declined by 5.1% in 1983. Eleven Texas law enforcement officers were killed in the line of duty by criminal action in 1983; six died in duty related accidents; and there were 3,870 assaults upon officers. **COURTS** The basic structure of the present court system of Texas was established by an 1891 constitutional amendment. APPELLATE COURTS The amendment established the Supreme Court, which is the highest state appellate court for civil and juvenile matters and the Court of Criminal Appeals, which makes the final determination in criminal matters. There are now 14 intermediate Courts of Appeals which, since September 1, 1981, exercise intermediate appellate jurisdiction in both civil and criminal cases. Prior to that date, those courts had jurisdiction in intermediate civil appellate cases only. TRIAL COURTS The state trial courts of general jurisdiction are the 347 District Courts. The geographical jurisdiction of each District Court is established by the specific statute creating that court. In addition to these State courts the Texas Constitution provides for county courts in each county and not less than four and no more than eight justices of the peace courts in each county. The Legislature has established 49 additional "statutory" county courts to relieve the case load in the more populous counties. The Legislature has also established municipal courts in incorporated cities, which have jurisdiction over violations of city ordinances and concurrent criminal jurisdiction with the justice of the peace courts over state law violations. Municipal courts do not have jurisdiction. With a few exceptions, trials in the justice of the peace courts

and the municipal courts are not of record; appeals therefrom are to the county courts for a new trial. Appellate Courts do not try cases, have jurors, or hear witnesses. Rather they review actions and decisions of the lower courts on questions of law or allegations of procedural error. They are usually restricted to the evidence and exhibits presented at the trial level courts. Trial courts are those courts in which witnesses are heard, testimony is received, exhibits offered into evidence and a verdict is rendered. In a civil case, the verdict determines which party to a lawsuit prevails; in a criminal case, the verdict determines whether the defendant is guilty or not guilty of the crime with which he or she is charged. In all cases, parties have the right to a trial by jury of either six or 12 citizens of the locale. Except in capital murder cases the right to trial by jury may be waived. Determinations made in the trial courts can be appealed for review by the appellate courts. The district courts are the general trial courts for the state, having original jurisdiction in all felony cases, divorce cases, titles to land, contested elections and all civil matters wherein the amount at controversy is $500 or more. The district courts have concurrent jurisdiction with constitutional county courts in cases involving less than $1,000 and with statutory county courts in cases involving less than $5,000. Most district courts exercise both civil and criminal jurisdiction; however in metropolitan areas there is a tendency for courts to specialize in either civil, criminal or family law matters. District courts also have both original and appellate jurisdiction in probate matters. SUPREME COURT On 1/1/82 there were 49 regular causes (cases where there is an oral argument and a written opinion) pending in the Supreme Court. During 1982, 119 cases were added to the docket, 117 cases were disposed of, leaving 51 pending in 12/31/82. On 1/1/82 there were 180 applications for writs of error pending. During 1982, 765 new applications were filed, 113 were granted, there were 664 other dispositions and 184 were left pending on 12/31/82. On 1/1/82, 40 other writs and motions were pending. During 1982, 714 were filed; 709 were disposed of and 45 were pending on 12/31/82. The Supreme Court wrote 152 opinions during 1982. COURT OF CRIMINAL APPEALS On 1/1/82 there were 2,470 cases pending. During 1982 414 cases were added to the docket, 1,497 were disposed of, leaving 1,400 cases pending on 12/31/82. This court acquired the right of discretionary review on 9/1/81. Of the 33 cases filed in 1981, 27 were pending in 1/1/82. During 1982 1,060 new petitions were filed, 200 were granted, 724 were refused and 154 were pending on 12/31/82. On 1/1/82 311 writs of habeas corpus and other motions were still pending. During 1982, 1,745 new writs were filed, 1,840 were disposed of, leaving 216 pending on 12/31/82. The Court of Criminal Appeals considered 745 motions and wrote 1,397 opinions in 1982. The Courts of Appeals (formerly the Courts of Civil Appeals). In the 14 Courts of Appeal, staffed by 78 judges, there were 1,954 civil cases and 4,166 criminal cases pending on 1/1/82. During 1982, 2,920 civil cases were added to the docket, 2,442 cases were disposed of, and 2,432 were left pending on 12/31/82. Also during 1982, 4,691 criminal cases were added to the docket, 4,395 were disposed of, leaving 4,463 pending on 12/31/82. The Courts of Appeal wrote 6,509 opinions in 1982. In the 342 District Courts throughout the State, there were 425,687 civil cases and 80,078 criminal cases pending on 1/1/82. During the year 350,317 civil cases were added to the docket, 312,506 were disposed of, leaving 463,697 pending on 12/31/82. Also during 1982, 108,385 criminal cases were added to the docket, there were 58,757 convictions and 35,249 other dispositions, leaving 87,162 criminal cases pending on 12/31/82. There were 8,215 juvenile cases pending in the District Courts on 1/1/82. During 1982, 11,859 were added to the docket, 11,530 cases were disposed of, leaving 5,280 pending on 12/31/82.

JAILS Persons convicted and confined on misdemeanor charges serve their sentences in county jails. County jails are also used for holding persons awaiting trial if they have not been released on bail. In 1984 all but 12 of Texas' 254 counties have county jails and an additional twelve counties have closed their jails because they were not in compliance with the Texas Commission on Jail Standards. Many county jails are lacking in rehabilitation programs which would involve educational instruction, job training and counseling and the high cost of county jail construction makes it difficult to avoid overcrowded conditions. The Commission on Jail Standards exists to correct problems and to provide technical assistance to counties. There are 64 counties with prisons that are not in compliance with jail standards (there are 638 points of compliance) and 178 county prisons are in compliance. In April, 1984 all Dallas County prisons were found to provide a safe and sanitary environment. Dallas County has the second largest inmate population after Harris County which is not in compliance with the Texas Commission of Jail Standards. The Texas Commission on Jail Standards reported that at the end of 1983 there were 19,568 jail bunks in the state and an average jail population of 15,519, 79 percent of total capacity. In 1983 46 jails began new construction or renovation as 15 new jails opened and 14 jails completed renovation. The Commission received 73 complaints (a reduction of 29 percent over 1982). Also the Commission conducted 266 jail inspections with every operating jail, lock-up and low-risk facility inspected at least once during 1983. (The Texas Minimum Jail Standards can be found in the Texas Register Volume I, Number 97, December 17, 1976). In 1975 the Texas Legislature created the Texas Commssion on Jail Standards in recognition of the necessity of regulating county jails in order to avoid federal intervention in the jail system. The Commission publishes rules of minimum standards for the construction and operation of county jails, the number of jail supervisory personnel and the programs and services for prisoners. In addition to county jails there are 303 city jails which are not monitored or regulated by a state commission. The attorney general's office released statistics in 1984 on the number of suicides In Texas county and city jails for the period September, 1983 through mid-May, 1984. Of the twenty-one suicides that occurred during this time period, 11 were ages 21-30, 20 were male, nine occurred under three hours after being put in jail and ten cases involved drinking. PRISONS The Texas State Prison System is operated by the Texas Department of Corrections (TDC) and houses adults who are convicted felons. As of August 31, 1983 there were 24 state prison units located primarily in East Texas with 36,769 inmates, a 56% increase since 1973. In fiscal year 1983, 8,588 prisoners were paroled, 1,997 were discharges and 17,981 entered the prison system. Ninety-five percent of prisoners were men, five percent were women. By category of race, 44 percent were Black, 38 percent were White and 19 percent Mexican-American. A breakdown of prisoners by age shows that 21 percent were between the ages of 17 and 22, 32 percent were between the ages of 23 and 28, 23 percent were between the ages of 29 and 34, 12 percent were between the ages of 35 and 40, six percent were between the ages of 41 and 46, three percent between 47 and 52, two percent between 53 and 61 and one percent 62 and over. In terms of the length of maximum sentence that inmates are serving, 43.5 percent are serving three to nine years, 24.8 percent are serving 10 to 19 years and 10.5 percent are serving 20 to 29 years, 13.4 percent are serving 30 to 80 plus years and 8.8 percent are serving life terms. In 1983 Texas was second in the United States (after Florida) with 163 persons on death row. Inmates who are in prison for the first time make up 77 percent of the prison population. The average sentence of inmates was 20.33 years in 1983. The state prison units vary in size, function and type of offender incarcerated. The type of unit is different according to whether the inmate is a young first offender or older first offender, a repeat offender, a male or female offender and an offender with special medical needs. The daily cost per inmate was $14.57 in fiscal year 1983 compared to $3.89 in fiscal year 1973. This is an increase in daily costs of 73 percent per inmate during the past ten years. The yearly maintenance cost per prisoner was $5,318.05 in 1983 compared to $1,419.85 per inmate in 1973. The cost of construction (a separate item from prisoner maintenance) was $25,000 per in fiscal year 1982. The ratio of inmates to employees was 5.3 to 1 in fiscal year 1983, an improvement over fiscal year 1973 when the ratio was 6.1 to 1. There were 6,876 TDC employees in 1984. In fiscal year 1984, $321,083,232 was appropriated by the Texas Legislature for the TDC. The costs of the state prison system are significantly reduced by the labor contribution of prisoners in the work areas of agriculture (44,774 acres of crops) construction and maintenance and industry (metalwork, woodwork, textiles, furniture, highways signs and license plates, shoes, mattresses, etc.). The crops grown and livestock raised meet nearly three-fourths of the food needs of the state prison system. Texas has one of the least expensive prison systems in the United States. Nevertheless, two private prisons will open in Texas to handle illegal aliens and more private prisons may be established because of cost efficiencies in private prisons. Also the Texas prison system is only one of nine prison systems in the United States that is not filled to capacity. The once overcrowded state prison systems is operating in 1984 at 91 percent capacity after the TDC went to an early release program to lessen the overcrowding. Under this program inmates concited of non-violent crimes and who have good disciplinary records while in prison are freed 180 days early. In 1983, 7,118 prisoners were released early. A study by the State Board of Pardons and Paroles revealed that early release prisoners are not likely to commit crimes compared to prisoners released normally, but they are more likely to violate their parole. The early release program has allowed the TDC to phase out the use of tents which at one time housed 3,763 inmates in 380 tents because of overcrowding. A U.S. district court judge in 1980 ordered the TDC to allow each inmate 40 square feet of livig space. Prior to this some prisoners were held in cells as small as 45 square feet for three prisoners. However, there has been an increase in violence between inmates and against guards. In 1982 there were four suicides, six slaying, 399 assaults with weapons and 20,915 rule violations. In 1983 there were 11 suicides (a 125 percent increase), 10 slayings (a 66 percent increase), 601 assaults with weapons (a 51 percent increase) and 24,255 rule violations (a 16 percent increase). The January through March, 1983 period had 114 assaults on guards compared to the January through March, 1984 period which had 165 occurrences (a 45 percent increase). The filing of lawsuits by prisoners also has increased. In the Houston and Galveston federal districts these lawsuits cost the Texas taxpayer at least $630,000 in 1983. Over 1,000 prisoner lawsuits were pending court action; 60 percent were civil rights lawsuits and 40 percent habeas corpus complaints. **ATTORNEYS** According to a 1984 U.S. Census Bureau report, Texas ranked third in the 1982 dollar amount of legal service revenue, $2.3 billion. The number of law offices in Texas in 1982 was 6,962, the annual payroll was $779,278,000 and the number of paid employees was 33,458. The State Bar of Texas, created in 1939, is the association for all licensed attorneys who automatically become members when licensed by the Texas Supreme Court. In 1982 there were 35,591 bar members residing in Texas. Attorneys must conform to the rules of the State Bar and pay dues to cover all of the State Bar's operational expenses (no public monies are given to the State Bar). In return for the payment of dues the members of the State Bar can benefit from a well-developed program of continuing legal education which enables lawyers to keep up-to-date in their profession. The State Bar is an administrative agency of the judicial branch, its principal objective is to educate and inform its members and has helped the Texas Supreme Court establish the Rules of Civil Procedure which are the basis for all civil actions in state courts. The State Bar in 1973 also helped revise the Penal Code which defines crimes and penalties. Texas is divided into 17 State Bar districts within which there is at least one grievance committee composed of local attorneys and nonlawyers who respond to complaints regarding violation of the standards of conduct for lawyers defined in the Code of Professional Responsibility. The State Bar has the power to discipline (a public or private reprimand), suspend and disbar attorneys who are found in violation of professional ethics after an investigation, hearing and formal report. In Texas an accused attorney must agree with the decision of the grievance committee. Otherwise a formal complaint may be filed in a county district court and a civil suit is underway. The State Bar employs a general counsel (located in the central offices at Austin) to help grievance committees. Estimates of the number of cases before grievance committees in any one year range from 2,000 to 3,000 and the *TEXAS BAR JOURNAL* claims that one-third of all grievances result from poor communications between lawyers and their clients or from delays in handling cases. Almost one-fifth of the grievances regard fees. In May, 1984 the U.S. Supreme Court *(Hoover v. Ronwin)* upheld the power of all state bar associations to regulate the number of new attorneys through administering state bar examinations. To practice law in a state a person must (among other things) pass a bar examination and only a specified number of applicants pass. The attorney general of Texas filed a "friend of the court" brief arguing that bar examinations should not be exempt from federal anti-competition laws. The Texas Supreme Court came out against the attorney general's opinion. By a narrow 4 to 3 vote the U.S. Supreme Court upheld the present licensing system controlled by state bar association still exempt from anti-trust law. The Texas State Bar also operates a Lawyer Referral Service which receives 2,700 calls per month from people who are in need of legal services and an attorney. There is a Prepaid Legal Services Program which makes legal help available to policyholders at an affordable price. The Texas Lawyers Care program provides legal help to low-income clients. **INSURANCE** The State Board of Insurance regulates the insurance and fire prevention industries according to the provisions of the Texas Insurance Code and other relevant laws. The primary objective is to promote financial soundness in the insurance industry and to protect the insurance-buying public. An estimated $14 billion in premiums are paid each year in Texas. The State Board of Insurance meets once a year to set rates for home and auto insurance. This State Board also licenses insurance companies, conducts statewide building inspections and arson investigations, approves new life, accident and health insurance policies, reviews advertising by insurance companies, examines the financial condition of insurance companies and answers insurance-consumer questions and complaints. On the basis of consumer complaints more than $10 million in additional claim payments were collected for policyholders in fiscal year 1983. Also this State Board collects the Texas tax on insurance premiums. Revenues from this premium tax amounted to over $201 million in fiscal year 1983. At the end of fiscal year 1982 (August 31, 1982) there were 2,021 insurance companies operating in Texas with 144,948 licensed agents. In fiscal year 1982 the state of Texas collected $214,211,734 in taxed and fees from insurance companies. Two federal insurance programs operate in Texas. The Federal Crop Insurance Program was in effect in 247 counties in 1980 and insured such crops as barley, citrus, wheat, corn, cotton, grain sorghum oats, peanuts, rice, soybeans, sugar beets and sugar cane. The National Flood Insurance Program provides insurance for residence, business, religious and agricultural structures in flood-prone areas. In mid-1982, 771 Texas committees were participating in

this program and there were 281, 742 policies in effect. Texas has a Mandatory Auto Liability Law which became effective January 1, 1982. This law requires Texas motorists to show evidence of financial responsibility by providing evidence of liability insurance when requested by a law enforcement officer. There is judicial conflict over the interpretation of this law: is the law violated when you do not provide evidence of insurance when requested or is it violated when you fail to maintain minimum insurance coverage? In 1981 there were 1,054 companies selling life insurance and Texas ranked second in the nation in the number of persons who purchased life insurance in 1981. As regards health insurance 71 percent of Texans under age 65 in 1980 were covered by hospital expense insurance, 66 percent had surgical expense insurance and 61 percent had physicians' expense insurance. Health insurance premiums have increased substantially in recent years and Texas ranked second in the nation in health insurance premiums paid to insurance companies in 1980. **UTILITIES** Texas leads the nation in the consumption of energy. In 1981 Texans consumed 11 percent of all energy used in the United States and a total of 8,300 trillion BTUs (British thermal units). Texas was fourth in per capita energy consumption at 464 million BTUs. Texas has many energy intensive industries as 50.5 percent of energy consumption goes to industry compared to 39.6 percent going to industry throughout the United States. In Texas transportation consumes 23.1 percent of all energy, residential users account for 16.7 percent and commercial users 9.7 percent. The natural gas utility industry had 3,319,000 customers in 1982 of which 91.3 percent were residential, 8.1 percent commercial and .6 percent industrial. The average natural gas price per MFC (thousand cubic feet) per residential customer was $5.09 in 1982 which was slightly above the national average of $4.97. The electric utility industry produced 206.4 billion kwh (kilowatt hours) in 1982 and sold 186.1 billion kWh as 32.6 percent went to residential users, 25.2 percent went to commercial users and 42.2 to industrial users. For the most part electricity in Texas is generated by fossil-fired steam or hydroelectric plants. Four nuclear plants are under construction, two at Glen Rose (Comanche Peak Steam Electrical Station, Units 1 and 2) and two at Bay City South Texas Nuclear Project, Units 1 and 2). The Comanche Peak plant (Unit 1) was expected to be in commercial operation in 1984 but a large number of unresolved safety-related issues are pending before a federal licensing board and it is unlikely that a license will be issued before April, 1985. Texas Utilities officials have said they will begin fuel-loading in August or September of 1984 in order to begin commercial operations by the end of 1984. The Public Utilities Commission (PUC) created in 1975 is a three-member commission that regulated utility companies. Prior to the PUC, Texas cities set rates for electric power, natural gas, water and telephone service. Today the PUC sets rates for all telephone service, for natural gas and electricity (if a city council votes to give up this power), water (when private or investor owned) and for electric service outside cities. When PUC decisions are appealed in natural gas rate cases, they go to the Texas Railroad Commission and then to state courts. In electric rate cases appeals from the PUC go directly to state courts. The PUC functions as a consumer-oriented body. Water rates are set locally by the Texas Water Commission does hear appeals regarding water rates and water rights. There has been a dispute between the city of Dallas and cities in the suburbs around Dallas concerning increasing water rates and this dispute has entered the state courts. In 1981 the state of Texas consumed 23.3 billion gallons of water and the percapita consumption per day was 206.7 gallons. There has been concern raised around the state that groundwater supplies are diminishing and existing supplies are being polluted. The total estimated amount of water accounted for distribution in 1981 was 256,920,824,000 gallons.

TEXAS TODAY

RECREATION Even though Texas is a vast state, one is never far from a State Recreation Property. Most properties have some facilities available, such as camping, picnicking, groceries, campsites with electricity and sewage, water, restrooms, showers, fishing, swimming, boat ramps, museums, exhibits, screened shelters, nature and hiking trails and historic structures. The size of these areas varies from the 38,500 acre Choke Canyon, to the burial site of Davy Crockett's wife. As of July 1983, there were 36 State Parks, 35 State Recreation Areas, 16 State Historical Parks, 18 State Natural Historical Sites, four State Historical Structures, three State Natural Areas and three State Fishing Piers. State Park and Recreation Areas made up approximately 189,000 acres in 1982. In East Texas there are 665,034 acres of federally owned land scattered intermittently across 12 counties. This land makes up Angelina, Sabine, Davy Crockett and Sam Houston National Forests. In addition to the forests, Texas has other federal facilities such as wildlife refuges, recreation areas and parks such as Big Bend National Park. Texas is also a land of many lakes. The state has more than 4,790 square miles of inland water and its lakes offer various amenities to help Texans enjoy their water activities. **SPORTS** Texas has its share of professional sports teams as well as semiprofessional clubs. Texans can go to professional football, basketball, baseball or soccer games as well as professional golf or tennis tournaments and see the major stars of the day. Texas has well defined athletic programs throughout its educational systems and its teams compete favorably in all divisions and categories of sports. In addition to watching athletic contests, many Texans participate in recreational activities themselves. **HUNTING/FISHING** Hunting and fishing are two of the most popular outdoor activities. Texas has nearly three million fishermen and 1.3 million hunters, and it is estimated that they spend $2.5 billion annually. The Wildlife Conservation Act of 1983 placed all counties in Texas under the regulatory responsibility of the Parks and Wildlife Commission; however, all current general laws and special statutes remain in effect from the date of the act until changed by Commission action. The following information is general in nature and may not reflect recent changes in regulations. Detailed information about game and fish regulations is available from local game wardens and offices of the Texas Parks and Wildlife Department. Texans may also call the Texas Parks and Wildlife Department's toll-free number, 1-800-792-1112, for information about game and fish regulations. All licenses issued by the Department, regardless of the month issued, are valid during the period of September 1st through August 31st of the following year, except for those licenses issued for a specific number of days. A combination hunting and fishing license is available for $12 to Texas residents who meet the requirements for resident hunting and fishing licenses. (A resident is defined as a person with American citizenship who has resided in Texas for more than six months immediately preceding application for a license.) A resident fishing license is $8.00 and is required of all persons who fish in Texas waters except persons under 17 or over 65 who are Texas residents, and non-residents from states granting similar age exemptions to Texas residents. Persons fishing on property they or members of their immediate family own or on which they reside are exempt. Other exemptions include persons fishing in the county of their residence with a trotline, throwline or ordinary pole and line without a reel or other winding device, those with a Texas commercial fishing license, members of a visiting tourist group of 25 or more fishing as a group, residents of a hospital or state school when fishing is part of approved therapy under the immediate supervision of an employee or other approved supervisor of the hospital or school, and persons holding a $1.25 exempt fishing license available to certain disabled veterans or the blind. A non-resident fishing license is $15 and a temporary (five days) non-resident license is $7. For Lake

Texoma, permits are available for $5.75 to fish in either Texas or Oklahoma waters. The permit is good until December 31 following the date of issuance. A temporary (14-day) sport fishing license is available for $5 to Texas residents only. A $20 license is required for any person who takes mussels, clams or naiads, or their shells, from public waters. A $45 fee is required for using a dredge. Texas has a reciprocal license agreement with Louisiana that allows resident sport fishermen of either state who are properly licensed or exempt because of age to fish common boundary lakes and rivers between Louisiana and Texas. The Texas Parks and Wildlife Department should be contacted in regard to specific saltwater fishing regulations. Texas has more than 600 public reservoirs, 16,000 miles of streams, rivers and tributary waters and 370 miles of coastline encompassing four million acres of saline waters that are managed by the Texas Parks and Wildlife Department. Texas, however, does not have a significant amount of public land for hunter use. Most of Texas is privately owned, so hunters must secure a hunting lease from land owners in order to hunt on the property. Fees and duration of the leases vary. Inquiries should be made locally about the leasing practices. A resident hunting license is available for $8, and is required of all Texas residents who hunt outside the county of their residence or who hunt deer or turkey anywhere in the state, with these exceptions: residents under 17 years of age or 65 years of age and over, residents hunting on land where they reside, and certain disabled veterans, may hunt deer or turkey if they obtain a $5 Resident Exempt Hunting License. Members of the United States armed forces may purchase a resident license if they furnish proof of active duty assignment at any federal installation within the state for more than 30 days. Other licenses include a combination hunting and fishing license for $12. Texas residents who are eligible and required to have a resident hunting or fishing license may obtain this combination license which is valid for both. An archery stamp for $6 is required, in addition to a valid regular or exempt hunting license, of all persons who hunt wild deer, bear, turkey and javelina during any archery-only open season. The stamp must be signed on its face by the person using it. A Texas waterfowl stamp for $5 is required, in addition to a valid Federal "Duck Stamp" and a valid regular or exempt hunting license, of all persons who hunt waterfowl. A white-winged dove stamp for $6 is required, in addition to a valid regular or exempt hunting license, of all persons who hunt white-winged doves. The stamp must be signed on its face by the person using it. A non-resident general license for $100.75 is valid for any animal or bird that may be legally taken. A non-resident small game license for $37.75 is valid for all non-game animals and all game birds that may be legally taken except turkey. (Not valid for any game animals except squirrel.) A trapper license for a resident is $10.75; non-resident, $200.75. It is required for taking, hunting or shooting fur-bearing animals or their pelts. A valid hunting license is also required for all non-residents and for residents taking furbearers outside the county where they reside. No person may hunt pronghorn antelope or antlerless deer without first obtaining a legal permit from the landowner or agent of the tract where hunting. In Duval, Maverick, Webb and Zapata Counties, a permit is required for hunting buck deer with forked antlers during the regular season only. This permit is required in addition to a properly filled out tag for buck deer from the hunting license. In Brewster, Culberson, El Paso, Hudspeth, Jeff Davis, Pecos, Presidio, Reeves and Terrell Counties, a permit is required for hunting elk. There are some permit exceptions in certain counties where the bag limit for deer is specified "antlerless by permit;" population or habitat conditions may be such that no permits will be issued. In counties where the bag limit is specified "either sex;" an antlerless deer tag, secured from the landowner or agent of the land where hunting, must be attached to all antlerless deer taken during the regular hunting season. This tag is required in addition to a properly filled out tag for antlerless deer from the hunting license. No permit is required for taking antlerless deer during archery only seasons. No permit is required to hunt antlerless deer on the Aransas National Wildlife Refuge in Aransas County or on the Laguna Atascosa National Wildlife Refuge in Cameron County. The following are general hunting regulations for Texas: Firearms; taking of game animals and game birds is limited to rifles, shotguns and other legal firearms and longbows and arrows. Firearms are further restricted as follows: it is illegal to use a jet gun or rocket gun or any firearm using rimfire ammunition in taking deer, antelope and elk. These methods are also prohibited in certain Panhandle counties fo taking aoudad sheep. It is illegal to shoot prairie chickens with a rifle. It is illegal to shoot migratory game birds with any firearm other than a shotgun that is permanently plugged to a three-shell capacity, including one in the chamber. Archery equipment; in taking game animals and game birds, the bow must be capable of shooting a hunting arrow equipped with a broadhead hunting point for a distance of 130 yards; broadhead hunting point must be at least seven-eighth inch in width and not more than one and one-half inches in width, and arrows must be marked with the name and address of the user in some non-water-soluble medium. Arrows may not be poisoned, drugged or explosive. Crossbows are not legal for taking game animals and game birds at any time. Shotguns with shells having shot no larger than number four may be possessed during the open archery only season but may not be used for taking deer, javelina or turkey. Legal archery equipment may be used for taking any game animal or game bird during any open season. Restricted devices; animals and birds not classified as migratory may be hunted from a motor vehicle, powerboat, or sailboat, or from any other floating device within the boundaries of private property or upon private water if no attempt is made to hunt any wild bird or wild animal on any part of the road system or public waters of this state. Calling devices, except recordings and electrically amplified calls, are permitted. Artificial light of any form may not be used to take game animals and game birds. Cables, chains, ropes or other devices connected between moving objects may not be used when hunting pheasant. Restricted areas; hunting is prohibited on any area designated as a wildlife sanctuary, refuge, nesting or propagation area and in state or federal parks except as may be provided by special state or federal regulations. Hunting is prohibited on any public road or road right-of-way. Hunting is prohibited on any lands of the Lowe Colorado River Authority. It is illegal to hunt or fish on privately owned lands or waters without the consent of the owner or the owner's agent. It is illegal to shoot or take turkeys from a roost by any means. Game animals and game birds: all of the following wild species listed are game animals or game birds and may be taken only during the seasons provided or as otherwise restricted; antelope, black bear, deer, desert bighorn sheep, javelina (collared peccary) and squirrel (gray or cat and fox or red squirrel); in Armstrong, Briscoe, Donley, Floyd, Hall, Motley, Randall and Swisher Counties only, aoudad sheep; in Brewster, Culberson, El Paso, Hudspeth, Jeff Davis, Pecos, Presidio, Reeves and Terrell Counties only, elk; and in Bexar County only, non-individually owned wild axis deer. In all counties, a buck deer is a deer with a hardened antler protruding through the skin and all other deer are antlerless or doe deer. Spike bucks are legal buck deer in all counties. All wild varieties of turkey, grouse, prairie chickens, pheasants, partridge, bobwhite quail, scaled quail, Mearn's quail, Gambel's quail, chachalacas, and all migratory game birds. Migratory game birds include all wild varieties of ducks, geese, brant, coot, rail, gallinules, plovers, Wilson's snipe (jack snipe) woodcock, mourning doves, white-winged doves, white-doves, red-billed pigeons, band-tailed pigeons, shore birds and sandhill cranes. Fur-bearing animals; trapper's license is required for taking all fur-bearing animals which include beaver, otter, mink, ring-tailed cat, badger, skunk, racoon, muskrat, opossum, fox, weasel, nutria and civet cat. A valid hunting license is also required for any person taking furbearers in any county other than the county of their residence. Landowners' or their agents are not required to have this license if these animals are found to be causing loss or damage to agricultural crops, livestock, poultry or personal property on their land. No person may hunt, take, possess, transport, sell or offer for sale or ship any of the following species or goods made from these species within the State of Texas. Holders of valid Scientific or Zoological permits issued by the Texas Parks and Wildlife Department are excepted within the restrictions of the permit. Endangered mammals; Blue whale, finback whale, right whale, sperm whale, black-footed ferret, jaguar, jaguarundi, margay, ocelot, red wolf, gray wolf, Mexican wolf, West Indian manatee, bighorn sheep. Protected mammals; lesser yellow bat, Rafinsque's big-eared bat, southeastern bat, spotted bat, bridled dolphin, rough-toothed dolphin, spotted dolphin, Palo Duro mouse, Texas kangaroo rat, dwarf sperm whale, false killer whale, goose-beaked whale, Gulf Stream beaked whale, killer whale, shortfinned pilot whale, pygmy killer whale, pygmy sperm whale. Endangered birds; brown pelican, southern bald eagle, American peregrine falcon, Arctic peregrine falcon, Attwater's greater prairie chicken, whooping crane, Eskimo curlew, interior least tern, ivory-billed woodpecker, red-cockaded woodpecker, Bachman's warbler. Protected birds; reddish egret, aplomado falcon, black hawk, gray hawk, white-tailed hawk, zone-tailed hawk, white-faced ibis, swallow-tailed kite, osprey, ferruginous owl, wood stork, least tern, golden-cheeked warbler. Endangered reptiles; speckled racer, Harter's water snake, Atlantic ridley turtle, hawksbill turtle, leatherback turtle, American alligator. Protected reptiles; Atlantic loggerhead, Texas tortoise, Atlantic green turtle, Big Bend mud turtle, Big Bend gecko, Big Bend canyon lizard, Presidio canyon lizard, reticulate collared lizard, Texas horned lizard, mountain short-horned lizard, Trans-Pecos copperhead, gray-banded kingsnake, rock rattlesnake, black-striped snake, northern cat-eyed snake, Texas indigo snake, Texas lyre snake, Big Bend milk snake, central plains milk snake, Louisiana milk snake, Mexican milk snake, Louisiana pine snake, Baird's rat snake, Trans-Pecos rat snake. Endangered amphibians; Cascade Cavern salamander, Texas blind salamander, Houston toad. Protected amphibians; Mexican cliff frog, Mexican tree frog, Rio Grand frog, white-lipped frog, black-spotted newt, Fern Bank salamander, Honey Creek salamander, mole salamander, San Marcos salamander, Valdina Farms salamander, Rio Grande siren, giant toad, Mexican burrowing toad. Endangered fishes; paddlefish, shovelnose sturgeon, Amistad gambusia, San Marcos gambusia, Big Bend gambusia, Clear Creek gambusia, Pecos gambusia, Comanche Springs pupfish, Leon Springs pupfish, fountain darter, bluntnose shiner. Protected fishes; toothless blindcat, widemouth blindcat, Rio Grande chub, Rio Grande darter, river darter, western sand darter, blotched gambusia, Devils Riber minnow, Conchos pupfish, Chihuahua shiner, Kiamichi shiner, proserpine shiner, Mexican stoneroller, blue sucker. Endangered plants; Texas wildrice, Parks (Navasota) ladiesstresses, Texas poppymallow, Tocusch fishhook cactus, Nellie Cory cactus, Sneed pinchushion cactus, Lloyd's hedgehog cactus, Black lace cactus, Davis green pitaya. Threatened plants; Bunched Cory cactus, Lloyd's Mariposa cactus, Pointed hedeoma. Other protected species; hawks, owls, eagles and most other nongame birds are protected by various state and federal laws. Only the following birds are not protected by State Law; European starlings, English sparrows, feral pigeons, grackles, ravens, redwinged blackbirds, cowbirds and crows.

TEXAS GOVERNMENT

CONSTITUTION OF TEXAS The present Constitution, Texas' seventh, was written in 1875 and adopted by Texas voters on February 15, 1876. The Texas Constitution is about 63,000 words long (the third longest state constitution) and as of mid-1984 there have been 258 amendments. In 1974, the Texas Legislature met as a constitutional convention and drafted a new constitution, but on November 4, 1975 Texas voters rejected ratification. The Texas Constitution (Article 1) begins with a Bill of Rights: "That the general, great and essential principles of liberty and free government may be recognized and established . . ." As the fundamental law of the state, the Texas Constitution establishes three branches of state government—legislative, executive and judicial—and separates and distributes powers among these branches. The Texas Constitution also distributes power among the levels of government—state, county, municipal and special district governments.

LEGISLATIVE BRANCH

The two house Texas Legislature—Senate and House of Representatives—passes the laws for the state of Texas and is considered the strongest of the three branches of government. Modeled after the U.S. Congress, all revenue bills and impeachment proceedings must begin in the Texas House, while the approval of executive appointments and the trial of impeached officials must occur in the Texas Senate. The 150 members of the House are elected for a two-year term of office and the 31 members of the Senate are elected for a four-year term. The Legislature meets in regular session for not more than 140 calendar days starting the second Tuesday in January of every odd-numbered year. In 1985 the 69th Legislature will meet in Austin. Special sessions, lasting no more than 30 days, may be called only by the governor who alone controls the agenda. All business of the Legislature must be conducted in open session (the only exception may occur regarding executive appointment proceedings). Day-to-day business is conducted through a committee system in both houses: the Senate has nine standing (permanent) committees and the House has 31 standing committees. Each house is required to have a quorum of two-thirds of its membership present to conduct business and members may be compelled to attend. Also each house is required to publish a journal of its proceedings and votes. Besides its basic law-making power, the Texas Legislature controls the public purse by deciding what money will be spent and what taxes will be raised. The Legislature's budget proposal usually is adopted instead of the governor's budget proposal. State agencies are required to report periodically to the Legislature about their operations and finances. The Legislature has the investigative power to call witnesses, compel the submission of documents, make state agencies accountable and write remedial legislation. In recent years the Legislature has investigated child-care institutions, telephone companies and the Texas prison system. Both houses can propose amendents to the Texas Constitution which require a two-thirds vote of the entire membership of both houses and majority electoral approval by the people of Texas. Legislators have constitutional immunities: they cannot be sued for slander or otherwise held accountable for any statement made during a legislative proceeding; they cannot be arrested while attending or traveling to a legislative sesion, unless it be for "treason, felony, or breach of peace." The PRESIDENT OF THE SENATE (who is the elected lieutenant governor of Texas) is the presiding officer of the Senate and has the power to name some committee members and to name all committee chairmen. The President has a strong leadership role in the legislative process of the Senate, determining, for example, what committee a bill will be sent. The SPEAKER OF THE HOUSE is the presiding officer in the House of Representatives and is elected to this office by House members. All committee members and committee chairmen are appointed by the Speaker and the Speaker determines what committee will consider a bill. It is common in Texas to refer to the "Speaker's team", which is composed of a bloc of House members that support the Speaker and control most House activities. Both the Speaker of the House and the President of the Senate serve on the following bodies: LEGISLATIVE AUDIT COMMITTEE directs the State Auditor's Office to examine all accounts and financial reports of state agencies. The financial condition of the state, and the results of expenditures and revenue operations are determined. LEGISLATIVE BUDGET BOARD has the responsibility to present at each regular legislative session a recommended general appropriations bill and a performance report on the operations of state agencies. The board receives appropriations requests from all state agencies and cooperates with the Governor's Budget Office to prepare budget estimates (but each produces separate budget documents). The board also determines the constitutional spending ceiling for a two-year period based on the rate of growth projected for per capita income in Texas. TEXAS LEGISLATIVE COUNCIL gathers information for use by the Legislature in writing bills. A data-processing division aids legislators in carrying out their duties. LEGISLATIVE REDISTRICTING BOARD is required (when the Legislature fails) to apportion state senatorial and representative districts after each U.S. census every decade in order to adjust to population changes. The board has 90 days to complete the reapportionment after the closing of the regular legislative session. The board has been used in 1971 and 1981.

EXECUTIVE BRANCH

Under the Texas Constitution the GOVERNOR OF TEXAS has the executive power and responsibility to (1) be commander-in-chief of the military forces of the state and to declare martial law if necessary; (2) call special sessions of the Legislature and control the agenda of such sessions; (3) deliver the state of the state message explaining the governor's programs and accounting for public money spent by the state and raised by taxation; (4) appoint members of many state boards and commissions and fill vacancies in state and district elective offices (all appointments are subject to two-thirds majority Senate approval); and (5) sign or veto every bill, joint resolution, order or vote (except regarding adjournment) passed by the Legislature. The governor of Texas is elected for a four-year term of office. Before 1974, the governor's term of office was limited to two-year terms. There are no constitutional limits to the number of terms a governor may serve, but the tradition in Texas is two or three terms at most. OFFICE OF THE GOVERNOR The governor's office is organized into several functional sections: Administration, General Counsel, Legislative Staff, Appointments and Press. There are other divisions in the governor's office: Governor's Office of Budget and Planning which plans and submits the governor's budget to the Legislature; Governor's Office of Economic Development which develops policy and coordinates state activities affecting industrial growth and technological development; and Criminal Justice Division which develops policies and programs and proposes legislation for improving the administration of the criminal justice system. In recognition of the importance of Texas' natural resources, there are two advisory boards and two advisory commissions closely affiliated with the governor's office: Interstate Mining Commission which promotes interstate conservation practices by studying mining operations and recommending improvements; Southern States Energy Board which collects and publishes information relating to the civilian use of energy, encouraging the development of energy in a responsible manner; Interstate Oil Compact Commission which promotes the conservation and maximum recovery of oil and gas and reports its findings to several states; State Conservatorship Board which assumes all powers and duties of a state agency if the Legislative Audit Committee determines that a condition of gross fiscal mismanagement exists in an appointed (unelected) state agency. The LIEUTENANT GOVERNOR is elected for a four-year term of office and exercises the powers of the governor when the governor dies, resigns, is removed from office, impeached, unable to serve or is absent from the state. The lieutenant governor has a significant legislative role as president of the Texas Senate with the right to give the deciding vote if the Senate is equally divided. Texas Senate Rules give the lieutenant governor considerable authority in the management of the Senate and its affairs. By law the lieutenant governor is also chairman of the Legislative Budget Board, the Texas Legislative Council and the Legislative Audit Committee. The lieutenant governor is a member of the Foundation School Program Budget Committee and the Highway Cost Index Committee. The ATTORNEY GENERAL is elected for a four-year term of office and has the responsibility under the Texas Constitution to represent the state before the Texas Supreme Court. The attorney general provides legal advice to the governor, state and local officials and agencies. Legislators turn to the attorney general for advice on the constitutionality of proposed bills. The attorney general may issue legal opinions and other decisions which are publicly available upon request. The attorney general inquires into the charter rights of all private corporations, preventing them from exercising any power not authorized by law and seeking judicial forfeiture of such charters when necessary. All proposed public bond issues are approved or disapproved by the attorney general. The attorney general rules when requests are made for government documents under the Open Records Act and the attorney general provides child support enforcement services to the general public and primarily to welfare families.

TEXAS STATE BUDGET 1983

Expenditures

Education	$6,966,060,581	51.4%
Services (Welfare, Health, Corrections, Law Enforcement)	$3,328,592,673	24.6%
Improvements (Roads, Natural Resources, Parks)	$1,728,599,602	12.8%
Administration (State Government)	$495,019,010	3.6%
Employee Benefits	$463,501,468	3.4%
Grants to Local Government	$401,339,878	3.0%
All Other	$156,363,250	1.2%
Total	$13,539,476,462	100.0%

Revenues

Tax Collections	$8,497,817,125	58.1%
Federal Funding	$2,848,870,319	19.5%
Interest Income	$1,754,754,853	12.0%
Land Income	$582,362,433	4.0%
Licenses and Fees	$542,238,626	3.7%
All Other Sources	$393,559,412	2.7%
Total	$14,619,602,768	100.0%

The COMPTROLLER OF PUBLIC ACCOUNTS is elected for a four-year term of office and has responsibility in four major areas of state governmental activity. First, the comptroller is the state's chief accountant responsible for maintaining effective methods of accounting for the state's funds. Second, the comptroller serves as a member of the State Depository Board which supervises the investment of state funds. Third, the comptroller is the state's principal tax collector and tax administrator. There are 82 field offices and 59 enforcement offices for the reporting and collecting of 13 separate state taxes. Fourth, the comptroller is required to provide the research and statistics necessary for revenue estimating and certification. At the end of the fiscal year (August 31), the comptroller must provide the Legislature with a sworn financial statement showing the financial condition of the state, including an itemized estimate of probable revenues and expenditures for the next fiscal year. The comptroller also certifies that appropriations bills can be covered by available in state funds. In this respect, Texas is a balanced-budget, "pay-as-you-go" state. The STATE TREASURER, Treasury Department, is elected for a four-year term of office and has the general responsibility of receiving and investing state funds and paying state warrants. To pay the legal obligations of the state the treasurer uses funds appropriated by the Legislature and certified by the comptroller. The treasurer and the Treasury Department safeguard securities purchased for the state's investment funds. The department administers the state's depository program as state funds are deposited into officially-designated Texas banking institutions. Also the department directs the tax stamp program used to collect excise taxes on cigarettes and certain alcoholic beverages and manages the state's unclaimed property program. The COMMISSIONER OF AGRICULTURE, Texas Department of Agriculture, is elected for a four-year term of office as an advocate for farmers, ranchers and consumers. The department is the major agency enforcing agricultural laws, administering agricultural service programs and protecting consumers in regard to the weight, measure, packaging, labeling and marketing of agricultural products. The department has regulatory and inspection programs in the areas of pesticides, plant diseases, pest control, nurseries, seeds and grain warehouses. COMMISSIONER OF LAND OFFICE, Texas General Land Office, is elected to a four-year term of office which has the primary responsibility to manage all state lands which produce state revenue. The commissioner and the Land Office award oil, gas, sulphur and other hard mineral leases for exploration and production on state lands and in state riverbeds, tidelands, bays and inlets. Mineral accounting procedures in the Energy Resources Program guarantees maximum public benefit to the state from the lease and rental of state lands. The Land Resources Program administers the surface leasing of state lands for all non-oil and gas mineral production. The Veterans Land Program provides long-term, low interest, one-time loans up to $20,000 per individual to qualified Texas veterans for the purchase of land. The RAILROAD COMMISSION consists of three elected commissioners serving overlapping six-year terms of office. The Railroad Commission was created in 1891 to regulate intrastate railroads, but over the years its jurisdiction and responsibilities have greatly expanded. Besides still regulating railroads, the Oil and Gas Division of the commission regulates the oil and gas industries, setting allowable production rates based on market demand and enforcing statewide rules for conservation, waste management and water pollution. The Gas Utilities Division administers state law regarding the rates of natural gas utilities. Also regulated by the commission are liquified petroleum gas, surface mining for uranium, iron ore and lignite and geothermal energy. The Transportation Division regulates the licensing, scheduling and rate setting for all commercial motor vehicles within the state that transport persons or properties. The SECRETARY OF STATE is the only executive office under the Texas Constitution that is appointed by the governor and confirmed by the Senate. The Secretary of State is the chief election officer in Texas, verifying petitions for candidacy to office, certifying the ballot for all general elections and constitutional amendment elections, administering campaign reporting and disclosure laws and tabulating primary and general election returns for federal, state and county offices. Voter registration applications and the state's master voter file is kept by the Secretary of State. The Secretary of State files the state auditor's report and compiles, publishes and distributes the Texas Register (a collection of state agency rules, notices, appointments, executive orders and attorney general legal opinions, etc.). The Secretary of State grants charters to Texas corporations (excluding banks and insurance companies), issues permits to corporations outside Texas to conduct business in the state, registers trademarks and processes extradition agreements for the governor. As a constitutional duty the Secretary of State keeps the Great Seal of Texas.

GOVERNOR-APPOINTED AGENCIES

The governor of Texas appoints (subject to Senate approval) hundreds of members to serve on over 120 boards, departments and commissions. The major ones are listed and described in alphabetical order. ADJUTANT GENERAL'S DEPARTMENT supervises and administers the military organization, command, training and communications of the Texas Army National Guard, Texas Air National Guard and the Texas State Guard. Besides preparing for and coordinating with national wartime contingency plans, these state military forces provide for civil defense, disaster relief and other state emergencies. TEXAS DEPARTMENT ON AGING develops and strengthens services available for the aged by assisting area agencies to develop local programs, by conducting studies concerning how aging persons can lead productive lives and by establishing community older worker employment programs and community senior citizen volunteer programs. TEXAS AIR CONTROL BOARD administers Texas clean air laws in a manner consistent with human health and the economic development of the state. Its four functional programs are monitoring stations that collect and analyze air pollution samples, control strategies and regulations to achieve acceptable air quality, control and prevention programs which include investigating citizen complaints and educational activities regarding the board's policies and services. TEXAS ALCOHOLIC BEVERAGE COMMISSION has the power to grant, refuse, suspend or cancel permits and licenses in the alcoholic beverage industry. The commission assesses and collects taxes and fees and investigates and prosecutes violations of the alcoholic beverage control laws. TEXAS COMMISSION ON ALCOHOLISM provides a broad range of services including the study and publicity of alcohol abuse problems, the promotion of educational programs on alcoholism and the distribution of state and federal funds to organizations that provide programs of identification, referral, treatment and rehabilitation for alcoholics. The commission also certifies educational programs for driving-while-intoxicated offenders and licenses alcoholism health care facilities. TEXAS ANIMAL HEALTH COMMISSION is responsible for the eradication and control of harmful diseases or parasites in livestock, domestic animals and domestic fowl. The Commission conducts livestock market inspection, individual herd inspection and/or testing, livestock exhibition regulations, systematic inspection of livestock products and the use of veterinarians who issue official health certificates, conduct tests and vaccinate livestock. TEXAS COMMISSION ON THE ARTS serves the people of Texas through Texas arts organizations and artists to provide coordination, information and financial aid for arts programs and to act as a motivator for the development of quality arts in the state. TEXAS DEPARTMENT OF COMMUNITY AFFAIRS provides a broad range of services designed to aid communities in the delivery of essential public services. The specific services of this department are: serving as an advocate for local governments at the state and federal levels; collecting and publishing information in order to function as an information center and referral agency for local governments wanting to know about state and federal services and programs; administering and conducting educational and training programs for local government officials; and administering state responsibilities for federal programs in Texas. The kinds of public services funded and administered are local government aid in housing, rural development, financial and personnel management, public works improvements, the state weatherization programs, the energy crisis intervention program (for low income and elderly persons having difficulty paying utility bills), drug treatment and prevention programs and training and employment development programs. TEXAS COLLEGE AND UNIVERSITY SYSTEM COORDINATING BOARD was created in 1965 to be the highest authority in the state in public higher education. Excellence in education is achieved by providing leadership and coordination in the efficient use of all available educational resources. The board cooperates with the private sector in higher education. The board's primary responsibilities are in four areas. First, academic programs are approved or disapproved in public senior colleges and universities, public medical, dental or health-related institutions and public community colleges. Second, financial planning and administration in higher educational institutions is required to determine legislative appropriations, to prescribe a uniform system of financial reporting, to make contracts with two private medical and two dental institutions and to study future educational needs. Third, physical facilities and campus planning is supervised to make efficient use of construction funds and to meet the space requirements of public higher education. Fourth, student services are provided to determine student financial aid and state residency requirements. TEXAS DEPARTMENT OF CORRECTIONS has the responsibility to manage the state's correctional prison system. Its tasks are divided into the following categories. Treatment: a variety of rehabilitative programs exist such as educational and vocational opportunities, religious activities and recreation. Agriculture: prison inmates farm over 100,000 acres of state-owned land in order to learn job skills and to provide much of the food requirements for the prison system. Industry and construction: industrial projects provide vocational training and use prison labor to help maintain the prison facilities. Special Services: support services such as record keeping, data processing, security measures and personnel development are carried out. Business and Executive: all funds are held accountable and general administration services and public affairs are maintained. Health Services: the health of prison inmates is monitored and provided for. General Counsel: the department's legal responsibilities and obligations in its operations are coordinated with the Attorney General's Office and other state agencies. TEXAS ECONOMIC DEVELOPMENT COMMISSION has the purpose of promoting business and industrial growth in the state. The commission attracts new business and industry to Texas and provides assistance to firms already in the state. Its activities include matching the needs of expanding businesses with those Texas communities seeking to diversify their economic base and encouraging small and minority business enterprises. The development of commerce with other states and foreign countries is advanced through trade shows and trade missions. An extensive library with a computerized information system provides social and economic information of interest to the business community. TEXAS EDUCATION AGENCY administers the public schools. Prior to the 1984 special session of the Legislature it had an elected board (the State Board of Education) of 27 members, each one elected from a congressional district. The 1984 special session of the Legislature changed this board to 15 members appointed by the governor until 1988 when the board members will be elected. The policy-making powers of the TEA remain the same: preparation of a budget for its programs; appointment of a commissioner of education (with Senate approval) who is the chief executive officer of the TEA; approval of textbooks; approval of policy and standards for public schools; administration of teacher certification; preparation and submission of reports on education for the governor and Legislature. TEXAS EMPLOYMENT COMMISSION has the general responsibility to operate the automated employment service program, administer the Texas Unemployment Compensation Act and publish labor market information to provide guidance for the labor force. Its services include employment counseling, occupational aptitude and proficiency testing, an applicant referral clearance system and technical assistance to employers. STATE ETHICS ADVISORY COMMISSION renders legal opinions on ethical issues related to state officals, state employees, lobbyists and political candidates. Created by the Legislature in 1983, the commission will propose legislation regarding the ethical conduct of public officials. TEXAS DEPARTMENT OF HEALTH has general supervision and control over all matters concerning the health of citizens of Texas. In the area of environmental and consumer health protection, the Department of Health has a Bureau of Solid Waste Management to protect the health, welfare and physical property of the people; a Bureau of Environmental Health to monitor water, sanitation, industrial hygiene and safety; a Bureau of Radiation Control which does licensing, registration and inspection; and a Bureau of Consumer Health Protection regarding food, drug and other products affecting public health. Personal health services are maintained through a Bureau of Maternal and Child Health, a Bureau of Crippled Children's Services, a Bureau of Chronic Diseases, A Bureau of Dental Health and a Bureau of Emergency Management for emergency medical services. Preventable diseases are studied and controlled in a Bureau of Laboratories, a Bureau of Communicable Disease Services, a Bureau of Epidemiology (for infectious diseases) and a Bureau of Veterinary Public Health. Under special health services the Department of Health licenses, regulates and inspects nursing homes, custodial and personal care homes, adult day care facilities and long-term care institutions. A Bureau of Vital Statistics collects statewide data on births, deaths, marriages and divorces. STATE DEPARTMENT OF HIGHWAYS AND PUBLIC TRANSPORTATION is responsible for the construction and maintenance of interstate, US and state highways and also farm-to-market roads. This department administers state and federal highway and transportation funds and develops a state public transportation plan. The Texas Gulf Intracoastal Waterway System is also administered by this department in cooperation with the U.S. Corps of Engineers. TEXAS HISTORICAL COMMISSION provides information, services and leadership for all who are concerned about the preservation of historical heritage. The commisson administers the National Historical Preservation Act of 1966, initiates revitalization projects and directs state archeological programs. There is a program to mark and register historical structures, sites and objects. TEXAS HOUSING AGENCY was created in 1979 to meet the needs of low- and moderate-income families and individuals. This agency investigates housing conditions in order to consider means of improvement. Mortgage loans are made to housing sponsors in order to purchase, construct, remodel, improve or rehabilitate residential housing developments. TEXAS DEPARTMENT OF HUMAN RESOURCES is responsible for the development and administration of programs to help persons with inadequate economic resources, who are unable to deal with social problems or unable to finance required medical services. Eligibility is established by federal and state law. The department administers income-maintenance, disaster relief and food assistance programs. Social services provided are family self-support services, child protective services, care for the aged and disabled and community referral and information services. The department has responsibility for certifying social workers and for regulating and licensing child care facilities and child-placing agencies. STATE HUMAN RIGHTS COMMISSION was established in 1983 to carry out the policies of Title VII of the Federal Civil Rights Act of 1964. The commission's basic function is to secure freedom from discrimination in employment practices and to promote the interests, rights and privileges of individuals within the state. INDUSTRIAL ACCIDENT BOARD administers state

workers' compensation laws and, as if it were a court, conducts hearings on work injury cases, makes awards and reviews compromise settlements. The board keeps data on the number of accidents, the number of claims and the amount of compensation awarded. Also the board administers the Crime Victims Compensation Act, reviewing applications for compensation, conducting hearings and awarding payments (not to exceed $25,000) to crime victims. STATE BOARD OF INSURANCE was created by the Texas Insurance Code to have overall responsibility in the licensing and regulating of insurance companies, agents and adjusters. Uniform policies, rules, rates and endorsements are approved and claims and complaints about the business practices of insurance companies are investigated. This board conducts financial examinations and oversees the corporate activities of insurance companies. TEXAS ADVISORY COMMISSION ON INTERGOVERNMENTAL RELATIONS undertakes projects to improve coordination and cooperation between state and local governments and between the state and the federal government. Studies and recommendations are made regarding these intergovernmental relationships. Continuous evaluations are made of the impact of federal programs on the state of Texas and the state's role in helping local governments carry out their public responsibilities. TEXAS DEPARTMENT OF LABOR AND STANDARDS has the function of enforcing the Texas Minimum Wage Law and Prevailing Wage Law, the Texas Child Labor Law and the Semi-Monthly Pay Day Law. This department also administers laws relating to boxing and wrestling, auctioneering, labor agents and personnel employment services. The Manufactured Housing Division regulates the manufacture, sale and titling of all housing plants and retail and broker locations. The department has 14 field offices to do investigative work and to conduct inspections. TEXAS DEPARTMENT OF MENTAL HEALTH AND RETARDATION is responsible for the conservation and restoration of mental health, the improvement of services for the mentally retarded and the effective administration of mental health and mental retardation services at the state and local levels. There are 31 community mental health, mental retardation centers, eight state mental hospitals, 60 outpatient facilities, two state centers and the Waco Center for Youth. There are 13 state schools for the mentally retarded, three state centers and more than 140 outreach programs. PARKS AND WILDLIFE DEPARTMENT has the responsibility for regulating and managing the state's wildlife resources, the state's park system and the fisheries program. The department promotes the safety of persons and property in the operation of vessels on public waters. Lake and stream management and the marine resources of the Texas coast are under its control. Environmental protection programs, species management programs and resource studies programs are conducted. STATE PROPERTY TAX BOARD provides a wide range of services to improve and standardize the operation of the property tax system throughout the state. The board is required to conduct, sponsor or approve courses of instruction and training programs on the technical, legal and administrative aspects of property taxation. The board prepares and issues a general appraisal manual, a digest of all laws relating to property taxation and other publications that inform taxpayers. The board also develops and prescribes a uniform property tax record system and conducts biennial studies to determine the degree of uniformity in each property tax appraisal district. TEXAS DEPARTMENT OF PUBLIC SAFETY is the state policy agency responsible for three program areas. Under the Traffic Law Enforcement Division, traffic law enforcement is provided through the Highway Patrol Service, the Drivers License Service, the Vehicle Inspection Service, the License and Weight Service (for commercial motor vehicles) and the Safety Education Service. Under the Criminal Law Enforcement Division, there is specialized assistance to local law enforcement

TEXAS GOVERNMENT

agencies and cooperation with federal law enforcement agencies through the Texas Ranger Service which pursues major felony offenses, the Narcotics Service which combats illicit narcotic traffic, the Criminal Intelligence Service which is directed against organized crime and other criminal and security matters and the Motor Vehicle Theft Service that coordinates investigations concerning vehicle thefts. Under the Division of Emergency Management, there is the development of governmental relief and recovery operations during major emergenices and disasters. The Department of Public Safety also has a Driver and Vehicle Records Division which maintains driver record files. The Crime Records Division operates the fingerprint and criminal record files and keeps the statewide uniform crime reporting system. PUBLIC UTILITY COMMISSION was established on June 21, 1975 with the passage of the Public Utility Regulatory Act. The commission represents and protects the public interest through the evaluation of public utility rates and services. The commission has original control over the rates and services of all telephone utilities, electric utilities (except municipally-owned utilities) operating in unincorporated areas and privately- or investor-owned water utilities operating in unincorporated areas. By appeal the commission has control over other investor-owned electric utilities. The commission may serve as an advisory body to municipalities. The commission requires that public utilities keep certain records and accounts and report information the commission considers useful. The commission has additional tasks such as the development of a long-term statewide electrical energy forecast, the evaluation of management and business practices of all regulated utilities every decade, the holding of regional hearings to collect testimony when a utility requests a rate change and the identification of long-distance carriers and telecommunications markets which are subject to regulation because they dominate the marketplace. The commission has a Consumer Affairs Office which annually assists more than 10,000 consumers who have utility problems. TEXAS REHABILITATION COMMISSION is the principal state authority in the rehabilitation of physically or mentally handicapped and disabled individuals. It provides handicapped citizens with services to allow them to enter or return to productive employment. The commission makes a determination of disability for Texas citizens applying for federal benefits under the Social Security Disability Insurance Program and the Supplemental Security Income Program. Evaluation of work potential and counseling and guidance is provided. Financial aid for medical treatment, assistive devices, rehabilitation training and education is available based on economic need. Job placement and halfway house services are also available. OFFICE OF STATE AND FEDERAL RELATIONS coordinates state and federal programs by informing the governor and the Legislature of the existence of federal programs which may be carried out in Texas and which affect state programs. Also this office provides federal agencies and Congress with information about state policy and conditions in Texas that are of federal concern. The effect of federal programs on state and local government is measured. VETERAN'S AFFAIRS COMMISSION of the State of Texas assists eligible veterans and their dependents to secure federal and state military benefits. County veteran service officers are trained to provide information, services and facilities for veterans. Assistance is offered in actual claim filing. TEXAS DEPARTMENT OF WATER RESOURCES carries out the laws of Texas regarding water. Judicial functions are performed by the Water Commission which judges water rights claims, approves plans for constructing levees and weather modification activities, creates and supervises water districts and issues permits regarding waste water discharge, solid waste, surface water sites and industrial and municipal waste sites. The Water Development Board is responsible for a comprehensive State Water Plan and a Texas Water Quality Management

Plan. Basic data is collected on the quality and quantity of surface and groundwater resources and needs. TEXAS YOUTH COMMISSION administers the juvenile corrections system of Texas providing programs for the care, custody, rehabilitation and reintroduction into society of children committed by the courts because of delinquent behavior. Care is also provided for dependent and neglected children when referred by the courts.

THE JUDICIAL BRANCH

Under the Constitution of Texas the state's judicial power "shall be vested in one Supreme Court, in one Court of Criminal Appeals, in Courts of Appeals, in District Courts, in Commissioners Courts, in Courts of Justices of the Peace, and in such other courts as may be provided by law." The Constitution also gives the state Legislature the power to define the jurisdiction and organization of courts established by law. The function of state courts is to hear disputes involving laws of the Texas Constitution and the Texas Legislature. Some Texas courts hear only civil cases (i.e., disputes between two or more parties or between the state and citizens concerning non-criminal matters), while others are authorized to hear only criminal cases. Yet other Texas courts hear both civil and criminal cases.

THE TEXAS COURT SYSTEM

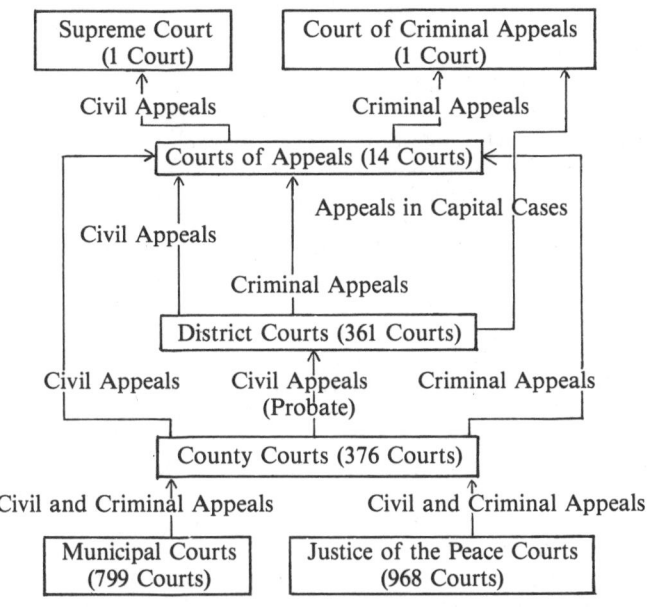

SUPREME COURT OF TEXAS The highest appellate court for civil cases, it has no jurisdiction over criminal cases. It serves as the final authority in proceedings for the involuntary retirement or removal of judges and sets the rules, procedures and policies to be followed in all Texas courts. The Supreme Court also has authority over several judicial agencies: it establishes rules for admission to the State Bar of Texas and appoints a board to administer these rules and approves the other rules and annual budget of the State Bar, as well as appoints some members of the State Bar Board of Directors and all members of State Bar Committees on Grievance Oversight, Professional Ethics and Unauthorized Practice of Law. The Supreme Court also determines the rules for the State Prosecutor Council, appoints the members of the Texas Court Reporters Certification Board and some of the members of the State Commission on Judicial Conduct. The Chief Justice has the special duty of certifying names of judges eligible for retirement benefits. The Supreme Court meets in Austin each year for a term beginning in October and ending in July. It consists of one Chief Justice and eight Justices. All nine are elected on a statewide basis for six-year, overlapping terms.

COURT OF CRIMINAL APPEALS The highest appellate court in the state for criminal cases, it holds a position over criminal appeals equal to that of the Supreme Court over civil appeals. With the exception of cases appealed from Municipal or Justice of the Peace Courts to County Courts in which the fine imposed does not exceed $100, the Court of Criminal Appeals has authority to review any criminal decision given by a lower court. All cases resulting in capital sentences are automatically heard on appeal by the Court of Criminal Appeals. The Court of Criminal Appeals meets in Austin each year from January through December. It consists of one presiding judge and eight other judges. All judges are elected on a statewide basis for six-year, overlapping terms. **SUPREME JUDICIAL DISTRICTS** Texas is divided into 14 Supreme Judicial Districts. COURTS OF APPEALS are located in each of these Districts. Each Court of Appeals has intermediate appellate jurisdiction over certain civil and criminal cases decided in District and County Courts. In civil cases the Courts of Appeals have appellate jurisdiction over all District and County Court decisions where the amount given in judgment exceeds $100 (not including interest or court costs). In criminal cases, the Courts of Appeals have appellate jurisdiction except for decisions appealed from Municipal and Justice of the Peace Courts to County Courts where the fine imposed does not exceed $100 and for decisions in which the death sentence is imposed. The number of Justices for each Court of Appeals varies from District to District. All Justices of the Courts of Appeals are elected by the voters of the District for six-year, overlapping terms. **DISTRICT COURTS** There are 361 District Courts in Texas. They are trial courts of general jurisdiction, usually over both criminal and civil matters. However, in metropolitan areas there is a tendency for the courts to specialize in criminal, civil or family law. In some cases the District Courts which specialize in criminal matters are officially known as Criminal District Courts. In criminal cases the District Courts have original jurisdiction over all felony case and over misdemeanors involving official misconduct. In civil cases the District Courts have original jurisdiction over cases of divorce, cases concerning land titles, cases contesting elections and all cases in which the amount in controversy is $5,000 or more. As a general rule they share jurisdiction with Statutory County Courts at Law in cases in which the amount in controversy is at least $500 but not more than $5,000. However the statute creating a particular County Court at Law may specify a different monetary level at which civil jurisdiction is shared with a District Court. In counties which have no statutory County Court at Law, District Courts have original jurisdiction over civil cases in which the amount in controversy is $1,000 or more and share jurisdiction with County Courts over cases in which the amount in controversy is at least $500 and not more than $1,000. District Courts have general original jurisdiction over all cases for which jurisdiction is not provided by the Texas Constitution or statutory law. The jurisdiction of District Courts over probate matters is both original and appellate (over decisions from County Courts and County Courts at Law). All judges of District Courts are elected by the voters of the District for four-year terms. **COUNTY COURTS** There are two kinds of courts at the county level in Texas. The Texas Constitution provides that there shall be a County Court in each county. These County Courts are sometimes referred to as Constitutional County Courts. The Texas Legislature also has the power to create special county courts, which are called County Courts at Law (and are sometimes referred to as Statutory County Courts at Law). Not all County Courts exercise judicial functions. In general, however, County Courts have both original and appellate jurisdiction over minor civil and criminal matters, as well as general control over probate matters. In civil cases where the contested amount is at least $200 but less than $500 County Courts share jurisdiction with Justice of the Peace

Courts. When the amount in question is at least $500 but less than $1,000 County Courts share jurisdiction with District Courts. In criminal cases County Courts generally have original jurisdiction over all misdemeanors when the fine to be imposed exceeds $200 or when a jail sentence may be imposed. Unless expressly provided by law, however, a County Court has no criminal jurisdiction in any county which has a Criminal District Court. Decisions of Justice of the Peace and Municipal Courts in both civil and criminal matters may be appealed to County Courts, but appeals generally take the form of new trials since most of these lower courts are not courts of records (i.e., transcripts of their proceedings are not made). Judges of County Courts are elected for four-year terms by the voters of the county. More than 100 County Courts at Law have been created by statute in some 50 counties, primarily in metropolitan areas, to relieve the constitutional County Courts of some or all of their judicial duties. The jurisdiction of County Courts at Law are defined by the statutes that created them. Some County Courts at Law handle civil cases, some handle wills and estates, some hear criminal misdemeanor cases and some hear cases appealed from Justice of the Peace and Municipal Courts. They are elected for four-year terms by the voters of the county. **JUSTICE OF THE PEACE** The Texas Constitution provides that each county is to be divided into from four to eight justice precincts, with each precinct having one Justice of the Peace. The Constitution also provides that if any justice precinct includes a city of 8,000 or more inhabitants, one additional Justice of the Peace shall be elected for that precinct. Justice of the Peace Courts have original jurisdiction in civil cases when the amount in dispute does not exceed $500. They also function as small claims courts in disputes over unpaid wages and salaries when the amount in question does not exceed $200 and in disputes over uncollected bills when the amount in question does not exceed $150. They have original jurisdiction in criminal cases when the fine to be imposed does not exceed $200. Justices of the Peace may also issue arrest and search warrants, conduct preliminary hearings, serve as ex officio notary publics, perform marriages and serve as coroners in counties which do not have medical examiners. Justices of the Peace are elected for four-year terms by the voters of the justice precinct. **MUNICIPAL COURTS** Statutes passed by the Texas Legislature have created 799 Municipal Courts. They have original jurisdiction in cases involving violations of city ordinances (generally traffic offenses). They also share jurisdiction with Justice of the Peace Courts in misdemeanor cases resulting from violations of state laws within city limits when punishment is a fine of $200 or less. The governing body of the incorporated city or town usually has authority to appoint Municipal Court judges. **JUDICIAL AGENCIES** The STATE BAR OF TEXAS provides rules for disciplining, suspending and disbarring attorneys in Texas, for State Bar operations and for the establishment of a professional code of ethics. The OFFICE OF COURT ADMINISTRATION OF THE TEXAS JUDICIAL SYSTEM promotes the efficient administration of justice in Texas. It assists the courts in fulfilling their administrative duties; examines and recommends improvements in business methods and systems employed in the offices of court clerks, court procedures and the expenditure of state funds; prepares and submits to the Legislature budget estimates for judicial operations; and performs additional duties as assigned by the Supreme Court. The COURT REPORTERS CERTIFICATION BOARD determines the qualifications of all persons applying for certification as court reporters; administers certification examinations; conducts hearings to examine charges of official misconduct by court reporters; and revokes or suspends certification of reporters following notice and hearing. The STATE COMMISSION ON JUDICIAL CONDUCT works to preserve the integrity of all judges in the state, to maintain public confidence in the judiciary and to maintain high standards of professional and personal conduct among judges. The Commission investigates complaints against judges, may initiate formal proceedings against them and takes appropriate disciplinary action. It may also issue private and public reprimands and public censure in cases of misconduct. It may require a judge to undergo a physical or mental examination and, when necessary, recommends to the Supreme Court the suspension, removal or retirement of a judge. the TEXAS JUDICIAL COUNCIL continuously studies and publishes annual reports on the organization of the courts of Texas; the rules and methods of procedure and the practice of the state's judicial system; the accomplishments of the courts; and the uniformity of the discretionary powers of the courts so that procedure may be simplified, judicial business expedited and justice better administered. The BOARD OF LAW EXAMINERS determines the moral fitness of candidates under examination for license to practice law in Texas and determines their eligibility for examination. Criteria for both these determinations are established by the Supreme Court. The PROSECUTOR COUNCIL is responsible for operations of prosecuting attorneys' offices throughout Texas. It has authority to develop minimum standards for operations of prosecutors' offices; provide techinical assistance to prosecutors; investigate complaints of incompetency or misconduct by prosecutors; and take such other actions as may be necessary for the improvement and more efficient administration of justice. The STATE PROSECUTING ATTORNEY represents the state in all proceedings before the Court of Criminal Appeals. He may also represent the state before any of the 14 Courts of Appeals when he judges that the interests of the state so require or when he is requested to do so by a district or county attorney. He also acts on behalf of the state in cases before the United States Supreme Court when requested to do so by the Attorney General. He may appoint one or more Assistant State Prosecuting Attorneys, whose duties and terms of office are the same as his own.

LOCAL TEXAS GOVERNMENTS

After counting the state government, the 1982 Census of Governments shows 4,180 other governments in Texas (the third largest number in the United States): 254 county governments, 1,121 municipal governments and 2,805 special districts (of which 1,124 are school districts). **COUNTY GOVERNMENT** Texas counties can be historically traced to Mexican *municipios* existing prior to the Texas Revolution for independence. The present Texas Constitution of 1876 restored county offices, rejecting revisions made during Reconstruction. Today counties are recognized by the Texas Constitution (Art. 11; Sec. 1) as legal subdivisions of the state. All county operations (unlike municipalities) must be authorized by state law and counties generally function as the administrative arm of the state serving state needs and purposes. In actuality, state supervision of counties is limited. Texas counties provide the following governmental functions: (1) conduct elections and register voters; (2) collect state and county taxes and fees; (3) administer portions of the court system (see the judicial branch); (4) provide some health care and welfare programs; (5) build and maintain roads; (6) keep vital statistics records (such as births and deaths); (7) sponsor some municipal-type public services such as libraries, hospitals, parks, museums, airports and prisons. The Texas Constitution establishes uniformity in county government as each one of the 254 counties has a commissioners court form of government and other specified elected officials. The commissioners court has no judicial functions. It does adopt a county budget and decides how revenue will be used to finance various programs and services. State law and the Texas Constitution define the kind of taxes and the maximum tax rate that the county commissioners court can set. The total legal limit for county taxes is $1.25 for every one hundred

dollars of property valuation (a county ad valorem tax). That $1.25 is divided into the following expenditure funds: 80 cents for the General Fund, the Road and Bridge Fund, the Jury Fund and the Permanent Improvement Fund; 30 cents for the Right-of-Way Fund (used for farm-to-market roads and flood control programs); and 15 cents for the special road and bridge fund. Some counties have been granted additional taxing power by two-thirds approval of their electorate to raise taxes for specific projects such as sea walls and sanitation. The other standard revenue sources are motor vehicle registration fees, fines and state and federal revenue-sharing. County indebtedness is limited by the Texas Constitution to 35 percent of a county's total assessed property valuation. The outstanding debt for all Texas counties in 1980-81 was $1,060,700,000.

GENERAL REVENUE, ALL TEXAS COUNTIES 1980-81
(in thousands)

Property Taxes	$893,900	50.8%
Fees, Fines and Misc.	$585,500	33.3%
Federal Revenue-Sharing	$120,500	6.8%
State Revenue-Sharing	$91,200	5.2%
Other Taxes	$68,700	3.9%
Total	$1,759,800	100.0%

DIRECT EXPENDITURES OF ALL TEXAS COUNTIES, 1980-81
(in thousands)

Health and Hospitals	$554,900	30.19%
Highways	$307,300	16.72%
Police/Fire Protection	$105,700	5.75%
Interest on Debt	$49,600	2.70%
Public Welfare	$41,900	2.27%
Education	$900	.05%
All Other	$777,900	42.32%
Total	$1,838,200	100.0%

ELECTED COUNTY OFFICIALS The Commissioners Court is composed of five members: COUNTY JUDGE is elected at-large to serve a four-year term of office and is the presiding officer of the commissioners court. As the chief executive officer of the county, the county judge represents the county at ceremonies, on boards and committees and on regional councils of government. In counties with fewer than 225,000 people, the county judge is the chief budget officer (otherwise a county auditor is appointed). In rural counties the county judge has judicial duties in the county court, but judicial responsibilities are few for county judges in major metropolitan areas. The county judge is responsible for filing with the secretary of state the final results of all election returns. All applications for beer licenses and waivers on mixed drink licenses are approved by the county judge. The county judge also serves as a notary public, may perform marriages and must sign delayed birth certificates. In counties having less than 3,000 school students, the county judge is *ex officio* school superintendent. The four COMMISSIONERS of the commissioners court are elected from four distinct precincts of the county to serve four-year terms of office. Individual commissioners supervise the maintenance of county roads within their precincts unless the county has established (fewer than 40 counties have by 1983) a "unit road system" under the Optional County Road Law of 1942. If county voters adopt the "unit road system", then a road department is established and a registered engineer is hired to administer and operate the road department. The commissioners court would still have a policy-making role regarding the road system. Besides budgetary responsibilities, the commissioners may issue bonds (with voter approval) to finance capital improvements. The commissioners can decide (without state authorization) to establish public services, regulate water wells, promote tourism and attract economic development to their county. COUNTY CLERK is elected for a four-year term of office to be the clerk of the county commissioners court. The county clerk is the recorder of legal documents (deeds, mortgages, contracts, etc.) and vital statistics (births, deaths, etc.). Many licensing requirements (marriages, hunting, fishing, etc.) are administered by the county clerk. The county clerk administers countywide special and general elections, certifying candidates and preparing the ballot. DISTRICT CLERK is elected for a four-year term of office to serve as clerk of the district court in counties with a population greater than 8,000 (otherwise the county clerk has the district clerk's functions and this is the case in some 76 rural counties). The district clerk is registrar, recorder, and custodian of all court activities and papers in any civil or criminal court in the county. The district clerk collects court filing fees and handles funds subject to court disposal. All divorces and annulments are reported by the district clerk to the Bureau of Vital Statistics of the Texas Department of Health. COUNTY SHERIFF is elected for a four-year term of office and serves as the chief law enforcement officer keeping the peace of the county. The sheriff appoints deputies, runs the county jail and is the security officer of county and district courts. The sheriff's department conducts criminal investigations, arrests offenders, serves warrants and civil papers and supplies bailiffs for all state courts. In counties with less than 10,000 people, the sheriff is tax assessor-collector unless the voters have approved a separate office for tax assessor-collector. COUNTY ATTORNEY is elected for a four-year term of office and forms part of the law enforcement team in a county. The county attorney represents the state in all criminal cases in county court and gives legal advice to county and precinct officials. In 17 counties there is no county attorney; an elected district attorney performs the duties of the county attorney. COUNTY TAX ASSESSOR-COLLECTOR is elected for a four-year term of office, having the task of assessing and collecting the county's property tax. The county tax assessor-collector must comply with state laws and regulations regarding assessment practices. In 1979 the state Legislature required counties to form one single countywide tax appraisal district. The tax assessor-collector also collects the sales tax on automobiles, issues and collects fees for automobile registrations and transfers of title and issues liquor, beer and wine licenses. COUNTY TREASURER is elected for a four-year term of office and receives and pays out all county funds according to the orders of the commissioners court. the treasurer prepares monthly financial reports for the commissioners court. This official keeps account of all revenues and expenditures of county funds and examines the financial records of all county officers who receive county funds. One CONSTABLE is elected from each justice of the peace precinct to serve a four-year term of office. The constable serves court actions called processes, attends justice of the peace courts and has the authority of a general peace officer who may make arrests. COUNTY SURVEYOR is elected for a four-year term of office and is paid only for specific jobs within the county. With the disappearance of open land requiring the work of a surveyor, this office is vacant in many counties. Otherwise, the county surveyor's duties would be the surveying of public lands. V.G. YOUNG INSTITUTE OF COUNTY GOVERNMENT was established in 1956 as part of the Texas Agricultural Extension Service at Texas A & M University. The objective of this Institute is to work daily with elected county officials to help them become more effective public servants. The Institute publishes a periodic newsletter and a variety of pamphlets and holds an annual conference for county officials. Conference topics have been county road construction and maintenance, judicial conduct, ways to improve public relations and a mock "Driving-While-Intoxicated Trial" for county judges. **APPOINTED COUNTY OFFICIALS** COUNTY AUDITOR

is required for any county with a population of at least 35,000 people or tax values in excess of $15 million. The district judge or judges of the county appoint a county auditor for a two-year term of office to function as the chief budget and finance officer of the county. The auditor examines the accounts and records of all county officers and departments, prepares the county budget, verifies funds received and funds spent and establishes the accounting system used for collecting county revenue. In many counties the auditor's work has expanded in practice to include many of the duties assigned by law to the county treasurer. COUNTY HEALTH OFFICER is appointed by the commissioners court for a two-year term of office to enforce public health requirements established by the State Board of Health. The state requires that all counties appoint a competent, state-licensed physician to serve in this office. Disease prevention, public sanitation, inspections, quarantine decisions and vital statistics gathering are some of the health officers functions. COUNTY ENGINEER is appointed by the commissioners court for a two-year term of office in order to have a person oversee the construction and maintenance of county roads, bridges and highways. The county engineer provides technical assistance regarding any county transportation project. There are about 40 appointed county engineers in Texas. JUVENILE BOARD AND OFFICER is determined by regulations in each county. All counties have juvenile officers and more than 50 percent of the counties have a juvenile board. Usually the county judge and one or more district court judges serve to ensure that juvenile cases are handled properly.

MUNICIPALITIES

The 1980 Census shows that Texas' population is 80 percent urban compared to an 80 percent rural population at the beginning of the twentieth century. Texas is the only state in the Union to have three cities among the nation's top ten in population. Texas has had the highest population growth rate of any state in the last 20 years. Consequently, the types and forms, functions and services of municipal government have become increasingly important. There are two types of municipalities by law: GENERAL LAW CITIES which have a population of 5,000 or less and are chartered or incorporated only under the general laws of Texas; HOME-RULE CITIES which have more than 5,000 people and have been adopted since 1912 when a majority of a city's electors so decide. SPECIAL LAW CITIES were chartered prior to 1912 but operate in the same manner as home-rule cities. If a general law city has its population increase to over 5,000 people or if a home-rule city has its population fall below 5,000, there is no automatic change in the city's legal status. Incorporation occurs when a people within a specific, defined boundary decide by majority election to become legally incorporated under the general laws of Texas. An incorporated area can then levy taxes and issue bonds for itself and provide certain public services. On the other hand, an unincorporated area has a government which (if desired) could contract privately for any services for that area. An unincorporated town does not have the legal power under the general laws of Texas to declare its area a wet or dry area as regards alcoholic beverages. The major difference between home-rule cities and general law cities is that home-rule cities are free to choose the form of government that best meets their local needs while general law cities are restricted to two forms of government: commission and city council (aldermanic) government. General law cities get specific grants of power from the state; home-rule cities only are limited in some of their powers by the state. Home-rule cities in Texas (in 1983 there were 236 of them) have chosen the mayor-council or council-manager form of government (only two home-rule cities have the commission form of government). **MUNICIPAL GOVERNMENT** CITY COUNCIL (aldermanic) consists of a mayor and from five to nine council members. The council (or board of aldermen) may provide for other city offices. Towns and villages are required to have an elected marshall who is *ex officio* police chief. COMMISSION form of government consists of a board of three commissioners (one may be an elected mayor as is the case in Corpus Christi) who share executive power and make policy. Each commissioner may be responsible for a department of government (public works, finance, etc.) and they must appoint a city clerk. Other officers may be appointed. MAYOR-COUNCIL form of government has two variations depending on whether the mayor is a strong or weak mayor. The strong mayor-council form of government is the predominant form of government in large cities across the United States, but it has not been adopted in most of the large cities of Texas. In a strong mayor-council government the mayor is elected at-large (thus representing the whole city), while council members are elected from single-member districts. The strong mayor has budgetary power (with council approval), can appoint and remove department heads and has veto power over council actions. In a weak mayor-council government the mayor is elected along with the other council members, the council makes most appointments and political administrative power is equal among the mayor and council members. The council can override the mayor's veto if he has one. The mayor has ceremonial power. In both weak and strong mayor-council governments, the council size varies from four to 11 members. COUNCIL-MANAGER form of government has been adopted in all the major cities of Texas (except for El Paso and Houston, although Houston's strong mayor-council government relies on a mayor-appointed administrator who functions similar to a manager). An elected council of five to nine members shares power equally, while a professional city manager is appointed by and responsible to the council. A weak mayor may be elected or the council choses the mayor to perform ceremonial functions with no veto power or special administrative functions. The professional city manager has administrative control of the city departments and appoints and removes department heads. Also the city manager prepares and carries out the budget which the council approves. The city manager does city planning and administers revenue sharing programs.

REVENUES OF ALL TEXAS MUNICIPALITIES, 1980-81
(in thousands)

Utility Revenue	$1,575,200	29.4%
Charges and Misc.	$1,208,700	22.5%
Property Taxes	$964,000	18.0%
Other Taxes	$814,300	15.2%
Federal Revenue Sharing	$595,400	11.1%
Employee Retirement Revenue	$124,500	2.3%
State and Other Revenue Sharing	$81,600	1.5%
Total	$5,363,700	100.0%

DIRECT EXPENDITURES OF ALL TEXAS MUNICIPALITIES, 1980-81
(in thousands)

Public Services (Airports, Parks, Libraries, etc.)	$1,935,300	34.441%
Utility Expenditures	$1,919,900	34.167%
Police/Fire Protection	$836,400	14.885%
Highways	$487,700	8.679%
Health/Hospitals	$192,500	3.426%
Interest on Debt	$167,800	2.986%
Employee Retirement Expend.	$68,200	1.214%
Public Welfare	$11,100	.198%
Education	$200	.004%
Total	$5,619,100	100.0%

BASIC MUNICIPAL FUNCTIONS AND SERVICES may be provided for residents (but are not required by law). The most basic services are personal and property protection (health and police safety), the building and maintaining of public facilities and the providing of public utilities (water, electricity, sewers). A municipality will also have administrative and financial functions (recordkeeping, issuing permits and licenses, collecting taxes, etc.). Most municipalities finance large capital improvements (parks, convention facilities, streets, sewers and water systems) by the sale of municipal bonds. In 1980-81 the outstanding debt of all Texas municipalities was $6,891,200,000. Budget limitations may prevent municipalities from providing a full range of services. Federal and state revenue sharing has concentrated on social services, community development and public transportation. SPECIAL DISTRICTS There are 2,805 special districts in Texas: 1,124 are school districts, 924 are water districts, 388 are housing authorities, 199 are soil and water conservation districts, 138 are active hospital districts and authorities, 47 are junior college districts and the rest include road districts, health districts, mosquito control districts, noxious weed control districts, rural fire prevention districts, wind erosion conservation districts, airport and mass transit authorities, a waste disposal authority and a municipal power agency. Special districts are created by an act of the Legislature (or in some cases by local ordinances) to provide a specific service. They are the fastest growing form of local government in Texas. They exist to meet public needs that cannot be met due to the constitutional restrictions imposed on the tax rates and functions of counties and municipalities. All special districts require voter approval in order to operate. Many special districts have some form of taxing power and some districts issue bonds but in both cases only after voter approval. Some state agencies serve and supervise special districts. For example, the Texas Education Agency helps distribute funds to school districts, the Texas Water Commission has the power to issue permits to water districts and the Texas Department of Water Resources reviews special water district legislation. PUBLIC SCHOOL DISTRICTS are established under state law to administer an educational program for students in specific areas. Most school districts are governed by a locally elected board of trustees consisting of five to seven members. Each school district is classified as a Regular Foundation School Program (FSP) District (the common form of school district eligible for state funding), a Special Public School District (near military bases and not administered by a state agency), and a State Administered Public School District (for the mentally retarded, blind, deaf and delinquent). Most school districts are known as "independent school districts" because they are controlled exclusively by a local board of trustees rather than under the general supervision of a county school board as are "common school districts". School boards have the power to employ teachers, administrators and support staff, determine curricula and design and build facilities. Certain educational requirements and minimum standards are set by state law and regulations. School boards are also authorized to levy and assess local property taxes to finance their operations. WATER DISTRICTS are organized to meet specific water needs and are independent of cities and counties in establishing policy or controls. Elected officers govern these districts and they may levy taxes and issue bonds after voter approval. Water districts can be created by a county commissioners court, a municipality or the Texas Water Commission. The state Legislature also can create a water district, subject to voter approval. Water districts supply water for domestic use, commercial or industrial use and irrigation. They may control water for navigation, recreation, flood prevention, soil conservation, power generation and sewage treatment. Some water districts engage in fire-fighting activities. Water districts ensure local control over water resources, but the state government supervises plans for development projects and their financial operations.

TEXAS BUSINESS REGULATIONS

AUTHORITY TO DO BUSINESS Under Texas law corporations for profit are permitted for lawful purpose and the authorization may be perpetual. Foreign corporations organized under the laws of the state enjoy the same rights and privileges of authorized domestic corporations. A corporation not presently doing business in Texas may apply for authorization with the Secretary of State. The company has the option of incorporating in Texas as a domestic corporation, or qualifying as a foreign corporation and obtaining a Certificate of Authority to do business in Texas. Secretary of State, Corporation Division, 6th Floor, Sam Houston State Office Building, P.O. Box 13697, Austin, Texas 78711, 512/475-5891. **LABOR LAWS** The Department of Labor and Standards, Labor Law Division, is responsible for the administration and enforcement of the labor laws such as child labor and semi-monthly pay days. In addition, the Division investigates and makes recommendations for the issuance of Texas non-profit corporation charters. Texas Department of Labor and Standards, E.O. Thompson State Office Building, 8th Floor, P.O. Box 12157, Austin, Texas 78711, 512/475-7001. **OCCUPATIONAL SAFETY** The Occupational Safety Board through the Department of Health offers free on-site safety and health inspections at the request of any Texas employer: Enforcement of the Texas Occupational Safety Act is conducted by the U.S. Occupational Safety and Health Administration. Employers taking advantage of the state inspections are exempt from OSHA enforcement for 12 months. Texas Department of Health, Occupational Safety Board, 1100 West 49th Street, Austin, Texas 78756, 512/458-7287. **OCCUPATIONAL HEALTH** The Occupational Health and Radiation Control Divisions of the Department of Health are responsible for safety control of x-ray equipment used in the state and issue licenses to persons intending to possess or handle radioactive substances. The Divisions have the responsibility for assuring a safe and healthful working environment for all employees of the state and they coordinate all Poison Control Centers in the state. In addition, they have the responsibility to provide effective controls against injury to citizens from electronic devices which are capable of emitting emissions, such as infrasonic, sonic and ultrasonic waves. Texas Department of Health, Radiation Control Division, 1212 E. Anderson Lane, 1100 West 49th Street (mail), Austin, Texas 78756, 512/835-7000. Texas Department of Health, Occupational Health Division, 1100 West 49th Street, Austin, Texas 78756, 512/458-7111. **PUBLIC WATER SUPPLY** Every person and firm intending to establish a drinking water supply for public use must submit completed plans and specifications to the Texas Department of Health, Division of Water Hygiene for approval. The Texas Board of Health sets standards and the Division of Water Hygiene maintains records of the quality of drinking water being supplied. Texas Department of Health, Division of Water Hygiene, 1100 West 49th Street, Austin, Texas 78756, 512/458-7111. **UNEMPLOYMENT INSURANCE** The Texas Employment Commission assigns an account number to any firm which employs one or more individuals during a portion of a day in each of 20 different weeks in a calendar year, or if it pays $1,500 or more in wages in a calendar quarter. The initial unemployment insurance rate is 2.7 percent of the first $7,000 paid in wages to each employee and it is collected quarterly for the first six calendar quarters. Eventually the rate is adjusted to the experience of the company. Texas Employment Commission, State Office Building, Status Section, Austin, Texas 78778, 512/397-4730. **WORKERS' COMPENSATION** Workers' Compensation Insurance, which is not mandatory in the state, is available through private insurance companies. The State Board of Insurance, which regulates all insurance rates, maintains a list of insurance companies qualified to write such policies. Accident claims causing an absence from work of more than one day must be filed with the Industrial Accident Board by employers with workers' compensation insurance. State Board of Insurance, Workers' Compensation Section, State Insurance Building, 1110 San Jacinto, Austin, Texas 78786, 512/475-2136. Industrial Accident Board, 200 E. Riverside Drive, 1st Floor, Austin, Texas 78704, 512/475-2251. **CONSTRUCTION STANDARDS** Texas has neither a statewide building code nor a statewide fire code. Building codes have been established by individual cities and city permits must be obtained. The Manufactured Housing Division of the Department of Labor and Standards administers the Texas Mobile Homes Standards Act, and the Boiler Inspection Division enforces laws concerning the construction, installation and operation of all boilers and some pressure vessels. Texas Department of Labor and Standards, E.O. Thompson State Office Building, P.O. Box 12157, Capitol Station, Austin, Texas 78711, 512/475-5712 (Mobile Homes), 512/475-4799 (Boilers). **ENVIRONMENTAL PROTECTION** The Air Control Board administers the control and prevention programs and enforces policies set by various state and federal agencies. All sources which contribute to or may tend to contribute to air contamination must obtain construction and operating permits from the Board prior to constructing new facilities or modifying existing processes. The industrial construction permit fee is 0.1% of the estimated capital cost of the project. The Board regularly inspects existing and possible future sources of air pollutants for compliance with air quality standards. Texas Air Control Board, 6330 Highway 290 East, Austin, Texas 78723, 512/451-5711. **POLLUTION ABATEMENT EQUIPMENT FINANCING** Regional Waste Disposal Act (Chapter 25 of the Texas Water Code) Under this Act, any district, city, or other political subdivision or agency of the state which has the power to own and operate waste collections, transportation, treatment, or disposal facilities or systems, and any joint board created under the provisions of Section 14, Chapter 114, Acts of the 50th Legislature (Article 46-d-14, Vernon's Texas Civil Statutes) has the authority to enter into contracts authorized by it and issue bonds for the construction, transportation, treatment, or disposal of waste materials. Clean Air Financing Act (Abatement). This Act is administered by the Texas Air Control Board (TACB). The goal of the TACB is to safeguard the air resources of the state by controlling or abating emissions of air contaminants. This Act authorizes cities, counties, and conservation districts to issue and sell revenue bonds to provide funds for the acquisition of air pollution abatement equipment. This equipment can then be sold or leased to private industries. **STATE LANDS** The General Land Office administers all state owned lands; issuing oil and gas leases, grazing and agricultural leases, mineral leases, and construction permits for the state owned submerged lands off the coast. General Land Office, 1700 N. Congress, Austin, Texas 78701, 512/475-4681. **WATER RESOURCES** The Department of Water Resources and its judicial arm, the Texas Water Commission issue permits for the diversion of public water. The Commission holds public hearings on applications for use of surface water, construction of water storage facilities, movement of water from one watershed to another, impoundment of water, creation of municipal water utility districts, construction of levees and the creation of underground water conservation districts. In addition the Department and Commission issue permits or registrations if wastes are to be discharged into the waters of the state, for hazardous waste disposal facilities and for shipping control for off-site hazardous waste disposal. They hold jurisdiction over the discharge of treated sewage and industrial waste water, discharges from agricultural operations, and the disposal of wastes via injection wells. Texas Department of Water Resources, Permits Division, P.O. Box 13087, Capitol Station, Austin, Texas 78711, 512/475-3345. **DISPOSAL OF DREDGED OR FILL MATERIAL** The U.S. Army Corps of Engineers is responsible for regulating the disposal of dredged or fill material in water

TEXAS BUSINESS REGULATIONS

site development fills, dams, levees and dikes, artificial islands, sanitary landfills, and property protection devices such as seawalls and breakwaters. U.S. Army Corps of Engineers, Permits Branch, P.O. Box 1229, Galveston, Texas 77553, 409/766-3925 or 3982 or 3941. **EQUAL OPPORTUNITY** Businesses involved in serving or selling to the general public may not discriminate on the basis of race, religion, national origin, sex or color. Credit discrimination on the above basis is strictly forbidden by Texas law. The U.S. Equal Employment Opportunity Commission is responsible for the prevention of discrimination in hiring, promotion, firing, wages, testing, training, apprenticeship and other conditions of employment. Office of Consumer Credit Commissioner, 1011 San Jacinto, Third Floor, P.O. Box 2107, Austin, Texas 78768, 512/475-2111. Equal Employment Opportunity Commission, 1900 Pacific Building, 13th Floor, Dallas, Texas 75201, 214/767-4607. Equal Employment Opportunity Commission, 727 E. Durango, Suite B-601, San Antonio, Texas 78206, 512/229-6051. Equal Employment Opportunity Commission, 405 Main, 6th Floor, Houston, Texas 77002, 713/226-2664. **MOTOR TRANSPORT** The Railroad Commission regulates the acts and services of motor carriers, motor transportation brokers and motor bus companies operating on any public highway in the state. A motor transportation broker must obtain a license issued by the Commission. Common carriers, specialized carriers and motor buses must be licensed by the Commission and no motor carrier can operate as a contract carrier without a permit for that operation. The carrier or bus company must register annually the vehicles they intend to operate. The Commission prescribes the rates to be charged by all rail and motor carriers engaged in intrastate trade. Texas Railroad Commission, Transportation Division, 1124 South I.H. 35, P.O. Drawer 12967, Austin, Texas 78711, 512/445-1343. **FUEL PERMITS** Interstate truckers operating gasoline or diesel powered vehicles in Texas must obtain special permits. Temporary permits are available if no more than five entries by the company or business are made into Texas in each calendar year. Various permits are required of Texas based vehicle fuels dealers. Comptroller of Public Accounts, Fuels Tax Division, 111 E. 17th Street, Austin, Texas 78774, 512/475-4334. Texas residents may call toll free at 1-800-252-5555. **MOTOR CARRIER LEASING** Any person who leases a commercial motor vehicle or truck-tractor must file a copy of the lease, memorandum or agreement with the Department of Public Safety. **HAZARDOUS MATERIALS** The transportation of hazardous materials is regulated by the Department of Public Safety. **MOTOR VEHICLE LICENSES** All motor vehicles must be registered annually through the County Tax Office. **DRIVERS' LICENSES** The Drivers' License Service of the Department of Public Safety issues drivers' licenses through their district office in each area. Texas Department of Public Safety, P.O. Box 4087, Austin, Texas 78773, 512/465-2000 (Drivers' Licenses), 512/465-2020 (Motor Vehicle Licenses), 512/465-2051 (Motor Carrier Leasing) and 512/465-2000 (Traffic Law Enforcement Division). **LICENSES ADMINISTERED BY STATE AGENCIES** A variety of businesses come under the jurisdiction of one or more state agencies. The agencies listed are those empowered to issue the necessary licenses, permits, charters or to impose standards in the operation of particular businesses. Certified Public Accountants and Public Accountants: Texas State Board of Public Accountancy, 1033 La Posada, Suite 340, Austin, Texas 78752-3894, 512/451-0241. Architects: Board of Architectural Examiners, 8213 Shoal Creek Blvd., #107, Austin, Texas 78758, 512/458-1363. Attorneys: State Bar of Texas, P.O. Box 12487, Capitol Station, Austin, Texas 78711, 512/475-1234. Auctioneers, Boiler Inspection, Boxing Matches, Employment Agencies, and Wrestling Matches: Texas Department of Labor and Standards, E.O. Thompson Building, 10th and Colorado, P.O. Box 12157, Capitol Station, Austin, Texas

78711, 512/475-3499. Barber Schools, Instructors and Barber Shops: State Board of Barber Examiners, 1300 E. Anderson Lane, Building C, Suite 275, Austin, Texas 78752, 512/835-2040. Beauty Salons, Cosmetology Specialists, Operators and Apprentices: Texas Cosmetology Commission, 1111 Rio Grande, Austin, Texas 78701, 512/475-3304. Beer Permits: Alcoholic Beverage Commission, 1600 West 38th Street, Austin, Texas 78731, 512/458-2500. Crabmeat Processing Plants, Wholesalers of Controlled Substances, Homes for the Aged or Infirm, Hospitals and Nursing Homes for the care of the sick, Medical Labs performing pre-marital blood tests, Shellfish Repackers, Social Psychotherapists and Solid Waste Disposal, Construction, Operation and Maintenance: Texas Department of Health, 1100 West 49th Street, Austin, Texas 78756, 512/458-7111. Funeral Directors and Embalmers: State Board of Morticians, 1513 South I.H. 35, Austin, Texas 78741, 512/442-6721. Business Schools: Texas Education Agency, 1200 East Anderson Lane, Austin, Texas 78752, 512/834-4000. Chauffeur Licenses, Commercial Driver Training Schools, Controlled Substances, Wholesalers, Manufacturers and Distributors and Repackers: Texas Department of Public Safety, 5805 North Lamar, P.O. Box 4087, Austin, Texas 78773, 512/465-2000. Child Care Facilities, Institutions, Group Homes and Day Care Centers: Department of Human Resources, 706 Banister Lane, P.O. Box 2960, Austin, Texas 78769, 512/441-3355. Chiropractors: Chiropractic Examiners Board, 1300 East Anderson Lane, Building C, Suite 245, Austin, Texas 78752, 512/835-2006. Blaster Licenses, Explosives, Hotels and Septic Tanks: Licenses issued by individual city authority. Amusement Machine Licenses: Texas Amusement Machine Commission, 1106 Clayton Lane, Suite 108E, P.O. Box 13226, Capitol Station, Austin, Texas 78711, 512/475-5651. Bingo Licenses, Cigarette, Cigar and Tobacco Permits, Cigarette Vending Machine Permits, Fuels Tax Permits. Gross Receipts Tax Permits, Interstate Motor Carrier Tax Permits, Manufactured Housing Sales Tax Permits, Sales Tax Permits and Vending Machines: Comptroller of Public Accounts, LBJ State Office Building, 111 East 17th Street, Austin, Texas 78774, 512/475-1914, 1-800-252-5555 toll free in Texas. Prepaid Funeral Contracts: Department of Banking, 2601 North Lamar, Austin, Texas 78705, 512/475-4451. Psychologists: Texas State Board of Examiners of Psychologists, 1300 East Anderson Lane, Suite C-270, Austin, Texas 78752, 512/835-2036. Credit Unions: Credit Union Department, 914 East Anderson Lane, Austin, Texas 78752, 512/837-9236. Dental Hygienists, Dental Labs, Dental Technicians and Dentists: Board of Dental Examiners, 411 West 13th Street, Suite 503, Austin, Texas 78701, 512/475-2443. Antifreeze Manufacturers, Economic Poisons, Egg Handlers, Fresh Flower Dealers, Fruit Dealers-Wholesale, Grain Warehouses-Commercial, Grocery Stores, Liquefied Petroleum Dealers and Transporters, Milk and Milk Products (Grade A) Transporters, Nursery Stock, Ornamental Plant Dealers, Pest Control and Plant Disease Control, Pesticide Operators-Commercial, Seed Retailers and Wholesalers, Vegetable Dealers-Wholesalers, Public Warehouses and Weighers: Texas Department of Agriculture, 9th Floor, Stephen F. Austin State Office Building, P.O. Box 12847, Capitol Station, Austin, Texas 78711, 512/475-6346. Public Surveyors, Real Estate Brokers and Salesmen: Real Estate Commission, 1101 Camino La Costa (78752), P.O. Box 12188, Capitol Station, Austin, Texas 78711, 512/459-6544. Engineers: State Board of Registration for Professional Engineers, 1917 I.H. 35 South (78741), P.O. Box 18329, Austin, Texas 78760, 512/475-3141. Freight and Passenger Transporters, Gas and Oilwell Drilling, Liquefied Petroleum Dealers and Transporters: Railroad Commission of Texas, P.O. Box 12967, Capitol Station, Austin, Texas 78711, 512/445-1343. Savings and Loan Associations: Savings and Loan Department, 1004 Lavaca (78701), P.O. Box 1089, Austin, Texas 78767, 512/475-7991. Veterinarians: State Board of Veterinary Medical Examiners, 3810 Medical Parkway, Suite 119, Austin, Texas 78756, 512/458-1183. Crabmeat Processing Plants, Fur Buyers, Fur Processors, Fur Trappers, Hunting and Fishing Licenses, Shellfish Repackers and Shooting Preservers: Texas Parks and Wildlife Department, 4200 Smith School Road, Austin, Texas 78744, 512/479-4800. Investment Advisors, Security Broker-Dealers and Salesmen: State Securities Board, 1800 San Jacinto, P.O. Box 13167, Capitol Station, Austin, Texas 78711, 512/474-2233. Burial Associations, Insurance: Adjustors (Independent and Public), Agents, Companies, Rating Bureaus, and Surplus Line Brokers: State Board of Insurance, State Insurance Building, 1110 San Jacinto, Austin, Texas 78786, 512/475-2444. Beehive Licenses: State Entomologist, Texas A&M University, Entomology Department, BSDE, College Station, Texas 77843-2475, 409/845-2516. State Land Surveyors: Texas Board of Land Surveying, Twin Towers Office Building, 1106 Clayton Lane, Suite 210-W, Austin, Texas 78723, 512/452-9427. Landscape Architects: Texas State Board of Landscape Architects, 8213 Shoal Creek Blvd., Suite 107, Austin, Texas 78758, 512/458-4126. Hearing Aid Dispensers: Texas Board of Examiners in the Fitting and Dispensing of Hearing Aids, 1212 Guadalupe, Room 105, Austin, Texas 78701, 512/475-3429. Water Well Driller: Texas Department of Water Resources, Stephen F. Austin State Office Building, P.O. Box 13087, Capitol Station, Austin, Texas 78711, 512/475-3187. Private Investigators and Private Security Agencies: Board of Private Investigators and Private Security Agencies, 510 South Congress, Suite 116, P.O. Box 13509, Austin, Texas 78711, 512/475-3944. Insurance Premium Finance Companies, Loan and Investment Companies, Small Loan Companies and Pawnbrokers: Office of the Consumer Credit Commissioner, 1011 San Jacinto, 3rd Floor, P.O. Box 2107, Austin, Texas 78768, 512/475-2111. Polygraph Examiners: Polygraph Examiners Board, 6121 North Lamar Blvd., P.O. Box 4143, Austin, Texas 78765, 512/465-2058. Milk and Milk Products (Grade A) Distributors, Processors, Producers and Transporters, Food Services, Frozen Food Plants, Grocery Stores, Restaurants and Septic Tanks: Licenses, permits, regulations issued by local area health authorities. Motor Vehicle Dealers, Distributors and Manufacturers: Texas Motor Vehicle Commission, 815 Brazos, Suite 302, P.O. Box 2293, Austin, Texas 78768, 512/476-3587. Nurses, Vocational: Board of Vocational Nurse Examiners, 1300 East Anderson Lane, Building C, Suite 285, Austin, Texas 78752, 512/835-2071. Nurses, Registered: Board of Nurse Examiners for the State of Texas, 1300 East Anderson Lane, Building C, Suite 225, Austin, Texas 78752, 512/835-4880. Nursing Home Administrators: Texas Board of Licensure for Nursing Home Administrators, 3407 I.H. 35 North, Austin, Texas 78722, 512/479-0922. Opthalmologists, Osteopaths and Physicians: Texas State Board of Medical Examiners, 1101 Camino La Costa, Suite 201 (78752), P.O. Box 13562, Capitol Station, Austin, Texas 78711, 512/475-0741. Optometrists: Texas Optometry Board, 1300 East Anderson Lane, Suite C-240, Austin, Texas 78752, 512/835-1938. Pesticide Operators, Commercial: Structural Pest Control Board, 1300 East Anderson Lane, Building C., Suite 250, Austin, Texas 78752, 512/835-4066. Pharmaceutical Manufacturers, Pharmacies and Pharmacists: State Board of Pharmacy, Southwest Tower, Suite 1121, 211 East 7th Street, Austin, Texas 78701, 512/478-9827. Physical Therapists and Assistants: Texas Board of Physical Therapy Examiners, 1300 East Anderson Lane, Building C, Suite 260, Austin, Texas 78752, 512/835-1846. Plumbers and Plumbing Contractors: Texas State Board of Plumbing Examiners, 929 East 41st Street, P.O. Box 4200, Austin, Texas 78765, 512/458-2145. Podiatrists: State Board of Podiatry Examiners, 411 West 13th Street, Suite 504, Austin, Texas 78701, 512/475-1770. **ECONOMIC DEVELOPMENT COMMISSION** The purpose of the Economic Development Commission is to promote business and industrial growth in the state by attracting new business and industry to Texas and by providing assistance to firms already established in the state. BUSINESS DEVELOPMENT The Business Development Department provides technical assistance to communities in developing their capacity to attract industry. Assistance is provided by: 1) identifying federal funding sources 2) developing local programs through clinics, planning seminars and sales team training 3) assisting small and minority businesses with buying patterns, purchasing procedures and contract opportunities 4) registering small and minority contractors and suppliers with the appropriate procuring agencies 5) providing assistance in accessing capital from private and public lenders and 6) providing access to education and training resources. INTERNATIONAL DEVELOPMENT The International Development Department is responsible for assisting Texas business in developing commerce for international markets. The staff provides import-export information, counsels individual companies, recruits and coordinates Texas company participation in foreign trade shows and organizes and conducts foreign trade missions to advance the export of Texas products. The department also provides foreign investment information and conducts foreign investment missions. The department provides computerized trade leads gathered worldwide which are delivered to Texas manufacturers. The State of Texas Office in Mexico City, a part of the International Development Department, provides assistance, guidance, and trade information to Texas businessmen doing business in Mexico. RESEARCH AND DATA SERVICES The Research and Data Services Department maintains an extensive library and computerized information system. The department compiles and publishes social and economic information of interest to the business community. FINANCIAL ASSISTANCE The Commission is responsible for approving industrial revenue bonds issued by local industrial development corporations under provisions of the Development Corporation Act of 1979. Published rules and regulations governing the issuance of revenue bonds, including special rules which apply to commercial projects, may be obtained from the Commission. The Commission is also responsible for administering a rural loan program under the Rural Industrial Development Act. Under the rural loan program, a local industrial development agency can obtain a direct loan from the state for up to 40% of the eligible costs of a manufacturing or industrial project located in a rural area. Texas Economic Development Commission, 410 East 5th Street, P.O. Box 12728, Capitol Station, Austin, Texas 78711, 512/472-5059. **U.S. SMALL BUSINESS ADMINISTRATION** The Small Business Administration (SBA) provides business counseling and financial assistance under a variety of programs. In Texas the SBA can be contacted at the following addresses: Regional Office, 1720 Regal Row, Room 230, Dallas, Texas 75235, 214/767-7643. 1100 Commerce Street, Room 3C36, Dallas, Texas 75242, 214/767-0605. 100 South Washington Street, Room G-12, Marshall, Texas 75670, 214/935-5257. 2525 Murworth, Suite 112, Houston, Texas 77054, 713/660-4401. 1611 10th Street, Suite 200, Lubbock, Texas 79401, 806/743-7466. 4100 Rio Bravo, Suite 300, El Paso, Texas 79902, 915/541-7586. 222 East Van Buren Street, Suite 500, Harlingen, Texas 78550, 512/423-8934. 3105 Leopard Street, Box 9253, Corpus Christi, Texas 78408, 512/888-3303. 727 East Durango Street, Room A-513, San Antonio, Texas 78206, 512/229-6250. 300 East 8th Street, Austin, Texas 78701, 512/482-5288. **U.S. HOUSING AND URBAN DEVELOPMENT** The following programs can be used to assist in business financing: Urban Development Action Grants, Community Development Block Grants, the 312 Program, the 108 Program and the Neighborhood Self-Help Program. HUD, P.O. Box 9163, 800 Dolorosa, San Antonio, Texas 78285, 512/229-6781. HUD (CPD), P.O. Box 2905, 221 W. Lancaster, Fort Worth, Texas 76113, 817/870-5483.

REGIONAL COUNCILS

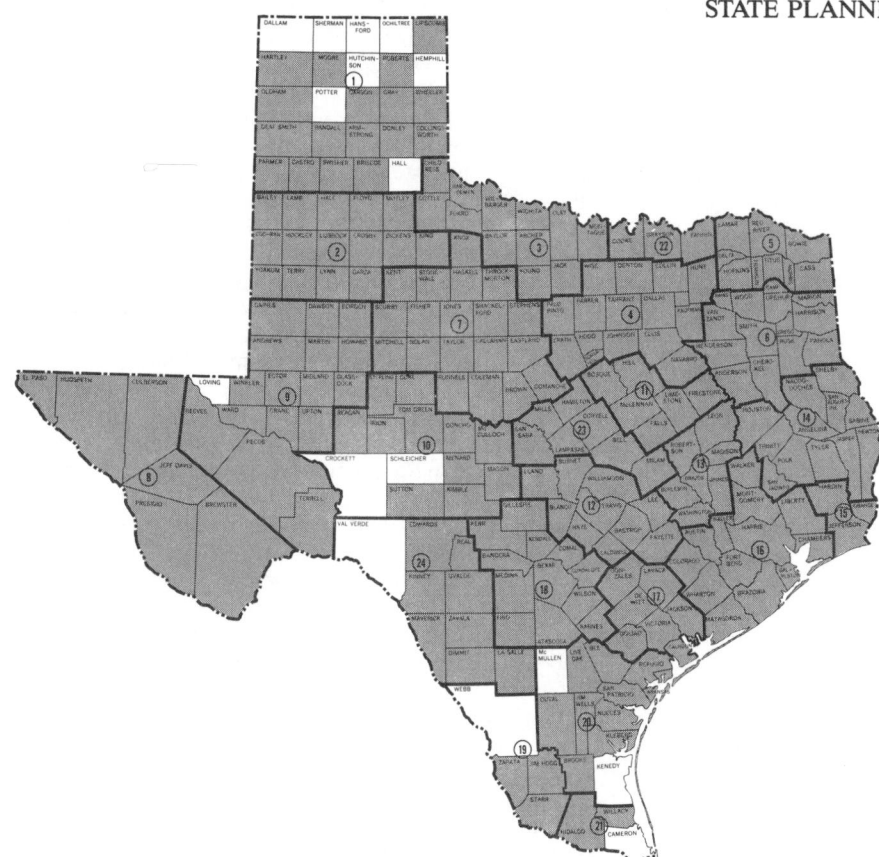

STATE PLANNING REGIONS AND REGIONAL COUNCIL

1. Panhandle Regional Planning Commission
2. South Plains Association of Governments
3. Nortex Regional Planning Commission
4. North Central Texas Council of Governments
5. ARK-TEX Council of Governments
6. East Texas Council of Governments
7. West Central Texas Council of Governments
8. West Texas Council of Governments
9. Permian Basin Regional Planning Commission
10. Concho Valley Council of Governments
11. Heart of Texas Council of Governments
12. Capital Area Planning Council
13. Brazos Valley Development Council
14. Deep East Texas Council of Governments
15. South East Texas Regional Planning Commission
16. Houston-Galveston Area Council
17. Golden Crescent Regional Planning Commission
18. Alamo Area Council of Governments
19. South Texas Development Council
20. Coastal Bend Council of Governments
21. Lower Rio Grande Valley Development Council
22. Texoma Regional Planning Commission
23. Central Texas Council of Governments
24. Middle Rio Grande Development Council

No single definition is comprehensive enough to cover all regional governments and agencies in Texas. While all of them include more than one local government in their geographical area, their organization, legal authorities, duties and purposes vary. Some, such as the Regional Councils, function purely as planning bodies and have no regulatory powers. Others, such as the River Authorities, have regulatory powers and may even levy taxes. Yet others fall somewhere between these two extremes. **REGIONAL COUNCILS** The term most commonly used to indicate voluntary associations of local governments formed to deal with problems and planning needs that require the attention of more than one local government is Regional Council. While Regional Councils in Texas have various names, these do not reflect legal distinctions. The 24 Regional Councils of Texas serve state planning regions, each of which includes several counties. Participating local governments design their regional council to meet specific local needs. Each council has its own bylaws or articles of agreement and the structure of the councils varies. The council's activities stem from planning and development programs delegated to them by the state or federal governments. These programs may involve the development of comprehensive regional plans. They may also be specialized plans for such areas as employment and training, drug abuse, criminal justice, aging, economic development, alcoholism, health, early childhood development, local resource management, transportation, water quality and rural development. The Councils also provide technical assistance, service and training to member local governments, as well as review of and comment on local government grant applications. State law requires that at least two-thirds of the members of the governing body of each Regional Council must be local elected officials. The Regional Councils of Government (COGs) represent areas with similar social and economic characteristics and, in most cases, correspond with the market

areas in the state. However, population, employment and income data vary from region to region. The Houston-Galveston Area Council encompasses the most population (3,276,236) and the Middle Rio Grande Development Council has the least (125,077). On the other hand, the Panhandle Regional Planning Commission oversees the largest area (24,900 square miles) and the South East Texas Regional Planning Commission has the smallest (2,196 square miles). Per capita income is the highest in North Central Texas, the Gulf Coast and Permian Basin, reflecting the influence of the metropolitan areas within each region. The regional boundaries are subject to review and revision. FUNDING Regional Councils receive funding from local, state and federal governments. At the local level funding is generally composed of dues paid by member governments. In fiscal year 1982 the Regional Councils received $1,414,104 in local dues, $4,772,068 in state grants, $52,355,753 (56%) in state administered federal funds and $36,589,343 (39%) in direct federal grants. The U.S. Department of Labor provided the largest portion (65%) of the direct federal funds and the Texas Department on Aging provided 61% of the federal funds administered by the state. Alamo Area Council of Governments, 118 Broadway, Suite 400, San Antonio, 78205, 512/225-5201. Ark-Tex Council of Governments, P.O. Box 5307, Texarkana, 75501, 501/774-3481. Brazos Valley Development Council, P.O. Box 4128, Bryan, 77801, 713/822-7421. Capital Area Planning Council, 2520 Interstate 35 South, Suite 100, Austin, 78704, 512/443-7653. Central Texas Council of Governments, P.O. Box 729, Belton, 76513, 817/939-1801, ext. 32. Coastal Bend Council of Governments, P.O. Box 9909, Corpus Christi, 78408. Concho Valley Council of Governments, 5002 Knickerbocker Road, San Angelo, 76901, 915/944-9666. Deep East Texas Council of Governments, P.O. Drawer 1170, Jasper, 75951, 713/384-5704. East Texas Council of Governments, Stoneridge Plaza Office Building, 3800 Stone Road, Kilgore,

75662, 214/984-8641. Golden Crescent Council of Governments, P.O. Box 2028, Victoria, 77901, 512/578-1587. Heart of Texas Council of Governments, 320 Franklin Ave., Waco, 76701, 817/756-6631. Houston-Galveston Area Council, P.O. Box 22777, Houston, 77027, 713/627-3200. Lower Rio Grande Valley Development Council, First National Bank Building, Suite 207, McAllen, 78501, 512/682-3481. Middle Rio Grande Development Council, P.O. Box 702, Carrizo Springs, 78834, 512/876-3533. North Central Texas Council of Governments, P.O. Drawer COG, Arlington, 76011. Nortex Regional Planning Commission, 2101 Kemp Blvd., Wichita Falls, 76309, 817/322-5281. Panhandle Regional Planning Commission, P.O. Box 9257, Amarillo, 79105, 806/372-3381. Permian Basin Regional Planning Commission, P.O. Box 6391, Midland, 79701, 915/563-1061. South East Texas Regional Planning Commission, P.O. Drawer 1387, Nederland, 77627, 713/727-2384. South Plains Association of Governments, P.O. Box 2787, Lubbock, 79408, 806/762-8721. South Texas Development Council, P.O. Box 2187, Laredo, 78041, 512/722-3995. Texoma Regional Planning Commission, 10000 Grayson Dr., Denison, 75020, 214/786-2955. West Central Texas Council of Governments, P.O. Box 3195, Abilene, 79604, 915/672-8544. West Texas Council of Governments, 2 Civic Center Plaza, El Paso, 79999, 915/541-4681. **METROPOLITAN PLANNING ORGANIZATIONS** They fulfill requirements under federal law that planning for transportation in urban areas be carried on cooperatively by state and local governments. Federal law also requires that responsible local officials be consulted formally in the process of locating a transportation corridor and in designing projects for particular corridors. Metropolitan Planning Organizations have been designated in 25 urbanized areas of Texas. In 18 of these areas, independent Metropolitan Planning Organizations have been designated. In the other seven urbanized areas the Regional Councils also serve as the designated Metropolitan Planning Organization. The following are, or function as, independent Metropolitan Planning Organizatons: the city of Abilene; the City of Amarillo; the Austin Urban Transportation Study Policy Advisory Committee; the City of Brownsville; the Bryan-College Station Urban Transportation Study Steering Committee; the City of Corpus Christi; the City of El Paso; the City of Harlingen; the Laredo Urban Transportation Study Steering Committee; the City of Longview; the Lubbock Urban Transportation Study Steering Committee; the McAllen, Pharr, Edinburg Urban Transportation Study Steering Committee; the City of San Angelo; the San Antonio Urban Transportation Study Steering Committee; the City of Tyler; the City of Victoria; the City of Waco; and the City of Wichita Falls. The following seven Regional Councils also function as designated Metropolitan Planning Orgaizations (the urbanized area served follows in parenthesis): the South East Texas Regional Planning Commission (Beaumont and Port Arthur); the North Central Texas Council of Governments (Dallas and Fort Worth); the Houston-Galveston Area Council (Houston, Galveston, Texas City and La Marque); The Central Texas Council of Governments (Killeen and Temple); The Permian Basin Regional Planning Commission (Midland and Odessa); the Texoma Regional Planning Commission (Sherman and Denison); and the Ark-Tex Council of Governments (Texarkana). **ECONOMIC DEVELOPMENT AGENCIES OF TEXAS** Originally designated by the Governor, these Agencies are organized under the mandate of federal law. They are designed to assist designated areas in attracting industry and jobs to improve the overall economic status of the residents of the area. The Agencies are directly funded by the Economic Development Administration of the United States Department of Commerce. Three Economic Development Agencies have been established as independent agencies: The Central Texas Economic Development District in Waco; the Pecan Valley Economic Development District in Brownwood; and the Northeast Texas Economic Development District in Texarkana. The following Regional Councils also function as Economic Development Agencies: the Alamo Area Council of Governments; the Brazos Valley Development Council; the Capital Area Planning Council; the Coastal Bend Council of Governments; the Deep East Texas Council of Governments; the Lower Rio Grande Valley Development Council; the Middle Rio Grande Development Council; the Panhandle Regional Planning Commission; the South Plains Association of Governments; the South Texas Development Corporation; the Texoma Regional Planning Commission; and the West Texas Council of Governments. **RIVER AUTHORITIES** In 1929, some four years before the federal government created the Tennessee Valley Authority, Texas created its first River Authority. There are currently 29 state governmental agencies recognized as River Authorities, either because they are classified as such by the Texas Department of Water Resources or because they are members of the River Authorities Panel of the Texas Water Conservation Association. Created at various times between 1929 and 1977 under the authority of article XVI, section 59 of the Texas Constitution, which provides broad power for the creation of conservation and reclamation districts to manage the waters of Texas rivers and streams, the River Authorities of Texas vary so broadly in their methods of selection and specific major functions that it is necessary to discuss each authority separately. The chart identifies the River Authorities of Texas by their official names (the name of the city that follows in parentheses is the location of the Authority's main office) and provides codes which indicate the method by which the Authorities' members are selected and the major functions the Authorities perform. The key to these codes is as follows: Method of Selection—A = appointed by Governor with Senate confirmation, B = elected from district, C = appointed by Texas Water Development Board, D = appointed by governing bodies of member local governments; Major Functions—1 = flood control, 2 = water quality and sewage treatment, 3 = parks and recreation, 4 = water conservation and supply, 5 = hydroelectric power, 6 = thermal power, 7 = water resource data collection, 8 = navigation, 9 = solid waste disposal. Angelina and Neches River Authority (Lufkin) A 2. Brazos River Authority (Waco) A 1,2,3,4,5,7. Canadian River Municipal Water Authority (Sanford) D 1,3,4. Central Colorado River Authority (Coleman) A 4. Chambers-Liberty County Navigation District (Anahuac) D 8. Colorado River Municipal Water District (Big Spring) D 1,2,3,4,7,9. Galveston County Water Authority (Texas City) D 4. Guadalupe-Blanco River Authority (Seguin) A* 1,2,3,4,5,7. Gulf Coast Waste Disposal Authority (Houston) D 2,7,9. Lavaca-Navidad River Authority (Edna) A 3,4. Lower Colorado River Authority (Austin) A 1,2,3,4,5,6,7,8. Lower Neches Valley Authority (Beaumont) C 2,4,7. Lower Nueces River Water Suply District (Corpus Christi) B 4. North-East Texas Municipal Water District (Dangerfield) D 4,7. North Texas Municipal Water District (Wylie) D 2,4. Nueces River Authority (Uvalde) A 4. Palo Duro River Authority (Spearman) D 1,3,4. Red Bluff Water Power Control District (Pecos) B 2,3,4,5,7. Red River Authority OF Texas (Wichita Falls) A 2,4. Sabine River Authority (Orange) A 2,3,4,5,7. San Antonio River Authority (San Antonio) B 1,2,3,4,7,8,9. San Jacinto River Authority (Conroe) C 2,4,7. Titus County Fresh Water Supply District No. 1 (Mount Pleasant) B 4,7. Trinity River Authority of Texas (Arlington) A 1,2,3,4,5,7,9. Upper Colorado River Authority (Ballinger) A 1,4. Upper Guadalupe River Authority (Kerrville) A 1,2,4,7. Upper Neches River Municipal Water Authority (Palestine) A 2,4,7. West Central Texas Municipal Water District (Abilene) D 4,7. White River Municipal Water District (Spur) D 3,4.

*Governor's appointments are made upon recommendation of the Texas Water Development Board.

ECONOMIC REGIONS

Source: Texas Comptroller of Public Accounts

THE METROPLEX
THE PLAINS
EAST TEXAS
THE BORDER
THE CENTRAL CORRIDOR
THE GULF COAST

Texas joined the United States under the condition that it could divide into five separate states at any time. The diversity of geology, climate, culture and economy provide ample reasons for dividing the state into regions, if not states. Many state agencies have divided Texas into a variety of regions for administrative purposes and, in order to assess more accurately the economy of Texas, the Comptroller of Public Accounts has divided the state into six economic regions. The 1984 economic recovery has not spread evenly throughout the State of Texas. Each economic region has taken a different path on the road to recovery, primarily the result of the importance of petroleum and the Mexican peso to the region's economy and the closeness of the region's link with the United States economy. The Central Corridor is predicted by several sources to have the fastest economic and population growth, compared with the other regions in the state, between 1982 and 2007. **EAST TEXAS** Primarily a nonmetropolitan region dependent on timber, oil and coal, agriculture and manufacturing are becoming more important to the economy of East Texas. Over 80% of the total timber production in Texas comes from this region, providing employment for about 20,000 in lumbering and the manufacture of wood products. In 1981 East Texas produced 68% of the coal, 12% of the crude oil and 9% of the natural gas produced in Texas. Poultry production has contributed significantly to the economy of the region in recent years as have the cattle and dairy industries. When rising oil prices and interest rates caused a slowdown in construction between 1979 and 1981 the lumber industry went into a recession while the petroleum industry was expanding rapidly. However, in 1981 and 1982 the lumber and oil prices declined together and nonagricultural employment fell by 4%. When mortgage interest rates began to fall in 1982 construction was stimulated and lumber prices began to rise. By mid 1983 the lumber industry was able to offset the effects of the continued slide in the oil industry. The economic outlook for East Texas is mixed. Nonagricultural employment is expected to increase by

an average 3.2% per year during 1984 and 1985 and the petroleum industry has shown signs of a slight recovery; however, lumber prices have slowed their climb as mortgage rates turned upward in late 1983. Trade, services and finance are expected to lead the economy. **METROPLEX** With abundant natural resources and land well-suited to agriculture the Dallas-Fort Worth Metroplex region is dominated by manufacturing, commerce, services and finance. It is the most diversified of the regions; the manufacturing sector provides over 2% of the region's employment (the highest percentage of all the regions), the wholesale trade employs 6% and finance, insurance and real estate provide 7.5% of the total employment (higher than the other regions). The production of electronic, aerospace and military hardware is important to the economy with defense expenditures of $4.5 billion in 1983. Tourism is also significant to the economy—Dallas is a convention and trade show host and one of the most visited cities in Texas. The Metroplex economy maintained a relatively steady growth between 1978 and 1984. In 1982 the nonagricultural employment averaged 1.6 million, 3% more than in 1981. The diversified manufacturing sector continued to attract new firms and workers. The region is the least dependent on the petroleum industry and the economic outlook is good. Nonagricultural employment in the Metroplex is forecast to increase an average 4.5% per year during 1984-1985. **THE PLAINS** The oil and gas industry, centered in Midland and Odessa, dominates the economy of the west central and southwestern areas of The Plains Region. The discovery of the west Texas oilfields in the 1930s plus a strong demand for petroleum products led to rapid economic growth. In 1981 about 65% of the oil and 42% of the gas produced in Texas came from this region. Intensive irrigation of farmlands with water from the Ogallaha Aquifer produced massive amounts of cotton, sorghum, wheat, corn and other feed grains in the northwestern part of the region, from Lubbock north toward Amarillo. In addition this area is a national leader in feedlot cattle production. Farming in the southeastern part of the region is smaller in scale and less dependent on irrigation with more cattle and sheep ranching. Low agricultural prices, a soft demand for petroleum products and declining water supplies will determine the future economic health of the Plains Region. Eight percent of the region's income in 1980 was from agriculture and almost 13% of the nonagricultural employment was in the oil and gas industry. Manufacturing provides for only 14% of the Plains employment (the statewide average is 18%). During 1982, with the collapse in drilling activity, oil and gas employment fell by 21%. Lower agricultural exports drove agricultural prices down while production costs rose and by 1982 the real net farm income had fallen to 60% of its 1979 level. Although the federal Payment-in-Kind (PIK) program increased farm receipts in 1983, a drought in the Plains Region has damaged both crops and farm income. The strong dollar and increases in interest rates may forestall any long term improvement in agricultural income. Nonagricultural employment is forecast up an average 2.9% per year during 1984-85. **THE BORDER** The economic turmoil in Mexico has severely affected this region. The recent devaluations of the Mexican peso against the U.S. dollar, high unemployment and rampant inflation in Mexico have severely restricted retail sales to Mexicans all along the border. The trade sector employs almost 30% of the labor force in the Border Region and, as a result, the unemployment rate in the border metropolitan areas skyrocketed. In the McAllen-Pharr-Edinburg Metropolitan Area unemployment rates rose from 13.6% in 1980 to 24.5% in 1983. Laredo is more dependent on trade with Mexico than El Paso, which has a substantial government payroll, diversified manufacturing, ore smelting and irrigated agriculture. Over a million acres in the region are irrigated with water from the Rio Grande and underground aquifers, so that agriculture provides substantial income and employment in the area. Oil and gas production also contributes substantially to the income of the region: Kleberg County is a major Texas producer of natural gas. The 1980 Census reported that agriculture and mining employed about 9% of the workers in the Border Region. The region suffered further losses in the December, 1983 freeze which destroyed millions of dollars in citrus and vegetable crops. An estimated 20,000 persons were put out of work, an estimated 3,600 growers sustained losses by that freeze and 42 counties were designated disaster areas. During the first half of 1984 as the Border Region struggled to recover from those economic losses and a lack of rain withered dry land crops, the Falcon and Amistad Reservoirs which supply irrigation water dropped to their lowest level in 10 years. Some growers will have used up their water allotments before the end of the summer. However, the peso devaluation has increased tourism to Mexico from the United States and as a result the economy in the border counties with ports of entry has improved. The lowered Mexican wages have made investment along the border more profitable and interest in the Twin Plant program has increased. The *Maquiladoras,* as they are known in Mexico, are thriving along the border as American firms operate Mexican subsidiaries. The American owned plants in Mexico assemble components manufactured in U.S. factories into final products which are then shipped back to the United States for sale. Most of the *Maquiladoras* (a Spanish word for assembly plants) produce electronic equipment, machinery components or textiles. The number of Twin Plants has grown to 600 factories employing 130,000 Mexican workers in the last 20 years. There were 178 Twin Plants along the Texas/Mexico border in 1978 and by spring 1983 there were 232, a 30% increase. The Twin Plant program began when the Mexican government invited foreign businesses to take advantage of Mexico's low-cost work force in an effort to increase Mexico's economic stability. Before the 1982 peso devaluations, the U.S. dollar was worth about 25 pesos and a Mexican worker earned about $5 an hour. In 1983 the dollar was worth about 155 pesos and a Mexican worker could be hired

for $5 a day. For the first time since the Mexican revolution, Mexican majority ownership is not a prerequisite for doing business in Mexico. In fact, Mexico assured foreign companies that the companies would retain 100% ownership of any newly established Mexican subsidiaries. Most of the American-owned plants are located in large, Mexican-built, Mexican-owned industrial parks. The program has been critized by American labor unions claiming that American jobs are being exported to Mexico; however, the participating companies claim that without the low labor cost they would not be able to compete with the less expensive foreign goods. Border city officials support the program, pointing to the number of jobs created on the American side of the border. A recent Texas Department of Community Affairs study concluded that a 10% increase in Twin Plant employment in Mexico causes a two to three percent increase in employment in El Paso and McAllen and a three to four percent increase in Brownsville and Laredo. The border economy forecast shows a weak recovery during 1984-1985 with nonagricultural employment growing at an average rate of 2.4% each year. **CENTRAL CORRIDOR** The operation of military installations in this region and the large amount of both public and private services have acted as a buffer against economic downturns. The area has prospered independently of its natural resources and geology with several principal economic centers linked by Interstate Highway 35 (except Bryan-College Station). The services sector, led by health and education, in 1980 provided 40% of the Central Corridor's employment and government employment accounted for 23%. The manufacturing employment of 13.5% (the smallest percentage of the state's regions) and the petroleum industry with 2% of the regional employment were affected by the downturn in the economy and the soft demand for petroleum products during 1981 and 1982, but the regional economy did not suffer as a result. The Central Corridor is fast becoming a growth center for high technology design and manufacturing. As a result the Central Corridor Region is expected to lead all the regions in nonagricultural employment growth with an average 5.2% growth each year during 1984 and 1985, compared to a statewide forecast of 3.1% growth. **GULF COAST** The discovery of oil at Spindletop near Beaumont in 1901 was the beginning of the oil industry dominance of the economy of this region. Houston became a center for oil refining, petroleum transportation and the manufacture of oil drilling equipment. In 1982, 77% of the employment in Texas in the petroleum and petrochemical industries and 48% of the state's mining employment were in this region. The Houston Metropolitan Area has the most diversified economy in the region with banking, trade and manufacturing, but it is still dominated by the petroleum and petrochemical industries. The regional employment includes shipbuilding, steel production, port activity, fishing and agricultural production. The most dramatic economic highs and lows in Texas during the 1979-1983 period were experienced in this region. From the first quarter of 1979 through the first quarter of 1982 the petroleum industry expanded rapidly, with the nonagricultural employment in the region expanding by almost 17%. Population growth and increased trade with Mexico also contributed to the growth. In early 1982, when the petroleum industry went into a steep decline and the Mexican peso began its slide in value, the regional employment fell by over five percent. By the end of 1982 manufacturing employment had dropped by nearly 18%. During 1983, as the economy struggled to recover, Hurricane Alicia battered the Gulf Coast damaging businesses and homes and further disrupting the area economy. Oil prices stabilized in late 1983 and employment is growing at a slow rate. However, with excess office, hotel and factory space it will take time for this region to recover. The nonagricultural employment forecast shows an expected average growth rate of 1.4% each year during 1984 and 1985.

LAND RESOURCE REGIONS

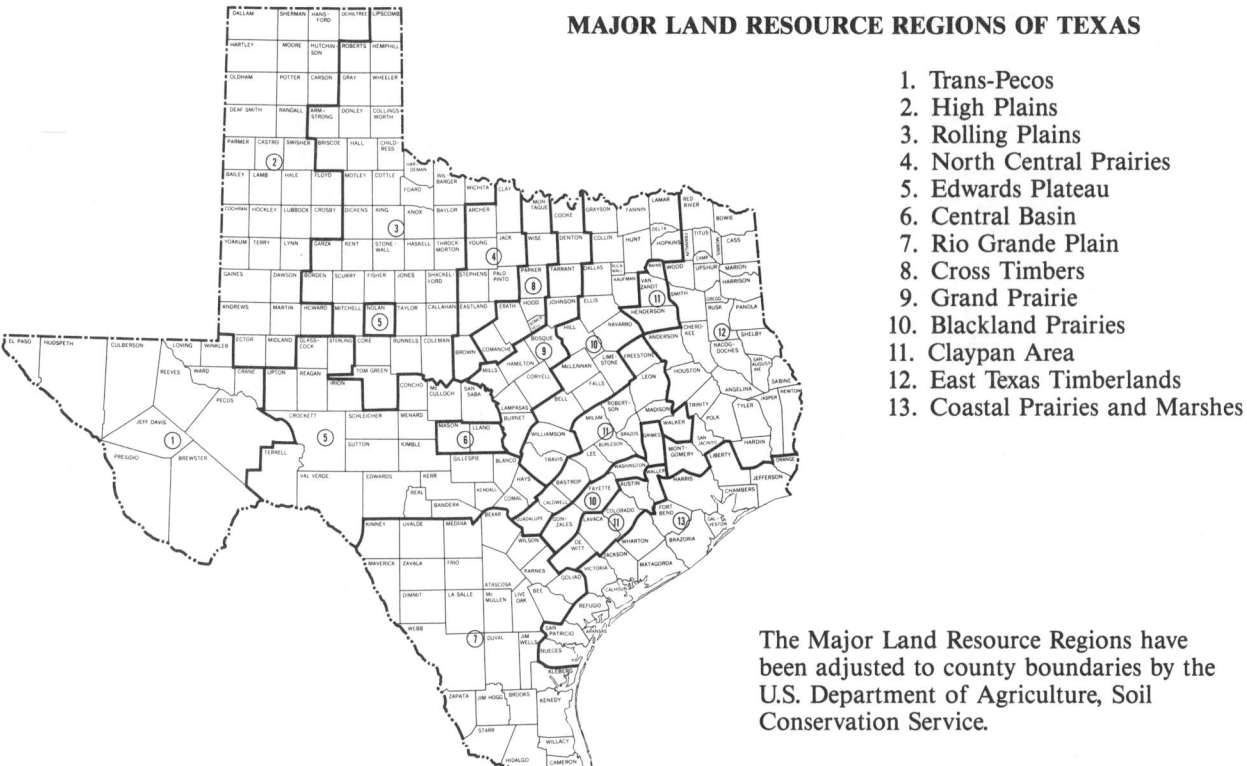

MAJOR LAND RESOURCE REGIONS OF TEXAS

1. Trans-Pecos
2. High Plains
3. Rolling Plains
4. North Central Prairies
5. Edwards Plateau
6. Central Basin
7. Rio Grande Plain
8. Cross Timbers
9. Grand Prairie
10. Blackland Prairies
11. Claypan Area
12. East Texas Timberlands
13. Coastal Prairies and Marshes

The Major Land Resource Regions have been adjusted to county boundaries by the U.S. Department of Agriculture, Soil Conservation Service.

The Major Land Resource Regions of Texas vary in soil types, amounts of precipitation and vegetation. There are approximately 800 different soils in Texas. The annual rainfall varies from over 56 inches in East Texas to less than eight inches in parts of West Texas and the vegetation ranges from pine and hardwood forests to desert shrubs. The state has been divided into 13 Major Land Resource Regions, each having similar soils, vegetation and climate. **TRANS-PECOS** The total land area is about 18.5 million acres, with broad desert basins and valleys bordered by gently to strongly sloping hillsides. Steep mountain ranges running north and south and many small plateaus are in the western part of the region. Elevations in the area range from 2,400 to over 7,900 feet. The soils are deep to very shallow clayey loams, clays and desert sands. The annual rainfall ranges from eight to 18 inches. The area supports desert grasses, cacti, giant and mesa dropseed, along with scattered shrubs such as sand sagebrush, creosotebush, tarbush, catclaw and javalinabush. Giant sacation and vine-mesquite grow in drainageways and depressions, while juniper, pinyon, ponderosa pine and Douglasfir can be found on the upper mountain slopes. **HIGH PLAINS** The total land area is about 18.8 million acres with smooth, gently sloping plains except along major rivers where breaks are very steep. Elevations range from 2,000 to 5,000 feet and the soils vary from deep, clayey loams to sands. The annual rainfall ranges from 14 to 21 inches. The area's vegetation is made up of short grasses such as blue grama and buffalograss, mid grasses such as sideoats grama on the more open soils and tall grasses like sand bluestem, little bluestem and Indiangrass with shinnery oak and sand sagebrush on the sandy soils. A wide range of perennial forbs grow on the sandier soils and are characterized by dotted gayfeather, pitchersage, sagewort, bushsunflower and daleas. **ROLLING PLAINS** The total land area is about 22.6 million acres with the elevation ranging from 1,500 to 2,750 feet. The area consists mainly of gently sloping plains that increase in

height gradually from the east to west. In the valleys, slopes are short and steep. Soils are deep sandy loams, clayey loams and clays. The annual rainfall ranges from 18 to 28 inches. The area supports mid and tall grasses such as sand and little bluestem and sand sagebrush on the coarse textured soils and little bluestem, gramas and associated grasses and forbs on the finer textured soils. **NORTH CENTRAL PRAIRIES** The total land area is about 7.1 million acres. The area consists mainly of undulating prairies with narrow, steep-sided valleys. Elevations range from 500 to 2,000 feet. Soils are deep, sandy loams and clayey loams with some stony areas. The annual rainfall ranges from 25 to 32 inches. The savannah vegetation is fairly uniform throughout the area despite the variation in soils. Little and big bluestem, Indiangrass, sideoats, hairy grama and Texas wintergrass are the dominant grasses. Post and blackjack oak, sumacs, bumelias and elm are the dominant trees. There are numerous perennial forbs, including Maximilian sunflower, heath aster, bushsunflower and Engelmann-daisy. **EDWARDS PLATEAU** The total land area is about 23.1 million acres. The valleys are narrow to broad and have gently sloping to steep walls and smooth floors. Their elevation ranges from 600 to 1,500 feet. The elevation of hills and plateaus ranges from 1,200 to 3,650 feet. Hills are sloping to very steep and plateaus are broad and nearly level. The soils are shallow to very shallow stony clays and clayey loams. The annual rainfall ranges from 12 to 32 inches. This region supports a plant community ranging from desert shrub, mid and short grasses and an abundance of low-growing woody plants in the west, to a mixed oak savannah with tall and mid grasses in the east. The savannah has nearly open grasslands with scattered trees mixed with grasses and forbs in great abundance. **CENTRAL BASIN** The total land area is about 1.7 million acres with elevations ranging from 600 to 1,200 feet. The broad valleys have moderately sloping walls and smooth to undulating floors, the hills are moderately sloping to steep and the plateaus

FLYING THE COLORS: TEXAS ©JOHN CLEMENTS 1984

are broad and gently sloping. Soils are gravelly and stony or sandy and loamy. The annual rainfall ranges from 25 to 30 inches. This region supports a mixed oak savannah vegetation of live, post and blackjack oak with tall and mid grasses such as little pinhole and bluestem, sideoats grama, Indiangrass, switchgrass, sand and plains lovegrass, green sprangletop, purpletop and plains bristlegrass. Such forbs as orange zexmania, bushsunflower, Englemann-daisy and trailing ratany grow throughout the area. **RIO GRANDE PLAIN** This region is broken into four divisions: northern, western, central and lower with elevations ranging from sea level to 600 feet. The northern division has a total land area of about 4.5 million acres, and is a gently undulating plain with smooth hills and gently undulating valleys. Soils are deep to shallow clayey to sandy loams. The annual rainfall ranges from 17 to 21 inches. It supports open grassland with scattered mesquite, live oak and other trees. Little bluestem, sideoats grama, lovegrass tridens, fourflower trichloris, Arizona cottontop, plains bristlegrass and other mid grasses are dominant on the deeper soils. On the shallow soils the grasslands have scattered low-growing brush, such as guajillo, blackbrush, elbowbush, and kidneywood, and mid grasses such as Arizona cottontop, sideoats grama, green sprangletop, and twoflower trichloris. The western division has a total land area of about 4.5 million acres. It is a gently undulating plain where soils are deep to shallow clayey loams and sandy loams with some shallow soils being gravelly. Annual rainfall ranges from 17 to 21 inches. Mid grasses such as alkali sacation, twoflower trichloris, pink whiplash and pappusgrass, white tredens and vine-mesquite are dominant on the deep, clayey soils. The more gravelly soils support semiopen grassland vegetation of mid grasses interspersed with low-growing shrubs. The central division has a total land area of about 5.1 million acres. It is a gently undulating plain where soils are deep, sandy loams and sands. The annual rainfall ranges from 21 to 26 inches. The major vegetation on soils with deep, fine, sandy surfaces are tall and mid grasses such as seacoast bluestem Indiangrass, crinkleawn, tanglehead and an abundant variety of perennial legumes and forbs. On the loamy soils there are mid grasses such as Arizona cottontop, fourflower trichloris, tanglehead, plains lovegrass, and pinhole bluestem. Many forbs and low-growing shrubs, including condalias, vine ephedra and guajillo grow with these grasses. The lower division has a total land area of about 2.0 million acres. A nearly level plain, the soils are deep clayey loams, clays and sandy loams. The annual rainfall ranges from 17 to 28 inches. Twoflower and fourflower trichloris, plains bristlegrass and lovegrass tridens are among the dominant grasses. Desert yaupon, spiny hackberry and blackbrush are the major woody plants. Tall and mid grasses such as switchgrass, giant sacaton, fourflower trichloris, big sandbur, little bluestem and southwestern bristlegrass are dominant on bottom lands with hackberry and elm the major trees. **CROSS TIMBERS** This region is broken into two divisions, east and west with elevations ranging from 250 to 2,000 feet. The west division has a total land area of about 2.5 million acres. It is a gently rolling plain with narrow stream valleys that have steep sides. The soils are sandy loams, loamy sands and sands. The annual rainfall ranges from 25 to 32 inches. Little and big bluestem, purpletop tridens, Indiangrass, switchgrass, sand lovegrass, post and blackjack oak, elm, coralberry, greenbrier and elbowbush are the dominant vegetation. The east division has a total land area of about 0.7 million acres. It is a gently rolling plain with narrow, steep-sided valleys. The soils are loamy sands and sandy loams. The annual rainfall ranges from 34 to 39 inches. Little and big bluestem, purpletop tridens, Indiangrass, switchgrass, post and blackjack oak, elm, coralberry, American beautyberry, bumelia, greenbrier and elbowbush are some of the dominant vegetation. Engelmann-daisy and trailing wildbeans are among the numerous perennial forbs. **GRAND PRAIRIE** The total land area is about 6.5 million acres with elevations ranging from 250 to 2,000 feet. Dominated by rolling to hilly prairies with stream valleys that are shallow and narrow in their upper reaches, but deep and broad near the eastern edge of the area. The soils are deep to shallow, stony, clayey loams and clays. The annual rainfall ranges from 30 to 35 inches. Little and big bluestem, Indiangrass, and switchgrass are typical grasses with sideoats and tall grama, scattered shrub, live oak and juniper trees on the very shallow soils and along steep slopes. **BLACKLAND PRAIRIES** The total land area is about 12.7 million acres with elevations ranging from 250 to 1,000 feet. The area is a nearly level to gently rolling plain with gently sloping uplands. Large rivers cross the area in broad and shallow valleys. Significant tracts of hilly land run along the west near Austin. The soils are deep, clay loams and clays. The annual rainfall ranges from 30 to 45 inches. This region supports true prairie vegetation in which little bluestem is dominant. Indiangrass, big bluestem, switchgrass, and eastern gamagrass are the major species with many forbs. Oak, elm, cottonwood, hackberry and pecan trees produce a scattered hardwood cover. **CLAYPAN AREA** The total land area is about 6.2 million acres with elevations ranging from 250 to 1,000 feet. The area is nearly level to gently rolling with the valleys of large streams shallow and wide flood plains bordered by level uplands. The soils have thin sandy, loamy surfaces and dense, clayey subsoils. The annual rainfall ranges from 40 to 45 inches. Little bluestem is dominant in all areas, along with Indiangrass, brownseed paspalum, beaked panicum, switchgrass and big bluestem. Some mixed pine-hardwood forests are in the southwest and east. Hardwood forests of oak, elm, pecan and other species grow on the wet bottom lands. **EAST TEXAS TIMBERLANDS** This region is made up of two divisions, rolling woods and flatwoods. The rollingwoods division has a total land area of about 15.3 million acres. It is a gently rolling to hilly area where soils are deep, sandy loams, loamy sands and sands. The annual rainfall is 40-56 inches. Loblolly pine and shortleaf pine grow with sweetgum, post, southern red and white oak and flowering dogwood. American beautyberry, greenbriar, hawthorns and others make up the woody undergrowth. Little and pinhole bluestem are the dominant grasses plus beaked panicum, longleaf uniola, spike uniola and yellow Indiangrass. The flatwoods division has a total land area of about 2.2 million acres of nearly level to gently sloping land. The soils are sandy loams and sands. The annual rainfall ranges from 46 to 55 inches. It supports pine and hardwood forest characterized by the longleaf pine. Sweetgum, blackgum, post, blackjack and southern red oak are the principal hardwood species. Mid and tall grasses are dominant in open areas with little pinhole and big bluestems, switchgrass and Indiangrass. In shady areas the longleaf uniola, Virginia wildrye and several low-growing panicums and paspalums are the principal grasses. **COASTAL PRAIRIES AND MARSHES** This region has two divisions, the coastal prairies and the coastal marshes with the elevation ranging from sea level to 250 feet. The coastal prairies have a total land area of about 9.3 million acres of nearly level prairie with clayey loams and clay soils. The annual rainfall ranges from 28 to 56 inches. This area supports a true prairie plant community with little and big bluestem, Indiangrass and switchgrass dominant. A few groves of live oak dot the landscape. The coastal marshes have a total land area of about 1.5 million acres of nearly level marshes or semimarsh areas with some sand dunes along the beaches. Soils are clayey loams, beach sand and clays. The annual rainfall ranges from 40 to 55 inches. The more saline soils support a plant community of gulf cordgrass and smaller amounts of little bluestem, switchgrass, seashore saltgrass, inland saltgrass, bushy sea-oxeye, marshhay cordgrass, rushes, sedges and pickleweed. The less saline sandy soils support a plant community of little bluestem and lesser amounts of switchgrass, gulfdune paspalum and marshhay cordgrass.

REGIONS OF CLIMATE

CLIMATIC ATLAS OF TEXAS 1983, TEXAS DEPARTMENT OF WATER RESOURCES

REGIONS OF CLIMATE CLASSIFICATION IN TEXAS

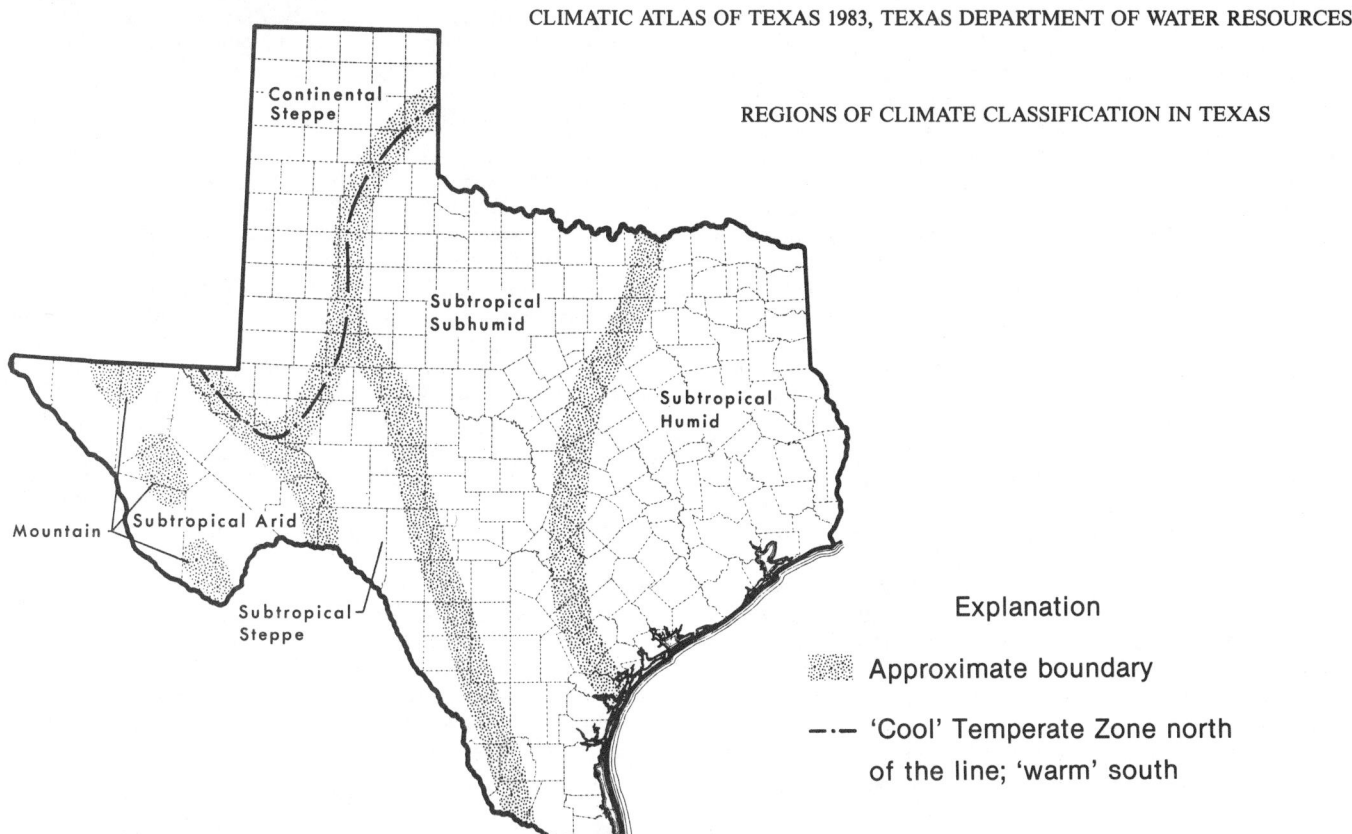

Explanation

▦ Approximate boundary

—·— 'Cool' Temperate Zone north of the line; 'warm' south

The seasonal progression of weather in Texas is much like a symphony: beginning in the fall is the overture with rather gentle, but distinct weather changes being noted, then in winter the weather changes are more frequent and more abrupt, reaching a crescendo or climax with the clashing of cymbals typified by the thunderstorms and hailstorms of late winter and spring. Following this a marked decrease in frontal activity in late spring is a prelude to the quiet period of the Texas summer, which is generally hot and dry. The only areas of relief from the heat at this time is along the Texas coast from Galveston and Corpus Christi to Brownsville, and in far north and west Texas and the Edwards Plateau Region where the nights are somewhat cooler due primarily to higher elevations and drier air. By the time of the autumnal equinox (September 22) almost without exception temperatures will reflect a change from those of the summer extremes of July and August. The first perceptible change will be noted in the lower minimum temperatures rather than a significant change in the average daily maximum temperatures. Occasional frontal passages begin to occur in late August and early September. In winter daily temperature changes are larger and sharp temperature variations may be expected with frequent frontal passages. Sometimes the cloud band associated with a front may be less than 20 miles, or as wide as 100 miles. Fast moving cold fronts will produce greater lifting of the air, therefore greater instability, more turbulence and heavier thunderstorms with stronger winds. During spring Texas weather not only has warmed significantly from its winter freezes and low minimum temperatures, a new phase has begun. As cold Continental Polar air clashes with the warming and more humid Maritime Tropical air, the temperature contrasts are greater in the atmosphere and more violent types of weather are the result. Severe thunderstorms with hail and the possibility of a tornado will exist in the spring storm systems as they move rapidly across the state. **SUBTROPICAL HUMID** Texas lies within both the "cool" and "warm" sections of the Temperate Zone in the northern

hemisphere and has five climatic regions. The eastern one-third of Texas is most noted for its warm, humid summers. The prevailing airmass during the summer is Maritime Tropical with its characteristic high humidity and conditional instability that requires only a small amount of lifting by fronts or only daily afternoon heating, to become unstable. When this occurs it usually results in cumulus clouds which may grow into rainshowers and thunderstorms. In this region large amounts of precipitation may accrue in a given location as thunderstorm cells tend to move slowly in tropical airmasses. Beginning in September, fronts begin to push through bringing refreshing relief in the form of drier air, cooler temperatures and rainfall. As the season progresses thunderstorms may become heavier and cold fronts more frequent. Winters are cool and dry, with a rare injection of Continental Arctic air bringing severe freezes to the area in January. Snow in winter is rare except in the northern portions of East Texas where a few inches will fall. A variety of weather phenomena reach their maximum frequency and intensity during spring. Thunderstorms will occasionally become severe, with accompanying damaging winds, large hail and even a tornado is at risk at this time. Duststorms also move across the region in spring. Dust is picked up in New Mexico and West Texas by dry Pacific fronts and carried aloft up to one mile above the ground by the winds which carry the dust eastward through the entire state and beyond. In the case of major duststorms, visibilities can be reduced to one mile or less. Fog can be a problem spring and fall. Fog will fall into one of three categories: (1) radiation fog, usually after a rain, during a clear, cool night (2) advection fog, when warmer air with higher dewpoints is carried by winds to an area of lower dewpoints and brings the air to saturation (3) sea fog which is very erratic and may improve during the evening or before daybreak. Tropical storms and hurricanes are at risk, especially in the immediate coastal areas from June through October. The hurricanes will decrease in intensity after crossing from the Gulf of Mexico onto land because they loose the warm, moist Gulf and slightly cooler, drier air is drawn into the circulation pattern. Besides the damage of hurricane force winds and rain, tornadoes may be found primarily near the "eye" or center of the hurricane. Wide spread flooding may occur in association with slow moving storms. **SUBTROPICAL SUBHUMID** The central one-third of Texas falls into this category and is characterized by hot summers and dry winters. Precipitation is greater during fall and spring. In summer there is an infusion of Continental Tropical air from Mexico. During fall and spring there is an increased frequency of Maritime Pacific air. This air has been dried as it passes over the mountain ranges to the west, but as it reaches this region of Texas with its generally moist air, thunderstorms may develop along the leading edge as it invades the region. Although summers are dry, airmass thunderstorms may occur and some areas may receive rain while others nearby will receive none. As frontal activity begins to move through the area with some regularity in the fall the precipitation distribution becomes more general. Winters in this zone are generally dry: most of the snowfall is during January from the Edwards Plateau, Temple, Palestine, Longview line northward. Thunderstorms, a particular feature of this region, can occur any month of the year, but reach a maximum in spring. Thunderstorms move across the region generally from west to east and frequently in lines of over 150 miles in length and 25 to 50 miles in width. The tops of such "line squall" thunderstorms may reach as high as 50,000 feet. These are severe thunderstorms and will contain damaging surface winds, large hail and possible tornadoes. In this region a particular feature known as "the dry line" (a dew point discontinuity line) divides the Maritime Tropical air to the east and the Maritime Pacific air to the west. Some 25 to 50 miles east of the dry line thunderstorms will suddenly form parallel to the "dry line", moving eastward or northeastward with the "steering winds". The band of thunderstorms usually form along a line from Childress to Abilene, to east of San Angelo, Texas. They will move eastward at speeds of about 30 miles per hour to the coastal and eastern most section of the state within a 24 hour period. Fog may be a problem in this zone on occasions and especially in the central and southern areas from late fall to early spring. The greatest occurrence of fog is in the early morning hours from before daybreak until about 10 A.M. Sea fog which is quite variable forms in late afternoon and early evening off shore in the cold water belt and moves inland about dark. Flooding in this region is somewhat rare but does occur as a result of "flash flooding" due to extremely heavy rains that persist for hours at a time. This action may be in association with tropical storms, formerly hurricanes, that move very slowly across an area bringing 15 to 20 inches of rain in one or two days, or may be triggered by slow moving tropical air thunderstorms with rainfall rates in excess of one inch of rainfall per hour. **SUBTROPICAL STEPPE** This region is characterized by semi-arid to arid conditions. The prevailing airmasses are Continental Tropical and Maritime Tropical in summer and Maritime Tropical in winter with frequent infusions of Maritime Pacific and an occasional entry of Continental Polar air. This area is characterized by sub-marginal precipitation and very hot summers with temperatures exceeding 100 °F on most days of July and August. Frontal passages will be experienced ten months of the year, except for July and August. On the average most of the rainfall occurs during the month of September and is most likely to be associated with weakening tropical hurricanes or tropical storms. precipitation from frontal passages although heavy at times is sparse and brief. Snowfall is rare in this area. Thunderstorms in this area include severe storms that may contain unusually large hail. Fog in this region is less likely to be a problem because of the relative dryness of the airmasses involved. Duststorms will move across the area especially in spring with visibilities reduced

from one to three miles. Floods are rare, but when they do occur they most likely will be of the "flash flood" type. **SUBTROPICAL ARID** The basin and plateau region of the Trans-Pecos features a subtropical arid climate that is characterized by hot summers and relatively cool nights. Precipitation patterns vary widely, with heavier amounts in the mountainous regions and almost none in the lowlands. The dryness of this zone is due to two important factors: the heating and drying effects of air flowing down from higher elevations known as the "down slope effect" or adiabatic heating and the location and altitude which precludes the invasion of Maritime Tropical air in most cases. Continental Tropical air, which is very hot and dry, prevails during summer. Due to the dryness of the air and the altitude of the region, daily temperature changes are large enough to bring relief from the heat at night. Continental Polar air invades the region from time to time during winter. Thunderstorms do occur and may become severe with locally heavy rains, large hail and "flash flooding", but precipitation is sparse. When the area does receive general rain it will occur as a result of a weakening tropical storm moving through the region from Mexico. Snow does occur in winter in association with migratory winter storm systems moving through far western Texas and northern Mexico. Snow, like rainfall, accumulates far less at the lower elevations and due to the dryness of the air will disappear quickly. Duststorms during late winter and spring are common. Surface winds may exceed 55 miles per hour as strong fronts pass through the area with visibilities reduced to nearly zero at times. **CONTINENTAL STEPPE** The region with the coldest climate in the state, it is a plateau region marked by irregular summer precipitation and semi-arid to arid conditions which are usually associated with areas to the lee side of mountain ranges. Maritime Tropical air occurs far less than in the Subtropical Subhumid region. Continental Tropical air during the summer produces hot, dry summers. Continental Polar and Maritime Pacific airmasses will penetrate this region rarely during summer, but will begin to do so with regularity in September, reaching a maximum during winter and early spring. Maritime Pacific air passes over the mountains to the west and northwest, drying and warming somewhat in the process so that precipitation is light and temperatures relatively mild. Continental Arctic air which is extremely cold may reach this area during the winter and may be associated with heavy snows and near blizzard conditions brought about as deepening lows or storm centers develop on the lee side of the Southern Rocky Mountains of Colorado. Winds will increase, snow will blow, visibilities will be reduced to near zero, and temperatures will drop to well below freezing. These severe winter storms will move along storm tracks "guided" by the jetstream, a fast moving current of air meandering through the atmosphere between 25,000 and 45,000 feet. The average storm track guides the storms from southern Colorado over northern portions of Texas and eastward across western Oklahoma. During spring severe thunderstorms will occur along and south of this track with damaging winds, hail, dust and even a few tornadoes. Duststorms at times will become a major consideration as these strong winds drive dust from New Mexico and West Texas eastward across all of Texas and much of the nation. During the height of severe duststorms, surface winds will exceed 50 miles per hour and visibilities may be reduced to near zero. Fog is usually associated with relatively cool, moist air and frequently occurs during the night following a slow moving cold front which has produced rain. Although hurricanes do not reach this area, weakening tropical storms do migrate through the southern sections of this region from Mexico. Much needed rain may be brought to this area in this way in late summer. Flooding of the "flash flood" type may result from heavy thunderstorms which move slowly during summer.

WATER RESOURCES

Texas Department of Water Resources

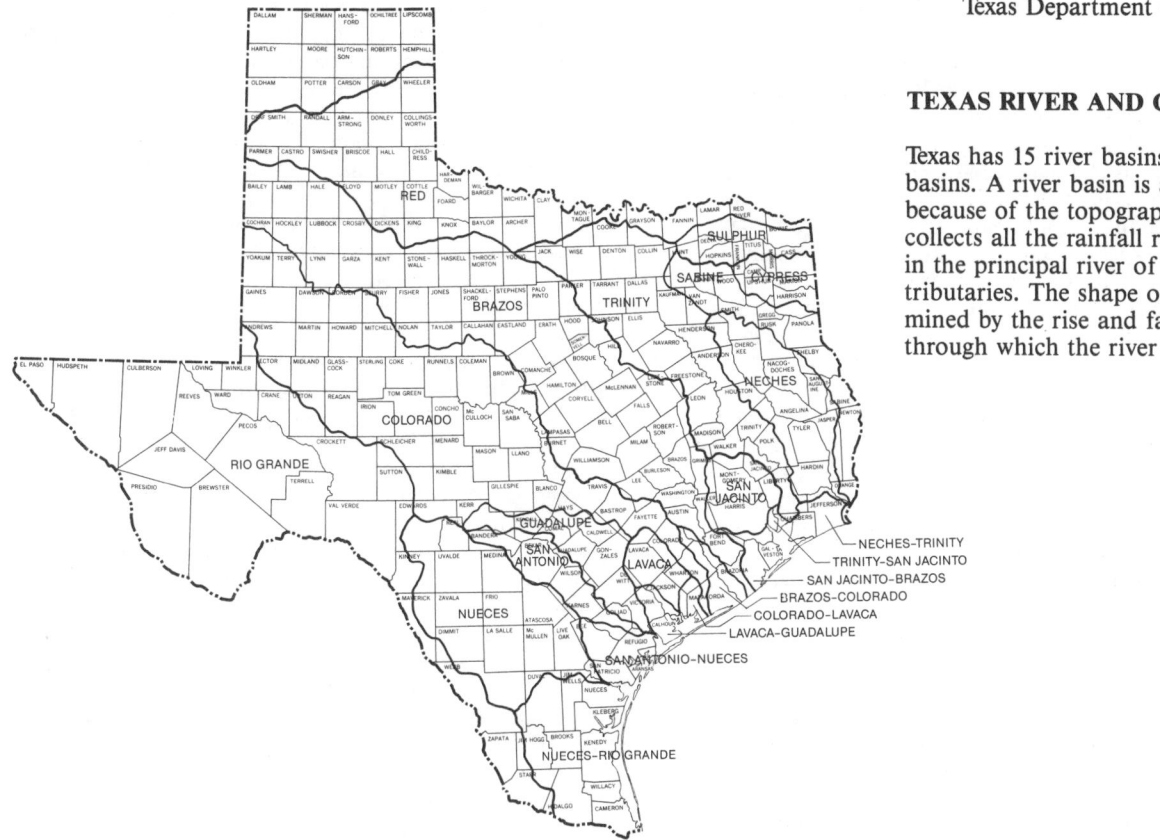

TEXAS RIVER AND COASTAL BASINS

Texas has 15 river basins and eight coastal basins. A river basin is an area which, because of the topography of the land, collects all the rainfall runoff in the basin in the principal river of the basin and its tributaries. The shape of a basin is determined by the rise and fall of the land through which the river flows.

Texans use enough water each year to cover the 18 million acres of the High Plains Region of Texas with a foot of water. For over two years a drought has held parts of west and central Texas in its grip. By July, 1984 the drought had spread to the majority of Texas with farming and ranching affected in all except 20 of the 254 counties. Rainfall was 30 to 50% below normal for most of the state in the first half of 1984 with 55 counties suffering severe drought. For the first time in 20 years the Guadalupe River stopped flowing into Canyon Lake and by mid July 68 towns and cities in central and south Texas were under mandatory water rationing. Water consumption was at record levels in many areas during early July; San Antonio's underground water supply, the Edward's aquifer, was at is lowest in 17 years and Corpus Christi officials were forced to release water from the new Choke Canyon Dam. Over half of Texas is underlaid by seven major aquifers (underground water supplies) and 17 minor aquifers of local importance. Groundwater supplies 70% of the water used in Texas, most of which is used in irrigated agriculture, with the balance from surface water supplies. In addition there ar 3,700 designated streams and tributaries with 80,000 miles of streambeds. Since 1930 over 100 major reservoirs, each with a capacity of over 5,000 acre feet of water, have been constructed in Texas. The total water supply storage capacity is 32.3 million acre feet. Even in a critical drought period the major reservoirs will supply 10 million acre feet annually. Rapid population expansion, economic development and a heavy reliance on irrigated agriculture have resulted in numerous existing and anticipated water supply shortages in Texas. There is little excess surface storage capacity in many areas to meet water demands during periods of drought. Groundwater, which has historically supplied large areas with water, is being consumed more rapidly than it is being replaced through natural recharge. Heavy industrialization and population increases in the metropolitan areas have resulted in steadily rising water requirements, with the cities of San Antonio and Corpus Christi facing short-term water supply problems.

The population of rural areas is on the increase after decades of decline, and rural systems are having difficulties providing dependable, uninterrupted service and meeting drinking water standards. The small size of these systems often means high costs per customer. Heavy pumping from the fresh water aquifers has resulted in water level declines and in some areas a deterioration in water quality. The Carrizo Aquifer in south Texas, for example, has experienced extreme water level declines as has the Gulf Coast Aquifer in Jackson County on the central Texas coast. The extensive pumping of the Hensell and Hosston Aquifers in the mid Brazo River Basin has led to severe water level declines and saline water encroachment. Groundwater from the Ogallala Aquifer is the primary source of water for the High Plains area. Severe water level declines have occurred and it is expected that the Ogallala will be exhausted in 20 to 50 years. Problems of water quality and pollution in Texas are caused both by natural occurrences and human activity. Natural salinity is a severe problem in the upper Colorado River Basin and in the Brazos River Basin, and in some instances improper oil well drilling or plugging have allowed saline waters into fresh water supplies. Much of the surface water pollution originates in the metropolitan areas; however, small amounts of a variety of pesticides are widely distributed in the surface waters of Texas. Flooding is a common problem across Texas. In East Texas the streams flow through broad, flat valleys and floods are generally broad, slow moving and inundate the land for prolonged periods, adversely affecting agriculture. In the central and western areas heavy rainfall causes flash floods. Coastal areas are subjected to flooding from heavy rain and from tidal surge and many urban and agricultural areas in the Gulf Region have drainage problems. In fact much of the eastern third of the state has poor drainage, with an estimated 6 million acres affected. Salinity is a major problem in irrigated agricultural areas from the Gulf to the High Plains. An estimated 5 to 20% of the irrigated areas are affected, except in the western Rio Grande plain along the coast to Beaumont, which has about 50% saline soils. Most of the state is susceptible to water erosion, with extensive gully erosion in central and east Texas. Shoreline erosion along the Gulf Coast can cause loss of land and the destruction of piers, buildings and highways. **LAND SUBSIDENCE** Land subsidence is a serious problem along the coast, especially in the Houston-Galveston area, where large groundwater withdrawals have drastically reduced the artesia pressure in the Gulf Coast Aquifer, causing considerable compaction of the clays. In an area of 2,500 square miles the land has subsided from one to nine feet. Subsidence has caused considerable damage to buildings, sewers, pipelines, underground cables, streets, bridges, railroads and airport runways in Harris County. Along the western shore of Galveston Bay lands which 30 years ago were above high tide are now permanently beneath the water of the Bay. **SALINE WATER** The most serious occurrences of saline water entering fresh water supplies is along the Gulf Coast. In general, fresh to slightly saline groundwater both underlies and overlies a saline groundwater. When the layers of fresh water are excessively pumped, the saline groundwater seeps into the fresh water aquifers. Houston, Galveston, Texas City, Freeport, Port Lavaca and other cities in the area have all been forced to reduce pumping, move wells and/or develop surface water supplies. The potential for saline water encroachment is very high in Kleberg, Calhoun and Jackson Counties, the San Antonio (Edwards Aquifer) and the Winter Garden District in Dimmit, Zavala, Frio and LaSalle Counties (Carrizo-Wilcox Aquifer). **RIO GRANDE REGION** To achieve an equitable apportionment of the waters of the Rio Grande River the states of Texas, New Mexico and Colorado entered into a compact in 1938. In addition, New Mexico and Texas entered into a compact in 1948 to apportion the waters of the Pecos River. A watermaster is responsible for daily allocations of water to diverters holding rights to water from the Rio Grande. Water diverted for irrigation accounts for the largest use of streamflow and variations in streamflow require water storage to assure a dependable supply. The water is used and reused by the three states and Mexico. Salts from leaching are usually returned to the streams along with municipal and industrial effluents so the water quality deteriorates downstream. Groundwater is an important part of the region's water supply. The water quality varies from acceptable to brackish and withdrawals must be carefully controlled to prevent encroachment of brackish water into fresh water pools. Some groundwater is available in the lower Rio Grande Valley but is generally too saline for municipal or industrial use. Use of the groundwater for irrigation has resulted in severe soil salinity problems. Increasing demands exceed existing reliable supplies throughout this region. **PECOS RIVER AREA** A saline supply of surface water from the Red Bluff Reservoir on the Pecos River is used in small quantities for irrigation in Reeves, Pecos, Loving and Ward Counties, but groundwater is the principal source of irrigation water. The groundwater supply is declining as pumpage exceeds the natural recharge rates to the aquifers and it is becoming more saline. A number of areas in Reeves County are no longer cultivated due to the poor quality and inadequate amounts of water, although heavy water applications on salt tolerant crops such as cotton permit some irrigated agriculture. The deterioration of the water quality of the Pecos River is due primarily to natural brine emissions in New Mexico and the McMillan Delta project is operated to alleviate the salinity problems. The increased costs of energy to pump irrigation water have caused additional problems—the price increases plus a requirement of up to 44 inches of water to leach the salts from the soil have made it impossible for many farmers to produce at a profitable level. **LOWER RIO GRANDE VALLEY** The counties of Starr, Willacy, Hidalgo, and Cameron encompass 4,241 square miles. A favorable climate and port facilities encouraged this area to expand its irrigated agriculture, petroleum

refining, petrochemical production, synthetic textile production and food processing—all of which are water intensive. Water supplies available include a small quantity of groundwater and Rio Grande water from the Amista and Falcon Reservoirs. The groundwater is saline and widespread use for irrigation has caused soil salinity problems. In addition, overapplication of irrigation water has resulted in local drainage problems. Municipal and industrial water use is approximately 65 million gallons per day (72,809 acre feet per year) with steam electric power plants consuming an additional 5,000 acre feet annually. In addition to individual industries which have developed water supplies, there are 39 purveyors of municipal, domestic and industrial water supplies, several irrigation districts which also supply water to a number of small communities and 42 communities (about 20% of the Valley population) which are not served by a public water supply system. Inferior water quality and problems with insufficient piant capacity plague most of the Valley population. By the year 2000 studies indicate that water shortages could occur 70% of the time. **EL PASO** There are four major sources of fresh water in El Paso County; the Hueco Bolson, the La Mesa Bolson, the Rio Grande groundwater and the Rio Grande River. The city of Juarez, across the Rio Grande River in Mexico, also draws its water from the Hueco Bolson. About 80% of the water is pumped for municipal use and 20% by various industries. The Hueco Bolson is being depleted and saline water encroachment is a problem. The surface water supplies are used for irrigated agriculture and also have water quality problems. **RURAL** Approximately 600 public water systems may be in violation of the U.S. Safe Drinking Water Act. A significant number of Texans (an estimated 6%) are affected. The relatively small size of these water systems could create financial problems in providing and operating either the necessary treatment facilities or developing alternative sources of supply. An estimated 504 systems do not comply with fluoride requirements and a large number of systems suffer from nitrate contamination. **BEAUMONT-PORT ARTHUR** Orange and Jefferson Counties contain large population centers which are highly industrialized and thousands of acres of irrigated cropland. Large diversions of water from the Neches River have created water quality problems. Salt water from the Gulf migrates up the Neches, requiring the construction of a salt water barrier upstream of Beaumont, and urban returns often constitute the majority of the flow in the river. Water is supplied in Jefferson County primarily by the Lower Neches Valley Authority (LNVA) and the city of Beaumont. A system of canals serves much of the county and during the rice growing season the LNVA supplies water to irrigate approximately 78.5 million acres in Jefferson, Liberty and Chambers Counties. With the salt water barriers in place, the Neches River essentially becomes a waste disposal channel. **UPPER TRINITY RIVER BASIN** Collin, Cooke, Dallas, Denton, Ellis, Hood, Hunt, Johnson, Kaufman, Parker, Tarrant and Wise Counties are within the upper Trinity River Basin. The population and economic base of the area are in rapid expansion, creating heavy demands on water supplies. The majority of the water is supplied by surface water sources with about 74,000 acre feet pumped each year from the Trinity Group and Woodbine Aquifers. Excessive fluoride concentrations are a problem in many parts of the aquifers. The most severe groundwater problem in the area, however, is the declining pumping levels (pumping lifts exceed 1,000 feet in many wells) causing a shift to surface water supplies. Twenty-seven major reservoirs currently serve this area, with three used exclusively for steam electric power plants. Water supplies in the area, except in local areas with rapid expansion, are adequate for the next 20 years unless a drought occurs. The Trinity River in the Dallas-Fort Worth area suffers from pollution and, although the river tends to purify itself as it flows downstream, some water quality

WATER RESOURCES

problems are experienced all the way downstream to Lake Livingston. **HOUSTON METROPOLITAN AREA** The wastes from both domestic and indusrial sources, the periodic lack of dissolved oxygen in surface waters and salt water encroachment due to excessive groundwater pumpage have caused water quality problems. The metropolitan area is drained almost entirely by the Buffalo Bayou which has been channelized in its lower reaches into the Houston Ship Channel. Houston, the Houston Ship Channel industrial complex and the ports of Galveston, Texas City and Houston have undergone tremendous growth. The channels and bays have received large quantities of wastes which, together with the sluggish flows of the waterways and the tidal action, have overloaded the natural purification of the estuary. Historically the area has obtained the majority of its water supply from the Gulf Coast Aquifer. However excessive pumping has caused a decline in the water level of over 400 feet, allowing salt water to enter the fresh water supply. The Texas City and Galveston areas are both affected by this problem. The land has subsided between one and 8.5 feet, permanently inundating lands previously above high tides, and surface drainage has become less effective, causing a severe flood risk in the area. Surface waters from the Trinity River Basin and the Brazos River are being diverted for use in southern Harris County to reduce the use of ground water and slow the rate of land subsidence. **HASKELL AND JONES COUNTIES** The Seymour Aquifer has high concentrations of nitrogen and the salinity has increased in recent years. The high nitrate content renders it unsafe for human consumption and, when extremely high, for livestock. Both problems increase the costs for water treatment when the water is used for municipal purposes. **BRAZOS BASIN ABOVE POSSUM KINGDOM RESERVOIR** Full utilization of the water resources of the main stem of the Brazos River is not possible at present due to the high salinity from natural salt pollution. Numerous salt flats are located within the drainage system. Sulfate from gypsum bearing rock formations is also a problem. In critical years cities such as Waco and Marlin have been forced to use the Brazos River as a supplemental water supply. In the lower reaches of the Brazos the water is used for irrigation and industrial purposes due to large inflows of good quality water in that region. However, during some periods the flow remains of poor quality even in the lower reaches of the river. **CARRIZO AQUIFER, WINTER GARDEN AREA** The area consists of all or part of Atascosa, Bexar, Caldwell, Dimmit, Frio, Gonzales, Guadalupe, Karnes, LaSalle, Live Oak, McMullen, Maverick, Medina, Uvalde, Webb, Wilson and Zavala Counties. The Carrizo Aquifer is heavily pumped, with an average of 172,000 acre feet pumped in excess of recharge each year. The water levels are declining and the water quality in Dimmit, Zavala and eastern Maverick Counties has been affected. In Dimmit, for example, saline water from the Bigford Formation is leaking through old well bores and contaminating the Carrizo Aquifer. The large declines in the water level has reduced well yields causing deeper wells, larger motors and new wells to meet demands. **EDWARDS (BALCONES FAULT ZONE) AQUIFER** The San Antonio metropolitan area is the largest urban area in the nation which depends solely on groundwater for its municipal and industrial needs. Although studies show that the Edwards Aquifer is capable of meeting the needs of San Antonio, the declining water level is adversely affecting Comal Springs, San Marcos Springs and agriculture. It is also reducing the fresh water inflows to San Antonio Bay. Poor quality water may be drawn into the southern limits of the Edwards Aquifer if water levels are lowered significantly below their lowest historic level. The aquifer extends from central Kinney County through Uvalde, Medina, Bexar, Comal and Hays Counties. Canyon Reservoir on the Guadalupe River is the source of surface water in the area and other reservoirs are planned. **JACKSON COUNTY** The Gulf Coast Aquifer is the only source of fresh water in Jackson County and portions of Lavaca, Wharton and Matagorda. Pumping exceeds the natural recharge and the water levels are falling. An estimated 95 million acre feet of fresh water is in storage under Jackson County, but most of it cannot be used because it occurs at great depths. **CORPUS CHRISTI** The city of Corpus Christi and the surrounding Coastal Bend area obtain their water supply exclusively from surface water in the Nueces River Basin. Impoundment is necessary as the natural flow of the Nueces River varies from floods to no flow during dry periods. Water demand has been steadily increasing and now matches the annual dependable supply of Lake Corpus Christi. Groundwater withdrawals exceed the estimated safe yields from local aquifers. **UPPER COLORADO RIVER** Saline water problems in Scurry, Mitchell, Howard and Coke Counties are the result of saline water in the Upper Colorado River Basin below Lake J.B. Thomas. The salt is both natural and man made. Early oil field operation included the construction of over 200 salt water evaporation pits from which salt water seeped into the fresh water aquifers. The early wells were improperly plugged and allowed saline water from deeper formations to seep into the fresh water aquifers. Naturally occurring saline water from the Santa Rosa Aquifer also discharges into the Colorado River and Beals Creek, a large tributary, has its headwaters in Natural Dam Salt Lake. The water in E.V. Spence Reservoir is marginal for most municipal and industrial uses without treatment due to the salinity. **MID BRAZOS RIVER BASIN** The problem area covers 18 counties in the central part of the Brazos Basin. Groundwater comes from the Henzel and Hosston Aquifer. Since 1900 the water level has dropped over 400 feet because pumping has exceeded recharge. Due to the reduction in the pressure, numerous cities such as Waco, Temple and Hillsboro have been forced to convert their supply to surface water sources. However, the salt pollution in the Brazos River at Waco makes the water unsuitable for use unless blended with high quality water. **COASTAL BAYS AND ESTUARIES** Texas has one of the most diverse coastal regions in the nation and one of the most productive ecosystems in the world. There are seven major estuarine systems. One fundamental aspect in maintaining the health of the systems is the timing, magnitude and quality of the fresh water inflows from the 15 major Texas river basins. Bays and estuaries may be altered in the future as water requirements change the fresh water flows into the estuarine systems. **HIGH PLAINS** The Ogallala Aquifer occurs at or near the surface over much of the 42 county High Plains area of northwest Texas. It ranges from a few feet to over 500 feet thick; north and west of Lubbock it is 100 to 300 feet, south of Lubbock it is 25 to 150 feet and north of Amarillo it is over 500 feet thick. The Ogallaha is one of the most intensely developed aquifers in the United States, supporting over 65% of the irrigated acres in Texas. The pumping is considerably in excess of the annual natural recharge and water levels are declining. The Ogallala will not support the present amount of irrigation much longer. Increasing pumping costs and the declining water levels will substantially reduce the water supplies within 20 to 30 years. Detailed investigations are being conducted as this is one of the most serious water supply problems facing Texas. **WATER FOR TEXAS: PLANNING FOR THE FUTURE** In 1983 the Texas Department of Water Resources reported that currently there are 1,092 public municipal water supply systems, 800 rural water supply corporations and 750 investor-owned public water supply systems operating in Texas. In addition there are 28 river authorities and regional water supply districts that provide water supply and distribution, flood control and water quality protection services, 950 water supply and municipal utility districts, 45 flooding and drainage organizations, 56 drainage districts, eight groundwater conservation districts, one subsidence district and the Gulf Coast Waste Disposal Authority. Thousands of individuals and businesses also develop water supplies, use water, and are engaged in treating wastewater. From 1940 through 1970, statewide runoff averaged 57 million acre feet per year during the wettest period (1940-1950), and 23 million acre feet per year during the severe drought of the early and mid-1950s. There are currently 179 major reservoirs (27 federal and 152 non-federal) with 5,000 acre feet or greater total capacity. In addition, there are 10 reservoirs presently under construction (seven federal and three non-federal). Conservation storage capacity in major existing reservoirs and those under construction total about 32.3 million acre feet. The dependable water supply—the uniform yield that can be withdrawn annually through extended drought periods from major reservoirs—is about 11 million acre feet annually. This supply, however, will not meet all of the projected municipal and industrial needs of many central, south, north central and west Texas cities. Projections also show that many cities in eastern portions of the state will need additional surface water supplies in the immediate future. Of the estimated current water use in the SMSAs, approximately 38 percent or 1.4 million acre feet is supplied from groundwater resources and about 62 percent or 2.2 million acre feet is obtained from developed surface water sources. By the year 2000, because of physical and economic problems related to overdraft or mining of groundwater, approximately 80 percent of the 6.5 million acre feet of the water requirements for SMSAs will have to be supplied from developed surface water resources, some of which are located in neighboring river basins. By the year 2000, between 6.0 and 9.8 million acre feet of additional water will be needed each year for irrigation. About one-half of this total will be needed to maintain current levels of irrigated acreage in the future; the remainder would be needed to support agricultural growth. Statewide, water use for livestock purposes was estimated to total about 244 thousand acre feet in 1980. Requirements for livestock watering purposes throughout the state are projected to be 288 and 332 thousand acre feet per year in 1980 and 2000, respectively. By the year 2000, total Statewide water requirements are projected to range between 19.8 and 25.8 million acre feet annually. About 63 percent of the dependable yield of Texas reservoirs is being used to meet current needs; the remainder is committed for expanding municipal and industrial needs of the next 20 to 30 years in areas which can be served by these supplies. These supplies, however, will not meet the projected future needs within their respective locations, with a few exceptions, and of course cannot meet all future needs in neighboring and more distant locations. Texas has 65 potential major reservoir project sites. Of this total, 19 are authorized federal projects, seven are planned state/local projects, six are planned federal/state/local projects needed to meet projected year 2000 water requirements in areas near the locations of these projects, and 33 are potential projects needed to meet the projected water requirements beyond the year 2000. About 5.3 million acre feet per year of additional dependable surface water yield and capturable treated sewage return flows (4.3 million acre feet of yield and 1.0 million acre feet of capturable return flows) can be developed with construction of these 65 potential reservoir projects. Development of the remaining 65 major reservoir sites will add about 39 percent to existing dependable yields and an additional one million acre feet, or nine percent, of water yield from recapturable, treated wastewater return flows. However, parts of sites suitable for reservoirs are being converted to other uses that could conflict with future water development. Like surface water supplies, groundwater resources are unevenly distributed across Texas and aquifers are recharged at unequal rates. The Edwards (Balcones Fault Zone) Aquifer, for example, has limited volumes of groundwater available but high recharge rates, so that water withdrawn from storage can be recovered rapidly during high rainfall periods. Over the whole of Texas, however, the continued long term development and use of ground water is limited by the fact that more groundwater is being removed in many areas of the state than is being replaced by natural recharge. Nonetheless, groundwater will continue to be an important source of water in the future. In planning for meeting the future water requirements in Texas it is anticipated that approximately 3,800 new municipal wells will be required between 1984 and the year 2000. This estimated number of wells does not account for additional wells developed privately for industrial purposes, nor does it include an estimate for new irrigation wells needed during this time.

COST ESTIMATES 1984-2030 Since 1956, federal funds have been appropriated and awarded as grants to the states to allocate to local governments for the construction of domestic wastewater treatment facilities. While these grants currently provide 75% of construction costs of eligible projects, this share will be reduced to 55% by 1985 and possibly eliminated by 1990. Given the anticipated reduction in federal funding for water management programs and the requirements to meet water quality standards, local and state governments will be forced to assume a larger share of these costs. Local governments borrow funds for water purposes through the sale of general obligation bonds and the sale of revenue bonds backed by the expected income from the sale of water and sewage treatment services. State assistance can be in the form of loan insurance or guarantees, acquisition of a part of the conservation storage or a combination of those methods. Rural water supply corporations, as non-profit organizations, cannot qualify for loans or grants from either of the state water financing funds mentioned above. While the Farmers Home Administration (FmHA) of the U.S. Department of Agriculture has provided funding in the past, this type of funding assistance is declining and will be reduced further in the future. Approximately 270 sewerage treatment projects will be required throughout Texas over the period 1984-1989, 2,100 in the 1990s and an additional 9,700 between 2000 and 2030. For those municipalities that are expected to obtain their future supply of water from groundwater sources, approximately 1,700 new wells will have to be developed between 1984 and 1989. Eighteen pipeline and conveyance facilities will be needed by the year 2000 to bring raw water from sources of supply and 14 new raw water treatment facilities will be needed between 1984 and 2000. In order to meet future water supply requirements, 28 reservoirs, two channel dams, one salt water barrier and seven (natural salt chloride) control projects need to be developed between 1984 and 2005. Estimated total capital requirements for 1984-85 are $2 billion. Wastewater collection and treatment facilities account for $841 million of the total and estimated capital costs for reservoirs total $428 million. Estimated capital requirements for the period 1984 through 2005 total $40.2 billion in inflated dollars at an annual inflation rate of eight percent ($14.9 billion in 1983 dollars). Wastewater treatment facilities account for $20.5 billion of the total $40.2 billion needed and construction accounts for $11.6 billion, with the remaining $8.1 billion going to water conveyance, water treatment and wells. The estimated annual per capita investment costs, at eight percent inflation, for the period 1984 through 2005 total $46.40 for wastewater treatment facilities, $25.80 for reservoirs, and $19.40 for water conveyance, water treatment and wells. With inflation at eight percent per annum, estimated state financial assistance needs for the 1984 through 2005 time period include $4.5 billion for reservoirs, $9.7 billion for wastewater collection treatment facilities and $1.5 billion of funding for raw water conveyance, treatment facilities and well fields. Debt service loans for four reservoir projects in the Brazos River Basin would add $677 million to the estimated total state financial assistance needed. At zero inflation rate, cost estimates total $4.0 billion for reservoirs, $7.5 billion for wastewater collection and treatment facilities, and $3.7 billion for water conveyance, treatment facilities and well fields.

COUNTY LOCATION CHART

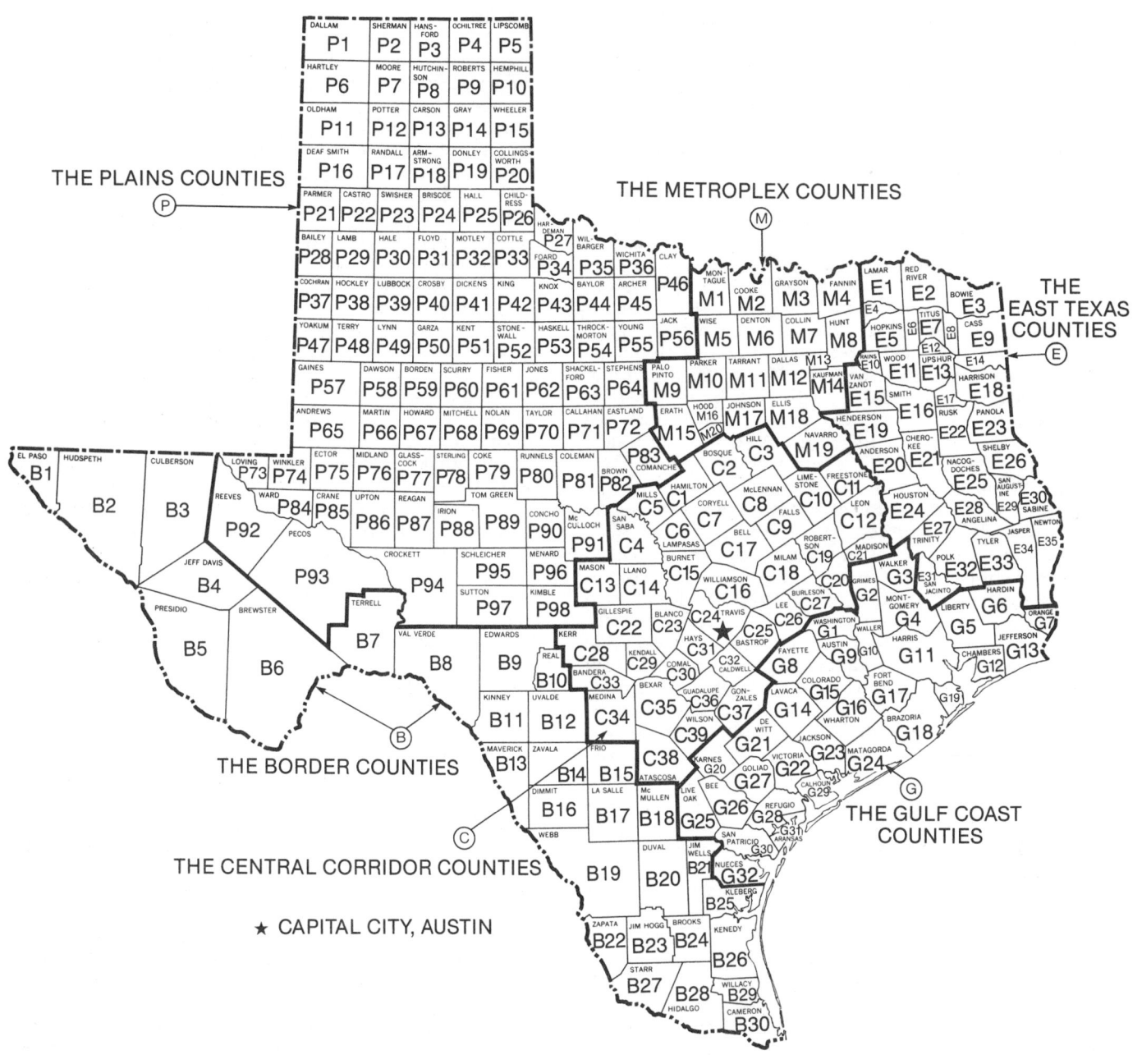

THE PLAINS COUNTIES ⓟ

THE METROPLEX COUNTIES ⓜ

THE EAST TEXAS COUNTIES Ⓔ

THE BORDER COUNTIES Ⓑ

THE CENTRAL CORRIDOR COUNTIES ©

THE GULF COAST COUNTIES Ⓖ

★ CAPITAL CITY, AUSTIN

County	Chart Location	1980 Co. Pop.	County Seat	County	Chart Location	1980 Co. Pop.	County Seat	County	Chart Location	1980 Co. Pop.	County Seat
Anderson	E20	38,381	Palestine	Gillespie	C22	13,532	Fredericksburg	Moore	P7	16,575	Dumas
Andrews	P65	13,323	Andrews	Glasscock	P77	1,304	Garden City	Morris	E8	14,629	Daingerfield
Angelina	E28	64,172	Lufkin	Goliad	G27	5,193	Goliad	Motley	P32	1,950	Matador
Aransas	G31	14,260	Rockport	Gonzales	C37	16,949	Gonzales	Nacogdoches	E25	46,786	Nacogdoches
Archer	P45	7,266	Archer City	Gray	P14	26,386	Pampa	Navarro	M19	35,323	Corsicana
Armstrong	P18	1,994	Claude	Grayson	M3	89,796	Sherman	Newton	E35	13,254	Newton
Atascosa	C38	25,055	Jourdanton	Gregg	E17	99,495	Longview	Nolan	P69	17,359	Sweetwater
Austin	G9	17,726	Bellville	Grimes	G2	13,580	Anderson	Nueces	G32	268,215	Corpus Christi
Bailey	P28	8,168	Muleshoe	Guadalupe	C36	46,708	Seguin	Ochiltree	P4	9,588	Perryton
Bandera	C33	7,084	Bandera	Hale	P30	37,592	Plainview	Oldham	P11	2,283	Vega
Bastrop	C25	24,726	Bastrop	Hall	P25	5,594	Memphis	Orange	G7	83,838	Orange
Baylor	P44	4,919	Seymour	Hamilton	C1	8,297	Hamilton	Palo Pinto	M9	24,062	Palo Pinto
Bee	G26	26,030	Beeville	Hansford	P3	6,209	Spearman	Panola	E23	20,724	Carthage
Bell	C17	157,820	Belton	Hardeman	P27	6,368	Quanah	Parker	M10	44,609	Weatherford
Bexar	C35	988,798	San Antonio	Hardin	G6	40,721	Kountze	Parmer	P21	11,038	Farwell
Blanco	C23	4,681	Johnson City	Harris	G11	2,409,547	Houston	Pecos	P93	14,618	Fort Stockton
Borden	P59	859	Gail	Harrison	E18	52,265	Marshall	Polk	E32	24,407	Livingston
Bosque	C2	13,401	Meridian	Hartley	P6	3,987	Channing	Potter	P12	98,637	Amarillo
Bowie	E3	75,301	Boston	Haskell	P53	7,725	Haskell	Presidio	B5	5,188	Marfa
Brazoria	G18	169,587	Angleton	Hays	C31	40,594	San Marcos	Rains	E10	4,839	Emory
Brazos	C20	93,588	Bryan	Hemphill	P10	5,304	Canadian	Randall	P17	75,062	Canyon
Brewster	B6	7,573	Alpine	Henderson	E19	42,606	Athens	Reagan	P87	4,135	Big Lake
Briscoe	P24	2,579	Silverton	Hidalgo	B28	283,323	Edinburg	Real	B10	2,469	Leakey
Brooks	B24	8,428	Falfurrias	Hill	C3	25,024	Hillsboro	Red River	E2	16,101	Clarksville
Brown	P82	33,057	Brownwood	Hockley	P38	23,230	Levelland	Reeves	P92	15,801	Pecos
Burleson	C27	12,313	Caldwell	Hood	M16	17,714	Granbury	Refugio	G28	9,289	Refugio
Burnet	C15	17,803	Burnet	Hopkins	E5	25,247	Sulphur Springs	Roberts	P9	1,187	Miami
Caldwell	C32	23,637	Lockhart	Houston	E24	22,299	Crockett	Robertson	C19	14,653	Franklin
Calhoun	G29	19,574	Port Lavaca	Howard	P67	33,142	Big Spring	Rockwall	M13	14,528	Rockwall
Callahan	P71	10,992	Baird	Hudspeth	B2	2,728	Sierra Blanca	Runnels	P80	11,872	Ballinger
Cameron	B30	209,727	Brownsville	Hunt	M8	55,248	Greenville	Rusk	E22	41,382	Henderson
Camp	E12	9,275	Pittsburg	Hutchinson	P8	26,304	Stinnett	Sabine	E30	8,702	Hemphill
Carson	P13	6,672	Panhandle	Irion	P88	1,386	Mertzon	San Augustine	E29	8,785	San Augustine
Cass	E9	29,430	Linden	Jack	P56	7,408	Jacksboro	San Jacinto	E31	11,434	Coldspring
Castro	P22	10,556	Dimmit	Jackson	G23	13,352	Edna	San Patricio	G30	58,013	Sinton
Chambers	G12	18,538	Anahuac	Jasper	E34	30,781	Jasper	San Saba	C4	6,204	San Saba
Cherokee	E21	38,127	Rusk	Jeff Davis	B4	1,647	Fort Davis	Schleicher	P95	2,820	Eldorado
Childress	P26	6,950	Childress	Jefferson	G13	250,938	Beaumont	Scurry	P60	18,192	Snyder
Clay	P46	9,582	Henrietta	Jim Hogg	B23	5,168	Hebbronville	Shackelford	P63	3,915	Albany
Cochran	P37	4,825	Morton	Jim Wells	B21	36,498	Alice	Shelby	E26	23,084	Center
Coke	P79	3,196	Robert Lee	Johnson	M17	67,649	Cleburne	Sherman	P2	3,174	Stratford
Coleman	P81	10,439	Coleman	Jones	P62	17,268	Anson	Smith	E16	128,366	Tyler
Collin	M7	144,576	McKinney	Karnes	G20	13,593	Karnes City	Somervell	M20	4,154	Glen Rose
Collingsworth	P20	4,648	Wellington	Kaufman	M14	39,029	Kaufman	Starr	B27	27,266	Rio Grande City
Colorado	G15	18,823	Columbus	Kendall	C29	10,635	Boerne	Stephens	P64	9,926	Breckenridge
Comal	C30	36,446	New Braunfels	Kenedy	B26	543	Sarita	Sterling	P78	1,206	Sterling City
Comanche	P83	12,617	Comanche	Kent	P51	1,145	Jayton	Stonewall	P52	2,406	Aspermont
Concho	P90	2,915	Paint Rock	Kerr	C28	28,780	Kerrville	Sutton	P97	5,130	Sonora
Cooke	M2	27,656	Gainesville	Kimble	P98	4,063	Junction	Swisher	P23	9,723	Tulia
Coryell	C7	56,767	Gatesville	King	P42	425	Guthrie	Tarrant	M11	860,880	Fort Worth
Cottle	P33	2,947	Paducah	Kinney	B11	2,279	Brackettville	Taylor	P70	110,932	Abilene
Crane	P85	4,600	Crane	Kleberg	B25	33,358	Kingsville	Terrell	B7	1,595	Sanderson
Crockett	P94	4,608	Ozona	Knox	P43	5,329	Benjamin	Terry	P48	14,581	Brownfield
Crosby	P40	8,859	Crosbyton	Lamar	E1	42,156	Paris	Throckmorton	P54	2,053	Throckmorton
Culberson	B3	3,315	Van Horn	Lamb	P29	18,669	Littlefield	Titus	E7	21,442	Mount Pleasant
Dallam	P1	6,531	Dalhart	Lampasas	C6	12,005	Lampasas	Tom Green	P89	84,784	San Angelo
Dallas	M12	1,556,390	Dallas	La Salle	B17	5,514	Cotulla	Travis	C24	419,573	★Austin
Dawson	P58	16,184	Lamesa	Lavaca	G14	19,004	Hallettsville	Trinity	E27	9,450	Groveton
Deaf Smith	P16	21,165	Hereford	Lee	C26	10,952	Giddings	Tyler	E33	16,223	Woodville
Delta	E4	4,839	Cooper	Leon	C12	9,594	Centerville	Upshur	E13	28,595	Gilmer
Denton	M6	143,126	Denton	Liberty	G5	47,088	Liberty	Upton	P86	4,619	Rankin
De Witt	G21	18,903	Cuero	Limestone	C10	20,224	Groesbeck	Uvalde	B12	22,441	Uvalde
Dickens	P41	3,539	Dickens	Lipscomb	P5	3,766	Lipscomb	Val Verde	B8	35,910	Del Rio
Dimmit	B16	11,367	Carrizo Springs	Live Oak	G25	9,606	George West	Van Zandt	E15	31,426	Canton
Donley	P19	4,075	Clarendon	Llano	C14	10,144	Llano	Victoria	G22	68,807	Victoria
Duval	B20	12,517	San Diego	Loving	P73	91	Mentone	Walker	G3	41,789	Huntsville
Eastland	P72	19,480	Eastland	Lubbock	P39	211,651	Lubbock	Waller	G10	19,798	Hempstead
Ector	P75	115,374	Odessa	Lynn	P49	8,605	Tahoka	Ward	P84	13,976	Monahans
Edwards	B9	2,033	Rocksprings	McCulloch	P91	8,735	Brady	Washington	G1	21,998	Brenham
Ellis	M18	59,743	Waxahachie	McLennan	C8	170,755	Waco	Webb	B19	99,258	Laredo
El Paso	B1	479,899	El Paso	McMullen	B18	789	Tilden	Wharton	G16	40,242	Wharton
Erath	M15	22,560	Stephenville	Madison	C21	10,649	Madisonville	Wheeler	P15	7,137	Wheeler
Falls	C9	17,946	Marlin	Marion	E14	10,360	Jefferson	Wichita	P36	121,082	Wichita Falls
Fannin	M4	24,285	Bonham	Martin	P66	4,684	Stanton	Wilbarger	P35	15,931	Vernon
Fayette	G8	18,832	La Grange	Mason	C13	3,683	Mason	Willacy	B29	17,495	Raymondville
Fisher	P61	5,891	Roby	Matagorda	G24	37,828	Bay City	Williamson	C16	76,507	Georgetown
Floyd	P31	9,834	Floydada	Maverick	B13	31,398	Eagle Pass	Wilson	C39	16,756	Floresville
Foard	P34	2,158	Crowell	Medina	C34	23,164	Hondo	Winkler	P74	9,944	Kermit
Fort Bend	G17	130,846	Richmond	Menard	P96	2,346	Menard	Wise	M5	26,575	Decatur
Franklin	E6	6,893	Mount Vernon	Midland	P76	82,636	Midland	Wood	E11	24,697	Quitman
Freestone	C11	14,830	Fairfield	Milam	C18	22,732	Cameron	Yoakum	P47	8,299	Plains
Frio	B15	13,785	Pearsall	Mills	C5	4,477	Goldthwaite	Young	P55	19,083	Graham
Gaines	P57	13,150	Seminole	Mitchell	P68	9,088	Colorado City	Zapata	B22	6,628	Zapata
Galveston	G19	195,940	Galveston	Montague	M1	17,410	Montague	Zavala	B14	11,666	Crystal City
Garza	P50	5,336	Post	Montgomery	G4	128,487	Conroe				

COUNTIES

ANDERSON (E-20)

THE LAND

Southeast of Dallas on U.S. Highways 287, 79 and 84 in the East Texas Timberlands Region, Anderson County covers 1,077 square miles of grass and woodlands divided by a mineral ridge. The elevation ranges from 400 to 525 feet. In the east the land is undulating to rolling with loamy acidic surface soils low in plant nutrients and reddish or mottled clayey or loamy subsoils. The subsoils have a high capacity to shrink and swell. Around Palestine the land is nearly level with moderately-well to poorly drained, acidic, loamy to sandy soils and yellow to red mottled or reddish clayey subsoils. To the west the land is nearly level with slightly acidic loamy soils and deep reddish to mottled subsoils. Along the Trinity River are grayish, cracking, clayey soils with a high capacity to shrink and swell and reddish brown loamy alluvial soil. The Pineywoods of East Anderson has pine trees (longleaf, shortleaf, loblolly and slash) and hardwoods such as oaks, hickory, elms, magnolia, sweet and black gum, tupelo and maple, forage plants such as Indiangrass, shrubs and brush. The Post Oak Savannah in the west is primarily grasslands with tall grasses, elm, post and blackjack oak trees, plus walnut and pecan trees along streams. Less than 10% of the land in the county is considered prime farmland. **CLIMATE** Subtropical humid, warm and moist. The average annual temperature is 66°F. Temperatures in January range from an average low of 35° to an average high of 56°F and in July range from 72° to 95°F. The average annual precipitation is 42 inches, with an average relative humidity of 84% at 6 A.M. and 56% at 6 P.M. The average annual snowfall is only a trace. The growing season averages 264 days per year, with the last freeze in early March and the first freeze in late November. The sun shines during the year on the average 65% of the daylight hours.

THE PEOPLE

The 1982 estimated population of 42,200 indicates a continuation of the strong growth rate begun in the 1970s which reversed the steady population decrease between 1940 and 1970. Almost 70% of the growth between 1970 and 1980 was in rural areas. The age groups with the largest gains were ages 20 to 34 and birth to five years. The largest ancestry groups are persons of English descent (26%), Black (21%), Irish descent (16%) and those of German descent (10%). **REGISTERED VOTERS** As of November 2, 1982 there were 16,764 registered voters (0.3% of the state total). The 1982 general election had a 51% voter turnout, compared to a 67% turnout in the 1980 general election. In the 1982 primary 97% voted Democratic and 3% Republican, with 5,711 votes cast.

THE ECONOMY

AGRICULTURE Good pasture and timberland. In 1982, 52% of the land was in farms and ranches, with 9% of the farmland under cultivation. Anderson ranked 149th in the state in highest agricultural receipts with 91% from livestock and livestock products. Primary crops: hay, wheat, peanuts, oats and sorghum. Primary vegetables: watermelons. Primary fruits and nuts: peaches and pecans. Primary livestock and products: cattle, milk and hogs. Improper grassland management, inadequate cropping systems and improper woodland management are the current conservation problems. **BUSINESS** Total number of business establishments in the county: 741. Retail sales during the first quarter of 1984 increased 20%. In 1980, 10% of the labor force were self-employed, 18% were employed in professional or related services, 15% in manufacturing, 21% in wholesale and retail trade, 11% in transportation, communications, and other public utilities, 12% were employed in other counties and there were 3,641 retired workers. The industries with the most employment: oil and gas extraction, aluminum smelting, meat packing, construction and the manufacture of furniture, glass containers, men's work clothing and women's dresses. The nonfarm earnings in 1981 totaled $326,873,000. The retired workers received an average monthly Social Security payment of $289. **FINANCE** On June 30, 1983 six commercial banks had total deposits of $217,260,000 and total assets of $244,153,000. There are four branches of state savings and loan associations and five credit unions in the county. **HOUSING** Average value of homes in 1980: $28,500. Permits for new, privately owned housing units decreased in 1982: 93 permits were issued with a total construction cost of $2,974,270. Of those permits, 77 were for single family houses. Between 1970 and 1980 the number of housing units increased by 31%. Seventy-two percent of all units in the county are air-conditioned, 73% are heated by gas and 19% by electricity. **NATURAL RESOURCES** Ceramic, clay, limonite iron, salt domes, industrial sand, sand and gravel, oil and gas. In 1982 a total of 10,787,612 thousand cubic feet of gas well gas, 245,893 barrels of condensate, 3,562,207 barrels of crude oil and 7,145,621 thousand cubic feet of casinghead gas were produced. Current production of other minerals and products includes aluminum, aluminum chloride, hydrochloric acid and clay. Pine and hardwood production in 1981 totaled 6,815,252 cubic feet: 5,424,902 cubic feet of pine and 1,390,350 cubic feet of hardwood. **TOURISM** Travel expenditures of $17,004,000 in 1982 (an increase of 12% over 1981) generated 398 jobs and $3,260,000 in payroll. Lodging: six hotels, motels and tourist courts. **ALCOHOLIC BEVERAGES** Packaged distilled spirits, beer, ale, malt liquor and wine are legal in parts of the county. **FEDERAL EXPENDITURES** The federal government had direct expenditures or obligations of $73,642,000 in the county during fiscal year 1983, including $3,159,000 by the U.S. Department of Defense. In addition, the federal government provided $3,347,000 in grant awards, paid $3,598,000 in salaries and wages, made direct payments to individuals of $61,652,000 including $46,254,000 in retirement and disability payments, awarded $4,755,000 in procurement contracts and spent $290,000 in other expenditures or obligations. The federal government also provided $44,000 in direct loans and $5,498,000 in guaranteed loans and insurance.

COMMUNICATION

Newspapers–Daily: Palestine Herald-Press, ave. eve. circ. 10,726. Weekly: The Frankston Citizen. Radio: KNET-AM, KYYK-FM and KLIS-FM Stereo (Palestine). Cable TV. Telephone companies: Continental Telephone and United Telephone. **TRANSPORTATION** Total public road mileage: 1,418. In 1982 there were 33,353 registered vehicles and 987 reported traffic accidents including 21 fatalities. Intercity bus service is available. Motor freight: 10 local and intrastate carriers. Rail: Two main and one branch line carry freight through the county. One of the main lines carries annually five to 10 million tons of freight and the other carries 10 to 20. The branch line carries annually five to 10 million tons of freight. Aircraft: 27 are registered in the county. Airports: Palestine Municipal Airport provides general aviation service and serves as a base for 22 aircraft.

COMMUNITY SERVICES

EDUCATION Seven school districts with 13 elementary, two middle and seven high schools. The average daily attendance in 1981-82 was 6,701, with expenditures per pupil of $3,215 including 438 classroom teachers with an average annual salary of $15,824. Forty percent of the 492 high school graduates planned to attend college. In 1982-83, 74% of the students were White, 5% Hispanic, 21% Black, 0.3% Asian and 0.1% American Indian. Vocational education: Anderson College Center, a division of Henderson County Junior College (Palestine). **PUBLIC LIBRARIES** Palestine Carnegie Library: 45,500 volumes. **CHILD CARE** 37 day care and 17 twenty-four hour care licensed facilities. **HEALTH CARE** 38 physicians and 13 dentists. Hospitals: one with a capacity of 124. Ambulance services: two fire departments and one volunteer emergency company. Mental health: one county clinic. Nursing homes: seven with a combined capacity of 613 nursing care and 16 custodial care. The average cost per day for private patients in 1982 was $30.31. **CHURCHES** 94 churches have an estimated combined membership of 22,239. The largest denominations are Southern Baptist, United Methodist and Catholic. **SOCIAL SERVICES** In fiscal year 1983 a total of $1,149,551 in food stamps was distributed, with an average of 2,592 persons receiving food stamps each month. Aid to Families with Dependent Children (AFDC) totaled $291,690 with an average of 206 families receiving AFDC each month. Medical assistance benefits for the aged and disabled of $3,948,983 and for families and children of $323,810 brought the county benefit total to $5,714,034. **FIRE PROTECTION** One paid and 11 volunteer fire departments. **LAW ENFORCEMENT** The County Sheriff has 35 commissioned officers. Three police departments have a combined force of 60. **CRIME** 130 violent crimes (murder, forcible rape, robbery and aggravated assault) and 1,420 nonviolent crimes (burglary, larceny-theft and motor vehicle theft) were reported in 1982. **JUDICIAL SYSTEM** Three District Courts and Judges, two County Courts and Judges and four Justices of the Peace. In the District Courts a total of 2,795 cases were pending on 1/1/82, 1,322 new cases were filed and 898 cases were disposed of during the year leaving 3,224 cases pending on 12/31/82. There were 632 criminal cases on the docket, 109 convictions, 18 persons committed to prison and three committed to jail and 369 cases left pending. In the County Courts 1,874 cases were pending on 1/1/82, 914 new cases were filed and 1,545 cases were disposed of during the year leaving 1,335 cases pending on 12/31/82. There were 2,399 criminal cases on the docket, 404 convictions, 76 persons committed to jail, and 1,121 cases left pending. **JAILS** One jail, capacity 28. **PRISONS** BETO I, on 3,774 acres south of Tennessee Colony, had an inmate population of 2,330 in 1983. It has agricultural operations and a highway sign factory. BETO II, on 1,866 acres west of Palestine, had 1,039 inmates, a records conversion facility and livestock production. Coffield, on 17,300 acres southwest of Tennessee Colony, had 3,987 inmates, agricultural operations, a meat packing plant, a sawmill, a records conversion facility, a metal fabrication plant and a dump-bed body factory. **ATTORNEYS AT LAW** 45. **UTILITIES** 85% of the residents are connected to a public or privately owned water system and 54% are connected to a public sewer system. Natural gas is distributed to the county by Entex, Inc. and Lone Star Gas Co., a division of Enserch. The average annual residential bill for natural gas in 1982 for the Entex distribution system was $390.31, an increase of 26% over 1981 and for Lone Star Gas it was $405.91, an increase of 35%. Electricity is distributed to the county by Houston County Electric Coop., Inc., New Era Electric Coop., Inc., Texas Power and Light Co. and Cochran Power and Light Co. and is generated primarily by gas and coal. The typical residential electric bill is $165.24 per month for an all-electric house using 2,500 kwh. **TAXES** The county has 12 units with taxing authority: seven school districts, three cities, one county and one college district.

RECREATION/ENTERTAINMENT

NATIONAL REGISTER OF HISTORIC PLACES Palestine: Sacred Heart Catholic Church and School and Link House. Palestine vicinity: Pace McDonald Site. **STATE** Fanthorp Inn State Historic Site covers one acre and is closed to the public as of July, 1983. **COUNTY/MUNICIPAL PARKS** 1,649 acres in one county and 13 municipal parks. These parks contain 12 miles of hiking trails, seven playgrounds, two football and soccer fields, 15 baseball and softball fields, nine tennis courts, one swimming pool and shore fishing facilities. **SCENIC DRIVES** The Texas Forest Trail runs through this county. This trail explores the farming, ranching and oilfield areas of the East Texas Pineywoods. **BOATING/FISHING** Lakes/reservoirs: Bass Haven (520 acres), Calhoun (42 acres), Circle R #1 (57 acres), Circle R #2 (25 acres), Creek #1 (14 acres), Creek #2 (24 acres), Crystal (36 acres), CWM (63 acres), Duggeys (30 acres), Elkhart (20 acres), Fisherman Paradise (107 acres), Francis (34 acres), Frankston (185 acres), Gator (71 acres), Haverlah (34 acres), Ioni (60 acres), JDM (69 acres), Lakeview (27 acres), Lost Prairie (70 acres), Lower City (28 acres), Palestine (25,560 acres), Pineywoods (36 acres), Riley (55 acres), Wilson (57 acres) and Wolf Creek (44 acres). Major rivers: Neches and Trinity. Primary streams: Coon, Stills, Spring, Sand, Brushy, Wolf, Box, Mitchell, Catfish, Clem Mill, Mound Prairie, Ioni, Crooked, Hurricane and Basset. **WILDLIFE REFUGES** Gus Engeling State Wildlife Management Area covers 10,941 acres. **HUNTING** Fall and winter seasons on deer. Late fall, winter and spring seasons on squirrel. Spring season on turkey in certain areas. Winter seasons on quail, muskrat, beaver, otter, opossum, mink, ring-tailed cat, badger, fox, raccoon, skunk and civet cat. No closed season on coyotes, nutria and bobcats. In 1983 duck, coot, geese, woodcock and jacksnipe seasons occurred during the winter months. Teal duck, rail and gallinule seasons occurred in the fall. Mourning dove seasons occurred at various times during the fall and winter months. **MUSEUMS** Palestine: Howard House Museum. **SPECIAL EVENTS** Dogwood Trails Festival, Palestine, March/April; Anderson County Fair, Palestine, May; Fall Fair Festival, Palestine, October; Christmas Homes Pilgrimage, Palestine, December.

COMMUNITIES

COUNTY SEAT Palestine, County Courthouse, 75801; County Clerk's Office, 214/729-7170. **INCORPORATED COMMUNITIES** (1980 population and ZIP Code) Elkhart (1,317) 75839, Frankston (1,255) 75763 and Palestine (15,948) 75801. **UNINCORPORATED COMMUNITIES** (and ZIP Code) Bethel 75861, Blackfoot 75853, Bois D'Arc 75801, Bradford (Hawks Store) 75853, Broyles 75801, Brushy Creek 75801, Carroll Springs 75767, Cayuga 75832, Cooks Store 75861, Crystal Lake 75801, Denson Springs 75844, Elmwood 75801, Frankston Lake 75763, Grays Chapel 75801, Harmony 75801, Kickapoo 75763, Lone Pine 75801, Long Lake 75801, Massey Lake 75861, Montalba 75853, Mound City 75844, Neches 75779, Pert 75801, Salmon 75839, Slocum 75839, Springfield 75853, Swanson Hill 75801, Tennessee Colony 75861, Todd City 75801, Tucker 75801, Walston Springs 75801 and Yard (Greens Bluff) 75861. **FOR ADDITIONAL LOCAL INFORMATION** S. Anderson Co. Chamber of Commerce, Drawer 109, Elkhart, 75839 and Palestine Chamber of Commerce, Drawer I, Palestine, 75801, 214/729-6066.

ANDREWS (P-65)

THE LAND

Bordering New Mexico northwest of Odessa on U.S. Highway 385 in the High Plains Region, Andrews County covers 1,501 square miles with the elevation ranging from 3,000 to 3,500 feet. The nearly level soils are loamy with clayey subsoils and a high shrink-swell potential. In the southeast there is a lime accumulation in the subsoils, at times within 20 inches of the surface. Treeless, the principal vegetation is buffalo grass and blue grama. The loamy soils have such grasses as western wheatgrass and Indiangrass. Mesquite, sand sagebrush, cacti, shinnery oak and yucca are problem plants. Less than 1% of the land is considered

COUNTIES

ANDREWS (continued)

prime farmland. **CLIMATE** Continental Steppe with dry, cold, windy winters and warm summers. The average annual temperature is 63°F. Temperatures in January range from an average low of 27°F to an average high of 57°F and in July range from 68° to 95°F. The average annual precipitation is 14 inches, with an average relative humidity of 70% at 6 A.M. and 34% at 6 P.M. The average annual snowfall is four inches. The growing season averages 213 days per year, with the last freeze in early April and the first freeze in early November. The sun shines during the year on the average 76% of the daylight hours.

THE PEOPLE
The 1982 estimated population of 15,000 indicates a continuation of the growth rate begun in the 1970s which reversed the population decrease between 1960 and 1970. The county is one of the most sparsely populated in the state. Rural and urban areas between 1970 and 1980 grew equally with an urban growth of 28% and rural growth of 30%. The age groups with the largest gains were ages birth to five years and ages 20 to 34. Andrews County has one of the highest birth rates in the state and one of the highest percentages of population under 18 with 34% of the residents in that category. The largest ancestry groups are Hispanic (22%) and persons of English descent (21%). **REGISTERED VOTERS** As of November 2, 1982 there were 5,943 registered voters (0.1% of the state total). The 1982 general election had a 46% voter turnout, compared to a 71% turnout in the 1980 general election. In the 1982 primary 97% voted Democratic and 3% Republican, with 2,386 votes cast.

THE ECONOMY
AGRICULTURE Ranchland. In 1982, 93% of the land was in farms and ranches, with 7% of the farmland under cultivation and 18% irrigated. Andrews ranked 201st in the state in highest agricultural receipts with 65% from crops. Undesirable brush and weeds, overgrazing and wind erosion are current conservation problems. Primary crops: cotton, sorghum and wheat. Primary livestock and products: cattle. **BUSINESS** Total number of business establishments in the county: 311. Retail sales during the first quarter of 1984 increased 9%. In 1980, 7% of the labor force were self-employed, 18% were employed in professional or related services, 8% in manufacturing, 15% in wholesale and retail trade, 30% in agriculture, forestry, fisheries and mining, 8% were employed in other counties and there were 679 retired workers. The industries with the most employment: oil and gas extraction, agribusiness, heavy construction and the manufacture of vacuum cleaners. The nonfarm earnings in 1981 totaled $153,827,000. The retired workers received an average monthly Social Security payment of $349. **FINANCE** On June 30, 1983, three commercial banks had total deposits of $82,831,000 and total assets of $92,904,000. On December 31, 1982 one state savings and loan association and one federal association branch had assets of $60,675,033. In addition there are two credit unions in the county. **HOUSING** Average value of homes in 1980: $28,000. Permits for new, privately owned housing units increased in 1982: 154 permits were issued with a total construction cost of $6,018,690. Of those permits, 60 were for single family houses. Between 1970 and 1980 the number of housing units increased by 26%. Eighty-five percent of all units in the county are air-conditioned, 81% are heated by gas and 18% by electricity. **NATURAL RESOURCES** Caliche, oil, gas and brine wells. In 1982 a total of 3,806,356 thousand cubic feet of gas well gas, 15,539 barrels of condensate, 39,456,766 barrels of crude oil and 29,055,808 thousand cubic feet of casinghead gas were produced. Current production of other minerals and products includes brine, caliche and sulphur. **TOURISM** Travel

expenditures of $4,023,000 in 1982 (an increase of 11% over 1981) generated 96 jobs and $779,000 in payroll. Convention/meeting facilities: Andrews-Mustang Stadium, Brazoria County Fair Association. **ALCOHOLIC BEVERAGES** Totally dry. **MILITARY INSTITUTIONS** Odessa Radar Site, Andrews, one acre, electronics site. **FEDERAL EXPENDITURES** The federal government had direct expenditures or obligations of $14,750,000 in the county during fiscal year 1983, including $350,000 by the U.S. Department of Defense. In addition, the federal government provided $224,000 in grant awards, paid $1,066,000 in salaries and wages, made direct payments to individuals of $9,997,000 including $8,308,000 in retirement and disability payments, awarded $9,000 in procurement contracts and spent $3,453,000 in other expenditures or obligations. The federal government also provided $2,515,000 in direct loans and $7,676,000 in guaranteed loans and insurance.

COMMUNICATION
Newspapers–Weekly: Andrews County News (Andrews). Radio: KACT-AM & FM (Andrews). Cable TV. Telephone companies: Continental Telephone and Southwestern Bell. **TRANSPORTATION** Total public road mileage: 576. In 1982 there were 15,122 registered vehicles and 402 reported traffic accidents including 12 fatalities. Intercity bus service is available. Motor freight: eight local and intrastate carriers. Aircraft: 28 are registered in the county. Airports: Andrews County Airport at Andrews provides general aviation service and serves as a base for 20 aircraft.

COMMUNITY SERVICES
EDUCATION One school district with five elementary, one middle and one high school. The average daily attendance in 1981-82 was 2,913, with expenditures per pupil of $4,160 including 206 classroom teachers with an average annual salary of $23,542. Forty-four percent of the 151 high school graduates planned to attend college. In 1982-83, 64% of the students were White, 33% Hispanic, 2% Black, 1% Asian and 0.3% American Indian. **PUBLIC LIBRARIES** Andrews County Library (Andrews): 27,367 volumes. **CHILD CARE** 17 day care and three twenty-four hour care licensed facilities. **HEALTH CARE** 16 physicians and four dentists. Hospitals: one with a capacity of 104. Clinics: One public health clinic. Ambulance services: one police department service. Mental health: one county clinic. Nursing homes: one nursing home has a capacity of 98 nursing care residents. The average cost per day for private patients in 1982 was $33.76. **CHURCHES** 22 churches have an estimated combined membership of 8,565. The largest denominations are Southern Baptist, United Methodist and Assembly of God. **SOCIAL SERVICES** In fiscal year 1983 a total of $111,977 in food stamps was distributed with an average of 233 persons receiving food stamps each month. Aid to Families with Dependent Children (AFDC) totaled $20,872 with an average of 40 families receiving AFDC each month. Medical assistance benefits for the aged and disabled of $491,221 and for families and children of $32,863 brought the county benefit total to $656,933. **FIRE PROTECTION** One volunteer fire department. **LAW ENFORCEMENT** The County Sheriff has 14 commissioned officers. One police department has a force of 15. One college has a campus police department with one officer. **CRIME** 17 violent crimes (murder, forcible rape, robbery and aggravated assault) and 394 nonviolent crimes (burglary, larceny-theft and motor vehicle theft) were reported in 1982. **JUDICIAL SYSTEM** One District Court and Judge, one County Court and Judge and two Justices of the Peace. In the District Court a total of 415 cases were pending on 1/1/82, 538 new cases were filed and 403 cases were disposed of during the year leaving 550 cases pending on 12/31/82. There were 281 criminal cases on the docket, 26 convictions, five persons committed to prison and 215 cases left pending. In the County

Court 367 cases were pending on 1/1/82, 402 new cases were filed and 428 cases were disposed of during the year leaving 341 cases pending on 12/31/82. There were 714 criminal cases on the docket, 284 convictions, 17 persons committed to jail, and 317 cases left pending. **JAILS** One jail, capacity 46. **ATTORNEYS AT LAW** 11. **UTILITIES** 84% of the residents are connected to a public or privately owned water system and 84% are connected to a public sewer system. Natural gas is distributed to the county by Andrews Gas Co. Electricity is distributed to the county by Texas Electric Service Co., Caprock Electric Coop., Inc. and Lyntegar Electric Coop., Inc. and is generated primarily by gas. The typical residential electric bill is $154.69 per month for an all-electric house using 2,500 kwh. **TAXES** The county has three units with taxing authority: one school district, one city and one county.

RECREATION/ENTERTAINMENT
NATIONAL REGISTER OF HISTORIC PLACES Andrews: The Andrews Lake Site. **COUNTY/MUNICIPAL PARKS** 201 acres in one county and nine municipal parks. These parks contain five playgrounds, one golf course, one football and soccer field, five baseball and softball fields, one tennis court and two swimming pools. Developed campsites: 46. **HUNTING** Fall season on antelope. Fall and winter seasons on javelina. No closed seasons on coyotes, bobcats and squirrel. Late fall to early winter seasons on quail. Winter seasons on muskrat, beaver, opossum, ring-tailed cat, badger, fox, weasel, raccoon, skunk and civet cat. In 1983 sandhill crane, duck, coot, geese, woodcock and jacksnipe seasons occurred during the winter months. Teal duck, rail and gallinule seasons occurred in the fall. Mourning dove seasons occurred intermittently during the fall and winter months. **SPECIAL EVENTS** Junior Rodeo, Andrews, June; Fourth of July Celebration, Andrews, July.

COMMUNITIES
COUNTY SEAT Andrews, County Courthouse, 79714; County Clerk's Office, 915/523-2285. **INCORPORATED COMMUNITIES** (1980 population and ZIP Code) Andrews (11,061) 79714. **UNINCORPORATED COMMUNITIES** (and ZIP Code) Florey 79732 and Frankel City 79737. **FOR ADDITIONAL LOCAL INFORMATION** Andrews Co. Chamber of Commerce, 700 W. Broadway, Andrews, 79714, 915/523-2695.

ANGELINA (E-28)

THE LAND
Northeast of Houston on U.S. Highways 59 and 69 in the East Texas Timberlands Region, Angelina County covers 807 square miles that rise to a central ridge. The ridge forms two watersheds, with drainage flowing east to the Angelina River and west to the Neches River. The elevation ranges from 200 to 350 feet. The land is gently rolling to hilly with reddish, loamy, acidic soils low in plant nutrients and mostly very deep, reddish, clayey subsoils high in iron with a high potential to shrink and swell. Along the northern border the soils are light-colored, loamy to sandy. In the Pineywoods Region, the pine tree is the principal timber (longleaf, shortleaf, loblolly and slash pines). Hardwoods include oaks, hickory, sweet and blackgum, elm, magnolia and tupelo. The primary forage plants include such grasses as Canada and Virginia wildryes, bluestems, lovegrasses and legumes. Shrubs and brush have invaded the area. Between 21 and 30% of the land is considered prime farmland. **CLIMATE** Subtropical humid, moist and mild. The average annual temperature is 67°F. Temperatures in January range from an average low of 37° to an average high of 59°F and in July range from 72° to 94°F. The average annual precipitation is 43 inches, with an average relative humidity of 86% at 6 A.M. and 56% at 6 P.M. The average annual snowfall is only a trace. The growing season averages 245 days per year, with the last freeze mid March and the first freeze mid November. The sun shines during the year on the average of 65% of the daylight hours.

THE PEOPLE
The 1982 estimated population of 67,600 indicates a continuation of the strong growth rate begun in the 1960s. From 1970 to 1980 rural population increased 34% with a slightly lower growth rate experienced by urban areas. The age groups with the largest gains were ages 20 to 34 and 62 and over. The county's divorce rate of 3 per 1,000 population is one of the lowest in the state. The largest ancestry groups are persons of English descent (24%), Irish descent (20%) and Black (15%). **REGISTERED VOTERS** As of November 2, 1982 there were 31,450 registered voters (0.5% of the state total). The 1982 general election had a 47% voter turnout, compared to a 67% turnout in the 1980 general election. In the 1982 primary 99% voted Democratic and 1% Republican, with 12,714 votes cast.

THE ECONOMY
AGRICULTURE Major timber products area. In 1982, 25% of the land was in farms and ranches, with 11% of the farmland under cultivation. Angelina ranked 211th in the state for agricultural receipts, 82% from livestock and livestock products. Overgrazing, fertilization, inadequate timber harvesting systems and undesirable woody vegetation are current conservation problems. Primary crops: hay and rye. Primary vegetables: potatoes, sweet potatoes, tomatoes and watermelons. Primary fruits and nuts: peaches and pecans. Primary livestock and products: cattle, milk and hogs. **BUSINESS** Total number of business establishments in the county: 1,293. Retail sales during the first quarter of 1984 increased 14%. In 1980 7% of the labor force were self-employed, 18% were employed in professional or related services, 30% in manufacturing, 22% in wholesale and retail trade, 9% in construction, 7% were employed in other counties and there were 4,898 retired workers. The industries with the most employment: general construction, lumber and paper mills, poultry processing, iron and steel foundries and the manufacture of candy, wood products, construction machinery and truck trailers. The nonfarm earnings in 1981 totaled $589,309,000. The retired workers received an average monthly Social Security payment of $328. **FINANCE** On June 30, 1983, seven commercial banks had total deposits of $344,827,000 and total assets of $400,279,000. On December 31, 1982 two state savings and loan associations, one federal association, three state branches and two federal branches had combined assets of $295,368,657. In addition there are 11 credit unions in the county. **HOUSING** Average value of homes in 1980: $32,200. Permits for new, privately owned housing units increased in 1982: 299 permits were issued with a total construction cost of $7,934,294. Of those permits, 75 were for single family houses. Housing permits in Lufkin increased from 83 in 1981 to 286 in 1982 with 213 of the permits issued for apartments and condominiums. Between 1970 and 1980 the number of housing units increased by 42%. Seventy-nine percent of all units in the county are air-conditioned, 73% are heated by gas and 23% by electricity. **NATURAL RESOURCES** Clay, industrial sand, oil and gas. In 1982 a total of 1,976,469 thousand cubic feet of gas well gas, 17,201 barrels of condensate, 1,005 barrels of crude oil and 22 thousand cubic feet of casinghead gas were produced. Current production of other minerals and products includes bentonite, clay, fire clay and drilling mud. Pine and hardwood production in 1981 totaled 22,736,959 cubic feet: 19,076,222 cubic feet of pine and 3,660,737 cubic feet of hardwood. **TOURISM** Travel expenditures of $36,936,000 in 1982 (an increase of 11% over 1981) generated 939

COUNTIES

ANGELINA (continued)

jobs and $7,529,000 in payroll. Lodging: 12 hotels, motels and tourist courts. **ALCOHOLIC BEVERAGES** Totally dry. **FEDERAL EXPENDITURES** The federal government had direct expenditures or obligations of $93,623,000 in the county during fiscal year 1983, including $3,894,000 by the U.S. Department of Defense. In addition, the federal government provided $1,993,000 in grant awards, paid $9,322,000 in salaries and wages, made direct payments to individuals of $82,001,000 including $64,804,000 in retirement and disability payments, awarded $102,000 in procurement contracts and spent $265,000 in other expenditures or obligations. The federal government also provided $6,807,000 in guaranteed loans and insurance.

COMMUNICATION

Newspapers–Daily: Lufkin Daily News, ave. eve. circ. 14,632. Weekly: Free Press (Diboll) and The Zavalla Herald. Radio: KIPR-AM and FM (Diboll), KLNX-AM, KRBA-AM, KDEY-FM and KYKS-FM (Lufkin). Television: KTRE-Ch. 9 (Lufkin). Cable TV. Telephone companies: Continental Telephone, Southwestern Bell, Colmesneil Telephone and Lufkin Telephone Exchange. **TRANSPORTATION** Total public road mileage: 1,336. In 1982 there were 66,686 registered vehicles and 1,592 reported traffic accidents including 25 fatalities. Taxi cabs: two companies in Lufkin. Intercity bus service is available. Motor freight: 30 local and intrastate carriers. Rail: five branch lines carry freight through the county. Three of the lines carry annually 10 to 20 million tons of freight each. One carries one to five and the other carries less than one million. Aircraft: 45 are registered in the county. Airports: Angelina County Airport at Lufkin is a basic transportation airport with commuter service. It serves as a base for 51 aircraft.

COMMUNITY SERVICES

EDUCATION Seven school districts with 15 elementary, seven middle, seven high schools and three special education. The average daily attendance in 1981-82 was 12,835, with expenditures per pupil of $2,097 including 746 classroom teachers with an average annual salary of $15,861. Thirty-seven percent of the 688 high school graduates planned to attend college. In 1982-83, 71% of the students were White, 9% Hispanic, 20% Black and 0.2% Asian. Sports championships: 1983 AA baseball, 1984 AA girls' basketball, Pollock Central H.S. Private schools: 315 students enrolled in one elementary school. Angelina College is located in Lufkin. Established in 1968 it is a vocational and two year academic college under state and local control. Enrollment in 1982 was 2,035 with in state undergraduate tuition and fees of $252 per semester. Vocational education: Richard and Josephs Beauty College (Lufkin). **PUBLIC LIBRARIES** TLL Temple Memorial Library (Diboll): 19,000 volumes. Kurth Memorial Library (Lufkin): 44,847 volumes. **CHILD CARE** 65 day care and 12 twenty-four hour care licensed facilities. **HEALTH CARE** 82 physicians and 25 dentists. Hospitals: two with a combined capacity of 416. Clinics: one public health clinic. Ambulance services: one fire department service. Mental health: one county clinic, one state school with capacity of 652, one center with capacity of 60. Nursing homes: Five nursing homes with a combined capacity of 504 nursing care residents. The average cost per day for private patients in 1982 was $27.67. **CHURCHES** 117 churches have an estimated combined membership of 38,142. The largest denominations are Southern Baptist, Baptist Missionary and United Methodist. **SOCIAL SERVICES** In fiscal year 1983 a total of $2,874,574 in food stamps was distributed, with an average of 6,041 persons receiving food stamps each month. Aid to Families with Dependent Children (AFDC) totaled $561,861 with an average of 365 families receiving AFDC each month. Medical assistance benefits for the aged and disabled of $5,628,786 and for families and children of $747,749 brought the county benefit total to $9,812,969. **FIRE PROTECTION** One paid and eight volunteer fire departments. **LAW ENFORCEMENT** The County Sheriff has 32 commissioned officers. Five police departments have a combined force of 72. **CRIME** 276 violent crimes (murder, forcible rape, robbery and aggravated assault) and 2,724 nonviolent crimes (burglary, larceny-theft and motor vehicle theft) were reported in 1982. **JUDICIAL SYSTEM** Two District Courts and Judges, two County Courts and Judges and five Justices of the Peace. In the District Courts a total of 3,039 cases were pending on 1/1/82, 1,913 new cases were filed and 1,462 cases were disposed of during the year leaving 3,490 cases pending on 12/31/82. There were 759 criminal cases on the docket, 250 convictions, 74 persons committed to prison and 24 committed to jail and 366 cases left pending. In the County Courts 4,294 cases were pending on 1/1/82, 2,392 new cases were filed and 3,091 cases were disposed of during the year leaving 3,595 cases pending on 12/31/82. There were 4,462 criminal cases on the docket, 786 convictions, 127 persons committed to jail, and 1,672 cases left pending. **JAILS** One jail, capacity 45. Opened the new jail in 1983. **ATTORNEYS AT LAW** 84. **UTILITIES** 90% of the residents are connected to a public or privately owned water system and 56% are connected to a public sewer system. Natural gas is distributed to the county by Entex, Inc. The average annual residential bill for natural gas in 1982 for the Entex distribution system was $390.31, an increase of 26% over 1981. Electricity is distributed to the county by Texas Power and Light Co., Jasper and Newton Electric Coop., Inc., Houston County Electric Coop. and Sam Houston Electric Coop., Inc. and is generated primarily by oil and gas. The typical residential electric bill is $165.24 per month for an all-electric house using 2,500 kwh. **TAXES** The county has 11 units with taxing authority: six school districts, three cities, one county and one college district.

RECREATION/ENTERTAINMENT

FEDERAL Angelina National Forest covers 154,916 acres in parts of four counties and includes eight recreation areas. **STATE** Cassells Boykin Park covers 265 acres. **MUNICIPAL PARKS** 809 acres in 12 municipal parks. These parks contain two miles of hiking trails, 12 playgrounds, one golf course, four football and soccer fields, 17 baseball and softball fields, 17 tennis courts, seven multi-use courts, four swimming pools and shore fishing facilities. **SCENIC DRIVES** The Texas Forest Trail runs through this county. This trail explores the farming, ranching and wildlife areas of the East Texas Pineywoods. **BOATING/FISHING** Lakes/reservoirs: Little Cedar (50 acres), Fiberboard (341 acres), Kurth (770 acres) and Sam Rayburn (114,500 acres). Major rivers: Angelina and Neches. Primary streams: Cedar and White Oak. **HUNTING** Late fall and early winter seasons for deer. Late fall through early winter and spring seasons for squirrel. Winter seasons for quail, muskrat, nutria, beaver, otter, opossum, mink, ring-tailed cat, badger, fox, raccoon, skunk and civet cat. No closed seasons for coyotes and bobcats. In 1983 duck, coot, geese, woodcock and jacksnipe seasons occurred during the winter months. Teal duck, rail and gallinule seasons occurred in the fall. Mourning dove seasons occurred intermittently during the fall and winter months. **MUSEUMS** Lufkin: Lufkin Historical and Creative Arts Center and Texas Forestry Museum. Zavalla: Havard Home Museum. **ZOO** Lufkin: Ellen Trout Zoo. **SPECIAL EVENTS** Southern Hushpuppy Olympics, Lufkin, May; East Texas Folklife Festival, Lufkin, October; Christmas Parade, Lufkin; December.

COMMUNITIES

COUNTY SEAT Lufkin, County Courthouse, 75901; County Clerk's Office, 409/634-8339.

INCORPORATED COMMUNITIES (1980 population and ZIP Code) Burke (322) 75941, Diboll (5,227) 75941, Fullersprings (1,470) 75901, Hudson (1,659) 75901, Huntington (1,672) 75949, Lufkin (28,562) 75901 and Zavalla (762) 75980. **UNINCORPORATED COMMUNITIES** (and ZIP Code) Bald Hill 75901, Cedar Grove 75901, Central 75969, Clawson 75901, Davisville 75901, Gilbert 75901, Homer 75901, Moffett 75901, Pine Valley 75941, Pollok 75969, Providence 75901, Redland 75901, Redtown 75901, Shady Grove 75941, Shawnee Prairie (Flournoy) 75901, Sulphur Springs (Nancy) 75980 and Woodlawn 75901. **FOR ADDITIONAL LOCAL INFORMATION** Angelina Co. Chamber of Commerce, 515 S. First, P.O. Box 1606, Lufkin, 75901, 409/634-6644.

ARANSAS (G31)

THE LAND

On the Gulf Coast northeast of Corpus Christi on State Highway 35 in the Coastal Prairie Region, Aransas County covers 280 square miles with the elevation ranging from sea level to 50 feet. The level land is somewhat poorly drained, with saline, dark, loamy soils over cracking clayey subsoils. Also, there are sandy soils of beaches. In the northwest the loamy acidic surface layers have cracking, clayey subsoils. The Gulf marshes vegetation consists primarily of cordgrass, sedges, rushes, seashore saltgrass, marsh millet and maidencane. The saltgrasses begin at tidewater and further inland the tall grasses of the Gulf Prairie begin. Some hardwoods such as oaks and elms can be found, especially along streams, along with post oaks. Between 11 and 20% of the land in the county is considered prime farmland. **CLIMATE** Subtropical humid with warm summers. Tropical storms and possible hurricanes are a risk June through October. The average annual temperature is 71°F. Temperatures in January range from an average low of 46° to an average high of 63°F and in July range from 76° to 91°F. The average annual precipitation is 36 inches, with an average relative humidity of 95% at 6 A.M. and 75% at 6 P.M. There is no snowfall. The growing season averages 305 days per year, with the last freeze in mid December and the first freeze in early February. The sun shines during the year on the average 66% of the daylight hours.

THE PEOPLE

The 1982 estimated population of 16,000 indicates a continuation of the high growth rate (60%) begun in 1970 which made Aransas one of the most rapidly growing counties in the state. Between 1970 and 1980 the rural population increased 126%, one of the largest rural growth rates in the state, while urban growth declined by 1%. The age groups with the largest gains were birth to five years and ages 20 to 34. The county's marriage rate of 18 per 1,000 population is one of the highest in the state. The largest ancestry groups are persons of English descent (26%) and Hispanic (19%). **REGISTERED VOTERS** As of November 2, 1982 there were 6,985 registered voters (0.1% of the state total). The 1982 general election had a 54% voter turnout, compared to a 69% turnout in the 1980 general election. In the 1982 primary 83% voted Democratic and 17% Republican, with 1,966 votes cast.

THE ECONOMY

AGRICULTURE In 1982, 33% of the land was in farms and ranches, with 14% of the farmland under cultivation. Aransas ranked 253rd in the state in highest agricultural receipts, with 69% from crops. Overgrazing, undesirable brush and weeds, drainage and shoreline erosion are current conservation problems. Primary crops: sorghum. Primary fruits and nuts: peaches and pecans. Primary livestock and products: cattle. **BUSINESS** Total number of business establishments in the county: 320. Retail

sales during the first quarter of 1984 increased 19%. In 1980, 16% of the labor force were self-employed, 13% were employed in professional or related services, 10% in manufacturing, 22% in wholesale and retail trade, 13% in agriculture, forestry, fisheries and mining, 33% were employed in other counties and there were 1,520 retired workers. The industries with the most employment: agribusiness, tourism, oil and gas extraction, fish packaging and ship building and repairing. The nonfarm earnings in 1981 totaled $127,926,000. The retired workers received an average monthly Social Security payment of $323. **FINANCE** On June 30, 1983, two commercial banks had total deposits of $95,028,000 and total assets of $103,354,000. There are four branches of state savings and loan associations in the county. **HOUSING** Average value of homes in 1980: $36,600. Permits for new, privately owned housing units increased in 1982: 89 permits were issued with a total construction cost of $3,585,889. Of those permits, 35 were for single family houses. Between 1970 and 1980 the number of housing units increased by 79%. Seventy-four percent of all units in the county are air-conditioned, 70% are heated by gas and 28% by electricity. **NATURAL RESOURCES** Industrial sand. In 1982 a total of 16,741,234 thousand cubic feet of gas well gas, 115,125 barrels of condensate, 542,332 barrels of crude oil and 1,271,449 thousand cubic feet of casinghead gas were produced. **TOURISM** Travel expenditures of $41,591,000 in 1982 (an increase of 12% over 1981) generated 926 jobs and $7,784,000 in payroll. Lodging: 11 hotels, motels and tourist courts. **ALCOHOLIC BEVERAGES** Packaged distilled spirits, beer, ale, malt liquor and wine are legal. Sale of mixed beverages is legal in all or parts of the county. **FEDERAL EXPENDITURES** The federal government had direct expenditures or obligations of $25,806,000 in the county during fiscal year 1983, including $4,088,000 by the U.S. Department of Defense. In addition, the federal government provided $2,032,000 in grant awards, paid $452,000 in salaries and wages, made direct payments to individuals of $22,351,000 including $19,157,000 in retirement and disability payments, awarded $935,000 in procurement contracts and spent $35,000 in other expenditures or obligations. The federal government also provided $2,000 in direct loans and $174,923,000 in guaranteed loans and insurance.

COMMUNICATION

Newspapers–Weekly: The Toast of the Coast Herald (Rockport) and the Rockport Herald-Spanish. Cable TV. Telephone companies: General Telephone and Southwestern Bell. **TRANSPORTATION** Total public road mileage: 291. In 1982 there were 13,026 registered vehicles and 413 reported traffic accidents including 10 fatalities. Taxi cabs: one company in Rockport. Intercity bus service is available. Motor freight: four carriers. Rail: one branch line carries annually less than one million tons of freight through the county. Aircraft: 32 are registered in the county. Airports: Aransas County Airport is a basic transportation airport. It serves as a base for 25 aircraft. Also serving this area are Mustang Beach Airport at Port Aransas and Aransas Pass Municipal Airport. Waterborne commerce: (See Nueces County.) The Channel to Aransas Pass carried freight traffic of 9,953 short tons of domestic shipment in 1981. Rockport had freight traffic that totaled 210,055 short tons of domestic shipment.

COMMUNITY SERVICES

EDUCATION One school district with three elementary, one middle and one high school. The average daily attendance in 1981-82 was 2,260, with expenditures per pupil of $3,951 including 157 classroom teachers with an average annual salary of $16,989. Forty-seven percent of the 139 high school graduates planned to attend college. In 1982-83, 62% of the students were White, 31% Hispanic, 3% Black and 5% Asian. Private schools: 53 students enrolled in two elementary schools.

COUNTIES

ARANSAS (continued)

PUBLIC LIBRARIES Aransas County Public Library (Rockport): 25,384 volumes. **CHILD CARE** 16 day care and two twenty-four hour care licensed facilities. **HEALTH CARE** 16 physicians and three dentists. Ambulance services: two county services. **CHURCHES** 17 churches have an estimated combined membership of 7,005. The largest denominations are Catholic, Southern Baptist and United Methodist. **SOCIAL SERVICES** In fiscal year 1983 a total of $715,211 in food stamps was distributed, with an average of 1,381 persons receiving food stamps each month. Aid to Families with Dependent Children (AFDC) totaled $130,078, with an average of 92 families receiving AFDC each month. Medical assistance benefits for the aged and disabled of $239,606 and for families and children of $141,733 brought the county benefit total to $1,226,627. **FIRE PROTECTION** Four volunteer fire departments. **LAW ENFORCEMENT** The County Sheriff has 17 commissioned officers. One police department has a force of eight. **CRIME** 79 violent crimes (murder, forcible rape, robbery and aggravated assault) and 570 nonviolent crimes (burglary, larceny-theft and motor vehicle theft) were reported in 1982. **JUDICIAL SYSTEM** Two District Courts and Judges, one County Court and Judge and four Justices of the Peace. In the District Courts a total of 312 cases were pending on 1/1/82, 510 new cases were filed and 510 cases were disposed of during the year leaving 312 cases pending on 12/31/82. There were 196 criminal cases on the docket, 105 convictions, 26 persons committed to prison and four committed to jail and 49 cases left pending. In the County Court 1,147 cases were pending on 1/1/82, 882 new cases were filed and 721 cases were disposed of during the year leaving 1,308 cases pending on 12/31/82. There were 1,949 criminal cases on the docket, 286 convictions, 43 persons committed to jail, and 1,246 cases left pending. **JAILS** One jail, capacity 39. **ATTORNEYS AT LAW** 17. **UTILITIES** 85% of the residents are connected to a public or privately owned water system and 47% are connected to a public sewer system. Natural gas is distributed to the county by Aransas Natural Gas Co. Electricity is distributed to the county by Central Power and Light Co., Cochran Power and Light Co., and San Miguel Electric Coop., Inc. and is generated primarily by gas, oil and coal. The typical residential electric bill is $162.15 per month for an all-electric house using 2,500 kwh. **TAXES** The county has six units with taxing authority: one school district, two cities, one county and two special districts.

RECREATION/ENTERTAINMENT

NATIONAL REGISTER OF HISTORIC PLACES Aransas Pass: Aransas Pass Light Station. Fulton Beach: Fulton Mansion. Rockport: T.H. Mathis House. **STATE** Fulton Mansion State Historic Structure covers two acres and is closed to the public as of July, 1983. Goose Island State Recreation Area covers 307 acres with facilities which include camping and trailer sites as well as swimming and boat ramp areas. **COUNTY/ MUNICIPAL PARKS** 37 acres in five municipal parks. These parks contain four playgrounds, two football and soccer fields, four baseball and softball fields, two tennis courts, one boat ramp and shore fishing facilities. **BOATING/FISHING** Lakes/reservoirs: Burgentine (100 acres), Reynolds Metals Co. (113 acres) and Tailing Ponds (1,000 acres). Major rivers: Aransas. Primary streams: Salt, Copano, Cavasso, Cedar Bayou, Mesquite Bay, Redfish Bay and Aransas Bay. **STATE FISHING PIERS** Copano Bay. **SALTWATER FISHING** for speckled trout, redfish and flounders is usually good in Redfish Bay, Aransas Bay, Mesquite Bay, Copano Bay and St. Charles Bay. Surf-fishing is very good from the Gulf of Mexico side of St. Joseph Island. Shrimp, oysters and crabs may be taken but, like other saltwater fish, under specific regulations. **WILDLIFE REFUGES** Aransas

National Wildlife Refuge covers 90,069 acres. **HUNTING** Fall and winter seasons on deer. No closed season for javelina, squirrel, nutria, coyotes and bobcats. Late fall through early winter season on quail. Fall and winter seasons on turkey. Winter seasons on muskrat, beaver, otter, opossum, mink, ring-tailed cat, badger, fox, raccoon, skunk and civet cat. In 1983 duck, coot, geese, woodcock and jacksnipe seasons occurred during the winter months. Teal duck, rail and gallinule seasons occurred in the fall. Mourning dove seasons occurred intermittently during the fall and winter months. **MUSEUMS** Rockport: Marine Laboratory and Museum. **THEATERS** Rockport: Alpha-Omega Players. **SPECIAL EVENTS** Oysterfest, Fulton, March; Art Festival, Rockport, July; Seafair and Parade, Rockport, October.

COMMUNITIES

COUNTY SEAT Rockport, County Courthouse, 78382; County Clerk's Office, 512/729-7430. **INCORPORATED COMMUNITIES** (1980 population and ZIP Code) Aransas Pass (7,173: 860 in Aransas Co., 6,308 in San Patricio Co. and five in Nueces Co.) 78336, Fulton (424) 78358 and Rockport (3,686) 78382. **UNINCORPORATED COMMUNITIES** (and ZIP Code) Copano Village 78382, Estes 78382, Fulton Beach 78358 and Lamar 78382. **FOR ADDITIONAL LOCAL INFORMATION** Aransas Pass Chamber of Commerce, 452 Cleveland Blvd., Aransas Pass, 78336, 512/758-2750, Port Aransas Area Chamber of Commerce, P.O. Box 356, Port Aransas, 78373, 512/749-5919 and Rockport Area Chamber of Commerce, 404 Broadway, P.O. Box 1055, Rockport, 78382, 512/729-6445 or 729-9952.

ARCHER (P45)

THE LAND

South of Wichita Falls on U.S. Highways 281 and 82/277 in the North Central Prairies Region, Archer County covers 907 square miles of level land highlighted by hills along river tributaries. The elevation ranges from 950 to 1,250 feet. The undulating to hilly land has moderately deep to deep soils acidic to alkaline with loamy surface layers and clayey subsoils. Some areas have light colored, well drained soils and there are some that have hardened calcium deposits in the subsoils. In the Cross Timbers and Prairies vegetation area, prairie-type mid to short grasses such as: wildryes, bluestems, gramas and Indiangrass have been invaded by woody brush such as mesquite and juniper. There are a few live oak, post oak and blackjack oak trees. Between 21 and 30% of the land in the county is considered prime farmland. **CLIMATE** Subtropical subhumid with hot summers. The average annual temperature is 63°F. Temperatures in January range from an average low of 28° to an average high of 53°F and in July range from 73° to 98°F. The average annual precipitation is 27 inches, with an average relative humidity of 76% at 6 A.M. and 46% at 6 P.M. The average annual snowfall is five inches. The growing season averages 220 days per year, with the last freeze the first of April and the first freeze in early November. The sun shines during the year on the average 68% of the daylight hours.

THE PEOPLE

This county is one of the most sparsely populated in the state with an average of eight persons per square miles. The 1982 estimated population of 7,500 indicates a continuation of the steady growth rate begun in the 1970s which reversed the population decline between 1930 and 1970. Almost 17% of the growth between 1970 and 1980 was in the rural areas. The age groups with the largest gains were birth to five years and ages 20 to 34. The largest ancestry groups are persons of German descent (28%) and those of English descent (23%). **REGISTERED VOTERS** As of November 2, 1982 there were 4,092 registered voters (0.1% of the state total). The 1982 general election had a 59% voter turnout, compared to a 76% turnout in the 1980 general election. In the 1982 primary 96% voted Democratic and 4% Republican, with 1,331 votes cast.

THE ECONOMY

AGRICULTURE

Wheat and dairy area. In 1982, 93% of the land was in farms and ranches, with 18% of the farmland under cultivation and 2% irrigated. Archer ranked 83rd in the state in highest agricultural receipts, with 83% from livestock and livestock products. Overgrazing, undesirable brush and weeds, water erosion and difficulties with grass establishment are current conservation problems. Primary crops: wheat, oats and cotton. Primary fruits and nuts: peaches and pecans. Primary livestock and products: sixth in the state for milk production, cattle and hogs. **BUSINESS** Total number of business establishments in the county: 169. Retail sales during the first quarter of 1984 increased 22%. In 1980 17% of the labor force were self-employed, 15% were employed in professional or related services, 9% in manufacturing, 17% in wholesale and retail trade, 30% in agriculture, forestry, fisheries and mining, 47% were employed in other counties and there were 597 retired workers. The industries with the most employment: oil and gas extraction and agribusiness. The nonfarm earnings in 1981 totaled $71,552,000. The retired workers received an average monthly Social Security payment of $307. **FINANCE** On June 30, 1983, one commercial bank had total deposits of $22,212,000 and total assets of $25,041,000. There are two branches of state savings and loan associations and 19 credit unions in the county. **HOUSING** Average value of homes in 1980: $27,500. Permits for new, privately owned housing units increased in 1982: 35 permits were issued with a total construction cost of $876,408. Of those permits, 30 were for single family houses. Between 1970 and 1980 the number of housing units increased by 39%. Eight-six percent of all units in the county are air-conditioned, 69% are heated by gas and 27% by electricity. **NATURAL RESOURCES** Oil, gas, clay and sand, and gravel. In 1982 a total of 4,131 thousand cubic feet of gas well gas, 3,789,505 barrels of crude oil and 737,482 thousand cubic feet of casinghead gas were produced. Current production of other minerals and products includes crushed sandstone. **TOURISM** Travel expenditures of $4,574,000 in 1982 (an increase of 18% over 1981) generated 70 jobs and $749,000 in payroll. **ALCOHOLIC BEVERAGES** Packaged distilled spirits, beer, ale, malt liquor and wine are legal in parts of the county. **FEDERAL EXPENDITURES** The federal government had direct expenditures or obligations of $28,883,000 in the county during fiscal year 1983, including $12,965,000 by the U.S. Department of Defense. In addition, the federal government provided $586,000 in grant awards, paid $2,132,000 in salaries and wages, made direct payments to individuals of $15,957,000 including $12,195,000 in retirement and disability payments, awarded $9,706,000 in procurement contracts and spent $503,000 in other expenditures or obligations. The federal government also provided $2,312,000 in direct loans and $2,422,000 in guaranteed loans and insurance.

COMMUNICATION

Newspapers–Weekly: Archer County News (Archer City). Cable TV. Telephone companies: Continental Telephone, General Telephone, Southwestern Bell, Brazos Telephone Coop. and Community Telephone. **TRANSPORTATION** Total public road mileage: 740. In 1982 there were 7,936 registered vehicles and 147 reported traffic accidents including five fatalities. Intercity bus service is available. Motor freight: three carriers. Rail: one line carries annually less than one million tons of freight through the county. Aircraft: 13 are registered in the county. Airports: Archer City Municipal Airport.

COMMUNITY SERVICES

EDUCATION Four school districts with four elementary and four high schools. The average daily attendance in 1981-82 was 1,576, with expenditures per pupil of $2,340 including 104 classroom teachers with an average annual salary of $15,507. Forty-five percent of the 130 high school graduates planned to attend college. In 1982-83, 98% of the students were White, 2% Hispanic, 1% Black and 0.1% American Indian. **PUBLIC LIBRARIES** Archer County Public Library (Archer City): 5,800 volumes. **CHILD CARE** Nine day care and three twenty-four hour care licensed facilities. **HEALTH CARE** One physician and one dentist. Hospitals: one with a capacity of 26. Ambulance services: one county, one commercial and one volunteer fire deparment service. Mental health: one county clinic. Nursing homes: one nursing home with a combined capacity of 46 nursing care residents. The average cost per day for private patients in 1982 was $30. **CHURCHES** 24 churches have an estimated combined membership of 5,501. The largest denominations are Southern Baptist, Catholic and Christian Methodist Episcopal. **SOCIAL SERVICES** In fiscal year 1983 a total of $69,149 in food stamps was distributed, with an average of 157 persons receiving food stamps each month. Aid to Families with Dependent Children (AFDC) totaled $8,095, with an average of five families receiving AFDC each month. Medical assistance benefits for the aged and disabled of $252,399 and for families and children of $7,118 brought the county benefit total to $336,761. **FIRE PROTECTION** Two paid and four volunteer fire departments. **LAW ENFORCEMENT** The County Sheriff has seven commissioned officers. One police department in the county with one officer. **CRIME** Five violent crimes (murder, forcible rape, robbery and aggravated assault) and 115 nonviolent crimes (burglary, larceny-theft and motor vehicle theft) were reported in 1982. **JUDICIAL SYSTEM** One District Court and Judge, one County Court and Judge and four Justices of the Peace. In the District Court a total of 239 cases were pending on 1/1/82, 186 new cases were filed and 260 cases were disposed of during the year leaving 165 cases pending on 12/31/82. There were 95 criminal cases on the docket, 10 convictions, five persons committed to prison and 22 cases left pending. In the County Court 528 cases were pending on 1/1/82, 565 new cases were filed and 570 cases were disposed of during the year leaving 523 cases pending on 12/31/82. There were 1,041 criminal cases on the docket, 310 convictions, 51 persons committed to jail, and 486 cases left pending. **JAILS** One jail, capacity 12. **ATTORNEYS AT LAW** Five. **UTILITIES** 87% of the residents are connected to a public or privately owned water system and 50% are connected to a public sewer system. Natural gas is distributed to the county by Lone Star Gas Co., Division of Enserch. The average annual residential bill for natural gas in 1982 for the Lone Star distribution system was $405.91, an increase of 35%. Electricity is distributed to the county by Texas Electric Service, B-K Electric Coop., Inc., J-A-C Electric Coop., Inc. and Fort Belknap Electric Coop., Inc. and is generated primarily by gas. The typical residential electric bill is $106.53 per month for an all-electric house using 2,500 kwh. **TAXES** The county has nine units with taxing authority: four school districts, four cities and one county.

RECREATION/ENTERTAINMENT

NATIONAL REGISTER OF HISTORIC PLACES Archer City: Archer County Courthouse and Jail. STATE: Lake Arrowhead State Recreation Area (see Clay County). **COUNTY/ MUNICIPAL PARKS** 320 acres in one county and 11 municipal parks. These parks contain four playgrounds, two baseball and

COUNTIES

ARCHER (continued)

softball fields, two tennis courts, one multi-use court, one swimming pool, three beaches and three boat ramps. **BOATING/FISHING** Lakes/reservoirs: Archer City (57 acres), Diversion (3,419 acres), Cooper (250 acres), Kickapoo (6,200 acres), Megargel Creek (14 acres), Olney (215 acres) and Scotland (70 acres). Major rivers: Wichita, North Fork Little Wichita, Little Wichita and South Fork Little Wichita. Primary streams: Carver and Mesquite. **HUNTING** Fall and winter seasons on deer. No closed seasons on squirrel, nutria, coyotes and bobcats. Fall, winter and spring seasons on turkey. Winter seasons on quail, muskrat, beaver, otter, opossum, mink, ring-tailed cat, badger, fox, raccoon, skunk and civet cat. In 1983 duck, coot, geese, woodcock and jacksnipe seasons occurred during the winter months. Teal duck, rail and gallinule seasons occurred in the fall. Mourning dove seasons occurred intermittently during the fall and winter months. **MUSEUMS** Archer City: Archer County Historical Museum. Windthorst: Archer County Museum. **SPECIAL EVENTS** Rattlesnake Hunt, Archer City, April; Rodeo and Parade, Archer City, June; Arts and Crafts Festival, Holliday, June; Annual German Sausage Supper, Windthorst, June; Scotland Picnic, Scotland, July; Annual Dance and Picnic, Megargel, August; Turkey Shoot, Archer City, November/December; and Christmas Parade, Archer City, December.

COMMUNITIES
COUNTY SEAT Archer City, County Courthouse, 76351; County Clerk's Office, 817/574-4615. **INCORPORATED COMMUNITIES** (1980 population and ZIP Code) Archer City (1,862) 76351, Holliday (1,349) 76366, Lakeside City (515) 76308, Megargel (381) 76370, Scotland (367: 365 in Archer Co. and 2 in Clay) 76379 and Windthorst (409: 401 in Archer Co. and 8 in Clay Co.) 76389. **UNINCORPORATED COMMUNITIES** (and ZIP Code) Dundee 76358 and Mankins 76366. **FOR ADDITIONAL LOCAL INFORMATION** Archer Co. Chamber of Commerce, P.O. Box 877, Archer, 76351, 817/574-4212 and Wichita Falls, Board of Community and Industry, 8th and Lamar, P.O. Box 1860, Wichita Falls, 76307, 817/723-2741.

ARMSTRONG (P18)

THE LAND
In the Texas Panhandle southeast of Amarillo on U.S. Highway 287 in the Rolling Plains Region, Armstrong County covers 910 square miles of level to rolling land broken by the Palo Duro Canyon. The elevation ranges from 2,400 to 3,000 feet. The red to brown loamy slightly acidic to alkaline soils cover limestone in most areas. In the northwest and southwest the soils are loamy with clayey subsoils. The southeastern half of Armstrong is in the Rolling Plains vegetation area with mesquite woodlands and prairie. The tall grasses such as bluestems and Indiangrass have been invaded by tumblegrass, sandburs, ragweed, yucca, sand sagebrush and mesquite. The northwestern half is in the High Plains vegetation area and switchgrass, buffalograss, wheatgrass, bluestems and blue grama grasses are prominent. Mesquite, juniper, yucca and sagebrush have also invaded this area. Between 41 and 50% of the land in the county is considered prime farmland. **CLIMATE** Continental Steppe with dry, cold, windy winters and warm summers. The average annual temperature is 59°F. Temperatures in January range from an average low of 23° to an average high of 51°F and in July range from 66° to 93°F. The average annual precipitation is 21 inches, with an average relative humidity of 69% at 6 A.M. and 39% at 6 P.M. The average annual snowfall is 15 inches. The growing season averages 202 days per year, with the last freeze in early April and the first freeze in early November. The sun shines during the year on the average 75% of the daylight hours.

THE PEOPLE
This county is one of the most sparsely populated in the state with an average of two persons per square mile. The 1982 estimated population of 1,900 indicates a slight reversal of the growth during the 1970s. The majority of residents live in rural areas. The age group with the largest gain between 1970 and 1980 was birth to five years, while the group with the largest decrease was ages five to 14 years. The largest ancestry groups are persons of Irish descent (27%) and those of English descent (26%). **REGISTERED VOTERS** As of November 2, 1982 there were 1,260 registered voters (0.01% of the state total). The 1982 general election had a 70% voter turnout, compared to a 77% turnout in the 1980 general election. In the 1982 primary 95% voted Democratic and 5% Republican, with 505 votes cast.

THE ECONOMY
AGRICULTURE Wheat area. In 1982, 97% of the land was in farms and ranches, with 26% of the farmland under cultivation and 10% irrigated. Armstrong ranked 177th in the state in highest agricultural receipts, with 51% from livestock and livestock products. Overgrazing, water and wind erosion, decreasing irrigation, water supply and noxious weeds are current conservation problems. Primary crops: wheat, sorghum, sunflowers and cotton. Primary vegetables: sweet potatoes and tomatoes. Primary fruits and nuts: pecans. Primary livestock and products: cattle and hogs. **BUSINESS** Total number of business establishments in the county: 39. Retail sales during the first quarter of 1984 increased 10%. In 1980, 24% of the labor force were self-employed, 18% were employed in professional or related services, 14% in manufacturing, 16% in wholesale and retail trade, 25% in agriculture, forestry, fisheries and mining, 39% were employed in other counties and there were 242 retired workers. The industries with the most employment: road construction and agribusiness. The nonfarm earnings in 1981 totaled $16,381,000. The retired workers received an average monthly Social Security payment of $322. **FINANCE** On June 30, 1983, one commercial bank had total deposits of $11,951,000 and total assets of $13,365,000. **HOUSING** Average value of homes in 1980: $26,400. Between 1970 and 1980 the number of housing units increased by 12%. Seventy-four percent of all units in the county are air-conditioned, 93% are heated by gas and 6% by electricity. **NATURAL RESOURCES** Caliche and gypsum. Current production of minerals includes sand and gravel. **TOURISM** Travel expenditures of $1,824,000 in 1982 (an increase of 11% over 1981) generated 47 jobs and $370,000 in payroll. **ALCOHOLIC BEVERAGES** Totally dry. **FEDERAL EXPENDITURES** The federal government had direct expenditures or obligations of $5,896,000 in the county during fiscal year 1983, including $77,000 by the U.S. Department of Defense. In addition, the federal government provided $31,000 in grant awards, paid $159,000 in salaries and wages, made direct payments to individuals of $3,523,000 including $2,555,000 in retirement and disability payments, awarded $61,000 in procurement contracts and spent $2,122,000 in other expenditures or obligations. The federal government also provided $5,753,000 in direct loans and $3,641,000 in guaranteed loans and insurance.

COMMUNICATION
Newspapers–Weekly: Claude News. Telephone companies: General Telephone, Southwestern Bell and Midplains Rural Telephone Coop. **TRANSPORTATION** Total public road

mileage: 574. In 1982 there were 2,774 registered vehicles and 54 reported traffic accidents including one fatality. Intercity bus service is available. Motor freight: two carriers. Rail: One main line carries annually over 30 million tons of freight through the county. Aircraft: six are registered in the county.

COMMUNITY SERVICES

EDUCATION One school district with one elementary and one high school. The average daily attendance in 1981-82 was 307, with expenditures per pupil of $2,820 including 21 classroom teachers with an average annual salary of $15,606. Seventy-eight percent of the 27 high school graduates planned to attend college. In 1982-83, 93% of the students were White, 7% Hispanic and 0.3% Asian. **PUBLIC LIBRARIES** Claude Public Library: 6,200 volumes. **CHILD CARE** Two twenty-four hour care licensed facilities. **HEALTH CARE** Two physicians. Ambulance services: one volunteer service. Nursing homes: one nursing home has a capacity of 54 nursing care residents. The average cost per day for private patients in 1982 was $38. **CHURCHES** Eight churches have an estimated combined membership of 1,521. The largest denominations are Southern Baptist, United Methodist and Catholic. **SOCIAL SERVICES** In fiscal year 1983 a total of $12,862 in food stamps was distributed, with an average of 33 persons receiving food stamps each month. Aid to Families with Dependent Children (AFDC) payments totaled $223. Medical assistance benefits for the aged and disabled of $268,115 and for families and children of $25,861 brought the county benefit total to $307,061. **FIRE PROTECTION** Two volunteer fire departments. **LAW ENFORCEMENT** The County Sheriff has two commissioned officers. **CRIME** 18 nonviolent crimes (burglary, larceny-theft and motor vehicle theft) were reported in 1982. **JUDICIAL SYSTEM** One District Court and Judge, one County Court and Judge and one Justice of the Peace. In the District Court a total of 32 cases were pending on 1/1/82, 30 new cases were filed and 41 cases were disposed of during the year leaving 21 cases pending on 12/31/82. There were five criminal cases on the docket, two convictions, one committed to jail and three cases left pending. In the County Court 20 cases were pending on 1/1/82, 22 new cases were filed and 28 cases were disposed of during the year leaving 14 cases pending on 12/31/82. There were 33 criminal cases on the docket, 16 convictions, four persons committed to jail, and eight cases left pending. **ATTORNEYS AT LAW** Two. **UTILITIES** 61% of the residents are connected to a public or privately owned water system and 51% are connected to a public sewer system. Natural gas is distributed to the county by Producers Utilities Corp. Electricity is distributed to the county by Southwestern Public Service Co., Greenbelt Electric Coop., Inc. and Swisher Electric Coop., Inc. and is generated primarily by gas and coal. **TAXES** The county has five units with taxing authority: one school district, one city, one county and two special districts.

RECREATION/ENTERTAINMENT

NATIONAL REGISTER OF HISTORIC PLACES Claude: JA Ranch (National Historic Landmark). **STATE** Palo Duro Canyon State Park (see Randall County). **MUNICIPAL PARKS** Three acres in one municipal park. This park contains one playground and one baseball and softball field. **SCENIC DRIVES** The Texas Plains Trail runs through this county. Texas 207 provides one of the most impressive drives in the state through agricultural areas and into the Palo Duro Canyon, a nine-mile canyon carved by the Prairie Dog Town Fork of the Red River. Major rivers: Prairie Dog Town Fork Red and Salt Fork Red. Primary streams: Mulberry. **HUNTING** Fall season on antelope. Early and mid-winter seasons on aoudad sheep. Fall and winter seasons on deer and mule deer. Summer and late fall seasons on squirrel. Fall, winter and spring seasons on turkey. Winter seasons on pheasant, quail, muskrat, beaver, opossum, ring-tailed cat, badger, fox, weasel, raccoon, skunk and civet cat. No closed seasons for coyotes and bobcats. In 1983 sandhill crane, duck, coot, geese, woodcock and jacksnipe seasons occurred during the winter months. Teal duck, rail and gallinule seasons occurred in the fall. Mourning dove seasons occurred intermittently during the fall and winter months. **SPECIAL EVENTS** Old Settler's Reunion, Claude, July; Cowboy Breakfast, Claude, May-September.

COMMUNITIES

COUNTY SEAT Claude, County Courthouse, 79019; County Clerk's Office, 806/226-2081. **INCORPORATED COMMUNITIES** (1980 population and ZIP Code) Claude (1,112) 79019. **UNINCORPORATED COMMUNITIES** (and ZIP Code) Goodnight 79226, Paloduro 79226, Washburn 79019, Wayside 79094. **FOR ADDITIONAL LOCAL INFORMATION** Claude Chamber of Commerce, P.O. Box 328, Claude, 79109, 806/226-2621.

ATASCOSA (C38)

THE LAND

South of San Antonio on Interstate Highway 37 in the Rio Grande Plain Region, Atascosa County covers 1,218 square miles of level to rolling land. The elevation ranges from 350 to 700 feet. The soils are deep with loamy surface layers and clayey subsoils. Along the southern border the light colored soils have limestone near the surface. In some areas the soils are gray to black, cracking and clayey with a high shrink-swell potential. In the South Texas Plains vegetation area, the subtropical dryland vegetation is primarily cactus, weeds, grasses, thorny shrubs and some small trees such as mesquite, live oak and post oak. As much of the area is covered by a dense mixture of brush, the region is known as "brush country". Many of the open grassland areas have been seeded with buffalograss. Between 41 and 50% of the land in the county is considered prime farmland. **CLIMATE** Subtropical subhumid with mild winters and hot summers. The average annual temperature is 70°F. Temperatures in January range from an average low of 40° to an average high of 65°F and in July range from 74° to 97°F. The average annual precipitation is 27 inches, with an average relative humidity of 84% at 6 A.M. and 51% at 6 P.M. There is no significant snowfall. The growing season averages 282 days per year, with the last freeze in late February and the first freeze in early December. The sun shines during the year on the average 65% of the daylight hours.

THE PEOPLE

In 1980 this county ranked 40th among all U.S. counties in percent of persons of Spanish origin. The 1982 estimated population of 26,100 indicates a continuation of the strong growth rate begun in the 1970s. The county has a history of reversals in growth with increases in population from 1930 to 1950 followed by a decline from 1950 to 1970. The 45% urban growth rate between 1970 and 1980 was one of the highest in the state. The age groups with the largest gains were ages 62 and over and 30 to 34. The largest ancestry groups are persons of Hispanic (48%), German descent (15%) and those of English descent (14%). **REGISTERED VOTERS** As of November 2, 1982 there were 13,418 registered voters (0.2% of the state total). The 1982 general election had a 34% voter turnout, compared to a 63% turnout in the 1980 general election. In the 1982 primary 98% voted Democratic and 2% Republican, with 4,923 votes cast.

COUNTIES

ATASCOSA (continued)

THE ECONOMY

AGRICULTURE Diversified products. In 1982, 93% of the land was in farms and ranches, with 17% of the farmland under cultivation and 35% irrigated. Atascosa ranked 51st in the state in highest agricultural receipts with 71% from livestock and livestock products. Overgrazing, water erosion and inefficient irrigation systems are current conservation problems. Primary crops: fourth in the state for peanuts. Oats, hay, wheat and sorghum. Primary vegetables: eighth in the state for watermelons. Primary fruits and nuts: seventh in the state for peaches. Pecans. Primary livestock and products: fourth in the state for beef cows that have calved. Cattle, milk and hogs. **BUSINESS** Total number of business establishments in the county: 400. Retail sales during the first quarter of 1984 increased 17%. In 1980 12% of the labor force were self-employed, 16% were employed in professional or related services, 7% in manufacturing, 19% in wholesale and retail trade, 21% in agriculture, forestry, fisheries and mining, 35% were employed in other counties and there were 1,796 retired workers. The industries with the most employment: oil and gas extraction, general construction and agribusiness. The nonfarm earnings in 1981 totaled $181,579,000. The retired workers received an average monthly Social Security payment of $273. **FINANCE** On June 30, 1983, six commercial banks had total deposits of $110,415,000 and total assets of $128,018,000. On December 31, 1982 one state savings and loan association and three state branches had assets of $34,880,160. **HOUSING** Average value of homes in 1980: $20,200. Permits for new, privately owned housing units decreased in 1982: 62 permits were issued with a total construction cost of $2,004,662. Of those permits, all were for single family houses. Between 1970 and 1980 the number of housing units increased by 50%. Fifty-nine percent of all units in the county are air-conditioned, 76% are heated by gas and 19% by electricity. **NATURAL RESOURCES** Clay, industrial sand, uranium, sand and gravel, oil and gas. In 1982 a total of 25,135,305 thousand cubic feet of gas well gas, 81,555 barrels of condensate, 1,619,391 barrels of crude oil and 6,333,523 thousand cubic feet of casinghead gas were produced. Current production of other minerals and products includes caliche, clay, lignite coal, construction and industrial sand, recovered sulphur and uranium. **TOURISM** Travel expenditures of $7,405,000 in 1982 (an increase of 14% over 1981) generated 142 jobs and $1,272,000 in payroll. **ALCOHOLIC BEVERAGES** Packaged distilled spirits, beer, ale, malt liquor and wine are legal in parts of the county. **FEDERAL EXPENDITURES** The federal government had direct expenditures or obligations of $32,953,000 in the county during fiscal year 1983, including $2,460,000 by the U.S. Department of Defense. In addition, the federal government provided $1,043,000 in grant awards, paid $1,267,000 in salaries and wages, made direct payments to individuals of $30,365,000 including $23,396,000 in retirement and disability payments, awarded $45,000 in procurement contracts and spent $234,000 in other expenditures or obligations. The federal government also provided $140,000 in direct loans and $7,066,000 in guaranteed loans and insurance.

COMMUNICATION

Newspapers–Weekly: Pleasanton Express. Radio: KBOP-AM and KBOP-FM (Pleasanton). Cable TV. Telephone companies: Continental Telephone, General Telephone, Southwestern Bell and Valley Telephone Coop. **TRANSPORTATION** Total public road mileage: 1,149. In 1982 there were 20,357 registered vehicles and 435 reported traffic accidents including seven fatalities. Intercity bus service is available. Motor freight: six local and intrastate carriers. Rail: The Eagle provides passenger service on the Amtrack route. Two branch lines carry freight through the county; one carries five to 10 million tons annually and the other carries one to five. Aircraft: 43 are registered in the county. Airports: Pleasanton Municipal Airport is a basic utility airport providing general aviation services. It serves as a base for 15 aircraft.

COMMUNITY SERVICES

EDUCATION Five school districts with eight elementary, five middle and five high schools. The average daily attendance in 1981-82 was 5,604, with expenditures per pupil of $2,220 including 362 classroom teachers with an average annual salary of $15,444. Thirty-four percent of the 386 high school graduates planned to attend college. In 1982-83, 41% of the students were White, 58% Hispanic, 0.4% Black and 0.3% Asian. Private schools: 34 students enrolled in one elementary and one high school. **PUBLIC LIBRARIES** Jourdanton Community Library: 7,500 volumes. Lytle Public Library: 5,000 volumes. Pleasanton Public Library: 22,000 volumes. Poteet Public Library: 11,685 volumes. **CHILD CARE** 18 day care and three twenty-four hour care licensed facilities. **HEALTH CARE** 11 physicians and eight dentists. Hospitals: one with a capacity of 65. Clinics: one for treatment of drug abuse, one outpatient clinic and one public health clinic. Ambulance services: three volunteer services, one commercial and one funeral home service. Mental health: one clinic and one county clinic. Nursing homes: five nursing homes with a combined capacity of 327 nursing care residents. The average cost per day for private patients in 1982 was $30.66. **CHURCHES** 45 churches have an estimated combined membership of 18,175. The largest denominations are Catholic, Southern Baptist and United Methodist. **SOCIAL SERVICES** In fiscal year 1983 a total of $2,060,977 in food stamps was distributed, with an average of 4,346 persons receiving food stamps each month. Aid to Families with Dependent Children (AFDC) totaled $384,404 with an average of 243 families receiving AFDC each month. Medical assistance benefits for the aged and disabled of $2,542,295 and for families and children of $536,563 brought the county benefit total to $5,524,239. **FIRE PROTECTION** Nine volunteer fire departments. **LAW ENFORCEMENT** The County Sheriff has 37 commissioned officers. Four police departments have a combined force of 28. **CRIME** 68 violent crimes (murder, forcible rape, robbery and aggravated assault) and 333 nonviolent crimes (burglary, larceny-theft and motor vehicle theft) were reported in 1982. **JUDICIAL SYSTEM** Two District Courts and Judges, one County Court and Judge and four Justices of the Peace. In the District Courts a total of 519 cases were pending on 1/1/82, 528 new cases were filed and 502 cases were disposed of during the year leaving 545 cases pending on 12/31/82. There were 357 criminal cases on the docket, 113 convictions, 34 persons committed to prison and three committed to jail and 149 cases left pending. In the County Court 529 cases were pending on 1/1/82, 337 new cases were filed and 244 cases were disposed of during the year leaving 622 cases pending on 12/31/82. There were 638 criminal cases on the docket, 116 convictions and 410 cases left pending. **JAILS** One jail, capacity 26. **ATTORNEYS AT LAW** 15. **UTILITIES** 76% of the residents are connected to a public or privately owned water system and 59% are connected to a public sewer system. Natural gas is distributed to the county by Entex, Inc. The average annual residential bill for natural gas in 1982 for the Entex distribution system was $390.31, an increase of 26% over 1981. Electricity is distributed to the county by Central Power and Light Co., Karnes Electric Coop., Inc., Medina Coop., Inc. Cochran Power and Light Co. and San Antonio City Public Service Board and is generated primarily by gas, oil and coal. The typical residential electric bill is $162.15 per month for an all-electric house using 2,500 kwh. **TAXES** The county has 15 units with taxing authority: five school districts, six cities, one county and three special districts.

RECREATION/ENTERTAINMENT

MUNICIPAL PARKS 120 acres in 10 municipal parks. These parks contain five playgrounds, seven baseball and softball fields, six tennis courts, two multi-use courts and two swimming pools. **BOATING/FISHING** Lakes/reservoirs: Bonita (20 acres), Pilgrim (49 acres) and Rips (20 acres). Major rivers: Atascosa. Primary streams: Bonita. **HUNTING** Fall and winter seasons on deer. No closed seasons on javelina, squirrel, coyotes and bobcats. Fall, winter and spring seasons on turkey. Winter season on quail, muskrat, beaver, opossum, ring-tailed cat, badger, fox, weasel, raccoon, skunk and civet cat. In 1983 sandhill crane, duck, coot, geese, woodcock and jacksnipe seasons occurred during the winter months. Teal duck, rail and gallinule seasons occurred in the fall. Mourning dove season occurred intermittently during the fall and winter months with a fall season on white-winged doves. **MUSEUMS** Pleasanton: Longhorn Museum. **SPECIAL EVENTS** Strawberry Festival, Poteet, April; Jourdanton Days Celebration, Jourdanton, May; Cowboy Homecoming and Rodeo, Pleasanton, August.

COMMUNITIES

COUNTY SEAT Jourdanton, County Courthouse, 78026; County Clerk's Office, 512/769-2511. **INCORPORATED COMMUNITIES** (1980 population and ZIP Code) Campbellton (279*) 78008, Charlotte (1,443) 78011, Christine (392) 78012, Jourdanton (2,743) 78026, Lytle (1,920: 1,544 in Atascosa Co., 17 in Bexar Co. and 359 in Medina Co.), Pleasanton (6,346) 78064 and Poteet (3,086) 78065. *Est., Incorp. inactive. **UNINCORPORATED COMMUNITIES** (and ZIP Code) Coughran 78064, Davisville 78001, Dobrowolski 78026, Fashing 78020, Hindes 78026, Kyote 78005, Leming 78050, McCoy 78053, Peggy 78062, Rossville 78065 and Verdi 78064. **FOR ADDITIONAL LOCAL INFORMATION** Jourdanton Community Chamber of Commerce, P.O. Box 747, Jourdanton, 78026, 512/769-3275; Greater Lytle Chamber of Commerce, P.O. Box 640, Lytle, 78052, 512/772-3692 and Pleasanton Chamber of Commerce, 605 Second, P.O. Box 153, Pleasanton, 78064, 512/569-2163.

AUSTIN (G9)

THE LAND

West of Houston on Interstate Highway 10 in the Claypan Area, Austin County covers 656 square miles with the elevation ranging from 125 to 400 feet. The northern third of the county has undulating alkaline to slightly acidic soils. The deep, dark, cracking, clayey soils have a high potential to shrink and swell and cover chalk. The central one-third has nearly level to undulating light colored, acidic soils with loamy surface layers and mottled gray and red to yellow cracking, clayey subsoils with a high potential to shrink and swell. The level soils in the southern third are somewhat poorly drained with loamy surface layers and cracking, clayey, acidic subsoils. The northern third of the county is in the Blackland Prairie vegetation area, with a variety of trees along streams such as oaks, elms, pecans and mesquite. Most grasslands are under cultivation, with buffalograss, Texas grama and legumes in pastures. The central third is in the Post Oak Savannah with tall grasses, some oak and elm trees plus walnuts and pecans along streams. The southern third is in the Gulf Prairie area with tall grasses including bluestems, wintergrass and Indiangrass. A few oak and elm trees grow along streams. Between 11 and 20% of the land in the county is considered prime farmland. **CLIMATE** Subtropical humid with mild winters and hot summers. The average annual temperature is 58°F. Temperatures in January range from an average low of 41° to an average high of 61°F and in July range from 73° to 96°F. The average annual precipitation is 42 inches, with an average relative humidity of 86% at 6 A.M. and 56% at 6 P.M. There is no significant snowfall. The growing season averages 283 days per year, with the last freeze in late February and the first freeze in early December. The sun shines during the year on the average 68% of the daylight hours.

THE PEOPLE

The 1982 estimated population of 19,300 indicates a continuation of the strong growth rate begun in the 1970s. The urban growth rate of 151% between 1970 and 1980 was one of the highest in the state. The age group with the largest gain was ages 20 to 39. The county's population is older than average and the 1980 marriage rate of six per 1,000 residents is one of the lowest in the state. The largest ancestry groups are persons of German descent (49%) and Black (15%). **REGISTERED VOTERS** As of November 2, 1982 there were 8,104 registered voters (0.1% of the state total). The 1982 general election had a 55% voter turnout, compared to a 71% turnout in the 1980 general election. In the 1982 primary 85% voted Democratic and 15% Republican, with 1,514 votes cast.

THE ECONOMY

AGRICULTURE Cattle area. In 1982, 83% of the land was in farms and ranches, with 17% of the farmland under cultivation and 10% irrigated. Austin ranked 100th in the state in highest agricultural receipts, with 83% from livestock and livestock products. Overgrazing, water erosion, inefficient irrigation systems and drainage are current conservation problems. Primary crops: hay, sorghum, corn, rice and oats. Primary vegetables: potatoes, sweet potatoes and watermelons. Primary fruits and nuts: peaches and pecans. Primary livestock and products: cattle and hogs. **BUSINESS** Total number of business establishments in the county: 411. Retail sales during the first quarter of 1984 increased 5%. In 1980 15% of the labor force were self-employed, 14% were employed in professional or related services, 15% in manufacturing, 23% in wholesale and retail trade, 13% in agriculture, forestry, fisheries and mining, 33% were employed in other counties and there were 2,041 retired workers. The industries with the most employment: general and heavy construction, agribusiness and steel mills. The nonfarm earnings in 1981 totaled $176,815,000. The retired workers received an average monthly Social Security payment of $284. **FINANCE** On June 30, 1983, six commercial banks had total deposits of $186,509,000 and total assets of $212,283,000. There are three state savings and loan association branches and one federal association branch in the county. **HOUSING** Average value of homes in 1980: $38,700. Permits for new, privately owned housing units decreased in 1982: 63 permits were issued with a total construction cost of $2,589,319. Of those permits, 43 were for single family houses. Between 1970 and 1980 the number of housing units increased by 43%. Sixty-four percent of all units in the county are air-conditioned, 65% are heated by gas and 27% by electricity. **NATURAL RESOURCES** Salt domes, sand and gravel, oil and gas. In 1982 a total of 5,582,162 thousand cubic feet of gas well gas, 79,771 barrels of condensate, 648,175 barrels of crude oil and 489,609 thousand cubic feet of casinghead gas were produced. Current production of other minerals and products includes construction sand. **TOURISM** Travel expenditures of $4,358,000 in 1982 (an increase of 13% over 1981) generated 92 jobs and $787,000 in payroll. Convention/meeting facilities: Bellville-Austin County Fair Grandstand. **ALCOHOLIC BEVERAGES** Packaged distilled spirits, beer, ale, malt liquor and wine are legal. Sale of mixed beverages is legal in all or parts of the county. **FEDERAL EXPENDITURES** The federal government had direct expenditures or obligations of $31,090,000 in the county during fiscal year 1983, including $616,000 by the U.S. Department of Defense. In addition, the federal government

AUSTIN (continued)

provided $251,000 in grant awards, paid $1,227,000 in salaries and wages, made direct payments to individuals of $28,789,000 including $19,831,000 in retirement and disability payments, awarded $56,000 in procurement contracts and spent $766,000 in other expenditures or obligations. The federal government also provided $99,000 in direct loans and $7,613,000 in guaranteed loans and insurance.

COMMUNICATION

Newspapers–Weekly: The New Ulm Enterprise, Sealy News and the Wallis News Review. Cable TV. Telephone companies: General Telephone, Southwestern Bell and Industry Telephone. **TRANSPORTATION** Total public road mileage: 877. In 1982 there were 18,084 registered vehicles and 470 reported traffic accidents including 10 fatalities. Intercity bus service is available. Motor freight: four carriers. Rail: four main lines and one branch line carry freight through the county. Two of the main lines carry annually over 30 million tons of freight each; one carries 20 to 30 million tons and the other carries one to five. The branch line annually carries 20 to 30 million tons of freight. Aircraft: 22 are registered in the county. Airports: Grawunder Field in Bellville is a basic utility airport providing general aviation service. It serves as a base for 15 aircraft. For emergency use Bellville Memorial Hospital Heliport at Bellville is available.

COMMUNITY SERVICES

EDUCATION Three school districts with six elementary, three middle and three high schools. The average daily attendance in 1981-82 was 3,697, with expenditures per pupil of $3,660 including 246 classroom teachers with an average annual salary of $16,057. Fifty-three percent of the 248 high school graduates planned to attend college. In 1982-83, 73% of the students were White, 10% Hispanic, 17% Black and 0.1% Asian. **PUBLIC LIBRARIES** Bellville Public Library: 14,887 volumes. Virgil and Josephine Gordon Memorial Library (Sealy): 9,415 volumes. Knoy Memorial Library (Wallis): 17,012 volumes. **CHILD CARE** 39 day care and seven twenty-four hour care licensed facilities. **HEALTH CARE** 11 physicians and six dentists. Hospitals: two with a combined capacity of 57. Ambulance services: one county service. Nursing homes: three nursing homes have a combined capacity of 326 nursing care residents. The average cost per day for private patients in 1982 was $29.29. **CHURCHES** 34 churches have an estimated combined membership of 9,004. The largest denominations are Catholic, American Lutheran and United Methodist. **SOCIAL SERVICES** In fiscal year 1983 a total of $639,768 in food stamps was distributed, with an average of 1,321 persons receiving food stamps each month. Aid to Families with Dependent Children (AFDC) totaled $178,599 with an average of 122 families receiving AFDC each month. Medical assistance benefits for the aged and disabled of $1,517,677 and for families and children of $247,943 brought the county benefit total to $2,583,986. **FIRE PROTECTION** Ten volunteer fire departments. **LAW ENFORCEMENT** The County Sheriff has 24 commissioned officers. Four police departments have a combined force of 25. **CRIME** 59 violent crimes (murder, forcible rape, robbery and aggravated assault) and 282 nonviolent crimes (burglary, larceny-theft and motor vehicle theft) were reported in 1982. **JUDICIAL SYSTEM** One District Court and Judge, one County Court and Judge and four Justices of the Peace. In the District Court a total of 475 cases were pending on 1/1/82, 411 new cases were filed and 424 cases were disposed of during the year leaving 462 cases pending on 12/31/82. There were 193 criminal cases on the docket, 48 convictions, nine persons committed to prison and 86 cases left pending. In the County Court

400 cases were pending on 1/1/82, 450 new cases were filed and 309 cases were disposed of during the year leaving 541 cases pending on 12/31/82. There were 645 criminal cases on the docket, 95 convictions, 15 persons committed to jail, and 398 cases left pending. **JAILS** One jail, capacity 39. **ATTORNEYS AT LAW** 25. **UTILITIES** 47% of the residents are connected to a public or privately owned water system and 42% are connected to a public sewer system. Natural gas is distributed to the county by Entex, Inc. The average annual residential bill for natural gas in 1982 for the Entex distribution system was $390.31, an increase of 26% over 1981. Electricity is distributed to the city of Bellville by the Bellville Light and Power System and to the rest of the county by Houston Lighting and Power Co., Fayette Electric Coop., Inc., Bluebonnet Electric Coop., Inc. and San Bernard Electric Coop., Inc. and is generated primarily by water and gas. The typical residential electric bill is $201.39 per month for an all-electric house using 2,500 kwh. **TAXES** The county has eight units with taxing authority: four school districts, three cities and one county.

RECREATION/ENTERTAINMENT

NATIONAL REGISTER OF HISTORIC PLACES Bellville: Austin County Jail. Wallis vicinity: Allens Creek Ossuary Site. **STATE** Stephen F. Austin State Historical Park covers 667 acres with facilities which include camping and trailer sites as well as areas for fishing, swimming and golfing. The historical section offers a museum and a replica of Austin's dog-run log cabin amid numerous markers and monuments. **COUNTY/MUNICIPAL PARKS** 21 acres in one county and three municipal parks. These parks contain two playgrounds, three baseball and softball fields, one tennis court and one boat ramp. **SCENIC DRIVES** The Texas Independence Trail runs through this county. This trail not only surveys the historic sites of southeastern Texas but also includes modern visitor attractions such as the Johnson Space Center. **BOATING/FISHING** Lakes/reservoirs: Allens Creek (5,037 acres) and Butler (30 acres). Major rivers: San Bernard and Brazos. Primary streams: Allen and Black Walnut. **HUNTING** Fall and winter seasons on deer. No closed season on coyotes, bobcats and squirrel. Winter season on quail, muskrat, beaver, opossum, ring-tailed cat, badger, fox, weasel, raccoon, skunk and civet cat. In 1983 sandhill crane, duck, coot, geese, woodcock and jacksnipe seasons occurred during the winter months. Teal duck, rail and gallinule seasons occurred in the fall. Mourning dove seasons occured intermittently during the fall and winter months. **SPECIAL EVENTS** Country Livin' Festival, Bellville, April; Czech Day, Wallis, June; Old Time Fun Festival, Wallis, July; Harvest Festival, Wallis, September; Austin County Fair, Bellville, varies; Poultry Festival, Shelby, September.

COMMUNITIES

COUNTY SEAT Bellville, County Courthouse, 77418; County Clerk's Office, 409/865-3158. **INCORPORATED COMMUNITIES** (1980 population and ZIP Code) Bellville (2,860) 77418, San Felipe (532) 77473, Sealy (3,875) 77474 and Wallis (1,138) 77485. **UNINCORPORATED COMMUNITIES** (and ZIP Code) Bleiblerville 78931, Buckhorn 77418, Burleigh 77418, Cat Spring 78933, Cochran 77418, Frydek 77474, Industry 78944, Kenney 77452, Millheim 77474, Nelsonville 77418, New Ulm 78950, New Wehdem 77833, Peters 77474, Postoak Point 78950, Raccoon Bend 77418, Rockhouse 78950, Schoenau 78950, Shelby 78940 and Welcome 78944. **FOR ADDITIONAL LOCAL INFORMATION** Bellville Chamber of Commerce, P.O. Box 670, Bellville, 77418, 409/865-3407 and Sealy Chamber of Commerce, P.O. Box 586, Sealy, 77474, 409/885-3222.

BAILEY (P28)

THE LAND

Bordering New Mexico northwest of Lubbock on U.S. Highway 84 in the High Plains Region, Bailey County covers 827 square miles of level land. The elevation ranges from 3,700 to 4,000 feet. The soils are mostly loamy with clayey subsoils. Some soils have limestone or powdery lime within 20 inches of the surface. In the High Plains vegetation area, blue grama, switchgrass, buffalograss, wheatgrass, blue stems and Indiangrass have been invaded by yucca, sagebrush and mesquite. Between one and 10% of the land in the county is considered prime farmland. **CLIMATE** Continental Steppe with dry, cold, windy winters and warm summers. The average annual temperature is 57°F. Temperatures in January range from an average low of 20° to an average high of 52°F and in July range from 64° to 92°F. The average annual precipitation is 16 inches, with an average relative humidity of 68% at 6 A.M. and 36% at 6 P.M. The average annual snowfall is nine inches. The growing season averages 180 days per year, with the last freeze in mid April and the first freeze in early October. The sun shines during the year on the average 75% of the daylight hours.

THE PEOPLE

The 1982 estimated population of 8,300 indicates a slight growth in population, a reversal of the steady population decrease which began in the 1960s. The urban areas grew between 1970 and 1980 while rural areas had population loses. The age group with the largest decrease was ages five to 14 with a slight increase among ages 62 and over. The largest ancestry groups are Hispanic (34%) and those of English descent (22%). **REGISTERED VOTERS** As of November 2, 1982 there were 3,666 registered voters (0.1% of the state total). The 1982 general election had a 55% voter turnout, compared to a 71% turnout in the 1980 general election. In the 1982 primary 94% voted Democratic and 6% Republican, with 1,163 votes cast.

THE ECONOMY

AGRICULTURE Diversified products. In 1982, 95% of the land was in farms and ranches, with 59% of the farmland under cultivation and 57% irrigated. Bailey ranked 36th in the state in highest agricultural receipts, with 57% from crops. Wind, erosion and decreasing irrigation water supplies are current conservation problems. Primary crops: sixth in the state for corn and fourth for sunflowers. Cotton, sorghum, wheat and soybeans. Primary vegetables: potatoes, onions and processed vegetables including beets, cucumbers for pickles, snapbeans, spinach, sweet corn and tomatoes. Primary fruits and nuts: peaches and pecans. Primary livestock and products: cattle, milk, sheep and wool. **BUSINESS** Total number of business establishments in the county: 202. Retail sales during the first quarter of 1984 increased 5%. In 1980, 18% of the labor force were self-employed, 18% were employed in professional or related services, 5% in manufacturing, 21% in wholesale and retail trade, 30% in agriculture, forestry, fisheries and mining, 15% were employed in other counties and there were 662 retired workers. The industry with the most employment is agribusiness. The nonfarm earnings in 1981 totaled $65,738,000. The retired workers received an average monthly Social Security payment of $326. **FINANCE** On June 30, 1983, two commercial banks had total deposits of $61,683,000 and total assets of $70,851,000. There is one state savings and loan association branch. **HOUSING** Average value of homes in 1980: $25,100. Permits for new, privately owned housing units decreased in 1982: 13 permits were issued with a total construction cost of $354,500. Of those permits, 13 were for single family houses. Between 1970 and 1980 the number of housing units increased by 2%. Seventy-four per-

cent of all units in the county are air-conditioned, 91% are heated by gas and 8% by electricity. **NATURAL RESOURCES** Caliche, oil and gas. Current production of other minerals and products includes sand and gravel. **TOURISM** Travel expenditures of $6,156,000 in 1982 (an increase of 18% over 1981) generated 87 jobs and $911,000 in payroll. **ALCOHOLIC BEVERAGES** Totally dry. **FEDERAL EXPENDITURES** The federal government had direct expenditures or obligations of $20,810,000 in the county during fiscal year 1983, including $118,000 by the U.S. Department of Defense. In addition, the federal government provided $189,000 in grant awards, paid $719,000 in salaries and wages, made direct payments to individuals of $8,915,000 including $6,457,000 in retirement and disability payments, awarded $2,000 in procurement contracts and spent $10,986,000 in other expenditures or obligations. The federal government also provided $5,897,000 in direct loans and $22,134,000 in guaranteed loans and insurance.

COMMUNICATION

Newspapers–Weekly: Muleshoe Journal and the Bailey County Journal (Muleshoe). Radio: KMUL-AM and KMUL-FM (Muleshoe). Cable TV. Telephone companies: General Telephone, Five-Area Telephone Coop. and West Texas Rural Telephone Coop. **TRANSPORTATION** Total public road mileage: 1,097. In 1982 there were 8,035 registered vehicles and 165 reported traffic accidents including three fatalities. Intercity bus service is available. Motor freight: three carriers. Rail: one main line carries annually 20 to 30 million tons of freight through the county. Aircraft: 39 are registered in the county. Airports: Edward Warren Field in Muleshoe is a basic utility airport providing general aviation service. It serves as a base for 24 aircraft. Also serving this area is Williams Field at Goodland.

COMMUNITY SERVICES

EDUCATION Two school districts with three elementary, one middle and two high schools. The average daily attendance in 1981-82 was 1,723, with expenditures per pupil of $2,568 including 118 classroom teachers with an average annual salary of $15,900. Sixty-four percent of the 112 high school graduates planned to attend college. In 1982-83, 48% of the students were White, 50% Hispanic, 3% Black and 0.1% Asian. Sports championships: 1982 AAA Boys' Cross Country, Muleshoe H.S. **PUBLIC LIBRARIES** Muleshoe Area Public Library: 16,956 volumes. **CHILD CARE** 16 day care and four twenty-four hour care licensed facilities. **HEALTH CARE** Four physicians and five dentists. Hospitals: one with a capacity of 31. Ambulance services: one funeral home service. Mental health: one clinic. Nursing homes: one nursing home has a capacity of 57 nursing care residents. The average cost per day for private patients in 1982 was $27.60. **CHURCHES** 24 churches have an estimated combined membership of 7,232. The largest denominations are Southern Baptist, Catholic and United Methodist. **SOCIAL SERVICES** In fiscal year 1983 a total of $376,857 in food stamps was distributed, with an average of 793 persons receiving food stamps each month. Aid to Families with Dependent Children (AFDC) totaled $46,188 with an average of 29 families receiving AFDC each month. Medical assistance benefits for the aged and disabled of $284,996 and for families and children of $44,309 brought the county benefit total to $752,350. **FIRE PROTECTION** Four volunteer fire departments. **LAW ENFORCEMENT** The County Sheriff has five commissioned officers. One police department has a force of eight. **CRIME** 29 violent crimes (murder, forcible rape, robbery and aggravated assault) and 262 nonviolent crimes (burglary, larceny-theft and motor vehicle theft) were reported in 1982. **JUDICIAL SYSTEM** One District Court and Judge, one County Court and Judge and

BAILEY (continued)

two Justices of the Peace. In the District Court a total of 202 cases were pending on 1/1/82, 217 new cases were filed and 208 cases were disposed of during the year leaving 211 cases pending on 12/31/82. There were 81 criminal cases on the docket, 33 convictions, five persons committed to prison and 33 cases left pending. In the County Court 366 cases were pending on 1/1/82, 235 new cases were filed and 437 cases were disposed of during the year leaving 164 cases pending on 12/31/82. There were 514 criminal cases on the docket, 97 convictions, 34 persons committed to jail, and 121 cases left pending. **JAILS** One jail, capacity 22. **ATTORNEYS AT LAW** Five. **UTILITIES** 63% of the residents are connected to a public or privately owned water system and 61% are connected to a public sewer system. Natural gas is distributed to the county by Energas Company. The average annual residential bill for natural gas in 1982 for the Energas distribution system was $371.63, an increase of 23% over 1981. Electricity is distributed to the county by Southwestern Public Service, Bailey Co. Electric Coop. and Lamb Co. Electric Coop., Inc. and is generated primarily by gas. The typical residential electric bill is $170.44 per month for an all-electric house using 2,500 kwh. **TAXES** The county has five units with taxing authority: two school districts, one city, one county and one special district.

RECREATION/ENTERTAINMENT

MUNICIPAL PARKS 130 acres in five municipal parks. These parks contain two playgrounds, four baseball and softball fields, four tennis courts and one swimming pool. **SCENIC DRIVES** The Texas Plains Trail runs through this county. This trail spans a vast area of the High Plains region of Texas slicing through the southernmost extension of the Great Plains of the United States. The land is flat except where erosion has carved canyon landscapes. **BOATING/FISHING** Lakes/reservoirs: Baileyboro (150 acres) and Coyote (100 acres). **WILDLIFE REFUGES** Muleshoe National Wildlife Refuge covers 5,809 acres. **HUNTING** Summer and fall to early winter seasons on squirrel. Winter season on pheasant,quail, muskrat, beaver, opossum, ring-tailed cat, badger, fox, weasel, raccoon, skunk and civet cat. No closed season on coyotes and bobcats. In 1983 sandhill crane, duck, coot, geese, woodcock and jacksnipe seasons occurred during the winter months. Teal duck, rail and gallinule seasons occurred in the fall and winter months. Mourning dove season occurred intermittently during the fall and winter months. **SPECIAL EVENTS** Junior Livestock Show, Muleshoe, February; Old Settlers Reunion and Festivities, Muleshoe, July; World Championship Muleshoe Pitch, Muleshoe, July; Christmas Bazaar and Parade, Muleshoe, December.

COMMUNITIES

COUNTY SEAT Muleshoe, County Courthouse, 79347; County Clerk's Office, 806/272-3044. **INCORPORATED COMMUNITIES** (1980 population and ZIP Code) Muleshoe (4,842) 79347. **UNINCORPORATED COMMUNITIES** (and ZIP Code) Baileyboro 79371, Bula 79320, Circle Back 79371, Enochs 79324, Fairview 79371, Goodland 79327, Maple 79344, Needmore 79371, Progress 79347 and Stegal 79327. **FOR ADDITIONAL LOCAL INFORMATION** Muleshoe Chamber of Commerce, P.O. Box 356, Muleshoe, 79347, 806/272-4248.

BANDERA (C33)

THE LAND

Northwest of San Antonio on State Highways 173 and 16 in the Edwards Plateau Region, Bandera County covers 793 square miles with the elevation ranging from 1,200 to 2,300 feet. The undulating to hilly alkaline soils are shallow to deep loamy layers over deep, limy cracking, clayey or loamy subsoils. The vegetation is primarily grasses such as bluestems, grama, buffalograss, wintergrass and wildryes. Cedar, live oak and mesquite dominate, with cypress along major streams. Between 11% and 20% of the land in the county is considered prime farmland. **CLIMATE** Subtropical subhumid with mild winters and warm summers. The average annual temperature is 66°F. Temperatures in January range from an average low of 36° to an average high of 69°F and in July range from 69° to 95°F. The average annual precipitation is 29 inches, with an average relative humidity of 76% at 6 A.M. and 45% at 6 P.M. There is no significant snowfall. The growing season averages 235 days per year, with the last freeze in late March and the first freeze in mid November. The sun shines during the year on the average 65% of the daylight hours.

THE PEOPLE

The 1982 estimated population of 7,500 indicates a continuation of the strong growth rate begun in the 1960s. The 49% gain from 1970 to 1980 made this county one of the fastest growing in the state. The majority of residents live in rural areas. The age groups with the largest increases were ages 20 to 24 and 65 and over and the median age lowered from 42 in 1970 to 41 in 1980. The largest ancestry groups are persons of German descent (29%), Irish descent (26%) and English descent (26%). **REGISTERED VOTERS** As of November 2, 1982 there were 4,490 registered voters (0.1% of the state total). The 1982 general election had a 59% voter turnout, compared to a 76% turnout in the 1980 general election. In the 1982 primary 82% voted Democratic and 18% Republican, with 1,842 votes cast.

THE ECONOMY

AGRICULTURE In 1982, 82% of the land was in farms and ranches, with 4% under cultivation. Bandera ranked 238th in the state in highest agricultural receipts, with 95% from livestock and livestock products. Undesirable brush and weeds, wind and water erosion and water conservation are current conservation problems. Primary crops: oats, hay, wheat and sorghum. Primary fruits and nuts: peaches and pecans. Primary livestock and products: cattle, sheep, wool, angora goats and mohair. **BUSINESS** Total number of business establishments in the county: 118. Retail sales during the first quarter of 1984 increased 10%. In 1980 19% of the labor force were self-employed, 22% were employed in professional or related services, 7% in manufacturing, 19% in wholesale and retail trade, 16% in construction, 37% were employed in other counties and there were 907 retired workers. The industries with the most employment: the manufacture of women's leather handbags and tourism. The nonfarm earnings in 1981 totaled $63,665,000. The retired workers received an average monthly Social Security payment of $292. **FINANCE** On June 30, 1983, two commercial banks had total deposits of $34,840,000 and total assets of $38,384,000. There are two state savings and loan association branches in the county. **HOUSING** Average value of homes in 1980: $34,800. Between 1970 and 1980 the number of housing units increased by 40%. Fifty-seven percent of all units in the county are air-conditioned, 52% are heated by gas and 29% by electricity. **NATURAL RESOURCES** Dolomite, oil and gas. Current production of other minerals and products includes sand and gravel. **TOURISM** Travel expenditures of $4,073,000 in 1982 (an increase of 14% over 1981) generated 83 jobs and $725,000 in payroll. **ALCOHOLIC BEVERAGES** Packaged distilled spirits, beer, ale, malt liquor and wine are legal in parts of the county. Sale of mixed beverages is legal in all or parts of the county. **FEDERAL EXPENDITURES** The federal government had direct expenditures or obligations of $20,936,000 in the county during fiscal year 1983, including $4,198,000 by the U.S. Department of Defense. In addition, the federal government provided $83,000 in grant awards, paid $2,051,000 in salaries and wages, made direct payments to individuals of $16,031,000 including $13,631,000 in retirement and disability payments, awarded $2,546,000 in procurement contracts and spent $226,000 in other expenditures or obligations. The federal government also provided $33,000 in direct loans and $5,643,000 in guaranteed loans and insurance.

COMMUNICATION

Newspapers–Weekly: Bandera Bulletin. Cable TV. Telephone companies: Southwestern Bell, Hill Country Telephone Coop. and SW Texas Telephone. **TRANSPORTATION** Total public road mileage: 607. In 1982 there were 7,691 registered vehicles and 190 reported traffic accidents including five fatalities. Intercity bus service is available. Motor freight: two carriers. Aircraft: 33 are registered in the county. Airports: Flying L Ranch Airport in Bandera, Circle R Resort Ranch Airport at Medina, Freedom Springs Ranch Airport and Medina River Ranch Airport at Pipe Creek.

COMMUNITY SERVICES

EDUCATION Two school districts with two elementary, one middle and two high schools. The average daily attendance in 1981-82 was 1,192, with expenditures per pupil of $2,381 including 75 classroom teachers with an average annual salary of $16,527. Forty-seven percent of the 103 high school graduates planned to attend college. In 1982-83, 88% of the students were White, 12% Hispanic, 0.3% Black and 0.2% Asian. **PUBLIC LIBRARIES** Bandera County Library (Bandera): 19,387 volumes. **CHILD CARE** Five day care and two twenty-four hour care licensed facilities. **HEALTH CARE** Six physicians and two dentists. Ambulance service: one county service. Nursing homes: one nursing home has a capacity of 62 nursing care residents. The average cost per day for private patients in 1982 was $26.31. **CHURCHES** 15 churches have an estimated combined membership of 3,319. The largest denominations are Southern Baptist, Catholic and United Methodist. **SOCIAL SERVICES** In fiscal year 1983 a total of $119,754 in food stamps was distributed, with an average of 238 persons receiving food stamps each month. Aid to Families with Dependent Children (AFDC) totaled $17,139 with an average of 13 families receiving AFDC each month. Medical assistance benefits for the aged and disabled of $320,350 and for families and children of $29,868 brought the county benefit total to $487,111. **FIRE PROTECTION** Six volunteer fire departments. **LAW ENFORCEMENT** The County Sheriff has 14 commissioned officers. One police department has a force of seven. **CRIME** Six violent crimes (murder, forcible rape, robbery and aggravated assault) and 162 nonviolent crimes (burglary, larceny-theft and motor vehicle theft) were reported in 1982. **JUDICIAL SYSTEM** One District Court and Judge, one County Court and Judge and four Justices of the Peace. In the District Court a total of 181 cases were pending on 1/1/82, 162 new cases were filed and 164 cases were disposed of during the year leaving 179 cases pending on 12/31/82. There were 118 criminal cases on the docket, 22 convictions, seven persons committed to prison and 55 cases left pending. In the County Court 44 cases were pending on 1/1/82, 73 new cases were filed and 72 cases were disposed of during the year leaving 45 cases pending on 12/31/82. There were 88 criminal cases on the docket, 41 convictions, one person committed to jail, and 25 cases left pending. **JAILS** One jail, capacity 15. **ATTORNEYS AT LAW** 10. **UTILITIES** 31% of the residents are connected to a public or privately owned water system and 20% are connected to a public sewer system. Natural gas is distributed to the county by Lone Star Gas Co., Division of Enserch. The average annual rseidential bill for natural

gas in 1982 for the Lone Star distribution system was $405.91, an increase of 35% over 1981. Electricity is distributed to the county by Bandera Electric Coop., Inc. and is generated primarily by oil, water and coal. **TAXES** The county has eight units with taxing authority: three school districts, one city, one county and three special districts.

RECREATION/ENTERTAINMENT

NATIONAL REGISTER OF HISTORIC PLACES Bandera: Bandera County Courthouse and Jail, Old Bandera County Courthouse and Jureczki House. **STATE** Hill Country Natural Area covers 4,753 acres in this county and is closed to the public as of July, 1983. Lost Maples State Natural Area covers 2,174 acres and offering facilities which include camping and trailer sites as well as areas for swimming, fishing and nature hiking. **COUNTY/MUNICIPAL PARKS** 50 acres in one county and one municipal park. This park contains one playground, four baseball and softball fields and one beach. **SCENIC DRIVES** The Texas Hill Country Trail runs through this county. Hill country landscapes exist throughout the county such as on Texas 173. Dramatic blue hills surround Texas 16 and F.M. 470 West. **BOATING/FISHING** Lakes/reservoirs: Alkek (13 acres), Clements (19 acres), Medina (5,575 acres), Montague (25 acres), Mosher Big (27 acres), Ross Cliff (41 acres), Voss (15 acres) and Walton (15 acres). Major rivers: Medina. Primary streams: San Julian, Verde, English Hollow, Bandera, Spires, Simpson and South Fork San Geronimo. **HUNTING** Fall and winter seasons on deer. No closed season on javelina, squirrel, coyotes and bobcats. Fall, winter and spring seasons on turkey. Winter season on quail, muskrat, beaver, opossum, ring-tailed cat, badger, fox, weasel, raccoon, skunk and civet cat. In 1983 sandhill crane, duck, coot, geese, woodcock and jacksnipe seasons occurred during the winter months. Teal duck, rail and gallinule seasons occurred in the fall. Mourning dove season occurred intermittently during the fall and winter months with a fall season on white-winged doves. **MUSEUMS** Bandera: Frontier Times Museum. **SPECIAL EVENTS** Funtier Days, Bandera, May; Bandera County Fair, Bandera, July; Miss Bandera Pageant, Bandera, July; and Great Gumbo Cookoff, Lake Hills, September.

COMMUNITIES

COUNTY SEAT Bandera, County Courthouse, 78003; County Clerk's Office, 512/796-3332. **INCORPORATED COMMUNITIES** (1980 population and ZIP Code) Bandera (947) 78003. **UNINCORPORATED COMMUNITIES** (and ZIP Code) Bandera Falls 78063, Lakehills (North Lake) 78063, Medina 78055, Pipe Creek (Pipecreek) 78063, Tarpley 78883 and Vanderpool 78885. **FOR ADDITIONAL LOCAL INFORMATION** Bandera Co. Chamber of Commerce, 503 Main St., P.O. Box 171, Bandera, 78003, 512/796-4312.

BASTROP (C25)

THE LAND

East of Austin on State Highways 71, 95, 21 and 304 in the Claypan Area, Bastrop County covers 895 square miles with the elevation ranging from 400 to 600 feet. Along the Colorado River the soil is somewhat poorly to moderately well drained, cracking and clayey. The poorly drained soils have loamy alkaline surface layers and cracking clayey subsoils. The rest of the county has very deep, reddish subsoil or reddish mottles in the subsoil. In the northeast corner and along the northwest border are undulating, noncalcareous and alkaline cracking, clayey soils and slightly acidic soils with loamy surface layers and cracking, clayey subsoils. In the southwestern corner are slightly acidic soils with

BASTROP (continued)

loamy surface layers and cracking, clayey subsoils and acidic cracking, clayey soils. In the north central and eastern one-fourth of the county the soils are nearly level to undulating, light-colored and medium to slightly acidic. Here soils have loamy surface layers and mottled gray and red to yellow cracking, clayey subsoils. Throughout the county there is a high shrink-swell potential. Most of the county is located in the Post Oak Savannah vegetation region with tall grasses somewhat invaded by mesquite. There are post oak, elm, pecan and cottonwood trees forming a 30% cover. Along the northwest border and central southeastern border the Blackland Prairies vegetation area has tall grasses and hardwood trees along rivers and streams. Between 11% and 20% of the land in the county is considered prime farmland. **CLIMATE** Subtropical humid with mild winters and hot summers. The average annual temperature is 69°F. Temperatures in January range from an average low of 40° to an average high of 60°F and in July range from 73° to 96°F. The average annual precipitation is 37 inches, with an average relative humidity of 85% at 6 A.M. and 54% at 6 P.M. There is no significant snowfall. The growing season averages 270 days per year, with the last freeze in early March and the first freeze in late November. The sun shines during the year on the average 65% of the daylight hours.

THE PEOPLE

The 1982 estimated population of 28,200 indicates a continuation of the growth rate which began at a moderate level between 1960 and 1970 and accelerated to a rate of 43% between 1970 and 1980, making this county one of the fastest-growing in the state. The 75% rural growth rate was one of the state's highest for that category. Since the age groups with the largest gains from 1970 to 1980 were those ages 20 to 34 and birth to five years, the median age decreased from 36 in 1970 to 32 in 1980. The largest ancestry groups are persons of German descent (26%) and English descent (20%). **REGISTERED VOTERS** As of November 2, 1982 there were 13,703 registered voters (0.2% of the state total). The 1982 general election had a 50% voter turnout, compared to a 64% turnout in the 1980 general election. In the 1982 primary 97% voted Democratic and 3% Republican, with 5,478 votes cast.

THE ECONOMY

AGRICULTURE Cattle area. In 1982, 79% of the land was in farms and ranches, with 12% of the farmland under cultivation and 2% irrigated. Bastrop ranked 137th in the state in highest agricultural receipts, with 88% from livestock and livestock products. Overgrazing, undesirable brush, water erosion, noxious weeds, difficulties with grass establishment and flooding are the current conservation problems. Primary crops: hay, sorghum, wheat, oats and corn. Primary vegetables: potatoes, sweet potatoes, tomatoes and watermelons. Primary fruits and nuts: peaches and pecans. Primary livestock and products: cattle and hogs. **BUSINESS** Total number of business establishments in the county: 374. Retail sales during the first quarter of 1984 increased 22%. In 1980, 12% of the labor force were self-employed, 21% were employed in professional or related services, 15% in manufacturing, 20% in wholesale and retail trade, 10% in public administration, 44% were employed in other counties and there were 2,659 retired workers. The industries with the most employment: agribusiness, oil and gas extraction and the manufacture of household furniture, brick and clay tile and fabricated structural metal products. The nonfarm earnings in 1981 totaled $187,444,000. The retired workers received an average

monthly Social Security payment of $288. **FINANCE** On June 30, 1983, five commercial banks had total deposits of $124,864,000 and total assets of $139,087,000. On December 31, 1982 two state savings and loan associations and two state branches had combined assets of $49,776,006. **HOUSING** Average value of homes in 1980: $27,200. Permits for new, privately owned housing units decreased in 1982: 76 permits were issued with a total construction cost of $2,333,826. Of those permits, 72 were for single family houses. Housing permits for Smithville increased from 21 in 1981 to 47 in 1982. Between 1970 and 1980 the number of housing units increased by 58%. Sixty percent of all units in the county are air-conditioned, 71% are heated by gas and 19% by electricity. **NATURAL RESOURCES** Industrial sand, sand and gravel, oil, gas and ceramic clay. In 1982 a total of 51,635 thousand cubic feet of gas well gas, 125,698 barrels of crude oil and 96,457 thousand cubic feet of casinghead gas were produced. Current production of other minerals and products includes brick, fire clay, miscellaneous clay, sand and gravel. **TOURISM** Travel expenditures of $2,890,000 in 1982 (an increase of 12% over 1981) generated 65 jobs and $542,000 in payroll. **ALCOHOLIC BEVERAGES** Packaged distilled spirits, beer, ale, malt liquor and wine are legal. **FEDERAL EXPENDITURES** The federal government had direct expenditures or obligations of $50,645,000 in the county during fiscal year 1983, including $4,361,000 by the U.S. Department of Defense. In addition, the federal government provided $874,000 in grant awards, paid $7,265,000 in salaries and wages, made direct payments to individuals of $41,695,000 including $31,385,000 in retirement and disability payments, awarded $458,000 in procurement contracts and spent $353,000 in other expenditures or obligations. The federal government also provided $49,000 in direct loans and $5,465,000 in guaranteed loans and insurance.

COMMUNICATION

Newspapers–Weekly: Bastrop Advertiser and County News, Elgin Courier and the Bastrop County Times (Smithville). Radio: KELG-AM (Elgin). Cable TV. Telephone companies: Continental Telephone, General Telephone, Southwestern Bell and Guadalupe Valley Telephone Coop. **TRANSPORTATION** Total public road mileage: 1,120. In 1982 there were 22,697 registered vehicles and 621 reported traffic accidents including 10 fatalities. Intercity bus service is available. Motor freight: four carriers. Rail: Three main and three branch lines carry freight through the county. One main line carries 20 to 30 million tons of freight annually while the other two carry 10 to 20 each. All three branch lines carry annually one to five million tons of freight each. Aircraft: 29 are registered in the county. Airports: Smithville Municipal Airport, attended part time.

COMMUNITY SERVICES

EDUCATION Four school districts with seven elementary, three middle and three high schools. The average daily attendance in 1981-82 was 5,151, with expenditures per pupil of $2,081 including 346 classroom teachers with an average annual salary of $14,495. Thirty-five percent of the 328 high school graduates planned to attend college. In 1982-83, 62% of the students were White, 19% Hispanic, 19% Black, 0.2% Asian and 0.1% American Indian. **PUBLIC LIBRARIES** Bastrop Public Library: 15,000 volumes. Smithville Public Library: 13,000 volumes. **CHILD CARE** 53 day care and nine twenty-four hour care licensed facilities. **HEALTH CARE** 17 physicians and seven dentists. Hospitals: two with a combined capacity of 60. Ambulance services: three commercial services. Mental health: one county clinic. Nursing homes: three nursing homes with a combined capacity of 212 nursing care residents. The average cost per day for private patients in 1982 was $32.35. **CHURCHES** 55 churches have an estimated combined membership of 9,381. The largest denominations are Southern Baptist, United Methodist and American Lutheran. **SOCIAL SERVICES** In fiscal year 1983 a total of $1,228,551 in food stamps was distributed, with an average of 2,536 persons receiving food stamps each month. Aid to Families with Dependent Children (AFDC) totaled $291,349 with an average of 192 families receiving AFDC each month. Medical assistance benefits for the aged and disabled of $2,262,247 and for families and children of $439,691 brought the county benefit total to $4,221,838. **FIRE PROTECTION** 10 volunteer fire departments. **LAW ENFORCEMENT** The County Sheriff has 10 commissioned officers. Three police departments have a combined force of 23. **CRIME** 71 violent crimes (murder, forcible rape, robbery and aggravated assault) and 692 nonviolent crimes (burglary, larceny-theft and motor vehicle theft) were reported in 1982. **JUDICIAL SYSTEM** Two District Courts and Judges, one County Court and Judge and four Justices of the Peace. In the District Courts a total of 1,352 cases were pending on 1/1/82, 784 new cases were filed and 597 cases were disposed of during the year leaving 1,539 cases pending on 12/31/82. There were 371 criminal cases on the docket, 63 convictions, 15 persons committed to prison and one committed to jail and 216 cases left pending. In the County Court 636 cases were pending on 1/1/82, 504 new cases were filed and 475 cases were disposed of during the year leaving 665 cases pending on 12/31/82. There were 956 criminal cases on the docket, 108 convictions, 52 persons committed to jail, and 534 cases left pending. **JAILS** One jail, capacity 20. **ATTORNEYS AT LAW** 27. **UTILITIES** 83% of the residents are connected to a public or privately owned water system and 45% are connected to a public sewer system. Natural gas is distributed to the county by Entex, Inc. The average annual residential bill for natural gas in 1982 for the Entex distribution system was $390.31, an increase of 26% over 1981. Electricity is distributed to the city of Bastrop by the Bastrop Electric Dept. and to Smithville by the Smithville Light and Water Dept. and to the rest of the county by Texas Power and Light, Fayette Electric Coop., Inc. and Bluebonnet Electric Coop., Inc. and is generated primarily by gas, coal and oil. The typical residential electric bill is $165.24 per month for an all-electric house using 2,500 kwh. **TAXES** The county has eight units with taxing authority: four school districts, three cities and one county.

RECREATION/ENTERTAINMENT
NATIONAL REGISTER OF HISTORIC PLACES Bastrop: Allen-Bell House, Bastrop County Courthouse and Jail and Crocheran-McDowell House. Hills Prairie vicinity: A.W. Hills House. Smithville: Smithville Commercial Historic District. **STATE** Bastrop State Park covers 3,504 acres with camping and trailer sites and areas which offer swimming, boat ramps, nature trails, scenic drives, golfing and rental boats. Buescher State Park covers 1,017 acres with camping and trailer sites as well as areas offering fishing and scenic drives. **MUNICIPAL PARKS** 62 acres in 11 municipal parks. These parks contain one playground, nine baseball and softball fields, five tennis courts, one multi-use court, one swimming pool and one boat ramp. **SCENIC DRIVES** The Texas Independence Trail and the Texas Brazos Trail run through this county. The Independence Trail not only surveys the historic sites of southeastern Texas but also includes many modern visitor attractions such as the Johnson Space Center. The Brazos Trail moves through a beautiful and historic section of Central Texas revealing forested landscapes filled with wildlife and wild flowers. **BOATING/FISHING** Lakes/reservoirs: Bastrop (906 acres), Double D (28 acres), Droemer (38 acres), Indian (40 acres) and Rod (18 acres). Major rivers: Colorado. Primary streams: Spicer, Gravelly, Line, Cedar and Walnut. **HUNTING** Fall and winter seasons on deer. No closed season on squirrel, coyotes and bobcats. Spring season on turkey. Winter season on quail, muskrat, beaver, opossum, ring-tailed cat,

badger, fox, weasel, raccoon, skunk and civet cat. In 1983 sandhill crane, duck, coot, geese, woodcock and jacksnipe seasons occurred during the winter months. Teal duck, rail and gallinule seasons occurred in the fall. Mourning dove season occurred intermittently during the fall and winter months. **MUSEUMS** Bastrop: Bastrop County Historical Society Museum. Elgin: Elgin Log Cabin Museum. McDade: McDade Museum. Smithville: Smithville Heritage Society Museum. **SPECIAL EVENTS** Jamboree, Smithville, April; Annual Firemen's Barbeque, Smithville, May; Watermelon Festival, McDade, July; Western Days Festival, Elgin, July; Championship Barbeque Cookoff, Smithville, July; Rodeo, Bastrop, August.

COMMUNITIES
COUNTY SEAT Bastrop, County Courthouse, 78602; County Clerk's Office, 512/321-2311. **INCORPORATED COMMUNITIES** (1980 population and ZIP Code) Bastrop (3,789) 78602, Elgin (4,535) 78621 and Smithville (3,470) 78957. **UNINCORPORATED COMMUNITIES** (and ZIP Code) Alum Creek 78602, Bateman (Coxville) 78662, Butler 78621, Calvin 78602, Cedar Creek 78612, Clearview 78602, Hill (Hills Prairie) 78602, Jeddo 78953, Kovar 78941, McDade 78650, Paige 78659, Phelan 78602, Red Rock 78662, Rockne 78602, Rosanky 78953, Sayers (Sayersville) 78602, Shiloh 78602, String Prairie 78953, Togo 78957, Type 78621, Upton 78957 and Utley 78602. **FOR ADDITIONAL LOCAL INFORMATION** Bastrop Chamber of Commerce, P.O. Box 681, Bastrop, 78602, 512/321-2419, Cedar Creek Lake Chamber of Commerce, Rt. 5, P.O. Box 229, Kemp, 75143 214/432-3152, Elgin Chamber of Commerce, 15 N. Main, P.O. Box 408, Elgin, 78621, 512/285-4515 and Smithville Chamber of Commerce, 317 Main, P.O. Box 716, Smithville, 78957 512/237-2313.

BAYLOR (P64)

THE LAND
Southwest of Wichita Falls on U.S. Highways 277/82 and 183/283 in the Rolling Plains Region, Baylor County covers 862 square miles of mostly level land. The elevation ranges from 1,200 to 1,400 feet. The county has rolling to level, red to brown, well drained soils. Also, there are soils with loamy surface layers and cracking clayey subsoils with some areas having lime accumulations in the subsoils. Most of the vegetation of the county is of the Rolling Plains vegetation area consisting of short to mid grasses, mesquite trees and some cacti. In the southeast corner of the county the Cross Timbers and Prairies vegetation area includes short and mid grasses, tall grasses, mesquite and live oak trees. Between 41% and 50% of the land in the county is considered prime farmland. **CLIMATE** Subtropical subhumid with dry, cold winters and hot summers. The average annual temperature is 63°F. Temperatures in January range from an average low of 28° to an average high of 55°F and in July range from 72° to 98°F. The average annual precipitation is 25 inches, with an average relative humidity of 74% at 6 A.M. and 45% at 6 P.M. The average annual snowfall is six inches. The growing season averages 218 days per year, with the last freeze in early April and the first freeze in early November. The sun shines during the year on the average 76% of the daylight hours.

THE PEOPLE
With a median age of 42 Baylor ranks 51st among all U.S. counties in percent of population 65 and over. The 1982 estimated

BAYLOR (continued)

population of 5,200 indicates a slight increase in population following a steady decline since 1940. The greatest change between 1970 to 1980 was in the rural population, which declined 28%. The age groups with the largest losses were ages five to nine and 45 to 54. The largest ancestry groups are persons of English descent (24%) and Irish descent (21%). **REGISTERED VOTERS** As of November 2, 1982 there were 3,405 registered voters (0.1% of the state total). The 1982 general election had a 49% voter turnout, compared to a 71% turnout in the 1980 general election. In the 1982 primary 95% voted Democratic and 5% Republican, with 838 votes cast.

THE ECONOMY

AGRICULTURE Wheat area. In 1982, 92% of the land was in farms and ranches, with 26% of the farmland under cultivation and 3% irrigated. Baylor ranked 181st in the state in highest agricultural receipts, with 69% from crops. Overgrazing, undesirable brush, noxious weeds and water erosion are current conservation problems. Primary crops: wheat, cotton, hay and oats. Primary vegetables: sweet potatoes and watermelons. Primary fruits and nuts: peaches and pecans. Primary livestock and products: cattle. **BUSINESS** Total number of business establishments in the county: 152. Retail sales during the first quarter of 1984 increased 7%. In 1980 21% of the labor force were self-employed, 17% were employed in professional or related services, 12% in manufacturing, 22% in wholesale and retail trade, 19% in agriculture, forestry, fisheries and mining, 3% were employed in other counties and there were 794 retired workers. The industries with the most employment: agribusiness and heavy construction. The nonfarm earnings in 1981 totaled $50,466,000. The retired workers received an average monthly Social Security payment of $292. **FINANCE** On June 30, 1983, two commercial banks had total deposits of $52,786,000 and total assets of $59,894,000. There is one state savings and loan association branch in the county. **HOUSING** Average value of homes in 1980: $22,500. Permits for new, privately owned housing units decreased in 1982: six permits were issued with a total construction cost of $410,000. Of those permits, all were for single family houses. Between 1970 and 1980 the number of housing units increased 3%. Eighty-three percent of all units in the county are air-conditioned, 94% are heated by gas and 3% by electricity. **NATURAL RESOURCES** Oil, gas and bituminous coal. In 1982 a total of 405,689 barrels of crude oil and 62,709 thousand cubic feet of casinghead gas were produced. **TOURISM** Travel expenditures of $4,664,000 in 1982 (an increase of 13% over 1981) generated 105 jobs and $874,000 in payroll. **ALCOHOLIC BEVERAGES** Only 4% beer is legal in parts of the county. **FEDERAL EXPENDITURES** The federal government had direct expenditures or obligations of $13,877,000 in the county during fiscal year 1983, including $175,000 by the U.S. Department of Defense. In addition, the federal government provided $69,000 in grant awards, paid $563,000 in salaries and wages, made direct payments to individuals of $11,191,000 including $7,840,000 in retirement and disability payments, awarded $30,000 in procurement contracts and spent $2,025,000 in other expenditures or obligations. The federal government also provided $7,184,000 in direct loans and $4,186,000 in guaranteed loans and insurance.

COMMUNICATION

Newspapers–Weekly: Baylor County Banner (Seymour). Radio: KSEY-AM, KSEY-FM (Seymour). Cable TV. Telephone companies: Continental Telephone, General Telephone and Santa Rosa Telephone Coop. **TRANSPORTATION** Total public road mileage: 619. In 1982 there were 6,050 registered vehicles and 129 reported traffic accidents including six fatalities. Intercity bus service is available. Motor freight: two carriers. Rail: One line carries annually less than one million tons of freight through the county. Aircraft: 34 are registered in the county. Airports: Cooper Municipal in Seymour is a basic utility airport providing general aviation service. It serves as a base for 10 aircraft.

COMMUNITY SERVICES

EDUCATION One school district with one elementary, one middle and one high school. The average daily attendance in 1981-82 was 809, with expenditures per pupil of $2,133 including 48 classroom teachers with an average annual salary of $17,077. Fifty-eight percent of the 67 high school graduates planned to attend college. In 1982-83, 81% of the students were White, 11% Hispanic, 7% Black and 0.6% Asian. **PUBLIC LIBRARIES** Baylor County Free Library (Seymour): 14,550 volumes. **CHILD CARE** 13 day care and three twenty-four hour care licensed facilities. **HEALTH CARE** Four physicians and one dentist. Hospitals: one with a capacity of 49. Ambulance services: one commercial and one city service. Nursing homes: one nursing home with a capacity of 100 nursing care residents. The average cost per day for private patients in 1982 was $31.04. **CHURCHES** 18 churches have an estimated combined membership of 4,374. The largest denominations are Southern Baptist, United Methodist and Catholic. **SOCIAL SERVICES** In fiscal year 1983 a total of $156,408 in food stamps was distributed, with an average of 378 persons receiving food stamps each month. Aid to Families with Dependent Children (AFDC) totaled $15,885 with an average of 13 families receiving AFDC each month. Medical assistance benefits for the aged and disabled of $497,482 and for families and children of $25,825 brought the county benefit total to $695,600. **FIRE PROTECTION** One volunteer fire department. **LAW ENFORCEMENT** The County Sheriff has three commissioned officers. One police department has a force of four. **CRIME** Seven violent crimes (murder, forcible rape, robbery and aggravated assault) and 146 nonviolent crimes (burglary, larceny-theft and motor vehicle theft) were reported in 1982. **JUDICIAL SYSTEM** One District Court and Judge, one County Court and Judge and two Justices of the Peace. In the District Court a total of 91 cases were pending on 1/1/82, 122 new cases were filed and 29 cases were disposed of during the year leaving 184 cases pending on 12/31/82. There were 65 criminal cases on the docket, 20 convictions, five persons committed to prison and 36 cases left pending. In the County Court 140 cases were pending on 1/1/82, 157 new cases were filed and 144 cases were disposed of during the year leaving 153 cases pending on 12/31/82. There were 242 criminal cases on the docket, 77 convictions, 14 persons committed to jail, and 98 cases left pending. **JAILS** One jail, capacity 15. **ATTORNEYS AT LAW** Four. **UTILITIES** 61% of the residents are connected to a public or privately owned water system and 58% are connected to a public sewer system. Natural gas is distributed to the county by Lone Star Gas Co., Division of Enserch. The average annual residential bill for natural gas in 1982 for the Lone Star distribution system was $405.91, an increase of 35% over 1981. Electricity is distributed to the city of Seymour partially by Seymour Power and Light and to the rest of the county by Texas Electric Service, B-K Electric Coop., Inc. and is generated primarily by gas, oil and water. The typical residential electric bill is $178.91 per month for an all-electric house using 2,500 kwh. **TAXES** The county has three units with taxing authority: one school district, one city and one county.

RECREATION/ENTERTAINMENT

MUNICIPAL PARKS 36,077 acres in three municipal parks. These parks contain one playground, four baseball and softball fields, one swimming pool, one beach and five boat ramps. **BOATING/FISHING** Lakes/reservoirs: Cowan (27 acres), Hunt (25 acres), Kemp (16,540 acres), Millers Creek (1,900 acres), Peacock (17 acres) and Waggoner (48 acres). Major rivers: North

Fork Little Wichita, Big Wichita, Wichita and Brazos. Primary streams: Horse, Millers and Coffee. **HUNTING** Fall and winter seasons on deer. No closed season on javelina, squirrel, nutria, coyotes and bobcats. Spring season on turkey. Winter season on quail, muskrat, beaver, otter, opossum, mink, ring-tailed cat, badger, fox, raccoon, skunk and civet cat. In 1983 duck, coot, geese, woodcock and jacksnipe seasons occurred during the winter months. Teal duck, rail and gallinule seasons occurred in the fall. Mourning dove season occurred intermittently during the fall and winter months. **SPECIAL EVENTS** Fish Days, Seymour, April/May; Old Settlers Reunion, Seymour, July.

COMMUNITIES
COUNTY SEAT Seymour, County Courthouse, 76380; County Clerk's Office, 817/888-3322. **INCORPORATED COMMUNITIES** (1980 population and ZIP Code) Seymour (3,657) 76380. **UNINCORPORATED COMMUNITIES** (and ZIP Code) Bomarton 76353, Mabelle 76380, Red Springs 76378 and Westover 76380. **FOR ADDITIONAL LOCAL INFORMATION** Seymour Chamber of Commerce, 301½ Washington St., P.O. Box 1379, Seymour, 76380, 817/888-2921.

BEE (G26)

THE LAND
North of Corpus Christi on U.S. Highways 181 and 59 in the Rio Grande Plain Region, Bee County covers 880 square miles that slope gently toward the coast. The elevation ranges from 200 to 300 feet. A small portion of the southwest corner of the county has soils with somewhat poorly to moderately well-drained, cracking, clayey soils and poorly drained soils with loamy surface layers and cracking clayey subsoil. These soils are strongly acidic to moderately alkaline on the surface with increasing alkalinity in the subsoils. The northern two-thirds of the county has nearly level to undulating soils that are poorly drained, alkaline and dark, with loamy surface layers and clayey subsoils. The rest of the county has light-colored, slightly acidic soils with loamy surface layers and clayey subsoils. All of the county has a high corrosion potential and the northern two-thirds and the southwest corner have a high shrink-swell potential. Most of the county is in the South Texas Plains vegetation region with open grasslands and scattered shrubs and cacti. The southeastern corner of the county has Gulf Prairies grasslands. Between 41 and 50% of the land in the county is considered prime farmland. **CLIMATE** Subtropical humid with mild winters and warm summers. From June through October a risk exists for tropical storms or hurricanes. The average annual temperature is 71°F. Temperatures in January range from an average low of 42° to an average high of 65°F and in July range from 73° to 96°F. The average annual precipitation is 30 inches, with an average relative humidity of 89% at 6 A.M. and 60% at 6 P.M. There is no snowfall. The growing season averages 275 days per year, with the last freeze in late February and the first freeze in early December. The sun shines during the year on the average 66% of the daylight hours.

THE PEOPLE
The county ranks 49th among all U.S. counties in the highest percent of persons of Spanish origins. The 1982 estimated population of 27,200 indicates a continuation of the steady growth rate begun in the 1970s. Rural areas experienced a population gain of 24% between 1970 and 1980. The age groups with the largest increases were those of ages 25 to 29 and birth to five years. Both the median age of 26 and the death rate of six per 1,000 population are lower than average. The largest ancestry groups are Hispanic (46%), persons of English descent (16%) and those of German descent (16%). **REGISTERED VOTERS** As of November 2, 1982 there were 11,185 registered voters (0.2% of the state total). The 1982 general election had a 48% voter turnout, compared to a 65% turnout in the 1980 general election. In the 1982 primary 90% voted Democratic and 10% Republican, with 1,923 votes cast.

THE ECONOMY
AGRICULTURE In 1982, 93% of the land was in farms and ranches, with 17% of the farmland under cultivation and 5% irrigated. Bee ranked 139th in the state in highest agricultural receipts with 63% from livestock and livestock products. Water erosion and moisture conservation on cropland are current conservation problems. Primary crops: sorghum, corn, hay, wheat and oats. Primary vegetables: 10th in the state for watermelons. Primary fruits and nuts: peaches. Primary livestock and products: cattle, milk, sheep, wool and hogs. **BUSINESS** Total number of business establishments in the county: 491. Retail sales during the first quarter of 1984 increased 17%. In 1980 8% of the labor force were self-employed, 21% were employed in professional or related services, 4% in manufacturing, 20% in wholesale and retail trade, 19% in agriculture, forestry, fisheries and mining, 13% were employed in other counties and there were 1,507 retired workers. The industries with the most employment: oil and gas extraction, heavy construction, agribusiness and the manufacture of fabricated metal products. The nonfarm earnings in 1981 totaled $206,200,000. The retired workers received an average monthly Social Security payment of $289. **FINANCE** On June 30, 1983, three commercial banks had total deposits of $149,196,000 and total assets of $168,991,000. There are five state savings and loan association branches and two credit unions in the county. **HOUSING** Average value of homes in 1980: $27,500. Permits for new, privately owned housing units decreased in 1982: 133 permits were issued with a total construction cost of $3,061,075. Of those permits, 67 were for single family houses. Between 1970 and 1980 the number of housing units increased by 23%. Sixty-four percent of all units in the county are air-conditioned, 70% are heated by gas and 27% by electricity. **NATURAL RESOURCES** Caliche, oil, gas and uranium. In 1982 a total of 23,951,445 thousand cubic feet of gas well gas, 138,535 barrels of condensate, 861,323 barrels of crude oil and 1,578,717 thousand cubic feet of casinghead gas were produced. Current production of other minerals and products includes uranium, caliche, sand and gravel. **TOURISM** Travel expenditures of $7,125,000 in 1982 (an increase of 11% over 1981) generated 171 jobs and $1,382,000 in payroll. Lodging: three hotels, motels and tourist courts. **ALCOHOLIC BEVERAGES** Packaged distilled spirits, beer, ale, malt liquor and wine are legal. Sale of mixed beverages is legal in all or parts of the county. **MILITARY INSTALLATIONS** Chase Field, Naval Air Station, Beeville, 2,501 personnel, 7,032 acres, flight training; Goliad, Naval Auxiliary Field, Beeville, 1,570 acres, auxiliary training field. **FEDERAL EXPENDITURES** The federal government had direct expenditures or obligations of $74,912,000 in the county during fiscal year 1983, including $45,670,000 by the U.S. Department of Defense. In addition, the federal government provided $1,477,000 in grant awards, paid $42,623,000 in salaries and wages, made direct payments to individuals of $27,841,000 including $20,790,000 in retirement and disability payments, awarded $1,754,000 in procurement contracts and spent $1,217,000 in other expenditures or obligations. The federal government also provided $417,000 in direct loans and $16,256,000 in guaranteed loans and insurance.

COUNTIES

BEE (continued)

COMMUNICATION

Newspapers–Weekly: Beeville Bee-Picayune. Radio: KIBL-AM, KACO-AM and KCWW-FM (Beeville). Cable TV. Telephone companies: Southwestern Bell/Central Telephone-Midstate. **TRANSPORTATION** Total public road mileage: 783. In 1982 there were 19,584 registered vehicles and 451 reported traffic accidents including 13 fatalities. Intercity bus service is available. Motor freight: eight local and intrastate carriers. Rail: three branch lines carry annually one to five million tons of freight each through the county. Aircraft: 49 are registered in the county. Airports: Beeville Municipal Airport is a general utility airport providing general aviation service. It serves as a base for 30 aircraft.

COMMUNITY SERVICES

EDUCATION Four school districts with eight elementary, two middle and four high schools. The average daily attendance in 1981-82 was 4,884, with expenditures per pupil of $2,299 including 317 classroom teachers with an average annual salary of $15,758. Forty-two percent of the 307 high school graduates planned to attend college. In 1982-83, 39% of the students were White, 59% Hispanic, 2.0% Black and 0.7% Asian. Private schools: 415 students enrolled in four elementary schools. Bee County College is located in Beeville. Established in 1965 it is a vocational and two year academic college under state and local control. Enrollment in 1982 was 1,976 with in state undergraduate tuition and fees of $230 per semester. **PUBLIC LIBRARIES** Bee County Public Library (Beeville): 29,283 volumes. **CHILD CARE** 27 day care and 13 twenty-four hour care licensed facilities. **HEALTH CARE** 14 physicians and four dentists. Hospitals: one with a capacity of 73. Clinics: one for treatment of drug abuse. Ambulance services: one volunteer service and one volunteer fire department service. Mental health: one county clinic. Nursing homes: two nursing homes with a combined capacity of 220 nursing care residents. The average cost per day for private patients in 1982 was $31.67. **CHURCHES** 45 churches have an estimated combined membership of 15,748. The largest denominations are Catholic, Southern Baptist and United Methodist. **SOCIAL SERVICES** In fiscal year 1983 a total of $1,698,218 in food stamps was distributed, with an average of 3,707 persons receiving food stamps each month. Aid to Families with Dependent Children (AFDC) totaled $412,703 with an average of 274 families receiving AFDC each month. Medical assistance benefits for the aged and disabled of $2,169,239 and for families and children of $705,367 brought the county benefit total to $4,985,527. **FIRE PROTECTION** Seven volunteer fire departments. **LAW ENFORCEMENT** The County Sheriff has 34 commissioned officers. One police department has a force of 28. **CRIME** 27 violent crimes (murder, forcible rape, robbery and aggravated assault) and 786 nonviolent crimes (burglary, larceny-theft and motor vehicle theft) were reported in 1982. **JUDICIAL SYSTEM** Two District Courts and Judges, one County Court and Judge and four Justices of the Peace. In the District Courts a total of 3,018 cases were pending on 1/1/82, 626 new cases were filed and 759 cases were disposed of during the year leaving 2,885 cases pending on 12/31/82. There were 233 criminal cases on the docket, 89 convictions, 28 persons committed to prison and three committed to jail and 117 cases left pending. In the County Court 312 cases were pending on 1/1/82, 614 new cases were filed and 471 cases were disposed of during the year leaving 455 cases pending on 12/31/82. There were 825 criminal cases on the docket, 219 convictions, 25 persons committed to jail, and 384 cases left pending. **JAILS** One jail, capacity 26. **ATTORNEYS AT LAW** 28. **UTILITIES** 67% of the residents are connected to a public or privately owned water system and 65% are connected to a public sewer system. Natural gas is distributed to the county by Entex, Inc. The average annual residential bill for natural gas in 1982 for the Entex distribution system was $390.31, an increase of 26% over 1981. Electricity is distributed to the county by San Patricio Electric Coop., Inc., Central Power and Light Co. and Karnes Electric Coop., Inc. and is generated primarily by gas, oil and water. The typical residential electric bill is $162.15 per month for an all-electric house using 2,500 kwh. **TAXES** The county has eight units with taxing authority: four school districts, one city, one county, one college district and one special district.

RECREATION/ENTERTAINMENT

NATIONAL REGISTER OF HISTORIC PLACES Beeville: Praeger Building. **MUNICIPAL PARKS** 266 acres in 10 municipal parks. These parks contain nine playgrounds, one golf course, five baseball and softball fields, two tennis courts and one swimming pool. Developed campsites: 16. **BOATING/FISHING** Lakes/reservoirs: Dougherty (22 acres). Major rivers: Aransas. Primary streams: Medio. **HUNTING** Fall and winter seasons on deer. No closed season on javelina, squirrel, bobcats and coyotes. Fall, winter and spring seasons on turkey. Winter season on quail, muskrat, beaver, opossum, ring-tailed cat, badger, fox, weasel, raccoon, skunk and civet cat. Special regulations on state owned river beds of the Aransas and the Poeseta Rivers which are game sanctuaries. In 1983 sandhill crane, duck, coot, geese, woodcock and jacksnipe seasons occurred during the winter months. Teal duck, rail and gallinule seasons occurred in the fall. Mourning dove season occurred intermittently during the fall and winter months with a fall season on white-winged doves. **MUSEUMS** Skidmore: Skidmore Historical Society Museum. **COLLEGIATE FINE ARTS** Beeville: Cultural events offered by Bee County College. **SPECIAL EVENTS** Fourth of July Celebration and Rodeo, Beeville, July; Western Week Celebration, Beeville, October.

COMMUNITIES

COUNTY SEAT Beeville, County Courthouse, 78102; County Clerk's Office, 512/358-3664. **INCORPORATED COMMUNITIES** (1980 population and ZIP Code) Beeville (14,574) 78102. **UNINCORPORATED COMMUNITIES** (and ZIP Code) Blanconia 78102, Cadiz 78102, Caesar 78119, Clareville 78102, Mineral 78125, Monteola 78119, Normanna 78142, Oaks 78119, Olmos 78389, Orangedale 78102, Papalote 78387, Pawnee 78145, Pettus 78146, Skidmore 78389, Tuleta 78162, Tulsita 78119 and Tynan 78391. **FOR ADDITIONAL LOCAL INFORMATION** Bee Co. Chamber of Commerce, 1705 N. St. Marys, P.O. Box 99, Beeville, 78102, 512/358-3267.

BELL (C17)

THE LAND

Between Austin and Waco on Interstate Highway 35 in the Blackland Prairies Region, Bell County covers 1,055 square miles of rolling to rough terrain. The elevation ranges from 350 to 1,050 feet. Starting from the east, one-half of the county's soil is undulating, slightly acidic, with loamy surface layers and cracking, clayey subsoils and acidic, cracking, clayey soils. They have a high corrosion and shrink-swell potential. The rest of the county has undulating to hilly light colored, well drained soils, and very dark, loamy surfaces over loamy subsoils that have accumulations of lime. The western half of the county is in the cross timbers and prairies vegetation region consisting of tall grasses and a large influx of mesquite and other woody species. The eastern half consists of Blackland Prairies vegetation which is tall grasses and hardwood trees along rivers and streams. Between 41 and 50% of the land in the county is considered prime farmland. **CLIMATE** Subtropical humid to subhumid with mild winters and hot summers. The average annual temperature is 67°F. Temperatures in January range from an average low of 36° to an average high of 59°F and in July range from 72° to 96°F. The average annual precipitation is 34 inches, with an average relative humidity of 82% at 6 A.M. and 52% at 6 P.M. There is no significant snowfall. The growing season averages 258 days per year, with the last freeze in mid March and the first freeze in late November. The sun shines during the year on the average 65% of the daylight hours.

THE PEOPLE

This county is one of the most densely populated in the state and ranks 37th among all U.S. counties in the highest birth rate. It also ranks as one of the six counties in Texas having the lowest percent of residents who are native Texans. The 1982 estimated population of 164,100 indicates a continuation of the strong growth rate begun in the 1940s. Rural areas experienced a population gain of 60% between 1970 and 1980. The age groups with the largest increases were ages 30 to 34 and 62 and over causing the county's low median age to rise from 23 in 1970 to 25 in 1980. The largest ancestry groups are persons of English descent (21%), German descent (20%), Black (16%) and Hispanic (11%). **REGISTERED VOTERS** As of November 2, 1982 there were 47,902 registered voters (0.7% of the state total). The 1982 general election had a 46% voter turnout, compared to a 69% turnout in the 1980 general election. In the 1982 primary 91% voted Democratic and 9% Republican, with 10,710 votes cast.

THE ECONOMY

AGRICULTURE Wheat and sorghum area. In 1982, 80% of the land was in farms and ranches, with 38% of the farmland under cultivation and 1% irrigated. Bell ranked 79th in the state in highest agricultural receipts with 55% from livestock and livestock products. Overgrazing, undesirable brush and weeds and water erosion are current conservation problems. Primary crops: wheat, sorghum, hay, oats, corn and cotton. Primary vegetables: watermelons. Primary fruits and nuts: peaches and pecans. Primary livestock and products: cattle, sheep, wool and hogs. **BUSINESS** Total number of business establishments in the county: 2,589. Retail sales during the first quarter of 1984 increased 14%. In 1980 7% of the labor force were self-employed, 25% were employed in professional or related services, 14% in manufacturing, 23% in wholesale and retail trade, 8% in public administration, 5% were employed in other counties and there were 8,499 retired workers. The industries with the most employment: agribusiness, general and heavy construction, aluminum foundries, lumber mills, soft drink bottling and canning and the manufacture of men's work clothing, metal office furniture, paper bags, plastic products, mineral wool and electronic computer equipment. The nonfarm earnings in 1981 totaled $1,394,572. The retired workers received an average monthly Social Security payment of $287. **FINANCE** On June 30, 1983, 16 commercial banks had total deposits of $622,829,000 and total assets of $714,695,000. On December 31, 1982 two state savings and loan associations, one federal association, 19 state branches and two federal branches had combined assets of $404,427,329. In addition there are eight credit unions in the county. **HOUSING** Average value of homes in 1980: $36,900. Permits for new, privately owned housing units increased in 1982: 1,419 permits were issued with a total construction cost of $51,790,445. Of those permits, 945 were for single family houses. Housing permits increased in Harker Heights from 43 in 1981 to 175 in 1982, in Killeen from 496 to 909, in Temple from 117 to 195 and in Troy

from 11 to 32. Between 1970 and 1980 the number of housing units increased by 56%. Eighty-four percent of all units in the county are air-conditioned, 62% are heated by gas and 37% by electricity. **NATURAL RESOURCES** Limestone, oil, gas, sand and gravel, and dolomite. In 1982 a total of 89 barrels of crude oil and eight thousand cubic feet of casinghead gas were produced. Current production of other minerals and products includes crushed limestone, rock wool, sand and gravel. **TOURISM** Travel expenditures of $100,434,000 in 1982 (an increase of 9% over 1981) generated 2,237 jobs and $20,948,000 in payroll. Lodging: 21 hotels, motels and tourist courts. Convention/meeting facilities: Killeen-Killeen Community Center, Killeen Exhibit Hall, Central Texas College, one large room, Harker Heights Community Center and one hotel has facilities for large gatherings; Temple-Frank W. Mayborn Civic and Convention Center. **ALCOHOLIC BEVERAGES** Packaged distilled spirits, beer, ale, malt liquor and wine are legal in parts of the county. Sale of mixed beverages is legal in all or parts of the county. **MILITARY INSTALLATIONS** Fort Hood, Killeen, 43,205 personnel, 216,946 acres, 1st Cavalry Division 2nd Armored Division. **FEDERAL EXPENDITURES** The federal government had direct expenditures or obligations of $1,067,258,000 in the county during fiscal year 1983, including $836,544,000 by the U.S. Department of Defense. In addition, the federal government provided $9,999,000 in grant awards, paid $722,338,000 in salaries and wages, made direct payments to individuals of $199,203,000 including $167,578,000 in retirement and disability payments, awarded $133,811,000 in procurement contracts and spent $1,907,000 in other expenditures or obligations. The federal government also provided $7,730,000 in direct loans and $50,006,000 in guaranteed loans and insurance.

COMMUNICATION

Newspapers–Daily: Killeen Daily Herald, ave. morning circ. 15,454 and the Temple Daily Telegram, ave. morning circ. 25,493. Weekly: Bartlett Tribune, Belton Journal and the Holland Progress. Radio: KTON-AM (Belton), KIIZ-AM, KREM-AM, KPLE-FM (Temple), KIXS-FM and KNCT-FM Stereo (Killeen). TV: KCEN-CH. 6 (Temple). Cable TV. Telephone companies: Continental Telephone, Southwestern Bell, Central Telephone and Central Telephone-Midstate. **TRANSPORTATION** Total public road mileage: 2,110. In 1982 there were 131,916 registered vehicles and 4,138 reported traffic accidents including 31 fatalities. Taxi cabs: two companies in Killeen and one in Temple. Municipal transit systems: One intercity bus system provides some intracity service to Temple, Belton, Killeen and Fort Hood in Bell county, and the Copperas Cove area in Coryell county. Intercity bus service is available. Motor freight: 36 local and intrastate carriers. Rail: The Eagle provides passenger service on the Amtrak route. Six main lines carry freight through the county; three of them carry annually over 30 million tons each, one carries 20 to 30 and two carry 10 to 20 each. Aircraft: 146 are registered in the county. Airports: Draughon-Miller Municipal Airport at Temple is a basic transportation airport with commuter service. It serves as a base for 62 aircraft. Killeen Municipal Airport is a basic transportation airport with commuter service. It serves as a base for 90 aircraft. Salado Airport at Salado. Also available are heliports at Scott and White Memorial Hospital and the Veteran Administration Center at Temple.

COMMUNITY SERVICES

EDUCATION Nine school districts with 39 elementary, nine middle and 13 high schools. The average daily attendance in 1981-82 was 28,203, with expenditures per pupil of $2,032 including 1,841 classroom teachers with an average annual salary of $15,455. Fifty-nine percent of the 1,665 high school graduates planned

COUNTIES

BELL (continued)

to attend college. In 1982-83, 64% of the students were White, 14% Hispanic, 19% Black, 3% Asian and 0.2% American Indian. Sports championships: 1983 A Boys' Golf Team, Salado H.S. Private schools: 756 students enrolled in four elementary and one high school. Central Texas College is located in Killeen. Established in 1965 it is a vocational and two year academic college under local control. Enrollment in 1982 was 4,776 with in state undergraduate tuition and fees of $270 per semester. Temple Junior College is located in Temple. Established in 1926 it is under local control. Enrollment in 1982 was 2,368 with in state undergraduate tuition and fees of $260 per semester. University of Mary Hardin-Baylor is located in Belton. Established in 1845 it is affiliated with the Southern Baptist Church. Enrollment in 1982 was 1,034 with in state undergraduate tuition and fees of $2,050 per semester. The highest degree offered is: Bachelor. American Technological Institute is located in Killeen. Established in 1973 it is an independent nonprofit institution. Enrollment in 1982 was 765 with in state undergraduate tuition and fees of $1,674 per semester. The highest degree offered is Master (no lower division). Vocational education: Killeen Beauty College and Beneficial Tax Preparation School (Killeen). **PUBLIC LIBRARIES** Teinert Memorial Public Library (Bartlett): 16,211 volumes. Belton City Library: 29,931 volumes. Harker Heights Library. Killeen Public Library: 54,340 volumes. Morgan's Point Library. Temple Public Library: 65,915 volumes. **CHILD CARE** 261 day care and 49 twenty-four hour care licensed facilities. **HEALTH CARE** 470 physicians and 74 dentists. Hospitals: four with a combined capacity of 815. Specialized hospitals: one army hospital with capacity of 250 and one veterans center with capacity of 575. Clinics: one youth clinic, one dialysis clinic, one public health clinic and one minor emergency center. Ambulance services: three commercial, four volunteer services, two fire departments, one air and one city service. Mental health: two clinics and two county clinics. Nursing homes: 12 nursing homes with a combined capacity of 1,135 nursing care residents. The average cost per day for private patients in 1982 was $31.66. **CHURCHES** 154 churches have an estimated combined membership of 64,117. The largest denominations are Southern Baptist, Catholic and United Methodist. **SOCIAL SERVICES** In fiscal year 1983 a total of $5,623,726 in food stamps was distributed, with an average of 11,262 persons receiving food stamps each month. Aid to Families with Dependent Children (AFDC) totaled $1,746,804 with an average of 1,172 families receiving AFDC each month. Medical assistance benefits for the aged and disabled of $9,084,777 and for families and children of $1,836,523 brought the county benefit total to $18,291,829. **FIRE PROTECTION** One paid, one partly paid and 14 volunteer fire departments. **LAW ENFORCEMENT** The County Sheriff has 33 commissioned officers. Ten police departments have a combined force of 294. Two colleges have campus police departments with a combined force of 14 officers. **CRIME** 720 violent crimes (murder, forcible rape, robbery and aggravated assault) and 7,766 nonviolent crimes (burglary, larceny-theft and motor vehicle theft) were reported in 1982. **JUDICIAL SYSTEM** Four District Courts and Judges, three County Courts and Judges and six Justices of the Peace. In the District Courts a total of 3,315 cases were pending on 1/1/82, 5,362 new cases were filed and 5,306 cases were disposed of during the year leaving 3,371 cases pending on 12/31/82. There were 1,526 criminal cases on the docket, 526 convictions, 186 persons committed to prison and 25 committed to jail and 690 cases left pending. In the County Courts 5,694 cases were pending on 1/1/82, 7,693 new cases were filed and 7,385 cases were disposed of during the year leaving 6,002 cases pending on 12/31/82. There were 11,168 criminal cases on the docket, 3,854 convictions, 756 persons committed to jail, and

4,744 cases left pending. **JAILS** One jail, capacity 114. New jail under construction, capacity 500. Lost certification in 1983 due to crowded conditions. **ATTORNEYS AT LAW** 186. **UTILITIES** 96% of the residents are connected to a public or privately owned water system and 81% are connected to a public sewer system. Natural gas is distributed to the county by Lone Star Gas Co., Division of Enserch. The average annual residential bill for natural gas in 1982 for the Lone Star distribution system was $405.91, an increase of 35% over 1981. Electricity is distributed to the city of Bartlett by the Bartlett Municipal Light Dept. and to the rest of the county by Texas Power and Light Co., Wood County Electric Coop., Inc. Bartlett Electric Coop., Inc. Belfalls Electric Coop., Inc., McLennan Co. Electric Coop., Inc. and Pedernales Electric Coop., Inc. and is generated primarily by gas and coal. The typical residential electric bill is $165.24 per month for an all-electric house using 2,500 kwh. **TAXES** The county has 33 units with taxing authority: 10 school districts, 11 cities, one county, two college districts and nine special districts.

RECREATION/ENTERTAINMENT

NATIONAL REGISTER OF HISTORIC PLACES Bartlett: Bartlett Commercial Historic District. Belton: Bell County Courthouse and Old St. Luke's Church. Salado: Major A.J. Rose House. Temple: Ferguson House. **COUNTY/MUNICIPAL PARKS** 1,047 acres in two county and 47 municipal parks. These parks contain two miles of hiking trails, 43 playgrounds, two golf courses, two football and soccer fields, 33 baseball and softball fields, 18 tennis courts, one multi-use court, seven swimming pools and two boat ramps. **SCENIC DRIVES** The Texas Brazos Trail runs through this county. This trail moves through a beautiful and historic section of Central Texas revealing forested landscapes filled with wildlife and wild flowers. **BOATING/FISHING** Lakes/reservoirs: Belton (12,300 acres), Donahoe Creek Soil Conservation Service Lakes 5, 6, and 7 (99 acres), Engineer (24 acres), Polk (22 acres), Stillhouse Hollow (6,430 acres) and Temple (223 acres). Major rivers: Leon and Lampassas. Primary streams: Pennington, Flag, Donohoe, Nolan, Bird and Salado. **HUNTING** Fall and winter seasons on deer. No closed season on squirrel, nutria, coyotes and bobcats. Winter and spring seasons on turkey. Winter season on quail, muskrat, beaver, otter, opossum, mink, ring-tailed cat, badger, fox, raccoon, skunk and civet cat. Special regulations on the land or water of Stillhouse Hollow Reservoir where all hunting, except for birds, is prohibited. In 1983 sandhill crane, duck, coot, geese, woodcock and jacksnipe seasons occurred during the winter months. Teal duck, rail and gallinule seasons occurred in the fall. Mourning dove season occurred intermittently during the fall and winter months. **MUSEUMS** Belton: Bell County Museum and Sid Richardson Museum of Mary Hardin-Baylor College. Fort Hood: 2nd Armored Division Museum and First Cavalry Museum. Salado: Central Texas Area Museum. Temple: SPIST (Czech) Museum and Railroad and Pioneer Museum. **THEATERS** Temple: Temple Civic Theatre. **ZOO** Belton: Bell County Zoo. **PLANETARIUM** Killeen: Central Texas College Planetarium. **OBSERVATORY** Belton: University of Mary Hardin-Baylor Observatory. Killeen: Central Texas College Observatory. **COLLEGIATE FINE ARTS** Cultural events offered by Central Texas College in Killeen. Mary Hardin-Baylor College in Belton and Temple Junior College in Temple. **SPECIAL EVENTS** Youth Fair and Junior Stock Show, Temple, February; Annual Jackpot Open Benefit Horse Show, Temple, February; International Fair, Killeen, variable; Pilgrimage to Old Salado, Salado, April; Arts and Crafts Festival, Killeen, April; Rodeo, Killeen, May; Corn Festival, Holland, June; Pioneer Day Celebration, Temple, June; Fourth of July Celebration, Belton,

July; Chisholm Trail Annual Junior Golf Classic, Belton, July; Salado Art Fair, Salado, August; Sailboat Races, Temple, October; Gathering of the Scottish Clans, Salado, November; Christmas Parade, Temple, December; Candlelight Christmas in Old Salado, Salado, December.

COMMUNITIES

COUNTY SEAT Belton, County Courthouse, 76513; County Clerk's Office, 817/939-3521. **INCORPORATED COMMUNITIES** (1980 population and ZIP Code) Bartlett (1,567: 696 in Bell Co. and 871 in Williamson Co.) 76511, Belton (10,660) 76513, Harker Heights (7,345) 76541, Holland (863) 76534, Killeen (46,296) 76541, Little River Academy (1,155) 76513, Morgan's Point Resort (1,082) 76513, Nolanville (1,308) 76559, Rogers (1,242) 76569, Temple (42,483) 76501 and Troy (1,353) 76579. **UNINCORPORATED COMMUNITIES** (and ZIP Code) Airville 76501, Belfalls 76579, Burgess (Reed Lake) 76569, Cyclone 76519, Ding Dong 76544, Dogridge 76513, Edgeworth 76569, Heidenheimer 76533, Lakeview 76513, Leedale (Gindale) 76569, McNair Village 76546, Maxdale 76544, Meador Grove 76557, Meeks 76519, Moffatt 76501, Oenaville 76501, Oscar 76501, Pendleton 76564, Prairie Dell 76571, Ratibor 76501, Red Ranger 76569, Salado 76571, Seaton 76501, Sparks 76534, Stampede 76557, Vilas 76534, West Cliff 76513, White Hall 76557, Willow Grove (Willow Springs) 76557, Youngsport 76544 and Zabcikville (Marekville) 76501. **FOR ADDITIONAL LOCAL INFORMATION** Bartlett Area Chamber of Commerce, P.O. Box 564, Bartlett, 76511, 817/527-3219, 527-3319; Belton Area Chamber of Commerce, 106 S. East, P.O. Box 659, Belton, 76513, 817/939-3551; Greater Killeen Chamber of Commerce, P.O. Box 548, 507 N. 8th St., Killeen, 76540, 817/526-9551; Salado Chamber of Commerce, P.O. Box 81, Salado, 76571, 817/947-5040; and Temple Chamber of Commerce, P.O. Box 158, Two N. 5th, Temple, 75603, 817/773-2105.

BEXAR (C35)

THE LAND

Interstate Highways 10, 35 and 37 intersect at San Antonio. Bexar County, in the Rio Grande Plain Region, covers 1,248 square miles. The hilly northwest portion of the county is the source of numerous springs and artesian wells. The elevation ranges from 600 to 1,200 feet. The northern one-third of the county has undulating to hilly alkaline soils over limestone and limy earths with shallow to deep loamy soils. The rest of the county has very dark, loamy soils with some clayey subsoils and gray to black, cracking clayey soils with a high shrink-swell potential. A narrow strip of nearly level to undulating soils to the south are deep with loamy surface layers and loamy to clayey subsoils. The northern quarter of the county has Edwards Plateau vegetation of tall and mid grasses, live oaks, juniper and mesquite trees. A central strip has Blackland Prairie vegetation consisting of tall grasses. The rest of the county has South Texas Plains vegetation of tall grasses, mid grasses, a few live oak, mesquite trees, thorny bushes and cacti. Between 21 and 30% of the land in the county is considered prime farmland. **CLIMATE** Subtropical subhumid with mild winters and hot summers. The average annual temperature is 70°F. Temperatures in January range from an average low of 39° to an average high of 62°F and in July range from 73° to 96°F. The average annual precipitation is 31 inches, with an average relative humidity of 84% at 6 A.M. and 52% at 6 P.M. There is no significant snowfall. The growing season averages 265 days per year, with the last freeze in early March and the first freeze in late November. The sun shines during the year on the average 65% of the daylight hours.

THE PEOPLE

Bexar County ranks 26th in the U.S. in population and is one of the state's most densely populated counties. The 1982 estimated population of 1,052,100 indicates a continuation of the steady growth rate since 1930. Although the population is primarily urban, the greatest change between 1970 and 1980 occurred in the rural areas with a growth rate of 24%. The age groups with the largest gains were ages 20 to 44 and 62 and over. Therefore, the low median age rose from 24 in 1970 to 27 in 1980. Bexar ranks 46th among all U.S. counties in the highest percent of residents of Spanish origin. The largest ancestry groups are Hispanic (47%), persons of German descent (16%) and English descent (15%). **REGISTERED VOTERS** As of November 2, 1982 there were 425,668 registered voters (7% of the state total). The 1982 general election had a 46% voter turnout, compared to a 67% turnout in the 1980 general election. In the 1982 primary 81% voted Democratic and 19% Republican, with 96,167 votes cast.

THE ECONOMY

AGRICULTURE Diversified products. In 1982, 66% of the land was in farms and ranches, with 27% of the farmland under cultivation and 14% irrigated. Bexar ranked 53rd in the state in highest agricultural receipts, with 61% from livestock and livestock products. Overgrazing, undesirable brush and weeds, water erosion and flooding are current conservation problems. Primary crops: oats, sorghum, hay, corn and wheat. Primary vegetables: sixth in the state for carrots and eighth for cabbage. Watermelons and potatoes. Primary fruits and nuts: peaches and 10th in the state for pecans. Primary livestock and products: cattle, milk, sheep, wool and hogs. **BUSINESS** Total number of business establishments in the county: 18,747. Retail sales during the first quarter of 1984 increased 20%. In 1980, 6% of the labor force were self-employed, 21% were employed in professional or related services, 11% in manufacturing, 24% in wholesale and retail trade, 10% in public administration, 2% were employed in other counties and there were 60,392 retired workers. The industries with the most employment: tourism, oil and gas extraction, production of malt beverages, general and heavy construction, soft drink canning and bottling, commercial printing, bookbinding, lumber mills, iron and steel mills and the manufacture of men's and women's clothing, household furniture, curtains and draperies, paperboard boxes, pharmaceutical drugs, shoes, ready-mixed concrete, construction machinery, aircraft and aircraft parts and electronic computers. The nonfarm earnings in 1981 totaled $9,609,598,000. The retired workers received an average monthly Social Security payment of $297. **FINANCE** On June 30, 1983, 55 commercial banks had total deposits of $5,978,306,000 and total assets of $6,993,286,000. On December 31, 1982 seven state savings and loan associations, two federal associations, 72 state branches and 12 federal branches had combined assets of $2,957,315,493. In addition there are 74 credit unions in the county. **HOUSING** Average value of homes in 1980: $32,800. Permits for new, privately owned housing units increased in 1982: 14,025 permits were issued with a total construction cost of $308,887,511. Of those permits, 3,040 were for single family houses. Housing permits increased in Alamo Heights from 58 in 1981 to 90 in 1982, in Balcones Heights from one to 20, in Converse from 48 to 130, in Leon Valley from 124 to 541, with 538 of the permits issued for apartments and condominiums, in Live Oak from 28 to 152 with 120 of the permits issued for apartments and condominiums, in Olmos Park

COUNTIES

from one to 61 with 59 of the permits issued for apartments and condominiums, in San Antonio from 5,975 to 11,822 with 9,582 of the permits issued for apartments and condominiums and in Universal City from 49 to 451 with 338 of the permits issued for apartments and condominiums. Between 1970 and 1980 the number of housing units increased by 39%. Seventy-eight percent of all units in the county are air-conditioned, 82% are heated by gas and 17% by electricity. **NATURAL RESOURCES** Ceramic clay, limestone, industrial sand, sand and gravel, oil, gas and lignite coal. In 1982 a total of 19,133 thousand cubic feet of gas well gas, 515,346 barrels of crude oil and 17,256 thousand cubic feet of casinghead gas were produced. Current production of other minerals and products includes brick, cement, clay, lime, crushed limestone, perlite, construction sand, sand and gravel and vermiculite. **TOURISM** Travel expenditures of $804,949,000 in 1982 (an increase of 9% over 1981) generated 18,101 jobs and $167,320,000 in payroll. Lodging: 106 hotels, motels and tourist courts. Convention/meeting facilities: San Antonio-Convention Center, Joe and Harry Freeman Coliseum, St. Mary's University Stadium and Gym, San Antonio Independent School District with one gym and stadium, Trinity University's Laurie Auditorium, Villita Assembly Building and 12 hotels with facilities for large gatherings. **ALCOHOLIC BEVERAGES** Packaged distilled spirits, beer, ale, malt liquor and wine are legal. Sale of mixed beverages is legal in all or parts of the county. **MILITARY INSTALLATIONS** Camp Bullis, San Antonio, 27,000 acres, Reserve Training; Fort Sam Houston, San Antonio, 14,804 personnel, 2,995 acres, Medical Training Headquarters; Camp Stanley, San Antonio, 4,000 acres, Storage; Brooks Air Force Base, San Antonio, 2,574 personnel, 1,310 acres, Aerospace Medical Division; Kelly Air Force Base, San Antonio, 30,848 personnel, 4,721 acres, Air Logistics Center; Lackland Air Force Base, San Antonio, 9,306 personnel, 6,784 acres, Basic Training School; Randolph Air Force Base, Universal City, 7,626 personnel, 3,771 acres, Flying Training Wing; Randolph Communications Site, Universal City, four acres, Communications; San Antonio Air Force Station, San Antonio, seven acres, Communications. **FEDERAL EXPENDITURES** The federal government had direct expenditures or obligations of $3,570,913,000 in the county during fiscal year 1983, including $2,112,207,000 by the U.S. Department of Defense. In addition, the federal government provided $95,420,000 in grant awards, paid $1,574,151,000 in salaries and wages, made direct payments to individuals of $1,510,981,000 including $1,271,533,000 in retirement and disability payments, awarded $387,034,000 in procurement contracts and spent $3,327,000 in other expenditures or obligations. The federal government also provided $2,001,000 in direct loans and $267,001,000 in guaranteed loans and insurance.

COMMUNICATION

Newspapers–Daily: San Antonio Express, ave. morn. circ. 83,291. San Antonio News, ave. eve. circ. 73,762. San Antonio Light, ave eve. circ. 120,464. Weekly: Herald-News and the North San Antonio Times. Radio: KDRY-AM (Alamo Heights), KAPE-AM, KBUC-AM, KCOR-AM, KEDA-AM, KFHM-AM, KKYX-AM, KLLS-AM, KMAC-AM, KONO-AM, KTSA-AM, KVAR-AM, WOAI-AM, KAJA-FM, KESI-FM, KISS-FM, KLLS-FM, KRTU-FM, KSLR-FM, KSYM-FM, KVAR-FM, KBUC-FM Stereo, KITY-FM Stereo, KOXT-FM Stereo and KTFM-FM Stereo (San Antonio). Television: KENS-CH. 5, KMOL-CH4, KSAT-CH. 12, KWEX-CH. 41-Spanish (San Antonio). Cable TV. Telephone companies: Continental Telephone, General Telephone, Southwestern Bell and Guadalupe Valley Telephone Coop. **TRANSPORTATION** Total public road mileage: 5,383.

In 1982 there were 723,620 registered vehicles and 31,940 reported traffic accidents including 197 fatalities. Taxi cabs: 23 companies in San Antonio and one in Universal City. Municipal transit systems: one metropolitan bus system in San Antonio with scheduled routes. Intercity bus service is available. Motor freight: 200 local and intrastate carriers. Rail: The Eagle and Sunset Limited provide passenger service on the Amtrak route. Five main and three branch lines carry freight through the county. Two of the main lines carry annually over 30 million tons of freight each, one carries 10 to 20, one carries five to 10 and the other carries one to five million. Two of the branch lines carry annually one to five million tons of freight each and the other branch line carries less than one million. Aircraft: 991 are registered in the county. Airports: San Antonio International Airport serves as a base for 350 aircraft and is a medium haul and medium sized hub airport with carrier service. Stinson Municipal Airport at San Antonio, a reliever airport to San Antonio International, serves as a base for 150 aircraft and is a general utility airport. Also serving the area are Triple "R" Airport, Twin Oaks Airport, Horizon Airport and West Side Airport. Heliports in San Antonio are Helicab Heliport, International Airport Helipad, Baptist Memorial Hospital, Bexar County Hospital, Methodist Hospital, Northeast Baptist Hospital and Santa Rosa Medical Center Heliport. Domestic and foreign exports by air from San Antonio average about 100 thousand pounds per month. Imports by air to San Antonio average about 25 thousand pounds per month.

COMMUNITY SERVICES

EDUCATION 15 school districts with 184 elementary, 55 middle, 35 high schools and 19 special education. The average daily attendance in 1981-82 was 181,028, with expenditures per pupil of $2,240 including 10,415 classroom teachers with an average annual salary of $17,763. Fifty-five percent of the 12,382 high school graduates planned to attend college. In 1982-83, 35% of the students were White, 58% Hispanic, 7% Black, 0.9% Asian and 0.1% American Indian. Sports championships: 1983 AAAA Girls' Tennis Doubles, Alamo Heights H.S.; 1983 AAAAA Football, Converse Judson; 1984 Girls' Swimming and Diving, San Antonio Churchill H.S. Private schools: 26,312 students enrolled in 74 elementary and 24 high schools. Sports championships: 1982 AAA Boys' Soccer, St. Anthony H.S. Seminary; 1983 AAA Boy's Tennis, St. Anthony H.S. Seminary; 1984 AAAA Boys' Basketball, Central Catholic H.S.; 1984 AAAA Girls' Basketball, Incarnate Word H.S.; 1983 AAAA Girls' Softball, St. Gerard H.S.; 1983 AAAA Girls' Volleyball, Incarnate Word H.S.; and 1983 AAAA Girls' Track, Ursuline Academy. Trinity University is located in San Antonio. Established in 1869 it is an independent nonprofit institution. Enrollment in 1982 was 3,256 with in state undergraduate tuition and fees of $3,622 per semester. The highest degree offered is Master. University of Texas Health Science Center at San Antonio was established in 1959 and is under state control. Enrollment in 1982 was 2,212. The highest degree offered is Doctorate. Saint Mary's University is located in San Antonio. Established in 1852 it is affiliated with the Catholic Church. Enrollment in 1982 was 3,324 with in state undergraduate tuition and fees of $2,880 per semester. The highest degree offered is Master. San Antonio Community College is located in San Antonio (two campuses). Established in 1925 it is a vocational and two year academic college under local control. Enrollment in 1982 was 27,035 with in state undergraduate tuition and fees of $173 per semester. Oblate College of the Southwest is located in San Antonio. Established in 1903 it is affiliated with the Catholic Church. Enrollment in 1982 was 52. Our Lady of the Lake University of San Antonio was established in 1911 and is affiliated with the Catholic Church. Enrollment in 1982 was

1,768 with in state undergraduate tuition and fees of $2,700 per semester. The highest degree offered is Master. University of Texas at San Antonio was established in 1969 and is under state control. Enrollment in 1982 was 9,831 with in state undergraduate tuition and fees of $364 per semester. The highest degree offered is Master. Baylor University Army Medical Service School is located in San Antonio. Established in 1903 it is an independent nonprofit institution. Incarnate Word College is located in San Antonio. Established in 1881 it is affiliated with the Catholic Church. Enrollment in 1982 was 1,573 with in state undergraduate tuition and fees of $2,770 per semester. The highest degree offered is Master. Vocational education: San Antonio-Alamo Beauty College, American Beauty College, Audie and Joyce School of Hair Design, Baptist Memorial Hospital School of X-Ray Technology and School of Nursing, Broadway Automotive Technical Institute, Inc., Computer and Business Management Education Center, Durham's Business College of San Antonio Texas, Inc., Easons Institute of Technology, Hallmark Aero Technology, Hicks Beauty School, Johnson's School of Cosmetic Arts and Sciences, Lewis Barber College, Mims Classic Beauty College, San Antonio Barber College, San Antonio Beauty College, San Antonio College of Med-Dental Assistants, San Antonio School of Vocational Nursing, San Antonio State Chest Hospital School of Medical Lab Technology, San Antonio Trade School, Southwest School of Medical Assistants, Texas Vocational School, San Antonio School of Vocational Nursing, Vogue Beauty College, Barbizon School of San Antonio, CBM Education Center of San Antonio, Inc., Control Data Learning Center, Fermon's Floral Designing School, International Bartending Institute, International Travel Training Systems, Lincoln Institute, R.N. State Board Review, Sales Training Institute and Southwest Paramedical School. Universal City—Lee's School of Business and Rets Electronic School. **PUBLIC LIBRARIES** Leon Valley Library. San Antonio Public Library and Information Center: 1,207,133 volumes and 12 branches.**CHILD CARE** 1,728 day care and 198 twenty-four hour care licensed facilities. **HEALTH CARE** 2,589 physicians and 710 dentists. Hospitals: 14 with a combined capacity of 4,873. Specialized hospitals: one veterans hospital with capacity of 670, one army hospital with capacity of 658, one for treatment of alcohol abuse with capacity of 45, one children's center with capacity of 64, one state chest hospital with capacity of 150, one air force medical center with capacity of 1,000, one women's hospital under construction, one Ambulance Surgical Center with a capacity of two. Clinics: 14 minor emergency clinics, 11 outpatient clinics, five for the treatment of alcohol and/or drug abuse, three dialysis clinics, one dental clinic, one physical therapy clinic, one air force clinic and one public health clinic. Ambulance services: eight commercial, three fire departments, three hospital-based and one volunteer service. Mental health: 15 county clinics, one state hospital with capacity of 994, one state school with capacity of 405 and one center with capacity of 60. Nursing homes: 43 nursing homes with a combined capacity of 5,399 nursing care, 110 custodial care and 127 personal care residents. The average cost per day for private patients in 1982 was $30.98. **CHURCHES** 514 churches have an estimated combined membership of 591,177. The largest denominations are Catholic, Southern Baptist and United Methodist. **SOCIAL SERVICES** In fiscal year 1983 a total of $58,980,163 in food stamps was distributed, with an average of 117,035 persons receiving food stamps each month. Aid to Families with Dependent Children (AFDC) totaled $16,473,739 with an average of 10,528 families receiving AFDC each month. Medical assistance benefits for the aged and disabled of $62,073,546 and for families and children of $33,900,068 brought the county benefit total to $171,427,516. **FIRE PROTECTION** Six paid, two partly paid and 30 volunteer fire departments. **LAW ENFORCEMENT** The County Sheriff has 1,052

commissioned officers. Nineteen police departments have a combined force of 1,501. One college and two universities have campus police departments with a combined force of 59 officers. There are 76 San Antonio Park Rangers. The San Antonio Airport has 43 officers. **CRIME** 6,387 violent crimes (murder, forcible rape, robbery and aggravated assault) and 68,066 nonviolent crimes (burglary, larceny-theft and motor vehicle theft) were reported in 1982. **JUDICIAL SYSTEM** 19 District Courts and Judges, seven County Courts and Judges and eight Justices of the Peace. In the District Courts a total of 40,997 cases were pending on 1/1/82, 30,142 new cases were filed and 25,492 cases were disposed of during the year leaving 45,647 cases pending on 12/31/82. There were 8,070 criminal cases on the docket, 2,793 convictions, 1,084 persons committed to prison and 109 committed to jail and 3,567 cases left pending. In the County Courts 23,214 cases were pending on 1/1/82, 21,765 new cases were filed and 17,839 cases were disposed of during the year leaving 27,140 cases pending on 12/31/82. There were 25,866 criminal cases on the docket, 5,274 convictions, 1,377 persons committed to jail, and 12,181 cases left pending. **JAILS** One jail, capacity 739. New jail under construction, capacity 1,400. **ATTORNEYS AT LAW** 2,640. **UTILITIES** 98% of the residents are connected to a public or privately owned water system and 93% are connected to a public sewer system. Natural gas is distributed to the county by Entex, Inc. and West End Gas Company. The average annual residential bill for natural gas in 1982 for the Entex distribution system was $390.31, an increase of 26% over 1981. Electricity is distributed to the county by San Antonio City Public Service Board, Texas Power and Light Co., West Texas Utilities Co., Bandera Electric Coop., Inc. and Pedernales Electric Coop., Inc. and is generated primarily by gas and oil. The typical residential electric bill is $178.33 per month for an all-electric house using 2,500 kwh. **TAXES** The county has 48 units with taxing authority: 12 school districts, 22 cities, one county, one college district and 12 special districts.

RECREATION/ENTERTAINMENT
PROFESSIONAL SPORTS San Antonio: San Antonio Spurs Basketball Team (Hemisfair Arena), San Antonio Gunslingers Football Team (Alamo Stadium). **TEXAS LEAGUE BASEBALL** The city of San Antonio has a team in the Western Division of the League. **FEDERAL** San Antonio Missions National Historical Park contains four Catholic frontier missions which were part of a system that stretched across the Spanish Southwest in the eighteenth century. Included in the park are a related historic dam and aqueduct system. The old missions are still centers of worship. **NATIONAL REGISTER OF HISTORIC PLACES** Leon Springs: Aue Stagecoach Inn. Live Oak vicinity: Live Oak Park Site. San Antonio: Alamo Methodist Church, L.B. Clegg House, Main and Military Plazas Historic District, San Pedro Springs Park, Salado Battlefield and Archeological Site, Source of the River Archeological District, San Antonio Casino Club Building, The Alamo (National Historic Landmark), Alamo Plaza Historic District, Alamo Portland and Roman Cement Works, Bexar County Courthouse, James Butler Bonham Elementary School, Espada Aqueduct (National Historic Landmark), Fest-Steves Block, Fort Sam Houston, Fourth Ward School, Hangar 9, International and Great Northern Railroad Station, King William Historic District, La Villita Historic District, Old Lone Star Brewery, Majestic Theatre, Menger Soap Works, Mission Concepcion (National Historic Landmark), Mission Espada, Mission Parkway Historic District, Mission San Jose (National Historic Landmark), Mission San Juan Capistrano, Jose Antonio Navarro Elementary School #8, Navarro House, Old First National Bank, Pershing House, Post Chapel, The Quadrangle, San Fernando Cathedral, San Antonio

COUNTIES

BEXAR (continued)

Loan and Trust Building, Schroeder-Yturri House, South Pacific Depot Historic District, Southern Pacific Railroad Sation, Spanish Governor's Palace (National Historic Landmark), Daniel J. Sullivan Stable and Carriage House, U.S. Arsenal District, Ursuline Academy, Bushnell, Central Trust Company Building, City of San Antonio Municipal Auditorium, San Antonio Water Works Pump Station No. 2, Emil Elmendorf House, Stack Brothers Building and Ximenes Chapel. San Antonio vicinity: Maverick-Altgelt Ranch and Fenstermaker-Fromme Farm. **STATE** Jose Antonio Navarro State Historic Site covers 0.3 acres with a museum and historic structure. The limestone structures built around 1850 were the home and office of a Texas patriot and signer of the Texas Declaration of Independence. **COUNTY/MUNICIPAL PARKS** 7,019 acres in eight county and 147 municipal parks. These parks contain 24 miles of hiking trails, 108 playgrounds, four golf courses, 29 football and soccer fields, 97 baseball and softball fields, 149 tennis courts, 44 multi-use courts, 26 swimming pools and one boat ramp. Developed campsites: 10. **SCENIC DRIVES** The Texas Independence Trail and the Texas Hill Country Trail run through this county. The Independence Trail not only surveys the historic sites of southeastern Texas but also includes many modern visitor attractions such as the Johnson Space Center. The Hill Country Trail winds through a scenic region of South-Central Texas, spanning a vast ranching area abundant with wildlife in a landscape of deeply-sculptured valleys and hills. **BOATING/FISHING** Lakes/reservoirs: Blue Wing (250 acres), Braunig (1,350 acres), three Soil Conservation Service lakes on Calaveras Creek (42 acres), Cassin (25 acres), Martinez Creek Soil Conservation Service Lakes 1, 2, 4, 5 and 6A (58 acres) and Mitchell (660 acres). Major rivers: San Antonio and Medina. Primary streams: Arroyo Seco, Calaveras, Hondo, Chupaderas, Sauz, Minita, Martinez, Helotes, Salitrillo, Olmos Creek, Lorence, Salado and Cibolo. **HUNTING** Fall and winter seasons on deer. No closed season on javelina, squirrel, bobcat and coyote. Fall, winter and spring seasons on turkey. Winter season on quail, muskrat, beaver, opossum, ringtailed cat, badger, fox, weasel, raccoon, skunk and civet cat. In 1983 sandhill crane, duck, coot, geese, woodcock and jacksnipe seasons occurred during the winter months. Teal duck, rail and gallinule seasons occurred in the fall. Mourning dove season occurred intermittently during the fall and winter months with a fall season on white-winged dove. **MUSEUMS** Lackland Air Force Base: History and Traditions Museum. San Antonio: San Antonio Museum of Art, Buckhorn Hall of Horns, Hall of Texas History, Hangar 9 Museum of Flight, Edward H. White Memorial Museum, Institute of Texan Cultures, McNay Art Institute, O. Henry House, Official Grand Lodge Museum I.O.O.F., Jersey Lilley Hospitality Center, Water Museum, Old San Antonio Museum, San Antonio Museum of Transportation, Steves Homestead, Witte Memorial Museum, Hertzberg Circus Collection of the San Antonio Public Library, History and Traditions Museum, Marion Koogler McNay Art Institute, Pioneer Hall, Spanish Governor's Palace, South Texas Health Education Center, U.S.A.F. Security Police Museum, Yturri Edmunds Home and Old Mill, San Antonio Conservation Society, Fort Sam Houston Museum and the Memorial Building. **THEATERS** San Antonio: Remember the Alamo Theatre, San Antonio Convention Center, Tuesday Musical Club, First Repertory Company of San Antonio, Hacienda Dinner Playhouse, San Antonio Little Theatre and Academy, Brackenridge Park Sunken Garden Theater and Arneson River Theatre. **ORCHESTRAS** San Antonio: Symphony Society, Symphony Orchestra and Youth Orchestra. **OPERA** San Antonio: Grand Opera Festival and Symphony. **DANCE** San Antonio: Ballet Folklorico De San Antonio, Ballet Company and Texas Civic Ballet. **BOTANIC GARDENS** San Antonio: Botanical Center and Brackenridge Chinese Sunken Garden. **ZOO** San Antonio: Zoological Garden. **AQUARIUM** San Antonio: Aquarium. **PLANETARIUM** San Antonio: College Planetarium and Observatory. **COLLEGIATE FINE ARTS** San Antonio: Cultural events offered by Incarnate Word College, Our Lady of the Lake College, Saint Mary's University, Saint Phillips College, San Antonio College and Trinity University. **SPECIAL EVENTS** Junior Stock Show and Rodeo, San Antonio, January; Los Pastores, San Antonio, January; Great Country River Festival, San Antonio, January; Stock Show and Rodeo, San Antonio, February; Alamo Trailhikers Volksmarch, San Antonio, February; Volkssport Festival, San Antonio, February; Texas Wanderers Volksmarch, San Antonio, February; Fiesta, San Antonio, April; Home and Garden Show and Pilgrimage, San Antonio, April/May; Charity Horse Show, San Antonio, April; Cornyval Festival, Helotes, April/May; Polo Matches, San Antonio, April-November; Starving Artists Show, San Antonio, April; Governor's Cup Polo, San Antonio, May; Nite in Ole Live Oak, Live Oak, May; Fair, Kirby, May/June; Performing Arts Festival, San Antonio, May/June; Memorial Weekend Celebration, San Antonio, May; Fiesta Noche del Rio, San Antonio, June-August; Funtier Nights, San Antonio, July-August; Texas Folklife Festival, San Antonio, August; La Feria del Rio, San Antonio, September; Mexican-American Friendship Week, San Antonio, September; Night in Ole Converse, Converse, September/October; The River Art Show, San Antonio, October; Greek Funstival, San Antonio, October; Veterans Day Celebration and Parade, Universal City, November; Las Posadas, San Antonio, December, Fiesta de las Luminarias, San Antonio, December; and Fiesta Navidena in El Mercado, San Antonio, December.

COMMUNITIES

COUNTY SEAT San Antonio, County Courthouse, 78205; County Clerk's Office, 512/220-2216. **INCORPORATED COMMUNITIES** (1980 population and ZIP Code) Alamo Heights (6,252) 78209, Balcones Heights (2,556) 78201, Castle Hills (4,773) 78213, China Grove (434) 78223, Converse (4,907) 78109, Elmendorf (492) 78112, Grey Forest (442) 78023, Helotes (2,100 est., incorp. inactive) 78023, Hill Country Village (972) 78232, Hollywood Park (3,231) 78232, Kirby (6,385) 78219, Leon Valley (8,951) 78238, Live Oak (8,183) 78233, Lytle (1,920: 17 in Bexar Co., 1,544 in Atascosa Co. and 359 in Medina Co.) 78052, Olmos Park (2,069) 78212, Saint Hedwig (690 est. incorp. inactive) 78152, San Antonio (785,880) 78201, All-America cities award 1949, 1951 and 1982-83. With All-America Cities Honorable Mention 1952. Schertz (7,262: 2 in Bexar Co., 26 in Comal Co. and 7,234 in Guadalupe Co.) 78154, Selma (528: 283 in Bexar Co., 88 in Comal Co. and 157 in Guadalupe Co.) 78209, Shavano Park (1,448) 78213, Somerset (1,102) 78069, Terrell Hills (4,644) 78209, Universal City (10,720) 78148 and Windcrest (5,332) 78239. **UNINCORPORATED COMMUNITIES** (and ZIP Code) Adkins (Sayers) 78101, Airport City 78108, Atascosa 78002, Buena Vista 78221, Camp Bullis 78236, Helotes Park Estates 78023, Helotes Ranch Acres 78023, Leon Springs 78006, Lone Oak 78101, Losoya 78221, Macdona 78054, Natural Bridge Caverns 78218, San Geronimo 78023, Seglar 78002, Senior 78073, Southton 78221, Thelma 78221, Van Raub 78006 and Von Ormy 78073. **FOR ADDITIONAL LOCAL INFORMATION** Greater San Antonio Chamber of Commerce, 602 E. Commerce, P.O. Box 1628, San Antonio, 78296, 512/229-2100, San Antonio Mexican Chamber of Commerce, 112 Auditorium Cir., 602 E. Commerce, San Antonio, 78205, 512/225-0462, North San Antonio Chamber of Commerce, 45 NE Loop 410, Suite 100, San Antonio, 78216, 512/344-4848 and Greater Randolph Area Chamber of Commerce, 2117 Pat Booker Rd., Universal City, 78148, 512/658-6281.

BLANCO (C23)

THE LAND

North of San Antonio on U.S. Highways 290 and 281 in the Edwards Plateau Region, Blanco County covers 714 square miles of mostly hills. The elevation ranges from 720 to 1,600 feet. The northwest border and center of the county have undulating to rolling, dark red soils mainly over consolidated rock with loamy surface layers and clayey subsoils. There are some shallow soils over limestone and deep loamy soils over sandstone. These soils are mildly alkaline on the surface and calcareous below. It is 10 to 40 inches to bedrock throughout the area. The rest of the county is undulating to hilly with light colored, well drained soils. Also, there are very dark, loamy surfaces over clayey or loamy subsoils that have accumulations of lime. The county lies in the Edwards Plateau vegetation area consisting of tall and mid grasses, live oak, some mesquite trees, shrubs and cacti. Between 11 and 20% of the land in the county is considered prime farmland. **CLIMATE** Subtropical subhumid with mild winters and warm summers. The average annual temperature is 67°F. Temperatures in January range from an average low of 34° to an average high of 60°F and in July range from 71° to 96°F. The average annual precipitation is 32 inches, with an average relative humidity of 80% at 6 A.M. and 48% at 6 P.M. The average annual snowfall is only a trace. The growing season averages 242 days per year, with the last freeze in late March and the first freeze in mid November. The sun shines during the year on the average 65% of the daylight hours.

THE PEOPLE

The 1982 estimated population of 4,900 indicates a continuation of a steady growth rate begun in the 1970s, which reversed the population decrease between 1940 and 1970. The majority of residents live in rural areas. The age group with the greatest increases between 1970 and 1980 was ages 20 to 39. Therefore the high median age decreased from 43 in 1970 to 39 in 1980. The high death rate and low birth rate also reflect the county's older population. The largest ancestry groups are persons of German descent (35%) and those of English descent (24%). **REGISTERED VOTERS** As of November 2, 1982 there were 2,970 registered voters (0.04% of the state total). The 1982 general election had a 63% voter turnout, compared to an 80% turnout in the 1980 general election. In the 1982 primary 72% voted Democratic and 28% Republican, with 426 votes cast.

THE ECONOMY

AGRICULTURE In 1982, 89% of the land was in farms and ranches, with 4% of the farmland under cultivation. Blanco ranked 210th in the state in highest agricultural receipts with 87% from livestock and livestock products. Overgrazing, undesirable brush and weeds and water erosion are current conservation problems. Primary crops: hay, oats, wheat and sorghum. Primary fruits and nuts: peaches and pecans. Primary livestock and products: cattle, milk, sheep, wool, angora goats, mohair and hogs. **BUSINESS** Total number of business establishments in the county: 102. Retail sales during the first quarter of 1984 increased 18%. In 1980, 21% of the labor force were self-employed, 16% were employed in professional or related services, 8% in manufacturing, 22% in wholesale and retail trade, 18% in agriculture, forestry, fisheries and mining, 27% were employed in other counties and there were 666 retired workers. The industries with the most employment: tourism, agribusiness and construction. The nonfarm earnings in 1981 totaled $37,441,000. The retired workers received an average monthly Social Security payment of $293. **FINANCE** On June 30, 1983, two commercial banks had total deposits of $32,960,000 and total assets of $37,096,000. On December 31, 1982 one state savings and loan association and two state branches had assets of $5,666,389. **HOUSING** Average value of homes in 1980: $32,800. In 1982 two permits were issued for new single family houses. Between 1970 and 1980 the number of housing units increased by 48%. Fifty-eight percent of all units in the county are air-conditioned, 50% are heated by gas, 30% by electricity and 1% by other fuels. **NATURAL RESOURCES** Lead, oil, gas, industrial sand and dolomite. **TOURISM** Travel expenditures of $4,759,000 in 1982 (an increase of 13% over 1981) generated 107 jobs and $891,000 in payroll. **ALCOHOLIC BEVERAGES** Packaged distilled spirits, beer, ale, malt liquor and wine are legal in parts of the county. Sale of mixed beverages is legal in all or parts of the county. **FEDERAL EXPENDITURES** The federal government had direct expenditures or obligations of $12,515,000 in the county during fiscal year 1983, including $2,109,000 by the U.S. Department of Defense. In addition, the federal government provided $49,000 in grant awards, paid $1,214,000 in salaries and wages, made direct payments to individuals of $9,802,000 including $7,613,000 in retirement and disability payments, awarded $1,104,000 in procurement contracts and spent $347,000 in other expenditures or obligations. The federal government also provided $580,000 in guaranteed loans and insurance.

COMMUNICATION

Newspapers–Weekly: Blanco County News and The Record-Courier (Johnson City). Cable TV. Telephone companies: General Telephone, Southwestern Bell and Guadalupe Valley Telephone Coop. **TRANSPORTATION** Total public road mileage: 448. In 1982 there were 5,532 registered vehicles and 133 reported traffic accidents. Intercity bus service is available. Motor freight: three carriers. Aircraft: 18 are registered in the county.

COMMUNITY SERVICES

EDUCATION Two school districts with two elementary and two high schools. The average daily attendance in 1981-82 was 898, with expenditures per pupil of $1,931 including 49 classroom teachers with an average annual salary of $15,640. Thirty-six percent of the 67 high school graduates planned to attend college. In 1982-83, 81% of the students were White, 17% Hispanic, 2% Black and 0.5% Asian. **PUBLIC LIBRARIES** Blanco Library 6,750 volumes. Johnson City Library: 14,207 volumes. **CHILD CARE** Eight day care and four twenty-four hour care licensed facilities. **HEALTH CARE** Six physicians and two dentists. Hospitals: one with a capacity of 15. Ambulance services: two volunteer services. Nursing homes: three nursing homes with a combined capacity of 102 nursing care residents. The average cost per day for private patients in 1982 was $28. **CHURCHES** 15 churches have an estimated combined membership of 3,286. The largest denominations are Southern Baptist, United Methodist and Catholic. **SOCIAL SERVICES** In fiscal year 1983 a total of $61,106 in food stamps was distributed, with an average of 141 persons receiving food stamps each month. Aid to Families with Dependent Children (AFDC) totaled $8,417 with an average of seven families receiving AFDC each month. Medical assistance benefits for the aged and disabled of $638,529 and for families and children of $20,086 brought the county benefit total to $728,138. **FIRE PROTECTION** Two volunteer fire departments. **LAW ENFORCEMENT** The County Sheriff has 17 commissioned officers. Two police departments have a combined force of six. **CRIME** Eight violent crimes (murder, forcible rape, robbery and aggravated assault) and 58 nonviolent crimes (burglary, larceny-theft and motor vehicle theft) were reported in 1982.

COUNTIES

BLANCO (continued)

JUDICIAL SYSTEM One District Court and Judge, one County Court and Judge and two Justices of the Peace. In the District Courts a total of 111 cases were pending on 1/1/82, 83 new cases were filed and 68 cases were disposed of during the year leaving 126 cases pending on 12/31/82. There were 70 criminal cases on the docket, 16 convictions, 10 persons committed to prison and 42 cases left pending. In the County Courts 100 cases were pending on 1/1/82, 116 new cases were filed and 125 cases were disposed of during the year leaving 91 cases pending on 12/31/82. There were 200 criminal cases on the docket, 29 convictions, three persons committed to jail, and 87 cases left pending. **JAILS** One jail, capacity 10. **ATTORNEYS AT LAW** 10. **UTILITIES** 42% of the residents are connected to a public or privately owned water system and 35% are connected to a public sewer system. Electricity is distributed to the county by Central Texas Electric Cooperative Inc. and is generated primarily by oil, water and coal. **TAXES** The county has five units with taxing authority: two school districts, two cities and one county.

RECREATION/ENTERTAINMENT

FEDERAL Lyndon B. Johnson National Historic Park (see Gillespie County). **NATIONAL REGISTER OF HISTORIC PLACES** Blanco: The Adrian Edwards Conn House. Johnson City: The Boyhood Home of Lyndon Baines Johnson (National Historic Site). Round Mountain: Round Mountain Stage Coach Inn and Stable. **STATE** Blanco State Recreation Area covers 105 acres with areas for camping, fishing and swimming. Pedernales Falls State Park covers 4,860 acres with camping and trailer sites as well as areas for fishing and swimming. **MUNICIPAL PARKS** Six acres in two municipal parks. These parks contain one baseball and softball field, four tennis courts and one swimming pool. **SCENIC DRIVES** Texas Hill Country Trail runs through this county along F.M. 1323, U.S. 281 and U.S. 290. R.M. 32 in southern Blanco county follows a scenic ridge called the "Devil's Backbone". **BOATING/FISHING** Lakes/reservoirs: Johnson City (58 acres). Major rivers: Pedernales and Blanco. **HUNTING** Fall and winter seasons on deer and javelina. No closed season on squirrel, bobcat and coyote. Fall, winter and spring seasons on turkey. Winter season on quail, muskrat, beaver, opossum, ring-tailed cat, badger, fox, weasel, raccoon, skunk and civet cat. In 1983 duck, coot, geese, woodcock and jacksnipe seasons occurred during the winter months with a winter season on sandhill cranes in some parts of the county. Teal duck, rail and gallinule seasons occurred in the fall. Mourning dove season occurred intermittently during the fall and winter months with a fall season on white-winged doves. **MUSEUMS** Johnson City: Lyndon B. Johnson National Historic Site. **SPECIAL EVENTS** Bluebonnet Trail, Blanco, April; Blanco Valley Jamboree, Blanco, June; Chili Cookoff and Old Fiddlers Contest, Blanco, June; Annual Hill Country Artists Show, Blanco, October; Hunter's Ball, Blanco, November.

COMMUNITIES

COUNTY SEAT Johnson City, County Courthouse, 78636; County Clerk's Office, 512/868-7357. **INCORPORATED COMMUNITIES** (1980 population and ZIP Code) Blanco (1,179) 78606 and Johnson City (872) 78636. **UNINCORPORATED COMMUNITIES** (and ZIP Code) Cypress Mill 78654, Hye 78635, Pleasant Hill 78636, Round Mountain 78663 and Sandy 78665. **FOR ADDITIONAL LOCAL INFORMATION** Blanco Chamber of Commerce, P.O. Box 626, Blanco, 78606, 512/833-5101.

BORDEN (P59)

THE LAND

South of Lubbock on U.S. Highway 180 in the Rolling Plains Region, Borden County covers 900 square miles with the elevation ranging from 2,400 to 3,000 feet. The northwest corner of the county has nearly level soils with loamy surface layers and clayey subsoils. Some have hardened to powdery lime within 20 inches of the surface. The rest of the county has level to undulating, red to brown soils with loamy surface layers and cracking clayey to loamy subsoils. The soils are neutral in the upper part and moderately alkaline below. Most of the vegetation is of the Rolling Plains area consisting of short and mid grasses with mesquite and cacti. In the northwest and southwest corners of the county the High Plains vegetation area consists of short and mid grasses, small mesquite trees, thorny shrubs and cacti. Between 21 and 30% of the land in the county is considered prime farmland. **CLIMATE** Mostly dry, with dust and thunderstorms during the spring. The average annual temperature is 62°F. Temperatures in January range from an average low of 25° to an average high of 55°F and in July range from 68° to 94°F. The average annual precipitation is 18 inches, with an average relative humidity of 72% at 6 A.M. and 42% at 6 P.M. The average annual snowfall is eight inches. The growing season averages 214 days per year, with the last freeze in late March and the first freeze in mid November. The sun shines during the year on the average 75% of the daylight hours.

THE PEOPLE

Borden is one of the most sparsely populated counties in the state and has a low birth rate. The 1982 estimated population of 1,000 indicates a slight increase in population following a steady decline since the 1930s. The majority of the residents live in rural areas. The age group with the largest decrease between 1970 and 1980 was ages five to 14. Therefore the median age rose from 30 in 1970 to 32 in 1980. The largest ancestry groups are persons of English descent (32%) and Hispanic (15%). **REGISTERED VOTERS** As of November 2, 1982 there were 593 registered voters. The 1982 general election had a 57% voter turnout, compared to a 81% turnout in the 1980 general election. In the 1982 primary 99% voted Democratic and 0.3% Republican, with 381 votes cast.

THE ECONOMY

AGRICULTURE Ranchland. In 1982, 95% of the land was in farms and ranches, with 6% of the farmland under cultivation and 6% irrigated. Borden ranked 227th in the state in highest agricultural receipts, with 67% from crops. Overgrazing, undesirable brush and weeds, water and wind erosion are current conservation problems. Primary crops: cotton, wheat and hay. Primary fruits and nuts: peaches and pecans. Primary livestock and products: cattle, sheep and wool. **BUSINESS** Total number of business establishments in the county: 5. In 1980, 32% of the labor force were self-employed, 21% were employed in professional or related services, 3% in manufacturing, 5% in wholesale and retail trade, 51% in agriculture, forestry, fisheries and mining, 25% were employed in other counties and there were 27 retired workers. The industries with the most employment: agribusiness and construction. The nonfarm earnings in 1981 totaled $6,774,000. The retired workers received an average monthly Social Security payment of $333. **HOUSING** Average value of homes in 1980: $13,100. Between 1970 and 1980 the number of housing units increased by 41%. Seventy-five percent of all units in the county are air-conditioned, 84% are heated by gas and 13% by electricity. **NATURAL RESOURCES**

Caliche, oil and gas. In 1982 a total of 7,620,746 barrels of crude oil and 6,501,534 thousand cubic feet of casinghead gas were produced. Current production of other minerals and products includes sand and gravel. **TOURISM** Travel expenditures of $1,703,000 in 1982 (an increase of 19% over 1981) generated 21 jobs and $237,000 in payroll. **ALCOHOLIC BEVERAGES** Totally dry. **FEDERAL EXPENDITURES** The federal government had direct expenditures or obligations of $2,874,000 in the county during fiscal year 1983, including $7,000 by the U.S. Department of Defense. In addition, the federal government provided $21,000 in grant awards, paid $29,000 in salaries and wages, made direct payments to individuals of $386,000 including $293,000 in retirement and disability payments and spent $2,437,000 in other expenditures or obligations. The federal government also provided $4,234,000 in direct loans and $3,573,000 in guaranteed loans and insurance.

COMMUNICATION
Newspapers–Weekly: The Borden Star (Gail). Telephone companies: Southwestern Bell, Poka-Lambro Rural Telephone Coop. and Wes-Tex Telephone Coop. **TRANSPORTATION** Total public road mileage: 399. In 1982 there were 1,226 registered vehicles and 13 reported traffic accidents including two fatalities. Motor freight: one carrier. Aircraft: one is registered in the county.

COMMUNITY SERVICES
EDUCATION One school district with one elementary and one high school. The average daily attendance in 1981-82 was 205, with expenditures per pupil of $8,500 including 20 classroom teachers with an average annual salary of $17,655. Fifty-three percent of the 19 high school graduates planned to attend college. In 1982-83, 77% of the students were White, 23% Hispanic and 0.4% Black. **HEALTH CARE** Ambulance services: one volunteer fire department service. **CHURCHES** six churches have an estimated combined membership of 513. The largest denominations are Southern Baptist, Catholic and Churches of Christ. **SOCIAL SERVICES** In fiscal year 1983 a total of $16,468 in food stamps was distributed, with an average of 35 persons receiving food stamps each month. Medical assistance benefits for the aged and disabled of $801 and for families and children of $148 brought the county benefit total to $17,417. **FIRE PROTECTION** one volunteer fire department. **LAW ENFORCEMENT** The County Sheriff has one commissioned officer. **CRIME** Two violent crimes (murder, forcible rape, robbery and aggravated assault) and 13 nonviolent crimes (burglary, larceny-theft and motor vehicle theft) were reported in 1982. **JUDICIAL SYSTEM** One District Court and Judge, one County Court and Judge and one Justice of the Peace. In the District Court a total of 16 cases were pending on 1/1/82, 29 new cases were filed and 21 cases were disposed of during the year leaving 24 cases pending on 12/31/82. There were two criminal cases on the docket and two convictions. In the County Court 13 cases were pending on 1/1/82, and 10 cases were disposed of during the year leaving three cases pending on 12/31/82. There were 13 criminal cases on the docket, and three cases left pending. **UTILITIES** 30% of the residents are connected to a public or privately owned water system and 8% are connected to a public sewer system. Electricity is distributed to the county by Texas Power and Light Co., Cap Rock Electric Coop., Inc., Lonewolf Electric Coop., Inc., Lyntegar Electric Coop., Inc. and Midwest Electric Coop., Inc. and is generated primarily by gas and oil. The typical residential electric bill is $165.24 per month for an all-electric house using 2,500 kwh. **TAXES** The county has two units with taxing authority: one school district and one county.

RECREATION/ENTERTAINMENT
SCENIC DRIVES The Texas Plains Trail runs through this

county. F.M. 669 in north central Borden County ascends the Texas High Plains which are the southernmost extension of the Great Plains of the United States. **BOATING/FISHING** Lakes/reservoirs: County Tank (53 acres), Johnson Tank (19 acres), Jones (26 acres) and Thomas J.B. (7,820 acres). Major rivers: Colorado. Primary streams: Bull and Salt. **HUNTING** Fall season on antelope. Fall and winter season on deer and mule deer. No closed season on coyotes, bobcats and squirrel. Fall, winter and spring seasons on turkey. Winter season on quail, muskrat, beaver, opossum, ring-tailed cat, badger, fox, weasel, raccoon, skunk and civet cat. In 1983 sandhill crane, duck, coot, geese, woodcock and jacksnipe seasons occurred during the winter months. Teal duck, rail and gallinule seasons occurred in the fall. Mourning dove season occurred intermittently during the fall and winter months. **MUSEUMS** Gail: Borden County Historical Museum.

COMMUNITIES
COUNTY SEAT Gail, County Courthouse, 79738; County Clerk's Office, 915/856-4312. **UNINCORPORATED COMMUNITIES** (and ZIP Code) Gail 79738 and Mesquite 79351.

BOSQUE (C2)

THE LAND
Northwest of Waco on State Highways 174, 144, 22, and 6 in the Grand Prairie Region, Bosque County covers 989 square miles which include flat topped hills in the northern and western portions of the county. The elevation ranges from 500 to 1,200 feet. Most of the county has undulating to hilly, alkaline loamy, soils over limestone. In the very northwest corner of the county the land is nearly level, light-colored and medium to slightly acidic, with loamy surface layers and mottled gray and red to yellow cracking clayey subsoils. The county is in the Cross Timbers and Prairies vegetation area consisting of live oak, post oak and tall grass savanna. Juniper and mesquite are spreading out onto the prairie. Between 31 and 40% of the land in the county is considered prime farmland. **CLIMATE** Subtropical humid with mild winters and hot summers. The average annual temperature is 66°F. Temperatures in January range from an average low of 33° to an average high of 58°F and in July range from 72° to 97°F. The average annual precipitation is 31 inches, an average relative humidity of 77% at 6 A.M. and 48% at 6 P.M. The average annual snowfall is two inches. The growing season averages 243 days per year, with the last freeze in late March and the first freeze in late November. The sun shines during the year on the average 65% of the daylight hours.

THE PEOPLE
Bosque ranks 14th among all U.S. counties with high percentages of those aged 65 and over. The 1982 estimated population of 13,600 indicates a continuation of a steady growth rate begun in the 1970s which reversed a decline in population since 1940. The greatest change occurred in rural areas which experienced a 23% population gain between 1970 and 1980. The age groups with the largest increases were ages birth to five years and 20 to 34. Therefore the high median age decreased from 48 in 1970 to 45 in 1980. The largest ancestry groups are persons of English descent (26%) and Irish descent (25%). **REGISTERED VOTERS** As of November 2, 1982 there were 7,420 registered voters (0.1% of the state total). The 1982 general election had a 58% voter turnout, compared to a 73% turnout in the 1980 general election. In the 1982 primary 97% voted Democratic and 3% Republican, with 3,535 votes cast.

BOSQUE (continued)

THE ECONOMY

AGRICULTURE A leading turkey producer. In 1982, 88% of the land was in farms and ranches, with 18% of the farmland under cultivation and 2% irrigated. Bosque ranked 107th in the state in highest agricultural receipts, with 87% from livestock and livestock products. Overgrazing, undesirable brush and weeds, water erosion and livestock waste management are current conservation problems. Primary crops: seventh in the state for oats. Hay, wheat and sorghum. Primary vegetables: potatoes, sweet potatoes and watermelons. Primary fruits and nuts: Peaches and pecans. Primary livestock and products: fourth in the state for turkeys. Cattle, milk, sheep, wool, angora goats, mohair and hogs. **BUSINESS** Total number of business establishments in the county: 221. Retail sales during the first quarter of 1984 increased 22%. Morgan had a 14% decrease while Meridian posted a 101% increase. In 1980, 17% of the labor force were self-employed, 18% were employed in professional or related services, 20% in manufacturing, 17% in wholesale and retail trade, 13% in construction, 28% were employed in other counties and there were 2,522 retired workers. The industries with the most employment: grain mills, lumber mills, agribusiness, lime production and the manufacture of men's work clothing and oilfield machinery. The nonfarm earnings in 1981 totaled $125,771,000. The retired workers received an average monthly Social Security payment of $290. **FINANCE** On June 30, 1983, five commercial banks had total deposits of $106,245,000 and total assets of $121,420,000. There is one state savings and loan association branch in the county. **HOUSING** Average value of homes in 1980: $23,700. Permits for new, privately owned housing units increased in 1982: 19 permits were issued with a total construction cost of $796,021. Of those permits, 15 were for single family houses. Between 1970 and 1980 the number of housing units increased by 32%. Seventy-four percent of all units in the county are air-conditioned, 75% are heated by gas and 18% by electricity. **NATURAL RESOURCES** Limestone, industrial sand, oil, gas, sand and gravel. Current production of other minerals and products includes lime, and crushed limestone. **TOURISM** Travel expenditures of $4,418,000 in 1982 (an increase of 16% over 1981) generated 72 jobs and $698,000 in payroll. **ALCOHOLIC BEVERAGES** Packaged distilled spirits, beer, ale, malt liquor and wine are legal in parts of the county. **FEDERAL EXPENDITURES** The federal government had direct expenditures or obligations of $34,579,000 in the county during fiscal year 1983, including $1,984,000 by the U.S. Department of Defense. In addition, the federal government provided $274,000 in grant awards, paid $1,601,000 in salaries and wages, made direct payments to individuals of $32,388,000 including $23,522,000 in retirement and disability payments, awarded $5,000 in procurement contracts and spent $311,000 in other expenditures or obligations. The federal government also provided $78,000 in direct loans and $1,988,000 in guaranteed loans and insurance.

COMMUNICATION

Newspapers–Weekly: The Clifton Record, Iredell Times, Meridian Tribune and Valley Mills Tribune. Telephone companies: Continental Telephone, Southwestern Bell, Central Telephone-Midstate and Texas-Midland Telephone. **TRANSPORTATION** Total public road mileage: 1,106. In 1982 there were 12,881 registered vehicles and 198 reported traffic accidents including four fatalities. Intercity bus service is available. Motor freight: two carriers. Rail: The Eagle provides passenger service on the Amtrak route. One main line carries over 30 million tons of freight through the county annually. Aircraft: 34 are registered in the county. Airports: Clifton Municipal Airport is a basic utility airport providing general aviation service. It serves as a base for 10 aircraft. Also serving the area are Flat Top Ranch Airport at Walnut Springs and Valley Mills Municipal Airport.

COMMUNITY SERVICES

EDUCATION Eight school districts with eight elementary, and eight high schools. The average daily attendance in 1981-82 was 2,102, with expenditures per pupil of $2,034 including 153 classroom teachers with an average annual salary of $14,923. Fifty-two percent of the 145 high school graduates planned to attend college. In 1982-83, 87% of the students were White, 10% Hispanic, 3% Black, 0.1% Asian and 0.1% American Indian. Sports championships: 1983 A Baseball, Valley Mills H.S. **PUBLIC LIBRARIES** Clifton Library. **CHILD CARE** 44 day care and three twenty-four hour care licensed facilities. **HEALTH CARE** 12 physicians and five dentists. Hospitals: two with a combined capacity of 104. Ambulance services: two hospital-based and one commercial service. Mental health: one county clinic. Nursing homes: three nursing homes with a combined capacity of 333 nursing care residents. The average cost per day for private patients in 1982 was $37.91. **CHURCHES** 53 churches have an estimated combined membership of 10,388. The largest denominations are Southern Baptist, United Methodist and American Lutheran. **SOCIAL SERVICES** In fiscal year 1983 a total of $291,180 in food stamps was distributed, with an average of 681 persons receiving food stamps each month. Aid to Families with Dependent Children (AFDC) totaled $34,347, with an average of 25 families receiving AFDC each month. Medical assistance benefits for the aged and disabled of $2,237,912 and for families and children of $30,547 brought the county benefit total to $2,593,986. **FIRE PROTECTION** 11 volunteer fire departments. **LAW ENFORCEMENT** The County Sheriff has 12 commissioned officers. Six police departments have a combined force of seven. **CRIME** 29 violent crimes (murder, forcible rape, robbery and aggravated assault) and 269 nonviolent crimes (burglary, larceny-theft and motor vehicle theft) were reported in 1982. **JUDICIAL SYSTEM** One District Court and Judge, one County Court and Judge and four Justices of the Peace. In the District Court a total of 179 cases were pending on 1/1/82, 283 new cases were filed and 262 cases were disposed of during the year leaving 200 cases pending on 12/31/82. There were 112 criminal cases on the docket, 10 convictions, one person committed to prison and 63 cases left pending. In the County Court 100 cases were pending on 1/1/82, 131 new cases were filed and 109 cases were disposed of during the year leaving 122 cases pending on 12/31/82. There were 186 criminal cases on the docket, 34 convictions, nine persons committed to jail, and 81 cases left pending. **JAILS** one jail, capacity eight. **ATTORNEYS AT LAW** 12. **UTILITIES** 76% of the residents are connected to a public or privately owned water system and 34% are connected to a public sewer system. Natural gas is distributed to the county by Lone Star Gas Co., Division of Enserch. The average annual residential bill for natural gas in 1982 for the Lone Star distribution system was $405.91, an increase of 35% over 1981. Electricity is distributed to the county by Texas New-Mexico Power Co., Erath County Electric Coop., Assn., Johnson Co. Electric Coop., Assn., and McLennan Co. Electric Coop., Inc. and is generated primarily by gas, oil and water. The typical residential electric bill is $168.05 per month for an all-electric house using 2,500 kwh. **TAXES** The county has 16 units with taxing authority: eight school districts, seven cities and one county.

RECREATION/ENTERTAINMENT

NATIONAL REGISTER OF HISTORIC PLACES Meridian: Bosque County Courthouse and Jail and First National Bank Building. Meridian vicinity: Bridges-Johnson House. Mosheim vicinity: Hog Creek Archeological District. **STATE** Meridian

State Recreation Area covers 502 acres with camping and trailer sites as well as areas offering swimming, boat ramps, fishing and nature trails. **MUNICIPAL PARKS** 64 acres in six municipal parks. These parks contain four playgrounds, one football and soccer field, three baseball and softball fields, two tennis courts and one beach. **SCENIC DRIVES** The Texas Brazos Trail and the Texas Lakes Trail run through this county. The Brazos Trail moves through a beautiful and historic section of Central Texas revealing forested landscapes filled with wildlife and wild flowers. The Lakes Trail includes some 30 blue-water recreational areas in a variety of settings throughout North-Central Texas. **BOATING/FISHING** Lakes/reservoirs: Big (50 acres), Campbell (17 acres), El Colina #2 (18 acres), El Colina (17 acres) Flag Branch (20 acres), Hog Creek Soil Conservation Service Lake 1 (74 acres), Meridian (41 acres), Mustang (20 acres), Old (20 acres), Polnac (20 acres), Reed 1 (18 acres), Reed 4 (27 acres), Roberts (63 acres), Stufflbeme (21 acres), Taylor (14 acres) and Whitney (23,750 acres). Major rivers: East Bosque and Brazos. Primary streams: Tuggle, Steele, Mesquite, Flag, Hog, Bee, Rough, Spring, Hill and Childress. **HUNTING** Fall and winter seasons on deer. No closed season on squirrel, nutria, bobcat, and coyote. Fall, winter and spring seasons on turkey. Winter season on quail, muskrat, beaver, otter, opossum, mink, ring-tailed cat, badger, fox, raccoon, skunk and civet cat. In 1983 duck, coot, geese, woodcock and jacksnipe seasons occurred during the winter months. Teal duck, rail and gallinule seasons occurred in the fall. Mourning dove season occurred intermittently during the fall and winter months. **MUSEUMS** Clifton: Bosque Memorial Museum. **SPECIAL EVENTS** Annual Bosque County Talent Show, Clifton, March; Rattlesnake Roundup, Walnut Springs, March; Central Texas Poultry Show, Clifton, March; Easter Morning Sunrise Service, Clifton/Lake Village, April; Frontier Days Celebration, Iredell, May; July 4 Celebration, Valley Mills, July; Bosque Valley Arts and Crafts Festival, Meridian, July; Central Texas Fair, Clifton, August; Volunteer Fire Dept. Fish Fry, Laguna Park, September; Bosque County Conservatory of Fine Arts, Labor Day Art Show, Clifton, September; Septemberfest, Cranfills Gap, September; Street Dance and Firemen's Barbecue, Meridian, October; Bosque County Bass Club Bass Tournament, Lake Whitney, October; Central Texas Polled Hereford Show, Clifton, November; Norse Smorgasbord, Norse/Clifton, November; Womack Brotherhood Homemade Sausage Supper, Womack/Clifton, November; Annual Lutefisk Feast, Cranfills Gap, December; Holiday Homes Tour, Clifton, December.

COMMUNITIES

COUNTY SEAT Meridian, County Courthouse, 76665; County Clerk's Office, 817/435-2201. **INCORPORATED COMMUNITIES** (1980 population and ZIP Code) Clifton (3,063) 76634, Cranfills Gap (341) 76637, Iredell (407) 76649, Meridian (1,330) 76665, Morgan (485) 76671, Valley Mills (1,236: 1,226 in Bosque Co. and 10 in McLennan Co.) 76689 and Walnut Springs (613) 76690. **UNINCORPORATED COMMUNITIES** (and ZIP Code) Brazos Point 76652, Cayote 76689, Eulogy 76652, Fairview 76689, Kimball 76652, Kopperl 76652, Laguna Park 76634, Lakeside Village 76671, Lakewood Harbor 76634, Mosheim 76689, Norse 76634, Poesville 76671, Roswell 76634, Smiths Bend 76634, Union Hill 76652 and Womack 76634. **FOR ADDITIONAL LOCAL INFORMATION** Clifton Chamber of Commerce, P.O. Box 104, Clifton, 76634, 817/675-3720.

BOWIE (E3)

THE LAND

Bordering Arkansas and Oklahoma on Interstate Highway 30 in the East Texas Timberlands Region, Bowie County covers 891 square miles of rich bottom lands and abundant forests. The elevation ranges from 200 to 450 feet. In the very northern part of the county the soil is level, with loamy surface layers and clayey, mottled to gray, or loamy subsoils. South and along the southwest border is a strip of nearly level to undulating, light-colored, medium to slightly acidic soils with sandy surface layers and mottled yellow to red and gray, clayey to loamy subsoils. The rest of the county has mostly acidic, light-colored, undulating to rolling soils with loamy surface layers and very deep, reddish mottled, clayey subsoils. The entire county has a high shrink-swell potential. The southeastern one-third of the county is in the Pineywoods vegetation area with pines and hardwoods such as oak, elm, hickory, sweet and black gum, magnolia and tupelo. The rest of the county has the tall grasses of the Post Oak Savanna vegetation area with some post oak, elm, and blackjack oak along rivers and streams. Between 41 and 50% of the land in the county is considered prime farmland. **CLIMATE** is subtropical humid, moist and mild. The average annual temperature is 51°F. Temperatures in January range from an average low of 30° to an average high of 52°F and in July range from 70° to 94°F. The average annual precipitation is 47 inches, with an average relative humidity of 84% at 6 A.M. and 57% at 6 P.M. The average annual snowfall is two inches. The growing season averages 235 days per year, with the last freeze in late March and the first freeze near November 11th. The sun shines during the year on the average 67% of the daylight hours.

THE PEOPLE

The 1982 estimated population of 76,500 indicates a continuation of a steady growth in population. The greatest change between 1970 and 1980 was a 12% increase in urban areas. The age group with the largest gain was ages 65 and over and the largest decrease occurred in ages five to 14. Therefore the median age rose from 30 in 1970 to 31 in 1980. The largest ancestry groups are persons of English descent (24%) and Black (22%) **REGISTERED VOTERS** As of November 2, 1982 there were 37,063 registered voters (0.6% of the state total). The 1982 general election had a 46% voter turnout, compared to a 68% turnout in the 1980 general election. In the 1982 primary 99% voted Democratic and 1% Republican, with 15,004 votes cast.

THE ECONOMY

AGRICULTURE Timberland. In 1982, 51% of the land was in farms and ranches, with 29% of the farmland under cultivation and 4% irrigated. Bowie ranked 127th in the state in highest agricultural receipts, with 80% from livestock and livestock products. Overgrazing, water erosion, improper woodland management and flooding are current conservation problems. Primary crops: third in the state for hay, wheat, soybeans, sorghum and rice. Primary vegetables: sweet corn, potatoes, sweet potatoes, tomatoes and watermelons. Primary fruits and nuts: peaches and pecans. Primary livestock and products: cattle, milk and hogs. **BUSINESS** Total number of business establishments in the county: 1,608. Retail sales during the first quarter of 1984 increased 13%. In 1980, 7% of the labor force were self-employed, 18% were employed in professional or related services, 26% in manufacturing, 22% in wholesale and retail trade, 7% in public administration, 20% were employed in other counties and there were 6,809 retired workers. The industries with the most employment: tourism, the processing of dairy products, agribusiness, heavy construction, soft drink canning and bottling, fruit and vegetable canning and the manufacture of wood containers, mobile homes, household furniture and ammunition. The nonfarm earnings in 1981 totaled $682,858,000. The retired workers received an average monthly Social Security payment of $282. **FINANCE** On June 30, 1983, nine commercial banks had total

COUNTIES

BOWIE (continued)

deposits of $387,048,000 and total assets of $439,563,000. On December 31, 1982 three state savings and loan associations, and four state branches had combined assets of $138,818,058. In addition there are 12 credit unions in the county. **HOUSING** Average value of homes in 1980: $30,500. Permits for new, privately owned housing units increased in 1982: 258 permits were issued with a total construction cost of $8,200,414. Of those permits, 82 were for single family houses. Housing permits in Texarkana increased from 61 in 1981 to 199 in 1982. Between 1970 and 1980 the number of housing units increased by 22%. Seventy-eight percent of all units in the county are air-conditioned, 79% are heated by gas and 17% by electricity. **NATURAL RESOURCES** Ceramic clay, oil, gas, and lignite coal. In 1982 a total of 432,538 thousand cubic feet of gas well gas, 27,451 barrels of condensate, 7,918 barrels of crude oil and 1,619 thousand cubic feet of casinghead gas were produced. Current production of other minerals and products includes sand and gravel, and recovered sulphur. Pine and hardwood production in 1981 totaled 10,292,035 cubic feet: 7,853,223 cubic feet of pine and 2,438,812 cubic feet of hardwood. **TOURISM** Travel expenditures of $28,809,000 in 1982 (an increase of 11% over 1981) generated 714 jobs and $5,847,000 in payroll. Lodging: 12 hotels, motels and tourist courts. Convention/meeting facilities: Texarkana — Four States Fair Exhibition Area, Perot Theatre, Texarkana College Auditorium Hall. **ALCOHOLIC BEVERAGES** Totally dry. **MILITARY INSTALLATIONS** Lone Star Army Ammunition Plant, Texarkana, 1,386 personnel, 16,546 acres, ammunition production; Red River Army Depot, Texarkana, 6,606 personnel, 19,081 acres, logistics depot. **FEDERAL EXPENDITURES** The federal government had direct expenditures or obligations of $441,704,000 in the county during fiscal year 1983, including $269,994,000 by the U.S. Department of Defense. In addition, the federal government provided $25,255,000 in grant awards, paid $145,188,000 in salaries and wages, made direct payments to individuals of $133,966,000 including $107,147,000 in retirement and disability payments, awarded $134,953,000 in procurement contracts and spent $2,342,000 in other expenditures or obligations. The federal government also provided $1,935,000 in direct loans and $19,325,000 in guaranteed loans and insurance.

COMMUNICATION
Newspapers–Daily: Texarkana Gazette, ave. morn. circ. 30,690. Weekly: The De Kalb News, Hooks Reporter, The Bowie County News (New Boston) and the News-Digest/TV Today (Texarkana). Radio: KNBO-AM (New Boston), KADO-AM, KCMC-AM, KOSY-AM, KTFS-AM, KADO-FM, KOSY-FM and KTAL-FM (Texarkana). Television: KTAL-Ch. 6 (Texarkana). Telephone companies: General Telephone, Southwestern Bell, Avery Telephone, Century Telephone and Lakeside Telephone. **TRANSPORTATION** Total public road mileage: 1,674. In 1982 there were 68,125 registered vehicles and 1,878 reported traffic accidents including 20 fatalities. Taxi cabs: two companies in Texarkana. Intercity bus service is available. Motor freight: 29 local and intrastate carriers. Rail: The Eagle provides passenger service on the Amtrak route. Four main and one branch line carry freight through the county. One of the main lines carries over 30 million tons of freight annually, two carry 20 to 30 and the other one carries 10 to 20. The branch line carries less than one million tons of freight annually. Aircraft: 138 are registered in the county. Airports: Texarkana Municipal Airport provides commuter and general aviation services

COMMUNITY SERVICES
EDUCATION 13 school districts with 23 elementary, eight middle, eight high schools and one special education. The average

daily attendance in 1981-82 was 14,789, with expenditures per pupil of $1,905 including 894 classroom teachers with an average annual salary of $15,911. Fifty-five percent of the 1,003 high school graduates planned to attend college. In 1982-83, 70% of the students were White, 0.4% Hispanic, 30% Black and 0.3% Asian. Sports championships: 1984 AAA Boys' Basketball, New Boston H.S. Private schools: 130 students enrolled in one elementary school. Texarkana Community College is located in Texarkana. Established in 1927 it is a vocational and two year academic college under local control. Enrollment in 1982 was 3,223 with in state undergraduate tuition and fees of $270 per semester. East Texas State University at Texarkana was established in 1971 and is under state control. Enrollment in 1982 was 1,248 with in state undergraduate tuition and fees of $256 per semester. The highest degree offered is master (no lower division). Vocational education: Wadley Hospital School of X-Ray Technology (Texarkana). **PUBLIC LIBRARIES** New Boston Library and Texarkana Library. **CHILD CARE** 83 day care and 22 twenty-four hour care licensed facilities. **HEALTH CARE** 160 physicians and 38 dentists. Hospitals: three with a combined capacity of 531. Clinics: one public health clinic. Ambulance services: two commercial, one city, one fire department, one police department, and one volunteer service. Mental health: one clinic. Nursing homes: six nursing homes with a combined capacity of 639 nursing care residents. The average cost per day for private patients in 1982 was $29.34. **CHURCHES** 145 churches have an estimated combined membership of 48,152. The largest denominations are Southern Baptist, United Methodist and Churches of Christ. **SOCIAL SERVICES** In fiscal year 1983 a total of $4,796,546 in food stamps was distributed, with an average of 9,718 persons receiving food stamps each month. Aid to Families with Dependent Children (AFDC) totaled $1,424,687 with an average of 924 families receiving AFDC each month. Medical assistance benefits for the aged and disabled of $5,998,479 and for families and children of $1,866,319 brought the county benefit total to $14,086,030. **FIRE PROTECTION** One paid, one partly paid and nine volunteer fire departments. **LAW ENFORCEMENT** The County Sheriff has 53 commissioned officers. seven police departments have a combined force of 104. **CRIME** 350 violent crimes (murder, forcible rape, robbery and aggravated assault) and 3,539 nonviolent crimes (burglary, larceny-theft and motor vehicle theft) were reported in 1982. **JUDICIAL SYSTEM** Three District Courts and Judges, one County Court and Judge and seven Justices of the Peace. In the District Courts a total of 1,866 cases were pending on 1/1/82, 3,281 new cases were filed and 2,549 cases were disposed of during the year leaving 2,598 cases pending on 12/31/82. There were 1,657 criminal cases on the docket, 760 convictions, 63 persons committed to prison and 41 committed to jail and 590 cases left pending. In the County Court 28 cases were pending on 1/1/82, and 28 cases were left pending on 12/31/82. **JAILS** One jail, capacity 54 with new construction at Texarkana, capacity 130. **ATTORNEYS AT LAW** 118. **UTILITIES** 77% of the residents are connected to a public or privately owned water system and 67% are connected to a public sewer system. Natural gas is distributed to the county by Arkla, Inc. The average annual residential bill for natural gas in 1982 for the Arkla distribution system was $316.69, an increase of 23% over 1981. Electricity is distributed to the county by Bowie-Cass Electric Coop., Inc., and Southwestern Electric Service and is generated primarily by gas, oil and water. The typical residential electric bill is $196.85 per month for an all-electric house using 2,500 kwh. **TAXES** The county has 23 units with taxing authority: 13 school districts, eight cities, one county, and one college district.

RECREATION/ENTERTAINMENT
NATIONAL REGISTER OF HISTORIC PLACES Boston:

Bowie County Courthouse and Jail. Texarkana: Draughn-Moore House, Offenhauser Building, Saenger Theatre, Hotel McCartney, Rialto Building and Whitaker House. Texarkana vicinity: Roseburough Lake Site. **MUNICIPAL PARKS** 341 acres in 16 municipal parks. These parks contain one mile of hiking trails, 13 playgrounds, 16 baseball and softball fields, four tennis courts, two multi-use courts, two swimming pools and shore fishing facilities. **BOATING/FISHING** Lakes/reservoirs: Blackman #1 (45 acres), Blackman #2 (55 acres), Bringle (263 acres), Caney Creek (67 acres), Elliott Creek (121 acres), Kennedy (44 acres) and Wright Patman (20,300 acres). Major rivers: Sulphur and Red. Primary streams: Daniels, Holly, Clear, Caney, Elliott and Crutchers. **HUNTING** Fall and winter seasons on deer. Summer, fall and winter seasons on squirrel. Winter season on quail, muskrat, beaver, otter, opossum, mink, ring-tailed cat, badger, fox, raccoon, skunk and civet cat. No closed season on coyotes, nutria and bobcats. In 1983 duck, coot, geese, woodcock and jacksnipe seasons occurred during the winter months. Teal duck, rail and gallinule seasons occurred in the fall. Mourning dove season occurred intermittently during the fall and winter months. **MUSEUMS** Texarkana: Texarkana Historical Society and Museum. **ZOO** Texarkana: Spring Lake Park Zoo. **COLLEGIATE FINE ARTS** Texarkana: Cultural events offered by Texarkana College. **SPECIAL EVENTS** Miss Texarkana Pageant, Texarkana, April; Senior Citizens' Health Fair, Texarkana, May; Bluegrass Festival, Texarkana, May; Bass Tourney, Texarkana, May; Crystal Springs Splash Day, Maud, May; Pioneer Days, New Boston, June; Quadrangle Festival, Texarkana, September; Octoberfest, De Kalb, October; Four States Fair and Rodeo, Texarkana, October/November.

COMMUNITIES

COUNTY SEAT Boston, County Courthouse, 75557; County Clerk's Office, 214/628-2571. **INCORPORATED COMMUNITIES** (1980 population and ZIP Code) De Kalb (2,217) 75559, Hooks (2,507) 75561, Leary (253) 75501, Maud (1,059) 75567, Nash (2,022) 75569, New Boston (4,628) 75570, Texarkana (31,271) 75501 and Wake Village (3,865) 75501. **UNINCORPORATED COMMUNITIES** (and ZIP Code) Almont 75559, Barkman 75561, Bassett 75574, Beaver Dam 75559, Bethlehem 75559, Boston 75570, Burns 75561, Carbondale 75567, College Hill 75559 Corley 75567, Dalby Springs 75559, Eylau 75501, Garland 75559, Hodgson 75559, Macedonia 75501, Malta 75570, Oak Grove 75554, Oak Ridge 75559, Old Boston 75570, Old Union (POER) 75574, Redbank 75561, Redlick 75501, Red Springs 75501, Redwater 75573, Siloam 75559, Simms 75574, Smith Hill 75561, South Texarkana 75501, Spring Hill 75559, Victory City 75561, Wamba 75501 Wards Creek (Needmore) 75574 and Whaley 75570. **FOR ADDITIONAL LOCAL INFORMATION** New Boston Chamber of Commerce, 109 N. Ellis, New Boston, 75570, 214/628-2581 and Texarkana Chamber of Commerce, P.O. Box 1468, Texarkana 75504, 214/792-7191.

BRAZORIA (G18)

THE LAND

On the Gulf Coast south of Houston on State Highways 35, 36, 288 and 332 in the Coastal Prairie Region, Brazoria County covers 1,407 square miles. The elevation ranges from sea level to 60 feet. The eastern half of the county has level soils. They are somewhat poorly to moderately-well drained, cracking, clayey soils with loamy surface layers and clayey subsoils. They have very slow permeability, high sodium, a high shrink-swell and corrosion potential. The western half has a high shrink-swell and corrosion potential and occasional flooding. Along the coast is a strip of saline, clayey and loamy soils of the marshes and the sandy soils of beaches. The county is located in the Gulf Prairies and Marshes vegetation area consisting of tall grasses, live oaks and hardwood trees along rivers and streams with tall grasses. Along the coast are cordgrasses other bunchgrasses and sedges. Between 61 and 70% of the land in the county is considered prime farmland. **CLIMATE** Subtropical humid, moist and mild. There is a risk of a tropical storm or hurricane moving across the area during months of June through October. The average annual temperature is 69°F. Temperatures in January range from an average low of 43° to an average high of 62°F and in July range from 74° to 92°F. The average annual precipitation is 52 inches, with an average relative humidity of 90% at 6 A.M. and 70% at 6 P.M. There is no snowfall. The growing season averages 268 days per year, with the last freeze in early March and the first freeze in late November. The sun shines during the year on the average 69% of the daylight hours.

THE PEOPLE

The 1982 estimated population of 178,400 indicates a continuation of the strong growth rate since the 1940s. The 57% population increase between 1970 and 1980 was one of the highest in the state. Although the population is primarily urban, rural areas experienced a gain of 62%. The age groups with the largest increases were ages 20 to 39 and 60 and over. Consequently the county's median age increased from 26 in 1970 to 27 in 1980. The largest ancestry groups are persons of English descent (23%), Irish descent (20%) and Hispanic (13%). **REGISTERED VOTERS** As of November 2, 1982 there were 67,487 registered voters (1% of the state total). The 1982 general election had a 52% voter turnout, compared to a 68% turnout in the 1980 general election. In the 1982 primary 74% voted Democratic and 26% Republican, with 15,785 votes cast.

THE ECONOMY

AGRICULTURE A leading rice producer. In 1982, 72% of the land was in farms and ranches, with 18% of the farmland under cultivation and 5%irrigated. Brazoria ranked 54th in the state in highest agricultural receipts with 58% from crops. Overgrazing, undesirable weeds and brush, drainage, and difficulties in grass establishment are current conservation problems. Primary crops: fourth in the state for rice. Soybeans, sorghum, hay, cotton and cowpeas. Primary vegetables: watermelons, potatoes and sweet potatoes. Primary fruits and nuts: oranges, peaches and pecans. Primary livestock and products: cattle, milk and hogs. **BUSINESS** Total number of business establishments in the county: 2,785. Retail sales during the first quarter of 1984 increased 21% with a gain of 57% in Brazoria. In 1980, 5% of the labor force were self-employed, 14% were employed in professional or related services, 27% in manufacturing, 18% in wholesale and retail trade, 16% in construction, 23% were employed in other counties and there were 6,849 retired workers. The industries with the most employment: agribusiness, heavy and general construction, oil and gas extraction, petroleum refining, lumber mills, ship building and repairing, the mining of vanadium ore, the refining of primary nonferrous metals and the manufacturing of industrial organic chemicals, plastics and resins, x-ray apparatus and opthalmic goods. The nonfarm earnings in 1981 totaled $1,791,337,000. The retired workers received an average monthly Social Security payment of $356. **FINANCE** On June 30, 1983, 23 commercial banks had total deposits of $789,766,000 and total assets of $899,820,000. On December 31, 1982 three state savings and loan associations, 17 state branches and four federal association branches had combined assets of $835,186,748. In addition there are eight credit unions in the county. **HOUSING** Average value of homes in 1980: $49,800. Permits for new, privately owned housing units decreased in 1982: 1,474 permits were issued with a total construction cost of

COUNTIES

BRAZORIA (continued)

$64,532,648. Of those permits, 1,091 were for single family houses. Housing permits increased in Alvin from 110 in 1981 to 194 in 1982 with 160 of the permits issued for apartments and condominiums, and in Pearland from 70 to 296. Between 1970 and 1980 the number of housing units increased by 74%. Ninety percent of all units in the county are air-conditioned, 67% are heated by gas and 31% by electricity. **NATURAL RESOURCES** Salt domes, industrial sand, oil and gas. In 1982 a total of 105,101,882 thousand cubic feet of gas well gas, 605,373 barrels of condensate, 8,925,715 barrels of crude oil and 11,155,309 thousand cubic feet of casinghead gas were produced. Current production of other minerals and products includes brine, lime, crushed limestone, magnesium, molybdenum, salt, construction sand, sand and gravel, recovered sulphur, and vanadium. **TOURISM** Travel expenditures of $66,699,000 in 1982 (an increase of 10% over 1981) generated 1,371 jobs and $13,468,000 in payroll. Lodging: 16 hotels, motels and tourist courts. **ALCOHOLIC BEVERAGES** Packaged distilled spirits, beer, ale, malt liquor and wine are legal in parts of the county. Sale of mixed beverages is legal in all or parts of the county. **FEDERAL EXPENDITURES** The federal government had direct expenditures or obligations of $248,169,000 in the county during fiscal year 1983, including $110,867,000 by the U.S. Department of Defense. In addition, the federal government provided $12,759,000 in grant awards, paid $9,720,000 in salaries and wages, made direct payments to individuals of $114,961,000 including $95,320,000 in retirement and disability payments, awarded $105,180,000 in procurement contracts and spent $5,550,000 in other expenditures or obligations. The federal government also provided $6,439,000 in direct loans and $1,236,464,000 in guaranteed loans and insurance.

COMMUNICATION

Newspapers–Daily: The Alvin Sun, ave. eve. circ. 8,676, The Angleton Times, ave. morn. circ. 4,227 and The Brazosport Facts (Clute) ave. eve. circ. 19,580. Weekly: The Brazorian News (Lake Jackson) and The Brazoria County News (West Columbia). Radio: KBRZ-AM (Freeport). Cable TV. Telephone companies: Continental Telephone, General Telephone, Southwestern Bell, Brazoria Telephone, Central Telephone-Midstate, and Sweeny-Old Ocean Telephone. **TRANSPORTATION** Total public road mileage: 2,097. In 1982 there were 159,960 registered vehicles and 4,172 reported traffic accidents including 63 fatalities. Taxi cabs: one company in Freeport. Intercity bus service is available. Motor freight: 37 local and intrastate carriers. Rail: six main and one branch line carry freight through the county. Two of the main lines carry annually over 30 million tons of freight each; one carries 20 to 30, two carry 10 to 20 each and one carries five to 10 million tons. The branch line carries less than one million tons of freight annually. Aircraft: 318 are registered in the county. Airports: Angleton-Lake Jackson Airport is a general transportation airport with commuter service. It serves as a base for 50 aircraft. Alvin Airpark at Alvin provides general aviation service and serves as a base for 30 aircraft. Also serving the area are Cameron Airport at Angleton, Bailes Airport at Angleton, Joseph Ross Scherdin at Richwood, Wolfe Airpark at Manvel, Skyway Manor at Pearland and Pearland Airport. Heliports in the area are Welling Heliport in Alvin, Pearland Heliport and The Deport Heliport at Pearland. Waterborne commerce: Chocolate Bayou freight traffic in 1981 totaled 4,301,199 short tons of domestic shipments, The San Bernard River freight traffic totaled 660,291 short tons of domestic freight and Freeport Harbor freight traffic totaled 23,357,106 short tons: 12,894,323 in foreign imports, 1,199,855 in foreign exports, and 9,262,928 in domestic shipments.

COMMUNITY SERVICES

EDUCATION Eight school districts with 36 elementary, 14 middle, eight high schools and one special education. The average daily attendance in 1981-82 was 33,156, with expenditures per pupil of $3,137 including 2,034 classroom teachers with an average annual salary of $18,916. Fifty percent of the 2,049 high school graduates planned to attend college. In 1982-83, 75% of the students were White, 17% Hispanic, 7% Black, 0.5% Asian and 0.1% American Indian. Private schools: 217 students enrolled in two elementary schools. Brazosport College is located in Lake Jackson. Established in 1948 it is a vocational and two year academic college under local control. Enrollment in 1982 was 3,660 with in state undergraduate tuition and fees of $166 per semester. Alvin Community College is located in Alvin. Established in 1948 it is a vocational and two year academic college under local control. Enrollment in 1982 was 3,024 with in state undergraduate tuition and fees of $160 per semester. Vocational education: Brazosport Beauty College (Freeport) and Attitudes (Lake Jackson). **PUBLIC LIBRARIES** Brazoria County Library System (Angleton): 219,920 volumes and 10 branches. **CHILD CARE** 272 day care and 33 twenty-four hour care licensed facilities. **HEALTH CARE** 108 physicians and 64 dentists. Hospitals: four with a combined capacity of 325. Clinics: one public health clinic. Ambulance services: eleven commercial, five volunteer services, three city, one air, and one fire department service. Mental health: three clinics and one development center with a capacity of 120. Nursing homes: 10 nursing homes with a combined capacity of 1,001 nursing care and 20 personal care residents. The average cost per day for private patients in 1982 was $29.08. **CHURCHES** 161 churches have an estimated combined membership of 86,358. The largest denominations are Southern Baptist, Catholic and United Methodist. **SOCIAL SERVICES** In fiscal year 1983 a total of $3,386,134 in food stamps was distributed, with an average of 6,602 persons receiving food stamps each month. Aid to Families with Dependent Children (AFDC) totaled $529,085 with an average of 344 families receiving AFDC each month. Medical assistance benefits for the aged and disabled of $6,747,559 and for families and children of $690,060 brought the county benefit total to $11,352,837. **FIRE PROTECTION** One partly paid and 32 volunteer fire departments. **LAW ENFORCEMENT** The County Sheriff has 145 commissioned officers. Twenty police departments have a combined force of 308. Two colleges have campus police departments with a combined force of 16. **CRIME** 472 violent crimes (murder, forcible rape, robbery and aggravated assault) and 6,138 nonviolent crimes (burglary, larceny-theft and motor vehicle theft) were reported in 1982. **JUDICIAL SYSTEM** Four District Courts and Judges, three County Courts and Judges and eight Justices of the Peace. In the District Courts a total of 4,525 cases were pending on 1/1/82, 4,867 new cases were filed and 4,899 cases were disposed of during the year leaving 4,493 cases pending on 12/31/82. There were 1,126 criminal cases on the docket, 443 convictions, 155 persons committed to prison and 41 committed to jail and 511 cases left pending. In the County Courts 1,297 cases were pending on 1/1/82, 4,148 new cases were filed and 3,937 cases were disposed of during the year leaving 1,508 cases pending on 12/31/82. There were 3,954 criminal cases on the docket, 1,882 convictions, 340 persons committed to jail, and 852 cases left pending. **JAILS** One jail, capacity 144 with new jail under construction, capacity 240. Lost certification in 1983 due to overcrowding. **PRISONS** Clemens, on 8,116 acres south of Brazoria, had an inmate population 1,018 in 1983. It has agricultural operations. Darrington, on 6,770 acres north of Rosharon, had 2,130 inmates, agricultural operations and a tire recapping plant. Ramsey I located four miles west of FM 521 on FM 655 shares 16,844 acres with Ramsey II and III. In 1983 it had 1,572 inmates, agricultural operations and a furniture refinishing plant. Ramsey II located four miles west of FM 521 on FM 655, had 1,190 inmates and agricultural operations. Ramsey III located four miles west of FM 521 on FM 655 had 960 inmates and agricultural operations. Retrieve, on 6,754 acres south of Angleton, had 938 inmates and agricultural operations. **ATTORNEYS AT LAW** 181. **UTILITIES** 71% of the residents are connected to a public or privately owned water system and 66% are connected to a public sewer system. Natural gas is distributed to the county by Entex, Inc. The average annual residential bill for natural gas in 1982 for the Entex distribution system was $390.31, an increase of 26% over 1981. Electricity is distributed to the county by Jackson Electric Coop., Inc., Texas New-Mexico Power Co. and Houston Lighting and Power Co. and is generated primarily by gas and oil. The typical residential electric bill is $201.39 per month for an all-electric house using 2,500 kwh. **TAXES** The county has 48 units with taxing authority: eight school districts, 18 cities, one county, two college districts and 19 special districts.

RECREATION/ENTERTAINMENT

NATIONAL REGISTER OF HISTORIC PLACES Angleton: Old Brazoria County Courthouse. Brazoria vicinity: Ellerslie Plantation. East Columbia: Ammon Underwood House. Jones Creek: Durazno Plantation and McCroskey Log Cabin. West Columbia vicinity: Varner-Hogg Plantation. **STATE** Bryan Beach State Recreation Area covers 878 acres with an undeveloped Gulf beach. Varner-Hogg Plantation State Historical Park covers 66 acres with a museum, a historic structure and guided tours. The main feature is a Greek Revival plantation home built in the 1830s and later owned by James Stephen Hogg, first native-born governor of Texas. **COUNTY/MUNICIPAL PARKS** 1,706 acres in seven county and 60 municipal parks. These parks contain seven miles of hiking trails, 37 playgrounds, one golf course, 10 football and soccer fields, 28 baseball and softball fields, 19 tennis courts, one multi-use court, six swimming pools, three beaches, five boat ramps and shore fishing facilities. **SCENIC DRIVES** The Texas Independence Trail runs through the county. This trail not only surveys the historic sites of southeastern Texas but also includes many modern visitor attractions such as the Johnson Space Center. **BOATING/FISHING** Lakes/reservoirs: Amoco (291 acres), Angleton Club (625 acres), Archer (443 acres), Baker (300 acres), Bar X Ranch (275 acres), Beal (258 acres), Bieri 3 (111 acres), Bieri 4 (208 acres), Bintliff (600 acres), Black Ranch (285 acres), Blackwell (600 acres), Brazoria City (438 acres), Brazoria (1,865 acres), Brock (105 acres), Brown (83 acres), Buffalo Camp Bayou (167 acres), Clemens 1 (149 acres), Clemens 2 (119 acres), Coale (78 acres), Dacus (111 acres), Dingle 1 (345 acres), Dingle 2 (125 acres) Division (218 acres), Duck (893 acres), Evans (138 acres), Fontaine (833 acres), Garrett (277 acres), Griffith (205 acres), Harris (1,663 acres), Hudeck (156 acres), Lazy C-Z (109 acres), Lemon (125 acres), Lostak (258 acres), Mann (1,250 acres), Markle (179 acres), McCormack 1 (383 acres), McCormack 2 (138 acres) McCormack 3 (230 acres), McCormack 4 (543 acres), McCullough (116 acres), Monsanto (481 acres), Mowery (98 acres), Mustang East (502 acres), Mustang West (518 acres), North (71 acres), San Bernard 1 (278 acres), San Bernard 2 (471 acres), San Bernard 3 (500 acres), Tenneco 1 (335 acres), Tenneco 2 (275 acres), Turner (367 acres), Williams 1 (128 acres) and Williams 2 (100 acres). Major rivers: San Bernard and Brazos. Primary streams: Chocolate Bayou, Bastrop Bayou, South Texas Canal, Mill Bayou, Flores Bayou, Mound, San Bernard, Big Slough, Buffalo Camp Bayou, Austin Bayou, Middle Bayou, Oyster, Briscoe Canal, Mustang Bayou, Clear and Cedar Lake. **SALTWATER FISHING** for speckled trout, redfish and flounders is usually good around Freeport which is best known for its nearness to excellent offshore fishing. Bay, jetty and surf-fishing is excellent throughout the county especially around Follets Island. Shrimp, oysters and crabs may be taken but, like other saltwater fish, under specific regulations. **WILDLIFE REFUGES** Brazoria National Wildlife Refuge covers 9,978 acres. San Bernard National Wildlife Refuge spans 19,382 acres. **HUNTING** Fall and winter seasons on deer. Fall, winter and spring seasons on squirrel. Winter season on quail, muskrat, beaver, otter, opossum, mink, ring-tailed cat, badger, fox, raccoon, skunk and civet cat. No closed season on coyote, nutria and bobcat. In 1983 sandhill crane, duck, coot, geese, woodcock and jacksnipe seasons occurred during the winter months. Teal duck, rail and gallinule seasons occurred in the fall. Mourning dove season occurred intermittently during the fall and winter months. **MUSEUMS** Clute: Brazosport Museum of Natural Science and Brazosport Art Gallery and Museum. West Columbia: Replica of first capitol of Texas Republic. **THEATERS** Clute: Brazosport Little Theater and Music Theater. **AQUARIUM** Clute: Brazosport Museum of Natural Science **COLLEGIATE FINE ARTS** Cultural events offered by Alvin Junior College in Alvin and Brazosport College in Lake Jackson. **SPECIAL EVENTS** San Jacinto Festival, West Columbia, April; Spring Fling, Clute, April; Mexican Fiesta, Pearland, May; Youth Rodeo, Alvin, May; Frontier Days, Alvin, May; Fishing Fiesta, Freeport, July; Fireworks Display, Alvin, July 4; Great Texas Mosquito Festival and Parade, Clute, July; Founders Day Celebration, Pearland, September; County Fair and Rodeo, Angleton, October; Bluegrass and Gospel Fall Festival, Brazoria, October.

COMMUNITIES

COUNTY SEAT Angleton, County Courthouse, 77515; County Clerk's Office, 409/849-5711. **INCORPORATED COMMUNITIES** (1980 population and ZIP Code) Alvin (16,515) 77511, Angleton (13,929) 77515, Bailey's Prairie (353) 77515, Bonney (94) 77515, Brazoria (3,025) 77422, Brookside Village (1,453) 77581, Clute (9,577) 77531, Danbury (1,357) 77534, Freeport (13,444) 77541, Hillcrest (771) 77511, Holiday Lakes (787, est. incorp. inactive) 77515, Iowa Colony (585) 77583, Jones Creek (2,634) 77541, Lake Jackson (19,102) 77566, Liverpool (602) 77577, Manvel (3,549) 77578, Oyster Creek (1,473) 77541, Pearland (13,248: 12,461 in Brazoria Co. and 787 in Harris Co.) 77581, Quintana (30) 77541, Richwood (2,591) 77531, Surfside Beach (577) 77541, Sweeny (3,538) 77480 and West Columbia (4,109) 77486. **UNINCORPORATED COMMUNITIES** (and ZIP Code) Anchor 77515, Bastrop Bayou 77515, Bastrop Beach 77515, Chocolate Bayou 77511, Churchill Bridge 77422, Damon 77430, Danciger 77431, East Columbia 77486, Four Corners 77422, Hinkles Ferry 77422, Lake Alaska 77515, Lake Jackson Farms 77566, Lochridge 77583, McBeth 77515, Old Brazoria 77422, Old Ocean 77463, Otey 77583, Perry Landing 77541, Rosharon 77583, Sandy Point 77583, Stratton Ridge 77541, The Heights 77511 and Wild Peach Village 77422. **FOR ADDITIONAL LOCAL INFORMATION** Alvin-Manvel Area Chamber of Commerce, 316 W. Willis, P.O. Box 191, Alvin 77512, 409/585-3359 or 331-3944, Greater Angleton Co. Chamber of Commerce, 445 E. Mulberry, P.O. Box 47 Angleton 77515, 409/849-6443, Brazosport Chamber of Commerce, P.O. Box 2470, Freeport 77541, 409/265-2505, Pearland Area Chamber of Commerce, 3501 Liberty Dr., Pearland 77581, 409/485-3634, Sweeny Chamber of Commerce, 112 N. Main, P.O. Box 338, Sweeny, 77480, 409/548-3249, West Columbia Chamber of Commerce, P.O. Box 837, West Columbia, 77486, 409/345-3921.

BRAZOS (C20)

THE LAND

Northwest of Houston on U.S. Highway 190 in the Claypan area,

COUNTIES

BRAZOS (continued)

Brazos county covers 588 square miles of rolling prairie and woodland. The elevation ranges from 200 to 350 feet. The soils have acidic, loamy, dark surface layers and mottled, gray and red to yellow, cracking, clayey subsoils. Along the northern border the soils are cracking and clayey with some loamy surface layers. In the southwest along the Brazos River the level soils are somewhat poorly drained, cracking, clayey soils with some loamy surface layers. The northern third of the county is in the Blackland Prairie vegetation area with a variety of elms, oaks, pecans and mesquite trees along streams. Originally grassland with tall bunchgrasses, most of the land is now under cultivation. The remainder of the county is in the Post Oak Savannah vegetation area with tall bunchgrasses, blackjack and post oak trees plus walnuts and pecans along streams. Between 11 and 20% of the land in the county is considered prime farmland. **CLIMATE** Subtropical humid, moist and mild. The average annual temperature is 68°F. Temperatures in January range from an average low of 39° to an average high of 60°F and in July range from 73° to 95°F. The average annual precipitation is 39 inches, with an average relative humidity of 87% at 6 A.M. and 56% at 6 P.M. There is no significant snowfall. The growing season averages 268 days per year, with the last freeze in early March and the first freeze in late November. The sun shines during the year on the average 65% of the daylight hours.

THE PEOPLE

Brazos county ranks as one of the most densely populated in the state. The 1982 estimated population of 112,100 indicates a continuation of the strong growth rate since the 1930s. The 61% increase in population from 1970 to 1980 was one of the highest in the state. Urban areas experienced a population gain of 62% between 1970 and 1980. The age groups with the largest gains were ages 20 to 39 and 65 and over. However the county's population remained young with a median age of 23. The largest ancestry groups are persons of English descent (25%) and German descent (22%). **REGISTERED VOTERS** As of November 2, 1982 there were 34,681 registered voters (0.5% of the state total). The 1982 general election had a 56% voter turnout, compared to a 85% turnout in the 1980 general election. In the 1982 primary 95% voted Democratic and 5% Republican, with 11,417 votes cast.

THE ECONOMY

AGRICULTURE Beef and dairy products. In 1982, 67% of the land was in farms and ranches, with 18% of the farmland under cultivation and 20% irrigated. Brazos ranked 118th in the state in highest agricultural receipts, with 80% from livestock and livestock products. Water erosion and flooding are the current conservation problems. Primary crops: hay, cotton, sorghum, oats and wheat. Primary vegetables: potatoes, sweet potatoes and watermelons. Primary fruits and nuts: peaches and pecans. Primary livestock and products: cattle, milk and hogs. **BUSINESS** Total number of business establishments in the county: 1,859. Retail sales during the first quarter of 1984 increased 9%. In 1980, 6% of the labor force were self-employed, 38% were employed in professional or related services, 8% in manufacturing, 20% in wholesale and retail trade, 8% in construction, 7% were employed in other counties and there were 4,274 retired workers. The industries with the most employment: agribusiness, oil and gas extraction, construction and the manufacture of household furniture, business forms, rubber products, dairy products, metal doors, farm machinery, electronic computing equipment, ready-mixed concrete and radio and TV communication equipment. The nonfarm earnings in 1981 totaled $785,803,000. The retired workers received an average monthly Social Security payment of $312. **FINANCE** On

June 30, 1983, nine commercial banks had total deposits of $611,232,000 and total assets of $670,456,000. On December 31, 1982 three state savings and loan associations, one federal association and seven state branches had combined assets of $560,288,312. In addition there are two credit unions in the county. **HOUSING** Average value of homes in 1980: $47,000. Permits for new, privately owned housing units increased in 1982: 3,389 permits were issued with a total construction cost of $101,028,686. Of those permits, 896 were for single family houses. Between 1970 and 1980 the number of housing units increased by 92%. Eighty-six percent of all units in the county are air-conditioned, 65% are heated by gas and 34% by electricity. **NATURAL RESOURCES** Clay, salt domes, sand and gravel, oil, gas, and lignite coal. In 1982 a total of 1,535,138 thousand cubic feet of gas well gas, 75,207 barrels of condensate, 6,730,858 barrels of crude oil and 7,970,135 thousand cubic feet of casinghead gas were produced. Current production of other minerals and products includes sand and gravel. **TOURISM** Travel expenditures of $58,109,000 in 1982 (an increase of 11% over 1981) generated 1,470 jobs and $12,085,000 in payroll. Lodging: 13 hotels, motels and tourist courts. Convention/meeting facilities: Bryan-Civic Auditorium; College Station-Community center; the cities of Bryan and College Station have two hotels with facilities for large gatherings. **ALCOHOLIC BEVERAGES** Packaged distilled spirits, beer, ale, malt liquor and wine are legal. Sale of mixed beverages is legal in all or parts of the county. **FEDERAL EXPENDITURES** The federal government had direct expenditures or obligations of $164,516,000 in the county during fiscal year 1983, including $19,822,000 by the U.S. Department of Defense. In addition, the federal government provided $43,408,000 in grant awards, paid $22,079,000 in salaries and wages, made direct payments to individuals of $77,929,000 including $59,176,000 in retirement and disability payments, awarded $19,517,000 in procurement contracts and spent $1,583,000 in other expenditures or obligations. The federal government also provided $4,565,000 in direct loans and $45,627,000 in guaranteed loans and insurance.

COMMUNICATION

Newspapers–Daily: Bryan-College Station Eagle, ave. morn. circ. 21,751. Radio: KAGC-AM, KTAM-AM, WTAW-AM, KORA-FM and WTAW-FM Stereo (Bryan) and KAMU-FM (College Station). Television: KBTX-Ch. 3 (Bryan) and KAMU-Ch. 15 PBS (College Station). Cable TV. Telephone companies: Continental Telephone, General Telephone and United Telephone. **TRANSPORTATION** Total public road mileage: 1,219. In 1982 there were 74,789 registered vehicles and 3,496 reported traffic accidents including 31 fatalities. Taxi cabs: three companies in Bryan-College Station. Intercity bus service is available. Motor freight: 26 local and intrastate carriers. Rail: Five main lines carry freight through the county. One of the lines carries over 30 million tons of freight annually, three carry 10 to 20 each and the other one carries five to 10. Aircraft: 137 are registered in the county. Airports: Coulter Field in Bryan is a general utility airport. It serves as a base for 30 aircraft. Easterwood Field at College Station is a general transportation airport providing commuter service. It serves as a base for 60 aircraft. In emergency, St. Joseph Hospital Heliport is available.

COMMUNITY SERVICES

EDUCATION Two school districts with 14 elementary, three middle and two high schools. The average daily attendance in 1981-82 was 13,354, with expenditures per pupil of $2,139 including 741 classroom teachers with an average annual salary of $15,441. Fifty-nine percent of the 802 high school graduates planned to attend college. In 1982-83, 65% of the students were White, 15% Hispanic, 20% Black, 1% Asian and 0.1% American Indian.

Sports championships: 1984 AAAAA Boys' Basketball, Bryan H.S.; 1982 AAAA Boys' Cross Country, College Station A&M Consolidated H.S. Private schools: 425 students enrolled in five elementary and three high schools. Texas A&M University is located in College Station. Established in 1876 it is under state control. Enrollment in 1982 was 33,499 with in state undergraduate tuition and fees of $500 per semester. The highest degree offered is doctorate. Texas A&M University College of Medicine located in College Station, was established in 1977. Vocational education: Bryan—Bryan School of Vocational Nursing, Britten Auction Academy, Charles and Sue's School of Hair Design, McKenzie-Baldwin Business College. College Station—Texas Engineering Extension Service (The Texas A&M University System.) **PUBLIC LIBRARIES** Bryan Public Library: 102,747 volumes. **CHILD CARE** 232 day care and 18 twenty-four hour care licensed facilities. **HEALTH CARE** 120 physicians and 33 dentists. Hospitals: two with a combined capacity of 213. Specialized hospitals: one for treatment of drug abuse with a capacity of 76. Clinics: two outpatient clinics, one dialysis clinic, and one public health clinic. Ambulance services: two commercial, two fire departments, and one hospital-based service. Mental health: one clinic and one center with capacity of 40. Nursing homes: four nursing homes with a combined capacity of 603 nursing care residents. The average cost per day for private patients in 1982 was $33.94. **CHURCHES** 69 churches have an estimated combined membership of 35,636. The largest denominations are Southern Baptist, Catholic and United Methodist. **SOCIAL SERVICES** In fiscal year 1983 a total of $1,833,317 in food stamps was distributed, with an average of 3,791 persons receiving food stamps each month. Aid to Families with Dependent Children (AFDC) totaled $523,831 with an average of 349 families receiving AFDC each month. Medical assistance benefits for the aged and disabled of $3,864,307 and for families and children of $710,919 brought the county benefit total to $6,932,374. **FIRE PROTECTION** Two paid and six volunteer fire departments. **LAW ENFORCEMENT** The County Sheriff has 40 commissioned officers. Two police departments have a combined force of 159. One university has a campus police department with 43 officers. The Texas Forest Service has 10 officers. **CRIME** 386 violent crimes (murder, forcible rape, robbery and aggravated assault) and 6,380 nonviolent crimes (burglary, larceny-theft and motor vehicle theft) were reported in 1982. **JUDICIAL SYSTEM** Two District Courts and Judges, two County Courts and Judges and seven Justices of the Peace. In the District Courts a total of 1,500 cases were pending on 1/1/82, 2,118 new cases were filed and 1,741 cases were disposed of during the year leaving 1,877 cases pending on 12/31/82. There were 962 criminal cases on the docket, 223 convictions, 98 persons committed to prison and five committed to jail and 523 cases left pending. In the County Courts 2,800 cases were pending on 1/1/82, 2,501 new cases were filed and 2,220 cases were disposed of during the year leaving 3,081 cases pending on 12/31/82. There were 3,781 criminal cases on the docket, 1,007 convictions, 246 persons committed to jail, and 1,896 cases left pending. **JAILS** One jail, capacity 79, under renovation. **ATTORNEYS AT LAW** 156. **UTILITIES** 94% of the residents are connected to a public or privately owned water system and 88% are connected to a public sewer system. Natural gas is distributed to the county by Lone Star Gas Co., Division of Enserch. The average annual residential bill for natural gas in 1982 for the Lone Star distribution system was $405.91, an increase of 35% over 1981. Electricity is distributed to the city of College Station by College Station Utilities and to the rest of the county by the Bryan Municipal Electric System, Texas-New Mexico Power Co., and Mid-South Electric Coop. and is generated primarily by gas and oil. The typical residential electric bill is $102.88 per month for an all-electric house using 2,500 kwh. **TAXES** The county has five units with taxing authority: two school districts, two cities, and one county.

RECREATION/ENTERTAINMENT

NATIONAL REGISTER OF HISTORIC PLACES Bryan: Bryan Carnegie Library and Cavitt House. **COUNTY/MUNICIPAL PARKS** 792 acres in 42 municipal parks. These parks contain five miles of hiking trails, 25 playgrounds, one golf course, 14 football and soccer fields, 26 baseball and softball fields, 20 tennis courts, six multi-use courts, five swimming pools, two boat ramps and shore fishing facilities. **SCENIC DRIVES** The Texas Brazos Trail runs through this county. This trail moves through a beautiful and historic section of Central Texas revealing forested landscapes filled with wildlife and wild flowers. **BOATING/FISHING** Lakes/reservoirs: Bryan Utilities (829 acres), Carter (38 acres), Clifty Creek (13 acres), Frierson (37 acres), Herring #2 (91 acres), Oakland (34 acres), Prescott (34 acres) and Wheeler (46 acres). Major rivers: Navasota, Brazos. Primary streams: Thompsons, Carter, Clifty, Peach, Allcorn and Hudson. **HUNTING** Fall and winter seasons on deer. No closed season on coyotes, bobcats and squirrel. Winter season on quail, muskrat, beaver, opossum, ring-tailed cat, badger, fox, weasel, raccoon, skunk and civet cat. In 1983 duck, coot, geese, woodcock and jacksnipe seasons occurred during the winter months. Teal duck, rail and gallinule seasons occurred in the fall. Mourning dove season occurred intermittently during the fall and winter months. **MUSEUMS** Bryan: Junior Museum of Natural History and Brazos Valley Museum of Natural Science. College Station: Texas A&M University Art Exhibits. **PLANETARIUM** College Station: Texas A&M Planetarium. **SPECIAL EVENTS** Hunters Pistol Matches, College Station, January-December; Clay Pigeon Open Matches, College Station, January-December; International Festival, College Station, February; Juried Art Show, College Station, February; Texas Autorama, Bryan, February; Skeet Open Matches, College Station, March/April; Kite Flying Contest, College Station, March; Triathlon, College Station, April; Juried Spring Art Show, Bryan, April; Brazos de Dios Rodeo and Western Fiesta, Bryan, April; Spring Arts Festival and Music in the Park, College Station, May; "Texans Only" Art Celebration, Bryan, May/June; Heritage Needlework Festival, Bryan, July; Jazz Fest, College Station, July; Septemberfest, Bryan, September; Texas Race of Champions and Chili Cookoff, College Station, October; Christmas in Old Bryan, Bryan, December; Christmas Holiday Parade, Bryan/College Station, December.

COMMUNITIES

COUNTY SEAT Bryan, County Courthouse, 77801; County Clerk's Office, 409/775-7400. **INCORPORATED COMMUNITIES** (1980 population and ZIP Code) Bryan (44,337) 77801 and College Station (37,272) 77840. **UNINCORPORATED COMMUNITIES** (and ZIP Code) Allenfarm 77868, Cawthon 77868, Edge 77801, Harvey 77801, Kurten 77862, Law 77801, Macy 77882, Millican 77866, Mooring (Steeles Store) 77801, Mudville 77801, Reliance 77801, Rye 77832, Smetana 77801, Steep Hollow 77801, Tabor 77801, Varisco 77801 and Wellborn 77881. **FOR ADDITIONAL LOCAL INFORMATION** Bryan-College Station Chamber of Commerce, P.O. Box 726, Bryan, 77806, 409/779-2278.

BREWSTER (B6)

THE LAND

Bordering Mexico southwest of Odessa on U.S. Highways 67/90 and 385 in the Transpecos Region, Brewster County covers 6,169 square miles of rough terrain and mountains. The elevation ranges from 1,700 to 7,835 feet. The eastern half of the county is

COUNTIES

BREWSTER (continued)

undulating to hilly. Loamy to sandy soils cover limestone, with areas of exposed rock. The rest of the county has limestone and igneous rock outcrops, mostly shallow, sandy to loamy soils with a few areas of deep soils with loamy surface layers and clayey subsoils. The vegetation is drought resistant with short, sparse grasses, desert shrubs, some mesquite, cacti and several poisonous plants. The higher mountain elevations support some pinion pine, juniper and ponderosa pine. Less than 1% of the land in the county is considered prime farmland. **CLIMATE** Subtropical arid with wide-ranging daily temperature fluctuations. The average annual temperature is 63°F. Temperatures in January range from an average low of 34° to an average high of 60°F and in July range from 67° to 95°F. The average annual precipitation is 12 inches, with an average relative humidity of 69% at 6 A.M. and 33% at 6 P.M. The average annual snowfall is three inches. The growing season averages 239 days per year, with the last freeze in mid March and the first freeze in early November. The sun shines during the year on the average 73% of the daylight hours.

THE PEOPLE
Brewster County ranks 53rd in land area among all U.S. counties and is one of the most sparsely populated counties in Texas. The 1982 estimated population of 7,700 indicates a slight increase in county population. Rural areas experienced a 17% growth from 1970 and 1980. The age groups with the largest gains were ages 65 and over, with the largest decrease occurring in those aged 20 to 24. Brewster ranks 59th among all U.S. counties in the highest percent of population of Spanish origin. The largest ancestry groups are Hispanic (43%) and persons of English descent (43%). **REGISTERED VOTERS** As of November 2, 1982 there were 3,879 registered voters (0.1% of the state total). The 1982 general election had a 54% voter turnout, compared to a 67% turnout in the 1980 general election. In the 1982 primary 92% voted Democratic and 8% Republican, with 1,639 votes cast.

THE ECONOMY
AGRICULTURE Ranchland. In 1982, 71% of the land was in farms and ranches, with less than 1% of the farmland under cultivation. Brewster ranked 195th in the state in highest agricultural receipts, with 95% from livestock and livestock products. Overgrazing and undesirable brush and weeds are current conservation problems. Primary crop: hay. Primary fruits and nuts: peaches and pecans. Primary livestock and products: cattle, sheep, wool, angora goats and mohair. **BUSINESS** Total number of business establishments in the county: 188. Retail sales during the first quarter of 1984 increased 12%. In 1980, 11% of the labor force were self-employed, 28% were employed in professional or related services, 3% in manufacturing, 26% in wholesale and retail trade, 10% in public administration, 6% were employed in other counties and there were 648 retired workers. The industries with the most employment: tourism and oil and gas extraction. The nonfarm earnings in 1981 totaled $62,202,000. The retired workers received an average monthly Social Security payment of $310. **FINANCE** On June 30, 1983, one commercial bank had total deposits of $40,407,000 and total assets of $46,442,000. There is one state savings and loan association branch in the county. **HOUSING** Average value of homes in 1980: $26,000. Permits for new, privately owned housing units increased in 1982: 27 permits were issued with a total construction cost of $836,000. Of those permits, all were for single family houses. Housing permits in Alpine increased from seven in 1981 to 27 in 1982. Between 1970 and 1980 the number of housing units increased by 20%. Sixty-two percent of all units in the county are air-conditioned, 83% are heated by gas and 14% by

electricity. **NATURAL RESOURCES** Limestone, volcanic rock, uranium, mercury, silver, lead, copper, zinc, molybdenum, fluorspar, leonardite, bituminous coal, oil and gas. Current production of other minerals and products includes agate, fluorspar, crushed limestone, sand and gravel and crushed rhyolite. **TOURISM** Travel expenditures of $12,585,000 in 1982 (an increase of 12% over 1981) generated 305 jobs and $2,483,000 in payroll. Lodging: five hotels, motels and tourist courts. Convention/meeting facilities: Alpine-Sul Ross State University Stadium and Gymnasium. **ALCOHOLIC BEVERAGES** Packaged distilled spirits, beer, ale, malt liquor and wine are legal. Sale of mixed beverages is legal in all or parts of the county. **FEDERAL EXPENDITURES** The federal government had direct expenditures or obligations of $14,134,000 in the county during fiscal year 1983, including $504,000 by the U.S. Department of Defense. In addition, the federal government provided $332,000 in grant awards, paid $2,820,000 in salaries and wages, made direct payments to individuals of $10,706,000 including $7,698,000 in retirement and disability payments, awarded $127,000 in procurement contracts and spent $150,000 in other expenditures or obligations. The federal government also provided $140,000 in direct loans and $11,322,000 in guaranteed loans and insurance.

COMMUNICATION
Newspapers–Weekly: Alpine Avalanche. Radio: KULF-AM (Alpine). Cable TV. Telephone companies: Southwestern Bell and Big Bend Telephone. **TRANSPORTATION** Total public road mileage: 965. In 1982 there were 5,970 registered vehicles and 175 reported traffic accidents. Intercity bus service is available. Motor freight: three carriers. Rail: The Sunset Limited provides passenger service on the Amtrak route. Two main and one branch line carry freight through the county. The two main lines carry annually over 30 million tons of freight each. The branch line carries annually one to five million tons of freight. Aircraft: 36 are registered in the county. Airports: Alpine Municipal Airport is a general utility airport providing general aviation service. It serves as a base for 28 aircraft. Also serving the area are Terlingua Airport, Terlingua Ranch Airport and Lajitas Airport.

COMMUNITY SERVICES
EDUCATION Four school districts with four elementary, one middle and two high schools. The average daily attendance in 1981-82 was 1,281, with expenditures per pupil of $2,992 including 122 classroom teachers with an average annual salary of $16,291. Six percent of the 83 high school graduates planned to attend college. In 1982-83, 47% of the students were White, 52% Hispanic, 0.8% Black, 0.4% Asian and 0.1% American Indian. Private schools: one elementary school. Sul Ross State University is located in Alpine. Established in 1917 it is under state control. Enrollment in 1982 was 2,143 with in state undergraduate tuition and fees of $284 per semester. The highest degree offered is Master. **PUBLIC LIBRARIES** Alpine Public Library: 44,250 volumes and one branch. **CHILD CARE** 11 day care and one twenty-four hour care licensed facilities. **HEALTH CARE** 12 physicians. Hospitals: one with a capacity of 50. Ambulance services: two commercial and two volunteer services. Mental health: one clinic. Nursing homes: one nursing home has a capacity of 59 nursing care residents. The average cost per day for private patients in 1982 was $28.98. **CHURCHES** 18 churches have an estimated combined membership of 4,114. The largest denominations are Catholic, Southern Baptist and United Methodist. **SOCIAL SERVICES** In fiscal year 1983 a total of $251,341 in food stamps was distributed, with an average of 540 persons receiving food stamps each month. Aid to Families with Dependent Children (AFDC) totaled $36,945 with an average of 25 families receiving AFDC each month. Medical assistance benefits

for the aged and disabled of $508,827 and for families and children of $37,624 brought the county benefit total to $834,737. **FIRE PROTECTION** Two volunteer fire departments. **LAW ENFORCEMENT** The County Sheriff has three commissioned officers. One police department has a force of 11. One university has a campus police department with a force of six officers. **CRIME** 14 violent crimes (murder, forcible rape, robbery and aggravated assault) and 174 nonviolent crimes (burglary, larceny-theft and motor vehicle theft) were reported in 1982. **JUDICIAL SYSTEM** One District Court and Judge, one County Court and Judge and three Justices of the Peace. In the District Court a total of 258 cases were pending on 1/1/82, 188 new cases were filed and 183 cases were disposed of during the year leaving 263 cases pending on 12/31/82. There were 116 criminal cases on the docket, 40 convictions, two persons committed to prison and 35 cases left pending. In the County Court 227 cases were pending on 1/1/82, 271 new cases were filed and 336 cases were disposed of during the year leaving 162 cases pending on 12/31/82. There were 440 criminal cases on the docket, 118 convictions and 142 cases left pending. **JAILS** One jail, capacity 17. **ATTORNEYS AT LAW** Nine. **UTILITIES** 78% of the residents are connected to a public or privately owned water system and 76% are connected to a public sewer system. Natural gas is distributed to the county by Southwest Texas Municipal Gas Corp. Electricity is distributed to the county by West Texas Utilities Co. and Rio Grande Electric Cooperative Inc. and is generated primarily by gas, oil and coal. The typical residential electric bill is $145.78 per month for an all-electric house using 2,500 kwh. **TAXES** The county has six units with taxing authority: four school districts, one city and one county.

RECREATION/ENTERTAINMENT

FEDERAL BIG BEND NATIONAL PARK encompasses 708,118 acres in the great bend of the Rio Grande River. It provides magnificent scenery with mountains contrasting with desert and a variety of unusual geological formations. Variations in elevation and temperature make the area an ideal year round park. Over 1,100 plant types can be found, the most common animals being deer, coyotes, javelinas, skunks, raccoons and jackrabbits. Over 350 bird species have been identified. Basic facilities include a Visitor Center, campgrounds, trailer parks and store-gas stations. Limited lodging is available. Also offered are nature walks, hiking trails, scenic drives and horseback riding. RIO GRANDE WILD AND SCENIC RIVER is a 191-mile strip on the American shore of the Rio Grande in the Chihuahuan Desert. It begins in Big Bend National Park and continues downstream to the Terrell-Val Verde County Line. The area encompasses 9,600 acres outside Big Bend National Park. No federal facilities are available. **NATIONAL REGISTER OF HISTORIC PLACES** Alpine: Brewster County Courthouse and Jail Building. Big Bend National Park: Castalon Historic District, Hot Springs, Luna Jacal, Marsical Mine, Sublett Farm-Rancho Estelle and Homer Wilson Ranch **COUNTY/MUNICIPAL PARKS** 33 acres in one county and four municipal parks. These parks contain three playgrounds, one baseball and softball field, two multi-use fields and one swimming pool. Developed campsites: three. **SCENIC DRIVES** The Texas Mountain Trail runs through this county. Desert and mountain landscapes along Texas 118 toward Big Bend National Park where El Camino del Rio and F.M. 170 provides one of the nation's most spectacular drives. Primary streams: Terlingua and San Francisco. **WILDLIFE REFUGES** Blackgap State Wildlife Management Area covers 102,258 acres. **HUNTING** Fall season on antelope. Fall and winter seasons on deer and mule deer. No closed season on elk, javelina, coyote and bobcat. Winter season on quail, muskrat, beaver, opossum, ringtailed cat, badger, fox, weasel, raccoon, skunk and civet cat. In 1983 sandhill crane, duck, coot, geese, woodcock and jacksnipe

seasons occurred during the winter months. Teal duck, rail and gallinule seasons occurred in the fall. Mourning dove season occurred intermittently during the fall and winter months with a fall season on white-winged dove. **MUSEUMS** Alpine: Museum of the Big Bend. Marathon: Marathon Museum. **THEATERS** Alpine: Alpine Amphitheater. **PLANETARIUM** Alpine: Sul Ross State University Planetarium. **COLLEGIATE FINE ARTS** Alpine: Cultural events offered by Sul Ross State University. **SPECIAL EVENTS** Annual Cookie Chilloff, Piethon and 10K Race, Terlingua, February; Outdoor Summer Theatre, Alpine, July (Thurs.-Sat.); Paisano Day, Big Bend National Park, October; World Championship Chili Cookoff, Terlingua, November.

COMMUNITIES

COUNTY SEAT Alpine, County Courthouse, 79830; County Clerk's Office, 915/837-3366. **INCORPORATED COMMUNITIES** (1980 population and ZIP Code) Alpine (5,465) 79830. **UNINCORPORATED COMMUNITIES** (and ZIP Code) Basin 79834, Boquillas 79834, Castolon 79852, Lajitas 79852, Marathon 79842, Study Butte 79852 and Terlingua 79852. **FOR ADDITIONAL LOCAL INFORMATION** Alpine Chamber of Commerce, 106 N. Third, P.O. Box 209, Alpine, 79831, 915/837-2326.

BRISCOE (P24)

THE LAND

In the Texas Panhandle northeast of Lubbock on State Highways 207, 86 and 256 in the Rolling Plains Region, Briscoe County covers 887 square miles of varied topography. The plains in the southwestern portion of the county are separated from the rest of the county by the Cap Rock Escarpment. Elevation ranges from 2,200 to 3,200 feet with changes of 1,000 feet experienced in just a few miles along the Tule Canyon. Ruins of irrigation canals or stockades of a Pre-Columbian people and fossil remains of sea turtles and mastodons are found in the area. The red to brown alkaline soils have loamy surface layers and compact clayey to loamy subsoils. In some areas the soils are a shallow covering over limestone. From the center of the county toward the southwest the soils are more level with loamy surface layers and clayey subsoils. The northeast portion of the county is in the Rolling Plains vegetation area with grasses, mesquite and yucca, while the southwest portion lies in the High Plains vegetation with grama and buffalograss, sagebrush, mesquite and yucca. Between 41 and 50% of the land in the county is considered prime farmland. **CLIMATE** Borders continental steppe and subtropical subhumid. It is characterized by wide-ranging daily temperature fluctuations. The average annual temperature is 59°F. Temperatures in January range from an average low of 24° to an average high of 52°F and in July range from 66° to 94°F. The average annual precipitation is 20 inches, with an average relative humidity of 72% at 6 A.M. and 40% at 6 P.M. The average annual snowfall is nine inches. The growing season averages 216 days per year, with the last freeze near April 8th and the first freeze near November 10th. The sun shines during the year on the average 75% of the daylight hours.

THE PEOPLE

The 1982 estimated population of 2,500 indicates a continuation of the steady decline in population which has existed since 1930. The majority of residents live in rural areas. The age group with the most loss between 1970 and 1980 was that of ages five to 14. The median age is 33. The largest ancestry groups are persons of English descent (45%), Irish descent (20%) and Hispanic (16%). **REGISTERED VOTERS** As of November 2, 1982 there

BRISCOE (continued)

were 1,509 registered voters (0.02% of the state total). The 1982 general election had a 63% voter turnout, compared to a 71% turnout in the 1980 general election. In the 1982 primary 99% voted Democratic and 1% Republican, with 686 votes cast.

THE ECONOMY

AGRICULTURE Cotton and wheat area. In 1982, 96% of the land was in farms and ranches, with 30% of the farmland under cultivation and 34% irrigated. Briscoe ranked 197th in the state in highest agricultural receipts, with 74% from crops. Overgrazing, undesirable brush and weeds, water and wind erosion and decreasing irrigation water supplies are the current conservation problems. Primary crops: wheat, cotton, sorghum and soybeans. Primary vegetables: watermelons. Primary fruits and nuts: pecans. Primary livestock and products: cattle and wool. **BUSINESS** Total number of business establishments in the county: 54. Retail sales during the first quarter of 1984 increased 34% with a gain of 204% in Quitaque. In 1980, 38% of the labor force were self-employed, 9% were employed in professional or related services, 4% in manufacturing, 19% in wholesale and retail trade, 40% in agriculture, forestry, fisheries and mining, 9% were employed in other counties and there were 291 retired workers. The industry with the most employment: agribusiness. The nonfarm earnings in 1981 totaled $18,741,000. The retired workers received an average monthly Social Security payment of $309. **FINANCE** On June 30, 1983, two commercial banks had total deposits of $33,653,000 and total assets of $39,905,000. There is one state savings and loan association branch in the county. **HOUSING** Average value of homes in 1980: $20,500. Between 1970 and 1980 the number of housing units decreased by 4%. Seventy-seven percent of all units in the county are air-conditioned, 92% are heated by gas and 7% by electricity. **NATURAL RESOURCES** Caliche, gypsum, oil and gas. In 1982 a total of 3,554 barrels of crude oil and 1,550 thousand cubic feet of casinghead gas were produced. Current production of other minerals and products includes caliche, sand and gravel. **TOURISM** Travel expenditures of $614,000 in 1982 (an increase of 17% over 1981) generated 9 jobs and $92,000 in payroll. **ALCOHOLIC BEVERAGES** Totally dry. **FEDERAL EXPENDITURES** The federal government had direct expenditures or obligations of $8,355,000 in the county during fiscal year 1983, including $64,000 by the U.S. Department of Defense. In addition, the federal government provided $48,000 in grant awards, paid $257,000 in salaries and wages, made direct payments to individuals of $4,785,000 including $3,553,000 in retirement and disability payments, awarded $1,000 in procurement contracts and spent $3,263,000 in other expenditures or obligations. The federal government also provided $4,558,000 in direct loans and $3,115,000 in guaranteed loans and insurance.

COMMUNICATION

Newspapers–Weekly: The Valley Tribune (Quitaque) and The Briscoe County News (Silverton). Cable TV. Telephone companies: General Telephone, Southwestern Bell and Midplains Rural Telephone Coop. **TRANSPORTATION** Total public road mileage: 583. In 1982 there were 2,891 registered vehicles and 31 reported traffic accidents. Motor freight: one carrier. Rail: one branch line carries annually one to five million tons of freight through the county. Aircraft: seven are registered in the county.

COMMUNITY SERVICES

EDUCATION One school district with one elementary and one high school. The average daily attendance in 1981-82 was 259, with expenditures per pupil of $3,258 including 23 classroom teachers with an average annual salary of $16,421. Seventy-four percent of the 19 high school graduates planned to attend college. In 1982-83, 68% of the students were White, 29% Hispanic and 4% Black. **PUBLIC LIBRARIES** Silverton Public Library: 2,300 volumes. **CHILD CARE** Three day care licensed facilities. **HEALTH CARE** One physician. Ambulance services: one volunteer service and one volunteer fire department service. **CHURCHES** Nine churches have an estimated combined membership of 2,312. The largest denominations are Southern Baptist, Churches of Christ and United Methodist. **SOCIAL SERVICES** In fiscal year 1983 a total of $98,393 in food stamps was distributed, with an average of 227 persons receiving food stamps each month. Aid to Families with Dependent Children (AFDC) totaled $11,074 with an average of seven families receiving AFDC each month. Medical assistance benefits for the aged and disabled of $65,826 and for families and children of $26,207 brought the county benefit total to $201,500. **FIRE PROTECTION** Two volunteer fire departments. **LAW ENFORCEMENT** The County Sheriff has five commissioned officers. One police department has a force of four. **CRIME** One violent crime (murder, forcible rape, robbery and aggravated assault) and 19 nonviolent crimes (burglary, larceny-theft and motor vehicle theft) were reported in 1982. **JUDICIAL SYSTEM** One District Court and Judge, one County Court and Judge and two Justices of the Peace. In the District Court a total of 95 cases were pending on 1/1/82, 28 new cases were filed and 32 cases were disposed of during the year leaving 91 cases pending on 12/31/82. There were 20 criminal cases on the docket, three convictions, one person committed to prison, and 16 cases left pending. In the County Court 59 cases were pending on 1/1/82, 35 new cases were filed and 22 cases were disposed of during the year leaving 72 cases pending on 12/31/82. There were 90 criminal cases on the docket, 21 convictions, two persons committed to jail, and 69 cases left pending. **ATTORNEYS AT LAW** One. **UTILITIES** 70% of the residents are connected to a public or privately owned water system and 64% are connected to a public sewer system. Natural gas is distributed to the county by Energas Company. The average annual residential bill for natural gas in 1982 for the Energas distribution system was $371.63, an increase of 23% over 1981. Electricity distributed to the county by Lighthouse Electric Coop., Inc. and Swisher Electric Coop., Inc. and is generated primarily by gas and oil. **TAXES** The county has five units with taxing authority: one school district, two cities, one county and one special district.

RECREATION/ENTERTAINMENT

REGISTER OF HISTORIC PLACES Quitaque vicinity: Lake Theo Folsom Site and Quitaque Railway Tunnel. Silverton vicinity: Mayfield Dugout. **STATE** Caprock Canyons State Park covers 13,655 acres with areas offering fishing, swimming and boat ramps. **MUNICIPAL PARKS** 12 acres in four municipal parks. These parks contain three playgrounds, two baseball and softball fields and two tennis courts. **SCENIC DRIVES** The Texas Plains Trail runs through this county. This trail spans a vast area of the High Plains region of Texas slicing through the southernmost extension of the Great Plains of the United States. The land is flat except where erosion has carved canyon landscapes. **BOATING/FISHING** Lakes/reservoirs: Burson (12 acres), Grahamo (29 acres), Kent Creek Soil Conservation Service Lake (20 acres), Mackenzie (911 acres), Puckett (20 acres) and Theo (48 acres). Major rivers: Prairie Dog Town Fork Red and Little Red. Primary streams: Bluff, Little Cottonwood, Kent, Tule, Holmes, Indian, Battle, Mulberry, Barrel, Coon and Mexican. **HUNTING** Winter season on aoudad sheep, pheasant, quail, muskrat, beaver, opossum, ring-tailed cat, badger, fox, weasel, raccoon, skunk and civet cat. Fall and winter seasons on deer and mule deer. Fall, winter and spring seasons on squirrel. No closed season on coyote and bobcat. Fall, winter and spring seasons on turkey. In 1983 sandhill crane, duck, coot, geese, woodcock and jacksnipe seasons occurred during the winter months. Teal duck, rail and gallinule seasons occurred in the fall. Mourning dove season occurred intermittently during the fall and winter months. **MUSEUMS** Silverton: Briscoe County Museum. **SPECIAL EVENTS** Rodeo and Parade, Silverton, August; Pioneer Days Celebration, Silverton, August.

COMMUNITIES

COUNTY SEAT Silverton, County Courthouse, 79257; County Clerk's Office, 806/823-2325. **INCORPORATED COMMUNITIES** (1980 population and ZIP Code) Quitaque (696) 79255 and Silverton (918) 79257. **UNINCORPORATED COMMUNITIES** (and ZIP Code) Gasoline 79255 and Rock Creek 79257.

BROOKS (B24)

THE LAND

Southwest of Corpus Christi on U.S. Highway 281 in the Rio Grande Plain Region, Brooks County covers 942 square miles of brushy mesquite land. The elevation ranges from 100 to 400 feet. The nearly level to undulating soils are poorly drained, dark and loamy throughout or sandy with dunes possible. In the northeast corner of the county the soils are light-colored with loamy surface layers and clayey subsoils. In the South Texas Plains vegetation area, small trees, brush, weeds, cacti and grasses dominate. Between 1 and 10% of the land in the county is considered prime farmland. **CLIMATE** Subtropical subhumid with the possibility of tropical storms or hurricanes June through October. The average annual temperature is 73°F. Temperatures in January range from an average low of 44° to an average high of 69°F and in July range from 73° to 97°F. The average annual precipitation is 25 inches, with an average relative humidity of 86% at 6 A.M. and 60% at 6 P.M. There is no snowfall. The growing season averages 310 days per year, with the last freeze near February 10th and the first freeze near December 10th. The sun shines during the year on the average 66% of the daylight hours.

THE PEOPLE

Brooks county ranks seventh among all U.S. counties in the highest percent of population of Spanish origin. It also ranks among the top 11 Texas counties in percent of county residents who are native Texans. The 1982 estimated population of 8,800 indicates a continuation of the growth begun in the 1970s which reversed the steady population decline between 1950 and 1970. The rural population between 1970 and 1980 grew 41%, a high rate among Texas counties. The age group with the largest gains was ages 65 and over, while the largest decrease occurred in ages five to 14. The largest ancestry groups are Hispanic (86%) and persons of English descent (6%). **REGISTERED VOTERS** As of November 2, 1982 there were 5,882 registered voters (0.1% of the state total). The 1982 general election had a 50% voter turnout, compared to a 54% turnout in the 1980 general election. In the 1982 primary 100% voted Democratic, with 3,314 votes cast.

THE ECONOMY

AGRICULTURE A leading watermelon producer. In 1982, 95% of the land was in farms and ranches, with 3% of the farmland under cultivation and 50% irrigated. Brooks ranked 182nd in the state in highest agricultural receipts, with 80% from livestock and livestock products. Overgrazing, undesirable brush and weeds and inefficient tillage are the current conservation problems.

Primary crops: sorghum and hay. Primary vegetables: second in the state for watermelons and 10th for total fresh market vegetables. Primary fruits and nuts: oranges and peaches. Primary livestock and products: cattle and milk. **BUSINESS** Total number of business establishments in the county: 157. Retail sales during the first quarter of 1984 declined 1%. In 1980, 10% of the labor force were self-employed, 21% were employed in professional or related services, 6% in manufacturing, 22% in wholesale and retail trade, 17% in agriculture, forestry, fisheries and mining, 16% were employed in other counties and there were 533 retired workers. The industry with the most employment is oil and gas extraction. The nonfarm earnings in 1981 totaled $50,442,000. The retired workers received an average monthly Social Security payment of $261. **FINANCE** On June 30, 1983, one commercial bank had total deposits of $31,543,000 and total assets of $36,674,000. On December 31, 1982 one state savings and loan association had assets of $18,605,824. **HOUSING** Average value of homes in 1980: $16,800. In 1982 four permits were issued for single family houses. Between 1970 and 1980 the number of housing units in the county increased by 17%. Fifty-two percent of all units are air-conditioned, 84% are heated by gas and 14% by electricity. **NATURAL RESOURCES** Caliche, salt domes, oil and gas. In 1982 a total of 90,434,098 thousand cubic feet of gas well gas, 520,482 barrels of condensate, 739,581 barrels of crude oil and 2,392,340 thousand cubic feet of casinghead gas were produced. **TOURISM** Travel expenditures of $2,842,000 in 1982 (an increase of 14% over 1981) generated 58 jobs and $502,000 in payroll. **ALCOHOLIC BEVERAGES** Packaged distilled spirits, beer, ale, malt liquor and wine are legal in parts of the county. **FEDERAL EXPENDITURES** The federal government had direct expenditures or obligations of $10,996,000 in the county during fiscal year 1983, including $249,000 by the U.S. Department of Defense. In addition, the federal government provided $856,000 in grant awards, paid $943,000 in salaries and wages, made direct payments to individuals of $9,021,000 including $6,639,000 in retirement and disability payments, awarded $2,000 in procurement contracts and spent $176,000 in other expenditures or obligations. The federal government also provided $200,000 in direct loans and $7,035,000 in guaranteed loans and insurance.

COMMUNICATION

Newspapers–Weekly: Falfurrias Facts. Radio: KPSO-AM (Falfurrias). Telephone companies: General Telephone, Southwestern Bell, Riviera Telephone and Valley Telephone Coop. **TRANSPORTATION** Total public road mileage: 255. In 1982 there were 5,785 registered vehicles and 205 reported traffic accidents including two fatalities. Intercity bus service is available. Motor freight: two carriers. Rail: one branch line carries annually one to five million tons of freight through the county. Aircraft: six are registered in the county. Airports: Brooks County Airport in Falfurrias is a basic transportation airport and serves as a base for 18 aircraft.

COMMUNITY SERVICES

EDUCATION One school district with three elementary, one middle and one high school. The average daily attendance in 1981-82 was 1,806, with expenditures per pupil of $3,828 including 152 classroom teachers with an average annual salary of $18,038. Sixty-nine percent of the 109 high school graduates planned to attend college. In 1982-83, 8% of the students were White, 92% Hispanic and 0.1% Asian. Private schools: 29 students enrolled in one elementary school. **PUBLIC LIBRARIES** Brooks County Library (Falfurrias): 45,803 volumes. **CHILD CARE** Six day care licensed facilities. **HEALTH CARE** Four physicians and one dentist. Hospitals: one with a capacity of 31. Ambulance services: one

BROOKS (continued)

commercial service. Mental health: one clinic. Nursing homes: one nursing home has a capacity of 100 nursing care residents. The average cost per day for private patients in 1982 was $27.71. **CHURCHES** 17 churches have an estimated combined membership of 6,694. The largest denominations are Catholic, Southern Baptist and United Methodist. **SOCIAL SERVICES** In fiscal year 1983 a total of $1,291,195 in food stamps was distributed, with an average of 2,673 persons receiving food stamps each month. Aid to Families with Dependent Children (AFDC) totaled $233,330 with an average of 161 families receiving AFDC each month. Medical assistance benefits for the aged and disabled of $1,086,652 and for families and children of $319,086 brought the county benefit total to $2,930,263. **FIRE PROTECTION** One volunteer fire department. **LAW ENFORCEMENT** The County Sheriff has nine commissioned officers. One police department has a force of seven. **CRIME** Nine violent crimes (murder, forcible rape, robbery and aggravated assault) and 197 nonviolent crimes (burglary, larceny-theft and motor vehicle theft) were reported in 1982. **JUDICIAL SYSTEM** One District Court and Judge, one County Court and Judge and four Justices of the Peace. In the District Court a total of 317 cases were pending on 1/1/82, 208 new cases were filed and 209 cases were disposed of during the year leaving 316 cases pending on 12/31/82. There were 136 criminal cases on the docket, 41 convictions, eight persons committed to prison, and 81 cases left pending. In the County Court 706 cases were pending on 1/1/82, 318 new cases were filed and 235 cases were disposed of during the year leaving 789 cases pending on 12/31/82. There were 977 criminal cases on the docket and 742 cases left pending. **JAILS** One jail, capacity 12. **ATTORNEYS AT LAW** Four. **UTILITIES** 79% of the residents are connected to a public or privately owned water system and 71% are connected to a public sewer system. Electricity is distributed to the county by Central Power and Light Co., Cochran Power and Light Co., Medina Electric Coop., Inc. and Nueces Electric Coop., Inc. and is generated primarily by gas, oil, coal and water. The typical residential electric bill is $162.15 per month for an all-electric house using 2,500 kwh. **TAXES** The county has three units with taxing authority: one school district, one county and one city.

RECREATION/ENTERTAINMENT

MUNICIPAL PARKS 66 acres in four municipal parks. These parks contain three playgrounds, one golf course, four baseball and softball fields and two tennis courts. **SCENIC DRIVES** The Texas Tropical Trail runs through this county. This trail is charted through the state's southernmost wedge meandering through ranchland, resort areas on the Gulf of Mexico and fertile farmlands. **BOATING/FISHING** Primary streams: Baluarte, Los Olmos, Palo Blanco and Vargas. **HUNTING** Fall and winter seasons on deer. No closed season on javelina, squirrel, coyote and bobcat. Winter season on quail, muskrat, beaver, opossum, ring-tailed cat, badger, fox, weasel, raccoon, skunk and civet cat. Fall, winter and spring seasons on turkey. In 1983 duck, coot, geese, woodcock and jacksnipe seasons occurred during the winter months with a winter season on sandhill cranes in some parts of the county. Teal duck, rail and gallinule seasons occurred in the fall. Mourning dove seasons occurred intermittently during the fall and winter months with a fall season on white-winged dove. **MUSEUMS** Falfurrias: Heritage Museum at Falfurrias. **SPECIAL EVENTS** Fiesta Ranchera, Falfurrias, May; Watermelon Roundup, Falfurrias, June; Mexican Village Celebration, Falfurrias, June; Fourth of July Rodeo, Falfurrias, July.

COMMUNITIES

COUNTY SEAT Falfurrias, County Courthouse, 78355; County Clerk's Office, 512/325-3053. **INCORPORATED COMMUNITIES** (1980 population and ZIP Code) Falfurrias (6,103) 78355. **UNINCORPORATED COMMUNITIES** (and ZIP Code) Encino 78353, Flowella 78355 and Rachal 78353. **FOR ADDITIONAL LOCAL INFORMATION** Falfurrias Chamber of Commerce, 124 N. St. Mary's, P.O. Box 476, Falfurrias, 78355, 512/325-3333.

BROWN (P82)

THE LAND

Southeast of Abilene on U.S. Highways 67/377 and 84/183 in the North Central Prairies Region, Brown County covers 936 square miles of fairly level to hilly land. The elevation ranges from 1,380 to 1,770 feet. Mineral water can be found throughout the county. In the northeast corner of the county the land is nearly level with light-colored soils of loamy to sandy surface layers and mottled, cracking, clayey subsoils. Along the eastern border and in the southeast the undulating to hilly alkaline soils are loamy over limestone. The rest of the county is undulating to hilly with loamy to clayey soils over shale or sandstone. In the center of the county and toward the southwest, the soils are mostly loamy throughout. In the Cross Timbers and Prairie vegetation area, woody brush such as mesquite and juniper have invaded the grasslands. Some blackjack, post and live oak trees grow in the area. Between 21 and 30% of the land in the county is considered prime farmland. **CLIMATE** Subtropical subhumid with wide-ranging daily temperature fluctuations. The average annual temperature is 64°F. Temperatures in January range from an average low of 31° to an average high of 56°F and in July range from 70° to 96°F. The average annual precipitation is 26 inches, with an average relative humidity of 79% at 6 A.M. and 46% at 6 P.M. The average annual snowfall is three inches. The growing season averages 232 days per year, with the last freeze in late March and the first freeze in the middle of November. The sun shines during the year on the average 68% of the daylight hours.

THE PEOPLE

The 1982 estimated population of 34,500 indicates a continuation of the strong growth rate of the 1970s. Almost 61% of the growth between 1970 and 1980 was in rural areas. The age groups with the largest gains were ages 20 to 34 and birth to five years, dropping the high median age from 37 in 1970 to 32 in 1980. The largest ancestry groups are persons of English descent (37%) and Irish descent (24%). **REGISTERED VOTERS** As of November 2, 1982 there were 14,500 registered voters (0.2% of the state total). The 1982 general election had a 56% voter turnout, compared to a 75% turnout in the 1980 general election. In the 1982 primary 96% voted Democratic and 4% Republican, with 5,178 votes cast.

THE ECONOMY

AGRICULTURE In 1982, 90% of the land was in farms and ranches, with 13% of the farmland under cultivation and 42% irrigated. Brown ranked 117th in the state in highest agricultural receipts, with 87% from livestock and livestock products. Overgrazing, undesirable brush and weeds, water erosion and difficulties in grass establishment are the current conservation problems. Primary crops: 10th in the state for peanuts. Wheat, oats, hay, sorghum and rye. Primary fruits and nuts: peaches and pecans. Primary livestock and products: eighth in the state for turkeys. Cattle, milk, sheep, wool, angora goats, mohair and hogs. **BUSINESS** Total number of business establishments in the county: 751. Retail sales during the first quarter of 1984 increased 17%. In 1980, 11% of the labor force were self-employed, 21% were employed in professional or related services, 19% in manufacturing, 21% in wholesale and retail trade, 9% in transportation, communications and other public utilities, 6% were employed in other counties and there were 4,164 retired workers. The industries with the most employment: meat packing, commercial printing and the manufacture of leather gloves, plastic products, plumbing fixtures, construction equipment and oilfield machinery. The nonfarm earnings in 1981 totaled $287,603,000. The retired workers received an average monthly Social Security payment of $297. **FINANCE** On June 30, 1983, five commercial banks had total deposits of $210,047,000 and total assets of $227,841,000. On December 31, 1982 one state savings and loan association and four state branches had assets of $202,665,942. In addition there are three credit unions in the county. **HOUSING** Average value of homes in 1980: $25,500. Permits for new, privately owned housing units increased in 1982: 141 permits were issued with a total construction cost of $4,028,200. Of those permits, 137 were for single family houses. Between 1970 and 1980 the number of housing units increased by 40%. Seventy-seven percent of all units in the county are air-conditioned, 77% are heated by gas and 19% by electricity. **NATURAL RESOURCES** Ceramic clay, limestone, industrial sand, gas, oil and bituminous coal. In 1982 a total of 5,115,720 thousand cubic feet of gas well gas, 8,187 barrels of condensate, 444,930 barrels of crude oil and 2,570,297 thousand cubic feet of casinghead gas were produced. Current production of other minerals and products includes brick, clay, crushed limestone and industrial sand. **TOURISM** Travel expenditures of $53,177,000 in 1982 (an increase of 10% over 1981) generated 1,352 jobs and $11,146,000 in payroll. Lodging: six hotels, motels and tourist courts. Convention/meeting facilities: Brownwood—Brownwood Coliseum and Howard Payne University Stadium and Gym. **ALCOHOLIC BEVERAGES** Packaged distilled spirits, beer, ale, malt liquor and wine are legal in parts of the county. **FEDERAL EXPENDITURES** The federal government had direct expenditures or obligations of $66,134,000 in the county during fiscal year 1983, including $2,559,000 by the U.S. Department of Defense. In addition, the federal government provided $647,000 in grant awards, paid $3,826,000 in salaries and wages, made direct payments to individuals of $61,584,000 including $44,578,000 in retirement and disability payments and spent $880,000 in other expenditures or obligations. The federal government also provided $2,524,000 in direct loans and $12,424,000 in guaranteed loans and insurance.

COMMUNICATION

Newspapers–Daily: Brownwood Bulletin, ave. eve. circ. 10,309. Weekly: Brown County Gazette (Bangs). Radio: KBWD-AM, KXYL-AM, KXYL-FM, KOXE-FM and KPSM-FM (Brownwood). Cable TV. Telephone companies: Continental Telephone, General Telephone, Central Texas Telephone Coop., Coleman County Telephone Coop and Comanche County Telephone. **TRANSPORTATION** Total public road mileage: 1,227. In 1982 there were 34,162 registered vehicles and 963 reported traffic accidents including 12 fatalities. Taxi cabs: one company in Brownwood. Intercity bus service is available. Motor freight: 11 local and intrastate carriers. Rail: Three main lines carry freight through the county. One of the main lines carries annually over 30 million tons of freight; one carries 20 to 30 million and one carries 10 to 20 million. Aircraft: 58 are registered in the county. Airports: Brownwood Municipal Airport is a basic transportation airport with commuter service. It serves as a base for 22 aircraft. Bowie Memorial Airport at Brownwood includes a Helipad.

COMMUNITY SERVICES

EDUCATION Eight school districts with 10 elementary, four middle, seven high schools and one special education. The average

daily attendance in 1981-82 was 5,912, with expenditures per pupil of $2,195 including 373 classroom teachers with an average annual salary of $15,656. Thirty-one percent of the 339 high school graduates planned to attend college. In 1982-83, 81% of the students were White, 12% Hispanic, 7% Black, 0.5% Asian and 0.1% American Indian. Sports championships: 1983 AAAA Boys' Tennis Singles, Brownwood H.S. and 1983 AAAA Boys' Tennis Doubles, Brownwood H.S. Howard Payne University is located in Brownwood. Established in 1889 it is affiliated with the Southern Baptist Church. Enrollment in 1982 was 1,201 with in state undergraduate tuition and fees of $1,920 per semester. The highest degree offered is Bachelor. Vocational education: Brownwood—Brownwood School of Vocational Nursing, Central Texas Commercial College and Gary's Beauty College. **PUBLIC LIBRARIES** Brownwood Public Library: 54,307 volumes. **CHILD CARE** 92 day care and nine twenty-four hour care licensed facilities. **HEALTH CARE** 34 physicians and 15 dentists. Hospitals: one with a capacity of 218. Clinics: one dialysis clinic and one public health clinic. Ambulance services: one commercial and one volunteer fire department service. Mental health: one clinic and one development center with bed capacity of 112. Nursing homes: six nursing homes with a combined capacity of 458 nursing care residents. The average cost per day for private patients in 1982 was $30.85. **CHURCHES** 65 churches have an estimated combined membership of 22,989. The largest denominations are Southern Baptist, United Methodist and Catholic. **SOCIAL SERVICES** In fiscal year 1983 a total of $1,304,572 in food stamps was distributed, with an average of 2,738 persons receiving food stamps each month. Aid to Families with Dependent Children (AFDC) totaled $264,287 with an average of 174 families receiving AFDC each month. Medical assistance benefits for the aged and disabled of $5,176,968 and for families and children of $360,515 brought the county benefit total to $7,106,342. **FIRE PROTECTION** One paid and six volunteer fire departments. **LAW ENFORCEMENT** The County Sheriff has eight commissioned officers. Three police departments have a combined force of 35. **CRIME** 42 violent crimes (murder, forcible rape, robbery and aggravated assault) and 1,351 nonviolent crimes (burglary, larceny-theft and motor vehicle theft) were reported in 1982. **JUDICIAL SYSTEM** One District Court and Judge, one County Court and Judge and three Justices of the Peace. In the District Court a total of 780 cases were pending on 1/1/82, 1,086 new cases were filed and 1,032 cases were disposed of during the year leaving 834 cases pending on 12/31/82. There were 354 criminal cases on the docket, 155 convictions, 43 persons committed to prison, eight committed to jail and 121 cases left pending. In the County Court 2,041 cases were pending on 1/1/82, 1,500 new cases were filed and 1,365 cases were disposed of during the year leaving 2,176 cases pending on 12/31/82. There were 3,209 criminal cases on the docket, 565 convictions, 58 persons committed to jail, and 2,027 cases left pending. **JAIL** One jail, capacity 72. **ATTORNEYS AT LAW** 44. **UTILITIES** 88% of the residents are connected to a public or privately owned water system and 67% are connected to a public sewer system. Natural gas is distributed to the county by Lone Star Gas Co., Division of Enserch. The average annual residential bill for natural gas in 1982 for the Lone Star distribution system was $405.91, an increase of 35% over 1981. Electricity is distributed to the county by Texas Power and Light Co., Comanche Co. Electric Coop., Inc. and McCulloch Electric Coop., Inc. and is generated primarily by gas, oil, water and coal. The typical residential electric bill is $165.24 per month for an all-electric house using 2,500 kwh. **TAXES** The county has 12 units with taxing authority: seven school districts, four cities and one county.

BROWN (continued)

RECREATION/ENTERTAINMENT
NATIONAL REGISTER OF HISTORIC PLACES
Brownwood: Saint John's Episcopal Church, Santa Fe Railroad Station, J.A. Walters House and R.B. Rogers House. **STATE** Lake Brownwood State Recreation Area covers 537 acres with camping and trailer sites, swimming, fishing and boat ramps. **COUNTY/MUNICIPAL PARKS** 223 acres in one county and 18 municipal parks. These parks contain eight playgrounds, five football and soccer fields, nine baseball and softball fields, 11 tennis courts, three swimming pools and one boat ramp. Developed campsites: 28. **SCENIC DRIVES** The Texas Forts Trail runs through this county. This trail leads to eight of the famous frontier forts of West Central Texas and an ancient presidio of the Spanish colonial period. **BOATING/FISHING** Lakes/reservoirs: Brownwood (2,604 acres), Brownwood Laterals Soil Conservation Service Lake 3 (15 acres), Brownwood Municipal Lower (50 acres), Brownwood Municipal Upper (37 acres), Clear Creek Soil Conservation Service Lakes 1, 3 and 6 (62 acres), Coggin (34 acres) and Turkey Creek Soil Conservation Service Lake 12 (12 acres). Major rivers: Colorado. Primary streams: Blanket, Clear, Dooley, Turkey, Pecan Bayou, West Fork Clear and Willis. **HUNTING** Fall and winter seasons on deer. No closed seasons on squirrel, nutria, bobcat and coyote. Winter seasons on quail, muskrat, beaver, otter, opossum, mink, ring-tailed cat, badger, fox, raccoon, skunk and civet cat. Fall, winter and spring seasons on turkey. In 1983 duck, coot, geese, woodcock and jacksnipe seasons occurred during the winter months. Teal duck, rail and gallinule seasons occurred in the fall. Mourning dove seasons occurred intermittently during the fall and winter months. **MUSEUMS** Brownwood: Douglas MacArthur Academy of Freedom. **COLLEGIATE FINE ARTS** Brownwood: Cultural events offered by Howard Payne University. **SPECIAL EVENTS** Stage Band Festival, Brownwood, February; Domino Tourney, Brownwood, March; Rattlesnake Roundup, Brownwood, March; Annual Golf Scramble, Brownwood, June; Rodeo, Brownwood, July; and Pecan Valley Arts Festival, Brownwood, September.

COMMUNITIES
COUNTY SEAT Brownwood, County Courthouse, 76801; County Clerk's Office, 915/643-2594. **INCORPORATED COMMUNITIES** (1980 population and ZIP Code) Bangs (1,716) 76823, Blanket (388) 76432, Brownwood (19,396) 76801 and Early (2,313) 76801. **UNINCORPORATED COMMUNITIES** (and ZIP Code) Brookesmith 76827, Byrds 76847, Cross Cut 76801, Dulin 76827, Grosvenor 76801, Indian Creek 76801, Lake Brownwood 76801, Lake Shore 76801, May 76857, Owens 76857, Shamrock Shores 76801, Thrifty 76801, Williams 76857, Winchell 76827 and Zephyr 76890. **FOR ADDITIONAL LOCAL INFORMATION** Brownwood Chamber of Commerce, 521 E. Baker, P.O. Box 880, Brownwood, 76801, 915/646-9535.

BURLESON (C27)

THE LAND
Northwest of Houston on State Highways 21 and 36 in the Claypan Area, Burleson County covers 668 square miles with the elevation ranging from 225 to 475 feet. Artesian water is found in areas of the county. The northern one-fourth of the county has nearly level to undulating, light-colored, medium to slightly acidic soils, with loamy or sandy surface layers and red or mottled clayey to loamy subsoils. A narrow strip runs through Caldwell of undulating, alkaline to slightly acidic, cracking, clayey soils with loamy surface layers. The rest of the county is nearly level to undulating with light-colored, sandy surface layers and cracking, clayey subsoils. Along the Brazos River the soils have loamy to clayey surfaces with cracking, clayey subsoils. East to west through the center of the county are the tall grasses, mesquite and other scrubby trees of the Blackland Prairies vegetation area. North and south of that are the hardwood forests and shade tolerant tall grasses of the Post Oak Savannah vegetation area. Between 21 and 30% of the land in the county is considered prime farmland. **CLIMATE** Subtropical subhumid and generally mild. The average annual temperature is 68°F. Temperatures in January range from an average low of 39° to an average high of 60°F and in July range from 73° to 95°F. The average annual precipitation is 37 inches, with an average relative humidity of 84% at 6 A.M. and 54% at 6 P.M. The average annual snowfall is less than one inch. The growing season averages 268 days per year, with the last freeze the first of March and the first freeze in late November. The sun shines during the year on the average 68% of the daylight hours.

THE PEOPLE
The 1982 estimated population of 14,700 indicates a continuation of the strong growth rate begun in the 1970s which reversed the steady population decrease since 1930. The age groups with the largest gains between 1970 and 1980 were ages 20 to 24 and birth to five years, lowering the high median age from 37 in 1970 to 34 in 1980. The high death rate in the county reflects the older than average population. The largest ancestry groups are Black (22%), and persons of German descent (18%). **REGISTERED VOTERS** As of November 2, 1982 there were 6,946 registered voters (0.1% of the state total). The 1982 general election had a 49% voter turnout, compared to a 64% turnout in the 1980 general election. In the 1982 primary 98% voted Democratic and 2% Republican, with 2,068 votes cast.

THE ECONOMY
AGRICULTURE In 1982, 77% of the land was in farms and ranches, with 16% of the farmland under cultivation and 27% irrigated. Burleson ranked 144th in the state in highest agricultural receipts, with 75% from livestock and livestock products. Overgrazing, undesirable brush and weeds, water erosion and flooding are the current conservation problems. Primary crops: hay, cotton, sorghum, oats and wheat. Primary vegetables: watermelons. Primary fruits and nuts: peaches and pecans. Primary livestock and products: cattle and hogs. **BUSINESS** Total number of business establishments in the county: 267. Retail sales during the first quarter of 1984 increased 9% with a gain of 23% in Caldwell, a decrease of 32% in Somerville, and a 9% decrease in Snook. In 1980, 13% of the labor force were self-employed, 20% were employed in professional or related services, 17% in manufacturing, 17% in wholesale and retail trade, 14% in agriculture, forestry, fisheries and mining, 32% were employed in other counties and there were 1,413 retired workers. The industries with the most employment: oil and gas extraction, agribusiness and the manufacture of metal household furniture and steel wire. The nonfarm earnings in 1981 totaled $113,036,000. The retired workers received an average monthly Social Security payment of $271. **FINANCE** On June 30, 1983, five commercial banks had total deposits of $116,461,000 and total assets of $129,109,000. On December 31, 1982 one state savings and loan association and one state branch had assets of $10,031,404. **HOUSING** Average value of homes in 1980: $22,500. Permits for new, privately owned housing units decreased in 1982: 89 permits were issued with a total construction cost of $2,898,233. Of those permits, 36 were for single family houses. Between 1970 and 1980 the number of housing units increased by 51%. Sixty-one percent of all units in the county are air-conditioned, 79% are heated by gas and 10% by electricity. **NATURAL RESOURCES** Clay, sand and gravel, oil, gas and lignite coal.

In 1982 a total of 28,882,841 thousand cubic feet of gas well gas, 1,009,821 barrels of condensate, 17,013,055 barrels of crude oil and 67,879,464 thousand cubic feet of casinghead gas were produced. Current production of other minerals and products includes crushed sandstone, and sand and gravel. **TOURISM** Travel expenditures of $4,546,000 in 1982 (an increase of 12% over 1981) generated 103 jobs and $857,000 in payroll. **ALCOHOLIC BEVERAGES** Packaged distilled spirits, beer, ale, malt liquor and wine are legal in parts of the county. **FEDERAL EXPENDITURES** The federal government had direct expenditures or obligations of $24,928,000 in the county during fiscal year 1983, including $1,644,000 by the U.S. Department of Defense. In addition, the federal government provided $143,000 in grant awards, paid $1,068,000 in salaries and wages, made direct payments to individuals of $21,677,000 including $15,750,000 in retirement and disability payments, awarded $667,000 in procurement contracts and spent $1,373,000 in other expenditures or obligations. The federal government also provided $936,000 in direct loans and $1,919,000 in guaranteed loans and insurance.

COMMUNICATION

Newspapers–Weekly: Burleson County Citizen Tribune (Caldwell) and the Somerville Tribune. Cable TV. Telephone companies: General Telephone and Southwestern Bell. **TRANSPORTATION** Total public road mileage: 731. In 1982 there were 13,079 registered vehicles and 529 reported traffic accidents including 15 fatalities. Intercity bus service is available. Motor freight: five local and intrastate carriers. Rail: six main lines carry freight through the county. Five of the main lines carry annually over 30 million tons of freight each and one carries 10 to 20 million. Aircraft: 20 are registered in the county. Airports: Caldwell Municipal Airport.

COMMUNITY SERVICES

EDUCATION Three school districts with four elementary, two middle, and three high schools. The average daily attendance in 1981-82 was 2,653, with expenditures per pupil of $2,582 including 162 classroom teachers with an average annual salary of $15,094. Forty-four percent of the 157 high school graduates planned to attend college. In 1982-83, 59% of the students were White, 14% Hispanic and 27% Black. Sports championships: 1984 A Boys' Basketball, Snook H.S. **PUBLIC LIBRARIES** Harrie P. Woodson Memorial Library (Caldwell): 11,000 volumes. **CHILD CARE** 14 day care and eight twenty-four hour care licensed facilities. **HEALTH CARE** Four physicians and one dentist. Hospitals: one with a capacity of 37. Ambulance services: two commercial and one county service. Mental health: one county clinic. Nursing homes: one nursing home has a capacity of 156 nursing care residents. The average cost per day for private patients in 1982 was $35.65. **CHURCHES** 31 churches have an estimated combined membership of 5,419. The largest denominations are Southern Baptist, Catholic and United Methodist. **SOCIAL SERVICES** In fiscal year 1983 a total of $541,187 in food stamps was distributed, with an average of 1,144 persons receiving food stamps each month. Aid to Families with Dependent Children (AFDC) totaled $197,764 with an average of 124 families receiving AFDC each month. Medical assistance benefits for the aged and disabled of $1,370,195 and for families and children of $163,569 brought the county benefit total to $2,272,714. **FIRE PROTECTION** Six volunteer fire departments. **LAW ENFORCEMENT** The County Sheriff has 13 commissioned officers. Two police departments have a combined force of 38. **CRIME** 28 violent crimes (murder, forcible rape, robbery and aggravated assault) and 267 nonviolent crimes (burglary, larceny-theft and motor vehicle theft) were reported in 1982. **JUDICIAL SYSTEM** Two District Courts and Judges, one County Court and Judge and four Justices of the Peace. In the

District Courts a total of 652 cases were pending on 1/1/82, 593 new cases were filed and 429 cases were disposed of during the year leaving 816 cases pending on 12/31/82. There were 255 criminal cases on the docket, 118 convictions, 39 persons committed to prison and 9 committed to jail and 97 cases left pending. In the County Court 544 cases were pending on 1/1/82, 279 new cases were filed and 371 cases were disposed of during the year leaving 452 cases pending on 12/31/82. There were 699 criminal cases on the docket, 147 convictions, 65 persons committed to jail, and 408 cases left pending. **JAILS** One jail, capacity 12. **ATTORNEYS AT LAW** 19. **UTILITIES** 70% of the residents are connected to a public or privately owned water system and 37% are connected to a public sewer system. Natural gas is distributed to the county by Lone Star Gas Co., Division of Enserch. The average annual residential bill for natural gas in 1982 for the Lone Star distribution system was $405.91, an increase of 35% over 1981. Electricity is distributed to the city of Caldwell by the Caldwell Municipal Light Dept. and to the rest of the county by Gulf State Utilities Co., Bluebonnet Electric Coop., Inc., and Bartlett Electric Coop., Inc. and is generated primarily by gas, oil and water. **TAXES** The county has eight units with taxing authority: three school districts, two cities, one county, and two special districts.

RECREATION/ENTERTAINMENT

STATE Lake Somerville State Recreation Area covers 5,200 acres with camping, trailer sites, swimming, fishing, boat ramps, nature and horseback trails. **COUNTY/MUNICIPAL PARKS** 324 acres in two county and five municipal parks. These parks contain two playgrounds, three baseball and softball fields, four tennis courts and three boat ramps. **SCENIC DRIVES** The Texas Brazos Trail runs through this county. This trail moves through a beautiful and historic section of Central Texas revealing forested landscapes filled with wildlife and wild flowers. **BOATING/FISHING** Lakes/reservoirs: Balcar (30 acres), Bowers (15 acres), Cade (50 acres), East-West (98 acres), Somerville (11,460 acres) and Woodrow (15 acres). Major rivers: Brazos. Primary streams: Cottonwood, Davidson, Second Davidson, East Yegua, Sweet Gum and Yegua. **WILDLIFE REFUGES:** Somerville State Wildlife Management Area covers 1,800 acres in this county. **HUNTING** Fall and winter seasons on deer. No closed seasons on coyotes, bobcats and squirrels. Winter season on quail, muskrat, beaver, opossum, ring-tailed cat, badger, fox, weasel, raccoon, skunk and civet cat. In 1983, duck, coot, geese, woodcock and jacksnipe seasons occurred during the winter months. Teal duck, rail and gallinule seasons occurred in the fall. Mourning dove seasons occurred intermittently during the fall and winter months. **MUSEUMS** Caldwell: Burleson County Historical Museum. **SPECIAL EVENTS** Go Texan Day, Caldwell, January; Spring Festival, Caldwell, March; Annual Class A Quarter Horse Show, Caldwell, April; Bass Fishing Tourney, Caldwell, May; Fishing Tourney, Somerville, May; Farmer's Square, Caldwell, June; Youth Rodeo, Caldwell, July; Barbecue Cookoff, Caldwell, September; County Fair and Parade, Caldwell, September; Arts and Crafts Festival, Caldwell, December.

COMMUNITIES

COUNTY SEAT Caldwell, County Courthouse, 77836; County Clerk's Office, 409/567-4326. **INCORPORATED COMMUNITIES** (1980 population and ZIP Code) Caldwell (2,953) 77836, Snook (408) 77878 and Somerville (1,814) 77879. **UNINCORPORATED COMMUNITIES** (and ZIP Code) Birch 77879, Center Line 77879, Chances Store (Chance) 77879, Chriesman 77838, Clay 77839, Cooks Point 77836, Deanville 77852, Fosters Store 77836, Frenstat 77836, Hix 77857, Hogg 77836, Lyons 77863, Merle 77855, Rita 77857, Tunis 77836 and Wilcox 77879.

COUNTIES

BURLESON (continued)

FOR ADDITIONAL LOCAL INFORMATION Caldwell Chamber of Commerce, 119 Buck, P.O. Box 126, Caldwell 77836, 409/567-3218 or 567-7979 and Somerville Chamber of Commerce, P.O. Box 352, Somerville 77879, 409/596-2383.

BURNET (C15)

THE LAND

Northwest of Austin on U.S. Highways 281 and 183 in the Grand Prairie Region, Burnet County covers 994 square miles of gentle to broken hills. The elevation ranges from 700 to 1,770 feet. The southwest corner of the county has deep, dark red soils with loamy surface layers and clayey subsoils. In some areas shallow soils cover limestone or sandstone. The remainder of the county has loamy soils. The northeastern portion of the county is in the Crosstimbers and Prairie vegetation area with mid to tall grasses, live oaks and some juniper and mesquite. The southwest is in the Edwards Plateau vegetation area with tall to mid grasses, live oaks, scrubby post oaks, mesquite, shrubs and cacti. Between 11 and 20% of the land in the county is considered prime farmland. **CLIMATE** Subtropical subhumid with hot summers and mild winters. The average annual temperature is 66°F. Temperatures in January range from an average low of 37° to an average high of 59°F and in July range from 71° to 96°F. The average annual precipitation is 30 inches, with an average relative humidity of 76% at 6 A.M. and 46% at 6 P.M. The average annual snowfall is three inches. The growing season averages 234 days per year, with the last freeze in late March and the first freeze in mid November. The sun shines during the year on the average 66% of the day-light hours.

THE PEOPLE

Burnet County ranks 70th among all U.S. counties in percent of population aged 65 and over. The 1982 estimated population of 19,200 indicates a continuation of the strong growth rate begun in the 1960s. The urban growth rate of 133% between 1970 and 1980 was one of the highest in the state. The age groups with the largest gains from 1970 to 1980 were ages birth to five and 20 to 34, lowering the high median age from 43 in 1970 to 42 in 1980. The largest ancestry groups are persons of English descent (34%) and Irish descent (30%). **REGISTERED VOTERS** As of November 2, 1982 there were 11,203 registered voters (0.2% of the state total). The 1982 general election had a 51% voter turnout, compared to a 75% turnout in the 1980 general election. In the 1982 primary 94% voted Democratic and 6% Republican, with 3,969 votes cast.

THE ECONOMY

AGRICULTURE In 1982, 88% of the land was in farms and ranches, with 4% of the farmland under cultivation. Burnet ranked 188th in the state in highest agricultural receipts, with 94% from livestock and livestock products. Overgrazing, undesirable brush and weeds, water erosion and the cultivation of marginal lands are the current conservation problems. Primary crops: hay, oats and wheat. Primary fruits and nuts: peaches and pecans. Primary livestock and products: cattle, sheep, wool, angora goats, mohair and hogs. **BUSINESS** Total number of business establishments in the county: 417. Retail sales during the first quarter of 1984 increased 18% with a gain of 32% in Marble Falls and a decline of 8% in Bertram and 3% in Burnet. In 1980, 17% of the labor force were self-employed, 15% were employed in professional or related services, 8% in manufacturing, 21% in wholesale and retail trade, 17% in construction, 24% were employed in other counties and there were 3,036 retired workers. The industries with the most employment: the quarrying of limestone, agribusiness, general construction and the manufacture of wood kitchen cabinets and switchgear and switchboard apparatus. The nonfarm earnings in 1981 totaled $183,214,000. The retired workers received an average monthly Social Security payment of $320. **FINANCE** On June 30, 1983, five commercial banks had total deposits of $181,334,000 and total assets of $201,264,000. On December 31, 1982 one state savings and loan association and two state branches had assets of $25,464,800. **HOUSING** Average value of homes in 1980: $34,200. Permits for new, privately owned housing units increased in 1982: 172 permits were issued with a total construction cost of $6,984,300. Of those permits, 52 were for single family houses. Between 1970 and 1980 the number of housing units increased by 67%. Seventy-five percent of all units in the county are air-conditioned, 61% are heated by gas and 29% by electricity. **NATURAL RESOURCES** Granite, limestone, industrial sand, silver, serpentine, graphite, gold, copper, lead, zinc, fluorspar, iron, molybdenum, oil and gas. Current production of other minerals and products includes crushed dolomite, block granite, dimension granite, terrazzo granite, flake graphite, lime, crushed limestone, fieldstone limestone, terrazzo limestone, fieldstone marble, terrazzo marble, sand and gravel, fieldstone sandstone and terrazzo serpentine. **TOURISM** Travel expenditures of $23,198,000 in 1982 (an increase of 11% over 1981) generated 586 jobs and $4,656,000 in payroll. **ALCOHOLIC BEVERAGES** Packaged distilled spirits, beer, ale, malt liquor and wine are legal in parts of the county. Sale of mixed beverages is legal in all or parts of the county. **FEDERAL EXPENDITURES** The federal government had direct expenditures or obligations of $62,947,000 in the county during fiscal year 1983, including $5,141,000 by the U.S. Department of Defense. In addition, the federal government provided $912,000 in grant awards, paid $1,074,000 in salaries and wages, made direct payments to individuals of $60,518,000 including $50,031,000 in retirement and disability payments, awarded $67,000 in procurement contracts and spent $376,000 in other expenditures or obligations. The federal government also provided $1,737,000 in direct loans and $6,766,000 in guaranteed loans and insurance.

COMMUNICATION

Newspapers–Weekly: Burnet Bulletin and The Highlander (Marble Falls). Radio: KHLB-AM, KMRB-FM (Burnet). Cable TV. Telephone companies: Continental Telephone, General Telephone, Southwestern Bell and Central Telephone. **TRANSPORTATION** Total public road mileage: 995. In 1982 there were 19,832 registered vehicles and 480 reported traffic accidents including nine fatalities. Intercity bus service is available. Motor freight: two carriers. Rail: three branch lines carry freight through the county. Two of the branch lines carry annually one to five million tons of freight each and one carries less than one million. Aircraft: 55 are registered in the county. Airports: Kate Craddock Field in Burnet is a general utility airport with general aviation service. It serves as a base for 35 aircraft. Also serving the area are Barnhill II Airport at Lake Victor, Granite Shoals Municipal Airport and Horseshoe Bay Airport at Marble Falls

COMMUNITY SERVICES

EDUCATION Two school districts with three elementary, three middle and two high schools. The average daily attendance in 1981-82 was 3,168, with expenditures per pupil of $2,450 including 200 classroom teachers with an average annual salary of $15,136. Fifty percent of the 202 high school graduates planned to attend college. In 1982-83, 85% of the students were White, 12% Hispanic, 3% Black, 0.3% Asian and 0.3% American Indian. Sports championships: 1983 AAA Girls' Tennis Doubles, Marble Falls H.S. **PUBLIC LIBRARIES** Herman Brown Free

Library (Burnet): 44,071 volumes and four branches. **CHILD CARE** 37 day care and three twenty-four hour care licensed facilities. **HEALTH CARE** 27 physicians and 13 dentists. Hospitals: one with a capacity of 92. Ambulance services: five commercial, four volunteer services, two funeral homes, and one city service. Mental health: one county clinic. Nursing homes: three nursing homes with a combined capacity of 194 nursing care residents. The average cost per day for private patients in 1982 was $43.84. **CHURCHES** 47 churches have an estimated combined membership of 10,329. The largest denominations are Southern Baptist, Churches of Christ and United Methodist. **SOCIAL SERVICES** In fiscal year 1983 a total of $466,572 in food stamps was distributed, with an average of 978 persons receiving food stamps each month. Aid to Families with Dependent Children (AFDC) totaled $124,888 with an average of 83 families receiving AFDC each month. Medical assistance benefits for the aged and disabled of $1,276,391 and for families and children of $246,898 brought the county benefit total to $2,114,748. **FIRE PROTECTION** Ten volunteer fire departments. **LAW ENFORCEMENT** The County Sheriff has 21 commissioned officers. Three police departments have a combined force of 23. **CRIME** 35 violent crimes (murder, forcible rape, robbery and aggravated assault) and 495 nonviolent crimes (burglary, larceny-theft and motor vehicle theft) were reported in 1982. **JUDICIAL SYSTEM** One District Court and Judge, one County Court and Judge and four Justices of the Peace. In the District Court a total of 470 cases were pending on 1/1/82, 537 new cases were filed and 481 cases were disposed of during the year leaving 526 cases pending on 12/31/82. There were 191 criminal cases on the docket, 27 convictions, five persons committed to prison and one committed to jail and 145 cases left pending. In the County Court 225 cases were pending on 1/1/82, 520 new cases were filed and 593 cases were disposed of during the year leaving 152 cases pending on 12/31/82. There were 689 criminal cases on the docket, 247 convictions, 44 persons committed to jail, and 132 cases left pending. **JAILS** One jail, capacity 40. **ATTORNEYS AT LAW** 36. **UTILITIES** 66% of the residents are connected to a public or privately owned water system and 36% are connected to a public sewer system. Natural gas is distributed to the county by Lone Star Gas Co., Division of Enserch. The average annual residential bill for natural gas in 1982 for the Lone Star distribution system was $405.91, an increase of 35% over 1981. Electricity is distributed to the city of Burnet by Burnet Utilities and to the rest of the county by Pedernales Electric Coop., Inc. The typical residential electric bill is $141.05 per month for an all-electric house using 2,500 kwh. **TAXES** The county has eight units with taxing authority: two school districts, four cities, one county and one special district.

RECREATION/ENTERTAINMENT
NATIONAL REGISTER OF HISTORIC PLACES Marble Falls: Roper Hotel. Marble Falls vicinity: Louis Page Archeological Site. Spicewood vicinity: Krause Spring. **STATE** Inks Lake State Park covers 1,201 acres with camping and trailer sites as well as areas offering swimming, fishing, boat ramps, nature trails, golf and rental boats. Longhorn Cavern State Park covers 639 acres with fishing, boat ramps, nature trails, golf and daily tours of the world's third largest cavern. **COUNTY/ MUNICIPAL PARKS** 69 acres in two county and 25 municipal parks. These parks contain 18 playgrounds, one football and soccer field, four baseball and softball fields, two tennis courts, five swimming pools, four beaches and 10 boat ramps. Developed campsites: 10. **SCENIC DRIVES** The Texas Hill Country Trail runs through this county. Texas 29 and RM 2341 to Spider Mountain is considered one of Texas' most scenic drives. Also noteworthy are the picturesque Hoover Valley Road below Inks

Lake State Park and R.M. 2342 both of which offer landscape views. **BOATING/FISHING** Lakes/reservoirs: Buchanan (23,060 acres), Inks (803 acres), Lyndon B. Johnson (6,375 acres), Marble Falls (780 acres), Oak Hollow (41 acres) and Sulphur Creek Soil Conservation Service Lake 4 (6 acres). Major rivers: Colorado, Lampasas, North Fork San Gabriel and Russell Fork. Primary streams: Beaver, Pillar Bluff and South Rocky. **HUNTING** Fall and winter seasons on deer. No closed seasons on coyote, bobcat and squirrel. Winter season on quail, muskrat, beaver, opossum, ring-tailed cat, badger, fox, weasel, raccoon, skunk and civet cat. Fall, winter and spring seasons on turkey. In 1983 duck, coot, geese, woodcock and jacksnipe seasons occurred during the winter months. Teal duck, rail and gallinule seasons occurred in the fall. Mourning dove seasons occurred intermittently during the fall and winter months. **MUSEUMS** Burnet: Fort Croghan Museum, Longhorn Cavern Museum and Pioneer Museum. **OTHER** Burnet: Old Mormon Colony and Mill. **SPECIAL EVENTS** Howdy Roo Festival, Marble Falls, April; Highland Lakes Bluebonnet Trail, Marble Falls/Burnet, April; Annual Dairy Goat Assn. Show, Burnet, April; Junior Rodeo, Marble Falls, May; Junior Rodeo, Burnet, May; Rodeo and Parade, Burnet, July; Rodeo, Marble Falls, July; Texas Old Time Fiddlers' Contest, Burnet, August; Oatmeal Festival, Bertram/ Oatmeal, August; County Fair, Burnet, August; Main Street Fiesta, Marble Falls, September; Roping Contests, Burnet, October; Highland Lakes Arts and Crafts Festival, Burnet, October.

COMMUNITIES
COUNTY SEAT Burnet, County Courthouse, 78611; County Clerk's Office, 512/756-4601. **INCORPORATED COMMUNITIES** (1980 population and ZIP Code) Bertram (824) 78605, Burnet (3,410) 78611, Granite Shoals (634) 78654 and Marble Falls (3,252) 78654. **UNINCORPORATED COMMUNITIES** (and ZIP Code) Briggs 78608, Fairland 78654, Hoovers Valley 78611, Jappa 78605, Lake Victor 76550, Mahomet 78605, Naruna 76550, Oakalla 76541, Oatmeal 78605, Sherwood Shores 78654, Smithwick 78654, Spicewood 78669, Tamega 78605 and Watson 76550. **FOR ADDITIONAL LOCAL INFORMATION** Burnet Chamber of Commerce, 306 W. Polk, Drawer M, Burnet, 78611, 512/756-4297 and Marble Falls Chamber of Commerce, 801 Hwy. 281, Marble Falls, 78654, 512/693-4449.

CALDWELL (C32)

THE LAND
South of Austin on U.S. Highway 183 in the Claypan Area, Caldwell County covers 546 square miles. Level prairies are found in the northern portion of the county with hills in the southeast and broken valleys in the southwestern portion. The elevation ranges from 375 to 500 feet. The northwest one-third has slightly acidic, dark loamy to clayey soils with cracking, clayey subsoils. The middle one-third of the county has dark, cracking, clayey soils with some loamy surfaces. There is a high shrink-swell potential. The southeastern corner has sandy soils with cracking, clayey subsoils. The northwest half of the county is in the Blackland Prairie vegetation area and has tall grasses, mesquite and other scrubby trees. The southeast half has tall grasses and hardwood trees such as oak and elm. Between 21 and 30% of the land in the county is considered prime farmland. **CLIMATE** is subtropical humid and generally mild. The average annual temperature is 68°F. Temperatures in January range from an average low of 38° to an average high of 61°F and in July range from 72° to 96°F. The average annual precipitation is 35 inches, with an average relative humidity of 85% at 6 A.M. and 55% at 6 P.M. There is no significant snowfall. The growing season

averages 274 days per year, with the last freeze in late February and the first freeze in late November. The sun shines during the year on the average 66% of the daylight hours.

THE PEOPLE

The 1982 estimated population of 24,800 indicates a continuation of the steady growth begun in the 1960s, which reversed a loss in population of over 24,000 between 1930 and 1960. Urban areas experienced a population gain of 16% between 1970 and 1980. The age group with the largest gain was ages 20 to 39, while the largest decrease occurred in persons aged 15 to 19. Therefore the median age increased from 23 in 1970 to 27 in 1980. The largest ancestry groups Hispanic (33%), Black (17%), persons of English descent (16%) and German descent (16%). **REGISTERED VOTERS** As of November 2, 1982 there were 10,381 registered voters (0.2% of the state total). The 1982 general election had a 50% voter turnout, compared to a 60% turnout in the 1980 general election. In the 1982 primary 94% voted Democratic and 6% Republican, with 3,216 votes cast.

THE ECONOMY

AGRICULTURE In 1982, 83% of the land was in farms and ranches, with 20% of the farmland under cultivation. Caldwell ranked 125th in the state in highest agricultural receipts, with 84% from livestock and livestock products. Overgrazing, undesirable brush and weeds, water erosion and soil compaction are the current conservation problems. Primary crops: sorghum, hay, oats, cotton, wheat and corn. Primary vegetables: watermelons. Primary fruits and nuts: peaches and pecans. Primary livestock and products: fifth in the state for egg production and sixth for hens and pullets, cattle and hogs. **BUSINESS** Total number of business establishments in the county: 459. Retail sales during the first quarter of 1984 increased 9% with a gain of 13% in Lockhart. In 1980, 11% of the labor force were self-employed, 23% were employed in professional or related services, 13% in manufacturing, 19% in wholesale and retail trade, 12% in agriculture, forestry, fisheries and mining, 38% were employed in other counties and there were 2,077 retired workers. The industries with the most employment: oil and gas extraction, poultry processing and the manufacture of women's apparel, engineering and scientific instruments and wood products. The nonfarm earnings in 1981 totaled $183,245,000. The retired workers received an average monthly Social Security payment of $289. **FINANCE** On June 30, 1983, four commercial banks had total deposits of $108,785,000 and total assets of $121,255,000. On December 31, 1982 one state savings and loan association, one federal association and one state branch had combined assets of $75,116,799. **HOUSING** Average value of homes in 1980: $23,500. Permits for new, privately owned housing units decreased in 1982: 97 permits were issued with a total construction cost of $3,148,687. Of those permits, 67 were for single family houses. Between 1970 and 1980 the number of housing units increased by 28%. Sixty-one percent of all units in the county are air-conditioned, 78% are heated by gas and 16% by electricity. **NATURAL RESOURCES** Clay, industrial sand, sand and gravel, oil and gas. In 1982 a total of 27,621 thousand cubic feet of gas well gas, 692 barrels of condensate, 2,542,405 barrels of crude oil and 1,628,530 thousand cubic feet of casinghead gas were produced. Current production of other minerals and products includes sand and gravel. **TOURISM** Travel expenditures of $2,038,000 in 1982 (an increase of 13% over 1981) generated 37 jobs and $338,000 in payroll. **ALCOHOLIC BEVERAGES** Only 4% beer is legal in parts of the county. **FEDERAL EXPENDITURES** The federal government had direct expenditures or obligations of $36,791,000 in the county during fiscal year 1983, including $2,379,000 by the U.S. Department of Defense. In addition, the federal govern-

ment provided $2,375,000 in grant awards, paid $1,521,000 in salaries and wages, made direct payments to individuals of $31,941,000 including $22,678,000 in retirement and disability payments, awarded $134,000 in procurement contracts and spent $821,000 in other expenditures or obligations. The federal government also provided $332,000 in direct loans and $5,524,000 in guaranteed loans and insurance.

COMMUNICATION

Newspapers–Weekly: Lockhart Post-Register (Bilingual) and the Luling Newsboy and Signal. Radio: KCLT-AM (Lockhart). Cable TV. Telephone companies: Continental Telephone, Southwestern Bell, Guadalupe Valley Telephone Coop. and San Marcos Telephone. **TRANSPORTATION** Total public road mileage: 722. In 1982 there were 18,640 registered vehicles and 510 reported traffic accidents including 11 fatalities. Taxi cabs: one comany in Lockhart. Intercity bus service is available. Motor freight: five local and intrastate carriers. Rail: one main and one branch line carry freight through the county. The main line carries annually over 30 million tons of freight, and the branch line carries one to five million. Aircraft: 18 are registered in the county. Airports: Lockhart Municipal Airport and the Carter Memorial Airport at Luling.

COMMUNITY SERVICES

EDUCATION Three school districts with five elementary, one middle and three high schools. The average daily attendance in 1981-82 was 3,910, with expenditures per pupil of $2,300 including 262 classroom teachers with an average annual salary of $15,385. Thirty-two percent of the 237 high school graduates planned to attend college. In 1982-83, 43% of the students were White, 47% Hispanic, 10% Black, 0.2% Asian. **PUBLIC LIBRARIES** Dr. Eugene Clark Library (Lockhart): 20,000 volumes. Luling Public Library: 22,108 volumes. **CHILD CARE** 34 day care and five twenty-four hour care licensed facilities. **HEALTH CARE** 18 physicians and eight dentists. Hospitals: two with a combined capacity of 74. Clinics: one alcohol counseling and recovery clinic. Ambulance services: two city services. Mental health: one county clinic. Nursing homes: five nursing homes with a combined capacity of 412 nursing care residents. The average cost per day for private patients in 1982 was $29.47. **CHURCHES** 47 churches have an estimated combined membership of 10,559. The largest denominations are Southern Baptist, Catholic and United Methodist. **SOCIAL SERVICES** In fiscal year 1983 a total of $1,331,220 in food stamps was distributed, with an average of 2,907 persons receiving food stamps each month. Aid to Families with Dependent Children (AFDC) totaled $327,733 with an average of 214 families receiving AFDC each month. Medical assistance benefits for the aged and disabled of $2,901,484 and for families and children of $422,988 brought the county benefit total to $4,983,425. **FIRE PROTECTION** Nine volunteer fire departments. **LAW ENFORCEMENT** The County Sheriff has 18 commissioned officers. Two police departments have a combined force of 32. **CRIME** 86 violent crimes (murder, forcible rape, robbery and aggravated assault) and 487 nonviolent crimes (burglary, larceny-theft and motor vehicle theft) were reported in 1982. **JUDICIAL SYSTEM** Three District Courts and Judges, one County Court and Judge and four Justices of the Peace. In the District Courts a total of 638 cases were pending on 1/1/82, 613 new cases were filed and 577 cases were disposed of during the year leaving 674 cases pending on 12/31/82. There were 415 criminal cases on the docket, 118 convictions, 35 persons committed to prison and one committed to jail and 160 cases left pending. In the County Court 654 cases were pending on 1/1/82, 531 new cases were filed and 450 cases were disposed of during the year leaving 735 cases pending on 12/31/82. There were 1,091 criminal cases on the docket, 373 convictions, 53 persons

CALDWELL-CALHOUN

committed to jail, and 650 cases left pending. **JAILS** One jail, capacity 32, opened in 1983. **ATTORNEYS AT LAW** 23. **UTILITIES** 87% of the residents are connected to a public or privately owned water system and 59% are connected to a public sewer system. Natural gas is distributed to the county by Arkla Inc. The average annual residential bill for natural gas in 1982 for the Arkla distribution system was $316.69, an increase of 23% over 1981. Electricity is distributed to the city of Lockhart by Lockhart Utilities, Luling by Luling Utilities and to the rest of the county by Bluebonnet Electric Coop., Inc. and Pedernales Electric Coop., Inc. and is generated primarily by oil, water and coal. The typical residential electric bill is $141.38 per month for an all-electric house using 2,500 kwh. **TAXES** The county has seven units with taxing authority: three school districts, two cities, one county and one special district.

RECREATION/ENTERTAINMENT
NATIONAL REGISTER OF HISTORIC PLACES Lockhart: Caldwell County Courthouse Historic District, Emmanuel Episcopal Church and M.A. Withers Residence. **STATE** Lockhart State Recreation Area covers 264 acres with camping, swimming, and golf. **MUNICIPAL PARKS** 131 acres in eight municipal parks. These parks contain one mile of hiking trails, seven playgrounds, one golf course, two baseball and softball fields, six tennis courts, three multi-use courts and three swimming pools. **SCENIC DRIVES** The Texas Independence Trail runs through this county. This trail not only surveys the historic sites of eastern Texas but also includes many modern visitor attractions such as the Johnson Space Center. **BOATING/FISHING** Lakes/reservoirs: Plum Creek Lower Soil Conservation Service Lake 34 (10 acres). Major rivers: San Marcos. Primary streams: Dry and Plum. **HUNTING** Fall and winter seasons on deer and javelina. No closed seasons on coyote, bobcat, nutria and squirrel. Winter season on quail, muskrat, beaver, otter, mink, opossum, ring-tailed cat, badger, fox, raccoon, skunk and civet cat. Spring season on turkey. In 1983 sandhill crane, duck, coot, geese, woodcock and jacksnipe seasons occurred during the winter months. Teal duck, rail and gallinule seasons occurred in the fall. Mourning dove seasons occurred intermittently during the fall and winter months. **BOTANIC GARDENS** Luling: Palmetto State Park. **SPECIAL EVENTS** Chisholm Trail Round-up, Lockhart, May; Rodeo, Lockhart, June; Watermelon Thump, Luling, June; and Arts and Crafts Fair, Lockhart, August and October.

COMMUNITIES
COUNTY SEAT Lockhart, County Courthouse, 78644; County Clerk's Office, 512/398-2424. **INCORPORATED COMMUNITIES** (1980 population and ZIP Code) Lockhart All-America Cities Honorable Mention 1968 (7,953) 78644, Luling (5039) 78648 and Martindale (926) 78655. **UNINCORPORATED COMMUNITIES** (and ZIP Code) Blanks 78644, Brownsboro 78644, Dale 78616, Delhi 78953, Fentress 78622, Joliet 78648, Lytton Springs 78616, McMahan 78616, McNeil 78648, Maxwell 78656, Mendoza 78644, Neiderwald (also in Hays Co.) 78640, Prairie Lea 78661, Reedville 78656, Seawillow (Sea Willow) 78644, Stairtown 78648, Taylorsville 78662, Tilman 78616 and Uhland (also in Hays Co.) 78640. **FOR ADDITIONAL LOCAL INFORMATION** Lockhart Chamber of Commerce, Drawer 840, Lockhart, 78644, 512/398-2818 and Luling Chamber of Commerce, Drawer 710, 308 N. Magnolia, Luling, 78648, 512/875-3214.

CALHOUN (G29)

THE LAND
On the Gulf Coast northeast of Corpus Christi on U.S. Highway 87 in the Coastal Prairie Region, Calhoun County covers 540 square miles of which about one-fourth is water. The elevation ranges from sea level to 50 feet. The county has level, somewhat poorly to moderately-well drained soils, with loamy surface layers and cracking, clayey subsoils. In a wide strip along the coast the soils are saline, clayey and loamy in the marshes and sandy with dunes on the beaches. The Gulf Prairies and Marshes vegetation area consists of tall grasses and live oaks with cordgrasses and sedges along the coast. Between 21 and 30% of the land in the county is considered prime farmland. **CLIMATE** Subtropical humid, moist and mild. A possibility of a tropical storm or hurricane will exist during the months of June through October. The average annual temperature is 71°F. Temperatures in January range from an average low of 44° to an average high of 63°F and in July range from 76° to 92°F. The average annual precipitation is 40 inches, with an average relative humidity of 90% at 6 A.M. and 70% at 6 P.M. There is no snowfall. The growing season averages 305 days per year, with the last freeze in mid February and the first freeze in mid December. The sun shines during the year on the average 68% of the daylight hours.

THE PEOPLE
The 1982 estimated population of 21,300 continues a growth rate which has steadily climbed since the 1950s. Rural areas experienced a population gain of 18% between 1970 and 1980. The age group with the largest increase was ages 65 and over, while the greatest decrease occurred in the age group of five to 14. Therefore the low median age rose from 23 in 1970 to 28 in 1980. The largest ancestry groups are Hispanic (34%), persons of German descent (18%) and English descent (18%). **REGISTERED VOTERS** As of November 2, 1982 there were 9,450 registered voters (0.1% of the state total). The 1982 general election had a 57% voter turnout, compared to a 68% turnout in the 1980 general election. In the 1982 primary 96% voted Democratic and 4% Republican, with 3,565 votes cast.

THE ECONOMY
AGRICULTURE Sorghum area. In 1982, 70% of the land was in farms and ranches, with 30% of the farmland under cultivation and 34% irrigated. Calhoun ranked 168th in the state in highest agricultural receipts, with 60% from crops. Inefficient irrigation systems, soil compaction, drainage and shoreline erosion are the current conservation problems. Primary crops: sorghum, rice, corn and soybeans. Primary fruits and nuts: pecans. Primary livestock and products: cattle. **BUSINESS** Total number of business establishments in the county: 380. Retail sales during the first quarter of 1984 were up 7%, with an increase of 16% in Port Lavaca, a decline of 41% in Port Comfort and a decline of 47% in Seadrift. In 1980, 10% of the labor force were self-employed, 14% were employed in professional or related services, 22% in manufacturing, 19% in wholesale and retail trade, 16% in construction, 12% were employed in other counties and there were 1,010 retired workers. The industries with the most employment: oil and gas extraction, fish packaging, heavy construction and the manufacture of industrial chemicals. The nonfarm earnings in 1981 totaled $196,895,000. The retired workers received an average monthly Social Security payment of $327. **FINANCE** On June 30, 1983, four commercial banks had total deposits of $137,362,000 and total assets of $152,751,000. On December 31, 1982 one state savings and loan association and one state branch had assets of $10,231,678. In addition there are three credit unions in the county. **HOUSING** Average value of homes in 1980: $30,000. Permits for new, privately owned housing units increased in 1982: 77 permits were issued with a total construction cost of $3,251,748. Of those permits, 73 were for single family houses. Between 1970 and 1980 the number of housing units increased by 33%. Sixty-nine percent

CALHOUN (continued)

of all units in the county are air-conditioned, 80% are heated by gas and 19% by electricity. **NATURAL RESOURCES** Industrial sand, oil and gas. In 1982 a total of 43,787,907 thousand cubic feet of gas well gas, 313,318 barrels of condensate, 849,240 barrels of crude oil and 2,439,971 thousand cubic feet of casing-head gas were produced. Current production of other minerals and products includes alumina and lime. **TOURISM** Travel expenditures of $18,068,000 in 1982 (an increase of 16% over 1981) generated 317 jobs and $3,006,000 in payroll. Lodging: eight hotels, motels and tourist courts. **ALCOHOLIC BEVERAGES** Packaged distilled spirits, beer, ale, malt liquor and wine are legal in parts of the county. Sale of mixed beverages is legal in all or parts of the county. **FEDERAL EXPENDITURES** The federal government had direct expenditures or obligations of $20,831,000 in the county during fiscal year 1983, including $1,908,000 by the U.S. Department of Defense. In addition, the federal government provided $428,000 in grant awards, paid $932,000 in salaries and wages, made direct payments to individuals of $15,902,000 including $12,888,000 in retirement and disability payments, awarded $709,000 in procurement contracts and spent $2,859,000 in other expenditures or obligations. The federal government also provided $2,692,000 in direct loans and $138,234,000 in guaranteed loans and insurance.

COMMUNICATION

Newspapers–Daily: The Port Lavaca Wave, ave. eve. circ. 4,193. Radio: KGUL-AM (Port Lavaca). Cable TV. Telephone companies: General Telephone and Laward Telephone. **TRANSPORTATION** Total public road mileage: 427. In 1982 there were 16,786 registered vehicles and 463 reported traffic accidents including nine fatalities. Taxi cabs: one company in Port Lavaca. Intercity bus service is available. Motor freight: five local and intrastate carriers. Rail: two branch lines carry freight through the county. Each of the lines carries annually less than one million tons of freight. Aircraft: 48 are registered in the county. Airports: Calhoun County Airport at Port Lavaca is a general utility airport with general aviation service. It serves as a base for 22 aircraft. Tanner Airport at Port Lavaca is a Sea Plane Base. Waterborne commerce: Matagorda Ship Channel traffic in 1981 totaled 4,148,664 short tons: 3,347,547 in foreign imports, 153,501 in foreign exports and 647,616 in domestic shipments.

COMMUNITY SERVICES

EDUCATION One school district with eight elementary, three middle and one high school. The average daily attendance in 1981-82 was 4,131, with expenditures per pupil of $3,235 including 316 classroom teachers with an average annual salary of $19,038. Thirty-three percent of the 239 high school graduates planned to attend college. In 1982-83, 52% of the students were White, 43% Hispanic, 3% Black and 2% Asian. Vocational education: B.A. Bull Welding School (Port Lavaca). **PUBLIC LIBRARIES** Calhoun County Library (Port Lavaca): 52,443 volumes and two branches. **CHILD CARE** 26 day care and one twenty-four hour care licensed facilities. **HEALTH CARE** 12 physicians and seven dentists. Hospitals: one with a capacity of 75. Clinics: one public health clinic. Ambulance services: three commercial, three volunteer fire departments, one fire department, and one funeral home service. Nursing homes: one nursing home with a capacity of 120 nursing care residents. The average cost per day for private patients in 1982 was $32.15. **CHURCHES** 30 churches have an estimated combined membership of 18,846. The largest denominations are Catholic, Southern Baptist and United Methodist. **SOCIAL SERVICES** In fiscal year 1983 a total of $1,009,028 in food stamps was distributed, with an average of 2,018 persons receiving food stamps each month. Aid to Families

with Dependent Children (AFDC) totaled $192,798 with an average of 128 families receiving AFDC each month. Medical assistance benefits for the aged and disabled of $1,021,508 and for families and children of $383,560 brought the county benefit total to $2,606,894. **FIRE PROTECTION** One partly paid and four volunteer fire departments. **LAW ENFORCEMENT** The County Sheriff has 31 commissioned officers. Four police departments have a combined force of 45. **CRIME** 66 violent crimes (murder, forcible rape, robbery and aggravated assault) and 829 nonviolent crimes (burglary, larceny-theft and motor vehicle theft) were reported in 1982. **JUDICIAL SYSTEM** Three District Courts and Judges, one County Court and Judge and five Justices of the Peace. In the District Courts a total of 603 cases were pending on 1/1/82, 639 new cases were filed and 552 cases were disposed of during the year leaving 690 cases pending on 12/31/82. There were 410 criminal cases on the docket, 79 convictions, 22 persons committed to prison and six committed to jail and 245 cases left pending. In the County Court 933 cases were pending on 1/1/82, 523 new cases were filed and 543 cases were disposed of during the year leaving 913 cases pending on 12/31/82. There were 910 criminal cases on the docket, 245 convictions, 38 persons committed to jail, and 482 cases left pending. **JAILS** One jail, capacity 41. **ATTORNEYS AT LAW** 15. **UTILITIES** 83% of the residents are connected to a public or privately owned water system and 63% are connected to a public sewer system. Natural gas is distributed to the county by Entex, Inc. The average annual residential bill for natural gas in 1982 for the Entex distribution system was $390.31, an increase of 26% over 1981. Electricity is distributed to the county by Central Power and Light, Cochran Power and Light, Jackson Electric Coop., Inc., and Victoria Electric Coop., Inc. and is generated primarily by gas, oil and coal. The typical residential electric bill is $162.15 per month for an all-electric house using 2,500 kwh. **TAXES** The county has 11 units with taxing authority: one school district, three cities, one county and six special districts.

RECREATION/ENTERTAINMENT

STATE Matagorda Island State Park covers 7,325 acres. **COUNTY/MUNICIPAL PARKS** 129 acres in ten county and ten municipal parks. These parks contain six playgrounds, seven baseball and softball fields, one tennis court, two multi-use courts, three swimming pools, three beaches, ten boat ramps and shore fishing facilities. Developed campsites: 20. **SCENIC DRIVES** The Texas Independence Trail runs through this county, this trail not only surveys the historic sites of eastern Texas but also includes many modern visitor attractions such as the Johnson Space Center. **BOATING/FISHING** Lakes/reservoirs: Cox's Creek (406 acres), Dredge Spoil (166 acres), Evaporation #1 (42 acres), Evaporation #2 (119 acres), Evaporation #3 (87 acres), Mud #4 (469) acres, Operating Basins #1 (388 acres), #4 (151 acres) #5 (123 acres) and #31 (136 acres), Raw Water (256 acres) and Station 1886 (136 acres). Major rivers: Guadalupe. Primary streams: Cox's, Huisache, Goff Bayou and North Caloma. **STATE FISHING PIERS** Port Lavaca. **SALTWATER FISHING** for speckled trout, redfish and flounders is usually good out of Port Lavaca and Port O'Connor. Other excellent areas include San Antonio Bay, Lavaca Bay, Matagorda Bay and Espiritu Santo Bay. Shrimp, oysters and crabs may be taken but, like other saltwater fish, under specific regulations. **WILDLIFE REFUGES** Matagorda Island State Wildlife Management Area covers 36,568 acres. Aransas National Wildlife Refuge, also in Calhoun County, covers 90,069 acres. **HUNTING** Fall and winter seasons on deer and javelina. No closed seasons on coyote, bobcat, nutria and squirrel. Winter seasons on quail, muskrat, beaver, otter, opossum, ring-tailed cat, badger, fox, raccoon, skunk and civet cat. Fall and winter seasons on turkey. In 1983 duck, coot, geese, woodcock and jacksnipe seasons occurred during the winter months. Teal duck, rail and gallinule seasons occurred in the fall. Mourning dove seasons occurred intermittently during the fall and winter months. **MUSEUMS** Port Lavaca: "Jail" Museum. **SPECIAL EVENTS** Celebrate Austin Music Festival, Port Lavaca, April; Sea Fest, Port Lavaca, May; Texas Water Safari, Port Lavaca, June; Shrimp-Fest, Seadrift, July; Fishing Derby, Port Lavaca, August; Youth Rodeo, Port Lavaca, August; Christmas Parade and Drill Team Competition, Port Lavaca, December; Calhoun County Fair, Port Lavaca, October.

COMMUNITIES
COUNTY SEAT Port Lavaca, County Courthouse, 77979; County Clerk's Office, 512/552-2954. **INCORPORATED COMMUNITIES** (1980 population and ZIP Code) Point Comfort (1,125) 77978, Port Lavaca (10,911) 77979 and Seadrift (1,277) 77983. **UNINCORPORATED COMMUNITIES** (and ZIP Code) Clarks 77979, Green Lake 77979, Indianola 77979, Kamey 77979, Long Mott 77972, Magnolia Beach 77979, Olivia 77979, Port Alto 77979 and Port O'Connor 77982. **FOR ADDITIONAL LOCAL INFORMATION** Pt. Lavaca–Calhoun Co. Chamber of Commerce, P.O. Box 528, Port Lavaca, 77979, 512/552-2959 and Port O'Connor Chamber of Commerce, P.O. Box 701, Port O'Connor, 77982, 512/983-2870.

CALLAHAN (P71)

THE LAND
East of Abilene on Interstate Highway 20 in the Rolling Plains Region, Callahan County covers 899 square miles of grassy prairies. The County is divided by a low range of hills that drain the land north toward the Brazos River and south toward the Colorado River. The elevation ranges from 1,500 to 1,900 feet. The light to dark loamy soils have clayey to loamy subsoils with some accumulations of lime in the subsoils. In the southeast the soils are light colored with loamy to sandy surfaces and clayey subsoils. The eastern one-fourth has Cross Timbers and Prairies vegetation consisting of grasses with some mesquite, post oak, and live oak. The rest of the county has short and mid grasses, except for the southwest corner which has tall grasses. Live oak, mesquite, juniper and cacti dot the area. Between 21 and 30% of the land in the county is considered prime farmland. **CLIMATE** Subtropical subhumid with wide-ranging daily temperatures, mild winters and warm summers. The average annual temperature is 64°F. Temperatures in January range from an average low of 31° to an average high of 56°F and in July range from 71° to 96°F. The average annual precipitation is 25 inches, with an average relative humidity of 75% at 6 A.M. and 45% at 6 P.M. The average annual snowfall is six inches. The growing season averages 230 days per year, with the last freeze in late March and the first freeze near November 11th. The sun shines during the year on the average 68% of the daylight hours.

THE PEOPLE
The 1982 estimated population of 11,700 indicates a continuation of a steady growth rate begun in the 1970s. The age groups with the largest gains were ages 20 to 34 and birth to five years, lowering the high median age from 42 in 1970 to 37 in 1980. The high death rate and low birth rate are related to the older than average county population. The largest ancestry groups are persons of English descent (35%) and those of Irish descent (30%) **REGISTERED VOTERS** As of November 2, 1982 there were 6,181 registered voters (0.1% of the state total). The 1982 general election had a 52% voter turnout, compared to a 69% turnout in the 1980 general election. In the 1982 primary 96% voted Democratic and 4% Republican, with 1,576 votes cast.

THE ECONOMY
AGRICULTURE In 1982, 91% of the land was in farms and ranches, with 18% of the farmland under cultivation and 4% irrigated. Callahan ranked 180th in the state in highest agricultural receipts, with 73% from livestock and livestock products. Overgrazing, undesirable brush and weeds, water erosion, a lack of potable water and salinity are the current conservation problems. Primary crops: wheat, oats, hay, sorghum and peanuts. Primary vegetables: watermelons. Primary fruits and nuts: peaches and pecans. Primary livestock and products: cattle, sheep, wool and hogs. **BUSINESS** Total number of business establishments in the county: 174. Retail sales during the first quarter of 1984 increased 17%. In 1980, 15% of the labor force were self-employed, 18% were employed in professional or related services, 13% in manufacturing, 21% in wholesale and retail trade, 14% in agriculture, forestry, fisheries and mining, 55% were employed in other counties and there were 1,401 retired workers. The industries with the most employment: agribusiness, oil and gas extraction and the manufacture of fabricated metal products. The nonfarm earnings in 1981 totaled $97,794,000. The retired workers received an average monthly Social Security payment of $290. **FINANCE** On June 30, 1983, three commercial banks had total deposits of $69,635,000 and total assets of $79,496,000. There are three state savings and loan association branches in the county. **HOUSING** Average value of homes in 1980: $23,500. Permits for new, privately owned housing units decreasd in 1982: 23 permits were issued with a total construction cost of $869,500. Of those permits, all were for single family houses. Between 1970 and 1980 the number of housing units increased by 41%. Seventy-eight percent of all units in the county are air-conditioned, 81% are heated by gas and 14% by electricity. **NATURAL RESOURCES** Limestone, industrial sand, oil, gas dolomite and bituminous coal. In 1982 a total of 3,507,377 thousand cubic feet of gas well gas, 18,001 barrels of condensate, 1,404,778 barrels of crude oil and 2,922,126 thousand cubic feet of casinghead gas were produced. Current production of other minerals and products includes crushed limestone. **TOURISM** Travel expenditures of $1,520,000 in 1982 (an increase of 11% over 1981) generated 35 jobs and $290,000 in payroll. **ALCOHOLIC BEVERAGES** Packaged distilled spirits, beer, ale, malt liquor and wine are legal in parts of the county. **FEDERAL EXPENDITURES** The federal government had direct expenditures or obligations of $20,862,000 in the county during fiscal year 1983, including $1,277,000 by the U.S. Department of Defense. In addition, the federal government provided $296,000 in grant awards, paid $612,000 in salaries and wages, made direct payments to individuals of $19,659,000 including $14,033,000 in retirement and disability payments, awarded $23,000 in procurement contracts and spent $272,000 in other expenditures or obligations. The federal government also provided $350,000 in direct loans and $2,040,000 in guaranteed loans and insurance.

COMMUNICATION
Newspapers–Weekly: Callahan County Star (Baird), Clyde Journal and the Cross Plains Review. Cable TV. Telephone companies: Continental Telephone, Southwestern Bell and Taylor Telephone. **TRANSPORTATION** Total public road mileage: 839. In 1982 there were 13,892 registered vehicles and 275 reported traffic accidents including nine fatalities. Intercity bus service is available. Motor freight: three carriers. Rail: one main line carries annually 10 to 20 million tons of freight through the county. Aircraft: six are registered in the county.

COMMUNITY SERVICES
EDUCATION Four school districts with five elementary, one middle and four high schools. The average daily attendance in 1981-82 was 2,253, with expenditures per pupil of $2,000

COUNTIES

CALLAHAN (continued)

including 126 classroom teachers with an average annual salary of $15,570. Forty-seven percent of the 141 high school graduates planned to attend college. In 1982-83, 96% of the students were White, 4% Hispanic and 0.1% Black. **PUBLIC LIBRARIES** Callahan County Library (Baird): 17,000 volumes. Clyde Library. Cross Plains Library. **CHILD CARE** 24 day care and six twenty-four hour care licensed facilities. **HEALTH CARE** Four physicians and two dentists. Hospitals: one with a capacity of 26. Ambulance services: two commercial services. Nursing homes: three nursing homes with a combined capacity of 168 nursing care residents. The average cost per day for private patients in 1982 was $29.80. **CHURCHES** 31 churches have an estimated combined membership of 6,505. The largest denominations are Southern Baptist, United Methodist and Churches of Christ. **SOCIAL SERVICES** In fiscal year 1983 a total of $241,557 in food stamps was distributed, with an average of 559 persons receiving food stamps each month. Aid to Families with Dependent Children (AFDC) totaled $36,945, with an average of 22 families receiving AFDC each month. Medical assistance benefits for the aged and disabled of $1,194,333 and for families and children of $75,549 brought the county benefit total to $1,548,384. **FIRE PROTECTION** Four volunteer fire departments. **LAW ENFORCEMENT** The County Sheriff has six commissioned officers. Three police departments have a combined force of five. **CRIME** Nine violent crimes (murder, forcible rape, robbery and aggravated assault) and 111 nonviolent crimes (burglary, larceny-theft and motor vehicle theft) were reported in 1982. **JUDICIAL SYSTEM** One District Court and Judge, one County Court and Judge and four Justices of the Peace. In the District Court a total of 375 cases were pending on 1/1/82, 268 new cases were filed and 183 cases were disposed of during the year leaving 460 cases pending on 12/31/82. There were 71 criminal cases on the docket, 15 convictions, five persons committed to prison and 46 cases left pending. In the County Court 283 cases were pending on 1/1/82, 697 new cases were filed and 525 cases were disposed of during the year leaving 455 cases pending on 12/31/82. There were 915 criminal cases on the docket, 167 convictions, 59 persons committed to jail, and 392 cases left pending. **JAILS** One jail, capacity 10. **ATTORNEYS AT LAW** Four. **UTILITIES** 62% of the residents are connected to a public or privately owned water system and 51% are connected to a public sewer system. Natural gas is distributed to the county by Lone Star Gas Co., Division of Enserch. The average annual residential bill for natural gas in 1982 for the Lone Star distribution system was $405.91, an increase of 35% over 1981. Electricity is distributed to the county by West Texas Utilities, Comanche Co. Electric Coop., Inc., and Taylor Electric Coop., Inc. and is generated primarily by gas, oil and water. The typical residential electric bill is $165.76 per month for an all-electric house using 2,500 kwh. **TAXES** The county has seven units with taxing authority: three school districts, three cities and one county.

RECREATION/ENTERTAINMENT

MUNICIPAL PARKS 45 acres in two municipal parks. These parks contain two playgrounds, two baseball and softball fields, one swimming pool, one beach and one boat ramp. Developed campsites: 10. **BOATING/FISHING** Lakes/reservoirs: Baird (129 acres), Baird Railroad (46 acres), Clyde (449 acres), La Reata (108 acres) and Upper Soil Conservation Service 2 and 18A Pecan Lakes (20 acres). Primary streams: Mexia, Deep, North Pecan Bayou, East Fork Brushy, South Pecan Bayou and West Burnt. **HUNTING** Fall and winter seasons on deer. No closed season on coyote, bobcat and squirrel. Winter seasons on quail, muskrat, beaver, opossum, ring-tailed cat, badger, fox, weasel, raccoon, skunk and civet cat. Fall, winter and spring seasons on turkey.

In 1983 duck, coot, geese, woodcock and jacksnipe seasons occurred during the winter months. Teal duck, rail and gallinule seasons occurred in the fall. Mourning dove seasons occurred intermittently during the fall and winter months. **MUSEUMS** Baird: Callahan County Pioneer Museum. **SPECIAL EVENTS** July 4th Celebration, Baird, July.

COMMUNITIES

COUNTY SEAT Baird, County Courthouse, 79504; County Clerk's Office, 915/854-1217. **INCORPORATED COMMUNITIES** (1980 population and ZIP Code) Baird (1,696) 79504, Clyde (2,562) 79510, Cross Plains (1,240) 76443, and Putnam (116) 76469. **UNINCORPORATED COMMUNITIES** (and ZIP Code) Admiral 79504, Atwell 76437, Cottonwood 79504, Denton 79510, Dudley 79601, Eula 79501, Oplin 79510 and Rowden 79504. **FOR ADDITIONAL LOCAL INFORMATION** Baird Chamber of Commerce, P.O. Box 846, Baird, 79504, 915/854-2003 and Clyde Chamber of Commerce, P.O. Box 257, Clyde, 79510, 915/893-4221.

CAMERON (B30)

THE LAND

Bordering Mexico and the Gulf Coast on U.S. Highways 281 and 83/77 in the Rio Grande Plain Region, Cameron County covers 905 square miles with an elevation range from sea level to 60 feet. The nearly level land has brownish to reddish soils with loamy to clayey surface layers and clayey subsoils. Along the eastern border the soils are sandy and saline with some cracking, clayey soils. Along the coast the land is in the Gulf Prairie and Marsh vegetation area. Marsh and salt grasses grow at tidewater while further inland there are tall grasses, bluestems and grama grasses plus some oaks and elms along streams. The remainder of the county is in the South Texas Plains area with small trees, brush, weeds and grasses. Mesquite, live oak, post oak and shrubs grow densely. Between 41 and 50% of the land in the county is considered prime farmland. **CLIMATE** is subtropical subhumid with hot summers and mild winters. The risk of a tropical storm or hurricane exists from June through October. Another concern is the risk of freezing weather in late December and January. The average annual temperature is 74°F. Temperatures in January range from an average low of 50° to an average high of 69°F and in July range from 75° to 94°F. The average annual precipitation is 26 inches, with an average relative humidity of 90% at 6 A.M. and 70% at 6 P.M. There is no snowfall. The growing season averages 320 days per year, with the last freeze in late January and the first freeze in mid December. The sun shines during the year on the average 68% of the daylight hours.

THE PEOPLE

Cameron County is one of the most densely populated in the state and ranks 16th among all U.S. counties in the highest percent of persons of Spanish origin. The 1982 estimated population of 230,500 indicates a continuation of the strong growth rate since the 1930s, (except for a decrease of 7% between 1960 and 1970.) The population gain between 1970 and 1980 was one of the highest in the state, with an urban growth of 52% and a rural growth of 40%. The age groups with the largest gains were ages 65 and over and 20 to 34 years causing the low median age to rise from 22 in 1970 to 25 in 1980. The largest ancestry groups are persons of English descent (8%) and Hispanic (77%). **REGISTERED VOTERS** As of November 2, 1982 there were 81,094 registered voters (1% of the state total). The 1982 general election had a 42% voter turnout, compared to a 59% turnout in the 1980 general election. In the 1982 primary 97% voted Democratic and 3% Republican, with 27,299 votes cast.

THE ECONOMY

AGRICULTURE A leading cotton, vegetable and citrus fruit producer in the lower Rio Grande Valley. In 1982, 83% of the land was in farms and ranches, with 50% of the farmland under cultivation and 90% irrigated. Cameron ranked 19th in the state in highest agricultural receipts, with 75% from crops. Inefficient irrigation systems, salinity, drainage, flooding and difficulties in grass establishment are the current conservation problems. Primary crops: fourth in the state for cotton and 10th for sorghum. Corn, sugarcane, hay and soybeans. Primary vegetables: ninth in the state for onions, third for cabbage, seventh for cantaloupes and ninth for total fresh market vegetables. Bell peppers, sweet corn, watermelons, cucumbers, carrots, honeydew melons and tomatoes. Primary fruits and nuts: grapefruit, oranges and pecans. Primary livestock and products: cattle, milk and hogs. **BUSINESS** Total number of business establishments in the county: 3,932. Retail sales during the first quarter of 1984 were up 14%, with an increase of 56% in Santa Rosa, a decrease of 23% in Combes and a decrease of 17% in Rio Hondo. In 1980, 8% of the labor force were self-employed, 21% were employed in professional or related services, 16% in manufacturing, 24% in wholesale and retail trade, 7% in construction, 5% were employed in other counties and there were 12,327 retired workers. The industries with the most employment: tourism, agribusiness, barite mining, cotton seed oil mills, general construction, meat packing, sugar refining, fish packaging, ship building and repairing, soft drink bottling and canning, baking, and the manufacture of men and women's apparel, paper bags, industrial chemicals, abrasive products, oilfield machinery, metal doors, food products machinery, electronic components, motor vehicles and car bodies and sporting goods. The nonfarm earnings in 1981 totaled $1,319,182,000. The retired workers received an average monthly Social Security payment of $290. **FINANCE** On June 30, 1983, 20 commercial banks had total deposits of $1,291,439,000 and total assets of $1,451,999,000. On December 31, 1982 four state savings and loan associations, 17 state branches and one federal branch had combined assets of $194,783,021. In addition there are 15 credit unions in the county. **HOUSING** Average value of homes in 1980: $24,700. Permits for new, privately owned housing units decreased in 1982: 2,276 permits were issued with a total construction cost of $114,561,721. Of those permits, 1,091 were for single family houses. Housing permits in Harlingen increased from 257 in 1981 to 494 in 1982. Between 1970 and 1980 the number of housing units increased by 59%. Fifty-six percent of all units in the county are air-conditioned, 66% are heated by gas and 29% by electricity. **NATURAL RESOURCES** Oil and gas. In 1982 a total of 2,424,550 thousand cubic feet of gas well gas, 4,239 barrels of crude oil and 4,670 thousand cubic feet of casinghead gas were produced. Current production of other minerals and products includes barite, celestite, chromium, bentonite clay, fluorspar, manganese and phosphate. **TOURISM** Travel expenditures of $301,484,000 in 1982 (an increase of 11% over 1981) generated 7,082 jobs and $60,515,000 in payroll. Lodging: 43 hotels, motels and tourist courts. Convention/meeting facilities: Brownsville—Brown Auditorium, Herbert L. Stokely Hall, Stillman Town Hall, Robert E. Lee Youth Center, Fort Brown Women's Center, International Friendship Pavilion, and six hotels with facilities for large gatherings; Harlingen—Casa De Sol, Casa De Amistad, Municipal facilities auditorium, J. Lewis Boggus Stadium and two hotels with facilities for large gatherings. **ALCOHOLIC BEVERAGES** Packaged distilled spirits, beer, ale, malt liquor and wine are legal. Sale of mixed beverages is legal in all or parts of the county. **FEDERAL EXPENDITURES** The federal government had direct expenditures or obligations of $266,998,000 in the county during fiscal year 1983, including $18,324,000 by the U.S. Department of Defense. In addition, the federal government provided $27,604,000 in grant awards, paid $26,748,000 in salaries and wages, made direct payments to individuals of $192,599,000 including $152,575,000 in retirement and disability payments, awarded $10,051,000 in procurement contracts and spent $9,996,000 in other expenditures or obligations. The federal government also provided $5,785,000 in direct loans and $287,424,000 in guaranteed loans and insurance.

COMMUNICATION

Newspapers–Daily: The Brownsville Herald, ave. eve. circ. 13,999 and the Valley Morning Star (Harlingen), ave. morn. circ. 23,275. Weekly: The Brownsville Times, LaFeria News, Port Isabel-South Padre Press, San Benito News. Radio: KBOR-AM, KRIX-FM and KDUV FM-Stereo (Brownsville) and KGBT-AM, KELT-FM and KIWW-FM (Harlingen). Television: KBGT-CH 4 (Harlingen) and KZLN-CH 60 (San Benito). Cable TV. Telephone companies: General Telephone, Southwestern Bell and Valley Telephone Coop. **TRANSPORTATION** Total public road mileage: 2,083. In 1982 there were 125,242 registered vehicles and 5,206 reported traffic accidents including 64 fatalities. Taxi cabs: 13 companies in Brownsville, one in Harlingen and one in San Benito. Municipal transit systems: one intracity bus system in Brownsville, with scheduled routes. Intercity bus service is available. Motor freight: 41 local and intrastate carriers. Rail: eight branch lines carry freight through the county. Three of the branch lines carry annually one to five million tons of freight each and five carry less than one million tons each. Aircraft: 436 are registered in the county. Airports: Rio Grande Valley International Airport at Harlingen serves as a base for 100 aircraft and provides carrier service. South Padre Island International Airport at Brownsville serves as a base for 50 aircraft and provides carrier service. Port Isabel County Airport serves as a base for 15 aircraft and provides general aviation service. San Benito Municipal Airport. Domestic and foreign exports by air from Brownsville average 210 thousand pounds per month. Imports average 13 thousand pounds per month. Waterborne commerce: Intercoastal Waterway to Port Harlington freight traffic totaled 655,127 short tons of domestic shipments in 1981. Brownsville shipped 2,810,018 short tons of freight: 391,307 in foreign imports, 977,294 in foreign exports and 1,441,417 in domestic shipments. Port Isabel shipped 313,036 short tons: 65 in foreign imports, 55 in foreign exports and 312,916 in domestic shipments.

COMMUNITY SERVICES

EDUCATION 11 school districts with 60 elementary, 13 middle, 11 high schools and three special education. The average daily attendance in 1981-82 was 53,997, with expenditures per pupil of $1,768 including 2,886 classroom teachers with an average annual salary of $15,427. Fifty-seven percent of the 2,449 high school graduates planned to attend college. In 1982-83, 10% of the students were White, 90% Hispanic, 0.3% Black and 0.1% Asian. Private schools: 3,720 enrolled in 11 elementary and five high schools. Sports championships: 1983 AAA Boys' Swimming, Saint Joseph Academy. Texas Southmost College is located in Brownsville. Established in 1926 it is a vocational and two year academic college under state and local control. Enrollment in 1982 was 4,283 with in state undergraduate tuition and fees of $221 per semester. Vocational education: Brownfield—Brownfield Regional Medical Center School of Vocational Nursing. Harlingen—De Lynn's College of the Valley, Texas State Technical Institute Harlingen Campus, Valley Baptist Medical Center School of Vocational Nursing, Valley Barber College, Professional Advancement, Incorporated. Brownsville—Texas Language and Commercial Academy. **PUBLIC LIBRARIES** Arnulfo L. Oliveira Memorial Library (Brownsville): 96,424 volumes. Harlingen Public Library: 65,367. Bailey H. Dunlap

COUNTIES

CAMERON (continued)

Memorial Library (La Feria): 13,430. Laguna Vista Library. Ethel L. Whipple Memorial Library (Los Fresnos): 12,292. Port Isabel Public Library: 9,582. Rio Hondo Library. San Benito Public Library: 22,963. **CHILD CARE** 190 day care and 48 twenty-four hour care licensed facilities. **HEALTH CARE** 222 physicians and 66 dentists. Hospitals: four with a combined capacity of 574. Specialized hospitals: one state chest hospital with capacity of 109 and one eye clinic-hospital. Clinics: two dialysis clinics, one x-ray clinic, one medical electronics clinic, one family health clinic and one public health clinic. Ambulance services: two commercial, two air, two police departments, one city, one county and one volunteer service. Mental health: four clinics, one state center with capacity of 160 and one development center with bed capacity of 74. Nursing homes: eight nursing homes with a combined capacity of 842 nursing care residents. The average cost per day for private patients in 1982 was $34.26. **CHURCHES** 161 churches have an estimated combined membership of 151,254. The largest denominations are Catholic, Southern Baptist and United Methodist. **SOCIAL SERVICES** In fiscal year 1983 a total of $32,072,273 in food stamps was distributed, with an average of 64,697 persons receiving food stamps each month. Aid to Families with Dependent Children (AFDC) totaled $4,678,994, with an average of 3,003 families receiving AFDC each month. Medical assistance benefits for the aged and disabled of $15,144,181 and for families and children of $5,702,342 brought the county benefit total to $57,597,789. **FIRE PROTECTION** Two paid, one partly paid and nine volunteer fire departments. **LAW ENFORCEMENT** The County Sheriff has 76 commissioned officers. 14 police departments have a combined force of 258. Two colleges have campus police departments with a combined force of 15 officers. Harlingen Airport has five police officers. **CRIME** 951 violent crimes (murder, forcible rape, robbery and aggravated assault) and 12,355 nonviolent crimes (burglary, larceny-theft and motor vehicle theft) were reported in 1982. **JUDICIAL SYSTEM** Four District Courts and Judges, three County Courts and Judges and 11 Justices of the Peace. In the District Courts a total of 14,335 cases were pending on 1/1/82, 9,396 new cases were filed and 3,332 cases were disposed of during the year leaving 20,399 cases pending on 12/31/82. There were 2,265 criminal cases on the docket, 518 convictions, 125 persons committed to prison and eight committed to jail and 1,360 cases left pending. In the County Courts 4,172 cases were pending on 1/1/82, 5,447 new cases were filed and 4,814 cases were disposed of during the year leaving 4,805 cases pending on 12/31/82. There were 6,934 criminal cases on the docket, 1,736 convictions, 569 persons committed to jail, and 2,792 cases left pending. **JAILS** One jail, capacity 278. New low risk facility for 200 under construction. **ATTORNEYS AT LAW** 284. **UTILITIES** 90% of the residents are connected to a public or privately owned water system and 80% are connected to a public sewer system. Natural gas is distributed to the county by Rio Grande Valley Gas Co. The average annual residential bill for natural gas in 1982 for the Rio Grande distribution system was $245.19, an increase of 25% over 1981. Electricity is distributed to the county by Central Power and Light Co., the City of Brownsville Public Utilities Board, Cochran Power and Light and Magic Valley Electric Coop., Inc. and is generated primarily by gas, oil and coal. The typical residential electric bill is $178.33 per month for an all-electric house using 2,500 kwh. **TAXES** The county has 32 units with taxing authority: 10 school district, 11 cities, one county and 10 special districts.

RECREATION/ENTERTAINMENT

FEDERAL PALO ALTO BATTLEFIELD HISTORIC SITE is a 50 acre park which contains the site of the first of two important Mexican War battles fought on American soil. General Zachary Taylor's victory here made the invasion of Mexico possible. **NATIONAL REGISTER OF HISTORIC PLACES** Brazos Island: Brazos Santiago Depot. Brownsville: Browne-Wagner Residence, Fort Brown, Palo Alto Battlefield (National Historic Landmark), Resaca de la Palma Battlefield (National Historic Landmark), Immaculate Conception Church, Southern Pacific Railroad Passenger Depot and Charles Stillman House. Brownsville vicinity: Old Brulay Plantation. Port Isabel: Port Isabel Lighthouse. Port Isabel vicinity: Garcia Pasture. **STATE** Brazos Island State Recreation Area covers 217 acres with camping, fishing and swimming on an undeveloped Gulf beach. Port Isabel Lighthouse State Historic Structure covers 0.5 acres with a museum and a historic structure. Built in 1853 and remaining in use until 1905, the lighthouse offers an excellent view from the top of Laguna Madre to South Padre Island. Resaca de la Palma State Park Site covers 1,100 acres and is closed to the public as of July, 1983. **COUNTY/MUNICIPAL PARKS** 1,490 acres in five county and 44 municipal parks. These parks contain one mile of hiking trails, 36 playgrounds, one golf course, three football and soccer fields, 19 baseball and softball fields, 34 tennis courts, two multi-use courts, 10 swimming pools, five beaches, six boat ramps and shore fishing facilities. Developed campsites: 722. **SCENIC DRIVES** The Texas Tropical Trail runs through this county. This trail is charted through the state's southernmost wedge meandering through ranchland, resort areas on the Gulf of Mexico and fertile farmlands. **BOATING/FISHING** Lakes/reservoirs: Adams Garden (113 acres), Cain 1 (86 acres), Cain 2 (66 acres), four Cameron County lakes (1,394 acres), Cuates (94 acres), Dana-Tule Levee 1 (123 acres), Dana-Tule Levee 2 (88 acres), Dixieland (283 acres), Esperanza Farms (77 acres), Hext Levee (100 acres), La Feria (299 acres), Main (833 acres), McCloud-Hood (83 acres), Mercer Dry (536 acres), Mercer 1 (193 acres), Mercer 2 (248 acres), Montgomery (45 acres), Noriega Plantation (417 acres), Port Isabel (386 acres), Rancho Viejo (105 acres), Reba Bass (200 acres), Roos Dam A (229 acres), Roos Dam C (85 acres), Russel Dam 1 (134 acres), Sweeney East (1,375 acres), Sweeney West (1,031 acres) and Wardner (100 acres). Major rivers: Rio Grande. Primary streams: Resaca De Los Fresnos, Resaca De Los Cuates, Resaca Del Rancho Veijo, Harlingen Main Canals, Arroyo Colorado, Resaca De La Palma and Laguna Vista. **STATE FISHING PIERS** Queen Isabella. **SALTWATER FISHING** for speckled trout, redfish and flounders is usually good around Brownsville and Port Isabel. Shrimp, oysters and crabs may be taken but, like other saltwater fish, under specific regulations. **WILDLIFE REFUGES** Las Palomas State Wildlife Management Area covers 468 acres in this county. Laguna Atascosa National Wildlife Refuge is also located in Cameron County, spanning 45,204 acres. **HUNTING** Fall and winter seasons on deer. No closed seasons on nutria, javelina, coyote, bobcat and squirrel. Winter seasons on chachalaca, quail, muskrat, beaver, otter, opossum, mink, ring-tailed cat, badger, fox, raccoon, skunk and civet cat. In 1983 duck, coot, geese, woodcock and jacksnipe seasons occurred during the winter months with a winter season on sandhill cranes in some parts of the county. Teal duck, rail and gallinule seasons occurred in the fall. Mourning dove seasons occurred intermittently during the fall and winter months with a fall season on white-winged dove. **MUSEUMS** Brownsville: Brownsville Art League and Stillman House Museum. Harlingen: Confederate Air Force Museum, Lon C. Hill Home and Rio Grande Valley Museum. **THEATERS** Brownsville: Friendship Garden Pavilion and Jacob Brown Auditorium at Fort Brown Memorial Center and Camille Playhouse. **ZOO** Brownsville: Gladys Porter Zoo. **COLLEGIATE FINE ARTS** Brownsville: Cultural events offered by Texas Southmost College. **OTHER** Brownsville: Palmito Hill Battlefield and Palo Alto Battlefield. **SPECIAL EVENTS** Tourist

Festival and Shuffleboard Tourney, San Benito, January; Winter Olympics, Port Isabel, January; Cameron County Livestock Show, San Benito, January; Golden Glove Boxing, Brownsville, January; Charro Days, Brownsville, February; Winter Texan Fishing Tourney, Port Isabel, February; Valley Music Festival, Harlingen, February; Tip O' Texas Wildcat Show, Brownsville, February; Little Bit of Mexico, Brownsville, February; All-Valley Winter Texans Gold Tourney, Brownsville, March; Riofest, Harlingen, March; Bellas Artes, Brownsville, June; July 4th Celebration, South Padre Island, July; Blessing of the Shrimp Fleet, Port Isabel, July; Texas International Fishing Tourney, Port Isabel-South Padre Island, August; Seafest, Port Isabel-South Padre Island, September; Fiesta Internacional, Brownsville, September; Confederate Air Force Airshow, Harlingen, October; and Welcome Home Winter Texans Party, Brownsville, November.

COMMUNITIES
COUNTY SEAT Brownsville, County Courthouse, 78520; County Clerk's Office, 512/544-0815. **INCORPORATED COMMUNITIES** (1980 population and ZIP Code) Bayview (291) 78566, Brownsville (84,997) 78520, Combes (1,488) 78535, Harlingen (43,543) 78550, Indian Lake (917*) 78586, La Feria (3,495) 78559, Laguna Vista (632) 78578, Los Fresnos (2,173) 78,566, Palm Valley (935*) 78550, Port Isabel (3,769) 78578, Primera (1,380) 78550, Rancho Viejo (275*) 78361, Rangerville (80*) 78586, Rio Hondo (1,673) 78583, San Benito (17,988) 78586, Santa Rosa (1,889) 78593 and South Padre Island (791) 78578 (*est., incorp. inactive). **UNINCORPORATED COMMUNITIES** (and ZIP Code) Adams Gardens 78550, Bahia Mar 78578, Bluetown 78592, Carricitos 78586, Colaboz 78586, El Jardin 78520, Keller Corner 78520, Kennedy Shores 78520, Kopernik Shores 78520, Laguna Heights 78578, Landrum 78586, La Paloma 78586, Las Rusias 78586, Laureles 78586, Los Cuates 78586, Los Indios 78567, Lozano 78568, Olmito 78575, Ranchito (Encantada) 78586, Santa Maria 78592, Stuart Place 78550, Villa Cavazos 78520, Villa Nueva 78520 and Yescas (Las Yescas) 78586. **FOR ADDITIONAL LOCAL INFORMATION** Brownsville Chamber of Commerce, P.O. Box 752, Brownsville, 78520, 512/542-4341, Harlingen Chamber of Commerce, P.O. Box 189, Harlingen, 78551, 512/423-5440, La Feria Chamber of Commerce, P.O. Box 365, La Feria, 78559, 512/797-1829, San Benito Area Chamber of Commerce, 210 E. Heywood, Drawer 1623, San Benito, 78586, 512/399-5321 and Port Isabel-South Padre Island Chamber of Commerce, P.O. Box 209B, Padre Island, 78597, 512/943-2092 or 943-2262.

CAMP (E12)

THE LAND
East of Dallas on U.S. Highway 271 in the East Texas Timberlands Region, Camp County covers 203 square miles with an elevation range of 350 to 500 feet. The undulating to rolling land has acid, light-colored soils low in plant nutrients with loamy to sandy surface layers and reddish mottled clayey subsoils, with a high potential for shrinking and swelling. The Pineywoods vegetation area includes the longleaf, shortleaf and loblolly pine, plus hickory, elm, oaks, sweet and blackgum and magnolia trees. The grasslands include species of wildryes, bluestems and legumes. Between 31 and 40% of the land in the county is considered prime farmland. **CLIMATE** Subtropical humid, moist and mild. The average annual temperature is 63°F. Temperatures in January range from an average low of 30° to an average high of 54°F and in July range from 71° to 94°F. The average annual precipitation is 44 inches, with an average relative humidity of 83% at 6 A.M. and 58% at 6 P.M. The average annual snowfall is two inches. The growing season averages 240 days per year, with

the last freeze in late March and the first freeze in mid November. The sun shines during the year on the average 67% of the daylight hours.

THE PEOPLE
The 1982 estimated population of 9,800 indicates a continuation of the slow growth rate begun in the 1960s. This growth trend reversed the steady population decrease between 1940 and 1960. Over 21% of the growth between 1970 and 1980 was in rural areas, with 10% in urban areas. The age group with the largest gains was ages 20 to 39 with the largest decrease occurring among ages 10 to 14. The high median age dropped from 35 in 1970 to 32 in 1980. The largest ancestry groups are persons of English descent (28%), Black (26%) and persons of Irish descent (16%). **REGISTERED VOTERS** As of November 2, 1982 there were 5,130 registered voters (0.1% of the state total). The 1982 general election had a 54% voter turnout, compared to a 69% turnout in the 1980 general election. In the 1982 primary 100% voted Democratic with 2,349 votes cast.

THE ECONOMY
AGRICULTURE Forest production area. In 1982, 54% of the land was in farms and ranches, with 18% of the farmland under cultivation Camp ranked 66th in the state in highest agricultural receipts, with 97% from livestock and livestock products. Overgrazing, water erosion and improper woodland management are the current conservation problems. Primary crops: hay. Primary vegetables: watermelons and sweet potatoes. Primary fruits and nuts: peaches and pecans. Primary livestock and products: second in the state for hens and pullets, second for eggs and fourth for commercial broiler production. Cattle and milk. **BUSINESS** Total number of business establishments in the county: 186. Retail sales during the first quarter of 1984 increased 10%. In 1980, 10% of the labor force were self-employed, 11% were employed in professional or related services, 33% in manufacturing, 22% in wholesale and retail trade, 9% in construction, 37% were employed in other counties and there were 1,091 retired workers. The industries with the most employment: agribusiness and the manufacture of pipes and pipe fittings and children's clothes. The nonfarm earnings in 1981 totaled $83,012,000. The retired workers received an average monthly Social Security payment of $290. **FINANCE** On June 30, 1983, two commercial banks had total deposits of $63,492,000 and total assets of $71,672,000. On December 31, 1982 one state savings and loan association and one state branch had assets of $17,987,668. **HOUSING** Average value of homes in 1980: $24,600. Permits for new, privately owned housing units increased in 1982: 80 permits were issued with a total construction cost of $2,314,910. Of those permits, 33 were for single family houses. Between 1970 and 1980 the number of housing units increased by 29%. Sixty-eight percent of all units in the county are air-conditioned, 75% are heated by gas and 19% by electricity. **NATURAL RESOURCES** Ceramic clay, industrial sand, oil, gas and lignite coal. In 1982 a total of 4,322,947 thousand cubic feet of gas well gas, 125 barrels of condensate, 435,159 barrels of crude oil and 36,317 thousand cubic feet of casinghead gas were produced. Current production of other minerals and products includes brick, clay, lignite coal and industrial sand. Pine and hardwood production in 1981 totaled 2,168,053 cubic feet: 1,858,761 cubic feet of pine and 309,292 cubic feet of hardwood. **TOURISM** Travel expenditures of $1,084,000 in 1982 (an increase of 11% over 1981) generated 24 jobs and $200,000 in payroll. **ALCOHOLIC BEVERAGES** Packaged distilled spirits, beer, ale, malt liquor and wine are legal in parts of the county. Sale of mixed beverages is legal in all or parts of the county. **FEDERAL EXPENDITURES** The federal government had direct expenditures or obligations of $16,919,000 in the county during fiscal year 1983,

COUNTIES

CAMP (continued)

including $637,000 by the U.S. Department of Defense. In addition, the federal government provided $124,000 in grant awards, paid $554,000 in salaries and wages, made direct payments to individuals of $16,149,000 including $11,435,000 in retirement and disability payments, awarded $6,000 in procurement contracts and spent $86,000 in other expenditures or obligations. The federal government also provided $7,000 in direct loans and $613,000 in guaranteed loans and insurance.

COMMUNICATION

Newspapers–Weekly: The Pittsburg Gazette. Cable TV. Telephone companies: General Telephone, Southwestern Bell, ETEX Telephone Corp. and Peoples Telephone Corp. **TRANSPORTATION** Total public road mileage: 353. In 1982 there were 8,863 registered vehicles and 196 reported traffic accidents including nine fatalities. Motor freight: four carriers. Rail: four main lines carry freight through the county. Two of the lines carry annually 20 to 30 million tons of freight each and two carry five to 10 each. Aircraft: six are registered in the county.

COMMUNITY SERVICES

EDUCATION One school district with two elementary, one middle and one high school. The average daily attendance in 1981-82 was 1,866, with expenditures per pupil of $1,937 including 96 classroom teachers with an average annual salary of $15,893. Twenty-six percent of the 141 high school graduates planned to attend college. In 1982-83, 67% of the students were White, 2% Hispanic and 32% Black. **PUBLIC LIBRARIES** Camp County Library (Pittsburg): 21,986 volumes. **CHILD CARE** Nine day care and one twenty-four hour care licensed facilities. **HEALTH CARE** Nine physicians and three dentists. Hospitals: one with a capacity of 90. Ambulance services: one commercial service. Nursing homes: two nursing homes with a combined capacity of 130 nursing care residents. The average cost per day for private patients in 1982 was $29.50. **CHURCHES** 41 churches have an estimated combined membership of 7,437. The largest denominations are Southern Baptist, Christian Methodist Episcopal and Baptist Missionary. **SOCIAL SERVICES** In fiscal year 1983 a total of $553,158 in food stamps was distributed, with an average of 1,321 persons receiving food stamps each month. Aid to Families with Dependent Children (AFDC) totaled $124,418, with an average of 90 families receiving AFDC each month. Medical assistance benefits for the aged and disabled of $1,364,579 and for families and children of $207,548 brought the county benefit total to $2,249,702. **FIRE PROTECTION** Two volunteer fire departments. **LAW ENFORCEMENT** The County Sheriff has eight commissioned officers. One police department has a force of seven. **CRIME** Eight violent crimes (murder, forcible rape, robbery and aggravated assault) and 195 nonviolent crimes (burglary, larceny-theft and motor vehicle theft) were reported in 1982. **JUDICIAL SYSTEM** Two District Courts and Judges, one County Court and Judge and four Justices of the Peace. In the District Courts a total of 633 cases were pending on 1/1/82, 303 new cases were filed and 269 cases were disposed of during the year leaving 667 cases pending on 12/31/82. There were 138 criminal cases on the docket, 19 convictions, 10 persons committed to prison, and 75 cases left pending. In the County Court 481 cases were pending on 1/1/82, 327 new cases were filed and 211 cases were disposed of during the year leaving 597 cases pending on 12/31/82. There were 763 criminal cases on the docket, 135 convictions, one person committed to jail, and 557 cases left pending. **JAILS** One jail, capacity 14. **ATTORNEYS AT LAW** Eight. **UTILITIES** 70% of the residents are connected to a public or privately owned water system and 46% are connected to a public sewer system. Electricity is distributed to the county by Southwestern Electric Service, Wood County Electric Coop., Inc. and Upshur Rural Electric Coop., Inc. and is generated primarily by gas and oil. The typical residential electric bill is $152.08 per month for an all-electric house using 2,500 kwh. **TAXES** The county has three units with taxing authority: one school district, one city and one county.

RECREATION/ENTERTAINMENT

MUNICIPAL PARKS 23 acres in two municipal parks. These parks contain two playgrounds, six baseball and softball fields and two tennis courts. **BOATING/FISHING** Lakes/reservoirs: Bob Sandlin (8,081 acres), Ferndale (272 acres) and Highland Club (33 acres). Primary streams: Cypress, North Lilly and Reeves. **HUNTING** Fall and winter seasons on deer. Fall, winter and spring seasons on squirrel. Winter seasons on quail, muskrat, beaver, otter, opossum, mink, ring-tailed cat, badger, fox, raccoon, skunk and civet cat. No closed seasons on bobcat, nutria and coyote. In 1983 duck, coot, geese, woodcock and jacksnipe seasons occurred during the winter months. Teal duck, rail and gallinule seasons occurred in the fall. Mourning dove seasons occurred intermittently during the fall and winter months. **SPECIAL EVENTS** Junior Stock Show, Pittsburg, March; Rodeo and Parade, Pittsburg, May; Pioneer Days, Pittsburg, September; and Christmas Parade, Pittsburg, December.

COMMUNITIES

COUNTY SEAT Pittsburg, County Courthouse, 75686; County Clerk's Office, 214/856-2731. **INCORPORATED COMMUNITIES** (1980 population and ZIP Code) Pittsburg (4,245) 75686 and Rocky Mound (123) 75686. **UNINCORPORATED COMMUNITIES** (and ZIP Code) Center Point 75686, County Line 75686, Ebenezer 75686, Faker 75686, Harvard 75686, Leesburg 75451, Matinburg (Fairview) 75686, Miller Grove 75686, New Mine 75686, Newsome 75686 and Pine 75686. **FOR ADDITIONAL LOCAL INFORMATION** Camp Co. Chamber of Commerce, 202 Jefferson, Pittsburg, 75686, 214/856-3442.

CARSON (P13)

THE LAND

In the Texas Panhandle east of Amarillo on U.S. Highway 60 in the High Plains Region, Carson County covers 924 square miles of mostly grassy prairie. The elevation ranges from 3,000 to 3,500 feet. The soils in the northern half of the county have alkaline, loamy surface layers and cracking, clayey subsoils with some limestone. In the southern half the nearly level land has very dark loamy soils and cracking, clayey subsoils. The northern half of the county is in the Rolling Plains vegetation region with prairie grasslands and mesquite trees. Tall bunchgrasses, bluestems and wildryes compete with tumblegrass, yucca and sandburs. The southern half is in the High Plains vegetation area with such grasses as buffalograss, bluegrama, wheatgrass and Indiangrass competing with sagebrush, yucca and mesquite. Between 51 and 60% of the land in the county is considered prime farmland. **CLIMATE** Continental steppe and among the coldest in the state, with wide-ranging daily and seasonal temperature changes. The average annual temperature is 59°F. Temperatures in January range from an average low of 23° to an average high of 51°F and in July range from 67° to 93°F. The average annual precipitation is 19 inches, with an average relative humidity of 72% at 6 A.M. and 40% at 6 P.M. The average annual snowfall is 16 inches. The growing season averages 198 days per year, with the last freeze near April 17th and the first freeze in late October. The sun shines during the year on the average 72% of the daylight hours.

THE PEOPLE

The 1982 estimated population of 7,100 indicates a continuation of the growth rate begun in the 1970s which reversed the decline in population between 1960 and 1970. There were slight changes within population age groups between 1970 and 1980, with the largest gain among ages 20 to 24 and the largest loss among ages 10 to 14. The median age of 32 remained unchanged from 1970 to 1980. The largest ancestry groups are persons of English descent (29%), Irish descent (26%) and German descent (23%). **REGISTERED VOTERS** As of November 2, 1982 there were 3,965 registered voters (0.1% of the state total). The 1982 general election had a 62% voter turnout, compared to a 75% turnout in the 1980 general election. In the 1982 primary 88% voted Democratic and 12% Republican, with 1,640 votes cast.

THE ECONOMY

AGRICULTURE High Plains wheat area. In 1982, 97% of the land was in farms and ranches, with 47% of the farmland under cultivation and 54% irrigated. Carson ranked 93rd in the state in highest agricultural receipts, with 70% from crops. Noxious weeds, overgrazing, wind erosion and decreasing irrigation water supplies are the current conservation problems. Primary crops: ninth in the state for sorghum. Wheat, hay and corn. Primary livestock and products: cattle. **BUSINESS** Total number of business establishments in the county: 116. Retail sales during the first quarter of 1984 decreased 6% with a 7% increase in Panhandle. In 1980, 16% of the labor force were self-employed, 17% were employed in professional or related services, 18% in manufacturing, 15% in wholesale and retail trade, 22% in agriculture, forestry, fisheries and mining, 32% were employed in other counties and there were 567 retired workers. The industries with the most employment: oil and gas extraction and the manufacture of weapons. The nonfarm earnings in 1981 totaled $73,527,000. The retired workers received an average monthly Social Security payment of $362. **FINANCE** On June 30, 1983, three commercial banks had total deposits of $43,558,000 and total assets of $48,746,000. There are two state savings and loan association branches and two credit unions in the county. **HOUSING** Average value of homes in 1980: $25,000. Permits for new, privately owned housing units increased in 1982: 42 permits were issued with a total construction cost of $1,845,530. Of those permits, all were for single family houses. Between 1970 and 1980 the number of housing units increased by 13%. Seventy-three percent of all units in the county are air-conditioned, 94% are heated by gas and 5% by electricity. **NATURAL RESOURCES** Caliche, oil and gas. In 1982 a total of 43,457,646 thousand cubic feet of gas well gas, 658 barrels of condensate, 1,376,964 barrels of crude oil and 33,269,191 thousand cubic feet of casinghead gas were produced. Current production of other minerals and products includes caliche, sand and gravel. **TOURISM** Travel expenditures of $2,726,000 in 1982 (an increase of 11% over 1981) generated 70 jobs and $554,000 in payroll. **ALCOHOLIC BEVERAGES** Packaged distilled spirits, beer, ale, malt liquor and wine are legal in parts of the county. **FEDERAL EXPENDITURES** The federal government had direct expenditures or obligations of $14,739,000 in the county during fiscal year 1983, including $311,000 by the U.S. Department of Defense. In addition, the federal government provided $99,000 in grant awards, paid $390,000 in salaries and wages, made direct payments to individuals of $8,973,000 including $6,552,000 in retirement and disability payments, awarded $2,000 in procurement contracts and spent $5,275,000 in other expenditures or obligations. The federal government also provided $19,482,000 in direct loans and $6,251,000 in guaranteed loans and insurance.

COMMUNICATION

Newspapers–Weekly: The Groom News, Panhandle Herald and The White Deer News. Cable TV. Telephone companies: Continental Telephone, General Telephone Southwestern Bell and Midplains Rural Telephone Coop. **TRANSPORTATION** Total public road mileage: 940. In 1982 there were 7,427 registered vehicles and 200 reported traffic accidents including five fatalities. Intercity bus service is available. Motor freight: five local and intrastate carriers. Rail: four main and two branch lines carry freight through the county. Three of the main lines carry annually over 30 million tons of freight each and one carries 10 to 20. The two branch lines carry annually less than one million tons of freight each. Aircraft: 22 are registered in the county. Airports: Carson County Airport at Panhandle. Skellytown Airport at Skellytown.

COMMUNITY SERVICES

EDUCATION Three school districts with four elementary, two middle and three high schools. The average daily attendance in 1981-82 was 1,393, with expenditures per pupil of $3,860 including 112 classroom teachers with an average annual salary of $17,818. Fifty-nine percent of the 107 high school graduates planned to attend college. In 1982-83, 95% of the students were White, 5% Hispanic, 0.4% Black and 0.1% Asian. **PUBLIC LIBRARIES** Carson County Public Library (Panhandle): 83,633 volumes and three branches. **CHILD CARE** Six day care and four twenty-four hour care licensed facilities. **HEALTH CARE** One physician and one dentist. Ambulance services: two volunteer services and one volunteer fire department service. Nursing homes: one nursing home has a capacity of 52 nursing care residents. The average cost per day for private patients in 1982 was $23.22. **CHURCHES** 20 churches have an estimated combined membership of 5,964. The largest denominations are Southern Baptist, United Methodist and Catholic. **SOCIAL SERVICES** In fiscal year 1983 a total of $61,198 in food stamps was distributed, with an average of 135 persons receiving food stamps each month. Aid to Families with Dependent Children (AFDC) totaled $11,575, with an average of nine families receiving AFDC each month. Medical assistance benefits for the aged and disabled of $145,931 and for families and children of $15,558 brought the county benefit total to $234,262. **FIRE PROTECTION** Four volunteer fire departments. **LAW ENFORCEMENT** The County Sheriff has 67 commissioned officers. One police department has a force of 11. **CRIME** Four violent crimes (murder, forcible rape, robbery and aggravated assault) and 64 nonviolent crimes (burglary, larceny-theft and motor vehicle theft) were reported in 1982. **JUDICIAL SYSTEM** One District Court and Judge, one County Court and Judge and three Justices of the Peace. In the District Court a total of 103 cases were pending on 1/1/82, 172 new cases were filed and 142 cases were disposed of during the year leaving 133 cases pending on 12/31/82. There were 53 criminal cases on the docket, 23 convictions, 10 persons committed to prison and, 26 cases left pending. In the County Court 71 cases were pending on 1/1/82, 150 new cases were filed and 140 cases were disposed of during the year leaving 81 cases pending on 12/31/82. There were 220 criminal cases on the docket, 77 convictions, and 81 cases left pending. **JAILS** One jail, capacity 24. In 1983 lost certification due to supervision. **ATTORNEYS AT LAW** Five. **UTILITIES** 83% of the residents are connected to a public or privately owned water system and 76% are connected to a public sewer system. Natural gas is distributed to the county by Producers Utilities Corp. and Energas Company. The average annual residential bill for natural gas in 1982 for the Energas distribution system was $371.63, an increase of 23% over 1981. Electricity is distributed to the county by Southwestern Public Service Company and is generated primarily by gas and oil. **TAXES** The county has nine units with taxing authority: three school districts, four cities, one county and one special district.

COUNTIES

RECREATION/ENTERTAINMENT

NATIONAL REGISTER OF HISTORIC PLACES Panhandle: Square House. **MUNICIPAL PARKS** 10 acres in three municipal parks. These parks contain two playgrounds and one swimming pool. **SCENIC DRIVES** The Texas Plains Trail Runs through this county. This trail spans a vast area of the HighPlains region of Texas slicing through the Southernmost extension of the Great Plains of the United States. The land is flat except where erosion has carved canyon landscapes. **BOATING/FISHING** Lakes/reservoirs: McClellan Creek and Soil Conservation Service Lake 1 (19 acres). Primary streams: McClellan. **HUNTING** Fall season on antelope. Fall and winter seasons on deer and mule deer. Summer, fall and winter seasons on squirrel. Winter seasons on pheasant, quail, muskrat, beaver, opossum, ring-tailed cat, badger, fox, weasel, raccoon, skunk and civet cat. No closed seasons on bobcat and coyote. Fall, winter and spring seasons on turkey. In 1983 sandhill crane, duck, coot, geese, woodcock and jacksnipe seasons occurred during the winter months. Teal duck, rail and gallinule seasons occurred in the fall. Mourning dove seasons occurred intermittently during the fall and winter months. **MUSEUMS** Panhandle: Carson County Square House Museum. **SPECIAL EVENTS** Rodeo, White Deer, April/May; and Independence Day Celebration, Panhandle, July.

COMMUNITIES

COUNTY SEAT Panhandle, County Courthouse, 79068; County Clerk's Office, 806/537-3873. **INCORPORATED COMMUNITIES** (1980 population and ZIP Code) Groom (736) 79039, Panhandle (2,226) 79068, Skellytown (899) 79080 and White Deer (1,210) 79097. **UNINCORPORATED COMMUNITIES** (and ZIP Code) Conway 79068, Lark 79039 and Pantex 79069. **FOR ADDITIONAL LOCAL INFORMATION** Panhandle Chamber of Commerce, P.O. Box 1021, Panhandle, 79068, 806/537-3477.

CASS (E9)

THE LAND

Bordering Arkansas and Louisiana on U.S. Highway 59 in the East Texas Timberlands Region, Cass County covers 937 square miles of woodland. The elevation ranges from 250 to 400 feet. The undulating to rolling land has acidic, light-colored soils low in plant nutrients with loamy to sandy surface layers and reddish mottled, cracking, clayey subsoils. In the Pineywoods vegetation area, the pine (longleaf, shortleaf, loblolly and slash) is the principal timber along with hardwoods such as oaks, elms, hickory, tupelo, sweet and blackgum, magnolia and maple. The grasslands include species of blackseed, needlegrass, switchcane and wildryes. Between 21 and 30% of the land in the county is considered prime farmland. **CLIMATE** Subtropical humid, mild and moist. The average annual temperature is 64°F. Temperatures in January range from an average low of 31° to an average high of 53°F and in July range from 70° to 94°F. The average annual precipitation is 46 inches, with an average relative humidity of 85% at 6 A.M. and 59% at 6 P.M. The average annual snowfall is two inches. The growing season averages 237 days per year, with the last freeze near March 19th and the first freeze near November 11th. The sun shines during the year on the average 67% of the daylight hours.

THE PEOPLE

The 1982 estimated population of 30,600 indicates a continuation of the growth rate since the 1970s. This growth reversed the steady population decline between 1940 and 1970. Almost 25% of the growth between 1970 and 1980 was in urban areas with a 21% gain in rural areas. The age groups with the largest increases were ages 20 to 24 and 62 and over. However, the median age of 33 remained unchanged from 1970 to 1980. The largest ancestry groups are Black (22%), persons of English descent (24%) and Irish descent (17%). **REGISTERED VOTERS** As of November 2, 1982 there were 16,092 registered voters (0.3% of the state total). The 1982 general election had a 48% voter turnout, compared to a 66% turnout in the 1980 general election. In the 1982 primary 98% voted Democratic and 2% Republican, with 6,769 votes cast.

THE ECONOMY

AGRICULTURE Major forest production area. In 1982, 47% of the land was in farms and ranches, with 10% of the farmland under cultivation. Cass ranked 202nd in the state in highest agricultural receipts, with 80% from livestock and livestock products. Water erosion on the forestland and undesirable woody vegetation are the current conservation problems. Primary crops: hay and wheat. Primary vegetables: sweet potatoes and watermelons. Primary fruits and nuts: peaches and pecans. Primary livestock and products: cattle, milk and hogs. **BUSINESS** Total number of business establishments in the county: 451. Retail sales during the first quarter of 1984 increased 15%. Atlanta had an increase of 57%, while Domino posted a 76% decrease. In 1980, 9% of the labor force were self-employed, 18% were employed in professional or related services, 29% in manufacturing, 17% in wholesale and retail trade, 9% in construction, 38% were employed in other counties and there were 2,920 retired workers. The industries with the most employment: agribusiness, oil and gas extraction, metal mining, paperboard mills, sawmills and the manufacture of leather gloves. The nonfarm earnings in 1981 totaled $220,736,000. The retired workers received an average monthly Social Security payment of $293. **FINANCE** On June 30, 1983, six commercial banks had total deposits of $132,820,000 and total assets of $148,846,000. On December 31, 1982 one federal savings and loan association, one state savings and loan assocation branch and one federal branch had assets of $76,777,249. In addition there are two credit unions in the county. **HOUSING** Average value of homes in 1980: $26,000. Permits for new, privately owned housing units decreased in 1982: 26 permits were issued with a total construction cost of $599,127. Of those permits, 20 were for single family houses. Between 1970 and 1980 the number of housing units increased by 35%. Seventy-four percent of all units in the county are air-conditioned, 73% are heated by gas and 18% by electricity. **NATURAL RESOURCES** Ceramic clay, granite, industrial sand, oil, gas, iron and lignite coal. In 1982 a total of 24,977,620 thousand cubic feet of gas well gas, 113,383 barrels of condensate, 835,913 barrels of crude oil and 2,045,149 thousand cubic feet of casinghead gas were produced. Current production of other minerals and products includes clay, iron magnetite, ironsiderite, construction sand, sand and gravel, and recovered sulphur. Pine and hardwood production in 1981 totaled 16,920,041 cubic feet: 13,466,097 cubic feet of pine and 3,453,944 cubic feet of hardwood. **TOURISM** Travel expenditures of $6,214,000 in 1982 (an increase of 11% over 1981) generated 152 jobs and $1,219,000 in payroll. Lodging: five hotels, motels and tourist courts. **ALCOHOLIC BEVERAGES** Packaged distilled spirits, beer, ale, malt liquor and wine are legal in parts of the county. **FEDERAL EXPENDITURES** The federal government had direct expenditures or obligations of $53,515,000 in the county during fiscal year 1983, including $2,202,000 by the U.S. Department of Defense. In addition, the federal government provided $2,262,000 in grant awards, paid $1,573,000 in salaries and wages, made direct payments to individuals of $49,330,000 including $37,956,000 in retirement and disability payments, awarded $95,000 in procurement contracts and spent $256,000 in other expenditures or obligations. The federal government also provided $1,017,000 in direct loans and $3,051,000 in guaranteed loans and insurance.

COMMUNICATION

Newspapers–Weekly: The Atlanta Times, Citizens Journal (Atlanta) and the Cass County Sun (Linden). Radio: KALT-AM (Atlanta). Cable TV. Telephone companies: General Telephone, Southwestern Bell, Caddoan Telephone, ETEX Telephone Coop., Lakeside Telephone and SW Arkansas Telephone Coop. **TRANSPORTATION** Total public road mileage: 1,377. In 1982 there were 22,593 registered vehicles and 481 reported traffic accidents including seven fatalities. Taxi cabs: one company in Atlanta. Intercity bus service is available. Motor freight: five local and intrastate carriers. Rail: The Eagle provides passenger service on the Amtrak route. Four main lines carry freight through the county with one carrying annually over 30 million tons of freight, one 20 to 30, one 10 to 20 and one 5 to 10 million tons. Aircraft: 37 are registered in the county. Airports: Atlanta Municipal Airport is a basic utility airport with general aviation service and serves as a base for 23 aircraft. McKenzie Field at Avinger is unattended.

COMMUNITY SERVICES

EDUCATION Eight school districts with 10 elementary, four middle, seven high schools and one special education. The average daily attendance in 1981-82 was 5,698, with expenditures per pupil of $2,653 including 358 classroom teachers with an average annual salary of $15,677. Forty-two percent of the 390 high school graduates planned to attend college. In 1982-83, 72% of the students were White, 0.8% Hispanic, 27% Black and 0.1% American Indian. **PUBLIC LIBRARIES** Atlanta Library. **CHILD CARE** 31 day care and 15 twenty-four hour care licensed facilities. **HEALTH CARE** 21 physicians and 13 dentists. Hospitals: three with a combined capacity of 183. Clinics: one public health clinic. Ambulance services: three volunteer services and one fire department. Mental health: one clinic. Nursing homes: five nursing homes with a combined capacity of 453 nursing care residents. The average cost per day for private patients in 1982 was $29.52. **CHURCHES** 105 churches have an estimated combined membership of 23,198. The largest denominations are Southern Baptist, United Methodist and Christian Methodist Episcopal. **SOCIAL SERVICES** In fiscal year 1983 a total of $1,944,855 in food stamps was distributed, with an average of 4,195 persons receiving food stamps each month. Aid to Families with Dependent Children (AFDC) totaled $505,699, with an average of 341 families receiving AFDC each month. Medical assistance benefits for the aged and disabled of $3,281,522 and for families and children of $530,697 brought the county benefit total to $6,262,773. **FIRE PROTECTION** One partly paid and nine volunteer fire departments. **LAW ENFORCEMENT** The County Sheriff has eight commissioned officers. Five police departments have a combined force of 42. **CRIME** 35 violent crimes (murder, forcible rape, robbery and aggravated assault) and 344 nonviolent crimes (burglary, larceny-theft and motor vehicle theft) were reported in 1982. **JUDICIAL SYSTEM** One District Court and Judge, one County Court and Judge and four Justices of the Peace. In the District Court a total of 1,064 cases were pending on 1/1/82, 1,298 new cases were filed and 1,388 cases were disposed of during the year leaving 974 cases pending on 12/31/82. There were 1,143 criminal cases on the docket, 445 convictions, 17 persons committed to prison and 40 committed to jail and 54 cases left pending. **JAILS** One jail, capacity 24. Major renovation completed in 1983. **ATTORNEYS AT LAW** 18. **UTILITIES** 52% of the residents are connected to a public or privately owned water system and 40% are connected to a public sewer system. Natural gas is distributed to the county

by Arkla, Inc. and McLedd Gas Co. The average annual residential bill for natural gas in 1982 for the Arkla distribution system was $316.69, an increase of 23% over 1981. Electricity is distributed to the county by Southwestern Electric Power Co., Bowie-Cass Electric Coop., Inc. and Upshur-rural Electric Coop., Corp. and is generated primarily by gas and oil. The typical residential electric bill is $152.08 per month for an all-electric house using 2,500 kwh. **TAXES** The county has 15 units with taxing authority: eight school districts, six cities and one county.

RECREATION/ENTERTAINMENT

NATIONAL REGISTER OF HISTORIC PLACES Linden: Cass County Courthouse. Queen City: Mathews-Powell House. **STATE** Atlanta State Recreation Area covers 1,475 acres with camping and trailer sites as well as areas offering fishing, swimming, boat ramps and nature trails. **MUNICIPAL PARKS** 54 acres in six municipal parks. These parks contain one playground, four baseball and softball fields, three tennis courts and one swimming pool. **BOATING/FISHING** Lakes/reservoirs: Arrowhead (63 acres), Foreman (37 acres), Iron Ore (138 acres), Rhyue (22 acres), Simpson (162 acres) and Wright Patman. Major rivers: Sulphur. Primary streams: White Oak, Bowman, Jim Bayou, Alley, Frazier and Cypress. **HUNTING** Fall and winter seasons on deer. Summer, fall and winter seasons on squirrel. Winter seasons on quail, muskrat, beaver, otter, opossum, mink, ringtailed cat, badger, raccoon, skunk and civet cat. No closed season for nutria, coyote and bobcat. In 1983 duck, coot, geese, woodcock and jacksnipe seasons occurred during the winter months. Teal duck, rail and gallinule seasons occurred in the fall. Mourning dove seasons occurred intermittently during the fall and winter months. **SPECIAL EVENTS** Wildflower Trails, Hughes Springs, April; Miss Wild Flower Pageant, Linden, April; Bluegrass Festival, Hughes Springs, June; Forest Festival and Parade, Atlanta, August; Hughes Springs Bluegrass Festival, Hughes Springs, September; and Cullen Baker Country Fair, Bloomburg, November.

COMMUNITIES

COUNTY SEAT Linden, County Courthouse, 75563; County Clerk's Office, 214/756-5071. **INCORPORATED COMMUNITIES** (1980 population and ZIP Code) Atlanta (6,272) 75551, Avinger (671) 75630, Bloomburg (419) 75556, Domino (249) 75572, Douglassville (228) 75560, Hughes Springs (2,196) 75656. Linden (2,443) 75563, Marietta (169) 75566 and Queen City (1,748) 75572. **UNINCORPORATED COMMUNITIES** (and ZIP Code) Antioch 75551, Bivins 75555, Bogus Springs 75555, Bryans Mill 75560, Carterville 75563, Cass 75556, Cornett 75568, Cusseta 75566, Dalton 75568, Doss 75563, Galloway 75551, Huffines 75555, Kildare 75562, Kildare Junction 75555, Lanark 75572, Lanier 75563, Love Chapel 75656, McLeod 75565, New Colony 75563, Nickleberry 75566, O'Farrell 75551, Patman (Turkey Creek) 75630, Pruitt 75657, Red Hill 75563, Smyrna 75551, Springdale 75572, Walton 71082 and Wiggins 75555. **FOR ADDITIONAL LOCAL INFORMATION** Atlanta Chamber of Commerce, Drawer –29, 305 E. Hiram, Atlanta, 75551, 214/796-3296, Bloomburg Area Chamber of Commerce, P.O. Box 262, Bloomburg, 75556, 214/728-5222, Hughes Springs Chamber of Commerce, P.O. Box 218, Hughes Springs, 75656, 214/639-2351 and Linden Chamber of Commerce, P.O. Box 429, 104 S. Main, Linden, 75563, 214/756-5741.

CASTRO (P22)

THE LAND

In the Texas Panhandle southwest of Amarillo on U.S. Highway 385 in the High Plains Region, Castro County covers 899 square

COUNTIES

CASTRO (continued)

miles with the elevation ranging from 3,500 to 4,000 feet. The nearly level soils are loamy with clayey subsoils that have a high potential to shrink and swell. In some areas limestone or powdery lime have accumulated in the subsoils. In the High Plains vegetation area, the primary grasses are short buffalograss and blue grama. Mesquite, yucca and sagebrush have become a problem in some areas. Castro County has more land considered prime farmland than any other county in Texas—between 91 and 100% of the land in the county is considered prime farmland. **CLIMATE** Continental steppe, generally cool and dry with wide-ranging daily and seasonal temperature fluctuations. The average annual temperature is 57°F. Temperatures in January range from an average low of 21° to an average high of 51°F and in July range from 64° to 93°F. The average annual precipitation is 17 inches, with an average relative humidity of 70% at 6 A.M. and 38% at 6 P.M. The average annual snowfall is 12 inches. The growing season averages 193 days per year, with the last freeze in mid April and the first freeze in late October. The sun shines during the year on the average 74% of the daylight hours.

THE PEOPLE

In 1980 Castro County ranked 65th among all U.S. counties in the highest percent of population of Spanish origin. The 1982 estimated population of 10,600 indicates no population growth following moderate growth since the 1940s. Almost 16% of the population increase between 1970 and 1980 was in urban aras, with rural areas experiencing a 9% decline. The age group with the largest gain was ages 62 and over, raising the low median age from 21 in 1970 to 25 in 1980. The county has a high percent of population under 18 and a low death rate. The largest ancestry groups are Hispanic (39%), persons of English descent (17%) and those of Irish descent (17%). **REGISTERED VOTERS** As of November 2, 1982 there were 4,659 registered voters (0.1% of the state total). The 1982 general election had a 55% voter turnout, compared to a 70% turnout in the 1980 general election. In the 1982 primary 95% voted Democratic and 5% Republican, with 1,958 votes cast.

THE ECONOMY

AGRICULTURE Prime farmland with diversified products. In 1982, 98% of the land was in farms and ranches, with 71% of the farmland under cultivation and 83% irrigated. Castro ranked fourth in the state in highest agricultural receipts, with 59% from crops. Wind erosion and decreasing irrigation water supplies are the current conservation problems. Primary crops: eighth in the state for wheat, first for corn, seventh for soybeans and 10th for sunflowers. Cotton, sorghum and sugarbeets. Primary vegetables: third in the state for carrots and fifth for total fresh market vegetables. Potatoes, onions and processed vegetables including beets, cucumbers for pickles, snapbeans, spinach, sweet corn and tomatoes. Primary fruits and nuts: pecans. Primary livestock and products: sixth in the state for cattle and seventh for fed cattle marketings. Milk, sheep, wool and hogs. **BUSINESS** Total number of business establishments in the county: 215. Retail sales during the first quarter of 1984 increased 16%. In 1980, 19% of the labor force were self-employed, 18% were employed in professional or related services, 9% in manufacturing, 16% in wholesale and retail trade, 36% in agriculture, forestry, fisheries and mining, 7% were employed in other counties and there were 497 retired workers. The industries with the most employment: agribusiness, grain mills and the manufacture of fertilizers. The nonfarm earnings in 1981 totaled $60,091,000. The retired workers received an average monthly Social Security payment of $324. **FINANCE** On June 30, 1983, two commercial banks had total deposits of $48,590,000 and total assets of $55,441,000. There

are two state savings and loan association branches in the county. **HOUSING** Average value of homes in 1980: $29,600. Between 1970 and 1980 the number of housing units increased by 11%. Seventy-three percent of all units in the county are air-conditioned, 91% are heated by gas and 8% by electricity. **NATURAL RESOURCES** Caliche, oil and gas. **TOURISM** Travel expenditures of $8,625,000 in 1982 (an increase of 17% over 1981) generated 137 jobs and $1,346,000 in payroll. **ALCOHOLIC BEVERAGES** Packaged distilled spirits, beer, ale, malt liquor and wine are legal in parts of the county. **FEDERAL EXPENDITURES** The federal government had direct expenditures or obligations of $23,055,000 in the county during fiscal year 1983, including $173,000 by the U.S. Department of Defense. In addition, the federal government provided $259,000 in grant awards, paid $510,000 in salaries and wages, made direct payments to individuals of $6,972,000 including $5,357,000 in retirement and disability payments, awarded $25,000 in procurement contracts and spent $15,289,000 in other expenditures or obligations. The federal government also provided $41,744,000 in direct loans and $20,065,000 in guaranteed loans and insurance.

COMMUNICATION

Newspapers–Weekly: Castro County News (Dimmitt) and Heart Beat. Radio: KDHN-AM (Dimmitt). Cable TV. Telephone companies: Continental Telephone, Five-Area Telephone Coop., Midplains Rural Telephone Coop., South Plains Telephone Coop. and West Texas Rural Telephone Coop. **TRANSPORTATION** Total public road mileage: 1,184. In 1982 there were 9,880 registered vehicles and 188 reported traffic accidents including eight fatalities. Motor freight: seven local and intrastate carriers. Rail: one main and one branch line carry freight through the county. The main line carries annually over 30 million tons of freight and the branch carries less than one million. Aircraft: 43 are registered in the county. Airports: Dimmitt Municipal Airport is a basic utility airport providing general aviation service. It serves as a base for 32 aircraft.

COMMUNITY SERVICES

EDUCATION Three school districts with three elementary, one middle and three high schools. The average daily attendance in 1981-82 was 2,422, with expenditures per pupil of $2,506 including 181 classroom teachers with an average annual salary of $15,843. Sixty-five percent of the 144 high school graduates planned to attend college. In 1982-83, 38% of the students were White, 58% Hispanic and 3% Black. Sports championships: 1984 A Girls' Basketball, Nazareth H.S. **PUBLIC LIBRARIES** Rhodes Memorial Library (Dimmitt): 22,000 volumes. **CHILD CARE** 23 day care and five twenty-four hour care licensed facilities. **HEALTH CARE** Four physicians and two dentists. Hospitals: one with a capacity of 46. Ambulance services: one hospital-based service. Mental health: one clinic. Nursing homes: one nursing home has a capacity of 118 nursing care residents. The average cost per day for private patients in 1982 was $32.74. **CHURCHES** 22 churches have an estimated combined membership of 8,620. The largest denominations are Southern Baptist, Catholic and United Methodist. **SOCIAL SERVICES** In fiscal year 1983 a total of $877,159 in food stamps was distributed, with an average of 1,805 persons receiving food stamps each month. Aid to Families with Dependent Children (AFDC) totaled $90,745, with an average of 59 families receiving AFDC each month. Medical assistance benefits for the aged and disabled of $385,089 and for families and children of $91,191 brought the county benefit total to $1,444,183. **FIRE PROTECTION** Three volunteer fire departments. **LAW ENFORCEMENT** The County Sheriff has five commissioned officers. Two police departments have a combined force of 11. **CRIME** 24 violent crimes (murder, forcible rape, robbery and aggravated assault) and 212 nonviolent crimes (burglary, larceny-theft and motor vehicle theft) were reported in 1982. **JUDICIAL SYSTEM** Two District Courts and Judges, one County Court and Judge and one Justice of the Peace. In the District Courts a total of 277 cases were pending on 1/1/82, 168 new cases were filed and 163 cases were disposed of during the year leaving 282 cases pending on 12/31/82. There were 162 criminal cases on the docket, 38 convictions, three persons committed to prison and eight committed to jail and 85 cases left pending. In the County Court 713 cases were pending on 1/1/82, 389 new cases were filed and 174 cases were disposed of during the year leaving 928 cases pending on 12/31/82. There were 951 criminal cases on the docket, 140 convictions, 62 persons committed to jail, and 783 cases left pending. **JAILS** One jail, capacity 18. **ATTORNEYS AT LAW** Six. **UTILITIES** 66% of the residents are connected to a public or privately owned water system and 64% are connected to a public sewer system. Natural gas is distributed to the county by Energas Company. The average annual residential bill for natural gas in 1982 for the Energas distribution system was $371.63, an increase of 23% over 1981. Electricity is distributed to the county by Southwestern Public Service, Bailey County Electric Coop., Deafsmith Electric Coop., Inc., Lamb Co. Electric Coop., Inc. and Swisher Electric Coop., Inc. and is generated primarily by gas and oil. The typical residential electric bill is $170.44 per month for an all-electric house using 2,500 kwh. **TAXES** The county has nine units with taxing authority: three school districts, three cities, one county and two special districts.

RECREATION/ENTERTAINMENT

MUNICIPAL PARKS 16 acres in three municipal parks. These parks contain two playgrounds, three baseball and softball fields and one tennis court. **SCENIC DRIVES** The Texas Plains Trail runs through this county. This trail spans a vast area of the High Plains region of Texas slicing through the southernmost extension of the Great Plains of the United States. The land is flat except where erosion has carved canyon landscapes. **BOATING/ FISHING** Lakes/reservoirs: Running Water Draw Soil Conservation Service Lake (98 acres). **HUNTING** Summer, fall and winter seasons on squirrel. Winter seasons on pheasant, quail, muskrat, beaver, opossum, ring-tailed cat, badger, fox, weasel, raccoon, skunk and civet cat. No closed seasons on coyote and bobcat. In 1983 sandhill crane, duck, coot, geese, woodcock and jacksnipe seasons occurred during the winter months. Teal duck, rail and gallinule seasons occurred in the fall. Mourning dove seasons occurred intermittently during the fall and winter months. **MUSEUMS** Dimmitt: Castro County Historical Museum. **SPECIAL EVENTS** Hart Days, Hart, June/July; Harvest Days Celebration, Dimmitt, September; County Fair, Dimmitt, September; Old Settlers Reunion, Dimmitt, September/ October; German Sausage Festival, Nazareth, October; and Christmas Parade, Dimmitt, December.

COMMUNITIES

COUNTY SEAT Dimmitt, County Courthouse, 79027; County Clerk's Office, 806/647-3338. **INCORPORATED COMMUNITIES** (1980 population and ZIP Code) Dimmitt (5,019) 79207, Hart (1,008) 79043 and Nazareth (299) 79063. **UNINCORPORATED COMMUNITIES** (and ZIP Code) Arney 79042, Easter 79045, Flagg 79027, Summerfield 79085 and Sunnyside 79027. **FOR ADDITIONAL LOCAL INFORMATION** Dimmitt Chamber of Commerce, 201 E. Jones, P.O. Box 924, Dimmitt, 79027, 806/647-2524.

CHAMBERS (G12)

THE LAND

East of Houston on Interstate Highway 10 in the Coastal Prairie Region, Chambers County covers 616 square miles which slope toward the Gulf of Mexico. The elevation ranges from sea level to 50 feet. The soils in the eastern two-thirds of the county are sandy, clayey to loamy and somewhat poorly drained. Along the Trinity River to the west the soils are loamy with cracking, clayey subsoils. To the south the soils become saline clays with loamy soils in the marshes and sandy toward the Gulf. The Gulf Prairies and Marshes vegetation area has tall grasses with live oaks and hardwood trees along rivers and streams. Between 11 and 20% of the land in the county is considered prime farmland. **CLIMATE** Subtropical humid, generally mild. Sea fog may be a concern occasionally during winter and spring and from June through October tropical storms and hurricanes may occur. The average annual temperature is 69°F. Temperatures in January range from an average low of 44° to an average high of 61°F and in July range from 75° to 91°F. The average annual precipitation is 48 inches, with an average relative humidity of 90% at 6 A.M. and 70% at 6 P.M. There is no snowfall. The growing season averages 261 days per year, with the last freeze in early March and the first freeze in mid November. The sun shines during the year on the average 65% of the daylight hours.

THE PEOPLE

The 1982 estimated population of 19,100 indicates a continuation of the strong growth rate begun in the 1970s. Chambers experienced one of the highest growth rates in the state between 1970 and 1980, with a 52% gain in rural population. The age groups with the largest gains were ages 20 to 34 and birth to five years. The largest ancestry groups are persons of English descent (27%), those of Irish descent (17%) and Black (14%). **REGISTERED VOTERS** As of November 2, 1982 there were 9,476 registered voters (0.1% of the state total). The 1982 general election had a 48% voter turnout, compared to a 63% turnout in the 1980 general election. In the 1982 primary 99% voted Democratic and 1% Republican, with 3,489 votes cast.

THE ECONOMY

AGRICULTURE Forest products area along with rice and soybeans. In 1982, 90% of the land was in farms and ranches, with 30% of the farmland under cultivation and 62% irrigated. Chambers ranked 104th in the state in highest agricultural receipts, with 78% from crops. Overgrazing, inefficient irrigation systems, drainage, improper woodland management and water erosion are the current conservation problems. Primary crops: fifth in the state for both soybeans and rice. Primary vegetables: potatoes. Primary fruits and nuts: peaches and pecans. Primary livestock and products: cattle. **BUSINESS** Total number of business establishments in the county: 288. Retail sales during the first quarter of 1984 increased 16%. In 1980, 8% of the labor force were self-employed, 15% were employed in professional or related services, 21% in manufacturing, 17% in wholesale and retail trade, 15% in construction, 42% were employed in other counties and there were 786 retired workers. The industries with the most employment: oil and gas extraction, agribusiness, petroleum refining and the manufacture of plastics and resins. The nonfarm earnings in 1981 totaled $184,304,000. The retired workers received an average monthly Social Security payment of $344. **FINANCE** On June 30, 1983, four commercial banks had total deposits of $107,228,000 and total assets of $119,685,000. There are two state savings and loan

CHAMBERS (continued)

association branches and three credit unions in the county. **HOUSING** Average value of homes in 1980: $40,600. Permits for new, privately owned housing units decreased in 1982: six permits were issued with a total construction cost of $255,774. Of those permits, all were for single family houses. Between 1970 and 1980 the number of housing units increased by 56%. Eighty-three percent of all units in the county are air-conditioned, 64% are heated by gas and 33% by electricity. **NATURAL RESOURCES** Salt domes, industrial sand, oil and gas. In 1982 a total of 36,223,773 thousand cubic feet of gas well gas, 452,436 barrels of condensate, 7,762,738 barrels of crude oil and 32,337,363 thousand cubic feet of casinghead gas were produced. Current production of other minerals and products includes brine, clay and construction sand. Pine and hardwood production in 1981 totaled 1,063,464 cubic feet: 562,377 cubic feet of pine and 501,087 cubic feet of hardwood. **TOURISM** Travel expenditures of $15,619,000 in 1982 (an increase of 18% over 1981) generated 222 jobs and $2,384,000 in payroll. **ALCOHOLIC BEVERAGES** Packaged distilled spirits, beer, ale, malt liquor and wine are legal in parts of the county. **FEDERAL EXPENDITURES** The federal government had direct expenditures or obligations of $22,722,000 in the county during fiscal year 1983, including $840,000 by the U.S. Department of Defense. In addition, the federal government provided $411,000 in grant awards, paid $807,000 in salaries and wages, made direct payments to individuals of $13,692,000 including $10,810,000 in retirement and disability payments, awarded $814,000 in procurement contracts and spent $6,998,000 in other expenditures or obligations. The federal government also provided $4,124,000 in direct loans and $48,409,000 in guaranteed loans and insurance.

COMMUNICATION

Newspapers–Weekly: Anahuac Progress. Cable TV. Telephone companies: General Telephone, Southwestern Bell, Cameron Telephone and Trinity Valley Telephone. **TRANSPORTATION** Total public road mileage: 573. In 1982 there were 21,582 registered vehicles and 577 reported traffic accidents including 12 fatalities. Intercity bus service is available. Motor freight: six local and intrastate carriers. Rail: one branch line carries annually less than one million tons of freight through the county. Aircraft: 45 are registered in the county. Airports: Chambers County Airport at Anahuac is a general utility airport providing general aviation service. It serves as a base for 25 aircraft. Also serving the area are Chambers County Airport at Winnie, Baytown Municipal Airport and R.W.J. Airpark at Baytown. San Jacinto Methodist Hospital has a heliport for emergencies. Waterborne commerce: (See Galveston County.) Anahuac Channel had total freight of 219,702 short tons of domestic freight in 1981. Double Bayou shipped 26,136 short tons of domestic freight.

COMMUNITY SERVICES

EDUCATION Three school districts with four elementary, three middle and three high schools. The average daily attendance in 1981-82 was 3,615, with expenditures per pupil of $4,730 including 261 classroom teachers with an average annual salary of $21,033. Forty percent of the 225 high school graduates planned to attend college. In 1982-83, 78% of the students were White, 5% Hispanic, 17% Black and 0.1% Asian. **PUBLIC LIBRARIES** Chambers County Library (Anahuac): 43,093 volumes and two branches. **CHILD CARE** 21 day care and four twenty-four hour care licensed facilities. **HEALTH CARE** Seven physicians and five dentists. Hospitals: two with a combined capacity of 106. Clinics: one public health clinic. Ambulance services: three volunteer services and two volunteer fire department services. Nursing homes: one nursing home has a capacity of 100 nursing

care residents. The average cost per day for private patients in 1982 was $34.57. **CHURCHES** 27 churches have an estimated combined membership of 9,418. The largest denominations are Southern Baptist, Catholic and United Methodist. **SOCIAL SERVICES** In fiscal year 1983 a total of $989,883 in food stamps was distributed, with an average of 1,894 persons receiving food stamps each month. Aid to Families with Dependent Children (AFDC) totaled $197,362, with an average of 132 families receiving AFDC each month. Medical assistance benefits for the aged and disabled of $636,486 and for families and children of $348,969 brought the county benefit total to $2,172,699. **FIRE PROTECTION** 11 volunteer fire departments. **LAW ENFORCEMENT** The County Sheriff has 17 commissioned officers. Two police departments have a combined force of four. **CRIME** 54 violent crimes (murder, forcible rape, robbery and aggravated assault) and 361 nonviolent crimes (burglary, larceny-theft and motor vehicle theft) were reported in 1982. **JUDICIAL SYSTEM** Two District Courts and Judges, one County Court and Judge and six Justices of the Peace. In the District Courts a total of 739 cases were pending on 1/1/82, 589 new cases were filed and 548 cases were disposed of during the year leaving 780 cases pending on 12/31/82. There were 504 criminal cases on the docket, 116 convictions, 27 persons committed to prison and five committed to jail and 296 cases left pending. In the County Court 214 cases were pending on 1/1/82, 659 new cases were filed and 387 cases were disposed of during the year leaving 486 cases pending on 12/31/82. There were 794 criminal cases on the docket, 222 convictions, six persons committed to jail, and 429 cases left pending. **JAILS** One jail, capacity 52. Opened in 1983. **ATTORNEYS AT LAW** 13. **UTILITIES** 71% of the residents are connected to a public or privately owned water system and 45% are connected to a public sewer system. Natural gas is distributed to the county by Entex, Inc. The average annual residential bill for natural gas in 1982 for the Entex distribution system was $390.31, an increase of 26% over 1981. Electricity is distributed to the county by Gulf State Utilities and Houston Lighting and Power Co. and is generated primarily by gas and oil. The typical residential electric bill is $157.00 per month for an all-electric house using 2,500 kwh. **TAXES** The county has 11 units with taxing authority: four school districts, two cities, one county and four special districts.

RECREATION/ENTERTAINMENT

NATIONAL REGISTER OF HISTORIC PLACES Anahuac: Chambersea and Fort Anahuac. Baytown vicinity: Cedar Bayou Archeological District. Houston vicinity: Anahuac Archeological Site and Orcoquisac Archeological District. Wallisville: Old Wallisville Town Site. **COUNTY/MUNICIPAL PARKS** 261 acres in 12 county and one municipal park. These parks contain nine playgrounds, six baseball and softball fields, four tennis courts, one multi-use court, one swimming pool and 12 boat ramps and shore fishing facilities. Developed campsites: 53. **BOATING/FISHING** Lakes/reservoirs: Anahuac (2,000 acres), Cedar Bayou (4,813 acres), Frost (186 acres), Marshall No. 1 (98 acres), Marshall No. 2 (148 acres), Martrac Farms (173 acres), E.W. Monteith –1 (299 acres), E.W. Monteith –2 (317 acres), E.W. Monteith –3 (293 acres) and Stanolind (234 acres). Primary streams: Turtle Bayou, Cedar Bayou, Hickory Gulley, Spindletop Bayou, East Bay Bayou, Willow Marsh and Elm Bayou. **SALTWATER FISHING** for speckled trout, redfish and flounders is usually good around Trinity Bay, East Bay and Galveston Bay, all of which border the county. Shrimp, oysters and crabs may be taken but, like other saltwater fish, under specific regulations. **WILDLIFE REFUGES** Anahuac National Wildlife Refuge covers 9,837 acres. Moody National Wildlife Refuge, spanning 714 acres, is also in this county. **HUNTING** Fall and winter seasons on deer. Summer, fall and winter seasons on squirrel. Winter seasons on quail, muskrat, beaver, otter, opossum, mink, ring-tailed cat, badger, fox, raccoon, skunk and civet cat. No closed season on coyote, nutria and bobcat. Special regulations on Lake Anahuac, the Trinity River, Wallisville Reservoir and Oyster Bay Bayou. In 1983 duck, coot, geese, woodcock and jacksnipe seasons occurred during the winter months. Teal duck, rail and gallinule seasons occurred in the fall. Mourning dove seasons occurred intermittently during the fall and winter months. **MUSEUMS** Anahuac: Dr. Nicholas T. Schilling Medical Office Building. **SPECIAL EVENTS** Rice Festival, Winnie, September/October.

COMMUNITIES

COUNTY SEAT Anahuac, County Courthouse, 77514; County Clerk's Office, 409/267-3471. **INCORPORATED COMMUNITIES** (1980 population and ZIP Code) Anahuac (1,840) 77514, Baytown (56,923: 6 in Chambers Co. and 56,917 in Harris Co.) 77520, Beach City (977) 77520, Cove (645) 77520, Mont Belvieu (1,730) 77580 and Old River Winfree (1,058) 77514. **UNINCORPORATED COMMUNITIES** (and ZIP Code) Cedar Point 77520, Double Bayou 77514, Figridge 77661, Hankamer 77560, Monroe City 77579, Oak Island 77514, Shoreacres 77571, Smith Point 77514, Stowell 77661, Turtle Bayou 77514, Wallisville 77597, Whites Ranch 77661, Winfree 77535 and Winnie 77665. **FOR ADDITIONAL LOCAL INFORMATION** Baytown Chamber of Commerce, P.O. Box 330, Baytown, 77522, 409/422-8359 or 420-3353, La Porte-Bayshore Chamber of Commerce, P.O. Box 996, Shoreacres, 77571, 409/471-1123 and Winnie Chamber of Commerce, P.O. Box 147, Winnie, 77665, 409/296-2231.

CHEROKEE (E21)

THE LAND

Southeast of Dallas on U.S. Highways 175, 79, 84 and 69 in the East Texas Timberlands Region, Cherokee County covers 1,052 square miles of grass and woodlands. The elevation ranges from 225 to 600 feet. To the east are nearly level, moderately-well to poorly drained, sandy to loamy soils with yellow and red mottled or gray subsoils. To the west are rolling to hilly soils with loamy surfaces and a very deep, reddish subsoil. The county is in the Pineywoods vegetation area which consists of a mixture of pine and hardwoods such as oak, elm, hickory, magnolia, sweet and black gum and tupelo. Between 21 and 30% of the land in the county is considered prime farmland. **CLIMATE** Subtropical humid, moist and mild. The average annual temperature is 65°F. Temperatures in January range from an average low of 35° to an average high of 56°F and in July range from 71° to 95°F. The average annual precipitation is 44 inches, with an average relative humidity of 85% at 6 A.M. and 56% at 6 P.M. The average annual snowfall is only a trace. The growing season averages 260 days per year, with the last freeze in early March and the first freeze in late November. The sun shines during the year on the average 67% of the daylight hours.

THE PEOPLE

The 1982 estimated population of 38,500 indicates a continuation of the growth rate begun in the 1970s which reversed the steady population decrease between 1940 and 1970. Rural areas had an increase of 22% between 1970 and 1980, while urban areas grew 16%. The age groups with the largest gains were ages 20 to 34 and ages 65 and over. The high median age lowered from 38 in 1970 to 34 in 1980. The largest ancestry groups are persons of English descent (23%), Black (19%) and persons of Irish descent (18%). **REGISTERED VOTERS** As of November 2, 1982 there were 17,207 registered voters (0.3% of the state total). The 1982 general election had a 54% voter turnout, compared to a 63% turnout in the 1980 general election. In the 1982 primary 97% voted Democratic and 3% Republican, with 5,950 votes cast.

THE ECONOMY

AGRICULTURE Major forest productions and dairy area. In 1982, 50% of the land was in farms and ranches, with 10% of the farmland under cultivation. Cherokee ranked 45th in the state in highest agricultural receipts, with 64% from livestock and livestock products. Overgrazing, undesirable brush and weeds, difficulties in grass establishment and fertilization of the grasslands are the current conservation problems. Primary crops: hay, wheat, oats and rye. Primary vegetables: watermelons and tomatoes. Primary fruits and nuts: peaches and pecans. Primary livestock and products: ninth in the state for milk production. Cattle and hogs. **BUSINESS** Total number of business establishments in the county: 655. Retail sales during the first quarter of 1984 increased 13%. In 1980, 10% of the labor force were self-employed, 26% were employed in professional or related services, 22% in manufacturing, 18% in wholesale and retail trade, 8% in construction, 17% were employed in other counties and there were 4,256 retired workers. The industries with the most employment: oil and gas extraction, agribusiness and the manufacture of wood containers, womens' apparel, plastic products, farm machinery and equipment, refrigeration and heating equipment and surgical and medical instruments. The nonfarm earnings in 1981 totaled $304,522,000. The retired workers received an average monthly Social Security payment of $292. **FINANCE** On June 30, 1983, six commercial banks had total deposits of $201,753,000 and total assets of $225,307,000. On December 31, 1982 two state savings and loan associations, one federal associations one state branch and two federal branches had combined assets of $177,212,979. In addition there are two credit unions in the county. **HOUSING** Average value of homes in 1980: $23,000. Permits for new, privately owned housing units decreased in 1982: 54 permits were issued with a total construction cost of $1,571,543. Of those permits, 38 were for single family houses. Between 1970 and 1980 the number of housing units increased by 31%. Sixty-nine percent of all units in the county are air-conditioned, 79% are heated by gas and 14% by electricity. **NATURAL RESOURCES** Glauconite, iron, salt domes, industrial sand, oil, gas and lignite coal. In 1982 a total of 9,311,292 thousand cubic feet of gas well gas, 87,312 barrels of condensate, 1,205,429 barrels of crude oil and 1,076,727 thousand cubic feet of casinghead gas were produced. Current production of other minerals and products includes ball clay, iron limonite and industrial sand. Pine and hardwood production in 1981 totaled 17,361,063 cubic feet: 12,719,205 cubic feet of pine and 4,641,858 cubic feet of hardwood. **TOURISM** Travel expenditures of $14,370,000 in 1982 (an increase of 11% over 1981) generated 350 jobs and $2,815,000 in payroll. Lodging: five hotels, motels and tourist courts. **ALCOHOLIC BEVERAGES** Totally dry. **FEDERAL EXPENDITURES** The federal government had direct expenditures or obligations of $63,631,000 in the county during fiscal year 1983, including $2,957,000 by the U.S. Department of Defense. In addition, the federal government provided $1,159,000 in grant awards, paid $1,906,000 in salaries and wages, made direct payments to individuals of $59,999,000 including $43,003,000 in retirement and disability payments, awarded $257,000 in procurement contracts and spent $310,000 in other expenditures or obligations. The federal government also provided $100,000 in direct loans and $2,386,000 in guaranteed loans and insurance.

COMMUNICATION

Newspapers–Daily: Jacksonville Daily Progress, ave. eve. circ. 6,871. Weekly: The Alto Herald, Cherokee County Banner (Rusk) and The Cherokeean (Rusk). Radio: KEBE-AM and KOOI-FM (Jacksonville). KTLU-AM and KWRW-FM (Rusk). Cable TV. Telephone companies: Continental Telephone, General Telephone, United Telephone, Alto Telephone, EASTEX Telephone

COUNTIES

CHEROKEE (continued)

and Lufkin Telephone Exchange. **TRANSPORTATION** Total public road mileage: 1,548. In 1982 there were 31,827 registered vehicles and 836 reported traffic accidents including 13 fatalities. Taxi cabs: one company in Jacksonville. Intercity bus service is available. Motor freight: seven local and intrastate carriers. Rail: two main lines carry freight through the county. One of the lines carries annually 10 to 20 million tons of freight and one carries five to 10 million. Aircraft: 43 are registered in the county. Airports: Cherokee County Airport at Jacksonville is a basic transportation airport with general aviation service. It serves as a base for 20 aircraft. Maxwell Lumber Airport at Mount Selman.

COMMUNITY SERVICES

EDUCATION Six school districts with nine elementary, two middle, six high schools and one special education. The average daily attendance in 1981-82 was 6,054, with expenditures per pupil of $2,208 including 377 classroom teachers with an average annual salary of $15,822. Forty-nine percent of the 363 high school graduates planned to attend college. In 1982-83, 72% of the students were White, 4% Hispanic, 25% Black and 0.3% Asian. Private schools: 111 enrolled in one elementary school. Lon Morris College is located in Jacksonville. Established in 1873 it is a vocational and two year academic college affiliated with the Methodist Church. Enrollment in 1982 was 338 with in state undergraduate tuition and fees of $1,600 per semester. Jacksonville College is located in Jacksonville. Established in 1899 it is a vocational and two year academic college affiliated with the Baptist Church. Enrollment in 1982 was 279 with in state undergraduate tuition and fees of $810 per semester. **PUBLIC LIBRARIES** Stella Hill Memorial Library (Alto): 9,300 volumes. Jacksonville Public Library: 30,472 volumes. Singletary Memorial Library (Rusk): 17,052 volumes. Wells Library. **CHILD CARE** 69 day care and eight twenty-four hour care licensed facilities. **HEALTH CARE** 51 physicians and 15 dentists. Hospitals: three with a combined capacity of 259. Clinics: one outpatient clinic, one for treatment of alcohol and/or drug abuse and one public health clinic. Ambulance services: three commercial and two hospital-based services. Mental health: one county clinic and one state hospital with a capacity of 1,053. Nursing homes: seven nursing homes with a combined capacity of 585 nursing care residents. The average cost per day for private patients in 1982 was $31.48. **CHURCHES** 131 churches have an estimated combined membership of 26,048. The largest denominations are Southern Baptist, Baptist Missionary and United Methodist. **SOCIAL SERVICES** In fiscal year 1983 a total of $1,760,868 in food stamps was distributed, with an average of 3,902 persons receiving food stamps each month. Aid to Families with Dependent Children (AFDC) totaled $386,867, with an average of 250 families receiving AFDC each month. Medical assistance benefits for the aged and disabled of $5,102,147 and for families and children of $702,034 brought the county benefit total to $7,951,916. **FIRE PROTECTION** Two partly paid and four volunteer fire departments. **LAW ENFORCEMENT** The County Sheriff has 35 commissioned officers. Five police departments have a combined force of 35. **CRIME** 56 violent crimes (murder, forcible rape, robbery and aggravated assault) and 869 nonviolent crimes (burglary, larceny-theft and motor vehicle theft) were reported in 1982. **JUDICIAL SYSTEM** One District Court and Judge, one County Court and Judge and four Justices of the Peace. In the District Court a total of 2,049 cases were pending on 1/1/82, 1,064 new cases were filed and 1,240 cases were disposed of during the year leaving 1,873 cases pending on 12/31/82. There were 639 criminal cases on the docket, 80 convictions, 32 persons committed to prison and five committed to jail and 447 cases left pending. In the County Court 665 cases were pending on 1/1/82, 607 new cases were filed and 720 cases were disposed of during the year leaving 552 cases pending on 12/31/82. There were 1,065 criminal cases on the docket, 240 convictions, 123 persons committed to jail, and 448 cases left pending. **JAILS** One jail, capacity 28. **ATTORNEYS AT LAW** 39. **UTILITIES** 82% of the residents are connected to a public or privately owned water system and 44% are connected to a public sewer system. Natural gas is distributed to the county by Entex, Inc. The average annual residential bill for natural gas in 1982 for the Entex distribution system was $390.31, an increase of 26% over 1981. Electricity is distributed to the county by Southwestern Electric Service, Texas Power and Light, Central Texas Electric Coop., Inc., Houston Co. Electric Coop., Inc. and Rusk Co. Electric Coop., Inc. and is generated primarily by gas, oil and coal. The typical residential electric bill is $155.87 per month for an all-electric house using 2,500 kwh. **TAXES** The county has 13 units with taxing authority: seven school districts, five cities and one county.

RECREATION/ENTERTAINMENT

NATIONAL REGISTER OF HISTORIC PLACES Alto vicinity: George C. Davis Site and George C. Davis Site Addition. Jacksonville: William Walter Newton House. **STATE** Caddoan Mounds State Historical Site covers 94 acres and is closed to the public as of July, 1983. I.D. Fairchild State Forest covers 2,896 acres with acres offering fishing and hiking trails. Jim Hogg State Historical Park covers 177 acres with nature trails, exhibits and a historic structure. The park is a memorial to James Stephen Hogg, first native-born governor of Texas. Texas State Railroad State Historical Park covers 507 acres with a museum and an operating vintage railroad. Contact park for schedule of runs. **COUNTY/MUNICIPAL PARKS** 182 acres in one county and 10 municipal parks. These parks contain one mile of hiking trails, 10 playgrounds, five football and soccer fields, five baseball and softball fields, four tennis courts, one multi-use court, one swimming pool, one beach and two boat ramps and shore fishing facilities. Developed campsites: 95. **SCENIC DRIVES** Forested hills and streams can be viewed along U.S. 69 and Texas 21 (El Camino Real). F.M. 747 and F.M. 2138 around Lake Jacksonville offer lake scenery. **BOATING/FISHING** Lakes/reservoirs: Acker (74 acres), Cherokee (33 acres), Duren (303 acres), Jacksonville (1,320 acres), Palestine (25,560 acres), Pine Crest (58 acres), Rusk City (18 acres), Rusk State Hospital (18 acres) and Striker (2,400 acres). Major rivers: Neches and Angelina. Primary streams: Merrits, Beans, Gum, Keyes, College, Eye and Striker. **HUNTING** Fall and winter seasons on deer. Summer, fall and winter seasons on squirrel. Winter seasons on quail, muskrat, ring-tailed cat, badger, fox, opossum, mink, beaver, otter, raccoon, skunk and civet cat. No closed seasons on nutria, coyote and bobcat. In 1983 duck, coot, geese, woodcock and jacksnipe seasons occurred during the winter months. Teal duck, rail and gallinule seasons occurred in the fall. Mourning dove seasons occurred intermittently during the fall and winter months. **MUSEUMS** Jacksonville: Jacksonville Public Library Museum. Rusk: James S. Hogg Memorial Museum. **COLLEGIATE FINE ARTS** Jacksonville: cultural events offered by Jacksonville College and Lon Morris College. **SPECIAL EVENTS** Old Settlers Reunion, Rusk, May; Getaway Weekend, Jacksonville, July; Western Week and Tops in Texas Rodeo, Jacksonville, July; Western Week, Rusk, August; Black Gold Stampede Rodeo, Rusk, August; Indian Summer Festival with Arts and Crafts Fair, Rusk, October; County Fair, Jacksonville, October, and Old Fashioned Christmas Pageant, Jacksonville, December.

COMMUNITIES

COUNTY SEAT Rusk, County Courthouse, 75785; County Clerk's Office, 214/683-2350.

INCORPORATED COMMUNITIES (1980 population and ZIP Code) Alto (1,203) 75925, Bullard (681: 59 in Cherokee Co. and 622 in Smith Co.) 75757, Gallatin (132) 75764, Jacksonville (12,264) 75766, New Summerfield (Summerfield) (319) 75780, Reklaw (305: 191 in Cherokee Co. and 114 in Rusk Co.) 75784, Rusk (4,681) 75785, Troup (1,911: 64 in Cherokee Co. and 1,847 in Smith Co.) 75789 and Wells (926) 75976. **UNINCORPORATED COMMUNITIES** (and ZIP Code) Atoy 75785, Black Jack 75789, Brunswick 75925, Central 75925, Circle 75785, Concord 75789, Cove Spring 75766, Craft 75766, Cuney 75759, Dialville 75761, Elm Grove 75785, Enterprise 75766, Forest 75945, Griffin 75789, Henrys Chapel 75789, Holcombs Store 75785, Ironton 75766, Linwood 75925, Maydelle 75772, Mixon 75789, Morrill 75925, Mount Selman 75757, Neches Indian Village 75925, New Hope 75766, North Rusk 75785, Oakland 75785, Old Larissa 75757, Pine Hill 75766, Pierces Chapel 75766, Ponta 75766, Redlawn 75925, Reese 75766, Shady Grove 75785, Tecula 75766, Turney 75766 and Weeping Mary 75925. **FOR ADDITIONAL LOCAL INFORMATION** Alto Chamber of Commerce, P.O. Box 536, Alto, 75925, 409/858-4713, Jacksonville Chamber of Commerce, P.O. Box 1231, Jacksonville, 75766, 214/586-2217, Rusk Chamber of Commerce, P.O. Box 67, Rusk, 75785, 214/683-4242 and Troup Chamber of Commerce, 106 E. Duval, P.O. Box 336, Troup, 75789, 214/842-4113.

CHILDRESS (P26)

THE LAND
In the Texas Panhandle southeast of Amarillo on U.S. Highways 287 and 62/83 in the Rolling Plains Region, Childress County covers 707 square miles. The elevation ranges from 1,600 to 1,900. The land is level to undulating with red to brown soils with loamy surface layers and cracking, clayey or loamy subsoils. Some areas have shallow soils over hardened calcium deposits. In the Rolling Plains vegetation area, there are mid and tall grasses, mesquite trees and cacti. In the southwest corner of the county are short and mid grasses and live oak trees. Between 41 and 50% of the land in the county is considered prime farmland. **CLIMATE** Generally dry, windy and cool. Dust, thunderstorms and hail may be a problem in the spring. The average annual temperature is 62°F. Temperatures in January range from an average low of 26° to an average high of 52°F and in July range from 71° to 96°F. The average annual precipitation is 21 inches, with an average relative humidity of 73% at 6 A.M. and 43% at 6 P.M. The average annual snowfall is 12 inches. The growing season averages 215 days per year, with the last freeze in early April and the first freeze in early November. The sun shines during the year on the average 75% of the daylight hours.

THE PEOPLE
The 1982 estimated population of 6,900 indicates a retardation of the moderate growth rate begun in the 1970s which reversed the steady population decreases between 1930 and 1970. Urban areas experienced an 8% gain, while rural areas had a 5% population loss between 1970 and 1980. Slight increases occurred in age groups birth to five and 20 to 34. The high median age dropped from 43 in 1970 to 38 in 1980. The low birth rate and high death rate are related to the high median age. The largest ancestry groups are persons of English descent (35%), those of Irish descent (28%) and those of German descent (14%). **REGISTERED VOTERS** As of November 2, 1982 there were 3,465 registered voters (0.1% of the state total). The 1982 general election had a 54% voter turnout, compared to a 72% turnout in the 1980 general election. In the 1982 primary 93% voted Democratic and 7% Republican, with 833 votes cast.

THE ECONOMY
AGRICULTURE Wheat and cotton area. In 1982, 96% of the land was in farms and ranches, with 26% of the farmland under cultivation and 5% irrigated. Childress ranked 164th in the state in highest agricultural receipts, with 81% from crops. Water and wind erosion are the current conservation problems. Primary crops: wheat, cotton and sorghum. Primary livestock and products: cattle. **BUSINESS** Total number of business establishments in the county: 197. Retail sales during the first quarter of 1984 increased 3%. In 1980, 15% of the labor force were self-employed, 15% were employed in professional or related services, 16% in manufacturing, 22% in wholesale and retail trade, 14% in transportation, communications and other public utilities, 4% were employed in other counties and there were 1,013 retired workers. The industries with the most employment: agribusiness and the manufacture of mobile homes and women's clothing. The nonfarm earnings in 1981 totaled $57,787,000. The retired workers received an average monthly Social Security payment of $295. **FINANCE** On June 30, 1983, two commercial banks had total deposits of $35,983,000 and total assets of $40,860,000. On December 31, 1982 one federal savings and loan associations and one state savings and loan association branch had assets of $37,834,419. In addition there is one credit union in the county. **HOUSING** Average value of homes in 1980: $19,900. Permits for new, privately owned housing units increased in 1982: 27 permits were issued with a total construction cost of $1,133,050. Of those permits, all were for single family houses. Between 1970 and 1980 the number of housing units increased by 4%. Eighty-seven percent of all units in the county are air-conditioned, 92% are heated by gas and 7% by electricity. **NATURAL RESOURCES** Gypsum, saltbeds, oil and gas. In 1982 a total of 8,472 barrels of crude oil and 2,113 thousand cubic feet of casinghead gas were produced. Current production of other minerals and products includes sand and gravel. **TOURISM** Travel expenditures of $6,205,000 in 1982 (an increase of 13% over 1981) generated 135 jobs and $1,144,000 in payroll. **ALCOHOLIC BEVERAGES** Packaged distilled spirits, beer, ale, malt liquor and wine are legal in parts of the county. **FEDERAL EXPENDITURES** The federal government had direct expenditures or obligations of $20,475,000 in the county during fiscal year 1983, including $313,000 by the U.S. Department of Defense. In addition, the federal government provided $149,000 in grant awards, paid $1,110,000 in salaries and wages, made direct payments to individuals of $14,212,000 including $9,766,000 in retirement and disability payments, awarded $80,000 in procurement contracts and spent $4,924,000 in other expenditures or obligations. The federal government also provided $3,908,000 in direct loans and $2,668,000 in guaranteed loans and insurance.

COMMUNICATION
Newspapers–Weekly: Childress Index. Radio: KETX-AM (Childress). Cable TV. Telephone companies: General Telephone, Southwestern Bell and Santa Rosa Telephone Coop. **TRANSPORTATION** Total public road mileage: 737. In 1982 there were 7,312 registered vehicles and 163 reported traffic accidents including six fatalities. Taxi cabs: one company in the city of Childress. Intercity bus service is available. Motor freight: three carriers. Rail: two main and one branch line carry freight through the county. The two main lines carry annually over 30 million tons of freight each and the one branch line carries less than one million. Aircraft: 17 are registered in the county. Airports: Childress Municipal Airport is a general utility airport providing general aviation service. It serves as a base for 11 aircraft.

COMMUNITY SERVICES
EDUCATION One school district with one elementary, one middle and one high school. The average daily attendance in 1981-82

CHILDRESS (continued)

was 1,063, with expenditures per pupil of $1,740 including 61 classroom teachers with an average annual salary of $15,428. Forty-eight percent of the 97 high school graduates planned to attend college. In 1982-83, 76% of the students were White, 18% Hispanic, 6% Black and 0.2% Asian. **PUBLIC LIBRARIES** Childress Public Library: 17,846 volumes. **CHILD CARE** 12 day care and two twenty-four hour care licensed facilities. **HEALTH CARE** Nine physicians and three dentists. Hospitals: one with a capacity of 75. Clinics: one dialysis clinic. Ambulance services: one commercial and one hospital-based service. Mental health: one clinic. Nursing homes: two nursing homes with a combined capacity of 180 nursing care residents. The average cost per day for private patients in 1982 was $31.35. **CHURCHES** 20 churches have an estimated combined membership of 5,430. The largest denominations are Southern Baptist, Catholic and United Methodist. **SOCIAL SERVICES** In fiscal year 1983 a total of $205,113 in food stamps was distributed, with an average of 514 persons receiving food stamps each month. Aid to Families with Dependent Children (AFDC) totaled $26,923, with an average of 20 families receiving AFDC each month. Medical assistance benefits for the aged and disabled of $952,642 and for families and children of $28,446 brought the county benefit total to $1,213,124. **FIRE PROTECTION** One volunteer fire department. **LAW ENFORCEMENT** The County Sheriff has six commissioned officers. One police department has a force of eight. **CRIME** 21 violent crimes (murder, forcible rape, robbery and aggravated assault) and 122 nonviolent crimes (burglary, larceny-theft and motor vehicle theft) were reported in 1982. **JUDICIAL SYSTEM** One District Court and Judge, one County Court and Judge and two Justices of the Peace. In the District Court a total of 193 cases were pending on 1/1/82, 197 new cases were filed and 159 cases were disposed of during the year leaving 231 cases pending on 12/31/82. There were 91 criminal cases on the docket, 30 convictions, four persons committed to prison, 34 cases left pending. In the County Court 565 cases were pending on 1/1/82, 233 new cases were filed and 220 cases were disposed of during the year leaving 578 cases pending on 12/31/82. There were 650 criminal cases on the docket, 120 convictions, 43 persons committed to jail, and 443 cases left pending. **JAILS** One jail, capacity 18. **ATTORNEYS AT LAW** 11. **UTILITIES** 97% of the residents are connected to a public or privately owned water system and 84% are connected to a public sewer system. Natural gas is distributed to the county by Lone Star Gas Co., Division of Enserch. The average annual residential bill for natural gas in 1982 for the Lone Star distribution system was $405.91, an increase of 35% over 1981. Electricity is distributed to the county by West Texas Utilities, Gate City Electric Coop., Inc., Greenbelt Electric Coop. and Lighthouse Electric Coop., Inc. and is generated primarily by gas and oil. The typical residential electric bill is $145.78 per month for an all-electric house using 2,500 kwh. **TAXES** The county has four units with taxing authority: one school district, one city, one county and one hospital district.

RECREATION/ENTERTAINMENT

MUNICIPAL PARKS 765 acres in three municipal parks. These parks contain two playgrounds, one football and soccer field, four tennis courts, one swimming pool, one beach and one boat ramp and shore fishing facility. Developed campsites: 212. **BOATING/FISHING** Lakes/reservoirs: Baylor (610 acres), Childress (134 acres), Scott (26 acres) and Williams (25 acres). Major rivers: Prairie Dog Town Fork Rea and Pease. Primary streams: Baylor, Scatterbranch, East Salt, Spiller and Cousins. **HUNTING** Fall and winter seasons on deer and mule deer. Summer, fall and winter seasons on squirrel. Winter seasons on pheasant, quail, muskrat, beaver, opossum, ring-tailed cat, badger, fox, weasel, raccoon, skunk and civet cat. Fall, winter and spring seasons on turkey. No closed seasons on coyote and bobcat. In 1983 sandhill crane, duck, coot, geese, woodcock and jacksnipe seasons occurred during the winter months. Teal duck, rail and gallinule seasons occurred in the fall. Mourning dove seasons occurred intermittently during the fall and winter months. **MUSEUMS** Childress: Childress County Heritage Museum. **ZOO** Childress: Childress City Park Zoo. **SPECIAL EVENTS** Old Settlers Reunion, Childress, July; Fourth of July Celebration, Childress, July; World Championship Ice Cream Freeze-Off, Childress, July; and Greenbelt Bowl, Childress, August.

COMMUNITIES

COUNTY SEAT Childress, County Courthouse, 79201; County Clerk's Office, 817/937-3491. **INCORPORATED COMMUNITIES** (1980 population and ZIP Code) Childress (5,817) 79201. **UNINCORPORATED COMMUNITIES** (and ZIP Code) Arlie 79201, Carey 79222, Garden Valley 79238, Kirkland 79238, Loco 79201 and Tell 79259. **FOR ADDITIONAL LOCAL INFORMATION** Childress Chamber of Commerce, P.O. Box 35, Childress, 79201, 817/937-2567.

CLAY (P46)

THE LAND

East of Wichita Falls on U.S. Highways 287 and 82 in the North Central Prairie Region, Clay County covers 1,085 square miles of woodland and prairies. The elevation ranges from 900 to 1,100 feet. The undulating to hilly soils over shale or sandstone have moderately deep to deep, loamy surface layers and clayey subsoils. The county is primarily in the Cross Timbers and Prairie vegetation area consisting of short and mid grasses, mesquite and post oak trees. In the northwest corner is Rolling Plains vegetation area with mid and tall grasses, mesquite trees and cacti. Between 21 and 30% of the land in the county is considered prime farmland. **CLIMATE** Mild and dry. The average annual temperature is 64°F. Temperatures in January range from an average low of 28° to an average high of 53°F and in July range from 73° to 98°F. The average annual precipitation is 28 inches, with an average relative humidity of 79% at 6 A.M. and 49% at 6 P.M. The average annual snowfall is six inches. The growing season averages 229 days per year, with the last freeze in late March and the first freeze in mid November. The sun shines during the year on the average 67% of the daylight hours.

THE PEOPLE

The 1982 estimated population of 9,700 indicates a continuation of the growth rate begun in the 1970s which reversed the steady population decrease between 1930 and 1970. Almost 24% of the growth between 1970 and 1980 was in rural areas, with urban areas experiencing a 9% gain. The age groups with the largest increases were birth to five years and ages 20 to 24. The high median age lowered from 38 in 1970 to 36 in 1980. The largest ancestry groups are persons of English descent (27%) those of Irish descent (27%) and those of German descent (20%). **REGISTERED VOTERS** As of November 2, 1982 there were 5,899 registered voters (0.1% of the state total). The 1982 general election had a 58% voter turnout, compared to a 72% turnout in the 1980 general election. In the 1982 primary 98% voted Democratic and 2% Republican, with 3,064 votes cast.

THE ECONOMY

AGRICULTURE Cattle area. In 1982, 88% of the land was in farms and ranches, with 18% of the farmland under cultivation and 3% irrigated. Clay ranked 76th in the state in highest agricultural receipts, with 78% from livestock and livestock products. Overgrazing, undesirable brush and weed, water erosion and difficulties in grass establishment are the current conservation problems. Primary crops: wheat, hay, oats, cotton and sorghum. Primary vegetables: sweet potatoes and watermelons. Primary fruits and nuts: peaches and pecans. Primary livestock and products: cattle and milk. **BUSINESS** Total number of business establishments in the county: 124. Retail sales during the first quarter of 1984 increased 5%. In 1980, 18% of the labor force were self-employed, 16% were employed in professional or related services, 15% in manufacturing, 21% in wholesale and retail trade, 18% in agriculture, forestry, fisheries and mining, 53% were employed in other counties and there were 1,019 retired workers. The industries with the most employment: agribusiness and the manufacture of mobile homes. The nonfarm earnings in 1981 totaled $93,644,000. The retired workers received an average monthly Social Security payment of $294. **FINANCE** On June 30, 1983, two commercial banks had total deposits of $54,470,000 and total assets of $61,457,000. There is one state savings and loan association branch and one federal association branch in the county. **HOUSING** Average value of homes in 1980: $23,600. Permits for new, privately owned housing units increased in 1982: 15 permits were issued with a total construction cost of $444,795. Of those permits, 13 were for single family houses. Between 1970 and 1980 the number of housing units increased by 32%. Eighty-one percent of all units in the county are air-conditioned, 72% are heated by gas and 22% by electricity. **NATURAL RESOURCES** Sand and gravel, oil, gas, and bituminous coal. In 1982 a total of 439,070 thousand cubic feet of gas well gas, 4,039 barrels of condensate, 2,839,850 barrels of crude oil and 3,444,375 thousand cubic feet of casinghead gas were produced. Current production of other minerals and products includes sand and gravel. **TOURISM** Travel expenditures of $1,861,000 in 1982 (an increase of 15% over 1981) generated 39 jobs and $383,000 in payroll. **ALCOHOLIC BEVERAGES** Totally dry. **FEDERAL EXPENDITURES** The federal government had direct expenditures or obligations of $16,273,000 in the county during fiscal year 1983, including $689,000 by the U.S. Department of Defense. In addition, the federal government provided $152,000 in grant awards, paid $625,000 in salaries and wages, made direct payments to individuals of $14,432,000 including $10,086,000 in retirement and disability payments, awarded $4,000 in procurement contracts and spent $1,060,000 in other expenditures or obligations. The federal government also provided $2,106,000 in direct loans and $2,132,000 in guaranteed loans and insurance.

COMMUNICATION

Newspapers–Weekly: Bellevue News, Bellevue Times and the Clay County Leader. Cable TV. Telephone companies: Southwestern Bell, Byers-Petrolia Telephone, Community Telephone, Nocona Telephone and Santa Rosa Telephone Coop. **TRANSPORTATION** Total public road mileage: 1,200. In 1982 there were 8,744 registered vehicles and 251 reported traffic accidents including seven fatalities. Intercity bus service is available. Motor freight: two carriers. Rail: one main line carries annually over 30 million tons of freight through the county. Aircraft: 10 are registered in the county.

COMMUNITY SERVICES

EDUCATION Five school districts with five elementary, one middle and five high schools. The average daily attendance in 1981-82 was 1,661, with expenditures per pupil of $2,556 including 128 classroom teachers with an average annual salary of $15,257. Fifty-four percent of the 136 high school graduates planned to attend college. In 1982-83, 97% of the students were White,

2% Hispanic, 0.5% Black and 0.5% Asian. **PUBLIC LIBRARIES** Edwards Public Library (Henrietta): 22,944 volumes. **CHILD CARE** 10 day care and one twenty-four hour care licensed facility. **HEALTH CARE** Three physicians and one dentist. Hospitals: One with a capacity of 50. Ambulance services: one commercial service. Mental health: one county clinic. Nursing homes: two nursing homes with a combined capacity of 150 nursing care residents The average cost per day for private patients in 1982 was $29.10. **CHURCHES** 30 churches have an estimated combined membership of 6,467. The largest denominations are Southern Baptist, United Methodist and Churches of Christ. **SOCIAL SERVICES** In fiscal year 1983 a total of $138,898 in food stamps was distributed, with an average of 330 persons receiving food stamps each month. Aid to Families with Dependent Children (AFDC) totaled $18,902, with an average of 12 families receiving AFDC each month. Medical assistance benefits for the aged and disabled of $670,194 and for families and children of $18,252 brought the county benefit total to $846,246. **FIRE PROTECTION** Six volunteer fire departments. **LAW ENFORCEMENT** The County Sheriff has 17 commissioned officers. There is one police officer in the only police department in the county. **CRIME** 20 violent crimes (murder, forcible rape, robbery and aggravated assault) and 317 nonviolent crimes (burglary, larceny-theft and motor vehicle theft) were reported in 1982. **JUDICIAL SYSTEM** One District Court and Judge, one County Court and Judge and four Justices of the Peace. In the District Court a total of 229 cases were pending on 1/1/82, 241 new cases were filed and 249 cases were disposed of during the year leaving 221 cases pending on 12/31/82. There were 103 criminal cases on the docket, eight convictions, three persons committed to prison and 49 cases left pending. In the County Court 736 cases were pending on 1/1/82, 230 new cases were filed and 158 cases were disposed of during the year leaving 808 cases pending on 12/31/82. There were 737 criminal cases on the docket, 70 convictions, 21 persons committed to jail, and 582 cases left pending. **JAILS** One jail, capacity 16. **ATTORNEYS AT LAW** Five. **UTILITIES** 69% of the residents are connected to a public or privately owned water system and 50% are connected to a public sewer system. Natural gas is distributed to the county by Lone Star Gas Co., Division of Enserch. The average annual residential bill for natural gas in 1982 for the Lone Star distribution system was $405.91, an increase of 35% over 1981. Electricity is distributed to the county by J-A-C Electric Coop., Inc., and Texas Electric Service and is generated primarily by gas and water. The typical residential electric bill is $154.69 per month for an all-electric house using 2,500 kwh. **TAXES** The county has 12 units with taxing authority: five school districts, four cities, one county, and two special districts.

RECREATION/ENTERTAINMENT

NATIONAL REGISTER OF HISTORIC PLACES The Clay County Courthouse and Jail. **STATE** Lake Arrowhead State Recreation Area covers 524 acres with facilities which include camping and trailer sites, as well as swimming, a boat ramp and horseback areas. **MUNICIPAL PARKS** 1,503 acres in 45 municipal parks. These parks contain three playgrounds, three tennis courts, one swimming pool, 32 beaches, five boat ramps and shore fishing facilities. **BOATING/FISHING** Lakes/reservoirs: Arrowhead (16,200 acres), Burns (23 acres), Henrietta (40 acres), Lively (20 acres), Petrolia (26 acres) and Windthorst (66 acres). Major rivers: Little Wichita, Red and Wichita. Primary streams: Turkey, Dry Fork, Hay and East Post Oak. **HUNTING** Fall and winter seasons on deer. No closed seasons on coyote, bobcat and squirrel. Winter seasons on quail, muskrat, beaver, opossum, ring-tailed cat, badger, fox, weasel, raccoon, skunk and civet cat. Fall, winter and spring seasons on turkey. In 1983,

COUNTIES

CLAY (continued)

duck, coot, geese, woodcock and jacksnipe seasons occurred during the winter months. Teal duck, rail and gallinule seasons occurred in the fall. Mourning dove seasons occurred intermittently during the fall and winter months. **SPECIAL EVENTS** Pioneer Reunion Festival, Henrietta, September; Junior Stock Show, Henrietta, October.

COMMUNITIES

COUNTY SEAT Henrietta, County Courthouse, 76365; County Clerk's Office, 817/538-4631. **INCORPORATED COMMUNITIES** (1980 population and ZIP Code) Bellevue (352) 76228, Byers (556) 76357, Dean (Dean/Dale) (212) 76301, Henrietta (3,149) 76365, Jolly (174) 76301 and Petrolia (755) 76377. **UNINCORPORATED COMMUNITIES** (and ZIP Code) Bluegrove 76352, Buffalo Springs 76228, Charlie 76308, Deer Creek 76365, Hurnville 76365, Joy 76365, Newport 76254, Shannon 76365, Stanfield 76365, Thornberry 76308, Vashti 76228. **FOR ADDITIONAL LOCAL INFORMATION** Henrietta and Clay County Chamber of Commerce, P.O. Box 75, Henrietta, 76365 817/538-5261.

COCHRAN (P37)

THE LAND

Bordering New Mexico west of Lubbock on State Highways 214, 114, and 125 in the High Plains Region, Cochran County covers 775 square miles of level grassland. The elevation ranges from 3,500 to 3,800 feet. In the northeast half of the county the soils have loamy surface layers and clayey subsoils. Some areas have limestone within 20 inches of the surface. In the southwest half the soils are usually dry with sandy surface layers and loamy subsoils, or sandy throughout. The High Plains vegetation area consists of short and mid grasses, small mesquite trees, thorny shrubs and cacti. Between 1 and 10% of the land in the county is considered prime farmland. **CLIMATE** Climate cool and dry. Dust storms may be significant during the spring. The average annual temperature is 58°F. Temperatures in January range from an average low of 22° to an average high of 54°F and in July range from 64° to 92°F. The average annual precipitation is 17 inches, with an average relative humidity of 67% at 6 A.M. and 35% at 6 P.M. The average annual snowfall is 12 inches. The growing season averages 184 days per year, with the last freeze in mid April and the first freeze in late October. The sun shines during the year on the average 75% of the daylight hours.

THE PEOPLE

The 1982 estimated population of 4,900 indicates a slight growth since 1980, after a population decrease between 1960 and 1980. Rural areas declined in population between 1970 and 1980 by 17%, while urban areas declined 2%. The age group with the greatest decrease was ages five to 14. The young median age rose from 25 in 1970 to 26 in 1980. The largest ancestry groups are persons of English descent (24%), Irish descent (16%) and those of Hispanic descent (35%). **REGISTERED VOTERS** As of November 2, 1982 there were 2,445 registered voters (0.03% of the state total). The 1982 general election had a 58% voter turnout, compared to a 68% turnout in the 1980 general election. In the 1982 primary 99% voted Democratic and 0.3% Republican, with 1,185 votes cast.

THE ECONOMY

AGRICULTURE Cotton area. In 1982, 93% of the land was in farms and ranches, with 65% of the farmland under cultivation and 34% irrigated. Cochran ranked 69th in the state in highest agricultural receipts, with 75% from crops. Water and wind erosion, cultivation of marginal lands and noxious weeds are the current conservation problems. Primary crops: seventh in the state for sorghum. Cotton and wheat. Primary vegetables: sweet potatoes, tomatoes and watermelons. Primary livestock and products: cattle. **BUSINESS** Total number of business establishments in the county: 72. Retail sales during the first quarter of 1984 increased 18%. In 1980, 17% of the labor force were self-employed, 22% were employed in professional or related services, 6% in manufacturing, 13% in wholesale and retail trade, 37% in agriculture, forestry, fisheries and mining, 11% were employed in other counties and there were 340 retired workers. The industries with the most employment: agribusiness. The nonfarm earnings in 1981 totaled $30,739,000. The retired workers received an average monthly Social Security payment of $312. **FINANCE** On June 30, 1983, one commercial bank had total deposits of $26,058,000 and total assets of $29,715,000. There is one state savings and loan association branch in the county. **HOUSING** Average value of homes in 1980: $15,300. Permits for new, privately owned housing units increaed in 1982: six permits were issued with a total construction cost of $286,000. Of those permits, all were for single family houses. Between 1970 and 1980 the number of housing units decreased by 3%. Seventy percent of all units in the county are air-conditioned, 94% are heated by gas and 6% by electricity. **NATURAL RESOURCES** Caliche, oil and gas. In 1982 a total of 2,510,094 thousand cubic feet of gas well gas, 16,733 barrels of condensate, 11,059,176 barrels of crude oil and 6,097,976 thousand cubic feet of casinghead gas were produced. **TOURISM** Travel expenditures of $4,841,000 in 1982 (an increase of 16% over 1981) generated 81 jobs and $775,000 in payroll. **ALCOHOLIC BEVERAGES** Totally dry. **FEDERAL EXPENDITURES** The federal government had direct expenditures or obligations of $14,119,000 in the county during fiscal year 1983, including $63,000 by the U.S. Department of Defense. In addition, the federal government provided $183,000 in grant awards, paid $423,000 in salaries and wages, made direct payments to individuals of $4,785,000 including $3,383,000 in retirement and disability payments, awarded $1,000 in procurement contracts and spent $8,727,000 in other expenditures or obligations. The federal government also provided $4,668,000 in direct loans and $10,511,000 in guaranteed loans and insurance.

COMMUNICATION

Newspapers–Weekly: Morning Tribune. Radio: KRAN-AM (Morton). Cable TV. Telephone companies: General Telphone, Five-Area Telephone Coop., Romain Telephone, and South Plains Telephone Coop. **TRANSPORTATION** Total public road mileage: 783. In 1982 there were 4,468 registered vehicles and 53 reported traffic accidents including one fatality. Intercity bus service is available. Motor freight: two carriers. Rail: one branch line carries annually less than one million tons of freight through the county. Aircraft: 23 are registered in the county. Airports: Cochran County Airport at Morton is a general utility airport providing general aviation service. It serves as a base for 14 aircraft.

COMMUNITY SERVICES

EDUCATION Three school districts with three elementary, one middle and three high schools. The average daily attendance in 1981-82 was 1,238, with expenditures per pupil of $3,702 including 90 classroom teachers with an average annual salary of $16,241. Twenty-two percent of the 78 high school graduates planned to attend college. In 1982-83, 44% of the students were White, 46% Hispanic, 11% Black and 0.1% Asian. **PUBLIC LIBRARIES** Cochran County Library (Morton): 14,937 volumes. **CHILD CARE** One day care and three twenty-four hour care licensed facilities. **HEALTH CARE** Three physicians. Hospitals: One with a capacity of 30. Ambulance services: three volunteer services. Nursing homes: One nursing home has a capacity of 30 nursing care residents. The average cost per day for private patients in 1982 was $28.94. **CHURCHES** 13 churches have an estimated combined membership of 4,280. The largest denominations are Southern Baptist, Catholic and United Methodist. **SOCIAL SERVICES** In fiscal year 1983 a total of $368,845 in food stamps was distributed, with an average of 785 persons receiving food stamps each month. Aid to Families with Dependent Children (AFDC) totaled $48,789, with an average of 33 families receiving AFDC each month. Medical assistance benefits for the aged and disabled of $269,985 and for families and children of $67,851 brought the county benefit total to $755,480. **FIRE PROTECTION** Three volunteer fire departments. **LAW ENFORCEMENT** The County Sheriff has 12 commissioned officers. **CRIME** Three violent crimes (murder, forcible rape, robbery and aggravated assault) and 108 nonviolent crimes (burglary, larceny-theft and motor vehicle theft) were reported in 1982. **JUDICIAL SYSTEM** One District Court and Judge, one County Court and Judge and two Justices of the Peace. In the District Court a total of 135 cases were pending on 1/1/82, 82 new cases were filed and 71 cases were disposed of during the year leaving 146 cases pending on 12/31/82. There were 22 criminal cases on the docket, nine convictions, five persons committed to prison and nine cases left pending. In the County Court 90 cases were pending on 1/1/82, 77 new cases were filed and 64 cases were disposed of during the year leaving 103 cases pending on 12/31/82. There were 142 criminal cases on the docket, 38 convictions, 10 persons committed to jail, and 85 cases left pending. **JAILS** One jail, capacity 12. **ATTORNEYS AT LAW** Three. **UTILITIES** 70% of the residents are connected to a public or privately owned water system and 65% are connected to a public sewer system. Natural gas is distributed to the county by Bledso Natural Gas Co. Electricity is distributed to the county by Southwestern Public Service, and Cochran Power and Light Co. and is generated primarily by gas. The typical residential electric bill is $123.79 per month for an all-electric house using 2,500 kwh. **TAXES** The county has eight units with taxing authority: three school districts, two cities, one county and two special districts.

RECREATION/ENTERTAINMENT

COUNTY/MUNICIPAL PARKS 65 acres in one county and four municipal parks. These parks contain three playgrounds, three baseball and softball fields and one swimming pool. **SCENIC DRIVES** The Texas Plains Trail runs through this county. This trail spans a vast area of the High Plains region of Texas slicing through the southernmost extension of the United States. The land is flat except where erosion has carved canyon landscapes. **HUNTING** Fall season on antelope. No closed seasons on coyote, bobcat and squirrel. Fall season on prairie chicken. Winter seasons on quail, muskrat, beaver, opossum, ring-tailed cat, badger, fox, weasel, raccoon, skunk and civet cat. In 1983 sandhill crane, duck, coot, geese, woodcock and jacksnipe seasons occurred during the winter months. Teal duck, rail and gallinule seasons occurred in the fall. Mourning dove seasons occurred intermittently during the fall and winter months. **MUSEUMS** Morton: Cochran County Museum. **SPECIAL EVENTS** Last Frontier Days Rodeo and Barbecue, Morton, August; Cochran County Fair, Morton, October.

COMMUNITIES

COUNTY SEAT Morton, County Courthouse, 79346; County Clerk's Office, 806/266-5450. **INCORPORATED COMMUNITIES** (1980 population and ZIP Code) Morton (2,674) 79346 and Whiteface (463) 79379. **UNINCORPORATED COMMUNITIES** (and ZIP Code) Bledsoe 79314, Griffith (Oasis)

79346, Lehman 79346. **FOR ADDITIONAL LOCAL INFORMATION** Morton Area Chamber of Commerce, 106 S.W. 1st, Morton, 79346, 806/266-5200.

COKE (P79)

THE LAND

Southwest of Abilene on U.S. Highway 277 in the Rolling Plains Region, Coke County covers 908 square miles of level to broken terrain. The elevation ranges from 1,800 to 2,500 feet. The eastern third of the county has shallow to moderately deep red to brown alkaline soils with loamy surface layers and clayey subsoils with hardened calcium deposits. To the west the undulating to hilly alkaline soils are shallow and loamy with areas of exposed rock. The eastern half of the county is in the Rolling Plains vegetation area with prairie grasses, mesquite trees and cacti. The western half is in the Edwards Plateau vegetation area with a combination of grasses, desert shrubs, and small trees such as live oak, cedar and shinnery oak. Between 21 and 30% of the land in the county is considered prime farmland. **CLIMATE** Mild and dry. Dust storms may be a problem during spring. The average annual temperature is 65°F. Temperatures in January range from an average low of 31° to an average high of 56°F and in July range from 71° to 96°F. The average annual precipitation is 20 inches, with an average relative humidity of 73% at 6 A.M. and 43% at 6 P.M. The average annual snowfall is four inches. The growing season averages 225 days per year, with the last freeze in early April and the first freeze in the first half of November. The sun shines during the year on the average 75% of the daylight hours.

THE PEOPLE

Coke County ranks 42nd among all U.S. counties in the highest percent of population over age 64. The high median age rose from 39 in 1970 to 44 in 1980. The 1982 estimated population of 3,500 continues the increase in population since 1970, which reversed Coke County's population decline from 5,253 in 1930 to 3,087 in 1970. The majority of residents live in rural areas. The age groups with the largest gains were ages 62 and over. The largest ancestry groups are persons of English descent (34%) and those of Irish descent (28%). **REGISTERED VOTERS** As of November 2, 1982 there were 2,227 registered voters (0.03% of the state total). The 1982 general election had a 54% voter turnout, compared to a 74% turnout in the 1980 general election. In the 1982 primary 98% voted Democratic and 2% Republican, with 1,217 votes cast.

THE ECONOMY

AGRICULTURE Sheep area. In 1982, 96% of the land was in farms and ranches, with 6% of the farmland under cultivation and 3% irrigated. Coke ranked 214th in the state in highest agricultural receipts, with 95% from livestock and livestock products. Overgrazing, undesirable brush and water erosion are the current conservation problems. Primary crops: wheat, oats, hay and sorghum. Primary vegetables: watermelons. Primary fruits and nuts: peaches and pecans. Primary livestock and products: cattle, sheep, wool, angora goats, mohair and hogs. **BUSINESS** Total number of business establishments in the county: 57. Retail sales during the first quarter of 1984 increased 9%. In 1980, 17% of the labor force were self-employed, 21% were employed in professional or related services, 9% in manufacturing, 14% in wholesale and retail trade, 23% in agriculture, forestry, fisheries and mining, 24% were employed in other counties and there were 527 retired workers. The industries with the most employment: oil and gas extraction and agribusiness. The nonfarm earnings in 1981 totaled $27,377,000. The retired workers received an average monthly Social Security payment of $302.

COUNTIES

COKE (continued)

FINANCE On June 30, 1983, two commercial banks had total deposits of $31,956,000 and total assets of $34,836,000. There is one state savings and loan association branch in the county. **HOUSING** Average value of homes in 1980: $21,900. Permits for new, privately owned housing units decreased in 1982: six permits were issued with a total construction cost of $251,675. Of those permits, all were for single family houses. Between 1970 and 1980 the number of housing units increased by 32%. Seventy-six percent of all units in the county are air-conditioned, 82% are heated by gas and 13% by electricity. **NATURAL RESOURCES** Gypsum, industrial sand, oil, gas and dolomite. In 1982 a total of 1,619,355 thousand cubic feet of gas well gas, 7,204 barrels of condensate, 2,242,955 barrels of crude oil and 8,714,523 thousand cubic feet of casinghead gas were produced. Current production of other minerals and products includes sand and gravel. **TOURISM** Travel expenditures of $1,058,000 in 1982 (an increase of 12% over 1981) generated 25 jobs and $205,000 in payroll. **ALCOHOLIC BEVERAGES** Totally dry. **FEDERAL EXPENDITURES** The federal government had direct expenditures or obligations of $7,586,000 in the county during fiscal year 1983, including $218,000 by the U.S. Department of Defense. In addition, the federal government provided $406,000 in grant awards, paid $270,000 in salaries and wages, made direct payments to individuals of $6,162,000 including $4,530,000 in retirement and disability payments, awarded $2,000 in procurement contracts and spent $745,000 in other expenditures or obligations. The federal government also provided $15,000 in direct loans and $451,000 in guaranteed loans and insurance.

COMMUNICATION

Newspapers–Weekly: The Bronte Enterprise (Spanish), and the Robert Lee Observer (Spanish). Cable TV. Telephone companies: General Telephone and Taylor Telephone. **TRANSPORTATION** Total public road mileage: 490. In 1982 there were 4,459 registered vehicles and 72 reported traffic accidents including three fatalities. Intercity bus service is available. Motor freight: two carriers. Rail: one branch line carries annually less than one million tons of freight through the county. Aircraft: three are registered in the county. Airports: Robert Lee Airport at Robert Lee.

COMMUNITY SERVICES

EDUCATION Two school districts with two elementary and two high schools. The average daily attendance in 1981-82 was 591, with expenditures per pupil of $3,597 including 47 classroom teachers with an average annual salary of $16,867. Seventy-four percent of the 47 high school graduates planned to attend college. In 1982-83, 80% of the students were White, 20% Hispanic and 0.2% Asian. **PUBLIC LIBRARIES** Coke County Library (Robert Lee): 10,240 volumes. **CHILD CARE** Four day care and one twenty-four hour care licensed facilities. **HEALTH CARE** One physician and one dentist. Hospitals: One with a capacity of 26. Ambulance services: one county and one hospital-based service. Nursing homes: two nursing homes with a combined capacity of 84 nursing care residents. The average cost per day for private patients in 1982 was $29.00. **CHURCHES** 18 churches have an estimated combined membership of 2,471. The largest denominations are Southern Baptist, Churches of Christ and United Methodist. **SOCIAL SERVICES** In fiscal year 1983 a total of $59,265 in food stamps was distributed, with an average of 135 persons receiving food stamps each month. Aid to Families with Dependent Children (AFDC) totaled $12,001, with an average of seven families receiving AFDC each month. Medical assistance benefits for the aged and disabled of $718,596 and

for families and children of $17,395 brought the county benefit total to $807,257. **FIRE PROTECTION** Two volunteer fire departments. **LAW ENFORCEMENT** The County Sheriff has four commissioned officers. **CRIME** Two violent crimes (murder, forcible rape, robbery and aggravated assault) and 56 nonviolent crimes (burglary, larceny-theft and motor vehicle theft) were reported in 1982. **JUDICIAL SYSTEM** One District Court and Judge, one County Court and Judge and four Justices of the Peace. In the District Court a total of 33 cases were pending on 1/1/82, 77 new cases were filed and 63 cases were disposed of during the year leaving 47 cases pending on 12/31/82. There were 24 criminal cases on the docket, 10 convictions, one person committed to prison, seven cases left pending. In the County Court 32 cases were pending on 1/1/82, 116 new cases were filed and 77 cases were disposed of during the year leaving 71 cases pending on 12/31/82. There were 138 criminal cases on the docket, 22 convictions, two persons committed to jail, and 63 cases left pending. **JAILS** One jail, capacity two. **ATTORNEYS AT LAW** One. **UTILITIES** 68% of the residents are connected to a public or privately owned water system and 49% are connected to a public sewer system. Natural gas is distributed to the county by Lone Star Gas Co., Division of Enserch. The average annual residential bill for natural gas in 1982 for the Lone Star distribution system was $405.91, an increase of 35% over 1981. Electricity is distributed to the county by West Texas Utilities, Bailey Co. Electric Coop., and Lamb Co. Electric Coop., Inc. and is generated primarily by gas, oil and coal. **TAXES** The county has eight units with taxing authority: two school districts, two cities, one county, two hospital districts and one special district.

RECREATION/ENTERTAINMENT

NATIONAL REGISTER OF HISTORIC PLACES Bronte vicinity: Fort Chadbourne. **COUNTY/MUNICIPAL PARKS** 228 acres in two county and four municipal parks. These parks contain one playground, two golf courses, ten baseball and softball fields, four tennis courts, two swimming pools, one beach, three boat ramps and shore fishing facilities. **SCENIC DRIVES** The Texas Forts Trail runs through this county. This trail leads to eight of the famous frontier forts of West Central Texas and an ancient presidio of the Spanish colonial period. **BOATING/FISHING** Lakes/reservoirs: Kickapoo Creek Soil conservation Service Lakes 4 and 5 (28 acres), Mountain Creek (49 acres), Oak Creek (2,375 acres), Rawling Tank (32 acres) and E.V. Spence (14,950 acres). Major rivers: Colorado and North Concho. Primary streams: Middle Kickapoo, Mountain, Oak and Turkey. **HUNTING** Winter season on antelope. Fall and winter seasons on deer and javelina. No closed seasons on coyote, bobcat and squirrel. Winter seasons on quail, muskrat, beaver, opossum, ring-tailed cat, badger, fox, weasel, raccoon, skunk and civet cat. Fall, winter and spring seasons on turkey. In 1983 duck, coot, geese, woodcock and jacksnipe seasons occurred during the winter months with a winter season on sandhill crane in some parts of the county. Teal duck, rail and gallinule seasons occurred in the fall. Mourning dove seasons occurred intermittently during the fall and winter months. **SPECIAL EVENTS** Ole Coke County Pageant, Robert Lee, July; Rodeo, Bronte, July.

COMMUNITIES

COUNTY SEAT Robert Lee, County Courthouse, 76945; County Clerk's Office, 915/453-2631. **INCORPORATED COMMUNITIES** (1980 population and ZIP Code) Blackwell (286: 21 in Coke Co. and 265 in Nolan Co.) 79506, Bronte (983) 76933 and Robert Lee (1,202) 76945. **UNINCORPORATED COMMUNITIES** (and ZIP Code) Divide 76945, Edith 76945, Sanco 76945, Silver 76949, Tennyson 76953.

COLEMAN (P81)

THE LAND

Southeast of Abilene on U.S. Highways 283 and 67/84 in the Rolling Plains Region, Coleman County covers 1,277 square miles. The County has hilly limestone ridges, many valleys and wide bottom lands. The elevation ranges from 1,550 to 2,350 feet. Along the Eastern border of the county the moderately deep to deep soils have loamy surface layers and clayey subsoils. In some areas the soils are shallow and clayey over shale or sandstone. The rest of the county has soils that are mostly loamy throughout, with some limestone bedrock and some clayey subsoils. In the Rolling Plains vegetation area, grasses include bluestems, Indiangrass, and sideoats grama with a few blackjack oaks, post oaks and sumacs. Between 21 and 30% of the land in the county is considered prime farmland. **CLIMATE** Mild and dry. Dust storms may be a problem during spring. The average annual temperature is 65°F. Temperatures in January range from an average low of 32° to an average high of 58°F and in July range from 71° to 96°F. The average annual precipitation is 25 inches, with an average relative humidity of 76% at 6 A.M. and 42% at 6 P.M. The average annual snowfall is four inches. The growing season averages 230 days per year, with the last freeze in late March and the first freeze in mid November. The sun shines during the year on the average 70% of the daylight hours.

THE PEOPLE

Coleman County ranks 19th among all U.S. counties in the highest percent of population age 65 and over. The 1982 estimated population of 10,500 indicates a continuation of the slow growth rate begun in the 1970s which reversed the steady population decline between 1930 and 1970. Urban areas grew, while rural areas declined in population by 4%, between 1970 and 1980. The age groups with the largest gains were ages birth to five and 20 to 24, lowering the high median age from 46 in 1970 to 43 in 1980. The largest ancestry groups are persons of English descent (27%) and those of Irish descent (25%). **REGISTERED VOTERS** As of November 2, 1982 there were 5,804 registered voters (0.1% of the state total). The 1982 general election had a 52% voter turnout, compared to a 67% turnout in the 1980 general election. In the 1982 primary 94% voted Democratic and 6% Republican, with 1,268 votes cast.

THE ECONOMY

AGRICULTURE Sheep and wheat area. In 1982, 93% of the land was in farms and ranches, with 20% of the farmland under cultivation and 2% irrigated. Coleman ranked 159th in the state in highest agricultural receipts, with 75% from livestock and livestock products. Overgrazing, undesirable brush and weeds and water erosion are the current conservation problems. Primary crops: second in the state for oats, wheat, sorghum, hay and cotton. Primary vegetables: sweet potatoes and watermelons. Primary fruits and nuts: peaches and pecans. Primary livestock and products: cattle, milk, sheep, wool and hogs. **BUSINESS** Total number of business establishments in the county: 242. Retail sales during the first quarter of 1984 increased 24% with a decrease of 8% in Santa Anna. In 1980, 21% of the labor force were self-employed, 18% were employed in professional or related services, 10% in manufacturing, 18% in wholesale and retail trade, 23% in agriculture, forestry, fisheries and mining, 16% were employed in other counties and there were 1,787 retired workers. The industries with the most employment: agribusiness, oil and extraction and the manufacture of apparel, wood office furniture and ceramic wall and floor tile. The nonfarm earnings in 1981 totaled $88,215,000. The retired workers received an average monthly Social Security payment of $285. **FINANCE** On June 30, 1983, three commercial banks had total deposits of $95,094,000 and total assets of $104,448,000. There are two state savings and loan association branches in the county. **HOUSING** Average value of homes in 1980: $15,500. Permits for new, privately owned housing units decreased in 1982: 11 permits were issued with a total construction cost of $309,900. Of those permits, all were for single family houses. Between 1970 and 1980 the number of housing units increased by 9%. Sixty-one percent of all units in the county are air-conditioned, 89% are heated by gas and 7% by electricity. **NATURAL RESOURCES** Clay, limestone, industrial sand oil, and gas, dolomite, and bituminous coal. In 1982 a total of 6,601,652 thousand cubic feet of gas well gas, 12,778 barrels of condensate, 982,099 barrels of crude oil and 3,428,040 thousand cubic feet of casinghead gas were produced. Current production of other minerals and products includes brick, caliche and clay. **TOURISM** Travel expenditures of $4,108,000 in 1982 (an increase of 11% over 1981) generated 98 jobs and $796,000 in payroll. **ALCOHOLIC BEVERAGES** Packaged distilled spirits, beer, ale, malt liquor and wine are legal in parts of the county. **FEDERAL EXPENDITURES** The federal government had direct expenditures or obligations of $27,499,000 in the county during fiscal year 1983, including $1,249,000 by the U.S. Department of Defense. In addition, the federal government provided $521,000 in grant awards, paid $1,054,000 in salaries and wages, made direct payments to individuals of $24,431,000 including $16,233,000 in retirement and disability payments, awarded $481,000 in procurement contracts and spent $1,011,000 in other expenditures or obligations. The federal government also provided $322,000 in direct loans and $1,514,000 in guaranteed loans and insurance.

COMMUNICATION

Newspapers–Weekly: Coleman County Chronicle, The Coleman Democrat-Voice and the Santa Anna News. Radio: KSTA-AM, KSTA-FM (Coleman). Cable TV. Telephone companies: Continental Telephone, General Telephone, Coleman County Telephone Coop. and Taylor Telephone. **TRANSPORTATION** Total public road mileage: 1,284. In 1982 there were 10,793 registered vehicles and 231 reported traffic accidents including two fatalities. Taxi cabs: one company in the city of Coleman. Intercity bus service is available. Motor freight: two carriers. Rail: two main and one branch line carry freight through the county. One of the main lines carries annually over 30 million tons of freight and one carries 20 to 30 million. The one branch line carries annually one to five million tons of freight. Aircraft: 20 are registered in the county. Airports: Coleman Municipal Airport is a basic utility airport providing general aviation service. It serves as a base for 16 aircraft.

COMMUNITY SERVICES

EDUCATION Five school districts with six elementary, one middle and five high schools. The average daily attendance in 1981-82 was 1,602, with expenditures per pupil of $2,682 including 128 classroom teachers with an average annual salary of $15,538. Forty-six percent of the 143 high school graduates planned to attend college. In 1982-83, 75% of the students were White, 19% Hispanic, 6% Black, 0.2% Asian. Sports championships: 1983 A Boys' Tennis Doubles, Santa Anna H.S.; 1983 AAA Boys' Tennis Doubles, Coleman H.S. **PUBLIC LIBRARIES** Coleman Public Library: 20,866 volumes, Santa Anna City Library: 5,200 volumes. **CHILD CARE** 10 day care and one twenty-four hour care licensed facilities. **HEALTH CARE** Seven physicians and four dentists. Hospitals: Two with a combined capacity of 80. Ambulance services: two funeral homes and one commercial service. Mental health: one clinic. Nursing homes: three nursing homes with a combined capacity of 208 nursing care residents. The average cost per day for private patients in 1982 was $30.04. **CHURCHES** 52 churches have an estimated combined

COLEMAN (continued)

membership of 8,199. The largest denominations are Southern Baptist, United Methodist and Catholic. **SOCIAL SERVICES** In fiscal year 1983 a total of $396,134 in food stamps was distributed, with an average of 886 persons receiving food stamps each month. Aid to Families with Dependent Children (AFDC) totaled $89,518, with an average of 58 families receiving AFDC each month. Medical assistance benefits for the aged and disabled of $1,601,266 and for families and children of $107,855 brought the county benefit total to $2,194,773. **FIRE PROTECTION** Seven volunteer fire departments. **LAW ENFORCEMENT** The County Sheriff has 10 commissioned officers. Four police departments have a combined force of 18. **CRIME** Seven violent crimes (murder, forcible rape, robbery and aggravated assault) and 107 nonviolent crimes (burglary, larceny-theft and motor vehicle theft) were reported in 1982. **JUDICIAL SYSTEM** One District Court and Judge, one County Court and Judge and two Justices of the Peace. In the District Court a total of 209 cases were pending on 1/1/82, 235 new cases were filed and 214 cases were disposed of during the year leaving 230 cases pending on 12/31/82. There were 69 criminal cases on the docket, 22 convictions, seven persons committed to prison and one committed to jail and 28 cases left pending. In the County Court 321 cases were pending on 1/1/82, 387 new cases were filed and 383 cases were disposed of during the year leaving 325 cases pending on 12/31/82. There were 648 criminal cases on the docket, 181 convictions, 47 persons committed to jail, and 277 cases left pending. **JAILS** One jail, capacity 15. **ATTORNEYS AT LAW** Eight. **UTILITIES** 80% of the residents are connected to a public or privately owned water system and 64% are connected to a public sewer system. Natural gas is distributed to the county by Lone Star Gas Co., Division of Enserch. The average annual residential bill for natural gas in 1982 for the Lone Star distribution system was $405.91, an increase of 35% over 1981. Electricity is distributed to the city of Coleman by the Coleman Municipal Power and Light Dept. and to the rest of the county by Gulf State Utilities, West Texas Utilities, Coleman Co. Electric Coop., Inc., and McCulloch Electric Coop., Inc., and is generated primarily by gas and oil. The typical residential electric bill is $167.55 per month for an all-electric house using 2,500 kwh. **TAXES** The county has nine units with taxing authority: five school districts, three cities and one county.

RECREATION/ENTERTAINMENT

MUNICIPAL PARKS 445 acres in seven municipal parks. These parks contain two playgrounds, six baseball and softball fields, 15 tennis courts, two swimming pools, three beaches and one boat ramp. Developed campsites: 15. **BOATING/FISHING** Lakes/reservoirs: Coleman (2,000 acres), Home Creek Soil Conservation Service Lakes 4, 7A and 13 (541 acres), Jim Ned Creek Soil Conservation Service Lakes 12, 20 and 26 (42 acres), Miller (11 acres) Mukewater Soil Conservation Service Lakes 4 and 10A (34 acres), Northwest Lateral Soil Conservation Service Lake 5A (9 acres), Novice City (14 acres), Upper Pecan Bayou Soil Conservation Service Lake 24 (14 acres), Sealy (50 acres), Scarborough (89 acres), San Tana (43 acres) and Talpa City (40 acres). Major rivers: Colorado. Primary streams: Jim Ned, Wildcat, Loss, Red Bank, Hords, Buck, Watts, Indian, Hay, Mukewater, Elm, Little Pecan, Mud and Grape. **HUNTING** Fall and winter seasons on deer. No closed seasons on coyote, bobcat and squirrel. Winter seasons on quail, muskrat, beaver, opossum, ring-tailed cat, badger, fox, weasel, raccoon, skunk and civet cat. Fall, winter and spring seasons on turkey. In 1983 sandhill crane, duck, coot, geese, woodcock and jacksnipe seasons occurred during the winter months. Teal duck, rail and gallinule seasons occurred in the fall. Mourning dove seasons occurred intermittently during the fall and winter months. **MUSEUMS** Coleman: Coleman County Museum. Santa Anna: Old Rock House. **SPECIAL EVENTS** Coleman County Stock Show, Coleman, January; Fun Fest, Coleman, July; Rodeo, Coleman, July; Junior Rodeo, Coleman, August; Fiesta de la Paloma, Coleman, September.

COMMUNITIES

COUNTY SEAT Coleman, County Courthouse, 76834; County Clerk's Office, 915/625-2889. **INCORPORATED COMMUNITIES** (1980 population and ZIP Code) Coleman (5,960) 76834, Novice (201) 79538, Santa Anna (1,535) 76878 and Talpa (122) 76882. **UNINCORPORATED COMMUNITIES** (and ZIP Code) Burkett 76828, Echo 76834, Fisk 76834, Glen Cove 76843, Goldsboro 79519, Gouldbusk 76845, Leaday 76851, Mozelle 76834, Rockwood 76873, Shields 76878, Silver Valley 76834, Trickham 76878, Valera 76884, Voss 76888, Webbville 76828 and Whon 75889. **FOR ADDITIONAL LOCAL INFORMATION** Coleman Chamber of Commerce, P.O. Box 796, Coleman, 76834, 915/625-2329, Santa Anna Chamber of Commerce, P.O. Box 275, Santa Anna, 76878, 915/348-3535.

COLLIN (M7)

THE LAND

North of Dallas on U.S. Highways 380 and 75 in the Blackland Prairies Region, Collin County covers 851 square miles of rolling terrain with the elevation ranging from 500 to 750 feet. The dark soils are slightly acidic with loamy surface layers and cracking, clayey subsoils. In the Blackland Prairie vegetation area, a variety of trees such as pecan, elm, oak, bois d'arc and mesquite thrive along streams. Originally covered by tall bunchgrasses, the pastures now are primarily buffalograss and Texas grama. Between 51 and 60% of the land in the county is considered prime farmland. **CLIMATE** Mild and moist. Thunderstorms with hail may present a problem during late spring and early summer. The average annual temperature is 65°F. Temperatures in January range from an average low of 32° to an average high of 55°F and in July range from 73° to 96°F. The average annual precipitation is 36 inches, with an average relative humidity of 80% at 6 A.M. and 53% at 6 P.M. The average annual snowfall is four inches. The growing season averages 230 days per year, with the last freeze in late March and the first freeze in mid November. The sun shines during the year on the average 70% of the daylight hours.

THE PEOPLE

Collin County ranks 25th among all U.S. counties in the highest growth rate between 1970 and 1980. It also ranks as one of the most densely populated counties in the state and is one of the lowest counties in the percent of residents who are native Texans. The 1982 estimated population of 160,900 indicates a continuation of the strong growth rate begun in the 1970s. Between 1970 and 1980 the population increased from 66,920 to 144,576. Urban areas had an outstanding growth rate of 195%. The age groups with the largest gains were ages 35 to 39, increasing over 250%, and ages five to 19, which doubled. The largest ancestry groups are persons of English descent (30%), Irish descent (24%) and those of German descent (21%). **REGISTERED VOTERS** As of November 2, 1982 there were 75,122 registered voters (1% of the state total). The 1982 general election had a 53% voter turnout, compared to a 75% turnout in the 1980 general election. In the 1982 primary 53% voted Democratic and 47% Republican, with 10,998 votes cast.

THE ECONOMY

AGRICULTURE Wheat and sorghum area. In 1982, 79% of

the land was in farms and ranches, with 58% of the farmland under cultivation and 2% irrigated. Collin ranked 67th in the state in highest agricultural receipts, with 51% from livestock and livestock products. Overgrazing, water erosion, noxious weeds, flooding and urban encroachment are the current conservation problems. Primary crops: wheat, sorghum, hay, oats, cotton and corn. Primary vegetables: cantaloupes, potatoes, tomatoes and watermelon. Primary fruits and nuts: peaches and pecans. Primary livestock and products: cattle, milk and hogs. **BUSINESS** Total number of business establishments in the county: 2,388. Retail sales during the first quarter of 1984 increased 38% with Lucas having a 195% increase and Princeton a 98% increase. In 1980, 7% of the labor force were self-employed, 15% were employed in professional or related services, 25% in manufacturing, 23% in wholesale and retail trade, 8% in construction, 59% were employed in other counties and there were 6,573 retired workers. The industries with the most employment: agribusiness, meat packing, general construction and the manufacture of men's work clothing, children's clothes, wood kitchen cabinets, leather goods, plumbing fittings, insulated wire, valves and pipefittings, communication equipment and vehicle lighting equipment. The nonfarm earnings in 1981 totaled $1,608,454,000. The retired workers received an average monthly Social Security payment of $310. **FINANCE** On June 30, 1983, 22 commercial banks had total deposits of $729,666,000 and total assets of $814,364,000. On December 31, 1982 three state savings and loan associations, 18 state branches and two federal branches had combined assets of $162,149,948. In addition there are four credit unions in the county. **HOUSING** Average value of homes in 1980: $67,900. Permits for new, privately owned housing units increased in 1982: 3,342 permits were issued with a total construction cost of $185,258,135. Of those permits, 1,850 were for single family houses. Housing permits increased in Frisco from 24 in 1981 to 68 in 1982 with 48 of the permits issued for single family houses, in McKinney from 55 to 120 with 100 of the permits issued for single family houses and in Plano from 1,473 to 2,819. Between 1970 and 1980 the number of housing units increased by 114%. Ninety percent of all units in the county are air-conditioned, 71% are heated by gas and 28% by electricity. **NATURAL RESOURCE PRODUCTION** Limestone, sand and gravel. **TOURISM** Travel expenditures of $9,302,000 in 1982 (an increase of 15% over 1981) generated 238 jobs and $2,677,000 in payroll. Lodging: six hotels, motels and tourist courts. **ALCOHOLIC BEVERAGES** Packaged distilled spirits, beer, ale, malt liquor and wine are legal in parts of the county. **FEDERAL EXPENDITURES** The federal government had direct expenditures or obligations of $158,818,000 in the county during fiscal year 1983, including $23,523,000 by the U.S. Department of Defense. In addition, the federal government provided $6,667,000 in grant awards, paid $10,287,000 in salaries and wages, made direct payments to individuals of $126,544,000 including $88,013,000 in retirement and disability payments, awarded $13,775,000 in procurement contracts and spent $1,545,000 in other expenditures or obligations. The federal government also provided $5,098,000 in direct loans and $101,692,000 in guaranteed loans and insurance.

COMMUNICATION

Newspapers–Daily: McKinney Courier-Gazette, ave. eve. circ. 6,691 and the Plano Daily Star-Courier ave. eve. circ. 15,684. Weekly: Allen American, Celina Record, Farmersville Times, Frisco Enterprize (Spanish), Princeton Herald, Royce City American, and the Wylie News. Radio: KXYI-AM (Plano), KMMK-FM Stereo (McKinney). Cable TV. Telephone companies: Continental Telephone, General Telephone and Southwestern Bell. **TRANSPORTATION** Total public road mileage: 2,233. In 1982 there were 124,671 registered vehicles

and 3,349 reported traffic accidents including 34 fatalities. Taxi cabs: one company in McKinney. Intercity bus service is available. Motor freight: 22 local and intrastate carriers. Rail: six main and three branch lines carry freight through the county. One of the main lines carries annually 10 to 20 million tons of freight, three carry 5 to 10 each and two carry one to five million each. Two of the branch lines carry annually one to five million tons of freight each and one carries less than one million. Aircraft: 226 are registered in the county. Airports: McKinney Municipal Airport is a general utility airport providing general aviation service. It serves as a base for 88 aircraft. Also serving this area are McKinney Aero Country Airport, J.S.I. Airport at Princeton and Dallas North Airport at Plano.

COMMUNITY SERVICES

EDUCATION 15 school districts with 37 elementary, 15 middle and 17 high schools. The average daily attendance in 1981-82 was 35,261, with expenditures per pupil of $2,666 including 2,149 classroom teachers with an average annual salary of $17,345. Sixty-one percent of the 2,185 high school graduates planned to attend college. In 1982-83, 89% of the students were White, 6% Hispanic, 5% Black, 1% Asian and 0.2% American Indian. Sports championships: 1983 AA Girls' Track, Frisco H.S.; 1982 AAA Girls' Cross Country, Frisco H.S. Private schools: 430 enrolled in three elementary and two high schools. Vocational education: Collin Memorial Hospital School of X-Ray Technology (McKinney). National Beauty School (Plano). **PUBLIC LIBRARIES** Allen Public Library: 24,000 volumes. Farmersville Library. McKinney Memorial Public Library: 36,204 volumes. Plano Public Library System: 102,357, volumes, two branches. Wyle Public Library: 13,513 volumes. **CHILD CARE** 248 day care and 19 twenty-four hour care licensed facilities. **HEALTH CARE** 246 physicians and 69 dentists. Hospitals: four with a combined capacity of 455. Specialized hospitals: one obstetrics hospital with capacity of eight. Clinics: two minor emergency centers, one outpatient clinic, one for treatment of alcohol and/or drug abuse, and one public health clinic. Ambulance services: three volunteer services, two fire departments, and one funeral home service. Mental health: one clinic, one child guidance clinic, and one county clinic. Nursing homes: eight nursing homes with a combined capacity of 906 nursing care residents. The average cost per day for private patients in 1982 was $33.05. **CHURCHES** 171 churches have an estimated combined membership of 64,915. The largest denominations are Southern Baptist, Catholic and United Methodist. **SOCIAL SERVICES** In fiscal year 1983 a total of $1,905,008 in food stamps was distributed, with an average of 4,110 persons receiving food stamps each month. Aid to Families with Dependent Children (AFDC) totaled $629,657, with an average of 414 families receiving AFDC each month. Medical assistance benefits for the aged and disabled of $5,691,299 and for families and children of $1,280,361 brought the county benefit total to $9,506,324. **FIRE PROTECTION** One paid, one partly paid and 19 volunteer fire departments. **LAW ENFORCEMENT** The County Sheriff has 92 commissioned officers. 13 police departments have a combined force of 24. **CRIME** 376 violent crimes (murder, forcible rape, robbery and aggravated assault) and 5,027 nonviolent crimes (burglary, larceny-theft and motor vehicle theft) were reported in 1982. **JUDICIAL SYSTEM** Three District Courts and Judges, three County Courts and Judges and five Justices of the Peace. In the District Courts a total of 2,819 cases were pending on 1/1/82, 4,509 new cases were filed and 3,847 cases were disposed of during the year leaving 3,481 cases pending on 12/31/82. There were 1,062 criminal cases on the docket, 579 convictions, 91 persons committed to prison and 13 committed to jail and 377 cases left pending. In the County Courts 1,021 cases were pending on 1/1/82, 3,464 new cases were filed and 2,900 cases were

COUNTIES

COLLIN (continued)

disposed of during the year leaving 1,585 cases pending on 12/31/82. There were 3,471 criminal cases on the docket, 1,414 convictions, 349 persons committed to jail, and 1,086 cases left pending. **JAILS** One jail, capacity 109, planning third floor. **ATTORNEYS AT LAW** 200. **UTILITIES** 97% of the residents are connected to a public or privately owned water system and 83% are connected to a public sewer system. Natural gas is distributed to the county by Lone Star Gas Co., Division of Enserch. The average annual residential bill for natural gas in 1982 for the Lone Star distribution system was $405.91, an increase of 35% over 1981. Electricity is distributed to the city of Farmersville by Farmersville Municipal Light and Power and to the rest of the county by Texas Power and Light, Houston Lighting and Power Co., Grayson-Collin Electric Coop., Inc., and Hunt and Collin Electric Coop., Inc. and is generated primarily by gas and coal. The typical residential electric bill is $165.24 per month for an all-electric house using 2,500 kwh. **TAXES** The county has 37 units with taxing authority: 15 school districts, 20 cities, one county and one utility district.

RECREATION/ENTERTAINMENT

PROFESSIONAL SPORTS Plano: Dallas Americans Soccer Team (Clark Stadium). **NATIONAL REGISTER OF HISTORIC PLACES** Farmersville vicinity: Sister Grove Creek Site. McKinney: Collin McKinney Cabin. Plano: Ammie Wilson House. **MUNICIPAL PARKS** 2,265 acres in 86 municipal parks. These parks contain 15 miles of hiking trails, 57 playgrounds, four golf courses, 18 football and soccer fields, 19 baseball and softball fields, 62 tennis courts, six multi-use courts and three swimming pools. **SCENIC DRIVES** The Texas Lakes Trail runs through this county. This trail introduces some 30 blue-water recreational areas in a variety of settings in North-Central Texas. **BOATING/FISHING** Lakes/reservoirs: East Fork Lavon Soil Conservation Service Lakes 2A, 4, 46, 47, 8H, 3B, 42, 43, 8G, 11, 14, 15, and 16 (155 acres), Lavon (11,080 acres), Moores (20 acres), Pilot Grove Creek Soil Conservation Service Lakes 82 and 29 (84 acres), Rowlett Creek Soil Conservation Service 4 and 7 (27 acres) and Sister Grove Soil Conservation Service Lakes 17, 9, 10 and 12 (48 acres). Major rivers: Elm Fork Trinity and East Fork Trinity. Primary streams: Stover, Franklin, Slayter, Throckmorton, Honey, Hurricane, Bluff, Elm, Lick, Muddy, Maxwell, Sister Grove and Stiff. **HUNTING** No closed seasons on nutria, coyote, bobcat and squirrel. Winter seasons on quail, muskrat, beaver, otter, opossum, mink, ring-tailed cat, badger, fox, raccoon, skunk and civet cat. Special regulations on Lake Lavon. In 1983 duck, coot, geese, woodcock and jacksnipe seasons occurred during the winter months. Teal duck, rail and gallinule seasons occurred in the fall. Mourning dove seasons occurred intermittently during the fall and winter months. **MUSEUMS** McKinney: Heard Natural Science Museum and Bolin Museum; Plano: Heritage Center Farmstead Museum. **SPECIAL EVENTS** Roundup Craft Fair, Plano, April; Blackland Jamboree, Plano, May; May Fair, McKinney, May; On-the-Water Fireworks, Clear Lake, July; Fourth of July Parade, McKinney, July; Star-Spangled Spectacular, Plano, July; Lunar Festival, Clear Lake, July; Blessing of the Fleet, Clear Lake, August; Hot Air Balloon Rally and Celebration, Plano, August/September; Shrimporee, Clear Lake, August/September; Chili/Crafts Fest, McKinney, August/September; Heritage Day Fair, Plano, October; Old Time Saturday, Farmersville, October; Heritage Tour of Homes, McKinney, December; Christmas Boat Lane Parade, Clear Lake, December.

COMMUNITIES

COUNTY SEAT McKinney, County Courthouse, 75069; County Clerk's Office, 214/542-9441. **INCORPORATED COMMUNITIES** (1980 population and ZIP Code) Allen (8,314) 75002, Altoga (269) 75069, Anna (855) 75003, Blue Ridge (442) 75004, Celina (1,520) 75009, Dallas (904,078: 1,357 in Collin Co., 101 in Denton Co., 902,619 in Dallas Co. and 1 in Kaufman Co.) 75200, Fairview (893) 75069, Farmersville (2,360) 75031, Frisco (3,499: 3,335 in Collin Co. and 85 in Denton Co.) 75034, Josephine (416) 75064, Lavon (185) 75066, Lowry Crossing (443) 75069, Lucas (1,371) 75069, McKinney (16,256) 75069, Melissa (604) 75071, Murphy (1,150) 75074, Nevada (200 est. incorp. inactive) 75073, New Hope (331) 75069, Parker (1,098) 75002, Plano (72,331) 75074, Princeton (3,408) 75077, Prosper (675) 75078, Richardson (72,496: 6,780 in Collin Co. and 65,716 in Dallas Co.) 75080, Royse City (1,566: 172 in Collin Co. and 1,394 Rockwall Co.) 75089, Sachse (1,640: 29 in Collin Co. and 1,611 in Dallas Co.) 75040, St. Paul (363) 75098, Westminster (278) 75096, Weston (405) 75097 and Wylie (3,152) 75098. **UNINCORPORATED COMMUNITIES** (and ZIP Code) Beverly Hills 75069, Bloomdale 75069, Branch 75069, Chambersville 75069, Chambliss 75003, Clear Lake 75069, Climax 75077, Copeville 75018, Culleoka 75069, Deep Water Point Estates 75018, Desert 75004, Fayburg 75004, Foncine 75069, Foot 75069, Forest Grove 75069, Frognot 75004, Kelly 75003, Lavon Beach Estates 75031, Lavon Shores Estates 75069, Lebanon 75034, Lolaville 75034, Marilee 75058, Milligan 75069, Millwood 75089, Pebble Beach-Sunset Acres 75018, Pike 75004, Rhea Mills 75069, Rockhill 75069, Sedalia 75095, Snow Hill 75031, Trinity Park 75098, Valdasta 75004, Verona 75004, Walnut Grove 75069, Yucote Acres 75069. **FOR ADDITIONAL LOCAL INFORMATION** Metrocrest Chamber of Commerce, 1204 Metrocrest Dr., Carrollton, 75006, 214/245-0444, Frisco Chamber of Commerce, P.O. Box 1074, Frisco, 75034, 214/377-9522, Farmersville Chamber of Commerce, P.O. Box 366, Farmersville, 75031, 214/782-6234, McKinney Chamber of Commerce, 2055 W. Louisiana, P.O. Box 621, McKinney, 75069, Plano Chamber of Commerce, 1200 E. 15th, Plano, 75074, 214/424-7547 or 424-7540, Richardson Chamber of Commerce, 411 Belle Grove Dr., Richardson, 75080, 214/234-4141, Royse City Chamber of Commerce, P.O. Box 547, Royse City, 75089, 214/635-9051, Wylie Area Chamber of Commerce, 113 N. Ballard, P.O. Box 918, Wylie, 75098, 214/442-2804.

COLLINGSWORTH (P20)

THE LAND

In the Texas Panhandle east of Amarillo on U.S. Highway 83 in the Rolling Plains Region, Collingsworth County covers 909 square miles of level to rolling terrain. The elevation ranges from 1,800 to 2,600 feet. The red to brown soils have loamy to sandy surface layers and clayey or loamy subsoils. In the Rolling Plains vegetation area, the prairie grasses have been invaded by mesquite, yucca and sagebrush. Between 11 and 20% of the land in the county is considered prime farmland. **CLIMATE** Borderline continental steppe and subtropical subhumid, generally cool and dry. The average annual temperature is 60°F. Temperatures in January range from an average low of 23° to an average high of 52°F and in July range from 69° to 97°F. The average annual precipitation is 22 inches, with an average relative humidity of 74% at 6 A.M. and 42% at 6 P.M. The average annual snowfall is 12 inches. The growing season averages 215 days per year, with the last freeze in early April and the first freeze in early November. The sun shines during the year on the average 75% of the daylight hours.

THE PEOPLE

The 1982 estimated population of 4,500 indicates a decline in residents since 1980 and is a continuation of the steady population decrease since 1930. However the rate of decline lowered from 24% between 1960 and 1970 to 2% between 1970 and 1980. Rural areas experienced population losses between 1970 and 1980, while urban areas increased 6%. The age groups with the greatest decreases were ages 60 to 64 and 45 to 59, lowering the high median age from 42 in 1970 to 36 in 1980. The largest ancestry groups are persons of English descent (25%), Irish descent (23%) and those of German descent (14%). **REGISTERED VOTERS** As of November 2, 1982 there were 2,595 registered voters (0.04% of the state total). The 1982 general election had a 53% voter turnout, compared to a 68% turnout in the 1980 general election. In the 1982 primary 100% voted Democratic, with 1,190 votes cast.

THE ECONOMY

AGRICULTURE Cotton and wheat area. In 1982, 95% of the land was in farms and ranches, with 27% of the farmland under cultivation and 12% irrigated. Collingsworth ranked 167th in the state in highest agricultural receipts, with 56% from crops. Overgrazing, undesirable brush and weeds and water and wind erosion are the current conservation problems. Primary crops: cotton, wheat, sorghum and hay. Primary vegetables: watermelons. Primary fruits and nuts: peaches. Primary livestock and products: cattle and hogs. **BUSINESS** Total number of business establishments in the county: 93. Retail sales during the first quarter of 1984 increased 5%. In 1980, 25% of the labor force were self-employed, 18% were employed in professional or related services, 4% in manufacturing, 14% in wholesale and retail trade, 31% in agriculture, forestry, fisheries and mining, 13% were employed in other counties and there were 580 retired workers. The industries with the most employment: agribusiness and steel mills. The nonfarm earnings in 1981 totaled $30,581,000. The retired workers received an average monthly Social Security payment of $300. **FINANCE** On June 30, 1983, two commercial banks had total deposits of $43,736,000 and total assets of $49,388,000. There is one federal savings and loan association branch in the county. **HOUSING** Average value of homes in 1980: $19,100. In 1982 four permits were issued for single family houses. Between 1970 and 1980 the number of housing units increased by 6%. Seventy-four percent of all units in the county are air-conditioned, 92% are heated by gas and 7% by electricity. **NATURAL RESOURCES** Caliche, gypsum, oil and gas. In 1982 a total of 2,747,143 thousand cubic feet of gas well gas, 322 barrels of condensate, 12,784 barrels of crude oil and 120,717 thousand cubic feet of casinghead gas were produced. Current production of other minerals and products includes caliche. **TOURISM** Travel expenditures of $1,274,000 in 1982 (an increase of 13.1% over 1981) generated 27 jobs and $233,000 in payroll. **ALCOHOLIC BEVERAGES** Totally dry. **FEDERAL EXPENDITURES** The federal government had direct expenditures or obligations of $14,033,000 in the county during fiscal year 1983, including $283,000 by the U.S. Department of Defense. In addition, the federal government provided $99,000 in grant awards, paid $562,000 in salaries and wages, made direct payments to individuals of $8,363,000 including $5,405,000 in retirement and disability payments, awarded $1,000 in procurement contracts and spent $5,007,000 in other expenditures or obligations. The federal government also provided $2,179,000 in direct loans and $3,403,000 in guaranteed loans and insurance.

COMMUNICATION

Newspapers–Weekly: Wellington Leader. Cable TV. Telephone companies: General Telephone and Southwestern Bell. **TRANSPORTATION** Total public road mileage: 802. In 1982 there were 4,462 registered vehicles and 75 reported traffic accidents including one fatality. Motor freight: two carriers. Rail: one branch line carries annually less than one million tons of freight through the county. Aircraft: 14 are registered in the county. Airports: Marian Municipal Airport at Wellington is a basic utility airport providing general aviation service. It serves as a base for 13 aircraft.

COMMUNITY SERVICES

EDUCATION Two school districts with two elementary, one middle and two high schools. The average daily attendance in 1981-82 was 777, with expenditures per pupil of $2,506 including 51 classroom teachers with an average annual salary of $15,773. Sixty-nine percent of the 49 high school graduates planned to attend college. In 1982-83, 64% of the students were White, 24% Hispanic, 12% Black, 0.1% Asian and 0.5% American Indian. **PUBLIC LIBRARIES** Collingsworth County Library (Wellington): 20,044 volumes. **CHILD CARE** Five day care licensed facilities. **HEALTH CARE** Three physicians and three dentists. Hospitals: one with a capacity of 27. Ambulance services: one volunteer service. Mental health: one clinic. Nursing homes: one nursing home has a capacity of 84 nursing care residents. The average cost per day for private patients in 1982 was $25.87. **CHURCHES** 18 churches have an estimated combined membership of 3,769. The largest denominations are Southern Baptist, United Methodist and Churches of Christ. **SOCIAL SERVICES** In fiscal year 1983 a total of $164,463 in food stamps was distributed, with an average of 377 persons receiving food stamps each month. Aid to Families with Dependent Children (AFDC) totaled $20,557, with an average of 12 families receiving AFDC each month. Medical assistance benefits for the aged and disabled of $488,757 and for families and children of $37,427 brought the county benefit total to $711,204. **FIRE PROTECTION** Two volunteer fire departments. **LAW ENFORCEMENT** The County Sheriff has 48 commissioned officers. **CRIME** 93 nonviolent crimes (burglary, larceny-theft and motor vehicle theft) were reported in 1982. **JUDICIAL SYSTEM** One District Court and Judge, one County Court and Judge and one Justice of the Peace. In the District Courts a total of 73 cases were pending on 1/1/82, 158 new cases were filed and 128 cases were disposed of during the year leaving 103 cases pending on 12/31/82. There were 64 criminal cases on the docket, 14 convictions, five persons committed to prison and 27 cases left pending. In the County Courts 68 cases were pending on 1/1/82, 96 new cases were filed and 124 cases were disposed of during the year leaving 40 cases pending on 12/31/82. There were 132 criminal cases on the docket, 44 convictions, three persons committed to jail, and 30 cases left pending. **JAILS** One jail, capacity 17, planning new construction as lost certification in 1983 due to structural reasons. **ATTORNEYS AT LAW** Three. **UTILITIES** 84% of the residents are connected to a public or privately owned water system and 67% are connected to a public sewer system. Natural gas is distributed to the county by Lone Star Gas Co., Division of Enserch. The average annual residential bill for natural gas in 1982 for the Lone Star distribution system was $405.91, an increase of 35% over 1981. Electricity is distributed to the county by Greenbelt Electric Coop., Lighthouse Electric Coop., Inc., and West Texas Utilities Co. and is generated primarily by gas and oil. The typical residential electric bill is $145.78 per month for an all-electric house using 2,500 kwh. **TAXES** The county has seven units with taxing authority: three school districts, two cities, one county, and one hospital district.

RECREATION/ENTERTAINMENT

COUNTY/MUNICIPAL PARKS 73 acres in one county and four municipal parks. These parks contain two playgrounds, one golf course, one multi-use field, one multi-use court and one swimming pool. Developed campsites: 27. **BOATING/FISHING** Lakes/reservoirs: Allred-Sessions Lake (25 acres), Atteberry (15

COUNTIES

COLLINGSWORTH (continued)

acres), Brookhollow Club (73 acres) and Evans (17 acres). Major rivers: Salt Fork Red and Red. Primary streams: Sand, Dry Salt, Jonah, Spiller, Wolf and Elm. **HUNTING** Fall and winter seasons on deer. Summer, fall and winter seasons on squirrel. Fall season on prairie chicken. Winter season on pheasant, quail, muskrat, beaver, opossum, ring-tailed cat, badger, fox, weasel, raccoon, skunk and civet cat. No closed season for coyote and bobcat. Fall, winter and spring seasons on turkey. In 1983 sandhill crane, duck, coot, geese, woodcock and jacksnipe seasons occurred during the winter months. Teal duck, rail and gallinule seasons occurred in the fall. Mourning dove season occurred intermittently during the fall and winter months. **MUSEUMS** Wellington: Collingsworth County Historical Museum. **SPECIAL EVENTS** Collingsworth County Fair, Wellington, September; Rodeos and Related Events, Wellington, Variable dates.

COMMUNITIES

COUNTY SEAT Wellington, County Courthouse, 79095; County Clerk's Office, 806/447-2408. **INCORPORATED COMMUNITIES** (1980 population and ZIP Code) Dodson (185) (Dodsonville) 79230 and Wellington (3,043) 79095. **UNINCORPORATED COMMUNITIES** (and ZIP Code) Aberdeen 79095, Dozier 79079, Lillie (Lilly) 79095, Lutie 79079, Quail 79251, Rolla 79095, Samnorwood 79077.

COLORADO (G15)

THE LAND

West of Houston on Interstate Highway 10 in the Claypan Area, Colorado County covers 964 square miles. The terrain varies from low level land to rolling woodland with the elevation ranging from 150 to 425 feet. In the northeast and southwest corners of the county the light colored soils have sandy surfaces and clayey subsoils. The soils toward the center of the county have loamy surface layers and mottled gray and red to yellow, cracking, clayey subsoils. In the center and along the Colorado River the soils are somewhat poorly drained, cracking clayey soils with some loamy surface layers. In the Post Oak Savannah vegetation area, the principal trees are post oak, black jack oak and elm with pecans and walnuts along streams. The original tall grasses have been replaced with buffalograss and Texas grama. Between 11 and 20% of the land in the county is considered prime farmland. **CLIMATE** Subtropical humid, generally mild. The average annual temperature is 69°F. Temperatures in January range from an average low of 41° to an average high of 63°F and in July range from 73° to 96°F. The average annual precipitation is 41 inches, with an average relative humidity of 87% at 6 A.M. and 60% at 6 P.M. There is little accumulation of snow. The growing season averages 280 days per year, with the last freeze in first of March and the first freeze in early December. The sun shines during the year on the average 68% of the daylight hours.

THE PEOPLE

The 1982 estimated population of 19,500 indicates a continuation of the growth rate begun in the 1970s, which reversed a steady population decrease between 1970 and 1980. Over 13% of the growth between 1970 and 1980 was in urban areas with a 3% gain in rural areas. The age groups with the largest increase was ages 20 to 34, while the group with the largest decrease was ages five to 14. The high median age of 34 remained unchanged. The largest ancestry groups are persons of German descent (35%), Black (18%) and Hispanic (14%). **REGISTERED VOTERS** As of November 2, 1982 there were 9,013 registered voters (0.1% of the state total). The 1982 general election had a 48% voter turnout, compared to a 68% turnout in the 1980 general election. In the 1982 primary 94% voted Democratic and 6% Republican, with 2,275 votes cast.

THE ECONOMY

AGRICULTURE Rice area. In 1982, 94% of the land was in farms and ranches, with 20% of the farmland under cultivation and 60% irrigated. Colorado ranked 35th in the state in highest agricultural receipts, with 56% from crops. Overgrazing, undesirable brush and weeds, inefficient irrigation systems and water erosion are the current conservation problems. Primary crops: third in the state for rice. Corn, hay, soybeans, oats and sorghum. Primary vegetables: potatoes, sweet potatoes and watermelons. Primary fruits and nuts: peaches and pecans. Primary livestock and products: eighth in the state for hogs, cattle and milk. **BUSINESS** Total number of business establishments in the county: 497. Retail sales during the first quarter of 1984 increased 17%. In 1980, 15% of the labor force were self-employed, 15% were employed in professional or related services, 9% in manufacturing, 22% in wholesale and retail trade, 22% in agriculture, forestry, fisheries and mining, 20% were employed in other counties and there were 2,065 retired workers. The industries with the most employment: agribusiness, sand and gravel, and the manufacture of prepared agricultural feeds and gaskets, packing and sealing devices. The nonfarm earnings in 1981 totaled $186,444,000. The retired workers received an average monthly Social Security payment of $289. **FINANCE** On June 30, 1983, five commercial banks had total deposits of $165,849,000 and total assets of $197,589,000. On December 31, 1982 one federal savings and loan association, one state savings and loan association branch and one federal branch had assets of $167,484,499. In addition there is one credit union in the county. **HOUSING** Average value of homes in 1980: $28,700. Permits for new, privately owned housing units increased in 1982: 48 permits were issued with a total construction cost of $1,853,847. Of those permits, 46 were for single family houses. Housing permits in Eagle Lake increased from 17 in 1981 to 35 in 1982 with 33 of the permits issued for single family houses. Between 1970 and 1980 the number of housing units increased by 28%. Sixty-one percent of all units in the county are air-conditioned, 73% are heated by gas and 21% by electricity. **NATURAL RESOURCES** Sand and gravel, oil and gas. In 1982 a total of 38,459,485 thousand cubic feet of gas well gas, 317,480 barrels of condensate, 445,757 barrels of crude oil and 1,670,523 thousand cubic feet of casinghead gas were produced. Current production of other minerals and products includes industrial sand, sand and gravel. **TOURISM** Travel expenditures of $24,573,000 in 1982 (an increase of 11% over 1981) generated 612 jobs and $4,886,000 in payroll. Lodging: five hotels, motels and tourist courts. **ALCOHOLIC BEVERAGES** Packaged distilled spirits, beer, ale, malt liquor and wine are legal. Sale of mixed beverages is legal in all or parts of the county. **FEDERAL EXPENDITURES** The federal government had direct expenditures or obligations of $38,638,000 in the county during fiscal year 1983, including $781,000 by the U.S. Department of Defense. In addition, the federal government provided $297,000 in grant awards, paid $1,496,000 in salaries and wages, made direct payments to individuals of $28,905,000 including $20,569,000 in retirement and disability payments, awarded $4,000 in procurement contracts and spent $7,936,000 in other expenditures or obligations. The federal government also provided $988,000 in direct loans and $6,876,000 in guaranteed loans and insurance.

COMMUNICATION

Newspaper–Weekly: The Colorado County Citizen (Columbus), Eagle Lake Headlight and The Weimar Mercury. Radio:

KVLM-FM (Columbus). Cable TV. Telephone companies: General Telephone, Southwestern Bell, Colorado Valley Telephone Coop. and Industry Telephone. **TRANSPORTATION** Total public road mileage: 990. In 1982 there were 20,207 registered vehicles and 494 reported traffic accidents including 25 fatalities. Intercity bus service is available. Motor freight: 15 local and intrastate carriers. Rail: the Sunset Limited provides passenger service on the Amtrak Route. Five main and seven branch lines carry freight through the county. Three of the main lines carry annually 20 to 30 million tons of freight each one carries 10 to 20 and one carries one to five million tons. One of the branch lines carries annually 20 to 30 million tons of freight, four carry one to five each and two carry less than one million each. Aircraft: 41 are registered in the county. Airports: Robert E. Wells Airport at Columbus is a basic utility airport providing general aviation service. It serves as a base for 15 aircraft. Eagle Lake Municipal Airport and Renz Ranch Airport are at Eagle Lake.

COMMUNITY SERVICES

EDUCATION Three school districts with five elementary, three middle and three high schools. The average daily attendance in 1981-82 was 3,143, with expenditures per pupil of $2,562 including 211 classroom teachers with an average annual salary of $16,479. Fifty-four percent of the 256 high school graduates planned to attend college. In 1982-83, 54% of the students were White, 23% Hispanic and 23% Black. Sports championships: 1983 AAA Girls' Golf Singles and Team, Columbus H.S.. Private schools: total enrollment of 348 students enrolled in three elementary schools. **PUBLIC LIBRARIES** Nesbitt Memorial Library (Columbus): 12,388 volumes. Eula and David Winterman Library (Eagle Lake): 11,000 volumes. Veterans Memorial Library (Garwood): 5,977 volumes. Sheridan Library. Weimar Public Library: 13,625. **CHILD CARE** 24 day care and six twenty-four hour care licensed facilities. **HEALTH CARE** 21 physicians and seven dentists. Hospitals: three with a combined capacity of 113. Ambulance services: two commercial, one volunteer service, one funeral home and one volunteer fire department service. Mental health: one county clinic. Nursing homes: four nursing homes with a combined capacity of 390 nursing care and 16 personal care residents. The average cost per day for private patients in 1982 was $28.74. **CHURCHES** 46 churches have an estimated combined membership of 12,455. The largest denominations are Catholic, Southern Baptist and United Methodist. **SOCIAL SERVICES** In fiscal year 1983 a total of $792,906 in food stamps was distributed, with an average of 1,682 persons receiving food stamps each month. Aid to Families with Dependent Children (AFDC) totaled $187,899, with an average of 133 families receiving AFDC each month. Medical assistance benefits for the aged and disabled of $2,373,786 and for families and children of $303,176 brought the county benefit total to $3,657,766. **FIRE PROTECTION** Seven volunteer fire departments. **LAW ENFORCEMENT** The County Sheriff has 21 commissioned officers. Three police departments have a combined force of 21. **CRIME** 48 violent crimes (murder, forcible rape, robbery and aggravated assault) and 380 nonviolent crimes (burglary, larceny-theft and motor vehicle theft) were reported in 1982. **JUDICIAL SYSTEM** Two District Courts and Judges, one County Court and Judge and seven Justices of the Peace. In the District Courts a total of 573 cases were pending on 1/1/82, 485 new cases were filed and 446 cases were disposed of during the year leaving 612 cases pending on 12/31/82. There were 277 criminal cases on the docket, 31 convictions, six persons committed to prison and one committed to jail and 188 cases left pending. In the County Court 407 cases were pending on 1/1/82, 242 new cases were filed and 188 cases were disposed of during the year leaving 461 cases pending on 12/31/82. There were 524 criminal cases on the docket, 71 convictions and 370 cases left pending. **JAILS** One jail, capacity 19. **ATTORNEYS AT LAW** 18. **UTILITIES** 58% of the residents are connected to a public or privately owned water system and 53% are connected to a public sewer system. Natural gas is distributed to the county by Southwest Gas Distributors, Inc. Electricity is distributed to the city of Weimar by Weimar Electric Utilities and to the rest of the county by Central Power and Light Co., Cochran Power and Light, Bluebonnet Electric Coop., Inc., San Bernard Electric Coop., Inc., and Fayette Electric Coop., Inc. and is generated primarily by gas, oil and coal. The typical residential electric bill is $162.15 per month for an all-electric house using 2,500 kwh. **TAXES** The county has ten units with taxing authority: four school districts, three cities, one county, and two special districts.

RECREATION/ENTERTAINMENT

NATIONAL REGISTER OF HISTORIC PLACES Columbus: Colorado County Courthouse, Colorado County Courthouse District, Old Stafford Ranch and Stafford Opera House. Columbus vicinity: Zimmberscheidt—Leyendecker House. **MUNICIPAL PARKS** 243 acres in five municipal parks. These parks contain three playgrounds, three golf courses, four baseball and softball fields, two tennis courts and two swimming pools. **BOATING/FISHING** Lakes/reservoirs: Eagle (1,000 acres), Engstrom (75 acres), Kallina (78 acres) and Sheridan (47 acres). Major rivers: Colorado and San Bernard. Primary streams: Bucksnag, Pinoak and Crooked. **WILDLIFE REFUGES** Attwater Prairie Chicken National Wildlife Refuge covers 2,109 acres. **HUNTING** Fall and winter seasons on deer. No closed season on nutria, coyote, bobcat and squirrel. Winter season on quail, muskrat, beaver, otter, opossum, mink, ring-tailed cat, badger, fox, raccoon, skunk and civet cat. In 1983 sandhill crane, duck, coot, geese, woodcock and jacksnipe seasons occurred during the winter months. Teal duck, rail and gallinule seasons occurred in the fall. Mourning dove season occurred intermittently during the fall and winter months. **MUSEUMS** Columbus: Koliba Home Museum, Tate-Senftenberg-Brandon House and Alley Log Cabin. **THEATERS** Columbus: Stafford Opera House. **OTHER** Eagle Lake: Attwater Prairie Chicken Refuge. **SPECIAL EVENTS** Magnolia Homes Tours, Columbus, May; July 4th Celebration, Columbus, July; Colorado County Fair, Columbus, September.

COMMUNITIES

COUNTY SEAT Columbus, County Courthouse, 78934; County Clerk's Office, 409/732-2155. **INCORPORATED COMMUNITIES** (1980 population and ZIP Code) Columbus (3,923) 78934, Eagle Lake (3,921) 77434, Weimar (2,128) 78962. **UNINCORPORATED COMMUNITIES** (and ZIP Code) Alleyton 78935, Altair 77412, Bernardo 78933, Borden 78962, Chesterville 77435 (also in Wharton Co.), Frelsburg 78950, Garwood 77442, Glidden 78943, Hillcrest 78934, Mentz 78935, Nada 77460, Oakland 78951, Provident City 77455, Ramsey 78935, Rock Island 77470, Sheridan 77475, Slutter 78935. **FOR ADDITIONAL LOCAL INFORMATION** Columbus Chamber of Commerce, P.O. Box 343, Columbus, 78934, 409/732-5881, Eagle Lake Chamber of commerce, P.O. Box 216, Eagle Lake, 77434, 409/234-2780, Weimar Chamber of Commerce, P.O. Box 90, Weimar, 78962, 409/725-8561.

COMAL (C30)

THE LAND

North of San Antonio on Interstate 35 in the Edwards Plateau Region, Comal County covers 555 square miles. The elevation ranges from 675 to 1,500 feet with the Balcones Escarpment dividing the county into a high northern and a lower southern

COMAL (continued)

section. Water flowing from the base of the escarpment forms the Comal River. Along the southeast border are cracking, clayey soils with some loamy surfaces. The rest of the county has loamy soils with some clayey subsoils. Along the southeast border of the county the vegetation is of the Blackland Prairie vegetation area consisting of tall grasses. The rest of the county is in the Edwards Plateau vegetation area consisting of tall and mid grasses, live oak, juniper and some mesquite trees. Between 11 and 20% of the land in the county is considered prime farmland. **CLIMATE** Subtropical moist. The average annual temperature is 69°F. Temperatures in January range from an average low of 36° to an average high of 61°F and in July range from 73° to 95°F. The average annual precipitation is 33 inches, with an average relative humidity of 83% at 6 A.M. and 53% at 6 P.M. Snow seldom accumulates. The growing season averages 265 days per year, with the last freeze the first of March and the first freeze in late November. The sun shines during the year on the average 67% of the daylight hours.

THE PEOPLE
The 1982 estimated population of 39,400 indicates a continued growth. Comal's population growth rate between 1970 and 1980 was one of the highest in the state, with rural areas increasing 121% and urban areas increasing 26%. The age groups with the largest gains were ages 62 to over and ages 20 to 34, raising the median age from 31 in 1970 to 34 in 1980. The largest ancestry groups are persons of German descent (36%), Hispanic (24%) and persons of English descent (21%). **REGISTERED VOTERS** As of November 2, 1982 there were 19,191 registered voters (0.3% of the state total). The 1982 general election had a 54% voter turnout, compared to a 75% turnout in the 1980 general election. In the 1982 primary 38% voted Democratic and 62% Republican, with 5,030 votes cast.

THE ECONOMY
AGRICULTURE In 1982, 82% of the land was in farms and ranches, with 8% of the farmland under cultivation. Comal ranked 228th in the state in highest agricultural receipts, with 87% from livestock and livestock products. Overgrazing, undesirable brush and weeds, water erosion flooding and water conservation are the current conservation problems. Primary crops: hay, sorghum, oats and wheat. Primary vegetables: potatoes and sweet potatoes. Primary fruits and nuts: pecans. Primary livestock and products: cattle, sheep, wool, angora goats, mohair and hogs. **BUSINESS** Total number of business establishments in the county: 884. Retail sales during the first quarter of 1984 increased 23%. In 1980, 10% of the labor force were self-employed, 18% were employed in professional or related services, 19% in manufacturing, 21% in wholesale and retail trade, 12% in construction, 35% were employed in other counties and there were 4,234 retired workers. The industries with the most employment: limestone quarrying, textile mills, road construction, tourism and the manufacture of women's clothing, household furniture, plastic products, concrete products and fabricated metal products. The nonfarm earnings in 1981 totaled $393,995,000. The retired workers received an average monthly Social Security payment of $317. **FINANCE** On June 30, 1983, four commercial banks had total deposits of $181,695,000 and total assets of $198,471,000. On December 31, 1982 one state savings and loan association, one federal association, one state branch and one federal branch had combined assets of $210,492,179. **HOUSING** Average value of homes in 1980: $42,700. Permits for new, privately owned housing units increased in 1982: 747 permits were issued with a total construction cost of $33,471,329. Of those permits, 439 were for single family

houses. Housing permits in New Braunfels increased from 150 in 1981 to 446 in 1982. Between 1970 and 1980 the number of housing units increased by 65%. Eighty percent of all units in the county are air-conditioned, 53% are heated by gas and 42% by electricity. **NATURAL RESOURCES** Limestone and dolomite. Current production of other minerals and products includes cement, lime, crushed limestone, perlite, sand and gravel. **TOURISM** Travel expenditures of $35,610,000 in 1982 (an increase of 11% over 1981) generated 878 jobs and $7,107,000 in payroll. Lodging: 15 hotels, motels and tourist courts. **ALCOHOLIC BEVERAGES** Packaged distilled spirits, beer, ale, malt liquor and wine are legal. Sale of mixed beverages is legal in all or part of the county. **FEDERAL EXPENDITURES** The federal government had direct expenditures or obligations of $78,889,000 in the county during fiscal year 1983, including $14,029,000 by the U.S. Department of Defense. In addition, the federal government provided $3,799,000 in grant awards, paid $3,305,000 in salaries and wages, made direct payments to individuals of $71,022,000 including $60,994,000 in retirement and disability payments, awarded $534,000 in procurement contracts and spent $229,000 in other expenditures or obligations. The federal government also provided $26,710,000 in guaranteed loans and insurance.

COMMUNICATION
Newspapers–Daily: New Braunfels Herald-Zeitung, ave. eve. circ. 6,292. Weekly: Times Guardian (Canyon Lake). Radio: KGNB-AM KNBT-FM Stereo (New Braunfels). Cable TV. Telephone companies: General Telephone, Southwestern Bell, Guadalupe Valley Telephone Coop. and San Marcos Telephone. **TRANS-PORTATION** Total public road mileage: 896. In 1982 there were 33,135 registered vehicles and 1,131 reported traffic accidents including 16 fatalities. Taxi cabs: one company in New Braunfels. Intercity bus service is available. Motor freight: 11 local and intra-state carriers. Rail: The Eagle provides passenger service on the Amtrak route. Two main and two branch lines carry freight through the county. The two main lines carry annually 10 to 20 million tons of freight each and the two branch lines carry one to five million tons each. Aircraft: 36 are registered in the county. Airports: New Braunfels Municipal Airport is a basic transportation airport providing general aviation service. It serves as a base for 40 aircraft.

COMMUNITY SERVICES
EDUCATION Two school districts with eight elementary, four middle, three high schools and one special education. The average daily attendance in 1981-82 was 7,459, with expenditures per pupil of $2,525 including 495 classroom teachers with an average annual salary of $17,258. Forty-seven percent of the 592 high school graduates planned to attend college. In 1982-83, 68% of the students were White, 31% Hispanic, 1% Black and 0.1% Asian. Private schools: 216 enrolled in one elementary school. Vocational education: New Braunfels School of Vocational Nursing (New Braunfels). **PUBLIC LIBRARIES** The Preston Memorial Library (Canyon Lake): 15,176 volumes. Dittlinger Memorial Library (New Braunfels): 40,792 volumes. **CHILD CARE** 42 day care and nine twenty-four hour care licensed facilities. **HEALTH CARE** 51 physicians and 29 dentists. Hospitals: one with a capacity of 86. Ambulance services: one volunteer service, one fire department and one volunteer fire department service. Mental health: one county clinic and one center with a combined capacity of 160. Nursing homes: three nursing homes with a combined capacity of 467 nursing care residents. The average cost per day for private patients in 1982 was $34.85. **CHURCHES** 34 churches have an estimated combined membership of 22,236. The largest denominations are Catholic, Southern Baptist and United Church of Christ. **SOCIAL SERVICES** In fiscal year 1983 a

total of $790,824 in food stamps was distributed, with an average of 1,714 persons receiving food stamps each month. Aid to Families with Dependent Children (AFDC) totaled $190,672, with an average of 129 families receiving AFDC each month. Medical assistance benefits for the aged and disabled of $4,580,835 and for families and children of $256,816 brought the county benefit total to $5,819,146. **FIRE PROTECTION** One partly paid and seven volunteer fire departments. **LAW ENFORCEMENT** The County Sheriff has 72 commissioned officers. Two police departments have a combined force of 48. **CRIME** 121 violent crimes (murder, forcible rape, robbery and aggravated assault) and 1,373 nonviolent crimes (burglary, larceny-theft and motor vehicle theft) were reported in 1982. **JUDICIAL SYSTEM** Three District Courts and Judges, two County Courts and Judges and four Justices of the Peace. In the District Courts a total of 791 cases were pending on 1/1/82, 785 new cases were filed and 709 cases were disposed of during the year leaving 867 cases pending on 12/31/82. There were 344 criminal cases on the docket, 129 convictions, 34 persons committed to prison and nine committed to jail and 145 cases left pending. In the County Courts 1,533 cases were pending on 1/1/82, 2,068 new cases were filed and 1,786 cases were disosed of during the year leaving 1,815 cases pending on 12/31/82. There were 2,743 criminal cases on the docket, 904 convictions, 159 persons committed to jail, and 1,265 cases left pending. **JAILS** One jail, capacity 28. New jail under construction, capacity 97. **ATTORNEYS AT LAW** 66. **UTILITIES** 82% of the residents are connected to a public or privately owned water system and 58% are connected to a public sewer system. Natural gas is distributed to the county by Entex Inc. The average annual residential bill for natural gas in 1982 for the Entex distribution system was $390.31, an increase of 26% over 1981. Electricity is distributed to the city of New Braunfels by New Braunfels Utilities and to the rest of the county by San Antonio City Public Service Board and Pedernales Electric Coop., Inc. and is generated primarily by oil, water and coal. The typical residential electric bill is $124.98 per month for an all-electric house using 2,500 kwh. **TAXES** The county has 10 units with taxing authority: two school districts, three cities, one county and four special districts.

RECREATION/ENTERTAINMENT
NATIONAL REGISTER OF HISTORIC PLACES Gruene: Gruene Historic District. New Braunfels: Guadalupe-Schmitz Hotel, Stephen Klein House, Lindheimer House, First Protestant Church and the Andreas Breustedt House. **STATE** Guadalupe River State Park covers 1,900 acres with facilities which include camping and trailer sites as well as fishing areas for swimming, fishing and hiking on nature trails. **COUNTY/ MUNICIPAL PARKS** 368 acres in eight county and 12 municipal parks. These parks contain seven playgrounds, one golf course, eight football and soccer fields, 11 baseball and softball fields, four tennis courts, eight multi-use courts, two swimming pools, four beaches and eight boat ramps. **SCENIC DRIVES** The Texas Hill Country Trail runs through this county. This trail winds through a scenic region of South-Central Texas, spanning a vast ranching area abundant with wildlife in a landscape of deeply-sculptured valleys and hills. **BOATING/FISHING** Lakes/reservoirs: Canyon (8,240 acres), Comal Creek Soil Conservation Service Lake 4 (14 acres), Shaefer Koeter Lake #2 (19 acres) and York Creek Soil Conservation Service Lake 4 (13 acres). Major rivers: Guadalupe and Comal. Primary streams: Bear, Rebecca, Mesquite and Cibolo. **HUNTING** Fall and winter seasons on deer and javelina. No closed season on coyote, bobcat and squirrel. Fall, winter and spring seasons on turkey. Winter seasons on muskrat, beaver, opossum, ring-tailed cat, badger, fox, weasel, raccoon, skunk and civet cat. In 1983 sandhill crane, duck, coot, geese, woodcock and jacksnipe seasons occurred during the winter months. Teal duck, rail and gallinule seasons occurred in the fall. Mourning dove season occurred intermittently during the fall and winter months with a fall season on white-winged dove. **MUSEUMS** New Braunfels: Sophienburg Memorial Museum and Lindheimer Home. **ZOO** New Braunfels: Otto M. Locke Nursery. **SPECIAL EVENTS** Texas Junior Miss Pageant, New Braunfels, January; Fair at Lyonesse, New Braunfels, June/July; Independence Day Parade, New Braunfels, July; Wurstfest, New Braunfels, November; March-Und-Wandergruppe Walkfest, New Braunfels, November; and Comal County Fair, New Braunfels, variable.

COMMUNITIES
COUNTY SEAT New Braunfels, County Courthouse, 78130; County Clerk's Office, 512/625-4121. **INCORPORATED COMMUNITIES** (1980 population and ZIP Code) Garden Ridge (647) 78218, New Braunfels (22,402: 22,375 in Comal Co. and 27 in Guadalupe Co.) 78130, Schertz (7,262: 2 in Bexar Co., 26 in Comal Co. and 7,234 in Guadalupe Co.) 78154 and Selma (528: 88 in Comal Co., 157 in Guadalupe Co. and 283 in Bexar Co.) 78209. **UNINCORPORATED COMMUNITIES** (and ZIP Code) Bracken 78218, Bulverde 78163, Canyon Lake (Canyon City) 78130, Comal 78130, Dittlinger 78130, Fischer 78623, Gruene 78130, Hunter 78130, Mission Valley 78130, Sattler 78623, Selma (528: 88 in Comal Co., 157 in Guadalupe Co. and 283 in Bexar Co.) 78209, Solms 78130, Spring Branch 78070 and Startzville 78130. **FOR ADDITIONAL LOCAL INFORMATION** Greater New Braunfels Chamber of Commerce, P.O. Box 180, New Braunfels, 78130, 512/625-2385.

COMANCHE (P83)

THE LAND
Southwest of Fort Worth on U.S. Highway 67/377 in the Cross Timbers Region, Comanche County covers 930 square miles of level to partly broken terrain. The elevation ranges from 1,200 to 1,400 feet. In the southeast corner and northwest one-third of the county there are nearly level to undulating, light-colored, medium to slightly acid soils with sandy surface layers and mottled gray and red, to yellow cracking, clayey subsoils. The rest of the county has undulating to hilly alkaline, loamy soils over limestone. The county is in the Cross Timbers and Prairies vegetation region consisting of post oak and tall grass savannah in the northwestern one-third, while the rest of the county has tall and mid grasses, live oak, juniper and some mesquite trees. Between 11 and 20% of the land in the county is considered prime farmland. **CLIMATE** Subtropical subhumid with wide-ranging daily temperature changes. The average annual temperature is 64°F. Temperatures in January range from an average low of 30° to an average high of 56°F and in July range from 72° to 96°F. The average annual precipitation is 28 inches, with an average relative humidity of 77% at 6 A.M. and 46% at 6 P.M. The average annual snowfall is four inches. The growing season averages 238 days per year, with the last freeze in late March and the first freeze in late November. The sun shines during the year on the average 68% of the daylight hours.

THE PEOPLE
Comanche County ranks 43rd among all U.S. counties in the highest percent of population aged 65 and over. The 1982 estimated population of 12,900 indicates a continuation of the small growth in population which began in the 1970s, reversing a steady population decline. The percent of growth increased from 0.3% between 1960 and 1970 to 6% between 1970 and 1980. The age group with the largest gain was ages 25 to 39, with slight losses occurring among ages five to 14. Although the median

COMANCHE (continued)

age lowered from 43 in 1970 to 40 in 1980, the population remained older than average. The largest ancestry groups are persons of English descent (31%) and those of Irish descent (22%). **REGISTERED VOTERS** As of November 2, 1982 there were 7,050 registered voters (0.1% of the state total). The 1982 general election had a 54% voter turnout, compared to a 66% turnout in the 1980 general election. In the 1982 primary 99% voted Democratic and 1% Republican, with 3,290 votes cast.

THE ECONOMY

AGRICULTURE Diversified products. In 1982, 88% of the land was in farms and ranches, with 26% of the farmland under cultivation and 15% irrigated. Comanche County ranked 27th in the state in highest agricultural receipts, with 80% from livestock and livestock products. Overgrazing, undesirable brush and weeds, water and wind erosion and inefficient tillage systems are the current conservation problems. Primary crops: second in the state for both peanuts and rye. Hay, oats, wheat and sorghum. Primary vegetables: watermelons. Primary fruits and nuts: a leader in the state for pears, fifth for peaches and eighth for pecans. Primary livestock and products: fourth in the state for milk production. Cattle, sheep, wool, angora goats, mohair and hogs. **BUSINESS** Total number of business establishments in the county: 266. Retail sales during the first quarter of 1984 were up 23%, with an increase of 29% in Comanche and a decrease of 21% in Gustine. In 1980, 22% of the labor force were self-employed, 18% were employed in professional or related services, 13% in manufacturing, 21% in wholesale and retail trade, 23% in agriculture, forestry, fisheries and mining, 17% were employed in other counties and there were 1,958 retired workers. The industries with the most employment: agribusiness and the manufacture of prepared agricultural feeds and men and women's belts. The nonfarm earnings in 1981 totaled $103,299,000. The retired workers received an average monthly Social Security payment of $277. **FINANCE** On June 30, 1983, four commercial banks had total deposits of $118,673,000 and total assets of $131,513,000. There are two state savings and loan association branches and one credit union in the county. **HOUSING** Average value of homes in 1980: $19,900. Permits for new, privately owned housing units increased in 1982: 22 permits were issued with a total construction cost of $704,650. Of those permits, 13 were for single family houses. Between 1970 and 1980 the number of housing units increased by 18%. Seventy-two percent of all units in the county are air-conditioned, 82% are heated by gas and 13% by electricity. **NATURAL RESOURCES** Limestone, industrial sand, oil, gas, dolomite and bituminous coal. In 1982 a total of 2,373,942 thousand cubic feet of gas well gas, 6,975 barrels of condensate, 83,357 barrels of crude oil and 483,589 thousand cubic feet of casinghead gas were produced. Current production of other minerals and products includes brick, clay, terrazzo, limestone, sand and gravel. **TOURISM** Travel expenditures of $2,955,000 in 1982 (an increase of 13% over 1981) generated 62 jobs and $531,000 in payroll. **ALCOHOLIC BEVERAGES** Packaged distilled spirits, beer, ale, malt liquor and wine are legal in parts of the county. **FEDERAL EXPENDITURES** The federal government had direct expenditures or obligations of $29,295,000 in the county during fiscal year 1983, including $1,315,000 by the U.S. Department of Defense. In addition, the federal government provided $965,000 in grant awards, paid $1,201,000 in salaries and wages, made direct payments to individuals of $25,619,000 including $17,692,000 in retirement and disability payments, awarded $729,000 in procurement contracts and spent $782,000 in other expenditures or obligations. The federal government also provided $72,000 in direct loans and $10,140,000 in guaranteed loans and insurance.

COMMUNICATION

Newspapers–Weekly: Comanche Chief and the De Leon Free Press. Radio: KCOM-AM (Comanche). Cable TV. Telephone companies: Continental Telephone, General Telephone, United Telephone, Alenco Communications, Central Texas Telephone Coop. and Comanche County Telephone. **TRANSPORTATION** Total public road mileage: 1,263. In 1982 there were 12,583 registered vehicles and 285 reported traffic accidents including two fatalities. Intercity bus service is available. Motor freight: two carriers. Rail: one main line carries annually 10 to 20 million tons of freight through the county. Aircraft: 13 are registered in the county. Airports: Comanche County-City Airport at Comanche is a general utility airport providing general aviation service. It serves as a base for 14 aircraft. Also serving this area is De Leon Municipal Airport.

COMMUNITY SERVICES

EDUCATION Four school districts with four elementary, one middle and four high schools. The average daily attendance in 1981-82 was 2,100, with expenditures per pupil of $1,933 including 139 classroom teachers with an average annual salary of $15,034. Forty-four percent of the 139 high school graduates planned to attend college. In 1982-83, 77% of the students were White, 22% Hispanic, 0.8% Black and 0.1% American Indian. **PUBLIC LIBRARIES** Comanche Public Library: 18,530 volumes. De Leon Public Library: 6,017 volumes. **CHILD CARE** Nine day care licensed facilities. **HEALTH CARE** Nine physicians and six dentists. Hospitals: two with a combined capacity of 65. Ambulance services: one county and one hospital-based service. Mental health: one clinic. Nursing homes: three nursing homes with a combined capacity of 321 nursing care residents. The average cost per day for private patients in 1982 was $28.86. **CHURCHES** 50 churches have an estimated combined membership of 7,970. The largest denominations are Southern Baptist, United Methodist and Churches of Christ. **SOCIAL SERVICES** In fiscal year 1983 a total of $380,864 in food stamps was distributed, with an average of 855 persons receiving food stamps each month. Aid to Families with Dependent Children (AFDC) totaled $41,279, with an average of 30 families receiving AFDC each month. Medical assistance benefits for the aged and disabled of $1,985,839 and for families and children of $113,557 brought the county benefit total to $2,521,539. **FIRE PROTECTION** Five volunteer fire departments. **LAW ENFORCEMENT** The County Sheriff has seven commissioned officers. Two police departments have a combined force of 14. **CRIME** 12 violent crimes (murder, forcible rape, robbery and aggravated assault) and 170 nonviolent crimes (burglary, larceny-theft and motor vehicle theft) were reported in 1982. **JUDICIAL SYSTEM** One District Court and Judge, one County Court and Judge and three Justices of the Peace. In the District Court a total of 285 cases were pending on 1/1/82, 469 new cases were filed and 363 cases were disposed of during the year leaving 391 cases pending on 12/31/82. There were 167 criminal cases on the docket, 30 convictions, 12 persons committed to prison, and 70 cases left pending. In the County Court 442 cases were pending on 1/1/82, 566 new cases were filed and 588 cases were disposed of during the year leaving 420 cases pending on 12/31/82. There were 853 criminal cases on the docket, 164 convictions, four persons committed to jail, and 284 cases left pending. **JAILS** One jail, capacity 21. **ATTORNEYS AT LAW** 12. **UTILITIES** 57% of the residents are connected to a public or privately owned water system and 53% are connected to a public sewer system. Natural gas is distributed to the county by Lone Star Gas Co., Division of Enserch. The average annual residential bill for natural gas in 1982 for the Lone Star distribution system was $405.91, an increase of 35% over 1981. Electricity is distributed to the county by Texas Power and Light Co., Texas-New Mexico Power Co.,

Comanche Co. Electric Coop., Inc., Erath Co. Electric Coop., Assn. and Hamilton Co. Electric Coop., Inc. and is generated primarily by gas, oil and coal. The typical residential electric bill is $165.24 per month for an all-electric house using 2,500 kwh. **TAXES** The county has 11 units with taxing authority: four school districts, three cities, one county and three special districts.

RECREATION/ENTERTAINMENT
COUNTY/MUNICIPAL PARKS 39 acres in two municipal parks. These parks contain two playgrounds, two swimming pools and one boat ramp. Developed campsite: one. **SCENIC DRIVES** The Texas Forts Trail runs through this county. This trail leads to eight of the famous frontier forts of West Central Texas and an ancient presidio of the Spanish colonial period. **BOATING/FISHING** Lakes/reservoirs: Comanche (273 acres), Eanes (78 acres), Gibson (25 acres), Guilder (25 acres), Nabors (38 acres), Proctor (4,610 acres), Rush Creek Soil Conservation Service Lakes 2, 4, 9, 10, 11, 12 and 13 (185 acres) and Wolfe Creek Soil Conservation Service Lake 1 (30 acres). Major rivers: Leon and South Leon. Primary streams: Mercer, Sipe Spring, Fade, Copperas, Martins, Jimmys, Rabbit and Sweetwater. **HUNTING** Fall and winter seasons on deer. No closed season on coyote, bobcat and squirrel. Winter season on quail, muskrat, beaver, opossum, ring-tailed cat, badger, fox, weasel, raccoon, skunk and civet cat. Fall, winter and spring seasons on turkey. In 1983 duck, coot, geese, woodcock and jacksnipe seasons occurred during the winter months. Teal duck, rail and gallinule seasons occurred in the fall. Mourning dove season occurred intermittently during the fall and winter months. **MUSEUMS** Comanche: Burks Museum and Comanche County Historical Museum. **SPECIAL EVENTS** Flower Show, Comanche, April; Indian Pow Wow, Comanche, June; Rodeo, Comanche, June; Peach and Melon Festival, De Leon, July; Tomato and Flower Show, Comanche, July; County Fair, Comanche, August; and Airshow, Comanche, August.

COMMUNITIES
COUNTY SEAT Comanche, County Courthouse, 76442; County Clerk's Office, 915/356-2655. **INCORPORATED COMMUNITIES** (1980 population and ZIP Code) Comanche, (4,075) 76442, De Leon (2,478) 76444 and Gustine (416) 76455. **UNINCORPORATED COMMUNITIES** (and ZIP Code) Beattie 76442, Comyn 76444, Cross Roads 76474, Democrat 76442, Downing 76442, Duster 76444, Energy 76452, Hasse 76456, Lamkin 76460, Mercers Gap 76442, Newburg 76442, Pettit 76455, Proctor 76468, Rucker 76444, Sidney 76474, Siloam 76455, Sipe Springs 76442, Sweetwater 76442 and Vandyke 76442. **FOR ADDITIONAL LOCAL INFORMATION** Comanche Chamber of Commerce, P.O. Box 65, 110 W. Central Ave., Comanche, 76442, 915/356-3233.

CONCHO (P90)

THE LAND
East of San Angelo on U.S. Highways 83 and 87 in the Edwards Plateau Region, Concho County covers 992 square miles with the elevation ranging from 1,600 to 2,100 ft. The county is divided into a northern section of rolling land and a southern section which is rough and broken. On one part of the cliffs of the Concho River are ancient Indian pictographs. In the northwest corner of the county are mostly deep soils with loamy surface layers and clayey subsoils. The rest of the county has loamy soils over limestone. Bedrock is found at 10 to 40 inches in some areas. In the northwest corner on the Rolling Plains the vegetation is short and mid grasses, mesquite and cacti. The rest of the county is the Edwards Plateau vegetation area with short and mid grasses,

tall grasses, live oak and some mesquite and juniper trees. Between 11 and 20% of the land in the county is considered prime farmland. **CLIMATE** Mild and dry. The average annual temperature is 65°F. Temperatures in January range from an average low of 33° to an average high of 61°F and in July range from 70° to 97°F. The average annual precipitation is 23 inches, with an average relative humidity of 76% at 6 A.M. and 43% at 6 P.M. The average annual snowfall is three inches. The growing season averages 228 days per year, with the last freeze in late March and the first freeze near November 12th. The sun shines during the year on the average 67% of the daylight hours.

THE PEOPLE
The 1982 estimated population of 3,000 indicates a slight increase over the 1980 population. The population continuously declined from 7,645 in 1930 to 2,915 in 1980, with a 20% decrease between 1960 and 1970. The age group with the largest decrease was ages 45 to 54. The high median age lowered from 43 in 1970 to 37 in 1980. The majority of the residents live in rural areas. The largest ancestry groups are Hispanic (28%), persons of Irish descent (21%), those of English descent (19%) and those of German descent (19%). **REGISTERED VOTERS** As of November 2, 1982 there were 1,887 registered voters (0.02% of the state total). The 1982 general election had a 57% voter turnout, compared to a 72% turnout in the 1980 general election. In the 1982 primary 84% voted Democratic and 16% Republican, with 202 votes cast.

THE ECONOMY
AGRICULTURE Sheep and wheat area. In 1982, 95% of the land was in farms and ranches, with 20% of the farmland under cultivation and 7% irrigated. Concho ranked 161st in the state in highest agricultural receipts, with 57% from crops. Overgrazing, undesirable brush and weeds, water erosion, inefficient irrigation systems, moisture conservation and salinity are the current conservation problems. Primary crops: wheat, sorghum, cotton and oats. Primary fruits and nuts: pecans. Primary livestock and products: fourth in the state for both sheep and wool production. Cattle, angora goats, mohair and hogs. **BUSINESS** Total number of business establishments in the county: 55. Retail sales during the first quarter of 1984 increased 9%. In 1980, 30% of the labor force were self-employed, 19% were employed in professional or related services, 9% in manufacturing, 17% in wholesale and retail trade, 29% in agriculture, forestry, fisheries and mining, 29% were employed in other counties and there were 415 retired workers. The industry with the most employment is agribusiness. The nonfarm earnings in 1981 totaled $18,187,000. The retired workers received an average monthly Social Security payment of $289. **FINANCE** On June 30, 1983, two commercial banks had total deposits of $23,511,000 and total assets of $26,177,000. There is one state savings and loan association branch in the county. **HOUSING** Average value of homes in 1980: $19,100. Between 1970 and 1980 the number of housing units increased by 9%. Seventy percent of all units in the county are air-conditioned, 82% are heated by gas and 12% by electricity. **NATURAL RESOURCES** Caliche, limestone, oil, gas, dolomite and bituminous coal. In 1982 a total of 1,982,444 thousand cubic feet of gas well gas, 11,533 barrels of condensate, 218,748 barrels of crude oil and 252,126 thousand cubic feet of casinghead gas were produced. **TOURISM** Travel expenditures of $348,000 in 1982 (an increase of 10% over 1981) generated 5 jobs and $46,000 in payroll. **ALCOHOLIC BEVERAGES** Only 4% beer is legal in parts of the county. **FEDERAL EXPENDITURES** The federal government had direct expenditures or obligations of $8,833,000 in the county during fiscal year 1983, including $174,000 by the U.S. Department of Defense. In addition, the federal government provided $48,000 in grant awards, paid $370,000 in salaries and wages, made direct payments to indi-

CONCHO (continued)

viduals of $5,579,000 including $3,652,000 in retirement and disability payments, awarded $21,000 in procurement contracts and spent $2,814,000 in other expenditures or obligations. The federal government also provided $1,997,000 in direct loans and $1,784,000 in guaranteed loans and insurance.

COMMUNICATION

Newspapers–Weekly: The Eden Echo and The Concho-Herald (Paint Rock). Cable TV. Telephone companies: General Telephone, Central Texas Telephone Coop. and Coleman County Telephone Coop. **TRANSPORTATION** Total public road mileage: 651. In 1982 there were 3,218 registered vehicles and 84 reported traffic accidents. Intercity bus service is available. Motor freight: two carriers. Aircraft: four are registered in the county.

COMMUNITY SERVICES

EDUCATION Two school districts with two elementary and two high schools. The average daily attendance in 1981-82 was 565, with expenditures per pupil of $2,804 including 40 classroom teachers with an average annual salary of $14,049. Fifty-one percent of the 35 high school graduates planned to attend college. In 1982-83, 56% of the students were White and 44% Hispanic. **PUBLIC LIBRARIES** Eden Library. Paint Rock Library. **CHILD CARE** Six day care licensed facilities. **HEALTH CARE** Two physicians. Hospitals: one with a capacity of 20. Ambulance services: one volunteer fire department service. Nursing homes: one nursing home has a capacity of 82 nursing care residents. The average cost per day for private patients in 1982 was $35.58. **CHURCHES** 17 churches have an estimated combined membership of 1,534. The largest denominations are Southern Baptist, United Methodist and Churches of Christ. **SOCIAL SERVICES** In fiscal year 1983 a total of $93,775 in food stamps was distributed, with an average of 201 persons receiving food stamps each month. Aid to Families with Dependent Children (AFDC) totaled $7,601, with an average of six families receiving AFDC each month. Medical assistance benefits for the aged and disabled of $361,987 and for families and children of $18,637 brought the county benefit total to $482,000. **FIRE PROTECTION** Five volunteer fire departments. **LAW ENFORCEMENT** The County Sheriff has three commissioned officers. One police department has a force of one. **CRIME** Five violent crimes (murder, forcible rape, robbery and aggravated assault) and 26 nonviolent crimes (burglary, larceny-theft and motor vehicle theft) were reported in 1982. **JUDICIAL SYSTEM** Two District Courts and Judges, one County Court and Judge and two Justices of the Peace. In the District Courts a total of 50 cases were pending on 1/1/82, 76 new cases were filed and 35 cases were disposed of during the year leaving 91 cases pending on 12/31/82. There were 22 criminal cases on the docket, eight convictions, one person committed to prison and, 14 cases left pending. In the County Court 36 cases were pending on 1/1/82, 89 new cases were filed and 65 cases were disposed of during the year leaving 60 cases pending on 12/31/82. There were 120 criminal cases on the docket, 31 convictions, one person committed to jail, and 57 cases left pending. **ATTORNEYS AT LAW** Two. **UTILITIES** 69% of the residents are connected to a public or privately owned water system and 26% are connected to a public sewer system. Natural gas is distributed to the county by Lone Star Gas Co., Division of Enserch. The average annual residential bill for natural gas in 1982 for the Lone Star distribution system was $405.91, an increase of 35% over 1981. Electricity is distributed to the county by West Texas Utilities, Coleman Co. Electric Coop., Inc. Concho Valley Electric Coop., Inc., McCulloch Co. Electric Coop., Inc. and Southwest Texas Electric Coop., Inc. and is generated primarily by gas and oil. **TAXES** The county has nine units with taxing authority: three school districts, two cities, one county, one hospital district and two special districts.

RECREATION/ENTERTAINMENT

NATIONAL REGISTER OF HISTORIC PLACES Paint Rock: Concho County Courthouse and Paint Rock Pictographs. Salt Gap vicinity: The Bishop Site. **MUNICIPAL PARKS** 31 acres in six municipal parks. These parks contain two playgrounds, two football and soccer fields, three baseball and softball fields, one multi-use court, one swimming pool and one beach. Developed campsites: five. **BOATING/FISHING** Lakes/reservoirs: Allison (113 acres), Brady Creek Soil Conservation Service Lakes 20, 21, 28 and 32 (55 acres) and Locket (28 acres). Major rivers: Concho. Primary streams: South Brady, Brady, Fitzgerald, Reubes, Mustang and Kickapoo. **HUNTING** Fall and winter seasons on deer and javelina. No closed season on coyote, bobcat and squirrel. Winter season on quail, muskrat, beaver, opossum, ring-tailed cat, badger, fox, weasel, raccoon, skunk and civet cat. In 1983 duck, coot, geese, woodcock and jacksnipe seasons occurred during the winter months. Teal duck, rail and gallinule seasons occurred in the fall. Mourning dove season occurred intermittently during the fall and winter months. **SPECIAL EVENTS** Annual Lion's Club Festival, Eden, August; and Concho County Fair, Eden, August/September.

COMMUNITIES

COUNTY SEAT Paint Rock, County Courthouse, 76866; County Clerk's Office, 915/732-4322. **INCORPORATED COMMUNITIES** (1980 population and ZIP Code) Eden (1,294) 76837 and Paint Rock (256) 76866. **UNINCORPORATED COMMUNITIES** (and ZIP Code) Concho 76866, Eola 76937, Henderson Chapel 76866, Lowake 76855, Millersview 76862 and Vick 76955. **FOR ADDITIONAL LOCAL INFORMATION** Eden Chamber of Commerce, P.O. Box 103, Eden, 76837.

COOKE (M2)

THE LAND

North of Fort Worth on Interstate 35 in the Grand Prairie Region, Cooke County covers 893 square miles of gently rolling hills. The elevation ranges from 700 to 1,000 feet. Along the northwest corner, the tip of the southwest corner and running north and south on the eastern border of the county are light-colored, medium to slightly acid soils with loamy surface layers and mottled gray and red, to yellow cracking, clayey subsoils. The rest of the county has loamy alkaline soils over limestone with some moderately deep cracking, clayey subsoils. Bedrock is often reached at 10 to 40 inches. The vegetation of the county is of the Cross Timbers and Prairies area consisting of post oak, tall grass in the southwest corner and eastern border, and tall and mid grasses, live oak, juniper and mesquite trees in the rest of the county. Between 21 and 30% of the land in the county is considered prime farmland. **CLIMATE** Subtropical subhumid with hot summers. The average annual temperature is 64°F. Temperatures in January range from an average low of 29° to an average high of 53°F and in July range from 72° to 97°F. The average annual precipitation is 34 inches, with an average relative humidity of 83% at 6 A.M. and 53% at 6 P.M. The average annual snowfall is six inches. The growing season averages 226 days per year, with the last freeze in late March and the first freeze near the first of November. The sun shines during the year on the average 67% of the daylight hours.

THE PEOPLE

The 1982 estimated population of 28,600 indicates a continuation of a growth rate begun in the 1970s. Rural areas experienced a 41% growth between 1970 and 1980. The age groups with the largest gains were ages 20 to 34 and ages 62 and over. The median age remained unchanged at 31. The largest ancestry groups are persons of German descent (29%), those of English descent (24%) and those of Irish descent (24%). **REGISTERED VOTERS** As of November 2, 1982 there were 14,337 registered voters (0.2% of the state total). The 1982 general election had a 52% voter turnout, compared to a 74% turnout in the 1980 general election. In the 1982 primary 95% voted Democratic and 5% Republican, with 3,395 votes cast.

THE ECONOMY

AGRICULTURE Cattle and wheat area. In 1982, 82% of the land was in farms and ranches, with 25% of the farmland under cultivation and 3% irrigated. Cooke County 72nd in the state in highest agricultural receipts, with 84% from livestock and livestock products. Overgrazing, undesirable brush and weeds, water erosion, inefficient tillage systems and the cultivation of marginal lands are the current conservation problems. Primary crops: fifth in the state for both oats and barley. Wheat, hay and sorghum. Primary vegetables: watermelons. Primary fruits and nuts: peaches and pecans. Primary livestock and products: cattle, milk and hogs. **BUSINESS** Total number of business establishments in the county: 680. Retail sales during the first quarter of 1984 decreased 1%. In 1980, 13% of the labor force were self-employed, 13% were employed in professional or related services, 29% in manufacturing, 19% in wholesale and retail trade, 13% in agriculture, forestry, fisheries and mining, 11% were employed in other counties and there were 2,707 retired workers. The industries with the most employment: oil and gas extraction, agribusiness, iron and steel foundries and the manufacture of women's apparel, mobile homes, paints, aircraft and aircraft parts, plastic products, machine tool accessories and pumps and pumping equipment. The nonfarm earnings in 1981 totaled $286,524,000. The retired workers received an average monthly Social Security payment of $310. **FINANCE** On June 30, 1983, five commercial banks had total deposits of $227,054,000 and total assets of $250,004,000. There are four state savings and loan association branches and four credit unions in the county. **HOUSING** Average value of homes in 1980: $32,500. Permits for new, privately owned housing units increased in 1982: 65 permits were issued with a total construction cost of $2,503,820. Of those permits, 29 were for single family houses. Between 1970 and 1980 the number of housing units increased by 36%. Eighty-three percent of all units in the county are air-conditioned, 73% are heated by gas and 22% by electricity. **NATURAL RESOURCES** Limestone, industrial sand, sand and gravel, oil, gas and bituminous coal. In 1982 a total of 299,711 thousand cubic feet of gas well gas, 2,209 barrels of condensate, 4,285,755 barrels of crude oil and 1,411,579 thousand cubic feet of casinghead gas were produced. Current production of other minerals and products includes crushed limestone, sand and gravel. **TOURISM** Travel expenditures of $9,627,000 in 1982 (an increase of 11% over 1981) generated 237 jobs and $1,896,000 in payroll. **ALCOHOLIC BEVERAGES** Packaged distilled spirits, beer, ale, malt liquor and wine are legal in parts of the county. **FEDERAL EXPENDITURES** The federal government had direct expenditures or obligations of $43,115,000 in the county during fiscal year 1983, including $2,010,000 by the U.S. Department of Defense. In addition, the federal government provided $470,000 in grant awards, paid $1,887,000 in salaries and wages, made direct payments to individuals of $40,102,000 including $30,494,000 in retirement and disability payments, awarded $116,000 in procurement contracts and spent $539,000 in other expenditures or obligations. The federal government also provided $1,069,000 in direct loans and $15,175,000 in guaranteed loans and insurance.

COMMUNICATION

Newspapers–Daily: Gainesville Daily Register, ave. eve. circ. 8,349. Weekly: The Voice (Lindsay) and The Muenster Enterprise. Radio: KGAF-AM and KDNG-FM (Gainesville). Cable TV. Telephone companies: General Telephone, Southwestern Bell, Central Telephone-Midstate, Muenster Telephone and Valley View Telephone. **TRANSPORTATION** Total public road mileage: 1,266. In 1982 there were 26,418 registered vehicles and 859 reported traffic accidents including 10 fatalities. Taxi cabs: one company in Gainesville. Intercity bus service is available. Motor freight: two carriers. Rail: one main line carries annually over 30 million tons of freight through the county. Aircraft: 50 are registered in the county. Airports: Gainesville Municipal Airport is a general utility airport providing general aviation service. It serves as a base for 35 aircraft.

COMMUNITY SERVICES

EDUCATION Eight school districts with 13 elementary, three middle and six high schools. The average daily attendance in 1981-82 was 4,322, with expenditures per pupil of $2,381 including 284 classroom teachers with an average annual salary of $17,061. Sixty-one percent of the 309 high school graduates planned to attend college. In 1982-83, 91% of the students were White, 3% Hispanic, 6% Black, 0.4% Asian and 0.3% American Indian. Private schools: 422 enrolled in two elementary and one high schools. Cooke County College is located in Gainesville. Established in 1924 it is a vocational and two year academic college under state and local control. Enrollment in 1982 was 1,525 with in state undergraduate tuition and fees of $365 per semester. **PUBLIC LIBRARIES** Cooke County Library (Gainesville): 48,200 volumes. Muenster Public Library: 14,796. **CHILD CARE** 24 day care and four twenty-four hour care licensed facilities. **HEALTH CARE** 20 physicians and nine dentists. Hospitals: two with a combined capacity of 132. Ambulance services: one county service. Mental health: one clinic. Nursing homes: four nursing homes with a combined capacity of 316 nursing care residents. The average cost per day for private patients in 1982 was $29.88. **CHURCHES** 61 churches have an estimated combined membership of 17,365. The largest denominations are Southern Baptist, Catholic and United Methodist. **SOCIAL SERVICES** In fiscal year 1983 a total of $853,678 in food stamps was distributed, with an average of 1,729 persons receiving food stamps each month. Aid to Families with Dependent Children (AFDC) totaled $103,656, with an average of 73 families receiving AFDC each month. Medical assistance benefits for the aged and disabled of $1,821,754 and for families and children of $156,902 brought the county benefit total to $2,935,989. **FIRE PROTECTION** One partly paid and six volunteer fire departments. **LAW ENFORCEMENT** The County Sheriff has 24 commissioned officers. Three police departments have a combined force of 40. **CRIME** 54 violent crimes (murder, forcible rape, robbery and aggravated assault) and 811 nonviolent crimes (burglary, larceny-theft and motor vehicle theft) were reported in 1982. **JUDICIAL SYSTEM** One District Court and Judge, one County Court and Judge and five Justices of the Peace. In the District Court a total of 1,058 cases were pending on 1/1/82, 783 new cases were filed and 912 cases were disposed of during the year leaving 929 cases pending on 12/31/82. There were 281 criminal cases on the docket, 98 convictions, 45 persons committed to prison and seven committed to jail and 135 cases left pending. In the County Court 864 cases were pending on 1/1/82, 1,143 new cases were filed and 1,450 cases were disposed of during the year leaving 557 cases pending on 12/31/82. There were 1,746 criminal cases on the docket, 360 convictions, 30 persons committed to jail, and 432 cases left pending. **JAILS** One jail, capacity 19. **ATTORNEYS AT LAW** 26. **UTILITIES** 82% of the residents are connected to a public or privately owned water system and 65% are con-

COUNTIES

COOKE (continued)

nected to a public or privately owned water system and 65% are connected to a public sewer system. Natural gas is distributed to the county by Lone Star Gas Co., Division of Enserch. The average annual residential bill for natural gas in 1982 for the Lone Star distribution system was $405.91, an increase of 35% over 1981. Electricity is distributed to the county by Texas Power and Light, Cooke Co., Electric Coop., Assn. and Denton Co. Electric Coop., Inc. and is generated primarily by gas and coal. The typical residential electric bill is $165.24 per month for an all-electric house using 2,500 kwh. **TAXES** The county has 13 units with taxing authority: eight school districts, two cities, one county, one college district and one hospital district.

RECREATION/ENTERTAINMENT
NATIONAL REGISTER OF HISTORIC PLACES Era: Thomason-Scott House. Gainesville: Cloud-Stark House. Lindsay: Saint Peter's Roman Catholic Church. **MUNICIPAL PARKS** 1,643 acres in eight municipal parks. These parks contain one mile of hiking trails, six playgrounds, one golf course, three football and soccer fields, 12 baseball and softball fields, two tennis courts, two multi-use courts, three swimming pools, one beach and two boat ramps and shore fishing facilities. **SCENIC DRIVES** The Texas Lakes Trail runs through this county providing views of the Cross Timbers region. Off the trail northwest of Gainesville via F.M. 1201 is Moss Lake. **BOATING/FISHING** Lakes/reservoirs: Clear Creek Soil Conservation Service Lakes 36, 47 and 52 (36 acres), Elm Fork Soil Conservation Service Lakes 7A, 7C, 9, 18 and 19 (359 acres), Kiowa (560 acres) and Hubert H. Moss (1,125 acres). Major rivers: Red and Elm Fork Trinity. Primary streams: Dixon, Flat, Little Duck, Dry Elm, Montague, Persimmon, Brushy Elm, Indian and Fish. **HUNTING** Fall and winter seasons on deer. No closed season on nutria, coyote, bobcat and squirrel. Winter season on quail, muskrat, beaver, otter, opossum, mink, ring-tailed cat, badger, fox, raccoon, skunk and civet cat. In 1983 duck, coot, geese, woodcock and jacksnipe seasons occurred during the winter months. Teal duck, rail and gallinule seasons occurred in the fall. Mourning dove season occurred intermittently during the fall and winter months. **MUSEUMS** Gainesville: Cooke County Heritage Museum. COLLEGIATE FINE ARTS Gainesville: Cultural events offered by Cooke County Junior College. **SPECIAL EVENTS** Junior Livestock Show, Gainesville, March; Germanfest, Muenster, April/May; Heritage Days and Tours of Homes, Gainesville, June; and Cooke County Fair, Gainesville, August.

COMMUNITIES
COUNTY SEAT Gainesville, County Courthouse, 76240; County Clerk's Office, 817/665-2132. **INCORPORATED COMMUNITIES** (1980 population and ZIP Code) Callisburg (281) 76240, Gainesville (14,081) 76240, Lindsay (581) 76250, Muenster (1,408) and Valley View (514) 76252. **UNINCORPORATED COMMUNITIES** (and ZIP Code) Bloomfield 76258, Bulcher 76252, Burns 76258, Dexter 76240, Era 76238, Freemound 76252, Hood 76240, Lake Kiowa 76240, Leo 76234, Lois 76272, Marysville 76252, Mountain Springs 76258, Myra 76253, Prairie Point 76239, Rosston 76263, Sivells Bend 76240, Sturgeon 76273, Tylers Bluff 76265 and Woodbine 76240. **FOR ADDITIONAL LOCAL INFORMATION** Gainesville Chamber of Commerce, 101 S. Culberson, P.O. Box 518, Gainesville, 76240, 817/665-2831.

CORYELL (C7)

THE LAND
West of Waco on U.S. Highway 84 in the Grand Prairie Region,

Coryell County covers 1,057 square miles of plateaus and grasslands. The elevation ranges from 600 to 1,200 feet. All of the county has undulating to hilly alkaline soils over limestone and limy earths with very dark, loamy surfaces over loamy subsoils, and light colored, brownish to reddish, well drained soils. The vegetation of the county is of the Cross Timbers and Prairies area and consists of tall and mid grasses, live oak, mesquite and juniper trees. Between 41 and 50% of the land in the county is considered prime farmland. **CLIMATE** Mild in winter and warm in summer. The average annual temperature is 66°F. Temperatures in January range from an average low of 33° to an average high of 59°F and in July range from 72° to 97°F. The average annual precipitation is 32 inches, with an average relative humidity of 82% at 6 A.M. and 53% at 6 P.M. The average annual snowfall is two inches. The growing season averages 244 days per year, with the last freeze in late March and the first freeze in late November. The sun shines during the year on the average 67% of the daylight hours.

THE PEOPLE
The 1982 estimated population of 59,809 indicates a continuation of the population growth which began in the 1950s. The growth from 1970 to 1980 was one of the largest in the state. Rural areas experienced a growth of 79% from 1970 to 1980. The age groups with the largest gains were ages 25 to 39 and birth to nine years. The county's median age of 22 is young. The largest ancestry groups are persons of English descent (22%), those of German descent (21%) and Black (19%). **REGISTERED VOTERS** As of November 2, 1982 there were 14,218 registered voters (0.2% of the state total). The 1982 general election had a 43% voter turnout, compared to a 67% turnout in the 1980 general election. In the 1982 primary 93% voted Democratic and 7% Republican, with 4,121 votes cast.

THE ECONOMY
AGRICULTURE Cattle area. In 1982, 88% of the land was in farms and ranches, with 20% of the farmland under cultivation. Coryell ranked 97th in the state in highest agricultural receipts, with 80% from livestock and livestock products. Overgrazing, undesirable brush and weeds, water erosion, inefficient tillage systems and the cultivation of marginal lands are the current conservation problems. Primary crops: fourth in the state for oats. Wheat, sorghum and hay. Primary vegetables: potatoes and sweet potatoes. Primary fruits and nuts: peaches and pecans. Primary livestock and products: fifth in the state for turkeys. Cattle, sheep, wool, angora goats, mohair and hogs. **BUSINESS** Total number of business establishments in the county: 447. Retail sales during the first quarter of 1984 increased 28%. In 1980, 10% of the labor force were self-employed, 21% were employed in professional or related services, 11% in manufacturing, 23% in wholesale and retail trade, 13% in public administration, 80% were employed in other counties and there were 2,140 retired workers. The industries with the most employment: agribusiness and the manufacture of women's apparel and truck trailers. The nonfarm earnings in 1981 totaled $357,536,000. The retired workers received an average monthly Social Security payment of $277. **FINANCE** On June 30, 1983, six commercial banks had total deposits of $148,799,000 and total assets of $168,196,000. On December 31, 1982 two state savings and loan associations, one state branch and one federal association branch had combined assets of $91,924,378. **HOUSING** Average value of homes in 1980: $33,300. Permits for new, privately owned housing units increased in 1982: 371 permits were issued with a total construction cost of $10,622,665. Of those permits, 177 were for single family houses. Housing permits increased in Copperas Cove from 95 in 1981 to 328 in 1982 and in Gatesville from seven to 43 with 39 of the permits issued for single family houses.

Between 1970 and 1980 the number of housing units increased by 86%. Eighty-three percent of all units in the county are air-conditioned, 70% are heated by gas and 27% by electricity. **NATURAL RESOURCES** Limestone, industrial sand and dolomite. Current production of other minerals and products includes crushed limestone, sand and gravel. **TOURISM** Travel expenditures of $2,702,000 in 1982 (an increase of 11% over 1981) generated 64 jobs and $519,000 in payroll. **ALCOHOLIC BEVERAGES** Totally dry. **FEDERAL EXPENDITURES** The federal government had direct expenditures or obligations of $65,016,000 in the county during fiscal year 1983, including $20,119,000 by the U.S. Department of Defense. In addition, the federal government provided $851,000 in grant awards, paid $4,662,000 in salaries and wages, made direct payments to individuals of $57,529,000 including $47,036,000 in retirement and disability payments, awarded $1,119,000 in procurement contracts and spent $854,000 in other expenditures or obligations. The federal government also provided $188,000 in direct loans and $11,959,000 in guaranteed loans and insurance.

COMMUNICATION

Newspapers–Weekly: Copperas Cove Leader-Press and the Gatesville Messenger and Star-Forum. Radio: KOOV-FM and KPEP-FM (Gatesville). Cable TV. Telephone companies: Continental Telephone, Southwestern Bell, United Telephone, Central Telephone, Central Telephone-Midstate and Central Texas Telephone Coop. **TRANSPORTATION** Total public road mileage: 989. In 1982 there were 27,652 registered vehicles and 655 reported traffic accidents including five fatalities. Taxi cabs: two companies in Copperas Cove and one company in Gatesville. Municipal transit systems: one intercity bus system provides some intracity service to Temple, Belton, Killeen and Fort Hood in Bell County, and the Copperas Cove area in Coryell County. Intercity bus service is available. Motor freight: five local and intrastate carriers. Rail: one main and one branch line carry freight through the county. The main line carries annually 20 to 30 million tons of freight and the branch line carries less than one million. Aircraft: 24 are registered in the county. Airports: Gatesville City-County Airport is a basic utility airport providing general aviation service. It serves as a base for 10 aircraft.

COMMUNITY SERVICES

EDUCATION Five school districts with 11 elementary, three middle and five high schools. The average daily attendance in 1981-82 was 7,072, with expenditures per pupil of $1,843 including 438 classroom teachers with an average annual salary of $14,517. Forty-eight percent of the 504 high school graduates planned to attend college. In 1982-83, 83% of the students were White, 6% Hispanic, 8% Black, 3% Asian and 0.2% American Indian. Vocational education: Gatesville School of Vocational Nursing (Gatesville). **PUBLIC LIBRARIES** Copperas Cove Public Library: 26,689 volumes. Gatesville Public Library: 16,305 volumes. **CHILD CARE** 81 day care and 18 twenty-four hour care licensed facilities. **HEALTH CARE** 12 physicians and 12 dentists. Hospitals: one with a capacity of 55. Ambulance services: two commercial and one hospital-based service. Mental health: two clinics. Nursing homes: four nursing homes with a combined capacity of 503 nursing care residents. The average cost per day for private patients in 1982 was $40.54. **CHURCHES** 68 churches have an estimated combined membership of 16,986. The largest denominations are Southern Baptist, United Methodist and Churches of Christ. **SOCIAL SERVICES** In fiscal year 1983 a total of $1,105,947 in food stamps was distributed, with an average of 2,462 persons receiving food stamps each month. Aid to Families with Dependent Children (AFDC) totaled $254,355, with an average of 176 families receiving AFDC each month. Medical assistance benefits for the aged and disabled of

$2,926,616 and for families and children of $251,078 brought the county benefit total to $4,537,616. **FIRE PROTECTION** One partly paid and five volunteer fire departments. **LAW ENFORCEMENT** The County Sheriff has 11 commissioned officers. Three police departments have a combined force of 53. **CRIME** 91 violent crimes (murder, forcible rape, robbery and aggravated assault) and 1,044 nonviolent crimes (burglary, larceny-theft and motor vehicle theft) were reported in 1982. **JUDICIAL SYSTEM** One District Court and Judge, one County Court and Judge and four Justices of the Peace. In the District Court a total of 580 cases were pending on 1/1/82, 1,151 new cases were filed and 1,142 cases were disposed of during the year leaving 589 cases pending on 12/31/82. There were 320 criminal cases on the docket, 84 convictions, 32 persons committed to prison and one committed to jail and 117 cases left pending. In the County Court 799 cases were pending on 1/1/82, 1,729 new cases were filed and 1,447 cases were disposed of during the year leaving 1,081 cases pending on 12/31/82. There were 2,317 criminal cases on the docket, 417 convictions, two persons committed to jail, and 879 cases left pending. **JAILS** One jail, capacity 20. **PRISONS** Gatesville, on 1,244 acres north of Gatesville, had an inmate population (females only) of 914 in 1983. It has agricultural operations and a garment factory. It also tests and classifies all female inmates before they are transferred to their permanent unit. Hilltop, on 1,240 acres north of Gatesville, had 978 inmates, agricultural operations and a garment factory. Mountain View, on 97 acres north of Gatesville, had 693 female inmates and is a psychiatric treatment and prerelease center. It has an industrial operation involving Braille facilities. **ATTORNEYS AT LAW** 18. **UTILITIES** 91% of the residents are connected to a public or privately owned water system and 78% are connected to a public sewer system. Natural gas is distributed to the county by Southern Union Company and Lone Star Gas Company, Division of Enserch. The average annual residential bill for natural gas in 1982 for the Southern Union distribution system was $355.85, an increase of 23% over 1981 and for Lone Star it was $405.91, an increase of 35%. Electricity is distributed to the county by Texas Power and Light Co., Erath Co. Electric Coop., Assn. and Hamilton Co. Electric Coop., Assn. and is generated primarily by gas, coal and water. The typical residential electric bill is $168.05 per month for an all-electric house using 2,500 kwh. **TAXES** The county has 10 units with taxing authority: five school districts, three cities, one college district and one county.

RECREATION/ENTERTAINMENT

NATIONAL REGISTER OF HISTORIC PLACES Copperas Cove vicinity: Copperas Cove Stagestop and Post Office. Gatesville: Coryell County Courthouse. Mosheim vicinity: Hogg Creek Archeological District (see Bosque County). **STATE** Mother Neff State Park covers 259 acres with facilities which include camping and trailer sites as well as fishing areas. **MUNICIPAL PARKS** 149 acres in five municipal parks. These parks contain six playgrounds, nine golf courses, two football and soccer fields, seven baseball and softball fields, 10 tennis courts and two swimming pools. **SCENIC DRIVES** The Texas Brazos Trail runs through this county. F.M. 182, F.M. 107 and F.M. 116 traverse a countryside of Spanish oaks, cedars and wild flowers in season. **BOATING/FISHING** Lakes/reservoirs: Peni-Bilt (20 acres) and Woodward (18 acres). Major rivers: Leon. Primary streams: Cowhouse, Settlement and Shoal. **HUNTING** Fall and winter seasons on deer. No closed season on nutria, coyote, bobcat and squirrel. Winter season on quail, muskrat, beaver, otter, opossum, mink, ring-tailed cat, badger, fox, raccoon, skunk and civet cat. Fall, winter and spring seasons on turkey. In 1983 duck, coot, geese, woodcock and jacksnipe seasons occurred during the winter months. Teal duck, rail and

COUNTIES

CORYELL (continued)

gallinule seasons occurred in the fall. Mourning dove season occurred intermittently during the fall and winter months. **SPECIAL EVENTS** Junior Stock Show and Homemaking Show, Copperas Cove, January; Rabbit Fest, Copperas Cove, May; Trail Ride, Gatesville, June; Shivaree, Gatesville, June; Rodeo, Gatesville, June; Junior Rodeo, Gatesville, July; Shivaree, Gatesville, August; Octoberfest, Copperas Cove, October; Jackpot Roping, Gatesville, October.

COMMUNITIES

COUNTY SEAT Gatesville, County Courthouse, 76528; County Clerk's Office, 817/865-5016. **INCORPORATED COMMUNITIES** (1980 population and ZIP Code) Copperas Cove (19,469) 76522, Evant 425 (356 Coryell Co. and 69 Hamilton Co.) 76525, Fort Gates (777) 76528, Gatesville (6,260) 76528 and Oglesby (470) 76561. **UNINCORPORATED COMMUNITIES** (and ZIP Code) Ames 76528, Arnett 76528, Ater 76528, Bee House 76512, Cavitt 76561, Coryell 76689, Flat 76526, Hurst Springs 76634, Ireland 76528, Jonesboro (also in Hamilton Co.) 76538, Kay Bee Heights 76546, King 76563, Leon Junction 76552, Levita 76528, Mound 75844, Mountain 76528, Montague Village (West Fort Hood) 76544, Osage 76528, Pancake 76538, Pearl 76563, Pecan Grove (Pecangrove) 76561, Pidcoke 76528, Purmela 76566, South Purmela 76566, The Grove 76576, Topsey 76522, Turnersville 76580, White Hall 76528, and Whitson 76557. **FOR ADDITIONAL LOCAL INFORMATION** Copperas Cove Chamber of Commerce, Drawer C, 311 S. First, Copperas Cove 76522 817/547-7571, Greater Gatesville Chamber of Commerce, 2401 Hwy. 36 S., P.O. Box 206, Gatesville 76528, 817/865-2617.

COTTLE (P33)

THE LAND

West of Wichita Falls on U.S. Highways 62/83 and 70 in the Rolling Plains Region, Cottle County covers 895 square miles with an elevation range of 1,600 to 2,100 feet. The soils are loamy with cracking, clayey subsoils or shallow soils over limestone. The red to brown soils are nearly level to undulating and moderately alkaline. In the Rolling Plains vegetation area, the original prairie grasses have been replaced by short to mid grasses, mesquite trees, yucca and some live oaks. Sandburs, tumblegrass, ragweed and other weeds have become a problem in some areas. Between 21 and 30% of the land is considered prime farmland. **CLIMATE** Mild on the whole, but contains variable temperature extremes. The average annual temperature is 63 °F. Temperatures in January range from an average low of 27 ° to an average high of 53 °F and in July range from 72 ° to 96 °F. The average annual precipitation is 22 inches, with an average relative humidity of 74% at 6 A.M. and 42% at 6 P.M. The average annual snowfall is nine inches. The growing season averages 215 days per year, with the last freeze in early April and the first freeze in early November. The sun shines during the year on the average 75% of the daylight hours.

THE PEOPLE

The 1982 estimated population of 2,800 indicates a continuation of the steady decline in population from 9,395 in 1930 to 2,947 in 1980. However the rate of decrease lowered from 24% between 1960 and 1970 to 8% between 1970 and 1980. The majority of the residents live in rural areas. The age groups with the largest losses between 1970 and 1980 were ages five to 14, 20 to 24 and 45 to 54. The high median age increased from 37 in 1970 to 38 in 1980. The largest ancestry groups are persons of English descent (27%), Irish descent (20%) and Hispanic

(14%). **REGISTERED VOTERS** As of November 2, 1982 there were 1,778 registered voters (0.02% of the state total). The 1982 general election had a 56% voter turnout, compared to a 67% turnout in the 1980 general election. In the 1982 primary 100% voted Democratic, with 655 votes cast.

THE ECONOMY

AGRICULTURE Cotton area. In 1982, 94% of the land was in farms and ranches, with 19% of the farmland under cultivation and 6% irrigated. Cottle ranked 185th in the state in highest agricultural receipts, with 63% from crops. Overgrazing, undesirable brush and weeds, water and wind erosion and a lack of potable water are the current conservation problems. Primary crops: cotton, sorghum and wheat. Primary vegetables: sweet potatoes and watermelons. Primary fruits and nuts: peaches. Primary livestock and products: cattle. **BUSINESS** Total number of business establishments in the county: 78. Retail sales during the first quarter of 1984 increased 6%. In 1980, 25% of the labor force were self-employed, 16% were employed in professional or related services, 2% in manufacturing, 20% in wholesale and retail trade, 33% in agriculture, forestry, fisheries and mining, 4% were employed in other counties and there were 429 retired workers. The industry with the most employment: agribusiness. The nonfarm earnings in 1981 totaled $21,919,000. The retired workers received an average monthly Social Security payment of $298.00. **FINANCE** On June 30, 1983, one commercial bank had total deposits of $26,973,000 and total assets of $32,556,000. There is one state savings and loan association branch in the county. **HOUSING** Average value of homes in 1980: $19,600. Permits for new, privately owned housing units decreased in 1982: seven permits were issued with a total construction cost of $289,500. Of those permits, all were for single family houses. Between 1970 and 1980 the number of housing units decreased by 5%. Eighty-four percent of all units in the county are air-conditioned, 94% are heated by gas and 4% by electricity. **NATURAL RESOURCES** Gypsum, saltbeds, oil, gas and bituminous coal. In 1982 a total of 3,104,915 thousand cubic feet of gas well gas, 28,032 barrels of condensate, 148,876 barrels of crude oil and 83,620 thousand cubic feet of casinghead gas were produced. Current production of other minerals and products includes sand and gravel. **TOURISM** Travel expenditures of $4,949,000 in 1982 (an increase of 15% over 1981) generated 95 jobs and $854,000 in payroll. **ALCOHOLIC BEVERAGES** Totally dry. **FEDERAL EXPENDITURES** The federal government had direct expenditures or obligations of $11,248,000 in the county during fiscal year 1983, including $46,000 by the U.S. Department of Defense. In addition, the federal government provided $41,000 in grant awards, paid $320,000 in salaries and wages, made direct payments to individuals of $5,489,000 including $3,590,000 in retirement and disability payments and spent $5,399,000 in other expenditures or obligations. The federal government also provided $2,672,000 in direct loans and $6,267,000 in guaranteed loans and insurance.

COMMUNICATION

Newspapers–Weekly: The Paducah Post. Cable TV. Telephone companies: General Telephone, Cap Rock Telephone and Santa Rosa Telephone Coop. **TRANSPORTATION** Total public road mileage: 527. In 1982 there were 3,029 registered vehicles and 35 reported traffic accidents. Motor freight: two carriers. Aircraft: 14 are registered in the county. Airports: Dan E. Richardson Municipal Airport at Paducah is a basic utility airport providing general aviation service. It serves as a base for six aircraft.

COMMUNITY SERVICES

EDUCATION One school district with one elementary and one high school. The average daily attendance in 1981-82 was 480, with expenditures per pupil of $2,916 including 33 classroom teachers with an average annual salary of $14,149. Seventy-two percent of the 32 high school graduates planned to attend college. In 1982-83, 64% of the students were White, 22% Hispanic, 15% Black and 0.4% Asian. **PUBLIC LIBRARIES** Paducah Library. **CHILD CARE** Five day care and one twenty-four hour care licensed facility. **HEALTH CARE** Three physicians and one dentist. Hospitals: one with a capacity of 20. Ambulance services: one commercial service. Mental health: one clinic. Nursing homes: one nursing home has a capacity of 46 nursing care residents. **CHURCHES** 13 churches have an estimated combined membership of 2,986. The largest denominations are Southern Baptist, Catholic and Baptist Missionary. **SOCIAL SERVICES** In fiscal year 1983 a total of $179,083 in food stamps was distributed, with an average of 398 persons receiving food stamps each month. Aid to Families with Dependent Children (AFDC) totaled $32,058 with an average of 21 families receiving AFDC each month. Medical assistance benefits for the aged and disabled of $451,074 and for families and children of $97,193 brought the county benefit total to $759,408. **FIRE PROTECTION** One volunteer fire department. **LAW ENFORCEMENT** The County Sheriff has one commissioned officer. **CRIME** Three violent crimes (murder, forcible rape, robbery and aggravated assault) and five nonviolent crimes (burglary, larceny-theft and motor vehicle theft) were reported in 1982. **JUDICIAL SYSTEM** One District Court and Judge, one County Court and Judge and one Justice of the Peace. In the District Court a total of 44 cases were pending on 1/1/82, 49 new cases were filed and 43 cases were disposed of during the year leaving 50 cases pending on 12/31/82. There were 28 criminal cases on the docket, 12 convictions, two persons committed to prison, and 14 cases left pending. In the County Court 61 cases were pending on 1/1/82, 34 new cases were filed and 31 cases were disposed of during the year leaving 64 cases pending on 12/31/82. There were 82 criminal cases on the docket, 26 convictions, and 51 cases left pending. **JAILS** One jail, capacity seven. **ATTORNEYS AT LAW** Five. **UTILITIES** 94% of the residents are connected to a public or privately owned water system and 70% are connected to a public sewer system. Natural gas is distributed to the county by Lone Star Gas Co., Division of Enserch. The average annual residential bill for natural gas in 1982 for the Lone Star distribution system was $405.91, an increase of 35% over 1981. Electricity is distributed to the county by West Texas Utilities, Gate City Electric Coop. and Lighthouse Electric Coop., Inc. and is generated primarily by gas and oil. **TAXES** The county has three units with taxing authority: one school district, one city and one county.

RECREATION/ENTERTAINMENT

MUNICIPAL PARKS 13 acres in one municipal park. This park contains one playground, one multi-use field, one multi-use court and one swimming pool. **BOATING/FISHING** Major rivers: North Pease, South Pease, North Wichita and Middle Pease. **WILDLIFE REFUGES** Matador State Wildlife Management Area covers 28,183 acres. **HUNTING** Fall season on antelope. Fall and winter seasons on deer and mule deer. Summer, fall and winter seasons on squirrel. Winter season on quail, pheasant, muskrat, beaver, badger, fox, weasel, raccoon, skunk and civet cat, opossum, ring-tailed cat. No closed season on bobcat and coyote. Fall, winter and spring seasons on turkey. In 1983 sandhill crane, duck, coot, geese, woodcock and jacksnipe seasons occurred during the winter months. Teal duck, rail and gallinule seasons occurred in the fall. Mourning dove season occurred intermittently during the fall and winter months. **MUSEUMS** Paducah: Bicentennial City-County Museum. **SPECIAL EVENTS** Old Settlers Reunion and Rodeo, Paducah, April; Cotton Festival, Paducah, September.

COMMUNITIES

COUNTY SEAT Paducah, County Courthouse, 79248; County Clerk's Office, 806/492-3823. **INCORPORATED COMMUNITIES** (1980 population and ZIP Code) Paducah (2,216) 79248. **UNINCORPORATED COMMUNITIES** (and ZIP Code) Cee Vee 79223, Chalk 79224, Delwin 79248, Dunlap 79248, Hackberry (Stewart) 79248, Lazare (also in Hardeman Co.) 79238, Sneedville 79248 and Swearingen 79248. **FOR ADDITIONAL LOCAL INFORMATION** Paducah Chamber of Commerce, P. O. Box 863, Paducah, 79248, 806/492-2044.

CRANE (P85)

THE LAND

West of San Angelo on U.S. Highway 385 in the Trans-Pecos Region, Crane County covers 782 square miles with an elevation range of 2,400 to 2,900 feet. The sandy soils are nearly level to undulating with a few dunes. There are localized areas of either loamy or clayey soils, and areas with accumulations of gypsum or powdery lime. Along the Pecos River the soils are saline and shallow with loamy deposits from the mountains. In the Trans-Pecos, Mountains and Basins vegetation area, most of the land is native rangeland with a variety of grasses, yucca, shinnery oak, sandsage, desert shrub and mesquite. Less than 1% of the land in the county is considered prime farmland. **CLIMATE** Mild and dry. The average annual temperature is 65 °F. Temperatures in January range from an average low of 30 ° to an average high of 60 °F and in July range from 71 ° to 96 °F. The average annual precipitation is 12 inches, with an average relative humidity of 72% at 6 A.M. and 33% at 6 P.M. The average annual snowfall is three inches. The growing season averages 228 days per year, with the last freeze in late March and the first freeze in mid November. The sun shines during the year on the average 75% of the daylight hours.

THE PEOPLE

The 1982 estimated population of 5,000 continues the moderate growth of the 1970s. Almost 31% of the growth between 1970 and 1980 was in rural areas. The groups with the largest gains were ages 20 to 34 and ages 62 and over. The median age of 27 in 1980 shifted from average in 1970 to younger than average in 1980. The high birth rate of 25 per 1,000 persons reflects this shift. The largest ancestry groups are persons of English descent (28%), Hispanic (25%) and persons of Irish descent (20%). **REGISTERED VOTERS** As of November 2, 1982 there were 2,654 registered voters (0.04% of the state total). The 1982 general election had a 60% voter turnout, compared to a 70% turnout in the 1980 general election. In the 1982 primary 98% voted Democratic and 2% Republican, with 1,084 votes cast.

THE ECONOMY

AGRICULTURE Ranchland. In 1982, 88% of the land was farms and ranches. Crane ranked 251st in the state in highest agricultural receipts, with 100% from livestock and livestock products. Overgrazing and undesirable brush and weeds are the current conservation problems. Primary livestock and products: cattle, sheep and wool. **BUSINESS** Total number of business establishments in the county: 121. Retail sales during the first quarter of 1984 decreased 16%. In 1980, 5% of the labor force were self-employed, 16% were employed in professional or related services, 7% in manufacturing, 17% in wholesale and retail trade, 35% in agriculture, forestry, fisheries and mining, 11% were employed in other counties and there were 268 retired workers. The industries with the most employment: oil and gas extraction and trucking. The nonfarm earnings in 1981 totaled $57,004,000. The retired workers received an average monthly

COUNTIES

CRANE (continued)

Social Security payment of $354.00. **FINANCE** On June 30, 1983, one commercial bank had total deposits of $15,013,000 and total assets of $18,398,000. There is one state savings and loan association branch and one credit union in the county. **HOUSING** Average value of homes in 1980: $22,300. Five permits for new, privately owned housing units, with a total construction cost of $315,000 were issued in 1982. Of those permits, all were for single family houses. Between 1970 and 1980 the number of housing units increased by 14%. Eighty percent of all units in the county are air-conditioned, 89% are heated by gas and 9% by electricity. **NATURAL RESOURCES** Caliche, sand, gravel, oil and gas. In 1982 a total of 46,682,693 thousand cubic feet of gas well gas, 62,050 barrels of condensate, 26,117,537 barrels of crude oil and 127,208,293 thousand cubic feet of casinghead gas were produced. Current production of other minerals and products includes brine, sand, gravel and recovered sulpher. **TOURISM** Travel expenditures of $1,854,000 in 1982 (an increase of 11% over 1981) generated 47 jobs and $372,000 in payroll. **ALCOHOLIC BEVERAGES** Packaged distilled spirits, beer, ale, malt liquor and wine are legal in parts of the county. **FEDERAL EXPENDITURES** The federal government had direct expenditures or obligations of $4,419,000 in the county during fiscal year 1983, including $61,000 by the U.S. Department of Defense. In addition, the federal government provided $116,000 in grant awards, paid $195,000 in salaries and wages, made direct payments to individuals of $4,076,000 including $3,166,000 in retirement and disability payments, and spent $32,000 in other expenditures or obligations. The federal government also provided $494,000 in guaranteed loans and insurance.

COMMUNICATION

Newspapers–Weekly: The Crane News. Radio: KXOI-AM (Crane). Cable TV. Telephone companies: Southwestern Bell. **TRANSPORTATION** Total public road mileage: 265. In 1982 there were 5,748 registered vehicles and 116 reported traffic accidents including two fatalities. Intercity bus service is available. Motor freight: four local and intrastate carriers. Rail: one mainline carries annually five to 10 million tons of freight through the county. Aircraft: 20 are registered in the county. Airports: Crane County Airport at Crane is a basic utility airport providing general aviation service. It serves as a base for 12 aircraft.

COMMUNITY SERVICES

EDUCATION One school district with one elementary, one middle and one high school. The average daily attendance in 1981-82 was 1,136, with expenditures per pupil of $4,243 including 85 classroom teachers with an average annual salary of $22,218. None of the 66 high school graduates planned to attend college. In 1982-83, 62% of the students were White, 35% Hispanic, 3.0% Black and 0.3% Asian. **PUBLIC LIBRARIES** Crane County Library (Crane): 22,253 volumes. **CHILD CARE** Three day care licensed facilities. **HEALTH CARE** Three physicians and one dentist. Hospitals: one with a capacity of 28. Ambulance services: one volunteer fire department service. Nursing homes: one nursing home has a capacity of 30 nursing care residents. The average cost per day for private patients in 1982 was $30.00. **CHURCHES** Seven churches have an estimated combined membership of 2,860. The largest denominations are Southern Baptist, United Methodist, Christian Churches and Churches of Christ. **SOCIAL SERVICES** In fiscal year 1983 a total of $41,382 in food stamps was distributed, with an average of 83 persons receiving food stamps each month. Aid to Families with Dependent Children (AFDC) totaled $12,544 with an average of 10 families receiving AFDC each month. Medical assistance benefits for the aged and disabled of $151,296 and for families

and children of $21,738 brought the county benefit total to $226,960. **FIRE PROTECTION** One volunteer fire department. **LAW ENFORCEMENT** The County Sheriff has five commissioned officers. One police department has a combined force of nine. **CRIME** Seven violent crimes (murder, forcible rape, robbery and aggravated assault) and 83 nonviolent crimes (burglary, larceny-theft and motor vehicle theft) were reported in 1982. **JUDICIAL SYSTEM** One District Court and Judge, one County Court and Judge and four Justices of the Peace. In the District Court a total of 136 cases were pending on 1/1/82, 131 new cases were filed and 84 cases were disposed of during the year leaving 183 cases pending on 12/31/82. There were 87 criminal cases on the docket, eight convictions, four persons committed to prison, 64 cases left pending. In the County Court 112 cases were pending on 1/1/82, 345 new cases were filed and 295 cases were disposed of during the year leaving 162 cases pending on 12/31/82. There were 405 criminal cases on the docket, 187 convictions, five persons committed to jail, and 124 cases left pending. **JAILS** one jail, capacity 16. **ATTORNEYS AT LAW** Three. **UTILITIES** 97% of the residents are connected to a public or privately owned water system and 84% are connected to a public sewer system. Natural gas is distributed to the county by Southern Union Company. The average annual residential bill for natural gas in 1982 for the Southern Union distribution system was $355.85, an increase of 23% over 1981. Electricity is distributed to the county by Texas Electric Service Co. and is generated primarily by gas. The typical residential electric bill is $154.69 per month for an all-electric house using 2,500 kwh. **TAXES** The county has three units with taxing authority: one school district, one city and one county.

RECREATION/ENTERTAINMENT

COUNTY PARKS 54 acres in three county parks. These parks contain two playgrounds, three tennis courts, five multi-use fields and two swimming pools. **BOATING/FISHING** Major rivers: Pecos. **HUNTING** Fall and winter seasons on deer, mule deer and javelina. No closed season on squirrel, bobcat and coyote. Winter season on quail, muskrat, beaver, opossum, ring-tailed cat, badger, fox, weasel, raccoon, skunk and civet cat. Fall, winter and spring seasons on turkey. In 1983 sandhill crane, duck, coot, geese, woodcock and jacksnipe seasons occurred during the winter months. Teal duck, rail and gallinule seasons occurred in the fall. Mourning dove season occurred intermittently during the fall and winter months. **SPECIAL EVENTS** 4-H Livestock Show, Crane, January; Annual Cancer Theatre, Crane, March; Community Banquet, Crane, November.

COMMUNITIES

COUNTY SEAT Crane, County Courthouse, 79731; County Clerk's Office, 915/558-3581. **INCORPORATED COMMUNITIES** (1980 population and ZIP Code) Crane (3,622) 79731. **UNINCORPORATED COMMUNITIES** (and ZIP Code) Rio Pecos (79740) **FOR ADDITIONAL LOCAL INFORMATION** Crane Co. Chamber of Commerce, 409 S. Gaston, Crane 79731, 915/558-2311.

CROCKETT (P94)

THE LAND

Southwest of San Angelo on Interstate Highway 10 in the Edwards Plateau Region, Crockett County cover 2,806 square miles with an elevation range of 1,600 to 2,700 feet. The land varies from undulating to steep hills with loamy, alkaline soils over limestone. In some areas bedrock is within 20 inches of the surface with stoniness on steep slopes. In the Edwards Plateau vegetation area, there is a variety of short and mid grasses, desert shrub and scrubby live oak trees. Less than 1% of the land in the county is considered prime farmland. **CLIMATE** Mild and dry. The average annual temperature is 67 °F. Temperatures in January range from an average low of 34° to an average high of 61 °F and in July range from 70° to 96 °F. The average annual precipitation is 18 inches, with an average relative humidity of 74% at 6 A.M. and 37% at 6 P.M. The average annual snowfall will average less than 2 inches. The growing season averages 233 days per year, with the last freeze in late March and the first freeze in mid November. The sun shines during the year on the average 75% of the daylight hours.

THE PEOPLE

Crockett County is one of the most sparsely poplulated in the state. It ranks 51st among all U.S. counties in the highest percent of population of Spanish origin. The 1982 estimated population of 5,100 continues the moderate growth rate begun in the 1970's. Urban areas experienced a population gain of 32% between 1970 and 1980. The age groups with the largest increases were ages 20 to 34 and 65 and over. The largest ancestry groups are Hispanic (45%), persons of English descent (20%) and Irish descent (16%). **REGISTERED VOTERS** As of November 2, 1982 there were 2,592 registered voters (0.04% of the state total). The 1982 general election had a 35% voter turnout, compared to a 55% turnout in the 1980 general election. In the 1982 primary 100% voted Democratic with 641 votes cast.

THE ECONOMY

AGRICULTURE Sheep ranches. In 1982, 94% of the land was in farms and ranches, with less than 1% of the farmland under cultivation. Crockett ranked 190th in the state in highest agricultural receipts, with 99% from livestock and livestock products. Overgrazing, undersirable brush and weeds, water erosion and water conservation are the current conservation problems. Primary crops: wheat. Primary fruits and nuts: peaches. Primary livestock and products: second in the state for both sheep and woll production and sixth for both angora goats and mohair production. Cattle. **BUSINESS** Total number of business establishments in the county: 114. In 1980, 15% of the labor force were self-employed, 13% were employed in professional or related services, 2% in manufacturing, 21% in wholesale and retail trade, 33% in agriculture, forestry, fisheries and mining, 9% were employed in other counties and there were 278 retired workers. The industry with the most employment: oil and gas extraction. The nonfarm earnings in 1981 totaled $49,048,000. The retired workers received an average monthly Social Security payment of $320.00. **FINANCE** On June 30, 1983, two commercial banks had total deposits of $52,143,000 and total assets of $62,073,000. There is one state savings and loan association branch in the county. **HOUSING** Average value of homes in 1980: $27,600. Between 1970 and 1980 the number of housing units increased by 14%. Eighty-three percent of all units in the county are air-conditioned, 86% are heated by gas and 11% by electricity. **NATURAL RESOURCES** Limestone, salt beds, oil & gas. In 1982 a total of 77,057,572 thousand cubic feet of gas well gas, 301,845 barrels of condensate, 4,627,931 barrels of crude oil and 10,782,604 thousand cubic feet of casinghead gas were produced. Current production of other minerals and products includes brine, crushed limestone, sand & gravel. **TOURISM** Travel expenditures of $7,379,000 in 1982 (an increase of 13% over 1981) generated 162 jobs and $1,367,000 in payroll. Lodging: five hotels, motels and tourist courts. **ALCOHOLIC BEVERAGES** Totally dry. **FEDERAL EXPENDITURES** The federal government had direct expenditures or obligations of $6,250,000 in the county during fiscal year 1983, including $145,000 by the U.S. Department of Defense. In addition, the federal government provided $116,000 in grant awards, paid $351,000 in salaries and wages,

made direct payments to individuals of $3,688,000 including $2,769,000 in retirement and disability payments, awarded $1,000 in procurement contracts and spent $2,093,000 in other expenditures or obligations. The federal government also provided $1,000 in direct loans and $244,000 in guaranteed loans and insurance.

COMMUNICATION

Newspapers–Weekly: Ozona Stockman, Radio: KRCT-FM (Ozona). Cable TV. Telephone companies: General Telephone, Southwestern Bell and Big Bend Telephone. **TRANSPORTATION** Total public road mileage: 725. In 1982 there were 4,943 registered vehicles and 178 reported traffic accidents including seven fatalities. Intercity bus service is available. Motor freight: two carriers. Rail: one branch line carries annually one to five million tons of freight through the county. Aircraft: 42 are registered in the county. Airports: Ozona Municipal Airport is a general utility airport providing general aviation service. It serves as a base for 12 aircraft.

COMMUNITY SERVICES

EDUCATION one school district with two elementary, one middle and one high school. The average daily attendance in 1981-82 was 1,044 with expenditures per pupil of $3,050 including 71 classroom teachers with an average annual salary of $16,906. Seventy-five percent of the 67 high school graduates planned to attend college. In 1982-83, 41% of the students were White, 57% Hispanic and 1% Black. **PUBLIC LIBRARIES** Crockett County Library (Ozona): 4,433 volumes. **CHILD CARE** Five day care and two twenty-four hour care licensed facilities. **HEALTH CARE** Two physicians and three dentists. Hospitals: one with a capacity of 20. Ambulance services: onc county service. Nursing homes: one nursing home has a capacity of 36 nursing care residents. The average cost per day for private patients in 1982 was $37.14 **CHURCHES** Nine churches have an estimated combined membership of 4,296. The largest denominations are Catholic, Southern Baptist and United Methodist. **SOCIAL SERVICES** In fiscal year 1983 a total of $76,024 in food stamps was distributed, with an average of 168 persons receiving food stamps each month. Aid to Families with Dependent Children (AFDC) totaled $31,177 with an average of 19 families receiving AFDC each month. Medical assistance benefits for the aged and disabled of $178,386 and for families and children of $48,102 brought the county benefit total to $333,689. **FIRE PROTECTION** One volunteer fire department. **LAW ENFORCEMENT** The County Sheriff has 10 commissioned officers. **CRIME** 24 violent crimes (murder, forcible rape, robbery and aggravated assault) and 174 nonviolent crimes (burglary, larceny-theft and motor vehicle theft) were reported in 1982. **JUDICIAL SYSTEM** One District Court and Judge, one County Court and Judge and one Justice of the Peace. In the District Court a total of 192 cases were pending on 1/1/82, 190 new cases were filed and 108 cases were disposed of during the year leaving 274 cases pending on 12/31/82. There were 101 criminal cases on the docket, four convictions, two persons committed to prison and 75 cases left pending. In the County Court 73 cases were pending on 1/1/82, 192 new cases were filed and 63 cases were disposed of during the year leaving 202 cases pending on 12/31/82. There were 257 criminal cases on the docket, 20 convictions, two persons committed to jail, and 194 cases left pending. **JAILS** One jail, capacity 30. **ATTORNEYS AT LAW** Four. **UTILITIES** 94% of the residents are connected to a public or privately owned water system and 91% are connected to a public sewer system. Natural gas is distributed to the county by Energas Company. The average annual residential bill for natural gas in 1982 for the Energas distribution system was $371.63, an increase of 23% over 1981. Electricity is distributed to the county by West Texas Utilities

COUNTIES

CROCKETT (continued)

Co., Rio Grande Electric Coop., Inc. and Southwest Texas Electric Coop., Inc. and is generated primarily by gas, oil, coal and water. The typical residential electric bill is $145.78 per month for an all-electric house using 2,500 kwh. **TAXES** The county has two units with taxing authority: one school district and one county.

RECREATION/ENTERTAINMENT
NATIONAL REGISTER OF HISTORIC PLACES Ozona: Crockett County Courthouse. Ozona vicinity: Turkey Roost Petroglyph Site. **STATE** Fort Lancaster State Historic Site covers 82 acres with a modern visitor center and a historic structure. The fort was established in 1855 by 1st U.S. Infantry and housed two companies. **COUNTY PARKS** 29 acres in seven county parks. These parks contain one playground, six baseball and softball fields and three swimming pools. **SCENIC DRIVES** The Pecos Trail runs through this county. This trail rambles through the vast region of southwest and west Texas with landscapes varying from raw, arid regions to green valley. In addition Lancaster Hill on U.S. 290 near Ozona overlooks the Pecos River Valley. **BOATING/FISHING** Lakes/reservoirs: Johnson Draw Soil Conservation Service Lake 4 (nine acres), Major rivers: Pecos. Primary streams: Live Oak. **HUNTING** Fall and winter seasons on deer and mule deer. No closed season on javelina, squirrel, bobcat and coyote. Winter season on quail, muskrat, beaver, opossum, ring-tailed cat, badger, fox, weasel, raccoon, skunk and civet cat. Fall, winter and spring seasons on turkey. In 1983 sandhill crane, duck, coot, geese, woodcock and jacksnipe seasons occurred during the winter months. Teal duck, rail and gallinule seasons occurred in the fall. Mourning dove season occurred intermittently during the fall and winter months with a fall season on white-winged doves. **MUSEUMS** Ozona: Crockett County Museum. **SPECIAL EVENTS** "Biggest Little Race in Texas", Ozona, May; Junior Rodeo, Ozona, July; Pecan Show and Pecan Foods Fest, Ozona, November.

COMMUNITIES
COUNTY SEAT Ozona, County Courthouse, 76943; County Clerk's Office, 915/392-2022. **UNINCORPORATED COMMUNITIES** (and ZIP Code) Ozona 76943. **FOR ADDITIONAL LOCAL INFORMATION** Ozona Chamber of Commerce, P. O. Box 1135, 1110 Ave. E., Ozona, 76943, 915/392-3066 or 392-3043.

CROSBY (P40)

THE LAND
East of Lubbock on U.S. Highway 62/82 in the High Plains Region, Crosby County covers 898 square miles with an elevation range of 2,250 to 3,200 feet. To the west, south and southeast and along the White River the land is level to undulating, with loamy surfaces and clayey subsoils. In the north the nearly level soils are dark and loamy with clayey subsoils. In some area bedrock is within 20 inches of the surface. Between 51 and 60% of the land in the county is considered prime farmland. The northern half of Crosby is in the High Plains vegetation area and the dominant grasses are buffalograss and blue grama. The southern half of the county is in the Rolling Plains vegetation area with mid to tall grasses, mesquite trees, some cacti and to the west thorny shrubs. **CLIMATE** Mild and dry. Duststorms and thunderstorms will occur in spring. The average annual temperature is 61 °F. Temperatures in January range from an average low of 26° to an average high of 53 °F and in July range from 67° to 95 °F. The average annual precipitation is 20 inches, with an average relative humidity of 73% at 6 A.M. and 38%

at 6 P.M. The average annual snowfall is 11 inches. The growing season averages 209 days per year, with the last freeze in mid April and the first freeze in early November. The sun shines during the year on the average 75% of the daylight hours.

THE PEOPLE
In 1980 Crosby County ranked 69th among all U.S. counties in the percent of population of Spanish origin. The 1982 estimated population of 8,700 indicates a slight decrease since 1980. The population declined 12% between 1960 and 1970 and continued to decrease at a slower rate from 1970 to 1980. The age group with the largest decrease between 1970 and 1980 was ages 5 to 14. The majority of the residents live in rural areas. The largest ancestry groups are Hispanic (37%), persons of English descent (24%) and those of Irish descent (16%). **REGISTERED VOTERS** As of November 2, 1982 there were 4,049 registered voters (0.1% of the state total). The 1982 general election had a 49% voter turnout, compared to a 66% turnout in the 1980 general election. In the 1982 primary 98% voted Democratic and 2% Republican, with 1,339 votes cast.

THE ECONOMY
AGRICULTURE Cotton area. In 1982, 95% of the land was in farms and ranches, with 55% of the farmland under cultivation and 41% irrigated. Crosby ranked 75th in the state in highest agricultural receipts with 90% from crops. Undersirable brush and weeds, water and wind erosion and decreasing irrigation water supplies are the current conservation problems. Primary crops: sixth in the state for sunflowers. Cotton, sorghum, wheat and soybeans. Primary vegetables: fifth in the state for onions. Cantaloupes, cucumbers and bell peppers. Primary fruits and nuts: pecans. Primary livestock and products: cattle. **BUSINESS** Total number of business establishments in the county: 154. Retail sales during the first quarter of 1984 increase 5%. In 1980, 22% of the labor force were self-employed, 20% were employed in professional or related services, 7% in manufacturing, 16% in wholesale and retail trade, 33% in agriculture, forestry, fisheries and mining, 14% were employed in other counties and there were 759 retired workers. The industries with the most employment: agribusiness and textile mills. The nonfarm earnings in 1981 totaled $60,600,000. The retired workers received an average monthly Social Security payment of $311.00. **FINANCE** On June 30, 1983, three commercial banks had total deposits of $58,236,000 and total assets of $67,591,000. There is one state savings and loan association branch, one federal association branch and one credit union in the county. **HOUSING** Average value of homes in 1980: $20,600. Permits for new, privately owned housing units decreased in 1982: 20 permits were issued with a total construction cost of $632,250. Of those permits, all were for single family houses. Between 1970 and 1980 the number of housing units increased by 3%. Seventy-three percent of all units in the county are air-conditioned, 91% are heated by gas and 8% by electricity. **NATURAL RESOURCES** Caliche, oil and gas. In 1982 1,252,868 barrels of crude oil and 41,111 thousand cubic feet of casinghead gas were produced. Current production of other minerals and products includes sand and gravel. **TOURISM** Travel expenditures of $6,586,000 in 1982 (an increase of 16% over 1981) generated 114 jobs and $1,073,000 in payroll. **ALCOHOLIC BEVERAGES** Totally dry. **FEDERAL EXPENDITURES** The federal government had direct expenditures or obligations of $30,258,000 in the county during fiscal year 1983, including $76,000 by the U.S. Department of Defense. In addition, the federal government provided $652,000 in grant awards, paid $513,000 in salaries and wages, made direct payments to individuals of $10,294,000 including $7,119,000 in retirement and disability payments, awarded $1,000 in procurement contracts and spent $18,797,000 in other expenditures or obligations. The

federal government also provided $5,409,000 in direct loans and $19,978,000 in guaranteed loans and insurance.

COMMUNICATION

Newspapers–Weekly: Crosbyton Review, Lorenzo Leader and the Ralls Banner. Radio: KCLR-AM (Ralls). Cable TV. Telephone companies: General Telephone, Southwestern Bell, Cap Rock Telephone and South Plains Telephone Coop. **TRANSPORTATION** Total public road mileage: 1,049. In 1982 there were 7,310 registered vehicles and 130 reported traffic accidents including four fatalities. Intercity bus service is available. Motor freight: two carriers. Rail: One branch line carries annually less than one million tons of freight through the county. Aircraft: 31 are registered in the county. Airports: Crosbyton Municipal Airport is a basic utility airport providing general aviation service. It serves as a base for 10 aircraft. Cone Airport at Ralls. Paudler Airport at Crosbyton serves as a base for dusting, spraying and seeding operations.

COMMUNITY SERVICES

EDUCATION three school districts with three elementary, two middle and three high schools. The average daily attendance in 1981-82 was 1,834, with expenditures per pupil of $3,096 including 152 classroom teachers with an average annual salary of $14,420. Fifty percent of the 115 high school graduates planned to attend college. In 1982-83, 36% of the students were White, 58% Hispanic, 6% Black and 0.1% Asian.**PUBLIC LIBRARIES** Crosby County Library (Crosbyton): 22,000 volumes. **CHILD CARE** Nine day care and three twenty-four hour care licensed facilities. **HEALTH CARE** four physicians and two dentists. Hospitals: one with a capacity of 50. Ambulance services: two volunteer services and one commercial service. Nursing homes: two nursing homes with a combined capacity of 108 nursing care residents. The average cost per day for private patients in 1982 was $30.56. **CHURCHES** 20 churches have an estimated combined membership of 8,241. The largest denominations are Southern Baptist, Catholic and United Methodist. **SOCIAL SERVICES** In fiscal year 1983 a total of $836,327 in food stamps was distributed, with an average of 1,784 persons receiving food stamps each month. Aid to Families with Dependent Children (AFDC) totaled $85,246 with an average of 49 families receiving AFDC each month. Medical assistance benefits for the aged and disabled of $687,053 and for families and children of $90,046 brought the county benefit total to $1,698,671. **FIRE PROTECTION** three volunteer fire departments. **LAW ENFORCEMENT** The County Sheriff has six commissioned officers. Three police departments have a combined force of four. **CRIME** seven violent crimes (murder, forcible rape, robbery and aggravated assault) and 74 nonviolent crimes (burglary, larceny-theft and motor vehicle theft) were reported in 1982. **JUDICIAL SYSTEM** One District Court and Judge, one County Court and Judge and two Justices of the Peace. In the District Court a total of 446 cases were pending on 1/1/82, 142 new cases were filed and 111 cases were disposed of during the year leaving 477 cases pending on 12/31/82. There were 79 criminal cases on the docket, 23 convictions, seven persons committed to prison and 49 cases left pending. In the County Court 194 cases were pending on 1/1/82, 242 new cases were filed and 203 cases were disposed of during the year leaving 233 cases pending on 12/31/82. There were 379 criminal cases on the docket, 137 convictions, 39 persons committed to jail, and 182 cases left pending. **JAILS** One jail, capacity 11. **ATTORNEYS AT LAW** Seven. **UTILITIES** 75% of the residents are connected to a public or privately owned water system and 70% are connected to a public sewer system. Natural gas is distributed to the county by Energas Company. The average annual residential bill for natural gas in 1982 for the Energas distribution system was $371.63, an increase of 23% over 1981.

Electricity is distributed to the city of Crosbyton partially by the Crosbyton Power and Light System and to the rest of the county by Southwestern Public Service, Dickens Electric Coop., Inc., Lighthouse Electric Coop., Inc. and South Plains Electric Coop., Inc. and is generated primarily by gas and oil. **TAXES** The county has eight units with taxing authority: three school districts, three cities, one county and one special district.

RECREATION/ENTERTAINMENT

MUNICIPAL PARKS 14 acres in six municipal parks. These parks contain three playgrounds, three baseball and softball fields, three tennis courts and two swimming pools. **SCENIC DRIVES** The Texas Plains Trail runs through this county. This trail spans a vast area of the High Plains region of Texas slicing through the southernmost extension of the Great Plains of the United States. The land is flat except where erosion has carved canyon landscapes. **BOATING/FISHING** Major rivers: White and Brazos. **HUNTING** Fall season on antelope. Fall and winter seasons on deer and mule deer. No closed season on squirrel, coyote and bobcat. Winter seasons on quail, muskrat, beaver, opossum, ring-tailed cat, badger, fox, weasel, raccoon, skunk and civet cat. In 1983 sandhill crane, duck coot, geese, woodcock and jacksnipe seasons occurred during the winter months. Teal duck, rail and gallinule seasons occurred in the fall. Mourning dove season occurred intermittently during the fall and winter months. **MUSEUMS** Crosbyton: Crosby County Pioneer Memorial Museum. Ralls: Ralls Historical Museum. **SPECIAL EVENTS** St. Mary's Church Homecoming, Robertson, October; and Fall Fantasy, Ralls, November.

COMMUNITIES

COUNTY SEAT Crosbyton, County Courthouse, 79401; County Clerk's Office, 806/675-2334. **INCORPORATED COMMUNITIES** (1980 population and ZIP Code) Crosbyton (2,289) 79322, Lorenzo (1,394) 79343 and Ralls (2,422) 79357. **UNINCORPORATED COMMUNITIES** (and ZIP Code)Broadway 79322, Canyon Valley 79356, Cap Rock 79357, Cone 79321, Estacado 79343, Farmer 79357, Kalgary (Watson) 79356, Mount Blanco 79322, Owens 79357, Robertson 79343, Savage 79357 and Wake 79243. **FOR ADDITIONAL LOCAL INFORMATION** Crosbyton Chamber of Commerce, 115 S. Ayrshire, Crosbyton, 79322 (806) 675-2261 and Ralls Chamber of Commerce, P.O. Box 807, Ralls, 79357, (806) 253-2342.

CULBERSON (B3)

THE LAND

East of El Paso on Interstate Highway 10 in the Trans-Pecos Region, Culberson County covers 3,815 square miles. The elevation ranges in this mountainous county from 3,000 feet to the highest point in Texas which is the 8,751 foot Guadalupe Peak. The soils vary from nearly level to undulating, shallow and loamy with limestone and igneous rock outcrops to valleys with deep loamy soils over clayey subsoils to steep mountainous slopes with thin layers of clayey or loamy soil and over 90% of the surface exposed igneous rocks. Most of the soils have accumulations of gypsum or powdery lime and are saline. In the Trans-Pecos Mountains and Basins vegetation area, grass is short, sparse and drought-resistant. Desert shrubs such as creosote-tarbrush, yucca, cenizo and some mesquite dot the area. In the mountains pinon pine, juniper and some ponderosa pine are found at higher elevations. Less than 1% of the land in the county is considered prime farmland. **CLIMATE** Mild and dry. The average annual temperature is 62 °F. Temperatures in January range from an average low of 30° to an average high of 56 °F and in July range from 67° to 94 °F. The average annual precipitation is 10 inches,

COUNTIES

CULBERSON (continued)

with an average relative humidity of 65% at 6 A.M. and 31% at 6 P.M. The average annual snowfall is three inches. The growing season averages 224 days per year, with the last freeze the first of April and the first freeze in early November. The sun shines during the year on the average 75% of the daylight hours.

THE PEOPLE

Culberson County is one of the most sparsely populated in the state. Among all the U.S. Counties, it ranks 37th in the highest birth rate and 25th in the highest percent of population of Spanish origin. The 1982 estimated population of 3,400 indicates a slight increase since 1980. The county's population has continuously increased since 1930 except for a 3% decline between 1970 and 1980. Almost 84% of the decline between 1970 and 1980 was in rural areas. The age group with the largest decrease was ages five to 14. The young median age rose from 22 in 1970 to 24 in 1980. The largest ancestry groups are Hispanics (63%), persons of English descent (16%), and those of Irish descent (12%). **REGISTERED VOTERS** As of November 2, 1982 there were 1,736 registered voters (0.02% of the state total). The 1982 general election had a 53% voter turnout, compared to a 58% turnout in the 1980 general election. In the 1982 primary 94% voted Democratic and 6% Republican, with 630 votes cast.

THE ECONOMY

AGRICULTURE Ranchland. In 1982, 85% of the land was in farms and ranches, with less than 1% of the farmland under cultivation. Most of the cropland and some of the rangeland was irrigated. Culberson ranked 237th in the state in highest agricultural receipts, with 61% from livestock and livestock products. Overgrazing, undesirable brush, decreasing irrigation water supplies and salinity are the current conservation problems. Primary crops: hay, wheat, cotton and sorghum. Primary vegetables: onions. Primary fruits and nuts: peaches and pecans. Primary livestock and products: cattle, sheep and wool. **BUSINESS** Total number of business establishments in the county: 90. Retail sales during the first quarter of 1984 incresed 36%. In 1980, 8% of the labor force were self-employed, 14% were employed in professional or related services, 5% in manufacturing, 23% in wholesale and retail trade, 23% in agriculture, forestry, fisheries and mining, 12% were employed in other counties and there were 195 retired workers. The industries with the most employment: agribusiness and tourism. The nonfarm earnings in 1981 totaled $24,271,000. The retired workers received an average monthly Social Security payment of $297.00. **FINANCE** On June 30, 1983, one commercial bank had total deposits of $9,954,000 and total assets of $11,519,000. THere is one state savings and loan association branch in the county. **HOUSING** Average value of homes in 1980: $18,300. Permits for new, privately owned housing units increased in 1982: eight permits were issued with a total construction cost of $147,000. Of those permits, all were for single family houses. Between 1970 and 1980 the number of housing units increased by 9%. Eighty-three percent of all units in the county are air-conditioned, 91% are heated by gas and 6% by electricity. **NATURAL RESOURCES** Dolomite, gypsum, limestone, salt, oil, gas, silver, copper, lead, zinc, barite and molybdenum. In 1982 a total of 2,666,772 thousand cubic feet of gas well gas, 1,416 barrels of condensate, 1,101,607 barrels of crude oil and 2,249,453 thousand cubic feet of casinghead gas were produced. Current production of other minerals and products includes copper, gypsum, brucitic marble, mica, molybdenum, crushed rhyolite, silver, frasch sulphur and talc. **TOURISM** Travel expenditures of $17,432,000 in 1982 (an increase of 11% over 1981) generated 443 jobs and $3,514,000 in payroll. Lodging: nine hotels, motels and tourist courts. **ALCOHOLIC BEVERAGES** Packaged distilled spirits, beer, ale, malt liquor and wine are legal. **FEDERAL EXPENDITURES** The federal government had direct expenditures or obligations of $7,651,000 in the county during fiscal year 1983, including $110,000 by the U.S. Department of Defense. In addition, the federal government provided $79,000 in grant awards, paid $939,000 in salaries and wages, made direct payments to individuals of $4,802,000 including $3,958,000 in retirement and disability payments, awarded $1,406,000 in procurement contracts and spent $425,000 in other expenditures or obligations. The federal government also provided $532,000 in direct loans and $2,205,000 in guaranteed loans and insurance.

COMMUNICATION

Newspapers–Weekly: Van Horn Advocate. Cable TV. Telephone companies: Continental Telephone and Dell Telephone Coop. **TRANSPORTATION** Total public road mileage: 597. In 1982 there were 2,725 registered vehicles and 134 reported traffic accidents including three fatalities. Intercity bus service is available. Motor freight: five local and intrastate carriers. Rail: The Sunset Limited provides passenger service on the amtrak route. Four main and one branch line carry freight through the county. One of the main lines carries annually over 30 million tons of freight, one carries five to 10, and two carry one to five million each. The branch line carries annually less than one million tons. Aircraft: 11 are registered in the county. Airports: Culberson County Airport at Van Horn is a general utility airport providing general aviation service. It serves as a base for 15 aircraft. County Hospital provides a Heliport for emergency use.

COMMUNITY SERVICES

EDUCATION One school district with two elementary, one middle and one high school. The average daily attendance in 1981-82 was 857, with expenditures per pupil of $2,962 including 63 classroom teachers with an average annual salary of $17,076. None of the 63 high school graduates planned to attend college. In 1982-83, 26% of the students were White, 73% Hispanic, 0.1% Black, 0.3% Asian and 0.3% American Indian. **PUBLIC LIBRARIES** Van Horn City-County Library: 12,491 volumes. **CHILD CARE** One day care licensed facility. **HEALTH CARE** Two physicians. Hospitals: one with a capacity of 25. Ambulance services: one county service. Mental health: one clinic. **CHURCHES** 11 churches have an estimated combined membership of 3,299. The largest denominations are Catholic, Southern Baptist and United Methodist. **SOCIAL SERVICES** In fiscal year 1983 a total of $210,892 in food stamps was distributed, with an average of 481 persons receiving food stamps each month. Aid to Families with Dependent Children (AFDC) totaled $17,723 with an average of 12 families receiving AFDC each month. Medical assistance benefits for the aged and disabled of $57,228 and for families and children of $49,959 brought the county benefit total to $335,802. **FIRE PROTECTION** One volunteer fire department. **LAW ENFORCEMENT** The County Sheriff has eight commissioned officers. **CRIME** Nine violent crimes (murder, forcible rape, robbery and aggravated assault) and 34 nonviolent crimes (burglary, larceny-theft and motor vehicle theft) were reported in 1982. **JUDICIAL SYSTEM** Three District Courts and Judges, one County Court and Judge and four Justices of the Peace. In the District Courts a total of 217 cases were pending on 1/1/82, 90 new cases were filed and 54 cases were disposed of during the year leaving 253 cases pending on 12/31/82. There were 26 criminal cases on the docket, five convictions, four persons committed to prison and 16 cases left pending. In the County Court 174 cases were pending on 1/1/82, 56 new cases were filed and 35 cases were disposed of during the year leaving 195 cases pending on 12/31/82. There were 172 criminal cases on the docket, 16 convictions, 13 persons committed to jail, and 140 cases left pending. **JAILS** one jail, capacity 17. Renovating bookkeeping-processing facilities. **ATTORNEYS AT LAW** Two. **UTILITIES** 89% of the residents are connected to a public or privately owned water system and 85% are connected to a public sewer system. Natural gas is distributed to the county by Southern Union Company and Texas Western Municipal Gas Corp. The average annual residential bill for natural gas in 1982 for the Southern Union distribution system was $355.85, an increase of 23% over 1981. Electricity is distributed to the county by El Paso Electric Co., and Rio Grande Electric Coop., Inc. and is generated primarily by gas, oil and coal. The typical residential electric bill is $183.69 per month for an all-electric house using 2,500 kwh. **TAXES** The county has three units with taxing authority: one school district, one city, and one county.

RECREATION/ENTERTAINMENT
FEDERAL GUADALUPE MOUNTAINS NATIONAL PARK was dedicated in 1972 and contains 76,293 acres including the Guadalupe Peak, the highest point in Texas. Rising from the desert, these mountains contain four of the state's highest peaks and a rare mixture of plant and animal life. Facilities include camping and trailer sites as well as hiking trails. **NATIONAL REGISTER OF HISTORIC PLACES** Guadalupe Mountains National Park: Guadalupe Ranch, Pinery Station and Wallace Pratt Lodge. Toyah vicinity: Granado Cave. Van Horn: Clark Hotel and First Presbyterian Church. **COUNTY/MUNICIPAL PARKS** 14 acres in one county and one municipal park. These parks contain one baseball and softball field. **SCENIC DRIVES** The Texas Mountain Trail runs through this county. This trail offers an adventurous route through West Texas, a remote region of stark majesty with its secluded canyons and high peaks. **BOATING/FISHING** Lakes/reservoirs: Big Charley Tank (19 acres) and Levinson (53 acres). Primary streams: Cottonwood and Delaware. **WILDLIFE REFUGES** Culberson State Wildlife Management Area covers 7,791 acres. **HUNTING** Fall season on antelope. Fall and winter seasons on deer and mule deer. No closed season on elk, javelina, coyote and bobcat. Winter season on quail, muskrat, beaver, opossum, ring-tailed cat, badger, fox, weasel, raccoon, skunk and civet cat. In 1983 sandhill crane, duck, coot, geese, woodcock and jacksnipe seasons occurred during the winter months. Teal duck, rail and gallinule season occurred in the fall. Mourning dove season occurred intermittently during the fall and winter months with a fall season in white-winged dove in some parts of the county. **MUSEUMS** Van Horn: Honeycutt House and Culberson County Historical Museum. **SPECIAL EVENTS** Big Country Celebration, Van Horn, June.

COMMUNITIES
COUNTY SEAT Van Horn, County Courthouse, 79855; County Clerk's Office, 915/283-2058. **INCORPORATED COMMUNITIES** (1980 population and ZIP Code) Van Horn (2,772) 79855. **UNICORPORATED COMMUNITIES** (and ZIP Code) Kent 79855, Lobo 79855, Nickel Creek 88220, Pine Springs 88220, Plateau 79855 and Wild Horse 79855. **FOR ADDITIONAL LOCAL INFORMATION** Van Horn Chamber of Commerce, P. O. Box 762, Van Horn, 79855 915/283-2043.

DALLAM (P1)

THE LAND
In the northwest corner of the Texas Panhandle on U.S. Highways 385, 54 and 87 in the High Plains Region, Dallam County covers 1,505 square miles with an elevation range of 3,800 to 4,600 feet. The county has nearly level, loamy soils with clayey subsoils.

In the High Plains vegetation area, Dallam has short to tall prairie grasses with live oak and small mesquite trees, yucca, thorny shrubs and cacti. Between 11 and 20% of the land in the county is considered prime farmland. **CLIMATE** Continental Steppe and the coolest in the state. The average annual temperature is 55 °F. Temperatures in January range from an average low of 18 ° to an average high of 46 °F and in July range from 63 ° to 91 °F. The average annual precipitation is 16 inches, with an average relative humidity of 70% at 6 A.M. and 40% at 6 P.M. The average annual snowfall is 15 inches. The growing season averages 178 days per year, with the last freeze in late April and the first freeze in mid October. The sun shines during the year on the average 75% of the daylight hours.

THE PEOPLE
The 1982 estimated population of 6,700 indicates a continuation of the growth pattern begun in the 1970s which reversed the steady population decrease from 1950 to 1970. Over 17% of the growth between 1970 and 1980 occured in rural areas. The age group with the largest gain was ages 20 to 34. The median age lowered from 30 in 1970 to 29 in 1980. The largest ancestry groups are those of English descent (27%), Irish descent (19%), German descent (18%) and Hispanic (17%). **REGISTERED VOTERS** As of November 2, 1982 there were 2,569 registered voters (0.04% of the state total). The 1982 general election had a 54% voter turnout, compared to a 62% turnout in the 1980 general election. In the 1982 primary 89% voted Democratic and 11 Republican, with 1,132 votes cast.

THE ECONOMY
AGRICULTURE Wheat, cattle, and sorghum area. In 1982, 98% of the land was in farms and ranches, with 39% of the farmland under cultivation and 57% irrigated. Dallam ranked 31st in the state in highest agricultural receipts with 72% from crops. Overgrazing, undesirable brush and weeds, wind erosion, decreasing irrigation water supplies and difficulties in grass establishment are the current conservation problems. Primary crops: fourth in the state for wheat, fifth for corn and seventh for cowpeas. Sorgham and hay. Primary livestock and products: ninth in the state for cattle. Hogs. **BUSINESS** Total number of business establishments in the county: 227. Retail sales during the first quarter of 1984 increased 17%. In 1980, 20% of the labor force were self-employed, 13% were employed in professional or related services, 5% in manufacturing, 28% in wholesale and retail trade, 24% in agriculture, forestry, fisheries and mining, 15% were employed in other counties and there were 760 retired workers. The industries with the most employment: meat packing and agribusiness. The non farm earnings in 1981 totaled $64,123,000. The retired workers received an average monthly Social Security payment of $313.00. **FINANCE** On June 30, 1983, three commercial banks had total deposits of $86,175,000 and total assets of $99,489,000. On December 31, 1982 one federal savings and loan association, one state savings and loan association branch and one federal branch had assets of $45,556,753. **HOUSING** Average value of homes in 1980: $18,900. Permits for new, privately owned housing units increased in 1982: 56 permits were issued with a total construction cost of $2,184,700. Of those permits, all were for single family houses. Housing permits in Dalhart increased from 31 in 1981 to 56 in 1982. Between 1970 and 1980 the number of housing units increased by 21%. Seventy percent of all units in the county are air-conditioned, 97% are heated by gas and 3% by electricity. **NATURAL RESOURCES** Caliche, oil and gas. In 1982 a total of 58,467 thousand cubic feet of gas well gas were produced. Current production of other minerals and products includes caliche. **TOURISM** Travel expenditures of $14,194,000 in 1982 (an increase of 11% over 1981) generated 360 jobs and $2,854,000 in payroll.

COUNTIES

DALLAM (continued)

Lodging: eight hotels, motels and tourist courts. **ALCOHOLIC BEVERAGES** Packaged distilled spirits, beer, ale, malt liquor and wine are legal in parts of the county. **FEDERAL EXPENDITURES** The federal government had direct expenditures or obligations of $19,409,000 in the county during fiscal year 1983, including $247,000 by the U.S. Department of Defense. In addition, the federal government provided $177,000 in grant awards, paid $782,000 in salaries and wages, made direct payments to individuals of $10,343,000 including $7,337,000 in retirement and disability payments, awarded $3,000 in procurement contracts and spent $8,105,000 in other expenditures or obligations. The federal government also provided $28,406,000 in direct loans and $7,305,000 in guaranteed loans and insurance.

COMMUNICATION

Newspapers–Daily: Dalhart Daily Texan, ave. eve. circ. 2,764. Radio: KXIT-AM, KXIT-FM, (Dalhart) Cable TV. Telephone companies: General Telephone and XIT Rural Telephone Coop. **TRANSPORTATION** Total public road mileage: 791. In 1982 there were 7,090 registered vehicles and 189 reported traffic accidents including six fatalities. Intercity bus service is available. Rail: four main lines carry freight through the county with two carrying annually over 30 million tons each and two carrying one to five each. Aircraft: 85 are registered in the county. Airports: Dalhart Municipal Airport is a basic transportation airport providing general aviation service. It serves as a base for 86 aircraft. Miller Airfield at Dalhart.

COMMUNITY SERVICES

EDUCATION Two school districts with two elementary, one middle and two high schools. The average daily attendance in 1981-82 was 1,658, with expenditures per pupil of $2,581 including 120 classroom teachers with an average annual salary of $16,884. Four percent of the 118 high school graduates planned to attend college. In 1982-83, 80% of the students were White, 17% Hispanic, 2% Black and Asian 0.7% Private schools: 98 students enrolled in one elementary school. **PUBLIC LIBRARIES** Dallam County Library (Dalhart): 20,000 volumes. **CHILD CARE** 20 day care and three twenty-four hour care licensed facilities. **HEALTH CARE** Five physicians and two dentists. Ambulance services: two volunteer services. Mental health: one clinic. **CHURCHES** 20 churches have an estimated combined membership of 7,491. The largest denominations are Southern Baptist, Catholic and United Methodist. **SOCIAL SERVICES** In fiscal year 1983 a total of $164,804 in food stamps was distributed, with an average of 361 persons receiving food stamps each month. Aid to Families with Dependent Children (AFDC) totaled $12,955 with an average of eight families receiving AFDC each month. Medical assistance benefits for the aged and disabled of $163,956 and for families and children of $16,285 brought the county benefit total to $358,000. **FIRE PROTECTION** Two volunteer fire departments. **LAW ENFORCEMENT** The County Sheriff has three commissioned officers. One police department have a combined force of 11. **CRIME** 12 violent crimes (murder, forcible rape, robbery and aggravated assault) and 209 nonviolent crimes (burglary, larceny-theft and motor vehicle theft) were reported in 1982. **JUDICIAL SYSTEM** One District Court and Judge, one County Court and Judge and three Justices of the Peace. In the District Court a total of 128 cases were pending on 1/1/82, 189 new cases were filed and 216 cases were disposed of during the year leaving 101 cases pending on 12/31/82. There were 47 criminal cases on the docket, 25 convictions, nine persons committed to prison and seven cases left pending. In the County Court 85 cases were pending on 1/1/82, 131 new cases were filed and 175 cases were disposed of during the year leav-

ing 41 cases pending on 12/31/82. There were 173 criminal cases on the docket, 62 convictions, 13 persons committed to jail, and 29 cases left pending. **JAILS** One jail, capacity 15, opened in 1983. **ATTORNEYS AT LAW** 12. **UTILITIES** 82% of the residents are connected to a public or privately owned water system and 76% are connected to a public sewer system. Natural gas is distributed to the county by Energas Company and People Natural Gas Co. The average annual residential bill for natural gas in 1982 for the Energas distribution system was $371.63, an increase of 23% over 1981. Electricity is distributed to the county by Rita Blanco Electric Coop., Inc. and Southwestern Public Service Co. and is generated primarily by gas and coal. The typical residential electric bill is $123.79 per month for an all-electric house using 2,500 kwh. **TAXES** The county has five units with taxing authority: two school district, two cities, and one county.

RECREATION/ENTERTAINMENT

MUNICIPAL PARKS 4 acres in 2 municipal parks. These parks contain one playground. **BOATING/FISHING** Primary streams: Carrizo, Coldwater and Rita Blanco. **HUNTING** Fall season on antelope. Fall and winter seasons on mule deer. Summer, fall and winter seasons on squirrel. Winter season on pheasant, quail, muskrat, beaver, opossum, ring-tailed cat, badger, fox, weasel raccoon, skunk and civet cat. No closed season for coyote and bobcat. Fall, winter and spring seasons for turkey. In 1983 sandhill crane, duck, coot, geese, woodcock and jacksnipe seasons occurred during the winter months. Teal duck, rail and gallinule seasons occurred in the fall. Mourning dove season occurred intermittently during the fall and winter months. **MUSEUMS** Dalhart: Dallam-Hartley Counties XIT Museum. **SPECIAL EVENTS** Bicounty Junior Livestock Show, Dalhart, February; XIT Rodeo and Reunion, Dalhart, August; Inter-State Fair, Dalhart, September.

COMMUNITIES

COUNTY SEAT Dalhart, County Courthouse, 79022; County Clerk's Office, 806/249-4751. **INCORPORATED COMMUNITIES** (1980 population and ZIP Code) Dalhart (68541: 4,571 in Dallam Co. and 2,283 in Hartley Co.) 79022 and Texline (477) 79087. **UNINCORPORATED COMMUNITIES** (and ZIP Code) Conlen 79022, Kerrick 79051, Perico 79087. **FOR ADDITIONAL LOCAL INFORMATION** Dalhart Chamber of Commerce, P. O. Box 967, Dalhart, 79022, 806/249-5646.

DALLAS (M12)

THE LAND

At the intersection of Interstate Highways 35 East, 30 and 45 in the Blackland Prairies Region, Dallas county covers 880 square miles with an elevation range of 450 to 750 feet. Along the western border and in the eastern two-thirds of the county are undulating, slightly acidic soils with loamy surfaces and cracking, clayey subsoils as well as acidic, cracking clayey soils all of which have a high shrink-swell potential. The rest of the county has undulating, alkaline, mostly loamy soils. In the Blackland Prairies vegetation area, the county has tall grasses with oak, pecan and elm trees along streams with mesquite in the prairies. Between 31 and 40% of the land in the county is considered prime farmland. **CLIMATE** Subtropical subhumid and subtropical humid with wide-ranging seasonal changes. The average annual temperature is 66 °F. Temperatures in January range from an average low of 33 ° to an average high of 56 °F and in July range from 73 ° to 97 °F. The average annual precipitation is 34 inches, with an average relative humidity of 83% at 6 A.M. and 53% at 6 P.M. The average annual snowfall is four inches. The growing season averages 235 days per year, with the last freeze the first of April and the first freeze in mid November. The sun shines during the year on the average 66% of the daylight hours.

THE PEOPLE

Among all U.S. counties, Dallas County ranks 69th in the most people per square mile and 11th in the largest population. The 1982 estimated population of 1,641,400 indicates a continuation of the strong growth rate established in the 1940's. The population increased 40% between 1960 and 1970, then slowed to 17% between 1970 and 1980. Urban areas grew 18% from 1970 to 1980, while rural areas lost 28% of their population. The age groups with the largest gains were ages 20 to 34 and 65 and over with the largest decreases occurring in ages five to nine. The median age rose from 26 in 1970 to 28 in 1980. The largest ancestry groups are persons of English descent (26%), Black (19%), Irish descent (18%) and German descent (15%). **REGISTERED VOTERS** As of November 2, 1982 there were 675,890 registered voters (11% of the state total). The 1982 general election had a 51% voter turnout, compared to a 68% turnout in the 1980 general election. In the 1982 primary 51% voted Democratic and 49% Republican, with 120,391 votes cast.

THE ECONOMY

AGRICULTURE In 1982, 23% of the land was in farms and ranches, with 56% of the farmland under cultivation. Dallas ranked 111th in the state in highest agricultural receipts, with 73% from crops. Water erosion, flooding and urban encroachment are the current conservation problems. Primary crops: hay, wheat, sorghum, oats and cotton. Primary vegetables: cabbage and sweet potatoes. Primary fruits and nuts: peaches and pecans. Primary livestock and products: cattle, milk and hogs. **BUSINESS** Total number of business establishments in the county: 43,747. Retail sales during the first quarter of 1984 increased 24%. In 1980, 6% of the labor force were self-employed, 16% were employed in professional or related services, 20% in manufacturing, 23% in wholesale and retail trade, 9% in finance, insurance and real estate, 5% were employed in other counties and there were 91,928 retired workers. The industries with the most employment: oil and gas extraction, tourism, general construction, soft drink bottling and canning, commercial printing, steel foundries, fruit and vegetable processing and the manufacture of dairy products, bakery products, men's and women's apparel, kitchen cabinets, household and office furniture, cardboard boxes, industrial and agricultural chemicals, asphalt, fabricated rubber products, ceramic tile, tools, heating and plumbing equipment, fabricated structural metal products, ammunition, oilfield machinery, pumps and pumping equipment, electronic computing equipment, communication equipment for radio and television, electronic components, refrigeration equipment, motor vehicles and equipment, aircraft and aircraft parts. The nonfarm earnings in 1981 totaled $21,859,624,000. The retired workers received an average monthly Social Security payment of $346.00. **FINANCE** On June 30, 1983, 140 commercial banks had total deposits of $23,859,297,000 and total assets of $35,503,834,000. On December 31, 1982, 16 state savings and loan associations, four federal associations, 167 state branches and 37 federal branches had combined assets of $6,232,556,338. In addition there are 193 credit unions in the county. **HOUSING** Average value of homes in 1980: $48,800. Permits for new, privately owned housing units increased in 1982: 31,340 permits were issued with a total construction cost of $1,129,055,070. Of those permits, 8,585 were for single family houses. Housing permits increased in Addison from 244 in 1981 to 393 in 1982, in Balch Springs for 24 to 232 with 197 of the permits issued for apartments and condominiums, in Cedar Hill from 126 to 278 with 232 of the permits issued for single family houses, in Coppell from 138 to 349 with all of the permits issued for single family houses, in Dallas from

7,612 to 12,336 with 9,730 of the permits issued for apartments and condominiums, in Desoto from 55 to 671 with 547 of the permits issued for apartments and condominiums, in Garland from 1,790 to 4, 388 with 3,228 of the permits issued for apartments and condominiums, in Grand Prairie from 1,055 to 2,600 with 1,890 of the permits issued for apartments and condominiums, in Irving from 1,975 to 4,844 with 4,128 of the permits issued for apartments and condominiums, in Lancaster from 72 to 165 with 155 of the permits issued for single family houses, in Mesquite from 744 to 2,215, in Sachse from 41 to 115 and in Seagoville from 16 to 33 with all permits issued for single family houses. Between 1970 and 1980 the number of housing units increased by 39%. Ninety-three percent of all units in the county are air-conditioned, 68% are heated by gas and 32% by electricity. **NATURAL RESOURCES** Limestone, sand and gravel, oil, gas and shale. Current production of other minerals and products includes cement, clay, crushed limestone, lightweight aggregate, construction sand, sand and gravel and shale. **TOURISM** Travel expenditures of $3,103,918,000 in 1982 (an increase of 8% over 1981) generated 59,350 jobs and $699,242,000 in payroll. Lodging: 177 hotels, motels and tourist courts. Convention/meeting facilities: Carrollton-Buffalo Park Speedway, Dallas-Apparel Mart, Bishop College's Stadium, Dallas Baptist College's Fieldhouse, Dallas Convention Center, Market Hall, Reunion Arena, Southern Methodist University has two Theatres and a Coliseum, Stars over Texas, Texas State Fair has a Coliseum, Music Hall and Stadium, and 35 hotels have facilities for large gatherings; and Irving-Texas Stadium. **ALCOHOLIC BEVERAGES** Packaged distilled spirits, beer, ale, malt liquor and wine are legal in parts of the county. Sale of mixed beverages is legal in all or parts of the county. **MILITARY INSTALLATIONS** Garland Air National Guard Base, Garland, 176 personnel, four acres, Air National Guard Activities; Dallas Naval Air Station, Dallas, 3,864 personnel, 795 acres, Reserve Air Training; Naval Weapons Industrial Plant, Dallas, 315 acres, Aircraft Parts Production. **FEDERAL EXPENDITURES** The federal government had direct expenditures or obligations of $3,972,289,000 in the county during fiscal year 1983, including $1,742,512,000 by the U.S. Department of Defense. In addition, the federal government provided $172,281,000 in grant awards, paid $595,807,000 in salaries and wages, made direct payments to individuals of $1,389,644,000 including $1,099,623,000 in retirement and disability payments, awarded $1,719,411,000 in procurement contracts and spent $95,146,000 in other expenditures or obligations. The federal government also provided $11,275,000 in direct loans and $579,909,000 in guaranteed loans and insurance.

COMMUNICATION

Newspapers–Daily: The Dallas Morning News, ave. morn. circ. 317,279, Dallas Times Herald, ave. daily circ. 269,409, Garland Daily News ave. eve. circ. 6,514, Irving Daily News ave. eve. circ. 10,940, News (Mesquite) ave. eve. circ. 4,045 and the Richardson Daily News ave. eve. circ. 5,895. Weekly: Balch Springs Sentinel (Seagoville), Carrollton Chronicle, Cedar Hill Chronicle, Oak Cliff Tribune, Post Tribune, Park Cities News, Suburban Tribune, The White Rocker, DeSoto News Advertiser, DeSoto Leader (Lancaster), DeSota Journal, Duncanville Suburban, Farmers Branch Times, Suburban News (Farmers Branch), The Grapevine Sun, The Leader in Lancaster, North Dallas/Addison Today and Suburbia News (Seagoville). Radio: KKDA-AM (Grand Prairie), KPBC-AM (Irving), KBOX-AM, KRLD-AM, KSKY-AM, KVIL-AM, WFAA-AM and KAAM-AM (Dallas), KKDA-FM (Grand Prairie), KCHU-FM, KCBI-FM, KERA-FM, KLVU-FM, KMGC-FM, KNON-FM, KRSM-FM, KUTT-FM, WRR-FM, KAFM-FM, and KMEZ-FM Stereo, KOAX-FM Stereo, KVIL-FM Stereo and KZEW-FM Stereo (Dallas). Television: KDFW-

COUNTIES

DALLAS (continued)

CH. 4, KERA (PBS) CH. 13, KNBN CH. 33, KTWS CH. 27, KXTX CH. 39, WFAA CH. 8 (Dallas). Cable TV. Telephone companies: Continental Telephone, General Telephone and Southwestern Bell. **TRANSPORTATION** Total public road mileage: 8,594. In 1982 there were 1,475,542 registered vehicles and 45,528 reported traffic accidents including 298 fatalities. Taxi cabs: four companies in the city of Dallas, one in Irving and one in Grand Pairie. Municipal transit systems: one bus system in the city of Dallas, with scheduled routes and one Surtran Shuttle system between the Dallas-Fort Worth Airport and the central business areas and major hotels and motels. Intercity bus service is available. Motor freight: 560 local and intrastate carriers. Rail: the Eagle provides passenger service on the Amtrak route. Ten main and four branch lines carry freight through the county. One of the main lines carries annually over 30 million tons of freight, two carry 20 to 30 each, two carry 10 to 20 each, three carry five to ten each, one carries one to five and one carries less than one million tons. Two of the branch lines carry annually one to five million tons of freight each and two carry less than one each. Aircraft: 2,695 are registered in the county. Airports: Dallas-Fort Worth Regional Airport is located centrally between the two cities and provides full carrier service. It is a large hub for long haul flights. Dallas Love Field in Dallas serves as a base for 871 aircraft and is a large hub for medium haul flights with carrier service. Grand Prairie Municipal Airport serves as a base for 210 aircraft and is a general utility airport with general aviation service. Lancaster Municipal Airport serves as a base for 161 aircraft and is a basic transportation airport with general aviation service. Also serving the area are Addison Municipal Airport at Addison, Carroll Airpark at DeSoto, Red Bird Airport at Dallas, Dallas Airpark, Doan East at Dallas, Phillips Flying Ranch at Dallas, Phil L. Hudson Airport at Mesquite, Seagoville Airport at Seagoville, Addison (North-South) at Dallas, Dallas Love Field Heliport at Dallas, DFW Airport Heliport at Dallas, North Park Inn Heliport at Dallas, Southland Center Heliport at Dallas, Texas Helicopters Heliport at Irving, Seena Heliport at Grand Prairie and Presbyterian Hospital Heliport at Dallas. Dallas-Fort Worth ships by air about 1.5 million pounds of domestic and foreign exports each month. Import shipments average about two million pounds per month.

COMMUNITY SERVICES

EDUCATION 15 school districts with 284 elementary, 69 middle, 62 high schools and six special education. The average daily attendance in 1981-82 was 260,368, with expenditures per pupil of $2,687 including 15,628 classroom teachers with an average annual salary of $19,132. Sixty-two percent of the 17,810 high school graduates planned to attend college. In 1982-83, 57% of the students were White, 14% Hispanic, 26% Black, 2% Asian and 0.4% American Indian. Sports championships: 1983 Boys' Soccer Champion, Richardson Pearce H.S.; 1983 Girls' Soccer Champion, Dallas Kimble H.S.; 1983 AAAAA Boy's Track, Dallas Roosevelt H.S.; 1982 AAAAA Girls' Cross Country, Highland Park H.S. Private schools: 30,927 students enrolled in 106 elementary and 36 high schools. Sports championships: 1983 AAAA Boy's Baseball, Soccer, Tennis, Jesuit College Preparatory H.S.; 1983 AAAA Girls' Tennis and Swimming, Ursuline Acadamy; 1983 AAAA Boys' Golf, Jesuit College Preparatory H.S. and Tarrant County's Nolan H.S. (tie). Baylor College of Dentistry is located in Dallas. Established in 1905 it is an independent nonprofit institution. Enrollment in 1982 was 534 with in state undergraduate tuition and fees of $900 per quarter. The highest degree offered is: Doctorate. Baylor University School of Nursing is also located in Dallas. Bishop College is located in Dallas. Established in 1881 it is affiliated with the Baptist Church. Enrollment in 1982 was 945 with in state undergraduate tuition and fees of $2,400 per semester. The highest degree offered: Bachelor. Dallas Baptist College is located in Dallas. Established in 1965 it is affiliated with the Southern Baptist Church. Enrollment in 1982 was 1,134 with in state undergraduate tuition and fees of $2,100 per semester. The highest degree offered is: Bachelor. Dallas Bible College is located in Dallas. Established in 1941 it is an independent nonprofit institution. Enrollment in 1982 was 235 with in state undergraduate tuition and fees of $1,962 per semester. The highest degree offered is: Bachelor. Dallas Christian College is located in Dallas. Established in 1950 it is affiliated with the Churches of Christ. Enrollment in 1982 was 147. The highest degree offered is: Bachelor. Dallas County Community College System is located in Dallas (7 campuses). Established in 1965 it is a vocational and two year academic college under state control. Enrollment in 1982 was 42,432 with in state undergraduate tuition and fees of $204 per semester. Dallas Theological Seminary is located in Dallas. Established in 1924 it is an independent nonprofit institution. Enrollment in 1982 was 1,036. The highest degree offered is: Doctorate (no undergraduates). Devry Institute of Technology is located in Irving. Established in 1969 it is a profit making institution. Enrollment in 1982 was 1,076 with in state undergraduate tuition and fees of $3,845 per trimester. The highest degree offered is: Bachelor. Southern Methodist University is located in Dallas. Established in 1911 it is affiliated with the Methodist Church. Enrollment in 1982 wa 9,112 with in state undergraduate tuition and fees of $4,910 per semester. The highest degree offered is: Doctorate. Sport championships; (Southwest Conference) 1983 Men's Tennis. University of Dallas is located in Irving. Established in 1956 it is affiliated with the Catholic Church. Enrollment in 1982 was 2,688 with in state undergraduate tuition and fees of $3,272 per semester. The highest degree offered is: Doctorate. University of Texas at Dallas is located in Richardson. Established in 1969 it is under state control. Enrollment in 1982 was 6,368 with in state undergraduate tuition and fees of $394 per semester. The highest degree offered is: Doctorate (no lower division). University of Texas Health Science Center at Dallas was established in 1943 and is under state control. Enrollment in 1982 was 1,322. The highest degree offered is: Doctorate (no lower division). Amber University (formerly Abilene Christian University at Dallas) is located in Dallas. Established in 1971 it is an independant nonprofit institution. Enrollment in 1982 was 931 with in state undergraduate tuition and fees of $1,584 per semester. The highest degree offered is: Master. Vocational education: Dallas-Academy of Barbering, Allstate Business College, American Trades Institute, Control Data Institute, Control Data Learning Center, Cosmetology Career Center, Dallas Christian College, Dallas Institute of Funeral Services, Elkins Institute, Executive Secretarial School, Fashion and Art Institute, Industrial Trade School, Lincoln Technical Institute, Methodist Hospital School of Respiratory Therapy, National Beauty School, Miss Wades Fashion College, National Institute of Technology, Neilson Beauty College, Renee's Cosmetology Center, Texas Barber College, Texas College of Medical and Dental Assistants, Texas Institute, Velma B's Beauty Academy, Video Technical Institute, Academy for Medical and Dental Assistants, Inc. Auston's Professional Modeling of Dallas, Barbizon School of Modeling, Bartending Academy of Texas, Inc., Bradford School, Court Reporting Institute, Dallas Word Processing Institute, H & R Block Income Tax School, International Aviation and Travel Academy, International Bartending Institute, KD Studio, Stanley H. Kaplan Educational Center, Learning Techniques, Metroplex Institute of Business and Technology, National Institute for Continuing Professional Development, Nurses Aide Academy, Inc.,

Pittman Business College, John Robert Powers College, Prep Tutoring Service, John Sexton Test Preparation Center/Dallas, Inc., Texas Continuing Education Services for Nurses, Inc. United Electronics Institute, Viking Travel Careers, TACS, Inc., Evelyn Wood Reading Dynamics. Duncanville—Verbatim Court Reporting College. Garland—National Beauty School, Broadcast Media Institute. Irving—Irving Barber College, Irving Beauty Academy, Lindsey-Cooper Refrigeration School, National Beauty School, International Travel Institute, Northlake College. Lancaster—Cedar Valley College. Mesquite—Eastfield College, Metroplex Beauty School, National Beauty School. Richardson—Professional Court Reporting, Texas Teller Schools of America. **PUBLIC LIBRARIES** Carrollton Public Library: 40,000 volumes. Dallas County Public Library (Dallas): 220,404 volumes, 11 branches. Dallas Public Library: 1,884,827 volumes, 18 branches. Duncanville Public Library: 41,700 volumes. Farmers Branch Public Library: 56,000 volumes. Nicholson Memorial Library (Garland): 184,336 volumes, two branches. Grand Prairie Memorial Library: 80,538 volumes. Highland Park Library: 28,500 volumes. Irving Public Library System: 231,325 volumes, two branches. Mesquite Public Library: 94,407 volumes. Richardson Public Library: 132,836 volumes. **CHILD CARE** 2,050 day care and 367 twenty-four hour care licensed facilities. **HEALTH CARE** 3,657 physicians and 1,117 dentists. Hospitals: 35 with a combined capacity of 7,474. Specialized hospitals: two rehabilitation centers with capacity of 127, one children's medical hospital with capacity of 158, one cancer and research hospital with capacity of 110, one center for treatment of alcohol abuse with capacity of 26, one crippled children's hospital with capacity of 125, and one veterans medical center with capacity of 685. Clinics: 12 minor emergency centers, eight for treatment of alcohol and/or drug abuse, five dialysis clinics, three youth clinics, three community clinics, two public health clinics, one dental clinic, and one cancer research clinic. Ambulance services: 15 fire departments, 13 commercial, seven volunteer services, five funeral homes, one air, one hospital based, and one police department service. Mental health: eight clinics and four centers with capacity of 458. Nursing homes: 66 nursing homes with a combined capacity of 8,233 nursing care, 465 custodial care and 60 personal care residents. The average cost per day for private patients in 1982 was $33.68. **CHURCHES** 984 churches have an estimated combined membership of 769,821. The largest denominations are Southern Baptist, Catholic and United Methodist. **SOCIAL SERVICES** In fiscal year 1983 a total of $46,270,733 in food stamps was distributed, with an average of 89,098 persons receiving food stamps each month. Aid to Families with Dependent Children (AFDC) totaled $15,564,819 with an average of 10,244 families receiving AFDC each month. Medical assistance benefits for the aged and disabled of $62,633,957 and for families and children of $21,244,836 brought the county benefit total to $145,714,345. **FIRE PROTECTION** 11 paid, 4 partly paid and 10 volunteer fire departments. **LAW ENFORCEMENT** The County Sheriff has 576 commissioned officers. Twenty-four police departments have a combined force of 3,282. One university and eight colleges have campus police departments with a combined force of 67 officers. Dallas Park Police force has 75 officers. Irving Park Police force has five officers. Dallas-Forth Worth Airport has 204 officers. Dallas Love Field Security has 185 officers. Dallas County Municipal Utilities District I has five officers. **CRIME** 15,138 violent crimes (murder, forcible rape, robbery and aggravated assault) and 143,432 non-violent crimes (burglary, larceny-theft and motor vehicle theft) were reported in 1982. **JUDICIAL SYSTEM** 31 District Courts and Judges, 21 County Courts and Judges and 12 Justices of the Peace. In the District Courts a total of 31,003 cases were pending on 1/1/82, 55,882 new cases were filed and 51,799 cases were disposed of during the year leaving 35,086 cases pending on

12/31/82. There were 22,308 criminal cases on the docket, 9,496 convictions, 4,007 persons committed to prison, 602 committed to jail and 8,379 cases left pending. In the County Courts 61,604 cases were pending on 1/1/82, 83,606 new cases were filed and 78,191 cases were disposed of during the year leaving 67,019 cases pending on 12/31/82. There were 122,356 criminal cases on the docket, 21,259 convictions, 10,373 persons committed to jail and 57,796 cases left pending. **JAILS** Four jails, capacity 3004. Opened a new jail in 1983, and renovated bunks. **ATTORNEYS AT LAW** 7,445. **UTILITIES** 99% of the residents are connected to a public or privately owned water system and 98% are connected to a public sewer system. Natural gas is distributed to the county by Lone Star Gas Co., Division of Enserch. The average annual residential bill for natural gas in 1982 for the Lone Star distribution system was $405.91, an increase of 35% over 1981. Electricity is distributed to the city of Garland by the Garland Power and Light System and to the rest of the county by Dallas Power and Light Co., Texas Power and Light, Texas Utilities Co., Hill Co. Electric Coop., Inc., West Texas Utilities and Farmers Electric Coop., Inc. and is generated primarily by oil, gas and water. The typical residential electric bill is $165.24 per month for an all-electric house using 2,500 kwh. **TAXES** The county has 49 units with taxing authority: 15 school districts, 25 cities, one county, one hospital district, one college district and six special districts.

RECREATION/ENTERTAINMENT

PROFESSIONAL SPORTS Dallas: Dallas Mavericks Basketball Team (Reunion Arena), Side Kicks Soccer Team (Reunion Arena); Irving: Dallas Cowboys Football Team (Texas Stadium). **NATIONAL REGISTER OF HISTORIC PLACES** Dallas: John Hickman Miller House, Alfred H. Belo House, Dallas County Courthouse, Dallas Union Terminal, De Golyer Estate, El Centro College, Magnolia Building, Munger Place Historic District, South Boulevard Park Row Historic District, Swiss Avenue Historic District, Trinity Methodist Episcopal Church, Waples-Platter Coffee Roaster, Westend Historic District, Wilson Block, Dallas Scottish Rite Temple, Majestic Theatre, Waples-Platter Buildings, Wilson Building, Number 4 Hook and Ladder Company and the following structures at Southern Methodist University in Dallas: Clements Hall, Fred Florence Hall, Hyer Hall, McFarlin Memorial Auditorium, Jordan C. Ownby Stadium, Stanley Patterson Hall, Dallas Hall, Perkins Hall of Administration, Snider Hall and Virginia Hall. Lancaster: Randlett House, Capt. R.A. Rawlins House and W.A. Strain House. **COUNTY/MUNICIPAL PARKS** 28,152.5 acres in one county and 572 municipal parks. These parks contain 28 miles of hiking trails, 408 playgrounds, nine golf courses, 287 football and soccer fields, 350 baseball and softball fields, 438 tennis courts, 142 multi-use courts, 66 swimming pools and 10 boat ramps and shore fishing facilities. Developed Campsites: 22 **SCENIC DRIVES** The Texas Lakes Trail runs through this county. This trail introduces some 30 blue-water recreational areas in a variety of settings in North-Central Texas. **BOATING/FISHING** Lakes/reservoirs: Bachman (68 acres), Carolyn (171 acres), Columbia Club (30 acres), Dallas Hunting and Fishing Lower Club (96 acres), Dallas Hunting and Fishing Upper Club (54 acres), Fin and Feather Club (100 acres), Ray Hubbard (22,745 acres), Lancaster Club (109 acres), Lemon (179 acres), Mountain Creek (1,078 acres), North (800 acres), Number Nine (22 acres), Parkdale Storage Pond (179 acres), Rowlett Creek Soil Conservation Service Lake 10 (15 acres), Texaco (24 acres), Vilbig (100 acres), and White Rock (1,119 acres). Major rivers: Trinity, West Fork Trinity, Elm Fork Trinity and East Fork Trinity. Primary streams: Bachman, Hutlon, Prairie, Mountain, South Fork Grapevine, Hickory and White Rock. **HUNTING** No closed season on nutria, squirrel, bobcat and coyote. Winter season on quail, muskrat, beaver, otter, opossum,

COUNTIES

DALLAS (continued)

mink, ring-tailed cat, badger, fox, raccoon, skunk and civet cat. In 1983 duck, coot, geese, woodcock and jacksnipe seasons occurred during the winter months. Teal duck, rail and gallinule seasons occurred in the fall. Mourning dove season occurred during the fall and winter months. **MUSEUMS** Carrollton: A.W. Perry Homestead Museum. Dallas: Dallas Historical Society, Age of Steam Railroad Museum. Dallas Health and Science Museum, Dallas Museum of Fine Arts, Dallas Museum of Natural History, Meadows Museum, Old City Park, Texas Hall of State, International Museum of Cultures, Biblical Arts Center, Mexican American Cultural Heritage Center, McCord Theatre Collection, and The Museum of African-American Life and Culture. Grand Prairie: Jordan-Bowles Home, Fire Museum of Texas and Southwestern Historical Wax Museum. Irving: Irving Municipal Museum. Richardson: La Napoule Art Foundation, Henry Clews Memorial and History of Aviation Collection. Garland: Landmark Museum. **THEATERS** Dallas: Caruth Auditorium, Dallas Convention Center, Dallas Theater Center Kalita Humphreys Theater, Bob Hope Theatre, Margo Jones Experimental Theatre, McFarlin Memorial Auditorium, Majestic Theatre, Theatre Three, Music Hall at Fair Park, Reunion Arena, Alpha Omega Players Repertory Theatre of America, Crystal Palace Dinner Theatre, Dallas Summer Musicals, Granny's Dinner Playhouse, Harlequin Players, Junior Players Guild, National Children's Theatre Association and Shakespeare Festival of Dallas. **ORCHESTRAS** Dallas: Dallas Chamber Music Society, Dallas Civic Symphony, Dallas Symphony Association and Greater Dallas Youth Orchestra. Irving: Irving Symphony Orchestra. Richardson: Richardson Symphony Orchestra. **OPERA** Dallas: Dallas Civic Opera, High Noon Opera and Dallas Opera. **DANCE** Dallas: Dallas Ballet Theatre, Dallas Civic Ballet, Dallas Metropolitan Ballet, Dance Ensemble, Dance Repertory Theatre of Dallas, The Dancers Workshop, Stage West and Texas Civic Ballet of Dallas. Garland: Ballet Classique and Texas Baroque Ensemble. Irving: Irving Ballet. **BOTANIC GARDENS** Dallas: Dallas Arboretum and Botanical Garden and Dallas Civic Garden Center. **ZOO** Dallas Zoo. **AQUARIUM** Dallas: The Dallas Aquarium. **PLANETARIUM** Dallas: Dallas Health and Science Museum and Planetarium, Highland Park Planetarium, Richland College Cosmic Theatre, St. Mark's Planetarium and Observatory and the Science Place. Grand Prairie: Grand Prairie I.S.D. Planetarium. Irving: Irving I.S.D. Planetarium. Richardson: Richardson I.S.D. Planetarium. **OBSERVATORY** Garland: Northview Observatory. Richardson: University of Texas at Dallas. **COLLEGIATE FINE ARTS** Dallas: Cultural events offered by Bishop College, Southern Methodist University, Dallas Baptist College, Dallas Bible College, Eastfield College, El Centro College, Mountain View College, Richland College and University of Dallas. **OTHER** Dallas: Dallas Civic Chorus. Garland: Carland Civic Chorus. **SPECIAL EVENTS** Cotton Bowl Football and Parade, Dallas, January; Hearts and Flowers Festival, Dallas, February; Dallas Trekkers Volks March, Dallas, March; Rodeo, Mesquite, April-November; Prairie Dog Chili Cookoff, Grand Prairie, April; Byron Nelson Golf Classic, Dallas, April; Spring Festival, Lancaster, May; Folk Festival, Mesquite, May; Miniature Mayfest, Dallas, May; Western Days, Grand Prairie, May; Spring Flowers Festival, Dallas, May; Cinco de Mayo Fiesta, Grand Prairie, May; Artfest, Dallas, May; Traders Village Barrel Racing Futurity, Grand Prairie, May; Fireworks at the Cotton Bowl, Dallas, July; Arts and Crafts Fair, Dallas, July/August; Shakespeare Festival, Dallas, July; Firework Celebration, DeSoto, July; Fourth of July Celebration, Duncanville, July; Dallas Grand Prix, Dallas, July; Texas Spectacular Rodeo, Dallas, August/September; Fall Harvest Festival, Dallas, August; National Championship Indian Pow-Wow, Grand Prairie, September, Cityfest, Dallas, September/October; Clown and Circus Days, Grand Prairie, October; Octoberfest, Garland, October; Octoberfest, Grand Prairie, October; State Fair of Texas , Dallas, October; Christmas Jamboree, Dallas, September.

COMMUNITIES

COUNTY SEAT Dallas, County Courthouse, 75202; County Clerk's Office, 214/749-8131. **INCORPORATED COMMUNITIES** (1980 population and ZIP Code) Addison (5,553: 5,553 in Dallas Co.) 75001, Balch Springs (13,746) 75180, Buckingham (159) 75080, Carrollton (40,595: 26,853 in Dallas Co. and 13,742 in Denton Co.) 75006, Cedar Hill (6,849: 6,847 in Dallas Co. and 2 in Ellis Co.) 75104, Cockrell Hill (3,262) 75211, Combine (688: 560 in Kaufman Co. and 128 in Dallas, Co.) 75159, Coppell (3,826) 75019, Dallas (904,078: 902,619 in Dallas Co. and 1,357 in Collin Co., one in Kaufman Co. and 101 in Denton Co.) 75200, All-America Cities Award 1970, DeSoto (15,538) 75115, Duncanville (27,781) 75116, Farmers Branch (24,863) 75234, All-America Cities Honorable Mention 1963, Garland (138,857) 75040, Glenn Heights (1033: 1,008 in Dallas Co. and 25 in Ellis Co.) 75115, All-America Cities Award 1974-1975, Grand Prairie (71,462: 65,726 in Dallas Co., 5 in Ellis Co. and 5,731 in Tarrant Co.) 75050, Grapevine (11,801: 39 in Dallas Co. and 11,762 in Tarrant Co.) 76051, Highland Park (8,909) 75205, Hutchins (2,837) 75141, Irving (109,943) 75060, Lancaster (14,807) 75146, Mesquite (67,053) 75149, Ovilla (1,067: 45 in Dallas Co. and 1,022 in Ellis Co.) 76065, Richardson (72,496: 65,716 in Dallas Co. and 6,780 in Collin Co.) 75080, Rowlett (7,522: 6,348 in Dallas Co. and 1,174 in Rockwall Co.) 75088, Sachse (1,640: 1,611 in Dallas Co. and 29 in Collin Co.) 75040, Seagoville (7,298 in Dallas Co. and 6 in Kaufman Co.) 75159, Sunnyvale (1,404) 75149, University Park (22,254) 75205 and Wilmer (2,367) 75172. **UNINCORPORATED COMMUNITIES** (and ZIP Code) Carl Range 75062, Greenview Hills 75060, Lakeland Heights 75050, Lawson 75149, Ledbetter Hills 75211, Liberty Grove 75087, Patrick 75125, Pleasant Valley 75040. **FOR ADDITIONAL LOCAL INFORMATION** Metrocrest Chamber of Commerce, 1204 Metrocrest Dr., Addison, 75006, 214/245-0444; Balch Springs Chamber of Commerce, P. O. Box 80095, Balch Springs, 75180, 214/557-0988; Cedar Hill Chamber of Commerce, 712 Cedar, P. O. Box 355, Cedar Hill, 75104, 214/291-4624; Dallas Chamber of Commerce, 1507 Pacific Ave., Dallas, 75201, 214/954-1111; East Dallas Chamber of Commerce, 9543 Losa Drive, Dallas, 75218, 214/321-6446; Irving Chamber of Commerce, 1309 W. Airport Freeway, P.O. Box 445, Irving, 75060, 214/252-8484; Dallas Hispanic Chamber of Commerce, 4343 Maple Ave., Dallas, 75214, 214/522-6490; North Dallas Chamber of Commerce, 10707 Preston Rd., Dallas, 75230 214/368-6485; Oak Cliff Chamber of Commerce, 660 S. Zang Blvd., Dallas, 75208, 214/943-4567; Southeast Dallas Chamber of Commerce, P. O. Box 17132, Dallas, 75217, 214/398-6489 or 398-0601; DeSoto Chamber of Commerce, P. O. Box 100, DeSoto, 75115, 214/224-3565; Duncanville Chamber of Commerce, P. O. Box 36, Duncanville, 75116, 214/298-6128; Farmers Branch Chamber of Commerce, P. O. Box 344267, Farmers Branch, 75234, Garland Chamber of Commerce, 914 S. Garland, P. O. Box 460939, Garland, 75040, 214/272-7551; Grand Prairie Chamber of Commerce, 306 W. Main, P. O. Box 531227, Grand Prairie, 75053, 214/264-1558; , Grapevine Chamber of Commerce, P. O. Box 368, Grapevine, 76051, 817/481-1522; Lancaster Chamber of Commerce,zP. O. Box 32, Lancaster, 75146, 214/227-2579; Mesquite Chamber of Commerce, P. O. Box 115, Mesquite, 75149, 214/285-0211 and Rowlett Chamber of Commerce, P. O. Box 610, Rowlett, 75088, 214/475-3200; Seagoville Chamber of Commerce, 107 Hall, Seagoville, 75159, 214/287-5184.

DAWSON (P58)

THE LAND

South of Lubbock on U.S. Highway 87 in the High Plains Region, Dawson County covers 903 square miles with an elevation range of 2,600 to 3,150 feet. The soils of the county are nearly level to undulating with the western one-forth being dry, sandy and acidic. The rest of the county has soils with loamy surface layers and clayey subsoils with lime accumulations. Dawson lies in the High Plains vegetation area with prairie grasses and shinnery oak, some mesquite trees, yucca and thorny shrubs. Between one and 10% of the land in the county is considered prime farmland. **CLIMATE** Mild and dry. The average annual temperature is 62°F. Temperatures in January range from an average low of 26° to an average high of 56°F and in July range from 71° to 94°F. The average annual precipitation is 16 inches, with an average relative humidity of 77% at 6 A.M. and 36% at 6 P.M. The average annual snowfall is seven inches. The growing season averages 212 days per year, with the last freeze in early April and the first freeze in early November. The sun shines during the year on the average 75% of the daylight hours.

THE PEOPLE

Dawson county ranks 68th among all U.S. Counties in the percent of population of Spanish origin. The 1982 estimated population of 16,700 continues the slight increase in residents since 1980. Between 1970 and 1980 the rural areas declined 13% in residents while the population in urban areas increased 2%. The age group with the largest decrease was ages five to 14. The median age rose from 27 in 1970 to 29 in 1980. The largest ancestry groups are Hispanics (38%), persons of English descent (26%) and Irish descent (15%). **VOTERS** As of November 2, 1982 there were 7,826 registered voters (0.1% of the state total). The 1982 general election had a 49% voter turnout, compared to a 69% turnout in the 1980 general election. In the 1982 primary 97% voted Democratic and 3% Republican, with 3,106 votes cast.

THE ECONOMY

AGRICULTURE Cotton area. In 1982, 95% of the land was in farms and ranches, with 56% of the farmland under cultivation and 11% irrigated. Dawson ranked 17th in the state in highest agricultural receipts, with 98% from crops. Undesirable brush and weeds, water and wind erosion, decreasing irrigation water supplies and inefficient tillage systems are the current conservation problems. Primary crops: second in the state for cotton. Sorghum and wheat. Primary vegetables: watermelons. Primary fruits and nuts: peaches and pecans. Primary livestock and products: cattle and hogs. **BUSINESS** Total number of business establishments in the county: 406. Retail sales during the first quarter of 1984 decreased 2%. In 1980, 20% of the labor force were self-employed, 19% were employed in professional or related services, 5% in manufacturing, 22% in wholesale and retail trade, 29% in agriculture, forestry, fisheries and mining, 9% were employed in other counties and there were 1,407 retired workers. The industries with the most employment: agribusiness, oil and gas field servicing, cottonseed oil mills and the manufacture of women's suits and coats. The nonfarm earnings in 1981 totaled $132,621,000. The retired workers received an average monthly Social Security payment of $321.00. **FINANCE** On June 30, 1983, two commercial banks had total deposits of $154,107,000 and total assets of $173,908,000. On December 31, 1982 one federal savings and loan association and one state savings and loan association branch had assets of $87,881,765. In addition there are two credit unions in the county. **HOUSING** Average value of homes in 1980: $23,300. Permits for new, privately owned housing units increased in 1982: six permits were issued with a total construction cost of $185,000. Of those permits, all were for single

family houses. Between 1970 and 1980 the number of housing units increased by 2%. Eighty-four percent of all units in the county are air-conditioned, 87% are heated by gas and 13% by electricity. **NATURAL RESOURCES** Caliche, limestone, oil and gas. In 1982 a total of 6,769,189 barrels of crude oil and 3,753,015 thousand cubic feet of casinghead gas were produced. Current production of other minerals and products includes caliche, crushed limestone, and recovered sulphur. **TOURISM** Travel expenditures of $12,267,000 in 1982 (an increase of 17% over 1981) generated 180 jobs and $1,846,000 in payroll. **ALCOHOLIC BEVERAGES** Only 4% beer is legal in parts of the county. **FEDERAL EXPENDITURES** The federal government had direct expenditures or obligations of $40,648,000 in the county during fiscal year 1983, including $311,000 by the U.S. Department of Defense. In addition, the federal government provided $1,276,000 in grant awards, paid $1,023,000 in salaries and wages, made direct payments to individuals of $19,257,000 including $13,532,000 in retirement and disability payments, awarded $12,000 in procurement contracts and spent $19,080,000 in other expenditures or obligations. The federal government also provided $15,764,000 in direct loans and $15,463,000 in guaranteed loans and insurance.

COMMUNICATION

Newspapers–Weekly: Lamesa Press-Reporter (Spanish) and the Index Press (O'Donnell). Radio: KPET-AM, KCOT-FM (Lamesa). Cable TV. Telephone companies: General Telephone, Poka-Lambro Rural Telephone Coop. and Wes-Tex Telephone Coop. **TRANSPORTATION** Total public road mileage: 1,358. In 1982 there were 16,305 registered vehicles and 385 reported traffic accidents including eight fatalities. Taxi cabs: one company in Lamesa. Intercity bus service is available. Motor freight: nine local and intrastate carriers. Rail: one branch line carries annually less than one million tons of freight through the county. Aircraft: 48 are registered in the county. Airports: Lamesa Municipal Airport is a basic utility airport providing general aviation service. It serves as a base for 30 aircraft. Also serving this area are Thorp Airport at Lamesa and Askew Farms Airport at O'Donnell.

COMMUNITY SERVICES

EDUCATION Four school districts with six elementary, two middle and four high schools. The average daily attendance in 1981-82 was 3,559, with expenditures per pupil of $3,243 including 254 classroom teachers with an average annual salary of $16,862. Forty-seven percent of the 221 high school graduates planned to attend college. In 1982-83, 38% of the students were White, 57% Hispanic, 5% Black and 0.3% Asian. **PUBLIC LIBRARIES** Dawson County Public Library (Lamesa): 35,350 volumes. **CHILD CARE** 14 day care and three twenty-four hour care licensed facilities. **HEALTH CARE** eight physicians and four dentists. Hospitals: one with a capacity of 72. Clinics: one public health clinic. Ambulance services: one commercial service. Mental health: one county clinic. Nursing homes: two nursing homes with a combined capacity of 128 nursing care residents. The average cost per day for private patients in 1982 was $39.05. **CHURCHES** 46 churches have an estimated combined membership of 14,975. The largest denominations are Southern Baptist, Catholic and United Methodist **SOCIAL SERVICES** In fiscal year 1983 a total of $1,260,064 in food stamps was distributed, with an average of 2,714 persons receiving food stamps each month. Aid to Families with Dependent Children (AFDC) totaled $187,505, with an average of 121 families receiving AFDC each month. Medical assistance benefits for the aged and disabled of $866,499 and for families and children of $207,470 brought the county benefit total to $2,521,538. **FIRE PROTECTION** one partly paid and one volunteer fire

COUNTIES

DAWSON (continued)

departments. **LAW ENFORCEMENT** The County Sheriff has seven commissioned officers. One police department has a force of 15. **CRIME** 42 violent crimes (murder, forcible rape, robbery and aggravated assault) and 522 nonviolent crimes (burglary, larceny-theft and motor vehicle theft) were reported in 1982. **JUDICIAL SYSTEM** one District Court and Judge, one County Court and Judge and one Justice of the Peace. In the District Court a total of 438 cases were pending on 1/1/82, 451 new cases were filed and 341 cases were disposed of during the year leaving 548 cases pending on 12/31/82. There were 241 criminal cases on the docket, 86 convictions, 13 persons committed to prison and 139 cases left pending. In the County Court 186 cases were pending on 1/1/82, 368 new cases were filed and 316 cases were disposed of during the year leaving 238 cases pending on 12/31/82. There were 493 criminal cases on the docket, 169 convictions, 35 persons committed to jail, and 199 cases left pending. **JAILS** one jail, capacity 22. **ATTORNEYS AT LAW** 13. **UTILITIES** 82% of the residents are connected to a public or privately owned water system and 77% are connected to a public sewer system. Natural gas is distributed to the county by Energas Company. The average annual residential bill for natural gas in 1982 for the Energas distribution system was $371.63, an increase of 23% over 1981. Electricity is distributed to the county by Texas Electric Service, Cap Rock Electric Coop., Inc. and Lyntegar Electric Coop., Inc. and is generated primarily by gas and coal. The typical residential electric bill is $154.69 per month for an all-electric house using 2,500 kwh. **TAXES** The county has five units with taxing authority: three school districts, one city, and one county.

RECREATION/ENTERTAINMENT

MUNICIPAL PARKS 173 acres in 10 municipal parks. These parks contain 11 playgrounds, nine golf courses, 10 baseball and softball fields, seven tennis courts and one swimming pool. Developed campsites: eight. **HUNTING** Fall season on antelope. No closed season on squirrel, bobcat and coyote. Winter season on quail, muskrat, beaver, opossum, ring-tailed cat, badger, fox, weasel, raccoon, skunk and civet cat. Fall, winter and spring seasons on turkey. In 1983 sandhill crane, duck, coot, geese, woodcock and jacksnipe seasons occurred during the winter months. Teal duck, rail and gallinule seasons occurred in the fall. Mourning dove season occurred intermittently during the fall and winter months. **MUSEUMS** Lamesa: Lamesa-Dawson County Museum and Art Center. **SPECIAL EVENTS** Rodeo, Lamesa, August; Dawson County Fair, Lamesa, September.

COMMUNITIES

COUNTY SEAT Lamesa, County Courthouse, 79331; County Clerk's Office, 806/872-3778. **INCORPORATED COMMUNITIES** (1980 population and ZIP Code) Ackerly (317: 225 in Dawson Co. and 92 in Martin Co.) 79713, Lamesa (11,790) 79331 and O'Donnell (1,200: 124 in Dawson Co. and 1,076 in Lynn Co.) 79351. **UNINCORPORATED COMMUNITIES** (and ZIP Code) Arvana 79331, Grandview 79331, Hancock 79331, Key 79331, Klondike 79331, Midway 79331, Mungerville 79331, Patricia 79331, Pumpkin Center (Lou) 79331, Sand 7931, Sparenberg 79331 and Welch 79377. **FOR ADDITIONAL LOCAL INFORMATION** Lamesa Chamber of Commerce and Bd. of City, 307 N. Houston, Drawer J, Lamesa, 79331, 806/872-2181.

DEAF SMITH (P16)

THE LAND

In the High Plains Region of the Texas Panhandle west of Amarillo on U.S. Highways 385 and 60, Deaf Smith County covers 1,497 square miles with an elevation range of 3,200 to 4,200 feet. The majority of soils are nearly level with loamy, alkaline surfaces and clayey subsoils over limestone. In the High Plains vegetation area, the most abundant grasses are short buffalograss and blue gramas with some tall bunchgrasses, mesquite, shinnery oak and sagebrush. Between 61 and 70% of the land in the county is considered prime farmland. **CLIMATE** Cool and dry. The average annual temperature is 56 °F. Temperatures in January range from an average low of 20° to an average high of 56 °F and in July range from 63° to 91 °F. The average annual precipitation is 16 inches, with an average relative humidity of 70% at 6 A.M. and 37% at 6 P.M. The average annual snowfall is 15 inches. The growing season averages 185 days per year, with the last freeze in late April and the first freeze in late October. The sun shines during the year on the average 75% of the daylight hours.

THE PEOPLE

Deaf Smith ranks 62nd among all U.S. counties in the percent of population of Spanish origin. The 1982 estimated population of 20,400 indicates a decline in population since 1980, the first population decline in 50 years. Over 18% of the population growth between 1970 and 1980 was in urban areas while rural areas experienced a 5% loss. The age groups with the largest increases were ages 65 and over and 20 to 34. The young median age rose from 23 in 1970 to 25 in 1980. The largest ancestry groups are Hispanic (41%), those of English descent (19%) and Irish descent (14%). **REGISTERED VOTERS** As of November 2, 1982 there were 8,514 registered voters (0.1% of the state total). The 1982 general election had a 53% voter turnout, compared to a 65% turnout in the 1980 general election. In the 1982 primary 95% voted Democratic and 5% Republican, with 2,676 votes cast.

THE ECONOMY

AGRICULTURE Diversified products. In 1982, 97% of the land was in farms and ranches, with 42% of the farmland under cultivation and 65% irrigated. Deaf Smith ranked second in the state in highest agricultural receipts, with 73% from livestock and livestock products. Overgrazing, water and wind erosion, decreasing irrigation water supplies and inefficient tillage systems are the current conservation problems. Primary crops: first in the state for wheat, ninth for both corn and sunflowers and second for barley. Sorghum, sugarbeets and cotton. Primary vegetables: fourth in the state for carrots, sixth for total fresh market vegetables and 10th for cabbage. Potatoes, lettuce, cantaloupes, onions and cucumbers. Primary fruits and nuts: pecans. Primary livestock and products: first in the state for both cattle and fed cattle marketings. Milk and hogs. **BUSINESS** Total number of business establishments in the county: 459. Retail sales during the first quarter of 1984 increased 16%. In 1980, 16% of the labor force were self-employed, 16% were employed in professional or related services, 15% in manufacturing, 21% in wholesale and retail trade, 21% in agriculture, forestry, fisheries and mining, 8% were employed in other counties and there were 1,177 retired workers. The industries with the most employment: agribusiness, meat packing, grain mills, road construction, beet sugar refining and the manufacture of women's apparel and farm machinery. The nonfarm earnings in 1981 totaled $160,541,000. The retired workers received an average monthly Social Security payment of $325. **FINANCE** On June 30, 1983, two commercial banks had total deposits of $122,297,000 and total assets of $140,518,000. On December 31, 1982 one state savings and loan association and one federal branch association had assets of $36,299,265. In addition there is one credit union in the county. **HOUSING** Average value of homes in 1980: $32,100. In 1982 four permits were issued for new single family houses. Between

1970 and 1980 the number of housing units increased by 14%. Seventy-four percent of all units in the county are air-conditioned, 88% are heated by gas and 12% by electricity. **NATURAL RESOURCES** Caliche, oil and gas. Current production of other minerals and products includes caliche and lime. **TOURISM** Travel expenditures of $17,372,000 in 1982 (an increase of 17% over 1981) generated 281 jobs and $2,811,000 in payroll. Lodging: three hotels, motels and tourist courts. **ALCOHOLIC BEVERAGES** Totally dry. **FEDERAL EXPENDITURES** The federal government had direct expenditures or obligations of $29,540,000 in the county during fiscal year 1983, including $202,000 by the U.S. Department of Defense. In addition, the federal government provided $537,000 in grant awards, paid $1,399,000 in salaries and wages, made direct payments to individuals of $16,054,000 including $12,339,000 in retirement and disability payments, awarded $14,000 in procurement contracts and spent $11,535,000 in other expenditures or obligations. The federal government also provided $32,419,000 in direct loans and $27,115,000 in guaranteed loans and insurance.

COMMUNICATION

Newspapers–Daily: Hereford Brand, ave. eve. circ. 3,369. Radio: KPAN-AM, KPAN-FM (Hereford). Telephone companies: Continental Telephone, Southwestern Bell and West Texas Rural Telephone Coop. **TRANSPORTATION** Total public road mileage: 1,243. In 1982 there were 17,204 registered vehicles and 415 reported traffic accidents including five fatalities. Intercity bus service is available. Motor freight: 19 local and intrastate carriers. Rail: one main line carries annually over 30 million tons of freight through the county. Aircraft: 56 are registered in the county. Airports: Hereford Municipal Airport is a general utility airport providing general aviation service. It serves as a base for 60 aircraft.

COMMUNITY SERVICES

EDUCATION Two school districts with seven elementary, two middle and one high school. The average daily attendance in 1981-82 was 4,490, with expenditures per pupil of $2,490 including 324 classroom teachers with an average annual salary of $16,407. Sixty percent of the 323 high school graduates planned to attend college. In 1982-83, 38% of the students were White, 60% Hispanic, 2% Black, 0.1% Asian. Private schools: 233 students enrolled in one elementary school. **PUBLIC LIBRARIES** Deaf Smith County Library (Hereford): 55,339 volumes. **CHILD CARE** 51 day care and six twenty-four hour care licensed facilities. **HEALTH CARE** Nine physicians and five dentists. Hospitals: one with a capacity of 77. Ambulance services: one hospital-based service. Mental health: one clinic. Nursing homes: one nursing home has a capacity of 79 nursing care residents. The average cost per day for private patients in 1982 was $36.86. **CHURCHES** 28 churches have an estimated combined membership of 15,619. The largest denominations are Catholic, Southern Baptist and United Methodist. **SOCIAL SERVICES** In fiscal year 1983 a total of $1,544,527 in food stamps was distributed, with an average of 3,167 persons receiving food stamps each month. Aid to Families with Dependent Children (AFDC) totaled $247,991 with an average of 159 families receiving AFDC each month. Medical assistance benefits for the aged and disabled of $569,252 and for families and children of $294,054 brought the county benefit total to $2,655,824. **FIRE PROTECTION** Four volunteer fire departments. **LAW ENFORCEMENT** The County Sheriff has 36 commissioned officers. One police department has a force of 20. **CRIME** 152 violent crimes (murder, forcible rape, robbery and aggravated assault) and 718 nonviolent crimes (burglary, larceny-theft and motor vehicle theft) were reported in 1982. **JUDICIAL SYSTEM** One District Court and Judge, one County Court and Judge and one Justice of the Peace.

In the District Court a total of 333 cases were pending on 1/1/82, 584 new cases were filed and 535 cases were disposed of during the year leaving 382 cases pending on 12/31/82. There were 211 criminal cases on the docket, 67 convictions, 12 persons committed to prison and six committed to jail and 92 cases left pending. In the County Court 423 cases were pending on 1/1/82, 558 new cases were filed and 548 cases were disposed of during the year leaving 433 cases pending on 12/31/82. There were 734 criminal cases on the docket, 255 convictions, 64 persons committed to jail, and 250 cases left pending. **JAILS** One jail, capacity 72, under renovation. **ATTORNEYS AT LAW** 29. **UTILITIES** 80% of the residents are connected to a public or privately owned water system and 78% are connected to a public sewer system. Natural gas is distributed to the county by Energas Company. The average annual residential bill for natural gas in 1982 for the Energas distribution system was $371.63, an increase of 23% over 1981. Electricity is distributed to the county by Deaf Smith Electric Co. and Southwestern Public Service and is generated primarily by gas and coal. The typical residential electric bill is $170.44 per month for an all-electric house using 2,500 kwh. **TAXES** The county has seven units with taxing authority: two school districts, one city, one county, one hospital district and two special districts.

RECREATION/ENTERTAINMENT

NATIONAL REGISTER OF HISTORIC PLACES Hereford: E.B. Black Residence. **MUNICIPAL PARKS** 480 acres in 14 municipal parks. These parks contain one mile of hiking trails, seven playgrounds, 36 golf courses, two baseball and softball fields, two tennis courts and one swimming pool. **SCENIC DRIVES** The Texas Plains Trail runs through this county. This trail spans a vast area of the High Plains Region of Texas slicing through the southernmost extension of the Great Plains of the United States. The land is flat except where erosion has carved canyon landscapes. **BOATING/FISHING** Primary streams: Palo Duro, North Palo Duro and Tierra Blanca. **HUNTING** Fall season on antelope. Fall and winter seasons on mule deer. Summer, fall and winter seasons on squirrel. Winter season on pheasant, quail, muskrat, beaver, otter, opossum, mink, ring-tailed cat, badger, fox, raccoon, skunk and civet cat. No closed season on nutria, coyote and bobcat. In 1983 sandhill crane, duck, coot, geese, woodcock and jacksnipe seasons occurred during the winter months. Teal duck, rail and gallinule seasons occurred in the fall. Mourning dove season occurred intermittently during the fall and winter months. **MUSEUMS** Hereford: Deaf Smith County Historical Museum and National Cowgirl Hall of Fame. **SPECIAL EVENTS** Miss Hereford Pageant, Hereford, August; Town and Country Jubilee, Hereford, August; National Cowgirl Hall of Fame's All-Girl Rodeo, Hereford, August.

COMMUNITIES

COUNTY SEAT Hereford, County Courthouse, 79045; County Clerk's Office, 806/364-1746. **INCORPORATED COMMUNITIES** (1980 population and ZIP Code) Hereford (15,853) 79045. **UNINCORPORATED COMMUNITIES** (and ZIP Code) Dawn 79025, Glenrio 88423 and Westway 79045. **FOR ADDITIONAL LOCAL INFORMATION** Deaf Smith Co. Chamber of Commerce, P. O. Box 192, Hereford, 79045, 806/364-3333.

DELTA (E4)

THE LAND

Northeast of Dallas on State Highway 24 in the Blackland Prairies Region, Delta County covers 278 square miles with elevation range of 400 to 500 feet. The undulating land has dark, deep, cracking clayey soils with some loamy surfaces. In the Blackland

COUNTIES

DELTA (continued)

Prairies vegetation area, there is abundant timber along streams, such as oaks, elms, pecan, bois d'arc and mesquite. Tall bunchgrass, buffalograss and Texas grama are the primary grasses. Between 51 and 60% of the land in the county is considered prime farmland. **CLIMATE** Mild and moist. Thunderstorms occur in spring and early summer. The average annual temperature is 63 °F. Temperatures in January range from an average low of 31 ° to an average high of 52 °F and in July range from 71 ° to 95 °F. The average annual precipitation is 44 inches, with an average relative humidity of 83% at 6 A.M. and 56% at 6 P.M. The average annual snowfall is two inches. The growing season averages 233 days per year, with the last freeze in late March and the first freeze in mid November. The sun shines during the year on the average 67% of the daylight hours.

THE PEOPLE

Delta County ranks 15th among all U.S. counties in the percent of population aged 65 and over. The 1982 estimated population of 4,800 shows a slight decrease since 1980. Delta's population has steadily decreased since 1930, with a decline of 16% from 1960 to 1970. The majority of residents live in rural areas. The age groups with the greatest decreases between 1970 and 1980 were birth to five and 50 to 64. The high median age lowered from 47 in 1970 to 42 in 1980. The largest ancestry groups are persons of Irish decent (25%) and English descent (22%). **REGISTERED VOTERS** As of November 2, 1982 there were 2,921 registered voters (0.04% of the state total). The 1982 general election had a 52% voter turnout, compared to a 70% turnout in the 1980 general election. In the 1982 primary 99% voted Democratic and 1% Republican, with 1,319 votes cast.

THE ECONOMY

AGRICULTURE Wheat area. In 1982, 81% of the land was in farms and ranches, with 51% of the farmland under cultivation and 7% irrigated. Delta ranked 176th in the state in highest agricultural receipts, with 73% from livestock and livestock products. Overgrazing, water erosion and inefficient tillage systems are the current conservation problems. Primary crops: wheat, hay, sorghum, soybeans and cotton. Primary fruits and nuts: peaches and pecans. Primary livestock and products: cattle and milk. **BUSINESS** Total number of business establishments in the county: 60. Retail sales during the first quarter of 1984 remained constant with pecan gap showing a 37% decline. In 1980 17% of the labor force were self-employed, 18% were employed in professional or related services, 24% in manufacturing, 16% in wholesale and retail trade, 15% in agriculture, forestry, fisheries and mining, 42% were employed in other counties and there were 875 retired workers. The industry with the most employment is agribusiness. The nonfarm earnings in 1981 totaled $33,274,000. The retired workers received an average monthly Social Security payment of $269.00. **FINANCE** On June 30, 1983, three commercial banks had total deposits of $30,475,000 and total assets of $34,339,000. **HOUSING** Average value of homes in 1980: $16,800. In 1982 four permits were issued for new single family houses. Between 1970 and 1980 the number of housing units increased by 5%. Fifty-eight percent of all units in the county are air-conditioned, 83% are heated by gas and 13% by electricity. **NATURAL RESOURCES** Limestone. **TOURISM** Travel expenditures of $731,000 in 1982 (an increase of 17% over 1981) generated 10 jobs and $108,000 in payroll. **ALCOHOLIC BEVERAGES** Totally dry. **FEDERAL EXPENDITURES** The federal government had direct expenditures or obligations of $14,225,000 in the county during fiscal year 1983, including $479,000 by the U.S. Department of Defense. In addition, the federal government provided $577,000 in grant awards,

paid $542,000 in salaries and wages, made direct payments to individuals of $10,851,000 including $7,008,000 in retirement and disability payments, awarded $131,000 in procurement contracts and spent $2,123,000 in other expenditures or obligations. The federal government also provided $1,331,000 in direct loans and $9,843,000 in guaranteed loans and insurance.

COMMUNICATION

Newspapers–Weekly: Cooper Review. Telephone companies: Continental Telephone, General Telephone and United Telephone. **TRANSPORTATION** Total public road mileage: 442. In 1982 there were 4,735 registered vehicles and 76 reported traffic accidents including two fatalities. Intercity bus service is available. Motor freight: two carriers. Rail: one main line carries annually one to five million tons of freight through the county. Aircraft: nine are registered in the county.

COMMUNITY SERVICES

EDUCATION Two school districts with two elementary, one middle and two high schools. The average daily attendance in 1981-82 was 993, with expenditures per pupil of $1,824 including 62 classroom teachers with an average annual salary of $15,177. Forty-nine percent of the 81 high school graduates planned to attend college. In 1982-83, 77% of the students were White and 23% Black. **CHILD CARE** Four day care licensed facilities. **HEALTH CARE** One physician and one dentist. Ambulance services: one commercial service. Nursing homes: two nursing homes with a combined capacity of 138 nursing care and 24 personal care residents. The average cost per day for private patients in 1982 was $23.57. **CHURCHES** 27 churches have an estimated combined membership of 4,026. The largest denominations are Southern Baptist, United Methodist and Churches of Christ. **SOCIAL SERVICES** In fiscal year 1983 a total of $222,923 in food stamps was distributed, with an average of 564 persons receiving food stamps each month. Aid to Families with Dependent Children (AFDC) totaled $46,625 with an average of 34 families receiving AFDC each month. Medical assistance benefits for the aged and disabled of $1,032,089 and for families and children of $71,182 brought the county benefit total to $1,372,819. **FIRE PROTECTION** Three volunteer fire departments. **LAW ENFORCEMENT** The County Sheriff has three commissioned officers. One police department has a force of two. **CRIME** 13 violent crimes (murder, forcible rape, robbery and aggravated assault) and 98 nonviolent crimes (burglary, larceny-theft and motor vehicle theft) were reported in 1982. **JUDICIAL SYSTEM** Two District Courts and Judges, one County Court and Judge and one Justice of the Peace. In the District Courts a total of 346 cases were pending on 1/1/82, 120 new cases were filed and 120 cases were disposed of during the year leaving 346 cases pending on 12/31/82. There were 73 criminal cases on the docket, 50 convictions, nine persons committed to prison, and 19 cases left pending. In the County Court 151 cases were pending on 1/1/82, 124 new cases were filed and 35 cases were disposed of during the year leaving 240 cases pending on 12/31/82. There were 263 criminal cases on the docket, 27 convictions, eight persons committed to jail, and 228 cases left pending. **JAILS** One jail, capacity six. **ATTORNEYS AT LAW** three. **UTILITIES** 95% of the residents are connected to a public or privately owned water system and 52% are connected to a public sewer system. Natural gas is distributed to the county by Lone Star Gas Co., Division of Enserch. The average annual residential bill for natural gas in 1982 for the Lone Star distribution system was $405.91, an increase of 35% over 1981. Electricity is distributed to the county by Farmer Electric Co. and Lamar Co. Electric Coop., Assn. and is generated primarily by gas and coal. **TAXES** The county has five units with taxing authority: two school districts, two cities, and one county.

RECREATION/ENTERTAINMENT
MUNICIPAL PARKS 15 acres in one municipal park. This park contains one playground, two baseball and softball fields and two multi-use courts. **SCENIC DRIVES** The Texas Lakes Trail runs through this county. This trail introduces some 30 blue-water recreational areas in a variety of settings in North-Central Texas. **BOATING/FISHING** Major rivers: North Sulphur and South Sulphur. **HUNTING** Fall and winter seasons on deer. Summer, fall and winter seasons on squirrel. Winter season on quail, muskrat, beaver, otter, opossum, mink, ring-tailed cat, badger, fox, raccoon, skunk and civet cat. No closed season on bobcat, nutria and coyote. In 1983 duck, coot, geese, woodcock and jacksnipe seasons occurred during the winter months. Teal duck, rail and gallinule seasons occurred in the fall. Mourning dove season occurred intermittently during the fall and winter months. **MUSEUMS** Cooper: Patterson Memorial County Library and Museum. **SPECIAL EVENTS** Rodeo and Parade, Cooper, May; Chili Cookoff, Cooper, July/August; and Christmas Parade, Cooper, December.

COMMUNITIES
COUNTY SEAT Cooper, County Courthouse, 75432; County Clerk's Office, 214/395-4110. **INCORPORATED COMMUNITIES** (1980 population and ZIP Code) Cooper (2,338) 75432, Enloe (113 est., incorp. inactive) 75441 and Pecan Gap (250: 234 in Delta Co. and 16 in Fannin Co.) 75469. **UNINCORPORATED COMMUNITIES** (and ZIP Code) Amy 75432, Antioch 75432, Ben Franklin 75415, Charleston 75424, Crossroads (Clem) 75432, Horton 75428, Jot-Em-Down (also in Hunt Co.) 75449, Kensing 75450, Klondike 75448, Lake Creek 75450, Mount Joy 75432, Pacio 75450, Prattville 75432, Price 75432, Racetrack 75432, Rattan 75432, Vasco 75450, Yowell (also in Hunt Co.) 75428. **FOR ADDITIONAL LOCAL INFORMATION** Delta Co. Chamber of Commerce, P. O. Box 457, Cooper, 75432, 214/395-4314.

DENTON (M6)

THE LAND
North of the Dallas-Fort Worth area on Interstate Highway 35 in the Grand Prairie Region, Denton County covers 911 square miles with an elevation range of 550 to 850 feet. The western one-third of the county has limestone under undulating to hilly loamy soils. The central one-third has level to undulating, light-colored, medium to slightly acidic, soils with loamy surface layers and cracking, clayey subsoils. The rest of the county has slightly acidic soils with loamy surfaces and cracking, clayey subsoils or acidic, cracking, clayey soils. Denton lies in the Cross Timbers and Prairies vegetation area with tall and mid grasses, live oak, post oak, juniper and some mesquite trees. Between 51 and 60% of the land in the county is considered prime farmland. **CLIMATE** Subtropical subhumid and generally mild, but seasonal changes are widely variable. The average annual temperature is 65 °F. Temperatures in January range from an average low of 30 ° to an average high of 55 °F and in July range from 73 ° to 96 °F. The average annual precipitation is 33 inches, with an average relative humidity of 83% at 6 A.M. and 53% at 6 P.M. The average annual snowfall is four inches. The growing season averages 230 days per year, with the last freeze the last of March and the first freeze near mid November. The sun shines during the year on the average 66% of the daylight hours.

THE PEOPLE
Denton is one of the state's most densely populated counties. The 1982 estimated population of 157,300 indicates a continuation of the strong growth rate, with an increase of 60% from 1960 to 1970 and 89% from 1970 to 1980. The county ranks 53rd among all U.S. counties in highest growth rate from 1970 to 1980. The urban growth of 127% between 1970 and 1980 was one of the highest in the state. The age groups with the largest gains were ages 25 to 39, which tripled in size, and birth to five. Denton's median age rose from 24 in 1970 to 27 in 1980. The largest ancestry groups are persons of English descent (29%), Irish descent (23%) and German descent (21%). **REGISTERED VOTERS** As of November 2, 1982 there were 66,231 registered voters (1% of the state total). The 1982 general election had a 51% voter turnout, compared to a 72% turnout in the 1980 general election. In the 1982 primary 59% voted Democratic and 41% Republican, with 10,003 votes cast.

THE ECONOMY
AGRICULTURE Wheat and cattle area. In 1982, 81% of the land was in farms and ranches, with 40% of the farmland under cultivation and 3% irrigated. Denton County ranked 42nd in the state in highest agricultural receipts, with 68% from livestock and livestock products. Overgrazing, water erosion, flooding and urban encroachment are the current conservation problems. Primary crops: 10th in the state for oats. Wheat, sorghum, hay, cotton and peanuts. Primary vegetables: sweet potatoes. Primary fruits and nuts: peaches and pecans. Primary livestock and products: fourth in the state for both hens and pullets and egg production. Cattle, milk, sheep, wool and hogs. **BUSINESS** Total number of business establishments in the county: 2,281. Retail sales during the first quarter of 1984 increased 35%. In 1980, 7% of the labor force were self-employed, 22% were employed in professional or related services, 22% in manufacturing, 22% in wholesale and retail trade, 8% in transportation, communications and other public utilities, 47% were employed in other counties and there were 6,722 retired workers. The industries with the most employment: agribusiness, construction and the manufacture of women's lingerie, business forms, metal doors, metal working machinery, radio and television communication equipment, motor vehicles and equipment and jewelry. The nonfarm earnings in 1981 totaled $1,400,803,000. The retired workers received an average monthly Social Security payment of $330. **FINANCE** On June 30, 1983, 15 commercial banks had total deposits of $595,074,000 and total assets of $657,155,000. On December 31, 1982 one state savings and loan association and 20 state branches had assets of $83,279,329. In addition there are six credit unions in the county. **HOUSING** Average value of homes in 1980: $58,200. Permits for new, privately owned housing units increased in 1982: 1,911 permits were issued with a total construction cost of $81,378,742. Of those permits, 1,186 were for single family houses. Housing permits in the city of Denton increased from 243 in 1981 to 575 in 1982. Between 1970 and 1980 the number of housing units increased by 117%. Ninety-two percent of all units in the county are air-conditioned, 65% are heated by gas and 34% by electricity. **NATURAL RESOURCES** Limestone, sand and gravel, oil, gas, clay and bituminous coal. In 1982 a total of 1,359,075 thousand cubic feet of gas well gas, 824 barrels of condensate, 15,375 barrels of crude oil and 218 thousand cubic feet of casinghead gas were produced. Current production of other minerals and products includes brick, clay, crushed limestone, construction sand, sand and gravel. **TOURISM** Travel expenditures of $38,867,000 in 1982 (an increase of 13% over 1981) generated 878 jobs and $7,733,000 in payroll. Lodging: 12 hotels, motels and tourist courts. Convention/meeting facilities: North Texas State University Stadium and Arena (Denton). **ALCOHOLIC BEVERAGES** Packaged distilled spirits, beer, ale, malt liquor and wine are legal in parts of the county. Sale of mixed beverages is legal in all or parts of the county. **FEDERAL EXPENDITURES** The federal government had direct expenditures or obligations of $250,731,000 in the county during fiscal year 1983, including

DENTON (continued)

$127,649,000 by the U.S. Department of Defense. In addition, the federal government provided $5,619,000 in grant awards, paid $15,581,000 in salaries and wages, made direct payments to individuals of $110,689,000 including $87,437,000 in retirement and disability payments, awarded $117,651,000 in procurement contracts and spent $1,191,000 in other expenditures or obligations. The federal government also provided $2,288,000 in direct loans and $112,799,000 in guaranteed loans and insurance.

COMMUNICATION

Newspapers–Daily: Denton Record-Chronicle, ave. eve. circ. 15,047 and The Daily Leader (Lewisville), ave. eve. circ. 5,277. Weekly: Lewisville News-Advertiser, Post Signal (Pilot Point) and the Sanger Courier. Radio: KDNT-AM and KNTU-FM (Denton). Cable TV. Telephone companies: General Telephone, Southwestern Bell, Central Telephone-Midstate and Lake Dallas Telephone. **TRANSPORTATION** Total public road mileage: 2,070. In 1982 there were 130,820 registered vehicles and 4,552 reported traffic accidents including 29 fatalities. Taxi cabs: three companies in the city of Denton. Intercity bus service is available. Motor freight: 24 local and intrastate carriers. Rail: five main and two branch lines carry freight through the county. One of the main lines carries annually over 30 million tons of freight, one carries 20 to 30 and three carry 10 to 20 million each. The two branch lines carry annually one to five million tons of freight each. Aircraft: 365 are registered in the county. Airports: Denton Municipal Airport is a basic transportation airport providing reliever service for Dallas/Fort Worth Airport. It serves as a base for 119 aircraft. Also serving the area are Hartlee Field at Denton, Aero Valley Airport at Roanoke, Palmer Field and Deussen Field at Ponder, Flying S Farm Airstrip at Justin, Richards Field at Krum, Lakeview Airport at Lake Dallas and Lane Field at Sanger.

COMMUNITY SERVICES

EDUCATION 11 school districts with 31 elementary, 12 middle, 11 high schools and one special education. The average daily attendance in 1981-82 was 24,836, with expenditures per pupil of $3,184 including 1,466 classroom teachers with an average annual salary of $16,600. Forty-four percent of the 1,544 high school graduates planned to attend college. In 1982-83, 89% of the students were White, 5% Hispanic, 5% Black, 0.9% Asian and 0.3% American Indian. Private schools: 500 enrolled in five elementary and three high schools. Texas Woman's University is located in Denton. Established in 1901 it is under state control. Enrollment in 1982 was 7,935 with in state undergratuate tuition and fees of $389 per semester. The highest degree offered is Doctorate. North Texas State University is located in Denton. Established in 1890 it is under state control. Enrollment in 1982 was 17,158 with in state undergraduate tuition and fees of $438 per semester. The highest degree offered is Doctorate. Sports championships: (Southland Conference) 1983 Football (tie with Northeast Louisiana). Vocational education: Jessies Beauty College (Denton). **PUBLIC LIBRARIES** Denton Public Library: 111,266 volumes. Lake Dallas Library. Lewisville Public Library: 36,503 volumes. Pilot Point Library. Roanoke Library. The Colony Library. **CHILD CARE** 382 day care and 46 twenty-four hour care licensed facilities. **HEALTH CARE** 170 physicians and 51 dentists. Hospitals: five with a combined capacity of 497. Clinics: one osteopathic clinic, one dialysis clinic, one public health clinic and one minor emergency center. Ambulance services: five volunteer fire departments, three fire departments, two city, two funeral homes and two commercial services. Mental health: three centers with capacity of 369, one state school with capacity of 942 and one county clinic. Nursing homes: seven

nursing homes with a combined capacity of 612 nursing care residents. The average cost per day for private patients in 1982 was $35.57. **CHURCHES** 155 churches have an estimated combined membership of 53,692. The largest denominations are Southern Baptist, Catholic and United Methodist. **SOCIAL SERVICES** In fiscal year 1983 a total of $1,512,416 in food stamps was distributed, with an average of 3,050 persons receiving food stamps each month. Aid to Families with Dependent Children (AFDC) totaled $364,558 with an average of 247 families receiving AFDC each month. Medical assistance benefits for the aged and disabled of $9,186,609 and for families and children of $797,984 brought the county benefit total to $11,861,567. **FIRE PROTECTION** One paid, one partly paid and 17 volunteer fire departments. **LAW ENFORCEMENT** The County Sheriff has 59 commissioned officers. 17 police departments have a combined force of 279. Two universities have campus police departments with a combined force of 36 officers. **CRIME** 371 violent crimes (murder, forcible rape, robbery and aggravated assault) and 7,080 nonviolent crimes (burglary, larceny-theft and motor vehicle theft) were reported in 1982. **JUDICIAL SYSTEM** Three District Courts and Judges, three County Courts and Judges and five Justices of the Peace. In the District Courts a total of 9,275 cases were pending on 1/1/82, 6,049 new cases were filed and 6,261 cases were disposed of during the year leaving 9,063 cases pending on 12/31/82. There were 1,402 criminal cases on the docket, 300 convictions, 89 persons committed to prison and 14 committed to jail and 628 cases left pending. In the County Courts 4,313 cases were pending on 1/1/82, 6,074 new cases were filed and 5,384 cases were disposed of during the year leaving 5,003 cases pending on 12/31/82. There were 8,910 criminal cases on the docket, 1,521 convictions, 87 persons committed to jail, and 3,778 cases left pending. **JAILS** One jail, capacity 52. Constructing a new jail, capacity 250. In 1983 lost certification due to overcrowding. **ATTORNEYS AT LAW** 136. **UTILITIES** 92% of the residents are connected to a public or privately owned water system and 83% are connected to a public sewer system. Natural gas is distributed to the county by Lone Star Gas Co., Division of Enserch. The average annual residential bill for natural gas in 1982 for the Lone Star distribution system was $405.91, an increase of 35% over 1981. Electricity is distributed to the city of Denton by Denton Municipal Utilities, Sanger by the Sanger Electric System and to the rest of the county by Texas Power and Light Co., Texas-New Mexico Power Co., Tri Co. Electric Coop., Inc., Denton Co. Electric Coop., Inc. and Cooke Co. Electric Coop., Assn. and is generated primarily by gas, water, oil and coal. The typical residential electric bill is $168.05 per month for an all-electric house using 2,500 kwh. **TAXES** The county has 38 units with taxing authority: 12 school districts, 18 cities, one county and seven special districts.

RECREATION/ENTERTAINMENT

NATIONAL REGISTER OF HISTORIC PLACES Denton: The Denton County Courthouse. Denton vicinity: Cranston Site, J.C. Lambert Site, Roark-Griffith Site, A.H. Serien Site and Wilson-Donaldson Site. **STATE** Lake Lewisville State Park covers 721 acres with fishing, swimming and boat ramp facilities. **MUNICIPAL PARKS** 2,048 acres in 44 municipal parks. These parks contain five miles of hiking trails, 31 playgrounds, one golf course, 13 football and soccer fields, 29 baseball and softball fields, 40 tennis courts, 15 multi-use courts, three swimming pools, two beaches, seven boat ramps and shore fishing facilities. Developed campsites: 67. **SCENIC DRIVES** The Texas Lakes Trail runs through this county. This trail introduces some 30 blue-water recreational areas in a variety of settings in North-Central Texas. **BOATING/FISHING** Lakes/reservoirs: Burger (22 acres), Clear Creek Soil Conservation Service Lakes 41, 50 and 53 (40 acres), Deussen (116 acres), Grapevine (7,380 acres), Lewisville (20,300 acres), Paddock (20 acres) and Turner (31 acres). Major rivers: Elm Fork Trinity. Primary streams: White, Boom, Clear, Willow, Denton, Ranger and Marshall. **HUNTING** Fall and winter seasons on deer. No closed season on nutria, coyote, bobcat and squirrel. Winter season on quail, muskrat, beaver, otter, opossum, mink, ring-tailed cat, badger, fox, raccoon, skunk and civet cat. In 1983 duck, coot, geese, woodcock and jacksnipe seasons occurred during the winter months. Teal duck, rail and gallinule seasons occurred in the fall. Mourning dove season occurred intermittently during the fall and winter months. **MUSEUMS** Denton: Texas Woman's University Art Galleries, D.A.R. Museum, North Texas State U. Fashion Collection, North Texas State U. Historical Collection and Denton County Musuem. Lewisville: Lewisville Historical Museum. **THEATERS** Denton: Denton Community Theater. **COLLEGIATE FINE ARTS** Denton: Cultural events offered by North Texas State University and Texas Woman's University. **SPECIAL EVENTS** Youth Fair and Rodeo, Denton, March; Spring Arts Festival, Denton, April; Wild Flower Days, Denton, April; Art Fiesta, Carrollton, April; Fun Run and Fireworks, Denton, July 4; North Texas State Fair, Denton, August; Festival of Carols, Denton, November; and Victorian Christmas on the Square, Denton, December.

COMMUNITIES

COUNTY SEAT County Courthouse, Denton; County Clerk's Office, 76201; 817/382-9729. **INCORPORATED COMMUNITIES** (1980 population and ZIP Code) Argyle (1,111) 76226, Aubrey (948) 76227, Bartonville (441) 76226, Carrollton (40,591: 26,853 in Dallas Co. and 13,742 in Denton Co.) 75006, Copper Canyon (465) 76201, Corinth (1,264) 76201, Corral City (85) 76226, Cross Roads (302) 76227, Dallas (904,078: 101 in Denton Co., 902,619 in Dallas Co., 1,357 in Collin Co. and 1 in Kaufman Co.) 75200, Denton (48,063) 76201, Double Oak (836) 76226, Eastvale (503) 75067, Flower Mound (4,402) 75067, Frisco (3,499: 85 in Denton Co. and 3,335 in Collin Co.) 75034, Hebron (385) 75067, Hickory Creek (1,422) 75065, Highland Village (3,246) 75067, Justin (920) 76247, Krugerville (469) 76227, Krum (917) 76249, Lake Dallas (3,177) 75065, Lakewood Village (165) 76201, Lewisville (24,273) 75067, Lincoln Park (39) 76227, Little Elm (926) 75068, Northlake (143) 76247, Oak Point (387) 75034, Pilot Point (2,211) 76258, Ponder (297) 76259, Roanoke (910) 76262, Sanger (2,574) 76266, Shadyshores (813) 76201, Southlake (2,808: 16 in Denton Co. and 2,792 in Tarrant Co.) 76051, The Colony (11,586) 76056 and Westlake (214: 64 in Denton Co. and 150 in Tarrant Co.) 76248. **UNINCORPORATED COMMUNITIES** (and ZIP Code) Bolivar 76266, Camey 75034, Camp Dallas 75034, Drop 76247, Green Valley 76227, Hickory Grove 75065, Mayhill 76201, Mustang 76258, Navo 75034, Parvin 75009, Stony 76259 and Trophy Club 75261. **FOR ADDITIONAL LOCAL INFORMATION** Denton Chamber of Commerce, 414 Parkway, Drawer P, Denton, 76202, 817/382-9693, Lake Cities Chamber of Commerce, P.O. Box 1028, Lake Dallas, 75065, 817/497-3097, Greater Lewisville Chamber of Commerce, P.O. Box 416, Lewisville, 75067, 214/436-9571, Pilot Point Chamber of Commerce, 206 S. Washington, P.O. Box 497, Pilot Point, 76258, 817/686-5385, Sanger Area Chamber of Commerce, P.O. Box 537, Sanger, 76266, 817/458-7702, and The Colony Chamber of Commerce, 5204 S. Colony Blvd., Suite 250, The Colony, 76056.

DE WITT (G21)

THE LAND

Southeast of San Antonio on U.S Highways 183 and 87 in the Claypan Area, De Witt County covers 910 square miles with an elevation range of 150 to 400 feet. In the northeast the undulating land has deep to shallow, alkaline, dark, clayey soils over chalk. In the northwest the dark soils are either cracking, clay or slightly acidic loam over cracking, red clay subsoils. In the southeast the land is more level, lighter in color, and slightly acidic. The loamy surface layer covers cracking, clayey subsoils. In the southwest the soils are dark and deep with loamy surface layers and loamy or clayey subsoils. However in some areas bedrock is at shallow depth. The vegetation in the east is the Post Oak Savannah with tall grasses plus oaks, elms and pecans along streams. In the north it is Blackland Prairie vegetation with tall grasses, mesquite and a variety of trees along streams. In the southwest the vegetation is the South Texas Plains with short to mid grasses, small trees and shrubs. Between 21 and 30% of the land in the county is considered prime farmland. **CLIMATE** Subtropical humid with the possibility of a tropical storm or hurricane June through September. The average annual temperature is 70 °F. Temperatures in January range from an average low of 43 ° to an average high of 65 °F and in July range from 73 ° to 96 °F. The average annual precipitation is 33 inches, with an average relative humidity of 88% at 6 A.M. and 53% at 6 P.M. The growing season averages 270 days per year, with the last freeze in early March and the first freeze in late November. The sun shines during the year on the average 67% of the daylight hours.

THE PEOPLE

De Witt County ranks as one of the highest in the state in percent of residents who are native Texans. The 1982 estimated population of 20,000 indicates a continuation of the slight increase in population begun in the 1970s which reversed the steady population decrease from 1930 to 1970. About 2% of the growth between 1970 and 1980 was in the rural areas. The age group with the largest gain was ages 20 to 24. The county's median age, which is older than average, lowered from 39 in 1970 to 37 in 1980. The largest ancestry groups are persons of German descent (36%), Hispanic (23%) and Irish descent (13%). **REGISTERED VOTERS** As of November 2, 1982 there were 8,482 registered voters (0.1% of the state total). The 1982 general election had a 55% voter turnout, compared to a 67% turnout in the 1980 general election. In the 1982 primary 88% voted Democratic and 12% Republican, with 2,733 votes cast.

THE ECONOMY

AGRICULTURE Cattle area. In 1982, 93% of the land was in farms and ranches, with 10% of the farmland under cultivation. De Witt ranked 99th in the state in highest agricultural receipts, with 91% from livestock and livestock products. Overgrazing, undesirable brush, noxious weeds, and water erosion are the current conservation problems. Primary crops: hay, oats, corn, sorghum and wheat. Primary vegetables: potatoes, sweet potatoes and tomatoes. Primary fruits and nuts: peaches and pecans. Primary livestock and products: ninth in the state for beef cows that have calved. Cattle, milk, sheep, wool and hogs. **BUSINESS** Total number of business establishments in the county: 399. Retail sales during the first quarter of 1984 increased 5%. In 1980, 14% of the labor force were self-employed, 18% were employed in professional or related services, 15% in manufacturing, 20% in wholesale and retail trade, 18% in agriculture, forestry, fisheries and mining, 23% were employed in other counties and there were 2,169 retired workers. The industries with the most employment: oil and gas extraction, lumber mills, agribusiness, cotton weaving, and the manufacture of leather goods and plastic products. The nonfarm earnings in 1981 totaled $159,876,000. The retired workers received an average monthly Social Security payment of $265. **FINANCE** On June 30, 1983, eight commercial banks had total deposits of $219,479,000 and total assets of $242,589,000. On December 31, 1982 two federal savings and loan associations, two state branches and one federal branch had

COUNTIES

DE WITT (continued)

combined assets of $127,927,089. In addition there are two credit unions in the county. **HOUSING** Average value of homes in 1980: $22,600. Permits for new, privately owned housing units increased in 1982: 58 permits were issued with a total construction cost of $1,563,462. Of those permits, 42 were for single family houses. Housing permits increased in Cuero from 13 in 1981 to 32 in 1982 and in Yorktown from 12 to 26 with all permits issued for single family houses. Between 1970 and 1980 the number of housing units increased by 16%. Fifty percent of all units in the county are air-conditioned, 79% are heated by gas and 15% by electricity. **NATURAL RESOURCES** Clay, sand and gravel, oil and gas. In 1982 a total of 20,710,110 thousand cubic feet of gas well gas, 282,535 barrels of condensate, 359,007 barrels of crude oil and 745,438 thousand cubic feet of casinghead gas were produced. Current production of other minerals and products includes sand and gravel. **TOURISM** Travel expenditures of $9,972,000 in 1982 (an increase of 11% over 1981) generated 242 jobs and $1,953,000 in payroll. **ALCOHOLIC BEVERAGES** Packaged distilled spirits, beer, ale, malt liquor and wine are legal in parts of the county. Sale of mixed beverages is legal in all or parts of the county. **FEDERAL EXPENDITURES** The federal government had direct expenditures or obligations of $31,339,000 in the county during fiscal year 1983, including $1,438,000 by the U.S. Department of Defense. In addition, the federal government provided $244,000 in grant awards, paid $1,141,000 in salaries and wages, made direct payments to individuals of $29,666,000 including $20,440,000 in retirement and disability payments, awarded $61,000 in procurement contracts and spent $227,000 in other expenditures or obligations. The federal government also provided $14,000 in direct loans and $5,643,000 in guaranteed loans and insurance.

COMMUNICATION

Newspapers–Weekly: Cuero Record, Herald Times (Yoakum) Yorktown News and De Witt County View (Yorktown). Radio: KEWS-AM (Cuero). Cable TV. Telephone companies: Continental Telephone, Southwestern Bell and Guadalupe Valley Telephone Coop. **TRANSPORTATION** Total public road mileage: 1,143. In 1982 there were 17,676 registered vehicles and 435 reported traffic accidents including six fatalities. Taxi cabs: one company in Cuero. Intercity bus service is available. Motor freight: five local and intrastate carriers. Rail: one branch line carries annually five to 10 million tons of freight through the county. Aircraft: 19 are registered in the county. Airports: Cuero Municipal Airport is a general utility airport providing general aviation service. It serves as a base for 10 aircraft. Yoakum Municipal Airport at the Lavaca/Dewitt County Line. Heliports for emergency use are available at the Cuero Community Hospital and Yorktown Memorial Hospital at Yorktown.

COMMUNITY SERVICES

EDUCATION Six school districts with eight elementary, three middle, four high schools and one special education. The average daily attendance in 1981-82 was 4,050, with expenditures per pupil of $3,469 including 299 classroom teachers with an average annual salary of $15,768. Twenty-five percent of the 291 high school graduates planned to attend college. In 1982-83, 57% of the students were White, 31% Hispanic, 12% Black and 0.1% Asian. Private schools: 145 students enrolled in one elementary school. **PUBLIC LIBRARIES** Cuero Public Library: 18,000 volumes. Yorktown Public Library: 11,723 volumes. **CHILD CARE** 30 day care and nine twenty-four hour care licensed facilities. **HEALTH CARE** 10 physicians and seven dentists. Hospitals: two with a combined capacity of 94. Clinics: one public health clinic. Ambulance services: one hospital-based, one funeral home, one commercial and one fire department service. Nursing homes: five nursing homes with a combined capacity

of 444 nursing care residents. The average cost per day for private patients in 1982 was $31.18. **CHURCHES** 37 churches have an estimated combined membership of 12,776. The largest denominations are Catholic, American Lutheran and Southern Baptist. **SOCIAL SERVICES** In fiscal year 1983 a total of $1,263,600 in food stamps was distributed, with an average of 2,822 persons receiving food stamps each month. Aid to Families with Dependent Children (AFDC) totaled $259,235 with an average of 176 families receiving AFDC each month. Medical assistance benefits for the aged and disabled of $3,014,867 and for families and children of $342,875 brought the county benefit total to $4,880,577. **FIRE PROTECTION** One partly paid and six volunteer fire departments. **LAW ENFORCEMENT** The County Sheriff has 14 commissioned officers. Two police departments have a combined force of 16. **CRIME** 51 violent crimes (murder, forcible rape, robbery and aggravated assault) and 264 nonviolent crimes (burglary, larceny-theft and motor vehicle theft) were reported in 1982. **JUDICIAL SYSTEM** Three District Courts and Judges, one County Court and Judge and five Justices of the Peace. In the District Courts a total of 358 cases were pending on 1/1/82, 557 new cases were filed and 428 cases were disposed of during the year leaving 487 cases pending on 12/31/82. There were 176 criminal cases on the docket, 99 convictions, 10 persons committed to prison and 71 cases left pending. In the County Court 426 cases were pending on 1/1/82, 679 new cases were filed and 631 cases were disposed of during the year leaving 474 cases pending on 12/31/82. There were 856 criminal cases on the docket, 299 convictions, 72 persons committed to jail, and 303 cases left pending. **JAILS** One jail, capacity 23. **ATTORNEYS AT LAW** 13. **UTILITIES** 62% of the residents are connected to a public or privately owned water system and 60% are connected to a public sewer system. Natural gas is distributed to the county by Arkla, Inc. and Entex, Inc. The average annual residential bill for natural gas in 1982 for the Arkla distribution system was $316.69, an increase of 23% over 1981 and for Entex it was $309.31, an increase of 26%. Electricity is distributed to the city of Cuero by Cuero Electric Utility, Yoakum by Yoakum Municipal Utilities and to the rest of the county by Cochran Power & Light Co., De Witt Electric Coop., Inc. and Victoria Co. Electric Coop., Inc. and is generated primarily by gas, oil, water and coal. The typical residential electric bill is $136.35 per month for an all-electric house using 2,500 kwh. **TAXES** The county has 14 units with taxing authority: six school districts, four cities, one county, one hospital district and two special districts.

RECREATION/ENTERTAINMENT

NATIONAL REGISTER OF HISTORIC PLACES Cuero: De Witt County Courthouse. Cuero vicinity: Cuero I Archeological District and Hydroelectric Plant. Yorktown: Eckhardt Stores. **MUNICIPAL PARKS** 162 acres in six municipal parks. These parks contain seven playgrounds, one golf course, one football and soccer field, 14 baseball and softball fields, four tennis courts and one swimming pool. **BOATING/FISHING** Lakes/reservoirs: Cuero (49 acres). Major rivers: Guadalupe. Primary streams: Coleto. **HUNTING** Fall and winter seasons on deer. Fall and winter seasons on javalina. No closed season on nutria, squirrel, bobcat and coyote. Winter season on quail, muskrat, beaver, otter, opossum, mink, ring-tailed cat, badger, fox, raccoon, skunk, and civet cat. In 1983 sandhill crane, duck, coot, geese, woodcock and jacksnipe seasons occurred during the winter months. Teal duck, rail and gallinule seasons occurred in the fall. Mourning dove season occurred intermittently during the fall and winter months. **MUSEUMS** Cuero: De Witt County Historical Museum. Yorktown: Yorktown Historical Museum. **SPECIAL EVENTS** Western Days Celebration, Yorktown, October; and Turkeyfest, Cuero, October.

COMMUNITIES

COUNTY SEAT Cuero, County Courthouse, 77954; County Clerk's Office, 512/275-3724. **INCORPORATED COMMUNITIES** (1980 population and ZIP Code) Cuero (7,124) 77954, All-America Cities Award 1969, Nordheim (369) 78141, Yoakum (6,148: 2,325 in De Witt Co. and 3,823 in Lavaca Co.) 77995 and Yorktown (2,498) 78164. **UNINCORPORATED COMMUNITIES** (and ZIP Code) Arneckeville 77954, Clinton 77954, Concrete 77954, Edgar 77954, Garfield 78164, Gruenau 78164, Hochheim 77967, Lindenau 77954, Meyersville 77974, Nopal 78164, Pearl City 77995, Petersville 77995, Stratton 77954, Terryville 77995, Thomaston 77989, Upper Meyersville 78164, Valley View 77954, Verhelle 77954 and Westhoff 77994. **FOR ADDITIONAL LOCAL INFORMATION** Cuero Chamber of Commerce, 103 N. Esplanade, Cuero, 77954, 512/275-2112, Yoakum Chamber of Commerce, 105 Huck, P. O. Box 591, Yoakum, 77995, 512/293-2149 and Yorktown Chamber of Commerce, P.O. Box 488, Yorktown, 78164, 512/564-2661.

DICKENS (P41)

THE LAND

East of Lubbock on U.S. Highway 82 in the Rolling Plains Region, Dickens County covers 907 square miles with the elevation ranging from 2,000 to 3,000 feet. The northern portion of the western border has nearly level, alkaline soils with loamy surface layers and clayey subsoils. Along the eastern border and in a strip to the center of the county are level to undulating, red to brown, alkaline soils with loamy surface layers and clayey subsoils. The rest of the county has mostly loamy soils with some clayey subsoils. The county is in the Rolling Plains vegetation area with tall to mid grasses, such as little bluestem, big bluestem, sideoats grama, Indiangrass, switchgrass, hairy grama, bluegrama, wildryes, tobosa and buffalograss. Between 21 and 30% of the land in the county is considered prime farmland. **CLIMATE** Mild and dry with thunderstorms and duststorms in the spring and early summer. The average annual temperature is 61°F. Temperatures in January range from an average low of 26° to an average high of 54°F and in July range from 69° to 95°F. The average annual precipitation is 21 inches, with an average relative humidity of 73% at 6 A.M. and 40% at 6 P.M. The average annual snowfall is 11 inches. The growing season averages 217 days per year, with the last freeze in early April and the first freeze in early November. The sun shines during the year on the average 75% of the daylight hours.

THE PEOPLE

The 1982 estimated population of 3,300 indicates a pattern of continuing decline which began as early as 1930. However, between 1970 and 1980 the population decreased only 5%. The age groups with the largest losses from 1970 to 1980 were ages 10 to 14 and 60 to 64. The county's median age, which is older than average, lowered from 42 in 1970 to 38 in 1980. The largest ancestry groups are persons of English descent (26%), Irish descent (24%) and Hispanic (17%). **REGISTERED VOTERS** As of November 2, 1982 there were 2,028 registered voters (0.03% of the state total). The 1982 general election had a 56% voter turnout, compared to a 67% turnout in the 1980 general election. In the 1982 primary 100% voted Democratic, with 1,189 votes cast.

THE ECONOMY

AGRICULTURE Cotton area. In 1982, 95% of the land was in farms and ranches, with 17% of the farmland under cultivation and 16% irrigated. Dickens ranked 163rd in the state in highest agricultural receipts, with 64% from livestock and livestock products. Overgrazing, undesirable brush and weeds, water and wind erosion and difficulties in grass establishment are the current conservation problems. Primary crops: cotton, wheat and sorghum. Primary fruits and nuts: pecans. Primary livestock and products: cattle and wool. **BUSINESS** Total number of business establishments in the county: 65. Retail sales during the first quarter of 1984 decreased 16%. In 1980, 30% of the labor force were self-employed, 13% were employed in professional or related services, 8% in manufacturing, 17% in wholesale and retail trade, 34% in agriculture, forestry, fisheries and mining, 9% were employed in other counties and there were 549 retired workers. The industries with the most employment: agribusiness, oil and gas extraction, heavy construction, petroleum refining and the manufacture of men's work clothing. The nonfarm earnings in 1981 totaled $23,836,000. The retired workers received an average monthly Social Security payment of $273. **FINANCE** On June 30, 1983, one commercial bank had total deposits of $17,657,000 and total assets of $19,867,000. **HOUSING** Average value of homes in 1980: $15,000. Between 1970 and 1980 the number of housing units decreased by 4%. Eighty percent of all units in the county are air-conditioned, 91% are heated by gas and 7% by electricity. **NATURAL RESOURCES** Caliche, gypsum, salt, volcanic ash, oil and gas. In 1982 a total of 93,150 barrels of crude oil and 4,282 thousand cubic feet of casinghead gas were produced. Current production of other minerals and products includes caliche, sand and gravel. **TOURISM** Travel expenditures of $2,752,000 in 1982 (an increase of 14% over 1981) generated 57 jobs and $495,000 in payroll. **ALCOHOLIC BEVERAGES** Packaged distilled spirits, beer, ale, malt liquor and wine are legal in parts of the county. **FEDERAL EXPENDITURES** The federal government had direct expenditures or obligations of $11,126,000 in the county during fiscal year 1983, including $69,000 by the U.S. Department of Defense. In addition, the federal government provided $606,000 in grant awards, paid $389,000 in salaries and wages, made direct payments to individuals of $6,566,000 including $4,150,000 in retirement and disability payments, awarded $1,000 in procurement contracts and spent $3,564,000 in other expenditures or obligations. The federal government also provided $815,000 in direct loans and $12,413,000 in guaranteed loans and insurance.

COMMUNICATION

Newspapers–Weekly: The Texas Spur. Cable TV. Telephone companies: General Telephone, Caprock Telephone and South Plains Telephone Coop. **TRANSPORTATION** Total public road mileage: 637. In 1982 there were 3,267 registered vehicles and 46 reported traffic accidents including one fatality. Intercity bus service is available. Motor freight: two carriers. Aircraft: eight are registered in the county. Airports: Spur Municipal Airport.

COMMUNITY SERVICES

EDUCATION Three school districts with three elementary and three high schools. The average daily attendance in 1981-82 was 591, with expenditures per pupil of $3,078 including 54 classroom teachers with an average annual salary of $15,031. Forty-one percent of the 37 high school graduates planned to attend college. In 1982-83, 62% of the students were White, 31% Hispanic, 7% Black, 0.3% Asian and 0.5% American Indian. **PUBLIC LIBRARIES** Spur Library. **CHILD CARE** Five day care and one twenty-four hour care licensed facilities. **HEALTH CARE** One physician. Ambulance services: one county service. Nursing homes: one nursing home has a capacity of 40 nursing care residents. The average cost per day for private patients in 1982 was $26.10. **CHURCHES** 19 churches have an estimated combined membership of 3,396. The largest denominations are Southern Baptist, United Methodist and Catholic.

COUNTIES

DICKENS (continued)

SOCIAL SERVICES In fiscal year 1983 a total of $159,405 in food stamps was distributed, with an average of 349 persons receiving food stamps each month. Aid to Families with Dependent Children (AFDC) totaled $21,652 with an average of 14 families receiving AFDC each month. Medical assistance benefits for the aged and disabled of $292,614 and for families and children of $33,032 brought the county benefit total to $506,703. **FIRE PROTECTION** Two volunteer fire departments. **LAW ENFORCEMENT** The County Sheriff has four commissioned officers. One police department has a force of two. **CRIME** Six violent crimes (murder, forcible rape, robbery and aggravated assault) and 75 nonviolent crimes (burglary, larceny-theft and motor vehicle theft) were reported in 1982. **JUDICIAL SYSTEM** One District Court and Judge, one County Court and Judge and two Justices of the Peace. In the District Court a total of 332 cases were pending on 1/1/82, 66 new cases were filed and 69 cases were disposed of during the year leaving 329 cases pending on 12/31/82. There were 26 criminal cases on the docket, 12 convictions, one person committed to prison, and nine cases left pending. In the County Court 406 cases were pending on 1/1/82, 163 new cases were filed and 76 cases were disposed of during the year leaving 493 cases pending on 12/31/82. There were 511 criminal cases on the docket, 52 convictions, and 439 cases left pending. **JAILS** One jail, capacity six. Completed major renovation in 1983. **ATTORNEYS AT LAW** Four. **UTILITIES** 75% of the residents are connected to a public or privately owned water system and 62% are connected to a public sewer system. Electricity is distributed to the county by Dickens Electric Coop., Inc., Gate City Electric Coop., Inc., Lighthouse Electric Coop., Inc. and West Texas Utilities Co. and is generated primarily by gas and oil. **TAXES** The county has seven units with taxing authority: three school districts, two cities, one county and one special district.

RECREATION/ENTERTAINMENT

NATIONAL REGISTER OF HISTORIC PLACES Dickens: Dickens County Courthouse and Jail. **MUNICIPAL PARKS** 383 acres in four municipal parks. These parks contain one playground, one golf course and one swimming pool. Developed campsites: 40. **BOATING/FISHING** Lakes/reservoirs: Duck Creek Soil Conservation Service Lakes 1, 3, 5, 7 and 8 (158 acres). Primary streams: Croton, Cottonwood, Dockum and Duck. **HUNTING** Fall and winter seasons on deer and mule deer. No closed season on coyote, bobcat and squirrel. Winter season on quail, muskrat, beaver, opossum, ring-tailed cat, badger, fox, weasel, raccoon, skunk and civet cat. Fall, winter and spring seasons on turkey. In 1983 sandhill crane, duck, coot, geese, woodcock and jacksnipe seasons occurred during the winter months. Teal duck, rail and gallinule seasons occurred in the fall. Mourning dove season occurred intermittently during the fall and winter months. **MUSEUMS** Dickens: Dickens County Museum. Spur: Margaret A. Elliot Museum. **SPECIAL EVENTS** Dickens Homecoming, Dickens, July; Junior Rodeo, Dickens, July; Spur Homecoming and Celebration, Spur, October; Christmas Parade, Spur, December.

COMMUNITIES

COUNTY SEAT Dickens, County Courthouse, 79229; County Clerk's Office, 806/623-5531. **INCORPORATED COMMUNITIES** (1980 population and ZIP Code) Dickens (409) 79229 and Spur (1,690) 79370. **UNINCORPORATED COMMUNITIES** (and ZIP Code) Afton 79220, Croton 79232, Dumont (also in King Co.) 79232, East Afton 79220, Gilpin 79370, Glenn 79220 and McAdoo 79243.

DIMMIT (B16)

THE LAND

Southwest of San Antonio on U.S. Highway 83 in the Rio Grande Plain Region, Dimmit County covers 1,307 square miles with an elevation range of 500 to 800 feet. Artesian water is found in the county. The nearly level soils are poorly drained in some areas and loamy with limestone within 40 inches of the surface. The south central area soils are alkaline and loamy to clayey with a high shrink-swell potential. In the South Plains vegetation area there are mid to short grasses, mesquite and small trees, thorny brush and cacti. Less than 1% of the land in the county is considered prime farmland. **CLIMATE** Subtropical steppe and relatively dry. The average annual temperature is 72°F. Temperatures in January range from an average low of 40° to an average high of 66°F and in July range from 74° to 99°F. The average annual precipitation is 22 inches, with an average relative humidity of 80% at 6 A.M. and 43% at 6 P.M. There is no snowfall. The growing season averages 290 days per year, with the last freeze in mid February and the first freeze in early December. The sun shines during the year on the average 67% of the daylight hours.

THE PEOPLE

Dimmit County ranks 14th among all U.S. counties in the highest percent of persons of Spanish origin. The 1982 estimated population of 11,800 indicates a continuation of the growth begun in the 1970s which reversed a population decline. Between 1970 and 1980 the population had a 26% increase, with a 28% growth in the urban areas and a 22% growth in rural areas. The age groups with the largest gains were ages 25 to 34 and 50 to 54. Therefore, the county's young median age rose from 21 in 1970 to 25 in 1980. The largest ancestry groups are Hispanic (78%), persons of English descent (9%) and Irish descent (7%). **REGISTERED VOTERS** As of November 2, 1982 there were 6,445 registered voters (0.1% of the state total). The 1982 general election had a 45% voter turnout, compared to a 53% turnout in the 1980 general election. In the 1982 primary 99% voted Democratic and 0.1% Republican, with 3,224 votes cast.

THE ECONOMY

AGRICULTURE Ranchland in the lower Rio Grande Valley. In 1982, 89% of the land was in farms and ranches, with 2% of the farmland under cultivation, most of which was irrigated. Dimmit ranked 153rd in the state in highest agricultural receipts, with 65% from livestock and livestock products. Overgrazing, undesirable brush and salinity are the current conservation problems. Primary crops: sorghum, cotton, wheat and oats. Primary vegetables: fifth in the state for carrots, fourth for cantaloupes and sixth for cabbage. Onions, cucumbers and spinach. Primary fruits and nuts: grapefruit, oranges and pecans. Primary livestock and products: cattle and hogs. **BUSINESS** Total number of business establishments in the county: 170. Retail sales during the first quarter of 1984 decreased 7%. In 1980, 9% of the labor force were self-employed, 24% were employed in professional or related services, 9% in manufacturing, 18% in wholesale and retail trade, 20% in agriculture, forestry, fisheries and mining, 15% were employed in other counties and there were 647 retired workers. The industries with the most employment: agribusiness, oil and gas field servicing, trucking, heavy construction and the manufacture of men's and boy's apparel. The nonfarm earnings in 1981 totaled $63,739,000. The retired workers received an average monthly Social Security payment of $252. **FINANCE** On June 30, 1983, two commercial banks had total deposits of $46,698,000 and total assets of $51,747,000. There is one state savings and loan association branch in the county. **HOUSING** Average value of homes in 1980: $14,700.

Permits for new, privately owned housing units increased in 1982: 46 permits were issued with a total construction cost of $1,221,611. Of those permits, 34 were for single family houses. Housing permits in Big Wells increased from one in 1981 to 13 in 1982 with all permits issued for single family houses. Between 1970 and 1980 the number of housing units increased by 33%. Fifty-one percent of all units in the county are air-conditioned, 84% are heated by gas and 11% by electricity. **NATURAL RESOURCES** Caliche, industrial sand, sand and gravel, oil, gas, and lignite coal. In 1982 a total of 5,896,799 thousand cubic feet of gas well gas, 37,967 barrels of condensate, 3,891,382 barrels of crude oil and 4,112,645 thousand cubic feet of casinghead gas were produced. Current production of other minerals and products includes recovered sulphur. **TOURISM** Travel expenditures of $5,372,000 in 1982 (an increase of 16% over 1981) generated 89 jobs and $858,000 in payroll. **ALCOHOLIC BEVERAGES** Packaged distilled spirits, beer, ale, malt liquor and wine are legal in parts of the county. Sale of mixed beverages is legal in all or parts of the county. **FEDERAL EXPENDITURES** The federal government had direct expenditures or obligations of $11,993,000 in the county during fiscal year 1983, including $255,000 by the U.S. Department of Defense. In addition, the federal government provided $1,199,000 in grant awards, paid $1,032,000 in salaries and wages, made direct payments to individuals of $9,443,000 including $6,961,000 in retirement and disability payments, awarded $1,000 in procurement contracts and spent $318,000 in other expenditures or obligations. The federal government also provided $23,000 in direct loans and $902,000 in guaranteed loans and insurance.

COMMUNICATION

Newspapers–Weekly: Carrizo Springs Javelin. Radio: KBEN-AM (Carrizo Springs). Telephone companies: Southwestern Bell and Valley Telephone Coop. **TRANSPORTATION** Total public road mileage: 437. In 1982 there were 7,718 registered vehicles and 106 reported traffic accidents including two fatalities. Intercity bus service is available. Motor freight: five local and intrastate carriers. Rail: one branch line carries annually less than one million tons of freight through the county. Aircraft: 19 are registered in the county. Airports: Dimmit County Airport at Carrizo Springs is a basic transportation airport providing general aviation service. It serves as a base for 16 aircraft. Price Ranch Airport at Big Wells. Dimmit Memorial Hospital provides a heliport for emergency use.

COMMUNITY SERVICES

EDUCATION Two school districts with five elementary, one middle and two high schools. The average daily attendance in 1981-82 was 3,180, with expenditures per pupil of $2,555 including 223 classroom teachers with an average annual salary of $15,673. Forty percent of the 208 high school graduates planned to attend college. In 1982-83, 14% of the students were White, 85% Hispanic, 0.8% Black and 0.1% Asian. **PUBLIC LIBRARIES** Carrizo Springs Library. **CHILD CARE** Six day care licensed facilities. **HEALTH CARE** Six physicians and one dentist. Hospitals: one with a capacity of 49. Clinics: one public health clinic. Ambulance services: one volunteer service and one hospital-based service. Mental health: one county clinic. Nursing homes: one nursing home has a capacity of 100 nursing care and 24 personal care residents. The average cost per day for private patients in 1982 was $21.39. **CHURCHES** 15 churches have an estimated combined membership of 9,863. The largest denominations are Catholic, Southern Baptist and United Methodist. **SOCIAL SERVICES** In fiscal year 1983 a total of $2,114,172 in food stamps was distributed, with an average of 4,247 persons receiving food stamps each month. Aid to Families with Dependent Children (AFDC) totaled $338,395 with an average of 211 families receiving AFDC each month. Medical assistance benefits for the aged and disabled of $1,145,383 and for families and children of $523,162 brought the county benefit total to $4,121,112. **FIRE PROTECTION** Four volunteer fire departments. **LAW ENFORCEMENT** The County Sheriff has seven commissioned officers. One police department has a force of one. **CRIME** 12 violent crimes (murder, forcible rape, robbery and aggravated assault) and 57 nonviolent crimes (burglary, larceny-theft and motor vehicle theft) were reported in 1982. **JUDICIAL SYSTEM** One District Court and Judge, one County Court and Judge and four Justices of the Peace. In the District Court a total of 436 cases were pending on 1/1/82, 256 new cases were filed and 430 cases were disposed of during the year leaving 262 cases pending on 12/31/82. There were 117 criminal cases on the docket, 24 convictions, seven persons committed to prison and one committed to jail and 48 cases left pending. In the County Court 764 cases were pending on 1/1/82, 404 new cases were filed and 461 cases were disposed of during the year leaving 707 cases pending on 12/31/82. There were 1,008 criminal cases on the docket, 232 convictions and 553 cases left pending. **JAILS** One jail, capacity 11. **ATTORNEYS AT LAW** 10. **UTILITIES** 88% of the residents are connected to a public or privately owned water system and 53% are connected to a public sewer system. Electricity is distributed to the county by Central Power and Light Co., Cochran Power and Light Co., Medina Electric Coop., Inc., and is generated primarily by gas, oil and coal. The typical residential electric bill is $162.15 per month for an all-electric house using 2,500 kwh. **TAXES** The county has six units with taxing authority: two school districts, three cities, and one county.

RECREATION/ENTERTAINMENT

COUNTY/MUNICIPAL PARKS 60 acres in four county and three municipal parks. These parks contain one playground, two baseball and softball fields, one swimming pool, one beach and two boat ramps. **BOATING/FISHING** Lakes/reservoirs: Bermuda (85 acres), Bookout (47 acres), Boynton (276 acres), Burro (3,500 acres), Chip Briscoe (86 acres), Dolph Briscoe (21 acres), Espantosa (364 acres), Marion (136 acres), Reynolds and Wilson (59 acres) and Soldier (100 acres). Major rivers: Nueces. Primary streams: Los Tablas, El Moro, Stag Hollow, Soldier Slough and Sam Rogue. **WILDLIFE REFUGES** Chaparral State Wildlife Management Area covers 8,000 acres in the county. **HUNTING** Fall and winter seasons on deer. No closed season on javelina, coyote, bobcat and squirrel. Winter season on quail, muskrat, beaver, opossum, ring-tailed cat, badger, fox, weasel, raccoon, skunk, turkey and civet cat. Special regulations on game animals, game birds or fur-bearing animals in state-owned river beds. In 1983 sandhill crane, duck, coot, geese, woodcock and jacksnipe seasons occurred during the winter months. Teal duck, rail and gallinule seasons occurred in the fall. Mourning dove season occurred intermittently during the fall and winter months with a fall season on white-winged dove. **SPECIAL EVENTS** Junior Stock Show, Carrizo Springs, January; Miss Carizzo Springs Pageant, Carrizo Springs, January; World Championship Slingshot Tourney, Carrizo Springs, October.

COMMUNITIES

COUNTY SEAT Carrizo Springs, County Courthouse, 78834; County Clerk's Office, 512/876-3569. **INCORPORATED COMMUNITIES** (1980 population and ZIP Code) Asherton (1,574) 78827, Big Wells (939) 78830 and Carrizo Springs (6,886) 78834. **UNINCORPORATED COMMUNITIES** (and ZIP Code) Brundage 78834, Catarina 78836, Valley Wells 78830 and Winter Haven 78839. **FOR ADDITIONAL LOCAL INFORMATION** Dimmit County Chamber of Commerce, 307 N. 5th St., Carrizo Springs, 78834, 512/876-2616.

COUNTIES

DONLEY (P19)

THE LAND

East of Amarillo in the Texas Panhandle on U.S. Highway 287 in the Rolling Plains Region, Donley County covers 929 square miles. The elevation ranges from 1,980 to 2,850 feet with breaks of the Mulberry Canyon in the southwest and the escarpment of the Llano Estacado in the north. The northwest and southern borders have level to undulating, red to brown, alkaline soils with loamy surface layers and clayey or loamy subsoils. The rest of the county has soils ranging from sandy to loamy with some clayey subsoils. Donley is in the Rolling Plains vegetation area with tall to mid grasses, such as big, little, sand and silver bluestems, buffalograss, wildryes, sideoats, Indiangrass and switchgrass. Mesquite, shinnery oak and sage have moved into the sandy regions. Between one and 10% of the land in the county is considered prime farmland. **CLIMATE** Mild and dry, but temperature extremes can be expected. The average annual temperature is 59°F. Temperatures in January range from an average low of 26° to an average high of 51°F and in July range from 67° to 95°F. The average annual precipitation is 21 inches, with an average relative humidity of 73% at 6 A.M. and 40% at 6 P.M. The average annual snowfall is 15 inches. The growing season averages 206 days per year, with the last freeze in early April and the first freeze in early November. The sun shines during the year on the average 75% of the daylight hours.

THE PEOPLE

The 1982 estimated population of 4,200 indicates a continuation of the small growth rate begun in the 1970s which reversed the steady population decrease between 1930 and 1970. The majority of residents live in rural areas. The age groups with the largest gains between 1970 and 1980 were ages birth to five years. Therefore the median age lowered from 43 in 1970 to 40 in 1980. However, the county's population remains older than average. The largest ancestry groups are persons of English descent (32%), Irish descent (22%) and German descent (14%). **REGISTERED VOTERS** As of November 2, 1982 there were 2,481 registered voters (0.03% of the state total). The 1982 general election had a 52% voter turnout, compared to a 74% turnout in the 1980 general election. In the 1982 primary 100% voted Democratic, with 1,064 votes cast.

THE ECONOMY

AGRICULTURE Cotton area. In 1982, 97% of the land was in farms and ranches, with 13% of the farmland under cultivation and 19% irrigated. Donley ranked 192nd in the state in highest agricultural receipts, with 56% from livestock and livestock products. Overgrazing, undesirable brush and weeds, wind erosion, cultivation of marginal lands and inefficient tillage systems are the current conservation problems. Primary crops: cotton, sorghum and wheat. Primary vegetables: watermelons. Primary fruits and nuts: peaches and pecans. Primary livestock and products: cattle. **BUSINESS** Total number of business establishments in the county: 84. Retail sales during the first quarter of 1984 increased 6%, with a 53% rise in Howardwick. In 1980, 21% of the labor force were self-employed, 23% were employed in professional or related services, 6% in manufacturing, 18% in wholesale and retail trade, 26% in agriculture, forestry, fisheries and mining, 15% were employed in other counties and there were 616 retired workers. The industry with the most employment: agribusiness. The nonfarm earnings in 1981 totaled $33,591,000. The retired workers received an average monthly Social Security payment of $295. **FINANCE** On June 30, 1983, three commercial banks had total deposits of $49,018,000 and total assets of $54,660,000. **HOUSING** Average value of homes in 1980: $21,200. In 1982 one permit was issued for a new single family

house. Between 1970 and 1980 the number of housing units increased by 28%. Seventy-seven percent of all units in the county are air-conditioned, 95% are heated by gas and 3% by electricity. **NATURAL RESOURCES** Caliche, gypsum, oil and gas. In 1982 a total of 32,949 thousand cubic feet of gas well gas were produced. Current production of other minerals and products includes sand and gravel. **TOURISM** Travel expenditures of $1,707,000 in 1982 (an increase of 12% over 1981) generated 38 jobs and $318,000 in payroll. **ALCOHOLIC BEVERAGES** Packaged distilled spirits, beer, ale, malt liquor and wine are legal in parts of the county. Sale of mixed beverages is legal in all or parts of the county. **FEDERAL EXPENDITURES** The federal government had direct expenditures or obligations of $11,575,000 in the county during fiscal year 1983, including $191,000 by the U.S. Department of Defense. In addition, the federal government provided $268,000 in grant awards, paid $311,000 in salaries and wages, made direct payments to individuals of $8,384,000 including $5,468,000 in retirement and disability payments, awarded $1,000 in procurement contracts and spent $2,613,000 in other expenditures or obligations. The federal government also provided $1,885,000 in direct loans and $1,898,000 in guaranteed loans and insurance.

COMMUNICATION

Newspapers–Weekly: The Clarendon Press and the Hedley Informer. Cable TV. Telephone companies: General Telephone and Southwestern Bell. **TRANSPORTATION** Total public road mileage: 611. In 1982 there were 4,964 registered vehicles and 121 reported traffic accidents including one fatality. Intercity bus service is available. Motor freight: one carrier. Rail: two main lines carry freight through the county with one carrying annually over 30 million tons of freight and one carrying 10 to 20 million. Aircraft: 13 are registered in the county. Airports: Sleepy Springs Airport at Howardwick. Clarendon Municipal Airport.

COMMUNITY SERVICES

EDUCATION Two school districts with two elementary and two high schools. The average daily attendance in 1981-82 was 652, with expenditures per pupil of $2,313 including 45 classroom teachers with an average annual salary of $16,518. Seventy-seven percent of the 61 high school graduates planned to attend college. In 1982-83, 86% of the students were White, 7% Hispanic and 8% Black. Clarendon College is located in Clarendon. Established in 1898 it is a vocational and two year academic college under state and local control. Enrollment in 1982 was 951 with in state undergratuate tuition and fees of $196 per semester. **PUBLIC LIBRARIES** Gabie Betts Burton Memorial Library (Clarendon): 12,413 volumes. **CHILD CARE** Nine day care and one twenty-four hour care licensed facilities. **HEALTH CARE** Two physicians and two dentists. Ambulance services: one city service. Mental health: one clinic. Nursing homes: one nursing home has a capacity of 43 nursing care residents. The average cost per day for private patients in 1982 was $36.01. **CHURCHES** 16 churches have an estimated combined membership of 2,955. The largest denominations are Southern Baptist, United Methodist and Churches of Christ. **SOCIAL SERVICES** In fiscal year 1983 a total of $154,920 in food stamps was distributed, with an average of 322 persons receiving food stamps each month. Aid to Families with Dependent Children (AFDC) totaled $32,885 with an average of 22 families receiving AFDC each month. Medical assistance benefits for the aged and disabled of $313,724 and for families and children of $18,330 brought the county benefit total to $519,859. **FIRE PROTECTION** Three volunteer fire departments. **LAW ENFORCEMENT** The County Sheriff has 23 commissioned officers. **CRIME** Nine violent crimes (murder, forcible rape, robbery and aggravated assault) and 99 nonviolent crimes (burglary, larceny-theft and motor vehicle theft) were reported in 1982. **JUDICIAL SYSTEM** One District Court and Judge, one County Court and Judge and two Justices of the Peace. In the District Court a total of 41 cases were pending on 1/1/82, 83 new cases were filed and 65 cases were disposed of during the year leaving 59 cases pending on 12/31/82. There were 51 criminal cases on the docket, 17 convictions, two persons committed to prison and 24 cases left pending. In the County Court 57 cases were pending on 1/1/82, 354 new cases were filed and 328 cases were disposed of during the year leaving 83 cases pending on 12/31/82. There were 392 criminal cases on the docket, 317 convictions and 65 cases left pending. **JAILS** One jail, capacity five. **ATTORNEYS AT LAW** Seven. **UTILITIES** 74% of the residents are connected to a public or privately owned water system and 58% are connected to a public sewer system. Natural gas is distributed to the county by Lone Star Gas Co., Division of Enserch. The average annual residential bill for natural gas in 1982 for the Lone Star distribution system was $405.91, an increase of 35% over 1981. Electricity is distributed to the county by West Texas Utilities, Greenbelt Electric Coop., Inc., and Lighthouse Electric Coop., Inc. and is generated primarily by gas and oil. **TAXES** The county has seven units with taxing authority: two school districts, two cities, one county, one hospital district and one college district.

RECREATION/ENTERTAINMENT
NATIONAL REGISTER OF HISTORIC PLACES Clarendon: Donley County Courthouse and Jail. **MUNICIPAL PARKS** 8 acres in one municipal park. This park contains one playground. **SCENIC DRIVES** In southern Donley County rugged canyon country can be viewed on Texas 70 which skirts the edge of the High Plains known as the Cap Rock. **BOATING/FISHING** Lakes/reservoirs: Clarendon (100 acres), Greenbelt (2,025 acres) and Lakeview Soil Conservation Service Lakes 1 and 2 (84 acres). Major rivers: Salt Fork Red. Primary streams: Brushy, Whitefish, Saddlers, Big Sandy, Mulberry, Indian, Oaks, E. Bitter and W. Bitter. **HUNTING** Fall season on antelope and prairie chicken. Winter season on aoudad sheep, pheasant, quail, muskrat, beaver, opossum, ring-tailed cat, badger, fox, weasel, raccoon, skunk and civet cat. Fall and winter seasons on deer and mule deer. Fall, winter and spring seasons on turkey. No closed season on bobcat and coyote. In 1983 sandhill crane, duck, coot, geese, woodcock and jacksnipe seasons occurred during the winter months. Teal duck, rail and gallinule seasons occurred in the fall. Mourning dove season occurred intermittently during the fall and winter months. **SPECIAL EVENTS** Miss Texas Teenager Pageant, Clarendon, May; Pre-Teen Pageant, Clarendon, June; July 4th Celebration and Rodeo, Clarendon, July; Saint's Roost Celebration, Clarendon, July.

COMMUNITIES
COUNTY SEAT Clarendon, County Courthouse, 79226; County Clerk's Office, 806/874-3436. **INCORPORATED COMMUNITIES** (1980 population and ZIP Code) Clarendon (2,220) 79226, Hedley (380) 79237 and Howardwick (165) 79226. **UNINCORPORATED COMMUNITIES** (and ZIP Code) Ashtola 79226, Giles 79237, Jericho 79226 and Lelia Lake 79240. **FOR ADDITIONAL LOCAL INFORMATION** Clarendon Chamber of Commerce, P.O. Box 730, Clarendon 79226, 806/874-2421.

DUVAL (B20)

THE LAND
West of Corpus Christi on U.S. Highway 59 in the Rio Grande Plain Region, Duval County covers 1,795 square miles with the elevation ranging from 250 to 800 feet. The northern half of the county has nearly level to undulating, alkaline, poorly drained, loamy soils and well drained, dark clayey soils. A high shrink-swell potential exists. The southern half has light colored, loamy surfaces over deep red or mottled clayey subsoils. Limestone lies within 40 inches of the surface in some areas. Duval is in the South Texas Plains vegetation area with mesquite, post and live oak trees, and cacti. The main grasses consist of silver bluestem, Arizona cottontop and buffalograss. Less than 1% of the land in the county is considered prime farmland. **CLIMATE** Subtropical subhumid with hot summers. The average annual temperature is 72°F. Temperatures in January range from an average low of 43° to an average high of 67°F and in July range from 73° to 98°F. The average annual precipitation is 24 inches, with an average relative humidity of 85% at 6 A.M. and 55% at 6 P.M. Snow accumulation is extremely rare. The growing season averages 298 days per year, with the last freeze in mid February and the first freeze in mid December. The sun shines during the year on the average 66% of the daylight hours.

THE PEOPLE
Duval County ranks 8th among all U.S. counties in the highest percent of residents of Spanish origin and ranks as one of the highest in the state in percent of persons who are native Texans. The 1982 estimated population of 12,900 indicates a continuation of a small growth rate begun in the 1970s which reversed the steady population decrease between 1940 and 1970. Almost 15% of the growth between 1970 and 1980 was in urban areas, while rural areas declined 4% in population. The age groups with the largest gains were ages 20 to 24 and 65 and over. Therefore the median age rose from 26 in 1970 to 28 in 1980. This county's population is younger than average and has a high birth rate. The largest ancestry groups are Hispanic (86%), persons of English descent (7%), German descent (5%) and Irish descent (5%). **REGISTERED VOTERS** As of November 2, 1982 there were 8,615 registered voters (0.1% of the state total). The 1982 general election had a 46% voter turnout, compared to a 60% turnout in the 1980 general election. In the 1982 primary 100% voted Democratic, with 5,280 votes cast.

THE ECONOMY
AGRICULTURE Cattle ranches. In 1982, 87% of the land was in farms and ranches, with 4% of the farmland under cultivation and 8% irrigated. Duval ranked 135th in the state in highest agricultural receipts, with 92% from livestock and livestock products. Undesirable brush and weeds, water and wind erosion cultivation of marginal lands and a lack of potable water are the current conservation problems. Primary crops: sorghum, hay, oats and wheat. Primary vegetables: watermelons. Primary fruits and nuts: ninth in the state for peaches. Oranges. Primary livestock and products: cattle and milk. **BUSINESS** Total number of business establishments in the county: 185. Retail sales during the first quarter of 1984 increased 34%. In 1980, 8% of the labor force were self-employed, 21% were employed in professional or related services, 2% in manufacturing, 14% in wholesale and retail trade, 31% in agriculture, forestry, fisheries and mining, 23% were employed in other counties and there were 946 retired workers. The industries with the most employment: agribusiness, oil and gas extraction and general construction. The nonfarm earnings in 1981 totaled $88,996,000. The retired workers received an average monthly Social Security payment of $260. **FINANCE** On June 30, 1983, two commercial banks had total deposits of $34,389,000 and total assets of $40,023,000. On December 31, 1982 one state savings and loan association and one federal association branch had assets of $4,976,588. In addition there are two credit unions in the county. **HOUSING** Average value of homes in 1980: $14,500. Between 1970 and 1980 the number of housing units in the county are air-conditioned,

DUVAL (continued)

86% are heated by gas and 10% by electricity. **NATURAL RESOURCES** Caliche, clay, salt domes, sandstone, uranium, oil and gas. In 1982 a total of 43,065,544 thousand cubic feet of gas well gas, 115,622 barrels of condensate, 3,557,249 barrels of crude oil and 3,046,067 thousand cubic feet of casinghead gas were produced. Current production of other minerals and products includes caliche, salt, sand and gravel, crushed sandstone and uranium. **TOURISM** Travel expenditures of $3,519,000 in 1982 (an increase of 13% over 1981) generated 79 jobs and $659,000 in payroll. **ALCOHOLIC BEVERAGES** Packaged distilled spirits, beer, ale, malt liquor and wine are legal. Sale of mixed beverages is legal in all or parts of the county. **FEDERAL EXPENDITURES** The federal government had direct expenditures or obligations of $16,208,000 in the county during fiscal year 1983, including $210,000 by the U.S. Department of Defense. In addition, the federal government provided $1,208,000 in grant awards, paid $489,000 in salaries and wages, made direct payments to individuals of $13,967,000 including $9,909,000 in retirement and disability payments, awarded $3,000 in procurement contracts and spent $541,000 in other expenditures or obligations. The federal government also provided $197,000 in direct loans and $5,815,000 in guaranteed loans and insurance.

COMMUNICATION

Cable TV. Telephone companies: Southwestern Bell and Valley Telephone Coop. **TRANSPORTATION** Total public road mileage: 772. In 1982 there were 8,373 registered vehicles and 227 reported traffic accidents including three fatalities. Intercity bus service is available. Motor freight: five local and intrastate carriers. Aircraft: 14 are registered in the county. Airports: Freer Municipal Airport.

COMMUNITY SERVICES

EDUCATION Four school districts with six elementary, three middle and three high schools. The average daily attendance in 1981-82 was 3,162, with expenditures per pupil of $3,645 including 238 classroom teachers with an average annual salary of $16,298. Sixty percent of the 216 high school graduates planned to attend college. In 1982-83, 9% of the students were White, 91% Hispanic and 0.1% Black. **PUBLIC LIBRARIES** Freer-Government Wells Library: 7,023 volumes. **CHILD CARE** Four day care licensed facilities. **HEALTH CARE** Five physicians and one dentist. Ambulance services: two commercial, one volunteer fire department, and one funeral home service. Mental health: one clinic. The average cost per day for private patients in 1982 was $36.06. **CHURCHES** 16 churches have an estimated combined membership of 4,160. The largest denominations are Catholic, Southern Baptist and United Methodist. **SOCIAL SERVICES** In fiscal year 1983 a total of $1,799,430 in food stamps was distributed, with an average of 3,883 persons receiving food stamps each month. Aid to Families with Dependent Children (AFDC) totaled $318,451 with an average of 208 families receiving AFDC each month. Medical assistance benefits for the aged and disabled of $1,783,291 and for families and children of $655,148 brought the county benefit total to $4,556,320. **FIRE PROTECTION** Three volunteer fire departments. **LAW ENFORCEMENT** The County Sheriff has 21 commissioned officers. Three police departments have a combined force of 10. **CRIME** 32 violent crimes (murder, forcible rape, robbery and aggravated assault) and 221 nonviolent crimes (burglary, larceny-theft and motor vehicle theft) were reported in 1982. **JUDICIAL SYSTEM** One District Court and Judge, one County Court and Judge and eight Justices of the Peace. In the District Court a total of 1,040 cases

were pending on 1/1/82, 348 new cases were filed and 326 cases were disposed of during the year leaving 1,062 cases pending on 12/31/82. There were 189 criminal cases on the docket, 35 convictions, five persons committed to prison and 113 cases left pending. In the County Court 569 cases were pending on 1/1/82, 204 new cases were filed and 130 cases were disposed of during the year leaving 643 cases pending on 12/31/82. There were 628 criminal cases on the docket, 116 convictions and 501 cases left pending. **JAILS** One jail, capacity 14. **ATTORNEYS AT LAW** Nine. **UTILITIES** 81% of the residents are connected to a public or privately owned water system and 68% are connected to a public sewer system. Natural gas is distributed to the county by Entex, Inc. The average annual residential bill for natural gas in 1982 for the Entex distribution system was $390.31, an increase of 26% over 1981. Electricity is distributed to the county by Central Power and Light Co., Cochran Power and Light, and Medina Electric Coop., Inc. and is generated primarily by gas, oil and coal. The typical residential electric bill is $162.15 per month for an all-electric house using 2,500 kwh. **TAXES** The county has seven units with taxing authority: four school districts, one county and two special districts.

RECREATION/ENTERTAINMENT

COUNTY/MUNICIPAL PARKS 155 acres in six county and two municipal parks. These parks contain four playgrounds, five baseball and softball fields and five tennis courts. **SCENIC DRIVES** The Texas Tropical Trail runs through this county. This trail is charted through the state's southernmost wedge meandering through ranchland, resort areas by the Gulf of Mexico and fertile farmlands. **BOATING/FISHING** Lakes/reservoirs: Chiltipia-San Fernando Creek Soil Conservation Service Lake 2 (17 acres), San Diego-Rosa Soil Conservation Service Lake 1 (16 acres) and San Diego-Rosita Creek Soil Conservation Service Lakes 2, 4, 7 and 9 (62 acres). Primary streams: Chiltipia, San Diego, Tarancahuas, Rosita, Las Animas, Los Olmos and Macho. **HUNTING** Fall and winter seasons on deer and turkey. No closed season on javelina, coyote, bobcat and squirrel. Winter season on quail, muskrat, beaver, opossum, ring-tailed cat, badger, fox, weasel, raccoon, skunk and civet cat. In 1983 sandhill crane, duck, coot, geese, woodcock and jacksnipe seasons occurred during the winter months. Teal duck, rail and gallinule seasons occurred in the fall. Mourning dove season occurred intermittently during the fall and winter months with a fall season on white-winged dove. **SPECIAL EVENTS** Rattlesnake Roundup, Freer, April; Freer C-C, Freer, April; Old Fiddlers Contest, Freer, July.

COMMUNITIES

COUNTY SEAT San Diego, County Courthouse, 78384; County Clerk's Office, 512/279-3322. **INCORPORATED COMMUNITIES** (1980 population and ZIP Code) Benavides (1,978) 78341, Freer (3,213) 78357 and San Diego 5,225 (4,331 in Duval Co. and 894 in Jim Wells Co.) 78384. **UNINCORPORATED COMMUNITIES** (and ZIP Code) Bess 78322, Concepcion 78349, Cruz Calle (Santa Cruz) 78349, Guajillo 78332, Humble Government Wells Camp 78357, Ramirez 78376, Realitos 78376, Rios 78349, Rosita 78384, San Jose 78332, Sejita 78376 and Seven Sisters 78357. **FOR ADDITIONAL LOCAL INFORMATION** Freer Chamber of Commerce, P.O. Box 717, Freer, 78357, 512/394-6891, San Diego Chamber of Commerce, San Diego, 78384.

EASTLAND (P72)

THE LAND

East of Abilene on Interstate Highway 20 in the North Central

Prairies Region, Eastland County covers 924 square miles with the elevation ranging from 1,200 to 1,800 feet. The southern one-fourth of the county has nearly level to undulating, light-colored, acidic soils with loamy surface layers and mottled gray and red or yellow cracking clayey subsoils. The rest of the county has undulating to hilly soils over shale or sandstone. The soils are moderately deep to deep with loamy surface layers and clayey subsoils. The vegetation is of the Cross Timbers and Prairie area with mid to short grasses and dense brush of mostly post and blackjack oak. Between 11 and 20% of the land in the county is considered prime farmland. **CLIMATE** Mild and dry with wide-ranging extremes. The average annual temperature is 64°F. Temperatures in January range from an average low of 30° to an average high of 56°F and in July range from 71° to 96°F. The average annual precipitation is 27 inches, with an average relative humidity of 74% at 6 A.M. and 47% at 6 P.M. The average annual snowfall is five inches. The growing season averages 229 days per year, with the last freeze in late March and the first freeze in early November. The sun shines during the year on the average 68% of the daylight hours.

THE PEOPLE

Eastland County ranks 57th among U.S. counties in highest percent of population 65 and over. The 1982 estimated population of 20,700 indicates a continuation of the moderate growth begun in the 1970s which reversed the steady population decrease between 1930 and 1970. About 9% of the growth between 1970 and 1980 was in the urban areas, with a 5% growth in rural areas. The age groups with the largest gains were ages 20 to 34 and birth to five years. Therefore the median age lowered from 44 in 1970 to 39 in 1980. However, the county's population remains older than average and has a high death rate. The largest ancestry groups are persons of English descent (33%), Irish descent (28%) and German descent (15%). **REGISTERED VOTERS** As of November 2, 1982 there were 10,952 registered voters (0.2% of the state total). The 1982 general election had a 50% voter turnout, compared to a 74% turnout in the 1980 general election. In the 1982 primary 96% voted Democratic and 4% Republican, with 3,325 votes cast.

THE ECONOMY

AGRICULTURE In 1982, 82% of the land was in farms and ranches, with 20% of the farmland under cultivation and 17% irrigated. Eastland ranked 134th in the state in highest agricultural receipts, with 66% from livestock and livestock products. Overgrazing, undesirable brush and weeds, water and wind erosion and inefficient tillage systems are the current conservation problems. Primary crops: fifth in the state for peanuts and third for rye. Hay, wheat, oats and sorghum. Primary vegetables: watermelons. Primary fruits and nuts: fourth in the state for peaches. Pecans. Primary livestock and products: cattle, milk, sheep, wool, angora goats, mohair and hogs. **BUSINESS** Total number of business establishments in the county: 501. Retail sales during the first quarter of 1984 increased 22%. In 1980, 18% of the labor force were self-employed, 21% were employed in professional or related services, 13% in manufacturing, 20% in wholesale and retail trade, 17% in agriculture, forestry, fisheries and mining, 11% were employed in other counties and there were 3,234 retired workers. The industries with the most employment: oil and gas extraction, construction, commercial printing, agribusiness and the manufacture of prepared agricultural feeds, men's clothing, rubber products and prefabricated metal buildings. The nonfarm earnings in 1981 totaled $163,958,000. The retired workers received an average monthly Social Security payment of $292. **FINANCE** On June 30, 1983, five commercial banks had total deposits of $131,225,000 and total assets of $146,200,000. There are four state savings and loan association branches and one credit union in the county. **HOUSING** Average value of homes in 1980: $18,200. Permits for new, privately owned housing units increased in 1982: 58 permits were issued with a total construction cost of $1,345,409. Of those permits, all were for single family houses. Housing permits increased in Cisco from three in 1981 to 17 in 1982, and in Ranger from three to 39. Between 1970 and 1980 the number of housing units increased by 13%. Seventy-eight percent of all units in the county are air-conditioned, 83% are heated by gas and 13% by electricity. **NATURAL RESOURCES** Ceramic clay, limestone, industrial sand, gas, oil, shale and bituminous coal. In 1982 a total of 8,737,664 thousand cubic feet of gas well gas, 24,141 barrels of condensate, 2,463,831 barrels of crude oil and 9,234,543 thousand cubic feet of casinghead gas were produced. Current production of other minerals and products includes brick, clay, lightweight agregate, crushed limestone, construction sand, sand and gravel and shale. **TOURISM** Travel expenditures of $6,773,000 in 1982 (an increase of 14% over 1981) generated 137 jobs and $1,196,000 in payroll. Lodging: three hotels, motels and tourist courts. **ALCOHOLIC BEVERAGES** Packaged distilled spirits, beer, ale, malt liquor and wine are legal in parts of the county. Sale of mixed beverages is legal in all or parts of the county. **FEDERAL EXPENDITURES** The federal government had direct expenditures or obligations of $47,786,000 in the county during fiscal year 1983, including $1,662,000 by the U.S. Department of Defense. In addition, the federal government provided $268,000 in grant awards, paid $1,616,000 in salaries and wages, made direct payments to individuals of $45,441,000 including $29,447,000 in retirement and disability payments, awarded $176,000 in procurement contracts and spent $285,000 in other expenditures or obligations. The federal government also provided $12,944,000 in direct loans and $5,375,000 in guaranteed loans and insurance.

COMMUNICATION

Newspapers–Weekly: The Cisco Press, Eastland Telegram, Gorman Progress, Ranger Times and The Rising Star. Radio: KERC-AM (Eastland). Television: KNCT CH.46 (Eastland) PBS. Cable TV. Telephone companies: Continental Telephone, Southwestern Bell and Comanche County Telephone. **TRANSPORTATION** Total public road mileage: 1,287. In 1982 there were 19,991 registered vehicles and 497 reported traffic accidents including 11 fatalities. Intercity bus service is available. Motor freight: 12 local and intrastate carriers. Rail: one main line carries annually 10 to 20 million tons of freight through the county. Aircraft: 36 are registered in the county. Airports: Cisco Municipal Airport is a basic utility airport providing general aviation service. It serves as a base for 25 aircraft. Also serving this area are Ranger Municipal Airport and Eastland Municipal Airport. Gorman Airport at Gorman is for emergency use only.

COMMUNITY SERVICES

EDUCATION Six school districts with seven elementary, two middle and six high schools. The average daily attendance in 1981-82 was 3,044, with expenditures per pupil of $2,303 including 187 classroom teachers with an average annual salary of $15,259. Fifty-four percent of the 221 high school graduates planned to attend college. In 1982-83, 90% of the students were White, 8% Hispanic, 1% Black, 1% Asian and 0.2% American Indian. Ranger Junior College is located in Ranger. Established in 1926 it is a vocational and two year academic college under local control. Enrollment in 1982 was 717 with in state undergraduate tuition and fees of $290 per semester. Cisco Junior College is located in Cisco. Established in 1940 it is a vocational and two year academic college under state control. Enrollment in 1982 was 1,714 with in state undergraduate tuition and fees of $308 per semester. **PUBLIC LIBRARIES** Cisco Public Library: 15,000

COUNTIES

EASTLAND (continued)

volumes. Centennial Memorial Library (Eastland): 19,000 volumes. Ranger Community Library: 13,066 volumes. **CHILD CARE** 41 day care and four twenty-four hour care licensed facilities. **HEALTH CARE** 15 physicians and six dentists. Hospitals: four with a combined capacity of 190. Ambulance services: two commercial, two hospital-based, one volunteer fire department, and one city service. Mental health: one clinic and one development center with capacity of 54. Nursing homes: six nursing homes with a combined capacity of 518 nursing care residents. The average cost per day for private patients in 1982 was $30.39. **CHURCHES** 70 churches have an estimated combined membership of 14,672. The largest denominations are Southern Baptist, Churches of Christ and United Methodist. **SOCIAL SERVICES** In fiscal year 1983 a total of $405,778 in food stamps was distributed, with an average of 910 persons receiving food stamps each month. Aid to Families with Dependent Children (AFDC) totaled $45,583 with an average of 31 families receiving AFDC each month. Medical assistance benefits for the aged and disabled of $3,725,667 and for families and children of $72,887 brought the county benefit total to $4,249,915. **FIRE PROTECTION** Eight volunteer fire departments. **LAW ENFORCEMENT** The County Sheriff has nine commissioned officers. Five police departments have a combined force of 30. **CRIME** 31 violent crimes (murder, forcible rape, robbery and aggravated assault) and 354 nonviolent crimes (burglary, larceny-theft and motor vehicle theft) were reported in 1982. **JUDICIAL SYSTEM** One District Court and Judge, one County Court and Judges and five Justices of the Peace. In the District Court a total of 1,012 cases were pending on 1/1/82, 1,323 new cases were filed and 1,315 cases were disposed of during the year leaving 1,020 cases pending on 12/31/82. There were 722 criminal cases on the docket, 302 convictions, 28 persons committed to prison and 62 committed to jail and 128 cases left pending. In the County Court 19 cases were pending on 1/1/82, 29 new cases were filed and 41 cases were disposed of during the year leaving seven cases pending on 12/31/82. There were 48 criminal cases on the docket, 22 convictions, 20 persons committed to jail, and seven cases left pending. **JAILS** One jail, capacity 26. **ATTORNEYS AT LAW** 29. **UTILITIES** 84% of the residents are connected to a public or privately owned water system and 67% are connected to a public sewer system. Natural gas is distributed to the county by Lone Star Gas Co., Division of Enserch. The average annual residential bill for natural gas in 1982 for the Lone Star distribution system was $405.91, an increase of 35% over 1981. Electricity is distributed to the county by West Texas Utilities, Texas Electric Service, Texas-New Mexico Power Co., Comanche Co. Electric Coop., Inc., Erath Co. Electric Coop., Inc., and Taylor Electric Coop., Inc. and is generated primarily by gas and oil. The typical residential electric bill is $154.69 per month for an all-electric house using 2,500 kwh. **TAXES** The county has 20 units with taxing authority: six school districts, six cities, one county, two college districts, three hospital districts and two special districts.

RECREATION/ENTERTAINMENT

NATIONAL REGISTER OF HISTORIC PLACES Cisco: Mobley Hotel. **MUNICIPAL PARKS** 1,333 acres in 10 municipal parks. These parks contain four playgrounds, one golf course, two baseball and softball fields, three tennis courts, three swimming pools, two beaches, three boat ramps and shore fishing facilities. **SCENIC DRIVES** The Texas Forts Trail runs through this county. This trail leads to eight of the famous frontier forts of West Central Texas and an ancient presidio of the Spanish colonial period. **BOATING/FISHING** Lakes/reservoirs: Bernie (30 acres), Cisco (445 acres), Dickey (21 acres), Duran (26 acres),

Eastland (145 acres), Hagaman (72 acres), Hanson (32 acres), Leon (1,590 acres), Olden (130 acres), Perrin (30 acres), Phill Pe Co (20 acres), Ringling (30 acres), Twin (20 acres) and Warren (29 acres). Major rivers: Leon, North Fork Leon and Sabana. Primary streams: Sandy, West Fork Palo Pinto, Ellison Springs, Palo Pinto, Nash, Salt, Brawshaw and Sandy. **HUNTING** Fall and winter seasons on deer. No closed season on coyote, bobcat and squirrel. Winter season on quail, muskrat, beaver, opossum, ring-tailed cat, badger, fox, weasel, raccoon, skunk and civet cat. Fall, winter and spring seasons on turkey. In 1983 duck, coot, geese, woodcock and jacksnipe seasons occurred during the winter months. Teal duck, rail and gallinule seasons occurred in the fall. Mourning dove season occurred intermittently during the fall and winter months. **MUSEUMS** Eastland: Kendrick Religious Museum. **THEATERS** Eastland: Kendrick Amphitheater. **COLLEGIATE FINE ARTS** Cultural events offered by Cisco Junior College in Cisco and Ranger Junior College in Ranger. **SPECIAL EVENTS** Easter Pageant, Cisco, April; Frontier Jubilee, Cisco, April; Folklife Festival, Cisco, May; Life of Christ Pageant, Cisco, June-August; Rodeo, Ranger, July; Roaring Ranger Day, Ranger, November.

COMMUNITIES

COUNTY SEAT Eastland, County Courthouse, 76448; County Clerk's Office, 817/629-1583. **INCORPORATED COMMUNITIES** (1980 population and ZIP Code) Carbon (281) 76435, Cisco (4,517) 76437, Eastland (3,747) 76448, Gorman (1,258) 76454, Ranger (3,142) 76470 and Rising Star (1,204) 76471. **UNINCORPORATED COMMUNITIES** (and ZIP Code) Branton 76471, Chuckville 76471, Desdemona 76445, Dothan 76437, Kokomo 76454, Long Branch 76435, Mangum 76448, Morton Valley 76448, Nimrod 76437, Okra 76435, Olden 76466, Pioneer 76471, Pleasant Hill 76437, Pumpkin Center 76448, Romney 76471, Sabanna 76437, Scranton 76473, Staff 76448 and Yellow Mound 76448. **FOR ADDITIONAL LOCAL INFORMATION** Cisco Chamber of Commerce, 619 Conrad Hamilton Ave., Cisco, 76437, 817/442-2537, Eastland Chamber of Commerce, 102 S. Seaman, Eastland, 76448, 817/629-2332, Gorman Chamber of Commerce, P.O. Box 266, Gorman, 76454, 817/734-2317, Ranger Chamber of commerce, Main and Commerce, P.O. Box 57, Ranger, 76470, 817/647-3091, Rising Star Chamber of Commerce, P.O. Box 65, Rising Star, 76471, 817/643-1161.

ECTOR (P75)

THE LAND

At the intersection of Interstate Highway 20 and State Highway 385 in the High Plains Region, Ector County covers 903 square miles with the elevation ranging from 2,650 to 3,250 feet. In the northwest is a strip of nearly level, acidic usually dry soils with sandy surfaces and loamy subsoils. A wide central strip has alkaline soils, mostly loamy throughout with lime accumulations in the subsoil and some clayey subsoils. This area has a high shrink-swell potential. To the southeast is a small strip of soils with loamy surface layers and clayey subsoils. In the southeast corner are undulating to hilly alkaline soils over limestone with stoney surfaces. In the southwest corner are sandy soils. The northern part of Ector is in the High Plains vegetation area with prairie grasses of which buffalograss and blue grama are most abundant. Shinnery oak, sagebrush, mesquite trees and yucca plants are found throughout. The southern part of Ector consists of Trans-Pecos, Mountains and Basins vegetation with cacti, desert shrub and scrub mesquite trees. Less than 1% of the land in the county is considered prime farmland. **CLIMATE** Warm and dry with winds and dust in the spring. The average annual temperature is 64°F. Temperatures in January range from an average low of 29° to an average high of 58°F and in July range from 70° to 96°F. The average annual precipitation is 14 inches, with an average relative humidity of 70% at 6 A.M. and 33% at 6 P.M. The average annual snowfall is four inches. The growing season averages 217 days per year, with the last freeze in early April and the first freeze in early November. The sun shines during the year on the average 75% of the daylight hours.

THE PEOPLE

The 1982 estimated population of 134,200 indicates a continuation of the strong growth rate begun in the 1930s. Almost 42% of the growth between 1970 and 1980 was in rural areas. The age groups with the largest increases were ages 20 to 34 and 65 and over. Therefore, the median age rose from 26 in 1970 to 27 in 1980. The county's population is younger than average and has a high birth rate. The largest ancestry groups are persons of English descent (23%), Hispanic (22%) and Irish descent (19%). **REGISTERED VOTERS** As of November 2, 1982 there were 49,421 registered voters (0.8% of the state total). The 1982 general election had a 48% voter turnout, compared to a 71% turnout in the 1980 general election. In the 1982 primary 68% voted Democratic and 32% Republican, with 9,889 votes cast.

THE ECONOMY

AGRICULTURE Ranchland. In 1982, 81% of the land was in farms and ranches, with 1% of the farmland under cultivation, most of which was irrigated. Ector ranked 245th in the state in highest agricultural receipts, with 97% from livestock and livestock products. Overgrazing, undesirable brush and weeds, and difficulties in grass establishment are the current conservation problems. Primary crops: oats. Primary fruits and nuts: peaches and pecans. Primary livestock and products: cattle, milk and hogs. **BUSINESS** Total number of business establishments in the county: 3,639. Retail sales during the first quarter of 1984 decreased 1%. In 1980, 6% of the labor force were self-employed, 14% were employed in professional or related services, 17% in manufacturing, 25% in wholesale and retail trade, 13% in agriculture, forestry, fisheries and mining, 11% were employed in other counties and there were 5,427 retired workers. The industries with the most employment: agribusiness, oil and gas extraction, heavy construction, petroleum refining, and the manufacture of mineral wool, oil field machinery, structural metal products, pumps and pumping equipment, electrical industrial equipment, motor vehicles and equipment. The non-farm earnings in 1981 totaled $1,512,200,000. The retired workers received an average monthly Social Security payment of $349. **FINANCE** On June 30, 1983, nine commercial banks had total deposits of $800,664,000 and total assets of $906,003,000. On December 31, 1982 three state savings and loan associations, 12 state branches and one federal association branch had combined assets of $534,338,488. In addition there are 19 credit unions in the county. **HOUSING** Average value of homes in 1980: $33,900. Permits for new, privately owned housing units decreased in 1982: 1,947 permits were issued with a total construction cost of $53,667,139. Of those permits, 416 were for single family houses. Between 1970 and 1980 the number of housing units increased by 39%. Ninety-two percent of all units in the county are air-conditioned, 78% are heated by gas and 21% by electricity. **NATURAL RESOURCES** Bismuth, brine, caliche, limestone, oil and gas. In 1982 a total of 61,963,546 thousand cubic feet of gas well gas, 58,677 barrels of condensate, 46,125,521 barrels of crude oil and 46,668,103 thousand cubic feet of casinghead gas were produced. Current production of other minerals and products includes brine, caliche, cement, crushed limestone and recovered sulphur. **TOURISM** Travel expenditures of $98,011,000 in 1982 (an increase of 11% over 1981) generated 2,499 jobs and $20,049,000 in payroll. Lodging: 19 hotels, motels and

tourist courts. Convention/meeting facilities: Odessa-Ector County Coliseum and two hotels with facilities for large gatherings. **ALCOHOLIC BEVERAGES** Packaged distilled spirits, beer, ale, malt liquor and wine are legal in parts of the county. Sale of mixed beverages is legal in all or parts of the county. **FEDERAL EXPENDITURES** The federal government had direct expenditures or obligations of $97,351,000 in the county during fiscal year 1983, including $4,104,000 by the U.S. Department of Defense. In addition, the federal government provided $3,956,000 in grant awards, paid $8,964,000 in salaries and wages, made direct payments to individuals of $82,067,000 including $68,062,000 in retirement and disability payments, awarded $2,114,000 in procurement contracts and spent $251,000 in other expenditures or obligations. The federal government also provided $150,000 in direct loans and $27,329,000 in guaranteed loans and insurance.

COMMUNICATION

Newspapers–Daily: The Odessa American, ave. eve. circ. 36,284. Radio: KJJT-AM, KOYL-AM, KOZA-AM, KRIG-AM, KYXX-AM, KUFO-FM, KOIP-FM Stereo (Odessa). Television: KOSA CH.7 (Odessa). Cable TV. Telephone companies: Southwestern Bell. **TRANSPORTATION** Total public road mileage: 1,225. In 1982 there were 131,792 registered vehicles and 6,492 reported traffic accidents including 68 fatalities. Taxi cabs: one company in Odessa. Intercity bus service is available. Motor freight: 66 local and intrastate carriers. Rail: one main line carries annually five to 10 million tons of freight through the county. Aircraft: 368 are registered in the county. Airports: Schlemeyer Field at Odessa is a basic transportation airport providing general aviation service. It serves as a base for 135 aircraft.

COMMUNITY SERVICES

EDUCATION One school district with 24 elementary, six middle, two high schools and one special education. The average daily attendance in 1981-82 was 22,568, with expenditures per pupil of $3,039 including 1,331 classroom teachers with an average annual salary of $20,411. Forty-four percent of the 1,297 high school graduates planned to attend college. In 1982-83, 61% of the students were White, 32% Hispanic, 6% Black, 0.7% Asian and 0.2% American Indian. Private schools: 1,306 students enrolled in six elementary and three high schools. University of Texas of the Permian Basin is located in Odessa. Established in 1969 it is under state control. Enrollment in 1982 was 1,580 with in state undergraduate tuition and fees of $300 per semester. The highest degree offered is Master (now lower division). Odessa College, established in 1946, is a vocational and two year academic college under local control. Enrollment in 1982 was 3,822 with in state undergraduate tuition and fees of $286 per semester. Vocational education: Aladdin Beauty College, American Commercial College (Odessa). **PUBLIC LIBRARIES** Ector County Library (Odessa): 159,355 volumes. **CHILD CARE** 218 day care and 25 twenty-four hour care licensed facilities. **HEALTH CARE** 127 physicians and 42 dentists. Hospitals: one with a capacity of 376. Specialized hospitals: one women's and children's hospital with a capacity of 114. Clinics: one for the treatment of alcohol and/or drug abuse, one dialysis center, one public health clinic, and one minor emergency center. Ambulance services: two commercial, one volunteer fire department, and one fire department service. Mental health: one clinic. Nursing homes: four nursing homes with a combined capacity of 450 nursing care residents. The average cost per day for private patients in 1982 was $32.03. **CHURCHES** 96 churches have an estimated combined membership of 70,385. The largest denominations are Southern Baptist, Catholic and United Methodist. **SOCIAL SERVICES** In fiscal year 1983 a total of $2,646,858 in food stamps was distributed, with an average of

COUNTIES

ECTOR (continued)

5,384 persons receiving food stamps each month. Aid to Families with Dependent Children (AFDC) totaled $574,051 with an average of 365 families receiving AFDC each month. Medical assistance benefits for the aged and disabled of $3,641,301 and for families and children of $646,861 brought the county benefit total to $7,509,070. **FIRE PROTECTION** One paid and three volunteer fire departments. **LAW ENFORCEMENT** The County Sheriff has 146 commissioned officers. 10 police departments have a combined force of 347. One college campus has a police department with a force of three officers. **CRIME** 865 violent crimes (murder, forcible rape, robbery and aggravated assault) and 12,440 nonviolent crimes (burglary, larceny-theft and motor vehicle theft) were reported in 1982. **JUDICIAL SYSTEM** Three District Courts and Judges, two County Courts and Judges and four Justices of the Peace. In the District Courts a total of 5,025 cases were pending on 1/1/82, 5,556 new cases were filed and 4,058 cases were disposed of during the year leaving 6,523 cases pending on 12/31/82. There were 1,830 criminal cases on the docket, 577 convictions, 165 persons committed to prison and 67 committed to jail and 757 cases left pending. In the County Courts 11,815 cases were pending on 1/1/82, 6,010 new cases were filed and 4,613 cases were disposed of during the year leaving 13,212 cases pending on 12/31/82. There were 15,617 criminal cases on the docket, 1,109 convictions, 410 persons committed to jail, and 11,578 cases left pending. **JAILS** One jail, capacity 165 under renovation. **ATTORNEYS AT LAW** 180. **UTILITIES** 77% of the residents are connected to a public or privately owned water system and 80% are connected to a public sewer system. Natural gas is distributed to the county by B&W Gas Company, and Energas Company. The average annual residential bill for natural gas in 1982 for the Energas distribution system was $371.63, an increase of 23% over 1981. Electricity is distributed to the county by Texas Electric Service, and Cap Rock Electric Coop., Inc. and is generated primarily by gas. The typical residential electric bill is $154.69 per month for an all-electric house using 2,500 kwh. **TAXES** The county has six units with taxing authority: one school district, two cities, one county, one college district and one utility district.

RECREATION/ENTERTAINMENT
NATIONAL REGISTER OF HISTORIC PLACES Odessa: White-Pool House. **COUNTY PARKS** 291 acres in 32 county parks. These parks contain 0.4 miles of hiking trails, 27 playgrounds, two football and soccer fields, 24 baseball and softball fields, 23 tennis courts, 17 multi-use courts and five swimming pools. **SCENIC DRIVES** The Texas Pecos Trail runs through this county. This trail rambles through the vast region of southwest and west Texas with landscapes varying from raw, arid regions to green valleys. **HUNTING** Fall season on antelope. Fall and winter seasons on deer, mule deer and javelina. No closed season on coyote, bobcat and squirrel. Winter season on quail, muskrat, beaver, opossum, ring-tailed cat, badger, fox, weasel, raccoon, skunk and civet cat. Fall, winter and spring seasons on turkey. In 1983 sandhill crane, duck, coot, geese, woodcock and jacksnipe seasons occurred during the winter months. Teal duck, rail and gallinule seasons occurred in the fall. Mourning dove season occurred intermittently during the fall and winter months. **MUSEUMS** Odessa: Odessa College Museum of the Permian Basin, Odessa Meteorite Museum and Presidential Museum. **THEATERS** Odessa: Globe of the Great Southwest Theatre, Permian Playhouse and Ector County Coliseum. **ORCHESTRAS** Odessa: Symphony orchestra and chorale. **PLANETARIUM** Odessa: Odessa College Planetarium. **COLLEGIATE FINE ARTS** Odessa: Cultural events offered by Odessa College. **SPECIAL EVENTS** Sandhills Hereford and Quarter Horse Show and Rodeo, Odessa, January; Shakespeare Festival, Odessa, February-March; Balloon Festival, Odessa, February; Fiesta del Arte, Odessa, April; Shakespearean Renaissance Fair, Odessa, April-May; Boom Town Days Festival, Odessa, May; Twelve-Hour Grand Prix Race, Odessa-Midland, April/May; Junior Rodeo, Odessa, August; Permian Basin Fair, Odessa, September.

COMMUNITIES
COUNTY SEAT Odessa, County Courthouse, 79760; County Clerk's Office, 915/332-8271. **INCORPORATED COMMUNITIES** (1980 population and ZIP Code) Goldsmith (409) 79741 and Odessa (90,027) 79760. **UNINCORPORATED COMMUNITIES** (and ZIP Code) Country Club Estates 79760, Gardendale 79758, Greenfield Acres 79760, Harrisdale 79760, Notrees 79759, Penwell 79776, Pleasant Farms 79763, Sunset Heights 79760, West Odessa 79760 and Westover 79760. **FOR ADDITIONAL LOCAL INFORMATION** Odessa Chamber of Commerce, P.O. Box 3626, Odessa, 79760, 915/332-9111.

EDWARDS (B9)

THE LAND
West of San Antonio on U.S. Highway 377 in the Edwards Plateau Region, Edwards County covers 2,120 square miles with an elevation range of 1,500 to 2,500 feet. In the southwest corner of the county are undulating to hilly, alkaline shallow to deep loamy soils with rock outcrops. The rest of the county has loamy soils over limestone. The county is in the Edwards Plateau vegetation area with short to mid grasses, desert shrub and scrubby live oak in the southwest corner. The rest of the county has tall to mid grasses, live oaks and some mesquite trees. Less than one percent of the land in the county is considered prime farmland. **CLIMATE** Warm and dry. The average annual temperature is 67°F. Temperatures in January range from an average low of 34° to an average high of 62°F and in July range from 71° to 97°F. The average annual precipitation is 22 inches, with an average relative humidity of 77% at 6 A.M. and 43% at 6 P.M. Snowfall is very rare. The growing season averages 250 days per year, with the last freeze in mid March and the first freeze in late November. The sun shines during the year on the average 66% of the daylight hours.

THE PEOPLE
Edwards county ranks 42nd among all U.S. counties in the highest percent of residents of Spanish origin. The 1982 estimated population of 2,100 indicates a slight increase since 1980. However, the number of residents has steadily declined since 1940. The majority of residents live in rural areas. The age group with the largest decrease between 1970 and 1980 were birth to nine years. The median age rose from 28 in 1970 to 30 in 1980. The largest ancestry groups are Hispanic (48%), persons of English descent (27%) and Irish descent (16%). **REGISTERED VOTERS** As of November 2, 1982 there were 1,116 registered voters (0.01% of the state total). The 1982 general election had a 51% voter turnout, compared to a 71% turnout in the 1980 general election. In the 1982 primary 100% voted Democratic, with 421 votes cast.

THE ECONOMY
AGRICULTURE Sheep and angora goat ranches. In 1982, 87% of the land was in farms and ranches, with 1% of the farmland under cultivation. Edwards ranked 203rd in the state in highest agricultural receipts, with 99% from livestock and livestock products. Overgrazing, undesirable brush and weeds and water erosion are the current conservation problems. Primary crops: hay.

Primary fruits and nuts: peaches and pecans. Primary livestock and products: first in the state in both angora goats and mohair production. Cattle, sheep, wool and hogs. **BUSINESS** Total number of business establishments in the county: 44. Retail sales during the first quarter of 1984 increased 85%. In 1980, 24% of the labor force were self-employed, 15% were employed in professional or related services, 2% in manufacturing, 17% in wholesale and retail trade, 37% in agriculture, forestry, fisheries and mining, 9% were employed in other counties and there were 206 retired workers. The industries with the most employment: agribusiness. The nonfarm earnings in 1981 totaled $16,134,000. The retired workers received an average monthly Social Security payment of $306. **FINANCE** On June 30, 1983, one commercial bank had total deposits of $10,668,000 and total assets of $12,812,000. **HOUSING** Average value of homes in 1980: $17,800. Between 1970 and 1980 the number of housing units increased by 34%. Thirty percent of all units in the county are air-conditioned, 86% are heated by gas and 9% by electricity. **NATURAL RESOURCES** Limestone, oil and gas. In 1982 a total of 7,535,125 thousand cubic feet of gas well gas, 2,847 barrels of condensate, 12,799 barrels of crude oil and 2,711 thousand cubic feet of casinghead gas were produced. **TOURISM** Travel expenditures of $5,626,000 in 1982 (an increase of 15% over 1981) generated 104 jobs and $948,000 in payroll. **ALCOHOLIC BEVERAGES** Packaged distilled spirits, beer, ale, malt liquor and wine are legal in parts of the county. **FEDERAL EXPENDITURES** The federal government had direct expenditures or obligations of $6,019,000 in the county during fiscal year 1983, including $162,000 by the U.S. Department of Defense. In addition, the federal government provided $46,000 in grant awards, paid $227,000 in salaries and wages, made direct payments to individuals of $2,861,000 including $2,019,000 in retirement and disability payments, awarded $1,000 in procurement contracts and spent $2,885,000 in other expenditures or obligations. The federal government also provided $42,000 in guaranteed loans and insurance.

COMMUNICATION
Newspapers–Weekly: Mohair Weekly (Rocksprings). Cable TV. Telephone companies: General Telephone, Southwestern Bell, Big Bend Telephone, Hill Country Telephone Coop. and SW Texas Telephone. **TRANSPORTATION** Total public road mileage: 456. In 1982 there were 2,070 registered vehicles and 36 reported traffic accidents. Intercity bus service is available. Motor freight: two carriers. Aircraft: two are registered in the county. Airports: Edwards County Airport and Mayfield Ranch Airport at Rocksprings. For emergency use a Heliport is provided at Edwards County Memorial Hospital.

COMMUNITY SERVICES
EDUCATION Three school districts with three elementary and two high schools. The average daily attendance in 1981-82 was 783, with expenditures per pupil of $2,754 including 58 classroom teachers with an average annual salary of $16,058. Eighty-five percent of the 47 high school graduates planned to attend college. In 1982-83, 43% of the students were White, 57% Hispanic, 0.7% Asian. Sports championships: 1983 A Boys' Tennis Singles; Barksdale Nueces Canyon H.S. **PUBLIC LIBRARIES** Barksdale Library. Rocksprings Library. **HEALTH CARE** One physician. Hospitals: one with a capacity of eight. Ambulance services: one hospital-based service. **CHURCHES** Nine churches have an estimated combined membership of 1,573. The largest denominations are Catholic, Southern Baptist and United Methodist. **SOCIAL SERVICES** In fiscal year 1983 a total of $237,105 in food stamps was distributed, with an average of 488 persons receiving food stamps each month. Aid to Families with Dependent Children (AFDC) totaled $29,397 with an average of 18 families receiving AFDC each month. Medical assistance benefits for the aged and disabled of $87,978 and for families and children of $43,332 brought the county benefit total to $397,812. **FIRE PROTECTION** One volunteer fire department. **LAW ENFORCEMENT** The County Sheriff has eight commissioned officers. **CRIME** Eight violent crimes (murder, forcible rape, robbery and aggravated assault) and 19 nonviolent crimes (burglary, larceny-theft and motor vehicle theft) were reported in 1982. **JUDICIAL SYSTEM** One District Court and Judge, one County Court and Judge and one Justice of the Peace. In the District Court a total of 52 cases were pending on 1/1/82, 73 new cases were filed and 35 cases were disposed of during the year leaving 90 cases pending on 12/31/82. There were 14 criminal cases on the docket, two convictions and 10 cases left pending. In the County Court 104 cases were pending on 1/1/82, 82 new cases were filed and 67 cases were disposed of during the year leaving 119 cases pending on 12/31/82. There were 162 criminal cases on the docket, 59 convictions, and 100 cases left pending. **JAILS** One jail, capacity five. **ATTORNEYS AT LAW** Two. **UTILITIES** 54% of the residents are connected to a public or privately owned water system and 9% are connected to a public sewer system. Electricity is distributed to the county by Cochran Power and Light Co., Rio Grande Electric Coop., Inc., Kimble Co. Electric Coop., Inc., Medina Electric Coop., Inc. and Southwest Texas Electric Coop., Inc. and is generated primarily by gas, oil and coal. **TAXES** The county has five units with taxing authority: three school districts, one city, and one county.

RECREATION/ENTERTAINMENT
NATIONAL REGISTER OF HISTORIC PLACES Rocksprings: Edwards County Courthouse and Jail. **COUNTY/MUNICIPAL PARKS** 20 acres in one county and one municipal park. These parks contain one playground, one baseball and softball field, three multi-use fields, and one beach. **SCENIC DRIVES** The Texas Pecos Trail runs through this county. This trail rambles through the vast region of southwest and west Texas with landscapes varying from raw, arid regions to green valleys. **BOATING/FISHING** Lakes/reservoirs: Terramar (40 acres). Major rivers: West Nueces, South Llano, Nueces. Primary streams: Indian. **HUNTING** Fall and winter seasons on deer. No closed season on javelina, coyote, bobcat and squirrel. Winter season on quail, muskrat, beaver, opossum, ring-tailed cat, badger, fox, weasel, raccoon, skunk and civet cat. Fall, winter and spring seasons on turkey. In 1983 sandhill crane, duck, coot, geese, woodcock and jacksnipe seasons occurred during the winter months. Teal duck, rail and gallinule seasons occurred in the fall. Mourning dove season occurred intermittently during the fall and winter months with a fall season on white-winged dove. **MUSEUMS** Rocksprings: Angora Goat Breeders' Association Museum. **OTHER** Barksdale: Camp Wood, a pre-Civil War U.S. military post. **SPECIAL EVENTS** Top-of-the-World Festival, Rocksprings, May; Fourth of July Rodeo and Parade, Rocksprings, July.

COMMUNITIES
COUNTY SEAT Rocksprings, County Courthouse, 78880; County Clerk's Office, 512/683-2235. **INCORPORATED COMMUNITIES** (1980 population and ZIP Code) Rocksprings (1,317) 78880. **UNINCORPORATED COMMUNITIES** (and ZIP Code) Barksdale 78828 and Carta Valley 78835. **FOR ADDITIONAL LOCAL INFORMATION** Edwards Chamber of Commerce, P.O. Box 267, Rocksprings, 78880, 512/683-3567.

ELLIS (M18)

THE LAND
South of Dallas on Interstate Highways 35 East and 45 in the

COUNTIES

ELLIS (continued)

Blackland Prairies Region, Ellis County covers 939 square miles with an elevation range of 350 to 650 feet. A narrow strip of undulating, dark, alkaline, loamy soils lie in the western part of the county. The rest of the soils in the county are slightly acidic with loamy surface layers and cracking, clayey subsoils or dark, cracking, clayey soils. Ellis lies in the Blackland Prairies vegetation area consisting of grasses such as little bluestem, big bluestem, Indiangrass, switchgrass, sideoats grama and Texas wintergrass. Post and blackjack oak trees are found throughout. Between 41 and 50% of the land in the county is considered prime farmland. **CLIMATE** Mild, but seasonal extremes vary widely. The average annual temperature is 66°F. Temperatures in January range from an average low of 33° to an average high of 56°F and in July range from 73° to 97°F. The average annual precipitation is 36 inches, with an average relative humidity of 80% at 6 A.M. and 57% at 6 P.M. The average annual snowfall is three inches. The growing season averages 245 days per year, with the last freeze in mid March and the first freeze in mid November. The sun shines during the year on the average 65% of the daylight hours.

THE PEOPLE

The 1982 estimated population of 62,500 indicates a continuation of the strong growth rate begun in the 1960s which reversed the steady population decrease between 1930 and 1960. Rural areas experienced a 35% population gain from 1970 to 1980. The age group with the largest increase was ages 20 to 34. The largest ancestry groups are persons of English descent (23%), Irish descent (18%) and Black (12%). **REGISTERED VOTERS** As of November 2, 1982 there were 28,809 registered voters (0.4% of the state total). The 1982 general election had a 44% voter turnout, compared to a 67% turnout in the 1980 general election. In the 1982 primary 93% voted Democratic and 7% Republican, with 6,874 votes cast.

THE ECONOMY

AGRICULTURE Wheat area. In 1982, 81% of the land was in farms and ranches, with 52% of the farmland under cultivation and 2% irrigated. Ellis ranked 65th in the state in highest agricultural receipts, with 53% from crops. Overgrazing, undesirable brush and weeds, water erosion, a lack of potable water and flooding are the current conservation problems. Primary crops: wheat, sorghum, hay, cotton, oats and corn. Primary vegetables: potatoes and tomatoes. Primary fruits and nuts: peaches and pecans. Primary livestock and products: cattle, milk and hogs. **BUSINESS** Total number of business establishments in the county: 987. Retail sales during the first quarter of 1984 were up 52%, with an increase of 84% in Ennis. In 1980, 8% of the labor force were self-employed, 14% were employed in professional or related services, 28% in manufacturing, 19% in wholesale and retail trade, 9% in construction, 38% were employed in other counties and there were 5,606 retired workers. The industries with the most employment: agribusiness, construction, steel mills and the manufacture of women's apparel, household furniture, business forms, paving and roofing materials, women's handbags, hydraulic cement, mineral wool, structural metal products, oilfield machinery, refrigeration equipment and engine electrical equipment. The nonfarm earnings in 1981 totaled $579,298,000. The retired workers received an average monthly Social Security payment of $302. **FINANCE** On June 30, 1983, 12 commercial banks had total deposits of $322,553,000 and total assets of $374,291,000. On December 31, 1982 two state savings and loan associations, one state branch and three federal association branches had combined assets of $94,871,734. In addition there are four credit unions in the county.

HOUSING Average value of homes in 1980: $33,200. Permits for new, privately owned housing units increased in 1982: 400 permits were issued with a total construction cost of $11,801,612. Of those permits, 186 were for single family houses. Between 1970 and 1980 the number of housing units increased by 33%. Seventy-eight percent of all units in the county are air-conditioned, 75% are heated by gas and 23% by electricity. **NATURAL RESOURCES** Limestone, construction sand, oil and gas. In 1982 a total of 23,238 barrels of crude oil and 163 thousand cubic feet of casinghead gas were produced. Current production of other minerals and products includes clay, cement, brick, crushed limestone, sand and gravel. **TOURISM** Travel expenditures of $6,433,000 in 1982 (an increase of 13% over 1981) generated 128 jobs and $1,116,000 in payroll. **ALCOHOLIC BEVERAGES** Packaged distilled spirits, beer, ale, malt liquor and wine are legal in parts of the county. **FEDERAL EXPENDITURES** The federal government had direct expenditures or obligations of $89,178,000 in the county during fiscal year 1983, including $4,292,000 by the U.S. Department of Defense. In addition, the federal government provided $1,917,000 in grant awards, paid $3,714,000 in salaries and wages, made direct payments to individuals of $79,076,000 including $57,672,000 in retirement and disability payments, awarded $2,504,000 in procurement contracts and spent $1,967,000 in other expenditures or obligations. The federal government also provided $7,387,000 in direct loans and $19,496,000 in guaranteed loans and insurance.

COMMUNICATION

Newspapers–Daily: The Ennis Daily News, ave. eve. circ. 4,427 and the Waxahachie Daily Light ave. eve. circ. 5510. Weekly: Weekly Press (Ennis), Ennis Local, Ferris Wheel, The Italy News-Herald, The Midlothian Mirror, Midlothian Reporter, The Milford Press and the Palmer Rustler. Radio: KBEC-AM (Waxahachie). Cable TV. Telephone companies: Continental Telephone, General Telephone and Southwestern Bell. **TRANSPORTATION** Total public road mileage: 1,789. In 1982 there were 55,726 registered vehicles and 1,334 reported traffic accidents including 23 fatalities. Taxi cabs: four companies in Ennis and one in Waxahachie. Intercity bus service is available. Motor freight: 21 local and intrastate carriers. Rail: seven main and one branch line carry freight through the county. One of the main lines carries annually over 30 million tons of freight, one carries 10 to 20 and five carry five to 10 million each. The one branch line carries annually less than one million tons of freight. Aircraft: 72 are registered in the county. Airports: Ennis Municipal Airport is a general utility airport providing general aviation service. It serves as a base for 29 aircraft. Also serving this area Bee Creek Airport at Maypearl.

COMMUNITY SERVICES

EDUCATION 10 school districts with 15 elementary, six middle and 10 high schools. The average daily attendance in 1981-82 was 12,507, with expenditures per pupil of $2,116 including 749 classroom teachers with an average annual salary of $15,569. Forty-eight percent of the 832 high school graduates planned to attend college. In 1982-83, 71% of the students were White, 13% Hispanic, 16% Black, 0.3% Asian and 0.1% American Indian. Private schools: 484 students enrolled in two elementary and two high schools. Southwestern Assemblies of God Junior College is located in Waxahachie. Established in 1927 it is affiliated with the Assemblies of God Church. Enrollment in 1982 was 693 with in state undergratuate tuition and fees of $1,652 per semester. The highest degree offered is Bachelor. **PUBLIC LIBRARIES** Ennis Public Library: 16,373 volumes. Ferris Public Library: 8,109 volumes. S M Dunlap Memorial Library (Italy): 8,262 volumes. Midlothian Library. Nicholas P. Sims Library (Waxahachie): 50,602 volumes. **CHILD CARE** 90 day care and

20 twenty-four hour care licensed facilities. **HEALTH CARE** 32 physicians and 17 dentists. Hospitals: two with a combined capacity of 121. Ambulance services: three volunteer fire departments, three commercial, one fire department and one volunteer service. Mental health: two county clinics. Nursing homes: seven nursing homes with a combined capacity of 632 nursing care residents. The average cost per day for private patients in 1982 was $30.98. **CHURCHES** 123 churches have an estimated combined membership of 36,197. The largest denominations are Southern Baptist, United Methodist and Baptist Missionary. **SOCIAL SERVICES** In fiscal year 1983 a total of $2,007,436 in food stamps was distributed, with an average of 4,415 persons receiving food stamps each month. Aid to Families with Dependent Children (AFDC) totaled $485,781 with an average of 315 families receiving AFDC each month. Medical assistance benefits for the aged and disabled of $4,721,645 and for families and children of $606,168 brought the county benefit total to $7,821,030. **FIRE PROTECTION** One paid, one partly paid and 16 volunteer fire departments. **LAW ENFORCEMENT** The County Sheriff has 32 commissioned officers. Eleven police departments have a combined force of 163. **CRIME** 242 violent crimes (murder, forcible rape, robbery and aggravated assault) and 2,129 nonviolent crimes (burglary, larceny-theft and motor vehicle theft) were reported in 1982. **JUDICIAL SYSTEM** One District Court and Judge, one County Court and Judge and five Justices of the Peace. In the District Court a total of 2,317 cases were pending on 1/1/82, 1,437 new cases were filed and 1,078 cases were disposed of during the year leaving 2,676 cases pending on 12/31/82. There were 416 criminal cases on the docket, 144 convictions, 51 persons committed to prison and three committed to jail and 263 cases left pending. In the County Court 1,536 cases were pending on 1/1/82, 2,925 new cases were filed and 2,265 cases were disposed of during the year leaving 2,196 cases pending on 12/31/82. There were 3,926 criminal cases on the docket, 2,058 convictions, 1,276 persons committed to jail, and 1,677 cases left pending. **JAILS** One jail, capacity 65 under renovation. **ATTORNEYS AT LAW** 49. **UTILITIES** 94% of the residents are connected to a public or privately owned water system and 64% are connected to a public sewer system. Natural gas is distributed to the county by Lone Star Gas Co., Division of Enserch. The average annual residential bill for natural gas in 1982 for the Lone Star distribution system was $405.91, an increase of 35% over 1981. Electricity is distributed to the county by Texas Power and Light Co., West Texas Utilities, Hill Co. Electric Coop., Inc., Johnson Co. Electric Coop., Assn., and Navarro Co. Electric Coop., Inc. and is generated primarily by gas and oil. The typical residential electric bill is $165.24 per month for an all-electric house using 2,500 kwh. **TAXES** The county has 27 units with taxing authority: 10 school districts, 13 cities, one county, and three special districts.

RECREATION/ENTERTAINMENT

NATIONAL REGISTER OF HISTORIC PLACES Waxahachie: Chataugua Auditorium, Ellis County Courthouse Historic District, Williams-Erwin House and Rosemont House. **MUNICIPAL PARKS** 455 acres in 25 municipal parks. These parks contain one mile of hiking trails, 20 playgrounds, one football and soccer field, 15 baseball and softball fields, one multiuse court, one swimming pool, three beaches, five boat ramps and shore fishing facilities. **BOATING/FISHING** Lakes/reservoirs: Bardwell (3,570 acres), Bell Branch (18 acres) Chambers Creek Soil Conservation Service Lakes 1, 102, 106, 111, 113, 2F, 53, 54, 56, 7, 75B, 82, 85B, 97, 98, 98A, 99 and 117 (502 acres), Clark (102 acres), Clopton (22 acres), Ennis Old City (41 acres), Gifford-Hill (13 acres), Mountain Creek Soil Conservation Service Lakes 9 and 10 (61 acres), Waxahachie (690 acres) and Waxahachie Country Club (22 acres). Major rivers: West Fork Trinity.

Primary streams: Waxahachie, Bell, North Prong, Mill, Big Onion, Little Onion, North Prong Waxahachie, East Fork Chambers, Oak, Valley, Chambers, Elm, Little Mustang, Red Oak, Mustang, Bedford, Cottonwood, Newton, South Prong and Mountain. **HUNTING** Fall and winter seasons on deer. No closed season on nutria, coyote, bobcat and squirrel. Winter season on quail, muskrat, beaver, opossum, mink, ring-tailed cat, badger, fox, otter, raccoon, skunk and civet cat. In 1983 duck, coot, geese, woodcock and jacksnipe seasons occurred during the winter months. Teal duck, rail and gallinule seasons occurred in the fall. Mourning dove season occurred intermittently during the fall and winter months. **MUSEUMS** Waxahachie: Ellis County Historical Museum and Gallery. **THEATERS** Waxahachie: Chautagua Auditorium. **COLLEGIATE FINE ARTS** Waxahachie: Cultural events offered by Southwestern Assemblies of God Junior College. **SPECIAL EVENTS** Bluebonnet Trails, Ennis, April; Scarborough Renaissance Faire, Waxahachie, April/May; National Polka Festival, Ennis, May; Miss Red Oak Pageant, Red Oak, April/May; Art Club Spring Show, Ennis, May; Gingerbread Trail, Waxahachie, June; Italian Festival, Italy, June; Founders Day, Red Oak, August; Christmas Parade and Tour of Homes, Waxahachie, December.

COMMUNITIES

COUNTY SEAT Waxahachie, County Courthouse, 75165; County Clerk's Office, 214/937-1290. **INCORPORATED COMMUNITIES** (1980 population and ZIP Code) Alma (171) 75119, Bardwell (335) 75101, Cedar Hill (6,849: two in Ellis Co. and 6,847 in Dallas Co.) 75104, Ennis (12,110) 75119, Ferris (2,228) 75125, Garrett (220) 75119, Glenn Heights (1,033: 25 in Ellis Co. and 1,008 in Dallas Co.) 75115, Grand Prairie (71,462: five in Ellis County, 65,726 in Dallas County and 5,731 in Tarrant Co.) 75050, Italy (1,306) 76651, Maypearl (626) 76064, Midlothian (3,219) 76065, Milford (681) 76670, Ovilla (1,067: 1,022 in Ellis Co. and 45 in Dallas Co.) 76065, Palmer (1,187) 75152, Red Oak (1,882) 75154, Rice (439: seven in Ellis Co., 432 in Navarro Co.) 75155 and Waxahachie (14,624) 75165. **UNINCORPORATED COMMUNITIES** (and ZIP Code) Alsdorf 75119, Auburn 76050, Avalon 76623, Bell Branch 76651, Bethel 75165, Boyce 75165, Boz 75165, Bristol 75119, Britton (also in Tarrant Co.) 76063, Byrd 75119, Center Point 76651, Creechville 75119, Crisp 75119, Ensign 75119, Five Points 75165, Forreston 76041, Griffith 76084, Howard 75165, Ike 75165, India 75125, Lone Cedar 76641, Lone Elm 75165, Mountain Peak 76065, Nash 76041, Neals Valley 75119, Oak Grove 75119, Rankin 75119, Reagor Springs 75165, Rockett 75165, Sand Lake (Sandlake) 75119, Sardis (76065), Sterrett 75165, Telico 75119, Trumbull 75125 and Walnut Springs 75125. **FOR ADDITIONAL LOCAL INFORMATION** Ennis Chamber of Commerce, 304C E. Ennis Ave., P.O. Box 1177, Ennis, 75119, 214/875-2625, Ferris Area Chamber of Commerce, Train Depot on Sq., Ferris, 75125, 214/544-2222, Italy Chamber of Commerce, P.O. Box 160, Italy, 76651, 214/483-6271, Midlothian Chamber of Commerce, P.O. Box 609, Midlothian, 76065, 214/775-8500 and Waxahachie Chamber of Commerce, 431 N. College, Waxahachie, 75165, 214/937-2390.

EL PASO (B1)

THE LAND

Bordering Mexico and New Mexico on Interstate Highway 10 in the Trans-Pecos Region, El Paso County is the furthest west of all Texas Counties. It covers 1,014 square miles of mountainous terrain with an elevation range of 3,600 to 7,100 feet. Cave remains of ancient dwellers have been found. The desertic soils are generally shallow, saline and sandy with deep, loamy surface layers over clayey subsoils in some valleys and outcrops of

COUNTIES

EL PASO (continued)

limestone and igneous rocks in the mountains and hills. To the west the soils are the loamy and clayey soils of the Rio Grande River flood plain. Along the river the soils are saline and have a high shrink-swell potential. In the Trans-Pecos, Mountains and Basins vegetation area, the grasses are short and sparse with desert shrub and cacti, a few juniper and scrub oak. Pine trees grow at the higher mountain elevations. On the flood plains are salt tolerant grasses, salt cedar, cottonwood trees and cacti. Less than 1% of the land in the county is considered prime farmland. **CLIMATE** Subtropical arid, mild, dry and quite windy in spring. The average annual temperature is 63°F. Temperatures in January range from an average low of 30° to an average high of 58°F and in July range from 69° to 96°F. The average annual precipitation is eight inches, with an average relative humidity of 53% at 6 A.M. and 20% at 6 P.M. The average annual snowfall is five inches. The growing season averages 246 days per year, with the last freeze in early March and the first freeze in early November. The sun shines during the year on the average 80% of the daylight hours, the highest percentage in the state.

THE PEOPLE

El Paso County ranks as one of the most densely populated counties in the state and is 27th among all U.S. counties in the highest percent of persons who are of Spanish origin. The 1982 estimated population of 513,400 indicates a continuation of the strong growth rate begun in the 1940s. The population increased 34% between 1970 and 1980. The age groups with the largest gains were ages 65 and over and 20 to 34. Therefore the median age rose from 23 in 1970 to 25 in 1980. The population is younger than average and has a low percent of persons who are native Texans. The largest ancestry groups are Hispanic (62%) and persons of English descent (11%). **REGISTERED VOTERS** As of November 2, 1982 there were 150,749 registered voters (2% of the state total). The 1982 general election had a 47% voter turnout, compared to a 66% turnout in the 1980 general election. In the 1982 primary 82% voted Democratic and 18% Republican, with 40,417 votes cast.

THE ECONOMY

AGRICULTURE Dairy and cotton area. In 1982, 74% of the land was in farms and ranches, with 10% of the farmland under cultivation. Most of the cropland and some commercial pecan groves were irrigated. El Paso ranked 64th in the state in highest agricultural receipts, with 54% from crops. A lack of potable water, salinity, decreasing irrigation water supplies and urban encroachment are the current conservation problems. Primary crops: first in the state for American-Pima cotton. Hay, wheat, upland cotton and sorghum. Primary vegetables: lettuce, onions, tomatoes and watermelons. Primary fruits and nuts: peaches and first in the state for pecans. Primary livestock and products: 10th in the state for milk production. Cattle and hogs. **BUSINESS** Total number of business establishments in the county: 8,156. Retail sales during the first quarter of 1984 increased 23%. In 1980, 5% of the labor force were self-employed, 21% were employed in professional or related services, 19% in manufacturing, 23% in wholesale and retail trade, 9% in transportation, communications, and other public utilities, 4% were employed in other counties and there were 21,641 retired workers. The industries with the most employment: agribusiness, construction, meat packing, lumber mills, lead and copper smelting, steel mills, fruit and vegetable canning, soft drink bottling and canning, petroleum refining, book printing, textile mills and the manufacture of pet food, bakery products, dairy products, men's and women's apparel, structural metal products, calculating machines, telephone equipment, motor vehicles and equipment

and optical instruments and lenses. The nonfarm earnings in 1981 totaled $3,651,595,000. The retired workers received an average monthly Social Security payment of $305. **FINANCE** On June 30, 1983, 26 commercial banks had total deposits of $2,424,023,000 and total assets of $2,773,765,000. On December 31, 1982 four state savings and loan associations, one federal association, 16 state branches and three federal branches had combined assets of $530,911,179. In addition there are 38 credit unions in the county. **HOUSING** Average value of homes in 1980: $38,400. Permits for new, privately owned housing units increased in 1982: 4,075 permits were issued with a total construction cost of $112,736,819. Of those permits, 1,941 were for single family houses. Housing permits in El Paso increased from 2,293 in 1981 to 4,050 in 1982. Between 1970 and 1980 the number of housing units increased by 46%. Eighty-nine percent of all units in the county are air-conditioned, 87% are heated by gas and 11% by electricity. **NATURAL RESOURCES** Copper, dolomite, iron, limestone, rhyolite, sand and gravel, tin and tungsten. Current production of other minerals and products includes cement, crushed limestone, dimension limestone, crushed rhyolite, industrial sand, sand and gravel, and recovered sulphur. **TOURISM** Travel expenditures of $346,181,000 in 1982 (an increase of 9% over 1981) generated 7,565 jobs and $73,487,000 in payroll. Lodging: 54 hotels, motels and tourist courts. Convention/meeting facilities: El Paso-Dudley Field, El Paso Civic Center, El Paso County Coliseum, University of Texas Special Events Center and nine hotels with facilities for large gatherings. **ALCOHOLIC BEVERAGES** Packaged distilled spirits, beer, ale, malt liquor and wine are legal. Sale of mixed beverages is legal in all or parts of the county. **MILITARY INSTALLATIONS** Fort Bliss, El Paso, 24,722 personnel, 118,218 acres, Air Defense Center and School. **FEDERAL EXPENDITURES** The federal government had direct expenditures or obligations of $1,165,493,000 in the county during fiscal year 1983, including $585,161,000 by the U.S. Department of Defense. In addition, the federal government provided $41,464,000 in grant awards, paid $457,392,000 in salaries and wages, made direct payments to individuals of $543,441,000 including $460,141,000 in retirement and disability payments, awarded $96,719,000 in procurement contracts and spent $26,478,000 in other expenditures or obligations. The federal government also provided $25,046,000 in direct loans and $115,048,000 in guaranteed loans and insurance.

COMMUNICATION

Newspapers–Daily: El Paso Times, ave. morn. circ. 55,420 and El Paso Herald-Post ave. eve. circ. 32,191. Weekly: The Valley Independent (Fabens). Radio: KAMA-AM, KHEY-AM, KISO-AM, KKOL-AM, KROD-AM, KSET-AM, KSET-FM Stereo (El Paso). Television: KCIK-CH. 14, KCOS-CH. 13, KDBC-CH. 4, KTSM-CH. 9 and KVIA-CH. 7 (El Paso). Cable TV. Telephone companies: Continental and Southwestern Bell. **TRANSPORTATION** Total public road mileage: 1,958. In 1982 there were 296,161 registered vehicles and 13,055 reported traffic accidents including 103 fatalities. Taxi cabs: three companies in the city of El Paso. Municipal transit systems: one intracity bus system in the city of El Paso, with scheduled routes. Intercity bus service is available. Motor freight: 94 local and intrastate carriers. Rail: The Sunset Limited provides passenger service on the Amtrak Route. Five main lines carry freight through the county. Three of the main lines carry annually over 30 million tons of freight each and two carry five to 10 each. Aircraft: 420 are registered in the county. Airports: El Paso International Airport serves as a base for 390 aircraft, is a medium size hub for medium hauls and has carrier service. Also serving this area are El Paso County Airport at Fabens and West Texas Airport at El Paso. Domestic and foreign exports by air from El Paso average about one thousand pounds per month and imports average about two thousand pounds per month.

COMMUNITY SERVICES

EDUCATION Nine school districts with 94 elementary, 21 middle, 21 high schools and three special education. The average daily attendance in 1981-82 was 106,340, with expenditures per pupil of $2,216 including 5,734 classroom teachers with an average annual salary of $16,072. Fifty-two percent of the 6,628 high school graduates planned to attend college. In 1982-83, 22% of the students were White, 74% Hispanic, 3% Black, 0.6% Asian and 0.2% American Indian. Private schools: 7,619 students enrolled in 20 elementary and nine high schools. Sports championships: 1983 AAAA Boys' Swimming, Cathedral H.S. The University of Texas at El Paso was established in 1913 and is under state control. Enrollment in 1982 was 15,750 with in state undergraduate tuition and fees of $396 per semester. The highest degree offered is Doctorate. El Paso County Community College is located in El Paso. Established in 1969 it is a vocational and two year academic college under local control. Enrollment in 1982 was 10,830 with in state undergraduate tuition and fees of $270 per semester. Vocational education: El Paso—Aladdin Beauty College, Durham's Business College, El Paso Barber College, International Business College-Bond Office, Investigators Training Academy, Mannequin Manor Fashion Career School, Pipo Academy of Hair Design, Southwest Beauty College, Inc., Tri-State Beauty School, Conley's Watch and Jewelry Repair, El Paso Trade School, Inc. **PUBLIC LIBRARIES** El Paso Public Library: 480,000 volumes, nine branches. El Paso County Library (Fabens): 34,366 volumes. **CHILD CARE** 527 day care and 112 twenty-four hour care licensed facilities. **HEALTH CARE** 698 physicians and 175 dentists. Hospitals: 16 with a combined capacity of 2,439. Specialized hospitals: one Army medical center with capacity of 483 and one obstetrics hopsital with capacity of 32. Clinics: four outpatient clinics, two for treatment of alcohol/drug abuse, one cancer treatment clinic, one diagnostic clinic and one public health clinic. Ambulance services: two commercial, one air and one city service. Mental health: 10 clinics and one development center with capacity of 167. Nursing homes: nine nursing homes with a combined capacity of 1,050 nursing care residents. The average cost per day for private patients in 1982 was $34.08. **CHURCHES** 236 churches have an estimated combined membership of 205,221. The largest denominations are Catholic, Southern Baptist and United Methodist. **SOCIAL SERVICES** In fiscal year 1983 a total of $39,550,833 in food stamps was distributed, with an average of 81,892 persons receiving food stamps each month. Aid to Families with Dependent Children (AFDC) totaled $5,887,510 with an average of 3,814 families receiving AFDC each month. Medical assistance benefits for the aged and disabled of $17,695,769 and for families and children of $8,143,754 brought the county benefit total to $71,277,865. **FIRE PROTECTION** Three paid and four volunteer fire departments. **LAW ENFORCEMENT** The County Sheriff has 276 commissioned officers. Four police departments have a combined force of 661. El Paso International Airport Security has 21 officers. **CRIME** 4,154 violent crimes (murder, forcible rape, robbery and aggravated assault) and 27,017 nonviolent crimes (burglary, larceny-theft and motor vehicle theft) were reported in 1982. **JUDICIAL SYSTEM** Ten District Courts and Judges, six County Courts and Judges and six Justices of the Peace. In the District Courts a total of 16,759 cases were pending on 1/1/82, 11,895 new cases were filed and 11,400 cases were disposed of during the year leaving 17,254 cases pending on 12/31/82. There were 4,397 criminal cases on the docket, 938 convictions, 357 persons committed to prison and 12 committed to jail and 2,995 cases left pending. In the County Courts 15,710 cases were pending on 1/1/82, 12,265 new cases were filed

and 8,480 cases were disposed of during the year leaving 19,495 cases pending on 12/31/82. There were 18,875 criminal cases on the docket, 1,843 convictions, 481 persons committed to jail, and 12,730 cases left pending. **JAILS** One jail, capacity 1,024, opened in 1983. **ATTORNEYS AT LAW** 754. **UTILITIES** 98% of the residents are connected to a public or privately owned water system and 93% are connected to a public sewer system. Natural gas is distributed to the county by Southern Union Company. The average annual residential bill for natural gas in 1982 for the Southern Union distribution system was $355.85, an increase of 23% over 1981. Electricity is distributed to the county by El Paso Electric Co. and Rio Grande Electric Coop., Inc. and is generated primarily by gas, oil and coal. The typical residential electric bill is $183.69 per month for an all-electric house using 2,500 kwh. **TAXES** The county has 20 units with taxing authority: nine school districts, three cities, one county, one college district, one hospital district and five special districts.

RECREATION/ENTERTAINMENT

TEXAS LEAGUE BASEBALL The city of El Paso has a team in the Western Division of the League. **FEDERAL** CHAMIZAL NATIONAL MEMORIAL is a tribute to the amicable settlement in 1963 of a longstanding border dispute between Texas and Mexico. The memorial is located in an area by the Rio Grande where a new channel marks the adjusted international boundary. Facilities include a visitor center as well as exhibits. **NATIONAL REGISTER OF HISTORIC PLACES** El Paso: Abdou Building, O.T. Bassett Tower, Richard Caples Building, W.S. Hills Commercial Structure, Hotel Cortez, Hotel Paso del Norte, Manhattan Heights Historic District, J.J. Newberry Company, Palace Theatre, Plaza Hotel, Popular Department Store, Roberts-Banner Building, Singer Sewing Company, State National Bank, White House Department Store, Hotel McCoy, Chamizal National Memorial, El Paso Union Station, First Mortgage Co. Building, Magoffin Homestead, Mexican Consulate, Old Fort Bliss, Toltec Club, Henry C. Trost House, Northgate Site, Women's Club of El Paso and Ysleta Mission. El Paso vicinity: Sgt. Doyle Archeological Site, Fusselman Canyon Rock Art District, Hot Well Archeological Site and Hueco Tanks. Fort Bliss vicinity: Castner Range Archeological District. San Elizario: Presidio Chapel of San Elizario. Socorro: Mission Socorro. **STATE** Franklin Mountains State Park covers 8,897 acres with no facilities available—pedestrian access only. Hueco Tanks State Historical Park covers 860 acres with camping and trailer sites as well as Indian pictographs. Magoffin Home State Historic Site covers two acres with a museum and a historic structure—a replica of an early El Paso home which was an early political and social center. **COUNTY/ MUNICIPAL PARKS** 5,743 acres in 11 county and 91 municipal parks. These parks contain three miles of hiking trails, 86 playgrounds, one golf course, six football and soccer fields, 49 baseball and softball fields, 46 tennis courts, 25 multi-use courts, 12 swimming pools, three boat ramps and shore fishing facilities. Developed campsites: 67. **SCENIC DRIVES** The Texas Mountain Trail runs through the Franklin Mountains in this county. This trail offers an adventurous route through West Texas, a remote region of stark majesty with its secluded canyons and high peaks. In addition Loop 375 climbs through Smuggler's Gap, offering views of mountain-desert scenery. **BOATING/ FISHING** Lakes/reservoirs: Cottonwood (63 acres), Fabens (24 acres), Mesa Drain (33 acres), Northeast Oxidation Ponds 1 (129 acres), 2 (117 acres), 3 (98 acres) and 4 (127 acres), Rattlesnake (31 acres), Riverside Diversion (109 acres) and Thorn (22 acres). Major rivers: Rio Grande. Primary streams: San Felipe Arroyo and Herrera Main Lateral. **HUNTING** Fall season on antelope. Fall and winter seasons on mule deer. No closed seasons on elk, javelina, coyote and bobcat. Winter seasons on quail, muskrat, beaver, opossum, ring-tailed cat, badger, fox, weasel, raccoon,

COUNTIES

EL PASO (continued)

skunk and civet cat. In 1983 sandhill crane, duck, coot, geese, woodcock and jacksnipe seasons occurred during the winter months. Teal duck, rail and gallinule seasons occurred in the fall. Mourning dove seasons occurred intermittently during the fall and winter months with a fall season on white-winged doves. **MUSEUMS** El Paso: El Paso Museum of History, Insights—El Paso Science Center, Chamizal National Memorial Museum, El Paso Calvary Museum, Wilderness Park Museum, El Paso Centennial Museum, Bullfight Museum, El Paso Museum of Art and Ysleta Del Sur Pueblo Museum. Fort Bliss: Fort Bliss Replica Museum, U.S. Army Defense Artillery and 3rd Cavalry Museum and the U.S. Army Museum of the Noncommissioned Officer. San Elizario: Museo de San Elizario. **THEATERS** El Paso: Civic Center Theatre. San Elizario: Adobe Horseshoe Theatre Restaurant. **ORCHESTRAS** El Paso: Symphony Orchestra and Youth Symphony. **ZOO** El Paso: Zoological Park. **PLANETARIUM** El Paso: Public Schools Planetarium. **COLLEGIATE FINE ARTS** El Paso: Cultural events offered by University of Texas-El Paso. **SPECIAL EVENTS** Fort Bliss Wind Walkers Volksmarch, El Paso, January; Southwest Stock Show and Rodeo, El Paso, February; Volksmarch, El Paso, April; Tigua St. Anthony's Day Ceremony, El Paso, June; "Viva El Paso" Historial Musical, El Paso, June; Street Festival, El Paso, July; Indian Dancing, Tigua Reservation, El Paso, July; Fiesta de la San Lorenzo, El Paso, July; Chili Cookoff, El Paso, August/September; Border Folk Festival, El Paso, October; Thanksgiving Day Parade, El Paso, November; Sun Bowl Festival, El Paso, November/December.

COMMUNITIES

COUNTY SEAT El Paso, County Courthouse, 79901; County Clerk's Office, 915/546-2071. **INCORPORATED COMMUNITIES** (1980 population and ZIP Code) Anthony (2,640) 88021, Clint (1,314) 79836, El Paso (425, 259) 79901, All-America Cities Award 1969 and Vinton (350, est. incorp. inactive) 88021. **UNINCORPORATED COMMUNITIES** (and ZIP Code) Aero Vista 79918, Alamo Alto 79853, Borderland 79940, Canutillo 79835, Casey 79836, Cuadrilla 79836, Fabens 79838, Horizon City 79907, La Isla 79838, Mesa 79838, Newman 79924, Nuway 88021, San Elizario 79849, Socorro 79927, Tigua Indian Reservation 79917, Tornillo 79853 and Westway 79835. **FOR ADDITIONAL LOCAL INFORMATION** El Paso Chamber of Commerce, P.O. Box 9738, El Paso, 79987, 915/544-7880.

ERATH (M15)

THE LAND

Southwest of Fort Worth on U.S. Highways 281, 377 and 67 in the Cross Timbers Region, Erath County covers 1,080 square miles with an elevation range of 1,000 to 1,600 feet. To the east the soils are undulating to hilly, alkaline, moderately deep, loamy to clayey soils over limestone. Along the eastern border and to the west the soils are more level, light-colored and acidic with loamy surface layers and mottled clay subsoils. In the northwest the hilly soils have shale or sandstone bedrock. In the Cross Timbers and Prairies vegetation area, the grasses are tall with live oak, juniper and mesquite trees. Between 21 and 30% of the land in the county is considered prime farmland. **CLIMATE** Mild and dry. The average annual temperature is 65°F. Temperatures in January range from an average low of 32° to an average high of 55°F and in July range from 73° to 96°F. The average annual precipitation is 30 inches, with an average relative humidity of 77% at 6 A.M. and 48% at 6 P.M. The average annual snowfall is five inches. The growing season averages 238 days per year, with the last freeze in late March and the first freeze in mid November. The sun shines during the year on the average 67% of the daylight hours.

THE PEOPLE

The 1982 estimated population of 23,500 indicates a continuation of the moderate growth begun in the 1960s which reversed the steady population decrease between 1930 and 1960. Over 31% of the growth between 1970 and 1980 was in rural areas with urban areas experiencing a 21% growth rate. The age groups with the largest gains were ages 25 to 34 and birth to five years. Therefore the median age lowered from 38 in 1970 to 33 in 1980. The largest ancestry groups are persons of English descent (37%), Irish descent (26%) and German descent (14%). **REGISTERED VOTERS** As of November 2, 1982 there were 12,081 registered voters (0.2% of the state total). The 1982 general election had a 55% voter turnout, compared to a 70% turnout in the 1980 general election. In the 1982 primary 97% voted Democratic and 3% Republican, with 4,170 votes cast.

THE ECONOMY

AGRICULTURE Cattle and dairy area. In 1982, 88% of the land was in farms and ranches, with 14% of the farmland under cultivation and 9% irrigated. Erath ranked 15th in the state in highest agricultural receipts, with 91% from livestock and livestock products. Overgrazing, undesirable brush and weeds, water erosion and livestock waste management are the current conservation problems. Primary crops: seventh in the state for hay and eighth for peanuts. Oats, wheat, sorghum and rye. Primary vegetables: watermelons. Primary fruits and nuts: peaches and pecans. Primary livestock and products: second in the state for milk production. Cattle, sheep, wool, angora goats, mohair and hogs. **BUSINESS** Total number of business establishments in the county: 490. Retail sales during the first quarter of 1984 increased 7%. In 1980, 16% of the labor force were self-employed, 22% were employed in professional or related services, 11% in manufacturing, 21% in wholesale and retail trade, 16% in agriculture, forestry, fisheries and mining, 14% were employed in other counties and there were 3,056 retired workers. The industries with the most employment: agribusiness, oil and gas extraction and the manufacture of women's apparel, abrasive products and oilfield machinery. The nonfarm earnings in 1981 totaled $201,261,000. The retired workers received an average monthly Social Security payment of $287. **FINANCE** On June 30, 1983, four commercial banks had total deposits of $200,582,000 and total assets of $224,837,000. On December 31, 1982 one state savings and loan association and four state branches had assets of $98,043,609. In addition there is one credit union in the county. **HOUSING** Average value of homes in 1980: $29,000. Permits for new, privately owned housing units in the county increased in 1982: 223 permits were issued with a total construction cost of $4,809,200. Of those permits, 49 were for single family houses. Housing permits in Stephenville increased from 55 in 1981 to 216 in 1982 with 150 of the permits issued for apartments and condominiums. Between 1970 and 1980 the number of housing units increased by 32%. Seventy-eight percent of all units in the county are air-conditioned, 73% are heated by gas and 24% by electricity. **NATURAL RESOURCES** Clay, coal, limestone, industrial sand, oil, gas and bituminous coal. In 1982 a total of 4,524,216 thousand cubic feet of gas well gas, 4,979 barrels of condensate, 12,819 barrels of crude oil and 89,566 thousand cubic feet of casinghead gas were produced. Current production of other minerals and products includes clay and bituminous coal. **TOURISM** Travel expenditures of $8,123,000 in 1982 (an increase of 12% over 1981) generated 193 jobs and $1,598,000 in payroll. Lodging: four hotels, motels and tourist courts. Convention/meeting facilities: Stephenville—Tarlton State University Stadium and two gyms. **ALCOHOLIC BEVERAGES** Totally dry. **FEDERAL EXPENDITURES** The federal government had direct expenditures or obligations of $48,465,000 in the county during fiscal year 1983, including $2,600,000 by the U.S. Department of Defense. In addition, the federal government provided $931,000 in grant awards, paid $2,474,000 in salaries and wages, made direct payments to individuals of $43,103,000 including $30,073,000 in retirement and disability payments, awarded $1,649,000 in procurement contracts and spent $307,000 in other expenditures or obligations. The federal government also provided $17,000 in direct loans and $6,276,000 in guaranteed loans and insurance.

COMMUNICATION

Newspapers–Daily: Stephenville Empire-Tribune, ave. eve. circ. 4,641. Weekly: The Dublin Progress. Radio: KSTV-AM and KWWM-FM (Stephenville). Cable TV. Telephone companies: Continental Telephone, Southwestern Bell, United Telephone, Alenco Communications, Comanche County Telephone and Texas-Midland Telephone. **TRANSPORTATION** Total public road mileage: 1,250. In 1982 there were 22,284 registered vehicles and 658 reported traffic accidents including eight fatalities. Taxi cabs: one company in Stephenville. Intercity bus service is available. Motor freight: seven local and intrastate carriers. Rail: two main lines carry freight through the county with one carrying 10 to 20 million tons of freight annually and the other carrying five to 10 million. Aircraft: 51 are registered in the county. Airports: Clark Field at Stephenville is a basic utility airport providing general aviation service and serves as a base for 25 aircraft. Dublin Municipal Airport is a basic utility airport providing general aviation service and serves as a base for 10 aircraft. Campbell Ranch Airport at Dublin and J.F. Ranch Airport at Clairette.

COMMUNITY SERVICES

EDUCATION Seven school districts with eight elementary, two middle and four high schools. The average daily attendance in 1981-82 was 3,246, with expenditures per pupil of $2,349 including 204 classroom teachers with an average annual salary of $15,681. Sixty-four percent of the 207 high school graduates planned to attend college. In 1982-83, 92% of the students were White, 7% Hispanic, 0.4% Black, 0.5% Asian and 0.2% American Indian. Tarleton State University is located in Stephenville. Established in 1899 it is under state control. Enrollment in 1982 was 3,592 with in state undergraduate tuition and fees of $374 per semester. The highest degree offered is Master. Vocational education: Stephenville Beauty School and Stephenville General Hospital LVN School (Stephenville). **PUBLIC LIBRARIES** Dublin Public Library: 7,632 volumes. Stephenville Public Library: 33,204 volumes. **CHILD CARE** 34 day care and four twenty-four hour care licensed facilities. **HEALTH CARE** 22 physicians and 12 dentists. Hospitals: two with a combined capacity of 125. Ambulance services: one police department and one fire department service. Mental health: one clinic. Nursing homes: six nursing homes with a combined capacity of 538 nursing care residents. The average cost per day for private patients in 1982 was $30.23. **CHURCHES** 60 churches have an estimated combined membership of 15,964. The largest denominations are Southern Baptist, United Methodist and Churches of Christ. **SOCIAL SERVICES** In fiscal year 1983 a total of $427,436 in food stamps was distributed, with an average of 970 persons receiving food stamps each month. Aid to Families with Dependent Children (AFDC) totaled $68,989 with an average of 47 families receiving AFDC each month. Medical assistance benefits for the aged and disabled of $4,005,626 and for families and children of $231,949 brought the county benefit total to $4,734,000. **FIRE PROTECTION** One partly paid and three volunteer fire departments. **LAW ENFORCEMENT** The County Sheriff has 20 commissioned officers. Two police departments have a combined

force of 40. One university campus has a police department with a force of 10 officers. **CRIME** 23 violent crimes (murder, forcible rape, robbery and aggravated assault) and 546 nonviolent crimes (burglary, larceny-theft and motor vehicle theft) were reported in 1982. **JUDICIAL SYSTEM** One District Court and Judge, one County Court and Judge and two Justices of the Peace. In the District Court a total of 507 cases were pending on 1/1/82, 799 new cases were filed and 607 cases were disposed of during the year leaving 699 cases pending on 12/31/82. There were 185 criminal cases on the docket, 75 convictions, 23 persons committed to prison and one committed to jail and 54 cases left pending. In the County Court 1,545 cases were pending on 1/1/82, 612 new cases were filed and 1,155 cases were disposed of during the year leaving 1,002 cases pending on 12/31/82. There were 1,936 criminal cases on the docket, 369 convictions, 79 persons committed to jail, and 837 cases left pending. **JAILS** One jail, capacity 20. Planning a renovation. **ATTORNEYS AT LAW** 22. **UTILITIES** 66% of the residents are connected to a public or privately owned water system and 63% are connected to a public sewer system. Natural gas is distributed to the county by Lone Star Gas Co., Division of Enserch. The average annual residential bill for natural gas in 1982 for the Lone Star distribution system was $405.91, an increase of 35% over 1981. Electricity is distributed to the county by Erath Co. Electric Coop., Inc. and Texas Power and Light and is generated primarily by gas, coal and water. The typical residential electric bill is $193.64 per month for an all-electric house using 2,500 kwh. **TAXES** The county has 11 units with taxing authority: seven school districts, two cities, one county and one special district.

RECREATION/ENTERTAINMENT

NATIONAL REGISTER OF HISTORIC PLACES Bluff Dale: Bluff Dale Suspension Bridge. Stephenville: Erath County Courthouse and Berry House. Thurber: Thurber Historic District. **MUNICIPAL PARKS** 109 acres in three municipal parks. These parks contain seven miles of hiking trails, five playgrounds, six football and soccer fields, 12 baseball and softball fields, four tennis courts, two multi-use courts and two swimming pools. Developed campsites: 25. **BOATING/FISHING** Lakes/reservoirs: Upper Bosque Soil Conservation Service Lakes 17, 10, 11, 13, 18, 19, 2, 6, 20, 21, 24, 25, 3 and 9 (443 acres), Collier (13 acres), Cross (27 acres), Gilmore Creek (22 acres), Green Creek Soil Conservation Service Lakes 1, 8, 10, 12 and 13 (108 acres), Horseshoe (20 acres), House (27 acres), Leon River Tributary Soil Conservation Service Lakes 1, 5 and 7 (45 acres), Lesley (41 acres), Mitchell (19 acres), Paluxy River Soil Conservation Service Lake 20 (7 acres), Spindor (19 acres) and Turber (60 acres). Major rivers: North Fork North Bosque, Bosque South Fork, North Bosque, East Bosque and North Paluxy. Primary streams: Goose, Indian, Sims, Dry, Live Oak, Round Hole, Spring, Scarborough, Henshaw, Sycamore, Gilmore, Henning, Lallah, Pony, Elmir, Gibson, Green, Bell, Heavenly, South Fork Little Green, Black Spring, Mitchell, Armstrong and Hackberry. **HUNTING** Fall and winter seasons on deer. No closed seasons on coyote, bobcat and squirrel. Winter seasons on quail, muskrat, beaver, opossum, ring-tailed cat, badger, fox, weasel, raccoon, skunk and civet cat. Fall, winter and spring seasons on turkey. In 1983 duck, coot, geese, woodcock and jacksnipe seasons occurred during the winter months. Teal duck, rail and gallinule seasons occurred in the fall. Mourning dove seasons occurred intermittently during the fall and winter months. **MUSEUMS** Dublin: Lyon Museum. Stephenville: Stephenville Historical House Museum. **COLLEGIATE FINE ARTS** Stephenville: Cultural events offered by Tarleton State University. **SPECIAL EVENTS** Junior Stock Show, Stephenville, March; St. Patrick's Day Celebration, Dublin, March.

COUNTIES

ERATH (continued)

COMMUNITIES

COUNTY SEAT Stephenville, County Courthouse, 76401; County Clerk's Office, 817/965-3219. **INCORPORATED COMMUNITIES** (1980 population and ZIP Code) Dublin (2,723) 76446 and Stephenville (11,881) 76401. **UNINCORPORATED COMMUNITIES** (and ZIP Code) Alexander 76446, Bluff Dale 76433, Bunyan 76446, Chalk Mountain 76401, Clairette 76447, Duffau 76447, Edna Hill 76446, Hannibal 76401, Harbin 76446, Highland 76446, Huckabay 76401, Johnsville 76457, Lingleville 76461, Morgan Mill 76465, Oak Dale 76401, Patilo (Patillo) 76462, Purves 76446, Selden 76401, Smith Springs 76401, Thurber 76463 and Welcome Valley 76401. **FOR ADDITIONAL LOCAL INFORMATION** Dublin Chamber of Commerce, 213 E. Blackjack, Dublin, 76446, 817/445-3422 and Stephenville Chamber of Commerce, 161 S. Loop, P.O. Box 306, Stephenville, 76401, 817/965-5313 or 965-5323.

FALLS (C9)

THE LAND

South of Waco on Interstate Highway 35 in the Blackland Prairies Region, Falls County covers 770 square miles with an elevation range of 350 to 550 feet. Mineral waters are found in the county. The soils are undulating and slightly acidic with loamy surface layers and cracking, clayey subsoils or cracking clay throughout. Along the Brazos River are clayey and loamy deposits with a high shrink-swell potential. In the Blackland Prairies vegetation area, there are a variety of trees such as elms, oaks, mesquite, Bois d'arc and pecans along streams and grasses such as buffalograss and Texas grama. Between 41 and 50 % of the land in the county is considered prime farmland. **CLIMATE** Subtropical humid and generally mild. The average annual temperature is 65°F. Temperatures in January range from an average low of 37° to an average high of 59°F and in July range from 73° to 97°F. The average annual precipitation is 36 inches, with an average relative humidity of 82% at 6 A.M. and 53% at 6 P.M. The average annual snowfall is one inch or less. The growing season averages 257 days per year, with the last freeze near mid March and the first freeze in late November. The sun shines during the year on the average 66% of the daylight hours.

THE PEOPLE

Falls County ranks 60th among U.S. counties in highest percent of population 65 and over and has a high percent of native Texans. The 1982 estimated population of 18,200 indicates a continuation of the growth rate begun in the 1970s which reversed the steady population decrease between 1930 and 1970. Almost 12% of the growth between 1970 and 1980 was in urban areas. The age group with the largest gains was ages 20 to 34. Therefore the median age lowered from 41 in 1970 to 39 in 1980. The county's population is older than average and has a high death rate. The largest ancestry groups are Black (27%), persons of German descent (21%), English descent (16%) and Irish descent (16%). **REGISTERED VOTERS** As of November 2, 1982 there were 9,505 registered voters (0.1% of the state total). The 1982 general election had a 45% voter turnout, compared to a 63% turnout in the 1980 general election. In the 1982 primary 99% voted Democratic and 1% Republican, with 2,999 votes cast.

THE ECONOMY

AGRICULTURE Cattle area. In 1982, 84% of the land was in farms and ranches, with 49% of the farmland under cultivation and 3% irrigated. Falls ranked 101st in the state in highest agricultural receipts, with 63% from livestock and livestock products. Overgrazing, undesirable brush and weeds, water erosion and flooding are the current conservation problems. Primary crops: oats, wheat, sorghum, hay, cotton and corn. Primary vegetables: sweet corn, potatoes, sweet potatoes, tomatoes and watermelons. Primary fruits and nuts: peaches and pecans. Primary livestock and products: eighth in the state for cattle. Hogs. **BUSINESS** Total number of business establishments in the county: 280. Retail sales during the first quarter of 1984 increased 23%. In 1980, 14% of the labor force were self-employed, 24% were employed in professional or related services, 17% in manufacturing, 21% in wholesale and retail trade, 12% in agriculture, forestry, fisheries and mining, 23% were employed in other counties and there were 2,337 retired workers. The industries with the most employment: agribusiness and the manufacture of carpets and business forms. The nonfarm earnings in 1981 totaled $128,057,000. The retired workers received an average monthly Social Security payment of $264. **FINANCE** On June 30, 1983, six commercial banks had total deposits of $130,972,000 and total assets of $144,551,000. On December 31, 1982 one state savings and loan association and one state branch had assets of $167,101,669. In addition there is one credit union in the county. **HOUSING** Average value of homes in 1980: $17,600. Permits for new, privately owned housing units increased in 1982: 14 permits were issued with a total construction cost of $431,900. Of those permits, all were for single family houses. Between 1970 and 1980 the number of housing units increased by 15%. Sixty-one percent of all units in the county are air-conditioned, 87% are heated by gas and 9% by electricity. **NATURAL RESOURCES** Limestone, sand, gravel, oil and gas. In 1982 a total of 90,906 thousand cubic feet of gas well gas, 198 barrels of condensate, 9,859 barrels of crude oil and 820 thousand cubic feet of casinghead gas were produced. Current production of other minerals and products includes crushed limestone. **TOURISM** Travel expenditures of $2,680,000 in 1982 (an increase of 13% over 1981) generated 57 jobs and $495,000 in payroll. **ALCOHOLIC BEVERAGES** Packaged distilled spirits, beer, ale, malt liquor and wine are legal in parts of the county. Sale of mixed beverages is legal in all or parts of the county. **FEDERAL EXPENDITURES** The federal government had direct expenditures or obligations of $44,935,000 in the county during fiscal year 1983, including $1,075,000 by the U.S. Department of Defense. In addition, the federal government provided $329,000 in grant awards, paid $8,288,000 in salaries and wages, made direct payments to individuals of $34,988,000 including $24,045,000 in retirement and disability payments, awarded $384,000 in procurement contracts and spent $946,000 in other expenditures or obligations. The federal government also provided $778,000 in direct loans and $23,274,000 in guaranteed loans and insurance.

COMMUNICATION

Newspapers–Daily: Marlin Daily Democrat, ave. eve. circ. 3,223. Weekly: Marlin Weekly Democrat and The Rosebud News. Radio: KLMT-FM (Marlin). Cable TV. Telephone companies: Continental Telephone, Southwestern Bell, United Telephone and Central Telephone-Midstate. **TRANSPORTATION** Total public road mileage: 1,179. In 1982 there were 17,444 registered vehicles and 294 reported traffic accidents including six fatalities. Taxi cabs: two companies in Marlin. Intercity bus service is available. Motor freight: three carriers. Rail: four main and one branch line carry freight through the county. Two of the main lines carry annually over 30 million tons of freight each and two carry 10 to 20 million each. Aircraft: 10 are registered in the county. Airports: Marlin Municipal Airport is a basic utility airport providing general aviation service. It serves as a base for 10 aircraft.

COMMUNITY SERVICES

EDUCATION Four school districts with six elementary, three middle and three high schools. The average daily attendance in 1981-82 was 2,893, with expenditures per pupil of $2,128 including 203 classroom teachers with an average annual salary of $14,959. Forty-two percent of the 211 high school graduates planned to attend college. In 1982-83, 44% of the students were White, 14% Hispanic, 42% Black, 0.4% Asian and 0.1% American Indian. Private schools: one elementary school. Vocational education: Marlin School of Vocational Nursing (Marlin). **PUBLIC LIBRARIES** Marlin Public Library: 11,376 volumes. D. Brown Memorial Library (Rosebud): 12,500 volumes. **CHILD CARE** 12 day care and five twenty-four hour care licensed facilities. **HEALTH CARE** 17 physicians and five dentists. Hospitals: two with a combined capacity of 168. Specialized hospitals: one veterans medical center with capacity of 197. Ambulance services: two funeral homes and one commercial service. Mental health: one county clinic. Nursing homes: three nursing homes with a combined capacity of 361 nursing care residents. The average cost per day for private patients in 1982 was $27.75. **CHURCHES** 53 churches have an estimated combined membership of 11,901. The largest denominations are Southern Baptist, United Methodist and Catholic. **SOCIAL SERVICES** In fiscal year 1983 a total of $1,146,682 in food stamps was distributed, with an average of 2,446 persons receiving food stamps each month. Aid to Families with Dependent Children (AFDC) totaled $310,620 with an average of 208 families receiving AFDC each month. Medical assistance benefits for the aged and disabled of $2,684,583 and for families and children of $369,337 brought the county benefit total to $4,511,222. **FIRE PROTECTION** One partly paid and seven volunteer fire departments. **LAW ENFORCEMENT** The County Sheriff has 13 commissioned officers. Three police departments have a combined force of 19. **CRIME** 36 violent crimes (murder, forcible rape, robbery and aggravated assault) and 272 nonviolent crimes (burglary, larceny-theft and motor vehicle theft) were reported in 1982. **JUDICIAL SYSTEM** One District Court and Judge, one County Court and Judge and four Justices of the Peace. In the District Court a total of 745 cases were pending on 1/1/82, 742 new cases were filed and 571 cases were disposed of during the year leaving 916 cases pending on 12/31/82. There were 710 criminal cases on the docket, 118 convictions, 13 persons committed to prison and five committed to jail and 419 cases left pending. **JAILS** One jail, capacity 16. **ATTORNEYS AT LAW** 14. **UTILITIES** 89% of the residents are connected to a public or privately owned water system and 59% are connected to a public sewer system. Natural gas is distributed to the county by Lone Star Gas Co., Division of Enserch. The average annual residential bill for natural gas in 1982 for the Lone Star distribution system was $405.91, an increase of 35% over 1981. Electricity is distributed to the county by Southwest Electric Service, Texas Power and Light Co., Limestone Co. Electric Coop., Inc., McLennan Co. Electric Coop., Inc. and Robertson Electric Coop., Inc. and is generated primarily by gas, oil, coal and water. The typical residential electric bill is $155.87 per month for an all-electric house using 2,500 kwh. **TAXES** The county has 10 units with taxing authority: five school districts, three cities, one county and one special district.

RECREATION/ENTERTAINMENT

COUNTY/MUNICIPAL PARKS 717 acres in one county and eight municipal parks. These parks contain six playgrounds, one baseball and softball field, six tennis courts, one swimming pool and two boat ramps. Developed campsites: nine. **SCENIC DRIVES** The Texas Brazos Trail runs through this county. This trail moves through a beautiful and historic section of Central Texas revealing forested landscapes filled with wildlife and wildflowers. **BOATING/FISHING** Lakes/reservoirs: Cow Bayou Soil Conservation Service Lakes 7, 15, 16 and 30 (127 acres), New Marlin (197 acres), Old Marlin (77 acres), Rosebud (20 acres) and Spring (32 acres). Major rivers: Brazos. Primary streams: Cow Bayou, Long, Lavalla, Big Sandy, Pond and Poole. **HUNTING** Fall and winter seasons on deer. No closed seasons on nutria, coyote, bobcat and squirrel. Winter seasons on quail, muskrat, beaver, otter, opossum, mink, ring-tailed cat, badger, fox, raccoon, skunk and civet cat. Special regulations regarding hunting on state-owned lands. In 1983 duck, coot, geese, woodcock and jacksnipe seasons occurred during the winter months. Teal duck, rail and gallinule seasons occurred in the fall. Mourning dove seasons occurred intermittently during the fall and winter months. **MUSEUMS** Marlin: Highlands Mansion. **SPECIAL EVENTS** Festival Days, Marlin, April/May.

COMMUNITIES

COUNTY SEAT Marlin, County Courthouse, 76661; County Clerk's Office, 817/883-2061. **INCORPORATED COMMUNITIES** (1980 population and ZIP Code) Bruceville-Eddy (1,038: nine in Falls Co. and 1,029 in McLennan Co.) 76630, Golinda (335: 292 in Falls Co. and 43 in McLennan Co.) 76655, Lott (865) 76656, Marlin (7,099) 76661 and Rosebud (2,076) 76570. **UNINCORPORATED COMMUNITIES** (and ZIP Code) Alto Springs 76653, Barclay 76656, Blevins 76524, Blue Ridge 76680, Cedar Springs 76570, Cego 76524, Chilton 76632, Cottonwood 76655, Denny 76653, Dot 76524, Durango 76656, Eloise 76680, Goodville (Tomlinson Hill) 76656, Highbank 76644, McClanahan 76661, Mooresville (Mooreville) 76632, North Prairie 76632, Otto 76675, Perry 76677, Pleasant Grove 76570, Reagan 76680, Rocky Hill 76661, Rosedale 76680, Saint Paul 76661, Satin 76685, Stranger 76653, Sunrise 76661, Terrys Chapel (Terry Chapel) 76570, Travis 76656, Westphalia 76656, Wilderville 76570 and Zipperlenville (Zipperlandville) 76570. **FOR ADDITIONAL LOCAL INFORMATION** Marlin Chamber of Commerce, 245 Coleman St., P.O. Box 369, Marlin, 76661, 817/883-2171 and Rosebud Chamber of Commerce, P.O. Box 369, Rosebud, 76570, 817/583-7979.

FANNIN (M4)

THE LAND

Bordering Oklahoma northeast of Dallas on U.S. Highway 82 in the Blackland Prairies Region, Fannin County covers 895 square miles with an elevation range of 500 to 700 feet. Along the Red River the soils are loamy with clayey or loamy subsoils. Southeast of the river, the soils become sandy with loamy subsoils. The center of the county has cracking, clayey soils or loam over cracking clay. In the southern half the soils are slightly acidic with some loamy surface layers over cracking clay. The vegetation is the prairie grasses of the Blackland Prairies with abundant trees along streams. Between 41 and 50% of the land in the county is considered prime farmland. **CLIMATE** Mild and moist with wide-ranging seasonal changes. The average annual temperature is 64°F. Temperatures in January range from an average low of 31° to an average high of 53°F and in July range from 72° to 95°F. The average annual precipitation is 42 inches, with an average relative humidity of 82% at 6 A.M. and 54% at 6 P.M. The average annual snowfall is three inches. The growing season averages 230 days per year, with the last freeze in late March and the first freeze in mid November. The sun shines during the year on the average 67% of the daylight hours.

THE PEOPLE

The 1982 estimated population of 24,100 indicates a slight decrease in population since 1980, following a moderate growth which began in the 1970s. Almost 13% of the growth between 1970 and 1980 was in rural areas. The age group with the largest gains was ages 20 to 34. Therefore the median age lowered from

COUNTIES

FANNIN (continued)

42 in 1970 to 40 in 1980. However, the county's population remained older than average. The largest ancestry groups are persons of English descent (27%), Irish descent (22%) and German descent (11%). **REGISTERED VOTERS** As of November 2, 1982 there were 13,564 registered voters (0.2% of the state total). The 1982 general election had a 54% voter turnout, compared to a 63% turnout in the 1980 general election. In the 1982 primary 97% voted Democratic and 3% Republican, with 5,602 votes cast.

THE ECONOMY

AGRICULTURE Wheat and cattle area. In 1982, 79% of the land was in farms and ranches, with 62% of the farmland under cultivation and 5% irrigated. Fannin ranked 70th in the state in highest agricultural receipts, with 62% from livestock and livestock products. Water erosion, cultivation of marginal lands and flooding are the current conservation problems. Primary crops: ninth in the state for peanuts. Wheat, hay, sorghum and soybeans. Primary vegetables: sweet potatoes, tomatoes and watermelons. Primary fruits and nuts: peaches and pecans. Primary livestock and products: cattle, milk and hogs. **BUSINESS** Total number of business establishments in the county: 410. Retail sales during the first quarter of 1984 increased 10%. In 1980, 13% of the labor force were self-employed, 18% were employed in professional or related services, 29% in manufacturing, 17% in wholesale and retail trade, 8% in construction, 26% were employed in other counties and there were 3,524 retired workers. The industries with the most employment: agribusiness and the manufacture of women's apparel, mobile homes, agricultural chemicals, insulated wire and refrigeration machinery. The nonfarm earnings in 1981 totaled $182,635,000. The retired workers received an average monthly Social Security payment of $274. **FINANCE** On June 30, 1983, seven commercial banks had total deposits of $155,163,000 and total assets of $179,263,000. On December 31, 1982 one state savings and loan association and one state branch had assets of $43,804,563. In addition there are three credit unions in the county. **HOUSING** Average value of homes in 1980: $18,900. Permits for new, privately owned housing units decreased in 1982: 26 permits were issued with a total construction cost of $899,422. Of those permits, 18 were for single family houses. Between 1970 and 1980 the number of housing units increased by 13%. Sixty-nine percent of all units in the county are air-conditioned, 76% are heated by gas and 16% by electricity. **NATURAL RESOURCES** Limestone, oil and gas. **TOURISM** Travel expenditures of $1,728,000 in 1982 (an increase of 14% over 1981) generated 23 jobs and $239,000 in payroll. **ALCOHOLIC BEVERAGES** Packaged distilled spirits, beer, ale, malt liquor and wine are legal in parts of the county. **FEDERAL EXPENDITURES** The federal government had direct expenditures or obligations of $71,189,000 in the county during fiscal year 1983, including $3,141,000 by the U.S. Department of Defense. In addition, the federal government provided $2,184,000 in grant awards, paid $9,221,000 in salaries and wages, made direct payments to individuals of $49,746,000 including $34,774,000 in retirement and disability payments, awarded $3,952,000 in procurement contracts and spent $6,087,000 in other expenditures or obligations. The federal government also provided $6,557,000 in direct loans and $26,381,000 in guaranteed loans and insurance.

COMMUNICATION

Newspapers–Daily: Favorite (Bonham), ave. eve. circ. 3,808. Weekly: Bonham Herald, Signal Citizen (Honey Grove), Ladonia News, the Leonard Graphic, Trenton Tribune and the Whitewright Sun. Radio: KFYN-AM and KFYZ-FM (Bonham). Cable TV. Telephone companies: Continental Telephone, General Telephone and Southwestern Bell. **TRANSPORTATION** Total public road mileage: 1,510. In 1982 there were 21,474 registered vehicles and 415 reported traffic accidents including three fatalities. Taxi cabs: one company in Bonham. Intercity bus service is available. Motor freight: two carriers. Rail: three branch lines carry freight through the county with one carrying annually one to five million tons and two carrying less than one million each. Aircraft: 41 are registered in the county. Airports: Jones Field at Bonham is a basic utility airport providing general aviation service. It serves as a base for 27 aircraft.

COMMUNITY SERVICES

EDUCATION Nine school districts with 10 elementary, two middle and nine high schools. The average daily attendance in 1981-82 was 3,896, with expenditures per pupil of $2,202 including 271 classroom teachers with an average annual salary of $15,215. Fifty-four percent of the 285 high school graduates planned to attend college. In 1982-83, 90% of the students were White, 1% Hispanic, 9% Black, 0.2% Asian and 0.1% American Indian. **PUBLIC LIBRARIES** Bonham Public Library: 21,944 volumes. Honey Grove Memorial Library: 12,000 volumes. **CHILD CARE** 20 day care and 10 twenty-four hour care licensed facilities. **HEALTH CARE** 22 physicians and eight dentists. Hospitals: one with a capacity of 65. Specialized hospitals: veterans medical center with capacity of 403. Ambulance services: one volunteer service, one commercial, one city, one funeral home and one volunteer fire department service. Mental health: one clinic. Nursing homes: seven nursing homes with a combined capacity of 635 nursing care residents. The average cost per day for private patients in 1982 was $28.86. **CHURCHES** 117 churches have an estimated combined membership of 17,586. The largest denominations are Southern Baptist, United Methodist and Churches of Christ. **SOCIAL SERVICES** In fiscal year 1983 a total of $954,632 in food stamps was distributed, with an average of 2,236 persons receiving food stamps each month. Aid to Families with Dependent Children (AFDC) totaled $209,326 with an average of 150 families receiving AFDC each month. Medical assistance benefits for the aged and disabled of $4,507,426 and for families and children of $318,557 brought the county benefit total to $5,989,940. **FIRE PROTECTION** 11 volunteer fire departments. **LAW ENFORCEMENT** The County Sheriff has 21 commissioned officers. Seven police departments have a combined force of 28. Bonham Park Police have two officers. **CRIME** 30 violent crimes (murder, forcible rape, robbery and aggravated assault) and 324 nonviolent crimes (burglary, larceny-theft and motor vehicle theft) were reported in 1982. **JUDICIAL SYSTEM** One District Court and Judge, one County Court and Judge and four Justices of the Peace. In the District Court a total of 747 cases were pending on 1/1/82, 1,284 new cases were filed and 842 cases were disposed of during the year leaving 1,189 cases pending on 12/31/82. There were 159 criminal cases on the docket, 40 convictions, 19 persons committed to prison, and 71 cases left pending. In the County Court 389 cases were pending on 1/1/82, 685 new cases were filed and 667 cases were disposed of during the year leaving 407 cases pending on 12/31/82. There were 970 criminal cases on the docket, 208 convictions, 205 persons committed to jail, and 310 cases left pending. **JAILS** One jail, capacity 30. **ATTORNEYS AT LAW** 16. **UTILITIES** 84% of the residents are connected to a public or privately owned water system and 60% are connected to a public sewer system. Natural gas is distributed to the county by Lone Star Gas Co., Division of Enserch. The average annual residential bill for natural gas in 1982 for the Lone Star distribution system was $405.91, an increase of 35% over 1981. Electricity is distributed to the county by Texas Power and Light Co., Hunt-Collin Electric Coop., Inc., Lamar Co. Electric Coop., Inc., Texas-New Mexico Power Co. and Fannin Co. Electric Coop. and is generated primarily by gas and coal. The typical residential electric bill is $165.24 per month for an all-electric house using 2,500 kwh. **TAXES** The county has 22 units with taxing authority: 10 school districts, nine cities, one county and two special districts.

RECREATION/ENTERTAINMENT
NATIONAL REGISTER OF HISTORIC PLACES Bonham: Nunn House, Clendenen-Carlton House, Haden House, Ladonia-Haden House and Sam Rayburn House (National Historic Landmark). **STATE** Bonham State Recreation Area covers 261 acres with camping and trailer sites as well as areas offering fishing, swimming, golf and rental boats. **MUNICIPAL PARKS** 1,474 acres in 10 municipal parks. These parks contain two miles of hiking trails, seven playgrounds, one golf course, six baseball and softball fields, five tennis courts, one beach, two boat ramps and shore fishing facilities. Developed campsites: 60. **SCENIC DRIVES** The Texas Lakes Trail runs through this county. This trail introduces some 30 blue-water recreational areas in a variety of settings in North-Central Texas. **BOATING/FISHING** Lakes/reservoirs: Bonham (1,020 acres), Bonham State Park (41 acres), Caney Creek Soil Conservation Service Lakes 15 and 7 (72 acres), Canoe (25 acres), Coffee Mill (650 acres), Crockett (232 acres), Fannin (28 acres), Honey Grove City (35 acres), Pilot Grove Soil Conservation Service Lakes 38, 39 and 40 (43 acres), Quail Haven (38 acres), Tx. No Name No. 32 (28 acres), Valley (1,080 acres) and Williams Lake (29 acres). Major rivers: Red and Sulphur. Primary streams: Timber, Bois D'Arc, Little Caney, Post Oak, Coffee Mill, Sandy, Honey Grove, Dog, Indian, Bailey, Spoonamore, Freeman, Brushy and Pickle. **HUNTING** Fall and winter seasons on deer. Spring, fall and winter seasons on squirrel. No closed seasons on coyote, bobcat and nutria. Winter seasons on quail, muskrat, beaver, opossum, otter, ring-tailed cat, badger, fox, weasel, raccoon, skunk and civet cat. In 1983 duck, coot, geese, woodcock and jacksnipe seasons occurred during the winter months. Teal duck, rail and gallinule seasons occurred in the fall. Mourning dove seasons occurred intermittently during the fall and winter months. **MUSEUMS** Bonham: Fannin County Museum, Fort Inglish and Sam Rayburn Library. Honey Grove: Richard F. Voyer Museum. **SPECIAL EVENTS** Kueckelhan Rodeo, Bonham, July; Annual Picnic, Parade, Barbecue, Leonard, July; Creative Arts Fair, Bonham, October; County Fair, Bonham, October.

COMMUNITIES
COUNTY SEAT Bonham, County Courthouse, 75418; County Clerk's Office, 214/583-3711. **INCORPORATED COMMUNITIES** (1980 population and ZIP Code) Bailey (185) 75413, Bonham (7,338) 75418, Dodd City (286) 75438, Ector (573) 75439, Honey Grove (1,973) 75446, Ladonia (761) 75449, Leonard (1,421) 75452, Pecan Gap (250: 16 in Fannin Co. and 234 in Delta Co.) 75469, Ravenna (186, est. incorp. inactive) 75476, Savoy (855) 75479, Trenton (691) 75490, Whitewright (1,760: 9 in Fannin Co. and 1,751 in Grayson Co.) 75491 and Windom (276) 75492. **UNINCORPORATED COMMUNITIES** (and ZIP Code) Allens Chapel 75492, Allens Point 75446, Bagby 75446, Bartley-Woods 75492, Boyd 75418, Bug Tussle 75449, Carson 75488, Cotton Center 75418, Dial 75407, Duplex 75447, Edhube 75418, Elwood 75488, Ely 75439, Gober 75443, Hail (Hale) 75492, Ivanhoe 75447, Lamasco 75488, Lannius 75438, Midway 75418, Monkstown 75488, Moore's Chapel 75418, Mulberry 75476, Nobility 75452, Orangeville 75491, Randolph 75475, Ridings 75476, Riverby 75488, Sash 75446, Selfs 75446, Sowells Bluff 75476, Taylorville 75452, Telephone 75488, Tulip 75447 and Valleycreek (Valley Creek) 75452. **FOR ADDITIONAL LOCAL INFORMATION** Bonham Chamber of Commerce, 510 N. Main, Bonham, 75418, 214/583-4811, Honey Grove Chamber of Commerce, 808 N. 11th Street, Honey Grove, 75446, 214/378-7237,

Ladonia Chamber of Commerce, P.O. Box 188, Ladonia, 75449, Leonard Chamber of Commerce, P.O. Box 157, Leonard, 75452, 214/587-2253 and Whitewright Chamber of Commerce, P.O. Box 189, Whitewright, 75491, 214/364-2115.

FAYETTE (G8)

THE LAND
Southeast of Austin on Interstate Highway 10 in the Blackland Prairies Region, Fayette County covers 950 square miles with an elevation range of 200 to 500 feet. Along the Colorado River the soils are clayey and loamy with a high shrink-swell potential. From the southeast to the southwest the alkaline, loamy to clayey soils vary from deep to shallow over chalk. From the northeast to the northwest the light colored, acidic soils have sandy surfaces and clayey subsoils. The vegetation is mixed with Post Oak Savannah areas and Blackland Prairies: tall grasses, mesquite trees, oaks and elms. Between 11 and 20% of the land in the county is considered prime farmland. **CLIMATE Subtropical humid and generally mild.** The average annual temperature is 69°F. Temperatures in January range from an average low of 41° to an average high of 62°F and in July range from 73° to 96°F. The average annual precipitation is 38 inches, with an average relative humidity of 87% at 6 A.M. and 60% at 6 P.M. The average annual snowfall is less than one inch. The growing season averages 277 days per year, with the last freeze in early March and the first freeze in early December. The sun shines during the year on the average 65% of the daylight hours.

THE PEOPLE
Fayette County ranks 45th among all U.S. counties in highest percent of population aged 65 and over and has a high percent of residents who are native Texans. The 1982 estimated population of 20,500 indicates a continuation of the moderate growth begun in the 1970s which reversed the steady population decrease from 1930 to 1970. Population in urban areas increased 22% between 1970 and 1980. The age group with the largest gain was ages 20 to 24. Therefore the median age lowered from 47 in 1970 to 42 in 1980. However the population is older than average. The largest ancestry groups are persons of German descent (44%), English descent (10%) and Black (9%). **REGISTERED VOTERS** As of November 2, 1982 there were 10,009 registered voters (0.2% of the state total). The 1982 general election had a 55% voter turnout, compared to a 77% turnout in the 1980 general election. In the 1982 primary 97% voted Democratic and 3% Republican, with 4,348 votes cast.

THE ECONOMY
AGRICULTURE Cattle area. In 1982, 84% of the land was in farms and ranches, with 15% of the farmland under cultivation and 3% irrigated. Fayette ranked 50th in the state in highest agricultural receipts, with 87% from livestock and livestock products. Overgrazing, undesirable brush and weeds, and water erosion are the current conservation problems. Primary crops: hay, corn, sorghum, oats and wheat. Primary vegetables: potatoes, sweet potatoes, tomatoes and watermelons. Primary fruits and nuts: peaches and pecans. Primary livestock and products: second in the state for hogs and third for both hens and pullets and egg production. Cattle and milk. **BUSINESS** Total number of business establishments in the county: 600. Retail sales during the first quarter of 1984 increased 2%. In 1980, 18% of the labor force were self-employed, 12% were employed in professional or related services, 13% in manufacturing, 25% in wholesale and retail trade, 18% in agriculture, forestry, fisheries and mining, 16% were employed in other counties and there were 2,968 retired workers. The industries with the most employment:

COUNTIES

FAYETTE (continued)

agribusiness, oil and gas extraction and the manufacture of structural metal products, toys and games and measuring and controlling instruments. The nonfarm earnings in 1981 totaled $190,366,000. The retired workers received an average monthly Social Security payment of $260. **FINANCE** On June 30, 1983, eight commercial banks had total deposits of $208,092,000 and total assets of $232,475,000. On December 31, 1982 one state savings and loan association, one federal association branch and two state branches and had assets of $26,272,543. In addition there is one credit union in the county. **HOUSING** Average value of homes in 1980: $30,600. Permits for new, privately owned housing units decreased in 1982: 33 permits were issued with a total construction cost of $1,930,201. Of those permits, all were for single family houses. Between 1970 and 1980 the number of housing units increased by 20%. Fifty-eight percent of all units in the county are air-conditioned, 67% are heated by gas and 19% by electricity. **NATURAL RESOURCES** Clay, sand, gravel, oil, gas and lignite coal. In 1982 a total of 17,872,078 thousand cubic feet of gas well gas, 687,210 barrels of condensate, 6,561,622 barrels of crude oil and 12,824,908 thousand cubic feet of casinghead gas were produced. Current production of other minerals and products includes bentonite clay, clay, sand and gravel. **TOURISM** Travel expenditures of $8,561,000 in 1982 (an increase of 12% over 1981) generated 200 jobs and $1,639,000 in payroll. Lodging: nine hotels, motels and tourist courts. Convention/meeting facilities: La Grange-Fayette Country Fair Grandstand and Arena. **ALCOHOLIC BEVERAGES** Packaged distilled spirits, beer, ale, malt liquor and wine are legal in parts of the county. Sale of mixed beverages is legal in all or parts of the county. **FEDERAL EXPENDITURES** The federal government had direct expenditures or obligations of $41,502,000 in the county during fiscal year 1983, including $1,115,000 by the U.S. Department of Defense. In addition, the federal government provided $326,000 in grant awards, paid $1,715,000 in salaries and wages, made direct payments to individuals of $38,426,000 including $24,911,000 in retirement and disability payments, awarded $576,000 in procurement contracts and spent $459,000 in other expenditures or obligations. The federal government also provided $4,534,000 in direct loans and $1,550,000 in guaranteed loans and insurance.

COMMUNICATION

Newspapers–Weekly: The Flatonia Argus, The Fayette County Record (La Grange), La Grange Journal, and The Schulenburg Sticker. Radio: KVLG-AM, KMUZ-FM (La Grange). Cable TV. Telephone companies: General Telephone, Southwestern Bell, Colorado Valley Telephone Coop., Guadalupe Valley Telephone Coop. and Industry Telephone. **TRANSPORTATION** Total public road mileage: 1,309. In 1982 there were 20,944 registered vehicles and 579 reported traffic accidents including 20 fatalities. Intercity bus service is available. Motor freight: six local and intrastate carriers. Rail: The Sunset Limited provides passenger service on the Amtrak Route. Four main and one branch line carry freight through the county. Two of the main lines carry annually over 30 million tons of freight each and two carry 20 to 30 each. The one branch line carries annually five to 10 million tons of freight. Aircraft: 21 are registered in the county. Airports: Guenther Field at La Grange is a basic utility airport providing general aviation service and serves as a base for 10 aircraft. Also serving this area are Flatonia Municipal Airport, Rocky Creek Ranch at La Grange, Bakers Acres Ranch at Warrenton, Cherry Spraying Services Airport at Muldoon, LaPaisano Airport at Round Top and Marty Ranch Airport at Schulenberg.

COMMUNITY SERVICES

EDUCATION Five school districts with five elementary, one middle and five high schools. The average daily attendance in 1981-82 was 2,892, with expenditures per pupil of $2,501 including 175 classroom teachers with an average annual salary of $15,493. Forty percent of the 239 high school graduates planned to attend college. In 1982-83, 77% of the students were White, 9% Hispanic, 14% Black and 0.2% Asian. Private schools: 321 students enrolled in two elementary and one high school. **PUBLIC LIBRARIES** Fayette Public Library (La Grange): 13,500 volumes. Schulenberg Public Library: 7,563 volumes. Warrenton Library. **CHILD CARE** 31 day care and three twenty-four hour care licensed facilities. **HEALTH CARE** 22 physicians and eight dentists. Hospitals: one with a capacity of 60. Ambulance services: one county service. Mental health: one county clinic. Nursing homes: three nursing homes with a combined capacity of 278 nursing care residents. The average cost per day for private patients in 1982 was $29.58. **CHURCHES** 56 churches have an estimated combined membership of 15,066. The largest denominations are Catholic, American Lutheran and Lutheran-Missouri Synod. **SOCIAL SERVICES** In fiscal year 1983 a total of $413,219 in food stamps was distributed, with an average of 1,025 persons receiving food stamps each month. Aid to Families with Dependent Children (AFDC) totaled $81,277 with an average of 59 families receiving AFDC each month. Medical assistance benefits for the aged and disabled of $2,422,012 and for families and children of $131,535 brought the county benefit total to $3,048,042. **FIRE PROTECTION** Nine volunteer fire departments. **LAW ENFORCEMENT** The County Sheriff has 15 commissioned officers. Six police departments have a combined force of 13. **CRIME** Nine violent crimes (murder, forcible rape, robbery and aggravated assault) and 102 nonviolent crimes (burglary, larceny-theft and motor vehicle theft) were reported in 1982. **JUDICIAL SYSTEM** One District Court and Judge, one County Court and Judge and four Justices of the Peace. In the District Court a total of 509 cases were pending on 1/1/82, 488 new cases were filed and 325 cases were disposed of during the year leaving 672 cases pending on 12/31/82. There were 125 criminal cases on the docket, 26 convictions, five persons committed to prison and two committed to jail and 87 cases left pending. In the County Court 424 cases were pending on 1/1/82, 633 new cases were filed and 566 cases were disposed of during the year leaving 491 cases pending on 12/31/82. There were 957 criminal cases on the docket, 373 convictions and 394 cases left pending. **JAILS** One jail, capacity 10. Planning a new jail, capacity 45. **ATTORNEYS AT LAW** 23. **UTILITIES** 49% of the residents are connected to a public or privately owned water system and 41% are connected to a public sewer system. Natural gas is distributed to the county by Entex, Inc. The average annual residential bill for natural gas in 1982 for the Entex distribution system was $390.31, an increase of 26% over 1981. Electricity is distributed to the city of Flatonia by the Flatonia Electric Dept., La Grange by La Grange Utilities, Schulenburg by the Schulenberg Utilities Dept. and to the rest of the county by Bluebonnet Electric Coop. Inc., and Fayette Electric Coop. Inc., and is generated primarily by oil, water and coal. The typical residential electric bill is $127.94 per month for an all-electric house using 2,500 kwh. **TAXES** The county has 14 units with taxing authority: six school districts, six cities, one county and one special district.

RECREATION/ENTERTAINMENT

NATIONAL REGISTER OF HISTORIC PLACES Dubina: Simon Pytlovany House. Flatonia vicinity: Buckner's Creek Bridge. La Grange: Fayette County Courthouse and Jail and St. James Episcopal Church. La Grange vicinity: Kreische House and Brewery, Mount Eliza and Winedale Inn Complex. Round

Top: Bethlehem Lutheran Church and Cummins Creek Bridge. Schulenburg: Mulberry Creek Bridge and Schulenburg Cotton Press. Warrenton: William Neese House. **STATE** Kreische Brewery State Historic Site covers 36 acres and is closed to the public as of July, 1983. Monument Hill State Historic Site covers four acres with a historic structure. The park is the final resting place of those who died following the Mier Expedition against Mexico and those who were massacred at Salado Creek. **MUNICIPAL PARKS** 124 acres in seven municipal parks. These parks contain one mile of hiking trails, five playgrounds, four baseball and softball fields, two tennis courts, one multi-use court, one swimming pool, one beach and one boat ramp. **SCENIC DRIVES** The Texas Independence Trail runs through this county. This trail not only surveys the historic sites of southeastern Texas but also includes many modern visitor attractions such as the Johnson Space Center. An additional scenic drive in Fayette County is F.M. 153 from U.S. 77 which traverses the Colorado River Valley. **BOATING/FISHING** Lakes/reservoirs: Baylor Creek (1,050 acres), Cedar Creek (1,750 acres), Cummins Creek Soil Conservation Service Lakes 4, 6, 7, 9, 10 and 15 (136 acres), Ellisor (28 acres) and No Name No. 53 (21 acres). Major rivers: Colorado. Primary streams: Baylor, Cedar, Mile, Flat, Shaw, Jacks, Barton and Ross. **HUNTING** Fall and winter seasons on deer. No closed seasons on nutria, coyote, bobcat and squirrel. Winter seasons on quail, muskrat, beaver, otter, opossum, mink, ring-tailed cat, badger, fox, weasel, raccoon, skunk and civet cat. In 1983 sandhill crane, duck, coot, geese, woodcock and jacksnipe seasons occurred during the winter months. Teal duck, rail and gallinule seasons occurred in the fall. Mourning dove seasons occurred intermittently during the fall and winter months. **MUSEUMS** La Grange: Fayette Heritage Museum and N.W. Faison Home and Museum. Round Top: University of Texas Winedale Museum and Henkel Square. **SPECIAL EVENTS** Special Concerts, Round Top, Monthly; Antique Fair, Round Top, March; Junior Livestock Show, La Grange, March; Spring Festival and Crafts Fair, Round Top, April; Trail Ride to Ellinger and Parade, Round Top, May; Bluegrass Festival, Round Top, May; Heritage Days, La Grange, May; Eeyore's Birthday at Winedale, Round Top, May; July 4th Celebration and Parade, Round Top, July; Festival Days, Schulenburg, August; Shakespeare at Winedale Festival, Round Top, August; Praha Annual Feast of St. Mary's Church, Praha, August; Fayette County Country Fair, La Grange, August/September; St. Rose of Lima Church Festival, Schulenburg, August; Octoberfest, Round Top, October; Czhilispiel, Flatonia, October; Christmas at Winedale, Round Top, December.

COMMUNITIES
COUNTY SEAT La Grange, County Courthouse, 78945; County Clerk's Office, 409/968-3251. **INCORPORATED COMMUNITIES** (1980 population and ZIP Code) Carmine (239) 78932, Fayetteville (356) 78940, Flatonia (1,070) 78941, La Grange (3,768) 78945, Round Top (87) 78954 and Schulenburg (2,469) 78956. **UNINCORPORATED COMMUNITIES** (and ZIP Code) Ammansville 78945, Cistern 78941, Colony 78941, Dubina 78956, Ellinger 78938, Elm Grove 78959, Engle 78956, Floy 78941, Freyburg 78956, Halsted 78945, High Hill 78956, Holman 78962, Hostyn 78945, Kirtley 78957, Ledbetter 78946, Lena 78963, Muldoon 78949, Mullins Prairie 78945, Nechanitz 78946, Oldenburg 78945, O'Quinn 78945, Park 78945, Plum 78952, Praha 78941, Rabbs Prairie 78945, Rek Hill 78940, Rutersville 78945, Stellar 78949, Swiss Alp 78956, Waldeck 78946, Walhalla 78954, Warda 78960, Warrenton 78961, West Point 78963, Willow Springs 78940, Winchester 78964 and Winedale 77835. **FOR ADDITIONAL LOCAL INFORMATION** Ellinger Chamber of Commerce, P.O. Box 37, Ellinger, 78938, 409/732-5233, Flatonia Chamber of Commerce, P.O. Box 651, Flatonia, 78941, 512/865-3920, La Grange Area Chamber of Commerce, 316 N. Jefferson, Suite One, La Grange, 78945, 409/968-5756 and Schulenburg Chamber of Commerce, P.O. Box 65, Schulenburg, 78956, 409/743-3023.

FISHER (P61)

THE LAND
West of Abilene on U.S. Highway 180 in the Rolling Plains Region, Fisher County covers 897 square miles with an elevation range of 1,800 to 2,400 feet. The county consists of level to undulating, red to brown, loamy to clayey soils. There is a high shrink-swell potential. Fisher lies in the Rolling Plains vegetation area with mid to short grasses, some mesquite trees and cacti. Between 51 and 60% of the land in the county is considered prime farmland. **CLIMATE** Subtropical Subhumid, mild and dry. High winds and dust may occur in spring. The average annual temperature is 63°F. Temperatures in January range from an average low of 28° to an average high of 56°F and in July range from 70° to 96°F. The average annual precipitation is 22 inches, with an average relative humidity of 73% at 6 A.M. and 40% at 6 P.M. The average annual snowfall is five inches. The growing season averages 222 days per year, with the last freeze in early April and the first freeze in early November. The sun shines during the year on the average 70% of the daylight hours.

THE PEOPLE
The 1982 estimated population of 5,900 indicates a continuation of the population decline which has existed since 1930. The majority of the residents live in rural areas. The age groups with the largest decreases between 1970 and 1980 were ages five to 14 and 50 to 59. Although the median age lowered from 39 in 1970 to 38 in 1980, the county population remains older than average. The largest ancestry groups are persons of English descent (27%), Irish descent (24%) and Hispanic (19%). **REGISTERED VOTERS** As of November 2, 1982 there were 3,787 registered voters (0.1% of the state total). The 1982 general election had a 50% voter turnout, compared to a 65% turnout in the 1980 general election. In the 1982 primary 100% voted Democratic, with 1,986 votes cast.

THE ECONOMY
AGRICULTURE Cotton area. In 1982, 94% of the land was in farms and ranches, with 27% of the farmland under cultivation and 2% irrigated. Fisher ranked 102nd in the state in highest agricultural receipts, with 73% from crops. Undesirable brush and weeds, water and wind erosion and salinity are the current conservation problems. Primary crops: cotton, wheat, sorghum, hay and oats. Primary vegetables: cantaloupes, tomatoes and watermelons. Primary fruits and nuts: peaches and pecans. Primary livestock and products: cattle, milk and hogs. **BUSINESS** Total number of business establishments in the county: 97. Retail sales during the first quarter of 1984 decreased 2%. In 1980, 23% of the labor force were self-employed, 18% were employed in professional or related services, 13% in manufacturing, 13% in wholesale and retail trade, 31% in agriculture, forestry, fisheries and mining, 23% were employed in other counties and there were 727 retired workers. The industries with the most employment: agribusiness, oil and gas extraction and the manufacture of gypsum products. The nonfarm earnings in 1981 totaled $45,908,000. The retired workers received an average monthly Social Security payment of $298. **FINANCE** On June 30, 1983, two commercial banks had total deposits of $39,422,000 and total assets of $43,956,000. There is one state savings and loan association branch in the county. **HOUSING** Average value

FISHER (continued)

of homes in 1980: $18,600. Between 1970 and 1980 the number of housing units decreased by 5%. Eighty percent of all units in the county are air-conditioned, 87% are heated by gas and 11% by electricity. **NATURAL RESOURCES** Caliche, gypsum, oil, gas, and bituminous coal. In 1982 a total of 433,037 thousand cubic feet of gas well gas, 3,025 barrels of condensate, 3,880,527 barrels of crude oil and 5,161,396 thousand cubic feet of casinghead gas were produced. Current production of other minerals and products includes clay, gypsum, sand and gravel. **TOURISM** Travel expenditures of $5,853,000 in 1982 (an increase of 17% over 1981) generated 93 jobs and $914,000 in payroll. **ALCOHOLIC BEVERAGES** Totally dry. **FEDERAL EXPENDITURES** The federal government had direct expenditures or obligations of $19,099,000 in the county during fiscal year 1983, including $136,000 by the U.S. Department of Defense. In addition, the federal government provided $275,000 in grant awards, paid $489,000 in salaries and wages, made direct payments to individuals of $9,810,000 including $6,569,000 in retirement and disability payments, awarded $2,000 in procurement contracts and spent $8,522,000 in other expenditures or obligations. The federal government also provided $3,544,000 in direct loans and $11,759,000 in guaranteed loans and insurance.

COMMUNICATION

Newspapers–Weekly: Advance Star Record (Rotan). Cable TV. Telephone companies: Continental Telephone, Southwestern Bell and Taylor Telephone. **TRANSPORTATION** Total public road mileage: 961. In 1982 there were 5,838 registered vehicles and 103 reported traffic accidents including five fatalities. Motor freight: one carrier. Rail: two main and one branch line carry freight through the county. One of the main lines carries annually 20 to 30 million tons of freight and the other one carries 10 to 20 million. The one branch carries annually less than one million tons of freight. Aircraft: 18 are registered in the county. Airports: Fisher County Airport between Roby and Rotan. Hamlin Municipal Airport.

COMMUNITY SERVICES

EDUCATION Four school districts with four elementary, one middle and three high schools. The average daily attendance in 1981-82 was 968, with expenditures per pupil of $2,785 including 65 classroom teachers with an average annual salary of $15,484. Seventy percent of the 77 high school graduates planned to attend college. In 1982-83, 55% of the students were White, 37% Hispanic, 8% Black, 0.1% Asian and 0.1% American Indian. **PUBLIC LIBRARIES** Rotan Public Library: 11,802 volumes. **CHILD CARE** Six day care and one twenty-four hour care licensed facilities. **HEALTH CARE** Five physicians and one dentist. Hospitals: one with a capacity of 30. Ambulance services: one county service. Nursing homes: three nursing homes with a combined capacity of 117 nursing care residents. The average cost per day for private patients in 1982 was $28.95. **CHURCHES** 23 churches have an estimated combined membership of 5,379. The largest denominations are Southern Baptist, Catholic and United Methodist. **SOCIAL SERVICES** In fiscal year 1983 a total of $257,256 in food stamps was distributed, with an average of 549 persons receiving food stamps each month. Aid to Families with Dependent Children (AFDC) totaled $33,752 with an average of 20 families receiving AFDC each month. Medical assistance benefits for the aged and disabled of $652,171 and for families and children of $47,903 brought the county benefit total to $991,082. **FIRE PROTECTION** Two volunteer fire departments. **LAW ENFORCEMENT** The County Sheriff has four commissioned officers. One police department has a force of four. **CRIME** 11 violent crimes (murder, forcible rape, robbery and aggravated assault) and 63 nonviolent crimes (burglary, larceny-theft and motor vehicle theft) were reported in 1982. **JUDICIAL SYSTEM** One District Court and Judge, one County Court and Judge and two Justices of the Peace. In the District Court a total of 174 cases were pending on 1/1/82, 135 new cases were filed and 123 cases were disposed of during the year leaving 186 cases pending on 12/31/82. There were 49 criminal cases on the docket, eight convictions, three persons committed to prison and 36 cases left pending. In the County Court 119 cases were pending on 1/1/82, 149 new cases were filed and 158 cases were disposed of during the year leaving 110 cases pending on 12/31/82. There were 237 criminal cases on the docket, 79 convictions, and 79 cases left pending. **JAILS** One jail, capacity 15. **ATTORNEYS AT LAW** Two. **UTILITIES** 92% of the residents are connected to a public or privately owned water system and 52% are connected to a public sewer system. Natural gas is distributed to the county by Lone Star Gas Co., division of Enserch. The average annual residential bill for natural gas in 1982 for the Lone Star distribution system was $405.91, an increase of 35% over 1981. Electricity is distributed to the county by West Texas Utilities, Lonewolf Electric Coop., Inc., Midwest Electric Coop., Inc., and Stamford Electric Coop., Inc. and is generated primarily by gas and oil. The typical residential electric bill is $134.05 per month for an all-electric house using 2,500 kwh. **TAXES** The county has nine units with taxing authority: four school districts, two cities, one county, one hospital district and one special district.

RECREATION/ENTERTAINMENT

MUNICIPAL PARKS 26 acres in two municipal parks. These parks contain two playgrounds, one golf course, two baseball and softball fields, two tennis courts and two swimming pools. **BOATING/FISHING** Lakes/reservoirs: Moore (113 acres), West Moore (30 acres) and Plasterco (30 acres). Major rivers: Double Mountain Fork Brazos, Brazos and Clear Fork. Primary streams: California and Rough. **HUNTING** Fall and winter seasons on deer and mule deer. No closed seasons on coyote, bobcat and squirrel. Winter seasons on quail, muskrat, beaver, opossum, ring-tailed cat, badger, fox, weasel, raccoon, skunk and civet cat. Fall, winter and spring seasons on turkey. In 1983 sandhill crane, duck, coot, geese, woodcock and jacksnipe seasons occurred during the winter months. Teal duck, rail and gallinule seasons occurred in the fall. Mourning dove seasons occurred intermittently during the fall and winter months.

COMMUNITIES

COUNTY SEAT Roby, County Courthouse, 79543; County Clerk's Office, 915/776-2401. **INCORPORATED COMMUNITIES** (1980 population and ZIP Code) Roby (814) 79543 and Rotan (2,284) 79546. **UNINCORPORATED COMMUNITIES** (and ZIP Code) Busby 79543, Claytonville 79556, Eskota 79561, Hobbs 79526, Longworth 79543, McCaulley 79534, Palava 79556, Royston 79543 and Sylvester 79560. **FOR ADDITIONAL LOCAL INFORMATION** Rotan Chamber of Commerce, 807 E. Lee, Rotan, 79546, 915/735-3145.

FLOYD (P31)

THE LAND

Northeast of Lubbock on U.S. Highway 70 in the High Plains Region, Floyd County covers 992 square miles with an elevation range of 2,600 to 3,300 feet. The northeast corner of the county has level to undulating soils that are mostly loamy throughout, with some clayey subsoils. The rest of the county has nearly level, alkaline soils with dark loamy surfaces and clayey subsoils. There is a high shrink-swell potential. Floyd is in the High Plains vegetation area with mid to tall grasses and mesquite trees. Between 71 and 80% of the land in the county is considered prime farmland. **CLIMATE** Subtropical subhumid, mild and dry. Temperatures vary and are subject to sudden changes. Significant dust and wind will occur during spring. The average annual temperature is 60°F. Temperatures in January range from an average low of 24° to an average high of 53°F and in July range from 67° to 94°F. The average annual precipitation is 19 inches, with an average relative humidity of 73% at 6 A.M. and 39% at 6 P.M. The average annual snowfall is 11 inches. The growing season averages 213 days per year, with the last freeze in early April and the first freeze in early November. The sun shines during the year on the average 75% of the daylight hours.

THE PEOPLE

The 1982 estimated population of 9,500 indicates a slight decrease since 1980. The population declined 11% between 1970 and 1980. The greatest losses occurred in the rural areas which decreased 19% from 1970 to 1980. The age groups with the largest decrease was ages five to 14. Therefore the median age rose from 29 in 1970 to 30 in 1980. The largest ancestry groups are Hispanic (34%), persons of English descent (23%), and Irish descent (19%). **REGISTERED VOTERS** As of November 2, 1982 there were 4,693 registered voters (0.1% of the state total). The 1982 general election had a 46% voter turnout, compared to a 74% turnout in the 1980 general election. In the 1982 primary 95% voted Democratic and 5% Republican, with 1,102 votes cast.

THE ECONOMY

AGRICULTURE Cotton and wheat area. In 1982, 98% of the land was in farms and ranches, with 70% of the farmland under cultivation and 59% irrigated. Floyd ranked 21st in the state in highest agricultural receipts, with 75% from crops. Water and wind erosion, decreasing irrigation water supplies and noxious weeds are the current conservation problems. Primary crops: second in state for soybeans and first for sunflowers. Cotton, wheat, sorghum and corn. Primary vegetables: third in state for onions and seventh for total fresh market vegetables. Bell peppers and cucumbers. Primary fruits and nuts: pecans. Primary livestock and products: cattle, milk and hogs. **BUSINESS** Total number of business establishments in the county: 189. Retail sales during the first quarter of 1984 increased 3%. In 1980, 24% of the labor force were self-employed, 19% were employed in professional or related services, 6% in manufacturing, 19% in wholesale and retail trade, 34% in agriculture, forestry, fisheries and mining, 9% were employed in other counties and there were 894 retired workers. The industries with the most employment: agribusiness and the manufacture of farm equipment and machinery. The nonfarm earnings in 1981 totaled $68,652,000. The retired workers received an average monthly Social Security payment of $324. **FINANCE** On June 30, 1983, two commercial banks had total deposits of $64,504,000 and total assets of $74,844,000. There is one state savings and loan association branch and one credit union in the county. **HOUSING** Average value of homes in 1980: $20,200. In 1982 two permits were issued for new, single family houses. Between 1970 and 1980 the number of housing units decreased by 6%. Seventy-two percent of all units in the county are air-conditioned, 92% are heated by gas and 8% by electricity. **NATURAL RESOURCES** Caliche, oil and gas. In 1982, 2,192 barrels of crude oil and 610 thousand cubic feet of casinghead gas were produced. Current production of other minerals and products includes crushed limestone. **TOURISM** Travel expenditures of $6,279,000 in 1982 (an increase of 18% over 1981) generated 86 jobs and $918,000 in payroll. **ALCOHOLIC BEVERAGES** Totally dry. **FEDERAL EXPENDITURES** The federal government had direct expenditures or obligations of $37,042,000 in the county during fiscal year 1983, including $96,000 by the U.S. Department of Defense. In addition, the federal government provided $171,000 in grant awards, paid $752,000 in salaries and wages, made direct payments to individuals of $12,184,000 including $8,251,000 in retirement and disability payments, awarded $622,000 in procurement contracts and spent $23,313,000 in other expenditures or obligations. The federal government also provided $15,871,000 in direct loans and $47,195,000 in guaranteed loans and insurance.

COMMUNICATION

Newspapers–Weekly: Floyd County Hesperian (Floydada) and Lockney Beacon. Radio: KFBA-AM (Floydada). Cable TV. Telephone companies: General Telephone, Southwestern Bell, Cap Rock Telephone and Midplains Rural Telephone Coop. **TRANSPORTATION** Total public road mileage: 1,376. In 1982 there were 9,782 registered vehicles and 128 reported traffic accidents including one fatality. Motor freight: three carriers. Rail: five branch lines carry freight through the county. Three of the lines carry annually one to five million tons of freight each and two carry less than one million each. Aircraft: 27 are registered in the county. Airports: Floydada Municipal Airport is a basic utility airport providing general aviation service. It serves as a base for 24 aircraft.

COMMUNITY SERVICES

EDUCATION Four school districts with five elementary, two middle and two high schools. The average daily attendance in 1981-82 was 2,057, with expenditures per pupil of $2,494 including 151 classroom teachers with an average annual salary of $15,381. Twenty-two percent of the 127 high school graduates planned to attend college. In 1982-83, 41% of the students were White, 54% Hispanic, 5% Black and 0.3% Asian. **PUBLIC LIBRARIES** Floyd County Library (Floydada): 36,000 volumes, one branch. **CHILD CARE** Six day care and two twenty-four hour care licensed facilities. **HEALTH CARE** Seven physicians and two dentists. Hospitals: two with a combined capacity of 60. Ambulance services: one commercial and one city service. Mental health: one clinic. Nursing homes: two nursing homes with a combined capacity of 104 nursing care residents. The average cost per day for private patients in 1982 was $29.16. **CHURCHES** 28 churches have an estimated combined membership of 8,997. The largest denominations are Southern Baptist, Catholic and United Methodist. **SOCIAL SERVICES** In fiscal year 1983 a total of $821,692 in food stamps was distributed, with an average of 1,760 persons receiving food stamps each month. Aid to Families with Dependent Children (AFDC) totaled $112,399 with an average of 71 families receiving AFDC each month. Medical assistance benefits for the aged and disabled of $688,500 and for families and children of $135,017 brought the county benefit total to $1,757,607. **FIRE PROTECTION** Two volunteer fire departments. **LAW ENFORCEMENT** The County Sheriff has 10 commissioned officers. Two police departments have a combined force of 13. **CRIME** Five violent crimes (murder, forcible rape, robbery and aggravated assault) and 102 nonviolent crimes (burglary, larceny-theft and motor vehicle theft) were reported in 1982. **JUDICIAL SYSTEM** One District Court and Judge, one County Court and Judge and two Justices of the Peace. In the District Court a total of 305 cases were pending on 1/1/82, 202 new cases were filed and 220 cases were disposed of during the year leaving 287 cases pending on 12/31/82. There were 88 criminal cases on the docket, 25 convictions, six persons committed to prison and 52 cases left pending. In the County Court 211 cases were pending on 1/1/82, 196 new cases were filed and 137 cases were disposed of during the year leaving 270 cases pending on 12/31/82. There were 346 criminal cases on the docket, 124 convictions, and 220 cases left pending. **JAILS** One jail, capacity nine. **ATTORNEYS AT LAW** Six. **UTILITIES** 70%

FLOYD (continued)

of the residents are connected to a public or privately owned water system and 65% are connected to a public sewer system. Natural gas is distributed to the county by Energas Company. The average annual residential bill for natural gas in 1982 for the Energas distribution system was $371.63, an increase of 23% over 1981. Electricity is distributed to the city of Floydada by the Floydada Electric Dept. and to the rest of the county by Lighthouse Electric Coop., Inc., Texas Power and Light Co., and Southwestern Public Service and is generated primarily by gas and coal. The typical residential electric bill is $149 per month for an all-electric house using 2,500 kwh. **TAXES** The county has 11 units with taxing authority: four school districts, two cities, one county, two hospitals and two special districts.

RECREATION/ENTERTAINMENT

NATIONAL REGISTER OF HISTORIC PLACES Floydada vicinity: Floydada Country Club Site. **MUNICIPAL PARKS** 44 acres in five municipal parks. These parks contain four playgrounds, four baseball and softball fields, four tennis courts and two swimming pools. **SCENIC DRIVES** The Texas Plains Trail runs through this county. This trail spans a vast area of the High Plains region of Texas slicing through the southern-most extension of the Great Plains of the United States. The land is flat except where erosion has carved canyon landscapes. **BOATING/FISHING** Lakes/reservoirs: Cogdell (10 acres). Major rivers: White. Primary streams: Wilson and Quitaque. **HUNTING** Fall season on antelope. Fall and winter seasons on deer and mule deer. No closed season on coyote and bobcat. Winter season on auodad sheep, pheasant, quail, muskrat, beaver, opossum, ring-tailed cat, badger, fox, weasel, raccoon, skunk and civet cat. Summer, fall and winter seasons on squirrel. Fall, winter and spring seasons on turkey. In 1983 sandhill crane, duck, coot, geese, woodcock and jacksnipe seasons occurred during the winter months. Teal duck, rail and gallinule seasons occurred in the fall. Mourning dove seasons occurred intermittently during the fall and winter months. **MUSEUMS** Floydada: Floyd County Historical Museum. **SPECIAL EVENTS** Old Settlers Day Reunion, Floydada, May; Floyd County Fair, Lockney, Variable.

COMMUNITIES

COUNTY SEAT Floydada, County Courthouse, 79235; County Clerk's Office, 806/983-3236. **INCORPORATED COMMUNITIES** (1980 population and ZIP Code) Floydada (4,193) 79235 and Lockney (2,334) 79241. **UNINCORPORATED COMMUNITIES** (and ZIP Code) Aiken 79221, Barwise 79235, Cedar Hill (Alcino) 79241, Dougherty 79231, Lakeview 79235, Lone Star 79241, McCoy 79235, Mickey 79241, Muncy 79241, Sandhill 79235, South Plains 79258 and Sterley 79241. **FOR ADDITIONAL LOCAL INFORMATION** Floydada Chamber of Commerce, 105 W. California, P.O. Box 147, Floydada, 79235, 806/983-3434 and Lockney Chamber of Commerce, P.O. Box 85, Lockney, 79241, 806/652-3813.

FOARD (P34)

THE LAND

West of Wichita Falls on U.S. Highway 70 in the Rolling Plains Region, Foard County covers 703 square miles with an elevation range of 1,400 to 1,750 feet. The soils are loamy with clayey subsoils. Foard is in the Rolling Plains vegetaton area with short to tall grasses, mesquite and some live oak trees. Between 41 and 50% of the land in the county is considered prime farmland. **CLIMATE** The average annual temperature is 63°F.

Temperatures in January range from an average low of 25° to an average high of 54°F and in July range from 72° to 98°F. The average annual precipitation is 24 inches, with an average relative humidity of 75% at 6 A.M. and 44% at 6 P.M. The average annual snowfall is seven inches. The growing season averages 219 days per year, with the last freeze in early April and the first freeze in early November. The sun shines during the year on the average 72% of the daylight hours.

THE PEOPLE

Foard County ranks 24th among all U.S. counties in the highest percent of population age 65 and over. The 1982 estimated population of 2,000 indicates a continuation of a decline in the population which has existed since 1930. However the decline slowed to 2% between 1970 and 1980. The age group with the largest decrease was ages 50 to 64. Although the median age lowered from 46 in 1970 to 42 in 1980, the population is older than average. The largest ancestry groups are persons of English descent (24%), Irish descent (19%) and German descent (15%). **REGISTERED VOTERS** As of November 2, 1982 there were 1,413 registered voters (0.02% of the state total). The 1982 general election had a 57% voter turnout, compared to a 68% turnout in the 1980 general election. In the 1982 primary 98% voted Democratic and 2% Republican, with 611 votes cast.

THE ECONOMY

AGRICULTURE Wheat area. In 1982, 95% of the land was in farms and ranches, with 28% of the farmland under cultivation and 4% irrigated. Foard ranked 217th in the state in highest agricultural receipts, with 72% from crops. Overgrazing, undesirable brush and weeds, water and wind erosion are the current conservation problems. Primary crops: wheat, cotton, hay and oats. Primary vegetables: sweet potatoes and watermelons. Primary fruits and nuts: peaches. Primary livestock and products: cattle. **BUSINESS** Total number of business establishments in the county: 40. Retail sales during the first quarter of 1984 increased 30%. In 1980, 29% of the labor force were self-employed, 22% were employed in professional or related services, 7% in manufacturing, 12% in wholesale and retail trade, 29% in agriculture, forestry, fisheries and mining, 13% were employed in other counties and there were 347 retired workers. The industries with the most employment: agribusiness and the manufacture of hats and caps. The nonfarm earnings in 1981 totaled $16,332,000. The retired workers received an average monthly Social Security payment of $311. **FINANCE** On June 30, 1983, one commercial bank had total deposits of $15,322,000 and total assets of $16,999,000. There are two state savings and loan association branches in the county. **HOUSING** Average value of homes in 1980: $17,000. In 1982 one permit was issued for a new single family house. Between 1970 and 1980 the number of housing units increased by 2%. Eighty-one percent of all units in the county are air-conditioned, 93% are heated by gas and 5% by electricity. **NATURAL RESOURCES** Copper, gypsum, oil, gas and bituminous coal. In 1982 a total of 126,989 thousand cubic feet of gas well gas, 493,234 barrels of crude oil and 29,572 thousand cubic feet of casinghead gas were produced. **TOURISM** Travel expenditures of $1,286,000 in 1982 (an increase of 13% over 1981) generated 28 jobs and $236,000 in payroll. **ALCOHOLIC BEVERAGES** Totally dry. **FEDERAL EXPENDITURES** The federal government had direct expenditures or obligations of $7,076,000 in the county during fiscal year 1983, including $31,000 by the U.S. Department of Defense. In addition, the federal government provided $170,000 in grant awards, paid $208,000 in salaries and wages, made direct payments to individuals of $4,714,000 including $3,171,000 in retirement and disability payments and spent $1,983,000 in other expenditures or obligations. The federal government also provided $3,674,000 in direct loans and $4,541,000 in guaranteed loans and insurance.

COMMUNICATION

Newspapers–Weekly: The Foard County News and Crowell Index. Cable TV. Telephone companies: General Telephone, Southwestern Bell and Santa Rosa Telephone Coop. **TRANS-PORTATION** Total public road mileage: 540. In 1982 there were 2,090 registered vehicles and 37 reported traffic accidents. Motor freight: two carriers. Rail: one branch line carries annually less than one million tons of freight through the county. Aircraft: nine are registered in the county. Airports: Foard County Airport at Crowell is a basic utility airport providing general aviation service. It serves as a base for 18 aircraft.

COMMUNITY SERVICES

EDUCATION One school district with one elementary and one high school. The average daily attendance in 1981-82 was 353, with expenditures per pupil of $2,619 including 25 classroom teachers with an average annual salary of $15,655. Fifty-nine percent of the 27 high school graduates planned to attend college. In 1982-83, 68% of the students were White, 20% Hispanic, 12% Black and 0.3% Asian. **PUBLIC LIBRARIES** Foard County Library (Crowell): 4,761 volumes. **CHILD CARE** Six day care licensed facilities. **HEALTH CARE** One physician. Hospitals: one with a capacity of 24. Ambulance services: one commercial service. Nursing homes: one nursing home has a capacity of 80 nursing care residents. **CHURCHES** 10 churches have an estimated combined membership of 1,876. The largest denominations are Southern Baptist, United Methodist and Churches of Christ. **SOCIAL SERVICES** In fiscal year 1983 a total of $69,481 in food stamps was distributed, with an average of 170 persons receiving food stamps each month. Aid to Families with Dependent Children (AFDC) totaled $11,278 with an average of eight families receiving AFDC each month. Medical assistance benefits for the aged and disabled of $331,762 and for families and children of $10,436 brought the county benefit total to $422,957. **FIRE PROTECTION** One volunteer fire department. **LAW ENFORCEMENT** The County Sheriff has three commissioned officers. **CRIME** 12 nonviolent crimes (burglary, larceny-theft and motor vehicle theft) were reported in 1982. **JUDICIAL SYSTEM** One District Court and Judge, one County Court and Judge and one Justice of the Peace. In the District Court a total of 88 cases were pending on 1/1/82, 33 new cases were filed and 15 cases were disposed of during the year leaving 106 cases pending on 12/31/82. There were 36 criminal cases on the docket, three convictions, and 33 cases left pending. In the County Court 65 cases were pending on 1/1/82, 44 new cases were filed and 30 cases were disposed of during the year leaving 79 cases pending on 12/31/82. There were 101 criminal cases on the docket, 18 convictions, two persons committed to jail, and 72 cases left pending. **JAILS** One jail, capacity eight. **ATTORNEYS AT LAW** Four. **UTILITIES** 87% of the residents are connected to a public or privately owned water system and 62% are connected to a public sewer system. Natural gas is distributed to the county by Texas Natural Gas Co. Electricity is distributed to the county by West Texas Utilities, B-K Electric Coop., Inc., and Gate City Coop., Inc. and is generated primarily by gas, oil and water. **TAXES** The county has three units with taxing authority: one school district, one city, and one county.

RECREATION/ENTERTAINMENT

MUNICIPAL PARKS 30 acres in one municipal park. This park contains one playground and one multi-use field. **BOATING/FISHING** Lakes/reservoirs: Crowell City (26 acres). Major rivers: North Wichita and Pease. Primary streams: Raggedy. **HUNTING** Fall and winter seasons on deer. Summer, fall and winter seasons on squirrel. No closed seasons on coyote and bobcat. Winter seasons on quail, muskrat, beaver, opossum, ringtailed cat, badger, fox, weasel, raccoon, skunk and civet cat. Fall, winter and spring seasons on turkey. In 1983 sandhill crane, duck, coot, geese, woodcock and jacksnipe seasons occurred during the winter months. Teal duck, rail and gallinule seasons occurred in the fall. Mourning dove seasons occurred intermittently during the fall and winter months. **MUSEUMS** Crowell: Foard County Courthouse Museum, Foard County Museum-McAdams Ranch, and Fire Hall Museum. **SPECIAL EVENTS** 4-H and FFA Livestock Show, Crowell, February; Veterans Memorial Service, Crowell, November.

COMMUNITIES

COUNTY SEAT Crowell, County Courthouse, 79227; County Clerk's Office, 817/684-1365. **INCORPORATED COMMUNITIES** (1980 population and ZIP Code) Crowell (1,509) 79227. **UNINCORPORATED COMMUNITIES** (and ZIP Code) Foard City 79227, Margaret 79227, Rayland 76384 and Thalia 79227.

FORT BEND (G17)

THE LAND

Southwest of Houston on U.S. Highway 59 in the Coastal Prairie Region, Fort Bend County covers 876 square miles with an elevation range of 80 to 200 feet. The county has level, acidic, somewhat poorly to moderately well drained, cracking, clayey soils and poorly drained soils with dark, loamy surfaces and cracking clayey subsoils. Along the Brazos River are clayey and loamy alkaline soils. There is a high shrink-swell potential. Fort Bend is in the Gulf Prairies vegetation area with tall grasses and a variety of brusy trees along streams. Between 61 and 70% of the land in the county is considered prime farmland. **CLIMATE** Subtropical, moist and humid. Chance of a tropical storm or hurricane from June through October. The average annual temperature is 69°F. Temperatures in January range from an average low of 41° to an average high of 62°F and in July range from 73° to 94°F. The average annual precipitation is 44 inches, with an average relative humidity of 88% at 6 A.M. and 65% at 6 P.M. Small amounts of snow may occur on rare occasions. The growing season averages 275 days per year, with the last freeze in mid February and the first freeze in early December. The sun shines during the year on the average 75% of the daylight hours.

THE PEOPLE

The 1982 estimated population of 154,500 indicates a continuation of the strong growth rate begun in the 1970s. The population increased 150% between 1970 and 1980, ranking Fort Bend 12th among all U.S. counties in rate of growth. The greatest population growth was in urban areas where the increase of 234% was one of the highest in the state. The age group of 25 to 39 quadrupled between 1970 and 1980. The median age lowered from 37 in 1970 to 30 in 1980. The largest ancestry groups are Hispanic (20%), those of German descent (18%), English descent (18%) and Black (16%). **REGISTERED VOTERS** As of November 2, 1982 there were 57,211 registered voters (0.9% of the state total). The 1982 general election had a 49% voter turnout, compared to a 67% turnout in the 1980 general election. In the 1982 primary 53% voted Democratic and 47% Republican, with 8,199 votes cast.

THE ECONOMY

AGRICULTURE Cotton and rice area. In 1982, 84% of the land was in farms and ranches, with 35% of the farmland under cultivation and 20% irrigated. Fort Bend ranked 32nd in the state in highest agricultural receipts, with 73% from crops.

COUNTIES

FORT BEND (continued)

Overgrazing, water erosion, decreasing irrigation water supplies, soil compaction and drainage are the current conservation problems. Primary crops: ninth in the state for rice. Sorghum, cotton, soybeans and corn. Primary vegetables: watermelons, cabbage, sweet corn, potatoes, sweet potatoes and tomatoes. Primary fruits and nuts: peaches and pecans. Primary livestock and products: cattle and hogs. **BUSINESS** Total number of business establishments in the county: 1,765. Retail sales during the first quarter of 1984 increased 21%. In 1980, 6% of the labor force were self-employed, 18% were employed in professional or related services, 20% in manufacturing, 18% in wholesale and retail trade, 10% in construction, 63% were employed in other counties and there were 3,329 retired workers. The industries with the most employment: agribusiness, oil and gas extraction, heavy construction, sugar cane refining, soft drink canning and bottling, sulfur mining and the manufacture of chemical preparations, insulated wire, oil field machinery, valves and pipe fittings and electronic computing equipment. The nonfarm earnings in 1981 totaled $1,388,696,000. The retired workers received an average monthly Social Security payment of $333. **FINANCE** On June 30, 1983, 13 commercial banks had total deposits of $428,512,000 and total assets of $487,438,000. On December 31, 1982 one state savings and loan association, one federal association, 15 state branches and two federal branches had combined assets of $236,849,606. In addition there are four credit unions in the county. **HOUSING** Average value of homes in 1980: $63,800. Permits for new, privately owned housing units increased in 1982: 1,892 permits were issued with a total construction cost of $81,071,217. Of those permits, 1,303 were for single family houses. Housing permits increased in Richmond from 74 in 1981 to 219 in 1982 with 169 of the permits issued for apartments and condominiums, and in Sugar Land from 217 to 488 with all permits issued for single family houses. Between 1970 and 1980 the number of housing units increased by 187%. Eighty-nine percent of all units in the county are air-conditioned, 61% are heated by gas and 38% by electricity. **NATURAL RESOURCES** Oil and gas, salt domes, sand and gravel and sulphur. In 1982 a total of 41,294,292 thousand cubic feet of gas well gas, 353,084 barrels of condensate, 7,019,885 barrels of crude oil and 7,312,359 thousand cubic feet of casinghead gas were produced. Current production of other minerals and products includes clay, lightweight aggregate, salt, construction sand, sand and gravel, and recovered sulphur. **TOURISM** Travel expenditures of $54,189,000 in 1982 (an increase of 6% over 1981) generated 768 jobs and $12,613,000 in payroll. Lodging: six hotels, motels and tourist courts. Convention/meeting facilities: Rosenberg-Fort Bend County Fair Grandstand and Exhibit Area. **ALCOHOLIC BEVERAGES** Packaged distilled spirits, beer, ale, malt liquor and wine are legal. Sale of mixed beverages is legal in all or parts of the county. **FEDERAL EXPENDITURES** The federal government had direct expenditures or obligations of $95,731,000 in the county during fiscal year 1983, including $7,281,000 by the U.S. Department of Defense. In addition, the federal government provided $7,282,000 in grant awards, paid $6,928,000 in salaries and wages, made direct payments to individuals of $85,495,000 including $50,890,000 in retirement and disability payments, awarded $1,992,000 in procurement contracts. The federal government also provided $4,235,000 in direct loans and $3,426,729,000 in guaranteed loans and insurance.

COMMUNICATION

Newspapers–Daily: The Herald-Coaster (Rosenberg), ave. eve. circ. 7,165. Weekly: Katy Times, Fort Bend Mirror (Missouri City) and Gulf Coast Tribune (Needville). Radio: KFRD-AM, KFRD-FM (Rosenberg). Cable TV. Telephone companies: Continental Telephone, General Telephone, Southwestern Bell, Fort Bend Telephone and Sugar Land Telephone. **TRANSPORTATION** Total public road mileage: 1,463. In 1982 there were 107,241 registered vehicles and 3,080 reported traffic accidents including 28 fatalities. Intercity bus service is available. Motor freight: 24 local and intrastate carriers. Rail: The Sunset Limited provides passenger service on the Amtrak Route. Eight main and five branch lines carry freight through the county. Five of the main lines carry annually over 30 million tons of freight each, two carry 20 to 30 each and one carries 10 to 20 million. One branch line carries annually 20 to 30 million tons of freight, one carries one to five million and three carry less than one million. Aircraft: 116 are registered in the county. Airports: Lane Airpark at Rosenberg.

COMMUNITY SERVICES

EDUCATION Five school districts with 26 elementary, eight middle, eight high schools and one special education school. The average daily attendance in 1981-82 was 30,151, with expenditures per pupil of $2,567 including 1,686 classroom teachers with an average annual salary of $17,485. Fifty percent of the 1,466 high school graduates planned to attend college. In 1982-83, 53% of the students were White, 24% Hispanic, 19% Black, 5% Asian and 0.1% American Indian. Private schools: 736 students enrolled in four elementary and one high school. Vocational education: Rosenberg Beauty College (Rosenberg). National Center for Montessori Education-Houston (Missouri City). **PUBLIC LIBRARIES** Fort Bend County Library (Richmond): 158,420 volumes, two branches. **CHILD CARE** 182 day care and 25 twenty-four hour care licensed facilities. **HEALTH CARE** 99 physicians and 45 dentists. Hospitals: two with a combined capacity of 199 and one new hospital under construction. Clinics: one for treatment of alcohol and/or drug abuse, one dialysis clinic and one public health clinic. Ambulance services: two commercial, one county and one fire department service. Mental health: one county clinic and one state school with capacity of 1,000. Nursing homes: six nursing homes with a combined capacity of 568 nursing care residents. The average cost per day for private patients in 1982 was $33.10. **CHURCHES** 86 churches have an estimated combined membership of 49,336. The largest denominations are Catholic, Southern Baptist and United Methodist. **SOCIAL SERVICES** In fiscal year 1983 a total of $2,964,567 in food stamps was distributed, with an average of 6,016 persons receiving food stamps each month. Aid to Families with Dependent Children (AFDC) totaled $547,099 with an average of 335 families receiving AFDC each month. Medical assistance benefits for the aged and disabled of $3,244,760 and for families and children of $717,771 brought the county benefit total to $7,474,196. **FIRE PROTECTION** One partly paid and 13 volunteer fire departments. **LAW ENFORCEMENT** The County Sheriff has 161 commissioned officers. 21 police departments have a combined force of 352. **CRIME** 450 violent crimes (murder, forcible rape, robbery and aggravated assault) and 4,761 nonviolent crimes (burglary, larceny-theft and motor vehicle theft) were reported in 1982. **JUDICIAL SYSTEM** Three District Courts and Judges, two County Courts and Judges and four Justices of the Peace. In the District Courts a total of 2,967 cases were pending on 1/1/82, 3,676 new cases were filed and 3,134 cases were disposed of during the year leaving 3,509 cases pending on 12/31/82. There were 1,379 criminal cases on the docket, 292 convictions, 79 persons committed to prison and 45 committed to jail and 703 cases left pending. In the County Courts 1,133 cases were pending on 1/1/82, 1,929 new cases were filed and 1,706 cases were disposed of during the year leaving 1,356 cases pending on 12/31/82. There were 2,304 criminal cases on the docket, 374 convictions, 105 persons committed to jail, and 991 cases left pending. **JAILS** One jail, capacity 106.

PRISONS Central, on 4,459 acres south of Sugar Land, had an inmate population of 899 in 1983. It has agricultural operations including a Central Agricultural Commissary, a soap and detergent factory and operates a Central Industrial Distribution Warehouse. Jester I, II, III, on 5,012 acres East of Richmond, had a total inmate population of 1,672 in 1983. They have agricultural operations and Jester I has the Pre-Release and Work-Release programs for male inmates. **ATTORNEYS AT LAW** 217. **UTILITIES** 83% of the residents are connected to a public or privately owned water system and 82% are connected to a public sewer system. Natural gas is distributed to the county by Entex, Inc. The average annual residential bill for natural gas in 1982 for the Entex distribution system was $390.31, an increase of 26% over 1981. Electricity is distributed to the county by Houston Lighting and Power Co. and is generated primarily by gas. The typical residential electric bill is $201.39 per month for an all-electric house using 2,500 kwh. **TAXES** The county has 73 units with taxing authority: five school districts, 13 cities, one county, two utility districts, one college district and 51 special districts.

RECREATION/ENTERTAINMENT
NATIONAL REGISTER OF HISTORIC PLACES Richmond: Fort Bend County Courthouse. **STATE** Brazos Bend State Park covers 4,897 acres and is closed to the public as of July 1983. **COUNTY/MUNICIPAL PARKS** 149 acres in one county and 15 municipal parks. These parks contain one mile of hiking trails, 11 playgrounds, eight baseball and softball fields, 11 tennis courts, two multi-use courts and three swimming pools. **SCENIC DRIVES** The Texas Independence Trail runs through this county. This trail not only surveys the historic sites of southeastern Texas but also includes many modern visitor attractions such as the Johnson Space Center. **BOATING/FISHING** Lakes/reservoirs: Fort Bend Old Soil Conservation Service Lake 1 (208 acres), Fort Bend Soil Conservation Service Lakes 1, 2 and 3 (1,583 acres), Harlem (243 acres), Kitty Hollow (308 acres), Paw Paw (43 acres), Smithers (2,480 acres) and Worthington (300 acres). Major rivers: Brazos and San Bernard. Primary streams: Oyster, Big, Dry and Rabb Bayou. **HUNTING** Fall and winter seasons on deer. Summer, fall and winter seasons on squirrel. No closed seasons on coyote, bobcat and nutria. Winter seasons on quail, muskrat, beaver, otter, opossum, mink, ring-tailed cat, badger, fox, raccoon, skunk and civet cat. In 1983 duck, coot, geese, woodcock and jacksnipe seasons occurred during the winter months with a winter season on sandhill crane in some parts of the county. Teal duck, rail and gallinule seasons occurred in the fall. Mourning dove seasons occurred intermittently during the winter months. **MUSEUMS** Richmond: Fort Bend County Historical Museum and Confederate Museum. **SPECIAL EVENTS** Czech Fest, Rosenberg, May; Rodeo, Simonton, Weekly, January-December; County Fair, Rosenberg, October.

COMMUNITIES
COUNTY SEAT Richmond County Courthouse, 77469; County Clerk's Office, 713/342-3411. **INCORPORATED COMMUNITIES** (1980 population and ZIP Code) Beasley (410) 77417, Fulshear (594) 77441, Houston (1,595,138: 16,270 in Fort Bend Co., 1,578,849 in Harris Co. and 19 in Montgomery Co.) 77001, All-America Cities Honorable Mention 1952, Katy (5,660: 517 in Fort Bend Co., 4,475 in Harris Co. and 668 in Waller Co.) 77450, Kendleton (606) 77451, Missouri City (24,533: 3,936 in Harris Co. and 20,597 in Fort Bend Co.) 77459, Needville (1,417) 77461, Orchard (408) 77464, Pleak (365) 77469, Richmond (9,692) 77469, Rosenberg (17,995) 77471, Simonton (603) 77476, Stafford (4,755: 4,526 in Fort Bend Co. and 229 in Harris Co.) 77477, Sugar Land (8,826) 77478 and Thompsons (240) 77481. **UNINCORPORATED COMMUNITIES** (and ZIP Code) Arcola 77583, Booth 77421, Clodine 77469, Crabb 77469, Dewalt

77433, Duke 77583, Fairchilds 77461, Foster 77469, Fresno 77545, Guy 77444, Juliff 77583, Long Point 77461, Powell Point 77451, Tavener 77435, The Meadows 77477 and Valley Lodge 77476. **FOR ADDITIONAL LOCAL INFORMATION** Rosenberg-Richmond Chamber of Commerce, 4120 Avenue H, Rosenberg, 77471, 409/342-5464 and East Fort Bend Chamber of Commerce, 9920 Hwy. 90A, Sugar Land, 77478, 409/491-0800.

FRANKLIN (E6)

THE LAND
Northeast of Dallas on Interstate Highway 30 in the East Texas Timberlands Region, Franklin County covers 294 square miles with an elevation range of 300 to 500 feet. The northern one-third of the county has undulating, cracking, clayey soils with some loamy surface layers. To the south is a narrow strip of sandy soils with cracking, clayey subsoils. The remainder of the county has rolling to hilly soils with loamy surfaces and reddish mottled clayey subsoils. The northern part of the county is in the Blackland Prairies vegetation area with prairie grasses like little bluestem, Indiangrass, silver bluestem and Texas wintergrass. There are post and blackjack oak and mesquite. The southern part of the county is in the Post Oak Savannah vegetation area with tall grasses, post and blackjack oak trees. Between 11 and 20% of the land in the county is considered prime farmland. **CLIMATE** Mild and moist. The average annual temperature is 63°F. Temperatures in January range from an average low of 30° to an average high of 53°F and in July range from 70° to 94°F. The average annual precipitation is 44 inches, with an average relative humidity of 83% at 6 A.M. and 57% at 6 P.M. The average annual snowfall is two inches. The growing season averages 239 days per year, with the last freeze in late March and the first freeze in mid November. The sun shines during the year on the average 66% of the daylight hours.

THE PEOPLE
The 1982 estimated population of 7,100 indicates a continuation of the growth rate begun in the 1960s which reversed the steady population decrease between 1930 and 1960. Almost 36% of the population gains between 1970 and 1980 were in rural areas. The age groups with the largest gains were ages birth to five and 20 to 34 years. The median age lowered from 41 in 1970 to 37 in 1980, however the population remained older than average with a high percent of residents 65 and older. The largest ancestry groups are persons of English descent (33%), German descent (20%) and Irish descent (11%). **REGISTERED VOTERS** As of November 2, 1982 there were 3,590 registered voters (0.1% of the state total). The 1982 general election had a 52% voter turnout, compared to a 70% turnout in the 1980 general election. In the 1982 primary 97% voted Democratic and 3% Republican, with 956 votes cast.

THE ECONOMY
AGRICULTURE Forest production area. In 1982, 69% of the land was in farms and ranches, with 22% of the farmland under cultivation. Franklin ranked 132nd in the state in highest agricultural receipts, with 96% from livestock and livestock products. Overgrazing, water erosion and improper woodland management are the current conservation problems. Primary crops: hay, wheat and sorghum. Primary vegetables: sweet potatoes and watermelons. Primary fruits and nuts: peaches and pecans. Primary livestock and products: cattle and milk. **BUSINESS** Total number of business establishments in the county: 93. Retail sales during the first quarter of 1984 increased 19%. In 1980, 16% of the labor force were self-employed, 18% were employed in professional or related services, 14% in

FRANKLIN (continued)

manufacturing, 18% in wholesale and retail trade, 15% in agriculture, forestry, fisheries and mining, 45% were employed in other counties and there were 634 retired workers. The industries with the most employment: agribusiness and the manufacture of women's apparel and household furniture. The nonfarm earnings in 1981 totaled $47,018,000. The retired workers received an average monthly Social Security payment of $287. **FINANCE** On June 30, 1983, two commercial banks had total deposits of $42,425,000 and total assets of $48,189,000. There is one state savings and loan association branch in the county. **HOUSING** Average value of homes in 1980: $24,800. Permits for new, privately owned housing units decreased in 1982: 12 permits were issued with a total construction cost of $434,000. Of those permits, all were for single family houses. Between 1970 and 1980 the number of housing units increased by 48%. Seventy-nine percent of all units in the county are air-conditioned, 71% are heated by gas and 22% by electricity. **NATURAL RESOURCES** Oil, gas, limestone and lignite coal. In 1982 a total of 12,394,986 thousand cubic feet of gas well gas, 1,733,174 barrels of crude oil and 50,451 thousand cubic feet of casinghead gas were produced. Current production of other minerals and products includes recovered sulphur. Pine and hardwood production in 1981 totaled 1,073,412 cubic feet: 742,984 cubic feet of pine and 330,428 cubic feet of hardwood. **TOURISM** Travel expenditures of $2,733,000 in 1982 (an increase of 11% over 1981) generated 70 jobs and $554,000 in payroll. **ALCOHOLIC BEVERAGES** Totally dry. **FEDERAL EXPENDITURES** The federal government had direct expenditures or obligations of $9,870,000 in the county during fiscal year 1983, including $850,000 by the U.S. Department of Defense. In addition, the federal government provided $88,000 in grant awards, paid $245,000 in salaries and wages, made direct payments to individuals of $9,270,000 including $6,868,000 in retirement and disability payments, awarded $1,000 in procurement contracts and spent $266,000 in other expenditures or obligations. The federal government also provided $321,000 in direct loans and $1,763,000 in guaranteed loans and insurance.

COMMUNICATION

Newspapers–Weekly: Mt Vernon Optic Herald and The Winnsboro News. Telephone companies: Continental Telephone, General Telephone, Southwestern Bell and Peoples Telephone Coop. **TRANSPORTATION** Total public road mileage: 402. In 1982 there were 5,453 registered vehicles and 115 reported traffic accidents including three fatalities. Taxi cabs: one company in Mount Vernon. Intercity bus service is available. Motor freight: three carriers. Rail: two main lines carry freight through the county with one carrying annually five to 10 million tons and one carrying one to five million. Aircraft: two are registered in the county. Airports: Mackay Heliport in Mount Vernon for emergency use only.

COMMUNITY SERVICES

EDUCATION One school district with one elementary, one middle and one high school. The average daily attendance in 1981-82 was 1,007, with expenditures per pupil of $2,461 including 62 classroom teachers with an average annual salary of $15,557. Sixty-six percent of the 71 high school graduates planned to attend college. In 1982-83, 89% of the students were White, 1% Hispanic, 10% Black, 0.2% Asian and 0.1% American Indian. **PUBLIC LIBRARIES** Mount Vernon Library. **CHILD CARE** Four day care and one twenty-four hour care licensed facilities. **HEALTH CARE** Four physicians and three dentists. Hospitals: one with a capacity of 51. Ambulance services: one hospital-based service. Nursing homes: two nursing homes with a combined capacity of 127 nursing care residents. The average cost per day for private patients in 1982 was $28.71. **CHURCHES** 27 churches have an estimated combined membership of 4,848. The largest denominations are Southern Baptist, United Methodist and Catholic. **SOCIAL SERVICES** In fiscal year 1983 a total of $129,209 in food stamps was distributed, with an average of 312 persons receiving food stamps each month. Aid to Families with Dependent Children (AFDC) totaled $12,940 with an average of eight families receiving AFDC each month. Medical assistance benefits for the aged and disabled of $1,038,768 and for families and children of $22,108 brought the county benefit total to $1,203,025. **FIRE PROTECTION** Two volunteer fire departments. **LAW ENFORCEMENT** The County Sheriff has 10 commissioned officers. **CRIME** One violent crime (murder, forcible rape, robbery and aggravated assault) and 114 nonviolent crimes (burglary, larceny-theft and motor vehicle theft) were reported in 1982. **JUDICIAL SYSTEM** Two District Courts and Judges, one County Court and Judge and one Justice of the Peace. In the District Courts a total of 169 cases were pending on 1/1/82, 149 new cases were filed and 172 cases were disposed of during the year leaving 146 cases pending on 12/31/82. There were 53 criminal cases on the docket, 44 convictions, 14 persons committed to prison and two committed to jail and six cases left pending. In the County Court 184 cases were pending on 1/1/82, 283 new cases were filed and 248 cases were disposed of during the year leaving 219 cases pending on 12/31/82. There were 376 criminal cases on the docket, 95 convictions, nine persons committed to jail, and 136 cases left pending. **JAILS** One jail, capacity 12. **ATTORNEYS AT LAW** Four. **UTILITIES** 84% of the residents are connected to a public or privately owned water system and 42% are connected to a public sewer system. Natural gas is distributed to the county by Arkla Inc. The average annual residential bill for natural gas in 1982 for the Arkla distribution system was $316.69, an increase of 23% over 1981. Electricity is distributed to the county by Southwestern Electric Power Co., Wood County Electric Coop., Inc., and Bowie-Cass Electric Coop., Inc. and is generated primarily by gas and coal. The typical residential electric bill is $125.48 per month for an all-electric house using 2,500 kwh. **TAXES** The county has six units with taxing authority: three school districts, one city, one county, and one special district.

RECREATION/ENTERTAINMENT

NATIONAL REGISTER OF HISTORIC PLACES Mount Vernon vicinity: Rogers-Drummond House. **MUNICIPAL PARKS** nine acres in two municipal parks. These parks contain one baseball and softball field and one swimming pool. **SCENIC DRIVES** Texas 37 and F.M. 21 in southern Franklin County offer views of rolling wooded areas. **BOATING/FISHING** Lakes/reservoirs: Cypress Springs (3,400 acres), Franklin (31 acres), Mt. Vernon City (30 acres), Paradise (116 acres), Romal (169 acres) and Zachry (21 acres). Major rivers: Sulphur. Primary streams: Mitchell, Lick, Blair, Brushy, Big Cypress, Glade, Denton and White Oak. **HUNTING** Fall and winter seasons on deer. Summer, fall and winter seasons on squirrel. No closed seasons on coyote, bobcat and nutria. Winter seasons on quail, muskrat, beaver, otter, opossum, mink, ring-tailed cat, badger, fox, raccoon, skunk and civet cat. In 1983 duck, coot, geese, woodcock and jacksnipe seasons occurred during the winter months. Teal duck, rail and gallinule seasons occurred in the fall. Mourning dove seasons occurred intermittently during the fall and winter months. **SPECIAL EVENTS** County Fair, Mount Vernon, October; Rodeo, Mount Vernon, June; Christmas Parade, Mount Vernon, December.

COMMUNITIES

COUNTY SEAT Mount Vernon, County Courthouse, 75457;

County Clerk's Office, 214/537-4252. **INCORPORATED COMMUNITIES** (1980 population and ZIP Code) Mount Vernon (2,025) 75457 and Winnsboro (3,458: 862 in Franklin Co. and 2,596 in Wood Co.) 75494. **UNINCORPORATED COMMUNITIES** (and ZIP Code) Cypress 75494, Daphane (Daphne) 75455, Hagansport 75487, Hopewell 75457, Macon 75455, Majors 75457, Purley 75457, Scroggins 75480 and Yale 75457. **FOR ADDITIONAL LOCAL INFORMATION** Franklin County Chamber of Commerce, 101 S. Kaufman, P.O. Box 554, Mount Vernon, 75457 and Winnsboro Chamber of Commerce, 201 W. Broadway, Winnsboro, 75494, 214/342-6066.

FREESTONE (C11)

THE LAND

South of Dallas on Interstate Highway 45 in the Claypan Area, Freestone County covers 888 square miles with an elevation range of 300 to 500 feet. The nearly level to undulating soils are light colored sandy to loamy with mottled, cracking, clayey subsoils. Along the Trinity River the soils are loamy with clay subsoils. The vegetation is primarily Post Oak Savannah with tall grasses and trees such as post and blackjack oak along streams. Between 11 and 20% of the land in the county is considered prime farmland. **CLIMATE** Subtropical Humid and generally mild. The average annual temperature is 66 °F. Temperatures in January range from an average low of 35° to an average high of 56°F and in July range from 72° to 95°F. The average annual precipitation is 40 inches, with an average relative humidity of 84% at 6 A.M. and 54% at 6 P.M. Snowfall may amount to one inch, however some years none will be recorded. The growing season averages 261 days per year, with the last freeze in early March and the first freeze in late November. The sun shines during the year on the average 66% of the daylight hours.

THE PEOPLE

The 1982 estimated population of 15,800 indicates a continuation of the growth begun in the 1970s which reversed the steady population decline between 1930 and 1970. The population shifted from a 11% decrease between 1960 and 1970 to a 33% increase between 1970 and 1980. Population in the urban areas of Freestone county increased 141%, one of the highest urban growth rates in the state. The age group with the largest gain was ages 20 to 34 which doubled in size. The median age lowered from 43 in 1970 to 35 in 1980, however the population remained older than average with a high percent of residents over 65. The largest ancestry groups are persons of English descent (33%), Black (22%) and Irish descent (21%). **REGISTERED VOTERS** As of November 2, 1982 there were 7,686 registered voters (0.1% of the state total). The 1982 general election had a 43% voter turnout, compared to a 67% turnout in the 1980 general election. In the 1982 primary 97% voted Democratic and 3% Republican, with 2,359 votes cast.

THE ECONOMY

AGRICULTURE In 1982, 71% of the land was in farms and ranches, with 11% of the farmland under cultivation and 2% irrigated. Freestone ranked 165th in the state in highest agricultural receipts, with 93% from livestock and livestock products. Overgrazing, undesirable brush and weeds, fertilization and erosion are the current conservation problems. Primary crops: hay, oats and wheat. Primary vegetables: potatoes, sweet potatoes, tomatoes and watermelons. Primary fruits and nuts: peaches and pecans. Primary livestock and products: cattle and hogs. **BUSINESS** Total number of business establishments in the county: 254. Retail sales during the first quarter of 1984 increased 17%. In 1980, 12% of the labor force were self-employed, 21% were employed in professional or related services, 9% in manufacturing, 16% in wholesale and retail trade, 17% in transportation, communications, and other public utilities, 26% were employed in other counties and there were 1,773 retired workers. The industries with the most employment: oil and gas extraction and agribusiness. The nonfarm earnings in 1981 totaled $128,663,000. The retired workers received an average monthly Social Security payment of $277. **FINANCE** On June 30, 1983, five commercial banks had total deposits of $91,243,000 and total assets of $101,550,000. There are two state savings and loan association branches and two credit unions in the county. **HOUSING** Average value of homes in 1980: $25,600. Permits for new, privately owned housing units decreased in 1982: 35 permits were issued with a total construction cost of $1,507,530. Of those permits, 27 were for single family houses. Between 1970 and 1980 the number of housing units increased by 39%. Sixty-nine percent of all units in the county are air-conditioned, 76% are heated by gas and 17% by electricity. **NATURAL RESOURCES** Clay, salt domes, industrial sand, sand and gravel, oil, gas, and lignite coal. In 1982 a total of 42,682,586 thousand cubic feet of gas well gas, 104,156 barrels of condensate, 293,848 barrels of crude oil and 374,992 thousand cubic feet of casinghead gas were produced. Current production of other minerals and products includes brick, clay, lignite coal, industrial sand, crushed sandstone and recovered sulphur. **TOURISM** Travel expenditures of $2,255,000 in 1982 (an increase of 12% over 1981) generated 49 jobs and $410,000 in payroll. Lodging: four hotels, motels and tourist courts. **ALCOHOLIC BEVERAGES** Totally dry. **FEDERAL EXPENDITURES** The federal government had direct expenditures or obligations of $28,093,000 in the county during fiscal year 1983, including $586,000 by the U.S. Department of Defense. In addition, the federal government provided $312,000 in grant awards, paid $2,624,000 in salaries and wages, made direct payments to individuals of $24,831,000 including $17,565,000 in retirement and disability payments, awarded $77,000 in procurement contracts and spent $248,000 in other expenditures or obligations. The federal government also provided $268,000 in direct loans and $1,488,000 in guaranteed loans and insurance.

COMMUNICATION

Newspapers–Weekly: Fairfield Recorder, The Teague Chronicle and the News Tribune (Teague). Cable TV. Telephone companies: Continental Telephone and Southwestern Bell. **TRANSPORTATION** Total public road mileage: 1,040. In 1982 there were 13,663 registered vehicles and 317 reported traffic accidents including eight fatalities. Intercity bus service is available. Motor freight: five local and intrastate carriers. Rail: three main lines carry freight through the county with one carrying annually over 30 million tons and two carrying five to 10 million each. Aircraft: 11 are registered in the county. Airports: Stewart Field at Teague provides general aviation services.

COMMUNITY SERVICES

EDUCATION Four school districts with five elementary, two middle and three high schools. The average daily attendance in 1981-82 was 2,630, with expenditures per pupil of $2,938 including 180 classroom teachers with an average annual salary of $15,787. Forty-eight percent of the 149 high school graduates planned to attend college. In 1982-83, 72% of the students were White, 4% Hispanic, 24% Black, 0.6% Asian and 0.1% American Indian. Vocational education: Fairfield Barber College (Fairfield). **PUBLIC LIBRARIES** Fairfield Library Association, Inc.: 16,747 volumes. Teague City Library: 13,173 volumes. **CHILD CARE** 26 day care and nine twenty-four hour care licensed facilities. **HEALTH CARE** Nine physicians and four dentists. Hospitals: three with a combined capacity of 109. Ambulance

COUNTIES

FREESTONE (continued)

services: one commercial and one hospital-based service. Mental health: one county clinic. Nursing homes: four nursing homes with a combined capacity of 376 nursing care residents. The average cost per day for private patients in 1982 was $28.12. **CHURCHES** 52 churches have an estimated combined membership of 8,175. The largest denominations are Southern Baptist, Baptist Missionary and United Methodist. **SOCIAL SERVICES** In fiscal year 1983 a total of $547,007 in food stamps was distributed, with an average of 1,230 persons receiving food stamps each month. Aid to Families with Dependent Children (AFDC) totaled $119,618 with an average of 79 families receiving AFDC each month. Medical assistance benefits for the aged and disabled of $2,844,223 and for families and children of $162,872 brought the county benefit total to $3,673,719. **FIRE PROTECTION** Five volunteer fire departments. **LAW ENFORCEMENT** The County Sheriff has 33 commissioned officers. Two police departments have a combined force of 20. **CRIME** 37 violent crimes (murder, forcible rape, robbery and aggravated assault) and 285 nonviolent crimes (burglary, larceny-theft and motor vehicle theft) were reported in 1982. **JUDICIAL SYSTEM** Two District Courts and Judges, one County Court and Judge and four Justices of the Peace. In the District Courts a total of 580 cases were pending on 1/1/82, 469 new cases were filed and 371 cases were disposed of during the year leaving 678 cases pending on 12/31/82. There were 242 criminal cases on the docket, 109 convictions, 35 persons committed to prison and one committed to jail and 116 cases left pending. In the County Court 342 cases were pending on 1/1/82, 420 new cases were filed and 330 cases were disposed of during the year leaving 432 cases pending on 12/31/82. There were 652 criminal cases on the docket, 294 convictions, 58 persons committed to jail, and 332 cases left pending. **JAILS** One jail, capacity 23. **ATTORNEYS AT LAW** 15. **UTILITIES** 85% of the residents are connected to a public or privately owned water system and 55% are connected to a public sewer system. Natural gas is distributed to the county by Lone Star Gas Co., Division of Enserch. The average annual residential bill for natural gas in 1982 for the Lone Star distribution system was $405.91, an increase of 35% over 1981. Electricity is distributed to the county by Southwestern Electric Service, Texas Power and Light, Navarro Co. Electric Coop., Inc., Houston Co. Electric Coop., Inc., Limestone Co. Electric Coop., and Robertson Electric Coop., Inc. and is generated primarily by gas, oil and coal. The typical residential electric bill is $155.87 per month for an all-electric house using 2,500 kwh. **TAXES** The county has nine units with taxing authority: four school districts, four cities, and one county district.

RECREATION/ENTERTAINMENT

NATIONAL REGISTER OF HISTORIC PLACES Teague: Trinity and Brazos Valley Railroad Depot and Office Building. **STATE** Fairfield Lake State Recreation Area covers 1,460 acres with camping and trailer sites as well as areas offering fishing, swimming, boat ramps and nature trails. **MUNICIPAL PARKS** 28 acres in two municipal parks. These parks contain two playgrounds, two baseball and softball fields, three tennis courts, one multi-use court and one swimming pool. **BOATING/FISHING** Lakes/reservoirs: Blue (20 acres), Burleson (27 acres), Fairfield (2,350 acres), Hunt Ranch (20 acres), Indian Creek (144 acres), Lipsey (26 acres), Little Red (29 acres), Lower Club (50 acres), Neal (49 acres), Plum Creek (23 acres), Red (68 acres), Snyder (50 acres), Teague City (100 acres), Upper Club (30 acres) and Wortham (25 acres). Major rivers: Trinity. Primary streams: Gaston, Jelly Slough, Big Brown, Bee, Indian, Keechi, Jeter, Batsmith, Plum, Dottie, Holman, Jackson and Tehuacana.

HUNTING Fall and winter seasons on deer. Summer, fall and winter seasons on squirrel. No closed seasons on coyote, bobcat and nutria. Winter seasons on quail, muskrat, beaver, otter, opossum, ring-tailed cat, badger, fox, mink, raccoon, skunk and civet cat. In 1983 duck, coot, geese, woodcock and jacksnipe seasons occurred during the winter months. Teal duck, rail and gallinule seasons occurred in the fall. Mourning dove seasons occurred intermittently during the fall and winter months. **MUSEUMS** Fairfield: Freestone County Historical Museum, Stewart Mills Country Store and Moody-Bradley House. Teague: Burlington-Rock Island Railroad Museum. **SPECIAL EVENTS** HIstorical Pilgrimage, Fairfield, May; Rodeo, Teague, July; County Fair, Fairfield, August; Christmas Tour of Homes, Fairfield, December.

COMMUNITIES

COUNTY SEAT Fairfield, County Courthouse, 75840; County Clerk's Office, 214/389-2635. **INCORPORATED COMMUNITIES** (1980 population and ZIP Code) Fairfield (3,505) 75840, Kirvin (107) 75848, Streetman (415: 396 in Freestone Co. and 19 in Navarro Co.) 75859, Teague (3,390) 75860 and Wortham (1,187) 76693. **UNINCORPORATED COMMUNITIES** (and ZIP Code) Butler 75855, Cotton Gin 75860, Dew 75831, Donie 75838, Freestone 75842, Furney-Richardson 75860, Grindstone 75840, Lanely 75831, Postoak 75860, Red Lake 75855, Simsboro 75860, Stewards Mills 75859, Turlington 75840, Ward Prairie 75840, Winkler (also in Navarro Co.) 75859 and Young 75840. **FOR ADDITIONAL LOCAL INFORMATION** Fairfield Chamber of Commerce, 820 E. Commerce, P.O. Box 956, Fairfield, 75840, 214/389-5792 and Teague Chamber of Commerce, 205 S. 5th Ave., Teague, 75860, 817/739-2061.

FRIO (B15)

THE LAND

Southwest of San Antonio on Interstate Highway 35 in the Rio Grande Plain Region, Frio County covers 1,133 square miles with an elevation range of 400 to 700 feet. To the northeast the soils are deep with loamy surfaces and clayey subsoils. The rest of the county has deep to moderately deep, light colored loamy surfaces and clayey subsoils with limestone. In the South Texas Plains vegetation area, the grasses include bluestems, gramas, buffalograss and Texas wintergrass with a variety of brushy plants. Between 41 and 50% of the land in the county is considered prime farmland. **CLIMATE** Subtropical Subhumid with hot summers. The average annual temperature is 70°F. Temperatures in January range from an average low of 39° to an average high of 64°F and in July range from 74° to 98°F. The average annual precipitation is 25 inches, with an average relative humidity of 83% at 6 A.M. and 48% at 6 P.M. Snowfall of less than one inch may accumulate. The growing season averages 276 days per year, with the last freeze in late February and the first freeze in early December. The sun shines during the year on the average 66% of the daylight hours.

THE PEOPLE

In 1980 Frio County ranked 23rd among all U.S. counties in the highest percent of persons of Spanish origin. The 1982 estimated population of 14,300 indicates a continuation of the moderate growth begun in the 1960s. Almost 80% of the growth between 1970 and 1980 was in urban areas with rural areas declining 32%. The age groups with the largest gains were ages 20 to 34 and 62 and over. The population is younger than average with a median age of 25 and has a high birth rate. The largest ancestry groups are Hispanic (68%), persons of Irish descent (10%) and English descent (9%). **REGISTERED VOTERS** As of November

2, 1982 there were 7,253 registered voters (0.1% of the state total). The 1982 general election had a 47% voter turnout, compared to a 63% turnout in the 1980 general election. In the 1982 primary 99% voted Democratic and 1% Republican, with 3,021 votes cast.

THE ECONOMY

AGRICULTURE In 1982, 93% of the land was in farms and ranches, with 17% of the farmland under cultivation and 68% irrigated. Frio ranked 40th in the state in highest agricultural receipts, with 55% from crops. Undesirable brush and weeds, water erosion and water conservation are the current conservation problems. Primary crops: first in the state for peanuts. Wheat, oats and sorghum. Primary vegetables: first in the state for watermelons, fifth in the state for cabbage and third for total fresh market vegetables. Spinach, potatoes, cucumbers and honeydew melons. Primary fruits and nuts: peaches and pecans. Primary livestock and products: cattle and milk. **BUSINESS** Total number of business establishments in the county: 233. Retail sales during the first quarter of 1984 decreased 4%. In 1980, 15% of the labor force were self-employed, 18% were employed in professional or related services, 2% in manufacturing, 23% in wholesale and retail trade, 26% in agriculture, forestry, fisheries and mining, 11% were employed in other counties and there were 814 retired workers. The industries with the most employment: oil and gas extraction and agribusiness. The nonfarm earnings in 1981 totaled $78,496,000. The retired workers received an average monthly Social Security payment of $267. **FINANCE** On June 30, 1983, two commercial banks had total deposits of $71,766,000 and total assets of $82,456,000. There is one state savings and loan association branch and one credit union in the county. **HOUSING** Average value of homes in 1980: $18,800. Permits for new, privately owned housing units increased in 1982: 59 permits were issued with a total construction cost of $1,493,399. Of those permits, 52 were for single family houses. Between 1970 and 1980 the number of housing units increased by 41%. Fifty-seven percent of all units in the county are air-conditioned, 77% are heated by gas and 19% by electricity. **NATURAL RESOURCES** Industrial sand, sand and gravel, oil and gas. In 1982 a total of 2,164,929 thousand cubic feet of gas well gas, 10,574 barrels of condensate, 3,334,012 barrels of crude oil and 2,084,165 thousand cubic feet of casinghead gas were produced. **TOURISM** Travel expenditures of $6,911,000 in 1982 (an increase of 12% over 1981) generated 160 jobs and $1,319,000 in payroll. **ALCOHOLIC BEVERAGES** Packaged distilled spirits, beer, ale, malt liquor and wine are legal in parts of the county. Sale of mixed beverages is legal in all or parts of the county. **FEDERAL EXPENDITURES** The federal government had direct expenditures or obligations of $15,018,000 in the county during fiscal year 1983, including $380,000 by the U.S. Department of Defense. In addition, the federal government provided $1,259,000 in grant awards, paid $682,000 in salaries and wages, made direct payments to individuals of $12,484,000 including $8,945,000 in retirement and disability payments, awarded $1,000 in procurement contracts and spent $591,000 in other expenditures or obligations. The federal government also provided $495,000 in direct loans and $6,034,000 in guaranteed loans and insurance.

COMMUNICATION

Newspapers–Weekly: Dilley Herald and Pearsall Leader. Radio: KVWG-AM (Pearsall). Cable TV. Telephone companies: General Telephone, Southwestern Bell and Valley Telephone Coop. **TRANSPORTATION** Total public road mileage: 732. In 1982 there were 8,759 registered vehicles and 217 reported traffic accidents including five fatalities. Taxi cabs: one company in Pearsall. Intercity bus service is available. Motor freight: five local and intrastate carriers. Rail: the Eagle provides passenger service on the Amtrak Route. One main line carries annually five to 10 million tons of freight through the county. Aircraft: 30 are registered in the county. Airports: McKinley Field at Pearsall is a basic utility airport providing general aviation service and serves as a base for 16 aircraft. Kennels Airport at Bigfoot and Municipal Airpark at Dilley.

COMMUNITY SERVICES

EDUCATION Two school districts with three elementary, two middle and two high schools. The average daily attendance in 1981-82 was 3,147, with expenditures per pupil of $2,593 including 204 classroom teachers with an average annual salary of $15,193. Forty-nine percent of the 163 high school graduates planned to attend college. In 1982-83, 17% of the students were White, 83% Hispanic, 0.3% Black and 0.1% Asian. **PUBLIC LIBRARIES** Frio Public Library (Pearsall): 46,400 volumes. **CHILD CARE** 15 day care and two twenty-four hour care licensed facilities. **HEALTH CARE** Six physicians and one dentist. Hospitals: two with a combined capacity of 57. Ambulance services: one county and one volunteer fire department service. Mental health: one mobile clinic. Nursing homes: two nursing homes with a combined capacity of 156 nursing care residents. The average cost per day for private patients in 1982 was $30.31. **CHURCHES** 25 churches have an estimated combined membership of 8,271. The largest denominations are Catholic, Southern Baptist and United Methodist. **SOCIAL SERVICES** In fiscal year 1983 a total of $1,924,582 in food stamps was distributed, with an average of 4,117 persons receiving food stamps each month. Aid to Families with Dependent Children (AFDC) totaled $509,584 with an average of 322 families receiving AFDC each month. Medical assistance benefits for the aged and disabled of $1,513,877 and for families and children of $895,200 brought the county benefit total to $4,843,243. **FIRE PROTECTION** Three volunteer fire departments. **LAW ENFORCEMENT** The County Sheriff has 25 commissioned officers. Two police departments have a combined force of seven. **CRIME** 31 violent crimes (murder, forcible rape, robbery and aggravated assault) and 115 nonviolent crimes (burglary, larceny-theft and motor vehicle theft) were reported in 1982. **JUDICIAL SYSTEM** Two District Courts and Judges, one County Court and Judge and four Justices of the Peace. In the District Courts a total of 459 cases were pending on 1/1/82, 516 new cases were filed and 431 cases were disposed of during the year leaving 544 cases pending on 12/31/82. There were 363 criminal cases on the docket, 99 convictions, 27 persons committed to prison and 196 cases left pending. In the County Court 568 cases were pending on 1/1/82, 968 new cases were filed and 909 cases were disposed of during the year leaving 627 cases pending on 12/31/82. There were 1,185 criminal cases on the docket, 446 convictions, and 367 cases left pending. **JAILS** One jail, capacity 22. **ATTORNEYS AT LAW** Nine. **UTILITIES** 84% of the residents are connected to a public or privately owned water system and 68% are connected to a public sewer system. Electricity is distributed to the county by Central Power and Light Co., Cochran Power and Light Co., and Medina Electric Coop., Inc. and is generated primarily by gas, oil and coal. The typical residential electric bill is $162.15 per month for an all-electric house using 2,500 kwh. **TAXES** The county has six units with taxing authority: two school districts, two cities, one county, and one special district.

RECREATION/ENTERTAINMENT

NATIONAL REGISTER OF HISTORIC PLACES Pearsall: Old Frio County Jail. **COUNTY/MUNICIPAL PARKS** 16 acres in four county and three municipal parks. These parks contain two playgrounds, three baseball and softball fields, 11 tennis courts, two multi-use courts and one swimming pool.

FRIO (continued)

BOATING/FISHING Lakes/reservoirs: Burns (205 acres), Cox (30 acres), Derby (49 acres), Holcomb (27 acres) and Miracle (75 acres). Major rivers: Frio. Primary streams: Martin, Chacon, Elm, Live Oak, San Miguel and Hondo. **HUNTING** Fall and winter seasons on deer. No closed seasons on javelina, coyote, bobcat and squirrel. Winter seasons on quail, muskrat, beaver, opossum, ring-tailed cat, badger, fox, weasel, raccoon, skunk and civet cat. Fall, winter and spring seasons on turkey. In 1983 sandhill crane, duck, coot, geese, woodcock and jacksnipe seasons occurred during the winter months. Teal duck, rail and gallinule seasons occurred in the fall. Mourning dove seasons occurred intermittently during the fall and winter months with a fall season on white-winged dove. **MUSEUMS** Bigfoot: Bigfoot Wallace Museum. Pearsall: Frio Pioneer Jail Museum. **SPECIAL EVENTS** Spring Arts and Crafts Festival, Pearsall, April; Steer Tripping and Barbecue, Dilley, April; Wintergarden Rodeo and Parade, Dilley, May; Fall Arts and Crafts Festival, Pearsall, October; Christmas Parade, Pearsall, December.

COMMUNITIES

COUNTY SEAT Pearsall, County Courthouse, 78061; County Clerk's Office, 512/334-2214. **INCORPORATED COMMUNITIES** (1980 population and ZIP Code) Dilley (2,579) 78017 and Pearsall (7,383) 78061. **UNINCORPORATED COMMUNITIES** (and ZIP Code) Bigfoot 78005, Derby 78017, Divot 78017, Frio Town 78061, Gold Finch (Goldfinch) 78005, Miguel 78005, Moore 78057, Ratama 78017 and Schattel 78005. **FOR ADDITIONAL LOCAL INFORMATION** Pearsall Chamber of Commerce, 309 E. San Marcos, Pearsall, 78061, 512/334-2242.

GAINES (P57)

THE LAND

Bordering New Mexico and north of Odessa on U.S Highways 385 and 62/180 in the High Plains Region, Gaines County covers 1,504 square miles with an elevation range of 3,000 to 3,600 feet. The usually dry, nearly level soils are sandy with some loamy soils in the north and east. In the High Plains vegetation area, the grasses are mid to tall with a few mesquite trees, shinnery oaks, yucca and sagebrush. Less than 1% of the land in the county is considered prime farmland. **CLIMATE** Mild and dry with dust and wind significant features of weather patterns during spring. The average annual temperature is 61°F. Temperatures in January range from an average low of 25° to an average high of 56°F and in July range from 65° to 94°F. The average annual precipitation is 16 inches, with an average relative humidity of 70% at 6 A.M. and 35% at 6 P.M. The average annual snowfall is 10 inches. The growing season averages 210 days per year, with the last freeze in early April and the first freeze in early November. The sun shines during the year on the average 75% of the daylight hours.

THE PEOPLE

The 1982 estimated population of 13,700 indicates a continuation of the moderate growth begun in the 1970s. Although the urban areas experienced a growth of 73% between 1970 and 1980 the rural population declined 32%. The age groups with the largest gains were ages 20 to 34 and 65 and over. The population is younger than average and has a high birth rate. The largest ancestry groups are Hispanic (30%), persons of English descent (24%) and Irish descent (16%). **REGISTERED VOTERS** As of November 2, 1982 there were 5,251 registered voters (0.1% of the state total). The 1982 general election had a 41% voter turnout, compared to a 65% turnout in the 1980 general election.

In the 1982 primary 97% voted Democratic and 3% Republican, with 1,573 votes cast.

THE ECONOMY

AGRICULTURE Cotton and peanuts area. In 1982, 94% of the land was in farms and ranches, with 58% of the farmland under cultivation and 61% irrigated. Gaines ranked 10th in the state in highest agricultural receipts, with 97% from crops. Overgrazing, wind erosion, decreasing irrigation water supplies and the cultivation of marginal lands are the current conservation problems. Primary crops: first in the state for cotton and third for peanuts. Sorghum and wheat. Primary vegetables: watermelons, potatoes and processed vegetables including beets, cucumbers for pickles, snapbeans, spinach, sweet corn and tomatoes. Primary fruits and nuts: peaches and pecans. Primary livestock and products: cattle, sheep, wool and hogs. **BUSINESS** Total number of business establishments in the county: 263. Retail sales during the first quarter of 1984 increased 11%, with an increase of 19% in Seminole and a decrease of 21% in Seagraves. In 1980, 15% of the labor force were self-employed, 16% were employed in professional or related services, 5% in manufacturing, 18% in wholesale and retail trade, 36% in agriculture, forestry, fisheries and mining, 15% were employed in other counties and there were 767 retired workers. The industries with the most employment: oil and gas extraction, agribusiness, construction and the manufacture of machinery. The nonfarm earnings in 1981 totaled $104,595,000. The retired workers received an average monthly Social Security payment of $322. **FINANCE** On June 30, 1983, three commercial banks had total deposits of $79,915,000 and total assets of $94,273,000. There are two state savings and loan association branches, one federal association and one credit union in the county. **HOUSING** Average value of homes in 1980: $25,400. Permits for new, privately owned housing units increased in 1982: 73 permits were issued with a total construction cost of $2,778,961. Of those permits, 33 were for single family houses. Between 1970 and 1980 the number of housing units increased by 18%. Eighty-four percent of all units in the county are air-conditioned, 18% are heated by gas and 11% by electricity. **NATURAL RESOURCES** Caliche, oil, gas, brine wells and potash. In 1982 a total of 2,429,543 thousand cubic feet of gas well gas, 1,859 barrels of condensate, 47,523,651 barrels of crude oil and 34,235,224 thousand cubic feet of casinghead gas were produced. Current production of other minerals and products includes brine, caliche, sand and gravel, sodium sulfate and recovered sulphur. **TOURISM** Travel expenditures of $5,184,000 in 1982 (an increase of 14% over 1981) generated 102 jobs and $940,000 in payroll. **ALCOHOLIC BEVERAGES** Totally dry. **FEDERAL EXPENDITURES** The federal government had direct expenditures or obligations of $36,533,000 in the county during fiscal year 1983, including $161,000 by the U.S. Department of Defense. In addition, the federal government provided $332,000 in grant awards, paid $559,000 in salaries and wages, made direct payments to individuals of $10,150,000 including $7,683,000 in retirement and disability payments, awarded $2,000 in procurement contracts and spent $25,490,000 in other expenditures or obligations. The federal government also provided $19,174,000 in direct loans and $19,887,000 in guaranteed loans and insurance.

COMMUNICATION

Newspapers–Weekly: Gaines County News (Seagraves) and The Seminole Sentinel (Spanish). Radio: KIKZ-AM (Seminole). Cable TV. Telephone companies: Continental Telephone, General Telephone, Southwestern Bell, Poka-Lambro Rural Telephone Coop. and Romain Telephone. **TRANSPORTATION** Total public road mileage: 1,235. In 1982 there were 12,402 registered vehicles and 318 reported traffic accidents including four fatalities. Intercity bus service is available. Motor freight: six local and intrastate carriers. Rail: one branch line carries annually less than one million tons of freight through the county. Aircraft: 55 are registered in the county. Airports: Gaines County Airport at Seminole is a general utility airport providing general aviation service. It serves as a base for 12 aircraft. Seagraves Airport at Seagraves.

COMMUNITY SERVICES

EDUCATION Three school districts with five elementary, two middle and three high schools. The average daily attendance in 1981-82 was 2,732, with expenditures per pupil of $3,866 including 199 classroom teachers with an average annual salary of $19,401. Forty-seven percent of the 151 high school graduates planned to attend college. In 1982-83, 50% of the students were White, 46% Hispanic, 4% Black and 0.3% Asian. **PUBLIC LIBRARIES** Gaines County Library (Seminole): 34,000 volumes and one branch. **CHILD CARE** 10 day care and four twenty-four hour care licensed facilities. **HEALTH CARE** Six physicians and three dentists. Hospitals: one with a capacity of 49. Clinics: one public health clinic. Ambulance services: one commercial, one county and one volunteer fire department service. Mental health: one county clinic. Nursing homes: one nursing home has a capacity of 32 nursing care residents. **CHURCHES** 28 churches have an estimated combined membership of 8,808. The largest denomination is Southern Baptist. **SOCIAL SERVICES** In fiscal year 1983 a total of $421,487 in food stamps was distributed, with an average of 992 persons receiving food stamps each month. Aid to Families with Dependent Children (AFDC) totaled $62,402 with an average of 38 families receiving AFDC each month. Medical assistance benefits for the aged and disabled of $309,816 and for families and children of $113,859 brought the county benefit total to $907,564. **FIRE PROTECTION** Two volunteer fire departments. **LAW ENFORCEMENT** The County Sheriff has eight commissioned officers. Two police departments have a combined force of 12. **CRIME** 21 violent crimes (murder, forcible rape, robbery and aggravated assault) and 433 nonviolent crimes (burglary, larceny-theft and motor vehicle theft) were reported in 1982. **JUDICIAL SYSTEM** One District Court and Judge, one County Court and Judge and two Justices of the Peace. In the District Court a total of 378 cases were pending on 1/1/82, 635 new cases were filed and 366 cases were disposed of during the year leaving 647 cases pending on 12/31/82. There were 174 criminal cases on the docket, 48 convictions, 11 persons committed to prison and four committed to jail and 95 cases left pending. In the County Court 158 cases were pending on 1/1/82, 309 new cases were filed and 203 cases were disposed of during the year leaving 264 cases pending on 12/31/82. There were 380 criminal cases on the docket, 115 convictions, 39 persons committed to jail, and 190 cases left pending. **JAILS** One jail, capacity 32. **ATTORNEYS AT LAW** Nine. **UTILITIES** 73% of the residents are connected to a public or privately owned water system and 70% are connected to a public sewer system. Natural gas is distributed to the county by Energas Company. The average annual residential bill for natural gas in 1982 for the Energas distribution system was $371.63, an increase of 23% over 1981. Electricity is distributed to the county by Southwestern Public Service and Lyntegar Electric Coop., Inc. and is generated primarily by gas and coal. The typical residential electric bill is $170.44 per month for an all-electric house using 2,500 kwh. **TAXES** The county has seven units with taxing authority: three school districts, two cities, one county and one hospital district.

RECREATION/ENTERTAINMENT

COUNTY/MUNICIPAL PARKS 33 acres in three county and two municipal parks. These parks contain two playgrounds, one golf course and three tennis courts. Developed campsites: three. **BOATING/FISHING** Lakes/reservoirs: McKenzie (100 acres). **HUNTING** Fall season on antelope. No closed seasons on coyote, bobcat and squirrel. Winter seasons on quail, muskrat, beaver, opossum, ring-tailed cat, badger, fox, weasel, raccoon, skunk and civet cat. In 1983 sandhill crane, duck, coot, geese, woodcock and jacksnipe seasons occurred during the winter months. Teal duck, rail and gallinule seasons occurred in the fall. Mourning dove seasons occurred intermittently during the fall and winter months. **MUSEUMS** Seagraves: Gaines County Museum and Art Center. **SPECIAL EVENTS** Independence Day Celebration, Seminole, July.

COMMUNITIES

COUNTY SEAT Seminole, County Courthouse, 79360; County Clerk's Office, 915/758-3521. **INCORPORATED COMMUNITIES** (1980 population and ZIP Code) Seagraves (2,596) 79359 and Seminole (6,080) 79360. **UNINCORPORATED COMMUNITIES** (and ZIP Code) Ashmore 79342, Higginbotham 79323 and Loop 79342. **FOR ADDITIONAL LOCAL INFORMATION** Seagraves Area Chamber of Commerce, 401 Main, P.O. Box 1257, Seagraves, 79359, 806/546-2609 and Seminole Area Chamber of Commerce, P.O. Box 1198, Seminole, 79360, 915/758-2352.

GALVESTON (G19)

THE LAND

Bordering the Gulf of Mexico and south of Houston on Interstate Highway 45 in the Coastal Prairie Region, Galveston County covers 399 square miles with an elevation ranging from sea level to 50 feet. Along the Gulf coast the soils are saline with clayey and loamy soils in marshes and sandy soils along the coastline. To the north the soils are somewhat poorly drained, cracking, clayey soils with areas of loam. In the Gulf Prairies and Marshes vegetation area, the salt marshes have cordgrass, saltgrass and marsh millet. Further inland are tall bunchgrasses and a few mesquite, oak, prickly pear and acacia trees. Between 11 and 20% of the land in the county is considered prime farmland. **CLIMATE** Subtropical humid and mild with tropical storms and a chance of hurricanes June through October. The average annual temperature is 70°F. Temperatures in January range from an average low of 46° to an average high of 60°F and in July range from 78° to 88°F. The average annual precipitation is 44 inches, with an average relative humidity of 95% at 6 A.M. and 70% at 6 P.M. Snowfall is extremely rare. The growing season averages 265 days per year, with the last freeze the first of March and the first freeze in mid December. The sun shines during the year on the average 66% of the daylight hours.

THE PEOPLE

Galveston County is one of the most densely populated in the state. The 1982 estimated population of 207,600 indicates a continuation of the steady growth which has existed since 1930. The age groups with the largest gains were ages 20 to 34 and 65 and over. The largest ancestry groups are persons of English descent (20%), Black (19%), Irish descent (18%) and German descent (17%). **REGISTERED VOTERS** As of November 2, 1982 there were 98,887 registered voters (1% of the state total). The 1982 general election had a 48% voter turnout, compared to a 67% turnout in the 1980 general election. In the 1982 primary 88% voted Democratic and 12% Republican, with 20,165 votes cast.

THE ECONOMY

AGRICULTURE In 1982, 38% of the land was in farms and ranches, with 15% of the farmland under cultivation and 86%

COUNTIES

Galveston (continued)

irrigated. Galveston ranked 235th in the state in highest agricultural receipts, with 62% from livestock and livestock products. Primary crops: rice, hay and soybeans. Primary vegetables: watermelons. Primary fruits and nuts: oranges and pecans. Primary livestock and products: cattle, milk and hogs. **BUSINESS** Total number of business establishments in the county: 3,479. Retail sales during the first quarter of 1984 increased 13%, with Crystal Beach showing a 76% increase and League City showing a 47% increase. In 1980, 6% of the labor force were self-employed, 23% were employed in professional or related services, 17% in manufacturing, 18% in wholesale and retail trade, 10% in construction, 24% were employed in other counties and there were 12,363 retired workers. The industries with the most employment: agribusiness, oil and gas extraction, construction, food packaging, ship building and repairing, petroleum refining, metal coating and the manufacture of industrial chemicals, primary nonferrous metals, pipe and pipe fittings and measuring and controlling instruments. The nonfarm earnings in 1981 totaled $2,360,587,000. The retired workers received an average monthly Social Security payment of $347. **FINANCE** On June 30, 1983, 20 commercial banks had total deposits of $986,719,000 and total assets of $1,133,832,000. On December 31, 1982 five state savings and loan associations, one federal association, nine state branches and seven federal branches had combined assets of $838,959,930. In addition there are 29 credit unions in the county. **HOUSING** Average value of homes in 1980: $42,900. Permits for new, privately owned housing units increased in 1982: 2,877 permits were issued with a total construction cost of $117,618,129. Of those permits, 2,081 were for single family houses. Housing permits increased in Friendswood from 137 in 1981 to 221 in 1982 with all permits issued for single family houses in Galveston from 419 to 1,177 and in League City from 474 to 766 with 706 of the permits issued for single family houses. Between 1970 and 1980 the number of housing units increased by 34%. Eighty-four percent of all units in the county are air-conditioned, 74% are heated by gas and 26% by electricity. **NATURAL RESOURCES** Oil, gas, clay and construction sand. In 1982 a total of 57,542,540 thousand cubic feet of gas well gas, 539,543 barrels of condensate, 3,411,424 barrels of crude oil and 14,853,465 thousand cubic feet of casinghead gas were produced. Current production of other minerals and products includes clay, sand and gravel, and recovered sulphur. **TOURISM** Travel expenditures of $217,127,000 in 1982 (an increase of 10% over 1981) generated 5,102 jobs and $43,563,000 in payroll. Lodging: 31 hotels, motels and tourist courts. Convention/meeting facilities: Galveston—Moody Center Theatre and Exhibit Area and four hotels with facilities for large gatherings. **ALCOHOLIC BEVERAGES** Packaged distilled spirits, beer, ale, malt liquor and wine are legal in parts of the county. Sale of mixed beverages is legal in all or parts of the county. **FEDERAL EXPENDITURES** The federal government had direct expenditures or obligations of $279,754,000 in the county during fiscal year 1983, including $41,466,000 by the U.S. Department of Defense. In addition, the federal government provided $23,571,000 in grant awards, paid $26,508,000 in salaries and wages, made direct payments to individuals of $205,499,000 including $164,249,000 in retirement and disability payments, awarded $22,671,000 in procurement contracts and spent $1,504,000 in other expenditures or obligations. The federal government also provided $2,808,000 in direct loans and $2,329,735,000 in guaranteed loans and insurance.

COMMUNICATION
Newspapers–Daily: The Galveston Daily News, ave. morn. circ. 27,829 and The Texas City Sun, ave. morn. circ. 12,625. Weekly: Suburban Journal (Dickenson), Friendswood Journal, The News (Friendswood) and The LaMarque Times. Radio: KGBC-AM, KILE-AM, KXKX-FM (Galveston) and KYST-AM (Texas City). Cable TV. Telephone companies: General Telephone, Southwestern Bell and Cameron Telephone. **TRANSPORTATION** Total public road mileage: 1,466. In 1982 there were 156,915 registered vehicles and 6,762 reported traffic accidents including 70 fatalities. Municipal transit systems: one intracity bus system in the city of Galveston, with scheduled routes. Intercity bus service is available. Motor freight: 45 local and intrastate carriers. Rail: six main lines carry freight through the county with one carrying annually 20 to 30 million tons, three carrying 10 to 20 each and two carrying five to 10 million each. Aircraft: 228 are registered in the county. Airports: Scholes Field at Galveston is a general transportation airport providing commuter service and serves as a base for 110 planes. Johnie Volk Field at Hitchcock and Ellis Airport at San Leon. The University of Texas Medical Branch Hospital at Galveston and Texas City Hospital at La Marque provide a Heliport for emergency use. Domestic and foreign exports by air from Texas City average three thousand pounds per month. Imports average 40,000 pounds per month. Imports to Galveston average 10,000 pounds per month. Waterborne Commerce: The Texas City Channel at Texas City had total freight traffic in 1981 of 27,852,242 short tons: 11,170,366 in foreign imports, 722,010 in foreign exports and 15,959,866 in domestic shipments. Galveston Channel freight traffic totaled 11,268,337 short tons: 1,904,371 in foreign imports, 7,543,887 in foreign exports and 1,820,079 in domestic shipments. Dickenson Bayou freight traffic totaled 23,275 short tons of domestic shipments.

COMMUNITY SERVICES
EDUCATION Nine school districts with 42 elementary, 14 middle, 10 high schools and two special education. The average daily attendance in 1981-82 was 48,167, with expenditures per pupil of $2,698 including 3,027 classroom teachers with an average annual salary of $19,369. Forty-nine percent of the 3,547 high school graduates planned to attend college. In 1982-83, 70% of the students were White, 11% Hispanic, 17% Black, 2% Asian and 0.1% American Indian. Sports championships: 1983 AAAA Girls' Tennis Singles, Friendswood H.S.; 1984 Boys' Swimming and Diving, League City Clear Lake H.S. Private schools: 3,147 students enrolled in 14 elementary and three high schools. Galveston College is located in Galveston. Established in 1966 it is a vocational and two year academic college under state and local control. Enrollment in 1982 was 1,652 with in state undergraduate tuition and fees of $142 per semester. University of Texas Medical Branch at Galveston was established in 1881 and is under state control. Enrollment in 1982 was 1,586. Texas A&M University at Galveston was established in 1971 and is under state control. Enrollment in 1982 was 593 with in state undergraduate tuition and fees of $279 per semester. The highest degree offered is Bachelor. College of the Mainland is located in Galveston. Established in 1966 it is a vocational and two year academic college under local control. Enrollment in 1982 was 2,501 with in state undergraduate tuition and fees of $135 per semester. Vocational education: John's Mainland Beauty College and Metils, Inc. (Texas City). Financial Careers School, Inc. (Dickenson). **PUBLIC LIBRARIES** Dickenson Public Library: 18,984 volumes. Friendswood Public Library: 35,000 volumes. Rosenberg Library (Galveston): 286,013 volumes. Hitchcock Library. La Marque Public Library: 24,000 volumes. League City Public Library: 48,200 volumes. Santa Fe Library. Moore Memorial Public Library (Texas City): 80,000 volumes. **CHILD CARE** 281 day care and 39 twenty-four hour care licensed facilities. **HEALTH CARE** 719 physicians and 84 dentists.

GALVESTON

Hospitals: four with a combined capacity of 1,576. Specialized hospitals: one children's burn center with capacity of 30. Clinics: two community clinics, one dialysis clinic and one public health clinic. Ambulance services: five commercial, five volunteer services, one city and one county service. Mental health: three clinics. Nursing homes: nine nursing homes with a combined capacity of 956 nursing care residents. The average cost per day for private patients in 1982 was $34.41. **CHURCHES** 163 churches have an estimated combined membership of 94,943. The largest denominations are Catholic, Southern Baptist and United Methodist. **SOCIAL SERVICES** In fiscal year 1983 a total of $9,003,088 in food stamps was distributed, with an average of 16,800 persons receiving food stamps each month. Aid to Families with Dependent Children (AFDC) totaled $2,003,995 with an average of 1,313 families receiving AFDC each month. Medical assistance benefits for the aged and disabled of $8,250,496 and for families and children of $2,313,423 brought the county benefit total to $21,571,001. **FIRE PROTECTION** Three paid and 14 volunteer fire departments. **LAW ENFORCEMENT** The County Sheriff has 193 commissioned officers. 31 police departments have a combined force of 677. One college and one university campus have police departments with a combined force of 13 officers. **CRIME** 1,364 violent crimes (murder, forcible rape, robbery and aggravated assault) and 11,829 nonviolent crimes (burglary, larceny-theft and motor vehicle theft) were reported in 1982. **JUDICIAL SYSTEM** Five District Courts and Judges, five County Courts and Judges and nine Justices of the Peace. In the District Courts a total of 9,684 cases were pending on 1/1/82, 6,197 new cases were filed and 5,289 cases were disposed of during the year leaving 10,592 cases pending on 12/31/82. There were 1,554 criminal cases on the docket, 513 convictions, 231 persons committed to prison and seven committed to jail and 724 cases left pending. In the County Courts 3,779 cases were pending on 1/1/82, 7,095 new cases were filed and 5,545 cases were disposed of during the year leaving 5,329 cases pending on 12/31/82. There were 8,051 criminal cases on the docket, 2,036 convictions, 313 persons committed to jail, and 3,121 cases left pending. **JAILS** One jail, capacity 330. Completed major renovation in 1983. **PRISONS** Texas Department of Corrections Hospital located on the east side of John Sealy Hospital on Strand Street in Galveston. In 1983 the inmate population was 53. Inmates requiring specialized treatment, major surgery or acute care are treated here. **ATTORNEYS AT LAW** 314. **UTILITIES** 93% of the residents are connected to a public or privately owned water system and 89% are connected to a public sewer system. Natural gas is distributed to the county by Entex, Inc.. The average annual residential bill for natural gas in 1982 for the Entex distribution system was $390.31, an increase of 26% over 1981. Electricity is distributed to the county by Gulf State Utilities, Texas-New Mexico Power Co. and Houston Lighting and Power Co. and is generated primarily by gas and oil. The typical residential electric bill is $201.39 per month for an all-electric house using 2,500 kwh. **TAXES** The county has 44 units with taxing authority: nine school districts, 12 cities, one county and 22 special districts.

RECREATION/ENTERTAINMENT
NATIONAL REGISTER OF HISTORIC PLACES Galveston: Galvez Hotel, Daniel Webster Kempner House, Trinity Protestant Episcopal Church, John Hagemann House, First Presbyterian Church, Galveston Orphans Home, Ashton Villa, Henry Beissner House, Bishop's Palace, East End Historic District, Galveston Causeway, Galveston Maritime Site, Galveston Orphans Home, Galveston Seawall, Garten Verein Pavillon, Grace Episcopal Church, Grand Opera House, McKinney-McDonald House, Michel B. Menard House, Old Customs House, "Old Red", Powhatan House, El Paso High School, St. Joseph's Church, St. Mary's Cathedral, George Sealy Home, Strand Historic District, Sweeney-Royston House, Trueheart-Adriance Building and Samuel May Williams House. Galveston vicinity: U.S.S. Hatteras. Galveston Island: Elissa. Port Bolivar: Port Bolivar Lighthouse. Texas City: Frank B. Davison Home. **STATE** Galveston Island State Park covers 1,944 acres with camping and trailer sites as well as areas for fishing, swimming and nature trails. The "Lone Star" a dramatic production is performed during the summer months. **COUNTY/MUNICIPAL PARKS** 4,539 acres in 31 county and 76 municipal parks. These parks contain five miles of hiking trails, 57 playgrounds, two golf courses, three football and soccer fields, 39 baseball and softball fields, 42 tennis courts, 25 multi-use courts, five swimming pools, 19 beaches, 20 boat ramps and shore fishing facilities. Developed campsites: 506. **SCENIC DRIVES** The Texas Independence Trail runs through this county. This trail not only surveys the historic sites of southeastern Texas but also includes many modern visitor attractions such as the Johnson Space Center. **BOATING/FISHING** Lakes/reservoirs: Galveston County (812) acres. Primary streams: Dickenson Bayou and Highland Bayou. **SALTWATER FISHING** Speckled trout, redfish and flounder is usually good around West Bay near Galveston Island. The North and South Jetties at Galveston are nationally known for good fishing. San Luis Pass, at the west end of Galveston Island, ranks as one of the finest natural fish passes on the entire Western Gulf coast. Shrimp, oysters and crabs may be taken but, like other saltwater fish, under specific regulations. **HUNTING** Summer, fall and winter seasons on squirrel. Winter seasons on quail, muskrat, beaver, otter, opossum, mink, ringtailed cat, badger, fox, raccoon, skunk and civet cat. No closed seasons on nutria, bobcat and coyote. In 1983 duck, coot, geese, woodcock and jacksnipe seasons occurred during the winter months. Teal duck, rail and gallinule seasons occurred in the fall. Mourning dove seasons occurred intermittently during the fall and winter months. **MUSEUMS** Friendswood: Frank J. Brown Heritage Museum. Galveston: Galveston County Historical Museum, Rosenberg Library, Trube House, Galveston Historical Foundation, American National Archives, Ashton Villa, The Bishop's Palace, Powhaten House and the Sweeney-Royston House. **THEATERS** League City: Clear Creek Community Theatre. **DANCE** Galveston Civic Ballet and Ballet of the Bay. **COLLEGIATE FINE ARTS** Texas City: Cultural events offered by College of the Mainland. **OTHER** Galveston: Sea-Arama Marineworld. **SPECIAL EVENTS** Battle of Galveston Re-enactment, Galveston, January and April; Marathon Run, Galveston, March; Baseball Day Activities, Friendswood, April; Festival on the Strand, Galveston, April; Village Fair, League City, May; Trinity Auction Gala, Galveston, May; Historical Homes Tour, Galveston, May; Outdoor Drama at State Park, Galveston, May-August; Galveston County Fair, Santa Fe, May; Rainbow Festival, Galveston, May; Strawberry Festival, Dickenson, May; International Seafood Gumbo Cookoff, Galveston, June; Tackle Time Fishing Tourney, Texas City, June; Fireworks Display, Texas City, July 4; Fourth of July Celebration and Parade, Friendswood, July 4; On-the-Water-Fireworks, Kemah, July 4; Annual Famly Picnic and Ice Cream Crank-off, Galveston; July; Annual Blessing of the Fleet, Seabrook-Kemah, August; Good Ole Days Celebration, Hitchcock, August; Annual Shrimp Boil, Texas City, August; Buttermilk Junction, La Marque, August; Heritage Festival, Santa Fe, October; Arts and Crafts Fair, Texas City, November; Glow of Christmas at Ashton Villa, Galveston, December.

COMMUNITIES
COUNTY SEAT Galveston, County Courthouse, 77550; County Clerk's Office, 409/766-2200. **INCORPORATED COMMUNITIES** (1980 population and ZIP Code) Clear Lake Shores (755)

COUNTIES

GALVESTON (continued)

77565, Crystal Beach (776) 77650, Dickenson (Dickenson Village) (7,505) 77539, Friendswood (10,719) 77546, All-America Cities Award 1961 and Honorable Mention 1960, Galveston (61,902) 77550, Hitchcock (6,655) 77563, Jamaica Beach (365) 77550, Kemah (1,304) 77565, La Marque (15,372) 77568, League City (16,578) 77573, Santa Fe (6,172) 77550 and Texas City (41,403) 77590. **UNINCORPORATED COMMUNITIES** (and ZIP Code) Algoa 77511, Bacliff (Bay View) 77518, Caplen 77617, Gilchrist 77617, High Island 77623, Highland Bayou 77563, Port Bolivar 77650, San Leon 77539, Tiki Island 77551, Virginia Point 77550 and West Galveston 77550. **FOR ADDITIONAL LOCAL INFORMATION** Dickenson Chamber of Commerce, P.O. Box 426, Dickenson, 77539, 409/337-3434, Friendswood Chamber of Commerce, 416 W. Friendswood Drive, P.O. Box 11, Friendswood, 77546, 409/482-3329, Galveston Chamber of Commerce, 315 Tremont, Galveston, 77550, 409/763-5326, Galveston Mexican Chamber of Commerce, 1801 Avenue L, Galveston, 77550, 409/763-3980, Hitchcock Chamber of Commerce, P.O. Box 389, Hitchcock, 77563, 409/986-5222 and Texas City-La Marque Chamber of Commerce, P.O. Box 3330, Texas City, 77590, 409/935-1408.

GARZA (P50)

THE LAND

Southeast of Lubbock on U.S. Highway 84 in the Rolling Plains Region, Garza County covers 895 square miles with an elevation range of 2,300 to 3,000 feet. Along the northern half of the western border are nearly level, alkaline soils with loamy surface layers and clayey subsoils, some with hardened lime within 20 inches of the surface. The southern half of the county has red to brown soils with loamy surface layers and clayey or loamy subsoils and cracking, clayey soils. There is a high shrink-swell potential. The rest of the county has loamy soils with some clayey subsoils. Garza is in the Rolling Plains vegetation area with short to tall grass, some small mesquite, thorny shrubs and cacti. Between 21 and 30% of the land in the county is considered prime farmland. **CLIMATE** Mild and dry, with thunderstorms, duststorms and high winds possible during spring and early summer. The average annual temperature is 61°F. Temperatures in January range from an average low of 25° to an average high of 54°F and in July range from 68° to 93°F. The average annual precipitation is 19 inches, with an average relative humidity of 72% at 6 A.M. and 38% at 6 P.M. The average annual snowfall is 10 inches. The growing season averages 216 days per year, with the last freeze in early April and the first freeze early November. The sun shines during the year on the average 75% of the daylight hours.

THE PEOPLE

The 1982 estimated population of 5,600 indicates a continuation of the growth rate begun in the 1970s which reversed the population decrease of 20% between 1960 and 1970. While urban areas grew slightly from 1970 to 1980, population in rural areas declined. The age group with the largest gain was ages 20 to 34 with the largest loss among ages five to 14. The largest ancestry groups are persons of English descent (30%), Hispanic (24%) and Irish descent (15%). **REGISTERED VOTERS** As of November 2, 1982 there were 2,642 registered voters (0.04% of the state total). The 1982 general election had a 40% voter turnout, compared to a 68% turnout in the 1980 general election. In the 1982 primary 98% voted Democratic and 2% Republican, with 900 votes cast.

THE ECONOMY

AGRICULTURE Cotton area. In 1982, 94% of the land was in farms and ranches, with 11% of the farmland under cultivation and 13% irrigated. Garza ranked 171st in the state in highest agricultural receipts, with 53% from crops. Overgrazing, undesirable brush and weeds, water erosion, decreasing irrigation water supplies and noxious weeds are the current conservation problems. Primary crops: cotton, sorghum, wheat and hay. Primary livestock and products: eighth in the state for egg production and ninth for hens and pullets. Cattle. **BUSINESS** Total number of business establishments in the county: 115. Retail sales during the first quarter of 1984 decreased 3%. In 1980, 19% of the labor force were self-employed, 14% were employed in professional or related services, 22% in manufacturing, 12% in wholesale and retail trade, 28% in agriculture, forestry, fisheries and mining, 11% were employed in other counties and there were 546 retired workers. The industries with the most employment: agribusiness, oil and gas extraction and textile mills. The non-farm earnings in 1981 totaled $50,762,000. The retired workers received an average monthly Social Security payment of $311. **FINANCE** On June 30, 1983, one commercial bank had total deposits of $38,710,000 and total assets of $42,944,000. There is one savings and loan association branch in the county. **HOUSING** Average value of homes in 1980: $19,400. Permits for new, privately owned housing units increased in 1982: 35 permits were issued with a total construction cost of $1,404,879. Of those permits, three were for single family houses. Between 1970 and 1980 the number of housing units increased by 1%. Eighty percent of all units in the county are air-conditioned, 92% are heated by gas and 7% by electricity. **NATURAL RESOURCES** Caliche, oil and gas. In 1982 a total of 7,742,995 barrels of crude oil and 1,220,391 thousand cubic feet of casinghead gas were produced. **TOURISM** Travel expenditures of $1,236,000 in 1982 (an increase of 13% over 1981) generated 27 jobs and $227,000 in payroll. **ALCOHOLIC BEVERAGES** Packaged distilled spirits, beer, ale, malt liquor and wine are legal in parts of the county. **FEDERAL EXPENDITURES** The federal government had direct expenditures or obligations of $12,118,000 in the county during fiscal year 1983, including $97,000 by the U.S. Department of Defense. In addition, the federal government provided $128,000 in grant awards, paid $413,000 in salaries and wages, made direct payments to individuals of $7,152,000 including $4,971,000 in retirement and disability payments, awarded $744,000 in procurement contracts and spent $3,680,000 in other expenditures or obligations. The federal government also provided $357,000 in direct loans and $1,993,000 in guaranteed loans and insurance.

COMMUNICATION

Newspapers–Weekly: The Post Dispatch. Radio: KPOS-AM (Post). Cable TV. Telephone companies: General Telephone, Southwestern Bell, Cap Rock Telephone and Poka-Lambro Rural Telephone Coop. **TRANSPORTATION** Total public road mileage: 504. In 1982 there were 4,880 registered vehicles and 180 reported traffic accidents including four fatalities. Intercity bus service is available. Motor freight: two carriers. Rail: one main line carries annually over 30 million tons of freight through the county. Aircraft: 12 are registered in the county. Airports: Post-Garza County Municipal Airport is a basic utility airport providing general aviation service. It serves as a base for 15 aircraft.

COMMUNITY SERVICES

EDUCATION Two school districts with two elementary, one middle and two high schools. The average daily attendance in 1981-82 was 1,225, with expenditures per pupil of $3,441 including 86 classroom teachers with an average annual salary of $17,235. Thirty-eight percent of the 80 high school graduates planned to

GARZA-GILLESPIE

attend college. In 1982-83, 56% of the students were White, 37% Hispanic, 7% Black and 0.1% Asian. **PUBLIC LIBRARIES** Post Public Library: 13,194 volumes. **CHILD CARE** One day care and three twenty-four hour care licensed facilities. **HEALTH CARE** Four physicians and two dentists. Hospitals: one with a capacity of 26. Ambulance services: one volunteer service. Mental health: one county clinic. Nursing homes: two nursing homes with a combined capacity of 99 nursing care residents. The average cost per day for private patients in 1982 was $28.24. **CHURCHES** 21 churches have an estimated combined membership of 3,472. The largest denominations are Southern Baptist, United Methodist and Churches of Christ. **SOCIAL SERVICES** In fiscal year 1983 a total of $264,444 in food stamps was distributed, with an average of 589 persons receiving food stamps each month. Aid to Families with Dependent Children (AFDC) totaled $48,030 with an average of 32 families receiving AFDC each month. Medical assistance benefits for the aged and disabled of $498,418 and for families and children of $45,651 brought the county benefit total to $856,533. **FIRE PROTECTION** One volunteer fire department. **LAW ENFORCEMENT** The County Sheriff has seven commissioned officers. **CRIME** 14 violent crimes (murder, forcible rape, robbery and aggravated assault) and 140 nonviolent crimes (burglary, larceny-theft and motor vehicle theft) were reported in 1982. **JUDICIAL SYSTEM** One District Court and Judge, one County Court and Judge and two Justices of the Peace. In the District Court a total of 268 cases were pending on 1/1/82, 126 new cases were filed and 129 cases were disposed of during the year leaving 265 cases pending on 12/31/82. There were 85 criminal cases on the docket, 26 convictions, three persons committed to prison, and 44 cases left pending. In the County Court 132 cases were pending on 1/1/82, 247 new cases were filed and 239 cases were disposed of during the year leaving 140 cases pending on 12/31/82. There were 369 criminal cases on the docket, 187 convictions, four persons committed to jail, and 134 cases left pending. **JAILS** One jail, capacity 10. **ATTORNEYS AT LAW** Four. **UTILITIES** 78% of the residents are connected to a public or privately owned water system and 74% are connected to a public sewer system. Natural gas is distributed to the county by Energas Company. The average annual residential bill for natural gas in 1982 for the Energas distribution system was $371.63, an increase of 23% over 1981. Electricity is distributed to the county by Southwestern Public Service, Dickens Electric Coop., Inc, Lyntegar Electric Coop., Inc. and Midwest Electric Coop., Inc. and is generated primarily by gas and coal. The typical residential electric bill is $170.44 per month for an all-electric house using 2,500 kwh. **TAXES** The county has five units with taxing authority: two school districts, one city, one county and one hospital district.

RECREATION/ENTERTAINMENT
NATIONAL REGISTER OF HISTORIC PLACES Post: Agerita Hotel and Post Sanitarium. Post vicinity: Cooper's Canyon Site, Post-Montgomery Site and Post West Dugout. **MUNICIPAL PARKS** 32 acres in one municipal park. This park contains one playground, one multi-use court and one swimming pool. Developed campsites: six. **SCENIC DRIVES** The Texas Plains Trail runs through this county. In southern Garza County F.M. 669 reaches the edge of Texas High Plains and descends where the plains end travelling through views of steep cliffs and canyons. **BOATING/FISHING** Lakes/reservoirs: Justiceburg (35 acres). Major rivers: North Fork Double Mountain Fork Brazos, Double Mountain Fork Brazos, Salt Fork Brazos and White. Primary streams: Coon. **HUNTING** Fall season on antelope. Fall and winter seasons on deer and mule deer. No closed seasons on coyote, bobcat and squirrel. Winter seasons on quail, muskrat, beaver, opossum, ring-tailed cat, badger, fox, weasel, raccoon, skunk and civet cat. Fall, winter

and spring seasons on turkey. In 1983 sandhill crane, duck, coot, geese, woodcock and jacksnipe seasons occurred during the winter months. Teal duck, rail and gallinule seasons occurred in the fall. Mourning dove seasons occurred intermittently during the fall and winter months. **MUSEUMS** Post: Garza County Historical Museum. **SPECIAL EVENTS** Junior Stock Show and Fair, Post, March; Taba'na Yuan'e, Post, March; Fourth of July Celebration, Post, July; Stampede Rodeo and Parade, Post, August.

COMMUNITIES
COUNTY SEAT Post, County Courthouse, 79356; County Clerk's Office, 806/495-3352. **INCORPORATED COMMUNITIES** (1980 population and ZIP Code) Post (3,961) 79356 and Southland (168, est. incorp. inactive) 79368. **UNINCORPORATED COMMUNITIES** (and ZIP Code) Close City (Ragtown) 79356, Graham (Graham Chapel) 79356, Justiceburg 79330 and Pleasant Valley 79356. **FOR ADDITIONAL LOCAL INFORMATION** Post Chamber of Commerce, 106 S. Broadway, Post, 79356, 806/495-3461.

GILLESPIE (C22)

THE LAND
West of Austin on U.S. Highways 290 and 87 in the Edwards Plateau Region, Gillespie County covers 1,061 square miles with an elevation range of 1,110 to 2,100 feet. Along the northern border and the Pedernales River from the eastern border to the center of the county are deep to shallow soils with loamy surface layers and clayey to loamy subsoils over granite, schist or sandstone. The remainder of the county has alkaline, shallow to deep, loamy soils with some clayey subsoils. Gillespie is in the Edwards Plateau vegetation area with tall and mid grasses, live oaks, scrubby post oak, mesquite, shrubs and cacti. Between 11 and 20% of the land in the county is considered prime farmland. **CLIMATE** Subtropical Subhumid with hot summer days and cool nights. The average annual temperature is 66°F. Temperatures in January range from an average low of 35° to an average high of 61°F and in July range from 69° to 96°F. The average annual precipitation is 28 inches, with an average relative humidity of 78% at 6 A.M. and 48% at 6 P.M. The average annual snowfall is two inches. The growing season averages 219 days per year, with the last freeze in early April and the first freeze in early November. The sun shines during the year on the average 65% of the daylight hours.

THE PEOPLE
Gillespie County population is older than average and ranks 75th among all U.S. counties in the highest percent of population 65 and over. The 1982 estimated population of 14,200 indicates a continuation of a moderate growth rate begun in the 1960s reversing the steady population decline between 1930 and 1960. The population grew 28% between 1970 and 1980. Almost 36% of the growth was in rural areas. The age groups with the largest gains were ages 20 to 34 and 62 and over. The largest ancestry groups are persons of German descent (23%) English descent (18%) and Irish descent (10%). **REGISTERED VOTERS** As of November 2, 1982 there were 7,429 registered voters (0.1% of the state total). The 1982 general election had a 61% voter turnout, compared to an 82% turnout in the 1980 general election. In the 1982 primary 42% voted Democratic and 58% Republican, with 1,094 votes cast.

THE ECONOMY
AGRICULTURE Diversified products. In 1982, 95% of the land was in farms and ranches, with 10% of the farmland under cultivation and 3% irrigated. Gillespie ranked 124th in the state

GILLESPIE (continued)

in highest agricultural receipts, with 92% from livestock and livestock products. Overgrazing, water erosion and water conservation are the current conservation problems. Primary crops: ninth in the state for oats. Wheat, hay and sorghum. Primary vegetables: potatoes, sweet potatoes, tomatoes and watermelons. Primary fruits and nuts: first in the state for peaches and a leader in both apples and plums. Pecans. Primary livestock and products: second in the state for turkeys, sixth for hogs and 10th for both angora goats and mohair production. Cattle, milk, sheep and wool. **BUSINESS** Total number of business establishments in the county: 415. Retail sales during the first quarter of 1984 increased 12%. In 1980, 19% of the labor force were self-employed, 20% were employed in professional or related services, 9% in manufacturing, 25% in wholesale and retail trade, 14% in construction, 13% were employed in other counties and there were 2,137 retired workers. The industries with the most employment: agribusiness, tourism, construction and processing poultry. The nonfarm earnings in 1981 totaled $140,421,000. The retired workers received an average monthly Social Security payment of $304. **FINANCE** On June 30, 1983, four commercial banks had total deposits of $139,469,000 and total assets of $155,863,000. There are two state savings and loan association branches, one branch of a federal association and one credit union in the county. **HOUSING** Average value of homes in 1980: $41,300. Permits for new, privately owned housing units decreased in 1982: 73 permits were issued with a total construction cost of $3,304,700. Of those permits, 53 were for single family houses. Between 1970 and 1980 the number of housing units increased by 39%. Fifty-eight percent of all units in the county are air-conditioned, 71% are heated by gas and 17% by electricity. **NATURAL RESOURCES** Copper, dolomite, sand, serpentine, talc, gypsum, granite, lead, vermiculite, oil and gas. Current production of other minerals and products includes dimension granite, gypsum, crushed limestone, dimension limestone, sand and gravel and terrazzo serpentine. **TOURISM** Travel expenditures of $9,636,000 in 1982 (an increase of 14% over 1981) generated 189 jobs and $1,700,000 in payroll. Lodging: five hotels, motels and tourist courts. Convention/meeting facilities: Fredericksburg—Gillespie County Fair Grandstand and Exhibit Area. **ALCOHOLIC BEVERAGES** Packaged distilled spirits, beer, ale, malt liquor and wine are legal in parts of the county. Sale of mixed beverages is legal in all or parts of the county. **FEDERAL EXPENDITURES** The federal government had direct expenditures or obligations of $34,542,000 in the county during fiscal year 1983, including $3,902,000 by the U.S. Department of Defense. In addition, the federal government provided $198,000 in grant awards, paid $2,149,000 in salaries and wages, made direct payments to individuals of $29,036,000 including $22,317,000 in retirement and disability payments, awarded $1,935,000 in procurement contracts and spent $1,224,000 in other expenditures or obligations. The federal government also provided $22,000 in direct loans and $5,603,000 in guaranteed loans and insurance.

COMMUNICATION

Newspapers–Weekly: Fredericksburg Standard, The Radio Post (Fredericksburg) and The Harper Herald. Radio: KNAF-AM and KFAN-FM (Fredericksburg). Cable TV. Telephone companies: General Telephone, Hill Country Telephone Coop. and Kerrville Telephone. **TRANSPORTATION** Total public road mileage: 779. In 1982 there were 15,145 registered vehicles and 315 reported traffic accidents including nine fatalities. Taxi cabs: one company in Fredericksburg. Intercity bus service is available. Motor freight: four carriers. Aircraft: 20 are registered in the county. Airports: Gillespie County Airport at Fredericksburg is a general utility airport providing general aviation service. It serves as a base for 15 aircraft.

COMMUNITY SERVICES

EDUCATION Three school districts with four elementary, one middle and two high schools The average daily attendance in 1981-82 was 2,173, with expenditures per pupil of $2,665 including 167 classroom teachers with an average annual salary of $16,056. Thirty-six percent of the 192 high school graduates planned to attend college. In 1982-83, 80% of the students were White, 20% Hispanic, 0.5% Black and 0.4% Asian. Private schools: 163 students enrolled in one elementary school. Vocational education: Fredericksburg School of Vocational Nursing (Fredericksburg). **PUBLIC LIBRARIES** Pioneer Memorial City-County Library (Fredericksburg): 34,227 volumes. **CHILD CARE** 44 day care licensed facilities. **HEALTH CARE** 18 physicians and nine dentists. Hospitals: one with a capacity of 61. Ambulance services: one hospital-based and one volunteer fire department service. Mental health: one clinic. Nursing homes: four nursing homes with a combined capacity of 365 nursing care residents. The average cost per day for private patients in 1982 was $27.09. **CHURCHES** 22 churches have an estimated combined membership of 10,251. The largest denominations are American Lutheran, Churches of Christ and United Methodist. **SOCIAL SERVICES** In fiscal year 1983 a total of $221,260 in food stamps was distributed, with an average of 495 persons receiving food stamps each month. Aid to Families with Dependent Children (AFDC) totaled $33,793 with an average of 23 families receiving AFDC each month. Medical assistance benefits for the aged and disabled of $1,680,472 and for families and children of $46,938 brought the county benefit total to $1,982,463. **FIRE PROTECTION** Five volunteer fire departments. **LAW ENFORCEMENT** The County Sheriff has nine commissioned officers. One police department has a force of 12. **CRIME** Three violent crimes (murder, forcible rape, robbery and aggravated assault) and 194 nonviolent crimes (burglary, larceny-theft and motor vehicle theft) were reported in 1982. **JUDICIAL SYSTEM** One District Court and Judge, one County Court and Judge and one Justice of the Peace. In the District Court a total of 134 cases were pending on 1/1/82, 196 new cases were filed and 174 cases were disposed of during the year leaving 156 cases pending on 12/31/82. There were 64 criminal cases on the docket, 15 convictions, three persons committed to prison, and 31 cases left pending. In the County Court 70 cases were pending on 1/1/82, 246 new cases were filed and 264 cases were disposed of during the year leaving 52 cases pending on 12/31/82. There were 297 criminal cases on the docket, 160 convictions, 46 persons committed to jail, and 40 cases left pending. **JAILS** One jail, capacity 15. **ATTORNEYS AT LAW** 25. **UTILITIES** 56% of the residents are connected to a public or privately owned water system and 53% are connected to a public sewer system. Natural gas is distributed to the county by Lone Star Gas Co., Division of Enserch. The average annual residential bill for natural gas in 1982 for the Lone Star distribution system was $405.91, an increase of 35% over 1981. Electricity is distributed to the city of Fredericksburg by the Fredericksburg Electric Utility and to the rest of the county by Central Texas Electric Coop., Inc. and Pedernales Electric Coop., Inc. and is generated primarily by oil, water and coal. The typical residential electric bill is $117.35 per month for an all-electric house using 2,500 kwh. **TAXES** The county has six units with taxing authority: three school districts, one city, one county and one special district.

RECREATION/ENTERTAINMENT

FEDERAL LYNDON B. JOHNSON NATIONAL HISTORIC PARK encompasses 1,478 acres and contains the birthplace, boyhood home and ranch of the 36th President of the United

States as well as the ranch of his grandparents. **NATIONAL REGISTER OF HISTORIC PLACES** Fredericksburg: Fredericksburg Historic District and Fredericksburg Memorial Library. Fredericksburg vicinity: Fort Martin Scott. Stonewall vicinity: LBJ National Historic Site. **STATE** Admiral Nimitz State Historical Park covers nine acres with a museum and a historic structure. Enchanted Rock State Natural Area covers 1,643 acres with camping facilities. The park includes a massive dome of solid granite which, according to Indian legend, was said to be the site of human sacrifices. Lyndon B. Johnson State Historical Park covers 718 acres with areas offering fishing, swimming and nature trails. Historic buildings depict the frontier days of the Texas Hill Country. Wildlife displays include Texas Longhorns, white-tailed deer and buffalo. **MUNICIPAL PARKS** 193 acres in three municipal parks. These parks contain two playgrounds, one golf course, six baseball and softball fields, six tennis courts, two multi-use courts, one swimming pool, two beaches and one boat ramp. Developed campsites: 113. **SCENIC DRIVES** The Texas Hill Country Trail runs through this county. This trail winds through a scenic region of South-Central Texas, spanning a vast ranching area abundant with wildlife in a landscape of deeply-sculptured valleys and hills. **BOATING/FISHING** Lakes/reservoirs: Voigt (32 acres). Major rivers: Pedernales. Primary streams: Crabapple, Mayer and Threadgill. **HUNTING** Fall and winter seasons on deer and javelina. No closed seasons on coyote, bobcat and squirrel. Winter seasons on quail, muskrat, beaver, opossum, ring-tailed cat, badger, fox, weasel, raccoon, skunk and civet cat. Fall, winter and spring seasons on turkey. In 1983 sandhill crane, duck, coot, geese, woodcock and jacksnipe seasons occurred during the winter months. Teal duck, rail and gallinule seasons occurred in the fall. Mourning dove seasons occurred intermittently during the fall and winter months. **MUSEUMS** Fredericksburg: Admiral Nimitz Center and Pioneer Museum. Stonewall: LBJ State Park Visitor Center. **SPECIAL EVENTS** Junior Stock Show, Fredericksburg, January; Wild Game Dinner for Men, Fredericksburg, March; Easter Fire Pageant and Homes Tour, Fredericksburg, April; HCHC Rodeo, Fredericksburg, April; Founders Day Celebration, Fredericksburg, May; Walkfest, Fredericksburg, June; Swimfest, Fredericksburg, June; Peach Jamboree and Rodeo, Stonewall, June; Patriotic Celebration, Fredericksburg, July; Fourth of July Race Festival, Fredericksburg, July; Night in Old Fredericksburg, Fredericksburg, July; Bundes Schuetzenfest, Fredericksburg, July; County Fair, Fredericksburg, August; Das 1st Alles Fest, Fredericksburg, September; Ima Hogg Memorial Texas State Ladies Chili Bust, Luckenbach, October; Octoberfest, Fredericksburg, October; Waltzfest, Fredericksburg, October; Turkey Shoot, Fredericksburg, November; Kristkindl Market and Candlelight Tour, Fredericksburg, December.

COMMUNITIES

COUNTY SEAT Fredericksburg, County Courthouse, 78624; County Clerk's Office, 512/997-2955. **INCORPORATED COMMUNITIES** (1980 population and ZIP Code) Fredericksburg (6,412) 78624. **UNINCORPORATED COMMUNITIES** (and ZIP Code) Albert 78601, Blumenthal 78624, Cain City 78647, Cherry Spring 78624, Doss 78618, Eckert 78675, Gold 78624, Harper 78631, Luckenbach (Luckenbach) 78624, Morris Ranch 78624, Stonewall 78671, Tivydale 78624 and Willow City 78675. **FOR ADDITIONAL LOCAL INFORMATION** Fredericksburg Chamber of Commerce, P.O. Box 506, Fredericksburg, 78624, 512/997-3444 and Stonewall Chamber of Commerce, P.O. Box One, Stonewall, 78671, 512/644-2304.

GLASSOCK (P77)

THE LAND

East of Midland on State Highways 158, 137 and 33 in the Edwards Plateau Region, Glassock County covers 900 square miles with an elevation range of 2,400 to 2,600 feet. In the northwest corner of the county are mostly level soils with loamy surfaces and clayey subsoils. The rest of the county has undulating to hilly alkaline, loamy soils over limestone. Up to 90% of the area is exposed rock. The northwest corner of the county is in the High Plains vegetation area with short and mid grasses, small mesquite trees, thorny shrubs and cacti. The rest of the county is in the Edwards Plateau vegetation area with tall or mid grasses, brushey mesquite, juniper, live oak and shinnery oak trees. Less than 1% of the land in the county is considered prime farmland. **CLIMATE** Mild and dry with dust storms and high winds possible during spring. The average annual temperature is 65°F. Temperatures in January range from an average low of 30° to an average high of 59°F and in July range from 71° to 95°F. The average annual precipitation is 16 inches, with an average relative humidity of 73% at 6 A.M. and 37% at 6 P.M. The average annual snowfall is four inches. The growing season averages 222 days per year, with the last freeze in early April and the first freeze in mid November. The sun shines during the year on the average 75% of the daylight hours.

THE PEOPLE

Glassock County is one of the most sparsely populated in the state. The 1982 estimated population of 1,200 indicates a decline in population since 1980. Rural areas increased 13% in population from 1970 to 1980. The age group with the largest gain was ages 20 to 34, with the young median age lowering from 27 in 1970 to 25 in 1980. The largest ancestry groups are persons of German descent (32%), Hispanic (29%) and Irish descent (19%). **REGISTERED VOTERS** As of November 2, 1982 there were 712 registered voters (0.01% of the state total). The 1982 general election had a 62% voter turnout, compared to a 81% turnout in the 1980 general election. In the 1982 primary 100% voted Democratic with 354 votes cast.

THE ECONOMY

AGRICULTURE Cotton area. In 1982, 95% of the land was in farms and ranches, with 15% of the farmland under cultivation and 45% irrigated. Glassock ranked 121st in the state in highest agricultural receipts, with 87% from crops. Overgrazing, undesirable brush and weeds, wind erosion, decreasing irrigation water supplies and inadequate cropping systems are the current conservation problems. Primary crops: cotton, sorghum and wheat. Primary vegetables: cantaloupes, tomatoes and watermelons. Primary fruits and nuts: pecans. Primary livestock and products: cattle, sheep, wool and hogs. **BUSINESS** Total number of business establishments in the county: 14. In 1980, 40% of the labor force were self-employed, 10% were employed in professional or related services, 2% in manufacturing, 10% in wholesale and retail trade, 60% in agriculture, forestry, fisheries and mining, 28% were employed in other counties and there were 64 retired workers. The industries with the most employment: agribusiness and oil and gas extraction. The nonfarm earnings in 1981 totaled $12,479,000. The retired workers received an average monthly Social Security payment of $313. **HOUSING** Average value of homes in 1980: $25,400. Between 1970 and 1980 the number of housing units increased by 33%. Sixty percent of all units in the county are air-conditioned, 77% are heated by gas and 22% by electricity. **NATURAL RESOURCES** Caliche, limestone, salt, oil and gas. In 1982 a total of 181,321 thousand cubic feet of gas well gas, 35,747 barrels of condensate, 4,317,767 barrels of crude oil and 11,151,304 thousand cubic feet of

GLASSOCK (continued)

casinghead gas were produced. **TOURISM** Travel expenditures of $1,272,000 in 1982 (an increase of 19% over 1981) generated 16 jobs and $178,000 in payroll. **ALCOHOLIC BEVERAGES** Totally dry. **FEDERAL EXPENDITURES** The federal government had direct expenditures or obligations of $6,924,000 in the county during fiscal year 1983, including $10,000 by the U.S. Department of Defense. In addition, the federal government provided $32,000 in grant awards, paid $38,000 in salaries and wages, made direct payments to individuals of $935,000 including $687,000 in retirement and disability payments and spent $5,919,000 in other expenditures or obligations. The federal government also provided $4,280,000 in direct loans and $7,073,000 in guaranteed loans and insurance.

COMMUNICATION

Telephone companies: General Telephone, Southwestern Bell and Wes-Tex Telephone Coop. **TRANSPORTATION** Total public road mileage: 316. In 1982 there were 1,527 registered vehicles and 29 reported traffic accidents including three fatalities. Intercity bus service is available. Motor freight: two carriers. Aircraft: six are registered in the county.

COMMUNITY SERVICES

EDUCATION One school district with one elementary and one high school. The average daily attendance in 1981-82 was 345, with expenditures per pupil of $5,366 including 29 classroom teachers with an average annual salary of $18,555. None of the 27 high school graduates planned to attend college. In 1982-83, 58% of the students were White and 42% Hispanic. **HEALTH CARE** Ambulance services: one volunteer service. **CHURCHES** Four churches have an estimated combined membership of 895. The largest denominations are Catholic and Southern Baptist. **SOCIAL SERVICES** In fiscal year 1983 a total of $40,033 in food stamps was distributed, with an average of 73 persons receiving food stamps each month. Aid to Families with Dependent Children (AFDC) totaled $7,223. Medical assistance benefits for the aged and disabled of $4,615 and for families and children of $12,537 brought the county benefit total to $64,408. **FIRE PROTECTION** Three volunteer fire departments. **LAW ENFORCEMENT** The County Sheriff has three commissioned officers. **CRIME** Eight nonviolent crimes (burglary, larceny-theft and motor vehicle theft) were reported in 1982. **JUDICIAL SYSTEM** One District Court and Judge, one County Court and Judge and one Justice of the Peace. In the District Court a total of 32 cases were pending on 1/1/82, 24 new cases were filed and 17 cases were disposed of during the year leaving 257 cases pending on 12/31/82. There were seven criminal cases on the docket, two convictions, two persons committed to prison, and five cases left pending. In the County Court nine cases were pending on 1/1/82, 11 new cases were filed and 16 cases were disposed of during the year leaving four cases pending on 12/31/82. There were 20 criminal cases on the docket, 10 convictions, and four cases left pending. **JAILS** One jail, capacity 12. **UTILITIES** 3% of the residents are connected to a public or privately owned water system and 3% are connected to a public sewer system. Electricity is distributed to the county by Cap Rock Electric Coop., Inc. and Concho Valley Electric Coop., Inc. and is generated primarily by gas and oil. **TAXES** The county has three units with taxing authority: one school district, one county and one special district.

RECREATION/ENTERTAINMENT

BOATING/FISHING Lakes/reservoirs: Currie (50 acres) and Dewey (100 acres). Major rivers: North Concho. Primary streams: Lacy. **HUNTING** Fall season on antelope. Fall and winter seasons

on deer and javelina. No closed seasons on coyote, bobcat and squirrel. Winter seasons on quail, muskrat, beaver, opossum, ring-tailed cat, badger, fox, weasel, raccoon, skunk and civet cat. In 1983 sandhill crane, duck, coot, geese, woodcock and jacksnipe seasons occurred during the winter months. Teal duck, rail and gallinule seasons occurred in the fall. Mourning dove seasons occurred intermittently during the fall and winter months.

COMMUNITIES

COUNTY SEAT Garden City, County Courthouse, 79739; County Clerk's Office, 915/354-2371. **UNINCORPORATED COMMUNITIES** (and ZIP Code) Garden City 79739, Lees (Lee Store) 79720 and Saint Lawrence 79739.

GOLIAD (G27)

THE LAND

North of Corpus Christi on U.S. Highways 59 and 183 in the Rio Grande Plain Region, Goliad County covers 859 square miles with an elevation range of 100 to 250 feet. The county has level to undulating loamy to clayey soils over limestone. To the east the soils have sandy surfaces. The northeastern corner of the county lies in the Post Oak Savannah vegetation area with tall grasses and post and blackjack oak trees. The rest of the county is in the South Texas Plains vegetation area with short to tall grasses, some mesquite, thorny shrubs and cacti. Between 31 and 40% of the land in the county is considered prime farmland. **CLIMATE** Borders Subtropical Humid and Subtropical Subhumid and is generally mild. The average annual temperature is 71 °F. Temperatures in January range from an average low of 43° to an average high of 66 °F and in July range from 74° to 95 °F. The average annual precipitation is 36 inches, with an average relative humidity of 87% at 6 A.M. and 60% at 6 P.M. There is no snowfall. The growing season averages 285 days per year, with the last freeze in late February and the first freeze in early November. The sun shines during the year on the average 67% of the daylight hours.

THE PEOPLE

In 1980 Goliad County ranked 75th among all U.S. counties in the highest percent of persons of Spanish origin. The 1982 estimated population of 5,400 indicates a continuation of the growth begun in the 1970s which reversed the steady population decline from 1930 to 1970. The age group with the largest gain was ages 20 to 34. The largest ancestry groups are Hispanic (36%), persons of German descent (25%) and English descent (13%). **REGISTERED VOTERS** As of November 2, 1982 there were 3,176 registered voters (0.04% of the state total). The 1982 general election had a 56% voter turnout, compared to a 72% turnout in the 1980 general election. In the 1982 primary 100% voted Democratic with 880 votes cast.

THE ECONOMY

AGRICULTURE In 1982, 90% of the land was in farms and ranches, with 5% of the farmland under cultivation and 8% irrigated. Goliad ranked 155th in the state in highest agricultural receipts, with 84% from livestock and livestock products. Overgrazing, undesirable brush and weeds, water erosion and inefficient tillage systems are the current conservation problems. Primary crops: hay, corn, oats and sorghum. Primary vegetables: seventh in the state for watermelons. Primary fruits and nuts: peaches and pecans. Primary livestock and products: cattle, milk, sheep, wool and hogs. **BUSINESS** Total number of business establishments in the county: 79. Retail sales during the first quarter of 1984 increased 30%. In 1980, 13% of the labor force were self-employed, 22% were employed in professional or related services, 7% in manufacturing, 13% in wholesale and retail trade, 18% in agriculture, forestry, fisheries and mining, 34% were employed in other counties and there were 460 retired workers. The industries with the most employment: oil and gas extraction and tourism. The nonfarm earnings in 1981 totaled $41,339,000. The retired workers received an average monthly Social Security payment of $272. **FINANCE** On June 30, 1983, one commercial bank had total deposits of $25,064,000 and total assets of $28,321,000. On December 31, 1982 one state savings and loan association had assets of $10,407,743. **HOUSING** Average value of homes in 1980: $24,500. Seven permits for new, privately owned housing units with a total construction cost of $265,000 were issued in 1982. Of those permits, all were for single family houses. Between 1970 and 1980 the number of housing units increased by 14%. Fifty-six percent of all units in the county are air-conditioned, 72% are heated by gas and 22% by electricity. **NATURAL RESOURCES** Caliche, sand and gravel, oil and gas. In 1982 a total of 19,476,372 thousand cubic feet of gas well gas, 88,094 barrels of condensate, 704,365 barrels of crude oil and 1,063,774 thousand cubic feet of casinghead gas were produced. **TOURISM** Travel expenditures of $454,000 in 1982 (an increase of 11% over 1981) generated 10 jobs and $82,000 in payroll. **ALCOHOLIC BEVERAGES** Packaged distilled spirits, beer, ale, malt liquor and wine are legal in parts of the county. Sale of mixed beverages is legal in all or parts of the county. **FEDERAL EXPENDITURES** The federal government had direct expenditures or obligations of $8,685,000 in the county during fiscal year 1983, including $604,000 by the U.S. Department of Defense. In addition, the federal government provided $130,000 in grant awards, paid $535,000 in salaries and wages, made direct payments to individuals of $7,700,000 including $5,308,000 in retirement and disability payments, awarded $66,000 in procurement contracts and spent $254,000 in other expenditures or obligations. The federal government also provided $64,000 in direct loans and $3,050,000 in guaranteed loans and insurance.

COMMUNICATION
Newspapers–Weekly: Advance-Guard (Goliad). Telephone companies: Southwestern Bell and Central Telephone-Midstate. **TRANSPORTATION** Total public road mileage: 538. In 1982 there were 4,597 registered vehicles and 139 reported traffic accidents including one fatality. Intercity bus service is available. Motor freight: three carriers. Aircraft: seven are registered in the county.

COMMUNITY SERVICES
EDUCATION One school district with one elementary, one middle and one high school. The average daily attendance in 1981-82 was 1,101, with expenditures per pupil of $3,733 including 102 classroom teachers with an average annual salary of $15,831. None of the 71 high school graduates planned to attend college. In 1982-83, 44% of the students were White, 48% Hispanic and 8% Black. **PUBLIC LIBRARIES** Goliad County Library (Goliad): 10,800 volumes. **CHILD CARE** Five day care and four twenty-four hour care licensed facilities. **HEALTH CARE** One physician and one dentist. Hospitals: one with a capacity of 34. Ambulance services: one volunteer service. Nursing homes: one nursing home has a capacity of 60 nursing care residents. The average cost per day for private patients in 1982 was $30.29. **CHURCHES** 18 churches have an estimated combined membership of 3,416. The largest denominations are Catholic, Lutheran Church of America and Southern Baptist. **SOCIAL SERVICES** In fiscal year 1983 a total of $459,397 in food stamps was distributed, with an average of 1,021 persons receiving food stamps each month. Aid to Families with Dependent Children (AFDC) totaled $68,016 with an average of 49 families receiving

AFDC each month. Medical assistance benefits for the aged and disabled of $655,188 and for families and children of $103,153 brought the county benefit total to $1,285,754. **FIRE PROTECTION** Three volunteer fire departments. **LAW ENFORCEMENT** The County Sheriff has 17 commissioned officers. One police department has a force of nine. **CRIME** 11 violent crimes (murder, forcible rape, robbery and aggravated assault) and 85 nonviolent crimes (burglary, larceny-theft and motor vehicle theft) were reported in 1982. **JUDICIAL SYSTEM** Three District Courts and Judges, three County Courts and Judges and four Justices of the Peace. In the District Courts a total of 186 cases were pending on 1/1/82, 155 new cases were filed and 182 cases were disposed of during the year leaving 159 cases pending on 12/31/82. There were 100 criminal cases on the docket, 45 convictions, 31 persons committed to prison and three committed to jail and 44 cases left pending. In the County Courts 114 cases were pending on 1/1/82, 191 new cases were filed and 189 cases were disposed of during the year leaving 116 cases pending on 12/31/82. There were 267 criminal cases on the docket, 125 convictions, 26 persons committed to jail, and 108 cases left pending. **JAILS** One jail, capacity nine. **ATTORNEYS AT LAW** Four. **UTILITIES** 43% of the residents are connected to a public or privately owned water system and 37% are connected to a public sewer system. Electricity is distributed to the county by San Miguel Electric Coop., Inc., Cochran Power and Light and Dewitt Co. Electric Coop., Inc. and is generated primarily by gas, oil, coal and water. **TAXES** The county has three units with taxing authority: one school district, one city and one county.

RECREATION
NATIONAL REGISTER OF HISTORIC PLACES Goliad: Goliad County Courthouse Historic District, Mission Rosario, Old Market House, Captain Barton Peck House and Presidio La Bahia. Goliad vicinity: Nuestra Senora del Espiritu Santa de Zuniga. **STATE** Fannin Battleground State Historic Site covers 13 acres with a historic monument which marks the site where Fannin surrendered to a Mexican army following the Battle of Coleto Creek on March 20, 1836. Goliad State Historical Park covers 184 acres with camping and trailer sites as well as fishing areas. The park features the restored Mission Espiritu Santo and a museum. **SCENIC DRIVES** The Texas Independence Trail runs through this county. This trail not only surveys historic sites of southeastern Texas but also includes many modern visitor attractions such as the Johnson Space Center. Major rivers: San Antonio and Sarco. Primary streams: Coleto, Blanco, Perdido and Manahuilla. **HUNTING** Fall and winter seasons on deer and javelina. No closed seasons on coyote, bobcat, nutria and squirrel. Winter seasons on quail, muskrat, beaver, opossum, otter, mink, ring-tailed cat, badger, fox, raccoon, skunk and civet cat. Fall, winter and spring seasons on turkey. In 1983 sandhill crane, duck, coot, geese, woodcock and jacksnipe seasons occurred during the winter months. Teal duck, rail and gallinule seasons occurred in the fall. Mourning dove seasons occurred intermittently during the fall and winter months. **MUSEUMS** Goliad: Presidio La Bahia Museum. **OTHER** Goliad: Mission Rosario (Ruins) and General Zaragoza State Historic Site. **SPECIAL EVENTS** Quarterhorse Racing, Goliad, March; Goliad Day, Goliad, March; County Fair and Rodeo, Goliad, March; Fiesta Zaragoza, Goliad, April; Cinco de Mayo, Goliad, May; Longhorn Stampede and Chili Cookoff, Goliad, July.

COMMUNITIES
COUNTY SEAT Goliad, County Courthouse, 77963; County Clerk's Office, 512/645-3294. **INCORPORATED COMMUNITIES** (1980 population and ZIP Code) Goliad (1,990) 77963. **UNINCORPORATED COMMUNITIES** (and ZIP Code) Ander 77963, Berclair 78107, Charco 77963, Cologne 77901,

COUNTIES

GOLIAD (continued)

Fannin 77960, Sarco 77963, Schroeder 77963, Weesatche 77993 and Weser 77963. **FOR ADDITIONAL LOCAL INFORMATION** Goliad Chamber of Commerce, P.O. Box 606, Goliad, 77963, 512/645-3563.

GONZALES (C37)

THE LAND
East of San Antonio on U.S. Highways 90, 183 and 87 in the Blackland Prairies Region, Gonzales County covers 1,068 square miles with an elevation range of 200 to 400 feet. The northwestern one-third of the county has nearly level to undulating, light colored, sandy soils with cracking, clayey subsoils. In the southern corner of the county are deep, loamy soils with some clayey subsoils. The rest of the county has undulating cracking, clayey soils and soils with loamy surfaces and cracking, clayey subsoils. Along the north, the northwestern border and the southeastern border Gonzales has vegetation of the Post Oak Savannah area, with tall grasses, post and blackjack oak trees. The rest of the county has vegetation of the Blackland Prairies area with tall grasses, mesquite and other scrubby deciduous trees. Between 11 and 20% of the land in the county is considered prime farmland. **CLIMATE** Subtropical moist. There is a possibility of tropical storms June through October. The average annual temperature is 70°F. Temperatures in January range from an average low of 37° to an average high of 63°F and in July range from 73° to 95°F. The average annual precipitation is 35 inches, with an average relative humidity of 87% at 6 A.M. and 60% at 6 P.M. There is no yearly snowfall. The growing season averages 276 days per year, with the last freeze the end of February and and the first freeze in early December. The sun shines during the year on the average 68% of the daylight hours.

THE PEOPLE
The 1982 estimated population of 18,500 indicates continued growth which began in the 1970s reversing the continuous population losses from 1930 to 1970. While urban areas grew 22% between 1970 and 1980 rural areas decreased 8%. The age group with the largest increase was ages 20 to 34 lowering the median age from 35 in 1970 to 33 in 1980. The largest ancestry groups are Hispanic (29%), persons of German descent (22%) and English descent (18%). **REGISTERED VOTERS** As of November 2, 1982 there were 8,941 registered voters (0.1% of the state total). The 1982 general election had a 41% voter turnout, compared to a 64% turnout in the 1980 general election. In the 1982 primary 97% voted Democratic and 3% Republican, with 2,796 votes cast.

THE ECONOMY
AGRICULTURE Diversified products. In 1982, 93% of the land was in farms and ranches, with 12% of the farmland under cultivation and 8% irrigated. Gonzales ranked fifth in the state in highest agricultural receipts, with 96% from livestock and livestock products. Overgrazing, undesirable brush and weeds and water erosion are the current conservation problems. Primary crops: 10th in the state for hay. Sorghum, oats, corn and wheat. Primary vegetables: third in the state for watermelons. Primary fruits and nuts: peaches and seventh in the state for pecans. Primary livestock and products: first in the state for hens and pullets, egg production and turkeys; second for beef cows that have calved and commercial broiler production; seventh for cattle; and a leading hog producer. **BUSINESS** Total number of business establishments in the county: 411. Retail sales during the first quarter of 1984 decreased 6%. In 1980, 16% of the labor

force were self-employed, 16% were employed in professional or related services, 12% in manufacturing, 20% in wholesale and retail trade, 25% in agriculture, forestry, fisheries and mining, 14% were employed in other counties and there were 2,028 retired workers. The industries with the most employment: oil and gas extraction, petroleum refining, agribusiness, poultry processing, the manufacture of prepared agricultural feeds and mining. The nonfarm earnings in 1981 totaled $133,171,000. The retired workers received an average monthly Social Security payment of $267. **FINANCE** On June 30, 1983, four commercial banks had total deposits of $102,122,000 and total assets of $118,808,000. On December 31, 1982 two state savings and loan associations and two federal branches had combined assets of $192,929,641. In addition there is one credit union in the county. **HOUSING** Average value of homes in 1980: $20,400. Permits for new, privately owned housing units decreased in 1982: 71 permits were issued with a total construction cost of $2,238,770. Of those permits, 20 were for single family houses. Housing permits in Nixon increased from four in 1981 to 26 in 1982. Between 1970 and 1980 the number of housing units increased by 16%. Sixty percent of all units in the county are air-conditioned, 69% are heated by gas and 25% by electricity. **NATURAL RESOURCES** Clay, industrial sand, sand and gravel, oil, gas, uranium and pumicite. In 1982 a total of 2,405,981 thousand cubic feet of gas well gas, 100,459 barrels of condensate, 5,212,205 barrels of crude oil and 4,339,398 thousand cubic feet of casinghead gas were produced. Current production of other minerals and products includes bentonite clay, refractory clay, crushed sandstone and uranium. **TOURISM** Travel expenditures of $5,309,000 in 1982 (an increase of 12% over 1981) generated 124 jobs and $1,018,000 in payroll. Lodging: four hotels, motels and tourist courts. **ALCOHOLIC BEVERAGES** Packaged distilled spirits, beer, ale, malt liquor and wine are legal in parts of the county. **FEDERAL EXPENDITURES** The federal government had direct expenditures or obligations of $30,468,000 in the county during fiscal year 1983, including $1,715,000 by the U.S. Department of Defense. In addition, the federal government provided $1,145,000 in grant awards, paid $1,837,000 in salaries and wages, made direct payments to individuals of $27,124,000 including $18,091,000 in retirement and disability payments, awarded $65,000 in procurement contracts and spent $296,000 in other expenditures or obligations. The federal government also provided $1,000 in direct loans and $10,248,000 in guaranteed loans and insurance.

COMMUNICATION
Newspapers–Daily: Daily Inquirer (Gonzales), ave. eve. circ. 3,315. Weekly: The Gonzales Inquirer, Nixon News and Home Paper (Waelder). Radio: KCTI-AM (Gonzales). Cable TV. Telephone companies: General Telephone, Southwestern Bell/Guadalupe Valley Telephone Coop. **TRANSPORTATION** Total public road mileage: 1,196. In 1982 there were 14,359 registered vehicles and 526 reported traffic accidents including seven fatalities. Taxi cabs: three companies in the city of Gonzales. Intercity bus service is available. Motor freight: 13 local and intrastate carriers. Rail: the Sunset Limited provides passenger service on the Amtrak route. Two main and one branch line carries freight through the county. The two main lines carry annually over 30 million tons of freight each and the one branch line carries less than one million. Aircraft: 14 are registered in the county. Airports: Gonzales Municipal Airport is a geneal utility airport providing general aviation service. It serves as a base for 10 aircraft.

COMMUNITY SERVICES
EDUCATION Three school districts with five elementary, two middle and three high schools. The average daily attendance in

1981-82 was 3,408, with expenditures per pupil of $2,599 including 238 classroom teachers with an average annual salary of $15,631. Thirty-six percent of the 226 high school graduates planned to attend college. In 1982-83, 45% of the students were White, 43% Hispanic, 12% Black, 0.1% Asian and 0.1% American Indian. **PUBLIC LIBRARIES** Gonzales Public Library: 18,200 volumes. Nixon Public Library: 3,725 volumes. Stella Hart Memorial Public Library (Smiley): 7,000 volumes. Waelder Public Library: 5,235 volumes. **CHILD CARE** 23 day care and two twenty-four hour care licensed facilities. **HEALTH CARE** 11 physicians and four dentists. Hospitals: one with a capacity of 42. Specialized hospitals: one rehabilitation hospital with capacity of 68. Ambulance services: two volunteer services. Mental health: one county clinic. Nursing homes: three nursing homes with a combined capacity of 277 nursing care residents. The average cost per day for private patients in 1982 was $28.94. **CHURCHES** 44 churches have an estimated combined membership of 11,338. The largest denominations are Southern Baptist, Catholic and United Methodist. **SOCIAL SERVICES** In fiscal year 1983 a total of $1,196,631 in food stamps was distributed, with an average of 2,691 persons receiving food stamps each month. Aid to Families with Dependent Children (AFDC) totaled $247,814 with an average of 165 families receiving AFDC each month. Medical assistance benefits for the aged and disabled of $2,502,446 and for families and children of $309,141 brought the county benefit total to $4,256,032. **FIRE PROTECTION** Four volunteer fire departments. **LAW ENFORCEMENT** The County Sheriff has 47 commissioned officers. Two police departments have a combined force of 11. **CRIME** 79 violent crimes (murder, forcible rape, robbery and aggravated assault) and 421 nonviolent crimes (burglary, larceny-theft and motor vehicle theft) were reported in 1982. **JUDICIAL SYSTEM** Two District Courts and Judges, one County Court and Judge and three Justices of the Peace. In the District Courts a total of 550 cases were pending on 1/1/82, 648 new cases were filed and 531 cases were disposed of during the year leaving 667 cases pending on 12/31/82. There were 327 criminal cases on the docket, 69 convictions, 20 persons committed to prison and two committed to jail and 172 cases left pending. In the County Court 336 cases were pending on 1/1/82, 538 new cases were filed and 511 cases were disposed of during the year leaving 363 cases pending on 12/31/82. There were 763 criminal cases on the docket, 276 convictions, one person committed to jail and 275 cases left pending. **JAILS** One jail, capacity 18. In 1983 lost certification due to supervision deficiencies. **ATTORNEYS AT LAW** 16. **UTILITIES** 73% of the residents are connected to a public or privately owned water system and 55% are connected to a public sewer system. Electricity is distributed to the city of Gonzales by the Gonzales Electric System and to the rest of the county by Cochran Power and Light and Guadalupe Valley Electric Coop., Inc. and is generated primarily by gas and oil. The typical residential electric bill is $137.75 per month for an all-electric house using 2,500 kwh. **TAXES** The county has 12 units with taxing authority: four school districts, four cities, one county, two hospital districts and one special district.

RECREATION/ENTERTAINMENT
NATIONAL REGISTER OF HISTORIC PLACES Cuero I Archeological District (see De Witt County). Gonzales: Gonzales County Courthouse, Gonzales County Jail and Kennard House. Gonzales vicinity: Braches Home. Leesville vicinity: Leesville School House. **STATE** Palmetto State Park covers 264 acres with camping and trailer sites as well as areas for fishing, swimming and nature trails. **MUNICIPAL PARKS** 164 acres in four municipal parks. These parks contain two playgrounds, one golf course, four baseball and softball fields, four tennis courts and one swimming pool. **SCENIC DRIVES** The Texas Indepen-

dence Trail runs through this county. This trail not only surveys the historic sites of southeastern Texas but also includes many modern visitor attractions such as the Johnson Space Center. **BOATING/FISHING** Lakes/reservoirs: Gonzales 4-H (696 acres), Gonzales (60 acres), Quien Sabe (45 acres), Wade (240 acres) and Wood (345 acres). Major rivers: Guadalupe. Primary streams: Oneal. **HUNTING** Fall and winter seasons on deer and javelina. No closed seasons on coyote, nutria, bobcat and squirrel. Winter seasons on quail, muskrat, beaver, otter, opossum, mink, ring-tailed cat, badger, fox, raccoon, skunk and civet cat. Spring season on turkey. In 1983 sandhill crane, duck, coot, geese, woodcock and jacksnipe seasons occurred during the winter months. Teal duck, rail and gallinule seasons occurred in the fall. Mourning dove seasons occurred intermittently during the fall and winter months. **MUSEUMS** Gonzales: Gonzales Museum, Eggleston House and 1887 Jail (currently headquarters for the Chamber of Commerce). **SPECIAL EVENTS** Feather Fest, Nixon, September; Come-and-Take-It Days, Gonzales, September.

COMMUNITIES
COUNTY SEAT Gonzales, County Courthouse, 78629; County Clerk's Office, 512/672-2435. **INCORPORATED COMMUNITIES** (1980 population and ZIP Code) Gonzales (7,152) 78629, Nixon (2,008) 78140, Smiley (439) 78159 and Waelder (942) 78959. **UNINCORPORATED COMMUNITIES** (and ZIP Code) Bebe 78603, Belmont 78604, Cheapside 77952, Cost 78614, Dewville 78140, Dilworth 78629, Dreyer 77984, Glaze City 77984, Hamon 78629, Harwood 78632, Hickston 78959, Leesville 78122, Maurin 78629, Monthalia 78614, Nickel 78629, Oak Forest (Quinton) 78629, Ottine 78658, Sandy Fork 78632, Saturn 78959, School Land (Schoolland) 78140, Stieren 78632, Summerville 78629, Thompsonville (Cranz) 78959 and Wrightsboro 78677. **FOR ADDITIONAL LOCAL INFORMATION** Gonzales Chamber of Commerce, 414 St. Lawrence, P.O. Box 134, Gonzales, 78629, 512/672-6532 and Nixon Area Chamber of Commerce, 207 N. Nixon Ave., Nixon, 78140, 512/582-1711.

GRAY (P14)

THE LAND
East of Amarillo on Interstate Highway 40 in the Rolling Plains Region, Gray County covers 921 square miles with an elevation range of 2,800 to 3,200 feet. In the southeast the soils are level to undulating, red to brown and loamy with some sandy areas and some areas with clayey subsoils. The central area has alkaline, loamy and cracking, clayey soils over limestone. To the north and west the more level soils have dark, loamy surfaces and clayey subsoils over limestone. The mid to tall grasses, mesquite and oak trees of the Rolling Plains vegetation area in the south become the short grasses, mesquite and yucca of the High Plains vegetation area in the north. Between 31 and 40% of the land in the county is considered prime farmland. **CLIMATE** Moderate and dry. Cold fronts are active most of the year and can be associated with sudden temperature changes. The average annual temperature is 58°F. Temperatures in January range from an average low of 28° to an average high of 50°F and in July range from 67° to 94°F. The average annual precipitation is 20 inches, with an average relative humidity of 73% at 6 A.M. and 40% at 6 P.M. The average annual snowfall is 16 inches. The growing season averages 205 days per year, with the last freeze in mid April and the first freeze in late October. The sun shines during the year on the average 75% of the daylight hours.

THE PEOPLE
Although the population of Gray County has declined over the past 20 years, the reduction rate lowered from 15% between 1960

COUNTIES

GRAY (continued)

and 1970 to 2% between 1970 and 1980. The 1982 estimated population of 27,700, however, reflects a 5% population growth between 1980 and 1982. Between 1970 and 1980 the greatest loss was in the rural areas. The age group with the largest reduction was ages five to 14, with slight increases in ages 20 to 34 and 65 and over. The largest ancestry groups are persons of English descent (33%), Irish descent (24%) and German descent (17%). **REGISTERED VOTERS** As of November 2, 1982 there were 13,740 registered voters (0.2% of the state total). The 1982 general election had a 56% voter turnout, compared to a 74% turnout in the 1980 general election. In the 1982 primary 77% voted Democratic and 23% Republican, with 3,014 votes cast.

THE ECONOMY

AGRICULTURE Fed cattle and wheat area. In 1982, 97% of the land was in farms and ranches, with 26% of the farmland under cultivation and 24% irrigated. Gray ranked 61st in the state in highest agricultural receipts, with 78% from livestock and livestock products. Overgrazing, undesirable brush, noxious weeds and wind erosion are the current conservation problems. Primary crops: wheat, sorghum and hay. Primary vegetables: watermelons. Primary livestock and products: cattle and hogs. **BUSINESS** Total number of business establishments in the county: 809. Retail sales during the first quarter of 1984 increased 9%. In 1980, 10% of the labor force were self-employed, 15% were employed in professional or related services, 17% in manufacturing, 24% in wholesale and retail trade, 17% in agriculture, forestry, fisheries and mining, 9% were employed in other counties and there were 2,701 retired workers. The industries with the most employment: agribusiness, oil and gas extraction, heavy construction and the manufacture of industrial chemicals and oil field machinery. The nonfarm earnings in 1981 totaled $327,588,000. The retired workers received an average monthly Social Security payment of $350. **FINANCE** On June 30, 1983, three commercial banks had total deposits of $208,329,000 and total assets of $235,323,000. On December 31, 1982 one federal savings and loan association, one state savings and loan association branch and one federal branch had assets of $255,749,355. In addition there are seven credit unions in the county. **HOUSING** Average value of homes in 1980: $24,400. Permits for new, privately owned housing units increased in 1982: 90 permits were issued with a total construction cost of $6,759,695. Of those permits, 84 were for single family houses. Between 1970 and 1980 the number of housing units increased by 6%. Seventy-eight percent of all units in the county are air-conditioned, 94% are heated by gas and 5% by electricity. **NATURAL RESOURCES** Caliche, gypsum, oil and gas. In 1982 a total of 22,045,081 thousand cubic feet of gas well gas, 3,313 barrels of condensate, 3,769,646 barrels of crude oil and 16,190,219 thousand cubic feet of casinghead gas were produced. Current production of other minerals and products includes sand and gravel. **TOURISM** Travel expenditures of $16,512,000 in 1982 (an increase of 11% over 1981) generated 405 jobs and $3,288,000 in payroll. **ALCOHOLIC BEVERAGES** Packaged distilled spirits, beer, ale, malt liquor and wine are legal in parts of the county. **FEDERAL EXPENDITURES** The federal government had direct expenditures or obligations of $45,310,000 in the county during fiscal year 1983, including $4,035,000 by the U.S. Department of Defense. In addition, the federal government provided $373,000 in grant awards, paid $2,447,000 in salaries and wages, made direct payments to individuals of $37,043,000 including $27,797,000 in retirement and disability payments, awarded $3,480,000 in procurement contracts and spent $1,967,000 in other expenditures or obligations. The federal government also provided $6,326,000 in direct loans and $3,240,000 in guaranteed loans and insurance.

COMMUNICATION

Newspapers–Daily: News (Pampa), ave. eve. circ. 8,079. Weekly: The McLean News. Radio: KGRO-AM, KSZN-AM and KOMX-FM (Pampa). Cable TV. Telephone companies: General Telephone and Southwestern Bell. **TRANSPORTATION** Total public road mileage: 1,120. In 1982 there were 31,695 registered vehicles and 934 reported traffic accidents including 21 fatalities. Taxi cabs: one company in Pampa. Intercity bus service is available. Motor freight: 25 local and intrastate carriers. Rail: three main lines carry freight through the county with two carrying annually over 30 million tons each and one carrying 10 to 20. Aircraft: 52 are registered in the county. Airports: Perry Lefors Field at Pampa is a basic transportation airport providing general aviation service and is a base for 60 aircraft. Gray County Airport at McLean.

COMMUNITY SERVICES

EDUCATION Five school districts with 10 elementary, one middle and three high schools. The average daily attendance in 1981-82 was 4,375, with expenditures per pupil of $2,454 including 311 classroom teachers with an average annual salary of $16,976. Forty-seven percent of the 259 high school graduates planned to attend college. In 1982-83, 86% of the students were White, 8% Hispanic, 6% Black, 0.3% Asian and 0.2% American Indian. Private schools: 159 students enrolled in two elementary and one high school. **PUBLIC LIBRARIES** Lovett Memorial Library (McLean): 11,578 volumes. Lovett Memorial Library (Pampa): 66,000 volumes. **CHILD CARE** 30 day care and 12 twenty-four hour care licensed facilities. **HEALTH CARE** 32 physicians and 11 dentists. Hospitals: one with a capacity of 126. Ambulance services: two volunteer services, one commercial, one fire department and one community service. Mental health: one clinic. Nursing homes: three nursing homes with a combined capacity of 279 nursing care residents. The average cost per day for private patients in 1982 was $30.90. **CHURCHES** 47 churches have an estimated combined membership of 21,074. The largest denominations are Southern Baptist, United Methodist and Churches of Christ. **SOCIAL SERVICES** In fiscal year 1983 a total of $402,621 in food stamps was distributed, with an average of 907 persons receiving food stamps each month. Aid to Families with Dependent Children (AFDC) totaled $53,633 with an average of 38 families receiving AFDC each month. Medical assistance benefits for the aged and disabled of $1,208,339 and for families and children of $103,901 brought the county benefit total to $1,768,494. **FIRE PROTECTION** One paid and two volunteer fire departments. **LAW ENFORCEMENT** The County Sheriff has 12 commissioned officers. One police department has a force of 31. **CRIME** 217 violent crimes (murder, forcible rape, robbery and aggravated assault) and 1,299 nonviolent crimes (burglary, larceny-theft and motor vehicle theft) were reported in 1982. **JUDICIAL SYSTEM** Two District Courts and Judges, one County Court and Judge and two Justices of the Peace. In the District Courts a total of 945 cases were pending on 1/1/82, 823 new cases were filed and 696 cases were disposed of during the year leaving 1,072 cases pending on 12/31/82. There were 229 criminal cases on the docket, 67 convictions, seven persons committed to prison, and 100 cases left pending. In the County Court 664 cases were pending on 1/1/82, 408 new cases were filed and 428 cases were disposed of during the year leaving 644 cases pending on 12/31/82. There were 817 criminal cases on the docket, 153 convictions, 13 persons committed to jail, and 401 cases left pending. **JAILS** One jail, capacity 24. **ATTORNEYS AT LAW** 30. **UTILITIES** 93% of the residents are connected to a public or privately owned water system and 90% are connected to a public sewer system. Electricity is distributed to the county by Southwestern Public Service and Greenbelt Electric Coop., Inc. and is generated primarily by gas and oil. The typical residential electric bill is $170.44 per month for an all-electric house using 2,500 kwh. **TAXES** The county has 10 units with taxing authority: five school districts, three cities, one county and one special district.

RECREATION/ENTERTAINMENT

MUNICIPAL PARKS 256 acres in 22 municipal parks. These parks contain three miles of hiking trails, 13 playgrounds, four baseball and softball fields, five tennis courts, one multi-use court and two swimming pools. Developed campsites: six. **BOATING/FISHING** Lakes/reservoirs: McClellan (325 acres). Major rivers: North Fork Red. Primary streams: Cantonment and McClellan. **HUNTING** Fall seasons on antelope and prairie chicken. Fall and winter seasons on deer and mule deer. Summer, fall and winter seasons on squirrel. Winter seasons on pheasant, quail, muskrat, beaver, opossum, ring-tailed cat, badger, fox, weasel, raccoon, skunk and civet cat. No closed seasons on bobcat and coyote. Fall, winter and spring seasons on turkey. In 1983 sandhill crane, duck, coot, geese, woodcock and jacksnipe seasons occurred during the winter months. Teal duck, rail and gallinule seasons occurred in the fall. Mourning dove seasons occurred intermittently during the fall and winter months. **MUSEUMS** McLean: Alanreed-McLean Area Museum. Pampa: White Deer Land Museum. **THEATERS** Pampa: M.K. Brown Municipal Auditorium and Pampa Fine Arts Association. **DANCE** Pampa: Civic Ballet and Ballet of the Golden Spread. **SPECIAL EVENTS** Top O'Texas Junior Stock Show and Top O'Texas Hereford Breeders Show, Pampa, March; Top O'Texas Rodeo, Pampa, July; Top O'Texas Golf Tournament, Pampa, September.

COMMUNITIES

COUNTY SEAT Pampa, County Courthouse, 79065; County Clerk's Office, 806/665-2308. **INCORPORATED COMMUNITIES** (1980 population and ZIP Code) Lefors (829) 79054, McLean (1,160) 79057 and Pampa (21,396) 79065. **UNINCORPORATED COMMUNITIES** (and ZIP Code) Alanreed 79002, Boydston 79039, Coltexo 79054, Hoover 79065, Kings Mill (Kingsmill) 79065 and Laketon 79065. **FOR ADDITIONAL LOCAL INFORMATION** Pampa Chamber of Commerce, Hughes Bldg., P.O. Box 1942, Pampa, 79065, 806/669-3241.

GRAYSON (M3)

THE LAND

North of Dallas on U.S. Highways 75, 82 and 377 in the Blackland Prairies Region, Grayson County covers 934 square miles with an elevation range of 600 to 800 feet. Along the northern and western borders the soils are light colored and acidic with loamy to sandy surfaces and mottled, cracking, clayey subsoils. North and west of Sherman the darker, cracking, clayey soils have some surfaces of loam. Southeast of Sherman the dark, loamy surfaces have cracking, clayey subsoils. In the north the vegetation includes bluestems, gramas, legumes, oaks, mesquite and juniper of the Cross Timbers and Prairies vegetation area. To the south the Blackland Prairies vegetation area has a variety of timber along streams, tall bunchgrasses, buffalograsses and Texas grama. Between 31 and 40% of the land in the county is considered prime farmland. **CLIMATE** Mild and moist. The average annual temperature is 64°F. Temperatures in January range from an average low of 30° to an average high of 53°F and in July range from 73° to 96°F. The average annual precipitation is 37 inches, with an average relative humidity of 83% at 6 A.M. and 53% at 6 P.M. The average annual snowfall is five inches. The growing season averages 227 days per year, with the last freeze in late March and the first freeze in early November. The sun shines during the year on the average 66% of the daylight hours.

THE PEOPLE

The 1982 estimated population of 92,300 indicates a continuation of the steady growth which has occurred since 1930. Rural areas grew faster than urban areas from 1970 to 1980. The age groups with the largest gains were ages 20 to 24 and 65 and over. The county has a high concentration of residents over age 64 and a median age of 33. The largest ancestry groups are persons of English descent (27%), German descent (24%) and Irish descent (14%). **REGISTERED VOTERS** As of November 2, 1982 there were 42,538 registered voters (0.7% of the state total). The 1982 general election has a 50% voter turnout, compared to a 71% turnout in the 1980 general election. In the 1982 primary 91% voted Democratic and 9% Republican, with 5,931 votes cast.

THE ECONOMY

AGRICULTURE Wheat and cattle area. In 1982, 78% of the land was in farms and ranches, with 39% of the farmland under cultivation and 3% irrigated. Grayson ranked 109th in the state in highest agricultural receipts, with 69% from livestock and livestock products. Overgrazing, undesirable brush and weeds, water erosion, inefficient tillage systems and the cultivation of marginal lands are the current conservation problems. Primary crops: wheat, sorghum, hay, oats and peanuts. Primary vegetables: potatoes, sweet potatoes and watermelons. Primary fruits and nuts: peaches and pecans. Primary livestock and products: cattle, milk and hogs. **BUSINESS** Total number of business establishments in the county: 1,912. Retail sales during the first quarter of 1984 increased 22%. In 1980, 9% of the labor force were self-employed, 18% were employed in professional or related services, 31% in manufacturing, 19% in wholesale and retail trade, 8% in transportation, communication and other public utilities, 8% were employed in other counties and there were 10,082 retired workers. The industries with the most employment: agribusiness, tourism, oil and gas extraction, aluminum smelting, construction, meat processing, flour mills, textile mills and the manufacture of cooking oils, asbestos products, men's and women's clothing, structural metal products, oil field machinery, radio and televiion communication equipment, electronic components and surgical appliances and supplies. The nonfarm earnings in 1981 totaled $886,957,000. The retired workers received an average monthly Social Security payment of $298. **FINANCE** On June 30, 1983, 15 commercial banks had total deposits of $664,965,000 and total assets of $722,211,000. On December 31, 1982 two state savings and loan associations and seven state branches had combined assets of $154,992,463. In addition there are 12 credit unions in the county. **HOUSING** Average value of homes in 1980: $28,100. Permits for new, privately owned housing units increased in 1982: 186 permits were issued with a total construction cost of $5,886,003. Of those permits, 72 were for single family houses. Between 1970 and 1980 the number of housing units increased by 25%. Eighty percent of all units in the county are air-conditioned, 79% are heated by gas and 18% by electricity. **NATURAL RESOURCES** Limestone, sand and gravel, oil, gas and bituminous coal. In 1982 a total of 5,836,158 thousand cubic feet of gas well gas, 93,044 barrels of condensate, 3,603,851 barrels of crude oil and 5,147,199 thousand cubic feet of casinghead gas were produced. Current production of other minerals and products includes sand and gravel and crushed limestone. **TOURISM** Travel expenditures of $33,976,000 in 1982 (an increase of 11% over 1981) generated 853 jobs and $7,014,000 in payroll. Lodging: 12 hotels, motels and tourist courts. Convention/meeting facilities: Sherman—Austin College Sid Richardson Center and Louis Caulder Stadium, Kidd-Key Auditorium and Municipal Ballroom. **ALCOHOLIC BEVERAGES** Packaged distilled spirits, beer, ale, malt liquor and wine are legal in parts of the county. **FEDERAL EXPENDITURES** The federal government had direct expenditures or obligations of $246,196,000 in the county during fiscal year 1983, including $84,627,000 by the U.S. Department of Defense. In

COUNTIES

addition, the federal government provided $3,571,000 in grant awards, paid $6,553,000 in salaries and wages, made direct payments to individuals of $160,726,000 including $123,067,000 in retirement and disability payments, awarded $73,400,000 in procurement contracts and spent $1,947,000 in other expenditures or obligations. The federal government also provided $5,871,000 in direct loans and $21,397,000 in guaranteed loans and insurance.

COMMUNICATION

Newspapers–Daily: The Denison Herald, ave. eve. circ. 13,170 and the Sherman Democrat, ave. eve. circ. 19,564. Weekly: The Howe Enterprise, Van Alstyne Leader and The News-Record (Whitesboro). Radio: KDSX-AM and KGCC-FM (Denison) and KIKM-AM, KTXO-AM and KIKM-FM (Sherman). Television: KXII-Ch. 12 (Sherman). Cable TV. Telephone companies: Continental Telephone, General Telephone and Southwestern Bell. **TRANSPORTATION** Total public road mileage: 2,366. In 1982 there were 88,911 registered vehicles and 2,518 reported traffic accidents including 23 fatalities. Taxi cabs: two companies in Denison and one in Sherman. Intercity bus service is available. Motor freight: 35 local and intrastate carriers. Rail: six main and four branch lines carry freight through the county. Three of the main lines carry annually 10 to 20 million tons of freight each and three carry five to 10 each. One of the branch lines carries annually one to five million tons of freight and three carry less than one million each. Aircraft: 132 are registered in the county. Airports: Grayson County Airport between Sherman and Denison is a basic transportation airport providing general aviation service and serves as a base for 86 aircraft. Sherman Municipal Airport is a basic utility airport providing general aviation service and serves as a base for 29 aircraft. Loe's Highport Resort Airport at Pottsboro.

COMMUNITY SERVICES

EDUCATION 13 school districts with 25 elementary, nine middle, 12 high schools and one special education. The average daily attendance in 1981-82 was 15,156, with expenditures per pupil of $2,383 including 950 classroom teachers with an average annual salary of $17,451. Forty-eight percent of the 1,105 high school graduates planned to attend college. In 1982-83, 89% of the students were White, 1% Hispanic, 9% Black, 0.4% Asian and 0.3% American Indian. Private schools: 334 students enrolled in three elementary and one high school. Grayson County Junior College is located in Grayson. Established in 1963 it is a vocational and two year academic college under state and local control. Enrollment in 1982 was 3,622 with in state undergraduate tuition and fees of $210 per semester. Austin College is located in Sherman. Established in 1849 it is affiliated with the Presbyterian Church. Enrollment in 1982 was 1,189. The highest degree offered is: Master. Vocational education: Aladdin Beauty College (Sherman). **PUBLIC LIBRARIES** Denison Public Library: 69,502 volumes. Howe Library. Sherman Public Library: 68,357 volumes. Van Alstyne Library. Whitesboro Public Library: 16,386 volumes. Whitewright Public Library: 11,200 volumes. **CHILD CARE** 141 day care and 22 twenty-four hour care licensed facilities. **HEALTH CARE** 157 physicians and 52 dentists. Hospitals: five with a combined capacity of 682. Clinics: one dialysis clinic and one public health clinic. Ambulance services: three volunteer services, two fire departments, one funeral home, one commercial and one city service. Mental health: two clinics and one development center with capacity of 66. Nursing homes: 12 nursing homes with a combined capacity of 1,374 nursing care and 12 custodial care residents. The average cost per day for private patients in 1982 was $30.40. **CHURCHES** 195 churches have an estimated combined membership of 60,802.

The largest denominations are Southern Baptist, United Methodist and Churches of Christ. **SOCIAL SERVICES** In fiscal year 1983 a total of $2,430,158 in food stamps was distributed, with an average of 4,900 persons receiving food stamps each month. Aid to Families with Dependent Children (AFDC) totaled $591,652 with an average of 418 families receiving AFDC each month. Medical assistance benefits for the aged and disabled of $10,573,418 and for families and children of $913,501 brought the county benefit total to $14,508,728. **FIRE PROTECTION** Two paid and 13 volunteer fire departments. **LAW ENFORCEMENT** The County Sheriff has 75 commissioned officers. 12 police departments have a combined force of 116. Two college campuses have police departments with a combined police force of 12 officers. **CRIME** 526 violent crimes (murder, forcible rape, robbery and aggravated assault) and 4,694 nonviolent crimes (burglary, larceny-theft and motor vehicle theft) were reported in 1982. **JUDICIAL SYSTEM** Two District Courts and Judges, three County Courts and Judges and seven Justices of the Peace. In the District Courts a total of 2,957 cases were pending on 1/1/82, 4,191 new cases were filed and 2,200 cases were disposed of during the year leaving 4,948 cases pending on 12/31/82. There were 1,079 criminal cases on the docket, 307 convictions, 98 persons committed to prison, and 599 cases left pending. In the County Courts 5,903 cases were pending on 1/1/82, 5,626 new cases were filed and 5,198 cases were disposed of during the year leaving 6,331 cases pending on 12/31/82. There were 10,461 criminal cases on the docket, 2,106 convictions, 268 persons committed to jail, and 5,740 cases left pending. **JAILS** One jail, capacity 92. Constructing addition for 75. **ATTORNEYS AT LAW** 119. **UTILITIES** 93% of the residents are connected to a public or privately owned water system and 77% are connected to a public sewer system. Natural gas is distributed to the county by Lone Star Gas Co., Division of Enserch. The average annual residential bill for natural gas in 1982 for the Lone Star distribution system was $405.91, an increase of 35% over 1981. Electricity is distributed to the city of Whitesboro by the Whitesboro Light and Power Dept. and to the rest of the county by Texas Power and Light, Cooke Co. Electric Coop., Assn., Denton Co. Electric Coop., Inc., Fanin Co. Electric Coop., Inc. and Grayson-Collin Electric Co. and is generated primarily by gas, coal, oil and water. The typical residential electric bill is $205.81 per month for an all-electric house using 2,500 kwh. **TAXES** The county has 28 units with taxing authority: 13 school districts, 12 cities, one county, one college district and one special district.

RECREATION/ENTERTAINMENT

NATIONAL REGISTER OF HISTORIC PLACES Denison: George Braun House and Ernst Martin Kohl Building. **STATE** Eisenhower Birthplace State Historic Site covers three acres with a museum and a historic structure. The two-story white frame house has been restored to its 1890 appearance. Eisenhower State Recreation Area covers 457 acres with camping and trailer sites as well as areas offering fishing, swimming, boat ramps, nature trails and a marina. **COUNTY/MUNICIPAL PARKS** 749 acres in one county and 39 municipal parks. These parks contain two miles of hiking trails, 37 playgrounds, one football and soccer field, 23 baseball and softball fields, 19 tennis courts, seven swimming pools and one boat ramp. Developed campsites: 10. **SCENIC DRIVES** The Texas Lakes Trail runs through this county. This trail introduces some 30 blue-water recreational areas in a variety of settings in North-Central Texas. **BOATING/ FISHING** Lakes/reservoirs: Choctaw Creek Soil Conservation Service Lakes 10A and 15 (54 acres), Waterloo (29 acres), Denison Rod and Gun Club (19 acres), Lavon East Fork Soil Conservation Service Lakes 18, 20 and 39 (35 acres), Little Elm Soil Conservation Service Lake 4 (17 acres), Loy (37 acres), Pilot Grove Soil Conservation Service Lake 30 (12 acres), Randell (311 acres),

Russell (20 acres), Sherman Country Club (38 acres), Sister Grove Soil Conservation Service Lakes 28, 31 and 32 (37 acres), Stern (18 acres) and Texoma (89,000 acres). Major rivers: East Fork Trinity and Red. Primary streams: Sand, Cedar, Iron Ore, Shawnee, East Prong, Whites, Little Elm, Loy, Desert, Big Mineral, Elba, West Sister Grove, East Sister Grove and Mill. **WILDLIFE REFUGES** Hagerman National Wildlife Refuge covers 11,320 acres. **HUNTING** No closed seasons on nutria, coyote, bobcat and squirrel. Winter seasons on quail, muskrat, beaver, otter, opossum, ring-tailed cat, badger, fox, raccoon, skunk and civet cat. In 1983 duck, coot, geese, woodcock and jacksnipe seasons occurred during the winter months. Teal duck, rail and gallinule seasons occurred in the fall. Mourning dove seasons occurred intermittently during the fall and winter months. **MUSEUMS** Denison: Thompson House. Sherman: Sherman Historical Museum. Van Alstyne: Van Alstyne Museum. Whitewright: Whitewright Museum. **THEATERS** Sherman: Sherman Community Players and Sherman Community Series. **ORCHESTRAS** Sherman: Symphony Orchestra. **COLLEGIATE FINE ARTS** Sherman: Cultural events offered by Austin College in Sherman and by Grayson County Junior College in Denison. **OTHER** Sherman: Civic Chorus. **SPECIAL EVENTS** Junior Stock Show, Sherman, March; Junior Stock Show, Denison, March; County Stock Show, Sherman, April; Four Corners Balloon Rally, Farmington, May; State and National Fink Day, Fink, June; July Fourth Celebration, Sherman, July; Quarterhorse Assn. Rodeo and Parade, Sherman, July; Western Days, Denison, July; Red River Valley Arts Fest, Sherman, September; Miss West Grayson County Pageant, Whitesboro, October; Peanut Festival, Whitesboro, October; Veterans Day Parade, Denison, November; Chili Cookoff, Sherman, November; Christmas Pilgrimage of Homes, Sherman, December.

COMMUNITIES

COUNTY SEAT Sherman, County Courthouse, 75090; County Clerk's Office, 214/892-8109. **INCORPORATED COMMUNITIES** (1980 population and ZIP Code) Bells (846) 75414, Collinsville (860) 76233, Denison (23,884) 75020, All-America Cities Honorable Mention 1958, Dorchester (205) 75030, Gunter (849) 75058, Howe (2,072) 75059, Luella (371) 75090, Pottsboro (895) 75076, Sadler (329) 76264, Sherman (30,413) 75090, All-America Cities Award 1979-1980, Southmayd (318) 76268, Tioga (511) 76271, Tom Bean (811) 75489, Van Alstyne (1,860) 75095, Whitesboro (3,197) 76273 and Whitewright (1,760: 1,751 in Grayson Co. and nine in Fannin Co.) 75491. **UNINCORPORATED COMMUNITIES** (and ZIP Code) Ambrose 75414, Basin Springs 76264, Cannon 75095, Cedar Mills 76264, Dixie 76273, Elmont 75095, Ethel 76233, Farmington 75058, Fink 75076, Gordonville 76245, Highland Acres 75076, Hiland Shores 75076, Ida 75491, Kentuckytown (Kentucky Town) 75491, Locust 75076, Penland 75414, Pilot Grove 75491, Preston Shores (Preston) 75076, Sandusky 76273, Smith Oaks 75090, South Gale 75020, White Mound 75090 and White Rock 75020. **FOR ADDITIONAL LOCAL INFORMATION** Denison Area Chamber of Commerce, P.O. Box 325, Denison, 75020, 214/465-1551, Sherman Area Chamber of Commerce, 306 N. Travis, P.O. Box 1029, Sherman, 75090, 214/893-1184, Van Alstyne Chamber of Commerce, P.O. Box 698, Van Alstyne, 75095, 214/482-5234 and Whitesboro Chamber of Commerce, 101 W. Main, P.O. Box 522, Whitesboro, 76273, 214/564-3331.

GREGG (E17)

THE LAND

East of Dallas on Interstate Highway 20 in the East Texas Timberlands Region, Gregg County covers 273 square miles with an elevation range of 300 to 500 feet. The acidic, light colored soils are undulating to rolling with loamy or sandy surfaces and reddish clay subsoils. In the Pineywoods vegetation area the pine and hardwood forests include the loblolly, short and longleaf pines and such hardwoods as oaks, hickory and maple. Indiangrass, legumes and shrubs are typical. Between one and 10% of the land in the county is considered prime farmland. **CLIMATE** Subtropical Humid. Mild and moist with May as the wettest month. Thunderstorms are frequent in spring. The average annual temperature is 64°F. Temperatures in January range from an average low of 34° to an average high of 55°F and in July range from 72° to 94°F. The average annual precipitation is 46 inches, with an average relative humidity of 84% at 6 A.M. and 57% at 6 P.M. The average annual snowfall is two inches. The growing season averages 247 days per year, with the last freeze in mid March and the first freeze in mid November. The sun shines during the year on the average 66% of the daylight hours.

THE PEOPLE

Gregg County is one of the most densely populated in the state. The 1982 estimated population of 109,700 indicates a continuation of the strong growth which has occurred since the 1930s. Urban areas grew 42% between 1970 and 1980 while rural areas experienced little change. The age groups with the largest gains were ages 20 to 34 and 65 and over. The median age of 29 remained unchanged. The largest ancestry groups are persons of English descent (26%), Irish descent (20%) and Black (18%). **REGISTERED VOTERS** As of November 2, 1982 there were 46,496 registered voters (0.7% of the state total). The 1982 general election had a 51% voter turnout, compared to a 71% turnout in the 1980 general election. In the 1982 primary 84% voted Democratic and 16% Republican, with 11,794 votes cast.

THE ECONOMY

AGRICULTURE Forest production area. In 1982, 39% of the land was in farms and ranches, with 11% of the farmland under cultivation. Gregg ranked 247th in the state in highest agricultural receipts, with 81% from livestock and livestock products. Undesirable brush, water erosion, improper woodland management and the reclamation of oil and gas drilling sites are the current conservation problems. Primary crops: hay. Primary vegetables: sweet potatoes. Primary fruits and nuts: peaches and pecans. Primary livestock and products: cattle, milk and hogs. **BUSINESS** Total number of business establishments in the county: 3,162. Retail sales during the first quarter of 1984 increased 7%. In 1980, 7% of the labor force were self-employed, 16% were employed in professional or related services, 22% in manufacturing, 24% in wholesale and retail trade, 8% in construction, 13% were employed in other counties and there were 8,510 retired workers. The industries with the most employment: oil and gas extraction, construction, tourism, petroleum refining, ship building and repairing, textile mills, soft drink bottling and canning, iron and steel foundries and the manufacture of women's apparel, plumbing fixtures, hats, metal cans, structural metal products, construction and oil field machinery, motor vehicles and equipment, malt beverages and travel trailers and campers. The nonfarm earnings in 1981 totaled $1,147,783,000. The retired workers received an average monthly Social Security payment of $329. **FINANCE** On June 30, 1983, 16 commercial banks had total deposits of $980,384,000 and total assets of $1,124,700,000. On December 31, 1982 three state savings and loan associations, three federal associations, nine state branches and two federal branches had combined assets of $440,659,376. In addition there are 19 credit unions in the county. **HOUSING** Average value of homes in 1980: $40,000. Permits for new, privately owned housing units increased in 1982: 1,282 permits were issued with a total construction cost of $56,923,440. Of those permits, 550 were for

COUNTIES

GREGG (continued)

single family houses. Housing permits increased in Gladewater from 11 in 1981 to 31 in 1982 with 27 of the permits issued for single family houses, in Longview from 438 to 1,097 and in White Oak from 22 to 78 with 56 of the permits issued for single family houses. Between 1970 and 1980 the number of housing units increased by 45%. Eighty-five percent of all units in the county are air-conditioned, 76% are heated by gas and 24% by electricity. **NATURAL RESOURCES** Industrial sand, oil, gas and lignite coal. In 1982 a total of 11,770,255 thousand cubic feet of gas well gas, 108,720 barrels of condensate, 39,124,405 barrels of crude oil and 13,829,515 thousand cubic feet of casinghead gas were produced. Current production of other minerals and products includes sand and gravel. Pine and hardwood production in 1981 totaled 2,638,443 cubic feet: 2,400,582 cubic feet of pine and 237,861 cubic feet of hardwood. **TOURISM** Travel expenditures of $55,082,000 in 1982 (an increase of 11% over 1981) generated 1,373 jobs and $11,083,000 in payroll. Lodging: 22 hotels, motels and tourist courts. Convention/meeting facilities: Longview—Le Tourneau College Gym, Maude Cobb Activity Center and two hotels with facilities for large gatherings. **ALCOHOLIC BEVERAGES** Packaged distilled spirits, beer, ale, malt liquor and wine are legal in parts of the county. **FEDERAL EXPENDITURES** The federal government had direct expenditures or obligations of $155,174,000 in the county during fiscal year 1983, including $9,522,000 by the U.S. Department of Defense. In addition, the federal government provided $9,535,000 in grant awards, paid $11,570,000 in salaries and wages, made direct payments to individuals of $131,031,000 including $100,917,000 in retirement and disability payments, awarded $2,760,000 in procurement contracts and spent $279,000 in other expenditures or obligations. The federal government also provided $96,163,000 in guaranteed loans and insurance.

COMMUNICATION

Newspapers–Daily: Kilgore News Herald, ave. eve. circ. 6,047, Longview Morning Journal, ave. morn. circ. 16,804 and the Longview News, ave. eve. circ. 16,000. Weekly: Gladewater Mirror. Radio: KEES-AM (Gladewater), KOCA-AM, KKTX-FM (Kilgore) and KFRO-AM, KLUE-AM and KYKX-FM Stereo (Longview). Cable TV. Telephone companies: General Telephone and Southwestern Bell. **TRANSPORTATION** Total public road mileage: 1,178. In 1982 there were 121,868 registered vehicles and 4,633 reported traffic accidents including 36 fatalities. Taxi cabs: two companies in Longview and one in Kilgore. Municipal transit systems: one minibus system in Longview, with limited service on scheduled routes. Intercity bus service is available. Motor freight: 32 local and intrastate carriers. Rail: The Eagle provides passenger service on the Amtrak route. Three main and one branch line carry freight through the county. One of the main lines carries annually over 30 million tons of freight, one carries 20 to 30 and one carries 10 to 20 million. The branch line carries annually one to five million tons of freight. Aircraft: 205 are registered in the county. Airports: Gregg County Airport at Longview serves as a base for 92 aircraft and is a general transportation airport with commuter service. Also serving the area are East Side Airport at Longview and Gladewater Municipal Airport.

COMMUNITY SERVICES

EDUCATION Seven school districts with 21 elementary, 11 middle, seven high schools and one special education. The average daily attendance in 1981-82 was 20,360 with expenditures per pupil of $3,315 including 1,316 classroom teachers with an average annual salary of $17,602. Seventy-one percent of the 1,322 high school graduates planned to attend college. In 1982-83, 76% of the students were White, 1% Hispanic, 23% Black, 0.5% Asian and 0.1% American Indian. Private schools: 795 students enrolled in five elementary and two high schools. Kilgore College is located in Kilgore. Established in 1935 it is a vocational and two year academic college under local control. Enrollment in 1982 was 4,095 with in state undergraduate tuition and fees of $330 per semester. Le Tourneau College is located in Longview. Established in 1946 it is an independent nonprofit institution. Enrollment in 1982 was 1,037 with in state undergraduate tuition and fees of $3,203 per semester. The highest degree offered is: Bachelor. Vocational education: Longview—Aladdin Beauty College, Bish Mathis Institute, Good Shepherd Hospital School of Radiologic Technology, Michaels University of Beauty Culture. **PUBLIC LIBRARIES** Lee Public Library (Gladewater): 23,834 volumes. Kilgore Public Library: 34,646 volumes and one branch. Nicholson Memorial Public Library (Longview): 62,182 volumes and two branches. **CHILD CARE** 263 day care and 32 twenty-four hour care licensed facilities. **HEALTH CARE** 145 physicians and 78 dentists. Hospitals: five with a combined capacity of 540. Clinics: one for the treatment of alcohol and/or drug abuse. Ambulance services: two fire departments and one city service. Mental health: one clinic. Nursing homes: 10 nursing homes with a combined capacity of 1,022 nursing care residents. The average cost per day for private patients in 1982 was $30.74. **CHURCHES** 141 churches have an estimated combined membership of 60,552. The largest denominations are Southern Baptist, United Methodist and Churches of Christ. **SOCIAL SERVICES** In fiscal year 1983 a total of $3,899,384 in food stamps was distributed, with an average of 7,950 persons receiving food stamps each month. Aid to Families with Dependent Children (AFDC) totaled $1,088,256 with an average of 730 families receiving AFDC each month. Medical assistance benefits for the aged and disabled of $7,651,584 and for families and children of $1,359,521 brought the county benefit total to $13,998,745. **FIRE PROTECTION** One paid, one partly paid and seven volunteer fire departments. **LAW ENFORCEMENT** The County Sheriff has 93 commissioned officers. Five police departments have a combined force of 205. One college has a campus police department with a force of 13 officers. The County Airport Police force has five officers. **CRIME** 609 violent crimes (murder, forcible rape, robbery and aggravated assault) and 6,635 nonviolent crimes (burglary, larceny-theft and motor vehicle theft) were reported in 1982. **JUDICIAL SYSTEM** Three District Courts and Judges, two County Courts and Judges and four Justices of the Peace. In the District Courts a total of 4,852 cases were pending on 1/1/82, 3,136 new cases were filed and 3,982 cases were disposed of during the year leaving 4,006 cases pending on 12/31/82. There were 850 criminal cases on the docket, 235 convictions, 100 persons committed to prison and three committed to jail and 375 cases left pending. In the County Courts 2,671 cases were pending on 1/1/82, 3,739 new cases were filed and 3,278 cases were disposed of during the year leaving 3,132 cases pending on 12/31/82. There were 4,029 criminal cases on the docket, 1,040 convictions, 353 persons committed to jail, and 1,792 cases left pending. **JAILS** One jail, capacity 199. **ATTORNEYS AT LAW** 194. **UTILITIES** 95% of the residents are connected to a public or privately owned water system and 80% are connected to a public sewer system. Natural gas is distributed to the county by Entex, Inc. and Southern Gas Co. The average annual residential bill for natural gas in 1982 for the Entex distribution system was $390.31, an increase of 26% over 1981. Electricity is distributed to the county by Southwestern Electric Power Co., Rusk Co. Electric Coop., Inc., Upshur-Rural Electric Coop., Corp. and is generated primarily by gas and coal. The typical residential electric bill is $125.48 per month for an all-electric house using 2,500 kwh. **TAXES** The county has 18 units with taxing authority: seven school districts, seven cities, one county, one college district and two special districts.

RECREATION/ENTERTAINMENT

NATIONAL REGISTER OF HISTORIC PLACES Longview: Northcutt House, Everett Building and Whaley House. **COUNTY/MUNICIPAL PARKS** 383 acres in one county and 34 municipal parks. These parks contain five miles of hiking trails, 27 playgrounds, one football and soccer field, 18 baseball and softball fields, 32 tennis courts, 14 multi-use courts, six swimming pools, one boat ramp and shore fishing facilities. **SCENIC DRIVES** The Texas Forest Trail runs through this county. This trail explores the farming, ranching and oilfield areas of the East Texas Pineywoods. **BOATING/FISHING** Lakes/reservoirs: Cherokee (3,987 acres), Deverina (51 acres), Forest (25 acres), Griffin (29 acres), Lamond (35 acres) and Le Tourneau (75 acres). Major rivers: Sabine. Primary streams: Cherokee Bayou, Campbells, Johnson, Wynns Bayou, Grace and Bullhide Slough. **HUNTING** Fall and winter seasons on deer. Summer, fall and winter seasons on squirrel. Winter seasons on quail, muskrat, beaver, otter, opossum, mink, ring-tailed cat, badger, fox, raccoon, skunk and civet cat. No closed season on nutria, coyote and bobcat. In 1983 duck, coot, geese, woodcock and jacksnipe seasons occurred during the winter months. Teal duck, rail and gallinule seasons occurred in the fall. Mourning dove seasons occurred intermittently during the fall and winter months. **MUSEUMS** Kilgore: East Texas Oil Museum and Rangerette Showcase. Longview: Caddo Indian Museum, Longview Museum and Art Center and R.G. Le Tourneau Museum. **ORCHESTRAS** Longview: Symphony Orchestra. **DANCE** Longview: Ballet Theatre. **COLLEGIATE FINE ARTS** Kilgore: Cultural events offered by Kilgore College. **SPECIAL EVENTS** Rodeo, Gladewater, June; Arts and Crafts Outdoor Festival, Gladewater, September; County Fair, Longview, September.

COMMUNITIES

COUNTY SEAT Longview, County Courthouse, 75601; County Clerk's Office, 214/758-6181. **INCORPORATED COMMUNITIES** (1980 population and ZIP Code) Clarksville City (525) 75647, Easton (333: 265 in Gregg Co. and 68 in Rusk Co.) 75641, Gladewater (6,548: 4,311 in Gregg Co. and 2,237 in Upshur Co.) 75647, Kilgore (10,968: 8,425 in Gregg Co. and 2,543 in Rusk Co.) 75662, Lakeport (835) 75601, Liberty City (1,121) 75647, Longview (62,762: 61,085 in Gregg Co. and 1,677 in Harrison Co.) 75601, Rolling Meadows (252) 75601, Warren City (281: 279 in Gregg Co. and two in Upshur Co.) 75647 and White Oak (4,415) 75693. **UNINCORPORATED COMMUNITIES** (and ZIP Code) Camps 75601, Danville 75662, Fredonia 75662, Judson 75660, Lake Cherokee 75652, Pleasant Green 75604, Spring Hill 75601 and Swamp City 75647. **FOR ADDITIONAL LOCAL INFORMATION** Kilgore Chamber of Commerce, 107 S. Martin, P.O. Box 1582, Kilgore, 75662, 214/984-5022 and Longview Chamber of Commerce, P.O. Box 472, Longview, 75606, 214/757-3333.

GRIMES (G2)

THE LAND

Northwest of Houston on State Highways 30, 90 and 105 in the Blackland Prairies Region, Grimes County covers 799 square miles with an elevation range of 200 to 400 feet. Along the Brazos River the soils are cracking and clayey with some loamy surfaces. In the south the gently rolling to hilly soils are light colored, acidic and loamy with reddish clay subsoils. Except for a strip of darker, alkaline, clayey soils over chalk in the south central area, the central and northwest areas have dark, deep to shallow, clayey soils over chalk. The northeastern soils are lighter, more level and slightly acidic with sandy surfaces and mottled, clayey subsoils. The vegetation is a combination of Post Oak Savannah in the northwest and Blackland Prairies with tall grasses and oaks, mesquite, pecans along streams. Between one and 10% of the land in the county is considered prime farmland. **CLIMATE** Subtropical Humid. Thunderstorms may occur at any time, but are most frequent in late spring and early summer. The average annual temperature is 68°F. Temperatures in January range from an average low of 39° to an average high of 60°F and in July range from 73° to 95°F. The average annual precipitation is 40 inches, with an average relative humidity of 87% at 6 A.M. and 58% at 6 P.M. The average annual snowfall is less than one inch. The growing season averages 275 days per year, with the last freeze in early March and the first freeze in early December. The sun shines during the year on the average 67% of the daylight hours.

THE PEOPLE

The population patterns in Grimes County have shifted over the past 20 years. The 1982 estimated population of 15,500 indicates a continuation of strong growth begun in the 1970s, which reversed the steady population decrease between 1930 and 1970. Growth was greater in the urban areas than in the rural areas between 1970 and 1980. The age groups with the largest gains were ages 20 to 34 and birth to five years, lowering the median age from 36 in 1970 to 32 in 1980. The largest ancestry groups are Black (28%), persons of English descent (18%) and German descent (18%). **REGISTERED VOTERS** As of November 2, 1982 there were 7,710 registered voters (0.1% of the state total). The 1982 general election had a 44% voter turnout, compared to a 62% turnout in the 1980 general election. In the 1982 primary 97% voted Democratic and 3% Republican, with 2,838 votes cast.

THE ECONOMY

AGRICULTURE Forest production area and cattle. In 1982, 69% of the land was in farms and ranches, with 12% of the farmland under cultivation. Grimes ranked 78th in the state in highest agricultural receipts, with 93% from livestock and livestock products. Overgrazing, undesirable brush, water erosion, flooding and inefficient tillage systems are the current conservation problems. Primary crops: hay, corn and oats. Primary vegetables: potatoes, sweet potatoes and watermelons. Primary fruits and nuts: peaches and pecans. Primary livestock and products: cattle, milk and hogs. **BUSINESS** Total number of business establishments in the county: 286. Retail sales during the first quarter of 1984 increased 12%. In 1980, 16% of the labor force were self-employed, 15% were employed in professional or related services, 22% in manufacturing, 19% in wholesale and retail trade, 15% in agriculture, forestry, fisheries and mining, 20% were employed in other counties and there were 1,614 retired workers. The industries with the most employment: metal heat treating, iron and steel forging, and the manufacture of mobile homes, tanks, valves and pipe fittings. The nonfarm earnings in 1981 totaled $128,897,000. The retired workers received an average monthly Social Security payment of $277. **FINANCE** On June 30, 1983, seven commercial banks had total deposits of $98,771,000 and total assets of $112,676,000. There is one state savings and loan association branch and one federal association branch in the county. **HOUSING** Average value of homes in 1980: $24,500. Permits for new, privately owned housing units increased in 1982: 78 permits were issued with a total construction cost of $4,317,327. Of those permits, 22 were for single family houses. Housing permits in Navasota increased from 31 in 1981 to 78 in 1982. Between 1970 and 1980 the number of housing units increased by 29%. Sixty-one percent of all units in the county are air-conditioned, 79% are heated by gas and 13% by electricity. **NATURAL RESOURCES** Clay, sand, gravel, oil, gas, and lignite coal. In 1982 a total of 17,299,244 thousand cubic feet of gas well gas, 515,242 barrels of condensate, 139,058 barrels of crude oil and 286,291 thousand cubic feet of casinghead

GRIMES (continued)

gas were produced. Current production of other minerals and products includes lignite coal, sand and gravel and crushed sandstone. Pine and hardwood production in 1981 totaled 6,422,932 cubic feet: 6,388,772 cubic feet of pine and 34,160 cubic feet of hardwood. **TOURISM** Travel expenditures of $2,173,000 in 1982 (an increase of 12% over 1981) generated 50 jobs and $413,000 in payroll. **ALCOHOLIC BEVERAGES** Packaged distilled spirits, beer, ale, malt liquor and wine are legal in parts of the county. Sale of mixed beverages is legal in all or parts of the county. **FEDERAL EXPENDITURES** The federal government had direct expenditures or obligations of $25,845,000 in the county during fiscal year 1983, including $1,001,000 by the U.S. Department of Defense. In addition, the federal government provided $307,000 in grant awards, paid $859,000 in salaries and wages, made direct payments to individuals of $24,048,000 including $16,610,000 in retirement and disability payments, awarded $398,000 in procurement contracts and spent $233,000 in other expenditures or obligations. The federal government also provided $4,879,000 in guaranteed loans and insurance.

COMMUNICATION
Newspapers–Weekly: The Navasota Examiner and Grimes County Review (Navasota). Radio: KWBC-AM (Navasota). Cable TV. Telephone companies: Continental Telephone, Southwestern Bell, United Telephone and Conroe Telephone. **TRANSPORTATION** Total public road mileage: 795. In 1982 there were 14,077 registered vehicles and 378 reported traffic accidents including three fatalities. Taxi cabs: one company in Navasota. Intercity bus service is available. Motor freight: three carriers. Rail: six main lines carry freight through the county with one carrying annually 20 to 30 million tons of freight and five carry 10 to 20 million each. Aircraft: 24 are registered in the county. Airports: Navasota Municipal Airport.

COMMUNITY SERVICES
EDUCATION Four school districts with four elementary, one middle and four high schools. The average daily attendance in 1981-82 was 2,836, with expenditures per pupil of $2,367 including 199 classroom teachers with an average annual salary of $14,829. Forty percent of the 178 high school graduates planned to attend college. In 1982-83, 58% of the students were White, 13% Hispanic, 29% Black and 0.1% Asian. **PUBLIC LIBRARIES** Grimes County Library (Navasota): 20,000 volumes. **CHILD CARE** 19 day care and one twenty-four hour care licensed facilities. **HEALTH CARE** Nine physicians and six dentists. Hospitals: one with a capacity of 57. Ambulance services: one hospital-based and one county service. Mental health: one county clinic. Nursing homes: one nursing home has a capacity of 174 nursing care residents. The average cost per day for private patients in 1982 was $21.10. **CHURCHES** 51 churches have an estimated combined membership of 9,490. The largest denominations are Catholic, Southern Baptist and United Methodist. **SOCIAL SERVICES** In fiscal year 1983 a total of $883,742 in food stamps was distributed, with an average of 1,866 persons receiving food stamps each month. Aid to Families with Dependent Children (AFDC) totaled $259,997 with an average of 168 families receiving AFDC each month. Medical assistance benefits for the aged and disabled of $1,591,717 and for families and children of $320,314 brought the county benefit total to $3,055,769. **FIRE PROTECTION** Five volunteer fire departments. **LAW ENFORCEMENT** The County Sheriff has 15 commissioned officers. One police department has a force of 12. **CRIME** 44 violent crimes (murder, forcible rape, robbery and aggravated assault) and 523 nonviolent crimes (burglary, larceny-theft and motor vehicle theft) were reported in 1982.

JUDICIAL SYSTEM Two District Courts and Judges, one County Court and Judge and six Justices of the Peace. In the District Courts a total of 670 cases were pending on 1/1/82, 424 new cases were filed and 408 cases were disposed of during the year leaving 686 cases pending on 12/31/82. There were 206 criminal cases on the docket, 50 convictions, 24 persons committed to prison and 115 cases left pending. In the County Court 514 cases were pending on 1/1/82, 422 new cases were filed and 173 cases were disposed of during the year leaving 763 cases pending on 12/31/82. There were 781 criminal cases on the docket, 124 convictions, 40 persons committed to jail, and 624 cases left pending. **JAILS** One jail, capacity 22. **PRISONS** Pack I, on 3,913 acres southwest of Navasota, had an inmate population in 1983 of 409. It has agricultural operations. Pack II, on 2,090 acres southwest of Navasota, had 1,058 inmates, agricultural operations and a stainless steel factory. **ATTORNEYS AT LAW** 14. **UTILITIES** 60% of the residents are connected to a public or privately owned water system and 40% are connected to a public sewer system. Electricity is distributed to the county by Gulf State Utilities, Mid-South Electric Coop., Assn. and San Benard Electric Coop., Inc. and is generated primarily by gas, oil, coal and water. The typical residential electric bill is $198.32 per month for an all electric house using 2,500 kwh. **TAXES** The county has seven units with taxing authority: four school districts, one city, one county and one special district.

RECREATION/ENTERTAINMENT
NATIONAL REGISTER OF HISTORIC PLACES Anderson: Anderson Historic District. Anderson vicinity: Piedmont Springs Archeological Site. Navasota: P.A. Smith Hotel and Steele House. Navasota vicinity: Foster House. **STATE** Fanthorp Inn State Historic Site (see Anderson County). **MUNICIPAL PARKS** 51 acres in four municipal parks. These parks contain four playgrounds, one golf course, three baseball and softball fields and one tennis court. **SCENIC DRIVES** The Texas Brazos Trail runs through this county. This trail moves through a beautiful and historic section of Central Texas revealing forested landscapes filled with wildlife and wild flowers. **BOATING/FISHING** Lakes/reservoirs: Carr (110 acres), Gibbons Creek (2,490 acres), Hideaway Hills (27 acres), K-Ranch (36 acres), Bedias (35 acres), Irine (50 acres), Wayne (36 acres), Waltrip Ranch (33 acres) and Yarboro (22 acres). Major rivers: Navasota and Brazos. Primary streams: Gibbons, Nebletts, Rocky, Pine and Hurricane. **HUNTING** Fall and winter seasons on deer. No closed seasons on nutria, coyote, bobcat and squirrel. Winter seasons on quail, muskrat, beaver, otter, opossum, mink, ring-tailed cat, badger, fox, raccoon, skunk and civet cat. In 1983 duck, coot, geese, woodcock and jacksnipe seasons occurred during the winter months. Teal duck, rail and gallinule seasons occurred in the fall. Mourning dove seasons occurred during the fall and winter months. **MUSEUMS** Anderson: Steinhagen Log Cabin. **SPECIAL EVENTS** Nostalgia Days, Navasota, April/May; Anderson Texas Trek, Anderson, May; County Fair, Anderson, June; Texas Renaissance Festival, Plantersville, October-November.

COMMUNITIES
COUNTY SEAT Anderson, County Courthouse, 77830; County Clerk's Office, 409/873-2662. **INCORPORATED COMMUNITIES** (1980 population and ZIP Code) Navasota (5,971) 77868 and Todd Mission (225, est. incorp. inactive) 77363. **UNINCORPORATED COMMUNITIES** (and ZIP Code) Anderson 77830, Apolonia 77830, Bedias 77831, Carlos 77830, Courtney 77868, Cross 77861, Erwin 77830, Iola 77861, Keith 77861, Piedmont 77830, Plantersville 77363, Richards 77873, Roans Prairie 77875, Shiro 77876, Singleton 77877, Stoneham 77868, White Hall (Wallace Prairie) 77868 and Yarboro 77868. **FOR ADDITIONAL LOCAL INFORMATION** Grimes Co. Chamber of Commerce, P.O. Box 530, Navasota, 77868, 409/825-6600.

GUADALUPE (C36)

THE LAND

East of San Antonio on Interstate Highway 10 in the Claypan Area, Guadalupe County covers 713 square miles with an elevation range of 450 to 800 feet. The northwest has undulating, slightly acidic soils with loamy surfaces and cracking, clayey subsoils. The north central area has cracking, clayey soils with loamy surfaces in some spots. Toward the south the soils become deep loam with some clay subsoils or limestone bedrock. In the southeast the soils are loamy with deep, reddish, clayey subsoils. The vegetation is the Blackland Prairies in the northwest and Post Oak Savannah to the southeast with tall grasses and such trees as oaks and mesquite along streams. Between 31 and 40% of the land in the county is considered prime farmland. **CLIMATE** Subtropical mild. Thunderstorms may occur at any time, but are more frequent in late spring and early summer. The average annual temperature is 69°F. Temperatures in January range from an average low of 38° to an average high of 62°F and in July range from 73° to 96°F. The average annual precipitation is 33 inches, with an average relative humidity of 86% at 6 A.M. and 53% at 6 P.M. The average annual snowfall is less than one inch. The growing season averages 275 days per year, with the last freeze in early March and the first freeze in early December. The sun shines during the year on the average 67% of the daylight hours.

THE PEOPLE

The 1982 estimated population of 49,400 indicates a continuation of the steady growth begun in the 1950s. Almost 53% of the growth between 1970 and 1980 was in rural areas. The age groups with the largest gains were ages 20 to 34 and 15 to 19. The median age rose from 28 in 1970 to 30 in 1980. The largest ancestry groups are persons of German descent (33%), Hispanic (25%) and English descent (18%). **REGISTERED VOTERS** As of November 2, 1982 there were 21,759 registered voters (0.3% of the state total). The 1982 general election had a 56% voter turnout, compared to a 74% turnout in the 1980 general election. In the 1982 primary 78% voted Democratic and 22% Republican, with 6,347 votes cast.

THE ECONOMY

AGRICULTURE In 1982, 80% of the land was in farms and ranches, with 29% of the farmland under cultivation and 7% irrigated. Guadalupe ranked 145th in the state in highest agricultural receipts, with 71% from livestock and livestock products. Overgrazing, undesirable brush and weeds, water erosion and flooding are the current conservation problems. Primary crops: sorghum, hay, oats, wheat and corn. Primary vegetables: watermelons. Primary fruits and nuts: peaches and sixth in the state for pecans. Primary livestock and products: cattle, milk and hogs. **BUSINESS** Total number of business establishments in the county: 819. Retail sales during the first quarter of 1984 increased 21%. In 1980, 10% of the labor force were self-employed, 17% were employed in professional or related services, 20% in manufacturing, 22% in wholesale and retail trade, 9% in construction, 46% were employed in other counties and there were 3,421 retired workers. The industries with the most employment: agribusiness, poultry processing, textile mills, oil and gas extraction and the manufacture of radio and television sets, farm machinery and equipment and structural metal products. The nonfarm earnings in 1981 totaled $384,811,000. The retired workers received an average monthly Social Security payment of $286. **FINANCE** On June 30, 1983, six commercial banks had total deposits of $240,070,000 and total assets of $268,167,000. On December 31, 1982 one state savings and loan association and three state branches had assets of $46,129,197. **HOUSING** Average value of homes in 1980: $34,600. Permits

for new, privately owned housing units increased in 1982: 300 permits were issued with a total construction cost of $7,134,645,000. Of those permits, 136 were for single family houses. Housing permits in Schertz increased from four in 1981 to 69 in 1982 with 40 of the permits issued for two family structures. Between 1970 and 1980 the number of housing units increased by 51%. Seventy-two percent of all units in the county are air-conditioned, 58% are heated by gas and 37% by electricity. **NATURAL RESOURCES** Ceramic clay, industrial sand, sand and gravel, oil, gas and lignite coal. In 1982 a total of 98,422 thousand cubic feet of gas well gas, 1,567 barrels of condensate, 1,693,730 barrels of crude oil and 878,401 thousand cubic feet of casinghead gas were produced. Current production of other minerals and products includes brick, ball clay, sand and gravel. **TOURISM** Travel expenditures of $17,818,000 in 1982 (an increase of 14% over 1981) generated 359 jobs and $3,303,000 in payroll. Lodging: five hotels, motels and tourist courts. Convention/meeting facilities: Seguin-Texas Lutheran College Theatre, Stadium and Jesse Jones Complex. **ALCOHOLIC BEVERAGES** Packaged distilled spirits, beer, ale, malt liquor and wine are legal in parts of the county. Sale of mixed beverages is legal in all or parts of the county. **MILITARY INSTALLATIONS** Seguin Auxiliary Air Field, Seguin, 826 acres, Auxiliary Training Field. **FEDERAL EXPENDITURES** The federal government had direct expenditures or obligations of $80,872,000 in the county during fiscal year 1983, including $17,425,000 by the U.S. Department of Defense. In addition, the federal government provided $1,207,000 in grant awards, paid $4,159,000 in salaries and wages, made direct payments to individuals of $74,682,000 including $61,678,000 in retirement and disability payments, awarded $302,000 in procurement contracts and spent $523,000 in other expenditures or obligations. The federal government also provided $703,000 in direct loans and $48,650,000 in guaranteed loans and insurance.

COMMUNICATION

Newspapers–Daily: Gazette Enterprise (Seguin) ave. eve. circ. 4,949. Weekly: The Seguin Citizen. Radio: KWED-AM and KWED-FM (Seguin). Cable TV. Telephone companies: Continental Telephone, Southwestern Bell, Central Telephone-Midstate, Guadalupe Valley Telephone Coop. and San Marcos Telephone. **TRANSPORTATION** Total public road mileage: 1,210. In 1982 there were 38,571 registered vehicles and 1,114 reported traffic accidents including 25 fatalities. Intercity bus service is available. Motor freight: eight local and intrastate carriers. Rail: The Sunset Limited provides passenger service on the Amtrak Route. One main line carries annually over 30 million tons of freight through the county. Aircraft: 63 are registered in the county. Airports: Geronimo Field at Seguin, Kardy's Airport at Cibolo, H.M. Ranch Airport at Marion and Glen Beicker Ranch at Seguin. Guadalupe Hospital Heliport at Seguin is for emergency use.

COMMUNITY SERVICES

EDUCATION Four school districts with 11 elementary, five middle and four high schools. The average daily attendance in 1981-82 was 9,494, with expenditures per pupil of $2,063 including 637 classroom teachers with an average annual salary of $15,851. Fifty-eight percent of the 760 high school graduates planned to attend college. In 1982-83, 58% of the students were White, 34% Hispanic, 7% Black, 0.8% Asian and 0.1% American Indian. Private schools: 332 students enrolled in two elementary schools. Texas Lutheran College is located in Seguin. Established in 1891 it is affiliated with the American Lutheran Church. Enrollment in 1982 was 1,342. The highest degree offered is Bachelor. **PUBLIC LIBRARIES** Schertz Public Library: 14,000 volumes. Seguin-Guadalupe County Public Library: 36,000 volumes.

COUNTIES

CHILD CARE 64 day care and 16 twenty-four hour care licensed facilities. **HEALTH CARE** 33 physicians and 20 dentists. Hospitals: one with a capacity of 75. Clinics: one for treatment of alcohol and/or drug abuse and one dialysis clinic. Ambulance services: two funeral homes, one volunteer service, and one city service. Mental health: one county clinic. Nursing homes: four nursing homes with a combined capacity of 364 nursing care and 96 custodial care residents. The average cost per day for private patients in 1982 was $30.47. **CHURCHES** 44 churches have an estimated combined membership of 23,433. The largest denominations are Catholic, Southern Baptist and American Lutheran. **SOCIAL SERVICES** In fiscal year 1983 a total of $1,784,051 in food stamps was distributed, with an average of 3,848 persons receiving food stamps each month. Aid to Families with Dependent Children (AFDC) totaled $398,504 with an average of 280 families receiving AFDC each month. Medical assistance benefits for the aged and disabled of $3,272,878 and for families and children of $483,324 brought the county benefit total to $5,938,757. **FIRE PROTECTION** One partly paid and seven volunteer fire departments. **LAW ENFORCEMENT** The County Sheriff has 75 commissioned officers. Six police departments have a combined force of 45. **CRIME** 200 violent crimes (murder, forcible rape, robbery and aggravated assault) and 1,633 nonviolent crimes (burglary, larceny-theft and motor vehicle theft) were reported in 1982. **JUDICIAL SYSTEM** Three District Courts and Judges, two County Courts and Judges and four Justices of the Peace. In the District Courts a total of 1,030 cases were pending on 1/1/82, 1,076 new cases were filed and 982 cases were disposed of during the year leaving 1,124 cases pending on 12/31/82. There were 408 criminal cases on the docket, 134 convictions, 44 persons committed to prison and 140 cases left pending. In the County Courts 3,387 cases were pending on 1/1/82, 2,454 new cases were filed and 1,676 cases were disposed of during the year leaving 4,165 cases pending on 12/31/82. There were 5,425 criminal cases on the docket, 957 convictions, 43 persons committed to jail and 3,842 cases left pending. **JAILS** One jail, capacity 31. **ATTORNEYS AT LAW** 42. **UTILITIES** 83% of the residents are connected to a public or privately owned water system and 56% are connected to a public sewer system. Natural gas is distributed to the county by Entex, Inc. The average annual residential bill for natural gas in 1982 for the Entex distribution system was $390.31, an increase of 26% over 1981. Electricity is distributed to the city of Seguin by the Seguin Electric System, New Braunfels by New Braunfels utilities and to the rest of the county by Bluebonnet Electric Coop., Inc., Guadalupe Valley Electric Coop., Inc., Pedernales Electric Coop., Inc. and San Antonio City Public Service Board and is generated primarily by oil, water and coal. The typical residential electric bill is $170.80 per month for an all-electric house using 2,500 kwh. **TAXES** The county has 11 units with taxing authority: four school districts, five cities, one county, and one special district.

RECREATION/ENTERTAINMENT
NATIONAL REGISTER OF HISTORIC PLACES Seguin: Erskine-Hollamon House, Joseph F. Johnson House, Los Nogales, Sebastopol, Robert Hall House, Saffold Dam and Park Hotel. Seguin vicinity: Wilson Utility Pottery Kilns District. **STATE** Sebastopol House State Historic Structure is closed to the public as of July 1983. **MUNICIPAL PARKS** 352 acres in 13 municipal parks. These parks contain one mile of hiking trails, eight playgrounds, one golf course, 12 baseball and softball fields, eight tennis courts, two multi-use courts and four swimming pools. **SCENIC DRIVES** The Texas Independence Trail runs through this county. This trail not only surveys the historic sites of southeastern Texas but also includes many modern visitor attractions such as the Johnson Space Center. **BOATING/FISHING** Lakes/reservoirs: Dunlap (410 acres), Meadow (144 acres), McQueeny (396 acres), Placid (260 acres), Salt (120 acres), Max Starcke Park (50 acres) and York Creek Soil Conservation Service Lakes 7, 10, 13, 14 and 15 (136 acres). Major rivers: Guadalupe and San Marcos. Primary streams: Cibolo, Cottonwood, Long and York. **HUNTING** Fall and winter seasons on deer and javelina. No closed seasons on coyote, bobcat and squirrel. Winter seasons on quail, muskrat, beaver, opossum, ring-tailed cat, badger, fox, weasel, raccoon, skunk and civet cat. In 1983 sandhill crane, duck, coot, geese, woodcock and jacksnipe seasons occurred during the winter months. Teal duck, rail and gallinule seasons occurred in the fall. Mourning dove seasons occurred intermittently during the fall and winter months. **MUSEUMS** Seguin: A.M. and Alma Fiedler Memorial Museum, Sebastopol House State Historic Structure and Los Nogales Museum. **COLLEGIATE FINE ARTS** Seguin: Cultural events offered by Texas Lutheran College. **SPECIAL EVENTS** Mayfest, Seguin, May; Senior Citizen's Day, Schertz, May; Freedom Fiesta, Seguin, July; July 4th Jubilee, Schertz, July; Heimfest, Marion, September; County Fair, Seguin, October; Pecan Show, Seguin, November.

COMMUNITIES
COUNTY SEAT Seguin, County Courthouse, 78155; County Clerk's Office, 512/379-0418. **INCORPORATED COMMUNITIES** (1980 population and ZIP Code) Cibolo (549) 78108, Marion (674) 78124, New Berlin (253) 78155, New Braunfels (22,402: 27 in Guadalupe Co. and 22,375 in Comal Co.) 78130, Schertz (7,264: 7,234 in Guadalupe Co., 2 in Bexar Co. and 26 in Comal Co.) 78154, Seguin (17,854) 78155 and Selma (528: 88 in Comal Co., 157 in Guadalupe Co. and 283 in Bexar Co.) 78209. **UNINCORPORATED COMMUNITIES** (and ZIP Code) Barbarosa 78130, Behring Store 78155, Camp Willow 78130, Clear Spring 78130, Galle 78638, Geronimo 78115, Kingsbury 78638, Lake Placid 78155, McQueeney 78123, Parkview Estates 78155, Redwood 78666, Schumansville 78130, Spring Hill 78155, Staples 78670, Sullivan 78638, Weinert 78638, Zippville (Zipp) 78155, Zorn 78666 and Zuehl 78124. **FOR ADDITIONAL LOCAL INFORMATION** Seguin and Guadalupe Co., Chamber of Commerce, P.O. Box 710, Seguin, 78155, 512/379-6382.

HALE (P30)

THE LAND
North of Lubbock on Interstate Highway 27 in the High Plains Region, Hale County covers 1,005 square miles with an elevation range of 3,200 to 3,600 feet. The nearly level soils have loamy surfaces and clayey subsoils. In some areas lime may be found within 20 inches of the surface. In the High Plains vegetation area the principal grasses are blue grama and buffalograss with some shinnery oak, mesquite, sagebrush and yucca. Between 81 and 90% of the land in the county is considered prime farmland. **CLIMATE** Mild and dry. Thunderstorms, a few severe with hail, and duststorms may be expected in spring. The average annual temperature is 59°F. Temperatures in January range from an average low of 23° to an average high of 52°F and in July range from 66° to 92°F. The average annual precipitation is 19 inches, with an average relative humidity of 70% at 6 A.M. and 38% at 6 P.M. The average annual snowfall is 11 inches. The growing season averages 211 days per year, with the last freeze in early April and the first freeze in early November. The sun shines during the year on the average 75% of the daylight hours.

THE PEOPLE
The 1982 estimated population of 38,000 indicates a

continuation of the steady growth begun in the 1970s. Almost 16% of the growth was in urban areas. The age groups with the largest gains were ages 20 to 24 and 62 and over. The county's population is younger than average (median age 27) and has a high birth rate. The largest ancestry groups are Hispanic (34%), persons of English descent (28%) and Irish descent (16%). **REGISTERED VOTERS** As of November 2, 1982 there were 14,176 registered voters (0.2% of the state total). The 1982 general election had a 53% voter turnout, compared to a 70% turnout in the 1980 general election. In the 1982 primary 89% voted Democratic and 11% Republican, with 3,009 votes cast.

THE ECONOMY

AGRICULTURE Prime farmland with diversified products. In 1982, 98% of the land was in farms and ranches, with 80% of the farmland under cultivation and 90% irrigated. Hale ranked sixth in the state in highest agricultural receipts, with 84% from crops. Water erosion, decreasing irrigation water supplies and inadequate cropping systems are the current conservation problems. Primary crops: seventh in the state for cotton, first for soybeans, third for corn and eighth for sunflowers. Wheat and sorghum. Primary vegetables: fifth in the state for onions. Potatoes, cucumbers and processed vegetables including beets, snapbeans, spinach, sweet corn and tomatoes. Primary fruits and nuts: pecans. Primary livestock and products: 10th in the state for hogs. Cattle, milk, sheep and wool. **BUSINESS** Total number of business establishments in the county: 850. Retail sales during the first quarter of 1984 increased 15%. In 1980, 16% of the labor force were self-employed, 19% were employed in professional or related services, 13% in manufacturing, 23% in wholesale and retail trade, 18% in agriculture, forestry, fisheries and mining, 9% were employed in other counties and there were 2,911 retired workers. The industries with the most employment: agribusiness, heavy construction, meat packing and the manufacture of metal containers and men's work clothing. The nonfarm earnings in 1981 totaled $305,259,000. The retired workers received an average monthly Social Security payment of $328. **FINANCE** On June 30, 1983, six commercial banks had total deposits of $239,993,000 and total assets of $268,289,000. On December 31, 1982 one state savings and loan association, five state branches and one federal association branch had assets of $150,000,945. In addition there are three credit unions in the county. **HOUSING** Average value of homes in 1980: $27,500. Permits for new, privately owned housing units decreased in 1982: 15 permits were issued with a total construction cost of $959,587. Of those permits, all were for single family houses. Between 1970 and 1980 the number of housing units increased by 14%. Seventy-six percent of all units in the county are air-conditioned, 91% are heated by gas and 8% by electricity. **NATURAL RESOURCES** Caliche, oil and gas. In 1982 a total of 4,510,073 barrels of crude oil and 683,013 thousand cubic feet of casinghead gas were produced. **TOURISM** Travel expenditures of $19,721,000 in 1982 (an increase of 14% over 1981) generated 393 jobs and $3,454,000 in payroll. Convention/meeting facilities: Plainview-Jaycee Park and Wayland Baptist College Hutchinson Center and Stadium. **ALCOHOLIC BEVERAGES** Totally dry. **FEDERAL EXPENDITURES** The federal government had direct expenditures or obligations of $81,145,000 in the county during fiscal year 1983, including $912,000 by the U.S. Department of Defense. In addition, the federal government provided $4,652,000 in grant awards, paid $3,463,000 in salaries and wages, made direct payments to individuals of $41,920,000 including $29,821,000 in retirement and disability payments, awarded $1,792,000 in procurement contracts and spent $29,318,000 in other expenditures or obligations. The federal government also provided $40,940,000 in direct loans and $34,337,000 in guaranteed loans and insurance.

COMMUNICATION

Newspapers–Daily: Plainview Daily Herald, ave. eve. circ. 9,533. Weekly: Abernathy Weekly Review, Hale Center American and the Petersburg Post. Radio: KKYN-AM, KVOP-AM and KATX-FM (Plainview). Cable TV. Telephone companies: General Telephone and Southwestern Bell. **TRANSPORTATION** Total public road mileage: 1,942. In 1982 there were 34,149 registered vehicles and 841 reported traffic accidents including eight fatalities. Intercity bus service is available. Motor freight: 17 local and intrastate carriers. Rail: two main and four branch lines carry freight through the county. The two main lines carry annually 10 to 20 million tons of freight each. One branch line carries annually one to five million tons of freight and three carry less than one million each. Aircraft: 133 are registered in the county. Airports: Hale County Airport at Plainview serves as a base for 196 aircraft and is a basic transportation airport with general aviation service. Abernathy Municipal Airport.

COMMUNITY SERVICES

EDUCATION Five school districts with 11 elementary, five middle and five high schools. The average daily attendance in 1981-82 was 7,630, with expenditures per pupil of $2,547 including 527 classroom teachers with an average annual salary of $17,346. Forty-one percent of the 504 high school graduates planned to attend college. In 1982-83, 41% of the students were White, 51% Hispanic, 8% Black and 0.3% Asian. Sports championships: 1984 AAA Girls' Basketball, Abernathy H.S. Wayland Baptist College is located in Plainview. Established in 1908 it is affiliated with the Southern Baptist Church. Enrollment in 1982 was 1,256. The highest degree offered is Bachelor. Vocational education: Plainview-Central Plains General Hospital School of X-Ray Technology, Gregg School of Auctioneering, Lippert Court Reporting College. **PUBLIC LIBRARIES** Abernathy Public Library: 9,418 volumes. Hale Center Public Library: 5,677 volumes. Petersburg Library. Unger Memorial Library (Plainview): 40,745 volumes. **CHILD CARE** 47 day care and 17 twenty-four hour care licensed facilities. **HEALTH CARE** 45 physicians and 13 dentists. Hospitals: three with a combined capacity of 218. Clinics: one public health clinic. Ambulance services: three volunteer services and one commercial service. Mental health: two clinics. Nursing homes: four nursing homes with a combined capacity of 276 nursing care residents. The average cost per day for private patients in 1982 was $28.53. **CHURCHES** 71 churches have an estimated combined membership of 32,055. The largest denominations are Southern Baptist, Catholic and United Methodist. **SOCIAL SERVICES** In fiscal year 1983 a total of $2,412,867 in food stamps was distributed, with an average of 5,086 persons receiving food stamps each month. Aid to Families with Dependent Children (AFDC) totaled $381,221 with an average of 238 families receiving AFDC each month. Medical assistance benefits for the aged and disabled of $2,063,739 and for families and children of $535,940 brought the county benefit total to $5,393,767. **FIRE PROTECTION** One paid and six volunteer fire departments. **LAW ENFORCEMENT** The County Sheriff has 56 commissioned officers. Four police departments have a combined force of 37. **CRIME** 148 violent crimes (murder, forcible rape, robbery and aggravated assault) and 1,303 non-violent crimes (burglary, larceny-theft and motor vehicle theft) were reported in 1982. **JUDICIAL SYSTEM** Two District Courts and Judges, one County Court and Judge and two Justices of the Peace. In the District Courts a total of 1,678 cases were pending on 1/1/82, 1,085 new cases were filed and 1,210 cases were disposed of during the year leaving 1,553 cases pending on 12/31/82. There were 642 criminal cases on the docket, 177 convictions, 54 persons committed to prison and one committed to jail and 290 cases left pending. In the County Court 1,739 cases were pending on 1/1/82, 1,488 new cases were filed and

COUNTIES

HALE (continued)

1,729 cases were disposed of during the year leaving 1,498 cases pending on 12/31/82. There were 2,667 criminal cases on the docket, 658 convictions, 111 persons committed to jail and 1,239 cases left pending. **JAILS** One jail, capacity 86. **ATTORNEYS AT LAW** 30. **UTILITIES** 79% of the residents are connected to a public or privately owned water system and 75% are connected to a public sewer system. Natural gas is distributed to the county by Energas Co. The average annual residential bill for natural gas in 1982 for the Energas distribution system was $371.63, an increase of 23% over 1981. Electricity is distributed to the county by Swisher Electric Coop., Inc., Lighthouse Electric Coop., Inc., Southwestern Public Service and South Plains Electric Coop., Inc. and is generated primarily by coal, gas and oil. The typical residential electric bill is $170.44 per month for an all-electric house using 2,500 kwh. **TAXES** The county has 12 units with taxing authority: five school districts, five cities, one county, and one special district.

RECREATION/ENTERTAINMENT

NATIONAL REGISTER OF HISTORIC PLACES Plainview vicinity: Plainview Site. **MUNICIPAL PARKS** 315 acres in 13 municipal parks. These parks contain two miles of hiking trails, six playgrounds, one golf course, seven baseball and softball fields, two tennis courts, two multi-use courts and four swimming pools. Developed campsites: 40. **BOATING/FISHING** Lakes/reservoirs: Lower Runningwater Soil Conservation Service Lake (38 acres). **HUNTING** Summer, fall and winter seasons on squirrel. No closed seasons on coyote and bobcat. Winter seasons on pheasant, quail, muskrat, beaver, opossum, ring-tailed cat, badger, fox, weasel, raccoon, skunk and civet cat. In 1983 sandhill crane, duck, coot, geese, woodcock and jacksnipe seasons occurred during the winter months. Teal duck, rail and gallinule seasons occurred in the fall. Mourning dove seasons occurred intermittently during the fall and winter months. **MUSEUMS** Plainview: Llano Estacado Museum. **ORCHESTRAS** Plainview: Symphony Orchestra. **COLLEGIATE FINE ARTS** Cultural events offered by Wayland Baptist College. **OTHER** Plainview: Wayland Baptist College Meteorite Display. **SPECIAL EVENTS** 4-H Stock Show, Plainview, March; Pioneer Roundup, Plainview, May; All-American Fiddlers Contest, Hale Center, July; Bar None Rodeo and Parade, Plainview, July; Babe Ruth Baseball Tourney, Plainview, August; Arts and Crafts Festival, Plainview, October; Queens Classic Basketball Tourney, Plainview, November.

COMMUNITIES

COUNTY SEAT Plainview, County Courthouse, 79072; County Clerk's Office, 806/293-8481. **INCORPORATED COMMUNITIES** (1980 population and ZIP Code) Abernathy (2904: 2,205 in Hale Co. and 699 in Lubbock Co.) 79311, Edmonson (291) 79032, Hale Center (2,297) 79041, Petersburg (1,633) 79250 and Plainview (22,187) 79072. **UNINCORPORATED COMMUNITIES** (and ZIP Code) Cotton Center 79021, County Line (also in Lubbock Co.) 79363, Finney 79072, Halfway 79072, Happy Union 79072 and Seth Ward 79072. **FOR ADDITIONAL LOCAL INFORMATION** Abernathy Chamber of Commerce, P.O. Box 539, Abernathy, 79311, 806/298-4038, Hale Chamber of Commerce, 702 Main, P.O. Box 487, Hale Center, 79041, 806/839-2642 and Plainview Chamber of Commerce, 710 W. 5th, P.O. Box 340, Plainview, 79072, 806/296-7431.

HALL (P25)

THE LAND

In the Rolling Plains Region of the Texas Panhandle southeast of Amarillo on U.S. Highway 287, Hall County covers 876 square miles with an elevation range of 1,800 to 2,400 feet. In the northeast the red to brown soils are loamy with some sandy areas and areas with clayey subsoils. Along the Prairie Dog Town Fork of the Red River and to the southwest the brownish to reddish soils have some loamy surfaces and some areas with shallow soils over hardened calcium deposits. In the Rolling Plains vegetation area the grasses include bluestems, gramas, wild ryes, buffalograsses and wheatgrasses. Mesquite, shinnery oak, sandsage, sandburs, tumblegrass and ragweed are problems in some areas. Between 21 and 30% of the land in the county is considered prime farmland. **CLIMATE** Mild and dry. A few thunderstorms with hail, dust, and high winds may be expected in the spring. The average annual temperature is 61°F. Temperatures in January range from an average low of 25° to an average high of 53°F and in July range from 69° to 95°F. The average annual precipitation is 21 inches, with an average relative humidity of 72% at 6 A.M. and 40% at 6 P.M. The average annual snowfall is 13 inches. The growing season averages 213 days per year, with the last freeze in early April and the first freeze in early November. The sun shines during the year on the average 75% of the daylight hours.

THE PEOPLE

The population of Hall County is largely rural and has been declining since 1930. The 1982 estimated population of 5,200 indicates a continuation of that pattern. Urban areas grew slightly in population from 1970 to 1980, but the rural areas had a 20% loss. The age groups with the largest reductions were ages 50 to 54 and five to 19. The county's median age is older than average with a high concentraton of residents over age 64. The largest ancestry groups are persons of English descent (31%), Irish descent (20%) and Hispanic (15%). **REGISTERED VOTERS** As of November 2, 1982 there were 2,977 registered voters (0.04% of the state total). The 1982 general election had a 56% voter turnout, compared to a 70% turnout in the 1980 general election. In the 1982 primary 97% voted Democratic and 3% Republican, with 1,333 votes cast.

THE ECONOMY

AGRICULTURE Cotton area. In 1982, 95% of the land was in farms and ranches, with 22% of the farmland under cultivation and 12% irrigated. Hall ranked 141st in the state in highest agricultural receipts, with 78% from crops. Water and wind erosion are the current conservation problems. Primary crops: cotton, wheat, sorghum and rye. Primary fruits and nuts: peaches. Primary livestock and products: cattle. **BUSINESS** Total number of business establishments in the county: 134. Retail sales during the first quarter of 1984 increased 14%. In 1980, 24% of the labor force were self-employed, 16% were employed in professional or related services, 2% in manufacturing, 19% in wholesale and retail trade, 29% in agriculture, forestry, fisheries and mining, 10% were employed in other counties and there were 764 retired workers. The industry with the most employment: agribusiness. The nonfarm earnings in 1981 totaled $41,819,000. The retired workers received an average monthly Social Security payment of $306. **FINANCE** On June 30, 1983, three commercial banks had total deposits of $53,495,000 and total assets of $60,782,000. There is one state savings and loan association branch and one federal association branch in the county. **HOUSING** Average value of homes in 1980: $19,900. Between 1970 and 1980 the number of housing units increased by 0.6%. Eighty-one percent of all units in the county are air-conditioned, 93% are heated by gas and 6% by electricity. **NATURAL RESOURCES** Gypsum, sand and gravel, oil and gas. Current production of other minerals and products includes sand and gravel. **TOURISM** Travel expenditures of $5,622,000 in 1982 (an increase of 15% over 1981) generated 103 jobs and $943,000 in payroll. **ALCOHOLIC BEVERAGES** Packaged distilled spirits, beer, ale, malt liquor and wine are legal in parts of the county. **FEDERAL EXPENDITURES** The federal government had direct expenditures or obligations of $18,419,000 in the county during fiscal year 1983, including $90,000 by the U.S. Department of Defense. In addition, the federal government provided $123,000 in grant awards, paid $538,000 in salaries and wages, made direct payments to individuals of $11,009,000 including $7,298,000 in retirement and disability payments, awarded $2,000 in procurement contracts and spent $6,747,000 in other expenditures or obligations. The federal government also provided $3,300,000 in direct loans and $7,142,000 in guaranteed loans and insurance.

COMMUNICATION
Newspapers–Weekly: Memphis Democrat. Radio: KLSR-AM (Memphis). Cable TV. Telephone companies: General Telephone, Cap Rock Telephone and South Plains Telephone Coop. **TRANSPORTATION** Total public road mileage: 648. In 1982 there were 5,515 registered vehicles and 114 reported traffic accidents including three fatalities. Intercity bus service is available. Motor freight: two carriers. Rail: two main and one branch line carry freight through the county. The two main lines carry annually over 30 million tons of freight each and one branch carries one to five million. Aircraft: 10 are registered in the county. Airports: Memphis Municipal Airport serves as a base for 10 aircraft and is a basic utility airport with general aviation service.

COMMUNITY SERVICES
EDUCATION Four school districts with five elementary, one middle and three high schools. The average daily attendance in 1981-82 was 1,058 with expenditures per pupil of $2,679 including 84 classroom teachers with an average annual salary of 14,679. Seventy-three percent of the 70 high school graduates planned to attend college. In 1982-83, 60% of the students were White, 26% Hispanic and 15% Black. **PUBLIC LIBRARIES** Memphis Public Library: 10,050 volumes. **CHILD CARE** Six day care and two twenty-four hour care licensed facilities. **HEALTH CARE** Four physicians and one dentist. Hospitals: one with a capacity of 46. Ambulance service: one city and one volunteer fire department service. Mental health: one clinic. Nursing homes: one nursing home with a capacity of 80 nursing care residents. The average cost per day for private patients in 1982 was $28.08. **CHURCHES** 24 churches have an estimated combined membership of 5,419. The largest denominations are Southern Baptist, United Methodist and Churches of Christ. **SOCIAL SERVICES** In fiscal year 1983 a total of $357,364 in food stamps was distributed, with an average of 773 persons receiving food stamps each month. Aid to Families with Dependent Children (AFDC) totaled $56,867 with an average of 34 families receiving AFDC each month. Medical assistance benefits for the aged and disabled of $500,015 and for families and children of $20,594 brought the county benefit total to $934,840. **FIRE PROTECTION** Four volunteer fire departments. **LAW ENFORCEMENT** The County Sheriff has five commissioned officers. Two police departments have a combined force of four. **CRIME** Three violent crimes (murder, forcible rape, robbery and aggravated assault) and 81 nonviolent crimes (burglary, larceny-theft and motor vehicle theft) were reported in 1982. **JUDICIAL SYSTEM** One District Court and Judge, one County Court and Judge and two Justices of the Peace. In the District Court a total of 102 cases were pending on 1/1/82, 132 new cases were filed and 147 cases were disposed of during the year leaving 87 cases pending on 12/31/82. There were 26 criminal cases on the docket, 14 convictions, three persons committed to prison and nine cases left pending. In the County Court 66 cases were pending on 1/1/82, 123 new cases

were filed and 171 cases were disposed of during the year leaving 18 cases pending on 12/31/82. There were 170 criminal cases on the docket, 94 convictions, and 10 cases left pending. **JAILS** One jail, capacity nine. **ATTORNEYS AT LAW** Four. **UTILITIES** 94% of the residents are connected to a public or privately owned water system and 78% are connected to a public sewer system. Natural gas is distributed to the county by Lone Star Gas Co., Division of Enserch. The average annual residential bill for natural gas in 1982 for the Lone Star distribution system was $405.91, an increase of 35% over 1981. Electricity is distributed to the county by Gate City Electric Coop., Inc., Lighthouse Electric Coop., Inc. and West Texas Utilities and is generated primarily by gas and oil. The typical residential electric bill is $145.78 per month for an all-electric house using 2,500 kwh. **TAXES** The county has nine units with taxing authority: four school districts, four cities and one county district.

RECREATION/ENTERTAINMENT
MUNICIPAL PARKS 12 acres in two municipal parks. These parks contain one playground, one baseball and softball field, one tennis court and one swimming pool. **SCENIC DRIVES** The Texas Plains Trail runs through this county. In addition Texas 256 traverses rolling country, threads among sections of the High Plains and ascends the Cap Rock in a drive amid cliffs and canyons. **BOATING/FISHING** Lakes/reservoirs: Lakeview Soil Conservation Service Lakes 3, 4, 5, 6, 7 and 8 (237 acres). Major rivers: Little Red, Wind, North Pease and Prairie Dog Town Fork Red. Primary streams: T-Bar Canyon, Mulberry, Mountain, Rustlers, N. Baylor, Running Water and Cottonwood. **HUNTING** Fall and winter seasons on deer and mule deer. No closed seasons on coyote and bobcat. Winter seasons on aoudad sheep, pheasant, quail, muskrat, beaver, opossum, ring-tailed cat, badger, fox, weasel, raccoon, skunk and civet cat. Summer, fall and winter seasons on squirrel. Fall, winter and spring seasons on turkey. In 1983 sandhill crane, duck, coot, geese, woodcock and jacksnipe seasons occurred during the winter months. Teal duck, rail and gallinule seasons occurred in the fall. Mourning dove seasons occurred intermittently during the fall and winter months. **MUSEUMS** Memphis: Hall County Heritage Hall. **SPECIAL EVENTS** Big Tom's Country Roundup, Memphis, Monthly; Bob Wills Day, Turkey, April; Cotton Boll Enduro, Memphis, October.

COMMUNITIES
COUNTY SEAT Memphis, County Courthouse, 79245; County Clerk's Office, 806/259-2627. **INCORPORATED COMMUNITIES** (1980 population and ZIP Code) Estelline (258) 79233, Lakeview (244) 79239, Memphis (3,352) 79245 and Turkey (644) 79261. **UNINCORPORATED COMMUNITIES** (and ZIP Code) Brice 79226, Eli 79245, Lesley 79239, Newlin 79245, Parnell 79233, Plaska 79245, South Brice 79226 and Wolf Flat 79261. **FOR ADDITIONAL LOCAL INFORMATION** Memphis Chamber of Commerce, P.O. Box 789, Memphis, 79245, 806/259-3144.

HAMILTON (C1)

THE LAND
West of Waco on U.S. Highway 281 in the Grand Prairie Region, Hamilton County covers 836 square miles with an elevation range of 950 to 1,600 feet. The undulating to hilly soils are loamy with limestone bedrock under most of the area. In the northeastern corner the light colored sandy soils have cracking, clayey subsoils. In the Cross Timbers and Prairies vegetation area, the primary grasses are bluestems, Indiangrass, wildrye, sideoats and hairy grama. Dense brush of post and blackjack oak occurs in some

HAMILTON (continued)

areas. Between 41 and 50% of the land in the county is considered prime farmland. **CLIMATE** Generally mild and moist, but can be quite dry during the summer months. The average annual temperature is 65°F. Temperatures in January range from an average low of 32° to an average high of 58°F and in July range from 72° to 97°F. The average annual precipitation is 28 inches, with an average relative humidity of 77% at 6 A.M. and 50% at 6 P.M. The average annual snowfall is two inches. The growing season averages 239 days per year, with the last freeze in late March and the first freeze in late November. The sun shines during the year on the average 65% of the daylight hours.

THE PEOPLE
Hamilton County ranks 7th among all U.S. counties in the highest percent of population age 65 and over. The 1982 estimated population of 8,100 indicates a continuation of the moderate growth rate begun in the 1970s which reversed the population losses of the previous 40 years. Urban and rural areas grew at an equal rate from 1970 to 1980. The age groups with the largest gains were ages 20 to 34 and birth to five years, lowering the median age from 50 in 1970 to 46 in 1980. The largest ancestry groups are persons of English descent (32%), Irish descent (26%) and German descent (24%). **REGISTERED VOTERS** As of November 2, 1982 there were 5,060 registered voters (0.1% of the state total). The 1982 general election had a 50% voter turnout, compared to a 66% turnout in the 1980 general election. In the 1982 primary 98% voted Democratic and 2% Republican, with 2,003 votes cast.

THE ECONOMY
AGRICULTURE Cattle area. In 1982, 89% of the land was in farms and ranches, with 19% of the farmland under cultivation and 2% irrigated. Hamilton ranked 103rd in the state in highest agricultural receipts, with 88% from livestock and livestock products. Overgrazing, undesirable brush and weeds, water erosion, inefficient tillage systems and the cultivation of marginal lands are the current conservation problems. Primary crops: third in the state for oats and ninth for barley. Hay, wheat and sorghum. Primary fruits and nuts: peaches and pecans. Primary livestock and products: cattle, milk, sheep, wool, angora goats, mohair and hogs. **BUSINESS** Total number of business establishments in the county: 198. Retail sales during the first quarter of 1984 increased 7%. In 1980, 22% of the labor force were self-employed, 21% were employed in professional or related services, 13% in manufacturing, 18% in wholesale and retail trade, 17% in agriculture, forestry, fisheries and mining, 16% were employed in other counties and there were 1,638 retired workers. The industries with the most employment: agribusiness, construction, lumber mills and the manufacture of women's blouses and men's work clothing. The nonfarm earnings in 1981 totaled $61,321,000. The retired workers received an average monthly Social Security payment of $269. **FINANCE** On June 30, 1983, three commercial banks had total deposits of $77,298,000 and total assets of $85,849,000. There are two state savings and loan association branches in the county. **HOUSING** Average value of homes in 1980: $20,900. Permits for new, privately owned housing units increased in 1982: six permits were issued with a total construction cost of $380,612. Of those permits, all were for single family houses. Between 1970 and 1980 the number of housing units increased by 27%. Sixty-three percent of all units in the county are air-conditioned, 80% are heated by gas and 10% by electricity. **NATURAL RESOURCES** Dolomite, limestone, industrial sand, oil and gas. In 1982 a total of 214,109 thousand cubic feet of gas well gas, 76 barrels of condensate, 5,123 barrels of crude oil and 14,071 thousand cubic feet of casinghead gas

were produced. **TOURISM** Travel expenditures of $2,610,000 in 1982 (an increase of 13% over 1981) generated 55 jobs and $473,000 in payroll. **ALCOHOLIC BEVERAGES** Packaged distilled spirits, beer, ale, malt liquor and wine are legal in parts of the county. **FEDERAL EXPENDITURES** The federal government had direct expenditures or obligations of $21,574,000 in the county during fiscal year 1983, including $594,000 by the U.S. Department of Defense. In addition, the federal government provided $110,000 in grant awards, paid $719,000 in salaries and wages, made direct payments to individuals of $20,088,000 including $13,883,000 in retirement and disability payments, awarded $2,000 in procurement contracts and spent $655,000 in other expenditures or obligations. The federal government also provided $121,000 in direct loans and $3,381,000 in guaranteed loans and insurance.

COMMUNICATION
Newspapers–Weekly: Herald News (Hamilton) and The Hico News-Review. Radio: KCLW-AM (Hamilton). Cable TV. Telephone companies: United Telephone, Alenco Communications, Central Telephone-Midstate, Central Texas Telephone Coop. and Texas-Midland Telephone. **TRANSPORTATION** Total public road mileage: 916. In 1982 there were 8,396 registered vehicles and 130 reported traffic accidents including one fatality. Intercity bus service is available. Motor freight: one carrier. Aircraft: 31 are registered in the county. Airports: Hamilton Municipal Airport serves as a base for 11 aircraft and is a basic utility airport with general aviation service. Putty Ranch Airport at Hico.

COMMUNITY SERVICES
EDUCATION Three school districts with three elementary, one middle and three high schools. The average daily attendance in 1981-82 was 1,170, with expenditures per pupil of $2,316 including 99 classroom teachers with an average annual salary of $15,046. Twenty-nine percent of the 97 high school graduates planned to attend college. In 1982-83, 95% of the students were White, 4% Hispanic and 0.6% Asian. **PUBLIC LIBRARIES** Hamilton Library. **CHILD CARE** 27 day care and three twenty-four hour care licensed facilities. **HEALTH CARE** Eight physicians and six dentists. Hospitals: two with a combined capacity of 75. Ambulance service: two hospital-based services. Mental health: one clinic. Nursing homes: five nursing homes with a combined capacity of 357 nursing care residents. The average cost per day for private patients in 1982 was $29.68. **CHURCHES** 38 churches have an estimated combined membership of 5,989. The largest denominations are Southern Baptist, United Methodist and Churches of Christ. **SOCIAL SERVICES** In fiscal year 1983 a total of $188,851 in food stamps was distributed, with an average of 452 persons receiving food stamps each month. Aid to Families with Dependent Children (AFDC) totaled $33,174 with an average of 27 families receiving AFDC each month. Medical assistance benefits for the aged and disabled of $2,279,093 and for families and children of $92,038 brought the county benefit total to $2,593,156. **FIRE PROTECTION** Six volunteer fire departments. **LAW ENFORCEMENT** The County Sheriff has 12 commissioned officers. One police department has a force of four. **CRIME** 12 violent crimes (murder, forcible rape, robbery and aggravated assault) and 132 nonviolent crimes (burglary, larceny-theft and motor vehicle theft) were reported in 1982. **JUDICIAL SYSTEM** One District Court and Judge, one County Court and Judge and two Justices of the Peace. In the District Court a total of 118 cases were pending on 1/1/82, 174 new cases were filed and 135 cases were disposed of during the year leaving 157 cases pending on 12/31/82. There were 101 criminal cases on the docket, 17 convictions, two persons committed to prison and 64 cases left pending. In the County Court 201 cases were

pending on 1/1/82, 214 new cases were filed and 167 cases were disposed of during the year leaving 248 cases pending on 12/31/82. There were 368 criminal cases on the docket, 81 convictions, six persons committed to jail, and 204 cases left pending. **JAILS** One jail, capacity 10. **ATTORNEYS AT LAW** 10. **UTILITIES** 58% of the residents are connected to a public or privately owned water system and 51% are connected to a public sewer system. Natural gas is distributed to the county by Lone Star Gas Co., Division of Enserch. The average annual residential bill for natural gas in 1982 for the Lone Star distribution system was $405.91, an increase of 35% over 1981. Electricity is distributed to the county by Texas-New Mexico Power Co., Erath Co. Electric Coop., Assn. and McLennan Co. Electric Coop., Inc. and is generated primarily by gas, oil and water. The typical residential electric bill is $168.05 per month for an all-electric house using 2,500 kwh. **TAXES** The county has eight units with taxing authority: four school districts, three cities and one county.

RECREATION/ENTERTAINMENT
NATIONAL REGISTER OF HISTORIC PLACES Hamilton: Hamilton County Courthouse. **MUNICIPAL PARKS** 84 acres in six municipal parks. These parks contain two playgrounds, two baseball and softball fields and one swimming pool. Developed campsites: Eight. **BOATING/FISHING** Lakes/reservoirs: Upper Bosque Soil Conservation Service Lake 28 (12 acres), Edison (152 acres) and Hamilton City (31 acres). Major rivers: Leon, North Bosque River and Lampasas. Primary streams: Little Gilmore, Cowhouse and Two Mile. **HUNTING** Fall and winter seasons on deer. No closed seasons on coyote, bobcat and squirrel. Winter seasons on quail, muskrat, beaver, opossum, ringtailed cat, badger, fox, weasel, raccoon, skunk and civet cat. Fall, winter and spring seasons on turkey. In 1983 duck, coot, geese, woodcock and jacksnipe seasons occurred during the winter months. Teal duck, rail and gallinule seasons occurred in the fall. Mourning dove seasons occurred intermittently during the fall and winter months. **MUSEUMS** Hamilton County Museum. **SPECIAL EVENTS** Junior Stock Show, Hamilton, January; Old Settlers Reunion, Hico, July; Dove Festival and Parade, Hamilton, August; Christmas Tours and Activities, Hamilton, December.

COMMUNITIES
COUNTY SEAT Hamilton, County Courthouse, 76531; County Clerk's Office, 817/386-3518. **INCORPORATED COMMUNITIES** (1980 population and ZIP Code) Evant (425: 69 in Hamilton Co. and 356 in Coryell Co.) 76525, Hamilton (3,189) 76531 and Hico (1,375) 76457. **UNINCORPORATED COMMUNITIES** (and ZIP Code) Aleman 76531, Carlton 76436, Fairy (Martin Gap) 76457, Indian Gap 76531, Jonesboro (also in Coryell Co.) 76538, Lanham 76538, Olin 76457, Pottsville 76565, Shive 76531 and Whiteway (Whitesboro) 76536. **FOR ADDITIONAL LOCAL INFORMATION** Hamilton Chamber of Commerce, P.O. Box 429, Hamilton, 76531, 817/386-3216 and Civic Club Chamber of Commerce, P.O. Box 93, Hico, 76457.

HANSFORD (P3)

THE LAND
In the High Plains Region of the northernmost portion of the Texas Panhandle and bordering Oklahoma on State Highways 136 and 15, Hansford County covers 921 square miles with the elevation ranging from 2,900 to 3,300 feet. The nearly level soils are dark and loamy with clayey subsoils. In the High Plains vegetation area, the primary grasses are blue grama and buffalograss. There are some shinnery oaks, sage brush, mesquite

and yucca. Between 51 and 60% of the land in the county is considered prime farmland. **CLIMATE** Cool and dry. High winds, duststorms, and thunderstorms are possible during the spring. The average annual temperature is 57°F. Temperatures in January range from an average low of 19° to an average high of 49°F and in July range from 65° to 94°F. The average annual precipitation is 17 inches, with an average relative humidity of 72% at 6 A.M. and 42% at 6 P.M. The average annual snowfall is 15 inches. The growing season averages 186 days per year, with the last freeze in late April and the first freeze in late October. The sun shines during the year on the average 75% of the daylight hours.

THE PEOPLE
The population of Hansford County has been declining over the past decade, however, the 1982 estimated population of 6,400 indicates a slight growth since 1980. The majority of county residents live in urban areas. The age group with the largest loss was ages five to 19, raising the median age from 28 in 1970 to 30 in 1980. The largest ancestry groups are persons of English descent (28%), Irish descent (21%) and German descent (19%). **REGISTERED VOTERS** As of November 2, 1982 there were 3,162 registered voters (0.04% of the state total). The 1982 general election had a 54% voter turnout, compared to a 77% turnout in the 1980 general election. In the 1982 primary 89% voted Democratic and 11% Republican, with 885 votes cast.

THE ECONOMY
AGRICULTURE Wheat and fed cattle area. In 1982, 98% of the land was in farms and ranches, with 61% of the farmland under cultivation and 64% irrigated. Hansford ranked 13th in the state in highest agricultural receipts, with 64% from livestock and livestock products. Overgrazing, undesirable brush and weeds, water and wind erosion and decreasing irrigation water supplies are the current conservation problems. Primary crops: third in the state for wheat and sixth for both sorghum and barley. Corn and hay. Primary livestock and products: fourth in the state for fed cattle marketings and fifth for cattle. Hogs. **BUSINESS** Total number of business establishments in the county: 184. Retail sales during the first quarter of 1984 increased 1%. In 1980, 21% of the labor force were self-employed, 15% were employed in professional or related services, 3% in manufacturing, 20% in wholesale and retail trade, 33% in agriculture, forestry, fisheries and mining, 11% were employed in other counties and there were 397 retired workers. The industries with the most employment: agribusiness and oil and gas extraction. The nonfarm earnings in 1981 totaled $56,725,000. The retired workers received an average monthly Social Security payment of $348. **FINANCE** On June 30, 1983, two commercial banks had total deposits of $64,061,000 and total assets of $75,518,000. There is one state savings and loan association branch in the county. **HOUSING** Average value of homes in 1980: $32,600. Permits for new, privately owned housing units increased in 1982: 11 permits were issued with a total construction cost of $557,500. Of those permits, all were for single family houses. Between 1970 and 1980 the number of housing units increased by 17%. Eighty-five percent of all units in the county are air-conditioned, 93% are heated by gas and 6% by electricity. **NATURAL RESOURCES** Caliche, oil and gas. In 1982 a total of 26,091,168 thousand cubic feet of gas well gas, 37,068 barrels of condensate, 482,326 barrels of crude oil and 2,891,866 thousand cubic feet of casinghead gas were produced. Current production of other minerals and products includes caliche and helium. **TOURISM** Travel expenditures of $1,256,000 in 1982 (an increase of 11% over 1981) generated 27 jobs and $227,000 in payroll. **ALCOHOLIC BEVERAGES** Totally dry. **FEDERAL EXPENDITURES** The federal government had direct expenditures or obligations of

COUNTIES

HANSFORD (continued)

$16,568,000 in the county during fiscal year 1983, including $71,000 by the U.S. Department of Defense. In addition, the federal government provided $116,000 in grant awards, paid $400,000 in salaries and wages, made direct payments to individuals of $6,417,000 including $4,860,000 in retirement and disability payments, awarded $2,000 in procurement contracts and spent $9,633,000 in other expenditures or obligations. The federal government also provided $30,990,000 in direct loans and $4,782,000 in guaranteed loans and insurance.

COMMUNICATION

Newspapers–Weekly: Gruver Statesman, Hansford Plainsman (Spearman) and the Spearman Reporter. Radio: KRDF-FM Stereo (Spearman). Cable TV. Telephone companies: Continental Telephone, General Telephone, Southwestern Bell and Panhandle Telephone Coop. **TRANSPORTATION** Total public road mileage: 762. In 1982 there were 8,445 registered vehicles and 110 reported traffic accidents. Intercity bus service is available. Motor freight: one carrier. Rail: two branch lines carry freight through the county with one carrying annually one to five million tons and one carrying less than one million. Aircraft: 59 are registered in the county. Airports: Spearman Municipal Airport serves as a base for 32 aircraft and is a basic utility airport with general aviation service. Gruver Municipal Airport serves as a base for 23 aircraft and is a basic utility airport with general aviation service. Cluck Airport at Gruver.

COMMUNITY SERVICES

EDUCATION Three school districts with three elementary, two middle and two high schools. The average daily attendance in 1981-82 was 1,319, with expenditures per pupil of $3,582 including 106 classroom teachers with an average annual salary of $19,303. Twenty-seven percent of the 94 high school graduates planned to attend college. In 1982-83, 79% of the students were White, 21% Hispanic, 0.1% Asian and 0.1% American Indian. **PUBLIC LIBRARIES** Gruver City Library: 8,560 volumes. Hansford County Library (Spearman): 15,971 volumes. **CHILD CARE** Three day care and two twenty-four hour care licensed facilities. **HEALTH CARE** Five physicians and one dentist. Hospitals: one with a capacity of 28. Ambulance services: one volunteer service and one volunteer fire department service. Nursing homes: one nursing home has a capacity of 39 nursing care residents. The average cost per day for private patients in 1982 was $39.03. **CHURCHES** 15 churches have an estimated combined membership of 4,837. The largest denominations are Southern Baptist and United Methodist. **SOCIAL SERVICES** In fiscal year 1983 a total of $50,351 in food stamps was distributed, with an average of 125 persons receiving food stamps each month. Aid to Families with Dependent Children (AFDC) totaled $9,061 with an average of five families receiving AFDC each month. Medical assistance benefits for the aged and disabled of $121,526 and for families and children of $13,005 brought the county benefit total to $193,943. **FIRE PROTECTION** Three volunteer fire departments. **LAW ENFORCEMENT** The County Sheriff has six commissioned officers. Two police departments have a combined force of 11. **CRIME** 13 violent crimes (murder, forcible rape, robbery and aggravated assault) and 105 nonviolent crimes (burglary, larceny-theft and motor vehicle theft) were reported in 1982. **JUDICIAL SYSTEM** One District Court and Judge, one County Court and Judge and one Justice of the Peace. In the District Court a total of 233 cases were pending on 1/1/82, 192 new cases were filed and 120 cases were disposed of during the year leaving 305 cases pending on 12/31/82. There were 74 criminal cases on the docket, 11 convictions, one person committed to prison and two committed to jail and 52 cases left pending. In the County Court 197 cases were pending on 1/1/82, 177 new cases were filed and 153 cases were disposed of during the year leaving 221 cases pending on 12/31/82. There were 264 criminal cases on the docket, 102 convictions, 15 persons committed to jail, and 112 cases left pending. **JAILS** One jail, capacity nine. **ATTORNEYS AT LAW** Seven. **UTILITIES** 80% of the residents are connected to a public or privately owned water system and 76% are connected to a public sewer system. Electricity is distributed to the county by West Texas Utilities Co., Texas-New Mexico Power Co., Southwestern Public Service, Rita Blanca Electric Coop., Inc. and North Plains Electric Coop., Inc and is generated primarily by gas and oil. The typical residential electric bill is $168.05 per month for an all-electric house using 2,500 kwh. **TAXES** The county has nine units with taxing authority: three school districts, two cities, one county, one hospital district, two special districts.

RECREATION/ENTERTAINMENT

MUNICIPAL PARKS 16 acres in five municipal parks. These parks contain five playgrounds, two multi-use courts and one swimming pool. **BOATING/FISHING** Primary streams: Coldwater, North Palo Duro and Palo Duro. **HUNTING** Fall season on antelope. Fall and winter seasons on deer. Summer, fall and winter seasons on squirrel. No closed seasons on coyote and bobcat. Winter seasons on pheasant, quail, muskrat, beaver, opossum, ring-tailed cat, badger, fox, weasel, raccoon, skunk and civet cat. Fall, winter and spring seasons on turkey. In 1983 sandhill crane, duck, coot, geese, woodcock and jacksnipe seasons occurred during the winter months. Teal duck, rail and gallinule seasons occurred in the fall. Mourning dove seasons occurred intermittently during the fall and winter months. **MUSEUMS** Spearman: Stationmaster's House Museum. **SPECIAL EVENTS** Hansford Roundup, Spearman, May; Fun Day, Spearman, July.

COMMUNITIES

COUNTY SEAT Spearman, County Courthouse, 79081; County Clerk's Office, 806/659-2666. **INCORPORATED COMMUNITIES** (1980 population and ZIP Code) Gruver (1,216) 79040 and Spearman (3,413) 79801. **UNINCORPORATED COMMUNITIES** (and ZIP Code) Hitchland 79342, McKibben 79081, Morse 79062 and Phillips Camp 79040. **FOR ADDITIONAL LOCAL INFORMATION** Spearman Chamber of Commerce and Board of City Development, 211 Main, P.O. Box 161, Spearman, 79081, 806/659-5555.

HARDEMAN (P27)

THE LAND

West of Wichita Falls on U.S. Highway 287 in the Rolling Plains Region, Hardeman County covers 688 square miles with an elevation range of 1,300 to 1,700 feet. The red to brown soils have loamy surface layers and clayey or loamy subsoils. The vegetation is the mid to tall grasses of the Rolling Plains with some mesquite and shinnery oak. Between 31 and 40% of the land in the county is considered prime farmland. **CLIMATE** Cool and dry, but hot in summer. Thunderstorms, duststorms and high winds may be experienced in the spring. The average annual temperature is 62°F. Temperatures in January range from an average low of 24° to an average high of 52°F and in July range from 72° to 98°F. The average annual precipitation is 23 inches, with an average relative humidity of 76% at 6 A.M. and 45% at 6 P.M. The average annual snowfall is seven inches. The growing season averages 220 days per year, with the last freeze in late March and the first freeze in early November. The sun shines during the year on the average 72% of the daylight hours.

THE PEOPLE

The 1982 estimated population of 6,500 indicates a slight increase in population since 1980, following years of decline. The greatest decrease in population between 1970 and 1980 was in rural areas. The age groups with the largest reductions were ages 45 to 59 and five to 19. The population is older than average with a median age which fell from 42 in 1970 to 39 in 1980. The county's population is primarily urban with a high concentration of residents over age 64. The largest ancestry groups are persons of English descent (30%), Irish descent (25%) and German descent (13%). **REGISTERED VOTERS** As of November 2, 1982 there were 3,222 registered voters (0.1% of the state total). The 1982 general election had a 50% voter turnout, compared to a 69% turnout in the 1980 general election. In the 1982 primary 98% voted Democratic and 2% Republican, with 1,367 votes cast.

THE ECONOMY

AGRICULTURE Wheat area. In 1982, 96% of the land was in farms and ranches, with 40% of the farmland under cultivation and 8% irrigated. Hardeman ranked 160th in the state in highest agricultural receipts, with 78% from crops. Overgrazing, undesirable brush and weeds, water and wind erosion are the current conservation problems. Primary crops: wheat, cotton, hay and oats. Primary vegetables: watermelons. Primary fruits and nuts: peaches and pecans. Primary livestock and products: cattle. **BUSINESS** Total number of business establishments in the county: 132. Retail sales during the first quarter of 1984 increased 4%. In 1980, 22% of the labor force were self-employed, 18% were employed in professional or related services, 20% in manufacturing, 18% in wholesale and retail trade, 18% in agriculture, forestry, fisheries and mining, 8% were employed in other counties and there were 923 retired workers. The industries with the most employment: construction, agribusiness and the manufacture of gypsum products. The nonfarm earnings in 1981 totaled $52,684,000. The retired workers received an average monthly Social Security payment of $312. **FINANCE** On June 30, 1983, three commercial banks had total deposits of $57,923,000 and total assets of $63,193,000. There is one state savings and loan association branch in the county. **HOUSING** Average value of homes in 1980: $16,900. In 1982 two permits were issued for new, single family houses. Between 1970 and 1980 the number of housing units decreased by 9%. Seventy-nine percent of all units in the county are air-conditioned, 92% are heated by gas and 7% by electricity. **NATURAL RESOURCES** Copper, gypsum, salt, oil, gas, sand, gravel and bituminous coal. In 1982 a total of 3,060 thousand cubic feet of gas well gas, 1,717,984 barrels of crude oil and 768,389 thousand cubic feet of casinghead gas were produced. Current production of other minerals and products includes gypsum, sand and gravel. **TOURISM** Travel expenditures of $4,767,000 in 1982 (an increase of 13% over 1981) generated 106 jobs and $890,000 in payroll. **ALCOHOLIC BEVERAGES** Totally dry. **FEDERAL EXPENDITURES** The federal government had direct expenditures or obligations of $17,865,000 in the county during fiscal year 1983, including $277,000 by the U.S. Department of Defense. In addition, the federal government provided $442,000 in grant awards, paid $584,000 in salaries and wages, made direct payments to individuals of $13,423,000 including $9,043,000 in retirement and disability payments, awarded $1,000 in procurement contracts and spent $3,415,000 in other expenditures or obligations. The federal government also provided $7,631,000 in direct loans and $3,389,000 in guaranteed loans and insurance.

COMMUNICATION

Newspapers–Weekly: Valley News (Chillicothe) and the Tribune-Chief (Quanah). Radio: KIXC-AM (Quanah). Cable TV. Telephone companies: Southwestern Bell. **TRANSPORTATION** Total public road mileage: 789. In 1982 there were 6,140 registered vehicles and 140 reported traffic accidents. Intercity bus service is available. Motor freight: two carriers. Rail: four main and two branch lines carry freight through the county. The four main lines carry annually over 30 million tons of freight each and the two branches carry less than one million. Aircraft: 25 are registered in the county. Airports: Quanah Municipal Airport serves as a base for 34 aircraft and is a basic utility airport with general services.

COMMUNITY SERVICES

EDUCATION Two school districts with two elementary, one middle and two high schools. The average daily attendance in 1981-82 was 1,150, with expenditures per pupil of $2,581 including 88 classroom teachers with an average annual salary of $15,013. Seventy-seven percent of the 65 high school graduates planned to attend college. In 1982-83, 73% of the students were White, 16% Hispanic, 11% Black, 0.3% Asian and 0.2% American Indian. **PUBLIC LIBRARIES** Hardeman County Public Library (Quanah): 17,704 volumes. **CHILD CARE** 14 day care licensed facilities. **HEALTH CARE** Six physicians and two dentists. Hospitals: two with a combined capacity of 84. Ambulance services: one commercial and one county service. Mental health: one clinic. Nursing homes: two nursing homes with a combined capacity of 108 nursing care residents. The average cost per day for private patients in 1982 was $29.17. **CHURCHES** 22 churches have an estimated combined membership of 4,997. The largest denominations are Southern Baptist, United Methodist and Churches of Christ. **SOCIAL SERVICES** In fiscal year 1983 a total of $207,625 in food stamps was distributed, with an average of 497 persons receiving food stamps each month. Aid to Families with Dependent Children (AFDC) totaled $37,322 with an average of 26 families receiving AFDC each month. Medical assistance benefits for the aged and disabled of $691,793 and for families and children of $68,740 brought the county benefit total to $1,005,450. **FIRE PROTECTION** Two volunteer fire departments. **LAW ENFORCEMENT** The County Sheriff has four commissioned officers. Two police departments have a combined force of six. **CRIME** Six violent crimes (murder, forcible rape, robbery and aggravated assault) and 126 nonviolent crimes (burglary, larceny-theft and motor vehicle theft) were reported in 1982. **JUDICIAL SYSTEM** One District Court and Judge, one County Court and Judge and two Justices of the Peace. In the District Court a total of 121 cases were pending on 1/1/82, 140 new cases were filed and 123 cases were disposed of during the year leaving 138 cases pending on 12/31/82. There were 55 criminal cases on the docket, 14 convictions, four persons committed to prison and one committed to jail and 30 cases left pending. In the County Court 280 cases were pending on 1/1/82, 182 new cases were filed and 107 cases were disposed of during the year leaving 355 cases pending on 12/31/82. There were 399 criminal cases on the docket, 89 convictions, three persons committed to jail, and 293 cases left pending. **JAILS** One jail, capacity eight. **ATTORNEYS AT LAW** Five. **UTILITIES** 90% of the residents are connected to a public or privately owned water system and 73% are connected to a public sewer system. Natural gas is distributed to the county by Lone Star Gas Co., Division of Enserch. The average annual residential bill for natural gas in 1982 for the Lone Star distribution system was $405.91, an increase of 35% over 1981. Electricity is distributed to the county by Gate City Electric Coop., Inc., and West Texas Utilities and is generated primarily by gas and oil. The typical residential electric bill is $145.78 per month for an all-electric house using 2,500 kwh. **TAXES** The county has seven units with taxing authority: two school districts, two cities, one county and two hospital districts.

COUNTIES

HARDEMAN (continued)

RECREATION/ENTERTAINMENT
NATIONAL REGISTER OF HISTORIC PLACES Quanah: Quanah, Acme and Pacific Depot. **STATE** Copper Breaks State Park covers 1,889 acres with camping and trailer sites as well as fishing, swimming, boat ramps, nature trails and a horseback area. Exhibits can also be found in the park. **MUNICIPAL PARKS** 13 acres in two municipal parks. These parks contain three baseball and softball fields, three tennis courts and two swimming pools. **BOATING/FISHING** Lakes/reservoirs: Copper Breaks (28 acres) and Pauline (516 acres). Major rivers: Pease and Prairie Dog Town Fork Red. Primary streams: Devils and Wanderers. **HUNTING** Fall and winter seasons on deer. Summer, fall and winter seasons on squirrel. No closed seasons on coyote and bobcat. Winter seasons on pheasant, quail, muskrat, beaver, opossum, ring-tailed cat, badger, fox, weasel, raccoon, skunk and civet cat. Fall, winter and spring seasons on turkey. In 1983 sandhill crane, duck, coot, geese, woodcock and jacksnipe seasons occurred during the winter months. Teal duck, rail and gallinule seasons occurred in the fall. Mourning dove seasons occurred intermittently during the fall and winter months. **MUSEUMS** Quanah: Hardeman County Historical Commission. **SPECIAL EVENTS** Old-Timers Rodeo, Quanah, June; Rodeo and Parade, Quanah, August.

COMMUNITIES
COUNTY SEAT Quanah, County Courthouse, 79252; County Clerk's Office, 817/663-2901. **INCORPORATED COMMUNITIES** (1980 population and ZIP Code) Chillicothe (1,052) 79225 and Quanah (3,890) 79252. **UNINCORPORATED COMMUNITIES** (and ZIP Code) Goodlett 79252, Lazare (also in Cottle Co.) 79238, Medicine Mound 79252, North Groesbeck 79252 and Pauline 79252. **FOR ADDITIONAL LOCAL INFORMATION** Quanah Chamber of Commerce, P.O. Box 158, Quanah, 79252, 817/663-2222.

HARDIN (G6)

THE LAND
Northwest of Beaumont on U.S. Highway 69/287 in the East Texas Timberlands Region, Hardin County covers 898 square miles with an elevation range of 50 to 150 feet. The undulating to rolling soils are loamy with very deep cracking clayey subsoils. In the Pineywoods vegetation area there are pine and hardwood forests, shrubs and grasses such as Indiangrass and native legumes. Between 21 and 30% of the land in the county is considered prime farmland. **CLIMATE** Subtropical Humid. Tropical storms and hurricanes are possible June through October. The average annual temperature is 68°F. Temperatures in January range from an average low of 39° to an average high of 61°F and in July range from 72° to 93°F. The average annual precipitation is 48 inches, with an average relative humidity of 88% at 6 A.M. and 65% at 6 P.M. Snowfall is rare. The growing season averages 246 days per year, with the last freeze in mid March and the first freeze in mid November. The sun shines during the year on the average 68% of the daylight hours.

THE PEOPLE
The population of Hardin County has consistently increased over the past 50 years and the 1982 estimated population of 42,100 indicates a continuation of that growth. The county's urban growth rate of 108% from 1970 to 1980 was one of the highest in the state, however the majority of residents live in rural areas. The age groups with the largest gains were ages 65 and over and 20 to 34, raising the median age from 28 in 1970 to 30 in 1980.

The largest ancestry groups are persons of English descent (26%), Irish descent (23%), German descent (13%) and French descent (11%). **REGISTERED VOTERS** As of November 2, 1982 there were 24,798 registered voters (0.4% of the state total). The 1982 general election had a 39% voter turnout, compared to a 59% turnout in the 1980 general election. In the 1982 primary 98% voted Democratic and 2% Republican, with 8,210 votes cast.

THE ECONOMY
AGRICULTURE Major forest producton area. In 1982, 21% of the land was in farms and ranches, with 6% of the farmland under cultivation and 29% irrigated. Hardin ranked 244th in the state in highest agricultural receipts, with 82% from crops. Overgrazing, undesirable brush, inefficient irrigation systems, improper woodland management and flooding are the current conservation problems. Primary crops: soybeans, rice and hay. Primary vegetables: sweet potatoes, tomatoes and watermelons. Primary fruits and nuts: peaches and pecans. Primary livestock and products: cattle. **BUSINESS** Total number of business establishments in the county: 540. Retail sales during the first quarter of 1984 increased 8%. In 1980, 6% of the labor force were self-employed, 14% were employed in professional or related services, 25% in manufacturing, 21% in wholesale and retail trade, 10% in transportation, communications, and other public utilities, 54% were employed in other counties and there were 2,625 retired workers. The industries with the most employment: oil and gas extraction, general construction, petroleum refining and the manufacture of oil field machinery, softwood veneer, plywood, wood pallets and skids. The nonfarm earnings in 1981 totaled $365,395,000. The retired workers received an average monthly Social Security payment of $341. **FINANCE** On June 30, 1983, five commercial banks had total deposits of $116,641,000 and total assets of $130,538,000. On December 31, 1982 two state savings and loan associations, three state branches and two federal association branches had combined assets of $82,904,294. In addition there is one credit union in the county. **HOUSING** Average value of homes in 1980: $32,900. 15 permits for new, privately owned housing units with a total construction cost of $561,388 were issued in 1982. Of those permits, all were for single family houses. Between 1970 and 1980 the number of housing units increased by 50%. Eighty percent of all units in the county are air-conditioned, 60% are heated by gas and 35% by electricity. **NATURAL RESOURCES** Salt domes, sand, gravel, oil and gas. In 1982 a total of 14,412,508 thousand cubic feet of gas well gas, 673,065 barrels of condensate, 3,313,838 barrels of crude oil and 2,746,837 thousand cubic feet of casinghead gas were produced. Current production of other minerals and products includes industrial sand. Pine and hardwood production in 1981 totaled 23,158,957 cubic feet: 18,745,686 cubic feet of pine and 4,413,271 cubic feet of hardwood. **TOURISM** Travel expenditures of $4,085,000 in 1982 (an increase of 15% over 1981) generated 59 jobs and $600,000 in payroll. **ALCOHOLIC BEVERAGES** Packaged distilled spirits, beer, ale, malt liquor and wine are legal in parts of the county. **FEDERAL EXPENDITURES** The federal government had direct expenditures or obligations of $47,605,000 in the county during fiscal year 1983, including $1,824,000 by the U.S. Department of Defense. In addition, the federal government provided $395,000 in grant awards, paid $1,822,000 in salaries and wages, made direct payments to individuals of $45,066,000 including $35,986,000 in retirement and disability payments, awarded $69,000 in procurement contracts and spent $252,000 in other expenditures or obligations. The federal government also provided $98,000 in direct loans and $42,261,000 in guaranteed loans and insurance.

COMMUNICATION
Newspapers–Weekly: Kountze News-Visitor and The Silsbee Bee.

Radio: KKAS-AM and KWDX-FM (Silsbee). Cable TV. Telephone companies: Continental Telephone, Southwestern Bell, Eastex Telephone Coop. and Santa Rosa Telephone Coop. **TRANSPORTATION** Total public road mileage: 804. In 1982 there were 38,862 registered vehicles and 739 reported traffic accidents including 16 fatalities. Taxi cabs: two companies in Silsbee. Intercity bus service is available. Motor freight: seven local and intrastate carriers. Rail: seven main lines carry freight through the county with two carrying annually 10 to 20 million tons each, three carry five to 10 million tons each and two carry one to five each. Aircraft: 26 are registered in the county. Airports: Hawthorne Field between Kountze and Silsbee serves as a base for 13 aircraft and is a general utility airport with general aviation service.

COMMUNITY SERVICES

EDUCATION Five school districts with 10 elementary, five middle and five high schools. The average daily attendance in 1981-82 was 9,237, with expenditures per pupil of $2,484 including 583 classroom teachers with an average annual salary of $17,473. Thirty-eight percent of the 668 high school graduates planned to attend college. In 1982-83, 84% of the students were White, 1% Hispanic, 14% Black and 0.1% Asian. Sports championships: 1983 AAA Girls' Volleyball Kountze H.S.; 1983 AAA Boys' Golf Singles and Team, Sour Lake Hardin-Jefferson H.S. **PUBLIC LIBRARIES** Kountze Public Library: 21,026 volumes. Silsbee Public Library: 41,313 volumes. Alma M. Carpenter Public Library (Sour Lake): 11,460 volumes. **CHILD CARE** 48 day care and nine twenty-four hour care licensed facilities. **HEALTH CARE** 14 physicians and seven dentists. Hospitals: two with a combined capacity of 106. Clinics: one public health clinic. Ambulance services: three commercial and two volunteer fire department services. Mental health: one county clinic. Nursing homes: three nursing homes with a combined capacity of 248 nursing care residents. The average cost per day for private patients in 1982 was $28.58. **CHURCHES** 62 churches have an estimated combined membership of 20,990. The largest denominations are Southern Baptist, United Methodist and Catholic. **SOCIAL SERVICES** In fiscal year 1983 a total of $1,839,450 in food stamps was distributed, with an average of 3,537 persons receiving food stamps each month. Aid to Families with Dependent Children (AFDC) totaled $441,357 with an average of 283 families receiving AFDC each month. Medical assistance benefits for the aged and disabled of $3,101,710 and for families and children of $734,193 brought the county benefit total to $6,116,709. **FIRE PROTECTION** Eight volunteer fire departments. **LAW ENFORCEMENT** The County Sheriff has 37 commissioned officers. Five police departments have a combined force of 30. **CRIME** 94 violent crimes (murder, forcible rape, robbery and aggravated assault) and 850 nonviolent crimes (burglary, larceny-theft and motor vehicle theft) were reported in 1982. **JUDICIAL SYSTEM** One District Court and Judge, one County Court and Judge and six Justices of the Peace. In the District Court a total of 2,257 cases were pending on 1/1/82, 1,489 new cases were filed and 1,256 cases were disposed of during the year leaving 2,490 cases pending on 12/31/82. There were 787 criminal cases on the docket, 39 convictions, 27 persons committed to prison, two committed to jail and 636 cases left pending. In the County Court 1,640 cases were pending on 1/1/82, 955 new cases were filed and 1,078 cases were disposed of during the year leaving 1,517 cases pending on 12/31/82. There were 2,380 criminal cases on the docket, 48 convictions, 15 persons committed to jail and 1,314 cases left pending. **JAILS** One jail, capacity 31. **ATTORNEYS AT LAW** 28. **UTILITIES** 67% of the residents are connected to a public or privately owned water system and 46% are connected to a public sewer system. Natural gas is distributed to the county by Entex, Inc. The average annual residential bill for natural gas in 1982 for the Entex distribution system was $390.31, an increase of 26% over 1981. Electricity is distributed to the county by Gulf State Utilities Co. and Sam Houston Electric Coop., Inc. and is generated primarily by gas and oil. The typical residential electric bill is $198.32 per month for an all-electric house using 2,500 kwh. **TAXES** The county has 13 units with taxing authority: five school districts, four cities, one county, one utility district and two special districts.

RECREATION/ENTERTAINMENT

FEDERAL BIG THICKET NATIONAL PRESERVE encompasses 84,550 acres and was established to protect the area's unique ecological system which is a mingling of diverse plant life resulting in a large variety of species. Study and research opportunities are excellent. Facilities are limited. **NATIONAL REGISTER OF HISTORIC PLACES** Batson: Ada Belle Oil Well. **STATE** Village Creek State Park covers 942 acres and is closed to the public as of July 1983. **MUNICIPAL PARKS** 32 acres in three municipal parks. These parks contain one mile of hiking trails, two playgrounds, two baseball and softball fields and four tennis courts. **BOATING/FISHING** Lakes/reservoirs: Kimble (37 acres). Major rivers: Neches. Primary streams: Kimball, Little Pine Island Bayou and Pine Island Bayou. **HUNTING** Fall and winter seasons on deer. Summer, fall and winter seasons on squirrel. No closed seasons on coyote, bobcat and nutria. Winter seasons on quail, muskrat, beaver, otter, opossum, mink, ring-tailed cat, badger, fox, raccoon, skunk and civet cat. In 1983 duck, coot, geese, woodcock and jacksnipe seasons occurred during the winter months. Teal duck, rail and gallinule seasons occurred in the fall. Mourning dove seasons occurred intermittently during the fall and winter months. **MUSEUMS** Saratoga: Big Thicket Museum. **SPECIAL EVENTS** Brer' Rabbit Run, Silsbee, April; Big Thicket Parade, Saratoga, April; Saratoga Day, Saratoga, April; Big Thicket Day, Saratoga, June; Fourth of July Celebration, Silsbee, July; Chili Cookoff, Silsbee, November.

COMMUNITIES

COUNTY SEAT Kountze, County Courthouse, 77625; County Clerk's Office, 409/246-3371. **INCORPORATED COMMUNITIES** (1980 population and ZIP Code) Grayburg (194) 77618, Kountze (2,716) 77625, Lumberton (2,480) 77656, Rose Hill Acres (460) 77656, Silsbee (7,684) 77656 and Sour Lake (1,807) 77659. **UNINCORPORATED COMMUNITIES** (and ZIP Code) Ariola 77625, Batson 77519, Fresenius 77656, Glad Tidings 77625, Hardin 77625, Honey Island 77625, Kirby Town 77656, Lillard 77656, Loeb 77656, Nona 77625, Pine Ridge 77625, Pinewood Estates 77706, Saratoga 77585, Thicket 77374, Village Mills (Long Station) 77663, Votaw 77376, Wildwood (also in Tyler Co.) 77663. **FOR ADDITIONAL LOCAL INFORMATION** Kountze Chamber of Commerce, P.O. Box 878, Kountze, 77625, 409/246-2761, Lumberton Chamber of Commerce, 2310 Hwy. 96 S., P.O. Box 8574, Lumberton, 77711 409/755-0554 and Silsbee Chamber of Commerce, 835 Hwy. 96 S., Silsbee, 77656, 409/385-5562.

HARRIS (G11)

THE LAND

Along the southeast portion of the Gulf Coast area on Interstate Highways 45 and 10 in the Coastal Prairie Region, Harris County covers 1,734 square miles with an elevation ranging from sea level to 200 feet. Most of the county has level, somewhat poorly to moderately well drained, cracking, clayey soils, or poorly drained soils with loamy surfaces and cracking, clayey subsoils. In the central portion and along Spring Creek in the northeastern

COUNTIES

HARRIS (continued)

portion of the county there are light colored loamy surfaces over very deep reddish clayey or loamy subsoils with hardened calcium deposits in the subsoils. The northern quarter of the county lies in the Pineywoods vegetation area with loblolly, shortleaf, longleaf and slash pines as well as oaks, hickory, maple and other hardwoods and bluestem, Indiangrass and other grasses. The rest of the county located in the Gulf Prairies and Marshes vegetation area has cord grasses and other bunch grasses, sedges and marsh millet with some mesquite, oak and prickly pear trees. Between 31 and 40% of the land in the county is considered prime farmland. **CLIMATE** Subtropical Humid. Occasional thunderstorms in spring and summer, chance of tropical storms June through October. The average annual temperature is 69°F. Temperatures in January range from an average low of 40° to an average high of 62°F and in July range from 73° to 94°F. The average annual precipitation is 48 inches, with an average relative humidity of 87% at 6 A.M. and 65% at 6 P.M. Snowfall for the year is rare. The growing season averages 270 days per year, with the last freeze in early March and the first freeze in early December. The sun shines during the year on the average 70% of the daylight hours.

THE PEOPLE

Harris County ranks third among all U.S. counties in the largest population and is one of the most densely populated in the state. The 1982 estimated population of 2,684,100 indicates a continuation of the very strong growth. Almost 40% of the growth from 1970 to 1980 was in urban areas where the population is concentrated. The age groups with the largest gains were ages 20 to 34 and 65 and over. The county's median age is younger than average. The largest ancestry groups are persons of English descent (20%), Black (20%), Irish descent (15%) and those of German descent (15%). **REGISTERED VOTERS** As of November 2, 1982 there were 1,022,500 registered voters (16% of the state total). The 1982 general election had a 46% voter turnout, compared to a 69% turnout in the 1980 general election. In the 1982 primary 59% voted Democratic and 41% Republican, with 143,654 votes cast.

THE ECONOMY

AGRICULTURE Forest production area along with rice and soybeans. In 1982, 42% of the land was in farms and ranches, with 22% of the farmland under cultivation and 28% irrigated. Harris ranked 44th in the state in highest agricultural receipts, with 63% from crops. Flooding, land subsidence and solid waste management are the current conservation problems. Primary crops: 10th in the state for rice. Soybeans, hay, corn and sorghum. Primary vegetables: cantaloupes, sweet corn, cucumbers, potatoes, sweet potatoes and tomatoes. Primary fruits and nuts: peaches and pecans. Primary livestock and products: cattle, milk and hogs. **BUSINESS** Total number of business establishments in the county: 59,359. Retail sales during the first quarter of 1984 increased 9%. In 1980, 5% of the labor force were self-employed, 17% were employed in professional or related services, 18% in manufacturing, 21% in wholesale and retail trade, 10% in construction, 3% were employed in other counties and there were 99,492 retired workers. The industries with the most employment: tourism, agribusiness, oil and gas extraction, ship building and repair, general and heavy construction, rice mills, metal coating, soft drink bottling and canning, paper mills, commercial printing, petroleum refining, steel mills and foundries, iron and steel forgings and the manufacture of metal containers, oil field machinery, valves and pipe fittings, radio and television equipment, paint, plastics and synthetics, malt beverages, roasted coffee, bakery products, industrial and agricultural chemicals, structural metal products, metal working machinery, pumps and pumping equipment, electronic components, aircraft equipment, measuring and controlling instruments, railroad equipment, switchgear and switchboard apparatus, engines, fabricated rubber products, ready-mixed concrete and gaskets packing and sealing devices. The nonfarm earnings in 1981 totaled $35,437,885,000. The retired workers received an average monthly Social Security payment of $354.00. **FINANCE** On June 30, 1983, 216 commercial banks had total deposits of $30,480,598,000 and total assets of $41,423,631,000. On December 31, 1982, 26 state savings and loan associations, 309 state branches and 21 federal branches had combined assets of $13,187,948,268. In addition there are 231 credit unions in the county. **HOUSING** Average value of homes in 1980: $55,400. Permits for new, Permits for new, privately owned housing units increased in 1982: 67,974 permits were issued with a total construction cost of $2,010,624,905. Of those permits, 25,431 were for single family houses. Housing permits increased in Deer Park from 76 in 1981 to 199 in 1982 with all permits issued for single family houses, in El Lago from 16 to 46 with 36 of the permits issued for apartments and condominiums, in La Porte from 294 to 553 with 395 of the permits issued for single family houses, in Pasadena from 390 to 1,053 with 714 of the permits issued for apartments and condominiums, in Seabrook from three to 226 with 216 of the permits issued for apartments and condominiums in Tomball from 67 to 133 and in Webster from 181 to 352 with 347 of the permits issued for apartments and condominiums. Between 1970 and 1980 the number of housing units increased by 66%. Ninety-two percent of all units in the county are air-conditioned, 64% are heated by gas and 35% by electricity. **NATURAL RESOURCES** Clay, salt domes, sand & gravel, oil & gas. In 1982 a total of 29,310,003 thousand cubic feet of gas well gas, 247,264 barrels of condensate, 8,812,152 barrels of crude oil and 29,982,132 thousand cubic feet of casinghead gas were produced. Current production of other minerals and products includes brick, brine, cement chlorine, clay, hydrogen sulfide, lime, salt, construction sand, sand and gravel, recovered sulphur and sulphur dioxide. Pine and hardwood production in 1981 totaled 3,268,691 cubic feet: 3,088,285 cubic feet of pine and 180,406 cubic feet of hardwood. **TOURISM** Travel expenditures of $3,301,511,000 in 1982 (an increase of 8% over 1981) generated 66,089 jobs and $714,380,000 in payroll. Lodging: 227 hotels, motels and tourist courts. Convention/meeting facilities: Deerpark-Abshier Stadium; Houston-Astrodome-Astrohall Stadium, Civic Center Complex, Delmar Stadium Complex, Houston Baptist University Gym, Rice University Stadium and Gym, the Summit Arena, University of Houston Hofheinz Pavillion, Robertson Stadium and 35 hotels with facilities for large gatherings. **ALCOHOLIC BEVERAGES** Packaged distilled spirits, beer, ale, malt liquor and wine are legal in parts of the county. Sale of mixed beverages is legal in all or parts of the county. **MILITARY INSTALLATIONS** Ellington Air National Guard Base, Houston, 1,280 personnel, 2,281 acres, Air National Guard Activities; La Porte Air National Guard Station, La Porte, 115 personnel, 12 acres, Air National Guard Activities. **FEDERAL EXPENDITURES** The federal government had direct expenditures or obligations of $3,732,953,000 in the county during fiscal year 1983, including $661,392,000 by the U.S. Department of Defense. In addition, the federal government provided $312,784,000 in grant awards, paid $661,862,000 in salaries and wages, made direct payments to individuals of $1,645,377,000 including $1,324,211,000 in retirement and disability payments, awarded $1,101,067,000 in procurement contracts and spent $11,863,000 in other expenditures or obligations. The federal government also provided $60,507,000 in direct loans and $7,009,314,000 in guaranteed loans and insurance.

FLYING THE COLORS: TEXAS ©JOHN CLEMENTS 1984

COMMUNICATION

Newspapers–Daily: The Baytown Sun ave. eve. circ. 17,412, the Citizen (Clear Lake City), ave. morn. circ. 6,101, Houston Chronicle, ave. daily circ. 419,869, the Houston Post, ave. morn. circ. 376,455 and the Pasadena Citizen, ave. morn. circ. 10,769. Weekly: The Sentinel (Channelview), Community News (Crosby), Deer Park Progress, Community News (Channelview), The Highland Star, Southwest Suburbia Reporter, Forward Times, Houston Informer, The Texas Tribune (Houston), The Sun (Houston), Humble Echo, The Bay Shore Sun (La Porte), North Freeway Leader (Houston), The Leader (Houston), North Harris County News (Spring) and the Westside Suburbia Reporter (Houston). Radio: KBUK-AM (Baytown), KCOH-AM, KENR-AM, KEYH-AM, KIKK-AM, KILT-AM, KKBQ-AM, KLAT-AM, KLVL-AM, KNUZ-AM, KPRC-AM, KTRH-AM, KXYZ-AM, KYOK-AM, KFMK-FM, KGOL-FM, KHCB-FM, KILT-FM, KKBQ-FM, KODA-FM, KQUE-FM, KRLY-FM, KSRR-FM, KTSU-FM, KUHF-FM, KIKK-FM, KLEF-FM, KLOL-FM, KMJQ-FM, KPFT-FM, KRBE-FM, (Houston) KJIC-FM (Pasadena), KTRU-FM Stereo (Houston). Television: KHOU CH. 11, KHTV CH. 39, KPRC CH. 2, KRN CH. 26, KTRK CH. 13, (PBS) KUHT CH. 5 (Houston). Cable TV. Telephone companies: Continental Telephone, General Telephone, Southwestern Bell, Central Telephone and Fort Bend Telephone. **TRANSPORTATION** Total public road mileage: 11,785. In 1982 there were 2,075,088 registered vehicles and 100,464 reported traffic accidents including 683 fatalities. Taxi cabs: 26 taxi and 43 limousine companies in Houston. Municipal transit systems: one metropolitan bus system in Houston, with scheduled routes. Intercity bus service is available. Motor freight: 687 local and intrastate carriers. Rail: The Sunset Limited provides passenger service on the Amtrak route. Fourteen main and two branch lines carry freight through the county. One of the mainlines carries annually over 30 million tons of freight each, two carry 20 to 30 each, eight carry 10 to 20 each, two carry five to 10 each and one carries one to five million tons. One of the branch lines carries annually over 30 million tons of freight and one carries one to five million. Aircraft: 3211 are registered in the county. Airports: Intercontinental Airport at Houston serves as a base for 130 aircraft and is a large hub with long haul flights providing carrier service. William P. Hobby Field at Houston serves as a base for 660 aircraft and is a large hub with short haul flights providing carrier service. David Wayne Hooks Memorial Airport at Houston serves as a base for 250 aircraft. Lakeside Airport in Houston serves as a base for 200 aircraft. Baytown Municipal Airport, a reliever airport to Houston Intercontinental Airport, serves as a base for 200 aircraft. LaPorte Municipal Airport, a reliever airport to Houston Intercontinental Airport, serves as a base for 200 aircraft. Also serving the area Andrau Airpark, Beaman Airpark, Clover Field, Houston Gulf, Hull Field, May Airport, Southwest Airpark, Ward Airpark, Weiser Airpark, Westheimer Airpark and Williams Field at Houston, R.J.W. Airpark at Baytown, Genoa Airport at Genoa and Harbican Airpark at Katy. Heliports serving the area are Executive Airlines at Allen Center, Executive Airlines Greenway Plaza, Powers Airport/Heliport and Regency Square Helistop at Houston, Strock Farms Heliport at Spring, Hickory Hollow Heliport at Tomball, Citizens General Hospital Heliport, John S. Dunn Herman Hospital Heliport and Medical Center Heliport at Houston. Hooks Memorial at Houston is a Sea Plane Base. Domestic and foreign exports by air from Houston average about 4 million pounds per month. Imports average about 1.5 million pounds per month. Waterborne commerce: Houston Ship Channel traffic in 1981 totaled 100,966,741 short tons: 27,698,682 in foreign imports, 22,819,011 in foreign exports and 50,449,048 in domestic products. Cedar Bayau Harbor shipped 231,485 short tons of domestic freight.

COMMUNITY SERVICES

EDUCATION 20 school districts with 363 elementary, 101 middle, 69 high schools and seven special education. The average daily attendance in 1981-82 was 432,227, with expenditures per pupil of $3,043 including 25,361 classroom teachers with an average annual salary of $19,328. Fifty-five percent of the 26,155 high school graduates planned to attend college. In 1982-83, 52% of the students were White, 20% Hispanic, 25% Black, 4% Asian and 0.1% American Indian. Sports championships: 1983 AAAAA Girls' Track, Houston Smiley H.S., 1983 AAAAA Girls' Golf Team, Houston Cypress Creek. Private schools: 36,306 students enrolled in 120 elementary and 36 high schools. Sports championships: 1984 AAA Boy's Basketball, Marian Christian H.S.; 1982 AAA Boys' Track, Marian Christian H.S.; 1983 AAA Boys' Baseball, Saint Pius X H.S.; 1983 AAA Girls' Softball, Saint Pius X H.S.; 1983 AAA Girls' Swimming, Duchesne Academy; 1983 AAAA Boys' Track, Strake Jesuit College Preparatory; 1983 AAA Boys' Football, Saint Pius X H.S.; 1983 AAAA Boys' Cross Country, Strake Jesuit; 1983 AAAA Boys' Football, Saint Thomas H.S.; 1983 AAAA Girls; Cross Country, Saint Agnes Academy. University of Texas Health Science Center at Houston was established in 1972 and is under state control. Enrollment in 1982 was 2,734 with in state undergraduate tuition and fees of $340 per quarter. The highest degree offered is: Doctorate. Gulf Coast Bible College is located in Houston. Established in 1953 it is affiliated with the Church of God. Enrollment in 1982 was 337 with in state undergraduate tuition and fees of $2,287 per semester. The highest degree offered is: Bachelor. Baylor College of Medicine is located in Houston. Established in 1903 it is an independent nonprofit institution. Enrollment in 1982 was 863 with in state undergraduate tuition and fees of $3,340 per quarter. The highest degree offered is: Doctorate. Houston Baptist University is located in Houston. Established in 1960 it is affiliated with the Southern Baptist Church. Enrollment in 1982 was 4,159 with in state undergraduate tuition and fees of $3,135 per quarter. The highest degree offered is: Master. Houston Community College is located in Houston. Established in 1971 it is a vocational and two year academic college under state control. Enrollment in 1982 was 18,280 with in state undergraduate tuition and fees of $372 per semester. Lee College is located in Baytown. Established in 1934 it is a vocational and two year academic college under state and local control. Enrollment in 1982 was 4,896 with in state undergraduate tuition and fees of $180 per semester. North Harris County College is located in Houston. Established in 1972 it is a vocational and two year academic college under state and local control. Enrollment in 1982 was 6,523 with in state undergraduate tuition and fees of $276 per semester. Rice University is located in Houston. Established in 1891 it is an independent nonprofit institution. Enrollment in 1982 was 3,476 with in state undergraduate tuition and fees of $3,200 per semester. The highest degree offered is: Doctorate. South Texas College of Law is located in Houston. Established in 1923 it is an independant nonprofit institution. Enrollment in 1982 was 1,248. San Jacinto College is located in Pasadena. Established in 1960 it is a vocational and two year academic college under state and local control. Enrollment in 1982 was 12,307 with in state undergraduate tuition and fees of $175 per semester. Southern Bible College is located in Houston. Established in 1958 it is a Protestant affiliated institution. Enrollment in 1982 was 125 with in state undergraduate tuition and fees of $1,800 per semester. The highest degree offered is: Bachelor. Texas Chiropractic College is located in Houston. Established in 1908 it is an independant nonprofit institution. Enrollment in 1982 was 432. Texas Southern University is located in Houston. Established in 1947 it is under state control. Enrollment in 1982 was 8,100 with in state undergraduate tuition and fees of $532 per semester. The highest degree offered

HARRIS (continued)

is: Doctorate. University of Houston Central Campus is located in Houston. Established in 1927 it is under state control. Enrollment in 1982 was 30,693 with in state undergraduate tuition and fees of $400 per semester. The highest degree is: Doctorate. University of Houston Downtown College is located in Houston. Established in 1974 it is under state control. Enrollment in 1982 was 5,055 with in state undergraduate tuition and fees of $380 per semester. The highest degree offered is: Bachelor. University of Saint Thomas is located in Houston. Established in 1947 it is affiliated with the Catholic Church. Enrollment in 1982 was 1,940 with in state undergraduate tuition and fees of $2,500 per semester. The highest degree offered is: Master. Sport championships: (Southwest Conference) 1984 Mens' Basketball, 1984 Womens' Indoor Track, 1983 Womens' Outdoor Track. University of Houston at Clear Lake City is located in Clear Lake City. Established in 1971 it is under state control. Enrollment in 1982 was 5,592 with in state undergraduate tuition and fees of $400 per semester. The highest degree offered is: Master (No lower division). Vocational education: Baytown-Baytown Industrial Welding School, Lonnie School of Hair Design, San Jacinto Methodist Hospital School of X-Ray Technicians. Houston-Action Training, Agnew Beauty Academy, Airco Technical Institute, Art Institute of Houston, Baldwin Beauty School, Bryman School, Commonwealth College of Funeral Services, Elkins Institute, Espanolas Beauty College, Franklin Beauty School, Hargest Vocational and Technical College, Hermann Hospital School of Practical Nursing, Houston Technical College, Industrial Drafting and Design School, Massey Business College, Memorial Hospital School of X-Ray Technology, Metils Inc., Modern Barber College, Norris of Houston-Edgebrook Barber College, Ocean Corporation, Professional Beauty College of North East, R. S. Institute, R/S Barber College, Southwestern Paralegal Institute, Spring Branch Beauty College, Texas Academy of Art, Vogue Beauty College, Academy School of Nurse Assistant, American Teller Schools, Auston's Professional Modeling of Houston, Barbizon School of Houston, Bradford School of Business, The Bryman School, Clerical Arts Academy, Control Data Institute, Control Data Learning Center, Doolin Technical College, Dorothy Smith Education Foundation, Inc., Energy Education Institute of Houston, Inc., Goodwill Industries of Houston, Halco School of Modeling, Bess High School of Floral Design, Raymond J. Horn School of Drafting, Houston Galveston Psychoanalytic Institute Inc., Houston Montessori Center, International Bartending Institute of Houston, International Travel Institute, Kellow Technical College, Inc., Loyle Leonard's Training Schools, Inc. Lollie Lowe's Career College, The Mayo-Hill School of Modeling, Microcomputer Technology Institute, Professional Bartenders School, Inc., Shelton School of Floral Design, South Houston Area Training School, Southwest School of Polygraph, Texas Dental Technology School, Texas Montessori Institute, Texas Travel School, Texas Word Processing Institute, Inc., Train America, Inc., Zorn Business College, Nursing Review Course, Pages Parkes School of Modeling, Printing Industries of the Gulf Coast-Technical Training Center. Stamford-Stamford Memorial Hospital School for Vocational Nursing. Pasadena-Special"T" of Houston Training Center. **PUBLIC LIBRARIES** Sterling Municipal Library (Baytown): 108,667 volumes. Bellaire City Library: 45,291 volumes. Deer Park Public Library: 45,328 volumes. Harris County Public Library (Houston): 451,763 volumes, 17 branches. Houston Public Library: 2,704,300 volumes, 31 branches. Pasadena Public Library: 164,354 volumes. **CHILD CARE** 3,330 day care and 557 twenty-four hour care licensed facilities. **HEALTH CARE** 5,810 physicians and 1,472 dentists. Hospitals: 54 with a combined capacity of 14,129. Specialized hospitals:

three rehabilitation and research centers with a combined capacity of 153, two children's hospitals with a combined capacity of 368, two women's hospitals with a combined capacity of 220, one veterans medical center with capacity of 1,103, and one out patient surgical center under construction. Clinics: 20 minor emergency centers, 16 for treatment of alcohol and/or drug abuse, eight outpatient clinics, six dialysis clinics, two radiology clinics, two public health clinics, one children's clinic, one obstetrical clinic, one dental clinic and one family services clinic. Ambulance services: 46 commercial, 16 volunteer services, four fire departments, four county, three city, three funeral homes, three hospital-based, one air and one police department service. Mental health: 24 clinics, seven centers with a combined capacity of 828, one county center with a combined capacity of 65, and one state residential institute with capacity of 60. Nursing homes: 65 nursing homes with a combined capacity of 8,081 nursing care and 245 custodial care residents. The average cost per day for private patients in 1982 was $32.87. **CHURCHES** 1,105 churches have an estimated combined membership of 1,027,768. The largest denominations are Catholic, Southern Baptist and United Methodist. **SOCIAL SERVICES** In fiscal year 1983 a total of $107,290,608 in food stamps was distributed, with an average of 192,426 persons receiving food stamps each month. Aid to Families with Dependent Children (AFDC) totaled $27,805,945 with an average of 17,744 families receiving AFDC each month. Medical assistance benefits for the aged and disabled of $75,563,721 and for families and children of $43,067,381 brought the county benefit total to $253,727,654. **FIRE PROTECTION** Three paid, two partly paid and 62 volunteer fire departments. **LAW ENFORCEMENT** The County Sheriff has 1583 commissioned officers. 61 police departments have a combined force of 8,194. Six universities and four college campuses have police departments with a combined total of 172 officers. **CRIME** 22,045 violent crimes (murder, forcible rape, robbery and aggravated assault) and 196,243 nonviolent crimes (burglary, larceny-theft and motor vehicle theft) were reported in 1982. **JUDICIAL SYSTEM** 55 District Courts and Judges, 18 County Courts and Judges and 16 Justices of the Peace. In the District Courts a total of 97,403 cases were pending on 1/1/82, 91,709 new cases were filed and 79,607 cases were disposed of during the year leaving 109,505 cases pending on 12/31/82. There were 33,251 criminal cases on the docket, 14,476 convictions, 4,609 persons committed to prison and 2,868 committed to jail and 13,944 cases left pending. In the County Courts 26,344 cases were pending on 1/1/82, 63,784 new cases were filed and 63,631 cases were disposed of during the year leaving 26,497 cases pending on 12/31/82. There were 68,718 criminal cases on the docket, 33,274 convictions, 24,907 persons committed to jail, and 25,216 cases left pending. **JAILS** Seven jails, capacity 4006. Two jails, five lockups and two floors under construction. **ATTORNEYS AT LAW** 11,285. **UTILITIES** 96% of the residents are connected to a public or privately owned water system and 95% are connected to a public sewer system. Natural gas is distributed to the county by Entex, Inc. The average annual residential bill for natural gas in 1982 for the Entex distribution system was $390.31, an increase of 26% over 1981. Electricity is distributed to the county by Houston Lighting & Power Co., San Benard Electric Coop., Inc. and Texas New-Mexico Power Co. and is generated primarily by gas oil, coal and water. The typical residential electric bill is $201.39 per month for an all-electric house using 2,500 kwh. **TAXES** The county has 437 units with taxing authority: 20 school districts, 29 cities, one county, three college districts and 384 special districts.

RECREATION/ENTERTAINMENT

PROFESSIONAL SPORTS Houston: Houston Oilers Football Team (Astrodome), Houston Astros Baseball Team (Astrodome), Houston Rockets Basketball Team (The Summit), Houston

Gamblers' Football Team (Rice Stadium), Houston Dynamos Soccer Team (Butler Stadium). **NATIONAL REGISTER OF HISTORIC PLACES** Baytown vicinity: Cedar Bayou Archeological District. (See Chambers County). Houston: Bayou Bend, Broadacres Historic District, Christ Church Complex, State National Bank Building, Harris County Courthouse of 1910, John Milroy House, Kennedy Bakery, Paul Building, Paul Allen House, Broadacres Historic District, Merchants and Manufacturers Building, Scanlan Building, Church, Antioch Missionary Baptist Church, W. L. Foley Building, Hogg Building, 1879 Houston Waterworks, Julia Ideson Building, Kellum-Noble House, Mansfield Street Archeological Site, Old Cotton Exchange, Old Houston National Bank, The Old Sixth Ward District, Pillot Building, Rice Hotel, San Jacinto Battle Field (National Historic Landmark), C. H. Sewall House, South Texas National Bank, Sweeney, Combs and Fredericks Building, Union Station, U.S. Custom House, U.S.S. Texas (National Historic Landmark) and the following residences in Courtlandt Place: James L. Autry House, J. J. Carroll House, W. T. Carter, Jr. House, A.S. Cleveland House, T. J. Donoghue House, J. M. Dorrance, Jones-Hunt House, Sterling Myer House, C.L. Neuhaus House, John W. Parker House and Judson L. Taylor House. Houston Vicinity: Harris County Boys School Site. Pasadena vicinity: Armand Bayou Archeological District. **STATE** Lake Houston State Park Site covers 2,190 acres and is closed to the public as of July, 1983. San Jacinto Battleground State Historical Park covers 327 acres with fishing facilities, a museum and a historic structure. The park is located on the site where Texas won its independence from Mexico on 1836. The Battleship Texas is moored in a permanent slip at the Battleground. **COUNTY/MUNICIPAL PARKS** 22,027 acres in 83 county and 399 municipal parks. These parks contain 83 miles of hiking trails, 357 playgrounds, 11 golf courses, 113 football and soccer fields, 320 baseball and softball fields, 330 tennis courts, 29 multi-use courts, 67 swimming pools, two beaches, 17 boat ramps and shore fishing facilities. Developed campsites: 100 **SCENIC DRIVES** The Texas Independence Trail runs through this county. This trail not only surveys the historic sites of southeastern Texas but also includes many modern visitor attractions such as the Johnson Space Center. **BOATING/FISHING** Lakes/reservoirs: Cedar Bayou (114 acres), Cypress Farms 1 (63 acres), Cypress Farms 2 (95 acres), Dennison (178 acres), Hegar (300 acres), Highlands (8 acres), Houston (12,240 acres), Longenbaugh (181 acres), Lynchburgh (336 acres), Nelson (408 acres), Seaburg #2 (119 acres), Seaberg #3 (63 acres), Seaburg #4 (130 acres), Sheldon (1,700 acres), Smith (125 acres), Southhard (158 acres), Sludge Fill Pond (33 acres) and Warren (64 acres). Major rivers: Harris: San Jacinto and West Fork. Primary streams: Hunting Bayou, Vince Bayou, Berry Bayou, Sims Bayou, Brays Bayou, Spring Creek, Whiteoak Bayou, Cole, Halls Bayou, Keegans Bayou, Greens Bayou, Mayde and Langhams, Buffalo Bayou, Cedar Bayou, Langham, Mound, Goose, Cypress, Clear, Carpenters Bayou, Cypress, Little Cypress and Rock Hollow. State fishing piers: Saltwater fishing for speckled trout, redfish and flounders is usually good around Baytown, La Porte, San Leon, Seabrook and Kemah. Trinity and Galveston Bay waters that lap on Harris County offer speckled trout fishing. Shrimp, oysters and crabs may be taken but, like other saltwater fish, under specific regulations. **WILDLIFE REFUGES** Sheldon State Wildlife Management Area covers 2,503 acres. **HUNTING** Fall and winter seasons on deer. Summer, fall and winter seasons on squirrel. Winter seasons on quail, muskrat, beaver, otter, opossum, mink, ring-tailed cat, badger, fox, raccoon, skunk and civet cat. No closed season on nutria, coyote and bobcat. Various special regulations in force. In 1983 duck, coot, geese, woodcock and jacksnipe seasons occurred during the winter months. Teal duck, rail and gallinule seasons occured in the fall. Mourning dove seasons occurred intermittently during the fall and winter months. **MUSEUMS** Baytown: Baytown Historical Museum. Houston: Battleship Texas, Art League of Houston Gallery, Bayou Bend Collection of the Museum of Fine Arts, Classic Showcase, Contemporary Arts Museum, Harris County Heritage Society, Houston Museum of Natural Arts-Rice University, Railroad Train Museum, Texas Gulf Coast Historical Association, Sewell Art Gallery-Rice University, Sarah Campbell Blaffer Gallery, Lyndon B. Johnson Space Center, Old Ben Milam Hotel, Rice Museum, Environmental Science Center, Institute for the Arts at Rice University, Memorial Log Cabin, Museum of American Architecture and Decorative Arts, Museum of Fine Arts, Museum of Medical Science and Houston Museum of Natural Science. La Porte: San Jacinto Museum of History Association. Tomball: Magdalene Charlton Memorial Museum and Griffin Memorial House. Pasadena: Pasadena Historical Museum. **THEATERS** Houston: Jones Hall for Performing Arts, Black Arts Center Theatre, Channing Hall of First Unitarian Church, Houston Music Hall, Kaplan Theatre, Theatre Suburbia, Jewish Community Center of Houston Society for the Performing Arts, Alley Theatre, Channing Players, Theatre Under the Stars, Windmill Dinner Theatre and Miller Outdoor Theatre. **ORCHESTRAS** Baytown: Baytown Community Orchestra. Houston: Houston Youth Symphony, Houston Pops Orchestra, Houston Symphony Orchestra, Clear Lake Symphony, Symphony North of Houston and Texas Chamber of Orchestra. **OPERA** Houston: Houston Grand Opera Association, Texas Opera Theatre and Houston Opera Studio. **DANCE** Bellaire: Dance Arts Company. Houston: Discovery Dance Group, Houston Allegro Ballet, Houston Ballet, Houston Jazz-Ballet Company and Houston Youth Ballet. **BOTANIC GARDENS** Houston: Houston Arboretum and Botanical Garden and Armand Bayou Nature Center. **ZOO** Houston: Houston Zoological Gardens. **PLANETARIUM** Houston: Burke-Baker Planetarium. **COLLEGIATE FINE ARTS** Houston: Cultural events offered by Rice University, University of Saint Thomas, South Texas Junior College, Texas Southern University, Dominican College, San Jacinto College, North Houston Baptist University and University of Houston (Central Campus and Downtown Campus). Baytown: Lee College. Pasadena: San Jacinto College. **OTHER** Houston: Gilbert and Sullivan Society, Hope Development Black Arts Center, Houston Symphony Chorale, Houston Tidelanders Barbershop Chorus and Quartets and Tuesday Musical Club. **SPECIAL EVENTS** Bayou Bend Museum Open House, Houston, Monthly; Tenneco Marathon, Houston, January; Stock Show and Rodeo, Houston, February/March; Annual Azalea Trail, Houston, March; Ethnic Folk Festival, Bellaire, March; Festival, Houston, March; St. Patrick's Parade and Irish Stew Cookoff, Webster, March; The Bayou Bash, Houston, March; Astroworld, Houston, Spring-Fall, Strawberry Festival, Pasadena, April; Antique Festival, Bellaire, April; "Good Oil Days" Festival, Humble, April, Sylvan Beach Festival, La Porte, April; San Jacinto Day Parade, Pasadena, April; Holland Festival, Houston, May; Solo Autocross, Houston, May; Pet Parade, Houston, May; County Fair, Spring, May; Arts Festival, Bellaire, May; Gathering of the Clams, Irish Feis, Houston, May; Square and Round Dance Festival, Houston, June; Street Festival, Houston, June; Celebration at Sam Houston Park, Houston, July; Old Market Square Art and Folk Festival, Houston, Varies; 4th of July Celebration, Tomball, July; 4th of July Celebration, Bellaire, July; G. B. Shaw Festival, Houston, July; Old Tyme Days, Crosby, August; Will Roger's Day, Houston, August; Volks Wurstfest, Houston, August; Stock Show and Rodeo, Pasadena, September; 5-Mile Fun Run and Chili Cookoff, Deer Park, October; Autumn Festival, Alief, October; Fall Festival, Deer Park, October; Heritage Holiday, Spring, October; Rice Harvest Festival, Katy,

COUNTIES

HARRIS (continued)

October; Family Festival, Pasadena, October; Festival, Seabrook, October; Armand Bayou Nature Center Festival, Houston, October; County Fair Pasadena, October; Westheimer Art Festival, Houston, October; Relics & Antique Festival, Bellaire, November; Christmas Parade and Pageant, Tomball, November; Lone Star Sampler, Houston, November; Thanksgiving Day Parade, Houston, November; Bluebonnet Bowl Football, Houston, December.

COMMUNITIES

COUNTY SEAT Houston, County Courthouse, 77002; County Clerk's Office, 713/221-6411. **INCORPORATED COMMUNITIES** (1980 population and ZIP Code) Baytown (56,923: 56,917 in Harris Co. and 6 in Chambers Co.) 77520, Bellaire, (14,950) 77401, Bunker Hill Village (3,750) 77024, Deer Park (22,648) 77536, El Lago (3,129) 77586, Galena Park (9,879) 77547, Hedwig Village (2,506) 77024, Hilshire Village (621) 77055, Houston (1,595,138: 1,578,849 in Harris Co., 16,270 in Fort Bend Co. and 19 in Montgomery Co.) 77001, Humble (6,729) 77338, Hunters Creek Village (4,215) 77024, Jacinto City (8,953) 77029, Jersey Village (4,084) 77040, Katy (5,660: 4,475 in Harris Co., 668 in Waller Co. and 517 in Fort Bend Co.) 77450, La Porte (14,062) 77571, Lomax (2,991) 77571, Missouri City (24,533: 20,597 in Fort Bend Co. and 3,936 in Harris Co.) 77459, Morgan's Point (428) 77571, Nassau Bay (4,526) 77058, Pasadena (112,560) 77501, Pearland (13,248: 12,461 in Bazoria Co. and 787 in Harris Co.) 77581, Piney Point Village (2,958) 77024, Seabrook (4,670) 77586, Shore Acres (1,260) 77571, South Houston (13,293) 77587, Southside Place (1,366) 77005, Spring Valley (3,353) 77024, Stafford (4,755: 4,526 in Fort Bend Co. and 229 in Harris Co.) 77477, Taylor Lake Village (3,669) 77586, Tomball (3,996) 77375, Waller (1,241: 164, in Harris Co. and 1,077 in Waller Co.) 77484, Webster (2,405) 77598 and West University Place (12,010) 77005. **UNINCORPORATED COMMUNITIES** (and ZIP Code) Addicks 77079, Aldine (Estates, Gardens and Meadows) 77039, Alief 77411, Bammel 77040, Barker 77413, Barrett 77532, Bayside Terrace 77571, Beaumont Place 77049, Bellaire West 77072, Channelview 77530, Channelwood 77530, Clear Lake City 77058, Cloverleaf 77015, Coady 77520, Crosby 77532, Cypress 77429, Cypress Bend 77040, Cypress Creek Estates 77429, Dyersdale 77016, East River (Also in Montgomery Co.) 77327, Garth 77520, Gatewood 77039, Hidden Valley 77018, Highlands 77562, Hillside Gardens 77039, Hockley 77447, Hockley Mine 77447, Houmont Park 77044, Howellville 77411, Huffman 77336, Hufsmith 77337, Humble Heights 77338, Kenwood Place 77039, Kingwood 77339, Kinwood 77052, Klein 77373, Kohrville 77040, Lake Cypress 77429, La Porte 77571, Lynchburg 77520, Lyncrest 77016, Magnolia Gardens 77044, McNair 77520, Moonshine Hill 77338, Mount Houston 77016, Newport 77532, North Houston 77018, North Houston Heights 77016, Northline Terrace 77022, Old River Terrace 77530, Park Glen 77072, Rose Hill 77375, River Terrace 77327, Satsuma 77040, Shadow Glen 77530, Sheldon 77028, Spring 77379, Thompson 77040, Timberlake 77429, Westfield 77090, Westgate 77429.**FOR ADDITIONAL LOCAL INFORMATION** Alief-SW Houston Chamber of Commerce, P.O. Box 235, Alief, 77411, 713/498-6071, Bellaire/SW Houston Chamber of Commerce, P.O. Box 788, Bellaire 77401, 409/666-1521, Crosby Area Chamber of Commerce, P.O. Box 452, 210 Kernohan, Crosby, 77532 (409) 328-6984, Deer Park Chamber of Commerce, P.O. Box 153, 1605 Center, Deer Park, 77536, 409/479-1559, Humble Area Chamber of Commerce, 19506 Eastex Frwy., P.O. Box 3337, Humble, 77338, 409/446-2128, Galena Park Chamber of Commerce, P. O. Box 427, Galena Park, 77547, (409) 672-6443, Houston Chamber of Commerce, 1100 Milam Bldg. 25th Flr., Houston, 77002,

713/651-1313, Clear Lake Area Chamber of Commerce, 1201 Nasa Rd. One, Houston, 77058, 713/488-7676, Houston Northwest Chamber of Commerce, 3730 FM 1960 W., Suite 114, Houston, 77068, 713/440-4160, North Channel Area Chamber of Commerce, 911C Federal Rd., P.O. Box 9652, Houston 77213, 713/455-3860, Spring Branch Memorial Chamber of Commerce, 9235 Katy Frwy., Suite 102, Houston, 77024, 713/461-1408, La Porte-Bayshore Chamber of Commerce, P.O. Box 996, La Porte, 77571, (409) 471-1123, Pasadena Chamber of Commerce, 4334 Fairmont Pkwy., Pasadena, 77504, 409/487-7871, Greater South Houston Chamber of Commerce, P.O. Box 75, S. Houston, 77034, 713/943-0244, Tomball Area Chamber of Commerce, P.O. Box 516, Tomball, 77375 (409) 351-7222 and Waller Chamber of Commerce, P.O. Box 53, Waller, 77484, (409) 372-2410 or 372-3676.

HARRISON (E18)

THE LAND

East of Dallas bordering Louisiana on Interstate Highway 20 in the East Texas Timberlands Region, Harrison County covers 908 square miles with an elevation range of 200 to 400 feet. The county has mostly acidic, light colored soils which are undulating to rolling with loamy or sandy surfaces covering reddish mottled or reddish throughout subsoils. The county, located in the Pineywoods vegetation area, has loblolly, shortleaf, long leaf and slash pines as well as oak, hickory, maple and other hardwoods with bluestem, Indiangrasses and other grasses. Between 21 and 30 of the land in the county in considered prime farmland. **CLIMATE** Subtropical humid. A few severe storms may be experienced during spring months. The average annual temperature is 64°F. Temperatures in January range from an average low of 33° to an average high of 55°F and in July range from 71° to 94°F. The average annual precipitation is 46 inches, with an average relative humidity of 86% at 6 A.M. and 58% at 6 P.M. The average annual snowfall is one inch. The growing season averages 245 days per year, with the last freeze in mid March and the first freeze in mid November. The sun shines during the year on the average 65% of the daylight hours.

THE PEOPLE

Harrison County experienced a surge in population with a 16% increase between 1970 and 1980. The 1982 estimated population of 55,500 indicates a continuation of that growth. Urban and rural growth between 1970 and 1980 was approximately equal. The age groups with the greatest gains were ages 20 to 34 and 65 and over. The largest ancestry groups are Black (32%) persons of English descent (22%) and Irish descent (17%). **REGISTERED VOTERS** As of November 2, 1982 there were 24,818 registered voters (0.4% of the state total). The 1982 general election had a 48% voter turnout, compared to a 64% turnout in the 1980 general election. In the 1982 primary 98 voted Democratic and 2% Republican, with 9,340 votes cast.

THE ECONOMY

AGRICULTURE Forest production area. In 1982, 38% of the land was in farms and ranches, with 14% of the farmland under cultivation. Harrison ranked 183rd in the state in highest agricultural receipts, with 88% from livestock and livestock products. Overgrazing, water erosion, improper woodland management and undesirable woody vegetation in the forestlands are the current conservation problems. Primary crops: hay, rye, wheat and oats. Primary vegetables: sweet potatoes and watermelons. Primary fruits and nuts: peaches and pecans. Primary livestock and products: cattle, milk and hogs. **BUSINESS** Total number of business establishments in the county: 827. Retail sales during

HARRISON

the first quarter of 1984 increased 10%. In 1980, 8% of the labor force were self-employed, 18% were employed in professional or related services, 27% in manufacturing, 20% in wholesale and retail trade, 8% in construction, 28% were employed in other counties and there were 4,162 retired workers. The industries with the most employment: oil and gas extraction, logging, iron and steel foundries and the manufacture of industrial chemicals, insulated wire, structural metal products, small arms ammunition, railroad equipment, ceramic tile and pottery. The nonfarm earnings in 1981 totaled $451,539,000. The retired workers received an average monthly Social Security payment of $298.00. **FINANCE** On June 30, 1983, six commercial banks had total deposits of $266,814,000 and total assets of $291,133,000. On December 31, 1982 one state savings and loan association, one federal association, three state branches and one federal branch had combined assets of $69,776,543. In addition there are six credit unions in the county. **HOUSING** Average value of homes in 1980: $29,900. Permits for new, privately owned housing units increased in 1982: 292 permits were issued with a total construction cost of $9,138,285. Of those permits, 77 were for single family houses. Housing permits increased in Hallsville from 29 in 1981 to 57 in 1982 and in Marshall from 129 to 235. Between 1970 and 1980 the number of housing units increased by 29%. seventy-five percent of all units in the county are air-conditioned, 80% are heated by gas and 16% by electricity. **NATURAL RESOURCES** Ceramic clay, copper, industrial sand, oil, gas and lignite coal. In 1982 a total of 36,605,314 thousand cubic feet of gas well gas, 222,327 barrels of condensate, 872,282 barrels of crude oil and 1,592,521 thousand cubic feet of casinghead gas were produced. Current production of other minerals and products includes brick, fireclay, lignite coal and sand and gravel. Pine and hardwood production in 1981 totaled 12,015,087 cubic feet: 9,771,458 cubic feet of pine and 2,243,629 cubic feet of hardwood. **TOURISM** Travel expenditures of $34,893,000 in 1982 (an increase of 11% over 1981) generated 883 jobs and $7,162,000 in payroll. Lodging: 11 hotels, motels and tourist courts. Convention/meeting facilities: Marshall-East Texas Baptist College Gym, Marshall Civic Center. **ALCOHOLIC BEVERAGES** Packaged distilled spirits, beer, ale, malt liquor and wine are legal in parts of the county. **MILITARY INSTALLATIONS** Longhorn Army Ammunition Plant, Marshall, 843 personnel, 8,493 acres, Ammunition Production. **FEDERAL EXPENDITURES** The federal government had direct expenditures or obligations of $131,041,000 in the county during fiscal year 1983, including $55,257,000 by the U.S. Department of Defense. In addition, the federal government provided $2,025,000 in grant awards, paid $4,963,000 in salaries and wages, made direct payments to individuals of $73,929,000 including $53,919,000 in retirement and disability payments, awarded $49,798,000 in procurement contracts and spent $326,000 in other expenditures or obligations. The federal government also provided $104,000 in direct loans and $5,354,000 in guaranteed loans and insurance.

COMMUNICATION
Newspapers–Daily: Marshall News Messenger, ave. eve. circ. 10,393. Weekly: Hallsville Herald and the Waskom Weekly Review. Radio: KKYR-AM, KMHT-AM, KBWC-FM, KMHT-FM (Marshall). Cable TV. Telephone companies: General Telephone, Southwestern Bell, Century Telephone, Eastex Telephone Coop. and Etex Telephone. **TRANSPORTATION** Total public road mileage: 1,457. In 1982 there were 42,288 registered vehicles and 1,504 reported traffic accidents including 22 fatalities. Taxi cabs: five companies in Marshall. Municipal transit systems: one mini-bus service in Longview. Intercity bus service is available. Motor freight: eight local and intrastate carriers. Rail: The Eagle provides passenger service on the Amtrak route. Four main and one branch line carry freight through the

county. Two of the main lines carry annually over 30 million tons of freight each and two carry five to ten and the one branch carries on to five million tons. Aircraft: 34 are registered in the county. Airports: Harrison County Airport at Marshall serves as a base for 43 aircraft and is a general utility airport with general aviation service. Beers Caddo Lake Airport at Uncertain.

COMMUNITY SERVICES
EDUCATION Six school districts with 12 elementary, seven middle and seven high schools. The average daily attendance in 1981-82 was 10,639, with expenditures per pupil of $2,822 including 646 classroom teachers with an average annual salary of $16,289. Forty-eight percent of the 792 high school graduates planned to attend college. In 1982-83, 64% of the students were White, 0.7% Hispanic, 35% Black, 0.1% Asian. Sports championships: 1984 AAAAA Girl's Basketball, Longview H.S. Private schools: 370 students enrolled in two elementary schools. Wiley College is located in Marshall. Established in 1873 it is affiliated with the Methodist Church. Enrollment in 1982 was 664 with in state undergraduate tuition and fees of $2,100 per semester. The highest degree offered is Bachelor. East Texas Baptist College is located in Marshall. Established in 1912 it is affiliated with The Southern Baptist Church. Enrollment in 1982 was 916 with in state undergraduate tuition and fees of $1,770 per semester. The highest degree offered is Bachelor. Vocational education: Marshall College of Beauty (Marshall). **PUBLIC LIBRARIES** Marshall Public Library: 72,000 volumes. **CHILD CARE** 86 day care and 18 twenty-four hour care licensed facilities. **HEALTH CARE** 44 physicians and 15 dentists. Hospitals: one with a capacity of 145. Clinics: one public health clinic. Ambulance services: one commercial and one fire department service. Mental health: one clinic. Nursing homes: four nursing homes with a combined capacity of 543 nursing care residents. The average cost per day for private patients in 1982 was $29.47. **CHURCHES** 115 churches have an estimated combined membership of 30,921. The largest denominations are Southern Baptist, United Methodist and Christian Methodist Episcopal. **SOCIAL SERVICES** In fiscal year 1983 a total of $3,021,309 in food stamps was distributed, with an average of 6,291 persons receiving food stamps each month. Aid to Families with Dependent Children (AFDC) totaled $1,017,280 with an average of 670 families receiving AFDC each month. Medical assistance benefits for the aged and disabled of $4,782,255 and for families and children of $1,266,416 brought the county benefit total to $10,087,260. **FIRE PROTECTION** One paid and six volunteer fire departments. **LAW ENFORCEMENT** The County Sheriff has 35 commissioned officers. Four police departments have a combined force of 52. **CRIME** 140 violent crimes (murder, forcible rape, robbery and aggravated assault) and 2,066 nonviolent crimes (burglary, larceny-theft and motor vehicle theft) were reported in 1982. **JUDICIAL SYSTEM** One District Court and Judge, two County Courts and Judges and seven Justices of the Peace. In the District Court a total of 1598 cases were pending on 1/1/82, 1,631 new cases were filed and 1,273 cases were disposed of during the year leaving 1,956 cases pending on 12/31/82. There were 267 criminal cases on the docket, 115 convictions, 53 persons committed to prison and one committed to jail and 109 cases left pending. In the County Courts 2,292 cases were pending on 1/1/82, 1,376 new cases were filed and 857 cases were disposed of during the year leaving 2,811 cases pending on 12/31/82. There were 2,960 criminal cases on the docket, 386 convictions, 35 persons committed to jail, and 2,249 cases left pending. **JAILS** One jail, capacity 57. **ATTORNEYS AT LAW** 68. **UTILITIES** 75% of the residents are connected to a public or privately owned water system and 52% are connected to a public sewer system. Natural gas is distributed to the county by Entex, Inc. The average annual residential bill for natural gas

COUNTIES

HARRISON (continued)

in 1982 for the Entex distribution system was $390.31, an increase of 26% over 1981. Electricity is distributed to the county by Panola and Harrison Electric Coop., Inc. and Upshur-Rural Electric Coop., Corp. and is generated primarily by gas. The typical residential electric bill is $170.44 per month for an all-electric house using 2,500 kwh. **TAXES** The county has 10 units with taxing authority: six school districts, three cities and one county.

RECREATION/ENTERTAINMENT

NATIONAL REGISTER OF HISTORIC PLACES Jonesville: Locust Grove. Leigh: Mimosa Hall. Marshall: Arnot House, John R. Stinson House, James Turner House, First Methodist Church, Starr House, Fry-Barry House, Ginocchio Historic District, Hagerty House, Harrison County Courthouse, Magnolia Hall and Marshall Arsenal. Marshall vicinity: Dial-Williamson House and Edgemont. **STATE** Caddo Lake State Park covers 480 acres with camping and trailer sites as well as areas offering fishing, swimming, boat ramps, nature trails and a recreational hall. Starr Mansion State Historic Site covers one acre and is closed to the public as of July 1983. **MUNICIPAL PARKS** 56 acres in eight municipal parks. These parks contain seven playgrounds, three baseball and softball fields, six tennis courts and three multi-use courts. **SCENIC DRIVES** The Texas Forest Trail runs through this county. This trail explores the farming, ranching and oil field areas of the East Texas Pineywoods. **BOATING/FISHING** Lakes/reservoirs: Big Rock (30 acres), Caddo (25,400 acres), Deerwood Estates (22 acres), Ferguson Creek (245 acres), Fern (33 acres), Highway (18 acres), Holmes (78 acres), Mason Creek (330 acres), Mitchell (19 acres), Shadowood (127 acres) and Tanyard Branch (62 acres). Major rivers: Harrison: Sabine. Primary streams: Page, Little Cypress Bayou, Ferguson, Pienitt, Clarks, Eight Mile, Grays, Mason, Haggerty, Deboldin and Tanyard. **HUNTING** Fall and winter seasons on deer. Summer, fall and winter seasons on squirrel. Winter seasons on quail, muskrat, beaver, otter, opossum, mink, ring-tailed cat, badger, fox, raccoon, skunk and civet cat. No closed seasons on nutria, bobcat and coyote. In 1983 duck, coot, geese, woodcock and jacksnipe seasons occurred during the winter months. Teal duck, rail and gallinule seasons occurred in the fall. Mourning dove seasons occurred intermittently during the fall and winter months. **MUSEUMS** Marshall: Harrison County Historical Museum, Franks Museum and Allen House Museum. Waskon: T.C. Lindsey and Co. General Store and Museum. **ORCHESTRAS** Marshall: Marshall Symphony Orchestra. **COLLEGIATE FINE ARTS** Marshall: cultural events offered by East Texas Baptist College and Wiley College. **SPECIAL EVENTS** Farm/City Week, Marshall, April; Stagecoach Days, Marshall, May; Championship Junior Barrel Race, Marshall, May; Central East Texas Fair, Marshall, September; Fireant Festival, Marshall, October; Water Parade, Uncertain, December.

COMMUNITIES

COUNTY SEAT Marshall, County Courthouse, 75670; County Clerk's Office, 214/938-4385. **INCORPORATED COMMUNITIES** (1980 population and ZIP Code) Hallsville (1,556) 75650, Longview (62,762: 1,677 in Harrison Co. and 61,085 in Gregg Co.) 75601, Marshall (24,921) 75670, All-America Cities Award 1975-1976, Nesbitt (129) 75670, Scottsville (245) 75688, Uncertain (176) 75661 and Waskom (1,821) 75692. **UNINCORPORATED COMMUNITIES** (and ZIP Code) Baldwin 75661, Blocker 75670, Crossroads 75670, Darco (Cave Springs) 75670, Eight Mile 75670, Elysian Fields 75642, Estes 75601, Gill 75670, Grange Hall 75670, Gum Springs 75601, Harleton 75651, Jonesville 75659, Karnack 75661, Leigh 75661, Long Point 75661, Longview Heights 75601, Morton 75640, New Hebron 75685,

Walkers Mill 75650 Woodlawn 75694 and Woodley 75670.**FOR ADDITIONAL LOCAL INFORMATION** Hallsville Area Chamber of Commerce, P.O. Box 535, Hallsville, 75650, 214/668-2592, Greater Marshall Chamber of Commerce, 213 W. Austin, P.O. Box 520, Marshall, 75670, 214/935-7868, Waskom Chamber of Commerce, P.O. Box 666, Waskom, 75692, 214/687-3337.

HARTLEY (P6)

THE LAND

Northwest of Amarillo bordering New Mexico on U.S. Highways 385, 87 and 54 in the High Plains Region, Hartley County covers 1,462 square miles with an elevation range of 3,400 to 4,200 feet. The level to undulating, alkaline, red to brown soils along the southern border have loamy surfaces with clayey or loamy subsoils or shallow soils over calcium deposits. The soil in the rest of the county has loamy surfaces with clayey subsoils which creates a high shrink-swell potential in some areas. In many sections soils have hardened to powdery lime within 20 inches of the surface. Lying in the Rolling Plains vegetation area of Hartley County the southern one-third has prairie grasses with mesquite and live oak trees. The rest of the county is in the High Plains vegetation area. With short and mid grasses, small mesquite trees, thorny shrubs and cacti. Between 11 and 20% of the land in the county is considered prime farmland.. **CLIMATE** Cool and Dry. A few severe thunderstorms with hail and high winds may be experienced during spring. The average annual temperature is 55 °F. Temperatures in January range from an average low of 18 ° to an average high of 49 °F and in July range from 63 ° to 91 °F. The average annual precipitation is 16 inches, with an average relative humidity of 70% at 6 A.M. and 40% at 6 P.M. The average annual snowfall is 16 inches. The growing season averages 184 days per year, with the last freeze in late April and the first freeze in late October. The sun shines during the year on the average 75% of the daylight hours.

THE PEOPLE

Hartley County has had continuous population growth since the 1940s although the 1982 estimated population of 3,700 indicates a decline since 1980. Urban areas grew 67% between 1970 and 1980, while rural areas increased 20%. The age groups with the largest gains were ages 30 to 34, 65 and over and birth to five years. The largest ancestry groups are persons of English descent (34%), German decent (26%) and Irish descent (26%). **REGISTERED VOTERS** As of November 2, 1982 there were 2,152 registered voters (0.03% of the state total). The 1982 general election had a 61% voter turnout, compared to a 74% turnout in the 1980 general election. In the 1982 primary 89% voted Democratic and 11% Republican, with 824 votes cast.

THE ECONOMY

AGRICULTURE Wheat and fed cattle area. in 1982, 98% of the land was in farms and ranches, with 18% of the farmland under cultivation and 73% irrigated. Hartley ranked 20th in the state in highest agricultural receipts, with 80% from livestock and livestock products. Overgrazing, undesirable brush and weeds, wind erosion and decreasing irrigation water supplies are the current conservation problems. Primary crops: wheat, sorghum, corn, hay and rye. Primary vegetables: sweet potatoes. Primary livestock and products: third in the state for fed cattle marketings. Milk and hogs. **BUSINESS** Total number of business establishments in the county: 45. Retail sales during the first quarter of 1984 decreased 12%. In 1980, 27% of the labor force were self-employed, 19% were employed in professional or related services, 3% in manufacturing, 20% in wholesale and retail trade,

31% in agriculture, forestry, fisheries and mining, 48% were employed in other counties and there were 113 retired workers. The industry with the most employment is agribusiness. The non-farm earnings in 1981 totaled $21,901,000. The retired workers received an average monthly Social Security payment of $336.00. **HOUSING** Average value of homes in 1980: $47,200. Between 1970 and 1980 the number of housing units increased by 53%. Eighty-six percent of all units in the county are air-conditioned, 91% are heated by gas and 9% by electricity. **NATURAL RESOURCES** Caliche, oil and gas. In 1982 a total of 6,592,406 thousand cubic feet of gas well gas was produced. **TOURISM** Travel expenditures of $7,600,000 in 1982 (an increase of 11% over 1981) generated 196 jobs and $1,546,000 in payroll. **ALCOHOLIC BEVERAGES** Only 4% beer is legal in parts of the county. **FEDERAL EXPENDITURES** The federal government had direct expenditures or obligations of $6,864,000 in the county during fiscal year 1983, including $14,000 by the U.S. Department of Defense. In addition, the federal government provided $42,000 in grant awards, paid $240,000 in salaries and wages, made direct payments to individuals of $1,914,000 including $1,522,000 in retirement and disability payments, and spent $4,668,000 in other expenditures or obligations. The federal government also provided $15,185,000 in direct loans and $3,040,000 in guaranteed loans and insurance.

COMMUNICATION
Cable TV. Telephone companies: Continental Telephone, General Telephone and XIT Rural Telephone Coop. **TRANSPORTATION** Total public road mileage: 566. In 1982 there were 4,329 registered vehicles and 96 reported traffic accidents including three fatalities. Intercity bus service is available. Rail: two main and one branch line carry freight through the county. One main line carries annually over 30 million tons of freight and the other one carries one to five million with the branch carrying less than one million tons. Aircraft: seven are registered in the county.

COMMUNITY SERVICES
EDUCATION Two school districts with two elementary and two high schools. The average daily attendance in 1981-82 was 283, with expenditures per pupil of $4,898 including 31 classroom teachers with an average annual salary of $16,613. Forty percent of the 20 high school graduates planned to attend college. In 1982-83, 87% of the students were White, 13% Hispanic, 0.3% Black. **HEALTH CARE** Hospitals: one with a capacity of 60. Ambulance services: two volunteer fire department services. Nursing homes: one nursing home has capacity of 57 nursing care, 31 custodial care residents. The average cost per day for private patients in 1982 was $28.61. **CHURCHES** Seven churches have an estimated combined membership of 1,343. The largest denominations are United Methodist and Southern Baptist. **SOCIAL SERVICES** In fiscal year 1983 a total of $3,110 in food stamps was distributed, with an average of 13 persons receiving food stamps each month. Medical assistance benefits for the aged and disabled of $66,892 and for families and children of $36 brought the county benefit total to $70,038. **FIRE PROTECTION** Two volunteer fire departments. **LAW ENFORCEMENT** The County Sheriff has three commissioned officers. **CRIME** Twelve nonviolent crimes (burglary, larceny-theft and motor vehicle theft) were reported in 1982. **JUDICIAL SYSTEM** One District Court and Judge, one County Court and Judge and three Justices of the Peace. In the District Court a total of 27 cases were pending on 1/1/82, 61 new cases were filed and 54 cases were disposed of during the year leaving 34 cases pending on 12/31/82. There were 16 criminal cases on the docket, 12 convictions, one person committed to prison and two cases left pending. In the County Court 119 cases were pending on 1/1/82, 117 new cases were filed and 80 cases were disposed of during the

year leaving 156 cases pending on 12/31/82. There were 210 criminal cases on the docket, 44 convictions, four persons committed to jail, and 145 cases left pending. **JAILS** One jail, capacity seven. **UTILITIES** 79% of the residents are connected to a public or privately owned water system and 60% are connected to a public sewer system. Natural gas is distributed to the county by Energas Company. The average annual residential bill for natural gas in 1982 for the Energas distribution system was $371.63, an increase of 23% over 1981. Electricity is distributed to the county by Rita Blanca Electric Coop., Inc. and Southwestern Public Service and is generated primarily by gas and coal. The typical residential electric bill is $170.44 per month for an all-electric house using 2,500 kwh. **TAXES** The county has seven units with taxing authority: two school districts, one city, one county, two hospital districts and one special district.

RECREATION/ENTERTAINMENT
COUNTY/MUNICIPAL PARKS 1,253 acres in one county and two municipal parks. These parks contain two playgrounds, three baseball and softball fields, four tennis courts, two multi-use courts, one swimming pool, five beaches, one boat ramp and shore fishing facilities. Developed campsites: 32. **SCENIC DRIVES** The Texas Plains Trail runs through this county. this trail spans a vast area of the High Plains region of Texas slicing through the southernmost extension of the Great Plains of the United States. The land is flat except where erosion has carved canyon landscapes. **BOATING/FISHING** Lakes/reservoirs: Rita Blanca (524 acres). Primary streams: Rita Blanca and Punta de Agua. **HUNTING** Fall season on antelope. Fall and winter season on mule deer. Summer, fall and winter seasons on squirrel. Winter seasons on quail, pheasant, muskrat, beaver, opossum, ring-tailed cat, badger, fox, weasel, raccoon, skunk and civet cat. Fall, winter and spring seasons on turkey. No closed season on bobcat and coyote. In 1983 sandhill crane, duck, coot, geese, woodcock and jacksnipe seasons occurred during the winter months. Teal duck, rail and gallinule seasons occurred in the fall. Mourning dove seasons occurred intermittently during the fall and winter seasons. **SPECIAL EVENTS** Health Fair, Dalhart, April; XIT Rodeo and Reunion, Dalhart, July/August; Matador Cowboy Reunion, Channing, August; Chili Cookoff, Dalhart, variable dates; Interstate Fair, Dalhart, September.

COMMUNITIES
COUNTY SEAT Channing, County Courthouse, 79018; County Clerk's Office, 806/235-3582. **INCORPORATED COMMUNITIES** (1980 population and ZIP Code) Channing (304) 79018, Dalhart (6,854: in Hartley Co. and 4,571 in Dallam Co.) 79022. **UNINCORPORATED COMMUNITIES** (and ZIP Code) Hartley 79044, Middle Water 79060 and Romero 79022.

HASKELL (P53)

THE LAND
North of Abilene on U.S. Highways 277 and 380 in the Rolling Plains Region, Haskell County covers 901 square miles with an elevation range of 1,400 to 1,600 feet. The soils of the county are light colored and well drained as well as very dark, loamy soils over clayey subsoils with hardened calcium deposits in some areas. Lying in the Rolling Plains vegetation area, Haskell County has short and mid grasses, with some mesquite trees and cacti. Between 51 and 60% of the land in the county is considered prime farmland. **CLIMATE** Generally mild, but extremes in temperatures may be encountered. The average annual temperature is 64°F. Temperatures in January range from an average low of 29° to an average high of 54°F and in July range from 72° to 97°F. The average annual precipitation is 24 inches,

COUNTIES

with an average relative humidity of 76% at 6 A.M. and 46% at 6 P.M. The average annual snowfall is six inches. The growing season averages 230 days per year, with the last freeze in late March and the first freeze in mid November. The sun shines during the year on the average 70% of the daylight hours.

THE PEOPLE

Haskell County ranks 70th among all U.S. counties in the highest percent of population over age 64. The 1982 estimated population of 7,600 continues the steady population losses which have occurred since 1930. Urban areas grew 1% between 1970 and 1980, while rural populations declined 18%. The age groups with the greatest decreases were ages 10 to 14 and 55 to 59. Since the population is older than average, the county has a low birth rate and a high death rate. The largest ancestry groups are persons of English descent (32%), Irish descent (19 %) and Hispanic (16%). **REGISTERED VOTERS** As of November 2, 1982 there were 4,624 registered voters (0.1% of the state total). The 1982 general election had a 50% voter turnout, compared to a 70% turnout in the 1980 general election. In the 1982 primary 100% voted Democratic with 1,660 votes cast.

THE ECONOMY

AGRICULTURE Cotton and wheat area. In 1982, 93% of the land was in farms and ranches, with 52% of the farmland under cultivation and 5% irrigated. Haskell ranked 115th in the state in highest agricultural receipts, with 86% from crops. Overgrazing, undesirable brush and weeds, water erosion and inefficient tillage systems are the current conservation problems. Primary crops: cotton, wheat and sorghum. Primary vegetables: watermelons. Primary fruits and nuts: peaches and pecans. Primary livestock and products: cattle. **BUSINESS** Total number of business establishments in the county: 185. Retail sales during the first quarter of 1984 decreased 3%. In 1980, 27% of the labor force were self-employed, 19% were employed in professional or related services, 3% in manufacturing, 21% in wholesale and retail trade, 30% in agriculture, forestry, fisheries and mining, 7% were employed in other counties and there were 1,171 retired workers. The industries with the most employment: oil and gas extraction and agribusiness. The nonfarm earnings in 1981 totaled $61,360,000. The retired workers received an average monthly Social Security payment of $298.00. **FINANCE** On June 30, 1983, three commercial banks had total deposits of $70,455,000 and total assets of $76,835,000. There is one state savings and loan association branch and one credit union. **HOUSING** Average value of homes in 1980: $18,400. Permits for new, privately owned housing units increased in 1982: 12 permits were issued with a total construction cost of $244,800. Of those permits, seven were for single family houses. Between 1970 and 1980 the number of housing units decreased by 1%. Eighty percent of all units in the county are air-conditioned, 89% are heated by gas and 8% by electricity, 1% by other fuels. **NATURAL RESOURCES** Limestone, oil, gas, and bituminous coal. In 1982 a total of 22,136 thousand cubic feet of gas well gas, 1,474,245 barrels of crude oil and 382,921 thousand cubic feet of casinghead gas were produced. **TOURISM** Travel expenditures of $2,781,000 in 1982 (an increase of 13% over 1981) generated 59 jobs and $503,000 in payroll. **ALCOHOLIC BEVERAGES** Packaged distilled spirits, beer, ale, malt liquor and wine are legal in parts of the county. **FEDERAL EXPENDITURES** The federal government had direct expenditures or obligations of $26,896,000 in the county during fiscal year 1983, including $536,000 by the U.S. Department of Defense. In addition, the federal government provided $598,000 in grant awards, paid $737,000 in salaries and wages, made direct payments to individuals of $15,131,000 including $10,177,000 in retirement and disability payments, awarded $2,000 in procurement contracts and spent $10,427,000 in other expenditures or obligations. The federal government also provided $5,598,000 in direct loans and $6,942,000 in guaranteed loans and insurance.

COMMUNICATION

Newspapers–Weekly: The Haskell Free Press, Twin Cities News (Rochester-Rule) and the Stamford American. Radio: KURP-FM (Haskell). Cable TV. Telephone companies: General Telephone and Southwestern Bell. **TRANSPORTATION** Total public road mileage: 1,122. In 1982 there were 9,941 registered vehicles and 98 reported traffic accidents including five fatalities. Intercity bus service is available. Motor freight: one carrier. Rail: one branch line carries annually less than one million tons of freight through the county. Aircraft: 26 are registered in the county. Airports: Haskell Municipal Airport serves as a base for 15 aircraft and is a basic utility airport with general aviation service.

COMMUNITY SERVICES

EDUCATION Five school districts with five elementary and five high schools. The average daily attendance in 1981-82 was 1,203, with expenditures per pupil of $2,519 including 95 classroom teachers with an average annual salary of $14,902. Twenty-two percent of the 97 high school graduates planned to attend college. In 1982-83, 66% of the students were White, 27% Hispanic, 7% Black, 0.2% Asian. **PUBLIC LIBRARIES** Haskell County Library (Haskell): 10,660 volumes. **CHILD CARE** 15 day care licensed facilities. **HEALTH CARE** Five physicians and three dentists. Hospitals: one with a capacity of 30. Ambulance services: one volunteer service. Mental health: one clinic. Nursing homes: two nursing homes with a combined capacity of 150 nursing care residents. The average cost per day for private patients in 1982 was $32.49. **CHURCHES** 36 churches have an estimated combined membership of 7,901. The largest denomination is Southern Baptist. **SOCIAL SERVICES** In fiscal year 1983 a total of $274,903 in food stamps was distributed, with an average of 632 persons receiving food stamps each month. Aid to Families with Dependent Children (AFDC) totaled $56,613, with an average of 36 families receiving AFDC each month. Medical assistance benefits for the aged and disabled of $970,885 and for families and children of $46,579 brought the county benefit total to $1,348,980. **FIRE PROTECTION** Six volunteer fire departments. **LAW ENFORCEMENT** The County Sheriff has three commissioned officers. Two police departments have a combined force of four. **CRIME** Six violent crimes (murder, forcible rape, robbery and aggravated assault) and 66 nonviolent crimes (burglary, larceny-theft and motor vehicle theft) were reported in 1982. **JUDICIAL SYSTEM** One District Court and Judge, one County Court and Judge and three Justices of the Peace. In the District Court a total of 379 cases were pending on 1/1/82, 117 new cases were filed and 111 cases were disposed of during the year leaving 385 cases pending on 12/31/82. There were 70 criminal cases on the docket, 13 convictions, one person committed to prison and 52 cases left pending. In the County Court 1,522 cases were pending on 1/1/82, 256 new cases were filed and 109 cases were disposed of during the year leaving 1,669 cases pending on 12/31/82. There were 1,556 criminal cases on the docket, seven convictions and 1,447 cases left pending. **JAILS** One jail, capacity 16, planning a renovation. **ATTORNEYS AT LAW** Eight. **UTILITIES** 81% of the residents are connected to a public or privately owned water system and 73% are connected to a public sewer system. Natural gas is distributed to the county by Lone Star Bas Co., Division of Enserch. The average annual residential bill for natural gas in 1982 for the Lone Star distribution system was $405.91, an increase of 35% over 1981. Electricity is distributed to the county by West Texas Utilities Co., R-K Electric Coop., Inc. and Stamford Electric Coop., Inc. and is generated primarily by gas, oil and water. The typical residential electric bill is $145.78 per month for an all-electric house using 2,500 kwh. **TAXES** The county has 14 units with taxing authority: five school districts, five cities, one county, one hospital district and two special districts.

RECREATION/ENTERTAINMENT

COUNTY/MUNICIPAL PARKS 133 acres in one county and four municipal parks. These parks contain three playgrounds, two baseball and softball fields, one swimming pool, two beaches and two boat ramps. Developed campsites: 55. **BOATING/FISHING** Lakes/reservoirs: Elm Creek (38 acres) and Stamford (4,690 acres). Major rivers: Clear Fork Brazos and Double Mountain Fork Brazos. Primary streams: California, Elm, Millers, Mule and Paint. **HUNTING** Fall and winter seasons on deer and mule deer. No closed season on squirrel, bobcat and coyote. Winter season on quail, muskrat, beaver, opossum, ringtailed cat, badger, fox, weasel, raccoon, skunk and civet cat. Fall, winter and spring seasons on turkey. In 1983 sandhill crane, duck, coot, geese, woodcock and jacksnipe seasons occurred during the winter months. Teal duck, rail and gallinule seasons occurred in the fall. Mourning dove seasons occurred intermittently during the fall and winter months. **MUSEUMS** Haskell: Haskell County Railroad Museum and J. U. and Florence B. Fields Museum of Fine Living. **SPECIAL EVENTS** Frontier Days Celebration and Rodeo, Haskell, May; Jubilee, Rule, July; Haskell County Fair, Haskell, September; Country Dinner Theatre, Haskell, October; Veterans' Celebration, Rochester, November; Night Christmas Parade, Haskell, December.

COMMUNITIES

COUNTY SEAT Haskell, County Courthouse, 79521; County Clerk's Office, 817/864-2451. **INCORPORATED COMMUNITIES** (1980 population and ZIP Code) Haskell (3,782) 79521, O'Brien (212) 79539, Rochester (492) 79544, Rule (1,015) 79547, Stamford (4,542: 45 in Haskell Co. and 4,497 in Jones Co.) 79553 and Weinert (253) 76388. **UNINCORPORATED COMMUNITIES** (and ZIP Code) Jud 79544, Sagerton 79548. **FOR ADDITIONAL LOCAL INFORMATION** Haskell Chamber of Commerce, P.O. Box 713, Haskell, 79521, 817/864-2477, Rule Chamber of Commerce, 5th and Union, P.O. Box 607, Rule, 79547, 817/997-2214 and Stamford Chamber of Commerce, P.O. Box 1206, Stamford, 79553, 915/773-2411.

HAYS (C31)

THE LAND

Southwest of Austin on Interstate Highway 35 in the Edwards Plateau Region, Hays County covers 678 square miles with an elevation range of 400 to 1,400 feet. Along the southeastern border of the county are undulating, slightly acidic soils with loamy surfaces over cracking, clayey subsoils and acidic, cracking, clayey soils all of which have a high shrink-swell potential. The rest of the county has light colored, well drained soils and very dark, loamy soils over clayey subsoils or loamy subsoils that have accumulations of lime. The southeastern one-forth of the county lies in the Blackland Prairies vegetation area which has tall prairie grasses with some mesquite and oak trees. The rest of the county is in the Edwards Plateau vegetation area which has tall and mid grasses and live oak savannah with some mesquite and juniper. Between 11 and 20% of the land in the county is considered prime farmland. **CLIMATE** Subtropical humid. Thunderstorms may be expected at any time, but are most frequent in late spring. The average annual temperature is 67 °F.

Temperatures in January range from an average low of 36° to an average high of 60°F and in July range from 72° to 95°F. The average annual precipitation is 33 inches, with an average relative humidity of 85% at 6 A.M. and 53% at 6 P.M. The average annual snowfall is less than one inch. The growing season averages 255 days per year, with the last freeze in early March and the first freeze in early December. The sun shines during the year on the average 68% of the daylight hours.

THE PEOPLE

Hays County has been rapidly growing over the past 20 years with the 1982 estimated population of 43,700 indicating a continuation of that strong growth rate. Rural areas increased in population nearly 96% from 1970 to 1980, with urban areas experiencing a growth of 24%. The age groups with the largest gains were ages 20 to 34 and 15 to 19. The county's population is young with a median age of 23. The largest ancestry groups are Hispanic (30%), persons of English descent (23%) and German descent (21%). **REGISTERED VOTERS** As of November 2, 1982 there were 19,466 registered voters (0.3% of the state total). The 1982 general election had a 49% voter turnout, compared to a 65% turnout in the 1980 general election. In the 1982 primary 91% voted Democratic and 9% Republican, with 5,157 votes cast.

THE ECONOMY

AGRICULTURE In 1982, 82% of the land was in farms and ranches, with 10% of the farmland under cultivation. Hays ranked 206th in the state in highest agricultural receipts, with 80% from livestock and livestock products. Overgrazing, undesirable brush and weeds, water erosion, soil compaction and water conservation are the current conservation problems. Primary crops: hay, oats, sorghum, wheat and corn. Primary vegetables: potatoes. Primary fruits and nuts: peaches and pecans. Primary livestock and products: cattle, sheep, wool, angora, goats and mohair. **BUSINESS** Total number of business establishments in the county: 758. Retail sales during the first quarter of 1984 increased by 35%. In 1980, 8% of the labor force were self-employed, 31% were employed in professional or related services, 11% in manufacturing, 21% in wholesale and retail trade, 9% in construction, 30% were employed in other counties and there were 2,306 retired workers. The industries with the most employment: tourism, agribusiness, road construction and the manufacture of hydraulic cement, motors and generators and lighting equipment. The nonfarm earnings in 1981 totaled $314,285,000. The retired workers received an average monthly Social Security payment of $310.00. **FINANCE** On June 30, 1983, seven commercial banks had total deposits of $161,033,000 and total assets of $182,597,000. On December 31, 1982 one state savings and loan association, three state branches and two federal association branches had combined assets of $15,771,336. In addition there are three credit unions in the county. **HOUSING** Average value of homes in 1980: $44,400. Permits for new, privately owned housing units decreased in 1982: 482 permits were issued with a total construction cost of $10,756,580. Of those permits, 60 were for single family houses. Between 1970 and 1980 the number of housing units increased by 75%. Seventy-seven percent of all units in the county are air-conditioned, 55% are heated by gas and 39% by electricity. **NATURAL RESOURCES** dolomite, limestone, industrial sand, and sand and gravel. Current production of other minerals and products includes cement, crushed limestone, sand and gravel and shale. **TOURISM** Travel expenditures of $29,479,000 in 1982 (an increase of 9% over 1981) generated 558 jobs and $5,495,000 in payroll. Lodging: eight hotels, motels and tourist courts. Convention/meeting facilities: San Marcos-Southwest Texas State University Gym and Stadium. **ALCOHOLIC BEVERAGES** Packaged distilled spirits, beer, ale, malt liquor and wine are legal in parts of the county. Sale of

HAYS (continued)

mixed beverages is legal in all or parts of the county. **FEDERAL EXPENDITURES** The federal government had direct expenditures or obligations of $71,810,000 in the county during fiscal year 1983, including $7,756,000 by the U.S. Department of Defense. In addition, the federal government provided $1,277,000 in grant awards, paid $3,619,000 in salaries and wages, made direct payments to individuals of $41,880,000 including $32,296,000 in retirement and disability payments, awarded $24,715,000 in procurement contracts and spent $319,000 in other expenditures or obligations. The federal government also provided $524,000 in direct loans and $19,241,000 in guaranteed loans and insurance.

COMMUNICATION

Newspapers–Daily: San Marco Daily Record, ave. eve. circ. 4,590. Weekly: The Wimberley View. Radio: KCNY-AM (San Marcos). Cable TV. Telephone companies: Continental Telephone, General Telephone, Southwestern Bell, Guadalupe Valley Telephone Coop. and San Marcos Telephone. **TRANSPORTATION** Total public road mileage: 872. In 1982 there were 30,687 registered vehicles and 1,441 reported traffic accidents including 16 fatalities. Taxi cabs: one company in San Marcos. Intercity bus service is available. Motor freight: nine local and intrastate carriers. Rail: the Eagle provides passenger service on the Amtrak route. Two main and two branch lines carry freight through the county. The two mainlines carry annually 10 to 20 million tons of freight each and the two branches carry one to five million each. Aircraft: 65 are registered in the county. Airports: San Marcos Municipal Airport serves as a base for 30 aircraft and is a basic transportation airport with general aviation service. Robert Lowman Airport at San Marcos.

COMMUNITY SERVICES

EDUCATION three school districts with eight elementary, two middle, three high schools. The average daily attendance in 1981-82 was 7,254, with expenditures per pupil of $2,438 including 499 classroom teachers with an average annual salary of $15,626. Twenty percent of the 485 high school graduates planned to attend college. In 1982-83, 50% of the students were White, 47% Hispanic, 3% Black, 0.6% Asian and 0.1% American Indian. Private schools: 562 students enrolled in two elementary and one high school. Southwest Texas State University is located in San Marcos. Established in 1899 it is under state control. Enrollment in 1982 was 15,450 with in state undergratuate tuition and fees of $426 per semester. The highest degree offered is Master. Sports championships: (Lone Star Conference) 1983 Football, 1984 Women's Basketball (tie with Abilene Christian), 1983 Men's Tennis, 1983 Men's Golf. **PUBLIC LIBRARIES** Kyle Community Library: 14,242 volumes. San Marcos Public Library: 35,835. Village Library (Wimberly): 6,000. **CHILD CARE** 55 day care and five twenty-four hour care licensed facilities. **HEALTH CARE** 42 physicians and 18 dentists. Hospitals: one with a capacity of 40. Clinics: one for treatment of alcohol abuse, one dialysis clinic, and one public health clinic. Ambulance services: one volunteer service and one commercial service. Mental health: one county clinic and one school with a combined capacity of 265. Nursing homes: two nursing homes with a combined capacity of 281 nursing care residents. The average cost per day for private patients in 1982 was $37.07. **CHURCHES** 44 churches have an estimated combined membership of 17,186. The largest denominations are Southern Baptist, Catholic and United Methodist. **SOCIAL SERVICES** In fiscal year 1983 a total of $1,527,203 in food stamps was distributed, with an average of 3,265 persons receiving food stamps each month. Aid to Families with Dependent Children (AFDC) totaled $398,954 with an average of 254 families receiving AFDC each month. Medical

assistance benefits for the aged and disabled of $2,122,579 and for families and children of $557,639 brought the county benefit total to $4,606,375. **FIRE PROTECTION** One partly paid and eight volunteer fire departments. **LAW ENFORCEMENT** The County Sheriff has 52 commissioned officers. Three police departments have a combined force of 40. One university campus has a police force of 16 officers. **CRIME** 181 violent crimes (murder, forcible rape, robbery and aggravated assault) and 2,199 nonviolent crimes (burglary, larceny-theft and motor vehicle theft) were reported in 1982. **JUDICIAL SYSTEM** Three District Courts and Judges, two County Courts and Judges and six Justices of the Peace. In the District Courts a total of 773 cases were pending on 1/1/82, 618 new cases were filed and 559 cases were disposed of during the year leaving 832 cases pending on 12/31/82. There were 306 criminal cases on the docket, 96 convictions, 32 persons committed to prison and eight committed to jail and 139 cases left pending. In the County Courts 3,110 cases were pending on 1/1/82, 2,290 new cases were filed and 1,608 cases were disposed of during the year leaving 3,792 cases pending on 12/31/82. There were 4,857 criminal cases on the docket, 574 convictions, 135 persons committed to jail, and 3,334 cases left pending. **JAILS** One jail, capacity 27, planning an addition; lost certification in 1983 due to crowded conditions. **ATTORNEYS AT LAW** 74. **UTILITIES** 82% of the residents are connected to a public or privately owned water system and 59% are connected to a public sewer system. Natural gas is distributed to the county by Entex, Inc. The average annual residential bill for natural gas in 1982 for the Entex distribution system was $390.31, an increase of 26% over 1981. Electricity is distributed to the county by Bluebonnet Electric Coop., Inc., Pendernales Electric Coop., Inc. and Lower Colorado River Authority and is generated primarily by oil, water and coal. The typical residential electric bill is $123.05 per month for an all-electric house using 2,500 kwh. **TAXES** The county has 16 units with taxing authority: three school districts, five cities, one county, one utility district and six special districts.

RECREATION/ENTERTAINMENT

NATIONAL REGISTER OF HISTORIC PLACES Kyle vicinity: Claiborne Kyle Log House. San Marcos: Burleson-Knispel House, Cock House First United Methodist Church and Hays County Courthouse. San Marcos vicinity: Harry Freeman Site and Ruskin C. Norman Site. **COUNTY/MUNICIPAL PARKS** 198 acres in two county and 11 municipal parks. These parks contain one mile of hiking trails, five playgrounds, one football and soccer field, 14 baseball and softball fields, six tennis courts, one multi-use court, one swimming pool and one beach.**SCENIC DRIVES** The Texas Hill Country Trail runs through this county. This trail winds through a scenic region of South-Central Texas, spanning a vast ranching area abundant with wildlife in a landscape of deeply-sculptured valleys and hills. Also scenic in Hays County is F.M. 12 to R.M. 32, the winding edge route known as the "Devil's Backbone". **BOATING/ FISHING** Lakes/reservoirs: Pierce (25 acres), Plum Creek Soil Conservation Service Lake 11 (17 acres) and York Creek Soil Conservation Service Lake 5 (36 acres). Major rivers: Hays: Blanco and San Marcos. Primary streams: Brushy, York and Onion. **HUNTING** Fall and winter seasons on deer and javelina. No closed seasons on squirrel, bobcat and coyote. Winter season on quail, muskrat, beaver, opossum, ring-tailed cat, badger, fox, weasel, raccoon, skunk and civet cat. Fall, winter and spring seasons on turkey. In 1983 sandhill crane, duck, coot, geese, woodcock and jacksnipe seasons occurred during the winter months. Teal duck, rail and gallinule seasons occurred in the fall. Mourning dove seasons occurred intermittently during the fall and winter seasons. **MUSEUMS** San Marcos: Mission San Fransico Xavier, Texas Museum of History, Dr. Eli T. Merriman Home and General Edward Burleson Museum. Wimberley: Pioneer Town. **COLLEGIATE FINE ARTS** Cultural events offered by Southwest Texas State University. **SPECIAL EVENTS** River Arts Festival, San Marcos, April; Spring Fest, San Marcos, April; Hillaceous 10 K Run, Wimberley, April; Volksmarch, Wimberley, April; Central Texas Golf Fest, San Marcos, April; Fun Fest, Wimberly, April; Cinco de Mayo, San Marcos, May; Heritage Tours of Distinction, San Marcos, May; Rectangles on the Square, San Marcos, May; Water Safari, San Marcos, June; Juneteenth Celebration, San Marcos, June; Rodeo, Wimberley, July; Chilympiad, San Marcos, September; Fair on the Square, Kyle, October.

COMMUNITIES
COUNTY SEAT San Marcos, County Courthouse, 78666; County Clerk's Office, 512/392-2601. **INCORPORATED COMMUNITIES** (1980 population and ZIP Code) Buda (597) 78610, Dripping Springs (650) Est. incorporation inactive. 78620, Hays (286) 78666, Kyle (2,093) 78640 and San Marcos (23,420) 78666. **UNINCORPORATED COMMUNITIES** (and ZIP Code) Driftwood 78619, Fitzhugh 78703, Henley 78620, Mount Sharp 78620, Niederwald (Also in Caldwell Co.) 78640, Pioneer Town 78676, Uhland (Also in Caldwell Co.) 78640 and Wimberly 78676.**FOR ADDITIONAL LOCAL INFORMATION** San Marcos Chamber of Commerce, P. O. Box 2310, San Marcos, 78666, 512/396-2495, Wimberly Chamber of Commerce, P. O. Box 12, Wimberly, 78676 512/847-2201.

HEMPHILL (P10)

THE LAND
Northeast of Amarillo and bordering Oklahoma on U.S. Highways 60 and 83, in the Rolling Plains Region. Hemphill County covers 903 square miles with an elevation range of 2,300 to 2,800 feet. All of the county has light colored, well drained soils and loamy soils over clayey or loamy subsoils that have calcium deposits or accumulations of lime with the exception of the southern border from U.S. Highway 83 to the eastern end of the county. This area has mostly loamy soils throughout, but some have sandy surfaces or clayey subsoils. Hemphill is located in the Rolling Plains vegetation area with short to tall grasses, mesquite and live oak trees and cacti. Less than one percent of the land in the county is considered prime farmland. **CLIMATE** Cool and dry, but subject to extreme swings in temperatures from winter to summer as well as sudden changes particularly in winter. The average annual temperature is 57 °F. Temperatures in January range from an average low of 20° to an average high of 48 °F and in July range from 67 ° to 95 °F. The average annual precipitation is 21 inches, with an average relative humidity of 73% at 6 A.M. and 43% at 6 P.M. The average annual snowfall is 17 inches. The growing season averages 204 days per year, with the last freeze near April 10th and the first freeze in late October. The sun shines during the year on the average 75% of the daylight hours.

THE PEOPLE
The 1982 estimated population of 6,300 indicates a continuation of the growth begun in the 1970s reversing a steady population decline. The age groups with the largest increases were ages 20 to 34 and birth to five years, lowering the median age form 32 in 1970 to 26 in 1980. The county has a high birth rate and a low death rate. The largest ancestry groups are persons of Irish descent (18%), English descent (16%) and German descent (13%). **REGISTERED VOTERS** As of November 2, 1982 there were 2,407 registered voters (0.03% of the state total). The 1982 general election had a 55% voter turnout, compared to a 72%

turnout in the 1980 general election. In the 1982 primary 83% voted Democratic and 17% Republican, with 723 votes cast.

THE ECONOMY
AGRICULTURE Wheat and cattle area. In 1982, 98% of the land was in farms and ranches, with 9% of the farmland under cultivation and 6% irrigated. Hemphill ranked 126th in the state in highest agricultural receipts, with 90% from livestock and livestock products. Undesirable brush and weeds, water and wind erosion, decreasing irrigation water supplies and the reclamation of oil and gas drilling sites are the current conservation problems. Primary crops: wheat, sorghum and hay. Primary livestock and products: cattle, milk, sheep, wool and hogs. **BUSINESS** Total number of business establishments in the county: 172. Retail sales during the first quarter of 1984 increased by 1%. In 1980, 13% of the labor force were self-employed, 14% were employed in professional or related services, 10% in manufacturing, 17% in wholesale and retail trade, 26% in agriculture, forestry, fisheries and mining, 9% were employed in other counties and there were 280 retired workers. The industry with the most employment: oil & gas extraction. The nonfarm earnings in 1981 totaled $61,871,000. The retired workers received an average monthly Social Security payment of $336.00. **FINANCE** On June 30, 1983, two commercial banks had total deposits of $81,873,000 and total assets of $90,733,000. There is one state savings and loan association branch in the county. **HOUSING** Average value of homes in 1980: $38,600. Permits for new, privately owned housing units decreased in 1982: eight permits were issued with a total construction cost of $438,000. Of those permits, all were for single family houses. Between 1970 and 1980 the number of housing units increased by 73%. Eighty-two percent of all units in the county are air-conditioned, 93% are heated by gas and 7% by electricity. **NATURAL RESOURCES** Caliche, oil and gas. In 1982 a total of 140,361,712 thousand cubic feet of gas well gas, 881,092 barrels of condensate, 532,845 barrels of crude oil and 9,967,776 thousand cubic feet of casinghead gas were produced. **TOURISM** Travel expenditures of $4,171,000 in 1982 (an increase of 11% over 1981) generated 106 jobs and $840,000 in payroll. **ALCOHOLIC BEVERAGES** Totally dry. **FEDERAL EXPENDITURES** The federal government had direct expenditures or obligations of $5,064,000 in the county during fiscal year 1983, including $76,000 by the U.S. Department of Defense. In addition, the federal government provided $147,000 in grant awards, paid $309,000 in salaries and wages, made direct payments to individuals of $4,196,000 including $2,996,000 in retirement and disability payments, awarded $1,000 in procurement contracts and spent $412,000 in other expenditures or obligations. The federal government also provided $1,241,000 in direct loans and $1,010,000 in guaranteed loans and insurance.

COMMUNICATION
Newspapers–Weekly: The Canadian Record. Cable TV. Telephone companies: General Telephone and Southwestern Bell. **TRANSPORTATION** Total public road mileage: 469. In 1982 there were 6,387 registered vehicles and 142 reported traffic accidents including three fatalities. Motor freight: eight local and intrastate carriers. Rail: one main line carries annually over 30 million tons of freight through the county. Aircraft: 42 are registered in the county. Airports: Hemphill County Airport at Canadian serves as a base for 12 aircraft and is a basic utility airport with general aviation service.

COMMUNITY SERVICES
EDUCATION One school district with one elementary, one middle and one high school. The average daily attendance in 1981-82 was 1,013, with expenditures per pupil of $4,229 including 67 classroom teachers with an average annual salary of $18,267.

COUNTIES

HEMPHILL (continued)

None of the 54 high school graduates planned to attend college. In 1982-83, 86% of the students were White, 13% Hispanic, 0.3% Black, 0.2% Asian and 0.3% American Indian. **PUBLIC LIBRARIES** Hemphill County Library (Canadian): 19,366 volumes. **CHILD CARE** Four day care and three twenty-four hour care licensed facilities. **HEALTH CARE** Three physicians and one dentist. Hospitals: one with a capacity of 26. Ambulance services: one city service. Mental health: one clinic. Nursing homes: one nursing home has a capacity of 59 nursing care residents. The average cost per day for private patients in 1982 was $31.77. **CHURCHES** 11 churches have an estimated combined membership of 2,676. The largest denominations are Southern Baptist, United Methodist and Churches of Christ. **SOCIAL SERVICES** In fiscal year 1983 a total of $32,488 in food stamps was distributed, with an average of 76 persons receiving food stamps each month. Aid to Families with Dependent Children (AFDC) totaled $6,571 with an average of five families receiving AFDC each month. Medical assistance benefits for the aged and disabled of $166,858 and for families and children of $5,599 brought the county benefit total to $211,516. **FIRE PROTECTION** Two volunteer fire departments. **LAW ENFORCEMENT** The County Sheriff has five commissioned officers. One police department has a force of three. **CRIME** 11 violent crimes (murder, forcible rape, robbery and aggravated assault) and 132 nonviolent crimes (burglary, larceny-theft and motor vehicle theft) were reported in 1982. **JUDICIAL SYSTEM** One District Court and Judge, one County Court and Judge and one Justice of the Peace. In the District Court a total of 339 cases were pending on 1/1/82, 166 new cases were filed and 127 cases were disposed of during the year leaving 378 cases pending on 12/31/82. There were 26 criminal cases on the docket, seven convictions and 15 cases left pending. In the County Court 240 cases were pending on 1/1/82, 95 new cases were filed and 61 cases were disposed of during the year leaving 274 cases pending on 12/31/82. There were 234 criminal cases on the docket, 23 convictions, 10 persons committed to jail, and 180 cases left pending. **JAILS** One jail, capacity 18. **ATTORNEYS AT LAW** Nine. **UTILITIES** 77% of the residents are connected to a public or privately owned water system and 60% are connected to a public sewer system. Natural gas is distributed to the county by High Plains Natural Gas Co. Electricity is distributed to the county by Southwestern Public Service, Greenbelt Electric Coop., Inc. and North Plains Electric Coop., Inc. and is generated primarily by gas and oil. The typical residential electric bill is $170.44 per month for an all-electric house using 2,500 kwh. **TAXES** The county has four units with taxing authority: two school districts, one city and one county.

RECREATION/ENTERTAINMENT

MUNICIPAL PARKS 263 acres in five municipal parks. These parks contain three playgrounds, one golf course, two baseball and softball fields, two tennis courts and one swimming pool. Developed campsites: 15. **BOATING/FISHING** Lakes/reservoirs: Hutson-Stickley (46 acres), Kiowa (32 acres), Loretta Cooper Bowers (21 acres), Marvin (69 acres) and Washita River Upper Soil Conservation Service Lakes 1, 2, 10, 11, 25, 27 and 32 (100 acres). Major rivers: Washita and Canadian. Primary streams: Hackberry, Boggy, Gageby, Red Deer and Dads. **WILDLIFE REFUGES** Gene Howe State Wildlife Management Area covers 5,821 acres. **HUNTING** Fall season on antelope and prairie chicken. Fall and winter seasons on mule deer and deer. Summer, fall and winter seasons on squirrel. Winter seasons on pheasant, quail, muskrat, beaver, opossum, ring-tailed cat, badger, fox weasel, raccoon, skunk and civet cat. No closed season on coyote and bobcat. Fall, winter and spring seasons on

turkey. In 1983 sandhill crane, duck, coot, geese, woodcock and jacksnipe seasons occurred during the winter months. Teal, duck, rail and gallinule seasons occurred in the fall. Mourning dove seasons occurred intermittently during the fall and winter months. **MUSEUMS** Canadian: Hemphill County Pioneer Museum. **SPECIAL EVENTS** Annual Rodeo and Parade, Canadian, July; Music Festival, Canadian, August.

COMMUNITIES

COUNTY SEAT Canadian, County Courthouse, 79014; County Clerk's Office, 806/323-6212. **INCORPORATED COMMUNITIES** (1980 population and ZIP Code) Canadian (3,491) 79014. **UNINCORPORATED COMMUNITIES** (and ZIP Code) Dreyfoos 79046, Glazier 79037, Zybach (Also in Wheeler Co.) 79011 **FOR ADDITIONAL LOCAL INFORMATION** Canandian-Hemphill Co. Chamber of Commerce, P.O. Box 365, 3rd & Main, Canadian, 79014, 806/323-6234.

HENDERSON (E19)

THE LAND

Southeast of Dallas on U.S. Highway 175 in the Claypan Area, Henderson County covers 888 square miles with an elevation range of 300 to 600 feet. The eastern two-thirds of the county has light colored, undulating to rolling soils with loamy surfaces and reddish, mottled, clayey subsoils high in iron. Adjacent is a narrow strip of level to undulating soils with sandy surfaces and mottled gray and red or yellow cracking, clayey subsoils. Along the Trinity River are grayish, cracking, clayey soils. In the very northwest corner of the county are cracking, clayey soils and slightly acidic soils with loamy surfaces and cracking, clayey subsoils. The eastern end of the county lies in the Pineywood vegetation area with loblolly, shortleaf, longleaf and slash pines as well as hardwoods, such as oak, hickory and maple. Bluestem and Indiangrass along with other grasses make up the rest of the vegetation. The western border is in the Blackland Prairie vegetation area with prairie grasses such as little bluestem, big bluestem, Indiangrass and Texas wintergrass. Post oak and blackjack oak can be found along the streams. The rest of the county is in the Post Oak Savannah vegetation area with tall grasses and post oak, blackjack oak and elm trees. Mesquite is a problem in some areas. Between 11 and 20% of the land in the county is considered prime farmland. **CLIMATE** Subtropical mild and humid. A few severe thunderstorms may occur in spring. The average annual temperature is 65 °F. Temperatures in January range from an average low of 34° to an average high of 56 °F and in July range from 72° to 95 °F. The average annual precipitation is 40 inches, with an average relative humidity of 84% at 6 A.M. and 55% at 6 P.M. The average annual snowfall is two inches. The growing season averages 260 days per year, with the last freeze in mid March and the first freeze in late November. The sun shines during the year on the average 66% of the daylight hours.

THE PEOPLE

The growth rate of the population of Henderson County nearly tripled from 22% between 1960 and 1970 to 61% between 1970 and 1980. The 1982 estimated population of 45,600 indicates a continuation of that growth. The majority of county residents live in rural areas, which increased 92% in population between 1970 and 1980. The age groups with the largest gains were ages 20 to 34 and 62 and over. The county's population is older than average with a median age of 38 in 1980. The largest ancestry groups are persons of English descent (26%), Irish descent (20%), German descent (11%) and Black (11%). **REGISTERED VOTERS** As of November 2, 1982 there were 24,200 registered voters (0.4% of the state total). The 1982 general election had a 50% voter turnout, compared to a 69% turnout in the 1980 general election. In the 1982 primary 95% voted Democratic and 5% Republican, with 7,592 votes cast.

THE ECONOMY

AGRICULTURE Cattle area. In 1982, 56% of the land was in farms and ranches, with 17% of the farmland under cultivation. and 3% irrigated. Henderson ranked 94th in the state in highest agricultural receipts, with 78% from livestock and livestock products. Overgrazing, water erosion, the cultivation of marginal lands and the reestablishment of timberlands are the current conservation problems. Primary crops: fifth in the state for both hay and rye. Oats, sorghum and wheat. Primary vegetables: watermelons, sweet potatoes and tomatoes. Primary fruits and nuts: peaches and pecans. Primary livestock and products: 10th in the state for cattle. Milk and hogs. **BUSINESS** Total number of business establishments in the county: 619. Retail sales during the first quarter of 1984 increased by 34%. In 1980, 12% of the labor force were self-employed, 15% were employed in professional or related services, 21% in manufacturing, 21% in wholesale and retail trade, 12% in construction, 34% were employed in other counties and there were 4,149 retired workers. The industries with the most employment: agribusiness, oil and gas extraction, construction and the manufacture of women's lingerie, mobile homes, brick and clay tile, radio and television sets and medical instruments. The nonfarm earnings in 1981 totaled $315,452,000. The retired workers received an average monthly Social Security payment of $306. **FINANCE** On June 30, 1983, eight commercial banks had total deposits of $216,569,000 and total assets of $241,933,000. There are five state savings and loan association branches, one federal association branch and one credit union in the county. **HOUSING** Average value of homes in 1980: $32,500. Permits for new, privately owned housing units increased in 1982: 229 permits were issued with a total construction cost of $7,789,840. Of those permits, 92 were for single family houses. Housing permits increased in Athens from 23 in 1981 to 90 in 1982 and in Malakoff from three to 30 with 24 of the permits issued for apartments and condominiums. Between 1970 and 1980 the number of housing units increased by 105%. Seventy-eight percent of all units in the county are air-conditioned, 65% are heated by gas and 29% by electricity. **NATURAL RESOURCES** Clay, lignite coal, limonite iron, salt domes, industrial sand, sand and gravel, oil and gas. In 1982 a total of 44,585,974 thousand cubic feet of gas well gas, 59,613 barrels of condensate, 3,079,552 barrels of crude oil and 16,655,344 thousand cubic feet of casinghead gas were produced. Current production of other minerals and products includes brick, clay, limonite iron, sand and gravel, and recovered sulphur. **TOURISM** Travel expenditures of $14,549,000 in 1982 (an increase of 13% over 1981) generated 316 jobs and $2,671,000 in payroll. Lodging: six hotels, motels and tourist courts. **ALCOHOLIC BEVERAGES** Packaged distilled spirits, beer, ale, malt liquor and wine are legal in parts of the county. **FEDERAL EXPENDITURES** The federal government had direct expenditures or obligations of $65,777,000 in the county during fiscal year 1983, including $3,303,000 by the U.S. Department of Defense. In addition, the federal government provided $1,832,000 in grant awards, paid $2,018,000 in salaries and wages, made direct payments to individuals of $61,581,000 including $48,738,000 in retirement and disability payments, awarded $27,000 in procurement contracts and spent $319,000 in other expenditures or obligations. The federal government also provided $1,462,000 in direct loans and $4,416,000 in guaranteed loans and insurance.

COMMUNICATION

Newspapers–Daily: Athens Daily Review, ave. eve. circ. 6,025. Weekly: Athens Weekly Review and the Malakoff News. Radio: KBVD-AM (Athens). Cable TV. Telephone companies: Southwestern Bell and United Telephone. **TRANSPORTATION** Total public road mileage: 1,436. In 1982 there were 42,110 registered vehicles and 952 reported traffic accidents including 12 fatalities. Intercity bus service is available. Motor freight: 10 local and intrastate carriers. Rail: two main and one branch line carry freight through the county. The two main lines carry annually 20 to 30 million tons of freight each and the one branch carries less than one million. Aircraft: 35 are registered in the county. Airports: Jones Municipal Airport serves as a base for 27 aircraft and is a basic utility airport with general aviation service.

COMMUNITY SERVICES

EDUCATION Eight school districts with 12 elementary, four middle and seven high schools. The average daily attendance in 1981-82 was 6,494, with expenditures per pupil of $2,722 including 412 classroom teachers with an average annual salary of $15,776. Fifty-one percent of the 438 high school graduates planned to attend college. In 1982-83, 81% of the students were White, 1% Hispanic, 17% Black, 0.1% Asian and 0.1% American Indian. Private schools: 43 students enrolled in one elementary and one high school. Henderson County Junior College is located in Athens. Established in 1946 it is a vocational and two year academic college under state and local control. Enrollment in 1982 was 2,993 with in state undergraduate tuition and fees of $300 per semester. Sports championships: (Texas Junior College Football Conference) 1983 and (Texas Eastern Junior College Basketball Conference) 1983 Men's Championship. **PUBLIC LIBRARIES** Henderson County, Clint W. Murchison Memorial Library (Athens): 34,773 volumes and one branch. Malakoff Public Library: 22,268 volumes. **CHILD CARE** 47 day care and 10 twenty-four hour care licensed facilities. **HEALTH CARE** 24 physicians and 15 dentists. Hospitals: one with a capacity of 85. Ambulance services: one commercial and one volunteer fire department service. Mental health: one regional clinic and one development center with a capacity of 60. Nursing homes: four nursing homes with a combined capacity of 400 nursing care residents. The average cost per day for private patients in 1982 was $27.96. **CHURCHES** 100 churches have an estimated combined membership of 21,188. The largest denominations are Southern Baptist, United Methodist and Baptist Missionary. **SOCIAL SERVICES** In fiscal year 1983 a total of $1,460,096 in food stamps was distributed, with an average of 3,205 persons receiving food stamps each month. Aid to Families with Dependent Children (AFDC) totaled $375,502 with an average of 266 families receiving AFDC each month. Medical assistance benefits for the aged and disabled of $4,595,882 and for families and children of $534,117 brought the county benefit total to $6,965,597. **FIRE PROTECTION** One partly paid and 20 volunteer fire departments. **LAW ENFORCEMENT** The County Sheriff has 39 commissioned officers. 13 police departments have a combined force of 105. One college campus has a police department with a force of three officers. **CRIME** 92 violent crimes (murder, forcible rape, robbery and aggravated assault) and 1,243 nonviolent crimes (burglary, larceny-theft and motor vehicle theft) were reported in 1982. **JUDICIAL SYSTEM** Two District Courts and Judges, two County Courts and Judges and six Justices of the Peace. In the District Courts a total of 2,899 cases were pending on 1/1/82, 1,608 new cases were filed and 1,513 cases were disposed of during the year leaving 2,994 cases pending on 12/31/82. There were 566 criminal cases on the docket, 129 convictions, 20 persons committed to prison and 10 committed to jail and 329 cases left pending. In the County Courts 774 cases were pending on 1/1/82, 825 new cases were filed and 385 cases were disposed of during the year leaving 1,214 cases pending on 12/31/82. There were 1,291 criminal cases on the

HENDERSON (continued)

docket, 186 convictions, 78 persons committed to jail, and 956 cases left pending. **JAILS** One jail, capacity 44. **ATTORNEYS AT LAW** 34. **UTILITIES** 79% of the residents are connected to a public or privately owned water system and 32% are connected to a public sewer system. Natural gas is distributed to the county by Lone Star Gas Co., Division of Enserch. The average annual residential bill for natural gas in 1982 for the Lone Star distribution system was $405.91, an increase of 35% over 1981. Electricity is distributed to the county by Texas Power and Light Co., Kaufman Co. Electric Coop. Inc. and New Era Electric Coop., Inc. and is generated primarily by gas & coal. The typical residential electric bill is $165.24 per month for an all-electric house using 2,500 kwh. **TAXES** The county has 21 units with taxing authority: nine school districts, eight cities, one county, one college district and two special districts.

RECREATION/ENTERTAINMENT
NATIONAL REGISTER OF HISTORIC PLACES Athens: Faulk and Gaunt Building. **COUNTY/MUNICIPAL PARKS** 192 acres in six county and 12 municipal parks. These parks contain one mile of hiking trails, seven playgrounds, one golf course, two football and soccer fields, five baseball and softball fields, five tennis courts, two multi-use courts, two swimming pools, five beaches, 10 boat ramps and shore fishing facilities. Developed campsites: 27. **SCENIC DRIVES** The Texas Forest Trail and the Texas Lakes Trail run through this county. The Forest Trail explores the farming, ranching and oil field areas of the East Texas Pineywoods. The Lakes Trail introduces some 30 blue-water recreational areas in a variety of settings in North-Central Texas. **BOATING/FISHING** Lakes/reservoirs: Alder Creek (48 acres), Anding (79 acres), Athens (1,520 acres), Caddo Creek (284 acres), Catfish Creek Ranch (107 acres), Cedar Creek (33,750 acres), Closuit (71 acres), Creslenn Ranch (263 acres), Dennis (56 acres), Dragert (38 acres), Echo (148 acres), Fincastle (23 acres), Forest Grove (1,113 acres), Frontier City (27 acres), Hall (72 acres), Hollywood (49 acres), Jonsson (66 acres), Koon Kreek (267 acres), Koon Kreek Klub (89 acres), Mabank City (22 acres), Mawsy (24 acres), Murchison (90 acres), Palestine (25,560 acres), Perryman (31 acres), Rainbo (252 acres), Shelton (69 acres), Sportsmans (39 acres), Staway Ranch (95 acres), Trinidad City (68 acres), Trinidad (740 acres), Trinidad River East Laterals Soil Conservation Service Lakes 2, 3 and 4 (196 acres) and Underwood (68 acres). Major rivers: Trinity and Neches. Primary streams: Alder, Anding, Flat, Caddo, Catfish, Cedar, Little Alder, Bailey, Caney, Turkey, Selfs, Coon, North Twin, Shelton Mill, Prairie, Clear, Kite and Daniel. **HUNTING** Fall and winter seasons on deer. Summer, fall and winter seasons on squirrel. Winter season on quail, muskrat, beaver, otter, opossum, mink, ring-tailed cat, badger, fox, raccoon, skunk and civet cat. No closed season on nutria, bobcat and coyote. Spring season on turkey. In 1983 duck, coot, geese, woodcock and jacksnipe seasons occurred during the winter months. Teal duck, rail and gallinule seasons occurred in the fall. Mourning dove seasons occurred intermittently during the fall and winter months. **COLLEGIATE FINE ARTS** Athens: Cultural events offered by Henderson County Junior College. **SPECIAL EVENTS** Championship Hamburger Cookoff, Athens, March; Old Fiddlers Reunion, Athens, May; Black-eyed Pea Jamboree, Athens, July; Harvest Festival, Eustace, October.

COMMUNITIES
COUNTY SEAT Athens, County Courthouse, 75751; County Clerk's Office, 214/675-6141. **INCORPORATED COMMUNITIES** (1980 population and ZIP Code) Athens (10,197) 75751, Berryville (513) 75763, Brownsboro (582) 75756, Caney City (312) 75148, Chandler (1,308) 75758, Coffee City (254) 75763, Enchanted Oaks (212) 75147, Eustace (541) 75124, Gun Barrel City (2,118) 75147, Mabank (1,443: 156 in Henderson Co. and 1,287 in Kaufman Co.) 75147, Malakoff (2,082) 75148, Moore Station (335) 75770, Murchison (513) 75778, Payne Springs (422) 75124, Poynor (272) 75782, Seven Points (647) 75143, Star Harbor (310) 75148, Tool (1,591) 75143 and Trinidad (1,130) 75163. **UNINCORPORATED COMMUNITIES** (and ZIP Code) Aley 75143, Antioch 75758, Ash 75751, Baxter 75751, Bethel 75751, Blue Water Key 75758, Crescent Heights (Midway) 75751, Cross Roads 75148, Fincastle 75763, Forest Grove 75758, Larue 75770, Leagueville 75778, Mankin 75163, New Hope 75756, New York 75770, Opelika 75778, Pauline 75124, Pickens 75751, Stockard 75751 and Tri Cities 75751. **FOR ADDITIONAL LOCAL INFORMATION** Athens Chamber of Commerce, P.O. Box 608, Athens, 75751, 214/675-5181, Eustace Area Chamber of Commerce, P.O. Box 333, Edgar and Wheeler, Eustace, 75124, 214/425-3031, Mabank Chamber of Commerce, P.O. Box 201, Mabank, 75147, 214/887-0010, Malakoff Area Chamber of Commerce, P.O. Box 1042, Malakoff, 75148, 214/489-1518 and Cedar Creek Lake Chamber of Commerce, Seven Points, 75143, 214/432-3152.

HILDALGO (B28)

THE LAND
Bordering Mexico and southwest of Corpus Christi on U.S. Highways 281 and 83 in the Rio Grande Plain Region, Hidalgo county covers 1,569 square miles with an elevation range of 40 to 200 feet. The northern portion of the county has sandy soils and light colored loamy soils over deep reddish or mottled, clayey subsoils. To the south is a strip of loamy soils over deep reddish or mottled, clayey subsoils with limestone within 40 inches of the surface in some areas. The southern part of the county has loamy surfaces tht are deep to moderately deep over clayey subsoils. Along the Rio Grande River are high shrink-swell potential, brown to red soils with loamy surfaces and cracking, clayey subsoils or brown to red cracking and clayey soils. Hidalgo is in the South Texas Plains vegetation area with mid and tall grasses, mesquite and live oak trees. Mid to short grasses are in the north with mesquite, thorny shrubs and cacti in the rest of the county. Between 51 and 60% of the land in the county is considered prime farmland. **CLIMATE** Subtropical subhumid and Steppe with semi-arid conditions and hot summers. The average annual temperature is 73 °F. Temperatures in January range from an average low of 47 ° to an average high of 70 °F and in July range from 73 ° to 96 °F. The average annual precipitation is 23 inches, with an average relative humidity of 88% at 6 A.M. and 60% at 6 P.M. There is no yearly snowfall. The growing season averages 320 days per year, with the last freeze in early February and the first freeze in early December. The sun shines during the year on the average 68% of the daylight hours.

THE PEOPLE
Hidalgo County ranks 64th among all U.S. counties in the highest birth rate and 12th in highest percent of persons of Spanish origin. It is one of the most densely populated counties in the state. The 1982 estimated population of 315,100 indicates a continuation of the steady growth since 1930. Two-thirds of the county residents live in urban areas. The age groups with the largest gains were ages 62 and over and 20 to 24, with a median age of 24 in 1980. The largest ancestry groups are Hispanic (81%), persons of English descent (6%) and German descent (5%). **REGISTERED VOTERS** As of November 2, 1982 there were 108,708 registered voters (2% of the state total). The 1982 general election had a 45% voter turnout, compared to a 58% turnout in

the 1980 general election. In the 1982 primary 95% voted Democratic and 5% Republican, with 29,847 votes cast.

THE ECONOMY

AGRICULTURE The leading county in agricultural production. In 1982, 91% of the land was in farms and ranches, with 52% of the farmland under cultivation and 85% irrigated. Hidalgo ranked first in the state in highest agricultural receipts, with 94% from crops. Undesirable brush and weeds, wind erosion, inefficient irrigation systems and drainage are the current conservation problems. Primary crops: third in the state for sorghum, ninth for cotton and 10th for corn. Primary vegetables: first in the state for total fresh market vegetables and processed vegetables. First for cabbage, onions, cantaloupes and carrots, and fourth for watermelons. Primary fruits and nuts: grapefruit, oranges and pecans. Primary livestock and products: cattle, milk and hogs. **BUSINESS** Total number of business establishments in the county: 4,481. Retail sales during the first quarter of 1984 increased by 17%. In 1980, 8% of the labor force were self-employed, 21% were employed in professional or related services, 11% in manufacturing, 25% in wholesale and retail trade, 13% in agriculture, forestry, fisheries and mining, 5% were employed in other counties and there were 15,868 retired workers. The industries with the most employment: agribusiness, tourism, oil and gas field servicing, construction, meat packing, soft drink bottling and canning, the manufacturing of men's and women's clothing, cardboard boxes, men's leather shoes, gaskets, packing and sealing devices, farm machinery and equipment, surgical and medical equipment, concrete, gypsum and plaster products and the processing of canned, dehydrated and frozen fruits and vegetables. The nonfarm earnings in 1981 totaled $1,575,879,000. The retired workers received an average monthly Social Security payment of $282. **FINANCE** On June 30, 1983, 23 commercial banks had total deposits of $1,658,961,000 and total assets of $1,873,731,000. On December 31, 1982 three state savings and loan associations, one federal association, 15 state branches and six federal branches had combined assets of $682,373,777. In addition there are 12 credit unions in the county. **HOUSING** Average value of homes in 1980: $24,200. Permits for new, privately owned housing units decreased in 1982: 2,639 permits were issued with a total construction cost of $106,340,675. Of those permits, 1,363 were for single family houses. Between 1970 and 1980 the number of housing units increased by 76%. Fifty-four percent of all units in the county are air-conditioned, 70% are heated by gas and 30% by electricity. **NATURAL RESOURCES** Caliche, sand, gravel, oil and gas. In 1982 a total of 98,487,211 thousand cubic feet of gas well gas, 1,101,666 barrels of condensate, 139,995 barrels of crude oil and 515,784 thousand cubic feet of casinghead gas were produced. Current production of other minerals and products includes caliche, sand and gravel. **TOURISM** Travel expenditures of $188,823,000 in 1982 (an increase of 13% over 1981) generated 3,971 jobs and $34,777,000 in payroll. Lodging: 25 hotels, motels and tourist courts. Convention/meeting facilities: Edinburg-Pan American University Fieldhouse and Stadium; McAllen-International Civic Center and four hotels with facilities for large gathers; Mercedes-Rio Grande Valley Livestock Show Exhibit Area and Arena. **ALCOHOLIC BEVERAGES** Packaged distilled spirits, beer, ale, malt liquor and wine are legal. Sale of mixed beverages is legal in all or parts of the county. **FEDERAL EXPENDITURES** The federal government had direct expenditures or obligations of $360,570,000 in the county during fiscal year 1983, including $53,025,000 by the U.S. Department of Defense. In addition, the federal government provided $37,071,000 in grant awards, paid $27,705,000 in salaries and wages, made direct payments to individuals of $242,074,000 including $190,184,000 in retirement and disability payments, awarded $45,905,000 in procurement

contracts and spent $7,816,000 in other expenditures or obligations. The federal government also provided $12,740,000 in direct loans and $185,381,000 in guaranteed loans and insurance.

COMMUNICATION

Newspapers–Daily: Hidalgo Review (Edinburg), ave. eve. circ. 5,050 and The Monitor (McAllen) ave. eve. circ. 21,880. Weekly: The Mercedes Enterprise, Pharr Press and the Weslaco Mid Valley News. Radio: KJAV-FM (Alamo), KURV-AM (Edinburg), KIRT-AM, KRIO-AM, KOXX-FM, KBFM-FM Stereo (McAllen), KUMV-FM (Pharr), KRGV-AM (Weslaco). Television: KRGV CH. 5 (Weslaco). Telephone companies: General Telephone, Southwestern Bell and Valley Telephone Coop. **TRANSPORTATION** Total public road mileage: 3,091. In 1982 there were 184,921 registered vehicles and 5,964 reported traffic accidents including 75 fatalities. Taxi cabs: 22 companies in McAllen, six in Edinburg; three each in Pharr, the city of Hidalgo and Weslaco; two each in Mission, San Juan and Mercedes; and one in Donna. Municipal transit systems: one intercity bus system headquartered in Harlingen (Cameron County) provides some service as an intracity carrier, primarily in McAllen. This system operates in the McAllen-Pharr-Edinburg area. Intercity bus service is available. Motor freight: 47 local and intrastate carriers. Rail: three branch lines carry freight through the county with all three branches carrying annually less than one million tons of freight each. Aircraft: 405 are registered in the county. Airports: Mid Valley Municipal Airport at Weslaco serves as a base for 25 aircraft and is a general utility airport with general aviation service. Others serving the area are International Airport at Edinburg, Norman and White Airport at Edinburg, Burch Airstrip at Edinburg, Miller International Airport at McAllen and Old Reb Airport at Mercedes. Domestic and foreign exports by air from Hidalgo average 325 thousand pounds per month and imports average 25 thousand pounds per month.

COMMUNITY SERVICES

EDUCATION 15 school districts with 82 elementary, 18 middle and 12 high schools. The average daily attendance in 1981-82 was 76,487, with expenditures per pupil of $2,247 including 4,374 classroom teachers with an average annual salary of $15,338. Forty-four percent of the 4,040 high school graduates planned to attend college. In 1982-83, 7% of the students were White, (93%) Hispanic and (0.1%) Black. Private schools: 2,803 students enrolled in 16 elementary and two high schools. Pan American University is located in Edinburg. Established in 1927 it is under state control. Enrollment in 1982 was 9,450 with in state undergraduate tuition and fees of $290 per semester. The highest degree offered is Master. Vocational education: McAllen-Barber College, Vogue Beauty School, Vivian Harmon School of Modeling, Phyllis Jennings School of Modeling, Pharr Vocational School, Valley School of Business, Inc. Weslaco-Knapp Memorial Methodist Hospital School of Vocational Nursing. **PUBLIC LIBRARIES** Alamo Library. Donna Public Library: 21,000 volumes. Edinburg Public Library: 40,000 volumes. Elsa Public Library: 14,822 volumes. Hidalgo County Library System (McAllen): 351,860 volumes. McAllen Memorial Library: 136,607 volumes. Mercedes Memorial Library: 20,447 volumes. Speer Memorial Library (Mission): 40,000 volumes. Pharr Memorial Library: 41,019 volumes. Weslaco Public Library: 25,880 volumes. **CHILD CARE** 365 day care and 33 twenty-four hour care licensed facilities. **HEALTH CARE** 254 physicians and 62 dentists. Hospitals: five with a combined capacity of 834. Specialized hospitals: one obstetrics hospital with capacity of six. Clinics: one cancer treatment clinic, one dialysis clinic, one public health clinic and one minor emergency center. Ambulance services: seven commercial, two volunteer services, one city, one funeral home, one fire department, one hospital based and one air service.

COUNTIES

HIDALGO (continued)

Mental health: nine clinics and one center with capacity of 10. Nursing homes: 12 nursing homes with a combined capacity of 1,009 nursing care residents. The average cost per day for private patients in 1982 was $32.21. **CHURCHES** 211 churches have an estimated combined membership of 188,894. The largest denominations are Catholic and Southern Baptist. **SOCIAL SERVICES** In fiscal year 1983 a total of $52,068,195 in food stamps was distributed, with an average of 103,269 persons receiving food stamps each month. Aid to Families with Dependent Children (AFDC) totaled $7,107,190 with an average of 4,531 families receiving AFDC each month. Medical assistance benefits for the aged and disabled of $18,432,628 and for families and children of $8,575,350 brought the county benefit total to $86,183,362. **FIRE PROTECTION** One paid, two partly paid and 12 volunteer fire departments. **LAW ENFORCEMENT** The County Sheriff has 167 commissioned officers. 30 police departments have a combined force of 602. One university campus has a police department with a force of 12 officers. **CRIME** 1,195 violent crimes (murder, forcible rape, robbery and aggravated assault) and 13,276 nonviolent crimes (burglary, larceny-theft and motor vehicle theft) were reported in 1982. **JUDICIAL SYSTEM** Six District Courts and Judges, four County Courts and Judges and nine Justices of the Peace. In the District Courts a total of 4,521 cases were pending on 1/1/82, 5,216 new cases were filed and 4,914 cases were disposed of during the year leaving 4,823 cases pending on 12/31/82. There were 1,451 criminal cases on the docket, 489 convictions, 127 persons committed to prison and 20 committed to jail and 669 cases left pending. In the County Courts 1,568 cases were pending on 1/1/82, 4,943 new cases were filed and 3,222 cases were disposed of during the year leaving 3,289 cases pending on 12/31/82. There were 6,511 criminal cases on the docket, 1,662 convictions, 434 persons committed to jail, and 3,289 cases left pending. **JAILS** One jail, capacity 213, completed major renovation in 1983. **ATTORNEYS AT LAW** 326. **UTILITIES** 94% of the residents are connected to a public or privately owned water system and 73% are connected to a public sewer system. Natural gas is distributed to the county by Rio Grande Valley Gas Co. The average annual residential bill for natural gas in 1982 for the Rio Grande distribution system was $245.19, an increase of 25% over 1981. Electricity is distributed to the county by Central Power and Light, Cochran Power and Light Co. and Magic Valley Electric Coop., Inc. and is generated primarily by gas, oil and coal. The typical residential electric bill is $162.15 per month for an all-electric house using 2,500 kwh. **TAXES** The county has 41 units with taxing authority: 16 school districts, 15 cities, one county and nine special districts.

RECREATION/ENTERTAINMENT

NATIONAL REGISTER OF HISTORIC PLACES Hidalgo: Old Hidalgo Courthouse and Building and Old Hidalgo School, La Lomita Historic District. Linn vicinity: El Sal Del Rey Archeological District. **STATE** Bentsen-Rio Grande State Park covers 588 acres with camping and trailer sites as well as fishing and nature trails. **COUNTY/MUNICIPAL PARKS** 1,596 acres in six county and 91 municipal parks. These parks contain seven miles of hiking trails, 70 playgrounds, three golf courses, two football and soccer fields, 31 baseball and softball fields, 41 tennis courts, 14 multi-use courts, 13 swimming pools, one boat ramp and shore fishing facilities. **SCENIC DRIVES** The Texas Tropical Trail runs through this county. This trail is charted through the state's southernmost wedge meandering through ranchland, resort areas on the Gulf of Mexico and fertile farmlands. **BOATING/FISHING** Lakes/reservoirs: Boeye (90 acres), Carlson Settling Basin (161 acres), Delta 1 (531 acres), Delta 2 (2,371 acres), Donna 1 (305 acres), Donna 2 (108 acres), Engelman Gardens (52 acres), La Joya (243 acres), Mercedes Settling Basin (1,050 acres), Penitas (70 acres), Retama (2,462 acres) and Valley Acres (906 acres). Major rivers: Rio Grande. Primary streams: Main Branch Northeast Canal and La Joya. **WILDLIFE REFUGES** Las Palomas State Wildlife Management area covers 409 acres in this county. Also located in Hidalgo County is Santa Ana National Wildlife Refuge, spanning 2,430 acres. **HUNTING** Fall and winter season on deer. No closed season on javelina, squirrel, coyote and bobcat. Winter seasons on chachalaca, quail, muskrat, beaver, opossum, ring-tailed cat, badger, fox, weasel, raccoon, skunk and civet cat. Spring season on turkey. In 1983 sandhill crane, duck, coot, geese, woodcock and jacksnipe seasons occurred during the winter months. Teal duck, rail and gallinule seasons occurred in the fall. Mourning dove seasons occurred intermittently during the fall and winter months with a fall season on white-winged dove. **MUSEUMS** Alamo: Live Steam Museum. Donna: Donna Hooks Fletcher Museum. Edinburg: Hidalgo County Historical Museum. McAllen: McAllen International Museum. Mission: La Lomita Museum and Farms. Pharr: Old Clock Museum. Weslaco: Bi-Cultural Museum and World's Smallest Telephone Museum. **DANCE** McAllen: Rio Grande Valley Ballet Foundation and Rio Grande Valley Civic Ballet. **COLLEGIATE FINE ARTS** Edinburg: Cultural events offered by Pan American University. **OTHER** San Juan: Shrine of La Virgen de San Juan del Valle. **SPECIAL EVENTS** Texas Citrus Fiesta, Mission, January; South Texas Lamb and Sheep Exposition, Donna, January; Winter Texan Week, Pharr, February; Pool Tourney, Pharr, February; Sport Shirt Festival, San Juan, February; Square Dance Jamboree, Pharr, February; Illinois Picnic, McAllen, February; Sugarfest, Weslaco, February; Junior Stock Show, Mercedes, February; Michigan/Texas Picnic, McAllen, February; Rio Ramblers Volksmarch, Pharr, February; Rodeo, Mission, February; Rio Grande Valley Stock Show, Mercedes, March; Fiesta Hidalgo, Edinburg, March; Taste of the Valley, McAllen, March; Fajita Cookoff, McAllen, July; Pan American Bronco Days and Rodeo, Edinburg, November; All-Valley Winter Vegetable Show and Parade, Pharr, December; Poinsettia Show, Mission, December.

COMMUNITIES

COUNTY SEAT Edinburg, County Courthouse, 78539; County Clerk's Office, 512/383-2751. **INCORPORATED COMMUNITIES** (1980 population and ZIP Code) Alamo (5,831) 78516, Alton (2,732) 78572, Donna (9,952) 78537, Edcouch (3,092) 78538, Edinburg (24,075) 78539, All-America cities award 1968, Elsa (5,061) 78543, Hidalgo (2,288) 78557, La Joya (2,018) 78560, LaVilla (1,442) 78562, McAllen (66,281) 78501, Mercedes (11,851) 78570, Mission (22,589) 78572, Palmhurst (364) 78572, Palmview (683) 78539, Pharr (21,381) 78577, Progreso Lakes (222, est. incorp. inactive) 78579, San Juan (7,608) 78589 and Weslaco (19,331) 78596. **UNINCORPORATED COMMUNITIES** (and ZIP Code) Abram 78572, Campo Alto 78516, Chihuahua 78572, Citrus City 78572, Curvitas (Cuevitas) 78565, El Gato 78516, Engelman (Engelman Gardens) 78543, Faysville 78539, Granjeno 78572, Hargill 78549, Havana 78572, Heidelberg 78570, La Blanca 78558, La Tijera (Scissors) 78537, Las Milpas 78577, Linn 78563, Lopezville 78589, Los Ebanos 78565, Lull 78539, Madero 78572, McCook 78539, Monte Alto 78538, Penitas 78576, Perezville 78572, Progreso 78579, Puerto Rico 78563, Red Gate 78539, Relampago 78570, Rio Farms 78538, Rio Rico 78570, Rogerslacy 78593, Small 75117, San Carlos 78539, San Juan Community 78539, Stockholm 78569, Sullivan City 78595 and Thayer 78570. **FOR ADDITIONAL LOCAL INFORMATION** Donna Chamber of Commerce, 129 S. 8th, Donna, 78537, 512/464-3272, Edinburg Chamber of Commerce, P.O. Box 85, Edinburg, 78539, 512/383-4974, Hidalgo Chamber of Commerce, P.O. Box 309,

Hidalgo, 78557, 512/843-2734, McAllen Chamber of Commerce, P.O. Box 790, McAllen, 78502, 512/682-2871, Mecedes Chamber of Commerce, 534 E. 2nd St., Mercedes, 78570, 512/565-2221, Mission Chamber of Commerce, P.O. Box 431, Mission, 78572, 512/585-2727, Pharr Chamber of Commerce, P.O. Drawer X, Pharr, 78577, 512/787-1481 and Weslaco Chamber of Commerce, 519 S. Texas, Weslaco, 78596, 512/968-2102.

HILL (C3)

THE LAND

North of Waco on Interstate Highway 35 in the Blackland Prairies Region, Hill County covers 968 square miles with an elevation range of 500 to 800 feet. The eastern and west central portions of the county have undulating slightly acidic soils with dark loamy surfaces over clayey subsoils and acidic, clayey soils. The area has a high shrink-swell potential. The central part of the county has very dark loamy soils and in the west are level to undulating soils that have loamy or sandy surfaces over red or mottled, clayey or loamy subsoils. Along the Brazos River are undulating to hilly, alkaline soils that are light colored and well drained or very dark, loamy soils throughout with lime accumulations in the subsoils. The western part of Hill is in the Cross Timbers and Prairies vegetation area with tall and mid grasses and live oak, mesquite and juniper trees. The eastern part is in the Blackland Prairies vegetation area with tall grasses and mesquite, pecan, oak and elm trees along streams. Between 41 and 50% of the land in the county is considered prime farmland. **CLIMATE** Generally mild with hot summers. The average annual temperature is 66°F. Temperatures in January range from an average low of 33° to an average high of 57°F and in July range from 73° to 97°F. The average annual precipitation is 34 inches, with an average relative humidity of 83% at 6 A.M. and 53% at 6 P.M. The average annual snowfall is two inches. The growing season averages 260 days per year, with the last freeze in late March and the first freeze in late November. The sun shines during the year on the average 66% of the daylight hours.

THE PEOPLE

The 1982 estimated population of 25,800 continues the moderate growth which began in the 1970s. The majority of residents live in rural areas which experienced a growth of 15% between 1970 and 1980. The county population is older than average although the median age lowered from 41 in 1970 to 39 in 1980. The largest ancestry groups are persons of English descent (26%), Irish descent (25%) and German descent (13%). **REGISTERED VOTERS** As of November 2, 1982 there were 13,142 registered voters (0.2% of the state total). The 1982 general election had a 50% voter turnout, compared to a 66% turnout in the 1980 general election. In the 1982 primary 98% voted Democratic and 2% Republican, with 5,000 votes cast.

THE ECONOMY

AGRICULTURE Sorghum and wheat area. In 1982, 79% of the land was in farms and ranches, with 51% of the farmland under cultivation and 1% irrigated. Hill ranked 37th in the state in highest agricultural receipts, with 52% from livestock and livestock products. Overgrazing, water erosion and inefficient tillage systems are the current conservation problems. Primary crops: Sorghum, wheat, hay, cotton, oats and peanuts. Primary vegetables: potatoes, sweet potatoes, tomatoes and watermelons. Primary fruits and nuts: peaches and pecans. Primary livestock and products: sixth in the state for turkeys. Cattle, milk and hogs. **BUSINESS** Total number of business establishments in the county: 473. Retail sales during the first quarter of 1984 increased 13%. In 1980, 16% of the labor force were self-employed, 20%

were employed in professional or related services, 21% in manufacturing, 20% in wholesale and retail trade, 10% in agriculture, forestry, fisheries and mining, 24% were employed in other counties and there were 3,894 retired workers. The industries with the most employment: agribusiness, heavy construction, and the manufacture of women's clothing, mattresses and bedsprings, lime, copper wire, residential lighting fixtures and asbestos products. The nonfarm earnings in 1981 totaled $198,358,000. The retired workers received an average monthly Social Security payment of $287. **FINANCE** On June 30, 1983, seven commercial banks had total deposits of $139,875,000 and total assets of $164,344,000. There are three state savings and loan association branches and one federal association branch in the county. **HOUSING** Average value of homes in 1980: $20,000. Permits for new, privately owned housing units increased in 1982: 17 permits were issued with a total construction cost of $805,855. Of those permits, 15 were for single family houses. Between 1970 and 1980 the number of housing units increased by 24%. Seventy-One percent of all units in the county are air-conditioned, 81% are heated by gas and 15% by electricity. **NATURAL RESOURCES** Limestone, sand and gravel, oil and gas. In 1982 a total of 1,914 barrels of crude oil and 92 thousand cubic feet of casinghead gas were produced. Current production of other minerals and products includes lime and crushed limestone. **TOURISM** Travel expenditures of $4,301,000 in 1982 (an increase of 14% over 1981) generated 82 jobs and $733,000 in payroll. **ALCOHOLIC BEVERAGES** Packaged distilled spirits, beer, ale, malt liquor and wine are legal in parts of the county. **FEDERAL EXPENDITURES** The federal government had direct expenditures or obligations of $60,524,000 in the county during fiscal year 1983, including $4,454,000 by the U.S. Department of Defense. In addition, the federal government provided $1,709,000 in grant awards, paid $1,859,000 in salaries and wages, made direct payments to individuals of $52,557,000 including $37,447,000 in retirement and disability payments, awarded $2,759,000 in procurement contracts and spent $1,638,000 in other expenditures or obligations. The federal government also provided $1,285,000 in direct loans and $4,196,000 in guaranteed loans and insurance.

COMMUNICATION

Newspapers–Weekly: The Reporter (Hillsboro), The Hubbard City News, Itasca Item, Whitney Messenger and The Whitney Star. Radio: KHBR-AM and KHBR-FM (Hillsboro). Cable TV. Telephone companies: Continental Telephone, General Telephone, Southwestern Bell and Texas-Midland Telephone. **TRANSPORTATION** Total public road mileage: 1,746. In 1982 there were 25,097 registered vehicles and 510 reported traffic accidents including eight fatalities. Taxi cabs: one company in Hillsboro. Intercity bus service is available. Motor freight: six local and intrastate carriers. Rail: The Eagle provides passenger service on the Amtrak Route. Three main and two branch lines carry freight through the county. One of the main lines carries annually over 30 million tons of freight, one carries 20 to 30 and the other one carries 10 to 20. The two branches carry annually less than one million tons of freight each. Aircraft: 28 are registered in the county. Airports: Hillsboro Municipal Airport serves as a base for 10 aircraft and is a basic utility airport with general aviation service. Also serving the area are Lake Whitney State Park at Whitney and Reece Ranch Airport at Itasca.

COMMUNITY SERVICES

EDUCATION 12 school districts with 14 elementary, four middle and 10 high schools. The average daily attendance in 1981-82 was 4,163, with expenditures per pupil of $2,273 including 281 classroom teachers with an average annual salary of $14,929. Sixty-eight percent of the 295 high school graduates planned to

HILL (continued)

attend college. In 1982-83, 76% of the students were White, 9% Hispanic, 15% Black and 0.2% Asian. Hill Junior College is located in Hillsboro. Established in 1962 it is a vocational and two year academic college under local control. Enrollment in 1982 was 702 with in state undergraduate tuition and fees of $380 per semester. **PUBLIC LIBRARIES** Hillsboro City Library: 22,998 volumes. Mount Calm Library. **CHILD CARE** 48 day care and nine twenty-four hour care licensed facilities. **HEALTH CARE** 20 physicians and seven dentists. Hospitals: three with a combined capacity of 194. Ambulance services: two hospital-based, one funeral home and one city service. Mental health: one county clinic. Nursing homes: six nursing homes with a combined capacity of 575 nursing care residents. The average cost per day for private patients in 1982 was $29.50. **CHURCHES** 84 churches have an estimated combined membership of 15,375. The largest denominations are Southern Baptist, United Methodist and Catholic. **SOCIAL SERVICES** In fiscal year 1983 a total of $1,309,987 in food stamps was distributed, with an average of 2,897 persons receiving food stamps each month. Aid to Families with Dependent Children (AFDC) totaled $267,861 with an average of 174 families receiving AFDC each month. Medical assistance benefits for the aged and disabled of $4,270,906 and for families and children of $398,859 brought the county benefit total to $6,247,613. **FIRE PROTECTION** One partly paid and 13 volunteer fire departments. **LAW ENFORCEMENT** The County Sheriff has 29 commissioned officers. Nine police departments have a combined force of 37. **CRIME** 46 violent crimes (murder, forcible rape, robbery and aggravated assault) and 655 nonviolent crimes (burglary, larceny-theft and motor vehicle theft) were reported in 1982. **JUDICIAL SYSTEM** One District Court and Judge, one County Court and Judge and four Justices of the Peace. In the District Court a total of 1,633 cases were pending on 1/1/82, 1,412 new cases were filed and 1,182 cases were disposed of during the year leaving 1,863 cases pending on 12/31/82. There were 1,717 criminal cases on the docket, 470 convictions, 25 persons committed to prison and 43 committed to jail and 938 cases left pending. **JAILS** One jail, capacity 22, constructing new jail, capacity 40. **ATTORNEYS AT LAW** 25. **UTILITIES** 91% of the residents are connected to a public or privately owned water system and 51% are connected to a public sewer system. Natural gas is distributed to the county by Lonestar Gas Co., Division of Enserch. The average annual residential bill for natural gas in 1982 for the Lone Star distribution system was $405.91, an increase of 35% over 1981. Electricity is distributed to the county by Texas Power and Light Co., Texas-New Mexico Power Co., Limestone Co. Electric Coop., Inc. and Navarro Co. Electric Coop., Inc. and is generated primarily by gas, coal, oil and water. The typical residential electric bill is $165.24 per month for an all-electric house using 2,500 kwh. **TAXES** The county has 26 units with taxing authority: 12 school districts, eleven cities, one county, one college district and one special district.

RECREATION/ENTERTAINMENT
NATIONAL REGISTER OF HISTORIC PLACES Blum vicinity: Sheep Cave. Hillsboro: Missouri-Kansas-Texas Company Railroad Station and Hill County Courthouse and Jail. Hillsboro vicinity: McKenzie Site. Itasca vicinity: Joe E. Turner House. Lake Whitney vicinity: Bear Creek Shelter, Buzzard Cave, Kyle Shelter and Pictograph Cave. **STATE** Jeff Davis State Recreation Area covers 38 acres. Lake Whitney State Recreation Area covers 955 acres with camping sites as well as areas offering fishing, swimming, boat ramps and airstrips. **COUNTY/MUNICIPAL PARKS** 567 acres in two county and 10 municipal parks. These parks contain five miles of hiking trails, seven playgrounds, one football and soccer field, three baseball and softball fields, three tennis courts, one multi-use court, five beaches, five boat ramps and shore fishing facilities. Developed campsites: 25. **SCENIC DRIVES** The Texas Lakes Trail runs through this county. This trail introduces some 30 blue-water recreational areas in a variety of settings in North-Central Texas. **BOATING/FISHING** Lakes/reservoirs: Aquilla (3,280 acres), Chambers Creek Soil Conservation Service Lakes 65A, 67B, 72 and 74 (65 acres), Katy (30 acres), Keenan (21 acres), Richland Creek Soil Conservation Service Lakes 38, 63, 82 and 93 (53 acres), Tehuacana Creek Soil Conservation Service Lakes 1A, 1 and 7 (41 acres) and Lake Whitney (23,750 acres). Major rivers: Brazos Primary streams: Aquilla, Island, Majors, Itasca, Bond, Bear, Richland, Grove, Ash, Cottonwood, Tehuacana and Wolf. **HUNTING** Fall and winter seasons on deer. No closed seasons on nutria, squirrel, coyote and bobcat. Winter seasons on quail, muskrat, beaver, otter, opossum, mink, ring-tailed cat, badger, fox, raccoon, skunk and civet cat. In 1983 duck, coot, geese, woodcock and jacksnipe seasons occurred during the winter months. Teal duck, rail and gallinule seasons occurred in the fall. Mourning dove seasons occurred intermittently during the fall and winter months. **MUSEUMS** Hillsboro: Confederate Researach Center and Gun Museum. Itasca: Itasca Museum and Recreation Center. **COLLEGIATE FINE ARTS** Hillsboro: Cultural events offered by Hill Junior College. **SPECIAL EVENTS** Lake Whitney Beauty Pageant, Whitney, Spring; County Fair, Hillsboro, March; Arts and Crafts Show, Hillsboro, June; Rodeo, Whitney, June; Quarter Horse Show, Hillsboro, June; Hill County Roundup and Rodeo, Hillsboro, July; Pioneer Day Celebration and Parade, Whitney, October.

COMMUNITIES
COUNTY SEAT Hillsboro, County Courthouse, 76645; County Clerk's Office, 817/582-2161. **INCORPORATED COMMUNITIES** (1980 population and ZIP Code) Abbott (359) 76621, Aquilla (130) 76622, Blum (357) 76627, Bynum (232) 76631, Covington (259) 76636, Hillsboro (7,397) 76645, Hubbard (1,676) 76648, Itasca (16,000) 76055, Malone (315) 76660, Mertens (133) 76673, Mount Calm (393) 7673, Penelope (235) 76676 and Whitney (1,631) 76692. **UNINCORPORATED COMMUNITIES** (and ZIP Code) Bethlehem 76692, Birome 76625, Bonanza 76692, Brandon 76628, Chat (Chatt) 76645, Files Valley 76055, Huron 76692, Irene 76650, Iverson 76670, Liberty Hill 76692, Lovelace 76645, Mayfield 76055, Menlow 76621, Midway 76645, Osceola 76055, Peoria 76645, Tarver 76692, Vaughan 76645, Woodbury 76645, Yetes 76692. **FOR ADDITIONAL LOCAL INFORMATION** Hillsboro Chamber of Commerce, P.O. Box 358, Hillsboro, 76645, 817/582-2481 or 582-9197 and Whitney Chamber of Commerce, P.O. Box 604, Whitney, 76645, 817/694-2540.

HOCKLEY (P38)

THE LAND
West of Lubbock on U.S. Highway 385 in the High Plains Region, Hockley County covers 908 square miles with an elevation range of 3,300 to 3,500 feet. The county has nearly level soils with mostly loamy surfaces and clayey subsoils. Some of the soils have hardened calcium or powdery lime within 20 inches of the surface. Hockley lies in the High Plains vegetation area with short and mid grasses interspersed with mesquite, thorny shrubs and cacti. Between 21 and 30% of the land in the county is considered prime farmland. **CLIMATE** Continental Steppe characterized by rapid changes in wind, temperature and precipitation, especially in winter and spring. The average annual temperature is 59°F. Temperatures in January range from an average low of

23° to an average high of 54°F and in July range from 65° to 92°F. The average annual precipitation is 17 inches, with an average relative humidity of 70% at 6 A.M. and 37% at 6 P.M. The average annual snowfall is 11 inches. The growing season averages 196 days per year, with the last freeze in mid April and the first freeze in late October. The sun shines during the year on the average 75% of the daylight hours.

THE PEOPLE

The pattern of gradual population growth in Hockley County was restored in the 1970s after a short period of decline. The 1982 estimated population of 24,100 continues that growth rate. Residents in urban areas increased 21% between 1970 and 1980, while rural areas grew at a slower rate. The county's population is younger than average with a median age of 26. The largest ancestry groups are Hispanic (27%), persons of English descent (21%) and Irish descent (19%). **REGISTERED VOTERS** As of November 2, 1982 there were 11,758 registered voters (0.2% of the state total). The 1982 general election had a 39% voter turnout, compared to a 65% turnout in the 1980 general election. In the 1982 primary 98% voted Democratic and 2% Republican, with 3,473 votes cast.

THE ECONOMY

AGRICULTURE Cotton area. In 1982, 94% of the land was in farms and ranches, with 74% of the farmland under cultivation and 47% irrigated. Hockley ranked 47th in the state in highest agricultural receipts, with 91% from crops. Wind erosion, decreasing irrigation water supplies, moisture conservation and noxious weeds are the current conservation problems. Primary crops: fifth in the state for sorghum, cotton, wheat, sunflowers and soybeans. Primary vegetables: cucumbers, onions, bell peppers, sweet potatoes and watermelons. Primary fruits and nuts: peaches and pecans. Primary livestock and products: cattle and hogs. **BUSINESS** Total number of business establishments in the county: 470. Retail sales during the first quarter of 1984 increased 16%. In 1980, 14% of the labor force were self-employed, 18% were employed in professional or related services, 5% in manufacturing, 18% in wholesale and retail trade, 33% in agriculture, forestry, fisheries and mining, 16% were employed in other counties and there were 1,429 retired workers. The industries with the most employment: agribusiness, oil and gas extraction, heavy construction and cottonseed oil mills. The nonfarm earnings in 1981 totaled $202,233,000. The retired workers received an average monthly Social Security payment of $326. **FINANCE** On June 30, 1983, five commercial banks had total deposits of $231,985,000 and total assets of $258,398,000. On December 31, 1982 one federal savings and loan association, one state branch and one federal branch had assets of $59,080,159. In addition there is one credit union in the county. **HOUSING** Average value of homes in 1980: $29,200. Permits for new, privately owned housing units increased in 1982: 172 permits were issued with a total construction cost of $5,623,418. Of those permits, 65 were for single family houses. Housing permits in Levelland increased from 51 in 1981 to 151 in 1982 with 107 of the permits issued for apartments and condominiums. Between 1970 and 1980 the number of housing units increased by 20%. Eight-four percent of all units in the county are air-conditioned, 90% are heated by gas and 10% by electricity. **NATURAL RESOURCES** Brine, caliche, limestone, oil, gas and potash. In 1982 a total of 521,410 thousand cubic feet of gas well gas, 5,318 barrels of condensate, 39,220,773 barrels of crude oil and 18,075,624 thousand cubic feet of casinghead gas were produced. Current production of other minerals and products includes brine, crushed limestone, sand and gravel, and sulphur. **TOURISM** Travel expenditures of $10,722,000 in 1982 (an increase of 16% over 1981) generated 176 jobs and $1,711,000

in payroll. **ALCOHOLIC BEVERAGES** Totally dry. **FEDERAL EXPENDITURES** The federal government had direct expenditures or obligations of $51,680,000 in the county during fiscal year 1983, including $621,000 by the U.S. Department of Defense. In addition, the federal government provided $3,415,000 in grant awards, paid $1,282,000 in salaries and wages, made direct payments to individuals of $23,158,000 including $17,115,000 in retirement and disability payments, awarded $3,000 in procurement contracts and spent $23,822,000 in other expenditures or obligations. The federal government also provided $14,070,000 in direct loans and $40,550,000 in guaranteed loans and insurance.

COMMUNICATION

Newspapers–Weekly: Anton Star and The Levelland and Hockley County News-Press. Radio: KLVT-AM and KHOC-FM (Levelland). Cable TV. Telephone companies: General Telephone, Five-Area Telephone Coop., Poka-Lambro Rural Telephone Coop. and South Plains Telephone Coop. **TRANSPORTATION** Total public road mileage: 1,628. In 1982 there were 23,296 registered vehicles and 614 reported traffic accidents including 10 fatalities. Intercity bus service is available. Motor freight: 12 local and intrastate carriers. Rail: one main and two branch lines carry freight through the county. The main line carries annually 20 to 30 million tons of freight and the two branches carry less than one million each. Aircraft: 54 are registered in the county. Airports: Levelland Municipal Airport serves as a base for 40 aircraft and is a general utility airport with general aviation services. McNabb Farms Airport at Ropesville.

COMMUNITY SERVICES

EDUCATION Six school districts with nine elementary, four middle and six high schools. The average daily attendance in 1981-82 was 4,675, with expenditures per pupil of $3,788 including 380 classroom teachers with an average annual salary of $18,224. Sixty-four percent of the 301 high school graduates planned to attend college. In 1982-83, 57% of the students were White, 38% Hispanic, 5% Black, 0.1% Asian and 0.1% American Indian. Sports championships: 1983 A Girls' Golf Team, Sundown H.S. Private schools: 136 students enrolled in one elementary school. South Plains College is located in Levelland. Established in 1957 it is a vocational and two year academic college under state control. Enrollment in 1982 was 2,841 with in state undergraduate tuition and fees of $201 per semester. **PUBLIC LIBRARIES** Hockley County Memorial Library (Levelland): 23,600 volumes. **CHILD CARE** 32 day care and 12 twenty-four hour care licensed facilities. **HEALTH CARE** 10 physicians and five dentists. Hospitals: one with a capacity of 74. Clinics: one public health clinic. Ambulance services: three volunteer fire departments and one commercial service. Mental health: one clinic and one development center with capacity of 42. Nursing homes: one nursing home has a capacity of 89 nursing care residents. The average cost per day for private patients in 1982 was $31.23. **CHURCHES** 51 churches have an estimated combined membership of 16,992. The largest denominations are Southern Baptist, United Methodist and Catholic. **SOCIAL SERVICES** In fiscal year 1983 a total of $916,365 in food stamps was distributed, with an average of 1,987 persons receiving food stamps each month. Aid to Families with Dependent Children (AFDC) totaled $158,009 with an average of 104 families receiving AFDC each month. Medical assistance benefits for the aged and disabled of $1,154,734 and for families and children of $302,797 brought the county benefit total to $2,531,904. **FIRE PROTECTION** Six volunteer fire departments. **LAW ENFORCEMENT** The County Sheriff has 26 commissioned officers. Four police departments have a combined force of 33. One college campus has a police department with a force of six officers. **CRIME** 198 violent crimes (murder, forcible rape, robbery and aggravated assault) and 847

COUNTIES

HOCKLEY (continued)

nonviolent crimes (burglary, larceny-theft and motor vehicle theft) were reported in 1982. **JUDICIAL SYSTEM** One District Court and Judge, one County Court and Judge and four Justices of the Peace. In the District Court a total of 531 cases were pending on 1/1/82, 691 new cases were filed and 592 cases were disposed of during the year leaving 630 cases pending on 12/31/82. There were 199 criminal cases on the docket, 71 convictions, seven persons committed to prison and five committed to jail and 48 cases left pending. In the County Court 1,923 cases were pending on 1/1/82, 1,543 new cases were filed and 1,130 cases were disposed of during the year leaving 2,336 cases pending on 12/31/82. There were 2,838 criminal cases on the docket, 677 convictions, 79 persons committed to jail, and 1,773 cases left pending. **JAILS** One jail, capacity 25, constructing new jail, capacity 62. **ATTORNEYS AT LAW** 21. **UTILITIES** 78% of the residents are connected to a public or privately owned water system and 75% are connected to a public sewer system. Natural gas is distributed to the county by Energas Company. The average annual residential bill for natural gas in 1982 for the Energas distribution system was $371.63, an increase of 23% over 1981. Electricity is distributed to the county by Lamb Co. Electric Coop., Inc., Lyntegar Electric Coop., Inc., Southwestern Public Service and Southplains Electric Coop., Inc. and is generated primarily by gas and coal. The typical residential electric bill is $170.44 per month for an all-electric house using 2,500 kwh. **TAXES** The county has 14 units with taxing authority: six school districts, five cities, one county, one college district and one special district.

RECREATION/ENTERTAINMENT

MUNICIPAL PARKS 234 acres in 17 municipal parks. These parks contain 12 playgrounds, one golf course, four football and soccer fields, four baseball and softball fields, two tennis courts and two swimming pools. **SCENIC DRIVES** The Texas Plains Trail runs through this county. This trail spans a vast area of the High Plains region of Texas slicing through the southernmost extension of the Great Plains of the United States. The land is flat except where erosion has carved canyon landscapes. **BOATING/FISHING** Lakes/reservoirs: Silver (100 acres). Major rivers: Yellowhouse. **HUNTING** Fall season on antelope and prairie chicken. No closed seasons on squirrel, coyote and bobcat. Winter seasons on quail, muskrat, beaver, opossum, ringtailed cat, badger, fox, weasel, raccoon, skunk and civet cat. In 1983 sandhill crane, duck, coot, geese, woodcock and jacksnipe seasons occurred during the winter months. Teal duck, rail and gallinule seasons occurred in the fall. Mourning dove seasons occurred intermittently during the fall and winter months. **MUSEUMS** Levelland: South Plains Museum and South Plains College Art Museum. **DANCE** Levelland: Lubbock Area Square and Round Dance Federation. **COLLEGIATE FINE ARTS** Levelland: cultural events offered by South Plains College. **SPECIAL EVENTS** Country Caravan Music Extravaganza, Levelland, May-July; Early Settlers Reunion and Festivities, Levelland, July; Marigold Arts and Crafts Fair, Levelland, October/November.

COMMUNITIES

COUNTY SEAT Levelland, County Courthouse, 79336; County Clerk's Office, 806/894-3185. **INCORPORATED COMMUNITIES** (1980 population and ZIP Code) Anton (1,180) 79313, Levelland (13,809) 79336, Ropesville (489) 79358 and Sundown (1,511) 79372. **UNINCORPORATED COMMUNITIES** (and ZIP Code) Arnett 79336, Busterville 79358, Clauene 79336, Dean 79363, Lockettville 79358, Oklahoma Flat 79339, Opdyke 79336, Pep 79353, Pettit 79354, Roundup 79313, Smyer 79367 and Witharral 79380. **FOR ADDITIONAL LOCAL INFORMATION** Levelland Area Chamber of Commerce, 1101 Avenue H, Levelland, 79336, 806/894-3157.

HOOD (M16)

THE LAND

Southwest of Fort Worth on U.S. Highway 377 in the Cross Timbers Region, Hood County covers 425 square miles with an elevation range of 600 to 1,000 feet. To the east and in the western central portion of Hood County the undulating to hilly soils are either light colored browns and reds or very dark, loamy surfaces over loamy subsoils with an accumulation of lime. The remainder of the county has light colored soils with loamy or sandy surfaces and deep, red or mottled, clayey subsoils. In the Cross Timbers and Prairies vegetation area, the main prairie grasses are bluestems, Indiangrass and gramas. Brushy plants such as mesquite, oaks and juniper are heavy in areas. Between 31 and 40% of the land in the county is considered prime farmland. **CLIMATE** Subtropical subhumid, mild and dry with extremes in high and low temperatures from summer to winter. The average annual temperature is 66°F. Temperatures in January range from an average low of 33° to an average high of 56°F and in July range from 72° to 97°F. The average annual precipitation is 30 inches, with an average relative humidity of 78% at 6 A.M. and 52% at 6 P.M. The average annual snowfall is three inches. The growing season averages 240 days per year, with the last freeze in late March and the first freeze in mid November. The sun shines during the year on the average 67% of the daylight hours.

THE PEOPLE

Hood Conty ranks 6th among all U.S. counties in the highest growth rate between 1970 and 1980. The 1982 estimated population of 19,900 continues that strong growth rate of 178% between 1970 and 1980. From 1970 to 1980 rural areas experienced a population gain of 126%. The age groups with the largest gains were ages 20 to 34, which quadrupled in size, and birth to 19 years, which doubled in size. The county's population is older than average although the median age lowered from 38 in 1970 to 35 in 1980. The largest ancestry groups are persons of English descent (32%), Irish descent (27%) and German descent (15%). **REGISTERED VOTERS** As of November 2, 1982 there were 9,657 registered voters (0.2% of the state total). The 1982 general election had a 62% voter turnout, compared to a 74% turnout in the 1980 general election. In the 1982 primary 93% voted Democratic and 7% Republican, with 4,637 votes cast.

THE ECONOMY

AGRICULTURE In 1982, 84% of the land was in farms and ranches, with 30% of the farmland under cultivation and 6% irrigated. Hood ranked 186th in the state in highest agricultural receipts, with 74% from livestock and livestock products. Overgrazing, undesirable brush and weeds, water and wind erosion and livestock waste management are the current conservation problems. Primary crops: hay, wheat, oats and peanuts. Primary vegetables: potatoes. Primary fruits and nuts: peaches and first in the state for pecans. Primary livestock and products: cattle and milk. **BUSINESS** Total number of business establishments in the county: 330. Retail sales during the first quarter of 1984 increased 23%. In 1980, 12% of the labor force were self-employed, 12% were employed in professional or related services, 15% in manufacturing, 18% in wholesale and retail trade, 24% in construction, 49% were employed in other counties and there were 2,101 retired workers. The industries with the most employment: agribusiness, tourism and the manufacture of women's clothing and agricultural fertilizers. The nonfarm earnings in 1981 totaled $172,408,000. The retired workers received an average monthly Social Security payment of $321. **FINANCE** On June 30, 1983, three commercial banks had total deposits of $105,646,000 and total assets of $114,657,000. There are three state savings and loan association branches in the county. **HOUSING** Average value of homes in 1980: $44,000. Permits for new, privately owned housing units increased in 1982: 40 permits were issued with a total construction cost of $1,721,000. Of those permits, 24 were for single family houses. Housing permits in Granbury increased from eight in 1981 to 40 in 1982. Between 1970 and 1980 the number of housing units increased by 235%. Eighty-seven percent of all units in the county are air-conditioned, 59% are heated by gas and 37% by electricity. **NATURAL RESOURCES** Limestone, industrial sand, sand and gravel, oil and gas. In 1982 a total of 2,450,195 thousand cubic feet of gas well gas, 2,843 barrels of condensate, 74 barrels of crude oil and 17,389 thousand cubic feet of casinghead gas were produced. Current production of other minerals and products includes crushed limestone, sand and gravel. **TOURISM** Travel expenditures of $5,937,000 in 1982 (an increase of 12% over 1981) generated 129 jobs and $1,089,000 in payroll. **ALCOHOLIC BEVERAGES** Packaged distilled spirits, beer, ale, malt liquor and wine are legal in parts of the county. **FEDERAL EXPENDITURES** The federal government had direct expenditures or obligations of $38,059,000 in the county during fiscal year 1983, including $4,166,000 by the U.S. Department of Defense. In addition, the federal government provided $2,220,000 in grant awards, paid $1,186,000 in salaries and wages, made direct payments to individuals of $33,007,000 including $29,036,000 in retirement and disability payments, awarded $1,498,000 in procurement contracts and spent $149,000 in other expenditures or obligations. The federal government also provided $9,000 in direct loans and $4,954,000 in guaranteed loans and insurance.

COMMUNICATION
Newspapers–Weekly: The Granbury Tablet. Radio: KPAR-AM (Granbury). Cable TV. Telephone companies: Continental Telephone, Southwestern Bell, Lipan Telephone and Texas-Midland Telephone. **TRANSPORTATION** Total public road mileage: 592. In 1982 there were 19,633 registered vehicles and 428 reported traffic accidents including four fatalities. Intercity bus service is available. Motor freight: two carriers. Rail: two main and one branch line carry freight through the county. The two main lines carry annually five to 10 million tons of freight each and the one branch carries five to 10 million tons. Aircraft: 45 are registered in the county. Airports: Cherry Field Municipal Airport at Granbury serves as a base for 20 aircraft and is a basic utility airport with general aviation service. Bourland Field at Cresson.

COMMUNITY SERVICES
EDUCATION Three school districts with five elementary, one middle and three high schools. The average daily attendance in 1981-82 was 2,995, with expenditures per pupil of $1,947 including 177 classroom teachers with an average annual salary of $16,178. Sixty-nine percent of the 199 high school graduates planned to attend college. In 1982-83, 95% of the students were White, 4% Hispanic, 0.1% Black, 0.5% Asian and 0.1% American Indian. **PUBLIC LIBRARIES** Hood County Public Library (Granbury): 19,000 volumes. **CHILD CARE** 15 day care and five twenty-four hour care licensed facilities. **HEALTH CARE** 19 physicians and seven dentists. Hospitals: one with a capacity of 63. Ambulance services: one volunteer service, one hospital-based and one volunteer fire department service. Mental health: one clinic. Nursing homes: two nursing homes with a combined capacity of 209 nursing care residents. The average cost per day for private

patients in 1982 was $27.86. **CHURCHES** 32 churches have an estimated combined membership of 7,354. The largest denominations are Southern Baptist and United Methodist. **SOCIAL SERVICES** In fiscal year 1983 a total of $316,363 in food stamps was distributed, with an average of 637 persons receiving food stamps each month. Aid to Families with Dependent Children (AFDC) totaled $67,909 with an average of 47 families receiving AFDC each month. Medical assistance benefits for the aged and disabled of $1,662,709 and for families and children of $188,998 brought the county benefit total to $2,235,979. **FIRE PROTECTION** Eight volunteer fire departments. **LAW ENFORCEMENT** The County Sheriff has 24 commissioned officers. Two police departments have a combined force of 11. **CRIME** 12 violent crimes (murder, forcible rape, robbery and aggravated assault) and 434 nonviolent crimes (burglary, larceny-theft and motor vehicle theft) were reported in 1982. **JUDICIAL SYSTEM** One District Court and Judge, one County Court and Judge and two Justices of the Peace. In the District Court a total of 680 cases were pending on 1/1/82, 548 new cases were filed and 549 cases were disposed of during the year leaving 679 cases pending on 12/31/82. There were 153 criminal cases on the docket, 52 convictions, 19 persons committed to prison, and 46 cases left pending. In the County Court 1,737 cases were pending on 1/1/82, 928 new cases were filed and 2,121 cases were disposed of during the year leaving 544 cases pending on 12/31/82. There were 2,512 criminal cases on the docket, 116 convictions, 101 persons committed to jail, and 405 cases left pending. **JAILS** One jail, capacity 22. **ATTORNEYS AT LAW** 19. **UTILITIES** 78% of the residents are connected to a public or privately owned water system and 31% are connected to a public sewer system. Natural gas is distributed to the county by Lone Star Gas Co., Division of Enserch. The average annual residential bill for natural gas in 1982 for the Lone Star distribution system was $405.91, an increase of 35% over 1981. Electricity is distributed to the city of Granbury by the Granbury Municipal Electric Dept. and to the county by Erath Co. Electric Coop., Assn. and Johnson Electric Coop., Assn. and is generated primarily by water. **TAXES** The county has seven units with taxing authority: three school districts, two cities, one county and one utility district.

RECREATION/ENTERTAINMENT
NATIONAL REGISTER OF HISTORIC PLACES Granbury: Hood County Courthouse Historic District and Wright-Henderson-Duncan House. **STATE** Acton State Historic Site covers 0.006 acres and is the burial site of Davy Crockett's wife. **MUNICIPAL PARKS** 10 acres in three municipal parks. These parks contain three playgrounds, 30 baseball and softball fields, one swimming pool and one beach. **SCENIC DRIVES** The Texas Lakes Trail runs through this county. This trail introduces some 30 blue-water recreational areas in a variety of settings in North-Central Texas. **BOATING/FISHING** Lakes/reservoirs: Engler (22 acres), Granbury (8,700 acres), Smelley (28 acres) and Star Hollow (65 acres). Major rivers: Brazos. Primary streams: Fall, Robinson, Star Hollow and Weaver. **HUNTING** Fall and winter seasons on deer. No closed seasons on coyote, bobcat and squirrel. Winter seasons on quail, muskrat, beaver, opossum, ringtailed cat, badger, fox, weasel, raccoon, skunk and civet cat. Fall, winter and spring seasons on turkey. In 1983 duck, coot, geese, woodcock and jacksnipe seasons occurred during the winter months. Teal duck, rail and gallinule seasons occurred in the fall. Mourning dove seasons occurred intermittently during the fall and winter months. **THEATERS** Granbury: Granbury Opera House. **SPECIAL EVENTS** Bass Tourney, Granbury, April; Arts and Crafts Festival, Granbury, April; Junior Rodeo, Granbury, June; Independence Day Celebration, Granbury, July; Harvest of Arts Festival, Granbury, October.

COUNTIES

HOOD (continued)

COMMUNITIES

COUNTY SEAT Granbury, County Courthouse, 76048; County Clerk's Office, 817/573-1767. **INCORPORATED COMMUNITIES** (1980 population and ZIP Code) Granbury (3,332) 76048; Lipan (435) 76462 and Tolar (415) 76476. **UNINCORPORATED COMMUNITIES** (and ZIP Code) Acton 76048, Center Mill 76048, Cresson (also in Johnson Co.) 76035, Fairview 76048, Fort Spunky 76031, Hill City 76476, Mambrino 76048, Paluxy 76467, Thorp Spring 76048 and Waples 76048. **FOR ADDITIONAL LOCAL INFORMATION** Lake Granbury Area Chamber of Commerce, P.O. Box 277, Granbury, 76048, 817/573-1622.

HOPKINS (E5)

THE LAND

Northeast of Dallas on Interstate Highway 30 in the Blackland Prairies Region, Hopkins County covers 789 square miles with an elevation range of 350 to 650 feet. In the north and west the undulating soils are gray to black, cracking and clayey with some light colored, loamy surfaces. There is a high shrink-swell potential. Toward the southeast the nearly level to undulating soils are light colored and sandy with mottled, clayey subsoils. The north and west is in the Blackland Prairies vegetation area with a variety of trees along streams and grasses such as buffalograss and Texasgrama. The remainder of the county is in the Post Oak Savannah vegetation area with post and blackjack oak trees, tall grasses and some brush. Between 11 and 20% of the land in the county is considered prime farmland. **CLIMATE** Subtropical, generally mild and humid. Heavy thunderstorms in the spring and early summer. The average annual temperature is 63°F. Temperatures in January range from an average low of 31° to an average high of 54°F and in July range from 71° to 94°F. The average annual precipitation is 44 inches, with an average relative humidity of 83% at 6 A.M. and 56% at 6 P.M. The average annual snowfall is two inches. The growing season averages 234 days per year, with the last freeze in late March and the first freeze in mid November. The sun shines during the year on the average 67% of the daylight hours.

THE PEOPLE

The 1982 estimated population of 26,300 continues the steady growth begun in the 1960s. Gains in rural areas betwen 1970 and 1980 were slightly larger than those in urban areas. The county's population is older than average, although the median age lowered from 36 in 1970 to 33 in 1980. The largest ancestry groups are persons of English descent (30%), Irish descent (20%) and Black (10%). **REGISTERED VOTERS** As of November 2, 1982 there were 11,793 registered voters (0.2% of the state total). The 1982 general election had a 53% voter turnout, compared to a 68% turnout in the 1980 general election. In the 1982 primary 97% voted Democratic and 3% Republican, with 4,010 votes cast.

THE ECONOMY

AGRICULTURE Cattle and dairy area. In 1982, 74% of the land was in farms and ranches, with 25% of the farmland under cultivation. Hopkins ranked seventh in the state in highest agricultural receipts, with 98% from livestock and livestock products. Overgrazing and difficulties in grass establishment are the current conservation problems. Primary crops: first in the state for hay. Wheat, soybeans, oats, rye and sorghum. Primary vegetables: sweet potatoes, tomatoes and watermelons. Primary fruits and nuts: peaches and pecans. Primary livestock and products: first in the state in milk production and second for cattle.

Hogs. **BUSINESS** Total number of business establishments in the county: 465. Retail sales during the first quarter of 1984 increased 25%. In 1980, 16% of the labor force were self-employed, 15% were employed in professional or related services, 22% in manufacturing, 20% in wholesale and retail trade, 16% in agriculture, forestry, fisheries and mining, 11% were employed in other counties and there were 2,860 retired workers. The industries with the most employment: agribusiness, road construction, lumber mills, coal mining, dairy production, trucking and the manufacture of men's work clothing and valves and pipefittings. The nonfarm earnings in 1981 totaled $203,558,000. The retired workers received an average monthly Social Security payment of $289. **FINANCE** On June 30, 1983, four commercial banks had total deposits of $186,983,000 and total assets of $207,041,000. On December 31, 1982 one state savings and loan association and one federal association branch had assets of $47,727,646. **HOUSING** Average value of homes in 1980: $25,200. Permits for new, privately owned housing units decreased in 1982: 166 permits were issued with a total construction cost of $4,507,555. Of those permits, 88 were for single family houses. Between 1970 and 1980 the number of housing units increased by 31%. Seventy-six percent of all units in the county are air-conditioned, 67% are heated by gas and 27% by electricity. **NATURAL RESOURCES** Clay, lignite coal, industrial sand, oil, gas, glauconite and phosphorite. In 1982 a total of 2,834,317 thousand cubic feet of gas well gas, 28,091 barrels of condensate, 1,279,370 barrels of crude oil and 1,675,998 thousand cubic feet of casinghead gas were produced. Current production of other minerals and products includes fireclay, lignite coal and recovered sulphur. **TOURISM** Travel expenditures of $5,104,000 in 1982 (an increase of 11% over 1981) generated 123 jobs and $1,033,000 in payroll. Lodging: five hotels, motels and tourist courts. **ALCOHOLIC BEVERAGES** Totally dry. **FEDERAL EXPENDITURES** The federal government had direct expenditures or obligations of $45,064,000 in the county during fiscal year 1983, including $1,545,000 by the U.S. Department of Defense. In addition, the federal government provided $149,000 in grant awards, paid $1,805,000 in salaries and wages, made direct payments to individuals of $39,912,000 including $28,538,000 in retirement and disability payments, awarded $71,000 in procurement contracts and spent $3,127,000 in other expenditures or obligations. The federal government also provided $616,000 in direct loans and $4,777,000 in guaranteed loans and insurance.

COMMUNICATION

Newspapers–Daily: Sulphur Springs News-Telegram, ave. eve. circ. 6,551. Weekly: Hopkins County Echo (Sulphur Springs). Radio: KSST-AM (Sulphur Springs). Cable TV. Telephone companies: Continental Telephone, General Telephone, Cumby Telephone Coop. and Peoples Telephone Coop. **TRANSPORTATION** Total public road mileage: 1,334. In 1982 there were 22,649 registered vehicles and 546 reported traffic accidents including nine fatalities. Taxi cabs: one company in Sulphur Springs. Intercity bus service is available. Motor freight: 18 local and intrastate carriers. Rail: four main lines carry freight through the county. With one carrying annually five to 10 millon tons of freight and three carrying one to five million each. Aircraft: 24 are registered in the county. Airports: Sulphur Springs Municipal Airport serves as a base for 29 aircraft and is a general utility airport with general aviation service.

COMMUNITY SERVICES

EDUCATION Seven school districts with 12 elementary, one middle and seven high schools. The average daily attendance in 1981-82 was 4,448, with expenditures per pupil of $2,187 including 285 classroom teachers with an average annual salary of $15,516.

Forty-nine percent of the 276 high school graduates planned to attend college. In 1982-83, 86% of the students were White, 2% Hispanic, 12% Black and 0.2% Asian. Vocational education: Sulphur Springs School of Vocational Nursing. **PUBLIC LIBRARIES** Sulphur Springs Public Library: 35,647 volumes. **CHILD CARE** 19 day care and seven twenty-four hour care licensed facilities. **HEALTH CARE** 24 physicians and 10 dentists. Hospitals: one with a capacity of 100. Ambulance services: two fire departments and one hospital-based service. Mental health: one county clinic. Nursing homes: four nursing homes with a combined capacity of 395 nursing care residents. The average cost per day for private patients in 1982 was $29.56. **CHURCHES** 96 churches have an estimated combined membership of 17,635. The largest denominations are Southern Baptist, United Methodist and Baptist Missionary. **SOCIAL SERVICES** In fiscal year 1983 a total of $574,866 in food stamps was distributed, with an average of 1,424 persons receiving food stamps each month. Aid to Families with Dependent Children (AFDC) totaled $99,214 with an average of 72 families receiving AFDC each month. Medical assistance benefits for the aged and disabled of $2,809,408 and for families and children of $190,097 brought the county benefit total to $3,673,584. **FIRE PROTECTION** One partly paid and eight volunteer fire departments. **LAW ENFORCEMENT** The County Sheriff has 19 commissioned officers. Two police departments have a combined force of 31. **CRIME** 43 violent crimes (murder, forcible rape, robbery and aggravated assault) and 820 nonviolent crimes (burglary, larceny-theft and motor vehicle theft) were reported in 1982. **JUDICIAL SYSTEM** Two District Courts and Judges, one County Court and Judge and four Justices of the Peace. In the District Courts a total of 981 cases were pending on 1/1/82, 678 new cases were filed and 610 cases were disposed of during the year leaving 1,049 cases pending on 12/31/82. There were 218 criminal cases on the docket, 176 convictions, 44 persons committed to prison and three committed to jail and 34 cases left pending. In the County Court 2,459 cases were pending on 1/1/82, 756 new cases were filed and 325 cases were disposed of during the year leaving 2,890 cases pending on 12/31/82. There were 3,025 criminal cases on the docket, 182 convictions, 69 persons committed to jail, and 2,715 cases left pending. **JAILS** One jail, capacity 45. In 1983 opened a new jail. **ATTORNEYS AT LAW** 22. **UTILITIES** 89% of the residents are connected to a public or privately owned water system and 55% are connected to a public sewer system. Natural gas is distributed to the county by Lone Star Gas Co., Division of Enserch. The average annual residential bill for natural gas in 1982 for the Lone Star distribution system was $405.91, an increase of 35% over 1981. Electricity is distributed to the county by Gulf State Utilities, Wood Co. Electric Coop., Inc. and Farmers Electric Coop., Inc. and is generated primarily by gas and coal. The typical residential electric bill is $165.24 per month for an all-electric house using 2,500 kwh. **TAXES** The county has 12 units with taxing authority: seven school districts, three cities, one county and one hospital district.

RECREATION/ENTERTAINMENT

NATIONAL REGISTER OF HISTORIC PLACES Sulphur Springs: Hopkins County Courthouse. **MUNICIPAL PARKS** 610 acres in eight municipal parks. These parks contain two miles of hiking trails, three playgrounds, three football and soccer fields, nine baseball and softball fields, seven tennis courts, four multi-use courts, one swimming pool, five boat ramps and shore fishing facilities. **BOATING/FISHING** Lakes/reservoirs: Century (613 acres), Coleman (49 acres), Helm (21 acres) and Sulphur Springs (1,134 acres). Major rivers: South Sulphur. Primary streams: White Oak and Rock. **HUNTING** Fall and winter seasons on deer. Summer, fall and winter seasons on squirrel.

Winter seasons on quail, muskrat, beaver, otter, mink, opossum, ring-tailed cat, badger, fox, raccoon, skunk and civet cat. No closed seasons on nutria, bobcat and coyote. In 1983 duck, coot, geese, woodcock and jacksnipe seasons occurred during the winter months. Teal duck, rail and gallinule seasons occurred in the fall. Mourning dove seasons occurred intermittently during the fall and winter months. **MUSEUMS** Sulphur Springs: Hopkins County Museum and Heritage Park. **SPECIAL EVENTS** CRA Rodeo, Sulphur Springs, April; Dairy Festival, Sulphur Springs, May; Fall Festival, Sulphur Springs, September.

COMMUNITIES

COUNTY SEAT Sulphur Springs, County Courthouse, 75482; County Clerk's Office, 214/885-3929. **INCORPORATED COMMUNITIES** (1980 population and ZIP Code) Como (254) 75431, Cumby (647) 75433, Sulphur Springs (12,804) 75482 and Tira (249) 75482. **UNINCORPORATED COMMUNITIES** (and ZIP Code) Addran 75482, Arbala 75482, Askew 75431, Birthright 75482, Blackoak 75431, Bonanza 75420, Brashear 75420, Caney 75482, Cornersville 75494, Crossroads 75482, Dike 75437, Emblem 75482, Flora 75437, Greenview 75420, Greenwood (Penn) 75478, Hatchetville 75437, Mahoney 75482, Martin Springs 75482, Miller Grove 75433, Nelta 75437, Peerless 75482, Pickton 75471, Pine Forest 75431, Posey 75482, Reilly Springs 75482, Ridgeway 75482, Saltillo 75478, Seymore 75482, Shirley 75482, Sulphur Bluff 75481, Thermo 75482, Weaver 75478 and Weirville (Weir) 75482. **FOR ADDITIONAL LOCAL INFORMATION** Hopkins Co. Chamber of Commerce, P.O. Box 347, Sulphur Springs, 75482, 214/885-6515.

HOUSTON (E24)

THE LAND

East of Waco on U.S. Highway 287 in the East Texas Timberlands Region, Houston County covers 1,234 square miles with an elevation range of 200 to 400 feet. The soils are gently rolling to hilly, with light colored, loamy surfaces and very deep reddish, clayey subsoils high in iron. To the west and in the southwest the soils are sandy with clayey subsoils. Along the Trinity River the soils have very dark, loamy surfaces with cracking, clayey subsoils. In the Pineywoods vegetation area the primary timber species are longleaf, shortleaf, loblolly pines and hardwoods such as oaks, hickory and elm. Between 21 and 30% of the land in the county is considered prime farmland. **CLIMATE** Subtropical Humid, warm and moist. The average annual temperature is 66 °F. Temperatures in January range from an average low of 36° to an average high of 58°F and in July range from 71° to 94°F. The average annual precipitation is 42 inches, with an average relative humidity of 86% at 6 A.M. and 57% at 6 P.M. The average annual snowfall is less than one inch. The growing season averages 260 days per year, with the last freeze in early March and the first freeze in late November. The sun shines during the year on the average 65% of the daylight hours.

THE PEOPLE

Houston County is in a period of population growth for the first time in 30 years. The 1982 estimated population of 23,700 continues that growth which began in the 1970s. Gains in rural areas from 1970 to 1980 were larger than in urban areas. The age groups with the greatest increase were ages 20 to 34 and birth to five years. The largest ancestry groups are Black (32%), persons of English descent (25%) and Irish descent (18%). **REGISTERED VOTERS** As of November 2, 1982 there were 10,632 registered voters (0.2% of the state total). The 1982 general election had a 45% voter turnout, compared to a 67% turnout in the 1980

COUNTIES

HOUSTON (continued)

general election. In the 1982 primary 98% voted Democratic and 2% Republican, with 4,367 votes cast.

THE ECONOMY

AGRICULTURE Forest production area and cattle. In 1982, 55% of the land was in farms and ranches, with 14% of the farmland under cultivation and 3% irrigated. Houston ranked 91st in the state in highest agricultural receipts, with 86% from livestock and livestock products. Overgrazing, water erosion, improper woodland management and urban encroachment are the current conservation problems. Primary crops: sixth in the state for rye. Hay, cotton, oats, sorghum, wheat and peanuts. Primary vegetables: watermelons. Primary fruits and nuts: peaches and pecans. Primary livestock and products: eighth in the state for beef cows that have calved. Cattle, milk and hogs. **BUSINESS** Total number of business establishments in the county: 368. Retail sales during the first quarter of 1984 increased 17%. In 1980, 14% of the labor force were self-employed, 20% were employed in professional or related services, 19% in manufacturing, 18% in wholesale and retail trade, 11% in agriculture, forestry, fisheries and mining, 11% were employed in other counties and there were 2,641 retired workers. The industries with the most employment: oil and gas extraction, lumber mills, and the manufacture of men's work clothing, children's clothing, aircraft equipment and structural metal products. The nonfarm earnings in 1981 totaled $183,021,000. The retired workers received an average monthly Social Security payment of $282. **FINANCE** On June 30, 1983, seven commercial banks had total deposits of $118,370,000 and total assets of $131,734,000. There are three state savings and loan association branches and two credit unions in the county. **HOUSING** Average value of homes in 1980: $25,500. Permits for new, privately owned housing units increased in 1982: 36 permits were issued with a total construction cost of $783,100. Of those permits, 14 were for single family houses. Housing permits in Crockett increased from 17 in 1981 to 34 in 1982. Between 1970 and 1980 the number of housing units increased by 40%. Sixty-three percent of all units in the county are air-conditioned, 75% are heated by gas and 16% by electricity. **NATURAL RESOURCES** Lignite coal, iron, glauconite, salt domes, sand and gravel, oil and gas. In 1982 a total of 7,384,380 thousand cubic feet of gas well gas, 110,644 barrels of condensate, 847,541 barrels of crude oil and 782,305 thousand cubic feet of casinghead gas were produced. Current production of other minerals and products includes sand and gravel and crushed sandstone. Pine and hardwood production in 1981 totaled 13,681,382 cubic feet: 12,507,970 cubic feet of pine and 1,173,412 cubic feet of hardwood. **TOURISM** Travel expenditures of $12,471,000 in 1982 (an increase of 11% over 1981) generated 299 jobs and $2,423,000 in payroll. **ALCOHOLIC BEVERAGES** Totally dry. **FEDERAL EXPENDITURES** The federal government had direct expenditures or obligations of $40,378,000 in the county during fiscal year 1983, including $1,434,000 by the U.S. Department of Defense. In addition, the federal government provided $806,000 in grant awards, paid $1,617,000 in salaries and wages, made direct payments to individuals of $37,009,000 including $25,926,000 in retirement and disability payments, awarded $327,000 in procurement contracts and spent $619,000 in other expenditures or obligations. The federal government also provided $824,000 in direct loans and $3,013,000 in guaranteed loans and insurance.

COMMUNICATION

Newspapers–Weekly: Grapeland Messenger and the Crockett Houston County Courier. Radio: KIVY-AM and KIVY-FM (Crockett). Cable TV. Telephone companies: Continental Telephone, General Telephone and Lufkin Telephone Exchange.

TRANSPORTATION Total public road mileage: 1,210. In 1982 there were 16,475 registered vehicles and 367 reported traffic accidents including five fatalities. Taxi cabs: one company in Crockett. Intercity bus service is available. Motor freight: eight local and intrastate carriers. Rail: one main line carries annually 10 to 20 million tons of freight through the county. Aircraft: 22 are registered in the county. Airports: Houston County Airport at Crockett serves as a base for 14 aircraft and is a basic utility airport with general aviation services.

COMMUNITY SERVICES

EDUCATION Five school districts with six elementary, two middle and five high schools. The average daily attendance in 1981-82 was 3,428, with expenditures per pupil of $2,681 including 258 classroom teachers with an average annual salary of $15,164. Fifty percent of the 211 high school graduates planned to attend college. In 1982-83, 58% of the students were White, 1% Hispanic, 41% Black, 0.3% Asian and 0.1% American Indian. Vocational education: Houston County Hospital School of Vocational Nursing (Crockett). **PUBLIC LIBRARIES** Crockett Public Library: 60,000 volumes. **CHILD CARE** 15 day care and six twenty-four hour care licensed facilities. **HEALTH CARE** 15 physicians and 10 dentists. Hospitals: two with a combined capacity of 117. Ambulance services: two funeral homes, one community service and one fire department service. Nursing homes: four nursing homes with a combined capacity of 319 nursing care residents. The average cost per day for private patients in 1982 was $31.70. **CHURCHES** 70 churches have an estimated combined membership of 10,883. The largest denominations are Southern Baptist and United Methodist. **SOCIAL SERVICES** In fiscal year 1983 a total of $1,308,658 in food stamps was distributed, with an average of 2,801 persons receiving food stamps each month. Aid to Families with Dependent Children (AFDC) totaled $417,993 with an average of 285 families receiving AFDC each month. Medical assistance benefits for the aged and disabled of $3,265,687 and for families and children of $530,745 brought the county benefit total to $5,523,083. **FIRE PROTECTION** Eight volunteer fire departments. **LAW ENFORCEMENT** The County Sheriff has seven commissioned officers. One police department has a force of 14. **CRIME** 40 violent crimes (murder, forcible rape, robbery and aggravated assault) and 376 nonviolent crimes (burglary, larceny-theft and motor vehicle theft) were reported in 1982. **JUDICIAL SYSTEM** Two District Courts and Judges, two County Courts and Judges and four Justices of the Peace. In the District Courts a total of 794 cases were pending on 1/1/82, 440 new cases were filed and 343 cases were disposed of during the year leaving 891 cases pending on 12/31/82. There were 201 criminal cases on the docket, 31 convictions, six persons committed to prison, and 128 cases left pending. In the County Courts 356 cases were pending on 1/1/82, 210 new cases were filed and 345 cases were disposed of during the year leaving 221 cases pending on 12/31/82. There were 384 criminal cases on the docket, 97 convictions, three persons committed to jail, and 161 cases left pending. **JAILS** One jail, capacity 21. **PRISONS** Eastham, on 13,073 acres west of Trinity, had an inmate population of 3,090 in 1983. It has agricultural operations including a feedmill, poultry house and hog operation and operates a garment factory. **ATTORNEYS AT LAW** 17. **UTILITIES** 77% of the residents are connected to a public or privately owned water system and 40% are connected to a public sewer system. Natural gas is distributed to the county by Entex, Inc. The average annual residential bill for natural gas in 1982 for the Entex distribution system was $390.31, an increase of 26% over 1981. Electricity is distributed to the county by Houston Co. Electric Coop., Inc. and Houston Lighting and Power Co. and is generated primarily by gas and oil. The typical residential electric bill is $165.24 per month for an all-electric house using

2,500 kwh. **TAXES** The county has 12 units with taxing authority: five school districts, four cities, one county, one hospital district and one special district.

RECREATION/ENTERTAINMENT

FEDERAL DAVY CROCKETT NATIONAL FOREST covers 161,497 acres in Houston and Trinity Counties and includes five recreation areas. **NATIONAL REGISTER OF HISTORIC PLACES** Crockett: Downes-Aldrich House and Monroe-Crook House. Kennard vicinity: Westerman Mound. **STATE** Mission Tejas State Historical Park covers 118 acres with camping sites as well as areas offering fishing, swimming and nature trails. A landmark in the park is a replica of the first Spanish mission in East Texas, built in 1690 to stem the tide of French settlement. **MUNICIPAL PARKS** 36 acres in two municipal parks. These parks contain one playground, two multi-use fields and four tennis courts. **SCENIC DRIVES** The Texas Forest Trail runs through this county. This trail explores the farming, ranching and oilfield areas of the East Texas Pineywoods. **BOATING/FISHING** Lakes/reservoirs: Broxson (27 acres), Eastham (123 acres), Garden (21 acres), Grapeland (76 acres), Houston County (1,282 acres), Moore (24 acres), Murchison (123 acres), Northcutt (18 acres), Ratcliff (50 acres) and Spring Creek Club (35 acres). Major rivers: Trinity and Neches. Primary streams: Tantabogue, San Pedro, Little Elkhart, Miles, Gail, Lee, Spring, Big Elkhart, Hickory, Cochino Bayou and Hurricane Bayou. **HUNTING** Fall and winter seasons on deer. Summer, fall and winter seasons on squirrel. Winter seasons on quail, muskrat, beaver, otter, opossum, mink, ring-tailed cat, badger, fox, raccoon, skunk and civet cat. Spring season on turkey. No closed season on nutria, coyote and bobcat. In 1983 duck, coot, geese, woodcock and jacksnipe seasons occurred during the winter months. Teal duck, rail and gallinule seasons occurred in the fall. Mourning dove seasons occurred intermittently during the fall and winter months. **MUSEUMS** Crockett: Monroe-Crook House. **SPECIAL EVENTS** Love Festival, Lovelady, February; County Fair and Stock Show, Crockett, April; Bass Fishing Tourney, Crockett, April/May; Family and Friends Day, Fodice, May; Championship Rodeo and Parade, Crockett, June; Fiddlers and Bluegrass Festival, Crockett, June; Annual Birthday Party for Houston County, Crockett, June; Trail Ride and Barbecue, Austonio, July; Bluegrass Festival, Grapeland, August; Pilgrimage to Mission Tejas, Crockett, October; Fall Festival, Crockett, October; Peanut Festival, Grapeland, October; Christmas Tour of Homes, Crockett, December.

COMMUNITIES

COUNTY SEAT Crockett, County Courthouse, 75835; County Clerk's Office, 409/544-3263. **INCORPORATED COMMUNITIES** (1980 population and ZIP Code) Crockett (7,405) 75835, Grapeland (1,634) 75844, Kennard (424) 75847, Latexo (312) 75849 and Lovelady (509) 75851. **UNINCORPORATED COMMUNITIES** (and ZIP Code) Antioch 75851, Arbor 75847, Ash 75835, Augusta 75844, Austonio 75835, Belott 75835, Cut 75835, Dalys 75844, Daniel 75835, Fodice 75851, Holly 75851, Hopewell 75835, James 75847, Mapleton (Stumpville) 75835, Pearsons Chapel (Post Oak) 75851, Percilla 75844, Porter Springs 75835, Ratcliff 75858, Refuge 75844, Reynard 75844, Sand Ridge 75835, Smith Grove 75851, Tadmor 75847, Vistula 75851, Weches 75844 and Weldon 75863. **FOR ADDITIONAL LOCAL INFORMATION** Crockett Chamber of Commerce, P.O. Box 307, 700 E. Houston, Crockett, 75835, 409/544-2359.

HOWARD (P67)

THE LAND

West of Abilene on Interstate Highway 20 in the High Plains

Region, Howard County covers 901 square miles with an elevation range of 2,200 to 2,550 feet. The soils range from light to very dark loamy surfaces with some deep, clayey subsoils. In areas there are accumulations of lime in the subsoils. In the south central portion of the county the limestone bedrock comes close to the surface with areas of exposed rock. In the High Plains vegetation area, the most abundant grasses are buffalograss and blue grama. Between 41 and 50% of the land in the county is considered prime farmland. **CLIMATE** Borderline of Continental Steppe and Subtropical Subhumid, mild and dry. Duststorms, thunderstorms and high winds occur mostly in spring and early summer. The average annual temperature is 64°F. Temperatures in January range from an average low of 29° to an average high of 57°F and in July range from 71° to 95°F. The average annual precipitation is 18 inches, with an average relative humidity of 73% at 6 A.M. and 38% at 6 P.M. The average annual snowfall is four inches. The growing season averages 217 days per year, with the last freeze in early April and the first freeze in early November. The sun shines during the year on the average 75% of the daylight hours.

THE PEOPLE

The 1982 estimated population of 36,500 is a 10% increase in population since the 1980 census. The number of county residents had declined between 1960 and 1980. Population reductions from 1970 to 1980 were greater in urban areas than rural areas. The age group with the largest loss was ages 10 to 14. The county's median age rose from 27 in 1970 to 31 in 1980. The largest ancestry groups are persons of English descent (23%), Hispanic (21%) and Irish descent (18%). **REGISTERED VOTERS** As of November 2, 1982 there were 15,343 registered voters (0.2% of the state total). The 1982 general election had a 55% voter turnout, compared to a 71% turnout in the 1980 general election. In the 1982 primary 94% voted Democratic and 6% Republican, with 4,428 votes cast.

THE ECONOMY

AGRICULTURE Cotton area. In 1982, 91% of the land was in farms and ranches, with 21% of the farmland under cultivation and 9% irrigated. Howard ranked 73rd in the state in highest agricultural receipts, with 89% from crops. Overgrazing, undesirable brush and weeds, water and wind erosion are the current conservation problems. Primary crops: cotton, sorghum and wheat. Primary vegetables: cantaloupes, tomatoes and watermelons. Primary fruits and nuts: pecans. Primary livestock and products: cattle, sheep and wool. **BUSINESS** Total number of business establishments in the county: 833. Retail sales during the first quarter of 1984 decreased 15%. In 1980, 11% of the labor force were self-employed, 26% were employed in professional or related services, 14% in manufacturing, 22% in wholesale and retail trade, 12% in agriculture, forestry, fisheries and mining, 4% were employed in other counties and there were 2,992 retired workers. The industries with the most employment: agribusiness, oil and gas extraction, heavy construction, petroleum refining and the manufacture of men's and women's clothing, wood pallets and skids, mobile homes and plastic products. The nonfarm earnings in 1981 totaled $356,186,000. The retired workers received an average monthly Social Security payment of $322. **FINANCE** On June 30, 1983, four commercial banks had total deposits of $268,055,000 and total assets of $301,341,000. On December 31, 1982 one federal savings and loan association and two state branches had assets of $132,138,281. In addition there are six credit unions in the county. **HOUSING** Average value of homes in 1980: $24,000. Permits for new, privately owned housing units increased in 1982: 56 permits were issued with a total construction cost of $2,141,280. Of those permits, 46 were for single family houses. Housing permits in Big

COUNTIES

HOWARD (continued)

Spring increased from 29 in 1981 to 56 in 1982 with 46 of the permits issued for single family houses. Between 1970 and 1980 the number of housing units increased by 8%. Eighty-seven percent of all units in the county are air-conditioned, 85% are heated by gas and 14% by electricity. **NATURAL RESOURCES** Caliche, limestone, oil and gas. In 1982 a total of 267,781 thousand cubic feet of gas well gas, 7,392 barrels of condensate, 13,459,742 barrels of crude oil and 7,484,798 thousand cubic feet of casinghead gas were produced. Current production of other minerals and products includes caliche, crushed limestone, sand and gravel and recovered sulphur. **TOURISM** Travel expenditures of $23,816,000 in 1982 (an increase of 11% over 1981) generated 587 jobs and $4,756,000 in payroll. Lodging: nine hotels, motels and tourist courts. Convention/meeting facilities: Big Spring-Dorothy Garrett Coliseum, Howard County Fair outdoor and indoor arenas and the Spring City Theatre. **ALCOHOLIC BEVERAGES** Packaged distilled spirits, beer, ale, malt liquor and wine are legal in parts of the county. **FEDERAL EXPENDITURES** The federal government had direct expenditures or obligations of $77,287,000 in the county during fiscal year 1983, including $4,321,000 by the U.S. Department of Defense. In addition, the federal government provided $864,000 in grant awards, paid $14,175,000 in salaries and wages, made direct payments to individuals of $49,468,000 including $39,589,000 in retirement and disability payments, awarded $2,869,000 in procurement contracts and spent $9,911,000 in other expenditures or obligations. The federal government also provided $6,156,000 in direct loans and $36,296,000 in guaranteed loans and insurance.

COMMUNICATION

Newspapers–Daily: Big Spring Herald, ave. eve. circ. 10,598. Radio: KBST-AM, KBYG-AM, KKIK-AM and KWKI-FM (Big Spring). Cable TV. Telephone companies: General Telephone, Southwestern Bell and Wes-Tex Telephone Coop. **TRANSPORTATION** Total public road mileage: 1,044. In 1982 there were 35,607 registered vehicles and 1,224 reported traffic accidents including 12 fatalities. Taxi cabs: one company in Big Spring. Intercity bus service is available. Motor freight: 20 local and intrastate carriers. Rail: one main line carries annually five to 10 million of tons of freight through the county. Aircraft: 84 are registered in the county. Airports: Big Spring Airport serves as a base for 65 aircraft and is a basic transportation airport with general aviation services.

COMMUNITY SERVICES

EDUCATION Three school districts with nine elementary, three middle and three high schools. The average daily attendance in 1981-82 was 5,923, with expenditures per pupil of $3,149 including 414 classroom teachers with an average annual salary of $18,841. Forty-three percent of the 376 high school graduates planned to attend college. In 1982-83, 63% of the students were White, 31% Hispanic, 6% Black, 0.4% Asian and 0.1% American Indians. Private schools: 444 students enrolled in three elementary schools. Howard County Junior College is located in Big Spring. Established in 1945 it is a vocational and two year academic college under state and local control. Enrollment in 1982 was 1,076 with in state undergraduate tuition and fees of $250 per semester. Vocational education: Aladdin Beauty College, Malone-Hogan Hospital School of Radiologic Technology (Big Spring). **PUBLIC LIBRARIES** Howard County Library (Big Spring): 47,151 volumes. **CHILD CARE** 35 day care and five twenty-four hour care licensed facilities. **HEALTH CARE** 67 physicians and 15 dentists. Hospitals: three with a combined capacity of 238. Specialized hospitals: one veterans medical center

with capacity of 263. Clinics: one public health clinic. Ambulance services: three commercial services. Mental health: one county clinic and one state hospital with capacity of 458. Nursing homes: two nursing homes with a combined capacity of 292 nursing care residents. The average cost per day for private patients in 1982 was $34.50. **CHURCHES** 68 churches have an estimated combined membership of 27,113. The largest denominations are Southern Baptist, Catholic and United Methodist. **SOCIAL SERVICES** In fiscal year 1983 a total of $1,420,391 in food stamps was distributed, with an average of 2,933 persons receiving food stamps each month. Aid to Families with Dependent Children (AFDC) totaled $340,284 with an average of 226 families receiving AFDC each month. Medical assistance benefits for the aged and disabled of $2,203,427 and for families and children of $471,368 brought the county benefit total to $4,435,470. **FIRE PROTECTION** One paid and five volunteer fire departments. **LAW ENFORCEMENT** The County Sheriff has 27 commissioned officers. Two police departments have a combined force of 53. **CRIME** 417 violent crimes (murder, forcible rape, robbery and aggravated assault) and 1,978 nonviolent crimes (burglary, larceny-theft and motor vehicle theft) were reported in 1982. **JUDICIAL SYSTEM** One District Court and Judge, one County Court and Judge and three Justices of the Peace. In the District Court a total of 1,173 cases were pending on 1/1/82, 1,112 new cases were filed and 1,121 cases were disposed of during the year leaving 1,164 cases pending on 12/31/82. There were 492 criminal cases on the docket, 140 convictions, 42 persons committed to prison, and 261 cases left pending. In the County Court 948 cases were pending on 1/1/82, 1,226 new cases were filed and 1,195 cases were disposed of during the year leaving 979 cases pending on 12/31/82. There were 1,853 criminal cases on the docket, 191 convictions, 50 persons committed to jail, and 743 cases left pending. **JAILS** One jail, capacity 29. **ATTORNEYS AT LAW** 36. **UTILITIES** 86% of the residents are connected to a public or privately owned water system and 78% are connected to a public sewer system. Natural gas is distributed to the county by Energas. The average annual residential bill for natural gas in 1982 for the Energas distribution system was $371.63, an increase of 23% over 1981. Electricity is distributed to the county by Texas Electric Service Co., Cap Rock Electric Coop., Inc. and Lonewolf Electric Coop., Inc. and is generated primarily by gas. The typical residential electric bill is $154.69 per month for an all-electric house using 2,500 kwh. **TAXES** The county has nine units with taxing authority: three school districts, three cities, one county, one college district and one special district.

RECREATION/ENTERTAINMENT

NATIONAL REGISTER OF HISTORIC PLACES Big Spring: Potton-Hayden House. **STATE** Big Spring State Recreation Area covers 370 acres with nature trails, scenic drives and exhibits. **MUNICIPAL PARKS** 425 acres in 10 municipal parks. These parks contain two miles of hiking trails, five playgrounds, one golf course, seven baseball and softball fields, 13 tennis courts, two swimming pools, one beach, one boat ramp and shore fishing facilities. Developed campsites: 26. **BOATING/FISHING** Lakes/reservoirs: Cosden (47 acres), Fourmile (50 acres), Latan (20 acres), Moss Creek (183 acres), Onemile (100 acres), Powell (122 acres), Refinery (22 acres) and Threemile (30 acres). Major rivers: North Concho. Primary streams: Beals, Dugout, Moss, Powell, Morgan and Wild Horse. **HUNTING** Fall season on antelope. Fall and winter seasons on javelina and deer. No closed season on coyote, bobcat and squirrel. Winter seasons on quail, muskrat, beaver, opossum, ring-tailed cat, badger, fox, weasel, raccoon, skunk and civet cat. Fall, winter and spring seasons on turkey. In 1983 sandhill crane, duck, coot, geese, woodcock and jacksnipe seasons occurred during the winter months. Teal duck, rail and gallinule seasons occurred in the fall. Mourning dove seasons occurred intermittently during the fall and winter months. **MUSEUMS** Big Spring: Heritage Museum. **THEATERS** Big Spring: Dorothy Garrett Coliseum and Comanche Trail Park Amphitheater. **PLANETARIUM** Big Spring: Big Spring High School Planetarium. **COLLEGIATE FINE ARTS** Big Spring: cultural events offered by Howard College. **SPECIAL EVENTS** Junior Stock Show, Big Spring, January; Rattlesnake Roundup, Big Spring, March; Square Dance Festival, Big Spring, May; Pro-Am Golf Tourney, Big Spring, May; Annual Cowboy Reunion and Rodeo, Big Spring, June; Texas-Style Domino Tourney, Big Spring, July; Junior Rodeo, Big Spring, August; Old Settlers Reunion, Big Spring, August; County Fair, Big Spring, September; Arts and Crafts Festival, Big Spring, October; Christmas Parade, Big Spring, December.

COMMUNITIES

COUNTY SEAT Big Spring, County Courthouse, 79720; County Clerk's Office, 915/267-2881. **INCORPORATED COMMUNITIES** (1980 population and ZIP Code) Big Spring (24,804) 79720, Coahoma (1,069) 79511 and Forsan (239) 79733. **UNINCORPORATED COMMUNITIES** (and ZIP Code) Center Point 79720, Fairview 79720, Knott 79748, Lomax 79720, Luther 79720, Otis Chalk 79733, Ross City 79720, Sand Springs 79720, Vealmoor 79720 and Vincent 79511. **FOR ADDITIONAL LOCAL INFORMATION** Big Spring Area Chamber of Commerce, 215 W. 3rd Street, P.O. Box 1391, Big Spring, 79721, 915/263-7641.

HUDSPETH (B2)

THE LAND

Bordering New Mexico, Mexico and east of El Paso on Interstate Highway 10 in the Trans-Pecos Region, Hudspeth County covers 4,566 square miles with an elevation range of 3,200 to 7,500 feet. The desertic soils are alkaline and loamy with clayey subsoils over limestone in some areas. The mountains and hills are over 90% exposed rock with thin, alkaline, loamy soils. To the southwest the soils are sandy throughout with accumulations of gypsum or lime. Along the Rio Grande River the soils are brown to red and loamy to clayey. In the Trans-Pecos, Mountains and Basins vegetation area, the grasses are short and sparse with creosote-tarbush, desert shrub, cacti and some mesquite. On the higher mountain slopes are pine trees and juniper. Less than one percent of the land in the county is considered prime farmland. **CLIMATE** Subtropical Arid, warm and dry. The average annual temperature is 62°F. Temperatures in January range from an average low of 29° to an average high of 56°F and in July range from 67° to 94°F. The average annual precipitation is less than 10 inches, with an average relative humidity of 65% at 6 A.M. and 30% at 6 P.M. The average annual snowfall is four inches. The growing season averages 230 days per year, with the last freeze in late March and the first freeze in early November. The sun shines during the year on the average 80% of the daylight hours.

THE PEOPLE

Hudspeth County is one of the most sparsely populated in Texas and ranks 30th among all U.S. counties in the highest percent of residents of Spanish origin. The 1982 estimated population of 2,900 continues the moderate growth rate begun in the 1970s which reversed a steady population decline between 1950 and 1970. The population is younger than average although the median age rose from 24 in 1970 to 25 in 1980. The largest ancestry groups are persons of Hispanic (58%), persons of English descent (8%), German descent (6%) and Irish descent

(6%). **REGISTERED VOTERS** As of November 2, 1982 there were 1,255 registered voters (0.01% of the state total). The 1982 general election had a 46% voter turnout, compared to a 66% turnout in the 1980 general election. In the 1982 primary 98% voted Democratic and 2% Republican, with 626 votes cast.

THE ECONOMY

AGRICULTURE Ranchland. In 1982, 86% of the land was in farms and ranches, with 1% of the farmland under cultivation. Most of the cropland and some of the rangeland was irrigated. Hudspeth ranked 166th in the state in highest agricultural receipts, with 57% from crops. Overgrazing, decreasing irrigation water supplies, salinity and urban encroachment are the current conservation problems. Primary crops: ninth in the state for hay and second for American-pima cotton. Upland cotton and sorghum. Primary vegetables: ninth in the state for cantaloupes. Tomatoes and watermelons. Primary fruits and nuts: peaches and pecans. Primary livestock and products: cattle, sheep, wool and hogs. **BUSINESS** Total number of business establishments in the county: 35. Retail sales during the first quarter of 1984 increased 17%. In 1980, 18% of the labor force were self-employed, 9% were employed in professional or related services, 2% in manufacturing, 17% in wholesale and retail trade, 41% in agriculture, forestry, fisheries and mining, 9% were employed in other counties and there were 126 retired workers. The industries with the most employment: agribusiness and tourism. The nonfarm earnings in 1981 totaled $14,527,000. The retired workers received an average monthly Social Security payment of $278. **FINANCE** On June 30, 1983, one commercial bank had total deposits of $4,646,000 and total assets of $5,259,000. **HOUSING** Average value of homes in 1980: $13,300. Between 1970 and 1980 the number of housing units increased by 14%. Fifty-five percent of all units in the county are air-conditioned, 88% are heated by gas and 8% by electricity. **NATURAL RESOURCES** Beryllium, coal, copper, fluorspar, gold, gypsum, lead, limestone, mica, clay, salt, silver, talc, zinc and bituminous coal. Current production of other minerals and products includes gypsum, crushed limestone, mica, crushed rhyolite, sand, gravel and talc. **TOURISM** Travel expenditures of $5,237,000 in 1982 (an increase of 13% over 1981) generated 112 jobs and $956,000 in payroll. **ALCOHOLIC BEVERAGES** Packaged distilled spirits, beer, ale, malt liquor and wine are legal. Sale of mixed beverages is legal in all or parts of the county. **FEDERAL EXPENDITURES** The federal government had direct expenditures or obligations of $8,067,000 in the county during fiscal during fiscal year 1983, including $94,000 by the U.S. Department of Defense. In addition, the federal government provided $91,000 in grant awards, paid $1,521,000 in salaries and wages, made direct payments to individuals of $2,304,000 including $1,734,000 in retirement and disability payments, awarded $2,970,000 in procurement contracts and spent $1,180,000 in other expenditures or obligations. The federal government also provided $407,000 in direct loans and $4,975,000 in guaranteed loans and insurance.

COMMUNICATION

Newspapers–Weekly: Hudspeth County Herald and Dell Valley Review (Dell City). Telephone companies: Continental Telephone and Dell Telephone Coop. **TRANSPORTATION** Total public road mileage: 742. In 1982 there were 2,121 registered vehicles and 177 reported traffic accidents including seven fatalities. Intercity bus service is available. Motor freight: four carriers. Rail: The Sunset Limited provides passenger service on the Amtrak route. Three main lines carry freight through the county with two carrying annually over 30 million tons each and one carrying one to five million. Aircraft: 21 are registered in the

COUNTIES

HUDSPETH (continued)

county. Airports: Dell City Municipal Airport, Mayfield Ranch at Cornudas and a heliport near Dell City.

COMMUNITY SERVICES

EDUCATION Four school districts with four elementary and three high schools. The average daily attendance in 1981-82 was 744, with expenditures per pupil of $2,525 including 53 classroom teachers with an average annual salary of $14,772. Forty-seven percent of the 34 high school graduates planned to attend college. In 1982-83, 32% of the students were White, 68% Hispanic and 0.1% Black. **PUBLIC LIBRARIES** Dell City Library. **CHILD CARE** Two day care licensed facilities. **HEALTH CARE** One physician. Ambulance services: one volunteer service. **CHURCHES** 12 churches have an estimated combined membership of 2,518. The largest denominations are Catholic and Southern Baptist. **SOCIAL SERVICES** In fiscal year 1983 a total of $230,592 in food stamps was distributed, with an average of 463 persons receiving food stamps each month. Aid to Families with Dependent Children (AFDC) totaled $27,594 with an average of 15 families receiving AFDC each month. Medical assistance benefits for the aged and disabled of $57,943 and for families and children of $21,910 brought the county benefit total to $338,039. **FIRE PROTECTION** Three volunteer fire departments. **LAW ENFORCEMENT** The County Sheriff has seven commissioned officers. **CRIME** Seven violent crimes (murder, forcible rape, robbery and aggravated assault) and 25 nonviolent crimes (burglary, larceny-theft and motor vehicle theft) were reported in 1982. **JUDICIAL SYSTEM** Three District Courts and Judges, one County Court and Judge and five Justices of the Peace. In the District Courts a total of 300 cases were pending on 1/1/82, 74 new cases were filed and 70 cases were disposed of during the year leaving 304 cases pending on 12/31/82. There were 122 criminal cases on the docket, 13 convictions, three persons committed to prison, and 90 cases left pending. In the County Court 177 cases were pending on 1/1/82, 309 new cases were filed and 202 cases were disposed of during the year leaving 284 cases pending on 12/31/82. There were 435 criminal cases on the docket, 70 convictions, 21 persons committed to jail, and 248 cases left pending. **JAILS** One jail, capacity nine. New jail under construction, capacity 25. **UTILITIES** 66% of the residents are connected to a public or privately owned water system and 25% are connected to a public sewer system. Natural gas is distributed to the county by Southern Union Company. The average annual residential bill for natural gas in 1982 for the Southern Union distribution system was $355.85, an increase of 23% over 1981. Electricity is distributed to the county by Rio Grande Electric Coop., Inc. and is generated primarily by gas, oil and coal. **TAXES** The county has eight units with taxing authority: four school districts, one city, one county and two special districts.

RECREATION/ENTERTAINMENT

FEDERAL Guadalupe Mountains National Park (see Culberson County). **NATIONAL REGISTER OF HISTORIC PLACES** Allamoore vicinity: Red Rock Archeological Complex. Sierra Blanca: Hudspeth County Courthouse. Sierra Blanca vicinity: Rod Johnson Site and Tinaja de las Palmas Battle Site. **COUNTY PARKS** 19 acres in three county parks. These parks contain two playgrounds, two multi-use fields, one multi-use court and one swimming pool. **SCENIC DRIVES** The Texas Mountain Trail runs through this county. In addition F.M. 1111 to U.S. 62/180 provides views of flat, ranching areas edged by mountains on the horizon. Profuse stands of yuccas which bloom in March and April exist. **BOATING/FISHING** Lakes/reservoirs: Alamo Arroyo Soil Conservation Service Lake 1 (16 acres),

Diablo Arroyo Soil Conservation Service Lakes 1 and 2 (37 acres), Fort Quitman Lake (50 acres) and No Name 47 (88 acres). Major rivers: Rio Grande and Green. Primary streams: Alamo Arroyo and Diablo Arroyo. **HUNTING** Fall season on antelope. Fall and winter seasons on mule deer. No closed seasons on elk, javelina, coyote and bobcat. Winter seasons on quail, muskrat, beaver, opossum, ring-tailed cat, badger, fox, weasel, raccoon, skunk and civet cat. In 1983 sandhill crane, duck, coot, geese, woodcock and jacksnipe seasons occurred during the winter months. Teal duck, rail and gallinule seasons occurred in the fall. Mourning dove seasons occurred intermittently during the fall and winter months with a fall season on white-winged dove in some parts of the county. **MUSEUMS** McNary: Covered Wagon Trading Post and Fort Quitman Replica. Sierra Blanca: E.A. Dogie Wright Collection. **SPECIAL EVENTS** Hudspeth County Fair, Dell City, September.

COMMUNITIES

COUNTY SEAT Sierra Blanca, County Courthouse, 79851; County Clerk's Office, 915/369-2301. **INCORPORATED COMMUNITIES** (1980 population and ZIP Code) Dell City (495) 79837. **UNINCORPORATED COMMUNITIES** (and ZIP Code) Acala 79839, Allamoore (Allamore) 79855, Cornudas 79847, Esperanza 79841, Fort Hancock 79839, Mile High 79851, McNary 79841, Salt Flat (Ables) 79847 and Sierra Blanca 79851. **FOR ADDITIONAL LOCAL INFORMATION** Dell Valley Chamber of Commerce, P.O. Box 709, Dell City, 79837, 915/964-2524 or 964-2840.

HUNT (M8)

THE LAND

Northeast of Dallas on U.S. Highway 67 in the Blackland Prairies Region, Hunt County covers 840 square miles with an elevation range of 400 to 700 feet. In the west central, northeast and northwest corners of the county are undulating, slightly acidic soils with dark, loamy surfaces over cracking, clayey subsoils and black to gray, acidic clayey soils. The rest of the county has gray to black, cracking, clayey soils and slightly acidic soils with loamy surfaces and cracking, clayey subsoils. The county's soils have a high shrink-swell potential. Hunt is in the Blackland Prairies vegetation area with tall grasses and mesquite, oak, elm and pecan trees along streams. Between 21 and 30% of the land in the county is considered prime farmland. **CLIMATE** Subtropical moist. Heavy thunderstorms are possible in the spring. The average annual temperature is 64°F. Temperatures in January range from an average low of 31° to an average high of 95°F and in July range from 72° to 95°F. The average annual precipitation is 40 inches, with an average relative humidity of 83% at 6 A.M. and 56% at 6 P.M. The average annual snowfall is five inches. The growing season averages 238 days per year, with the last freeze in late March and the first freeze in mid November. The sun shines during the year on the average 67% of the daylight hours.

THE PEOPLE

The 1982 estimated population of 59,300 indicates a continuation of the steady growth begun in the 1960s which reversed a population decline. Although the rural areas experienced population gains of 52% from 1970 to 1980, urban areas had a loss of 4%. The population's median age rose from 28 in 1970 to 32 in 1980. The largest ancestry groups are persons of English descent (26%), Irish descent (19%), Black (13%) and German descent (12%). **REGISTERED VOTERS** As of November 2, 1982 there were 25,318 registered voters (0.4% of the state total). The 1982 general election had a 49% voter turnout, compared to a

71% turnout in the 1980 general election. In the 1982 primary 92% voted Democratic and 8% Republican, with 7,282 votes cast.

THE ECONOMY

AGRICULTURE Wheat area. In 1982, 80% of the land was in farms and ranches, with 44% of the farmland under cultivation and 2% irrigated. Hunt ranked 84th in the state in highest agricultural receipts, with 59% from livestock and livestock products. Water erosion is the current conservation problem. Primary crops: wheat, hay, sorghum, cotton and oats. Primary vegetables: cantaloupes, potatoes, sweet potatoes and tomatoes. Primary fruits and nuts: peaches and pecans. Primary livestock and products: cattle, milk and hogs. **BUSINESS** Total number of business establishments in the county: 1,027. Retail sales during the first quarter of 1984 increased 20%. In 1980, 9% of the labor force were self-employed, 21% were employed in professional or related services, 29% in manufacturing, 17% in wholesale and retail trade, 7% in construction, 22% were employed in other counties and there were 5,888 retired workers. The industries with the most employment: agribusiness, oil and gas extraction, general construction, lumber mills, bakery products, cottonseed oil mills, commercial printing, bookbinding, and the manufacture of mobile homes, chemical products, fabricated rubber products, mining machinery, transformers, motor vehicle parts and accessories, aircraft and aircraft parts and plastic products. The nonfarm earnings in 1981 totaled $497,774,000. The retired workers received an average monthly Social Security payment of $301. **FINANCE** On June 30, 1983, 10 commercial banks had total deposits of $323,815,000 and total assets of $361,709,000. On December 31, 1982 one state savings and loan association, two federal associations, two state branches and one federal branch had combined assets of $169,649,765. In addition there are five credit unions in the county. **HOUSING** Average value of homes in 1980: $25,800. Permits for new, privately owned housing units increased in 1982: 282 permits were issued with a total construction cost of $9,528,710. Of those permits, 131 were for single family houses. Housing permits in Greenville increased from 69 in 1981 to 265 in 1982. Between 1970 and 1980 the number of housing units increased by 26%. Eighty-one percent of all units in the county are air-conditioned, 78% are heated by gas and 19% by electricity. **NATURAL RESOURCES** Limestone, glauconite, oil, gas and phosphorite. In 1982 a total of 113,927 thousand cubic feet of gas well gas, 2,553 barrels of condensate, 16,235 barrels of crude oil and 35 thousand cubic feet of casinghead gas were produced. Current production of other minerals and products includes crushed limestone. **TOURISM** Travel expenditures of $36,418,000 in 1982 (an increase of 8% over 1981) generated 596 jobs and $7,827,000 in payroll. Lodging: five hotels, motels and tourist courts. Convention/meeting facilities: Commerce—East Texas State University Fieldhouse. **ALCOHOLIC BEVERAGES** Packaged distilled spirits, beer, ale, malt liquor and wine are legal in parts of the county. **FEDERAL EXPENDITURES** The federal government had direct expenditures or obligations of $364,868,000 in the county during fiscal year 1983, including $271,296,000 by the U.S. Department of Defense. In addition, the federal government provided $3,826,000 in grant awards, paid $8,037,000 in salaries and wages, made direct payments to individuals of $86,052,000 including $63,791,000 in retirement and disability payments, awarded $265,787,000 in procurement contracts and spent $1,165,000 in other expenditures or obligations. The federal government also provided $3,099,000 in direct loans and $13,831,000 in guaranteed loans and insurance.

COMMUNICATION

Newspapers–Daily: Herald-Banner (Greenville), ave. morn. circ. 12,235. Weekly: Commerce Journal and the Tawakoni News (Quinlan). Radio: KGVL-AM, KIKT-FM (Greenville) and KETR-FM (Commerce). Cable TV. Telephone companies: Continental Telephone, Southwestern Bell, United Telephone, Campbell Telephone Coop., Cumby Telephone Coop. and Peoples Telephone Coop. **TRANSPORTATION** Total public road mileage: 1,907. In 1982 there were 48,750 registered vehicles and 1,455 reported traffic accidents including 16 fatalities. Taxi cabs: one company in Commerce and one in Greenville. Intercity bus service is available. Motor freight: 14 local and intrastate carriers. Rail: five main and five branch lines carry freight through the county. One main line carries annually five to 10 million tons of freight and four carry one to five million each. One branch line carries five to 10 million tons of freight, three carry one to five each and one carries less than one million. Aircraft: 82 are registered in the county. Airports: Majors Field at Greenville serves as a base for 28 aircraft and is a basic transportation airport with commuter service. Commerce Municipal Airport serves as a base for 10 aircraft and is a basic utility airport with general aviation service. Caddo Mills Municipal Airport serves as a base for 15 aircraft and is a basic utility airport with general aviation service. Flyers Field at Greenville.

COMMUNITY SERVICES

EDUCATION 10 school districts with 19 elementary, five middle and 10 high schools. The average daily attendance in 1981-82 was 9,713, with expenditures per pupil of $3,006 including 606 classroom teachers with an average annual salary of $15,902. Forty-eight percent of the 679 high school graduates planned to attend college. In 1982-83, 79% of the students were White, 3% Hispanic, 17% Black, 0.6% Asian and 0.2% American Indian. Private schools: 138 students enrolled in one elementary and one high school. East Texas State Univeristy is located in Commerce. Established in 1917 it is under state control. Enrollment in 1982 was 8,317 with in state undergraduate tuition and fees of $316 per semester. The highest degree offered is: Doctorate. Sports championships: (Lone Star Conference) 1983 Women's Football. **PUBLIC LIBRARIES** Commerce Public Library: 22,732 volumes. Walworth Harrison Public Library (Greenville): 45,023 volumes. Wolfe City Public Library: 5,150 volumes. **CHILD CARE** 90 day care and 16 twenty-four hour care licensed facilities. **HEALTH CARE** 44 physicians and 25 dentists. Hospitals: two with a combined capacity of 126. Clinics: one outpatient clinic, one dialysis clinic and one public health clinic. Ambulance services: two fire departments, two commercial and one funeral home service. Mental health: two clinics. Nursing homes: seven nursing homes with a combined capacity of 654 nursing care residents. The average cost per day for private patients in 1982 was $30.38. **CHURCHES** 131 churches have an estimated combined membership of 33,142. The largest denominations are Southern Baptist, United Methodist and Churches of Christ. **SOCIAL SERVICES** In fiscal year 1983 a total of $2,289,649 in food stamps was distributed, with an average of 4,687 persons receiving food stamps each month. Aid to Families with Dependent Children (AFDC) totaled $628,257 with an average of 430 families receiving AFDC each month. Medical assistance benefits for the aged and disabled of $4,464,096 and for families and children of $760,636 brought the county benefit total to $8,142,637. **FIRE PROTECTION** One paid, one partly paid and six volunteer fire departments. **LAW ENFORCEMENT** The County Sheriff has 29 commissioned officers. Eight police departments have a combined force of 84. One university campus has a police department with a force of 16 officers. **CRIME** 429 violent crimes (murder, forcible rape, robbery and aggravated assault) and 2,826 nonviolent crimes (burglary, larceny-theft and motor vehicle theft) were reported in 1982. **JUDICIAL SYSTEM** One District Court and Judge, two County Courts and Judges and five Justices of the Peace.

COUNTIES

HUNT (continued)

In the District Court a total of 1,386 cases were pending on 1/1/82, 1,462 new cases were filed and 1,286 cases were disposed of during the year leaving 1,562 cases pending on 12/31/82. There were 544 criminal cases on the docket, 223 convictions, 61 persons committed to prison and nine committed to jail and 194 cases left pending. In the County Courts 3,628 cases were pending on 1/1/82, 3,206 new cases were filed and 3,368 cases were disposed of during the year leaving 3,466 cases pending on 12/31/82. There were 6,070 criminal cases on the docket, 519 convictions, 117 persons committed to jail, and 3,128 cases left pending. **JAILS** One jail, capacity 63. New jail under construction, capacity 99. **ATTORNEYS AT LAW** 39. **UTILITIES** 96% of the residents are connected to a public or privately owned water system and 65% are connected to a public sewer system. Natural gas is distributed to the county by Lone Star Gas Co., Division of Enserch. The average annual residential bill for natural gas in 1982 for the Lone Star distribution system was $405.91, an increase of 35% over 1981. Electricity is distributed to the city of Greenville by the Greenville Municipal Light and Power Dept. and to the rest of the county by Texas Power and Light Co., Fanin Electric Coop., Inc., Kaufman Co. Electric Coop., Inc., Farmers Electric Coop., Inc. and Hunt and Collin Electric Coop., Inc. and is generated primarily by gas, coal, oil and water. The typical residential electric bill is $223.17 per month for an all-electric house using 2,500 kwh. **TAXES** The county has 22 units with taxing authority: 11 school districts, eight cities, one county, one hospital district and one special district.

RECREATION/ENTERTAINMENT

NATIONAL REGISTER OF HISTORIC PLACES Greenville: Post Office. **MUNICIPAL PARKS** 217 acres in 13 municipal parks. These parks contain 10 playgrounds, one golf course, two football and soccer fields, 13 baseball and softball fields, four tennis courts, one multi-use court, one swimming pool, one boat ramp and shore fishing facilities. **SCENIC DRIVES** The Texas Lakes Trail runs through this county. This trail introduces some 30 blue-water recreational areas in a variety of settings in North Central Texas. **BOATING/FISHING** Lakes/reservoirs: Greenville Club (187 acres), Greenville #3 (52 acres), Greenville #4 (327 acres), Greenville #5 (288 acres), Tawakoni (36,700 acres), Upper Lake Fork Creek Soil Conservation Service Lake 1 (30 acres), Wolfe City #1 (39 acres) and Wolfe City #2 (40 acres). Major rivers: Sabine, South Fork Sabine, South Sulphur and Cowleech Fork Sabine River. Primary streams: Cedar, Lake Fork, North Fork Turkey and Turkey. **HUNTING** Summer, fall and winter seasons on squirrel. No closed seasons on nutria, coyote and bobcat. Winter seasons on quail, muskrat, beaver, opossum, otter, mink, ring-tailed cat, badger, fox, raccoon, skunk and civet cat. In 1983 duck, coot, geese, woodcock and jacksnipe seasons occurred during the winter months. Teal duck, rail and gallinule seasons occurred in the fall. Mourning dove seasons occurred intermittently during the fall and winter months. **MUSEUMS** Greenville: Ende-Gaillard House. **COLLEGIATE FINE ARTS** Commerce: cultural events offered by East Texas State University. **SPECIAL EVENTS** Hunt County Fair, Greenville, August; Western Days Festival and Rodeo, Wolfe City, August; Cotton Pickin' Arts and Crafts Jubilee, Greenville, November.

COMMUNITIES

COUNTY SEAT Greenville, County Courthouse, 75401; County Clerk's Office, 214/455-6460. **INCORPORATED COMMUNITIES** (1980 population and ZIP Code) Caddo Mills (1,060) 75005, Campbell (549) 75422, Celeste (716) 75423, Commerce (8,136) 75428, Greenville (22,161) 75401, Lone Oak (467) 75453, Newlandville (168) 75401, Quinlan (1,002) 75474, West Tawakoni (840) 75474 and Wolfe City (1,594) 75496. **UNINCORPORATED COMMUNITIES** (and ZIP Code) Aberfoyle 75496, Blue Haven Estates 75169, Burrow 75089, Cash 75401, Center Point 75401, Clinton 75005, Concord 75401, Dickson Cove 75474, Dixon 75401, Donelton 75453, Fairlie 75428, Floyd 75401, Hickory Creek 75423, Highland Acres 75453, Holiday Estates 75169, Jacobia 75401, Jardin 75428, Jot-Em-Down (also in Delta Co.) 75449, Kingston 75401, Lane 75423, Melton 75401, Merit 75072, Mexico 75474, Muddig 75449, Panorama Estates 75169, Rolling Hills 75453, Shawnee Shores Estates 75474, South Sulphur 75496, Tidwell 75401, Union Valley 75089, White Rock 75423, Wieland 75401, Yancy 75401 and Yowell (also in Delta Co.) 75428. **FOR ADDITIONAL LOCAL INFORMATION** Commerce Chamber of Commerce, P.O. Box 290, 1107½ Main St., Commerce, 75428, 214/886-3950, Greenville Chamber of Commerce, P.O. Box 1055, Greenville, 75401, 214/455-1510, Lake Tawakoni Area Chamber of Commerce, Drawer 1810, Quinlan, 75474, 214/356-2454 and Wolfe City Chamber of Commerce, P.O. Box 8, Wolfe City, 75496, 214/496-2251.

HUTCHINSON (P8)

THE LAND

Northeast of Amarillo on State Highways 207 and 152 in the High Plains Region, Hutchinson County covers 871 square miles with an elevation range of 2,800 to 3,400 feet. The county has nearly level soils with very dark, loamy surfaces over clayey subsoils and hardened calcium deposits or powdery lime. The northern part of the county lies in the High Plains vegetation area with short grasses, mesquite, shinnery oak and some cacti. The rest of the county is in the Rolling Plains vegetation area with short and mid grasses, mesquite and cacti. Between 21 and 30% of the land in the county is considered prime farmland. **CLIMATE** Continental Steppe, cool and dry. Thunderstorms, duststorms and hail are significant weather features which primarily occur during the spring. The average annual temperature is 59°F. Temperatures in January range from an average low of 21° to an average high of 51°F and in July range from 67° to 94°F. The average annual precipitation is 18 inches, with an average relative humidity of 72% at 6 A.M. and 41% at 6 P.M. The average annual snowfall is 17 inches. The growing season averages 187 days per year, with the last freeze in late April and the first freeze in late October. The sun shines during the year on the average 75% of the daylight hours.

THE PEOPLE

Within the past 50 years the population of Hutchinson County has had significant shifts, from a strong growth between 1930 and 1960 to a 29% decrease between 1960 and 1970. The 1982 estimated population of 29,200 continues the growth of the 1970s. Rural areas experienced a 35% population gain between 1970 and 1980 while the urban population slightly declined. The county's median age lowered from 34 in 1970 to 32 in 1980. The largest ancestry groups are persons of English descent (35%), Irish descent (22%) and German descent (15%). **REGISTERED VOTERS** As of November 2, 1982 there were 13,294 registered voters (0.2% of the state total). The 1982 general election had a 57% voter turnout, compared to a 78% turnout in the 1980 general election. In the 1982 primary 84% voted Democratic and 16% Republican, with 3,748 votes cast.

THE ECONOMY

AGRICULTURE Wheat area. In 1982, 98% of the land was in farms and ranches, with 14% of the farmland under cultivation and 79% irrigated. Hutchinson ranked 205th in the state in highest agricultural receipts, with 53% from crops. Overgrazing, undesirable brush and weeds, water and wind erosion and decreasing irrigation water supplies are the current conservation problems. Primary crops: wheat and sorghum. Primary livestock and products: cattle and hogs. **BUSINESS** Total number of business establishments in the county: 629. Retail sales during the first quarter of 1984 increased 2%. In 1980, 8% of the labor force were self-employed, 13% were employed in professional or related services, 26% in manufacturing, 21% in wholesale and retail trade, 12% in agriculture, forestry, fisheries and mining, 4% were employed in other counties and there were 2,289 retired workers. The industries with the most employment: oil and gas extraction, construction, petroleum refining and the manufacture of synthetic rubber, agricultural chemicals and carbon black. The nonfarm earnings in 1981 totaled $352,524,000. The retired workers received an average monthly Social Security payment of $380. **FINANCE** On June 30, 1983, four commercial banks had total deposits of $217,716,000 and total assets of $248,643,000. On December 31, 1982 two state savings and loan associations, had combined assets of $54,267,489. In addition there are seven credit unions in the county. **HOUSING** Average value of homes in 1980: $23,500. Permits for new, privately owned housing units increased in 1982: 145 permits were issued with a total construction cost of $5,665,185. Of those permits, 59 were for single family houses. Housing permits in Borger increased from 72 in 1981 to 124 in 1982. Between 1970 and 1980 the number of housing units increased by 13%. Eighty-five percent of all units in the county are air-conditioned, 94% are heated by gas and 6% by electricity. **NATURAL RESOURCES** Caliche, sand, gravel, oil and gas. In 1982 a total of 22,583,798 thousand cubic feet of gas well gas, 4,584 barrels of condensate, 3,002,551 barrels of crude oil and 25,290,755 thousand cubic feet of casinghead gas were produced. Current production of other minerals and products includes brine, caliche, sand, gravel and recovered sulphur. **TOURISM** Travel expenditures of $6,664,000 in 1982 (an increase of 11% over 1981) generated 169 jobs and $1,400,000 in payroll. Lodging: seven hotels, motels and tourist courts. **ALCOHOLIC BEVERAGES** Packaged distilled spirits, beer, ale, malt liquor and wine are legal in parts of the county. **FEDERAL EXPENDITURES** The federal government had direct expenditures or obligations of $37,432,000 in the county during fiscal year 1983, including $855,000 by the U.S. Department of Defense. In addition, the federal government provided $333,000 in grant awards, paid $2,059,000 in salaries and wages, made direct payments to individuals of $32,007,000 including $25,663,000 in retirement and disability payments, awarded $159,000 in procurement contracts and spent $2,873,000 in other expenditures or obligations. The federal government also provided $9,662,000 in direct loans and $4,569,000 in guaranteed loans and insurance.

COMMUNICATION

Newspapers–Daily: Borger News-Herald, ave. eve. circ. 8,226. Radio: KQTY-AM, KBBB-AM and KDKQ-FM (Borger). Cable TV. Telephone companies: Continental Telephone, General Telephone and Southwestern Bell. **TRANSPORTATION** Total public road mileage: 748. In 1982 there were 34,767 registered vehicles and 924 reported traffic accidents including 11 fatalities. Intercity bus service is available. Motor freight: 12 local and intrastate carriers. Rail: four branch lines carry freight through the county with one carrying annually one to five million tons and three carrying less than one million each. Aircraft: 61 are registered in the county. Airports: Hutchinson County Airport at Borger serves as a base for 74 aircraft and is a basic transportation airport with general aviation service.

COMMUNITY SERVICES

EDUCATION Six school districts with eight elementary, two middle and four high schools. The average daily attendance in 1981-82 was 4,518, with expenditures per pupil of $2,984 including 317 classroom teachers with an average annual salary of $18,180. Thirty-five percent of the 293 high school graduates planned to attend college. In 1982-83, 88% of the students were White, 8% Hispanic, 4% Black, 0.2% Asian and 0.1% American Indian. Private schools: 136 students enrolled in one elementary school. Frank Phillips College is located in Borger. Established in 1948 it is a vocational and two year academic college under local control. Enrollment in 1982 was 923 with in state undergraduate tuition and fees of $300 per semester. **PUBLIC LIBRARIES** Hutchinson County Library (Borger): 46,932 volumes and two branches. **CHILD CARE** 32 day care and 11 twenty-four hour care licensed facilities. **HEALTH CARE** 17 physicians and 11 dentists. Hospitals: one with a capacity of 99. Ambulance services: one volunteer service, one fire department and one volunteer fire department service. Mental health: one clinic. Nursing homes: two nursing homes with a combined capacity of 178 nursing care residents. The average cost per day for private patients in 1982 was $27.86. **CHURCHES** 47 churches have an estimated combined membership of 19,344. The largest denominations are Southern Baptist, United Methodist and Churches of Christ. **SOCIAL SERVICES** In fiscal year 1983 a total of $248,082 in food stamps was distributed, with an average of 543 persons receiving food stamps each month. Aid to Families with Dependent Children (AFDC) totaled $38,050 with an average of 24 families receiving AFDC each month. Medical assistance benefits for the aged and disabled of $731,809 and for families and children of $78,278 brought the county benefit total to $1,096,219. **FIRE PROTECTION** Two paid and three volunteer fire departments. **LAW ENFORCEMENT** The County Sheriff has 31 commissioned officers. Three police departments have a combined force of 31. **CRIME** 55 violent crimes (murder, forcible rape, robbery and aggravated assault) and 719 nonviolent crimes (burglary, larceny-theft and motor vehicle theft) were reported in 1982. **JUDICIAL SYSTEM** Two District Courts and Judges, one County Court and Judge and three Justices of the Peace. In the District Courts a total of 742 cases were pending on 1/1/82, 913 new cases were filed and 745 cases were disposed of during the year leaving 910 cases pending on 12/31/82. There were 329 criminal cases on the docket, 109 convictions, 20 persons committed to prison and 11 committed to jail and 155 cases left pending. In the County Court 7,193 cases were pending on 1/1/82, 1,499 new cases were filed and 1,327 cases were disposed of during the year leaving 7,365 cases pending on 12/31/82. There were 8,056 criminal cases on the docket, 595 convictions, 117 persons committed to jail and 6,753 cases left pending. **JAILS** One jail, capacity 41. The new jail was opened in 1983. **ATTORNEYS AT LAW** 25. **UTILITIES** 96% of the residents are connected to a public or privately owned water system and 84% are connected to a public sewer system. Natural gas is distributed to the county by Southern Union Company, U-Grove Distribution System, and Energas Company. The average annual residential bill for natural gas in 1982 for the Southern Union distribution system was $355.85, an increase of 23% over 1981 and for Energas it was $371.63, an increase of 23%. Electricity is distributed to the county by Southwestern Public Service, North Plains Electric Coop., Inc. and Rita Blanca Electric Coop., Inc. and is generated primarily by gas and oil. The typical residential electric bill is $170.44 per month for an all-electric house using 2,500 kwh. **TAXES** The county has 13 units with taxing authority: six school districts, four cities, one county, one college district and one special district.

RECREATION/ENTERTAINMENT

FEDERAL LAKE MEREDITH RECREATION AREA, a popular water-activity center in the Southwest, occupies 44,994 acres. Facilities include a marina, boat ramps and camp sites

HUTCHINSON(continued)

as well as swimming and fishing areas. **NATIONAL REGISTER OF HISTORIC PLACES** Fritch vicinity: Antelope Creek Archeological District. Stinnett vicinity: Adobe Walls. **MUNICIPAL PARKS** 96 acres in 23 municipal parks. These parks contain 21 playgrounds, four baseball and softball fields, seven tennis courts, three multi-use fields and three swimming pools. Developed campsites: 19. **SCENIC DRIVES** The Texas Plains Trail runs through this county. Canyon-cut landscapes of the Canadian River and views of Lake Meredith can be seen along Texas 136, F.M. 139 and F.M. 687 in southwestern Hutchinson County. **BOATING/FISHING** Lakes/reservoirs: Meredith (16,504 acres) and Pantex (20 acres). Major rivers: Canadian. Primary streams: Patton, Dixon, Spring, White Deer, Carson and Moose. **HUNTING** Fall season on antelope. Fall and winter seasons on deer and mule deer. No closed seasons on coyote and bobcat. Summer, fall and winter seasons on squirrel. Winter seasons on pheasant, quail, muskrat, beaver, opossum, ring-tailed cat, badger, fox, weasel, raccoon, skunk and civet cat. Fall, winter and spring seasons on turkey. In 1983 sandhill crane, duck, coot, geese, woodcock and jacksnipe seasons occurred during the winter months. Teal duck, rail and gallinule seasons occurred in the fall. Mourning dove seasons occurred intermittently during the fall and winter months. **MUSEUMS** Borger: Hutchinson County Museum. Fritch: Lake Meredith Aquatic and Wildlife Museum. Stinnett: Isaac McCormick Pioneer Cottage. **COLLEGIATE FINE ARTS** Borger: Cultural events offered by Frank Phillips College. **OTHER** Stinnett: Site of Battle of Adobe Walls. **SPECIAL EVENTS** World's Largest Fish Fry, Borger, June; Annual birthday Celebration, Borger, June; July 4th Fireworks, Fritch, July; Crafts Festival, Borger, September/October.

COMMUNITIES

COUNTY SEAT Stinnett, County Courthouse, 79083; County Clerk's Office, 806/878-2829. **INCORPORATED COMMUNITIES** (1980 population and ZIP Code) Borger (15,837) 79007 All-America Cities Award 1969, Fritch (2,299) 79036, Sanford (249) 79078 and Stinnett (2,222) 79083. **UNINCORPORATED COMMUNITIES** (and ZIP Code) Bunavista 79007, Dial 79026, Electric City 79006, Phillips 79071, Philview Camp 79007, Pringle 79083 and Texroy 79080. **FOR ADDITIONAL LOCAL INFORMATION** Borger Chamber of Commerce, P.O. Box 490, Borger, 79007, 806/274-2211.

IRION (P88)

THE LAND

West of San Angelo on U.S. Highway 67 in the Edwards Plateau Region, Irion County covers 1,052 square miles with an elevation range of 2,100 to 2,600 feet. The county has undulating to hilly soils with loamy surfaces and loamy or clayey subsoils. Limestone is within 40 inches of the surface and in some areas about 90% of the land is exposed rock. In the Edwards Plateau vegetation area the grasses are mid to tall with junipers, live and shinnery oak and mesquite. Between 11 and 20% of the land in the county is considered prime farmland. **CLIMATE** Subtropical Steppe, mild and dry. During spring high winds and dust occur with regularity. The average annual temperature is 66°F. Temperatures in January range from an average low of 32° to an average high of 60°F and in July range from 71° to 96°F. The average annual precipitation is 18 inches, with an average relative humidity of 74% at 6 A.M. and 40% at 6 P.M. The average annual snowfall is four inches. The growing season averages 232 days per year, with the last freeze in late March and

the first freeze in late October. The sun shines during the year on the average 70% of the daylight hours.

THE PEOPLE

Irion County is one of the most sparsely populated in the state. The 1982 estimated population of 1,600 continues the moderate growth rate begun in the 1970s, which reversed a population decline. The age groups with the largest gains were ages 15 to 19 and 20 to 34. The median age lowered from 36 in 1970 to 32 in 1980. The largest ancestry groups are persons of English descent (24%), Irish descent (21%), Hispanic (19%) and German descent (18%). **REGISTERED VOTERS** As of November 2, 1982 there were 794 registered voters (0.01% of the state total). The 1982 general election had a 68% voter turnout, compared to a 80% turnout in the 1980 general election. In the 1982 primary 85% voted Democratic and 15% Republican, with 281 votes cast.

THE ECONOMY

AGRICULTURE Sheep ranches. In 1982, 95% of the land was in farms and ranches, with less than 1% of the farmland under cultivation, most of which was irrigated. Irion ranked 234th in the state in highest agricultural receipts, with 98% from livestock and livestock products. Overgrazing, undesirable brush and weeds, water and wind erosion and decreasing irrigation water supplies are the current conservation problems. Primary fruits and nuts: pecans. Primary livestock and products: cattle, sheep, wool, angora goats and mohair. **BUSINESS** Total number of business establishments in the county: 24. Retail sales during the first quarter of 1984 increased 13%. In 1980, 16% of the labor force were self-employed, 12% were employed in professional or related services, 4% in manufacturing, 15% in wholesale and retail trade, 40% in agriculture, forestry, fisheries and mining, 29% were employed in other counties and there were 127 retired workers. The industry with the most employment: oil and gas extraction. The nonfarm earnings in 1981 totaled $13,569,000. The retired workers received an average monthly Social Security payment of $331. **FINANCE** On June 30, 1983, one commercial bank had total deposits of $28,523,000 and total assets of $32,697,000. **HOUSING** Average value of homes in 1980: $26,400. Between 1970 and 1980 the number of housing units increased by 33%. Fifty-six percent of all units in the county are air-conditioned, 82% are heated by gas and 13% by electricity. **NATURAL RESOURCES** Dolomite, limestone, salt beds, oil and gas. In 1982 a total of 6,695,432 thousand cubic feet of gas well gas, 132,947 barrels of condensate, 3,293,892 barrels of crude oil and 15,397,902 thousand cubic feet of casinghead gas were produced. **TOURISM** Travel expenditures of $120,000 in 1982 (an increase of 7% over 1981) generated 3 jobs and $22,000 in payroll. **ALCOHOLIC BEVERAGES** Only 4% beer is legal in parts of the county. **FEDERAL EXPENDITURES** The federal government had direct expenditures or obligations of $2,699,000 in the county during fiscal year 1983, including $70,000 by the U.S. Department of Defense. In addition, the federal government provided $36,000 in grant awards, paid $74,000 in salaries and wages, made direct payments to individuals of $2,045,000 including $1,461,000 in retirement and disability payments, awarded $1,000 in procurement contracts and spent $542,000 in other expenditures or obligations. The federal government also provided $57,000 in direct loans and $188,000 in guaranteed loans and insurance.

COMMUNICATION

Telephone companies: General Telephone. **TRANSPORTATION** Total public road mileage: 269. In 1982 there were 1,671 registered vehicles and 57 reported traffic accidents including four fatalities. Intercity bus service is available. Motor freight: one carrier. Rail: one branch line carries annually one to five million tons of freight through the county. Aircraft: eight are registered in the county.

COMMUNITY SERVICES

EDUCATION One school district with one elementary and one high school. The average daily attendance in 1981-82 was 295, with expenditures per pupil of $6,011 including 18 classroom teachers with an average annual salary of $19,843. Thirty-one percent of the 26 high school graduates planned to attend college. In 1982-83, 77% of the students were White and 23% Hispanic. **PUBLIC LIBRARIES** Irion County Public Library (Mertzon): 1,025 volumes. **CHILD CARE** One day care licensed facility. **HEALTH CARE** Ambulance services: one volunteer fire department service. **CHURCHES** Six churches have an estimated combined membership of 737. The largest denominations are Southern Baptist and United Methodist. **SOCIAL SERVICES** In fiscal year 1983 a total of $20,426 in food stamps was distributed, with an average of 45 persons receiving food stamps each month. Aid to Families with Dependent Children (AFDC) totaled $2,696. Medical assistance benefits for the aged and disabled of $27,763 and for families and children of $9,634 brought the county benefit total to $60,519. **FIRE PROTECTION** Three volunteer fire departments. **LAW ENFORCEMENT** The County Sheriff has three commissioned officers. **CRIME** Four nonviolent crimes (burglary, larceny-theft and motor vehicle theft) were reported in 1982. **JUDICIAL SYSTEM** One District Court and Judge, one County Court and Judge and one Justice of the Peace. In the District Court a total of 24 cases were pending on 1/1/82, 47 new cases were filed and 38 cases were disposed of during the year leaving 33 cases pending on 12/31/82. There were 10 criminal cases on the docket, eight convictions and one person was committed to prison. In the County Court 85 cases were pending on 1/1/82, 104 new cases were filed and 86 cases were disposed of during the year leaving 103 cases pending on 12/31/82. There were 175 criminal cases on the docket, 16 convictions, five persons committed to jail, and 91 cases left pending. **UTILITIES** 37% of the residents are connected to a public or privately owned water system and 32% are connected to a public sewer system. Electricity is distributed to the county by West Texas Utilities Cap Rock Electric Coop., Inc., Cocho Valley Electric Coop., Inc. and Southwest Texas Electric Coop., Inc. and is generated primarily by gas and oil. **TAXES** The county has three units with taxing authority: one school district, one city, and one county.

RECREATION/ENTERTAINMENT

NATIONAL REGISTER OF HISTORIC PLACES Sherwood: Irion County Courthouse. **MUNICIPAL PARKS** 30 acres in two municipal parks. These parks contain one playground, one baseball and softball field, one swimming pool and one beach. Major rivers: Concho and Middle Concho. Primary streams: Live Oak, West Rocky, Lopez, Spring, Dove and Kiowa. **HUNTING** Fall season on antelope. Fall and winter seasons on deer and javelina. No closed season on coyote, bobcat and squirrel. Winter seasons on quail, muskrat, beaver, opossum, ring-tailed cat, badger, fox, weasel, raccoon, skunk and civet cat. Fall, winter and spring seasons on turkey. In 1983 sandhill crane, duck, coot, geese, woodcock and jacksnipe seasons occurred during the winter months. Teal duck, rail and gallinule seasons occurred in the fall. Mourning dove seasons occurred intermittently during the fall and winter months.

COMMUNITIES

COUNTY SEAT Mertzon, County Courthouse, 76941; County Clerk's Office, 915/835-2421. **INCORPORATED COMMUNITIES** (1980 population and ZIP Code) Mertzon (687) 76941.

UNINCORPORATED COMMUNITIES (and ZIP Code) Arden 76901, Barnhart 76930 and Sherwood 76941.

JACK (P56)

THE LAND

Southeast of Wichita Falls on U.S. Highways 281 and 380 in the North Central Prairies Region, Jack County covers 920 square miles with an elevation range of 1,000 to 1,600 feet. The land is undulating to hilly with light colored, loamy soils over very deep, reddish clayey subsoils, shale and sandstone. Jack is in the Cross Timbers and Prairies vegetation area with prairie grasses, post oak and mesquite trees. Between 11 and 20% of the land in the county is considered prime farmland. **CLIMATE** Subtropical Subhumid, generally mild and dry. Wide variations in temperatures from winter to summer will be experienced. The average annual temperature is 65°F. Temperatures in January range from an average low of 31° to an average high of 57°F and in July range from 73° to 97°F. The average annual precipitation is 29 inches, with an average relative humidity of 78% at 6 A.M. and 47% at 6 P.M. The average annual snowfall is six inches. The growing season averages 222 days per year, with the last freeze in early April and the first freeze in early November. The sun shines during the year on the average 72% of the daylight hours.

THE PEOPLE

The 1982 estimated population of 7,800 indicates a continuation of the growth in population which began in the 1970s, reversing the steady population decrease between 1940 and 1970. Urban areas grew faster than rural areas between 1970 and 1980. The median age lowered from 39 in 1970 to 35 in 1980. The largest ancestry groups are persons of English descent (35%), Irish descent (24%) and German descent (14%). **REGISTERED VOTERS** As of November 2, 1982 there were 4,193 registered voters (0.1% of the state total). The 1982 general election had a 50% voter turnout, compared to a 66% turnout in the 1980 general election. In the 1982 primary 95% voted Democratic and 5% Republican, with 1,320 votes cast.

THE ECONOMY

AGRICULTURE In 1982, 87% of the land was in farms and ranches, with 4% of the farmland under cultivation. Jack ranked 198th in the state in highest agricultural receipts, with 94% from livestock and livestock products. Overgrazing, undesirable brush and weeds, water erosion, a lack of potable water and difficulties in grass establishment are the current conservation problems. Primary crops: wheat, oats and hay. Primary vegetables: sweet potatoes and watermelons. Primary fruits and nuts: peaches and pecans. Primary livestock and products: cattle and hogs. **BUSINESS** Total number of business establishments in the county: 181. Retail sales during the first quarter of 1984 increased 7%. In 1980, 14% of the labor force were self-employed, 16% were employed in professional or related services, 9% in manufacturing, 17% in wholesale and retail trade, 27% in agriculture, forestry, fisheries and mining, 20% were employed in other counties and there were 948 retired workers. The industries with the most employment: oil and gas extraction and the manufacture of structure metal products and oil field machinery. The nonfarm earnings in 1981 totaled $76,208,000. The retired workers received an average monthly Social Security payment of $303. **FINANCE** On June 30, 1983, three commercial banks had total deposits of $81,275,000 and total assets of $89,590,000. There is one state savings and loan association branch in the county. **HOUSING** Average value of homes in 1980: $22,000. Permits for new, privately owned housing units

COUNTIES

JACK (continued)

decreased in 1982: 11 permits were issued with a total construction cost of $568,998. Of those permits, all were for single family houses. Between 1970 and 1980 the number of housing units increased by 17%. Seventy-nine percent of all units in the county are air-conditioned, 83% are heated by gas and 12% by electricity. **NATURAL RESOURCES** Clay, limestone, oil, gas and bituminous coal. In 1982 a total of 25,237,681 thousand cubic feet of gas well gas, 189,185 barrels of condensate, 2,748,082 barrels of crude oil and 13,181,868 thousand cubic feet of casinghead gas were produced. Current production of other minerals and products includes crushed limestone. **TOURISM** Travel expenditures of $910,000 in 1982 (an increase of 12% over 1981) generated 19 jobs and $161,000 in payroll. **ALCOHOLIC BEVERAGES** Totally dry. **FEDERAL EXPENDITURES** The federal government had direct expenditures or obligations of $15,119,000 in the county during fiscal year 1983, including $1,092,000 by the U.S. Department of Defense. In addition, the federal government provided $758,000 in grant awards, paid $613,000 in salaries and wages, made direct payments to individuals of $13,616,000 including $9,581,000 in retirement and disability payments, awarded $5,000 in procurement contracts and spent $125,000 in other expenditures or obligations. The federal government also provided $10,000 in direct loans and $390,000 in guaranteed loans and insurance.

COMMUNICATION

Newspapers–Weekly: Jack County Herald (Jacksboro) and the Gazette-News (Jacksboro). Cable TV. Telephone companies: General Telephone, Southwestern Bell, United Telephone, Brazos Telephone Coop., Central Telephone-Midstate and Palo Pinto Telephone. **TRANSPORTATION** Total public road mileage: 705. In 1982 there were 8,114 registered vehicles and 172 reported traffic accidents including seven fatalities. Intercity bus service is available. Motor freight: three carriers. Aircraft: 11 are registered in the county. Airports: Jacksboro Municipal Airport serves as a base for 10 aircraft and is a basic utility airport with general aviation service.

COMMUNITY SERVICES

EDUCATION Three school districts with three elementary, two middle and three high schools. The average daily attendance in 1981-82 was 1,414, with expenditures per pupil of $2,550 including 88 classroom teachers with an average annual salary of $16,396. Forty-one percent of the 111 high school graduates planned to attend college. In 1982-83, 97% of the students were White, 2% Hispanic, 0.8% Black and 0.1% Asian. **PUBLIC LIBRARIES** Jacksboro Library. **CHILD CARE** Seven day care licensed facilities. **HEALTH CARE** Four physicians and four dentists. Hospitals: one with a capacity of 49. Ambulance services: one commercial and one police department service. Mental health: one county clinic. Nursing homes: two nursing homes with a combined capacity of 158 nursing care residents. The average cost per day for private patients in 1982 was $31.14. **CHURCHES** 35 churches have an estimated combined membership of 5,277. The largest denominations are Southern Baptist and United Methodist. **SOCIAL SERVICES** In fiscal year 1983 a total of $112,699 in food stamps was distributed, with an average of 234 persons receiving food stamps each month. Aid to Families with Dependent Children (AFDC) totaled $17,389 with an average of 15 families receiving AFDC each month. Medical assistance benefits for the aged and disabled of $643,108 and for families and children of $48,921 brought the county benefit total to $822,117. **FIRE PROTECTION** Six volunteer fire departments. **LAW ENFORCEMENT** The County Sheriff has four commissioned officers. One police department has a force of seven.

CRIME Seven violent crimes (murder, forcible rape, robbery and aggravated assault) and 155 nonviolent crimes (burglary, larceny-theft and motor vehicle theft) were reported in 1982. **JUDICIAL SYSTEM** One District Court and Judge, one County Court and Judge and two Justices of the Peace. In the District Court a total of 540 cases were pending on 1/1/82, 208 new cases were filed and 305 cases were disposed of during the year leaving 443 cases pending on 12/31/82. There were 41 criminal cases on the docket, 12 convictions, six persons committed to prison, and 21 cases left pending. In the County Court 302 cases were pending on 1/1/82, 292 new cases were filed and 252 cases were disposed of during the year leaving 342 cases pending on 12/31/82. There were 465 criminal cases on the docket, 125 convictions, 41 persons committed to jail, and 220 cases left pending. **JAILS** One jail, capacity 15. **ATTORNEYS AT LAW** Six. **UTILITIES** 64% of the residents are connected to a public or privately owned water system and 61% are connected to a public sewer system. Natural gas is distributed to the county by Brazos River Gas Co. Electricity is distributed to the county by Texas Power and Light Co., Fort Belknap Electric Coop., Inc., J-A-C Electric Coop., Inc. and Tri Co. Electric Coop. Inc. and is generated primarily by gas, coal and water. The typical residential electric bill is $165.24 per month for an all-electric house using 2,500 kwh. **TAXES** The county has eight units with taxing authority: three school districts, two cities, one county, and two special districts.

RECREATION/ENTERTAINMENT

NATIONAL REGISTER OF HISTORIC PLACES Jacksboro: Fort Richardson (National Historic Landmark) and James W. Knox House. **STATE** Fort Richardson State Historical Park covers 389 acres with camping and trailer sites as well as fishing areas. The post hospital now serves as a Western museum. Also existing are the officers' quarters and the bakery. **COUNTY/MUNICIPAL PARKS** 14 acres in one county and two municipal parks. These parks contain one playground, four tennis courts, one swimming pool, one boat ramp and shore fishing facilities. Developed campsites: nine. **SCENIC DRIVES** The Texas Forts Trail runs through this county. This trail leads to eight of the famous frontier forts of West Central Texas and an ancient presidio of the Spanish colonial period. **BOATING/FISHING** Lakes/reservoirs: Bryson (96 acres), Cherryhomes (11 acres), Conners (24 acres), Craft (42 acres), Grace (15 acres), Ida (32 acres), Jacksboro (86 acres), Johnson (29 acres), Keechi Creek Soil Conservation Service Lakes 1, 2, 5 and 6 (58 acres), North Creek Soil Conservation Lake 16 (13 acres) and Worthington (20 acres). Major rivers: West Fork Trinity and Little Cleveland. Primary streams: East Rock, Howard, Lost, Crooked, North Fork Crooked, Little Cleveland, West Fork Keechi, Two Bush and Henderson. **HUNTING** Fall and winter seasons on deer. No closed season on coyote, bobcat and squirrel. Winter seasons on quail, muskrat, beaver, opossum, ring-tailed cat, badger, fox, weasel, raccoon, skunk and civet cat. Fall, winter and spring seasons on turkey. In 1983 duck, coot, geese, woodcock and jacksnipe seasons occurred during the winter months. Teal duck, rail and gallinule seasons occurred in the fall. Mourning dove seasons occurred intermittently during the fall and winter months. **SPECIAL EVENTS** County Fair and Stock Show, Jacksboro, February; Snake Safari, Jacksboro, March; Weekend in Ole Mesquiteville, Jacksboro, June; Quarter Horse Show, Jacksboro, September.

COMMUNITIES

COUNTY SEAT Jacksboro, County Courthouse, 76056; County Clerk's Office, 817/567-2111. **INCORPORATED COMMUNITIES** (1980 population and ZIP Code) Bryson (579) 76027 and Jacksboro (4,000) 76056. **UNINCORPORATED COMMUNITIES** (and ZIP Code) Antelope 76350, Bartons Chapel

76056, Cundiff 76056, Gibtown 76075, Jermyn 76057, Joplin 76056, Newport (also in Clay Co.) 76254, Perrin 76075, Postoak 76230, Truce (Friendship Church) 76254, Vineyard 76085 and Wizard Wells 76056. **FOR ADDITIONAL LOCAL INFORMATION** Jacksboro Chamber of Commerce, Belknap and Main, P.O. Box 606, Jacksboro, 76056, 817/567-2602.

JACKSON (G23)

THE LAND

Southwest of Houston on U.S. Highway 59 in the Coastal Prairies Region, Jackson County covers 844 square miles with an elevation ranging from sea level to 150 feet. The level soils of the county are light colored and loamy, with very deep, reddish subsoils in the northwestern one-third. Light to dark loamy surfaces with clayey subsoils or gray to black cracking, clayey soils with a high shrink-swell potential are in the rest of the county. Jackson is in the Gulf Prairies and Marshes vegetation area with tall grasses, post oak and bunchgrasses. Mesquite are on the prairie with marsh millet, saltgrass and cordgrasses in the marshes. Between 41 and 50% of the land in the county is considered prime farmland. **CLIMATE** Subtropical Humid. Tropical storms and hurricanes are possible June through October. The average annual temperature is 70°F. Temperatures in January range from an average low of 43° to an average high of 63°F and in July range from 75° to 94°F. The average annual precipitation is 40 inches, with an average relative humidity of 90% at 6 A.M. and 65% at 6 P.M. There is no yearly snowfall. The growing season averages 285 days per year, with the last freeze in late February and the first freeze in early December. The sun shines during the year on the average 68% of the daylight hours.

THE PEOPLE

The 1982 estimated population of 13,700 continues a growth in population which began in the 1970s, reversing a population decrease between 1960 and 1970. Urban areas grew at a faster rate than rural areas between 1970 and 1980. The county has a high percentage of residents over age 64, although the population's median age was 31 in 1980. The largest ancestry groups are persons of German descent (20%), Hispanic (19%), English descent (16%) and Irish descent (16%). **REGISTERED VOTERS** As of November 2, 1982 there were 6,909 registered voters (0.1% of the state total). The 1982 general election had a 59% voter turnout, compared to a 63% turnout in the 1980 general election. In the 1982 primary 98% voted Democratic and 2% Republican, with 2,435 votes cast.

THE ECONOMY

AGRICULTURE Sorghum area. In 1982, 90% of the land was in farms and ranches, with 30% of the farmland under cultivation and 35% irrigated. Jackson ranked 59th in the state in highest agricultural receipts, with 70% from crops. Overgrazing, undesirable brush and weeds, water erosion, inefficient irrigation systems, drainage and flooding are the current conservation problems. Primary crops: sixth in the state for rice, sorghum, corn, hay and cotton. Primary vegetables: potatoes, sweet potatoes and watermelons. Primary fruits and nuts: peaches and pecans. Primary livestock and products: cattle. **BUSINESS** Total number of business establishments in the county: 288. Retail sales during the first quarter of 1984 decreased 1%. In 1980, 14% of the labor force were self-employed, 14% were employed in professional or related services, 11% in manufacturing, 23% in wholesale and retail trade, 22% in agriculture, forestry, fisheries and mining, 33% were employed in other counties and there were 1,172 retired workers. The industries with the most employment: oil and gas extraction, concrete production and heavy

construction. The nonfarm earnings in 1981 totaled $124,865,000. The retired workers received an average monthly Social Security payment of $303. **FINANCE** On June 30, 1983, three commercial banks had total deposits of $117,242,000 and total assets of $130,831,000. On December 31, 1982 one state savings and loan association and one state branch had assets of $19,598,117. In addition there are two credit unions in the county. **HOUSING** Average value of homes in 1980: $28,600. Permits for new, privately owned housing units decreased in 1982: 37 permits were issued with a total construction cost of $1,451,711. Of those permits, 21 were for single family houses. Between 1970 and 1980 the number of housing units increased by 19%. Sixty-six percent of all units in the county are air-conditioned, 76% are heated by gas and 20% by electricity. **NATURAL RESOURCES** Oil and gas. In 1982 a total of 18,352,810 thousand cubic feet of gas well gas, 108,264 barrels of condensate, 6,662,923 barrels of crude oil and 11,166,409 thousand cubic feet of casinghead gas were produced. **TOURISM** Travel expenditures of $1,953,000 in 1982 (an increase of 12% over 1981) generated 42 jobs and $357,000 in payroll. **ALCOHOLIC BEVERAGES** Packaged distilled spirits, beer, ale, malt liquor and wine are legal in parts of the county. Sale of mixed beverages is legal in all or parts of the county. **FEDERAL EXPENDITURES** The federal government had direct expenditures or obligations of $26,290,000 in the county during fiscal year 1983, including $496,000 by the U.S. Department of Defense. In addition, the federal government provided $335,000 in grant awards, paid $854,000 in salaries and wages, made direct payments to individuals of $17,327,000 including $13,109,000 in retirement and disability payments, awarded $98,000 in procurement contracts and spent $7,675,000 in other expenditures or obligations. The federal government also provided $4,255,000 in direct loans and $16,405,000 in guaranteed loans and insurance.

COMMUNICATION

Newspapers–Weekly: Edna Herald and the Ganado Tribune. Cable TV. Telephone companies: General Telephone, Southwestern Bell, Ganado Telephone and La Ward Telephone. **TRANSPORTATION** Total public road mileage: 776. In 1982 there were 14,094 registered vehicles and 278 reported traffic accidents including three fatalities. Intercity bus service is available. Motor freight: five local and intrastate carriers. Rail: two main and one branch line carry freight through the county. One of the main lines carries annually 10 to 20 million tons of freight and the other one carries five to 10 million with the branch line carrying one to five million tons. Aircraft: 31 are registered in the county. Airports: Jackson County Airport at Edna serves as a base for 20 aircraft and is a basic utility airport with general aviation service. Also serving the area are Hahns Airport at Edna and White's Airport at La Ward.

COMMUNITY SERVICES

EDUCATION Three school districts with seven elementary, two middle and three high schools. The average daily attendance in 1981-82 was 2,866, with expenditures per pupil of $2,822 including 205 classroom teachers with an average annual salary of $17,225. Forty-four percent of the 212 high school graduates planned to attend college. In 1982-83, 64% of the students were White, 24% Hispanic, 11% Black and 0.2% Asian. **PUBLIC LIBRARIES** Jackson County Library (Edna): 11,106 volumes. **CHILD CARE** 12 day care and six twenty-four hour care licensed facilities. **HEALTH CARE** 10 physicians and five dentists. Hospitals: two with a combined capacity of 85. Clinics: one public health clinic. Ambulance services: two volunteer fire department services, one commercial and one volunteer service. Nursing homes: two nursing homes with a combined capacity of 118 nursing care residents. The average cost per day for private patients in 1982 was $29.49.

COUNTIES

JACKSON (continued)

CHURCHES 34 churches have an estimated combined membership of 8,599. The largest denominations are Southern Baptist, Catholic and United Methodist. **SOCIAL SERVICES** In fiscal year 1983 a total of $676,833 in food stamps was distributed, with an average of 1,439 persons receiving food stamps each month. Aid to Families with Dependent Children (AFDC) totaled $181,717 with an average of 131 families receiving AFDC each month. Medical assistance benefits for the aged and disabled of $1,273,239 and for families and children of $222,074 brought the county benefit total to $2,353,862. **FIRE PROTECTION** Five volunteer fire departments. **LAW ENFORCEMENT** The County Sheriff has 26 commissioned officers. Two police departments have a combined force of 10. **CRIME** 28 violent crimes (murder, forcible rape, robbery and aggravated assault) and 138 nonviolent crimes (burglary, larceny-theft and motor vehicle theft) were reported in 1982. **JUDICIAL SYSTEM** Three District Courts and Judges, one County Court and Judge and four Justices of the Peace. In the District Courts a total of 354 cases were pending on 1/1/82, 302 new cases were filed and 309 cases were disposed of during the year leaving 347 cases pending on 12/31/82. There were 200 criminal cases on the docket, 87 convictions, 24 persons committed to prison and one committed to jail and 71 cases left pending. In the County Court 213 cases were pending on 1/1/82, 526 new cases were filed and 383 cases were disposed of during the year leaving 356 cases pending on 12/31/82. There were 614 criminal cases on the docket, 211 convictions, one person committed to jail, and 281 cases left pending. **JAILS** One jail, capacity 29. **ATTORNEYS AT LAW** 15. **UTILITIES** 64% of the residents are connected to a public or privately owned water system and 62% are connected to a public sewer system. Natural gas is distributed to the county by Entex, Inc. The average annual residential bill for natural gas in 1982 for the Entex distribution system was $390.31, an increase of 26% over 1981. Electricity is distributed to the county by Central Power and Light Co., Cochran Power and Light Co., DeWitt Co. Electric Coop., Inc., Jackson Electric Coop., Inc. and Victoria Co. Electric Coop. Inc. and is generated primarily by gas, oil, coal and water. The typical residential electric bill is $162.15 per month for an all-electric house using 2,500 kwh. **TAXES** The county has 13 units with taxing authority: four school districts, two cities, one county, one hospital district and five special districts.

RECREATION/ENTERTAINMENT
NATIONAL REGISTER OF HISTORIC PLACES Edna: Texana Presbyterian Church. **STATE** Lake Texana State Park covers 575 acres with camping and trailer sites as well as areas offering fishing, swimming and boat ramps. **COUNTY/MUNICIPAL PARKS** 92 acres in six county and two municipal parks. These parks contain two playgrounds, three baseball and softball fields, one swimming pool, three beaches, four boat ramps and shore fishing facilities. **SCENIC DRIVES** The Texas Independence Trail runs through this county. This trail not only surveys the historic sites of southeastern Texas but also includes many modern visitor attractions such as the Johnson Space Center. **BOATING/FISHING** Lakes/reservoirs: Texana (11,000 acres). Major rivers: Navidad and Lavaca. Primary streams: Carancahua, West Carancahua, Garcitas, Arenosa and Sandy. **SALT WATER FISHING** for speckled trout, redfish and flounders is usually good around Lavaca Bay and Carancahua Bay. Shrimp, oysters and crabs may be taken but, like other saltwater fish, under specific regulations. **HUNTING** Fall and winter seasons on deer. No closed season on nutria, squirrel, coyote and bobcat. Winter seasons on quail, muskrat, beaver, otter, opossum, mink, ring-tailed cat, badger, fox, weasel, raccoon, skunk and civet cat. In 1983 duck, coot, geese, woodcock and jacksnipe seasons occurred during the winter months. Winter season on sandhill cranes in some parts of the county. Teal duck, rail and gallinule seasons occurred in the fall. Mourning dove seasons occurred intermittently during the fall and winter months. **MUSEUMS** Edna: Texana Museum and Library. **SPECIAL EVENTS** Texana Days, Edna, date varies; Jackson County Fair, Edna, September/October.

COMMUNITIES
COUNTY SEAT Edna, County Courthouse, 77957; County Clerk's Office, 512/782-3563. **INCORPORATED COMMUNITIES** (1980 population and ZIP Code) Edna (5,650) 77957, Ganado (1,770) 77962 and La Ward (218) 77970. **UNINCORPORATED COMMUNITIES** (and ZIP Code) Carancahua 77465, Cordele 77957, El Toro 77957, Francitas 77961, La Salle 77969, Lolita 77971, Morales 77957, Vanderbilt 77991 and Weedhaven 77979. **FOR ADDITIONAL LOCAL INFORMATION** Jackson County Chamber of Commerce, 317 W. Main, P.O. Box 788, Edna, 77957, 512/782-2382.

JASPER (E34)

THE LAND
Northeast of Houston on U.S. Highways 190 and 96 in the East Texas Timberlands Region, Jasper County covers 921 square miles with an elevation ranging from 25 to 400 feet. The soils along the northern border and southern one-third of the county are gently rolling to hilly with light colored loamy surfaces over very deep, reddish, clayey or loamy subsoils. The rest of the county has nearly level, moderately well to poorly drained, light colored, acidic, sandy to loamy surfaces with very deep, mottled or reddish throughout, subsoils. These soils are deficient in plant nutrients. In the Pineywoods vegetation area the prime timber species are loblolly, shortleaf, longleaf and slash pines, and hardwoods such as oak, hickory and maple with Indiangrass, native legumes and occasional shrubs. Between 31 and 40% of the land in the county is considered prime farmland. **CLIMATE** Subtropical Humid. Annual rainfall is among the highest in the state. The average annual temperature is 67 °F. Temperatures in January range from an average low of 37° to an average high of 59°F and in July range from 72° to 93°F. The average annual precipitation is 52 inches, with an average relative humidity of 87% at 6 A.M. and 65% at 6 P.M. Snowfall in winter is rare. The growing season averages 229 days per year, with the last freeze in mid March and the first freeze in early November. The sun shines during the year on the average 62% of the daylight hours.

THE PEOPLE
The population of Jasper County has grown steadily since 1930. The 1982 estimated population of 31,200 indicates a continuation of that growth rate. Greater gains in population occurred in rural areas between 1970 and 1980 than in urban areas. The population has a high percentage of residents who are over age 64, although the median age is 31. The largest ancestry groups are persons of English descent (30%), Irish descent (21%) and Black (19%). **REGISTERED VOTERS** As of November 2, 1982 there were 16,100 registered voters (0.3% of the state total). The 1982 general election had a 43% voter turnout, compared to a 64% turnout in the 1980 general election. In the 1982 primary 98% voted Democratic and 2% Republican, with 6,619 votes cast.

THE ECONOMY
AGRICULTURE Major forest production area. In 1982, 20% of the land was in farms and ranches, with 1% of the farmland under cultivation. Jasper ranked 229th in the state in highest agricultural receipts, with 80% from livestock and livestock

products. Overgrazing, undesirable brush and weeds, inadequate cropping systems, water erosion and flooding are the current conservation problems. Primary crops: hay. Primary vegetables: cabbage, sweet potatoes, tomatoes and watermelons. Primary fruits and nuts: peaches and pecans. Primary livestock and products: cattle and hogs. **BUSINESS** Total number of business establishments in the county: 546. Retail sales during the first quarter of 1984 increased 14%. In 1980, 9% of the labor force were self-employed, 17% were employed in professional or related services, 27% in manufacturing, 20% in wholesale and retail trade, 11% in construction, 29% were employed in other counties and there were 2,754 retired workers. The industries with the most employment: agribusiness, heavy construction, poultry processing, lumber mills, sawmills and paperboard mills. The nonfarm earnings in 1981 totaled $269,734,000. The retired workers received an average monthly Social Security payment of $323. **FINANCE** On June 30, 1983, four commercial banks had total deposits of $118,678,000 and total assets of $134,243,000. On December 31, 1982 one state savings and loan association, one federal association and one federal branch had combined assets of $125,281,221. In addition there are two credit unions in the county. **HOUSING** Average value of homes in 1980: $24,900. Permits for new, privately owned housing units increased in 1982: 31 permits were issued with a total construction cost of $841,350. Of those permits, all were for single family houses. Housing permits in Jasper increased from 12 in 1981 to 26 in 1982 with all permits issued for single family houses. Between 1970 and 1980 the number of housing units increased by 47%. Seventy-three percent of all units in the county are air-conditioned, 66% are heated by gas and 24% by electricity. **NATURAL RESOURCES** Clay, industrial sand, oil and gas. In 1982 a total of 1,004,551 thousand cubic feet of gas well gas, 37,677 barrels of condensate, 552,899 barrels of crude oil and 1,072,090 thousand cubic feet of casinghead gas were produced. Current production of other minerals and products includes clay, industrial sand, sand and gravel and crushed sandstone. Pine and hardwood production in 1981 totaled 23,060,677 cubic feet: 18,925,330 cubic feet of pine and 4,135,347 cubic feet of hardwood. **TOURISM** Travel expenditures of $5,528,000 in 1982 (an increase of 12% over 1981) generated 117 jobs and $995,000 in payroll. **ALCOHOLIC BEVERAGES** Packaged distilled spirits, beer, ale, malt liquor and wine are leal in parts of the county. **FEDERAL EXPENDITURES** The federal government had direct expenditures or obligations of $46,490,000 in the county during fiscal year 1983, including $2,953,000 by the U.S. Department of Defense. In addition, the federal government provided $1,367,000 in grant awards, paid $2,290,000 in salaries and wages, made direct payments to individuals of $42,177,000 including $32,444,000 in retirement and disability payments, awarded $518,000 in procurement contracts and spent $138,000 in other expenditures or obligations. The federal government also provided $5,000 in direct loans and $3,152,000 in guaranteed loans and insurance.

COMMUNICATION

Newspapers–Weekly: News Boy-Spanish (Jasper) and the Kirbyville Banner. Radio: KTXJ-AM and KWYX-FM (Jasper). Cable TV. Telephone companies: Southwestern Bell and Colmesneil Telephone. **TRANSPORTATION** Total public road mileage: 1,023. In 1982 there were 29,974 registered vehicles and 480 reported traffic accidents including 16 fatalities. Taxi cabs: two companies in the city of Jasper. Intercity bus service is available. Motor freight: six local and intrastate carriers. Rail: three main and two branch lines carry freight through the county. Two of the main lines carry annually five to 10 million tons of freight each and the other one carries one to five. The two branch lines carry one to five million tons of freight each. Aircraft: 31 are registered in the county. Airports: Bell Field at Jasper serves as a base for 23 aircraft and is a general utility airport with general aviation service. Also serving the area are Pineywoods Airport at Jasper and County Airport at Kirbyville.

COMMUNITY SERVICES

EDUCATION Five school districts with six elementary, three middle and five high schools. The average daily attendance in 1981-82 was 6,583, with expenditures per pupil of $2,285 including 388 classroom teachers with an average annual salary of $16,579. Thirty-three percent of the 466 high school graduates planned to attend college. In 1982-83, 72% of the students were White, 1% Hispanic, 27% Black and 0.1% Asian. Private schools: 72 students enrolled in one elementary school. Vocational education: Jasper Memorial Hospital School of Vocational Nursing. **PUBLIC LIBRARIES** Jasper Public Library: 16,759 volumes. Kirbyville Public Library: 6,809 volumes. **CHILD CARE** 16 day care and 11 twenty-four hour care licensed facilities. **HEALTH CARE** 25 physicians and eight dentists. Hospitals: four with a combined capacity of 198. Clinics: one public health clinic. Ambulance services: two funeral homes, one commercial and one city service. Mental health: one county clinic. Nursing homes: three nursing homes with a combined capacity of 270 nursing care residents. The average cost per day for private patients in 1982 was $28.63. **CHURCHES** 78 churches have an estimated combined membership of 18,827. The largest denominations are Southern Baptist, United Methodist and Baptist Missionary. **SOCIAL SERVICES** In fiscal year 1983 a total of $2,275,109 in food stamps was distributed, with an average of 4,507 persons receiving food stamps each month. Aid to Families with Dependent Children (AFDC) totaled $525,374 with an average of 349 families receiving AFDC each month. Medical assistance benefits for the aged and disabled of $2,834,011 and for families and children of $715,175 brought the county benefit total to $6,349,668. **FIRE PROTECTION** Four volunteer fire departments. **LAW ENFORCEMENT** The County Sheriff has 21 commissioned officers. Two police departments have a combined force of 22. **CRIME** 61 violent crimes (murder, forcible rape, robbery and aggravated assault) and 644 nonviolent crimes (burglary, larceny-theft and motor vehicle theft) were reported in 1982. **JUDICIAL SYSTEM** Two District Courts and Judges, one County Court and Judge and six Justices of the Peace. In the District Courts a total of 1,170 cases were pending on 1/1/82, 948 new cases were filed and 870 cases were disposed of during the year leaving 1,248 cases pending on 12/31/82. There were 358 criminal cases on the docket, 81 convictions, 18 persons committed to prison, and 166 cases left pending. In the County Court 2,076 cases were pending on 1/1/82, 625 new cases were filed and 909 cases were disposed of during the year leaving 1,792 cases pending on 12/31/82. There were 2,510 criminal cases on the docket, 282 convictions, 21 persons committed to jail, and 1,607 cases left pending. **JAILS** One jail, capacity 12. New jail under construction. **ATTORNEYS AT LAW** 27. **UTILITIES** 57% of the residents are connected to a public or privately owned water system and 36% are connected to a public sewer system. Natural gas is distributed to the county by Entex, Inc. The average annual residential bill for natural gas in 1982 for the Entex distribution system was $390.31, an increase of 26% over 1981. Electricity is distributed to the city of Jasper by the Jasper Electric System, Kirbyville by the Kirbyville Light and Power Co. and to the rest of the county by Jasper-Newton Electric Coop., Inc. and Deep East Texas Electric Coop., Inc. and is generated primarily by gas and oil. The typical residential electric bill is $140.81 per month for an all-electric house using 2,500 kwh. **TAXES** The county has 11 units with taxing authority: five school districts, two cities, one county, one hospital district and two special districts.

COUNTIES

JASPER (continued)

RECREATION/ENTERTAINMENT

FEDERAL BIG THICKET NATIONAL PRESERVE (See Hardin County). ANGELINA NATIONAL FOREST covers 154,916 acres in four counties and includes eight recreation areas. SABINE NATIONAL FOREST covers 188,220 acres in five counties and includes seven recreation areas. **NATIONAL REGISTER OF HISTORIC PLACES** Jasper: Blake-Beaty-Orton House. Jasper vicinity: Andrew Smyth House and Randolph C. Doom House. Roganville: Turner-White-McGee House. **STATE** Martin Dies, Jr. State Park covers 705 acres with camping and trailer sites, fishing, swimming, boat ramps and nature trails. **MUNICIPAL PARKS** Eight acres in two municipal parks with one playground. **SCENIC DRIVES** The Texas Forest Trail runs through this county. This trail explores the farming, ranching and oilfield areas of the East Texas Pineywoods. **BOATING/FISHING** Lakes/reservoirs: B.A. Steinhagen (13,700 acres). Major rivers: Angelina and Neches. **WILDLIFE REFUGES** Angelina-Neches Scientific Area is a State Wildlife Management Area covering 4,042 acres. Dam B State Wildlife Management Area covers 6,500 acres. **HUNTING** Fall and winter seasons on deer. Summer, fall and winter seasons on squirrel. No closed seasons on coyote, bobcat and nutria. Winter seasons on quail, muskrat, beaver, otter, opossum, mink, ring-tailed cat, badger, fox, raccoon, skunk and civet cat. Fall, winter and spring seasons on turkey. In 1983 duck, coot, geese, woodcock and jacksnipe seasons occurred during the winter months. Teal duck, rail and gallinule seasons occurred in the fall. Mourning dove seasons occurred intermittently during the fall and winter months. **MUSEUMS** Jasper: Jasper County Museum. **SPECIAL EVENTS** Azalea Trail, Jasper, March/April; Rodeo, Jasper, May; Fireworks Display, Jasper, July 4; Indian Summer Arts and Crafts Festival, Jasper, October; Christmas Parade, Jasper, December.

COMMUNITIES

COUNTY SEAT Jasper, County Courthouse, 75951; County Clerk's Office, 409/384-2632. **INCORPORATED COMMUNITIES** (1980 population and ZIP Code) Browndell (228) 75931, Jasper (6,959) 75951 and Kirbyville (1,972) 75956. **UNINCORPORATED COMMUNITIES** (and ZIP Code) Bessmay 77612, Bon Ami 75956, Buna 77612, Call (Call Junction) (also in Newton Co.) 75933, Curtis 75951, Erin 75951, Evadale 77615, Friendship 75966, Harrisburg 75951, Holly Springs 75951, Magnolia Springs 75957, Mount Union 75956, Parkwood 77612, Roganville 75971 and Sam Rayburn (Rayburn Country) 75951. **FOR ADDITIONAL LOCAL INFORMATION** Jasper Chamber of Commerce, 790 S. Wheeler, P.O. Box 638, Jasper, 75951, 409/384-2762 and Kirbyville Chamber of Commerce, P.O. Box 417, Kirbyville, 75956, 409/423-2284.

JEFF DAVIS (B4)

THE LAND

Southeast of El Paso on U.S. Highway 90 in the Trans-Pecos Region, Jeff Davis County covers 2,258 square miles with an elevation range of 3,800 to 6,000 feet. About 90% of the interior portion of this mountainous county is exposed rock with very dark loamy soils over clayey subsoils in the valleys. In the southwest and along the fringe of the county are alkaline, loamy soils over clayey subsoils with limestone bedrock. Jeff Davis is in the Trans-Pecos, Mountains and Basins vegetation area with desert shrub, salt tolerant grasses, cacti, juniper, pinon pine and oak. Less than 1% of the land in the county is considered prime farmland. **CLIMATE** Subtropical Arid with warm, dry winters. The average annual temperature is 63 °F. Temperatures in January range from an average low of 32° to an average high of 54°F and in July range from 63° to 90°F. The average annual precipitation is 18 inches, with an average relative humidity of 65% at 6 A.M. and 33% at 6 P.M. The average annual snowfall is six inches. The growing season averages 225 days per year, with the last freeze in late March and the first freeze in early November. The sun shines during the year on the average 77% of the daylight hours.

THE PEOPLE

Jeff Davis County is one of the most sparsely populated in the state and ranks 44th among all U.S. counties in the highest percent of residents who are of Spanish origin. The 1982 estimated population of 1,600 indicates a decline in population since 1980. The majority of residents live in rural areas. The largest ancestry groups are Hispanic (47%) persons of English descent (22%), German descent (14%) and Irish descent (14%). **REGISTERED VOTERS** As of November 2, 1982 there were 981 registered voters (0.01% of the state total). The 1982 general election had a 56% voter turnout, compared to a 70% turnout in the 1980 general election. In the 1982 primary 100% voted Democratic, with 232 votes cast.

THE ECONOMY

AGRICULTURE Ranchland. In 1982, 86% of the land was in farms and ranches, with 1% of the farmland under cultivation, most of which was irrigated. Jeff Davis ranked 230th in the state in highest agricultural receipts, with 90% from livestock and livestock products. Overgrazing and decreasing irrigation water supplies are the current conservation problems. Primary crops: 10th in the state for barley. Wheat. Primary fruits and nuts: peaches and pecans. Primary livestock and products: cattle, angora goats and mohair. **BUSINESS** Total number of business establishments in the county: 27. In 1980, 14% of the labor force were self-employed, 18% were employed in professional or related services, 2% in manufacturing, 16% in wholesale and retail trade, 25% in agriculture, forestry, fisheries and mining, 9% were employed in other counties and there were 158 retired workers. The industries with the most employment: tourism and oil and gas extraction. The nonfarm earnings in 1981 totaled $12,022,000. The retired workers received an average monthly Social Security payment of $297. **FINANCE** On June 30, 1983, one commercial bank had total deposits of $5,945,000 and total assets of $7,169,000. There is one state savings and loan association branch in the county. **HOUSING** Average value of homes in 1980: $14,400. Between 1970 and 1980 the number of housing units increased by 5%. Fifty-two percent of all units in the county are air-conditioned, 77% are heated by gas and 10% by electricity. **NATURAL RESOURCES** Barite, kaolin clay, lead, limestone, manganese, rhyolite and silver. **TOURISM** Travel expenditures of $2,071,000 in 1982 (an increase of 12% over 1981) generated 50 jobs and $404,000 in payroll. **ALCOHOLIC BEVERAGES** Packaged distilled spirits, beer, ale, malt liquor and wine are legal in parts of the county. **FEDERAL EXPENDITURES** The federal government had direct expenditures or obligations of $3,291,000 in the county during fiscal year 1983, including $164,000 by the U.S. Department of Defense. In addition, the federal government provided $14,000 in grant awards, paid $318,000 in salaries and wages, made direct payments to individuals of $2,416,000 including $1,879,000 in retirement and disability payments, awarded $392,000 in procurement contracts and spent $151,000 in other expenditures or obligations. The federal government also provided $1,379,000 in guaranteed loans and insurance.

COMMUNICATION

Cable TV. Telephone companies: Continental Telephone,

Southwestern Bell and Big Bend Telephone. **TRANSPORTA-TION** Total public road mileage: 409. In 1982 there were 1,650 registered vehicles and 57 reported traffic accidents including two fatalities. Intercity bus service is available. Motor freight: two carriers. Rail: the Sunset Limited provides passenger service on the Amtrak Route. Two main lines carry freight through the county with one carrying annually over 30 million tons and the other carrying one to five million. Aircraft: 10 are registered in the county.

COMMUNITY SERVICES

EDUCATION Two school districts with two elementary and two high schools. The average daily attendance in 1981-82 was 308, with expenditures per pupil of $2,852 including 24 classroom teachers with an average annual salary of $15,403. Fifty-three percent of the 15 high school graduates planned to attend college. In 1982-83, 49% of the students were White, 51% Hispanic and 0.3% Asian. Sports championships: 1983 A Girls' Tennis Doubles, Fort Davis H.S. **PUBLIC LIBRARIES** Fort Davis Library. **CHILD CARE** Two twenty-four hour care licensed facilities. **HEALTH CARE** One physician and one dentist. Ambulance services: one volunteer service and one volunteer fire department service. **CHURCHES** Nine churches have an estimated combined membership of 2,246. The largest denominations is the Christian Methodist Episcopal. **SOCIAL SERVICES** In fiscal year 1983 a total of $70,501 in food stamps was distributed, with an average of 153 persons receiving food stamps each month. Aid to Families with Dependent Children (AFDC) totaled $7,242. Medical assistance benefits for the aged and disabled of $41,898 and for families and children of $4,714 brought the county benefit total to $124,355. **FIRE PROTECTION** Four volunteer fire departments. **LAW ENFORCEMENT** The County Sheriff has five commissioned officers. **JUDICIAL SYSTEM** One District Court and Judge, one County Court and Judge and three Justices of the Peace. In the District Court a total of 56 cases were pending on 1/1/82, 49 new cases were filed and 22 cases were disposed of during the year leaving 83 cases pending on 12/31/82. There were seven criminal cases on the docket, four convictions, and three cases left pending. In the County Court 23 cases were pending on 1/1/82, 51 new cases were filed and 40 cases were disposed of during the year leaving 34 cases pending on 12/31/82. There were 67 criminal cases on the docket, seven convictions, and 32 cases left pending. **UTILITIES** 49% of the residents are connected to a public or privately owned water system and 32% are connected to a public sewer system. Natural gas is distributed to the county by Southwest Texas Municipal Gas Corp. Electricity is distributed to the county by Rio Grande Electric Cooperative Inc. and is generated primarily by gas, oil and coal. **TAXES** The county has three units with taxing authority: two school districts, and one county.

RECREATION/ENTERTAINMENT

FEDERAL FORT DAVIS NATIONAL HISTORIC SITE is considered the most extensive and impressive existing example of Southwestern frontier forts. Spanning 460,000 acres, the fort was built in 1854 as a stronghold for western travellers and became a key post in the West Texas defensive system. Facilities include a museum in reconstructed barracks and a sound re-creation of a military retreat parade from the previous century. **NATIONAL REGISTER OF HISTORIC PLACES** Fort Davis: Fort Davis (National Historic Landmark) and Grierson-Sprowl House. **STATE** Davis Mountains (Indian Lodge) State Park covers 1,869 acres with camping and trailer sites as well as swimming, nature trails, scenic drives and exhibits. **SCENIC DRIVES** The Texas Mountain Trail runs through this county. In addition State Highways 17, 166 and 118 around Fort Davis form a 74-mile loop

through the Davis Mountains and Madera Canyon offering a host of mountain landscapes. **BOATING/FISHING** Primary streams: Van Horn. **HUNTING** Fall season on antelope. Fall and winter seasons on deer and mule deer. No closed seasons on javelina, elk, coyote and bobcat. Fall and winter seasons on quail. Winter seasons on muskrat, beaver, opossum, ring-tailed cat, badger, fox, weasel, raccoon, skunk and civet cat. In 1983 sandhill crane, duck, coot, geese, woodcock and jacksnipe seasons occurred during the winter months. Teal duck, rail and gallinule seasons occurred in the fall. Mourning dove seasons occurred intermittently during the fall and winter months with a fall season on white-winged dove. **MUSEUMS** Fort Davis: Interpretive Center, Neill Museum and Overland Trail Museum. **OBSERVATORY** Fort Davis: McDonald Observatory. **SPECIAL EVENTS** New Year's Day Celebration, Fort Davis, January; Three-Day Independence Celebration, Fort Davis, July.

COMMUNITIES

COUNTY SEAT Fort Davis, County Courthouse, 79734; County Clerk's Office, 915/426-3251. **INCORPORATED COMMUNITIES** (1980 population and ZIP Code) Valentine (328) 79854. **UNINCORPORATED COMMUNITIES** (and ZIP Code) Fort Davis 79734. **FOR ADDITIONAL LOCAL INFORMATION** Fort Davis Chamber of Commerce, P.O. Box 378, Fort Davis, 79734, 915/426-3441.

JEFFERSON (G13)

THE LAND

Bordering Louisiana and the Gulf of Mexico on Interstate Highway 10 in the Coastal Prairies Region, Jefferson County covers 937 square miles with an elevation ranging from sea level to 50 feet. Along the coast are the sandy soils of beaches and the dark, saline, loamy surfaces over clayey subsoils of marshes. Along the northern border are light colored, loamy soils over very deep, reddish clayey or loamy subsoils that have hardened calcium deposits. The rest of the county has light to dark loamy surfaces over clayey subsoils or gray to black cracking, clayey soils with a high shrink-swell potential. The county lies in the Gulf Prairies and Marshes vegetation area with tall grasses, bunchgrasses, post oak, mesquite, marsh millet, seashore saltgrass and cordgrasses. Between one and 10% of the land in the county is considered prime farmland. **CLIMATE** Subtropical Humid, with warm, moist summers. There is a possibility of tropical storms and hurricanes June through October. The average annual temperature is 69°F. Temperatures in January range from an average low of 43° to an average high of 61°F and in July range from 75° to 91°F. The average annual precipitation is 53 inches, with an average relative humidity of 90% at 6 A.M. and 70% at 6 P.M. There is no snowfall. The growing season averages 255 days per year, with the last freeze in early March and the first freeze in mid November. The sun shines during the year on the average 60% of the daylight hours.

THE PEOPLE

Jefferson County is one of the most densely populated in the state with 94% of its residents living in urban areas. The 1982 estimated population of 257,400 represents a slight increase since 1980. The growth rate began to slow during the 1960s. Between 1970 and 1980 rural areas grew faster than urban areas. The median age rose from 28 in 1970 to 30 in 1980. The largest ancestry groups are Black (28%), persons of English descent (22%), Irish descent (17%), French descent (16%) and German descent (12%). **REGISTERED VOTERS** As of November 2, 1982 there were 122,000 registered voters (2% of the state total). The 1982 general election had a 48% voter turnout, compared to a

JEFFERSON (continued)

67% turnout in the 1980 general election. In the 1982 primary 97% voted Democratic and 3% Republican, with 41,950 votes cast.

THE ECONOMY

AGRICULTURE Forest production and rice area. In 1982, 64% of the land was in farms and ranches, with 21% of the farmland under cultivation and 81% irrigated. Jefferson ranked 123rd in the state in highest agricultural receipts, with 75% from crops. Overgrazing, inefficient irrigation systems and drainage are the current conservation problems. Primary crops: seventh in the state for rice and 10th for soybeans. Primary fruits and nuts: peaches and pecans. Primary livestock and products: cattle. **BUSINESS** Total number of business establishments in the county: 5,318. Retail sales during the first quarter of 1984 increased 11%. In 1980, 5% of the labor force were self-employed, 19% were employed in professional or related services, 24% in manufacturing, 22% in wholesale and retail trade, 9% in transportation, communications and other public utilities, 6% were employed in other counties and there were 19,043 retired workers. The industries with the most employment: agribusiness, bakery products, oil and gas field servicing, construction, soft drink bottling and canning, commercial printing, petroleum refining, iron and steel foundries, metal coating, ship building and repairing, and the manufacture of engineering and scientific instruments, oil field machinery, metal containers, synthetic rubber, industrial chemicals, plastics and resins, electrical wiring devices, structural metal products, valves and pipe fittings, optical instruments, nuts and bolts. The nonfarm earnings in 1981 totaled $3,057,522,000. The retired workers received an average monthly Social Security payment of $368. **FINANCE** On June 30, 1983, 17 commercial banks had total deposits of $1,685,467,000 and total assets of $1,947,727,000. On December 31, 1982 five state savings and loan associations, one federal association, 18 state branches and five federal branches had combined assets of $675,289,331. In addition there are 46 credit unions in the county. **HOUSING** Average value of homes in 1980: $30,600. Permits for new, privately owned housing units decreased in 1982: 1,113 permits were issued with a total construction cost of $50,544,083. Of those permits, 645 were for single family houses. Housing permits increased in Groves from 25 in 1981 to 86 in 1982 with 54 of the permits issued for apartments and condominiums, and in Port Neches from 26 to 50 with all permits issued for single family houses. Between 1970 and 1980 the number of housing units increased by 18%. Eighty-six percent of all units in the county are air-conditioned, 75% are heated by gas and 25% by electricity. **NATURAL RESOURCES** Brine, clay, salt domes, industrial sand, oil and gas. In 1982 a total of 76,663,975 thousand cubic feet of gas well gas, 1,494,321 barrels of condensate, 3,296,208 barrels of crude oil and 4,686,683 thousand cubic feet of casinghead gas were produced. Current production of other minerals and products includes brine, construction sand, sand and gravel, frasch sulphur and recovered sulphur. Pine and hardwood production in 1981 totaled 1,806,960 cubic feet: 759,473 cubic feet of pine and 1,047,487 cubic feet of hardwood. **TOURISM** Travel expenditures of $173,645,000 in 1982 (an increase of 9% over 1981) generated 3,770 jobs and $33,623,000 in payroll. Lodging: 32 hotels, motels and tourist courts. Convention/meeting facilities: Beaumont-Civic Center Complex, Speedway 90 Stadium, Julie Rogers Theatre, Fairpark Coliseum, Harvest Club and four hotels with facilities for large gatherings; Port Arthur-Civic Center. **ALCOHOLIC BEVERAGES** Packaged distilled spirits, beer, ale, malt liquor and wine are legal in parts of the county. Sale of mixed beverages is legal in all or parts of the county.

MILITARY INSTALLATIONS Nederland Air National Guard Station, Nederland, 102 personnel, nine acres, Air National Guard Activities. **FEDERAL EXPENDITURES** The federal government had direct expenditures or obligations of $631,657,000 in the county during fiscal year 1983, including $272,991,000 by the U.S. Department of Defense. In addition, the federal government provided $23,459,000 in grant awards, paid $34,586,000 in salaries and wages, made direct payments to individuals of $303,552,000 including $232,269,000 in retirement and disability payments, awarded $262,428,000 in procurement contracts and spent $7,633,000 in other expenditures or obligations. The federal government also provided $9,154,000 in direct loans and $1,166,075,000 in guaranteed loans and insurance.

COMMUNICATION

Newspapers–Daily: The Beaumont Enterprise, ave. morn. circ. 65,294, The Beaumont Journal, ave. eve. circ., 10,633 and the Port Arthur News, ave. eve. circ., 24,628. Weekly: Groves Chronicle, Nederland Review and Mid Chronicle (Port Neches). Radio: KALO-AM, KAYC-AM, KLVI-AM, KTLK-AM, KQXY-FM, KVLU-FM, KWIC-FM, KZZB-FM and KAYD-FM Stereo (Beaumont), KOLE-AM, KTXC-AM, KHYS-FM, KYKR-FM (Port Arthur) and KDLF-AM, KGUL-FM (Port Neches). Television: KBMT-CH. 12, KFDM-CH. 6 (Beaumont), KJAC-CH. 4 (Port Arthur). Cable TV. Telephone companies: Southwestern Bell, Cameron Telephone and Trinity Valley Telephone. **TRANSPORTATION** Total public road mileage: 2,005. In 1982 there were 222,441 registered vehicles and 9,266 reported traffic accidents including 64 fatalities. Taxi cabs: 13 companies in Port Arthur, four in Beaumont, one in Nederland and one in Port Neches. Municipal transit systems: one intracity bus system in Port Arthur and one in Beaumont, both with scheduled routes. Intercity bus service is available. Motor freight: 68 local and intrastate carriers. Rail: The Sunset Limited provides passenger service on the Amtrak Route. Thirteen main and one branch line carry freight through the county. Three of the main lines carry annually 20 to 30 million tons of freight each, one carries 10 to 20, six carry five to 10 each, one carries one to five and two carry less than one million tons each. The one branch carries annually less than one million tons of freight. Aircraft: 245 are registered in the county. Airports: Jefferson County Airport between Port Arthur and Beaumont serves as a base for 95 aircraft and is a non-hub airport with short haul flights and carrier service. Beaumont Municipal Airport serves as a base for 70 aircraft and is a general utility airport with general aviation service. Park Place Hospital at Port Arthur provides a Heliport for emergency use. Waterborne commerce: Beaumont Port shipped 40,358,920 short tons in 1981: 15,644,921 in foreign imports, 3,528,188 in foreign exports and 21,185,622 in domestic products. Port Arthur shipped 26,037,529 short tons: 11,189,200 in foreign imports, 2,879,094 in foreign exports and 11,951,235 in domestic products. Sabine-Pass Harbor shipped 1,063,238 short tons: 11,051 in foreign exports and 1,052,187 in domestic products. Sabine-Neches Waterway shipped 27,008,243 short tons of domestic products.

COMMUNITY SERVICES

EDUCATION Seven school districts with 42 elementary, 15 middle, 12 high schools and one special education. The average daily attendance in 1981-82 was 39,951, with expenditures per pupil of $3,352 including 2,625 classroom teachers with an average annual salary of $20,956. Forty-eight percent of the 3,224 high school graduates planned to attend college. In 1982-83, 54% of the students were White, 4% Hispanic, 39% Black and 3% Asian. Sports championships: 1984 AAAA Boys' Basketball, Port Arthur Lincoln H.S.; 1983 AAAAA Baseball, Port Arthur

Jefferson H.S. Private schools: 3,736 students enrolled in 14 elementary and four high schools. Sports championships: 1982 AAA Boys' Golf, Kelly H.S. Lamar University is located in Beaumont. Established in 1923 it is under state control. Enrollment in 1982 was 13,526 with in state undergraduate tuition and fees of $516 per semester. The highest degree offered is Doctorate. Sports championships: (Southland conference) 1983 Men's Cross Country, 1983 Men's Indoor Track, 1983 Women's Volleyball, 1983 Men's Outdoor Track, 1983 Women's Tennis, 1983 Men's Golf, 1984 Men's Basketball. Lamar University at Port Arthur was established in 1975 and is under state control. Vocational education: Beaumont-Baptist Hospital of Southeast Texas, Metils, Inc., Chenier Business College, Lonnie's Beauty College. Port Arthur-Broussard's School Inc. **PUBLIC LIBRARIES** Beaumont Public Library System: 191,046 volumes, three branches. Groves Library. D. Bob Henson Memorial Library (Nederland): 26,181 volumes. Jefferson County Library (Nederland): 40,916 volumes. Port Arthur Public Library: 107,838 volumes, one branch. Effie and Wilton Hebert Public Library (Port Neches): 32,365 volumes. **CHILD CARE** 306 day care and 62 twenty-four hour care licensed facilities. **HEALTH CARE** 427 physicians and 138 dentists. Hospitals: seven with a combined capacity of 1,758. Clinics: two for treatment of drug abuse, two public health clinics, one outpatient clinic, and one dialysis clinic. Ambulance services: seven commercial, five funeral homes, one city, and one volunteer fire department service. Mental health: two clinics, one state outreach clinic, one hospital with a capacity of 93, one center with a capacity of 130 and one state development center with a capacity of 56. Nursing homes: 12 nursing homes with a combined capacity of 1,613 nursing care and 40 custodial care residents. The average cost per day for private patients in 1982 was $31.52. **CHURCHES** 222 churches have an estimated combined membership of 171,181. The largest denominations are Catholic, Southern Baptist and United Methodist. **SOCIAL SERVICES** In fiscal year 1983 a total of $13,133,689 in food stamps was distributed, with an average of 24,453 persons receiving food stamps each month. Aid to Families with Dependent Children (AFDC) totaled $3,244,167 with an average of 2,108 families receiving AFDC each month. Medical assistance benefits for the aged and disabled of $16,498,013 and for families and children of $5,391,232 brought the county benefit total to $38,267,101. **FIRE PROTECTION** Three paid, two partly paid and 10 volunteer fire departments. **LAW ENFORCEMENT** The County Sheriff has 80 commissioned officers. Seven police departments have a combined force of 383. One university campus has a police department with a force of 10 officers. **CRIME** 2,589 violent crimes (murder, forcible rape, robbery and aggravated assault) and 16,075 nonviolent crimes (burglary, larceny-theft and motor vehicle theft) were reported in 1982. **JUDICIAL SYSTEM** Eight District Courts and Judges, three County Courts and Judges and eight Justices of the Peace. In the District Courts a total of 6,416 cases were pending on 1/1/82, 9,202 new cases were filed and 9,013 cases were disposed of during the year leaving 6,605 cases pending on 12/31/82. There were 3,784 criminal cases on the docket, 767 convictions, 563 persons committed to prison and 16 committed to jail and 2,511 cases left pending. In the County Courts 10,872 cases were pending on 1/1/82, 7,437 new cases were filed and 6,434 cases were disposed of during the year leaving 11,875 cases pending on 12/31/82. There were 13,756 criminal cases on the docket, 1,911 convictions, 1,049 persons committed to jail and 9,177 cases left pending. **JAILS** Two jails, capacity 352. An addition to increase capacity by 163 is being built as certification was lost in 1983 due to overcrowding. **ATTORNEYS AT LAW** 494. **UTILITIES** 97% of the residents are connected to a public or privately owned water system and 95% are connected to a public sewer system. Natural gas is distributed to the county by Entex, Inc. and Southern Union Company. The average annual residential bill for natural gas in 1982 for the Entex distribution system was $390.31, an increase of 26% over 1981 and for Southern Union it was $355.85, an increase of 23%. Electricity is distributed to the county by Gulf State Utilities Co. and is generated primarily by gas and oil. The typical residential electric bill is $198.32 per month for an all-electric house using 2,500 kwh. **TAXES** The county has 26 units with taxing authority: seven school districts, six cities, one county, and 12 special districts.

RECREATION/ENTERTAINMENT

TEXAS LEAGUE BASEBALL The city of Beaumont has a team in the Western Division of the League. **FEDERAL** Big Thicket National Preserve (See Hardin County). **NATIONAL REGISTER OF HISTORIC PLACES** Beaumont: Jefferson County Courthouse, Beaumont Y.M.C.A., Beaumont Commercial District, French Home Trading Post, Hinchee House, Idle Hours, Jefferson Theatre, McFaddin House complex, Mildred Buildings and Sanders House. Beaumont vicinity: Lucas Gusher (National Historic Landmark). Port Arthur: Rose Hill Pompeiian Villa and Gates Memorial Library. **STATE** Sabine Pass Battleground State Historical Park covers 56 acres with fishing and boat ramp facilities. The park is the site of a union attempt to invade Texas during the Civil War. Dominating today's park is a statue of Dick Dowling, leader of the Confederate defense. Sea Rim State Park covers 15,109 acres with camping and trailer sites as well as fishing, swimming, boat ramps, nature hikes, air boat rides and exhibits. **COUNTY/MUNICIPAL PARKS** 4,100 acres in one county and 78 municipal parks. These parks contain three miles of hiking trails, 61 playgrounds, three golf courses, one football and soccer field, 42 baseball and softball fields, 64 tennis courts, 24 multi-use courts, seven swimming pools, one beach, eight boat ramps and shore fishing facilities. Developed campsites: 174. **BOATING/FISHING** Lakes/reservoirs: Crawford (100 acres), Fisher (500 acres), Fontenot (300 acres), Little (300 acres), McBride (126 acres), McFaddin (1,000 acres), J.D. Murphree (10,000 acres), Ogden (200 acres), Port Arthur Club (500 acres), Russells (150 acres), Spindletop (500 acres), Taylor (100 acres) and Viterbo Reservoir (200 acres). Major rivers: Neches. Primary streams: Salt Bayou, Elm Bayou, Taylor Bayou, Hillbrandt and Pine Island Bayou. **SALTWATER FISHING** Speckled trout, redfish and flounder fishing is usually good around Port Arthur and Beaumont. Jefferson County offers easy access to the Sabine Jetties which are offshore waters for those who like deepsea fishing. Shrimp, oysters and crabs may be taken but, like other saltwater fish, under specific regulations. **WILDLIFE REFUGES** J.D. Murphree State Wildlife Management Area covers 8,048 acres. **HUNTING** Fall and winter seasons on deer. Summer, fall and winter seasons on squirrel. No closed seasons on coyote, bobcat and nutria. Winter seasons on pheasant, quail, muskrat, beaver, otter, opossum, mink, ring-tailed cat, badger, fox, raccoon, skunk and civet cat. In 1983 duck, coot, geese, woodcock and jacksnipe seasons occurred during the winter months. Teal duck, rail and gallinule seasons occurred in the fall. Mourning dove seasons occurred intermittently during the fall and winter months. **MUSEUMS** Beaumont: Art Museum, Brown-Scurlock Galleries, Babe Didrickson, Zaharias Memorial Museum, John Jay French Trading Post, Port of Beaumont Visitor Center, Spindletop Museum, Temple to the Brave and Lucas Gusher Monument. Nederland: Dutch Windmill Museum and La Maison Des Acadiens. Port Arthur: Historical Museum and Pompeiian Villa. Sabine Pass: Sea Rim State Visitor Center. **THEATERS** Beaumont: City Auditorium and Jefferson Theater. **ORCHESTRAS** Beaumont: Symphony Orchestra. **OPERA** Beaumont: Civic Opera. **DANCE** Beaumont: Civic Ballet. **PLANETARIUM** Jefferson: Port Neches I.S.D. Planetarium. **COLLEGIATE FINE ARTS** Beaumont: cultural

COUNTIES

JEFFERSON (continued)

events offered by Lamar University. **SPECIAL EVENTS** Triangle Trekkers Volksmarch, Beaumont, January; Southwest Texas Woodcarvers Show, Beaumont, January; Heritage Festival, Nederland, March; YMBL Rodeo, Beaumont, April; Neches River Festival, Beaumont, April; May Fete, Beaumont, May; Kaleidoscope Arts Festival, Beaumont, May; Beaumont Charity Horse Show, Beaumont, May; Saltwater Anglers Fishing Tourney, Port Arthur, May; Pow Wow Festival, Port Neches, May; Jazz Festival, Beaumont, July; Spindletop Boom Days, Beaumont, September; Mexican Festival, Port Arthur, September; Pecan Festival, Groves, September; South Texas Fair, Beaumont, October; CavOilcade, Port Arthur, October; Halloween Parade, Groves, October; Polderfaire Arts and Crafts Show, Nederland, November; Arts and Crafts Fair, Groves, November; Christmas Parade and Tree Lighting, Groves, December.

COMMUNITIES

COUNTY SEAT Beaumont, County Courthouse, 77701; County Clerk's Office, 409/835-8475. **INCORPORATED COMMUNITIES** (1980 population and ZIP Code) Beaumont (118,102) 77701, Bevil Oaks (1,306) 77706, China (1,351) 77613, Griffing Park (1,802) 77640, Groves (17,090) 77619, Nederland (16,855) 77627, Nome (550) 77629, Port Arthur (61,251) 77640, All-America Cities Award in 1973 and Honorable Mention 1970 and Port Neches (13,944) 77651. **UNINCORPORATED COMMUNITIES** (and ZIP Code) Beaux Art Gardens 77705, Central Gardens 77627, Central Heights 77627, Cheek 77705, Clayton 77627, Del Monte 77627, Fannett 77705, Hamshire 77622, Hillebrant 77705, Hollywood 77627, Lovell Lake 77706, Meeker 77706, Pine Island 77706, Peterson 77627, Price 77627 and Ridgecrest 77627. **FOR ADDITIONAL LOCAL INFORMATION** Beaumont Chamber of Commerce, 595 Orleans, P.O. Box 3150, Beaumont, 77704, 409/838-6581, Groves Chamber of Commerce, 6221 Coolidge Groves, 77619, 409/962-3631, Nederland Chamber of Commerce, 1515 Boston Ave., P.O. Box 891, Nederland, 77627, 409/722-0279, Greater Port Arthur Chamber of Commerce, Fidelity Tower, #300N, 4749 Twin City Hwy., Port Arthur, 77640, 409/963-1107 and Port Neches Chamber of Commerce, 1207 Pt. Neches Ave., Port Neches, 77651, 409/722-9154.

JIM HOGG (B23)

THE LAND

Southwest of Corpus Christi on State Highways 1017 and 16 in the Rio Grande Plains Region, Jim Hogg County covers 1,136 square miles with an elevation range of 200 to 800 feet. To the east the nearly level soils are sandy with areas of light colored, loamy surfaces over very deep reddish or mottled, clayey subsoils. The rest of the county has loamy surfaces over deep reddish or mottled clayey subsoils with limestone within 40 inches of the surface in some areas. Jim Hogg is in the South Texas Plains vegetation area with grasslands, mesquite, post and live oak and cacti. Less than 1% of the land in the county is considered prime farmland. **CLIMATE** Subtropical Humid. An occasional tropical storm or weakening hurricane will move inland from the gulf. The average annual temperature is 73°F. Temperatures in January range from an average low of 44° to an average high of 69°F and in July range from 73° to 99°F. The average annual precipitation is 23 inches, with an average relative humidity of 88% at 6 A.M. and 55% at 6 P.M. There is no snowfall. The growing season averages 305 days per year, with the last freeze in mid February and the first freeze in mid December. The sun shines during the year on the average 67% of the daylight hours.

THE PEOPLE

Jim Hogg County ranks 3rd among all U.S. counties in the highest percent of residents who are of Spanish origin. The 1982 estimated population of 5,500 indicates a continuation of the moderate growth which began in the 1970s, reversing a steady population decline between 1940 and 1970. 87% of the residents live in urban areas which had a 15% population gain between 1970 to 1980, while the population in rural areas decreased. The largest ancestry group is Hispanic (90%). **REGISTERED VOTERS** As of November 2, 1982 there were 4,027 registered voters (0.1% of the state total). The 1982 general election had a 44% voter turnout, compared to a 52% turnout in the 1980 general election. In the 1982 primary 100% voted Democratic, with 2,295 votes cast.

THE ECONOMY

AGRICULTURE Ranchland. In 1982, 94% of the land was in farms and ranches, with 2% of the farmland under cultivation and 21% irrigated. Jim Hogg ranked 189th in the state in highest agricultural receipts, with 88% from livestock and livestock products. Overgrazing, undesirable brush and weeds and difficulties in grass establishment are the current conservation problems. Primary crops: sorghum and hay. Primary vegetables: watermelons and onions. Primary livestock and products: cattle, milk, sheep and hogs. **BUSINESS** Total number of business establishments in the county: 91. In 1980, 11% of the labor force were self-employed, 18% were employed in professional or related services, 3% in manufacturing, 18% in wholesale and retail trade, 26% in agriculture, forestry, fisheries and mining, 25% were employed in other counties and there were 390 retired workers. The industry with the most employment: oil and gas extraction. The nonfarm earnings in 1981 totaled $36,155,000. The retired workers received an average monthly Social Security payment of $244. **FINANCE** On June 30, 1983, one commercial bank had total deposits of $29,531,000 and total assets of $34,928,000. There is one state savings and loan association branch in the county. **HOUSING** Average value of homes in 1980: $17,000. Between 1970 and 1980 the number of housing units increased by 16%. Forty-two percent of all units in the county are air-conditioned, 83% are heated by gas and 16% by electricity. **NATURAL RESOURCES** Caliche, clay, uranium, oil and gas. In 1982 a total of 12,047,688 thousand cubic feet of gas well gas, 113,875 barrels of condensate, 596,516 barrels of crude oil and 1,443,974 thousand cubic feet of casinghead gas were produced. Current production of other minerals and products includes uranium. **TOURISM** Travel expenditures of $1,105,000 in 1982 (an increase of 12% over 1981) generated 25 jobs and $209,000 in payroll. **ALCOHOLIC BEVERAGES** Packaged distilled spirits, beer, ale, malt liquor and wine are legal. Sale of mixed beverages is legal in all or parts of the county. **FEDERAL EXPENDITURES** The federal government had direct expenditures or obligations of $7,467,000 in the county during fiscal year 1983, including $112,000 by the U.S. Department of Defense. In addition, the federal government provided $759,000 in grant awards, paid $946,000 in salaries and wages, made direct payments to individuals of $5,698,000 including $4,084,000 in retirement and disability payments, awarded $2,000 in procurement contracts and spent $63,000 in other expenditures or obligations. The federal government also provided $5,000 in direct loans and $703,000 in guaranteed loans and insurance.

COMMUNICATION

Newspapers–Weekly: Hebbronville Enterprise. Cable TV. Telephone companies: General Telephone, Southwestern Bell and Valley Telephone Coop. **TRANSPORTATION** Total public road mileage: 209. In 1982 there were 3,940 registered vehicles and 91 reported traffic accidents including one fatality. Intercity bus service is available. Motor freight: four carriers. Aircraft: nine are registered in the county. Airports: Jim Hogg County Airport at Hebbronville.

COMMUNITY SERVICES

EDUCATION One school district with one elementary, one middle and one high school. The average daily attendance in 1981-82 was 1,122, with expenditures per pupil of $4,821 including 76 classroom teachers with an average annual salary of $16,605. Sixty-four percent of the 70 high school graduates planned to attend college. In 1982-83, 7% of the students were White and 93% Hispanic. **PUBLIC LIBRARIES** Jim Hogg County Public Library (Hebbronville): 16,071 volumes. **CHILD CARE** Three day care licensed facilities. **HEALTH CARE** Four physicians. Ambulance services: one county service. Mental health: one clinic. **CHURCHES** 13 churches have an estimated combined membership of 4,453. The largest denomination is Catholic. **SOCIAL SERVICES** In fiscal year 1983 a total of $492,095 in food stamps was distributed, with an average of 1,175 persons receiving food stamps each month. Aid to Families with Dependent Children (AFDC) totaled $71,366 with an average of 51 families receiving AFDC each month. Medical assistance benefits for the aged and disabled of $343,722 and for families and children of $75,388 brought the county benefit total to $982,570. **FIRE PROTECTION** Two volunteer fire departments. **LAW ENFORCEMENT** The County Sheriff has 12 commissioned officers. **CRIME** 10 violent crimes (murder, forcible rape, robbery and aggravated assault) and 24 nonviolent crimes (burglary, larceny-theft and motor vehicle theft) were reported in 1982. **JUDICIAL SYSTEM** One District Court and Judge, one County Court and Judge and four Justices of the Peace. In the District Court a total of 152 cases were pending on 1/1/82, 98 new cases were filed and 103 cases were disposed of during the year leaving 147 cases pending on 12/31/82. There were 58 criminal cases on the docket, 25 convictions, and 24 cases left pending. In the County Court 54 cases were pending on 1/1/82, 74 new cases were filed and 38 cases were disposed of during the year leaving 90 cases pending on 12/31/82. There were 88 criminal cases on the docket, 23 convictions, two persons committed to jail, and 55 cases left pending. **JAILS** One jail, capacity 18. **ATTORNEYS AT LAW** Six. **UTILITIES** 93% of the residents are connected to a public or privately owned water system and 78% are connected to a public sewer system. Natural gas is distributed to the county by Entex, Inc. The average annual residential bill for natural gas in 1982 for the Entex distribution system was $390.31, an increase of 26% over 1981. Electricity is distributed to the county by Cochran Power and Light Co. and Medina Electric Coop., Inc. and is generated primarily by gas and water. The typical residential electric bill is $162.15 per month for an all-electric house using 2,500 kwh. **TAXES** The county has three units with taxing authority: one school district, one county and one special district.

RECREATION/ENTERTAINMENT

COUNTY PARKS 26 acres in four county parks. These parks contain two miles of hiking trails, two playgrounds, one baseball and softball field, three tennis courts, one multi-use court and one swimming pool. **SCENIC DRIVES** The Texas Tropical Trail runs through this county. This trail is charted through the state's southernmost wedge meandering through ranchland, resort areas on the Gulf of Mexico and fertile farmlands. **BOATING/FISHING** Primary streams: Arroyo Los Palos, Arroyo Baluarte, Palo Blanco and Noriacitas. **HUNTING** Fall and winter seasons on deer. No closed seasons on javelina, coyote, bobcat and squirrel. Winter seasons on quail, muskrat, beaver, opossum, ring-tailed cat, badger, fox, weasel, raccoon, skunk and civet cat. Fall, winter and spring seasons on turkey. In 1983

sandhill crane, duck, coot, geese, woodcock and jacksnipe seasons occurred during the winter months. Teal duck, rail and gallinule seasons occurred in the fall. Mourning dove seasons occurred intermittently during the fall and winter months with a fall season on white-winged dove. **SPECIAL EVENTS** Chamber of Commerce Festival, Hebbronville, September/October; Jim Hogg County Fair, Hebbronville, December/January.

COMMUNITIES

COUNTY SEAT Hebbronville, County Courthouse, 78361; County Clerk's Office, 512/527-4031. **UNINCORPORATED COMMUNITIES** (and ZIP Code) Agua Nueva 78361, Guerra 78360, Hebbronville (4,079 est. incorp. inactive) 78361, Kelsay 78353 and Rancho Viejo 78361. **FOR ADDITIONAL LOCAL INFORMATION** Hebbronville Chamber of Commerce, 210 N. Smith, Hebbronville, 78361, 512/527-3024.

JIM WELLS (B21)

THE LAND

West of Corpus Christi on U.S. Highway 281 in the Rio Grande Plain Region, Jim Wells County covers 867 square miles with an elevation range of 200 to 400 feet. The nearly level soils are light to dark, with loamy surfaces over reddish, clayey subsoils and limestone 40 inches from the surface. There are some gray to black, cracking, clayey soils with a high shrink-swell potential. Jim Wells is in the South Texas Plains vegetation area with grasslands, mesquite, post and live oak and cacti. Between 41 and 50% of the land in the county is considered prime farmland. **CLIMATE** Subtropical Humid with heavy rains from weakening tropical storms and/or hurricanes June through October. The average annual temperature is 72 °F. The January temperatures range from an average low of 44 °F to an average high of 68 °F. and in July range from 74° to 96 °F. The average precipitation for the year is 28 inches, with an average relative humidity of 88% at 6 A.M. and 60% at 6 P.M. There is no snowfall. The growing season averages 304 days per year, with the last freeze in mid February and the first freeze in early December. The sun shines during the year on the average 68% of the daylight hours.

THE PEOPLE

Jim Wells County ranks 24th among all U.S. counties in the highest percent of persons who are of Spanish origin. The 1982 estimated population of 38,200 indicates a continuation of the growth in population which began in the 1970s. The greatest growth from 1970 to 1980 occurred in rural areas, with a population gain of 31%. The median age rose from 24 in 1970 to 27 in 1980. The largest ancestry groups are Hispanic (67%) persons of English descent (11%), German descent (10%) and Irish descent (9%). **REGISTERED VOTERS** As of November 2, 1982 there were 20,949 registered voters (0.3% of the state total). The 1982 general election had a 43% voter turnout, compared to a 58% turnout in the 1980 general election. In the 1982 primary 99% voted Democratic and 1% Republican, with 9,128 votes cast.

THE ECONOMY

AGRICULTURE Sorghum area. In 1982, 87% of the land was in farms and ranches, with 31% of the farmland under cultivation and 10% irrigated. Jim Wells ranked 110th in the state in highest agricultural receipts, with 58% from livestock and livestock products. Overgrazing, undesirable brush and weeds, water erosion and inefficient tillage systems are the current conservation problems. Primary crops: sorghum, hay, corn, wheat and cotton. Primary vegetables: ninth in the state for watermelons. Primary fruits: grapefruit and oranges. Primary

COUNTIES

JIM WELLS (continued)

livestock and products: cattle and milk. **BUSINESS** Total number of business establishments in the county: 833. Retail sales during the first quarter of 1984 increased 10%. In 1980, 8% of the labor force were self-employed, 18% were employed in professional or related services, 7% in manufacturing, 20% in wholesale and retail trade, 23% in agriculture, forestry, fisheries and mining, 17% were employed in other counties and there were 2,193 retired workers. The industries with the most employment: oil and gas extraction, agribusiness, metal mining, heavy construction and trucking. The nonfarm earnings in 1981 totaled $339,236,000. The retired workers received an average monthly Social Security payment of $298. **FINANCE** On June 30, 1983, six commercial banks had total deposits of $250,928,000 and total assets of $290,226,000. On December 31, 1982 one state savings and loan association, one state branch and one federal association branch had assets of $44,391,006. In addition there are two credit unions in the county. **HOUSING** Average value of homes in 1980: $23,200. Permits for new, privately owned housing units decreased in 1982: 141 permits were issued with a total construction cost of $4,518,178. Of those permits, 110 were for single family houses. Between 1970 and 1980 the number of housing units increased by 20%. Sixty-four percent of all units in the county are air-conditioned, 79% are heated by gas and 19% by electricity. **NATURAL RESOURCES** Caliche, industrial sand, oil and gas. In 1982 a total of 71,145,452 thousand cubic feet of gas well gas, 323,170 barrels of condensate, 1,071,617 barrels of crude oil and 5,712,202 thousand cubic feet of casinghead gas were produced. Current production of other minerals and products includes caliche, sand and gravel. **TOURISM** Travel expenditures of $23,994,000 in 1982 (an increase of 11% over 1981) generated 590 jobs and $4,769,000 in payroll. Lodging: six hotels, motels and tourist courts. Convention/meeting facilities: Alice-Jim Wells County Fair Grandstand. **ALCOHOLIC BEVERAGES** Packaged distilled spirits, beer, ale, malt liquor and wine are legal in parts of the county. Sale of mixed beverages is legal in all or parts of the county. **MILITARY INSTALLATIONS** Orange Naval Auxiliary Field, Orange Grove, 1,596 acres, Auxiliary Training Field. **FEDERAL EXPENDITURES** The federal government had direct expenditures or obligations of $46,701,000 in the county during fiscal year 1983, including $2,396,000 by the U.S. Department of Defense. In addition, the federal government provided $7,047,000 in grant awards, paid $3,335,000 in salaries and wages, made direct payments to individuals of $34,812,000 including $26,946,000 in retirement and disability payments, awarded $13,000 in procurement contracts and spent $1,494,000 in other expenditures or obligations. The federal government also provided $2,103,000 in direct loans and $15,673,000 in guaranteed loans and insurance.

COMMUNICATION

Newspapers–Daily: Echo-News (Alice), ave. eve. circ. 7,200. Radio: KOPY-AM, KDSI-FM, and KBIC-FM Stereo (Alice). Cable TV. Telephone companies: General Telephone, Southwestern Bell and Valley Telephone Coop. **TRANSPORTATION** Total public road mileage: 937. In 1982 there were 31,245 registered vehicles and 915 reported traffic accidents including 14 fatalities. Intercity bus service is available. Motor freight: 21 local and intrastate carriers. Rail: one branch carries annually one to five million tons of freight through the county. Aircraft: 89 are registered in the county. Airports: Alice International Airport serves as a base for 25 aircraft and is a general utility airport with general aviation service.

COMMUNITY SERVICES

EDUCATION Five school districts with 12 elementary, six middle and four high schools. The average daily attendance in 1981-82 was 7,954 with expenditures per pupil of $2,352 including 510 classroom teachers with an average annual salary of $16,232. Fifty-seven percent of the 484 high school graduates planned to attend college. In 1982-83, 24% of the students were White, 76% Hispanic, 0.5% Black and 0.1% Asian. Private schools: 316 students enrolled in two elementary schools. **PUBLIC LIBRARIES** Alice Public Library: 90,000 volumes, two branches. **CHILD CARE** 21 day care and five twenty-four hour care licensed facilities. **HEALTH CARE** 27 physicians and five dentists. Hospitals: one with a capacity of 131. Clinics: one dialysis clinic. Ambulance services: two commercial, one funeral home, and one volunteer service. Mental health: one clinic. Nursing homes: four nursing homes with a combined capacity of 434 nursing care and 15 personal care residents. The average cost per day for private patients in 1982 was $33.34. **CHURCHES** 43 churches have an estimated combined membership of 21,305. The largest denominations are Catholic, Southern Baptist and United Methodist. **SOCIAL SERVICES** In fiscal year 1983 a total of $3,587,575 in food stamps was distributed, with an average of 7,702 persons receiving food stamps each month. Aid to Families with Dependent Children (AFDC) totaled $644,334 with an average of 430 families receiving AFDC each month. Medical assistance benefits for the aged and disabled of $5,167,415 and for families and children of $1,591,105 brought the county benefit total to $10,990,428. **FIRE PROTECTION** One paid and three volunteer fire departments. **LAW ENFORCEMENT** The County Sheriff has 46 commissioned officers. Three police departments have a combined force of 42. **CRIME** 124 violent crimes (murder, forcible rape, robbery and aggravated assault) and 2,155 nonviolent crimes (burglary, larceny-theft and motor vehicle theft) were reported in 1982. **JUDICIAL SYSTEM** One District Court and Judge, one County Court and Judge and five Justices of the Peace. In the District Court a total of 1,409 cases were pending on 1/1/82, 1,142 new cases were filed and 1,070 cases were disposed of during the year leaving 1,481 cases pending on 12/31/82. There were 379 criminal cases on the docket, 181 convictions, 54 persons committed to prison and one committed to jail and 103 cases left pending. In the County Court 1,210 cases were pending on 1/1/82, 1,651 new cases were filed and 991 cases were disposed of during the year leaving 1,870 cases pending on 12/31/82. There were 2,421 criminal cases on the docket, 152 convictions, 30 persons committed to jail and 1,481 cases left pending. **JAILS** One jail, capacity 30. Completed major renovation in 1983. **ATTORNEYS AT LAW** 44. **UTILITIES** 80% of the residents are connected to a public or privately owned water system and 72% are connected to a public sewer system. Natural gas is distributed to the county by Entex, Inc. The average annual residential bill for natural gas in 1982 for the Entex distribution system was $390.31, an increase of 26% over 1981. Electricity is distributed to the county by Central Power and Light Co., Nueces Electric Coop., Inc. and San Patricio Electric Coop., Inc. and is generated primarily by gas, oil and water. The typical residential electric bill is $162.15 per month for an all-electric house using 2,500 kwh. **TAXES** The county has 11 units with taxing authority: five school distircts, three cities, one county, and two special districts.

RECREATION/ENTERTAINMENT

NATIONAL REGISTER OF HISTORIC PLACES Alice vicinity: Hinojosa Archeological Site. **STATE** Lake Corpus Christi State Recreation Area (see San Patricio County). **MUNICIPAL PARKS** 232 acres in eight municipal parks. These parks contain four playgrounds, one golf course, seven baseball and softball fields, three multi-use courts and two swimming pools. **SCENIC DRIVES** The Texas Tropical Trail runs through this county. This trail is charted through the state's southernmost wedge meandering through ranchland, resort areas by the Gulf of Mexico and fertile farm lands. **BOATING/FISHING** Lakes/reservoirs: Alice (409 acres), Chiltipin-San Fernando Soil Conservation Service Lakes 1 and 4 (80 acres), and Corpus Christi (19,336 acres). Major rivers: Nueces. Primary streams: Chiltipin, Amargosa, San Diego, San Fernando, Salado and Escondido. **HUNTING** Fall and winter seasons on deer. No closed seasons on javelina, coyote, bobcat and squirrel. Winter seasons on quail, muskrat, beaver, opossum, ring-tailed cat, badger, fox, weasel, raccoon, skunk and civet cat. Fall, winter and spring seasons on turkey. In 1983 sandhill crane, duck, coot, geese, woodcock and jacksnipe seasons occurred during the winter months. Teal duck, rail and gallinule seasons occurred in the fall. Mourning dove seasons occurred intermittently during the fall and winter months with a fall season on white-winged dove. **MUSEUMS** Alice: South Texas Museum. **SPECIAL EVENTS** Fiesta Bandana Celebration, Alice, April; Youth Rodeo, Alice, June; County Fair, Alice, October.

COMMUNITIES
COUNTY SEAT Alice, County Courthouse, 78332; County Clerk's Office, 512/664-9522. **INCORPORATED COMMUNITIES** (1980 population and ZIP Code) Alice (20,961) 78332, Orange Grove (1,212) 78372, Premont (2,984) 78375 and San Diego (5,225: 4,331 in Duval Co. and 894 in Jim Wells Co.) 78384. **UNINCORPORATED COMMUNITIES** (and ZIP Code) Alfred 78332, Ben Bolt 78342, Palito Blanco (Eva) 78332, Sandia 78383 and Springfield 78332. **FOR ADDITIONAL LOCAL INFORMATION** Alice Chamber of Commerce, P.O. Box 1609, 612 E. Main, Alice, 78332, 512/664-3454 and Premont Chamber of Commerce, P.O. Box 706, Premont, 78375, 512/348-3912.

JOHNSON (M17)

THE LAND
South of Fort Worth on Interstate Highway 35W in the Grand Prairie Region, Johnson County covers 731 square miles with an elevation range of 600 to 900 feet. The western half of the county has undulating to hilly, alkaline, light to dark, well drained, loamy soils with accumulations of lime in the subsoil. The central part has nearly level to undulating, light colored soils with loamy or sandy surfaces over reddish or mottled clayey or loamy subsoils. To the east the undulating, slightly acidic soils have dark, loamy or clayey surfaces and cracking, clayey subsoils. Johnson is in the Cross Timbers and Prairies vegetation area with tall and mid grasses, live and post oak, junipers and some mesquite. Between 21 and 30% of the land in the county is considered prime farmland. **CLIMATE.** Subtropical Humid with wide-ranging temperatures from winter to summer and thunderstorms in the spring. The average annual temperature is 66°F. Temperatures in January range from an average low of 33° to an average high of 57°F and in July range from 73° to 97°F. The average annual precipitation is 32 inches, with an average relative humidity of 78% at 6 A.M. and 53% at 6 P.M. The average annual snowfall is two inches. The growing season averages 235 days per year, with the last freeze in late March and the first freeze in mid November. The sun shines during the year on the average 66% of the daylight hours.

THE PEOPLE
The population of Johnson County has doubled in size since the 1950s. The 1982 estimated population of 73,200 continues that strong growth rate. Urban areas grew slightly faster than rural areas from 1970 to 1980. The age groups with the largest gains were ages 20 to 34 and birth to five years. The median age of 30 remained unchanged from 1970 to 1980. The largest ancestry groups are persons of English descent (31%), Irish descent (23%) and German descent (14%). **REGISTERED VOTERS** As of November 2, 1982 there were 30,293 registered voters (0.5% of the state total). The 1982 general election had a 56% voter turnout, compared to a 72% turnout in the 1980 general election. In the 1982 primary 90% voted Democratic and 10% Republican, with 6,868 votes cast.

THE ECONOMY
AGRICULTURE Dairy area. In 1982, 78% of the land was in farms and ranches, with 24% of the farmland under cultivation and 4% irrigated. Johnson ranked 58th in the state in highest agricultural receipts, with 87% from livestock and livestock products. Overgrazing, undesirable brush and weeds, water erosion and flooding are the current conservation problems. Primary crops: wheat, hay, oats, sorghum and cotton. Primary vegetables: potatoes, sweet potatoes, tomatoes and watermelons. Primary fruits and nuts: peaches and pecans. Primary livestock and products: fifth in the state for milk production. Cattle and hogs. **BUSINESS** Total number of business establishments in the county: 1,131. Retail sales during the first quarter of 1984 increased 24%. In 1980, 8% of the labor force were self-employed, 15% were employed in professional or related services, 27% in manufacturing, 19% in wholesale and retail trade, 11% in construction, 44% were employed in other counties and there were 5,267 retired workers. The industries with the most employment: agribusiness, construction, lime production and the manufacture of men's work clothing, textile products, mobile homes, household furniture, cardboard boxes, explosives, plastics products, mineral wool, conveyors, small household electrical appliances and truck trailers. The nonfarm earnings in 1981 totaled $668,503,000. The retired workers received an average monthly Social Security payment of $302. **FINANCE** On June 30, 1983, 10 commercial banks had total deposits of $404,147,000 and total assets of $445,842,000. There are three state savings and loan association branches, one federal association branch and three credit unions in the county. **HOUSING** Average value of homes in 1980: $38,300. Permits for new, privately owned housing units increased in 1982: 266 permits were issued with a total construction cost of $10,345,928. Of those permits, 186 were for single family houses. Between 1970 and 1980 the number of housing units increased by 54%. Eighty-six percent of all units in the county are air-conditioned, 67% are heated by gas and 31% by electricity. **NATURAL RESOURCES** Limestone, sand and gravel. Current production includes lime, crushed limestone, industrial sand, sand and gravel. **TOURISM** Travel expenditures of $6,449,000 in 1982 (an increase of 11% over 1981) generated 130 jobs and $1,170,000 in payroll. **ALCOHOLIC BEVERAGES** Totally dry. **FEDERAL EXPENDITURES** The federal government had direct expenditures or obligations of $98,700,000 in the county during fiscal year 1983, including $6,447,000 by the U.S. Department of Defense. In addition, the federal government provided $865,000 in grant awards, paid $4,319,000 in salaries and wages, made direct payments to individuals of $91,948,000 including $72,870,000 in retirement and disability payments, awarded $999,000 in procurement contracts and spent $571,000 in other expenditures or obligations. The federal government also provided $4,785,000 in direct loans and $31,599,000 in guaranteed loans and insurance.

COMMUNICATION
Newspapers–Daily: Cleburne Times-Review, ave. eve. circ. 9,344. Weekly: Alvardo Bulletin, Burleson Star, Grandview Tribune, Johnson County News (Cleburne), Joshua Tribune, Weekly Chronicle (Keene) and the Mansfield News-Mirror. Radio: KCLE-AM (Cleburne) and KSUC-FM (Keene). Cable TV. Telephone companies: Continental Telephone, Southwestern Bell

JOHNSON (continued)

and Texas-Midland Telephone. **TRANSPORTATION** Total public road mileage: 1,505. In 1982 there were 64,125 registered vehicles and 1,856 reported traffic accidents including 21 fatalities. Intercity bus service is available. Motor freight: 22 local and intrastate carriers. Rail: Five main and one branch line carry freight through the county. Two of the main lines carry annually over 30 million tons of freight each, one carries 20 to 30 and two carry 10 to 20 million tons each. The branch carries annually five to 10 million tons of freight. Aircraft: 122 are registered in the county. Airports: Cleburne Municipal Airport serves as a base for 103 aircraft and is a basic transportation airport with general aviation service. Also serving this area are Blackwood Airpark at Cleburne, Bourland Field at Cresson, Coppenger Farm Airport at Godley, McElroy Ranch Airport near Grandview, Southwest Adventist College Airport at Keene and Smith Ranch First State Bank Airport at Rio Vista.

COMMUNITY SERVICES

EDUCATION 11 school districts with 20 elementary, five middle and eight high schools. The average daily attendance in 1981-82 was 13,802, with expenditures per pupil of $2,333 including 830 classroom teachers with an average annual salary of $16,134. Thirty-two percent of the 901 high school graduates planned to attend college. In 1982-83, 91% of the students were White, 6% Hispanic, 3% Black, 0.4% Asian and 0.1% American Indian. Sports championships: 1983 A Girls' Tennis Singles, Venus H.S. Private schools: 636 students enrolled in two elementary and two high schools. Southwestern Adventist College is located in Keene. Established in 1893 it is affiliated with the Seventh Day Adventists Church. Enrollment in 1982 was 700 with in state undergraduate tuition and fees of $4,084 per semester. The highest degree offered is Bachelor. Vocational education: Aladdin Beauty College (Cleburne). **PUBLIC LIBRARIES** Burleson Public Library: 18,000 volumes. Cleburne Public Library: 42,321 volumes. **CHILD CARE** 89 day care and 23 twenty-four hour care licensed facilities. **HEALTH CARE** 54 physicians and 23 dentists. Hospitals: one with a capacity of 186. Clinics: one outpatient clinic. Ambulance services: three volunteer fire departments, one fire department, one hospital-based, one commercial and one city service. Mental health: one county clinic. Nursing homes: eight nursing homes with a combined capacity of 821 nursing care residents. The average cost per day for private patients in 1982 was $32.68. **CHURCHES** 106 churches have an estimated combined membership of 39,096. The largest denominations are Southern Baptist, United Methodist and Seventh Day Adventist. **SOCIAL SERVICES** In fiscal year 1983 a total of $1,649,709 in food stamps was distributed, with an average of 3,391 persons receiving food stamps each month. Aid to Families with Dependent Children (AFDC) totaled $389,768 with an average of 259 families receiving AFDC each month. Medical assistance benefits for the aged and disabled of $6,421,380 and for families and children of $694,510 brought the county benefit total to $9,155,367. **FIRE PROTECTION** One paid and nine volunteer fire departments. **LAW ENFORCEMENT** The County Sheriff has 27 commissioned officers. Nine police departments have a combined force of 102. **CRIME** 154 violent crimes (murder, forcible rape, robbery and aggravated assault) and 2,518 nonviolent crimes (burglary, larceny-theft and motor vehicle theft) were reported in 1982. **JUDICIAL SYSTEM** Two District Courts and Judges, one County Court and Judge and four Justices of the Peace. In the District Courts a total of 6,914 cases were pending on 1/1/82, 4,913 new cases were filed and 3,997 cases were disposed of during the year leaving 7,830 cases pending on 12/31/82. There were 8,200 criminal cases on the docket, 865 convictions, 60

persons committed to prison, three committed to jail and 5,443 cases left pending. **JAILS** One jail, capacity 27 with new facilities under construction. **ATTORNEYS AT LAW** 51. **UTILITIES** 91% of the residents are connected to a public or privately owned water system and 60% are connected to a public sewer system. Natural gas is distributed to the county by Lone Star Gas Co., Division of Enserch. The average annual residential bill for natural gas in 1982 for the Lone Star distribution system was $405.91, an increase of 35% over 1981. Electricity is distributed to the county by Texas Power and Light Co., Texas Electric Service Co., Hill County Electric Coop., Inc. and Johnson Co. Electric Coop., Assn. and is generated primarily by gas and coal. The typical residential electric bill is $154.69 per month for an all-electric house using 2,500 kwh. **TAXES** The county has 23 units with taxing authority: 11 school districts, nine cities, one county and two special districts.

RECREATION/ENTERTAINMENT

NATIONAL REGISTER OF HISTORIC PLACES Cleburne: Cleburne Carnegie Library. Rio Vista: Meredith Hart House. Rio Vista vicinity: Ham Creek Site. **STATE** Cleburne State Recreation Area covers 529 acres with camping and trailer sites as well as fishing, swimming and boat ramps. **MUNICIPAL PARKS** 412 acres in 19 municipal parks. These parks contain three miles of hiking trails, 13 playgrounds, one golf course, 29 football and soccer fields, 16 baseball and softball fields, 10 tennis courts, two multi-use courts, three swimming pools, two beaches and three boat ramps. Developed campsites: 11. **BOATING/FISHING** Lakes/reservoirs: Alvarado (264 acres), Chambers Creek Soil Conservation Service Lakes 43A, 44, 57 and 64A (52 acres), Charca (19 acres), Cleburne State Park (58 acres) and Pat Cleburne (1,550 acres). Major rivers: Nolan. Primary streams: Turkey, North Fork Chambers, Middle Fork Chambers, Station and West Fork Camp. **HUNTING** Fall and winter seasons on deer. No closed season on coyote, bobcat and squirrel. Winter seasons on quail, muskrat, beaver, opossum, ring-tailed cat, badger, fox, weasel, raccoon, skunk and civet cat. In 1983 duck, coot, geese, woodcock and jacksnipe seasons occurred during the winter months. Teal duck, rail and gallinule seasons occurred in the fall. Mourning dove seasons occurred intermittently during the fall and winter months. **MUSEUMS** Burleson: Burleson Library. Cleburne: Layland Museum. Cresson: Hal S. Smith Farm Machinery Museum and Sturdy's Prairie Box House Museum. **COLLEGIATE FINE ARTS** Keene: Cultural events offered by Southwestern Adventist College. **SPECIAL EVENTS** Junior Stock Show and Youth Fair, Cleburne, March; Spring Arts and Crafts Show, Cleburne, May; Rodeo and Parade, Cleburne, June; 4th of July Celebration, Cleburne, July; Pioneers and Old Settlers Reunion and Parade, Cleburne/Alvarado, August; Christmas Candlewalk, Cleburne, December.

COMMUNITIES

COUNTY SEAT Cleburne, County Courthouse, 76031; County Clerk's Office, 817/645-2292. **INCORPORATED COMMUNITIES** (1980 population and ZIP Code) Alvarado (2,701) 76009, Briar Oaks (592) 76028, Burleson (11,734: 10,611 in Johnson Co. and 1,123 in Tarrant Co.) 76028, Cleburne (19,218) 76031, Godley (614) 76044, Grandview (1,205) 76050, Joshua (1,470) 76058, Keene (3,013) 76059, Mansfield (8,102: 22 in Johnson Co. and 8,080 in Tarrant Co.) 76063, Rio Vista (509) 76093 and Venus (518) 76084. **UNINCORPORATED COMMUNITIES** (and ZIP Code) Bono 76031, Cresson (also in Hood Co.) 76035, Cuba (Sand Flat) 76031, Egan 76031, Happy Hill 76009, Lane Prairie 76031, Lillian 76061, Oak Hill 76031, Parker 76050, Pleasant Point 76009, Prairie Springs 76028 and Retta (also in Tarrant Co.) 76028. **FOR ADDITIONAL LOCAL INFORMATION**

Burleson Area Chamber of Commerce, 1044 S.W. Wilshire, P.O. Box 9, Burleson 76028, 817/295-6121, Cleburne Chamber of Commerce, P.O. Box 701, 1511 W. Henderson, Cleburne, 76031, 817/645-2455 and Mansfield Chamber of Commerce, 1305 E. Broad Street, P.O. Box 363, Mansfield, 76063, 817/477-3331.

JONES (P62)

THE LAND

North of Abilene on U.S. Highways 277 and 180 in the Rolling Plains Region, Jones County covers 931 square miles with an elevation range of 1,600 to 1,900 feet. The county has light to dark, well drained, loamy soils with very deep clayey, mottled subsoils. Jones is in the Rolling Plains vegetation area with tall and mid grasses and mesquite. Between 51 and 60% of the land in the county is considered prime farmland. **CLIMATE** Subtropical Subhumid with significant temperature extremes between winter, summer and spring thunderstorms. The average annual temperature is 63°F. Temperatures in January range from an average low of 30° to an average high of 56°F and in July range from 71° to 96°F. The average annual precipitation is 23 inches, with an average relative humidity of 74% at 6 A.M. and 43% at 6 P.M. The average annual snowfall is six inches. The growing season averages 230 days per year, with the last freeze in late March and the first freeze in mid November. The sun shines during the year on the average 72% of the daylight hours.

THE PEOPLE

The 1982 estimated population of 17,600 indicates a continuation of the growth in population which began in the 1970s, reversing the steady population decrease from 1930 to 1970. Rural areas grew faster than urban areas from 1970 to 1980. Although the median age lowered from 39 in 1970 to 36 in 1980, the county's population is older than average. The largest ancestry groups are persons of English descent (24%), Irish descent (23%) and Hispanic (15%). **REGISTERED VOTERS** As of November 2, 1982 there were 8,523 registered voters (0.1% of the state total). The 1982 general election had a 53% voter turnout, compared to a 68% turnout in the 1980 general election. In the 1982 primary 96% voted Democratic and 4% Republican, with 2,797 votes cast.

THE ECONOMY

AGRICULTURE Wheat and cotton area. In 1982, 94% of the land was in farms and ranches, with 52% of the farmland under cultivation and 4% irrigated. Jones ranked 56th in the state in highest agricultural receipts, with 85% from crops. Undesirable brush and weeds and water erosion are the current conservation problems. Primary crops: wheat, cotton, sorghum, hay and oats. Primary vegetables: watermelons. Primary fruits and nuts: peaches and pecans. Primary livestock and products: cattle, sheep, wool and hogs. **BUSINESS** Total number of business establishments in the county: 367. Retail sales during the first quarter of 1984 increased 7%. In 1980, 16% of the labor force were self-employed, 20% were employed in professional or related services, 9% in manufacturing, 19% in wholesale and retail trade, 21% in agriculture, forestry, fisheries and mining, 35% were employed in other counties and there were 2,149 retired workers. The industries with the most employment: trucking and agribusiness, oil and gas extraction and the manufacture of gypsum products. The nonfarm earnings in 1981 totaled $148,748,000. The retired workers received an average monthly Social Security payment of $301. **FINANCE** On June 30, 1983, four commercial banks had total deposits of $99,587,000 and total assets of $111,896,000. On December 31, 1982 one state savings and loan association and three state branches had assets of $122,232,132. In addition there are 13 credit unions in the county. **HOUSING** Average value of homes in 1980: $19,100. Permits for new, privately owned housing units decreased in 1982: 17 permits were issued with a total construction cost of $723,403. Of those permits, all were for single family houses. Between 1970 and 1980 the number of housing units increased by 11%. Eighty-five percent of all units in the county are air-conditioned, 85% are heated by gas and 12% by electricity. **NATURAL RESOURCES** Limestone, sand and gravel, oil, gas, and bituminous coal. In 1982 a total of 83,976 thousand cubic feet of gas well gas, 690 barrels of condensate, 2,622,406 barrels of crude oil and 1,395,505 thousand cubic feet of casinghead gas were produced. Current production of other minerals and products includes dimension limestone, crushed limestone, sand and gravel. **TOURISM** Travel expenditures of $6,191,000 in 1982 (an increase of 11% over 1981) generated 168 jobs and $1,456,000 in payroll. Lodging: three hotels, motels and tourist courts. **ALCOHOLIC BEVERAGES** Totally dry. **FEDERAL EXPENDITURES** The federal government had direct expenditures or obligations of $66,876,000 in the county during fiscal year 1983, including $24,347,000 by the U.S. Department of Defense. In addition, the federal government provided $2,499,000 in grant awards, paid $3,577,000 in salaries and wages, made direct payments to individuals of $52,166,000 including $41,601,000 in retirement and disability payments, awarded $5,000 in procurement contracts and spent $8,629,000 in other expenditures or obligations. The federal government also provided $4,727,000 in direct loans and $8,596,000 in guaranteed loans and insurance.

COMMUNICATION

Newspapers–Weekly: Western Observer (Anson) and Hamlin Herald. Radio: KDWT-AM (Stamford). Cable TV. Telephone companies: Continental Telephone, Southwestern Bell and Taylor Telephone. **TRANSPORTATION** Total public road mileage: 1,424. In 1982 there were 17,242 registered vehicles and 384 reported traffic accidents including seven fatalities. Intercity bus service is available. Motor freight: nine local and intrastate carriers. Rail: two branch lines annually carry less than one million tons of freight each through the county. Aircraft: 37 are registered in the county. Airports: Arledge Field at Stamford serves as a base for 20 aircraft and is a basic utility airport with general aviation service. Hamlin Municipal Airport.

COMMUNITY SERVICES

EDUCATION Five school districts with six elementary, two middle and five high schools. The average daily attendance in 1981-82 was 3,129, with expenditures per pupil of $2,421 including 243 classroom teachers with an average annual salary of $15,302. Forty-four percent of the 225 high school graduates planned to attend college. In 1982-83, 67% of the students were White, 26% Hispanic, 6% Black, 0.4% Asian and 0.1% American Indian. **PUBLIC LIBRARIES** Anson Public Library: 10,366 volumes. Stamford Carnegie Library: 13,000 volumes. **CHILD CARE** 34 day care and 10 twenty-four hour care licensed facilities. **HEALTH CARE** 15 physicians and five dentists. Hospitals: three with a combined capacity of 144. Ambulance services: one hospital-based, one commercial and one funeral home service. Mental health: one clinic and one center with a capacity of 102. Nursing homes: four nursing homes with a combined capacity of 318 nursing care residents. The average cost per day for private patients in 1982 was $30.34. **CHURCHES** 57 churches have an estimated combined membership of 14,715. The largest denominations are Southern Baptist, Catholic and United Methodist. **SOCIAL SERVICES** In fiscal year 1983 a total of $627,111 in food stamps was distributed, with an average of 1,389 persons receiving food stamps each month. Aid to Families with Dependent Children (AFDC) totaled $130,100 with an average of 82 families receiving AFDC each month. Medical assistance

COUNTIES

JONES (continued)

benefits for the aged and disabled of $3,295,239 and for families and children of $295,658 brought the county benefit total to $4,348,107. **FIRE PROTECTION** One partly paid and four volunteer fire departments. **LAW ENFORCEMENT** The County Sheriff has 19 commissioned officers. Four police departments have a combined force of 40. **CRIME** 34 violent crimes (murder, forcible rape, robbery and aggravated assault) and 225 nonviolent crimes (burglary, larceny-theft and motor vehicle theft) were reported in 1982. **JUDICIAL SYSTEM** One District Court and Judge, one County Court and Judge and three Justices of the Peace. In the District Court a total of 1,455 cases were pending on 1/1/82, 1,154 new cases were filed and 611 cases were disposed of during the year leaving 1,998 cases pending on 12/31/82. There were 1,546 criminal cases on the docket, 159 convictions, seven persons committed to prison and 24 committed to jail and 1,182 cases left pending. **JAILS** One jail, capacity 15, lost certification in 1983 due to deficiencies in supervision. **ATTORNEYS AT LAW** 11. **UTILITIES** 88% of the residents are connected to a public or privately owned water system and 59% are connected to a public sewer system. Natural gas is distributed to the county by Lone Star Gas Co., Division of Enserch. The average annual residential bill for natural gas in 1982 for the Lone Star distribution system was $405.91, an increase of 35% over 1981. Electricity is distributed to the county by West Texas Utilities, Midwest Electric Coop., Inc., Stamford Electric Coop., Inc. and Taylor Electric Coop., Inc. and is generated primarily by gas and oil. The typical residential electric bill is $145.78 per month for an all-electric house using 2,500 kwh. **TAXES** The county has 15 units with taxing authority: six school districts, five cities, one county, two hospital districts and one special district.

RECREATION/ENTERTAINMENT
NATIONAL REGISTER OF HISTORIC PLACES Abilene vicinity: Fort Phantom Hill. Noodle vicinity: Steadman Site. **MUNICIPAL PARKS** 409 acres in 10 municipal parks. These parks contain five playgrounds, one golf course, four baseball and softball fields, two tennis courts, two swimming pools, one beach, one boat ramp and shore fishing facilities. Developed campsites: four. **SCENIC DRIVES** The Texas Forts Trail runs through this county. This trail leads to eight of the famous frontier forts of West Central Texas and an ancient presidio of the Spanish colonial period. **BOATING/FISHING** Lakes/reservoirs: Anson City (56 acres), Anson North (169 acres), Fort Phantom Hill (4,246 acres), Red (50 acres), Sayles (69 acres), Shackelford (47 acres) and South (170 acres). Major rivers: Clear Fork Brazos. Primary streams: Carter, Thompson, Big Elm, Turkey Paint, Mulberry, Dry California and Cedar. **HUNTING** Fall and winter seasons on deer and mule deer. No closed season on coyote, bobcat and squirrel. Winter seasons on quail, muskrat, beaver, opossum, ring-tailed cat, badger, fox, weasel, raccoon, skunk and civet cat. Fall, summer and spring seasons on turkey. In 1983 sandhill crane, duck, coot, geese, woodcock and jacksnipe seasons occurred during the winter months. Teal duck, rail and gallinule seasons occurred in the fall. Mourning dove seasons occurred intermittently during the fall and winter months. **MUSEUMS** Abilene: Fine Arts Museum. Stamford: Buie's General Store and Cowboy Country Museum. **ZOO** Abilene: Zoological Gardens. **PLANETARIUM** Abilene: Morgan Jones Jr. Planetarium. **OBSERVATORY** Abilene: Abilene Christian University Observatory. **SPECIAL EVENTS** Annual Texas Cowboy Reunion and Rodeo, Stamford, July; County Fair and Parade, Anson, August; Fall Festival, Anson, October; Cowboys Christmas Ball, Anson, December (see Abilene, Taylor Co.).

COMMUNITIES
COUNTY SEAT Anson, County Courthouse, 79501; County Clerk's Office, 915/823-3762. **INCORPORATED COMMUNITIES** (1980 population and ZIP Code) Abilene (98,315: 503 in Jones Co. and 97,812 in Taylor Co.) 79601 All-America Cities Honorable Mention 1959, Anson (2,831) 79501, Hamlin (3,248) 79520, Hawley (679) 79525, Lueders (420) 79533 and Stamford 4,542 (4,497 in Jones Co. and 45 in Haskell Co.) 79553. **UNINCORPORATED COMMUNITIES** (and ZIP Code) Avoca 79503, Corinth 79553, East Stamford 79553, Funston 79501, Hodges 79525, Neinda 79520, New Hope 79553, Noodle 79536, Nugent 79601, Radium 79501, Stith 79536, Truby 79525 and Tuxedo 79553. **FOR ADDITIONAL LOCAL INFORMATION** Anson Chamber of Commerce, 1051 12th St., P.O. Box 351, Anson, 79501, 915/823-3259 or 823-3144, Lueders Chamber of Commerce, P.O. Box 158, Lueders, 79533, 915/228-4565 and Hamlin Board of Community Development, P.O. Box 402, Hamlin, 79520, 915/576-3501.

KARNES (G20)

THE LAND
Southeast of San Antonio on U.S. Highway 181 in the Rio Grande Plain Region, Karnes County covers 753 square miles with an elevation range of 180 to 400 feet. The northwestern half of the county has nearly level to undulating, deep soils with light colored, loamy surfaces and clayey subsoils. The rest of the county has light to dark, loamy surfaces over reddish, clayey subsoils with limestone within 40 inches of the surface, and gray to black, cracking, clayey soils with a high shrink-swell potential. Karnes is in the South Texas Plains vegetation area with grasslands, mesquite, live oak, post oak, some brush and cacti. Between 71 and 80% of the land in the county is considered prime farmland. **CLIMATE** Subtropical Humid with warm summers. The average annual temperature is 62 °F. Temperatures in January range from an average low of 41° to an average high of 65°F and in July range from 74° to 96°F. The average annual precipitation is 32 inches, with an average relative humidity of 87% at 6 A.M. and 55% at 6 P.M. Snowfall during winter is rare. The growing season averages 280 days per year, with the last freeze in late February and the first freeze in early December. The sun shines during the year on the average 67% of the daylight hours.

THE PEOPLE
Karnes County ranks 58th among all U.S. counties in the highest percent of persons who are of Spanish origin and ranks high among Texas counties in percent of residents who are native Texans. The 1982 estimated population of 13,700 suggests that the steady population decrease since 1930 has ended. Urban areas experienced an 8% growth between 1970 and 1980 while rural areas declined in population. The county has a higher than average percent of residents who are over 64. The largest ancestry groups are Hispanic (43%), persons of German descent (19%), English descent (11%) and Irish descent (10%). **REGISTERED VOTERS** As of November 2, 1982 there were 7,047 registered voters (0.1% of the state total). The 1982 general election had a 49% voter turnout, compared to a 69% turnout in the 1980 general election. In the 1982 primary 100% voted Democratic, with 2,244 votes cast.

THE ECONOMY
AGRICULTURE Cattle area. In 1982, 86% of the land was in farms and ranches, with 23% of the farmland under cultivation and 1% irrigated. Karnes ranked 116th in the state in highest agricultural receipts, with 82% from livestock and livestock products. Overgrazing, undesirable brush and weeds, water erosion

and inefficient tillage systems are the current conservation problems. Primary crops: hay, wheat, corn, sorghum and oats. Primary vegetables: sweet corn and watermelons. Primary fruits and nuts: peaches and pecans. Primary livestock and products: ninth in the state for hogs. Cattle and milk. **BUSINESS** Total number of business establishments in the county: 337. Retail sales during the first quarter of 1984 increased 27%. In 1980, 12% of the labor force were self-employed, 18% were employed in professional or related services, 10% in manufacturing, 20% in wholesale and retail trade, 23% in agriculture, forestry, fisheries and mining, 15% were employed in other counties and there were 1,341 retired workers. The industries with the most employment: oil and gas production and extraction, road construction, flour mills, the manufacture of farm machinery and equipment and the mining of uranium. The nonfarm earnings in 1981 totaled $110,609,000. The retired workers received an average monthly Social Security payment of $259. **FINANCE** On June 30, 1983, four commercial banks had total deposits of $95,378,000 and total assets of $107,410,000. On December 31, 1982 one state savings and loan association and one state branch had assets of $49,389,941. In addition there are two credit unions in the county. **HOUSING** Average value of homes in 1980: $21,100. Permits for new, privately owned housing units decreased in 1982: 19 permits were issued with a total construction cost of $467,395. Of those permits, all were for single family houses. Between 1970 and 1980 the number of housing units increased by 17%. Fifty-four percent of all units in the county are air-conditioned, 81% are heated by gas and 16% by electricity. **NATURAL RESOURCES** Caliche, clay, sand and gravel, uranium, oil and gas. In 1982 a total of 16,426,667 thousand cubic feet of gas well gas, 234,738 barrels of condensate, 634,169 barrels of crude oil and 4,223,531 thousand cubic feet of casinghead gas were produced. Current production of other minerals and products includes crushed sandstone, recovered sulphur and uranium. **TOURISM** Travel expenditures of $6,956,000 in 1982 (an increase of 12% over 1981) generated 156 jobs and $1,303,000 in payroll. **ALCOHOLIC BEVERAGES** Packaged distilled spirits, beer, ale, malt liquor and wine are legal. **FEDERAL EXPENDITURES** The federal government had direct expenditures or obligations of $22,098,000 in the county during fiscal year 1983, including $825,000 by the U.S. Department of Defense. In addition, the federal government provided $979,000 in grant awards, paid $949,000 in salaries and wages, made direct payments to individuals of $19,761,000 including $13,390,000 in retirement and disability payments, awarded $38,000 in procurement contracts and spent $371,000 in other expenditures or obligations. The federal government also provided $58,000 in direct loans and $5,267,000 in guaranteed loans and insurance.

COMMUNICATION

Newspapers–Weekly: The Karnes Citation-Spanish (Karnes City) and the Kenedy Advance Times. Radio: KAML-AM (Kenedy). Cable TV. Telephone companies: Continental Telephone, General Telephone and Southwestern Bell. **TRANSPORTATION** Total public road mileage: 937. In 1982 there were 11,983 registered vehicles and 208 reported traffic accidents including five fatalities. Intercity bus service is available. Motor freight: nine local and intrastate carriers. Rail: one branch carries annually one to five million tons of freight through the county. Aircraft: 28 are registered in the county. Airports: Karnes County Airport at Kenedy serves as a base for 15 aircraft and is a basic utility airport with general aviation service. Otto Kaiser Hospital at Kenedy provides a heliport for emergency use.

COMMUNITY SERVICES

EDUCATION Four school districts with seven elementary, two middle and four high schools. The average daily attendance in

1981-82 was 2,631, with expenditures per pupil of $2,934 including 175 classroom teachers with an average annual salary of $15,831. Thirty-five percent of the 218 high school graduates planned to attend college. In 1982-83, 39% of the students were White, 57% Hispanic, 4% Black, 0.1% Asian and 0.1% American Indian. Sports championships: 1983 AAA Baseball, Kenedy H.S. **PUBLIC LIBRARIES** Karnes City Public Library: 14,500 volumes. Karnes County Library System (Kenedy): 51,025 volumes. Runge Public Library: 7,870 volumes. **CHILD CARE** 15 day care and two twenty-four hour care licensed facilities. **HEALTH CARE** Eight physicians and five dentists. Hospitals: two with a combined capacity of 62. Ambulance services: one funeral home and one volunteer service. Mental health: one county clinic. Nursing homes: four nursing homes with a combined capacity of 252 nursing care and 21 personal care residents. The average cost per day for private patients in 1982 was $26.33. **CHURCHES** 37 churches have an estimated combined membership of 11,868. The largest denominations are Catholic and Southern Baptist. **SOCIAL SERVICES** In fiscal year 1983 a total of $1,266,211 in food stamps was distributed, with an average of 2,772 persons receiving food stamps each month. Aid to Families with Dependent Children (AFDC) totaled $235,557 with an average of 150 families receiving AFDC each month. Medical assistance benefits for the aged and disabled of $2,173,169 and for families and children of $304,732 brought the county benefit total to $3,979,669. **FIRE PROTECTION** Four volunteer fire departments. **LAW ENFORCEMENT** The County Sheriff has 19 commissioned officers. Two police departments have a combined force of 17. **CRIME** Three violent crimes (murder, forcible rape, robbery and aggravated assault) and 81 nonviolent crimes (burglary, larceny-theft and motor vehicle theft) were reported in 1982. **JUDICIAL SYSTEM** Two District Courts and Judges, one County Court and Judge and five Justices of the Peace. In the District Courts a total of 441 cases were pending on 1/1/82, 319 new cases were filed and 367 cases were disposed of during the year leaving 393 cases pending on 12/31/82. There were 226 criminal cases on the docket, 68 convictions, 29 persons committed to prison and 140 cases left pending. In the County Court 414 cases were pending on 1/1/82, 307 new cases were filed and 285 cases were disposed of during the year leaving 436 cases pending on 12/31/82. There were 683 criminal cases on the docket, 165 convictions and 398 cases left pending. **JAILS** One jail, capacity 15. **ATTORNEYS AT LAW** 10. **UTILITIES** 73% of the residents are connected to a public or privately owned water system and 61% are connected to a public sewer system. Natural gas is distributed to the county by Lone Star Gas Co., Division of Enserch. The average annual residential bill for natural gas in 1982 for the Lone Star distribution system was $405.91, an increase of 35% over 1981. Electricity is distributed to the county by Central Power and Light, Cochran Power and Light, Floresville Electric Light and Power and Dewitt Co. Electric Coop., Inc. and is generated primarily by gas, oil and coal. The typical residential electric bill is $135.47 per month for an all-electric house using 2,500 kwh. **TAXES** The county has 13 units with taxing authority: four school districts, four cities, one county, one hospital district and three special districts.

RECREATION/ENTERTAINMENT

NATIONAL REGISTER OF HISTORIC PLACES Helena: John Ruckman House. Panna Maria: Panna Maria Historic District. **MUNICIPAL PARKS** 44 acres in six municipal parks. These parks contain two playgrounds, four baseball and softball fields, one beach and shore fishing facilities. **SCENIC DRIVES** The Texas Independence Trail runs through this county. This trail not only surveys the historic sites of southeastern Texas but also includes many modern visitor attractions such as the Johnson Space Center. **BOATING/FISHING** Lakes/reservoirs:

KARNES (continued)

Escondido Creek Soil Conservation Service Lakes 1, 3, 4, 6, 8, 9, 10, 11 and 13 (219 acres), Hondo Creek Soil Conservation Service Lake 1 (13 acres) and Uranium (55 acres). Major rivers: San Antonio. Primary streams: Panther, Doe, Bucker, Olmos, Escondido, Dry Escondido, Hondo and Scared Dog. **HUNTING** Fall and winter seasons on deer. No closed season on javelina, coyote, bobcat and squirrel. Winter seasons on quail, muskrat, beaver, opossum, ring-tailed cat, badger, fox, weasel, raccoon, skunk and civet cat. Fall, winter and spring seasons on turkey. In 1983 sandhill crane, duck, coot, geese, woodcock and jacksnipe seasons occurred during the winter months. Teal duck, rail and gallinule seasons occurred in the fall. Mourning dove seasons occurred intermittently during the fall and winter months with a fall season on white-winged dove. **MUSEUMS** Helena: Courthouse Museum, Runge: Runge Museum. **SPECIAL EVENTS** Chili Cookoff, Karnes City, April; Bluebonnet Days, Kenedy, May; Town and Country Days and Parade, Karnes City, September; Indian Summer Festival, Helena, October.

COMMUNITIES

COUNTY SEAT Karnes City, County Courthouse, 78118; County Clerk's Office, 512/780-3938. **INCORPORATED COMMUNITIES** (1980 population and ZIP Code) Falls City (580) 78113, Karnes City (3,296) 78118, Kenedy (4,356) 78119 and Runge (1,244) 78151. **UNINCORPORATED COMMUNITIES** (and ZIP Code) Bainville 78119, Burnell 78119, Choate 78119, Coy City 78110, Cestohowa 78113, Ecleto 78111, El Oso 78119, Gillett 78116, Green 78119, Helena 78118, Hobson 78117, Lenz 78118, Panna Maria 78144, Pawelekville 78113 and Zunkerville 78119. **FOR ADDITIONAL LOCAL INFORMATION** Falls City Chamber of Commerce, P.O. Box 289, Falls City, 78113, 512/254-3242, Community Chamber of Commerce, 314 E. Calvert, Karnes City, 78118, 512/780-3112 and Kenedy Chamber of Commerce, P.O. Box 1929, Kenedy, 78119, 512/583-3223.

KAUFMAN (M14)

THE LAND

East of Dallas on Interstate Highway 20 in the Blackland Prairies Region, Kaufman County covers 788 square miles with an elevation range of 300 to 500 feet. The county has undulating, slightly acidic soils with dark to light, loamy surfaces and cracking, clayey subsoils and gray to black cracking clayey soils. These soils have a high shrink-swell potential. In the Blackland Prairies vegetation area there are prairie grasses, mesquite, oak, pecan and elm trees along streams. Between 31 and 40% of the land in the county is considered prime farmland. **CLIMATE** Subtropical Humid, but widely varying temperatures may be expected from winter to summer. The average annual temperature is 65°F. Temperatures in January range from an average low of 33° to an average high of 54°F and in July range from 72° to 97°F. The average annual precipitation is 39 inches, with an average relative humidity of 82% at 6 A.M. and 54% at 6 P.M. The average annual snowfall is three inches. The growing season averages 245 days per year, with the last freeze in late March and the first freeze in late November. The sun shines during the year on the average 65% of the daylight hours.

THE PEOPLE

The population of Kaufman County has regained its size of 1930. The 1982 estimated population of 42,300 continues a growth in population which began in the 1960s, reversing a steady population decrease. Gains in rural areas were high between 1970 to 1980, while the population in urban areas decreased slightly. The median age lowered from 34 in 1970 to 32 in 1980. The largest ancestry groups are persons of English descent (24%), Black (19%), Irish descent (17%) and German descent (10%). **REGISTERED VOTERS** As of November 2, 1982 there were 18,697 registered voters (0.3% of the state total). The 1982 general election had a 51% voter turnout, compared to a 65% turnout in the 1980 general election. In the 1982 primary 95% voted Democratic and 5% Republican, with 6,004 votes cast.

THE ECONOMY

AGRICULTURE Cattle area. In 1982, 81% of the land was in farms and ranches, with 29% of the farmland under cultivation and 1% irrigated. Kaufman ranked 105th in the state in highest agricultural receipts, with 84% from livestock and livestock products. Overgrazing, undesirable brush and weeds and water erosion are the current conservation problems. Primary crops: wheat, hay, oats, sorghum and cotton. Primary vegetables: cantaloupes, potatoes, sweet potatoes, tomatoes and watermelons. Primary fruits and nuts: peaches and pecans. Primary livestock and products: ninth in the state for beef cows that have calved. Cattle and hogs. **BUSINESS** Total number of business establishments in the county: 799. Retail sales during the first quarter of 1984 increased 12%. In 1980, 10% of the labor force were self-employed, 21% were employed in professional or related services, 20% in manufacturing, 18% in wholesale and retail trade, 10% in construction, 41% were employed in other counties and there were 5,252 retired workers. The industries with the most employment: agribusiness, general construction, knitting mills and the manufacture of tools, metal doors, architectural metal work, curtains and draperies, furniture partitions and fixtures and ice cream and frozen desserts. The nonfarm earnings in 1981 totaled $381,111,000. The retired workers received an average monthly Social Security payment of $313. **FINANCE** On June 30, 1983, nine commercial banks had total deposits of $296,239,000 and total assets of $326,095,000. On December 31, 1982 one federal savings and loan association, five state branches had assets of $23,341,970. In addition there are three credit unions in the county. **HOUSING** Average value of homes in 1980: $28,400. Permits for new, privately owned housing units decreased in 1982: 130 permits were issued with a total construction cost of $4,876,238. Of those permits, 104 were for single family houses. Between 1970 and 1980 the number of housing units increased by 34%. Seventy-seven percent of all units in the county are air-conditioned, 74% are heated by gas and 23% by electricity. **NATURAL RESOURCES** Limestone, sand and gravel, oil and gas. In 1982 a total of 377,910 thousand cubic feet of gas well gas, 46,701 barrels of condensate, 261,613 barrels of crude oil and 130,209 thousand cubic feet of casinghead gas were produced. Current production of other minerals and products includes crushed limestone. **TOURISM** Travel expenditures of $8,315,000 in 1982 (an increase of 11% over 1981) generated 220 jobs and $1,997,000 in payroll. **ALCOHOLIC BEVERAGES** Packaged distilled spirits, beer, ale, malt liquor and wine are legal in parts of the county. **FEDERAL EXPENDITURES** The federal government had direct expenditures or obligations of $78,022,000 in the county during fiscal year 1983, including $4,666,000 by the U.S. Department of Defense. In addition, the federal government provided $2,839,000 in grant awards, paid $3,615,000 in salaries and wages, made direct payments to individuals of $70,227,000 including $54,445,000 in retirement and disability payments, awarded $387,000 in procurement contracts and spent $953,000 in other expenditures or obligations. The federal government also provided $3,045,000 in direct loans and $13,675,000 in guaranteed loans and insurance.

COMMUNICATION

Newspapers–Daily: The Terrell Tribune, ave. eve. circ. 5,591.

Weekly: The Forney Messenger, The Kaufman Herald, Cedar Creek Pilot (Kemp) and The Kemp News. Radio: KTER-AM and KTLR-FM (Terrell). Cable TV. Telephone companies: Continental Telephone, Southwestern Bell, United Telephone and Texas-Midland Telephone. **TRANSPORTATION** Total public road mileage: 1,219. In 1982 there were 37,612 registered vehicles and 1,064 reported traffic accidents including 24 fatalities. Taxi cabs: one company in Terrell. Intercity bus service is available. Motor freight: five local and intrastate carriers. Rail: the Eagle provides passenger service on the Amtrak Route. One main line carries annually 20 to 30 million tons of freight through the county. Aircraft: 72 are registered in the county. Airports: Terrell Municipal Airport serves as a base for 56 aircraft and is a general utility airport with general aviation service. Also serving the area are Flying G Airport at Kaufman, Smith Field at Forney, Parker Airport and Wallace Airport at Terrell.

COMMUNITY SERVICES

EDUCATION Seven school districts with 12 elementary, six middle, seven high schools and one special education. The average daily attendance in 1981-82 was 9,113, with expenditures per pupil of $2,375 including 589 classroom teachers with an average annual salary of $15,664. Forty-four percent of the 551 high school graduates planned to attend college. In 1982-83, 74% of the students were White, 5% Hispanic, 20% Black, 0.5% Asian and 0.1% American Indian. Southwestern Christian College is located in Terrell. Established in 1949 it is a vocational and two year academic college affiliated with Churches of Christ. Enrollment in 1982 was 285 with in state undergraduate tuition and fees of $2,096 per semester. **PUBLIC LIBRARIES** Kaufman County Library (Kaufman): 24,000 volumes. Carnegie Public Library (Terrell): 29,123 volumes. **CHILD CARE** 75 day care and 12 twenty-four hour care licensed facilities. **HEALTH CARE** 55 physicians and 14 dentists. Hospitals: four with a combined capacity of 192. Ambulance services: one commercial, one hospital-based and one volunteer fire department service. Mental health: one county clinic and one state hospital with capacity of 1,034. Nursing homes: nine nursing homes with a combined capacity of 720 nursing care and 28 personal care residents. The average cost per day for private patients in 1982 was $30.05. **CHURCHES** 88 churches have an estimated combined membership of 23,088. The largest denominations are Southern Baptist, United Methodist and Baptist Missionary. **SOCIAL SERVICES** In fiscal year 1983 a total of $1,347,691 in food stamps was distributed, with an average of 2,956 persons receiving food stamps each month. Aid to Families with Dependent Children (AFDC) totaled $396,262 with an average of 274 families receiving AFDC each month. Medical assistance benefits for the aged and disabled of $5,217,319 and for families and children of $791,171 brought the county benefit total to $7,752,443. **FIRE PROTECTION** Nine volunteer fire departments. **LAW ENFORCEMENT** The County Sheriff has 32 commissioned officers. Six police departments have a combined force of 64. **CRIME** 137 violent crimes (murder, forcible rape, robbery and aggravated assault) and 1,276 nonviolent crimes (burglary, larceny-theft and motor vehicle theft) were reported in 1982. **JUDICIAL SYSTEM** One District Court and Judge, one County Court and Judge and four Justices of the Peace. In the District Court a total of 2,155 cases were pending on 1/1/82, 1,599 new cases were filed and 2,227 cases were disposed of during the year leaving 1,527 cases pending on 12/31/82. There were 381 criminal cases on the docket, 336 convictions, 102 persons committed to prison and 58 committed to jail and 17 cases left pending. In the County Court 778 cases were pending on 1/1/82, 817 new cases were filed and 799 cases were disposed of during the year leaving 796 cases pending on 12/31/82. There were 1,335 criminal cases on the docket, 264 convictions, 130 persons committed to

jail and 723 cases left pending. **JAILS** One jail, capacity 16. A new jail is under construction. **ATTORNEYS AT LAW** 47. **UTILITIES** 94% of the residents are connected to a public or privately owned water system and 61% are connected to a public sewer system. Natural gas is distributed to the county by Lone Star Gas Co., Division of Enserch. The average annual residential bill for natural gas in 1982 for the Lone Star distribution system was $405.91, an increase of 35% over 1981. Electricity is distributed to the county by Kaufman Co. Electric Coop., Inc. and Texas Power and Light and is generated primarily by gas and coal. The typical residential electric bill is $165.24 per month for an all-electric house using 2,500 kwh. **TAXES** The county has 14 units with taxing authority: six school districts, six cities, one county, and one college district.

RECREATION/ENTERTAINMENT

NATIONAL REGISTER OF HISTORIC PLACES Terrell: Matthew Cartwright House and Warren-Crowell House. Terrell vicinity: Walter Porter Farm. **MUNICIPAL PARKS** 156 acres in seven municipal parks. These parks contain six playgrounds, seven football and soccer fields, nine baseball and softball fields, nine tennis courts and one swimming pool. **SCENIC DRIVES** The Texas Lakes Trail runs through this county. This trail introduces some 30 blue-water recreational areas in a variety of settings in North-Central Texas. **BOATING/FISHING** Lakes/reservoirs: Cedar Creek Soil Conservation Service Lakes 19 and 57 (54 acres), Coffee (21 acres), Dallas Storage (58 acres), Ray Hubbard (22,745 acres), Kaufman (131 acres), Kaufman City (41 acres), Kemp (27 acres), Lower East Fork, Soil Conservation Service Lakes 1, 10 and 2 (51 acres), Murphy (113 acres), Rosser-Trinidad (20 acres), Starbrand (19 acres), Tawakoni (88 acres), Terrell Country Club (101 acres), Terrell City (830 acres) and Nest (36 acres). Major rivers: East Fork Trinity and Trinity. Primary streams: Big Brushy, Egans, Bois D'Arc, Bachelor, Big Cottonwood, Kaufman, Cedar, Buffalo, Warsaw, Brushy, Kings, Muddy Cedar and Jones. **HUNTING** No closed seasons on nutria, coyote, bobcat and squirrel. Winter seasons on quail, muskrat, beaver, otter, opossum, ring-tailed cat, badger, fox, weasel, raccoon, skunk, mink and civet cat. In 1983 duck, coot, geese, woodcock and jacksnipe seasons occurred during the winter months. Teal duck, rail and gallinule seasons occurred in the fall. Mourning dove seasons occurred intermittently during the fall and winter months. **MUSEUMS** Terrell: Terrell Hospital Museum and Dr. L.E. Griffith Homeplace. **COLLEGIATE FINE ARTS** Terrell: Cultural events offered by Southwestern Christian College. **SPECIAL EVENTS** Spring Festival and Homes Tour, Terrell, April; Junior Stock Show, Kaufman, April; Annual Garden Club Show, Kaufman, May; Texas Greco-Roman Festival, Terrell, May; Kaufman County Fair, Kaufman, date varies; AJRA Rodeo, Scurry, August.

COMMUNITIES

COUNTY SEAT Kaufman, County Courthouse, 75142; County Clerk's Office, 214/932-2821. **INCORPORATED COMMUNITIES** (1980 population and ZIP Code) Combine (688: 128 in Dallas Co. and 560 in Kaufman Co.) 75159, Crandall (831) 75114, Dallas, (904,078: 1 in Kaufman Co., 902,619 in Dallas Co., 1,357 in Collin Co. and 101 in Denton Co.) 75200, Forney (2,483) 75126, Heath (1,459: 5 in Kaufman Co. and 1,454 in Rockwall Co.) 75087, Kaufman (4,658) 75142, Kemp (1,035) 75143, Lawrence (98 est., incorp. inactive) 75160, Mabank (1,443: 1,287 in Kaufman Co. and 156 in Henderson Co.) 75147, Oak Grove (319) 75142, Oak Ridge City (247) 75160, Post Oak Bend (878) 75142, Seagoville (7,304: 7,298 in Dallas Co. and 6 in Kaufman Co.) 75159 and Terrell (13,225) 75160. **UNINCORPORATED COMMUNITIES** (and ZIP Code) Ables Springs 75160, Abner 75160, Ashworth (Cedarvale) 75142, Becker 75142, Chief (Rand) 75142,

COUNTIES

KAUFMAN (continued)

Cobbs 75160, Elmo 75118, Gastonia 75114, Gossett 75143, Grays Prairie (Peed's Mill) 75158, Hiram 75169, Jiba 75142, Lively 75143, Lone Elm 75126, McCoy 75160, Ola 75142, Peeltown 75158, Poetry 75160, Prairieville 75147, Rand (Chief) 75142, Red Oak 75142, Rosser 75157, Scurry 75158, Styx 75143, Talty 75160, Tolosa 75143 and Warsaw 75142. **FOR ADDITIONAL LOCAL INFORMATION** Kaufman Chamber of Commerce, 112 S. Washington, Kaufman, 75142, 214/932-3118, Kemp Chamber of Commerce, P.O. Box 484, Kemp, 75143, 214/498-7731 and Greater Terrell Chamber of Commerce, 1314 W. Moore, Terrell, 75160, 214/563-5703.

KENDALL (C29)

THE LAND
Southwest of Austin on Interstate Highway 10 in the Edwards Plateau Region, Kendall County covers 663 square miles with an elevation range of 1,000 to 1,500 feet. The soils are alkaline, undulating to hilly, light colored and well drained, or very dark, loamy surfaces over clayey or loamy subsoils with accumulations of lime. Kendall is in the Edwards Plateau vegetation area with tall and mid grasses, live and shinnery oak, junipers and mesquite. Between 11 and 20% of the land in the county is considered prime farmland. **CLIMATE** Subtropical Subhumid with hot summers. The average annual temperature is 66°F. Temperatures in January range from an average low of 35° to an average high of 60°F and in July range from 69° to 94°F. The average annual precipitation is 32 inches, with an average relative humidity of 82% at 6 A.M. and 49% at 6 P.M. The average annual snowfall is not significant. The growing season averages 231 days per year, with the last freeze in late March and the first freeze in late November. The sun shines during the year on the average 67% of the daylight hours.

THE PEOPLE
The 1982 estimated population of 11,800 indicates a continuation of the strong growth rate which began in the 1970s and was one of the highest in the state. The age groups with the greatest gains between 1970 and 1980 were ages 15 to 34 and 62 and over. The county's population is older than average with a median age of 36 and a high percentage of persons who are over age 64. The largest ancestry groups are persons of German descent (41%), English descent (26%) and Irish descent (21%). **REGISTERED VOTERS** As of November 2, 1982 there were 5,967 registered voters (0.1% of the state total). The 1982 general election had a 63% voter turnout, compared to a 83% turnout in the 1980 general election. In the 1982 primary 28% voted Democratic and 72% Republican, with 1,144 votes cast.

THE ECONOMY
AGRICULTURE Sheep area. In 1982, 86% of the land was in farms and ranches, with 5% of the farmland under cultivation. Kendall ranked 216th in the state in highest agricultural receipts, with 94% from livestock and livestock products. Overgrazing, undesirable brush and weeds and water erosion are the current conservation problems. Primary crops: hay, oats, wheat and sorghum. Primary fruits and nuts: peaches and pecans. Primary livestock and products: cattle, milk, sheep, wool, angora goats, mohair and hogs. **BUSINESS** Total number of business establishments in the county: 288. Retail sales during the first quarter of 1984 increased 30%. In 1980, 15% of the labor force were self-employed, 17% were employed in professional or related services, 7% in manufacturing, 20% in wholesale and retail trade, 13% in construction, 48% were employed in other counties and

there were 1,288 retired workers. The industries with the most employment: agribusiness, oil and gas extraction and heavy construction. The nonfarm earnings in 1981 totaled $132,216,000. The retired workers received an average monthly Social Security payment of $297. **FINANCE** On June 30, 1983, three commercial banks had total deposits of $95,600,000 and total assets of $105,226,000. There are three state savings and loan association branches in the county. **HOUSING** Average value of homes in 1980: $50,000. Permits for new, privately owned housing units increased in 1982: 116 permits were issued with a total construction cost of $6,655,526. Of those permits, all were for single family houses. Housing permits increased in Boerne from 11 in 1981 to 34 in 1982 with all permits issued for single family houses. Between 1970 and 1980 the number of housing units increased by 45%. Fifty-seven percent of all units in the county are air-conditioned, 60% are heated by gas and 23% by electricity. **NATURAL RESOURCES** Dolomite and limestone. **TOURISM** Travel expenditures of $3,890,000 in 1982 (an increase of 17% over 1981) generated 57 jobs and $584,000 in payroll. **ALCOHOLIC BEVERAGES** Packaged distilled spirits, beer, ale, malt liquor and wine are legal. Sale of mixed beverages is legal in all or parts of the county. **FEDERAL EXPENDITURES** The federal government had direct expenditures or obligations of $24,582,000 in the county during fiscal year 1983, including $3,579,000 by the U.S. Department of Defense. In addition, the federal government provided $90,000 in grant awards, paid $683,000 in salaries and wages, made direct payments to individuals of $23,341,000 including $19,263,000 in retirement and disability payments, awarded $35,000 in procurement contracts and spent $433,000 in other expenditures or obligations. The federal government also provided $5,637,000 in guaranteed loans and insurance.

COMMUNICATION
Newspapers–Weekly: Boerne Star and the Comfort News. Radio: KNCI-AM (Boerne). Cable TV. Telephone companies: General Telephone, Guadalupe Valley Telephone Coop. and Hill Country Telephone Coop. **TRANSPORTATION** Total public road mileage: 453. In 1982 there were 11,044 registered vehicles and 296 reported traffic accidents including two fatalities. Taxi cabs: one company in Boerne. Intercity bus service is available. Motor freight: six local and intrastate carriers. Aircraft: 41 are registered in the county.

COMMUNITY SERVICES
EDUCATION Two school districts with three elementary, two middle and two high schools. The average daily attendance in 1981-82 was 2,392, with expenditures per pupil of $1,929 including 129 classroom teachers with an average annual salary of $16,523. Fifty-four percent of the 186 high school graduates planned to attend college. In 1982-83, 82% of the students were White, 17% Hispanic, 0.3% Black and 0.4% Asian. Private schools: 160 students enrolled in one elementary and one high school. **PUBLIC LIBRARIES** Boerne Public Library: 13,900 volumes. Comfort Public LIbrary: 19,000 volumes. Kendalia Public Library: 9,460 volumes. **CHILD CARE** 12 day care and two twenty-four hour care licensed facilities. **HEALTH CARE** 17 physicians and nine dentists. Hospitals: one with a capacity of 22. Ambulance services: one county service. Nursing homes: two nursing homes with a combined capacity of 203 nursing care residents. The average cost per day for private patients in 1982 was $26.97. **CHURCHES** 15 churches have an estimated combined membership of 5,514. The largest denominations are Catholic, Southern Baptist and American Lutheran. **SOCIAL SERVICES** In fiscal year 1983 a total of $139,326 in food stamps was distributed, with an average of 299 persons receiving food stamps each month. Aid to Families with Dependent Children

(AFDC) totaled $22,038 with an average of 15 families receiving AFDC each month. Medical assistance benefits for the aged and disabled of $873,846 and for families and children of $13,123 brought the county benefit total to $1,048,333. **FIRE PROTECTION** Three volunteer fire departments. **LAW ENFORCEMENT** The County Sheriff has 18 commissioned officers. One police department has a force of 13. **CRIME** 30 violent crimes (murder, forcible rape, robbery and aggravated assault) and 243 nonviolent crimes (burglary, larceny-theft and motor vehicle theft) were reported in 1982. **JUDICIAL SYSTEM** One District Court and Judge, one County Court and Judge and four Justices of the Peace. In the District Court a total of 248 cases were pending on 1/1/82, 208 new cases were filed and 219 cases were disposed of during the year leaving 237 cases pending on 12/31/82. There were 103 criminal cases on the docket, 37 convictions, 11 persons committed to prison and one committed to jail and 38 cases left pending. In the County Court 128 cases were pending on 1/1/82, 148 new cases were filed and 73 cases were disposed of during the year leaving 203 cases pending on 12/31/82. There were 217 criminal cases on the docket, 37 convictions, two persons committed to jail and 160 cases left pending. **JAILS** One jail, capacity seven. **ATTORNEYS AT LAW** 28. **UTILITIES** 47% of the residents are connected to a public or privately owned water system and 39% are connected to a public sewer system. Electricity is distributed to the city of Boerne by Boerne Utilities and to the rest of the county by Bandera Electric Coop., Inc., Central Texas Electric Coop., Inc. and Pedernales Electric Coop., Inc. and is generated primarily by oil, water and coal. **TAXES** The county has five units with taxing authority: two school districts, one city, one county and one special district.

RECREATION/ENTERTAINMENT
NATIONAL REGISTER OF HISTORIC PLACES Boerne: Kendall County Courthouse and Jail and Kendall Inn. Comfort: Comfort Historic District, Otto Brinkmann House and "Trueu der Union" Monument. Sisterdale: Sisterdale Valley District. **STATE** Guadalupe River State Park (see Comal County). **MUNICIPAL PARKS** 136 acres in four municipal parks. These parks contain three football and soccer fields, one baseball and softball field, one swimming pool, one beach and one boat ramp. **BOATING/FISHING** Lakes/reservoirs: Boerne City (112 acres), KWW Ranch (38 acres) and Oz (16 acres). Major rivers: Guadalupe. Primary streams: Cibolo, Walter and Frederick. **HUNTING** Fall and winter seasons on deer. No closed season on javelina, coyote, bobcat and squirrel. Fall, winter and spring seasons on turkey. Winter seasons on quail, muskrat, beaver, opossum, ring-tailed cat, badger, fox, weasel, raccoon, skunk and civet cat. In 1983 sandhill crane, duck, coot, geese, woodcock and jacksnipe seasons occurred during the winter months. Teal duck, rail and gallinule seasons occurred in the fall. Mourning dove seasons occurred intermittently during the fall and winter months with a fall season in some parts of the county on white-winged dove. **MUSEUMS** Boerne: Historical House, Theis House and King House. Comfort: Comfort Historical Museum. **THEATERS** Comfort: The Comfort Theater. **OTHER** Boerne: Cascade Caverns. **SPECIAL EVENTS** Volkssportverein's Easter Walk, Comfort, April; Berges Fest, Parade and Horse Races, Boerne, June; Independence Day Celebration, Comfort, July; County Fair, Boerne, September; Founders Day, Boerne, October.

COMMUNITIES
COUNTY SEAT Boerne, County Courthouse, 78006; County Clerk's Office, 512/249-2541. **INCORPORATED COMMUNITIES** (1980 population and ZIP Code) Boerne (3,229) 78006. **UNINCORPORATED COMMUNITIES** (and ZIP Code) Bankersmith 78624, Bergheim 78004, Camp Alzafar 78006, Comfort 78013, Kendalia 78027, Sisterdale 78006, Waring 78074

and Welfare 78006. **FOR ADDITIONAL LOCAL INFORMATION** Sisterdale Chamber of Commerce, Rt. 2, P.O. Box 2481G, Boerne, 78006, 512/324-2543 and Comfort Chamber of Commerce, P.O. BOx 777, Comfort, 78013, 512/995-3892.

KENEDY (B26)

THE LAND
Bordering the Gulf of Mexico south of Corpus Christi on U.S. Highway 77 in the Rio Grande Plain Region, Kenedy County covers 1,389 square miles with an elevation ranging from sea level to 100 feet. The nearly level to undulating soils are sandy with areas of light colored loamy surfaces over very deep, reddish or mottled, clayey subsoils. Along the Gulf Coast the soils are sandy and saline with areas of gray to black cracking clay. In the South Texas Plains vegetation area, the grasses are primarily bluestems with a variety of trees and shrubs such as post and live oak, acacias, and mesquite. Along the coast in the Gulf Prairies and Marshes vegetation area are tall bunchgrasses such as the seacoast bluestem with cordgrasses, saltgrass and marsh millet in the salt marshes. Less than 1% of the land in the county is considered prime farmland. **CLIMATE** Subtropical Humid with a risk of a tropical storm or hurricane June through October. The average annual temperature is 73°F. Temperatures in January range from an average low of 47° to an average high of 69°F and in July range from 74° to 96°F. The average annual precipitation is 26 inches, with an average relative humidity of 89% at 6 A.M. and 66% at 6 P.M. There is no snowfall. The growing season averages 319 days per year, with the last freeze in early February and the first freeze in late December. The sun shines during the year on the average 69% of the daylight hours.

THE PEOPLE
Kenedy County is one of the most sparsely populated in the state and ranks 10th among all U.S. counties in the highest percent of residents of Spanish origin. The 1982 estimated population of 500 indicates a slight decline since 1980. Although significant gains occurred between 1950 and 1960, population decreased 23% from 1960 to 1970 and 20% from 1970 to 1980. The county is comprised completely of rural areas. The age group with the largest reduction between 1970 and 1980 was ages five to 14. The largest ancestry groups are Hispanic (83%) and persons of Irish descent (5%). **REGISTERED VOTERS** As of November 2, 1982 there were 310 registered voters. The 1982 general election had a 63% voter turnout, compared to a 64% turnout in the 1980 general election. In the 1982 primary 98% voted Democratic and 2% Republican, with 199 votes cast.

THE ECONOMY
AGRICULTURE Ranchland. In 1982, 74% of the land was in farms and ranches, with less than 1% of the farmland under cultivation. Kenedy ranked 187th in the state in highest agricultural receipts, with 97% from livestock and livestock products. Overgrazing, undesirable brush and weeds and water erosion are the current conservation problems. Primary crops: hay. Primary vegetables: watermelons. Primary livestock and products: cattle and milk. **BUSINESS** Total number of business establishments in the county: 2. In 1980, 6% of the labor force were self-employed, 11% were employed in professional or related services, 3% in manufacturing, 7% in wholesale and retail trade, 68% in agriculture, forestry, fisheries and mining, 31% were employed in other counties and there were 42 retired workers. The industry with the most employment: agribusiness. The nonfarm earnings in 1981 totaled $7,197,000. The retired workers received an average monthly Social Security payment of $333. **HOUSING** Average value of homes in 1980: $11,700. Between 1970 and 1980 the

COUNTIES

KENEDY (continued)

number of housing units increased by 6%. Fifty percent of all units in the county are air-conditioned, 87% are heated by gas and 9% by electricity. **NATURAL RESOURCES** Oil and gas. In 1982 a total of 72,105,730 thousand cubic feet of gas well gas, 142,213 barrels of condensate, 420,856 barrels of crude oil and 786,058 thousand cubic feet of casinghead gas were produced. **ALCOHOLIC BEVERAGES** Packaged distilled spirits, beer, ale, malt liquor and wine are legal in parts of the county. **FEDERAL EXPENDITURES** The federal government had direct expenditures or obligations of $618,000 in the county during fiscal year 1983. In addition, the federal government provided $13,000 in grant awards, paid $34,000 in salaries and wages, made direct payments to individuals of $548,000 including $361,000 in retirement and disability payments and spent $24,000 in other expenditures or obligations. The federal government also provided $39,000 in direct loans and $12,000 in guaranteed loans and insurance.

COMMUNICATION

Telephone companies: General Telephone, Southwestern Bell and Riviera Telephone. **TRANSPORTATION** Total public road mileage: 53. In 1982 there were 360 registered vehicles and 44 reported traffic accidents including three fatalities. Intercity bus service is available. Motor freight: three carriers. Rail: one branch line carries annually five to 10 million tons of freight through the county. Aircraft: three are registered in the county.

COMMUNITY SERVICES

EDUCATION One school district with two elementary schools. The average daily attendance in 1981-82 was 34, with expenditures per pupil of $11,104 including 5 classroom teachers with an average annual salary of $18,178. In 1982-83, 2% of the students were White and 98% Hispanic. **CHILD CARE** One day care licensed facility. **CHURCHES** Two churches have an estimated combined membership of 483. The largest denomination is Catholic. **SOCIAL SERVICES** In fiscal year 1983 a total of $54,225 in food stamps was distributed, with an average of 147 persons receiving food stamps each month. Aid to Families with Dependent Children (AFDC) totaled $2,039. Medical assistance benefits for the aged and disabled of $14,102 and for families and children of $35 brought the county benefit total to $70,401. **LAW ENFORCEMENT** The County Sheriff has five commissioned officers. **CRIME** One violent crime (murder, forcible rape, robbery and aggravated assault) and two nonviolent crimes (burglary, larceny-theft and motor vehicle theft) were reported in 1982. **JUDICIAL SYSTEM** Two District Courts and Judges, one County Court and Judge and four Justices of the Peace. In the District Courts a total of 15 cases were pending on 1/1/82, four new cases were filed and nine cases were disposed of during the year leaving 10 cases pending on 12/31/82. In the County Court seven cases were pending on 1/1/82, six new cases were filed and seven cases were disposed of during the year leaving six cases pending on 12/31/82. There were 12 criminal cases on the docket, seven convictions, and five cases left pending. **JAILS** One jail, capacity 13. **ATTORNEYS AT LAW** One. **UTILITIES** 62% of the residents are connected to a public or privately owned water system and 39% are connected to a public sewer system. Natural gas is distributed to the county by Lone Star Gas Co., Division of Enserch. The average annual residential bill for natural gas in 1982 for the Lone Star distribution system was $405.91, an increase of 35% over 1981. Electricity is distributed to the county by Magic Valley Electric Coop., Inc., and Nueces Electric Coop., Inc. and is generated primarily by gas, oil and coal. **TAXES** The county has two units with taxing authority: one school district and one county.

RECREATION/ENTERTAINMENT

FEDERAL Padre Island National Seashore (see Kleberg County). **SCENIC DRIVES** The Texas Tropical Trail runs through this county. This trail is charted through the state's southernmost wedge meandering through ranch land, resort areas by the Gulf of Mexico and fertile farmlands. **BOATING/FISHING** Lakes/reservoirs: McGill (125 acres). Primary streams: Los Olmos. Saltwater fishing: speckled trout, redfish and flounders is usually good around Laguna Madre. Shrimp, oysters and crabs may be taken but, like other saltwater fish, under specific regulations. **HUNTING** Fall and winter seasons on deer. No closed seasons on nutria, javelina, coyote, bobcat and squirrel. Winter seasons on quail, muskrat, beaver, otter, opossum, mink, ring-tailed cat, badger, fox, raccoon, skunk and civet cat. Fall, winter and spring seasons on turkey. In 1983 duck, coot, geese, woodcock and jacksnipe seasons occurred during the winter months with a winter season on sandhill crane in some parts of the county. Teal duck, rail and gallinule seasons occurred in the fall. Mourning dove seasons occurred intermittently during the fall and winter months with a fall season on white-winged dove.

COMMUNITIES

COUNTY SEAT Sarita, County Courthouse, 78385; County Clerk's Office, 512/294-5220. **UNINCORPORATED COMMUNITIES** (and ZIP Code) Armstrong 78338, Norias 78338, Rudolph 78338 and Sarita 78385.

KENT (P51)

THE LAND

Southeast of Lubbock on U.S. Highway 380 in the Rolling Plains Region, Kent County covers 878 square miles with an elevation range of 2,000 to 2,400 feet. The soils range from light to very dark, loamy surfaces with very deep, reddish, clayey subsoils. Some areas have hardwood calcium deposits in the subsoils. In the Rolling Plains vegetation area, the tall to mid grasses have been invaded by problem plants such as ragweed and mesquite. Between 21 and 30% of the land in the county is considered prime farmland. **CLIMATE** Subtropical Subhumid with a risk of duststorms in spring and thunderstorms primarily during spring and summer. The average annual temperature is 62°F. Temperatures in January range from an average low of 24° to an average high of 54°F and in July range from 69° to 95°F. The average annual precipitation is 21 inches, with an average relative humidity of 72% at 6 A.M. and 40% at 6 P.M. The average annual snowfall is ten inches. The growing season averages 216 days per year, with the last freeze in early April and the first freeze in early November. The sun shines during the year on the average 75% of the daylight hours.

THE PEOPLE

Kent County is one of the most sparsely populated in the state. The 1982 estimated population of 1,200 indicates a slight gain since 1980, although steady population losses occurred the previous 50 years. A majority of the county residents live in rural areas. The age group with the largest decrease between 1970 and 1980 was ages five to 14 which declined 50%. The population is older than average with a median age of 41 in 1980. The largest ancestry groups are persons of English descent (36%), Irish descent (21%) and German descent (12%). **REGISTERED VOTERS** As of November 2, 1982 there were 833 registered voters (0.01% of the state total). The 1982 general election had a 69% voter turnout, compared to a 76% turnout in the 1980 general election. In the 1982 primary 100% voted Democratic, with 517 votes cast.

THE ECONOMY

AGRICULTURE Cotton area. In 1982, 94% of the land was in farms and ranches, with 8% of the farmland under cultivation and 5% irrigated. Kent ranked 225th in the state in highest agricultural receipts, with 56% from livestock and livestock products. Overgrazing, undesirable brush and weeds, water and wind erosion and difficulties in grass establishment are the current conservation problems. Primary crops: cotton, wheat and sorghum. Primary livestock and products: cattle. **BUSINESS** Total number of business establishments in the county: 12. In 1980, 30% of the labor force were self-employed, 17% were employed in professional or related services, 4% in manufacturing, 11% in wholesale and retail trade, 45% in agriculture, forestry, fisheries and mining, 15% were employed in other counties and there were 133 retired workers. The industry with the most employment is agribusiness. The nonfarm earnings in 1981 totaled $7,485,000. The retired workers received an average monthly Social Security payment of $286. **FINANCE** On June 30, 1983, one commercial bank had total deposits of $6,202,000 and total assets of $6,758,000. **HOUSING** Average value of homes in 1980: $17,300. Between 1970 and 1980 the number of housing units increased by 15%. Seventy-eight percent of all units in the county are air-conditioned, 86% are heated by gas and 12% by electricity. **NATURAL RESOURCES** Gypsum, salt, oil and gas. In 1982 10,525,000 barrels of crude oil and 6,291,975 thousand cubic feet of casinghead gas were produced. **TOURISM** Travel expenditures of $125,000 in 1982 (an increase of 7% over 1981) generated 3 jobs and $23,000 in payroll. **ALCOHOLIC BEVERAGES** Totally dry. **FEDERAL EXPENDITURES** The federal government had direct expenditures or obligations of $3,610,000 in the county during fiscal year 1983, including $181,000 by the U.S. Department of Defense. In addition, the federal government provided $29,000 in grant awards, paid $199,000 in salaries and wages, made direct payments to individuals of $1,884,000 including $1,264,000 in retirement and disability payments, awarded $1,000 in procurement contracts and spent $1,496,000 in other expenditures or obligations. The federal government also provided $712,000 in direct loans and $1,161,000 in guaranteed loans and insurance.

COMMUNICATION
Newspapers–Weekly: Jayton Chronicle. Telephone companies: Southwestern Bell and Cap Rock Telephone. **TRANSPORTATION** Total public road mileage: 375. In 1982 there were 1,666 registered vehicles and 17 reported traffic accidents including one fatality. Motor freight: one carrier. Aircraft: five are registered in the county. Airports: Kent County Airport at Jayton.

COMMUNITY SERVICES
EDUCATION One school district with one elementary and one high school. The average daily attendance in 1981-82 was 179, with expenditures per pupil of $8,289 including 22 classroom teachers with an average annual salary of $19,875. Ninety-four percent of the 16 high school graduates planned to attend college. In 1982-83, 84% of the students were White and 16% Hispanic. **PUBLIC LIBRARIES** Kent County Library (Jayton): 10,870 volumes. **HEALTH CARE** Ambulance services: one police department service. Nursing homes: one nursing home has a capacity of 33 nursing care residents. The average cost per day for private patients in 1982 was $26.19. **CHURCHES** Six churches have an estimated combined membership of 846. The largest denominations are Southern Baptist, United Methodist and Churches of Christ. **SOCIAL SERVICES** In fiscal year 1983 a total of $16,664 in food stamps was distributed, with an average of 43 persons receiving food stamps each month. Aid to Families with Dependent Children (AFDC) totaled $4,676. Medical assistance benefits for the aged and disabled of $185,817 and for families and children of $368 brought the county benefit total to $207,525. **FIRE PROTECTION** Three water trucks manned by volunteers. **LAW ENFORCEMENT** The County Sheriff has eight commissioned officers. **CRIME** One violent crime (murder, forcible rape, robbery and aggravated assault) and four nonviolent crimes (burglary, larceny-theft and motor vehicle theft) were reported in 1982. **JUDICIAL SYSTEM** One District Court and Judge, one County Court and Judge and one Justice of the Peace. In the District Court a total of 34 cases were pending on 1/1/82, 15 new cases were filed and 15 cases were disposed of during the year leaving 34 cases pending on 12/31/82. There were five criminal cases on the docket, one conviction. In the County Court 14 cases were pending on 1/1/82, 18 new cases were filed and 12 cases were disposed of during the year leaving 20 cases pending on 12/31/82. There were 19 criminal cases on the docket, nine convictions, and eight cases left pending. **ATTORNEYS AT LAW** One. **UTILITIES** 55% of the residents are connected to a public or privately owned water system and 9% are connected to a public sewer system. Electricity is distributed to the county by Dickens Electric Coop., Inc., and Midwest Electric Coop., Inc. and is generated primarily by gas and oil. **TAXES** The county has three units with taxing authority: one school district, one city and one county.

RECREATION/ENTERTAINMENT
COUNTY PARKS 96 acres in three county parks. These parks contain three playgrounds, one golf course and two baseball and softball fields. **BOATING/FISHING** Lakes/reservoirs: Cogdell Ranch (24 acres), Jayton City (25 acres) and So Relle (21 acres). Major rivers: Salt Fork Brazos, Double Mountain Fork Brazos and White. Primary streams: Cooper, Little Duck, Stinking, Salt, Maverick and ABC. **HUNTING** Fall season on antelope. Fall and winter seasons on deer and mule deer. No closed seasons on coyote, bobcat, nutria and squirrel. Winter seasons on quail, muskrat, beaver, otter, opossum, mink, ring-tailed cat, badger, fox, raccoon, skunk and civet cat. Fall, winter and spring seasons on turkey. In 1983 sandhill crane, duck, coot, geese, woodcock and jacksnipe seasons occurred during the winter months. Teal duck, rail and gallinule seasons occurred in the fall. Mourning dove seasons occurred intermittently during the fall and winter months.

COMMUNITIES
COUNTY SEAT Jayton, County Courthouse, 79528; County Clerk's Office, 806/237-3881. **INCORPORATED COMMUNITIES** (1980 population and ZIP Code) Jayton (638) 79528. **UNINCORPORATED COMMUNITIES** (and ZIP Code) Clairmont 79549, Girard 79518 and Polar 79515.

KERR (C28)

THE LAND
Northwest of San Antonio on Interstate Highway 10 in the Edwards Plateau Region, Kerr County covers 1,107 square miles with an elevation range of 1,500 to 2,000 feet. The undulating to hilly soils are dark and loamy over limestone northwest of Kerrville. To the south and east the soils vary with some areas having lighter colored brown to red soils, or very dark loamy soils, or loamy soils over clayey subsoils. In the Edwards Plateau vegetation area, the primary grasses are buffalograss, wildrye, switchgrass, bluestems and gramas with dense brushy areas of live oak, shinnery oak, junipers and mesquite. Between 1 and 10% of the land in the county is considered prime farmland. **CLIMATE** Subtropical subhumid with hot summers. The average annual temperature is 66°F. Temperatures in January range from an average low of 35° to an average high of 62°F and in July range from 69° to 96°F. The average annual precipitation is 26 inches, with an average relative humidity of 80% at 6 A.M. and 46% at 6 P.M. The average annual snowfall is two inches. The

KERR (continued)

growing season averages 218 days per year, with the last freeze in early April and the first freeze in early November. The sun shines during the year on the average 65% of the daylight hours.

THE PEOPLE

Kerr County ranks 43rd among all U.S. counties in the highest percent of residents over age 64. The 1982 estimated population of 30,200 continues the pattern of steady growth which has occurred since 1930. Kerr was one of the fastest growing counties in the state between 1970 and 1980 with a growth rate of 48%. The population in rural areas nearly doubled and urban areas grew 20%. The age groups with the greatest increases were ages 65 and over and 20 to 34 which doubled in size. The population is older than average. The largest ancestry groups are persons of English descent (30%), German descent (26%) and Irish descent (25%). **REGISTERED VOTERS** As of November 2, 1982 there were 15,728 registered voters (0.2% of the state total). The 1982 general election had a 58% voter turnout, compared to a 79% turnout in the 1980 general election. In the 1982 primary 27% voted Democratic and 73% Republican, with 5,213 votes cast.

THE ECONOMY

AGRICULTURE Sheep area. In 1982, 85% of the land was in farms and ranches, with 2% of the farmland under cultivation. Kerr ranked 226th in the state in highest agricultural receipts, with 97% from livestock and livestock products. Overgrazing, undesirable brush and weeds and water erosion are the current conservation problems. Primary crops: oats, hay, wheat and sorghum. Primary fruits and nuts: peaches and pecans. Primary livestock and products: cattle, sheep, wool, angora goats and mohair. **BUSINESS** Total number of business establishments in the county: 717. Retail sales during the first quarter of 1984 increased 31%. In 1980, 14% of the labor force were self-employed, 28% were employed in professional or related services, 8% in manufacturing, 20% in wholesale and retail trade, 11% in construction, 6% were employed in other counties and there were 4,893 retired workers. The industries with the most employment: general construction, tourism and the manufacture of plastics products, fabricated metal products, jewelry and aircraft. The nonfarm earnings in 1981 totaled $319,842,000. The retired workers received an average monthly Social Security payment of $317. **FINANCE** On June 30, 1983, five commercial banks had total deposits of $362,319,000 and total assets of $405,785,000. On December 31, 1982 one state savings and loan association and three state branches had assets of $26,556,539. In addition there are four credit unions in the county. **HOUSING** Average value of homes in 1980: $42,100. Permits for new, privately owned housing units decreased in 1982: 89 permits were issued with a total construction cost of $5,065,600. Of those permits, 76 were for single family houses. Between 1970 and 1980 the number of housing units increased by 66%. Seventy-six percent of all units in the county are air-conditioned, 56% are heated by gas and 35% by electricity. **NATURAL RESOURCES** Dolomite, limestone, sand, gravel, oil and gas. In 1982, 10,396 barrels of crude oil and 12 thousand cubic feet of casinghead gas were produced. Current production of other minerals and products includes crushed limestone, sand and gravel. **TOURISM** Travel expenditures of $72,138,000 in 1982 (an increase of 11% over 1981) generated 1,777 jobs and $14,484,000 in payroll. Lodging: eight hotels, motels and tourist courts. Convention/meeting facilities: Kerrville-Kerrville Municipal Auditorium and one hotel with facilities for large gatherings. **ALCOHOLIC BEVERAGES** Packaged distilled spirits, beer, ale, malt liquor and wine are legal in parts of the county. Sale of mixed beverages is legal in all or parts of the county. **FEDERAL EXPENDITURES** The federal government had direct expenditures or obligations of $94,913,000 in the county during fiscal year 1983, including $7,619,000 by the U.S. Department of Defense. In addition, the federal government provided $1,558,000 in grant awards, paid $15,584,000 in salaries and wages, made direct payments to individuals of $75,549,000 including $62,165,000 in retirement and disability payments, awarded $1,608,000 in procurement contracts and spent $613,000 in other expenditures or obligations. The federal government also provided $15,634,000 in guaranteed loans and insurance.

COMMUNICATION

Newspapers–Daily: Kerrville Daily Times, ave. eve. circ. 7,252. Weekly: Kerrville Mountain Sun. Radio: KERV-AM and KERV-FM (Kerrville). Cable TV. Telephone companies: General Telephone, Southwestern Bell, Hill Country Telephone Coop. and Kerrville Telephone. **TRANSPORTATION** Total public road mileage: 750. In 1982 there were 26,890 registered vehicles and 798 reported traffic accidents including 19 fatalities. Taxi cabs: one company in Kerrville. Intercity bus service is available. Motor freight: four carriers. Aircraft: 84 are registered in the county. Airports: Louis Schreiner Field at Kerrville serves as a base for 60 aircraft and is a basic transportation airport with general aviation service. Sky Harbor Airport at Mountain Home. The Veterans Administration Hospital at Kerrville provides a heliport for emergency use.

COMMUNITY SERVICES

EDUCATION Five school districts with seven elementary, one middle and three high schools. The average daily attendance in 1981-82 was 3,810, with expenditures per pupil of $3,854 including 266 classroom teachers with an average annual salary of $16,137. Fifty-four percent of the 295 high school graduates planned to attend college. In 1982-83, 74% of the students were White, 22% Hispanic, 4% Black, 0.5% Asian and 0.1% American Indian. Private schools: 306 students enrolled in two elementary schools. Schreiner College is located in Kerrville. Established in 1923 it is a vocational and two year academic college affiliated with the Presbyterian Church. Enrollment in 1982 was 474 with in state undergraduate tuition and fees of $2,560 per semester. Vocational education: Conlee College of Cosmetology (Kerrville). **PUBLIC LIBRARIES** Butt-Holdsworth Memorial Library (Kerrville): 59,000 volumes. **CHILD CARE** 62 day care and eight twenty-four hour care licensed facilities. **HEALTH CARE** 102 physicians and 31 dentists. Hospitals: two with a combined capacity of 162. Specialized hospitals: one for treatment of alcohol abuse with a capacity of 10 and one veterans medical center with a capacity of 291. Clinics: one dialysis clinic. Ambulance services: one commercial and one volunteer service. Mental health: three clinics and one state hospital with a capacity of 710. Nursing homes: four nursing homes with a combined capacity of 406 nursing care, 120 custodial care and 45 personal care residents. The average cost per day for private patients in 1982 was $28.82. **CHURCHES** 33 churches have an estimated combined membership of 14,134. The largest denominations are Southern Baptist, Catholic and United Methodist. **SOCIAL SERVICES** In fiscal year 1983 a total of $801,637 in food stamps was distributed, with an average of 1,583 persons receiving food stamps each month. Aid to Families with Dependent Children (AFDC) totaled $217,716 with an average of 145 families receiving AFDC each month. Medical assistance benefits for the aged and disabled of $1,821,494 and for families and children of $338,000 brought the county benefit total to $3,178,846. **FIRE PROTECTION** One paid and six volunteer fire departments. **LAW ENFORCEMENT** The County Sheriff has 12 commissioned officers. One police department has a force of 34. **CRIME** 42 violent crimes (murder, forcible rape, robbery and aggravated assault) and 843 nonviolent crimes (burglary, larceny-theft and motor vehicle theft) were reported in 1982. **JUDICIAL SYSTEM** Two District Courts and Judges, one County Court and Judge and four Justices of the Peace. In the District Courts a total of 690 cases were pending on 1/1/82, 878 new cases were filed and 817 cases were disposed of during the year leaving 751 cases pending on 12/31/82. There were 497 criminal cases on the docket, 110 convictions, 27 persons committed to prison and three committed to jail and 223 cases left pending. In the County Court 384 cases were pending on 1/1/82, 499 new cases were filed and 626 cases were disposed of during the year leaving 257 cases pending on 12/31/82. There were 776 criminal cases on the docket, 226 convictions, 37 persons committed to jail and 218 cases left pending. **JAILS** One jail, capacity 40. **ATTORNEYS AT LAW** 78. **UTILITIES** 77% of the residents are connected to a public or privately owned water system and 55% are connected to a public sewer system. Natural gas is distributed to the county by Lone Star Gas Co., Division of Enserch. The average annual residential bill for natural gas in 1982 for the Lone Star distribution system was $405.91, an increase of 35% over 1981. Electricity is distributed to the county by Bandera Electric Coop., Inc., Central Texas Electric Coop., Inc., Kimball Electric Coop., Inc. and Lower Colorado River Authority and is generated primarily by oil, water and coal. The typical residential electric bill is $123.05 per month for an all-electric house using 2,500 kwh. **TAXES** The county has nine units with taxing authority: five school districts, one city, one county and two special districts.

RECREATION/ENTERTAINMENT
NATIONAL REGISTER OF HISTORIC PLACES Camp Verde vicinity: Camp Verde. Kerrville: Charles A. Schreiner House. Kerrville vicinity: Tulahteka. **STATE** Kerrville State Recreation Area covers 517 acres with camping and trailer sites as well as fishing, swimming and boat ramps. **MUNICIPAL PARKS** 397 acres in seven municipal parks. These parks contain four playgrounds, one golf course, five baseball and softball fields, two tennis courts, one multi-use court, one swimming pool, one beach and one boat ramp. **SCENIC DRIVES** The Texas Hill Country Trail runs through this county. This trail winds through a scenic region of South-Central Texas, spanning a vast ranching area abundant with wildlife in a landscape of deeply-sculptured valleys and hills. **BOATING/FISHING** Lakes/reservoirs: Cedar (28 acres), Ingram (70 acres), Kerrville (90 acres), Poole (21 acres), River Ponding (105 acres), Roden (20 acres) and Walters (28 acres). Major rivers: North Fork Guadalupe, South Fork Guadalupe and Guadalupe. Primary streams: Fessenden, Bear Hollow, Palmer, Prison Canyon and Turtle. **WILDLIFE REFUGES** Kerr State Wildlife Management Area covers 6,493 acres. **HUNTING** Fall and winter seasons on deer. No closed seasons on javelina, coyote, bobcat and squirrel. Winter seasons on quail, muskrat, beaver, opossum, ring-tailed cat, badger, fox, weasel, raccoon, skunk and civet cat. Fall, winter and spring seasons on turkey. In 1983 sandhill crane, duck, coot, geese, woodcock and jacksnipe seasons occurred during the winter months. Teal duck, rail and gallinule seasons occurred in the fall. Mourning dove seasons occurred intermittently during the fall and winter months with a fall season on white-winged dove. **MUSEUMS** Kerrville: Hill Country Arts Foundation Art Gallery and Classic Car Showcase and Wax Museum. **THEATERS** Kerrville: Festival Outdoor Theatre and Kerrville Festivals. **ZOO** Hunt: Patio Ranch. **COLLEGIATE FINE ARTS** Kerrville: Cultural events offered by Schreiner College. **OTHER** Mountain Home: Y.O. Ranch Game Preserve. **SPECIAL EVENTS** Junior Stock Show, Kerrville, January; Winter Music Festival, Kerrville, January; Classical Winter Music Festival, Kerrville, February/March; Hill Country Bicycle Tour, Kerrville, April; Hill Country Chili Cookoff, Kerrville, April; Folk Festival, Kerrville, May; Texas State Arts and Crafts Fair, Kerrville, May/June; Summer Theatre, Ingram,

July; Morning-Star Fest, Kerrville, July; Summer Music Festival, Kerrville, July; County Fair, Kerrville, July; Southwestern Regional Fly-in, Kerrville, September; Camelot Faire Renaissance, Kerrville, September; Goodtime Music Festival, Kerrville, October; Christmas Parade, Kerrville, December.

COMMUNITIES
COUNTY SEAT Kerrville, County Courthouse, 78028; County Clerk's Office, 512/257-6181. **INCORPORATED COMMUNITIES** (1980 population and ZIP Code) Ingram (1,000 est. incorp. inactive) 78025 and Kerrville (15,276) 78028. **UNINCORPORATED COMMUNITIES** (and ZIP Code) Camp Scenic 78025, Camp Stewart 78024, Camp Verde 78010, Center Point 78010, Hunt 78024, Legion (Oak Park) 78028 and Mountain Home 78058. **FOR ADDITIONAL LOCAL INFORMATION** Kerrville Area Chamber of Commerce, P.O. Box 790, Kerrville, 78028, 512/896-1155.

KIMBLE (P98)

THE LAND
West of Austin on Interstate Highway 10 in the Edwards Plateau Region, Kimble County covers 1,250 square miles with an elevation range of 1,400 to 2,300 feet. The undulating to hilly, alkaline soils are very dark and loamy with limestone in the subsoils. Along the Llano River in the northeast the undulating to rolling soils are deep with loamy surfaces and clayey to loamy subsoils over limestone or sandstone. Between 11 and 20% of the land in the county is considered prime farmland. **CLIMATE** Subtropical subhumid with wide-ranging temperatures from summer to winter. The average annual temperature is 66°F. Temperatures in January range from an average low of 32° to an average high of 62°F and in July range from 69° to 96°F. The average annual precipitation is 22 inches, with an average relative humidity of 77% at 6 A.M. and 44% at 6 P.M. The average annual snowfall is three inches. The growing season averages 215 days per year, with the last freeze in early April and the first freeze in early November. The sun shines during the year on the average 67% of the daylight hours.

THE PEOPLE
The 1982 estimated population of 4,200 indicates a continuation of a growth in population which began in the 1970s after 30 years of population decline. The county's median age rose from 34 in 1970 to 38 in 1980. The population is older than average and includes a high percentage of residents who are over age 64. The largest ancestry groups are persons of Irish descent (28%), English descent (25%) and German descent (22%). **REGISTERED VOTERS** As of November 2, 1982 there were 2,303 registered voters (0.03% of the state total). The 1982 general election had a 50% voter turnout, compared to a 67% turnout in the 1980 general election. In the 1982 primary 96% voted Democratic and 4% Republican, with 697 votes cast.

THE ECONOMY
AGRICULTURE Sheep and angora goat area. In 1982, 93% of the land was in farms and ranches, with 1% of the farmland under cultivation some of which was irrigated. Kimble ranked 213th in the state in highest agricultural receipts, with 98% from livestock and livestock products. Overgrazing, undesirable brush and weeds and wind erosion are the current conservation problems. Primary crops: hay, wheat and oats. Primary fruits and nuts: peaches and pecans. Primary livestock and products: seventh in the state for both angora goats and mohair production. Cattle, sheep and wool. **BUSINESS** Total number of business establishments in the county: 108. Retail sales during

COUNTIES

KIMBLE (continued)

the first quarter of 1984 increased 1%. In 1980, 21% of the labor force were self-employed, 14% were employed in professional or related services, 11% in manufacturing, 23% in wholesale and retail trade, 23% in agriculture, forestry, fisheries and mining, 7% were employed in other counties and there were 548 retired workers. The industries with the most employment: tourism and textile mill products. The nonfarm earnings in 1981 totaled $31,839,000. The retired workers received an average monthly Social Security payment of $286. **FINANCE** On June 30, 1983, two commercial banks had total deposits of $26,547,000 and total assets of $30,099,000. There is one state savings and loan association branch in the county. **HOUSING** Average value of homes in 1980: $25,500. Permits for new, privately owned housing units decreased in 1982: seven permits were issued with a total construction cost of $281,000. Of those permits, all were for single family houses. Between 1970 and 1980 the number of housing units increased by 24%. Seventy-five percent of all units in the county are air-conditioned, 79% are heated by gas and 10% by electricity. **NATURAL RESOURCES** Dolomite, gypsum, limestone, sand, gravel, oil and gas. In 1982 a total of 295,406 thousand cubic feet of gas well gas, 2,388 barrels of crude oil and 7,523 thousand cubic feet of casinghead gas were produced. Current production of other minerals and products includes gypsum, crushed limestone, sand and gravel. **TOURISM** Travel expenditures of $8,918,000 in 1982 (an increase of 14% over 1981) generated 184 jobs and $1,594,000 in payroll. **ALCOHOLIC BEVERAGES** Packaged distilled spirits, beer, ale, malt liquor and wine are legal in parts of the county. **FEDERAL EXPENDITURES** The federal government had direct expenditures or obligations of $9,450,000 in the county during fiscal year 1983, including $370,000 by the U.S. Department of Defense. In addition, the federal government provided $82,000 in grant awards, paid $397,000 in salaries and wages, made direct payments to individuals of $7,649,000 including $5,435,000 in retirement and disability payments, awarded $51,000 in procurement contracts and spent $1,271,000 in other expenditures or obligations. The federal government also provided $1,545,000 in guaranteed loans and insurance.

COMMUNICATION

Newspapers–Weekly: The Junction Eagle. Radio: KMBL-AM (Junction). Cable TV. Telephone companies: General Telephone, Hill Country Telephone Coop. and Kerrville Telephone. **TRANSPORTATION** Total public road mileage: 497. In 1982 there were 4,983 registered vehicles and 123 reported traffic accidents including four fatalities. Intercity bus service is available. Motor freight: two carriers. Aircraft: 10 are registered in the county. Airports: Kimble County Airport at Junction serves as a base for 15 aircraft and is a general utility airport with general aviation service. F-6 Ranch Airfield at Junction.

COMMUNITY SERVICES

EDUCATION One school district with one elementary, one middle and one high school. The average daily attendance in 1981-82 was 741, with expenditures per pupil of $1,951 including 47 classroom teachers with an average annual salary of $14,551. Sixty-two percent of the 52 high school graduates planned to attend college. In 1982-83, 69% of the students were White and 31% Hispanic. Sports championships: 1983 AA Boys' Tennis Doubles, Junction H.S.; 1983 AA Girls' Tennis Singles, Junction H.S. **PUBLIC LIBRARIES** Kimble County Library (Junction): 17,650 volumes. **CHILD CARE** Five day care and one twenty-four hour care licensed facilities. **HEALTH CARE** One physician and three dentists. Hospitals: one with a capacity of 18. Ambulance services: one county service. Mental health: one clinic. Nursing homes: one nursing home has a capacity of 70

nursing care residents. The average cost per day for private patients in 1982 was $35.86. **CHURCHES** 12 churches have an estimated combined membership of 2,608. The largest denominations are Southern Baptist, Churches of Christ and United Methodist. **SOCIAL SERVICES** In fiscal year 1983 a total of $99,995 in food stamps was distributed, with an average of 210 persons receiving food stamps each month. Aid to Families with Dependent Children (AFDC) totaled $19,626 with an average of 14 families receiving AFDC each month. Medical assistance benefits for the aged and disabled of $554,565 and for families and children of $33,636 brought the county benefit total to $707,822. **FIRE PROTECTION** One volunteer fire department. **LAW ENFORCEMENT** The County Sheriff has two commissioned officers. **CRIME** Three violent crimes (murder, forcible rape, robbery and aggravated assault) and 37 nonviolent crimes (burglary, larceny-theft and motor vehicle theft) were reported in 1982. **JUDICIAL SYSTEM** One District Court and Judge, one County Court and Judge and two Justices of the Peace. In the District Court a total of 130 cases were pending on 1/1/82, 102 new cases were filed and 90 cases were disposed of during the year leaving 142 cases pending on 12/31/82. There were 95 criminal cases on the docket, 11 convictions, three persons committed to prison and 73 cases left pending. In the County Court 84 cases were pending on 1/1/82, 168 new cases were filed and 124 cases were disposed of during the year leaving 128 cases pending on 12/31/82. There were 234 criminal cases on the docket, 78 convictions, 17 persons committed to jail, and 113 cases left pending. **JAILS** One jail, capacity 19. **ATTORNEYS AT LAW** Nine. **UTILITIES** 63% of the residents are connected to a public or privately owned water system and 57% are connected to a public sewer system. Natural gas is distributed to the county by Junction Natural Gas Co. Electricity is distributed to the county by West Texas Utilities, Central Texas Electric Coop., Inc. and Kimble Electric Coop., Inc. and is generated primarily by gas, oil, coal and water. The typical residential electric bill is $145.78 per month for an all-electric house using 2,500 kwh. **TAXES** The county has six units with taxing authority: one school district, one city, one county, one hospital district and two special districts.

RECREATION/ENTERTAINMENT

NATIONAL REGISTER OF HISTORIC PLACES Junction: Brambletye. **MUNICIPAL PARKS** 25 acres in one municipal park. This park contains one playground, one baseball and softball field, one swimming pool, one beach and one boat ramp. Developed campsites: 10. **SCENIC DRIVES** The Texas Pecos Trail runs through this county. This trail rambles through the vast region of Southwest and West Texas with landscapes varying from raw, arid regions to green valleys. In addition U.S. 377 travelling along the south Llano River in Kimble County offers impressive scenery. **BOATING/FISHING** Lakes/reservoirs: Junction (60 acres) and Kimble County (44 acres). Major rivers: South Llano, East Fork James and North Llano. Primary streams: Red. **WILDLIFE REFUGES** South Llano River Site, owned by the Texas Parks and Wildlife Department, covers 509 acres. Also in this county is Walter Buck State Wildlife Management Area which covers 2,000 acres. **HUNTING** Fall and winter seasons on deer. No closed seasons on javelina, coyote, bobcat and squirrel. Winter seasons on quail, muskrat, beaver, opossum, ring-tailed cat, badger, fox, weasel, raccoon, skunk and civet cat. Fall, winter and spring seasons on turkey. In 1983 sandhill crane, duck, coot, geese, woodcock and jacksnipe seasons occurred during the winter months. Teal duck, rail and gallinule seasons occurred in the fall. Mourning dove seasons occurred intermittently during the fall and winter months with a fall season on white-winged dove in some parts of the county. **MUSEUMS** Junction: Kimble Historical Museum. **THEATERS** Junction: Amphitheater. **SPECIAL EVENTS** Easter Pageant, Junction,

April; Spring Races Meet, Junction, April; Race Meet, Billie Sale and Parade, Junction, August; Kimble County Kow Kick, Junction, September.

COMMUNITIES

COUNTY SEAT Junction, County Courthouse, 76849; County Clerk's Office, 915/446-3353. **INCORPORATED COMMUNITIES** (1980 population and ZIP Code) Junction (2,593) 76849. **UNINCORPORATED COMMUNITIES** (and ZIP Code) London 76854, Knoxville (New Knoxville) 76831, Roosevelt 76874, Segovia 76849, Telegraph 76883 and Yates (Yates Crossing) 76854. **FOR ADDITIONAL LOCAL INFORMATION** Kimble Co. Chamber of Commerce, 652 Main, Junction, 76849, 915/446-3190.

KING (P42)

THE LAND

Southwest of Wichita Falls on U.S. Highways 82 and 83 in the Rolling Plains Region, King County covers 914 square miles with an elevation range of 1,600 to 2,200 feet. The light colored, brownish to reddish soils are well drained. In the southeast corner there are areas of very dark, loamy soils over clayey subsoils and some hardened calcium deposits. In the northeast the loamy surfaces vary from light to dark with clayey subsoils and some limestone. In the Rolling Plains vegetation area, the prairie grasses have been invaded by mesquite. Between 31 and 40% of the land in the county is considered prime farmland. **CLIMATE** Subtropical Subhumid with high summer temperatures and cold winters. The average annual temperature is 62°F. Temperatures in January range from an average low of 27° to an average high of 53°F and in July range from 71° to 96°F. The average annual precipitation is 24 inches, with an average relative humidity of 73% at 6 A.M. and 42% at 6 P.M. The average annual snowfall is eight inches. The growing season averages 215 days per year, with the last freeze in early April and the first freeze in early November. The sun shines during the year on the average 75% of the daylight hours.

THE PEOPLE

King County is one of the most sparsely populated in the state. The 1982 estimated population of 400 continues 50 years of population decline. The county is comprised completely of rural areas. Between 1970 and 1980 the age groups with the greatest reductions were ages 10 to 19 and 50 to 59. The largest ancestry groups are persons of English descent (34%), Irish descent (18%) and German descent (12%). **REGISTERED VOTERS** As of November 2, 1982 there were 268 registered voters. The 1982 general election had a 74% voter turnout, compared to a 75% turnout in the 1980 general election. In the 1982 primary 100% voted Democratic, with 180 votes cast.

THE ECONOMY

AGRICULTURE Ranchland. In 1982, 96% of the land was in farms and ranches, with 4% of the farmland under cultivation and 10% irrigated. King ranked 220th in the state in highest agricultural receipts, with 86% from livestock and livestock products. Overgrazing, undesirable brush and weeds, and water and wind erosion are the current conservation problems. Primary crops: cotton, wheat and rye. Primary livestock and products: cattle and hogs. **BUSINESS** Total number of business establishments in the county: 5. In 1980, 23% of the labor force were self-employed, 12% were employed in professional or related services, .5% in manufacturing, 13% in wholesale and retail trade, 55% in agriculture, forestry, fisheries and mining, 18% were employed in other counties and there were 25 retired workers. The industry with the most employment: oil and gas extraction. The nonfarm earnings in 1981 totaled $3,929,000. The retired workers received an average monthly Social Security payment of $280. **HOUSING** Average value of homes in 1980: $14,600. Between 1970 and 1980 the number of housing units increased by 7%. Eighty-one percent of all units in the county are air-conditioned, 88% are heated by gas and 12% by electricity. **NATURAL RESOURCES** Copper, gypsum, oil and gas. In 1982 a total of 3,134,997 thousand cubic feet of gas well gas, 27,099 barrels of condensate, 3,495,929 barrels of crude oil and 771,983 thousand cubic feet of casinghead gas were produced. **TOURISM** Travel expenditures of $581,000 in 1982 (an increase of 17% over 1981) generated 8 jobs and $85,000 in payroll. **ALCOHOLIC BEVERAGES** Packaged distilled spirits, beer, ale, malt liquor and wine are legal in parts of the county. **FEDERAL EXPENDITURES** The federal government had direct expenditures or obligations of $1,523,000 in the county during fiscal year 1983, including $168,000 by the U.S. Department of Defense. In addition, the federal government provided $11,000 in grant awards, paid $55,000 in salaries and wages, made direct payments to individuals of $312,000 including $188,000 in retirement and disability payments, awarded $152,000 in procurement contracts and spent $994,000 in other expenditures or obligations. The federal government also provided $414,000 in direct loans and $552,000 in guaranteed loans and insurance.

COMMUNICATION

Cable TV. Telephone companies: General Telephone and Cap Rock Telephone. **TRANSPORTATION** Total public road mileage: 194. In 1982 there were 436 registered vehicles and 18 reported traffic accidents. Intercity bus service is available. Motor freight: two carriers.

COMMUNITY SERVICES

EDUCATION One school district with one elementary and one high school. The average daily attendance in 1981-82 was 94, with expenditures per pupil of $10,176 including 14 classroom teachers with an average annual salary of $15,400. None of the 5 high school graduates planned to attend college. In 1982-83, 81% of the students were White, 13% Hispanic and 7% Black. **CHURCHES** Three churches have an estimated combined membership of 212. The largest denomination is Southern Baptist. **SOCIAL SERVICES** In fiscal year 1983 a total of $11,743 in food stamps was distributed, with an average of 27 persons receiving food stamps each month. Aid to Families with Dependent Children (AFDC) totaled $340. Medical assistance benefits for the aged and disabled of $1,795 and for families and children of $42 brought the county benefit total to $13,920. **FIRE PROTECTION** One volunteer fire department. **LAW ENFORCEMENT** The County Sheriff has one commissioned officer. **CRIME** Six nonviolent crimes (burglary, larceny-theft and motor vehicle theft) were reported in 1982. **JUDICIAL SYSTEM** One District Court and Judge, one County Court and Judge and three Justices of the Peace. In the District Court a total of five cases were pending on 1/1/82, two new cases were filed and three cases were disposed of during the year leaving four cases pending on 12/31/82. In the County Court 56 cases were pending on 1/1/82, two new cases were filed during the year leaving 58 cases pending on 12/31/82. There were 44 criminal cases on the docket and 44 cases left pending. **JAILS** One jail, capacity three. **UTILITIES** 85% of the residents are connected to a public or privately owned water system and 12% are connected to a public sewer system. Electricity is distributed to the county by B-K Electric Coop., Inc., and Dickens Electric Coop., Inc. and is generated primarily by gas, oil and water. **TAXES** The county has two units with taxing authority: one school district and one county.

RECREATION/ENTERTAINMENT

BOATING/FISHING Lakes/reservoirs: Moorhouse (29 acres), Parramore (20 acres) and Snake Den Tank (15 acres). Major

COUNTIES

rivers: Middle Fork Wichita, Brazos and South Wichita. Primary streams: Little Croton, Pen, Farrer, Willow and North Croton. **HUNTING** Fall and winter seasons on deer and mule deer. No closed season on coyote, bobcat and squirrel. Winter seasons on quail, muskrat, beaver, opossum, ring-tailed cat, badger, fox, weasel, raccoon, skunk and civet cat. Fall, winter and spring seasons on turkey. In 1983 sandhill crane, duck, coot, geese, woodcock and jacksnipe seasons occurred during the winter months. Teal duck, rail and gallinule seasons occurred in the fall. Mourning dove seasons occurred intermittently during the fall and winter months.

COMMUNITIES
COUNTY SEAT Guthrie, County Courthouse, 79236; County Clerk's Office, 806/596-4412. **UNINCORPORATED COMMUNITIES** (and ZIP Code) Dumont (also in Dickens Co.) 79232, Finney 79248, Grow 79248 and Guthrie 79236.

KINNEY (B11)

THE LAND
Bordering Mexico west of San Antonio on U.S. Highway 90 in the Rio Grande Plain Region, Kinney County covers 1,359 square miles with an elevation range of 1,000 to 2,000 feet. The northern half of the county is rocky and hilly with some thin, loamy soils. There are areas with dark, loamy soils over limestone in the northeast corner. The southern half has gray to black, cracking, clayey soils over limestone with light colored loamy surfaces in some areas. In the South Texas Plains vegetation area, the grasses are short to mid height with thorny shrubs, cacti and mesquite. To the north in the Edwards Plateau vegetation area, the grasses are short with a few mesquite trees and cacti. Less than 1% of the land in the county is considered prime farmland. **CLIMATE** Subtropical, dry and mild in winter, hot in summer. The average annual temperature is 70°F. Temperatures in January range from an average low of 36° to an average high of 63°F and in July range from 74° to 97°F. The average annual precipitation is 22 inches, with an average relative humidity of 76% at 6 A.M. and 42% at 6 P.M. There is no snowfall. The growing season averages 272 days per year, with the last freeze in early March and the first freeze in late November. The sun shines during the year on the average 65% of the daylight hours.

THE PEOPLE
Kinney County is one of the most sparsely populated in the state and ranks 31st among all U.S. counties in the highest percent of residents who are of Spanish origin. The 1982 estimated population of 2,300 indicates a continuation of a moderate growth rate which began in the 1970s, reversing a steady population decrease. The county's median age rose from 28 in 1970 to 32 in 1980. The largest ancestry groups are Hispanic (58%), persons of English descent (14%) and German descent (9%). **REGISTERED VOTERS** As of November 2, 1982 there were 1,615 registered voters (0.02% of the state total). The 1982 general election had a 63% voter turnout, compared to a 66% turnout in the 1980 general election. In the 1982 primary 100% voted Democratic, with 761 votes cast.

THE ECONOMY
AGRICULTURE Sheep ranches. In 1982, 91% of the land was in farms and ranches, with 1% of the farmland under cultivation and most of which was irrigated. Kinney ranked 219th in the state in highest agricultural receipts, with 88% from livestock and livestock products. Overgrazing, undesirable brush and weeds, water erosion and inefficient irrigation systems are the current conservation problems. Primary crops: wheat, corn, hay and oats. Primary vegetables: onions and cantaloupes. Primary fruits and nuts: pecans. Primary livestock and products: fifth in the state for sheep and wool and ninth for angora goats and mohair. **BUSINESS** Total number of business establishments in the county: 30. Retail sales during the first quarter of 1984 increased 15%. In 1980, 16% of the labor force were self-employed, 14% were employed in professional or related services, 2% in manufacturing, 15% in wholesale and retail trade, 30% in agriculture, forestry, fisheries and mining, 8% were employed in other counties and there were 236 retired workers. The industries with the most employment: agribusiness and tourism. The nonfarm earnings in 1981 totaled $15,237,000. The retired workers received an average monthly Social Security payment of $275. **FINANCE** On June 30, 1983, one commercial bank had total deposits of $8,790,000 and total assets of $9,558,000. There is one state savings and loan association branch in the county. **HOUSING** Average value of homes in 1980: $18,300. In 1982 two permits were issued for new single family houses. Between 1970 and 1980 the number of housing units increased by 55%. Fifty-five percent of all units in the county are air-conditioned, 74% are heated by gas and 18% by electricity. **NATURAL RESOURCES** Limestone, sand, gravel, oil and gas. **TOURISM** Travel expenditures of $909,000 in 1982 (an increase of 11% over 1981) generated 23 jobs and $185,000 in payroll. **ALCOHOLIC BEVERAGES** Packaged distilled spirits, beer, ale, malt liquor and wine are legal. The sale of mixed beverages is legal in all or parts of the county. **FEDERAL EXPENDITURES** The federal government had direct expenditures or obligations of $6,934,000 in the county during fiscal year 1983, including $706,000 by the U.S. Department of Defense. In addition, the federal government provided $56,000 in grant awards, paid $430,000 in salaries and wages, made direct payments to individuals of $4,819,000 including $4,124,000 in retirement and disability payments, awarded $62,000 in procurement contracts and spent $1,566,000 in other expenditures or obligations. The federal government also provided $11,404,000 in guaranteed loans and insurance.

COMMUNICATION
Cable TV. Telephone companies: General Telephone and Southwestern Bell. **TRANSPORTATION** Total public road mileage: 303. In 1982 there were 1,966 registered vehicles and 42 reported traffic accidents. Intercity bus service is available. Motor freight: three carriers. Rail: The Sunset Limited provides passenger service on the Amtrak Route. Two main and one branch line carry freight through the county. The two main lines carry annually over 30 million tons of freight each and the one branch carries one to five million. Aircraft: nine are registered in the county.

COMMUNITY SERVICES
EDUCATION One school district with one elementary and one high school. The average daily attendance in 1981-82 was 555, with expenditures per pupil of $2,261 including 34 classroom teachers with an average annual salary of $15,585. Fifty-eight percent of the 33 high school graduates planned to attend college. In 1982-83, 29% of the students were White, 67% Hispanic, 3% Black, 0.2% Asian and 0.7% American Indian. **PUBLIC LIBRARIES** Kinney County Public Library (Brackettville): 12,307 volumes. **CHILD CARE** Two day care licensed facilities. **HEALTH CARE** One physician and one dentist. Ambulance services: one volunteer service. **CHURCHES** Seven churches have an estimated combined membership of 1,509. The largest denomination is Catholic. **SOCIAL SERVICES** In fiscal year 1983 a total of $255,965 in food stamps was distributed, with an average of 561 persons receiving food stamps each month. Aid to Families with Dependent Children (AFDC) totaled $31,454

with an average of 20 families receiving AFDC each month. Medical assistance benefits for the aged and disabled of $77,825 and for families and children of $54,053 brought the county benefit total to $419,297. **FIRE PROTECTION** One volunteer fire department. **LAW ENFORCEMENT** The County Sheriff has two commissioned officers. One police department has a force of two. **JUDICIAL SYSTEM** One District Court and Judge, one County Court and Judge and four Justices of the Peace. In the District Court a total of 126 cases were pending on 1/1/82, 54 new cases were filed and 102 cases were disposed of during the year leaving 78 cases pending on 12/31/82. There were 29 criminal cases on the docket, nine convictions, five persons committed to prison and six cases left pending. In the County Court 105 cases were pending on 1/1/82, 118 new cases were filed and 144 cases were disposed of during the year leaving 79 cases pending on 12/31/82. There were 181 criminal cases on the docket, 51 convictions, four persons committed to jail and 54 cases left pending. **JAILS** One jail, capacity 16. **ATTORNEYS AT LAW** One. **UTILITIES** 80% of the residents are connected to a public or privately owned water system and 67% are connected to a public sewer system. Electricity is distributed to the county by Cochran Power and Light Co., Kimble Electric Coop., Inc. and Rio Grande Electric Coop., Inc. and is generated primarily by gas, oil, coal and water. **TAXES** The county has four units with taxing authority: one school district, one city, one county and one special district.

RECREATION/ENTERTAINMENT

NATIONAL REGISTER OF HISTORIC PLACES Brackettville: Fort Clark Historic District. **COUNTY/MUNICIPAL PARKS** Seven acres in one county and one municipal park. These parks contain two playgrounds, one baseball and softball field, one tennis court and one swimming pool. **SCENIC DRIVES** The Texas Pecos Trail runs through this county. This trail rambles through the vast region of southwest and west Texas with landscapes varying from raw, arid regions to green valleys. **BOATING/FISHING** Major rivers: Rio Grande and West Nueces. Primary streams: Cow, East Fork Sycamore, Elm, Pinto and Tequesquite. **HUNTING** Fall and winter seasons on deer. No closed season on javelina, coyote, bobcat and squirrel. Winter seasons on quail, muskrat, beaver, opossum, ring-tailed cat, badger, fox, weasel, raccoon, skunk and civet cat. Fall, winter and spring seasons on turkey. In 1983 sandhill crane, duck, coot, geese, woodcock and jacksnipe seasons occurred during the winter months. Teal duck, rail and gallinule seasons occurred in the fall. Mourning dove seasons occurred intermittently during the fall and winter months with a fall season on white-winged dove. **SPECIAL EVENTS** Frontier Fair, Brackettville, March; Fort Clark Cavalry Days, Brackettville, April; Western Horse Races and Barbecue, Brackettville, September.

COMMUNITIES

COUNTY SEAT Brackettville, County Courthouse, 78832; County Clerk's Office, 512/563-2521. **INCORPORATED COMMUNITIES** (1980 population and ZIP Code) Brackettville (1,676) 78832 and Spofford (77) 78882. **FOR ADDITIONAL LOCAL INFORMATION** Brackettville Chamber of Commerce, P.O. Box 386, Brackettville, 78826, 512/563-2466.

KLEBERG (B25)

THE LAND

Bordering the Gulf of Mexico south of Corpus Christi on U.S. Highway 77 in the Rio Grande Plain Region, Kleberg County covers 853 square miles with an elevation ranging from sea level to 150 feet. The western half of the county has nearly level to undulating soils with light to dark loamy surfaces and reddish, cracking, clayey subsoils. Some subsoils have salts or hardened calcium deposits. In the east the soils vary from very dark, loamy surfaces with clayey subsoils to gray-black, cracking, clayey soils. Along the Gulf Coast are the sandy soils of beaches and the dark, loamy soils of marshes. The vegetation in the west is the mid to tall grasses, mesquite trees, thorny shrubs and cacti of the South Texas Plains vegetation area. In the east the vegetation is the tall grasses and live oaks of the Gulf Prairies and the bunchgrasses, cordgrasses and sedges of the marshes. Between 31 and 40% of the land in the county is considered prime farmland. **CLIMATE** Subtropical Subhumid with a risk of a tropical storm or hurricane June through October. The average annual temperature is 73°F. Temperatures in January range from an average low of 46° to an average high of 67°F and in July range from 74° to 95°F. The average annual precipitation is 27 inches, with an average relative humidity of 89% at 6 A.M. and 65% at 6 P.M. There is no snowfall. The growing season averages 314 days per year, with the last freeze in early February and the first freeze in mid December. The sun shines during the year on the average 69% of the daylight hours.

THE PEOPLE

Kleberg County ranks 35th among all U.S. counties in the highest percent of persons who are of Spanish origin. The 1982 estimated population of 34,400 indicates a continuation of the steady growth which has existed since 1930. The residents are younger than average, with a median age of 24 in 1980. The largest ancestry groups are Hispanic (52%), persons of English descent (14%), German descent (12%) and Irish descent (11%). **REGISTERED VOTERS** As of November 2, 1982 there were 13,312 registered voters (0.2% of the state total). The 1982 general election had a 49% voter turnout, compared to a 68% turnout in the 1980 general election. In the 1982 primary 97% voted Democratic and 3% Republican, with 5,251 votes cast.

THE ECONOMY

AGRICULTURE Cattle and sorghum area. In 1982, 95% of the land was in farms and ranches, with 16% of the farmland under cultivation and 2% irrigated. Kleberg ranked 85th in the state in highest agricultural receipts, with 67% from livestock and livestock products. Undesirable brush and weeds and water erosion are the current conservation problems. Primary crops: sorghum, cotton, hay and corn. Primary vegetables: cucumbers and watermelons. Primary fruits and nuts: oranges and pecans. Primary livestock and products: cattle, milk, sheep, wool and hogs. **BUSINESS** Total number of business establishments in the county: 546. Retail sales during the first quarter of 1984 increased 3%. In 1980, 5% of the labor force were self-employed, 26% were employed in professional or related services, 10% in manufacturing, 19% in wholesale and retail trade, 12% in agriculture, forestry, fisheries and mining, 17% were employed in other counties and there were 1,457 retired workers. The industries with the most employment: agribusiness, oil and gas field servicing and general construction. The nonfarm earnings in 1981 totaled $277,659,000. The retired workers received an average monthly Social Security payment of $303. **FINANCE** On June 30, 1983, three commercial banks had total deposits of $158,607,000 and total assets of $180,518,000. On December 31, 1982 one state savings and loan association and one state branch had assets of $21,418,340. In addition there are two credit unions in the county. **HOUSING** Average value of homes in 1980: $31,700. Permits for new, privately owned housing units increased in 1982: 53 permits were issued with a total construction cost of $2,505,670. Of those permits, 38 were for single family houses. Housing permits in Kingsville increased from 32 in 1981 to 53 in 1982 with 38 of the permits issued for single family houses. Between 1970

COUNTIES

KLEBERG (continued)

and 1980 the number of housing units increased by 17%. Seventy-three percent of all units in the county are air-conditioned, 76% are heated by gas and 23% by electricity. **NATURAL RESOURCES** Industrial sand, oil, gas and caliche. In 1982 a total of 202,712,617 thousand cubic feet of gas well gas, 341,983 barrels of condensate, 2,853,264 barrels of crude oil and 7,057,878 thousand cubic feet of casinghead gas were produced. **TOURISM** Travel expenditures of $20,512,000 in 1982 (an increase of 11% over 1981) generated 516 jobs and $4,160,000 in payroll. Lodging: six hotels, motels and tourist courts. **ALCOHOLIC BEVERAGES** Packaged distilled spirits, beer, ale, malt liquor and wine are legal in parts of the county. Sale of mixed beverages is legal in all or parts of the county. **MILITARY INSTALLATIONS** Kingsville Naval Air Station, Kingsville, 2,436 personnel, 3,986 acres, flight training. **FEDERAL EXPENDITURES** The federal government had direct expenditures or obligations of $195,507,000 in the county during fiscal year 1983, including $154,188,000 by the U.S. Department of Defense. In addition, the federal government provided $3,649,000 in grant awards, paid $137,730,000 in salaries and wages, made direct payments to individuals of $48,960,000 including $38,591,000 in retirement and disability payments, awarded $4,164,000 in procurement contracts and spent $1,005,000 in other expenditures or obligations. The federal government also provided $265,000 in direct loans and $31,301,000 in guaranteed loans and insurance.

COMMUNICATION
Newspapers–Weekly: Kingsville Record. Radio: KINE-AM, KINE-FM and KTAI-FM (Kingsville). Cable TV. Telephone companies: Southwestern Bell and Riviera Telephone. **TRANSPORTATION** Total public road mileage: 467. In 1982 there were 22,901 registered vehicles and 683 reported traffic accidents including 10 fatalities. Taxi cabs: one company in Kingsville. Intercity bus service is available. Motor freight: seven local and intrastate carriers. Rail: one branch line carries annually five to 10 million tons of freight through the county. Aircraft: 36 are registered in the county. Airports: Kleberg County Airport at Kingsville serves as a base for 60 aircraft and is a basic transportation airport with general aviation service.

COMMUNITY SERVICES
EDUCATION Five school districts with 11 elementary, two middle and two high schools. The average daily attendance in 1981-82 was 6,244, with expenditures per pupil of $2,916 including 446 classroom teachers with an average annual salary of $17,169. Forty-seven percent of the 438 high school graduates planned to attend college. In 1982-83, 31% of the students were White, 64% Hispanic, 3% Black and 1% Asian. Private schools: 546 students enrolled in three elementary and one high school. Texas Agricultural and Industrial University is located in Kingsville. Established in 1917 it is part of the University System of South Texas and is under state control. Enrollment in 1982 was 5,355 with in state undergraduate tuition and fees of $375 per semester. The highest degree offered is Doctorate. **PUBLIC LIBRARIES** Robert J. Kleberg Public Library (Kingsville): 71,765 volumes. **CHILD CARE** 21 day care and three twenty-four hour care licensed facilities. **HEALTH CARE** 33 physicians and 12 dentists. Hospitals: one with a capacity of 136. Ambulance services: one fire department and one volunteer fire department service. Mental health: one clinic. Nursing homes: one nursing home has a capacity of 198 nursing care residents. The average cost per day for private patients in 1982 was $30.84. **CHURCHES** 36 churches have an estimated combined membership of 21,531. The largest denominations are Catholic, Southern Baptist and United Methodist. **SOCIAL SERVICES** In fiscal year 1983 a total of

$2,873,721 in food stamps was distributed, with an average of 5,634 persons receiving food stamps each month. Aid to Families with Dependent Children (AFDC) totaled $685,536 with an average of 447 families receiving AFDC each month. Medical assistance benefits for the aged and disabled of $1,650,194 and for families and children of $1,415,140 brought the county benefit total to $6,624,590. **FIRE PROTECTION** One paid and three volunteer fire departments. **LAW ENFORCEMENT** The County Sheriff has 80 commissioned officers. One police department has a force of 39. One university campus has a police department with a force of 17 officers. **CRIME** 95 violent crimes (murder, forcible rape, robbery and aggravated assault) and 1,858 nonviolent crimes (burglary, larceny-theft and motor vehicle theft) were reported in 1982. **JUDICIAL SYSTEM** Two District Courts and Judges, one County Court and Judge and four Justices of the Peace. In the District Courts a total of 557 cases were pending on 1/1/82, 717 new cases were filed and 756 cases were disposed of during the year leaving 518 cases pending on 12/31/82. There were 196 criminal cases on the docket, 81 convictions, 24 persons committed to prison and 59 cases left pending. In the County Court 851 cases were pending on 1/1/82, 1,483 new cases were filed and 1,270 cases were disposed of during the year leaving 1,064 cases pending on 12/31/82. There were 1,969 criminal cases on the docket, 342 convictions, 49 persons committed to jail and 753 cases left pending. **JAILS** One jail, capacity 34. **ATTORNEYS AT LAW** 20. **UTILITIES** 94% of the residents are connected to a public or privately owned water system and 88% are connected to a public sewer system. Natural gas is distributed to the county by Entex, Inc. The average annual residential bill for natural gas in 1982 for the Entex distribution system was $390.31, an increase of 26% over 1981. Electricity is distributed to the county by Central Power and Light Co., Cochran Power and Light and Nueces Electric Coop., Inc. and is generated primarily by gas, oil and coal. The typical residential electric bill is $162.15 per month for an all-electric house using 2,500 kwh. **TAXES** The county has eight units with taxing authority: five school districts, one city, one county and one special district.

RECREATION/ENTERTAINMENT
FEDERAL PADRE ISLAND NATIONAL SEASHORE One of the last natural seashores in the nation, it spans 51,774 acres. This 80-mile stretch in the middle of the island offers wide sand beaches, fishing, bird and marine life, beach camping and a visitor information station. **NATIONAL REGISTER OF HISTORIC PLACES** Kingsville vicinity: King Ranch (National Historic Landmark). Padre Island: Dunn Ranch-Novillo Line Camp. **COUNTY PARKS** 567 acres in four county parks. These parks contain three playgrounds, one golf course, two baseball and softball fields, eight tennis courts, one boat ramp and shore fishing facilities. Developed campsites: 100. **SCENIC DRIVES** The Texas Tropical Trail runs through this county. This trail is charted through the state's southernmost wedge meandering through ranchland, resort areas by the Gulf of Mexico and fertile farmlands. **BOATING/FISHING** Lakes/reservoirs: Dairy Barn (46 acres), Escondido (198 acres), Falcon (106 acres), Patricio (61 acres), Paisano (48 acres), Iranquitas (198 acres) and Tulosa (88 acres). Primary streams: Santa Gertrudis, Escondido, Salado, Paisano, Tranquitas and San Fernando. **SALTWATER FISHING** Speckled trout, redfish and flounder fishing is usually good around Laguna Madre. Other fine fishing waters within the county are Laguna Salada, Baffin Bay, Alazan Bay and Padre Island. Shrimp, oysters and crabs may be taken but, like other saltwater fish, under specific regulations. **HUNTING** Fall season on deer. No closed season on nutria, javelina, coyote, bobcat and squirrel. Winter seasons on quail, muskrat, beaver, otter, opossum, mink, ring-tailed cat, badger, fox, raccoon, skunk and civet

cat. Fall, winter and spring seasons on turkey. In 1983 duck, coot, geese, woodcock and jacksnipe seasons occurred during the winter months with a winter season on sandhill crane in some parts of the county. Teal duck, rail and gallinule seasons occurred in the fall. Mourning dove seasons occurred intermittently during the fall and winter months with a fall season on white-winged dove. **MUSEUMS** Kingsville: John E. Conner Museum. **COLLEGIATE FINE ARTS** Kingsville: Cultural events offered by Texas Agricultural and Industrial University. **SPECIAL EVENTS** Intercollegiate Rodeo, Kingsville, March; County Fair and Stock Show, Kingsville, March; Young Performers Competition, Kingsville, March; Springfest, Kingsville, April; Fajita Cookoff, Kingsville, May; Youth Rodeo, Kingsville, June; Navy Relief Festival, Kingsville, July; Fiesta de Colores, Kingsville, October.

COMMUNITIES

COUNTY SEAT Kingsville, County Courthouse, 78363; County Clerk's Office, 512/592-6448. **INCORPORATED COMMUNITIES** (1980 population and ZIP Code) Kingsville (28,808) 78363. **UNINCORPORATED COMMUNITIES** (and ZIP Code) Loyola Beach 78379, Ricardo 78363, Riviera 78379, Riviera Beach 78379 and Vattmanville (Vattman) 78379. **FOR ADDITIONAL LOCAL INFORMATION** Kingsville Chamber of Commerce, P.O. Box 1030, Kingsville, 78363, 512/592-6438.

KNOX (P43)

THE LAND

Southwest of Wichita Falls on U.S. Highways 82 and 277 in the Rolling Plains Region, Knox County covers 845 square miles with an elevation range of 1,250 to 1,650 feet. The soils are light colored and brownish to reddish with loamy surfaces and reddish, clayey subsoils. In some areas the surfaces are dark and the subsoils have hardened calcium deposits. In the Rolling Plains vegetation area, the grasses are mid to tall with a few mesquite trees and cacti. Between 31 and 40% of the land in the county is considered prime farmland. **CLIMATE** Subtropical Subhumid with high temperatures in summer and cold in winter. The average annual temperature is 64°F. Temperatures in January range from an average low of 27° to an average high of 55°F and in July range from 71° to 98°F. The average annual precipitation is 24 inches, with an average relative humidity of 73% at 6 A.M. and 43% at 6 P.M. The average annual snowfall is eight inches. The growing season averages 217 days per year, with the last freeze in early April and the first freeze in early November. The sun shines during the year on the average 72% of the daylight hours.

THE PEOPLE

The 1982 estimated population of 5,600 represents an increase between 1980 and 1982 after a pattern of population losses which existed since 1930. A majority of the county residents live in rural areas. The age groups with the largest decreases were ages five to 14 and 50 to 59. The county's population is older than average with a median age of 40. The largest ancestry groups are persons of English descent (25%), Irish descent (19%) and German descent (15%). **REGISTERED VOTERS** As of November 2, 1982 there were 2,972 registered voters (0.04% of the state total). The 1982 general election had a 48% voter turnout, compared to a 66% turnout in the 1980 general election. In the 1982 primary 100% voted Democratic, with 1,135 votes cast.

THE ECONOMY

AGRICULTURE Wheat and cotton area. In 1982, 94% of the land was in farms and ranches, with 42% of the farmland under cultivation and 15% irrigated. Knox ranked 122nd in the state in highest agricultural receipts, with 76% from crops. Overgraz-

ing, water erosion, inefficient irrigation systems and drainage are the current conservation problems. Primary crops: wheat, cotton, sorghum and oats. Primary vegetables: potatoes. Primary fruits and nuts: a leader in the state for plums. Peaches and pecans. Primary livestock and products: cattle and hogs. **BUSINESS** Total number of business establishments in the county: 131. Retail sales during the first quarter of 1984 increased 3%. In 1980, 25% of the labor force were self-employed, 18% were employed in professional or related services, 4% in manufacturing, 19% in wholesale and retail trade, 33% in agriculture, forestry, fisheries and mining, 16% were employed in other counties and there were 768 retired workers. The industries with the most employment: oil and gas field servicing and agribusiness. The nonfarm earnings in 1981 totaled $42,954,000. The retired workers received an average monthly Social Security payment of $289. **FINANCE** On June 30, 1983, two commercial banks had total deposits of $40,845,000 and total assets of $45,412,000. **HOUSING** Average value of homes in 1980: $17,100. In 1982 three permits were issued for new, single family houses. Between 1970 and 1980 the number of housing units decreased by 9%. Eighty-one percent of all units in the county are air-conditioned, 90% are heated by gas and 8% by electricity. **NATURAL RESOURCES** Copper, gypsum, oil, gas and bituminous coal. In 1982 a total of 1,421,983 barrels of crude oil and 174,128 thousand cubic feet of casinghead gas were produced. Current production of other minerals and products includes sand and gravel. **TOURISM** Travel expenditures of $3,854,000 in 1982 (an increase of 17% over 1981) generated 58 jobs and $587,000 in payroll. **ALCOHOLIC BEVERAGES** Totally dry. **FEDERAL EXPENDITURES** The federal government had direct expenditures or obligations of $21,320,000 in the county during fiscal year 1983, including $4,664,000 by the U.S. Department of Defense. In addition, the federal government provided $570,000 in grant awards, paid $858,000 in salaries and wages, made direct payments to individuals of $10,882,000 including $7,075,000 in retirement and disability payments, awarded $4,296,000 in procurement contracts and spent $4,714,000 in other expenditures or obligations. The federal government also provided $8,181,000 in direct loans and $6,959,000 in guaranteed loans and insurance.

COMMUNICATION

Newspapers–Weekly: Knox County News (Knox City) and the Munday Courier. Cable TV. Telephone companies: General Telephone and Santa Rosa Telephone Coop. **TRANSPORTATION** Total public road mileage: 687. In 1982 there were 5,463 registered vehicles and 86 reported traffic accidents. Intercity bus service is available. Motor freight: two carriers. Rail: one branch line carries annually less than one million tons of freight through the county. Aircraft: 23 are registered in the county. Airports: Munday Municipal Airport serves as a base for 24 aircraft and is a basic utility airport with general aviation service. Also serving the area is Knox City Municipal Airport.

COMMUNITY SERVICES

EDUCATION Four school districts with four elementary, two middle and four high schools. The average daily attendance in 1981-82 was 1,043, with expenditures per pupil of $3,290 including 96 classroom teachers with an average annual salary of $15,060. Thirty-eight percent of the 71 high school graduates planned to attend college. In 1982-83, 56% of the students were White, 30% Hispanic, 15% Black and 0.2% Asian. Sports championships: 1983 A Football, Knox City H.S. **PUBLIC LIBRARIES** City-County Library (Munday): 11,500 volumes. **CHILD CARE** Nine day care licensed facilities. **HEALTH CARE** Three physicians and one dentist. Hospitals: one with a capacity of 28. Ambulance services: one city and one volunteer service. Nursing homes: two nursing homes with a combined capacity of 131 nursing care

KNOX (continued)

residents. The average cost per day for private patients in 1982 was $36.29. **CHURCHES** 32 churches have an estimated combined membership of 5,597. The largest denominations are Southern Baptist, United Methodist and Churches of Christ. **SOCIAL SERVICES** In fiscal year 1983 a total of $296,426 in food stamps was distributed, with an average of 684 persons receiving food stamps each month. Aid to Families with Dependent Children (AFDC) totaled $49,188 with an average of 35 families receiving AFDC each month. Medical assistance benefits for the aged and disabled of $849,668 and for families and children of $82,850 brought the county benefit total to $1,278,132. **FIRE PROTECTION** Four volunteer fire departments. **LAW ENFORCEMENT** The County Sheriff has 10 commissioned officers. Three police departments have a combined force of 11. **CRIME** 20 violent crimes (murder, forcible rape, robbery and aggravated assault) and 81 nonviolent crimes (burglary, larceny-theft and motor vehicle theft) were reported in 1982. **JUDICIAL SYSTEM** One District Court and Judge, one County Court and Judge and four Justices of the Peace. In the District Court a total of 211 cases were pending on 1/1/82, 99 new cases were filed and 76 cases were disposed of during the year leaving 234 cases pending on 12/31/82. There were 51 criminal cases on the docket, five convictions, two persons committed to prison and 46 cases left pending. In the County Court 236 cases were pending on 1/1/82, 80 new cases were filed and 84 cases were disposed of during the year leaving 232 cases pending on 12/31/82. There were 297 criminal cases on the docket, 24 convictions and 214 cases left pending. **JAILS** One jail, capacity 14. **ATTORNEYS AT LAW** Three. **UTILITIES** 75% of the residents are connected to a public or privately owned water system and 69% are connected to a public sewer system. Natural gas is distributed to the county by Lone Star Gas Co., Division of Enserch. The average annual residential bill for natural gas in 1982 for the Lone Star distribution system was $405.91, an increase of 35% over 1981. Electricity is distributed to the county by B-K Electric Coop., Inc., and West Texas Utilities and is generated primarily by gas, oil and water. **TAXES** The county has 12 units with taxing authority: four school districts, four cities, one county, one hospital district and two special districts.

RECREATION/ENTERTAINMENT

MUNICIPAL PARKS 135 acres in eight municipal parks. These parks contain four playgrounds, two baseball and softball fields, two tennis courts, one multi-use court and two swimming pools. **SCENIC DRIVES** U.S. 82 offers impressive views of the Wichita and Brazos Rivers. Farm and ranch landscapes in the northeast portion of the county are found along Texas 6, F.M. 1756 and F.M. 267. **BOATING/FISHING** Lakes/reservoirs: Bejamin (71 acres), Catarine (163 acres), Davis (585 acres), Horseshoe Tank (50 acres) and Truscott Brine (2,702 acres). Major rivers: North Wichita, Brazos and South Wichita. Primary streams: Dutchman, Hackberry, Bluff and Little Croton. **HUNTING** Fall and winter seasons on deer and mule deer. No closed season on coyote, bobcat and squirrel. Winter seasons on quail, muskrat, beaver, opossum, ring-tailed cat, badger, fox, weasel, raccoon, skunk and civet cat. Fall, spring and winter seasons on turkey. In 1983 sandhill crane, duck, coot, geese, woodcock and jacksnipe seasons occurred during the winter months. Teal duck, rail and gallinule seasons occurred in the fall. Mourning dove seasons occurred intermittently during the fall and winter months. **MUSEUMS** Benjamin: Knox County Museum. **SPECIAL EVENTS** Spring Arts and Crafts Show, Knox City, May/June; Knox County Vegetable Festival, Munday, June; Fall Festival and Chili Cookoff, Knox City, October; Christmas Parade, Munday, December.

COMMUNITIES

COUNTY SEAT Benjamin, County Courthouse, 79505; County Clerk's Office, 817/454-2441. **INCORPORATED COMMUNITIES** (1980 population and ZIP Code) Benjamin (257) 79505, Goree (524) 76363, Knox City (1,546) 79529 and Munday (1,738) 76371. **UNINCORPORATED COMMUNITIES** (and ZIP Code) Gilliland 79260, Hefner 76363, Rhineland 76371, Truscott 79260 and Vera 76383. **FOR ADDITIONAL LOCAL INFORMATION** Knox City Chamber of Commerce, P.O. Box 91, Knox, 79529, 817/658-3442 and Munday Chamber of Commerce, P.O. Drawer L, Munday, 76371, 817/422-4540.

LAMAR (E1)

THE LAND

Bordering Oklahoma west of Texarkana on U.S. Highways 82 and 271 in the Blackland Prairies Region, Lamar County covers 919 square miles with an elevation range of 400 to 600 feet. Along the Red River the soils are brownish to reddish with cracking, clayey areas and loamy areas. South of the river is an east-west strip of light colored, sandy soils with mottled, clayey subsoils. The remainder of the county has dark, loamy or clayey soils with cracking, clayey subsoils and a high shrink-swell potential. The vegetation to the north is the tall grasses and oak trees of the Post Oak Savannah vegetation area. In the south the vegetation is the tall grasses and scrubby trees of the Blackland Prairies vegetation area. Between 41 and 50% of the land in the county is considered prime farmland. **CLIMATE** Subtropical Subhumid with wide-ranging temperatures from winter to summer. The average annual temperature is 63°F. Temperatures in January range from an average low of 30° to an average high of 51°F and in July range from 72° to 94°F. The average annual precipitation is 45 inches, with an average relative humidity of 83% at 6 A.M. and 55% at 6 P.M. The average annual snowfall is three inches. The growing season averages 235 days per year, with the last freeze in late March and the first freeze in mid November. The sun shines during the year on the average 67% of the daylight hours.

THE PEOPLE

The population of Lamar County grew three times faster between 1970 and 1980 than in the previous decade. The 1982 estimated population of 43,000 indicates a continuation of that strong growth rate. Rural areas grew faster than urban areas from 1970 to 1980. The county's population is slightly older than average with a median age of 33 and there is a high percentage of persons over age 64. The largest ancestry groups are persons of English descent (26%), Irish descent (19%) and Black (15%). **REGISTERED VOTERS** As of November 2, 1982 there were 20,042 registered voters (0.3% of the state total). The 1982 general election had a 50% voter turnout, compared to a 64% turnout in the 1980 general election. In the 1982 primary 98% voted Democratic and 2% Republican, with 5,867 votes cast.

THE ECONOMY

AGRICULTURE Wheat and cattle area. In 1982, 78% of the land was in farms and ranches, with 36% of the farmland under cultivation and 4% irrigated. Lamar ranked 74th in the state in highest agricultural receipts, with 75% from livestock and livestock products. Water erosion, drainage, flooding and solid waste management are the current conservation problems. Primary crops: fourth in the state for hay, wheat, soybeans, sorghum, oats and cotton. Primary vegetables: potatoes, sweet potatoes, tomatoes and watermelons. Primary fruits and nuts: peaches and pecans. Primary livestock and products: cattle and milk. **BUSINESS** Total number of business establishments in the county: 832. Retail sales during the first quarter of 1984 increased 10%. In 1980, 11% of the labor force were self-employed, 19% were employed in professional or related services, 28% in manufacturing, 20% in wholesale and retail trade, 7% in construction, 6% were employed in other counties and there were 4,934 retired workers. The industries with the most employment: agribusiness, fruit and vegetable canning, and the manufacture of women's lingerie, business forms, metal containers, electrical equipment and supplies, fabricated plate and bakery products. The nonfarm earnings in 1981 totaled $336,023,000. The retired workers received an average monthly Social Security payment of $280. **FINANCE** On June 30, 1983, six commercial banks had total deposits of $202,714,000 and total assets of $232,620,000. On December 31, 1982 one state savings and loan association and one federal association had assets of $169,721,638. In addition there are 11 credit unions in the county. **HOUSING** Average value of homes in 1980: $21,500. Permits for new, privately owned housing units increased in 1982: 299 permits were issued with a total construction cost of $7,216,353. Of those permits, 127 were for single family houses. Housing permits increased in Deport from two in 1981 to 13 in 1982 and in Paris from 142 to 270. Between 1970 and 1980 the number of housing units increased by 28%. Seventy percent of all units in the county are air-conditioned, 70% are heated by gas and 22% by electricity. **NATURAL RESOURCES** Limestone, sand, gravel and phosphorite. Current production includes sand, gravel and crushed limestone. **TOURISM** Travel expenditures of $20,409,000 in 1982 (an increase of 11% over 1981) generated 499 jobs and $4,035,000 in payroll. Lodging: five hotels, motels and tourist courts. **ALCOHOLIC BEVERAGES** Packaged distilled spirits, beer, ale, malt liquor and wine are legal in parts of the county. Sale of mixed beverages is legal in all or parts of the county. **FEDERAL EXPENDITURES** The federal government had direct expenditures or obligations of $82,469,000 in the county during fiscal year 1983, including $4,620,000 by the U.S. Department of Defense. In addition, the federal government provided $1,467,000 in grant awards, paid $3,919,000 in salaries and wages, made direct payments to individuals of $70,985,000 including $51,339,000 in retirement and disability payments, awarded $1,279,000 in procurement contracts and spent $4,819,000 in other expenditures or obligations. The federal government also provided $7,734,000 in direct loans and $19,716,000 in guaranteed loans and insurance.

COMMUNICATION

Newspapers–Daily: The Paris News, ave. eve. circ. 13,277. Weekly: Deport Times and the Lamar County Echo (Paris). Radio: KPLT-AM, KPRE-AM and KTXU-FM (Paris). Cable TV. Telephone companies: Continental Telephone, Southwestern Bell and Blossom Telephone. **TRANSPORTATION** Total public road mileage: 1,509. In 1982 there were 38,077 registered vehicles and 1,126 reported traffic accidents including 13 fatalities. Taxi cabs: two companies in Paris. Intercity bus service is available. Motor freight: 19 local and intrastate carriers. Rail: three branch lines carry freight through the county with all three annually carrying less than one million tons each. Aircraft: 79 are registered in the county. Airports: Cox Field at Paris serves as a base for 37 aircraft and is a basic transportation airport with commuter service. Also serving the area are the Flying Tigers Airport at Flying Tigers Museum in Paris and Powderly Airport at Powderly.

COMMUNITY SERVICES

EDUCATION Six school districts with 10 elementary, four middle and six high schools. The average daily attendance in 1981-82 was 7,919, with expenditures per pupil of $1,977 including 493 classroom teachers with an average annual salary of $15,407. Forty-eight percent of the 504 high school graduates planned to attend college. In 1982-83, 77% of the students were White,

0.5% Hispanic, 21% Black, 0.4% Asian and 0.6% American Indian. Sports championships: 1983 AAAA Boys' Golf Team, Paris H.S. Private schools: 25 students enrolled in one elementary and one high school. Paris Junior College is located in Paris. Established in 1924 it is a vocational and two year academic college under state and local control. Enrollment in 1982 was 2,116 with in state undergraduate tuition and fees of $308 per semester. Vocational education: Paris Beauty School (Paris). **PUBLIC LIBRARIES** Paris Public Library: 37,904 volumes. **CHILD CARE** 60 day care and 11 twenty-four hour care licensed facilities. **HEALTH CARE** 68 physicians and 19 dentists. Hospitals: two with a combined capacity of 387. Clinics: one radiology clinic and one public health clinic. Ambulance services: one city and one commercial service. Mental health: one county clinic. Nursing homes: six nursing homes with a combined capacity of 690 nursing care and 22 personal care residents. The average cost per day for private patients in 1982 was $27.31. **CHURCHES** 104 churches have an estimated combined membership of 24,452. The largest denominations are Southern Baptist, United Methodist and Churches of Christ. **SOCIAL SERVICES** In fiscal year 1983 a total of $2,249,641 in food stamps was distributed, with an average of 5,030 persons receiving food stamps each month. Aid to Families with Dependent Children (AFDC) totaled $676,597 with an average of 452 families receiving AFDC each month. Medical assistance benefits for the aged and disabled of $5,871,341 and for families and children of $917,068 brought the county benefit total to $9,714,646. **FIRE PROTECTION** One paid and 12 volunteer fire departments. **LAW ENFORCEMENT** The County Sheriff has 31 commissioned officers. Four police departments have a combined force of 55. One college campus has a police department with a force of one. **CRIME** 342 violent crimes (murder, forcible rape, robbery and aggravated assault) and 2,668 nonviolent crimes (burglary, larceny-theft and motor vehicle theft) were reported in 1982. **JUDICIAL SYSTEM** Two District Courts and Judges, one County Court and Judge and six Justices of the Peace. In the District Courts a total of 1,229 cases were pending on 1/1/82, 1,257 new cases were filed and 1,240 cases were disposed of during the year leaving 1,246 cases pending on 12/31/82. There were 456 criminal cases on the docket, 134 convictions, 67 persons committed to prison, two committed to jail and 131 cases left pending. In the County Court 498 cases were pending on 1/1/82, 910 new cases were filed and 822 cases were disposed of during the year leaving 586 cases pending on 12/31/82. There were 1,211 criminal cases on the docket, 489 convictions, 63 persons committed to jail, and 404 cases left pending. **JAILS** One jail, capacity 48, under renovation. Lost certification in 1983 due to overcrowding. **ATTORNEYS AT LAW** 43. **UTILITIES** 92% of the residents are connected to a public or privately owned water system and 69% are connected to a public sewer system. Natural gas is distributed to the county by Lone Star Gas Co., Division of Enserch. The average annual residential bill for natural gas in 1982 for the Lone Star distribution system was $405.91, an increase of 35% over 1981. Electricity is distributed to the county by Houston Lighting and Power Co., Texas Electric Service, Texas-New Mexico Electric Coop., Inc., Fannin Co. Electric Coop., Inc. and Lamar Co. Electric Coop., Assn. and is generated primarily by gas and oil. The typical residential electric bill is $165.24 per month for an all-electric house using 2,500 kwh. **TAXES** The county has 13 units with taxing authority: six school districts, four cities, one county, one college district and one special district.

RECREATION/ENTERTAINMENT

NATIONAL REGISTER OF HISTORIC PLACES Faulkner vicinity: A.C. Mackin Archeological District. Paris: Samuel Bell Maxey House. Pin Hook vicinity: Ellis II Site, Emerson Site, Loma Alto Site, Swindle Site and McCarty Site. **STATE** Sam

COUNTIES

LAMAR (continued)

Bell Maxey House State Historic Structure covers 0.4 acres with a museum and a historic structure. Built in 1868 in High Victorian Italianate style, the home has been restored and refurnished. **MUNICIPAL PARKS** 2,508 acres in 11 municipal parks. These parks contain six playgrounds, nine baseball and softball fields, seven tennis courts, two multi-use courts, three beaches, three boat ramps and shore fishing facilities. **SCENIC DRIVES** The Texas Lakes Trail runs through this county. This trail introduces some 30 blue-water recreational areas in a variety of settings in North Central Texas. **BOATING/FISHING** Lakes/reservoirs: Crook (1,226 acres), Deport Creek Soil Conservation Service Lake 1 (15 acres), Gibbons (69 acres), Gordon (53 acres), Lamar (27 acres), Pat Mayse (5,993 acres), Ramsey (14 acres) and Willow (40 acres). Major rivers: Red and North Sulphur. Primary streams: Pine, Mustang, Cottonwood, Hicks, Sanders and Little Pine. **WILDLIFE REFUGES** Gambill Goose Refuge near the city of Paris covers 516 acres. Pat Mayse State Wildlife Management Area covers 8,317 acres. **HUNTING** Fall and winter seasons on deer. Summer, fall and winter seasons on squirrel. No closed season on coyote, bobcat and nutria. Winter seasons on quail, muskrat, beaver, otter, opossum, mink, ring-tailed cat, badger, fox, raccoon, skunk and civet cat. In 1983 duck, coot, geese, woodcock and jacksnipe seasons occurred during the winter months. Teal duck, rail and gallinule seasons occurred in the fall. Mourning dove seasons occurred intermittently during the fall and winter months. **MUSEUMS** Paris: Flying Tigers Air Museum and Sam Bell Maxey State Historic Structure. **COLLEGIATE FINE ARTS** Paris: Cultural events offered by Paris Junior College. **OTHER** Paris: John C. Gambill Canada Goose Refuge. **SPECIAL EVENTS** Salute to Wildflowers, Paris, May; AJRA Rodeo, Paris, May; Chisholm Trail Sports Car Rally, Paris, May; Young Farmers Annual Tractor Pull, Paris, July; Bastille Days Celebration, Paris, July; Red River Valley Exposition, Paris, date varies; Christmas Holiday Parade, Paris, December.

COMMUNITIES

COUNTY SEAT Paris, County Courthouse, 75460; County Clerk's Office, 214/785-7687. **INCORPORATED COMMUNITIES** (1980 population and ZIP Code) Blossom (1,487) 75416, Deport (724: 683 in Lamar Co. and 41 in Red River Co.) 75435, Paris (25,498) 75460, Reno (1,059) 75460, Roxton (735) 75477, Sun Valley (76) 75460 and Toco (164) 75421. **UNINCORPORATED COMMUNITIES** (and ZIP Code) Ambia 75421, Arthur City 75411, Atlas 75460, Belk 75411, Biardstown 75460, Broadway 75460, Broadway Junction 75460, Brookston 75421, Bunker Hill 75486, Caviness 75460, Chicota 75425, Clardy 75468, Cunningham 75434, Direct 75486, East Direct 75486, Emberson 75486, Faught 75460, Faulkner (Pin Hook) 75416, Forest Chapel 75411, Forest Hill 75446, Garretts Bluff 75411, Georgia 75486, Givens 75460, Globe 75486, Glory 75460, Harmon 75446, High 75421, Hinckley 75460, Howland 75460, Jennings 75460, Marvin 75460, Maxey 75421, Medill 75460, Milton 75435, Minter 75468, Noble 75470, Novice 75460, Pattonville 75468, Petty 75470, Postoak (Gantt) 75436, Powderly 75473, Ragtown 75411, Razor 75411, Slate Shoals 75460, Sumner 75486, Sylvan 75460, Taylor Town 75460, Tigertown (Cothrans Store) 75446 and Unity 75486. **FOR ADDITIONAL LOCAL INFORMATION** Paris Chamber of Commerce of Lamar Co., P.O. Box 1096, Paris, 75460, 214/784-2501.

LAMB (P29)

THE LAND

Northwest of Lubbock on U.S. Highways 84 and 385 in the High Plains Region, Lamb County covers 1,013 square miles with an elevation range of 3,400 to 3,800 feet. The nearly level soils are loamy with deep, clayey subsoils over limestone. In the High Plains vegetation area, the short to mid grasses have been invaded by small mesquite trees, thorny shrubs and cacti in some areas. Between 21 and 30% of the land in the county is considered prime farmland. **CLIMATE** Continental Steppe with wide-ranging temperatures from winter to summer. Duststorms and thunderstorms may cause problems during spring and early summer. The average annual temperature is 58°F. Temperatures in January range from an average low of 21° to an average high of 53°F and in July range from 69° to 92°F. The average annual precipitation is 17 inches, with an average relative humidity of 68% at 6 A.M. and 37% at 6 P.M. The average annual snowfall is 12 inches. The growing season averages 195 days per year, with the last freeze in mid April and the first freeze in early November. The sun shines during the year on the average 75% of the daylight hours.

THE PEOPLE

The 1982 estimated population of 18,500 reflects a small population loss since 1980. Urban areas grew faster than rural areas between 1970 and 1980. The population's death rate is higher than average and the county has a high percentage of residents over age 64. The largest ancestry groups are Hispanic (30%), persons of English descent (23%) and Irish descent (17%). **REGISTERED VOTERS** As of November 2, 1982 there were 8,984 registered voters (0.1% of the state total). The 1982 general election had a 41% voter turnout, compared to a 66% turnout in the 1980 general election. In the 1982 primary 98% voted Democratic and 2% Republican, with 3,257 votes cast.

THE ECONOMY

AGRICULTURE Fed cattle and cotton area. In 1982, 97% of the land was in farms and ranches, with 84% of the farmland under cultivation and 60% irrigated. Lamb ranked 11th in the state in highest agricultural receipts, with 67% from crops. Water erosion, decreasing irrigation water supplies and inadequate cropping systems are the current conservation problems. Primary crops: fourth in the state for both corn and soybeans, and fifth for sunflowers. Cotton, sorghum and wheat. Primary vegetables: potatoes and processed vegetables including beets, cucumbers for pickles, snapbeans, spinach, sweet corn and tomatoes. Primary fruits and nuts: pecans. Primary livestock and products: 10th in the state for fed cattle marketings. Hogs. **BUSINESS** Total number of business establishments in the county: 348. Retail sales during the first quarter of 1984 increased 26%. In 1980, 19% of the labor force were self-employed, 17% were employed in professional or related services, 12% in manufacturing, 20% in wholesale and retail trade, 26% in agriculture, forestry, fisheries and mining, 14% were employed in other counties and there were 1,708 retired workers. The industries with the most employment: agribusiness and cotton weaving mills. The nonfarm earnings in 1981 totaled $151,335,000. The retired workers received an average monthly Social Security payment of $310. **FINANCE** On June 30, 1983, six commercial banks had total deposits of $105,743,000 and total assets of $121,549,000. There are three state savings and loan association branches and one credit union in the county. **HOUSING** Average value of homes in 1980: $22,200. Permits for new, privately owned housing units decreased in 1982: 30 permits were issued with a total construction cost of $1,175,250. Of those permits, 24 were for single family houses. Between 1970 and 1980 the number of housing units decreased by 0.7%. Seventy-nine percent of all units in the county are air-conditioned, 91% are heated by gas and 8% by electricity. **NATURAL RESOURCES** Caliche, gas, oil and limestone. In 1982 a total of 1,118,811 barrels of crude oil and 169,196 thousand cubic feet of casinghead gas were produced. Current production of other minerals and products includes caliche and crushed limestone. **TOURISM** Travel expenditures of $10,690,000 in 1982 (an increase of 17% over 1981) generated 158 jobs and $1,613,000 in payroll. **ALCOHOLIC BEVERAGES** Totally dry. **FEDERAL EXPENDITURES** The federal government had direct expenditures or obligations of $48,122,000 in the county during fiscal year 1983, including $254,000 by the U.S. Department of Defense. In addition, the federal government provided $738,000 in grant awards, paid $1,013,000 in salaries and wages, made direct payments to individuals of $22,829,000 including $15,895,000 in retirement and disability payments, awarded $3,000 in procurement contracts and spent $23,539,000 in other expenditures or obligations. The federal government also provided $16,452,000 in direct loans and $34,838,000 in guaranteed loans and insurance.

COMMUNICATION

Newspapers–Weekly: Amherst Press, News-Sun (Earth), Lamb County Leader News (Littlefield), Olton Enterprise and the Sudan Beacon News. Radio: KZZN-AM (Littlefield). Cable TV. Telephone companies: General Telephone, Continental Telephone, Five-Area Telephone Coop. and South Plains Telephone Coop. **TRANSPORTATION** Total public road mileage: 1,678. In 1982 there were 16,805 registered vehicles and 301 reported traffic accidents including six fatalities. Intercity bus service is available. Motor freight: three carriers. Rail: one main line carries annually 20 to 30 million tons of freight through the county. Aircraft: 37 are registered in the county. Airports: Littlefield Municipal Airport serves as a base for 18 aircraft and is a basic utility airport with general aviation service. Also serving the area are H & M Agricultural Services Airport at Olton and Sudan Airfield at Sudan.

COMMUNITY SERVICES

EDUCATION Six school districts with eight elementary, three middle and six high schools. The average daily attendance in 1981-82 was 3,681, with expenditures per pupil of $3,745 including 269 classroom teachers with an average annual salary of $15,053. Forty-one percent of the 229 high school graduates planned to attend college. In 1982-83, 42% of the students were White, 48% Hispanic, 10% Black and 0.1% Asian. **PUBLIC LIBRARIES** Lamb County Library (Littlefield): 20,787 volumes, one branch. **CHILD CARE** 10 day care and 11 twenty-four hour care licensed facilities. **HEALTH CARE** 14 physicians and four dentists. Hospitals: two with a combined capacity of 110. Ambulance services: three volunteer services, one city and one hospital-based service. Mental health: one clinic. Nursing homes: three nursing homes with a combined capacity of 152 nursing care residents. The average cost per day for private patients in 1982 was $21.18. **CHURCHES** 44 churches have an estimated combined membership of 13,471. The largest denominations are Southern Baptist, United Methodist and Catholic. **SOCIAL SERVICES** In fiscal year 1983 a total of $1,372,759 in food stamps was distributed, with an average of 2,829 persons receiving food stamps each month. Aid to Families with Dependent Children (AFDC) totaled $186,058 with an average of 120 families receiving AFDC each month. Medical assistance benefits for the aged and disabled of $1,840,683 and for families and children of $425,027 brought the county benefit total to $3,824,527. **FIRE PROTECTION** Six volunteer fire departments. **LAW ENFORCEMENT** The County Sheriff has seven commissioned officers. Five police departments have a combined force of 19. **CRIME** 30 violent crimes (murder, forcible rape, robbery and aggravated assault) and 370 nonviolent crimes (burglary, larceny-theft and motor vehicle theft) were reported in 1982. **JUDICIAL SYSTEM** One District Court and Judge, one County Court and Judge and four Justices of the Peace. In the District Court a total of 497 cases were pending

on 1/1/82, 316 new cases were filed and 444 cases were disposed of during the year leaving 369 cases pending on 12/31/82. There were 139 criminal cases on the docket, 29 convictions, eight persons committed to prison and 52 cases left pending. In the County Court 264 cases were pending on 1/1/82, 474 new cases were filed and 463 cases were disposed of during the year leaving 275 cases pending on 12/31/82. There were 672 criminal cases on the docket, 193 convictions, 59 persons committed to jail and 231 cases left pending. **JAILS** One jail, capacity 23. **ATTORNEYS AT LAW** 11. **UTILITIES** 76% of the residents are connected to a public or privately owned water system and 71% are connected to a public sewer system. Natural gas is distributed to the county by Energas Company. The average annual residential bill for natural gas in 1982 for the Energas distribution system was $371.63, an increase of 23% over 1981. Electricity is distributed to the county by Southwestern Public Service, Baily Co. Electric Coop. and Lamb Co. Electric Coop., Inc. and is generated primarily by gas and oil. The typical residential electric bill is $170.44 per month for an all-electric house using 2,500 kwh. **TAXES** The county has 14 units with taxing authority: six school districts, six cities, one county and one special district.

RECREATION/ENTERTAINMENT

COUNTY PARKS 359 acres in 14 municipal parks. These parks contain six playgrounds, one golf course, 14 baseball and softball fields, two tennis courts, two swimming pools, four beaches and one boat ramp. Developed campsites: eight. **SCENIC DRIVES** The Texas Plains Trail runs through this county. This trail spans a vast area of the High Plains region of Texas slicing through the southernmost extension of the Great Plains of the United States. The land is flat except where erosion has carved canyon landscapes. **BOATING/FISHING** Lakes/reservoirs: Bull (500 acres). **HUNTING** Summer, fall and winter seasons on squirrel. No closed season on coyote, bobcat and nutria. Winter seasons on pheasant, quail, muskrat, beaver, opossum, ring-tailed cat, badger, fox, weasel, raccoon, skunk and civet cat. In 1983 sandhill crane, duck, coot, geese, woodcock and jacksnipe seasons occurred during the winter months. Teal duck, rail and gallinule seasons occurred in the fall. Mourning dove seasons occurred intermittently during the fall and winter months. **SPECIAL EVENTS** Sandhills Celebration, Olton, August.

COMMUNITIES

COUNTY SEAT Littlefield, County Courthouse, 79339; County Clerk's Office, 806/385-5173. **INCORPORATED COMMUNITIES** (1980 population and ZIP Code) Amherst (971) 79312, Earth (1,512) 79031, Littlefield (7,409) 79339 All-America Cities Honorable Mention 1965, Olton (2,235) 79064, Springlake (222) 79082 and Sudan (1,091) 79371. **UNINCORPORATED COMMUNITIES** (and ZIP Code) Bainer 79339, Beck 79371, Circle 79064, Corry 79041, Fieldton 79326, Friendship 79371, Hart Camp 79339, Lums Chapel 79339 and Spade 79369. **FOR ADDITIONAL LOCAL INFORMATION** Earth Chamber of Commerce, P.O. Box 496, Earth, 79031, 806/257-3365, Littlefield Chamber of Commerce, 301 E. 18th Street, P.O. Box 507, Littlefield, 79339, 806/385-4451 and Olton Chamber of Commerce, 518 8th St., P.O. Box 487, Olton, 79064, 806/285-2292.

LAMPASAS (C6)

THE LAND

Southwest of Waco on U.S. Highways 190 and 281 in the Grande Prairie Region, Lampasas County covers 714 square miles with an elevation range of 900 to 1,550 feet. The undulating to hilly

LAMPASAS (continued)

soils are light to dark, brownish to reddish and loamy with an accumulation of lime. Lampasas is in the Cross Timbers and Prairies vegetation area with tall and mid grasses, live and post oak, junipers and some mesquite. Between 11 and 20% of the land in the county is considered prime farmland. **CLIMATE** Subtropical Subhumid with wide-ranging temperatures from winter to summer. The average annual temperature is 65°F. Temperatures in January range from an average low of 30° to an average high of 58°F and in July range from 71° to 96°F. The average annual precipitation is 30 inches, with an average relative humidity of 80% at 6 A.M. and 50% at 6 P.M. The average annual snowfall is two inches. The growing season averages 225 days per year, with the last freeze in early April and the first freeze in early November. The sun shines during the year on the average 66% of the daylight hours.

THE PEOPLE

Lampasas County grew faster in the last decade than at any time in the past 50 years. The 1982 estimated population of 12,700 continues that strong growth rate. Rural areas grew by 72% between 1970 and 1980. The age groups with the largest gains were birth to nine years and 30 to 34, which doubled the size. The median age lowered from 35 in 1970 to 33 in 1980. The largest ancestry groups are persons of English descent (33%), Irish descent (24%) and German descent (20%). **REGISTERED VOTERS** As of November 2, 1982 there were 6,121 registered voters (0.1% of the state total). The 1982 general election had a 48% voter turnout, compared to a 70% turnout in the 1980 general election. In the 1982 primary 98% voted Democratic and 2% Republican, with 2,290 votes cast.

THE ECONOMY

AGRICULTURE Sheep area. In 1982, 92% of the land was in farms and ranches, with 9% of the farmland under cultivation. Lampasas ranked 172nd in the state in highest agricultural receipts, with 93% from livestock and livestock products. Overgrazing, undesirable brush and weeds and the cultivation of marginal lands are the current conservation problems. Primary crops: hay, wheat and oats. Primary vegetables: watermelons. Primary fruits and nuts: peaches and pecans. Primary livestock and products: cattle, sheep, wool, angora goats, mohair and hogs. **BUSINESS** Total number of business establishments in the county: 233. Retail sales during the first quarter of 1984 increased 17%. In 1980, 17% of the labor force were self-employed, 18% were employed in professional or related services, 7% in manufacturing, 25% in wholesale and retail trade, 12% in construction, 41% were employed in other counties and there were 1,371 retired workers. The industries with the most employment: agribusiness, general construction and the manufacture of prepared feeds and plastic products. The nonfarm earnings in 1981 totaled $96,045,000. The retired workers received an average monthly Social Security payment of $281. **FINANCE** On June 30, 1983, three commercial banks had total deposits of $114,541,000 and total assets of $124,694,000. On December 31, 1982 one federal savings and loan association and one state branch had assets of $26,839,911,000. **HOUSING** Average value of homes in 1980: $29,700. Permits for new, privately owned housing units increased in 1982: 82 permits were issued with a total construction cost of $2,416,600. Of those permits, 28 were for single family houses. Housing permits in the city of Lampasas increased from 8 in 1981 to 82 in 1982 with 52 of the permits issued for apartments and condominiums. Between 1970 and 1980 the number of housing units increased by 34%. Seventy-seven percent of all units in the county are air-conditioned, 70% are heated by gas and 23% by electricity. **NATURAL RESOURCES** Dolomite,

limestone and industrial sand. Current production includes crushed limestone, sand and gravel. **TOURISM** Travel expenditures of $1,880,000 in 1982 (an increase of 13% over 1981) generated 39 jobs and $334,000 in payroll. **ALCOHOLIC BEVERAGES** Totally dry. **FEDERAL EXPENDITURES** The federal government had direct expenditures or obligations of $27,333,000 in the county during fiscal year 1983, including $6,175,000 by the U.S. Department of Defense. In addition, the federal government provided $152,000 in grant awards, paid $849,000 in salaries and wages, made direct payments to individuals of $25,850,000 including $20,176,000 in retirement and disability payments, awarded $7,000 in procurement contracts and spent $475,000 in other expenditures or obligations. The federal government also provided $5,031,000 in direct loans and $5,107,000 in guaranteed loans and insurance.

COMMUNICATION

Newspapers–Weekly: Lampasas Record and the Lampasas Dispatch. Radio: KCYL-AM and KLTD-FM Stereo (Lampasas). Cable TV. Telephone companies: Southwestern Bell, Central Telephone, Central Telephone-Midstate and Central Texas Telephone Coop. **TRANSPORTATION** Total public road mileage: 693. In 1982 there were 10,596 registered vehicles and 270 reported traffic accidents including two fatalities. Intercity bus service is available. Motor freight: three carriers. Rail: two main and one branch line carry freight through the county. The two main lines carry annually 20 to 30 million tons of freight each and the one branch carries less than one million. Aircraft: 18 are registered in the county. Airports: Lampasas Municipal Airport serves as a base for 10 aircraft and is a basic utility airport with general aviation service. The Lometa Air Strip also serves the area.

COMMUNITY SERVICES

EDUCATION Two school districts with three elementary, one middle and two high schools. The average daily attendance in 1981-82 was 2,180, with expenditures per pupil of $1,943 including 118 classroom teachers with an average annual salary of $15,964. Fifty-one percent of the 156 high school graduates planned to attend college. In 1982-83, 82% of the students were White, 16% Hispanic, 2% Black and 1% Asian. **PUBLIC LIBRARIES** Lampasas Public Library: 18,241 volumes. **CHILD CARE** 27 day care and five twenty-four hour care licensed facilities. **HEALTH CARE** Four physicians and seven dentists. Hospitals: one with a capacity of 36. Ambulance services: one commercial service. Mental health: one clinic. Nursing homes: two nursing homes with a combined capacity of 164 nursing care residents. The average cost per day for private patients in 1982 was $37.57. **CHURCHES** 27 churches have an estimated combined membership of 6,471. The largest denominations are Southern Baptist, United Methodist and Churches of Christ. **SOCIAL SERVICES** In fiscal year 1983 a total of $486,974 in food stamps was distributed, with an average of 989 persons receiving food stamps each month. Aid to Families with Dependent Children (AFDC) totaled $83,151 with an average of 55 families receiving AFDC each month. Medical assistance benefits for the aged and disabled of $1,285,560 and for families and children of $161,642 brought the county benefit total to $2,017,327. **FIRE PROTECTION** Four volunteer fire departments. **LAW ENFORCEMENT** The County Sheriff has five commissioned officers. One police department has a force of seven. **CRIME** 33 violent crimes (murder, forcible rape, robbery and aggravated assault) and 293 nonviolent crimes (burglary, larceny-theft and motor vehicle theft) were reported in 1982. **JUDICIAL SYSTEM** One District Court and Judge, one County Court and Judge and three Justices of the Peace. In the District Court a total of 179 cases were pending on 1/1/82, 308 new cases were filed and 247 cases were disposed of during the year leaving 240 cases pending on 12/31/82. There were 120 criminal cases on the docket, 57 convictions, 20 persons committed to prison and 47 cases left pending. In the County Court 460 cases were pending on 1/1/82, 266 new cases were filed and 121 cases were disposed of during the year leaving 605 cases pending on 12/31/82. There were 602 criminal cases on the docket, 88 convictions, 26 persons committed to jail and 488 cases left pending. **JAILS** One jail, capacity 15. **ATTORNEYS AT LAW** 14. **UTILITIES** 73% of the residents are connected to a public or privately owned water system and 53% are connected to a public sewer system. Natural gas is distributed to the county by Lone Star Gas Co., Division of Enserch. The average annual residential bill for natural gas in 1982 for the Lone Star distribution system was $405.91, an increase of 35% over 1981. Electricity is distributed to the city of Lampasas by Lampasas Public Utilities and to the rest of the county by Texas Power and Light Co., Hamilton Co. Electric Coop., Assn. and Pedernales Electric Coop., Inc. and is generated primarily by gas, coal and water. The typical residential electric bill is $165.24 per month for an all-electric house using 2,500 kwh. **TAXES** The county has five units with taxing authority: two school districts, two cities and one county.

RECREATION/ENTERTAINMENT
NATIONAL REGISTER OF HISTORIC PLACES Lampasas: Lampasas County Courthouse. **MUNICIPAL PARKS** 144 acres in seven municipal parks. These parks contain four playgrounds, one golf course, five football and soccer fields, three baseball and softball fields, four tennis courts and one swimming pool. **BOATING/FISHING** Lakes/reservoirs: Jones (364 acres), Lometa (26 acres) and Sulphur Creek Soil Conservation Service Lakes 1, 2, 3 and 6 (48 acres). Major rivers: Lampasas and Colorado. Primary streams: Burleson, Salt, Donalson, Bean, Espy, School, Simms and Sulphur. **HUNTING** Fall and winter seasons on deer. No closed season on coyote, bobcat and squirrel. Winter seasons on quail, muskrat, beaver, opossum, ring-tailed cat, badger, fox, weasel, raccoon, skunk and civet cat. Fall, winter and spring seasons on turkey. In 1983 duck, coot, geese, woodcock and jacksnipe seasons occurred during the winter months. Teal duck, rail and gallinule seasons occurred in the fall. Mourning dove seasons occurred intermittently during the fall and winter months. **MUSEUMS** Lampasas: Cauthen House Museum and Keystone Square Museum. **SPECIAL EVENTS** Stock Show, Lometa, January; Junior Stock Show, Lometa, January; Diamondback Jubilee, Lometa, March; Highland Lakes Bluebonnet Trail, Lampasas, April; Memorial Golf Tourney, Lampasas, May; All-Western Roundup, Kempner, June; Spring Ho Festival, Lampasas, July; Rodeo, Lometa, July; Octoberfest, Kempner, October.

COMMUNITIES
COUNTY SEAT Lampasas, County Courthouse, 76550; County Clerk's Office, 512/556-5552. **INCORPORATED COMMUNITIES** (1980 population and ZIP Code) Lampasas (6,165) 76550 and Lometa (666) 76853. **UNINCORPORATED COMMUNITIES** (and ZIP Code) Adamsville 76510, Izoro 76522, Kempner 76539, Nix 76550 and Rumley 76539. **FOR ADDITIONAL LOCAL INFORMATION** Lampasas Co. Chamber of Commerce, 501 E. Second, P.O. Box 627, Lampasas, 76550, 512/556-5172 or 556-5301.

LA SALLE (B17)

THE LAND
Northwest of Corpus Christi on Interstate Highway 35 in the Rio Grande Plain Region, La Salle County covers 1,517 square miles with an elevation range of 400 to 600 feet. The northwestern half of the county has nearly level to undulating, deep to moderately deep, soils with light colored loamy surfaces over clayey subsoils and limestone within 40 inches of the surface in some areas. The southeastern half has light colored soils and gray to black, cracking, clayey soils that have a high shrink-swell potential. La Salle is in the South Texas Plains vegetation area with bunchgrasses, brush, mesquite, small live oak, post oak and cacti. Less than 1% of the land in the county is considered prime farmland. **CLIMATE** Subtropical Subhumid with dry, hot summers. The average annual temperature is 71°F. Temperatures in January range from an average low of 42° to an average high of 65°F and in July range from 74° to 99°F. The average annual precipitation is 22 inches, with an average relative humidity of 80% at 6 A.M. and 42% at 6 P.M. There is no snowfall. The growing season averages 288 days per year, with the last freeze in late February and the first freeze in early December. The sun shines during the year on the average 65% of the daylight hours.

THE PEOPLE
La Salle County ranks 21st among all U.S. counties in the highest percent of residents who are of Spanish origin. The 1982 estimated population of 5,800 indicates a continuation of the growth in population which began in the 1970s, reversing a steady population decline. Urban areas grew 15% between 1970 and 1980, while rural areas experienced little change. The population has a high birth rate and a median age of 27 in 1980. The largest ancestry groups are Hispanic (74%) and persons of English descent (9%). **REGISTERED VOTERS** As of November 2, 1982 there were 3,367 registered voters (0.1% of the state total). The 1982 general election had a 71% voter turnout, compared to a 60% turnout in the 1980 general election. In the 1982 primary 100% voted Democratic, with 1,545 votes cast.

THE ECONOMY
AGRICULTURE Cattle ranches. In 1982, 91% of the land was in farms and ranches, with 3% of the farmland under cultivation and 24% irrigated. La Salle ranked 148th in the state in highest agricultural receipts, with 87% from livestock and livestock products. Overgrazing, undesirable brush and weeds, water and wind erosion are the current conservation problems. Primary crops: sorghum, oats, wheat and hay. Primary vegetables: fifth in the state for watermelons. Primary fruits and nuts: peaches and pecans. Primary livestock and products: cattle, milk and hogs. **BUSINESS** Total number of business establishments in the county: 95. Retail sales during the first quarter of 1984 increased 34%. In 1980, 16% of the labor force were self-employed, 18% were employed in professional or related services, 3% in manufacturing, 17% in wholesale and retail trade, 22% in agriculture, forestry, fisheries and mining, 24% were employed in other counties and there were 429 retired workers. The industries with the most employment: agribusiness. The nonfarm earnings in 1981 totaled $30,906,000. The retired workers received an average monthly Social Security payment of $256. **FINANCE** On June 30, 1983, one commercial bank had total deposits of $15,218,000 and total assets of $17,214,000. There is one state savings and loan association branch in the county. **HOUSING** Average value of homes in 1980: $11,800. In 1982 four permits were issued for new single family houses. Between 1970 and 1980 the number of housing units increased by 27%. Forty-four percent of all units in the county are air-conditioned, 81% are heated by gas and 14% by electricity. **NATURAL RESOURCES** Sand and gravel, oil, gas and lignite coal. In 1982 a total of 4,668,423 thousand cubic feet of gas well gas, 32,936 barrels of condensate, 505,645 barrels of crude oil and 350,459 thousand cubic feet of casinghead gas were produced. **TOURISM** Travel expenditures of $5,302,000 in 1982 (an increase of 15% over 1981) generated 100 jobs and $903,000 in payroll. **ALCOHOLIC BEVERAGES** Packaged distilled spirits, beer, ale, malt liquor

LA SALLE (continued)

and wine are legal in parts of the county. Sale of mixed beverages is legal in all or parts of the county. **FEDERAL EXPENDITURES** The federal government had direct expenditures or obligations of $8,452,000 in the county during fiscal year 1983, including $219,000 by the U.S. Department of Defense. In addition, the federal government provided $907,000 in grant awards, paid $690,000 in salaries and wages, made direct payments to individuals of $6,429,000 including $4,478,000 in retirement and disability payments, awarded $1,000 in procurement contracts and spent $424,000 in other expenditures or obligations. The federal government also provided $544,000 in guaranteed loans and insurance.

COMMUNICATION

Newspapers–Weekly: Cotulla Record. Cable TV. Telephone companies: General Telephone, Southwestern Bell and Valley Telephone Co. **TRANSPORTATION** Total public road mileage: 487. In 1982 there were 3,405 registered vehicles and 105 reported traffic accidents including two fatalities. Intercity bus service is available. Motor freight: three carriers. Rail: the Eagle provides passenger service on the Amtrak Route. Two main and one branch line carry freight through the county. The two main lines annually carry five to 10 million tons of freight each and the one branch carries one to five million. Aircraft: 13 are registered in the county. Airports: Cotulla Municipal Airport.

COMMUNITY SERVICES

EDUCATION One school district with four elementary, one middle and one high school. The average daily attendance in 1981-82 was 1,252, with expenditures per pupil of $3,029 including 85 classroom teachers with an average annual salary of $15,327. Fifty-two percent of the 102 high school graduates planned to attend college. In 1982-83, 16% of the students were White, 84% Hispanic and 0.1% Black. **PUBLIC LIBRARIES** Alexander Memorial Library (Cotulla): 17,752 volumes. **CHILD CARE** Seven day care licensed facilities. **HEALTH CARE** One physician. Ambulance services: one commercial service. Mental health: one mobile clinic. **CHURCHES** 15 churches have an estimated combined membership of 4,777. The largest denominations are Catholic and Southern Baptist. **SOCIAL SERVICES** In fiscal year 1983 a total of $989,021 in food stamps was distributed, with an average of 2,071 persons receiving food stamps each month. Aid to Families with Dependent Children (AFDC) totaled $176,933 with an average of 116 families receiving AFDC each month. Medical assistance benefits for the aged and disabled of $726,929 and for families and children of $330,870 brought the county benefit total to $2,223,752. **FIRE PROTECTION** Three volunteer fire departments. **LAW ENFORCEMENT** The County Sheriff has 10 commissioned officers. **CRIME** Seven violent crimes (murder, forcible rape, robbery and aggravated assault) and 33 nonviolent crimes (burglary, larceny-theft and motor vehicle theft) were reported in 1982. **JUDICIAL SYSTEM** Two District Courts and Judges, one County Court and Judge and three Justices of the Peace. In the District Courts a total of 266 cases were pending on 1/1/82, 146 new cases were filed and 111 cases were disposed of during the year leaving 301 cases pending on 12/31/82. There were 65 criminal cases on the docket, 15 convictions, four persons committed to prison and 43 cases left pending. In the County Court 585 cases were pending on 1/1/82, 161 new cases were filed and 55 cases were disposed of during the year leaving 691 cases pending on 12/31/82. There were 682 criminal cases on the docket, 40 convictions and 634 cases left pending. **JAILS** One jail, capacity 14. **ATTORNEYS AT LAW** Two. **UTILITIES** 85% of the residents are connected to a public or privately owned water system and 65% are connected to a public sewer system. Electricity is distributed to the county by Central Power and Light Co., Cochran Power and Light Co. and Medina Electric Coop., Inc. and is generated primarily by gas, oil and coal. The typical residential electric bill is $162.15 per month for an all-electric house using 2,500 kwh. **TAXES** The county has three units with taxing authority: one school district, one city and one county.

RECREATION/ENTERTAINMENT

COUNTY/MUNICIPAL PARKS 45 acres in two county and three municipal parks. These parks contain one playground, one swimming pool and one beach. **BOATING/FISHING** Lakes/reservoirs: Allerkamp (32 acres), Big Alamo Tank (106 acres), Burns (74 acres), Burkett (60 acres), Cohenour (288 acres), Davis (80 acres), Dobie Ranch Tank (57 acres), Harris (63 acres), Holland #1 (663 acres), Holland #2 (160 acres), La Mata (30 acres), Macomber (35 acres) and Welder (35 acres). Major rivers: Nueces and Frio. Primary streams: Green, Martin, Cibolo, Piedro, Sauz, Quitania, Salem, Los Olmos, Caiman and Las Raices. **WILDLIFE REFUGES** Chaparral State Wildlife Management Area covers 7,000 acres in this county. **HUNTING** Fall and winter seasons on deer. No closed season on javelina, coyote, bobcat and squirrel. Winter seasons on quail, muskrat, beaver, opossum, ring-tailed cat, badger, fox, weasel, raccoon, skunk and civet cat. Fall, winter and spring seasons on turkey. Special regulations on state-owned river beds. In 1983 sandhill crane, duck, coot, geese, woodcock and jacksnipe seasons occurred during the winter months. Teal duck, rail and gallinule seasons occurred in the fall. Mourning dove seasons occurred intermittently during the fall and winter months with a fall season on white-winged dove. **SPECIAL EVENTS** County Fair and Wild Hog Cookoff, Cotulla, March.

COMMUNITIES

COUNTY SEAT Cotulla, County Courthouse, 78014; County Clerk's Office, 512/879-2117. **INCORPORATED COMMUNITIES** (1980 population and ZIP Code) Cotulla (3,912) 78014 and Encinal (704) 78019. **UNINCORPORATED COMMUNITIES** (and ZIP Code) Artesia Wells 78001, Atlee 78019, Fowlerton 78021, Gardendale 78014, Los Angeles 78051 and Millett 78014. **FOR ADDITIONAL LOCAL INFORMATION** Cotulla-La Salle Co. Chamber of Commerce, P.O. Box 515, Cotulla, 78014, 512/879-2326.

LAVACA (G14)

THE LAND

East of San Antonio on U.S. Highways 77 and Alt. 90 in the Claypan Area, Lavaca County covers 971 square miles of level to undulating land with an elevation range of 150 to 350 feet. In the southeast are light colored, loamy to sandy soils with very deep, reddish or mottled subsoils. To the northwest are shallow to deep, alkaline, clayey soils over chalk with a high shrink-swell potential. There are loamy surfaces in some areas. The northwestern portion of the county is in the Blackland Prairies vegetation area with tall grasses, mesquite, oak, pecan and elm trees along streams. The southeastern portion is in the Post Oak Savannah vegetation area with tall grasses, post and blackjack oak trees. Between 21 and 30% of the land in the county is considered prime farmland. **CLIMATE** Subtropical Humid, moist with warm summers. The average annual temperature is 70°F. Temperatures in January range from an average low of 41° to an average high of 64°F and in July range from 73° to 96°F. The average annual precipitation is 37 inches, with an average relative humidity of 87% at 6 A.M. and 59% at 6 P.M. There is no snowfall. The growing season averages 278 days per year, with the last freeze in early March and the first freeze in early

LAVACA

December. The sun shines during the year on the average 68% of the daylight hours.

THE PEOPLE
Twice as many people live in rural areas in Lavaca County than in urban areas. The 1982 estimated population of 18,400 reflects a decline in population since 1980, after a decade of growth. Urban areas grew faster than rural areas between 1970 and 1980. The age group with the largest increase was ages 20 to 34, which grew 50%. The population is older than average, although the median age lowered from 42 in 1970 to 38 in 1980. The county has a high percent of persons who are native Texans. The largest ancestry groups are persons of German descent (34%), English descent (12%) and Irish descent (10%). **REGISTERED VOTERS** As of November 2, 1982 there were 9,311 registered voters (0.1% of the state total). The 1982 general election had a 52% voter turnout, compared to a 66% turnout in the 1980 general election. In the 1982 primary 95% voted Democratic and 5% Republican, with 3,192 votes cast.

THE ECONOMY
AGRICULTURE Cattle and poultry area. In 1982, 85% of the land was in farms and ranches, with 10% of the farmland under cultivation and 16% irrigated. Lavaca ranked 81st in the state in highest agricultural receipts, with 89% from livestock and livestock products. Overgrazing, undesirable brush and weeds, water erosion and inefficient irrigation systems are the current conservation problems. Primary crops: hay, corn, sorghum, rice and oats. Primary vegetables: potatoes, sweet potatoes, tomatoes and watermelons. Primary fruits and nuts: peaches and pecans. Primary livestock and products: eighth in the state for hens and pullets and ninth for egg production. Cattle, milk and hogs. **BUSINESS** Total number of business establishments in the county: 458. Retail sales during the first quarter of 1984 increased 9%. In 1980, 16% of the labor force were self-employed, 17% were employed in professional or related services, 22% in manufacturing, 20% in wholesale and retail trade, 14% in agriculture, forestry, fisheries and mining, 26% were employed in other counties and there were 3,094 retired workers. The industries with the most employment: agribusiness, oil and gas extraction, construction, meat packing and the manufacture of apparel belts, leather goods and automatic vending machines. The nonfarm earnings in 1981 totaled $161,542,000. The retired workers received an average monthly Social Security payment of $254. **FINANCE** On June 30, 1983, four commercial banks had total deposits of $109,453,000 and total assets of $122,830,000. There are three state savings and loan association branches and one credit union in the county. **HOUSING** Average value of homes in 1980: $25,600. Permits for new, privately owned housing units decreased in 1982: 20 permits were issued with a total construction cost of $959,057. Of those permits, all were for single family houses. Between 1970 and 1980 the number of housing units increased by 17%. Fifty percent of all units in the county are air-conditioned, 73% are heated by gas and 14% by electricity. **NATURAL RESOURCES** Clay, oil, gas and sandstone. In 1982 a total of 44,344,646 thousand cubic feet of gas well gas, 334,819 barrels of condensate, 468,572 barrels of crude oil and 2,310,948 thousand cubic feet of casinghead gas were produced. **TOURISM** Travel expenditures of $8,293,000 in 1982 (an increase of 16% over 1981) generated 139 jobs and $1,329,000 in payroll. **ALCOHOLIC BEVERAGES** Packaged distilled spirits, beer, ale, malt liquor and wine are legal in parts of the county. Sale of mixed beverages is legal in all or parts of the county. **FEDERAL EXPENDITURES** The federal government had direct expenditures or obligations of $44,810,000 in the county during fiscal year 1983, including $677,000 by the U.S. Department of Defense. In addition, the federal government provided $888,000 in grant awards, paid $1,549,000 in salaries and wages, made direct payments to individuals of $40,928,000 including $26,603,000 in retirement and disability payments, awarded $154,000 in procurement contracts and spent $1,291,000 in other expenditures or obligations. The federal government also provided $182,000 in direct loans and $5,959,000 in guaranteed loans and insurance.

COMMUNICATION
Newspapers–Weekly: Lavaca County Tribune-Herald (Hallettsville), The Moulton Eagle and The Shiner Gazette. Radio: KRJH-AM (Hallettsville). Cable TV. Telephone companies: Southwestern Bell and Colorado Valley Telephone Coop. **TRANSPORTATION** Total public road mileage: 1,197. In 1982 there were 16,835 registered vehicles and 337 reported traffic accidents including four fatalities. Intercity bus service is available. Motor freight: three carriers. Rail: one branch line carries annually five to 10 million tons of freight through the county. Aircraft: 12 are registered in the county. Airports: Hallettsville Municipal Airport serves as a base for 10 aircraft and is a basic utility airport with general aviation service. Also serving the area are Yoakum Municipal Airport at the Lavaca/DeWitt County Line and Moulton Municipal Airport.

COMMUNITY SERVICES
EDUCATION Six school districts with six elementary, one middle and three high schools. The average daily attendance in 1981-82 was 1,758, with expenditures per pupil of $2,705 including 126 classroom teachers with an average annual salary of $16,624. Thirty-nine percent of the 140 high school graduates planned to attend college. In 1982-83, 78% of the students were White, 7% Hispanic, 15% Black and 0.2% Asian. Private schools: 754 students enrolled in three elementary and two high schools. **PUBLIC LIBRARIES** French Simpson Memorial Library (Hallettsville): 11,629 volumes. Yoakum Public Library: 13,453 volumes. **CHILD CARE** 50 day care and one twenty-four hour care licensed facilities. **HEALTH CARE** 16 physicians and eight dentists. Hospitals: three with a combined capacity of 106. Ambulance services: one volunteer service. Nursing homes: three nursing homes with a combined capacity of 340 nursing care residents. The average cost per day for private patients in 1982 was $28.32. **CHURCHES** 43 churches have an estimated combined membership of 15,343. The largest denominations are Catholic and Southern Baptist. **SOCIAL SERVICES** In fiscal year 1983 a total of $540,643 in food stamps was distributed, with an average of 1,236 persons receiving food stamps each month. Aid to Families with Dependent Children (AFDC) totaled $126,364 with an average of 84 families receiving AFDC each month. Medical assistance benefits for the aged and disabled of $3,023,317 and for families and children of $186,604 brought the county benefit total to $3,876,927. **FIRE PROTECTION** Four volunteer fire departments. **LAW ENFORCEMENT** The County Sheriff has 33 commissioned officers. Four police departments have a combined force of 33. **CRIME** 29 violent crimes (murder, forcible rape, robbery and aggravated assault) and 278 nonviolent crimes (burglary, larceny-theft and motor vehicle theft) were reported in 1982. **JUDICIAL SYSTEM** Two District Courts and Judges, one County Court and Judge and six Justices of the Peace. In the District Courts a total of 329 cases were pending on 1/1/82, 332 new cases were filed and 262 cases were disposed of during the year leaving 399 cases pending on 12/31/82. There were 152 criminal cases on the docket, 18 convictions, eight persons committed to prison and 109 cases left pending. In the County Court 232 cases were pending on 1/1/82, 290 new cases were filed and 195 cases were disposed of during the year leaving 327 cases pending on 12/31/82. There were 479 criminal cases on the docket, 98 convictions, 26 persons committed to jail, and 297 cases left pending. **JAILS** One jail, capacity 15, under

COUNTIES

LAVACA (continued)

renovation in kitchen area. **ATTORNEYS AT LAW** 21. **UTILITIES** 50% of the residents are connected to a public or privately owned water system and 48% are connected to a public sewer system. Natural gas is distributed to the county by Entex, Inc. and Arkla Inc. The average annual residential bill for natural gas in 1982 for the Entex distribution system was $390.31, an increase of 26% over 1981 and for Arkla it was $316.69, an increase of 23%. Electricity is distributed to the city of Hallettsville by the Hallettsville Municipal Utilities, Moulton by the Moulton Electric Dept., Shiner by the Shiner Light and Water Utilities, Yoakum by the Yoakum Municipal Utilities and to the rest of the county by DeWitt County Electric Coop., Inc., Fayette Electric Coop., Inc., Guadalupe Valley Electric Coop., Inc. and Jackson Electric Coop., Inc. and is generated primarily by oil, water and coal. The typical residential electric bill is $143.95 per month for an all-electric house using 2,500 kwh. **TAXES** The county has 14 units with taxing authority: eight school districts, three cities, one county, one hospital district and one special district.

RECREATION/ENTERTAINMENT
NATIONAL REGISTER OF HISTORIC PLACES Hallettsville: Lavaca County Courthouse and Lay-Bozka House. **MUNICIPAL PARKS** 290 acres in eight municipal parks. These parks contain six playgrounds, two golf courses, one football and soccer field, 13 baseball and softball fields, nine tennis courts and two swimming pools. Developed campsites: three. **BOATING/FISHING** Major rivers: Lavaca and Navidad. **HUNTING** Fall and winter seasons on deer. No closed seasons on nutria, coyote, bobcat and squirrel. Winter seasons on quail, muskrat, beaver, otter, opossum, mink, ring-tailed cat, badger, fox, raccoon, skunk and civet cat. In 1983 sandhill crane, duck, coot, geese, woodcock and jacksnipe seasons occurred during the winter months. Teal duck, rail and gallinule seasons occurred in the fall. Mourning dove seasons occurred intermittently during the fall and winter months. **MUSEUMS** Moulton: Community Heritage House. Shiner: Edwin Wolters Memorial Museum. **SPECIAL EVENTS** State Championship Domino Tourney, Hallettsville, January; Art and Hobby Fair, Shiner, February; Champion "42" Domino Tourney, Hallettsville, March; Easter Picnic, Moulton, April; Open Air Concerts, Moulton, April; Czech/German Polka and Waltz Festival, Moulton, May; State Championship Fiddlers Frolics, Hallettsville, April/May; Tom Tom Leather Festival, Yoakum, May; Half-Moon Days, Shiner, July; Youth Rodeo, Yoakum, July; Town and Country Jamboree, Moulton, July; St. Joseph's Annual Church Picnic, Moulton, September; Polka Festival, Shiner, October; County Fair, Hallettsville, October; Christmas Jubilee, Shiner, December.

COMMUNITIES
COUNTY SEAT Hallettsville, County Courthouse, 77964; County Clerk's Office, 512/798-2721. **INCORPORATED COMMUNITIES** (1980 population and ZIP Code) Hallettsville (2,865) 77964, Moulton (1,009) 77975, Shiner (2,213) 77984 and Yoakum (6,148: 3,823 in Lavaca Co. and 2,325 in DeWitt Co.) 77995. **UNINCORPORATED COMMUNITIES** (and ZIP Code) Breslau 77964, Ezzell 77964, Gleckler 78956, Henkhaus 77984, Hope 77995, Kinkler 77964, Koerth 77964, Midway 77984, Mont 77964, Moravia 78956, Mount Olive 77984, Novohrad 77975, Old Moulton 77975, Rabbs 77964, Speaks 77985, Sublime 77986, Sweet Home 77987, Vienna 77964, Wied 77964, Witting 77975, Williamsburg 77964 and Worthing 77964. **FOR ADDITIONAL LOCAL INFORMATION** Hallettsville Chamber of Commerce, N. La Grange and 4th, P.O. Box 313, Hallettsville, 77964, 214/668-2592, Moulton Chamber of Commerce, P.O. Box 482, Moulton, 77975, 512/596-7753, Shiner Chamber of Commerce, P.O. Box 596, Shiner, 77984, 512/594-3661, Yoakum Chamber of Commerce, Box 591, 105 Huck, Yoakum, 77995, 512/293-2149.

LEE (C26)

THE LAND
East of Austin on U.S. Highway 77 in the Claypan Area, Lee County covers 631 square miles with an elevation range of 270 to 970 feet. Along a strip in the northwest part of the county are light colored soils with loamy or sandy surfaces over mottled or reddish clayey or loamy subsoils. In the center of the county is a strip of gray to black, cracking, clayey soils or slightly acidic soils with light colored, loamy surfaces and very deep, reddish, clayey subsoils. These soils have a high shrink-swell potential. The rest of the county has light colored soils with sandy surfaces and mottled, clayey subsoils. The central part of Lee is in the Blackland Prairies vegetation area with tall grasses, mesquite and oak, pecan and elm trees along streams. The rest of the county is in the Post Oak Savannah vegetation area with tall grasses, post oak and blackjack oak. Between one and 10% of the land in the county is considered prime farmland. **CLIMATE** Subtropical humid with the heaviest precipitation during the months of May and September. The average annual temperature is 69°F. Temperatures in January range from an average low of 37° to an average high of 61°F and in July range from 73° to 96°F. The average annual precipitation is 36 inches, with an average relative humidity of 86% at 6 A.M. and 55% at 6 P.M. There is no snowfall. The growing season averages 273 days per year, with the last freeze in early December and the first freeze in early March. The sun shines during the year on the average 67% of the daylight hours.

THE PEOPLE
Between 1970 and 1980 Lee County experienced its first population gain in 50 years. The 1982 estimated population of 13,700 indicates a continuation of that growth. Urban areas grew slightly faster than rural areas between 1970 and 1980. The age groups with the largest gains were ages birth to five years and 15 to 29, lowering the median age from 41 in 1970 to 32 in 1980. The largest ancestry groups are persons of German descent (29%), Black (16%) and English descent (13%). **REGISTERED VOTERS** As of November 2, 1982 there were 5,847 registered voters (0.1% of the state total). The 1982 general election had a 48% voter turnout, compared to a 63% turnout in the 1980 general election. In the 1982 primary 100% voted Democratic, with 2,132 votes cast.

THE ECONOMY
AGRICULTURE Cattle area. In 1982, 78% of the land was in farms and ranches, with 16% of the farmland under cultivation and 2% irrigated. Lee ranked 119th in the state in highest agricultural receipts, with 92% from livestock and livestock products. Overgrazing, undesirable brush and weeds, water erosion and flooding are the current conservation problems. Primary crops: hay, oats, peanuts, wheat, sorghum and corn. Primary vegetables: potatoes, sweet potatoes, tomatoes and watermelons. Primary fruits and nuts: peaches and pecans. Primary livestock and products: seventh in the state for turkeys. Cattle and hogs. **BUSINESS** Total number of business establishments in the county: 359. Retail sales during the first quarter of 1984 increased 17%. In 1980, 16% of the labor force were self-employed, 18% were employed in professional or related services, 13% in manufacturing, 19% in wholesale and retail trade, 19% in agriculture, forestry, fisheries and mining, 19% were employed in other counties and there were 1,091 retired workers. The industries with the most employment: oil and gas extraction,

construction, boat building and repairing and the manufacture of wooden office furniture. The nonfarm earnings in 1981 totaled $107,978,000. The retired workers received an average monthly Social Security payment of $269. **FINANCE** On June 30, 1983, five commercial banks had total deposits of $144,700,000 and total assets of $161,925,000. On December 31, 1982 one state savings and loan association and four state branches had assets of $19,792,525. **HOUSING** Average value of homes in 1980: $30,100. Permits for new, privately owned housing units increased in 1982: 209 permits were issued with a total construction cost of $3,686,116. Of those permits, 35 were for single family houses. Housing permits in Giddings increased from 112 in 1981 to 209 in 1982 with 160 of the permits issued for apartments and condominiums. Between 1970 and 1980 the number of housing units increased by 31%. Sixty-two percent of all units in the county are air-conditioned, 75% are heated by gas and 13% by electricity. **NATURAL RESOURCES** Lignite coal, clay, ceramic clay, industrial sand, sand and gravel, oil and gas. In 1982 a total of 14,894,878 thousand cubic feet of gas well gas, 816,198 barrels of condensate, 9,984,813 barrels of crude oil and 31,380,100 thousand cubic feet of casinghead gas were produced. **TOURISM** Travel expenditures of $4,719,000 in 1982 (an increase of 11% over 1981) generated 119 jobs and $944,000 in payroll. **ALCOHOLIC BEVERAGES** Packaged distilled spirits, beer, ale, malt liquor and wine are legal in parts of the county. Sale of mixed beverages is legal in all or parts of the county. **FEDERAL EXPENDITURES** The federal government had direct expenditures or obligations of $16,743,000 in the county during fiscal year 1983, including $241,000 by the U.S. Department of Defense. In addition, the federal government provided $405,000 in grant awards, paid $660,000 in salaries and wages, made direct payments to individuals of $15,720,000 including $10,892,000 in retirement and disability payments, and spent $160,000 in other expenditures or obligations. The federal government also provided $22,000 in direct loans and $849,000 in guaranteed loans and insurance.

COMMUNICATION

Newspapers–Weekly: Times and News (Giddings). Cable TV. Telephone companies: General Telephone, Continental Telephone, Southwestern Bell and Industry Telephone. **TRANSPORTATION** Total public road mileage: 681. In 1982 there were 13,839 registered vehicles and 392 reported traffic accidents including 17 fatalities. Intercity bus service is available. Motor freight: seven local and intrastate carriers. Rail: two main and one branch line carry freight through the county. The two main lines carry annually over 30 million tons of freight each and the one branch carries one to five million. Aircraft: 16 are registered in the county. Airports: Lee County Airport at Giddings provides general aviation service and Lee Memorial Hospital has a Heliport.

COMMUNITY SERVICES

EDUCATION Three school districts with three elementary, two middle and three high schools. The average daily attendance in 1981-82 was 2,288, with expenditures per pupil of $4,038 including 162 classroom teachers with an average annual salary of $15,697. Twenty-eight percent of the 159 high school graduates planned to attend college. In 1982-83, 71% of the students were White, 9% Hispanic, 20% Black, 0.1% Asian and 0.1% American Indian. Private schools: 221 students enrolled in two elementary schools. **PUBLIC LIBRARIES** Rufus Young King Public Library (Giddings): 12,166 volumes. **CHILD CARE** 33 day care and five twenty-four hour care licensed facilities. **HEALTH CARE** Five physicians and five dentists. Hospitals: one with a capacity of 32. Clinics: one dialysis clinic. Ambulance services: one commercial service. Mental health: one county clinic. Nursing homes: two nursing homes with a combined capacity of 142 nursing care residents. The average cost per day for private

patients in 1982 was $30.42. **CHURCHES** 30 churches have an estimated combined membership of 7,154. The largest denominations are Lutheran-Missouri Synod and Southern Baptist. **SOCIAL SERVICES** In fiscal year 1983 a total of $236,112 in food stamps was distributed, with an average of 497 persons receiving food stamps each month. Aid to Families with Dependent Children (AFDC) totaled $65,351 with an average of 47 families receiving AFDC each month. Medical assistance benefits for the aged and disabled of $1,179,270 and for families and children of $116,165 brought the county benefit total to $1,596,898. **FIRE PROTECTION** Four volunteer fire departments. **LAW ENFORCEMENT** The County Sheriff has 13 commissioned officers. Two police departments have a combined force of 10. **CRIME** 35 violent crimes (murder, forcible rape, robbery and aggravated assault) and 341 nonviolent crimes (burglary, larceny-theft and motor vehicle theft) were reported in 1982. **JUDICIAL SYSTEM** Two District Courts and Judges, one County Court and Judge and five Justices of the Peace. In the District Courts a total of 810 cases were pending on 1/1/82, 701 new cases were filed and 460 cases were disposed of during the year leaving 1,051 cases pending on 12/31/82. There were 290 criminal cases on the docket, 77 convictions, 23 persons committed to prison and two committed to jail and 143 cases left pending. In the County Court 899 cases were pending on 1/1/82, 626 new cases were filed and 443 cases were disposed of during the year leaving 1,082 cases pending on 12/31/82. There were 1,128 criminal cases on the docket, 72 convictions, and 737 cases left pending. **JAILS** One jail, capacity 21, completed major renovation in 1983. **ATTORNEYS AT LAW** 15. **UTILITIES** 79% of the residents are connected to a public or privately owned water system and 47% are connected to a public sewer system. Natural gas is distributed to the county by Lone Star Gas Co., Division of Enserch. The average annual residential bill for natural gas in 1982 for the Lone Star distribution system was $405.91, an increase of 35% over 1981. Electricity is distributed to the city of Giddings by the Giddings Lighting and Power System, Lexington by the Lexington Municipal Electric Dept. and to the rest of the county by Bluebonnet Electric Coop., Inc. and Fayette Electric Coop., Inc. and is generated primarily by oil, water and coal. The typical residential electric bill is $114.15 per month for an all-electric house using 2,500 kwh. **TAXES** The county has six units with taxing authority: three school districts, two cities and one county.

RECREATION/ENTERTAINMENT

NATIONAL REGISTER OF HISTORIC PLACES Giddings: Lee County Courthouse, Schubert-Fletcher House and Droemer Brickyard Site. **STATE** Lake Somerville State Recreation Area (See Burleson County). **MUNICIPAL PARKS** 12 acres in two municipal parks. These parks contain one playground, two baseball and softball fields and three tennis courts. **SCENIC DRIVES** The Texas Brazos Trail runs through this county. This trail moves through a beautiful and historic section of Central Texas revealing forested landscapes filled with wildlife and wild flowers. **BOATING/FISHING** Lakes/reservoirs: Cedar Bluff (50 acres), Cummins Creek Soil Conservation Service Lakes 1 and 2 (237 acres), Phinney (54 acres), Crews (55 acres), Elverda (68 acres), Hayden (50 acres), Leon (74 acres), Limestone (8,770 acres), Normangee Park (41 acres), Red Oak (27 acres), Reed (70 acres), Rex Cauble (15 acres), Simms (37 acres) and Tankawa (75 acres). Primary streams: Middle Yegua, Cummins, West Fork, Brushy, Nails, East Yegua, Rabbs and West Yegua. **WILDLIFE REFUGES** Somerville State Wildlife Management Area covers 1,700 acres. **HUNTING** Fall and winter seasons on deer. No closed season on nutria, coyote, bobcat and squirrel. Winter seasons on quail, muskrat, beaver, otter, opossum, mink, ringtailed cat, badger, fox, raccoon, skunk and civet cat. In 1983

LEE (continued)

duck, coot, geese, woodcock and jacksnipe seasons occurred during the winter months with a winter season in some parts of the county on sandhill crane. Teal duck, rail and gallinule seasons occurred in the fall. Mourning dove seasons occurred intermittently during the fall and winter months. **MUSEUMS** Giddings: Lee County Museum. Serbin: Wendish Study Center and Museum. **SPECIAL EVENTS** Western Week, Giddings, May; Oil Appreciation Week, Giddings, June; Independence Day Picnic, Giddings, July; Geburstag Celebration, Giddings, October.

COMMUNITIES

COUNTY SEAT Giddings, County Courthouse, 78942; County Clerk's Office, 409/542-3684. **INCORPORATED COMMUNITIES** (1980 population and ZIP Code) Giddings (3,950) 78942 and Lexington (1,065) 78947. **UNINCORPORATED COMMUNITIES** (and ZIP Code) blue 78947, Dime Box 77853, Fedor 78947, Hills 78659, Leo 78947, Lincoln 78948, Loebau 78948, Manheim 78659, Northrup 78942, Old Dime Box 77853, Serbin 78942, Tanglewood 78947 and The Knobbs 78650. **FOR ADDITIONAL LOCAL INFORMATION** Giddings Chamber of Commerce, 195 E. Austin, P.O. Box 180, Giddings, 78942, 409/542-3455 and Lexington Chamber, P.O. Box 572, Lexington, 78947, 409/773-2255.

LEON (C12)

THE LAND

East of Waco on Interstate Highway 45 in the Claypan Area, Leon County covers 1,078 square miles with an elevation range of 150 to 500 feet. In the northwest corner and near the east and south borders are level to undulating, light colored, sandy soils with mottled, clayey subsoils. Along the south border are undulating, gray to black, clayey soils or slightly acidic soils with light colored, loamy surfaces and clayey subsoils with a high shrink-swell potential. Along the Trinity River are very dark loamy surfaces with mottled, gray, cracking, clayey subsoils. The rest of the county has light colored soils with loamy or sandy surfaces and mottled clayey or loamy subsoils. Leon is in the Post Oak Savannah vegetation area with pecan trees along streams, tall grasses, mesquite, oak and elm. Between one and 10% of the land in the county is considered prime farmland. **CLIMATE** Subtropical Humid with warm summers. The average annual temperature is 66°F. Temperatures in January range from an average low of 37° to an average high of 58°F and in July range from 72° to 95°F. The average annual precipitation is 40 inches, with an average relative humidity of 84% at 6 A.M. and 40% at 6 P.M. The average annual snowfall is less than one inch. The growing season averages 270 days per year, with the last freeze in early March and the first freeze in early December. The sun shines during the year on the average 66% of the daylight hours.

THE PEOPLE

Leon County ranks 45th among all U.S. counties in the highest percent of residents who are over age 64. The 1982 estimated population of 10,500 indicates a continuation of the moderate growth in population which began in the 1970s, reversing a steady population decline. The majority of county residents live in rural areas. The population is older than average with a median age of 42. The largest ancestry groups are persons of Irish descent (26%), English descent (25%), Black (20%) and German descent (11%). **REGISTERED VOTERS** As of November 2, 1982 there were 6,059 registered voters (0.1% of the state total). The 1982 general election had a 46% voter turnout, compared to a 66% turnout in the 1980 general election. In the 1982 primary 96% voted Democratic and 4% Republican, with 2,022 votes cast.

THE ECONOMY

AGRICULTURE Forest production and cattle area. In 1982, 62% of the land was in farms and ranches, with 11% of the farmland under cultivation. Leon ranked 87th in the state in highest agricultural receipts, with 93% from livestock and livestock products. Overgrazing, undesirable brush and weeds, and fertilization are the current conservation problems. Primary crops: sixth in the state for hay. Oats and wheat. Primary vegetables: watermelons. Primary fruits and nuts: peaches and pecans. Primary livestock and products: first in the state for beef cows that have calved. Cattle and hogs. **BUSINESS** Total number of business establishments in the county: 172. Retail sales during the first quarter of 1984 increased 26%. In 1980, 17% of the labor force were self-employed, 21% were employed in professional or related services, 15% in manufacturing, 17% in wholesale and retail trade, 14% in agriculture, forestry, fisheries and mining, 21% were employed in other counties and there were 1,707 retired workers. The industries with the most employment: steel mills, general construction, agribusiness and the manufacture of mobile homes. The nonfarm earnings in 1981 totaled $88,474,000. The retired workers received an average monthly Social Security payment of $278. **FINANCE** On June 30, 1983, five commercial banks had total deposits of $71,897,000 and total assets of $80,759,000. There are two state savings and loan association branches in the county. **HOUSING** Average value of homes in 1980: $21,800. Between 1970 and 1980 the number of housing units increased by 9%. Sixty-nine percent of all units in the county are air-conditioned, 73% are heated by gas and 17% by electricity. **NATURAL RESOURCES** Lignite coal, limestone, salt domes, industrial sand, sand and gravel, oil, gas and glauconite. In 1982 a total of 9,536,499 thousand cubic feet of gas well gas, 47,983 barrels of condensate, 345,814 barrels of crude oil and 248,768 thousand cubic feet of casinghead gas were produced. Current production of other minerals and products includes crushed limestone. Pine and hardwood production in 1981 totaled 1,562,067 cubic feet. **TOURISM** Travel expenditures of $3,328,000 in 1982 (an increase of 15% over 1981) generated 64 jobs and $574,000 in payroll. **ALCOHOLIC BEVERAGES** Packaged distilled spirits, beer, ale, malt liquor and wine are legal in parts of the county. **FEDERAL EXPENDITURES** The federal government had direct expenditures or obligations of $25,291,000 in the county during fiscal year 1983, including $602,000 by the U.S. Department of Defense. In addition, the federal government provided $98,000 in grant awards, paid $900,000 in salaries and wages, made direct payments to individuals of $23,966,000 including $17,083,000 in retirement and disability payments, awarded $7,000 in procurement contracts and spent $321,000 in other expenditures or obligations. The federal government also provided $1,182,000 in direct loans and $944,000 in guaranteed loans and insurance.

COMMUNICATION

Newspapers–Weekly: The Buffalo Press, The Leon County News (Centerville), The Jewett Messenger and the Normangee Star. Cable TV. Telephone companies: Continental Telephone and Southwestern Bell. **TRANSPORTATION** Total public road mileage: 867. In 1982 there were 9,758 registered vehicles and 269 reported traffic accidents including 12 fatalities. Intercity bus service is available. Motor freight: four carriers. Rail: four main lines carry freight through the county with one carrying annually 20 to 30 million tons and three carry five to 10 million tons each. Aircraft: 13 are registered in the county.

COMMUNITY SERVICES

EDUCATION Five school districts with five elementary, two middle and five high schools. The average daily attendance in 1981-82 was 2,162, with expenditures per pupil of $3,681 including 147 classroom teachers with an average annual salary of $15,359. Forty-three percent of the 154 high school graduates planned to attend college. In 1982-83, 75% of the students were White, 3% Hispanic, 22% Black and 0.1% Asian. Sports championships: 1983 A Girls' Volleyball Champion, Jewett Leon H.S. **PUBLIC LIBRARIES** Buffalo Library. Centerville Library. **CHILD CARE** 14 day care licensed facilities. **HEALTH CARE** 10 physicians and one dentist. Hospitals: one with a capacity of 36. Ambulance services: one volunteer fire department and one county service. Mental health: one county clinic. Nursing homes: two nursing homes with a combined capacity of 162 nursing care residents. The average cost per day for private patients in 1982 was $30.95. **CHURCHES** 52 churches have an estimated combined membership of 5,839. The largest denominations are Southern Baptist, United Methodist and Catholic. **SOCIAL SERVICES** In fiscal year 1983 a total of $482,635 in food stamps was distributed, with an average of 1,137 persons receiving food stamps each month. Aid to Families with Dependent Children (AFDC) totaled $77,461 with an average of 49 families receiving AFDC each month. Medical assistance benefits for the aged and disabled of $1,463,288 and for families and children of $98,691 brought the county benefit total to $2,122,075. **FIRE PROTECTION** Six volunteer fire departments. **LAW ENFORCEMENT** The County Sheriff has nine commissioned officers. Three police departments have a combined force of four. **CRIME** Six violent crimes (murder, forcible rape, robbery and aggravated assault) and 127 nonviolent crimes (burglary, larceny-theft and motor vehicle theft) were reported in 1982. **JUDICIAL SYSTEM** Three District Courts and Judges, one County Court and Judge and six Justices of the Peace. In the District Courts a total of 421 cases were pending on 1/1/82, 352 new cases were filed and 407 cases were disposed of during the year leaving 366 cases pending on 12/31/82. There were 201 criminal cases on the docket, 16 convictions, two persons committed to prison and 125 cases left pending. In the County Court 419 cases were pending on 1/1/82, 418 new cases were filed and 466 cases were disposed of during the year leaving 371 cases pending on 12/31/82. There were 718 criminal cases on the docket, 241 convictions, 55 persons committed to jail, and 257 cases left pending. **JAILS** One jail, capacity 13. **ATTORNEYS AT LAW** Six. **UTILITIES** 54% of the residents are connected to a public or privately owned water system and 33% are connected to a public sewer system. Natural gas is distributed to the county by Lone Star Gas Co., Division of Enserch. The average annual residential bill for natural gas in 1982 for the Lone Star distribution system was $405.91, an increase of 35% over 1981. Electricity is distributed to the county by Houston Co. Electric Coop., Inc. and Robertson Electric Coop., Inc. and is generated primarily by gas, coal and water. **TAXES** The county has ten units with taxing authority: five school districts, four cities and one county.

RECREATION/ENTERTAINMENT
NATIONAL REGISTER OF HISTORIC PLACES Centerville: Leon County Courthouse; Old Jail; 1918 Jail. **MUNICIPAL PARKS** 10 acres in one municipal park. **SCENIC DRIVES** The Texas Brazos Trail runs through this county. This trail moves through a beautiful and historic section of Central Texas revealing forested landscapes filled with wildlife and wild flowers. **BOATING/FISHING** Lakes/reservoirs: Bear Foot (85 acres), Bowie (30 acres), Cypress (163 acres), Duke (145 acres), Enderlin (136 acres), Frost #1 (161 acres), Frost #2 (97 acres), Frost #3 (86 acres), Josie (641 acres), Lovell #2 (139 acres), Maxwell (352 acres), Meche (110 acres), Pinoak (896 acres), Rusk (80 acres), Sam (20 acres) and Silver Bit (29 acres). Major rivers: Navasota and Trinity. Primary streams: North Fork Keechi, Buffalo, Boggy, Birch, Running, Right, Yellow, Upper Keechi and Beaver Dam. **HUNTING** Fall and winter seasons on deer. Summer, fall and winter seasons on squirrel. No closed seasons on coyote, bobcat and nutria. Winter seasons on quail, muskrat, beaver, otter, opossum, mink, ring-tailed cat, badger, fox, raccoon, skunk and civet cat. In 1983 duck, coot, geese, woodcock and jacksnipe seasons occurred during the winter months. Teal duck, rail and gallinule seasons occurred in the fall. Mourning dove seasons occurred intermittently during the fall and winter months. **SPECIAL EVENTS** Fourth of July Celebration, Centerville, July; Buffalo Stampede, Buffalo, September; Fall Frolics, Jewett, October.

COMMUNITIES
COUNTY SEAT Centerville, County Courthouse, 75833; County Clerk's Office, 214/536-2352. **INCORPORATED COMMUNITIES** (1980 population and ZIP Code) Buffalo (1,507) 75831, Centerville (799) 75833, Jewett (597) 75846, Leona (165) 75850, Marquez (231) 77865, Normangee (636: 580 in Leon Co. and 56 in Madison Co.) 77871 and Oakwood (606) 75855. **UNINCORPORATED COMMUNITIES** (and ZIP Code) Bear Grass (Evansville) 75846, Centerview 75833, Concord 77850, Corinth 75831, Davisville (Pleasant Springs) 75833, Flo 75831, Flynn 77855, Guys Store 75833, Hill Top Lakes 77871, Keechi 75831, Malvern 75854, Middleton 75833, Newby 75846, Nineveh 75831, Pleasant Ridge 75833, Redland 75833, Robbins 75846, Snow 77871, Spillers Store 75850, Spring Seat 75846, Vanetia 77865 and Wealthy 77871. **FOR ADDITIONAL LOCAL INFORMATION** Buffalo Chamber of Commerce, P.O. Box 207, Buffalo, 75831, 214/322-5636 or 322-5617, Centerville Chamber of Commerce, P.O. Box 97, Centerville, 75833, 214/536-2551, Jewett Area Chamber of Commerce, P.O. Box 220, Windmill Plaza, Jewett 75846, 214/626-4202, Normangee Chamber of Commerce, P.O. Box 265, Normangee, 77871, 409/396-2451 and Oakwood Chamber of Commerce, P.O. Box 96, Oakwood, 75855.

LIBERTY (G5)

THE LAND
Northeast of Houston on U.S. Highway 59 in the Coastal Prairie Region, Liberty County covers 1,174 square miles with an elevation range of 20 to 200 feet. In the southeast and along the Trinity River are undulating to rolling soils with very dark, loamy surfaces over gray, mottled, cracking, clayey subsoils. The northern part of the county has light colored, loamy surfaces over very deep, reddish clayey or loamy subsoils with hardened calcium deposits. The southwestern portion of the county has light to dark, loamy surfaces over clayey subsoils or gray to black, cracking, clayey soils with a high shrink-swell potential. The northern part of the county is in the Pineywoods vegetation area with loblolly, shortleaf, longleaf and slash pines and hardwoods such as oak, hickory and maple. There are occasional shrubs, Indiangrass and native legumes. The southern part is in the Gulf Prairies and Marshes vegetation area with tall prairie grasses, oak, mesquite and prickly pear. Between 41 and 50% of the land in the county is considered prime farmland. **CLIMATE** Subtropical Humid with warm summers. The average annual temperature is 68°F. Temperatures in January range from an average low of 39° to an average high of 62°F and in July range from 72° to 94°F. The average annual precipitation is 50 inches, with an average relative humidity of 88% at 6 A.M. and 67% at 6 P.M. There is no snowfall. The growing season averages 261 days per year, with the last freeze in early March and the first freeze in late November. The sun shines during the year on the average 68% of the daylight hours.

THE PEOPLE
The 1982 estimated population of 51,400 indicates a continuation of the strong growth pattern which began in the 1970s.

COUNTIES

LIBERTY (continued)

Rural areas grew twice as fast as urban areas between 1970 and 1980. The age groups with the largest gains were ages 20 to 39 and 65 and over. The county's median age rose from 29 in 1970 to 30 in 1980. The largest ancestry groups are persons of English descent (26%), Irish descent (22%), Black (14%) and French descent (12%). **REGISTERED VOTERS** As of November 2, 1982 there were 22,718 registered voters (0.4% of the state total). The 1982 general election had a 46% voter turnout, compared to a 64% turnout in the 1980 general election. In the 1982 primary 98% voted Democratic and 2% Republican, with 6,732 votes cast.

THE ECONOMY

AGRICULTURE Forest production area. In 1982, 52% of the land was in farms and ranches, with 36% of the farmland under cultivation and 34% irrigated. Liberty ranked 80th in the state in highest agricultural receipts, with 81% from crops. Inefficient irrigation systems, drainage and pest control are the current conservation problems. Primary crops: third in the state for soybeans and eighth for rice. Wheat and hay. Primary vegetables: watermelons. Primary fruits and nuts: peaches and pecans. Primary livestock and products: cattle. **BUSINESS** Total number of business establishments in the county: 954. Retail sales during the first quarter of 1984 increased 15%. In 1980, 9% of the labor force were self-employed, 16% were employed in professional or related services, 18% in manufacturing, 20% in wholesale and retail trade, 14% in construction, 36% were employed in other counties and there were 3,659 retired workers. The industries with the most employment: oil and gas extraction, the refining of sulphur, heavy construction and the manufacture of veneer and plywood, ready-mixed concrete, steel pipes, tubes and structural metal products. The nonfarm earnings in 1981 totaled $525,006,000. The retired workers received an average monthly Social Security payment of $325. **FINANCE** On June 30, 1983, seven commercial banks had total deposits of $298,727,000 and total assets of $334,399,000. On December 31, 1982 two state savings and loan associations, one federal association, one state branch and two federal branches had combined assets of $85,222,497. In addition there are two credit unions in the county. **HOUSING** Average value of homes in 1980: $31,100. Permits for new, privately owned housing units decreased in 1982: 563 permits were issued with a total construction cost of $24,602,832. Of those permits, 429 were for single family houses. Housing permits in Dayton increased from 13 in 1981 to 89 in 1982 with 64 of the permits issued for apartments and condominiums. Between 1970 and 1980 the number of housing units increased by 57%. Seventy-seven percent of all units in the county are air-conditioned, 72% are heated by gas and 22% by electricity. **NATURAL RESOURCES** Salt domes, sand and gravel, oil and gas. In 1982 a total of 6,250,400 thousand cubic feet of gas well gas, 80,921 barrels of condensate, 3,228,271 barrels of crude oil and 2,697,836 thousand cubic feet of casinghead gas were produced. Current production of other minerals and products includes construction sand, sand and gravel. Pine and hardwood production in 1981 totaled 14,488,840 cubic feet: 10,648,378 cubic feet of pine and 3,840,462 cubic feet of hardwood. **TOURISM** Travel expenditures of $10,299,000 in 1982 (an increase of 12% over 1981) generated 226 jobs and $1,889,000 in payroll. Lodging: eight hotels, motels and tourist courts. **ALCOHOLIC BEVERAGES** Packaged distilled spirits, beer, ale, malt liquor and wine are legal in parts of the county. **FEDERAL EXPENDITURES** The federal government had direct expenditures or obligations of $74,223,000 in the county during fiscal year 1983, including $1,977,000 by the U.S. Department of Defense. In addition, the federal government provided $7,750,000 in grant awards, paid $2,422,000 in salaries and wages, made direct payments to individuals of $57,424,000 including $44,468,000 in retirement and disability payments, awarded $295,000 in procurement contracts and spent $6,333,000 in other expenditures or obligations. The federal government also provided $384,000 in direct loans and $34,528,000 in guaranteed loans and insurance.

COMMUNICATION

Newspapers–Weekly: Cleveland Advocate and The Liberty Vindicator. Radio: KJCH-AM (Cleveland) and KPXE-AM (Liberty). Cable TV. Telephone companies: General Telephone, Continental Telephone, Southwestern Bell, Cameron Telephone and Eastex Telephone Coop. **TRANSPORTATION** Total public road mileage: 1,092. In 1982 there were 48,157 registered vehicles and 1,092 reported traffic accidents including 15 fatalities. Taxi cabs: one company in Cleveland and one in the city of Liberty. Intercity bus service is available. Motor freight: 24 local and intrastate carriers. Rail: The Sunset Limited provides passenger service on the Amtrak Route. Seven main lines carry freight through the county. Two of the lines carry annually 20 to 30 million tons of freight each and five carry 10 to 20 million each. Aircraft: 61 are registered in the county. Airports: Liberty Municipal Airport serves as a base for 22 aircraft and is a general utility airport with general aviaton service. Cleveland Municipal Airport serves as a base for 20 aircraft and is a basic utility airport with general aviation service. Waterborne commerce: The Trinity River Channel to Liberty had total freight traffic of 196,575 short tons in 1981.

COMMUNITY SERVICES

EDUCATION Seven school districts with 11 elementary, six middle, six high schools and one special education. The average daily attendance in 1981-82 was 10,252, with expenditures per pupil of $2,441 including 618 classroom teachers with an average annual salary of $17,477. Thirty-nine percent of the 648 high school graduates planned to attend college. In 1982-83, 82% of the students were White, 2% Hispanic, 16% Black, 0.1% Asian and 0.1% American Indian. Private schools: 117 students enrolled in one elementary and one high school. **PUBLIC LIBRARIES** Austin Memorial Library (Cleveland): 21,016 volumes. Dayton Library. Liberty Municipal Library: 24,109 volumes. **CHILD CARE** 35 day care and 15 twenty-four hour care licensed facilities. **HEALTH CARE** 23 physicians and 16 dentists. Hospitals: three with a combined capacity of 146. Ambulance services: three volunteer fire departments, three fire departments, three commercial, two county and one funeral home service. Mental health: two clinics. Nursing homes: four nursing homes with a combined capacity of 422 nursing care residents. The average cost per day for private patients in 1982 was $33.64. **CHURCHES** 91 churches have an estimated combined membership of 26,709. The largest denominations are Southern Baptist, Catholic and United Methodist. **SOCIAL SERVICES** In fiscal year 1983 a total of $2,776,691 in food stamps was distributed, with an average of 5,475 persons receiving food stamps each month. Aid to Families with Dependent Children (AFDC) totaled $574,817 with an average of 379 families receiving AFDC each month. Medical assistance benefits for the aged and disabled of $3,812,033 and for families and children of $797,211 brought the county benefit total to $7,960,751. **FIRE PROTECTION** One partly paid and 19 volunteer fire departments. **LAW ENFORCEMENT** The County Sheriff has 50 commissioned officers. Seven police departments have a combined force of 57. **CRIME** 328 violent crimes (murder, forcible rape, robbery and aggravated assault) and 1,603 nonviolent crimes (burglary, larceny-theft and motor vehicle theft) were reported in 1982. **JUDICIAL SYSTEM** Two District Courts and Judges, one County Court and Judge and seven Justices of the Peace. In the District Courts a total of 4,051 cases were pending on 1/1/82, 1,982 new cases were filed and

2,023 cases were disposed of during the year leaving 4,010 cases pending on 12/31/82. There were 1,388 criminal cases on the docket, 286 convictions, 62 persons committed to prison and four committed to jail and 541 cases left pending. In the County Court 4,209 cases were pending on 1/1/82, 2,093 new cases were filed and 1,239 cases were disposed of during the year leaving 5,063 cases pending on 12/31/82. There were 5,556 criminal cases on the docket, 595 convictions, one person committed to jail and 4,372 cases left pending. **JAILS** One jail, capacity 38, under renovation to increase capacity. **ATTORNEYS AT LAW** 49. **UTILITIES** 60% of the residents are connected to a public or privately owned water system and 41% are connected to a public sewer system. Natural gas is distributed to the county by Entex, Inc., Berry Gas Company, and Southwest Gas Distributors. The average annual residential bill for natural gas in 1982 for the Entex distribution system was $390.31, an increase of 26% over 1981. Electricity is distributed to the city of Liberty by the Liberty Municipal Electric System and to the rest of the county by Gulf State Utilities Co. and Sam Houston Electric Coop., Inc. and is generated primarily by gas, oil and coal. The typical residential electric bill is $198.32 per month for an all-electric house using 2,500 kwh. **TAXES** The county has 22 units with taxing authority: seven school districts, six cities, one county and eight special districts.

RECREATION/ENTERTAINMENT
FEDERAL Big Thicket National Preserve (See Hardin County). **NATIONAL REGISTER OF HISTORIC PLACES** Dayton vicinity: Site 41 LB4, historic Indian site. **MUNICIPAL PARKS** 199 acres in seven municipal parks. These parks contain five playgrounds, one football and soccer field, six baseball and softball fields, two multi-use fields and two swimming pools. **BOATING/FISHING** Major rivers: Trinity and East Fork San Jacinto. Primary streams: Mill, Davis Bayou, Menard, Cedar Bayou, Hickory Bayou, Josie Bayou, North Fork Long Island Bayou, Cow Island Bayou, Whites Bayou, Luce Bayou and Gaylor. **HUNTING** Fall and winter season on deer. Summer, fall and winter seasons on squirrel. No closed seasons on coyote, bobcat and nutria. Winter seasons on pheasant, quail, muskrat, beaver, otter, opossum, mink, ring-tailed cat, badger, fox, raccoon, skunk and civet cat. Special regulations apply on the Trinity River and Wallisville Reservoir. In 1983 duck, coot, geese, woodcock and jacksnipe seasons occurred during the winter months. Teal duck, rail and gallinule seasons occurred in the fall. Mourning dove seasons occurred intermittently during the fall and winter months. **MUSEUMS** Liberty: Geraldine D. Humphreys Museum and Sam Houston Regional Library and Research Center. **SPECIAL EVENTS** Mayhaw Festival, Hull-Daisetta, April/May; Trinity Valley Exposition and County Fair, Liberty, October; Santa Claus Parade, Liberty/Dayton, November/December.

COMMUNITIES
COUNTY SEAT Liberty, County Courthouse, 77575, County Clerk's Office, 409/336-6461. **INCORPORATED COMMUNITIES** (1980 population and ZIP Code) Ames (1,155) 77575, Cleveland (5,977) 77327, Daisetta (1,177) 77533, Dayton (4,908) 77535, Devers (507) 77538, Hardin (779) 77561, Kenefick (763) 77535, Liberty (7,945) 77575, North Cleveland (259) 77327 and Plum Grove (455) 77327. **UNINCORPORATED COMMUNITIES** (and ZIP Code) Clark 77327, Dolen 77327, Eastgate 77535, Hull 77564, Kevin 77327, King City 77327, La Cour 77575, Macedonia 77327, Moss Bluff 77575, Moss Hill 77575, Rayburn 77327, Raywood 77582, Romayor 77368, Rye 77369, Shiloh 77575, Stilson 77535 and Tarkington Prairie 77327. **FOR ADDITIONAL LOCAL INFORMATION** Greater Cleveland Chamber of Commerce, 222 S. Bonham Ave., Cleveland, 77327, 713/592-8786 and Liberty-Dayton Area Chamber of Commerce, 1915 Trinity, Liberty, 77575, 409/336-5736.

LIMESTONE (C10)

THE LAND
East of Waco on U.S. Highway 84 in the Blackland Prairies Region, Limestone County covers 931 square miles with an elevation range of 400 to 600 feet. The southeastern part of the county has level to undulating, light colored soils with sandy surfaces over mottled, clayey subsoils. The north central area has undulating, slightly acidic soils with dark, loamy surfaces and cracking, clayey subsoils or acidic gray to black, cracking, clayey soils. These soils have a high shrink-swell potential. The rest of the county has gray to black, cracking, clayey soils or light colored, loamy surfaces over very deep, reddish, cracking, clayey subsoils with a high shrink-swell potential. The northern part of the county is in the Blackland Prairies vegetation area with tall grasses, mesquite and oak, pecan and elm trees along streams. The southern part is in the Post Oak Savannah vegetation area with tall grasses, post oak and blackjack oak. Between 11 and 20% of the land in the county is considered prime farmland. **CLIMATE** Subtropical Humid with warm summers. The average annual temperature is 66°F. Temperatures in January range from an average low of 35° to an average high of 57°F and in July range from 72° to 96°F. The average annual precipitation is 38 inches, with an average relative humidity of 83% at 6 A.M. and 54% at 6 P.M. The average annual snowfall is one inch. The growing season averages 255 days per year, with the last freeze in mid March and the first freeze in late November. The sun shines during the year on the average 62% of the daylight hours.

THE PEOPLE
The population began growing in 1970 after 40 years of decline. The 1982 estimated population of 20,300 indicates a continuation of that growth. Although urban areas experienced a population increase of 76% between 1970 and 1980, rural areas decreased 20%. The county's population is older than average, with a median age of 37 in 1980. The largest ancestry groups are persons of English descent (25%), Black (23%) and Irish descent (20%). **REGISTERED VOTERS** As of November 2, 1982 there were 9,578 registered voters (0.1% of the state total). The 1982 general election had a 49% voter turnout, compared to a 59% turnout in the 1980 general election. In the 1982 primary 98% voted Democratic and 2% Republican, with 4,142 votes cast.

THE ECONOMY
AGRICULTURE Cattle area. In 1982, 85% of the land was in farms and ranches, with 24% of the farmland under cultivation and 2% irrigated. Limestone ranked 96th in the state in highest agricultural receipts, with 84% from livestock and livestock products. Overgrazing, undesirable brush and weeds, water erosion and flooding are the current conservation problems. Primary crops: Oats, wheat, hay and sorghum. Primary vegetables: watermelons. Primary fruits and nuts: seventh in the state for peaches. Pecans. Primary livestock and products: seventh in the state for beef cows that have calved and 10th for cattle. **BUSINESS** Total number of business establishments in the county: 338. Retail sales during the first quarter of 1984 increased 20%. In 1980, 12% of the labor force were self-employed, 35% were employed in professional or related services, 11% in manufacturing, 17% in wholesale and retail trade, 11% in agriculture, forestry, fisheries and mining, 16% were employed in other counties and there were 2,792 retired workers. The industries with the most employment: heavy construction, quarrying of industrial sand, textile mill, iron foundry, and the manufacture of women's blouses, structural metal products, motors and generators. The nonfarm earnings in 1981 totaled $147,306,000. The retired workers received an average monthly Social Security payment of $283. **FINANCE** On June 30, 1983, seven commercial banks had total deposits

COUNTIES

of $115,832,000 and total assets of $129,266,000. On December 31, 1982 one state savings and loan association, one state branch had assets of $84,510,468. In addition there are three credit unions in the county. **HOUSING** Average value of homes in 1980: $19,200. Permits for new, privately owned housing units increased in 1982: 62 permits were issued with a total construction cost of $2,329,893. Of those permits, 38 were for single family houses. Housing permits in Groesbeck increased from 12 in 1981 to 36 in 1982 with 24 of the permits issued for apartments and condomniums. Between 1970 and 1980 the number of housing units increased by 30%. Sixty-five percent of all units in the county are air-conditioned, 82% are heated by gas and 14% by electricity. **NATURAL RESOURCES** Kaolin clay, ceramic clay, clay, limestone, industrial sand, glauconite, lignite coal, oil and gas. In 1982 a total of 19,383,471 thousand cubic feet of gas well gas, 55,754 barrels of condensate, 168,465 barrels of crude oil and 8,448 thousand cubic feet of casinghead gas were produced. Current production of other minerals and products includes kaolin clay, clay, crushed limestone and industrial sand. **TOURISM** Travel expenditures of $4,866,000 in 1982 (an increase of 12% over 1981) generated 114 jobs and $933,000 in payroll. **ALCOHOLIC BEVERAGES** Beer, ale, malt liquor and wine not exceeding 14% alcoholic content are legal. **FEDERAL EXPENDITURES** The federal government had direct expenditures or obligations of $41,659,000 in the county during fiscal year 1983, including $899,000 by the U.S. Department of Defense. In addition, the federal government provided $411,000 in grant awards, paid $1,412,000 in salaries and wages, made direct payments to individuals of $39,270,000 including $27,247,000 in retirement and disability payments, awarded $8,000 in procurement contracts and spent $557,000 in other expenditures or obligations. The federal government also provided $260,000 in direct loans and $6,622,000 in guaranteed loans and insurance.

COMMUNICATION

Newspapers–Daily: Mexia Daily News, ave. eve. circ. 4,052. Weekly: The Groesbeck Journal. Radio: KBUS-AM (Mexia). Cable TV. Telephone companies: General Telephone, Continental Telephone, Southwestern Bell, United Telephone and Peeples Telephone. **TRANSPORTATION** Total public road mileage: 1,320. In 1982 there were 15,292 registered vehicles and 437 reported traffic accidents including 10 fatalities. Taxi cabs: two companies in Mexia. Intercity bus service is available. Motor freight: five local and intrastate carriers. Rail: three main lines carry annually over 30 million tons of freight each through the county. Aircraft: 16 are registered in the county. Airports: Limestone County Airport at Mexia serves as a base for 14 aircraft and is a general utility airport with general aviation service.

COMMUNITY SERVICES

EDUCATION Three school districts with three elementary, two middle and three high schools. The average daily attendance in 1981-82 was 3,048, with expenditures per pupil of $2,039 including 194 classroom teachers with an average annual salary of $15,909. Thirty-six percent of the 214 high school graduates planned to attend college. In 1982-83, 63% of the students were White, 5% Hispanic, 32% Black and 0.2% Asian. **PUBLIC LIBRARIES** Maffett Memorial Library (Groesbeck): 21,000 volumes. Gibbs Memorial Library (Mexia): 26,702 volumes. **CHILD CARE** 31 day care and eight twenty-four hour care licensed facilities. **HEALTH CARE** 20 physicians and six dentists. Hospitals: two with a combined capacity of 115. Clinics: two outpatient clinics. Ambulance services: one fire department, one commercial and one funeral home service. Mental health: one county clinic and one state school with a capacity of 1,215. Nursing homes: four

nursing homes with a combined capacity of 284 nursing care residents. The average cost per day for private patients in 1982 was $36.74. **CHURCHES** 52 churches have an estimated combined membership of 10,756. The largest denominations are Southern Baptist, United Methodist and Churches of Christ. **SOCIAL SERVICES** In fiscal year 1983 a total of $827,927 in food stamps was distributed, with an average of 1,887 persons receiving food stamps each month. Aid to Families with Dependent Children (AFDC) totaled $232,756 with an average of 154 families receiving AFDC each month. Medical assistance benefits for the aged and disabled of $2,718,835 and for families and children of $325,248 brought the county benefit total to $4,104,765. **FIRE PROTECTION** One partly paid and four volunteer fire departments. **LAW ENFORCEMENT** The County Sheriff has 21 commissioned officers. Five police departments have a combined force of 33. **CRIME** 80 violent crimes (murder, forcible rape, robbery and aggravated assault) and 595 nonviolent crimes (burglary, larceny-theft and motor vehicle theft) were reported in 1982. **JUDICIAL SYSTEM** Two District Courts and Judges, one County Court and Judge and four Justices of the Peace. In the District Courts a total of 947 cases were pending on 1/1/82, 690 new cases were filed and 586 cases were disposed of during the year leaving 1,051 cases pending on 12/31/82. There were 266 criminal cases on the docket, 82 convictions, 26 persons committed to prison and 112 cases left pending. In the County Court 1,457 cases were pending on 1/1/82, 448 new cases were filed and 727 cases were disposed of during the year leaving 1,178 cases pending on 12/31/82. There were 1,721 criminal cases on the docket, 143 convictions, 34 persons committed to jail, and 1,013 cases left pending. **JAILS** One jail, capacity 23. Completed major renovation in 1983. **ATTORNEYS AT LAW** 19. **UTILITIES** 83% of the residents are connected to a public or privately owned water system and 62% are connected to a public sewer system. Natural gas is distributed to the county by Lone Star Gas Co., Division of Enserch. The average annual residential bill for natural gas in 1982 for the Lone Star distribution system was $405.91, an increase of 35% over 1981. Electricity is distributed to the county by Southwestern Electric Power Co., Central Power and Light, Cochran Power and Light, Texas Power and Light Co., Limestone Co. Electric Coop. Inc., Navarro Co. Electric Coop., Inc. and Robertson Electric Coop., Inc. and is generated primarily by gas, oil and coal. The typical residential electric bill is $155.87 per month for an all-electric house using 2,500 kwh. **TAXES** The county has 12 units with taxing authority: three school districts, six cities, one county, one hospital district and one special district.

RECREATION/ENTERTAINMENT

NATIONAL REGISTER OF HISTORIC PLACES Mexia vicinity: Joseph E. Johnston Reunion Grounds, Camp No. 94 United Confederate Veterans. Tehuacana: Texas Hall at Old Trinity University Campus and Booker T. Washington Emancipation Proclamation Park. **STATE** Confederate Reunion State Historic Park covers 73 acres. Fort Parker State Recreation Area covers 1,485 acres with camping and trailer sites as well as areas offering fishing, swimming, boat ramps, golf and boat rentals. Old Fort Parker State Historic Site covers 11 acres with a museum and a historic structure. The fort was established in 1834 by the Parker family to protect a settlement of families. **MUNICIPAL PARKS** 58 acres in five municipal parks. These parks contain two playgrounds, one football and soccer field, seven baseball and softball fields, six tennis courts and two swimming pools. **SCENIC DRIVES** The Texas Brazos Trail runs through this county. This trail moves through a beautiful and historic section of Central Texas revealing forested landscapes filled with wildlife and wild flowers. **BOATING/FISHING** Lakes/reservoirs: Browns (34 acres), Duke (20 acres), Fort Parker State

Park (121 acres), Groesbeck (129 acres), Kennedy (27 acres), Limestone (8,770 acres), Mexia (1,220 acres), Oak Knoll (2,217 acres), Richland Creek Soil Conservation Service Lakes 7, 10 and 20 (114 acres) and Tehuacana Creek Soil Conservation Service Lake 19 (11 acres). Major rivers: Navasota. Primary streams: Chambers, Sand, Big, Steele, Munger, Elm and Williams. **HUNTING** Fall and winter seasons on deer. Summer, fall and winter seasons on squirrel. No closed season on coyote, bobcat and nutria. Winter seasons on quail, muskrat, beaver, otter, opossum, mink, ring-tailed cat, badger, fox, raccoon, skunk and civet cat. In 1983 duck, coot, geese, woodcock and jacksnipe seasons occurred during the winter months. Teal duck, rail and gallinule seasons occurred in the fall. Mourning dove seasons occurred intermittently during the fall and winter months. **MUSEUMS** Groesbeck: Old Fort Parker State Park and Limestone County Historical Museum. **SPECIAL EVENTS** Youth Stock Show, Groesbeck, April; Red Stocking Follies, Groesbeck, March; Arts and Crafts Fest, Groesbeck, March; Fiddle Festival, Groesbeck, May; County Fair, Groesbeck, Variable.

COMMUNITIES

COUNTY SEAT Groesbeck, County Courthouse, 76642; County Clerk's Office, 817/729-5504. **INCORPORATED COMMUNITIES** (1980 population and ZIP Code) Coolidge (810) 76635, Groesbeck (3,373) 76642, Kosse (484) 76653, Mexia (7,094) 76667, Tehuacana (265) 76686 and Thornton (498) 76687. **UNINCORPORATED COMMUNITIES** (and ZIP Code) Ben Hur 76664, Bighill (Big Hill) 76687, Billington 76624, Box Church 76642, Center 76642, Coit 76653, Davis Prairie 76687, Delia 76673, Doule (Doyle) 76642, Echols 76635, Fairoaks (Fair Oaks) 75838, Fallon 76667, Farrar 75838, Forest Glade 76667, Frosa 76678, Horn Hill 76642, Kirk 76664, Mustang 76635, Odds 76687, Old Union 76687, Oletha 76687, Personville 76642, Point Enterprise 76667, Prairie Grove 76667, Prairie Hill 76678, Shiloh 76667, Springfield 76667, Thelma 76642, Victoria 76664 and Watt 76664. **FOR ADDITIONAL LOCAL INFORMATION** Groesbeck Chamber of Commerce, 112½ N. Ellis, P.O. Box 326, Groesbeck, 76642, 817/729-3894 and Mexia Area Chamber of Commerce, 315 N. Sherman, Drawer 352, Mexia, 76667, 817/562-3761.

LIPSCOMB (P5)

THE LAND

In the Texas Panhandle bordering Oklahoma and northeast of Amarillo on U.S. Highway 60 in the Rolling Plains Region, Lipscomb County covers 933 square miles with an elevation range of 2,250 to 2,850 feet. The county has nearly level soils with light to very dark, loamy surfaces over clayey subsoils with hardened calcium deposits. Lipscomb is in the Rolling Plains vegetation area with tall and mid grasses, shinnery oak, mesquite and sandsage. Between 21 and 30% of the land in the county is considered prime farmland. **CLIMATE** Continental Steppe and generally dry. One of the coolest counties in the state with an average annual temperature of 57°F. Temperatures in January range from an average low of 20° to an average high of 47°F and in July range from 67° to 94°F. The average annual precipitation is 20 inches, with an average relative humidity of 73% at 6 A.M. and 43% at 6 P.M. The average annual snowfall is 15 inches. The growing season averages 202 days per year, with the last freeze in late October and the first freeze in early April. The sun shines during the year on the average 73% of the daylight hours.

THE PEOPLE

The majority of Lipscomb county residents live in rural areas. The 1982 estimated population of 4,300 continues the moderate growth in population which began in the 1960s. The population's median age lowered from 35 in 1970 to 31 in 1980. Lipscomb County has a low percentage of residents who are native Texans. The largest ancestry groups are persons of German descent (34%), English descent (33%) and Irish descent (18%). **REGISTERED VOTERS** As of November 2, 1982 there were 2,254 registered voters (0.03% of the state total). The 1982 general election had a 51% voter turnout, compared to a 77% turnout in the 1980 general election. In the 1982 primary 100% voted Democratic, with 1,005 votes cast.

THE ECONOMY

AGRICULTURE Wheat area. In 1982, 98% of the land was in farms and ranches, with 25% of the farmland under cultivation and 18% irrigated. Lipscomb ranked 170th in the state in highest agricultural receipts, with 53% from livestock and livestock products. Overgrazing, undesirable brush, noxious weeds, water erosion and the cultivation of marginal lands are the current conservation problems. Primary crops: wheat, hay, sorghum and oats. Primary livestock and products: cattle and hogs. **BUSINESS** Total number of business establishments in the county: 105. In 1980, 23% of the labor force were self-employed, 16% were employed in professional or related services, 6% in manufacturing, 22% in wholesale and retail trade, 29% in agriculture, forestry, fisheries and mining, 22% were employed in other counties and there were 323 retired workers. The industries with the most employment: oil and gas extraction and agribusiness. The nonfarm earnings in 1981 totaled $39,335,000. The retired workers received an average monthly Social Security payment of $307. **FINANCE** On June 30, 1983, four commercial banks had total deposits of $124,715,000 and total assets of $143,841,000. **HOUSING** Average value of homes in 1980: $27,800. Permits for new, privately owned housing units increased in 1982: 49 permits were issued with a total construction cost of $1,910,000. Of those permits, 17 were for single family houses. Between 1970 and 1980 the number of housing units increased by 12%. Eighty-five percent of all units in the county are air-conditioned, 88% are heated by gas and 10% by electricity. **NATURAL RESOURCES** Caliche, sand, gravel, oil and gas. In 1982 a total of 60,970,151 thousand cubic feet of gas well gas, 394,060 barrels of condensate, 1,549,499 barrels of crude oil and 7,727,089 thousand cubic feet of casinghead gas were produced. Current production of other minerals and products includes caliche, sand and gravel. **TOURISM** Travel expenditures of $3,693,000 in 1982 (an increase of 11% over 1981) generated 94 jobs and $744,000 in payroll. **ALCOHOLIC BEVERAGES** Packaged distilled spirits, beer, ale, malt liquor and wine are legal in parts of the county. **FEDERAL EXPENDITURES** The federal government had direct expenditures or obligations of $7,048,000 in the county during fiscal year 1983, including $86,000 by the U.S. Department of Defense. In addition, the federal government provided $93,000 in grant awards, paid $400,000 in salaries and wages, made direct payments to individuals of $4,582,000 including $3,019,000 in retirement and disability payments, awarded $2,000 in procurement contracts and spent $1,971,000 in other expenditures or obligations. The federal government also provided $4,145,000 in direct loans and $1,335,000 in guaranteed loans and insurance.

COMMUNICATION

Newspapers–Weekly: The Booker News and The Lipscomb County Limelight (Follett). Cable TV. Telephone companies: General Telephone and Southwestern Bell. **TRANSPORTATION** Total public road mileage: 643. In 1982 there were 5,110 registered vehicles and 61 reported traffic accidents. Motor freight: three carriers. Rail: one main and one branch line carry freight through the county. The main line carries annually over 30 million tons of freight and the branch carries less than one million. Aircraft: 40 are registered in the county. Airports: Lipscomb County

COUNTIES

LIPSCOMB (continued)

Airport at Follett, Lipscomb County Airport at Higgins and Mitchell Field at Booker.

COMMUNITY SERVICES

EDUCATION Four school districts with four elementary, one middle and four high schools. The average daily attendance in 1981-82 was 776, with expenditures per pupil of $7,574 including 79 classroom teachers with an average annual salary of $17,812. Seventy-three percent of the 49 high school graduates planned to attend college. In 1982-83, 87% of the students were White, 12% Hispanic, 0.1% Asian and 0.7% American Indian. **PUBLIC LIBRARIES** Higgins Public Library: 5,102 volumes. **CHILD CARE** Seven day care licensed facilities. **HEALTH CARE** One physician and one dentist. Ambulance services: two volunteer services and two volunteer fire department services. **CHURCHES** 18 churches have an estimated combined membership of 2,747. The largest denominations are United Methodist and Southern Baptist. **SOCIAL SERVICES** In fiscal year 1983 a total of $23,445 in food stamps was distributed, with an average of 54 persons receiving food stamps each month. Aid to Families with Dependent Children (AFDC) totaled $1,681. Medical assistance benefits for the aged and disabled of $47,653 and for families and children of $2,604 brought the county benefit total to $75,383. **FIRE PROTECTION** Five volunteer fire departments. **LAW ENFORCEMENT** The County Sheriff has seven commissioned officers. One police department has one officer. **CRIME** Two violent crimes (murder, forcible rape, robbery and aggravated assault) and 55 nonviolent crimes (burglary, larceny-theft and motor vehicle theft) were reported in 1982. **JUDICIAL SYSTEM** One District Court and Judge, one County Court and Judge and four Justices of the Peace. In the District Court a total of 132 cases were pending on 1/1/82, 106 new cases were filed and 76 cases were disposed of during the year leaving 162 cases pending on 12/31/82. There were 18 criminal cases on the docket, six convictions and 12 cases left pending. In the County Court 108 cases were pending on 1/1/82, 92 new cases were filed and 105 cases were disposed of during the year leaving 95 cases pending on 12/31/82. There were 178 criminal cases on the docket, 27 convictions, five persons committed to jail and 84 cases left pending. **JAILS** One jail, capacity 13. Major renovation completed in 1983. **ATTORNEYS AT LAW** Six. **UTILITIES** 81% of the residents are connected to a public or privately owned water system and 76% are connected to a public sewer system. Natural gas is distributed to the county by Consolidated Utilities, Inc. and High Plains Natural Gas Co. Electricity is distributed to the county by North Plains Electric Coop., Inc. and is generated primarily by gas and coal. **TAXES** The county has 15 units with taxing authority: four school districts, four cities, one county, five hospital districts and one special district.

RECREATION/ENTERTAINMENT

MUNICIPAL PARKS 35 acres in seven municipal parks. These parks contain five playgrounds, five baseball and softball fields and two tennis courts. **BOATING/FISHING** Primary streams: Kiowa, Mammoth, Skunk, Camp, Plum, Sand, Dugout, First, Second, Third, Fourth, Fifth and Wolf. **HUNTING** Fall seasons on antelope and prairie chicken. Fall and winter seasons on deer. Summer, fall and winter seasons on squirrel. No closed season on coyote and bobcat. Winter seasons on pheasant, quail, muskrat, beaver, opossum, ring-tailed cat, badger, fox, weasel, raccoon, skunk and civet cat. Fall, winter and spring seasons on turkey. In 1983 sandhill crane, duck, coot, geese, woodcock and jacksnipe seasons occurred during the winter months. Teal duck, rail and gallinule seasons occurred in the fall. Mourning dove seasons occurred intermittently during the fall and winter

months. **SPECIAL EVENTS** Deutches Fest, Darrouzett, July; Will Rogers Day, Higgins, August.

COMMUNITIES

COUNTY SEAT Lipscomb, County Courthouse, 79056; County Clerk's Office, 806/862-3091. **INCORPORATED COMMUNITIES** (1980 population and ZIP Code) Booker (1,219: 1,201 in Lipscomb Co. and 18 in Ochiltree Co.) 79005, Darrouzett (444) 79024, Follett (547) 79034 and Higgins (702) 79046. **UNINCORPORATED COMMUNITIES** (and ZIP Code) Lipscomb 79056.

LIVE OAK (G25)

THE LAND

Northwest of Corpus Christi on Interstate Highway 37 in the Rio Grande Plain Region, Live Oak County covers 1,057 square miles with an elevation of 70 to 400 feet. The eastern part of the county has light and dark soils with loamy surfaces over cracking, clayey subsoils. The northwestern part of the county has light colored soils with limestone within 40 inches of the surface, or gray to black clayey soils that have a high shrink-swell potential. The rest of the county has light to dark loamy surfaces over reddish, clayey subsoils with limestone within 40 inches of the surface, or gray to black, cracking, clayey soils with a high shrink-swell potential. Live Oak is in the South Texas Plains vegetation area with grasslands, post oak, blackbrush, small live oak, prickly pear and mesquite. Between 41 and 50% of the land in the county is considered prime farmland. **CLIMATE** Subtropical Subhumid with hot summers. June through October tropical storms and hurricanes are possible. The average annual temperature is 71 °F. Temperatures in January range from an average low of 42 ° to an average high of 66 °F and in July range from 73 ° to 96 °F. The average annual precipitation is 28 inches, with an average relative humdity of 88% at 6 A.M. and 55% at 6 P.M. There is no snowfall. The growing season averages 289 days per year, with the last freeze in late February and the first freeze in early December. The sun shines during the year on the average 66% of the daylight hours.

PEOPLE

The population of Live Oak County began growing in the 1970s after 30 years of decline. The 1982 estimated population of 9,900 indicates a continuation of that growth. The age groups with the largest increases between 1970 and 1980 were ages 20 to 29 and 65 and over. The largest ancestry groups are Hispanic (32%), persons of Irish descent (24%) and English descent (22%). **REGISTERED VOTERS** As of November 2, 1982 there were 6,009 registered voters (0.1% of the state total). The 1982 general election had a 40% voter turnout, compared to a 55% turnout in the 1980 general election. In the 1982 primary 96% voted Democratic and 4% Republican, with 1,885 votes cast.

THE ECONOMY

AGRICULTURE In 1982, 86% of the land was in farms and ranches, with 15% of the farmland under cultivation and 3% irrigated. Live Oak ranked 138th in the state in highest agricultural receipts, with 77% from livestock and livestock products. Undesirable brush, weeds and water erosion are the current conservation problems. Primary crops: corn, hay, sorghum and wheat. Primary vegetables: watermelons. Primary fruits and nuts: peaches and pecans. Primary livestock and products: cattle and hogs. **BUSINESS** Total number of business establishments in the county: 197. Retail sales during the first quarter of 1984 increased 24%. In 1980, 15% of the labor force were self-employed, 11% were employed in professional or related services, 8% in manufacturing, 21% in wholesale and retail trade,

29% in agriculture, forestry, fisheries and mining, 28% were employed in other counties and there were 674 retired workers. The industries with the most employment: gas and oil extraction, petroleum refining, agribusiness and construction. The non-farm earnings in 1981 totaled $81,355,000. The retired workers received an average monthly Social Security payment of $294. **FINANCE** On June 30, 1983, two commercial banks had total deposits of $72,511,000 and total assets of $82,415,000. There are two state savings and loan association branches and one credit union in the county. **HOUSING** Average value of homes in 1980: $27,700. Permits for new, privately owned housing units increased in 1982: 25 permits were issued with a total construction cost of $1,390,300. Of those permits, all were for single family houses. Between 1970 and 1980 the number of housing units increased by 59%. Sixty-seven percent of all units in the county are air-conditioned, 77% are heated by gas and 18% by electricity. **NATURAL RESOURCES** Caliche, clay, sand and gravel, uranium, oil and gas. In 1982 a total of 83,877,663 thousand cubic feet of gas well gas, 1,659,362 barrels of condensate, 778,381 barrels of crude oil and 999,477 thousand cubic feet of casinghead gas were produced. Current production of other minerals and products includes abrasives, caliche, construction sand, sand and gravel and crushed sandstone. **TOURISM** Travel expenditures of $3,771,000 in 1982 (an increase of 11% over 1981) generated 94 jobs and $750,000 in payroll. **ALCOHOLIC BEVERAGES** Packaged distilled spirits, beer, ale, malt liquor and wine are legal in parts of the county. **FEDERAL EXPENDITURES** The federal government had direct expenditures or obligations of $16,831,000 in the county during fiscal year 1983, including $433,000 by the U.S. Department of Defense. In addition, the federal government provided $725,000 in grant awards, paid $1,013,000 in salaries and wages, made direct payments to individuals of $10,550,000 including $7,912,000 in retirement and disability payments, awarded $3,508,000 in procurement contracts and spent $1,035,000 in other expenditures or obligations. The federal government also provided $202,000 in direct loans and $9,406,000 in guaranteed loans and insurance.

COMMUNICATION

Newspapers–Weekly: The Progress (George West). Cable TV. Telephone companies: General Telephone, Southwestern Bell and Valley Telephone Coop. **TRANSPORTATION** Total public road mileage: 785. In 1982 there were 9,394 registered vehicles and 298 reported traffic accidents including nine fatalities. Intercity bus service is available. Motor freight: three carriers. Rail: one main line carries annually one to five million tons of freight through the county. Aircraft: eight are registered in the county. Airports: Live Oak County Airport at George West.

COMMUNITY SERVICES

EDUCATION Two school districts with three elementary, two middle and two high schools. The average daily attendance in 1981-82 was 1,771, with expenditures per pupil of $3,005 including 114 classroom teachers with an average annual salary of $16,605. Fifty-two percent of the 122 high school graduates planned to attend college. In 1982-83, 58% of the students were White, 42% Hispanic and 0.2% Asian. Sports championships: 1983 AA Girls' Golf Singles, Three Rivers H.S. **PUBLIC LIBRARIES** Live Oak County Library (George West): 53,708 volumes. **CHILD CARE** 16 day care and one twenty-four hour care licensed facilities. **HEALTH CARE** Three physicians and one dentist. Clinics: one public health clinic. Ambulance services: two commercial services. Nursing homes: one nursing home has a capacity of 51 nursing care residents. The average cost per day for private patients in 1982 was $25.55. **CHURCHES** 24 churches have an estimated combined membership of 5,019. The largest denominations are Catholic and Southern Baptist. **SOCIAL SERVICES**

In fiscal year 1983 a total of $400,494 in food stamps was distributed, with an average of 866 persons receiving food stamps each month. Aid to Families with Dependent Children (AFDC) totaled $61,885 with an average of 43 families receiving AFDC each month. Medical assistance benefits for the aged and disabled of $601,977 and for families and children of $82,585 brought the county benefit total to $1,146,941. **FIRE PROTECTION** Four volunteer fire departments. **LAW ENFORCEMENT** The County Sheriff has 40 commissioned officers. Two police departments have a combined force of three. **CRIME** 13 violent crimes (murder, forcible rape, robbery and aggravated assault) and 260 nonviolent crimes (burglary, larceny-theft and motor vehicle theft) were reported in 1982. **JUDICIAL SYSTEM** Two District Courts and Judges, one County Court and Judge and four Justices of the Peace. In the District Courts a total of 313 cases were pending on 1/1/82, 289 new cases were filed and 322 cases were disposed of during the year leaving 280 cases pending on 12/31/82. There were 121 criminal cases on the docket, 47 convictions, 15 persons committed to prison and three committed to jail and 46 cases left pending. In the County Court 330 cases were pending on 1/1/82, 492 new cases were filed and 511 cases were disposed of during the year leaving 311 cases pending on 12/31/82. There were 778 criminal cases on the docket, 84 convictions, 27 persons committed to jail, and 272 cases left pending. **JAILS** One jail, capacity 25. **ATTORNEYS AT LAW** Seven. **UTILITIES** 51% of the residents are connected to a public or privately owned water system and 35% are connected to a public sewer system. Electricity is distributed to the county by Cochran Power and Light Co. and Karnes Electric Coop., Inc. and is generated primarily by gas and oil. **TAXES** The county has five units with taxing authority: two school districts, two cities and one county.

RECREATION/ENTERTAINMENT

STATE Lake Corpus Christi State Recreation Area (See San Patricio County). Tips State Recreation Area covers 31 acres with fishing facilities. **MUNICIPAL PARKS** 31 acres in one municipal park. Developed campsites: 17. **BOATING/FISHING** Lakes/reservoirs: Choke Canyon (16,509 acres), Corpus Christi (19,336 acres), Harris (51 acres), Lagarto (32 acres), Raschke (32 acres), Susquehanna Western (30 acres) and Three Rivers (47 acres). Major rivers: Frio, Nueces and Atascosa. Primary streams: Willow Hollow, Sulphur, Ramirena and Lagarto. **WILDLIFE REFUGES** James A. Daughtrey State Wildlife Management Area covers approximately 5,000 acres in this county. **HUNTING** Fall and winter seasons on deer. No closed season on coyote, bobcat, javelina and squirrel. Winter seasons on quail, muskrat, beaver, opossum, ring-tailed cat, badger, fox, weasel, raccoon, skunk and civet cat. Fall, winter and spring seasons on turkey. Special regulations on all state-owned river beds of the Nueces. In 1983 sandhill crane, duck, coot, geese, woodcock and jacksnipe seasons occurred during the winter months. Teal duck, rail and gallinule seasons occurred in the fall. Mourning dove seasons occurred intermittently during the fall and winter months with a fall season on white-winged dove. **MUSEUMS** George West: Cactus Park Museum and Live Oak County Museum. **SPECIAL EVENTS** County Fair, Three Rivers, March; County Fair, George West, April; Fiddlers Contest and Barbecue, George West, May.

COMMUNITIES

COUNTY SEAT George West, County Courthouse, 78022; County Clerk's Office, 512/449-1642. **INCORPORATED COMMUNITIES** (1980 population and ZIP Code) George West (2,627) 78022 and Three Rivers (2,133) 78071. **UNINCORPORATED COMMUNITIES** (and ZIP Code) Annarose 78022, Argenta 78368, Clegg 78022, Dinero 78350, Esseville 78075, Mount Lucas 78350, Nell 78119, Oakville 78060, Pernitas Point

COUNTIES

LIVE OAK (continued)

(also in Jim Wells Co.) 78383, Ray Point 78071, Simmons 78071, Sunniland 78071, Sweeny Switch 78368 and Whitsett 78075. **FOR ADDITIONAL LOCAL INFORMATION** George West Chamber of Commerce, Drawer F, George West, 78022, 512/449-1556 and Three Rivers Chamber of Commerce, P.O. Box 781, Three Rivers, 78071, 512/786-2591.

LLANO (C14)

THE LAND
Northwest of Austin on State Highway 29 in the Central Basin Region, Llano County covers 939 square miles with an elevation range of 1,100 to 1,800 feet. Along the northern border are undulating to hilly soils with very dark, loamy soils. The rest of the county has undulating to rolling soils with loamy surfaces over clayey subsoils, shallow soils over limestone, or deep loamy soils over sandstone. Llano is in the Edwards Plateau vegetation area with tall and mid grasses, live oak, shinnery oak, junipers and mesquite. Between one and 10% of the land in the county is considered prime farmland. **CLIMATE** Subtropical Subhumid with hot, dry summers. The average annual temperature is 66°F. Temperatures in January range from an average low of 32° to an average high of 60°F and in July range from 72° to 97°F. The average annual precipitation is 27 inches, with an average relative humidity of 83% at 6 A.M. and 48% at 6 P.M. The average annual snowfall is one inch. The growing season averages 229 days per year, with the last freeze in late March and the first freeze in mid November. The sun shines during the year on the average 66% of the daylight hours.

THE PEOPLE
Llano County ranks second among all U.S. counties in the highest percent of persons over age 64. The 1982 estimated population of 10,600 continues the high growth rate which began in the 1960s and reversed a steady population decrease. Between 1970 and 1980 rural areas grew at a high rate while urban areas experienced moderate growth. The age groups with the largest gains were 20 to 34 and 65 and over which increased 82%. The median age (the highest in the state) rose from 51 in 1970 to 56 in 1980. The largest ancestry groups are persons of English descent (35%), Irish descent (29%) and German descent (24%). **REGISTERED VOTERS** As of November 2, 1982 there were 6,553 registered voters (0.1% of the state total). The 1982 general election had a 67% voter turnout, compared to a 76% turnout in the 1980 general election. In the 1982 primary 87% voted Democratic and 13% Republican, with 2,763 votes cast.

THE ECONOMY
AGRICULTURE In 1982, 93% of the land was in farms and ranches, with 1% of the farmland under cultivation some of which was irrigated. Llano ranked 179th in the state in highest agricultural receipts, with 96% from livestock and livestock products. Overgrazing, undesirable brush and weeds and water erosion are the current conservation problems. Primary crops: hay and oats. Primary vegetables: potatoes, sweet potatoes and watermelons. Primary fruits and nuts: peaches and pecans. Primary livestock and products: fifth in the state for hogs. Cattle, sheep, wool, angora goats and mohair. **BUSINESS** Total number of business establishments in the county: 216. Retail sales during the first quarter of 1984 increased 23%. In 1980, 24% of the labor force were self-employed, 18% were employed in professional or related services, 6% in manufacturing, 25% in wholesale and retail trade, 12% in agriculture, forestry, fisheries and mining, 22% were employed in other counties and there were

2,378 retired workers. The industries with the most employment: tourism and heavy construction. The nonfarm earnings in 1981 totaled $99,000,000. The retired workers received an average monthly Social Security payment of $317. **FINANCE** On June 30, 1983, four commercial banks had total deposits of $121,742,000 and total assets of $139,264,000. On December 31, 1982 one state savings and loan association and four state branches had assets of $84,500,537. **HOUSING** Average value of homes in 1980: $38,400. Permits for new, privately owned housing units increased in 1982: nine permits were issued with a total construction cost of $564,284. Of those permits, all were for single family houses. Between 1970 and 1980 the number of housing units increased by 58%. Eighty-four percent of all units in the county are air-conditioned, 53% are heated by gas and 39% by electricity. **NATURAL RESOURCES** Bismuth, copper, dolomite, gold, granite, graphite, iron, limestone, magnesite, manganese, molybdenum, industrial sand, sand and gravel, serpentine, silver, talc, tungsten, vanadium, vermiculite, glauconite, feldspar, oil and gas. Current production includes dimension granite, riprap granite, graphite, crushed limestone, terrazzo marble and terrazzo serpentine. **TOURISM** Travel expenditures of $12,444,000 in 1982 (an increase of 13% over 1981) generated 263 jobs and $2,257,000 in payroll. **ALCOHOLIC BEVERAGES** Packaged distilled spirits, beer, ale, malt liquor and wine are legal in parts of the county. Sale of mixed beverages is legal in all or parts of the county. **FEDERAL EXPENDITURES** The federal government had direct expenditures or obligations of $32,833,000 in the county during fiscal year 1983, including $2,875,000 by the U.S. Department of Defense. In addition, the federal government provided $90,000 in grant awards, paid $741,000 in salaries and wages, made direct payments to individuals of $31,797,000 including $26,644,000 in retirement and disability payments, awarded $3,000 in procurement contracts and spent $202,000 in other expenditures or obligations. The federal government also provided $1,850,000 in guaranteed loans and insurance.

COMMUNICATION
Newspapers–Weekly: The Llano News. Telephone companies: General Telephone, Continental Telephone, Central Texas Telephone Coop. and Hill Country Telephone Coop. **TRANSPORTATION** Total public road mileage: 778. In 1982 there were 11,557 registered vehicles and 235 reported traffic accidents including five fatalities. Motor freight: three carriers. Rail: one branch line carries annually one to five million tons of freight through the county. Aircraft: 25 are registered in the county. Airports: Llano Municipal Airport, Estates Airport and Shirley Williams Airport at Kingsland.

COMMUNITY SERVICES
EDUCATION One school district with one elementary, one middle and one high school. The average daily attendance in 1981-82 was 934, with expenditures per pupil of $2,301 including 53 classroom teachers with an average annual salary of $16,203. Sixty percent of the 60 high school graduates planned to attend college. In 1982-83, 94% of the students were White, 6% Hispanic, 0.4% Black and 0.1% American Indian. Vocational education: Llano Memorial Hospital School of Vocational Nursing (Llano). **PUBLIC LIBRARIES** Llano County Public Library (Llano): 32,909 volumes, two branches. **CHILD CARE** 17 day care licensed facilities. **HEALTH CARE** Eight physicians and four dentists. Hospitals: one with a capacity of 30. Ambulance services: one county service. Nursing homes: three nursing homes with a combined capacity of 313 nursing care residents. The average cost per day for private patients in 1982 was $33.78. **CHURCHES** 27 churches have an estimated combined membership of 5,039. The largest denomination is Southern Baptist.

SOCIAL SERVICES In fiscal year 1983 a total of $106,146 in food stamps was distributed, with an average of 228 persons receiving food stamps each month. Aid to Families with Dependent Children (AFDC) totaled $11,977 with an average of nine families receiving AFDC each month. Medical assistance benefits for the aged and disabled of $1,719,764 and for families and children of $16,417 brought the county benefit total to $1,854,304. FIRE PROTECTION Six volunteer fire departments. LAW ENFORCEMENT The County Sheriff has 13 commissioned officers. Two police departments have a combined force of three. CRIME 12 violent crimes (murder, forcible rape, robbery and aggravated assault) and 162 nonviolent crimes (burglary, larceny-theft and motor vehicle theft) were reported in 1982. JUDICIAL SYSTEM One District Court and Judge, one County Court and Judge and four Justices of the Peace. In the District Court a total of 221 cases were pending on 1/1/82, 247 new cases were filed and 189 cases were disposed of during the year leaving 279 cases pending on 12/31/82. There were 131 criminal cases on the docket, 24 convictions, five persons committed to prison and one committed to jail and 93 cases left pending. In the County Court 520 cases were pending on 1/1/82, 297 new cases were filed and 257 cases were disposed of during the year leaving 560 cases pending on 12/31/82. There were 727 criminal cases on the docket, 142 convictions, 28 persons committed to jail and 481 cases left pending. JAILS One jail, capacity 10. ATTORNEYS AT LAW 21. UTILITIES 62% of the residents are connected to a public or privately owned water system and 28% are connected to a public sewer system. Natural gas is distributed to the county by Lone Star Gas Co., Division of Enserch. The average annual residential bill for natural gas in 1982 for the Lone Star distribution system was $405.91, an increase of 35% over 1981. Electricity is distributed to the city of Llano by Llano Utilities and to the rest of the county by Pedernales Electric Coop., Inc., Central Texas Electric Coop., Inc. and Hamilton Valley Electric Coop., Assn. and is generated primarily by oil, water and coal. The typical residential electric bill is $131.38 per month for an all-electric house using 2,500 kwh. TAXES The county has eight units with taxing authority: one school district, two cities, one county and four special districts.

RECREATION/ENTERTAINMENT
NATIONAL REGISTER OF HISTORIC PLACES Llano: County Courthouse and Jail, Southern Hotel and Badu Building. STATE Enchanted Rock State Natural Area (See Gillespie County). COUNTY/MUNICIPAL PARKS 113 acres in four county and eight municipal parks. These parks contain two playgrounds, one golf course, one baseball and softball field, two tennis courts, one swimming pool, two beaches, five boat ramps and shore fishing facilities. Developed campsites: 18. SCENIC DRIVES The Texas Hill Country Trail runs through this county. This trail winds through a scenic region of South Central Texas, spanning a vast ranching area abundant with wildlife in a landscape of deeply-sculptured valleys and hills. BOATING/FISHING Lakes/reservoirs: Buchanan (23,060 acres), Freight Development (21 acres), Inks (803 acres), Lyndon B. Johnson (6,375 acres) and Llano City (179 acres). Major rivers: Colorado and Llano. Primary streams: Lime Hollow, Pecan and Sandy. HUNTING Fall and winter seasons on deer. No closed season on coyote, bobcat and squirrel. Winter seasons on javelina, quail, muskrat, beaver, opossum, ring-tailed cat, badger, fox, weasel, raccoon, skunk and civet cat. Fall, winter and spring seasons on turkey. In 1983 duck, coot, geese, woodcock and jacksnipe seasons occurred during the winter months. Teal duck, rail and gallinule seasons occurred in the fall. Mourning dove seasons occurred intermittently during the fall and winter months. MUSEUMS Llano: County Historical Museum. SPECIAL EVENTS Old Time Fiddlers Fest, Llano, April;

Highland Lakes Bluebonnet Trail, Llano and Kingsland, April; Rodeo and Parade, Llano, June; Aqua-Boom Festival and Parade, Llano, July; Black Powder Shoot and Wild Game Cookoff, Llano, August.

COMMUNITIES
COUNTY SEAT Llano, County Courthouse, 78643; County Clerk's Office, 915/247-4455. INCORPORATED COMMUNITIES (1980 population and ZIP Code) Llano (3,071) 78643 and Sunrise Beach Village (420) 78643. UNINCORPORATED COMMUNITIES (and ZIP Code) Bluffton 78607, Buchanan Dam 78609, Castell 76831, Esbon 76885, Field Creek 76869, Granite Shoals Lake Estates 78639, Inks Lake Village 78609, Kingsland 78639, Lakeside Heights 78639, Lone Grove 78646, Oxford 78643, Sandy Harbor 78654, Tow 78672 and Valley Spring 76885. FOR ADDITIONAL LOCAL INFORMATION Lake Buchanan Chamber of Commerce, P.O. Box 282, Buchanan Dam, 78609, 512/793-2803, Kingsland Chamber of Commerce, P.O. Box 465, Hwy. 1431 East, Kingsland, 78639, 915/388-6211, 388-4237 and Llano Co. Chamber of Commerce, 700 Bessmer Ave., Llano, 78643, 915/247-5354.

LOVING (P73)

THE LAND
Bordering New Mexico west of Odessa on State Highway 302 in the Trans-Pecos Region, Loving County covers 671 square miles with the elevation ranging from 2,600 to 3,000 feet. The northeastern portion of the county has level to undulating, sandy soils or sandy surfaces over reddish, loamy subsoils. Limestone bedrock is within 40 inches of the surface. The rest of the county has alkaline, level to undulating, loamy soils, or loamy soils over clayey subsoils. Loving is in the Trans-Pecos Mountains and Basins vegetation area with desert shrub, grama grasses, yucca and juniper. Less than 1% of the land in the county is considered prime farmland. CLIMATE Continental Steppe and dry. The average annual temperature is 64 °F. Temperatures in January range from an average low of 28° to an average high of 58 °F and in July range from 69° to 98 °F. The average annual precipitation is 10 inches, with an average relative humidity of 68% at 6 A.M. and 33% at 6 P.M. The average annual snowfall is four inches. The growing season averages 222 days per year, with the last freeze in early April and the first freeze in early November. The sun shines during the year on the average 78% of the daylight hours.

THE PEOPLE
Loving is the least populated county in the United States. The 1982 estimated population of 83 continues the population decline which has existed since 1940. The age groups with the greatest losses were birth to 14 and 50 to 64. The county's population is older than average with a median age of 46 in 1980. The largest ancestry groups are persons of Irish ancestry (35%), Hispanic (18%) and English ancestry (12%). REGISTERED VOTERS As of November 2, 1982 there were 94 registered voters. The 1982 general election had a 61% voter turnout, compared to a 77% turnout in the 1980 general election. In the 1982 primary 100% voted Democratic with 62 votes cast.

THE ECONOMY
AGRICULTURE Ranchland. In 1982, 87% of the land was in farms and ranches. Loving ranked 254th in the state in highest agricultural receipts, with 100% from livestock and livestock products. Decreasing irrigation water supplies and salinity are the current conservation problems. Primary livestock and products: cattle and milk. BUSINESS Total number of business

COUNTIES

LOVING (continued)

establishments in the county: five. In 1980, 24% of the labor force were self-employed, 7% were employed in professional or related services, 4% in wholesale and retail trade, 70% in agriculture, forestry, fisheries and mining, 26% were employed in other counties and there were 11 retired workers. The industry with the most employment: gas and oil extraction. The nonfarm earnings in 1981 totaled $2,352,000. The retired workers received an average monthly Social Security payment of $364.00. **HOUSING** Average value of homes in 1980: $10,000. Between 1970 and 1980 the number of housing units decreased by 34%. Seventy-three percent of all units in the county are air-conditioned, 82% are heated by gas and 18% by electricity. **NATURAL RESOURCES** Caliche, sand and gravel, oil and gas. In 1982 a total of 54,841,771 thousand cubic feet of gas well gas, 70,639 barrels of condensate, 1,292,202 barrels of crude oil and 2,067,875 thousand cubic feet of casinghead gas were produced. Current production of other minerals and products includes brine. **ALCOHOLIC BEVERAGES** Packaged distilled spirits, beer, ale, malt liquor and wine are legal. Sale of mixed beverages is legal in all or parts of the county. **FEDERAL EXPENDITURES** The federal government had direct expenditures or obligations of $148,000 in the county during fiscal year 1983, including $8,000 by the U.S. Department of Defense. In addition, the federal government provided $2,000 in grant awards, paid $15,000 in salaries and wages, made direct payments to individuals of $124,000 including $114,000 in retirement and disability payments and spent $7,000 in other expenditures or obligations.

COMMUNICATION

Telephone companies: Continental Telephone. **TRANSPORTATION** Total public road mileage: 120. In 1982 there were 281 registered vehicles and nine reported traffic accidents.

COMMUNITY SERVICES

SOCIAL SERVICES In fiscal year 1983, $7,206 in food stamps, Aid to Families with Dependent Children and medical assistance benefits were distributed. **LAW ENFORCEMENT** The County Sheriff has one commissioned officer. **CRIME** Four nonviolent crimes (burglary, larceny-theft and motor vehicle theft) were reported in 1982. **JUDICIAL SYSTEM** One District Court and Judge, one County Court and Judge and four Justices of the Peace. In the District Court a total of 13 cases were pending on 1/1/82, 12 new cases were filed and six cases were disposed of during the year leaving 19 cases pending on 12/31/82. There were six criminal cases on the docket and six cases left pending. In the County Court one case was pending on 1/1/82, one new case was filed and two cases were disposed of during the year. There were two criminal cases on the docket with one conviction. **JAILS** One jail, capacity two. **UTILITIES** Seven percent of the residents are connected to a public or privately owned water system and 7% are connected to a public sewer system. **TAXES** The county has three units with taxing authority: one county and two special districts.

RECREATION/ENTERTAINMENT

BOATING/FISHING Lakes/reservoirs: Red Bluff (7,908 acres). Major rivers: Pecos. **HUNTING** Fall and winter seasons on deer and mule deer. Winter seasons on javelina, quail, muskrat, beaver, opossum, ring-tailed cat, badger, fox, weasel, raccoon, skunk and civet cat. No closed seasons on squirrel, bobcat and coyote. In 1983 sandhill crane, duck, coot, geese, woodcock and jacksnipe seasons occurred during the winter months. Teal duck, rail and gallinule seasons occurred in the fall. Mourning dove seasons occurred intermittently during the fall and winter months.

COMMUNITIES

COUNTY SEAT Mentone, County Courthouse, 79754; County Clerk's Office, 915/377-2441. **UNINCORPORATED COMMUNITIES** (and ZIP Code) Mentone 79754.

LUBBOCK (P39)

THE LAND

South of Amarillo on Interstate Highway 27 in the High Plains Region, Lubbock County covers 900 square miles with the elevation ranging from 3,000 to 3,400 feet. The county has nearly level soils with light colored, loamy surfaces over very deep, reddish or mottled, clayey subsoils, or very dark, loamy surfaces over clayey subsoils that have hardened calcium deposits. It is in the High Plains vegetation area with prairie grasses, junipers, mesquite and some yucca. Between 51 and 60% of the land in the county is considered prime farmland. **CLIMATE** Continental Steppe and dry. Thunderstorms and duststorms may be a problem in early spring to early summer. The average annual temperature is 60 °F. Temperatures in January range from an average low of 24 ° to an average high of 54 °F and in July range from 67 ° to 93 °F. The average annual precipitation is 18 inches, with an average relative humidity of 70% at 6 A.M. and 37% at 6 P.M. The average annual snowfall is 11 inches. The growing season averages 210 days per year, with the last freeze in mid April and the first freeze in early November. The sun shines during the year on the average 75% of the daylight hours.

THE PEOPLE

Lubbock County is one of the most densely populated in the state. The 1982 estimated population of 216,700 indicates a continuation of the strong growth rate which has occurred since the 1930s. About 80% of the county residents live in urban areas. The population is unusually young with a median age of 25 in 1980. The largest ancestry groups are persons of English descent (35%), Hispanic (20%), Irish descent (19%) and German descent (15%). **REGISTERED VOTERS** As of November 2, 1982 there were 85,791 registered voters (1% of the state total). The 1982 general election had a 54% voter turnout, compared to a 73% turnout in the 1980 general election. In the 1982 primary 85% voted Democratic and 15% Republican, with 21,140 votes cast.

THE ECONOMY

AGRICULTURE Fed cattle and cotton area. In 1982, 83% of the land was in farms and ranches, with 80% of the farmland under cultivation and 61% irrigated. Lubbock ranked 14th in the state in highest agricultural receipts, with 61% from crops. Water and wind erosion and decreasing irrigation water supplies are the current conservation problems. Primary crops: sixth in the state for cotton and second for sunflowers. Sorghum, wheat and soybeans. Primary vegetables: onions, watermelons and cucumbers. Primary fruits and nuts: pecans. Primary livestock and products: first in the state for hogs and 10th for hens and pullets and egg production. Cattle, milk, sheep and wool. **BUSINESS** Total number of business establishments in the county: 5,128. Retail sales during the first quarter of 1984 increased by 13%. In 1980, 8% of the labor force were self-employed, 23% were employed in professional or related services, 14% in manufacturing, 26% in wholesale and retail trade, 7% in transportation, communications and other public utilities, 4% were employed in other counties and there were 11,689 retired workers. The industries with the most employment: agribusiness, oil and gas field servicing, general construction, meat packing, cottonseed oil mills, soft drink bottling and canning, aluminum smelting and the manufacture of dairy products, watches and clocks, prepared agricultural feeds, bakery products, prepared

LUBBOCK

foods, wooden furniture, plastic products, ready-mixed concrete, structural metal products, fabricated pipes and fittings, farm machinery and equipment, construction machinery, pumps and pumping equipment, calculators, radio and television communication equipment, semiconductors, truck trailers, motor vehicle parts and accessories, speed changers, drives and gears and special industrial machinery. The nonfarm earnings in 1981 totaled $2,061,410,000. The retired workers received an average monthly Social Security payment of $333. **FINANCE** On June 30, 1983, 16 commercial banks had total deposits of $1,691,294,000 and total assets of $1,955,529,000. On December 31, 1982 three state savings and loan associations, one federal association, 14 state branches and three federal branches had combined assets of $469,638,853. In addition there are 17 credit unions in the county. **HOUSING** Average value of homes in 1980: $38,400. Permits for new, privately owned housing units decreased in 1982: 1,375 permits were issued with a total construction cost of $80,512,744. Of those permits, 841 were for single family houses. Housing permits in Wolfforth increased from 41 in 1981 to 70 in 1982 with all permits issued for single family houses. Between 1970 and 1980 the number of housing units increased by 37%. Eighty-six percent of all units in the county are air-conditioned, 80% are heated by gas and 19% by electricity. **NATURAL RESOURCES** Brine, caliche, sand and gravel, oil and gas. In 1982 a total of 1,896,310 barrels of crude oil and 177,816 thousand cubic feet of casinghead gas were produced. Current production of other minerals and products includes brine, caliche, sand and gravel. **TOURISM** Travel expenditures of $161,821,000 in 1982 (an increase of 10% over 1981) generated 3,866 jobs and $33,419,000 in payroll. Lodging: 26 hotels, motels and tourist courts. Convention/meeting facilities: Lubbock-Fair Park Coliseum, Memorial Civic Center, Municipal Auditorium and Coliseum, Texas Tech Jones Stadium and four hotels with facilities for large gatherings. **ALCOHOLIC BEVERAGES** Packaged distilled spirits, beer, ale, malt liquor and wine are legal in parts of the county. Sale of mixed beverages is legal in all or parts of the county. **MILITARY INSTALLATIONS** Reese Air Force Base, Lubbock, 3,000 personnel, 3,546 acres, Flight Training Wing. **FEDERAL EXPENDITURES** The federal government had direct expenditures or obligations of $361,497,000 in the county during fiscal year 1983, including $92,016,000 by the U.S. Department of Defense. In addition, the federal government provided $19,846,000 in grant awards, paid $98,344,000 in salaries and wages, made direct payments to individuals of $188,467,000 including $148,611,000 in retirement and disability payments, awarded $18,882,000 in procurement contracts and spent $35,957,000 in other expenditures or obligations. The federal government also provided $176,792,000 in direct loans and $140,149,000 in guaranteed loans and insurance.

COMMUNICATION

Newspapers–Daily: Lubbock Avalanche-Journal, ave. morn. circ. 58,202 and eve. 14,323. Weekly: Idalou Beacon, Suburban Today (Lubbock), West Texas Times (Lubbock) and The Slatonite (Slaton). Radio: KEND-AM, KFYO-AM, KKAM-AM, KLFB-AM, KRLB-AM, KSEL-AM, KWAZ-AM, KJAK-FM, KLBK-FM, KOHM-FM, KRLB-FM, KSEL-FM, KTXT-FM, KLLL-FM Stereo and KTEZ-FM Stereo (Lubbock) and KCAS-AM (Slaton). Television: KHMC-CH. 28, KCBB-CH. 11, KJAA-CH. 34, KLBK-CH. 13, KTXT-CH. 5 (Lubbock). Cable TV. Telephone companies: General Telephone, Southwestern Bell and South Plains Telephone Coop. **TRANSPORTATION** Total public road mileage: 2,794. In 1982 there were 176,109 registered vehicles and 7,447 reported traffic accidents including 59 fatalities. Taxi cabs: one company in the city of Lubbock. Municipal transit systems: one intracity bus systems in the city of Lubbock with scheduled routes. Intercity bus service is available. Motor freight: 71 local and intrastate carriers. Rail: four main and four branch lines carry freight through the county. Two of the main lines carry annually over 30 million tons of freight each, one carries 20 to 30 and one carries 10 to 20 million. One branch line carries annually one to five million tons of freight and three carry less than one million each. Aircraft: 331 are registered in the county. Airports: Lubbock International Airport serves as a base for 260 aircraft and is a small hub for short haul flights with carrier service. Slaton Municipal Airport serves as a base for 16 aircraft and is a basic utility airport with general aviation service. Also serving the area are the Town and Country Airpark at Lubbock and Shallowater Airport at Shallowater. Lubbock Methodist Hospital provides a heliport for emergency use.

COMMUNITY SERVICES

EDUCATION Eight school districts with 49 elementary, 13 middle, 12 high schools and four special education. The average daily attendance in 1981-82 was 35,295, with expenditures per pupil of $2,312 including 2,249 classroom teachers with an average annual salary of $17,030. Fifty-one percent of the 2,456 high school graduates planned to attend college. In 1982-83, 56% of the students were White, 31% Hispanic, 12% Black, 0.8% Asian and 0.1% American Indian. Sports championships: 1983 AAAA Boys' Track; Lubbock Estacado H.S. Private schools: 2,006 Students enrolled in nine elementary and four high schools. Texas Tech University is located in Lubbock. Established in 1923 it is under state control. Enrollment in 1982 was 23,063 with in state undergraduate tuition and fees of $430 per semester. The highest degree offered is Doctorate. Texas Tech University Health Science Center was established in 1969. Enrollment in 1982 was 282 and the highest degree offered is Doctorate. Lubbock Christian College is located in Lubbock. Established in 1957 it is affiliated with the Churches of Christ. Enrollment in 1982 was 1,239 with in state undergraduate tuition and fees of $2,675 per semester. The highest degree offered is Bachelor. Vocational education: Lubbock-Cinderella Beauty School, Jessie Lees Hair Design Institute, Lubbock Barber College, Methodist Hospital School of Nursing and School of X-Ray Technology, Metro Barber College, Texas Schools, Vogue Beauty College, American Commercial College, Sandi's School of Professional Modeling and Dance, The Robert Spence School. **PUBLIC LIBRARIES** Lubbock City-County Library: 302,264 volumes and three branches. **CHILD CARE** 581 day care and 97 twenty-four hour care licensed facilities. **HEALTH CARE** 502 physicians and 99 dentists. Hospitals: eight with a combined capacity of 1,546. Specialized hospitals: one air force hospital with a capacity of 20. Clinics: one dialysis clinic, one public health clinic and one minor emergency center. Ambulance services: two volunteer services, two county, one commercial, one hospital-based, one funeral home and one police department service. Mental health: two clinics and one state school with a capacity of 554. Nursing homes: 13 nursing homes with a combined capacity of 1,208 nursing care residents. The average cost per day for private patients in 1982 was $32.50. **CHURCHES** 199 churches have an estimated combined membership of 127,013. The largest denominations are Southern Baptist, Catholic and United Methodist. **SOCIAL SERVICES** In fiscal year 1983 a total of $8,130,689 in food stamps was distributed, with an average of 16,683 persons receiving food stamps each month. Aid to Families with Dependent Children (AFDC) totaled $1,303,020 with an average of 2,602 families receiving AFDC each month. Medical assistance benefits for the aged and disabled of $9,363,315 and for families and children of $2,504,573 brought the county benefit total to $21,301,596. **FIRE PROTECTION** One paid, 11 volunteer fire departments. **LAW ENFORCEMENT** The County Sheriff has 117 commissioned officers. Seven police departments have a combined force of 274. One college and one university have campus

COUNTIES

LUBBOCK (continued)

police departments with a combined force of 51. Lubbock Regional Airport police department has a force of 11. **CRIME** 1,914 violent crimes (murder, forcible rape, robbery and aggravated assault) and 17,465 nonviolent crimes (burglary, larceny-theft and motor vehicle theft) were reported in 1982. **JUDICIAL SYSTEM** Five District Courts and Judges, three County Courts and Judges and seven Justices of the Peace. In the District Courts a total of 6,699 cases were pending on 1/1/82, 4,909 new cases were filed and 3,787 cases were disposed of during the year leaving 7,821 cases pending on 12/31/82. There were 2,699 criminal cases on the docket, 559 convictions, 180 persons committed to prison and 53 committed to jail and 1,663 cases left pending. In the County Courts 9,404 cases were pending on 1/1/82, 9,617 new cases were filed and 8,550 cases were disposed of during the year leaving 10,471 cases pending on 12/31/82. There were 12,565 criminal cases on the docket, 1,469 convictions, 378 persons committed to jail and 6,288 cases left pending. **JAILS** One jail, capacity 278. **ATTORNEYS AT LAW** 454. **UTILITIES** 91% of the residents are connected to a public or privately owned water system and 90% are connected to a public sewer system. Natural gas is distributed to the county by Energas Co. The average annual residential bill for natural gas in 1982 for the Energas distribution system was $371.63, an increase of 23% over 1981. Electricity is distributed to the city of Lubbock by the Lubbock Power and Light Dept. and to the rest of the county by West Texas Utilities Service, Southwestern Public Service and South Plains Electric Coop., Inc. and is generated primarily by gas, oil and water. The typical residential electric bill is $170.44 per month for an all-electric house using 2,500 kwh. **TAXES** The county has 18 units with taxing authority: eight school districts, seven cities, one county, one hospital district and one special district.

RECREATION/ENTERTAINMENT

NATIONAL REGISTER OF HISTORIC PLACES Lubbock: Canyon Lakes Archelolgical District and Bacon, Warren and Myrta House. Lubbock vicinity: Lubbock Lake Site (National Historic Landmark). **STATE** McKenzie State Recreation Area covers 542 acres with camping sites, fishing, swimming and golf. **COUNTY/MUNICIPAL PARKS** 2,857 acres in four county and 62 municipal parks. These parks contain 10 miles of hiking trails, 44 playgrounds, two golf courses, nine football and soccer fields, 31 baseball and softball fields, 78 tennis courts, 15 multi-use courts, six swimming pools, three boat ramps and shore fishing facilities. Developed campsites: 30. **SCENIC DRIVES** The Texas Plains Trail runs through this county. This trail spans a vast area of the High Plains region of Texas slicing through the southernmost extension of the Great Plains of the United States. The land is flat except where erosion has carved canyon landscapes. **BOATING/FISHING** Lakes/reservoirs: Buffalo Springs (169 acres), Canyon #6 (48 acres), Clearwater (29 acres), Lubbock Terminal (78 acres) and Ransom Canyon (48 acres). Major rivers: Brazos, Double Mountain Fork Brazos, North Fork Double Mountain Fork, Brazos and Yellowstone. **HUNTING** Fall season on antelope. No closed season on squirrel, coyote and bobcat. Winter seasons on quail, muskrat, beaver, opossum, ring-tailed cat, badger, fox, weasel, raccoon, skunk and civet cat. In 1983 sandhill crane, duck, coot, geese, woodcock and jacksnipe seasons occurred during the winter months. Teal duck, rail and gallinule seasons occurred in the fall. Mourning dove seasons occcured intermittently during the fall and winter months. **MUSEUMS** Lubbock: Museum of Texas Tech University, Municipal Garden and Arts Center and Ranch Headquarters. Shallowater: Lubbock County Museum. Slaton: Slaton Museum. **THEATERS** Lubbock: Theatre Centre, Lubbock Community

Concert Association, Hayloft Dinner Theater and Lubbock Memorial Civic Center. **ORCHESTRAS** Lubbock: Symphony Orchestra. **DANCE** Lubbock: Ballet Theatre. **PLANETARIUM** Lubbock: Moody Planetarium. **COLLEGIATE FINE ARTS** Lubbock: Cultural events offered by Lubbock Christian College and Texas Tech University. **SPECIAL EVENTS** Jazz Band Festival, Lubbock, March; Rodeo and Livestock Show, Lubbock, March; Arts Festival, Lubbock, March/April; Scottish Gathering and Highland Games, Lubbock, June; Panhandle South Plains Fair, Lubbock, September.

COMMUNITIES

COUNTY SEAT Lubbock, County Courthouse, 79401; County Clerk's Office, 806/741-8034. **INCORPORATED COMMUNITIES** (1980 population and ZIP Code) Abernathy (2,904: 699 in Lubbock Co. and 2,205 in Hale Co.) 79311, Idalou (2,348) 79329, Lake Ransom Canyon (561) 79364, Lubbock All-America Cities Honorable Mention 1976-1977 (173,979) 79401, New Deal (637) 79350, Shallowater (1,932) 79363, Slaton (6,804) 79364 and Wolfforth (1,701) 79382. **UNINCORPORATED COMMUNITIES** (and ZIP Code) Acuff 79401, Becton 79343, Canyon 79401, Estacado 79250, Heckville 79329, Hurlwood 79328, Liberty 79401, Midway (McClung) 79364, Posey 79364, Reese Village 79401, Roosevelt 79401, Slide 79401, Tech 79409, Union 79364, West Carlisle (Carlisle) 79407, and Woodrow 79401. **FOR ADDITIONAL LOCAL INFORMATION** Lubbock Chamber of Commerce, P.O. Box 561, 14th and Ave. K, Lubbock, 79408, 806/763-4666, Lubbock Mexican-Americans, P.O. Box 886, Lubbock, 79408, 806/762-5059 and Slaton Chamber of Commerce, 200 W. Garza, P. O. Box 400, Slaton, 79364, 806/828-6238.

LYNN (P49)

THE LAND

South of Lubbock on U.S. Highways 87 and 380 in the High Plains Region, Lynn County covers 888 square miles with the elevation ranging from 2,700 to 3,300 feet. The soils are level throughout with sandy soils along parts of the western border. The rest of the county has light colored, loamy surfaces over very deep, reddish or mottled clayey subsoils, or very dark, loamy surfaces over clayey subsoils that have hardened calcium deposits. Lynn is in the High Plains vegetation area with prairie grasses, juniper, mesquite, yucca, sandsage and shinnery oak. Between 31 and 40% of the land in the county is considered prime farmland. **CLIMATE** Continental Steppe and dry. Thunderstorms and duststorms may be a problem from early spring to early summmer. The average annual temperature is 61 °F. Temperatures in January range from an average low of 25 ° to an average high of 54 °F and in July range from 66 ° to 94 °F. The average annual precipitation is 18 inches, with an average relative humidity of 70% at 6 A.M. and 37% at 6 P.M. The average annual snowfall is ten inches. The growing season averages 215 days per year, with the last freeze in early April and the first freeze in early November. The sun shines during the year on the average 75% of the daylight hours.

THE PEOPLE

Lynn County ranks 67th among all U.S. counties in the highest percent of residents of Spanish origin. The 1982 estimated population of 8,300 indicates a slight decrease since 1980, continuing a population decline since 1930. Gains occurred in urban areas from 1970 to 1980 while rural areas decreased in population. The age group with the largest decrease was ages five to 14. The largest ancestry groups are Hispanic (38%), persons of English descent (23%), Irish descent (17%) and German descent (14%). **REGISTERED VOTERS** As of November 2, 1982 there were 4,279 registered voters (0.1% of the state total). The 1982 general election had a 48% voter turnout, compared to a 67% turnout in the 1980 general election. In the 1982 primary 99% voted Democratic and 0.4% Republican, with 2,040 votes cast.

THE ECONOMY

AGRICULTURE Cotton area. In 1982, 95% of the land was in farms and ranches, with 59% of the farmland under cultivation and 12% irrigated. Lynn ranked 49th in the state in highest agricultural receipts, with 95% from crops. Undesirable brush, noxious weeds, water and wind erosion and decreasing irrigation water supplies are the current conservation problems. Primary crops: 10th in the state for cotton and third for sunflowers. Sorghum, wheat and soybeans. Primary vegetables: watermelons. Primary fruits and nuts: peaches and pecans. Primary livestock and products: cattle and hogs. **BUSINESS** Total number of business establishments in the county: 118. Retail sales during the first quarter of 1984 increased by 9%. In 1980, 24% of the labor force were self-employed, 16% were employed in professional or related services, 5% in manufacturing, 15% in wholesale and retail trade, 38% in agriculture, forestry, fisheries and mining, 23% were employed in other counties and there were 663 retired workers. The industry with the most employment is agribusiness. The nonfarm earnings in 1981 totaled $55,037,000. The retired workers received an average monthly Social Security payment of $330.00. **FINANCE** On June 30, 1983, three commercial banks had total deposits of $61,373,000 and total assets of $72,440,000. There is one state savings and loan association branch and one credit union in the county. **HOUSING** Average value of homes in 1980: $21,600. Permits for new, privately owned housing units increased in 1982: six permits were issued with a total construction cost of $269,942. Of those permits, all were for single family houses. Between 1970 and 1980 the number of housing units decreased by 8%. Eight percent of all units in the county are air-conditioned, 88% are heated by gas and 11% by electricity. **NATURAL RESOURCES** Limestone, caliche, oil and gas. In 1982 a total of 386,688 barrels of crude oil and 89,522 thousand cubic feet of casinghead gas were produced. Current production of other minerals and products includes caliche and crushed limestone. **TOURISM** Travel expenditures of $5,973,000 in 1982 (an increase of 18% over 1981) generated 81 jobs and $866,000 in payroll. **ALCOHOLIC BEVERAGES** Totally dry. **FEDERAL EXPENDITURES** The federal government had direct expenditures or obligations of $32,167,000 in the county during fiscal year 1983, including $70,000 by the U.S. Department of Defense. In addition, the federal government provided $928,000 in grant awards, paid $538,000 in salaries and wages, made direct payments to individuals of $10,011,000 including $6,837,000 in retirement and disability payments, awarded $1,000 in procurement contracts and spent $20,689,000 in other expenditures or obligations. The federal government also provided $4,552,000 in direct loans and $16,155,000 in guaranteed loans and insurance.

COMMUNICATION

Newspapers–Weekly: Lynn County News (Tahoka). Cable TV. Telephone companies: General Telephone, Southwestern Bell, Poka-Lambro Rural Telephone Coop. and South Plains Telephone Coop. **TRANSPORTATION** Total public road mileage: 1,321. In 1982 there were 8,228 registered vehicles and 99 reported traffic accidents including six fatalities. Intercity bus service is available. Motor freight: one carrier. Rail: one main and one branch line carry freight through the county with the main line carrying annually over 30 million tons of freight and the branch carries less than one million. Aircraft: 20 are registered in the county. Airports: T-Bar Municipal Airport at Tahoka and New Home Airport at New Home.

COMMUNITY SERVICES

EDUCATION Four school districts with five elementary, one middle and four high schools. The average daily attendance in 1981-82 was 1,745, with expenditures per pupil of $2,813 including 128 classroom teachers with an average annual salary of $15,696. Thirty-four percent of the 111 high school graduates planned to attend college. In 1982-83, 39% of the students were White, 57% Hispanic and 5% Black. **PUBLIC LIBRARIES** Tahoka Library. **CHILD CARE** Seven day care and three twenty-four hour care licensed facilities. **HEALTH CARE** Two physicians and three dentists. Hospitals: one with a capacity of 24. Ambulance services: one hospital-based and one volunteer service. Nursing homes: one nursing home has a capacity of 46 nursing care residents. The average cost per day for private patients in 1982 was $31.05. **CHURCHES** 27 churches have an estimated combined membership of 7,168. The largest denominations are Southern Baptist, United Methodist and Catholic. **SOCIAL SERVICES** In fiscal year 1983 a total of $647,310 in food stamps was distributed, with an average of 1,405 persons receiving food stamps each month. Aid to Families with Dependent Children (AFDC) totaled $91,285 with an average of 59 families receiving AFDC each month. Medical assistance benefits for the aged and disabled of $405,516 and for families and children of $85,356 brought the county benefit total to $1,229,466. **FIRE PROTECTION** Four volunteer fire departments. **LAW ENFORCEMENT** The County Sheriff has nine commissioned officers. Four police departments have a combined force of nine. **CRIME** 23 violent crimes (murder, forcible rape, robbery and aggravated assault) and 120 nonviolent crimes (burglary, larceny-theft and motor vehicle theft) were reported in 1982. **JUDICIAL SYSTEM** One District Court and Judge, one County Court and Judge and two Justices of the Peace. In the District Court a total of 361 cases were pending on 1/1/82, 237 new cases were filed and 131 cases were disposed of during the year leaving 467 cases pending on 12/31/82. There were 96 criminal cases on the docket, 24 convictions, eight persons committed to prison, one committed to jail and 57 cases left pending. In the County Court 186 cases were pending on 1/1/82, 138 new cases were filed and 231 cases were disposed of during the year leaving 93 cases pending on 12/31/82. There were 267 criminal cases on the docket, 65 convictions, eight persons committed to jail and 36 cases left pending. **JAILS** One jail, capacity 14. **ATTORNEYS AT LAW** Five. **UTILITIES** 64% of the residents are connected to a public or privately owned water system and 60% are connected to a public sewer system. Natural gas is distributed to the county by Energas Co. The average annual residential bill for natural gas in 1982 for the Energas distribution system was $371.63, an increase of 23% over 1981. Electricity is distributed to the county by Southwestern Public Service and South Plains Electric Coop., Inc. and is generated primarily by gas and oil. The typical residential electric bill is $170.44 per month for an all-electric house using 2,500 kwh. **TAXES** The county has 11 units with taxing authority: four school districts, four cities, one county, one hospital district and one special district.

RECREATION/ENTERTAINMENT

NATIONAL REGISTER OF HISTORIC PLACES Tahoka: Lynn County Courthouse. **MUNICIPAL PARKS** 36 acres in six municipal parks. These parks contain four playgrounds, four baseball and softball fields, three tennis courts and two swimming pools. **SCENIC DRIVES** The Texas Plains Trail runs through this county. This trail spans a vast area of the High Plains region of Texas slicing through the southernmost extension of the Great Plains of the United States. The land is flat except where

COUNTIES

LYNN (continued)

erosion has carved canyon landscapes. **BOATING/FISHING** Lakes/reservoirs: Double Lakes (1,000 acres), Gooch (100 acres), Guthrie (300 acres), Stewart (21 acres) and Tahoka (500 acres). Major rivers: Double Mountain Fork Brazos. **HUNTING** Fall season on antelope. No closed season on squirrel, coyote and bobcat. Winter seasons on quail, muskrat, beaver, opossum, ringtailed cat, badger, fox, weasel, raccoon, skunk and civet cat. Fall, winter and spring seasons on quail. In 1983 coot, geese, woodcock and jacksnipe seasons occurred during the winter months. Teal duck, rail and gallinule seasons occurred in the fall. Mourning dove seasons occurred intermittently during the fall and winter months. **MUSEUMS** O'Donnell: Museum. Tahoka: Pioneer Museum. **SPECIAL EVENTS** Rodeo, Tahoka, June; Old Settlers Reunion, Tahoka, June; Harvest Festival, Tahoka, October.

COMMUNITIES

COUNTY SEAT Tahoka, County Courthouse, 79373; County Clerk's Office, 806/998-4750. **INCORPORATED COMMUNITIES** (1980 population and ZIP Code) New Home (274) 79383, O'Donnel (1,200: 1,076 in Lynn Co. and 124 in Dawson Co.) 79351, Tahoka (3,262) 79373 and Wilson (578) 79381. **UNINCORPORATED COMMUNITIES** (and ZIP Code) Draw 79373, Gordon 79356, Grassland 79356, Lakeview 79345, New Lynn 79373, New Moore 79351, Petty 79373, Wayside 79381, Wells 79351 and West Point 79373.**FOR ADDITIONAL LOCAL INFORMATION** Tahoka Chamber of Commerce, P. O. Box 777, Tahoka, 79373 806/998-4761.

McCULLOCH (P91)

THE LAND

Southeast of Abilene on U.S. Highways 377, 190 and 283 in the Edwards Plateau Region, McCulloch County covers 1,071 square miles with the elevation ranging from 1,350 to 1,900 feet. In the southeastern corner are undulating to rolling soils with loamy surfaces and clayey subsoils over limestone or sandstone. In the northeast are undulating to hilly soils with light colored loamy surfaces over very deep, reddish or mottled, clayey subsoils. The rest of the county has very dark, loamy surfaces with accumulations of lime in the subsoils. McCulloch is in the Edwards Plateau vegetation area with tall and mid grasses, live oak, shinnery oak, junipers and mesquite. Between 21 and 30% of the land in the county is considered prime farmland. **CLIMATE** Subtropical Subhumid and somewhat dry. The average annual temperature is 65°F. Temperatures in January range from an average low of 31° to an average high of 59°F and in July range from 70° to 96°F. The average annual precipitation is 25 inches, with an average relative humidity of 73% at 6 A.M. and 45% at 6 P.M. The average annual snowfall is three inches. The growing season averages 226 days per year, with the last freeze the end of March and the first freeze in mid November. The sun shines during the year on the average 66% of the daylight hours.

THE PEOPLE

McCulloch County ranks 32nd among all U.S. counties in the highest percent of persons over the age of 64. The 1982 estimated population of 8,800 indicates a continuation of the moderate growth in population which began in the 1970's, reversing a steady population decline from the 1930s. Urban areas grew in population from 1970 to 1980 while rural areas had losses. The county's population is older than average with a median age of 40. The largest ancestry groups are persons of English descent (29%), Irish descent (23%) and Hispanic (19%). **REGISTERED VOTERS**

As of November 2, 1982 there were 4,905 registered voters (0.1% of the state total). The 1982 general election had a 56% voter turnout, compared to a 65% turnout in the 1980 general election. In the 1982 primary 97% voted Democratic and 3% Republican, with 2,033 votes cast.

THE ECONOMY

AGRICULTURE Sheep area. In 1982, 95% of the land was in farms and ranches, with 18% of the farmland under cultivation and 6% irrigated. McCulloch ranked 154th in the state in highest agricultural receipts, with 68% from livestock and livestock products. Overgrazing, undesirable brush and weeds, water erosion, inefficient irrigation systems and salinity are the current conservation problems. Primary crops: wheat, sorghum, oats, hay and cotton. Primary vegetables: watermelons. Primary fruits and nuts: pecans. Primary livestock and products: cattle, sheep, wool, angora goats, mohair and hogs. **BUSINESS** Total number of business establishments in the county: 212. Retail sales during the first quarter of 1984 increased by 12%. In 1980, 21% of the labor force were self-employed, 17% were employed in professional or related services, 13% in manufacturing, 26% in wholesale and retail trade, 16% in agriculture, forestry, fisheries and mining, 4% were employed in other counties and there were 1,415 retired workers. The industries with the most employment: industrial sand production, textile mills and the manufacture of truck trailers. The nonfarm earnings in 1981 totaled $74,170,000. The retired workers received an average monthly Social Security payment of $292.00. **FINANCE** On June 30, 1983, two commercial banks had total deposits of $75,865,000 and total assets of $84,190,000. On December 31, 1982 one state savings and loan association and one state branch had assets of $34,324,903. In addition there is one credit union in the county. **HOUSING** Average value of homes in 1980: $20,100. Permits for new, privately owned housing units decreased in 1982: six permits were issued with a total construction cost of $238,000. Of those permits, all were for single family houses. Between 1970 and 1980 the number of housing units increased by 11%. Seventy-five percent of all units in the county are air-conditioned, 89% are heated by gas and 6% by electricity. **NATURAL RESOURCES** Clay, dolomite, industrial sand, gas, oil and bituminous coal. In 1982 a total of 460,510 thousand cubic feet of gas well gas, 100 barrels of condensate, 5,176 barrels of crude oil and 60 thousand cubic feet of casinghead gas were produced. Current production of other minerals and products includes crushed limestone, industrial sand, sand and gravel. **TOURISM** Travel expenditures of $1,704,000 in 1982 (an increase of 13% over 1981) generated 34 jobs and $297,000 in payroll. **ALCOHOLIC BEVERAGES** Packaged distilled spirits, beer, ale, malt liquor and wine are legal in parts of the county. Sale of mixed beverages is legal in all or parts of the county. **FEDERAL EXPENDITURES** The federal government had direct expenditures or obligations of $21,347,000 in the county during fiscal year 1983, including $814,000 by the U.S. Department of Defense. In addition, the federal government provided $165,000 in grant awards, paid $968,000 in salaries and wages, made direct payments to individuals of $18,735,000 including $12,996,000 in retirement and disability payments, awarded $147,000 in procurement contracts and spent $1,330,000 in other expenditures or obligations. The federal government also provided $460,000 in direct loans and $4,684,000 in guaranteed loans and insurance.

COMMUNICATION

Newspapers–Weekly: The Brady Herald and The Brady Standard. Radio: KNEL-AM and KIXV-FM (Brady). Cable TV. Telephone companies: General Telephone, Central Texas Telephone Coop. and Hill Country Telephone Coop. **TRANSPORTATION** Total public road mileage: 804. In 1982 there were

8,907 registered vehicles and 212 reported traffic accidents including four fatalities. Intercity bus service is available. Motor freight: four carriers. Rail: one branch line carries annually less than one million tons of freight through the county. Aircraft: 15 are registered in the county. Airports: Curtis Field Municipal Airport at Brady serves as a base for 20 aircraft and is a general utility airport with general aviation service.

COMMUNITY SERVICES

EDUCATION Three school districts with five elementary, one middle and three high schools. The average daily attendance in 1981-82 was 1,534, with expenditures per pupil of $2,138 including 97 classroom teachers with an average annual salary of $16,095. Forty-five percent of the 88 high school graduates planned to attend college. In 1982-83, 60% of the students were White, 36% Hispanic, 4% Black, 0.1% Asian and 0.2% American Indian. **PUBLIC LIBRARIES** F.M. Richards Memorial Library (Brady): 25,000 volumes. **CHILD CARE** 12 day care and one twenty-four hour care licensed facilities. **HEALTH CARE** Six physicians and three dentists. Hospitals: one with a capacity of 50. Ambulance services: one city, one county and one funeral home service. Mental health: one clinic. Nursing homes: three nursing homes with a combined capacity of 237 nursing care residents. The average cost per day for private patients in 1982 was $32.51. **CHURCHES** 32 churches have an estimated combined membership of 5,149. The largest denominations are Southern Baptist, United Methodist and Churches of Christ. **SOCIAL SERVICES** In fiscal year 1983 a total of $396,025 in food stamps was distributed, with an average of 913 persons receiving food stamps each month. Aid to Families with Dependent Children (AFDC) totaled $64,192 with an average of 43 families receiving AFDC each month. Medical assistance benefits for the aged and disabled of $1,735,685 and for families and children of $128,040 brought the county benefit total to $2,323,942. **FIRE PROTECTION** Three volunteer fire departments. **LAW ENFORCEMENT** The County Sheriff has 16 commissioned officers. One police department has a force of six. **CRIME** 22 violent crimes (murder, forcible rape, robbery and aggravated assault) and 204 nonviolent crimes (burglary, larceny-theft and motor vehicle theft) were reported in 1982. **JUDICIAL SYSTEM** One District Court and Judge, one County Court and Judge and one Justice of the Peace. In the District Court a total of 321 cases were pending on 1/1/82, 251 new cases were filed and 250 cases were disposed of during the year leaving 322 cases pending on 12/31/82. There were 137 criminal cases on the docket, 36 convictions, 13 persons committed to prison and 69 cases left pending. In the County Court 143 cases were pending on 1/1/82, 349 new cases were filed and 342 cases were disposed of during the year leaving 150 cases pending on 12/31/82. There were 463 criminal cases on the docket, 282 convictions, 25 persons committed to jail and 121 cases left pending. **JAILS** One jail, capacity 28. **ATTORNEYS AT LAW** Nine. **UTILITIES** 85% of the residents are connected to a public or privately owned water system and 67% are connected to a public sewer system. Electricity is distributed to the city of Brady by Brady Water and Light Works and to the rest of the county by Central Texas Electric Coop., Inc. and McCulloch Electric Coop., Inc. and is generated primarily by gas, oil water and coal. **TAXES** The county has seven units with taxing authority: three school districts, two cities, one county and one special district.

RECREATION/ENTERTAINMENT

NATIONAL REGISTER OF HISTORIC PLACES Brady: McCulloch County Courthouse and Old McCulloch Jail. **MUNICIPAL PARKS** 628 acres in six municipal parks. These parks contain four playgrounds, one golf course, five baseball and softball fields, two tennis courts, two swimming pools, two beaches, three boat ramps and shore fishing facilities. Developed campsites: 94. **SCENIC DRIVES** The Texas Forts Trail runs through this county. This trail leads to eight of the famous frontier forts of West Central Texas and an ancient presidio of the Spanish colonial period. **BOATING/FISHING** Lakes/reservoirs: Brady (2,020 acres), Cedar Creek Tank (16 acres), Deep Creek Soil Conservation Service Lakes 1 and 5 (30 acres), Richards Park (63 acres) and Shroshire (38 acres). Major rivers: Colorado and San Saba. Primary streams: Brady, Cedar, Deep, Bluff, Cow, Little Saddle and Salt. **HUNTING** Fall and winter seasons on deer. Winter seasons on javelina, quail, muskrat, beaver, opposum, ring-tailed cat, badger, fox, weasel, raccoon, skunk and civet cat. Fall, winter and spring seasons on turkey. In 1983 duck, coot, geese, woodcock and jacksnipe seasons occurred during the winter months. Teal duck, rail and gallinule seasons occurred in the fall. Mourning dove seasons occurred intermittently during the fall and winter months. **OTHER** Brady: Camp San Saba Ruins. **SPECIAL EVENTS** Muzzle-Loaders Rifle Assn. "Frost on the Cactus" Shoot, Brady, February; Horse Races, Brady, Intermittent; Golf Tourney, Brady, May; State Championship Muzzle-Loaders Rifle Assn. Meet, Brady, June; Miss Heart of Texas Pageant, Brady, June; July Jubilee Celebration, Brady, July; Junior Rodeo, Brady, August; World Championship Goat Barbecue Cookoff, Brady, August; Arts and Crafts Fair, Brady, August; Muzzle-Loaders Rifle Assn. Fall Shoot, Brady, September/October.

COMMUNITIES

COUNTY SEAT Brady, County Courthouse, 76825; County Clerk's Office, 915/597-2355. **INCORPORATED COMMUNITIES** (1980 population and ZIP Code) Brady (5,969) 76825 and Melvin (202) 76858. **UNINCORPORATED COMMUNITIES** (and ZIP Code) Calf Creek 76825, Camp San Saba 76829, Doole 76836, Fife 76839, Lohn 76852, Mercury 76872, Milburn 76872 Pear Valley 76867, Placid 76868, Rochelle 76872, Salt Gap 76876, Stacy 76879, Voca 76887, Waldrip 76852 and Whiteland 76858. **FOR ADDITIONAL LOCAL INFORMATION** Brady Chamber of Commerce, 101 E. 1st, Brady, 76825, 915/597-2420.

McLENNAN (C8)

THE LAND

South of the Dallas-Fort Worth Metroplex on Interstate Highway 35 in the Blackland Prairies Region, McLennan County covers 1,031 square miles with the elevation ranging from 400 to 850 feet. In the central part of the county, running north to south, is a strip of undulating, very dark soil that is loamy throughout. Along the Brazos River are level, cracking, clayey or loamy soils. In the west are undulating to hilly, light colored, well drained soils, or very dark, loamy soils that have accumulations of lime. In the southeast the soils are black, cracking and clayey or light colored, loamy surfaces over very deep, reddish, cracking, clayey subsoils. There is a high shrink-swell potential. The west is in the Cross Timbers and Prairies vegetation area with tall and mid grasses, live oak, post oak, junipers and some mesquite. The rest of the county is in the Blackland Prairies vegetation area with tall grasses, mesquite, oak, pecan and elm trees along streams. Between 51 and 60% of the land in the county is considered prime farmland. **CLIMATE** Subtropical Humid and moist. Thunderstorms may produce significant precipitation early in the spring. The average annual temperature is 66 °F. Temperatures in January range from an average low of 37 ° to an average high of 58 °F and in July range from 75 ° to 97 °F. The average annual precipitation is 33 inches, with an average relative humidity of 80% at 6 A.M. and 53% at 6 P.M. The average annual snowfall is one inch. The growing season averages 253 days per year, with the last freeze in mid March and the first freeze in late November.

COUNTIES

MCLENNAN (continued)

The sun shines during the year on the average 65% of the daylight hours.

THE PEOPLE

McLennan County is one of the most densely populated in the state. The 1982 estimated population of 175,500 indicates a continuation of the steady growth rate begun in the 1970s which reversed the population decrease between 1960 and 1970. The greatest increases between 1970 and 1980 occurred in rural areas which grew twice as fast as urban areas where approximately 80% of the residents live. The county has a median age of 29. The largest ancestry groups are persons of English descent (24%), Irish descent (21%), German descent (19%) and Black (16%). **REGISTERED VOTERS** As of November 2, 1982 there were 82,105 registered voters (1% of the state total). The 1982 general election had a 51% voter turnout, compared to a 63% turnout in the 1980 general election. In the 1982 primary 93% voted Democratic and 7% Republican, with 25,993 votes cast.

THE ECONOMY

AGRICULTURE Wheat, cattle and turkey area. In 1982, 76% of the land was in farms and ranches, with 49% of the farmland under cultivation and 2% irrigated. McLennan ranked 26th in the state in highest agricultural receipts, with 59% from livestock and livestock products. Overgrazing, undesirable brush and weeds and water erosion are the current conservation problems. Primary crops: first in the state for oats. Sorghum, wheat, hay, corn and cotton. Primary vegetables: potatoes, sweet potatoes, tomatoes and watermelons. Primary fruits and nuts: peaches and pecans. Primary livestock and products: third in the state for turkeys. Cattle, milk, sheep, wool, angora goats, mohair and hogs. **BUSINESS** Total number of business establishments in the county: 3,725. Retail sales during the first quarter of 1984 increased by 18%. In 1980, 7% of the labor force were self-employed, 22% were employed in professional or related services, 22% in manufacturing, 23% in wholesale and retail trade, 6% in finance, insurance and real estate, 4% were employed in other counties and there were 16,346 retired workers. The industries with the most employment: agribusiness, sand and gravel production, general construction, road construction, lumber mills, poultry processing, soft drink bottling and canning, book binding, book publishing, commercial printing, trucking and the manufacture of prepared feeds, bakery products, candy, men's and women's clothing, mobile homes, furniture, mattresses and bedsprings, drapery hardware, tires, plastic products, glass containers, hydraulic cement, industrial trucks and trailers, refrigeration and heating equipment, telephone and telegraph equipment, dairy products, fabricated metal products, storage batteries, travel trailers and campers, surgical appliances and supplies, burial caskets, paper products, cardboard boxes, paperboard food containers, nuts and bolts. The nonfarm earnings in 1981 totaled $1,624,125,000. The retired workers received an average monthly Social Security payment of $302. **FINANCE** On June 30, 1983, 18 commercial banks had total deposits of $1,071,413,000 and total assets of $1,252,366,000. On December 31, 1982 one state savings and loan association, one federal association, 14 state branches and three federal branches had combined assets of $461,079,712. In addition there are 27 credit unions in the county. **HOUSING** Average value of homes in 1980: $29,300. Permits for new, privately owned housing units decreased in 1982: 896 permits were issued with a total construction cost of $28,223,410. Of those permits, 291 were for single family houses. Housing permits in Lacy-Lakeview increased from 9 in 1981 to 36 in 1982 and in Woodway from 28 to 48 with all permits issued for single family houses. Between 1970 and 1980 the number of housing units increased by 26%. Eighty-two percent of all units in the county are air-conditioned, 75% are heated by gas and 24% by electricity. **NATURAL RESOURCES** Limestone, sand and gravel, oil and gas. In 1982 a total of 7,832 barrels of crude oil and 156 thousand cubic feet of casinghead gas were produced. Current production of other minerals and products includes cement, clay, crushed limestone, construction sand, sand and gravel. **TOURISM** Travel expenditures of $113,912,000 in 1982 (an increase of 11% over 1981) generated 2,893 jobs and $23,679,000 in payroll. Lodging: 23 hotels, motels and tourist courts. Convention/meeting facilities: Waco-Baylor University Waco Hall and Baylor Stadium, Heart O' Texas Coliseum, Paul Quinn College Fieldhouse and Stadium, Waco Convention Center and two hotels with facilities for large gatherings. **ALCOHOLIC BEVERAGES** Packaged distilled spirits, beer, ale, malt liquor and wine are legal in parts of the county. Sale of mixed beverages is legal in all or parts of the county. **MILITARY INSTALLATIONS** Naval Weapons Industrial Reserve Plant, McGregor, 9,755 acres, rocket motors production. **FEDERAL EXPENDITURES** The federal government had direct expenditures or obligations of $416,934,000 in the county during fiscal year 1983, including $57,776,000 by the U.S. Department of Defense. In addition, the federal government provided $36,998,000 in grant awards, paid $65,164,000 in salaries and wages, made direct payments to individuals of $272,962,000 including $205,512,000 in retirement and disability payments, awarded $40,417,000 in procurement contracts and spent $1,392,000 in other expenditures or obligations. The federal government also provided $3,072,000 in direct loans and $50,262,000 in guaranteed loans and insurance.

COMMUNICATION

Newspapers–Daily: Waco Tribune-Herald, ave. daily circ. 51,519. Weekly: Mart Herald, McGregor Mirror, The Moody Courier, Riesel Rustler, Waco Messenger, Waco Citizen and The West News (West). Radio: KBBW-AM, KRZI-AM, KWTX-AM, KHOO-FM, KWBU-FM, KWTX-FM and KNFO-FM Stereo (Waco). Television: KWTX-CH.10 (Waco). Cable TV. Telephone companies: Continental Telephone, General Telephone, Southwestern Bell and Texas-Midland Telephone. **TRANSPORTATION** Total public road mileage: 2,596. In 1982 there were 146,649 registered vehicles and 5,207 reported traffic accidents including 41 fatalities. Taxi cabs: one company in Waco. Municipal transit systems: one intracity bus system in Waco, with scheduled routes. Intercity bus service is available. Motor freight: 41 local and intrastate carriers. Rail: The Eagle provides passenger service on the Amtrak route. Five main and three branch lines carry freight through the county. Two of the main lines carry annually over 30 million tons of freight each and three carry 10 to 20 each. The three branch lines carry annually less than one million tons of freight. Aircraft: 228 are registered in the county. Airports: Waco Madison-Cooper Airport at Waco serves as a base for 147 aircraft and is a basic transportation airport with commuter service. McGregor Municipal Airport serves as a base for 56 aircraft and is a general utility airport with general aviation service. Flying Heart Ranch, T.S.T.I. Airport and Wings For Christ International Flight Academy are at Waco. Rankins Roost Airport at Ross.

COMMUNITY SERVICES

EDUCATION 18 school districts with 41 elementary, 14 middle, 18 high schools and two special education. The average daily attendance in 1981-82 was 26,711, with expenditures per pupil of $2,309 including 1,736 classroom teachers with an average annual salary of $16,180. Forty-nine percent of the 1,964 high school graduates planned to attend college. In 1982-83, 64% of the students were White, 13% Hispanic, 23% Black, 0.5% Asian.

Sports championships: 1982 AAAA Girls' Cross Country, Waco Midway H.S.; 1984 AAAA Girls' Basketball, Waco Richfield H.S. Private schools: 2,055 students enrolled in 10 elementary and three high schools. McLennan Community College is located in Waco. Established in 1965 it is a vocational and two year academic college under state and local control. Enrollment in 1982 was 3,950 with in state undergraduate tuition and fees of $250 per semester. Paul Quinn College is located in Waco. Established in 1872 it is affiliated with the African Methodist Episcopal Church. Enrollment in 1982 was 438 with in state undergraduate tuition fees of $1,880 per semester. The highest degree offered is Bachelor. Baylor University is located in Waco. Established in 1845 it is affiliated with the Southern Baptist Church. Enrollment in 1982 was 10,125 with in state undergraduate tuition and fees of $2,400 per semester. The highest degree offered is Doctorate. Vocational education: Waco-A and C College of Beauty, Four C College, Texas State Technical Institute, Vogue Beauty College. West-Community Hospital School of Vocational Nursing. **PUBLIC LIBRARIES** McLennan County Library (Waco): 256,592 volumes and five branches. **CHILD CARE** 449 day care and 88 twenty-four hour care licensed facilities. **HEALTH CARE** 299 physicians and 88 dentists. Hospitals: three with a combined capacity of 662. Specialized hospitals: one veterans medical center with a capacity of 1,061. Clinics: one family counseling and children's service clinic, one dialysis clinic, and one public health clinic. Ambulance services: four commercial, two volunteer services, one funeral home and one hospital-based service. Mental health: three centers with a capacity of 206 and one center for youth with a capacity of 96. Nursing homes: 17 nursing homes with a combined capacity of 1,750 nursing care residents. The average cost per day for private patients in 1982 was $32.05. **CHURCHES** 229 churches have an estimated combined membership of 133,771. The largest denominations are Southern Baptist, Catholic and United Methodist. **SOCIAL SERVICES** In fiscal year 1983 a total of $7,875,926 in food stamps was distributed, with an average of 15,592 persons receiving food stamps each month. Aid to Families with Dependent Children (AFDC) totaled $2,170,001 with an average of 1,431 families receiving AFDC each month. Medical assistance benefits for the aged and disabled of $16,390,870 and for families and children of $2,750,944 brought the county benefit total to $29,187,740. **FIRE PROTECTION** One paid and 29 volunteer fire departments. **LAW ENFORCEMENT** The County Sheriff has 104 commissioned officers. 14 police departments have a combined force of 297. Two colleges and one university have campus police departments with a combined force of 34. **CRIME** 989 violent crimes (murder, forcible rape, robbery and aggravated assault) and 11,562 nonviolent crimes (burglary, larceny-theft and motor vehicle theft) were reported in 1982. **JUDICIAL SYSTEM** Four District Courts and Judges, three County Courts and Judges and eight Justices of the Peace. In the District Courts a total of 6,114 cases were pending on 1/1/82, 5,442 new cases were filed and 5,987 cases were disposed of during the year leaving 5,569 cases pending on 12/31/82. There were 819 criminal cases on the docket, 371 convictions, 234 persons committed to prison, five committed to jail and 272 cases left pending. In the County Courts 2,867 cases were pending on 1/1/82, 3,561 new cases were filed and 2,806 cases were disposed of during the year leaving 3,622 cases pending on 12/31/82. There were 3,179 criminal cases on the docket, 1,114 convictions, 501 persons committed to jail and 1,696 cases left pending. **JAILS** Two jails, capacity 239. **ATTORNEYS AT LAW** 389. **UTILITIES** 97% of the residents are connected to a public or privately owned water system and 84% are connected to a public sewer system. Natural gas is distributed to the county by Lone Star Gas Co., Division of Enserch. The average annual residential bill for natural gas in 1982 for the Lone Star distribution system was $405.91, an increase of 35% over 1981. Electricity is distributed to the county by Texas Power & Light Co., Hill Co. Electric Coop., Inc., Limestone Co. Electric Coop., Inc. and McLennan Co. Electric Coop., Inc. and is generated primarily by gas, coal and water. The typical residential electric bill is $201.39 per month for an all-electric house using 2,500 kwh. **TAXES** The county has 35 units with taxing authority: 16 school districts, 13 cities, one county, one college district and four special districts.

RECREATION/ENTERTAINMENT

NATIONAL REGISTER OF HISTORIC PLACES Waco: Earle-Napier-Kinnard House, East Terrace, Fort House, McCulloch House, McLennan County Courthouse, Rotan-Dossett House and Waco Suspension Bridge. Waco vicinity: Torrey's Trading House. **COUNTY/MUNICIPAL PARKS** 2,630 acres in three county and 57 municipal parks. These parks contain 15 miles of hiking trails, 38 playgrounds, one golf course, five football and soccer fields, 27 baseball and softball fields, 46 tennis courts, 12 multi-use courts, five swimming pools, two beaches, nine boat ramps and shore fishing facilities. Developed campsites: 209. **SCENIC DRIVES** The Texas Brazos Trail runs through this county. This trail moves through a beautiful and historic section of Central Texas revealing forested landscapes filled with wildlife and wild flowers. **BOATING/FISHING** Lakes/reservoirs: Battle (19 acres), Brazos (253 acres), Castleman Creek Soil Conservation Service Lake 1 (10 acres), Cow Bayou Soil Conservation Service Lake 2, 4 and 10 (34 acres), Lake Creek (550 acres), New Mart (52 acres), McGinnes (13 acres), Tehuacana Creek Soil Conservation Service Lakes 6, 8, 9, 10, 11, 15, 17, 21, 24, 25, 28 and 29 (210 acres), Tradinghouse Creek (2,010 acres) and Waco (7,270 acres). Major rivers: Brazos, North Bosque and Middle Bosque. Primary streams: Riggs, Castleman, South Fork Cow Bayou, Foster, North Cow Bayou, Manos, Tradinghouse, Sweet, Moose, Cottonwood, Rice, Post Oak, Little Tehuacana, Salt and Williams. **HUNTING** Fall and winter seasons on deer. No closed season on nutria, squirrel, coyote and bobcat. Winter seasons on quail, muskrat, beaver, otter, opossum, mink, ring-tailed cat, badger, fox, raccoon, skunk and civet cat. In 1983 duck, coot, geese, woodcock and jacksnipe seasons occurred during the winter months. Mourning dove seasons occurred intermittently during the fall and winter months. Teal duck, rail and gallinule seasons occurred in the fall. **MUSEUMS** Waco: Historic Waco Foundation, Armstrong Browning Library, Earle-Harrison House, Masonic Grand Lodge Library and Museum-A.F. and A.M., Strecker Museum, Youth Cultural Center, Sims Log Cabin, Lee Lockwood Texas Scottish Rite Library and Museum, Texas Ranger Hall of Fame and Museum, Texas History Collection at Baylor University and Waco Art Center. **THEATERS** Waco: Civic Theatre. **ORCHESTRAS** Waco: Symphony Orchestra. **ZOO** Waco: Central Texas Zoo. **COLLEGIATE FINE ARTS** Waco: Cultural events offered by Baylor University, McLennan Community College and Paul Quinn College. **SPECIAL EVENTS** Cotton Palace Pageant, Waco, April; Brazos River Festival, Waco, April; 500 Mile Ultramarathon Cycle Race, Waco, April; Highland Games, Waco, May; Heart O' Texas Truck and Tractor Pull, Waco, May; Freedom Frolic, Waco, July; Rodeo and Parade, West, August; Roundup Days, Bellmead, August; West Fest, West, September; Great Texas Raft Race, Waco, September; Hay Daze, Hewitt, September; Heart O' Texas Fair and Rodeo, Waco, October; Christmas on the Brazos Homes Tour, Waco, December.

COMMUNITIES

COUNTY SEAT Waco, County Courthouse, 76701; County Clerk's Office, 817/756-7171. **INCORPORATED COMMUNITIES** (1980 population and ZIP Code) Bellmead (7,569) 76705, Beverly Hills (2,083) 76711, Bruceville-Eddy (1,038: 1029 in

COUNTIES

MCLENNAN (continued)

McLennan Co. and 9 in Falls Co.) 76630, Crawford (610) 76638, Gholson (263) 76705, Golinda (335: 43 in McLennan Co. and 292 in Falls Co.) 76655, Hallsburg (455) 76705, Hewitt (5,247) 76643, Lacy-Lakeview (2,752) 76705, Leroy (253) 76654, Lorena (619) 76655, Mart (2,324) 76664, McGregor (4,513) 76657, Moody (1,385) 76557, Northcrest (1,944) 76705, Riesel (691) 76682, Robinson (6,074) 76706, Ross (200) 76684, Valley Mills (1,236: 10 in McLennan Co. and 1,226 in Bosque Co.) 76689, Waco (101,261) 76701, West (2,485) 76691 and Woodway (7,091) 76710. **UNINCORPORATED COMMUNITIES** (and ZIP Code) Asa 76707, Axtell 76624, Battle 76664, Chalk Bluff 76708, China Spring 76633, Downsville 76706, Elk 76624, Elm Mott 76640, Gerald 76640, Harrison 76682, Hoen 76673, Levi 76655, Oak Lake 76705, Ocee 76638, Patton 76689, Rock Creek 76708, Rogers Hill 76691, Rosenthal 76655, South Bosque 76710 Speegleville 76710, Spring Valley 76557, Tours 76691, Wiggins 76691 and Willow Grove 76710. **FOR ADDITIONAL LOCAL INFORMA-TION** Mart Chamber of Commerce, P. O. Box 59, Mart, 76664, 817/876-2231, McGregor Chamber of Commerce, 315 W. Third, McGregor, 76657, 817/840-2292, Moody Chamber of Commerce, P. O. Box 419, Moody, 76557, 817/853-2501, Waco Chamber of Commerce, P. O. Box 1220, Waco, 76703, 817/752-6551, Waco Centex Mexican-American Chamber of Commerce, 1075 18th, Waco, 76703, 817/754-1111 and West Chamber of Commerce, P. O. Box 123, West, 76691, 817/826-5721, 826-3411.

McMULLEN (B18)

THE LAND

South of San Antonio on State Highways 16 and 72 in the Rio Grande Plain Region, McMullen County covers 1,163 square miles with the elevation ranging from 150 to 450 feet. The county has nearly level to undulating soils with light to dark, loamy surfaces over reddish, clayey subsoils that have limestone within 40 inches of the surface and gray to black cracking, clayey soils with a high shrink-swell potential. McMullen is in the South Texas Plains vegetation area with short and mid grasses, mesquite, thorny shrubs and cacti. Less than 1% of the land in the county is considered prime farmland. **CLIMATE** Subtropical Subhumid and relatively dry. The average annual temperature is 71 °F. Temperatures in January range from an average low of 42° to an average high of 66 °F and in July range from 74° to 98 °F. The average annual precipitation is 24 inches, with an average relative humidity of 83% at 6 A.M. and 52% at 6 P.M. There is no snowfall. The growing season averages 290 days per year, with the last freeze in mid February and the first freeze in early December. The sun shines during the year on the average 67% of the daylight hours.

THE PEOPLE

McMullen County is one of the most sparsely populated in the state and has a high percent of residents who are native Texans. The 1982 estimated population of 800 indicates a slight growth in population since 1980 following decades of population decline. The majority of the residents live in rural areas. The age groups with the largest losses from 1970 and 1980 were ages birth to five years and five to 14, which dropped over 50%. The largest ancestry groups are Hispanic (35%), persons of Irish decent (25%), English descent (19%) and German descent (18%). **REGISTERED VOTERS** As of November 2, 1982 there were 596 registered voters. The 1982 general election had a 54% voter turnout, compared to a 62% turnout in the 1980 general

election. In the 1982 primary 100% voted Democratic with 172 votes cast.

THE ECONOMY

AGRICULTURE Ranchland. In 1982, 87% of the land was in farms and ranches, with 2% of the farmland under cultivation. McMullen ranked 224th in the state in highest agricultural receipts, with 93% from livestock and livestock products. Overgrazing, undesirable brush and weeds, water and wind erosion are the current conservation problems. Primary Crops: sorghum, hay and oats. Primary vegetables: watermelons. Primary livestock and products: cattle, milk and hogs. **BUSINESS** Total number of business establishments in the county: 19. In 1980, 24% of the labor force were self-employed, 14% were employed in professional or related services, 3% in manufacturing, 9% in wholesale and retail trade, 43% in agriculture, forestry, fisheries and mining, 25% were employed in other counties and there were 63 retired workers. The industry with the most employment is agribusiness. The nonfarm earnings in 1981 totaled $10,114,000. The retired workers received an average monthly Social Security payment of $302.00. **FINANCE** On June 30, 1983, one commercial bank had total deposits of $11,610,000 and total assets of $12,980,000. **HOUSING** Average value of homes in 1980: $18,000. Between 1970 and 1980 the number of housing units increased by 17%. Sixty-seven percent of all units in the county are air-conditioned, 77% are heated by gas and 17% by electricity. **NATURAL RESOURCES** Caliche, clay, lignite coal, salt domes, sand and gravel, uranium, oil and gas. In 1982 a total of 20,209,632 thousand cubic feet of gas well gas, 56,627 barrels of condensate, 899,661 barrels of crude oil and 639,355 thousand cubic feet of casinghead gas were produced. Current production of other minerals and products includes abrasives, caliche, gravel, crushed sandstone and recovered sulphur. **TOURISM** Travel expenditures of $1,197,000 in 1982 (an increase of 13% over 1981) generated 27 jobs and $224,000 in payroll. **ALCOHOLIC BEVERAGES** Only 4% beer is legal in parts of the county. **FEDERAL EXPENDITURES** The federal government had direct expenditures or obligations of $1,288,000 in the county during fiscal year 1983, including $20,000 by the U.S. Department of Defense. In addition, the federal government provided $19,000 in grant awards, paid $89,000 in salaries and wages, made direct payments to individuals of $936,000 including $564,000 in retirement and disability payments, awarded $14,000 in procurement contracts and spent $229,000 in other expenditures or obligations. The federal government also provided $1,755,000 in guaranteed loans and insurance.

COMMUNICATION

Telephone companies: General Telephone, Southwestern Bell and Valley Telephone Coop. **TRANSPORTATION** Total public road mileage: 300. In 1982 there were 1,141 registered vehicles and 30 reported traffic accidents including two fatalities. Motor freight: three carriers. Aircraft: one is registered in the county.

COMMUNITY SERVICES

EDUCATION One school district with one elementary and one high school. The average daily attendance in 1981-82 was 143, with expenditures per pupil of $5,728 including 17 classroom teachers with an average annual salary of $17,916. Seventy-three percent of the 11 high school graduates planned to attend college. In 1982-83, 51% of the students were White and 49% Hispanic. **HEALTH CARE** Ambulance services: one volunteer service. **CHURCHES** Three churches have an estimated combined membership of 317. The largest denominations are Southern Baptist and Catholic. **SOCIAL SERVICES** In fiscal year 1983 a total of $26,129 in food stamps was distributed, with an average of 59 persons receiving food stamps each month. Aid to Families with Dependent Children (AFDC) totaled $4,714 with an average of three families receiving AFDC each month. Medical assistance benefits for the aged and disabled of $12,362 and for families and children of $8,344 brought the county benefit total to $51,549. **FIRE PROTECTION** Two volunteer fire departments. **LAW ENFORCEMENT** The County Sheriff has seven commissioned officers. **CRIME** One violent crime (murder, forcible rape, robbery and aggravated assault) and seven nonviolent crimes (burglary, larceny-theft and motor vehicle theft) were reported in 1982. **JUDICIAL SYSTEM** Two District Courts and Judges, one County Court and Judge and two Justices of the Peace. In the District Courts a total of 22 cases were pending on 1/1/82, 17 new cases were filed and 11 cases were disposed of during the year leaving 28 cases pending on 12/31/82. There were five criminal cases on the docket, three convictions and two cases left pending. In the County Court 130 cases were pending on 1/1/82, 286 new cases were filed and 342 cases were disposed of during the year leaving 74 cases pending on 12/31/82. There were 412 criminal cases on the docket, 195 convictions and 73 cases left pending. **UTILITIES** 51% of the residents are connected to a public or privately owned water system and 2% are connected to a public sewer system. Electricity is distributed to the county by Karnes Electric Coop., Inc., Medina Electric Coop., Assn., and Nueces Electric Coop., Inc. and is generated primarily by gas, oil and coal. **TAXES** The county has three units with taxing authority: one school district, one county and one special district.

RECREATION/ENTERTAINMENT
NATIONAL REGISTER OF HISTORIC PLACES Calliham vicinity: Mustang Branch Site and Pagan Site. **BOATING/FISHING** Lakes/reservoirs: Big Mule Tank (34 acres), Big Tank (144 acres), Choke Canyon (16,509 acres), Horton (31 acres), Morton (32 acres), Paisano Ranch (34 acres), Red Gate Tank (30 acres) and Van Meter Tank (39 acres). Major rivers: Frio and Nueces. Primary streams: Galinda, Cow, Elm, Muerto, Little Leopard, Opossum, Leoncita, Ygnacio, Guadalupe and Esperanza. **WILDLIFE REFUGES** James A. Daughtrey State Wildlife Management Area covers approximately 20,000 acres in this county. **HUNTING** Fall and winter seasons on deer. No closed season on javelina, squirrel, bobcat and coyote. Winter seasons on quail, muskrat, beaver, opossum, ring-tailed cat, badger, fox, weasel, raccoon, skunk and civet cat. Fall, winter and spring seasons on turkey. Special regulations on state-owned river beds, In 1983 duck, coot, geese, woodcock and jacksnipe seasons occurred during the winter months. Teal duck, rail and gallinule seasons occurred in the fall. Mourning dove seasons occurred intermittently during the fall and winter months. **MUSEUMS** Tilden: McMullen County Museum and Archives. **SPECIAL EVENTS** Rodeo, Tilden, August.

COMMUNITIES
COUNTY SEAT Tilden, County Courthouse, 78072; County Clerk's Office, 512/274-3215. **UNINCORPORATED COMMUNITIES** (and ZIP Code) Calliham (New Calliham) 78007, Cross (Franklin Settlement) 78026, Lomo Alta 78072 and Tilden 78072.

MADISON (C21)

THE LAND
Southeast of Waco on Interstate Highway 45 in the Claypan area, Madison County covers 473 square miles with the elevation ranging from 200 to 350 feet. Along the northern border are undulating, gray to black, cracking, clayey soils that have a high shrink-swell potential and light colored, loamy soils with very deep, reddish, cracking, clayey subsoils. The rest of the county has nearly level to undulating soils with light colored, sandy surfaces and mottled, clayey subsoils. The northeast and south central parts of the county are in the Blackland Prairies vegetation area with tall grasses, mesquite, pecan, oak and elm trees along streams. The rest of the county is in the Post Oak Savannah vegetation area with tall grasses, post and blackjack oak. Between one an 10% of the land in the county is considered prime farmland. **CLIMATE** Subtropical Humid with warm summers. The average annual temperature is 68 °F. Temperatures in January range from an average low of 38° to an average high of 60 °F and in July range from 72° to 95 °F. The average annual precipitation is 40 inches, with an average relative humidity of 85% at 6 A.M. and 56% at 6 P.M. The average annual snowfall is just a trace. The growing season averages 272 days per year, with the last freeze in early March and the first freeze in early December. The sun shines during the year on the average 66% of the daylight hours.

THE PEOPLE
The 1982 estimated population of 11,500 continues the strong growth rate begun in the 1970s. The majority of county residents live in rural areas, which had a 45% population gain between 1970 and 1980. The age groups with the largest increases were ages 15 to 24, 25 to 34 and birth to five years. The county's median age lowered from 30 in 1970 to 24 in 1980. The largest ancestry groups are Black (25%), persons of English descent (22%) and Irish descent (20%). **REGISTERED VOTERS** As of November 2, 1982 there were 4,751 registered voters (0.1% of the state total). The 1982 general election had a 45% voter turnout, compared to a 60% turnout in the 1980 general election. In the 1982 primary 98% voted Democratic and 2% Republican, with 2,027 votes cast.

THE ECONOMY
AGRICULTURE In 1982, 74% of the land was in farms and ranches, with 11% of the farmland under cultivation. Madison ranked 106th in the state in highest agricultural receipts, with 54% from livestock and livestock products. Overgrazing and undesirable brush and weeds are the current conservation problems. Primary crops: hay, oats and sorghum. Primary vegetables: sweet potatoes and watermelons. Primary fruits and nuts: peaches and pecans. Primary livestock and products: cattle, milk and hogs. **BUSINESS** Total number of business establishments in the county: 181. Retail sales during the first quarter of 1984 increased by 8%. In 1980, 14% of the labor force were self-employed, 19% were employed in professional or related services, 8% in manufacturing, 19% in wholesale and retail trade, 20% in agriculture, forestry, fisheries and mining, 20% were employed in other counties and there were 1,004 retired workers. The industries with the most employment: oil and gas field servicing, general construction and the manufacture of men's clothing. The nonfarm earnings in 1981 totaled $69,750,000. The retired workers received an average monthly Social Security payment of $302.00. **FINANCE** On June 30, 1983, two commercial banks had total deposits of $104,754,000 and total assets of $113,254,000. There is one state savings and loan association branch in the county. **HOUSING** Average value of homes in 1980: $29,200. Between 1970 and 1980 the number of housing units increased by 37%. Sixty-six percent of all units in the county are air-conditioned, 77% are heated by gas and 17% by electricity. **NATURAL RESOURCES** Salt domes, sand and gravel, oil, gas and lignite coal. In 1982 a total of 6,652,239 thousand cubic feet of gas well gas, 93,384 barrels of condensate, 1,308,745 barrels of crude oil and 1,560,831 thousand cubic feet of casinghead gas were produced. Current production of other minerals and products includes sand and gravel. **TOURISM** Travel

MCMULLEN (continued)

expenditures of $1,794,000 in 1982 (an increase of 13% over 1981) generated 36 jobs and $312,000 in payroll. **ALCOHOLIC BEVERAGES** Totally dry. **FEDERAL EXPENDITURES** The federal government had direct expenditures or obligations of $14,660,000 in the county during fiscal year 1983, including $318,000 by the U.S. Department of Defense. In addition, the federal government provided $113,000 in grant awards, paid $522,000 in salaries and wages, made direct payments to individuals of $13,906,000 including $10,129,000 in retirement and disability payments, awarded $5,000 in procurement contracts and spent $114,000 in other expenditures or obligations. The federal government also provided $1,434,000 in guaranteed loans and insurance.

COMMUNICATION

Newspapers–Weekly: Madisonville Meteor. Cable TV. Telephone companies: Continental Telephone and Southwestern Bell. **TRANSPORTATION** Total public road mileage: 493. In 1982 there were 8,617 registered vehicles and 245 reported traffic accidents including six fatalities. Intercity bus service is available. Motor freight: two carriers. Rail: one main line carries annually 20 to 30 million tons of freight through the county. Aircraft: 10 are registered in the county. Airports: Madisonville Municipal Airport and Hensarling Flying Strip at Madisonville.

COMMUNITY SERVICES

EDUCATION Two school districts with three elementary, one middle and two high schools. The average daily attendance in 1981-82 was 1,662, with expenditures per pupil of $2,386 including 99 classroom teachers with an average annual salary of $15,603. Thirty-two percent of the 121 high school graduates planned to attend college. In 1982-83, 68% of the students were White, 6% Hispanic, 26% Black, 0.2% Asian. Vocational education: Madison County Medical Center School of Vocational Nursing (Madisonville). **PUBLIC LIBRARIES** Madison County Library (Madisonville): 230,000 volumes. **CHILD CARE** 13 day care licensed facilities. **HEALTH CARE** Seven physicians and three dentists. Hospitals: One with a capacity of 77. Ambulance services: one hospital-based service. Mental health: one county clinic. Nursing homes: two nursing homes with a combined capacity of 106 nursing care residents. The average cost per day for private patients in 1982 was $27.83. **CHURCHES** 26 churches have an estimated combined membership of 4,977. The largest denominations are Southern Baptist and United Methodist. **SOCIAL SERVICES** In fiscal year 1983 a total of $527,923 in food stamps was distributed, with an average of 1,097 persons receiving food stamps each month. Aid to Families with Dependent Children (AFDC) totaled $117,794 with an average of 80 families receiving AFDC each month. Medical assistance benefits for the aged and disabled of $915,299 and for families and children of $123,354 brought the county benefit total to $1,684,369. **FIRE PROTECTION** Two volunteer fire departments. **LAW ENFORCEMENT** The County Sheriff has seven commissioned officers. One police department has a force of seven. **CRIME** 53 violent crimes (murder, forcible rape, robbery and aggravated assault) and 296 nonviolent crimes (burglary, larceny-theft and motor vehicle theft) were reported in 1982. **JUDICIAL SYSTEM** Two District Courts and Judges, one County Court and Judge and four Justices of the Peace. In the District Courts a total of 249 cases were pending on 1/1/82, 286 new cases were filed and 298 cases were disposed of during the year leaving 237 cases pending on 12/31/82. There were 153 criminal cases on the docket, 33 convictions, 13 persons committed to prison and 98 cases left pending. In the County Court 591 cases were pending on 1/1/82, 374 new cases were filed and

191 cases were disposed of during the year leaving 774 cases pending on 12/31/82. There were 874 criminal cases on the docket, 143 convictions, 14 persons committed to jail and 684 cases left pending. **JAILS** One jail, capacity nine. **PRISONS** Ferguson on 4,355 acres northeast of Huntsville, had a inmate population of 2,462 in 1983. It has agricultural operations and a mop and broom factory. **ATTORNEYS AT LAW** Nine. **UTILITIES** 55% of the residents are connected to a public or privately owned water system and 44% are connected to a public sewer system. Natural gas is distributed to the county by Entex, Inc. and Lone Star Gas Co., Division of Enserch. The average annual residential bill for natural gas in 1982 for the Entex distribution system was $309.31, an increase of 26% over 1981, and for Lone Star it was $405.91, an increase of 35%. Electricity is distributed to the county by Gulf State Utilities Co., Houston Co. Electric Coop., Inc., Robertson Electric Coop., Inc. and Mid-South Electric Coop., Assn. and is generated primarily by gas, oil, coal and water. The typical residential electric bill is $198.32 per month for an all-electric house using 2,500 kwh. **TAXES** The county has four units with taxing authority: two school districts, one city and one county.

RECREATION/ENTERTAINMENT

NATIONAL REGISTER OF HISTORIC PLACES Madisonville: Shapira Hotel. **MUNICIPAL PARKS** 246 acres in one municipal park. This park contains two playgrounds, two tennis courts, four multi-use fields, one boat ramp and shore fishing facilities. **SCENIC DRIVES** The Texas Brazos Trail runs through this county. This trail moves through a beautiful and historic section of central Texas revealing forested landscapes filled with wildlife and wild flowers. **BOATING/FISHING** Lakes/reservoirs: Ferguson (113 acres), North Zulch (24 acres) and Town Branch Soil Conservation Service Lake 1 (30 acres). Major rivers: Trinity and Navasota. Primary streams: Shepherd, Town and Bedias. **HUNTING** Fall and winter seasons on deer, No closed season on nutria, squirrel, coyote and bobcat. Winter seasons on quail, muskrat, beaver, otter, opossum, mink, ring-tailed cat, badger, fox, raccoon, skunk and civet cat. In 1983 duck, coot, geese, woodcock and jacksnipe seasons occurred during the winter months. Teal duck, rail and gallinule seasons occurred in the fall. Mourning dove seasons occurred intermittently during the fall and winter months. **MUSEUMS** Madisonville: Yesteryear. **SPECIAL EVENTS** Madison County Fair, Madisonville, March; Sidewalk Cattlemen's Assn. Celebration, Madisonville, June; Fourth of July Celebration, Madisonville, July 4; Christmas Parade, Madisonville, December.

COMMUNITIES

COUNTY SEAT Madisonville, County Courthouse, 77864; County Clerk's Office, 409/348-2639. **INCORPORATED COMMUNITIES** (1980 population and ZIP Code) Madisonville (3,660) 77864 and Normangee (636: 56 in Madison Co. and 580 in Leon Co.) 77871. **UNINCORPORATED COMMUNITIES** (and ZIP Code) Antioch 75852, Connor 77864, Cottonwood 77872, Elwood 75852, George 77871, Hollis 77864, Island (Hopewell) 75852, Jozye 77864, Laceola 77871, Mecca 77871, Midway 75852 and North Zulch 77872. **FOR ADDITIONAL LOCAL INFORMATION** Madison Co. Chamber of Commerce, P. O. Box 358, Madisonville, 77864, 409/348-2658.

MARION (E14)

THE LAND

Bordering Louisiana north of Longview on U.S. Highway 59 in the East Texas Timberlands Region, Marion County covers 385 square miles with the elevation ranging from 200 to 500 feet. The county has sandy to loamy soils with very deep, mottled or reddish subsoils. The soils are deficient in plant nutrients. Marion is in the Pineywoods vegetation area with grasslands and loblolly, shortleaf, long leaf, and slash pines and hardwoods such as oak, hickory and maple. Between 11 and 20% of the land in the county is considered prime farmland. **CLIMATE** Subtropical Humid, warm and moist. The average annual temperature is 64 °F. Temperatures in January range from an average low of 32 ° to an average high of 54 °F and in July range from 71 ° to 93 °F. The average annual precipitation is 46 inches, with an average relative humidity of 85% at 6 A.M. and 57% at 6 P.M. The average annual snowfall is two inches. The growing season averages 236 days per year, with the last freeze in mid March and the first freeze in early November. The sun shines during the year on the average 66% of the daylight hours.

THE PEOPLE

Almost two-thirds of the residents in Marion County live in rural areas. The 1982 estimated population of 10,700 indicates a continuation of the growth in population which began in the 1960s. The greatest gains occurred in rural areas from 1970 to 1980, while urban areas declined in population. The median age of 35 is older than average. The largest ancestry groups are Black (35%), persons of English descent (22%) and Irish descent (16%). **REGISTERED VOTERS** As of November 2, 1982 there were 6,031 registered voters (0.1% of the state total). The 1982 general election had a 47% voter turnout, compared to a 61% turnout in the 1980 general election. In the 1982 primary 98% voted Democratic and 2% Republican, with 1,860 votes cast.

THE ECONOMY

AGRICULTURE Forest production area. In 1982, 32% of the land was in farms and ranches, with 12% of the farmland under cultivation. Marion ranked 246th in the state in highest agricultural receipts, with 78% from livestock and livestock products. Fertilization, water erosion and undesirable woody vegetation in the forestlands are the current conservation problems. Primary crops: hay. Primary vegetables: sweet potatoes and watermelons. Primary fruits and nuts: peaches and pecans. Primary livestock and products: cattle, milk and hogs. **BUSINESS** Total number of business establishments in the county: 121. Retail sales during the first quarter of 1984 increased by 15%. In 1980, 13% of the labor force were self-employed, 16% were employed in professional or related services, 29% in manufacturing, 17% in wholesale and retail trade, 8% in construction, 44% were employed in other counties and there were 915 retired workers. The industries with the most employment: tourism, oil and gas extraction and the manufacture of prepared foods and wood products. The nonfarm earnings in 1981 totaled $62,461,000. The retired workers received an average monthly Social Security payment of $280.00. **FINANCE** On June 30, 1983, one commercial bank had total deposits of $36,602,000 and total assets of $41,092,000. There is one state savings and loan assocaition branch and one credit union in the county. **HOUSING** Average value of homes in 1980: $23,500. Permits for new, privately owned housing units increased in 1982: 28 permits were issued with a total construction cost of $760,000. Of those permits, four were for single family houses. Between 1970 and 1980 the number of housing units increased by 55%. Seventy percent of all units in the county are air-conditioned, 75% are heated by gas and 15% by electricity. **NATURAL RESOURCES** Ceramic clay, iron, industrial sand, oil, gas and lignite coal. In 1982 a total of 3,987,033 thousand cubic feet of gas well gas, 37,181 barrels of condensate, 446,250 barrels of crude oil and 378,172 thousand cubic feet of casinghead gas were produced. Current production of other minerals includes clay. Pine and hardwood production in 1981 totaled 10,121,794 cubic feet: 7,455,839 cubic feet of pine and 2,665,955 cubic feet of

hardwood. **TOURISM** Travel expenditures of $4,706,000 in 1982 (an increase of 18% over 1981) generated 67 jobs and $697,000 in payroll. **ALCOHOLIC BEVERAGES** Packaged distilled spirits, beer, ale, malt liquor and wine are legal in parts of the county. **FEDERAL EXPENDITURES** The federal government had direct expenditures or obligations of $18,630,000 in the county during fiscal year 1983, including $2,848,000 by the U.S. Department of Defense. In addition, the federal government provided $167,000 in grant awards, paid $692,000 in salaries and wages, made direct payments to individuals of $15,900,000 including $11,917,000 in retirement and disability payments, awarded $1,759,000 in procurement contracts and spent $113,000 in other expenditures or obligations. The federal government also provided $30,000 in direct loans and $700,000 in guaranteed loans and insurance.

COMMUNICATION

Newspapers–Weekly: Jefferson Jimplecute. Cable TV. Telephone companies: General Telephone, Southwestern Bell, Caddoan Telephone and Etex Telephone Coop. **TRANSPORTATION** Total public road mileage: 520. In 1982 there were 8,530 registered vehicles and 198 reported traffic accidents including two fatalities. Intercity bus service is available. Motor freight: four carriers. Rail: The Eagle provides passenger service on the Amtrak route. Four main lines carry freight through the county with two carrying annually over 30 million tons of freight each and two carrying five to 10 million tons each. Aircraft: nine are registered in the county. Airports: Cypress River-Marion County Airport and Manning Field at Jefferson.

COMMUNITY SERVICES

EDUCATION One school district with one elementary, two middle and one high school. The average daily attendance in 1981-82 was 1,534, with expenditures per pupil of $2,427 including 111 classroom teachers with an average annual salary of $15,977. Thirty-eight percent of the 97 high school graduates planned to attend college. In 1982-83, 48% of the students were White, 0.3% Hispanic, 52% Black and 0.1% American Indian. Private schools: 63 students enrolled in one high school. **PUBLIC LIBRARIES** Carnegie Library (Jefferson): 10,000 volumes. **CHILD CARE** Four day care and three twenty-four hour care licensed facilities. **HEALTH CARE** Seven physicians and one dentist. Hospitals: two with a combined capacity of 62. Ambulance services: one hospital-based service. Nursing homes: two nursing homes with a combined capacity of 102 nursing care residents. The average cost per day for private patients in 1982 was $28.14. **CHURCHES** 37 churches have an estimated combined membership of 5,221. The largest denominations are Southern Baptist and United Methodist. **SOCIAL SERVICES** In fiscal year 1983 a total of $891,190 in food stamps was distributed, with an average of 1,853 persons receiving food stamps each month. Aid to Families with Dependent Children (AFDC) totaled $231,062, with an average of 162 families receiving AFDC each month. Medical assistance benefits for the aged and disabled of $965,449 and for families and children of $238,319 brought the county benefit total to $2,326,019. **FIRE PROTECTION** One volunteer fire department. **LAW ENFORCEMENT** The County Sheriff has 19 commissioned officers. One police department has a force of nine. **CRIME** 17 violent crimes (murder, forcible rape, robbery and aggravated assault) and 170 nonviolent crimes (burglary, larceny-theft and motor vehicle theft) were reported in 1982. **JUDICIAL SYSTEM** Two District Courts and Judges, one County Court and Judge and four Justices of the Peace. In the District Courts a total of 478 cases were pending on 1/1/82, 275 new cases were filed and 301 cases were disposed of during the year leaving 452 cases pending on 12/31/82. There were 352 criminal cases on the docket,

MARION (continued)

22 convictions, six persons committed to prison, three committed to jail and 46 cases left pending. In the County Court 115 cases were pending on 1/1/82, 305 new cases were filed and 257 cases were disposed of during the year leaving 163 cases pending on 12/31/82. There were 420 criminal cases on the docket, 161 convictions, two persons committed to jail and 163 cases left pending. **JAILS** One jail, capacity 12. **ATTORNEYS AT LAW** 389. **UTILITIES** 42% of the residents are connected to a public or privately owned water system and 22% are connected to a public sewer system. Natural gas is distributed to the county by Arkla, Inc. The average annual residential bill for natural gas in 1982 for the Arkla distribution system was $316.69, an increase of 23% over 1981. Electricity is distributed to the county by Southwestern Electric Power, and Upshur-Rural Electric Coop., Inc. and is generated primarily by gas and water. The typical residential electric bill is $152.08 per month for an all-electric house using 2,500 kwh. **TAXES** The county has four units with taxing authority: one school district, one city, one county and one hospital district.

RECREATION/ENTERTAINMENT
NATIONAL REGISTER OF HISTORIC PLACES Jefferson: Alley-Carlson House, Beard House, Excelsior Hotel, Epperson-McNutt House, Freeman Plantation, Jefferson Historic District, Jefferson Playhouse, The Magnolias, Capt. Perry House, Planters Bank and Warehouse, Old Post Office and Courts Building, Presbyterian Manse, Sedberry House, W.E. Singleton House and Perry Woods House. **COUNTY PARKS** Nine acres in four county parks. These parks contain one tennis court and three boat ramps. **SCENIC DRIVES** The Texas Forest Trail runs through this county. This trail explores the farming, ranching and oilfield areas of the East Texas Pineywoods. **BOATING/FISHING** Lakes/reservoirs: Caddo (25,400 acres), Johnson Creek (650 acres), Lake O' the Pines (18,700 acres) and A. H. Johnson (34 acres). Primary streams: Big Cypress, Little Cypress, Bayou and Johnson. **HUNTING** Fall and winter seasons on deer. Summer, fall and winter seasons on squirrel. Winter seasons on quail, muskrat, beaver, otter, opossum, mink, ring-tailed cat, badger, fox, raccoon, skunk and civet cat. No closed season on nutria, bobcat and coyote. In 1983 duck, coot, geese, woodcock and jacksnipe seasons occurred during the winter months. Teal duck, rail and gallinule seasons occurred in the fall. Mourning dove seasons occurred intermittently during the fall and winter months. **MUSEUMS** Jefferson: Jay Gould Private Railroad Car, Jefferson Historical Society Museum, Excelsior Hotel, Freeman Plantation, The Magnolias and House of the Seasons. **SPECIAL EVENTS** Historical Pilgrimage and Parade, Jefferson, April.

COMMUNITIES
COUNTY SEAT Jefferson, County Courthouse, 75657; County Clerk's Office, 214/665-3971. **INCORPORATED COMMUNITIES** (1980 population and ZIP Code) Jefferson (2,643) 75657. **UNINCORPORATED COMMUNITIES** (and ZIP Code) Berea 75657, Gethsemane 75657, Gray 75657, Hartzo 75657, Jackson 75657, Kellyville 75657, Lassater 75630, Lodi 75564, Lodwick 75657, Orrs 75630, Potters Point 75657, Prospect 75657, Smithland 75690, Sunview 75683 and Warlock 75630 **FOR ADDITIONAL LOCAL INFORMATION** Marion Co. Chamber of Commerce, 116 W. Austin, Jefferson, 75657, 214/665-2672.

MARTIN (P66)

THE LAND
South of Lubbock on State Highways 137 and 176 in the High Plains Region, Martin County covers 914 square miles with the elevation ranging from 2,600 to 3,000 feet. The land in the county is nearly level with sandy soils in the northwest corner over reddish, loamy subsoils. The rest of the county has light colored, loamy surfaces over very deep, reddish or mottled, clayey subsoils and very dark, loamy soils over clayey subsoils that have hardened calcium deposits. Martin is in the High Plains vegetation area with prairie grasses, some mesquite and yucca, junipers, sandsage and shinnery oak. Less than 1% of the land in the county is considered prime farmland. **CLIMATE** Continental Steppe and dry. Duststorms are a problem in spring. The average annual temperature is 63 °F. Temperatures in January range from an average low of 28 ° to an average high of 57 °F and in July range from 68 ° to 95 °F. The average annual precipitation is 16 inches, with an average relative humidity of 72% at 6 A.M. and 35% at 6 P.M. The average annual snowfall is four inches. The growing season averages 217 days per year, with the last freeze in early April and the first freeze in early November. The sun shines during the year on the average 75% of the daylight hours.

THE PEOPLE
The 1982 estimated population of 5,200 is a 12% increase in population since 1980, the first increase since the 1930s. The age group with the greatest loss between 1970 and 1980 was birth to five years. The median age rose from 27 in 1970 to 30 in 1980. The majority of the county residents live in rural areas. The largest ancestry groups are Hispanic (35%), persons of English descent (22%) and Irish descent (19%). **REGISTERED VOTERS** As of November 2, 1982 there were 2,462 registered voters (00.3% of the state total). The 1982 general election had a 44% voter turnout, compared to a 71% turnout in the 1980 general election. In the 1982 primary 98% voted Democratic and 2% Republican, with 940 votes cast.

THE ECONOMY
AGRICULTURE Cotton area. In 1982, 96% of the land was in farms and ranches, with 29% of the farmland under cultivation and 6% irrigated. Martin ranked 38th in the state in highest agricultural receipts, with 95% from crops. Overgrazing, undesirable brush and weeds, water and wind erosion and decreasing irrigation water supplies are the current conservation problems. Primary crops: fifth in the state for cotton. Sorghum, hay and wheat. Primary vegetables: watermelons. Primary fruits and nuts: pecans. Primary livestock and products: cattle and hogs. **BUSINESS** Total number of business establishments in the county: 79. Retail sales during the first quarter of 1984 decreased by 5%. In 1980, 21% of the labor force were self-employed, 17% were employed in professional or related services, 5% in manufacturing, 15% in wholesale and retail trade, 39% in agriculture, forestry, fisheries and mining, 23% were employed in other counties and there were 341 retired workers. The industries with the most employment: oil and gas extraction and agribusiness. The nonfarm earnings in 1981 totaled $44,572,000. The retired workers received an average monthly Social Security payment of $314.00. **FINANCE** On June 30, 1983, one commercial bank had total deposits of $37,217,000 and total assets of $42,152,000. There are three state savings and loan association branches in the county. **HOUSING** Average value of homes in 1980: $25,700. Permits for new, privately owned housing units increased in 1982: 14 permits were issued with a total construction cost of $298,500. Of those permits, all were for single family houses. Between 1970 and 1980 the number of housing units increased by 4%. Seventy-five percent of all units in the county are air-conditioned, 77% are heated by gas and 21% by electricity. **NATURAL RESOURCES** Caliche, oil and gas. In 1982 a total of 44,268 thousand cubic feet of gas well gas, 474 barrels of condensate, 8,880,907 barrels of crude oil and 14,651,865

thousand cubic feet of casinghead gas were produced. Current production of other minerals and products includes caliche. **TOURISM** Travel expenditures of $4,765,000 in 1982 (an increase of 16% over 1981) generated 79 jobs and $762,000 in payroll. **ALCOHOLIC BEVERAGES** Totally dry. **FEDERAL EXPENDITURES** The federal government had direct expenditures or obligations of $18,578,000 in the county during fiscal year 1983, including $128,000 by the U.S. Department of Defense. In addition, the federal government provided $157,000 in grant awards, paid $409,000 in salaries and wages, made direct payments to individuals of $4,842,000 including $3,509,000 in retirement and disability payments, awarded $1,000 in procurement contracts and spent $13,168,000 in other expenditures or obligations. The federal government also provided $4,903,000 in direct loans and $24,067,000 in guaranteed loans and insurance.

COMMUNICATION
Newspapers–Weekly: Stanton Reporter–Spanish. Cable TV. Telephone companies: Southwestern Bell, Poka-Lambro Rural Telephone Coop. and Wes-Tex Telephone Coop. **TRANSPORTATION** Total public road mileage: 715. In 1982 there were 6,174 registered vehicles and 116 reported traffic accidents including three fatalities. Intercity bus service is available. Motor freight: three carriers. Rail: One main line carries annually five to 10 million tons of freight through the county. Aircraft: 15 are registered in the county. Airports: Stanton Municipal Airport serves as a base for 12 aircraft and is a basic utility airport with general aviation service.

COMMUNITY SERVICES
EDUCATION Two school districts with two elementary, two middle and two high schools. The average daily attendance in 1981-82 was 1,050, with expenditures per pupil of $3,731 including 78 classroom teachers with an average annual salary of $18,543. Forty-three percent of the 44 high school graduates planned to attend college. In 1982-83, 45% of the students were White, 52% Hispanic and 3% Black. **PUBLIC LIBRARIES** Martin County Library (Stanton): 6,812 volumes. **CHILD CARE** 11 day care and two twenty-four hour care licensed facilities. **HEALTH CARE** Four physicians. Hospitals: one with a capacity of 26. Ambulance services: one hospital-based service. Nursing homes: one nursing home has a capacity of 65 nursing care residents. The average cost per day for private patients in 1982 was $31.67. **CHURCHES** 13 churches have an estimated combined membership of 3,882. The largest denominations are Catholic, Southern Baptist and United Methodist. **SOCIAL SERVICES** In fiscal year 1983 a total of $281,222 in food stamps was distributed, with an average of 623 persons receiving food stamps each month. Aid to Families with Dependent Children (AFDC) totaled $45,975 with an average of 29 families receiving AFDC each month. Medical assistance benefits for the aged and disabled of $404,170 for families and children of $89,753 brought the county benefit total to $821,120. **FIRE PROTECTION** Two volunteer fire departments. **LAW ENFORCEMENT** The County Sheriff has 13 commissioned officers. One police department has a force of four. **CRIME** Four violent crimes (murder, forcible rape, robbery and aggravated assault) and 73 nonviolent crimes (burglary, larceny-theft and motor vehicle theft) were reported in 1982. **JUDICIAL SYSTEM** One District Court and Judge, one County Court and Judge and two Justices of the Peace. In the District Court a total of 406 cases were pending on 1/1/82, 95 new cases were filed and 72 cases were disposed of during the year leaving 429 cases pending on 12/31/82. There were 87 criminal cases on the docket, six convictions, five persons committed to prison and 81 cases left pending. In the County Court 110 cases were pending on 1/1/82, 184 new cases were filed and 176 cases were disposed of during the year leaving 118 cases

pending on 12/31/82. There were 265 criminal cases on the docket, 79 convictions, 35 persons committed to jail and 92 cases left pending. **JAILS** One jail, capacity 16. **ATTORNEYS AT LAW** Two. **UTILITIES** 54% of the residents are connected to a public or privately owned water system and 52% are connected to a public sewer system. Natural gas is distributed to the county by Energas Company. The average annual residential bill for natural gas in 1982 for the Energas distribution system was $371.63, an increase of 23% over 1981. Electricity is distributed to the county by Cap Rock Electric Coop., Inc., and Lyntegar Electric Coop., Inc. and is generated primarily by gas and coal. **TAXES** The county has eight units with taxing authority: three school districts, two cities, one county, one hospital district and one special district.

RECREATION/ENTERTAINMENT
MUNICIPAL PARKS 25 acres in four municipal parks. These parks contain three playgrounds, one baseball and softball field, two tennis courts and one multi-use court. **BOATING/FISHING** Primary streams: Calf, Mustang and Sulphur Springs. **HUNTING** Fall season on antelope. Fall and winter seasons on javelina. No closed season on squirrel, bobcat and coyote. Winter seasons on quail, muskrat, beaver, opossum, ring-tailed cat, badger, fox, weasel, raccoon, skunk and civet cat. Fall, winter and spring seasons on turkey. In 1983 sandhill crane, duck, coot, geese, woodcock and jacksnipe seasons occurred during the winter months. Teal duck, rail and gallinule seasons occurred in the fall. Mourning dove seasons occurred intermittently during the fall and winter months. **MUSEUMS** Stanton: Martin County Historical Museum. **SPECIAL EVENTS** 4H and High School Agricultural Stock Show, Stanton, January; Old Settlers Reunion, Stanton, July; Martin County Fair, Stanton, August.

COMMUNITIES
COUNTY SEAT Stanton, County Courthouse, 79782; County Clerk's Office, 915/756-3412. **INCORPORATED COMMUNITIES** (1980 population and ZIP Code) Ackerly (317: 92 in Martin Co. and 225 in Dawson Co.) 79713 and Stanton (2,314) 79782. **UNINCORPORATED COMMUNITIES** (and ZIP Code) Lenorah 79749, Tarzan 79783 and Three Leagues 79713. **FOR ADDITIONAL LOCAL INFORMATION** Martin County Chamber of Commerce, P. O. Box 615, Courthouse Square, Stanton, 79782, 915/756-3386.

MASON (C13)

THE LAND
Northwest of Austin on U.S. Highways 87 and 377 in the Central Basin Region, Mason County covers 934 square miles with the elevation ranging from 1,400 to 2,200 feet. The northwestern and southwestern portion of the county have undulating to hilly soils with very dark, loamy soils with an accumulation of lime. The rest of the county has undulating to rolling soils, with loamy surfaces and clayey subsoils, limestone, or sandstone. Mason is in the Edwards Plateau vegetation area with tall and mid grasses, mesquite and shinnery oak. Between one and 10% of the land in the county is considered prime farmland. **CLIMATE** Subtropical Subhumid, dry and mild. The average annual temperature is 65 °F. Temperatures in January range from an average low of 32 ° to an average high of 60 °F and in July range from 70 ° to 97 °F. The average annual precipitation is 25 inches, with an average relative humidity of 77% at 6 A.M. and 45% at 6 P.M. The average annual snowfall is two inches. The growing season averages 217 days per year, with the last freeze in early April and the first freeze in early November. The sun shines during the year on the average 66% of the daylight hours.

MASON (continued)

THE PEOPLE

Mason County ranks 41st among all U.S. counties in the highest percent of population over age 64. The 1982 estimated population of 3,600 indicates a slight loss in population since 1980. The majority of county residents live in rural areas. The median age is older than average, although it lowered from 44 in 1970 to 42 in 1980. Consequently the county has a low birth rate and a high death rate. The largest ancestry groups are persons of German descent (44%), Irish descent (23%) and English descent (22%). **REGISTERED VOTERS** As of November 2, 1982 there were 2,287 registered voters (0.03% of the state total). The 1982 general election had a 54% voter turnout, compared to a 70% turnout in the 1980 general election. In the 1982 primary 73% voted Democratic and 26% Republican, with 644 votes cast.

THE ECONOMY

AGRICULTURE Sheep and angora goat area. In 1982, 93% of the land was in farms and ranches, with 3% of the farmland under cultivation, most of which was irrigated. Mason ranked 162nd in the state in highest agricultural receipts, with 80% from livestock and livestock products. Overgrazing, undesirable brush and weeds, wind and water erosion are the current conservation problems. Primary crops: seventh in the state for peanuts. Hay and oats. Primary vegetables: watermelons. Primary fruits and nuts: peaches and pecans. Primary livestock and products: 10th in the state for angora goats. Cattle, sheep, wool, mohair and hogs. **BUSINESS** Total number of business establishments in the county: 104. Retail sales during the first quarter of 1984 increased by 6%. In 1980, 24% of the labor force were self-employed, 21% were employed in professional or related services, 4% in manufacturing, 20% in wholesale and retail trade, 26% in agriculture, forestry, fisheries and mining, 8% were employed in other counties and there were 568 retired workers. The industry with the most employment is agribusiness. The nonfarm earnings in 1981 totaled $27,822,000. The retired workers received an average monthly Social Security payment of $289.00. **FINANCE** On June 30, 1983, two commercial banks had total deposits of $44,784,000 and total assets of $50,772,000. There is one state savings and loan association branch in the county. **HOUSING** Average value of homes in 1980: $23,700. Between 1970 and 1980 the number of housing units increased by 28%. Sixty-seven percent of all units in the county are air-conditioned, 70% are heated by gas and 17% by electricity. **NATURAL RESOURCES** Copper, dolomite, iron, manganese, industrial sand, tin, oil and gas. **TOURISM** Travel expenditures of $4,502,000 in 1982 (an increase of 14% over 1981) generated 90 jobs and $794,000 in payroll. **ALCOHOLIC BEVERAGES** Only 4% beer is legal in parts of the county. **FEDERAL EXPENDITURES** The federal government had direct expenditures or obligations of $8,837,000 in the county during fiscal year 1983, including $240,000 by the U.S. Department of Defense. In addition, the federal government provided $86,000 in grant awards, paid $226,000 in salaries and wages, made direct payments to individuals of $7,677,000 including $5,247,000 in retirement and disability payments, awarded $1,000 in procurement contracts and spent $846,000 in other expenditures or obligations. The federal government also provided $1,000 in direct loans and $660,000 in guaranteed loans and insurance.

COMMUNICATION

Newspapers–Weekly: Mason County News (Mason). Cable TV. Telephone companies: General Telephone and Hill Country Telephone Coop. **TRANSPORTATION** Total public road mileage: 512. In 1982 there were 3,770 registered vehicles and 74 reported traffic accidents including one fatality. Intercity bus service is available. Motor freight: three carriers. Aircraft: 19 are registered in the county. Airports: Mason County Airport at Mason.

COMMUNITY SERVICES

EDUCATION One school district with one elementary and one high school. The average daily attendance in 1981-82 was 613, with expenditures per pupil of $3,314 including 62 classroom teachers with an average annual salary of $15,569. Sixty-four percent of the 50 high school graduates planned to attend college. In 1982-83, 71% of the students were White, 29% Hispanic, 0.3% Black. **PUBLIC LIBRARIES** Mason County Library (Mason): 13,390 volumes. **CHILD CARE** 10 day care licensed facilities. **HEALTH CARE** One physician and one dentist. Hospitals: one with a capacity of 18. Ambulance services: one commercial service. Nursing homes: two nursing homes with a combined capacity of 74 nursing care residents. The average cost per day for private patients in 1982 was $26.89. **CHURCHES** 14 churches have an estimated combined membership of 2,837. The largest denominations are United Methodist, Southern Baptist and American Lutheran. **SOCIAL SERVICES** In fiscal year 1983 a total of $70,403 in food stamps was distributed, with an average of 167 persons receiving food stamps each month. Aid to Families with Dependent Children (AFDC) totaled $4,173 with an average of five families receiving AFDC each month. Medical assistance benefits for the aged and disabled of $485,772 and for families and children of $15,769 brought the county benefit total to $576,117. **FIRE PROTECTION** One volunteer fire department. **LAW ENFORCEMENT** The County Sheriff has five commissioned officers. One police department has a force of two. **CRIME** Seven violent crimes (murder, forcible rape, robbery and aggravated assault) and 32 nonviolent crimes (burglary, larceny-theft and motor vehicle theft) were reported in 1982. **JUDICIAL SYSTEM** One District Court and Judge, one County Court and Judge and one Justice of the Peace. In the District Court a total of 255 cases were pending on 1/1/82, 118 new cases were filed and 115 cases were disposed of during the year leaving 258 cases pending on 12/31/82. There were 228 criminal cases on the docket, 45 convictions, five persons committed to prison, five committed to jail and 161 cases left pending. **JAILS** One jail, capacity five. **ATTORNEYS AT LAW** Six. **UTILITIES** 51% of the residents are connected to a public or privately owned water system and 51% are connected to a public sewer system. Electricity is distributed to the county by Mason Utilities, McCulloch Electric Coop., Inc., Central Texas Electric Coop., Inc. and Kimble Electric Coop., Inc. and is generated primarily by gas, coal, oil and water. **TAXES** The county has four units with taxing authority: one school district, one city, one county and one special district.

RECREATION/ENTERTAINMENT

NATIONAL REGISTER OF HISTORIC PLACES Mason: Mason Historic District and Reynolds-Seaquist House. **COUNTY/MUNICIPAL PARKS** 102 acres in two municipal parks. These parks contain one playground, two baseball and softball fields and one swimming pool. **SCENIC DRIVES** The Texas Forts Trail runs through this county. This trail leads to eight of the famous frontier forts of west central Texas and an ancient presidio of the Spanish colonial period. **BOATING/FISHING** Major rivers: James, Llano and San Saba. Primary streams: Honey, Beaver, Martin, Schepp and Willow. **HUNTING** Fall and winter seasons on deer and javelina. No closed season on squirrel, bobcat and coyote. Winter seasons on quail, muskrat, beaver, opossum, ring-tailed cat, badger, fox, weasel, raccoon, skunk and civet cat. Fall, winter and spring seasons on turkey. In 1983 duck, coot, geese, woodcock and jacksnipe seasons occurred during the winter months. Teal duck, rail and gallinule seasons occurred in the fall. Mourning dove season occurred intermittently during the fall and winter months. **MUSEUMS** Mason: Mason County Museum, Seaquist House and Fort Mason. **SPECIAL EVENTS** Youth Stock Show, Mason, January; FFA Rodeo and Parade, Mason, May; Rodeo Roundup and Parade, Mason, July; County Fair, Mason, August.

COMMUNITIES
COUNTY SEAT Mason, County Courthouse, 76856; County Clerk's Office, 915/347-5253. **INCORPORATED COMMUNITIES** (1980 population and ZIP Code) Mason (2,153) 76856. **UNINCORPORATED COMMUNITIES** (and ZIP Code) Air (Camp Air) 76856, Art 76820, Fredonia 76842, Grit 76846, Hedwigs Hill 76856, Hilda 76856, Katemcy 76850, Koockville 76856, Loyal Valley 76856, Pontotoc 76869 and Streeter 76856. **FOR ADDITIONAL LOCAL INFORMATION** Mason Co. Chamber of Commerce, 108 Ft. McKavitt, Mason, 76856, 915/347-5758.

MATAGORDA (G24)

THE LAND
Bordering the Gulf of Mexico southwest of Houston on State Highways 35 and 60 in the Coastal Prairie Region, Matagorda County covers 1,127 square miles with the elevation ranging from sea level to 70 feet. Along the rivers the soils are brownish to reddish, cracking and clayey to loamy. The remainder of the county has light colored, shallow loam over clayey subsoils with areas of gray to black, cracking, clayey soils, especially in the marshes along the coast. Along the Gulf Coast the soils are sandy. The vegetation is the tall grasses and live oaks of the Gulf Prairies and the cordgrasses, sedges and saltgrasses of the Gulf Marshes. Between 31 and 40% of the land in the county is considered prime farmland. **CLIMATE** Subtropical Humid. June through October a risk of tropical storms and hurricanes exists. The average annual temperature is 70°F. Temperatures in January range from an average low of 44° to an average high of 64°F and in July range from 76° to 92°F. The average annual precipitation is 44 inches, with an average relative humidity of 90% at 6 A.M. and 70% at 6 P.M. There is no snowfall. The growing season averages 295 days per year, with the last freeze in mid February and the first freeze in mid December. The sun shines during the year on the average 66% of the daylight hours.

THE PEOPLE
The population growth in Matagorda County was more rapid between 1970 and 1980 than in the previous 40 years, however, the 1982 estimated population of 37,200 reflects a slight decrease in population since 1980. Urban areas grew faster than rural areas between 1970 and 1980. The age groups with the greatest gains were ages 20 to 34 and birth to five years. The largest ancestry groups are Hispanic (21%), persons of English descent (20%), German descent (16%) and Irish descent (16%). **REGISTERED VOTERS** As of November 2, 1982 there were 15,939 registered voters (0.2% of the state total). The 1982 general election had a 43% voter turnout, compared to a 63% turnout in the 1980 general election. In the 1982 primary 92% voted Democratic and 8% Republican, with 3,997 votes cast.

THE ECONOMY
AGRICULTURE Rice and sorghum area. In 1982, 80% of the land was in farms and ranches, with 28% of the farmland under cultivation and 40% irrigated. Matagorda ranked 23rd in the state in highest agricultural receipts, with 67% from crops. Drainage, flooding and stream bank erosion are the current conservation problems. Primary crops: second in the state for rice. Sorghum, soybeans, wheat, hay and cotton. Primary vegetables:

potatoes. Primary fruits and nuts: peaches and pecans. Primary livestock and products: cattle. **BUSINESS** Total number of business establishments in the county: 728. Retail sales during the first quarter of 1984 increased by 21%. In 1980, 9% of the labor force were self-employed, 13% were employed in professional or related services, 12% in manufacturing, 20% in wholesale and retail trade, 23% in construction, 16% were employed in other counties and there were 2,444 retired workers. The industries with the most employment: agribusiness, tourism, oil and gas field servicing, fish packaging and the manufacture of industrial chemicals. The nonfarm earnings in 1981 totaled $352,860,000. The retired workers received an average monthly Social Security payment of $321.00. **FINANCE** On June 30, 1983, four commercial banks had total deposits of $242,420,000 and total assets of $277,060,000. On December 31, 1982 one state savings and loan association, one federal association and one federal branch had combined assets of $171,365,000. In addition there are three credit unions in the county. **HOUSING** Average value of homes in 1980: $36,300. Permits for new, privately owned housing units decreased in 1982: 68 permits were issued with a total construction cost of $3,933,876. Of those permits, 66 were for single family houses. Between 1970 and 1980 the number of housing units increased by 48%. Seventy-five percent of all units in the county are air-conditioned, 76% are heated by gas and 23% by electricity. **NATURAL RESOURCES** Salt domes, brine, oil and gas. In 1982 a total of 97,440,054 thousand cubic feet of gas well gas, 1,083,410 barrels of condensate, 1,821,138 barrels of crude oil and 6,780,641 thousand cubic feet of casinghead gas were produced. Current production of other minerals and products includes brine. **TOURISM** Travel expenditures of $46,892,000 in 1982 (an increase of 16% over 1981) generated 793 jobs and $7,560,000 in payroll. Lodging: eight hotels, motels and tourist courts. **ALCOHOLIC BEVERAGES** Packaged distilled spirits, beer, ale, malt liquor and wine are legal in parts of the county. Sale of mixed beverages is legal in all or parts of the county. **FEDERAL EXPENDITURES** The federal government had direct expenditures or obligations of $53,940,000 in the county during fiscal year 1983, including $5,103,000 by the U.S. Department of Defense. In addition, the federal government provided $4,230,000 in grant awards, paid $2,460,000 in salaries and wages, made direct payments to individuals of $37,025,000 including $28,048,000 in retirement and disability payments, awarded $2,405,000 in procurement contracts and spent $7,820,000 in other expenditures or obligations. The federal government also provided $3,083,000 in direct loans and $146,388,000 in guaranteed loans and insurance.

COMMUNICATION
Newspapers–Daily: The Daily Tribune (Bay City), ave. eve. circ. 7,098. Weekly: Palacios Beacon. Radio: KIOX-AM (Bay City). Cable TV. Telephone companies: Continental Telephone, General Telephone and Southwestern Bell. **TRANSPORTATION** Total public road mileage: 952. In 1982 there were 31,083 registered vehicles and 820 reported traffic accidents including 14 fatalities. Taxi cabs: two companies in Bay City and one in Palacios. Intercity bus service is available. Motor freight: 16 local and intrastate carriers. Rail: Three main and five branch lines carry freight through the county. The three main lines carry annually 10 to 20 million tons of freight each and the five branch lines carry less than one million tons each. Aircraft: 74 are registered in the county. Airports: Bay City Municipal Airport serves as a base for 35 aircraft and is a basic transportation airport with general aviation service. Palacios Municipal Airport serves as a base for 15 aircraft and is a general utility airport with general aviation service. Also serving the area are Fehmel Dusting Service Airport at Bay City and Bay City Airport. Wagner General Hospital at Palacios provides a heliport for emergency use. Waterborne

COUNTIES

MATAGORDA (continued)

commerce: Colorado River and Flood Discharge Channels shipped 403,016 short tons of domestic freight in 1981. The Channel to Palacios shipped 100,293 short tons of domestic freight.

COMMUNITY SERVICES

EDUCATION Five school districts with 11 elementary, five middle and four high schools. The average daily attendance in 1981-82 was 6,814, with expenditures per pupil of $3,520 including 477 classroom teachers with an average annual salary of $18,349. Fifty-nine percent of the 461 high school graduates planned to attend college. In 1982-83, 52% of the students were White, 29% Hispanic, 17% Black, 2% Asian and 0.1% American Indian. Sports championships: 1984 AAAA Football, Bay City H.S. Private schools: 216 students enrolled in one elementary school. **PUBLIC LIBRARIES** Bay City Public Library: 20,500 volumes. Palacios Library, Inc.: 24,527 volumes. **CHILD CARE** 38 day care and 15 twenty-four hour care licensed facilities. **HEALTH CARE** 31 physicians and 10 dentists. Hospitals: two with a combined capacity of 153. Clinics: one public health clinic. Ambulance services: three commercial, three volunteer services and two funeral homes. Mental health: two county clinics. Nursing homes: three nursing homes with a combined capacity of 235 nursing care residents. The average cost per day for private patients in 1982 was $36.96. **CHURCHES** 55 churches have an estimated combined membership of 21,315. The largest denominations are Catholic, Southern Baptist and United Methodist. **SOCIAL SERVICES** In fiscal year 1983 a total of $1,765,285 in food stamps was distributed, with an average of 3,555 persons receiving food stamps each month. Aid to Families with Dependent Children (AFDC) totaled $394,949 with an average of 250 families receiving AFDC each month. Medical assistance benefits for the aged and disabled of $1,897,557 and for families and children of $542,968 brought the county benefit total to $4,600,759. **FIRE PROTECTION** Nine volunteer fire departments. **LAW ENFORCEMENT** The County Sheriff has 41 commissioned officers. Two police departments have a combined force of 48. **CRIME** 205 violent crimes (murder, forcible rape, robbery and aggravated assault) and 1,595 nonviolent crimes (burglary, larceny-theft and motor vehicle theft) were reported in 1982. **JUDICIAL SYSTEM** Two District Courts and Judges, one County Court and Judge and six Justices of the Peace. In the District Courts a total of 1,220 cases were pending on 1/1/82, 930 new cases were filed and 953 cases were disposed of during the year leaving 1,197 cases pending on 12/31/82. There were 267 criminal cases on the docket, 130 convictions, 26 persons committed to prison and 52 cases left pending. In the County Court 684 cases were pending on 1/1/82, 540 new cases were filed and 430 cases were disposed of during the year leaving 794 cases pending on 12/31/82. There were 919 criminal cases on the docket, 207 convictions, 65 persons committed to jail and 500 cases left pending. **JAILS** Two jails, capacity 59. New jail opened in 1983. **ATTORNEYS AT LAW** 39. **UTILITIES** 76% of the residents are connected to a public or privately owned water system and 66% are connected to a public sewer system. Natural gas is distributed to the county by Entex, Inc. and Markham Gas Corporation. The average annual residential bill for natural gas in 1982 for the Entex distribution system was $390.31, an increase of 26% over 1981. Electricity is distributed to the county by Cochran Power & Light Co., Central Power & Light Co., Jackson Electric Coop., Inc. and Wharton Co. Electric Coop., Inc. and is generated primarily by gas, oil and coal. The typical residential electric bill is $162.15 per month for an all-electric house using 2,500 kwh. **TAXES** The county has 13 units with taxing authority: six school districts, two cities, one county, two utility districts and two special districts.

RECREATION/ENTERTAINMENT

NATIONAL REGISTER OF HISTORIC PLACES Blessing: Hotel Blessing. **MUNICIPAL PARKS** 96 acres in 25 municipal parks. These parks contain 10 playgrounds, eight baseball and softball fields, eight tennis courts, one multi-use court, two swimming pools, one boat ramp and shore fishing facilities. **SCENIC DRIVES** The Texas Independence Trail runs through this county. This trail surveys the historic sites of southeastern Texas and includes many modern visitor attractions such as the Johnson Space Center. **BOATING/FISHING** Major rivers: Colorado. Primary streams: Cedar Lake, Linnville Bayou and Live Oak Bayou. Saltwater fishing: speckled trout, redfish and flounder fishing is usually good around Matagorda Bay, East Matagorda Bay and Tres Palacios Bay. Shrimp, oysters and crabs may be taken but, like other saltwater fish, under specific regulations. **WILDLIFE REFUGES** San Bernard National Wildlife Refuge covers 19,382 acres. **HUNTING** Fall and winter season on deer. No closed season on nutria, squirrel, bobcat and coyote. Winter seasons on quail, pheasant, muskrat, beaver, otter, oppossum, mink, ringtailed cat, badger, fox, raccoon, skunk and civet cat. Fall and winter seasons on turkey. In 1983 duck, coot, geese, woodcock and jacksnipe seasons occurred during the winter months with a winter season on sandhill crane in some parts of the county. Teal duck, rail and gallinule season occurred in the fall. Mourning dove seasons occurred intermittently during the fall and winter months. **MUSEUMS** Bay City: Matagorda County Historical Museum, Bay City Art Gallery and South Texas Project Visitors Center. **SPECIAL EVENTS** Valentine Parade and Pageant, Palacios, February; County Fair, Rodeo and Parade, Bay City, March; Springfling, Bay City, April; July 4th Boat Races and Carnival, Palacios, July; Rice Festival, Bay City, September; Bayfest, Palacios, November; Youth Rodeo, Bay City, November; Christmastime-by-the Sea Parade, Palacios, December.

COMMUNITIES

COUNTY SEAT Bay City, County Courthouse, 77414; County Clerk's Office, 409/245-8452. **INCORPORATED COMMUNITIES** (1980 population and ZIP Code) Bay City (17,837) 77414 and Palacios (4,667) 77465. **UNINCORPORATED COMMUNITIES** (and ZIP Code) Allenhurst 77414, Ashby 77465, Ashwood 77480, Beadle 77424, Blessing 77419, Buckeye 77414, Caney 77414, Cedar Lake 77414, Cedar Lane 77415, Clemville 77427, Collegeport 77428, Elmaton 77440, Hawkinsville 77425, Markham 77456, Matagorda 77457, Midfield 77458, Pledger 77468, Sargent 77414, Simpsonville 77465, Sugar Valley 77480, Van Vleck 77482 and Wadsworth 77483. **FOR ADDITIONAL LOCAL INFORMATION** Bay City Chamber of Commerce, 2420 7th St., Bay City, 77414, 409/245-8333 and Palacios Chamber of Commerce, P. O. Box 774, Palacios, 77465, 512/972-2615.

MAVERICK (B13)

THE LAND

Bordering Mexico southwest of San Antonio on U.S. Highways 57 and 277 in the Rio Grande Plain Region, Maverick County covers 1,287 square miles with the elevation ranging from 650 to 1,000 feet. The nearly level to undulating soils are gray to black, cracking and clayey with a high shrink-swell potential. In some areas the soils are light colored and loamy with limestone bedrock. In the South Plains vegetation area, the grasses are short to mid height with areas of dense brush. Less than 1% of the land in the county is considered prime farmland. **CLIMATE** Subtropical Steppe, warm and dry. The average annual temperature is 71 °F. Temperatures in January range from an average low of

39° to an average high of 64 °F and in July range from 75 ° to 99 °F. The average annual precipitation is 20 inches, with an average relative humidity of 77% at 6 A.M. and 42% at 6 P.M. There is no snowfall. The growing season averages 285 days per year, with the last freeze in mid February and the first freeze in early December. The sun shines during the year on the average 65% of the daylight hours.

THE PEOPLE
Among all U.S. counties Maverick County ranks fourth in the highest percent of persons who are of Spanish origin and 64th in the highest birth rate. The 1982 estimated population of 34,200 indicates a continuation of the steady growth which has existed since 1930. Population gains in rural areas between 1970 and 1980 reached 266%, one of the highest rural growth rates in the state. The age groups with the largest gains were ages 50 to 54 and 20 to 24, both of which doubled in size. With a median age of 22, the population is the youngest in the state. It ranks low among Texas counties in the percent of residents who are native Texans. The largest ancestry groups are Hispanic (90%), persons of English descent (3%) and Irish descent (2%). **REGISTERED VOTERS** As of November 2, 1982 there were 9,967 registered voters (0.2% of the state total). The 1982 general election had a 35% voter turnout, compared to a 48% turnout in the 1980 general election. In the 1982 primary 99% voted Democratic and 0.3% Republican, with 4,523 votes cast.

THE ECONOMY
AGRICULTURE Cattle ranches. In 1982, 88% of the land was in farms and ranches, with 2% of the farmland under cultivation, most of which was irrigated. Maverick ranked 108th in the state in highest agricultural receipts, with 89% from livestock and livestock products. Overgrazing, undesirable brush and weeds, inefficient irrigation systems and erosion are the current conservation problems. Primary crops: hay, oats and wheat. Primary vegetables: spinach. Primary fruits and nuts: peaches and fifth in the state for pecans. Primary livestock and products: cattle, milk, sheep, wool, angora goats, mohair and hogs. **BUSINESS** Total number of business establishments in the county: 440. Retail sales during the first quarter of 1984 increased by 15%. In 1980, 6% of the labor force were self-employed, 20% were employed in professional or related services, 19% in manufacturing, 21% in wholesale and retail trade, 10% in agriculture, forestry, fisheries and mining, 11% were employed in other counties and there were 1,397 retired workers. The industries with the most employment: gas and oil field services, tourism, agribusiness and men's work clothing. The nonfarm earnings in 1981 totaled $121,241,000. The retired workers received an average monthly Social Security payment of $242.00. **FINANCE** On June 30, 1983, two commercial banks had total deposits of $125,570,000 and total assets of $138,356,000. There are two state savings and loan association branches and two credit unions in the county. **HOUSING** Average value of homes in 1980: $25,600. Permits for new, privately owned housing units decreased in 1982: 114 permits were issued with a total construction cost of $2,304,800. Of those permits, 66 were for single family houses. Between 1970 and 1980 the number of housing units increased by 85%. Fifty-one percent of all units in the county are air-conditioned, 72% are heated by gas and 22% by electricity. **NATURAL RESOURCES** Bituminous coal, limestone, industrial sand, sand, gravel, oil and gas. In 1982 a total of 3,233,446 thousand cubic feet of gas well gas, 16,544 barrels of condensate, 1,448,838 barrels of crude oil and 654,298 thousand cubic feet of casinghead gas were produced. Current production of other minerals and products includes sand and gravel. **TOURISM** Travel expenditures of $16,506,000 in 1982 (an increase of 12% over 1981) generated 401 jobs and $3,239,000 in

payroll. Lodging: four hotels, motels and tourist courts. **ALCOHOLIC BEVERAGES** Packaged distilled spirits, beer, ale, malt liquor and wine are legal in parts of the county. Sale of mixed beverages is legal in all or parts of the county. **MILITARY INSTALLATIONS** Eagle Pass Auxiliary Air Field, Quemado, 824 acres, auxiliary training field. **FEDERAL EXPENDITURES** The federal government had direct expenditures or obligations of $28,865,000 in the county during fiscal year 1983, including $554,000 by the U.S. Department of Defense. In addition, the federal government provided $2,357,000 in grant awards, paid $4,959,000 in salaries and wages, made direct payments to individuals of $20,470,000 including $16,466,000 in retirement and disability payments, awarded $951,000 in procurement contracts and spent $128,000 in other expenditures or obligations. The federal government also provided $69,000 in direct loans and $2,666,000 in guaranteed loans and insurance.

COMMUNICATION
Newspapers–Weekly: Eagle Pass News-Guide. Radio: KEPS-AM and KINL-FM (Eagle Pass). Cable TV. Telephone companies: Southwestern Bell. **TRANSPORTATION** Total public road mileage: 324. In 1982 there were 15,972 registered vehicles and 379 reported traffic accidents including four fatalities. Taxi cabs: three companies in Eagle Pass. Municipal transit systems: two intracity bus systems in Eagle Pass with scheduled routes. Intercity bus service is available. Motor freight: two carriers. Rail: one branch line carries annually one to five million tons of freight through the county. Aircraft: 36 are registered in the county. Airports: Eagle Pass Municipal Airport is a basic transportation airport with general aviation service.

COMMUNITY SERVICES
EDUCATION One school district with eight elementary, one middle, one high school and one special education. The average daily attendance in 1981-82 was 8,033 with expenditures per pupil of $1,507 including 384 classroom teachers with an average annual salary of $15,110. Fifty-seven percent of the 430 high school graduates planned to attend college. In 1982-83, 4% of the students were White and 96% Hispanic. Private schools: 554 students enrolled in three elementary and one high school. **PUBLIC LIBRARIES** Eagle Pass Public Library: 40,500 volumes. Quemado Library. **CHILD CARE** 18 day care and one twenty-four hour care licensed facilities. **HEALTH CARE** 18 physicians and two dentists. Hospitals: one with a capacity of 77. Clinics: one dialysis clinic and one public health clinic. Ambulance services: one fire department and one hospital-based service. Mental health: one county clinic. Nursing homes: one nursing home has a capacity of 120 nursing care residents. The average cost per day for private patients in 1982 was $30.13. **CHURCHES** 21 churches have an estimated combined membership of 16,446. The largest denomination is Catholic. **SOCIAL SERVICES** In fiscal year 1983 a total of $6,091,959 in food stamps was distributed, with an average of 11,723 persons receiving food stamps each month. Aid to Families with Dependent Children (AFDC) totaled $754,959 with an average of 457 families receiving AFDC each month. Medical assistance benefits for the aged and disabled of $2,174,462 and for families and children of $1,082,366 brought the county benefit total to $10,103,744. **FIRE PROTECTION** One volunteer fire department. **LAW ENFORCEMENT** The County Sheriff has 17 commissioned officers. One police department has a force of 30. **CRIME** 91 violent crimes (murder, forcible rape, robbery and aggravated assault) and 1,244 nonviolent crimes (burglary, larceny-theft and motor vehicle theft) were reported in 1982. **JUDICIAL SYSTEM** One District Court and Judge, one County Court and Judge and five Justices of the Peace. In the District Court a total of 492 cases were pending on 1/1/82, 538 new cases

COUNTIES

MAVERICK (continued)

were filed and 744 cases were disposed of during the year leaving 286 cases pending on 12/31/82. There were 188 criminal cases on the docket, 93 convictions, 13 persons committed to prison, two committed to jail and 72 cases left pending. In the County Court 939 cases were pending on 1/1/82, 221 new cases were filed and 92 cases were disposed of during the year leaving 1,068 cases pending on 12/31/82. There were 1,072 criminal cases on the docket, 31 convictions, one person committed to jail and 989 cases left pending. **JAILS** One jail, capacity 44. Major renovation completed in 1983. **ATTORNEYS AT LAW** 15. **UTILITIES** 92% of the residents are connected to a public or privately owned water system and 73% are connected to a public sewer system. Natural gas is distributed to the county by Eagle Pass Natural Gas Co. Electricity is distributed to the county by Central Power and Light Co. and Rio Grande Electric Coop., Inc. and is generated primarily by gas, oil and coal. The typical residential electric bill is $162.15 per month for an all-electric house using 2,500 kwh. **TAXES** The county has four units with taxing authority: one school district, one city, one county and one hospital district.

RECREATION/ENTERTAINMENT

NATIONAL REGISTER OF HISTORIC PLACES Eagle Pass: Maverick County Courthouse and Fort Duncan. **COUNTY/ MUNICIPAL PARKS** 359 acres in one county and 13 municipal parks. These parks contain one mile of hiking trails, 12 playgrounds, one golf course, two football and soccer fields, seven baseball and softball fields, one tennis court, one multi-use court and three swimming pools. **BOATING/FISHING** Lakes/reservoirs: El Indio Farms (27 acres), Farias (254 acres), Goofy (48 acres), King Tank (48 acres), W. D. Ranch (21 acres), Winn Company 1 (237 acres), Winn Company 2 (96 acres), Winn 2 (117 acres) and Winn 3 (28 acres). Major rivers: Rio Grande. Primary streams: Comanche, Buck Hollow, Elm, Rosita, San Ambrosia, Picosa, Salado and Mula. **HUNTING** Fall and winter seasons on deer. No closed season on javelina, squirrel, bobcat and coyote. Winter seasons on quail, muskrat, beaver, opossum, ring-tailed cat, badger, fox, weasel, raccoon, skunk and civet cat. Fall and winter seasons on turkey. In 1983 sandhill crane, duck, coot, geese, woodcock and jacksnipe seasons occurred during the winter months. Teal duck, rail and gallinule seasons occurred in the fall. Mourning dove seasons occurred intermittently during the fall and winter months with a fall season on white-winged dove. **MUSEUMS** Eagle Pass: Fort Duncan Museum. **SPECIAL EVENTS** Maverick County Stock Show and Rodeo, Eagle Pass, January; International Friendship Festival, Eagle Pass, March; Fourth of July Celebration, Eagle Pass, July.

COMMUNITIES

COUNTY SEAT Eagle Pass, County Courthouse, 78852; County Clerk's Office, 512/773-2829. **INCORPORATED COMMUNITIES** (1980 population and ZIP Code) Eagle Pass (21,407) 78852. **UNINCORPORATED COMMUNITIES** (and ZIP Code) El Indio 78860, Normandy 78875, Quemado 78877 and Seco Mines (La Gloria) 78852. **FOR ADDITIONAL LOCAL INFORMATION** Eagle Pass Chamber of Commerce, 400 Garrison, Eagle Pass, 78853, 512/773-3224.

MEDINA (C34)

THE LAND

West of San Antonio on U.S. Highway 90 in the Rio Grande Plain Region, Medina County covers 1,331 square miles with the elevation ranging from 600 to 1,800 feet. The undulating to hilly soils are light colored, brownish to reddish and well drained with areas of dark loamy surfaces over clayey subsoils. In the southeast the more level soils are deep with light colored loam over mottled, clayey subsoils. The north is in the Edwards Plateau vegetation area with tall to mid grasses and brush, primarily junipers, mesquite, shinnery oak and some live oak. The remainder of Medina is in the South Texas Plains vegetation area with bluestems, buffalograss and Arizona cottontop grasses and post oak, live oak and mesquite trees. Between 41 and 50% of the land in the county is considered prime farmland. **CLIMATE** Subtropical Subhumid, with hot, dry summers. The average annual temperature is 67 °F. Temperatures in January range from an average low of 37 ° to an average high of 63 °F and in July range from 70 ° to 97 °F. The average annual precipitation is 28 inches, with an average relative humidity of 81% at 6 A.M. and 49% at 6 P.M. The annual snowfall is not significant. The growing season averages 275 days per year, with the last freeze in early March and the first freeze in late November. The sun shines during the year on the average 65% of the daylight hours.

THE PEOPLE

Medina County ranks 56th among all U.S. counties in the highest percent of persons of Spanish origin. The 1982 estimated population of 23,600 continues the moderate growth rate which has existed since the 1930s. The growth rate doubled from 7% between 1960 and 1970 to 14% between 1970 and 1980. Urban and rural areas grew at approximately the same pace between 1970 and 1980 with slightly higher gains in rural areas. The population has a median age of 31. The largest ancestry groups are Hispanic (43%), persons of German descent (43%), English descent (14%) and Irish descent (14%). **REGISTERED VOTERS** As of November 2, 1982 there were 11,843 registered voters (0.2% of the state total). The 1982 general election had a 49% voter turnout, compared to a 69% turnout in the 1980 general election. In the 1982 primary 94% voted Democratic and 6% Republican, with 3,959 votes cast.

THE ECONOMY

AGRICULTURE Cattle area. In 1982, 84% of the land was in farms and ranches, with 21% of the farmland under cultivation and 30% irrigated. Medina ranked 60th in the state in highest agricultural receipts, with 60% from livestock and livestock products. Overgrazing, undesirable brush and weeds, water erosion, inefficient irrigation systems and salinity are the current conservation problems. Primary crops: sorghum, corn, oats, wheat and hay. Primary vegetables: seventh in the state for carrots. Watermelons. Primary fruits and nuts: pecans. Primary livestock and products: cattle, milk, sheep, wool and hogs. **BUSINESS** Total number of business establishments in the county: 388. Retail sales during the first quarter of 1984 increased by 19%. In 1980, 14% of the labor force were self-employed, 17% were employed in professional or related services, 9% in manufacturing, 21% in wholesale and retail trade, 14% in agriculture, forestry, fisheries and mining, 37% were employed in other counties and there were 1,845 retired workers. The industries with the most employment: agribusiness, tourism, general construction and the manufacture of plumbing fixtures, aircraft engines and parts. The nonfarm earnings in 1981 totaled $165,334,000. The retired workers received an average monthly Social Security payment of $275.00. **FINANCE** On June 30, 1983, six commercial banks had total deposits of $76,006,000 and total assets of $86,962,000. On December 31, 1982 one state savings and loan association and four state branches had assets of $928,529,491. In addition there is one credit union in the county. **HOUSING** Average value of homes in 1980: $23,100. Permits for new, privately owned housing units decreased in 1982: 56 permits were issued with a total construction cost of $1,407,700. Of those permits, 16 were for single family houses. Housing permits in Castroville increased from three in 1981 to 44 in 1982 with 40 permits issued for apartments and condominiums. Between 1970 and 1980 the number of housing units increased by 23%. Fifty-three percent of all units in the county are air-conditioned, 79% are heated by gas and 14% by electricity. **NATURAL RESOURCES** Clay, limestone, industrial sand, sand and gravel, oil, gas and lignite coal. In 1982 a total of 115,529 thousand cubic feet of gas well gas, 20 barrels of condensate, 299,817 barrels of crude oil and 98,092 thousand cubic feet of casinghead gas were produced. Current production of other minerals and products includes brick, ceramic tile, structural clay products, crushed limestone, sand and gravel. **TOURISM** Travel expenditures of $10,384,000 in 1982 (an increase of 16% over 1981) generated 176 jobs and $1,672,000 in payroll. **ALCOHOLIC BEVERAGES** Packaged distilled spirits, beer, ale, malt liquor and wine are legal in parts of the county. Sale of mixed beverages is legal in all or parts of the county. **MILITARY INSTALLATIONS** Castroville Municipal Airport, and Hondo Municipal Airport are auxiliary training fields. **FEDERAL EXPENDITURES** The federal government had direct expenditures or obligations of $43,378,000 in the county during fiscal year 1983, including $10,936,000 by the U.S. Department of Defense. In addition, the federal government paid $1,613,000 in salaries and wages, made direct payments to individuals of $34,185,000 including $26,691,000 in retirement and disability payments, awarded $7,240,000 in procurement contracts and spent $506,000 in other expenditures or obligations. The federal government also provided $91,000 in direct loans and $18,633,000 in guaranteed loans and insurance.

COMMUNICATION

Newspapers– Weekly: The News Bulletin (Castroville), The Devine News-Spanish, Hondo Anvil Herald and Medina Valley Times (Devine). Radio: KRME-AM (Hondo). Cable TV. Telephone companies: Southwestern Bell, Hill Country Telephone Coop. and SW Texas Telephone. **TRANSPORTATION** Total public road mileage: 1,057. In 1982 there were 17,468 registered vehicles and 379 reported traffic accidents including 10 fatalities. Intercity bus service is available. Motor freight: seven local and intrastate carriers. Rail: The Eagle and Sunset Limited provide passenger service on the Amtrak route. Two main lines carry freight through the county with one carrying annually over 30 million tons of freight and one carrying five to 10 million tons. Aircraft: 40 are registered in the county. Airports: Hondo Municipal Airport serves as a base for 10 aircraft and is a general utility airport with general aviation service. Castroville Municipal Airport, a reliever airport for San Antonio International Airport, serves as a base for 25 aircraft and is a general utility airport. Devine Municipal Airport serves as a base for 20 aircraft and is a basic utility airport with general aviation service.

COMMUNITY SERVICES

EDUCATION Five school districts with five elementary, four middle and five high schools. The average daily attendance in 1981-82 was 5,227 with expenditures per pupil of $2,086 including 324 classroom teachers with an average annual salary of $15,394. Forty-seven percent of the 373 high school graduates planned to attend college. In 1982-83, 45% of the students were White, 54% Hispanic, 0.4% Black and 0.1% Asian. **PUBLIC LIBRARIES** Castroville Public Library: 9,819 volumes. Devine Public Library: 13,820 volumes. Hondo Public Library: 16,292 volumes. **CHILD CARE** 24 day care and two twenty-four hour care licensed facilities. **HEALTH CARE** Nine physicians and eight dentists. Hospitals: one with a capacity of 34. Clinics: one public health clinic. Ambulance services: two volunteer services and one city service. Mental health: two clinics. Nursing homes: four nursing homes with a combined capacity of 322 nursing

care and 18 personal care residents. The average cost per day for private patients in 1982 was $29.47. **CHURCHES** 36 churches have an estimated combined membership of 18,459. The largest denominations are Catholic, Southern Baptist and United Methodist. **SOCIAL SERVICES** In fiscal year 1983 a total of $1,434,025 in food stamps was distributed, with an average of 3,165 persons receiving food stamps each month. Aid to Families with Dependent Children (AFDC) totaled $319,524 with an average of 217 families receiving AFDC each month. Medical assistance benefits for the aged and disabled of $2,195,338 and for families and children of $479,378 brought the county benefit total to $4,428,265. **FIRE PROTECTION** Seven volunteer fire departments. **LAW ENFORCEMENT** The County Sheriff has 39 commissioned officers. Four police departments have a combined force of 20. **CRIME** 100 violent crimes (murder, forcible rape, robbery and aggravated assault) and 448 nonviolent crimes (burglary, larceny-theft and motor vehicle theft) were reported in 1982. **JUDICIAL SYSTEM** One District Court and Judge, two County Courts and Judges and four Justices of the Peace. In the District Court a total of 376 cases were pending on 1/1/82, 435 new cases were filed and 411 cases were disposed of during the year leaving 400 cases pending on 12/31/82. There were 202 criminal cases on the docket, 77 convictions, 7 persons committed to prison and 75 cases left pending. In the County Courts 830 cases were pending on 1/1/82, 742 new cases were filed and 688 cases were disposed of during the year leaving 884 cases pending on 12/31/82. There were 1,328 criminal cases on the docket, 232 convictions, 30 persons committed to jail and 684 cases left pending. **JAILS** One jail, capacity 26. **ATTORNEYS AT LAW** 17. **UTILITIES** 71% of the residents are connected to a public or privately owned water system and 54% are connected to a public sewer system. Natural gas is distributed to the county by Entex, Inc. and Westend Gas Company. The average annual residential bill for natural gas in 1982 for the Entex distribution system was $390.31, an increase of 26% over 1981. Electricity is distributed to the city of Castroville by the Castroville Utility System, to the city of Hondo by the Hondo Electric System and to the rest of the county by Central Power and Light Co., Cochran Power and Light Co., San Antonio City Public Service Board, Bandera Electric Coop., Inc. and Karnes Electric Coop., Inc. and is generated primarily by gas, oil and coal. The typical residential electric bill is $162.15 per month for an all-electric house using 2,500 kwh. **TAXES** The county has 12 units with taxing authority: five school districts, five cities, one county, and one special district.

RECREATION/ENTERTAINMENT

NATIONAL REGISTER OF HISTORIC PLACES Castroville: Castroville Historic District and Landmark Inn Complex. Castroville vicinity: Charles de Montel House. Devine: Devine Opera House. D'Hanis: Old D'Hanis Historic District. Mico vicinity: Medina Dam. Quihi: Saathoff House. **STATE** Hill Country Natural Area covers 2,000 acres and is closed to the public as of July 1983. Landmark Inn State Historic Site covers five acres with an historic inn which has been restored to the 1940s era and provides rooms for rent. **MUNICIPAL PARKS** 298 acres in 16 municipal parks. These parks contain two playgrounds, two golf courses, eight baseball and softball fields, six tennis courts and four swimming pools. Developed campsites: 20. **SCENIC DRIVES** The Texas Hill Country Trail runs through this county. This trail winds through a scenic region of south central Texas, spanning a vast ranching area abundant with wildlife in a landscape of deeply-sculptured valleys and hills. **BOATING/FISHING** Lakes/reservoirs: Chacon (183 acres), Medina (5,575 acres), Medina Diversion (89 acres), San Geronimo Concrete Recharge (18 acres), Seco Creek Soil Conservation Service Lake 11 (10 acres) and Wilson Lake (60 acres). Major rivers:

MEDINA (continued)

Medina. Primary streams: Chacon, San Geronimo, Parkers, Squirrel, Hondo, Seco and Verde. **HUNTING** Fall and winter seasons on deer. No closed season on javelina, squirrel, coyote and bobcat. Winter seasons on quail, muskrat, beaver, opossum, ring-tailed cat, badger, fox, weasel, raccoon, skunk and civet cat. Fall, winter and spring seasons on turkey. In 1983 sandhill crane, duck, coot, geese, woodcock and jacksnipe seasons occurred during the winter months. Teal duck, rail and gallinule seasons occurred in the fall. Mourning dove seasons occurred intermittently during the fall and winter months with a fall season on white-winged dove. **MUSEUMS** Devine: Bigfoot Wallace Museum. Hondo: Medina County Museum. **OTHER** Hondo: 777 Exotic Game Ranch. **SPECIAL EVENTS** Junior Stock Show, Hondo, January; Bass Tourney on Medina Lake, Hondo, April; Cinco de Mayo Celebration, Hondo, May; Museum Day Celebration, Hondo, May; Rodeo, Hondo, June; Senior Olympics, Hondo, June; Saint John's Festival, Hondo, July; Holy Cross Homecoming, Hondo, August; St. Louis Day, Castroville, August; County Fair and Rodeo, Hondo, September; Diez Y Seis Celebration, Hondo, September; Fall Festival, Devine, October; Pecan Show and Contests, Hondo, November; Old-Fashioned Christmas, Castroville, December.

COMMUNITIES

COUNTY SEAT Hondo, County Courthouse, 78861; County Clerk's Office, 512/426-2313. **INCORPORATED COMMUNITIES** (1980 population and ZIP Code) Castroville (1,821) 78009, Devine (3,756) 78016, Hondo (6057) 78861, La Coste (862) 78039, Lytle (1920: 359 in Medina Co., 17 in Bexar Co. and 1,544 in Atascosa Co.) 78052 and Natalia (1,264) 78059. **UNINCORPORATED COMMUNITIES** (and ZIP Code) Biry 78016, D'Hanis 78850, Dunlay 78861, Elstone 78861, Mico 78056, New Fountain 78861, Pearson 78016, Quihi 78018, Riomedina 78066, Vandenburg 78861 and Yancey 78886. **FOR ADDITIONAL LOCAL INFORMATION** Castroville Chamber of Commerce, P.O. Box 572, Castroville, 78009, 512/538-3142, Greater Devine Chamber of Commerce, 215 S. Bright, Devine, 78016, 512/663-2541, Hondo Chamber of Commerce, 1600 Avenue M, Hondo, 78861, 512/426-3037 and Natalia Chamber of Commerce, Natalia, 78059.

MENARD (P96)

THE LAND

Northwest of San Antonio on U.S. Highways 83 and 190 in the Edwards Plateau Region, Menard County covers 902 square miles with the elevation ranging from 1,700 to 2,400 feet. The undulating to hilly, alkaline soils are dark and loamy with an accumulation of lime in the subsoils. In the Edwards Plateau vegetation area, there are a variety of tall to mid grasses with some brushy plants such as live oak, juniper and mesquite. Between 1 and 10% of the land in the county is considered prime farmland. **CLIMATE** Subtropical Subhumid with dry winters and hot summers. The average annual temperature is 65°F. Temperatures in January range from an average low of 32° to an average high of 61°F and in July range from 69° to 97°F. The average annual precipitation is 22 inches, with an average relative humidity of 77% at 6 A.M. and 43% at 6 P.M. The average annual snowfall is two inches. The growing season averages 220 days per year, with the last freeze in late March and the first freeze in early November. The sun shines during the year on the average 66% of the daylight hours.

THE PEOPLE

Menard County ranks 61st among all U.S. counties in the highest percent of residents over age 64. The 1982 estimated population of 2,300 continues a pattern of population decline which has existed since the 1950s. The majority of county residents live in rural areas. The age group with the largest decrease was birth to nine years. The largest ancestry groups are Hispanic (29%) persons of English descent (24%) and Irish descent (20%). **REGISTERED VOTERS** As of November 2, 1982 there were 1,506 registered voters (0.02% of the state total). The 1982 general election had a 55% voter turnout, compared to a 67% turnout in the 1980 general election. In the 1982 primary 97% voted Democratic and 3% Republican, with 725 votes cast.

THE ECONOMY

AGRICULTURE Sheep area. In 1982, 94% of the land was in farms and ranches, with 2% of the farmland under cultivation and 27% irrigated. Menard ranked 204th in the state in highest agricultural receipts, with 96% from livestock and livestock products. Primary crops: wheat, hay, oats and sorghum. Primary vegetables: sweet potatoes and watermelons. Primary fruits and nuts: pecans. Primary livestock and products: sixth in the state for wool production and seventh for sheep. Cattle, angora goats and mohair. **BUSINESS** Total number of business establishments in the county: 54. Retail sales during the first quarter of 1984 increased by 5%. In 1980, 25% of the labor force were self-employed, 18% were employed in professional or related services, 2% in manufacturing, 20% in wholesale and retail trade, 31% in agriculture, forestry, fisheries and mining, 10% were employed in other counties and there were 390 retired workers. The industry with the most employment is agribusiness. The nonfarm earnings in 1981 totaled $20,911,000. The retired workers received an average monthly Social Security payment of $292.00. **FINANCE** On June 30, 1983, two commercial banks had total deposits of $19,824,000 and total assets of $24,152,000. There is one state savings and loan association branch in the county. **HOUSING** Average value of homes in 1980: $16,900. Between 1970 and 1980 the number of housing units increased by 12%. Seventy-two percent of all units in the county are air-conditioned, 77% are heated by gas and 13% by electricity. **NATURAL RESOURCES** Dolomite, oil and gas. In 1982 a total of 230,514 thousand cubic feet of gas well gas, 2,575 barrels of condensate, 168,374 barrels of crude oil and 152,318 thousand cubic feet of casinghead gas were produced. **TOURISM** Travel expenditures of $3,692,000 in 1982 (an increase of 15% over 1981) generated 68 jobs and $623,000 in payroll. **ALCOHOLIC BEVERAGES** Packaged distilled spirits, beer, ale, malt liquor and wine are legal in parts of the county. **FEDERAL EXPENDITURES** The federal government had direct expenditures or obligations of $6,497,000 in the county during fiscal year 1983, including $164,000 by the U.S. Department of Defense. In addition, the federal government provided $116,000 in grant awards, paid $180,000 in salaries and wages, made direct payments to individuals of $5,170,000 including $3,431,000 in retirement and disability payments and spent $1,031,000 in other expenditures or obligations. The federal government also provided $1,776,000 in guaranteed loans and insurance.

COMMUNICATION

Newspapers–Weekly: Menard News. Cable TV. Telephone companies: General Telephone, Central Texas Telephone Coop. and Hill Country Telephone Coop. **TRANSPORTATION** Total public road mileage: 341. In 1982 there were 5,085 registered vehicles and 42 reported traffic accidents. Motor freight: one carrier. Aircraft: four are registered in the county. Airports: Menard County Airport at Menard.

COMMUNITY SERVICES

EDUCATION One school district with one elementary and one high school. The average daily attendance in 1981-82 was 411, with expenditures per pupil of $3,735 including 49 classroom teachers with an average annual salary of $15,727. Fifty-five percent of the 42 high school graduates planned to attend college. In 1982-83, 52% of the students were White and 48% Hispanic. **PUBLIC LIBRARIES** Menard Public Library: 12,000 volumes. **CHILD CARE** Three day care licensed facilities. **HEALTH CARE** Four physicians and one dentist. Hospitals: one with a capacity of 30. Ambulance services: one city service. Nursing homes: one nursing home has a capacity of 40 nursing care residents. The average cost per day for private patients in 1982 was $29.64. **CHURCHES** 13 churches have an estimated combined membership of 1,685. The largest denominations are Southern Baptist and Catholic. **SOCIAL SERVICES** In fiscal year 1983 a total of $142,277 in food stamps was distributed, with an average of 324 persons receiving food stamps each month. Aid to Families with Dependent Children (AFDC) totaled $19,666 with an average of 13 families receiving AFDC each month. Medical assistance benefits for the aged and disabled of $450,055 and for families and children of $27,296 brought the county benefit total to $639,294. **FIRE PROTECTION** Two volunteer fire departments. **LAW ENFORCEMENT** The County Sheriff has three commissioned officers. **CRIME** Two violent crimes (murder, forcible rape, robbery and aggravated assault) and three nonviolent crimes (burglary, larceny-theft and motor vehicle theft) were reported in 1982. **JUDICIAL SYSTEM** One District Court and Judge, one County Court and Judge and one Justice of the Peace. In the District Court a total of 156 cases were pending on 1/1/82, 75 new cases were filed and 36 cases were disposed of during the year leaving 195 cases pending on 12/31/82. There were 47 criminal cases on the docket, four convictions and 39 cases left pending. In the County Court 87 cases were pending on 1/1/82, 97 new cases were filed and 45 cases were disposed of during the year leaving 139 cases pending on 12/31/82. There were 149 criminal cases on the docket, 38 convictions, one person committed to jail and 108 cases left pending. **JAILS** One jail, capacity six. **ATTORNEYS AT LAW** Three. **UTILITIES** 74% of the residents are connected to a public or privately owned water system and 41% are connected to a public sewer system. Electricity is distributed to the county by West Texas Utilitites, Kimble Electric Coop., Inc., Southwest Texas Electric Coop., Inc. and McCulloch Electric Coop., Inc. and is generated primarily by gas, oil, coal and water. **TAXES** The county has six units with taxing authority: one school district, one city, one county, one hospital district and two special districts.

RECREATION/ENTERTAINMENT

NATIONAL REGISTER OF HISTORIC PLACES Fort McKavett vicinity: Fort McKavett Historic District. Menard vicinity: Real Presidio de San Saba. **STATE** Fort McKavett State Historic Site covers 80 acres with a museum and an historic structure. A major restoration program is under way to rebuild this fort which was established in 1852 and provided stone barracks for eight companies. **COUNTY/MUNICIPAL PARKS** 99 acres in three county and one municipal park. These parks contain one golf course, one baseball and softball field, one swimming pool and two beaches. **SCENIC DRIVES** The Texas Forts Trail runs through this county. This trail leads to eight of the famous frontier forts of west central Texas and an ancient presidio of the Spanish colonial period. **BOATING/FISHING** Lakes/reservoirs: Clear Creek (50 acres). Major rivers: San Saba. Primary streams: Clear, Noyes Canal, Dry, Las Moras and Scalp. **HUNTING** Fall and winter seasons on deer. No closed season on javelina, squirrel, coyote and bobcat. Winter seasons on quail, muskrat, beaver, opossum, ring-tailed cat, badger, fox, weasel, raccoon, skunk and civet cat. Fall and winter seasons on turkey. In 1983 duck, coot, geese, woodcock and jacksnipe seasons

occurred during the winter months. Teal duck, rail and gallinule seasons occurred in the fall. Mourning dove seasons occurred intermittently during the fall and winter months. **MUSEUMS** Menard: Menard Museum. **SPECIAL EVENTS** Menardville Run, Menard, May; Barbecue Cookoff, Fort McKavett, May; Parade, Menard, November; Pecan Queen Contest, Menard, November.

COMMUNITIES

COUNTY SEAT Menard, County Courthouse, 76859; County Clerk's Office, 915/396-4682. **INCORPORATED COMMUNITIES** (1980 population and ZIP Code) Menard (1,697) 76859. **UNINCORPORATED COMMUNITIES** (and ZIP Code) Fort McKavett 76841 and Hext 76848. **FOR ADDITIONAL LOCAL INFORMATION** Menard Co. Chamber of Commerce, P. O. Box 64, Menard, 76859, 915/396-2365.

MIDLAND (P76)

THE LAND

South of Lubbock on Interstate Highway 20 in the High Plains Region, Midland County covers 902 square miles with the elevation ranging from 2,550 to 2,900 feet. In the northwest the nearly level soils are dark and loamy with clayey, limey subsoils. In the south the more undulating to hilly soils are loamy over limestone. The rest of Midland has more level, light to dark, loamy soils with reddish, clayey subsoils. The vegetation is the tall to mid grasses and brush of live oak, shinnery oak and mesquite of the Edwards Plateau vegetation area. Less than 1% of the land in the county is considered prime farmland. **CLIMATE** Continental Steppe with dry winters and warm summers. The average annual temperature is 64°F. Temperatures in January range from an average low of 30° to an average high of 59°F and in July range from 70° to 95°F. The average annual precipitation is 14 inches, with an average relative humidity of 72% at 6 A.M. and 36% at 6 P.M. The average annual snowfall is four inches. The growing season averages 220 days per year, with the last freeze in early April and the first freeze in early November. The sun shines during the year on the average 75% of the daylight hours.

THE PEOPLE

The 1982 estimated population of 97,400 indicates a continuation of the strong growth rate which began in the 1970s, dramatically reversing a population decline between 1960 and 1970 and re-establishing the pattern of growth between the 1930s and 1960. Almost 87% of the residents live in urban areas, but rural areas experienced one of the highest growth rates in the state between 1970 and 1980 with the population increasing 107%. The age groups with the largest gains were ages 20 to 34 and 65 and over. The largest ancestry groups are persons of English descent (27%), Irish descent (20%), German descent (17%) and Hispanic (15%). **REGISTERED VOTERS** As of November 2, 1982 there were 42,611 registered voters (0.7% of the state total). The 1982 general election had a 52% voter turnout, compared to a 77% turnout in the 1980 general election. In the 1982 primary 43% voted Democratic and 57% Republican, with 4,957 votes cast.

THE ECONOMY

AGRICULTURE Cotton area. In 1982, 90% of the land was in farms and ranches, with 9% of the farmland under cultivation and 36% irrigated. Midland ranked 156th in the state in highest agricultural receipts, with 66% from crops. Overgrazing, undesirable brush and weeds, wind erosion and inadequate cropping systems are the current conservation problems. Primary crops: cotton, hay, wheat and sorghum. Primary vegetables: watermelons. Primary fruits and nuts: pecans. Primary livestock and products: cattle, milk, sheep, wool and hogs.

COUNTIES

MIDLAND (continued)

BUSINESS Total number of business establishments in the county: 3,145. Retail sales during the first quarter of 1984 increased by 3%. In 1980, 9% of the labor force were self-employed, 14% were employed in professional or related services, 8% in manufacturing, 19% in wholesale and retail trade, 24% in agriculture, forestry, fisheries and mining, 8% were employed in other counties and there were 4,313 retired workers. The industries with the most employment: oil and gas extraction, general and heavy construction, agribusiness, trucking, commercial printing and the manufacture of men's work clothing, plastics products, metal pipe and fittings, oil field machinery and air and gas compressors. The nonfarm earnings in 1981 totaled $1,452,334,000. The retired workers received an average monthly Social Security payment of $348.00. **FINANCE** On June 30, 1983, nine commercial banks had total deposits of $1,702,105,000 and total assets of $2,373,294,000. On December 31, 1982 two state savings and loan associations, 14 state branches and one federal association branch had combined assets of $158,834,579. In addition there are 14 credit unions in the county. **HOUSING** Average value of homes in 1980: $48,100. Permits for new, privately owned housing units increased in 1982: 3,873 permits were issued with a total construction cost of $140,681,499. Of those permits, 1,230 were for single family houses. Between 1970 and 1980 the number of housing units increased by 37%. Ninety percent of all units in the county are air-conditioned, 78% are heated by gas and 21% by electricity. **NATURAL RESOURCES** Caliche, sand, gravel, oil and gas. In 1982 a total of 30,682,667 thousand cubic feet of gas well gas, 515,587 barrels of condensate, 7,094,082 barrels of crude oil and 24,947,027 thousand cubic feet of casinghead gas were produced. Current production of other minerals and products includes brine, caliche sand and gravel. **TOURISM** Travel expenditures of $112,411,000 in 1982 (an increase of 9% over 1981) generated 2,500 jobs and $23,788,000 in payroll. Lodging: 15 hotels, motels and tourist courts. Convention/meeting facilities: Midland-Chaparral Center of Midland College, Midland Center, Municipal Park Stadium and two hotels with facilities for large gatherings. **ALCOHOLIC BEVERAGES** Packaged distilled spirits, beer, ale, malt liquor and wine are legal in parts of the county. Sale of mixed beverages is legal in all or parts of the county. **FEDERAL EXPENDITURES** The federal government had direct expenditures or obligations of $86,709,000 in the county during fiscal year 1983, including $4,716,000 by the U.S. Department of Defense. In addition, the federal government provided $4,500,000 in grant awards, paid $14,831,000 in salaries and wages, made direct payments to individuals of $63,624,000 including $52,850,000 in retirement and disability payments, awarded $801,000 in procurement contracts and spent $2,953,000 in other expenditures or obligations. The federal government also provided $723,000 in direct loans and $35,372,000 in guaranteed loans and insurance.

COMMUNICATION

Newspapers–Daily: Midland Reporter-Telegram, ave. eve. circ. 23,150. Radio: KCRS-AM, KJBC-AM, KMND-AM, KWEL-AM, KKKK-FM, KWMJ-FM, KBAT-FM Stereo and KNFM-FM Stereo (Midland). Television: KMID-CH.2 (Midland). Cable TV. Telephone companies: Southwestern Bell and Wes-Tex Telephone Coop. **TRANSPORTATION** Total public road mileage: 1,282. In 1982 there were 106,095 registered vehicles and 4,387 reported traffic accidents including 34 fatalities. Taxi cabs: two companies in the city of Midland. Municipal transit systems: one intracity bus system in the city of Midland which provides monthly subscription service from home to work, a flex route service in the eastern part of the city and a demand response service throughout the city and county. Intercity bus service is available. Motor freight: 24 local and intrastate carriers. Rail: one main line carries annually five to 10 million tons of freight through the county. Aircraft: 500 are registered in the county. Airports: Midland Regional Airport serves as a base for 186 aircraft and is a small hub for medium haul flights with carrier service. Also servicing the area are Midland Air Park and Sky Ranch at Midland.

COMMUNITY SERVICES

EDUCATION Two school districts with 22 elementary, three middle and five high schools. The average daily attendance in 1981-82 was 15,424, with expenditures per pupil of $2,543 including 911 classroom teachers with an average annual salary of $20,395. Sixty-seven percent of the 945 high school graduates planned to attend college. In 1982-83, 65% of the students were White, 24% Hispanic, 10% Black, 0.8% Asian and 0.1% American Indian. Private schools: 1,614 students enrolled in four elementaries and one high school. Midland College is located in Midland. Established in 1969 it is a vocational and two year academic college under local control. Enrollment in 1982 was 2,698 with in state undergraduate tuition and fees of $245 per semester. Vocational education: Aladdin Beauty College (Midland). **PUBLIC LIBRARIES** Midland County Public Library (Midland): 138,472 volumes. **CHILD CARE** 171 day care and 20 twenty-four hour care licensed facilities. **HEALTH CARE** 112 physicians and 48 dentists. Hospitals: two with a combined capacity of 255. Clinics: two for the treatment of alcohol and/or drug abuse, two minor emergency centers and one public health clinic. Ambulance services: one fire department service. Mental health: one clinic. Nursing homes: five nursing homes with a combined capacity of 473 nursing care and 19 custodial care residents. The average cost per day for private patients in 1982 was $43.69. **CHURCHES** 69 churches have an estimated combined membership of 46,374. The largest denominations are Southern Baptist, United Methodist and Catholic. **SOCIAL SERVICES** In fiscal year 1983 a total of $1,745,396 in food stamps was distributed, with an average of 3,383 persons receiving food stamps each month. Aid to Families with Dependent Children (AFDC) totaled $457,921 with an average of 297 families receiving AFDC each month. Medical assistance benefits for the aged and disabled of $2,603,635 and for families and children of $618,371 brought the county benefit total to $5,425,322. **FIRE PROTECTION** One paid fire department. **LAW ENFORCEMENT** The County Sheriff has 44 commissioned officers. One police department has a force of 165. **CRIME** 533 violent crimes (murder, forcible rape, robbery and aggravated assault) and 5,016 nonviolent crimes (burglary, larceny-theft and motor vehicle theft) were reported in 1982. **JUDICIAL SYSTEM** Three District Courts and Judges, two County Courts and Judges and two Justices of the Peace. In the District Courts a total of 2,975 cases were pending on 1/1/82, 3,516 new cases were filed and 2,825 cases were disposed of during the year leaving 3,666 cases pending on 12/31/82. There were 1,579 criminal cases on the docket, 416 convictions, 157 persons committed to prison, two committed to jail and 696 cases left pending. In the County Courts 1,082 cases were pending on 1/1/82, 2,467 new cases were filed and 2,183 cases were disposed of during the year leaving 1,366 cases pending on 12/31/82. There were 2,535 criminal cases on the docket, 1,093 convictions, 157 persons committed to jail and 793 cases left pending. **JAILS** One jail, capacity 89. Planning a new jail with a capacity 225—lost certification in 1983 due to overcrowding. **ATTORNEYS AT LAW** 368. **UTILITIES** 86% of the residents are connected to a public or privately owned water system and 87% are connected to a public sewer system. Natural gas is distributed to the county by Energas Co. The average annual residential bill for natural gas in 1982 for the Energas distribution system was $371.63, an increase of 23% over 1981. Electricity is distributed to the county by Texas Electric Service and

Cap Rock Electric Coop., Inc. and is generated primarily by gas. The typical residential electric bill is $154.69 per month for an all-electric house using 2,500 kwh. **TAXES** The county has six units with taxing authority: two school districts, one city, one county, one college and one hospital district.

RECREATION/ENTERTAINMENT
TEXAS LEAGUE BASEBALL The city of Midland has a team in the Western Division of the League. **NATIONAL REGISTER OF HISTORIC PLACES** Midland: Brown-Dorsey House. **MUNICIPAL PARKS** 860 acres in 38 municipal parks. These parks contain two miles of hiking trails, 27 playgrounds, one golf course, 11 football and soccer fields, 37 baseball and softball fields, eight tennis courts, five multi-use courts and five swimming pools. Developed campsites: six. **SCENIC DRIVES** The Texas Pecos Trail runs through this county. This trail rambles through the vast region of southwest and west Texas with landscapes varying from raw, arid regions to green valleys. **HUNTING** Fall season on antelope. Fall and winter seasons on deer, mule deer, and javelina. No closed season on squirrel, coyote and bobcat. Winter seasons on quail, muskrat, beaver, opossum, ring-tailed cat, badger, fox, weasel, raccoon, skunk and civet cat. Fall, winter and spring seasons on turkey. In 1983 sandhill crane, duck, coot, geese, woodcock and jacksnipe seasons occurred during the winter months. Teal duck, rail and gallinule seasons occurred in the fall. Mourning dove season occurred intermittently during the fall and winter months. **MUSEUMS** Midland: Aeroplane Museum, Midland County Historical Museum, Museum of the Southwest, Permian Basin Petroleum Museum and Hall of Fame, Pliska Museum and Midland County Library (historical museum section). **ORCHESTRAS** Midland: Midland-Odessa Symphony and Chorale and West Texas Youth Orchestra. **DANCE** Midland: Permian Civic Ballet Association. **ZOO** Midland: Cole Park Zoo. **PLANETARIUM** Midland: Marian Blakemore Planetarium. **COLLEGIATE FINE ARTS** Midland: Cultural events offered by Midland College. **SPECIAL EVENTS** Twelve-Hour Grand Prix Race, Midland-Odessa, April/May; Mayfair, Midland, May; Septemberfest, Midland, September; Fall Festival, Midland, October/November; Arts and Crafts Festival, Midland, November.

COMMUNITIES
COUNTY SEAT Midland, County Courthouse, 79701; County Clerk's Office, 915/682-9481. **INCORPORATED COMMUNITIES** (1980 population and ZIP Code) Midland (70,525) 79701. **UNINCORPORATED COMMUNITIES** (and ZIP Code) Greenwood 79701, Spraberry 79704 and Valley View 79704. **FOR ADDITIONAL LOCAL INFORMATION** Midland Chamber of Commerce, 109 Main, Midland, 79702, 915/683-3381.

MILAM (C18)

THE LAND
Northeast of Austin on U.S. Highways 77, 190 and 79 in the Claypan area, Milam County covers 1,019 square miles with the elevation ranging from 400 to 600 feet. Along the Brazos River the soils are brownish to reddish and clayey to loamy. In the southeast the light colored, sandy loams have some clayey subsoils. In the northwest the slightly acidic soils have dark, loamy surfaces and cracking, clayey subsoils. The remainder of the county has areas of gray to black, cracking, clayey soils or light colored, sandy loams over very deep, cracking, clayey subsoils. The north is in the Blackland Prairies vegetation area with prairie grasses and some trees. The south is in the Post Oak Savannah vegetation area with tall grasses, post and blackjack oak trees. Between 41 and 50% of the land in the county is considered prime farm-

land. **CLIMATE** Subtropical Humid with warm summers. The average annual temperature is 68 °F. Temperatures in January range from an average low of 39° to an average high of 60 °F and in July range from 73° to 97 °F. The average annual precipitation is 35 inches, with an average relative humidity of 83% at 6 A.M. and 57% at 6 P.M. The average annual snowfall is less than one inch. The growing season averages 256 days per year, with the last freeze in mid March and the first freeze in late November. The sun shines during the year on the average 65% of the daylight hours.

THE PEOPLE
The population gain in Milam County between 1970 and 1980 offset the loss between 1960 and 1970. The 1982 estimated population of 23,000 indicates a continuation of the growth which began in the 1970s. Rural areas grew slightly faster than urban areas from 1970 to 1980. The county's median age lowered from 37 in 1970 to 34 in 1980. The largest ancestry groups are persons of German descent (33%), English descent (24%) and Irish descent (20%). **REGISTERED VOTERS** As of November 2, 1982 there were 11,431 registered voters (0.2% of the state total). The 1982 general election had a 51% voter turnout, compared to a 66% turnout in the 1980 general election. In the 1982 primary 99% voted Democratic and 1% Republican, with 5,209 votes cast.

THE ECONOMY
AGRICULTURE Cattle area. In 1982, 81% of the land was in farms and ranches, with 30% of the farmland under cultivation and 3% irrigated. Milam ranked 43rd in the state in highest agricultural receipts, with 73% from livestock and livestock products. Overgrazing, undesirable brush and weeds and water erosion are the current conservation problems. Primary crops: sorghum, wheat, hay, cotton, oats and corn. Primary vegetables: watermelons. Primary fruits and nuts: peaches and pecans. Primary livestock and products: third in the state for beef cows that have calved and seventh for hogs. Cattle and milk. **BUSINESS** Total number of business establishments in the county: 385. Retail sales during the first quarter of 1984 increased by 13%. In 1980, 12% of the labor force were self-employed, 15% were employed in professional or related services, 19% in manufacturing, 17% in wholesale and retail trade, 14% in agriculture, forestry fisheries and mining, 15% were employed in other counties and there were 2,601 retired workers. The industries with the most employment: agribusiness, aluminum smelting, cottonseed oil mills, lumber mills and the manufacture of children's clothing and furniture. The nonfarm earnings in 1981 totaled $194,847,000. The retired workers received an average monthly Social Security payment of $282.00. **FINANCE** On June 30, 1983, six commercial banks had total deposits of $153,313,000 and total assets of $178,023,000. On December 31, 1982 one state savings and loan association and two state branches had assets of $26,138,980. In addition there is one credit union in the county. **HOUSING** Average value of homes in 1980: $22,900. Permits for new, privately owned housing units increased in 1982: 76 permits were issued with a total construction cost of $2,174,750. Of those permits, 32 were for single family houses. Housing permits in Cameron increased from 16 in 1981 to 42 in 1982 with 32 permits issued for apartments and condominiums. Between 1970 and 1980 the number of housing units increased by 20%. Sixty-three percent of all units in the county are air-conditioned, 77% are heated by gas and 15% by electricity. **NATURAL RESOURCES** Clay, industrial sand, sand, gravel, oil, gas and lignite coal. In 1982 a total of 141,999 thousand cubic feet of gas well gas, 298,525 barrels of crude oil and 72,053 thousand cubic feet of casinghead gas were produced. Current production of other minerals and products includes aluminum, lightweight aggregate, roofing granules, lignite coal,

MILAM (continued)

sand and gravel. **TOURISM** Travel expenditures of $7,056,000 in 1982 (an increase of 12% over 1981) generated 157 jobs and $1,313,000 in payroll. Lodging: five hotels, motels and tourist courts. **ALCOHOLIC BEVERAGES** Packaged distilled spirits, beer, ale, malt liquor and wine are legal in parts of the county. **FEDERAL EXPENDITURES** The federal government had direct expenditures or obligations of $45,165,000 in the county during fiscal year 1983, including $1,640,000 by the U.S. Department of Defense. In addition, the federal government provided $2,050,000 in grant awards, paid $1,382,000 in salaries and wages, made direct payments to individuals of $39,746,000 including $27,067,000 in retirement and disability payments, awarded $497,000 in procurement contracts and spent $1,491,000 in other expenditures or obligations. The federal government also provided $2,015,000 in direct loans and $3,413,000 in guaranteed loans and insurance.

COMMUNICATION

Newspapers–Weekly: Cameron Herald, The Rockdale Reporter and Messenger and the Thorndale Champion. Radio: KMIL-AM (Cameron). Cable TV. Telephone companies: Continental Telephone, General Telephone, Southwestern Bell and Central Telephone-Midstate. **TRANSPORTATION** Total public road mileage: 1,207. In 1982 there were 22,051 registered vehicles and 576 reported traffic accidents including 11 fatalities. Taxi cabs: one company in Cameron. Intercity bus service is available. Motor freight: six local and intrastate carriers. Rail: four main and one branch line carry freight through the county. Two of the main lines carry annually over 30 million tons of freight each, two carry 10 to 20 each and the one branch carries less than one million tons. Aircraft: 24 are registered in the county. Airports: Cameron Municipal Airpark.

COMMUNITY SERVICES

EDUCATION Six school districts with eight elementary, two middle and five high schools. The average daily attendance in 1981-82 was 4,005, with expenditures per pupil of $2,318 including 268 classroom teachers with an average annual salary of $15,613. Forty-six percent of the 271 high school graduates planned to attend college. In 1982-83, 66% of the students were White, 17% Hispanic, 18% Black, 0.1% American Indian. Private schools: 62 students enrolled in one elementary school. **PUBLIC LIBRARIES** Cameron Public Library: 23,381 volumes. Lucy H. Patterson Memorial Library (Rockdale): 17,981 volumes. **CHILD CARE** 29 day care and seven twenty-four hour care licensed facilities. **HEALTH CARE** 12 physicians and nine dentists. Hospitals: three with a combined capacity of 168. Clinics: one public health clinic. Ambulance services: two volunteer services and one volunteer fire department service. Mental health: two clinics. Nursing homes: four nursing homes with a combined capacity of 246 nursing care residents. The average cost per day for private patients in 1982 was $29.04. **CHURCHES** 75 churches have an estimated combined membership of 14,295. The largest denominations are Southern Baptist, Catholic and United Methodist. **SOCIAL SERVICES** In fiscal year 1983 a total of $1,149,037 in food stamps was distributed, with an average of 2,507 persons receiving food stamps each month. Aid to Families with Dependent Children (AFDC) totaled $296,768 with an average of 199 families receiving AFDC each month. Medical assistance benefits for the aged and disabled of $2,568,160 and for families and children of $385,449 brought the county benefit total to $4,399,414. **FIRE PROTECTION** Eight volunteer fire departments. **LAW ENFORCEMENT** The County Sheriff has eight commissioned officers. Three police departments have a combined force of 21. **CRIME** 43 violent crimes (murder,

forcible rape, robbery and aggravated assault) and 453 nonviolent crimes (burglary, larceny-theft and motor vehicle theft) were reported in 1982. **JUDICIAL SYSTEM** One District Court and Judge, one County Court and Judge and six Justices of the Peace. In the District Court a total of 647 cases were pending on 1/1/82, 589 new cases were filed and 441 cases were disposed of during the year leaving 795 cases pending on 12/31/82. There were 354 criminal cases on the docket, 100 convictions, 33 persons committed to prison and 189 cases left pending. In the County Court 636 cases were pending on 1/1/82, 554 new cases were filed and 343 cases were disposed of during the year leaving 847 cases pending on 12/31/82. There were 1,107 criminal cases on the docket, 274 convictions, eight persons committed to jail and 796 cases left pending. **JAILS** One jail, capacity 18. **ATTORNEYS AT LAW** 21. **UTILITIES** 85% of the residents are connected to a public or privately owned water system and 57% are connected to a public sewer system. Natural gas is distributed to the county by Lone Star Gas Co., Division of Enserch. The average annual residential bill for natural gas in 1982 for the Lone Star distribution system was $405.91, an increase of 35% over 1981. Electricity is distributed to the county by Texas Power and Light Co., Bartlett Electric Coop., Inc. and Belfalls Electric Coop., Inc. and is generated primarily by gas, coal and water. The typical residential electric bill is $165.24 per month for an all-electric house using 2,500 kwh. **TAXES** The county has 13 units with taxing authority: six school district, four cities, one county and two special districts.

RECREATION/ENTERTAINMENT

NATIONAL REGISTER OF HISTORIC PLACES Cameron: Milam County Courthouse and Jail. Rockdale vicinity: San Xavier Mission Complex. **MUNICIPAL PARKS** 106 acres in 12 municipal parks. These parks contain two playgrounds, 11 baseball and softball fields, nine tennis courts, one multi-use court and three swimming pools. **BOATING/FISHING** Lakes/reservoirs: Alcoa (880 acres), Elm Creek (23 acres), Glaser (29 acres), Green (18 acres), Hobson (20 acres), Neusch (26 acres), Newton (50 acres), Young (28 acres) and Zalmanek (50 acres). Major rivers: Little, San Gabriel and Brazos. Primary streams: Sandy, Big Elm, Indian Hollow, Threemile, Mill, Foster, Bailey Hollow and Cedar. **HUNTING** Fall and winter seasons on deer. No closed season on nutria, squirrel, bobcat and coyote. Winter seasons on quail, muskrat, beaver, otter, opossum, mink, ring-tailed cat, badger, fox, raccoon, skunk and civet cat. In 1983 duck, coot, geese, woodcock and jacksnipe seasons occurred during the winter months. Teal ducks, rail and gallinule seasons occurred in the fall. Mourning dove seasons occurred intermittently during the fall and winter months. **MUSEUMS** Cameron: Milam County Historical Museum. **SPECIAL EVENTS** City Fair, Rockdale, May; Cinco de Mayo, Cameron, May; Folk Fete, Cameron, June; Arts and Crafts Fair, Cameron, October; Christmas Parade, Cameron, December.

COMMUNITIES

COUNTY SEAT Cameron, County Courthouse, 76520; County Clerk's Office, 817/697-6596. **INCORPORATED COMMUNITIES** (1980 population and ZIP Code) Buckholts (388) 76518, Cameron (5,721) 76520, Milano (468) 76556, Rockdale (5,611) 76567 and Thorndale (1,300: 1,296 in Milam Co. and 4 in Williamson Co.) 76577. **UNINCORPORATED COMMUNITIES** (and ZIP Code) Ad Hall 76520, Baileyville 76570, Ben Arnold 76517, Branchville 77837, Briary 76570, Burlington 76519, Crossroads 76520, Davilla 76523, Detmold 76577, Elevation 76556, Gause 77857, Handy 76567, Hanover 76520, Hoyte 76520, Jones Prairie 76520, Liberty Hill 76567, Lilac 76577, Maysfield 76555, Minerva 76567, New Clarkson 76570, Nile 76577, Pettibone 76520, Praesel 76567, Salty 76567, Sandy Creek 76556, San Gabriel 76577,

Sharp 76518, Silver City 76520, South Elm 76518, Tracy 76518, Val Verde 76518 and Yarrellton 76518. **FOR ADDITIONAL LOCAL INFORMATION** Cameron Area Chamber of Commerce, P.O. Drawer 432, Cameron, 76520, 817/697-2541, Rockdale Chamber of Commerce, 100 E. Cameron St., Rockdale, 76567, 512/446-2030 and Thorndale Chamber of Commerce, P. O. Box 428, Thorndale, 76577, 512/898-2826.

MILLS (C5)

THE LAND

West of Waco on U.S. Highways 84 and 84/183 in the Grand Prairie Region, Mills County covers 748 square miles with the elevation ranging from 1,200 to 1,700 feet. The undulating to hilly soils near the Colorado River are light colored and loamy with deep, reddish, clayey subsoils. The remainder of Mills County has loamy soils with light to dark surfaces and an accumulation of lime in the subsoils. Between 11 and 20% of the land in the county is considered prime farmland. **CLIMATE** Subtropical Humid with warm summers. The average annual temperature is 65 °F. Temperatures in January range from an average low of 31 ° to an average high of 57 °F and in July range from 71 ° to 97 °F. The average annual precipitation is 27 inches, with an average relative humidity of 78% at 6 A.M. and 50% at 6 P.M. The average annual snowfall is two inches. The growing season averages 230 days per year, with the last freeze at the end of March and the first freeze in mid November. The sun shines during the year on the average 65% of the daylight hours.

THE PEOPLE

Mills County ranks 10th among all U.S. counties in the highest percent of residents who are over age 64. The 1982 estimated population of 4,500 continues the pattern of growth begun in the 1970s which reversed the population decline since the 1930s. The majority of the county residents live in rural areas. Mills County is older than average with a median age which lowered from 49 in 1970 to 46 in 1980. The largest ancestry groups are persons of English descent (35%) and Irish descent (20%). **REGISTERED VOTERS** As of November 2, 1982 there were 2,807 registered voters (0.04% of the state total). The 1982 general election had a 51% voter turnout, compared to a 73% turnout in the 1980 general election. In the 1982 primary 100% voted Democratic, with 1,054 votes cast.

THE ECONOMY

AGRICULTURE Sheep and angora goat area. In 1982, 90% of the land was in farms and ranches, with 12% of the farmland under cultivation and 6% irrigated. Mills ranked 151st in the state in highest agricultural receipts, with 86% from livestock and livestock products. Overgrazing, undesirable brush and weeds, water erosion and difficulties in grass establishment are the current conservation problems. Primary crops: third in the state for oats. Hay, wheat and sorghum. Primary vegetables: potatoes, sweet potatoes, tomatoes and watermelons. Primary fruits and nuts: peaches and third in the state for pecans. Primary livestock and products: seventh in the state for both angora goats and mohair production. Cattle, milk, sheep, wool and hogs. **BUSINESS** Total number of business establishments in the county: 84. Retail sales during the first quarter of 1984 increased by 20%. In 1980, 27% of the labor force were self-employed, 21% were employed in professional or related services, 8% in manufacturing, 17% in wholesale and retail trade, 27% in agriculture, forestry, fisheries and mining, 15% were employed in other counties and there were 798 retired workers. The industries with the most employment: agribusiness, structural steel construction and the manufacture of artificial flowers. The

nonfarm earnings in 1981 totaled $35,849,000. The retired workers received an average monthly Social Security payment of $269. **FINANCE** On June 30, 1983, one commercial bank had total deposits of $51,998,000 and total assets of $58,261,000. There is one state savings and loan association branch in the county. **HOUSING** Average value of homes in 1980: $22,300. Between 1970 and 1980 the number of housing units increased by 15%. Sixty-two percent of all units in the county are air-conditioned, 76% are heated by gas and 6% by electricity. **NATURAL RESOURCES** Dolomite, limestone and industrial sand. **TOURISM** Travel expenditures of $2,142,000 in 1982 (an increase of 12% over 1981) generated 50 jobs and $411,000 in payroll. **ALCOHOLIC BEVERAGES** Packaged distilled spirits, beer, ale, malt liquor and wine are legal in parts of the county. **FEDERAL EXPENDITURES** The federal government had direct expenditures or obligations of $12,882,000 in the county during fiscal year 1983, including $313,000 by the U.S. Department of Defense. In addition, the federal government provided $522,000 in grant awards, paid $407,000 in salaries and wages, made direct payments to individuals of $10,550,000 including $7,167,000 in retirement and disability payments, awarded $1,000 in procurement contracts and spent $1,402,000 in other expenditures or obligations. The federal government also provided $13,000 in direct loans and $3,986,000 in guaranteed loans and insurance.

COMMUNICATION

Newspapers–Weekly: Goldthwaite Eagle. Cable TV. Telephone companies: General Telephone, Central Telephone-Midstate, Central Texas Telephone Coop. and Comanche County Telephone. **TRANSPORTATION** Total public road mileage: 680. In 1982 there were 4,976 registered vehicles and 93 reported traffic accidents including three fatalities. Intercity bus service is available. Motor freight: three carriers. Rail: one main line carries annually 20 to 30 million tons of freight through the county. Aircraft: six are registered in the county. Airports: Mills County Airport at Goldthwaite.

COMMUNITY SERVICES

EDUCATION Four school districts with four elementary, four high schools and one special education. The average daily attendance in 1981-82 was 760, with expenditures per pupil of $2,557 including 53 classroom teachers with an average annual salary of $15,537. Forty-six percent of the 61 high school graduates planned to attend college. In 1982-83, 87% of the students were White, 12% Hispanic and 0.7% Black. **CHILD CARE** One day care and two twenty-four hour care licensed facilities. **HEALTH CARE** Five physicians and two dentists. Hospitals: one with a capacity of 29. Ambulance services: one commercial service. Nursing homes: two nursing homes with a combined capacity of 194 nursing care residents. The average cost per day for private patients in 1982 was $30.25. **CHURCHES** 23 churches have an estimated combined membership of 3,828. The largest denominations are Southern Baptist, United Methodist and Churhes of Christ. **SOCIAL SERVICES** In fiscal year 1983 a total of $94,996 in food stamps was distributed, with an average of 215 persons receiving food stamps each month. Aid to Families with Dependent Children (AFDC) totaled $17,910 with an average of 13 families receiving AFDC each month. Medical assistance benefits for the aged and disabled of $958,657 and for families and children of $34,366 brought the county benefit total to $1,105,929. **FIRE PROTECTION** Two volunteer fire departments. **LAW ENFORCEMENT** The County Sheriff has four commissioned officers. **CRIME** Five violent crimes (murder, forcible rape, robbery and aggravated assault) and 50 nonviolent crimes (burglary, larceny-theft and motor vehicle theft) were reported in 1982. **JUDICIAL SYSTEM** One District Court and Judge, one County Court and Judge and two Justices of the Peace. In the District

COUNTIES

MILLS (continued)

Court a total of 69 cases were pending on 1/1/82, 80 new cases were filed and 79 cases were disposed of during the year leaving 70 cases pending on 12/31/82. There were 35 criminal cases on the docket, 13 convictions, two committed to jail and nine cases left pending. In the County Court 162 cases were pending on 1/1/82, 151 new cases were filed and 167 cases were disposed of during the year leaving 146 cases pending on 12/31/82. There were 311 criminal cases on the docket, 82 convictions, 14 persons committed to jail and 146 cases left pending. **JAILS** One jail, capacity seven. **ATTORNEYS AT LAW** Five. **UTILITIES** 48% of the residents are connected to a public or privately owned water system and 33% are connected to a public sewer system. Natural gas is distributed to the county by Lone Star Gas Co., Division of Enserch. The average annual residential bill for natural gas in 1982 for the Lone Star distribution system was $405.91, an increase of 35% over 1981. Electricity is distributed to the city of Goldthwaite by Goldthwaite Utilities and to the rest of the county by McCulloch Electric Coop., Inc. Comanche Co. Electric Coop., Inc. and Hamilton Valley Electric Coop., Inc. and is generated primarily by gas, coal, oil and water. **TAXES** The county has eight units with taxing authority: four school districts, two cities, one county and one special district.

RECREATION/ENTERTAINMENT
NATIONAL REGISTER OF HISTORIC PLACES Goldthwaite: Mills County Jailhouse and Regency Suspension Bridge. **MUNICIPAL PARK** 13 acres in one municipal park. This park contains one playground and one swimming pool. Developed campsites: five. **BOATING/FISHING** Lakes/reservoirs: Ashton (31 acres), Bennett Creek Soil Conservation Service Lakes 1, 2, 3 and 4 (62 acres), Blanket Creek Soil Conservation Service Lake 17A (33 acres), Brown-Mullin Soil Conservation Service Lake 2 (10 acres), Clayton (25 acres), Dennie Shelton (22 acres), Merritt (75 acres) and Shelton (20 acres). Major rivers: Colorado. Primary streams: Big Blanket, Middle Bennett, North Bennett, South Bennett, Mustang, Pompey, Mullin, Fisk, Herd Pen, Browns and Pecan Bayou. **HUNTING** Fall and winter seasons on deer. No closed season on squirrel, bobcat and coyote. Winter seasons on quail, muskrat, beaver, opossum, ring-tailed cat, badger, fox, weasel, raccoon, skunk and civet cat. Winter, fall and spring seasons on turkey. In 1983 duck, coot, geese, woodcock and jacksnipe seasons occurred during the winter months. Teal duck, rail and gallinule seasons occurred in the fall. Mourning dove seasons occurred intermittently during the fall and winter months. **MUSEUMS** Goldthwaite: Mills County Historical Museum. **SPECIAL EVENTS** County Fair and Stock Show, Goldthwaite, January; Annual Quarterhorse Show, Goldthwaite, April; Old Settlers Reunion, Goldthwaite, May; Old Fiddlers Contest, Goldthwaite, May; Farmers and Ranchers Appreciation Day, Goldthwaite, June; Gold-Tex Youth Finals Rodeo, Goldthwaite, August; Hunters Welcome Supper, Goldthwaite, November.

COMMUNITIES
COUNTY SEAT Goldthwaite, County Courthouse, 76844; County Clerk's Office, 915/648-2711. **INCORPORATED COMMUNITIES** (1980 population and ZIP Code) Goldthwaite (1,783) 76844 and Mullin (213) 76864. **UNINCORPORATED COMMUNITIES** (and ZIP Code) Bozar 76844, Caradan 76844, Center City 76844, Democrat 76442, Ebony 76864, Priddy 76870 Regency 76864, Ridge 76864, Scallorn 76853 and Star 76880.

MITCHELL (P68)

THE LAND
West of Abilene on Interstate 20 in the Rolling Plains Region,

Mitchell County covers 912 square miles with the elevation ranging from 2,000 to 2,400 feet. The soils have light colored, loamy surfaces with very deep, reddish, clayey subsoils. In areas the loamy surfaces are dark and have an accumulation of lime in the subsoils. In the Rolling Plains vegetation area, there are a variety of short to mid grasses, yucca and mesquite trees. Between 21 and 30% of the land in the county is considered prime farmland. **CLIMATE** Subtropical Subhumid. It is noted for duststorms in the spring and warm summers. The average annual temperature is 64°F. Temperatures in January range from an average low of 30° to an average high of 57°F and in July range from 71° to 95°F. The average annual precipitation is 20 inches, with an average relative humidity of 72% at 6 A.M. and 38% at 6 P.M. The average annual snowfall is five inches. The growing season averages 217 days per year, with the last freeze the first of April and the first freeze in early November. The sun shines during the year on the average 75% of the daylight hours.

THE PEOPLE
Mitchell County's population reduced significantly between 1950 and 1970, but a slight growth pattern began in the 1970s. The 1982 estimated population of 9,500 continues that trend. Urban areas grew slightly between 1970 and 1980 while rural areas had population losses. The county has a high percent of residents over age 64 and a median age of 34. The largest ancestry groups are persons of English descent (31%), Hispanic (25%), Irish descent (21%) and German descent (12%). **REGISTERED VOTERS** As of November 2, 1982 there were 4,434 registered voters (0.1% of the state total). The 1982 general election had a 52% voter turnout, compared to a 68% turnout in the 1980 general election. In the 1982 primary 100% voted Democratic, with 2,278 votes cast.

THE ECONOMY
AGRICULTURE Cotton area. In 1982, 96% of the land was in farms and ranches, with 16% of the farmland under cultivation and 6% irrigated. Mitchell ranked 175th in the state in highest agricultural receipts, with 71% from crops. Overgrazing, undesirable brush and weeds, water and wind erosion are the current conservation problems. Primary crops: cotton, wheat, sorghum, hay and oats. Primary vegetables: watermelons. Primary fruits and nuts: peaches and pecans. Primary livestock and products: cattle, sheep and wool. **BUSINESS** Total number of business establishments in the county: 192. Retail sales during the first quarter of 1984 increased by 15%. In 1980, 16% of the labor force were self-employed, 22% were employed in professional or related services, 8% in manufacturing, 19% in wholesale and retail trade, 25% in agriculture, forestry, fisheries and mining, 14% were employed in other counties and there were 1,193 retired workers. The industries with the most employment: agribusiness, oil and gas extraction and the manufacture of women's dresses. The nonfarm earnings in 1981 totaled $76,815,000. The retired workers received an average monthly Social Security payment of $310. **FINANCE** On June 30, 1983, three commercial banks had total deposits of $63,521,000 and total assets of $72,247,000. On December 31, 1982 one state savings and loan association and one state branch had assets of $22,447,999. In addition there is one credit union in the county. **HOUSING** Average value of homes in 1980: $17,200. Permits for new, privately owned housing units increased in 1982: 35 permits were issued with a total construction cost of $752,439. Of those permits, 11 were for single family houses. Between 1970 and 1980 the number of housing units increased by 11%. Eighty-seven percent of all units in the county are air-conditioned, 84% are heated by gas and 14% by electricity. **NATURAL RESOURCES** Caliche, salt beds, oil, gas and bituminous coal. In 1982 a total of 495,098 thousand cubic feet of gas well gas,

6,567,333 barrels of crude oil and 2,627,099 thousand cubic feet of casinghead gas were produced. Current production of other minerals and products includes sand and gravel. **TOURISM** Travel expenditures of $1,427,000 in 1982 (an increase of 12% over 1981) generated 31 jobs and $262,000 in payroll. **ALCOHOLIC BEVERAGES** Packaged distilled spirits, beer, ale, malt liquor and wine are legal in parts of the county. **FEDERAL EXPENDITURES** The federal government had direct expenditures or obligations of $23,415,000 in the county during fiscal year 1983, including $232,000 by the U.S. Department of Defense. In addition, the federal government provided $994,000 in grant awards, paid $617,000 in salaries and wages, made direct payments to individuals of $15,413,000 including $10,903,000 in retirement and disability payments, awarded $4,000 in procurement contracts and spent $6,387,000 in other expenditures or obligations. The federal government also provided $296,000 in direct loans and $2,735,000 in guaranteed loans and insurance.

COMMUNICATION
Newspapers–Weekly: Colorado City Record. Radio: KVMC (Colorado City). Cable TV. Telephone companies: Continental Telephone, General Telephone and Southwestern Bell. **TRANSPORTATION** Total public road mileage: 798. In 1982 there were 9,782 registered vehicles and 247 reported traffic accidents including three fatalities. Intercity bus service is available. Motor freight: three carriers. Rail: one main line carries annually five to 10 million tons of freight through the county. Aircraft: 14 are registered in the county. Airports: Colorado City Municipal Airport serves as a base for 12 aircraft and is a general utility airport with general aviation service. Trulock Ranch Airport near Colorado City.

COMMUNITY SERVICES
EDUCATION Three school districts with four elementary, one middle and three high schools. The average daily attendance in 1981-82 was 1,757, with expenditures per pupil of $3,288 including 125 classroom teachers with an average annual salary of $16,019. Fifty-four percent of the 106 high school graduates planned to attend college. In 1982-83, 50% of the students were White, 42% Hispanic, 8% Black, 0.2% Asian. **PUBLIC LIBRARIES** Mitchell County Public Library (Colorado City): 40,053 volumes. **CHILD CARE** 12 day care licensed facilities. **HEALTH CARE** Eight physicians and three dentists. Hospitals: one with a capacity of 39. Ambulance services: one volunteer fire department and one police department service. Mental health: one county clinic. Nursing homes: three nursing homes with a combined capacity of 228 nursing care residents. The average cost per day for private patients in 1982 was $32.24. **CHURCHES** 28 churches have an estimated combined membership of 7,369. The largest denominations are Southern Baptist, Catholic and United Methodist. **SOCIAL SERVICES** In fiscal year 1983 a total of $292,708 in food stamps was distributed, with an average of 728 persons receiving food stamps each month. Aid to Families with Dependent Children (AFDC) totaled $52,387, with an average of 36 families receiving AFDC each month. Medical assistance benefits for the aged and disabled of $1,404,328 and for families and children of $50,358 brought the county benefit total to $1,799,781. **FIRE PROTECTION** Three volunteer fire departments. **LAW ENFORCEMENT** The County Sheriff has 11 commissioned officers. Two police departments have a combined force of 14. **CRIME** 29 violent crimes (murder, forcible rape, robbery and aggravated assault) and 284 nonviolent crimes (burglary, larceny-theft and motor vehicle theft) were reported in 1982. **JUDICIAL SYSTEM** One District Court and Judge, one County Court and Judge and four Justices of the Peace. In the District Court a total of 516 cases were pending on 1/1/82, 314 new cases were

filed and 266 cases were disposed of during the year leaving 564 cases pending on 12/31/82. There were 228 criminal cases on the docket, 36 convictions, six persons committed to prison, three committed to jail and 136 cases left pending. In the County Court 126 cases were pending on 1/1/82, 155 new cases were filed and 112 cases were disposed of during the year leaving 169 cases pending on 12/31/82. There were 238 criminal cases on the docket, 36 convictions, 17 persons committed to jail and 158 cases left pending. **JAILS** One jail, capacity 27. **ATTORNEYS AT LAW** 11. **UTILITIES** 83% of the residents are connected to a public or privately owned water system and 64% are connected to a public sewer system. Natural gas is distributed to the county by Lone Star Gas Co., Division of Enserch. The average annual residential bill for natural gas in 1982 for the Lone Star distribution system was $405.91, an increase of 35% over 1981. Electricity is distributed to the county by Texas Electric Service Co., Midwest Electric Coop., Inc., Concho Valley Electric Coop., Inc., and Lone Wolf Electric Coop. Inc. and is generated primarily by gas and oil. The typical residential electric bill is $154.69 per month for an all-electric house using 2,500 kwh. **TAXES** The county has 11 units with taxing authority: six school districts, three cities, one county, and one hospital district.

RECREATION/ENTERTAINMENT
NATIONAL REGISTER OF HISTORIC PLACES Colorado City: Scott-Majors House. **STATE** Lake Colorado City State Recreation Area covers 500 acres with camping, trailer sites, fishing, swimming and boat ramps. **MUNICIPAL PARKS** 63 acres in four municipal parks. These parks contain two playgrounds, three baseball and softball fields, one swimming pool, one beach, one boat ramp and shore fishing facilities. Developed campsites: 28. **BOATING/FISHING** Lakes/reservoirs: Champion Creek (1,560 acres), Colorado River Off-Channel Storage (162 acres), Colorado City (1,612 acres) and Gregory (52 acres). Major rivers: Colorado. Primary streams: Champion, Morgan, Hasting, Willow, Beals, Wildhorse and Big Silver. **HUNTING** Fall season on antelope. Fall and winter seasons on deer and javelina. No closed seasons on squirrel, bobcat and coyote. Winter seasons on quail, muskrat, beaver, opossum, ring-tailed cat, badger, fox, weasel, raccoon, skunk and civet cat. Fall, winter and spring seasons on turkey. In 1983 sandhill crane, duck, coot, geese, woodcock and jacksnipe seasons occurred during the winter months. Teal duck, rail and gallinule seasons occurred in the fall. Mourning dove seasons occurred intermittently during the fall and winter. **MUSEUMS** Colorado City Museum. **SPECIAL EVENTS** AJRA Rodeo, Colorado City, June; Railhead Arts and Crafts Fair, Colorado City, October; County Fair, Colorado City, date varies.

COMMUNITIES
COUNTY SEAT Colorado City, County Courthouse, 79512; County Clerk's Office, 915/728-2522. **INCORPORATED COMMUNITIES** (1980 population and ZIP Code) Colorado City (5,405) 79512, Loraine (929) 79532 and Westbrook (298) 79565. **UNINCORPORATED COMMUNITIES** (and ZIP Code) Buford 79512, Cuthbert 79512, Hyman 79720, Iatan 79565 and Valley View 79512. **FOR ADDITIONAL LOCAL INFORMATION** Colorado City Area Chamber of Commerce, 157 W. 2nd St., Colorado, 79512, 915/728-3403.

MONTAGUE (M1)

THE LAND
Bordering Oklahoma east of Wichita Falls on U.S. Highways 81 and 82 in the Cross Timbers Region, Montague County covers 928 square miles with the elevation ranging from 800 to 1,250 feet.

MONTAGUE (continued)

To the north and west the undulating to hilly soils are deep to moderately deep with loamy surfaces and clayey subsoils over sandstone or shale. The light colored soils in the east are loamy to sandy with some red, clayey subsoils. In the Cross Timbers and Prairies vegetation area, the dominant grasses are the bluestems, Indiangrass, switchgrass, sideoats, wildrye and Texas wintergrass plus post and blackjack oak trees. Between 41 and 50% of the land in the county is considered prime farmland. **CLIMATE** Subtropical Subhumid with hot summers. The average annual temperature is 64°F. Temperatures in January range from an average low of 28° to an average high of 53°F and in July range from 71° to 99°F. The average annual precipitation is 29 inches, with an average relative humidity of 81% at 6 A.M. and 51% at 6 P.M. The average annual snowfall is five inches. The growing season averages 229 days per year, with the last freeze in late March and the first freeze in early November. The sun shines during the year on the average 68% of the daylight hours.

THE PEOPLE

The 1982 estimated population of 18,500 indicates a continuation of the growth rate begun in the 1960s which reversed the population decline from 1940 and 1960. Rural areas grew three times as fast as urban areas between 1970 and 1980. The county's population is older than average, with a median age of 39. The birth rate is low and the death rate is high. The largest ancestry groups are persons of English descent (31%), Irish descent (27%) and German descent (14%). **REGISTERED VOTERS** As of November 2, 1982 there were 9,611 registered voters (0.1% of the state total). The 1982 general election had a 50% voter turnout, compared to a 68% turnout in the 1980 general election. In the 1982 primary 99% voted Democratic and 1% Republican, with 3,475 votes cast.

THE ECONOMY

AGRICULTURE Wheat and cattle area. In 1982, 84% of the land was in farms and ranches, with 15% of the farmland under cultivation and 3% irrigated. Montague ranked 143rd in the state in highest agricultural receipts, with 82% from livestock and livestock products. Overgrazing, undesirable brush and weeds, water erosion, inefficient tillage systems and the cultivation of marginal lands are the current conservation problems. Primary crops: fourth in the state for rye. Wheat, hay, oats and sorghum. Primary vegetables: watermelons. Primary fruits and nuts: a leader in the state for apples and sixth for peaches. Pecans. Primary livestock and products: cattle, milk and hogs. **BUSINESS** Total number of business establishments in the county: 428. Retail sales during the first quarter of 1984 increased by 2%. In 1980, 17% of the labor force were self-employed, 16% were employed in professional or related services, 19% in manufacturing, 18% in wholesale and retail trade, 18% in agriculture, forestry, fisheries and mining, 16% were employed in other counties and there were 2,646 retired workers. The industries with the most employment: agribusiness, oil and gas field services and the manufacture of farm machinery and equipment, apparel belts and men's leather shoes. The nonfarm earnings in 1981 totaled $166,309,000. The retired workers received an average monthly Social Security payment of $293. **FINANCE** On June 30, 1983, five commercial banks had total deposits of $171,824,000 and total assets of $184,894,000. There are three state savings and loan association branches in the county. **HOUSING** Average value of homes in 1980: $23,200. Permits for new, privately owned housing units increased in 1982: 12 permits were issued with a total construction cost of $594,820. Of those permits, all were for single family houses. Between 1970 and 1980 the number of housing units increased by 28%. Seventy-seven percent of all units in the county are air-conditioned, 84% are heated by gas and 12% by electricity. **NATURAL RESOURCES** Limestone, sand, gravel, oil, gas and bituminous coal. In 1982 a total of 866,645 thousand cubic feet of gas well gas, 3,717 barrels of condensate, 2,452,053 barrels of crude oil and 3,980,284 thousand cubic feet of casinghead gas were produced. Current production of other minerals and products includes crushed limestone, sand and gravel. **TOURISM** Travel expenditures of $5,302,000 in 1982 (an increase of 13% over 1981) generated 113 jobs and $961,000 in payroll. **ALCOHOLIC BEVERAGES** Totally dry. **FEDERAL EXPENDITURES** The federal government had direct expenditures or obligations of $39,226,000 in the county during fiscal year 1983, including $1,551,000 by the U.S. Department of Defense. In addition, the federal government provided $229,000 in grant awards, paid $1,818,000 in salaries and wages, made direct payments to individuals of $36,527,000 including $26,307,000 in retirement and disability payments, awarded $190,000 in procurement contracts and spent $462,000 in other expenditures or obligations. The federal government also provided $148,000 in direct loans and $2,927,000 in guaranteed loans and insurance.

COMMUNICATION

Newspapers–Weekly: The Bowie News, Nocona News and the Saint Jo Tribune. Radio: KBAN-AM (Bowie). Cable TV. Telephone companies: Southwestern Bell, Central Telephone-Midstate, Muenster Telephone and Nocona Telephone. **TRANSPORTATION** Total public road mileage: 1,174. In 1982 there were 20,522 registered vehicles and 447 reported traffic accidents including three fatalities. Taxi cabs: one company in Bowie. Intercity bus service is available. Motor freight: 10 local and intrastate carriers. Rail: One main and one branch line carry freight through the county. The main line carries annually over 30 million tons of freight and the branch carries 20 to 30 million tons. Aircraft: 26 are registered in the county. Airports: Bowie Municipal Airport serves as a base for 17 aircraft and is a basic utility airport with general aviation service. Also serving the area are Nocona Municipal Airport and Nocona Hills Airport at Nocona.

COMMUNITY SERVICES

EDUCATION Seven school districts with eight elementary, two middle and one high school. The average daily attendance in 1981-82 was 2,928, with expenditures per pupil of $3,121 including 180 classroom teachers with an average annual salary of $15,770. Forty-two percent of the 217 high school graduates planned to attend college. In 1982-83, 97% of the students were White and 3% Hispanic. **PUBLIC LIBRARIES** Bowie Public Library: 13,900 volumes. Nocona Library. **CHILD CARE** 34 day care and two twenty-four hour care licensed facilities. **HEALTH CARE** 15 physicians and five dentists. Hospitals: two with a combined capacity of 107. Ambulance services: two funeral homes and one city service. Mental health: one county clinic. Nursing homes: five nursing homes with a combined capacity of 512 nursing care residents. The average cost per day for private patients in 1982 was $26.83. **CHURCHES** 58 churches have an estimated combined membership of 10,286. The largest denominations are Southern Baptist, United Methodist and Churches of Christ. **SOCIAL SERVICES** In fiscal year 1983 a total of $321,863 in food stamps was distributed, with an average of 679 persons receiving food stamps each month. Aid to Families with Dependent Children (AFDC) totaled $50,926 with an average of 33 families receiving AFDC each month. Medical assistance benefits for the aged and disabled of $2,829,906 and for families and children of $72,975 brought the county benefit total to $3,275,670. **FIRE PROTECTION** Seven volunteer fire departments. **LAW ENFORCEMENT** The County Sheriff has five commissioned officers. Three police departments have a combined force of 19. **CRIME** 23 violent crimes (murder, forcible rape, robbery and aggravated assault) and 433 nonviolent crimes (burglary, larceny-theft and motor vehicle theft) were reported in 1982. **JUDICIAL SYSTEM** One District Court and Judge, one County Court and Judge and four Justices of the Peace. In the District Court a total of 775 cases were pending on 1/1/82, 683 new cases were filed and 780 cases were disposed of during the year leaving 678 cases pending on 12/31/82. There were 210 criminal cases on the docket, 34 convictions, 13 persons committed to prison and 133 cases left pending. In the County Court 643 cases were pending on 1/1/82, 474 new cases were filed and 427 cases were disposed of during the year leaving 690 cases pending on 12/31/82. There were 986 criminal cases on the docket, 51 convictions, 21 persons committed to jail and 566 cases left pending. **JAILS** One jail, capacity 18. **ATTORNEYS AT LAW** 17. **UTILITIES** 68% of the residents are connected to a public or privately owned water system and 54% are connected to a public sewer system. Natural gas is distributed to the county by Lone Star Gas Co., Division of Enserch. The average annual residential bill for natural gas in 1982 for the Lone Star distribution system was $405.91, an increase of 35% over 1981. Electricity is distributed to the city of Bowie by Bowie Utilities and to the rest of the county by Texas New Mexico Power Co., Cooke Co. Electric Coop., Assn. and Wise Electric Coop., Inc. and is generated primarily by gas, oil and water. The typical residential electric bill is $168.05 per month for an all-electric house using 2,500 kwh. **TAXES** The county has 13 units with taxing authority: seven school district, three cities, one county, one hospital district and one special district.

RECREATION/ENTERTAINMENT

NATIONAL REGISTER OF HISTORIC PLACES Spanish Fort vicinity: Spanish Fort. **MUNICIPAL PARKS** 279 acres in nine municipal parks. These parks contain five playgrounds, one golf course, nine baseball and softball fields, eight tennis courts, two multi-use courts, one swimming pool, one beach, one boat ramp and shore fishing facilities. Developed campsites: 15. **BOATING/FISHING** Lakes/reservoirs: Big Sandy Creek Soil Conservation Service Lakes 8 and 22A (906 acres), Bowie (103 acres), Amon G. Carter (1,540 acres), Denton Creek Soil Conservation Service Lake 3A (12 acres), Elm Creek Soil Conservation Service Lake 5 (22 acres), Farmers Creek Soil Conservation Service Lakes 7 and 8 (30 acres), Katy (22 acres), Nocona (1,470 acres) and Leisure (26 acres). Major rivers: Red. Primary streams: Salt, Denton, West Fork Belknap, Kiel, Brushy, Big Sandy, Steelman, West Farmers, Mountain, Farmers and Barefoot. **HUNTING** Fall and winter seasons on deer. No closed season on squirrel, bobcat and coyote. Winter seasons on quail, muskrat, beaver, opossum, ring-tailed cat, badger, fox, raccoon, skunk and civet cat. Fall, winter and spring seasons on turkey. In 1983 duck, coot, geese, woodcock and jacksnipe seasons occurred during the winter months. Teal duck, rail and gallinule seasons occurred in the fall. Mourning dove seasons occurred intermittently during the fall and winter months. **MUSEUMS** Saint Jo: Stonewall Saloon Museum. Sunset: Old West Museum. **SPECIAL EVENTS** Jim Bowie Days, Bowie, June; Chisholm Trail Roundup Rodeo, Nocona, July; Amateur Rodeo, Saint Jo, August; Watermelon Festival, Forestburg, August; North Texas/South Oklahoma Pecan Festival, Nocona, November.

COMMUNITIES

COUNTY SEAT Montague, County Courthouse, 76251; County Clerk's Office, 817/894-2461. **INCORPORATED COMMUNITIES** (1980 population and ZIP Code) Bowie (5,610) 76230, Nocona (2,992) 76255 and Saint Jo (1,071) 76265.

UNINCORPORATED COMMUNITIES (and ZIP Code) Belcherville 76255, Bonita 76255, Capps Corner 76265, Dewey 76239, Dye (Dye Mound) 76265, Forestburg 76239, Fruitland 76230, Hardy 76265, Illinois Bend 76265, Mallard 76251, Montague 76251, New Harp (Newharp) 76239, Prairie Valley 76255, Salona 76230, Spanish Fort 76255, Stoneburg 76230 and Sunset 76270. **FOR ADDITIONAL LOCAL INFORMATION** Bowie Chamber of Commerce, 115 E. Tarrant, Bowie, 76230, 817/872-1173 and Nocona Chamber of Commerce, P. O. Box 27, Nocona, 76255, 817/825-3526.

MONTGOMERY (G4)

THE LAND

North of Houston on Interstate Highway 45 in the East Texas Timberlands Region, Montgomery County covers 1,047 square miles with the elevation ranging from 150 to 300 feet. To the south and west the light colored, loamy soils have very deep, reddish, clayey to loamy subsoils with hardened calcium deposits. The gently rolling to hilly soils in the remainder of the county are reddish with loamy surfaces and very deep, clayey subsoils. In the Pineywoods vegetation area, there are longleaf, shortleaf and loblolly pines, hickory, maple, sweet and black gum, oaks and magnolia trees. Between 31 and 40% of the land in the county is considered prime farmland. **CLIMATE** Subtropical Humid with warm summers. The average annual temperature is 68°F. Temperatures in January range from an average low of 39° to an average high of 61°F and in July range from 72° to 95°F. The average annual precipitation is 45 inches, with an average relative humidity of 88% at 6 A.M. and 60% at 6 P.M. There is no snowfall. The growing season averages 270 days per year, with the last freeze in the first of March and the first freeze late November. The sun shines during the year on the average 68% of the daylight hours.

THE PEOPLE

Montgomery County ranks ninth among all U.S. counties in the highest growth rate between 1970 and 1980. The 1982 estimated population of 148,700 indicates a continuation of that rapid growth. Over 77% of the residents live in rural areas which grew faster than urban areas between 1970 and 1980. The age groups with the largest gains were ages 20 to 34, 15 to 19 and birth to five years. The largest ancestry groups are persons of English descent (24%), Irish descent (24%) and German descent (20%). **REGISTERED VOTERS** As of November 2, 1982 there were 57,852 registered voters (0.9% of the state total). The 1982 general election had a 51% voter turnout, compared to a 68% turnout in the 1980 general election. In the 1982 primary 70% voted Democratic and 30 Republican, with 13,038 votes cast.

THE ECONOMY

AGRICULTURE Major forest production area. In 1982, 31% of the land was in farms and ranches, with 4% of the farmland under cultivation. Montgomery ranked 158th in the state in highest agricultural receipts, with 63% from crops. Undesirable woody vegetation in the forestlands, inadequate forest harvesting systems and erosion are the current conservation problems. Primary crops: hay. Primary vegetables: potatoes, sweet potatoes, tomatoes and watermelons. Primary fruits and nuts: peaches and pecans. Primary livestock and products: cattle and milk. **BUSINESS** Total number of business establishments in the county: 1,754. Retail sales during the first quarter of 1984 increased by 17%. In 1980, 8% of the labor force were self-employed, 15% were employed in professional or related services, 15% in manufacturing, 22% in wholesale and retail trade, 13% in construction, 55% were employed in other counties and there

COUNTIES

MONTGOMERY (continued)

were 6,028 retired workers. The industries with the most employment: Oil and gas extraction, general and heavy construction, sawmills, wood preservation and the manufacture of industrial chemicals, plastics products, metal pipe and fittings, construction machinery and oil field machinery. The nonfarm earnings in 1981 totaled $1,545,020,000. The retired workers received an average monthly Social Security payment of $341. **FINANCE** On June 30, 1983, 11 commercial banks had total deposits of $555,487,000 and total assets of $627,201,000. On December 31, 1982 one state savings and loan association, one federal association, 14 state branches and two federal branches had combined assets of $150,133,697. In addition there are three credit unions in the county. **HOUSING** Average value of homes in 1980: $58,300. Permits for new, privately owned housing units increased in 1982: 209 permits were issued with a total construction cost of $18,983,489. Of those permits, 153 were for single family houses. Housing permits in Willis increased from seven in 1981 to 46 in 1982 with 32 permits issued for apartments and condominiums. Between 1970 and 1980 the number of housing units increased by 171%. Eighty-nine percent of all units in the county are air-conditioned, 65% are heated by gas and 31% by electricity. **NATURAL RESOURCES** Industrial sand, sand, gravel, oil and gas. In 1982 a total of 5,576,350 thousand cubic feet of gas well gas, 84,597 barrels of condensate, 9,200,262 barrels of crude oil and 24,456,996 thousand cubic feet of casinghead gas were produced. Current production of other minerals and products includes construction sand, sand and gravel and crushed sandstone. Pine and hardwood production in 1981 totaled 22,399,040 cubic feet: 21,658,438 cubic feet of pine and 740,602 cubic feet of hardwood. **TOURISM** Travel expenditures of $26,253,000 in 1982 (an increase of 12% over 1981) generated 663 jobs and $5,763,000 in payroll. Lodging: three hotels, motels and tourist courts. **ALCOHOLIC BEVERAGES** Packaged distilled spirits, beer, ale, malt liquor and wine are legal in parts of the county. Sale of mixed beverages is legal in all or parts of the county. **FEDERAL EXPENDITURES** The federal government had direct expenditures or obligations of $124,201,000 in the county during fiscal year 1983, including $7,739,000 by the U.S. Department of Defense. In addition, the federal government provided $10,941,000 in grant awards, paid $9,274,000 in salaries and wages, made direct payments to individuals of $99,338,000 including $86,749,000 in retirement and disability payments, awarded $4,161,000 in procurement contracts and spent $486,000 in other expenditures or obligations. The federal government also provided $5,467,000 in direct loans and $166,582,000 in guaranteed loans and insurance.

COMMUNICATION

Newspapers–Daily: The Courier (Conroe), ave. eve. circ. 10,944. Radio: KIKR-AM and KJOJ-FM (Conroe). Cable TV. Telephone companies: General Telephone, Southwestern Bell, United Telephone, Central Telephone and Conroe Telephone. **TRANSPORTATION** Total public road mileage: 1,887. In 1982 there were 120,722 registered vehicles and 3,074 reported traffic accidents including 60 fatalities. Intercity bus service is available. Motor freight: 20 local and intrastate carriers. Rail: nine main lines carry freight through the county with one carrying annually 20 to 30 million tons, seven carry 10 to 20 each and one carries five to 10 million tons. Aircraft: 213 are registered in the county. Airports: Montgomery County Airport at Conroe serves as a base for 150 aircraft and is a basic transportation airport with general aviation service. Also serving the area are Cut and Shoot Airport near Conroe and Williams Airport at Porter. Heliflight Systems Heliport at Montgomery County Airport.

COMMUNITY SERVICES

EDUCATION Six school districts with 31 elementary, eight middle, eight high schools and two special education. The average daily attendance in 1981-82 was 30,262, with expenditures per pupil of $3,119 including 1,919 classroom teachers with an average annual salary of $16,895. Forty-three percent of the 1,790 high school graduates planned to attend college. In 1982-83, 91% of the students were White, 4% Hispanic, 5% Black, 0.4% Asian and 0.2% American Indian. Sports championships: 1982 AAAAA Boys' Cross Country, Conroe McCullough H.S. Private schools: 425 students enrolled in three elementary and two high school. Vocational education: Professional Beauty College of Conroe (Conroe). **PUBLIC LIBRARIES** Montgomery County Library (Conroe): 121,655 volumes and two branches. Splendora Library. **CHILD CARE** 137 day care and 33 twenty-four hour care licensed facilities. **HEALTH CARE** 83 physicians and 44 dentists. Hospitals: two with a combined capacity of 317. Clinics: one dialysis clinic and one public health clinic. Ambulance services: three volunteer fire departments, two commercial, one funeral home and one county service. Mental health: one county clinic and one psychiatric hospital with a capacity of 100. Nursing homes: four nursing homes with a combined capacity of 452 nursing care residents. The average cost per day for private patients in 1982 was $31.26. **CHURCHES** 112 churches have an estimated combined membership of 47,338. The largest denominations are Southern Baptist, Catholic and United Methodist. **SOCIAL SERVICES** In fiscal year 1983 a total of $2,433,523 in food stamps was distributed, with an average of 5,152 persons receiving food stamps each month. Aid to Families with Dependent Children (AFDC) totaled $445,088, with an average of 295 families receiving AFDC each month. Medical assistance benefits for the aged and disabled of $4,209,040 and for families and children of $764,052 brought the county benefit total to $7,851,702. **FIRE PROTECTION** One partly paid and 18 volunteer fire departments. **LAW ENFORCEMENT** The County Sheriff has 282 commissioned offers. 26 police departments have a combined force of 603. **CRIME** 427 violent crimes (murder, forcible rape, robbery and aggravated assault) and 4,105 nonviolent crimes (burglary, larceny-theft and motor vehicle theft) were reported in 1982. **JUDICIAL SYSTEM** Four District Courts and Judges, three County Courts and Judges and five Justices of the Peace. In the District Courts a total of 6,021 cases were pending on 1/1/82, 4,411 new cases were filed and 4,183 cases were disposed of during the year leaving 6,249 cases pending on 12/31/82. There were 1,143 criminal cases on the docket, 553 convictions, 150 persons committed to prison, 16 committed to jail and 430 cases left pending. In the County Courts 10,050 cases were pending on 1/1/82, 5,192 new cases were filed and 5,035 cases were disposed of during the year leaving 10,207 cases pending on 12/31/82. There were 14,009 criminal cases on the docket, 1,977 convictions, 321 persons committed to jail and 9,191 cases left pending. **JAILS** One jail, capacity 365. New jail opened in 1983. **ATTORNEYS AT LAW** 151. **UTILITIES** 68% of the residents are connected to a public or privately owned water system and 47% are connected to a public sewer system. Natural gas is distributed to the county by Moran Utilities Company. Electricity is distributed to the county by Gulf State Utilities Co. and Mid-South Electric Coop., Assn. and is generated primarily by gas and oil. The typical residential electric bill is $198.32 per month for an all-electric house using 2,500 kwh. **TAXES** The county has 69 units with taxing authority: seven school districts, 13 cities, one county, one hospital district and 47 special districts.

RECREATION/ENTERTAINMENT

FEDERAL SAM HOUSTON NATIONAL FOREST covers 160,401 acres in three counties and includes seven recreation areas.

NATIONAL REGISTER OF HISTORIC PLACES Montgomery: Arnold-Simonton House. Montgomery vicinity: Kirbee Kiln. **STATE** Lake Houston State Park Site covers 2,519 acres and was closed to the public as of July 1983. W. Goodrich Jones State Forest covers 1,725 acres with fishing, swimming and nature/hiking trails. **COUNTY/MUNICIPAL PARKS** 181 acres in four county and 13 municipal parks. These parks contain one mile of hiking trails, four playgrounds, two football and soccer fields, seven baseball and softball fields, four tennis courts and one boat ramp. **SCENIC DRIVES** The Texas Forest Trail runs through this county. This trail explores the farming, ranching and oilfield areas of the East Texas Pineywoods. **BOATING/FISHING** Lakes/reservoirs: Dunwoody (47 acres), Conroe (20,985 acres), Fish (14 acres), Flamingo (24 acres), Forest Falls (56 acres), Lewis Creek (1,010 acres), Moose Jaw (17 acres), Mount Pleasant (75 acres), Neidick (41 acres), Peach Creek (76 acres), Price (25 acres), Royal Rushing Spring (26 acres), Shadow (175 acres) and Stewart (31 acres). Major rivers: West Fork and San Jacinto. Primary streams: Little Caney, Caney, Base, Lewis, Mill, Peach, Rush, Sandy, Stewart and Spring. **HUNTING** Fall and winter seasons on deer. Summer, fall and winter seasons on squirrel. Winter seasons on quail, muskrat, beaver, otter, opossum, mink, ring-tailed cat, badger, fox, raccoon, skunk and civet cat. No closed season on nutria, bobcat and coyote. In 1983 duck, coot, geese, woodcock and jacksnipe seasons occurred during the winter months. Teal duck, rail and gallinule seasons occurred in the fall. Mourning dove seasons occurred intermittently during the fall and winter months. **SPECIAL EVENTS** Go Texan Parade, Conroe, February; Barbeque Cookoff, Conroe, March; County Fair and Rodeo, Conroe, March; Historical Trek, Montgomery, April; Main Street Festival, Conroe, June; Antique and Collectors Carnival, Conroe, October.

COMMUNITIES

COUNTY SEAT Conroe, County Courthouse, 77301; County Clerk's Office, 409/756-0571. **INCORPORATED COMMUNITIES** (1980 population and ZIP Code) Chateau Woods (590) 77301, Conroe (18,034) 77301, Cut and Shoot (568) 77301, Houston (1,594,086: 19 in Montgomery Co., 16,270 in Fort Bend Co. and 1,578,849 in Harris Co.) 77001, Magnolia (867) 77355, Montgomery (258) 77356, Oak Ridge North (2,504) 77301, Panorama Village (1,186) 77301, Patton Village (1,050) 77372, Roman Forest (929) 77357, Shenandoah (1,793) 77301, Splendora (721) 77372, Stage Coach (349) 77355, Willis (1,674) 77378, Woodbranch Village (720) 77357 and Woodloch (351) 77301. **UNINCORPORATED COMMUNITIES** (and ZIP Code) Beach 77301, Bobville 77333, Bonanza 77356, Dacus 77356, Decker Prairie 77355, Dobbin 77333, Egypt 77355, Four Corners 77301, Freeway Oaks Estates 77365, Grand Lake 77301, Grangerland 77302, Honea 77356, Johnstown 77301, Karen 77355, Keenan 77356, Lakeland 77301, Lake Estates 77356, Midline 77327, Midway 77327, Mostyn 77355, New Caney 77357, Oklahoma 77355, Pinehurst 77362, Pine Lake 77356, Piney Grove 77355, Pitts (Pittsville) 77338, Porter 77365, Porter Heights 77365, Rayford 77373 Security 77327, Sorters 77365, Tamina 77301, The Woodlands 77380, Timber Lake Acres 77365, Ventura 77355, White Oaks 77365, Wigginsville 77301 and Woody Acres 77365. **FOR ADDITIONAL LOCAL INFORMATION** Conroe-Montgomery Co. Chamber of Commerce, Drawer 2230, Conroe, 77301, 409/756-6644, West Montgomery Co. Chamber of Commerce, P.O. Box 1, Montgomery, 77356, 409/597-4155, East Montgomery Co. Chamber of Commerce, P. O. Box 967, New Caney, 77357, 409/354-2907, Splendora Chamber of Commerce, P. O. Box 967, New Caney, 77357, 409/354-2907 and S. Montgomery Co.-Woodlands Chamber of Commerce, 1400 Woodloch Forest Drive, #190, The Woodlands, 77380.

MOORE (P7)

THE LAND

North of Amarillo on U.S. Highways 287 and 87 in the High Plains Region, Moore County covers 905 square miles with the elevation ranging from 3,000 to 3,700 feet. The nearly level soils are very dark and loamy over clayey subsoils covering limestone. In the north the vegetation is the short grasses and few mesquite trees of the High Plains. In the south the vegetation is the taller grasses, mesquite and shinnery oak of the Rolling Plains vegetation area. Between 51 and 60% of the land in the county is considered prime farmland. **CLIMATE** Continental Steppe with wide-ranging daily and seasonal temperatures and irregular precipitation. The average annual temperature is 57 °F. Temperatures in January range from an average low of 20° to an average high of 49 °F and in July range from 65° to 93 °F. The average annual precipitation is 18 inches, with an average relative humidity of 68% at 6 A.M. and 40% at 6 P.M. The average annual snowfall is 16 inches. The growing season averages 185 days per year, with the last freeze in mid April and the first freeze in mid October. The sun shines during the year on the average 75% of the daylight hours.

THE PEOPLE

Nearly 74% of the residents on Moore County live in urban areas. The 1982 estimated population of 17,200 indicates a continuation of the growth in population which began in the 1970s, reversing the population decline between 1960 and 1970. The greatest growth between 1970 and 1980 was in urban areas with only slight increases in rural areas. The largest ancestry groups are persons of English descent (26%), Irish descent (22%), Hispanic (20%) and German descent (15%). **REGISTERED VOTERS** As of November 2, 1982 there were 7,542 registered voters (0.1% of the state total). The 1982 general election had a 49% voter turnout, compared to a 72% turnout in the 1980 general election. In the 1982 primary 96% voted Democratic and 4% Republican, with 2,914 votes cast.

THE ECONOMY

AGRICULTURE Wheat and fed cattle area. In 1982, 98% of the land was in farms and ranches, with 40% of the farmland under cultivation and 86% irrigated. Moore ranked 16th in the state in highest agricultural receipts, with 60% from livestock and livestock products. Overgrazing, water and wind erosion, decreasing irrigation water supplies and noxious weeds are the current conservation problems. Primary crops: 10th in the state for wheat, eighth for sorghum and third for barley. Corn and soybeans. Primary fruits and nuts: pecans. Primary livestock and products: sixth in the state for fed cattle marketings. Hogs. **BUSINESS** Total number of business establishments in the county: 390. Retail sales during the first quarter of 1984 increased by 13%. In 1980, 10% of the labor force were self-employed, 14% were employed in professional or related services, 23% in manufacturing, 20% in wholesale and retail trade, 16% in agriculture, forestry, fisheries and mining, 6% were employed in other counties and there were 908 retired workers. The industries with the most employment: agribusiness, oil and gas extraction, meat packing, petroleum refining and leather tanning. The nonfarm earnings in 1981 totaled $164,042,000. The retired workers received an average monthly Social Security payment of $366. **FINANCE** On June 30, 1983, three commercial banks had total deposits of $88,568,000 and total assets of $103,285,000. On December 31, 1982 one state savings and loan association, one state branch and one federal association branch had assets of $58,991,329. In addition there are three credit unions in the county. **HOUSING** Average value of homes in 1980: $30,300. Permits for new, privately owned housing units increased in 1982: 37 permits were

MOORE (continued)

issued with a total construction cost of $1,727,250. Of those permits, 34 were for single family houses. Between 1970 and 1980 the number of housing units increased by 24%. Eighty-three percent of all units in the county are air-conditioned, 89% are heated by gas and 11% by electricity. **NATURAL RESOURCES** Caliche, oil and gas. In 1982 a total of 117,477,283 thousand cubic feet of gas well gas, 2,396 barrels of condensate, 660,720 barrels of crude oil and 6,869,016 thousand cubic feet of casinghead gas were produced. Current production of other minerals and products includes helium, hydrochloric acid, recovered sulphur and potassium sulfate. **TOURISM** Travel expenditures of $13,204,000 in 1982 (an increase of 11% over 1981) generated 331 jobs and $2,637,000 in payroll. Lodging: four hotels, motels and tourist courts. **ALCOHOLIC BEVERAGES** Packaged distilled spirits, beer, ale, malt liquor and wine are legal. Sale of mixed beverages is legal in all or parts of the county. **FEDERAL EXPENDITURES** The federal government had direct expenditures or obligations of $26,368,000 in the county during fiscal year 1983, including $1,634,000 by the U.S. Department of Defense. In addition, the federal government provided $331,000 in grant awards, paid $2,839,000 in salaries and wages, made direct payments to individuals of $13,101,000 including $10,867,000 in retirement and disability payments, awarded $1,332,000 in procurement contracts and spent $8,767,000 in other expenditures or obligations. The federal government also provided $24,988,000 in direct loans and $10,029,000 in guaranteed loans and insurance.

COMMUNICATION

Newspapers–Weekly: The Moore County News-Press (Dumas). Radio: KDDD-AM and KMRE-FM (Dumas). Cable TV. Telephone companies: Continental Telephone and Southwestern Bell. **TRANSPORTATION** Total public road mileage: 615. In 1982 there were 17,859 registered vehicles and 406 reported traffic accidents including two fatalities. Intercity bus service is available. Motor freight: four carriers. Rail: Six branch lines carry freight through the county. Two of the branches carry annually five to 10 million tons of freight each and four carry less than one million each. Aircraft: 60 are registered in the county. Airports: Dumas City-County Airport serves as a base for 43 aircraft and is a general utility airport with general aviation service. Sunray Airport at Sunray serves as a base for 12 aircraft and is a basic utility airport with general aviation.

COMMUNITY SERVICES

EDUCATION Two school districts with six elementary, one middle and two high schools. The average daily attendance in 1981-82 was 3,537, with expenditures per pupil of $2,708 including 251 classroom teachers with an average annual salary of $18,510. Forty-two percent of the 208 high school graduates planned to attend college. In 1982-83, 66% of the students were White, 31% Hispanic, 0.3% Black, 3% Asian and 0.1% American Indian. **PUBLIC LIBRARIES** Killgore Memorial Library (Dumas): 34,821 volumes and one branch. **CHILD CARE** 19 day care and seven twenty-four hour care licensed facilities. **HEALTH CARE** 15 physicians and five dentists. Hospitals: one with a capacity of 80. Clinics: one outpatient clinic. Ambulance services: one hospital based and one volunteer fire department service. Mental health: one clinic. Nursing homes: one nursing home has a capacity of 47 nursing care residents. The average cost per day for private patients in 1982 was $34.28. **CHURCHES** 31 churches have an estimated combined membership of 10,914. The largest denominations are Southern Baptist, Catholic and United Methodist. **SOCIAL SERVICES** In fiscal year 1983 a total of $321,865 in food stamps was distributed, with an average of 654 persons receiving food stamps each month. Aid to Families with

Dependent Children (AFDC) totaled $44,576, with an average of 29 families receiving AFDC each month. Medical assistance benefits for the aged and disabled of $283,333 and for families and children of $78,868 brought the county benefit total to $728,462. **FIRE PROTECTION** Three volunteer fire departments. **LAW ENFORCEMENT** The County Sheriff has 13 commissioned officers. Three police departments have a combined force of 23. **CRIME** 17 violent crimes (murder, forcible rape, robbery and aggravated assault) and 405 nonviolent crimes (burglary, larceny-theft and motor vehicle theft) were reported in 1982. **JUDICIAL SYSTEM** One District Court and Judge, one County Court and Judge and three Justices of the Peace. In the District Court a total of 404 cases were pending on 1/1/82, 425 new cases were filed and 455 cases were disposed of during the year leaving 374 cases pending on 12/31/82. There were 43 criminal cases on the docket, 27 convictions, four persons committed to prison, three committed to jail and four cases left pending. In the County Court 167 cases were pending on 1/1/82, 520 new cases were filed and 491 cases were disposed of during the year leaving 196 cases pending on 12/31/82. There were 530 criminal cases on the docket, 239 convictions, 122 persons committed to jail and 145 cases left pending. **JAILS** One jail, capacity 26. **ATTORNEYS AT LAW** 15. **UTILITIES** 95% of the residents are connected to a public or privately owned water system and 92% are connected to a public sewer system. Electricity is distributed to the county by Southwestern Public Service and Rita Blanco Electric Coop., Inc. and is generated primarily by gas and coal. The typical residential electric bill is $170.44 per month for an all-electric house using 2,500 kwh. **TAXES** The county has nine units with taxing authority: two school districts, three cities, one county, one hospital district and two special districts.

RECREATION/ENTERTAINMENT

FEDERAL Lake Meredith Recreation Area (See Hutchinson County). **MUNICIPAL PARKS** 42 acres in 10 municipal parks. These parks contain nine playgrounds, four football and soccer fields, 11 baseball and softball fields and six tennis courts. Developed campsites 15. **SCENIC DRIVES** The Texas Plains Trail runs through this county. This trail spans a vast area of the High Plains region of Texas slicing through the southernmost extension of the Great Plains of the United States. The land is flat except where erosion has carved canyon landscapes. **BOATING/FISHING** Lakes/reservoirs: Dumas City (60 acres) and Meredith (16,504 acres). Major rivers: Canadian. Primary streams: Big Blue, Grapevine and Palo Duro. **HUNTING** Fall season on antelope. Fall and winter seasons on deer and mule deer. Summer, fall and winter seasons on squirrel. Winter seasons on pheasant, quail, muskrat, beaver, opossum, ring-tailed cat, badger, fox, weasel, raccoon, skunk and civet cat. Fall, winter and spring seasons on turkey. In 1983 sandhill crane, duck, coot, geese, woodcock and jacksnipe seasons occurred during the winter months. Teal duck, rail and gallinule seasons occurred in the fall. Mourning dove seasons occurred intermittently during the fall and winter months. **MUSEUMS** Dumas: Moore County Historical Museum. **SPECIAL EVENTS** Dogie Days, Dumas, June; County Fair, Dumas, September.

COMMUNITIES

COUNTY SEAT Dumas, County Courthouse, 79029; County Clerk's Office, 806/935-6164. **INCORPORATED COMMUNITIES** (1980 population and ZIP Code) Cactus (898) 79013, Dumas (12,194) 79029 and Sunray (1,952) 79086. **UNINCORPORATED COMMUNITIES** (and ZIP Code) Belle Plain 79029, Etter 79029, Exell 79058, Four Way 79018, Masterson 79058 and McKee 79086. **FOR ADDITIONAL LOCAL INFORMATION** Dumas Chamber of Commerce, 6th and Porter, Dumas, 79029, 806/935-2123.

MORRIS (E8)

THE LAND

Northwest of Longview on Interstate 30 in the East Texas Timerlands Region, Morris County covers 256 square miles with the elevation ranging from 250 to 500 feet. The light colored, acidic, sandy to loamy soils have deep reddish subsoils. Along the northern border the sandy soils have mottled, clayey subsoils. In the north the vegetation is the tall grasses and oak trees of the Post Oak Savannah vegetation area. In the south are the pine and hardwood forests of the Pineywoods vegetation area. Between 21 and 30% of the land in the county is considered prime farmland. **CLIMATE** Subtropical Humid. Thunderstorms may be locally heavy in spring. The average annual temperature is 63 °F. Temperatures in January range from an average low of 30 ° to an average high of 53 °F and in July range from 70 ° to 94 °F. The average annual precipitation is 46 inches, with an average relative humidity of 84% at 6 A.M. and 58% at 6 P.M. The average annual snowfall is two inches. The growing season averages 236 days per year, with the last freeze in mid March and the first freeze in mid November. The sun shines during the year on the average 66% of the daylight hours.

THE PEOPLE

Almost 80% of the residents in Morris County live in rural areas. The 1982 estimated population of 15,400 indicates a continuation of the growth rate begun in the 1970s, reversing the slight population decline between 1960 and 1970. Between 1970 and 1980 rural areas had a 20% population gain and urban areas had a 15% growth. The largest ancestry groups are persons of English descent (25%), Black (22%) and Irish descent (17%). **REGISTERED VOTERS** As of November 2, 1982 there were 8,292 registered voters (0.1% of the state total). The 1982 general election had a 50% voter turnout, compared to a 65% turnout in the 1980 general election. In the 1982 primary 99% voted Democratic and 1% Republican, with 3,374 votes cast.

THE ECONOMY

AGRICULTURE Forest production area. In 1982, 51% of the land was in farms and ranches, with 21% of the farmland under cultivation and 11% irrigated. Morris ranked 215th in the state in highest agricultural receipts, with 83% from livestock and livestock products. Overgrazing, water erosion and improper woodland management are the current conservation problems. Primary crops: hay, wheat and sorghum. Primary vegetables: watermelons and sweet potatoes. Primary fruits and nuts: peaches and pecans. Primary livestock and products: cattle and milk. **BUSINESS** Total number of business establishments in the county: 295. Retail sales during the first quarter of 1984 decreased by 3%, with an increase of 112% in Omaha and a decrease of 34% in Lone Star. In 1980, 8% of the labor force were self-employed, 17% were employed in professional or related services, 31% in manufacturing, 15% in wholesale and retail trade, 11% in transportation, communications and other public utilities, 21% were employed in other counties and there were 1,370 retired workers. The industries with the most employment: agribusiness, tourism, iron ore mining, oil and gas field services, heavy construction, steel mills and the manufacture of asphalt roofing materials. The nonfarm earnings in 1981 totaled $173,510,000. The retired workers received an average monthly Social Security payment of $304. **FINANCE** On June 30, 1983, four commercial banks had total deposits of $83,776,000 and total assets of $92,428,000. There are two state savings and loan branches, one federal branch and one credit union in the county. **HOUSING** Average value of homes in 1980: $27,300. Permits for new, privately owned housing units decreased in 1982: 24 permits were issued with a total construction cost of $901,600.

Of those permits, 20 were for single family houses. Between 1970 and 1980 the number of housing units increased by 31%. Seventy-eight percent of all units in the county are air-conditioned, 81% are heated by gas and 16% by electricity. **NATURAL RESOURCES** Clay, lignite coal, iron and industrial sand. Current production includes clay, magnetite iron, siderite iron and industrial sand. Pine and hardwood production in 1981 totaled 2,382,269 cubic feet: 1,725,971 cubic feet of pine and 656,298 cubic feet of hardwood. **TOURISM** Travel expenditures of $4,879,000 in 1982 (an increase of 11% over 1981) generated 119 jobs and $958,000 in payroll. **ALCOHOLIC BEVERAGES** Totally dry. **FEDERAL EXPENDITURES** The federal government had direct expenditures or obligations of $24,368,000 in the county during fiscal year 1983, including $1,088,000 by the U.S. Department of Defense. In addition, the federal government provided $625,000 in grant awards, paid $843,000 in salaries and wages, made direct payments to individuals of $22,593,000 including $17,212,000 in retirement and disability payments, awarded $186,000 in procurement contracts and spent $121,000 in other expenditures or obligations. The federal government also provided $10,000 in direct loans and $797,000 in guaranteed loans and insurance.

COMMUNICATION

Newspapers–Weekly: The Steel County Bee (Daingerfield) and The Monitor (Naples). Radio: KEGG-AM (Daingerfield). Cable TV. Telephone companies: General Telephone, Southwestern Bell and Etex Telephone Coop. **TRANSPORTATION** Total public road mileage: 420. In 1982 there were 18,373 registered vehicles and 304 reported traffic accidents including three fatalities. Intercity bus service is available. Motor freight: 16 local and intrastate carriers. Rail: three main lines carry freight through the county. One line carries annually 20 to 30 million tons of freight and two lines carry 5 to 10 million tons each. Aircraft: six are registered in the county. Airports: Greater Morris County Airport at Daingerfield. Hospital In The Pines at Lone Star provides an heliport for emergency use.

COMMUNITY SERVICES

EDUCATION Two school districts with four elementary, two middle and two high schools. The average daily attendance in 1981-82 was 3,014, with expenditures per pupil of $2,530 including 193 classroom teachers with an average annual salary of $16,562. Fifty-two percent of the 227 high school graduates planned to attend college. In 1982-83, 71% of the students were White, 1% Hispanic, 28% Black and 0.1% Asian. Sports championship: 1983 AAA Football, Daingerfield H.S. **PUBLIC LIBRARIES** Daingerfield Public Library: 16,342 volumes. **CHILD CARE** 11 day care and three twenty-four hour care licensed facilities. **HEALTH CARE** 13 physicians and four dentists. Hospitals: two with a combined capacity of 75. Clinics: one for treatment of alcohol and/or drug abuse. Ambulance services: two commercial and two volunteer services. Nursing homes: three nursing homes with a combined capacity of 257 nursing care residents. The average cost per day for private patients in 1982 was $27.76. **CHURCHES** 40 churches have an estimated combined membership of 8,890. The largest denominations are Southern Baptist, United Methodist and American Baptist. **SOCIAL SERVICES** In fiscal year 1983 a total of $799,250 in food stamps was distributed, with an average of 1,816 persons receiving food stamps each month. Aid to Families with Dependent Children (AFDC) totaled $213,743 with an average of 145 families receiving AFDC each month. Medical assistance benefits for the aged and disabled of $1,944,959 and for families and children of $254,127 brought the county benefit total to $3,212,078. **FIRE PROTECTION** Seven volunteer fire departments. **LAW ENFORCEMENT** The County Sheriff has 20 commissioned

COUNTIES

MORRIS (continued)

officers. Four police departments have a combined force of 33.
CRIME 49 violent crimes (murder, forcible rape, robbery and
aggravated assault) and 365 nonviolent crimes (burglary, larceny-
theft and motor vehicle theft) were reported in 1982. **JUDICIAL
SYSTEM** Two District Courts and Judges, one County Court
and Judge and four Justices of the Peace. In the District Courts
a total of 532 cases were pending on 1/1/82, 527 new cases were
filed and 537 cases were disposed of during the year leaving 522
cases pending on 12/31/82. There were 232 criminal cases on
the docket, 59 convictions, 20 persons committed to prison and
65 cases left pending. In the County Court 132 cases were pending on 1/1/82, 272 new cases were filed during the year leaving
404 cases pending on 12/31/82. There were 404 criminal cases
on the docket and 404 cases left pending. **JAILS** One jail, capacity
15. **ATTORNEYS AT LAW** Seven. **UTILITIES** 64% of the
residents are connected to a public or privately owned water
system and 55% are connected to a public sewer system. Natural
gas is distributed to the county by Arkla, Inc. The average annual
residential bill for natural gas in 1982 for the Arkla distribution
system was $316.69, an increase of 23% over 1981. Electricity
is distributed to the county by Southwestern Electric Power Co.,
Bowie-Cass Electric Coop., Inc. and Upshur-Rural Electric Coop.
and is generated primarily by gas and oil. The typical residential
electric bill is $152.08 per month for an all-electric house using
2,500 kwh. **TAXES** The county has seven units with taxing
authority: two school districts, four cities and one county.

RECREATION/ENTERTAINMENT

NATIONAL REGISTER OF HISTORIC PLACES Daingerfield: Old Morris County Courthouse. **STATE** Daingerfield State
Park covers 1,889 acres with camping and trailer sites, fishing,
swimming, boat ramps, nature trails, exhibits and horseback
areas. Texas Longhorns graze in the area. **MUNICIPAL PARKS**
16 acres in two municipal parks. These parks contain two
playgrounds, one football and soccer field, one baseball and softball field, one tennis court, one multi-use court, one beach,
court, one beach, one boat ramp and shore fishing facilities.
SCENIC DRIVES The Texas Forest Trail runs through this
county. This trail explores the farming, ranching and oilfield areas
of the East Texas Pineywoods. **BOATING/FISHING**
Lakes/reservoirs: Baines Creek (309 acres), Broseco #1 (55 acres),
Broseco #2 (75 acres), Daingerfield State Park (53 acres), Ellison
Creek (1,516 acres), Glass Club (38 acres) and Minor (32 acres).
Major rivers: Sulphur. Primary streams: Barnes, Murphy,
Brutons, Ellison, Village, Kelly and White Oak Bayou. **HUNT-
ING** Fall and winter seasons on deer. Summer, fall and winter
seasons on squirrel. Winter seasons on quail, muskrat, beaver,
otter, opossum, mink, ring-tailed cat, badger, fox, raccoon, skunk
and civet cat. No closed season on nutria, bobcat and coyote.
In 1983 duck, coot, geese, woodcock and jacksnipe seasons
occurred during the winter months. Teal duck, rail and gallinule
seasons occurred in the fall. Mourning dove seasons occurred
intermittently during the fall and winter months. **MUSEUMS**
Daingerfield: Morris County Museum. **SPECIAL EVENTS**
Junior Stock Show, Daingerfield, March; Rocky Branch Arts
and Crafts Show, Daingerfield, April; Beauty Pageant, Daingerfield, June; Grand Tour Motorcycle Show and Parade, Daingerfield, June.

COMMUNITIES

COUNTY SEAT Daingerfield, County Courthouse, 75638;
County Clerk's Office, 214/645-2321. **INCORPORATED
COMMUNITIES** (1980 population and ZIP Code) Daingerfield
(3,030) 75638, Lone Star (2,036) 75668 and Omaha (960) 75571.
UNINCORPORATED COMMUNITIES (and ZIP Code)

Cason 75636, Jenkins 75638, Naples 75568 and Rocky Branch
75568. **FOR ADDITIONAL LOCAL INFORMATION** Daingerfield Chamber of Commerce, 106½ Webb St., Daingerfield,
75638, 214/645-2646, Lone Star Chamber of Commerce, P. O.
Box 505, Lone Star, 75688, 214/656-3254, Naples Chamber of
Commerce, Drawer T, Naples, 75568, 214/897-2031 and Omaha
Chamber of Commerce, P.O. Box 816, Omaha, 75571,
214/884-2630.

MOTLEY (P32)

THE LAND

Northeast of Lubbock on U.S. Highway 62/70 in the Rolling
Plains Region, Motley County covers 959 square miles with the
elevation ranging from 2,000 to 3,000 feet. The loamy soils are
dark to light and alkaline with deep, reddish, clayey subsoils over
limestone. In the Rolling Plains vegetation area, the prairie grasses
are mid to tall with some mesquite trees and yucca. Between 11
and 20% of the land in the county is considered prime farmland.
CLIMATE Subtropical Subhumid with wide-ranging
temperatures from winter to summer. The average annual
temperature is 61 °F. Temperatures in January range from an
average low of 26° to an average high of 54 °F and in July range
from 69° to 96 °F. The average annual precipitation is 20 inches,
with an average relative humidity of 73% at 6 A.M. and 39%
at 6 P.M. The average annual snowfall is 11 inches. The growing
season averages 213 days per year, with the last freeze in early
April and the first freeze in early November. The sun shines during the year on the average 73% of the daylight hours.

THE PEOPLE

Motley County ranks 36th among all U.S. counties in the highest
percent of persons over age 64 and is one of the state's most
sparsely populated. The 1982 estimated population of 1,900 continues the decline in population which has existed since the 1930s.
The majority of the residents live in rural areas. The age groups
with the largest reductions between 1970 and 1980 were ages five
to 19 and 40 to 49. The population is older than average with
a median age of 42. The largest ancestry groups are persons of
English descent (36%), Irish descent (20%) and Hispanic (8%).
REGISTERED VOTERS As of November 2, 1982 there were
1,216 registered voters (0.01% of the state total). The 1982 general
election had a 56% voter turnout, compared to a 71% turnout
in the 1980 general election. In the 1982 primary 100% voted
Democratic with 564 votes cast.

THE ECONOMY

AGRICULTURE Cotton area. In 1982, 95% of the land was
in farms and ranches, with 13% of the farmland under cultivation and 9% irrigated. Motley ranked 184th in the state in highest
agricultural receipts, with 54% from livestock and livestock products. Undesirable brush and weeds, water and wind erosion,
inefficient tillage systems and the cultivation of marginal lands
are the current conservation problems. Primary crops: cotton,
wheat, sorghum, hay and rye. Primary vegetables: potatoes and
sweet potatoes. Primary fruits and nuts: peaches and pecans.
Primary livestock and products: cattle. **BUSINESS** Total number
of business establishments in the county: 38. Retail sales during
the first quarter of 1984 increased 30% in Roaring Springs. In
1980, 39% of the labor force were self-employed, 9% were
employed in professional or related services, .5% in manufacturing, 21% in wholesale and retail trade, 42% in agriculture,
forestry, fisheries and mining, 7% were employed in other counties and there were 282 retired workers. The industry with the
most employment is agribusiness. The nonfarm earnings in 1981
totaled $12,201,000. The retired workers received an average

monthly Social Security payment of $294. **FINANCE** On June 30, 1983, one commercial bank had total deposits of $6,729,000 and total assets of $8,597,000. There is one state savings and loan association branch in the county. **HOUSING** Average value of homes in 1980: $16,400. In 1982 one permit was issued for a new, single family house. Between 1970 and 1980 the number of housing units decreased by 8%. Eighty-four percent of all units in the county are air-conditioned, 84% are heated by gas and 13% by electricity. **NATURAL RESOURCES** Caliche, gypsum, salt, oil, gas and bituminous coal. In 1982 a total of 122,025 barrels of crude oil and 17,959 thousand cubic feet of casinghead gas were produced. Current production of other minerals and products includes sand, gravel and crushed sandstone. **TOURISM** Travel expenditures of $468,000 in 1982 (an increase of 16% over 1981) generated 8 jobs and $77,000 in payroll. **ALCOHOLIC BEVERAGES** Totally dry. **FEDERAL EXPENDITURES** The federal government had direct expenditures or obligations of $7,477,000 in the county during fiscal year 1983, including $61,000 by the U.S. Department of Defense. In addition, the federal government provided $232,000 in grant awards, paid $217,000 in salaries and wages, made direct payments to individuals of $4,151,000 including $2,578,000 in retirement and disability payments and spent $2,877,000 in other expenditures or obligations. The federal government also provided $1,710,000 in direct loans and $1,681,000 in guaranteed loans and insurance.

COMMUNICATION
Newspapers–Weekly: Matador Tribune. Cable TV. Telephone companies: General Telephone, Southwestern Bell and Cap Rock Telephone. **TRANSPORTATION** Total public road mileage: 425. In 1982 there were 2,218 registered vehicles and 25 reported traffic accidents. Motor freight: two carriers. Aircraft: two are registered in the county.

COMMUNITY SERVICES
EDUCATION One school district with one elementary and one high school. The average daily attendance in 1981-82 was 260, with expenditures per pupil of $3,613 including 29 classroom teachers with an average annual salary of $14,493. Eight percent of the 25 high school graduates planned to attend college. In 1982-83, 81% of the students were White, 11% Hispanic, 6% Black and 2% Asian. **PUBLIC LIBRARIES** Matador Library. **CHILD CARE** One twenty-four hour care licensed facility. **HEALTH CARE** One physician. Ambulance services: one hopital-based service. **CHURCHES** 15 churches have an estimated combined membership of 2,043. The largest denominations are Southern Baptist and United Methodist. **SOCIAL SERVICES** In fiscal year 1983 a total of $61,753 in food stamps was distributed, with an average of 137 persons receiving food stamps each month. Aid to Families with Dependent Children (AFDC) totaled $4,770. Medical assistance benefits for the aged and disabled of $80,395 and for families and children of $5,262 brought the county benefit total to $152,180. **FIRE PROTECTION** Three volunteer fire departments. **LAW ENFORCEMENT** The County Sheriff has four commissioned officers. **CRIME** One violent crime (murder, forcible rape, robbery and aggravated assault) and seven nonviolent crimes (burglary, larceny-theft and motor vehicle theft) were reported in 1982. **JUDICIAL SYSTEM** One District Court and Judge, one County Court and Judge and two Justices of the Peace. In the District Court a total of 32 cases were pending on 1/1/82, 17 new cases were filed and 18 cases were disposed of during the year leaving 31 cases pending on 12/31/82. There were eight criminal cases on the docket and eight cases left pending. In the County Court 230 cases were pending on 1/1/82, 36 new cases were filed and 44 cases were disposed of during the year leaving 232 cases pending on 12/31/82. There were 260 criminal cases on the docket,

10 convictions, five persons committed to jail and 216 cases left pending. **ATTORNEYS AT LAW** One. **UTILITIES** 78% of the residents are connected to a public or privately owned water system and 60% are connected to a public sewer system. Electricity is distributed to the county by West Texas Utilities, Dickens Electric Coop., Inc. and Lighthouse Electric Coop., Inc. and is generated primarily by gas and oil. **TAXES** The county has five units with taxing authority: one school district, two cities, one county and one hospital district.

RECREATION/ENTERTAINMENT
MUNICIPAL PARKS 0.1 acre in one municipal park. This park contains one playground. **SCENIC DRIVES** The Texas Plains Trail runs through this county. This trail spans a vast area of the High Plains Region of Texas slicing through the southernmost extension of the Great Plains of the United States. The land is flat except where erosion has carved canyon landscapes. **BOATING/FISHING** Lakes/reservoirs: Campbell South (17 acres) and Horner (62 acres). Major rivers: North Pease, South Pease, Middle Pease and Pease. Primary streams: Ballard, Cedar, Dutchman, Tee Pee, Quitaque, Turkey, Turtle Hole and Tom Ball. **HUNTING** Fall season on antelope. No closed season on bobcat and coyote. Winter seasons on aoudad sheep, pheasant, quail, muskrat, beaver, opossum, ring-tailed cat, badger, fox, weasel, raccoon, skunk and civet cat. Fall and winter seasons on deer and mule deer. Fall, winter and spring seasons on turkey. In 1983 sandhill crane, duck, coot, geese, woodcock and jacksnipe seasons occurred during the winter months. Teal duck, rail and gallinule seasons occurred in the fall. Mourning dove seasons occurred intermittently during the fall and winter months. **SPECIAL EVENTS** 4H Livestock Show, Matador, March; Old Settlers Reunion, Roaring Springs, August; Arts and Crafts Fair, Matador, December; Christmas Parade, Matador, December.

COMMUNITIES
COUNTY SEAT Matador, County Courthouse, 79244; County Clerk's Office, 806/347-2621. **INCORPORATED COMMUNITIES** (1980 population and ZIP Code) Matador (1,052) 79244 and Roaring Springs (315) 79256. **UNINCORPORATED COMMUNITIES** (and ZIP Code) Flomot 79234, Northfield 79246, Whiteflat 79234 and Whitestar 79234.

NACOGDOCHES (E25)

THE LAND
Southwest of Longview on U.S. Highways 59 and 259 in East Texas Timberlands Region, Nacogdoches County covers 939 square miles with the elevation ranging from 150 to 600 feet. The soils are light colored, acidic and nearly level with sandy to loamy surfaces and very deep, reddish, clayey subsoils. In the Pineywoods vegetation area, there are pine and hardwood forests. Between 21 and 30% of the land in the county is considered prime farmland. **CLIMATE** Subtropical Humid and mild. The average annual temperature is 65 °F. Temperatures in January range from an average low of 36° to an average high of 58 °F and in July range from 71° to 94 °F. The average annual precipitation is 45 inches, with an average relative humidity of 86% at 6 A.M. and 57% at 6 P.M. Snowfall is not significant. The growing season averages 245 days per year, with the last freeze in mid March and the first freeze in mid November. The sun shines during the year on the average 65% of the daylight hours.

THE PEOPLE
The population of Nacogdoches County has grown at approximately the same pace for the last 20 years. The 1982 estimated population of 48,700 indicates a continuation of the strong

COUNTIES

NACOGDOCHES (continued)

growth rate begun in the 1960s. Rural areas grew twice as fast as urban areas between 1970 and 1980. The age groups with the largest gains were ages 20 to 34, 62 and over and birth to five years. The county's population is younger than average with a median age of 26. The largest ancestry groups are persons of English descent (30%), Irish descent (19%) and Black (17%). **REGISTERED VOTERS** As of November 2, 1982 there were 21,523 registered voters (0.3% of the state total). The 1982 general election had a 44% voter turnout, compared to a 65% turnout in the 1980 general election. In the 1982 primary 97% voted Democratic and 3% Republican, with 6,839 votes cast.

THE ECONOMY

AGRICULTURE Timberland. In 1982, 43% of the land was in farms and ranches, with 15% of the farmland under cultivation. Nacogdoches ranked 12th in the state in highest agricultural receipts, with 98% from livestock and livestock products. Water erosion on the forestlands, flooding and undesirable brush and weeds are the current conservation problems. Primary crops: hay and oats. Primary vegetables: potatoes, sweet potatoes, tomatoes and watermelons. Primary fruits and nuts: peaches and pecans. Primary livestock and products: first in the state for commercial broiler production and seventh for hens, pullets and egg production. Cattle, milk and hogs. **BUSINESS** Total number of business establishments in the county: 897. Retail sales during the first quarter of 1984 increased by 29%. In 1980, 10% of the labor force were self-employed, 24% were employed in professional or related services, 22% in manufacturing, 22% in wholesale and retail trade, 7% in agriculture, forestry, fisheries and mining, 13% were employed in other counties and there were 3,954 retired workers. The industries with the most employment: oil and gas extraction, road construction, tourism, agribusiness, poultry processing, soft drink bottling and canning, sawmills, the printing of business forms and the maufacture of prepared agricultural feeds and fertilizers, metal furniture, valves and pipe fittings, transformers, motor vehicle parts and accessories, softwood veneer, plywood, wood pallets and skids. The nonfarm earnings in 1981 totaled $364,864,000. The retired workers received an average monthly Social Security payment of $298. **FINANCE** On June 30, 1983, eight commercial banks had total deposits of $355,717,000 and total assets of $393,322,000. On December 31, 1982 two state savings and loan associations, one federal association and one state branch had combined assets of $153,398,166. In addition there are five credit unions in the county. **HOUSING** Average value of homes in 1980: $34,600. Permits for new, privately owned housing units decreased in 1982: 273 permits were issued with a total construction cost of $9,026,616. Of those permits, 119 were for single family houses. Between 1970 and 1980 the number of housing units increased by 49%. Seventy-nine percent of all units in the county are air-conditioned, 69% are heated by gas and 26% by electricity. **NATURAL RESOURCES** Ceramic clay, lignite coal, iron, oil, gas and glauconite. In 1982 a total of 36,969,883 thousand cubic feet of gas well gas, 72,114 barrels of condensate, 32,143 barrels of crude oil and 205,402 thousand cubic feet of casinghead gas were produced. Current production of other minerals and products includes brick and structural tile. Pine and hardwood production in 1981 totaled 15,520,680 cubic feet: 12,700,931 cubic feet of pine and 2,819,749 cubic feet of hardwood. **TOURISM** Travel expenditures of $24,773,000 in 1982 (an increase of 11% over 1981) generated 610 jobs and $4,955,000 in payroll. Lodging: six hotels, motels and tourist courts. Convention/meeting facilities: Nacogdoches-Stephen Austin State University Coliseum and Stadium and Dragon Stadium. **ALCOHOLIC BEVERAGES** Packaged distilled spirits, beer, ale, malt liquor and wine are legal in parts of the county. **FEDERAL EXPENDITURES** The federal government had direct expenditures or obligations of $68,889,000 in the county during fiscal year 1983, including $3,858,000 by the U.S. Department of Defense. In addition, the federal government provided $2,179,000 in grant awards, paid $4,582,000 in salaries and wages, made direct payments to individuals of $61,684,000 including $45,188,000 in retirement and disability payments, awarded $106,000 in procurement contracts and spent $337,000 in other expenditures or obligations. The federal government also provided $420,000 in direct loans and $12,685,000 in guaranteed loans and insurance.

COMMUNICATION

Newspapers–Daily: The Daily Sentinel (Nacogdoches), ave. eve. circ. 9,150. Weekly: Cushing News and the Garrison News. Radio: KEEE-AM, KSFA-AM, KJCS-FM and KTBC-FM Stereo (Nacogdoches). Cable TV. Telephone companies: Continental Telephone, Southwestern Bell, Lufkin Telephone Exchange and Tri-County Telephone. **TRANSPORTATION** Total public road mileage: 1,276. In 1982 there were 34,399 registered vehicles and 1,237 reported traffic accidents including 25 fatalities. Taxi cabs: one company in the city of Nacogdoches. Intercity bus service is available. Motor freight: 12 local and intrastate carriers. Rail: two main lines carry annually 10 to 20 million tons of freight each through the county. Aircraft: 48 are registered in the county. Airports: East Texas Regional Airport at Nacogdoches serves as a base for 20 aircraft and is a basic utility airport with commuter service.

COMMUNITY SERVICES

EDUCATION Nine school districts with 12 elementary, one middle, eight high schools and one special education. The average daily attendance in 1981-82 was 6,872, with expenditures per pupil of $2,470 including 450 classroom teachers with an average annual salary of $15,512. Fifty-seven percent of the 438 high school graduates planned to attend college. In 1982-83, 69% of the students were White, 2% Hispanic, 29% Black, 0.5% Asian. Private schools: 410 students enrolled in four elementary schools and two high schools. Stephen F. Austin State University is located in Nacogdoches. Established in 1921 it is under state control. Enrollment in 1982 was 10,769 with in state undergraduate tuition and fees of $440 per semester. The highest degree offered is Doctorate. Sports championships: (Lone Star Conference) 1983 Men's Basketball. Vocational education: Massey Business College (Nacogdoches). **PUBLIC LIBRARIES** Hoya Memorial Library and Museum (Nacogdoches): 12,000 volumes. Nacogdoches Public Library: 40,000 volumes. **CHILD CARE** 67 day care and nine twenty-four hour care licensed facilities. **HEALTH CARE** 80 physicians and 21 dentists. Hospitals: two with a combined capacity of 334. Ambulance services: two volunteer services, one hospital-based and one commercial service. Mental health: one county clinic. Nursing homes: seven nursing homes with a combined capacity of 447 nursing care residents. The average cost per day for private patients in 1982 was $28.90. **CHURCHES** 105 churches have an estimated combined membership of 24,208. The largest denominations are Southern Baptist, Christian Methodist Episcopal and United Methodist. **SOCIAL SERVICES** In fiscal year 1983 a total of $1,708,968 in food stamps was distributed, with an average of 3,558 persons receiving food stamps each month. Aid to Families with Dependent Children (AFDC) totaled $497,558 with an average of 318 families receiving AFDC each month. Medical assistance benefits for the aged and disabled of $4,370,847 and for families and children of $730,767 brought the county benefit total to $7,308,140. **FIRE PROTECTION** One paid and 14 volunteer fire departments. **LAW ENFORCEMENT** The County Sheriff has 36 commissioned officers. One police department has a force of

48. One university campus has a police department with a force of 14 officers. **CRIME** 134 violent crimes (murder, forcible rape, robbery and aggravated assault) and 1,674 nonviolent crimes (burglary, larceny-theft and motor vehicle theft) were reported in 1982. **JUDICIAL SYSTEM** One District Court and Judge, two County Courts and Judges and four Justices of the Peace. In the District Court a total of 1,447 cases were pending on 1/1/82, 1,256 new cases were filed and 1,289 cases were disposed of during the year leaving 1,414 cases pending on 12/31/82. There were 735 criminal cases on the docket, 216 convictions, 39 persons committed to prison, seven committed to jail and 325 cases left pending. In the County Courts 1,648 cases were pending on 1/1/82, 1,271 new cases were filed and 1,210 cases were disposed of during the year leaving 1,709 cases pending on 12/31/82. There were 2,525 criminal cases on the docket, 756 convictions, 342 persons committed to jail and 1,415 cases left pending. **JAILS** One jail, capacity 49: lost certification in 1983 due to management deficiencies. **ATTORNEYS AT LAW** 69. **UTILITIES** 91% of the residents are connected to a public or privately owned water system and 59% are connected to a public sewer system. Natural gas is distributed to the county by South Rusk County Gas Co., Inc. and Entex Inc. The average annual residential bill for natural gas in 1982 for the Entex distribution system was $390.31, an increase of 26% over 1981. Electricity is distributed to the city of Garrison by the Garrison Electric Dept. and to the rest of the county by Texas Power and Light Co., Rusk Co. Electric Coop., Inc., Central Texas Electric Coop., Inc. and Deep East Texas Electric Coop., Inc. and is generated primarily by gas, oil, coal and water. The typical residential electric bill is $165.24 per month for an all-electric house using 2,500 kwh. **TAXES** The county has 15 units with taxing authority: nine school districts, three cities, one county, one hospital district and one special district.

RECREATION/ENTERTAINMENT
FEDERAL ANGELINA NATIONAL FOREST covers 154,916 acres in four counties and includes eight recreation areas. **NATIONAL REGISTER OF HISTORIC PLACES** Nacogdoches: Old Nacogdoches University and Adolphus Sterne House. Nacogdoches vicinity: Tol Barret House. Woden vicinity: Oil Springs Oil Field Discovery Well. **COUNTY/MUNICIPAL PARKS** 292 acres in one county and 15 municipal parks. These parks contain two miles of hiking trails, nine playgrounds, eight baseball and softball fields, six tennis courts, two swimming pools, three beaches and four boat ramps. Developed campsites: 49. **SCENIC DRIVES** The Texas Forest Trail runs through this county. This trail explores the farming, ranching and oilfield areas of the East Texas Pineywoods. **BOATING/FISHING** Lakes/reservoirs: Alazan (73 acres), Caro Pine (23 acres), Fern (40 acres), Nacogdoches (2,210 acres), Sam Rayburn (114,500 acres) and Scoggins (73 acres). Major rivers: East Fork and Angelina. Primary streams: Alazan, Boggy, Black Bayou, Bayou Loco, Black, Bayou La Nana and Attoyac Bayou. **HUNTING** Fall and winter seasons on deer. Summer, fall and spring seasons on squirrel. Winter seasons on quail, muskrat, beaver, otter, opossum, mink, ring-tailed cat, badger, fox, raccoon, skunk and civet cat. No closed season on nutria, bobcat and coyote. In 1983 duck, coot, geese, woodcock and jacksnipe seasons occurred during the winter months. Teal duck, rail and gallinule seasons occurred in the fall. Mourning dove seasons occurred intermittently during the fall and winter months. **MUSEUMS** Chireno: Halfway House. Nacogdoches: Hoya Memorial Library and Museum, Millard's Crossing Antiques and Texana Museum, Old University Building and Stone Fort Museum. **THEATERS** Nacogdoches: Lamp-Lite Players. **PLANETARIUM** Nacogdoches: Stephen F. Austin Planetarium. **OBSERVATORY** Nacogdoches: Stephen F. Austin Observatory. **COLLEGIATE**

FINE ARTS Nacogdoches: Cultural events offered by Stephen F. Austin State University. **SPECIAL EVENTS** Championship Rodeo, Nacogdoches, March; Bear Creek Annual Horse Show, Nacogdoches, April; Arabian Horse Show, Nacogdoches, April; Volksmarch, Nacogdoches, April; Heritage Festival, Nacogdoches, June; Nacogdoches County Exposition, Nacogdoches, October; Pineywoods Fair, Nacogdoches, October.

COMMUNITIES
COUNTY SEAT Nacogdoches, County Courthouse, 75963; County Clerk's Office, 409/564-0496. **INCORPORATED COMMUNITIES** (1980 population and ZIP Code) Appleby (453) 75961, Chireno (371) 75937, Cushing (518) 75760, Garrison (1,059) 75946 and Nacogdoches (27,149) 75961. **UNINCORPORATED COMMUNITIES** (and ZIP Code) Alazan 75961, Attoyac 75961, Caro 75961, Central Heights (Bonita) 75961, Douglass 75943, Etoile 75944, Fitze 75946, Henning 75946, Libby 75961, Lilbert 75760, Looneyville 75760, Mahl 75961, Martinsville 75958, Melrose 75961, Nat 75760, Oak Flat 75760, Oak Ridge 75961, Redfield 75961, Sacul 75788, Swift 75961, Trawick 75961, Union Springs 75961, Upshaw 75943 and Woden 75978 **FOR ADDITIONAL LOCAL INFORMATION** Nacogdoches Co. Chamber of Commerce, Drawer 1918, Nacogdoches, 75961, 409/564-7351.

NAVARRO (M19)

THE LAND
Southeast of Dallas on Interstate Highway 45 in the Blackland Prairies Region, Navarro County covers 1,068 square miles with the elevation ranging from 270 to 600 feet. Along the Trinity River the dark, loamy soils have cracking, clayey subsoils. To the northwest, west and south the soils are very dark and loamy throughout. The remainder of the county has gray to black, cracking, clayey soils with some light colored, loamy surfaces. In the Blackland Prairies vegetation area, the grasses are tall, primarily buffalograss and Texas grama and there are a variety of trees along streams including oaks, elms, pecans, bois d'arc and mesquite. Between 31 and 40% of the land in the county is considered prime farmland. **CLIMATE** Subtropical Humid with mild winters and warm summers. The average annual temperature is 66°F. Temperatures in January range from an average low of 34° to an average high of 55°F and in July range from 73° to 96°F. The average annual precipitation is 38 inches, with an average relative humidity of 83% at 6 A.M. and 53% at 6 P.M. The average annual snowfall is two inches. The growing season averages 255 days per year, with the last freeze in mid March and the first freeze in late November. The sun shines during the year on the average 65% of the daylight hours.

THE PEOPLE
The population of Navarro County had a 13% growth rate between 1970 and 1980. The 1982 estimated population of 36,700 indicates a continuation of that growth rate which reversed the population decline since the 1930's. Rural areas grew faster than urban areas from 1970 to 1980. The county's population has a high percent of residents who are over age 64 and a median age which lowered from 38 in 1970 to 35 in 1980. The largest ancestry groups are persons of English descent (29%), Irish descent (23%) and Black (20%). **REGISTERED VOTERS** As of November 2, 1982 there were 17,465 registered voters (0.3% of the state total). The 1982 general election had a 48% voter turnout, compared to a 68% turnout in the 1980 general election. In the 1982 primary 97% voted Democratic and 3% Republican, with 6,939 votes cast.

NAVARRO (continued)

THE ECONOMY

AGRICULTURE Cattle and wheat area. In 1982, 86% of the land was in farms and ranches, with 28% of the farmland under cultivation and 1% irrigated. Navarro ranked 77th in the state in highest agricultural receipts, with 75% from livestock and livestock products. Overgrazing, undesirable brush, noxious weeds, water erosion and difficulties in grass establishment are the current conservation problems. Primary crops: sixth in the state for oats. Wheat, hay, sorghum and cotton. Primary vegetables: potatoes and sweet potatoes. Primary fruits and nuts: peaches and pecans. Primary livestock and products: cattle, milk and hogs. **BUSINESS** Total number of business establishments in the county: 731. Retail sales during the first quarter of 1984 increased by 14%. In 1980, 12% of the labor force were self-employed, 21% were employed in professional or related services, 22% in manufacturing, 18% in wholesale and retail trade, 8% in finance, insurance and real estate, 10% were employed in other counties and there were 4,763 retired workers. The industries with the most employment: oil and gas extraction, road construction, meat packing, fruit and vegetable canning, the printing of business forms, iron foundry and the manufacture of prepared foods, men's hats, furniture, wood containers, chemical products, rubber products, oil field machinery, glass containers, mineral wool and women's leather handbags. The nonfarm earnings in 1981 totaled $335,819,000. The retired workers received an average monthly Social Security payment of $294. **FINANCE** On June 30, 1983, 10 commercial banks had total deposits of $291,353,000 and total assets of $334,979,000. There are two state savings and loan association branches, one federal branch and two credit unions in the county. **HOUSING** Average value of homes in 1980: $23,200. Permits for new, privately owned housing units decreased in 1982: 103 permits were issued with a total construction cost of $2,418,382. Of those permits, 62 were for single family houses. Between 1970 and 1980 the number of housing units increased by 20%. Seventy-one percent of all units in the county are air-conditioned, 85% are heated by gas and 13% by electricity. **NATURAL RESOURCES** Clay, limestone, sand, gravel, oil and gas. In 1982 a total of 7,853,549 thousand cubic feet of gas well gas, 127,690 barrels of condensate, 1,133,957 barrels of crude oil and 1,972,234 thousand cubic feet of casinghead gas were produced. Current production of other minerals and products includes clay, lightweight aggregate, crushed limestone, rock wool, sand and gravel, shale and recovered sulphur. **TOURISM** Travel expenditures of $7,000,000 in 1982 (an increase of 12% over 1981) generated 158 jobs and $1,357,000 in payroll. Lodging: one motel. **ALCOHOLIC BEVERAGES** Packaged distilled spirits, beer, ale, malt liquor and wine are legal in parts of the county. Sale of mixed beverages is legal in all or parts of the county. **FEDERAL EXPENDITURES** The federal government had direct expenditures or obligations of $74,467,000 in the county during fiscal year 1983, including $2,882,000 by the U.S. Department of Defense. In addition, the federal government provided $2,208,000 in grant awards, paid $3,682,000 in salaries and wages, made direct payments to individuals of $66,546,000 including $46,907,000 in retirement and disability payments, awarded $500,000 in procurement contracts and spent $1,531,000 in other expenditures or obligations. The federal government also provided $1,275,000 in direct loans and $6,103,000 in guaranteed loans and insurance.

COMMUNICATION

Newspapers–Daily: Corsicana Daily Sun, ave. eve. circ. 10,548. Weekly: The Blooming Grove Times, Corsicana Weekly Light, The Dawson Herald, Frost Enterprise and Kerens Tribune. Radio: KAND-AM and KXOI-AM (Corsicana). Cable TV. Telephone companies: Continental Telephone, General Telephone, Southwestern Bell and United Telephone. **TRANSPORTATION** Total public road mileage: 1,713. In 1982 there were 32,295 registered vehicles and 1,019 reported traffic accidents including 16 fatalities. Taxi cabs: one company in Corsicana. Intercity bus service is available. Motor freight: 17 local and intrastate carriers. Rail: five main lines and one branch carry freight through the county. Two of the main lines carry annually over 30 million tons of freight each, one carries 20 to 30 and two carry five to 10 million tons each. The one branch line carries annually less than one million tons of freight. Aircraft: 42 are registered in the county. Airports: Corsicana Municipal Airport serves as a base for 41 aircraft and is a basic transporation airport with general aviation service.

COMMUNITY SERVICES

EDUCATION Seven school districts with 11 elementary, two middle, six high schools and one special education. The average daily attendance in 1981-82 was 6,104, with expenditures per pupil of $3,465 including 407 classroom teachers with an average annual salary of $16,239. Fifty-nine percent of the 420 high school graduates planned to attend college. In 1982-83, 68% of the students were White, 5% Hispanic, 27% Black and 0.3% Asian. Private schools: 212 students enrolled in one elementary school. Navarro College is located in Corsicana. Established in 1946 it is a vocational and two year academic college under local control. Enrollment in 1982 was 2,260 with in state undergraduate tuition and fees of $408 per semester. Vocational education: Mr. Tomie's School of Cosmetology (Corsicana). **PUBLIC LIBRARIES** Corsicana Public Library: 53,349 volumes. **CHILD CARE** 77 day care and nine twenty-four hour care licensed facilities. **HEALTH CARE** 53 physicians and 14 dentists. Hospitals: one with a capacity of 177. Clinics: one public health clinic. Ambulance services: two volunteer services and one commercial service. Mental health: one clinic and one development center with a capacity of 71. Nursing homes: six nursing homes with a combined capacity of 538 nursing care residents. The average cost per day for private patients in 1982 was $40.58. **CHURCHES** 88 churches have an estimated combined membership of 23,561. The largest denominations are Southern Baptist, United Methodist and Churches of Christ. **SOCIAL SERVICES** In fiscal year 1983 a total of $1,430,782 in food stamps was distributed, with an average of 3,183 persons receiving food stamps each month. Aid to Families with Dependent Children (AFDC) totaled $401,316 with an average of 285 families receiving AFDC each month. Medical assistance benefits for the aged and disabled of $4,995,162 and for families and children of $396,923 brought the county benefit total to $7,224,182. **FIRE PROTECTION** One paid and 13 volunteer fire departments. **LAW ENFORCEMENT** The County Sheriff has 45 commissioned officers. Seven police departments have a combined force of 63. One college campus has a police department with two officers. **CRIME** 169 violent crimes (murder, forcible rape, robbery and aggravated assault) and 1,838 nonviolent crimes (burglary, larceny-theft and motor vehicle theft) were reported in 1982. **JUDICIAL SYSTEM** One District Court and Judge, one County Court and Judge and two Justices of the Peace. In the District Court a total of 839 cases were pending on 1/1/82, 1,052 new cases were filed and 1,007 cases were disposed of during the year leaving 884 cases pending on 12/31/82. There were 267 criminal cases on the docket, 197 convictions, 68 persons committed to prison, two committed to jail and 35 cases left pending. In the County Court 245 cases were pending on 1/1/82, 529 new cases were filed and 580 cases were disposed of during the year leaving 194 cases pending on 12/31/82. There were 753 criminal cases on the docket, 389 convictions, 126 persons committed to jail and 179 cases left pending. **JAILS** One jail, capacity 30. **ATTORNEYS AT LAW** 46. **UTILITIES** 94% of the residents are connected to a public or privately owned water system and 72% are connected to a public sewer system. Natural gas is distributed to the county by Lone Star Gas Co., Division of Enserch. The average annual residential bill for natural gas in 1982 for the Lone Star distribution system was $405.91, an increase of 35% over 1981. Electricity is distributed to the county by Navarro Co. Electric Coop., Inc., Houston Lighting and Power Co. and Texas Power and Light Co. and is generated primarily by gas, coal and water. The typical residential electric bill is $165.24 per month for an all-electric house using 2,500 kwh. **TAXES** The county has 15 units with taxing authority: seven school districts, six cities, one county and one college district.

RECREATION/ENTERTAINMENT

NATIONAL REGISTER OF HISTORIC PLACES Corsicana: Corsicana Oil Field Discovery Well. **MUNICIPAL PARKS** 321 acres in nine municipal parks. These parks contain eight playgrounds, two football and soccer fields, four baseball and softball fields, 19 tennis courts, one multi-use court, two swimming pools, three boat ramps and shore fishing facilities. Developed campsites: 25. **SCENIC DRIVES** The Texas Lakes Trail runs through this county. This trail introduces some 30 bluewater recreational areas in a variety of settings in north central Texas. **BOATING/FISHING** Lakes/reservoirs: Chambers Creek Soil Conservation Service Lakes 124, 128 and 129 (47 acres), Corsicana (556 acres), Dawson (30 acres), Grays Creek Soil Conservation Service Lakes 1 and 5 (35 acres), Halbert (650 acres), Kerens City (61 acres), Magnolia (83 acres), Navarro Mills (5,070 acres) and Richland Creek Soil Conservation Service Lakes 12, 100A, 101, 138, 31 and 98A (98 acres). Major rivers: Trinity. Primary streams: Chambers, Rice, Lockhart, Battle, Grays, Elm, Cow, Post Oak, Richland, Alligator, Hackberry, Briar, Board and Richland. **HUNTING** No closed season on nutria, bobcat and coyote. In 1983 duck, coot, geese, woodcock and jacksnipe seasons on occurred during the winter months. Teal duck, rail and gallinule seasons occurred in the fall. Mourning dove seasons occurred intermittently during the fall and winter months. **MUSEUMS** Corsicana: Pioneer Village. **THEATERS** Corsicana: Community Playhouse. **COLLEGIATE FINE ARTS** Corsicana: cultural events offered by Navarro College. **SPECIAL EVENTS** County Youth Exposition, Corsicana, March; Derrick Days, Corsicana, April; Arts and Crafts Fair, Corsicana, November; Christmas Parade, Corsicana, December.

COMMUNITIES

COUNTY SEAT Corsicana, County Courthouse, 75110; County Clerk's Office, 214/874-5201. **INCORPORATED COMMUNITIES** (1980 population and ZIP Code) Angus (244) 75110, Barry (192) 75102, Blooming Grove (823) 76626, Corsicana (21,712) 75110, Dawson (747) 76639, Emhouse (197) 75110, Frost (564) 76641, Goodlow (343) 75144, Kerens (1,582) 75144, Mustang (12) 75110, Powell (111) 75153, Purdon (133, est., incorp. inactive) 76679, Retreat (255) 75110, Rice (439: 7 in Ellis Co. and 432 in Navarro Co.) 75155, Richland (260) 76681 and Streetman (415: 19 in Navarro Co. and 396 in Freestone Co.) 75859. **UNINCORPORATED COMMUNITIES** (and ZIP Code) Bazette 75144, Chatfield 75105, Cheneyboro 75110, Corbet 75110, Cryer Creek 75102, Currie 76693, Drane 75110, Dresden 75102, Eldorado Center 76639, Emmett 76641, Eureka 75110, Goodnight 75144, Hester 75110, Jester 76679, Mildred 75110, Montfort 75156, Navarro 75151, Navarro Mills 76679, Pelham 76648, Pettys Chapel 75110, Pickett 75110, Pursley 76679, Raleigh 76641, Roane 75110, Rodney 76639, Round Prairie 75144, Rural Shade 75144, Rushing 76693, Rush Prairie 76641, Silver City 76679, Slay 76641, Spring Hill 76639, Timothy 75105, Tupelo 75155, Union High 76639 and Winkler (also in Freestone Co.) 75859.

FOR ADDITIONAL LOCAL INFORMATION Corsicana Chamber of Commerce, 120 N. 20th, Corsicana, 75110, 214/874-4731 and Kerens Chamber of Commerce, P. O. Box 117, Kerens, 75144, 214/396-2391.

NEWTON (E35)

THE LAND

Bordering Louisiana and northeast of Beaumont on U.S. Highway 190 in the East Texas Timberlands Region, Newton County covers 935 square miles with the elevation ranging from 30 to 400 feet. The undulating to rolling soils are light colored and acidic with sandy to loamy surfaces and reddish, clayey subsoils. In the Pineywoods vegetation area, there are pine and hardwood forests. Between 21 and 30% of the land in the county is considered prime farmland. **CLIMATE** Subtropical Humid with the second highest annual rainfall in the state. The average annual temperature is 67 °F. Temperatures in January range from an average low of 38 ° to an average high of 59 °F and in July range from 72 ° to 92 °F. The average annual precipitation is 54 inches, with an average relative humidity of 88% at 6 A.M. and 65% at 6 P.M. There is no snowfall. The growing season averages 230 days per year, with the last freeze in mid March and the first freeze in early November. The sun shines during the year on the average 63% of the daylight hours.

THE PEOPLE

The 1982 estimated population of 13,300 indicates a continuation of the growth rate begun in the 1960s which reversed the population decline from 1940 to 1960. The majority of county residents live in rural areas. The county's population has a median age which rose from 28 in 1970 to 30 in 1980. The largest ancestry groups are persons of English descent (25%), Black (24%) and Irish descent (19%). **REGISTERED VOTERS** As of November 2, 1982 there were 7,517 registered voters (0.1% of the state total). The 1982 general election had a 48% voter turnout, compared to a 59% turnout in the 1980 general election. In the 1982 primary 99% voted Democratic and 1% Republican, with 2,935 votes cast.

THE ECONOMY

AGRICULTURE Major forest production area. In 1982, 20% of the land was in farms and ranches, with 4% of the farmland under cultivation. Newton ranked 248th in the state in highest agricultural receipts, with 56% from crops. Overgrazing, undesirable brush and weeds, inadequate cropping systems, water erosion on the forestlands and flooding are the current conservation problems. Primary crops: hay. Primary vegetables: sweet potatoes, tomatoes and watermelons. Primary fruits and nuts: peaches and pecans. Primary livestock and products: cattle. **BUSINESS** Total number of business establishments in the county: 123. Retail sales during the first quarter of 1984 decreased by 1%. In 1980, 7% of the labor force were self-employed, 13% were employed in professional or related services, 33% in manufacturing, 16% in wholesale and retail trade, 14% in construction, 56% were employed in other counties and there were 916 retired workers. The industries with the most employment: logging, sawmills and the manufacture of softwood veneer and plywood. The nonfarm earnings in 1981 totaled $81,292,000. The retired workers received an average monthly Social Security payment of $293. **FINANCE** On June 30, 1983, one commercial bank had total deposits of $19,101,000 and total assets of $20,680,000. There is one federal savings and loan branch in the county. **HOUSING** Average value of homes in 1980: $18,500. Between 1970 and 1980 the number of housing units increased by 33%. Sixty-six percent of all units in the county are air-conditioned, 67% are heated by gas and 16% by electricity.

COUNTIES

NATURAL RESOURCES Industrial sand, sand, gravel, oil and gas. In 1982 a total of 1,250,481 thousand cubic feet of gas well gas, 95,940 barrels of condensate, 558,490 barrels of crude oil and 504,127 thousand cubic feet of casinghead gas were produced. Current production of other minerals and products includes construction sand, industrial sand, sand and gravel. Pine and hardwood production in 1981 totaled 24,462,998 cubic feet: 19,385,153 cubic feet of pine and 5,077,845 cubic feet of hardwood. **TOURISM** Travel expenditures of $4,669,000 in 1982 (an increase of 18% over 1981) generated 66 jobs and $691,000 in payroll. **ALCOHOLIC BEVERAGES** Packaged distilled spirits, beer, ale, malt liquor and wine are legal in parts of the county. **FEDERAL EXPENDITURES** The federal government had direct expenditures or obligations of $17,452,000 in the county during fiscal year 1983, including $572,000 by the U.S. Department of Defense. In addition, the federal government provided $593,000 in grant awards, paid $475,000 in salaries and wages, made direct payments to individuals of $16,207,000 including $11,919,000 in retirement and disability payments, awarded $40,000 in procurement contracts and spent $136,000 in other expenditures or obligations. The federal government also provided $54,000 in direct loans and $1,098,000 in guaranteed loans and insurance.

COMMUNICATION

Newspapers–Weekly: Newton County News. Telephone companies: Continental Telephone and Southwestern Bell. **TRANSPORTATION** Total public road mileage: 864. In 1982 there were 9,021 registered vehicles and 190 reported traffic accidents including 12 fatalities. Motor freight: two carriers. Rail: one branch line carries annually one to five million tons of freight through the county. Aircraft: four are registered in the county. Airports: Newton County Airport at Newton.

COMMUNITY SERVICES

EDUCATION Three school districts with four elementary, one middle and three high schools. The average daily attendance in 1981-82 was 2,688, with expenditures per pupil of $3,250 including 192 classroom teachers with an average annual salary of $16,185. Twenty-Eight percent of the 193 high school graduates planned to attend college. In 1982-83, 68% of the students were White, 0.3% Hispanic and 32% Black. **PUBLIC LIBRARIES** Newton Library. **CHILD CARE** Four day care and three twenty-four hour care licensed facilities. **HEALTH CARE** Four physicians and two dentists. Hospitals: one with a capacity of 48. Clinics: one public health clinic. Ambulance services: two commercial services. Nursing homes: one nursing home has a capacity of 82 nursing care residents. The average cost per day for private patients in 1982 was $28.88. **CHURCHES** 36 churches have an estimated combined membership of 6,038. The largest denominations are Southern Baptist and Christian Methodist Episcopal. **SOCIAL SERVICES** In fiscal year 1983 a total of $1,260,523 in food stamps was distributed, with an average of 2,484 persons receiving food stamps each month. Aid to Families with Dependent Children (AFDC) totaled $238,074 with an average of 157 families receiving AFDC each month. Medical assistance benefits for the aged and disabled of $1,140,039 and for families and children of $269,306 brought the county benefit total to $2,907,942. **FIRE PROTECTION** Five volunteer fire departments. **LAW ENFORCEMENT** The County Sheriff has 17 commissioned officers. One police department has a force of four. **CRIME** 16 violent crimes (murder, forcible rape, robbery and aggravated assault) and 149 nonviolent crimes (burglary, larceny-theft and motor vehicle theft) were reported in 1982. **JUDICIAL SYSTEM** Two District Courts and Judges, one County Court and Judge and four Justices of the Peace. In the District Courts a total of 334 cases were pending on 1/1/82, 303 new cases were filed and 306 cases were disposed of during the year leaving 331 cases pending on 12/31/82. There were 78 criminal cases on the docket, 35 convictions, nine persons committed to prison and 37 cases left pending. In the County Court 325 cases were pending on 1/1/82, 306 new cases were filed and 372 cases were disposed of during the year leaving 259 cases pending on 12/31/82. There were 589 criminal cases on the docket, 129 convictions 234 cases left pending. **JAILS** One jail, capacity 14. New jail opened in 1983. **ATTORNEYS AT LAW** Six. **UTILITIES** 33% of the residents are connected to a public or privately owned water system and 14% are connected to a public sewer system. Natural gas is distributed to the county by D and H Natural Gas Co. Electricity is distributed to the city of Newton by the Newton Municipal Utilities and to the rest of the county by Deep East Texas Electric Coop., Inc. and Jasper-Newton Electric Coop., Inc. and is generated primarily by gas, coal and oil. **TAXES** The county has six units with taxing authority: three school districts, one city, one county and one special district.

RECREATION/ENTERTAINMENT

FEDERAL SABINE NATIONAL FOREST covers 188,220 acres in five counties and includes seven recreation areas. **NATIONAL REGISTER OF HISTORIC PLACES** Newton: Newton County Courthouse. Old Salem vicinity: West Log House. **STATE** E. O. Siecke State Forest covers 1,722 acres with fishing and swimming. **COUNTY PARKS** Six acres in two county parks. These parks contain one playground and one multi-use court. **BOATING/FISHING** Lakes/reservoirs: Toledo Bend (109,730 acres). Major rivers: Sabine. Primary streams: Big Cow, Cypress, Nichols and Little Cow. **HUNTING** Fall and winter seasons on deer. Summer, fall and winter seasons on squirrel. Winter seasons on quail, muskrat, beaver, otter opossum, mink, ring-tailed cat, badger, fox, raccoon, skunk and civet cat. No closed season on nutria, coyote and bobcat. Spring season on turkey in some parts of the county. In 1983 duck, coot, geese, woodcock and jacksnipe seasons occurred during the winter months. Teal duck, rail and gallinule seasons occurred in the fall. Mourning dove seasons occurred intermittently during the fall and winter months. **BOTANIC GARDENS** Newton: Sylvan Nature Trail and Wild Azalea Canyons Trail. **SPECIAL EVENTS** Newton County Fair, Newton, April; Trailride, Newton to Jasper, May; Homecoming Celebration, Newton, October/November.

COMMUNITIES

COUNTY SEAT Newton, County Courthouse, 75966; County Clerk's Office, 409/379-5341. **INCORPORATED COMMUNITIES** (1980 population and ZIP Code) Newton (1,620) 75966. **UNINCORPORATED COMMUNITIES** (and ZIP Code) Adsul 75956, Belgrade 75928, Biloxi 75928, Bleakwood 75956, Bon Wier 75928, Buckhorn 75928, Burkeville 75932, Call 75933, Deweyville 77614, Farrsville 75977 Fawil 75928, Hartburg 77630, Indian Hill 75977, Jamestown 75966, Liberty 75966, Mattox 75977, Mayflower 75977, Old Laurel 77612, Old Salem (Salem) 75933, Pine Grove 75966, Quicksand 75966, Shepphard 77612, Shanklerville (Enterprise) 75932, Toledo 75932, Trout Creek 75933 and Wiergate 75977. **FOR ADDITIONAL LOCAL INFORMATION** Newton Co. Chamber of Commerce, Drawer 66, Newton, 75966, 409/379-8436.

NOLAN (P69)

THE LAND

West of Abilene on Interstate Highway 20 in the Edwards Plateau Region, Nolan County covers 915 square miles with the elevation ranging from 2,000 to 2,600 feet. The loamy soils vary from light to very dark with either deep, reddish, clayey subsoils or loamy subsoils with lime accumulations. In the Edwards Plateau vegetation area, the grasses are short to mid height with some mesquite trees and cacti. Between 21 and 30% of the land in the county is considered prime farmland. **CLIMATE** Subtropical Subhumid. Duststorms and thunderstorms will occur during spring. The average annual temperature is 64 °F. Temperatures in January range from an average low of 30 ° to an average high of 57 °F and in July range from 70 ° to 96 °F. The average annual precipitation is 22 inches, with an average relative humidity of 74% at 6 A.M. and 41% at 6 P.M. The average annual snowfall is six inches. The growing season averages 221 days per year, with the last freeze in early April and the first freeze in early November. The sun shines during the year on the average 72% of the daylight hours.

THE PEOPLE

The 1982 estimated population of 18,100 indicates a continuation of the moderate growth begun in the 1970s which reversed the population decline from 1950 to 1970. The majority of the growth from 1970 to 1980 was in rural areas with only slight gains made in urban areas where the majority of residents live. The median age is older than average although it lowered from 34 in 1970 to 32 in 1980. The largest ancestry groups are persons of English descent (27%), Irish descent (22%) and Hispanic (20%). **REGISTERED VOTERS** As of November 2, 1982 there were 7,697 registered voters (0.1% of the state total). The 1982 general election had a 55% voter turnout, compared to a 71% turnout in the 1980 general election. In the 1982 primary 97% voted Democratic and 3% Republican, with 3,281 votes cast.

THE ECONOMY

AGRICULTURE Cotton area. In 1982, 94% of the land was in farms and ranches, with 18% of the farmland under cultivation and 4% irrigated. Nolan ranked 131st in the state in highest agricultural receipts, with 53% from livestock and livestock products. Overgrazing, undesirable brush and weeds and water and wind erosion are the current conservation problems. Primary crops: cotton, wheat, sorghum and hay. Primary vegetables: sweet potatoes, tomatoes and watermelons. Primary fruits and nuts: peaches and pecans. Primary livestock and products: cattle, sheep, wool, angora goats, mohair and hogs. **BUSINESS** Total number of business establishments in the county: 415. Retail sales during the first quarter of 1984 increased by 4%. In 1980, 10% of the labor force were self-employed, 16% were employed in professional or related services, 17% in manufacturing, 21% in wholesale and retail trade, 14% in finance, insurance and real estate, 6% were employed in other counties and there were 1,963 retired workers. The industries with the most employment: oil and gas field services, heavy construction, agribusiness, cottonseed oil mills and the manufacture of women's clothing, plastics products and gypsum products. The nonfarm earnings in 1981 totaled $166,691,000. The retired workers received an average monthly Social Security payment of $310. **FINANCE** On June 30, 1983, three commercial banks had total deposits of $158,616,000 and total assets of $178,239,000. On December 31, 1982 one state savings and loan association and four state branches had assets of $169,767,445. **HOUSING** Average value of homes in 1980: $21,200. Permits for new, privately owned housing units increased in 1982: 18 permits were issued with a total construction cost of $568,450. Of those permits, 14 were for single family houses. Between 1970 and 1980 the number of housing units increased by 14%. Eighty-four percent of all units in the county are air-conditioned, 79% are heated by gas and 19% by electricity. **NATURAL RESOURCES** Caliche, celestite, dolomite, gypsum, limestone, salt, industrial sand, sand and gravel, oil, gas and bituminous coal. In 1982 a total of 2,547,191

thousand cubic feet of gas well gas, 24,490 barrels of condensate, 2,848,432 barrels of crude oil and 5,631,292 thousand cubic feet of casinghead gas were produced. Current production of other minerals and products includes cement, gypsum, lightweight aggregate, crushed limestone, sand and gravel and wallboard products. **TOURISM** Travel expenditures of $18,510,000 in 1982 (an increase of 11% over 1981) generated 469 jobs and $3,720,000 in payroll. Lodging: six hotels, motels and tourist courts. **ALCOHOLIC BEVERAGES** Packaged distilled spirits, beer, ale, malt liquor and wine are legal in parts of the county. **FEDERAL EXPENDITURES** The federal government had direct expenditures or obligations of $35,858,000 in the county during fiscal year 1983, including $741,000 by the U.S. Department of Defense. In addition, the federal government provided $1,520,000 in grant awards, paid $1,372,000 in salaries and wages, made direct payments to individuals of $27,998,000 including $19,859,000 in retirement and disability payments, awarded $41,000 in procurement contracts and spent $4,928,000 in other expenditures or obligations. The federal government also provided $886,000 in direct loans and $7,485,000 in guaranteed loans and insurance.

COMMUNICATION

Newspapers–Daily: Sweetwater Reporter, ave. eve. circ. 4,793. Weekly: Roscoe Times and The Nolan County News (Sweetwater). Radio: KXOX-AM, KXOX-FM (Sweetwater). Cable TV. Telephone companies: Continental Telephone, General Telephone, Southwestern Bell and Taylor Telephone. **TRANSPORTATION** Total public road mileage: 893. In 1982 there were 17,499 registered vehicles and 584 reported traffic accidents including nine fatalities. Intercity bus service is available. Motor freight: 13 local and intrastate carriers. Rail: six main lines and one branch carry freight through the county. Three of the main lines carry annually 20 to 30 million tons of freight each, one carries 10 to 20 million and two carry five to 10 million tons each. The one branch carries annually less than one million tons of freight. Aircraft: 35 are registered in the county. Airports: Sweetwater Municipal Airport serves as a base for 28 aircraft and is a general utility airport with general aviation service. Gesin Ranches Airport at Sweetwater.

COMMUNITY SERVICES

EDUCATION Five school districts with eight elementary, one middle and five high schools. The average daily attendance in 1981-82 was 3,404, with expenditures per pupil of $3,255 including 249 classroom teachers with an average annual salary of $16,084. Fifty-six percent of the 212 high school graduates planned to attend college. In 1982-83, 63% of the students were White, 31% Hispanic, 6% Black and 0.1% Asian. Sports championships: 1983 6-Man Football, Roscoe Highland H.S. Vocational education: Texas State Technical Institute (Sweetwater). **PUBLIC LIBRARIES** County-City Library (Sweetwater): 40,000 volumes. **CHILD CARE** 27 day care and eight twenty-four hour care licensed facilities. **HEALTH CARE** 12 physicians and 10 dentists. Hospitals: one with a capacity of 85. Clinics: one for treatment of alcohol and drug abuse and one public health clinic. Ambulance services: one volunteer fire department and one city service. Mental Health: one county clinic and one clinic. Nursing homes: three nursing homes have a combined capacity of 238 nursing care residents. The average cost per day for private patients in 1982 was $33.36. **CHURCHES** 41 churches have an estimated combined membership of 14,534. The largest denominations are Southern Baptist, Catholic and United Methodist. **SOCIAL SERVICES** In fiscal year 1983 a total of $606,324 in food stamps was distributed, with an average of 1,292 persons receiving food stamps each month. Aid to Families with Dependent Children (AFDC) totaled $136,064 with an average

COUNTIES

NOLAN (continued)

of 91 families receiving AFDC each month. Medical assistance benefits for the aged and disabled of $1,825,798 and for families and children of $114,799 brought the county benefit total to $2,682,984. **FIRE PROTECTION** One paid and three volunteer fire departments. **LAW ENFORCEMENT** The County Sheriff has 14 commissioned officers. Three police departments have a combined force of 21. One college campus has a police department with four officers. Sweetwater Park Police has one officer. **CRIME** 115 violent crimes (murder, forcible rape, robbery and aggravated assault) and 694 nonviolent crimes (burglary, larceny-theft and motor vehicle theft) were reported in 1982. **JUDICIAL SYSTEM** One District Court and Judge, two County Courts and Judges and two Justices of the Peace. In the District Court a total of 834 cases were pending on 1/1/82, 632 new cases were filed and 483 cases were disposed of during the year leaving 983 cases pending on 12/31/82. There were 427 criminal cases on the docket, 70 convictions, 23 persons committed to prison, three committed to jail and 321 cases left pending. In the County Courts 2,920 cases were pending on 1/1/82, 640 new cases were filed and 619 cases were disposed of during the year leaving 2,941 cases pending on 12/31/82. There were 3,257 criminal cases on the docket, 316 convictions, 21 persons committed to jail and 2,690 cases left pending. **JAILS** One jail, capacity 54. **ATTORNEYS AT LAW** 21. **UTILITIES** 92% of the residents are connected to a public or privately owned water system and 80% are connected to a public sewer system. Natural gas is distributed to the county by Lone Star Gas Co., Division of Enserch. The average annual residential bill for natural gas in 1982 for the Lone Star distribution system was $405.91, an increase of 35% over 1981. Electricity is distributed to the county by Texas Electric Service, Concho Valley Electric Coop., Inc., Midwest Electric Coop., Inc., Taylor Electric Coop., Inc. and Lonewolf Electric Coop., Inc. and is generated primarily by gas and oil. The typical residential electric bill is $154.69 per month for an all-electric house using 2,500 kwh. **TAXES** The county has 10 units with taxing authority: five school districts, three cities, one county and one special district.

RECREATION/ENTERTAINMENT
NATIONAL REGISTER OF HISTORIC PLACES Sweetwater: R.A. Ragland Building. **MUNICIPAL PARKS** 2,098 acres in seven municipal parks. These parks contain one mile of hiking trails, six playgrounds, one golf course, one football and soccer field, five baseball and softball fields, four tennis courts, two swimming pools, one beach, two boat ramps and shore fishing facilities. Developed campsites: 22. **BOATING/FISHING** Lakes/reservoirs: Headrick (56 acres), Santa Fe (26 acres), Sweetwater (630 acres), Trammell (123 acres) and Valley Creek Soil Conservation Service Lakes 1 and 5 (44 acres). Primary streams: Rock, Bitter, Sweetwater, Fish, North Fork Valley, Oak and Kildoogan. **HUNTING** Fall and winter seasons on deer and javelina. No closed season on squrrel, coyote and bobcat. Winter seasons on quail, muskrat, beaver, opossum, ring-tailed cat, badger, fox, weasel, raccoon, skunk and civet cat. Fall, winter and spring seasons on turkey. In 1983 sandhill crane, duck, coot, geese, woodcock and jacksnipe seasons occurred during the winter months. Teal duck, rail and gallinule seasons occurred in the fall. Mourning dove seasons occurred intermittently during the fall and winter months. **MUSEUMS** Roscoe: Roscoe Historical Museum. Sweetwater: Pioneer City-County Museum. **SPECIAL EVENTS** "World's Largest" Rattlesnake Roundup, Sweetwater, March; AJRA Rodeo, Sweetwater, April; Farm Show and Tractor Pull, Sweetwater, April; Lakefest, Sweetwater, June; Arts and Crafts Festival, Sweetwater, December.

COMMUNITIES
COUNTY SEAT Sweetwater, County Courthouse, 79556; County Clerk's Office, 915/235-2462. **INCORPORATED COMMUNITIES** (1980 population and ZIP Code) Blackwell (286: 265 in Nolan Co. and 21 in Coke Co.) 79506, Roscoe (1,628) 79545 and Sweetwater (12,242) 79556. **UNINCORPORATED COMMUNITIES** (and ZIP Code) Decker 79506, Hylton 79506, Maryneal 79535, Nolan 79537 and Wastella 79545. **FOR ADDITIONAL LOCAL INFORMATION** Sweetwater Chamber of Commerce, 104 W. 3rd., Sweetwater, 79556, 915/235-5488.

NUECES (G32)

THE LAND
Bordering the Gulf of Mexico southeast of San Antonio on U.S. Highway 77 in the Coastal Prairies Region, Nueces County covers 847 square miles with the elevation ranging from sea level to 180 feet. The very dark, nearly level soils have loamy surfaces with clayey subsoils, or gray to black, cracking clayey soils. To the west the soils are light to dark colored with loamy surfaces and clayey subsoils. Along the Gulf Coast are the sandy soils of the beaches and the very dark, loamy surfaces with clayey subsoils of the marshes. In the Gulf Prairies and Marshes vegetations area there are cordgrasses, saltgrasses and marsh millet along the coast and tall grasses with oaks, prickly pear, acacias and mesquite trees further inland. Between 61 and 70% of the land in the county is considered prime farmland. **CLIMATE** Subtropical Subhumid. hurricanes are a risk between June and October. The average annual temperature is 72 °F. Temperatures in January range from an average low of 47 ° to an average high of 66 °F and in July range from 79 ° to 93 °F. The average annual precipitation is 30 inches, with an average relative humidity of 90% at 6 A.M. and 65% at 6 P.M. There is no snowfall. The growing season averages 309 days per year, with the last freeze in early February and the first freeze in mid December. The sun shines during the year on the average 70% of the daylight hours.

THE PEOPLE
Nueces County ranks 38th among all U.S. counties in the highest percent of residents of Spanish origin and is one of the state's most densely populated. The 1982 estimated population of 283,100 continues the strong growth pattern which has existed since 1930. Rural areas grew at the same pace as urban areas, where 94% of the residents live. The largest ancestry groups are Hispanic (49%), persons of English descent (15%), German descent (12%) Irish descent (12%). **REGISTERED VOTERS** As of November 2, 1982 there were 128,297 registered voters (2% of the state total). The 1982 general election had a 50% voter turnout, compared to a 66% turnout in the 1980 general election. In the 1982 primary 91% voted Democratic and 9% Republican, with 39,217 votes cast.

THE ECONOMY
AGRICULTURE Sorghum area. In 1982, 85% of the land was in farms and ranches, with 77% of the farmland under cultivation and 1% irrigated. Nueces ranked 29th in the state in highest agricultural receipts, with 87% from crops. Overgrazing, undesirable brush and weeds, water erosion and inefficient tillage systems are the current conservation problems. Primary crops: first in the state for sorghum. Cotton, hay, corn and wheat. Primary vegetables: watermelons. Primary fruits and nuts: peaches and pecans. Primary livestock and products: cattle, milk and hogs. **BUSINESS** Total number of business establishments in the county: 6,425. Retail sales during the first quarter of 1984 increased by 7%. In 1980, 7% of the labor force were self-employed, 20% were employed in professional or related services,

12% in manufacturing, 23% in wholesale and retail trade, 10% in construction, 5% were employed in other counties and there were 14,911 retired workers. The industries with the most employment: tourism, agribusiness, general and heavy construction, oil and gas field services, meat packing, soft drink bottling and canning, commercial printing, petroleum refining, ship building and repairing, the refining of zinc and the manufacture of dairy products, bakery products, men's and women's clothing, plastics and resins, cement and ready-mixed concrete, prefabricated metal buildings, oil field machinery and electronic components. The nonfarm earnings in 1981 totaled $2,820,779,000. The retired workers received an average monthly Social Security payment of $320. **FINANCE** On June 30, 1983, 22 commercial banks had total deposits of $1,789,136,000 and total assets of $2,123,163,000. On December 31, 1982 two state savings and loan associations, one federal associatio and 27 state branches had combined assets of $243,679,668. In addition there are 31 credit unions in the county. **HOUSING** Average value of homes in 1980: $35,800. Permits for new, privately owned housing units increased in 1982: 3,608 permits were issued with a total construction cost of $132,369,018. Of those permits, 1,512 were for single family houses. Housing permits in Corpus Christi increased from 2,758 in 1981 to 3,247 in 1982. Between 1970 and 1980 the number of housing units increased by 26%. Seventy-three percent of all units in the county are air-conditioned, 72% are heated by gas and 27% by electricity. **NATURAL RESOURCES** Caliche, industrial sand, sand and gravel, oil and gas. In 1982 a total of 106,296,737 thousand cubic feet of gas well gas, 1,019,088 barrels of condensate, 2,551,161 barrels of crude oil and 6,692,052 thousand cubic feet of casinghead gas were produced. Current production of other minerals and products includes cement, lime, sand and gravel and recovered sulphur. **TOURISM** Travel expenditures of $274,484,000 in 1982 (an increase of 11% over 1981) generated 6,410 jobs and $54,100,000 in payroll. Lodging: 52 hotels, motels and tourist courts. Convention/meeting facilities: Corpus Christi-Bayfront Plaza Auditorium Theatre, Memorial Coliseum and Exposition Hall and ten hotels with facilities for large gatherings. **ALCOHOLIC BEVERAGES** Packaged distilled spirits, beer, ale, malt liquor and wine are legal in parts of the county. Sale of mixed beverages is legal in all or parts of the county. **MILITARY INSTALLATIONS** Corpus Christi Naval Air Station, Corpus Christi, 7,226 personnel, 2,618 acres, flight training; Cabaniss Naval Auxiliary Air Field, Nueces County, 692 acres, auxiliary training field; Waldron Naval Auxiliary Air Field, Corpus Christi, 763 acres, auxiliary training field; Corpus Christi Naval Regional Medical Center, 472 personnel, 32 acres, health care. **FEDERAL EXPENDITURES** The federal government had direct expenditures or obligations of $449,715,000 in the county during fiscal year 1983, including $136,554,000 by the U.S. Department of Defense. In addition, the federal government provided $26,241,000 in grant awards, paid $109,518,000 in salaries and wages, made direct payments to individuals of $260,784,000 including $211,104,000 in retirement and disability payments, awarded $46,410,000 in procurement contracts and spent $6,762,000 in other expenditures or obligations. The federal government also provided $4,215,000 in direct loans and $626,191,000 in guaranteed loans and insurance.

COMMUNICATION

Newspapers–Daily: Corpus Christi Caller, ave. morn. circ. 61,185 and The Corpus Christi Times ave. eve. circ. 23,678. Weekly: Bishop News, Portland News-Spanish, Robstown Record and the Port Aransas South Jetty. Radio: KFLZ-FM (Bishop), KCCT-AM, KCTA-AM, KEYS-AM, KIKN-AM, KRYS-AM, KSIX-AM, KUND-AM, KEXX-FM, KOUL-FM, KZFM-FM, KIOO-FM Stereo and KNCN-FM Stereo (Corpus Christi), KROB-AM and KROB-FM (Robstown). Television: KEDT CH.16, KIII CH.3,

KORO CH.28, KRIS CH.6, KZTV CH.10 (Corpus Christi). Cable TV. Telephone companies: General Telephone, Southwestern Bell and Mustang Telephone. **TRANSPORTATION** Total public road mileage: 2,558. In 1982 there were 211,036 registered vehicles and 8,835 reported traffic accidents including 70 fatalities. Taxi cabs: four companies in Corpus Christi and two in Aransas Pass. Municipal transit systems: one intracity bus systems in Corpus Christi with scheduled routes. Intercity bus service is available. Motor freight: 80 local and intrastate carriers. Rail: one main line and one branch carry freight through the county. The main line carries annually five to 10 million tons of freight and the branch carries five to 10 million. Aircraft: 316 are registered in the county. Airports: Corpus Christi International Airport serves as a base for 140 aircraft and is a short haul, small hub airport with carrier service. Nueces County Airport at Robstown serves as a base for 45 aircraft and is a general utility airport with general aviation service. Bishop Municipal Airport. Heliports in Corpus Christi are Corpus Christi Heliport, Memorial Medical Center, Physicians and Surgeons Hospital and Hospital Heliports. Waterborne commerce: Corpus Christi Ship Channel freight traffic totaled 39,148,522 short tons in 1981: 16,466,830 in foreign imports, 3,488,146 in foreign exports and 19,193,546 in domestic shipments. Harbor Island freight traffic totaled 2,868,208 short tons: 1,871,580 in foreign imports, 17,437 in foreign exports and 979,191 in domestic shipments.

COMMUNITY SERVICES

EDUCATION 13 school districts with 60 elementary, 20 middle, 15 high schools and six special education. The average daily attendance in 1981-82 was 51,537 with expenditures per pupil of $3,014 including 3,118 classroom teachers with an average annual salary of $17,650. Forty-Seven percent of the 3,292 high school graduates planned to attend college. In 1982-83, 34% of the students were White, 61% Hispanic, 5% Black, 0.6% Asian and 0.1% American Indian. Private schools: 6,607 students enrolled in 26 elementary and seven high schools. Sports championships: 1984 AAA Girls' Basketball, Incarnate Word Academy, 1983 AAA Girls' Track, Incarnate Word Academy, 1983 AAA Boys' Cross Country, Incarnate Word Academy, 1983 AAA Girls' Cross Country, Incarnate Word Academy. Corpus Christi State University is located in Corpus Christi. Established in 1971 it is part of the university system of South Texas and is under state control. Enrollment in 1982 was 2,918 with in state undergraduate tuition and fees of $304 per semester. The highest degree offered is Master (no lower division). Del Mar College is located in Corpus Christi. Established in 1935 it is a vocational and two year academic college under local control. Enrollment in 1982 was 8,286 with in state undergraduate tuition and fees of $220 per semester. Vocational education: Corpus Christi-Corpus Christi Beauty College, Memorial Medical Center Medical Lab Technician Certificate Program, Stevensons Advanced Beauty College, Vogue Beauty College, International Bartending Institute of Corpus Christi, Medical Transcription School, Metils Inc., Progress Welding School and South Texas Vocational Center. **PUBLIC LIBRARIES** Corpus Christi Public Libraries: 292,193 volumes, four branches. Port Aransas Library. Nueces County Library (Robstown): 44,951 volumes, one branch. **CHILD CARE** 282 day care and 64 twenty-four hour care licensed facilities. **HEALTH CARE** 529 physicians and 130 dentists. Hospitals: seven with a combined capacity of 1,646. Specialized hospitals: one children's hospital with a capacity of 155, one rehabilitation hopital with a capacity of 80, one women's surgical center with a capacity of 2, one surgical dental hospital with a capacity of 2 and one naval hospital with a capacity of 53. Clinics: three for treatment of alcohol and drug abuse, two minor emergency centers, one family planning clinic, one family counseling clinic, one veterans outpatient clinic, one dialysis clinic and one public

COUNTIES

NUECES (continued)

health clinic. Ambulance services: four commercial, two volunteer services and one fire department service. Mental health: five clinics, one development center with a capacity of 100 and one state school with capacity of 498. Nursing homes: 10 nursing homes with a combined capacity of 1,481 nursing care residents. The average cost per day for private patients in 1982 was $34.13. **CHURCHES** 202 churches have an estimated combined membership of 149,583. The largest denominations are Catholic, Southern Baptist and United Methodist. **SOCIAL SERVICES** In fiscal year 1983 a total of $16,637,409 in food stamps was distributed, with an average of 33,845 persons receiving food stamps each month. Aid to Families with Dependent Children (AFDC) totaled $3,656,296 with an average of 2,327 families receiving AFDC each month. Medical assistance benefits for the aged and disabled of $19,728,735 and for families and children of $6,297,039 brought the county benefit total to $46,319,479. **FIRE PROTECTION** Two paid and eight volunteer fire departments. **LAW ENFORCEMENT** The County Sheriff has 163 commissioned officers. Four police departments have a combined force of 418. One university has a police department with a force of nine. Corpus Christi Airport Police force has 15 officers. **CRIME** 2,080 violent crimes (murder, forcible rape, robbery and aggravated assault) and 22,337 nonviolent crimes (burglary, larceny-theft and motor vehicle theft) were reported in 1982. **JUDICIAL SYSTEM** Seven District Courts and Judges, four County Courts and Judges and nine Justices of the Peace. In the District Courts a total of 6,046 cases were pending on 1/1/82, 7,401 new cases were filed and 7,107 cases were disposed of during the year leaving 6,340 cases pending on 12/31/82. There were 2,048 criminal cases on the docket, 753 convictions, 262 persons committed to prison, 20 committed to jail and 868 cases left pending. In the County Courts 2,284 cases were pending on 1/1/82, 6,861 new cases were filed and 5,826 cases were disposed of during the year leaving 3,319 cases pending on 12/31/82. There were 5,790 criminal cases on the docket, 2,521 convictions, 755 persons committed to jail and 2,002 cases left pending. **JAILS** One jail, capacity 290. A major renovation has been completed and further construction is planned. Certification was lost in 1983 due to overcrowding. **ATTORNEYS AT LAW** 681. **UTILITIES** 98% of the residents are connected to a public or privately owned water system and 93% are connected to a public sewer system. Natural gas is distributed to the county by Entex, Inc. and Gulfside Gas Co. The average annual residential bill for natural gas in 1982 for the Entex distribution system was $390.31, an increase of 26% over 1981. Electricity is distributed to the county by Central Power and Light Co., Cochran Power and Light Co., Robstown Utility System and Nueces Electric Coop., Inc. and is generated primarily by gas, oil and coal. The typical residential electric bill is $221.90 per month for an all-electric house using 2,500 kwh. **TAXES** The county has 29 units with taxing authority: 13 school districts, six cities, one county, one college district, one hospital district and seven special districts.

RECREATION/ENTERTAINMENT
NATIONAL REGISTER OF HISTORIC PLACES King Ranch (See Kenedy County). Corpus Christi: Britton-Evans House and Nueces County Courthouse. Port Aransas: Tarpon Inn. Violet: Old Saint Anthony's Catholic Church. **STATE** Lipantitlan State Historic Site covers five acres. Mustang Island State Park covers 3,704 acres with camping and trailer sites, fishing, swimming and nature trails. **COUNTY/MUNICIPAL PARKS** 2,586 acres in 11 county and 162 municipal parks. These parks contain nine miles of hiking trails, 105 playgrounds, two golf courses, three football and soccer fields, 23 baseball and softball fields, 46 tennis courts, nine multi-use courts, 10 swimming pools, 11 beaches, eight boat ramps and shore fishing facilities. Developed campsites: 206. **SCENIC DRIVES** The Texas Tropical Trail runs through this county. This trail is charted through the state's southernmost wedge meandering through ranchland, resort areas by the Gulf of Mexico and fertile farmlands. **BOATING/FISHING** Lakes/reservoirs: Barney M. Davis (1,100 acres) and Calallen (430 acres). Major rivers: Nueces. Primary streams: Oso and San Fernando. Saltwater fishing: speckled trout, redfish and flounder fishing is usually good around Corpus Christi Bay, Nueces Bay and Mustang Island. Shrimp, oysters and crabs may be taken but, like other saltwater fish, under specific regulations. **HUNTING** Fall and winter seasons on deer. No closed season on nutria, javelina, squirrel, bobcat and coyote. Winter seasons on quail, muskrat, beaver, otter, opossum, mink, ring-tailed cat, badger, fox, raccoon, skunk and civet cat. Fall and winter seasons on turkey. In 1983 duck, coot, geese, woodcock and jacksnipe seasons occurred during the winter months with a winter season on sandhill crane in some parts of the county. Teal duck, rail and gallinule seasons occurred in the fall. Mourning dove seasons occurred intermittently during the fall and winter months with a fall season on white-winged dove. **MUSEUMS** Corpus Christi: Centennial House, Art Museum of South Texas, Corpus Christi Museum, South Texas Artmobile, Japanese Art Museum of Oriental Cultures and Sidbury and Lichtenstein Homes. Port Aransas: Natural History Specimen Collection and Marine Science Institute. **ORCHESTRAS** Corpus Christi: Symphony. **PLANETARIUM** Corpus Christi: Richard King High School Planetarium. **COLLEGIATE FINE ARTS** Cultural events offered by Corpus Christi State University and Del Mar College. **SPECIAL EVENTS** Annual Press Club Gridiron Show, Corpus Christi, January; Seafood and Game Dinner, Port Aransas, March; Fireworks on the Bayfront, Corpus Christi, April; Festival of Flowers, Corpus Christi, April; Chili Cookoff, Corpus Christi, April; Art Jamboree, Corpus Christi, April; Sr. Citizens Arts and Crafts Fair, Corpus Christi, May; Buccaneer Days, Corpus Christi, May; Bar Room Bicycle Race, Port Aransas, May; Navy Relief Festival, Corpus Christi, May; Spring Arts and Crafts Fair, Corpus Christi, May; Fijita Cookoff, Corpus Christi, May; Israel Independence Day Celebration, Corpus Christi, May; Miss Black Corpus Christi Pageant, Corpus Christi, June; Petticoat Fishing Tourney, Port Aransas, June; Jazz Festival, Corpus Christi, July; Independence Day Celebration, Corpus Christi, July; Deep-Sea Roundup, Port Aransas, July; Sand Dune Regatta, Port Aransas, July; Annual Outboard Fishing Tounrnament, Port Aransas, July; Volksmarch, Corpus Christi, July; Old Fiddlers Festival, Corpus Christi, August; Dean Hawn Billfish Tourney, Port Aransas, August; Feria de las Flores, Corpus Christi, August; Beach Olympics Port Aransas, August; Diez y Seis Celebration, Corpus Christi, September; Greyfest, Corpus Christi, September; Bayfest, Corpus Christi, September/October; Arts and Crafts Show Fair, Robstown, October; Festival of Arts and Crafts, Corpus Christi, October; Chili Cookoff, Port Aransas, November; Lighting of the Boats, Port Aransas, December; Christmas Celebration, Corpus Christi, December.

COMMUNITIES
COUNTY SEAT Corpus Christi, County Courthouse, 78401; County Clerk's Office, 512/888-0580. **INCORPORATED COMMUNITIES** (1980 population and ZIP Code) Agua Dulce (934) 78330, Aransas Pass (7,173: 5 in Nueces Co., 860 in Aransas Co. and 6,308 in San Patricio Co.) 78336, Bishop (3,706) 78343, Corpus Christi (231,999) 78401 All-America Cities Honorable Mention 1953 and 1963, Driscoll (648) 78351, Port Aransas (1,968) 78373, Robstown (12,100) 78380 and San Patricio (241: 31 in Nueces Co. and 210 in San Patricio Co.) 78368.

UNINCORPORATED COMMUNITIES (and ZIP Code) Banquete 78339, Bluntzer 78380, Chapman Ranch 78347, Palo Alto 78343, Petronila 78380, Rabb 78380, San Juan 78401, San Pedro 78380, Suntide 78409, Sycamore 75932, Viola 78409 and Violet 78380 FOR ADDITIONAL LOCAL INFORMATION Bishop Chamber of Commerce, County Bldg., 115 S. Ash, Bishop, 78343, 512/584-2214, Corpus Christi Chamber of Commerce, 1201 N. Shoreline Blvd., Corpus Christi, 78403, 512/882-6161, Corpus Christi Mexican Chamber of Commerce, P.O. Box 5523, Corpus Christi, 78405, 512/887-8531 and Robstown Chamber of Commerce, 110 N. Forth, Robstown, 78380, 512/387-3933.

OCHILTREE (P4)

THE LAND

Bordering Oklahoma northeast of Amarillo on U.S. Highway 83 in the High Plains Region, Ochiltree County covers 919 square miles with the elevation ranging from 2,600 to 3,100 feet. The nearly level, soils have very dark, loamy surfaces over clayey subsoils and limestone. To the east and south some of the soils are lighter in color with reddish clayey subsoils. In the High Plains vegetation area the primary grasses are buffalograss and blue grama with a few mesquite and yucca. Between 61 and 70% of the land in the county is considered prime farmland. CLIMATE Continental Steppe with wide-ranging temperatures on a daily basis, low relative humidity and irregular precipitation patterns. The average annual temperature is 58 °F. Temperatures in January range from an average low of 19° to an average high of 48°F and in July range from 66° to 95 °F. The average annual precipitation is 20 inches, with an average relative humidity of 73% at 6 A.M. and 42% at 6 P.M. The average annual snowfall is 16 inches. The growing season averages 190 days per year, with the last freeze in mid April and the first freeze in late October. The sun shines during the year on the average 75% of the daylight hours.

THE PEOPLE

The 1982 estimated population of 10,800 represents a 13% increase since 1980. Although the population declined between 1970 and 1980, sizeable growth occurred between 1940 and 1970 with the population increasing more than 50% from 1950 to 1960. Almost 84% of the residents live in urban areas which experienced slight growth from 1970 to 1980, while rural areas had a population loss of 16%. The age group with the greatest reduction was ages five to 14. Ochiltree has a low percent of residents who are native Texans. The largest ancestry groups are persons of English descent (26%), German descent (21%) and Irish descent (20%). REGISTERED VOTERS As of November 2, 1982 there were 4,623 registered voters (0.1% of the state total). The 1982 general election had a 59% voter turnout, compared to a 77% turnout in the 1980 general election. In the 1982 primary 92% voted Democratic and 8% Republican, with 1,265 votes cast.

THE ECONOMY

AGRICULTURE Wheat area. In 1982, 98% of the land was in farms and ranches, with 61% of the farmland under cultivation and 28% irrigated. Ochiltree ranked 46th in the state in highest agricultural receipts, with 51% from crops. Overgrazing, undesirable brush and weeds, water erosion and decreasing irrigation water supplies are the current conservation problems. Primary crops: second in the state for wheat. Sorghum and hay. Primary livestock and products: cattle, sheep, wool and hogs. BUSINESS Total number of business establishments in the county: 308. Retail sales during the first quarter of 1984 increased by 6%. In 1980, 14% of the labor force were self-employed, 13% were employed in professional or related services, 3% in

manufacturing, 23% in wholesale and retail trade, 37% in agriculture, forestry, fisheries and mining, 9% were employed in other counties and there were 556 retired workers. The industries with the most employment: agribusiness, meat packing, oil and gas field services, heavy construction and metal plate fabrication. The nonfarm earnings in 1981 totaled $118,504,000. The retired workers received an average monthly Social Security payment of $347. FINANCE On June 30, 1983, two commercial banks had total deposits of $97,117,000 and total assets of $112,843,000. On December 31, 1982 one state savings and loan association had assets of $58,156,194. In addition there is one credit union. HOUSING Average value of homes in 1980: $33,600. Permits for new, privately owned housing units decreased in 1982: 48 permits were issued with a total construction cost of $2,729,000. Of those permits, 46 were for single family houses. Between 1970 and 1980 the number of housing units increased by 17%. Seventy-six percent of all units in the county are air-conditioned, 91% are heated by gas and 8% by electricity. NATURAL RESOURCES Caliche, oil and gas. In 1982 a total of 31,105,142 thousand cubic feet of gas well gas, 141,824 barrels of condensate, 2,871,766 barrels of crude oil and 8,108,052 thousand cubic feet of casinghead gas were produced. TOURISM Travel expenditures of $8,334,000 in 1982 (an increase of 11% over 1981) generated 216 jobs and $1,744,000 in payroll. Lodging: four hotels, motels and tourist courts. ALCOHOLIC BEVERAGES Totally dry. FEDERAL EXPENDITURES The federal government had direct expenditures or obligations of $15,239,000 in the county during fiscal year 1983, including $155,000 by the U.S. Department of Defense. In addition, the federal government provided $73,000 in grant awards, paid $695,000 in salaries and wages, made direct payments to individuals of $7,752,000 including $5,796,000 in retirement and disability payments, awarded $4,000 in procurement contracts and spent $6,716,000 in other expenditures or obligations. The federal government also provided $19,060,000 in direct loans and $10,254,000 in guaranteed loans and insurance.

COMMUNICATION

Newspapers–Weekly: The Perryton Herald. Radio: KEYE-AM and KEYE-FM (Perryton). Cable TV. Telephone companies: General Telephone. TRANSPORTATION Total public road mileage: 892. In 1982 there were 13,180 registered vehicles and 335 reported traffic accidents including seven fatalities. Intercity bus service is available. Motor freight: six local and intrastate carriers. Rail: one branch line carries annually less than one million tons of freight through the county. Aircraft: 49 are registered in the county. Airports: Ochiltree County Airport at Perryton serves as a base for 28 aircraft and is a basic transportation airport with general aviation service. Also serving the area McLain Airport at Perryton and Mitchell Field at Booker.

COMMUNITY SERVICES

EDUCATION Two school districts with three elementary, one middle and one high school. The average daily attendance in 1981-82 was 1,765, with expenditures per pupil of $3,428 including 139 classroom teachers with an average annual salary of $19,364. None of the 92 high school graduates planned to attend college. In 1982-83, 83% of the students were White, 17% Hispanic, 0.2% Asian and 0.1% American Indian. PUBLIC LIBRARIES Perry Memorial Library (Perryton): 27,216 volumes. CHILD CARE 18 day care and four twenty-four hour care licensed facilities. HEALTH CARE Four physicians and four dentists. Hospitals: one with a capacity of 65. Ambulance services: one fire department. Mental health: one clinic. Nursing homes: one nursing home has a capacity of 60 nursing care residents. The average cost per day for private patients in 1982 was $36.06. CHURCHES 20 churches have an estimated combined membership of 5,647.

COUNTIES

OCHILTREE (continued)

The largest denominations are Southern Baptist and United Methodist. **SOCIAL SERVICES** In fiscal year 1983 a total of $67,129 in food stamps was distributed, with an average of 137 persons receiving food stamps each month. Aid to Families with Dependent Children (AFDC) totaled $14,622 with an average of 10 families receiving AFDC each month. Medical assistance benefits for the aged and disabled of $179,276 and for families and children of $27,057 brought the county benefit total to $288,084. **FIRE PROTECTION** Two volunteer fire departments. **LAW ENFORCEMENT** The County Sheriff has nine commissioned officers. One police department has a force of 11. **CRIME** 21 violent crimes (murder, forcible rape, robbery and aggravated assault) and 293 nonviolent crimes (burglary, larceny-theft and motor vehicle theft) were reported in 1982. **JUDICIAL SYSTEM** One District Court and Judge, one County Court and Judge and two Justices of the Peace. In the District Court a total of 314 cases were pending on 1/1/82, 447 new cases were filed and 351 cases were disposed of during the year leaving 410 cases pending on 12/31/82. There were 211 criminal cases on the docket, 81 convictions, 42 persons committed to prison, two committed to jail and 69 cases left pending. In the County Court 496 cases were pending on 1/1/82, 725 new cases were filed and 658 cases were disposed of during the year leaving 563 cases pending on 12/31/82. There were 1,061 criminal cases on the docket, 400 convictions, three persons committed to jail and 421 cases left pending. **JAILS** One jail, capacity 32. **ATTORNEYS AT LAW** 17. **UTILITIES** 87% of the residents are connected to a public or privately owned water system and 85% are connected to a public sewer system. Electricity is distributed to the county by North Plains Electric Coop., Inc. and Texas New-Mexico Power and is generated primarily by gas, oil and coal. The typical residential electric bill is $168.05 per month for an all-electric house using 2,500 kwh. **TAXES** The county has six units with taxing authority: two school districts, one city, one county, one hospital district and one special district.

RECREATION/ENTERTAINMENT

COUNTY/MUNICIPAL PARKS 850 acres in one county and six municipal parks. These parks contain four playgrounds, one golf course, two tennis courts, one swimming pool, three beaches, one boat ramp and shore fishing facilities. Developed campsites: 33. **BOATING/FISHING** Lakes/reservoirs: Fryer (47 acres) and Wheatheart (14 acres). Primary streams: Chiquita, Palo Duro and Wolf. **HUNTING** Fall seasons on antelope and prairie chicken. Fall and winter seasons on deer and mule deer. Summer, fall and winter seasons on squirrel. Winter seasons on pheasant, quail, muskrat, beaver, opossum, ring-tailed cat, badger, fox, weasel, raccoon, skunk and civet cat. No closed season on bobcat and coyote. Fall, winter and spring seasons on turkey. In 1983 sandhill crane, duck, coot, geese, woodcock and jacksnipe seasons occurred during the winter months. Teal duck, rail and gallinule seasons occurred in the fall. Mourning dove seasons occurred intermittently during the fall and winter months. **MUSEUMS** Perryton: Museum of the Plains. **SPECIAL EVENTS** Oil Patch Golf Tourney, Perryton, July; Fun Day in the Park, Perryton, July; Wheatheart Celebration, Perryton, August.

COMMUNITIES

COUNTY SEAT Perryton, County Courthouse, 79070; County Clerk's Office, 806/435-2562. **INCORPORATED COMMUNITIES** (1980 population and ZIP Code) Booker (1,219: 1,201 in Lipscomb Co. and 18 in Ochiltree Co.) 79005 and Perryton (7,991) 79070. **UNINCORPORATED COMMUNITIES** (and ZIP Code) Farnsworth 79033. Notla 79070, Twitchell 79070, Waka (Burnside) 79093. **FOR ADDITIONAL LOCAL INFORMATION**

Ochiltree Co. Chamber of Commerce, Nine S.E. 5th Ave., Perryton, 79070, 806/435-6575.

OLDHAM (P11)

THE LAND

In the High Plains Region of the Texas Panhandle bordering New Mexico west of Amarillo on Interstate Highway 40, Oldham County covers 1,485 square miles with the elevation ranging from 3,200 to 4,200 feet. The county has level to rolling soils with light colored, well drained surfaces or very dark, loamy surfaces over reddish, clayey subsoils that have hardened calcium deposits. Most of Oldham is in the Rolling Plains vegetation area with tall and mid grasses, mesquite and shinnery oak. Along the southern border the county has High Plains vegetation with prairie grasses, some cacti and mesquite trees. Between 11 and 20% of the land in the county is considered prime farmland. **CLIMATE** Continental Steppe, dry with wide temperature variations on a daily basis. The average annual temperature is 56 °F. Temperatures in January range from an average low of 19 ° to an average high of 49 °F and in July range from 63 ° to 91 °F. The average annual precipitation is 17 inches, with an average relative humidity of 68% at 6 A.M. and 36% at 6 P.M. The average annual snowfall is 15 inches. The growing season averages 186 days per year, with the last freeze in late April and the first freeze in late October. The sun shines during the year on the average 75% of the daylight hours.

THE PEOPLE

Oldham County is one of the most sparsely populated in the state, although the 1982 estimated population of 2,300 suggests a continuation of the slow growth which began in 1940. The majority of the county residents live in rural areas. This county has a young population with a high percent of its residents under age 18. However the median age rose from 22 in 1970 to 25 in 1980. The largest ancestry groups are persons of English descent (33%), Irish descent (25%) and German descent (19%). **REGISTERED VOTERS** As of November 2, 1982 there were 1,144 registered voters (00.1% of the state total). The 1982 general election had a 61% voter turnout, compared to a 76% turnout in the 1980 general election. In the 1982 primary 100% voted Democratic with 453 votes cast.

THE ECONOMY

AGRICULTURE Wheat area. In 1982, 97% of the land was in farms and ranches, with 15% of the farmland under cultivation and 19% irrigated. Oldham ranked 146th in the state in highest agricultural receipts, with 63% from livestock and livestock products. Undesirable brush, noxious weeds, water erosion, decreasing irrigation water supplies and a lack of potable water are the current conservation problems. Primary crops: wheat, sorghum and hay. Primary vegetables: tomatoes and watermelons. Primary livestock and products: cattle and hogs. **BUSINESS** Total number of business establishments in the county: 42. Retail sales during the first quarter of 1984 increased by 18%. In 1980, 20% of the labor force were self-employed, 22% were employed in professional or related services, 2% in manufacturing, 20% in wholesale and retail trade, 32% in agriculture, forestry, fisheries and mining, 13% were employed in other counties and there were 180 retired workers. The industry with the most employment is agribusiness. The nonfarm earnings in 1981 totaled $15,854,000. The retired workers received an average monthly Social Security payment of $328. **FINANCE** On June 30, 1983, one commercial bank had total deposits of $10,522,000 and total assets of $12,176,000. **HOUSING** Average value of homes in 1980: $24,500. Between 1970 and 1980 the number of housing units increased by 12%. Seventy-six percent of all units in the county are air-conditioned, 94% are heated by gas and 5% by electricity. **NATURAL RESOURCES** Caliche, oil and gas. In 1982 a total of 809,702 thousand cubic feet of gas well gas, 1,558,394 barrels of crude oil and 186,292 thousand cubic feet of casinghead gas were produced. Current production of other minerals and products includes caliche, sand and gravel. **TOURISM** Travel expenditures of $4,521,000 in 1982 (an increase of 11% over 1981) generated 117 jobs and $920,000 in payroll. **ALCOHOLIC BEVERAGES** Only 4% beer is legal in parts of the county. **FEDERAL EXPENDITURES** The federal government had direct expenditures or obligations of $4,379,000 in the county during fiscal year 1983, including $65,000 by the U.S. Department of Defense. In addition, the federal government provided $62,000 in grant awards, paid $235,000 in salaries and wages, made direct payments to individuals of $2,397,000 including $1,832,000 in retirement and disability payments and spent $1,685,000 in other expenditures or obligations. The federal government also provided $3,982,000 in direct loans and $2,258,000 in guaranteed loans and insurance.

COMMUNICATION
Newspapers–Weekly: The Vega Enterprise. Telephone companies: Continental Telephone. **TRANSPORTATION** Total public road mileage: 327. In 1982 there were 2,416 registered vehicles and 130 reported traffic accidents including three fatalities. Intercity bus service is available. Motor freight: one carrier. Rail: one main line carries annually over 30 million tons of freight through the county. Aircraft: 24 are registered in the county. Airports: Oldham County Airport at Vega serves as a base for 12 aircraft and is a basic utility airport with general aviation service.

COMMUNITY SERVICES
EDUCATION Three school districts with three elementary, and two high schools. The average daily attendance in 1981-82 was 457, with expenditures per pupil of $3,982 including 42 classroom teachers with an average annual salary of $16,897. Seventy-one percent of the 45 high school graduates planned to attend college. In 1982-83, 88% of the students were White, 10% Hispanic, 0.4% Black and 0.8% Asian. **CHILD CARE** Four day care and three twenty-four hour care licensed facilities. **HEALTH CARE** One physician. Clinics: one outpatient clinic. Ambulance services: two volunteer services and one volunteer fire department service. **CHURCHES** 10 churches have an estimated combined membership of 2,238. The largest denominations are Southern Baptist, United Methodist and Catholic. **SOCIAL SERVICES** In fiscal year 1983 a total of $20,637 in food stamps was distributed, with an average of 39 persons receiving food stamps each month. Aid to Families with Dependent Children (AFDC) totaled $3,184. Medical assistance benefits for the aged and disabled of $3,888 and for families and children of $3,635 brought the county benefit total to $31,344. **FIRE PROTECTION** Three volunteer fire departments. **LAW ENFORCEMENT** The County Sheriff has six commissioned officers. One police department has one officer. **CRIME** One violent crime (murder, forcible rape, robbery and aggravated assault) and 35 nonviolent crimes (burglary, larceny-theft and motor vehicle theft) were reported in 1982. **JUDICIAL SYSTEM** One District Court and Judge, one County Court and Judge and two Justices of the Peace. In the District Court a total of 41 cases were pending on 1/1/82, 37 new cases were filed and 43 cases were disposed of during the year leaving 35 cases pending on 12/31/82. There were 10 criminal cases on the docket, eight convictions, two persons committed to prison and two cases left pending. In the County Court 13 cases were pending on 1/1/82, 53 new cases were filed and 31 cases were disposed of during the year leaving 35 cases pending on 12/31/82. There were 60 criminal cases on the docket, 22 convictions, five persons committed to jail and 32 cases left

pending. **JAILS** One jail, capacity 10. **ATTORNEYS AT LAW** Two. **UTILITIES** 80% of the residents are connected to a public or privately owned water system and 60% are connected to a public sewer system. Natural gas is distributed to the county by Energas Company. The average annual residential bill for natural gas in 1982 for the Energas distribution system was $371.63, an increase of 23% over 1981. Electricity is distributed to the county by Deaf Smith Electric Coop., Inc. and Rita Blanca Electric Coop., Inc. and is generated primarily by gas and coal. **TAXES** The county has six units with taxing authority: three school districts, two cities and one county.

RECREATION/ENTERTAINMENT
NATIONAL REGISTER OF HISTORIC PLACES Adrian vicinity: Rocky Dell. Vega vicinity: Landergin Mesa. **MUNICIPAL PARKS** 12 acres in two municipal parks. These parks contain one playground, three tennis courts and one multi-use court. **SCENIC DRIVES** the Texas Plains Trail runs through this county. This trail spans a vast area of the High Plains region of Texas slicing through the southernmost extension of the Great Plains of the United States. The land is flat except where erosion has carved canyon landscapes. **BOATING/FISHING** Lakes/reservoirs: Rock Springs Tank (17 acres). Major rivers: Canadian. Primary streams: Las Arches, Minneosa, Pedarosa, Middle Alamosa, Trujillo, Morse, Drippings Springs, Sand, Horse, Romero, Agua de Piedra, West Alamosa, Sierrita de la Cruz, Alamocitos, Muares and Antelope. **HUNTING** Fall season on antelope. Fall and winter seasons on mule deer. Summer, fall and winter seasons on squirrel. Winter seasons on pheasant, quail, muskrat, beaver, opossum, ring-tailed cat, badger, fox, weasel, raccoon, skunk and civet cat. No closed season on coyote and bobcat. Fall, winter and spring seasons on turkey. In 1983 sandhill crane, duck, coot, geese, woodcock and jacksnipe seasons occurred during the winter months. Teal duck, rail and gallinule seasons occurred in the fall. Mourning dove seasons occurred intermittently during the fall and winter months. **MUSEUMS** Tascosa: Julian Bivins Museum. **SPECIAL EVENTS** Boys Ranch Rodeo, Tascosa, September.

COMMUNITIES
COUNTY SEAT Vega, County Courthouse, 79092; County Clerk's Office, 806/267-2667. **INCORPORATED COMMUNITIES** (1980 population and ZIP Code) Adrian (222) 79001 and Vega (900) 79092. **UNINCORPORATED COMMUNITIES** (and ZIP Code) Boys Ranch 79010 and Wildorado 79098.

ORANGE (G7)

THE LAND
Bordering Louisiana northeast of Houston on Interstate Highway 10 in the Coastal Prairie Region, Orange County covers 362 square miles with the elevation ranging from sea level to 30 feet. There are level soils in the south and central parts of the county, with light to dark loamy surfaces over clayey subsoils, or gray to black, cracking, clayey soils with a high shrink-swell potential. The rest of the county has soils with light colored, loamy surfaces over very deep, reddish, clayey or loamy subsoils that have hardened calcium deposits. Orange is in the Pineywoods vegetation area with grasslands and loblolly, shortleaf, longleaf and slash pines and hardwoods such as, oak, hickory and maple. The southern part of the county has Gulf Prairies vegetation with tall prairie grasses, mesquite and oak. Between 21 and 30% of the land in the county is considered prime farmland. **CLIMATE** Subtropical Humid with the highest annual rainfall average in the state. The average annual temperature is 68 °F. Temperatures in January range from an average low of 42 ° to an

COUNTIES

ORANGE (continued)

average high of 61 °F and in July range from 74° to 91 °F. The average annual precipitation is 56 inches, with an average relative humidity of 89% at 6 A.M. and 69% at 6 P.M. There is no snowfall. The growing season averages 240 days per year, with the last freeze in mid March and the first freeze in early November. The sun shines during the year on the average 60% of the daylight hours.

THE PEOPLE

Orange County is one of the most densely populated counties in the state and has experienced continuous growth since 1930: the population more than doubled between 1940 and 1950. The 1982 estimated population of 88,200 indicates a 5% gain in population since 1980. Almost 60% of the county residents live in urban areas which had a 9% population gain between 1970 and 1980 while rural areas experienced a 36% gain. The median age rose from 25 in 1970 to 28 in 1980. The largest ancestry groups are persons of English descent (26%), Irish descent (23%), French descent (20%) and German descent (15%). **REGISTERED VOTERS** As of November 2, 1982 there were 39,412 registered voters (0.6% of the state total). The 1982 general election had a 53% voter turnout, compared to a 71% turnout in the 1980 general election. In the 1982 primary 98% voted Democratic and 2% Republican, with 14,789 votes cast.

THE ECONOMY

AGRICULTURE Forest Production area. In 1982, 27% of the land was in farms and ranches, with 10% of the farmland under cultivation and 33% irrigated. Orange ranked 231st in the state in highest agricultural receipts, with 83% from crops. Overgrazing, undesirable brush and weeds, inefficient irrigation systems, drainage and improper woodland management are the current conservation problems. Primary crops: hay, rice and soybeans. Primary vegetables: potatoes and tomatoes. Primary fruits and nuts: peaches and pecans. Primary livestock and products: cattle. **BUSINESS** Total number of business establishments in the county: 1,156. Retail sales during the first quarter of 1984 increased by 13%. In 1980, 4% of the labor force were self-employed, 14% were employed in professional or related services, 33% in manufacturing, 18% in wholesale and retail trade, 12% in construction, 33% were employed in other counties and there were 4,218 retired workers. The industries with the most employment: agribusiness, oil and gas extraction, general construction, paperboard mills, steel foundries, ship building and repairing and the manufacture of paper bags, plastics and resins, synthetic rubber, industrial chemicals, cement, plastics products and fabricated structural metal products. The nonfarm earnings in 1981 totaled $899,154,000. The retired workers received an average monthly Social Security payment of $367. **FINANCE** On June 30, 1983, six commercial banks had total deposits of $252,351,000 and total assets of $286,491,000. On December 31, 1982 three state savings and loan associations and two state branches had combined assets of $179,453,036. In addition there are 11 credit unions in the county. **HOUSING** Average value of homes in 1980: $33,500. Permits for new, privately owned housing units decreased in 1982: 332 permits were issued with a total construction cost of $11,358,713. Of those permits, 258 were for single family houses. Between 1970 and 1980 the number of housing units increased by 38%. Eighty-eight percent of all units in the county are air-conditioned, 69% are heated by gas and 29% by electricity. **NATURAL RESOURCES** Salt domes, sand, gravel, oil and gas. In 1982 a total of 3,523,487 thousand cubic feet of gas well gas, 64,858 barrels of condensate, 756,520 barrels of crude oil and 617,031 thousand cubic feet of casinghead gas were produced. Current production of other minerals and products includes cement, clay, construction sand, sand and gravel. Pine and hardwood production in 1981 totaled 4,118,764 cubic feet: 3,332,373 cubic feet of pine and 786,391 cubic feet of hardwood. **TOURISM** Travel expenditures of $36,503,000 in 1982 (an increase of 11% over 1981) generated 898 jobs and $7,312,000 in payroll. Lodging: seven hotels, motels and tourist courts. **ALCOHOLIC BEVERAGES** Packaged distilled spirits, beer, ale, malt liquor and wine are legal in parts of the county. Sale of mixed beverages is legal in all or parts of the county. **FEDERAL EXPENDITURES** The federal government had direct expenditures or obligations of $86,536,000 in the county during fiscal year 1983, including $6,248,000 by the U.S. Department of Defense. In addition, the federal government provided $2,752,000 in grant awards, paid $5,138,000 in salaries and wages, made direct payments to individuals of $77,235,000 including $64,133,000 in retirement and disability payments, awarded $1,058,000 in procurement contracts and spent $353,000 in other expenditures or obligations. The federal government also provided $3,439,000 in direct loans and $163,824,000 in guaranteed loans and insurance.

COMMUNICATION

Newspapers–Daily: The Orange Leader, ave. eve. circ. 11,332. Weekly: Opportunity Valley News (Orange) and The Vidor Vidorian. Radio: KOGT-AM, KZOM-FM (Orange) and KIOC-FM Stereo (Vidor). Cable TV. Telephone companies: Southwestern Bell. **TRANSPORTATION** Total public road mileage: 763. In 1982 there were 73,945 registered vehicles and 2,253 reported traffic accidents including 25 fatalities. Taxi cabs: one company in the city of Orange and one in Vidor. Intercity bus service is available. Motor freight: 18 local and intrastate carriers. Rail: The Sunset limited provides passenger service on the Amtrak route. Five main lines and one branch carry freight through the county. Four of the main lines carry annually 20 to 30 million tons of freight each and one carries 10 to 20 million. The branch carries annually less than one million tons of freight. Aircraft: 50 are registered in the county. Airports: Orange County Airport at Orange serves as a base for 25 aircraft and is a basic transportation airport with general aviation service. Livingston Sea Plane Base at Orange. Waterborne commerce: Port traffic in Orange in 1981 totaled 484,942 short tons: five short tons in foreign imports, 33,602 short tons in foreign exports and 451,335 short tons in domestic products.

COMMUNITY SERVICES

EDUCATION Five school districts with 16 elementary, seven middle, six high schools and one special education. The average daily attendance in 1981-82 was 17,607, with expenditures per pupil of $2,827 including 1,109 classroom teachers with an average annual salary of $19,226. Forty-nine percent of the 1,345 high school graduates planned to attend college. In 1982-83, 87% of the students were White, 2% Hispanic, 10.1% Black, 1% Asian and 0.1% American Indian. Private schools: 311 students enrolled in three elementary schools. Lamar University at Orange was established in 1971 and is under state control. **PUBLIC LIBRARIES** Orange Public Library: 66,885 volumes. Vidor Public Library: 21,000 volumes. **CHILD CARE** 111 day care and 23 twenty-four hour care licensed facilities. **HEALTH CARE** 45 physicians and 29 dentists. Hospitals: one with a capacity of 205. Clinics: one for treatment of alcohol abuse and one public health clinic. Ambulance services: one commercial and one county service. Mental Health: one clinic and one center with a capacity of 40. Nursing homes: six nursing homes with a combined capacity of 597 nursing care residents. The average cost per day for private patients in 1982 was $27.27. **CHURCHES** 91 churches have an estimated combined membership of 53,480. The largest denominations are Southern Baptist, Catholic and

United Methodist. **SOCIAL SERVICES** In fiscal year 1983 a total of $3,783,080 in food stamps was distributed, with an average of 7,262 persons receiving food stamps each month. Aid to Families with Dependent Children (AFDC) totaled $763,730, with an average of 512 families receiving AFDC each month. Medical assistance benefits for the aged and disabled of $4,640,327 and for families and children of $1,271,240 brought the county benefit total to $10,458,376. **FIRE PROTECTION** One paid and eight volunteer fire departments. **LAW ENFORCEMENT** The County Sheriff has 48 commissioned officers. Seven police departments have a combined force of 545. **CRIME** 515 violent crimes (murder, forcible rape, robbery and aggravated assault) and 4,154 nonviolent crimes (burglary, larceny-theft and motor vehicle theft) were reported in 1982. **JUDICIAL SYSTEM** Three District Courts and Judges, two County Courts and Judges and four Justices of the Peace. In the District Courts a total of 2,268 cases were pending on 1/1/82, 2,258 new cases were filed and 2,495 cases were disposed of during the year leaving 2,031 cases pending on 12/31/82. There were 862 criminal cases on the docket, 183 convictions, 65 persons committed to prison, four committed to jail and 479 cases left pending. In the County Courts 3,903 cases were pending on 1/1/82, 3,262 new cases were filed and 2,304 cases were disposed of during the year leaving 4,861 cases pending on 12/31/82. There were 5,686 criminal cases on the docket, 521 convictions, 177 persons committed to jail and 4,148 cases left pending. **JAILS** One jail, capacity 44 The jail is under renovation as certification was lost in 1983 due to overcrowding. **ATTORNEYS AT LAW** 58. **UTILITIES** 67% of the residents are connected to a public or privately owned water system and 58% are connected to a public sewer system. Natural gas is distributed to the county by Entex, Inc. The average annual residential bill for natural gas in 1982 for the Entex distribution system was $390.31, an increase of 26% over 1981. Electricity is distributed to the county by Jasper and Newton Electric Coop., Inc., Gulf States Utilities Co., Texas Power and Light Co. and Southwestern Electric Service and is generated primarily by gas, coal and oil. The typical residential electric bill is $198.32 per month for an all-electric house using 2,500 kwh. **TAXES** The county has 22 units with taxing authority: five school districts, seven cities, one county and nine special districts.

RECREATION/ENTERTAINMENT
FEDERAL Big Thicket National Preserve (See Hardin County). **NATIONAL REGISTER OF HISTORIC PLACES** Orange: Lutcher Memorial Church Building, W.H. Stark House and Sims House. **COUNTY/MUNICIPAL PARKS** 573 acres in two county and 19 municipal parks. These parks contain seven miles of hiking trails, 14 playgrounds, two football and soccer fields, 10 baseball and softball fields, nine tennis courts, one swimming pool and two boat ramps. Developed campsites: nine. **BOATING/FISHING** Lakes/reservoirs: Dupont Plant (552 acres), Smiths (100 acres) and Tailings Pond (300 acres). Major rivers: Neches and Sabine. Primary streams: Adams Bayou and Caney. Saltwater fishing: speckled trout, redfish and flounder fishing is usually good where the county borders Sabine Lake. Shrimp, oysters and crabs may be taken but, like other saltwater fish, under specific regulations. **HUNTING** Fall and winter seasons on deer. Summer, fall and winter seasons on squirrel. Winter seasons on quail, muskrat, beaver, otter, opossum, mink, ring-tailed cat, badger, fox, raccoon, skunk and civet cat. No closed season on nutria, coyote and bobcat. In 1983 duck, coot, geese, woodcock and jacksnipe seasons occurred during the winter months. Teal duck, rail and gallinule seasons occurred in the fall. Mourning dove seasons occurred intermittently during the fall and winter months. **MUSEUMS** Orange: Heritage House of Orange County, Stark Museum of Art and Farmer's Mercantile. **THEATERS** Orange: Community Playhouse, Community Players and Lutcher Theatre for the Performing Arts. **SPECIAL EVENTS** Heritage Arts Festival, Orange, February/March; International Gumbo Cookoff, Orange, May; Star-Spangled Fourth, Orange, June.

COMMUNITIES
COUNTY SEAT Orange, County Courthouse, 77630; County Clerk's Office, 409/883-7740. **INCORPORATED COMMUNITIES** (1980 population and ZIP Code) Bridge City (7,667) 77611, Orange (23,628) 77630, Pine Forest (639) 77662, Pinehurst (3,055) 77630, Rose City (663) 77662, Vidor (12,117) 77662 and West Orange (4,610) 77630. **UNINCORPORATED COMMUNITIES** and ZIP Code) Bancroft 77630, Duncans Woods 77630, Echo 77630, Kinard Estates 77630, Lakeview 77662, Little Cypress 77630, Mauriceville 77626, North Vidor 77662, Oilla 77630, Orangefield 77639, Ridgecrest 77630, Victory Gardens 77630, West Bluff 77630, Westlawn 77630 and Winfree 77630. **FOR ADDITIONAL LOCAL INFORMATION** Bridge City Chamber of Commerce, 1860 Texas Avenue, Suite C, Bridge City, 77611, 409/735-5671, Greater Orange Area Chamber of Commerce, 1012 Green Ave., Orange, 77630, 409/883-3536 and Vidor Chamber of Commerce, P. O. Box 413, Vidor, 77662, 409/769-6339.

PALO PINTO (M9)

THE LAND
West of Fort Worth on Interstate Highway 20 in the North Central Prairies Region, Palo Pinto County covers 949 square miles with the elevation ranging from 900 to 1,200 feet. In the southeast corner of the county are nearly level to undulating soils with light colored, sandy surfaces over mottled, clayey subsoils. The rest of the county has undulating to hilly, light colored, loamy surfaces over very deep, reddish or mottled clayey subsoils. Palo Pinto is in the Cross Timbers and Prairies vegetation area with tall and mid grasses, live oak, post oak, junipers and mesquite. Between 11 and 20% of the land in the county is considered prime farmland. **CLIMATE** Subtropical Subhumid with mild winters and hot summers. The average annual temperature is 65 °F. Temperatures in January range from an average low of 32° to an average high of 56 °F and in July range from 73° to 97 °F. The average annual precipitation is 30 inches, with an average relative humidity of 77% at 6 A.M. and 49% at 6 P.M. The average annual snowfall is five inches. The growing season averages 225 days per year, with the last freeze in late March and the first freeze in early November. The sun shines during the year on the average 69% of the daylight hours.

THE PEOPLE
Although Palo Pinto County experienced a high growth rate between 1960 and 1970, a 17% population decline occurred between 1970 and 1980. The 1982 estimated population of 25,700, however, reflects a 7% increase in population since 1980. About 60% of the residents live in urban areas which had a 24% population loss between 1970 and 1980. The age groups with the largest reduction were birth to nine years and ages 20 to 24. The median age, which rose from 26 in 1970 to 34 in 1980, is older than average. The largest ancestry groups are persons of English descent (28%), Irish descent (24%) and German descent (13%). **REGISTERED VOTERS** As of November 2, 1982 there were 11,473 registered voters (0.2% of the state total). The 1982 general election had a 58% voter turnout, compared to a 73% turnout in the 1980 general election. In the 1982 primary 92% voted Democratic and 8% Republican, with 3,794 votes cast.

THE ECONOMY
AGRICULTURE In 1982, 78% of the land was in farms and

COUNTIES

PALO PINTO (continued)

ranches, with 7% of the farmland under cultivation. Palo Pinto ranked 208th in the state in highest agricultural receipts, with 90% from livestock and livestock products. Overgrazing, undesirable brush and weeds, water and wind erosion and difficulties in grass establishment are the current conservation problems: Primary crops: wheat, hay and oats. Primary vegetables: sweet potatoes. Primary fruits and nuts: 10th in the state for peaches. Pecans. Primary livestock and products: cattle, sheep, wool, angora goats, mohair and hogs. **BUSINESS** Total number of business establishments in the county: 564. Retail sales during the first quarter of 1984 increased 8%. In 1980, 11% of the labor force were self-employed, 14% were employed in professional or related services, 27% in manufacturing, 16% in wholesale and retail trade, 11% in agriculture, forestry, fisheries and mining, 16% were employed in other counties and there were 2,606 retired workers. The industries with the most employment: agribusiness, tourism, oil and gas extraction and the manufacture of radio and television communications equipment, women's clothing, electronic components, engineering and scientific equipment, oil field machinery, industrial machinery, plastics products, brick, structural clay and ceramic tile. The nonfarm earnings in 1981 totaled $227,489,000. The retired workers received an average monthly Social Security payment of $308. **FINANCE** On June 30, 1983, six commercial banks had total deposits of $185,856,000 and total assets of $206,225,000. On December 31, 1982 one state savings and loan association and two state branches had assets of $28,674,126. In addition there are four credit unions in the county. **HOUSING** Average value of homes in 1980: $23,400. Permits for new, privately owned housing units decreased in 1982: 16 permits were issued with a total construction cost of $775,200. Of those permits, 12 were for single family houses. Between 1970 and 1980 the number of housing units increased by 4%. Eighty-four percent of all units in the county are air-conditioned, 82% are heated by gas and 15% by electricity. **NATURAL RESOURCES** Limestone, industrial sand, oil, gas and bituminous coal. In 1982 a total of 28,547,922 thousand cubic feet of gas well gas, 119,241 barrels of condensate, 245,109 barrels of crude oil and 1,906,195 thousand cubic feet of casinghead gas were produced. Current production of other minerals and products includes brick, clay, crushed limestone, construction sand, sand and gravel, shale and ceramic tile. **TOURISM** Travel expenditures of $24,775,000 in 1982 (an increase of 11% over 1981) generated 614 jobs and $4,912,000 in payroll. Lodging: seven hotels, motels and tourist courts. **ALCOHOLIC BEVERAGES** Packaged distilled spirits, beer, ale, malt liquor and wine are legal in parts of the county. **FEDERAL EXPENDITURES** The federal government had direct expenditures or obligations of $47,666,000 in the county during fiscal year 1983, including $6,729,000 by the U.S. Department of Defense. In addition, the federal government provided $707,000 in grant awards, paid $2,207,000 in salaries and wages, made direct payments to individuals of $42,803,000 including $33,278,000 in retirement and disability payments, awarded $1,672,000 in procurement contracts and spent $277,000 in other expenditures or obligations. The federal government also provided $63,000 in direct loans and $4,572,000 in guaranteed loans and insurance.

COMMUNICATION
Newspapers–Daily: Index (Mineral Wells), ave. eve. circ. 5,102. Weekly: Mineral Wells Reporter and Palo Pinto County Star (Mineral Wells). Radio: KYXS-AM and KYXS-FM (Mineral Wells). Cable TV. Telephone companies: Southwestern Bell, United Telephone and Palo Pinto Telephone. **TRANSPORTATION** Total public road mileage: 906. In 1982 there were 26,393 registered vehicles and 838 reported traffic accidents including 13 fatalities. Intercity bus service is available. Motor freight: nine local and intrastate carriers. Rail: one main line carries annually 10 to 20 million tons of freight through the county. Aircraft: 78 are registered in the county. Airports: Mineral Wells Municipal Airport serves as a base for 56 aircraft and is a basic transportation airport with general aviation service. Possum Kingdom Airport at Possum Kingdom State Park.

COMMUNITY SERVICES
EDUCATION Six school districts with nine elementary, two middle and five high schools. The average daily attendance in 1981-82 was 4,366, with expenditures per pupil of $2,141 including 282 classroom teachers with an average annual salary of $15,595. Forty-five percent of the 296 high school graduates planned to attend college. In 1982-83, 85% of the students were White, 10% Hispanic, 4% Black and 1.4% Asian. Private schools: 35 students enrolled in one elementary and one high school. Vocational education: North Texas Farriers School (Mineral Wells). **PUBLIC LIBRARIES** Boyce Ditto Municipal Library (Mineral Wells): 35,000 volumes. **CHILD CARE** 25 day care and seven twenty-four hour care licensed facilities. **HEALTH CARE** 20 physicians and 10 dentists. Hospitals: one with a capacity of 80. Clinics: one for treatment of alcohol and drug abuse. Ambulance services: two city services, one fire department and one volunteer service. Mental health: one county clinic. Nursing homes: three nursing homes with a combined capacity of 280 nursing care residents. The average cost per day for private patients in 1982 was $34.56. **CHURCHES** 66 churches have an estimated combined membership of 15,524. The largest denominations are Southern Baptist, Catholic and United Methodist. **SOCIAL SERVICES** In fiscal year 1983 a total of $1,051,465 in food stamps was distributed, with an average of 2,198 persons receiving food stamps each month. Aid to Families with Dependent Children (AFDC) totaled $173,095 with an average of 119 families receiving AFDC each month. Medical assistance benefits for the aged and disabled of $2,268,181 and for families and children of $360,332 brought the county benefit total to $3,853,073. **FIRE PROTECTION** 10 volunteer fire departments. **LAW ENFORCEMENT** The County Sheriff has 39 commissioned officers. One police department has a force of 27. **CRIME** 47 violent crimes (murder, forcible rape, robbery and aggravated assault) and 1,078 nonviolent crimes (burglary, larceny-theft and motor vehicle theft) were reported in 1982. **JUDICIAL SYSTEM** One District Court and Judge, one County Court and Judge and seven Justices of the Peace. In the District Court a total of 975 cases were pending on 1/1/82, 914 new cases were filed and 797 cases were disposed of during the year leaving 1,092 cases pending on 12/31/82. There were 140 criminal cases on the docket, 79 convictions, 20 persons committed to prison and 25 cases left pending. In the County Court 1,134 cases were pending on 1/1/82, 1,659 new cases were filed and 1,682 cases were disposed of during the year leaving 1,111 cases pending on 12/31/82. There were 2,467 criminal cases on the docket, 510 convictions, 12 persons committed to jail and 936 cases left pending. **JAILS** One jail, capacity 29. Major renovation completed, now planning further construction. Lost certification in 1983 due to overcrowding. **ATTORNEYS AT LAW** 20. **UTILITIES** 84% of the residents are connected to a public or privately owned water system and 65% are connected to a public sewer system. Natural gas is distributed to the county by Lone Star Gas Co., Division of Enserch and Brazos River Gas Co. The average annual residential bill for natural gas in 1982 for the Lone Star distribution system was $405.91, an increase of 35% over 1981. Electricity is distributed to the county by Erath Co. Electric Coop., Inc. and Tri Co. Electric Coop., Inc. and is generated primarily by water. The typical residential electric bill is $119.09 per month

for an all-electric house using 2,500 kwh. **TAXES** The county has 16 units with taxing authority: six school districts, five cities, one county, one hospital district and three special districts.

RECREATION/ENTERTAINMENT

NATIONAL REGISTER OF HISTORIC PLACES Mineral Wells: Baker Hotel and First Presbyterian Church. Palo Pinto: Palo Pinto County Jail. **STATE** Possum Kingdom State Recreation Area covers 1,529 acres with camping and trailer sites, fishing, swimming, boat ramps and rental boats. Texas Longhorns graze in the area. **MUNICIPAL PARKS** 575 acres in four municipal parks. These parks contain three playgrounds, three football and soccer fields, 11 baseball and softball fields, nine tennis courts, two multi-use courts, two swimming pools and shore-fishing facilities. **SCENIC DRIVES** The Texas Forts Trail runs through this county. This trail leads to eight of the famous frontier forts of west central Texas and an ancient presidio of the Spanish colonial period. **BOATING/FISHING** Lakes/reservoirs: James (17 acres), Le Wallen (27 acres), Long (46 acres), Mingus (61 acres), Palo Pinto (2,661 acres), Lawrence Porter (10 acres), Possum Kingdom (17,700 acres), Richards (12 acres), Tucker (51 acres) and Waddell Ranch (20 acres). Major rivers: Brazos. Primary streams: Palo Pinto, Buck, Panther, Gibson, Big Sunday, Russell and Joes. **HUNTING** Fall and winter seasons on deer. No closed season on squirrel, coyote and bobcat. Winter seasons on quail, muskrat, beaver, opossum, ring-tailed cat, badger, fox, weasel, raccoon, skunk and civet cat. Fall, winter and spring seasons on turkey. In 1983 duck, coot, geese, woodcock and jacksnipe seasons occurred during the winter months. Teal duck, rail and gallinule seasons occurred in the fall. Mourning dove seasons occurred intermittently during the fall and winter months. **MUSEUMS** Mineral Wells: Palo Pinto Museum. **SPECIAL EVENTS** Palo Pinto County Rodeo, Mineral Wells, May; Crazy Water Festival, Mineral Wells, September.

COMMUNITIES

COUNTY SEAT Palo Pinto, County Courthouse, 76702; County Clerk's Office, 817/659-3651. **INCORPORATED COMMUNITIES** (1980 population and ZIP Code) Gordon (516) 76453, Graford (495) 76045, Mineral Wells (14,468: 14,348 in Palo Pinto Co. and 120 in Parker Co.) 76067, Mingus (212) 76463 and Strawn (694) 76475. **UNINCORPORATED COMMUNITIES** (and ZIP Code) Brad 76475, Brazos 76472, Live Oak 76462, Lone Camp 76072, Metcalf Gap 76475, New Salem 76472, Oran 76045, Palo Pinto 76072, Peadenville 76067, Pickwick 76045, Pleasant Valley 76067, Possum Kingdom 76045, Progress 76067, Salesville 76067, Santo 76472 and Sturdivant 76067. **FOR ADDITIONAL LOCAL INFORMATION** Mineral Wells Chamber of Commerce, P. O. Box 1408, Mineral Wells, 76067, 817/325-2557.

PANOLA (E23)

THE LAND

Bordering Louisiana southeast of Dallas on U.S. Highways 59 and 79 in the East Texas Timberlands Region, Panola County covers 812 square miles with the elevation ranging from 200 to 500 feet. The county has moderately well to poorly drained soils with light colored, acidic, sandy to loamy surfaces over very deep, reddish subsoils. These soils are deficient in plant nutrients. Panola is in the Pineywoods vegetation area with grasslands, loblolly, shortleaf, longleaf and slash pines and hardwoods such as oak, hickory and maple. Between 31 and 40% of the land in the county is considered prime farmland. **CLIMATE** Subtropical Humid with warm summers. The average annual temperature is 65 °F. Temperatures in January range from an average low of 34 ° to an average high of 56 °F and in July range

from 71 ° to 94 °F. The average annual precipitation is 48 inches, with an average relative humidity of 86% at 6 A.M. and 58% at 6 P.M. Snowfall is rare. The growing season averages 240 days per year, with the last freeze in mid March and the first freeze in mid November. The sun shines during the year on the average 65% of the daylight hours.

THE PEOPLE

Panola County experienced a strong growth rate between 1970 and 1980, reversing the pattern of population decline from 1930 to 1970. The 1982 estimated population of 22,000 indicates that the growth is continuing at the same pace. Almost 69% of the county residents live in rural areas which experienced a high growth rate between 1970 and 1980 while urban areas grew at a slower than average rate. The age groups with the largest gains were birth to five years and ages 20 to 29. The median age which lowered from 35 in 1970 to 32 in 1980 is slightly older than average. The largest ancestry groups are persons of English descent (24%), Black (20%) and Irish descent (9%). **REGISTERED VOTERS** As of November 2, 1982 there were 11,625 registered voters (0.2% of the state total). The 1982 general election had a 44% voter turnout, compared to a 65% turnout in the 1980 general election. In the 1982 primary 99% voted Democratic and 1% Republican, with 3,996 votes cast.

THE ECONOMY

AGRICULTURE Forest production area. In 1982, 42% of the land was in farms and ranches, with 12% of the farmland under cultivation. Panola ranked 112th in the state in highest agricultural receipts, with 94% from livestock and livestock products. Overgrazing, undesirable brush and weeds and improper woodland management are the current conservation problems. Primary crops: hay, wheat, rye and sorghum. Primary vegetables: sweet potatoes and watermelons. Primary fruits and nuts: peaches and pecans. Primary livestock and products: fifth in the state for commercial broiler production, cattle, milk and hogs. **BUSINESS** Total number of business establishments in the county: 377. Retail sales during the first quarter of 1984 increased by 13%. In 1980, 10% of the labor force were self-employed, 19% were employed in professional or related services, 16% in manufacturing, 15% in wholesale and retail trade, 17% in agriculture, forestry, fisheries and mining, 27% were employed in other counties and there were 1,780 retired workers. The industries with the most employment: coal mining, oil and gas extraction, general construction, poultry and egg processing, sawmills and the manufacture of plastics products. The non-farm earnings in 1981 totaled $173,581,000. The retired workers received an average monthly Social Security payment of $302. **FINANCE** On June 30, 1983, three commercial banks had total deposits of $124,274,000 and total assets of $141,104,000. On December 31, 1982 one federal savings and loan association and two state association branches had assets of $43,610,279. **HOUSING** Average value of homes in 1980: $27,600. Permits for new, privately owned housing units decreased in 1982: 19 permits were issued with a total construction cost of $967,303. Of those permits, all were for single family houses. Between 1970 and 1980 the number of housing units increased by 41%. Seventy-five percent of all units in the county are air-conditioned, 81% are heated by gas and 15% by electricity. **NATURAL RESOURCES** Ceramic clay, lignite coal, industrial sand, oil and gas. In 1982 a total of 130,800,053 thousand cubic feet of gas well gas, 1,009,336 barrels of condensate, 615,881 barrels of crude oil and 2,411,684 thousand cubic feet of casinghead gas were produced. Current production of other minerals and products includes lignite coal. Pine and hardwood production in 1981 totaled 13,398,162 cubic feet: 11,417,813 cubic feet of pine and 1,980,349 cubic feet of hardwood. **TOURISM** Travel expenditures of

COUNTIES

PANOLA (continued)

$1,662,000 in 1982 (an increase of 16% over 1981) generated 26 jobs and $254,000 in payroll. **ALCOHOLIC BEVERAGES** Totally dry. **FEDERAL EXPENDITURES** The federal government had direct expenditures or obligations of $31,828,000 in the county during fiscal year 1983, including $1,237,000 by the U.S. Department of Defense. In addition, the federal government provided $436,000 in grant awards, paid $1,255,000 in salaries and wages, made direct payments to individuals of $29,836,000 including $22,809,000 in retirement and disability payments, awarded $17,000 in procurement contracts and spent $283,000 in other expenditures or obligations. The federal government also provided $468,000 in direct loans and $1,202,000 in guaranteed loans and insurance.

COMMUNICATION

Newspapers–Weekly: Panola Watchman (Carthage) and Panola County Post (Carthage). Radio: KGAS-AM (Carthage). Cable TV. Telephone companies: Continental Telephone, General Telephone, Southwestern Bell, Colmesneil Telephone, Eastex Telephone Coop. and Tatum Telephone. **TRANSPORTATION** Total public road mileage: 982. In 1982 there were 18,225 registered vehicles and 495 reported traffic accidents including 10 fatalities. Intercity bus service is available. Motor freight: 13 local and intrastate carriers. Rail: one branch line carries annually one to five million tons of freight through the county. Aircraft: 28 are registered in the county. Airports: Panola County Airport (Sharpe Field) at Carthage serves as a base for 11 aircraft and is a basic utility airport with general aviation service. Pedro's Airport is two miles northeast of Panola.

COMMUNITY SERVICES

EDUCATION Three school districts with five elementary, three middle and three high schools. The average daily attendance in 1981-82 was 3,419, with expenditures per pupil of $3,688 including 233 classroom teachers with an average annual salary of $16,878. Forty percent of the 246 high school graduates planned to attend college. In 1982-83, 74% of the students were White, 0.2% Hispanic and 25% Black. Panola Junior College is located in Carthage. Established in 1947 it is a vocational and two year academic college under local control. Enrollment in 1982 was 973 with in state undergraduate tuition and fees of $184 per semester. **PUBLIC LIBRARIES** Service League library (Carthage): 16,719 volumes. **CHILD CARE** 31 day care and six twenty-four hour care licensed facilities. **HEALTH CARE** Eight physicians and six dentists. Hospitals: one with a capacity of 91. Ambulance services: one hospital-based service. Mental health: one clinic. Nursing homes: two nursing homes with a combined capacity of 204 nursing care residents. The average cost per day for private patients in 1982 was $38.49. **CHURCHES** 69 churches have an estimated combined membership of 11,436. The largest denominations are Southern Baptist, United Methodist and Catholic. **SOCIAL SERVICES** In fiscal year 1983 a total of $996,217 in food stamps was distributed, with an average of 2,150 persons receiving food stamps each month. Aid to Families with Dependent Children (AFDC) totaled $237,096 with an average of 160 families receiving AFDC each month. Medical assistance benefits for the aged and disabled of $1,969,735 and for families and children of $309,635 brought the county benefit total to $3,512,682. **FIRE PROTECTION** Four volunteer fire departments. **LAW ENFORCEMENT** The County Sheriff has 12 commissioned officers. Three police departments have a combined force of 15. **CRIME** 57 violent crimes (murder, forcible rape, robbery and aggravated assault) and 440 nonviolent crimes (burglary, larceny-theft and motor vehicle theft) were reported in 1982. **JUDICIAL SYSTEM** One District Court and Judge, one County Court and Judge and four Justices of the Peace. In the District Court a total of 1,481 cases were pending on 1/1/82, 696 new cases were filed and 445 cases were disposed of during the year leaving 1,732 cases pending on 12/31/82. There were 191 criminal cases on the docket, 57 convictions, 14 persons committed to prison, two committed to jail and 131 cases left pending. In the County Court 131 cases were pending on 1/1/82, 440 new cases were filed and 360 cases were disposed of during the year leaving 211 cases pending on 12/31/82. There were 503 criminal cases on the docket, 98 convictions, 10 persons committed to jail and 171 cases left pending. **JAILS** One jail, capacity 12. **ATTORNEYS AT LAW** 21. **UTILITIES** 65% of the residents are connected to a public or privately owned water system and 36% are connected to a public sewer system. Natural gas is distributed to the county by Entex, Inc. and Arkla, Inc. The average annual residential bill for natural gas in 1982 for the Entex distribution system was $390.31, an increase of 26% over 1981 and for Arkla it was $316.69, an increase of 23%. Electricity is distributed to the county by Southwestern Electric Power Co., Rusk Co. Electric Coop., Inc., Deep East Texas Electric Coop., Inc. and Panola and Harrison Electric Coop., Inc. and is generated primarily by gas and coal. The typical residential electric bill is $152.08 per month for an all-electric house using 2,500 kwh. **TAXES** The county has eight units with taxing authority: four school districts, two cities, one county and one college district.

RECREATION/ENTERTAINMENT

NATIONAL REGISTER OF HISTORIC PLACES Carthage: Panola County Jail. Carthage vicinity: Methodist Church. Deadwood vicinity: International Boundary Marker. **COUNTY/MUNICIPAL PARKS** 112 acres in six county and four municipal parks. These parks contain one mile of hiking trails, three playgrounds, five baseball and softball fields, one tennis court, one multi-use court, one swimming pool, two beaches, six boat ramps and shore fishing facilities. Developed campsites: 44. **BOATING/FISHING** Lakes/reservoirs: Dixie (109 acres), Moore (29 acres) and Murvaul (3,820 acres). Major rivers: Sabine. Primary streams: Little Sixmile, Hooker, Murvaul Bayou and Socagee. **HUNTING** Fall and winter seasons on deer. No closed season on nutria, bobcat and coyote. Summer, fall and winter seasons on squirrel. Winter seasons on quail, muskrat, beaver, otter, opossum, mink, ring-tailed cat, badger, fox, raccoon, skunk and civet cat. In 1983 duck, coot, geese, woodcock and jacksnipe seasons occurred during the winter months. Teal duck, rail and gallinule seasons occurred in the fall. Mourning dove seasons occurred intermittemtly during the fall and winter months. **THEATERS** Carthage: O.M. Martin Auditorium. **COLLEGIATE FINE ARTS** Cultural events offered by Panola Junior College. **SPECIAL EVENTS** Junior Rodeo, Carthage, May; Western Week, Carthage, July; Potlatch Festival, Carthage, October.

COMMUNITIES

COUNTY SEAT Carthage, County Courthouse, 75633; County Clerk's Office, 214/693-3382. **INCORPORATED COMMUNITIES** (1980 population and ZIP Code) Beckville (945) 75631, Carthage (6,447) 75633, Gary (Gary City) (322) 75643 and Tatum (1,339: 275 in Panola Co. and 1,064 in Rusk Co.) 75691. **UNINCORPORATED COMMUNITIES** (and ZIP Code) Bethany 71007 Buncomb 75633, Center Point 75691, Clayton 75637, Daniels 75633, Deadwood 75633, DeBerry 75639, Delray 75633, Dotson 75669, East Side 75639, Fair Play 75631, Front 75639, Gallaway 71049, Grand Bluff 75631, Halls Store 71007, Holland Quarters 75633, Horton 75639, Logan 71049, Long Branch 75699, McCoy 75643, Mount Calvary 75633, Midyett 75639, Panola (Latex) 75685, Pleasant Ridge 75633, Rehobeth

75633, Riderville 75633, River Hill 75633, Snap 75633 Tacoma 75633, Walnut Grove 75633 and Woods 75974 **FOR ADDITIONAL LOCAL INFORMATION** Panola Co. Chamber of Commerce, P. O. Box 207, Carthage, 75633, 214/693-6634.

PARKER (M10)

THE LAND
West of Fort Worth on Interstate Highway 20 in the Cross Timbers Region, Parker County covers 902 square miles with the elevation ranging from 700 to 1,200 feet. In the eastern part of the county are light colored, well drained soils and very dark, loamy soils with an accumulation of lime. The rest of the county has light colored, loamy or sandy surfaces over deep reddish or mottled subsoils. All the soils are undulating to hilly. Parker is in the Cross Timbers and Prairies vegetation area with tall grasses, mesquite, oak, pecan and elm trees are along streams. Between 21 and 30% of the land in the county is considered prime farmland. **CLIMATE** Subtropical Subhumid with warm summers. The average annual temperature is 64 °F. Temperatures in January range from an average low of 29° to an average high of 53 °F and in July range from 72° to 97 °F. The average annual precipitation is 29 inches, with an average relative humidity of 78% at 6 A.M. and 50% at 6 P.M. The average annual snowfall is four inches. The growing season averages 225 days per year, with the last freeze in late March and the first freeze in early November. The sun shines during the year on the average 68% of the daylight hours.

THE PEOPLE
Between 1960 and 1980 Parker County's population grew faster than in the previous 30 years. However, the growth rate lowered from 48% between 1960 and 1970 to 32% between 1970 and 1980. The 1982 estimated population of 47,900 indicates a continuation of that strong growth. Almost 70% of the residents live in rural areas which experienced strong growth between 1970 and 1980, while urban areas had a population decline. The age groups with the largest gains between 1970 and 1980 were ages 30 to 39 and 62 and over. Therefore, the median age rose from 28 in 1970 to 32 in 1980. The largest ancestry groups are persons of English descent (32%), Irish descent (26%) and German descent (17%). **REGISTERED VOTERS** As of November 2, 1982 there were 20,616 registered voters (0.3% of the state total). The 1982 general election had a 59% voter turnout, compared to a 77% turnout in the 1980 general election. In the 1982 primary 85% voted Democratic and 15% Republican, with 5,838 votes cast.

THE ECONOMY
AGRICULTURE Dairy Area. In 1982, 74% of the land was in farms and ranches, with 12% of the farmland under cultivation and 6% irrigated. Parker ranked 88th in the state in highest agricultural receipts, with 74% from livestock and livestock products. Overgrazing, undesirable brush and weeds, water and wind erosion are the current conservation problems. Primary crops: hay, oats, wheat, peanuts and sorghum. Primary vegetables: watermelons. Primary fruits and nuts: second in the state for peaches and a leader in pears. Pecans. Primary livestock and products: cattle, milk and hogs. **BUSINESS** Total number of business establishments in the county: 651. Retail sales during the first quarter of 1984 increased by 26%. In 1980, 12% of the labor force were self-employed, 15% were employed in professional or related services, 23% in manufacturing, 20% in wholesale and retail trade, 12% in construction, 52% were employed in other counties and there were 3,403 retired workers. The industries with the most employment: oil and gas field services, limestone quarrying, general construction and the

manufacture of rubber products and oil field machinery. The nonfarm earnings in 1981 totaled $391,757,000. The retired workers received an average monthly Social Security payment of $310. **FINANCE** On June 30, 1983, five commercial banks had total deposits of $219,568,000 and total assets of $243,537,000. On December 31, 1982 one state savings and loan association and four state branches had assets of $109,616,857. In addition there is one credit union in the county. **HOUSING** Average value of homes in 1980: $37,200. Permits for new, privately owned housing units increased in 1982: 83 permits were issued with a total construction cost of $2,853,818. Of those permits, 61 were for single family houses. Between 1970 and 1980 the number of housing units increased by 51%. Eight-three percent of all units in the county are air-conditioned, 71% are heated by gas and 25% by electricity. **NATURAL RESOURCES** Limestone, sand and gravel, oil, gas and bituminous coal. In 1982 a total of 32,600,897 thousand cubic feet of gas well gas, 74,394 barrels of condensate, 65,233 barrels of crude oil and 306,809 thousand cubic feet of casinghead gas were produced. Current production of other minerals and products includes brick, miscellaneous clay, crushed limestone, sand, gravel and shale. **TOURISM** Travel expenditures of $13,323,000 in 1982 (an increase of 17% over 1981) generated 222 jobs and $2,195,000 in payroll. **ALCOHOLIC BEVERAGES** Totally dry. **FEDERAL EXPENDITURES** The federal government had direct expenditures or obligations of $63,085,000 in the county during fiscal year 1983, including $8,804,000 by the U.S. Department of Defense. In addition, the federal government provided $779,000 in grant awards, paid $2,690,000 in salaries and wages, made direct payments to individuals of $59,166,000 including $47,320 in retirement and disability payments, awarded $208,000 in procurement contracts and spent $241,000 in other expenditures or obligations. The federal government also provided $31,000 in direct loans and $10,194,000 in guaranteed loans and insurance.

COMMUNICATION
Newspapers–Daily: The Weatherford Democrat, ave. eve. circ. 5,836. Weekly: Azle News Advertiser, Springtown Edigraph and the Parker County News (Weatherford). Radio: KZEE-AM, (Weatherford). Cable TV. Telephone companies: Continental Telephone, General Telephone, Southwestern Bell, United Telephone, Palo Pinto Telephone and Texas-Midland Telephone. **TRANSPORTATION** Total public road mileage: 1,583. In 1982 there were 40,608 registered vehicles and 1,129 reported traffic accidents including 35 fatalities. Intercity bus service is available. Motor freight: 15 local and intrastate carriers. Rail: two main lines carry annually 10 to 20 million tons of freight each through the county. Aircraft: 82 are registered in the county. Airports: Parker County Airport at Weatherford serves as a base for 64 aircraft and is a basic utility airport with general aviation service. Horseshoe Bend Airport at Weatherford.

COMMUNITY SERVICES
EDUCATION Eight school districts with 13 elementary, four middle, and seven high schools. The average daily attendance in 1981-82 was 7,767, with expenditures per pupil of $2,266 including 503 classroom teachers with an average annual salary of $15,834. Thirty-seven percent of the 521 high school graduates planned to attend college. In 1982-83, 95% of the students were White, 3% Hispanic, 1% Black, 0.5% Asian and 0.2% American Indian. Sports championships: 1983 AAA Girls' Tennis Singles, Springtown H.S. Private schools: 74 students enrolled in one elementary school. Weatherford Colledge is located in Weatherford. Established in 1869 it is a vocational and two year academic college under local control. Enrollment in 1982 was 1,596 with in state undergraduate tuition and fees of $208 per semester. **PUBLIC LIBRARIES** Weatherford Public Library: 34,316

PARKER (continued)

volumes. **CHILD CARE** 39 day care and 13 twenty-four hour care licensed facilities. **HEALTH CARE** 25 physicians and 11 dentists. Hospitals: one with a capacity of 97. Ambulance services: one air, one commerical and one fire department service. Mental health: one clinic and one county clinic. Nursing homes: four nursing homes with a combined capacity of 373 nursing care residents. The average cost per day for private patients in 1982 was $32.79. **CHURCHES** 91 churches have an estimated combined membership of 23,491. The largest denominations are Southern Baptist, United Methodist and Churches of Christ. **SOCIAL SERVICES** In fiscal year 1983 a total of $898,715 in food stamps was distributed, with an average of 1,904 persons receiving food stamps each month. Aid to Families with Dependent Children (AFDC) totaled $172,126 with an average of 118 families receiving AFDC each month. Medical assistance benefits for the aged and disabled of $2,510,137 and for families and children of $327,898 brought the county benefit total to $3,908,875. **FIRE PROTECTION** One partly paid and 17 volunteer fire departments. **LAW ENFORCEMENT** The County Sheriff has 32 commissioned officers. 14 police departments have a combined force of 85. **CRIME** 144 violent crimes (murder, forcible rape, robbery and aggravated assault) and 1,543 nonviolent crimes (burglary, larceny-theft and motor vehicle theft) were reported in 1982. **JUDICIAL SYSTEM** One District Court and Judge, one County Court and Judge and three Justices of the Peace. In the District Court a total of 784 cases were pending on 1/1/82, 1,526 new cases were filed and 1,548 cases were disposed of during the year leaving 762 cases pending on 12/31/82. There were 250 criminal cases on the docket, 77 convictions, 40 persons committed to prison, two committed to jail and 108 cases left pending. In the County Court 1,655 cases were pending on 1/1/82, 1,101 new cases were filed and 1,710 cases were disposed of during the year leaving 1,046 cases pending on 12/31/82. There were 2,298 criminal cases on the docket, 401 convictions, 71 persons committed to jail and 609 cases left pending. **JAILS** One jail, capacity 25: constructing an addition to increase capacity by 20. **ATTORNEYS AT LAW** 39. **UTILITIES** 59% of the residents are connected to a public or privately owned water system and 36 are connected to a public sewer system. Natural gas is distributed to the county by Brazos River Valley Gas Co. Electricity is distributed to the city of Weatherford by the Weatherford Municipal System and to the rest of the county by Texas Electric Service Co., Johnson Co., Electric Coop. Assn., Tri Co. Electric Coop. Inc., Houston Lighting and Power Co. and Texas-New Mexico Power Co. and is generated primarily by gas and water. The typical residential electric bill is $165.24 per month for an all-electric house using 2,500 kwh. **TAXES** The county has 14 units with taxing authority: nine school districts, one city, one county, one hospital district, one college district, and one utility district.

RECREATION/ENTERTAINMENT
NATIONAL REGISTER OF HISTORIC PLACES Tin Top vicinity: Tin Top Suspension Bridge. Weatherford: Parker County Courthouse. **STATE** Lake Mineral Wells State Park covers 2,853 acres with camping and trailer sites, fishing, swimming, boat ramps, nature trails and horseback areas. **MUNICIPAL PARKS** 302 acres in nine municipal parks. These parks contain two miles of hiking trails, seven playgrounds, 11 baseball and softball fields, six tennis courts, one swimming pool, three beaches and one boat ramp. Developed campsites: 11. **SCENIC DRIVES** The Texas Lakes Trail runs through this county. This trail introduces some 30 blue-water recreational areas in a variety of settings in north central Texas. **BOATING/FISHING** Lakes/reservoirs: Acme (23 acres), Clear Fork Trinity Soil Conservation Service Lakes 23,

24 and 31 (50 acres), Meeker (55 acres), Millsap (29 acres), Mineral Wells (646 acres), Moncrief (133 acres), Montex (53 acres), Mullett (30 acres), Sunshine (40 acres) and Weatherford (1,210 acres). Major rivers: Clear Fork Trinity and Brazos. Primary streams: Grassy Bayou, Squaw, Willow, Burgess, Rufe Evans Hollow, Willson, Rock, Turkey and Town. **HUNTING** Fall and winter seasons on deer. No closed season on squirrel, coyote and bobcat. Winter seasons on quail, muskrat, badger, opossum, ring-tailed cat, beaver, fox, weasel, raccoon, skunk and civet cat. Spring season on turkey. In 1983 duck, coot, geese, woodcock and jacksnipe seasons occurred during the winter months. Teal duck, rail and gallinule seasons occurred in the fall. Mourning dove seasons occurred intermittently during the fall and winter months. **MUSEUMS** Weatherford: H.B. Prather Museum and Texas Railroad Museum. **COLLEGIATE FINE ARTS** Weatherford: Cultural events offered by Weatherford College. **SPECIAL EVENTS** Spring Festival Tour of Homes and Parade, Weatherford, April; Frontier Days, Weatherford, July.

COMMUNITIES
COUNTY SEAT Weatherford, County Courthouse, 76086; County Clerk's Office, 817/594-7461. **INCORPORATED COMMUNITIES** (1980 population and ZIP Code) Aledo (1,027) 76008, Anneta (454) 76008, Anneta North (281) 76086, Anneta South (115) 76086, Azle (5,822: 896 in Parker Co. and 4,926 in Tarrant Co.) 76020, Briar (1,810: 349 in Parker Co., 642 in Wise Co. and 819 in Tarrant Co.) 76020, Cool (202) 76042, Hudson Oaks (309) 76025, Millsap (439) 76066, Mineral Wells (14,468: 120 in Parker Co. and 14,348 in Palo Pinto Co.) 76067, Reno (1,174) 76020, Sanctuary (250 est. incorp. inactive) 76020, Springtown (1,658) 76082, Weatherford (12,049) 76086 and Willow Park (1,113) 76086. **UNINCORPORATED COMMUNITIES** (and ZIP Code) Adell 76042, Agnes 76082, Authon 76042, Baker 76086, Bennett (Lakota) 76066, Bluff Springs 76020, Brock 76086, Brock Junction 76086, Buckner 76462, Center Point 76020, Dennis 76037, Dicey 76086, Fox 76086, Garner 76042, Greenwood 76086, Harmony 76086, Highland Addition 76082, La Junta 76020, Oak Ridge 76086, Peaster 76074, Poe Prairie 76066, Poolville 76076, Punkin Center 76086, Sabathany 76086, Soda Springs 76066, Tin Top 76086, Toto 76076, Veal Station 76082 and Whitt 76090. **FOR ADDITIONAL LOCAL INFORMATION** Azle Chamber of Commerce, P.O. Box 598, Azle, 76020, 817/444-1112 and Weatherford Chamber of Commerce, 100 Austin St., Weatherford, 76086, 817/594-3801.

PARMER (P21)

THE LAND
In the High Plains Region of the Texas Panhandle bordering New Mexico southwest of Amarillo on U.S. Highways 60 and 84, Parmer County covers 885 square miles with the elevation ranging from 3,800 to 4,100 feet. The county has light to very dark, loamy surfaces over very deep, reddish or mottled clayey subsoils. Some of the subsoils have hardened calcium deposits. Parmer is in the High Plains vegetation area with prairie grasses, some mesquite, juniper and yucca. Between 71 and 80% of the land in the county is considered prime farmland. **CLIMATE** Continental Steppe with large temperature variations on a daily basis. Thunderstorms and duststorms will be significant in the spring. The average annual temperature is 57 °F. Temperatures in January range from an average low of 19 ° to an average high of 51 °F and in July range from 63 ° to 91 °F. The average annual precipitation is 16.5 inches, with an average relative humidity of 68% at 6 A.M. and 36% at 6 P.M. The average annual snowfall is 13 inches. The growing season averages 183 days per year, with the last freeze in mid February and the first freeze in late

October. The sun shines during the year on the average 75% of the daylight hours.

THE PEOPLE

The 1982 estimated population of 11,100 indicates a continuation of the steady growth begun in the 1950s. Urban areas experienced population gains while rural areas declined slightly between 1970 and 1980. The number of residents under 18 is higher than average and the median age is 27. The largest ancestry groups are Hispanic (33%), persons of English descent (22%)and Irish descent (16%). **REGISTERED VOTERS** As of November 2, 1982 there were 4,315 registered voters (0.1% of the state total). The 1982 general election had a 56% voter turnout, compared to a 74% turnout in the 1980 general election. In the 1982 primary 93% voted Democratic and 7% Republican, with 1,404 votes cast.

THE ECONOMY

AGRICULTURE Prime farmland with diversfied products. In 1982, 98% of the land was in farms and ranches, with 84% of the farmland under cultivation and 72% irrigated. Parmer ranked third in the state in highest agricultural receipts, with 54% from crops. Wind erosion, moisture conservation, soil compaction and noxious weeds are the current conservation problems. Primary crops: fifth in the state for wheat, second for corn, eighth for soybeans, seventh for sunflowers and first for barley. Cotton and sorghum. Primary vegetables: 10th in the state for cabbage. Potatoes, lettuce, cucumbers and onions. Primary fruits and nuts: pecans. Primary livestock and products: second in the state for fed cattle marketings and fourth for cattle. Milk, sheep, wool and hogs. **BUSINESS** Total number of business establishments in the county: 200. Retail sales during the first quarter of 1984 increased by 15%. In 1980, 22% of the labor force were self-employed, 16% were employed in professional or related services, 11% in manufacturing, 18% in wholesale and retail trade, 35% in agriculture, forestry, fisheries and mining, 10% were employed in other counties and there were 638 retired workers. The industries with the most employment: meat packing and agribusiness. The nonfarm earnings in 1981 totaled $77,324,000. The retired workers received an average monthly Social Security payment of $334. **FINANCE** On June 30, 1983, three commercial banks had total deposits of $86,623,000 and total assets of $100,447,000. There are two state savings and loan association branches and two credit unions in the county. **HOUSING** Average value of homes in 1980: $26,900. Between 1970 and 1980 the number of housing units increased by 8%. Seven-six percent of all units in the county are air-conditioned, 87% are heated by gas and 12% by electricity. **NATURAL RESOURCES** Caliche, oil and gas. **TOURISM** Travel expenditures of $7,509,000 in 1982 (an increase of 19% over 1981) generated 95 jobs and $1,058,000 in payroll. **ALCOHOLIC BEVERAGES** Totally dry. **FEDERAL EXPENDITURES** The federal government had direct expenditures or obligations of $28,070,000 in the county during fiscal year 1983, including $170,000 by the U.S. Department of Defense. In addition, the federal government provided $616,000 in grant awards, paid $1,142,000 in salaries and wages, made direct payments to individuals of $8,893,000 including $6,857,000 in retirement and disability payments, awarded $92,000 in procurement contracts and spent $17,328,000 in other expenditures or obligations. The federal government also provided $40,592,000 in direct loans and $23,338,000 in guaranteed loans and insurance.

COMMUNICATION

Newspapers Weekly: Bovina Blade, The State Line Tribune (Farwell) and The Friona Star. Radio: KIJN-AM, (Farwell). Cable TV. Telephone companies: General Telephone, E.N.M.R. Telephone Coop., Five-Area Telephone Coop. and West Texas Rural Telephone Coop. **TRANSPORTATION** Total public road mileage: 1,355. In 1982 there were 11,488 registered vehicles and 166 reported traffic accidents including four fatalities. Intercity bus service is available. Motor freight: seven local and intrastate carriers. Rail: three main lines carry freight through the county. Two of the main lines carry annually over 30 million tons of freight each and one carries 20 to 30 million tons. Aircraft: 59 are registered in the county. Airports: Benger Airpark at Friona serves as a base for 23 aircraft and is a basic utility airport with general aviation services.

COMMUNITY SERVICES

EDUCATION Four school districts with five elementary, three middle and four high schools. The average daily attendance in 1981-82 was 2,369, with expenditures per pupil of $2,977 including 177 classroom teachers with an average annual salary of $15,722. Sixty-eight percent of the 151 high school graduates planned to attend college. in 1982-83, 50% of the students were White, 48% Hispanic, 2% Black and 0.1% Asian. **PUBLIC LIBRARIES** Friona Public Library: 12,827 volumes. **CHILD CARE** 13 day care and six twenty-four hour care licensed facilities. **HEALTH CARE** Three physicians and one dentist. Hospitals: one with a capacity of 34. Ambulance services: three volunteer services. Nursing homes: two nursing homes with a combined capacity of 160 nursing care residents. The average cost per day for private patients in 1982 was $28.51. **CHURCHES** 27 churches have an estimated combined membership of 9,473. The largest denominations are Southern Baptist, United Methodist and Catholic. **SOCIAL SERVICES** In fiscal year 1983 a total of $363,176 in food stamps was distributed, with an average of 806 persons receiving food stamps each month. Aid to Families with Dependent Children (AFDC) totaled $64,348 with an average of 41 families receiving AFDC each month. Medical assistance benefits for the aged and disabled of $527,897 and for families and children of $56,749 brought the county benefit total to $1,012,170. **FIRE PROTECTION** Four volunteer fire departments. **LAW ENFORCEMENT** The County Sheriff has six commissioned officers. Four police departments have a combined force of 18. **CRIME** 17 violent crimes (murder, forcible rape, robbery and aggravated assault) and 255 nonviolent crimes (burglary, larceny-theft and motor vehicle theft) were reported in 1982. **JUDICIAL SYSTEM** One District Court and Judge, one County Court and Judge and three Justices of the Peace. In the District Court a total of 311 cases were pending on 1/1/82, 287 new cases were filed and 312 cases were disposed of during the year leaving 286 cases pending on 12/31/82. There were 111 criminal cases on the docket, 28 convictions, two persons committed to prison, one committed to jail and 61 cases left pending. In the County Court 322 cases were pending on 1/1/82, 203 new cases were filed and 212 cases were disposed of during the year leaving 313 cases pending on 12/31/82. There were 394 criminal cases on the docket, 98 convictions, 12 persons committed to jail and 232 cases left pending. **JAILS** One jail, capacity 21. **ATTORNEYS AT LAW** five. **UTILITIES** 66% of the residents are connected to a public or privately owned water system and 64% are connected to a public sewer system. Natural gas is distributed to the county by Energas Company and Southern Union Company. The average annual residential bill for natural gas in 1982 for the Energas distribution system was $371.63, an increase of 23% over 1981 and for Southern Union it was $355.85, an increase of 23%. Electricity is distributed to the county by Southwestern Public Service, Bailey Co., Electric Coop. Inc., and Deaf Smith Electric Coop., Inc. and is generated primarily by gas and water. The typical residential electric bill is $170.44 per month for an all-electric house using 2,500 kwh. **TAXES** The county has 10 units with taxing authority: four school districts, three cities, one county, one hospital district, and one special district.

COUNTIES

RECREATION/ENTERTAINMENT

MUNICIPAL PARKS 20 acres in eight municipal parks. These parks contain one mile of hiking trails, six playgrounds, three baseball and softball fields and one swimming pool. **BOATING/FISHING** Lakes/reservoirs: Frye (72 acres), Mustang Lake Soil Conservation Service Lake 2 (64 acres) and Running-water Draw Soil Conservation Service Lake 3 (453 acres). **HUNT-ING** Summer, fall and winter seasons on squirrel. Winter seasons on pheasant, quail, muskrat, beaver, opossum, ring-tailed cat, badger, fox, weasel, raccoon, skunk and civet cat. No closed season on bobcat and coyote. In 1983 sandhill crane, duck, coot, geese, woodcock and jacksnipe seasons occurred during the winter months. Teal duck, rail and gallinule seasons occurred in the fall. Mourning dove seasons occurred intermittently during the fall and winter seasons. **SPECIAL EVENTS** July 4th Celebration, Friona, July; Border Town Days, Farwell, July; Maize Days, Friona, September.

COMMUNITIES

COUNTY SEAT Farwell, County Courthouse, 79325; County Clerk's Office, 806/481-3691. **INCORPORATED COMMUNI-TIES** (1980 population and ZIP Code) Bovina (1,499) 79009, Farwell (1,354) 79325 and Friona (3,809) 79035. **UNINCOR-PORATED COMMUNITIES** (and ZIP Code) Black 79004, Hub 79035, Lariat 79335, Lazbuddie 79053, Oklahoma Lane 79325 and Rhea 79035. **FOR ADDITIONAL LOCAL INFORMA-TION** Farwell Chamber of Commerce, P.O. Box 117, Farwell, 79325, 806/481-9456 and Friona Chamber of Commerce, 621 Main, Friona, 79035, 806/247-3491.

PECOS (P93)

THE LAND

South of Odessa on Interstate Highway 10 in the Trans-Pecos Region, Pecos County covers 4,776 square miles with the elevation ranging from 2,500 to 4,000 feet. The undulating to hilly soils to the south and east are dark and loamy over limestone with approximately 90% of the area exposed rock. The desertic soils of the north and west are alkaline, loamy and have some clayey subsoils over limestone bedrock. In the Trans-Pecos, Mountains and Basins vegetation area, the grasses are short and sparse with desert shrubs and cacti. To the southeast the vegetation is the slightly taller grasses, desert shrub and scrubby live oaks of the Edwards Plateau. Less than 1% of the land in the county is considered prime farmland. **CLIMATE** Subtropical Arid and affected by mountains resulting in wide ranging temperatures on a daily basis. The average annual temperature is 65°F. Temperatures in January range from an average low of 31° to an average high of 61°F and in July range from 69° to 96°F. The average annual precipitation is 13 inches, with an average relative humidity of 72% at 6 A.M. and 34% at 6 P.M. The average annual snowfall is three inches. The growing season averages 225 days per year, with the last freeze in late March and the first freeze in mid November. The sun shines during the year on the average 75% of the daylight hours.

THE PEOPLE

Pecos County ranks 39th among all U.S. counties in the highest percent of residents of Spanish origin. Since 1930 it has experienced steady increases in population with the most sizeable gains occurring between 1950 and 1970. The 1982 estimated population of 16,900 indicates a 15% increase since 1980. Rural areas grew faster than urban areas between 1970 and 1980. The median age of 25 indicates that the county's population is younger than average. The largest ancestry groups are Hispanic (49%), persons of English descent (19%) and Irish descent (13%). **REGISTERED VOTERS** As of November 2, 1982 there were 7,608 registered voters (0.1% of the state total). The 1982 general election had a 40% voter turnout, compared to a 59% turnout in the 1980 general election. In the 1982 primary 99% voted Democratic and 1% Republican, with 3,184 votes cast.

THE ECONOMY

AGRICULTURE Sheep ranches. In 1982, 86% of the land was in farms and ranches, with 1% of the farmland under cultivation. Most of the cropland and some of the rangeland was irrigated. Pecos ranked 136th in the state in highest agricultural receipts, with 57% from livestock and livestock products. Overgrazing, undesirable brush and weeds and inefficient irrigation systems are the current conservation problems. Primary crops: cotton, hay and wheat. Primary vegetables: third in the state for cantaloupes and ninth for carrots. Bell peppers and onions. Primary fruits and nuts: peaches and ninth in the state for pecans. Primary livestock and products: eighth in the state for sheep and ninth for wool production. Cattle, angora goats, mohair and hogs. **BUSINESS** Total number of business establishments in the county: 415. Retail sales during the first quarter of 1984 decreased 6%. In 1980, 9% of the labor force were self-employed, 15% were employed in professional or related services, 5% in manufacturing, 21% in wholesale and retail trade, 27% in agriculture, forestry, fisheries and mining, 6% were employed in other counties and there were 729 retired workers. The industries with the most employment: sulfur mining, agribusiness and oil and gas extraction. The nonfarm earnings in 1981 totaled $145,124,000. The retired workers received an average monthly Social Security payment of $313. **FINANCE** On June 30, 1983, three commercial banks had total deposits of $103,584,000 and total assets of $116,172,000. On December 31, 1982 one state savings and loan association had assets of $57,175,536. In addition there is one credit union in the county. **HOUSING** Average value of homes in 1980: $26,100. Permits for new, privately owned housing units increased in 1982: 31 permits were issued with a total construction cost of $1,038,314. Of those permits, all were for single family houses. Housing permits in Fort Stockton increased from 18 in 1981 to 31 in 1982. Between 1970 and 1980 the number of housing units increased by 17%. Eighty percent of all units in the county are air-conditioned, 87% are heated by gas and 12% by electricity. **NATURAL RESOURCES** Limestone, salt, sand and gravel, oil and gas. In 1982 a total of 274,741,143 thousand cubic feet of gas well gas, 239,047 barrels of condensate, 50,472,709 barrels of crude oil and 24,841,474 thousand cubic feet of casinghead gas were produced. Current production of other minerals and products includes brine, crushed limestone, sand and gravel, frasch sulphur and recovered sulphur. **TOURISM** Travel expenditures of $27,052,000 in 1982 (an increase of 11% over 1981) generated 675 jobs and $5,392,000 in payroll. Lodging: seven hotels, motels and tourist courts. Convention/meeting facilities: Fort Stockton-Pecos County Exhibit Building. **ALCOHOLIC BEVERAGES** Packaged distilled spirits, beer, ale, malt liquor and wine are legal in parts of the county. Sale of mixed beverages is legal in all or parts of the county. **FEDERAL EXPENDITURES** The federal government had direct expenditures or obligations of $14,000,000 in the county during fiscal year 1983, including $284,000 by the U.S. Department of Defense. In addition, the federal government provided $362,000 in grant awards, paid $961,000 in salaries and wages, made direct payments to individuals of $10,534,000 including $8,057,000 in retirement and disability payments, awarded $63,000 in procurement contracts and spent $2,079,000 in other expenditures or obligations. The federal government also provided $593,000 in direct loans and $1,541,000 in guaranteed loans and insurance.

COMMUNICATION
Newspapers–Weekly: The Fort Stockton Pioneer and the Iraan News. Radio: KFST-AM and KPJH-FM (Fort Stockton). Cable TV. Telephone companies: Continental Telephone, Southwestern Bell and Big Bend Telephone. **TRANSPORTATION** Total public road mileage: 1,345. In 1982 there were 14,717 registered vehicles and 542 reported traffic accidents including seven fatalities. Taxi cabs: one part time company in Fort Stockton. Intercity bus service is available. Motor freight: 10 local and intrastate carriers. Rail: The Sunset Limited provides passenger service on the Amtrak Route. One branch line carries annually one to five million tons of freight through the county. Aircraft: 67 are registered in the county. Airports: Pecos County Airport at Fort Stockton serves as a base for 53 aircraft and is a basic transportation airport with general aviation service.

COMMUNITY SERVICES
EDUCATION Three school districts with seven elementary, two middle and three high schools. The average daily attendance in 1981-82 was 3,706, with expenditures per pupil of $4,438 including 286 classroom teachers with an average annual salary of $19,782. Forty percent of the 217 high school graduates planned to attend college. In 1982-83, 40% of the students were White, 60% Hispanic, 0.3% Black and 0.3% Asian. Vocational education: Fort Stockton School of Vocational Nursing Midland College Extension (Fort Stockton). **PUBLIC LIBRARIES** Fort Stockton Public Library: 45,000 volumes. Imperial Library. Iraan Public Library: 14,830 volumes. **CHILD CARE** 11 day care and five twenty-four hour care licensed facilities. **HEALTH CARE** Eight physicians and four dentists. Hospitals: two with a combined capacity of 51. Ambulance services: two volunteer fire department services and one volunteer service. Mental health: one county clinic. Nursing homes: one nursing home as a capacity of 68 nursing care residents. The average cost per day for private patients in 1982 was $35.84. **CHURCHES** 31 churches have an estimated combined membership of 10,902. The largest denominations are Catholic, Southern Baptist and United Methodist. **SOCIAL SERVICES** In fiscal year 1983 a total of $578,741 in food stamps was distributed, with an average of 1,260 persons receiving food stamps each month. Aid to Families with Dependent Children (AFDC) totaled $83,784 with an average of 51 families receiving AFDC each month. Medical assistance benefits for the aged and disabled of $783,026 and for families and children of $100,729 brought the county benefit total to $1,546,279. **FIRE PROTECTION** Four volunteer fire departments. **LAW ENFORCEMENT** The County Sheriff has 14 commissioned officers. One police department has a force of 15. **CRIME** 88 violent crimes (murder, forcible rape, robbery and aggravated assault) and 574 nonviolent crimes (burglary, larceny-theft and motor vehicle theft) were reported in 1982. **JUDICIAL SYSTEM** Two District Courts and Judges, one County Court and Judge and five Justices of the Peace. In the District Courts a total of 615 cases were pending on 1/1/82, 409 new cases were filed and 401 cases were disposed of during the year leaving 623 cases pending on 12/31/82. There were 166 criminal cases on the docket, 53 convictions, 20 persons committed to prison, one committed to jail and 64 cases left pending. In the County Court 138 cases were pending on 1/1/82, 429 new cases were filed and 326 cases were disposed of during the year leaving 241 cases pending on 12/31/82. There were 514 criminal cases on the docket, 162 convictions, 54 persons committed to jail and 204 cases left pending. **JAILS** One jail, capacity 44. **ATTORNEYS AT LAW** 10. **UTILITIES** 80% of the residents are connected to a public or privately owned water system and 74% are connected to a

public sewer system. Natural gas is distributed to the county by D.J.B. Inc. Electricity is distributed to the county by Rio Grande Electric Coop., Inc., Texas-New Mexico Power Co. and West Texas Utilities and is generated primarily by gas, oil and coal. The typical residential electric bill is $168,05 per month for an all-electric house using 2,500 kwh. **TAXES** The county has nine units with taxing authority: three school districts, one city, one county and four special districts.

RECREATION/ENTERTAINMENT
NATIONAL REGISTER OF HISTORIC PLACES Fort Stockton: Fort Stockton Historic District. Sheffield vicinity: Canon Ranch Archeological District, Live Oak Creek Archeological District, Canon Ranch Railroad Eclipse Windmill. Fort Lancaster and Live Oak Creek Archeological site. Iraan vicinity: Camp Melvin and Petroglyph Site. **COUNTY/MUNICIPAL PARKS** 257 acres in six county and five municipal parks. These parks contain nine playgrounds, two golf courses, six baseball and softball fields, four tennis courts and five swimming pools. Developed campsites: 10. **SCENIC DRIVES** The Texas Pecos Trail runs through this county. This trail rambles through the vast region of southwest and west Texas with landscapes varying from raw, arid regions to green valleys. **BOATING/FISHING** Lakes/reservoirs: Comanche Creek (76 acres), Imperial (1,530 acres) and Leon Springs (381 acres). Major rivers: Pecos. Primary streams: Comanche, Leon, Courtney and Tunis. **HUNTING** Fall season on antelope. Fall and winter seasons on deer and mule deer. No closed season on elk, javelina, coyote, bobcat and squirrel. Winter seasons on quail, muskrat, beaver, opossum, ring-tailed cat, badger, fox, weasel, raccoon, skunk and civet cat. Fall, winter and spring seasons on turkey. In 1983 sandhill crane, duck, coot, geese, woodcock and jacksnipe seasons occurred during the winter months. Teal duck, rail and gallinule seasons occurred in the fall. Mourning dove seasons occurred intermittently during the fall and winter months with a fall season on white-winged dove in some parts of the county. **MUSEUMS** Fort Stockton: Annie Riggs Memorial Museum. Iraan: Iraan Archaeological and Historical Museum. Sheffield: Fort Lancaster Visitor Center. **SPECIAL EVENTS** County Stock Show, Ft. Stockton, January; AJRA Rodeo, Ft. Stockton, February; Comanche Relays, Ft. Stockton, February; West Texas Boys' Ranch Roping, Ft. Stockton, March; Alley Oop Celebration, Iraan, June; Fiesta de San Juan, Ft. Stockton, June; Miss Pecos County Pageant, Ft. Stockton, June; Festival and Water Carnival, Ft. Stockton, July; Miss Fort Stockton Pageant, Ft. Stockton, July; Arts and Crafts Fair, Ft. Stockton, October; Christmas Parade, Ft. Stockton, December.

COMMUNITIES
COUNTY SEAT Fort Stockton, County Courthouse, 79735; County Clerk's Office, 915/336-7555. **INCORPORATED COMMUNITIES** (1980 population and ZIP Code) Fort Stockton (8,688) 79735 All-America Cities Honorable Mention 1980-1981 and Iraan (1,358) 79744. **UNINCORPORATED COMMUNITIES** (and ZIP Code) Bakersfield 79717, Coyanosa 79730, Girvin 79740, Imperial 79743, Little Mexico 79735, Longfellow 79848 and Sheffield 79781. **FOR ADDITIONAL LOCAL INFORMATION** Fort Stockton Chamber of Commerce, 222 W. Dickinson, Fort Stockton, 79735, 915/336-2264 and Iraan Chamber of Commerce, 502 W. 6th, Iraan, 79744, 915/639-2232.

POLK (E32)

THE LAND
Northeast of Houston on U.S. Highways 190 and 59 in the East Texas Timberlands Region, Polk County covers 1,061 square miles

COUNTIES

with an elevation range of 100 to 300 feet. In the north the land is gently rolling to hilly with light colored, loamy surfaces and very deep, reddish, clayey subsoils. Central to south the land is more level with acidic, sandy to loamy surfaces and very deep, reddish, loamy to clayey subsoils. Along the Trinity River the soils are dark, with loamy surfaces and cracking clayey subsoils. In the Pineywoods vegetation area, there are pine and hardwood forests. Between 31 and 40% of the land in the county is considered prime farmland. **CLIMATE** Subtropical Humid with warm summers. The average annual temperature is 67°F. Temperatures in January range from an average low of 37° to an average high of 60°F and in July range from 71° to 94°F. The average annual precipitation is 48 inches, with an average relative humidity of 81% at 6 A.M. and 51% at 6 P.M. Snow is rare. The growing season averages 250 days per year, with the last freeze mid April and the first freeze in late October. The sun shines during the year on the average 65% of the daylight hours.

THE PEOPLE

Since 1970 Polk County has experienced rapid growth. The 1982 estimated population of 26,200 indicates a continuation of that growth pattern which began in the 1960s, reversing the population decline between 1940 and 1960. The growth rose significantly to 69% between 1970 and 1980. Almost 80% of the residents live in rural areas which grew three times as fast as urban areas from 1970 to 1980. The age groups with the largest gains were ages 20 to 24 and 30 to 39, both of which doubled in size. The median age of 35 is older than average. The largest ancestry groups are persons of English descent (28%), Irish descent (23%) and Black (16%). **REGISTERED VOTERS** As of November 2, 1982 there were 14,104 registered voters (0.2% of the state total). The 1982 general election had a 43% voter turnout, compared to a 61% turnout in the 1980 general election. In the 1982 primary 98% voted Democratic and 2% Republican, with 5,353 votes cast.

THE ECONOMY

AGRICULTURE The leader in forest production. In 1982, 27% of the land was in farms and ranches, with 9% of the farmland under cultivation. Polk ranked 218th in the state in highest agricultural receipts, with 77% from livestock and livestock products. Undesirable woody vegetation, inadequate harvesting systems on the forestlands and erosion are the current conservation problems. Primary crops: hay and oats. Primary vegetables: potatoes, sweet potatoes, tomatoes and watermelons. Primary fruits and nuts: peaches and pecans. Primary livestock and products: cattle, milk and hogs. **BUSINESS** Total number of business establishments in the county: 424. Retail sales during the first quarter of 1984 increased 32%. In 1980, 13% of the labor force were self-employed, 15% were employed in professional or related services, 22% in manufacturing, 21% in wholesale and retail trade, 11% in construction, 22% were employed in other counties and there were 3,006 retired workers. The industries with the most employment: oil and gas extraction, sawmills, tourism and the manufacture of softwood veneer and plywood. The nonfarm earnings in 1981 totaled $193,171,000. The retired workers received an average monthly Social Security payment of $327. **FINANCE** On June 30, 1983, four commercial banks had total deposits of $177,235,000 and total assets of $199,398,000. On December 31, 1982 one state savings and loan association and three state branches had assets of $47,175,200. **HOUSING** Average value of homes in 1980: $27,500. Permits for new, privately owned housing units increased in 1982: 22 permits were issued with a total construction cost of $1,036,000. Of those permits, 18 were for single family houses. Housing permits in

Livingston increased from 11 in 1981 to 22 in 1982. Between 1970 and 1980 the number of housing units increased by 133%. Seventy-eight percent of all units in the county are air-conditioned, 58% are heated by gas and 34% by electricity. **NATURAL RESOURCES** Clay, industrial sand, sand and gravel, oil and gas. In 1982 a total of 17,915,547 thousand cubic feet of gas well gas, 361,220 barrels of condensate, 703,007 barrels of crude oil and 767,243 thousand cubic feet of casinghead gas were produced. Current production of other minerals includes sand and gravel. Pine and hardwood production in 1981 totaled 38,425,225 cubic feet: 33,068,452 cubic feet of pine and 5,356,773 cubic feet of hardwood. **TOURISM** Travel expenditures of $13,905,000 in 1982 (an increase of 11% over 1981) generated 352 jobs and $2,813,000 in payroll. Lodging: three hotels, motels and tourist courts. **ALCOHOLIC BEVERAGES** Packaged distilled spirits, beer, ale, malt liquor and wine are legal in parts of the county. Sale of mixed beverages is legal in all or parts of the county. **FEDERAL EXPENDITURES** The federal government had direct expenditures or obligations of $49,576,000 in the county during fiscal year 1983, including $2,925,000 by the U.S. Department of Defense. In addition, the federal government provided $1,367,000 in grant awards, paid $1,361,000 in salaries and wages, made direct payments to individuals of $44,208,000 including $36,715,000 in retirement and disability payments, awarded $2,478,000 in procurement contracts and spent $162,000 in other expenditures or obligations. The federal government also provided $567,000 in direct loans and $12,799,000 in guaranteed loans and insurance.

COMMUNICATION

Newspapers–Weekly: Corrigan Times and the Polk County Enterprise (Livingston). Radio: KETX-AM and KETX-FM (Livingston). Cable TV. Telephone companies: Continental Telephone, Southwestern Bell, Eastex Telephone Coop., Lake Telephone, Livingston Telephone and Lufkin Telephone Exchange. **TRANSPORTATION** Total public road mileage: 877. In 1982 there were 24,795 registered vehicles and 673 reported traffic accidents including 21 fatalities. Intercity bus service is available. Motor freight: four carriers. Rail: two main lines carry annually 10 to 20 million tons of freight each through the county. Aircraft: 19 are registered in the county. Airports: Livingston Municipal Airport.

COMMUNITY SERVICES

EDUCATION Six school districts with six elementary, two middle and five high schools. The average daily attendance in 1981-82 was 4,395, with expenditures per pupil of $2,325 including 265 classroom teachers with an average annual salary of $15,788. Thirty-two percent of the 269 high school graduates planned to attend college. In 1982-83, 74% of the students were White, 4% Hispanic, 20% Black, 0.1% Asian and 2% American Indian. **PUBLIC LIBRARIES** Corrigan Public Library: 12,966 volumes. Murphy Memorial Library (Livingston): 25,000 volumes. **CHILD CARE** 23 day care and 17 twenty-four hour care licensed facilities. **HEALTH CARE** 12 physicians and five dentists. Hospitals: one with a capacity of 41. Ambulance services: one commercial, one volunteer service and one funeral home service. Mental health: one county clinic. Nursing homes: two nursing homes with a combined capacity of 172 nursing care residents. The average cost per day for private patients in 1982 was $26.11. **CHURCHES** 59 churches have an estimated combined membership of 11,642. The largest denominations are Southern Baptist, Baptist Missionary and United Methodist. **SOCIAL SERVICES** In fiscal year 1983 a total of $1,494,006 in food stamps was distributed, with an average of 2,983 persons receiving food stamps each month. Aid to Families with Dependent Children (AFDC) totaled $307,703 with an average of 201 families receiving AFDC each month. Medical assistance benefits for the aged and disabled of $1,957,092 and for families and children of $400,265 brought the county benefit total to $4,159,066. **FIRE PROTECTION** Nine volunteer fire departments. **LAW ENFORCEMENT** The County Sheriff has 28 commissioned officers. Three police departments have a combined force of 23. **CRIME** 53 violent crimes (murder, forcible rape, robbery and aggravated assault) and 766 nonviolent crimes (burglary, larceny-theft and motor vehicle theft) were reported in 1982. **JUDICIAL SYSTEM** Three District Courts and Judges, one County Court and Judge and four Justices of the Peace. In the District Courts a total of 1,275 cases were pending on 1/1/82, 811 new cases were filed and 732 cases were disposed of during the year leaving 1,354 cases pending on 12/31/82. There were 364 criminal cases on the docket, 109 convictions, 21 persons committed to prison, five committed to jail and 208 cases left pending. In the County Court 936 cases were pending on 1/1/82, 988 new cases were filed and 837 cases were disposed of during the year leaving 1,087 cases pending on 12/31/82. There were 1,768 criminal cases on the docket, 294 convictions, 12 persons committed to jail and 940 cases left pending. **JAILS** One jail, capacity 37. A new jail is the in planning stage. Certification was lost in 1983 due to over-crowding. **ATTORNEYS AT LAW** 22. **UTILITIES** 80% of the residents are connected to a public or privately owned water system and 26% are connected to a public sewer system. Natural gas is distributed to the county by Entex, Inc. The average annual residential bill for natural gas in 1982 for the Entex distribution system was $390.31, an increase of 26% over 1981. Electricity is distributed to the city of Livingston by the Livingston Municipal Light Dept. and to the rest of the county by Gulf State Utilities and Texas Power and Light Co. and is generated primarily by gas, oil and coal. The typical residential electric bill is $165.24 per month for an all-electric house using 2,500 kwh. **TAXES** The county has 15 units with taxing authority: six school districts, four cities, one county, two hospital districts, one utility district and one special district.

RECREATION/ENTERTAINMENT

FEDERAL BIG THICKET NATIONAL PRESERVE (See Hardin County). **STATE** Lake Livingston State Recreation Area covers 635 acres with camping and trailer sites, fishing, swimming, boat ramps and nature trails. **MUNICIPAL PARKS** 65 acres in three municipal parks. These parks contain three playgrounds, one golf course, four baseball and softball fields, two tennis courts, and one multi-use court. **SCENIC DRIVES** The Texas Forest Trail runs through this county. This trail explores the farming, ranching and oilfield areas of the East Texas Pineywoods. **BOATING/FISHING** Lakes/reservoirs: Duke (61 acres), Gerlach (46 acres), Livingston (82,600 acres), Londa Lynn (23 acres), Tombigbee (26 acres) and Taylor (105 acres). Major rivers: Trinity and Neches. Primary streams: Menard, Sally, Tombigbee, Big Sandy, Long King, Piney and Kickapoo. **HUNTING** Fall and winter seasons on deer. Summer, fall and winter seasons on squirrel. No closed season on coyote and bobcat. Winter seasons on quail, muskrat, beaver, otter, opossum, mink, nutria, ring-tailed cat, badger, fox, raccoon, skunk and civet cat. Spring season on turkey in some parts of the county. In 1983 duck, coot, geese, woodcock and jacksnipe seasons occurred during the winter months. Teal duck, rail and gallinule seasons occurred in the fall. Mourning dove seasons occurred intermittently during the fall and winter months. **MUSEUMS** Livingston: Alabama-Coushatta Indian Museum and Polk County Memorial Museum. **THEATERS** Livingston: Outdoor dramatic productions. **SPECIAL EVENTS** Miss Indian Texas Days and Pow-Wow, Livingston, April; Indian Pow-Wow, Livingston, June; "Beyond the Sundown" Indian Drama, Livingston, June; Youth Rodeo, Livingston, July; Folklife Festival, Livingston, October.

COMMUNITIES

COUNTY SEAT Livingston, County Courthouse, 77351; County Clerk's Office, 409/327-8210. **INCORPORATED COMMUNITIES** (1980 population and ZIP Code) Corrigan (1,770) 75939, Goodrich (350) 77335, Livingston (4,928) 77351, Onalaska (386) 77360 and Seven Oaks (300) 77350. **UNINCORPORATED COMMUNITIES** (and ZIP Code) Ace 77326, Alabama and Coushatta Indian Reservation 77351, Asia 75939, Barnes 75960, Barnum 75927, Blanchard 77351, Buck 77351, Camden 75934, Camp Ruby 77351, Carmona 75939, Dallardsville (Big Sandy) 77332, East Tempe 77351, Holly Grove 77351, Leggett 77350, Lily Island 75934, Marston 77351, Moscow 75960, New Willard 77350, Ollie 77350, Palestine (Darden) 75936, Pluck 75939, Pleasant Hill 75939, Providence (Camp Providence) 77351, Rock Island 75939, Schwab City 77351, Segno 77370, Soda 77351, Snow Hill 75939, Wakefield 75939 and West Temple 77351. **FOR ADDITIONAL LOCAL INFORMATION** Polk Co. Chamber of Commerce, 516 W. Church, Livingston 77351, 409/327-4929 and Onalaska Chamber of Commerce, P.O. Box 610, Onalaska, 77360, 409/646-5000.

POTTER (P12)

THE LAND

North of Lubbock on Interstate Highway 40 in the High Plains Region, Potter County covers 902 square miles with an elevation range of 3,200 to 3,800 feet. The light to dark loamy soils have some areas with reddish, clayey subsoils and lime accumulations. In the north the vegetation is the tall to mid grasses of the Rolling Plains. In the south the vegetation is the shorter prairie grasses of the High Plains vegetation area. Between 21 and 30% of the land in the county is considered prime farmland. **CLIMATE** Continental Steppe with large temperature variations on a daily basis. Thunderstorms and duststorms will be significant during spring. The average annual temperature is 57°F. Temperatures in January range from an average low of 23° to an average high of 49°F and in July range from 65° to 92°F. The average annual precipitation is 19 inches, with an average relative humidity of 72% at 6 A.M. and 38% at 6 P.M. The average annual snowfall is 15 inches. The growing season averages 190 days per year, with the last freeze in late April and the first freeze in late October. The sun shines during the year on the average 75% of the daylight hours.

THE PEOPLE

Nearly 94% of the residents in Potter county live in urban areas. The 1982 estimated population of 103,300 indicates a continuation of the growth begun in the 1970s which reversed the 22% population decline between 1960 and 1970. Between 1970 and 1980 rural areas experienced rapid increases while gains in urban areas were moderate. The largest ancestry groups are persons of English descent (26%), Irish descent (22%) and German descent (16%). **REGISTERED VOTERS** As of November 2, 1982 there were 35,374 registered voters (0.6% of the state total). The 1982 general election had a 53% voter turnout, compared to a 71% turnout in the 1980 general election. In the 1982 primary 82% voted Democratic and 18% Republican, with 10,286 votes cast.

THE ECONOMY

AGRICULTURE Wheat area. In 1982, 91% of the land was in farms and ranches, with 10% of the farmland under cultivation and 23% irrigated. Potter ranked 233rd in the state in highest agricultural receipts, with 51% from livestock and livestock products. Undesirable brush and weeds, water and wind erosion, decreasing irrigation water supplies and a lack of potable water

POTTER (continued)

are the current conservation problems. Primary crops: wheat and sorghum. Primary vegetables: sweet potatoes. Primary livestock and products: cattle. **BUSINESS** Total number of business establishments in the county: 3,469. Retail sales during the first quarter of 1984 increased 18%. In 1980, 6% of the labor force were self-employed, 17% were employed in professional or related services, 18% in manufacturing, 26% in wholesale and retail trade, 10% in transportation, communications and other public utilities, 17% were employed in other counties and there were 9,135 retired workers. The industries with the most employment: agribusiness, oil and gas extraction, heavy construction, meat packing, soft drink bottling and canning, lumber mills, commercial printing, petroleum refining, copper refining and the manufacture of dairy products, agricultural feeds, bakery products, prepared foods, glass, concrete, power transmission equipment as well as motor vehicles, parts and equipment. The nonfarm earnings in 1981 totaled $1,122,918,000. The retired workers received an average monthly Social Security payment of $328. **FINANCE** On June 30, 1983, eight commercial banks had total deposits of $1,648,541,000 and total assets of $1,993,292,000. On December 31, 1982 one federal savings and loan association, 12 state association branches and two federal association branches had assets of $210,448,692. In addition there are 21 credit unions in the county. **HOUSING** Average value of homes in 1980: $24,400. Permits for new, privately owned housing units increased in 1982: 1,518 permits were issued with a total construction cost of $67,130,331. Of those permits, 484 were for single family houses. Housing permits in Amarillo increased from 758 in 1981 to 1,518 in 1982 with 1,001 of the permits issued for apartments and condominiums. Between 1970 and 1980 the number of housing units increased by 12%. Seventy-five percent of all units in the county are air-conditioned, 92% are heated by gas and 8% by electricity. **NATURAL RESOURCES** Caliche, gas and oil. In 1982 a total of 48,476,960 thousand cubic feet of gas well gas, 766 barrels of condensate, 396,276 barrels of crude oil and 1,867,256 thousand cubic feet of casinghead gas were produced. Current production of other minerals and products includes caliche, cement, helium, sand and gravel, and recovered sulphur. **TOURISM** Travel expenditures of $165,218,000 in 1982 (an increase of 10% over 1981) generated 4,117 jobs and $34,014,000 in payroll. Lodging: 30 hotels, motels and tourist courts. Convention/meeting facilities: Amarillo-Civic Center, Tri State Fair Arena and Exhibit Area and five hotels with facilities for large gatherings. **ALCOHOLIC BEVERAGES** Packaged distilled spirits, beer, ale, malt liquor and wine are legal in parts of the county. Sale of mixed beverages is legal in all or parts of the county. **FEDERAL EXPENDITURES** The federal government had direct expenditures or obligations of $361,457,000 in the county during fiscal year 1983, including $28,082,000 by the U.S. Department of Defense. In addition, the federal government provided $19,264,000 in grant awards, paid $48,703,000 in salaries and wages, made direct payments to individuals of $150,542,000 including $114,242,000 in retirement and disability payments, awarded $141,999,000 in procurement contracts and spent $950,000 in other expenditures or obligations. The federal government also provided $2,493,000 in direct loans and $41,098,000 in guaranteed loans and insurance.

COMMUNICATION

Newspapers–Daily: Amarillo Daily News, ave. morn. circ. 44,040 and the Amarillo Globe Times, ave. eve. circ. 29,363. Radio: KIXZ-AM, KPUR-AM, KCNC-AM, KQIZ-AM, KDJW-AM, KZIP-AM (Amarillo), KMML-FM, KBUY-FM, KQIZ-FM, KWAS-FM and KGNC-FM Stereo (Amarillo). Television: KAMR-CH. 4, KFDA-CH. 10 and KVII-CH. 7 (Amarillo). Cable TV. Telephone companies: Continental Telephone and Southwestern Bell. **TRANSPORTATION** Total public road mileage: 1,113. In 1982 there were 92,635 registered vehicles and 5,491 reported traffic accidents including 31 fatalities. Municipal transit systems: one intracity bus system in Amarillo with scheduled routes. Intercity bus service is available. Motor freight: 64 local and intrastate carriers. Rail: five main lines and two branches carry freight through the county. Four of the main lines carry annually over 30 million tons of freight each and one carries 10 to 20 million. One branch line carries annually five to 10 million tons of freight and the other one carries one to five million. Aircraft: 301 are registered in the county. Airports: Amarillo International Airport serves as a base for 45 aircraft and is a small hub for short haul flights with carrier service. Tradewind Airport at Amarillo serves as a base for 166 aircraft and is a general utility airport with general aviaton service. Palo Duro Field at Amarillo. Amarillo Heliport at Amarillo.

COMMUNITY SERVICES

EDUCATION Four school districts with 35 elementary, 10 middle, five high schools, and one special education. The average daily attendance in 1981-82 was 25,004, with expenditures per pupil of $2,684 including 1,541 classroom teachers with an average annual salary of $17,582. Sixty percent of the 1,636 high school graduates planned to attend college. In 1982-83, 75% of the students were White, 14% Hispanic, 8% Black, 4% Asian and 0.1% American Indian. Sports championships: 1983 AAAAA Boys' Tennis Doubles, Amarillo Tascosa H.S.; 1983 AAAAA Girls' Tennis Doubles, Amarillo H.S. Private schools: 1,805 students enrolled in 10 elementary and three high schools. Amarillo College is located in Amarillo. Established in 1929 it is a vocational and two year academic college under state and local control. Enrollment in 1982 was 5,409 with in state undergraduate tuition and fees of $238 per semester. Vocational education: Amarillo-Texas State Technical Institute, Amarillo College of Hair Dressing, Amarillo Trade School Inc., Metro Barber College, Northwest Texas Hospital School of Nursing, West Texas Barber College, Panhandle School of Real Estate. **PUBLIC LIBRARIES** Amarillo Public Library: 389,007 volumes, three branches. **CHILD CARE** 370 day care and 46 twenty-four hour care licensed facilities. **HEALTH CARE** 320 physicians and 80 dentists. Hospitals: four with a combined capacity of 880. Specialized hospitals: one veterans center with capacity of 118. Clinics: one outpatient clinic, one dialysis clinic, one public health clinic and one minor emergency center. Ambulance services: four commercial and one fire department service. Mental health: one clinic, one district psychiatric hospital with capacity of 100, one child psychiatric center with capacity of 34 and one state center for human development with capacity of 40. Nursing homes: nine nursing homes with a combined capacity of 727 nursing care and 60 custodial care residents. The average cost per day for private patients in 1982 was $28.55. **CHURCHES** 117 churches have an estimated combined membership of 87,524. The largest denominations are Southern Baptist, Catholic and United Methodist. **SOCIAL SERVICES** In fiscal year 1983 a total of $3,394,776 in food stamps was distributed, with an average of 6,781 persons receiving food stamps each month. Aid to Families with Dependent Children (AFDC) totaled $554,855 with an average of 374 families receiving AFDC each month. Medical assistance benefits for the aged and disabled of $4,607,780 and for families and children of $959,967 brought the county benefit total to $9,517,377. **FIRE PROTECTION** One paid and six volunteer fire departments. **LAW ENFORCEMENT** The County Sheriff has 121 commissioned officers. Six police departments have a combined force of 390. Two college campuses have a police department with a combined force of 22. **CRIME** 887 violent crimes (murder, forcible rape, robbery and aggravated assault) and 10,533 non-violent crimes (burglary, larceny-theft and motor vehicle theft) were reported in 1982. **JUDICIAL SYSTEM** Five District Courts and Judges, three County Courts and Judges and two Justices of the Peace. In the District Courts a total of 2,716 cases were pending on 1/1/82, 3,778 new cases were filed and 3,685 cases were disposed of during the year leaving 2,809 cases pending on 12/31/82. There were 1,122 criminal cases on the docket, 414 convictions, 131 persons committed to prison, 60 committed to jail and 372 cases left pending. In the County Courts 2,419 cases were pending on 1/1/82, 4,176 new cases were filed and 4,308 cases were disposed of during the year leaving 2,287 cases 2,287 cases pending on 12/31/82. There were 4,347 criminal cases on the docket, 1,313 convictions, 617 persons committed to jail and 1,566 cases left pending. **JAILS** Four jails, capacity 318: additional low risk capacity under construction. **ATTORNEYS AT LAW** 448. **UTILITIES** 94% of the residents are connected to a public or privately owned water system and 94% are connected to a public sewer system. Natural gas is distributed to the county by Energas Company. The average annual residential bill for natural gas in 1982 for the Energas distribution system was $371.63, an increase of 23% over 1981. Electricity is distributed to the county by Southwestern Public Service Co. and Rita Blanca Electric Coop., Inc. and is generated primarily by gas, oil and coal. The typical residential electric bill is $170.44 per month for an all-electric house using 2,500 kwh. **TAXES** The county has 11 units with taxing authority: four school districts, one city, one county, two hospital districts, one college district and two special districts.

RECREATION/ENTERTAINMENT

FEDERAL ALIBATES FLINT QUARRIES NATIONAL MONUMENT covers 1,333 acres. Mined from about 10,000 B.C. to possibly the 1800s, these quarries yielded multicolored flint highly prized by ancient man for tools and weapons. Since the monument is still under development by the National Park Service, entry to the monument is by guided tours only. Lake Meredith Recreation Area (See Hutchinson County). **NATIONAL REGISTER OF HISTORIC PLACES** Amarillo: Mary Bivins Library, Landergin-Harrington House and Shelton-Houghton House. Lake Meredith vicinity: McBride Ranch House. **MUNICIPAL PARKS** 1,277 acres in 42 municipal parks. These parks contain three miles of hiking trails, 37 playgrounds, one golf course, 12 football and soccer fields, 14 baseball and softball fields, 40 tennis courts, 46 multi-use courts and two swimming pools. **SCENIC DRIVES** The Texas Plains Trail runs through this county. This trail spans a vast area of the High Plains region of Texas slicing through the southernmost extension of the Great Plains of the United States. The land is flat except where erosion has carved canyon landscapes. **BOATING/FISHING** Lakes/reservoirs: Amarillo Terminal (89 acres), Meredith (16,504 acres), Tecovas Pond (10 acres) and Whale Pond (14 acres). Major rivers: Canadian. Primary streams: Tecovas, Big Canyon, East Amarillo, Bonita, Box Canyon and West Amarillo. **HUNTING** Fall season on antelope. Fall and winter seasons on deer and mule deer. Summer, fall and winter seasons on squirrel. No closed season on coyote and bobcat. Winter seasons on pheasant, quail, muskrat, beaver, opossum, ring-tailed cat, badger, fox, weasel, raccoon, skunk and civet cat. Spring, fall and winter seasons on turkey. In 1983 sandhill crane, duck, coot, geese, woodcock and jacksnipe seasons occurred during the winter months. Teal duck, rail and gallinule seasons occurred in the fall. Mourning dove seasons occurred intermittently during the fall and winter months. **MUSEUMS** Amarillo: Art Center, Nielson Museum, Don Harrington Discovery Center and Museum Laws of Texas. **ORCHESTRAS** Amarillo: The Amarillo Symphony and the Greater Southwest Music Festival. **DANCE** Amarillo: Repertory Dance Company, Ballet Theater and the Lone Star Ballet.

BOTANIC GARDENS Amarillo: Garden Center. **PLANETARIUM** Amarillo: Don Harrington Discovery Center Planetarium. **COLLEGIATE FINE ARTS** Cultural events offered by Amarillo College. **SPECIAL EVENTS** Kwahadis Winter Ceremonials, Amarillo, January/February; Invitational Basketball Tourney, Amarillo, March; Greater Southwest Music Fest, Amarillo, April; Funfest, Amarillo, May; Will Rogers Rodeo, Amarillo, July; Tri-State Fair and Parade, Amarillo, September; Boys' Ranch Rodeo and Barbecue, Amarillo, September; National Old Timer Ropers Assn. Nationals, Amarillo, November; National Cutting Horse Finals, Amarillo, November; Annual Choir and Symphony Concert, Amarillo, December; Festival of Trees, Amarillo, December.

COMMUNITIES

COUNTY SEAT Amarillo, County Courthouse, 79101; County Clerk's Office, 806/372-3361. **INCORPORATED COMMUNITIES** (1980 population and ZIP Code) Amarillo (149,230: 93,019 in Potter Co. and 56,211 in Randall Co.) 79101. **UNINCORPORATED COMMUNITIES** (and ZIP Code) Ady 79010, Bushland 79012, Cliffside 79106, Pullman 79109, Soncy 79106, St. Francis 79107 and Summerfield 79101. **FOR ADDITIONAL LOCAL INFORMATION** Amarillo Chamber of Commerce, 1000 Polk, Amarillo, 79105, 806/374-5238.

PRESIDIO (B5)

THE LAND

Bordering Mexico southwest of Odessa on U.S. Highways 67 and 90 in the Trans-Pecos Region, Presidio County covers 3,857 square miles with an elevation range of 3,000 to 7,730 feet. The desertic soils vary from nearly level to mountainous with 90% of the land surface in the mountains exposed rock. The soils in the valleys and plains are alkaline and loamy with some clayey subsoils over limestone. In the Trans-Pecos Mountains and Basins vegetation area, the grasses are short and sparse with desert shrubs and cacti. Pine trees are found at higher mountain elevations. Less than 1% of the land in the county is considered prime farmland. **CLIMATE** Subtropical Arid with wide-ranging temperatures on a daily basis. The average annual temperature is 65°F. Temperatures in January range from an average low of 33° to an average high of 62°F and in July range from 68° to 98°F. The average annual precipitation is 12 inches, with an average relative humidity of 65% at 6 A.M. and 32% at 6 P.M. The average annual snowfall is two inches. The growing season averages 235 days per year, with the last freeze in mid March and the first freeze in mid November. The sun shines during the year on the average 78% of the daylight hours.

THE PEOPLE

Presidio County is one of the most sparsely populated in the state and ranks 17th among all U.S. counties in the highest percent of persons of Spanish origin. The 1982 estimated population of 5,500 indicates the continuation of a moderate growth rate begun in the 1970s which reversed the steady population decline between 1940 and 1970. The majority of the county residents live in rural areas. The largest ancestry groups are Hispanic (77%) and persons of English descent (10%). **REGISTERED VOTERS** As of November 2, 1982 there were 2,821 registered voters (0.04% of the state total). The 1982 general election had a 48% voter turnout, compared to a 59% turnout in the 1980 general election. In the 1982 primary 100% voted Democratic, with 1,023 votes cast.

THE ECONOMY

AGRICULTURE Ranchland. In 1982, 83% of the land was in

PRESIDIO (continued)

farms and ranches, with less than 1% of the farmland under cultivation. Most of the cropland and some of the rangeland was irrigated. Presidio ranked 174th in the state in highest agricultural receipts, with 68% from livestock and livestock products. Overgrazing, undesirable brush and weeds, decreasing irrigation water supplies, salinity and water erosion are the current conservation problems. Primary crops: wheat, hay and sorghum. Primary vegetables: eighth in the state for onions and fifth for cantaloupes. Honeydew melons and watermelons. Primary fruits and nuts: peaches. Primary livestock and products: cattle, sheep, wool, angora goats and mohair. **BUSINESS** Total number of business establishments in the county: 117. Retail sales during the first quarter of 1984 increased 17%. In 1980, 14% of the labor force were self-employed, 16% were employed in professional or related services, 3% in manufacturing, 23% in wholesale and retail trade, 20% in agriculture, forestry, fisheries and mining, 10% were employed in other counties and there were 481 retired workers. The industry with the most employment is agribusiness. The nonfarm earnings in 1981 totaled $33,657,000. The retired workers received an average monthly Social Security payment of $256. **FINANCE** On June 30, 1983, two commercial banks had total deposits of $29,576,000 and total assets of $33,435,000. There is one state savings and loan association branch. **HOUSING** Average value of homes in 1980: $16,000. In 1982 two permits were issued for new, single family houses. Between 1970 and 1980 the number of housing units increased by 19%. Fifty-seven percent of all units in the county are air-conditioned, 81% are heated by gas and 10% by electricity. **NATURAL RESOURCES** Subbituminous coal, fluorspar, gold, lead, limestone, manganese, mercury, perlite, rhyolite, silver, uranium, zinc, volcanic rock, oil and gas. Current production of other minerals and products includes perlite, crushed rhyolite, sand and gravel. **TOURISM** Travel expenditures of $1,045,000 in 1982 (an increase of 14% over 1981) generated 20 jobs and $181,000 in payroll. **ALCOHOLIC BEVERAGES** Packaged distilled spirits, beer, ale, malt liquor and wine are legal. Sale of mixed beverages is legal in all or parts of the county. **FEDERAL EXPENDITURES** The federal government had direct expenditures or obligations of $11,056,000 in the county during fiscal year 1983, including $143,000 by the U.S. Department of Defense. In addition, the federal government provided $152,000 in grant awards, paid $3,163,000 in salaries and wages, made direct payments to individuals of $7,514,000 including $5,413,000 in retirement and disability payments, awarded $86,000 in procurement contracts and spent $141,000 in other expenditures or obligations. The federal government also provided $1,364,000 in direct loans and $495,000 in guaranteed loans and insurance.

COMMUNICATION

Newspapers–Weekly: The Big Bend Sentinel (Marfa). Cable TV. Telephone companies: Southwestern Bell and Big Bend Telephone. **TRANSPORTATION** Total public road mileage: 748. In 1982 there were 3,885 registered vehicles and 97 reported traffic accidents including two fatalities. Intercity bus service is available. Motor freight: three carriers. Rail: The Sunset Limited provides passenger service on the Amtrak route. Two main lines and one branch carry freight through the county. The two main lines carry annually over 30 million tons of freight each and the branch carries one to five million. Aircraft: 33 are registered in the county. Airports: Marfa Municipal Airport serves as a base for 30 aircraft and is a general utility airport with general aviation service. Lely International Airport at Presidio is an immigration and customs entry airport. Also serving the area are Big Bend Ranch Airport at Presidio, Candelaria Airport at Candelaria and Hot Springs Airport at Ruidosa.

COMMUNITY SERVICES

EDUCATION Two school districts with four elementary, one middle and two high schools. The average daily attendance in 1981-82 was 1,163, with expenditures per pupil of $2,036 including 68 classroom teachers with an average annual salary of $14,846. Fifty percent of the 70 high school graduates planned to attend college. In 1982-83, 15% of the students were White, 85% Hispanic and 0.2% Black. Private schools: 117 students enrolled in one elementary. **PUBLIC LIBRARIES** Marfa Public Library: 16,694 volumes. **CHILD CARE** One day care licensed facility. **HEALTH CARE** Two physicians and three dentists. Ambulance services: one city and one volunteer service. **CHURCHES** 16 churches have an estimated combined membership of 4,047. The largest denominations are Catholic and Southern Baptist. **SOCIAL SERVICES** In fiscal year 1983 a total of $463,723 in food stamps was distributed, with an average of 964 persons receiving food stamps each month. Aid to Families with Dependent Children (AFDC) totaled $38,813 with an average of 29 families receiving AFDC each month. Medical assistance benefits for the aged and disabled of $215,144 and for families and children of $19,574 brought the county benefit total to $737,254. **FIRE PROTECTION** Two volunteer fire departments. **LAW ENFORCEMENT** The County Sheriff has three commissioned officers. One police department has a force of two. **CRIME** Seven violent crimes (murder, forcible rape, robbery and aggravated assault) and 24 nonviolent crimes (burglary, larceny-theft and motor vehicle theft) were reported in 1982. **JUDICIAL SYSTEM** One District Court and Judge, one County Court and Judge and two Justices of the Peace. In the District Court a total of 191 cases were pending on 1/1/82, 112 new cases were filed and 62 cases were disposed of during the year leaving 241 cases pending on 12/31/82. There were 58 criminal cases on the docket, 13 convictions, one person committed to prison and 36 cases left pending. In the County Court 248 cases were pending on 1/1/82, 94 new cases were filed and 106 cases were disposed of during the year leaving 236 cases pending on 12/31/82. There were 135 criminal cases on the docket, 84 convictions, two persons committed to jail and 31 cases left pending. **JAILS** One jail, capacity 31. **ATTORNEYS AT LAW** Seven. **UTILITIES** 79% of the residents are connected to a public or privately owned water system and 57% are connected to a public sewer system. Natural gas is distributed to the county by Southwest Texas Municipal Gas Co. Electricity is distributed to the county by West Texas Utilities Co. and Rio Grande Electric Coop., Inc. and is generated primarily by gas, oil and coal. **TAXES** The county has five units with taxing authority: two school districts, two cities and one county.

RECREATION/ENTERTAINMENT

NATIONAL REGISTER OF HISTORIC PLACES Marfa: El Paisano Hotel and Presidio County Courthouse. Presidio vicinity: Fort Leaton and La Junta de los Rios Archeological District. Redford vicinity: Tapalcomes. Shafter: Shafter Historic Mining District. Shafter vicinity: Fortin de la Cienega. **STATE** Fort Leaton State Historic Site covers 13 acres with a museum and a historic structure. The massive adobe fortress was built in 1848 immediately after the Mexican War. **COUNTY/MUNICIPAL PARKS** 147 acres in one county and three municipal parks. These parks contain one golf course, three baseball and softball fields and one swimming pool. **SCENIC DRIVES** The Texas Mountain Trail runs through this county. El Camino del Rio, F.M. 170, stretches from near Big Bend National Park into the Chinati Mountains. This modern highway, following the bed of the Rio Grande, is considered one of the most spectacular drives in the nation. **BOATING/FISHING** Lakes/reservoirs: Fowlkes Ranch (14 acres), San Esteban (155 acres) and Sutton (24 acres). Major rivers: Rio Grande. Primary streams: Paint, Alamito, Charco Becerro, Cibolo and Van Horn. **HUNTING** Fall season on antelope. Fall and winter seasons on deer and mule deer. No closed season on elk, javelina, coyote and bobcat. Winter seasons on quail, muskrat, beaver, opossum, ring-tailed cat, badger, fox, weasel, raccoon, skunk and civet cat. In 1983 sandhill crane, duck, coot, geese, woodcock and jacksnipe seasons occurred during the winter months. Teal duck, rail and gallinule seasons occurred in the fall. Mourning dove seasons occurred intermittently during the fall and winter months with a fall season on white-winged dove. **MUSEUMS** Marfa: Marfa-Presidio County Museum. **SPECIAL EVENTS** Highland Fair, Marfa, January; Highland Annual Bull Sale, Marfa, February; Folkloric Dancers, Marfa, April; Marfa Celebration, Marfa, May.

COMMUNITIES

COUNTY SEAT Marfa, County Courthouse, 79843; County Clerk's Office, 915/729-4812. **INCORPORATED COMMUNITIES** (1980 population and ZIP Code) Marfa (2,466) 79843 and Presidio (1,723: est. incorp. inactive) 79845. **UNINCORPORATED COMMUNITIES** (and ZIP Code) Candelaria 79843, Casa Piedra 79843, Chinati 79845, Indio 79845, Ochoa 79845, Porvenir 79854, Redford 79846, Ruidosa 79843 and Shafter 79850. **FOR ADDITIONAL LOCAL INFORMATION** Marfa Chamber of Commerce, P.O. Box 635, Marfa, 79843, 915/729-4942.

RAINS (E10)

THE LAND

East of Dallas on U.S. Highway 69 in the Claypan Area, Rains County covers 243 square miles with an elevation range of 300 to 500 feet. The eastern half of the county has undulating, light colored soils with sandy surfaces over mottled, clayey subsoils. The western half has undulating, cracking, gray to black clayey soils that have a high shrink-swell potential and slightly acidic soils with light colored, loamy surfaces over very deep, cracking, clayey subsoils. The eastern part of Rains lies in the Post Oak Savannah vegetation area with tall grasses, post and blackjack oak. The western part lies in the Blackland Prairies vegetation area with tall grasses and mesquite, oak, pecan and elm trees along streams. Between 21 and 30% of the land in the county is considered prime farmland. **CLIMATE** Subtropical Humid with warm summers. The average annual temperature is 64°F. Temperatures in January range from an average low of 32° to an average high of 54°F and in July range from 72° to 95°F. The average annual precipitation is 43 inches, with an average relative humidity of 83% at 6 A.M. and 53% at 6 P.M. The average annual snowfall is two inches. The growing season averages 245 days per year, with the last freeze in mid March and the first freeze in mid November. The sun shines during the year on the average 66% of the daylight hours.

THE PEOPLE

The steady population growth rate in Rains County between 1960 and 1980 and the 1982 estimated population of 5,200 indicate continued growth. The age groups with the largest gains were birth to five years and ages 62 and over. The county's population is older than average with a median age of 39. The majority of the county residents live in rural areas. The largest ancestry groups are persons of English descent (29%) and Irish descent (21%). **REGISTERED VOTERS** As of November 2, 1982 there were 3,241 registered voters (0.1% of the state total). The 1982 general election had a 57% voter turnout, compared to a 65%

turnout in the 1980 general election. In the 1982 primary 100% voted Democratic, with 1,331 votes cast.

THE ECONOMY

AGRICULTURE In 1982, 74% of the land was in farms and ranches, with 25% of the farmland under cultivation and 4% irrigated. Rains ranked 193rd in the state in highest agricultural receipts, with 90% from livestock and livestock products. Overgrazing and difficulties in grass establishment are the current conservation problems. Primary crops: hay, wheat and oats. Primary vegetables: sweet potatoes. Primary fruits and nuts: peaches and pecans. Primary livestock and products: cattle, milk and hogs. **BUSINESS** Total number of business establishments in the county: 64. Retail sales during the first quarter of 1984 decreased 6%, with an increase of 4% in Emory and a 25% decrease in East Tawakoni. In 1980, 13% of the labor force were self-employed, 11% were employed in professional or related services, 26% in manufacturing, 16% in wholesale and retail trade, 12% in agriculture, forestry, fisheries and mining, 50% were employed in other counties and there were 541 retired workers. The industries with the most employment: agribusiness and the manufacture of metal wire products. The nonfarm earnings in 1981 totaled $35,624,000. The retired workers received an average monthly Social Security payment of $283. **FINANCE** On June 30, 1983, two commercial banks had total deposits of $34,092,000 and total assets of $37,820,000. There is one state savings and loan association branch and one credit union in the county. **HOUSING** Average value of homes in 1980: $21,900. Permits for new, privately owned housing units decreased in 1982: nine permits were issued with a total construction cost of $242,950. Of those permits, all were for single family houses. Between 1970 and 1980 the number of housing units increased by 36%. Seventy-nine percent of all units in the county are air-conditioned, 75% are heated by gas and 18% by electricity. **NATURAL RESOURCES** Ceramic clay, lignite coal, glauconite and gas. In 1982 a total of 3,380,905 thousand cubic feet of gas well gas, 362 barrels of condensate were produced. Current production of other minerals and products includes clay. **TOURISM** Travel expenditures of $145,000 in 1982 (an increase of 8% over 1981) generated 4 jobs and $28,000 in payroll. **ALCOHOLIC BEVERAGES** Packaged distilled spirits, beer, ale, malt liquor and wine are legal in parts of the county. **FEDERAL EXPENDITURES** The federal government had direct expenditures or obligations of $9,006,000 in the county during fiscal year 1983, including $534,000 by the U.S. Department of Defense. In addition, the federal government provided $56,000 in grant awards, paid $484,000 in salaries and wages, made direct payments to individuals of $8,309,000 including $6,198,000 in retirement and disability payments, awarded $57,000 in procurement contracts and spent $100,000 in other expenditures or obligations. The federal government also provided $278,000 in direct loans and $584,000 in guaranteed loans and insurance.

COMMUNICATION

Newspapers–Weekly: Rains County Leader (Emory). Cable TV. Telephone companies: Continental Telephone. **TRANSPORTATION** Total public road mileage: 366. In 1982 there were 5,071 registered vehicles and 63 reported traffic accidents including two fatalities. Motor freight: one carrier.

COMMUNITY SERVICES

EDUCATION One school district with one elementary, one middle and one high school. The average daily attendance in 1981-82 was 802, with expenditures per pupil of $2,156 including 47 classroom teachers with an average annual salary of $15,221. Thirty-five percent of the 43 high school graduates planned to attend college. In 1982-83, 91% of the students were White, 1%

COUNTIES

RAINS (continued)

Hispanic, 8% Black and 0.1% Asian. **PUBLIC LIBRARIES** Emory Library. **CHILD CARE** Six day care and five twenty-four hour care licensed facilities. **HEALTH CARE** One physician and two dentists. Ambulance services: one volunteer fire department and one county service. **CHURCHES** 22 churches have an estimated combined membership of 3,476. The largest denominations are Southern Baptist and United Methodist. **SOCIAL SERVICES** In fiscal year 1983 a total of $127,109 in food stamps was distributed, with an average of 334 persons receiving food stamps each month. Aid to Families with Dependent Children (AFDC) totaled $21,293 with an average of 16 families receiving AFDC each month. Medical assistance benefits for the aged and disabled of $149,513 and for families and children of $45,097 brought the county benefit total to $343,012. **FIRE PROTECTION** Two volunteer fire departments. **LAW ENFORCEMENT** The County Sheriff has 12 commissioned officers. **CRIME** 10 violent crimes (murder, forcible rape, robbery and aggravated assault) and 154 nonviolent crimes (burglary, larceny-theft and motor vehicle theft) were reported in 1982. **JUDICIAL SYSTEM** One District Court and Judge, one County Court and Judge and four Justices of the Peace. In the District Court a total of 129 cases were pending on 1/1/82, 145 new cases were filed and 138 cases were disposed of during the year leaving 136 cases pending on 12/31/82. There were 84 criminal cases on the docket, 69 convictions, 19 persons committed to prison and five committed to jail and 13 cases left pending. In the County Court 49 cases were pending on 1/1/82, 77 new cases were filed and 27 cases were disposed of during the year leaving 99 cases pending on 12/31/82. There were 111 criminal cases on the docket, 19 convictions, two persons committed to jail, and 84 cases left pending. **ATTORNEYS AT LAW** Four. **UTILITIES** 84% of the residents are connected to a public or privately owned water system and 37% are connected to a public sewer system. Natural gas is distributed to the county by Lone Star Gas Co., Division of Enserch. The average annual residential bill for natural gas in 1982 for the Lone Star distribution system was $405.91, an increase of 35% over 1981. Electricity is distributed to the county by Wood County Electric Coop. Inc. and is generated primarily by gas and coal. **TAXES** The county has six units with taxing authority: one school district, three cities, one county and one special district.

RECREATION/ENTERTAINMENT

NATIONAL REGISTER OF HISTORIC PLACES Emory vicinity: Gilbert Site, Koons Site and Yandell Site. **MUNICIPAL PARKS** Three acres in one municipal park. This park contains one playground and one tennis court. **SCENIC DRIVES** The Texas Lakes Trail runs through this county. F.M. 47 which travels along Iron Bridge Dam and F.M. 35 which crosses Lake Tawakoni on the longest inland-water bridge in Texas offer scenic vistas of wood and water. **BOATING/FISHING** Lakes/reservoirs: Case (21 acres) and Tawakoni (36,700 acres). Major rivers: Sabine. Primary streams: Boardtree and Lake Fork. **HUNTING** Fall and winter seasons on deer. Summer, fall and winter seasons on squirrel. No closed seasons on coyote, bobcat and nutria. Winter seasons on quail, muskrat, beaver, otter, opossum, mink, ringtailed cat, badger, fox, raccoon, skunk and civet cat. In 1983 duck, coot, geese, woodcock and jacksnipe seasons occurred during the winter months. Teal duck, rail and gallinule seasons occurred in the fall. Mourning dove seasons occurred intermittently during the fall and winter months.

COMMUNITIES

COUNTY SEAT Emory, County Courthouse, 75440; County Clerk's Office, 214/473-2461. **INCORPORATED COMMUNITIES** (1980 population and ZIP Code) East Tawakoni (404) 75453, Emory (813) 75440 and Point (468) 75472. **UNINCORPORATED COMMUNITIES** (and ZIP Code) Bright Star 75410, Dougherty 75440, Dunbar Union 75440, Flats 75472, Ginger 75410, Grit 75410, Holiday Hills 75453, Pilgrims Rest 75440, Richland (Wattsville) 75472, Sand Flat 75440, Whispering Oaks 75453, Willow Springs 75440 and Woosley 75472.

RANDALL (P17)

THE LAND

In the High Plains Region of the Texas Panhandle north of Lubbock on Interstate Highway 27, Randall County covers 917 square miles with an elevation range of 3,000 to 3,800 feet. In the east central part of the county are light colored, well drained soils. The rest of the county has very dark, loamy surfaces over clay subsoils that have hardened calcium deposits. Randall is in the High Plains vegetation area with prairie grasses, junipers, some mesquite and yucca. Between 61 and 70% of the land in the county is considered prime farmland. **CLIMATE** Continental Steppe with wide-ranging daily temperature fluctuations. Duststorms and thunderstorms are significant in the spring. The average annual temperature is 58°F. Temperatures in January range from an average low of 23° to an average high of 53°F and in July range from 65° to 92°F. The average annual precipitation is 19 inches, with an average relative humidity of 69% at 6 A.M. and 38% at 6 P.M. The average annual snowfall is 15 inches. The growing season averages 200 days per year, with the last freeze in mid April and the first freeze in late October. The sun shines during the year on the average 75% of the daylight hours.

THE PEOPLE

Nearly 89% of the residents in Randall County live in urban areas. The 1982 estimated population of 79,300 indicates a continuation of the strong growth which has occurred since the 1930s. Rural areas grew faster than urban areas between 1970 and 1980. The age groups with the largest gains were ages 25 to 29 and 62 and over which doubled in size. Therefore the median age rose from 25 in 1970 to 28 in 1980. The largest ancestry groups are persons of English descent (36%), Irish descent (26%) and German descent (24%). **REGISTERED VOTERS** As of November 2, 1982 there were 38,800 registered voters (0.6% of the state total). The 1982 general election had a 59% voter turnout, compared to an 80% turnout in the 1980 general election. In the 1982 primary 62% voted Democratic and 38% Republican, with 9,672 votes cast.

THE ECONOMY

AGRICULTURE Fed cattle and wheat area. In 1982, 96% of the land was in farms and ranches, with 45% of the farmland under cultivation and 22% irrigated. Randall ranked 34th in the state in highest agricultural receipts, with 76% from livestock and livestock products. Overgrazing, water and wind erosion, decreasing irrigation water supplies and noxious weeds are the current conservation problems. Primary crops: wheat, sorghum and hay. Primary livestock and products: ninth in the state for fed cattle marketings. Milk and hogs. **BUSINESS** Total number of business establishments in the county: 987. Retail sales during the first quarter of 1984 increased 37%. In 1980, 9% of the labor force were self-employed, 21% were employed in professional or related services, 11% in manufacturing, 27% in wholesale and retail trade, 10% in transportation, communications, and other public utilities, 69% were employed in other counties and there were 3,194 retired workers. The industries with the most employment: agribusiness, general construction, road construction and the manufacture of men's work clothing, farm machinery and oil field machinery. The nonfarm earnings in 1981 totaled $785,039,000. The retired workers received an average monthly Social Security payment of $351. **FINANCE** On June 30, 1983, three commercial banks had total deposits of $110,953,000 and total assets of $121,392,000. On December 31, 1982 one state savings and loan association, five state branches and five federal association branches had assets of $25,633,013. **HOUSING** Average value of homes in 1980: $45,400. Permits for new, privately owned housing units increased in 1982: 86 permits were issued with a total construction cost of $4,724,180. Of those permits, 78 were for single family houses. Between 1970 and 1980 the number of housing units increased by 65%. Eighty-eight percent of all units in the county are air-conditioned, 87% are heated by gas and 13% by electricity. **NATURAL RESOURCES** Caliche. Current production of other minerals and products includes caliche. **TOURISM** Travel expenditures of $7,783,000 in 1982 (an increase of 11% over 1981) generated 189 jobs and $1,727,000 in payroll. Convention/meeting facilities: Canyon-West Texas State University Franks Kimbrough Memorial Stadium. (See Potter County for Amarillo). **ALCOHOLIC BEVERAGES** Packaged distilled spirits, beer, ale, malt liquor and wine are legal in parts of the county. Sale of mixed beverages is legal in all or parts of the county. **FEDERAL EXPENDITURES** The federal government had direct expenditures or obligations of $54,154,000 in the county during fiscal year 1983, including $2,723,000 by the U.S. Department of Defense. In addition, the federal government provided $3,418,000 in grant awards, paid $1,954,000 in salaries and wages, made direct payments to individuals of $45,362,000 including $39,432,000 in retirement and disability payments, awarded $29,000 in procurement contracts and spent $3,392,000 in other expenditures or obligations. The federal government also provided $9,388,000 in direct loans and $26,302,000 in guaranteed loans and insurance.

COMMUNICATION

(See Amarillo, Potter County). Radio: KHBJ-AM, KHBO-FM and KWTS-FM (Canyon). Cable TV. Telephone companies: General Telephone, Continental Telephone, Southwestern Bell and MidPlains Rural Telephone Coop. **TRANSPORTATION** Total public road mileage: 1,283. In 1982 there were 66,670 registered vehicles and 1,889 reported traffic accidents including 10 fatalities. Municipal transit systems: (see Amarillo, Potter County). Intercity bus service is available. Motor freight: 16 local and intrastate carriers. Rail: four main and two branch lines carry freight through the county. Three of the main lines carry annually over 30 million tons of freight each and one carries 10 to 20 million. One branch carries annually five to 10 million tons of freight and the other one carries one to five million. Aircraft: 59 are registered in the county. Airports: Rockwell Airport at Canyon and Gartrell Field at Canyon (see Amarillo, Potter County).

COMMUNITY SERVICES

EDUCATION One school district with four elementary, one middle and one high school. The average daily attendance in 1981-82 was 3,766, with expenditures per pupil of $2,177 including 218 classroom teachers with an average annual salary of $17,038. Sixty-seven percent of the 221 high school graduates planned to attend college. In 1982-83, 93% of the students were White, 6% Hispanic, 0.8% Black, 0.7% Asian and 0.2% American Indian. (The Texas Education Agency reported Amarillo Independent School District statistics under Potter County-see Potter County). Sports championships: (see Amarillo, Potter County). (For Amarillo College, see Potter County). West Texas State University is located in Canyon. Established in 1909 it is under state control. Enrollment in 1982 was 6,559 with in state

undergraduate tuition and fees of $434 per semester. The highest degree offered is Master. Vocational education: (see Amarillo, Potter County). **PUBLIC LIBRARIES** Canyon Public Library: 22,661 volumes. Amarillo Public Library: 389,007 volumes, three branches. **CHILD CARE** 293 day care and 40 twenty-four hour care licensed facilities. **HEALTH CARE** Nine physicians and five dentists. Hospitals: one with a capacity of 49. Ambulance services: one city and one volunteer service. Nursing homes: three nursing homes with a combined capacity of 252 nursing care residents. The average cost per day for private patients in 1982 was $32.75. **CHURCHES** 43 churches have an estimated combined membership of 28,428. The largest denominations are Southern Baptist, United Methodist and Catholic. **SOCIAL SERVICES** In fiscal year 1983 a total of $305,847 in food stamps was distributed, with an average of 626 persons receiving food stamps each month. Aid to Families with Dependent Children (AFDC) totaled $43,319 with an average of 29 families receiving AFDC each month. Medical assistance benefits for the aged and disabled of $964,634 and for families and children of $81,561 brought the county benefit total to $1,395,361. **FIRE PROTECTION** Four volunteer fire departments. **LAW ENFORCEMENT** The County Sheriff has 33 commissioned officers. One police department has a force of nine. One university campus has a police department with a force of 10 officers. **CRIME** 33 violent crimes (murder, forcible rape, robbery and aggravated assault) and 348 nonviolent crimes (burglary, larceny-theft and motor vehicle theft) were reported in 1982. **JUDICIAL SYSTEM** Three District Courts and Judges, two County Courts and Judges and two Justices of the Peace. In the District Courts a total of 1,276 cases were pending on 1/1/82, 1,758 new cases were filed and 1,717 cases were disposed of during the year leaving 1,317 cases pending on 12/31/82. There were 547 criminal cases on the docket, 127 convictions, 45 persons committed to prison and 11 committed to jail and 218 cases left pending. In the County Courts 1,322 cases were pending on 1/1/82, 2,288 new cases were filed and 2,241 cases were disposed of during the year leaving 1,369 cases pending on 12/31/82. There were 2,608 criminal cases on the docket, 837 convictions, 209 persons committed to jail, and 786 cases left pending. **JAILS** One jail, capacity 35, new jail being constructed, capacity 85. **ATTORNEYS AT LAW** 20. **UTILITIES** 91% of the residents are connected to a public or privately owned water system and 90% are connected to a public sewer system. Natural gas is distributed to the county by Energas Company. The average annual residential bill for natural gas in 1982 for the Energas distribution system was $371.63, an increase of 23% over 1981. Electricity is distributed to the county by Southwestern Public Service Co., Greenbelt Electric Coop., Inc. and Swisher Electric Coop., Inc. and is generated primarily by gas and oil. The typical residential electric bill is $170.44 per month for an all-electric house using 2,500 kwh. **TAXES** The county has 10 units with taxing authority: two school districts, two cities, one county, two hospital districts, one college district and two special districts.

RECREATION/ENTERTAINMENT

NATIONAL REGISTER OF HISTORIC PLACES Canyon: L.T. Lester House (see Amarillo, Potter County). **STATE** Palo Duro Canyon State Park covers 16,402 acres with camping and trailer sites as well as areas offering scenic drives, horseback trails, rental horses and exhibits. During the summer months, the musical drama "Texas" is performed. **MUNICIPAL PARKS** 3,297 acres in 15 municipal parks. These parks contain two miles of hiking trails, 14 playgrounds, 21 football and soccer fields, eight baseball and softball fields, seven tennis courts, 21 multi-use courts and three swimming pools. **SCENIC DRIVES** The Texas Plains Trail runs through this county. This trail spans a vast area of the High Plains region of Texas slicing through the southernmost

COUNTIES

RANDALL (continued)

extension of the Great Plains of the United States. The land is flat except where erosion has carved canyon landscapes. **BOATING/FISHING** Lakes/reservoirs: Bivins (379 acres), Buffalo (2,000 acres), Palo Duro Club (40 acres), Schaeffer (40 acres) and Tanglewood (191 acres). Major rivers: Prairie Dog Town Fork Red. Primary streams: Palo Duro, Tierra Blanca and South Ceta Canyon. **WILDLIFE REFUGES** Buffalo Lake National Wildlife Refuge covers 7,664 acres. **HUNTING** Fall and winter seasons on deer and mule deer. Summer, fall and winter seasons on squirrel. No closed seasons on coyote and bobcat. Winter seasons on aoudad sheep, pheasant, quail, muskrat, beaver, opossum, ring-tailed cat, badger, fox, weasel, raccoon, skunk and civet cat. Fall, winter and spring seasons on turkey. In 1983 sandhill crane, duck, coot, geese, woodcock and jacksnipe seasons occurred during the winter months. Teal duck, rail and gallinule seasons occurred in the fall. Mourning dove seasons occurred intermittently during the fall and winter months. **MUSEUMS** (for Amarillo facilities and events, see Potter County) Canyon: Panhandle-Plains Historical Museum. **THEATERS** Canyon: Pioneer Amphitheatre and Texas Panhandle Heritage Foundation, Inc. **COLLEGIATE FINE ARTS** Canyon: Cultural events offered by West Texas State University. **SPECIAL EVENTS** Miss Canyon Pageant, Canyon, April; Museum Family Day, Canyon, May; "Texas" Musical Drama, Canyon, June/August; Fourth of July Picnic, Canyon, July; Buffalo Day Roundup, Canyon, August; Annual Christmas Open House at the Museum, Canyon, December. (see Amarillo, Potter County).

COMMUNITIES

COUNTY SEAT Canyon, County Courthouse, 79015; County Clerk's Office, 806/655-2511. **INCORPORATED COMMUNITIES** (1980 population and ZIP Code) Amarillo (149,230: 56,211 in Randall Co. and 93,019 in Potter Co.) 79101, Canyon (10,724) 79015, Happy (674: 43 in Randall Co. and 631 in Swisher Co.) 79042 and Lake Tanglewood (485) 79105. **UNINCORPORATED COMMUNITIES** (and ZIP Code) Ogg 79042 and Umbarger 79091. **FOR ADDITIONAL LOCAL INFORMATION** Amarillo Chamber of Commerce, 1000 Polk, P.O. Box 9480, Amarillo, 79105, 806/374-5238 and Canyon Chamber of Commerce, P.O. Box Eight, Canyon 79015, 806/655-1183.

REAGAN (P87)

THE LAND

Southeast of Midland on U.S. Highway 67 in the Edwards Plateau Region, Reagan County covers 1,173 square miles with an elevation range of 2,400 to 2,600 feet. The county has loamy surface soils over subsoils with accumulations of lime, or limestone within 40 inches of the surface. Some areas are 90% exposed rock. Reagan is in the Edwards Plateau vegetation area with tall and mid grasses, shinnery and live oak, juniper and mesquite. Less than 1% of the land in the county is considered prime farmland. **CLIMATE** Subtropical Steppe with wide-ranging daily temperature fluctuations. Duststorms are significant during spring. The average annual temperature is 66°F. Temperatures in January range from an average low of 32° to an average high of 60°F and in July range from 71° to 95°F. The average annual precipitation is 16 inches, with an average relative humidity of 73% at 6 A.M. and 38% at 6 P.M. The average annual snowfall is three inches. The growing season averages 229 days per year, with the last freeze in late March and the first freeze in mid November. The sun shines during the year on the average 71% of the daylight hours.

THE PEOPLE

Reagan County ranks 57th among all U.S. counties in the highest birth rate per 1,000 residents. It has a 1982 estimated population of 4,700 and experienced a sizeable growth rate between 1970 and 1980 which offset the 14% population decline between 1960 and 1970. Nearly 82% of the county residents live in urban areas, but rural areas experienced a 77% population increase between 1970 and 1980. The age groups with the largest gains were birth to five years which nearly doubled in size and ages 20 to 34. Therefore the county's population shifted from one of average age to one younger than average with a median age of 25. The largest ancestry groups are Hispanic (32%), persons of Irish descent (21%), English descent (20%) and German descent (15%). **REGISTERED VOTERS** As of November 2, 1982 there were 2,042 registered voters (0.03% of the state total). The 1982 general election had a 50% voter turnout, compared to a 66% turnout in the 1980 general election. In the 1982 primary 100% voted Democratic, with 883 votes cast.

THE ECONOMY

AGRICULTURE Sheep ranches. In 1982, 94% of the land was in farms and ranches, with 5% of the farmland under cultivation, most of which was irrigated. Reagan ranked 222nd in the state in highest agricultural receipts, with 62% from crops. Overgrazing, undesirable brush and weeds, wind erosion, inefficient irrigation systems and water erosion are the current conservation problems. Primary crops: cotton, wheat, sorghum and sunflowers. Primary vegetables: potatoes, sweet potatoes, tomatoes and watermelons. Primary fruits and nuts: pecans. Primary livestock and products: cattle, sheep, wool, angora goats and mohair. **BUSINESS** Total number of business establishments in the county: 104. Retail sales during the first quarter of 1984 increased 18%. In 1980, 9% of the labor force were self-employed, 10% were employed in professional or related services, 2% in manufacturing, 15% in wholesale and retail trade, 46% in agriculture, forestry, fisheries and mining, 15% were employed in other counties and there were 192 retired workers. The industry with the most employment is oil and gas extraction. The non-farm earnings in 1981 totaled $44,574,000. The retired workers received an average monthly Social Security payment of $349. **FINANCE** On June 30, 1983, one commercial bank had total deposits of $30,595,000 and total assets of $33,826,000. There is one state savings and loan association branch. **HOUSING** Average value of homes in 1980: $24,100. Permits for new, privately owned housing units decreased in 1982: 19 permits were issued with a total construction cost of $1,685,603. Of those permits, all were for single family houses. Between 1970 and 1980 the number of housing units increased by 25%. Eighty-one percent of all units in the county are air-conditioned, 89% are heated by gas and 11% by electricity. **NATURAL RESOURCES** Caliche, limestone, salt, gas and oil. In 1982 a total of 1,276,563 thousand cubic feet of gas well gas, 17,109 barrels of condensate, 7,437,347 barrels of crude oil and 28,780,666 thousand cubic feet of casinghead gas were produced. Current production of other minerals and products includes recovered sulphur. **TOURISM** Travel expenditures of $1,937,000 in 1982 (an increase of 14% over 1981) generated 38 jobs and $339,000 in payroll. **ALCOHOLIC BEVERAGES** Packaged distilled spirits, beer, ale, malt liquor and wine are legal. **FEDERAL EXPENDITURES** The federal government had direct expenditures or obligations of $5,634,000 in the county during fiscal year 1983, including $58,000 by the U.S. Department of Defense. In addition, the federal government provided $104,000 in grant awards, paid $271,000 in salaries and wages, made direct payments to individuals of $2,560,000 including $2,027,000 in retirement and disability payments, awarded $2,000 in procurement contracts and spent $2,697,000 in other expenditures or obligations. The federal government also provided $1,200,000 in direct loans and $1,920,000 in guaranteed loans and insurance.

COMMUNICATION

Newspapers–Weekly: The Big Lake Wildcat. Radio: KWGH-AM (Big Lake). Cable TV. Telephone companies: General Telephone, Southwestern Bell and Wes-Tex Telephone Coop. **TRANSPORTATION** Total public road mileage: 361. In 1982 there were 4,716 registered vehicles and 118 reported traffic accidents including one fatality. Intercity bus service is available. Motor freight: one carrier. Rail: one branch line carries annually one to five million tons of freight through the county. Aircraft: 13 are registered in the county. Airports: Reagan County Airport at Big Lake.

COMMUNITY SERVICES

EDUCATION One school district with one elementary, one middle and one high school. The average daily attendance in 1981-82 was 1,012, with expenditures per pupil of $3,392 including 69 classroom teachers with an average annual salary of $19,694. Thirty-six percent of the 58 high school graduates planned to attend college. In 1982-83, 51% of the students were White, 46% Hispanic, 3% Black, 0.2% Asian and 0.3% American Indian. Sports championships: 1983 AA Girls' Golf Team, Reagan County H.S. **PUBLIC LIBRARIES** Reagan County Library (Big Lake): 14,925 volumes. **CHILD CARE** Nine day care and one twenty-four hour care licensed facilities. **HEALTH CARE** Three physicians. Hospitals: one with a capacity of 29. Ambulance services: one volunteer fire department service. **CHURCHES** Nine churches have an estimated combined membership of 2,669. The largest denominations are Southern Baptist and Catholic. **SOCIAL SERVICES** In fiscal year 1983 a total of $53,440 in food stamps was distributed, with an average of 129 persons receiving food stamps each month. Aid to Families with Dependent Children (AFDC) totaled $12,190 with an average of seven families receiving AFDC each month. Medical assistance benefits for the aged and disabled of $30,922 and for families and children of $29,801 brought the county benefit total to $126,353. **FIRE PROTECTION** Two volunteer fire departments. **LAW ENFORCEMENT** The County Sheriff has five commissioned officers. **CRIME** Nine violent crimes (murder, forcible rape, robbery and aggravated assault) and 91 nonviolent crimes (burglary, larceny-theft and motor vehicle theft) were reported in 1982. **JUDICIAL SYSTEM** Two District Courts and Judges, one County Court and Judge and three Justices of the Peace. In the District Courts a total of 198 cases were pending on 1/1/82, 112 new cases were filed and 84 cases were disposed of during the year leaving 226 cases pending on 12/31/82. There were 88 criminal cases on the docket, 19 convictions, four persons committed to prison and 63 cases left pending. In the County Court 81 cases were pending on 1/1/82, 124 new cases were filed and 124 cases were disposed of during the year leaving 81 cases pending on 12/31/82. There were 178 criminal cases on the docket, 65 convictions, 24 persons committed to jail, and 58 cases left pending. **JAILS** One jail, capacity nine. **ATTORNEYS AT LAW** Two. **UTILITIES** 83% of the residents are connected to a public or privately owned water system and 81% are connected to a public sewer system. Electricity is distributed to the county by West Texas Utilities Co., Cap Rock Electric Coop., Inc., Concho Valley Electric Coop., Inc., and Southwest Texas Electric Coop., Inc. and is generated primarily by gas and oil. **TAXES** The county has five units with taxing authority: one school district, one city, one county, one hospital district and one special district.

RECREATION/ENTERTAINMENT

NATIONAL REGISTER OF HISTORIC PLACES Stiles: Old Reagan County Courthouse. **COUNTY PARKS** 57 acres in two county parks. These parks contain two playgrounds, four baseball and softball fields, one tennis court and two swimming pools. Developed campsites: six. **BOATING/FISHING** Lakes/reservoirs: Big Lake (1,000 acres). Major rivers: Middle Concho. **HUNTING** Fall season on antelope. Fall and winter seasons on deer, mule deer and javelina. No closed seasons on coyote, bobcat and squirrel. Winter seasons on quail, muskrat, beaver, opossum, ring-tailed cat, badger, fox, weasel, raccoon, skunk and civet cat. Fall, winter and spring seasons on turkey. In 1983 sandhill crane, duck, coot, geese, woodcock and jacksnipe seasons occurred during the winter months. Teal duck, rail and gallinule seasons occurred in the fall. Mourning dove seasons occurred intermittently during the fall and winter months. **SPECIAL EVENTS** Junior Stock Show and Barbecue, Big Lake, January; 4-H Junior Stock Show, Big Lake, July; Chili Cookoff, Big Lake, October.

COMMUNITIES

COUNTY SEAT Big Lake, County Courthouse, 76932; County Clerk's Office, 915/884-2442. **INCORPORATED COMMUNITIES** (1980 population and ZIP Code) Big Lake (3,404) 76932. **UNINCORPORATED COMMUNITIES** (and ZIP Code) Best 76931, Stiles 76932 and Texon 76954. **FOR ADDITIONAL LOCAL INFORMATION** Big Lake Chamber of Commerce, P.O. Box 905, Big Lake, 76932, 915/884-2980.

REAL (B10)

THE LAND

Northwest of San Antonio on U.S. Highway 83 in the Edwards Plateau Region, Real County covers 697 square miles with an elevation range of 1,500 to 2,400 feet. The county has light colored, well drained soils and very dark, loamy surfaces over clayey or loamy subsoils with accumulations of lime. Real is in the Edwards Plateau vegetation area with tall and mid grasses, shinnery and live oak, junipers and mesquite. Less than 1% of the land in the county is considered prime farmland. **CLIMATE** Mild and dry. The average annual temperature is 68°F. Temperatures in January range from an average low of 35° to an average high of 62°F and in July range from 70° to 96°F. The average annual precipitation is 26 inches, with an average relative humidity of 78% at 6 A.M. and 46% at 6 P.M. The average annual snowfall is one inch. The growing season averages 235 days per year, with the last freeze in late March and the first freeze in mid November. The sun shines during the year on the average 65% of the daylight hours.

THE PEOPLE

The 1982 estimated population of 2,600 indicates a continuation of the moderate growth rate established in the 1970s which reversed the population decline from 1940 to 1970. The age groups with the largest gains from 1970 to 1980 were ages 62 and over and 15 to 19. The county has a high number of residents who are over age 64. The high median age rose from 32 to 1970 to 35 in 1980. The majority of the county residents live in rural areas. The largest ancestry groups are persons of English descent (31%), Irish descent (22%), Hispanic (22%) and German descent (18%). **REGISTERED VOTERS** As of November 2, 1982 there were 1,969 registered voters (0.03% of the state total). The 1982 general election had a 69% voter turnout, compared to a 73% turnout in the 1980 general election. In the 1982 primary 96% voted Democratic and 4% Republican, with 875 votes cast.

THE ECONOMY

AGRICULTURE Sheep ranches. In 1982, 83% of the land was in farms and ranches, with 2% of the farmland under

REAL (continued)

cultivation. Real ranked 241st in the state for highest agricultural receipts, with 97% from livestock and livestock products. Overgrazing, undesirable brush and weeds and water erosion are the current conservation problems. Primary crops: hay and sorghum. Primary fruits and nuts: pecans. Primary livestock and products: cattle, sheep, wool, angora goats and mohair. **BUSINESS** Total number of business establishments in the county: 37. Retail sales during the first quarter of 1984 increased 18%. In 1980, 27% of the labor force were self-employed, 14% were employed in professional or related services, 3% in manufacturing, 21% in wholesale and retail trade, 26% in agriculture, forestry, fisheries and mining, 20% were employed in other counties and there were 281 retired workers. The industry with the most employment is tourism. The nonfarm earnings in 1981 totaled $15,158,000. The retired workers received an average monthly Social Security payment of $278. **FINANCE** On June 30, 1983, one commercial bank had total deposits of $9,358,000 and total assets of $10,558,000. There are two state savings and loan association branches in the county. **HOUSING** Average value of homes in 1980: $20,200. In 1982 three permits were issued for new, single family houses. Between 1970 and 1980 the number of housing units increased by 49%. Fifty-three percent of all units in the county are air-conditioned, 61% are heated by gas and 15% by electricity. **NATURAL RESOURCES** Caliche, limestone, kaolin clay, oil and gas. **TOURISM** Travel expenditures of $8,119,000 in 1982 (an increase of 14% over 1981) generated 171 jobs and $1,469,000 in payroll. **ALCOHOLIC BEVERAGES** Totally dry. **FEDERAL EXPENDITURES** The federal government had direct expenditures or obligations of $5,423,000 in the county during fiscal year 1983, including $347,000 by the U.S. Department of Defense. In addition, the federal government provided $244,000 in grant awards, paid $136,000 in salaries and wages, made direct payments to individuals of $4,734,000 including $3,815,000 in retirement and disability payments, awarded $2,000 in procurement contracts and spent $308,000 in other expenditures or obligations. The federal government also provided $4,000 in direct loans and $529,000 in guaranteed loans and insurance.

COMMUNICATION
Newspapers–Weekly: Real County American (Leakey). Telephone companies: General Telephone, Frio Canyon Telephone, Hill Country Telephone Coop. and SW Texas Telephone. **TRANSPORTATION** Total public road mileage: 236. In 1982 there were 2,694 registered vehicles and 13 reported traffic accidents. Motor freight: two carriers. Aircraft: four are registered in the county. Airports: Real County Airport at Leakey and Lewis Ranch Airport near Leakey.

COMMUNITY SERVICES
EDUCATION One school district with one elementary and one high school. The average daily attendance in 1981-82 was 262, with expenditures per pupil of $2,404 including 17 classroom teachers with an average annual salary of $14,553. Forty-six percent of the 24 high school graduates planned to attend college. In 1982-83, 78% of the students were White and 22% Hispanic. **CHILD CARE** Four day care licensed facilities. **HEALTH CARE** One physician and one dentist. Ambulance services: two volunteer services. **CHURCHES** Nine churches have an estimated combined membership of 1,791. The largest denominations are Southern Baptist and Catholic. **SOCIAL SERVICES** In fiscal year 1983 a total of $198,443 in food stamps was distributed, with an average of 397 persons receiving food stamps each month. Aid to Families with Dependent Children (AFDC) totaled $25,365 with an average of 18 families receiving AFDC

each month. Medical assistance benefits for the aged and disabled of $104,866 and for families and children of $33,531 brought the county benefit total to $362,205. **FIRE PROTECTION** Three volunteer fire departments. **LAW ENFORCEMENT** The County Sheriff has five commissioned officers. **CRIME** Three violent crimes (murder, forcible rape, robbery and aggravated assault) and 35 nonviolent crimes (burglary, larceny-theft and motor vehicle theft) were reported in 1982. **JUDICIAL SYSTEM** one District Court and Judge, one County Court and Judge and three Justices of the Peace. In the District Court a total of 47 cases were pending on 1/1/82, 74 new cases were filed and 79 cases were disposed of during the year leaving 42 cases pending on 12/31/82. There were 35 criminal cases on the docket, nine convictions, two persons committed to prison and 11 cases left pending. In the County Court 22 cases were pending on 1/1/82, 45 new cases were filed and 49 cases were disposed of during the year leaving 18 cases pending on 12/31/82. There were 63 criminal cases on the docket, 31 convictions, two persons committed to jail, and 18 cases left pending. **JAILS** One jail, capacity three. **ATTORNEYS AT LAW** One. **UTILITIES** 49% of the residents are connected to a public or privately owned water system and 10% are connected to a public sewer system. Electricity is distributed to the county by Bandera Electric Coop., Inc., Central Texas Electric Coop., Inc., Kimble Electric Coop., Inc. and Medina Electric Coop., Inc. and is generated primarily by oil, water and coal. **TAXES** The county has three units with taxing authority: one school district, one county and one college district.

RECREATION/ENTERTAINMENT
NATIONAL REGISTER OF HISTORIC PLACES Camp Wood: San Lorenzo de la Santa Cruz. **MUNICIPAL PARKS** Three acres in two municipal parks. These parks contain one playground. **SCENIC DRIVES** The Texas Hill Country Trail runs through this county on F.M. 337, U.S. 83 and Texas 39. Additional Hill Country views can be found in the county's western-portion on Texas 55, F.M. 335, Texas 41 and F.M. 336. **BOATING/FISHING** Major rivers: Frio and East Frio. **HUNTING** Fall and winter seasons on deer. No closed seasons on javelina, coyote, bobcat and squirrel. Winter seasons on quail, muskrat, beaver, opossum, ring-tailed cat, badger, fox, weasel, raccoon, skunk and civet cat. Fall, winter and spring seasons on turkey. In 1983 sandhill crane, duck, coot, geese, woodcock and jacksnipe seasons occurred during the winter months. Teal duck, rail and gallinule seasons occurred in the fall. Mourning dove seasons occurred intermittently during the fall and winter months with a fall season on white-winged dove. **SPECIAL EVENTS** July Jubilee (Parade, Events), Leakey, July; Old Settlers Reunion, Camp Wood, August.

COMMUNITIES
COUNTY SEAT Leakey, County Courthouse, 78873; County Clerk's Office, 512/232-5202. **INCORPORATED COMMUNITIES** (1980 population and ZIP Code) Camp Wood (728) 78833 and Leakey (468) 78873. **UNINCORPORATED COMMUNITIES** (and ZIP Code) Prade Ranch 78058, Rio Frio 78879 and Vance 78828. **FOR ADDITIONAL LOCAL INFORMATION** Nueces Canyon Chamber of Commerce, P.O. Box 369, Camp Wood, 78833, 512/597-3974 and Frio Canyon Chamber of Commerce, P.O. Box 743, Leakey, 78873, 512/232-6757.

RED RIVER (E2)

THE LAND
Bordering Oklahoma west of Texarkana on U.S. Highway 82 in the East Texas Timberlands Region, Red River County covers 1,054 square miles with an elevation range of 300 to 500 feet. In

the west central portion of the county are slightly acidic soils with light or dark colored loamy surfaces and cracking, clayey subsoils and gray to black, cracking, clayey soils with a high shrink-swell potential. In the southeastern part of the county are light colored soils with loamy surfaces over reddish clayey subsoils high in iron. Along the Red River are brownish to reddish, cracking, clayey soils, or loamy soils. The rest of the county has light colored soils with sandy surfaces and mottled, clayey subsoils. The southwestern part of the county is in the Blackland Prairies vegetation area with tall grasses, mesquite, oak, pecan and elm trees along streams. The rest of the county is in the Post Oak Savannah vegetation area with tall grasses, post and blackjack oak. Between 21 and 30% of the land in the county is considered prime farmland. **CLIMATE** Subtropical Humid, mild with above average precipitation. The average annual temperature is 63°F. Temperatures in January range from an average low of 30° to an average high of 52°F and in July range from 71° to 94°F. The average annual precipitation is 46 inches, with an average relative humidity of 83% at 6 A.M. and 57% at 6 P.M. The average annual snowfall is four inches. The growing season averages 234 days per year, with the last freeze in late March and the first freeze in mid November. The sun shines during the year on the average 67% of the daylight hours.

THE PEOPLE
The 1982 estimated population of 15,800 indicates a reversal of the population growth experienced from 1970 to 1980 when urban areas had a 47% population gain. Although the median age lowered from 40 in 1970 to 36 in 1980 the population remains older than average. The largest ancestry groups are persons of English descent (22%), Black (20%) and Irish descent (18%). **REGISTERED VOTERS** As of November 2, 1982 there were 8,510 registered voters (0.1% of the state total). The 1982 general election had a 47% voter turnout, compared to a 64% turnout in the 1980 general election. In the 1982 primary 99% voted Democratic and 0.3% Republican, with 3,799 votes cast.

THE ECONOMY
AGRICULTURE Forest production and wheat area. In 1982, 70% of the land was in farms and ranches, with 34% of the farmland under cultivation and 1% irrigated. Red River ranked 129th in the state in highest agricultural receipts, with 70% from livestock and livestock products. Water erosion, improper woodland management, flooding and solid waste management are the current conservation problems. Primary crops: wheat, hay, soybeans and sorghum. Primary vegetables: tomatoes and processed vegetables including beets, cucumbers for pickles, snapbeans, spinach and sweet corn. Primary fruits and nuts: peaches and pecans. Primary livestock and products: cattle and hogs. **BUSINESS** Total number of business establishments in the county: 225. Retail sales during the first quarter of 1984 increased 4%. In 1980, 13% of the labor force were self-employed, 21% were employed in professional or related services, 31% in manufacturing, 15% in wholesale and retail trade, 9% in agriculture, forestry, fisheries and mining, 24% were employed in other counties and there were 2,038 retired workers. The industries with the most employment: agribusiness, lumber mills and the manufacture of men's work clothing, metal furniture and metal doors. The nonfarm earnings in 1981 totaled $104,037,000. The retired workers received an average monthly Social Security payment of $261. **FINANCE** On June 30, 1983, three commercial banks had total deposits of $59,454,000 and total assets of $66,223,000. There is one federal savings and loan association branch and two credit unions in the county. **HOUSING** Average value of homes in 1980: $15,900. Between 1970 and 1980 the number of housing units increased by 22%. Sixty-one percent of all units in the county are air-conditioned, 71% are

heated by gas and 13% by electricity. **NATURAL RESOURCES** Limestone, phosphorite, oil and gas. In 1982 a total of 65,066 barrels of crude oil and 3,123 thousand cubic feet of casinghead gas were produced. Current production of other minerals and products includes clay, industrial sand and chalk. Pine and hardwood production in 1981 totaled 4,736,264 cubic feet: 3,108,540 cubic feet of pine and 1,627,724 cubic feet of hardwood. **TOURISM** Travel expenditures of $1,537,000 in 1982 (an increase of 14% over 1981) generated 30 jobs and $264,000 in payroll. **ALCOHOLIC BEVERAGES** Packaged distilled spirits, beer, ale, malt liquor and wine are legal in parts of the county. **FEDERAL EXPENDITURES** The federal government had direct expenditures or obligations of $36,103,000 in the county during fiscal year 1983, including $678,000 by the U.S. Department of Defense. In addition, the federal government provided $284,000 in grant awards, paid $1,025,000 in salaries and wages, made direct payments to individuals of $31,687,000 including $21,913,000 in retirement and disability payments, awarded $27,000 in procurement contracts and spent $3,079,000 in other expenditures or obligations. The federal government also provided $4,886,000 in direct loans and $12,360,000 in guaranteed loans and insurance.

COMMUNICATION
Newspapers–Weekly: Bogata News, The Clarksville Times and The Woodland Sun. Radio: KCAR-AM (Clarksville). Cable TV. Telephone companies: General Telephone, Continental Telephone, Avery Telephone, Blossom Telephone and Century Telephone. **TRANSPORTATION** Total public road mileage: 1,038. In 1982 there were 13,152 registered vehicles and 235 reported traffic accidents including three fatalities. Taxi cabs: two companies in Clarksville. Intercity bus service is available. Motor freight: two carriers. Rail: one branch line carries annually less than one million tons of freight through the county. Aircraft: 35 are registered in the county. Airports: Red River County Airport at Clarksville serves as a base for 21 aircraft and is a basic utility airport with general aviation service. Shawnee Ranch Airport at Boxelder.

COMMUNITY SERVICES
EDUCATION Four school districts with seven elementary, one middle and four high schools. The average daily attendance in 1981-82 was 3,038, with expenditures per pupil of $2,282 including 206 classroom teachers with an average annual salary of $16,110. Forty-two percent of the 198 high school graduates planned to attend college. In 1982-83, 71% of the students were White, 1% Hispanic, 28% Black and 0.3 % American Indian. **PUBLIC LIBRARIES** Red River County Library (Clarksville): 25,958 volumes. **CHILD CARE** 13 day care and four twenty-four hour care licensed facilities. **HEALTH CARE** Eight physicians and three dentists. Hospitals: one with a capacity of 66. Ambulance services: one commercial service. Mental health: one clinic. Nursing homes: two nursing homes with a combined capacity of 286 nursing care residents. The average cost per day for private patients in 1982 was $28.07. **CHURCHES** 67 churches have an estimated combined membership of 10,699. The largest denominations are Southern Baptist, United Methodist and American Baptist. **SOCIAL SERVICES** In fiscal year 1983 a total of $990,537 in food stamps was distributed, with an average of 2,391 persons receiving food stamps each month. Aid to Families with Dependent Children (AFDC) totaled $246,139 with an average of 178 families receiving AFDC each month. Medical assistance benefits for the aged and disabled of $2,988,899 and for families and children of $368,966 brought the county benefit total to $4,594,540. **FIRE PROTECTION** Five volunteer fire departments. **LAW ENFORCEMENT** The County Sheriff has six commissioned officers. One police department has a force

COUNTIES

RED RIVER (continued)

of eight. **CRIME** 78 violent crimes (murder, forcible rape, robbery and aggravated assault) and 260 nonviolent crimes (burglary, larceny-theft and motor vehicle theft) were reported in 1982. **JUDICIAL SYSTEM** Two District Courts and Judges, one County Court and Judge and four Justices of the Peace. In the District Courts a total of 354 cases were pending on 1/1/82, 468 new cases were filed and 458 cases were disposed of during the year leaving 364 cases pending on 12/31/82. There were 170 criminal cases on the docket, 109 convictions, 22 persons committed to prison and four committed to jail and 37 cases left pending. In the County Court 61 cases were pending on 1/1/82, 112 new cases were filed and 100 cases were disposed of during the year leaving 73 cases pending on 12/31/82. There were 173 criminal cases on the docket, 96 convictions, and 73 cases left pending. **JAILS** One jail, capacity 12, constructing new jail, capacity 14. **ATTORNEYS AT LAW** 13. **UTILITIES** 81% of the residents are connected to a public or privately owned water system and 50% are connected to a public sewer system. Natural gas is distributed to the county by Lone Star Gas Co., Division of Enserch. The average annual residential bill for natural gas in 1982 for the Lone Star distribution system was $405.91, an increase of 35% over 1981. Electricity is distributed to the county by Bowie-Cass Electric Coop., Inc., Texas Power and Light Co. and Lamar Co. Electric Coop., Inc. and is generated primarily by gas and coal. The typical residential electric bill is $165.24 per month for an all-electric house using 2,500 kwh. **TAXES** The county has 11 units with taxing authority: four school districts, five cities, one county and one special district.

RECREATION/ENTERTAINMENT

NATIONAL REGISTER OF HISTORIC PLACES Blakeney vicinity: Sam Kaufman Site. Clarksville: Red River County Courthouse. Kanawha: Neely Site. Kiomatia vicinity: Kiomatia Mounds Archaeological District. **MUNICIPAL PARKS** 168 acres in one municipal park. This park contains one playground, three baseball and softball fields, one tennis court, three multi-use courts, three beaches, one boat ramp and shore fishing facilities. **BOATING/FISHING** Lakes/reservoirs: Arrowhead Ranch (16 acres), Clarksville Country Club (33 acres), Langford Creek (76 acres), Magic Valley (38 acres), South (70 acres) and River Crest (555 acres). Major rivers: Sulphur and Red. Primary streams: Pecan Bayou, Little Bayou, Langford, Sand, Pickett, Shawnee, Little Pine, Kickapoo, Denwiddie Bayou and Blanton. **HUNTING** Fall and winter seasons on deer. Summer, fall and winter seasons on squirrel. No closed seasons on coyote, bobcat and nutria. Winter seasons on quail, muskrat, beaver, otter, opossum, mink, ring-tailed cat, badger, fox, raccoon, skunk and civet cat. In 1983 duck, coot, geese, woodcock and jacksnipe seasons occurred during the winter months. Teal duck, rail and gallinule seasons occurred in the fall. Mourning dove seasons occurred intermittently during the fall and winter months. **SPECIAL EVENTS** County Fair, Clarksville, September; Rodeo, Clarksville, Variable dates.

COMMUNITIES

COUNTY SEAT Clarksville, County Courthouse, 75426; County Clerk's Office, 214/427-2401. **INCORPORATED COMMUNITIES** (1980 population and ZIP Code) Annona (471) 75550, Avery (520) 75554, Bogata (1,508) 75417, Clarksville (4,917) 75426, Deport 724: (41 in Red River Co. and 683 in Lamar Co.) 75435 and Detroit (805) 75436. **UNINCORPORATED COMMUNITIES** (and ZIP Code) Acworth 75426, Addielou 75412, Albion 75426, Bagwell 75412, Blakeney 75412, Boxelder 75550, Cuthand 75417, Davenport 75412, Dimple 75426, English 75426, Fulbright 75436, Greenwood 75426, Halesboro 75417,

Johntown 75417, Kanawha 75436, King 75550, Kiomatia (West Scrap) 75436, Lydia 75554, Mabry 75426, Manchester 75412, Negley (Mulberry) 75426, Peters Prairie (Petersburg) 75426, Rosalie 75417, Rugby 75435, Shadowland 75435, Sherry 75426, Siliver City 75426, Vandalia 75426, White Rock 75426 and Woodland 75436. **FOR ADDITIONAL LOCAL INFORMATION** Clarksville Chamber of Commerce, 101 N. Locust, Clarksville, 75426, 214/427-2645.

REEVES (P92)

THE LAND

East of El Paso on Interstate Highway 20 in the Trans-Pecos Region, Reeves County covers 2,626 square miles with an elevation range of 2,500 to 4,800 feet. The county has level to undulating soils which are alkaline and loamy throughout or loamy over clayey subsoils and limestone bedrock. Some areas are 90% exposed rock. Reeves is in the Trans-Pecos, Mountains and Basins vegetation area with desert shrub, grama grassland, juniper, some oak and yucca. Salt-tolerant plants are found in saline areas. Less than 1% of the land in the county is considered prime farmland. **CLIMATE** Subtropical Arid with wide-ranging daily temperatures. The average annual temperature is 64°F. Temperatures in January range from an average low of 29° to an average high of 58°F and in July range from 68° to 99°F. The average annual precipitation is 10 inches, with an average relative humidity of 67% at 6 A.M. and 33% at 6 P.M. The average annual snowfall is four inches. The growing season averages 226 days per year, with the last freeze in early April and the first freeze in mid November. The sun shines during the year on the average 77% of the daylight hours.

THE PEOPLE

Reeves County ranks 27th among all U.S. counties in the highest percent of residents who are of Spanish origin. The 1982 estimated population of 16,600 indicates an increase since 1980. However the population has steadily declined since the 1960s. Urban areas experienced a slight growth rate between 1970 and 1980 while rural areas had losses. The age group with the largest increase was ages 65 and over while the largest decrease was birth to nine years. Therefore the younger than average median age rose from 22 in 1970 to 25 in 1980. The largest ancestry groups are Hispanic (62%) persons of English descent (13%) and Irish descent (9%). **REGISTERED VOTERS** As of November 2, 1982 there were 7,983 registered voters (0.1% of the state total). The 1982 general election had a 47% voter turnout, compared to a 56% turnout in the 1980 general election. In the 1982 primary 100% voted Democratic, with 3,076 votes cast.

THE ECONOMY

AGRICULTURE Ranchland. In 1982, 87% of the land was in farms and ranches, with 2% of the farmland under cultivation. Most of the cropland and some of the rangeland was irrigated. Reeves ranked 90th in the state in highest agricultural receipts, with 81% from livestock and livestock products. Overgrazing, decreasing irrigation water supplies and salinity are the current conservation problems. Primary crops: fourth in the state for barley. Cotton, hay and wheat. Primary vegetables: onions and bell peppers. Primary fruits and nuts: peaches and pecans. Primary livestock and products: cattle and milk. **BUSINESS** Total number of business establishments in the county: 341. Retail sales during the first quarter of 1984 decreased 9%, with an increase in Toyah of 59% and a decrease in Pecos City of 10%. In 1980, 8% of the labor force were self-employed, 14% were employed in professional or related services, 5% in manufacturing, 17% in wholesale and retail trade, 25% in agriculture, forestry, fisheries and mining, 15% were employed in other counties and there were 881 retired workers. The industries with the most employment: tourism, oil and gas extraction, sulfur mining, cottonseed oil mills and agribusiness. The nonfarm earnings in 1981 totaled $115,235,000. The retired workers received an average monthly Social Security payment of $300. **FINANCE** On June 30, 1983, two commercial banks had total deposits of $90,830,000 and total assets of $103,781,000. There is one state savings and loan association branch and four credit unions in the county. **HOUSING** Average value of homes in 1980: $18,600. Permits for new, privately owned housing units decreased in 1982: 11 permits were issued with a total construction cost of $195,995. Of those permits, all were for single family houses. Between 1970 and 1980 the number of housing units increased by 5%. Eighty-three percent of all units in the county are air-conditioned, 86% are heated by gas and 12% by electricity. **NATURAL RESOURCES** Gypsum, limestone, salt, oil, gas and volcanic ash. In 1982 a total of 65,126,748 thousand cubic feet of gas well gas, 71,933 barrels of condensate, 1,252,686 barrels of crude oil and 3,566,674 thousand cubic feet of casinghead gas were produced. Current production of other minerals and products includes brine, sand and gravel and recovered sulphur. **TOURISM** Travel expenditures of $30,196,000 in 1982 (an increase of 12% over 1981) generated 691 jobs and $5,721,000 in payroll. Lodging: seven hotels, motels and tourist courts. **ALCOHOLIC BEVERAGES** Packaged distilled spirits, beer, ale, malt liquor and wine are legal in parts of the county. Sale of mixed beverages is legal in all or parts of the county. **FEDERAL EXPENDITURES** The federal government had direct expenditures or obligations of $16,122,000 in the county during fiscal year 1983, including $270,000 by the U.S. Department of Defense. In addition, the federal government provided $475,000 in grant awards, paid $1,294,000 in salaries and wages, made direct payments to individuals of $12,671,000 including $9,562,000 in retirement and disability payments, awarded $95,000 in procurement contracts and spent $1,587,000 in other expenditures or obligations. The federal government also provided $623,000 in direct loans and $5,564,000 in guaranteed loans and insurance.

COMMUNICATION

Newspapers–Daily: Pecos Enterprise, ave. eve. circ. 2,523. Radio: KIVN-AM (Pecos). Cable TV. Telephone companies: Continental Telephone and Big Bend Telephone. **TRANSPORTATION** Total public road mileage: 1,131. In 1982 there were 12,959 registered vehicles and 434 reported traffic accidents including eight fatalities. Taxi cabs: one part time company in Pecos. Intercity bus service is available. Motor freight: 13 local and intrastate carriers. Rail: two main and one branch line carry freight through the county. The two main lines carry annually five to 10 million tons of freight each and the one branch carries less than one million. Aircraft: 68 are registered in the county. Airports: Pecos Municipal Airport serves as a base for 45 aircraft and is a basic transportation airport with general aviation service. Balmorhea Airport at Balmorhea.

COMMUNITY SERVICES

EDUCATION Two school districts with six elementary, two middle and two high schools. The average daily attendance in 1981-82 was 4,039, with expenditures per pupil of $3,621 including 253 classroom teachers with an average annual salary of $17,818. Thirty-nine percent of the 207 high school graduates planned to attend college. In 1982-83, 23% of the students were White, 74% Hispanic, 3% Black, 0.3% Asian and 0.3% American Indian. **PUBLIC LIBRARIES** Balmorhea Public Library: 6,500 volumes. Reeves County Library (Pecos): 23,136 volumes. **CHILD CARE** Nine day care and three twenty-four hour care licensed facilities. **HEALTH CARE** Eight physicians and five dentists. Hospitals: one with a capacity of 62. Ambulance services: three volunteer services and one commercial service. Mental health: one county clinic. Nursing homes: one nursing home has a capacity of 60 nursing care residents. The average cost per day for private patients in 1982 was $34.11. **CHURCHES** 37 churches have an estimated combined membership of 11,809. The largest denominations are Catholic and Southern Baptist. **SOCIAL SERVICES** In fiscal year 1983 a total of $1,535,601 in food stamps was distributed, with an average of 3,356 persons receiving food stamps each month. Aid to Families with Dependent Children (AFDC) totaled $175,400 with an average of 116 families receiving AFDC each month. Medical assistance benefits for the aged and disabled of $796,590 and for families and children of $301,876 brought the county benefit total to $2,809,467. **FIRE PROTECTION** Three volunteer fire departments. **LAW ENFORCEMENT** The County Sheriff has 11 commissioned officers. One police department has a force of 16. **CRIME** 89 violent crimes (murder, forcible rape, robbery and aggravated assault) and 829 nonviolent crimes (burglary, larceny-theft and motor vehicle theft) were reported in 1982. **JUDICIAL SYSTEM** One District Court and Judge, two County Courts and Judges and four Justices of the Peace. In the District Court a total of 294 cases were pending on 1/1/82, 330 new cases were filed and 326 cases were disposed of during the year leaving 298 cases pending on 12/31/82. There were 156 criminal cases on the docket, 67 convictions, 14 persons committed to prison and 65 cases left pending. In the County Courts 276 cases were pending on 1/1/82, 884 new cases were filed and 753 cases were disposed of during the year leaving 407 cases pending on 12/31/82. There were 951 criminal cases on the docket, 144 convictions, 23 persons committed to jail, and 329 cases left pending. **JAILS** One jail, capacity 84. **ATTORNEYS AT LAW** 12. **UTILITIES** 97% of the residents are connected to a public or privately owned water system and 81% are connected to a public sewer system. Natural gas is distributed to the county by Southwest Texas Municipal Gas Corp. Electricity is distributed to the county by West Texas Utilities Co., Texas-New Mexico Power Co. and Rio Grande Electric Coop., Inc. and is generated primarily by gas, oil and coal. The typical residential electric bill is $168.05 per month for an all-electric house using 2,500 kwh. **TAXES** The county has eight units with taxing authority: two school districts, three cities, one county and two special districts.

RECREATION/ENTERTAINMENT

STATE Balmorhea State Recreation Area covers 46 acres with camping and trailer sites as well as swimming areas. A huge walled swimming pool is fed by the San Solomon Springs that flow 26 million gallons daily. **COUNTY/MUNICIPAL PARKS** 146 acres in three county and four municipal parks. These parks contain three playgrounds, one golf course, six baseball and softball fields, two multi-use courts and three swimming pools. **SCENIC DRIVES** The Texas Pecos Trail runs through this county. This trail rambles through the vast region of Southwest and West Texas with landscapes varying from raw, arid regions to green valleys. **BOATING/FISHING** Lakes/reservoirs: Balmorhea (573 acres) and Red Bluff (7,908 acres). Major rivers: Pecos. Primary streams: Sandia, Cottonwood and Toyah. **HUNTING** Fall season on antelope. Fall and winter seasons on deer and mule deer. No closed seasons on javelina, coyote, bobcat and elk. Winter seasons on quail, muskrat, beaver, opossum, ring-tailed cat, badger, fox, weasel, raccoon, skunk and civet cat. In 1983 sandhill crane, duck, coot, geese, woodcock and jacksnipe seasons occurred during the winter months. Teal duck, rail and gallinule seasons occurred in the fall. Mourning dove seasons occurred intermittently during the fall and winter months with a fall season on white-winged dove in some parts of the county. **MUSEUMS** Pecos: West of the Pecos Museum. **SPECIAL EVENTS** Rodeo Week, Pecos,

COUNTIES

REEVES (continued)

June; June Fest, Pecos, June; Night in Old Pecos, Pecos, June; Golden Girl of the West Pageant, Pecos, June; 1800's Parade, Pecos, June; 4th of July Parade, Pecos, July; Old Fiddlers Contest, Pecos, July; West of the Pecos Rodeo, Pecos, July; Frijole Cookoff, Balmorhea, August; Fall Fair Festival, Pecos, October.

COMMUNITIES

COUNTY SEAT Pecos, County Courthouse, 79772; County Clerk's Office, 915/4455-5467. **INCORPORATED COMMUNITIES** (1980 population and ZIP Code) Balmorhea (568) 79718, Pecos (12,855) 79772 and Toyah (165) 79785. **UNINCORPORATED COMMUNITIES** (and ZIP Code) Brogado 79718, Hermosa 79772, Orla 79770, Red Bluff 79770, Saragosa 79780, Toyahvale 79786 and Verhalen 79772. **FOR ADDITIONAL LOCAL INFORMATION** Pecos Chamber of Commerce, P.O. Box 27, Pecos, 79772, 915/445-2406.

REFUGIO (G28)

THE LAND

North of Corpus Christi on U.S. Highways 183 and 77 in the Coastal Prairies Region, Refugio County covers 771 square miles with an elevation range of sea level to 100 feet. The southwestern portion of the county has level to undulating soils with light or dark, loamy surfaces over cracking, clayey subsoils. In the northwestern part are level soils with light colored, loamy surfaces over very deep reddish or mottled subsoils. The rest of the county has very dark, loamy surfaces over clayey subsoils and gray to black, cracking, clayey soils with a high shrink-swell potential. Refugio is in the Gulf Prairies and Marshes vegetation area with tall prairie grasses, mesquite, oak and prickly pear. Between 51 and 60% of the land in the county is considered prime farmland. **CLIMATE** Subtropical Humid with mild temperatures and more than average precipitation. The risk of a tropical storm or hurricane exists June through October. The average annual temperature is 72°F. Temperatures in January range from an average low of 45° to an average high of 64°F and in July range from 76° to 93°F. The average annual precipitation is 37 inches, with an average relative humidity of 90% at 6 A.M. and 65% at 6 P.M. There is no snowfall. The growing season averages 309 days per year, with the last freeze in mid February and the first freeze in mid December. The sun shines during the year on the average 65% of the daylight hours.

THE PEOPLE

Refugio County ranks 66th among all U.S. counties in the highest percent of residents of Spanish origin and has one of the highest percents of persons who are native Texans. The 1982 estimated population of 9,200 indicates a continuation of the slow loss in population, which has occurred since the 1960s. Urban areas experienced a 10% population loss from 1970 to 1980 while rural areas grew 5%. The age group with the largest gain was ages 65 and over, while the most reduction occurred in ages five to 14. The largest ancestry groups are Hispanic (38%), persons of English descent (18%), Irish descent (18%) and German descent (18%). **REGISTERED VOTERS** As of November 2, 1982 there were 5,202 registered voters (0.1% of the state total). The 1982 general election had a 47% voter turnout, compared to a 74% turnout in the 1980 general election. In the 1982 primary 99% voted Democratic and 1% Republican, with 2,437 votes cast.

THE ECONOMY

AGRICULTURE In 1982, 91% of the land was in farms and ranches, with 18% of the farmland under cultivation. Refugio ranked 150th in the state in highest agricultural receipts, with 54% from livestock and livestock products. Overgrazing, undesirable brush, soil compaction, drainage, noxious weeds and shoreline erosion are the current conservation problems. Primary crops: sorghum, corn, cotton, wheat and hay. Primary vegetables: watermelons. Primary fruits and nuts: pecans. Primary livestock and products: cattle and hogs. **BUSINESS** Total number of business establishments in the county: 230. Retail sales during the first quarter of 1984 increased 13%. In 1980, 10% of the labor force were self-employed, 17% were employed in professional or related services, 7% in manufacturing, 19% in wholesale and retail trade, 26% in agriculture, forestry, fisheries and mining, 11% were employed in other counties and there were 783 retired workers. The industries with the most employment: oil and gas extraction and agribusiness. The nonfarm earnings in 1981 totaled $95,283,000. The retired workers received an average monthly Social Security payment of $331. **FINANCE** On June 30, 1983, two commercial banks had total deposits of $62,379,000 and total assets of $77,590,000. On December 31, 1982 one state savings and loan association had assets of $26,110,806. In addition there is one credit union in the county. **HOUSING** Average value of homes in 1980: $25,300. Permits for new, privately owned housing units increased in 1982: 16 permits were issued with a total construction cost of $549,760. Of those permits, all were for single family houses. Housing permits in Woodsboro increased from five in 1981 to 13 in 1982 with all permits issued for single family houses. Between 1970 and 1980 the number of housing units increased by 8%. Fifty-nine percent of all units in the county are air-conditioned, 83% are heated by gas and 14% by electricity. **NATURAL RESOURCES** Industrial sand, oil and gas. In 1982 a total of 56,470,457 thousand cubic feet of gas well gas, 39,920 barrels of condensate, 23,483,771 barrels of crude oil and 50,934,814 thousand cubic feet of casinghead gas were produced. **TOURISM** Travel expenditures of $3,205,000 in 1982 (an increase of 14% over 1981) generated 62 jobs and $550,000 in payroll. **ALCOHOLIC BEVERAGES** Packaged distilled spirits, beer, ale, malt liquor and wine are legal in parts of the county. **FEDERAL EXPENDITURES** The federal government had direct expenditures or obligations of $15,240,000 in the county during fiscal year 1983, including $365,000 by the U.S. Department of Defense. In addition, the federal government provided $229,000 in grant awards, paid $784,000 in salaries and wages, made direct payments to individuals of $11,764,000 including $8,732,000 in retirement and disability payments, awarded $663,000 in procurement contracts and spent $1,800,000 in other expenditures or obligations. The federal government also provided $1,780,000 in direct loans and $12,707,000 in guaranteed loans and insurance.

COMMUNICATION

Newspapers–Weekly: County Press (Refugio). Radio: KYOT-FM (Refugio). Cable TV. Telephone companies: General Telephone and Southwestern Bell. **TRANSPORTATION** Total public road mileage: 407. In 1982 there were 8,460 registered vehicles and 283 reported traffic accidents including 29 fatalities. Taxi cabs: one company in the city of Refugio. Intercity bus service is available. Motor freight: seven local and intrastate carriers. Rail: one main line carries annually five to 10 million tons of freight through the county. Aircraft: 38 are registered in the county. Airports: Rooke Field at Refugio which serves as a base for 32 aircraft with general aviation service, and Gulf Coast Airport at Tivoli. Waterborne commerce: (see San Patricio County and Calhoun County).

COMMUNITY SERVICES

EDUCATION Three school districts with four elementary, two middle and three high schools. The average daily attendance in 1981-82 was 1,904, with expenditures per pupil of $3,526 including

2,321 classroom teachers with an average annual salary of $18,312. Fifty-four percent of the 151 high school graduates planned to attend college. In 1982-83, 42% of the students were White, 48% Hispanic, 10% Black and 0.1% Asian. Sports championships: 1983 AAA Boys' Track, Refugio H.S.; 1983 AA Boys' Track, Woodsboro H.S. **PUBLIC LIBRARIES** Refugio County Public Library (Refugio): 19,656 volumes. **CHILD CARE** 12 day care licensed facilities. **HEALTH CARE** Six physicians and three dentists. Hospitals: one with a capacity of 60. Ambulance services: one hospital-based and one volunteer fire department service. Nursing homes: one nursing home has a capacity of 64 nursing care residents. The average cost per day for private patients in 1982 was $30. **CHURCHES** 30 churches have an estimated combined membership of 6,887. The largest denominations are Catholic and Southern Baptist. **SOCIAL SERVICES** In fiscal year 1983 a total of $556,299 in food stamps was distributed, with an average of 1,205 persons receiving food stamps each month. Aid to Families with Dependent Children (AFDC) totaled $136,739 with an average of 94 families receiving AFDC each month. Medical assistance benefits for the aged and disabled of $629,582 and for families and children of $144,991 brought the county benefit total to $1,467,610. **FIRE PROTECTION** Five volunteer fire departments. **LAW ENFORCEMENT** The County Sheriff has 10 commissioned officers. One police department has a force of 11. **CRIME** 14 violent crimes (murder, forcible rape, robbery and aggravated assault) and 244 nonviolent crimes (burglary, larceny-theft and motor vehicle theft) were reported in 1982. **JUDICIAL SYSTEM** Three District Courts and Judges, one County Court and Judge and four Justices of the Peace. In the District Courts a total of 127 cases were pending on 1/1/82, 178 new cases were filed and 169 cases were disposed of during the year leaving 136 cases pending on 12/31/82. There were 98 criminal cases on the docket, 51 convictions, 10 persons committed to prison and 42 cases left pending. In the County Court 329 cases were pending on 1/1/82, 552 new cases were filed and 432 cases were disposed of during the year leaving 449 cases pending on 12/31/82. There were 819 criminal cases on the docket, 174 convictions, 16 persons committed to jail, and 418 cases left pending. **JAILS** One jail, capacity 29. **ATTORNEYS AT LAW** 10. **UTILITIES** 80% of the residents are connected to a public or privately owned water system and 76% are connected to a public sewer system. Natural gas is distributed to the county by Entex, Inc. and Woodsboro Natural Gas Corp. The average annual residential bill for natural gas in 1982 for the Entex distribution system was $390.31, an increase of 26% over 1981. Electricity is distributed to the county by Central Power and Light Co., Cochran Power and Light Co. and Victoria Co. Electric Coop., Inc. and is generated primarily by gas, oil and coal. The typical residential electric bill is $162.15 per month for an all-electric house using 2,500 kwh. **TAXES** The county has 12 units with taxing authority: three school districts, four cities, one county, one hospital district and three special districts.

RECREATION/ENTERTAINMENT
MUNICIPAL PARKS 46 acres in six municipal parks. These parks contain three playgrounds, three baseball and softball fields, one tennis court, one swimming pool, one beach, two boat ramps and shore fishing facilities. **SCENIC DRIVES** The Texas Tropical Trail runs through this county. This trail is charted through the state's southernmost wedge meandering through ranchland, resort areas by the Gulf of Mexico and fertile farmlands. **BOATING/FISHING** Lakes/reservoirs: McGuill (75 acres), Melon (300 acres), Mustang (75 acres), Saint Nicholas North (100 acres), Saint Nicholas South (150 acres) and Twin Mott (50 acres). Major rivers: Rivers: Mission, Guadalupe, San Antonio and Aransas. Primary streams: Melon and Copano. Saltwater fishing: speckled trout, redfish and flounder fishing

is usually good in Copano Bay. Shrimp, oysters and crabs may be taken but, like other saltwater fish, under specific regulations. **WILDLIFE REFUGES** Aransas National Wildlife Refuge covers 90,069 acres. **HUNTING** Fall and winter seasons on deer and javelina. No closed seasons on nutria, coyote, bobcat and squirrel. Winter seasons on quail, muskrat, beaver, otter opossum, mink, ring-tailed cat, badger, fox, raccoon, skunk and civet cat. Fall, winter and spring seasons on turkey. In 1983 duck, coot, geese, woodcock and jacksnipe seasons occurred during the winter months with a winter season on sandhill crane in some parts of the county. Teal duck, rail and gallinule seasons occurred in the fall. Mourning dove seasons occurred intermittently during the fall and winter months with a fall season on white-winged dove. **SPECIAL EVENTS** Old-Fashioned Fourth, Refugio, July; State Frog-Jumping Contest, Refugio, July; County Fair, Refugio, October.

COMMUNITIES
COUNTY SEAT Refugio, County Courthouse, 78377; County Clerk's Office, 512/526-2233. **INCORPORATED COMMUNITIES** (1980 population and ZIP Code) Austwell (280) 77950, Bayside (381) 78340, Refugio (3,898) 78377 and Woodsboro (1,974) 78393. **UNINCORPORATED COMMUNITIES** (and ZIP Code) Bonnie View 78393, Tivoli 77990 and Vidauri 77992. **FOR ADDITIONAL LOCAL INFORMATION** Refugio Chamber of Commerce, P.O. Box 127, Refugio, 78377, 512/526-2835.

ROBERTS (P9)

THE LAND
In the Rolling Plains Region of the Texas Panhandle northeast of Amarillo on U.S. Highway 60, Roberts County covers 915 square miles with an elevation range of 2,500 to 3,200 feet. The county has light colored, well drained soils and very dark, loamy soils with clayey subsoils. Roberts is in the Rolling Plains vegetation area with tall and mid grasses, mesquite, live and shinnery oak. Between 11 and 20% of the land in the county is considered prime farmland. **CLIMATE** Continental Steppe with wide-ranging temperatures on a daily and seasonal basis. Duststorms and thunderstorms are experienced mostly during spring. The average annual temperature is 58°F. Temperatures in January range from an average low of 20° to an average high of 49°F and in July range from 67° to 94°F. The average annual precipitation is 20 inches, with an average relative humidity of 42% at 6 A.M. and 73% at 6 P.M. The average annual snowfall is 17 inches. The growing season averages 194 days per year, with the last freeze in mid April and the first freeze in late October. The sun shines during the year on the average 75% of the daylight hours.

THE PEOPLE
Roberts County is one of the most sparsely populated in the state. However it experienced a strong growth rate of 23% between 1970 and 1980 with a slight increase indicated by the 1982 estimated population of 1,200. The age groups with the largest increases between 1970 and 1980 were birth to nine years and ages 15 to 19. Therefore the high median age lowered from 33 in 1970 to 32 in 1980. The majority of the county residents live in rural areas. The largest ancestry groups are persons of Irish descent (25%), English descent (18%) and German descent (18%). **REGISTERED VOTERS** As of November 2, 1982 there were 715 registered voters (0.01% of the state total). The 1982 general election had a 59% voter turnout, compared to a 78% turnout in the 1980 general election. In the 1982 primary 84% voted Democratic and 16% Republican, with 256 votes cast.

COUNTIES

THE ECONOMY

AGRICULTURE Ranchland. In 1982, 98% of the land was in farms and ranches, with 9% of the farmland under cultivation and 18% irrigated. Roberts ranked 232nd in the state in highest agricultural receipts, with 77% from livestock and livestock products. Overgrazing, undesirable brush, noxious weeds and water and wind erosion are the current conservation problems. Primary crops: wheat, sorghum and hay. Primary livestock and products: cattle and hogs. **BUSINESS** Total number of business establishments in the county: 20. In 1980, 20% of the labor force were self-employed, 12% were employed in professional or related services, 3% in manufacturing, 16% in wholesale and retail trade, 41% in agriculture, forestry, fisheries and mining, 24% were employed in other counties and there were 87 retired workers. The industries with the most employment: oil and gas extraction and agribusiness. The nonfarm earnings in 1981 totaled $10,725,000. The retired workers received an average monthly Social Security payment of $333. **FINANCE** On June 30, 1983, one commercial bank had total deposits of $12,364,000 and total assets of $14,360,000. **HOUSING** Average value of homes in 1980: $27,400. Between 1970 and 1980 the number of housing units increased by 15%. Seventy-nine percent of all units in the county are air-conditioned, 90% are heated by gas and 9% by electricity. **NATURAL RESOURCES** Caliche, oil, gas and volcanic ash. In 1982 a total of 35,297,745 thousand cubic feet of gas well gas, 379,030 barrels of condensate, 796,473 barrels of crude oil and 6,634,764 thousand cubic feet of casinghead gas were produced. **TOURISM** Travel expenditures of $120,000 in 1982 (an increase of 7% over 1981) generated 3 jobs and $22,000 in payroll. **ALCOHOLIC BEVERAGES** Totally dry. **FEDERAL EXPENDITURES** The federal government had direct expenditures or obligations of $1,927,000 in the county during fiscal year 1983, including $36,000 by the U.S. Department of Defense. In addition, the federal government provided $30,000 in grant awards, paid $100,000 in salaries and wages, made direct payments to individuals of $1,270,000 including $919,000 in retirement and disability payments and spent $526,000 in other expenditures or obligations. The federal government also provided $1,770,000 in direct loans and $1,072,000 in guaranteed loans and insurance.

COMMUNICATION

Cable TV. Telephone companies: General Telephone and Southwestern Bell. **TRANSPORTATION** Total public road mileage: 355. In 1982 there were 1,791 registered vehicles and 31 reported traffic accidents including one fatality. Motor freight: two carriers. Rail: one main line carries annually over 30 million tons of freight through the county. Aircraft: 11 are registered in the county. Airports: Roberts County Airport at Miami.

COMMUNITY SERVICES

EDUCATION One school district with one elementary and one high school. The average daily attendance in 1981-82 was 229, with expenditures per pupil of $4,283 including 19 classroom teachers with an average annual salary of $17,814. Eighty-three percent of the 18 high school graduates planned to attend college. In 1982-83, 96% of the students were White, 4% Hispanic and 0.4% Black. **PUBLIC LIBRARIES** Roberts County Library (Miami): 11,500 volumes. **CHILD CARE** One twenty-four hour care licensed facility. **HEALTH CARE** One physician. **CHURCHES** Four churches have an estimated combined membership of 981. The largest denominations are Southern Baptist and United Methodist. **SOCIAL SERVICES** In fiscal year 1983 a total of $6,670 in food stamps, Aid to Families with Dependent Children (AFDC) and medical assistance benefits were distributed. **FIRE PROTECTION** One volunteer fire department. **LAW ENFORCEMENT** The County Sheriff has five commissioned officers. **CRIME** 12 nonviolent crimes (burglary, larceny-theft and motor vehicle theft) were reported in 1982. **JUDICIAL SYSTEM** One District Court and Judge, one County Court and Judge and one Justice of the Peace. In the District Court a total of 58 cases were pending on 1/1/82, 17 new cases were filed and 16 cases were disposed of during the year leaving 59 cases pending on 12/31/82. There were three criminal cases on the docket, two convictions, and one case left pending. In the County Court 17 cases were pending on 1/1/82, 16 new cases were filed and 11 cases were disposed of during the year leaving 22 cases pending on 12/31/82. There were 28 criminal cases on the docket, four convictions, and 20 cases left pending. **JAILS** One jail, capacity three. **UTILITIES** 62% of the residents are connected to a public or privately owned water system and 54% are connected to a public sewer system. Natural gas is distributed to the county by Consolidated Utilities, Inc. Electricity is distributed to the county by Greenbelt Electric Coop., Inc. and North Plains Electric Coop., Inc. and is generated primarily by gas and oil. **TAXES** The county has three units with taxing authority: one school district, one city and one county district.

RECREATION/ENTERTAINMENT

COUNTY/MUNICIPAL PARKS Seven acres in one county and two municipal parks. These parks contain one playground, one baseball and softball field, two tennis courts and one swimming pool. Developed campsites: seven. **BOATING/FISHING** Major rivers: Canadian. Primary streams: Reynolds, Tallahone, Chicken, Indian, Three Corrals, Horse, Home Ranch and Red Deer. **HUNTING** Fall season on antelope and prairie chicken. Fall and winter seasons on deer and mule deer. No closed seasons on coyote and bobcat. Winter seasons on pheasant, quail, muskrat, beaver, opossum, ring-tailed cat, badger, fox, weasel, raccoon, skunk and civet cat. Fall, winter and spring seasons on turkey. In 1983 sandhill crane, duck, coot, geese, woodcock and jacksnipe seasons occurred during the winter months. Teal duck, rail and gallinule seasons occurred in the fall. Mourning dove seasons occurred intermittently during the fall and winter months. **MUSEUMS** Miami: Roberts County Museum. **SPECIAL EVENTS** National Cow Calling Contest and Pioneer Roundup, Miami, June.

COMMUNITIES

COUNTY SEAT Miami, County Courthouse, 79059; County Clerk's Office, 806/868-2341. **INCORPORATED COMMUNITIES** (1980 population and ZIP Code) Miami (813) 79059. **FOR ADDITIONAL LOCAL INFORMATION** Miami Chamber of Commerce, P.O. Box 456, Miami, 79059, 806/868-3191.

ROBERTSON (C19)

THE LAND

Northeast of Austin on U.S. Highway 79/190 in the Claypan Area, Robertson County covers 864 square miles with an elevation range of 250 to 500 feet. Along the Trinity River are undulating to rolling soils with very dark, loamy surfaces over mottled, cracking clayey subsoils. Along the southern border are gray to black, cracking, clayey soils with a high shrink-swell potential and slightly acidic soils with light colored, loamy surfaces over very deep, reddish, cracking clayey subsoils. The rest of the county has level to undulating soils iwth light colored, loamy or sandy surfaces over clayey or loamy subsoils. Along the southern border Robertson has Blackland Prairies vegetation with tall grasses, mesquite, oak, pecan and elm trees along streams. The rest of the county is in the Post Oak Savannah vegetation area with tall grasses, blackjack and post oak. Between one and 10% of the land in the county is considered prime farmland. **CLIMATE** Subtropical Humid with above average annual precipitation. The average annual temperature is 68°F. Temperatures in January range from an average low of 38° to an average high of 59°F and in July range from 73° to 96°F. The average annual precipitation is 38 inches, with an average relative humidity of 83% at 6 A.M. and 54% at 6 P.M. The average annual snowfall is one inch. The growing season averages 265 days per year, with the last freeze in early March and the first freeze in early December. The sun shines during the year on the average 65% of the daylight hours.

THE PEOPLE
Robertson County has a high percent of residents who are native Texans. The 1982 estimated population of 15,300 suggests an increase in the moderate growth pattern begun in the 1970s. The population shifted from an 11% loss between 1960 and 1970 to a 2% gain between 1970 and 1980. Urban areas experienced slight growth while rural areas declined in population from 1970 to 1980. Since the county has a high percent of residents over age 64 the median age is older than average. The largest ancestry groups are Black (32%) persons of English descent (18%) and Irish descent (14%). **REGISTERED VOTERS** As of November 2, 1982 there were 8,115 registered voters (0.1% of the state total). The 1982 general election had a 47% voter turnout, compared to a 63% turnout in the 1980 general election. In the 1982 primary 100% voted Democratic, with 3,494 votes cast.

THE ECONOMY
AGRICULTURE Cattle area. In 1982, 70% of the land was in farms and ranches, with 23% of the farmland under cultivation and 26% irrigated. Robertson ranked 92nd in the state in highest agricultural receipts, with 70% from livestock and livestock products. Inefficient irrigation systems, water erosion and flooding are the current conservation problems. Primary crops: hay, oats, cotton, sorghum and wheat. Primary vegetables: watermelons and potatoes. Primary fruits and nuts: peaches and pecans. Primary livestock and products: cattle and hogs. **BUSINESS** Total number of business establishments in the county: 229. Retail sales during the first quarter of 1984 increased 7%. In 1980, 10% of the labor force were self-employed, 19% were employed in professional or related services, 13% in manufacturing, 21% in wholesale and retail trade, 14% in transportation, communications and other public utilities, 25% were employed in other counties and there were 1,812 retired workers. The industries with the most employment: agribusiness, lumber mills and the manufacture of plumbing fixtures and fabricated wire products. The non-farm earnings in 1981 totaled $112,416,000. The retired workers received an average monthly Social Security payment of $267. **FINANCE** On June 30, 1983, four commercial banks had total deposits of $79,617,000 and total assets of $89,307,000. On December 31, 1982 one state savings and loan association and one state branch had assets of $21,966,912. In addition there is one credit union in the county. **HOUSING** Average value of homes in 1980: $19,000. Permits for new, privately owned housing units increased in 1982: 67 permits were issued with a total construction cost of $1,408,210. Of those permits, 15 were for single family houses. Housing permits in Franklin increased from 23 in 1981 to 57 in 1982 with 36 permits issued for apartments and condominiums. Between 1970 and 1980 the number of housing units increased by 22%. Sixty-two percent of all units in the county are air-conditioned, 84% are heated by gas and 10% by electricity. **NATURAL RESOURCES** Clay, ceramic clay, industrial sand, sand and gravel, lignite coal, oil, gas and glauconite. In 1982 a total of 4,777,436 thousand cubic feet of gas well gas, 2,251 barrels of condensate, 31,045 barrels of crude

oil and 9,952 thousand cubic feet of casinghead gas were produced. Current production of other minerals and products includes lignite coal, industrial sand, sand and gravel. **TOURISM** Travel expenditures of $1,585,000 in 1982 (an increase of 15% over 1981) generated 28 jobs and $261,000 in payroll. **ALCOHOLIC BEVERAGES** Packaged distilled spirits, beer, ale, malt liquor and wine are legal in parts of the county. **FEDERAL EXPENDITURES** The federal government had direct expenditures or obligations of $32,761,000 in the county during fiscal year 1983, including $674,000 by the U.S. Department of Defense. In addition, the federal government provided $883,000 in grant awards, paid $952,000 in salaries and wages, made direct payments to individuals of $28,420,000 including $19,878,000 in retirement and disability payments, awarded $5,000 in procurement contracts and spent $2,501,000 in other expenditures or obligations. The federal government also provided $2,782,000 in direct loans and $3,891,000 in guaranteed loans and insurance.

COMMUNICATION
Newspapers–Weekly: Bremond Press, Franklin News Weekly and The Hearne Democrat. Cable TV. Telephone companies: General Telephone, Continental Telephone, Southwestern Bell and United Telephone. **TRANSPORTATION** Total public road mileage: 938. In 1982 there were 13,108 registered vehicles and 342 reported traffic accidents including four fatalities. Taxi cabs: one company in Hearne. Intercity bus service is available. Motor freight: three carriers. Rail: nine main lines carry freight through the county with three carrying over 30 million tons of freight each, three carry 10 to 20 each and three carry five to 10 million each. Aircraft: 20 are registered in the county. Airports: Hearne Municipal Airport serves as a base for 15 aircraft and is a general utility airport with general aviation service.

COMMUNITY SERVICES
EDUCATION Five school districts with six elementary, one middle and four high schools. The average daily attendance in 1981-82 was 2,890, with expenditures per pupil of $2,482 including 193 classroom teachers with an average annual salary of $14,710. Forty-five percent of the 187 high school graduates planned to attend college. In 1982-83, 47% of the students were White, 13% Hispanic, 40% Black and 0.1% Asian. Sports championships: 1983 A Boys' Track, Bremond H.S. Private schools: 86 students enrolled in one elementary school. **PUBLIC LIBRARIES** Katy Stricker Library (Calvert): 4,294 volumes. Robertson County Library (Franklin): 3,821 volumes. Smith-Welch Memorial Library (Hearne): 10,982 volumes. **CHILD CARE** 13 day care and three twenty-four hour care licensed facilities. **HEALTH CARE** Five physicians and five dentists. Hospitals: one with a capacity of 33. Ambulance services: one volunteer service, one funeral home and one volunteer fire department service. Mental health: one county clinic. Nursing homes: three nursing homes with a combined capacity of 262 nursing care residents. The average cost per day for private patients in 1982 was $29.46. **CHURCHES** 41 churches have an estimated combined membership of 6,660. The largest denominations is Southern Baptist. **SOCIAL SERVICES** In fiscal year 1983 a total of $1,461,648 in food stamps was distributed, with an average of 3,045 persons receiving food stamps each month. Aid to Families with Dependent Children (AFDC) totaled $440,823 with an average of 270 families receiving AFDC each month. Medical assistance benefits for the aged and disabled of $2,346,404 and for families and children of $469,674 brought the county benefit total to $4,718,549. **FIRE PROTECTION** Six volunteer fire departments. **LAW ENFORCEMENT** The County Sheriff has four commissioned officers. Four police departments have a combined force of 28. **CRIME** 94 violent crimes (murder, forcible rape, robbery and aggravated assault) and 591 nonviolent crimes (burglary,

COUNTIES

ROBERTSON (continued)

larceny-theft and motor vehicle theft) were reported in 1982. **JUDICIAL SYSTEM** One District Court and Judge, one County Court and Judge and four Justices of the Peace. In the District Court a total of 1,463 cases were pending on 1/1/82, 782 new cases were filed and 413 cases were disposed of during the year leaving 1,832 cases pending on 12/31/82. There were 837 criminal cases on the docket, 87 convictions, 12 persons committed to prison and three committed to jail and 634 cases left pending. **JAILS** One jail, capacity 14. **ATTORNEYS AT LAW** 10. **UTILITIES** 83% of the residents are connected to a public or privately owned water system and 56% are connected to a public sewer system. Natural gas is distributed to the county by Lone Star Gas Co., Division of Enserch. The average annual residential bill for natural gas in 1982 for the Lone Star distribution system was $405.91, an increase of 35% over 1981. Electricity is distributed to the city of Hearne by the Hearne Municipal Electric System and to the rest of the county by Gulf State Utilities, West Texas Utilities, Limestone Co. Electric Coop., Inc. and Robertson Electric Coop. Inc. and is generated primarily by gas, oil and water. The typical residential electric bill is $248.65 per month for an all-electric house using 2,500 kwh. **TAXES** The county has 10 units with taxing authority: five school districts, four cities and one county.

RECREATION/ENTERTAINMENT
NATIONAL REGISTER OF HISTORIC PLACES Calvert: Calvert Historic District and Hammond House. Franklin: Robertson County Courthouse and Jail. Hearne: Robert C. Allen House. **MUNICIPAL PARKS** 121 acres in five municipal parks. These parks contain three playgrounds, one golf course, one football and soccer field, three baseball and softball fields, two tennis courts and two swimming pools. **SCENIC DRIVES** The Texas Brazos Trail runs through this county. This trail moves through a beautiful and historic section of Central Texas revealing forested landscapes filled with wildlife and wild flowers. **BOATING/FISHING** Lakes/reservoirs: Antelope (26 acres), Artesian (27 acres), Mallard (58 acres), Camp Creek (750 acres), Kury (24 acres), Limestone (9,089 acres) and Twin Oak (1,458 acres). Major rivers: Navasota and Brazos. Primary streams: Bear, Steele, Camp, Mill and Duck. **HUNTING** Fall and winter seasons on deer. Summer, fall and winter seasons on squirrel. No closed seasons on coyote, bobcat and nutria. Winter seasons on quail, muskrat, beaver, otter, opossum, mink, ring-tailed cat, badger, fox, raccoon, skunk and civet cat. In 1983 duck, coot, geese, woodcock and jacksnipe seasons occurred during the winter months. Teal duck, rail and gallinule seasons occurred in the fall. Mourning dove seasons occurred intermittently during the fall and winter months. **OTHER** Easterly: Camp Cooley Ranch. **SPECIAL EVENTS** County Junior Stock Show, Hearne, March; Spring Homes Tour Pilgrimage, Calvert, April; Robertson County Fair, Hearne, April; Old Settlers Day, Franklin, August.

COMMUNITIES
COUNTY SEAT Franklin, County Courthouse, 77856; County Clerk's Office, 409/828-4130. **INCORPORATED COMMUNITIES** (1980 population and ZIP Code) Bremond (1,025) 76629, Calvert (1,732) 77837, Franklin (1,349) 77856 and Hearne (5,418) 77859. **UNINCORPORATED COMMUNITIES** (and ZIP Code) Astin 77859, Bald Prairie 77854, Benchley 77801, Box Quarter 77837, Easterly 77856, Eaton 77856, Elliott 77856, Hammond 76629, Headsville 76653, Marvin 77837, Mumford 77867, Nesbitt 76629, New Baden 77870, Owensville 77856, Petteway 76629, Ridge 77874, Seale 76687, Tidwell Prairie 76629 and Wheelock 77882. **FOR ADDITIONAL LOCAL INFORMATION**

Calvert Chamber of Commerce, P.O. Box 132, Calvert, 77837, 409/364-2559, Franklin Chamber of Commerce, P.O. Box 126, Franklin, 77856, 409/828-3276 and Hearne Chamber of Commerce, 103 Third St., P.O. Box 713, Hearne, 77859, 409/279-2351.

ROCKWALL (M13)

THE LAND
Northeast of Dallas on U.S. Highway 67 in the Blackland Prairies Region, Rockwall County covers 128 square miles with an elevation range of 400 to 550 feet. The county has undulating soils with slightly acidic, light to dark, loamy to clayey surfaces and cracking, clayey subsoils. The county is in the Blackland Prairies vegetation area with tall grasses, mesquite, oak, pecan and elm trees along streams. Between 71 and 80% of the land in the county is considered prime farmland. **CLIMATE** Subtropical moist with mild winters and warm summers. The average annual temperature is 65°F. Temperatures in January range from an average low of 32° to an average high of 54°F and in July range from 72° to 97°F. The average annual precipitation is 36 inches, with an average relative humidity of 82% at 6 A.M. and 54% at 6 P.M. The average annual snowfall is four inches. The growing season averages 236 days per year, with the last freeze in late March and the first freeze in mid November. The sun shines during the year on the average 66% of the daylight hours.

THE PEOPLE
Rockwall County has a 1982 estimated population of 16,700 and ranks 33rd among all U.S. counties in the highest growth rate between 1970 and 1980. Following 30 years of population decline the growth rate spiraled from 20% between 1960 and 1970 to 106% between 1970 and 1980. Urban areas grew faster than rural areas from 1970 to 1980. The age groups with the largest gains were ages 15 to 19, 25 to 44 and birth to five years. The median age is 31. The largest ancestry groups are persons of English descent (30%), Irish descent (23%) and German descent (18%). **REGISTERED VOTERS** As of November 2, 1982 there were 8,435 registered voters (0.1% of the state total). The 1982 general election had a 60% voter turnout, compared to a 75% turnout in the 1980 general election. In the 1982 primary 73% voted Democratic and 27% Republican, with 2,809 votes cast.

THE ECONOMY
AGRICULTURE In 1982, 73% of the land was in farms and ranches, with 48% of the farmland under cultivation and 3% irrigated. Rockwall ranked 240th in the state in highest agricultural receipts, with 71% from livestock and livestock products. Overgrazing, undesirable brush and weeds, water erosion and urban encroachment are the current conservation problems. Primary crops: wheat, hay, sorghum and oats. Primary vegetables: sweet potatoes. Primary fruits and nuts: pecans. Primary livestock and products: cattle and milk. **BUSINESS** Total number of business establishments in the county: 289. Retail sales during the first quarter of 1984 increased 56%. In 1980, 10% of the labor force were self-employed, 15% were employed in professional or related services, 22% in manufacturing, 22% in wholesale and retail trade, 10% in finance, insurance, and real estate, 65% were employed in other counties and there were 905 retired workers. The industries with the most employment: agribusiness and the manufacture of women's clothing and aluminum products. The nonfarm earnings in 1981 totaled $173,131,000. The retired workers received an average monthly Social Security payment of $315. **FINANCE** On June 30, 1983, four commercial banks had total deposits of $73,831,000 and total assets of $81,079,000. There is one federal savings and loan

association branch, one state association branch and one credit union in the county. **HOUSING** Average value of homes in 1980: $64,000. Permits for new, privately owned housing units increased in 1982: 258 permits were issued with a total construction cost of $17,324,712. Of those permits, 180 were for single family houses. Housing permits in the city of Rockwall increased from 102 in 1981 to 232 in 1982 with 158 permits issued for single family houses. Between 1970 and 1980 the number of housing units increased by 122%. Ninety percent of all units in the county are air-conditioned, 61% are heated by gas and 38% by electricity. **NATURAL RESOURCES** Sand and gravel, oil and gas. **TOURISM** Travel expenditures of $2,604,000 in 1982 (an increase of 13% over 1981) generated 58 jobs and $505,000 in payroll. **ALCOHOLIC BEVERAGES** Totally dry. **FEDERAL EXPENDITURES** The federal government had direct expenditures or obligations of $15,258,000 in the county during fiscal year 1983, including $1,372,000 by the U.S. Department of Defense. In addition, the federal government provided $120,000 in grant awards, paid $904,000 in salaries and wages, made direct payments to individuals of $13,946,000 including $10,820,000 in retirement and disability payments, awarded $119,000 in procurement contracts and spent $168,000 in other expenditures or obligations. The federal government also provided $513,000 in direct loans and $7,580,000 in guaranteed loans and insurance.

COMMUNICATION
Newspapers–Weekly: The Rockwall Texas Success. Cable TV. Telephone companies: General Telephone and Southwestern Bell. **TRANSPORTATION** Total public road mileage: 308. In 1982 there were 17,066 registered vehicles and 320 reported traffic accidents including four fatalities. Intercity bus service is available. Motor freight: seven local and intrastate carriers. Rail: one branch line carries annually one to five million tons of freight through the county. Aircraft: 42 are registered in the county. Airports: Rockwall Municipal Airport serves as a base for 99 aircraft and is a basic utility airport with general aviation service.

COMMUNITY SERVICES
EDUCATION Two school districts with five elementary, one middle and two high schools. The average daily attendance in 1981-82 was 3,526, with expenditures per pupil of $2,396 including 185 classroom teachers with an average annual salary of $16,022. Thirty-eight percent of the 251 high school graduates planned to attend college. In 1982-83, 90% of the students were White, 4% Hispanic, 6% Black and 0.5% Asian. **PUBLIC LIBRARIES** Rockwall County Library (Rockwall): 30,333 volumes. **CHILD CARE** 29 day care licensed facilities. **HEALTH CARE** 10 physicians and eight dentists. Ambulance services: one commercial service. Nursing homes: one nursing home has a capacity of 126 nursing care residents. The average cost per day for private patients in 1982 was $32.15. **CHURCHES** 25 churches have an estimated combined membership of 6,893. The largest denominations are Southern Baptist and United Methodist. **SOCIAL SERVICES** In fiscal year 1983 a total of $111,452 in food stamps was distributed, with an average of 245 persons receiving food stamps each month. Aid to Families with Dependent Children (AFDC) totaled $29,174 with an average of 18 families receiving AFDC each month. Medical assistance benefits for the aged and disabled of $879,804 and for families and children of $80,233 brought the county benefit total to $1,100,663. **FIRE PROTECTION** Five volunteer fire departments. **LAW ENFORCEMENT** The County Sheriff has 17 commissioned officers. Four police departments have a combined force of 17. **CRIME** 26 violent crimes (murder, forcible rape, robbery and aggravated assault) and 415 nonviolent crimes (burglary, larceny-theft and motor vehicle theft) were reported in 1982. **JUDICIAL SYSTEM** One District Court and Judge, one County Court and Judge and four

Justices of the Peace. In the District Court a total of 836 cases were pending on 1/1/82, 961 new cases were filed and 536 cases were disposed of during the year leaving 1,261 cases pending on 12/31/82. There were 110 criminal cases on the docket, 18 convictions, seven persons committed to prison and 52 cases left pending. In the County Court 326 cases were pending on 1/1/82, 290 new cases were filed and 409 cases were disposed of during the year leaving 207 cases pending on 12/31/82. There were 578 criminal cases on the docket, 190 convictions, 36 persons committed to jail, and 181 cases left pending. **JAILS** One jail, capacity 17. **ATTORNEYS AT LAW** 28. **UTILITIES** 98% of the residents are connected to a public or privately owned water system and 66% are connected to a public sewer system. Natural gas is distributed to the county by Lone Star Gas Co., Division of Enserch. The average annual residential bill for natural gas in 1982 for the Lone Star distribution system was $405.91, an increase of 35% over 1981. Electricity is distributed to the county by Texas Power and Light Co. and Houston Lighting and Power Co. and is generated primarily by gas and coal. The typical residential electric bill is $196.85 per month for an all-electric house using 2,500 kwh. **TAXES** The county has seven units with taxing authority: two school districts, four cities and one county.

RECREATION/ENTERTAINMENT
MUNICIPAL PARKS 49 acres in five municipal parks. These parks contain three playgrounds, two baseball and softball fields, two swimming pools, one beach, one boat ramp and shore fishing facility. **BOATING/FISHING** Lakes/reservoirs: Cedar Creek Soil Conservation Service Lakes 16A, 11, and 13 (63 acres) and Ray Hubbard (22,745 acres). Major rivers: Trinity. Primary streams: High Point, Hackberry and Berry. **HUNTING** No closed seasons on coyote, bobcat, nutria and squirrel. Winter seasons on quail, muskrat, beaver, otter, opossum, mink, ringtailed cat, badger, fox, raccoon, skunk and civet cat. In 1983 duck, coot, geese, woodcock and jacksnipe seasons occurred during the winter months. Teal duck, rail and gallinule seasons occurred in the fall. Mourning dove seasons occurred intermittently during the fall and winter months. **SPECIAL EVENTS** Arts and Crafts Fair, Rockwall, May; Christmas Parade, Rockwall, December.

COMMUNITIES
COUNTY SEAT Rockwall, County Courthouse, 75087; County Clerk's Office, 214/722-5141. **INCORPORATED COMMUNITIES** (1980 population and ZIP Code) Fate (263) 75032, Heath (1,459: 1,454 in Rockwall Co. and 5 in Kaufman Co.) 75087, McLendon-Chisholm (403) 75087, Rockwall (5,939) 75087, Rowlett (7,522: 1,174 in Rockwall Co. and 6,348 in Dallas Co.) 75088 and Royse City (1,566: 1,394 in Rockwall Co. and 172 in Collin Co.) 75089. **UNINCORPORATED COMMUNITIES** (and ZIP Code) Blackland 75089 and Munson 75089. **FOR ADDITIONAL LOCAL INFORMATION** Rockwall Chamber of Commerce, 2808 Ridge Rd., P.O. Box 92, Rockwall, 75087, 214/722-5733.

RUNNELS (P80)

THE LAND
South of Abilene on U.S. Highways 67 and 83 in the Rolling Plains Region, Runnels County covers 1,056 square miles with an elevation range of 1,600 to 2,000 feet. The southeastern part of the county has very dark, loamy soils with accumulations of lime. The rest of the county has very dark, loamy surfaces over reddish, clayey subsoils with hardened calcium deposits. The southeastern part of the county is in the Edwards Plateau vegetation area with tall or mid grasses, mesquite, junipers, live and

COUNTIES

shinnery oak. The rest of the county is in the Rolling Plains vegetation area with tall and mid grasses some mesquite and shinnery oak. Between 51 and 60% of the land in the county is considered prime farmland. **CLIMATE** Subtropical Subhumid with wide-ranging daily temperatures. The average annual temperature is 65°F. Temperatures in January range from an average low of 29° to an average high of 59°F and in July range from 71° to 96°F. The average annual precipitation is 24 inches, with an average relative humidity of 74% at 6 A.M. and 43% at 6 P.M. The average annual snowfall is five inches. The growing season averages 228 days per year, with the last freeze in late March and the first freeze in mid November. The sun shines during the year on the average 70% of the daylight hours.

THE PEOPLE

Although the 1982 estimated population of 12,100 indicates a gain since the 1980 census, the population in Runnels County consistently declined from 1930 to 1980. Urban areas experienced slight growth from 1970 to 1980 while rural areas had an 8% population loss. The age group with the largest increase was ages 20 to 24, while the largest reduction occurred in ages 10 to 14. The county's population is older than average although the median age lowered from 39 in 1970 to 37 in 1980. The largest ancestry groups are persons of English descent (24%), German descent (24%), Irish descent (21%) and Hispanic (19%). **REGISTERED VOTERS** As of November 2, 1982 there were 6,112 registered voters (0.1% of the state total). The 1982 general election had a 49% voter turnout, compared to a 66% turnout in the 1980 general election. In the 1982 primary 97% voted Democratic and 3% Republican, with 2,362 votes cast.

THE ECONOMY

AGRICULTURE Sheep, wheat and cotton area. In 1982, 94% of the land was in farms and ranches, with 39% of the farmland under cultivation and 3% irrigated. Runnels ranked 62nd in the state in highest agricultural receipts, with 52% from livestock and livestock products. Overgrazing, undesirable brush and weeds, water and wind erosion are the current conservation problems. Primary crops: wheat, sorghum, cotton, hay and oats. Primary vegetables: tomatoes and watermelons. Primary fruits and nuts: peaches and pecans. Primary livestock and products: seventh in the state for wool production. Cattle, milk, sheep, angora goats, mohair and hogs. **BUSINESS** Total number of business establishments in the county: 304. Retail sales during the first quarter of 1984 increased 6%. In 1980, 20% of the labor force were self-employed, 18% were employed in professional or related services, 18% in manufacturing, 17% in wholesale and retail trade, 23% in agriculture, forestry, fisheries and mining, 12% were employed in other counties and there were 1,663 retired workers. The industries with the most employment: oil and gas field services and the manufacture of architectural metal products and motor vehicle parts. The nonfarm earnings in 1981 totaled $106,396,000. The retired workers received an average monthly Social Security payment of $296. **FINANCE** On June 30, 1983, six commercial banks had total deposits of $139,577,000 and total assets of $153,889,000. There are four state savings and loan association branches in the county. **HOUSING** Average value of homes in 1980: $19,000. Permits for new, privately owned housing units increased in 1982: 26 permits were issued with a total construction cost of $824,500. Of those permits, all were for single family houses. Between 1970 and 1980 the number of housing units increased by 8%. Seventy-five percent of all units in the county are air-conditioned, 90% are heated by gas and 8% by electricity. **NATURAL RESOURCES** Caliche, dolomite, limestone sand and gravel, oil, gas and bituminous coal. In 1982

a total of 2,851,463 thousand cubic feet of gas well gas, 26,352 barrels of condensate, 2,344,858 barrels of crude oil and 3,926,806 thousand cubic feet of casinghead gas were produced. Current production of other minerals and products includes sand and gravel. **TOURISM** Travel expenditures of $6,181,000 in 1982 (an increase of 15% over 1981) generated 109 jobs and $1,014,000 in payroll. **ALCOHOLIC BEVERAGES** Packaged distilled spirits, beer, ale, malt liquor and wine are legal in parts of the county. **FEDERAL EXPENDITURES** The federal government had direct expenditures or obligations of $28,412,000 in the county during fiscal year 1983, including $921,000 by the U.S. Department of Defense. In addition, the federal government provided $239,000 in grant awards, paid $1,125,000 in salaries and wages, made direct payments to individuals of $22,871,000 including $15,420,000 in retirement and disability payments, awarded $3,000 in procurement contracts and spent $4,174,000 in other expenditures or obligations. The federal government also provided $3,617,000 in direct loans and $3,175,000 in guaranteed loans and insurance.

COMMUNICATION

Newspapers–Weekly: The Ballinger Ledger, Miles Messenger, Rowena Press and Winters Enterprise. Radio: KRUN-AM and KRUN-FM (Ballinger). Telephone companies: General Telephone and Taylor Telephone. **TRANSPORTATION** Total public road mileage: 1,247. In 1982 there were 13,489 registered vehicles and 220 reported traffic accidents including three fatalities. Taxi cabs: one company in Ballinger. Intercity bus service is available. Motor freight: four carriers. Rail: one branch line carries annually one to five million tons of freight through the county. Aircraft: 29 are registered in the county. Airports: Bruce Field at Ballinger serves as a base for 18 aircraft and is a basic utility airport with general aviation service. Winters Municipal Airport.

COMMUNITY SERVICES

EDUCATION Five school districts with five elementary, one middle and three high schools. The average daily attendance in 1981-82 was 2,275, with expenditures per pupil of $4,236 including 141 classroom teachers with an average annual salary of $15,498. Fifty-three percent of the 167 high school graduates planned to attend college. In 1982-83, 66% of the students were White, 32% Hispanic, 2% Black and 0.2% Asian. **PUBLIC LIBRARIES** Carnegie Public Library (Ballinger): 9,399 volumes. Winters Public Library: 10,000 volumes. **CHILD CARE** 36 day care and one twenty-four hour care licensed facilities. **HEALTH CARE** Nine physicians and six dentists. Hospitals: two with a combined capacity of 55. Ambulance services: one city and one county service. Nursing homes: three nursing homes with a combined capacity of 250 nursing care residents. The average cost per day for private patients in 1982 was $29.19. **CHURCHES** 49 churches have an estimated combined membership of 11,044. The largest denominations are Southern Baptist, Catholic and United Methodist. **SOCIAL SERVICES** In fiscal year 1983 a total of $354,099 in food stamps was distributed, with an average of 819 persons receiving food stamps each month. Aid to Families with Dependent Children (AFDC) totaled $76,913 with an average of 48 families receiving AFDC each month. Medical assistance benefits for the aged and disabled of $1,186,639 and for families and children of $114,979 brought the county benefit total to $1,732,630. **FIRE PROTECTION** Four volunteer fire departments. **LAW ENFORCEMENT** The County Sheriff has 12 commissioned officers. Two police departments have a combined force of 10. **CRIME** 13 violent crimes (murder, forcible rape, robbery and aggravated assault) and 102 nonviolent crimes (burglary, larceny-theft and motor vehicle theft) were reported in 1982. **JUDICIAL SYSTEM** One District Court and Judge, one County Court and Judge and four Justices of the Peace. In the District Court a total of 174 cases were pending on 1/1/84, 294 new cases were filed and 249 cases were disposed of during the year leaving 219 cases pending on 12/31/82. There were 69 criminal cases on the docket, 24 convictions, six persons committed to prison and two committed to jail and 25 cases left pending. In the County Court 632 cases were pending on 1/1/82, 545 new cases were filed and 443 cases were disposed of during the year leaving 734 cases pending on 12/31/82. There were 1,101 criminal cases on the docket, 263 convictions, 52 persons committed to jail, and 663 cases left pending. **JAILS** One jail, capacity 22. **ATTORNEYS AT LAW** 12. **UTILITIES** 81% of the residents are connected to a public or privately owned water system and 60% are connected to a public sewer system. Natural gas is distributed to the county by Lone Star Gas Co., Division of Enserch. The average annual residential bill for natural gas in 1982 for the Lone Star distribution system was $405.91, an increase of 35% over 1981. Electricity is distributed to the county by Coleman Co. Electric Coop., Inc. and West Texas Utilities and is generated primarily by gas and oil. The typical residential electric bill is $145.78 per month for an all-electric house using 2,500 kwh. **TAXES** The county has 14 units with taxing authority: six school districts, three cities, one county, one hospital district and three special districts.

RECREATION/ENTERTAINMENT

NATIONAL REGISTER OF HISTORIC PLACES Ballinger: Ballinger Carnegie Library and Van Pelt House. Miles: J. Thiele Building. **MUNICIPAL PARKS** 1,272 acres in six municipal parks. These parks contain two playgrounds, four baseball and softball fields, two tennis courts, two swimming pools and one boat ramp. Developed campsites: six. **SCENIC DRIVES** The Texas Forts Trail runs through this county. This trail leads to eight of the famous frontier forts of West Central Texas and an ancient presidio of the Spanish colonial period. **BOATING/FISHING** Lakes/reservoirs: Ballinger (317 acres), Country Club (20 acres), Elm Creek (45 acres), Kuhn (45 acres), Old Winters (30 acres) and Winters (163 acres). Major rivers: Colorado. Primary streams: Valley, Los Arroyos, Elm and Bluff. **HUNTING** Fall and winter seasons on deer and javelina. No closed season on coyote, bobcat and squirrel. Winter seasons on quail, muskrat, beaver, opossum, ring-tailed cat, badger, fox, weasel, raccoon, skunk and civet cat. Fall, winter and spring seasons on turkey. In 1983 duck, coot, geese, woodcock and jacksnipe seasons occurred during the winter months. Teal duck, rail and gallinule seasons occurred in the fall. Mourning dove seasons occurred intermittently during the fall and winter months. **THEATERS** Miles: Old Opera House. **SPECIAL EVENTS** Rattlesnake Roundup, Ballinger, March; Texas State Festival of Ethnic Cultures, Ballinger, April; Arts and Crafts Fair, Ballinger, April; Mayfest, Winters, May; Cotton Festival, Miles, September; Pinto Bean Cookoff, Ballinger, October; Miss Ballinger Pageant and Parade, Ballinger, December.

COMMUNITIES

COUNTY SEAT Ballinger, County Courthouse, 76821; County Clerk's Office, 915/365-2720. **INCORPORATED COMMUNITIES** (1980 population and ZIP Code) Ballinger (4,207) 76821, Miles (720) 76861 and Winters (3,061) 79567. **UNINCORPORATED COMMUNITIES** (and ZIP Code) Benoit 76882, Bethel 76821, Blanton 76821, Content (Tokeen) 79538, Crews 79567, Drasco 79567, Hatchel 76821, Marie 76933, Maverick 76865, Norton 76865, Olfen 76875, Pony 76821, Pumphrey 79567, Rowena 76875, Valley View 76821, Wilmeth 79567 and Wingate 79566. **FOR ADDITIONAL LOCAL INFORMATION** Ballinger Chamber of Commerce, 803 Hutchings Ave., P.O. Box 577, Ballinger, 76821, 915/365-2333 and Winters Area Chamber of Commerce, P.O. Box 698, Winters, 79567, 915/754-5210.

RUSK (E22)

THE LAND
Southwest of Longview on U.S. Highways 259 and 84 in the East Texas Timberlands Region, Rusk County covers 932 square miles with the elevation ranging from 300 to 600 feet. The light colored, acidic, sandy to loamy soils have very deep reddish, clayey subsoils. In the Pineywoods vegetation area, there are pine and hardwood forests. Between 11 and 20% of the land in the county is considered prime farmland. **CLIMATE** Subtropical Humid with May the wettest month. The average annual temperature is 65 °F. Temperatures in January range from an average low of 35° to an average high of 56 °F and in July range from 71° to 94 °F. The average annual precipitation is 45 inches, with an average relative humidity of 85% at 6 A.M. and 57% at 6 P.M. The average annual snowfall is two inches. The growing season averages 250 days per year, with the last freeze in mid March and the first freeze in mid November. The sun shines during the year on the average 66% of the daylight hours.

THE PEOPLE
During the last decade Rusk County began its first period of growth in 30 years. The 1982 estimated population of 42,600 indicates a continuation of that strong growth. Rural areas grew twice as fast as urban areas from 1970 to 1980. The county has a high percentage of residents over age 64. The population's high median age lowered from 37 in 1970 to 33 in 1980. The largest ancestry groups are persons of English descent (23%), Black (22%) and Irish descent (19%). **REGISTERED VOTERS** As of November 2, 1982 there were 22,519 registered voters (0.4% of the state total). The 1982 general election had a 42% voter turnout, compared to a 58% turnout in the 1980 general election. In the 1982 primary 94% voted Democratic and 6% Republican, with 7,078 votes cast.

THE ECONOMY
AGRICULTURE Forest production and cattle area. In 1982, 50% of the land was in farms and ranches, with 12% of the farmland under cultivation and 3% irrigated. Rusk ranked 140th in the state in highest agricultural receipts, with 90% from livestock and livestock products. Undesirable brush and weeds, water erosion and improper woodland management are the current conservation problems. Primary crops: hay, wheat and oats. Primary vegetables: watermelons. Primary fruits and nuts: peaches and pecans. Primary livestock and products: cattle and milk. **BUSINESS** Total number of business establishments in the county: 696. Retail sales during the first quarter of 1984 increased by 11%. In 1980, 9% of the labor force were self-employed, 17% were employed in professional or related services, 20% in manufacturing, 19% in wholesale and retail trade, 10% in agriculture, forestry, fisheries and mining, 35% were employed in other counties and there were 4,102 retired workers. The industries with the most employment: oil and gas extraction, metal plate fabricating, agribusiness, heavy construction, sawmills and the manufacture of brick and clay tile, metal office furniture and women's clothing. The nonfarm earnings in 1981 totaled $399,266,000. The retired workers received an average monthly Social Security payment of $307.00. **FINANCE** On June 30, 1983, six commercial banks had total deposits of $268,077,000 and total assets of $299,989,000. On December 31, 1982 two state savings and loan associations and three state branches had combined assets of $92,806,756. In addition there are three credit unions in the county. **HOUSING** Average value of homes in 1980: $28,100. Permits for new, privately owned housing units increased in 1982: 109 permits were issued with a total construction cost of $4,592,828. Of those permits, 53 were for single family houses. Housing permits in Henderson increased from 62 in 1981 to 108

COUNTIES

RUSK (continued)

in 1982. Between 1970 and 1980 the number of housing units increased by 26%. Seventy-five percent of all units in the county are air-conditioned, 81% are heated by gas and 14% by electricity. **NATURAL RESOURCES** Ceramic clay, magnetite iron, industrial sand, oil, gas, and lignite coal. In 1982 a total of 46,293,706 thousand cubic feet of gas well gas, 392,201 barrels of condensate, 14,747,682 barrels of crude oil and 8,148,364 thousand cubic feet of casinghead gas were produced. Current production of other minerals and products includes brick and kaolin clay. Pine and hardwood production in 1981 totaled 11,273,974 cubic feet: 8,544,937 cubic feet of pine and 2,729,037 cubic feet of hardwood. **TOURISM** Travel expenditures of $12,495,000 in 1982 (an increase of 13% over 1981) generated 254 jobs and $2,212,000 in payroll. Lodging: five hotels, motels and tourist courts. **ALCOHOLIC BEVERAGES** Totally dry. **FEDERAL EXPENDITURES** The federal government had direct expenditures or obligations of $63,880,000 in the county during fiscal year 1983, including $2,153,000 by the U.S. Department of Defense. In addition, the federal government provided $989,000 in grant awards, paid $2,143,000 in salaries and wages, made direct payments to individuals of $60,457,000 including $44,150,000 in retirement and disability payments, awarded $28,000 in procurement contracts and spent $263,000 in other expenditures or obligations. The federal government also provided $129,000 in direct loans and $9,915,000 in guaranteed loans and insurance.

COMMUNICATION

Newspapers–Daily: Henderson Daily News, ave. eve. circ. 6,307. Weekly: Mount Enterpise Progress and the Overton Press. Radio: KGRI-AM, KWRD-AM, KGRI-FM (Henderson). Cable TV. Telephone companies: Continental Telephone, General Telephone, Southwestern Bell, United Telephone, Eastex Telephone Coop., Tatum Telephone and Tri-County Telephone. **TRANSPORTATION** Total public road mileage: 1,664. In 1982 there were 37,022 registered vehicles and 829 reported traffic accidents including 16 fatalities. Taxi cabs: one company in Henderson. Intercity bus service is available. Motor freight: 14 local and intrastate carriers. Rail: two main and four branch lines carry freight through the county. The two main lines carry annually 10 to 20 million tons of freight each, one of the branch lines carries one to five and three branch lines carry less than one million tons each. Aircraft: 38 are registered in the county. Airports: Rusk County Airport at Henderson serves as a base for 30 aircraft and is a general utility airport with general aviation service.

COMMUNITY SERVICES

EDUCATION Eight school districts with 12 elementary, three middle, eight high schools and one special education. The average daily attendance in 1981-82 was 6,781, with expenditures per pupil of $2,984 including 499 classroom teachers with an average annual salary of $16,701. Forty-three percent of the 441 high school graduates planned to attend college. In 1982-83, 70% of the students were White, 3% Hispanic, 27% Black, 0.1% Asian and 0.1% American Indian. Sports championships: 1983 A Girls' Track, Price Carlisle H.S. **PUBLIC LIBRARIES** Rusk County Memorial Library (Henderson): 44,028 volumes. **CHILD CARE** 53 day care and eight twenty-four hour care licensed facilities. **HEALTH CARE** 26 physicians and 17 dentists. Hospitals: two with a combined capacity of 210. Ambulance services: two volunteer fire departments, one funeral home and one commercial service. Mental health: one clinic. Nursing homes: five nursing homes with a combined capacity of 555 nursing care residents. The average cost per day for private patients in 1982 was $29.88. **CHURCHES** 111 churches have an estimated combined membership of 22,864. The largest denominations are Southern Baptist, United Methodist and American Baptist. **SOCIAL SERVICES** In fiscal year 1983 a total of $1,892,109 in food stamps was distributed, with an average of 4,041 persons receiving food stamps each month. Aid to Families with Dependent Children (AFDC) totaled $489,315 with an average of 326 families receiving AFDC each month. Medical assistance benefits for the aged and disabled of $4,412,843 and for families and children of $630,559 brought the county benefit total to $7,424,826. **FIRE PROTECTION** One paid, one partly paid and five volunteer fire departments. **LAW ENFORCEMENT** The County Sheriff has 19 commissioned officers. Five police departments have a combined force of 43. **CRIME** 89 violent crimes (murder, forcible rape, robbery and aggravated assault) and 1,204 nonviolent crimes (burglary, larceny-theft and motor vehicle theft) were reported in 1982. **JUDICIAL SYSTEM** One District Court and Judge, one County Court and Judge and six Justices of the Peace. In the District Court a total of 2,596 cases were pending on 1/1/82, 1,090 new cases were filed and 845 cases were disposed of during the year leaving 2,841 cases pending on 12/31/82. There were 380 criminal cases on the docket, 188 convictions, 45 persons committed to prison, three committed to jail and 142 cases left pending. In the County Court 1,585 cases were pending on 1/1/82, 528 new cases were filed and 487 cases were disposed of during the year leaving 1,626 cases pending on 12/31/82. There were 1,828 criminal cases on the docket, 214 convictions, 86 persons committed to jail and 1,381 cases left pending. **JAILS** One jail, capacity 31. New construction planned as lost certification in 1983 due to overcrowding. **ATTORNEYS AT LAW** 36. **UTILITIES** 81% of the residents are connected to a public or privately owned water system and 40% are connected to a public sewer system. Natural gas is distributed to the county by Entex, Inc. and South Rusk County Gas Co., Inc. The average annual residential bill for natural gas in 1982 for the Entex distribution system was $390.31, an increase of 26% over 1981. Electricity is distributed to the county by Southwestern Electric Power, Rusk Co. Electric Coop. Inc., Central Texas Electric Coop. Inc., Upshur-Rural Electric Coop. Inc., and Deep East Texas Electric Coop. Inc. and is generated primarily by gas, oil, coal and water. The typical residential electric bill is $152.08 per month for an all-electric house using 2,500 kwh. **TAXES** The county has 16 units with taxing authority: nine school districts, four cities, one county, one college district and one special district.

RECREATION/ENTERTAINMENT

NATIONAL REGISTER OF HISTORIC PLACES Henderson: Poe-Jones-Richardson House. Tatum vicinity: Harmony Hill and Musgano Site. **STATE** Martin Creek Park Site State Recreation Area covers 216 acres with fishing, swimming and boat ramps. **MUNICIPAL PARKS** 206 acres in seven municipal parks. These parks contain seven playgrounds, one golf course, seven baseball and softball fields, four tennis courts, one multi-use court, three swimming pools, one boat ramp and shore fishing facilities. Developed campsites: seven. **SCENIC DRIVES** The Texas Forest Trail runs through this county. This trail explores the farming, ranching and oilfield areas of the East Texas Pineywoods. **BOATING/FISHING** Lakes/reservoirs: Attoyac Bayou Soil Conservation Service Lake 5 (76 acres), Cherokee (3,987 acres), Florey (21 acres), Jones (35 acres), Long Glade (34 acres), Mans (33 acres), Martin Creek (5,020 acres), Miller (43 acres), Morris (17 acres), Nix (102 acres), Willow (41 acres) and Striker (2,400 acres). Major rivers: Angelina and Sabine. Primary streams: Bowles, Caney, Cherokee Bayou, Wilds, Mill, Lee, Walker, Martin, Cooper, Barnhart, Wasson, Shawnee and Striker. **HUNTING** Fall and winter seasons on deer. Summer, fall and winter seasons on squirrel. Winter seasons on quail, muskrat, beaver, otter, opossum, mink, ring-tailed cat, badger, fox, raccoon, skunk and civet cat. No closed season on nutria, coyote and bobcat. In 1983 duck, coot, geese, woodcock and jacksnipe seasons occurred during winter months. Teal duck, rail and gallinule seasons occurred in the fall. Mourning dove seasons occurred intermittently during the fall and winter months. **MUSEUMS** Henderson: The Howard Dickson House. **SPECIAL EVENTS** G-Kart Assn. Texas Enduro, Henderson, March; Annual Juried Art Show, Henderson, March; Arts and Crafts Fair, Henderson, May; Livestock and Forage Field Day, Overton, May; Blowout, Overton, July.

COMMUNITIES

COUNTY SEAT Rusk, County Courthouse, 75652; County Clerk's Office, 214/657-2117. **INCORPORATED COMMUNITIES** (1980 population and ZIP Code) Easton (333: 265 in Gregg Co. and 68 in Rusk Co.) 75641, Henderson (11,473) 75652, Kilgore (10,968: 2,543 in Rusk Co. and 8,425 in Gregg Co.) 75662, Mount Enterprise (485) 75681, New London (942) 75682, Overton (2,420: 2,323 in Rusk Co. and 107 in Smith Co.) 75684, Reklaw (305: 114 in Rusk Co. and 191 in Cherokee Co.) 75784 and Tatum (1,339: 1,064 in Rusk Co. and 275 in Panola Co.) 75691. **UNINCORPORATED COMMUNITIES** (and ZIP Code) Anadarko 75667, Antioch 75652, Arlam 75946, Brachfield 75681, Caledonia 75975, Chapman 75652, Church Hill 75652, Concord 75681, Craig 75652, Cross Roads 75662, Dirgin 75691, Eulalie (Bryce) 75975, Fairview 75784, Flanagan 75691, Friar 75684, Fussel 75667, Glenfawn 75760, Harmony 75684, Harmony Hill 75691, Jacobs 75684, Joinerville 75658, Laird Hill 75666, Laneville 75667, Lawsonville 75681, Leveretts Chapel 75684, Liberty 75652, Mayflower 75691, McKnight 75652, Minden 75680, Monroe 75662, New Hope 75662, New Prospect 75652, New Salem 75652, Old London 75682, Oak Flat (Smyrna) 75681, Oak Hill 75652, Oakland 75652, Patrich 75681, Pinehill 75652, Pirtle 75684, Pitner Junction 75684, Pleasant Grove (Sardis) 75652, Pone 75667, Price (Carlisle) 75687, Selman City 75689, Sexton City 75684, Stewart 75652, Sulphur Springs 75760 and Turnertown 75689. **FOR ADDITIONAL LOCAL INFORMATION** Rusk Co. Chamber of Commerce, P. O. Box 432, Henderson, 75653, 214/657-5528 and Overton Chamber of Commerce, P. O. Box 6, Overton, 75684, 214/834-3542.

SABINE (E30)

THE LAND

Bordering Louisiana northeast of Houston on U.S. Highway 96 in the East Texas Timberlands Region, Sabine County covers 486 square miles with the elevation ranging from 150 to 350 feet. In the north the light colored, acidic, sandy to loamy soils have very deep, reddish, clayey subsoils. In the south the gently rolling to hilly soils have loamy surfaces with deep, reddish, clayey subsoils high in iron. In the Pineywoods vegetation area, there are pine and hardwood forests. Between 21 and 30% of the land in the county is considered prime farmland. **CLIMATE** Moist and mild. The average annual temperature is 66 °F. Temperatures in January range from an average low of 35 ° to an average high of 58 °F and in July range from 71 ° to 93 °F. The average annual precipitation is 52 inches, with an average relative humidity of 88% at 6 A.M. and 63% at 6 P.M. Snow is rare. The growing season averages 236 days per year, with the last freeze in late March and the first freeze in mid November. The sun shines during the year on the average 64% of the daylight hours.

THE PEOPLE

Sabine County is growing steadily after a long period of population decline. The 1982 estimated population of 9,000 indicates the continuation of that strong growth rate. A 2% population

loss between 1960 and 1970 was followed by a 21% gain between 1970 and 1980. The majority of county residents live in rural area. The population has high percentage of residents over age 64 and a high median age which rose from 33 in 1970 to 39 in 1980. The largest ancestry groups are persons of English descent (36%), Irish descent (22%) and Black (16%). **REGISTERED VOTERS** As of November 2, 1982 there were 7,031 registered voters (0.1% of the state total). The 1982 general election had a 35% voter turnout, compared to a 56% turnout in the 1980 general election. In the 1982 primary 99% voted Democratic and 1% Republican, with 3,066 votes cast.

THE ECONOMY

AGRICULTURE Forest production area. In 1982, 19% of the land was in farms and ranches, with 7% of the farmland under cultivation. Sabine ranked 221st in the state in highest agricultural receipts, with 89% from livestock and livestock products. Overgrazing, undesirable brush and weeds, water erosion, inadequate cropping systems and improper woodland management are the current conservation problems. Primary crops: hay. Primary vegetables: watermelons. Primary fruits and nuts: peaches and pecans. Primary livestock and products: ninth in the state for commercial broiler production. cattle. **BUSINESS** Total number of business establishments in the county: 133. Retail sales during the first quarter of 1984 increased by 1%. In 1980, 19% of the labor force were self-employed, 12% were employed in professional or related services, 22% in manufacturing, 19% in wholesale and retail trade, 13% in construction, 25% were employed in other counties and there were 1,323 retired workers. The industries with the most employment: the manufacture of plywood and softwood veneer. The nonfarm earnings in 1981 totaled $62,014,000. The retired workers received an average monthly Social Security payment of $320.00. **FINANCE** On June 30, 1983, two commercial banks had total deposits of $41,720,000 and total assets of $46,336,000. There is one state savings and loan association branch and two credit unions in the county. **HOUSING** Average value of homes in 1980: $18,800. In 1982 three permits were issued for new, single family houses. Between 1970 and 1980 the number of housing units increased by 112%. Seventy-five percent of all units in the county are air-conditioned, 71% are heated by gas and 16% by electricity. **NATURAL RESOURCES** Clay, ceramic clay, industrial sand, oil, gas and glauconite. In 1982 a total of 58,744 thousand cubic feet of gas well gas, 1483 barrels of condensate, 36,244 barrels of crude oil and 26,944 thousand cubic feet of casinghead gas were produced. Pine and hardwood production in 1981 totaled 13,487,783 cubic feet: 11,685,503 cubic feet of pine and 1,802,280 cubic feet of hardwood. **TOURISM** Travel expenditures of $11,498,000 in 1982 (an increase of 11% over 1981) generated 288 jobs and $2,299,000 in payroll. **ALCOHOLIC BEVERAGES** Only 4% beer is legal in parts of the county. **FEDERAL EXPENDITURES** The federal government had direct expenditures or obligations of $21,128,000 in the county during fiscal year 1983, including $766,000 by the U.S. Department of Defense. In addition, the federal government provided $313,000 in grant awards, paid $795,000 in salaries and wages, made direct payments to individuals of $19,833,000 including $15,910,000 in retirement and disability payments, awarded $125,000 in procurement contracts and spent $64,000 in other expenditures or obligations. The federal government also provided $415,000 in guaranteed loans and insurance.

COMMUNICATION

Newspapers–Weekly: The Sabine County Reporter (Hemphill). Radio: KAWS-AM, (Hemphill). Cable TV. Telephone companies: Continental Telephone and Southwestern Bell. **TRANSPORTATION** Total public road mileage: 639. In 1982 there were 8,107 registered vehicles and 106 reported traffic accidents including

SABINE (continued)

four fatalities. Intercity bus service is available. Motor freight: two carriers. Rail: one branch line carries annually one to five million tons of freight through the county. Aircraft: six are registered in the county. Airports: Pineland Municipal Airport at Pineland.

COMMUNITY SERVICES

EDUCATION Two school districts with two elementary and two high schools. The average daily attendance in 1981-82 was 1,372, with expenditures per pupil of $2,296 including 104 classroom teachers with an average annual salary of $16,368. Thirty-nine percent of the 106 high school graduates planned to attend college. In 1982-83, 78% of the students were White, 0.8 Hispanic, 21% Black, 0.1% Asian and 0.2% American Indian. **PUBLIC LIBRARIES** Arthur Temple Sr. Memorial Library (Pineland): 15,000 volumes. **CHILD CARE** One day care and two twenty-four hour care licensed facilities. **HEALTH CARE** Two physicians and two dentists. Hospitals: one with a capacity of 36. Ambulance services: one commercial service. Nursing homes: one nursing home has a capacity of 60 nursing care residents. The average cost per day for private patients in 1982 was $28.34. **CHURCHES** 41 churches have an estimated combined membership of 4,742. The largest denominations are Southern Baptist, United Methodist and Baptist Missionary. **SOCIAL SERVICES** In fiscal year 1983 a total of $462,348 in food stamps was distributed, with an average of 954 persons receiving food stamps each month. Aid to Families with Dependent Children (AFDC) totaled $116,334 with an average of 74 families receiving AFDC each month. Medical assistance benefits for the aged and disabled of $771,803 and for families and children of $121,825 brought the county benefit total to $1,472,310. **FIRE PROTECTION** five volunteer fire departments. **LAW ENFORCEMENT** The County Sheriff has seven commissioned officers. Two police departments have a combined force of two. **CRIME** 94 nonviolent crimes (burglary, larceny-theft and motor vehicle theft) were reported in 1982. **JUDICIAL SYSTEM** Two District Courts and Judges, one County Court and Judge and five Justices of the Peace. In the District Courts a total of 619 cases were pending on 1/1/82, 254 new cases were filed and 175 cases were disposed of during the year leaving 698 cases pending on 12/31/82. There were 175 criminal cases on the docket, 19 convictions, three persons committed to prison and 149 cases left pending. In the County Court 249 cases were pending on 1/1/82, 246 new cases were filed and 210 cases were disposed of during the year leaving 285 cases pending on 12/31/82. There were 495 criminal cases on the docket, 132 convictions and 285 cases left pending. **JAILS** One jail, capacity 17. New jail opened in 1983. **ATTORNEYS AT LAW** Five. **UTILITIES** 59% of the residents are connected to a public or privately owned water system and 30% are connected to a public sewer system. Electricity is distributed to the county by Southwestern Public Service, and Deep East Texas Electric Coop., Inc. and is generated primarily by gas, oil and coal. The typical residential electric bill is $170.44 per month for an all-electric house using 2,500 kwh. **TAXES** The county has six units with taxing authority: two school districts, two cities, one county and one hospital district.

RECREATION/ENTERTAINMENT

FEDERAL SABINE NATIONAL FOREST covers 188,220 acres in five counties and includes seven recreation areas. **NATIONAL REGISTER OF HISTORIC PLACES** Milam vicinity: Oliphant House. **MUNICIPAL PARKS** 43 acres in two municipal parks. These parks contain one playground, one baseball and softball field, four tennis courts and one swimming pool. **SCENIC DRIVES** The Texas Forest Trail runs through this county. This trail explores the farming, ranching and oilfield areas of the East

Texas Pineywoods. In Sabine County, stands of Virginia shortleaf pine can be seen at the community of Yellowpine via Texas 87. **BOATING/FISHING** Lakes/reservoirs: Red Hills (28 acres) and Toledo Bend (109,730 acres). Major rivers: Sabine. Primary streams: Corsey and Martinez Bayou. **WILDLIFE REFUGES** Moore Plantation Texas Wildlife Management Area covers 19,500 acres. **HUNTING** Fall and winter seasons on deer. Summer, fall and winter seasons on squirrel. Winter seasons on quail, muskrat, beaver, otter, opossum, mink, ring-tailed cat, badger, fox, raccoon, skunk and civet cat. No closed season on nutria, coyote and bobcat. In 1983 duck, coot, geese, woodcock and jacksnipe seasons occurred during the winter months. Teal duck, rail and gallinule seasons occurred in the fall. Mourning dove seasons occured intermittently during the fall and winter months. **SPECIAL EVENTS** Western Days, Hemphill, April; Sabine County Fair, Hemphill, October.

COMMUNITIES

COUNTY SEAT Hemphill, County Courthouse, 75948; County Clerk's Office, 409/787-3786. **INCORPORATED COMMUNITIES** (1980 population and ZIP Code) Bronson (254) 75930, Hemphill (1,353) 75948 and Pineland (1,111) 75968. **UNINCORPORATED COMMUNITIES** (and ZIP Code) Brookeland 75931, Fairmount 5948, Geneva 75947, Isla 75959, Magasco 75968, Milam 75959, Plainview 75968, Rosevine 75930, Sexton 75972, Strickland (Crossing) 75968, Sturgis Mill 75948, Yellowpine 75948. **FOR ADDITIONAL LOCAL INFORMATION** Sabine Co. Chamber of Commerce, P. O. Box 717, Hemphill, 75948, 409/787-2732.

SAN AUGUSTINE (E29)

THE LAND

Northeast of Houston on U.S. Highway 96 in the East Texas Timberlands Region, San Augustine County covers 524 square miles with the elevation ranging from 150 to 400 feet. In the north the light colored, acidic, sandy to loamy soils have very deep, reddish, clayey subsoils. In the south the gently rolling to hilly soils have loamy surfaces with deep, reddish, clayey subsoils high in iron. In the Pineywoods vegetation area, there are pine and hardwood forests, Between 21 and 30% of the land in the county is considered prime farmland. **CLIMATE** Mild and moist. The average annual temperature is 66 °F. Temperatures in January range from an average low of 36° to an average high of 58 °F and in July range from 71° to 94 °F. The average annual precipitation is 48 inches, with an average relative humidity of 88% at 6 A.M. and 61% at 6 P.M. The average annual snowfall is not significant. The growing season averages 238 days per year, with the last freeze in mid March and the first freeze in mid November. The sun shines during the year on the average 63% of the daylight hours.

THE PEOPLE

San Augustine County has been steadily growing since the 1960s. The 1982 estimated population of 9,000 indicates a continuation of that moderate growth. The growth rate rose from 2% between 1960 and 1970 to 12% between 1970 and 1980. Urban areas grew slightly faster than rural areas between 1970 and 1980. The county's population has a high percentage of residents over age 64 and a high median age which rose from 33 in 1970 to 37 in 1980. The largest ancestry groups are Black (30%), persons of English descent (25%) and Irish descent (18%). **REGISTERED VOTERS** As of November 2, 1982 there were 5,482 registered voters (0.1% of the state total). The 1982 general election had a 40% voter turnout, compared to a 65% turnout in the 1980 general elections. In the 1982 primary 100% voted Democratic with 2,680 votes cast.

THE ECONOMY

AGRICULTURE Forest production area. In 1982, 24% of the land was in farms and ranches, with 12% of the farmland under cultivation. San Augustine ranked 207th in the state in highest agricultural receipts, with 90% from livestock and livestock products. Overgrazing, undesirable brush and weeds, water erosion, inadequate cropping systems and improper woodland management are the current conservation problems. Primary crops: hay. Primary vegetables: sweet corn, potatoes and sweet potatoes. Primary fruits and nuts: peaches and pecans. Primary livestock and products: eighth in the state for commercial broiler production. Cattle. **BUSINESS** Total number of business establishments in the county: 139. Retail sales during the first quarter of 1984 increased by 5%. In 1980, 13% of the labor force were self-employed, 22% were employed in professional or related services, 24% in manufacturing, 15% in wholesale and retail trade, 11% in construction, 25% were employed in other counties and there were 1,011 retired workers. The industries with the most employment: sawmills and tourism. The nonfarm earnings in 1981 totaled $55,645,000. The retired workers received an average monthly Social Security payment of $284. **FINANCE** On June 30, 1983, two commercial banks had total deposits of $50,446,000 and total assets of $56,430,000. On December 31, 1982 one state savings and loan association had assets of $33,243,608. **HOUSING** Average value of homes in 1980: $20,200. In 1982 two permits were issued for new, single family houses. Between 1970 and 1980 the number of housing units increased by 45%. Sixty-five percent of all units in the county are air-conditioned, 72% are heated by gas and 16% by electricity. **NATURAL RESOURCES** Clay, ceramic clay, industrial sand, glauconite, oil, gas and lignite coal. In 1982 a total of 43,490 thousand cubic feet of gas well gas, 108 barrels of condensate, 483 barrels of crude oil and 15 thousand cubic feet of casinghead gas were produced. Pine and hardwood production in 1981 totaled 13,655,231 cubic feet: 11,050,101 cubic feet of pine and 2,605,130 cubic feet of hardwood. **TOURISM** Travel expenditures of $2,965,000 in 1982 (an increase of 11% over 1981) generated 72 jobs and $580,000 in payroll. Lodging: two hotels, motels and tourist courts. **ALCOHOLIC BEVERAGES** Packaged distilled spirits, beer, ale, malt liquor and wine are legal in parts of the county. **FEDERAL EXPENDITURES** The federal government had direct expenditures or obligations of $15,710,000 in the county during fiscal year 1983, including $316,000 by the U.S. Department of Defense. In addition, the federal government provided $99,000 in grant awards, paid $640,000 in salaries and wages, made direct payments to individuals of $14,837,000 including $10,996,000 in retirement and disability payments, awarded $19,000 in procurement contracts and spent $115,000 in other expenditures or obligations. The federal government also provided $162,000 in guaranteed loans and insurance.

COMMUNICATION

Newspapers–Weekly:San Augustine Tribune, and the San Augustine Rambler. Cable TV. Telephone companies: Continental Telephone and Southwestern Bell. **TRANSPORTATION** Total public road mileage: 645. In 1982 there were 7,869 registered vehicles and 101 reported traffic accidents including nine fatalities. Intercity bus service is available. Motor freight: two carriers. Rail: one branch line carries annually one to five million tons of freight through the county. Aircraft: two are registered in the county. Airports: San Augustine County Airport at San Augustine and Browns Ranch Airport at Broaddus.

COMMUNITY SERVICES

EDUCATION Two school districts with two elementary, two middle and two high schools. The average daily attendance in 1981-82 was 1,653, with expenditures per pupil of $1,941 including 91 classroom teachers with an average annual salary of $15,915. Nine percent of the 116 high school graduates planned to attend college. In 1982-83, 55% of the students were White, 1% Hispanic and 44% Black. **PUBLIC LIBRARIES** San Augustine Public Library: 15,000 volumes.**CHILD CARE** Two day care and two twenty-four hour care licensed facilities. **HEALTH CARE** Three physicians and four dentists. Hospitals: one with a capacity of 48. Ambulance services: two funeral home services. Mental health: one development center with a capacity of 56. Nursing homes: two nursing homes with a combined capacity of 128 nursing care residents. The average cost per day for private patients in 1982 was $30.17. **CHURCHES** 22 churches have an estimated combined membership of 3,869. The largest denominations are Southern Baptist, United Methodist and Baptist Missionary. **SOCIAL SERVICES** In fiscal year 1983 a total of $698,665 in food stamps was distributed, with an average of 1,545 persons receiving food stamps each month. Aid to Families with Dependent Children (AFDC) totaled $202,436 with an average of 135 families receiving AFDC each month. Medical assistance benefits for the aged and disabled of $2,274,717 and for families and children of $345,424 brought the county benefit total to $3,521,241. **FIRE PROTECTION** Four volunteer fire departments. **LAW ENFORCEMENT** The County Sheriff has six commissioned officers. One police department has a force of three. **CRIME** 16 violent crimes (murder, forcible rape, robbery and aggravated assault) and 21 nonviolent crimes (burglary, larceny-theft and motor vehicle theft) were reported in 1982. **JUDICIAL SYSTEM** Two District Courts and Judges, one County Court and Judge and four Justices of the Peace. In the District Courts a total of 445 cases were pending on 1/1/82, 226 new cases were filed and 152 cases were disposed of during the year leaving 519 cases pending on 12/31/82. There were 19 criminal cases on the docket, 11 convictions, two persons committed to prison and four cases left pending. In the County Court 54 cases were pending on 1/1/82, 250 new cases were filed and 249 cases were disposed of during the year leaving 55 cases pending on 12/31/82. There were 304 criminal cases on the docket, 197 convictions, three persons committed to jail and 55 cases left pending. **JAILS** One jail, capacity 30. **ATTORNEYS AT LAW** Six. **UTILITIES** 54% of the residents are connected to a public or privately owned water system and 27% are connected to a public sewer system. Electricity is distributed to the city of San Augustine by the San Augustine Light and Water Dept. and the the rest of the county by Deep East Texas Electric Coop. Inc. and is generated primarily by gas, oil and water. The typical residential electric bill is $104.49 per month for an all-electric house using 2,500 kwh. **TAXES** The county has five units with taxing authority: two school districts, one city, one county and one hospital district.

RECREATION/ENTERTAINMENT

FEDERAL ANGELINA NATIONAL FOREST covers 154,916 acres in four counties and includes eight recreation areas. SABINE NATIONAL FOREST covers 188,220 acres in five counties and includes seven recreation areas. **NATIONAL REGISTER OF HISTORIC PLACES** San Augustine: M. Cartwright House, Ezekiel Cullen House, Horn-Polk House and Mission Nuestra Senora de los Delores de los Amis. San Augustine vicinity: Capt. T. W. Blount House and William Garrett Plantation Home. **MUNICIPAL PARKS** Nine acres in two municipal parks. These parks contain one playground, one baseball and softball field, and one tennis court.**SCENIC DRIVES** The Texas Forest Trail runs through this county. This trail explores the farming, ranching and oilfield areas of the East Texas Pineywoods. **BOATING/FISHING** Lakes/reservoirs: San Augustine City (195 acres) and Sam Rayburn (114,500 acres). Major rivers: Angelina.

COUNTIES

SAN AUGUSTINE (continued)

Primary streams: Carrizo, Ayish Bayou and Attoyac Bayou. **WILDLIFE REFUGES** Bannister State Wildlife Management Area covers 20,700 acres. **HUNTING** Fall and winter seasons on deer. Summer, fall and winter seasons on squirrel. Winter seasons on quail, muskrat, beaver, otter, opossum, mink, ring-tailed cat, badger, fox, raccoon, skunk and civet cat. No closed season on nutria, bobcat and coyote. In 1983 duck, coot, geese, woodcock and jacksnipe seasons occured during the winter months. Teal duck, rail and gallinule seasons occurred in the fall. Mourning dove seasons occurred intermittently during the fall and winter months. **MUSEUMS** San Augustine: Ezekiel W. Cullen Home. **SPECIAL EVENTS** Tour of Medallion Homes and Historical Places, San Augustine, June; Rodeo, San Augustine, August.

COMMUNITIES

COUNTY SEAT San Augustine, County Courthouse, 75972; County Clerk's Office, 409/275-2452. **INCORPORATED COMMUNITIES** (1980 population and ZIP Code) Broaddus (225) 75929 and San Augustine (2,930) 75972. **UNINCORPORATED COMMUNITIES** (and ZIP Code) Bland Lake (Blandlake) 75972, Denning 75972, Fords Corner 75972, Macune 75972, Norwood 75972, Ratcliff 75972 and White Rock 75972. **FOR ADDITIONAL LOCAL INFORMATION** San Augustine Chamber of Commerce, 132-A W. Columbia, San Augustine, 75972, 409/275-3610.

SAN JACINTO (E31)

THE LAND

North of Houston on U.S. Highway 59 and 190 in the East Texas Timberlands Region, San Jacinto County covers 572 square miles with the elevation ranging from 100 to 300 feet. The light colored, acidic, sandy to loamy soils have very deep, reddish, clayey subsoils. Along the Trinity River are dark loamy to cracking clayey soils. In the Pineywoods vegetation area there are pine and hardwood forests. Between 21 and 30% of the land in the county is considered prime farmland. **CLIMATE** Mild and moist. The average annual temperature is 67 °F. Temperatures in January range from an average low of 38° to an average high of 60 °F and in July range from 71° to 95 °F. The average annual precipitation is 47 inches, with an average relative humidity of 88% at 6 A.M. and 62% at 6 P.M. The average annual snowfall is not significant. The growing season averages 260 days per year, with the last freeze in early March and the first freeze in mid November. The sun shines during the year on the average 63% of the daylight hours.

THE PEOPLE

San Jacinto County is one of the state's fastest growing counties. The 1982 estimated population of 11,900 indicates the continuation of that pattern of growth. The growth rate rose dramatically from 9% between 1960 and 1970 to 71% between 1970 and 1980. The majority of the county residents live in rural areas. The age groups with the largest gains between 1970 and 1980 were birth to five years and ages 20 to 34. The population's median age is 33. The largest ancestry groups are persons of English descent (24%), Irish descent (23%) and Black (21%). **REGISTERED VOTERS** As of November 2, 1982 there were 7,180 registered voters (0.1% of the state total). The 1982 general election had a 47% voter turnout, compared to a 57% turnout in the 1980 general election. In the 1982 primary 100% voted Democratic with 3,122 votes cast.

THE ECONOMY

AGRICULTURE Forest production area. In 1982, 25% of the land was in farms and ranches, with 10% of the farmland under cultivation. San Jacinto ranked 239th in the state in highest agricultural receipts, with 70% from livestock and livestock products. Undesirable woody vegetation on the forestlands, inadequate forestland harvesting systems and erosion are the current conservation problems. Primary crops: hay. Primary vegetables: sweet potatoes. Primary fruits and nuts: peaches and pecans. Primary livestock and products: cattle, milk and hogs. **BUSINESS** Total number of business establishments in the county: 94. Retail sales during the first quarter of 1984 increased by 13%. In 1980, 11% of the labor force were self-employed, 14% were employed in professional or related services, 16% in manufacturing, 20% in wholesale and retail trade, 19% in construction, 70% were employed in other counties and there were 868 retired workers. The industry with the most employment: agribusiness. The nonfarm earnings in 1981 totaled $71,286,000. The retired workers received an average monthly Social Security payment of $304.00. **FINANCE** On June 30, 1983, two commercial banks had total deposits of $27,151,000 and total assets of $30,436,000. There is one state savings and loan association branch. **HOUSING** Average value of homes in 1980: $25,900. Between 1970 and 1980 the number of housing units increased by 118%. Sixty-nine percent of all units in the county are air-conditioned, 59% are heated by gas and 27% by electricity. **NATURAL RESOURCES** Industrial sand, sand and gravel, oil and gas. In 1982 a total of 4,738,038 thousand cubic feet of gas well gas, 165,749 barrels of condensate, 91,742 barrels of crude oil and 78,964 thousand cubic feet of casinghead gas were produced. Current production of other minerals and products includes construction sand, sand and gravel. Pine and hardwood production in 1981 totaled 8,288,388 cubic feet; 7,611,720 cubic feet of pine and 676,668 cubic feet of hardwood. **TOURISM** Travel expenditures of $2,921,000 in 1982 (an increase of 11% over 1981) generated 72 jobs and $578,000 in payroll. **ALCOHOLIC BEVERAGES** Packaged distilled spirits, beer, ale, malt liquor and wine are legal in parts of the county. **FEDERAL EXPENDITURES** The federal government had direct expenditures or obligations of $15,976,000 in the county during fiscal year 1983, including $607,000 by the U.S. Department of Defense. In addition, the federal government provided $781,000 in grant awards, paid $504,000 in salaries and wages, made direct payments to individuals of $14,452,000 including $11,753,000 in retirement and disability payments, awarded $179,000 in procurement contracts and spent $61,000 in other expenditures or obligations. The federal government also provided $2,000 in direct loans and $1,608,000 in guaranteed loans and insurance.

COMMUNICATION

Newspapers–Weekly: San Jacinto News-Times (Shepherd). Telephone companies: General Telephone, Southwestern Bell, Conroe telephone, Eastex Telephone Coop. and Waterwood Communications. **TRANSPORTATION** Total public road mileage: 729. In 1982 there were 9,498 registered vehicles and 234 reported traffic accidents including three fatalities. Intercity bus service is available. Motor freight: four carriers. Rail: One main line carries annually 10 to 20 million tons of freight through the county. Aircraft: four are registered in the county. Airports: Lake Water Wheel Airport and Waterwood Airport at Waterwood.

COMMUNITY SERVICES

EDUCATION Two school districts with two elementary, two middle and two high schools. The average daily attendance in 1981-82 was 2,282, with expenditures per pupil of $3,217 including 154 classroom teachers with an average annual salary of $15,921.

Thirty-seven percent of the 137 high school graduates planned to attend college. In 1982-83, 74% of the students were White, 0.1% Hispanic, 26% Black and 0.2% American Indian. **PUBLIC LIBRARIES** Shepherd Library. **CHILD CARE** Four day care and two twenty-four hour care licensed facilities. **HEALTH CARE** Three physicians and four dentists. Clinics: one county health services clinic. Ambulance services: one county service. **CHURCHES** 29 churches have an estimated combined membership of 3,783. The largest denominations are Southern Baptist, United Methodist and Baptist Missionary. **SOCIAL SERVICES** In fiscal year 1983 a total of $1,033,422 in food stamps was distributed, with an average of 1,984 persons receiving food stamps each month. Aid to Families with Dependent Children (AFDC) totaled $194,548 with an average of 135 families receiving AFDC each month. Medical assistance benefits for the aged and disabled of $766,782 and for families and children of $194,718 brought the county benefit total to $2,189,470. **FIRE PROTECTION** Eight volunteer fire departments. **LAW ENFORCEMENT** The County Sheriff has 24 commissioned officers. **CRIME** Eight violent crimes (murder, forcible rape, robbery and aggravated assault) and 204 nonviolent crimes (burglary, larceny-theft and motor vehicle theft) were reported in 1982. **JUDICIAL SYSTEM** Three District Courts and Judges, one County Court and Judge and four Justices of the Peace. In the District Courts a total of 863 cases were pending on 1/1/82, 375 new cases were filed and 284 cases were disposed of during the year leaving 954 cases pending on 12/31/82. There were 141 criminal cases on the docket, 27 convictions, three persons committed to prison, three committed to jail and 103 cases left pending. In the County Court 890 cases were pending on 1/1/82, 811 new cases were filed and 717 cases were disposed of during the year leaving 984 cases pending on 12/31/82. There were 1,617 criminal cases on the docket, 278 convictions, 19 persons committed to jail and 901 cases left pending. **JAILS** One jail, capacity 28. **ATTORNEYS AT LAW** Seven. **UTILITIES** 58% of the residents are connected to a public or privately owned water system and 18% are connected to a public sewer system. Electricity is distributed to the county by Gulf State Utilities and Sam Houston Electric Coop., Inc. and is generated primarily by gas and coal. **TAXES** The county has seven units with taxing authority: two school districts, one city, one county and three special districts.

RECREATION/ENTERTAINMENT

FEDERAL SAM HOUSTON NATIONAL FOREST covers 160,401 acres in three counties with seven recreation areas. **NATIONAL REGISTER OF HISTORIC PLACES** Coldspring: San Jacinto County Jail. **SCENIC DRIVES** The Texas Forest Trail runs through this county. This trail explores the farming, ranching and oilfield areas of the East Texas Pineywoods. **BOATING/FISHING** Lakes/reservoirs: Livingston (82,600 acres). Major rivers: Trinity and San Jacinto. Primary streams: Big Creek and Winters Bayou. **HUNTING** Fall and winter seasons on deer. Summer, fall and winter seasons on squirrel. Winter seasons on quail, muskrat, otter, beaver, opossum, mink, ring-tailed cat, badger, fox, raccoon, skunk and civet cat. No closed season on nutria, coyote and bobcat. In 1983 duck, coot, geese, woodcock and jacksnipe seasons occurred during the winter months. Teal duck, rail and gallinule seasons occurred in the fall. Mourning dove seasons occurred intermittently during the fall and winter months. **SPECIAL EVENTS** Pioneer Days, Coldspring, April; County Fair, Coldspring, September.

COMMUNITIES

COUNTY SEAT Coldspring, County Courthouse, 77331; County Clerk's Office, 409/653-2324. **INCORPORATED COMMUNITIES** (1980 population and ZIP Code) Coldspring (569) 77331, Pointblank (325) 77364 and Shepherd (1,674) 77371.

UNINCORPORATED COMMUNITIES (and ZIP Code) Camilla 77331, Evergreen 77327, Everitt (Magnolia) 77327, Fish Branch 77371, Maynard 77358, New Hope 77327, Oakhurst 77359, Palmetto 77359, Pine Valley 77358, Pumpkin 77358, Stephen Creek 77331, Urbana 77371, Waterwood 77359, Waverly 77358 and Willow Springs 77331. **FOR ADDITIONAL LOCAL INFORMATION** Shepherd Chamber of Commerce, P.O. Box 520, Shepherd, 77371, 409/628-3505.

SAN PATRICIO (G30)

THE LAND

Southeast of San Antonio on Interstate Highway 37 in the Coastal Prairie Region, San Patricio County covers 693 square miles with the elevation ranging from sea level to 200 feet. The nearly level soils have light to dark, loamy surfaces with clayey subsoils. In some areas the soils are gray to black, cracking and clayey with a high shrink-swell potential. In the Gulf Prairies vegetation area the grasses are tall with some post oak and mesquite trees. Between 51 and 60% of the land in the county is considered prime farmland. **CLIMATE** Mild and moist. Tropical storms and hurricanes are a risk June through October. The average annual temperature is 72 °F. Temperatures in January range from an average low of 46 ° to an average high of 64 °F and in July range from 74 ° to 93 °F. The average annual precipitation is 33 inches, with an average relative humidity of 90% at 6 A.M. and 65% at 6 P.M. There is no snowfall. The growing season averages 303 days per year, with the last freeze in mid February and the first freeze in mid December. The sun shines during the year on the average 69% of the daylight hours.

THE PEOPLE

San Patricio County ranks 48th among all U.S. counties in the highest percent of residents of Spanish origin. The 1982 estimated population of 61,100 indicates a continuation of the moderate growth rate, which rose from 5% between 1960 and 1970 to 23% between 1970 and 1980. Urban areas experienced high population gains from 1970 to 1980 while rural areas had losses. The population's low median age rose from 23 in 1970 to 26 in 1980. The largest ancestry groups are Hispanic (46%), persons of English descent (17%), German descent (16%) and Irish descent (15%). **REGISTERED VOTERS** As of November 2, 1982 there were 28,518 registered voters (0.4% of the state total). The 1982 general election had a 42% voter turnout, compared to a 59% turnout in the 1980 general election. In the 1982 primary 95% voted Democratic and 5% Republican, with 8,241 votes cast.

THE ECONOMY

AGRICULTURE Sorghum and cotton area. In 1982, 93% of the land was in farms and ranches, with 61% of the farmland under cultivation and less than 1% irrigated. San Patricio ranked 28th in the state in highest agricultural receipts, with 68% from crops. Overgrazing, undesirable brush and weeds, water erosion, drainage and shoreline erosion are the current conservation problems. Primary crops: fourth in the state for sorghum and eighth for cotton. Corn and hay. Primary vegetables: 10th in the state for cabbage. Processed vegetables including beets, cucumbers for pickles, snapbeans, spinach, sweet corn and tomatoes. Primary fruits and nuts: peaches and pecans. Primary livestock and products: cattle and hogs. **BUSINESS** Total number of business establishments in the county: 953. Retail sales during the first quarter of 1984 increased by 8%. In 1980, 8% of the labor force were self-employed, 15% were employed in professional or related services, 15% in manufacturing, 19% in wholesale and retail trade, 13% in agriculture, forestry, fisheries and mining, 38% were employed in other counties and there

COUNTIES

SAN PATRICIO (continued)

were 3,286 retired workers. The industries with the most employment: shipbuilding and repairing, agribusiness, oil and gas extraction, heavy construction and the manufacture of industrial chemicals and nonferrous metal by-products. The nonfarm earnings in 1981 totaled $481,709,000. The retired workers received an average monthly Social Security payment of $317. **FINANCE** On June 30, 1983, 10 commercial banks had total deposits of $256,191,000 and total assets of $291,146,000. There are seven state savings and loan association branches and two credit unions in the county. **HOUSING** Average value of homes in 1980: $33,000. Permits for new, privately owned housing units decreased in 1982: 259 permits were issued with a total construction cost of $10,615,724. Of those permits, 216 were for single family houses. Between 1970 and 1980 the number of housing units increased by 28%. Sixty-five percent of all units in the county are air-conditioned, 76% are heated by gas and 23% by electricity. **NATURAL RESOURCES** Industrial sand, sand and gravel, caliche, oil and gas. In 1982 a total of 37,903,839 thousand cubic feet of gas well gas, 1,141,346 barrels of condensate, 2,506,860 barrels of crude oil and 4,761,743 thousand cubic feet of casinghead gas were produced. Current production of other minerals and products includes caliche, clay, sand and gravel. **TOURISM** Travel expenditures of $17,496,000 in 1982 (an increase of 13% over 1981) generated 354 jobs and $3,091,000 in payroll. Lodging: seven hotels, motels and tourist courts. **ALCOHOLIC BEVERAGES** Packaged distilled spirits, beer, ale, malt liquor and wine are legal in parts of the county. Sale of mixed beverages is legal in all or parts of the county. **FEDERAL EXPENDITURES** The federal government had direct expenditures or obligations of $70,195,000 in the county during fiscal year 1983, including $2,436,000 by the U.S. Department of Defense. In addition, the federal government provided $4,388,000 in grant awards, paid $2,245,000 in salaries and wages, made direct payments to individuals of $54,106,000 including $42,633,000 in retirement and disability payments, awarded $344,000 in procurement contracts and spent $9,111,000 in other expenditures or obligations. The federal government also provided $10,044,000 in direct loans and $116,932,000 in guaranteed loans and insurance.

COMMUNICATION

Newspapers–Weekly: Aransas Pass Progress, Ingleside Index, The Mathis News-Spanish, The Odem-Edroy Times-Spanish, The Odem-Edroy Times, San Patricio County News-Spanish (Sinton) and the Taft Tribune-Spanish. Cable TV. Telephone companies: General Telephone and Southwestern Bell. **TRANSPORTATION** Total public road mileage: 1,210. In 1982 there were 46,015 registered vehicles and 953 reported traffic accidents including 28 fatalities. Taxi cabs: one company in Sinton. Intercity bus service is available. Motor freight: 17 local and intrastate carriers. Rail: six main and four branch lines carry freight through the county. Three of the main lines carry annually five to 10 million tons of freight each and three carry one to five million each. One of the branch lines carries annually one to five million tons of freight and three carry less than one million each. Aircraft: 83 are registered in the county. Airports: San Patricio County Airport at Sinton serves as a base for 30 aircraft and is a general utility airport with general aviation service. Also serving the area are Hunt Airport at Portland and Hunt's Dusting Service Airport at Taft. Waterborne commerce: (see Nueces Co.).

COMMUNITY SERVICES

EDUCATION Seven school districts with 18 elementary, seven middle and seven high schools. The average daily attendance in 1981-82 was 14,349, with expenditures per pupil of $2,370 includ-

ing 920 classroom teachers with an average annual salary of $16,745. Fifty-one percent of the 882 high school graduates planned to attend college. In 1982-83, 44% of the students were White, 54% Hispanic, 2% Black and 0.3% Asian. Private Schools: 39 students enrolled in one elementary school. **PUBLIC LIBRARIES** Aransas Pass Public Library: 21,875 volumes. Gregory Public Library: 3,350 volumes. Ingleside Public Library: 15,000 volumes. Mathis Public Library: 4,585 volumes. Odem Public Library: 6,810 volumes. Bell Public Library (Portland): 15,000 volumes. San Patricio County Library System (Sinton): 103,791 volumes, eight branches. Sinton Public Library: 20,500 volumes. Taft Public Library: 11,878 volumes. **CHILD CARE** 70 day care and 12 twenty-four hour care licensed facilities. **HEALTH CARE** 35 physicians and 17 dentists. Hospitals: two with a combined capacity of 123. Clinics: one public health clinic. Ambulance services: two commercial, one police department, one volunteer service and one city serevice. Mental health: three county clinics. Nursing homes: four nursing homes with a combined capacity of 417 nursing care residents. The average cost per day for private patients in 1982 was $29.14. **CHURCHES** 84 churches have an estimated combined membership of 35,834. The largest denominations are Catholic, Southern Baptist and United Methodist. **SOCIAL SERVICES** In fiscal year 1983 a total of $5,061,339 in food stamps was distributed, with an average of 10,794 persons receiving food stamps each month. Aid to Families with Dependent Children (AFDC) totaled $964,009, with an average of 615 families receiving AFDC each month. Medical assistance benefits for the aged and disabled of $3,532,757 and for families and children of $1,412,662 brought the county benefit total to $10,970,765. **FIRE PROTECTION** Nine volunteer fire departments. **LAW ENFORCEMENT** The County Sheriff has 46 commissioned officers. Seven police departments have a combined force of 99. **CRIME** 175 violent crimes (murder, forcible rape, robbery and aggravated assault) and 1,898 nonviolent crimes (burglary, larceny-theft and motor vehicle theft) were reported in 1982. **JUDICIAL SYSTEM** Two District Courts and Judges, one County Court and Judge and seven Justices of the Peace. In the District Courts a total of 4,326 cases were pending on 1/1/82, 1,750 new cases were filed and 1,510 cases were disposed of during the year leaving 4,566 cases pending on 12/31/82. There were 392 criminal cases on the docket, 193 convictions, 57 persons committed to prison, eight committed to jail and 118 cases left pending. In the County Court 1,745 cases were pending on 1/1/82, 1,522 new cases were filed and 1,615 cases were disposed of during the year leaving 1,652 cases pending on 12/31/82. There were 3,062 criminal cases on the docket, 118 convictions, 27 persons committed to jail and 1,602 cases left pending. **JAILS** One jail, capacity 78. **ATTORNEYS AT LAW** 48. **UTILITIES** 87% of the residents are connected to a public or privately owned water system and 75% are connected to a public sewer system. Natural gas is distributed to the county by Entex, Inc. The average annual residential bill for natural gas in 1982 for the Entex distribution system was $390.31, an increase of 26% over 1981. Electricity is distributed to the county by Cochran Power and Light Co. and Central Power and Light Co. and is generated primarily by gas, oil and coal. The typical residential electric bill is $162.15 per month for an all-electric house using 2,500 kwh. **TAXES** The county has 19 units with taxing authority: seven school districts, eight cities, one county, one hospital district and two special districts.

RECREATION/ENTERTAINMENT

NATIONAL REGISTER OF HISTORIC PLACES San Patricio: James McGloin House. **STATE** Lake Corpus Christi State Recreation Area covers 365 acres with camping and trailer sites, fishing, swimming and a boat ramp. On the southeastern shore of the 14,000 acre lake, the state park offers a wide variety of land and water recreation. **MUNICIPAL PARKS** 647 acres in 32 municipal parks. These parks contain 10 playgrounds, one golf course, 15 baseball and softball fields, seven tennis courts, one multi-use court, three swimming pools and shore fishing facilities. Developed campsites: 12. **SCENIC DRIVES** The Texas Tropical Trail runs through this county. This trail is charted through the state's southern most wedge meandering through ranchland, resort areas by the gulf of Mexico and fertile farmlands. **BOATING/FISHING** Lakes/reservoirs: Corpus Christi (19,336 acres), Reynolds Metal Company (63 acres), Tailing Ponds No. 2 (1,000 acres) and Vahlsing (66 acres). Major rivers: Nueces and Aransas. Primary streams: Chilitpin. Saltwater fishing: speckled trout, redfish and flounder fishing is usually good around Corpus Christi Bay and Redfish Bay. Shrimp, oysters and crabs may be taken but, like other saltwater fish, under specific regulations. **HUNTING** Fall and winter seasons on deer. No closed season on nutria, javelina, squirrel, bobcat and coyote. Winter seasons on quail, muskrat, beaver, otter, opossum, mink, ring-tailed cat, badger, fox, raccoon, skunk and civet cat. Fall, winter and spring seasons on turkey. In 1983, duck coot, geese, woodcock and jacksnipe seasons occurred during the winter months with a winter season on sandhill crane in some parts of the county. Teal duck, rail and gallinule seasons occurred in the fall. Mourning dove seasons occurred intermittently during the fall and winter months with a fall season on white-winged dove in some parts of the county. **MUSEUMS** San Patricio: San Patricio Historical Museum. Sinton: Welder Wildlife Foundation. **OTHER** Sinton: Welder Wildlife Refuge. **SPECIAL EVENTS** World Championship Rattlesnake Races, San Patricio, March; Fish-A-Rama, Mathis, May; Shrimporee, Aransas Pass, May; Boll Weevil Festival, Taft, September; Old Fiddler's Festival, Sinton, October; Turkey Shoot, Mathis, November.

COMMUNITIES

COUNTY SEAT Sinton, County Courthouse, 78387; County Clerk's Office, 512/364-2490. **INCORPORATED COMMUNITIES** (1980 population and ZIP Code) Aransas Pass (7,173: 6,308 in San Patricio Co., 860 in Aransas Co. and 5 in Nueces Co.) 78336, Gregory (2,739) 78359, Ingleside (5,436) 78362, Lake City (431) 78387, Lakeside (276) 78368, Mathis (5,667) 78368, Odem (2,363) 78370, Portland (12,023) 78374, San Patricio (241: 210 in San Patricio Co. and 31 in Nueces Co.) 78368, Sinton (6,044) 78387 and Taft (3,686) 78390. **UNINCORPORATED COMMUNITIES** (and ZIP Code) Edroy 78352, Hubert 78368, Ingleside-on-the-Bay (McGloins Bluff) 78362, Midway 78390, Saint Paul 78387, Taft Southwest 78390 and West Sinton 78370. **FOR ADDITIONAL LOCAL INFORMATION** Ingleside Chamber of Commerce, 314 Dallas, Ingleside, 78362, 512/776-2906, Mathis Area Chamber of Commerce, 310 E. San Patricio, Mathis, 78368, 512/547-6112, Sinton Chamber of Commerce, 218 W. Sinton, Sinton, 78387, 512/364-2307 and Taft Chamber of Commerce, P. O. Box 65, Taft, 78390, 512/528-3230.

SAN SABA (C4)

THE LAND

Southwest of Waco on U.S. Highway 190 in the Edwards Plateau Region, San Saba County covers 1,136 square miles with the elevation ranging from 1,000 to 1,800 feet. The undulating to hilly soils in the south are very dark and loamy with accumulations of lime in the subsoils. In the north the soils are light colored with loamy surfaces over reddish, clayey subsoils. In the Edwards Plateau vegetation area the principal grasses are bluestems, gramas, wildryes, Indiangrasses and buffalograsses with oaks, cedar and mesquite trees along streams. Between 11 and 20%

of the land in the county is considered prime farmland. **CLIMATE** Subtropical Subhumid with wide-ranging daily tempurature variations. The average annual temperature is 66 °F. Temperatures in January range from an average low of 31 ° to an average high of 58 °F and in July range from 70 ° to 96 °F. The average annual precipitation is 26 inches, with an average relative humidity of 78% at 6 A.M. and 48% at 6 P.M. The average annual snowfall is two inches. The growing season averages 227 days per year, with the last freeze at end of March and the first freeze in mid November. The sun shines during the year on the average 65% of the daylight hours.

THE PEOPLE

San Saba County ranks 50th among all U.S. Counties in the highest percent of residents over age 64. The 1982 estimated population of 6,000 represents a decline in population since 1980. During the 1970s a population growth reversed the population decline from 1940 to 1960. Urban and rural areas grew at approximately the same rate from 1970 to 1980. The population is older than average although the median age lowered from 43 in 1970 to 40 in 1980. The largest ancestry groups are persons of English descent (30%), Irish descent (26%) and Hispanic (16%). **REGISTERED VOTERS** As of November 2, 1982 there were 3,053 registered voters (0.04% of the state total). The 1982 general election had a 56% voter turnout, compared to a 74% turnout in the 1980 general election. In the 1982 primary 100% voted Democratic with 1,281 votes cast.

THE ECONOMY

AGRICULTURE Livestock area. In 1982, 95% of the land was in farms and ranches, with 10% of the farmland under cultivation and 8% irrigated. San Saba ranked 133rd in the state in highest agricultural receipts, with 85% from livestock and livestock products. Overgrazing, undesirable brush and weeds and water erosion are the current conservation problems. Primary crops: wheat, hay, oats, peanuts and sorghum. Primary vegetables: watermelons. Primary fruits and nuts: peaches and fourth in the state for pecans. Primary livestock and products: ninth in the state for turkeys. Cattle, sheep, wool, angora goats, mohair and hogs. **BUSINESS** Total number of business establishments in the county: 128. Retail sales during the first quarter of 1984 increased by 3%. In 1980, 25% of the labor force were self-employed, 21% were employed in professional or related services, 7% in manufacturing, 16% in wholesale and retail trade, 24% in agriculture, forestry, fisheries and mining, 13% were employed in other counties and there were 907 retired workers. The industries with the most employment: stone quarring, agribusiness and tourism. The nonfarm earnings in 1981 totaled $40,366,000. The retired workers received an average monthly Social Security payment of $269.00. **FINANCE** On June 30, 1983, two commercial banks had total deposits of $39,177,000 and total assets of $44,170,000. On December 31, 1982 one state savings and loan association and one state branch had assets of $105,914,262. **HOUSING** Average value of homes in 1980: $19,800. Permits for new, privately owned housing units increased in 1982: eight permits were issued with a total construction cost of $241,000. Of those permits, all were for single family houses. Between 1970 and 1980 the number of housing units increased by 24%. Seventy-one percent of all units in the county are air-conditioned, 77% are heated by gas and 14% by electricity. **NATURAL RESOURCES** Dolomite, limestone, industrial sand and gas. In 1982 a total of 275,198 thousand cubic feet of gas well gas and 6,305 barrels of condensate were produced. Current production of other minerals and products includes crushed limestone, fieldstone, sand and gravel. **TOURISM** Travel expenditures of $4,157,000 in 1982 (an increase of 12% over 1981)

COUNTIES

SAN SABA (continued)

generated 99 jobs and $806,000 in payroll. **ALCOHOLIC BEVERAGES** Packaged distilled spirits, beer, ale, malt liquor and wine are legal in parts of the county. **FEDERAL EXPENDITURES** The federal government had direct expenditures or obligations of $14,976,000 in the county during fiscal year 1983, including $305,000 by the U.S. Department of Defense. In addition, the federal government provided $2,257,000 in grant awards, paid $470,000 in salaries and wages, made direct payments to individuals of $11,583,000 including $7,480,000 in retirement and disability payments, awarded $1,000 in procurement contracts and spent $666,000 in other expenditures or obligations. The federal government also provided $49,000 in direct loans and $1,037,000 in guaranteed loans and insurance.

COMMUNICATION

Newspapers–Weekly: The San Saba News and Star. Radio: KBAL-AM (San Saba). Cable TV. Telephone companies: General Telephone, Central Texas Telephone Coop. and Hill Country Telephone Corp. **TRANSPORTATION** Total public road mileage: 755. In 1982 there were 5,846 registered vehicles and 131 reported traffic accidents. Motor freight: two carriers. Rail: one branch line carries annually less than one million tons of freight through the county. Aircraft: seven are registered in the county. Airports: San Saba County Municipal Airport.

COMMUNITY SERVICES

EDUCATION Three school districts with four elementary, one middle and three high schools. The average daily attendance in 1981-82 was 1,048, with expenditures per pupil of $2,298 including 74 classroom teachers with an average annual salary of $15,205. Fifty-three percent of the 72 high school graduates planned to attend college. In 1982-83, 73% of the students were White, 27% Hispanic, 0.4% Black and 0.1% American Indian. Sports championships: 1983 AA Boys' Golf Singles and Team, San Saba H.S. **PUBLIC LIBRARIES** San Saba County Library (San Saba): 9,014 volumes. **CHILD CARE** 14 day care and two twenty-four hour care licensed facilities. **HEALTH CARE** Four physicians and three dentists. Hospitals: one with a capacity of 33. Ambulance services: one commercial service. Mental health: clinic. Nursing homes: two nursing homes with a combined capacity of 143 nursing care residents. The average cost per day for private patients in 1982 was $24.28. **CHURCHES** 24 churches have an estimated combined membership of 4,064. The largest denominations are Southern Baptist, Churches of Christ and United Methodist. **SOCIAL SERVICES** In fiscal year 1983 a total of $225,188 in food stamps was distributed, with an average of 519 persons receiving food stamps each month. Aid to Families with Dependent Children (AFDC) totaled $31,204 with an average of 22 families receiving AFDC each month. Medical assistance benefits for the aged and disabled of $1,090,906 and for families and children of $30,445 brought the county benefit total to $1,377,743. **FIRE PROTECTION** Three volunteer fire departments. **LAW ENFORCEMENT** The County Sheriff has seven commissioned officers. **CRIME** Five violent crimes (murder, forcible rape, robbery and aggravated assault) and 69 nonviolent crimes (burglary, larceny-theft and motor vehicle theft) were reported in 1982. **JUDICIAL SYSTEM** One District Court and Judge, one County Court and Judge and one Justice of the Peace. In the District Court a total of 204 cases were pending on 1/1/82, 141 new cases were filed and 135 cases were disposed of during the year leaving 210 cases pending on 12/31/82. There were 32 criminal cases on the docket, three convictions, two persons committed to prison and 29 cases left pending. In the County Court 41 cases were pending on 1/1/82, 108 new cases were filed and 94 cases were disposed of during the year leaving

55 cases pending on 12/31/82. There were 133 criminal cases on the docket, 44 convictions, nine persons committed to jail and 45 cases left pending. **JAILS** One jail, capacity 10. **ATTORNEYS AT LAW** Eight. **UTILITIES** 62% of the residents are connected to a public or privately owned water system and 52% are connected to a public sewer system. Natural gas is distributed to the county by Lone Star Gas Co., Division of Enserch. The average annual residential bill for natural gas in 1982 for the Lone Star distribution system was $405.91, an increase of 26% over 1981. Electricity is distributed to the county by Lower Colorado River Authority, McCulloch Electric Coop. Inc., Central Texas Electric Coop. Inc., Pedernales Electric Coop. Inc. and Hamilton Valley Electric Coop., Assn. and is generated primarily by gas, coal, oil and water. The typical residential electric bill is $123.05 per month for an all-electric house using 2,500 kwh. **TAXES** The county has seven units with taxing authority: three school districts, two cities, one county and one special district.

RECREATION/ENTERTAINMENT

NATIONAL REGISTER OF HISTORIC PLACES Regency Suspension Bridge. (see Mills County). **MUNICIPAL PARKS** 114 acres in three municipal parks. These parks contain one playground, one golf course, five baseball and softball fields, two tennis courts, one swimming pool, one beach, one boat ramp and shore fishing facilities. Developed campsites: 15. **BOATING/FISHING** Harlow (20 acres), Margery (12 acres) and Southeast Laterals Soil Conservation Service Lake 8A (42 acres). Major rivers: San Saba and Colorado. Primary streams: Harky Hollow, Bonnett, Wilbarger, Brady and Cherokee. **HUNTING** Fall and winter seasons on deer and javelina. No closed season on squirrel, coyote and bobcat. Winter seasons on quail, muskrat, beaver, opossum, ring-tailed cat, badger, fox, weasel, raccoon, skunk and civet cat. Fall, winter and spring seasons on turkey. In 1983 duck, coot, geese, woodcock and jacksnipe seasons occurred during the winter months. Teal duck, rail and gallinule seasons occurred in the fall. Mourning dove seasons occurred intermittently during the fall and winter months. **MUSEUMS** San Saba: San Saba County Historical Memorial Museum. **SPECIAL EVENTS** Junior Livestock Show, San Saba, January; Rodeo, Parade and Festival, San Saba, June; Annual Tractor Pull, San Saba, July; Pecan Festival, San Saba, November.

COMMUNITIES

COUNTY SEAT San Saba, County Courthouse, 76877; County Clerk's Office, 915/372-3614. **INCORPORATED COMMUNITIES** (1980 population and ZIP Code) Richland Springs (420) 76871 and San Saba (2,847) 76877. **UNINCORPORATED COMMUNITIES** (and ZIP Code) Algerita 76877, Bend 76824, Bowser 76860, Chappel 76877, Cherokee 76832, Elm Grove 76860, Hall 76871, Harkeyville 76877, Holt 76860, Locker 76871, McMillin 76877, Shaw Bend 76877, Skeeterville 76860 and Spring Creek 76871. **FOR ADDITIONAL LOCAL INFORMATION** San Saba Co. Chamber of Commerce, Courthouse, San Saba, 76877, 915/372-5141.

SCHLEICHER (P95)

THE LAND

South of Abilene on U.S. Highway 190 in the Edwards Plateau Region, Schleicher County covers 1,309 square miles with the elevation ranging from 2,100 to 2,400 feet. The undulating to hilly soils are very dark and loamy with lime accumulations in the subsoils. In the west the limestone bedrock is near the surface with areas of 90% exposed rock. In the Edwards Plateau vegetation area the tall grasses are bluestems, gramas, wildryes,

SCHLEICHER

Indiangrass and buffalograss with some oaks, cedars and mesquite trees. Between 11 and 20% of the land in the county is considered prime farmland. **CLIMATE** Subtropical Subhumid and relatively dry. The average annual temperature is 66 °F. Temperatures in January range from an average low of 32° to an average high of 61 °F and in July range from 69° to 96°F. The average annual precipitation is 20 inches, with an average relative humidity of 75% at 6 A.M. and 41% at 6 P.M. The average annual snowfall is two inches. The growing season averages 229 days per year, with the last freeze in late March and the first freeze in mid November. The sun shines during the year on the average 67% of the daylight hours.

THE PEOPLE
The population in Schleicher County is increasing after 40 years of gradual decline. The 1982 estimated population of 3,100 indicates a continuation of the growth which began in the 1970s. A majority of the county residents live in the rural areas. The population's median age lowered from 33 in 1970 to 30 in 1980. The largest ancestry groups are Hispanic (26%) persons of English descent (24%) and Irish descent (17%). **REGISTERED VOTERS** As of November 2, 1982 there were 1,490 registered voters (0.02% of the state total). The 1982 general election had a 55% voter turnout, compared to a 75% turnout in the 1980 general election. In the 1982 primary 100% voted Democratic with 655 votes cast.

THE ECONOMY
AGRICULTURE Sheep ranches. In 1982, 94% of the land was in farms and ranches, with 4% of the farmland under cultivation and 10% irrigated. Schleicher ranked 194th in the state in highest agricultural receipts, with 81% from livestock and livestock products. Overgrazing, undesirable brush and weeds, moisture conservation and water erosion are the current conservation problems. Primary crops: wheat, sorghum, cotton and oats. Primary vegetables: tomatoes. Primary fruits and nuts: pecans. Primary livestock and products: ninth in the state for sheep and 10th for wool production. Cattle, angora goats, mohair and hogs. **BUSINESS** Total number of business establishments in the county: 56. Retail sales during the first quarter of 1984 decreased by 39%. In 1980, 17% of the labor force were self-employed, 14% were employed in professional or related services, 2% in manufacturing, 13% in wholesale and retail trade, 44% in agriculture, forestry, fisheries and mining, 22% were employed in other counties and there were 275 retired workers. The industries with the most employment: oil and gas extracton, agribusiness, general construction and the manufacture of women's clothing. The nonfarm earnings in 1981 totaled $27,023,000. The retired workers received an average monthly Social Security payment of $305. **FINANCE** On June 30, 1983, one commercial bank had total deposits of $24,720,000 and total assets of $28,595,000. There is one state savings and loan association branch. **HOUSING** Average value of homes in 1980: $21,100. Permits for new, privately owned housing units increased in 1982: 13 permits were issued with a total construction cost of $475,000. Of those permits, seven were for single family houses. Between 1970 and 1980 the number of housing units increased by 17%. Sixty-eight percent of all units in the county are air-conditioned, 90% are heated by gas and 8% by electricity. **NATURAL RESOURCES** Dolomite, limestone, industrial sand, oil and gas. In 1982 a total of 16,585,286 thousand cubic feet of gas well gas, 136,925 barrels of condensate, 1,141,233 barrels of crude oil and 3,247,133 thousand cubic feet of casinghead gas were produced. **TOURISM** Travel expenditures of $1,815,000 in 1982 (an increase of 11% over 1981) generated 47 jobs and $369,000 in payroll. **ALCOHOLIC BEVERAGES** Packaged distilled spirits, beer, ale, malt liquor and wine are legal. **FEDERAL EXPENDITURES**

The federal government had direct expenditures or obligations of $5,445,000 in the county during fiscal year 1983, including $123,000 by the U.S. Department of Defense. In addition, the federal government provided $496,000 in grant awards, paid $157,000 in salaries and wages, made direct payments to individuals of $3,356,000 including $2,435,000 in retirement and disability payments, awarded $1,000 in procurement contracts and spent $1,437,000 in other expenditures or obligations. The federal government also provided $267,000 in direct loans and $5,578,000 in guaranteed loans and insurance.

COMMUNICATION
Cable TV. Telephone companies: General Telephone. **TRANSPORTATION** Total public road mileage: 426. In 1982 there were 3,523 registered vehicles and 88 reported traffic accidents. Intercity bus service is available. Motor freight: three carriers. Aircraft: 15 are registered in the county. Airports: Eldorado Municipal Airport.

COMMUNITY SERVICES
EDUCATION One school district with one elementary and one high school. The average daily attendance in 1981-82 was 616, with expenditures per pupil of $3,353 including 44 classroom teachers with an average annual salary of $17,860. Forty-six percent of the 46 high school graduates planned to attend college. In 1982-83, 57% of the students were White, 42% Hispanic, 1% Black and 0.1% American Indian. **PUBLIC LIBRARIES** Eldorado Public Library: 8,000 volumes. **CHILD CARE** Eight day care licensed facilities. **HEALTH CARE** Two physicians. Hospitals: one with a capacity of 16. Ambulance services: one volunteer service. Nursing homes: one nursing home has a capacity of 38 nursing care residents. The average cost per day for private patients in 1982 was $27.47. **CHURCHES** Nine churches have an estimated combined membership of 1,758. The largest denominations are Southern Baptist, Catholic and United Methodist. **SOCIAL SERVICES** In fiscal year 1983 a total of $78,800 in food stamps was distributed, with an average of 186 persons receiving food stamps each month. Aid to Families with Dependent Children (AFDC) totaled $7,188. Medical assistance benefits for the aged and disabled of $206,434 and for families and children of $6,181 brought the county benefit total to $298,603. **FIRE PROTECTION** Two volunteer fire departments. **LAW ENFORCEMENT** The County Sheriff has five commissioned officers. **CRIME** Five violent crimes (murder, forcible rape, robbery and aggravated assault) and 86 nonviolent crimes (burglary, larceny-theft and motor vehicle theft) were reported in 1982. **JUDICIAL SYSTEM** One District Court and Judge, one County Court and Judge and one Justice of the Peace. In the District Court a total of 23 cases were pending on 1/1/82, 97 new cases were filed and 69 cases were disposed of during the year leaving 51 cases pending on 12/31/82. There were 13 criminal cases on the docket, 10 convictions, two persons committed to prison, two committed to jail and two cases left pending. In the County Court 112 cases were pending on 1/1/82, 200 new cases were filed and 175 cases were disposed of during the year leaving 137 cases pending on 12/31/82. There were 298 criminal cases on the docket, 50 convictions, 11 persons committed to jail and 124 cases left pending. **JAILS** One jail, capacity 15. **ATTORNEYS AT LAW** Two. **UTILITIES** 72% of the residents are connected to a public or privately owned water system and 57% are connected to a public sewer system. Electricity is distributed to the county by Kimble Electric Coop. Inc., Houston Lighting and Power and Southwest Texas Electric Coop. Inc. and is generated primarily by gas, oil, coal and water. The typical residential electric bill is $201.39 per month for an all-electric house using 2,500 kwh. **TAXES** The county has four

COUNTIES

SCHLEICHER (continued)

units with taxing authority: one school district, one city, one county and one hospital district.

RECREATION/ENTERTAINMENT

COUNTY PARKS 90 acres in two county parks. These parks contain one playground, one golf course, one baseball and softball field and one swimming pool. **SCENIC DRIVES** The Texas Forts Trail runs through this county. This trail leads to eight of the famous frontier forts of west central Texas and an ancient presidio of the Spanish colonial period. **BOATING/FISHING** Lakes/reservoirs: Dry Devils and Lowrey Soil Conservation Service Lakes 1 and 2 (20 acres). Major rivers: Dry Devils and South Concho. Primary streams: Rocky. **HUNTING** Fall and winter seasons on deer. No closed season on javelina, squirrel, bobcat and coyote. Winter seasons on quail, muskrat, beaver, opossum, ring-tailed cat, badger, fox, weasel, raccoon, skunk and civet cat. Fall, winter and spring seasons on turkey. In 1983 sandhill crane, duck, coot, geese, woodcock and jacksnipe seasons occurred during the winter months. Teal duck, rail and gallinule seasons occurred in the fall. Mourning dove seasons occurred intermittently during the fall and winter months. **MUSEUMS** El Dorado: Schleicher County Museum. **SPECIAL EVENTS** Junior Rodeo, El Dorado, May/June; Mis Amigas Celebration, Eldorado, June; Schleicher County Days, El Dorado, June/July; Christmas Celebration, El Dorado, December.

COMMUNITIES

COUNTY SEAT El Dorado, County Courthouse, 76936; County Clerk's Office, 915/853-2833. **INCORPORATED COMMUNITIES** (1980 population and ZIP Code) Eldorado (2,061) 76936.

SCURRY (P60)

THE LAND

Southeast of Lubbock on U.S. Highways 180 and 84 in the Rolling Plains Region, Scurry County covers 900 square miles with the elevation ranging from 2,000 to 2,700 feet. The light to dark loamy soils have reddish, clayey subsoils with lime accumulations in some areas. In the Rolling Plains vegetation area, the bluestems, gramas, wildryes and wheatgrasses are tall to mid in height with mesquite trees in some areas. Between 41 and 50% of the land in the county is considered prime farmland. **CLIMATE** Subtropical Subhumid and relatively dry with wide-ranging daily temperature variations. The average annual temperature is 62 °F. Temperatures in January range from an average low of 26 ° to an average high of 55 °F and in July range from 69 ° to 95 °F. The average annual precipitation is 20 inches, with an average relative humidity of 73% at 6 A.M. and 40% at 6 P.M. The average annual snowfall is eight inches. The growing season averages 214 days per year, with the last freeze in early April and the first freeze in early November. The sun shines during the year on the average 74% of the daylight hours.

THE PEOPLE

The population of Scurry County is steadily regaining its size of the 1950s. The 1982 estimated population of 19,500 indicates a continuation of the growth begun in the 1970s. Rural areas grew slightly faster than urban areas from 1970 to 1980. The population's median age lowered from 32 in 1970 to 29 in 1980. The largest ancestry groups are persons of English descent (28%), Irish descent (23%) and Hispanic (19%). **REGISTERED VOTERS** As of November 2, 1982 there were 9,438 registered voters (0.1% of the state total). The 1982 general election had a 42% voter turnout, compared to a 60% turnout in the 1980

general election. In the 1982 primary 94% voted Democratic and 6% Republican, with 2,353 votes cast.

THE ECONOMY

AGRICULTURE Cotton area. In 1982, 95% of the land was in farms and ranches, with 19% of the farmland under cultivation and 4% irrigated. Scurry ranked 142nd in the state in highest agricultural receipts, with 68% from crops. Overgrazing, undesirable brush and weeds, water and wind erosion are the current conservation problems. Primary crops: cotton, sorghum, oats and wheat. Primary fruits and nuts: peaches and pecans. Primary livestock and products: cattle, sheep, wool and hogs. **BUSINESS** Total number of business establishments in the county: 510. Retail sales during the first quarter of 1984 increased by 7%. In 1980, 11% of the labor force were self-employed, 18% were employed in professional or related services, 8% in manufacturing, 18% in wholesale and retail trade, 27% in agriculture, forestry, fisheries and mining, 6% were employed in other counties and there were 1,413 retired workers. The industries with the most employment: oil and gas field services, agribusiness, heavy construction and the manufacture of small electric household appliances. The nonfarm earnings in 1981 totaled $191,566,000. The retired workers received an average monthly Social Security payment of $318. **FINANCE** On June 30, 1983, three commercial banks had total deposits of $167,602,000 and total assets of $190,044,000. On December 31, 1982 one state savings and loan association, one state branch and one federal association branch had assets of $29,458,183. In addition there is one credit union in the county. **HOUSING** Average value of homes in 1980: $25,800. Permits for new, privately owned housing units increased in 1982: 107 permits were issued with a total construction cost of $3,273,376. Of those permits, 45 were for single family houses. Between 1970 and 1980 the number of housing units increased by 17%. Eighty-three percent of all units in the county are air-conditioned, 84% are heated by gas and 14% by electricity. **NATURAL RESOURCES** Caliche, chlorine, magnesium, salt, oil, gas, volcanic ash and bituminous coal. In 1982 a total of 31,732,066 barrels of crude oil and 53,088,206 thousand cubic feet of casinghead gas were produced. Current production of other minerals and products includes brick, crushed limestone, sand and gravel. **TOURISM** Travel expenditures of $15,147,000 in 1982 (an increase of 15% over 1981) generated 288 jobs and $2,592,000 in payroll. Convention/meeting facilities: Snyder-Scurry County Coliseum and Agricultural Complex. **ALCOHOLIC BEVERAGES** Totally dry. **FEDERAL EXPENDITURES** The federal government had direct expenditures or obligations of $29,645,000 in the county during fiscal year 1983, including $399,000 by the U.S. Department of Defense. In addition, the federal government provided $458,000 in grant awards, paid $1,153,000 in salaries and wages, made direct payments to individuals of $20,948,000 including $15,170,000 in retirement and disability payments, awarded $4,000 in procurement contracts and spent $7,082,000 in other expenditures or obligations. The federal government also provided $426,000 in direct loans and $6,435,000 in guaranteed loans and insurance.

COMMUNICATION

Newspapers–Daily: News (Snyder), ave. eve. circ. 5,357. Radio: KSNY-AM and KSNY-FM (Snyder). Cable TV. Telephone companies: Continental Telephone and Southwestern Bell. **TRANSPORTATION** Total public road mileage: 1,052. In 1982 there were 20,747 registered vehicles and 514 reported traffic accidents including five fatalities. Intercity bus service is available. Motor freight: 16 local and intrastate carriers. Rail: two main lines carry freight through the county with one carrying over 30 million tons of freight and one carrying 20 to 30 million. Aircraft: 67 are registered in the county. Airports: Winston Field at Snyder serves as a base for 46 aircraft and is a basic transportation airport with general aviation service.

COMMUNITY SERVICES

EDUCATION Three school districts with eight elementary, one middle and three high schools. The average daily attendance in 1981-82 was 3,448, with expenditures per pupil of $2,872 including 254 classroom teachers with an average annual salary of $19,120. Seventy-one percent of the 220 high school graduates planned to attend college. In 1982-83, 66% of the students were White, 29% Hispanic, 4% Black and 0.5% Asian. Sports championships: 1983 AAAA Baseball, Snyder H.S. Private schools: 18 students enrolled in one elementary school. Western Texas College is located in Snyder. Established in 1969 it is a vocational and two year academic college under state and local control. Enrollment in 1982 was 1,163 with in state undergraduate tuition and fees of $200 per semester. **PUBLIC LIBRARIES** Scurry County Library (Snyder): 53,670 volumes. **CHILD CARE** 49 day care and 12 twenty-four hour care licensed facilities. **HEALTH CARE** 13 physicians and six dentists. Hospitals: one with a capacity of 128. Clinics: one public health clinic. Ambulance services: two commercial services. Mental health: one county clinic. Nursing homes: two nursing homes with a combined capacity of 197 nursing care residents. The average cost per day for private patients in 1982 was $40.59. **CHURCHES** 48 churches have an estimated combined membership of 15,042. The largest denominations are Southern Baptist, Catholic and United Methodist. **SOCIAL SERVICES** In fiscal year 1983 a total of $381,049 in food stamps was distributed, with an average of 874 persons receiving food stamps each month. Aid to Families with Dependent Children (AFDC) totaled $65,432 with an average of 40 families receiving AFDC each month. Medical assistance benefits for the aged and disabled of $1,121,425 and for families and children of $149,658 brought the county benefit total to $1,717,564. **FIRE PROTECTION** One partly paid and one volunteer fire department. **LAW ENFORCEMENT** The County Sheriff has nine commissioned officers. One police department has a force of 17. **CRIME** 38 violent crimes (murder, forcible rape, robbery and aggravated assault) and 508 nonviolent crimes (burglary, larceny-theft and motor vehicle theft) were reported in 1982. **JUDICIAL SYSTEM** One District Court and Judge, one County Court and Judge and four Justices of the Peace. In the District Court a total of 301 cases were pending on 1/1/82, 649 new cases were filed and 595 cases were disposed of during the year leaving 355 cases pending on 12/31/82. There were 244 criminal cases on the docket, 137 convictions, 45 persons committed to prison, 26 committed to jail and 68 cases left pending. In the County Court 458 cases were pending on 1/1/82, 645 new cases were filed and 648 cases were disposed of during the year leaving 455 cases pending on 12/31/82. There were 840 criminal cases on the docket, 460 convictions, 162 persons committed to jail and 228 cases left pending. **JAILS** One jail, capacity 53. **ATTORNEYS AT LAW** 17. **UTILITIES** 78% of the residents are connected to a public or privately owned water system and 69% are connected to a public sewer system. Natural gas is distributed to the county by Lone Star Gas Co., Division of Enserch. The average annual residential bill for natural gas in 1982 for the Lone Star distribution system was $405.91, an increase of 35% over 1981. Electricity is distributed to the county by Lonewolf Electric Coop., Inc. and Texas Electric Service and is generated primarily by gas. The typical residential electric bill is $154.69 per month for an all-electric house using 2,500 kwh. **TAXES** The county has six units with taxing authority: three school districts, one city, one county and one college district.

RECREATION/ENTERTAINMENT

COUNTY/MUNICIPAL PARKS 258 acres in three county and one municipal park. These parks contain five playgrounds, eight baseball and softball fields, three tennis courts and two swimming pools. **BOATING/FISHING** Lakes/reservoirs: J. B. Thomas (7,820 acres). Major rivers: Colorado. Primary streams: Deep Creek, Rough and Ennis. **HUNTING** Fall season on antelope. Fall and winter seasons on mule deer and deer. No closed season on squirrel, coyote and bobcat. Winter seasons on quail, muskrat, beaver, opossum, ring-tailed cat, badger, fox, weasel, raccoon, skunk and civet cat. Fall, winter and spring seasons on turkey. In 1983 sandhill crane, duck, coot, geese, woodcock and jacksnipe seasons occurred during the winter months. Teal duck, rail and gallinule seasons occurred in the fall. Mourning dove seasons occurred intermittently during the fall and winter months. **MUSEUMS** Snyder: Diamond M Foundation Museum and Scurry County Museum. **SPECIAL EVENTS** County Fair, Snyder, September; White Buffalo Day, Snyder, October.

COMMUNITIES

COUNTY SEAT Snyder, County Courthouse, 79549; County Clerk's Office, 915/573-5332. **INCORPORATED COMMUNITIES** (1980 population and ZIP Code) Snyder (12,705) 79545, All-America Cities Award 1968. **UNINCORPORATED COMMUNITIES** (and ZIP Code) Camp Springs 79526, China Grove 79526, Dermott 79515, Dunn 79516, Fluvanna 79517, Hermleigh 79526, Inadale 79545, Ira 79527, Knapp 79527, Lake Thomas 79527, Midway 79526, Pyron 79545 and Union 79549. **FOR ADDITIONAL LOCAL INFORMATION** Snyder Chamber of Commerce, 2302 Ave. R, Snyder, 79549, 915/573-3558.

SHACKELFORD (P63)

THE LAND

Northwest of Abilene on U.S. Highways 180 and 283 in the Rolling Plains Region, Shackelford County covers 915 square miles with the elevation ranging from 1,200 to 1,800 feet. The very dark, loamy soils have lime accumulations in the subsoils. Along the eastern border the loamy soils are lighter in color, with reddish, clayey subsoils. In the Rolling Plains vegetation area, the primary grasses are bluestems, gramas, wildryes and wheatgrass with some mesquite trees. Between 11 and 20% of the land in the county is considered prime farmland. **CLIMATE** Subtropical Subhumid with wide-ranging daily temperature variations. The average annual temperature is 63°F. Temperatures in January range from an average low of 27° to an average high of 56°F and in July range from 71° to 97°F. The average annual precipitation is 26 inches, with an average relative humidity of 74% at 6 A.M. and 45% at 6 P.M. The average annual snowfall is five inches. The growing season averages 226 days per year, with the last freeze in late March and the first freeze in early November. The sun shines during the year on the average 73% of the daylight hours.

THE PEOPLE

Population patterns have reversed in Shackelford County over the past two decades. The 1982 estimated population of 4,100 indicates a continuation of the growth begun in the 1970s. A 17% population loss between 1960 and 1970 was followed by an 18% gain between 1970 and 1980. The majority of the county residents live in rural areas. The population's high median age lowered significantly from 44 in 1970 to 34 in 1980. The largest ancestry groups are persons of English descent (33%), Irish descent (25%) and German descent (14%). **REGISTERED VOTERS** As of November 2, 1982 there were 2,401 registered voters (0.03% of the state total). The 1982 general election had a 48% voter turnout, compared to a 66% turnout in the 1980

SHACKELFORD (continued)

general election. In the 1982 primary 95% voted Democratic and 5% Republican, with 808 votes cast.

THE ECONOMY

AGRICULTURE Ranchland. In 1982, 92% of the land was in farms and ranches, with 10% of the farmland under cultivation and 2% irrigated. Shackelford ranked 196th in the state in highest agricultural receipts, with 76% from livestock and livestock products. Overgrazing, undesirable brush and weeds, water erosion, a lack of potable water and salinity are the current conservation problems. Primary crops: wheat, hay, oats, sorghum and cotton. Primary fruits and nuts: peaches and pecans. Primary livestock and products: cattle, milk, sheep and wool. **BUSINESS** Total number of business establishments in the county: 137. In 1980, 17% of the labor force were self-employed, 13% were employed in professional or related services, 7% in manufacturing, 13% in wholesale and retail trade, 41% in agriculture, forestry, fisheries and mining, 16% were employed in other counties and there were 461 retired workers. The industries with the most employment: oil and gas extraction and metal plate fabrication. The nonfarm earnings in 1981 totaled $44,933,000. The retired workers received an average monthly Social Security payment of $323. **FINANCE** On June 30, 1983, two commercial banks had total deposits of $33,886,000 and total assets of $39,590,000. There is one state savings and loan assocation branch. **HOUSING** Average value of homes in 1980: $21,700. Between 1970 and 1980 the number of housing units increased by 14%. Eighty-one percent of all units in the county are air-conditioned, 84% are heated by gas and 14% by electricity. **NATURAL RESOURCES** Limestone, sand and gravel, oil, gas and bituminous coal. In 1982 a total of 3,192,705 thousand cubic feet of gas well gas, 10,760 barrels of condensate, 2,055,071 barrels of crude oil and 4,177,445 thousand cubic feet of casinghead gas were produced. Current production of other minerals and products includes dimension limestone. **TOURISM** Travel expenditures of $610,000 in 1982 (an increase of 13% over 1981) generated 14 jobs and $113,000 in payroll. **ALCOHOLIC BEVERAGES** Totally dry. **FEDERAL EXPENDITURES** The federal government had direct expenditures or obligations of $7,474,000 in the county during fiscal year 1983, including $258,000 by the U.S. Department of Defense. In addition, the federal government provided $58,000 in grant awards, paid $242,000 in salaries and wages, made direct payments to individuals of $6,807,000 including $4,576,000 in retirement and disability and spent $367,000 in other expenditures or obligations. The federal government also provided $347,000 in direct loans and $990,000 in guaranteed loans and insurance.

COMMUNICATION

Newspapers–Weekly: The Albany News. Cable TV. Telephone companies: Continental Telephone, Southwestern Bell and Taylor Telephone. **TRANSPORTATION** Total public road mileage: 486. In 1982 there were 4,501 registered vehicles and 85 reported traffic accidents including two fatalities. Intercity bus service is available. Motor freight: one carrier. Aircraft: seven are registered in the county. Airports: Taylor Airport at Albany.

COMMUNITY SERVICES

EDUCATION Two school districts with two elementary, and two high schools. The average daily attendance in 1981-82 was 610, with expenditures per pupil of $2,713 including 42 classroom teachers with an average annual salary of $15,733. Sixty percent of the 43 high school graduates planned to attend college. In 1982-83, 87% of the students were White, 12% Hispanic, 0.9% Black and 0.3% Asian. **PUBLIC LIBRARIES** Shackelford

County Library (Albany): 6,150 volumes. **CHILD CARE** 12 day care licensed facilities. **HEALTH CARE** Two physicians and one dentist. Hospitals: one with a capacity of 24. Ambulance services: one county service. Nursing homes: one nursing home has a capacity of 80 nursing care residents. The average cost per day for private patients in 1982 was $48.86. **CHURCHES** 17 churches have an estimated combined membership of 2,822. The largest denominations are Southern Baptist and United Methodist. **SOCIAL SERVICES** In fiscal year 1983 a total of $48,312 in food stamps was distributed, with an average of 110 persons receiving food stamps each month. Aid to Families with Dependent Children (AFDC) totaled $5,099. Medical assistance benefits for the aged and disabled of $285,960 and for families and children of $3,898 brought the county benefit total to $343,269. **FIRE PROTECTION** Three volunteer fire departments. **LAW ENFORCEMENT** The County Sheriff has four commissioned officers. One police department has one officer. **CRIME** Eight violent crimes (murder, forcible rape, robbery and aggravated assault) and 83 nonviolent crimes (burglary, larceny-theft and motor vehicle theft) were reported in 1982. **JUDICIAL SYSTEM** One District Court and Judge, one County Court and Judge and one Justice of the Peace. In the District Court a total of 727 cases were pending on 1/1/82, 372 new cases were filed and 539 cases were disposed of during the year leaving 560 cases pending on 12/31/82. There were 766 criminal cases on the docket, 37 convictions, two persons committed to prison, 11 committed to jail and 312 cases left pending. **JAILS** One jail, capacity 12. **ATTORNEYS AT LAW** Three. **UTILITIES** 86% of the residents are connected to a public or privately owned water system and 57% are connected to a public sewer system. Natural gas is distributed to the county by Lone Star Gas Co., Division of Enserch. The average annual residential bill for natural gas in 1982 for the Lone Star distribution system was $405.91, an increase of 35% over 1981. Electricity is distributed to the county by Comanche Co. Electric Coop. Inc., West Texas Utilities and Taylor Electric Coop., Inc. and is generated primarily by water, gas and oil. **TAXES** The county has eight units with taxing authority: three school districts, two cities, one county one hospital district and one special district.

RECREATION/ENTERTAINMENT

NATIONAL REGISTER OF HISTORIC PLACES Albany: Shackelford County Courthouse District. Albany vicinity: Fort Griffin Brazos River Bridge and Fort Griffin. **STATE** Fort Griffin State Historical Park covers 506 acres with camping and trailer sites, fishing, exhibits and historic structures such as the ruins of several old fort buildings. A herd of Texas Longhorns grazes in the park. **MUNICIPAL PARKS** Five acres in one municipal park. This park contains one multi-use field, one playground and one swimming pool. **SCENIC DRIVES** The Texas Forts Trail runs through this county. This trail leads to eight of the famous frontier forts of west central Texas and an ancient presidio of the Spanish colonial period. **BOATING/FISHING** Lakes/reservoirs: De La Fosse (81 acres), McCarty (120 acres) and Nail #2 (22 acres). Major rivers: Clear Fork Brazos. Primary streams: Dry, Collins, Hubbard and Foyle. **HUNTING** Fall and winter seasons on deer. No closed season on squirrel, coyote and bobcat. Winter seasons on quail, muskrat, beaver, opossum, ringtailed cat, badger, fox, weasel, raccoon, skunk and civet cat. Fall, winter and spring seasons on turkey. In 1983 duck, coot, geese, woodcock and jacksnipe seasons occurred during the winter months with a winter season on sandhill crane in some parts of the county. Teal duck, rail and gallinule seasons occurred in the fall. Mourning dove seasons occurred intermittently during the fall and winter months. **MUSEUMS** Albany: Albany Museum, Ledbetter Picket House Museum and Old Jail Foundation and Art Research Center. **THEATERS** Albany:

Fort Griffin Fandangle Association Amphitheatre and Fort Griffin Fandangle Association. **SPECIAL EVENTS** Annual Fort Griffin Fandangle, Albany, June.

COMMUNITIES
COUNTY SEAT Albany, County Courthouse, 76430; County Clerk's Office, 915/762-2232. **INCORPORATED COMMUNITIES** (1980 population and ZIP Code) Albany (2,450) 76430 and Moran (344) 76464. **UNINCORPORATED COMMUNITIES** (and ZIP Code) Fort Griffin 76430. **FOR ADDITIONAL LOCAL INFORMATION** Albany Chamber of Commerce, P. O. Box 185, Albany, 76430, 915/762-2525.

SHELBY (E26)

THE LAND
Bordering Louisiana southeast of Longview on U.S. Highways 59 and 96 in the East Texas Timberlands Region, Shelby County covers 791 square miles with the elevation ranging from 150 to 400 feet. The soils are undulating to rolling with light colored, acidic, sandy to loamy surfaces and very deep reddish subsoils. The soils are deficient in plant nutrients. Shelby is in the Pineywoods vegetation area with grasslands, loblolly, shortleaf, longleaf and slash pine, and hardwoods such as oak, hickory and maple. Between 21 and 30% of the land in the county is considered prime farmland. **CLIMATE** Moist and mild. The average annual temperature is 65°F. Temperatures in January range from an average low of 34° to an average high of 57°F and in July range from 70° to 94°F. The average annual precipitation is 50 inches, with an average relative humidity of 88% at 6 A.M. and 60% at 6 P.M. The growing season averages 240 days per year, with the last freeze in mid March and the first freeze in mid November. The sun shines during the year on the average 65% of the daylight hours.

THE PEOPLE
The population of Shelby County is steadily regaining its size of the 1940s. The 1982 estimated population of 23,700 continues the population growth of the 1970s. A 4% population loss between 1960 and 1970 was followed by a 17% gain between 1970 and 1980. Almost 75% of the county residents live in rural areas. The county's population has a high percentage of residents over age 64 and a median age of 35. The largest ancestry groups are persons of English descent (27%), Black (21%) and Irish descent (19%). **REGISTERED VOTERS** As of November 2, 1982 there were 13,777 registered voters (0.2% of the state total). The 1982 general election had a 35% voter turnout, compared to a 62% turnout in the 1980 general election. In the 1982 primary 99% voted Democratic and 1% Republican, with 4,558 votes cast.

THE ECONOMY
AGRICULTURE Forest production area. In 1982, 44% of the land was in farms and ranches, with 9% of the farmland under cultivation. Shelby ranked 25th in the state in highest agricultural receipts, with 96% from livestock and livestock products. Overgrazing, undesirable brush and weeds, fertilization, improper woodland management and inadequate forestland harvesting systems are the current conservation problems. Primary crops: hay, wheat and oats. Primary vegetables: watermelons. Primary fruits and nuts: peaches and pecans. Primary livestock and products: third in the state for commercial broiler production, fifth for hens and pullets and sixth for egg production. Cattle. **BUSINESS** Total number of business establishments in the county: 404. Retail sales during the first quarter of 1984 increased by 15%. In 1980, 14% of the labor force were self-employed, 14% were employed in professional or related services, 24% in

manufacturing, 21% in wholesale and retail trade, 14% in agriculture, forestry, fisheries and mining, 23% were employed in other counties and there were 2,687 retired workers. The industries with the most employment: sawmills, poultry and egg processing, road construction, agribusiness, general construction and the manufacture of hardwood flooring, hardwood veneer and plywood. The nonfarm earnings in 1981 totaled $163,068,000. The retired workers received an average monthly Social Security payment of $280. **FINANCE** On June 30, 1983, five commercial banks had total deposits of $127,309,000 and total assets of $142,180,000. On December 31, 1982 two state savings and loan associations and four state branches had assets of $46,503,384. **HOUSING** Average value of homes in 1980: $20,900. Permits for new, privately owned housing units increased in 1982: 41 permits were issued with a total construction cost of $1,893,057. Of those permits, all were for single family houses. Housing permits in Center increased from seven in 1981 to 40 in 1982. Between 1970 and 1980 the number of housing units in the county increased by 39%. Sixty-nine percent of all units are air-conditioned, 81% are heated by gas and 12% by electricity. **NATURAL RESOURCES** Lignite coal, industrial sand, oil and gas. In 1982 a total of 6,858,807 thousand cubic feet of gas well gas, 31,098 barrels of condensate, 24,416 barrels of crude oil and 258,237 thousand cubic feet of casinghead gas were produced. Pine and hardwood production in 1981 totaled 14,867,416 cubic feet: 12,594,496 cubic feet of pine and 2,272,920 cubic feet of hardwood. **TOURISM** Travel expenditures of $1,581,000 in 1982 (an increase of 12% over 1981) generated 30 jobs and $266,000 in payroll. Lodging: three hotels, motels and tourist courts. **ALCOHOLIC BEVERAGES** Packaged distilled spirits, beer, ale, malt liquor and wine are legal in parts of the county. **FEDERAL EXPENDITURES** The federal government had direct expenditures or obligations of $45,495,000 in the county during fiscal year 1983, including $1,377,000 by the U.S. Department of Defense. In addition, the federal government provided $2,929,000 in grant awards, paid $1,865,000 in salaries and wages, made direct payments to individuals of $40,417,000 including $29,006,000 in retirement and disability payments, awarded $31,000 in procurement contracts and spent $252,000 in other expenditures or obligations. The federal government also provided $201,000 in direct loans and $1,044,000 in guaranteed loans and insurance.

COMMUNICATION
Newspapers–Weekly: East Texas Light (Center) and The Champion (Center). Radio: KDET-AM and KLCR-FM (Center). Cable TV. Telephone companies: Continental Telephone, Southwestern Bell and Eastex Telephone Coop. **TRANSPORTATION** Total public road mileage: 1,195. In 1982 there were 21,605 registered vehicles and 482 reported traffic accidents including seven fatalities. Taxi cabs: one company in Center. Intercity bus service is available. Motor freight: 15 local and intrastate carriers. Rail: two main and two branch lines carry freight through the county. The two main lines carry annually 10 to 20 million tons of freight each and the two branch lines carry one to five million each. Aircraft: 23 are registered in the county. Airports: Center Municipal Airport serves as a base for 22 aircraft and is a general utility airport with general aviation service.

COMMUNITY SERVICES
EDUCATION Six school districts with seven elementary, two middle, five high schools and two special education. The average daily attendance in 1981-82 was 4,151, with expenditures per pupil of $1,948 including 269 classroom teachers with an average annual salary of $15,509. Forty-nine percent of the 249 high school graduates planned to attend college. In 1982-83, 68% of the students were White, 1% Hispanic, 30% Black and 0.1% Asian. Sports championships: 1984 AA Basketball, Shelbyville H.S.

COUNTIES

SHELBY (continued)

Private schools: 94 students enrolled in one elementary and one high school. **PUBLIC LIBRARIES** Fannie Brown Booth Memorial Library (Center): 21,044 volumes. **CHILD CARE** 17 day care and five twenty-four hour care licensed facilities. **HEALTH CARE** 11 physicians and four dentists. Hospitals: two with a combined capacity of 99. Ambulance services: one funeral home, one hospital-based, one fire department and one volunteer service. Mental health: one county clinic. Nursing homes: two nursing homes with a combined capacity of 239 nursing care residents. The average cost per day for private patients in 1982 was $28.07. **CHURCHES** 97 churches have an estimated combined membership of 15,372. The largest denominations are Southern Baptist, American Baptist and United Methodist. **SOCIAL SERVICES** In fiscal year 1983 a total of $1,300,072 in food stamps was distributed, with an average of 2,822 persons receiving food stamps each month. Aid to Families with Dependent Children (AFDC) totaled $388,433 with an average of 263 families receiving AFDC each month. Medical assistance benefits for the aged and disabled of $3,165,080 and for families and children of $563,398 brought the county benefit total to $5,416,983. **FIRE PROTECTION** Five volunteer fire departments. **LAW ENFORCEMENT** The County Sheriff has five commissioned officers. Two police departments have a combined force of 13. **CRIME** 84 violent crimes (murder, forcible rape, robbery and aggravated assault) and 350 nonviolent crimes (burglary, larceny-theft and motor vehicle theft) were reported in 1982. **JUDICIAL SYSTEM** Two District Courts and Judges, one County Court and Judge and five Justices of the Peace. In the District Courts a total of 1,331 cases were pending on 1/1/82, 607 new cases were filed and 1,051 cases were disposed of during the year leaving 887 cases pending on 12/31/82. There were 762 criminal cases on the docket, 175 convictions, 45 persons committed to prison, two committed to jail and 276 cases left pending. In the County Courts 781 cases were pending on 1/1/82, 638 new cases were filed and 337 cases were disposed of during the year leaving 1,082 cases pending on 12/31/82. There were 1,314 criminal cases on the docket, 161 convictions, 34 persons committed to jail and 999 cases left pending. **JAILS** One jail, capacity 28. New jail under construction. **ATTORNEYS AT LAW** 24. **UTILITIES** 73% of the residents are connected to a public or privately owned water system and 27% are connected to a public sewer system. Natural gas is distributed to the county by Entex, Inc. and Farmers Natural Gas Company Co., Inc. The average annual residential bill for natural gas in 1982 for the Entex distribution system was $390.31, an increase of 26% over 1981. Electricity is distributed to the city of Timpson by the Timpson Light and Water Dept. and to the rest of the county by Southwestern Electric Power Co. and Deep East Texas Electric Corp., Inc. and is generated primarily by gas and coal. The typical residential electric bill is $152.08 per month for an all-electric house using 2,500 kwh. **TAXES** The county has 11 units with taxing authority: six school districts, four cities and one county.

RECREATION/ENTERTAINMENT

FEDERAL SABINE NATIONAL FOREST covers 188,220 acres in five counties with seven recreation areas. **NATIONAL REGISTER OF HISTORIC PLACES** Center: Shelby County Courthouse. **MUNICIPAL PARKS** 625 acres in four municipal parks. These parks contain two playgrounds, five baseball and softball fields, four tennis courts, one multi-use court and two boat ramps. **BOATING/FISHING** Lakes/reservoirs: Center (87 acres), Pinkston (298 acres), Timpson (147 acres) and Toledo Bend (109,730 acres). Major rivers: Sabine. Primary streams: Mill, Sandy, Blackwater and Attoyac Bayou. **HUNTING** Fall and winter seasons on deer. Summer, fall and winter seasons on squir-

rel. Winter seasons on quail, muskrat, beaver, otter, opossum, mink, ring-tailed cat, badger, fox, raccoon, skunk, and civet cat. No closed season on nutria, bobcat and coyote. In 1983 duck, coot, geese, woodcock and jacksnipe seasons occurred during the winter months. Teal duck, rail and gallinule seasons occurred in the fall. Mourning dove seasons occurred intermittently during the fall and winter months. **MUSEUMS** Center: Selby County Museum. **SPECIAL EVENTS** Texas Open Fox Hunt, Boles Field, March; Junior Livestock Show, Center, April; Take-A-Kid-Fishing Tournament, Toledo Bend, May; Shelby County 4-H Open Horse Show, Center, May; Texas State Fox Hunt, Boles Field, June; Shelby County Sheriff's Posse Rodeo, Center, July; East Texas Poultry Festival, Center, October; Heart-of-Texas Fox Hunt, Center, October; Christmas Parade, Center, December.

COMMUNITIES

COUNTY SEAT Center, County Courthouse, 75935; County Clerk's Office, 409/598-3611. **INCORPORATED COMMUNITIES** (1980 population and ZIP Code) Center (5,827) 75935, Huxley (341) 75973, Joaquin (917) 75954, Tenaha (1,005) 75974 and Timpson (1,164) 75975. **UNINCORPORATED COMMUNITIES** (and ZIP Code) Aiken 75935, Alexandera Store 75973, Antioch 75935, Arcadia (Toomey) 75935, Brady 75935, Campti 75935, Clever Creek 75935, Choice 75935, Dreka 75973, East Hamilton 75973, East Liberty 75935, Flat Fork 75974, Goober Hill 75973, Good Hope 75935, Grigsby 75935, Hanson 75954, Haslam 75954, Hurstown (Halbert) 75973, Jackson 75954, James 75935, Jericho 75935, Jordans Store 75973, Meldrum 75974, Neuville 75935, New Harmony 75973, New Prospect 75975, Patroon 75973, Paxton 75954, Ramah 75974, Shelbyville 75973, Short 75935, Silas 75975, Stockman 75975, Waterman 75935 and Willow Grove 75954. **FOR ADDITIONAL LOCAL INFORMATION** Center Chamber of Commerce, 321. Shelbyville, Center, 75935, 409/598-3682 and Timpson Chamber of Commerce, P.O. Box 424, Timpson, 75975, 409/254-2411.

SHERMAN (P2)

THE LAND

In the High Plains Region of the Texas Panhandle bordering Oklahoma and north of Amarillo on U.S. Highways 287 and 54, Sherman County covers 923 square miles with the elevation ranging from 3,200 to 3,800 feet. The county has nearly level soils with very dark, loamy surfaces over clayey subsoils with hardened calcium deposits. Sherman is in the High Plains vegetation area with prairie grasses, juniper, some mesquite and yucca. Between 41 and 50% of the land in the county is considered prime farmland. **CLIMATE** Continental Steppe: cool, dry and windy in spring. Duststorms and thunderstorms will occur in the spring. The average annual temperature is 56 °F. Temperatures in January range from an average low of 18° to an average high of 48 °F and in July range from 64° to 93 °F. The average annual precipitation is 17 inches, with an average relative humidity of 72% at 6 A.M. and 41% at 6 P.M. The average annual snowfall is 16 inches. The growing season averages 182 days per year, with the last freeze in late April and the first freeze in late October. The sun shines during the year on the average 75% of the daylight hours.

THE PEOPLE

The 1982 estimated population of 3,200 represents a 2% increase since 1980. Sherman County experienced population losses after a period of strong growth; a 40% population gain between 1960 and 1970 was followed by a 13% loss between 1970 and 1980. A majority of the county residents live in rural areas. The age group with the largest reduction between 1970 and 1980 was ages five to 14. The population's median age rose from 26 in 1970 to 32 in 1980. The largest ancestry groups are persons of English descent (26%), Irish descent (23%) and German descent (19%). **REGISTERED VOTERS** As of November 2, 1982 there were 1,754 registered voters (0.02% of the state total). The 1982 general election had a 59% voter turnout, compared to an 82% turnout in the 1980 general election. In the 1982 primary 93% voted Democratic and 7% Republican, with 842 votes cast.

THE ECONOMY

AGRICULTURE Wheat and fed cattle area. In 1982, 98% of the land was in farms and ranches, with 45% of the farmland under cultivation and 59% irrigated. Sherman ranked 22nd in the state in highest agricultural receipts, with 66% from livestock and livestock products. Overgrazing, water and wind erosion, decreasing irrigation water supplies and noxious weeds are the current conservation problems. Primary crops: seventh in the state for wheat and eighth for barley. Sorghum, corn and soybeans. Primary livestock and products: eighth in the state for fed cattle marketings. Hogs. **BUSINESS** Total number of business establishments in the county: 77. Retail sales during the first quarter of 1984 increased by 19%. In 1980, 25% of the labor force were self-employed, 12% were employed in professional or related services, 6% in manufacturing, 17% in wholesale and retail trade, 36% in agriculture, forestry, fisheries and mining, 16% were employed in other counties and there were 196 retired workers. The industries with the most employment: agribusiness and general construction. The nonfarm earnings in 1981 totaled $28,082,000. The retired workers received an average monthly Social Security payment of $347. **FINANCE** On June 30, 1983, one commercial bank had total deposits of $40,763,000 and total assets of $46,913,000. There is one state savings and loan association branch. **HOUSING** Average value of homes in 1980: $27,400. In 1982 two permits were issued for new, single family houses. Between 1970 and 1980 the number of housing units increased by 4%. Eighty-two percent of all units in the county are air-conditioned, 92% are heated by gas and 8% by electricity. **NATURAL RESOURCES** Caliche, oil and gas. In 1982 a total of 41,151,447 thousand cubic feet of gas well gas, 1,601 barrels of condensate, 102,037 barrels of crude oil and 284,923 thousand cubic feet of casinghead gas were produced. **TOURISM** Travel expenditures of $1,581,000 in 1982 (an increase of 12% over 1981) generated 30 jobs and $266,000 in payroll. **ALCOHOLIC BEVERAGES** Totally dry. **FEDERAL EXPENDITURES** The federal government had direct expenditures or obligations of $11,395,000 in the county during fiscal year 1983, including $43,000 by the U.S. Department of Defense. In addition, the federal government provided $49,000 in grant awards, paid $235,000 in salaries and wages, made direct payments to individuals of $2,753,000 including $2,038,000 in retirement and disability payments, awarded $2,000 in procurement contracts and spent $8,356,000 in other expenditures or obligations. The federal government also provided $24,581,000 in direct loans and $4,746,000 in guaranteed loans and insurance.

COMMUNICATION

Newspapers–Weekly: The Stratford Star. Cable TV. Telephone companies: Continental Telephone, General Telephone, Southwestern Bell and XIT Rural Telephone Coop. **TRANSPORTATION** Total public road mileage: 614. In 1982 there were 3,911 registered vehicles and 74 reported traffic accidents including three fatalities. Intercity bus service is available. Rail: one main and one branch line carry freight through the county with the one main line carrying annually one to five million tons and the branch line carrying five to 10 million. Aircraft: 24 are registered in the county. Airports: Stratford Field and Pronger Brothers Ranch Airport.

COMMUNITY SERVICES

EDUCATION Two school districts with two elementary, one middle and one high school. The average daily attendance in 1981-82 was 633, with expenditures per pupil of $3,725 including 51 classroom teachers with an average annual salary of $17,842. None of the 52 high school graduates planned to attend college. In 1982-83, 82% of the students were White, 18% Hispanic and 0.1% Asian. **PUBLIC LIBRARIES** Sherman County Public Library (Stratford): 15,008 volumes. **CHILD CARE** Four day care licensed facilities. **HEALTH CARE** One physician. Ambulance services: one volunteer service. Nursing homes: one nursing home has a capacity of 38 nursing care residents. The average cost per day for private patients in 1982 was $27.51. **CHURCHES** Eight churches have an estimated combined membership of 2,298. The largest denominations are Southern Baptist and United Methodist. **SOCIAL SERVICES** In fiscal year 1983 a total of $26,622 in food stamps was distributed, with an average of 53 persons receiving food stamps each month. Aid to Families with Dependent Children (AFDC) totaled $110. Medical assistance benefits for the aged and disabled of $144,395 brought the county benefit total to $171,127. **FIRE PROTECTION** Two volunteer fire departments. **LAW ENFORCEMENT** The County Sheriff has four commissioned officers. One police department has three officers. **CRIME** Six nonviolent crimes (burglary, larceny-theft and motor vehicle theft) were reported in 1982. **JUDICIAL SYSTEM** One District Court and Judge, one County Court and Judge and two Justices of the Peace. In the District Court a total of 56 cases were pending on 1/1/82, 96 new cases were filed and 60 cases were disposed of during the year leaving 92 cases pending on 12/31/82. There were 15 criminal cases on the docket, five convictions, three persons committed to prison and six cases left pending. In the County Court 94 cases were pending on 1/1/82, 175 new cases were filed and 170 cases were disposed of during the year leaving 99 cases pending on 12/31/82. There were 180 criminal cases on the docket, 103 convictions, four persons committed to jail, and 54 cases left pending. **JAILS** One jail, capacity 18. **ATTORNEYS AT LAW** Two. **UTILITIES** 77% of the residents are connected to a public or privately owned water system and 64% are connected to a public sewer system. Natural gas is distributed to the county by Southern Union Company. The average annual residential bill for natural gas in 1982 for the Southern Union distribution system was $355.85, an increase of 23% over 1981. Electricity is distributed to the county by Rita Blanca Electric Coop., Inc. and is generated primarily by gas and coal. **TAXES** The county has nine units with taxing authority: two school districts, two cities, one county, three hospital districts and one special district.

RECREATION/ENTERTAINMENT

MUNICIPAL PARKS Seven acres in four municipal parks. These parks contain two playgrounds and one baseball and softball field. **BOATING/FISHING** Major rivers: North Fork Canadian. Primary streams: North Palo Duro and Frisco. **HUNTING** Fall season on antelope. Fall and winter season on deer. Summer, fall and winter seasons on squirrel. Winter seasons on pheasant, quail, muskrat, beaver, opossum, ring-tailed cat, badger, fox weasel, raccoon, skunk and civet cat. No closed season on bobcat and coyote. Fall, winter and spring seasons on turkey. In 1983 sandhill crane, duck, coot, geese, woodcock and jacksnipe seasons occurred during the winter months. Mourning dove seasons occurred intermittently during the fall and winter months. Teal duck, rail and gallinule seasons occurred in the fall. **MUSEUMS** Stratford: Sherman House Museum and Art Gallery. **SPECIAL EVENTS** County Stock Show, Stratford, February; County Fair and Jamboree, Stratford, September.

COMMUNITIES

COUNTY SEAT Stratford, County Courthouse, 79084; County

COUNTIES

SHERMAN (continued)

Clerk's Office, 806/396-2371. **INCORPORATED COMMUNITIES** (1980 population and ZIP Code) Stratford (1,917) 79084 and Texhoma (358) 73949. **FOR ADDITIONAL LOCAL INFORMATION** Stratford Chamber of Commerce, 401 N. Third, Stratford, 79084, 806/396-2260.

SMITH (E16)

THE LAND

Southeast of Dallas on Interstate 20 in the East Texas Timberlands Region, Smith County covers 932 square miles with the elevation ranging from 300 to 600 feet. To the east and northwest the nearly level soils have light colored, acidic, sandy to loamy surfaces over very deep, mottled or reddish subsoils. These soils are deficient in plant nutrients. The rest of the county has gently rolling to hilly reddish soils with loamy surfaces over very deep, reddish, clayey subsoils that are high in iron. The eastern one-third of the county is in the Pineywoods vegetation area with grasslands, loblolly, shortleaf, longleaf and slash pine and hardwoods such as oak, hickory and maple. The rest of the county is in the Post Oak Savannah vegetation area with tall grasses, post and blackjack oak. Between one and 10% of the land in the county is considered prime farmland. **CLIMATE** Moist and mild. The average annual temperature is 65 °F. Temperatures in January range from an average low of 33 ° to an average high of 55 °F and in July range from 71 ° to 95 °F. The average annual precipitation is 44 inches, with an average relative humidity of 83% at 6 A.M. and 56% at 6 P.M. The average annual snowfall is two inches. The growing season averages 259 days per year, with the last freeze in early March and the first freeze in late November. The sun shines during the year on the average 65% of the daylight hours.

THE PEOPLE

The 1982 estimated population of 136,700 represents a 7% increase since 1980. Since 1970 Smith County has grown more rapidly than at any time in the previous 40 years. The growth rate more than doubled between 1960 and 1980 with a 12% increase from 1960 to 1970 rising to a 32% increase from 1970 to 1980. Rural areas grew twice as fast as urban areas between 1970 and 1980. The age groups with the largest gains were ages 62 and over and 20 to 29. The largest ancestry groups are persons of English descent (27%), Black (22%) and Irish descent (18%). **REGISTERED VOTERS** As of November 2, 1982 there were 62,178 registered voters (0.9% of the state total). The 1982 general election had a 52% voter turnout, compared to a 65% turnout in the 1980 general election. In the 1982 primary 75% voted Democratic and 25% Republican, with 13,351 votes cast.

THE ECONOMY

AGRICULTURE Forest production area. In 1982, 52% of the land was in farms and ranches, with 18% of the farmland under cultivation. Smith ranked 24th in the state in highest agricultural receipts, with 69% from crops. Overgrazing, water erosion, fertilization, improper woodland management and urban encroachment are the current conservation problems. Primary crops: eighth in the state for hay. Wheat, rye and corn. Primary vegetables: sweet potatoes and watermelons. Primary fruits and nuts: a leader in the state for blackberries and plums and third for peaches. Pecans. Primary livestock and products: cattle, milk and hogs. **BUSINESS** Total number of business establishments in the county: 3,247. Retail sales during the first quarter of 1984 increased by 21%. In 1980, 8% of the labor force were self-employed, 20% were employed in professional or related services, 22% in manufacturing, 22% in wholesale and retail trade, 7% in construction, 7% were employed in other counties and there were 11,252 retired workers. The industries with the most employment: agribusiness, oil and gas extraction, fruit and vegetable canning, soft drink bottling and canning, construction, petroleum refining, iron foundries, metal plate fabrication and the manufacture of refrigeration and heating equipment, sporting and athletic goods, women's clothing and other cloth products, plastics products, dairy products, bakery products, tires, brick and clay tile, plumbing fittings and brass goods, prefabricated metal buildings, oil field machinery, special industrial machinery prefabricated wooden buildings, household furniture, paper bags and cardboard boxes. The nonfarm earnings in 1981 totaled $1,368,991,000. The retired workers received an average monthly Social Security payment of $316. **FINANCE** On June 30, 1983, 14 commercial banks had total deposits of $1,310,838,000 and total assets of $1,502,163,000. On December 31, 1982 four state savings and loan associations, one federal association and seven state association branches had combined assets of $659,776,027. In addition there are 13 credit unions in the county. **HOUSING** Average value of homes in 1980: $38,000. Permits for new, privately owned housing units increased in 1982: 536 permits were issued with a total construction cost of $32,205,104. Of those permits, 296 were for single family houses. Between 1970 and 1980 the number of housing units increased by 51%. Eighty-two percent of all units in the county are air-conditioned, 74% are heated by gas and 24% by electricity. **NATURAL RESOURCES** Iron, salt domes, industrial sand, oil, gas and lignite coal. In 1982 a total of 9,729,412 thousand cubic feet of gas well gas, 72,936 barrels of condensate, 3,823,476 barrels of crude oil and 4,978,427 thousand cubic feet of casinghead gas were produced. Current production of other minerals and products includes fire clay, refractory clay products, industrial sand, sand and gravel and recovered sulphur. Pine and hardwood production in 1981 totaled 6,101,569 cubic feet: 5,396,015 cubic feet of pine and 705,554 cubic feet of hardwood. **TOURISM** Travel expenditures of $57,253,000 in 1982 (an increase of 11% over 1981) generated 1,487 jobs and $12,237,000 in payroll. Lodging: 23 hotels, motels and tourist courts. Convention/meeting facilities: Tyler-Caldwell Auditorium, Harvey Hall, Mayfair Auditorium, Rose Garden Center Building and Rose Stadium. **ALCOHOLIC BEVERAGES** Totally dry. **FEDERAL EXPENDITURES** The federal government had direct expenditures or obligations of $215,545,000 in the county during fiscal year 1983, including $28,798,000 by the U.S. Department of Defense. In addition, the federal government provided $7,836,000 in grant awards, paid $17,294,000 in salaries and wages, made direct payments to individuals of $166,052,000 including $129,338,000 in retirement and disability payments, awarded $23,658,000 in procurement contracts and spent $705,000 in other expenditures or obligations. The federal government also provided $80,000 in direct loans and $19,890,000 in guaranteed loans and insurance.

COMMUNICATION

Newspapers–Daily: Tyler Morning Telegraph, ave. morn. circ. 36,588 and Tyler Courier-Times ave. eve. circ. 8,688. Weekly: The Lindale News. Radio: KDOX-AM, KTBB-AM, KTYL-AM, KLEY-AM, KROZ-FM, KTYL-FM and KNUE-FM Stero (Tyler). Television: KLTV-CH. 7 (Tyler). Cable TV. Telephone companies: Continental Telephone, General Telephone, Southwestern Bell, United Telephone and Lakeside Telephone. **TRANSPORTATION** Total public road mileage: 2,199. In 1982 there were 112,713 registered vehicles and 4,093 reported traffic accidents including 30 fatalities. Taxi cabs: one company in Tyler. Municipal transit systems: one bus systems in Tyler, with scheduled routes. Intercity bus service is available. Motor freight: 32 local and intrastate carriers. Rail: four main and two branch lines carry freight through the county. Two of the main lines carry annually 20 to 30 million tons of freight each and two carry 10 to 20 million. The two branch lines carry annually less than one million tons of freight. Aircraft: 159 are registered in the county. Airports: Pounds Field at Tyler serves as a base for 130 aircraft and is a basic utility airport with commuter service.

COMMUNITY SERVICES

EDUCATION Eight school districts with 24 elementary, 11 middle, nine high schools and one special education. The average daily attendance in 1981-82 was 23,328, with expenditures per pupil of $2,504 including 1,412 classroom teachers with an average annual salary of $16,599. Forty percent of the 1,502 high school graduates planned to attend college. In 1982-83, 68% of the students were White, 4% Hispanic, 28% Black, 0.3% Asian and 0.1% American Indian. Private schools: 1,194 students enrolled in nine elementary and three high schools. Sports championships: 1983 AAA Girls' Tennis, T.K. Gorman H.S. Tyler Junior College is located in Tyler. Established in 1926 it is a vocational and two year academic college under state/local control. Enrollment in 1982 was 6,688 with in state undergraduate tuition and fees of $240 per semester. Sports championships: (Texas Eastern Junior College Basketball Conference) 1983 Women's Champion. Texas College is located in Tyler. Established in 1894 it is affiliated with the Christian Methodist Episcopal Church. Enrollment in 1982 was 476 with in state undergraduate tuition and fees of $1,800 per semester. The highest degree offered is Bachelor. University of Texas at Tyler was established in 1971 and is under state control. Enrollment in 1982 was 1,921 with in state undergraduate tuition fees of $324 per semester. The highest degree offered is: Master (no lower division). Vocational education: Troup-Pates Welding Trade School. Tyler-Barrow Beauty School, Richard and Joseph Artistic School of Hair, Tyler Commercial College. **PUBLIC LIBRARIES** Bullard Library. Tyler Public Library: 104,396 volumes. **CHILD CARE** 232 day care and 38 twenty-four hour care licensed facilities. **HEALTH CARE** 271 physicians and 87 dentists. Hospitals: four with a combined capacity of 705. Clinics: one for treatment of alcohol and drug abuse, one outpatient clinic, one dialysis clinic and one public health clinic. Ambulance services: one commercial, one city and one hospital based service. Mental health: one regional clinic. Nursing homes: 10 nursing homes with a combined capacity of 1,119 nursing care residents. The average cost per day for private patients in 1982 was $33.54. **CHURCHES** 191 churches have an estimated combined membership of 80,118. The largest denominations are Southern Baptist, United Methodist and Christian Methodist Episcopal. **SOCIAL SERVICES** In fiscal year 1983 a total of $4,387,228 in food stamps was distributed, with an average of 9,130 persons receiving food stamps each month. Aid to Families with Dependent Children (AFDC) totaled $1,360,281 with an average of 938 families receiving AFDC each month. Medical assistance benefits for the aged and disabled of $8,764,668 and for families and children of $1,869,709 brought the county benefit total to $16,381,885. **FIRE PROTECTION** 14 volunteer fire departments. **LAW ENFORCEMENT** The County Sheriff has 113 commissioned officers. Seven police departments have a combined force of 170. One college has a police department with six officers and the Tyler Park Police has three officers. **CRIME** 556 violent crimes (murder, forcible rape, robbery and aggravated assault) and 7,556 nonviolent crimes (burglary, larceny-theft and motor vehicle theft) were reported in 1982. **JUDICIAL SYSTEM** Four District Courts and Judges, three County Courts and Judges and five Justices of the Peace. In the District Courts a total of 4,123 cases were pending on 1/1/82, 3,556 new cases were filed and 3,269 cases were disposed of during the year leaving 4,410 cases pending on 12/31/82. There

were 1,474 criminal cases on the docket, 448 convictions, 139 persons committed to prison, and one committed to jail and 908 cases left pending. In the County Courts 5,815 cases were pending on 1/1/82, 4,409 new cases were filed and 5,010 cases were disposed of during the year leaving 5,214 cases pending on 12/31/82. There were 8,267 criminal cases on the docket, 1,306 convictions, 271 persons committed to jail and 4,435 cases left pending. **JAILS** One jail, capacity 152. New jail under construction, capacity 264. **ATTORNEYS AT LAW** 345. **UTILITIES** 91% of the residents are connected to a public or privately owned water system and 66% are connected to a public sewer system. Natural gas is distributed to the county by Entex, Inc. Lone Star Gas Co., Division of Enserch and Southern Union Company. The average annual residential bill for natural gas in 1982 for the Entex distribution system was $390.31, an increase of 26% over 1981 and for Lone Star it was $405.91, an increase of 35%, and for Southern Union it was $355.85, an increase of 23%. Electricity is distributed to the county by Texas Power and Light, Wood Co. Electric Coop. Inc., Central Texas Electric Coop. Inc. and Upshur-Rural Electric Coop. Inc. and is generated primarily by gas, oil and coal. The typical residential electric bill is $165.24 per month for an all-electric house using 2,500 kwh. **TAXES** The county has 17 units with taxing authority: seven school districts, seven cities, one county, one college district and one special district.

RECREATION/ENTERTAINMENT

NATIONAL REGISTER OF HISTORIC PLACES Teaselville: Col. John Dewberry House. Tyler: Carnegie Public Library, Goodman-LeGrand House and Whitaker-McClendon House. Tyler vicinity: 1894 Tyler Hydraulic-Fill Dam (1894 Tyler Waterworks Dam and Bellwood Lake Dam). **STATE** Tyler State Park covers 985 acres with camping and trailer sites, fishing, swimming, boat ramps, rental boats and nature trails. **COUNTY/MUNICIPAL PARKS** 1,034 acres in three county and 34 municipal parks. These parks contain seven miles of hiking trails, 23 playgrounds, two football and soccer fields, 19 baseball and softball fields, 17 tennis courts, three swimming pools, four beaches and nine boat ramps. Developed campsites: 12. **SCENIC DRIVES** The Texas Forest Trail runs through this county. This trail explores the farming, ranching and oilfield areas of the East Texas Pineywoods. **BOATING/FISHING** Lakes/reservoirs: Arp Club (39 acres), Bellwood (124 acres), Campbell (68 acres), Club Thirteen (23 acres), Green (20 acres), Greenbriar (75 acres), Hamrick (29 acres), Hide-Away #1 (86 acres), Hide-Away #2 (63 acres), Hitts (82 acres), Holiday Pines (31 acres), Holly Tree (18 acres), Horseshoe Club (21 acres), Howell Club (43 acres), Lost Pine (34 acres), Macs Creek (28 acres), West Mud Creek (16 acres), Park (63 acres), Pinedale (26 acres), Pleasure Acres (73 acres), Reynolds (18 acres), Sky (76 acres), Swan (19 acres), Timber (34 acres), Tyler (2,450 acres), Tyler East (2,570 acres), Tyler State Park (91 acres) and Van (82 acres). Major rivers: Sabine and Neches. Primary streams: Indian, Brushy, Butler, Sandy Botton, Hubbard, Hitts, Village, Born, Hankins, Macs, West Mud, Willow, Prairie, Duck, Chinquapin, East Prairie Mud and Little Saline. **HUNTING** Fall and winter seasons on deer. Summer, fall and winter seasons on squirrel. Winter seasons on quail, muskrat, beaver, otter, opossum, mink, ring-tailed cat, badger, fox, raccoon, skunk and civet cat. No closed season on nutria, bobcat and coyote. In 1983 duck, coot, geese, woodcock and jacksnipe seasons occurred during the winter months. Teal duck, rail and gallinule seasons occurred in the fall. Mourning dove seasons occurred intermittently during the fall and winter months. **MUSEUMS** Tyler: Goodman Museum, Tyler Museum of Art and World of Wildlife Museum. **THEATERS** Tyler: Wise Auditorium. **ORCHESTRAS** Tyler: East Texas Symphony Orchestra and the Tyler Youth Symphony Orchestra.

COUNTIES

SMITH (continued)

BOTANIC GARDENS Tyler: Municipal Rose Garden. **ZOO** Tyler: Caldwell Children's Zoo. **PLANETARIUM** Tyler: Hudnall Planetarium. **COLLEGIATE FINE ARTS** Tyler: Cultural events offered by Texas College and Tyler Junior College. **SPECIAL EVENTS** Spring Flower and Azalea Trail, Tyler, March/April; Yesteryear Celebration, Whitehouse, June; East Texas Fair, Tyler, September/October; Texas Rose Festival, Tyler, October; Lignite Country Festival, Troup, November; Christmas Parade, Tyler, December; Christmas Tour of Homes, Tyler, December.

COMMUNITIES

COUNTY SEAT Tyler, County Courthouse, 75702; County Clerk's Office, 214/595-4861. **INCORPORATED COMMUNITIES** (1980 population and ZIP Code) Arp (939) 75750, Bullard (681: 622 in Smith Co. and 59 in Cherokee Co.) 75757, Lindale (2,180) 75771, New Chapel Hill (618) 75701, Overton (2,430: 107 in Smith Co. and 2,323 in Rusk Co.) 75684, Troup (1,911: 1,847 in Smith Co. and 64 in Cherokee Co.) 75789, Tyler (70,508) 75701, Whitehouse (2,172) 75791 and Winona (443) 75792. **UNINCORPORATED COMMUNITIES** (and ZIP Code) Bascom 75705, Bellaire Addition 75701, Browning 75792, Carrol 75701 Coldhill 75701, Flint 75762, Friendship 75647, Garden Valley 75771, Gresham 75701, Joy 75647, Kirkpatrick Addition 75701, Midway 75792, Montgomery Gardens 75701, Mount Sylvan 75777, New Harmony 75701, New Hope 75701, Noonday 75762, Omen 75705, Owentown (Amigo) 75703, Red Springs 75771, Salem 75789, Shady Grove 75703, St. Clair City 75789, St. Louis 75701, Sandflat 75701, Sharon 75701, Starrville 75792, Swan 75701, Teaselville 75757, Thedford 75771, Walnut Grove 75789, Waters Bluff 75792, Wright City 75684 and Wood Springs 75771. **FOR ADDITIONAL LOCAL INFORMATION** Arp Area Chamber of Commerce, P. O. Box 146, Arp, 75750, 214/859-4621 and Tyler Area Chamber of Commerce, P. O. Box 390, Tyler, 75710, 214/592-1661.

SOMERVELL (M20)

THE LAND

Southwest of Fort Worth on U.S. Highway 67 in the Cross Timbers Region, Somervell County covers 188 square miles with the elevation ranging from 600 to 1,200 feet. In a strip in the southern part of the county and a small area of the northwest portion are nearly level to undulating soils with light colored, loamy or sandy surfaces over reddish or mottled clayey or loamy subsoils. The rest of the county has light colored, well drained soils and very dark, loamy soils. Between 31 and 40% of the land in the county is considered prime farmland. **CLIMATE** Subtropical Subhumid with warm summers. The average annual temperature is 66°F. Temperatures in January range from an average low of 33° to an average high of 56°F and in July range from 72° to 97°F. The average annual precipitation is 31 inches, with an average relative humidity of 78% at 6 A.M. and 51% at 6 P.M. The average annual snowfall is two inches. The growing season averages 236 days per year, with the last freeze in late March and the first freeze in mid November. The sun shines during the year on the average 66% of the daylight hours.

THE PEOPLE

Between 1970 and 1980 Somervell County was one of the state's fastest growing counties. The 1982 estimated population of 4,200 indicates a continuation of that growth. The growth rate rose from an 8% population increase between 1960 and 1970 to a 49% increase between 1970 and 1980. The majority of the residents live in rural areas. The age groups with the largest gains between 1970 and 1980 were ages 20 to 34 and birth to five years. Therefore, the population's median age lowered from 39 in 1970 to 30 in 1980. The largest ancestry groups are persons of English descent (34%), Irish descent (28%) and German descent (14%). **REGISTERED VOTERS** As of November 2, 1982 there were 2,471 registered voters (0.03 of the state total). The 1982 general election had a 55% voter turnout, compared to a 69% turnout in the 1980 general election. In the 1982 primary 97% voted Democratic and 3% Republican, with 1,103 votes cast.

THE ECONOMY

AGRICULTURE In 1982, 79% of the land was in farms and ranches, with 8% of the farmland under cultivation and 13% irrigated. Somervell ranked 249th in the state in highest agricultural receipts, with 84% from livestock and livestock products. Overgrazing, undesirable brush and weeds, water erosion and livestock waste management are the current conservation problems. Primary crops: hay, peanuts, wheat and oats. Primary vegetables: cantaloupes, sweet potatoes and watermelons. Primary fruits and nuts: peaches and pecans. Primary livestock and products: cattle, milk and hogs. **BUSINESS** Total number of business establishments in the county: 51. Retail sales during the first quarter of 1984 increased by 18%. In 1980, 10% of the labor force were self-employed, 15% were employed in professional or related services, 7% in manufacturing, 12% in wholesale and retail trade, 31% in construction, 18% were employed in other counties and there were 393 retired workers. The industries with the most employment: tourism and agribusiness. The nonfarm earnings in 1981 totaled $43,487,000. The retired workers received an average monthly Social Security payment of $275. **FINANCE** On June 30, 1983, one commercial bank had total deposits of $24,990,000 and total assets of $26,704,000. There is one state savings and loan association branch. **HOUSING** Average value of homes in 1980: $27,200. Between 1970 and 1980 the number of housing units increased by 50%. Eighty percent of all units in the county are air-conditioned, 78% are heated by gas and 19% by electricity. **NATURAL RESOURCES** Limestone, industrial sand, sand and gravel, gas and oil. In 1982 a total of 51,235 thousand cubic feet of gas well gas and 16 barrels of condensate were produced. Current production of other minerals and products includes industrial sand, sand and gravel and crushed sandstone. **TOURISM** Travel expenditures of $2,089,000 in 1982 (an increase of 11% over 1981) generated 54 jobs and $424,000 in payroll. **ALCOHOLIC BEVERAGES** Beer, ale, malt liquor and wine not exceeding 14% alcoholic content are legal. **FEDERAL EXPENDITURES** The federal government had direct expenditures or obligations of $5,846,000 in the county during fiscal year 1983, including $189,000 by the U.S. Department of Defense. In addition, the federal government provided $76,000 in grant awards, paid $338,000 in salaries and wages, made direct payments to individuals of $5,345,000 including $3,599,000 in retirement and disability payments, awarded $1,000 in procurement contracts and spent $86,000 in other expenditures or obligations. The federal government also provided $6,000 in direct loans and $1,305,000 in guaranteed loans and insurance.

COMMUNICATION

Newspapers–Weekly: Glen Rose Reporter. Cable TV. Telephone companies: Continental Telephone and Southwestern Bell. **TRANSPORTATION** Total public road mileage: 214. In 1982 there were 4,264 registered vehicles and 122 reported traffic accidents including two fatalities. Intercity bus service is available. Motor freight: one carrier. Aircraft: seven are registered in the county. Airports: Running M Airport at Glen Rose.

COMMUNITY SERVICES

EDUCATION One school district with one elementary, one middle and one high school. The average daily attendance in 1981-82 was 828, with expenditures per pupil of $3,364 including 53 classroom teachers with an average annual salary of $17,133. None of the 45 high school graduates planned to attend college. In 1982-83, 87% of the students were White, 12% Hispanic, 0.8% Asian and 0.2% American Indian. Private schools: 25 students enrolled in one elementary and one high school. **PUBLIC LIBRARIES** Glen Rose Library. **CHILD CARE** Seven day care and two twenty-four hour care licensed facilities. **HEALTH CARE** Two physicians. Hospitals: one with a capacity of 26. Ambulance services: one volunteer fire department service. Mental health: one county clinic. Nursing homes: one nursing home has a capacity of 42 nursing care residents. The average cost per day for private patients in 1982 was $31.43. **CHURCHES** 10 churches have an estimated combined membership of 2,170. The largest denomination is Southern Baptist. **SOCIAL SERVICES** In fiscal year 1983 a total of $102,122 in food stamps was distributed, with an average of 212 persons receiving food stamps each month. Aid to Families with Dependent Children (AFDC) totaled $22,915, with an average of 15 families receiving AFDC each month. Medical assistance benefits for the aged and disabled of $404,625 and for families and children of $68,170 brought the county benefit total to $597,832. **FIRE PROTECTION** One volunteer fire department. **LAW ENFORCEMENT** The County Sheriff has six commissioned officers. **CRIME** Eight violent crimes (murder, forcible rape, robbery and aggravated assault) and 74 nonviolent crimes (burglary, larceny-theft and motor vehicle theft) were reported in 1982. **JUDICIAL SYSTEM** Two District Courts and Judges, one County Court and Judge and four Justices of the Peace. In the District Courts a total of 187 cases were pending on 1/1/82, 92 new cases were filed and 105 cases were disposed of during the year leaving 174 cases pending on 12/31/82. There were 58 criminal cases on the docket, nine convictions, one person committed to prison and 48 cases left pending. In the County Court 790 cases were pending on 1/1/82, 171 new cases were filed and 244 cases were disposed of during the year leaving 717 cases pending on 12/31/82. There were 916 criminal cases on the docket, 74 convictions, four persons committed to jail, and 676 cases left pending. **JAILS** One jail, capacity 28. New jail under construction. **ATTORNEYS AT LAW** Three. **UTILITIES** 56% of the residents are connected to a public or privately owned water system and 52% are connected to a public sewer system. Electricity is distributed to the county by Erath Co. Electric Coop. Assn., Texas-New Mexico Power Co. and Johnson Co. Electric Coop. Assn. and is generated primarily by water, gas and oil. **TAXES** The county has three units with taxing authority: one school district, one city and one county.

RECREATION/ENTERTAINMENT

NATIONAL REGISTER OF HISTORIC PLACES Glen Rose: Somervell County Courthouse and Barnard's Mill. **STATE** Dinosaur Valley State Park covers 1,272 acres with camping and trailer sites, fishing and swimming areas. A herd of Texas Longhorns grazes in the park. Dinosaur footprints and replicas of the animals are on display. **SCENIC DRIVES** The Texas Lakes Trail runs through this county. This trail introduces some 30 blue-water recreational areas in a variety of settings in north central Texas. **BOATING/FISHING** Lakes/reservoirs: Arena (15 acres), Panther Branch (21 acres), Squaw Creek (3,240 acres) and Twin Arena (10 acres). Major rivers: Brazos and Paluxy. Primary streams: Rough, Panther and Squaw. **HUNTING** Fall and winter seasons on deer. No closed season on squirrel, bobcat and coyote. Winter seasons on quail, muskrat, beaver, opossum, ring-tailed cat, badger, fox, weasel, raccoon, skunk and civet cat. Fall, winter and spring seasons on turkey. In 1983 duck, coot, geese, woodcock and jacksnipe seasons occurred during the winter months. Teal duck, rail and gallinule seasons occurred in the fall. Mourning dove seasons occurred intermittently during the fall and winter months. **MUSEUMS** Glen Rose: Somervell County Museum. **SPECIAL EVENTS** Junior Livestock Show, Glen Rose, March; Bluegrass Jamboree, Glen Rose, May; July 4th Celebration, Glen Rose, July.

COMMUNITIES

COUNTY SEAT Glen Rose, County Courthouse, 76043; County Clerk's Office, 817/897-4427. **INCORPORATED COMMUNITIES** (1980 population and ZIP Code) Glen Rose (2,075) 76043. **UNINCORPORATED COMMUNITIES** (and ZIP Code) Glass 76090, Nemo 76070 and Rainbow 76077. **FOR ADDITIONAL LOCAL INFORMATION** Somervell Co. Chamber of Commerce, P. O. Box 605, Glen Rose, 76043, 817/897-2286.

STARR (B27)

THE LAND

Bordering Mexico Southwest of Corpus Christi on U.S. Highway 83 in the Rio Grande Plain Region, Starr County covers 1,226 square miles with the elevation ranging from 200 to 400 feet. The soils are nearly level to undulating. In the northeast the soils are sandy throughout or light colored and loamy over very deep, reddish or mottled, clayey subsoils. Some have limestone within 40 inches of the surface. In the central part of the county are light colored, deep to moderately deep, well drained soils. In the southwestern portion of the county are gray to black, cracking, clayey soils with a high shrink-swell potential. Limestone is found within 40 inches of the surface in some areas. Along the Rio Grande are brown to red loamy surfaces over cracking clayey soils. These soils have a high shrink-swell potential. Starr is in the South Texas Plains vegetation area with mid and short grasses, thorny shrubs, mesquite, cacti, live and post oak. Less than 1% of the land in the county is considered prime farmland. **CLIMATE** Subtropical Subhumid with mild winters and hot summers. The average annual temperature is 74 °F. Temperatures in January range from an average low of 44 ° to an average high of 70 °F and in July range from 73 ° to 99 °F. The average annual precipitation is 22 inches, with an average relative humidity of 84% at 6 A.M. and 55% at 6 P.M. There is no snowfall. The growing season averages 305 days per year, with the last freeze in mid February and the first freeze in mid December. The sun shines during the year on the average 65% of the daylight hours.

THE PEOPLE

Among all U.S. counties Starr County ranks first in the highest percent of persons of Spanish origin and 41st in the highest birth rate. The 1982 estimated population of 30,300 continues the steady growth which has exisited since 1930. Urban residents doubled in number from 1970 to 1980. The age groups with the largest gains were ages 25 to 34, 15 to 19 and birth to five years. The county's population is unusually young with a median age of 23. The largest ancestry group is Hispanic (97%). **REGISTERED VOTERS** As of November 2, 1982 there were 12,489 registered voters (0.2% of the state total). The 1982 general election had a 45% voter turnout, compared to a 52% turnout in the 1980 general election. In the 1982 primary 99% voted Democratic and 0.1% Republican, with 3,997 votes cast.

THE ECONOMY

AGRICULTURE Lower Rio Grande Valley vegetable and cattle area. In 1982, 80% of the land was in farms and ranches, with 17% of the farmland under cultivation and 19% irrigated. Starr

STARR (continued)

ranked 30th in the state in highest agricultural receipts, with 65% from crops. Overgrazing, undesirable brush and weeds, inefficient irrigation systems and water erosion are the current conservation problems. Primary crops: sorghum and hay. Primary vegetables: second in the state for total fresh market vegetables, cantaloupes and onions and fourth for cabbage. Lettuce, bell peppers and honeydew melons. Primary fruits and nuts: oranges. Primary livestock and products: cattle. **BUSINESS** Total number of business establishments in the county: 254. Retail sales during the first quarter of 1984 increased by 30%. In 1980, 9% of the labor force were self-employed, 27% were employed in professional or related services, 4% in manufacturing, 15% in wholesale and retail trade, 25% in agriculture, forestry, fisheries and mining, 12% were employed in other counties and there were 1,213 retired workers. The industries with the most employment: agribusiness, tourism and the manufacture of pleated textile products. The nonfarm earnings in 1981 totaled $89,487,000. The retired workers received an average monthly Social Security payment of $210.00. **FINANCE** On June 30, 1983, two commercial banks had total deposits of $65,851,000 and total assets of $73,053,000. There is one federal savings and loan association branch and two credit unions in the county. **HOUSING** Average value of homes in 1980: $12,900. Permits for new, privately owned housing units increased in 1982: 36 permits were issued with a total construction cost of $789,480. None of the permits were for single family houses. Between 1970 and 1980 the number of housing units increased by 57%. Forty-three percent of all units in the county are air-conditioned, 72% are heated by gas and 14% by electricity. **NATURAL RESOURCES** Caliche, clay, sand and gravel, oil and gas. In 1982 a total of 40,471,564 thousand cubic feet of gas well gas, 346,701 barrels of condensate, 1,642,590 barrels of crude oil and 4,696,580 thousand cubic feet of casinghead gas were produced. Current production of other minerals and products includes sand and gravel. **TOURISM** Travel expenditures of $10,289,000 in 1982 (an increase of 18% over 1981) generated 141 jobs and $1,504,000 in payroll. **ALCOHOLIC BEVERAGES** Packaged distilled spirits, beer, ale, malt liquor and wine are legal. Sale of mixed beverages is legal in all or parts of the county. **FEDERAL EXPENDITURES** The federal government had direct expenditures or obligations of $28,310,000 in the county during fiscal year 1983, including $404,000 by the U.S. Department of Defense. In addition, the federal government provided $3,814,000 in grant awards, paid $4,521,000 in salaries and wages, made direct payments to individuals of $18,565,000 including $13,961,000 in retirement and disability payments, awarded $30,000 in procurement contracts and spent $1,381,000 in other expenditures or obligations. The federal government also provided $1,053,000 in direct loans and $10,384,000 in guaranteed loans and insurance.

COMMUNICATION

Newspapers–Weekly: Rio Grande Herald (Rio Grande City) and the South Texas Reporter-Spanish (Roma-Los Saenz). Cable TV. Telephone companies: General Telephone, Southwestern Bell and Valley Telephone Coop. **TRANSPORTATION** Total public road mileage: 634. In 1982 there were 15,867 registered vehicles and 338 reported traffic accidents including 11 fatalities. Intercity bus service is available. Motor freight: four carriers. Rail: one branch line carries annually less than one million tons of freight through the county. Aircraft: five are registered in the county. Airports: Starr County Airport at Rio Grande City and Falcon State Park Airport at Roma-Los Saenz.

COMMUNITY SERVICES

EDUCATION Three school districts with 10 elementary, three middle and three high schools. The average daily attendance in 1981-82 was 7,988, with expenditures per pupil of $2,508 including 417 classroom teachers with an average annual salary of $15,411. Twenty-three percent of the 440 high school graduates planned to attend college. In 1982-83, 1% of the students were White and 99% Hispanic. Private schools: 181 students enrolled in one elementary school. **CHILD CARE** Eight day care and one twenty-four hour care licensed facilities. **HEALTH CARE** Seven physicians and two dentists. Hospitals: one with a capacity of 44. Clinics: one outpatient clinic. Ambulance services: one funeral home and one volunteer service. Mental health: one county clinic. Nursing homes: one nursing home has a capacity of 100 nursing care residents. The average cost per day for private patients in 1982 was $30.91. **CHURCHES** 20 churches have an estimated combined membership of 39,154. The largest denomination is Catholic. **SOCIAL SERVICES** In fiscal year 1983 a total of $6,290,110 in food stamps was distributed, with an average of 12,516 persons receiving food stamps each month. Aid to Families with Dependent Children (AFDC) totaled $621,656 with an average of 390 families receiving AFDC each month. Medical assistance benefits for the aged and disabled of $2,204,038 and for families and children of $676,351 brought the county benefit total to $9,792,154. **FIRE PROTECTION** Three volunteer fire departments. **LAW ENFORCEMENT** The County Sheriff has 27 commissioned officers. Two police departments have a combined force of nine. **CRIME** 22 violent crimes (murder, forcible rape, robbery and aggravated assault) and 359 nonviolent crimes (burglary, larceny-theft and motor vehicle theft) were reported in 1982. **JUDICIAL SYSTEM** One District Court and Judge, one County Court and Judge and six Justices of the Peace. In the District Court a total of 1,395 cases were pending on 1/1/82, 378 new cases were filed and 215 cases were disposed of during the year leaving 1,558 cases pending on 12/31/82. There were 219 criminal cases on the docket, 35 convictions, three persons committed to prison, one committed to jail and 154 cases left pending. In the County Court 671 cases were pending on 1/1/82, 563 new cases were filed and 542 cases were disposed of during the year leaving 692 cases pending on 12/31/82. There were 955 criminal cases on the docket, 189 convictions, two persons committed to jail and 419 cases left pending. **JAILS** One jail, capacity 24. **ATTORNEYS AT LAW** 17. **UTILITIES** 93% of the residents are connected to a public or privately owned water system and 41% are connected to a public sewer system. Electricity is distributed to the county by Central Power and Light Co., Cochran Power and Light, Magic Valley Electric Coop. Inc. and Medina Electric Coop. Inc. and is generated primarily by gas, oil and coal. The typical residential electric bill is $162.15 per month for an all-electric house using 2,500 kwh. **TAXES** The county has seven units with taxing authority: three school districts, two cities, one county and one hospital district.

RECREATION/ENTERTAINMENT

NATIONAL REGISTER OF HISTORIC PLACES Rio Grande City: La Borde House, Store and Hotel and Silverio de la Pena Drugstore and Post Office. Roma-Los Saenz: Roma Historic District. **STATE** Falcon State Recreation Area (See Zapata County). **COUNTY PARKS** 229 acres in seven county parks. These parks contain one playground and one baseball and softball field. Developed campsites: 40. **SCENIC DRIVES** The Texas Tropical Trail runs through this county, which circles the state's southernmost wedge meandering through ranchland, resort areas by the Gulf of Mexico and fertile farmlands. **BOATING/ FISHING** Lakes/reservoirs: International Falcon (87,210 acres) and Olmitos-Garcias Creek Soil Conservation Service Lakes 3, 5, 6 and 7 (87 acres). Major rivers: Rio Grande. Primary streams: Garcias, El Gato and Olmitas. **WILDLIFE REFUGES** Las Palomas State Wildlife Management Area covers 300 acres in this county. **HUNTING** Fall and winter seasons on deer. No closed season on javelina, squirrel, coyote and bobcat. Winter seasons on chachalaca, quail, muskrat, beaver, opossum, ring-tailed cat, badger, fox, weasel, raccoon, skunk and civet cat. In 1983 sandhill crane, duck, coot, geese, woodcock, and jacksnipe seasons occurred during the winter months. Teal duck, rail and gallinule seasons occurred in the fall. Mourning dove seasons occurred intermittently during the fall and winter months with a fall seasons on white-winged dove. **MUSEUMS** Rio Grande City: Our Lady of Lourdes Grotto. Roma-Los Saenz: Roma Historical Museum. **OTHER** Rio Grande City: Fort Ringgold. **SPECIAL EVENTS** Starr County Fair, Rio Grande City, March; Fourth of July Parade, Rio Grande City, July; Festival, Rio Grande City, December.

COMMUNITIES

COUNTY SEAT Rio Grande City, County Courthouse, 78582; County Clerk's Office, 512/487-2954. **INCORPORATED COMMUNITIES** (1980 population and ZIP Code) La Grulla (1,442) 78548 and Roma-Los Sauz (3,384) 78584. **UNINCORPORATED COMMUNITIES** (and ZIP Code) Delmita (Zaragosa) 78536, El Centro (Centro) 78536, El Sauz 78544, Escobares 78582, Falcon Heights 78545, Falcon Village 78545, Fronton 78546, Garceno 78582, Garciasville 78547, La Casita 78582, La Gloria 78591, La Reforma 78536, Rincon 78582, Rio Grande City 78582, Rosita 78582, Salineno 78585, San Isidro 78588, Santa Catarina 78582, Santa Cruz 78582, Santa Elena 78591, Viboras 78592 and Villareales 78582.

STEPHENS (P64)

THE LAND

Northeast of Abilene on U.S. Highways 183 and 180 in the North Central Plains Region, Stephens County covers 894 square miles with the elevation ranging from 1,000 to 1,600 feet. The undulating to hilly soils are light colored and well drained with loamy surfaces over very deep, reddish, clayey or mottled subsoils. Stephens is in the Cross Timbers and Prairies vegetation area with tall and mid grasses, mesquite, junipers, live and post oak. Between 11 and 20% of the land in the county is considered prime farmland. **CLIMATE** Subtropical Subhumid with wide-ranging daily temperature variations. The average annual temperature is 64°F. Temperatures in January range from an average low of 28° to an average high of 56°F and in July range from 72° to 97°F. The average annual precipitation is 27 inches, with an average relative humidity of 76% at 6 A.M. and 46% at 6 P.M. The average annual snowfall is four inches. The growing season averages 225 days per year, with the last freeze at the end of March and the first freeze in early November. The sun shines during the year on the average 69% of the daylight hours.

THE PEOPLE

Since 1970 Stephens County has been in a period of population growth for the first time in 40 years. The 1982 estimated population of 10,900 indicates a continuation of that growth. Almost 70% of the county residents live in urban areas. The county's population had a high median age of 40 in 1970 which lowered to 34 in 1980. The largest ancestry groups are persons of English descent (32%), Irish descent (24%) and German descent (10%). **REGISTERED VOTERS** As of November 2, 1982 there were 4,993 registered voters (0.1% of the state total). The 1982 general election had a 55% voter turnout, compared to a 67% turnout in the 1980 general election. In the 1982 primary 97% voted Democratic and 3% Republican, with 2,300 votes cast.

THE ECONOMY

AGRICULTURE In 1982, 90% of the land was in farms and ranches, with 9% of the farmland under cultivation and 2% irrigated. Stephens ranked 209th in the state in highest agricultural receipts, with 87% from livestock and livestock products. Overgrazing, undesirable brush and weeds, water erosion, a lack of potable water and salinity are the current conservation problems. Primary crops: wheat, hay, oats and sorghum. Primary vegetables: sweet potatoes and watermelons. Primary fruits and nuts: peaches and pecans. Primary livestock and products: cattle, sheep, wool, angora goats and mohair. **BUSINESS** Total number of business establishments in the county: 357. Retail sales during the first quarter of 1984 increased by 17%. In 1980, 13% of the labor force were self-employed, 18% were employed in professional or related services, 15% in manufacturing, 18% in wholesale and retail trade, 21% in agriculture, forestry, fisheries and mining, 9% were employed in other counties and there were 1,134 retired workers. The industries with the most employment: oil and gas extraction, agribusiness, trucking and the manufacture of mobile homes, aircraft and aircraft parts. The nonfarm earnings in 1981 totaled $98,544,000. The retired workers received an average monthly Social Security payment of $310. **FINANCE** On June 30, 1983, two commercial banks had total deposits of $130,727,000 and total assets of $144,754,000. On December 31, 1982 one federal savings and loan association and one state association branch had assets of $12,725,098. **HOUSING** Average value of homes in 1980: $24,000. Permits for new, privately owned housing units increased in 1982: 19 permits were issued with a total construction cost of $976,495. Of those permits, all were for single family houses. Between 1970 and 1980 the number of housing units increased by 32%. Eighty-five percent of all units in the county are air-conditioned, 81% are heated by gas and 17% by electricity. **NATURAL RESOURCES** Ceramic clay, limestone, industrial sand, oil, gas and bituminous coal. In 1982 a total of 9,227,609 thousand cubic feet of gas well gas, 31,863 barrels of condensate, 4,955,400 barrels of crude oil and 5,200,774 thousand cubic feet of casinghead gas were produced. Current production of other minerals and products: crushed limestone. **TOURISM** Travel expenditures of $5,238,000 in 1982 (an increase of 13% over 1981) generated 116 jobs and $971,000 in payroll. **ALCOHOLIC BEVERAGES** Only 4% beer is legal in parts of the county. **FEDERAL EXPENDITURES** The federal government had direct expenditures or obligations of $17,774,000 in the county during fiscal year 1983, including $1,025,000 by the U.S. Department of Defense. In addition, the federal government provided $155,000 in grant awards, paid $874,000 in salaries and wages, made direct payments to individuals of $16,443,000 including $11,357,000 in retirement and disability payments, awarded $153,000 in procurement contracts and spent $149,000 in other expenditures or obligations. The federal government also provided $22,000 in direct loans and $3,651,000 in guaranteed loans and insurance.

COMMUNICATION

Newspapers–Weekly: Breckenridge American. Radio: KSTB-AM (Breckenridge). Cable TV. Telephone companies: Continental Telephone, Southwestern Bell and Brazos Telephone Coop. **TRANSPORTATION** Total public road mileage: 681. In 1982 there were 11,876 registered vehicles and 328 reported traffic accidents including five fatalities. Taxi cabs: one company in Breckenridge. Intercity bus service is available. Motor freight: 13 local and intrastate carriers. Rail: one main line carries annually 10 to 20 million tons of freight through the county. Aircraft: 46 are registered in the county. Airports: Stephens County Airport at Breckenridge serves as a base for 29 aircraft and is a general utility airport with general aviation service.

COUNTIES

COMMUNITY SERVICES

EDUCATION One school district with three elementary, one middle and one high school. The average daily attendance in 1981-82 was 1,806 with expenditures per pupil of $2,183 including 91 classroom teachers with an average annual salary of $16,521. Fifty-eight percent of the 122 high school graduates planned to attend college. In 1982-83, 83% of the students were White, 11% Hispanic, 4% Black and 2% Asian. **PUBLIC LIBRARIES** Breckenridge Public Library: 10,000 volumes. **CHILD CARE** 33 day care and one twenty-four hour care licensed facilities. **HEALTH CARE** Five physicians and three dentists. Hospitals: one with a capacity of 54. Ambulance services: one city service. Mental health: one clinic. Nursing homes: two nursing homes with a combined capacity of 164 nursing care residents. The average cost per day for private patients in 1982 was $30.26. **CHURCHES** 25 churches have an estimated combined membership of 5,805. The largest denominations are Southern Baptist, United Methodist and Catholic. **SOCIAL SERVICES** In fiscal year 1983 a total of $213,478 in food stamps was distributed, with an average of 510 persons receiving food stamps each month. Aid to Families with Dependent Children (AFDC) totaled $32,047 with an average of 22 families receiving AFDC each month. Medical assistance benefits for the aged and disabled of $878,144 and for families and children of $68,255 brought the county benefit total to $1,191,924. **FIRE PROTECTION** One volunteer fire department. **LAW ENFORCEMENT** The County Sheriff has seven commissioned officers. One police department has a force of 11. Breckenridge Park Police has one officer. **CRIME** 13 violent crimes (murder, forcible rape, robbery and aggravated assault) and 257 nonviolent crimes (burglary, larceny-theft and motor vehicle theft) were reported in 1982. **JUDICIAL SYSTEM** One District Court and Judge, one County Court and Judge and two Justices of the Peace. In the District Court a total of 1,897 cases were pending on 1/1/82, 777 new cases were filed and 496 cases were disposed of during the year leaving 2,181 cases pending on 12/31/82. There were 2,178 criminal cases on the docket, 76 convictions, four persons committed to prison, one committed to jail and 1,425 cases left pending. **JAILS** One jail, capacity 27. **ATTORNEYS AT LAW** 13. **UTILITIES** 80% of the residents are connected to a public or privately owned water system and 62% are connected to a public sewer system. Natural gas is distributed to the county by Brazos River Gas Co. and Lone Star Gas Co., Division of Enserch. The average annual residential bill for natural gas in 1982 for the Lone Star distribution system was $405.91, an increase of 35% over 1981. Electricity is distributed to the county by Texas Electric Service Co. and Comanche Co. Electric Coop. and is generated primarily by gas and water. The typical residential electric bill is $154.69 per month for an all-electric house using 2,500 kwh. **TAXES** The county has four units with taxing authority: one school district, one city, one county and one special district.

RECREATION/ENTERTAINMENT

MUNICIPAL PARKS 82 acres in three municipal parks. These parks contain two baseball and softball fields, two multi-use fields, one swimming pool and one boat ramp. Developed campsites: eight. **BOATING/FISHING** Lakes/reservoirs: Atkins (64 acres), Conner (10 acres), Crystal Falls (108 acres), Daniel (924 acres), Grand (29 acres), Hubbard Creek (15,250 acres), Necessity (10 acres), Petroleum Corporation (69 acres), Powers (61 acres) and T P (38 acres). Major rivers: Clear Fork Brazos. Primary streams: Jones, Gonzales, Big, Hubbard, Cedar, Caddo and Gunsolus. **HUNTING** Fall and winter seasons on deer. No closed season on squirrel, bobcat and coyote. Winter seasons on quail, muskrat, beaver, opossum, ring-tailed cat, badger, fox, weasel, raccoon, skunk and civet cat. Fall, winter and spring seasons on turkey. In 1983 duck, coot, geese, woodcock and jacksnipe seasons occurred during the winter months. Teal duck, rail and gallinule seasons occurred in the fall. Mourning dove seasons occurred intermittently during the fall and winter months. **MUSEUMS** Breckenridge: Swenson Memorial Museum of Stephens County. **SPECIAL EVENTS** Junior Stock Show, Breckenridge, January; Junior Rodeo, Breckenridge, June; Miss Breckenridge Beauty Pageant, Breckenridge, July; County Fair, Breckenridge, October; Christmas Parade, Breckenridge, December.

COMMUNITIES

COUNTY SEAT Breckenridge, County Courthouse, 76024; County Clerk's Office, 817/559-3700. **INCORPORATED COMMUNITIES** (1980 population and ZIP Code) Breckenridge (6,921) 76024. **UNINCORPORATED COMMUNITIES** (and ZIP Code) Caddo 76029, Crystal Falls 76024, Eolian 76024, Frankell 76470, Gunsight 76437, Harpersville 76024, Ivan 76024, Necessity 76024 and South Hanlon 76024. **FOR ADDITIONAL LOCAL INFORMATION** Breckenridge Chamber of Commerce, 112 W. Walker, Breckenridge, 76024, 817/559-2301.

STERLING (P78)

THE LAND

East of Midland on U.S. Highway 87 in the Edwards Plateau Region, Sterling County covers 923 square miles with the elevation ranging from 2,200 to 2,600 feet. Along the northern border and east central portion are light to very dark, loamy, soils with reddish or mottled clayey subsoils. Some subsoils have lime accumulations. The rest of the county has undulating to hilly, loamy soils and limestone within 40 inches of the surface. About 90% of this area has exposed rock. Sterling is in the Edwards Plateau vegetation area with tall and mid grasses, mesquite, junipers, live and shinnery oak. Between 31 and 40% of the land in the county is considered prime farmland. **CLIMATE** Subtropical, dry with wide-ranging daily temperature fluctuations. The average annual temperature is 65 °F. Temperatures in January range from an average low of 31 ° to an average high of 59 °F and in July range from 71 ° to 95 °F. The average annual precipitation is 18 inches, with an average relative humidity of 73% at 6 A.M. and 39% at 6 P.M. The average annual snowfall is four inches. The growing season averages 226 days per year, with the last freeze in early April and the first freeze in early November. The sun shines during the year on the average 71% of the daylight hours.

THE PEOPLE

Sterling County is one of the most sparsely populated in the state. The 1982 estimated population of 1,400 indicates a continuation of the growth begun in the 1970s, which reversed the population decline of the previous 40 years. A majority of the residents live in rural areas. The largest ancestry groups are persons of English descent (36%), Irish descent (31%) and Hispanic (23%). **REGISTERED VOTERS** As of November 2, 1982 there were 772 registered voters (0.01% of the state total). The 1982 general election had a 61% voter turnout, compared to a 80% turnout in the 1980 general election. In the 1982 primary 95% voted Democratic and 5% Republican, with 357 votes cast.

THE ECONOMY

AGRICULTURE Ranchland. In 1982, 96% of the land was in farms and ranches, with 1% of the farmland under cultivation. Sterling ranked 242nd in the state in highest agricultural receipts, with 97% from livestock and livestock products. Overgrazing, undesirable brush and weeds, decreasing irrigation water supplies and inadequate cropping systems are the current conservation problems. Primary crops: wheat, barley and hay. Primary fruits and nuts: pecans. Primary livestock and products: cattle, sheep, wool, angora goats and mohair. **BUSINESS** Total number of business establishments in the county: 36. Retail sales during the first quarter of 1984 increased by 23%. In 1980, 13% of the labor force were self-employed, 18% were employed in professional or related services, 2% in manufacturing, 20% in wholesale and retail trade, 36% in agriculture, forestry, fisheries and mining, 3% were employed in other counties and there were 119 retired workers. The industries with the most employment: oil and gas extraction and agribusiness. The nonfarm earnings in 1981 totaled $12,166,000. The retired workers received an average monthly Social Security payment of $311. **FINANCE** On June 30, 1983, one commercial bank had total deposits of $20,278,000 and total assets of $23,188,000. **HOUSING** Average value of homes in 1980: $23,400. Between 1970 and 1980 the number of housing units increased by 27%. Eighty-two percent of all units in the county are air-conditioned, 94% are heated by gas and 4% by electricity. **NATURAL RESOURCES** Dolomite, limestone, salt, industrial sand, oil and gas. In 1982 a total of 7,636,295 thousand cubic feet of gas well gas, 47,562 barrels of condensate, 2,515,459 barrels of crude oil and 27,893,782 thousand cubic feet of casinghead gas were produced. Current production of other minerals: crushed limestone. **TOURISM** Travel expenditures of $494,000 in 1982 (an increase of 17% over 1981) generated 7 jobs and $73,000 in payroll. **ALCOHOLIC BEVERAGES** Totally dry. **FEDERAL EXPENDITURES** The federal government had direct expenditures or obligations of $2,220,000 in the county during fiscal year 1983, including $53,000 by the U.S. Department of Defense. In addition, the federal government paid $93,000 in salaries and wages, made direct payments to individuals of $1,613,000 including $1,516,000 in retirement and disability payments and spent $623,000 in other expenditures or obligations. The federal government also provided $181,000 in guaranteed loans and insurance.

COMMUNICATION
Newspapers–Weekly: Sterling City News-Record. Telephone companies: General Telephone. **TRANSPORTATION** Total public road mileage: 230. In 1982 there were 1,612 registered vehicles and 41 reported traffic accidents including four fatalities. Intercity bus service is available. Motor freight: two carriers. Aircraft: 12 are registered in the county.

COMMUNITY SERVICES
EDUCATION One school district with one elementary, one middle and one high school. The average daily attendance in 1981-82 was 270, with expenditures per pupil of $4,993 including 19 classroom teachers with an average annual salary of $21,733. Thirty-nine percent of the 18 high school graduates planned to attend college. In 1982-83, 65% of the students were White, 35% Hispanic and 0.6% Asian. **CHILD CARE** Two day care licensed facilities. **HEALTH CARE** One physician. Hospitals: one with a capacity of 16. Ambulance services: one county service. Nursing homes: one nursing home has a capacity of 29 nursing care residents. The average cost per day for private patients in 1982 was $44.04. **CHURCHES** Five churches have an estimated combined membership of 796. The largest denominations are Southern Baptist and United Methodist. **SOCIAL SERVICES** In fiscal year 1983 a total of $19,476 in food stamps was distributed, with an average of 39 persons receiving food stamps each month. Aid to Families with Dependent Children (AFDC) totaled $6,817. Medical assistance benefits for the aged and disabled of $108,809 and for families and children of $5,534 brought the county benefit total to $140,636. **FIRE PROTECTION**

One volunteer fire department. **LAW ENFORCEMENT** The County Sheriff has three commissioned officers. **CRIME** 22 nonviolent crimes (burglary, larceny-theft and motor vehicle theft) were reported in 1982. **JUDICIAL SYSTEM** One District Court and Judge, one County Court and Judge and four Justices of the Peace. In the District Court a total of 11 cases were pending on 1/1/82, 31 new cases were filed and 20 cases were disposed of during the year leaving 22 cases pending on 12/31/82. There were 13 criminal cases on the docket, two convictions, one committed to jail and nine cases left pending. In the County Court 53 cases were pending on 1/1/82, 68 new cases were filed and 94 cases were disposed of during the year leaving 27 cases pending on 12/31/82. There were 113 criminal cases on the docket, 41 convictions, two persons committed to jail and 26 cases left pending. **JAILS** One jail, capacity seven. **ATTORNEYS AT LAW** Three. **UTILITIES** 69% of the residents are connected to a public or privately owned water system and 1% are connected to a public sewer system. Electricity is distributed to the county by Concho Valley Electric Coop., Inc. and is generated primarily by gas and oil. **TAXES** The county has three units with taxing authority: one school district, one city and one county.

RECREATION/ENTERTAINMENT
COUNTY/MUNICIPAL PARKS Nine acres in one county and one municipal park. These parks contain one playground and two baseball and softball fields. **BOATING/FISHING** Major rivers: North Concho. Primary streams: Sterling, Gasconades, Forest, Lacy and Mulberry. **HUNTING** Fall season on antelope. Fall and winter seasons on deer and javelina. No closed season on squirrel, bobcat and coyote. Winter seasons on quail, muskrat, beaver, opossum, ring-tailed cat, badger, fox weasel, raccoon, skunk and civet cat. Fall, winter and spring seasons on turkey. In 1983 sandhill crane, duck, coot, geese, woodcock and jacksnipe seasons occurred during the winter months. Teal duck, rail and gallinule seasons occurred in the fall. Mourning dove seasons occurred intermittently during the fall and winter months.

COMMUNITIES
COUNTY SEAT Sterling City, County Courthouse, 76951; County Clerk's Office, 915/378-5191. **INCORPORATED COMMUNITIES** (1980 population and ZIP Code) Sterling City (915) 76951. **UNINCORPORATED COMMUNITIES** (and ZIP Code) Broome 76951.

STONEWALL (P52)

THE LAND
Northwest of Abilene on U.S. Highways 83 and 380 in the Rolling Plains Region, Stonewall County covers 925 square miles with the elevation ranging from 1,500 to 2,400 feet. The soils are light to very dark with loamy surfaces over clayey subsoils. Some of the subsoils have hardened calcium deposits. Stonewall is in the Rolling Plains vegetation area with tall and mid grasses, mesquite and shinnery oak. Between 21 and 30% of the land in the county is considered prime farmland. **CLIMATE** Subtropical with wide-ranging temperature variations. Relatively dry, duststorms will occur mostly during spring. The average annual temperature is 64 °F. Temperatures in January range from an average low of 27 ° to an average high of 55 °F and in July range from 70 ° to 96 °F. The average annual precipitation is 22 inches, with an average relative humidity of 74% at 6 A.M. and 42% at 6 P.M. The average annual snowfall is seven inches. The growing season averages 230 days per year, with the last freeze in early April and the first freeze in early November. The sun shines during the year on the average 72% of the daylight hours.

COUNTIES

STONEWALL (continued)

THE PEOPLE

The county's 1982 estimated population of 2,400 reverses the population increases of the 1970s. A 20% population loss between 1960 and 1970 was followed by a 4% gain between 1970 and 1980. A majority of the residents live in rural areas. The county's population is older than average with a median age of 40. The largest ancestry groups are persons of English descent (32%), Irish descent (19%) and German descent (11%). **REGISTERED VOTERS** As of November 2, 1982 there were 1,638 registered voters (0.02% of the state total). The 1982 general election had a 65% voter turnout, compared to a 74% turnout in the 1980 general election. In the 1982 primary 100% voted Democratic with 613 votes cast.

THE ECONOMY

AGRICULTURE Wheat area. In 1982, 94% of the land was in farms and ranches, with 18% of the farmland under cultivation and 6% irrigated. Stonewall ranked 200th in the state in highest agricultural receipts with 52% from crops. Overgrazing, undesirable brush and weeds, water and wind erosion are the current conservation problems. Primary crops: wheat, cotton, oats, sorghum, hay and peanuts. Primary vegetables: sweet potatoes and watermelons. Primary fruits and nuts: peaches. Primary livestock and products: cattle. **BUSINESS** Total number of business establishments in the county: 64. In 1980, 28% of the labor force were self-employed, 16% were employed in professional or related services, 0.9% in manufacturing, 16% in wholesale and retail trade, 37% in agriculture, forestry, fisheries and mining, 13% were employed in other counties and there were 310 retired workers. The industries with the most employment: oil and gas extraction and agribusiness. The nonfarm earnings in 1981 totaled $19,275,000. The retired workers received an average monthly Social Security payment of $294. **FINANCE** On June 30, 1983, one commercial bank had total deposits of $18,994,000 and total assets of $22,408,000. **HOUSING** Average value of homes in 1980: $20,000. Between 1970 and 1980 the number of housing units increased by 10%. Eighty-two percent of all units in the county are air-conditioned, 76% are heated by gas and 19% by electricity. **NATURAL RESOURCES** Copper, gypsum, sand, gravel, oil and gas. In 1982 a total of 4,420,375 barrels of crude oil and 1,704,306 thousand cubic feet of casinghead gas were produced. Current production of other minerals and products includes gypsum, sand and gravel. **TOURISM** Travel expenditures of $2,163,000 in 1982 (an increase of 12% over 1981) generated 51 jobs and $416,000 in payroll. **ALCOHOLIC BEVERAGES** Packaged distilled spirits, beer, ale, malt liquor and wine are legal in parts of the county. **FEDERAL EXPENDITURES** The federal government had direct expenditures or obligations of $5,513,000 in the county during fiscal year 1983, including $50,000 by the U.S. Department of Defense. In addition, the federal government provided $55,000 in grant awards, paid $269,000 in salaries and wages, made direct payments to individuals of $3,749,000 including $2,562,000 in retirement and disability payments, and spent $1,439,000 in other expenditures or obligations. The federal government also provided $1,304,000 in direct loans and $1,049,000 in guaranteed loans and insurance.

COMMUNICATION

Cable TV. Telephone companies: General Telephone, Southwestern Bell and Cap Rock Telephone. **TRANSPORTATION** Total public road mileage: 519. In 1982 there were 2,850 registered vehicles and 38 reported traffic accidents. Motor freight: one carrier. Rail: one branch line annually carries less than one million tons of freight through the county. Aircraft: five are registered in the county. Airports: Douglas Flying Service at Aspermont.

COMMUNITY SERVICES

EDUCATION Two school districts with two elementary, one middle and two high schools. The average daily attendance in 1981-82 was 341, with expenditures per pupil of $4,976 including 32 classroom teachers with an average annual salary of $15,073. Sixty-one percent of the 38 high school graduates planned to attend college. In 1982-83, 78% of the students were White, 18% Hispanic, 3% Black and 0.8% Asian. **PUBLIC LIBRARIES** Aspermont Library. **CHILD CARE** One day care and one twenty-four hour care licensed facilities. **HEALTH CARE** One physician. Hospitals: one with a capacity of 25. Ambulance services: one commercial service. Nursing homes: one nursing home has a capacity of 80 nursing care residents. The average cost per day for private patients in 1982 was $35.98. **CHURCHES** Nine churches have an estimated combined membership of 1,431. The largest denomination is Southern Baptist. **SOCIAL SERVICES** In fiscal year 1983 a total of $45,965 in food stamps was distributed, with an average of 111 persons receiving food stamps each month. Aid to Families with Dependent Children (AFDC) totaled $1,398. Medical assistance benefits for the aged and disabled of $502,596 and for families and children of $12,548 brought the county benefit total to $562,507. **FIRE PROTECTION** One volunteer fire department. **LAW ENFORCEMENT** The County Sheriff has six commissioned officers. **CRIME** Two violent crimes (murder, forcible rape, robbery and aggravated assault) and 27 nonviolent crimes (burglary, larceny-theft and motor vehicle theft) were reported in 1982. **JUDICIAL SYSTEM** One District Court and Judge, one County Court and Judge and one Justice of the Peace. In the District Court a total of 193 cases were pending on 1/1/82, 82 new cases were filed and 41 cases were disposed of during the year leaving 234 cases pending on 12/31/82. There were 43 criminal cases on the docket, three convictions, two persons committed to prison and 40 cases left pending. In the County Court 123 cases were pending on 1/1/82, 91 new cases were filed and 26 cases were disposed of during the year leaving 188 cases pending on 12/31/82. There were 141 criminal cases on the docket, 15 convictions and 116 cases left pending. **JAILS** One jail, capacity 10. **ATTORNEYS AT LAW** Two. **UTILITIES** 68% of the residents are connected to a public or privately owned water system and 52% are connected to a public sewer system. Electricity is distributed to the county by West Texas Utilities, B-K Electric Coop. Inc., Dickens Electric Coop. Inc. and Midwest Electric Coop. Inc. and is generated primarily by gas and oil. **TAXES** The county has six units with taxing authority: two school districts, one city, one county, one hospital district and one special district.

RECREATION/ENTERTAINMENT

BOATING/FISHING Lakes/reservoirs: Aspermont (20 acres) and Landreth (59 acres). Major rivers: Double Mountain Fork Brazos and Salt Fork Brazos. Primary streams: Tonk, South Camp Hollow, Salt Croton and Croton. **HUNTING** Fall season on antelope. Fall and winter seasons on mule deer and deer. No closed season on squirrel, bobcat and coyote. Winter seasons on quail, muskrat, beaver, opossum, ring-tailed cat, badger, fox, weasel, raccoon, skunk and civet cat. Fall, winter and spring seasons on turkey. In 1983 sandhill crane, duck, coot, geese, woodcock and jacksnipe seasons occurred during the winter months. Teal duck, rail and gallinule seasons occurred in the fall. Mourning dove seasons occurred intermittently during the fall and winter months. **SPECIAL EVENTS** Stonewall County Fair, Aspermont, June; Aspermont Township Homecoming, Aspermont, October.

COUNTY SEAT Aspermont, County Courthouse, 79502; County Clerk's Office, 817/989-2272. **INCORPORATED COMMUNITIES** (1980 population and ZIP Code) Aspermont (1,357) 79502. **UNINCORPORATED COMMUNITIES** (and ZIP Code) Old Glory 79540, Peacock 79542 and Swenson 79502.

SUTTON (P97)

THE LAND

Northwest of San Antonio on Interstate 10 in the Edwards Plateau Region, Sutton County covers 1,455 square miles with the elevation ranging from 1,900 to 2,300 feet. The land is undulating to hilly with loamy soils that have accumulations of lime. About 90% of the western quarter of the county is exposed rock. Sutton is in the Edwards Palteau vegetation area with tall and mid grasses, mesquite and shinnery oak. Between one and 10% of the land in the county is considered prime farmland. **CLIMATE** Subtropical Steppe with wide-ranging daily temperature fluctuations. The average annual temperature is 66°F. Temperatures in January range from an average low of 32° to an average high of 62°F and in July range from 69° to 96°F. The average annual precipitation is 20 inches, with an average relative humidity of 76% at 6 A.M. and 41% at 6 P.M. The average annual snowfall is two inches. The growing season averages 235 days per year, with the last freeze in late March and the first freeze in mid November. The sun shines during the year on the average 68% of the daylight hours.

THE PEOPLE

Among all U.S. counties Sutton County ranks 63rd in highest percent of residents of Spanish origin and 74th in highest birth rate. The 1982 estimated population of 5,700 continues the strong growth begun in the 1970s, which reversed the population decline of the previous 30 years. Population in rural areas lowered 60% between 1970 and 1980. The age groups with the largest gains were ages birth to five years and ages 20 to 34. The largest ancestry groups are Hispanic (40%) persons of English descent (25%), Irish descent (17%) and German descent (16%). **REGISTERED VOTERS** As of November 2, 1982 there were 2,439 registered voters (0.03% of the state total). The 1982 general election had a 28% voter turnout, compared to a 62% turnout in the 1980 general election. In the 1982 primary 97% voted Democratic and 3% Republican, with 714 votes cast.

THE ECONOMY

AGRICULTURE Sheep and angora goat ranches. In 1982, 93% of the land was in farms and ranches, with less than 1% of the farmland under cultivation. Sutton ranked 199th in the state in highest agricultural receipts with 99% from livestock and livestock products. Overgrazing, undesirable brush and weeds, water erosion, difficulties in grass establishment and rangeland loss to oil production are the current conservation problems. Primary crops: wheat. Primary fruits and nuts: pecans. Primary livestock and products: fourth in the state for angora goats and mohair production and 10th for sheep. Cattle. **BUSINESS** Total number of business establishments in the county: 150. Retail sales during the first quarter of 1984 decreased 14%. In 1980, 10% of the labor force were self-employed, 13% were employed in professional or related services, 2% in manufacturing, 19% in wholesale and retail trade, 33% in agriculture, forestry, fisheries and mining, 4% were employed in other counties and there were 253 retired workers. The industries with the most employment: oil and gas extraction and agribusiness. The nonfarm earnings in 1981 totaled $56,853,000. The retired workers received an average monthly Social Security payment of $324. **FINANCE**

On June 30, 1983, two commercial banks had total deposits of $41,512,000 and total assets of $47,876,000. There are two state savings and loan association branches. **HOUSING** Average value of homes in 1980: $25,700. Permits for new, privately owned housing units increased in 1982: 63 permits were issued with a total construction cost of $1,913,000. Of those permits, nine were for single family houses. Housing permits in Sonora increased from eight in 1981 to 63 in 1982 with 48 permits issued for apartments and condominiums. Between 1970 and 1980 the number of housing units increased by 54%. Eighty-eight percent of all units in the county are air-conditioned, 84% are heated by gas and 14% by electricity. **NATURAL RESOURCES** Dolomite, limestone, oil and gas. In 1982 a total of 56,380,657 thousand cubic feet of gas well gas, 125,803 barrels of condensate, 105,359 barrels of crude oil and 127,940 thousand cubic feet of casinghead gas were produced. Current production of other minerals and products includes crushed limestone. **TOURISM** Travel expenditures of $13,109,000 in 1982 (an increase of 11% over 1981) generated 335 jobs and $2,648,000 in payroll. **ALCOHOLIC BEVERAGES** Packaged distilled spirits, beer, ale, malt liquor and wine are legal. Sale of mixed beverages is legal in all or parts of the county. **FEDERAL EXPENDITURES** The federal government had direct expenditures or obligations of $6,707,000 in the county during fiscal year 1983, including $200,000 by the U.S. Department of Defense. In addition, the federal government provided $84,000 in grant awards, paid $819,000 in salaries and wages, made direct payments to individuals of $3,851,000 including $2,699,000 in retirement and disability payments, awarded $2,000 in procurement contracts and spent $1,951,000 in other expenditures or obligations. The federal government also provided $1,858,000 in guaranteed loans and insurance.

COMMUNICATION

Newspapers–Weekly: The Devil's River News (Sonora). Radio: KVRN-AM and KVRN-FM (Sonora). Cable TV. Telephone companies: General Telephone. **TRANSPORTATION** Total public road mileage: 417. In 1982 there were 6,271 registered vehicles and 220 reported traffic accidents including five fatalities. Intercity bus service is available. Motor freight: seven local and intrastate carriers. Aircraft: 23 are registered in the county. Airports: Sonora Municipal Airport, Allison Ranch Airport for emergency use only and Sonora Research Station Airport.

COMMUNITY SERVICES

EDUCATION One school district with one elementary, two middle and one high school. The average daily attendance in 1981-82 was 1,233, with expenditures per pupil of $2,932 including 80 classroom teachers with an average annual salary of $18,572. None of the 70 high school graduates planned to attend college. In 1982-83, 52% of the students were White, 48% Hispanic, 0.2% Black, 0.3% Asian and 0.1% American Indian. **PUBLIC LIBRARIES** Sonora Library. **CHILD CARE** Six day care and two twenty-four hour care licensed facilities. **HEALTH CARE** One physician and three dentists. Hospitals: One with a capacity of 21. Ambulance services: one county service. Nursing homes: one nursing home has a capacity of 39 nursing care residents. The average cost per day for private patients in 1982 was $29.90. **CHURCHES** 10 churches have an estimated combined membership of 3,154. The largest denominations are Catholic and Southern Baptist. **SOCIAL SERVICES** In fiscal year 1983 a total of $108,178 in food stamps was distributed, with an average of 287 persons receiving food stamps each month. Aid to Families with Dependent Children (AFDC) totaled $7,362 with an average of five families receiving AFDC each month. Medical assistance benefits for the aged and disabled of $243,362 and for families and children of $39,171 brought the county benefit total to

COUNTIES

SUTTON (continued)

$398,073. **FIRE PROTECTION** One volunteer fire department. **LAW ENFORCEMENT** The County Sheriff has six commissioned officers. One police department has a force of five. **CRIME** 14 violent crimes (murder, forcible rape, robbery and aggravated assault) and 157 nonviolent crimes (burglary, larceny-theft and motor vehicle theft) were reported in 1982. **JUDICIAL SYSTEM** One District Court and Judge, one County Court and Judge and one Justice of the Peace. In the District Court a total of 252 cases were pending on 1/1/82, 169 new cases were filed and 133 cases were disposed of during the year leaving 288 cases pending on 12/31/82. There were 41 criminal cases on the docket, 13 convictions, five persons committed to prison and 26 cases left pending. In the County Court 304 cases were pending on 1/1/82, 262 new cases were filed and 232 cases were disposed of during the year leaving 334 cases pending on 12/31/82. There were 539 criminal cases on the docket, 40 convictions, 22 persons committed to jail and 311 cases left pending. **JAILS** One jail, capacity 28. **ATTORNEYS AT LAW** Seven. **UTILITIES** 86% of the residents are connected to a public or privately owned water system and 78% are connected to a public sewer system. Natural gas is distributed to the county by Lone Star Gas Co., Division of Enserch. The average annual residential bill for natural gas in 1982 for the Lone Star distribution system was $405.91, an increase of 35% over 1981. Electricity is distributed to the city of Sonora by Sonora Municipal Power and Light and to the rest of the county by West Texas Utitities, Kimble Electric Coop., Inc. and Southwest Texas Electric Coop., Inc. and is generated primarily by gas, oil, water and coal. The typical residential electric bill is $145.78 per month for an all-electric house using 2,500 kwh. **TAXES** The county has three units with taxing authority: one school district, one city and one county.

RECREATION/ENTERTAINMENT
NATIONAL REGISTER OF HISTORIC PLACES Sonora: Old Mercantile Building and Sutton County Court House. **COUNTY/MUNICIPAL PARKS** 88 acres in one county and two municipal parks. These parks contain one golf course, one baseball and softball field, one swimming pool and one beach. Developed campsites: five. **SCENIC DRIVES** The Texas Pecos Trail runs through this county. This trail rambles through the vast region of southwest and west Texas with landscapes varying from raw, arid regions to green valleys. **BOATING/FISHING** Lakes/reservoirs: Dry Devils and Lowrey Soil Conservation Service Lakes 3 and 5 (23 acres). Major rivers: Dry Devils, Devils and North Llano. **HUNTING** Fall and winter seasons on deer. No closed season on javelina, squirrel, bobcat and coyote. Winter seasons on quail, muskrat, beaver, opossum, ring-tailed cat, badger, fox, weasel, raccoon, skunk and civet cat. Fall, winter and spring seasons on turkey. In 1983 sandhill crane, duck, coot, geese, woodcock and jacksnipe seasons occurred during the winter months. Teal duck, rail and gallinule seasons occurred in the fall. Mourning dove seasons occurred intermittently during the fall and winter months with a fall season on white-winged dove in some parts of the county. **MUSEUMS** Sonora: Miers Home Museum. **SPECIAL EVENTS** 4-H Food Fair, Sonora, March; Experiment Station Ram Sale and Field Day, Sonora, March; Hoot and Holler Goat Barbeque, Sonora, May; 4-H Junior Horse Show, Sonora, May; 4-H Wool Show, Sonora, June; Sutton County Days, Sonora, August; Game Dinner and Program, Sonora, November.

COMMUNITIES
COUNTY SEAT Sonora, County Courthouse, 76950; County Clerk's Office, 915/387-3815. **INCORPORATED COMMUNITIES** (1980 population and ZIP Code) Sonora (3,856) 76950.

FOR ADDITIONAL LOCAL INFORMATION Sonora Chamber of Commerce, P. O. Box 1172, Sonora, 76950, 915/387-2880.

SWISHER (P23)

THE LAND
In the High Plains Region of the Texas Panhandle south of Amarillo on Interstate Highway 27, Swisher County covers 902 square miles with the elevation ranging from 3,000 to 3,200 feet. In the east central part of the county are light colored, well drained soils. The rest of the county has nearly level, very dark, loamy surfaces over clayey subsoils with hardened calcium deposits. Swisher is in the High Plains vegetation area with prairie grasses, juniper, some mesquite and yucca. Between 81 and 90% of the land in the county is considered prime farmland. **CLIMATE** Continental Steppe with wide-ranging daily temperature fluctuations. During spring thunderstorms and duststorms will occur. The average annual temperature is 58 °F. Temperatures in January range from an average low of 22 ° to an average high of 52 °F and in July range from 65 ° to 93 °F. The average annual precipitation is 18 inches, with an average relative humidity of 70% at 6 A.M. and 38% at 6 P.M. The average annual snowfall is 12 inches. The growing season averages 205 days per year, with the last freeze in mid April and the first freeze in early November. The sun shines during the year on the average 75% of the daylight hours.

THE PEOPLE
The 1982 estimated population of 9,200 indicates a slight population decrease since 1980, following 50 years of reversals in growth. Population losses grew from 2% between 1960 and 1970 to 6% between 1970 and 1980. Rural and urban areas decreased in size equally between 1970 and 1980. The age groups with the greatest losses were ages five to 14 and 40 to 49. The largest ancestry groups are Hispanic (28%), persons of English descent (28%), Irish descent (21%) and German descent (14%). **REGISTERED VOTERS** As of November 2, 1982 there were 4,711 registered voters (0.1% of the state total). The 1982 general election had a 62% voter turnout, compared to a 74% turnout in the 1980 general election. In the 1982 primary 99% voted Democratic and 1% Republican, with 2,501 votes cast.

THE ECONOMY
AGRICULTURE Prime farmland with diversified products. In 1982, 97% of the land was in farms and ranches, with 78% of the farmland under cultivation and 60% irrigated. Swisher ranked ninth in the state in highest agricultural receipts with 53% from livestock and livestock products. Water and wind erosion, decreasing irrigation water supplies and noxious weeds are the current conservation problems. Primary crops: sixth in the state for wheat and soybeans and seventh for corn. Cotton and sorghum. Primary vegetables: potatoes, tomatoes and watermelons. Primary fruits and nuts: pecans. Primary livestock and products: third in the state for cattle and fifth for fed cattle marketings. Wool and hogs. **BUSINESS** Total number of business establishments in the county: 205. Retail sales during the first quarter of 1984 increased by 8%. In 1980, 23% of the labor force were self-employed, 16% were employed in professional or related services, 11% in manufacturing, 19% in wholesale and retail trade, 29% in agriculture, forestry, fisheries and mining, 11% were employed in other counties and there were 872 retired workers. The industries with the most employment: agribusiness and the manufacture of women's clothing. The nonfarm earnings in 1981 totaled $77,704,000. The retired workers received an average monthly Social Security payment of $333. **FINANCE**

On June 30, 1983, four commercial banks had total deposits of $100,586,000 and total assets of $115,744,000. On December 31, 1982 one state savings and loan association had assets of $69,105,258. In addition there is one credit union in the county. **HOUSING** Average value of homes in 1980: $25,600. In 1982 two permits were issued for new, single family houses. Between 1970 and 1980 the number of housing units increased by 3%. Sixty-seven percent of all units in the county are air-conditioned, 92% are heated by gas and 8% by electricity. **NATURAL RESOURCES** Caliche, volcanic ash, oil and gas. Current production includes caliche, sand and gravel. **TOURISM** Travel expenditures of $5,563,000 in 1982 (an increase of 15% over 1981) generated 102 jobs and $931,000 in payroll. **ALCOHOLIC BEVERAGES** Totally dry. **FEDERAL EXPENDITURES** The federal government had direct expenditures or obligations of $24,684,000 in the county during fiscal year 1983, including $148,000 by the U.S. Department of Defense. In addition, the federal government provided $154,000 in grant awards, paid $817,000 in salaries and wages, made direct payments to individuals of $11,817,000 including $8,431,000 in retirement and disability payments, awarded $1,000 in procurement contracts and spent $11,894,000 in other expenditures or obligations. The federal government also provided $23,055,000 in direct loans and $8,115,000 in guaranteed loans and insurance.

COMMUNICATION

Newspapers–Weekly: The Kress Chronicle and the Tulia Herald. Radio: KTUE-AM (Tulia). Cable TV. Telephone companies: Continental Telephone, General Telephone, Southwestern Bell, Mid-Plains Rural Telephone Coop. and South Plains Telephone Coop. **TRANSPORTATION** Total public road mileage: 1,285. In 1982 there were 9,544 registered vehicles and 208 reported traffic accidents including three fatalities. Intercity bus service is available. Motor freight: two carriers. Rail: one main and one branch line carry freight through the county with the main line carrying annually 10 to 20 million tons and the branch carrying less than one million. Aircraft: 46 are registered in the county. Airports: City of Tulia, Swisher County Airport serves as a base for 19 aircraft and is a basic utility airport with general aviation service. Joe Vaugh Spraying Airport at Kress.

COMMUNITY SERVICES

EDUCATION Three school districts with four elementary, one middle and three high schools. The average daily attendance in 1981-82 was 1,946, with expenditures per pupil of $3,071 including 159 classroom teachers with an average annual salary of $16,056. Sixty percent of the 141 high school graduates planned to attend college. In 1982-83, 52% of the students were White, 39% Hispanic, 8% Black, 0.3% Asian and 0.2% American Indian. **PUBLIC LIBRARIES** Swisher County Library (Tulia): 13,237 volumes. **CHILD CARE** 25 day care and one twenty-four hour care licensed facilities. **HEALTH CARE** Three physicians and three dentists. Hospitals: one with a capacity of 30. Ambulance services: one volunteer service and one volunteer fire department service. Mental health: one clinic. Nursing homes: one nursing home has a capacity of 52 nursing care residents. The average cost per day for private patients in 1982 was $31.72. **CHURCHES** 29 churches have an estimated combined membership of 7,627. The largest denominations are Southern Baptist, United Methodist and Catholic. **SOCIAL SERVICES** In fiscal year 1983 a total of $499,649 in food stamps was distributed, with an average of 1,102 persons receiving food stamps each month. Aid to Families with Dependent Children (AFDC) totaled $72,815 with an average of 47 families receiving AFDC each month. Medical assistance benefits for the aged and disabled of $293,832 and for families and children of $65,059 brought the county benefit total to $931,355. **FIRE PROTECTION** Three volunteer fire departments. **LAW ENFORCEMENT** The County Sheriff has 17 commissioned officers. Three police departments have a combined force of 20. **CRIME** 25 violent crimes (murder, forcible rape, robbery and aggravated assault) and 184 nonviolent crimes (burglary, larceny-theft and motor vehicle theft) were reported in 1982. **JUDICIAL SYSTEM** Two District Courts and Judges, one County Court and Judge and two Justices of the Peace. In the District Courts a total of 419 cases were pending on 1/1/82, 281 new cases were filed and 213 cases were disposed of during the year leaving 487 cases pending on 12/31/82. There were 94 criminal cases on the docket, 49 convictions, 18 persons committed to prison and 24 cases left pending. In the County Court 391 cases were pending on 1/1/82, 369 new cases were filed and 268 cases were disposed of during the year leaving 492 cases pending on 12/31/82. There were 556 criminal cases on the docket, 217 convictions, 51 persons committed to jail and 290 cases left pending. **JAILS** One jail, capacity 19. **ATTORNEYS AT LAW** Eight. **UTILITIES** 67% of the residents are connected to a public or privately owned water system and 68% are connected to a public sewer system. Natural gas is distributed to the county by Energas Company. The average annual residential bill for natural gas in 1982 for the Energas distribution system was $405.91, an increase of 35% over 1981. Electricity is distributed to the city of Tulia by Tulia Municipal Power and Light and to the rest of the county by Lighthouse Electric Coop., Inc. and Swisher Electric Coop., Inc. and is generated primarily by gas and coal. The typical residential electric bill is $190.15 per month for an all-electric house using 2,500 kwh. **TAXES** The county has nine units with taxing authority: three school districts, three cities, one county, one hospital district and one special district.

RECREATION/ENTERTAINMENT

MUNICIPAL PARKS 716 acres in five municipal parks. These parks contain three playgrounds, one golf course, two football and soccer fields, four baseball and softball fields, two tennis courts and one swimming pool. Developed campsites: two. **BOATING/FISHING** Lakes/reservoirs: Tule (48 acres) and Tulia Feedlot (43 acres). **HUNTING** Winter seasons on aoudad sheep, pheasant, quail, muskrat, beaver, opossum, ring-tailed cat, badger, fox, weasel, raccoon, skunk and civet cat. No closed season on coyote and bobcat. Fall and winter seasons on deer and mule deer. Fall, winter and spring seasons on turkey. Summer, fall and winter seasons on squirrel. In 1983 sandhill crane, duck, coot, geese, woodcock and jacksnipe seasons occurred during the winter months. Teal duck, rail and gallinule seasons occurred in the fall. Mourning dove seasons occurred intermittently during the fall and winter months. **MUSEUMS** Tulia: Swisher County Museum. **SPECIAL EVENTS** Swisher County Celebration, Tulia, July; Happy Days, Happy, August; County Fair, Tulia, September.

COMMUNITIES

COUNTY SEAT Tulia, County Courthouse, 79088; County Clerk's Office, 806/995-3294. **INCORPORATED COMMUNITIES** (1980 population and ZIP Code) Happy (674: 43 in Randall Co. and 631 in Swisher Co.) 79042, Kress (783) 79052 and Tulia (5,033) 79088. **UNINCORPORATED COMMUNITIES** (and ZIP Code) Claytonville 79052, Lakeview 79088 and Vigo Park 79088. **FOR ADDITIONAL LOCAL INFORMATION** Tulia Chamber of Commerce, P. O. Box 267, Tulia, 79088, 806/995-2296.

TARRANT (M11)

THE LAND
West of Dallas on Interstate Highways 20 and 35W in the Grand

TARRANT (continued)

Prairie Region, Tarrant County covers 868 square miles with the elevation ranging from 500 to 800 feet. In the east the light colored soils are sandy to loamy with clayey to loamy subsoils. Along the eastern border the soils are darker with some cracking, clayey soils. In the west the light to dark loamy soils are undulating to hilly with lime accumulations in the subsoils. In the Cross Timbers and Prairies vegetation area, the predominant tall grasses are bluestems, Indiangrass, wildryes, sideoats and Texas wintergrass with post, blackjack and live oak trees, mesquite, and juniper. Between 31 and 40% of the land in the county is considered prime farmland. **CLIMATE** Subtropical Subhumid with wide-ranging daily temperature variations and hot summers. The average annual temperature is 65 °F. Temperatures in January range from an average low of 33 ° to an average high of 55 °F and in July range from 74 ° to 97 °F. The average annual precipitation is 32 inches, with an average relative humidity of 78% at 6 A.M. and 52% at 6 P.M. The average annual snowfall is four inches. The growing season averages 235 days per year, with the last freeze in late March and the first freeze in mid November. The sun shines during the year on the average 66% of the daylight hours.

THE PEOPLE

Tarrant is one of the state's most densely populated counties and ranks 34th among all U.S. counties in largest population. The 1982 estimated population of 929,000 continues the strong growth which has existed since 1930. Almost 97% of the county residents live in urban areas. The median age rose from 27 in 1970 to 29 in 1980. The largest ancestry groups are persons of English descent (28%), Irish descent (22%) German descent (17%)and Black (12%). **REGISTERED VOTERS** As of November 2, 1982 there were 386,251 registered voters (6% of the state total). The 1982 general election had a 55% voter turnout, compared to a 76% turnout in the 1980 general election. In the 1982 primary 66% voted Democratic and 34% Republican, with 66,990 votes cast.

THE ECONOMY

AGRICULTURE In 1982, 42% of the land was in farms and ranches, with 37% of the farmland under cultivation. Tarrant ranked 130th in the state in highest agricultural receipts, with 79% from livestock and livestock products. Water erosion, flooding and urban encroachment are the current conservation problems. Primary crops: wheat, hay, sorghum and oats. Primary vegetables: cantaloupes, sweet corn, cucumbers, onions, tomatoes and watermelons. Primary fruits and nuts: peaches and pecans. Primary livestock and products: cattle, milk and hogs. **BUSINESS** Total number of business establishments in the county: 19,678. Retail sales during the first quarter of 1984 increased by 21%. In 1980, 6% of the labor force were self-employed, 16% were employed in professional or related services, 25% in manufacturing, 23% in wholesale and retail trade, 8% in transportation, communications and other public utilities, 19% were employed in other counties and there were 53,010 retired workers. The industries with the most employment: agribusiness, oil and gas extraction, construction sand and gravel, grain mills, commercial printing, book printing, metal plate fabrication, aluminum foundries steel mills, boat building and repair, iron and steel forgings, soft drink bottling and canning, construction, fruit and vegetable canning, the printing of business forms and the manufacture of sausages and other prepared meats, dairy products, pet food, refrigeration and heating equipment, industrial trucks and tractors, pumps and pumping equipment, lawn and garden equipment, industrial chemicals, pharmaceutical preparations, asphalt roofing materials, rubber products, plastics products, bakery products, candy, shortening and cooking oils, malt beverages, men's work clothing, women's and children's clothing, apparel belts, fabric bags, wood kitchen cabinets, wood pallets and skids, mobile homes, prefabricated wood buildings, household furniture, paper products, cardboard boxes, leather shoes, ceramic tile, ready-mixed concrete and cement, aluminum products, metal cans, hand tools, elevators, oil field machinery, conveyors, printing machinery, office machines, power transmission equipment, motors and generators, engineering and scientific equipment, measuring and controlling devices, sporting and athletic goods, artificial flowers, lighting equipment, communications equipment, motor vehicles, electronic components, railroad equipment, aircraft, prefabricated metal buildings, gaskets and sealing devices and prepared pickles, sauces and salad dressings. The nonfarm earnings in 1981 totaled $10,234,374,000. The retired workers received an average monthly Social Security payment of $333. **FINANCE** On June 30, 1983, 70 commercial banks had total deposits of $6,761,369,000 and total assets of $8,482,449,000. On December 31, 1982 five state savings and loan associations, 75 state branches and six federal association branches had combined assets of $735,214,456. In addition there are 73 credit unions in the county. **HOUSING** Average value of homes in 1980: $44,000. Permits for new, privately owned housing units increased in 1982: 17,278 permits were issued with a total construction cost of $665,383,920. Of those permits, 6,831 were for single family houses. Housing permits increased in Arlington from 3,790 in 1981 to 6,423 in 1982, in Bedford from 899 to 2,617 with 1,818 permits issued for apartments and condominiums, in Benbrook from 141 to 519 with 384 permits issued for apartments and condominiums, in Euless from 503 to 716 with 650 permits issued for single family houses, in Fort Worth from 2,255 to 4,327, in Grapevine from 221 to 499, in Haltom City from 38 to 192, in Hurst from 128 to 209, in Keller from 36 to 69 with 55 permits issued for single family houses, in Kennedale from 26 to 59 with 40 permits issued for two family structures, in Saginaw from 55 to 117 with 77 permits issued for single family houses, in Southlake from 65 to 96 with all permits issued for single family houses and in Watauga from 218 to 417 with all permits issued for single family houses and in White Settlement from 32 to 248 with 200 permits issued for apartments and condominiums. Between 1970 and 1980 the number of housing units increased by 40%. Ninety-three percent of all units in the county are air-conditioned, 68% are heated by gas and 32% by electricity. **NATURAL RESOURCES** Limestone, industrial sand, sand and gravel, oil, gas and bituminous coal. In 1982 a total of 90,249 thousand cubic feet of gas well gas were produced. Current production of other minerals and products includes cement, crushed limestone, construction sand, industrial sand, sand and gravel. **TOURISM** Travel expenditures of $1,240,727,000 in 1982 (an increase of 7% over 1981) generated 20,024 jobs and $273,831,000 in payroll. Lodging: 80 hotels, motels and tourist courts. Convention/meeting facilities: Arlington-Arlington Stadium, Six Flags over Texas Music theatre, University of Texas at Arlington Texas Hall, Community Center and six hotels with facilities for large gatherings; Fort Worth-Casa Manana Theatre, Cowtown Coliseum, Will Rogers Memorial Center Theatre, Exhibit Area and Arena, Tarrant County Convention Center, Texas Christian University, Amon G. Carter Stadium, Texas Wesleyan College two fieldhouses, and six hotels with facilities for large gatherings. **ALCOHOLIC BEVERAGES** Packaged distilled spirits, beer, ale, malt liquor and wine are legal in parts of the county. Sale of mixed beverages is legal in all or parts of the county. **MILITARY INSTALLATIONS** Saginaw Army Aircraft Plant, Fort Worth, 225 personnel, 155 acres, helicopter assemblies production; Carswell Air Force Base, Fort Worth, 7,082 personnel, 3,264 acres, 7th Bombardment Wing; Air Force Plant 4, Fort

Worth, 257 personnel, 515 acres, weapons systems production.
FEDERAL EXPENDITURES The federal government had direct expenditures or obligations of $4,169,743,000 in the county during fiscal year 1983, including $2,990,899,000 by the U.S. Department of Defense. In addition, the federal government provided $62,606,000 in grant awards, paid $391,467,000 in salaries and wages, made direct payments to individuals of $972,205,000 including $791,229,000 in retirement and disability payments, awarded $2,739,990,000 in procurement contracts and spent $3,475,000 in other expenditures or obligations. The federal government also provided $149,000 in direct loans and $501,663,000 in guaranteed loans and insurance.

COMMUNICATION

Newspapers–Daily: Arlington Daily News ave. eve. circ. 5,106, Fort Worth Star Telegram ave. morn. circ. 102,685 and eve. 127,875 and The Mid Cities Daily News (Hurst), ave. eve. circ. 7,415. Weekly: The Arlington Citizen-Journal, Crowley Beacon, Everman Times, White Settlement Bomber News, East Side News (Fort Worth), Fort Worth News Tribune, The North Fort Worth News and The Kennedale News. Radio: KLIF-AM, KPLX-FM, KWJS -FM Stereo (Arlington). KFJZ-AM, KJIM-AM, KSAX-AM, KUQQ-AM, KXOL-AM, WBAP-AM, KEGL-FM, KESS-FM, KNOX-FM, KSCS-FM and KTCU-FM (Fort Worth). Television: KTXA CH.21 (Arlington). KTVT CH.11, KXAS CH.5 (Fort Worth). Cable TV. Telephone companies: General Telephone and Southwestern Bell. **TRANSPORTATION** Total public road mileage: 5,578. In 1982 there were 804,028 registered vehicles and 32,490 reported traffic accidents including 171 fatalities. Taxi cabs: four companies in Fort Worth. Municipal transit systems: one intracity bus system in Fort Worth, with scheduled routes. Intercity bus service is available. Motor freight: 191 local and intrastate carriers. Rail: The Eagle provides passenger sevice on the Amtrak route. Eleven main lines and one branch carry freight through the county. One main line carries annually over 30 million tons of freight, four carry 20 to 30 each, three carry 10 to 20 each, two carry five to 10 each and one carries one to five millions tons of freight. The branch line carries less than one million tons of freight annually. Aircraft: 1,630 are registered in the county. Airports: Dallas-Fort Worth Regional Airport is located centrally between the two cities and provides full carrier service. It is a large hub for long haul flights. Meacham Field at Fort Worth serves as a base for 319 aircraft and is a general transportation airport with commuter service. Arlington Municipal Airport serves as a base for 160 aircraft with general aviation service. Grand Prairie Municipal Airport serves as a base for 210 aircraft and is a general utility airport with general aviation services. Also serving the area are Blue Mound Airport, Flying Oaks Airport, Luck Field, Mangham Field, Oak Grove Airport, Saginaw Airport, Sycamore Strip and Goode Airport at Keller. Heliport service is available at Plover Heliport at Crowley, Oak Grove Heliport, Tandy Heliport, City-County Health Department Heliport at Fort Worth, Sfena Heliport at Grand Prairie, 820 Northeast Heliport at Hurst, First State Bank Building at Bedford, Holiday Inn/Airport Freeway Heliport at Bedford, Glen View Hospital Heliport, John Peter Smith Hospital Heliport, St. Joseph Hospital Heliport and Harris Hospital Heliport at Fort Worth, Hurst-Euless-Bedford Hospital Heliport at Bedford and Arlington Community Hospital Heliport at Arlington.

COMMUNITY SERVICES

EDUCATION 17 school districts with 160 elementary, 50 middle, 34 high schools and 2 special education. The average daily attendance in 1981-82 was 148,766, with expenditures per pupil of $2,579 including 8,498 classroom teachers with an average annual salary of $18,165. Fifty-five percent of the 10,200 high

school graduates planned to attend college. In 1982-83, 71% of the students were White, 11% Hispanic, 16% Black, 2% Asian and 0.2% American Indian. Sports championships: 1983 AAAAA Girls' Volleyball Champion, Arlington H.S.; 1983 AAAA Girls' Track, Ft. Worth Polytechnic; 1983 AAAA Boys' Golf Singles, Mansfield H.S.; 1983 AAAAA Girls' Golf Singles, Arlington Heights H.S.; 1983 AAAA Girls' Golf Singles, Grapevine H.S. Private schools: 11,164 students enrolled in 45 elementary and 13 high schools. Sports championships: 1983 AAAA Boys' Golf, Nolan H.S. and Dallas County Jesuit College Preparatory H.S. (tie). University of Texas at Arlington was established in 1895 and is under state control. Enrollment in 1982 was 20,166 with in state undergraduate tuition and fees of $442 per semester. The highest degree offered is Doctorate. Southwestern Baptist Theological Seminary is located in Fort Worth. Established in 1908 it is affiliated with the Southern Baptist Church. Enrollment in 1982 was 3,447. The highest degree offered is Doctorate (no undergraduates). Tarrant County Junior College is located in Fort Worth. Established in 1965 it is a vocational and two year academic college under state and local control. Enrollment in 1982 was 20,798 with in state undergraduate tuition and fees of $140 per semester. Texas Christian University is located in Fort Worth. Established in 1873 it is affiliated with Christian Church (Disciples of Christ). Enrollment in 1982 was 6,283 with in state undergraduate tuition and fees of $3,390 per semester. The highest degree offered is Doctorate. Sports championships: (Southwestern Conference) 1983 Womens' Golf. Texas College of Osteopathic Medicine is located in Fort Worth. Established in 1966 it is under state control. Enrollment in 1982 was 330. Texas Wesleyan College is located in Fort Worth. Established in 1891 it is affiliated with the Methodist Church. Enrollment in 1982 was 1,667 with in state undergraduate tuition and fees of $2,800 per semester. The highest degree offered is Master. Arlington Baptist College is located in Arlington. Established in 1939 it is affiliated with the Baptist Church. Enrollment in 1982 was 467 with in state undergraduate tuition and fees of $1,500 per semester. The highest degree offered is Bachelor. Vocational education: Arlington-Alladin Beauty College, American Career Schools, Bauder Fashion College, Bryan Institute, Ogle School of Hair Design, Leonard's Training Programs, Fort Worth-Adult Education Center, Everybody's Hairstyling and Barber College, Fort Worth Beauty School, Fort Worth District Practical Nurse Program, Fort Worth School of Business, Fort Worth Trade Schools, Gene Prater Beauty School, Haltom City Beauty College, Harris Hospital Vocational Nursing, Miss Peggy Beauty College, One Hair Place of Hair Design, St. Joseph Hospital School of Vocational Nursing, University of Hair Design, Vogue Beauty College, Williams Barber College, Acme School of Aeronautics, Inc., Associated Auction School, Barbizon School of Modeling, Control Data Learning Center, Texas Court Reporting College, Fort Worth School of Floral Design, John Robert Powers School, Smith's Aircraft School, Stephen's Aircraft Mechanic School. Hurst-Aladdin Beauty College. Colleyville-The Hypnosis Institute. Southlake-North Texas Horseshoeing Institute. **PUBLIC LIBRARIES** Arlington Public Library: 185,617 volumes, three branches. Azle Public Library: 21,000 volumes. Bedford Public Library: 39,235 volumes. Euless Public Library: 39,767 volumes. Blue Mound Community Library (Ft. Worth): 10,000 volumes. Fort Worth Public Library: 787,570 volumes, eight branches. North Richland Hills Public Library (Ft. Worth): 35,776 volumes. Richland Hills Public Library (Ft. Worth): 30,000 volumes. Grapevine Public Library: 24,658 volumes. Haltom City Public Library: 57,520 volumes. Hurst Public Library: 85,940 volumes. Keller Library. Lake Worth Public Library: 13,884 volumes. Mansfield Public Library: 16,037 volumes. River Oaks Public Library: 18,000 volumes. Saginaw Public Library: 17,567 volumes. White

TARRANT (continued)

Settlement Library. **CHILD CARE** 1,601 day care and 239 twenty-four hour care licensed facilities. **HEALTH CARE** 1,505 physicians and 455 dentists. Hospitals: 22 with a combined capacity of 4,253. Specialized hospitals: two children's hospitals with a capacity of 169, one hospital for treatment of alcohol abuse with capacity of 34 and one Air Force Hospital with capacity of 115. Clinics: five outpatient clinics, four minor emergency centers, four for treatment of alcohol and drug abuse, two radiology clinics, two public health clinics, one osteopathic clinic, one obstetrical clinic, one children's clinic, one cancer clinic and one dialysis clinic. Ambulance services: twelve volunteer services, eleven fire departments, nine commercial, four funeral homes, three hospital-based and one air service. Mental health: six clinics, four centers with a capacity of 338 and one state school with a capacity of 555. Nursing homes: 57 nursing homes with a combined capacity of 6,372 nursing care and 18 custodial care residents. The average cost per day for private patients in 1982 was $32.57. **CHURCHES** 638 churches have an estimated combined membership of 429,742. The largest denominations are Southern Baptist, United Methodist and Catholic. **SOCIAL SERVICES** In fiscal year 1983 a total of $21,586,299 in food stamps was distributed, with an average of 42,756 persons receiving food stamps each month. Aid to Families with Dependent Children (AFDC) totaled $5,327,605 with an average of 3,596 families receiving AFDC each month. Medical assistance benefits for the aged and disabled of $46,337,645 and for families and children of $8,610,233 brought the county benefit total to $81,861,781. **FIRE PROTECTION** Three paid, eight partly paid and 29 volunteer fire departments. **LAW ENFORCEMENT** The County Sheriff has 219 commissioned officers. 62 police departments have a combined force of 2,200. Two colleges and one university have campus police departments with a combined force of 58 officers. **CRIME** 6,341 violent crimes (murder, forcible rape, robbery and aggravated assault) and 69,841 nonviolent crimes (burglary, larceny-theft and motor vehicle theft) were reported in 1982. **JUDICIAL SYSTEM** 17 District Courts and Judges, nine County Courts and Judges and eight Justices of the Peace. In the District Courts a total of 24,980 cases were pending on 1/1/82, 30,841 new cases were filed and 27,825 cases were disposed of during the year leaving 27,996 cases pending on 12/31/82. There were 9,328 criminal cases on the docket, 3,249 convictions, 1,105 persons committed to prison, 154 committed to jail and 4,592 cases left pending. In the County Courts 14,539 cases were pending on 1/1/82, 30,238 new cases were filed and 25,965 cases were disposed of during the year leaving 18,812 cases pending on 12/31/82. There were 34,548 criminal cases on the docket, 5,096 convictions, 102 persons committed to jail and 14,377 cases left pending. **JAILS** One jail, capacity 845. New jail under construction, capacity 525. **ATTORNEYS AT LAW** 1,823. **UTILITIES** 98% of the residents are connected to a public or privately owned water system and 94% are connected to a public sewer system. Natural gas is distributed to the county by Lone Star Gas Co., Division of Enserch. The average annual residential bill for natural gas in 1982 for the Lone Star distribution system was $405.91, an increase of 35% over 1981. Electricity is distributed to the county by Denton Co. Electric Coop. Inc., Johnson Co. Electric Coop. Inc., Tri Co. Electric Coop. Inc., Texas Electric Service Co. and Texas Power and Light Co. and is generated primarily by water. The typical residential electric bill is $154.69 per month for an all-electric house using 2,500 kwh. **TAXES** The county has 55 units with taxing authority: 17 school districts, 32 cities, one county and one utility district, one college district, one hospital district and two special districts.

RECREATION/ENTERTAINMENT

PROFESSIONAL SPORTS Arlington: Texas Rangers Baseball Team (Arlington Stadium). **NATIONAL REGISTER OF HISTORIC PLACES** Arlington vicinity: Marrow Bone Spring Archeological Site. Fort Worth: Neil P. Anderson Building, M.A. Benton House, Flatiron Building, Fort Worth Stockyards Historic District, Gulf, Colorado and Santa Fe Railroad Station, Knights of Pythias Building, Paddock Viaduct, Pollack-Capps House, Tarrant County Courthouse, Texas and Pacific Steam Locomotive 610, Texas and Pacific Steam Locomotive 610, Texas and Pacific Terminal Complex and Freight Buildings, Wharton-Scott House, Eddleman-McFarland House, Elizabeth Boulevard Historic District, Hotel Texas, W.T. Waggoner Building and Burk Burnett Building. **STATE** Eagle Mountain Lake State Recreation Area covers 401 acres and was closed to the public as of July 1983. **MUNICIPAL PARKS** 12,125 acres in 264 municipal parks. These parks contain 36 miles of hiking trails, 190 playgrounds, eight golf courses, 60 football and soccer fields, 160 baseball and softball fields, 145 tennis courts, 34 multi-use courts, 26 swimming pools, four beaches, 21 boat ramps and shore fishing facilities. Developed campsites: 34. **SCENIC DRIVES** The Texas Lakes Trail runs through this county. This trail introduces some 30 bluewater recreational areas in a variety of settings in north central Texas. **BOATING/FISHING** Lakes/reservoirs: Arlington (2,275 acres), Benbrook (3,770 acres), Cement Creek (100 acres), Eagle Mountain (5,602 acres), Grapevine (7,380 acres), Haywire #1 (24 acres), Haywire #2 (27 acres), Marine Creek (105 acres), Nutt (105 acres), TCWC (13 acres) and Worth (3,560 acres). Major rivers: Clear Fork Trinity and West Fork Trinity. Primary streams: Village, Cement, Denton, Silver, Marine and Deer. **HUNTING** Fall and winter seasons on deer. No closed season on nutria, squirrel, bobcat and coyote. Winter seasons on quail, muskrat, beaver, otter, opossum, mink, ring-tailed cat, badger, fox, raccoon, skunk and civet cat. In 1983 duck, coot, geese, woodcock and jacksnipe seasons occurred during the winter months. Teal duck, rail and gallinule seasons occurred in the fall. Mourning dove seasons occurred intermittently during the fall and winter months. **MUSEUMS** Arlington: University Art Gallery at the University of Texas-Arlington. Forth Worth: Amon Carter Museum of Western Art, Archaeology Museum, Southwestern Baptist Theological Seminary Museum, Fort Worth Art Museum, Fort Worth Museum of Science and History, Kimball Art Museum, The Western Company Museum, Museum of Aviation Group, Log Cabin Village, Pate Museum of Transportation, Texas Christian University Student Center Gallery and Thistle Hall. Grand Prairie: Texas Sports Hall of Fame. Grapevine: Grapevine Museum. Hurst: Heritage Room. **THEATERS** Fort Worth: Omni Theater, Casa Manana Theatre, William Edrington Scott Theatre, Greater Fort Worth Community Theatre and Will Rogers Memorial Coliseum Auditorium and Exhibit Buildings. **ORCHESTRAS** Fort Worth: Symphony Orchestra and Youth Orchestra of Greater Fort Worth. **OPERA** Fort Worth: Fort Worth Opera Association and Southwestern Opera Theater. **DANCE** Fort Worth: Ballet Concerto and Fort Worth Ballet. **BOTANIC GARDENS** Fort Worth: Botanic Garden. **ZOO** Fort Worth: Zoological Park. **AQUARIUM** Fort Worth: Aquarium. **PLANETARIUM** Arlington: The University of Texas at Arlington Planetarium. Fort Worth: Noble Planetarium. **OBSERVATORY** Fort Worth: Ames Observatory and Squaw Creek Valley Observatory. **COLLEGIATE FINE ARTS** Arlington: Cultural events offered by The University of Texas at Arlington. Fort Worth: cultural events offered by Fort Worth Christian College, Southwestern Baptist Theological Seminary, Tarrant County Junior College-South Camnpus, Texas Christian University and Texas Wesleyan College. Hurst: Cultural events offered by Tarrant County Junior College-Northeast Campus. **OTHER** Fort Worth: Texas Boys' Choir of Fort Worth and Texas Girls' Choir. **SPECIAL EVENTS** Southwestern Stock Show and Parade, Fort Worth, January; St. Patrick's Day Festivies and Parade, Fort

Worth, March; Mayfest, Fort Worth, May; Colonial National Golf Tourney, Fort Worth, May; Horse Shows, Haltom/Richland Hills, May; Cutting Horse Super Stakes, Fort Worth, May; Shakespeare in the Park, Fort Worth, June; Youth Rodeo, Halton/Richland Hills, June; Chisholm Trail Roundup, Fort Worth, June; Fourth of July Celebration, Halton/Richland Hills, July; Miss Texas Pageant, Fort Worth, July; July 4th Parade, Mansfield, July; Festival, Grapevine, July; 4th of July Celebration, Crowley, July; Good Ole Days Celebration, Saginaw, September; Pioneer Days, Fort Worth, September; Oktoberfest, Fort Worth, October; Christmas Parade and Tree Lighting, Grapevine, December; National Cutting Horse Futurity, Fort Worth, December.

COMMUNITIES

COUNTY SEAT Fort Worth, County Courthouse, 76102; County Clerk's Office, 817/334-1195. **INCORPORATED COMMUNITIES** (1980 population and ZIP Code) Arlington (160,113) 76010, Azle (5,822: 896 in Parker Co. and 4,926 in Tarrant Co.) 76020, Bedford (20,821) 76021, Benbrook (13,579) 76126, Blue Mound (2,169) 76131, Briar, (1,810: 819 in Tarrant Co. and 349 in Parker Co.) 76020, Burleson (11,734: 1,123 in Tarrant Co. and 10,611 in Johnson Co.) 76028, Colleyville (6,700) 76034, Crowley (5,852) 76036, Dalworthington Gardens (1,100) 76010, Edgecliff (2,695) 76134, Euless (24,002) 76039, Everman (5,387) 76140, Forest Hill (11,684) 76119, Fort Worth (385,164) 76101 All-America Cities Award 1964 and Honorable Mention 1980-1981, Grand Prairie (71,462: 5,731 in Tarrant Co., 65,726 in Dallas Co. and 5 in Ellis Co.) 75050, Grapevine (11,801: 39 in Dallas Co. and 11,762 in Tarrant Co.) 76051, Haltom City (29,014) 76117, Haslet (262) 76052, Hurst (31,420) 76053, Keller (4,156) 76248, Kennedale (2,594) 76060, Lakeside (957) 76108, Lakeworth (4,394) 76135, Mansfield (8,112: 8,080 in Tarrant Co. and 32 in Johnson Co.) 76063, North Richland Hills (30,592) 76118, Pantego (2,431: 76013, Richland Hills (7,977) 76118, River Oaks (6,890) 76114, Saginaw (5,736) 76179, Sansom Park Village (3,921) 76114, Southlake (2,808: 2,792 in Tarrant Co. and 16 in Denton Co.) 76051, Watauga (10,284) 76148, Westlake (214: 150 in Tarrant Co. and 64 in Denton Co.) 76248, Westover Hills (671) 76107, Westworth (3,651) 76114 and White Settlement (13,508) 76108. **UNINCORPORATED COMMUNITIES** (and ZIP Code) Avondale 76106, Bisbee 76063, Britton (also in Ellis Co.) 76063, Dido 76106, Eagle Mountain Acres 76060, Eagle Mountain 76135, Lakeview 76135, Linkwood Estates 76008, Minters Chapel 76051, Melody Hills 76111, Oaks 76114, Oak Grove 76028, Peden 76020, Pelican Bay 76020, Rendon 76028, Retta (also in Johnson Co.) 76028, St. Francis Village 76036, Southland Acres 76010, Sublett 76063, Webb 76010 and Wheatland 76116. **FOR ADDITIONAL LOCAL INFORMATION** Arlington Chamber of Commerce, P.O. Box 607, Arlington, 76010, 817/275-2613, Hurst-Euless-Bedford Chamber of Commerce, 1900 Airport Frwy., Bedford 76021, 817/283-1521, Colleyville Area Chamber of Commerce, 6610 Colleyville Blvd., Colleyville, 76034, 817/488-7148, Crowley Chamber of Commerce, P. O. Box 299, Crowley, 76036, 817/297-4211, Fort Worth Chamber of Commerce, 700 Throckmorton, Fort Worth, 76102, 817/336-2491, Fort Worth Hispanic Chamber of Commerce, 2315 N. Main, Suite 300, Fort Worth, 76106, 817/625-5411, Haltom-Richland Chamber of Commerce, P.O. Box 18518, Greater Richland, 76118, 817/281-9376, Greater Keller Chamber of Commerce, 217 N. Main, Keller 76248, 817/431-2169, Saginaw Chamber of Commerce, 201 N. Saginaw Blvd., Saginaw, 76179, 817/232-0050 and White Settlement Area Chamber of Commerce, P. O. Box 5461, White Settlement, 76108, 817/246-1121.

TAYLOR (P70)

THE LAND

Southwest of Fort Worth on Interstate Highway 20 in the Rolling Plains Region, Taylor County covers 917 square miles with the elevation ranging from 1,700 to 2,400 feet. The soils are reddish to brownish and light to very dark colored, with loamy surfaces and clayey subsoils. There are lime accumulations in most subsoils. In the Rolling Plains vegetation area the grasses are short to mid height with a few live oaks and mesquite. Between 41 and 50% of the land in the county is considered prime farmland. **CLIMATE** Subtropical Subhumid with wide-ranging daily temperature fluctuations and hot summers. The average annual temperature is 65 °F. Temperatures in January range from an average low of 31 ° to an average high of 57 °F and in July range from 72 ° to 96 °F. The average annual precipitation is 24 inches, with an average relative humidity of 74% at 6 A.M. and 43% at 6 P.M. The average annual snowfall is five inches. The growing season averages 229 days per year, with the last freeze near the end of March and the first freeze in mid November. The sun shines during the year on the average 69.5% of the daylight hours.

THE PEOPLE

Nearly 90% of the residents in Taylor County live in urban areas. The 1982 estimated population of 118,600 indicates a continuation of the moderate growth begun in the 1970s which reversed the slight population decline between 1960 and 1970. Rural areas grew much faster than urban areas from 1970 to 1980. The largest ancestry groups are persons of English descent (29%), Irish descent (21%) and German descent (16%). **REGISTERED VOTERS** As of November 2, 1982 there were 49,356 registered voters (.8% of the state total). The 1982 general election had a 56% voter turnout, compared to a 72% turnout in the 1980 general election. In the 1982 primary 90% voted Democratic and 10% Republican, with 10,299 votes cast.

THE ECONOMY

AGRICULTURE Wheat area. In 1982, 89% of the land was in farms and ranches, with 44% of the farmland under cultivation and 2% irrigated. Taylor ranked 55th in the state in highest agricultural receipts, with 67% from livestock and livestock products. Overgrazing, undesirable brush and weeds, water erosion and noxious weeds are the current conservation problems. Primary crops: wheat, sorghum, hay cotton and oats. Primary vegetables: sweet potatoes and watermelons. Primary fruits and nuts: peaches and pecans. Primary livestock and products: cattle, sheep, wool, angora goats, mohair and hogs. **BUSINESS** Total number of business establishments in the county: 3,150. Retail sales during the first quarter of 1984 increased by 14%. In 1980, 8% of the labor force were self-employed, 25% were employed in professional or related services, 11% in manufacturing, 25% in wholesale and retail trade, 8% in agriculture, forestry, fisheries and mining, 4% were employed in other counties and there were 8,948 retired workers. The industries with the most employment: agribusiness, oil and gas field services, general and heavy construction, meat packing, soft drink bottling and canning, commercial printing, petroleum refining and the manufacture of bakery products, men's clothing, metal cans, plumbing fittings and brass-goods, oil field machinery, metal working machinery, watches and clocks and aircraft equipment. The nonfarm earnings in 1981 totaled $1,251,210,000. The retired workers received an average monthly Social Security payment of $316.00. **FINANCE** On June 30, 1983, 12 commercial banks had total deposits of $1,449,369,000 and total assets of $1,750,611,000. On December 31, 1982 two state savings and loan associations and 15 state branches had assets of $156,402,627. In addition there is one credit union in the county. **HOUSING** Average value of

TAYLOR (continued)

homes in 1980: $33,600. Permits for new, privately owned housing units increased in 1982: 2,096 permits were issued with a total construction cost of $81,525,631. Of those permits, 748 were for single family houses. Housing permits in Abilene increased from 802 in 1981 to 2,063 in 1982 with 1,280 permits issued for apartments and condominiums. Between 1970 and 1980 the number of housing units increased by 23%. Eighty-seven percent of all units in the county are air-conditioned, 83% are heated by gas and 17% by electricity. **NATURAL RESOURCES** Dolomite, gypsum, limestone, industrial sand, sand and gravel, oil, gas, and bituminous coal. In 1982 a total of 295,339 thousand cubic feet of gas well gas, 4,541 barrels of condensate, 2,267,247 barrels of crude oil and 2,362,658 thousand cubic feet of casinghead gas were produced. Current production of other minerals and products includes brick, clay, crushed limestone, sand and gravel. **TOURISM** Travel expenditures of $90,558,000 in 1982 (an increase of 10% over 1981) generated 2,141 jobs and $18,620,000 in payroll. Lodging: 19 hotels, motels and tourist courts. Convention/meeting facilities: Abilene: Civic Center, Expo Center, McMurry College with two gyms and two hotels with facilities for large gatherings. **ALCOHOLIC BEVERAGES** Packaged distilled spirits, beer, ale, malt liquor and wine are legal in parts of the county. Sale of mixed beverages is legal in all or parts of the county. **MILITARY INSTALLATIONS** Dyess Air Force Base, Abilene, 5,826 personnel, 7,114 acres, 96th Bombardment Wing; Dyess Communications Annex, Tye, 20 acres, communications. **FEDERAL EXPENDITURES** The federal government had direct expenditures or obligations of $403,758,000 in the county during fiscal year 1983, including $254,362,000 by the U.S. Department of Defense. In addition, the federal government provided $6,677,000 in grant awards, paid $127,272,000 in salaries and wages, made direct payments to individuals of $128,141,000 including $95,055,000 in retirement and disability payments, awarded $139,830,000 in procurement contracts and spent $1,838,000 in other expenditures or obligations. The federal government also provided $2,634,000 in direct loans and $128,719,000 in guaranteed loans and insurance.

COMMUNICATION

Newspapers–Daily: Abilene Reporter-News, ave. morn. circ. 38,920 and eve. 16,123. Weekly: The Merkel Mail. Radio: KEAN-AM, KFMN-AM, KWKC-AM, KRBC-AM, KGNZ-FM, KORQ-FM, KEAN-FM Stereo, KFMN-FM Stereo (Abilene) and KMIO-AM (Merkel). Television: KRBC-CH. 9, KTAB-CH. 32 and KTXS-CH. 12 (Abilene). Cable TV. Telephone companies: Continental Telephone, Southwestern Bell and Taylor Telephone. **TRANSPORTATION** Total public road mileage: 1,617. In 1982 there were 107,328 registered vehicles and 4,305 reported traffic accidents including 26 fatalities. Taxi cabs: one company in Abilene. Municipal transit systems: one intracity bus system in Abilene, with scheduled routes. Intercity bus service is available. Motor freight: 37 local and intrastate carriers. Rail: four main and one branch line carry freight through the county. Two of the main lines carry annually 20 to 30 million tons of freight each and two carry 10 to 20 million each, with the one branch carrying less than one million. Aircraft: 252 are registered in the county. Airports: Abilene Municipal Airport serves as a base for 170 aircraft and is a short haul airport with air carrier service. Elmdale Airpark at Abilene.

COMMUNITY SERVICES

EDUCATION Five school districts with 25 elementary, nine middle, six high schools and three special education. The average daily attendance in 1981-82 was 18,445, with expenditures per pupil of $2,095 including 1,152 classroom teachers with an average

annual salary of $16,784. Forty-nine percent of the 1,147 high school graduates planned to attend college. In 1982-83, 72% of the students were White, 19% Hispanic, 8% Black, 1% Asian and 0.2% American Indian. Sports championships: 1983 AAAAA Boys' Golf Singles, Abilene H.S.; 1983 AAAAA Boys' Golf Team, Abilene H.S. Private schools: 759 students enrolled in three elementary and one high school. McMurry College is located in Abilene. Established in 1923 it is affiliated with the Methodist Church. Enrollment in 1982 was 1,494. The highest degree offered is Bachelor. Hardin-Simmons University is located in Abilene. Established in 1946 it is affiliated with the Southern Baptist Church. Enrollment in 1982 was 1,969 with in state undergraduate tuition and fees of $2,460 per semester. The highest degree offered is: Master. Abilene Christian University is located in Abilene. Established in 1906 it is an independent non profit institution. Enrollment in 1982 was 4,560 with in state undergraduate tuition and fees of $2,625 per semester. The highest degree offered is Master. Sports championships: (Lone Star Conference) 1983 Men's and Women's Cross Country; 1984 Womens' Basketball (tie with South West Texas State); 1983 Womens' Track. Vocational education: Abilene-Abilene Beauty College, American Commercial College, Hendrick Medical Center School of Radiography and School of Vocational Nursing, Stenograph Institute of Texas. **PUBLIC LIBRARIES** Abilene Public Library: 235,894 volumes and two branches. **CHILD CARE** 313 day care and 58 twenty-four hour care licensed facilities. **HEALTH CARE** 182 physicians and 64 dentists. Hospitals: two with a combined capacity of 579. Specialized hospitals: one air force hospital with capacity of 81. Clinics: one dialysis clinic and one public health clinic. Ambulance services: two commercial, one city and one volunteer fire department service. Mental health: four clinics and one state school with capacity of 1,214. Nursing homes: nine nursing homes with a combined capacity of 1,065 nursing care residents. The average cost per day for private patients in 1982 was $30.22. **CHURCHES** 146 churches have an estimated combined membership of 72,508. The largest denominations are Southern Baptist, Churches of Christ and United Methodist. **SOCIAL SERVICES** In fiscal year 1983 a total of $1,813,389 in food stamps was distributed, with an average of 3,962 persons receiving food stamps each month. Aid to Families with Dependent Children (AFDC) totaled $392,317 with an average of 259 families receiving AFDC each month. Medical assistance benefits for the aged and disabled of $6,713,643 and for families and children of $741,689 brought the county benefit total to $9,661,038. **FIRE PROTECTION** One paid and eight volunteer fire departments. **LAW ENFORCEMENT** The County Sheriff has 46 commissioned officers. Five police departments have a combined force of 156. Two universities have police departments with a combined force of 19 officers. Abilene Recreational Patrol has two officers. Abilene Municipal Airport police force has eight officers. **CRIME** 500 violent crimes (murder, forcible rape, robbery and aggravated assault) and 6,083 nonviolent crimes (burglary, larceny-theft and motor vehicle theft) were reported in 1982. **JUDICIAL SYSTEM** Three District Courts and Judges, two County Courts and Judges and five Justices of the Peace. In the District Courts a total of 3,779 cases were pending on 1/1/82, 3,751 new cases were filed and 3,216 cases were disposed of during the year leaving 4,314 cases pending on 12/31/82. There were 1,338 criminal cases on the docket, 576 convictions, 137 persons committed to prison and 109 committed to jail and 564 cases left pending. In the County Courts 8,524 cases were pending on 1/1/82, 5,054 new cases were filed and 3,360 cases were disposed of during the year leaving 10,218 cases pending on 12/31/82. There were 11,787 criminal cases on the docket, 1,115 convictions, 377 persons committed to jail, and 8,815 cases left pending. **JAILS** two jails, capacity 160. Constructing a new jail, capacity 250.

ATTORNEYS AT LAW 220. **UTILITIES** 97% of the residents are connected to a public or privately owned water system and 89% are connected to a public sewer system. Natural gas is distributed to the county by Lone Star Gas Co., Division of Enserch. The average annual residential bill for natural gas in 1982 for the Lone Star distribution system was $405.91, an increase of 35% over 1981. Electricity is distributed to the county by West Texas Utilities, Texas Power and Light Co. and Texas-New Mexico Power Co. and is generated primarily by gas, oil and coal. The typical residential electric bill is $145.78 per month for an all-electric house using 2,500 kwh. **TAXES** The county has 20 units with taxing authority: seven school districts, eight cities, one county and four special districts.

RECREATION/ENTERTAINMENT

NATIONAL REGISTER OF HISTORIC PLACES Abilene: U.S. Weather Bureau Building and Henry Sayles House. Buffalo Gap: Old Taylor County Courthouse and Jail. **STATE** Abilene State Recreation Area covers 621 acres with camping and trailer sites as well as swimming areas and hiking trails. **MUNICIPAL PARKS** 918 acres in 23 municipal parks. These parks contain 20 playgrounds, one golf course, two football and soccer fields, 19 baseball and softball fields, 18 tennis courts, two swimming pools, one beach and shore fishing facilities. Developed campsites: five. **SCENIC DRIVES** The Texas Forts Trail runs through this county. This trail leads to eight of the famous frontier forts of West Central Texas and an ancient presidio of the Spanish colonial period. **BOATING/FISHING** Lakes/reservoirs: Abilene (595 acres), Graham (95 acres), Jim Ned Creek Soil Conservation Service Lakes 12A and 19 (25 acres), Kirby (740 acres), Lawn (36 acres) and Lytle (106 acres). Primary streams: Elm, Bulger, Camp, Buffalo, Cedar, Red Bank and Lytle. **HUNTING** Fall and winter seasons on deer and javelina. No closed season on squirrel, bobcat and coyote. Winter season on quail, muskrat, beaver, opossum, ring-tailed cat, badger, fox, weasel, raccoon, skunk and civet cat. Fall, winter and spring seasons on turkey. In 1983 duck, coot, geese, woodcock and jacksnipe seasons occurred with a winter season on sandhill crane in some parts of the county. Teal duck, rail and gallinule seasons occurred in the fall. Mourning dove seasons occurred intermittently during the fall and winter months. **MUSEUMS** Abilene: Abilene Fine Arts Museum. Buffalo Gap: Taylor County Courthouse and Old Jail. **THEATERS** Abilene: Abilene Civic Center, Abilene Civic Theatre, Abilene Community Theatre, Teens and Children of Abilene Civic Theatre. **ORCHESTRAS** Abilene: Abilene Philharmonic Orchestra. **DANCE** Abilene: Abilene Metropolitan Ballet and Abilene Civic Ballet. **ZOO** Abilene: Nelson Park Zoo. **COLLEGIATE FINE ARTS** Abilene: Cultural events offered by Abilene Christian University, Hardin-Simmons University and McMurry College. **SPECIAL EVENTS** Parks and Beck Calf Roping, Abilene, March; Gun Show, Abilene, March; West Texas Arts and Crafts Show, Abilene, April; Junior Rodeo, Abilene, April; Marathon of the Great Southwest, Abilene, April; West Texas Barrel Racing Contest, Abilene, April; Intercollegiate Rodeo, Abilene, April; 4-H Rodeo, Abilene, June; Fun Day, Merkel, July; West Texas Fair and Rodeo, Abilene, September; Chili Super Bowl, Buffalo Gap, September; Lone Star Circuit Finals Rodeo, Abilene, November; Parks and Beck Calf Roping, Abilene, December.

COMMUNITIES

COUNTY SEAT Abilene, County Courthouse, 79602; County Clerk's Office, 915/677-1711. **INCORPORATED COMMUNITIES** (1980 population and ZIP Code) Abilene (98,315: 97,812 in Taylor Co. and 503 in Jones Co.) 79601, Buffalo Gap (387) 79508, Impact (54) 79603, Lawn (390) 79530, Merkel (2,493) 79536, Trent (313) 79561, Tuscola (660) 79562 and Tye (1,394)

79563. **UNINCORPORATED COMMUNITIES** (and ZIP Code) Blair 79536, Bradshaw 79567, Caps 79605, Elmdale 79605, Hamby 79601, Happy Valley 79566, Ovalo 79541, Potosi 79601, Shep 79566 and View 79564. **FOR ADDITIONAL LOCAL INFORMATION** Abilene Chamber of Commerce, P.O. Box 539, Abilene, 79604, 915/677-7241 and Merkel Chamber of Commerce, P.O. Box 536, Merkel, 79536, 915/928-5722.

TERRELL (B7)

THE LAND

Bordering Mexico south of Odessa on U.S. Highways 90 and 285 in the Edwards Plateau Region, Terrell County covers 2,357 square miles with the elevation ranging from 1,300 to 4,000 feet. The loamy soils are undulating to hilly with limestone near the surface. Nearly 80% of the area has exposed rock. In the Edwards Plateau vegetation area, the grasses are tall to mid height with live and shinnery oaks, mesquite and some cacti. Less than 1% of the land in the county is considered prime farmland. **CLIMATE** Subtropical Arid with wide-ranging daily temperatures. The average annual temperature is 66°F. Temperatures in January range from an average low of 34° to an average high of 62°F and in July range from 71° to 97°F. The average annual precipitation is 15 inches, with an average relative humidity of 73% at 6 A.M. and 36% at 6 P.M. The average annual snowfall is less than one inch. The growing season averages 237 days per year, with the last freeze near March 21st and the first freeze in mid November. The sun shines during the year on the average 75% of the daylight hours.

THE PEOPLE

Terrell County is one of the most sparsely populated in the state and ranks 57th among all U.S. counties in the highest percent of persons of Spanish origin. The 1982 estimated population of 1,500 reflects a slight population decline since 1980. The county's population declined between 1950 and 1980 with an 18% loss between 1970 and 1980. The majority of county residents live in rural areas. The age groups with the largest reduction between 1970 and 1980 were ages 50 to 54 and five and 14. The largest ancestry groups are Hispanic (43%), persons of Irish descent (17%), English descent (16%) and German descent (11%). **REGISTERED VOTERS** As of November 2, 1982 there were 1,025 registered voters (0.01% of the state total). The 1982 general election had a 57% voter turnout, compared to a 70% turnout in the 1980 general election. In the 1982 primary 100% voted Democratic, with 533 votes cast.

THE ECONOMY

AGRICULTURE Sheep and angora goat ranches. In 1982, 89% of the land was in farms and ranches. Terrell ranked 223rd in the state in highest agricultural receipts, with 100% from livestock and livestock products. Overgrazing, undesirable brush and weeds and water erosion are the current conservation problems. Primary fruits and nuts: pecans. Primary livestock and products: fifth in the state for angora goats and mohair production, sixth for sheep and eighth for wool production. Cattle. **BUSINESS** Total number of business establishments in the county: 22. In 1980, 15% of the labor force were self-employed, 13% were employed in professional or related services, 1% in manufacturing, 19% in wholesale and retail trade, 27% in transportation, communications and other public utilities, 14% were employed in other counties and there were 130 retired workers. The industry with the most employment is agribusiness. The nonfarm earnings in 1981 totaled $13,214,000. The retired workers received an average monthly Social Security payment of $277.00. **FINANCE** On June 30, 1983, one commercial bank had total deposits of $13,752,000

COUNTIES

TERRELL (continued)

and total assets of $15,387,000. There is one state savings and loan association branch in the county. **HOUSING** Average value of homes in 1980: $18,900. Between 1970 and 1980 the number of housing units increased by 11%. Fifty-two percent of all units in the county are air-conditioned, 92% are heated by gas and 7% by electricity. **NATURAL RESOURCES** Limestone, salt, oil and gas. In 1982 a total of 31,015,931 thousand cubic feet of gas well gas, 18,397 barrels of condensate, 47,330 barrels of crude oil and 398,170 thousand cubic feet of casinghead gas were produced. Current production of other minerals and products includes fieldstone and sandstone. **TOURISM** Travel expenditures of $1,576,000 in 1982 (an increase of 11% over 1981) generated 41 jobs and $320,000 in payroll. **ALCOHOLIC BEVERAGES** Packaged distilled spirits, beer, ale, malt liquor and wine are legal. **FEDERAL EXPENDITURES** The federal government had direct expenditures or obligations of $6,306,000 in the county during fiscal year 1983, including $53,000 by the U.S. Department of Defense. In addition, the federal government provided $33,000 in grant awards, paid $368,000 in salaries and wages, made direct payments to individuals of $2,464,000 including $1,757,000 in retirement and disability payments, awarded $2,213,000 in procurement contracts and spent $1,227,000 in other expenditures or obligations. The federal government also provided $95,000 in guaranteed loans and insurance.

COMMUNICATION
Newspapers–Weekly: Sanderson Times. Cable TV. Telephone companies: Southwestern Bell and Big Bend Telephone. **TRANSPORTATION** Total public road mileage: 288. In 1982 there were 1,632 registered vehicles and 41 reported traffic accidents. Intercity bus service is available. Motor freight: two carriers. Rail: the Sunset Limited provides passenger service on the Amtrak route. One main line carries annually over 30 million tons of freight through the county. Aircraft: seven are registered in the county. Airports: Terrel County Airport at Dryden.

COMMUNITY SERVICES
EDUCATION One school district with one elementary, one middle and one high school. The average daily attendance in 1981-82 was 334, with expenditures per pupil of $4,623 including 28 classroom teachers with an average annual salary of $16,816. Fifty-five percent of the 31 high school graduates planned to attend college. In 1982-83, 49% of the students were White, 51% Hispanic. **PUBLIC LIBRARIES** Sanderson Library. **HEALTH CARE** Ambulance services: one county service. **CHURCHES** Seven churches have an estimated combined membership of 1,478. The largest denominations are Catholic and Southern Baptist. **SOCIAL SERVICES** In fiscal year 1983 a total of $33,206 in food stamps was distributed, with an average of 80 persons receiving food stamps each month. Aid to Families with Dependent Children (AFDC) totaled $2,382. Medical assistance benefits for the aged and disabled of $46,283 and for families and children of $1,617 brought the county benefit total to $83,488. **FIRE PROTECTION** One volunteer fire department. **LAW ENFORCEMENT** The County Sheriff has three commissioned officers. **CRIME** One violent crime (murder, forcible rape, robbery and aggravated assault) and nine nonviolent crimes (burglary, larceny-theft and motor vehicle theft) were reported in 1982. **JUDICIAL SYSTEM** One District Court and Judge, one County Court and Judge and four Justices of the Peace. In the District Courts a total of 40 cases were pending on 1/1/82, 16 new cases were filed and 34 cases were disposed of during the year leaving 22 cases pending on 12/31/82. There were four criminal cases on the docket, one conviction, one person committed to prison and one

case left pending. In the County Courts 31 cases were pending on 1/1/82, 43 new cases were filed and 37 cases were disposed of during the year leaving 37 cases pending on 12/31/82. There were 63 criminal cases on the docket, 26 convictions, three persons committed to jail, and 27 cases left pending. **JAILS** One jail, capacity 10, the new jail was opened in 1983. **ATTORNEYS AT LAW** Two. **UTILITIES** 81% of the residents are connected to a public or privately owned water system and 5% are connected to a public sewer system. Electricity is distributed to the county by Texas-New Mexico Power Co. and Rio Grande Electric Coop., Inc. and is generated primarily by gas, oil and coal. **TAXES** The county has two units with taxing authority: one school district and one county.

RECREATION/ENTERTAINMENT
FEDERAL Rio Grande Wild and Scenic River (See Brewster County). **NATIONAL REGISTER OF HISTORIC PLACES** Dryden vicinity: Bullis Camp Site and Meyers Spring. Sanderson vicinity: Geddis Canyon Rock Art Site. **COUNTY PARKS** Two acres in one county and park. This park contains one playground and one swimming pool. **SCENIC DRIVES** The Texas Pecos Trail runs through this county. This trail rambles through the vast region of Southwest and West Texas with landscapes varying from raw, arid regions to green valleys. **BOATING/FISHING** Major rivers: Rio Grande and Pecos. Primary streams: Indian, Dry and Independence. **HUNTING** Fall season on antelope. No closed season on nutria, elk, javelina, squirrel, bobcat and coyote. Fall and winter seasons on deer and mule deer. Winter seasons on quail, muskrat, beaver, otter, opossum, mink, ring-tailed cat, badger, fox, raccoon, skunk and civet cat. Fall, winter and spring seasons on turkey. In 1983 sandhill crane, duck, coot, geese, woodcock, and jacksnipe seasons occurred during the winter months. Teal duck, rail and gallinule seasons occurred intermittently during the fall and winter months with a fall season on white-winged dove. **SPECIAL EVENTS** Rodeo, Sanderson, April/May; Street Dance, Sanderson, July; Terrell County Fair, Sanderson, December.

COMMUNITIES
COUNTY SEAT Sanderson, County Courthouse, 79848; County Clerk's Office, 915/345-2391. **UNINCORPORATED COMMUNITIES** (and ZIP Code) Dryden 78851 and Sanderson (est.) 79848.

TERRY (P48)

THE LAND
Southwest of Lubbock on U.S. Highways 385 and 380 in the High Plains region, Terry County covers 886 square miles with the elevation ranging from 3,200 to 3,600 feet. The nearly level soils are light colored with loamy surfaces and very deep, reddish, clayey subsoils. In some areas the soils are sandy thoughout. Along the northern border the soils are darker with loamy surfaces and clayey subsoils and limestone. In the High Plains vegetation area the principal grasses are buffalograss and blue grama, with brushy plants such as mesquite, shinnery oak and sage brush. Between 1 and 10% of the land in the county is considered prime farmland. **CLIMATE** Continental Steppe with wide-ranging daily temperatures. During spring duststorms and thunderstorms will be experienced. The average annual temperature is 60 °F. Temperatures in January range from an average low of 24° to an average high of 55 °F and in July range from 65° to 93 °F. The average annual precipitation is 17 inches, with an average relative humidity of 69% at 6 A.M. and 35% at 6 P.M. The average annual snowfall is ten inches. The growing season averages 208 days per year, with the last freeze near April 10th

and the first freeze in early November. The sun shines during the year on the average 76% of the daylight hours.

THE PEOPLE

After a brief period of decline, the population of Terry County is beginning to grow. The 1982 estimated population of 15,100 indicates a continuation of that growth begun in the 1970s. Urban areas gained in population from 1970 to 1980 while rural areas had losses. The population's median age rose form 25 in 1970 to 28 in 1980. The largest ancestry groups are Hispanic (34%), persons of English descent (20%) and Irish descent (15%). **REGISTERED VOTERS** As of November 2, 1982 there were 7,322 registered voters (0.1% of the state total). The 1982 general election had a 47% voter turnout, compared to a 68% turnout in the 1980 general election. In the 1982 primary 95% voted Democratic and 5% Republican, with 1,941 votes cast.

THE ECONOMY

AGRICULTURE Cotton area. In 1982, 96% of the land was in farms and ranches, with 84% of the farmland under cultivation and 25% irrigated. Terry ranked 18th in the state in highest agricultural receipts, with 98% from crops. Undesirable brush, wind erosion, decreasing irrigation water supplies, soil compaction and noxious weeds are the current conservation problems. Primary crops: third in the state for cotton. Sorghum, wheat and cowpeas. Primary vegetables: watermelons. Primary fruits and nuts: pecans. Primary livestock and products: cattle and hogs. **BUSINESS** Total number of business establishments in the county: 303. Retail sales during the first quarter of 1984 increased by 29%. In 1980, 16% of the labor force were self-employed, 18% were employed in professional or related services, 5% in manufacturing, 22% in wholesale and retail trade, 26% in agriculture, forestry, fisheries and mining, 7% were employed in other counties and there were 1,012 retired workers. The industries with the most employment: oil and gas extraction, heavy construction, agribusiness and the manufacture of sheet metal and oil field machinery. The nonfarm earnings in 1981 totaled $125,724,000. The retired workers received an average monthly Social Security payment of $316.00. **FINANCE** On June 30, 1983, two commercial banks had total deposits of $94,558,000 and total assets of $105,815,000. On December 31, 1982 one state savings and loan association and one federal association branch had assets of $50,071,216. In addition there is one credit union in the county. **HOUSING** Average value of homes in 1980: $26,800. Permits for new, privately owned housing units decreased in 1982: 15 permits were issued with a total construction cost of $831,500. Of those permits, 13 were for single family houses. Between 1970 and 1980 the number of housing units increased by 13%. Eighty percent of all units in the county are air-conditioned, 91% are heated by gas and 8% by electricity. **NATURAL RESOURCES** Caliche, potash, oil and gas. In 1982 a total of 1,842,433 thousand cubic feet of gas well gas, 14,262,852 barrels of crude oil and 3,626,920 thousand cubic feet of casinghead gas were produced. Current production of other minerals and products includes sodium sulfate. **TOURISM** Travel expenditures of $6,676,000 in 1982 (an increase of 18% over 1981) generated 87 jobs and $951,000 in payroll. **ALCOHOLIC BEVERAGES** Totally dry. **MILITARY INSTALLATIONS** Reese Auxiliary Air Field, Brownfield, 520 acres, Auxiliary Training Field. **FEDERAL EXPENDITURES** The federal government had direct expenditures or obligations of $39,845,000 in the county during fiscal year 1983, including $311,000 by the U.S. Department of Defense. In addition, the federal government provided $916,000 in grant awards, paid $945,000 in salaries and wages, made direct payments to individuals of $15,101,000 including $11,303,000 in retirement and disability payments, awarded $16,000 in procurement contracts and spent $22,867,000 in other

expenditures or obligations. The federal government also provided $11,351,000 in direct loans and $33,092,000 in guaranteed loans and insurance.

COMMUNICATION

Newspapers–Weekly: Country Press (Brownfield) and the Brownfield News. Radio: KKUB-AM (Brownfield). Cable TV. Telephone companies: General Telephone and Poka-Lambro Rural Telephone Coop. **TRANSPORTATION** Total public road mileage: 1,315. In 1982 there were 15,330 registered vehicles and 333 reported traffic accidents including six fatalities. Intercity bus service is available. Motor freight: eight local and intrastate carriers. Rail: one branch line carries annually less than one million tons of freight through the county. Aircraft: 41 are registered in the county. Airports: Terry County Airport at Brownfield serves as a base for 32 aircraft and is a general utility airport with general aviation service.

COMMUNITY SERVICES

EDUCATION Four school districts with six elementary, one middle and four high schools. The average daily attendance in 1981-82 was 2,959, with expenditures per pupil of $3,242 including 242 classroom teachers with an average annual salary of $17,237. Forty-nine percent of the 166 high school graduates planned to attend college. In 1982-83, 45% of the students were White, 50% Hispanic and 5% Black. **PUBLIC LIBRARIES** Kendrick Memorial Library (Brownfield): 26,008 volumes. **CHILD CARE** 33 day care and three twenty-four hour care licensed facilities. **HEALTH CARE** Nine physicians and three dentists. Hospitals: one with a capacity of 97. Clinics: one public health clinic. Ambulance services: one police department service. Mental health: one county clinic. Nursing homes: two nursing homes with a combined capacity of 170 nursing care residents. The average cost per day for private patients in 1982 was $29.34. **CHURCHES** 35 churches have an estimated combined membership of 10,791. The largest denominations are Southern Baptist, Catholic and United Methodist. **SOCIAL SERVICES** In fiscal year 1983 a total of $1,041,192 in food stamps was distributed, with an average of 2,114 persons receiving food stamps each month. Aid to Families with Dependent Children (AFDC) totaled $195,229 with an average of 131 families receiving AFDC each month. Medical assistance benefits for the aged and disabled of $983,710 and for families and children of $264,665 brought the county benefit total to $2,484,796. **FIRE PROTECTION** One paid and one volunteer fire department. **LAW ENFORCEMENT** The County Sheriff has 24 commissioned officers. One police department has a force of 32. **CRIME** 91 violent crimes (murder, forcible rape, robbery and aggravated assault) and 875 nonviolent crimes (burglary, larceny-theft and motor vehicle theft) were reported in 1982. **JUDICIAL SYSTEM** One District Court and Judge, one County Court and Judge and one Justice of the Peace. In the District Court a total of 519 cases were pending on 1/1/82, 394 new cases were filed and 404 cases were disposed of during the year leaving 509 cases pending on 12/31/82. There were 211 criminal cases on the docket, 76 convictions, 19 persons committed to prison and one committed to jail and 71 cases left pending. In the County Court 135 cases were pending on 1/1/82, 305 new cases were filed and 323 cases were disposed of during the year leaving 117 cases pending on 12/31/82. There were 385 criminal cases on the docket, 138 convictions, one person committed to jail, and 100 cases left pending. **JAILS** One jail, capacity 15. **ATTORNEYS AT LAW** 14. **UTILITIES** 81% of the residents are connected to a public or privately owned water system and 76% are connected to a public sewer system. Natural gas is distributed to the county by Energas Company. The average annual residential bill for natural gas in 1982 for the Energas distribution system was $371.63, an increase of 23% over 1981.

TERRY (continued)

Electricity is distributed to the city of Brownfield by Brownfield Municipal Light and Power Plant and to the rest of the county by Lyntegar Electric Coop., Inc. and is generated primarily by oil and gas. The typical residential electric bill is $148.00 per month for an all-electric house using 2,500 kwh. **TAXES** The county has eight units with taxing authority: four school districts, two cities, one county and one hospital district.

RECREATION/ENTERTAINMENT
COUNTY/MUNICIPAL PARKS 149 acres in seven county and two municipal parks. These parks contain eight playgrounds, one baseball and softball field, four tennis courts and two swimming pools. Developed campsites: seven. **BOATING/FISHING** Lakes/reservoirs: Mound (800 acres) and Rich (500 acres). **HUNTING** Fall season on antelope and prairie chicken. No closed season on squirrel, coyote and bobcat. Winter seasons on quail, muskrat, beaver, opossum, ring-tailed cat, badger, fox, weasel, raccoon, skunk and civet cat. In 1983 sandhill crane, duck, coot, geese, woodcock and jacksnipe seasons occurred during the winter months. Teal duck, rail and gallinule seasons occurred in the fall. Mourning dove seasons occurred intermittently during the fall and winter months. **MUSEUMS** Brownfield: Terry County Heritage Museum. **SPECIAL EVENTS** Country/Western Night, Meadow, April; Spring Art Show, Brownfield, April; Country/Western/Bluegrass/Gospel Extravaganza, Meadow, June; County Rodeo and Parade, Brownsfield, July; Pioneer Reunion, Brownfield, August; County Fair, Brownfield, October; Christmas Homes Tour, Brownfield, December.

COMMUNITIES
COUNTY SEAT Brownfield, County Courthouse, 79316; County Clerk's Office, 806/637-8551. **INCORPORATED COMMUNITIES** (1980 population and ZIP Code) Brownfield (10,387) 79316, Meadow (571) 79345 and Wellman (239) 79378. **UNINCORPORATED COMMUNITIES** (and ZIP Code) Foster (Forrester) 79316, Gomez 79316, Johnson 79316, Needmore 79345, Tokio 79376 and Union 79316. **FOR ADDITIONAL LOCAL INFORMATION** Brownfield Chamber of Commerce, P. O. Box 152, 221 Lubbock Rd., Brownfield, 79316, 806/637-2564.

THROCKMORTON (P54)

THE LAND
Northeast of Abilene on U.S. Highways 283 and 380 in the Rolling Plains region, Throckmorton County covers 912 square miles with the elevation ranging from 1,200 to 1,800 feet. The very dark loamy soils have lime accumulations in the subsoils. In the southeast, northeast and northwest the soils are lighter in color with clayey subsoils. In the Rolling Plains vegetation area the grasses are bluestems, gramas, wildryes and wheatgrass, with some mesquite trees. Between 21 and 30% of the land in the county is considered prime farmland. **CLIMATE** Subtropical Subhumid with wide-ranging daily temperatures and hot summers. The average annual temperature is 64 °F. Temperatures in January range from an average low of 28° to an average high of 55 °F and in July range from 72° to 98 °F. The average annual precipitation is 26 inches, with an average relative humidity of 75% at 6 A.M. and 45% at 6 P.M. The average annual snowfall is six inches. The growing season averages 225 days per year, with the last freeze the last of March and the first freeze in early November. The sun shines during the year on the average 69% of the daylight hours.

THE PEOPLE
Throckmorton County ranks 26th among U.S. counties in highest percent of residents over age 64. The 1982 estimated population of 2,200 indicates a slight increase in the population for the first time since 1930. The majority of the county residents live in rural areas. From 1970 to 1980 the age groups with the largest losses were ages 65 and over, 55 to 64 and 10 to 19. The county's population is older than average with a median age of 43. The largest ancestry groups are persons of English descent (37%) and Irish descent (30%). **REGISTERED VOTERS** As of November 2, 1982 there were 1,432 registered voters (0.02% of the state total). The 1982 general election had a 49% voter turnout, compared to a 61% turnout in the 1980 general election. In the 1982 primary 100% voted Democratic with 618 votes cast.

THE ECONOMY
AGRICULTURE Wheat area. In 1982, 93% of the land was in farms and ranches, with 20% of the farmland under cultivation and 3% irrigated. Throckmorton ranked 169th in the state in highest agricultural receipts, with 58% from livestock and livestock products. Overgrazing, undesirable brush and weeds, water erosion, inefficient tillage system and difficulties in grass establishment are the current conservation problems. Primary crops: wheat, cotton, hay, oats and sorghum. Primary fruits and nuts: peaches and pecans. Primary livestock and products: cattle. **BUSINESS** Total number of business establishments in the county: 63. Retail sales during the first quarter of 1984 increased by 12%. In 1980, 30% of the labor force were self-employed, 17% were employed in professional or related services, 11% in manufacturing, 11% in wholesale and retail trade, 35% in agriculture, forestry, fisheries and mining, 12% were employed in other counties and there were 333 retired workers. The industries with the most employment: oil and gas extraction and agribusiness. The nonfarm earnings in 1981 totaled $19,968,000. The retired workers received an average monthly Social Security payment of $294.00. **FINANCE** On June 30, 1983, two commercial banks had total deposits of $19,169,000 and total assets of $22,032,000. There are two state savings and loan association branches in the county. **HOUSING** Average value of homes in 1980: $16,900. Between 1970 and 1980 the number of housing units increased by 6%. Seventy-six percent of all units in the county are air-conditioned, 88% are heated by gas and 6% by electricity. **NATURAL RESOURCES** Limestone, sand and gravel, oil, gas and bituminous coal. In 1982 a total of 520,063 thousand cubic feet of gas well gas, 12,528 barrels of condensate, 1,778,477 barrels of crude oil and 2,196,741 thousand cubic feet of casinghead gas were produced. Current production of other minerals and products includes sand and gravel. **TOURISM** Travel expenditures of $145,000 in 1982 (an increase of 8% over 1981) generated 4 jobs and $28,000 in payroll. **ALCOHOLIC BEVERAGES** Totally dry. **FEDERAL EXPENDITURES** The federal government had direct expenditures or obligations of $5,982,000 in the county during fiscal year 1983, including $156,000 by the U.S. Department of Defense. In addition, the federal government provided $405,000 in grant awards, paid $250,000 in salaries and wages, made direct payments to individuals of $4,645,000 including $2,914,000 in retirement and disability payments, awarded $1,000 in procurement contracts and spent $681,000 in other expenditures or obligations. The federal government also provided $2,546,000 in direct loans and $558,000 in guaranteed loans and insurance.

COMMUNICATION
Newspapers–Weekly: Throckmorton Tribune. Cable TV. Telephone companies: General Telephone, Southwestern Bell and Brazos Telephone Coop. **TRANSPORTATION** Total public road mileage: 480. In 1982 there were 2,604 registered vehicles and

30 reported traffic accidents. Motor freight: two carriers. Aircraft: three are registered in the county. Airports: Throckmorton Municipal Airport.

COMMUNITY SERVICES

EDUCATION Two school districts with two elementary and two high schools. The average daily attendance in 1981-82 was 370, with expenditures per pupil of $3,363 including 28 classroom teachers with an average annual salary of $15,149. Sixty-nine percent of the 29 high school graduates planned to attend college. In 1982-83, 89% of the students were White and 11% Hispanic. **CHILD CARE** Four day care licensed facilities. **HEALTH CARE** One physician. Hospitals: one with a combined capacity of 30. Ambulance services: one hospital-based service. Nursing homes: one nursing home has a capacity of 58 nursing care residents. The average cost per day for private patients in 1982 was $32,61. **CHURCHES** 19 churches have an estimated combined membership of 2,574. The largest denominations is Southern Baptist. **SOCIAL SERVICES** In fiscal year 1983 a total of $51,500 in food stamps was distributed, with an average of 115 persons receiving food stamps each month. Aid to Families with Dependent Children (AFDC) totaled $5,741. Medical assistance benefits for the aged and disabled of $250,675 and for families and children of $3,696 brought the county benefit total to $311,612. **FIRE PROTECTION** Two volunteer fire departments. **LAW ENFORCEMENT** The County Sheriff has three commissioned officers. **CRIME** One violent crime (murder, forcible rape, robbery and aggravated assault) and 15 nonviolent crimes (burglary, larceny-theft and motor vehicle theft) were reported in 1982. **JUDICIAL SYSTEM** One District Court and Judge, one County Court and Judge and one Justice of the Peace. In the District Court a total of 219 cases were pending on 1/1/82, 53 new cases were filed and 64 cases were disposed of during the year leaving 208 cases pending on 12/31/82. There were 11 criminal cases on the docket and 11 cases left pending. In the County Court 241 cases were pending on 1/1/82, 22 new cases were filed and one case was disposed of during the year leaving 262 cases pending on 12/31/82. There were 190 criminal cases on the docket and 190 cases left pending. **ATTORNEYS AT LAW** Two. **UTILITIES** 66% of the residents are connected to a public or privately owned water system and 48% are connected to a public sewer system. Natural gas is distributed to the county by Alliance Gas Corporation. Electricity is distributed to the county by West Texas Utilities, Stamford Electric Coop., Inc., B-K Electric Coop., Inc. and Fork Belknap Electric Corp. and is generated primarily by gas, oil and water. **TAXES** The county has five units with taxing authority: two school districts, two cities and one county.

RECREATION/ENTERTAINMENT

NATIONAL REGISTER OF HISTORIC PLACES Throckmorton: Throckmorton County Courthouse and Jail. **MUNICIPAL PARKS** 13 acres in two municipal parks. These parks contain two playgrounds, one baseball and softball field, one swimming pool and one boat ramp. **SCENIC DRIVES** The Texas Forts Trail runs through this county. This trail leads to eight of the famous frontier forts of West Central Texas and an ancient presidio of the Spanish colonial period. **BOATING/FISHING** Lakes/reservoirs: Big Wolf Tank (24 acres), Elm Creek (50 acres), Throckmorton (120 acres) and Woodson (114 acres). Major rivers: Clear Fork Brazos and Brazos. Primary streams: Wolf, North Elm, Elm, Kings and Paint. **HUNTING** Fall and winter seasons on deer. No closed seasons on squirrel, bobcat and coytoe. Winter seasons on quail, muskrat, beaver, opossum, ring-tailed cat, badger, fox, weasel, raccoon, skunk and civet cat. Fall, winter and spring seasons on turkey. In 1983 duck, coot, geese, woodcock and jacksnipe seasons occurred during the winter months with winter season on sandhill crane in some parts of the county. Teal duck, rail and gallinule seasons occurred in the fall. Mourning dove seasons occurred intermittently during the fall and winter months. **SPECIAL EVENTS** Easter Egg Hunt and Festivities, Throckmorton, March/April; Pioneer Days, Throckmorton, June; Christmas Parade, Throckmorton, December.

COMMUNITIES

COUNTY SEAT Throckmorton, County Courthouse, 76083; County Clerk's Office, 817/849-2501. **INCORPORATED COMMUNITIES** (1980 population and ZIP Code) Throckmoreton (1,174) 76083 and Woodson (291) 76091. **UNINCORPORATED COMMUNITIES** (and ZIP Code) Elbert 76359, Lusk 76091 and Spring Creek 76370. **FOR ADDITIONAL LOCAL INFORMATION** Throckmorton Chamber of Commerce, P. O. Box 711, Throckmorton, 76083.

TITUS (E7)

THE LAND

Southwest of Texarkana on Interstate Highway 30 in the East Texas Timberlands Region, Titus County covers 412 square miles with the elevation ranging from 275 to 450 feet. The gently rolling to hilly soils are light colored and loamy with very deep reddish, clayey subsoils. Along the northern border and in the southeastern corner the surface layers are sandy. In the Post Oak Savannah vegetation area there are tall grasses with post and blackjack oaks, elms, pecans and walnuts along streams. Between 21 and 30% of the land in the county is considered prime farmland. **CLIMATE** Subtropical Humid with warm summers. The average annual temperature is 63 °F. Temperatures in January range from an average low of 30° to an average high of 53 °F and in July range from 70° to 94 °F. The average annual precipitation is 45 inches, with an average relative humidity of 83% at 6 A.M. and 58% at 6 P.M. The average annual snowfall is two inches. The growing season averages 236 days per year, with the last freeze in late March and the first freeze in early November. The sun shines during the year on the average 67% of the daylight hours.

THE PEOPLE

The population in Titus County began growing in 1970 after 30 years of decline. The 1982 estimated population of 22,300 indicates a continuation of that growth. Rural areas grew slightly faster than urban areas between 1970 and 1980. The age groups with the largest gains were birth to five years and ages 20 to 34, The median age lowered from 36 in 1970 to 32 in 1980. The largest ancestry groups are persons of English descent (31%), Irish descent (18%) and Black (14%). **REGISTERED VOTERS** As of November 2, 1982 there were 11,143 registered voters (0.2% of the state total). The 1982 general election had a 55% voter turnout, compared to a 61% turnout in the 1980 general election. In the 1982 primary 98% voted Democratic and 2% Republican, with 4,953 votes cast.

THE ECONOMY

AGRICULTURE Forest production area. In 1982, 67% of the land was in farms and ranches, with 16% of the farmland under cultivation and 4% irrigated. Titus ranked 128th in the state in highest agricultural receipts, with 94% from livestock and livestock products. Overgrazing, water erosion and improper woodland management are the current conservation problems. Primary crops: hay, wheat and sorghum. Primary vegetables: watermelons. Primary fruits and nuts: peaches and pecans. Primary livestock and products: seventh in the state for

TITUS (continued)

commercial broiler production. Cattle and milk. **BUSINESS** Total number of business establishments in the county: 514. Retail sales during the first quarter of 1984 increased by 18%. In 1980, 12% of the labor force were self-employed, 14% were employed in professional or related services, 19% in manufacturing, 24% in wholesale and retail trade, 10% in transportation, communications and other public utilities, 15% were employed in other counties and there were 2,292 retired workers. The industries with the most employment: coal mining, oil and gas extracton, poultry processing, agribusiness, lumber mills and petroleum refining. The nonfarm earnings in 1981 totaled $224,286,000. The retired workers received an average monthly Social Security payment of $292. **FINANCE** On June 30, 1983, four commercial banks had total deposits of $201,578,000 and total assets of $222,533,000. On December 31, 1982 one state savings and loan association and one state branch had assets of $35,258,832. **HOUSING** Average value of homes in 1980: $26,800. Permits for new, privately owned housing units decreased in 1982: 47 permits were issued with a total construction cost of $1,322,897. Of those permits, 31 were for single family houses. Between 1970 and 1980 the number of housing units increased by 34%. Seventynine percent of all units in the county are air-conditioned, 71% are heated by gas and 25% by electricity. **NATURAL RESOURCES** Ceramic clay, lignite coal, industrial sand, oil and gas. In 1982 a total of 2,044,850 barrels of crude oil and 21,349 thousand cubic feet of casinghead gas were produced. Current production of other minerals and products includes ball clay, lignite coal and recovered sulphur. Pine and hardwood production in 1981 totaled 789,314 cubic feet: 412,078 cubic feet of pine and 377,236 cubic feet of hardwood. **TOURISM** Travel expenditures of $15,415,000 in 1982 (an increase of 11% over 1981) generated 387 jobs and $3,080,000 in payroll. Lodging: three hotels, motels and tourist courts. **ALCOHOLIC BEVERAGES** Packaged distilled spirits, beer, ale, malt liquor and wine are legal in parts of the county. Sale of mixed beverages is legal in all or parts of the county. **FEDERAL EXPENDITURES** The federal government had direct expenditures or obligations of $38,625,000 in the county during fiscal year 1983, including $1,503,000 by the U.S. Department of Defense. In addition, the federal government provided $426,000 in grant awards, paid $2,298,000 in salaries and wages, made direct payments to individuals of $33,374,000 including $25,175,000 in retirement and disability payments, awarded $2,298,000 in procurement contracts and spent $229,000 in other expenditures or obligations. The federal government also provided $26,000 in direct loans and $2,747,000 in guaranteed loans and insurance.

COMMUNICATION

Newspapers–Daily: Mount Pleasant Daily Tribune, ave. eve. circ. 5,117. Weekly: Talco Times. Radio: KIMP-AM and KPXI-FM (Mount Pleasant). Cable TV. Telephone companies: General Telephone, Southwestern Bell and Peoples Telephone Coop. **TRANSPORTATION** Total public road mileage: 704. In 1982 there were 20,790 registered vehicles and 663 reported traffic accidents including 10 fatalities. Taxi cabs: one company in Mount Pleasant. Intercity bus service is available. Motor freight: six local and intrastate carriers. Rail: four main lines carry freight through the county with two carrying annually 20 to 30 million tons each, one carries five to 10 and one carries one to five million. Aircraft: 41 are registered in the county. Airports: Mount Pleasant Municipal Airport serves as a base for 29 aircraft and is a general utility airport with general aviation service.

COMMUNITY SERVICES

EDUCATION Four school districts with seven elementary, one middle and two high schools. The average daily attendance in 1981-82 was 3,732, with expenditures per pupil of $3,088 including 252 classroom teachers with an average annual salary of $16,557. Twenty-eight percent of the 231 high school graduates planned to attend college. In 1982-83, 76% of the students were White, 4% Hispanic, 20% Black, 0.1% Asian and 0.1% American Indian. Private schools: 138 students enrolled in one elementary and one high school. **PUBLIC LIBRARIES** Mount Pleasant Municipal Library: 34,000 volumes. **CHILD CARE** 32 day care and six twenty-four hour care licensed facilities. **HEALTH CARE** 27 physicians and 11 dentists. Hospitals: one with a capacity of 97. Ambulance services: one fire department and one hospital-based service. Mental health: one county clinic. Nursing homes: four nursing homes with a combined capacity of 347 nursing care residents. The average cost per day for private patients in 1982 was $32.31. **CHURCHES** 64 churches have an estimated combined membership of 13,664. The largest denominations are Southern Baptist, American Baptist and Churches of Christ. **SOCIAL SERVICES** In fiscal year 1983 a total of $777,483 in food stamps was distributed, with an average of 1,818 persons receiving food stamps each month. Aid to Families with Dependent Children (AFDC) totaled $189,072 with an average of 131 families receiving AFDC each month. Medical assistance benefits for the aged and disabled of $2,977,255 and for families and children of $432,099 brought the county benefit total to $4,375,908. **FIRE PROTECTION** Four volunteer fire departments. **LAW ENFORCEMENT** The County Sheriff has 25 commissioned officers. Two police departments have a combined force of 21. Titus County Freshwater Supervisory District has three officers. **CRIME** 36 violent crimes (murder, forcible rape, robbery and aggravated assault) and 492 nonviolent crimes (burglary, larceny-theft and motor vehicle theft) were reported in 1982. **JUDICIAL SYSTEM** Two District Courts and Judges, one County Court and Judge and four Justices of the Peace. In the District Courts a total of 1,733 cases were pending on 1/1/82, 605 new cases were filed and 437 cases were disposed of during the year leaving 1,901 cases pending on 12/31/82. There were 249 criminal cases on the docket, 48 convictions, 13 persons committed to prison and 106 cases left pending. In the County Courts 865 cases were pending on 1/1/82, 187 new cases were filed and 35 cases were disposed of during the year leaving 1,017 cases pending on 12/31/82. There were 861 criminal cases on the docket, 13 convictions, five persons committed to jail, and 834 cases left pending. **JAILS** One jail, capacity 25, opened the new jail in 1983. **ATTORNEYS AT LAW** 24. **UTILITIES** 78% of the residents are connected to a public or privately owned water system and 56% are connected to a public sewer system. Natural gas is distributed to the county by Arkla, Inc. The average annual residential bill for natural gas in 1982 for the Arkla distribution system was $316.69, an increase of 23% over 1981. Electricity is distributed to the county by Southwestern Electric Power Co., Wood County Electric Coop., Inc. and Bowie-Cass Electric Coop., Inc. and is generated primarily by gas and coal. The typical residential electric bill is $152.08 per month for an all-electric house using 2,500 kwh. **TAXES** The county has 11 units with taxing authority: five school districts, three cities, one county, one hospital district and one special district.

RECREATION/ENTERTAINMENT

COUNTY/MUNICIPAL PARKS 338 acres in one county and five municipal parks. These parks contain two playgrounds, nine baseball and softball fields, five tennis courts, two swimming pools, one beach and one boat ramp. Developed campsites; 30. **SCENIC DRIVES** The Texas Forest Trail runs through this county. This trail explores the farming, ranching and oilfield areas of the East Texas Pineywoods. **BOATING/FISHING** Lakes/reservoirs: Bob Sandlin (8,081 acres), J.D. Harlow (23 acres), Monticello (2,000 acres), Mount Pleasant New City (98 acres), Stephens (27 acres), Tankersley (199 acres) and Welsh (1,365 acres). Major rivers: Sulphur and Sabine. Primary streams: Big Cypress, Blundell, Hayes, Hart, Tankersley, Swauano and White Oak Bayou. **HUNTING** Fall and winter seasons on deer. Summer, fall and winter seasons on squirrel. Winter seasons on quail, muskrat, beaver, otter, opossum, ring-tailed cat, mink, badger, fox, raccoon, skunk and civet cat. No closed season on nutria, bobcat and coyote. In 1983 duck, coot, geese, woodcock and jacksnipe seasons occurred during the winter months. Teal duck, rail and gallinule seasons occurred in the fall. Mourning dove seasons occurred intermittently during the fall and winter months. **SPECIAL EVENTS** Arts and Crafts Festival, Mount Pleasant, April; Texas Bass Festival, Mount Pleasant, May; Rodeo, Mount Pleasant, June.

COMMUNITIES
COUNTY SEAT Mount Pleasant, County Courthouse, 75455; County Clerk's Office, 214/572-8891. **INCORPORATED COMMUNITIES** (1980 population and ZIP Code) Miller's Cove (61) 75455, Monticello (43) 75455, Mount Pleasant (11,003) 75455, Talco (751) 75487 and Winfield (349) 75493. **UNINCORPORATED COMMUNITIES** (and ZIP Code) Argo 75558, Blodgett 75686, Cookville 75558, Gladewater 75647, Green Hill 75455, Lone Star (Asander) 75558, Maple Springs 75455 and Midway 75455. **FOR ADDITIONAL LOCAL INFORMATION** Gladewater Chamber of Commerce, 215 N. Main, P.O. Box 1409, Gladewater 75647, 214/845-2626 and Mount Pleasant-Titus Co. Chamber of Commerce, 1604 N. Jefferson, Mount Pleasant, 75455, 214/572-8567.

TOM GREEN (P89)

THE LAND
Southwest of Abilene on U.S. Highways 277 and 67 in the Rolling Plains Region, Tom Green County covers 1,515 square miles with the elevation ranging from 1,600 to 2,500 feet. The soils have very dark, loamy surfaces with reddish, clayey subsoils and lime accumulations. In the northwest the limestone bedrock is near the surface with rocky areas. Along the northern border and in the south the soils are loamy throughout. In the Rolling Plains vegetation area the grasses are short to mid height with some mesquite trees and yucca. Between 31 and 40% of the land in the county is considered prime farmland. **CLIMATE** Subtropical dry. Duststorms will occur during spring and are sometimes preceded by thunderstorms. The average annual temperature is 66°F. Temperatures in January range from an average low of 32° to an average high of 59°F and in July range from 71° to 96°F. The average annual precipitation is 20 inches, with an average relative humidity of 75% at 6 A.M. and 40% at 6 P.M. The average annual snowfall is three inches. The growing season averages 235 days per year, with the last freeze in late March and the first freeze in mid November. The sun shines during the year on the average 70% of the daylight hours.

THE PEOPLE
The 1982 estimated poulation of 90,700 indicates a continuation of the steady increases since 1930. Population in rural areas increased 51% between 1970 and 1980. The county's population is of average age with a median age of 29 in 1980. The largest ancestry groups are persons of English descent (25%), Irish descent (21%), Hispanic (21%) and those of German descent (19%). **REGISTERED VOTERS** As of November 2, 1982 there were 34,799 registered voters (0.5% of the state total). The 1982 general election had a 57% voter turnout, compared to a 71%

turnout in the 1980 general election. In the 1982 primary 82% voted Democratic and 18% Republican, with 8,540 votes cast.

THE ECONOMY
AGRICULTURE Sheep and cotton area. In 1982, 94% of the land was in farms and ranches, with 17% of the farmland under cultivation and 22% irrigated. Tom Green ranked 41st in the state in highest agricultural receipts, with 55% from livestock and livestock products. Overgrazing, undesirable brush and weeds, water erosion, inefficient irrigation systems, moisture conservation and salinity are the current conservation problems. Primary crops: cotton, sorghum and wheat. Primary vegetables: cucumbers, sweet potatoes and watermelons. Primary fruits and nuts: peaches and pecans. Primary livestock and products: third in the state for both sheep and wool production. cattle, milk, angora goats, mohair and hogs. **BUSINESS** Total number of business establishments in the county: 2,123. Retail sales during the first quarter of 1984 decreased 2%. In 1980, 9% of the labor force were self-employed, 21% were employed in professional or related services, 15% in manufacturing, 23% in wholesale and retail trade, 9% in transportation, communications and other public utilities, 3% were employed in other counties and there were 7,434 retired workers. The industries with the most employment: agribusiness, tourism, oil and gas field services, general and heavy construction, meat packing, soft drink bottling and canning, lumber mills, book printing, structural steel fabrication, iron foundries and the manufacture of dairy products, bakery products, fats and oils, men's work clothing, men's leather shoes, transformers and surgical appliances and supplies. The nonfarm earnings in 1981 totaled $898,088,000. The retired workers received an average monthly Social Security payment of $313. **FINANCE** On June 30, 1983, seven commercial banks had total deposits of $734,720,000 and total assets of $837,980,000. On December 31, 1982 three state savings and loan associations, and eight state branches had assets of $469,866,613. In addition there are 15 credit unions in the county. **HOUSING** Average value of homes in 1980: $31,800. Permits for new, privately owned housing units increased in 1982: 1,547 permits were issued with a total construction cost of $32,114,370. Of those permits, 425 were for single family houses. Between 1970 and 1980 the number of housing units increased by 32%. Eighty-seven percent of all units in the county are air-conditioned, 72% are heated by gas and 27% by electricity. **NATURAL RESOURCES** Caliche, dolomite, limestone, salt, oil and gas. In 1982 a total of 1,353,760 thousand cubic feet of gas well gas, 13,363 barrels of condensate, 2,351,432 barrels of crude oil and 5,262,072 thousand cubic feet of casinghead gas were produced. Current production of other minerals and products includes crushed limestone, sand and gravel. **TOURISM** Travel expenditures of $52,632,000 in 1982 (an increase of 10% over 1981) generated 1,267 jobs and $10,870,000 in payroll. Lodging: 14 hotels, motels and tourist courts. Convention/meeting facilities: San Angelo Municipal Auditorium, San Angelo Coliseum, San Angelo Convention Center and one hotel with facilities for large gatherings. **ALCOHOLIC BEVERAGES** Packaged distilled spirits, beer, ale, malt liquor and wine are legal in parts of the county. **MILITARY INSTALLATIONS** Goodfellow Air Force Base, San Angelo, 1,321 personnel, 1,119 acres, 6,940 Security Wing. **FEDERAL EXPENDITURES** The federal government had direct expenditures or obligations of $195,816,000 in the county during fiscal year 1983, including $73,637,000 by the U.S. Department of Defense. In addition, the federal government provided $3,814,000 in grant awards, paid $46,514,000 in salaries and wages, made direct payments to individuals of $119,316,000 including $92,985,000 in retirement and disability payments, awarded $20,489,000 in procurement contracts and spent $5,684,000 in other expenditures or obligations. The federal government also

COUNTIES

provided $3,495,000 indirect loans and $29,561,000 in gauranteed loans and insurance.

COMMUNICATION

Newspapers-Daily: Standard (San Angelo) ave. morn. circ. 34,654, Times (San Angelo) ave. eve. circ. 6,530. Radio: KGKL-AM, KHOS-AM, KQSA-AM, KTWO-AM, WGKL-FM, KIXY-FM Stereo and KWLW-FM Stereo (San Angelo). Television: KACB-CH 3 and KLST-CH 8 (San Angelo). Cable TV. Telephone companies: General Telephone and Central Texas Telephone Coop. **TRANSPORTATION** Total public road mileage: 1,344. In 1982 there were 76,381 registered vehicles and 3,541 reported traffic accidents including 31 fatalities. Taxi cabs: four companies in San Angelo. Municipal transit systems: one intracity bus system in San Angelo, with scheduled routes. Intercity bus service is available. Motor freight: 29 local and intrastate carriers. Rail: three branch lines carry freight through the county with two carrying annually one to five million tons each and one carries less than one million. Aircraft: 202 are registered in the county. Airports: Mathis Field at San Angelo serves as a base for 151 aircraft and is a non-hub, short haul airport with carrier service. Also serving the area are Ducote Airpark and West Texas Boys Ranch Airport in San Angelo.

COMMUNITY SERVICES

EDUCATION Six school districts with 25 elementary, four middle and five high schools. The average daily attendance in 1981-82 was 14,321, with expenditures per pupil of $2,052 including 911 classroom teachers with an average annual salary of $16,120. Sixty-one percent of the 824 high school graduates planned to attend college. In 1982-83, 64% of the students were White, 31% Hispanic, 4% Black and 1% Asian. Private schools: 563 students enrolled in five elementary and in two high schools. Angelo State University is located in San Angelo. Established in 1926 it is under state control. Enrollment in 1982 was 5,705 with in state undergraduate tuition and fees of $420 per semester. The highest degree offered is master. Sports championships: (Lone Star Conference) 1983 Volleyball, 1983 Men's Track. Vocational education: San Angelo - American Commercial College, Jean's College of Beauty, San Angelo Barber College, Concho Trade School, Inc. **PUBLIC LIBRARIES** Tom Green County Library System (San Angelo): 175,903 volumes and two branches. **CHILD CARE** 221 day care and 32 twenty-four hour care licensed facilities. **HEALTH CARE** 147 physicians and 44 dentists. Hospitals: three with a total capacity of 483. Specialized hospitals: one long-term care (chronic) hospital with a capacity of 109. Clinics: one diagnostic clinic, one Air Force clinic, one public health clinic, and one minor emergency center. Ambulance services: one volunteer fire department, one volunteer service, and one city service. Mental health: two clinics and one development center with a capacity of 58. Nursing homes: five nursing homes with a combined capacity of 730 nursing care and 14 custodial care residents. The average cost per day for private patients in 1982 was $29.97. **CHURCHES** 92 churches have an estimated combined membership of 45,680. The largest denominations are Southern Baptist, Catholic and United Methodist. **SOCIAL SERVICES** In fiscal year 1983 a total of $1,864,583 in food stamps was distributed, with an average of 4,177 persons receiving food stamps each month. Aid to Families with Dependent Children (AFDC) totaled $454,595 with an average of 316 families receiving AFDC each month. Medical assistance benefits for the aged and disabled of $6,231,372 and for families and children of $890,968 brought the county benefit total to $9,441,517. **FIRE PROTECTION** One paid and five volunteer fire departments. **LAW ENFORCEMENT** The County Sheriff has 35 commis-

sioned officers. One police department has a force of 131. One university campus has a police department with a force of 10. San Angelo Lake Patrol has a force of six. San Angelo Municipal Airport has a force of five. San Angelo Municipal Court has a force of three. **CRIME** 452 violent crimes (murder, forcible rape, robbery and aggravated assault) and 4,910 nonviolent crimes (burglary, larceny-theft and motor vehicle theft) were reported in 1982. **JUDICIAL SYSTEM** Two District Courts and Judges, two County Courts and Judges and four Justices of the Peace. In the District Courts a total of 890 cases were pending on 1/1/82, 2,749 new cases were filed and 2,662 cases were disposed of during the year leaving 977 cases pending on 12/31/82. There were 848 criminal cases on the docket, 369 convictions, 83 persons committed to prison and 11 committed to jail and 218 cases left pending. In the County Courts 1,605 cases were pending on 1/1/82, 2,504 new cases were filed and 2,234 cases were disposed of during the year leaving 1,875 cases pending on 12/31/82. There were 3,352 criminal cases on the docket, 811 convictions, 130 persons committed to jail, and 1,473 cases left pending. **JAILS** One jail, capacity 91. Planning a new jail, capacity 80. **ATTORNEYS AT LAW** 154. **UTILITIES** 90% of the residents are connected to a public or privately owned water system and 86% are connected to a public sewer system. Natural gas is distributed to the county by Lone Star Gas Co., Division of Enserch. The average annual residential bill for natural gas in 1982 for the Lone Star distribution system was $405.91, an increase of 35% over 1981. Electricity is distributed to the county by West Texas Utilities, Cap Rock Electric Coop., Inc., McCulloch Electric Coop., Inc., Southwest Texas Electric Coop., Inc., and Concho Valley Electric Coop., Inc. and is generated primarily by gas, oil, coal and water. The typical residential electric bill is $145.78 per month for an all-electric house using 2,500 kwh. **TAXES** The county has eight units with taxing authority: six school districts, one city, and one county.

RECREATION/ENTERTAINMENT

NATIONAL REGISTER OF HISTORIC PLACES San Angelo: Fort Concho and Schwartz and Raas / San Angelo National Bank Buildings. **COUNTY/MUNICIPAL PARKS** 4,923 acres in 12 county and 32 municipal parks. These parks contain three miles of hiking trails, 28 playgrounds, one golf course, six baseball and softball fields, four tennis courts, 25 multi-use courts, two swimming pools, four beaches, nine boat ramps and shore fishing facilities. Developed campsites: 138. **SCENIC DRIVES** The Texas Forts Trail runs through this county. This trail leads to eight of the famous frontier forts of West Central Texas and an ancient presidio. **BOATING/FISHING** Lakes/reservoirs: Bell Street (45 acres), Ben Ficklin (44 acres), O.C. Fisher (5,440 acres), Jeschke (101 acres), Lone Wolf (80 acres), Metcalfe (362 acres), Nasworthy (1,596 acres) and Twin Buttes (9,080 acres). Major rivers: South Concho, Concho, Middle Concho and North Concho. Primary streams: Spring Creek, Dove Creek and Pecan Creek. **HUNTING** Fall and winter seasons on deer and javelina. No closed season on squirrel, bobcat and coyote. Winter seasons on quail, muskrat, beaver, opossum, ring-tailed cat, badger, fox, weasel, raccoon, skunk and civet cat. Fall, winter and spring seasons on turkey. In 1983 duck, coot, geese, woodcock and jacksnipe seasons occured during the winter months with a winter season on sandhill crane in some parts of the county. Teal duck, rail and gallinule seasons occured in the fall. Mourning dove seasons occurred intermittently during the fall and winter months. **MUSEUMS** San Angelo: Elmer H. Danner Museum of Telephony and Fort Concho Preservation and Museum. **THEATERS** San Angelo: San Angelo Coliseum, San Angelo Municipal Auditorium, San Angelo Entertainment Association and San Angelo Civic Theatre. **ORCHESTRAS** San Angelo: San Angelo Symphony Orchestra and Chorale. **COLLEGIATE FINE**

ARTS San Angelo: Cultural events offered by Angelo State University. **SPECIAL EVENTS** San Angelo Stock Show and Rodeo, San Angelo, March; Relays, San Angelo, March; Lamblast, San Angelo, April; Fiesta del Concho, San Angelo, June; Roping Festival, San Angelo, November. **COMMUNITIES COUNTY SEAT** San Angelo, County Courthouse, 76903; County Clerk's Office, 915/653-2385. **INCORPORATED COMMUNITIES** (1980 population and ZIP Code) San Angelo (73,240) 76901. **UNINCORPORATED COMMUNITIES** (and ZIP Code) Carlsbad 76934, Christoval 76935, Harriet 76901, Knickerbocker 76939, Mereta 76940, Orient 76901, Tankersly 76952, Vancourt 76955, Veribest 76886, Wall 76957 and Water Valley 76958 **FOR ADDITIONAL LOCAL INFORMATION** San Angelo Board of City Development and Chamber of Commerce, 500 Rio Concho Dr., San Angelo, 76903 915/655-4136.

TRAVIS (C24)

THE LAND

Northeast of San Antonio on Interstate Highway 35 in the Blackland Prairies Region, Travis County covers 989 square miles with the elevation ranging from 400 to 1,300 feet. In the west the undulating to hilly soils vary from light to dark in color with loamy surfaces and loamy to clayey subsoils with accumulations of lime. In the east the slightly acidic soils are dark, cracking and clayey with some loamy surfaces. Along the Colorado River the loamy and cracking clayey soils are brownish to reddish. In the west is the Edwards Plateau vegetation area, in the north the Cross Timbers and Prairies vegetation area and in the east the Blackland Prairies vegetation area. The grasses are tall with oaks, mesquite and pecan trees along streams. Between 21 and 30% of the land is considered prime farmland. **CLIMATE** Subtropical Humid in the east and subhumid in the west. Precipitation and humidity will vary widely from east to west across the county. The average annual temperature is 68 °F. Temperatures in January range from an average low of 38 ° to an average high of 60 °F and in July range from 73 ° to 96 °F. The average annual precipitation is 32 inches, with an average relative humidity of 84% at 6 A.M. and 53% at 6 P.M. The average annual snowfall is less than one inch. The growing season averages 270 days per year, with the last freeze in early March and the first freeze in late November. The sun shines during the year on the average 66% of the daylight hours.

THE PEOPLE

Travis County is one of the most densely populated in the state. The 1982 estimated population of 447,600 reflects a strong growth rate which rose from 39% between 1960 and 1970 to 42% between 1970 and 1980. Between 1970 and 1980 rural areas grew faster than urban areas. The age groups with the largest gains were ages 62 and over, 35 to 39 and 25 to 34 which doubled in size. The low median age rose from 24 in 1970 to 27 in 1980. The largest ancestry groups are persons of English descent (25%), Irish descent (22%) and those of German descent (21%). **REGISTERED VOTERS** As of November 2, 1982 there were 225,805 registered voters (4% of the state total). The 1982 general election had a 56% voter turnout, compared to a 71% turnout in the 1980 general election. In the 1982 primary 90% voted Democratic and 10% Republican, with 59,667 votes cast.

THE ECONOMY

AGRICULTURE In 1982, 63% of the land was in farms and ranches, with 23% of the farmland under cultivation and 2% irrigated. Travis ranked 147th in the state in highest agricultural receipts, with 66% from livestock and livestock products. Overgrazing, undersirable brush and weeds, water erosion and soil compaction are the current conservation problems. Primary crops: sorghum, wheat, hay, oats and cotton. Primary vegetables: potatoes and sweet potatoes. Primary fruits and nuts: peaches and pecans. Primary livestock and products: cattle, milk, sheep, wool and hogs. **BUSINESS** Total number of business establishments in the county: 10,504. Retail sales during the first quarter of 1984 increased by 28%. In 1980, 7% of the labor force were self-employed, 26% were employed in professional or related services, 12% in manufacturing, 20% in wholesale and retail trade, 12% in Government and Government Enterprises, 3% were employed in other counties and there were 22,336 retired workers. The industries with the most employment: agribusiness, oil and gas extraction, tourism, general and heavy construction, soft drink bottling and canning, book publishing, commercial printing, boat building and repairing and the manufacture of bakery products, prepared foods, household furniture, plastics products, concrete products, ready-mixed concrete, lime, fabricated metal products, oil field machinery, typewriters, computers, radio and television communication equipment, semiconductors, measuring and controlling devices, surgical and medical instruments, jewelry, and engineering and scientific instruments. The non-farm earnings in 1981 totaled $4,763,645,000. The retired workers received an average monthly Social Security payment of $340. **FINANCE** On June 30, 1983, 32 commercial banks had total deposits of $3,917,999,000 and total assets of $4,811,313,000. On December 31, 1982 six state savings and loan associations, one federal association, 60 state branches and 14 federal branches had combined assets of $1,604,863,753. In addition there are 42 credit unions in the county. **HOUSING** Average value of homes in 1980: $51,000. Permits for new, privately owned housing units increased in 1982: 10,368 permits were issued with a total construction cost of $495,636,730. Of those permits, 3,943 were for single family houses. Between 1970 and 1980 the number of housing units increased by 74%. Eighty-seven percent of all units in the county are air-conditioned, 72% are heated by gas and 27% by electricity. **NATURAL RESOURCES** Dolomite, limestone, industrial sand, sand and gravel, oil and gas. In 1982 8,438 barrels of crude oil and 96 thousand cubic feet of casinghead gas were produced. Current production of other minerals and products includes brick, lime, crushed limestone, construction sand, sand and gravel. **TOURISM** Travel expenditures of $358,200,000 in 1982 (an increase of 10% over 1981) generated 8,677 jobs and $74,247,000 in payroll. Lodging: 53 hotels, motels and tourist courts. Convention/meeting facilities: Austin - Lester E. Palmer Auditorium and Convention Center, Paramount Theatre for the Performing Arts, University of Texs Special Events Center and 11 hotels with facilities for large gatherings; Texas Manor, Downs Garden and Grandstand. **ALCOHOLIC BEVERAGES** Packaged distilled spirits, beer, ale, malt liquor and wine are legal. Sale of mixed beverages is legal in all or parts of the county. **MILITARY INSTALLATIONS** Camp Swift, Austin, 279 personnel, 11,740 acres, Army National Guard Activities; Bergstrom Air Force Base, Austin, 6,829 personnel, 3,936 acres, Tactical Reconnaissance Wing. **FEDERAL EXPENDITURES** The federal government had direct expenditures or obligations of $4,888,111,000 in the county during fiscal year 1983, including $433,615,000 by the U.S. Department of Defense. In addition, the federal government provided $3,211,886,000 in grant awards, paid $298,423,000 in salaries and wages, made direct payments to individuals of $1,152,925,000 including $381,397,000 in retirement and disability payments, awarded $223,022,000 in procurement contracts and spent $1,856,000 in other expenditures or obligations. The federal government also provided $7,003,000 in direct loans and $320,841,000 in guaranteed loans and insurance.

COUNTIES

COMMUNICATION

Newspapers–Daily: Austin American-Statesman ave. daily circ. 137,761. Weekly: The Bellville Times, Texas Posten (Swedish-English), Westlake Picayune (Austin), Onion Creek Free Press (Buda) and the Round Rock Leader. Radio: KIXL-AM, KLBJ-AM, KMMM-AM, KNOW-AM, KVET-AM, KASE-FM, KAZI-FM, KEYI-FM, KHFI-FM, KLBJ-FM, KMXX-FM, KOKE-FM, KRGT-FM, KMFA-FM Stereo (Austin) and KHCS-FM (Round Rock). Television: (PBS) KLRN-CH 9 and CH 18, KLRU-CH 18, KTBC-CH 7, KTVV-CH 36 and KVUE-CH 24 (Austin). Cable TV. Telephone companies: Continental Telephone, General Telephone and Southwestern Bell. **TRANSPORTATION** Total public road mileage: 2,945. In 1982 there were 344,806 registered vehicles and 17,801 reported traffic accidents including 90 fatalities. Taxi cabs: four companies in Austin. Municipal transit systems: one intracity bus system in Austin with scheduled routes. Intercity bus service is available. Motor freight: 81 local and intrastate carriers. Rail: the Eagle provides passenger service on the Amtrak route. Two main and three branch lines carry freight through the county. The two main lines carry annually 10 to 20 million tons of freight each and the three branches carry one to five million each. Aircraft: 549 are registered in the county. Airports: Robert Mueller Airport at Austin serves as a base for 223 aircraft and is a small hub for medium range flights with carrier service. Also serving the area are Executive Airpark, Bird's Nest Airport and Lakeway Airport/Heliport.

COMMUNITY SERVICES

EDUCATION Seven school districts with 72 elementary, 14 middle, 16 high schools and two special education. The average daily attendance in 1981-82 was 59,220, with expenditures per pupil of $3,010 including 4,004 classroom teachers with an average annual salary of $18,168. Fifty-nine percent of the 3,923 high school graduates planned to attend college. In 1982-83, 55% of the students were White, 26% Hispanic, 17.3% Black, 1% Asian and 0.1% American Indian. Sports championships: 1983 AAAAA Girls' Tennis Singles, Austin H.S.; 1983 AAAAA Boys' Tennis Singles, Austin H.S.; 1983 A Boys' Golf Singles, Lago Vista H.S. Private schools: 4,449 students enrolled in 24 elementary and five in high schools. Saint Edward's University is located in Austin. Established in 1885 it is an independent non profit institution. Enrollment in 1982 was 2,322. The highest degree offered is: Master. University of Texas at Austin was established in 1881 and is under state control. Enrollment in 1982 was 46,148 with in state undergraduate tuition and fees of $452 per semester. The highest degree offered is: Doctorate. Sports championships: (Southwest Conference) 1984 Women's Basketball, 1983 Volleyball, 1983 Football, 1984 Men's and Women's Swimming, 1983 Baseball, 1983 Women's Tennis and 1983 Men's Golf. Austin Presbyterian Theologial Seminary is located in Austin. Established in 1902 it is affiliated with the Presbyterian Church. Enrollment in 1982 was 149. The highest degree offered is: Doctorate (no undergraduate). Concordia Lutheran College is located in Austin. Established in 1926 it is affiliated with the Lutheran Church-Missouri Synod. Enrollment in 1982 was 360 with in state undergraduate tuition and fees of $1,950 per semester. The highest degree offered is Bachelor. Episcopal Theological Seminary of the Southwest is located in Austin. Established in 1952 it is affiliated with the Protestant Episcopal Church. Enrollment in 1982 was 76. The highest degree offered is Master (no undergraduate). Huston-Tillotson College is located in Austin. Established in 1876 it is affiliated with multiple Protestant denominations. Enrollment in 1982 was 692 with in state undergraduate tuition and fees of $2,040 per semester. The highest degree offered is Bachelor. Austin Community College is located in Austin. Established in 1972 it is a vocational and two year academic college under state and local control. Enrollment in 1982 was 12,527 with in state undergraduate tuition and fees of $312 per semester. Vocational education: Austin-A and C College of Beauty, Baldwin Beauty School, Brackenridge Hospital School of Nursing, Capital City Trade and Technical School, Durham Nixon-Clay Business College, Jacki Nell Executive Secretary School, Modern Barber College, Southwest School of Electronics, Vogue Beauty College, Control Data Learning Center, International Bartending Institute, Alicia Smith's Institute of Real Estate, Texas Institute for Paralegal Studies, Resource Control and Management Institute. **PUBLIC LIBRARIES** Austin Public Library: 704,652 volumes and 15 branches. Texas State Library (Austin): 1,287,223 volumes and two branches. **CHILD CARE** 1,465 day care and 106 twenty-four hour care licensed facilities. **HEALTH CARE** 909 physicians and 280 dentists. Hospitals: seven with a total capacity of 1,660. Specialized hospitals: one rehabilitation center for blind with a capacity of 51, one long-term care (chronic) hospital with a capacity of 70, and one Air Force hospital with capacity of 25. Clinics: seven for treatment of alcohol and drug abuse, five minor emergency centers, one cancer clinic, one dialysis clinic, and one public health clinic. Ambulance services: four commercial, one air, and one city service. Mental health: five clinics, two centers with a capacity of 168, two schools with a capacity of 241, two state schools with capacity of 1,826, and one state hospital with capacity of 1,020. Nursing homes: 25 nursing homes with a combined capacity of 2,678 nursing care residents. The average cost per day for private patients in 1982 was $32.12. **CHURCHES** 266 churches have an estimated combined membership of 194,194. The largest denominations are Catholic, Southern Baptist and United Methodist. **SOCIAL SERVICES** In fiscal year 1983 a total of $11,874,566 in food stamps was distributed, with an average of 22,885 persons receiving food stamps each month. Aid to Families with Dependent Children (AFDC) totaled $3,811,377, with an average of 2,494 families receiving AFDC each month. Medical assistance benefits for the aged and disabled of $24,748,378 and for families and children of $6,864,410 brought the county benefit total to $47,298,731. **FIRE PROTECTION** one paid and 20 volunteer fire departments. **LAW ENFORCEMENT** The County Sheriff has 205 commissioned officers. Six police departments have a combined force of 671. One college campus has a police department with a force of 17. Austin Park Rangers has a force of 19. Austin Airport Police has a force of 20. Lower Colorado River Authority has a force of 11. **CRIME** 1,858 violent crimes (murder, forcible rape, robbery and aggravated assault) and 34,426 nonviolent crimes (burglary, larceny-theft and motor vehicle theft) were reported in 1982. **JUDICIAL SYSTEM** 11 District Courts and Judges, five County Courts and Judges and five Justices of the Peace. In the District Courts a total of 24,514 cases were pending on 1/1/82, 17,859 new cases were filed and 16,057 cases were disposed of during the year leaving 26,316 cases pending on 12/31/82. There were 7,550 criminal cases on the docket, 1,648 convictions, 536 persons committed to prison and 174 committed to jail and 4,365 cases left pending. In the County Courts 36,622 cases were pending on 1/1/82, 19,470 new cases were filed and 13,980 cases were disposed of during the year leaving 42,112 cases pending on 12/31/82. There were 29,226 criminal cases on the docket, 3,056 convictions, 1,935 persons committed to jail, and 22,045 cases left pending. **JAILS** Two jails, capacity 415, constructing a new jail, capacity 257. **ATTORNEYS AT LAW** 3,049. **UTILITIES** 98% of the residents are connected to a public or privately owned water system and 87% are connected to a public sewer system. Natural gas is distributed to the county by Southern Union Company and Lone Star Gas Co., Division of Enserch. The average annual residential bill for natural gas

426

in 1982 for the Southern Union distribution system was $355.85, an increase of 23% over 1981 and for Lone Star it was $405.91 an increase of 35%. Electricity is distributed to the county by Texas Power and Light Co., the City of Austin Electric Dept., Bluebonnet Electric Coop., Inc. and Pedernales Electric Coop., Inc., and is generated primarily by water. The typical residential electric bill is $172.45 per month for an all-electric house using 2,500 kwh. **TAXES** The county has 39 units with taxing authority: nine school districts, eight cities, one county, and 21 special districts.

RECREATION/ENTERTAINMENT

NATIONAL REGISTER OF HISTORIC PLACES Austin: Austin "Moonlight" Towers, Battle Hall, Bremond Block Historic District, Brizendine House, Carrington-Covert House, Caswell Houses, Clarksville Historic District, Congress Avenue Historic District, Driskill Hotel, French Legation, Gethsemane Church, Goodman Building, Governor's Mansion, John Hancock House, Henry Hirshfeld House and Cottage, Laguna Gloria, Little Campus, Littlefield House, Mather-Kirkland House, Millett Opera House, McKinney Homestead, Neill Cochran House, Elizabet Ney Studio, O. Henry House, Old Land Office, Old Lundberg Bakery, Old Post Office and Federal Building, Michael Paggi House, Paramount Theatre, Raymond-Morley House, E. H. Rogers Site, St. David's Church, St. Edwards University, St. Mary's Cathedral, J. P. Schneider Store, Sheeks-Robertson House, Sixth Street Historic District, B. J. Smith House, Smith Rockshelter, Southwestern Telegraph and Telephone Building, Texas State Capitol, Wahrenberger House, "Woodlawn", Goodall Wooten House, Rather House, Scholz Garten, Smith-Clark and Smith-Bickler Houses, Westhill, Wooldridge Park, Youth Council Site, Boardman-Webb-Bugg House, Gilfillan House, Green Pastures, Stavely-Kunz-Johnson House, Aynsworth-Wright House, Evans Industrial Building (Hutson-Tillotson College Campus), George W. Sampson House and Richmond Kelley Smoot House. Austin vicinity: Walnut Creek Archeological District, Andrew Cox Ranch and Levi Rockshelter. **STATE** McKinney Falls State Park covers 726 acres with camping and trailer sites as well as fishing and hiking trails. An excellent visitor center, exhibits and ruins of the homestead of Thomas F. McKinney are also on the park site. **COUNTY/MUNICIPAL PARKS** 11,283 acres in 18 county and 153 municipal parks. These parks contain 26 miles of hiking trails, 71 playgrounds, four golf courses, 13 football and soccer fields, 58 baseball and softball fields, 95 tennis courts, 59 multi-use courts, 28 swimming pools, 15 beaches, 11 boat ramps and shore fishing facilities. Developed Campsites: 21. **SCENIC DRIVES** The Texas Brazos Trail and the Texas Hill Country Trail run through this county. **BOATING/FISHING** Lakes/reservoirs: Austin (1,830 acres), Long (1,269 acres), Town (135 acres) and Travis (18,930 acres). Major rivers: Colorado. Primary streams: Decker, Bull Creek, Boggy, Barton, Williamson, Shoal and Walnut. **HUNTING** Fall and winter seasons on deer. No closed season on squirrel, coyote and bobcat. Winter seasons on quail, muskrat, beaver, opossum, ring-tailed cat, badger, fox, weasel, raccoon, skunk and civet cat. Fall, winter and spring seasons on turkey. In 1983 duck, coot, geese, woodcock and jacksnipe seasons occurred during the winter months with a winter season on sandhill crane in some parts of the county. Teal duck, rail and gallinule seasons occurred in the fall. Mourning dove seasons occurred intermittently during the fall and winter months. **MUSEUMS** Austin: Archives Division-Texas State Library, Austin Natural Science Center, Daughters of the Confederacy and Daughters of the Republic of Texas Museum, The French Legation, Laguna Gloria Art Museum, Archer M. Huntington Art Gallery, Texas Confederate Museum, Leed's Gallery, Texas Memorial Museum, 36th Infantry Division War Museum,

University Art Museum-UT, Lorenzo De Zavala State Archives and Library Building, Swedish Pioneer Log Cabin, Elizabet Ney Museum, Harry Ransom Center, Neill-Cochran House, Michener Galleries, O. Henry Home Museum, LBJ Library and Museum and the Texas Historical Commission. **THEATERS** Austin: Austin Municipal Auditorium, Creek Theatre, Center State and Country Dinner Playhouse. **ORCHESTRAS** Austin: Austin Symphony Orchestra Society, Inc. **DANCE** Austin Ballet Theatre, Austin Civic Ballet, Sharir Dance Company, Deborah Hay Company and Ballet Austin. **PLANETARIUM** Austin: Austin Traveling Planetarium. **OBSERVATORY** Austin: University of Texas Public Telescope and University of Texas Solar Telescope Tour. **COLLEGIATE FINE ARTS** Austin: Cultural events offered by Huston-Tillotson College, Saint Edwards University and University of Texas-Austin. **SPECIAL EVENTS** Original Austin Gun Show, Austin, February; Horse Races, Manor, April-August; Austin-Travis County Livestock Show, Austin, April; Bluebonnet Trails, Austin, April; Bonsai Society Annual Show, Austin, April; Legends of Golf Tourney, Austin, April; Quilt Fair, Austin, April; Camel Parade, Austin, May; Flora Rama, Austin, May; Cinco de Mayo Celebration, Austin, May; Laguna Gloria Fiesta, Austin, May; Pflugerville Deutschen Pfest, Pflugerville, May; Pecan Street Festival, Austin, May; Folklife Festival, Austin, June; Juneteenth Celebration, Austin, June; Symphony Performance and Fireworks, Austin, July 4; Governor's Cup Sailing Regatta, Austin, July; Rodeo, Austin, July; Aqua Festival, Austin, August.

COMMUNITIES

COUNTY SEAT Austin, County Courthouse, 78767; County Clerk's Office, 512/473-9188. **INCORPORATED COMMUNITIES** (1980 population and ZIP Code) Austin (345,496: 345,109 in Travis Co. and 387 in Williamson Co.) 78701, Creedmoor (214, est. incorp. inactive) 78744, Lakeway (790) 78703, Manor (1,044) 78653, Pflugerville (745) 78660, Rollingwood (1,027) 78746, San Leanna (290) 78767, Sunset Valley (773) 78745 and West Lake Hills (2,166) 78746. **UNINCORPORATED COMMUNITIES** (and ZIP Code) Beecaves 78746, Bluff Springs 78744, Buffalo Gap 78746, Cedar Valley 78746, Cele 78653, Colton 78744, Daffan 78653, Del Valle 78617, Dessau 78751, Elroy 78617, Eubank Acres 78753, Ford Oaks 78704, Four Points (Hickmuntown) 78759, Garfield 78617, Gregg 78653, Heritage Hills 78753, Hornsby Bend (Mud)(Dunlay) 78702, Jonestown 78641, Kimbro 78653, Lago Vista 78641, Lakeland Hills 78746, Lakeland Park 78759, Littig 78621, Lund 78621, Manchaca 78652, Manda 78653, Marshall Ford 78759, McNeil 78651, Moores Crossing 78617, New Sweden 78653, North Oaks 78753, Oak Hill 78746, Pilot Knob 78744, River Hills 78759, Sprinkle 78751, Three Points 78664, Travis Peak 78654, Turnersville 78610, Volente (Dodd City) 78641, Walnut Forest 78753 and Webberville 78653. **FOR ADDITIONAL LOCAL INFORMATION** Austin Chamber of Commerce, P.O. Box 1967, Austin, 78767, 512/478-9383 and Austin Mexican Chamber of Commerce, P. O. Box 1173, Littlefield Mall, Austin, 78767, 512/476-7502.

TRINITY (E27)

THE LAND

North of Houston on U.S. Highway 287 in the East Texas Timberlands Region, Trinity County covers 692 square miles with an elevation range of 150 to 400 feet. The gently rolling to hilly, reddish soils have loamy surfaces and very deep, reddish, clayey subsoils high in iron. In the west the soils are light colored with sandy surfaces and clayey subsoils. In the Pineywoods vegetation area there are pine and hardwood forests. Between 21 and 30% of the land in the county is considered prime farmland. **CLIMATE** Subtropical Humid with warm summers. The average

COUNTIES

TRINITY (continued)

annual temperature is 67°F. Temperatures in January range from an average low of 38° to an average high of 59°F and in July range from 71° to 94°F. The average annual precipitation is 46 inches, with an average relative humidity of 87% at 6 A.M. and 59% at 6 P.M. The average annual snowfall is not significant. The growing season averages 260 days per year, with the last freeze in early March and the first freeze in mid November. The sun shines during the year on the average 66% of the daylight hours.

THE PEOPLE

The 1982 estimated population of 10,400 continues a pattern of strong growth which began in the 1960s, reversing the population decline between 1940 and 1960. Almost 72% of the county residents live in rural areas. Since the county has a high concentration of persons over age 64, the population's median age is high. The largest ancestry groups are persons of English descent (29%), Irish descent (20%) and Black (20%). **REGISTERED VOTERS** As of November 2, 1982 there were 8,041 registered voters (0.1% of the state total). The 1982 general election had a 39% voter turnout, compared to a 56% turnout in the 1980 general election. In the 1982 primary 100% voted Democratic, with 4,172 votes cast.

THE ECONOMY

AGRICULTURE Major forest production area. In 1982, 36% of the land was in farms and ranches, with 12% of the farmland under cultivation. Trinity ranked 212th in the state in highest agricultural receipts, with 83% from livestock and livestock products. Overgrazing, water erosion and improper woodland management are the current conservation problems. Primary crops: hay. Primary vegetables: sweet potatoes. Primary fruits and nuts: peaches and pecans. Primary livestock and products: cattle, milk and hogs. **BUSINESS** Total number of business establishments in the county: 170. Retail sales during the first quarter of 1984 increased 10%. In 1980, 15% of the labor force were self-employed, 19% were employed in professional or related services, 16% in manufacturing, 25% in wholesale and retail trade, 9% in construction, 37% were employed in other counties and there were 1,294 retired workers. The industries with the most employment: tourism, heavy construction, sawmills and the manufacture of fabricated metal products. The nonfarm earnings in 1981 totaled $65,006,000. The retired workers received an average monthly Social Security payment of $296. **FINANCE** On June 30, 1983, two commercial banks had total deposits of $46,430,000 and total assets of $51,898,000. There is one state savings and loan association branch in the county. **HOUSING** Average value of homes in 1980: $21,500. Permits for new, privately owned housing units decreased in 1982: five permits were issued with a total construction cost of $257,915. Of those permits, all were for single family houses. Between 1970 and 1980 the number of housing units increased by 85%. Sixty-five percent of all units in the county are air-conditioned, 67% are heated by gas and 23% by electricity. **NATURAL RESOURCES** Clay, lignite coal, industrial sand, sand and gravel, oil and gas. In 1982 a total of 8,438 barrels of crude oil and 96 thousand cubic feet of casinghead gas were produced. Pine and hardwood production in 1981 totaled 23,375,493 cubic feet: 22,402,453 cubic feet of pine and 973,040 cubic feet of hardwood. **TOURISM** Travel expenditures of $3,343,000 in 1982 (an increase of 11% over 1981) generated 81 jobs and $654,000 in payroll. **ALCOHOLIC BEVERAGES** Packaged distilled spirits, beer, ale, malt liquor and wine are legal. **FEDERAL EXPENDITURES** The federal government had direct expenditures or obligations of $21,090,000 in the county during fiscal year 1983, including $578,000 by the U.S. Department of Defense. In addition, the federal government

provided $611,000 in grant awards, paid $932,000 in salaries and wages, made direct payments to individuals of $19,087,000 including $14,490,000 in retirement and disability payments, awarded $375,000 in procurement contracts and spent $85,000 in other expenditures or obligations. The federal government also provided $272,000 in direct loans and $949,000 in guaranteed loans and insurance.

COMMUNICATION

Newspapers–Weekly: Groveton News and the Trinity Standard. Cable TV. Telephone companies: General Telephone Continental Telephone, Southwestern Bell and Lufkin Telephone Exchange. **TRANSPORTATION** Total public road mileage: 582. In 1982 there were 10,262 registered vehicles and 204 reported traffic accidents including 11 fatalities. Taxi cabs: one company in Groveton and one in the city of Trinity. Intercity bus service is available. Motor freight: three carriers. Rail: one main line carries annually 10 to 20 million tons of freight through the county. Aircraft: three are registered in the county. Airports: Groveton-Trinity County Airport.

COMMUNITY SERVICES

EDUCATION Four school districts with four elementary, one middle and four high schools. The average daily attendance in 1981-82 was 1,886, with expenditures per pupil of $1,916 including 108 classroom teachers with an average annual salary of $15,508. Twenty-nine percent of the 111 high school graduates planned to attend college. In 1982-83, 71% of the students were White, 0.5% Hispanic and 28% Black. **PUBLIC LIBRARIES** Groveton Library. Blance K. Werner Public Library (Trinity): 14,000 volumes. **CHILD CARE** Three day care and five twenty-four hour care licensed facilities. **HEALTH CARE** Eight physicians and one dentist. Hospitals: one with a capacity of 30. Ambulance services: one volunteer fire department, one funeral home and one commercial service. Mental health: one county clinic. Nursing homes: two nursing homes with a combined capacity of 60 nursing care residents. The average cost per day for private patients in 1982 was $28. **CHURCHES** 32 churches have an estimated combined membership of 4,712. The largest denominations are Southern Baptist, Churches of Christ and United Methodist. **SOCIAL SERVICES** In fiscal year 1983 a total of $638,802 in food stamps was distributed, with an average of 1,260 persons receiving food stamps each month. Aid to Families with Dependent Children (AFDC) totaled $178,751 with an average of 117 families receiving AFDC each month. Medical assistance benefits for the aged and disabled of $1,111,392 and for families and children of $220,891 brought the county benefit total to $2,149,835. **FIRE PROTECTION** Four volunteer fire departments. **LAW ENFORCEMENT** The County Sheriff has 12 commissioned officers. Two police departments have a combined force of 16. **CRIME** Seven violent crimes (murder, forcible rape, robbery and aggravated assault) and 89 nonviolent crimes (burglary, larceny-theft and motor vehicle theft) were reported in 1982. **JUDICIAL SYSTEM** Two District Courts and Judges, one County Court and Judge and four Justices of the Peace. In the District Courts a total of 416 cases were pending on 1/1/82, 267 new cases were filed and 275 cases were disposed of during the year leaving 408 cases pending on 12/31/82. There were 125 criminal cases on the docket, 51 convictions, 16 persons committed to prison and 34 cases left pending. In the County Court 330 cases were pending on 1/1/82, 450 new cases were filed and 256 cases were disposed of during the year leaving 524 cases pending on 12/31/82. There were 744 criminal cases on the docket, 92 convictions, one person committed to jail, and 489 cases left pending. **JAILS** One jail, capacity nine. **ATTORNEYS AT LAW** 10. **UTILITIES** 88% of the residents are connected to a public or privately owned water system and 42% are connected to a public sewer system. Natural gas is distributed to the county by

Entex, Inc. The average annual residential bill for natural gas in 1982 for the Entex distribution system was $390.31, an increase of 26% over 1981. Electricity is distributed to the county by Gulf State Utilities Co., Houston Co. Electric Coop., Inc. and Sam Houston Electric Coop., Inc. and is generated primarily by gas and oil. The typical residential electric bill is $198.32 per month for an all-electric house using 2,500 kwh. **TAXES** The county has nine units with taxing authority: four school districts, two cities, one county, one hospital district and one special district.

RECREATION/ENTERTAINMENT

FEDERAL DAVY CROCKETT NATIONAL FOREST covers 161,497 acres in Trinity and Houston counties and includes five recreation areas. **NATIONAL REGISTER OF HISTORIC PLACES** Riverside vicinity: Riverside Swinging Bridge. **MUNICIPAL PARKS** seven acres in two municipal parks. These parks contain one playground. **SCENIC DRIVES** The Texas Forest Trail runs through this county. This trail explores the ranching, farming and oilfield areas of the East Texas Pineywoods. **BOATING/FISHING** Lakes/reservoirs: Avery (51 acres), Blackcat (100 acres), Cameron (63 acres), Pennington (24 acres) and Westwood Shores (43 acres). Major rivers: Neches. Primary streams: Kickapoo, Dads, Louisville, White Rock, Caney and Piney. **WILDLIFE REFUGES** Alabama Creek State Wildlife Management Area covers 14,500 acres. **HUNTING** Fall and winter seasons on deer. Summer, fall and winter seasons on squirrel. No closed seasons on coyote, bobcat and nutria. Winter seasons on quail, muskrat, beaver, otter, opossum, mink, ringtailed cat, badger, fox, raccoon, skunk and civet cat. Spring season on turkey in some parts of the county. In 1983 duck, coot, geese, woodcock and jacksnipe seasons occurred during the winter months. Teal duck, rail and gallinule seasons occurred in the fall. Mourning dove seasons occurred intermittently during the fall and winter months. **SPECIAL EVENTS** Spring Festival, Trinity, May; Community Fair, Trinity, September.

COMMUNITIES

COUNTY SEAT Groveton, County Courthouse, 75845; County Clerk's Office, 409/642-1208. **INCORPORATED COMMUNITIES** (1980 population and ZIP Code) Groveton (1,262) 75845 and Trinity (2,620) 75862. **UNINCORPORATED COMMUNITIES** (and ZIP Code) Alabama Creek 75845, Apple Springs 75926, Carlisle 75862, Centerville 75845, Centralia 75834, Chita 75862, Crecy 75845, Friday 75845, Glendale 75862, Helmic 75845, Josserand 75845, Lacy 75845, Nigton 75926, Nogalus Prairie (Nogalus) 75845, North Cedar 75926, Pagoda 75862, Pennington 75856, Sebastopol 75862, Trevat 75845, Westville 75862 and Woodlake 75865. **FOR ADDITIONAL LOCAL INFORMATION** Groveton Chamber of Commerce, P.O. Box 366, Groveton, 75845, 409/642-1715 and Trinity Peninsula Chamber of Commerce, P.O. Box 549, 110 Robb St., Trinity, 75862, 409/594-3856, 594-2659.

TYLER (E33)

THE LAND

Northeast of Houston on U.S. Highways 69 and 190 in the East Texas Timberlands Region, Tyler County covers 922 square miles with the elevation ranging from 100 to 400 feet. The soils are light colored and acidic with sandy to loamy surfaces and reddish clayey subsoils. The hills are gently rolling with soils in the north and south which are light colored and loamy with very deep, reddish, clayey to loamy subsoils. In the Pineywoods vegetation area there are pine and hardwood forests. Between 21 and 30% of the land in the county in considered prime farmland. **CLIMATE** Subtropical humid with mild winters and warm summers. The average annual temperature is 67 °F. Temperatures in January range from an average low of 37 ° to an average high of 60 °F and in July range from 72 ° to 93 °F. The average annual precipitation is 49 inches, with an average relative humidity of 88% at 6 A.M. and 65% at 6 P.M. The average annual snowfall is not significant. The growing season averages 241 days per year, with the last freeze in mid March and the first freeze in mid November. The sun shines during the year on the average 63% of the daylight hours.

THE PEOPLE

Nearly 83% of the residents in Tyler County live in rural areas. The 1982 estimated population of 16,600 indicates a slowing down of the strong growth rate begun in the 1960s which reversed the pattern of population decline between 1940 and 1960. Rural areas experienced a 37% population gain between 1970 and 1980. The county's population has high concentration of persons over age 65 and a median age of 36. The largest ancestry groups are persons of Irish descent (27%), English descent (26%), Black (13%) and German descent (12%). **REGISTERED VOTERS** As of November 2, 1982 there were 10,458 registered voters (0.2% of the state total). The 1982 general election had a 41% voter turnout, compared to a 61% turnout in the 1980 general election. In the 1982 primary 99% voted Democratic and 1% Republican, with 3,931 votes cast.

THE ECONOMY

AGRICULTURE Second in the state in forest production. In 1982, 21% of the land was in farms and ranches, with 8% of the farmland under cultivation. Tyler ranked 236th in the state in highest agricultural receipts, with 61% from livestock and livestock products. Overgrazing, undesirable brush and weeds, fertilization, inadequate forestland harvesting systems and undesirable woody vegetation on the forestland are the current conservation problems. Primary crops: hay and soybeans. Primary vegetables: sweet corn, potatoes, sweet potatoes, tomatoes and watermelons. Primary fruits and nuts: peaches and pecans. Primary livestock and products: cattle, milk and hogs. **BUSINESS** Total number of business establishments in the county: 226. Retail sales during the first quarter of 1984 increased by 18%. In 1980, 13% of the labor force were self-employed, 19% were employed in professional or related services, 25% in manufacturing, 18% in wholesale and retail trade, 12% in construction, 38% were employed in other counties and there were 1,971 retired workers. The industries with the most employment: oil and gas extraction, logging and the manufacture of metal doors. The nonfarm earnings in 1981 totaled $118,145,000. The retired workers received an average monthly Social Security payment of $325. **FINANCE** On June 30, 1983, three commercial banks had total deposits of $53,421,000 and total assets of $59,450,000. On December 31, 1982 one state savings and loan association and one federal association branch had assets of $31,142,672. **HOUSING** Average value of homes in 1980: $24,300. In 1982 four permits were issued for new, single family houses. Between 1970 and 1980 the number of housing units increased by 43%. Seventy-one percent of all units in the county are air-conditioned, 60% are heated by gas and 25% by electricity. **NATURAL RESOURCES** Clay, industrial sand, oil and gas. In 1982 a total of 3,540,129 thousand cubic feet of gas well gas, 62,879 barrels of condensate, 278,775 barrels of crude oil and 330,168 thousand cubic feet of casinghead gas were produced. Current production of other minerals and products includes industrial sand. Pine and hardwood production in 1981 totaled 29,778,281 cubic feet: 26,048,391 cubic feet of pine and 3,729,890 cubic feet of hardwood. **TOURISM** Travel expenditures of $3,253,000 in 1982 (an increase of 12% over 1981) generated 75 jobs and $616,000 in payroll. **ALCOHOLIC BEVERAGES**

COUNTIES

TYLER (continued)

Totally dry. **FEDERAL EXPENDITURES** The federal government had direct expenditures or obligations of $34,099,000 in the county during fiscal year 1983, including $1,215,000 by the U.S. Department of Defense. In addition, the federal government provided $219,000 in grant awards, paid $985,000 in salaries and wages, made direct payments to individuals of $32,770,000 including $26,166,000 in retirement and disability payments, awarded $31,000 in procurement contracts and spent $94,000 in other expenditures or obligations. The federal government also provided $925,000 in direct loans and $658,000 in guaranteed loans and insurance.

COMMUNICATION

Newspapers–Weekly: Tyler County Booster (Woodville). Radio: KVLL-AM (Woodville). Cable TV. Telephone companies: Southwestern Bell, Colmesneil Telephone and Eastex Telephone Coop. **TRANSPORTATION** Total public road mileage: 813. In 1982 there were 13,436 registered vehicles and 254 reported traffic accidents including six fatalities. Municipal transit systems: one service in Tyler, uses vans on a fixed route. Intercity bus service is available. Motor freight: four carriers. Rail: one main line carries annually one to five million tons of freight through the county. Aircraft: 10 are registered in the county. Airports: Tyler County Airport at Woodville serves as a base for 10 aircraft and is a general utility airport with general aviation services.

COMMUNITY SERVICES

EDUCATION Five school districts with six elementary, two middle and five high schools. The average daily attendance in 1981-82 was 3,432, with expenditures per pupil of $2,908 including 216 classroom teachers with an average annual salary of $16,582. Twenty-five percent of the 254 high school graduates planned to attend college. In 1982-83, 79% of the students were White, 0.2% Hispanic, 19% Black, 0.1% Asian and 2% American Indian. **PUBLIC LIBRARIES** Allan Shivers Library (Woodville): 19,070 volumes. **CHILD CARE** Four day care and eight twenty-four hour care licensed facilities. **HEALTH CARE** Six physicians and six dentists. Hospitals: one with a capacity of 49. Ambulance services: one county service. Mental health: one county clinic. Nursing homes: two nursing homes with a combined capacity of 210 nursing care residents. The average cost per day for private patients in 1982 was $31.13. **CHURCHES** 58 churches have an estimated combined membership of 10,195. The largest denomination is Southern Baptist. **SOCIAL SERVICES** In fiscal year 1983 a total of $862,278 in food stamps was distributed, with an average of 1,858 persons receiving food stamps each month. Aid to Families with Dependent Children (AFDC) totaled $156,288 with an average of 99 families receiving AFDC each month. Medical assistance benefits for the aged and disabled of $1,647,101 and for families and children of $165,390 brought the county benefit total to $2,831,056. **FIRE PROTECTION** Six volunteer fire departments. **LAW ENFORCEMENT** The County Sheriff has 12 commissioned officers. One police department has a force of six. **CRIME** 15 violent crimes (murder, forcible rape, robbery and aggravated assault) and 205 nonviolent crimes (burglary, larceny-theft and motor vehicle theft) were reported in 1982. **JUDICIAL SYSTEM** Two District Courts and Judges, one County Court and Judge and four Justices of the Peace. In the District Courts a total of 590 cases were pending on 1/1/82, 407 new cases were filed and 376 cases were disposed of during the year leaving 621 cases pending on 12/31/82. There were 261 criminal cases on the docket, 15 convictions, 12 persons committed to prison and one committed to jail and 208 cases left pending. In the County Court 498 cases were pending on 1/1/82, 711 new cases were filed and 530 cases were disposed of during the year leaving 679 cases pending on 12/31/82. There were 1,134 criminal cases on the docket, 52 convictions, 12 persons committed to jail, and 613 cases left pending. **JAILS** One jail, capacity 12. **ATTORNEYS AT LAW** 13. **UTILITIES** 50% of the residents are connected to a public or privately owned water system and 20% are connected to a public sewer system. Natural gas is distributed to the county by Entex, Inc. and Doucette Gas Association. The average annual residential bill for natural gas in 1982 for the Entex distribution system was $390.31, an increase of 26% over 1981. Electricity is distributed to the county by Gulf State Utilities and is generated primarily by gas and oil. The typical residential electric bill is $198.32 per month for an all-electric house using 2,500 kwh. **TAXES** The county has seven units with taxing authority: five school districts, one city and one county.

RECREATION/ENTERTAINMENT

STATE Martin Dies, Jr. State Park. (See Jasper County). John Henry Kirby State Forest covers 600 acres. **MUNICIPAL PARKS** 10 acres in one municipal park. This parks contains one playground, one multi-use field and one multi-use court. **SCENIC DRIVES** The Texas Forest Trail runs through this county. This trail explores the farming, ranching and oilfield areas of the East Texas Pineywoods. **BOATING/FISHING** Lakes/reservoirs: Amanda (93 acres), B.A. Steinhagen (13,700 acres), Charmaine (54 acres), Frog Pond (54 acres), Galahad (87 acres), Richardson (20 acres), Sawyers (20 acres) and Tristan (69 acres). Major rivers: Neches. Primary streams: Wolf, Magnus, Caney, Russell, McGraw and Billiams. **WILDLIFE REFUGES** Dam B State Wildlife Management Area covers 6,583 acres in this county. **HUNTING** Fall and winter seasons on deer. Summer, fall and winter seasons on squirrel. Winter seasons on quail, muskrat, beaver, otter, opossum, mink, ring-tailed cat, badger, fox, raccoon, skunk and civet cat. Spring season on turkey in some parts of the county. No closed season on bobcat, coyote and nutria. In 1983 duck, coot, geese, woodcock and jacksnipe seasons occurred during the winter months. Teal duck, rail and gallinule seasons occurred in the fall. Mourning dove seasons occurred intermittently during the fall and winter months. **MUSEUMS** Chester: Kirby Memorial Chapel. Woodville: Allan Shivers Museum and Heritage Garden Village. **THEATERS** Woodville: Historical outdoor drama. **SPECIAL EVENTS** Neches Valley Gospel Singing Jubilee, Woodville, January; Miss Tyler County Pageant, Woodville, February; Dogwood Festival, Woodville, March/April; County Fair, Woodville, September/October.

COMMUNITIES

COUNTY SEAT Woodville, County Courthouse, 75979; County Clerk's Office, 409/283-2281. **INCORPORATED COMMUNITIES** (1980 population and ZIP Code) Chester (305) 75936, Colmesneil (553) 75938 and Woodville (2,821) 75979. **UNINCORPORATED COMMUNITIES** (and ZIP Code) Dies 75979, Dogwood 75979, Doucette 75942, Emille (Emilee) 75979, Fred 77616, Hampton 75936, Hillister 77624, Jeans 75970, Pedigo 75979, Rockland 75970, Spurger 77660, Town Bluff 75979, Warren 77664, William Spear Addition 75701 **FOR ADDITIONAL LOCAL INFORMATION** Tyler Co. Chamber of Commerce, 507 N. Pine St., Woodville, 75979, 409/283-2632.

UPSHUR (E13)

THE LAND

East of Dallas on U.S. Highway 271 in the East Texas Timberlands Region, Upshur County covers 587 square miles with the elevation ranging from 200 to 500 feet. The county has moderately well to poorly drained soils with light colored, acidic, sandy to loamy surfaces over very deep, reddish mottled subsoils. These soils are deficient in plant nutrients. Upshur is in the Pineywoods vegetation area with grasslands, loblolly, shortleaf, longleaf and slash pine and hardwoods such as oak, hickory and maple. Between 11 and 20% of the land in the county is considered prime farmland. **CLIMATE** Subtropical Humid with mild winters and warm summers. The average annual temperature is 64°F. Temperatures in January range from an average low of 32°F to an average high of 54°F and in July range from 71°F to 94°F. The average annual precipitation is 46 inches, with an average relative humidity of 85% at 6 A.M. and 57% at 6 P.M. The average annual snowfall is two inches. The growing season averages 245 days per year, with the last freeze in mid March and the first freeze in mid November. The sun shines during the year on the average 66% of the daylight hours.

THE PEOPLE

The growth rate of the population in Upshur County rose from 6% between 1960 and 1970 to 36% between 1970 and 1980. The 1982 estimated population of 31,100 indicates a continuation of those population gains. Nearly 74% of the county residents live in rural areas which has a 37% population gain between 1970 and 1980. The age groups with the largest increases were ages 20 to 34 and birth to five years. The largest ancestry groups are persons of English descent (28%), Irish descent (20%) and Black (15%). **REGISTERED VOTERS** As of November 2, 1982 there were 15,651 registered voters (0.2% of the state total). The 1982 general election had a 45% voter turnout, compared to a 63% turnout in the 1980 general election. In the 1982 primary 98% voted Democratic and 2% Republican, with 5,227 votes cast.

THE ECONOMY

AGRICULTURE Forest production and dairy area. In 1982, 45% of the land was in farms and ranches, with 14% of the farmland under cultivation and 4% irrigated. Upshur ranked 86th in the state in highest agricultural receipts, with 92% from livestock and livestock products. Undesirable brush and weeds, water erosion, improper woodland management, reclamation of oil and gas drilling sites and urban encroachment are the current conservation problems. Primary crops: hay. Primary vegetables: sweet potatoes and watermelons. Primary fruits and nuts: peaches and pecans. Primary livestock and products: sixth in the state for commercial broiler production and eight for milk production. Cattle. **BUSINESS** Total number of business establishments in the county: 333. Retail sales during the first quarter of 1984 increased by 18%. In 1980, 11% of the labor force were self-employed, 16% were employed in professional or related services, 24% in manufacturing, 19% in wholesale and retail trade, 11% in construction, 60% were employed in other counties and there were 2,546 retired workers. The industries with the most employment: sawmills, general construction, agribusiness and the manufacture of plumbing fixtures and electric wiring equipment. The nonfarm earnings in 1981 totaled $212,057,000. The retired workers received an average monthly Social Security payment of $301.00. **FINANCE** On June 30, 1983, four commercial banks had total deposits of $124,555,000 and total assets of $142,128,000. On December 31, 1982 one state savings and loan association and two state branches had assets of $20,779,770. In addition there are three credit unions in the county. **HOUSING** Average value of homes in 1980: $28,400. Permits for new, privately owned housing units decreased in 1982: 40 permits were issued with a total construction cost of $1,184,253. Of those permits, 35 were for single family houses. Between 1970 and 1980 the number of housing units increased by 54%. Seventy-seven percent of all units in the county are air-conditioned, 76% are heated by gas and 20% by electricity. **NATURAL RESOURCES**

Industrial sand, oil, gas and lignite coal. In 1982 a total of 24,514,652 thousand cubic feet of gas well gas, 359,659 barrels of condensate, 752,992 barrels of crude oil and 211,501 thousand cubic feet of casinghead gas were produced. Current production of other minerals and products includes industrial sand. Pine and hardwood production in 1981 totaled 14,421,380 cubic feet: 11,946,691 cubic feet of pine and 2,474,689 cubic feet of hardwood. **TOURISM** Travel expenditures of $3,739,000 in 1982 (an increase of 18% over 1981) generated 47 jobs and $523,000 in payroll. **ALCOHOLIC BEVERAGES** Packaged distilled spirits, beer, ale, malt liquor and wine are legal in parts of the county. **FEDERAL EXPENDITURES** The federal government had direct expenditures or obligations of $43,294,000 in the county during fiscal year 1983, including $2,035,000 by the U.S. Department of Defense. In addition, the federal government provided $578,000 in grant awards, paid $1,045,000 in salaries and wages, made direct payments to individuals of $41,473,000 including $32,128,000 in retirement and disability payments, awarded $5,000 in procurement contracts and spent $193,000 in other expenditures or obligations. The federal government also provided $524,000 in direct loans and $2,163,000 in guaranteed loans and insurance.

COMMUNICATION

Newspapers–Weekly: Big Sandy and Hawkins Journal and Tri-Area News and The Gilmer Mirror. Radio: KHYM-AM and KNIF-FM (Gilmer). Cable TV. Telephone companies: Continental Telephone, General Telephone, Southwestern Bell, Etex Telephone Coop. and Peoples Telephone Coop. **TRANSPORTATION** Total public road mileage: 991. In 1982 there were 24,955 registered vehicles and 569 reported traffic accidents including 17 fatalities. Motor freight: 10 local and intrastate carriers. Rail: four main lines carry annually 20 to 30 million tons of freight each through the county. Aircraft: 17 are registered in the county. Airports: Gilmir-Upshur County Airport at Gilmer serves as a base for 10 aircraft and is a basic utility airport with general aviation service. Ambassador Field at Big Sandy.

COMMUNITY SERVICES

EDUCATION Seven school districts with seven elementary, one middle and sevenhigh schools. The average daily attendance in 1981-82 was 5,098, with expenditures per pupil of $2,205 including 304 classroom teachers with an average annual salary of $15,757. Forty-three percent of the 330 high school graduates planned to attend college. In 1982-83, 83% of the students were White, 0.7% Hispanic, 17% Black and 0.1% Asian. Sports championships: 1983 AAA Girls' Track, Gilmer H.S. **PUBLIC LIBRARIES** Upshur County Library (Gilmer): 29,000 volumes. **CHILD CARE** 23 day care and 15 twenty-four hour care licensed facilities. **HEALTH CARE** Nine physicians and seven dentists. Hospitals: one with a capacity of 46. Clinics: one public health clinic. Ambulance services: two commercial and one volunteer fire department service. Mental health: one clinic. Nursing homes: two nursing homes with a combined capacity of 211 nursing care residents. The average cost per day for private patients in 1982 was $34.13. **CHURCHES** 83 churches have an estimated combined membership of 17,340. The largest denominations are Southern Baptist, Baptist Missionary and United Methodist. **SOCIAL SERVICES** In fiscal year 1983 a total of $1,285,895 in food stamps was distributed, with an average of 2,856 persons receiving food stamps each month. Aid to Families with Dependent Children (AFDC) totaled $296,650 with an average of 204 families receiving AFDC each month. Medical assistance benefits for the aged and disabled of $2,407,080 and for families and children of $468,525 brought the county benefit total to $4,458,150. **FIRE PROTECTION** 15 volunteer fire departments. **LAW ENFORCEMENT** The County

COUNTIES

UPSHUR (continued)

Sheriff has 21 commissioned officers. Three police departments have a combined force of 25. **CRIME** 97 violent crimes (murder, forcible rape, robbery and aggravated assault) and 751 nonviolent crimes (burglary, larceny-theft and motor vehicle theft) were reported in 1982. **JUDICIAL SYSTEM** One District Court and Judge, one County Court and Judge and five Justices of the Peace. In the District Court a total of 1,432 cases were pending on 1/1/82, 763 new cases were filed and 525 cases were disposed of during the year leaving 1,670 cases pending on 12/31/82. There were 307 criminal cases on the docket, 46 convictions, 20 persons committed to prison and one committed to jail and 165 cases left pending. In the County Court 787 cases were pending on 1/1/82, 1,229 new cases were filed and 773 cases were disposed of during the year leaving 1,243 cases pending on 12/31/82. There were 1,940 criminal cases on the docket, 151 convictions, 1,182 cases left pending. **JAILS** One jail, capacity 15, constructing new jail. Lost certification in 1983 due to overcrowding. **ATTORNEYS AT LAW** 16. **UTILITIES** 70% of the residents are connected to a public or privately owned water system and 36% are connected to a public sewer system. Natural gas is distributed to the county by Entex, Inc. The average annual residential bill for natural gas in 1982 for the Entex distribution system was $390.31, an increase of 26% over 1981. Electricity is distributed to the county by Wood County Electric Coop., Inc. and Southwestern Electric Power Co. and is generated primarily by gas and coal. The typical residential electric bill is $152.08 per month for an all-electric house using 2,500 kwh. **TAXES** The county has 12 units with taxing authority: seven school districts, four cities and one county.

RECREATION/ENTERTAINMENT

MUNICIPAL PARKS 60 acres in five municipal parks. These parks contain three playgrounds, 10 baseball and softball fields, five tennis courts, two multi-use courts, one swimming pool, one beach, two boat ramps and shore fishing facilities. Developed campsites: eight. **BOATING/FISHING** Lakes/reservoirs: Ambassador College (41 acres), Gladewater (800 acres), Glenwood Acres North (22 acres), Glenwood Acres West (20 acres), Lower Raintree (45 acres) and Upper Raintree (32 acres). Primary streams: Big Sandy, Glade, Bag, Horn Mill and Little Cypress. **HUNTING** Fall and winter seasons on deer. Summer, fall and winter seasons on squirrel. Winter seasons on quail, muskrat, beaver, otter, opossum, mink, ring-tailed cat, badger, fox, raccoon, skunk and civet cat. No closed season on nutria, coyote and bobcat. In 1983 duck, coot, geese, woodcock and jacksnipe seasons occurred during the winter months. Teal duck, rail and gallinule seasons occurred in the fall. Mourning dove seasons occurred intermittently during the fall and winter months. **SPECIAL EVENTS** Arts and Crafts Show and Fair, Gilmer, April; Health Fair, Gilmer, May; East Texas "Yamboree", Gilmer, October; "Possum" Festival, Rhonesboro, October; Christmas Parade, Gilmer, December.

COMMUNITIES

COUNTY SEAT Gilmer, County Courthouse, 75644; County Clerk's Office, 214/843-3118. **INCORPORATED COMMUNITIES** (1980 population and ZIP Codes) Big Sandy (1,258) 75755, East Mountain (855) 75644, Gilmer (5,167) 75644, Gladewater (6,548: 2,237 in Upshur Co. and 4,311 in Gregg Co.) 75647, Ore City (1,050) 75683, Union Grove (344) 75647, Warren City (281: 2 in Upshur Co. and 279 in Gregg Co.) 75647 and West Mountain (395) 75647. **UNINCORPORATED COMMUNITIES** (and ZIP Codes) Ashland 75640, Bethlehem 75644, Bettie 75632, Boxwood 75683, Brumley 75686, Cedar Springs 75683, Center Point 75755, Coffeville (Coffeyville) 75683, Cox 75644, Delrose 75644,

Diana (James) 75640, Enoch 75644, Ewell 75644, Glenwood 75644, Graceton 75644, Grice 75644, Indian Rock 75644, Kelsey 75644, La Fayette 75686, Latch 75644, Lone Mountain 75644, Midway 75686 Mings Chapel 75644, New Mountain 75644, Piney Grove 75686, Pinnacle 75755, Pleasant Grove 75755, Pritchett 75755, Rhonesboro 75755, Rosewood 75644, Sand Hill 75644, Seven Pines 75644, Shady Grove 75755, Soules Chapel 75644, Stamps 75644, Suffolk 75644, Summerfield 75644, Thomas 75686, Union Hill 75644, Valleyview (Valley View) 75644, Wallace Chapel 75686, Wilkins 75755 and Willow Oak 75644. **FOR ADDITIONAL LOCAL INFORMATION** Upshur Co. Chamber of Commerce, P.O. Box 854, Gilmer, 75644, 214/843-3981.

UPTON (P86)

THE LAND

South of Midland on U.S. Highway 67 in the Edwards Plateau Region, Upton County covers 1,243 square miles with the elevation ranging from 2,300 to 3,000 feet. Along parts of the western border are sandy soils with reddish loamy subsoils and some clay in the subsoils. There is limestone bedrock within 40 inches of the surface. The rest of the county has loamy soils with lime accumulations. In the southeast about 90% is exposed rock. Upton is in the Edwards Plateau vegetation area with tall and mid grasses, mesquite, desert shrub, scrubby live oak and yucca. Less than 1% of the land in the county is considered prime farmland. **CLIMATE** Mild and dry. High winds during spring are generally associated with duststorms. The average annual temperature is 65 °F. Temperatures in January range from an average low of 31 ° to an average high of 60 °F and in July range from 71 ° to 96 °F. The average annual precipitation is 14 inches, with an average relative humidity of 72% at 6 A.M. and 36% at 6 P.M. The average annual snowfall is three inches. The growing season averages 232 days per year, with the last freeze in late March and the first freeze in mid November. The sun shines during the year on the average 75% of the daylight hours.

THE PEOPLE

Following 20 years of steady population growth between 1940 and 1960 Upton County experienced a significant decline. However the estimated 1982 population of 5,300 indicates a strong increase since 1980. The majority of the county residents live in rural areas. The age group with the age group with the largest reduction between 1970 and 1980 was ages five to 14, while an increase occurred in ages 20 to 24. The largest ancestry groups are Hispanic (28%), persons of English descent (24%) and Irish descent (23%). **REGISTERED VOTERS** As of November 2, 1982 there were 2,285 registered voters (0.03% of the state total). The 1982 general election had a 46% voter turnout, compared to a 67% turnout in the 1980 general election. In the 1982 primary 100% voted Democratic with 773 votes cast.

THE ECONOMY

AGRICULTURE Sheep ranches. In 1982, 92% of the land was in farms and ranches, with 2% of the farmland under cultivation, most of which was irrigated. Upton ranked 243rd in the state in highest agricultural receipts, with 56% from crops. Overgrazing, undesirable brush and weeds, wind and water erosion and inefficient irrigation systems are the current conservation problems. Primary crops: cotton and wheat. Primary vegetables: watermelons. Primary fruits and nuts: pecans. Primary livestock and products: cattle, sheep and wool. **BUSINESS** Total number of business establishments in the county: 100. Retail sales during the first quarter of 1984 decreased by 8%. In 1980, 10% of the labor force were self-employed, 16% were employed in professional or related services, 3% in

UPTON

manufacturing, 13% in wholesale and retail trade, 40% in agriculture, forestry, fisheries and mining, 17% were employed in other counties and there were 308 retired workers. The industries with the most employment: oil and gas extraction and tourism. The nonfarm earnings in 1981 totaled $47,878,000. The retired workers received an average monthly Social Security payment of $341. **FINANCE** On June 30, 1983, two commercial banks had total deposits of $39,326,000 and total assets of $45,250,000. There is one state savings and loan association branch in the county. **HOUSING** Average value of homes in 1980: $16,200. Permits for new, privately owned housing units decreased in 1982: six permits were issued with a total construction cost of $192,000. Of those permits, all were for single family houses. Between 1970 and 1980 the number of housing units increased by 3%. Seventy-nine percent of all units in the county are air-conditioned, 93% are heated by gas and 7% by electricity. **NATURAL RESOURCES** Caliche, limestone, oil and gas. In 1982 a total of 12,123,576 thousand cubic feet of gas well gas, 458,366 barrels of condensate, 10,742,371 barrels of crude oil and 28,614,038 thousand cubic feet of casinghead gas were produced. Current production of other minerals and products includes brine and crushed limestone. **TOURISM** Travel expenditures of $2,209,000 in 1982 (an increase of 16% over 1981) generated 38 jobs and $361,000 in payroll. **ALCOHOLIC BEVERAGES** Packaged distilled spirits, beer, ale, malt liquor and wine are legal. **FEDERAL EXPENDITURES** The federal government had direct expenditures or obligations of $5,968,000 in the county during fiscal year 1983, including $108,000 by the U.S. Department of Defense. In addition, the federal government provided $115,000 in grant awards, paid $215,000 in salaries and wages, made direct payments to individuals of $4,278,000 including $3,169,000 in retirement and disability payments, awarded $2,000 in procurement contracts and spent $1,358,000 in other expenditures or obligations. The federal government also provided $373,000 in direct loans and $2,007,000 in guaranteed loans and insurance.

COMMUNICATION
Newspapers–Weekly: McCamey News and The Rankin News. Cable TV. Telephone companies: Southwestern Bell. **TRANSPORTATION** Total public road mileage: 449. In 1982 there were 4,962 registered vehicles and 115 reported traffic accidents including one fatality. Intercity bus service is available. Motor freight: three carriers. Rail: one branch line carries annually one to five million tons of freight through the county. Aircraft: 16 are registered in the county. Airports: Upton County Airport at McCamey and Upton County Airport at Rankin.

COMMUNITY SERVICES
EDUCATION Two school districts with two elementary, two middle and two high schools. The average daily attendance in 1981-82 was 1,108, with expenditures per pupil of $8,066 including 98 classroom teachers with an average annual salary of $19,434. Fifty percent of the 72 high school graduates planned to attend college. In 1982-83, 57% of the students were White, 42% Hispanic and 2% Black. **PUBLIC LIBRARIES** Upton County Public Library (McCamey): 14,615 volumes. Rankin Public Library: 15,763 volumes. **CHILD CARE** Four day care and one twenty-four hour care licensed facilities. **HEALTH CARE** Three physicians and one dentist. Hospitals: two with a combined capacity of 36. Ambulance services: one volunteer service and one hospital-based service. Mental Health: one county clinic. Nursing homes: one nursing home has a capacity of 13 nursing care residents. The average cost per day for private patients in 1982 was $27.45. **CHURCHES** 18 churches have an estimated combined membership of 3,642. The largest denominations are Southern Baptist and United Methodist. **SOCIAL SERVICES**

In fiscal year 1983 a total of $94,943 in food stamps was distributed, with an average of 196 persons receiving food stamps each month. Aid to Families with Dependent Children (AFDC) totaled $16,806 with an average of 10 families receiving AFDC each month. Medical assistance benefits for the aged and disabled of $81,982 and for families and children of $16,326 brought the county benefit total to $210,057. **FIRE PROTECTION** Two volunteer fire departments. **LAW ENFORCEMENT** The County Sheriff has seven commissioned officers. **CRIME** 29 violent crimes (murder, forcible rape, robbery and aggravated assault) and 102 nonviolent crimes (burglary, larceny-theft and motor vehicle theft) were reported in 1982. **JUDICIAL SYSTEM** Two District Courts and Judges, one County Court and Judge and four Justices of the Peace. In the District Courts a total of 354 cases were pending on 1/1/82, 150 new cases were filed and 78 cases were disposed of during the year leaving 426 cases pending on 12/31/82. There were 76 criminal cases on the docket, 11 convictions, three persons committed to prison and 62 cases left pending. In the County Court 241 cases were pending on 1/1/82, 138 new cases were filed and 71 cases were disposed of during the year leaving 308 cases pending on 12/31/82. There were 371 criminal cases on the docket, 45 convictions, 11 persons committed to jail, and 301 cases left pending. **JAILS** One jail, capacity 12. **ATTORNEYS AT LAW** Three. **UTILITIES** 90% of the residents are connected to a public or privately owned water system and 76% are connected to a public sewer system. Natural gas is distributed to the county by Southern Union Company. The average annual residential bill for natural gas in 1982 for the Southern Union distribution system was $355.85, an increase of 23% over 1981. Electricity is distributed to the county by West Texas Utilities, Cap Rock Electric Coop., Inc. and Southwest Texas Electric Coop., Inc. and is generated primarily by gas and oil. **TAXES** The county has eight units with taxing authority: two school districts, two cities, one county, two hospital districts and one special district.

RECREATION/ENTERTAINMENT
COUNTY/MUNICIPAL PARKS 182 acres in eight county and one municipal park. These parks contain three playgrounds, four baseball and softball fields and three swimming pools. **SCENIC DRIVES** The Texas Pecos Trail runs through this county. This trail rambles through the vast region of Southwest and West Texas with landscapes varying from raw, arid regions to green valleys. In Upton County the drive across King Mountain near the community of McCamey at U.S. 67 and U.S. 385 offers outstanding views. **BOATING/FISHING** Lakes/reservoirs: McElroy (44 acres). Primary streams: Fivemile and Rankin. **HUNTING** Fall and winter seasons on deer, mule deer and javelina. No closed seasons on squirrel, bobcat and coyote. Winter seasons on quail, muskrat, beaver, opossum, ring-tailed cat, badger, fox, weasel, raccoon, skunk and civet cat. Fall, winter and spring seasons on turkey. In 1983 sandhill crane, duck, coot, geese, woodcock and jacksnipe seasons occurred during the winter months. Teal duck, rail and gallinule seasons occurred in the fall. Mourning dove seasons occurred intermittently during the fall and winter months. **MUSEUMS** McCamey: Mendoza Trail Museum and Adrian House. Rankin: Rankin Museum. **SPECIAL EVENTS** County Livestock Show, Rankin, January; Junior Rodeo, Rankin, June; Christmas Parade, Rankin, December; Christmas Parade, McCamey, December.

COMMUNITIES
COUNTY SEAT Rankin, County Courthouse, 79778; County Clerk's Office, 915/693-2861. **INCORPORATED COMMUNITIES** (1980 population and ZIP Code) McCamey (2,436) 79752 and Rankin (1,216) 79778. **UNINCORPORATED COMMUNITIES** (and ZIP Code) Midkiff (Hadacol Corners) 79755.

UPTON (continued)

FOR ADDITIONAL LOCAL INFORMATION McCamey Chamber of Commerce, P.O. Box 906, McCamey, 79752, 915/652-8202.

UVALDE (B12)

THE LAND
West of San Antonio on U.S. Highways 83 and 90 in the Rio Grande Plain Region, Uvalde County covers 1,564 square miles with the elevation ranging from 750 to 2,000 feet. The northern part of the county has light to dark, well drained, loamy soils with accumulations of lime. Some areas along the western border are 90% exposed rock. The southern part of the county has light colored, well drained soils and gray to black cracking, clayey soils with a high shrink-swell potential. There are some areas with limestone within 40 inches of the surface. The northern part of Uvalde is in the Edwards Plateau vegetation area with tall and mid grasses, junipers, mesquite, live and shinnery oak. The southern part of the county is in the South Texas Plains vegetation area with short and mid grasses, mesquite, thorny shrubs and cacti. Less than 1% of the land in the county is considered prime farmland. **CLIMATE** Subtropical Subhumid with mild winters and hot summers. The average annual temperature is 69 °F. Temperatures in January range from an average low of 37° to an average high of 63°F and in July range from 71° to 98°F. The average annual precipitation is 24 inches, with an average relative humidity of 83% at 6 A.M. and 43% at 6 P.M. The average annual snowfall is not significant. The growing season averages 275 days per year, with the last freeze in early March and the first freeze in late November. The sun shines during the year on the average 65% of the daylight hours.

THE PEOPLE
Uvalde County ranks 34th among all U.S. counties in the highest percent of persons of Spanish origin. The 1982 estimated population of 23,000 indicates a continuation of the moderate growth since the 1930s. Nearly 63% of the county residnts live in urban areas. The age groups with the largest gains between 1970 and 1980 were ages 25 to 34 and 62 and over. The largest ancestry groups are Hispanic (55%), persons of English descent (15%) and Irish descent (13%). **REGISTERED VOTERS** As of November 2, 1982 there were 13,960 registered voters (0.2% of the state total). The 1982 general election had a 39% voter turnout, compared to a 62% turnout in the 1980 general election. In the 1982 primary 95% voted Democratic and 5% Republican, with 4,157 votes cast.

THE ECONOMY
AGRICULTURE Diversified ranchland. In 1982, 85% of the land was in farms and ranches, with 14% of the farmland under cultivation and 54% irrigated. Uvalde ranked 39th in the state in highest agricultural receipts, with 53% from crops. Undesirable brush and weeds, water erosion, inefficient irrigation systems, difficulties in grass establishment and flooding are the current conservation problems. Primary crops: wheat, oats, corn, hay, sorghum and cotton. Primary vegetables: second in the state for carrots and cabbage, third for processed vegetables, fourth for total fresh market vegtables and onion and sixth for cantaloupes. Primary fruits and nuts: peaches and pecans. Primary livestock and products: third in the state for both angora goats and mohair production and fourth for hogs. Cattle, sheep and wool. **BUSINESS** Total number of business establishments in the county: 466. Retail sales during the first quarter of 1984 increased 2% In 1980, 13% of the labor force were self-employed, 20%

were employed in professional or related services, 7% in manufacturing, 22% in wholesale and retail trade, 18% in agriculture, forestry, fisheries and mining, 9% were employed in other counties and there were 1,698 retired workers. The industries with the most employment: oil and gas extraction, heavy construction, agribusiness, the mining of nonmetallic minierals and the manufacture of men's work clothing. The nonfarm earnings in 1981 totaled $155,498,000. The retired workers received an average monthly Social Security payment of $292.00. **FINANCE** On June 30, 1983, four commercial banks had total deposits of $191,208,000 and total assets of $221,449,000. On December 31, 1982 two state savings and loan associations had assets of $83,905,002. In addition there are two credit unions in the county. **HOUSING** Average value of homes in 1980: $25,400. Permits for new, privately owned housing units decreased in 1982: 71 permits were issued with a total construction cost of $1,412,617. Of those permits, 42 were for single family houses. Between 1970 and 1980 the number of housing units increased by 33%. Sixty-one percent of all units in the county are air-conditioned, 71% are heated by gas and 21% by electricity. **NATURAL RESOURCES** Limestone, industrial sand, sand and gravel, lignite coal, oil and gas. Current production of other minerals and products includes asphaltic limestone, crushed limestone, sand and gravel and crushed basalt. **TOURISM** Travel expenditures of $16,785,000 in 1982 (an increase of 12% over 1981) generated 387 jobs and $3,191,000 in payroll. Lodging: six hotels, motels and tourist courts. **ALCOHOLIC BEVERAGES** Packaged distilled spirits, beer, ale, malt liquor and wine are legal in parts of the county. **FEDERAL EXPENDITURES** The federal government had direct expenditures or obligations of $32,096,000 in the county during fiscal year 1983, including $1,151,000 by the U.S. Department of Defense. In addition, the federal government provided $2,137,000 in grant awards, paid $1,966,000 in salaries and wages, made direct payments to individuals of $24,752,000 including $17,570,000 in retirement and disability payments and spent $3,246,000 in other expenditures or obligations. The federal government also provided $875,000 in direct loans and $8,831,000 in guaranteed loans and insurance.

COMMUNICATION
Newspapers–Weekly: The Sabinal Times and The Uvalde Leader News. Radio: KVOU-AM and KYUF-FM (Uvalde). Cable TV. Telephone companies: General Telephone, Southwestern Bell, Frio Canyon Telephone, Hill Country Telephone Coop., Knippa Telephone and SW Texas Telephone. **TRANSPORTATION** Total public road mileage: 702. In 1982 there were 16,861 registered vehicles and 440 reported traffic accidents including eight fatalities. Taxi cabs: one company in the city of Uvalde. Intercity bus service is available. Motor freight: nine local and intrastate carriers. Rail: the Sunset Limited provides passenger service on the Amtrak route. One main and one branch line carry freight through the county. The main line carries annually over 30 million tons of freight and the branch carries one to five million. Aircraft: 70 are registered in the county. Airports: Garner Field at Uvalde serves as a base for 40 aircraft and is a basic transportation airport with general aviation service. Uvalde Memorial Hospital Heliport provides emergency service.

COMMUNITY SERVICES
EDUCATION Four school districts with eight elementary, two middle and four high schools. The average daily attendance in 1981-82 was 4,843, with expenditures per pupil of $2,225 including 308 classroom teachers with an average annual salary of $15,219. Sixty-six percent of the 282 high school graduates planned to attend college. In 1982-83, 29% of the students were White, 71% Hispanic, 0.3% Black and 0.1% Asian. Sports championships: 1983 AA Girls' Tennis Doubles, Sabinal H.S. Private schools: 284

students enrolled in two elementary schools. Southwest Texas Junior College is located in Uvalde. Established in 1946 it is a vocational and two year academic college under local control. Enrollment in 1982 was 2,185 with in state undergratuate tuition and fees of $326 per semester. Vocational education: Henderson Technical Training Center (Uvalde). **PUBLIC LIBRARIES** El Progreso Memorial Library (Uvalde): 43,306 volumes and two branches. **CHILD CARE** 30 day care and five twenty-four hour care licensed facilities. **HEALTH CARE** 19 physicians and eight dentists. Hospitals: one with a capacity of 62. Clinics: one dialysis clinic and one public health clinic. Ambulance services: one volunteer service, one commercial service and one volunteer fire department service. Mental health: one mobile clinic. Nursing homes: two nursing homes with a combined capacity of 242 nursing care residents. The average cost per day for private patients in 1982 was $33.56. **CHURCHES** 38 churches have an estimated combined membership of 14,380. The largest denominations are Catholic, Southern Baptist and United Methodist. **SOCIAL SERVICES** In fiscal year 1983 a total of $2,162,180 in food stamps was distributed, with an average of 4,551 persons receiving food stamps each month. Aid to Families with Dependent Children (AFDC) totaled $362,381 with an average of 224 families receiving AFDC each month. Medical assistance benefits for the aged and disabled of $1,698,271 and for families and children of $541,680 brought the county benefit total to $4,764,512. **FIRE PROTECTION** Five volunteer fire departments. **LAW ENFORCEMENT** The County Sheriff has 27 commissioned officers. Two police departments have a combined force of 22. **CRIME** 64 violent crimes (murder, forcible rape, robbery and aggravated assault) and 614 nonviolent crimes (burglary, larceny-theft and motor vehicle theft) were reported in 1982. **JUDICIAL SYSTEM** One District Court and Judge, one County Court and Judge and five Justices of the Peace. In the District Court a total of 270 cases were pending on 1/1/82, 557 new cases were filed and 568 cases were disposed of during the year leaving 259 cases pending on 12/31/82. There were 278 criminal cases on the docket, 78 convictions, 14 persons committed to prison and 112 cases left pending. In the County Court 1,079 cases were pending on 1/1/82, 807 new cases were filed and 1,071 cases were disposed of during the year leaving 815 cases pending on 12/31/82. There were 1,562 criminal cases on the docket, 304 convictions, 56 persons committed to jail, and 519 cases left pending. **JAILS** One jail, capacity 45. **ATTORNEYS AT LAW** 28. **UTILITIES** 78% of the residents are connected to a public or privately owned water system and 64% are connected to a public sewer system. Electricity is distributed to the county by Central Power and Light, Cochran Power and Light, Rio Grande Electric Coop., Inc., Bandera Electric Coop., Inc. and Medina Electric Coop., Inc. and is generated primarily by gas, oil and coal. The typical residential electric bill is $162.15 per month for an all-electric house using 2,500 kwh. **TAXES** The county has nine units with taxing authority: three school districts, two cities, one county, one college district and two special districts.

RECREATION/ENTERTAINMENT

NATIONAL REGISTER OF HISTORIC PLACES Uvalde: John Nance Garner House and Ettie R. Garner Memorial Museum (National Historic Landmark) and Grand Opera House. Uvalde vicinity: Leona River Acheological Site, Taylor Slough Acheological Site, Uvalde Flint Quarry and Willingham Site. **STATE** Garner State Park covers 1,420 acres with camping and trailer sites as well as fishing, swimming, miniature golf and pedal boats. **COUNTY/MUNICIPAL PARKS** 248 acres in two county and 16 municipal parks. These parks contain six playgrounds, one golf course, one football and soccer field, nine baseball and softball fields, six tennis courts, one multi-use court, one swimming pool, five beaches and three boat ramps. Developed

campsites: 68. **SCENIC DRIVES** The Texas Hill Country Trail runs through this county. This trail winds through a scenic region of South-Central Texas, spanning a vast ranching area abundant with wildlife in a landscape of deeply-sculptured valleys and hills. Of particular interest in Uvalde County is the Frio River Canyon along U.S. 83, F.M. 1050 and Texas 127. **BOATING/FISHING** Lakes/reservoirs: Kincaid (29 acres), Nueses (50 acres), Nunley #1 (35 acres), Nunley #2 (34 acres), Smyth (42 acres), V-Bar (35 acres) and Willingham (45 acres). Major rivers: Leona, Nueces, Frio, Dry Frio and Sabinal. Primary streams: East Elm. **HUNTING** Fall and winter seasons on deer. No closed season on javelina, squirrel, bobcat and coyote. Winter seasons on quail, muskrat, beaver, opossum, ring-tailed cat, badger, fox, weasel, raccoon, skunk and civet cat. Fall, winter and spring seasons on turkey. Special regulation regarding state-owned river beds. In 1983 sandhill crane, duck, coot, geese, woodcock and jacksnipe seasons occurred during the winter months. Teal duck, rail and gallinule seasons occurred in the fall. Mourning dove seasons occurred intermittently during the fall and winter months. **MUSEUMS** Uvalde: Garner Memorial Museum. **THEATERS** Uvalde: Opera House. **COLLEGIATE FINE ARTS** Uvalde: Cultural events offered by Southwest Texas Junior College. **SPECIAL EVENTS** Cinco de Mayo Celebration, Uvalde, May; Catus Jack Festival, Uvalde, June; Cypress City Day, Uvalde, June; Sahawe Summer Ceremonials, Uvalde, July; Golf Tourney, Uvalde, July; Rodeo, Uvalde, August; Rabadillo Chili Cookoff, Uvalde, September; Diez y Seiz, Uvalde, September; An Evening in Old Uvalde, Uvalde, October; Intercollegiate Rodeo, Uvalde, October; Family Walkfest, Utopia, November; Hunters Roundup, Uvalde, November; Arts and Crafts Fair, Uvalde, November.

COMMUNITIES

COUNTY SEAT Uvalde, County Courthouse, 78801; County Clerk's Office, 512/278-6614. **INCORPORATED COMMUNITIES** (1980 population and ZIP Code) Sabinal (1,827) 78881 and Uvalde (14,178) 78801. **UNINCORPORATED COMMUNITIES** (and ZIP Code) Blewett 78801, Cline 78801, Concan 78838, Dabney 78801, Knippa 78870, Montell 78801, Reagan Wells 78801 and Utopia 78884 **FOR ADDITIONAL LOCAL INFORMATION** Sabinal Chamber of Commerce, P. O. Box 241, Sabinal 78881, 512/998-2634 and Uvalde Chamber of Commerce, 300 E. Main, P. O. Box 706, Uvalde, 78801, 512/278-3361

VAL VERDE (B8)

THE LAND

Bordering Mexico southeast of Odessa on U.S. Highways 90 and 277 in the Edwards Plateau Region, Val Verde County covers 3,150 square miles with the elevation ranging from 800 to 2,000 feet. In the southeastern corner are gray to black, cracking, clayey soils with a high shrink-swell potential. Limestone is found within 40 inches of the surface. The rest of the county has loamy soils with lime accumulations. About 90% of this area is exposed rock. Val Verde is in the Edwards Plateau vegetation area with short and mid grasses, mesquite, thorny shrubs and cacti. Less than 1% of the land in the county is considered prime farmland. **CLIMATE** Subtropical Steppe with a wide variation in the growing season from the northwest to the southeast portions. The average annual temperature is 68 °F. Temperatures in January range from an average low of 35 ° to an average high of 63 °F and in July range from 73 ° to 97 °F. The average annual precipitation is 17 inches, with an average relative humidity of 75% at 6 A.M. and 40% at 6 P.M. The average annual snowfall is not significant. The growing seasons averages 275 days per year, with the last freeze in mid February and the first freeze in early

COUNTIES

VAL VERDE (continued)

December. The sun shines during the year on the average 67% of the daylight hours.

THE PEOPLE

Val Verde County ranks 26th among all U.S. counties in the highest percent of persons within the population of Spanish origin. The 1982 estimated population of 37,900 indicates a continuation of the moderate growth between 1930 and 1980. The age groups with the largest increases were ages 25 to 34 and 62 and over. The largest ancestry groups are Hispanic (63%), persons of English descent (11%), Irish descent (8%) and German descent (8%). **REGISTERED VOTERS** As of November 2, 1982 there were 13,092 registered voters (0.2% of the state total). The 1982 general election had a 44% voter turnout, compared to a 68% turnout in the 1980 general election. In the 1982 primary 94% voted Democratic and 6% Republican, with 4,806 votes cast.

THE ECONOMY

AGRICULTURE Sheep and angora goat ranches. In 1982, 95% of the land was in farms and ranches, with less than 1% under cultivation. Val Verde ranked 191st in the state in highest agricultural receipts, with almost 100% from livestock and livestock products. Overgrazing, undesirable brush and weeds, difficulties in grass establishment and water erosion are the current conservation problems. Primary fruits and nuts: peaches and pecans. Primary livestock and products: first in the state for sheep and wool production, and second for angora goats and mohair production. Cattle. **BUSINESS** Total number of business establishments in the county: 608. Retail sales during the first quarter of 1984 increased by 4%. In 1980, 9% of the labor force were self-employed, 20% were employed in professional or related services, 9% in manufacturing, 23% in wholesale and retail trade, 12% in government and government enterprises, 5% were employed in other counties and there were 1,729 retired workers. The industries with the most employment: general constuction, agribusiness, tourism and the manufacture of men's clothing. The nonfarm earnings in 1981 totaled $241,582,000. The retired workers received an average monthly Social Security payment of $268.00. **FINANCE** On June 30, 1983, four commercial banks had total deposits of $180,090,000 and total assets of $201,267,000. On December 31, 1982 two state savings and loan associations and one state branch had combined assets of $46,406,498. In addition there are four credit unions in the county. **HOUSING** Average value of homes in 1980: $30,300. Permits for new, privately owned housing units decreased in 1982: 106 permits were issued with a total construction cost of $1,853,396. Of those permits, 86 were for single family houses. Between 1970 and 1980 the number of housing units increased by 46%. Seventy-seven percent of all units in the county are air-conditioned, 72% are heated by gas and 26% by electricity. **NATURAL RESOURCES** Limestone, manganese, sand, gravel, oil, gas and kaolin clay. In 1982 a total of 8,289,867 thousand cubic feet of gas well gas, 1,776 barrels of crude oil and 74 thousand cubic feet of casinghead gas were produced. Current production of other minerals and products includes barite, clay, crushed limestone, sand and gravel. **TOURISM** Travel expenditures of $28,463,000 in 1982 (an increase of 12% over 1981) generated 681 jobs and $5,540,000 in payroll. Lodging: 10 hotels, motels and tourist courts. **ALCOHOLIC BEVERAGES** Packaged distilled spirits, beer, ale, malt liquor and wine are legal in parts of the county. Sale of mixed beverages is legal in all or parts of the county. **MILITARY INSTALLATIONS** Laughlin Air Force Base, Del Rio, 3,068 personnel, 5,331 acres, Flying Training Wing. **FEDERAL EXPENDITURES** The federal govern-ment had direct expenditures or obligations of $125,158,000 in the county during fiscal year 1983, including $79,404,000 by the U.S. Department of Defense. In addition, the federal government provided $3,805,000 in grant awards, paid $70,440,000 in salaries and wages, made direct payments to individuals of $35,878,000 including $30,134,000 in retirement and disability payments, awarded $11,997,000 in procurement contracts and spent $3,037,000 in other expenditures or obligations. The federal government also provided $7,457,000 in guaranteed loans and insurance.

COMMUNICATION

Newspapers–Daily: News-Herald (Del Rio), ave. eve. circ. 6,050. Radio: KDLK-AM, KWMC-AM and KLKE-FM (Del Rio). Cable TV. Telephone companies: General Telephone, Big Bend Telephone and SW Texas Telephone. **TRANSPORTATION** Total public road mileage: 649. In 1982 there were 27,098 registered vehicles and 873 reported traffic accidents including nine fatalities. Taxi cabs: 10 companies in Del Rio. Municipal transit systems: two intracity bus systems in Del Rio with scheduled routes. Intercity bus service is available. Motor freight: seven local and intrastate carriers. Rail: The Sunset Limited provides passenger service on the Amtrak route. One main line carries annually over 30 million tons of freight through the county. Aircraft: 146 are registered in the county. Airports: Del Rio International Airport serves as a base for 58 aircraft and is a basic transportation airport with commuter service. Also serving the area are Davis Ranch Airport at Del Rio, Robertson Ranch Airport at Comstock and Mills Ranch Airport at Pandale. Val Verde Memorial Hospital at Del Rio provides a Heliport for emergency use.

COMMUNITY SERVICES

EDUCATION Three school districts with 10 elementary, one middle and two high schools. The average daily attendance in 1981-82 was 8,607, with expenditures per pupil of $1,903 including 506 classroom teachers with an average annual salary of $14,853. Thirty-nine percent of the 472 high school graduates planned to attend college. In 1982-83, 21% of the students were White, 77% Hispanic, 2% Black and 0.2% Asian. Private schools: 477 students enrolled in two elementary schools. Vocational education: A & C College of Beauty and Del Rio School of Vocational Nursing (Del Rio). **PUBLIC LIBRARIES** Val Verde County Library (Del Rio): 42,050 volumes. **CHILD CARE** 28 day care and two twenty-four hour care licensed facilities. **HEALTH CARE** 21 physicians and seven dentists. Hospitals: one with a combined capacity of 104. Specialized hospitals: one air force hospital with capacity of 28. Clinics: one youth counseling clinic and one public health clinic. Ambulance services: one city and one hospital based service. Mental health: one clinic. Nursing homes: two nursing homes with a combined capacity of 140 nursing care residents. The average cost per day for private patients in 1982 was $28.16. **CHURCHES** 25 churches have an estimated combined membership of 21,360. The largest denominations are Catholic and Southern Baptist. **SOCIAL SERVICES** In fiscal year 1983 a total of $4,099,894 in food stamps was distributed, with an average of 8,292 persons receiving food stamps each month. Aid to Families with Dependent Children (AFDC) totaled $593,268 with an average of 374 families receiving AFDC each month. Medical assistance benefits for the aged and disabled of $1,676,407 and for families and children of $749,007 brought the county benefit total to $7,118,574. **FIRE PROTECTION** One volunteer fire department. **LAW ENFORCEMENT** The County Sheriff has 45 commissioned officers. One police department has a force of 42. **CRIME** 142 violent crimes (murder, forcible rape, robbery and aggravated assault) and 1,490 nonviolent crimes (burglary, larceny-theft and motor vehicle theft) were reported in

1982. JUDICIAL SYSTEM One District Court and Judge, two County Courts and Judges and four Justices of the Peace. In the District Court a total of 806 cases were pending on 1/1/82, 688 new cases were filed and 622 cases were disposed of during the year leaving 872 cases pending on 12/31/82. There were 232 criminal cases on the docket, 54 convictions, 19 persons committed to prison and one committed to jail and 102 cases left pending. In the County Courts 2,192 cases were pending on 1/1/82, 930 new cases were filed and 1,040 cases were disposed of during the year leaving 2,082 cases pending on 12/31/82. There were 2,607 criminal cases on the docket, 82 convictions, 24 persons committed to jail, and 1,856 cases left pending. **JAILS** One jail, capacity 81. Completed major renovation in 1983 and is constructing new facilities. **ATTORNEYS AT LAW** 40. **UTILITIES** 90% of the residents are connected to a public or privately owned water system and 85% are connected to a public sewer system. Electricity is distributed to the county by Central Power and Light, Rio Grande Electric Coop., Inc., Cochran Power and Light, Farmers Electric Coop., Inc., and Southwest Texas Electric Coop., Inc. and is generated primarily by gas, oil and coal. The typical residential electric bill is $162.15 per month for an all-electric house using 2,500 kwh. **TAXES** The county has six units with taxing authority: three school districts, one city, one county and one hospital district.

RECREATION/ENTERTAINMENT
FEDERAL ANISTAD RECREATION AREA covering 62,452 acres, offers boating and watersports actitivties in the United States section of Amistad Reservoir on the Rio Grande River. **NATIONAL REGISTER OF HISTORIC PLACES** Comstock vicinity: Lower Pecos Canyon District and West of Pecos Railroad Camps District. Del Rio: Val Verde County Courthouse and Jail. Del Rio vicinity: San Felipe Creek Archeological District. Langtry vicinity: Mile Canyon Archeological District, Rattlesnake Canyon and Seminole Canyon District. **STATE** Seminole Canyon State Historical Park covers 2,172 acres with camping and trailer sites as well as nature trails. Esihibits explain the Indian pictographs found in the canyon. **MUNICIPAL PARKS** 83 acres in 11 municipal parks. These parks contain two miles of hiking trails, six playgrounds, five baseball and softball fields, six tennis courts, one multi-use court, two swimming pools and three beaches. **SCENIC DRIVES** The Texas Pecos Trail runs through this county. This trail rambles through the vast region of Southwest and West Texas with landscapes varying from raw, arid regions to green valleys. In Val Verde County on U.S. 90 east of Langtry, travellers can view the canyon of the Pecos River. **BOATING/FISHING** Lakes/reservoirs: Gillis East (78 acres) and International Amistad (64,900 acres). Major rivers: Rio Grande, Pecos, Devils and Dry Devils. Primary streams: Evans. **HUNTING** Fall and winter seasons on deer and mule deer. No closed seasons on javelina, squirrel, coyote and bobcat. Winter seasons on quail, muskrat, beaver, opossum, ring-tailed cat, badger, fox, weasel, raccoon, skunk and civet cat. Fall, winter and spring seasons on turkey. In 1983 sandhill crane, duck ,coot, geese, woodcock and jacksnipe seasons occurred during the winter months. Teal duck, rail and gallinule seasons occurred in the fall. Mourning dove seasons occurred intermittently during the fall and winter months with a fall season on white-winged dove. **MUSEUMS** Del Rio: Whitehead Memorial Museum. Langtry: Judge Roy Bean Visitor Center. **SPECIAL EVENTS** Miss Val Verde Pageant, Del Rio, January; Horse Races, Del Rio, Monthly; Rodeo, Del Rio, April; Pioneer Heritage Week, Del Rio, April/May; George Paul Memorial Bull Riding, Del Rio, May; Nights on Old San Felipe Del Rio, Del Rio, May; Cinco de Mayo Celebration, Del Rio, May; Amistad Navy Regatta, Del Rio, May; Diez y Seis Celebration, Del Rio, September; Fiesta Amistad,

Del Rio, October; Veterans Day Parade and Ceremony, Del Rio, November; Winter Texans Welcome Party, Del Rio, November.

COMMUNITIES
COUNTY SEAT Del Rio, County Courthouse, 78840; County Clerk's Office, 512/774-3611. **INCORPORATED COMMUNITIES** (1980 population and ZIP Code) Del Rio (30,034) 78840. **UNINCORPORATED COMMUNITIES** (and ZIP Code) Amistad 78840, Comstock 78837, Juno 76938, Langtry 78871, Loma Alta 78840, Pandale 76943 and Pumpville 78876. **FOR ADDITIONAL LOCAL INFORMATION** Del Rio Chamber of Commerce, 1915 Avenue F, Del Rio, 78840, 512/775-3551.

VAN ZANDT (E15)

THE LAND
East of Dallas on Interstate Highway 20 in the Claypan Area, Van Zandt County covers 855 square miles with the elevation ranging from 400 to 600 feet. The northwestern one-third of the county is undulating with gray to black, cracking, clayey soils that have a high shrink-swell potential and slightly acidic, light colored, loamy soils over very deep, reddish, cracking, clayey subsoils. The central one-third has light colored soils with sandy surfaces over mottled, clayey subsoils. The southeastern one-third has gently rolling to hilly, reddish soils with light colored, loamy surfaces over very deep, reddish, clayey subsoils that are high in iron. The eastern two-thirds of Van Zandt is in the Post Oak Savannah vegetation area with tall grasses, post and black jack oak. The western third is in the Blackland Prairies vegetation area with tall grasses, mesquite and oak, pecan and elm trees along streams. Between 11 and 20 % of the land in the county is considered prime farmland. **CLIMATE** Subtropical Humid with hot summers. The average annual temperature is 65°F. Temperatures in January range from an average low of 33° to an average high of 54°F and in July range from 72° to 97°F. The average annual precipitation is 43 inches, with an average relative humidity of 83% at 6 A.M. and 55% at 6 P.M. The average annual snowfall is three inches. The growing season averages 250 days per year, with the last freeze in mid March and the first freeze in late November. The sun shines during the year on the average 66% of the daylight hours.

THE PEOPLE
The population of VAn Zandt County has grown steadily with a 16% growth rate between 1960 and 1970 and a 42% growth rate between 1970 and 1980. The 1982 estimated population of 33,000 indicates a continuation of that strong growth. Nearly 74% of the county residents live in rural areas. The age groups with the largest gains between 1970 and 1980 were ages 25 to 39 and 15 to 19. The largest ancestry groups are persons of English descent (26%), Irish descent (23%) and German descent (11%). **REGISTERED VOTERS** As of November 2, 1982 there were 17,142 registered voters (0.3% of the state total). The 1982 general election had a 51% voter turnout, compared to a 65% turnout in the 1980 general election. In the 1982 primary 95% voted Democratic and 5% Republican, with 6,222 votes cast.

THE ECONOMY
AGRICULTURE Cattle area. In 1982, 74% of the land was in farms and ranches, with 22% of the farmland under cultivation and 3% irrigated. Van Zandt ranked 52nd in the state in highest agricultural receipts, with 78% from livestock and livestock products. Overgrazing, undesirable brush and weeds and water erosion are the current conservation problems. Primary crops: second in the state for hay, wheat, oats, rye and cotton. Primary vegetables: sweet potatoes, tomatoes and watermelons. Primary fruits and nuts: peaches and pecans. Primary livestock and

COUNTIES

products: fourth in the state for beef cows that have calved, cattle, milk and sheep. **BUSINESS** Total number of business establishments in the county: 465. Retail sales during the first quarter of 1984 increased by 22%. In 1980, 14% of the labor force were self-employed, 16% were employed in professional or related services, 20% in manufacturing, 21% in wholesale and retail trade, 11% in construction, 42% were employed in other counties and there were 4,061 retired workers. The industries with the most employment: tourism, oil and gas extration, construction and the manufacture of women's clothing, mobile homes, chemical preparations and metal doors. The nonfarm earnings in 1981 totaled $247,106,000. The retired workers received an average monthly Social Security payment of $300.00. **FINANCE** On June 30, 1983, eight commercial banks had total deposits of $113,220,000 and total assets of $127,592,000. There are two state savings and loan association branches, two federal association branches and one credit union in the county. **HOUSING** Average value of homes in 1980: $27,600. Permits for new, privately owned housing units decreased in 1982: 44 permits were issued with a total construction cost of $1,705,735. Of those permits, all were for single family houses. Between 1970 and 1980 the number of housing units increased by 50%. Seventy-four percent of all units in the county are air-conditioned, 71% are heated by gas and 22% by electricity. **NATURAL RESOURCES** Ceramic clay, lignite coal, iron salt domes, recovered sulphur, limestone, oil and gas. In 1982 a total of 12,652,758 thousand cubic feet of gas well gas, 27,509 barrels of condensate, 3,448,974 barrels of crude oil and 3,549,368 thousand cubic feet of casinghead gas were produced. Current production of other minerals and products includes clay, crushed limestone, salt and recovered sulphur. **TOURISM** Travel expenditures of $4,485,000 in 1982 (an increase of 12% over 1981) generated 94 jobs and $801,000 in payroll. Convention/meeting facilities: Canton-Van Zandt County Fair Arena. **ALCOHOLIC BEVERAGES** Totally dry. **FEDERAL EXPENDITURES** The federal government had direct expenditures or obligations of $60,757,000 in the county during fiscal year 1983, including $2,527,000 by the U.S. Department of Defense. In addition, the federal government provided $1,353,000 in grant awards, paid $1,578,000 in salaries and wages, made direct payments to individuals of $57,296,000 including $45,327,000 in retirement and disability payments, awarded $116,000 in procurement contracts and spent $414,000 in other expenditures or obligations. The federal government also provided $76,000 in direct loans and $3,535,000 in guaranteed loans and insurance.

COMMUNICATION

Newspapers–Weekly: Canton Herald, Edgewood Enterprise, The Grand Saline Sun, The Van Progress (Van) and the Wills Point Chronicle. Cable TV. Telephone companies: Continental Telephone, General Telephone, Southwestern Bell and United Telphone. **TRANSPORTATION** Total public road mileage: 1,527. In 1982 there were 30,444 registered vehicles and 624 reported traffic accidents including 17 fatalities. Intercity bus service is available. Motor freight: six local and intrastate carriers. Rail: The Eagle provides passenger service on the Amtrak route. One main line carries annually 20 to 30 million tons of freight through the county. Aircraft: 26 are registered in the county. Airports: Hackney Municipal at Canton and Wills Point Municipal Airport.

COMMUNITY SERVICES

EDUCATION Seven school districts with seven elementary, four middle and seven high schools. The average daily attendance in 1981-82 was 5,793, with expenditures per pupil of $2,126 including 348 classroom teachers with an average annual salary of $16,008. Fifty-five percent of the 385 high school graduates planned to attend college. In 1982-83, 92% of the students were White, 2% Hispanic, 6% Black, 0.3% Asian and 0.1% American Indian. Sports championships: 1983 AA Boys' Tennis Singles, Grand Saline H.S.; 1983 AAA Boys' Tennis Singles, Wills Point H.S. **PUBLIC LIBRARIES** Van Zandt County Library (Canton): 29,362 volumes. Grand Saline Public Library: 8,000 volumes. **CHILD CARE** 46 day care and 15 twenty-four hour care licensed facilities. **HEALTH CARE** 16 physicians and 12 dentists. Hospitals: one with a capacity of 52. Ambulance services: two commercial, one fire department, one volunteer fire department and one city service. Mental health: one regional clinic and one center with bed capacity of 38. Nursing homes: seven nursing homes with a combined capacity of 532 nursing care residents. The average cost per day for private patients in 1982 was $29.82. **CHURCHES** 108 churches have an estimated combined membership of 20,427. The largest denominations are Southern Baptist, Baptist Missionary and United Methodist. **SOCIAL SERVICES** In fiscal year 1983 a total of $850,750 in food stamps was distributed, with an average of 1,886 persons receiving food stamps each month. Aid to Families with Dependent Children (AFDC) totaled $151,551 with an average of 106 families receiving AFDC each month. Medical assistance benefits for the aged and disabled of $4,862,594 and for families and children of $298,498 brought the county benefit total to $6,163,392. **FIRE PROTECTION** Twelve volunteer fire departments. **LAW ENFORCEMENT** The County Sheriff has 24 commissioned officers. Five police departments have a combined force of 33. **CRIME** 74 violent crimes (murder, forcible rape, robbery and aggravated assault) and 695 nonviolent crimes (burglary, larceny-theft and motor vehicle theft) were reported in 1982. **JUDICIAL SYSTEM** One District Court and Judge, one County Court and Judge and four Justices of the Peace. In the District Court a total of 1,300 cases were pending on 1/1/82, 770 new cases were filed and 819 cases were disposed of during the year leaving 1,251 cases pending on 12/31/82. There were 289 criminal cases on the docket, 97 convictions, 35 persons committed to prison and 115 cases left pending. In the County Court 1,348 cases were pending on 1/1/82, 1,196 new cases were filed and 1,342 cases were disposed of during the year leaving 1,202 cases pending on 12/31/82. There were 2,132 criminal cases on the docket, 439 convictions, 25 persons committed to jail and 881 cases left pending. **JAILS** One jail, capacity 33. **ATTORNEYS AT LAW** 27. **UTILITIES** 74% of the residents are connected to a public or privately owned water system and 37% are connected to a public sewer system. Natural gas is distributed to the county by Lone Star Gas Co., Division of Enserch and Entex, Inc. The annual residential bill for natural gas in 1982 for the Lone Star distribution system was $405.91, an increase of 35% over 1981 and for Entex it was $390.31, an increase of 26%. Electricity is distributed to the county by Texas Power and Light, Texas New Mexico Power Co., Wood County Electric Coop., Inc. and Kaufman Co. Electric Coop., Inc. and is generated primarily by gas, oil and coal. The typical residential electric bill is $168.05 per month for an all-electric house using 2,500 kwh. **TAXES** The county has 15 units with taxing authority: seven school districts, five cities, one county and two college districts.

RECREATION/ENTERTAINMENT

STATE Purtis Creek Park Site covers 1,583 acres and is closed to the public as of July 1983. **MUNICIPAL PARKS** 470 acres in eight municipal parks. These parks contain three playgrounds, three football and soccer fields, eight baseball and softball fields, six tennis courts, one swimming pool, one beach, four boat ramps and shore fishing facilities. Developed campsites: two: **SCENIC DRIVES** The Texas Lakes Trail runs through this county. This trail introduces some 30 blue-water recreational areas in a variety of settings in North-Central Texas. **BOATING/FISHING** Lakes/reservoirs: Callendar (216 acres), Cedar Creek Soil Conservation Service Lakes 101, 104 and 140 (46 acres), Grand Saline City (31 acres), Club 20 (17 acres), Edgewood City (37 acres), Edgewood Old City (20 acres), Garden (38 acres), Metzger (28 acres), Metzger 3 (16 acres), Mill Creek Soil Conservation Service Lake #1 (123 acres), Neill (25 acres), Rhines (284 acres), Spring (32 acres), Tawakoni (36,700 acres), Willow (82 acres) and Wills Point (48 acres). Major rivers: Neches and Sabine. Primary streams: Slater, Wolf, Allen, Caney, Hoard, Village, Mill, Chinguapin, Wills and Magby. **HUNTING** Fall and winter season on deer. Summer, fall and winter seasons on squirrel. Winter seasons on quail, muskrat, beaver, otter, opossum, mink, ring-tailed cat, badger, fox, raccoon, skunk and civet cat. No closed seasons on nutria and coyote. In 1983 duck, coot, geese, woodcock and jacksnipe seasons occurred in the fall. Mourning dove seasons occurred intermittently during the fall and winter months. **SPECIAL EVENTS** Salt Festival and Rodeo, Grand Saline, June; County Fair and Rodeo, Canton, August; Bluegrass Festival, Canton, August; Christmas Parade, Grand Saline, December; First Monday, Canton.

COMMUNITIES

COUNTY SEAT Canton, County Courthouse, 75103; County Clerk's Office, 214/567-6503. **INCORPORATED COMMUNITIES** (1980 population and ZIP Code) Canton (2,845) 75103, Edgewood (1,413) 75117, Edom (250) 75756, Fruitvale (367) 75127, Grand Saline (2,709) 75140, Van (1,881) 75790 and Wills Point (2,631) 75169. **UNINCORPORATED COMMUNITIES** (and ZIP Code) Alsa 75169, Ben Wheeler 75754, Clifton 75169, Colfax 75103, Corinth 75140 Creagleville 75140, Dale Crest 75140, Enterprise 75169, Flatwood 75754, Friendship 75140, Hayden 75169, Jackson 75103, Johnstown 75169, Jones 75140, Lakeview Estates 75169, Lawrence Springs 75140, Martins Mills 75754, Myrtle Springs 75169, Oakland 75103, Odom 75147, Phalba 75147, Primrose 75754, Providence 75140, Pruitt 75140, Redland 75754, Roddy 75147, Rolling Oaks 75169, Sand Flat 75140, Sava (Bright Star) 75169, Scott 75169, Silver Lake 75140, Tundra 75103, Wallace (Ford) 75103, Walton 75751, Wentworth 75103, Whitton 75103. **FOR ADDITIONAL LOCAL INFORMATION** Canton Chamber of Commerce, 105 S. Buffalo St., Canton, 75103, 214/567-2991, Edgewood Chamber of Commerce, 207 E. Front, P.O. Box 438, Edgewood, 75117, 214/896-4241, Grand Saline Chamber of Commerce, 130 E. Frank, Grand Saline, 75140, 214/962-3555, Van Chamber of Commerce, P.O. Box 55, Van, 75790, 214/963-7216 and Wills Point Chamber of Commerce, 307 N. 4th, Wills Point, 75169, 214/873-3111.

VICTORIA (G22)

THE LAND

Southeast of San Antonio on U.S. Highways 87 and 59 in the Central Prairies Region, Victoria County covers 887 square miles with the elevation ranging from sea level to 200 feet. The northwestern part of the county has level to undulating, light colored soils with sandy surfaces and clayey subsoils. The central portion has level soils with light colored, loamy surfaces over very deep, reddish or mottled subsoils. The rest of the county has light colored, shallow, loamy surfaces over clayey subsoils and gray to black, cracking, clayey soils that have a high shrink-swell potential. Victoria is in the Gulf Prairies and Marshes vegetation area with tall grasses, mesquite, oak and tall bunchgrasses. Between 11 and 20% of the land in the county is considered prime farmland. **CLIMATE** Subtropical Humid. June through October tropical storms and hurricanes may be encountered. The average annual temperature is 71 °F. Temperatures in January range from an average low of 44 ° to an average high of 64 °F and in July range from 74 ° to 94 °F. The average annual precipitation is 38 inches, with an average relative humidity of 89% at 6 A.M. and 63% at 6 P.M. There is no snowfall. The growing season averages 290 days per year, with the last freeze in mid February and the first freeze in early December. The sun shines during the year on the average 60 to 65% of the daylight hours.

THE PEOPLE

The population of Victoria County has grown at steadily increasing rates since 1930. The pace accelerated from a 16% gain between 1960 and 1970 to a 28% gain between 1970 and 1980. The 1982 estimated population of 72,900 indicates a continuation of this strong growth pattern. Rural areas grew faster than urban areas from 1970 to 1980. The age groups with the largest gains were ages 20 to 29 and 62 and over. The largest ancestry groups are Hispanic (30%), persons of German descent (24%), English descent (16%) and Irish descent (16%). **REGISTERED VOTERS** As of November 2, 1982 there were 30,254 registered voters (0.5% of the state total). The 1982 general election had a 52% voter turnout, compared to a 68% turnout in the 1980 general election. In the 1982 primary 91% voted Democratic and 9% Republican, with 9,056 votes cast.

THE ECONOMY

AGRICULTURE In 1982, 86% of the land was in farms and ranches, with 21% of the farmland under cultivation and 8% irrigated. Victoria ranked 113th in the state in highest agricultural receipts, with 56% from livestock and livestock products. Undesirable brush, noxious weeds, inadequate cropping systems and drainage are the current conservation problems. Primary crops: sorghum, corn, rice and hay. Primary vegetables: potatoes. Primary fruits and nuts: peaches and pecans. Primary livestock and products: cattle and hogs. **BUSINESS** Total number of business establishments in the county: 1,774. Retail sales during the first quarter of 1984 increased by 9%. In 1980, 7% of the labor force were self-employed, 18% were employed in professional or related services, 16% in manufacturing, 23% in wholesale and retail trade, 11% in construction, 14% were employed in other counties and there were 3,944 retired workers. The industries with the most employment: agribusiness, construction sand and gravel, oil and gas field services, tourism, general and heavy construction, trucking and the maufacture of bakery products, industrial chemicals, concrete products, fabricated structural metal, construction machinery, oil field machinery and railroad equipment. The nonfarm earnings in 1981 totaled $802,133,000. The retired workers received an average monthly Social Security payment of $310. **FINANCE** On June 30, 1983, five commercial banks had total deposits of $923,006,000 and total assets of $1,104,461,000. On December 31, 1982 two state savings and loan associations, six state branches and one federal association branch had assets of $235,580,947. In addition there are four credit unions in the county. **HOUSING** Average value of homes in 1980: $38,800. Permits for new, privately owned housing units decreased in 1982: 574 permits were issued with a total construction cost of $30,074,879. Of those permits, 439 were for single family houses. Between 1970 and 1980 the number of housing units increased by 46%. Seventy-eight percent of all units in the county are air-conditioned, 63% are heated by gas and 34% by electricity. **NATURAL RESOURCES** Sand and gravel, oil and gas. In 1982 a total of 18,674,981 thousand cubic feet of gas well gas, 79,950 barrels of condensate, 1,984,139 barrels of crude oil and 2,851,790 thousand cubic feet of casinghead gas were produced. Current production of other minerals and products includes sand and gravel. **TOURISM** Travel expenditures of $37,661,000 in 1982

VICTORIA (continued)

(an increase of 11% over 1981) generated 945 jobs and $7,624,000 in payroll. Lodging: 12 hotels, motels and tourist courts. Convention/meeting facilities: Victoria-Community Center and two hotels with facilities for large gatherings. **ALCOHOLIC BEVERAGES** Packaged distilled spirits, beer, ale, malt liquor and wine are legal in parts of the county. Sale of mixed beverages is legal in all or parts of the county. **FEDERAL EXPENDITURES** The federal government had direct expenditures or obligations of $75,424,000 in the county during fiscal year 1983, including $4,196,000 by the U.S. Department of Defense. In addition, the federal government provided $2,649,000 in grant awards, paid $6,842,000 in salaries and wages, made direct payments to individuals of $63,621,000 including $50,191,000 in retirement and disability payments, awarded $648,000 in procurement contracts and spent $1,665,000 in other expenditures or obligations. The federal government also provided $103,000 in direct loans and $84,154,000 in guaranteed loans and insurance.

COMMUNICATION
Newspapers–Daily: The Victoria Advocate, ave. morn. circ. 35,144. Radio: KCWM-AM, KNAL-AM, KVIC-FM and KTXN-FM Stereo (Victoria). Television: KXIX-CH. 19 (Victoria). Cable TV. Telephone companies: General Telephone and Southwestern Bell. **TRANSPORTATION** Total public road mileage: 1,197. In 1982 there were 63,046 registered vehicles and 2,532 reported traffic accidents including 35 fatalities. Taxi cabs: one company in the city of Victoria. Intercity bus service is available. Motor freight: 31 local and intrastate carriers. Rail: Three main and six branch lines carry freight through the county. The three main lines carry annually five to 10 million tons of freight each. One of the branch lines carries annually five to 10 million tons of freight, one carries one to five and four carry less than one million each. Aircraft: 116 are registered in the county. Airports: Victoria Regional Airport at Victoria serves as a base for 60 aircraft and is a basic transportation airport with commuter service. Ball Airport at Victoria. Citizens Memorial Hospital at Victoria porvides a heliport for emegency use. Waterborne commerce: Channel To Victoria freight traffic in 1981 totaled 2,930,820 short tons of domestic freight.

COMMUNITY SERVICES
EDUCATION Four school districts with 21 elementary, four middle, three high schools and one special education. The average daily attendance in 1981-82 was 12,843, with expenditures per pupil of $2,156 including 759 classroom teachers with an average annual salary of $17,248. Forty-three percent of the 987 high school graduates planned to attend college. In 1982-83, 50% of the students were White, 41% Hispanic, 8% Black, 0.3% Asian and 0.1% American Indian. Private schools: 1,782 students enrolled in nine elementary and four high schools. Victoria College is located in Victoria. Established in 1925 it is a vocational and two year acedemic college under local control. Enrollment in 1982 was 2,362 with in state undergraduate tuition and fees of $140 per semester. University of Houston is located in Victoria. Established in 1973 it is under state control. Enrollment in 1982 was 803 with in state undergraduate tuition and fees of $252 per semester. The highest degree offered is: Master. Vocational education: Victoria-Citizen Memorial Hospital School of Radiologic Technology, Texas Vocational School of Victoria, Victoria Beauty College. **PUBLIC LIBRARIES** Victoria Public Library: 97,805 volumes. **CHILD CARE** 203 day care and 26 twenty-four hour care licensed facilities. **HEALTH CARE** 28 physicians and 34 dentists. Hospitals: four with a combined capacity of 665 and one hospital under construction. Clinics: one for treatment of alcohol and/or drug abuse and one public

health clinic. Ambulance services: one volunteer fire department, one commercial and one city service. Mental health: one clinic. Nursing homes: four nursing homes with a combined capacity of 560 nursing care residents. The average cost per day for private patients in 1982 was $33.02. **CHURCHES** 64 churches have an estimated combined membership of 43,850. The largest denominations are Catholic, Southern Baptist and United Methodist. **SOCIAL SERVICES** In fiscal year 1983 a total of $2,821,324 in food stamps was distributed, with an average of 6,040 persons receiving food stamps each month. Aid to Families with Dependent Children (AFDC) totaled $766,443 with an average of 513 families receiving AFDC each month. Medical assistance benefits for the aged and disabled of $4,533,027 and for families and children of $1,686,506 brought the county benefit total to $9,807,299. **FIRE PROTECTION** One paid, 12 volunteer fire departments. **LAW ENFORCEMENT** The County Sheriff has 92 commissioned officers. One police department has a force of 82. **CRIME** 342 violent crimes (murder, forcible rape, robbery and aggravated assault) and 4,665 nonviolent crimes (burglary, larceny-theft and motor vehicle theft) were reported in 1982. **JUDICIAL SYSTEM** Three District Courts and Judges, two County Courts and Judges and four Justices of the Peace. In the District Courts a total of 3,845 cases were pending on 1/1/82, 2,055 new cases were filed and 2,118 cases were disposed of during the year leaving 3,782 cases pending on 12/31/82. There were 602 criminal cases on the docket, 303 convictions, 90 persons committed to prison and four committed to jail and 255 cases left pending. In the County Courts 2,038 cases were pending on 1/1/82, 2,388 new cases were filed and 2,134 cases were disposed of during the year leaving 2,292 cases pending on 12/31/82. There were 3,308 criminal cases on the docket, 1,402 convictions, 83 persons committed to jail, and 1,610 cases left pending. **JAILS** Two jails, capacity 57, constructing a new jail, capacity 130. **ATTORNEYS AT LAW** 124. **UTILITIES** 80% of the residents are connected to a public or privately owned water system and 79% are connected to a public sewer system. Electricity is distributed to the county by Central Power and Light, DeWitt Co. Electric Coop. Inc. and Victoria Co. Electric Coop., Inc. and is generated primarily by gas, water, oil and coal. The typical residential electric bill is $135.47 per month for an all-electric house using 2,500 kwh. **TAXES** The county has 13 units with taxing authority: four school districts, one city, one county, one college district and six special districts.

RECREATION/ENTERTAINMENT
NATIONAL REGISTER OF HISTORIC PLACES Inez vicinity: Fort St. Louis. Mission vicinity: Willeke Site. Victoria: Callendar House, Mission Creek Dam and Acequia Site, Old Victoria County Courthouse, Tonkawa Bank Site and Victoria Grist Windmill. **COUNTY/MUNICIPAL PARKS** 731 acres in one county and 10 municipal parks. These parks contain nine playgrounds, one golf course, 14 baseball and softball fields, four beaches, two boat ramps and shore fishing facilities. Developed campsites: five. **SCENIC DRIVES** The Texas Independence Trail runs through this county. This trail not only surveys the historic sites of southeastern Texas but also includes many modern visitor attractions. **BOATING/FISHING** Lakes/reservoirs: Coleto Creek (3,100 acres) and Dupont (240 acres). Major rivers: Guadalupe and San Antonio. Primary streams: Coleto, Garcitas Creek, Placedo, Jackson and Arenosa. Saltwater fishing: speckled trout, redfish and flounder fishing is usually good around Lavaca Bay which is considered to be one of the better sports fishing bays along the Texas coast. Shrimp, oysters and crabs may be taken but, like other saltwater fish, under specific regulations. **HUNTING** Fall and winter seasons on deer and javeline. No closed seasons on nutria, squirrel, bobcat and coyote. Winter seasons on quail, muskrat, beaver, otter, opossum, mink, ring-

VICTORIA-WALKER

tailed cat, badger, fox, raccoon, skunk and civet cat. Spring season on turkey. In 1983 sandhill crane, duck, coot, geese, woodcock and jacksnipe seasons occurred during the winter months. Teal duck, rail and gallinule seasons occurred in the fall. Mourning dove seasons occurred intermittently during the fall and winter months. **MUSEUMS** Victoria: McNamara-O'Connor Historical and Fine Arts Museum and The Nave Museum. **ORCHESTRAS** Victoria: Victoria Symphony Orchestra. **ZOO** Victoria: The Texas Zoo. **COLLEGIATE FINE ARTS** Victoria: Cultural events offered by Victoria College. **SPECIAL EVENTS** Rodeo, Victoria, January; Six Flags Trail Ride to San Antonio, Victoria, February; Stock Show, Victoria, March; A Toast to Tradition, Victoria, April; South Texas Farm and Ranch Show, Victoria, May; Lone Star Super Bowl of Chili, Victoria, May; Bach Festival, Victoria, June; Women's Pro Golf Tourney, Victoria, June; Annual Texas Tour, Victoria, June; Fire Dept. Annual Barbecue, Dacosta, June; Food Fair, Victoria, August; Texas Zoofest, Victoria, August; Arts and Crafts Fair, Victoria, October; Veterans Day Parade, Victoria, November.

COMMUNITIES

COUNTY SEAT Victoria, County Courthouse, 77902; County Clerk's Office, 512/575-1478. **INCORPORATED COMMUNITIES** (1980 population and ZIP Code) Victoria (50,695) 77901. **UNINCORPORATED COMMUNITIES** (and ZIP Code) Aloe 77901, Bloomington 77951, Brentwood Manor 77901, Country Club Terrace 77901, Dacosta (Da Costa) 77901, Dernal 77901, Fordtran 77995, Garden Villas 77901, Guadalupe 77901, Highland Estates 77901, Inez 77968, McFaddin 77973, Mission Valley 77901, Northcrest Estates 77901, Northgate 77901, Nursery 77976, Placedo 77977, Raisin 77901, Spring Creek Acres 77901, Telferner 77988 and Tropical Acres 77901. **FOR ADDITIONAL LOCAL INFORMATION** Victoria Chamber of Commerce, 1106 E. Rio Grande, P. O. Box 2465, Victoria, 77902, 512/573-5277.

WALKER (G3)

THE LAND

North of Houston on Interstate Highway 45 in the Claypan Area, Walker County covers 786 square miles with the elevation ranging from 200 to 450 feet. The northern one-half of the county has light colored soils with sandy surfaces over clayey subsoils. The southern part has gently rolling to hilly, reddish soils with light colored loamy surfaces and very deep, reddish, clayey subsoils that are high in iron. The very southeastern corner of the county has clayey soils over chalk. These soils have a high shrink-swell potential, or light colored loamy surfaces over very deep, reddish, clayey subsoils. Along the Trinity River are very dark, loamy surfaces with mottled, cracking, clayey soils. Walker is in the Pineywoods vegetation area with grasslands, loblolly, shortleaf, longleaf and slash pine and hardwoods such as oak, hickory and maple. Between 21 and 30% of the land in the county is considered prime farmland. **CLIMATE** Subtropical Humid and mild. The average annual temperature is 67°F. Temperatures in January range from an average low of 39° to an average high of 60°F and in July range from 72° to 95°F. The average annual precipitation is 44 inches, with an average relative humidity of 88% at 6 A.M. and 58% at 6 P.M. The average annual snowfall is not significant. The growing season averages 265 days per year, with the last freeze in early March and the first freeze in late November. The sun shines during the year on the average 65% of the daylight hours.

THE PEOPLE

The population of Walker County has grown at steadily increasing rates since 1930. The pace accelerated from a 29% gain between 1960 and 1970 to a 51% gain between 1970 and 1980. The 1982 estimated population of 46,300 indicates a continuation of this strong growth pattern. Rural areas experienced a 77% population increase between 1970 and 1980. The age groups with the largest gains were ages 20 to 34 and 62 and over. The largest ancestry groups are Black (24%), persons of English descent (24%), Irish descent (19%) and German descent (14%). **REGISTERED VOTERS** As of November 2, 1982 there were 15,288 registered voters (0.2% of the state total). The 1982 general election had a 50% voter turnout, compared to a 69% turnout in the 1980 general election. In the 1982 primary 90% voted Democratic and 10% Republican, with 5,485 votes cast.

THE ECONOMY

AGRICULTURE Major forest production area. In 1982, 50% of the land was in farms and ranches, with 10% of the farmland under cultivation. Walker ranked 173rd in the state in highest agricultural receipts, with 70% from livestock and livestock products. Undesirable brush and weeds and fertilization are the current conservation problems. Primary crops: hay, oats, rye, cotton and sorghum. Primary vegetables: potatoes, sweet potatoes, tomatoes and watermelons. Primary fruits and nuts: peaches and pecans. Primary livestock and products: cattle, milk and hogs. **BUSINESS** Total number of business establishments in the county: 607. Retail sales during the first quarter of 1984 increased by 19%. In 1980, 8% of the labor force were self-employed, 27% were employed in professional or related services, 10% in manufacturing, 22% in wholesale and retail trade, 14% in government and government enterprises, 17% were employed in other counties and there were 2,390 retired workers. The industries with the most employment: agribusiness, general construction, logging, saw mills and the manufacture of cloth products, valves and pipe fittings, soft veneer and plywood. The nonfarm earnings in 1981 totaled $286,844,000. The retired workers received an average monthly Social Security payment of $310.00. **FINANCE** On June 30, 1983, five commercial banks had total deposits of $231,819,000 and total assets of $259,035,000. There are two state savings and loan association branches, one federal branch and two credit unions in the county. **HOUSING** Average value of homes in 1980: $43,100. Permits for new, privately owned housing units increased in 1982: 155 permits were issued with a total construction cost of $5,943,408. Of those permits, 19 were for single family houses. Between 1970 and 1980 the number of housing units increased by 82%. Eighty-one percent of all units in the county are air-conditioned, 65% are heated by gas and 32% by electricity. **NATURAL RESOURCES** Clay, industrial sand, sand and gravel, oil and gas. In 1982 a total of 856,503 thousand cubic feet of gas well gas, 8,943 barrels of condensate, 5,400 barrels of crude oil and 72 thousand cubic feet of casinghead gas were produced. Current production of other minerals and products includes bentonite clay, clay, industrial sand and crushed sandstone. Pine and hardwood production in 1981 totaled 16,825,111 cubic feet: 15,308,647 cubic feet of pine and 1,516,464 cubic feet of hardwood. **TOURISM** Travel expenditures of $17,339,000 in 1982 (an increase of 11% over 1981) generated 431 jobs and $3,516,000 in payroll. Lodging: seven hotels, motels and tourist courts. Convention/meeting facilities: Huntsville-Sam Houston State University Colisium. **ALCOHOLIC BEVERAGES** Packaged distilled spirits, beer, ale, malt liquor and wine are legal in parts of the county. Sale of mixed beverages is legal in all or parts of the county. **FEDERAL EXPENDITURES** The federal government had direct expenditures or obligations of $46,458,000 in the county during fiscal year 1983, including $3,925,000 by the U.S. Department of Defense. In addition, the federal government provided $1,688,000 in grant awards, paid $2,802,000 in salaries and wages, made direct payments to individuals of $41,640,000 including $32,278,000 in

WALKER (continued)

retirement and disability payments, awarded $76,000 in procurement contracts and spent $253,000 in other expenditures or obligations. The federal government also provided $2,000 in direct loans and $5,632,000 in guaranteed loans and insurance.

COMMUNICATION

Newspapers–Daily: The Huntsville Item, ave. eve. circ. 7,700. Radio: KSAM-AM, KHUN-FM, and KSHU-FM (Huntsville). Cable TV. Telephone companies: General Telephone, Southwestern Bell, United Telephone, Eastex Telephone Coop. and Waterwood Communications. **TRANSPORTATION** Total public road mileage: 934. In 1982 there were 26,373 registered vehicles and 976 reported traffic accidents including 17 fatalities. Taxi cabs: three companies in Huntsville. Intercity bus service is available. Motor freight: four carriers. Rail: two main and one branch line carry freight through the county. The two main lines carry annually 10 to 20 million tons of freight each and the branch line carries less than one million. Aircraft: 28 are registered in the county. Airports: Huntsville Municipal Airport serves as a base for 30 aircraft and is a basic transportation airport with commuter service.

COMMUNITY SERVICES

EDUCATION Two school districts with five elementary, one middle and two high schools. The average daily attendance in 1981-82 was 4,998, with expenditures per pupil of $2,381 including 303 classroom teachers with an average annual salary of $15,932. Four percent of the 294 high school graduates planned to attend college. In 1982-83, 66% of the students were White, 5% Hispanic, 28% Black, 0.6% Asian and 0.1% American Indian. Sam Houston State University is located in Huntsville. Established in 1879 it is under state control. Enrollment in 1982 was 9,341 with in state undergraduate tuition and fees of $420 per semester. The highest degree offered is Doctorate. Sports championships: (Lone Star Conference) 1983 Women's Tennis. Vocational education: Huntsville Memorial Hospital School of Vocational Nursing (Huntsville). **PUBLIC LIBRARIES** Huntsville Public Library: 33,012 volumes. **CHILD CARE** 39 day care and 10 twenty-four hour care licensed facilities. **HEALTH CARE** 50 physicians and 23 dentists. Hospitals: one with a capacity of 144. Specialized hospitals: one State Department of Corrections hospital with capacity of 97. Ambulance services: one commercial and one city service. Mental health: one county clinic. Nursing homes: two nursing homes with a combined capacity of 211 nursing care residents. The average cost per day for private patients in 1982 was $33.15. **CHURCHES** 41 churches have an estimated combined membership of 14,517. The largest denominations are Southern Baptist, United Methodist and Catholic. **SOCIAL SERVICES** In fiscal year 1983 a total of $1,424,689 in food stamps was distributed, with an average of 2,973 persons receiving food stamps each month. Aid to Families with Dependent Children (AFDC) totaled $458,141 with an average of 306 families receiving AFDC each month. Medical assistance benefits for the aged and disabled of $2,135,809 and for families and children of $589,912 brought the county benefit total to $4,608,550. **FIRE PROTECTION** Four volunteer fire departments. **LAW ENFORCEMENT** The County Sheriff has 31 commissioned officers. One police department has a force of 27. One university campus has a police department with a force of 12. **CRIME** 208 violent crimes (murder, forcible rape, robbery and aggravated assault) and 1,473 nonviolent crimes (burglary, larceny-theft and motor vehicle theft) were reported in 1982. **JUDICIAL SYSTEM** Two District Courts and Judges, two County Courts and Judges and four Justices of the Peace. In the District Courts a total of 513 cases were pending

on 1/1/82, 387 new cases were filed and 404 cases were disposed of during the year leaving 496 cases pending on 12/31/82. There were 290 criminal cases on the docket, 111 convictions, 52 persons committed to prison and 135 cases left pending. In the County Courts 4,430 cases were pending on 1/1/82, 1,132 new cases were filed and 675 cases were disposed of during the year leaving 4,887 cases pending on 12/31/82. There were 4,057 criminal cases on the docket, 190 convictions, one person committed to jail, and 3,806 cases left pending. **JAILS** One jail, capacity 66. **PRISONS** Diagnostic, on 50 acres north of Huntsville, had an inmate population of 1,203 in 1983. All male inmates are tested and classified at the diagnostic unit before being transferred to their permanent unit. Ellis I, on 11,672 acres north of Huntsville, had 2,309 inmates, agricultural operations including a syrup mill, farrowing barn and poultry and egg production and industrial operations including a dental lab, woodworking shop, shoe factory and bus repair facility. Ellis II, on 7,007 acres north of Huntsville, was under construction in 1983. Goree, on 889 acres south of Huntsville, had 1,065 inmates and a horse breeding operation. Huntsville, on 140 acres in Huntsville, had 2,266 inmates, a prison store, textile mill, the central infirmary, mechanical shop, print shop, prison rodeo arena, credit union and Windham Media Center. Wynne, on 1,433 acres in Huntsville, had 2,579 inmates with agricultural operations, a license plate plant, validation sticker plant, mattress factory, corrugated box factory, plastic sign shop, records conversion facility and transportation department. The Windham school system's offices and warehouse are located here. **ATTORNEYS AT LAW** 88. **UTILITIES** 82% of the residents are connected to a public or privately owned water system and 60% are connected to a public sewer system. Natural gas is distributed to the county by Entex, Inc. and Moran Utilities Company. The average annual residential bill for natural gas in 1982 for the Entex distribution system was $390.31, an increase of 26% over 1981. Electricity is distributed to the county by Gulf States Utilities Co., Houston Co. Electric Coop., Inc. and Mid-South Electric Coop., Assn. and is generated primarily by gas and oil. The typical residential electric bill is $198.32 per month for an all-electric house using 2,500 kwh. **TAXES** The county has nine units with taxing authority: three school districts, two cities, one county, one hospital and two special districts.

RECREATION/ENTERTAINMENT

FEDERAL SAM HOUSTON NATIONAL FOREST covers 160,401 acres in three counties and includes seven recreation areas. **NATIONAL REGISTER OF HISTORIC PLACES** Huntsville: John W. Thomason House and Sam Houston House. Riverside vicinity: Riverside Swinging Bridge. **STATE** Huntsville State Park covers 2,083 acres with camping and trailer sites as well as areas offering fishing, swimming, boat ramps, nature trails, rental boats and miniature golf. **COUNTY/MUNICIPAL PARKS** 51 acres in five municipal parks. These parks contain one mile of hiking trails, six playgrounds, four baseball and softball fields and one swimming pool. **SCENIC DRIVES** The Texas Forest Trail runs through this county. This trail explores the farming, ranching and oilfield areas of the East Texas Pineywoods. **BOATING/FISHING** Lakes/reservoirs: Elkins (100 acres), Ellis Reservoir (18 acres), Guerrant-Adams (25 acres), Hendricks (20 acres), Horseshoe (31 acres), Raven (86 acres) and Sunset (35 acres). Major rivers: Trinity and West Fork San Jacinto. Primary streams: Prairie, Turkey, School House, Era, Harmon, McDonald, Bedias and South Bedias. **HUNTING** Fall and winter seasons on deer. Summer, fall and winter seasons on squirrel. Winter seasons on quail, muskrat, beaver, otter, opossum, mink, ring-tailed cat, badger, fox, raccoon, skunk and civet cat. No closed season on nutria, bobcat and coyote. In 1983 duck, coot, geese, woodcock and jacksnipe seasons occurred during the winter months. Teal duck, rail and gallinule seasons occurred in the fall. Mourning dove seasons occurred intermittently during the fall and winter months. **MUSEUMS** Huntsville: Sam Houston Memorial Museum. **COLLEGIATE FINE ARTS** Huntsville: Cultural events offered by Sam Houston State University. **SPECIAL EVENTS** Confederate Heroes Day Celebration, Huntsville, January; Texas Independence Day Celebration, Huntsville, March; County Fair, Huntsville, April; Sam Houston State University Intercollegiate Rodeo, Huntsville, April; Elkins Lake Art and Craft Show, Huntsville, April; Texas Prison Rodeo, Huntsville, October.

COMMUNITIES

COUNTY SEAT Huntsville, County Courthouse, 77340; County Clerk's Office, 409/295-3811. **INCORPORATED COMMUNITIES** (1980 population and ZIP Code) Huntsville (23,936) 77340, New Waverly (824) 77358 and Riverside (425) 77367. **UNINCORPORATED COMMUNITIES** (and ZIP Code) Country Campus 77340, Crabbs Prairie 77340, Dodge 77334, Goshen 77340, Hawthorne 77358, Kittrell 77862, Loma (Gladstone) 77876, Phelps 77340, San Jacinto 77340 and Wesley Grove 77876. **FOR ADDITIONAL LOCAL INFORMATION** Huntsville-Walker Chamber of Commerce, 1327 11th Street, P. O. Box 538, Huntsville, 77340, 409/295-8113.

WALLER (G10)

THE LAND

West of Houston on Interstate Highway 10 in the Claypan Area, Waller County covers 514 square miles with the elevation ranging from 100 to 350 feet. The northern part of the county has gently rolling to hilly reddish soils with light colored, loamy surfaces and very deep, clayey subsoils that are high in iron. Along the Brazos River are brownish to reddish, cracking, clayey or loamy soils. The rest of the county has light colored, loamy surfaces over very deep, reddish or mottled subsoils. The southern third of Waller is in the Gulf Prairies and Marshes vegetation area with tall grasses, mesquite and post oak. The rest of the county is in the Post Oak Savannah vegetation area with tall grasses, post and blackjack oak. Between 31 and 40% of the land in the county is considered prime farmland. **CLIMATE** Subtropical Humid with mild winters and warm summers. The average annual temperature is 68°F. Temperatures in January range from an average low of 41° to an average high of 60°F and in July range from 72° to 95°F. The average annual precipitation is 42 inches, with an average relative humidity of 89% at 6 A.M. and 61% at 6 P.M. Snow is rare. The growing season averages 280 days per year, with the last freeze in late February and the first freeze in early December. The sun shines during the year on the average 68% of the daylight hours.

THE PEOPLE

The population of Waller County is growing, with an 18% gain between 1960 and 1970 and a 39% gain between 1970 and 1980. The 1982 estimated population of 21,700 indicates a continuation of that strong growth. Urban areas experienced a 107% increase in population between 1970 and 1980. The age groups with the largest gains were ages 25 to 39 and 65 and over. The largest ancestry groups are Black (42%), persons of German descent (15%) and English descent (14%). **REGISTERED VOTERS** As of November 2, 1982 there were 10,906 registered voters (0.2% of the state total). The 1982 general election had a 43% voter turnout, compared to a 63% turnout in the 1980 general election. In the 1982 primary 94% voted Democratic and 6% Republican, with 2,876 votes cast.

THE ECONOMY

AGRICULTURE Forest production and cattle area. In 1982, 81% of the land was in farms and ranches, with 33% of the farmland under cultivation and 23% irrigated. Waller ranked 95th in the state in highest agricultural receipts, with 53% from livestock and livestock products. Overgrazing, undesirable brush and weeds, inefficient tillage systems and flooding are the current conservation problems. Primary crops: soybeans, corn, hay and rice. Primary vegetables: watermelons. Primary fruits and nuts: peaches and pecans. Primary livestock and products: cattle, milk, sheep and hogs. **BUSINESS** Total number of business establishments in the county: 261. Retail sales during the first quarter of 1984 increased by 21%. In 1980, 10% of the labor force were self-employed, 28% were employed in professional or related services, 14% in manufacturing, 20% in wholesale and retail trade, 11% in construction, 45% were employed in other counties and there were 1,246 retired workers. The industries with the most employment: agribusiness, oil and gas extraction, heavy construction and the manufacture of fabricated metal products and oil field machinery. The nonfarm earnings in 1981 totaled $154,493,000. The retired workers received an average monthly Social Security payment of $293. **FINANCE** On June 30, 1983, three commercial banks had total deposits of $68,953,000 and total assets of $76,874,000. On December 31, 1982 one state savings and loan association and three state branches had assets of $3,539,789. In addition there is one credit union in the county. **HOUSING** Average value of homes in 1980: $40,500. Permits for new, privately owned housing units increased in 1982: 72 permits were issued with a total construction cost of $1,542,324. Of those permits, 11 were for single family houses. Between 1970 and 1980 the number of housing units increased by 53%. Seventy-two percent of all units in the county are air-conditioned, 73% are heated by gas and 22% by electricity. **NATURAL RESOURCES** Salt domes, sand, gravel, oil and gas. In 1982 a total of 139,264,619 thousand cubic feet of gas well gas, 61,748 barrels of condensate, 71,406 barrels of crude oil and 1,047,425 thousand cubic feet of casinghead gas were produced. Current production of other minerals and products includes sand, gravel and construction sand. Pine and hardwood production in 1981 totaled 1,921,210 cubic feet: 1,852,949 cubic feet of pine and 68,261 cubic feet of hardwood. **TOURISM** Travel expenditures of $1,954,000 in 1982 (an increase of 11% over 1981) generated 48 jobs and $387,000 in payroll. Conventions/meeting facilities: Prairie View-Prairie View A & M College Little Dome. **ALCOHOLIC BEVERAGES** Packaged distilled spirits, beer, ale, malt liquor and wine are legal in parts of the county. Sale of mixed beverages is legal in all or parts of the county. **FEDERAL EXPENDITURES** The federal government had direct expenditures or obligations of $35,939,000 in the county during fiscal year 1983, including $1,945,000 by the U.S. Department of Defense. In addition, the federal government provided $7,262,000 in grant awards, paid $2,045,000 in salaries and wages, made direct payments to individuals of $24,293,000 including $13,912,000 in retirement and disability payments, awarded $559,000 in procurement contracts and spent $1,781,000 in other expenditures or obligations. The federal government also provided $473,000 in direct loans and $6,006,000 in guaranteed loans and insurance.

COMMUNICATION

Newspapers–Weekly: Brookshire Banner and The Hempstead News Citizen. Radio: KPVU-FM (Hempstead). Cable TV. Telephone companies: Southwestern Bell and Fort Bend Telephone. **TRANSPORTATION** Total public road mileage: 736. In 1982 there were 25,807 registered vehicles and 607 reported traffic accidents including 13 fatalities. Intercity bus service is available. Motor freight: four carriers. Rail: one main line carries

WALLER (continued)

annually 10 to 20 million tons of freight through the county. Aircraft: 32 are registered in the county. Airports: Skylake Airport at Waller, Mikeska Field at Brookshire and Hempstead Airport.

COMMUNITY SERVICES

EDUCATION Three school districts with four elementary, four middle and three high schools. The average daily attendance in 1981-82 was 4,041, with expenditures per pupil of $2,723 including 264 classroom teachers with an average annual salary of $17,313. Forty-seven percent of the 268 high school graduates planned to attend college. In 1982-83, 58% of the students were White, 11% Hispanic, 31% Black, 0.4% Asian and 0.1% American Indian. Prairie View A & M University is located in Prairie View. Established in 1876 it is under state control. Enrollment in 1982 was 6,592 with in state undergraduate tuition and fees of $467 per semester. The highest degree offered is Master. **PUBLIC LIBRARIES** Waller County Library (Hempstead): 19,911 volumes. **CHILD CARE** 21 day care licensed facilities. **HEALTH CARE** 12 physicians and five dentists. Hospitals: one with a capacity of 34. Specialized hospitals: one state health center with a capacity of 43. Clinics: one state out patient clinic. Ambulance services: two volunteer services, one city, one hospital-based and one fire department service. Mental health: one county clinic. Nursing homes: two nursing homes with a combined capacity of 244 nursing care residents. The average cost per day for private patients in 1982 was $33.87. **CHURCHES** 37 churches have an estimated combined membership of 7,495. The largest denominations are Southern Baptist, Catholic and United Methodist. **SOCIAL SERVICES** In fiscal year 1983 a total of $1,076,130 in food stamps was distributed, with an average of 2,179 persons receiving food stamps each month. Aid to Families with Dependent Children (AFDC) totaled $279,459 with an average of 178 families receiving AFDC each month. Medical assistance benefits for the aged and disabled of $1,564,044 and for families and children of $333,645 brought the county benefit total to $3,253,278. **FIRE PROTECTION** Five volunteer fire departments. **LAW ENFORCEMENT** The County Sheriff has 21 commissioned officers. Four police departments have a combined force of 26. One university campus has a police department with a force of nine. **CRIME** 53 violent crimes (murder, forcible rape, robbery and aggravated assault) and 523 nonviolent crimes (burglary, larceny-theft and motor vehicle theft) were reported in 1982. **JUDICIAL SYSTEM** Two District Courts and Judges, one County Court and Judge and four Justices of the Peace. In the District Courts a total of 736 cases were pending on 1/1/82, 488 new cases were filed and 439 cases were disposed of during the year leaving 785 cases pending on 12/31/82. There were 223 criminal cases on the docket, 56 convictions, 19 persons committed to prison, two committed to jail and 112 cases left pending. In the County Court 177 cases were pending on 1/1/82, 409 new cases were filed and 347 cases were disposed of during the year leaving 239 cases pending on 12/31/82. There were 488 criminal cases on the docket, 136 convictions, 17 persons committed to jail and 198 cases left pending. **JAILS** One jail, capacity 21. New jail in planning stage as lost certification in 1983 due to overcrowding. **ATTORNEYS AT LAW** 15. **UTILITIES** 57% of the residents are connected to a public or privately owned water system and 45% are connected to a public sewer system. Natural gas is distributed to the county by Entex, Inc. The average annual residential bill for natural gas in 1982 for the Entex distribution system was $390.31, an increase of 26% over 1981. Electricity is distributed to the county by San Benard Electric Coop., Inc. and Houston Lighting & Power Co. and is generated primarily by gas. The typical residential electric bill is $201.39 per month for an all-electric house using 2,500 kwh. **TAXES** The county has 12 units with taxing authority: four school districts, five cities, one county and two special districts.

RECREATION/ENTERTAINMENT

NATIONAL REGISTER OF HISTORIC PLACES Hempstead vicinity: Liendo Plantation. Prairie View: Foster Hall. **COUNTY/MUNICIPAL PARKS** 28 acres in one county and three municipal parks. These parks contain one playground, five baseball and softball fields and two tennis courts. **BOATING/FISHING** Lakes/reservoirs: Becker (43 acres). Major rivers: Brazos. Primary streams: Clear, Buffalo Bayou and Spring. **HUNTING** Fall and winter seasons on deer. No closed seasons on nutria, squirrel, bobcat and coyote. Winter seasons on quail, muskrat, beaver, otter, opossum, mink, ring-tailed cat, badger, fox, raccoon, skunk and civet cat. In 1983 duck, coot, geese, woodcock and jacksnipe seasons occurred during the winter months with a winter season on sandhill crane in some parts of the county. Teal duck, rail and gallinule seasons occurred in the fall. Mourning dove seasons occurred intermittently during the fall and winter months. **MUSEUMS** Brookshire: Waller County Historical Museum. **COLLEGIATE FINE ARTS** Prairie View: Cultural events offered by Prairie View Agricultural and Mechanical College. **SPECIAL EVENTS** Koi Festival, Brookshire, May; Lotus Blossom Festival, Brookshire June; Waller County Festival, Brookshire, October.

COMMUNITIES

COUNTY SEAT Hempstead, County Courthouse, 77445; County Clerk's Office, 409/826-3357. **INCORPORATED COMMUNITIES** (1980 population and ZIP Code) Brookshire (2,175) 77423, Hempstead (3,456) 77445, Katy (5,660: 668 in Waller Co., 517 in Fort Bend Co. and 4,475 in Harris Co.) 77450, Pattison (318) 77466, Prairie View (3,993) 77445 and Waller (1,241: 1,077 in Waller Co. and 164 in Harris Co.) 77484. **UNINCORPORATED COMMUNITIES** (and ZIP Code) Cedar Creek 77445, Clemons 77423, Howth 77445, Monaville 77445, Mount Zion 77423, St. Paul 77445 and Sunny Side 77423. **FOR ADDITIONAL LOCAL INFORMATION** Hempstead Chamber of Commerce, P.O. Box 921, Hempstead, 77445, 409/826-6118.

WARD (P84)

THE LAND

Southwest of Odessa on Interstate Highway 20 in the Trans-Pecos Region, Ward County covers 836 square miles with an elevation range of 2,400 to 2,800 feet. The northern part of the county has nearly level soils with sandy surfaces over reddish, loamy to clayey subsoils. Limestone can be found within 40 inches of the surface. The rest of the county has alkaline, loamy soils with some clayey subsoils over limestone bedrock. Ward is in the Trans-Pecos, Mountains and Basins vegetation area with desert shrub, grama grasslands, juniper, and cacti. Less than 1% of the land in the county is considered prime farmland. **CLIMATE** Border line Subtropical Arid with wide-ranging daily and seasonal temperature variations. The average annual temperature is 64°F. Temperatures in January range from an average low of 29° to an average high of 60°F and in July range from 70° to 98°F. The average annual precipitation is 12 inches, with an average relative humidity of 70% at 6 A.M. and 33% at 6 P.M. The average annual snowfall is three inches. The growing season averages 223 days per year, with the last freeze in early April and the first freeze in early November. The sun shines during the year on the average 75% of the daylight hours.

THE PEOPLE

The 1982 estimated population of 16,000 indicates a continuation of the growth which began in the 1970s, reversing a population decline between 1960 and 1970. A 13% population loss between 1960 and 1970 was followed by a 7% gain between 1970 and 1980. Rural areas grew faster than urban areas from 1970 to 1980. The largest ancestry groups are Hispanic (27%), persons of English descent (27%), Irish descent (16%) and German descent (12%). **REGISTERED VOTERS** As of November 2, 1982 there were 6,915 registered voters (0.1% of the state total). The 1982 general election had a 46% voter turnout, compared to a 70% turnout in the 1980 general election. In the 1982 primary 99% voted Democratic and 1% Republican, with 3,391 votes cast.

THE ECONOMY

AGRICULTURE Ranchland. In 1982, 88% of the land was in farms and ranches, with less than 1% of the farmland under cultivation. Ward ranked 250th in the state in highest agricultural receipts, with 97% from livestock and livestock products. Overgrazing, decreasing irrigation water supplies and salinity are the current conservation problems. Primary vegetables: watermelons. Primary fruits and nuts: pecans. Primary livestock and products: cattle, milk and hogs. **BUSINESS** Total number of business establishments in the county: 346. In 1980, 7% of the labor force were self-employed, 15% were employed in professional or related services, 5% in manufacturing, 16% in wholesale and retail trade, 31% in agriculture, forestry, fisheries and mining, 19% were employed in other counties and there were 879 retired workers. The industry with the most employment is oil and gas extraction. The nonfarm earnings in 1981 totaled $158,613,000. The retired workers received an average monthly Social Security payment of $334. **FINANCE** On June 30, 1983, two commercial banks had total deposits of $101,108,000 and total assets of $113,165,000. On December 31, 1982 one state savings and loan association and one state branch had assets of $312,606,838. In addition there are three credit unions in the county. **HOUSING** Average value of homes in 1980: $22,000. Permits for new, privately owned housing units increased in 1982: 154 permits were issued with a total construction cost of $3,790,700. Of those permits, 27 were for single family houses. Between 1970 and 1980 the number of housing units increased by 19%. Eighty-three percent of all units in the county are air-conditioned, 92% are heated by gas and 8% by electricity. **NATURAL RESOURCES** Brine, caliche, sand and gravel, oil and gas. In 1982 a total of 122,242,679 thousand cubic feet of gas well gas, 484,129 barrels of condensate, 8,707,213 barrels of crude oil and 18,742,199 thousand cubic feet of casinghead gas were produced. Current production of other minerals and products includes brine, crushed limestone, sand and gravel and recovered sulphur. **TOURISM** Travel expenditures of $4,712,000 in 1982 (an increase of 11% over 1981) generated 118 jobs and $936,000 in payroll. **ALCOHOLIC BEVERAGES** Packaged distilled spirits, beer, ale, malt liquor and wine are legal in parts of the county. **FEDERAL EXPENDITURES** The federal government had direct expenditures or obligations of $16,384,000 in the county during fiscal year 1983, including $410,000 by the U.S. Department of Defense. In addition, the federal government provided $2,765,000 in grant awards, paid $666,000 in salaries and wages, made direct payments to individuals of $12,880,000 including $10,087,000 in retirement and disability payments, awarded $3,000 in procurement contracts and spent $70,000 in other expenditures or obligations. The federal government also provided $1,200,000 in guaranteed loans and insurance.

COMMUNICATION

Newspapers–Weekly: Monahans News. Radio: KVKM-AM (Monahans). Cable TV. Telephone companies: Continental Telephone and Southwestern Bell. **TRANSPORTATION** Total public road mileage: 610. In 1982 there were 15,697 registered vehicles and 496 reported traffic accidents including seven fatalities. Intercity bus service is available. Motor freight: eight local and intrastate carriers. Rail: two main and one branch line carry freight through the county. The two main lines carry annually five to 10 million tons of freight each and the branch line carries less than one million. Aircraft: 50 are registered in the county. Airports: Roy Hurd Memorial Airport at Monahans serves as a base for 20 aircraft and is a basic utility airport with general aviation service. Wilson Ranch Airport at Pyote.

COMMUNITY SERVICES

EDUCATION Two school districts with five elementary, two middle, two high schools and one special education. The average daily attendance in 1981-82 was 2,950, with expenditures per pupil of $4,748 including 207 classroom teachers with an average annual salary of $20,603. Fifty-one percent of the 172 high school graduates planned to attend college. In 1982-83, 60% of the students were White, 35% Hispanic, 4% Black, 0.2% Asian and 0.2% American Indian. Sports championships: 1983 AAAA Girls' Volleyball, Monahans H.S. **PUBLIC LIBRARIES** Ward County Library (Monahans): 41,266 volumes. **CHILD CARE** Nine day care and six twenty-four hour care licensed facilities. **HEALTH CARE** Seven physicians and three dentists. Hospitals: One with a capacity of 49. Ambulance services: one volunteer fire department and one commercial service. Mental health: one county clinic. Nursing homes: one nursing home has a capacity of 98 nursing care residents. The average cost per day for private patients in 1982 was $29.51. **CHURCHES** 32 churches have an estimated combined membership of 10,003. The largest denominations are Southern Baptist, Catholic and United Methodist. **SOCIAL SERVICES** In fiscal year 1983 a total of $375,792 in food stamps was distributed, with an average of 788 persons receiving food stamps each month. Aid to Families with Dependent Children (AFDC) totaled $54,795 with an average of 38 families receiving AFDC each month. Medical assistance benefits for the aged and disabled of $469,997 and for families and children of $85,961 brought the county benefit total to $986,545. **FIRE PROTECTION** Five volunteer fire departments. **LAW ENFORCEMENT** The County Sheriff has 18 commissioned officers. Nine police departments have a combined force of 35. **CRIME** 55 violent crimes (murder, forcible rape, robbery and aggravated assault) and 734 nonviolent crimes (burglary, larceny-theft and motor vehicle theft) were reported in 1982. **JUDICIAL SYSTEM** One District Court and Judge, one County Court and Judge and four Justices of the Peace. In the District Court a total of 297 cases were pending on 1/1/82; 506 new cases were filed and 547 cases were disposed of during the year leaving 256 cases pending on 12/31/82. There were 170 criminal cases on the docket, 65 convictions, eight persons committed to prison, one committed to jail and 56 cases left pending. In the County Court 590 cases were pending on 1/1/82, 350 new cases were filed and 410 cases were disposed of during the year leaving 530 cases pending on 12/31/82. There were 829 criminal cases on the docket, 130 convictions, 19 persons committed to jail and 465 cases left pending. **JAILS** One jail, capacity 68. **ATTORNEYS AT LAW** Nine. **UTILITIES** 81% of the residents are connected to a public or privately owned water system and 75% are connected to a public sewer system. Natural gas is distributed to the county by Southern Union Company. The average annual residential bill for natural gas in 1982 for the Southern Union distribution system was $355.85, an increase of 23% over 1981. Electricity is distributed to the county by Texas Electric Service and is generated primarily by gas. The typical residential electric bill is $106.53 per month for an all-

COUNTIES

WARD (continued)

electric house using 2,500 kwh. **TAXES** The county has eight units with taxing authority: two school districts, three cities, one county and two special districts.

RECREATION/ENTERTAINMENT

STATE Monahans Sandhills State Park covers 3,840 acres with camping and trailer sites as well as a modern museum and interpretive center. **COUNTY/MUNICIPAL PARKS** 159 acres in 10 county and five municipal parks. These parks contain 10 playgrounds, three golf courses, nine baseball and softball fields, eight tennis courts and five swimming pools. **SCENIC DRIVES** The Texas Pecos Trail runs through this county. This trail rambles through the vast region of southwest and west Texas with landscapes varying from raw, arid regions to green valleys. **BOATING/FISHING** Lakes/reservoirs: Ozark (20 acres). Major rivers: Pecos. **HUNTING** Fall and winter seasons on deer, mule deer and javelina. No closed season on coyote, bobcat and squirrel. Winter seasons on quail, muskrat, beaver, opossum, ringtailed cat, badger, fox, weasel, raccoon, skunk and civet cat. In 1983 sandhill crane, duck, coot, geese, woodcock and jacksnipe seasons occurred during the winter months. Teal duck, rail and gallinule seasons occurred in the fall. Mourning dove seasons occurred intermittently during the fall and winter months. **MUSEUMS** Monahans: Pyote Museum and Rattlesnake Bomber Base. **SPECIAL EVENTS** Freedom Fair, Monahans, July; Greenthumb Show, Monahans, July; AQHA Quarterhorse Show, Monahans, July; Miss Monahans Pageant, Monahans, July; Pecan Perfection Show, Monahans, November; Christmas Parade, Monahans, December; Fun Days, Grandfalls, Twice Yearly-Spring and Fall.

COMMUNITIES

COUNTY SEAT Monahans, County Courthouse, 79756; County Clerk's Office, 915/943-3294. **INCORPORATED COMMUNITIES** (1980 population and ZIP Code) Barstow (637) 79719, Grand Falls (635) 79742, Monahans (8,397: 8,393 in Ward Co. and 4 in Winkler Co.) 79756, Pyote (382) 79777, Thorntonville (717) 79756 and Wickett (689) 79788. **UNINCORPORATED COMMUNITIES** (and ZIP Code) Gulf Camp 79756 and Royalty 79779. **FOR ADDITIONAL LOCAL INFORMATION** Grandfalls-Royalty Chamber of Commerce, P.O. Box 269, Grand Falls, 79742, 915/547-2210 and Monahans Chamber of Commerce, P.O. Box 1058, Monahans, 79756, 915/943-2187.

WASHINGTON (G1)

THE LAND

East of Austin on Interstate Highway 290 in the Blackland Prairies Region, Washington County covers 610 square miles with an elevation range of 200 to 500 feet. Along the Brazos River are brownish to reddish, cracking, clayey soils and loamy soils. Along the northern border are light colored soils with sandy surfaces and mottled, clayey subsoils. The rest of the county has deep to shallow, clayey soils over chalk. The northwestern half of the county is in the Post Oak Savannah vegetation area with tall grasses, post and blackjack oak. The southeastern part of the county is in the Blackland Prairies vegetation area with tall grasses, mesquite, oak, pecan and elm trees along streams. Between 31 and 40% of the land in the county is considered prime farmland. **CLIMATE** Subtropical Humid with mild winters and hot summers. The average annual temperature is 68°F. Temperatures in January range from an average low of 39° to an average high of 61°F and in July range from 73° to 96°F. The average annual precipitation is 40 inches, with an average

relative humidity of 87% at 6 A.M. and 56% at 6 P.M. Snow is rare. The growing season averages 277 days per year, with the last freeze in early March and the first freeze in early December. The sun shines during the year on the average 66% of the daylight hours.

THE PEOPLE

Since 1970 the population of Washington County has grown steadily, reversing a pattern of continuous decreases between 1930 and 1970. The 1982 estimated population of 23,600 indicates a continuation of that growth. Urban areas experienced a 23% increase in population from 1970 to 1980 while rural areas had an 11% gain. The population's median age lowered from 37 in 1970 to 33 in 1980. The largest ancestry groups are persons of German descent (45%), Black (22%) and persons of English descent (13%). **REGISTERED VOTERS** As of November 2, 1982 there were 11,066 registered voters (0.2% of the state total). The 1982 general election had a 60% voter turnout, compared to a 69% turnout in the 1980 general election. In the 1982 primary 96% voted Democratic and 4% Republican, with 3,185 votes cast.

THE ECONOMY

AGRICULTURE Cattle area. In 1982, 87% of the land was in farms and ranches, with 14% of the farmland under cultivation. Washington ranked 114th in the state in highest agricultural receipts, with 90% from livestock and livestock products. Overgrazing, undesirable brush and weeds, water erosion and a lack of potable water are the current conservation problems. Primary crops: hay, oats, wheat and corn. Primary vegetables: potatoes, sweet potatoes and watermelons. Primary fruits and nuts: peaches and pecans. Primary livestock and products: cattle, milk and hogs. **BUSINESS** Total number of business establishments in the county: 555. Retail sales during the first quarter of 1984 decreased 2%. In 1980, 13% of the labor force were self-employed, 20% were employed in professional or related services, 19% in manufacturing, 24% in wholesale and retail trade, 10% in agriculture, forestry, fisheries and mining, 12% were employed in other counties and there were 2,632 retired workers. The industries with the most employment: agribusiness, general construction, tourism, weaving mills and the manufacture of ice cream, frozen desserts and household furniture. The nonfarm earnings in 1981 totaled $241,904,000. The retired workers received an average monthly Social Security payment of $280. **FINANCE** On June 30, 1983, five commercial banks had total deposits of $246,276,000 and total assets of $275,056,000. On December 31, 1982 two state savings and loan associations and three state branches had assets of $164,914,281. **HOUSING** Average value of homes in 1980: $39,100. Permits for new, privately owned housing units increased in 1982: 146 permits were issued with a total construction cost of $4,757,435. Of those permits, 75 were for single family houses. Between 1970 and 1980 the number of housing units increased by 31%. Seventy percent of all units in the county are air-conditioned, 73% are heated by gas and 21% by electricity. **NATURAL RESOURCES** Clay, salt domes, sand, gravel, oil, gas and lignite coal. In 1982 a total of 2,830,107 thousand cubic feet of gas well gas, 237,443 barrels of condensate, 460,056 barrels of crude oil and 1,593,703 thousand cubic feet of casinghead gas were produced. Current production of other minerals and products includes crushed limestone, sand and gravel. **TOURISM** Travel expenditures of $13,073,000 in 1982 (an increase of 11% over 1981) generated 321 jobs and $2,577,000 in payroll. Lodging: two hotels, motels and tourist courts. **ALCOHOLIC BEVERAGES** Packaged distilled spirits, beer, ale, malt liquor and wine are legal. Sale of mixed beverages is legal in all or parts of the county. **FEDERAL EXPENDITURES** The federal government had direct expenditures or obligations of $40,302,000 in the county during fiscal year 1983, including $1,596,000 by the U.S. Department of Defense. In addition, the federal government provided $499,000 in grant awards, paid $1,743,000 in salaries and wages, made direct payments to individuals of $37,449,000 including $25,606,000 in retirement and disability payments, awarded $397,000 in procurement contracts and spent $214,000 in other expenditures or obligations. The federal government also provided $28,000 in direct loans and $1,933,000 in guaranteed loans and insurance.

COMMUNICATION

Newspapers–Daily: Brenham Banner-Press, ave. eve. circ. 5,992. Radio: KTTX-AM and KWHI-FM (Brenham). Cable TV. Telephone companies: Continental Telephone, Southwestern Bell, United Telephone and Industry Telephone. **TRANSPORTATION** Total public road mileage: 917. In 1982 there were 21,865 registered vehicles and 686 reported traffic accidents including 19 fatalities. Taxi cabs: one company in Brenham. Intercity bus service is available. Motor freight: seven local and intrastate carriers. Rail: two main lines carry annually over 30 million tons of freight each through the county. Aircraft: 29 are registered in the county. Airports: Brenham Municipal Airport serves as a base for 15 aircraft and is a general utility airport with general aviation service.

COMMUNITY SERVICES

EDUCATION Two school districts with three elementary, two middle and two high schools. The average daily attendance in 1981-82 was 3,723, with expenditures per pupil of $2,016 including 219 classroom teachers with an average annual salary of $16,294. Fifty-nine percent of the 256 high school graduates planned to attend college. In 1982-83, 65% of the students were White, 3% Hispanic, 31% Black and 0.8% Asian. Sports championships: 1983 AAAA Girls' Golf Team, Brenham H.S. Private schools: 115 students enrolled in one elementary school. Blinn College is located in Brenham. Established in 1883 it is a vocational and two year academic college under state and local control. Enrollment in 1982 was 2,505 with in state undergraduate tuition and fees of $450 per semester. **PUBLIC LIBRARIES** Nancy Carol Roberts Memorial Library (Brenham): 32,040 volumes. **CHILD CARE** 44 day care and 10 twenty-four hour care licensed facilities. **HEALTH CARE** 25 physicians and 11 dentists. Hospitals: two with a combined capacity of 109. Ambulance services: one city service. Mental health: one county clinic and one state school with a capacity of 557. Nursing homes: two nursing homes with a combined capacity of 373 nursing care residents. The average cost per day for private patients in 1982 was $24.14. **CHURCHES** 34 churches have an estimated combined membership of 13,717. The largest denominations are American Lutheran, Catholic and Lutheran-Missouri Synod. **SOCIAL SERVICES** In fiscal year 1983 a total of $775,037 in food stamps was distributed, with an average of 1,736 persons receiving food stamps each month. Aid to Families with Dependent Children (AFDC) totaled $221,640 with an average of 150 families receiving AFDC each month. Medical assistance benefits for the aged and disabled of $2,660,996 and for families and children of $254,277 brought the county benefit total to $3,911,949. **FIRE PROTECTION** 10 volunteer fire departments. **LAW ENFORCEMENT** The County Sheriff has 11 commissioned officers. Two police departments have a combined force of 23. One college campus has a police department with one officer. **CRIME** 31 violent crimes (murder, forcible rape, robbery and aggravated assault) and 409 nonviolent crimes (burglary, larceny-theft and motor vehicle theft) were reported in 1982. **JUDICIAL SYSTEM** Two District Courts and Judges, one County Court and Judge and four Justices of the Peace. In the District Courts a total of 525 cases were

pending on 1/1/82, 575 new cases were filed and 455 cases were disposed of during the year leaving 645 cases pending on 12/31/82. There were 241 criminal cases on the docket, 111 convictions, 41 persons committed to prison, one committed to jail and 82 cases left pending. In the County Court 329 cases were pending on 1/1/82, 261 new cases were filed and 280 cases were disposed of during the year leaving 310 cases pending on 12/31/82. There were 404 criminal cases on the docket, 98 convictions and 167 cases left pending. **JAILS** One jail, capacity 17. **ATTORNEYS AT LAW** 26. **UTILITIES** 53% of the residents are connected to a public or privately owned water system and 46% are connected to a public sewer system. Electricity is distributed to the city of Brenham by the Brenham Municipal Light and Power System and to other parts of the county by Fayette Electric Coop., Inc. and is generated primarily by water. The typical residential electric bill is $125.65 per month for an all-electric house using 2,500 kwh. **TAXES** The county has seven units with taxing authority: two school districts, two cities, one county, one college district and one special district.

RECREATION/ENTERTAINMENT

NATIONAL REGISTER OF HISTORIC PLACES Brenham: Giddings-Wilkin House, Main Building (Blinn College), Pampell-day House and Giddings-Stone Mansion. Burton vicinity: Gantt-Jones House. Chappell Hill: W.W. Browning House and Stage Coach Inn. Gay Hill: Red House. Independence: Mrs. Sam Houston House. Independence vicinity: Asa Hoxey Home. Washington: J.M. Brown House and Hatfield Plantation. Wesley vicinity: Wesley Brethren Church. **STATE** Washington-on-the-Brazos State Historical Park covers 154 acres on which are located a reconstruction of Independence Hall, an auditorium for public use, an outdoor amphitheater and the home of Anson Jones, last president of the Republic of Texas. **COUNTY/MUNICIPAL PARKS** 151 acres in one county and seven municipal parks. These parks contain seven playgrounds, seven baseball and softball fields, six tennis courts, six mulit-use courts and one swimming pool. **SCENIC DRIVES** The Texas Independence Trail runs through this county. This trail not only surveys the historic sites of southeastern Texas but also includes many modern visitor attractions such as the Johnson Space Center. **BOATING/FISHING** Lakes/reservoirs: Butler (23 acres), Hughes (33 acres), Lang (30 acres) and Somerville (11,460 acres). Major rivers: Brazos. Primary streams: Old Yegua, East Mill, Yegua, Caney, Cedar and New Year. **HUNTING** Fall and winter seasons on deer. No closed season on nutria, coyote, bobcat and squirrel. Winter seasons on quail, muskrat, beaver, otter, opossum, mink, ring-tailed cat, badger, fox, raccoon, skunk and civet cat. In 1983 duck, coot, geese, woodcock and jacksnipe seasons occurred during the winter months with a winter season on sandhill crane in some parts of the county. Teal duck, rail and gallinule seasons occurred in the fall. Mourning dove seasons occurred intermittently during the fall and winter months. **MUSEUMS** Chappell Hill: Chappell Hill Historical Society Museum. Independence: Texas Baptist Historical Center Museum. Washington: Barrington, Star of the Republic Museum, Anson Jones Home and Independence Hall. **COLLEGIATE FINE ARTS** Brenham: Cultural events offered by Blinn College. **SPECIAL EVENTS** Texas Independence Day Celebration, Washington, March; Bluebell 10-K Fun Run, Brenham, April; Heritage Society Homes Tour, Brenham, April; Maifest, Brenham, May; July Fourth Celebration, Burton, July; Lions Fun Days, Burton, August; Washington County Fair, Brenham, September; Octoberfest, Washington, October.

COMMUNITIES

COUNTY SEAT Brenham, County Courthouse, 77833; County

COUNTIES

WASHINGTON (continued)

Clerk's Office, 409/836-4300. **INCORPORATED COMMUNITIES** (1980 population and ZIP Code) Brenham (10,966) 77833 and Burton (325) 77835. **UNINCORPORATED COMMUNITIES** (and ZIP Code) Berlin 77833, Chappell Hill (Chapel Hill) 77426, Daniels 77880, Earlywine 77833, Gay Hill 77833, Greenvine 77835, Independence 77833, Klump 77833, Latium 77835, Longpoint 77835, Mill Creek 77833, Muellersville 77833, Packery 77833, Phillipsburg 77833, Pleasant Hill 77833, Prairie Hill 77833, Quarry 77833, Sandy Hill 77833, Sauney Stand 77426, Washington (Washington-on-the-Brazos) 77880, Wesley 77833, Whitman 77833, William Penn 77833 and Zionsville (Zion) 77833. **FOR ADDITIONAL LOCAL INFORMATION** Washington Co. Chamber of Commerce, 314 S. Austin, Brenham, 77833, 409/836-3695 or 836-3696 and Burton Chamber of Commerce, Rt. 1 Box 23, Burton, 77835, 409/289-2454.

WEBB (B19)

THE LAND

Bordering Mexico and west of Corpus Christi on Interstate Highway 35, Webb County covers 3,363 square miles with an elevation range of 400 to 700 feet. The nearly level to undulating soils are gray to black, cracking and clayey with limestone bedrock and a high shrink-swell potential. In the northeast the soils are light colored and clayey, while in the southeast and along the north central border the light colored soils have loamy surfaces and clayey subsoils over limestone. Webb is in the South Texas Plains vegetation area with short and mid grasses, mesquite, thorny shrubs and cacti. Less than 1% of the land in the county is considered prime farmland. **CLIMATE** Subtropical Arid with mild winters and hot summers. The average annual temperature is 73°F. Temperatures in January range from an average low of 43° to an average high of 67°F and in July range from 74° to 100°F. The average annual precipitation is 20 inches, with an average relative humidity of 82% at 6 A.M. and 45% at 6 P.M. Snow is rare. The growing season averages 314 days per year, with the last freeze in mid February and the first freeze in mid December. The sun shines during the year on the average 65% of the daylight hours.

THE PEOPLE

Among all U.S. counties Webb County ranks second in the highest percent of persons of Spanish origin and 70th in the highest birth rate. The 1982 estimated population of 109,900 continues the steady growth which has occurred since 1930. A 13% population gain between 1960 and 1970 rose to a 36% gain between 1970 and 1980. Nearly 96% of the county residents live in urban areas. The age groups with the largest increases between 1970 and 1980 were birth to five years, 15 to 19 and 25 to 34. The largest ancestry groups are Hispanic (92%) and persons of English descent (2%). **REGISTERED VOTERS** As of November 2, 1982 there were 35,602 registered voters (0.6% of the state total). The 1982 general election had a 39% voter turnout, compared to a 49% turnout in the 1980 general election. In the 1982 primary 98% voted Democratic and 2% Republican, with 10,557 votes cast.

THE ECONOMY

AGRICULTURE Cattle ranches in the lower Rio Grande Valley vegetable area. In 1982, 95% of the land was in farms and ranches, with less than 1% of the farmland under cultivation, most of which was irrigated. Webb ranked 98th in the state in highest agricultural receipts, with 83% from livestock and livestock products. Undesirable brush, noxious weeds, water erosion, a lack of potable water and sedimentation are the current conservation problems. Primary crops: sorghum and hay. Primary vegetables: 10th in the state for onions and cantaloupes, eighth for carrots and seventh for cabbage. Watermelons. Primary fruits and nuts: Grapefruit, oranges and pecans. Primary livestock and products: fourth in the state for beef cows that have calved. Cattle. **BUSINESS** Total number of business establishments in the county: 2,061. Retail sales during the first quarter of 1984 increased 16%. In 1980, 8% of the labor force were self-employed, 19% were employed in professional or related services, 8% in manufacturing, 28% in wholesale and retail trade, 10% in transportation, communications and other public utilities, 3% were employed in other counties and there were 4,771 retired workers. The industries with the most employment: tourism, agribusiness, oil and gas extraction, general and heavy construction, meat packing, soft drink bottling and canning, trucking and the manufacture of men's, women's and children's clothing, leather shoes, electrical equipment and the mining of uranium. The nonfarm earnings in 1981 totaled $621,954,000. The retired workers received an average monthly Social Security payment of $261. **FINANCE** On June 30, 1983, six commercial banks had total deposits of $1,393,868,000 and total assets of $1,523,518,000. On December 31, 1982 two state savings and loan associations, one federal association and four state branches had assets of $127,124,215. In addition there are seven credit unions in the county. **HOUSING** Average value of homes in 1980: $29,600. Permits for new, privately owned housing units decreased in 1982: 546 permits were issued with a total construction cost of $15,123,502. Of those permits, 270 were for single family houses. Between 1970 and 1980 the number of housing units increased by 42%. Sixty percent of all units in the county are air-conditioned, 72% are heated by gas and 24% by electricity. **NATURAL RESOURCES** Caliche, clay, salt domes, bituminous coal, oil, gas, uranium and zeolite. In 1982 a total of 106,351,146 thousand cubic feet of gas well gas, 763,206 barrels of condensate, 871,615 barrels of crude oil and 602,983 thousand cubic feet of casinghead gas were produced. Current production of other minerals and products includes caliche, crushed limestone, sand and gravel, crushed sandstone, uranium and bituminous coal. **TOURISM** Travel expenditures of $107,530 in 1982 (an increase of 11% over 1981) generated 2,676 jobs and $21,590,000 in payroll. Lodging: 18 hotels, motels and tourist courts. Convention/meeting facilities: Laredo-Civic Center. **ALCOHOLIC BEVERAGES** Packaged distilled spirits, beer, ale, malt liquor and wine are legal. Sale of mixed beverages is legal in all or parts of the county. **FEDERAL EXPENDITURES** The federal government had direct expenditures or obligations of $128,445,000 in the county during fiscal year 1983, including $3,882,000 by the U.S. Department of Defense. In addition, the federal government provided $22,487,000 in grant awards, paid $17,462,000 in salaries and wages, made direct payments to individuals of $85,554,000 including $63,463,000 in retirement and disability payments, awarded $2,522,000 in procurement contracts and spent $419,000 in other expenditures or obligations. The federal government also provided $154,000 in direct loans and $15,454,000 in guaranteed loans and insurance.

COMMUNICATION

Newspapers–Daily: The Laredo News (Bilingual), ave. morn. circ. 22,991, The Laredo Times ave. morn. circ., 19,257. Weekly: The Laredo Citizen. Radio: KLAR-AM, KVOZ-AM, and KOYE-FM (Laredo). Television: KGNS-Ch. 8 and KVTV-Ch. 13 (Laredo). Cable TV. Telephone companies: General Telephone, Southwestern Bell and Valley Telephone Coop. **TRANSPORTATION** Total public road mileage: 999. In 1982 there were 64,477 registered vehicles and 2,739 reported traffic accidents including 11 fatalities. Taxi cabs: 21 companies in Laredo. Municipal transit systems: one intracity bus system in Laredo, with scheduled routes. Intercity bus service is available. Motor freight: 52 local and intrastate carriers. Rail: one main line carries annually five to 10 million tons of freight through the county. Aircraft: 93 are registered in the county. Airports: Laredo International Airport serves as a base for 65 aircraft and is a short haul, non-hub airport with carrier service. Domestic and foreign exports by air from Laredo average about 150 thousand pounds per month and imports average about 20 thousand pounds per month.

COMMUNITY SERVICES

EDUCATION Four school districts with 27 elementary, seven middle and six high schools. The average daily attendance in 1981-82 was 26,297, with expenditures per pupil of $2,518 including 1,437 classroom teachers with an average annual salary of $15,175. Fifty-nine percent of the 1,240 high school graduates planned to attend college. In 1982-83, 5% of the students were White, 95% Hispanic, 0.1% Black and 0.1% Asian. Private schools: 2,580 students enrolled in eight elementary and two high schools. Sports championships: 1983 Girls AAA Volleyball, Saint Augustine H.S. Laredo State University is located in Laredo. Established in 1969 it is part of the University System of South Texas and is under state control. Enrollment in 1982 was 816 with in state undergraduate tuition and fees of $244 per semester. The highest degree offered is Master. Laredo Junior College is located in Laredo. Established in 1946 it is a vocational and two year academic college under local control. Enrollment in 1982 was 3,120 with in state undergraduate tuition and fees of $299 per semester. Vocational education: Laredo Beauty College (Laredo). **PUBLIC LIBRARIES** Laredo Public Library: 50,152 volumes. **CHILD CARE** 103 day care and 11 twenty-four hour care licensed facilities. **HEALTH CARE** 78 physicians and 13 dentists. Hospitals: two with a combined capacity of 346. Clinics: one dialysis clinic and one public health clinic. Ambulance services: two commercial and one fire department service. Mental health: one county clinic. Nursing homes: two nursing homes with a combined capacity of 288 nursing care and 40 custodial care residents. The average cost per day for private patients in 1982 was $35.53. **CHURCHES** 47 churches have an estimated combined membership of 57,570. The largest denomination is Catholic. **SOCIAL SERVICES** In fiscal year 1983 a total of $17,776,006 in food stamps was distributed, with an average of 36,306 persons receiving food stamps each month. Aid to Families with Dependent Children (AFDC) totaled $1,933,136 with an average of 1,190 families receiving AFDC each month. Medical assistance benefits for the aged and disabled of $7,479,670 and for families and children of $2,999,750 brought the county benefit total to $30,188,562. **FIRE PROTECTION** One paid and three volunteer fire departments. **LAW ENFORCEMENT** The County Sheriff has 118 commissioned officers. One police department has a force of 148 and Laredo International Airport has a police force of six officers. **CRIME** 435 violent crimes (murder, forcible rape, robbery and aggravated assault) and 6,865 nonviolent crimes (burglary, larceny-theft and motor vehicle theft) were reported in 1982. **JUDICIAL SYSTEM** Two District Courts and Judges, two County Courts and Judges and five Justices of the Peace. In the District Courts a total of 1,480 cases were pending on 1/1/82, 1,833 new cases were filed and 1,226 cases were disposed of during the year leaving 2,087 cases pending on 12/31/82. There were 779 criminal cases on the docket, 204 convictions, 37 persons committed to prison, seven committed to jail and 380 cases left pending. In the County Courts 980 cases were pending on 1/1/82, 2,182 new cases were filed and 2,160 cases were disposed of during the year leaving 1,002 cases pending on 12/31/82. There were 1,608 criminal cases on the docket, 601

convictions, 10 persons committed to jail and 388 cases left pending. **JAILS** Two jails, capacity 343. New facilities are under construction and the current facilities are under renovation. **ATTORNEYS AT LAW** 140. **UTILITIES** 98% of the residents are connected to a public or privately owned water system and 92% are connected to a public sewer system. Natural gas is distributed to the county by Entex, Inc. The average annual residential bill for natural gas in 1982 for the Entex distribution system was $390.31, an increase of 26% over 1981. Electricity is distributed to the county by Central Power and Light Co., Cochran Power and Light, Medina Electric Coop., Inc. and Rio Grande Electric Coop., Inc. and is generated primarily by gas, oil and coal. The typical residential electric bill is $162.15 per month for an all-electric house using 2,500 kwh. **TAXES** The county has eight units with taxing authority: four school districts, one city, one county, one college district and one special district.

RECREATION/ENTERTAINMENT

NATIONAL REGISTER OF HISTORIC PLACES Laredo: Webb County Courthouse, Old Fort McIntosh Historic District and San Augustine de Laredo District. Laredo vicinity: Dolores Nuevo and Dolores Viejo. Mirando City vicinity: Los Ojuelos Ranch. **COUNTY/MUNICIPAL PARKS** 1,190 acres in six county and 30 municipal parks. These parks contain three miles of hiking trails, 18 playgrounds, one golf course, ten baseball and softball fields, 25 tennis courts, five swimming pools, two boat ramps and shore fishing facilities. Developed campsites: 16. **SCENIC DRIVES** The Texas Tropical Trail runs through this county. This trail is charted through the state's southernmost wedge meandering through ranchland resort areas by the Gulf of Mexico and fertile farm lands. **BOATING/FISHING** Lakes/reservoirs: Biel (200 acres), Casa Blanca (1,656 acres), Clark (24 acres), Flores (36 acres), Gates (27 acres), Link (47 acres), Manadas Creek (65 acres), Middle Pasture (105 acres), Nicholson Ranch (48 acres), Nunley (35 acres), Nunley #3 (68 acres), O'Keefe (124 acres), Retama (24 acres), San Ramon (60 acres), Spohn Ranch (220 acres), Vaquillas #1 (222 acres), Vaquillas #2 (34 acres), Zachary (88 acres) and Zachary #3 (26 acres). Major rivers: Rio Grande. Primary streams: Black, Chacon, Comal, Arroyo De Leon, San Idelfonso, North Sombrerito, Tordillo, Cochio, Reiser, Santa Lorenzo, Santa Isabel, Los Olmos, Salado, Black and Beccero. **HUNTING** Fall and winter seasons on deer. No closed season on javelina, coyote, bobcat and squirrel. Winter seasons on quail, muskrat, beaver, opossum, ring-tailed cat, badger, fox, weasel, raccoon, skunk and civet cat. Fall and winter seasons on turkey. Special regulations on equipment. In 1983 sandhill crane, duck, coot, geese, woodcock and jacksnipe seasons occurred during the winter months. Teal duck, rail and gallinule seasons occurred in the fall. Mourning dove seasons occurred intermittently during the fall and winter months with a fall season on white-winged dove. **MUSEUMS** Laredo: Nuevo Santander Museum and Republic of the Rio Grande Building. **THEATERS** Laredo: Civic Center. **ORCHESTRAS** Laredo: Philharmonic Orchestra. **DANCE** Laredo: Incarnate Word Ballet. **ZOO** Laredo: Mecom Ranch World Wildlife Preserve. **COLLEGIATE FINE ARTS** Laredo: Cultural events offered by Laredo Junior College. **SPECIAL EVENTS** Fiesta Caceria, Laredo, January; Washington's Birthday Celebration, Laredo, February; International Fair and Exposition, Laredo, March; Border Olympics, Laredo, March; Miss Laredo Pageant, Laredo, April; Frontier Days, Laredo, May; Borderfest, Laredo, June/July.

COMMUNITIES

COUNTY SEAT Laredo, County Courthouse, 78040; County Clerk's Office, 512/727-7272. **INCORPORATED COMMUNITIES** (1980 population and ZIP Code) Laredo (91,449) 78040.

COUNTIES

UNINCORPORATED COMMUNITIES (and ZIP Code) Aguilares 78369, Bruni 78344, Del Mar Hills 78040, Los Ojuelas (Ojuelas) 78369, Mirando 78369 and Oilton 78371. **FOR ADDITIONAL LOCAL INFORMATION** Laredo Chamber of Commerce, P.O. Box 790, Laredo, 78042, 512/722-9895.

WHARTON (G16)

THE LAND

Southwest of Houston on U.S. Highway 59 in the Coastal Prairie Region, Wharton County covers 1,086 square miles with an elevation range of 50 to 200 feet. The nearly level soils are light to dark colored, shallow, loamy surfaces over clayey subsoils or gray to black cracking, clayey soils with a high shrink-swell potential. Along the rivers the brownish to reddish, clayey to loamy, soils also have a high shrink-swell potential. Along the northern border the light colored, loamy surfaces have very deep reddish subsoils. The county is in the Gulf Prairies and Marshes vegetation area with tall prairie grasses, tall bunch grasses, mesquite and oak. Between 51 and 60% of the land in the county is considered prime farmland. **CLIMATE** Subtropical Humid. Tropical storms and hurricanes are a risk June through October. The average annual temperature is 69°F. Temperatures in January range from an average low of 42° to an average high of 63°F and in July range from 73° to 94°F. The average annual precipitation is 42 inches, with an average relative humidity of 89% at 6 A.M. and 65% at 6 P.M. The average annual snowfall is not significant. The growing season averages 268 days per year, with the last freeze in early March and the first freeze in late November. The sun shines during the year on the average 68% of the daylight hours.

THE PEOPLE

The 1982 estimated population of 40,900 indicates a continuation of a growth rate begun in the 1970s which reversed a population decline between 1960 and 1970. Urban areas experienced greater growth than rural areas from 1970 to 1980. The largest ancestry groups are Hispanic (22%), persons of German descent (18%), Black (17%) and English descent (13%). **REGISTERED VOTERS** As of November 2, 1982 there were 18,387 registered voters (0.3% of the state total). The 1982 general election had a 54% voter turnout, compared to a 66% turnout in the 1980 general election. In the 1982 primary 94% voted Democratic and 6% Republican, with 4,931 votes cast.

THE ECONOMY

AGRICULTURE Sorghum area. In 1982, 94% of the land was in farms and ranches, with 64% of the farmland under cultivation and 35% irrigated. Wharton ranked 8th in the state in highest agricultural receipts, with 81% from crops. Decreasing irrigation water supplies, soil compaction, drainage, noxious weeds and erosion are the current conservation problems. Primary crops: second in the state for sorghum, first for rice, ninth for soybeans, eighth for corn and seventh for rye. Cotton and hay. Primary vegetables: watermelons. Primary fruits and nuts: peaches and pecans. Primary livestock and products: cattle. **BUSINESS** Total number of business establishments in the county: 909. Retail sales during the first quarter of 1984 increased 10%. In 1980, 11% of the labor force were self-employed, 20% were employed in professional or related services, 11% in manufacturing, 19% in wholesale and retail trade, 21% in transportation, communications, and other public utilities, 19% were employed in other counties and there were 3,307 retired workers. The industries with the most employment: agribusiness,

oil and gas extraction, sulfur mining and the manufacture of ladies lingerie, wood kitchen cabinets and aluminum products. The nonfarm earnings in 1981 totaled $366,551,000. The retired workers received an average monthly Social Security payment of $298. **FINANCE** On June 30, 1983, seven commercial banks had total deposits of $292,861,000 and total assets of $330,295,000. There are three state savings and loan associaton branches, two federal association branches and four credit unions in the county. **HOUSING** Average value of homes in 1980: $33,700. Permits for new, privately owned housing units increased in 1982: 128 permits were issued with a total construction cost of $5,476,810. Of those permits, 58 were for single family houses. Housing permits in El Campo increased from 31 in 1981 to 90 in 1982. Between 1970 and 1980 the number of housing units increased by 25%. Sixty-nine percent of all units in the county are air-conditioned, 77% are heated by gas and 22% by electricity. **NATURAL RESOURCES** Salt domes, sand and gravel, oil and gas. In 1982 a total of 32,483,640 thousand cubic feet of gas well gas, 127,935 barrels of condensate, 3,328,171 barrels of crude oil and 8,650,641 thousand cubic feet of casinghead gas were produced. Current production of other minerals and products includes clay, and frasch sulfur. **TOURISM** Travel expenditures of $11,416,000 in 1982 (an increase of 11% over 1981) generated 272 jobs and $2,240,000 in payroll. **ALCOHOLIC BEVERAGES** Packaged distilled spirits, beer, ale, malt liquor and wine are legal in parts of the county. Sale of mixed beverages is legal in all or parts of the county. **FEDERAL EXPENDITURES** The federal government had direct expenditures or obligations of $65,389,000 in the county during fiscal year 1983, including $1,893,000 by the U.S. Department of Defense. In addition, the federal government provided $2,409,000 in grant awards, paid $2,641,000 in salaries and wages, made direct payments to individuals of $47,494,000 including $34,164,000 in retirement and disability payments, awarded $13,000 in procurement contracts and spent $12,421,000 in other expenditures or obligations. The federal government also provided $2,989,000 in direct loans and $27,609,000 in guaranteed loans and insurance.

COMMUNICATION

Newspapers–Weekly: East Bernard Tribune, El Campo Citizen, El Campo Leader-News and the Wharton Journal-Spectator. Radio: KULP-AM (El Campo) and KANI-AM (Wharton). Cable TV. Telephone companies: General Telephone, Continental Telephone, Southwestern Bell, Central Telephone-Midstate and Ganado Telephone. **TRANSPORTATION** Total public road mileage: 1,401. In 1982 there were 36,899 registered vehicles and 880 reported traffic accidents including 21 fatalities. Taxi cabs: two companies in El Campo and one in the city of Wharton. Intercity bus service is available. Motor freight: 23 local and intrastate carriers. Rail: The Sunset Limited provides passenger service on the Amtrak Route. One main and nine branch lines carry freight through the county. The main line carries annually 20 to 30 million tons of freight. The three branch lines carry annually one to five million tons each and six carry less than one million each. Aircraft: 156 are registered in the county. Airports: Wharton Municipal Airport serves as a base for 40 aircraft and is a general utility airport. Also serving the area are Lackley Aviation at Wharton and Thompson Flyers, Metro, Inc. and Coastal Airpark at El Campo.

COMMUNITY SERVICES

EDUCATION Five school districts with nine elementary, four middle and five high schools. The average daily attendance in 1981-82 was 7,753, with expenditures per pupil of $2,834 including 526 classroom teachers with an average annual salary of $18,283. Fifty-four percent of the 586 high school graduates planned to attend college. In 1982-83, 50% of the students were White, 30%

Hispanic and 20% Black. Sports championships: 1983 AA Girls' Volleyball, East Bernard H.S. Private schools: 309 students enrolled in one elementary school. Wharton County Junior College is located in Wharton. Established in 1946 it is a vocational and two year academic college under local control. Enrollment in 1982 was 2,089 with in state undergratuate tuition and fees of $200 per semester. **PUBLIC LIBRARIES** Wharton County Library (Wharton): 69,222 volumes, three branches. **CHILD CARE** 36 day care and 20 twenty-four hour care licensed facilities. **HEALTH CARE** 47 physicians and 14 dentists. Hospitals: three with a combined capacity of 221. Clinics: one physical and respiratory therapy clinic. Ambulance services: one volunteer service, one city, one fire department and one volunteer fire department service. Mental health: two county clinics. Nursing homes: three nursing homes with a combined capacity of 325 nursing care residents. The average cost per day for private patients in 1982 was $30.33. **CHURCHES** 64 churches have an estimated combined membership of 29,371. The largest denominations are Catholic, Southern Baptist and United Methodist. **SOCIAL SERVICES** In fiscal year 1983 a total of $1,652,371 in food stamps was distributed, with an average of 3,470 persons receiving food stamps each month. Aid to Families with Dependent Children (AFDC) totaled $367,430 with an average of 245 families receiving AFDC each month. Medical assistance benefits for the aged and disabled of $2,911,530 and for families and children of $412,088 brought the county benefit total to $5,343,419. **FIRE PROTECTION** 10 volunteer fire departments. **LAW ENFORCEMENT** The County Sheriff has 42 commissioned officers. Two police departments have a combined force of 48. One college campus has a police department with a force of six officers. **CRIME** 98 violent crimes (murder, forcible rape, robbery and aggravated assault) and 1,463 nonviolent crimes (burglary, larceny-theft and motor vehicle theft) were reported in 1982. **JUDICIAL SYSTEM** Two District Courts and Judges, one County Court and Judge and four Justices of the Peace. In the District Courts a total of 1,085 cases were pending on 1/1/82, 783 new cases were filed and 891 cases were disposed of during the year leaving 977 cases pending on 12/31/82. There were 217 criminal cases on the docket, 99 convictions, 41 persons committed to prison and two committed to jail and 49 cases left pending. In the County Court 1,951 cases were pending on 1/1/82, 897 new cases were filed and 701 cases were disposed of during the year leaving 2,147 cases pending on 12/31/82. There were 2,529 criminal cases on the docket, 439 convictions, five persons committed to jail, and 1,892 cases left pending. **JAILS** One jail, capacity 45. **ATTORNEYS AT LAW** 39. **UTILITIES** 63% of the residents are connected to a public or privately owned water system and 60% are connected to a public sewer system. Natural gas is distributed to the county by Entex, Inc. The average annual residential bill for natural gas in 1982 for the Entex distribution system was $390.31, an increase of 26% over 1981. Electricity is distributed to the county by Cochran Power and Light, Wharton Co. Electric Coop., Inc., Central Power and Light Co. and Houston Lighting and Power Co. and is generated primarily by gas, oil and coal. The typical residential electric bill is $201.39 per month for an all-electric house using 2,500 kwh. **TAXES** The county has 14 units with taxing authority: six school districts, two cities, one county, one college district and four special districts.

RECREATION/ENTERTAINMENT

MUNICIPAL PARKS 71 acres in 11 municipal parks. These parks contain one mile of hiking trails, 10 playgrounds, three football and soccer fields, nine baseball and softball fields, nine tennis courts, two multi-use courts and one swimming pool. **BOATING/FISHING** Lakes/reservoirs: Texas Gulf (538 acres). Major rivers: Colorado and San Bernard. Primary streams: West Bernard. **HUNTING** Fall and winter seasons on deer. No closed seasons on nutria, coyote, bobcat and squirrel. Winter seasons on quail, muskrat, beaver, otter, opossum, mink, ring-tailed cat, badger, fox, weasel, raccoon, skunk and civet cat with a winter season on pheasant in some parts of the county. In 1983 sandhill crane, duck, coot, geese, woodcock and jacksnipe seasons occurred during the winter months. Teal duck, rail and gallinule seasons occurred in the fall. Mourning dove seasons occurred intermittently during the fall and winter months. **MUSEUMS** Egypt: Northington-Heard Memorial Museum. El Campo: El Camp Museum and El Campo Big Game Trophy Museum. Wharton: Wharton County Historical Museum. **THEATERS** Wharton: Duson-Hanson Fine Arts Theater. **COLLEGIATE FINE ARTS** Wharton: Cultural events offered by Wharton County Junior College. **SPECIAL EVENTS** Wharton County Youth Fair and Exposition, Wharton, April; Grande Days Celebration), Wharton/El Campo, August; Square Fair, Wharton, October; Fun Run, Wharton, October; Christmas Parade, Wharton, December; Rodeos, Wharton, variable dates.

COMMUNITIES

COUNTY SEAT Wharton, County Courthouse, 77488; County Clerk's Office, 409/532-2381. **INCORPORATED COMMUNITIES** (1980 population and ZIP Code) El Campo (10,462) 77437 All-America Cities Honorable Mention 1955 and 1956, Wharton (9,033) 77488. **UNINCORPORATED COMMUNITIES** (and ZIP Code) Boling 77420, Burr 77488, Crescent 77488, Danevang 77432, Dinsmore 77488, East Bernard 77435, Egypt 77436, El Campo South 77437, Elm Grove 77434, Glen Flora 77443, Haid 77453, Hillje 77437, Hungerford 77448, Iago 77420, Jones Creek 77437, Lane City 77453, Lissie 77454, Louise 77455, Mackay 77488, Magnet 77488, Newgulf 77462, New Taiton 77437, Peach Creek 77488, Pierce 77467, Sandy Corner 77437, Sorrelle (Sorels) 77488, Southland 77437, Spanish Camp 77488 and Taiton 77437. **FOR ADDITIONAL LOCAL INFORMATION** East Bernard Chamber of Commerce, P.O. BOx 567, East Bernard, 77435, El Campo Chamber of Commerce, P.O. Box 446, El Campo, 77437, 409/543-2713, Louise-Hillje Chamber of Commerce, P.O. Box 156, Louise, 77455, 409/648-2323 and Wharton Chamber of Commerce, P.O. Box 868, 225 N. Richmond Road, Wharton, 77488, 409/532-1862.

WHEELER (P15)

THE LAND

In the Rolling Plains Region of the Texas Panhandle and east of Amarillo on Interstate Highway 40, Wheeler County covers 905 square miles with the elevation ranging from 2,100 to 2,700 feet. The light colored, sandy to loamy soils have very deep, reddish, clayey subsoils. In the northwest the very dark, loamy surfaces have reddish clayey subsoils over limestone. The county is in the Rolling Plains vegetation area with tall and mid grasses, mesquite and shinnery oak. Between one and 10% of the land in the county is considered prime farmland. **CLIMATE** Continental Steppe with cold winters and hot summers. The average annual temperature is 58°F. Temperatures in January range from an average low of 21° to an average high of 50°F and in July range from 67° to 96°F. The average annual precipitation is 23 inches, with an average relative humidity of 74% at 6 A.M. and 43% at 6 P.M. The average annual snowfall is 15 inches. The growing season averages 208 days per year, with the last freeze in early April and the first freeze in early November. The sun shines during the year on the average 75% of the daylight hours.

COUNTIES

THE PEOPLE

The 1982 estimated population of 7,800 indicates continuation of the growth which began in the 1970s reversing the steady population decline from 1930 to 1970. Rural areas grew faster than urban areas from 1970 to 1980. The population's high median age lowered from 40 in 1970 to 35 in 1980. The largest ancestry groups are persons of English descent (30%), Irish descent (24%) and German descent (14%). **REGISTERED VOTERS** As of November 2, 1982 there were 3,562 registered voters (0.1% of the state total). The 1982 general election had a 59% voter turnout, compared to a 68% turnout in the 1980 general election. In the 1982 primary 95% voted Democratic and 5% Republican, with 1,188 votes cast.

THE ECONOMY

AGRICULTURE Wheat and cattle area. In 1982, 95% of the land was in farms and ranches, with 26% of the farmland under cultivation and 7% irrigated. Wheeler ranked 120th in the state in highest agricultural receipts, with 73% from livestock and livestock products. Overgrazing, undesirable brush and weeds, water and wind erosion and inefficient tillage systems are the current conservation problems. Primary crops: first in the state for rye, wheat, sorghum, hay and cotton. Primary vegetables: cantaloupes, sweet potatoes and watermelons. Primary fruits and nuts: peaches and pecans. Primary livestock and products: cattle and hogs. **BUSINESS** Total number of business establishments in the county: 189. Retail sales during the first quarter of 1984 decreased 11%. In 1980, 21% of the labor force were self-employed, 18% were employed in professional or related services, 4% in manufacturing, 20% in wholesale and retail trade, 28% in agriculture, forestry, fisheries and mining, 13% were employed in other counties and there were 984 retired workers. The industries with the most employment: oil and gas extraction, agribusiness, heavy construction and the manufacture of carbon black. The nonfarm earnings in 1981 totaled $68,294,000. The retired workers received an average monthly Social Security payment of $296. **FINANCE** On June 30, 1983, four commercial banks had total deposits of $71,802,000 and total assets of $83,135,000. On December 31, 1982 one state savings and loan associations and one federal association branch had assets of $8,367,329. **HOUSING** Average value of homes in 1980: $21,700. Permits for new, privately owned housing units increased in 1982: 27 permits were issued with a total construction cost of $1,175,012. Of those permits, all were for single family houses. Between 1970 and 1980 the number of housing units increased by 11%. Eighty-one percent of all units in the county are air-conditioned, 94% are heated by gas and 5% by electricity. **NATURAL RESOURCES** Caliche, gypsum, oil and gas. In 1982 a total of 81,402,841 thousand cubic feet of gas well gas, 235,634 barrels of condensate, 820,749 barrels of crude oil and 1,249,918 thousand cubic feet of casinghead gas were produced. Current production of other minerals and products includes brine, caliche and sand and gravel. **TOURISM** Travel expenditures of $8,937,000 in 1982 (an increase of 11% over 1981) generated 219 jobs and $1,760,000 in payroll. **ALCOHOLIC BEVERAGES** Totally dry. **FEDERAL EXPENDITURES** The federal government had direct expenditures or obligations of $14,724,000 in the county during fiscal year 1983, including $323,000 by the U.S. Department of Defense. In addition, the federal government provided $142,000 in grant awards, paid $726,000 in salaries and wages, made direct payments to individuals of $12,632,000 including $8,380,000 in retirement and disability payments, awarded $4,000 in procurement contracts and spent $1,219,000 in other expenditures or obligations. The federal government also provided $1,241,000 in direct loans and $2,442,000 in guaranteed loans and insurance.

COMMUNICATION

Newspapers–Weekly: The Shamrock Texan and The Wheeler Times. Radio: KBYP-AM (Shamrock). Cable TV. Telephone companies: General Telephone and Southwestern Bell. **TRANSPORTATION** Total public road mileage: 873. In 1982 there were 8,034 registered vehicles and 197 reported traffic accidents including two fatalities. Intercity bus service is available. Motor freight: two carriers. Rail: one main line carries annually 10 to 20 million tons of freight through the county. Aircraft: 16 are registered in the county. Airports: Shamrock Municipal Airport serves as a base for 10 aircraft and is a basic utility airport with general aviation service. Holt Airport at Wheeler.

COMMUNITY SERVICES

EDUCATION Seven school districts with seven elementary, one middle and six high schools. The average daily attendance in 1981-82 was 1,249, with expenditures per pupil of $5,239 including 140 classroom teachers with an average annual salary of $16,176. Forty-two percent of the 72 high school graduates planned to attend college. In 1982-83, 90% of the students were White, 6% Hispanic, 3% Black, 0.8% Asian and 0.3% American Indian. Sports championships: 1983 A Girls' Golf Singles, Wheeler H.S. **PUBLIC LIBRARIES** Shamrock Public Library: 16,276 volumes. Wheeler Public Library: 24,421 volumes. **CHILD CARE** Six day care and two twenty-four hour care licensed facilities. **HEALTH CARE** Six physicians and five dentists. Hospitals: two with a combined capacity of 71. Ambulance services: one county service. Mental health: one clinic. Nursing homes: one nursing home has a capacity of 64 nursing care residents. The average cost per day for private patients in 1982 was $28.09. **CHURCHES** 29 churches have an estimated combined membership of 5,989. The largest denominations are Southern Baptist and United Methodist. **SOCIAL SERVICES** In fiscal year 1983 a total of $174,503 in food stamps was distributed, with an average of 373 persons receiving food stamps each month. Aid to Families with Dependent Children (AFDC) totaled $29,166 with an average of 19 families receiving AFDC each month. Medical assistance benefits for the aged and disabled of $518,413 and for families and children of $47,079 brought the county benefit total to $769,161. **FIRE PROTECTION** Six volunteer fire departments. **LAW ENFORCEMENT** The County Sheriff has five commissioned officers. One police department has a force of six. **CRIME** Eight violent crimes (murder, forcible rape, robbery and aggravated assault) and 150 nonviolent crimes (burglary, larceny-theft and motor vehicle theft) were reported in 1982. **JUDICIAL SYSTEM** One District Court and Judge, one County Court and Judge and three Justices of the Peace. In the District Court a total of 339 cases were pending on 1/1/82, 176 new cases were filed and 169 cases were disposed of during the year leaving 346 cases pending on 12/31/82. There were 23 criminal cases on the docket, five convictions, one person committed to prison and 13 cases left pending. In the County Court 436 cases were pending on 1/1/82, 167 new cases were filed and 124 cases were disposed of during the year leaving 479 cases pending on 12/31/82. There were 518 criminal cases on the docket, 102 convictions, 24 persons committed to jail, and 395 cases left pending. **JAILS** One jail, capacity 11, planning renovation. **ATTORNEYS AT LAW** Six. **UTILITIES** 76% of the residents are connected to a public or privately owned water system and 63% are connected to a public sewer system. Natural gas is distributed to the county by High Plains Natural Gas Co. Electricity is distributed to the county by West Texas Utilities, Greenbelt Electric Coop., Inc. and North Plains Electric Coop., Inc. and is generated primarily by gas and oil. The typical residential electric bill is $145.78 per month for an all-electric house using 2,500 kwh. **TAXES** The county has 13 units with taxing authority: seven school districts, three cities, one county and two hospital districts.

RECREATION/ENTERTAINMENT

MUNICIPAL PARKS 11 acres in three municipal parks. These parks contain two playgrounds, one baseball and softball field, two multi-use courts and two swimming pools. **BOATING/FISHING** Lakes/reservoirs: Fensterwald Soil Conservation Service Lake 21 (35 acres) and Washita River Upper Soil Conservation Lake 17 (15 acres). Major rivers: North Fork Red. Primary streams: Gageby and Sweetwater. **HUNTING** Fall and winter seasons on deer. Summer, fall and winter seasons on squirrel. Fall season on prairie chicken. Winter seasons on pheasant, quail, muskrat, beaver, opossum, ring-tailed cat, badger, fox, weasel, raccoon, skunk and civet cat. Fall, winter and spring seasons on turkey. In 1983 sandhill crane, duck, coot, geese, woodcock and jacksnipe seasons occurred during the winter months. Teal duck, rail and gallinule seasons occurred in the fall. Mourning dove seasons occurred intermittently during the fall and winter months. **MUSEUMS** Shamrock: Pioneer West Museum. Wheeler: Wheeler County Historical Museum and Old Mobeetie Museum. **SPECIAL EVENTS** St. Patrick's Day Celebration, Shamrock, March.

COMMUNITIES

COUNTY SEAT Wheeler, County Courthouse, 79096; County Clerk's Office, 806/826-5544. **INCORPORATED COMMUNITIES** (1980 population and ZIP Code) Mobeetie (291) 79061, Shamrock (2,834) 79079 and Wheeler (1,584) 79096. **UNINCORPORATED COMMUNITIES** (and ZIP Code) Allison 79003, Benonine 79068, Briscoe 79011, Heald 79057, Kellerville 79049, Kelton 79096, Lela 79079, New Mobeetie 79061, Old Mobeetie 79061, Pakan 79079, Twitty 79090 and Zybach 79011. **FOR ADDITIONAL LOCAL INFORMATION** Shamrock Chamber of Commerce, P.O. Box 588, 121 N. Main, Shamrock, 79079, 806/256-2501 and Wheeler Chamber of Commerce, P.O. Box 221, Wheeler, 79096, 806/826-3573.

WICHITA (P36)

THE LAND

Bordering Oklahoma northwest of the Dallas-Fort Worth metroplex on U.S. Highways 287 and 281 in the Rolling Plains Region, Wichita County covers 606 square miles with the elevation ranging from 900 to 1,200 feet. The light to dark loamy soils have very deep reddish, clayey subsoils with some lime accumulations. In the southeast the undulating to hilly soils are reddish to brownish, loamy surfaces over clayey subsoils. The county is in the Rolling Plains vegetation area with tall and mid grasses, mesquite and shinnery oak. Between 41 and 50% of the land in the county is considered prime farmland. **CLIMATE** Subtropical Subhumid with hot summers. The average annual temperature is 63°F. Temperatures in January range from an average low of 28° to an average high of 53°F and in July range from 72° to 98°F. The average annual precipitation is 27 inches, with an average relative humidity of 78% at 6 A.M. and 47% at 6 P.M. The average annual snowfall is six inches. The growing season averages 221 days per year, with the last freeze in early April and the first freeze in early November. The sun shines during the year on the average 71% of the daylight hours.

THE PEOPLE

Wichita County is one of the state's most densely populated. The 1982 estimated population of 125,500 indicates a reversal in the population losses from 1960 to 1980, which followed a 20 year period of rapid growth. Nearly 95% of the county residents live in urban areas. The age group with the largest gain between 1970 and 1980 was ages 25 to 29, while the largest decrease occurred among ages five to 14. The largest ancestry groups are persons of English descent (27%), Irish descent (22%) and German descent (19%). **REGISTERED VOTERS** As of November 2, 1982 there were 51,161 registered voters (0.8% of the state total). The 1982 general election had a 54% voter turnout, compared to a 76% turnout in the 1980 general election. In the 1982 primary 82% voted Democratic and 18% Republican, with 8,082 votes cast.

THE ECONOMY

AGRICULTURE Wheat area. In 1982, 87% of the land was in farms and ranches, with 32% of the farmland under cultivation and 6% irrigated. Wichita ranked 152nd in the state in highest agricultural receipts, with 58% from crops. Overgrazing, undesirable brush and weeds, water erosion, noxious weeds and salinity are the current conservation problems. Primary crops: wheat, cotton, hay, sorghum and oats. Primary vegetables: onions, sweet potatoes, tomatoes and watermelons. Primary fruits and nuts: peaches and pecans. Primary livestock and products: cattle, milk, sheep, wool and hogs. **BUSINESS** Total number of business establishments in the county: 3,121. Retail sales during the first quarter of 1984 increased 7%. In 1980, 9% of the labor force were self-employed, 20% were employed in professional or related services, 17% in manufacturing, 24% in wholesale and retail trade, 7% in construction, 2% were employed in other counties and there were 9,641 retired workers. The industries with the most employment: agribusiness, oil and gas extraction, general and heavy construction, soft drink bottling and canning, commercial printing, trucking, steel foundries and the manufacture of meat products, dairy products, men's work clothing, mobile homes, paper bags, plastics products, flat glass, mineral wool, fabricated structural metal, fabricated plate work, oil field machinery, power driven hand tools, commercial laundry equipment, refrigeration and heating equipment, industrial electrical controls, electronic capacitors, engine electrical equipment, motor vehicle parts, aircraft engines and parts, surgical appliances and supplies and sporting and athletic goods. The nonfarm earnings in 1981 totaled $1,418,377,000. The retired workers received an average monthly Social Security payment of $317. **FINANCE** On June 30, 1983, 10 commercial banks had total deposits of $1,096,268,000 and total assets of $1,299,171,000. On December 31, 1982 two state savings and loan associations, two federal associations, 11 state branches and two federal branches had combined assets of $318,038,120. In addition there are two credit unions in the county. **HOUSING** Average value of homes in 1980: $32,100. Permits for new, privately owned housing units increased in 1982: 846 permits were issued with a total construction cost of $19,435,914. Of those permits, 408 were for single family houses. Housing permits in Iowa Park increased from 23 in 1981 to 75 in 1982 with 48 permits issued for apartments and condominiums. Between 1970 and 1980 the number of housing units increased by 16%. Ninety-two percent of all units in the county are air-conditioned, 80% are heated by gas and 19% by electricity. **NATURAL RESOURCES** Sand and gravel, oil, gas, volcanic ash and bituminous coal. In 1982 a total of 5,287,922 barrels of crude oil and 255,652 thousand cubic feet of casinghead gas were produced. Current production of other minerals and products includes construction sand. **TOURISM** Travel expenditures of $80,476,000 in 1982 (an increase of 7% over 1981) generated 1,382 jobs and $17,360,000 in payroll. Lodging: 23 hotels, motels and tourist courts. Convention/meeting facilities: Wichita Falls-Midwestern State University Coliseum, Wichita Falls Activities Center and

COUNTIES

Memorial Auditorium, and two hotels with facilities for large gatherings. **ALCOHOLIC BEVERAGES** Packaged distilled spirits, beer, ale, malt liquor and wine are legal in parts of the county. **MILITARY INSTALLATIONS** Sheppard Air Force Base, Wichita Falls, 6,736 personnel, 5,258 acres, Technical Training Center. **FEDERAL EXPENDITURES** The federal government had direct expenditures or obligations of $385,960,000 in the county during fiscal year 1983, including $213,858,000 by the U.S. Department of Defense. In addition, the federal government provided $7,512,000 in grant awards, paid $158,915,000 in salaries and wages, made direct payments to individuals of $174,970,000 including $135,190,000 in retirement and disability payments, awarded $42,113,000 in procurement contracts and spent $2,451,000 in other expenditures or obligations. The federal government also provided $4,371,000 in direct loans and $117,656,000 in guaranteed loans and insurance.

COMMUNICATION

Newspapers–Daily: Wichita Falls Record-News, ave. morn. circ. 33,709, Wichita Falls Times, ave. eve. circ. 15,771. Weekly: Informer Star (Burkburnett) Iowa Park Leader and The Electra Star-News. Radio: KNIN-AM, KTRN-AM, KWFT-AM (Wichita Falls), KKQV-FM, KLUR-FM and KNIN-FM (Wichita Falls). Television: KAUZ-CH.6 and KFDX-CH.3 (Wichita Falls). Cable TV. Telephone companies: General Telephone, Continental Telephone, Southwestern Bell and Electra Telephone. **TRANSPORTATION** Total public road mileage: 1,355. In 1982 there were 112,987 registered vehicles and 3,679 reported traffic accidents including 27 fatalities. Taxi cabs: one company in Wichita Falls. Municipal transit systems: one intracity bus system in Wichita Falls, with scheduled routes. Intercity bus service is available. Motor freight: 46 local and intrastate carriers. Rail: one main and one branch line carry freight through the county with the main line carrying over 30 million tons of freight annually and the branch line carrying less than one million tons. Aircraft: 264 are registered in the county. Airports: Sheppard Air Force Base/Wichita Falls Airport serves as a base for 63 aircraft and is a short haul, non-hub airport with carrier service. Also serving the area are Kickapoo-Downtown, Wichita Valley and Tom Danaher.

COMMUNITY SERVICES

EDUCATION Five school districts with 26 elementary, seven middle, seven high schools and one special education. The average daily attendance in 1981-82 was 18,949, with expenditures per pupil of $2,365 including 1,224 classroom teachers with an average annual salary of $16,987. Fifty-three percent of the 1,354 high school graduates planned to attend college. In 1982-83, 77% of the students were White, 9% Hispanic, 12% Black, 2% Asian and 0.4% American Indian. Private schools: 849 students enrolled in five elementary and three high schools. Midwestern State University is located in Wichita Falls. Established in 1922 it is under state control. Enrollment in 1982 was 4,340 with in state undergraduate tuition and fees of $455 per semester. The highest degree offered is Master. Vocational education: Aladdin Beauty College, Wichita General School of Vocational Nursing (Wichita Falls). **PUBLIC LIBRARIES** Burkburnett Library: 19,364 volumes. Electra Public Library: 21,382 volumes. Iowa Park Library: 11,881 volumes. Kemp Public Library (Wichita Falls): 108,247 volumes. **CHILD CARE** 344 day care and 34 twenty-four hour care licensed facilities. **HEALTH CARE** 217 physicians and 77 dentists. Hospitals: three with a combined capacity of 528. Specialized hospitals: one Air Force hospital with a capacity of 140. Clinics: one for the treatment of alcohol abuse, one outpatient clinic, one dialysis clinic, and one public health clinic. Ambulance services: two commercial and one police department service. Mental health: one clinic, one psychiatric hospital with a capacity of 60 and one state hospital with capacity of 746. Nursing homes: 18 nursing homes with a combined capacity of 1,489 nursing care and 14 custodial care residents. The average cost per day for private patients in 1982 was $29.24. **CHURCHES** 133 churches have an estimated combined membership of 75,811. The largest denominations are Southern Baptist, United Methodist and Catholic. **SOCIAL SERVICES** In fiscal year 1983 a total of $3,318,302 in food stamps was distributed, with an average of 6,745 persons receiving food stamps each month. Aid to Families with Dependent Children (AFDC) totaled $688,145 with an average of 451 families receiving AFDC each month. Medical assistance benefits for the aged and disabled of $9,634,095 and for families and children of $1,009,877 brought the county benefit total to $14,650,418. **FIRE PROTECTION** One paid and nine volunteer fire departments. **LAW ENFORCEMENT** The County Sheriff has 24 commissioned officers. Four police departments have a combined force of 180. One university campus has a police department with a force of seven. **CRIME** 755 violent crimes (murder, forcible rape, robbery and aggravated assault) and 7,752 nonviolent crimes (burglary, larceny-theft and motor vehicle theft) were reported in 1982. **JUDICIAL SYSTEM** Three District Courts and Judges, two County Courts and Judges and five Justices of the Peace. In the District Courts a total of 4,119 cases were pending on 1/1/82, 3,756 new cases were filed and 3,453 cases were disposed of during the year leaving 4,422 cases pending on 12/31/82. There were 1,447 criminal cases on the docket, 271 convictions, 65 persons committed to prison and 11 committed to jail and 740 cases left pending. In the County Courts 1,967 cases were pending on 1/1/82, 4,002 new cases were filed and 3,248 cases were disposed of during the year leaving 2,721 cases pending on 12/31/82. There were 4,412 criminal cases on the docket, 1,099 convictions, 332 persons committed to jail and 1,940 cases left pending. **JAILS** One jail, capacity 110, construction began on a new jail in 1983. **ATTORNEYS AT LAW** 210. **UTILITIES** 99% of the residents are connected to a public or privately owned water system and 94% are connected to a public sewer system. Natural gas is distributed to the county by Lone Star Gas Co., Division of Enserch. The average annual residential bill for natural gas in 1982 for the Lone Star distribution system was $405.91, an increase of 35% over 1981. Electricity is distributed to the county by Texas Electric Service and Texas-New Mexico Power Co. and is generated primarily by gas and oil. The typical residential electric bill is $154.69 per month for an all-electric house using 2,500 kwh. **TAXES** The county has 11 units with taxing authority: five school districts, four cities, one county and one hospital district.

RECREATION/ENTERTAINMENT

NATIONAL REGISTER OF HISTORIC PLACES Wichita Falls: Weeks House, Frank Kell House and Wichita Falls Route Building. **MUNICIPAL PARKS** 2,872 acres in 60 municipal parks. These parks contain four miles of hiking trails, 52 playgrounds, three golf courses, 10 football and soccer fields, 23 baseball and softball fields, 33 tennis courts, 10 multi-use courts, four swimming pools, one beach, two boat ramps and shore fishing facilities. Developed campsites: five. **BOATING/FISHING** Lakes/reservoirs: Beaver Creek (67 acres), Burnett (55 acres), Gordon (41 acres), Iowa Park (178 acres), North Fork Buffalo Creek (1,500 acres), 77 Ranch (50 acres) and Wichita (2,200 acres). Major rivers: Wichita, Prairie and Red. Primary streams: Beaver, Turkey, Stevens, North Fork Buffalo and Holliday. **HUNTING** Fall and winter seasons on deer. No closed seasons on coyote, bobcat and squirrel. Winter seasons on quail, muskrat, beaver, opossum, ring-tailed cat, badger, fox, weasel, raccoon, skunk and civet cat. Fall, winter and spring seasons on turkey. In 1983 duck, coot, geese, woodcock and jacksnipe seasons occurred during the winter months. Teal duck, rail and gallinule seasons occurred in the fall. Mourning dove seasons occurred intermittently during the fall and winter months. **MUSEUMS** Wichita Falls: Wichita Falls Museum and Art Center. **ORCHESTRAS** Wichita Falls: Wichita Falls Symphony Orchestra. **OPERA** Wichita Falls: Red River Lyric Theater. **PLANETARIUM** Wichita Falls: Wichita Falls Museum and Art Center Planetarium. **COLLEGIATE FINE ARTS** Wichita Falls: Cultural events offered by Midwestern State University. **SPECIAL EVENTS** Arts and Crafts Festival and Goat Cookoff, Electra, April; Spring Fling, Wichita Falls, April; Red River Rodeo, Wichita Falls, June; Fast Pitch Tourney, Wichita Falls, June; North-of-the-Brazos Chili Cookoff, Wichita Falls, June; County Farmers Annual Tractor Pull, Wichita Falls, July; Oil Bowl, Wichita Falls, August; Texas Ranch Roundup, Wichita Falls, August; Hotter 'n Hell 100 Bicycle Ride and Festivities, Wichita Falls, August; Summerfest, Wichita Falls, August; Whoop-T-Do, Iowa Park, October.

COMMUNITIES

COUNTY SEAT Wichita Falls, County Courthouse, 76301; County Clerk's Office, 817/322-0721. **INCORPORATED COMMUNITIES** (1980 population and ZIP Code) Burkburnett (10,668) 76354, Electra (3,755) 76360, Iowa Park (6,184) 76367, Pleasant Valley (335) 76301 and Wichita Falls (94,201) 76301. **UNINCORPORATED COMMUNITIES** (and ZIP Code) Clara 76367, Haynesville (Mount Caramel) 76360, Kadane Corner 76360, Kamay (Kemp City) 76369, Valley View 76367 and Wichita Valley Farms 76701. **FOR ADDITIONAL LOCAL INFORMATION** Burkburnett Chamber of Commerce, 412 N. Ave. C., Burkburnett, 76354, 817/569-3393, Electra Chamber of Commerce, 112 W. Cleveland, Electra, 76360, 817/495-3577 and Iowa Park Chamber of Commerce, 103 E. Cash, P.O. Box 416, Iowa Park, 76367, 817/592-5441.

WILBARGER (P35)

THE LAND

Bordering Oklahoma and northwest of Wichita Falls on U.S. Highways 283 and 287 in the Rolling Plains Region, Wilbarger County covers 947 square miles with the elevation ranging from 1,200 to 1,400 feet. The light to dark, loamy soils have very deep, reddish, clayey subsoils with some lime accumulations. In the Rolling Plains vegetation area the tall grasses are primarily bluestems, gramas, and buffalograss. There are mesquite and shinnery oak trees. Between 41 and 50% of the land in the county is considered prime farmland. **CLIMATE** Subtropical Subhumid with hot summers. The average annual temperature is 63°F. Temperatures in January range from an average low of 28° to an average high of 54°F and in July range from 72° to 98°F. The average annual precipitation is 26 inches, with an average relative humidity of 77% at 6 A.M. and 45% at 6 P.M. The average annual snowfall is seven inches. The growing season averages 221 days per year, with the last freeze in late March and the first freeze in early November. The sun shines during the year on the average 71% of the daylight hours.

THE PEOPLE

The 1982 estimated population of 16,300 indicates a continuation of the growth begun in the 1970s which reversed the population decline from 1950 to 1970. Nearly 80% of the county residents live in urban areas, which experienced an 11% population growth from 1970 to 1980. The population's median age lowered from 40 in 1970 to 35 in 1980. The largest ancestry groups are persons of Irish descent (24%), English descent (24%) and German descent (16%). **REGISTERED VOTERS** As of November 2, 1982 there were 7,533 registered voters (0.1% of the state total). The 1982 general election had a 59% voter turnout, compared to a 73% turnout in the 1980 general election. In the 1982 primary 92% voted Democratic and 8% Republican, with 2,610 votes cast.

THE ECONOMY

AGRICULTURE Wheat area. In 1982, 93% of the land was in farms and ranches, with 41% of the farmland under cultivation and 9% irrigated. Wilbarger ranked 71st in the state in highest agricultural receipts, with 69% from crops. Overgrazing water erosion are the current conservation problems. Primary crops: ninth in the state for wheat and seventh for barley, cotton, hay and oats. Primary vegetables: watermelons. Primary fruits and nuts: peaches and pecans. Primary livestock and products: cattle and hogs. **BUSINESS** Total number of business establishments in the county: 380. Retail sales during the first quarter of 1984 increased 9%. In 1980, 16% of the labor force were self-employed, 26% were employed in professional or related services, 12% in manufacturing, 20% in wholesale and retail trade, 15% in agriculture, forestry, fisheries and mining, 5% were employed in other counties and there were 2,135 retired workers. The industries with the most employment: agribusiness, oil and gas extraction, meat packing, and the manufacture of men's work clothing and plastic materials and resins. The nonfarm earnings in 1981 totaled $154,810,000. The retired workers received an average monthly Social Security payment of $308. **FINANCE** On June 30, 1983, three commercial banks had total deposits of $165,794,000 and total assets of $183,108,000. On December 31, 1982 one state savings and loan association and one state branch had assets of $178,278,299. In addition there is one credit union in the county. **HOUSING** Average value of homes in 1980: $23,500. Permits for new, privately owned housing units decreased in 1982: 31 permits were issued with a total construction cost of $1,477,750. Of those permits, all were for single family houses. Between 1970 and 1980 the number of housing units increased by 6%. Eighty-six percent of all units in the county are air-conditioned, 90% are heated by gas and 9% by electricity. **NATURAL RESOURCES** Volcanic ash, sand and gravel, bituminous coal, oil and gas. In 1982 a total of 10,466 thousand cubic feet of gas well gas, 1,969,564 barrels of crude oil and 244,796 thousand cubic feet of casinghead gas were produced. Current production of other minerals and products includes sand and gravel. **TOURISM** Travel expenditures of $12,527,000 in 1982 (an increase of 11% over 1981) generated 304 jobs and $2,455,000 in payroll. Lodging: eight hotels, motels and tourist courts. Convention/meeting facilities: Vernon-Wilbarger Memorial Auditorium. **ALCOHOLIC BEVERAGES** Totally dry. **FEDERAL EXPENDITURES** The federal government had direct expenditures or obligations of $36,534,000 in the county during fiscal year 1983, including $1,000,000 by the U.S. Department of Defense. In addition, the federal government provided $261,000 in grant awards, paid $2,127,000 in salaries and wages, made direct payments to individuals of $28,019,000 including $19,602,000 in retirement and disability payments, awarded $7,000 in procurement contracts and spent $6,120,000 in other expenditures or obligations. The federal government also provided $10,454,000 in direct loans and $7,032,000 in guaranteed loans and insurance.

COMMUNICATION

Newspapers–Daily: The Vernon Daily Record, ave. eve. circ. 5,947. Radio: KVWC-AM and KVWC-FM (Vernon). Cable TV. Telephone companies: Continental Telephone and Santa Rosa Telephone Coop. **TRANSPORTATION** Total public road mileage: 1,023. In 1982 there were 15,113 registered vehicles and

COUNTIES

WILBARGER (continued)

425 reported traffic accidents. Taxi cabs: one company in Vernon. Intercity bus service is available. Motor freight: two carriers. Rail: one main and one branch line carry freight through the county with the main line carrying over 30 million tons of freight annually and the branch line carrying less than one million tons. Aircraft: 48 are registered in the county. Airports: Wilbarger County Airport at Vernon serves as a base for 32 aircraft and is a basic transportation airport with general aviation service.

COMMUNITY SERVICES

EDUCATION Three school districts with six elementary, one middle and three high schools. The average daily attendance in 1981-82 was 2,580, with expenditures per pupil of $3,684 including 192 classroom teachers with an average annual salary of $16,114. Thirty-eight percent of the 156 high school graduates planned to attend college. In 1982-83, 71% of the students were White, 15% Hispanic, 13% Black, 0.4% Asian and 0.3% American Indian. Vernon Regional Junior College is located in Vernon. Established in 1970 it is a vocational and two year academic college under state and local control. Enrollment in 1982 was 1,380 with in state undergraduate tuition and fees of $237 per semester. **PUBLIC LIBRARIES** Carnegie City-County Library (Vernon): 25,000 volumes. **CHILD CARE** 39 day care and four twenty-four hour care licensed facilities. **HEALTH CARE** 22 physicians and seven dentists. Hospitals: one with a capacity of 100. Ambulance services: one fire department service. Mental health: one clinic and one state psychiatric center with a capacity of 614. Nursing homes: two nursing homes with a combined capacity of 296 nursing care residents. The average cost per day for private patients in 1982 was $31.11. **CHURCHES** 38 churches have an estimated combined membership of 13,191. The largest denominations are Southern Baptist, United Methodist and Churches of Christ. **SOCIAL SERVICES** In fiscal year 1983 a total of $385,985 in food stamps was distributed, with an average of 928 persons receiving food stamps each month. Aid to Families with Dependent Children (AFDC) totaled $49,518 with an average of 38 families receiving AFDC each month. Medical assistance benefits for the aged and disabled of $1,872,166 and for families and children of $82,995 brought the county benefit total to $2,390,664. **FIRE PROTECTION** One partly paid and two volunteer fire departments. **LAW ENFORCEMENT** The County Sheriff has four commissioned officers. One police department has a force of 16. One college campus has a police department with a force of two. **CRIME** 38 violent crimes (murder, forcible rape, robbery and aggravated assault) and 372 nonviolent crimes (burglary, larceny-theft and motor vehicle theft) were reported in 1982. **JUDICIAL SYSTEM** One District Court and Judge, one County Court and Judge and two Justices of the Peace. In the District Court a total of 288 cases were pending on 1/1/82, 467 new cases were filed and 347 cases were disposed of during the year leaving 408 cases pending on 12/31/82. There were 155 criminal cases on the docket, 45 convictions, 16 persons committed to prison and one committed to jail and 79 cases left pending. In the County Court 467 cases were pending on 1/1/82, 302 new cases were filed and 376 cases were disposed of during the year leaving 393 cases pending on 12/31/82. There were 512 criminal cases on the docket, 180 convictions, 73 persons committed to jail, and 144 cases left pending. **JAILS** One jail, capacity 18. **ATTORNEYS AT LAW** 18. **UTILITIES** 88% of the residents are connected to a public or privately owned water system and 78% are connected to a public sewer system. Natural gas is distributed to the county by Lone Star Gas Co., Division of Enserch. The average annual residential bill for natural gas in 1982 for the Lone Star distribution system was $405.91, an increase of 35% over 1981. Electricity is distributed to the

city of Vernon by the Vernon Electric Dept. and to the rest of the county by West Texas Utilities and is generated primarily by gas and oil. The typical residential electric bill is $182.50 per month for an all-electric house using 2,500 kwh. **TAXES** The county has seven units with taxing authority: three school districts, one city, one county, one college district and one hospital district.

RECREATION/ENTERTAINMENT

NATIONAL REGISTER OF HISTORIC PLACES Doan's Crossing: Doan's Adobe House. **MUNICIPAL PARKS** 18 acres in two municipal parks. These parks contain two playgrounds, one baseball and softball field. **BOATING/FISHING** Lakes/reservoirs: Bitch Creek (52 acres), Electra (503 acres), Hamilton (38 acres) and Santa Rosa (1,500 acres). Major rivers: Red, Pease and Prairie Dog Town Fork Red. Primary streams: Bitch, Camp, South Beaver and Paradise. **HUNTING** Fall and winter seasons on deer. No closed seasons on coyote, bobcat and squirrel. Winter seasons on quail, muskrat, beaver, opossum, ring-tailed cat, badger, fox, weasel, raccoon, skunk and civet cat. Fall, winter and spring seasons on turkey. In 1983 duck, coot, geese, woodcock and jacksnipe seasons occurred during the winter months with a winter season on sandhill crane in some parts of the county. Teal duck, rail and gallinule seasons occurred in the fall. Mourning dove seasons occurred intermittently during the fall and winter months. **MUSEUMS** Vernon: R.L. More Sr. Bird Egg Collection and Red River Valley Museum. **SPECIAL EVENTS** Annual Doan's Crossing Picnic, Vernon, May; Santa Rosa Roundup and Rodeo, Vernon, May.

COMMUNITIES

COUNTY SEAT Vernon, County Courthouse, 76384; County Clerk's Office, 817/552-5486. **INCORPORATED COMMUNITIES** (1980 population and ZIP Code) Vernon (12,695) 76384. **UNINCORPORATED COMMUNITIES** (and ZIP Code) Doan's Crossing (Doans) 76384, Elliott 76364, Fargo 76384, Farmers Valley 76384, Grayback (Rock Crossing) 76360, Harrold 76364, Hines 76384, Kingola 76373, Lockett 76384, Odell 79247, Oklaunion 76373, Tolbert 76384 and White City 76384. **FOR ADDITIONAL LOCAL INFORMATION** Vernon Chamber of Commerce, P.O. Box 1538, Vernon, 76384, 817/552-2564.

WILLACY (B29)

THE LAND

Bordering the Gulf of Mexico and south of Corpus Christi on U.S. Highway 77 in the Rio Grande Plain Region, Willacy County covers 589 square miles with the elevation ranging from sea level to 50 feet. The nearly level to undulating soils have dark brown to red loamy surfaces with deep, clayey subsoils. Along the coast the soils are sandy and saline or cracking, clayey soils with a high shrink-swell potential. Along the coast the county is in the Gulf Prairies and Marshes vegetation area with cordgrasses, seashore saltgrass and marsh millet. The rest of the county is in the South Texas Plains vegetation area with mesquite, short and mid grasses, thorny shrubs and cacti. Between 51 and 60% of the land in the county is considered prime farmland. **CLIMATE** Subtropical Humid. June through October tropical storms and hurricanes are possible. The average annual temperature is 73°F. Temperatures in January range from an average low of 48° to an average high of 69°F and in July range from 74° to 95°F. The average annual precipitation is 27 inches, with an average relative humidity of 90% at 6 A.M. and 70% at 6 P.M. There is no snowfall. The growing season averages 318 days per year, with the last freeze in early February and the first freeze in mid December. The sun shines during the year on the average 68% of the daylight hours.

THE PEOPLE

Willacy County ranks 13th among all U.S. counties in the highest percent of persons of Spanish origin. The 1982 estimated population of 18,200 continues a growth rate begun in the 1970s, which reversed the population decline from 1950 to 1970. The population is unusually young with a median age which rose from 21 in 1970 to 24 in 1980. The largest ancestry groups are Hispanic (80%) and persons of English descent (6%). **REGISTERED VOTERS** As of November 2, 1982 there were 8,853 registered voters (0.1% of the state total). The 1982 general election had a 41% voter turnout, compared to a 58% turnout in the 1980 general election. In the 1982 primary 99% voted Democratic and 1% Republican, with 3,686 votes cast.

THE ECONOMY

AGRICULTURE Cotton area. In 1982, 76% of the land was in farms and ranches, with 57% of the farmland under cultivation and 18% irrigated. Willacy ranked 82nd in the state in highest agricultural receipts, with 91% from crops. Undesirable brush and weeds, decreasing irrigation water supplies, salinity, drainage and flooding are the current conservation problems. Primary crops: sorghum and cotton. Primary vegetables: onions, sweet corn, lettuce, watermelons and potatoes. Primary fruits and nuts: grapefruit, oranges and pecans. Primary livestock and products: cattle. **BUSINESS** Total number of business establishments in the county: 215. Retail sales during the first quarter of 1984 increased 1%. In 1980, 13% of the labor force were self-employed, 24% were employed in professional or related services, 11% in manufacturing, 14% in wholesale and retail trade, 23% in agriculture, forestry, fisheries and mining, 19% were employed in other counties and there were 1,104 retired workers. The industries with the most employment: agribusiness, oil and gas extraction and the manufacture of women's lingerie. The nonfarm earnings in 1981 totaled $87,173,000. The retired workers received an average monthly Social Security payment of $276. **FINANCE** On June 30, 1983, two commercial banks had total deposits of $74,949,000 and total assets of $87,423,000. There is one state savings and loan branch in the county. **HOUSING** Average value of homes in 1980: $15,800. Permits for new, privately owned housing units increased in 1982: 56 permits were issued with a total construction cost of $1,186,550. Of those permits, 54 were for single family houses. Between 1970 and 1980 the number of housing units increased by 13%. Forty percent of all units in the county are air-conditioned, 81% are heated by gas and 15% by electricity. **NATURAL RESOURCES** Caliche, oil and gas. In 1982 a total of 27,035,730 thousand cubic feet of gas well gas, 42,862 barrels of condensate, 1,496,880 barrels of crude oil and 10,299,152 thousand cubic feet of casinghead gas were produced. **TOURISM** Travel expenditures of $7,188,000 in 1982 (an increase of 15% over 1981) generated 131 jobs and $1,200,000 in payroll. **ALCOHOLIC BEVERAGES** Packaged distilled spirits, beer, ale, malt liquor and wine are legal in parts of the county. Sale of mixed beverages is legal in all or parts of the county. **FEDERAL EXPENDITURES** The federal government had direct expenditures or obligations of $26,368,000 in the county during fiscal year 1983, including $1,440,000 by the U.S. Department of Defense. In addition, the federal government provided $842,000 in grant awards, paid $764,000 in salaries and wages, made direct payments to individuals of $17,604,000 including $12,638,000 in retirement and disability payments, awarded $1,146,000 in procurement contracts and spent $6,012,000 in other expenditures or obligations. The federal government also provided $869,000 in direct loans and $24,866,000 in guaranteed loans and insurance.

COMMUNICATION

Newspapers–Weekly: Raymondville Chronicle and Willacy County News. Radio: KSOX-AM and KSOX-FM (Raymondville). Telephone companies: General Telephone and Valley Telephone Coop. **TRANSPORTATION** Total public road mileage: 756. In 1982 there were 11,232 registered vehicles and 216 reported traffic accidents including one fatality. Intercity bus service is available. Motor freight: five local and intrastate carriers. Rail: two branch lines carry freight through the county with one branch line carrying annually five to 10 million tons and one carrying one to five million. Aircraft: 36 are registered in the county. Airports: Navigaton District Airport at Port Mansfield, Fox Airport at Raymondville and P and G Farms Airport at Lyford. Waterborne commerce: Port Mansfield had freight traffic of 115,874 short tons of domestic shipments in 1981.

COMMUNITY SERVICES

EDUCATION Four school districts with eight elementary, two middle and three high schools. The average daily attendance in 1981-82 was 4,514, with expenditures per pupil of $2,739 including 320 classroom teachers with an average annual salary of $15,735. Sixty-seven percent of the 234 high school graduates planned to attend college. In 1982-83, 9% of the students were White, 91% Hispanic and 0.4% Black. **PUBLIC LIBRARIES** Reber Memorial Library (Raymondville): 42,579 volumes. **CHILD CARE** 12 day care and three twenty-four hour care licensed facilities. **HEALTH CARE** Six physicians and one dentist. Hospitals: one with a capacity of 24. Clinics: one family health services clinic. Ambulance services: one volunteer service. Mental health: one county clinic. Nursing homes: one nursing home has a capacity of 48 nursing care residents. The average cost per day for private patients in 1982 was $30.31. **CHURCHES** 30 churches have an estimated combined membership of 24,661. The largest denomination is Catholic. **SOCIAL SERVICES** In fiscal year 1983 a total of $3,272,733 in food stamps was distributed, with an average of 6,812 persons receiving food stamps each month. Aid to Families with Dependent Children (AFDC) totaled $350,725 with an average of 238 families receiving AFDC each month. Medical assistance benefits for the aged and disabled of $1,507,683 and for families and children of $375,045 brought the county benefit total to $5,506,186. **FIRE PROTECTION** Three volunteer fire departments. **LAW ENFORCEMENT** The County Sheriff has 23 commissioned officers. Two police departments have a combined force of 12. **CRIME** 24 violent crimes (murder, forcible rape, robbery and aggravated assault) and 586 nonviolent crimes (burglary, larceny-theft and motor vehicle theft) were reported in 1982. **JUDICIAL SYSTEM** Four District Courts and Judges, one County Court and Judge and six Justices of the Peace. In the District Courts a total of 298 cases were pending on 1/1/82, 389 new cases were filed and 302 cases were disposed of during the year leaving 385 cases pending on 12/31/82. There were 196 criminal cases on the docket, 80 convictions, 10 persons committed to prison and three committed to jail and 64 cases left pending. In the County Court 249 cases were pending on 1/1/82, 250 new cases were filed and 189 cases were disposed of during the year leaving 310 cases pending on 12/31/82. There were 466 criminal cases on the docket, 66 convictions, 23 persons committed to jail, and 300 cases left pending. **JAILS** One jail, capacity 12, completed major renovation in 1983. **ATTORNEYS AT LAW** 11. **UTILITIES** 95% of the residents are connected to a public or privately owned water system and 68% are connected to a public sewer system. Natural gas is distributed to the county by Rio Grande Valley Gas Co. The average annual residential bill for natural gas in 1982 for the Rio Grande distribution system was $245.19, an increase of 25% over 1981. Electricity is distributed to the county by Central Power and Light, Cochran Power and Light Co. and Magic Valley

COUNTIES

WILLACY (continued)

Electric Coop., Inc. and is generated primarily by gas, oil and coal. The typical residential electric bill is $162.15 per month for an all-electric house using 2,500 kwh. **TAXES** The county has 14 units with taxing authority: five school districts, three cities, one county, one hospital district, one utility district and three special districts.

RECREATION/ENTERTAINMENT

FEDERAL Padre Island National Seashore (See Kleberg County). **NATIONAL REGISTER OF HISTORIC PLACES** King Ranch (see Kenedy County) and Mansfield Cut Underwater Archaeological District (see Kenedy County). **MUNICIPAL PARKS** 65 acres in six municipal parks. These parks contain two playgrounds, one golf course, three baseball and softball fields and one swimming pool. **SCENIC DRIVES** The Texas Tropical Trail runs through this county. This trail is charted through the state's southernmost wedge meandering through ranchland, resort areas by the Gulf of Mexico and fertile farmlands. **BOATING/FISHING** Lakes/reservoirs: Armendaiz Levee (475 acres), Dry (67 acres) and Teniente (135 acres). Primary streams: Arroyo Colorado. Saltwater fishing: speckled trout, redfish and flounder fishing is usually good around Port Mansfield. Shrimp, oysters and crabs may be taken but, like other saltwater fish, under specific regulations. **WILDLIFE REFUGES** Las Palomas State Wildlife Management Area covers 35 acres in this county. **HUNTING** Fall and winter seasons on deer. No closed seasons on coyote, javelina, bobcat and squirrel. Winter seasons on quail, muskrat, beaver, opossum, ring-tailed cat, badger, fox, weasel, raccoon, skunk and civet cat. Fall, winter and spring seasons on turkey. In 1983 duck, coot, geese, woodcock and jacksnipe seasons occurred during the winter months with a winter season on sandhill crane in some parts of the county. Teal duck, rail and gallinule seasons occurred in the fall. Mourning dove seasons occurred intermittently during the fall and winter months with a fall season on white-winged dove. **MUSEUMS** Raymondville: Raymondville Historical and Community Center. **SPECIAL EVENTS** Willacy County Livestock Show, Raymondville, January; Our Little Miss of the Rio Grande Valley Pageant, Raymondville, March; Sidewalk Art Show, Raymondville, March; Port Mansfield Fishing Tournament, Port Mansfield, July; Winter Fun Festival, Raymondville, December.

COMMUNITIES

COUNTY SEAT Raymondville, County Courthouse, 78580; County Clerk's Office, 512/689-2710. **INCORPORATED COMMUNITIES** (1980 population and ZIP Code) Lyford (1,618) 78569, Raymondville (9,493) 78580 and San Perlita (475) 78590. **UNINCORPORATED COMMUNITIES** (and ZIP Code) Lasara 78561, Los Coyotes 78569, Porfirio 78580, Port Mansfield (Redfish Bay) 78598, Santa Monica 78580, Sebastian 78594 and Willamar 78580. **FOR ADDITIONAL LOCAL INFORMATION** Port Mansfield Chamber of Commerce, P.O. Box O, Port Mansfield, 78598, 512/944-2354 and Raymondville Chamber of Commerce, 427 S. 7th, Raymondville, 78580, 512/689-3171.

WILLIAMSON (C16)

THE LAND

North of Austin on Interstate 35 in the Blackland Prairies Region, Williamson County covers 1,137 square miles with an elevation range of 400 to 1,200 feet. In the west the undulating to hilly soils are light to dark and loamy with an accumulation of lime in the subsoils. In the east the dark, slightly acidic, soils are loamy to clayey with cracking, clayey subsoils. In the southeast corner the light colored soils have sandy surfaces and clayey subsoils. The western one-third of the county is in the Cross Timbers and Prairies vegetation area with tall and mid grasses, live and post oak, mesquite and junipers. The rest of the county is in the Blackland Prairies vegetation area with tall grasses, mesquite, oak, pecan and elm trees along streams. Between 21 and 30% of the land in the county is considered prime farmland. **CLIMATE** Subtropical, border line between Humid in the east and Subhumid in the west, and characterized by its mild winters and hot summers. The average annual temperature is 54°F. Temperatures in January range from an average low of 36° to an average high of 59°F and in July range from 72° to 96°F. The average annual precipitation is 33 inches, with an average relative humidity of 85% at 6 A.M. and 53% at 6 P.M. A trace of snow may fall. The growing season averages 258 days per year, with the last freeze in early March and the first freeze in late November. The sun shines during the year on the average 66% of the daylight hours.

THE PEOPLE

Williamson County ranks 34th among all U.S. counties in the highest population growth rate between 1970 and 1980. The 1982 estimated population of 85,700 indicates a continuation of that high growth rate. The age groups with the largest increases between 1970 and 1980 were ages 10 to 14 and 25 to 44. The largest ancestry groups are persons of German descent (27%), English descent (24%) and Irish descent (19%). **REGISTERED VOTERS** As of November 2, 1982 there were 38,484 registered voters (0.6% of the state total). The 1982 general election had a 49% voter turnout, compared to a 71% turnout in the 1980 general election. In the 1982 primary 87% voted Democratic and 13% Republican, with 8,938 votes cast.

THE ECONOMY

AGRICULTURE Livestock, cotton and wheat area. In 1982, 86% of the land was in farms and ranches, with 41% of the farmland under cultivation and 1% irrigated. Williamson ranked 33rd in the state in highest agricultural receipts, with 50% from crops. Overgrazing, undesirable brush and weeds, water erosion and urban encroachment are the current conservation problems. Primary crops: sorghum, wheat, cotton, hay and oats. Primary vegetables: sweet potatoes and watermelons. Primary fruits and nuts: peaches and pecans. Primary livestock and products: 10th in the state for turkeys. Cattle, milk, sheep, wool, angora goats, mohair and hogs. **BUSINESS** Total number of business establishments in the county: 1,344. Retail sales during the first quarter of 1984 increased 44%. In 1980, 9% of the labor force were self-employed, 20% were employed in professional or related services, 21% in manufacturing, 18% in wholesale and retail trade, 10% in construction, 54% were employed in other counties and there were 5,429 retired workers. The industries with the most employment: agribusiness, limestone quarrying, construction and the manufacture of padding and upholstery fillings, electrical motors and generators, oil field machinery, construction machinery, electronic components and pharmaceutical preparations. The nonfarm earnings in 1981 totaled $690,823,000. The retired workers received an average monthly Social Security payment of $300. **FINANCE** On June 30, 1983, 20 commercial banks had total deposits of $451,695,000 and total assets of $510,858,000. On December 31, 1982 three state savings and loan associations, 15 state branches and one federal association branch had combined assets of $111,080,461. In addition there is one credit union in the county. **HOUSING** Average value of homes in 1980: $50,800. Permits for new, privately owned housing units increased in 1982: 698 permits were issued with a total construction cost of $36,939,993. Of those permits, 464 were for single family houses.

Housing permits in Round Rock increased from 251 in 1981 to 455 in 1982 with 348 permits issued for single family houses. Between 1970 and 1980 the number of housing units increased by 114%. Seventy-eight percent of all units in the county are air-conditioned, 62% are heated by gas and 35% by electricity. **NATURAL RESOURCES** Dolomite, limestone, sand, gravel, oil and gas. In 1982 a total of 16,271 barrels of crude oil and 355 thousand cubic feet of casinghead gas were produced. Current production of other minerals and products includes crushed limestone, dimension limestone, fieldstone limestone, pulverulent limestone, sand and gravel. **TOURISM** Travel expenditures of $15,007,000 in 1982 (an increase of 12% over 1981) generated 329 jobs and $2,768,000 in payroll. **ALCOHOLIC BEVERAGES** Packaged distilled spirits, beer, ale, malt liquor and wine are legal in parts of the county. Sale of mixed beverages is legal in all or parts of the county. **FEDERAL EXPENDITURES** The federal government had direct expenditures or obligations of $102,638,000 in the county during fiscal year 1983, including $13,017,000 by the U.S. Department of Defense. In addition, the federal government provided $2,208,000 in grant awards, paid $5,094,000 in salaries and wages, made direct payments to individuals of $90,707,000 including $71,570,000 in retirement and disability payments, awarded $149,000 in procurement contracts and spent $4,479,000 in other expenditures or obligations. The federal government also provided $8,778,000 in direct loans and $46,211,000 in guaranteed loans and insurance.

COMMUNICATION

Newspapers–Daily: Taylor Daily Press, ave. eve. circ. 5,176. Weekly: Hill County News (Cedar Park), The Sunday Sun (Georgetown), The Williamson County Sun (Georgetown) and the Granger News (Taylor). Radio: KGTN-AM, KTAE-AM (Taylor) and KGTN-FM (Georgetown). Cable TV. Telephone companies: General Telephone, Continental Telephone and Central Telephone-Midstate. **TRANSPORTATION** Total public road mileage: 1,805. In 1982 there were 69,571 registered vehicles and 1,813 reported traffic accidents including 19 fatalities. Taxi cabs: one company in Round Rock and one in Taylor. Intercity bus service is available. Motor freight: 26 local and intrastate carriers. Rail: The Eagle provides passenger service on the Amtrak route. Seven main lines and one branch carry freight through the county. One of the main lines carries annually 20 to 30 million tons of freight, five carry 10 to 20 each and one carries one to five million tons. The branch line carries annually one to five million tons. Aircraft: 166 are registered in the county. Airports: Georgetown Municipal Airport serves as a base for 60 aircraft and is a basic transportation airport with general aviation service. Taylor Municipal Airport serves as a base for 16 aircraft and is a basic utility airport with general aviation service. Also serving the area are Bar-K Airport at Lago Vista, Sybert Farm Airport at Jarrell and Kittie Hill Airport in Leander.

COMMUNITY SERVICES

EDUCATION 11 school districts with 24 elementary, 10 middle and 11 high schools. The average daily attendance in 1981-82 was 20,835, with expenditures per pupil of $3,504 including 1,336 classroom teachers with an average annual salary of $15,900. Forty-eight percent of the 1,541 high school graduates planned to attend college. In 1982-83, 81% of the students were White, 14% Hispanic, 4% Black, 0.9% Asian and 0.1% American Indian. Private schools: 545 students enrolled in four elementary and one high school. Southwestern University is located in Georgetown. Established in 1840 it is affiliated with the Methodist Church. Enrollment in 1982 was 1,029 with in state undergraduate tuition and fees of $3,000 per semester. The highest degree offered is Bachelor. Vocational education: Taylor I.S.D. School of Vocational Nursing (Taylor). **PUBLIC LIBRARIES**

Cedar Park Library. Florence Library. Georgetown Public Library: 35,760 volumes. Round Rock Public Library: 24,000 volumes. Taylor Public Library: 29,000. **CHILD CARE** 283 day care and 34 twenty-four hour care licensed facilities. **HEALTH CARE** 49 physicians and 20 dentists. Hospitals: two with a combined capacity of 131 and one hospital under construction. Clinics: one public health clinic. Ambulance services: one county service. Mental health: two county clinics. Nursing homes: eight nursing homes with a combined capacity of 868 nursing care residents. The average cost per day for private patients in 1982 was $31.03. **CHURCHES** 102 churches have an estimated combined membership of 30,312. The largest denominations are Southern Baptist, United Methodist and Catholic. **SOCIAL SERVICES** In fiscal year 1983 a total of $1,748,997 in food stamps was distributed, with an average of 3,671 persons receiving food stamps each month. Aid to Families with Dependent Children (AFDC) totaled $483,132 with an average of 329 families receiving AFDC each month. Medical assistance benefits for the aged and disabled of $5,160,546 and for families and children of $642,082 brought the county benefit total to $8,034,756. **FIRE PROTECTION** Two partly paid and 12 volunteer fire departments. **LAW ENFORCEMENT** The County Sheriff has 47 commissioned officers. 10 police departments have a combined force of 89. **CRIME** 149 violent crimes (murder, forcible rape, robbery and aggravated assault) and 1,751 nonviolent crimes (burglary, larceny-theft and motor vehicle theft) were reported in 1982. **JUDICIAL SYSTEM** Two District Courts and Judges, one County Court and Judge and four Justices of the Peace. In the District Courts a total of 1,853 cases were pending on 1/1/82, 1,652 new cases were filed and 1,149 cases were disposed of during the year leaving 2,356 cases pending on 12/31/82. There were 637 criminal cases on the docket, 140 convictions, 56 persons committed to prison, four committed to jail and 424 cases left pending. In the County Court 1,770 cases were pending on 1/1/82, 2,152 new cases were filed and 2,724 cases were disposed of during the year leaving 1,198 cases pending on 12/31/82. There were 3,319 criminal cases on the docket, 901 convictions, 122 persons committed to jail and 958 cases left pending. **JAILS** One jail, capacity 55: completed renovation in 1983. **ATTORNEYS AT LAW** 103. **UTILITIES** 85% of the residents are connected to a public or privately owned water system and 58% are connected to a public sewer system. Natural gas is distributed to the county by Lone Star Gas Co., Division of Enserch. The average annual residential bill for natural gas in 1982 for the Lone Star distribution system was $405.81, an increase of 35% over 1981. Electricity is distributed to the city of Bartlett by the Bartlett Municipal Light Dept., Georgetown by the Georgetown Water and Light system and to the rest of the county by the city of Austin Electric Dept., Bartlett Electric Coop., Inc., Texas Power and Light and Bluebonnet Electric Coop. Inc. and is generated primarily by gas, oil, water and coal. The typical residential electric bill is $165.24 per month for an all-electric house using 2,500 kwh. **TAXES** The county has 29 units with taxing authority: 14 school districts, nine cities, one county and five special districts.

RECREATION/ENTERTAINMENT

NATIONAL REGISTER OF HISTORIC PLACES Georgetown: Southwestern University Administration Building and Mood Hall, Tinnen House, Williamson County Courthouse Historic District, Railroad Produce Depot and University Avenue-Elm Street Historic District. Liberty Hill vicinity: Bryson Stage Coach Stop. Round Rock: Cole House and Capt. N. Merrell House. Taylor: Taylor National Bank. Taylor vicinity: McFadin House. **MUNICIPAL PARKS** 384 acres in 28 municipal parks. These parks contain four miles of hiking trails, 17 playgrounds, five football and soccer fields, 18 baseball and softball fields, 21 tennis courts, two multi-use courts, seven

COUNTIES

WILLIAMSON (continued)

swimming pools and three beaches. **SCENIC DRIVES** The Texas Brazos Trail and the Texas Hill Country Trail run through this county. The Brazos Trail moves through a beautiful and historic section of central Texas revealing forested landscapes filled with wildlife and wild flowers. The Hill Country Trail winds through a scenic region of south central Texas, spanning a vast ranching area abundant with wildlife in a landscape of deeply sculptured valleys and hills. **BOATING/FISHING** Lakes/reservoirs: Donahoe Creek Soil Conservation Service Lake 2 (50 acres), Ganzert (12 acres), Granger (1,436 acres), Lower Brushy Creek Soil Conservation Service Lakes 3, 4A and 9 (120 acres), North Fork (576 acres), Smith (20 acres) and Upper Brushy Creek Soil Conservation Service Lakes 1, 4, 6, 7, 11, 14, 16, 25 and 29 (165 acres). Major rivers: North Fork San Gabriel, San Gabriel and South Fork San Gabriel. Primary streams: Long, Lake, Turkey, Spring, North Fork Brushy, Post Oak, Buttercup, South Brushy, Chandler, McNutt, Little Mustang, Battleground and Berry. **WILDLIFE REFUGES** There are four state wildlife areas in this county-Pecan Grove covers 630 acres, San Gabriel covers 2,640 acres, Sore Finger covers 1,496 acres and Willis Creek covers 1,950 acres. **HUNTING** Fall and winter seasons on deer. No closed season on nutria, coyote, bobcat and squirrel. Winter seasons on quail, muskrat, beaver, otter, opossum, mink, ring-tailed cat, badger, fox, raccoon, skunk and civet cat. Fall, winter and spring seasons on turkey. In 1983 duck, coot, geese, woodcock and jacksnipe seasons occurred during the winter months. Teal duck, rail and gallinule seasons occurred in the fall. Mourning dove seasons occurred intermittently during the fall and winter months. **MUSEUMS** Georgetown: Mood Heritage Museum. Round Rock: Washington Anderson-Irvin House Museum and El Milagro Museum. Taylor: Moody Museum. **COLLEGIATE FINE ARTS** Georgetown: Cultural events offered by Southwestern University at Georgetown. **SPECIAL EVENTS** Mayfair, Georgetown, May; Volksmarch, Round Rock, May; Sheriff's Posse Rodeo and Parade, Georgetown, June; Frontier Days Festival, Round Rock, July; Old Settlers' Days, Round Rock, July; Friendship Day Celebration, Florence, July; International Barbecue Cook-Off, Taylor, August; Cedar Chopper Festival, Cedar Park, September; County Fair, Georgetown, September.

COMMUNITIES

COUNTY SEAT Georgetown, County Courthouse, 78626; County Clerk's Office, 512/863-3585. **INCORPORATED COMMUNITIES** (1980 population and ZIP Code) Austin (345,496: 387 in Williamson Co. and 345,109 in Travis Co.) 78701, Bartlett (1,567: 871 in Williamson Co. and 696 in Bell co.) 76511, Cedar Park (3,474) 78613, Florence (744) 76527, Georgetown (9,468) 78626, Granger (1,236) 76530, Hutto (659) 78634, Leander (2,179) 78641, Round Rock (11,812) 78664, Taylor (10,619) 76574, Thorndale (1,300: 4 in Williamson Co. and 1,296 in Milam Co.) 76577 and Thrall (573) 78578. **UNINCORPORATED COMMUNITIES** (and ZIP Code) Andice 78626, Beaukiss 78621, Beversville (Beyersville) 78615, Circleville 76574, Coupland 78615, Frame Switch 76574, Friendship 76530, Gano 76577, Hare 76574, Hoxie 76574, Jarrell 76537, Jollyville 78664, Jonah 78626, Lago Vista 78641, Laneport 76574, Liberty Hill 78642, Monadale (Montadale) 78634, New Corn Hill 76537, Noack 76574, Norman's Crossing (Norman) 76574, Old Round Rock 78664, Rices Crossing 76574, Sandoval 76574, Schwertner 76573, Shiloh 76578, Siloam 78621, Structure 78621, Theon 76537, Type 78621, Walburg 78673, Waterloo 76574, Weir 78674 and Whitestone 78641. **FOR ADDITIONAL LOCAL INFORMATION** Florence Chamber of Commerce, P.O. Box 504, Florence, 76527, 817/793-2489, Georgetown Chamber of Commerce, 103 W. 9th,

Georgetown, 78626, 512/863-2251, Round Rock Chamber of Commerce, 212 E. Main, Round Rock, 78664, 512/255-5805 and Taylor Chamber of Commerce, P.O. Box 231, Taylor, 76574, 512/352-2342.

WILSON (C39)

THE LAND

Southeast of San Antonio on U.S. Highways 87 and 181 in the Rio Grande Plain Region, Wilson County covers 807 square miles with an elevation range of 300 to 600 feet. The nearly level to undulating soils are deep, light colored and loamy with mottled, clayey subsoils. The county is in the South Texas Plains vegetation area with short and mid grasses, mesquite, post and live oak, thorny shrubs and cacti. Between 31 and 40% of the land in the county is considered prime farmland. **CLIMATE** Subtropical Subhumid with mild winters and warm summers. The average annual temperature is 70°F. Temperatures in January range from an average low of 40° to an average high of 65°F and in July range from 74° to 96°F. The average annual precipitation is 29 inches, with an average relative humidity of 86% at 6 A.M. and 54% at 6 P.M. Snow is rare. The growing season averages 280 days per year, with the last freeze in late February and the first freeze in early December. The sun shines during the year on the average 65% of the daylight hours.

THE PEOPLE

Wilson County ranks 72nd among all U.S. counties in the highest percent of persons of Spanish origin. The 1982 estimated population of 17,300 indicates the continuation of a growth rate begun in the 1970s which reversed the population decline from 1930 to 1970. Nearly 74% of the county residents live in rural areas, which grew rapidly between 1970 and 1980. The age groups with the largest gains were ages 25 to 34 and 65 and over. The largest ancestry groups are Hispanic (37%), persons of German descent (23%), Irish descent (15%) and English descent (13%). **REGISTERED VOTERS** As of November 2, 1982 there were 10,706 registered voters (0.2% of the state total). The 1982 general election had a 45% voter turnout, compared to a 65% turnout in the 1980 general election. In the 1982 primary 97% voted Democratic and 3% Republican, with 4,310 votes cast.

THE ECONOMY

AGRICULTURE In 1982, 85% of the land was in farms and ranches, with 24% of the farmland under cultivation and 8% irrigated. Wilson ranked 68th in the state in highest agricultural receipts, with 75% from livestock and livestock products. Overgrazing, undesirable brush and weeds, water and wind erosion are the current conservation problems. Primary crops: sixth in the state for peanuts. Hay, sorghum, oats, wheat and corn. Primary vegetables: fifth in the state for watermelons. Primary fruits and nuts: peaches and pecans. Primary livestock and products: third in the state for hogs. Cattle and milk. **BUSINESS** Total number of business establishments in the county: 228. Retail sales during the first quarter of 1984 increased 7%. In 1980, 14% of the labor force were self-employed, 12% were employed in professional or related services, 13% in manufacturing, 21% in wholesale and retail trade, 18% in agriculture, forestry, fisheries and mining, 49% were employed in other counties and there were 1,270 retired workers. The industries with the most employment: agribusiness, oil and gas field services and the manufacture of structural clay products and fabricated metal plate work. The nonfarm earnings in 1981 totaled $101,416,000. The retired workers received an average monthly Social Security payment of $263. **FINANCE** On June 30, 1983, four commercial banks had total deposits of $80,350,000 and total assets of $90,916,000. **HOUSING** Average value of homes in 1980: $25,500. Permits for new, privately owned housing units decreased in 1982: 56 permits were issued with a total construction cost of $1,495,800. Of those permits, 24 were for single family houses. Between 1970 and 1980 the number of housing units increased by 43%. Fifty percent of all units in the county are air-conditioned, 76% are heated by gas and 18% by electricity. **NATURAL RESOURCES** Clay, industrial sand, sand and gravel, oil and gas. In 1982 a total of 1,053,572 thousand cubic feet of gas well gas, 28,369 barrels of condensate, 1,903,722 barrels of crude oil and 676,314 thousand cubic feet of casinghead gas were produced. Current production of other minerals and products includes brick, clay, sand and gravel and crushed sandstone. **TOURISM** Travel expenditures of $3,183,000 in 1982 (an increase of 11% over 1981) generated 74 jobs and $603,000 in payroll. **ALCOHOLIC BEVERAGES** Packaged distilled spirits, beer, ale, malt liquor and wine are legal. Sale of mixed beverages is legal in all or parts of the county. **FEDERAL EXPENDITURES** The federal government had direct expenditures or obligations of $22,627,000 in the county during fiscal year 1983, including $1,647,000 by the U.S. Department of Defense. In addition, the federal government provided $208,000 in grant awards, paid $838,000 in salaries and wages, made direct payments to individuals of $21,272,000 including $16,006,000 in retirement and disability payments, awarded $4,000 in procurement contracts and spent $306,000 in other expenditures or obligations. The federal government also provided $40,000 in direct loans and $5,556,000 in guaranteed loans and insurance.

COMMUNICATION

Newspapers–Weekly: Floresville Chronicle-Journal, La Vernia News and The Star (Stockdale). Radio: KWCB-FM (Floresville). Cable TV. Telephone companies: General Telephone, Continental Telephone and Central Telephone-Midstate. **TRANSPORTATION** Total public road mileage: 930. In 1982 there were 14,145 registered vehicles and 286 reported traffic accidents including eight fatalities. Intercity bus service is available. Motor freight: six local and intrastate carriers. Rail: one branch line carries annually one to five million tons of freight through the county. Aircraft: 30 are registered in the county.

COMMUNITY SERVICES

EDUCATION Four school districts with five elementary, three middle and four high schools. The average daily attendance in 1981-82 was 3,617, with expenditures per pupil of $1,940 including 200 classroom teachers with an average annual salary of $15,047. Fifty-one percent of the 146 high school graduates planned to attend college. In 1982-83, 55% of the students were White, 44% Hispanic, 1% Black and 0.1% Asian. Private schools: 146 students enrolled in one elementary school. **PUBLIC LIBRARIES** Wilson County Library (Floresville): 26,808 volumes. **CHILD CARE** 25 day care and four twenty-four hour care licensed facilities. **HEALTH CARE** Eight physicians and four dentists. Hospitals: one with a capacity of 44. Clinics: one public health clinic. Ambulance services: three volunteer services. Mental health: two clinics. Nursing homes: two nursing homes with a combined capacity of 152 nursing care residents. The average cost per day for private patients in 1982 was $29.49. **CHURCHES** 30 churches have an estimated combined membership of 10,910. The largest denominations are Catholic, Southern Baptist and American Lutheran. **SOCIAL SERVICES** In fiscal year 1983 a total of $733,324 in food stamps was distributed, with an average of 1,695 persons receiving food stamps each month. Aid to Families with Dependent Children (AFDC) totaled $143,716 with an average of 99 families receiving AFDC each month. Medical assistance benefits for the aged and disabled

of $1,695,513 and for families and children of $270,216 brought the county benefit total to $2,842,768. **FIRE PROTECTION** Five volunteer fire departments. **LAW ENFORCEMENT** The County Sheriff has 55 commissioned officers. One police department has a force of seven. **CRIME** 32 violent crimes (murder, forcible rape, robbery and aggravated assault) and 309 nonviolent crimes (burglary, larceny-theft and motor vehicle theft) were reported in 1982. **JUDICIAL SYSTEM** Two District Courts and Judges, one County Court and Judge and four Justices of the Peace. In the District Courts a total of 436 cases were pending on 1/1/82, 306 new cases were filed and 336 cases were disposed of during the year leaving 406 cases pending on 12/31/82. There were 304 criminal cases on the docket, 45 convictions, 16 persons committed to prison, one committed to jail and 194 cases left pending. In the County Court 378 cases were pending on 1/1/82, 772 new cases were filed and 588 cases were disposed of during the year leaving 562 cases pending on 12/31/82. There were 1,060 criminal cases on the docket, 141 convictions, 50 persons committed to jail and 501 cases left pending. **JAILS** One jail, capacity 16. **ATTORNEYS AT LAW** 10. **UTILITIES** 69% of the residents are connected to a public or privately owned water system and 43% are connected to a public sewer system. Natural gas is distributed to the county by Entex, Inc. The average annual residential bill for natural gas in 1982 for the Entex distribution system was $390.31, an increase of 26% over 1981. Electricity is distributed to the county by Guadalupe Valley Electric Coop., Inc., Karnes Electric Coop., Inc. and Floresville Electric Light and Power and is generated primarily by oil and water. The typical residential electric bill is $180.61 per month for an all-electric house using 2,500 kwh. **TAXES** The county has 14 units with taxing authority: four school districts, four cities, one county, one hospital district and four special districts.

RECREATION/ENTERTAINMENT

NATIONAL REGISTER OF HISTORIC PLACES Floresville: Wilson County Courthouse and Jail. Floresville vicinity: Rancho de las Cabras. Sutherland Springs vicinity: Whitehall. **STATE** Rancho de las Cabras State Historic Site covers 55 acres and was closed to the public as of July 1983. **MUNICIPAL PARKS** 54 acres in five municipal parks. These parks contain one mile of hiking trails, four playgrounds, two football and soccer fields, three baseball and softball fields, five tennis courts and two multiuse courts. **SCENIC DRIVES** The Texas Independence Trail runs through this county. This trail not only surveys the historic sites of southeastern Texas but also includes many modern visitor attractions such as the Johnson Space Center. **BOATING/FISHING** Lakes/reservoirs: Connally #1 (60 acres) and Connally #2 (44 acres). Major rivers: San Antonio. Primary streams: Cibola and Picosa. **HUNTING** Fall and winter seasons on deer. No closed season on javelina, coyote, bobcat and squirrel. Winter seasons on quail, muskrat, beaver, opossum, ringtailed cat, badger, fox, weasel, raccoon, skunk and civet cat. Fall, winter and spring seasons on turkey. In 1983 duck, coot, geese, woodcock and jacksnipe seasons occurred during the winter months. Teal duck, rail and gallinule seasons occurred in the fall. Mourning dove seasons occurred intermittently during the fall and winter months with a fall season on white-winged dove. **SPECIAL EVENTS** Arts and Crafts Fair, Floresville, May; Watermelon Jubilee and Rodeo, Stockdale, June; Peanut Festival, Floresville, October.

COMMUNITIES

COUNTY SEAT Floresville, County Courthouse, 78114; County Clerk's Office, 512/393-2845. **INCORPORATED COMMUNITIES** (1980 population and ZIP Code) Floresville (4,381) 78114, LaVernia (632) 78121, Poth (1,461) 78147 and Stockdale (1,265) 78160. **UNINCORPORATED COMMUNITIES** (and ZIP

WILSON (continued)

Code) Alum 78160, Calaveras 78114, Canada Verde 78114, Denhawken 78160, DeWees 78114, Fairview 78114, Graytown 78114, Kosciusko 78160, Labatt 78114, Loire 78064, Nockenut 78160, Pandora 78143, Saspamco 78153, Sutherland Springs (Old Sutherland) 78161 and Union Valley 78140. **FOR ADDITIONAL LOCAL INFORMATION** Floresville Chamber of Commerce, P.O. Box 220, Floresville, 78114, 512/393-3105, Poth Chamber of Commerce, P.O. Box 578, Poth, 78147 and Stockdale Chamber of Commerce, P.O. Box 366, Stockdale, 78160, 512/996-3866 or 996-3661.

WINKLER (P74)

THE LAND

Bordering New Mexico west of Odessa on State Highways 115 and 302 in the Trans-Pecos Region, Winkler County covers 840 square miles with an elevation range of 2,600 to 3,200 feet. The desertic soils have sandy surfaces, with reddish, loamy to clayey subsoils. Some areas are sandy throughout and other areas have limestone bedrock close to the surface. Along the west central border the soils are loamy with clayey subsoils over limestone. In the Trans-Pecos, Mountains and Basins vegetation area the grasses are short with desert shrubs and cacti. Less than 1% of the land in the county is considered prime farmland. **CLIMATE** Subtropical Arid. Duststorms may be experienced during spring. The average annual temperature is 64°F. Temperatures in January range from an average low of 28° to an average high of 59°F and in July range from 70° to 97°F. The average annual precipitation is 12 inches, with an average relative humidity of 70% at 6 A.M. and 33% at 6 P.M. The average annual snowfall is three inches. The growing season averages 220 days per year, with the last freeze in early April and the first freeze in early November. The sun shines during the year on the average 75% of the daylight hours.

THE PEOPLE

Winkler County has a history of reversals in population. Between 1940 and 1960 the population doubled in size, followed by a 29% loss between 1960 and 1970. The 1982 estimated population of 11,400 indicates a continuation of the growth of the 1970s. Nearly 81% of the county residents live in rural areas. The largest ancestry groups are Hispanic (26%), persons of English descent (21%) and Irish descent (15%). **REGISTERED VOTERS** As of November 2, 1982 there were 4,619 registered voters (0.1% of the state total). The 1982 general election had a 47% voter turnout, compared to a 68% turnout in the 1980 general election. In the 1982 primary 94% voted Democratic and 6% Republican, with 1,181 votes cast.

THE ECONOMY

AGRICULTURE Ranchland. In 1982, 88% of the land was in farms and ranches, with 1% of the farmland under cultivation. Winkler ranked 252nd in the state in highest agricultural receipts, with almost 100% from livestock. Overgrazing, decreasing irrigation water supplies and salinity are the current conservation problems. Primary fruits and nuts: pecans. Primary livestock and products: cattle, milk and hogs. **BUSINESS** Total number of business establishments in the county: 247. Retail sales during the first quarter of 1984 increased 29%. In 1980, 8% of the labor force were self-employed, 15% were employed in professional or related services, 5% in manufacturing, 17% in wholesale and retail trade, 30% in agriculture, forestry, fisheries and mining, 17% were employed in other counties and there were 638 retired workers. The industries with the most employment:

oil and gas extraction and agribusiness. The nonfarm earnings in 1981 totaled $110,524,000. The retired workers received an average monthly Social Security payment of $356. **FINANCE** On June 30, 1983, three commercial banks had total deposits of $79,710,000 and total assets of $89,797,000. On December 31, 1982 one state savings and loan association had assets of $11,915,947. In addition there are two credit unions in the county. **HOUSING** Average value of homes in 1980: $20,700. Permits for new, privately owned housing units decreased in 1982: 16 permits were issued with a total construction cost of $642,800. Of those permits, 11 were for single family houses. Between 1970 and 1980 the number of housing units increased by 8%. Eighty-nine percent of all units in the county are air-conditioned, 90% are heated by gas and 9% by electricity. **NATURAL RESOURCES** Caliche, brine, oil and gas. In 1982 a total of 99,074,269 thousand cubic feet of gas well gas, 333,114 barrels of condensate, 7,964,423 barrels of crude oil and 39,331,046 thousand cubic feet of casinghead gas were produced. Current production of other minerals and products includes brine and recovered sulfur. **TOURISM** Travel expenditures of $755,000 in 1982 (an increase of 12% over 1981) generated 15 jobs and $130,000 in payroll. **ALCOHOLIC BEVERAGES** Packaged distilled spirits, beer, ale, malt liquor and wine are legal. **FEDERAL EXPENDITURES** The federal government had direct expenditures or obligations of $10,296,000 in the county during fiscal year 1983, including $316,000 by the U.S. Department of Defense. In addition, the federal government provided $247,000 in grant awards, paid $652,000 in salaries and wages, made direct payments to individuals of $9,372,000 including $7,344,000 in retirement and disability payments, awarded $3,000 in procurement contracts and spent $22,000 in other expenditures or obligations. The federal government also provided $1,499,000 in guaranteed loans and insurance.

COMMUNICATION

Newspapers–Weekly: The Winkler County News (Kermit) and The Wink Bulletin. Radio: KERB-AM (Kermit). Cable TV. Telephone companies: Continental Telephone. **TRANSPORTATION** Total public road mileage: 357. In 1982 there were 10,963 registered vehicles and 303 reported traffic accidents including three fatalities. Intercity bus service is available. Motor freight: seven local and intrastate carriers. Rail: one branch line carries annually less than one million tons of freight through the county. Aircraft: 23 are registered in the county. Airports: Winkler County Airport at Wink serves as a base for 12 aircraft and is a basic utility airport with general aviation service. Robinson Airport at Kermit. Winkler County Heliport at Wink.

COMMUNITY SERVICES

EDUCATION Two school districts with three elementary, one middle and two high schools. The average daily attendance in 1981-82 was 2,272, with expenditures per pupil of $7,933 including 168 classroom teachers with an average annual salary of $19,231. Fifty-five percent of the 150 high school graduates planned to attend college. In 1982-83, 59% of the students were White, 39% Hispanic and 2% Black. Vocational education: Kermit School of Practical Nursing. **PUBLIC LIBRARIES** Winkler County Library (Kermit): 61,087 volumes, one branch. **CHILD CARE** Eight day care and seven twenty-four hour care licensed facilities. **HEALTH CARE** Eight physicians and one dentist. Hospitals: one with a capacity of 85. Ambulance services: one police department service. Nursing homes: one nursing home has a capacity of 100 nursing care residents. The average cost per day for private patients in 1982 was $30.50. **CHURCHES** 22 churches have an estimated combined membership of 8,544. The largest denominations are Southern Baptist and Catholic. **SOCIAL SERVICES** In fiscal year 1983 a total of $165,373 in food stamps was distributed, with an average of 361 persons receiving food stamps each month. Aid to Families with Dependent Children (AFDC) totaled $19,877 with an average of 14 families receiving AFDC each month. Medical assistance benefits for the aged and disabled of $481,761 and for families and children of $87,697 brought the county benefit total to $754,708. **FIRE PROTECTION** Two volunteer fire departments. **LAW ENFORCEMENT** The County Sheriff has eight commissioned officers. Two police departments have a combined force of 14. **CRIME** 24 violent crimes (murder, forcible rape, robbery and aggravated assault) and 278 nonviolent crimes (burglary, larceny-theft and motor vehicle theft) were reported in 1982. **JUDICIAL SYSTEM** One District Court and Judge, one County Court and Judge and four Justices of the Peace. In the District Court a total of 378 cases were pending on 1/1/82, 334 new cases were filed and 292 cases were disposed of during the year leaving 420 cases pending on 12/31/82. There were 184 criminal cases on the docket, 25 convictions, six persons committed to prison, two committed to jail and 74 cases left pending. In the County Court 555 cases were pending on 1/1/82, 400 new cases were filed and 397 cases were disposed of during the year leaving 558 cases pending on 12/31/82. There were 727 criminal cases on the docket, 95 convictions, 14 persons committed to jail and 404 cases left pending. **JAILS** One jail, capacity 23. **ATTORNEYS AT LAW** 10. **UTILITIES** 94% of the residents are connected to a public or privately owned water system and 92% are connected to a public sewer system. Natural gas is distributed to the county by West Texas Gas, Inc. Electricity is distributed to the county by Texas-New Mexico Power Co., and Texas Electric Service and is generated primarily by gas and oil. The typical residential electric bill is $168.05 per month for an all-electric house using 2,500 kwh. **TAXES** The county has five units with taxing authority: two school districts, two cities and one county.

RECREATION/ENTERTAINMENT
STATE Monahans Sandhills State Park (see Ward County). **COUNTY/MUNICIPAL PARKS** 130 acres in seven county and two municipal parks. These parks contain six playgrounds, one golf course, three baseball and softball fields, seven tennis courts and two swimming pools. **HUNTING** Fall season on antelope. Fall and winter seasons on mule deer and javelina. No closed season on coyote, bobcat and squirrel. Winter seasons on quail, muskrat, beaver, opossum, ring-tailed cat, badger, fox, weasel, raccoon, skunk and civet cat. In 1983 sandhill crane, duck, coot, geese, woodcock and jacksnipe seasons occurred during the winter months. Teal duck, rail and gallinule seasons occurred in the fall. Mourning dove seasons occurred during the fall and winter months. **MUSEUMS** Kermit: Medallion House Museum and outdoor museum at Pioneer Park. **SPECIAL EVENTS** Arts and Crafts Fair, Kermit, April; Fourth of July Celebration, Kermit, July; Kermit Krazy Daze, Kermit, July; Pride Days, Kermit, September; October Fair, Kermit, October; Christmas Parade, Kermit, December.

COMMUNITIES
COUNTY SEAT Kermit, County Courthouse, 79745; County Clerk's Office, 915/586-3401. **INCORPORATED COMMUNITIES** (1980 population and ZIP Code) Kermit (8,015) 79745, Monahans (8,397: 4 in Winkler Co. and 8,393 in Ward Co.) 79756 and Wink (1,182) 79789. **FOR ADDITIONAL LOCAL INFORMATION** Kermit Chamber of Commerce, 112 N. Poplar, Kermit, 79745, 915/586-2507 or 586-2508 and Wink Chamber of Commerce, P.O. Box 308, Wink, 79789, 915/527-4441.

WISE (M5)

THE LAND
Northwest of Fort Worth on U.S. Highways 81/287 and 380 in the Cross Timbers Region, Wise County covers 902 square miles with an elevation range of 650 to 1,300 feet. The eastern part of the county has undulating to hilly soils with light to very dark, loamy soils that have an accumulation of lime. The central part has nearly level to undulating, light colored soils with loamy or sandy surfaces over reddish or mottled clayey or loamy subsoils. The western part has undulating to hilly soils with light colored, loamy surfaces over very deep, reddish or mottled clayey subsoils. Wise is in the Cross Timbers and Prairies vegetation area with tall and mid grasses, live and post oak, some mesquite and juniper. Between 31 and 40% of the land in the county is considered prime farmland. **CLIMATE** Subtropical Subhumid with hot and dry summers. The average annual temperature is 64°F. Temperatures in January range from an average low of 29° to an average high of 55°F and in July range from 71° to 99°F. The average annual precipitation is 30 inches, with an average relative humidity of 79% at 6 A.M. and 51% at 6 P.M. The average annual snowfall is five inches. The growing season averages 220 days per year, with the last freeze in late March and the first freeze in early November. The sun shines during the year on the average 68% of the daylight hours.

THE PEOPLE
The population of Wise County had a 35% increase between 1970 and 1980 with the 1982 estimated population of 28,500 indicating a continuation of those gains. Over 70% of the county residents live in rural areas which experienced a 46% population increase from 1970 to 1980. The age groups with the largest gains were ages 20 to 39 and 65 and over. The largest ancestry groups are persons of English descent (29%), Irish descent (24%) and German descent (15%). **REGISTERED VOTERS** As of November 2, 1982 there were 13,187 registered voters (0.2% of the state total). The 1982 general election had a 51% voter turnout, compared to a 67% turnout in the 1980 general election. In the 1982 primary 94% voted Democratic and 6% Republican, with 3,582 votes cast.

THE ECONOMY
AGRICULTURE Dairy area. In 1982, 79% of the land was in farms and ranches, with 17% of the farmland under cultivation and 1% irrigated. Wise ranked 48th in the state in highest agricultural receipts, with 93% from livestock and livestock products. Undesirable brush and weeds, water erosion, the cultivation of marginal lands and flooding are the current conservation problems. Primary crops: hay, wheat, oats, sorghum and peanuts. Primary vegetables: watermelons. Primary fruits and nuts: peaches and pecans. Primary livestock and products: third in the state for milk production. Cattle and hogs. **BUSINESS** Total number of business establishments in the county: 437. Retail sales during the first quarter of 1984 increased 17%. In 1980, 13% of the labor force were self-employed, 14% were employed in professional or related services, 21% in manufacturing, 18% in wholesale and retail trade, 16% in agriculture, forestry, fisheries and mining, 32% were employed in other counties and there were 2,277 retired workers. The industries with the most employment: agribusiness, oil and gas extraction, the quarrying of construction sand, gravel, limestone and stone and the manufacture of women's clothing, carbon and graphite products. The nonfarm earnings in 1981 totaled $229,128,000. The retired workers received an average monthly Social Security payment of $299. **FINANCE** On June 30, 1983, six commercial banks had total deposits of $144,044,000 and total assets of $160,018,000. There are three state savings and loan association branches in the

COUNTIES

county. **HOUSING** Average value of homes in 1980: $28,900. Permits for new, privately owned housing units increased in 1982: 57 permits were issued with a total construction cost of $2,408,252. Of those permits, 49 were for single family houses. Between 1970 and 1980 the number of housing units increased by 48%. Eighty percent of all units in the county are air-conditioned, 78% are heated by gas and 18% by electricity. **NATURAL RESOURCES** Limestone, industrial sand, sand and gravel, oil, gas and bituminous coal. In 1982 a total of 74,971,018 thousand cubic feet of gas well gas, 221,818 barrels of conden-sate, 2,024,470 barrels of crude oil and 13,845,980 thousand cubic feet of casinghead gas were produced. Current production of other minerals and products includes brick, clay, crushed limestone, sand and gravel. **TOURISM** Travel expenditures of $4,155,000 in 1982 (an increase of 11% over 1981) generated 98 jobs and $797,000 in payroll. **ALCOHOLIC BEVERAGES** Only 4% beer is legal in parts of the county. **FEDERAL EXPEN-DITURES** The federal government had direct expenditures or obligations of $37,876,000 in the county during fiscal year 1983, including $2,380,000 by the U.S. Department of Defense. In addition, the federal government provided $490,000 in grant awards, paid $1,839,000 in salaries and wages, made direct payments to individuals of $34,860,000 including $25,905,000 in retirement and disability payments, awarded $354,000 in pro-curement contracts and spent $333,000 in other expenditures or obligations. The federal government also provided $50,000 in direct loans and $4,430,000 in guaranteed loans and insurance.

COMMUNICATION

Newspapers–Weekly: The Alvord News, The Bridgeport Index, Chico Texan, The Wise Times (Decatur) and the Wise County Messenger (Decatur). Cable TV. Telephone companies: General Telephone, Continental Telephone, United Telephone, Central Telephone-Midstate and Palo Pinto Telephone. **TRANSPORTA-TION** Total public road mileage: 1,242. In 1982 there were 27,821 registered vehicles and 722 reported traffic accidents including 10 fatalities. Intercity bus service is available. Motor freight: 14 local and intrastate carriers. Rail: one branch line carries annually 20 to 30 million tons of freight through the county. Aircraft: 45 are registered in the county. Airports: Decatur Municipal Air-port serves as a base for 17 aircraft and is a basic utility airport with general aviation service. Bridgeport Municipal Airport serves as a base for 24 aircraft and is a basic utility airport with general aviation service.

COMMUNITY SERVICES

EDUCATION Seven school districts with nine elementary, three middle and seven high schools. The average daily attendance in 1981-82 was 4,402, with expenditures per pupil of $3,267 including 296 classroom teachers with an average annual salary of $15,635. Thirty-nine percent of the 296 high school graduates planned to attend college. In 1982-83, 91% of the students were White, 8% Hispanic, 0.8% Black, 0.2% Asian and 0.2% American Indian. Sports championships: 1983 A Football, Boyd H.S. **PUBLIC LIBRARIES** Bridgeport Public Library: 21,000 volumes. Chico Library. Decatur Public Library: 17,567 volumes. **CHILD CARE** 31 day care and three twenty-four hour care licensed facilities. **HEALTH CARE** 15 physicians and five den-tists. Hospitals: two with a combined capacity of 94. Ambulance services: one hospital-based and one county service. Mental health: one county clinic. Nursing homes: four nursing homes with a combined capacity of 284 nursing care residents. The average cost per day for private patients in 1982 was $30.99. **CHURCHES** 81 churches have an estimated combined member-ship of 14,277. The largest denominations are Southern

Baptist, United Methodist and Churches of Christ. **SOCIAL SERVICES** In fiscal year 1983 a total of $499,234 in food stamps was distributed, with an average of 1,067 persons receiving food stamps each month. Aid to Families with Dependent Children (AFDC) totaled $92,199 with an average of 61 families receiving AFDC each month. Medical assistance benefits for the aged and disabled of $1,942,245 and for families and children of $138,916 brought the county benefit total to $2,672,594. **FIRE PROTEC-TION** 12 volunteer fire departments. **LAW ENFORCEMENT** The County Sheriff has 16 commissioned officers. Six police departments have a combined force of 27. **CRIME** Nine violent crimes (murder, forcible rape, robbery and aggravated assault) and 594 nonviolent crimes (burglary, larceny-theft and motor vehicle theft) were reported in 1982. **JUDICIAL SYSTEM** One District Court and Judge, two County Courts and Judges and four Justices of the Peace. In the District Court a total of 824 cases were pending on 1/1/82, 706 new cases were filed and 731 cases were disposed of during the year leaving 799 cases pend-ing on 12/31/82. There were 208 criminal cases on the docket, 57 convictions, 14 persons committed to prison, four committed to jail and 63 cases left pending. In the County Courts 2,778 cases were pending on 1/1/82, 1,582 new cases were filed and 1,439 cases were disposed of during the year leaving 2,921 cases pending on 12/31/82. There were 4,277 criminal cases on the docket, 665 convictions and 2,843 cases left pending. **JAILS** One jail, capacity 18. **ATTORNEYS AT LAW** 22. **UTILITIES** 55% of the residents are connected to a public or privately owned water system and 42% are connected to a public sewer system. Natural gas is distributed to the county by Lone Star Gas Co., Division of Enserch and Entex, Inc. The average annual residential bill for natural gas in 1982 for the Lone Star distribution system was $405.91, an increase of 35% over 1981 and for Entex it was $390.31, an increase of 26%. Electricity is distributed to the city of Bridgeport by the Bridgeport Light and Power system and to the rest of the county by Texas Power and Light Co., Cooke Co. Electric Coop., Assn., Denton Co. Electric Coop., Inc., and Wise Electric Coop., Inc. and is generated primarily by water and oil. The typical residential electric bill is $165.24 per month for an all-electric house using 2,500 kwh. **TAXES** The county has 19 units with taxing authority: eight school districts, eight cities, one county and two special districts.

RECREATION/ENTERTAINMENT

NATIONAL REGISTER OF HISTORIC PLACES Chico: J.T. Brown Hotel. Decatur: Administration Building (Decatur Bap-tist College), Waggoner Mansion and Wise County Courthouse. **COUNTY/MUNICIPAL PARKS** 149 acres in three county and five municipal parks. These parks contain three playgrounds, one baseball and softball field, two multi-use courts, one swim-ming pool, one beach and two boat ramps. Developed camp-sites: 12. **BOATING/FISHING** Lakes/reservoirs: Bridgeport (13,000 acres), Denton Creek Soil Conservation Service Lakes 12, 18, 21, 23 and 26 (58 acres) and Gifford-Hall (17 acres). Major rivers: West Fork Trinity. Primary streams: Cottonwood, Black, North Pecan, Catlett, Morris, Dry, Big Sandy and Denton. **HUNTING** Fall and winter seasons on deer. No closed season on coyote, bobcat and squirrel. Winter seasons on quail, muskrat, beaver, opossum, ring-tailed cat, badger, fox, weasel, raccoon, skunk and civet cat. Spring season on turkey. In 1983 duck, coot, geese, woodcock and jacksnipe seasons occurred during the winter months. Teal duck, rail and gallinule seasons occurred in the fall. Mourning dove seasons occurred intermittently dur-ing the fall and winter months. **MUSEUMS** Decatur: Wise County Heritage Museum. **SPECIAL EVENTS** Motorcycle Enduro at Runaway Bay, Bridgeport, March; Youth Fair and Rodeo, Decatur, April; Youth Rodeo, Bridgeport, April;

Historical Pageant, Decatur, May; Arts and Crafts Festival, Bridgeport, June; Wise County Old Settlers Reunion, Decatur, July; Rodeo, Decatur, July; Butterfield Stage Days, Bridgeport, July.

COMMUNITIES

COUNTY SEAT Decatur, County Courthouse, 76234; County Clerk's Office, 817/627-3351. **INCORPORATED COMMUNITIES** (1980 population and ZIP Code) Alvord (874) 76225, Aurora (376) 76078, Boyd (889) 76023, Briar (1,810: 642 in Wise Co., 349 in Parker Co. and 819 in Tarrant Co.) 76020, Bridgeport (3,737) 76026, Chico (890) 76030, Decatur (4,104) 76234, Fairview (180) 76078, Lake Bridgeport (271) 76026, Newark (466) 76071, Rhome (478) 76078 and Runaway Bay (504) 76234. **UNINCORPORATED COMMUNITIES** (and ZIP Code) Anneville 76023, Balsora 76026, Boonsville 76026, Cottondale 76073, Crafton 76030, Estes Addition 76071, Greenwood 76246, Garvin 76023, Keeter 76023, Lake 76026, Lucky Ridge 76023, Paradise 76073, Park Springs 76270, Slidell 76267, White City 76231 and Willow Point 76026. **FOR ADDITIONAL LOCAL INFORMATION** Bridgeport Chamber of Commerce, 1107 8th St., Bridgeport, 76026, 817/683-2076 and Decatur Chamber of Commerce, P.O. Box 474, Decatur, 76234, 817/627-3107.

WOOD (E11)

THE LAND

East of Dallas on U.S. Highway 80 in the East Texas Timberlands Region, Wood County covers 689 square miles with an elevation range of 250 to 600 feet. The eastern part of the county has nearly level, moderately well to poorly drained soils with light colored, acidic, sandy to loamy surfaces over very deep, reddish or mottled subsoils. The central part of the county has gently rolling to hilly, reddish soils with light colored, loamy surfaces over very deep, reddish, clayey subsoils that are high in iron. The western part of Wood has level to undulating soils with light colored sandy surfaces over mottled, clayey subsoils. The eastern part of the county is in the Pineywoods vegetation area with grasslands, loblolly, short leaf, longleaf and slash pine and hardwoods such as, oak, hickory and maple. The rest of the county is in the Post Oak Savannah vegetation area with tall grasses, post and blackjack oak. Between 11 and 20% of the land in the county is considered prime farmland. **CLIMATE** Subtropical, moist and mild. The average annual temperature is 64°F. Temperatures in January range from an average low of 32° to an average high of 54°F and in July range from 71° to 95°F. The average annual precipitation is 43 inches, with an average relative humidity of 83% at 6 A.M. and 56% at 6 P.M. The average annual snowfall is two inches. The growing season averages 246 days per year, with the last freeze in mid March and the first freeze in mid November. The sun shines during the year on the average 68% of the daylight hours.

THE PEOPLE

The 1982 estimated population of 25,600 indicates a continuation of the growth begun in the 1960s which reversed the population decline from 1940 to 1960. Over 72% of the county residents live in rural areas, which experienced rapid population growth between 1970 and 1980. The age groups with the largest gains were those of ages 25 to 39 and 65 and over. The largest ancestry groups are persons of English descent (30%), Irish descent (21%) and Black (10%). **REGISTERED VOTERS** As of November 2, 1982 there were 12,137 registered voters (0.2% of the state total). The 1982 general election had a 56% voter turnout, compared to a 68% turnout in the 1980 general election. In the 1982 primary 99% voted Democratic and 1% Republican, with 4,843 votes cast.

THE ECONOMY

AGRICULTURE Forest production and dairy area. In 1982, 52% of the land was in farms and ranches, with 17% of the farmland under cultivation and 5% irrigated. Wood ranked 89th in the state in highest agricultural receipts, with 89% from livestock and livestock products. Overgrazing, undesirable brush and weeds, water erosion, fertilization and improper woodland management are the current conservation problems. Primary crops: hay, wheat and rye. Primary vegetables: sweet potatoes and watermelons. Primary fruits and nuts: peaches and pecans. Primary livestock and products: seventh in the state for milk production and 10th for commercial broiler production. Cattle. **BUSINESS** Total number of business establishments in the county: 497. Retail sales during the first quarter of 1984 increased 12%. In 1980, 13% of the labor force were self-employed, 17% were employed in professional or related services, 18% in manufacturing, 21% in wholesale and retail trade, 12% in agriculture, forestry, fisheries and mining, 24% were employed in other counties and there were 3,698 retired workers. The industries with the most employment: oil and gas extraction, petroleum refining, agribusiness, tourism and the manufacture of motor vehicle parts, women's clothing and other cloth products. The nonfarm earnings in 1981 totaled $221,931,000. The retired workers received an average monthly Social Security payment of $297. **FINANCE** On June 30, 1983, seven commercial banks had total deposits of $200,990,000 and total assets of $224,205,000. On December 31, 1982 one federal savings and loan association, two state association branches and two federal branches had combined assets of $59,302,688. In addition there is one credit union in the county. **HOUSING** Average value of homes in 1980: $28,300. Permits for new, privately owned housing units decreased in 1982: 33 permits were issued with a total construction cost of $1,377,050. Of those permits, 29 were for single family houses. Between 1970 and 1980 the number of housing units increased by 49%. Seventy-nine percent of all units in the county are air-conditioned, 72% are heated by gas and 22% by electricity. **NATURAL RESOURCES** Ceramic clay, lignite coal, iron, salt domes, industrial sand, oil and gas. In 1982 a total of 17,235,565 thousand cubic feet of gas well gas, 120,980 barrels of condensate, 17,767,454 barrels of crude oil and 26,419,771 thousand cubic feet of casinghead gas were produced. Current production of other minerals and products includes fire clay, industrial sand and recovered sulfur. Pine and hardwood production in 1981 totaled 3,124,596 cubic feet: 2,234,762 cubic feet of pine and 889,834 cubic feet of hardwood. **TOURISM** Travel expenditures of $4,409,000 in 1982 (an increase of 12% over 1981) generated 100 jobs and $828,000 in payroll. **ALCOHOLIC BEVERAGES** Totally dry. **FEDERAL EXPENDITURES** The federal government had direct expenditures or obligations of $57,878,000 in the county during fiscal year 1983, including $3,090,000 by the U.S. Department of Defense. In addition, the federal government provided $2,311,000 in grant awards, paid $2,120,000 in salaries and wages, made direct payments to individuals of $52,570,000 including $39,544,000 in retirement and disability payments, awarded $514,000 in procurement contracts and spent $362,000 in other expenditures or obligations. The federal government also provided $2,782,000 in direct loans and $6,756,000 in guaranteed loans and insurance.

COMMUNICATION

Newspapers–Weekly: Mineola Monitor and The Wood County Democrat (Quitman). Radio: KMOO-AM and FM (Mineola). Cable TV. Telephone companies: General Telephone, Continental Telephone, Etex Telephone Coop. and Peoples Telephone Coop. **TRANSPORTATION** Total public road mileage: 1,155. In 1982 there were 24,719 registered vehicles and 439 reported traffic accidents including 11 fatalities. Taxi cabs: one

COUNTIES

WOOD (continued)

company in Winnsboro. Intercity bus service is available. Motor freight: eight local and intrastate carriers. Rail: The Eagle provides passenger service on the Amtrak route. Two main lines carry freight through the county with one line carrying annually 20 to 30 million tons of freight and one carrying five to 10. Aircraft: 38 are registered in the county. Airports: Winnsboro Municipal Airport serves as a base for 15 aircraft and is a general utility airport with general aviation service. Twin Oaks Airport at Winnsboro. Wisener Field at Mineola serves as a base for 15 aircraft and is a basic utility airport with general aviation service. Quitman Airport at Mineola.

COMMUNITY SERVICES

EDUCATION Six school districts with seven elementary, four middle and six high schools. The average daily attendance in 1981-82 was 4,373, with expenditures per pupil of $3,032 including 295 classroom teachers with an average annual salary of $16,593. Forty-one percent of the 299 high school graduates planned to attend college. In 1982-83, 89% of the students were White, 2% Hispanic, 9% Black, 0.3% Asian and 0.1% American Indian. Jarvis Christian College is located in Hawkins. Established in 1912 it is affiliated with the Christian Church (Disciples of Christ). Enrollment in 1982 was 619 with in state undergraduate tuition and fees of $1,500 per semester. The highest degree offered is Bachelor. **PUBLIC LIBRARIES** Mineola Memorial Library: 24,631 volumes. Quitman Public Library: 9,800 volumes. City Library (Winnsboro): 12,000 volumes. **CHILD CARE** 26 day care and eight twenty-four hour care licensed facilities. **HEALTH CARE** 18 physicians and nine dentists. Hospitals: three with a combined capacity of 88. Clinics: one community health clinic and one public health clinic. Ambulance services: two commercial, one volunteer fire department, and one county service. Mental health: one regional clinic. Nursing homes: eight nursing homes with a combined capacity of 617 nursing care residents. The average cost per day for private patients in 1982 was $26.73. **CHURCHES** 82 churches have an estimated combined membership of 16,965. The largest denominations are Southern Baptist, Baptist Missionary and United Methodist. **SOCIAL SERVICES** In fiscal year 1983 a total of $654,646 in food stamps was distributed, with an average of 1,551 persons receiving food stamps each month. Aid to Families with Dependent Children (AFDC) totaled $116,286 with an average of 87 families receiving AFDC each month. Medical assistance benefits for the aged and disabled of $4,226,577 and for families and children of $232,070 brought the county benefit total to $5,229,578. **FIRE PROTECTION** Six volunteer fire departments. **LAW ENFORCEMENT** The County Sheriff has 25 commissioned officers. 12 police departments have a combined force of 63. **CRIME** 32 violent crimes (murder, forcible rape, robbery and aggravated assault) and 436 nonviolent crimes (burglary, larceny-theft and motor vehicle theft) were reported in 1982. **JUDICIAL SYSTEM** Three District Courts and Judges, one County Court and Judge and four Justices of the Peace. In the District Courts a total of 1,420 cases were pending on 1/1/82, 687 new cases were filed and 841 cases were disposed of during the year leaving 1,266 cases pending on 12/31/82. There were 319 criminal cases on the docket, 42 convictions, 24 persons committed to prison, two committed to jail and 170 cases left pending. In the County Court 1,026 cases were pending on 1/1/82, 786 new cases were filed and 961 cases were disposed of during the year leaving 851 cases pending on 12/31/82. There were 1,673 criminal cases on the docket, 317 convictions, 32 persons committed to jail and 718 cases left pending. **JAILS** One jail, capacity 38: planning an addition. **ATTORNEYS AT LAW** 19. **UTILITIES** 81% of the residents connected to a public or privately owned water system and 44% are connected to a public sewer system. Natural gas is distributed to the county by Lone Star Gas Co., Division of Enserch, Entex, Inc. and South Bend Gas Supply, Inc. The average annual residential bill for natural gas in 1982 for the Lone Star distribution system was $405.91, an increase of 35% over 1981. Electricity is distributed to the county by Southwestern Electric Power, Wood County Electric Co. Inc. and Upshur-Rural Electric Coop., Inc. and is generated primarily by gas and coal. The typical residential electric bill is $152.08 per month for an all-electric house using 2,500 kwh. **TAXES** The county has 15 units with taxing authority: seven school districts, six cities, one county and one hospital district.

RECREATION/ENTERTAINMENT

NATIONAL REGISTER OF HISTORIC PLACES Alba vicinity: Sadler Site. Quitman vicinity: Howle Site and Osborn Site. **STATE** Governor Hogg Shrine State Historical Park covers 27 acres on which are located buildings, museums and momentos related to the Hogg family. **MUNICIPAL PARKS** 28 acres in four municipal parks. These parks contain one playground, two baseball and softball fields, four multi-use courts and two swimming pools. Developed campsites: 39. **SCENIC DRIVES** The Texas Forest Trail runs through this county. This trail explores the farming, ranching and oilfield areas of the East Texas Pineywoods. **BOATING/FISHING** Lakes/reservoirs: Big Woods Springs (75 acres), Brenda (18 acres), Brooks (50 acres), Brumley (1,431 acres), Garner (43 acres), Greenbriar (141 acres), Gunstream #1 (235 acres), Gunstream #2 (26 acres), Hawkins (776 acres), Holbrook (653 acres), Holly (26 acres), Indian Mound (45 acres), Lake Fork (21,387 acres), Louise (24 acres), Lydia (71 acres), Redland Acres (20 acres), Rock Falls (28 acres), Sundowner (44 acres), Timado (68 acres), Quitman (814 acres), West Lower (32 acres), West Upper (78 acres) and Winnsboro (806 acres). Major rivers: Sabine. Primary streams: Turkey, Two Mile, Boggy, Little Sandy, Four Mile, Greenbriar, Mill, Turman, Dry, Big Sandy, Keyes, Holly, Red, Lake Fork, Simpkins, Chinquapin, Lacey and Rock Falls. **HUNTING** Fall and winter seasons on deer. Summer, fall and winter seasons on squirrel. No closed season on coyote, bobcat and nutria. Winter seasons on quail, muskrat, beaver, otter, opossum, mink, ring-tailed cat, badger, fox, raccoon, skunk and civet cat. In 1983 duck, coot, geese, woodcock and jacksnipe seasons occurred during the winter months. Teal duck, rail and gallinule seasons occurred in the fall. Mourning dove seasons occurred intermittently during the fall and winter months. **MUSEUMS** Quitman: Miss Ima Hogg Museum and Honeymoon Cottage. **SPECIAL EVENTS** Dogwood Fiesta, Quitman, April; Rodeo, Winnsboro, May; Fiddlers' Contest, Winnsboro, July; Old Settlers Reunion, Quitman, August; Autumn Trails Festival, Winnsboro, October; Oil Festival, Hawkins, October; Christmas Parade, Mineola, December.

COMMUNITIES

COUNTY SEAT Quitman, County Courthouse, 75783; County Clerk's Office, 214/763-2711. **INCORPORATED COMMUNITIES** (1980 population and ZIP Code) Alba (568) 75410, Hawkins (1,302) 75765, Mineola (4,346) 75773, Quitman (1,893) 75783, Winnsboro (3,458: 2,596 in Wood Co. and 862 in Franklin Co.) 75494 and Yantis (210) 75497. **UNINCORPORATED COMMUNITIES** (and ZIP Code) Calvary 75773, Cartwright 75494, Coke 75431, Crow 75765, East Point 75494, Forest Hill 75783, Fouke 75765, Golden 75444, Hainesville 75773, Hoard 75773, Little Hope 75494, Mount Enterprise 75773, Musgrove (Chalybeate) 75494, New Hope 75773, Oak Grove 75783, Perryville 75644, Pine Mills 75733, Pineview 75494, Pleasant Grove 75494, Rock Hill 75783, Stormville 75783, Stout 75494 and West Mineola 75773. **FOR ADDITIONAL LOCAL INFORMATION**

Greater Hawkins Chamber of Commerce, P.O. Box 345, Hawkins, 75765, 214/769-3420, Mineola Chamber of Commerce, 101 E. Broad, Mineola, 75773, 214/569-2087 and Quitman Chamber of Commerce, 602 McAllister, Quitman, 75783, 214/763-4411.

YOAKUM (P47)

THE LAND

Bordering New Mexico southwest of Lubbock on U.S. Highway 82/380 in the High Plains Region, Yoakum County covers 800 square miles with an elevation range of 3,400 to 3,900 feet. The county has nearly level soils which are sandy over reddish, loamy subsoils. The county is in the High Plains vegetation area with prairie grasses, some mesquite, yucca, shinnery oak and sandsage. Less than 1% of the land in the county is considered prime farmland. **CLIMATE** Continental Steppe and dry with wide-ranging daily and seasonal temperature fluctuations. The average annual temperature is 59°F. Temperatures in January range from an average low of 23° to an average high of 55°F and in July range from 64° to 93°F. The average annual precipitation is 16 inches, with an average relative humidity of 68% at 6 A.M. and 34% at 6 P.M. The average annual snowfall is eight inches. The growing season averages 200 days per year, with the last freeze in mid April and the first freeze in late October. The sun shines during the year on the average 75% of the daylight hours.

THE PEOPLE

Yoakum County has a history of reversals in population. Between 1930 and 1940 the county's population quadrupled in size. After a decade of losses the growth rate between 1950 and 1960 caused a near doubling of the population. The 1982 estimated population of 8,500 indicates a continuation of a growth pattern begun in the 1970s. A 9% decrease between 1960 and 1970 was followed by a 13% increase between 1970 and 1980. The largest ancestry groups are Hispanic (28%), persons of English descent (25%) and Irish descent (17%). **REGISTERED VOTERS** As of November 2, 1982 there were 4,114 registered voters (0.1% of the state total). The 1982 general election had a 47% voter turnout, compared to a 74% turnout in the 1980 general election. In the 1982 primary 99% voted Democratic and 1% Republican, with 2,062 votes cast.

THE ECONOMY

AGRICULTURE Cotton area. In 1982, 93% of the land was in farms and ranches, with 44% of the farmland under cultivation and 34% irrigated. Yoakum ranked 57th in the state in highest agricultural receipts, with 95% from crops. Overgrazing, undesirable brush and weeds and wind erosion are the current conservation problems. Primary crops: cotton, sorghum, wheat, hay and corn. Primary vegetables: watermelons. Primary fruits and nuts: peaches and pecans. Primary livestock and products: cattle and hogs. **BUSINESS** Total number of business establishments in the county: 209. Retail sales during the first quarter of 1984 decreased 4%. In 1980, 15% of the labor force were self-employed, 15% were employed in professional or related services, 6% in manufacturing, 17% in wholesale and retail trade, 38% in agriculture, forestry, fisheries and mining, 6% were employed in other counties and there were 416 retired workers. The industries with the most employment: oil and gas extraction and agribusiness. The nonfarm earnings in 1981 totaled $82,280,000. The retired workers received an average monthly Social Security payment of $327. **FINANCE** On June 30, 1983, three commercial banks had total deposits of $56,908,000 and total assets of $66,645,000. There is one state savings and loan association branch and three credit unions in the county. **HOUSING** Average

value of homes in 1980: $28,600. Permits for new, privately owned housing units increased in 1982: 60 permits were issued with a total construction cost of $2,014,000. Of those permits, 12 were for single family houses. Housing permits in Denver City increased from two in 1981 to 56 in 1982. Between 1970 and 1980 the number of housing units increased by 23%. Eighty-four percent of all units in the county are air-conditioned, 90% are heated by gas and 10% by electricity. **NATURAL RESOURCES** Brine, caliche, oil and gas. In 1982 a total of 471,054 thousand cubic feet of gas well gas, 48,439,877 barrels of crude oil and 28,150,011 thousand cubic feet of casinghead gas were produced. Current production of other minerals and products includes chlorine, salt and sodium hydroxide. **TOURISM** Travel expenditures of $5,224,000 in 1982 (an increase of 13% over 1981) generated 111 jobs and $948,000 in payroll. **ALCOHOLIC BEVERAGES** Totally dry. **FEDERAL EXPENDITURES** The federal government had direct expenditures or obligations of $15,161,000 in the county during fiscal year 1983, including $67,000 by the U.S. Department of Defense. In addition, the federal government provided $194,000 in grant awards, paid $419,000 in salaries and wages, made direct payments to individuals of $5,458,000 including $4,135,000 in retirement and disability payments, awarded $3,000 in procurement contracts and spent $9,086,000 in other expenditures or obligations. The federal government also provided $9,257,000 in direct loans and $18,403,000 in guaranteed loans and insurance.

COMMUNICATION

Newspapers–Weekly: Denver City Press. Radio: KPLN-FM (Plains). Cable TV. Telephone companies: General Telephone, Poka-Lambro Rural Telephone Coop. and Romain Telephone. **TRANSPORTATION** Total public road mileage: 692. In 1982 there were 9,239 registered vehicles and 174 reported traffic accidents including four fatalities. Intercity bus service is available. Motor freight: two carriers. Aircraft: 39 are registered in the county. Airports: Denver City Airport serves as a base for 19 aircraft and is a basic utility airport with general aviation service. Yoakum County Airport at Plains.

COMMUNITY SERVICES

EDUCATION Two school districts with three elementary, three middle and two high schools. The average daily attendance in 1981-82 was 1,805, with expenditures per pupil of $6,132 including 162 classroom teachers with an average annual salary of $21,425. Forty-five percent of the 116 high school graduates planned to attend college. In 1982-83, 59% of the students were White, 39% Hispanic, 2% Black, 0.2% Asian and 0.1% American Indian. **PUBLIC LIBRARIES** Yoakum County Library (Denver City): 17,814 volumes. Yoakum County Library (Plains): 13,484 volumes. **CHILD CARE** Five day care and one twenty-four hour care licensed facilities. **HEALTH CARE** Two physicians and one dentist. Hospitals: one with a capacity of 43. Clinics: one public health clinic. Ambulance services: two volunteer fire departments and one police department service. Nursing homes: one nursing home has a capacity of 100 nursing care residents. The average cost per day for private patients in 1982 was $35.52. **CHURCHES** 16 churches have an estimated combined membership of 6,725. The largest denominations are Southern Baptist, Catholic and Christian Methodist Episcopal. **SOCIAL SERVICES** In fiscal year 1983 a total of $203,138 in food stamps was distributed, with an average of 418 persons receiving food stamps each month. Aid to Families with Dependent Children (AFDC) totaled $31,954 with an average of 20 families receiving AFDC each month. Medical assistance benefits for the aged and disabled of $352,417 and for families and children of $47,257 brought the county benefit total to $634,766. **FIRE PROTECTION** Two volunteer fire departments. **LAW ENFORCEMENT** The County Sheriff

YOAKUM (continued)

has 15 commissioned officers. One police department has a force of 13. **CRIME** Six violent crimes (murder, forcible rape, robbery and aggravated assault) and 219 nonviolent crimes (burglary, larceny-theft and motor vehicle theft) were reported in 1982. **JUDICIAL SYSTEM** One District Court and Judge, one County Court and Judge and two Justices of the Peace. In the District Court a total of 180 cases were pending on 1/1/82, 223 new cases were filed and 156 cases were disposed of during the year leaving 247 cases pending on 12/31/82. There were 55 criminal cases on the docket, 16 convictions, two persons committed to prison and 27 cases left pending. In the County Court 113 cases were pending on 1/1/82, 277 new cases were filed and 283 cases were disposed of during the year leaving 107 cases pending on 12/31/82. There were 333 criminal cases on the docket, 180 convictions, 73 persons committed to jail and 76 cases left pending. **JAILS** One jail, capacity nine. **ATTORNEYS AT LAW** Five. **UTILITIES** 78% of the residents are connected to a public or privately owned water system and 73% are connected to a public sewer system. Electricity is distributed to the county by Lyntegar Electric Coop., Inc. and Southwestern Public Service Co. and is generated primarily by gas and coal. The typical residential electric bill is $170.44 per month for an all-electric house using 2,500 kwh. **TAXES** The county has five units with taxing authority: two school districts, two cities and one county.

RECREATION/ENTERTAINMENT
COUNTY/MUNICIPAL PARKS 230 acres in five county and two municipal parks. These parks contain four playgrounds, one golf course, five baseball and softball fields and two swimming pools. Developed campsites: 12. **HUNTING** Fall seasons on antelope and prairie chicken. No closed season on coyote, bobcat and squirrel. Winter seasons on quail, muskrat, beaver, opossum, ring-tailed cat, badger, fox, weasel, raccoon, skunk and civet cat. In 1983 sandhill crane, duck, coot, geese, woodcock and jacksnipe seasons occurred during the winter months. Teal duck, rail and gallinule seasons occurred in the fall. Mourning dove seasons occurred intermittently during the fall and winter months. **MUSEUMS** Plains: Tsa Mo Ga Memorial Museum. **SPECIAL EVENTS** Old Settlers Reunion, Rodeo and Parade, Plains, August.

COMMUNITIES
COUNTY SEAT Plains, County Courthouse, 79355; County Clerk's Office, 806/456-2721. **INCORPORATED COMMUNITIES** (1980 population and ZIP Code) Denver City (4,704) 79323 and Plains (1,457) 79355. **UNINCORPORATED COMMUNITIES** (and ZIP Code) Bronco 79315. **FOR ADDITIONAL LOCAL INFORMATION** Denver City Chamber of Commerce, 104 W. 3rd St., Denver City, 79323, 806/592-3103 or 592-3978 and Yoakum Chamber of Commerce, 105 Huck, Yoakum 77995, 512/293-2149.

YOUNG (P55)

THE LAND
Northwest of Fort Worth on U.S. Highway 380 in the North Central Prairies Region, Young County covers 919 square miles with an elevation range of 1,000 to 1,200 feet. The county has light to dark loamy soils over reddish or mottled clayey subsoils. In the northwest corner hardened calcium deposits are in the subsoils. Young is in the Cross Timbers and Prairies vegetation area with tall and mid grasses, live and post oak, junipers and mesquite. Between 31 and 40% of the land in the county is considered prime farmland. **CLIMATE** Subtropical Subhumid with hot dry summers. The average annual temperature is 63°F. Temperatures in January range from an average low of 28° to an average high of 54°F and in July range from 72° to 98°F. The average annual precipitation is 17 inches, with an average relative humidity of 77% at 6 A.M. and 47% at 6 P.M. The average annual snowfall is five inches. The growing season averages 220 days per year, with the last freeze in early April and the first freeze in early November. The sun shines during the year on the average 70% of the daylight hours.

THE PEOPLE
The 1982 estimated population of 19,700 indicates a continuation of the growth rate begun in the 1970s. Nearly 69% of the county residents live in rural areas, which experienced strong growth in population from 1970 to 1980. The largest ancestry groups are persons of English descent (30%), Irish descent (24%) and German descent (13%). **REGISTERED VOTERS** As of November 2, 1982 there were 9,563 registered voters (0.1% of the state total). The 1982 general election had a 54% voter turnout, compared to a 72% turnout in the 1980 general election. In the 1982 primary 90% voted Democratic and 10% Republican, with 2,051 votes cast.

THE ECONOMY
AGRICULTURE Wheat area. In 1982, 90% of the land was in farms and ranches, with 19% of the farmland under cultivation and 2% irrigated. Young ranked 157th in the state in highest agricultural receipts, with 56% from livestock and livestock products. Undesirable brush and weeds, water erosion, a lack of potable water and reclamation of oil and gas drilling sites are the current conservation problems. Primary crops: wheat, oats, cotton, hay and sorghum. Primary vegetables: tomatoes and watermelons. Primary fruits and nuts: peaches and pecans. Primary livestock and products: cattle. **BUSINESS** Total number of business establishments in the county: 621. Retail sales during the first quarter of 1984 increased 5%. In 1980, 15% of the labor force were self-employed, 14% were employed in professional or related services, 20% in manufacturing, 16% in wholesale and retail trade, 23% in agriculture, forestry, fisheries and mining, 7% were employed in other counties and there were 2,455 retired workers. The industries with the most employment: agribusiness, oil and gas extraction, tourism, road construction and the manufacture of rubber and plastic hose and belting, metal foil and leaf, electronic components, aircraft and parts. The nonfarm earnings in 1981 totaled $228,181,000. The retired workers received an average monthly Social Security payment of $313. **FINANCE** On June 30, 1983, four commercial banks had total deposits of $190,226,000 and total assets of $215,279,000. On December 31, 1982 two state savings and loan associations and two state branches had combined assets of $521,691,265. **HOUSING** Average value of homes in 1980: $27,000. Permits for new, privately owned housing units decreased in 1982: 97 permits were issued with a total construction cost of $3,992,200. Of those permits, all were for single family houses. Between 1970 and 1980 the number of housing units increased by 28%. Eighty-seven percent of all units in the county are air-conditioned, 76% are heated by gas and 22% by electricity. **NATURAL RESOURCES** Ceramic clay, limestone, sand, gravel, oil, gas and bituminous coal. In 1982 a total of 4,914,391 thousand cubic feet of gas well gas, 29,357 barrels of condensate, 3,872,343 barrels of crude oil and 6,736,845 thousand cubic feet of casinghead gas were produced. Current production of other minerals and products includes crushed limestone, sand and gravel. **TOURISM** Travel expenditures of $11,561,000 in 1982 (an increase of 11% over 1981) generated 286 jobs and $2,289,000 in payroll. **ALCOHOLIC BEVERAGES** Totally dry. **FEDERAL EXPENDITURES** The federal government had direct expenditures or obligations

of $34,713,000 in the county during fiscal year 1983, including $1,714,000 by the U.S. Department of Defense. In addition, the federal government provided $244,000 in grant awards, paid $1,285,000 in salaries and wages, made direct payments to individuals of $31,844,000 including $22,486,000 in retirement and disability payments, awarded $634,000 in procurement contracts and spent $706,000 in other expenditures or obligations. The federal government also provided $4,234,000 in direct loans and $6,807,000 in guaranteed loans and insurance.

COMMUNICATION

Newspapers–Weekly: The Graham Leader and The Olney Enterprise. Radio: KSWA-AM and KWKQ-FM (Graham). Cable TV. Telephone companies: General Telephone and Brazos Telephone Coop. **TRANSPORTATION** Total public road mileage: 963. In 1982 there were 23,991 registered vehicles and 515 reported traffic accidents including nine fatalities. Taxi cabs: one company in Graham. Intercity bus service is available. Motor freight: seven local and intrastate carriers. Aircraft: 66 are registered in the county. Airports: Graham Municipal Airport serves as a base for 35 aircraft and is a general utility airport with general aviation service. Olney Municipal Airport serves as a base for 10 aircraft and is a general utility airport with general aviation service.

COMMUNITY SERVICES

EDUCATION Three school districts with five elementary, two middle and three high schools. The average daily attendance in 1981-82 was 3,392, with expenditures per pupil of $2,801 including 229 classroom teachers with an average annual salary of $16,116. Forty-seven percent of the 231 high school graduates planned to attend college. In 1982-83, 92% of the students were White, 6% Hispanic, 2% Black, 0.1% Asian and 0.1% American Indian. Private schools: 65 students enrolled in one elementary and one high school. Vocational education: Hamilton Vocational Nursing School (Olney). **PUBLIC LIBRARIES** Graham Public Library: 35,000 volumes. Olney Community Library and Arts Center: 25,477 volumes. **CHILD CARE** 63 day care and three twenty-four hour care licensed facilities. **HEALTH CARE** 17 physicians and 11 dentists. Hospitals: two with a combined capacity of 134. Ambulance services: one city and one county service. Mental health: one county clinic. Nursing homes: five nursing homes with a combined capacity of 412 nursing care residents. The average cost per day for private patients in 1982 was $34.34. **CHURCHES** 58 churches have an estimated combined membership of 13,874. The largest denominations are Southern Baptist, United Methodist and Churches of Christ. **SOCIAL SERVICES** In fiscal year 1983 a total of $353,075 in food stamps was distributed, with an average of 773 persons receiving food stamps each month. Aid to Families with Dependent Children (AFDC) totaled $47,612 with an average of 31 families receiving AFDC each month. Medical assistance benefits for the aged and disabled of $2,338,942 and for families and children of $54,442 brought the county benefit total to $2,794,072. **FIRE PROTECTION** Eight volunteer fire departments. **LAW ENFORCEMENT** The County Sheriff has seven commissioned officers. Three police departments have a combined force of 27. **CRIME** Eight violent crimes (murder, forcible rape, robbery and aggravated assault) and 251 nonviolent crimes (burglary, larceny-theft and motor vehicle theft) were reported in 1982. **JUDICIAL SYSTEM** One District Court and Judge, one County Court and Judge and two Justices of the Peace. In the District Court a total of 721 cases were pending on 1/1/82, 765 new cases were filed and 594 cases were disposed of during the year leaving 892 cases pending on 12/31/82. There were 427 criminal cases on the docket, 39 convictions, five persons committed to prison, one committed to jail and 297 cases left pending. In the County Court 835 cases were pending on

1/1/82, 1,139 new cases were filed and 890 cases were disposed of during the year leaving 1,084 cases pending on 12/31/82. There were 1,760 criminal cases on the docket, 450 convictions, 11 persons committed to jail and 915 cases left pending. **JAILS** One jail, capacity 20. **ATTORNEYS AT LAW** 30. **UTILITIES** 89% of the residents are connected to a public or privately owned water system and 74% are connected to a public sewer system. Natural gas is distributed to the county by Brazos River Gas Co. Lone Star Gas Co., Division of Enserch, and South Bend Supply, Inc. The average annual residential bill for natural gas in 1982 for the Lone Star distribution system was $405.91, an increase of 35% over 1981. Electricity is distributed to the county by Texas-New Mexico Power Co., Erath Co. Electric Coop., Inc. and Fort Belknap Electric Coop., Inc. and is generated primarily by gas, oil and water. The typical residential electric bill is $168.05 per month for an all-electric house using 2,500 kwh. **TAXES** The county has seven units with taxing authority: three school districts, three cities and one county.

RECREATION/ENTERTAINMENT

NATIONAL REGISTER OF HISTORIC PLACES Newcastle: Fort Belknap. South Bend: Harrell Site. **COUNTY/MUNICIPAL PARKS** 79 acres in one county and 10 municipal parks. These parks contain six playgrounds, one baseball and softball field, one tennis court, one multi-use court, two swimming pools and one boat ramp. Developed campsites: 14. **SCENIC DRIVES** The Texas Forts Trail runs through this county. This trail leads to eight of the famous frontier forts of west central Texas and an ancient presidio of the Spanish colonial period. **BOATING/FISHING** Lakes/reservoirs: Eddleman (587 acres), Graham (2,550 acres), Manning Vick (19 acres), Newcastle (16 acres), Old Eureka Mill (87 acres) and Whiskey Creek (48 acres). Major rivers: Clear Fork Brazos and Brazos. Primary streams: Flint, Salt, Ratcliff and Whiskey. **HUNTING** Fall and winter seasons on deer. No closed season on coyote, bobcat and squirrel. Winter seasons on quail, muskrat, beaver, opossum, ring-tailed cat, badger, fox, weasel, raccoon, skunk and civet cat. Fall, winter and spring seasons on turkey. In 1983 duck, coot, geese, woodcock and jacksnipe seasons occurred during the winter months. Teal duck, rail and gallinule seasons occurred in the fall. Mourning dove seasons occurred intermittently during the fall and winter months. **MUSEUMS** Newcastle: Fort Belknap Museum. **SPECIAL EVENTS** Possum Kingdom Relays and Junior Stock Show, Graham, March; Lake Country Art Festival, Graham, April/May; Spring Fever Tour for Vintage Autos, Graham, April; Possum Fair and Chili Cookoff, Graham, June; Pioneer Days Celebration, Olney, June.

COMMUNITIES

COUNTY SEAT Graham, County Courthouse, 76046; County Clerk's Office, 817/549-1227 **INCORPORATED COMMUNITIES** (1980 population and ZIP Code) Graham (9,170) 76046, New Castle (688) 76372 and Olney (4,060) 76374. **UNINCORPORATED COMMUNITIES** (and ZIP Code) Bunger 76046, Eliasville 76038, Flint Creek 76046, Fort Belknap Park 76372, Jean 76374, Loving 76062, Markley 76062, Murray 76046, Padgitt (Padgett) 76374, Proffit 76372 and South Bend 76081. **FOR ADDITIONAL LOCAL INFORMATION** Graham Chamber of Commerce, American Legion Bldg., Graham, 76046, 817/549-3355 and Olney Board of Industry and Community, 108 E. Main, Olney, 76374, 817/564-5445.

ZAPATA (B22)

THE LAND

Bordering Mexico southwest of Corpus Christi on U.S.

ZAPATA (continued)

Highway 83 in the Rio Grande Plain Region, Zapata County covers 999 square miles with the elevation ranging from 200 to 700 feet. The county has light colored, loamy soils over reddish or mottled, clayey subsoils with limestone and gray to black, cracking, clayey soils with a high shrink-swell potential and limestone within 40 inches of the surface. Zapata is in the South Texas Plains vegetation area with short and mid grasses, mesquite, thorny shrubs and cacti. Less than 1% of the land in the county is considered prime farmland. **CLIMATE** Subtropical Subhumid in the east and Subtropical Steppe in the west. Summers are dry and hot. The average annual temperature is 74°F. Temperatures in January range from an average low of 44° to an average high of 69°F and in July range from 75° to 100°F. The average annual precipitation is 19 inches, with an average relative humidity of 83% at 6 A.M. and 48% at 6 P.M. There is no snowfall. The growing season averages 295 days per year, with the last freeze in mid February and the first freeze in early December. The sun shines during the year on the average 65% of the daylight hours.

THE PEOPLE

Zapata County ranks 18th among all U.S. counties in the highest percent of persons of Spanish origin. The 1982 estimated population of 7,600 indicates a continuation of the strong growth which began in the 1970s. The age groups with the largest increases between 1970 and 1980 were ages 55 to 59 and 65 and over. The largest ancestry groups are Hispanic (76%) and persons of German descent (8%). **REGISTERED VOTERS** As of November 2, 1982 there were 4,286 registered voters (0.1% of the state total). The 1982 general election had a 43% voter turnout, compared to a 51% turnout in the 1980 general election. In the 1982 primary 100% voted Democratic, with 1,816 votes cast.

THE ECONOMY

AGRICULTURE Ranchland in the lower Rio Grande Valley vegetable area. In 1982, 88% of the land was in farms and ranches, with less than 1% of the farmland under cultivation. Zapata ranked 178th in the state in highest agricultural receipts, with 84% from livestock and livestock products. Undesirable brush and weeds, the cultivation of marginal lands, noxious weeds, a lack of potable water and urban encroachment are the current conservation problems. Primary crops: hay. Primary vegetables: eighth in the state for cantaloupes and ninth for carrots. Bell peppers, onions and watermelons. Primary fruits and nuts: oranges. Primary livestock and products: cattle, milk, sheep, wool and hogs. **BUSINESS** Total number of business establishments in the county: 78. In 1980, 11% of the labor force were self-employed, 18% were employed in professional or related services, 0.9% in manufacturing, 17% in wholesale and retail trade, 25% in agriculture, forestry, fisheries and mining, 9% were employed in other counties and there were 745 retired workers. The industry with the most employment: oil and gas extraction. The nonfarm earnings in 1981 totaled $34,086,000. The retired workers received an average monthly Social Security payment of $281. **FINANCE** On June 30, 1983, one commercial bank had total deposits of $32,117,000 and total assets of $35,661,000. There is one state savings and loan association branch in the county. **HOUSING** Average value of homes in 1980: $21,200. Between 1970 and 1980 the number of housing units increased by 83%. Fifty-three percent of all units in the county are air-conditioned, 63% are heated by gas and 29% by electricity. **NATURAL RESOURCES** Caliche, clay, lignite coal, sand, gravel, oil and gas. In 1982 a total of 96,076,758 thousand cubic feet of gas well gas, 131,181 barrels of condensate, 355,897 barrels of crude oil and 366,594 thousand cubic feet of casinghead gas were produced. **TOURISM**

Travel expenditures of $9,817,000 in 1982 (an increase of 13% over 1981) generated 223 jobs and $1,854,000 in payroll. Lodging: four hotels, motels and tourist courts. **ALCOHOLIC BEVERAGES** Packaged distilled spirits, beer, ale, malt liquor and wine are legal. Sale of mixed beverages is legal in all or parts of the county. **FEDERAL EXPENDITURES** The federal government had direct expenditures or obligations of $10,704,000 in the county during fiscal year 1983, including $638,000 by the U.S. Department of Defense. In addition, the federal government provided $145,000 in grant awards, paid $524,000 in salaries and wages, made direct payments to individuals of $9,814,000 including $8,034,000 in retirement and disability payments, awarded $71,000 in procurement contracts and spent $149,000 in other expenditures or obligations. The federal government also provided $40,000 in direct loans and $938,000 in guaranteed loans and insurance.

COMMUNICATION

Cable TV. Telephone companies: General Telephone and Valley Telephone Coop. **TRANSPORTATION** Total public road mileage: 243. In 1982 there were 5,736 registered vehicles and 118 reported traffic accidents including four fatalities. Intercity bus service is available. Motor freight: two carriers. Aircraft: five are registered in the county.

COMMUNITY SERVICES

EDUCATION One school district with three elementary, two middle and one high school. The average daily attendance in 1981-82 was 1,731, with expenditures per pupil of $3,355 including 120 classroom teachers with an average annual salary of $15,414. Sixty percent of the 96 high school graduates planned to attend college. In 1982-83, 12% of the students were White, 88% Hispanic, and 0.2% Asian. **CHILD CARE** Four day care and two twenty-four hour care licensed facilities. **HEALTH CARE** Four physicians. Clinics: one community clinic. Ambulance services: one volunteer fire department service. Mental health: one county clinic. **CHURCHES** 10 churches have an estimated combined membership of 3,058. The largest denomination is Catholic. **SOCIAL SERVICES** In fiscal year 1983 a total of $1,196,822 in food stamps was distributed, with an average of 2,354 persons receiving food stamps each month. Aid to Families with Dependent Children (AFDC) totaled $127,639 with an average of 87 families receiving AFDC each month. Medical assistance benefits for the aged and disabled of $505,910 and for families and children of $133,480 brought the county benefit total to $1,963,851. **FIRE PROTECTION** One volunteer fire department. **LAW ENFORCEMENT** The County Sheriff has 19 commissioned officers. **CRIME** 19 violent crimes (murder, forcible rape, robbery and aggravated assault) and 84 nonviolent crimes (burglary, larceny-theft and motor vehicle theft) were reported in 1982. **JUDICIAL SYSTEM** One District Court and Judge, one County Court and Judge and four Justices of the Peace. In the District Court a total of 135 cases were pending on 1/1/82, 139 new cases were filed and 85 cases were disposed of during the year leaving 189 cases pending on 12/31/82. There were 46 criminal cases on the docket, eight convictions, one person committed to prison and 36 cases left pending. In the County Court 138 cases were pending on 1/1/82, 129 new cases were filed and 141 cases were disposed of during the year leaving 126 cases pending on 12/31/82. There were 267 criminal cases on the docket, 115 convictions, one person committed to jail and 126 cases left pending. **JAILS** One jail, capacity 16. **ATTORNEYS AT LAW** Two. **UTILITIES** 92% of the residents are connected to a public or privately owned water system and 33% are connected to a public sewer system. Electricity is distributed to the county by Cochran Power and Light Co. and Medina Electric Coop., Inc. and is generated primarily by gas, oil and coal. **TAXES** The county has two units with taxing authority: one school district and one county.

RECREATION/ENTERTAINMENT
NATIONAL REGISTER OF HISTORIC PLACES San Ygnacio: San Ygnacio Historic District. San Ygnacio vicinity: Corralitos Ranch and San Francisco Ranch. **STATE** Falcon State Recreation Area covers 573 acres with camping and trailer sites, fishing, swimming and boat ramps. A 3,500 foot air strip is also located on the park site. **COUNTY PARKS** 146 acres in nine county parks. These parks contain two playgrounds, two baseball and softball fields, two multi-use fields, two tennis courts and one swimming pool. **SCENIC DRIVES** The Texas Tropical Trail runs through this county. This trail is charted through the state's southermost wedge meandering through ranchland resort areas by the Gulf of Mexico and fertile farmlands. **BOATING/FISHING** Lakes/reservoirs: Carlos Vela (39 acres), Garza 2 (46 acres), International Falcon (87,210 acres), McNeel 2 (26 acres), McNeel 5 (48 acres), Mecom Ranch (28 acres) and Vidaurri (41 acres). Major rivers: Rio Grande. Primary streams: Blancas, Salmoneno, Dolores, Salado, Arroyo Boleno, Arroyo Burro, Los Ovejos, Arroyo del Tigre, Arroyo Veleno and Arroyo Cabeza de Vaca. **HUNTING** Fall and winter seasons on deer. No closed season on javelina, coyote, bobcat and squirrel. Winter seasons on chachalaca, quail, muskrat, beaver, opossum, ringtailed cat, badger, fox, weasel, raccoon, skunk and civet cat. In 1983 sandhill crane, duck, coot, geese, woodcock and jacksnipe seasons occurred during the winter months. Teal duck, rail and gallinule seasons occurred in the fall. Mourning dove seasons occurred during the fall and winter months with a fall season on white-winged dove. **SPECIAL EVENTS** County Fair, Parade and Horse Races, Zapata, March.

COMMUNITIES
COUNTY SEAT Zapata, County Courthouse, 78076; County Clerk's Office, 512/765-4331. **INCORPORATED COMMUNITIES** (1980 population and ZIP Code) Zapata (3,831) 78076. **UNINCORPORATED COMMUNITIES** (and ZIP Code) Bustamante 78361, Escobas (Cuellar Store) 78361, Falcon 78584, Lopeno 78564, Ramireno 78067 and San Ygnacio 78067. **FOR ADDITIONAL LOCAL INFORMATION** Zapata County Chamber of Commerce, P.O. Box 1028, Zapata, 78076, 512/765-4871.

ZAVALA (B14)

THE LAND
Southwest of San Antonio on U.S. Highways 83 and 57 in the Rio Grande Plain Region, Zavala County covers 1,298 square miles with the elevation ranging from 550 to 850 feet. The northeastern part of the county has light colored, well drained soils. In the southeast and along most of the southern border the soils are deep to moderately deep, with light colored loamy surfaces over clayey subsoils that have limestone within 40 inches of the surface. The rest of the county has gray to black, cracking, clayey soils that have a high shrink-swell potential. Zavala is in the South Texas Plains vegetation area with short and mid grasses, mesquite, thorny shrubs and cacti. Less than 1% of the land in the county is considered prime farmland. **CLIMATE** Subtropical Subhumid with mild winters and hot summers. The average annual temperature is 71°F. Temperatures in January range from an average low of 40° to an average high of 65°F and in July range from 74° to 98°F. The average annual precipitation is 22 inches, with an average relative humidity of 80% at 6 A.M. and 44% at 6 P.M. There is no snowfall. The growing season averages 282 days per year, with the last freeze in late February and the first freeze in early December. The sun shines during the year on the average 65% of the daylight hours.

THE PEOPLE
Zavala County ranks fifth among all U.S. counties in highest percent of persons of Spanish origin. The 1982 estimated population of 12,000 indicates a continuation of the growth which began in the 1970s, reversing the population decline from 1960 to 1970. Nearly 71% of the county residents live in rural areas. The county's population is unusually young with a median age which rose from 21 in 1970 to 24 in 1980. The largest ancestry groups are Hispanic (89%) and persons of English descent (4%). **REGISTERED VOTERS** As of November 2, 1982 there were 7,022 registered voters (0.1% of the state total). The 1982 general election had a 37% voter turnout, compared to a 55% turnout in the 1980 general election. In the 1982 primary 100% voted Democratic, with 2,180 votes cast.

THE ECONOMY
AGRICULTURE Ranchland in the lower Rio Grande Valley vegetable area. In 1982, 94% of the land was in farms and ranches, with 9% of the farmland under cultivation. Most of the cropland and some of the rangeland was irrigated. Zavala ranked 63rd in the state in highest agricultural receipts, with 58% from crops. Overgrazing, undesirable brush and weeds and decreasing irrigation water supplies are the current conservation problems. Primary crops: wheat, sorghum, cotton, corn and oats. Primary vegetables: second in the state for processed vegetables, fifth for onions, ninth for carrots and eighth for cabbage and total fresh market vegetables. Spinach and watermelons. Primary fruits and nuts: peaches and pecans. Primary livestock and products: cattle, sheep, wool, angora goats, mohair and hogs. **BUSINESS** Total number of business establishments in the county: 135. Retail sales during the first quarter of 1984 increased 5%. In 1980, 8% of the labor force were self-employed, 22% were employed in professional or related services, 14% in manufacturing, 15% in wholesale and retail trade, 26% in agriculture, forestry, fisheries and mining, 17% were employed in other counties and there were 781 retired workers. The industries with the most employment: fruit and vegetable canning and agribusiness. The nonfarm earnings in 1981 totaled $51,567,000. The retired workers received an average monthly Social Security payment of $242. **FINANCE** On June 30, 1983, two commercial banks had total deposits of $20,001,000 and total assets of $22,918,000. **HOUSING** Average value of homes in 1980: $15,600. In 1982 two permits were issued for new single family homes. Between 1970 and 1980 the number of housing units increased by 11%. Forty-eight percent of all units in the county are air-conditioned, 79% are heated by gas and 13% by electricity. **NATURAL RESOURCES** Construction sand, sand and gravel, oil, gas, asphaltic sandstone and lignite coal. In 1982 a total of 12,332,437 thousand cubic feet of gas well gas, 28,028 barrels of condensate, 927,715 barrels of crude oil and 1,247,315 thousand cubic feet of casinghead gas were produced. **TOURISM** Travel expenditures of $3,416,000 in 1982 (an increase of 17% over 1981) generated 52 jobs and $523,000 in payroll. **ALCOHOLIC BEVERAGES** Packaged distilled spirits, beer, ale, malt liquor and wine are legal in parts of the county. Sale of mixed beverages is legal in all or parts of the county. **FEDERAL EXPENDITURES** The federal government had direct expenditures or obligations of $13,486,000 in the county during fiscal year 1983, including $111,000 by the U.S. Department of Defense. In addition, the federal government provided $1,230,000 in grant awards, paid $467,000 in salaries and wages, made direct payments to individuals of $9,375,000 including $6,526,000 in retirement and disability payments, awarded $63,000 in procurement contracts and spent $2,351,000 in other

ZAVALA (continued)

expenditures or obligations. The federal government also provided $372,000 in direct loans and $4,871,000 in guaranteed loans and insurance.

COMMUNICATION

Newspapers–Weekly: Zavala County Sentinel (Crystal City). Cable TV. Telephone companies: Valley Telephone Coop. **TRANSPORTATION** Total public road mileage: 496. In 1982 there were 5,680 registered vehicles and 166 reported traffic accidents including five fatalities. Intercity bus service is available. Motor freight: three carriers. Rail: three branch lines carry freight through the county. Two of the lines carry annually one to five million tons of freight each and one carries less than one million tons. Aircraft: 22 are registered in the county. Airports: Crystal City Municipal Airport.

COMMUNITY SERVICES

EDUCATION Two school districts with five elementary, one middle and two high schools. The average daily attendance in 1981-82 was 2,801, with expenditures per pupil of $2,409 including 156 classroom teachers with an average annual salary of $13,719. Fifty-five percent of the 189 high school graduates planned to attend college. In 1982-83, 4% of the students were White, 96% Hispanic and 0.2% Black. **PUBLIC LIBRARIES** Crystal City Library. **CHILD CARE** 10 day care licensed facilities. **HEALTH CARE** Five physicians and one dentist. Clinics: two outpatient clinics and one public health clinic. Ambulance services: one volunteer fire department and one county service. **CHURCHES** 22 churches have an estimated combined membership of 9,407. The largest denominations are Catholic and Southern Baptist. **SOCIAL SERVICES** In fiscal year 1983 a total of $2,556,747 in food stamps was distributed, with an average of 5,272 persons receiving food stamps each month. Aid to Families with Dependent Children (AFDC) totaled $359,134 with an average of 239 families receiving AFDC each month. Medical assistance benefits for the aged and disabled of $656,884 and for families and children of $383,368 brought the county benefit total to $3,956,133. **FIRE PROTECTION** Three volunteer fire departments. **LAW ENFORCEMENT** The County Sheriff has six commissioned officers. One police department has a force of 14. **CRIME** 32 violent crimes (murder, forcible rape, robbery and aggravated assault) and 106 nonviolent crimes (burglary, larceny-theft and motor vehicle theft) were reported in 1982. **JUDICIAL SYSTEM** One District Court and Judge, one County Court and Judge and four Justices of the Peace. In the District Court a total of 171 cases were pending on 1/1/82, 242 new cases were filed and 251 cases were disposed of during the year leaving 162 cases pending on 12/31/82. There were 101 criminal cases on the docket, 22 convictions, six persons committed to prison, one committed to jail and 61 cases left pending. In the County Court 305 cases were pending on 1/1/82, 251 new cases were filed and 142 cases were disposed of during the year leaving 414 cases pending on 12/31/82. There were 543 criminal cases on the docket, 73 convictions and 401 cases left pending. **JAILS** One jail, capacity 21. **ATTORNEYS AT LAW** Seven. **UTILITIES** 90% of the residents are connected to a public or privately owned water system and 57% are connected to a public sewer system. Natural gas is distributed to the county by Citizens Gas Co-Operative. Electricity is distributed to the county by Cochran Power and Light, Medina Electric Coop., Inc., Central Power and Light Co. and Rio Grande Electric Coop., Inc. and is generated primarily by gas, oil and coal. The typical residential electric bill is $162.15 per month for an all-electric house using 2,500 kwh. **TAXES** The county has five units with taxing authority: two school districts, one city, one county and one college district.

RECREATION/ENTERTAINMENT

COUNTY/MUNICIPAL PARKS 68 acres in nine county and seven municipal parks. These parks contain seven playgrounds, eight baseball and softball fields, two tennis courts, one multiuse courts, one swimming pool, five beaches and two boat ramps. **BOATING/FISHING** Lakes/reservoirs: Chaparrosa (37 acres), Johnson (24 acres) and Upper Nueces (316 acres). Major rivers: Nueces and Leona. Primary streams: Maverick, Chaparrosa, Comanche, Liveoak, Palo Blanco, Turkey and Tortuga. **HUNTING** Fall and winter seasons on deer. No closed season on javelina, coyote, bobcat and squirrel. Winter seasons on quail, muskrat, beaver, opossum, ring-tailed cat, badger, fox, weasel, raccoon, skunk and civet cat. Fall, winter and spring seasons on turkey. Special regulations on state-owned river beds. In 1983 sandhill crane, coot, geese, woodcock and jacksnipe seasons occurred during the winter months. Teal duck, rail and gallinule seasons occurred in the fall. Mourning dove seasons occurred intermittently during the fall and winter months with a fall season on white-winged dove. **SPECIAL EVENTS** Zavala County Fair, Crystal City, February/March; Cinco de Mayo Celebration, Crystal City, May; Fourth of July Celebration, Crystal City, July; Spinach Festival, Crystal City, November.

COMMUNITIES

COUNTY SEAT Crystal City, County Courthouse, 78839; County Clerk's Office, 512/374-2331. **INCORPORATED COMMUNITIES** (1980 population and ZIP Code) Crystal City (8,334) 78839. **UNINCORPORATED COMMUNITIES** (and ZIP Code) Asphalt Belt Junction (A.B. Junction) 78829, Batesville 78829, La Pryor 78872 and Loma Vista 78829. **FOR ADDITIONAL LOCAL INFORMATION** Zavala County Chamber of Commerce, 120 W. Uvalde, Crystal City, 78839, 512/374-2268 or 374-3478.

COUNTY LOCATION CHART

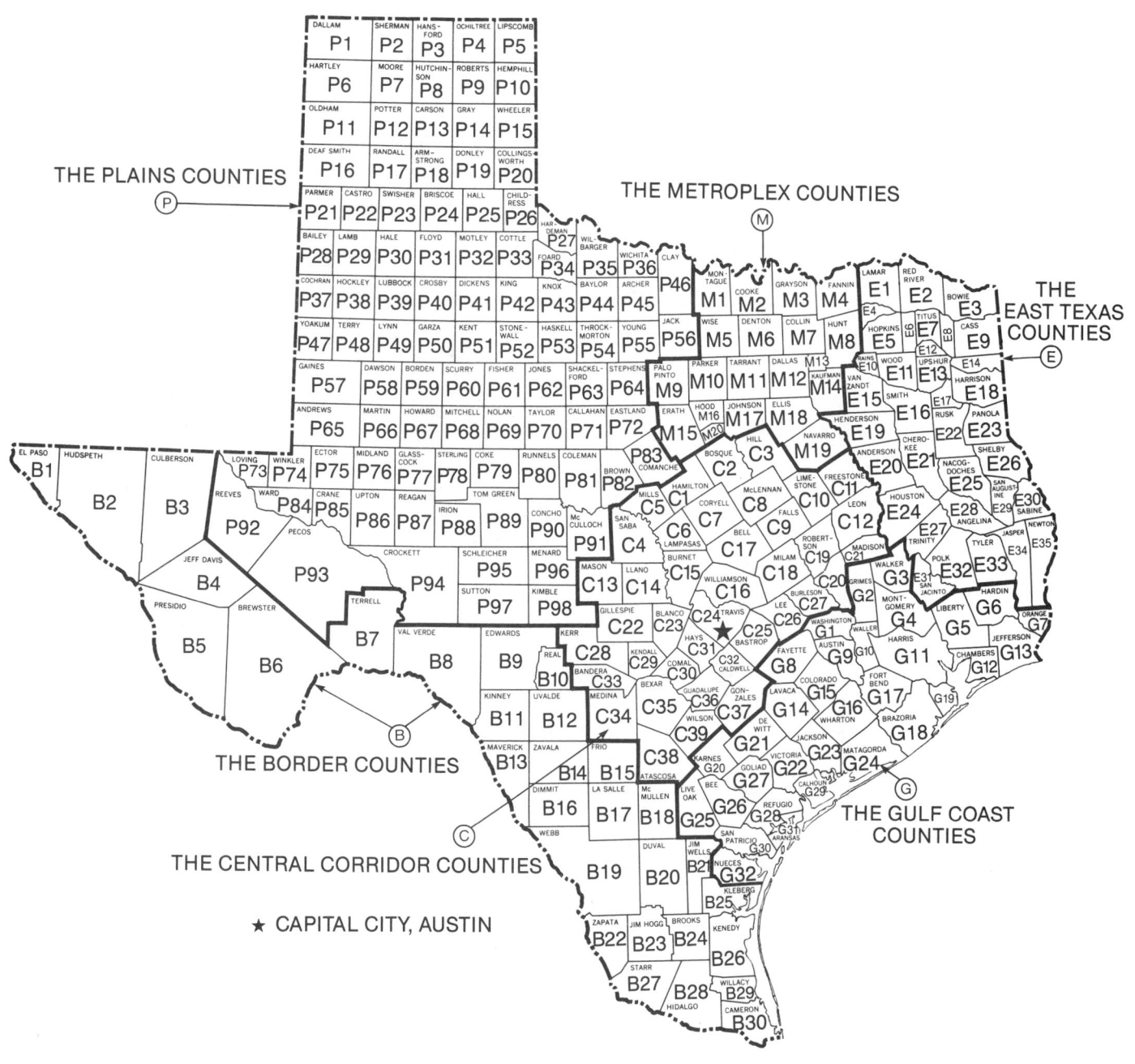

THE PLAINS COUNTIES (P)

THE METROPLEX COUNTIES (M)

THE EAST TEXAS COUNTIES (E)

THE BORDER COUNTIES (B)

THE CENTRAL CORRIDOR COUNTIES (C)

THE GULF COAST COUNTIES (G)

★ CAPITAL CITY, AUSTIN

COUNTY POPULATION

	STATE TOTALS	ANDERSON	ANDREWS	ANGELINA	ARANSAS	ARCHER	ARMSTRONG	ATASCOSA	AUSTIN	BAILEY
1982 Population[E]	15,418,900	40,457	13,930	67,421	15,375	7,637	2,021	26,692	18,684	8,283

1980 Population

	STATE TOTALS	ANDERSON	ANDREWS	ANGELINA	ARANSAS	ARCHER	ARMSTRONG	ATASCOSA	AUSTIN	BAILEY
1980 Census of Population	14,229,288	38,381	13,323	64,172	14,260	7,266	1,994	25,055	17,726	8,168
Rank in State		55	140	37	132	184	241	79	112	180
% Change 1970-80	27.1	38.1	28.5	30.0	60.2	26.2	5.2	34.0	28.2	-3.8
Urban Residents	11,333,017	15,948	11,061	33,789	4,546	515		12,175	6,735	4,842
% Change 1970-80	27.0	9.8	28.2	27.0	-1.3			44.6	150.8	7.0
Rural Residents	2,896,174	22,433	2,262	30,383	9,714	6,751	1,994	12,880	10,991	3,326
% Change 1970-80	27.3	69.1	29.5	33.6	126.1	17.2	5.2	25.3	-1.4	-16.1
Population Per Square Mile	54.3	35.6	8.9	79.5	50.9	8.0	2.2	20.6	27.0	9.9

	STATE TOTALS	ANDERSON	ANDREWS	ANGELINA	ARANSAS	ARCHER	ARMSTRONG	ATASCOSA	AUSTIN	BAILEY
Native Texans 1980 (%)[T]	67.8	82.4	64.7	82.4	66.4	80.6	77.0	88.1	87.9	71.1

Age 1980

	STATE TOTALS	ANDERSON	ANDREWS	ANGELINA	ARANSAS	ARCHER	ARMSTRONG	ATASCOSA	AUSTIN	BAILEY
Female (%)	50.8	46.6	50.0	51.2	50.9	49.9	51.1	49.9	51.1	50.7
Median Age	28.2	29.8	26.7	28.9	34.8	32.3	39.0	28.4	34.4	28.2
Under Age 5 (%)	8.2	7.2	10.1	8.6	7.4	7.5	6.8	8.9	7.3	9.3
Age 5-17 (%)	22.1	18.9	23.7	23.2	21.1	21.6	18.7	25.5	20.7	24.8
Age 18-64 (%)	60.1	58.7	58.7	56.6	56.4	57.0	55.6	53.6	53.2	54.0
Age 65 and Over (%)	9.6	15.2	7.5	11.6	15.1	13.9	18.9	12.0	18.8	11.9

	STATE TOTALS	ANDERSON	ANDREWS	ANGELINA	ARANSAS	ARCHER	ARMSTRONG	ATASCOSA	AUSTIN	BAILEY
Age 18 and Over (1980)	9,923,085	28,367	8,824	43,794	10,207	5,147	1,485	16,417	12,753	5,386
Registered Voters (11/2/82)	6,414,988	16,764	5,943	31,450	6,985	4,092	1,260	13,418	8,104	3,666

1980 Selected Ancestry Groups

	STATE TOTALS	ANDERSON	ANDREWS	ANGELINA	ARANSAS	ARCHER	ARMSTRONG	ATASCOSA	AUSTIN	BAILEY
Black	1,710,175	8,164	282	9,625	277	18	4	122	2,580	181
Hispanic	2,985,824	1,796	2,904	4,047	2,722	138	53	11,983	989	2,770
American Indian/Eskimo	40,975	87	63	84	49	38	6	55	14	9
Asian/Pacific Islander	120,313	84	125	137	239	6	7	48	40	5
English[F]	1,639,322	7,221	1,608	10,045	1,831	1,011	436	1,726	1,068	1,193
French[F]	152,072	251	59	696	149	38	30	112	62	47
German[F]	754,388	1,225	361	1,832	1,071	1,244	131	1,502	4,122	380
Irish[F]	572,732	1,953	625	3,949	906	527	145	849	506	447
Italian[F]	78,592	47	13	85	40	12	2	43	21	6
Polish[F]	70,688	27	5	116	77	35	5	253	395	12

	STATE TOTALS	ANDERSON	ANDREWS	ANGELINA	ARANSAS	ARCHER	ARMSTRONG	ATASCOSA	AUSTIN	BAILEY
Veterans 1980 (%)	11.9	21.6	16.4	16.1	21.0	18.3	20.0	13.9	14.2	10.8

1980 Family Characteristics

	STATE TOTALS	ANDERSON	ANDREWS	ANGELINA	ARANSAS	ARCHER	ARMSTRONG	ATASCOSA	AUSTIN	BAILEY
Households	4,929,267	12,386	4,423	21,781	5,168	2,644	750	8,036	6,434	2,681
Single Persons (Age 15+)	2,558,023	6,640	1,558	8,942	1,881	994	215	3,920	2,680	1,110
Families	3,677,865	9,442	3,668	17,177	4,099	2,099	583	6,442	4,836	2,202
Both Spouses Employed	1,360,111	2,954	1,454	5,855	906	714	201	1,906	1,805	699
With Children Under Age 18	1,992,484	4,422	2,024	9,078	1,756	1,022	253	3,529	2,366	1,212
Child. Living w/Two Parents (%)	77.9	76.4	82.1	78.2	88.2	88.9	92.7	83.0	78.2	80.1
Employed Mothers/Ages 0-5 (%)[M]	48.1	49.3	41.9	44.0	28.1	40.3	33.7	35.1	48.8	36.9
Age 3-4 in Nursery School (%)	31.6	23.1	22.5	26.1	22.5	18.1	11.4	17.8	20.1	20.0
Foreign Language in Home (%)[S]	21.8	5.7	22.2	6.3	19.1	3.7	3.1	46.9	20.3	31.1
Age 60+ Living Alone (%)	23.8	26.0	20.1	23.8	17.2	24.7	27.2	22.6	24.8	19.9

1980

	STATE TOTALS	ANDERSON	ANDREWS	ANGELINA	ARANSAS	ARCHER	ARMSTRONG	ATASCOSA	AUSTIN	BAILEY
School Dropouts Age 16-19 (%)	17.6	13.7	24.5	25.0	17.4	11.5	7.6	18.2	15.8	25.3
H.S. Graduates Age 25+ (%)	62.6	51.4	55.2	53.6	58.0	56.8	66.2	45.9	45.6	48.9
College Graduates Age 25+ (%)	16.9	8.4	11.0	11.1	12.0	8.2	14.3	8.7	7.6	9.0

1982

	STATE TOTALS	ANDERSON	ANDREWS	ANGELINA	ARANSAS	ARCHER	ARMSTRONG	ATASCOSA	AUSTIN	BAILEY
Birth Rate[R]	19.5	16.2	26.5	17.8	19.0	14.9	16.3	20.5	16.8	21.7
Death Rate[R]	7.3	11.4	6.8	8.3	9.4	8.9	12.4	8.4	11.3	6.6
Marriage Rate[R]	12.8	12.6	14.7	13.7	18.1	12.3	7.4	9.1	5.7	12.9
Divorce Rate[R]	6.4	1.7	7.5	2.8	6.3	6.8	5.9	1.7	5.4	5.1

Source: U.S. Department of Commerce, Bureau of Census/Secretary of State of Texas, Elections Division/Texas Department of Health, Division of Vital Statistics.
[E]Estimate.   [T]Born in Texas and residing in Texas in 1980.   [R]Per 1,000 population.   [1]Verified by the Bureau of Census   [2]Verified by the Elections Division
[M]Employed female with children ages 0-5   [S]Children ages 5+ who speak a language other than English at home.   [F]Those reporting single ancestry.

FLYING THE COLORS: TEXAS ©JOHN CLEMENTS 1984

	BANDERA	BASTROP	BAYLOR	BEE	BELL	BEXAR	BLANCO	BORDEN	BOSQUE	BOWIE	BRAZORIA	BRAZOS	BREWSTER	BRISCOE
	7,603	26,430	4,851	26,958	165,237	1,025,316	4,915	859	13,891	76,753	185,244	94,492	7,562	2,555
	7,084	24,726	4,919	26,030	157,820	988,798	4,681	859	13,401	75,301	169,587	93,588	7,573	2,579
	186	81	205	77	15	3	210	250	138	33	14	27	182	232
	49.2	42.9	−5.8	14.5	26.8	19.1	31.2	−3.3	22.2	9.3	56.6	61.4	−2.7	−7.7
		11,794	3,657	14,574	127,581	936,656			3,063	48,389	107,781	83,036	5,465	
		19.1	5.4	7.9	20.9	18.8			18.8	12.2	62.3	61.6	−8.5	
	7,084	12,932	1,262	11,456	30,308	52,144	4,681	859	10,338	26,912	61,806	10,552	2,108	2,579
	49.2	74.9	−28.0	24.1	60.1	23.5	31.2	−3.3	23.2	9.0	47.4	60.3	16.5	−7.7
	8.9	27.6	5.7	29.6	149.7	792.3	6.6	1.0	13.6	84.5	120.5	159.2	1.2	2.9
	77.5	81.6	83.8	77.3	51.6	67.7	81.7	82.0	84.3	61.6	68.2	69.4	73.0	86.2
	51.1	50.1	52.8	50.2	47.7	51.5	51.2	50.4	52.7	52.1	47.1	50.2	51.2	
	41.1	32.2	42.2	26.1	24.9	27.1	39.4	32.0	44.9	31.3	27.2	22.9	27.1	33.0
	5.6	7.8	6.1	10.0	9.8	8.5	5.7	8.3	5.5	7.9	8.8	6.8	6.8	8.0
	19.1	21.2	17.7	22.7	19.3	23.5	19.4	23.4	16.6	21.7	22.3	15.7	19.8	21.6
	56.8	54.8	52.7	57.2	63.0	59.3	54.7	57.6	51.4	57.1	62.8	70.7	62.0	53.5
	18.5	16.2	23.5	10.1	7.9	8.7	20.2	10.7	26.5	13.3	6.1	6.8	11.4	16.9
	5,337	17,561	3,745	17,511	111,813	672,227	3,503	[1]587	10,431	52,970	116,789	72,581	5,563	1,814
	4,490	13,703	3,405	11,185	47,902	425,688	2,970	[2]593	7,420	37,063	67,487	34,681	3,879	1,509
	20	4,259	179	673	25,873	69,201	77	3	296	16,498	13,152	10,350	58	120
	863	3,402	306	11,914	17,407	460,911	432	127	701	993	22,679	9,455	3,262	418
	20	63	13	91	590	2,332	3	4	37	172	512	168	20	4
	10	28	7	280	3,352	7,500	2		33	199	758	1,099	34	2
	744	2,555	748	2,126	16,825	61,549	470	172	1,816	11,755	18,465	11,355	833	858
	58	134	53	138	1,311	6,456	28	2	133	430	2,890	1,093	106	12
	810	3,405	258	1,618	12,214	58,915	978	41	1,171	2,239	9,844	7,295	465	106
	244	1,354	346	956	6,911	23,275	244	71	976	4,927	6,810	4,292	339	114
	38	27		40	792	6,007	2		22	248	1,021	1,724	14	
	120	32	6	105	504	8,883	6		23	65	920	761	7	
	20.1	17.1	15.3	15.1	20.9	18.6	20.5	13.6	17.8	18.6	18.5	10.9	17.1	12.4
	2,802	8,719	2,027	8,181	52,661	320,639	1,825	299	5,513	27,449	53,907	32,488	2,694	967
	943	3,898	537	4,384	27,528	192,789	621	105	1,600	10,935	27,068	34,110	1,949	330
	2,062	6,652	1,465	6,547	40,725	244,770	1,348	257	3,942	20,687	43,852	19,511	1,817	743
	553	2,209	572	2,198	14,495	79,779	513	70	1,267	6,728	17,511	8,327	561	194
	780	3,154	536	3,722	23,530	140,649	555	127	1,575	10,438	25,704	9,905	886	330
	79.4	80.9	85.5	77.6	79.6	75.0	79.3	88.6	85.7	71.2	84.4	78.4	76.4	88.5
	37.3	47.1	73.5	36.0	45.0	45.4	46.1	32.8	47.7	51.7	43.3	55.1	53.4	27.4
	24.4	28.6		32.8	24.3	30.7	25.0	11.8	26.0	23.7	36.7	41.9	19.4	2.2
	11.8	15.9	8.8	45.2	14.i	43.3	16.5	15.2	7.0	2.4	13.5	13.0	44.5	15.2
	27.2	25.3	27.4	22.9	24.7	22.9	26.4	22.9	24.5	25.8	19.9	23.1	28.5	27.1
	12.0	20.0	29.4	16.7	19.5	17.1	12.4	17.3	24.2	13.4	20.9	7.0	11.1	10.6
	64.9	49.0	50.3	50.3	67.1	63.1	54.3	51.2	48.2	59.9	65.2	69.1	67.5	53.0
	13.9	10.2	7.7	10.5	15.8	16.0	13.1	11.2	9.7	11.7	13.6	31.9	23.5	8.0
	10.1	19.7	15.7	17.7	28.4	19.7	14.0	7.0	13.0	16.0	19.0	21.6	16.4	12.9
	11.8	10.3	12.6	5.5	6.4	7.0	14.2	7.0	16.4	9.0	5.7	5.8	8.6	8.6
	16.2	10.6	14.0	13.6	19.8	13.4	11.8	4.7	12.2	12.2	11.8	12.1	13.6	6.7
	3.2	6.5	5.6	5.7	12.0	7.1	3.3	5.8	4.3	8.3	7.1	4.0	4.9	4.3

COUNTY POPULATION

	BROOKS	BROWN	BURLESON	BURNET	CALDWELL	CALHOUN	CALLAHAN	CAMERON	CAMP	CARSON	CASS
1982 Population[E]	8,580	34,642	12,794	19,294	24,146	19,893	11,750	229,139	9,641	6,752	30,683

1980 Population

	BROOKS	BROWN	BURLESON	BURNET	CALDWELL	CALHOUN	CALLAHAN	CAMERON	CAMP	CARSON	CASS
1980 Census of Population	8,428	33,057	12,313	17,803	23,637	19,574	10,992	209,727	9,275	6,672	29,430
Rank in State	177	65	145	111	86	100	152	11	170	189	69
% Change 1970-80	5.3	27.7	23.1	55.9	11.6	9.8	34.0	49.4	15.9	4.9	21.9
Urban Residents	6,103	19,396	2,953	6,662	12,992	10,911	2,562	165,577	4,245		6,272
% Change 1970-80	-4.0	11.7		132.6	15.9	4.0		52.2	10.4		25.3
Rural Residents	2,325	13,661	9,360	11,141	10,645	8,663	8,430	44,150	5,030	6,672	23,158
% Change 1970-80	40.9	60.5	-6.4	30.2	6.8	18.0	2.7	39.9	20.9	4.9	21.1
Population Per Square Mile	8.9	35.3	18.4	17.9	43.3	36.2	12.2	231.7	45.7	7.2	31.4

	BROOKS	BROWN	BURLESON	BURNET	CALDWELL	CALHOUN	CALLAHAN	CAMERON	CAMP	CARSON	CASS
Native Texans (%)[T]	91.2	82.7	89.2	76.3	81.0	80.9	82.9	64.9	84.3	68.1	75.0

Age 1980

	BROOKS	BROWN	BURLESON	BURNET	CALDWELL	CALHOUN	CALLAHAN	CAMERON	CAMP	CARSON	CASS
Female (%)	51.6	52.0	51.4	51.6	48.6	50.1	51.9	52.0	52.3	50.2	52.0
Median Age	28.4	32.3	34.5	41.5	27.2	28.0	36.8	25.0	32.7	32.5	32.5
Under Age 5 (%)	8.6	7.3	7.4	5.8	7.2	8.6	6.7	10.4	8.2	7.8	7.9
Age 5-17 (%)	25.1	20.6	20.6	19.0	24.2	24.1	19.9	27.9	20.6	22.2	22.1
Age 18-64 (%)	54.1	54.8	53.3	52.5	54.3	59.3	54.1	52.1	54.9	56.6	54.1
Age 65 and Over (%)	12.2	17.3	18.7	22.7	14.4	8.0	19.3	9.6	16.3	13.4	15.9

	BROOKS	BROWN	BURLESON	BURNET	CALDWELL	CALHOUN	CALLAHAN	CAMERON	CAMP	CARSON	CASS
Age 18 and Over (1980)	[1]5,587	23,855	8,873	13,400	16,256	13,168	8,064	129,327	6,601	4,668	20,605
Registered Voters (11/2/82)	[2]5,882	14,500	6,946	11,203	10,381	9,450	6,181	81,094	5,130	3,965	16,092

1980 Selected Ancestry Groups

	BROOKS	BROWN	BURLESON	BURNET	CALDWELL	CALHOUN	CALLAHAN	CAMERON	CAMP	CARSON	CASS
Black	6	1,571	2,693	277	3,867	629	4	722	2,369	20	6,460
Hispanic	7,247	2,608	1,274	1,258	7,790	6,651	371	161,654	125	264	336
American Indian/Eskimo	5	60	10	38	57	46	21	303	13	47	51
Asian/Pacific Islander	3	70	2	42	167	147	50	342	8	18	15
English[F]	276	8,450	1,064	3,158	1,915	1,495	2,288	7,735	1,893	1,010	4,648
French[F]	19	246	49	175	84	155	93	680	41	34	108
German[F]	97	1,620	1,077	1,433	1,555	1,231	494	3,752	232	510	503
Irish[F]	37	2,280	471	1,059	682	612	938	2,056	554	432	1,465
Italian[F]	12	73	52	67	6	17	22	484		4	28
Polish[F]		33	97	28	61	146	17	618		117	77

	BROOKS	BROWN	BURLESON	BURNET	CALDWELL	CALHOUN	CALLAHAN	CAMERON	CAMP	CARSON	CASS
Veterans 1980 (%)	11.4	15.7	15.6	18.8	11.9	18.1	17.9	12.4	17.7	17.6	17.3

1980 Family Characteristics

	BROOKS	BROWN	BURLESON	BURNET	CALDWELL	CALHOUN	CALLAHAN	CAMERON	CAMP	CARSON	CASS
Households	2,614	12,308	4,459	6,951	7,361	6,469	4,150	58,418	3,404	2,395	10,515
Single Persons (Age 15+)	1,583	4,852	1,977	1,967	5,561	2,998	1,277	37,617	1,162	866	3,944
Familes	2,161	9,052	3,355	5,456	5,563	5,220	3,251	48,796	2,579	1,882	8,192
Both Spouses Employed	560	3,269	1,178	1,556	1,879	1,753	1,083	13,734	884	674	2,350
With Children Under Age 18	1,187	4,211	1,511	2,084	2,793	2,928	1,445	30,086	1,196	913	4,018
Child. Living w/Two Parents (%)	81.6	78.3	75.0	83.6	68.0	86.5	88.0	78.2	77.6	87.7	78.5
Employed Mothers/Ages 0-5 (%)[M]	45.3	53.8	47.3	50.6	48.8	39.4	52.8	44.7	40.9	40.2	48.1
Age 3-4 in Nursery School (%)	23.7	32.3	16.7	26.2	22.4	20.7	17.8	23.0	11.5	9.5	18.8
Foreign Language in Home (%)[S]	83.6	8.2	15.6	8.9	33.2	31.5	4.8	76.6	1.9	4.9	1.6
Age 60+ Living Alone (%)	21.6	25.6	25.2	20.5	25.4	22.2	24.7	19.1	25.3	24.8	24.7

1980

	BROOKS	BROWN	BURLESON	BURNET	CALDWELL	CALHOUN	CALLAHAN	CAMERON	CAMP	CARSON	CASS
School Dropouts Age 16-19 (%)	22.1	16.2	16.9	20.1	52.8	16.6	11.2	19.1	17.2	7.6	14.9
H.S. Graduates Age 25+	40.7	57.2	42.3	51.7	47.2	53.7	54.5	43.8	50.8	62.8	52.5
College Graduates Age 25+	8.9	12.3	8.1	9.9	11.0	10.0	9.9	10.5	7.4	13.4	8.3

1982

	BROOKS	BROWN	BURLESON	BURNET	CALDWELL	CALHOUN	CALLAHAN	CAMERON	CAMP	CARSON	CASS
Birth Rate[R]	21.9	16.0	19.1	13.8	16.6	20.3	16.1	23.9	16.6	20.4	15.6
Death Rate[R]	8.9	10.5	14.8	11.9	8.1	7.3	12.8	5.7	12.6	9.3	11.3
Marriage Rate[R]	13.6	13.4	11.1	12.4	8.6	11.3	12.2	11.7	12.3	12.7	10.8
Divorce Rate[R]	1.8	4.9	5.5	6.7	3.7	5.5	6.2	3.9	5.3	3.0	7.1

[E]Estimate. [T]Born in Texas and residing in Texas in 1980. [R]Per 1,000 population. [1]Verified by the Bureau of Census [2]Verified by the Elections Division
[M]Employed female with children ages 0-5 [S]Children ages 5+ who speak a language other than English at home. [F]Those reporting single ancestry.

CASTRO	CHAMBERS	CHEROKEE	CHILDRESS	CLAY	COCHRAN	COKE	COLEMAN	COLLIN	COLLINGS-WORTH	COLORADO	COMAL	COMANCHE	CONCHO
10,925	20,247	39,520	7,029	9,933	4,876	3,204	10,457	165,067	4,644	19,031	39,564	12,778	2,939
10,556	18,538	38,127	6,950	9,582	4,825	3,196	10,439	144,576	4,648	18,823	36,446	12,617	2,915
156	108	56	187	167	208	226	157	16	211	106	60	143	229
1.6	52.1	19.1	5.2	18.6	−9.4	3.5	1.5	116.0	−2.3	6.7	50.8	6.0	−0.7
5,019	6	16,945	5,817	3,149	2,674		5,960	114,927	3,043	7,844	22,489	4,075	
16.0		15.7	7.6	8.7	−2.3		6.3	194.7	5.5	13.2	25.9	3.6	
5,537	18,532	21,182	1,133	6,433	2,151	3,196	4,479	29,649	1,605	10,979	13,957	8,542	2,915
−8.7	52.1	22.0	−5.3	24.1	−16.9	3.5	−4.3	6.2	−14.2	2.5	121.3	7.2	−0.7
11.7	30.1	36.2	9.8	8.8	6.2	3.5	8.2	169.9	5.1	19.5	65.7	13.6	2.9
78.6	72.2	84.9	76.2	79.5	77.9	84.0	85.0	55.8	73.1	87.7	74.2	85.8	89.2
49.7	49.7	51.3	52.8	51.0	49.1	52.1	52.9	50.5	52.2	50.9	51.4	52.1	51.8
24.7	27.8	33.9	38.7	36.3	26.5	44.3	42.4	28.2	35.4	34.4	34.2	40.7	37.5
10.9	9.3	7.1	7.3	6.5	9.6	6.0	6.8	8.7	7.1	7.4	6.6	6.1	7.4
28.9	23.7	20.5	18.4	19.6	27.2	17.4	17.6	26.5	21.3	19.8	20.9	18.7	20.2
52.5	59.1	54.8	52.0	56.0	52.5	52.7	50.0	58.2	50.2	55.3	57.7	51.4	50.6
7.7	7.9	17.6	22.3	17.9	10.7	23.9	25.6	6.6	21.4	17.5	14.8	23.8	21.8
6,358	12,421	27,629	5,167	7,080	3,049	2,450	7,888	93,620	3,328	13,703	26,427	9,484	2,111
4,659	9,476	17,207	3,465	5,899	2,445	2,227	5,804	75,122	2,595	9,013	19,191	7,050	1,887
336	2,658	7,039	364	67	281		397	6,260	341	3,436	383	3	
4,071	627	1,294	683	83	1,679	397	945	7,186	554	2,656	8,728	1,343	806
30	89	65	17	34	4	20	24	452	34	21	79	18	3
13	20	131	17	4	2	14	24	1,032	8	18	33	11	2
1,205	2,880	5,506	1,629	1,434	673	576	1,803	21,702	744	1,116	3,112	2,886	294
72	1,289	296	71	147	18	15	63	1,231	22	157	154	80	6
1,023	631	972	374	726	178	152	308	8,419	171	4,009	8,028	416	339
265	601	2,145	597	511	175	182	734	8,400	360	329	1,208	865	156
1	77	84	20	25		5	22	1,286		54	148	6	10
	53	8		13	3	7		707	21	79	145	13	
11.8	15.8	15.5	14.2	18.4	11.9	17.7	15.7	18.3	14.2	14.7	19.1	15.6	14.4
3,136	6,248	13,627	2,776	3,607	1,515	1,257	4,243	46,373	1,790	6,938	12,958	4,973	1,091
1,488	2,351	5,866	801	1,229	703	378	1,237	19,163	578	3,079	5,139	1,452	371
2,611	5,116	10,142	1,999	2,821	1,256	955	3,040	39,140	1,295	5,114	10,377	3,710	821
766	1,802	3,763	560	907	373	338	902	18,263	471	1,594	3,626	1,097	288
1,599	2,895	4,646	806	1,212	722	366	1,186	24,963	584	3,386	4,844	1,488	336
86.1	83.5	75.1	85.0	84.6	78.1	84.9	80.1	87.2	74.0	82.6'	80.8	84.3	91.4
31.6	37.6	54.9	43.1	44.0	26.8	39.6	49.1	47.2	52.7	36.8	50.5	43.8	59.1
12.8	28.4	27.6	3.9	18.4	16.2		21.8	49.6	21.7	9.5	33.3	16.0	26.4
37.6	7.0	4.3	9.1	1.6	33.0	12.3	8.6	6.4	11.7	18.5	31.8	10.0	29.6
22.2	25.4	25.9	27.4	25.7	23.9	23.1	26.4	23.3	27.0	26.7	20.1	26.4	26.2
19.3	18.7	22.1	28.7	16.2	14.0	10.6	24.2	14.8	16.2	14.2	10.8	23.8	7.5
52.3	57.5	49.6	47.7	50.3	47.8	52.7	44.4	76.0	53.3	42.3	60.0	44.7	48.6
13.2	10.0	10.3	7.9	6.9	10.2	10.5	7.3	26.9	13.6	8.5	15.0	8.4	12.3
19.0	16.6	14.3	12.8	12.7	13.5	14.7	14.1	17.3	11.8	18.7	14.8	12.3	14.6
5.7	5.8	11.1	15.2	10.9	6.8	17.2	17.1	4.9	13.8	11.9	9.4	13.9	16.0
8.8	25.8	11.1	27.5	12.7	10.0	13.7	11.0	10.0	20.7	9.9	12.7	11.8	10.9
2.1	4.5	5.7	7.0	5.4	4.1	2.8	3.9	6.1	3.0	4.6	3.8	4.2	4.8

COUNTY POPULATION

	COOKE	CORYELL	COTTLE	CRANE	CROCKETT	CROSBY	CULBERSON	DALLAM	DALLAS	DAWSON	DEAF SMITH
1982 Population[E]	28,463	59,809	2,895	4,741	4,824	9,064	3,616	6,645	1,606,720	16,159	22,134
1980 Population											
1980 Census of Population	27,656	56,767	2,947	4,600	4,608	8,859	3,315	6,531	1,556,390	16,184	21,165
Rank in State	72	40	228	214	213	172	225	191	2	122	96
% Change 1970-80	17.8	60.8	-8.0	10.3	18.6	-2.5	-3.3	8.6	17.2	-2.5	11.4
Urban Residents	14,081	39,484		3,622	3,766		2,772	4,571	1,547,093	11,790	15,853
% Change 1970-80	1.8	53.9		5.7	31.5			5.3	17.7	2.0	18.2
Rural Residents	13,575	17,283	2,947	978	842	8,859	543	1,960	9,297	4,394	5,312
% Change 1970-80	40.8	79.0	-8.0	31.3	-17.5	-2.5	-84.2	17.2	-28.2	-12.9	-4.9
Population Per Square Mile	31.0	53.7	3.3	5.9	1.6	9.9	0.9	4.3	1,768.6	17.9	14.1
Native Texans 1980[T]	78.0	33.9	86.1	71.9	76.1	87.9	75.3	57.0	64.3	85.5	73.0
Age 1980											
Female (%)	50.3	40.9	52.1	50.8	50.3	51.6	49.4	50.5	51.5	51.4	50.6
Median Age	30.8	22.6	38.5	27.0	27.3	28.7	24.3	29.0	28.4	29.1	25.3
Under Age 5 (%)	7.7	8.6	7.4	10.0	9.7	9.4	10.0	9.8	7.7	9.5	11.2
Age 5-17 (%)	21.2	18.9	19.1	24.5	24.5	25.1	29.0	23.3	21.2	23.8	27.2
Age 18-64 (%)	56.6	67.0	50.9	57.5	56.5	51.4	53.9	54.4	63.3	53.6	53.1
Age 65 and Over (%)	14.5	5.5	22.6	8.0	9.3	14.1	7.1	12.5	7.8	13.1	8.5
Age 18 and Over (1980)	19,659	41,147	2,166	3,015	3,031	5,804	2,024	4,368	1,106,830	10,794	13,047
Registered Voters (11/2/82)	14,337	14,218	1,778	2,654	2,592	4,049	1,736	2,569	675,390	7,826	8,514
1980 Selected Ancestry Groups											
Black	1,204	10,774	201	128	51	530		165	287,541	637	395
Hispanic	559	4,663	420	1,128	2,053	3,279	2,101	1,090	154,561	6,098	8,607
American Indian/Eskimo	146	342	2	7	20	5	6	43	6,487	11	36
Asian/Pacific Islander	76	1,261	6	12	3	4	8	28	15,034	36	37
English[F]	3,770	6,631	611	880	603	1,427	256	1,039	210,295	2,952	2,595
French[F]	178	648	27	26	12	32	8	16	12,704	60	118
German[F]	4,304	4,932	88	188	209	149	67	377	70,234	532	1,251
Irish[F]	1,709	2,372	240	324	206	340	66	303	67,388	824	884
Italian[F]	85	307		24		12		7	9,826		25
Polish[F]	59	243	3				8		6,676		34
Veterans 1980 (1980)	166	19.6	12.1	16.1	17.1	11.1	13.4	15.5	17.0	11.3	12.9
1980 Family Characteristics											
Households	10,078	14,090	1,164	1,552	1,558	2,920	987	2,386	577,701	5,483	6,487
Single Persons (Age 15+)	4,318	15,193	332	502	596	1,180	480	837	300,131	2,059	2,877
Families	7,669	11,836	854	1,271	1,219	2,330	832	1,774	401,364	4,394	5,433
Both Spouses Employed	2,741	3,946	255	365	372	672	233	547	169,973	1,334	1,924
With Children Under Age 18	3,716	7,467	375	784	692	1,276	546	954	216,518	2,155	3,331
Child. Living w/Two Parents (%)	80.5	84.2	88.6	85.4	83.6	84.4	81.4	82.8	72.9	83.3	85.6
Employed Mothers/Ages 0-5 (%)	48.9	39.9	31.8	28.0	27.8	31.9	47.0	35.6	55.8	43.6	38.2
Age 3-4 in Nursery School	14.2	18.3	26.7		24.4	26.2	9.4	5.7	42.8	29.6	25.0
Foreign Language In Home (%)[S]	3.4	11.6	13.7	22.8	46.8	35.7	69.4	14.2	11.4	36.0	40.4
Age 60+ Living Alone (%)	26.3	25.7	28.0	23.1	25.6	25.3	11.7	37.2	25.0	25.2	21.1
1980											
School Dropouts Age 16-19 (%)	18.2	15.5	30.9	29.7	29.5	21.4	15.7	20.7	19.0	21.0	21.7
H.S. Graduates Age 25+ (%)	58.1	72.2	41.9	57.6	50.3	45.3	44.3	58.1	71.2	42.9	51.4
College Graduates Age 25+	10.1	12.2	7.5	7.1	9.4	8.1	9.8	7.9	21.8	8.3	12.6
1982											
Birth Rate[R]	17.4	15.2	19.0	24.5	20.9	17.1	25.4	17.6	19.3	24.9	21.3
Death Rate[R]	9.3	3.9	16.2	7.0	9.1	11.8	5.3	9.9	6.8	10.2	5.8
Marriage Rate[R]	44.1	9.3	11.7	17.3	10.4	7.5	16.6	11.6	13.0	12.1	10.8
Divorce Rate[R]	5.4	4.2	3.5	4.2	2.5	2.8	1.7	3.3	7.6	4.1	3.6

[E]Estimate.   [T]Born in Texas and residing in Texas in 1980.   [R]Per 1,000 population.   [1]Verified by the Bureau of Census   [2]Verified by the Elections Division
[M]Employed female with children ages 0-5   [S]Children ages 5+ who speak a language other than English at home.   [F]Those reporting single ancestry.

FLYING THE COLORS: TEXAS ©JOHN CLEMENTS 1984

DELTA	DENTON	DE WITT	DICKENS	DIMMIT	DONLEY	DUVAL	EASTLAND	ECTOR	EDWARDS	ELLIS	EL PASO	ERATH	FALLS
4,848	160,821	19,016	3,518	11,957	4,178	12,842	19,762	121,052	2,127	62,839	513,302	23,518	18,039
4,839	143,126	18,903	3,539	11,367	4,075	12,517	19,480	115,374	2,033	59,743	479,899	22,560	17,946
207	17	104	224	150	218	144	101	22	240	38	5	91	110
−1.8	89.2	1.3	−5.3	25.8	11.9	6.8	7.7	24.5	−3.5	28.1	33.6	24.4	3.7
	111,281	9,449		6,886		7,544	11,406	100,957		29,960	461,084	14,604	7,099
	126.5	0.4		28.1		14.9	9.3	23.7		22.3	33.7	20.8	11.8
4,839	31,845	9,454	3,539	4,481	4,075	4,973	8,074	14,417	2,033	29,783	18,815	7,956	10,847
−1.8	20.2	2.2	−5.3	22.3	11.9	−3.6	5.4	41.9	−3.5	34.5	31.1	31.4	−0.9
17.4	157.1	20.8	3.9	8.7	4.4	7.0	21.1	127.8	1.0	63.6	473.3	20.9	23.3
85.1	59.0	91.6	86.1	76.2	78.3	91.5	83.5	68.9	82.4	81.0	49.9	81.7	91.1
53.2	50.8	52.5	51.8	50.8	52.3	51.0	51.8	50.1	51.5	51.1	51.0	51.7	52.4
42.7	27.0	36.8	38.4	24.7	39.7	28.2	39.2	27.1	29.7	30.2	25.0	32.6	38.9
5.0	8.0	7.0	7.6	10.7	6.0	9.2	6.3	9.3	8.7	7.9	9.4	6.5	6.6
20.0	21.2	20.0	20.1	28.0	17.2	25.5	16.5	21.7	27.1	23.4	25.8	16.7	19.4
48.6	64.4	57.9	49.8	51.3	55.0	51.4	54.0	62.0	49.4	55.7	58.2	57.0	51.0
26.4	6.4	21.1	22.5	10.0	21.8	13.9	23.2	7.0	14.8	13.0	6.6	19.8	23.0
3,633	101,450	13,809	2,561	6,970	3,131	[1]8,175	15,037	79,528	1,305	41,065	310,909	17,322	13,286
2,921	66,231	8,482	2,028	6,445	2,481	[2]8,615	10,952	49,421	1,116	28,809	150,749	12,081	9,505
397	6,173	2,054	163	67	174	10	371	5,154	2	7,433	18,151	181	4,883
20	6,402	4,363	587	8,845	150	10,735	929	24,831	967	5,774	297,001	920	1,690
22	586	9	2	20	8	12	46	535	12	134	1,515	33	26
4	1,507	8	3	14	2	2	33	444	2	73	4,053	70	21
741	20,587	1,373	601	557	907	468	4,030	13,485	481	8,958	25,053	5,681	2,000
25	1,365	84	48	65	59	20	158	736	17	316	2,192	228	33
108	9,006	4,631	46	181	182	295	951	4,390	93	2,111	15,475	1,218	2,252
500	7,822	638	232	176	414	227	1,490	4,112	97	3,117	8,075	1,738	845
4	977	26		4			26	348	8	101	2,689	62	112
	579	560		5			12	162	3	97	1,599	42	285
15.9	17.2	14.1	11.6	11.7	16.0	12.5	15.6	17.1	11.9	17.2	16.9	14.6	16.6
1,932	49,134	7,056	1,369	3,135	1,608	3,738	7,730	40,450	697	19,866	140,806	8,699	6,920
582	28,513	2,985	426	1,916	571	2,201	2,800	16,402	246	8,916	95,839	4,000	2,983
1,377	36,973	5,135	1,004	2,650	1,204	3,074	5,452	31,632	535	16,002	114,454	6,174	4,803
433	17,940	1,496	309	827	395	705	1,713	11,552	121	6,398	31,372	2,073	1,524
495	20,936	2,316	428	1,688	445	1,644	2,169	17,460	282	8,406	71,826	2,652	2,019
78.2	85.0	79.4	85.6	81.7	84.6	78.7	83.7	82.3	78.8	80.6	76.6	84.0	72.6
52.8	51.5	44.0	43.1	34.3	35.7	34.1	40.8	39.3	25.3	48.2	42.4	48.9	54.4
17.0	40.9	14.0	16.2	31.9	8.0	22.9	17.6	24.6	20.3	22.6	23.0	29.9	20.7
1.3	6.8	28.2	17.5	77.9	2.1	84.3	4.8	21.0	46.7	11.1	62.4	5.5	10.9
27.6	23.9	24.7	28.6	15.8	25.8	16.4	28.1	22.9	26.8	24.4	20.1	25.2	30.0
10.4	11.5	17.2	15.8	23.0	5.0	18.0	13.2	22.3	32.0	17.3	13.2	13.1	14.2
41.6	76.9	39.5	40.3	35.4	52.6	36.6	49.9	61.1	50.2	55.7	59.5	58.3	42.3
7.5	26.1	7.4	6.0	7.6	10.2	6.9	8.6	12.0	10.7	9.8	14.0	14.8	8.4
13.8	19.0	15.7	12.2	24.7	10.5	23.0	17.1	28.6	21.6	16.6	21.7	14.7	13.0
17.9	5.0	13.5	10.8	6.7	14.1	9.0	15.4	7.0	9.9	8.8	5.2	11.7	13.8
6.4	10.0	11.6	8.0	10.4	12.9	11.6	14.2	18.8	6.1	12.0	13.8	11.9	9.7
1.7	6.0	3.0	1.4	4.0	1.9	3.4	7.0	11.3	4.7	5.8	5.9	8.4	4.0

COUNTY POPULATION

	FANNIN	FAYETTE	FISHER	FLOYD	FOARD	FORT BEND	FRANKLIN	FREESTONE	FRIO	GAINES	GALVESTON
1982 Population[E]	24,643	19,106	5,860	10,017	2,119	151,665	7,322	15,930	14,554	13,546	201,474
1980 Population											
1980 Census of Population	24,285	18,832	5,891	9,834	2,158	130,846	6,893	14,830	13,785	13,150	195,940
Rank in State	84	106	195	162	238	18	188	126	134	142	12
% Change 1970-80	7.0	6.7	-7.1	-11.0	-2.4	150.1	30.3	33.4	23.5	13.4	15.4
Urban Residents	7,338	3,768		4,193		97,064	862	6,895	9,962	8,676	181,425
% Change 1970-80	-4.7	21.9	-100.0	2.0		233.9	0.8	140.5	79.7	73.3	19.6
Rural Residents	16,947	15,064	5,891	5,641	3,158	33,782	6,021	7,935	3,823	4,474	14,515
% Change 1970-80	12.9	3.5	-7.1	-18.7	-2.4	45.4	36.0	-3.8	-31.9	-32.1	-19.7
Population Per Square Mile	27.1	19.8	6.6	9.9	3.1	149.4	23.4	16.7	12.2	8.7	491.1
Native Texans 1980 (%)[T]	82.3	90.4	88.9	83.2	83.8	66.2	80.2	86.2	87.1	75.9	66.8
Age 1980											
Female (%)	51.8	51.0	51.5	50.9	52.5	48.9	51.7	52.4	51.2	50.4	50.8
Median Age	39.8	41.7	38.2	29.9	42.1	27.0	36.8	34.6	24.8	26.0	29.3
Under Age 5 (%)	6.0	6.3	6.9	8.8	6.5	9.9	7.3	7.8	11.0	10.1	8.1
Age 5-17 (%)	19.0	16.7	20.8	25.0	18.2	24.9	19.2	20.3	27.9	26.3	21.6
Age 18-64 (%)	52.7	53.3	51.3	51.7	50.0	60.2	54.0	51.2	50.6	54.5	61.2
Age 65 and Over (%)	22.3	23.7	21.0	14.5	25.3	5.0	19.5	20.7	10.5	9.1	9.1
Age 18 and Over (1980)	18,207	14,496	4,260	6,515	1,626	85,275	5,071	10,652	8,424	8,359	137,730
Registered Voters (11/2/82)	13,564	10,009	3,787	4,693	1,413	57,211	3,590	7,686	7,253	5,251	93,887
1980 Selected Ancestry Groups											
Black	1,824	1,687	246	401	132	20,420	409	3,198	62	357	36,328
Hispanic	324	968	1,107	3,333	238	26,656	78	301	9,427	4,028	23,557
Amerian Indian/Eskimo	61	26	10	23	4	276	18	22	23	30	525
Asian/Pacific Islander	26	12	6	12	2	3,725	10	35	17	17	1,762
English[F]	4,666	994	965	1,560	337	10,106	1,579	3,579	598	2,174	16,834
French[F]	97	61	66	77		1,455	35	124	82	106	2,854
German[F]	644	5,660	243	317	84	8,303	275	387	445	497	10,600
Irish[F]	1,868	422	478	469	116	3,234	313	1,105	444	557	7,543
Italian[F]	20	23	2	3		900	2	22	6	23	3,049
Polish[F]	52	73	12	5		1,246	6	23	54	7	797
Veterans 1980 (%)	19.4	15.1	13.9	11.9	15.1	16.8	17.2	14.9	10.9	12.1	18.7
1980 Family Characteristics											
Households	9,267	7,487	2,204	3,307	860	39,840	2,616	5,608	4,041	4,190	69,284
Single Persons (Age 15+)	3,246	3,003	767	1,276	283	19,102	744	1,860	2,090	1,753	34,044
Families	6,849	5,446	1,660	2,616	617	34,180	2,025	4,108	3,271	3,432	52,077
Both Spouses Employed	2,485	1,885	534	823	188	16,971	597	1,127	926	1,056	19,676
With Children Under Age 18	2,909	2,073	740	1,355	256	21,723	872	1,799	1,923	1,965	27,979
Child. Living w/Two Parents (%)	79.0	83.3	88.4	81.2	78.0	84.1	84.4	81.0	80.4	85.1	75.0
Employed Mothers/Ages 0-5 (%)[M]	51.4	49.5	47.0	34.5	49.0	54.5	36.8	41.6	42.3	24.7	52.4
Age 3-4 in Nursery School (%)	15.0	22.4	9.8	16.9	21.1	39.9	11.2	14.7	18.5	3.8	41.0
Foreign Language in Home (%)	2.3	26.8	18.0	32.9	11.3	23.1	2.5	2.9	67.9	32.3	11.8
Age 60+ Living Alone (%)	27.1	25.2	27.0	25.3	24.4	18.5	23.4	27.0	19.8	19.5	23.9
1980											
School Dropouts Age 16-19 (%)	12.6	7.7	13.8	18.5	7.7	20.0	23.3	12.4	33.1	25.1	17.5
H.S. Graduates Age 25+ (%)	47.0	39.8	47.0	45.1	47.5	71.6	51.0	49.3	40.7	50.9	65.3
College Graduates Age 25+	9.1	7.6	8.5	9.5	10.0	25.5	6.8	7.8	9.6	10.6	15.4
1982											
Birth Rate[R]	12.0	17.6	13.5	18.5	17.5	23.5	14.9	13.4	21.2	24.1	19.7
Death Rate[R]	13.8	16.5	14.2	11.4	14.2	4.3	13.4	12.1	6.8	5.6	8.2
Marriage Rate[R]	9.9	11.1	7.3	10.1	10.4	14.2	11.2	10.0	8.0	17.6	12.7
Divorce Rate[R]	6.0	4.0	4.1	3.3	3.8	5.0	3.8	5.1	2.8	6.7	3.4

[E] Estimate [T] Born in Texas and residing in Texas in 1980 [R] Per 1,000 population. [1] Verified by the Bureau of Census [2] Verified by the Elections Division
[M] Employed female with children ages 0-5 [S] Children ages 5+ who speak a language other than English at home. [F] Those reporting single ancestry.

GARZA	GILLESPIE	GLASSCOCK	GOLIAD	GONZALES	GRAY	GRAYSON	GREGG	GRIMES	GUADALUPE	HALE	HALL	HAMILTON	HANSFORD
5,384	14,151	1,339	5,307	17,068	26,158	90,830	104,690	13,986	50,021	38,657	5,535	8,542	6,178
5,336	13,532	1,304	5,193	16,949	26,386	89,796	99,495	13,580	46,708	37,592	5,594	8,297	6,209
198	137	246	201	118	75	28	24	136	45	58	196	179	193
0.9	28.2	12.9	6.7	3.1	-2.1	7.9	31.0	14.6	39.2	10.1	-7.0	15.3	-2.2
3,961	6,412			7,152	21,396	59,638	80,816	5,971	26,004	24,392	3,352	3,189	3,413
2.8	20.4			22.2	-1.5	2.3	41.5	16.8	30.1	16.1	3.9	15.5	-0.6
1,375	7,120	1,304	5,193	9,731	4,990	30,158	18,671	7,609	20,704	13,200	2,242	5,108	2,796
-4.2	36.2	12.9	6.7	-7.5	-4.5	20.8	-0.7	12.8	52.7	0.6	-19.6	15.1	-4.1
6.0	12.8	1.4	6.0	15.8	28.6	96.1	364.4	17.0	65.5	37.4	6.4	9.9	6.7
80.9	81.6	83.4	89.5	91.0	61.6	69.9	68.9	86.8	74.0	80.2	83.8	89.5	59.3
51.1	52.1	46.7	51.4	51.5	51.5	52.2	51.2	51.6	51.1	51.4	52.5	52.1	50.5
29.9	41.3	25.3	32.2	33.1	33.1	32.9	29.1	32.2	30.0	27.6	37.7	46.5	29.9
9.3	5.9	11.7	7.0	8.0	8.1	6.8	8.2	8.0	7.5	9.4	7.5	5.4	9.3
23.0	18.3	26.8	23.4	21.9	19.2	19.6	20.8	21.3	22.4	24.2	19.7	16.6	22.1
53.9	53.1	53.8	54.3	52.0	57.7	58.0	59.6	52.8	58.6	54.8	50.9	49.8	58.8
13.8	22.7	7.7	15.4	18.1	15.0	15.6	11.4	18.0	11.5	11.6	21.9	28.2	9.8
3,611	10,249	801	3,616	11,838	19,197	66,081	70,657	9,608	32,711	24,976	4,073	6,478	4,260
2,642	7,429	712	3,176	8,941	13,740	42,538	46,496	7,710	21,759	14,176	2,977	5,060	3,162
326	21	1	475	1,962	992	6,312	17,807	3,769	3,155	2,046	507		2
1,298	1,359	376	1,849	4,863	1,163	1,349	2,011	1,232	11,872	12,683	842	177	742
22	19	2	4	13	155	629	356	4	110	92	7	13	25
13	4	1	4	12	86	185	390	13	208	96	4	16	15
1,046	840	90	324	1,720	5,199	14,292	15,827	1,293	3,761	7,305	1,250	1,777	1,171
17	90		13	129	191	661	1,005	125	370	86	16	18	52
141	6,363	229	956	1,724	1,465	3,782	3,464	1,102	9,351	1,125	158	1,042	536
167	218	69	109	566	1,470	6,191	5,432	402	1,332	1,396	382	593	406
7	12	2		7	43	392	312	56	130	39			23
5	45		33	68	52	190	196	640	255	12		21	9
13.0	16.7	14.3	16.1	13.9	17.1	18.6	18.1	13.6	18.2	12.9	10.6	16.5	15.9
1,842	5,219	387	1,777	5,949	10,224	33,972	35,884	4,857	15,733	12,385	2,175	3,423	2,269
674	1,826	204	776	2,764	2,896	12,899	14,924	2,235	7,921	5,509	686	964	752
1,458	3,999	324	1,404	4,388	7,806	25,357	27,073	3,626	12,562	9,880	1,567	2,476	1,757
518	1,600	67	458	1,498	2,475	9,913	9,791	995	4,874	3,498	498	778	707
753	1,668	193	685	2,003	3,691	11,938	13,925	1,675	6,717	5,343	739	938	957
87.5	86.0	90.9	86.0	75.8	84.6	80.6	76.6	68.4	82.7	80.1	80.6	84.3	89.0
41.3	61.6	19.5	43.8	48.3	33.9	56.0	43.2	51.1	54.9	41.2	38.3	36.7	47.4
3.1	24.0	2.5	28.0	25.2	21.7	32.3	31.7	27.1	24.9	18.2	19.7	10.1	5.2
24.8	39.6	31.9	38.6	28.9	5.0	2.4	3.6	10.0	28.8	32.4	14.1	8.2	11.7
23.5	21.5	22.7	21.8	27.5	26.9	26.2	26.4	24.6	23.6	24.5	27.8	23.9	31.0
31.1	18.7	14.2	19.7	14.2	22.8	18.0	16.3	15.1	10.4	17.1	38.2	9.8	24.3
44.4	53.3	51.4	44.4	40.9	61.4	60.5	65.5	45.6	57.6	53.3	48.0	45.7	66.5
9.7	11.3	10.6	8.2	7.8	11.3	12.9	14.5	10.1	11.2	11.1	6.6	9.5	12.4
17.1	13.8	28.4	16.8	22.1	21.4	16.4	20.2	22.8	17.3	21.2	11.0	11.7	26.5
9.5	11.9	8.2	10.2	14.1	10.1	11.0	9.2	12.6	8.1	9.1	15.7	15.8	6.2
10.7	12.5	6.7	13.9	11.5	15.8	14.0	17.1	12.9	14.5	11.0	11.2	10.0	13.4
4.1	4.2	1.5	2.8	7.6	7.3	8.4	6.8	4.1	5.2	4.6	4.7	4.4	5.0

COUNTY POPULATION

	HARDEMAN	HARDIN	HARRIS	HARRISON	HARTLEY	HASKELL	HAYS	HEMPHILL	HENDERSON	HIDALGO	HILL
1982 Population[E]	6,350	43,398	2,571,295	53,923	4,266	7,588	41,180	5,873	46,704	311,966	25,515

1980 Population

	HARDEMAN	HARDIN	HARRIS	HARRISON	HARTLEY	HASKELL	HAYS	HEMPHILL	HENDERSON	HIDALGO	HILL
1980 Census of Population	6,368	40,721	2,409,547	52,265	3,987	7,725	40,594	5,304	42,606	283,323	25,024
Rank in State	192	51	1	42	220	181	52	200	47	7	80
% Change 1970-80	–6.3	35.8	38.3	16.6	43.3	–9.2	46.9	72.0	61.0	56.0	10.7
Urban Residents	3,890	16,027	2,322,988	26,598	2,283	3,827	23,420	3,491	10,197	212,481	7,397
% Change 1970-80	–1.5	108.1	39.6	16.0	67.3	1.1	24.2		6.4	58.0	2.4
Rural Residents	2,478	24,694	86,559	25,667	1,704	3,898	17,174	1,813	32,409	70,748	17,627
% Change 1970-80	–13.0	10.8	11.5	17.2	20.3	–17.5	95.6	–41.2	92.0	50.5	14.7
Population Per Square Mile	9.3	45.3	1,389.6	57.6	2.7	8.6	59.9	5.9	48.0	180.5	25.9

	HARDEMAN	HARDIN	HARRIS	HARRISON	HARTLEY	HASKELL	HAYS	HEMPHILL	HENDERSON	HIDALGO	HILL
Native Texans 1980 (%)[T]	79.5	79.0	59.3	75.0	61.0	89.4	76.4	62.6	79.6	65.2	85.5

Age 1980

	HARDEMAN	HARDIN	HARRIS	HARRISON	HARTLEY	HASKELL	HAYS	HEMPHILL	HENDERSON	HIDALGO	HILL
Female (%)	53.3	50.8	50.1	52.1	50.8	51.6	51.3	48.8	51.5	52.0	52.8
Median Age	38.7	29.5	27.5	30.3	32.8	40.7	22.9	26.5	37.6	24.1	39.1
Under Age 5 (%)	7.2	8.3	8.4	8.0	8.0	7.0	6.0	11.4	6.5	10.5	6.3
Age 5-17 (%)	19.9	24.0	21.7	22.4	23.3	19.4	18.6	21.2	19.4	28.8	19.1
Age 18-64 (%)	51.0	57.4	63.8	55.8	55.3	50.9	67.3	58.1	57.0	51.5	52.6
Age 65 and Over (%)	21.9	10.3	6.1	13.8	13.4	22.7	8.1	9.3	17.1	9.2	22.0

	HARDEMAN	HARDIN	HARRIS	HARRISON	HARTLEY	HASKELL	HAYS	HEMPHILL	HENDERSON	HIDALGO	HILL
Age 18 and Over (1980)	4,643	27,573	1,685,081	36,363	2,738	5,691	30,623	3,574	31,565	171,913	18,685
Registered Voters (11/2/82)	3,222	24,798	1,022,500	24,818	2,152	4,624	19,466	2,407	24,200	108,708	13,142

1980 Selected Ancestry Groups

	HARDEMAN	HARDIN	HARRIS	HARRISON	HARTLEY	HASKELL	HAYS	HEMPHILL	HENDERSON	HIDALGO	HILL
Black	520	4,138	473,695	16,447	20	345	1,102	8	4,620	544	2,551
Hispanic	510	572	369,007	802	178	1,195	12,386	545	619	230,212	1,414
American Indian/Eskimo	28	40	5,346	93	8	17	80	26	92	271	45
Asian/Pacific Islander	5	36	46,355	64	1	12	123	6	60	419	41
English[F]	1,344	6,792	222,499	7,705	767	1,693	4,505	439	7,001	8,326	3,969
French[F]	13	1,567	32,582	512	37	29	517	23	359	646	164
German[F]	259	1,426	116,232	1,520	294	496	3,597	170	1,298	5,131	1,220
Irish[F]	551	2,792	77,196	2,977	241	493	1,391	222	2,741	2,318	1,911
Italian[F]	9	128	23,224	61	4	8	261		83	399	33
Polish[F]	6	58	19,240	55	2	8	191		66	631	22

	HARDEMAN	HARDIN	HARRIS	HARRISON	HARTLEY	HASKELL	HAYS	HEMPHILL	HENDERSON	HIDALGO	HILL
Veterans 1980 (%)	15.9	18.0	16.5	16.9	16.8	13.8	11.5	14.3	18.6	10.0	15.8

1980 Family Characteristics

	HARDEMAN	HARDIN	HARRIS	HARRISON	HARTLEY	HASKELL	HAYS	HEMPHILL	HENDERSON	HIDALGO	HILL
Households	2,476	13,727	869,882	18,049	1,361	2,981	12,583	1,837	16,087	75,816	9,683
Single Persons (Age 15+)	780	5,150	469,757	8,033	435	921	14,837	621	5,234	51,855	3,459
Families	1,786	11,305	612,753	13,885	1,149	2,243	8,179	1,457	12,611	64,691	7,058
Both Spouses Employed	534	3,265	245,535	4,831	390	720	3,263	531	3,756	18,551	2,102
With Children Under Age 18	796	6,198	348,092	7,057	596	921	4,305	840	5,291	40,364	2,859
Child. Living w/Two Parents (%)	76.7	83.2	76.1	73.6	93.0	83.9	79.6	87.7	79.3	80.3	81.0
Employed Mothers/Ages 0-5 (%)[M]	38.5	32.0	49.0	48.7	38.2	40.9	54.4	40.1	48.1	46.8	47.7
Age 3-4 in Nursery School (%)	43.1	19.1	37.2	24.9	17.4	13.9	32.8	20.7	17.0	25.1	19.1
Foreign Language in Home (%)	7.6	2.5	17.4	3.4	5.3	16.1	30.3	7.2	2.3	80.4	8.1
Age 60+ Living Alone (%)	27.0	22.8	23.3	26.2	18.4	26.1	19.7	21.6	20.4	17.2	25.6

1980

	HARDEMAN	HARDIN	HARRIS	HARRISON	HARTLEY	HASKELL	HAYS	HEMPHILL	HENDERSON	HIDALGO	HILL
School Dropouts Age 16-19 (%)	14.2	16.8	20.7	16.8	8.2	21.7	6.1	32.8	17.3	19.8	15.7
H.S. Graduates Age 25+ (%)	47.2	56.7	70.5	56.4	73.0	44.1	62.1	56.4	50.7	41.1	45.5
College Graduates Age 25+ (%)	10.3	9.1	23.0	12.3	18.2	10.9	22.6	9.5	8.4	10.8	8.0

1982

	HARDEMAN	HARDIN	HARRIS	HARRISON	HARTLEY	HASKELL	HAYS	HEMPHILL	HENDERSON	HIDALGO	HILL
Birth Rate[R]	14.6	17.5	21.9	16.5	12.7	15.6	17.0	27.1	13.7	24.5	12.8
Death Rate[R]	13.1	7.7	6.0	10.6	8.7	14.5	6.1	4.9	10.9	5.4	14.2
Marriage Rate[R]	12.3	14.2	12.9	29.0	8.0	12.5	12.2	18.0	12.3	11.8	11.0
Divorce Rate[R]	4.3	13.3	8.1	6.3	2.8	5.8	4.0	2.6	3.0	3.8	5.6

[E]Estimate   [T]Born in Texas and residing in Texas in 1980   [R]Per 1,000 population.   [1]Verified by the Bureau of Census   [2]Verified by the Elections Division
[M]Employed female with children ages 0-5   [S]Children ages 5+ who speak a language other than English at home.   [F]Those reporting single ancestry.

FLYING THE COLORS: TEXAS ©JOHN CLEMENTS 1984

HOCKLEY	HOOD	HOPKINS	HOUSTON	HOWARD	HUDSPETH	HUNT	HUTCHINSON	IRION	JACK	JACKSON	JASPER	JEFF DAVIS	JEFFERSON
23,916	20,449	26,255	23,178	32,353	2,943	56,692	26,522	1,464	7,566	13,407	32,183	1,709	250,901
23,230	17,714	25,247	22,299	33,142	2,728	55,248	26,304	1,386	7,408	13,352	30,781	1,647	250,938
87	113	78	93	64	231	41	76	245	183	139	68	243	9
13.9	178.2	21.9	24.9	-12.3	14.0	15.2	7.6	29.5	10.4	2.9	24.7	7.9	1.8
13,809	3,332	12,804	7,405	24,804		30,297	15,837		4,000	5,650	6,959		236,664
20.7		20.3	11.9	-13.7		-4.1	-5.2		12.5	6.0	11.3		1.8
9,421	14,382	12,443	14,894	8,338	2,728	24,951	10,467	1,386	3,408	7,702	23,822	1,647	14,274
5.3	125.8	23.6	32.5	-8.0	14.0	52.4	35.4	29.5	8.0	0.8	29.2	7.9	15.3
25.6	41.7	32.0	18.1	36.8	0.6	65.8	30.2	1.3	8.1	15.8	33.4	0.7	267.8
80.8	68.9	83.8	86.3	76.6	57.2	77.3	59.8	81.7	84.6	88.6	81.5	75.0	67.0
49.8	50.3	51.7	45.2	50.6	48.1	51.6	50.2	49.9	51.4	51.1	51.5	50.6	51.5
25.8	35.3	33.3	33.3	31.7	25.5	32.0	32.0	32.0	35.2	30.9	31.3	33.0	29.7
10.3	6.7	7.4	6.1	7.7	10.7	6.7	8.8	7.1	7.5	8.2	7.8	8.0	7.8
23.4	18.6	20.2	18.3	20.8	26.7	20.2	19.0	23.5	18.8	21.8	23.6	20.7	20.6
56.5	60.3	54.7	57.8	59.1	54.4	58.5	59.8	53.7	54.6	56.2	54.8	56.7	60.4
9.8	14.4	17.7	17.8	12.3	8.2	14.6	12.4	15.7	19.1	13.8	13.8	14.6	11.2
15,403	13,231	18,268	16,862	23,693	1,707	40,400	19,002	961	5,466	9,351	21,124	1,174	179,731
11,758	9,657	11,793	10,632	15,343	1,255	25,318	13,294	794	4,193	6,909	16,100	981	122,000
929	18	2,552	7,213	1,330	11	7,006	687		71	1,376	5,942	2	70,810
6,279	475	397	809	6,977	1,589	1,321	1,262	257	97	2,494	382	777	10,279
72	61	36	36	120	12	174	219	2	33	11	30	3	449
12	36	28	24	164	4	152	86		13	6	22	1	2,652
2,983	3,233	5,548	4,044	4,712	157	9,257	5,670	162	1,809	1,227	6,545	180	29,513
97	178	133	201	232	7	385	262	4	45	122	802	10	19,827
1,092	732	694	596	1,129	102	1,629	1,364	89	326	1,092	753	74	7,323
1,213	1,234	1,428	1,553	1,616	82	2,888	1,705	85	474	554	1,519	27	9,602
25	118	63	94	63	10	140	55		12	36	72	4	3,628
4	15	2	53	15	4	129	40			113	12		461
12.7	22.0	14.6	17.0	17.5	11.8	17.4	19.2	15.1	15.6	15.3	15.3	17.3	16.7
7,522	6,759	9,528	7,204	11,965	822	20,331	9,837	507	2,894	4,685	10,708	592	90,245
3,497	1,990	3,079	3,999	4,684	395	9,473	3,116	191	821	2,105	4,041	221	43,499
6,098	5,430	7,278	5,351	9,139	680	14,921	7,727	393	2,183	3,636	8,501	458	67,876
1,912	1,543	2,453	1,546	3,013	158	5,669	2,463	126	703	983	2,329	133	20,946
3,363	2,297	3,333	2,154	4,602	421	7,056	3,672	209	978	1,881	4,267	210	34,071
84.1	84.7	81.0	68.7	77.9	83.8	77.3	85.7	86.1	92.0	78.7	81.2	88.3	74.7
33.0	27.3	51.3	42.3	39.7	29.9	55.9	35.4	43.8	39.5	31.0	36.3	33.6	45.8
13.8	26.5	18.2	20.3	33.4	3.9	26.0	19.3	9.4	5.9	8.7	8.2	23.6	34.5
26.4	3.7	2.1	4.3	21.2	61.2	3.6	5.1	19.0	2.3	20.4	1.9	49.5	7.9
24.2	17.7	24.6	24.7	25.7	17.8	26.4	20.8	29.2	25.2	24.8	23.7	20.5	23.6
22.1	17.1	25.9	15.8	14.8	22.8	15.7	18.6	15.5	16.1	14.4	14.3	13.1	9.0
51.6	62.4	51.3	48.5	54.3	46.3	56.6	64.4	59.1	49.3	45.5	51.6	55.0	63.5
9.9	13.1	10.3	7.8	10.0	9.3	13.7	12.4	11.6	6.7	8.8	7.7	22.4	13.6
23.6	13.9	15.2	12.0	23.1	18.7	14.6	23.2	18.4	16.8	20.9	17.3	7.0	18.7
7.2	9.2	11.9	12.1	10.8	3.7	10.2	9.5	8.2	14.1	11.1	10.3	7.6	9.2
12.4	13.7	10.7	9.0	17.0	9.2	12.0	17.0	15.0	13.3	11.3	11.9	11.7	12.7
6.2	1.2	7.0	3.9	3.6	2.7	6.3	9.1	2.7	7.7	3.8	7.3	2.9	6.8

COUNTY POPULATION

	JIM HOGG	JIM WELLS	JOHNSON	JONES	KARNES	KAUFMAN	KENDALL	KENEDY	KENT	KERR	KIMBLE
1982 Population[E]	5,372	37,473	73,071	17,541	13,635	40,714	11,439	590	1,111	30,768	4,083
1980 Population											
1980 Census of Population	5,168	36,498	67,649	17,268	13,593	39,029	10,635	543	1,145	28,780	4,063
Rank in State	203	59	36	117	135	54	155	252	249	70	219
% Change 1970-80	11.0	10.5	47.8	7.2	1.0	20.4	52.7	-19.9	-20.2	47.9	4.1
Urban Residents	4,684	24,839	35,565	11,079	7,652	17,890	3,229			15,276	2,593
% Change 1970-80	14.8	2.9	52.0	3.0	8.0	-1.7				20.5	-2.3
Rural Residents	484	11,659	32,084	6,189	5,941	21,125	7,406	543	1,145	13,504	1,470
% Change 1970-80	-15.8	31.0	43.4	15.7	-6.9	48.8	6.3	-19.9	-20.2	99.1	17.6
Population Per Square Mile	4.5	42.1	92.5	18.5	18.1	49.5	16.0	0.4	1.3	26.0	3.3
Native Texans 1980 (%)[T]	89.4	87.7	76.2	87.0	90.7	82.0	74.1	86.9	88.3	65.9	83.9
Age 1980											
Female (%)	51.3	50.7	51.2	52.1	51.5	51.6	51.9	49.9	49.2	52.9	50.8
Median Age (%)	28.0	26.8	30.5	35.8	30.0	32.1	36.1	30.1	40.7	42.3	38.4
Under Age 5 (%)	9.8	9.4	7.5	7.1	8.6	7.1	6.1	8.1	5.8	5.9	6.1
Age 5-17 (%)	25.5	25.7	23.2	21.3	22.9	22.4	21.8	22.6	19.0	16.9	20.9
Age 18-64 (%)	51.8	54.8	57.6	52.7	53.1	56.5	56.1	56.4	55.5	53.4	53.3
Age 65 and Over (%)	12.9	10.1	11.7	18.9	15.4	14.1	16.0	12.9	19.7	23.8	19.7
Age 18 and Over (1980)	3,344[1]	23,681	46,899	12,350	9,306	27,527	7,666	376	862	22,206	2,968
Registered Voters (11/2/82)	4,027[2]	20,949	30,293	8,523	7,047	18,697	5,967	310	883	15,728	2,303
1980 Selected Ancestry Groups											
Black		214	1,923	758	387	7,393	24		13	757	2
Hispanic	4,679	24,519	2,771	2,532	5,844	1,654	1,406	450	89	3,878	707
American Indian/Eskimo		38	129	41	9	66	26	4		62	2
Asian/Pacific Islander	1	41	133	58	16	86	20		1	66	1
English[F]	88	1,815	12,430	2,601	660	6,431	1,059	8	285	4,029	520
French[F]	27	187	402	104	71	218	54	5	6	245	47
German[F]	86	1,746	3,037	695	1,220	1,164	2,401	14	20	3,157	387
Irish[F]	55	864	4,034	1,331	359	2,090	331	7	78	1,366	368
Italian[F]		17	185	25	3	105	39		8	103	5
Polish[F]		175	163	11	1,326	60	6	4		103	
Veterans 1980 (%)	12.1	13.1	17.6	14.7	14.2	16.2	20.2	5.9	15.7	20.1	14.1
1980 Family Characteristics											
Households	1,564	11,165	23,122	6,367	4,522	13,154	3,801	169	431	11,171	1,564
Single Persons (Age 15+)	929	5,801	8,896	2,270	2,374	6,032	1,561	120	167	3,827	518
Families	1,319	9,251	18,817	4,813	3,539	10,261	2,975	135	341	8,285	1,171
Both Spouses Employed	345	2,727	7,508	1,519	1,110	4,339	1,022	41	124	2,525	386
With Children Under Age 18	732	5,309	10,264	2,168	1,749	5,240	1,450	81	149	3,101	551
Child. Living w/Two Parents	82.2	82.6	85.1	81.3	82.1	78.0	87.8	81.2	85.8	76.8	87.4
Employed Mothers/Ages 0-5 (%)[M]	36.3	37.5	46.4	43.7	43.2	55.3	40.5	29.5	34.0	55.1	41.8
Age 3-4 in Nursery School (%)	25.7	22.6	21.4	34.9	14.1	29.7	25.2		33.1		50.0
Foreign Language in Home (%)	89.0	66.5	4.8	14.5	49.8	4.8	19.2	88.2	9.5	16.4	20.6
Age 60+ Living Alone	20.9	21.1	23.2	27.0	24.0	24.9	21.9	8.0	21.5	19.0	24.2
1980											
School Dropouts Age 16-19 (%)	22.3	19.3	18.5	20.2	14.2	20.0	13.0	47.0	7.4	17.9	26.1
H.S. Graduates Age 25+ (%)	34.8	43.1	60.3	47.2	38.8	52.0	64.9	33.9	52.9	64.2	51.9
College Graduates Age 25+ (%)	9.4	8.8	10.5	9.9	8.6	10.7	17.2	16.6	9.8	16.8	8.0
1982											
Birth Rate[R]	22.0	23.4	16.9	14.6	17.4	16.0	12.9	5.1	17.1	12.4	15.9
Death Rate[R]	9.5	7.9	8.1	13.9	11.7	10.6	11.2	13.6	10.8	13.1	11.0
Marriage Rate[R]	3.7	11.8	12.0	12.8	7.6	21.7	10.6	10.2	9.0	11.0	12.7
Divorce Rate[R]	4.5	5.1	3.7	5.1	0.7	4.8	3.4		3.6	5.9	6.6

[E]Estimate   [T]Born in Texas and residing in Texas in 1980   [R]Per 1,000 population.   [1]Verified by the Bureau of Census   [2]Verified by the Elections Division
[M]Employed female with children ages 0-5   [S]Children ages 5+ who speak a language other than English at home.   [F]Those reporting single ancestry.

KING	KINNEY	KLEBERG	KNOX	LAMAR	LAMB	LAMPASAS	LA SALLE	LAVACA	LEE	LEON	LIBERTY	LIMESTONE	LIPSCOMB
432	2,409	33,743	5,243	43,532	18,976	12,628	5,656	19,201	11,639	9,859	50,768	20,602	3,864
425	2,279	33,358	5,329	42,156	18,669	12,005	5,514	19,004	10,952	9,594	47,088	20,224	3,766
253	237	63	199	48	107	146	197	103	153	165	43	98	222
-8.4	13.6	0.6	-10.8	16.9	5.1	28.8	10.0	6.1	36.1	9.8	42.6	11.7	8.0
		28,808		25,498	7,409	6,165	3,912	6,688	3,950		18,830	10,467	
		0.3		8.8	10.0	4.1	14.6	11.3	41.9		25.3	76.1	
425	2,279	4,550	5,329	16,658	11,260	5,840	1,602	12,316	7,002	9,594	28,258	9,757	3,766
-8.4	13.6	2.1	-10.8	32.0	2.1	71.7	0.2	3.6	33.0	9.8	57.1	-19.7	8.0
0.5	1.7	39.1	6.3	45.9	18.4	16.8	3.6	19.6	17.4	8.9	40.1	21.7	4.0
89.4	70.3	72.3	84.2	80.3	80.0	69.4	80.3	92.7	89.4	87.7	77.6	88.7	45.7
48.0	50.0	49.2	51.9	52.4	51.2	51.7	51.4	52.0	48.4	52.5	50.6	54.3	50.4
28.2	32.4	24.4	39.4	33.2	29.8	33.6	27.2	38.5	32.3	41.7	29.8	36.8	31.0
8.7	7.2	9.0	6.7	6.8	9.2	7.3	9.4	6.8	7.4	6.3	8.2	6.9	9.5
23.0	24.7	22.7	20.4	21.8	23.7	22.0	26.8	19.0	22.4	18.8	23.4	18.2	21.3
59.8	53.7	60.8	50.6	54.5	52.4	54.3	52.0	51.7	52.6	51.2	57.5	53.3	56.1
8.5	14.4	7.5	22.3	16.9	14.7	16.4	11.8	22.5	17.6	23.7	10.9	21.6	13.1
290	1,551	22,759	3,886	30,081	12,537	8,486	3,516	14,103	7,684	7,182	32,210	15,146	2,606
268	1,615	13,312	2,972	20,042	8,984	6,121	3,367	9,311	5,847	6,059	22,718	9,578	2,254
11	90	1,291	385	6,291	1,145	166	4	1,447	1,764	1,907	6,751	4,699	1
41	1,310	17,408	943	379	5,673	1,284	4,064	1,316	659	174	1,053	696	275
1	12	73	6	215	54	29	4	33	26	7	113	28	24
	3	469	4	93	18	101	6	34	20	6	57	37	9
101	204	2,202	902	7,393	2,729	2,445	302	1,357	748	1,567	7,679	3,502	743
	11	162	20	162	72	116	8	55	46	55	1,877	128	41
18	88	1,390	366	1,018	720	837	158	3,505	3,212	301	1,569	683	706
14	67	628	357	2,385	942	724	105	540	359	808	2,427	1,380	176
	5	77	6	62	34	42		11	17	29	169	31	2
3	4	73	10	55	11	38	12	109	57	16	172	92	2
16.5	16.1	14.6	12.5	16.5	13.0	19.7	8.1	16.1	15.2	13.7	16.7	12.4	15.4
154	771	10,280	2,042	15,710	6,408	4,414	1,726	7,150	3,856	3,826	16,227	7,421	1,402
43	399	7,579	689	5,948	2,412	1,579	958	3,161	1,975	1,192	6,149	3,989	435
121	598	7,876	1,531	11,621	5,090	3,341	1,348	5,288	2,919	2,720	12,946	15,118	1,093
45	170	2,841	473	4,149	1,728	1,039	425	1,830	1,044	688	3,741	1,879	440
63	286	4,522	630	5,483	3,557	1,735	819	2,330	1,389	1,085	6,970	2,139	546
92.6	84.0	82.9	80.9	74.3	82.9	79.6	75.7	86.0	71.4	79.1	81.6	66.6	92.2
51.9	41.8	46.4	39.4	53.7	37.5	46.4	36.6	56.0	50.8	38.2	37.7	62.2	46.4
	46.5	28.5	19.9	21.2	5.4	37.7	26.9	7.4	39.2	20.9	23.4	11.2	8.5
9.0	59.8	53.8	17.6	1.8	28.8	11.5	75.1	21.3	19.0	3.7	4.0	3.2	9.6
30.2	17.9	26.2	26.0	27.6	23.8	25.7	32.1	25.8	24.1	28.6	23.6	30.8	25.7
	10.2	13.0	13.5	19.6	21.3	10.5	34.7	12.5	11.5	12.9	22.0	23.0	19.7
67.4	40.1	58.8	45.7	53.1	46.5	56.9	29.7	38.6	43.5	45.3	50.1	42.6	64.2
8.1	7.4	18.1	9.5	10.0	10.1	13.2	7.8	8.1	9.6	8.7	8.1	7.1	16.2
13.9	10.8	22.7	18.3	15.6	18.7	13.8	23.9	15.9	21.1	17.4	18.9	14.9	24.8
6.9	9.5	5.7	15.4	12.1	10.5	12.7	7.4	14.6	10.7	15.8	9.0	14.5	8.5
6.9	15.8	14.5	9.9	14.1	9.2	13.0	11.1	9.0	14.1	17.1	17.1	11.7	9.3
4.6	3.3	6.0	3.8	7.0	3.8	2.9	2.5	2.4	5.7	5.2	7.8	7.4	5.4

COUNTY POPULATION

	LIVE OAK	LLANO	LOVING	LUBBOCK	LYNN	McCULLOCH	McLENNAN	McMULLEN	MADISON	MARION	MARTIN
1982 Population[E]	10,361	10,735	87	216,772	8,788	8,763	175,171	771	10,646	10,823	4,768
1980 Population											
1980 Census of Population	9,606	10,144	91	211,651	8,605	8,735	170,755	789	10,649	10,360	4,684
Rank in State	164	159	254	10	176	174	13	251	155	158	209
% Change 1970-80	43.4	45.4	-44.5	18.0	-5.5	1.9	15.7	-27.9	38.4	21.6	-1.9
Urban Residents	2,627	3,071		182,982	3,262	5,969	139,004		3,660	2,643	
% Change 1970-80		17.8		14.4	10.4	7.4	12.8		27.0	-7.8	
Rural Residents	6,979	7,073	91	28,669	5,343	2,766	31,751	789	6,989	7,717	4,684
% Change 1970-80	4.2	6.18	-44.5	48.3	-13.1	-8.2	30.4	-27.9	45.2	36.6	-1.9
Population Per Square Mile	9.1	10.8	0.1	235.2	9.7	8.2	165.6	0.7	22.5	26.9	5.1
Native Texans 1980 (%)[T]	84.4	73.0	83.5	73.0	89.4	88.6	79.9	92.1	85.9	73.9	87.6
Age 1980											
Female (%)	50.1	52.1	41.8	50.5	51.4	52.8	51.8	48.5	41.4	51.2	50.9
Median Age	30.9	55.4	45.3	25.5	28.9	39.9	29.3	36.9	24.6	35.0	29.9
Under Age 5 (%)	8.8	4.2		8.4	8.6	6.5	7.4	7.0	5.8	7.5	8.2
Age 5-17 (%)	21.3	12.2	13.2	20.4	26.1	19.9	19.3	18.2	17.6	20.5	25.6
Age 18-64 (%)	56.5	52.3	69.2	63.3	51.9	48.9	60.1	58.7	60.7	54.1	53.8
Age 65 and Over (%)	13.4	31.3	17.6	7.9	13.4	24.7	13.2	16.1	15.9	17.9	12.4
Age 18 and Over (1980)	6,715	8,481	[1]79	150,714	5,622	6,428	125,159	[1]590	8,154	7,453	3,099
Registered Voters (11/2/82)	6,009	6,553	[2]94	85,791	4,279	4,905	82,105	[2]596	4,751	6,031	2,426
1980 Selected Ancestry Groups											
Black	5	39		15,780	301	219	27,254	1	2,639	3,597	118
Hispanic	3,077	265	16	41,428	3,264	1,666	14,988	272	802	99	1,620
American Indian/Eskimo	20	38		546	20	16	305		30	28	6
Asian/Pacific Islander	12	16		1,646	4	17	552		27	9	1
English[F]	994	1,729	7	33,984	1,274	1,576	23,766	84	1,642	1,388	568
French[F]	71	99	2	1,670	33	51	1,213	2	85	63	63
German[F]	717	940	3	11,121	494	501	12,845	27	412	335	201
Irish[F]	639	572	20	10,525	438	489	9,354	77	744	301	245
Italian[F]	18	21		741	5	7	614		23	13	
Polish[F]	153	12		510			734	10	57		
Veterans 1980 (%)	15.1	20.9	13.4	14.2	12.0	14.4	17.4	16.6	11.8	16.7	13.7
1980 Family Characteristics											
Households	3,308	4,402	34	72,627	2,829	3,400	61,554	297	3,107	3,874	1,547
Single Persons (Age 15+)	1,297	959	17	46,387	1,261	1,081	34,683	134	2,995	1,548	605
Families	2,679	3,375	28	52,748	2,297	2,463	44,023	229	2,304	2,865	1,267
Both Spouses Employed	739	835	4	21,889	525	765	16,267	80	719	645	444
With Children Under Age 18	1,357	854	13	28,871	1,170	1,094	21,656	110	965	1,274	669
Child. Living w/Two Parents (%)	86.4	79.4	81.8	79.6	85.0	81.2	72.7	81.2	74.7	62.9	91.8
Employed Mothers/Ages 0-5 (%)[M]	41.9	51.5		51.7	28.8	44.7	55.0	43.8	56.9	42.5	41.7
Age 3-4 in Nursery School (%)	5.1	13.8		28.8	15.8	11.4	31.1		16.3	8.7	14.7
Foreign Language in Home (%)[S]	33.9	4.6	36.3	20.0	37.2	19.6	9.2	38.6	9.1	1.1	35.2
Age 60+ Living Alone (%)	23.6	17.6	15.0	22.9	22.2	27.7	25.4	21.9	30.5	26.2	23.0
1980											
School Dropouts Age 16-19 (%)	23.1	9.0	50.0	12.1	12.4	17.4	12.1	2.1	37.1	8.1	20.4
H.S. Graduates Age 25+ (%)	47.4	56.1	55.1	66.4	42.6	45.0	58.5	51.6	48.7	48.4	47.7
College Graduates Age 25+ (%)	10.3	12.9	4.3	20.1	10.0	11.0	14.5	15.4	11.7	6.5	6.7
1982											
Birth Rate[R]	12.3	9.3	23.0	19.2	15.9	16.2	16.9	16.9	11.1	16.3	25.0
Death Rate[R]	6.9	14.9	11.5	6.6	8.5	17.0	9.4	15.6	9.3	12.0	9.2
Marriage Rate[R]	9.7	12.1		13.3	10.1	12.4	12.2	5.1	11.5	13.5	14.3
Divorce Rate[R]	6.2	2.7		5.8	2.6	5.9	6.4		0.9	5.4	3.6

[E]Estimate [T]Born in Texas and residing in Texas in 1980 [R]Per 1,000 population. [1]Verified by the Bureau of Census [2]Verified by the Elections Division
[M]Employed female with children ages 0-5 [S]Children ages 5+ who speak a language other than English at home. [F]Those reporting single ancestry.

MASON	MATAGORDA	MAVERICK	MEDINA	MENARD	MIDLAND	MILAM	MILLS	MITCHELL	MONTAGUE	MONTGOMERY	MOORE	MORRIS	MOTLEY
3,729	40,331	35,640	23,878	2,329	86,718	23,373	4,524	9,180	17,829	148,705	17,100	15,145	1,919
3,683	37,828	31,398	23,164	2,346	82,636	22,732	4,477	9,088	17,410	128,487	16,575	14,629	1,950
223	57	67	88	235	31	90	215	171	115	19	120	128	242
9.7	35.5	73.5	14.4	-11.3	26.3	13.5	6.3	0.2	13.6	159.7	17.9	18.8	-10.5
	22,504	21,407	9,813		72,167	11,332		5,405	8,602	29,167	12,194	3,030	
	46.4	39.3	11.5		19.5	11.1		3.4	6.8	143.7	24.8	15.2	
3,683	15,324	9,991	13,351	2,346	10,469	11,400	4,479	3,683	8,808	99,320	4,381	11,599	1,950
9.7	22.2	266.1	16.6	-11.3	106.8	16.0	6.3	-4.2	21.2	164.8	2.1	19.8	-10.5
3.9	33.6	24.4	17.4	2.6	91.6	22.3	6.0	10.0	18.8	122.7	18.3	57.1	2.0
88.1	75.5	52.3	85.8	89.9	68.8	88.7	85.1	85.2	80.2	64.2	60.9	79.1	86.8
52.6	49.7	52.1	50.7	52.6	50.9	51.9	51.9	52.1	52.4	50.0	50.1	51.8	51.8
41.8	27.7	22.3	30.7	40.0	28.8	33.7	46.2	34.1	39.3	28.7	27.3	30.8	42.4
6.3	9.5	10.6	8.0	5.9	8.8	7.8	6.0	7.8	6.6	8.1	10.3	8.5	6.8
18.0	21.9	31.3	24.5	20.4	21.2	21.5	16.2	22.0	18.4	26.0	24.1	21.0	17.7
51.8	58.2	51.3	54.1	50.7	62.6	52.4	50.2	50.9	53.1	58.9	58.0	56.6	51.3
23.9	10.4	6.8	13.4	23.0	7.4	18.3	27.6	19.3	21.9	7.0	7.6	13.8	24.1
2,791	25,934	18,257	15,652	1,729	57,786	16,059	3,483	6,383	13,061	84,735	10,875	10,309	1,471
2,237	15,934	9,967	11,843	1,506	42,611	11,431	2,807	4,434	9,611	57,852	7,542	8,292	1,216
11	5,507	11	99	5	7,119	3,061	5	471	2	6,167	37	3,189	99
598	7,965	28,366	10,042	672	12,323	2,390	326	2,285	239	4,289	3,253	247	154
2	63	739	61	7	211	28	9	15	68	262	87	54	3
3	466	34	33	1	272	25	18	8	10	358	182	18	1
488	4,182	490	1,374	502	10,954	3,488	1,099	1,987	3,042	14,591	2,571	2,494	474
9	473	4	127	23	567	105	6	54	119	1,846	32	75	10
1,004	2,205	211	3,014	293	3,894	2,650	372	341	735	8,218	698	449	34
193	1,647	136	668	249	3,479	1,258	345	658	1,205	6,605	1,013	805	95
9	76	39	82		184	50	19		96	786	8	13	
2	298	54	60	4	189	28	11		18	1,049	1		
13.7	15.4	8.1	16.1	13.8	18.3	15.0	15.6	13.2	15.8	19.8	17.0	17.4	16.0
1,461	13,110	7,583	7,457	917	29,650	8,299	1,772	3,304	6,837	41,487	5,590	5,187	812
448	5,935	5,988	3,644	296	12,534	3,370	523	1,239	1,998	17,176	1,811	1,929	235
1,078	9,869	6,624	6,075	657	22,706	6,203	1,341	2,469	5,058	35,006	4,643	4,089	568
378	3,408	1,729	1,869	179	9,411	2,001	435	844	1,630	13,637	1,701	1,353	125
418	5,413	4,721	3,159	277	12,034	3,025	526	1,191	2,129	21,200	2,641	2,027	240
87.5	79.7	81.2	82.2	75.9	82.6	82.1	85.0	82.1	83.6	84.1	85.0	84.1	92.4
55.3	41.5	40.6	44.6	37.7	45.5	39.5	53.4	42.0	44.9	42.5	36.4	37.0	10.5
23.3	23.5	15.5	13.6	4.9	32.7	11.6	19.8	5.2	11.6	32.0	13.5	19.7	
21.5	20.3	91.5	45.7	27.7	15.1	14.1	8.2	24.8	1.8	4.6	18.7	2.2	8.0
26.0	28.2	16.4	21.7	28.0	24.1	27.0	22.6	26.5	24.8	21.2	23.9	25.9	31.1
14.0	19.7	22.7	19.0	12.6	16.3	13.2	17.4	23.9	17.9	16.4	21.3	17.0	4.6
50.5	53.6	32.2	45.4	44.5	72.5	45.4	45.3	47.1	46.2	65.8	59.7	54.0	51.8
14.5	10.9	8.4	7.5	12.6	24.3	7.7	11.5	8.1	7.5	15.4	11.1	9.7	10.5
11.0	19.1	22.4	15.8	16.7	28.0	16.0	7.5	16.0	13.9	18.9	24.7	17.4	6.3
12.1	8.4	4.3	8.4	15.9	7.0	11.9	13.9	11.9	11.7	6.1	5.8	11.3	13.0
8.9	11.9	12.9	7.7	12.5	16.5	12.6	11.0	9.5	11.0	14.6	15.7	9.7	10.4
5.4	5.7	3.2	3.9	3.4	6.7	3.3	4.4	4.5	7.3	4.7	7.9	6.1	2.1

	NACOG-DOCHES	NAVARRO	NEWTON	NOLAN	NUECES	OCHILTREE	OLDHAM	ORANGE	PALO PINTO	PANOLA	PARKER
1982 Population[E]	47,848	36,216	13,639	17,662	275,356	9,538	2,289	86,347	23,287	21,983	47,280
1980 Population											
1980 Census of Population	46,786	35,323	13,254	17,359	268,215	9,588	2,283	83,838	24,062	20,724	44,609
Rank in State	44	62	141	116	8	166	236	30	85	97	46
% Change 1970-80	28.7	13.4	13.7	7.0	12.9	−1.2	1.1	17.8	−16.9	30.4	31.6
Urban Residents	27,149	21,712		12,242	252,102	7,991		51,077	14,348	6,447	13,065
% Change 1970-80	20.4	8.7		1.8	12.9	2.3		8.3	−24.0	19.6	−16.6
Rural Residents	19,637	13,611	13,254	5,117	16,113	1,597	2,283	32,761	9,714	14,277	31,544
% Change 1970-80	42.1	21.8	13.7	21.8	12.9	−15.7	1.1	36.4	−3.6	35.9	73.2
Population Per Square Mile	49.8	33.1	14.2	19.0	316.7	10.4	1.5	231.6	25.4	25.5	49.5
Native Texans 1980 (%)[T]	79.5	85.2	78.4	84.8	74.9	53.5	68.1	66.1	74.9	77.0	75.6
Age 1980											
Female (%)	51.9	52.6	51.5	52.4	51.0	48.4	42.3	50.6	51.8	52.4	50.7
Median Age (%)	26.0	34.6	30.0	32.4	27.0	28.2	24.5	28.1	33.7	32.5	32.2
Under Age 5 (%)	6.9	6.9	8.1	8.0	9.2	9.7	6.6	8.6	6.8	8.0	6.9
Age 5-17 (%)	17.2	20.3	25.3	21.4	23.8	21.2	35.2	24.1	20.9	20.4	22.2
Age 18-64 (%)	63.9	53.2	53.2	54.4	58.7	60.0	49.7	59.8	56.4	55.7	59.0
Age 65 and Over (%)	12.0	19.6	13.4	16.2	8.3	9.1	8.5	7.5	15.9	15.9	11.9
Age 18 and Over (1980)	35,538	25,694	8,829	12,260	179,784	6,619	1,328	56,476	17,400	14,837	31,632
Registered Voters (11/2/82)	21,523	17,465	7,517	7,697	128,297	4,623	1,144	39,412	11,473	11,625	20,616
1980 Selected Ancestry Groups											
Black	8,024	7,117	3,197	810	12,338	2	13	6,860	827	4,125	393
Hispanic	1,320	1,462	109	3,394	131,247	897	117	1,762	1,363	343	1,355
American Indian/Eskimo	85	63	6	22	734	102	13	195	67	22	154
Asian/Pacific Islander	185	62	8	22	1,318	15	12	442	110	19	113
English[F]	9,468	6,579	2,463	2,762	18,979	1,394	487	11,812	4,334	3,389	8,140
French[F]	539	248	417	114	1,635	60	25	7,257	138	212	404
German[F]	1,947	1,190	285	713	10,691	836	152	3,090	1,043	446	2,190
Irish[F]	2,558	2,388	782	841	6,500	504	165	4,716	1,696	1,149	2,589
Italian[F]	232	73	28	10	662	33	8	430	117	22	157
Polish[F]	55	56	10	23	869	5		152	56	35	78
Veterans 1980 (%)	13.7	14.9	17.9	15.5	18.0	17.9	15.5	18.7	19.2	15.6	19.2
1980 Family Characteristics											
Households	16,457	13,331	4,470	6,446	86,989	3,486	674	27,918	8,977	7,434	15,640
Single Persons (Age 15+)	12,488	4,961	1,791	2,129	46,897	1,092	420	11,545	3,153	2,787	5,929
Families	11,226	9,791	3,582	4,901	67,555	2,732	551	23,106	6,799	5,796	12,722
Both Spouses Employed	4,118	3,352	692	1,717	24,203	934	264	6,928	2,304	1,641	4,609
With Children Under Age 18	5,388	4,303	1,891	2,317	38,321	1,461	299	13,182	3,131	2,745	6,502
Child. Living w/Two Parents (%)	74.7	72.6	76.2	83.6	77.0	87.0	53.8	82.3	81.3	78.5	86.1
Employed Mothers/Ages 0-5 (%)[M]	55.1	56.0	31.5	45.1	48.6	26.3	48.0	34.4	45.9	38.0	44.5
Age 3-4 in Nursery School (%)	30.1	27.8	4.7	17.1	30.0	12.8	35.2	25.4	17.6	27.3	29.5
Foreign Language in Home (%)[S]	4.5	4.6	1.2	20.0	45.4	9.8	2.6	4.8	6.7	2.9	4.1
Age 60+ Living Alone (%)	25.0	27.0	24.4	28.1	21.5	22.9	24.7	22.1	25.9	24.8	23.9
1980											
School Dropouts Age 16-19 (%)	10.0	22.7	19.0	19.7	19.2	28.3	5.7	14.0	23.3	16.8	16.6
H.S. Graduates Age 25+ (%)	57.9	48.6	45.2	49.4	59.0	66.5	63.5	62.2	53.9	52.3	59.3
College Graduates Age 25+ (%)	18.3	11.2	4.0	7.3	14.5	13.7	14.9	9.0	9.6	9.5	11.5
1982											
Birth Rate[R]	14.9	15.8	15.8	17.5	22.3	32.3	8.3	18.0	19.9	15.7	13.0
Death Rate[R]	8.7	13.2	9.1	11.6	7.0	8.6	8.3	7.0	12.0	9.7	8.0
Marriage Rate[R]	11.6	13.9	11.7	13.3	13.2	19.2	7.9	18.2	17.1	12.6	28.6
Divorce Rate[R]	4.1	6.5	4.5	5.9	7.2	8.9	9.2	9.3	10.8	6.2	6.7

[E]Estimate   [T]Born in Texas and residing in Texas in 1980   [R]Per 1,000 population.   [1]Verified by the Bureau of Census   [2]Verified by the Elections Division
[M]Employed female with children ages 0-5   [S]Children ages 5+ who speak a language other than English at home.   [F]Those reporting single ancestry.

PARMER	PECOS	POLK	POTTER	PRESIDIO	RAINS	RANDALL	REAGAN	REAL	RED RIVER	REEVES	REFUGIO	ROBERTS	ROBERTSON
11,345	15,107	27,036	100,194	5,343	5,109	79,339	4,363	2,539	16,546	15,953	9,276	1,250	14,723
11,038	14,618	24,407	98,637	5,188	4,839	75,062	4,135	2,469	16,101	15,801	9,289	1,187	14,653
151	129	83	26	202	206	34	217	233	123	125	169	248	127
5.0	6.3	68.8	9.0	7.1	29.0	39.3	27.7	22.7	12.6	-4.4	-2.2	22.8	1.8
3,809	8,688	4,928	93,019			66,935	3,404		4,917	12,855	3,898		5,418
22.4	4.9	25.6	7.6	-100.0		37.0			47.0	1.4	-10.2		8.8
7,229	5,930	19,479	5,618	5,188	4,839	8,127	731	2,469	11,184	2,946	5,391	1,187	9,235
-2.3	8.5	85.0	39.3	136.4	29.0	61.9	-77.4	22.7	2.1	-23.4	4.6	22.8	-1.8
12.5	3.1	23.0	109.4	1.3	19.9	81.9	3.5	3.5	15.3	6.0	12.0	1.3	17.0
67.0	73.5	80.0	65.4	73.7	85.4	65.3	76.1	81.7	85.1	75.6	90.4	72.1	91.4
50.4	49.7	51.1	51.9	51.9	50.5	51.3	48.1	51.6	52.6	50.6	50.1	50.8	52.8
26.8	25.4	35.2	28.8	29.7	39.0	28.4	24.8	35.5	36.1	25.0	30.8	31.3	35.1
10.2	10.1	7.8	8.9	7.6	6.7	7.9	12.6	5.6	6.9	10.4	8.0	8.2	7.6
26.1	26.9	20.8	19.9	27.9	18.3	20.8	24.5	24.6	21.1	27.5	23.2	24.8	21.9
54.1	55.8	54.2	59.4	50.0	56.1	64.3	57.1	53.5	51.4	54.0	55.4	54.3	49.6
9.6	7.2	17.2	11.8	14.5	18.8	7.0	5.7	16.3	20.6	8.1	13.4	12.7	20.9
7,034	9,219	17,445	70,306	3,345	3,625	53,501	2,597	[1]1,722	11,606	9,814	6,395	795	10,336
4,315	7,608	14,104	35,374	2,821	3,241	38,300	2,040	[2]1,969	8,570	7,933	5,202	715	8,115
203	68	3,861	7,895	1	270	634	163	1	3,263	375	777		4,699
3,606	7,099	903	11,538	3,989	58	3,359	1,301	552	280	9,790	3,556	26	1,372
17	25	603	542	8	19	207	18	13	72	23	7	3	12
4	35	10	1,261	1	1	332	2	1	17	33	7	2	13
1,510	2,033	4,337	15,185	331	1,010	14,268	467	454	2,386	1,535	728	275	1,788
11	113	333	751	9	31	896	38	8	48	86	56	9	57
581	499	893	4,881	76	93	5,689	237	175	324	396	635	64	391
533	674	1,928	5,018	91	349	4,368	239	130	1,079	539	317	71	641
15	15	131	305	5	4	322		2	11		17		148
18	8	85	302	3		319		7	2	11	23		718
11.9	13.0	16.0	17.7	14.3	18.2	17.8	17.4	17.1	16.3	11.9	14.2	12.4	14.2
3,489	4,567	8,909	37,769	1,680	1,911	26,709	1,305	900	6,042	4,789	3,168	426	5,518
1,396	2,116	3,024	14,834	963	519	12,511	417	341	2,168	2,392	1,614	119	2,290
2,917	3,740	6,934	26,426	1,270	1,490	20,974	1,109	695	4,484	3,890	2,444	343	3,795
732	1,243	1,577	9,103	292	395	9,528	295	238	1,269	944	719	106	1,021
1,674	2,199	2,958	13,322	698	598	11,230	72.8	324	2,048	2,363	1,245	183	1,753
87.5	87.1	79.7	74.8	81.0	79.0	87.5	79.7	80.0	75.0	83.3	77.6	91.9	64.9
21.4	38.1	35.7	49.0	36.1	40.4	46.6	18.3	37.1	45.4	27.4	36.7	27.2	41.4
8.6	11.3	15.9	28.2	19.3	8.5	32.8	8.6	43.5	12.5	17.6	13.1	5.4	10.7
30.1	48.3	6.7	12.7	80.4	0.6	5.5	30.6	22.0	3.1	62.7	36.4	1.4	11.8
20.6	24.4	21.9	28.6	26.0	24.3	25.1	18.1	25.6	27.4	29.3	22.9	26.4	32.3
17.4	23.8	20.9	24.5	18.2	19.8	8.6	20.8	14.1	12.8	29.0	15.4	14.6	12.3
51.7	49.3	46.0	60.1	41.1	42.7	81.7	55.1	46.9	43.6	44.5	43.6	64.4	40.0
9.5	9.3	9.1	10.3	12.2	5.0	24.1	9.1	7.9	8.9	8.7	9.5	14.1	7.1
18.2	26.1	14.1	21.4	16.1	14.1	16.0	33.0	13.4	13.1	29.1	17.7	9.6	20.1
7.4	5.6	12.4	9.7	8.4	11.2	4.9	5.0	12.2	14.6	7.8	10.8	8.0	15.4
9.0	14.0	13.5	17.4	10.3	11.5	8.9	12.4	12.6	14.5	13.7	12.1	11.2	10.1
4.1	7.1	2.1	10.1	2.4	8.0	6.7	3.7	7.1	6.7	4.1	5.6	0.8	4.1

COUNTY POPULATION

	ROCKWALL	RUNNELS	RUSK	SABINE	SAN AUGUSTINE	SAN JACINTO	SAN PATRICIO	SAN SABA	SCHLEICHER	SCURRY	SHACKELFORD
1982 Population[E]	16,427	11,903	43,218	9,011	8,960	12,696	60,579	6,361	2,949	18,686	4,083
1980 Population											
1980 Census of Population	14,528	11,872	41,382	8,702	8,785	11,434	58,013	6,204	2,820	18,192	3,915
Rank in State	131	147	50	175	173	149	39	194	230	109	221
% Change 1970-80	106.2	-1.9	21.3	21.1	11.8	70.6	22.7	12.0	23.8	15.4	17.8
Urban Residents	7,113	7,268	14,016		2,930		41,996	2,847		12,705	
% Change 1970-80	127.9	2.2	13.0		15.4		38.4	11.4		13.7	
Rural Residents	7,415	4,604	27,366	8,702	5,855	11,434	16,017	3,357	2,820	5,487	3,915
% Change 1970-80	88.9	-7.9	26.1	21.1	10.1	70.6	-5.5	12.5	23.8	19.6	17.8
Population Per Square Mile	113.5	11.2	44.4	17.9	16.8	20.0	83.7	5.5	2.2	20.2	4.3
Native Texans 1980 (%)[T]	66.4	89.2	80.8	80.3	89.5	81.5	79.5	88.6	79.4	83.3	84.7
Age 1980											
Female (%)	50.4	52.1	51.8	50.9	52.8	50.4	50.9	51.4	51.1	51.1	51.1
Median Age	31.1	36.8	33.2	39.4	36.9	33.2	26.4	40.1	29.9	29.4	34.0
Under Age 5 (%)	7.4	7.2	7.7	6.7	6.3	7.4	9.5	6.3	9.1	8.8	8.1
Age 5-17 (%)	24.3	20.8	20.5	19.3	22.1	23.2	26.8	20.4	21.9	21.3	19.7
Age 18-64 (%)	59.7	51.2	54.0	54.2	52.2	54.8	55.1	49.8	55.5	57.7	52.4
Age 65 and Over (%)	8.6	20.8	17.8	19.8	19.4	14.6	8.6	23.5	13.5	12.2	19.8
Age 18 and Over (1980)	9,914	8,547	29,710	6,439	6,295	7,932	36,946	4,543	1,944	12,715	2,830
Registered Voters (11/2/82)	8,435	6,112	22,519	7,031	5,482	7,180	28,518	3,053	1,490	9,438	2,401
1980 Selected Ancestry Groups											
Black	731	206	8,998	1,374	2,601	2,402	866	44	46	606	36
Hispanic	488	2,301	830	111	80	111	26,872	968	733	3,399	211
American Indian/Eskimo	21	15	77	19	17	41	133	13	6	33	6
Asian/Pacific Islander	47	22	50	2	4	5	122	10	4	12	4
English[F]	2,546	1,943	6,126	2,449	1,703	1,560	4,374	1,227	449	3,198	781
French[F]	143	53	436	124	40	168	385	43	28	98	26
German[F]	902	1,581	1,149	220	126	343	2,998	272	203	618	245
Irish[F]	832	792	2,798	699	739	722	1,684	512	164	1,196	279
Italian[F]	59	2	88	13	14	7	144	12	12	31	
Polish[F]	77	26	46	15		33	153	6	2		
Veterans 1980 (%)	19.1	15.6	16.8	15.5	11.3	19.4	16.2	15.1	13.9	15.7	16.0
1980 Family Characteristics											
Households	4,865	4,496	15,011	3,336	3,133	4,088	17,551	2,385	988	6,376	1,493
Single Persons (Age 15+)	1,949	1,547	5,496	1,088	1,338	1,467	8,753	760	329	2,449	437
Families	4,065	3,317	11,583	2,547	2,416	3,205	14,735	1,763	798	5,071	1,119
Both Spouses Employed	1,932	1,108	3,550	511	691	678	4,447	554	217	1,960	359
With Children Under Age 18	2,317	1,478	5,223	1,001	1,126	1,501	8,575	714	416	2,643	495
Child. Living w/Two Parents	87.5	81.3	79.5	78.7	63.3	77.9	81.4	84.4	84.1	84.6	87.8
Employed Mothers/Ages 0-5 (%)[M]	54.0	50.5	35.8	41.3	46.7	31.4	34.1	46.1	28.8	46.7	40.1
Age 3-4 in Nursery School (%)	56.9	20.7	28.3	6.2	22.5	9.2	24.3	22.8	9.5	15.4	10.2
Foreign Language in Home (%)[S]	5.7	20.5	2.4	2.5	1.9	2.9	44.8	14.1	28.1	17.6	5.5
Age 60+ Living Alone (%)	23.6	28.1	23.2	24.9	24.2	22.3	22.2	26.4	27.5	24.9	29.8
1980											
School Dropouts Age 16-19 (%)	10.5	19.8	15.9	20.2	20.4	25.2	17.6	16.3	29.4	23.2	29.9
H.S. Graduates Age 25+ (%)	70.3	42.2	53.1	41.7	38.2	43.9	51.6	49.7	54.7	55.5	51.7
College Graduates Age 25+ (%)	18.2	9.0	9.3	7.3	8.1	6.3	10.9	11.1	13.9	10.0	10.8
1982											
Birth Rate[R]	14.9	16.4	16.5	12.8	13.7	14.3	21.4	13.8	20.3	22.2	17.6
Death Rate[R]	5.9	11.4	11.3	13.6	12.8	8.3	7.0	15.6	9.5	8.6	11.0
Marriage Rate[R]	77.3	13.3	10.3	22.8	12.5	14.0	10.0	7.5	15.6	14.2	12.7
Divorce Rate[R]	6.9	5.3	6.7	3.2	0.7	6.9	4.1	5.0	4.4	7.5	6.9

[E]Estimate [T]Born in Texas and residing in Texas in 1980 [R]Per 1,000 population. [1]Verified by the Bureau of Census [2]Verified by the Elections Division
[M]Employed female with children ages 0-5 [S]Children ages 5+ who speak a language other than English at home. [F]Those reporting single ancestry.

SHELBY	SHERMAN	SMITH	SOMERVELL	STARR	STEPHENS	STERLING	STONEWALL	SUTTON	SWISHER	TARRANT	TAYLOR	TERRELL	TERRY
23,813	3,088	135,286	4,541	30,408	10,329	1,225	2,397	5,581	9,792	891,619	113,074	1,624	14,927
23,084	3,174	128,366	4,154	27,266	9,926	1,206	2,406	5,130	9,723	860,880	110,932	1,595	14,581
89	227	20	216	73	161	247	234	204	163	4	23	244	130
17.3	-13.2	32.2	48.7	54.0	18.0	14.2	0.4	61.6	-6.3	20.3	13.4	-17.8	3.3
5,827		72,927		12,314	6,921			3,856	5,033	833,800	99,260		10,387
16.8		22.0		116.9	16.4				-4.9	20.3	10.1		7.7
17,257	3,174	55,439	4,154	14,952	3,005	1,206	2,406	1,274	4,690	27,080	11,672	1,595	4,194
17.5	-13.2	48.6	48.7	24.3	21.7	14.2	0.4	-59.9	-7.7	16.8	52.1	-17.8	-6.2
29.2	3.4	137.7	22.1	22.2	11.1	1.3	2.6	3.5	10.8	991.8	121.0	0.7	16.5
84.5	58.8	75.9	73.6	72.5	83.0	84.1	89.0	84.3	85.7	65.3	69.5	84.7	80.8
52.0	50.4	52.0	49.6	51.4	52.4	51.3	52.7	50.1	51.3	51.0	51.3	48.2	51.2
34.8	31.7	30.0	30.0	22.8	34.3	29.9	40.5	27.1	29.9	28.8	27.4	31.8	27.8
6.8	7.7	7.7	9.0	10.3	7.7	9.1	7.2	10.1	8.7	7.6	8.2	8.9	9.8
21.3	22.8	21.3	20.2	31.3	19.6	22.2	17.7	23.9	24.7	21.1	19.6	22.3	24.8
53.4	57.3	58.5	56.5	49.5	55.6	54.1	53.0	58.4	53.7	62.8	61.5	55.8	53.7
18.5	12.2	12.5	14.3	8.9	17.1	14.6	22.1	7.6	12.9	8.5	10.7	13.0	11.7
16,597	2,206	91,181	2,944	15,929	7,221	829	1,805	3,385	6,480	613,762	80,057	1,098	9,536
13,777	1,754	62,178	2,471	12,489	4,993	772	1,638	2,439	4,711	386,251	49,356	1,025	7,322
4,905	4	28,215	3	3	349	5	73	3	465	101,183	6,707	2	535
260	364	4,037	287	26,428	562	279	196	2,071	2,678	67,632	13,203	691	4,956
75	1	233	26	26	12	3	4	16	9	3,050	307	2	32
19		353	10	14	16		5	3	7	6,465	751	1	22
4,541	405	21,185	910	117	2,328	211	613	845	1,775	121,470	18,274	124	2,031
150	29	1,050	44		23	4	15	41	26	7,419	959	2	81
509	183	5,035	131	13	278	41	120	405	446	43,138	5,631	25	397
1,510	201	6,523	408	30	649	83	192	243	577	42,829	5,999	66	750
4		367	13	7	9	2		10	21	4,611	383	9	
15		214	2	3	45			38		3,587	295	2	12
13.4	14.7	17.5	18.2	7.2	17.5	14.6	14.5	11.8	12.7	18.7	16.7	12.9	13.4
8,555	1,117	46,042	1,531	6,858	3,928	413	941	1,675	3,294	310,272	38,515	570	4,841
3,145	416	19,768	500	5,207	1,150	135	276	625	1,329	146,734	21,052	226	1,935
6,438	898	35,100	1,168	5,935	2,829	336	706	1,373	2,619	231,146	28,791	429	3,920
1,880	375	13,056	323	1,367	997	122	182	486	1,001	94,606	11,964	140	1,471
3,002	470	17,665	592	3,975	1,383	179	282	809	1,388	122,193	14,948	233	2,106
73.7	94.1	78.4	87.8	81.9	80.7	81.2	88.0	890	81.5	77.1	79.3	87.1	77.2
47.1	45.7	52.6	33.3	41.7	47.3	26.6	25.4	42.7	48.9	51.8	51.1	18.3	42.9
21.8	2.3	38.2	23.9	28.0	6.0	8.1	7.8	15.8	15.9	40.0	32.7	9.4	23.3
1.5	11.0	4.1	6.2	95.6	6.7	21.2	7.5	45.1	26.2	8.7	12.5	46.5	33.4
26.9	24.9	22.6	28.0	17.7	30.6	17.0	21.7	23.9	25.3	23.8	26.1	25.6	23.7
22.2	18.9	13.5	35.3	27.9	21.5	17.0	19.5	23.7	20.2	17.5	17.6	12.3	23.8
44.0	64.3	65.1	51.2	26.6	52.0	53.3	48.3	58.6	50.0	69.6	64.5	59.9	48.8
7.5	9.0	16.1	9.2	6.0	9.3	11.0	8.0	10.2	12.1	18.4	17.4	11.4	9.0
13.2	14.2	17.9	16.3	24.3	21.0	24.5	17.1	25.8	18.1	19.7	22.5	14.2	21.0
11.9	9.4	9.0	8.1	4.7	12.4	10.6	12.5	7.9	8.7	7.2	7.9	7.4	7.4
2.3	15.2	13.2	18.9	12.3	13.8	17.1	8.3	12.9	11.5	12.4	16.0	6.8	12.9
6.6	2.6	5.3	1.5	2.5	5.7	5.7	5.4	5.6	3.2	8.5	8.5	1.2	6.0

COUNTY POPULATION

	THROCK-MORTON	TITUS	TOM GREEN	TRAVIS	TRINITY	TYLER	UPSHUR	UPTON	UVALDE	VAL VERDE	VAN ZANDT
1982 Population[E]	2,040	22,554	87,655	442,839	9,901	17,181	30,553	4,687	23,890	38,379	33,807

1980 Population

	THROCK-MORTON	TITUS	TOM GREEN	TRAVIS	TRINITY	TYLER	UPSHUR	UPTON	UVALDE	VAL VERDE	VAN ZANDT
1980 Census of Population	2,053	21,442	84,784	419,573	9,450	16,223	28,595	4,619	22,441	35,910	31,426
Rank in State	239	95	29	6	168	121	71	212	92	61	66
% Change 1970-80	–6.9	28.4	19.3	42.0	23.9	30.7	36.3	–1.7	29.4	30.7	41.8
Urban Residents		11,003	73,994	370,046	2,620	2,821	7,404		14,178	33,028	8,185
% Change 1970-80		23.9	15.8	39.9	4.3	6.0	35.4	–100.0	31.7	33.2	210.5
Rural Residents	2,053	10,439	10,790	49,527	6,830	13,402	21,191	4,619	8,263	2,882	23,241
% Change 1970-80	–6.9	33.4	50.6	59.7	33.5	37.4	36.7	125.3	25.5	7.4	19.1
Population Per Square Mile	2.3	52.0	56.0	424.2	13.7	17.6	48.7	3.7	14.3	11.4	36.8

	THROCK-MORTON	TITUS	TOM GREEN	TRAVIS	TRINITY	TYLER	UPSHUR	UPTON	UVALDE	VAL VERDE	VAN ZANDT
Native Texans 1980 (%)[T]	87.6	81.9	73.9	66.8	86.0	80.7	78.2	73.9	79.4	57.8	82.5

Age 1980

	THROCK-MORTON	TITUS	TOM GREEN	TRAVIS	TRINITY	TYLER	UPSHUR	UPTON	UVALDE	VAL VERDE	VAN ZANDT
Female (%)	52.1	51.8	51.9	50.3	51.7	51.2	51.5	50.0	51.6	50.4	51.5
Median Age	42.4	31.5	28.9	26.7	39.1	35.9	31.9	26.5	27.4	24.6	37.1
Under Age 5 (%)	6.0	8.5	7.6	7.2	6.4	7.3	8.1	10.6	8.9	10.0	6.5
Age 5-17 (%)	17.3	21.0	19.7	18.4	20.2	21.7	21.8	23.9	25.5	27.5	20.5
Age 18-64 (%)	51.8	54.6	60.6	67.1	52.4	53.5	55.2	56.0	53.8	55.1	55.0
Age 65 and Over (%)	24.9	15.9	12.1	7.3	21.0	17.5	14.9	9.5	11.8	7.4	18.0

	THROCK-MORTON	TITUS	TOM GREEN	TRAVIS	TRINITY	TYLER	UPSHUR	UPTON	UVALDE	VAL VERDE	VAN ZANDT
Age 18 and Over (1980)	1,574	15,128	61,622	312,402	[1]6,944	11,523	20,050	3,024	14,721	22,474	22,944
Registered Voters (11/2/82)	1,432	11,143	34,799	225,805	[2]8,041	10,458	15,651	2,285	13,960	13,092	17,142

1980 Selected Ancestry Groups

	THROCK-MORTON	TITUS	TOM GREEN	TRAVIS	TRINITY	TYLER	UPSHUR	UPTON	UVALDE	VAL VERDE	VAN ZANDT
Black		2,994	3,386	44,988	1,909	2,097	4,403	92	78	748	1,284
Hispanic	115	608	17,953	72,288	84	134	215	1,295	12,394	22,601	558
American Indian/Eskimo	7	33	226	1,241	15	37	86	8	28	65	48
Asian/Pacific Islander	5	30	442	4,105	5	13	16		27	159	20
English[F]	469	4,642	10,839	49,540	1,860	2,709	5,473	819	1,565	2,076	5,260
French[F]	4	92	649	4,594	109	468	152	45	130	249	114
German[F]	63	425	6,047	33,808	280	505	826	399	984	1,319	812
Irish[F]	199	1,506	4,042	15,421	626	1,511	1,701	480	483	798	2,530
Italian[F]		26	216	2,727	16	9	37	18	37	183	39
Polish[F]			250	2,360	39	26	16		24	84	68

	THROCK-MORTON	TITUS	TOM GREEN	TRAVIS	TRINITY	TYLER	UPSHUR	UPTON	UVALDE	VAL VERDE	VAN ZANDT
Veterans 1980 (%)	14.8	16.2	16.9	15.4	17.4	16.1	18.1	14.6	12.8	12.7	18.4

1980 Family Characteristics

	THROCK-MORTON	TITUS	TOM GREEN	TRAVIS	TRINITY	TYLER	UPSHUR	UPTON	UVALDE	VAL VERDE	VAN ZANDT
Households	853	7,740	30,369	158,432	3,647	5,870	10,082	1,560	6,960	10,355	11,660
Single Persons (Age 15+)	238	2,683	15,449	112,710	1,256	1,973	3,697	558	3,715	5,837	3,751
Families	617	5,953	22,276	99,852	2,699	4,620	8,010	1,245	5,573	8,644	9,167
Both Spouses Employed	228	2,074	9,290	44,392	712	1,064	2,399	337	1,623	2,768	2,821
With Children Under Age 18	255	2,987	11,173	52,799	1,054	2,138	3,843	695	3,179	5,527	4,066
Child. Living w/Two Parents (%)	83.2	81.7	79.4	74.2	69.0	81.5	79.7	85.4	79.5	83.1	86.4
Employed Mothers/Ages 0-5 (%)[M]	45.4	41.9	58.9	61.6	41.7	27.8	40.8	28.5	35.1	42.1	46.1
Age 3-4 in Nursery School (%)	52.4	20.8	31.3	46.5	9.3	3.8	20.4		21.9	25.6	16.0
Foreign Language in Home (%)[S]	6.8	3.7	21.5	18.0	1.5	2.0	1.9	27.3	54.0	65.6	2.9
Age 60+ Living Alone	29.5	27.3	26.4	24.6	25.4	22.1	22.8	19.9	22.9	21.7	23.6

1980

	THROCK-MORTON	TITUS	TOM GREEN	TRAVIS	TRINITY	TYLER	UPSHUR	UPTON	UVALDE	VAL VERDE	VAN ZANDT
School Dropouts Age 16-19 (%)	15.3	17.6	18.7	13.2	15.4	21.4	17.0	22.9	24.1	25.5	16.6
H.S. Graduates Age 25+ (%)	50.2	52.9	59.8	75.4	45.0	49.8	54.0	52.9	46.7	51.1	49.3
College Graduates Age 25+ (%)	11.9	9.7	14.7	30.2	8.4	9.4	10.0	10.6	13.3	12.2	8.2

1982

	THROCK-MORTON	TITUS	TOM GREEN	TRAVIS	TRINITY	TYLER	UPSHUR	UPTON	UVALDE	VAL VERDE	VAN ZANDT
Birth Rate[R]	16.2	18.1	20.5	18.8	12.5	14.6	15.8	27.5	19.3	23.9	12.2
Death Rate[R]	16.7	11.6	9.2	5.8	17.7	11.6	9.0	9.4	8.4	5.9	11.4
Marriage Rate[R]	12.7	14.1	16.2	13.2	12.2	12.7	10.1	17.3	10.0	12.7	13.4
Divorce Rate[R]	2.9	1.2	5.6	7.7	1.8	5.2	5.5	3.6	4.7	4.8	5.5

[E]Estimate   [T]Born in Texas and residing in Texas in 1980   [R]Per 1,000 population.   [1]Verified by the Bureau of Census   [2]Verified by the Elections Division
[M]Employed female with children ages 0-5   [S]Children ages 5+ who speak a language other than English at home.   [F]Those reporting single ancestry.

VICTORIA	WALKER	WALLER	WARD	WASHINGTON	WEBB	WHARTON	WHEELER	WICHITA	WILBARGER	WILLACY	WILLIAMSON	WILSON	WINKLER
72,208	42,905	20,795	14,230	22,687	108,701	41,036	7,325	120,209	16,041	18,112	87,152	17,692	10,078
68,807	41,789	19,798	13,976	21,998	99,258	40,242	7,137	121,082	15,931	17,495	76,507	16,756	9,944
35	49	99	133	94	25	53	185	21	124	114	32	119	160
28.0	51.0	38.6	7.4	16.7	36.2	9.6	10.9	0.4	3.8	12.4	105.1	28.5	3.2
50,725	23,936	8,117	8,393	10,966	94,961	19,495	2,834	114,808	12,695	9,493	44,887	4,381	8,019
22.7	35.9	107.3	0.7	22.9	35.3	18.6	7.2	-1.4	10.8	18.9	138.5	18.2	1.7
18,082	17,853	11,681	5,583	11,032	4,297	20,747	4,303	6,274	3,236	8,002	31,634	12,375	1,925
45.6	77.3	12.7	19.1	11.2	61.4	2.3	13.5	16.7	-17.0	5.5	71.2	32.6	9.6
77.6	53.2	38.5	16.7	36.1	29.5	37.1	7.9	199.8	16.8	29.7	67.3	20.8	11.8
82.3	75.7	81.3	75.5	88.2	70.9	88.2	67.7	59.8	77.4	75.2	71.6	89.1	68.0
50.8	42.0	50.0	49.4	51.3	52.2	51.2	51.5	50.6	51.9	51.9	50.5	50.0	49.7
27.3	27.9	25.3	27.5	33.5	23.6	29.5	34.9	28.9	35.1	24.7	28.9	30.2	27.9
9.2	5.4	6.7	9.4	6.7	10.5	8.5	8.2	7.7	7.2	10.3	8.5	7.8	10.2
23.2	13.0	20.1	24.6	19.0	29.0	22.3	19.7	19.2	19.3	28.2	24.6	24.6	23.2
59.1	73.2	62.0	56.7	55.8	52.1	55.7	52.6	61.8	53.7	51.4	56.9	54.4	56.4
8.5	8.4	11.2	9.3	18.5	8.4	13.5	19.5	11.3	19.9	10.1	10.0	13.2	10.2
46,494	34,106	14,482	9,232	16,337	60,070	27,850	5,149	88,498	11,718	10,752	51,196	11,327	6,621
30,254	15,288	10,906	6,915	11,066	35,602	18,387	3,562	51,161	7,533	8,853	38,484	10,706	4,619
4,710	10,089	8,325	444	4,860	98	6,672	176	10,873	1,398	92	4,111	157	243
20,944	2,972	1,149	3,751	663	90,842	8,753	298	7,793	1,491	14,049	9,693	6,112	2,567
137	133	19	45	15	111	55	31	555	71	15	114	22	21
176	200	41	8	73	94	40	41	1,312	46	7	424	14	6
4,796	6,225	1,447	2,605	1,441	1,108	2,683	1,286	17,858	2,323	549	8,781	1,082	1,292
419	612	246	102	170	122	242	56	1,036	64	19	645	56	83
7,224	2,451	1,256	673	7,684	581	2,767	304	7,086	1,195	290	8,753	2,034	430
1,798	2,355	367	860	472	565	840	506	5,968	1,777	161	3,366	615	391
346	168	38	40	70	153	99	4	588	34	19	267	16	15
469	528	309	3	745	53	180	7	367	23	29	293	1,761	
16.6	16.8	13.1	14.8	14.1	10.5	13.7	13.9	18.6	15.2	10.1	18.1	14.7	16.7
22,988	11,813	5,726	4,765	7,817	25,896	13,887	2,740	43,134	5,983	4,760	24,932	5,429	3,411
11,119	12,645	5,602	1,806	4,534	20,002	6,900	851	21,362	2,224	3,154	11,418	2,737	1,146
18,161	7,541	4,464	3,779	5,772	22,047	10,503	2,089	32,179	4,335	4,011	20,449	4,443	2,761
6,754	2,915	1,862	1,154	2,390	5,729	3,843	612	12,465	1,580	1,074	9,837	1,610	801
10,135	3,671	2,286	2,115	2,473	14,382	5,475	961	16,475	1,897	2,350	12,314	2,416	1,512
81.3	74.6	78.3	80.6	78.5	79.2	81.6	84.7	79.4	76.2	78.2	85.5	88.0	88.1
40.4	52.2	52.5	36.5	63.0	43.4	47.5	38.6	51.0	53.0	48.3	60.0	50.1	30.9
23.7	40.1	15.3	12.1	24.1	21.6	24.1	16.8	31.6	14.6	24.7	42.5	21.5	10.1
28.9	10.0	7.2	26.0	11.3	92.7	25.4	5.1	7.7	7.9	79.7	16.7	43.1	23.7
24.4	26.7	26.2	30.7	27.8	18.7	26.4	24.6	27.6	26.0	20.7	22.8	25.3	22.6
17.2	11.8	5.6	34.2	16.6	20.6	13.5	18.8	14.9	19.4	28.7	10.55	15.8	34.9
58.4	60.8	58.1	58.2	48.3	41.5	48.3	54.6	65.4	50.2	33.6	65.5	45.2	52.9
12.0	17.7	16.3	8.4	11.3	9.8	10.8	10.7	14.4	10.9	8.9	19.4	6.6	7.7
23.4	13.0	17.1	26.6	18.5	25.9	18.6	25.3	19.4	16.8	24.1	17.1	16.4	29.7
7.5	5.7	7.8	8.3	13.3	5.4	9.4	11.3	8.8	13.8	7.8	6.7	8.4	7.5
12.1	11.1	9.5	14.8	11.9	11.3	11.7	33.4	20.8	24.7	9.4	8.7	7.7	13.8
7.2	4.5	4.9	7.4	3.7	0.1	4.5	7.0	9.2	7.4	2.2	4.3	4.2	4.1

COUNTY POPULATION

	WISE	WOOD	YOAKUM	YOUNG	ZAPATA	ZAVALA
1982 Population[E]	28,195	26,194	8,538	19,949	7,133	12,025

1980 Population

	WISE	WOOD	YOAKUM	YOUNG	ZAPATA	ZAVALA
1980 Census of Population	26,575	24,697	8,299	19,083	6,628	11,666
Rank in State	74	82	178	102	190	148
% Change 1970-80	35.0	32.9	13.0	23.9	52.3	2.6
Urban Residents	7,841	6,942	4,704	13,230	3,831	8,334
% Change 1970-80	14.4	13.2	13.8	19.2		2.8
Rural Residents	18,734	17,755	3,595	5,853	2,797	3,332
% Change 1970-80	46.0	42.6	12.0	36.1	-35.7	2.0
Population Per Square Mile	29.5	35.8	10.4	20.8	6.6	9.0

	WISE	WOOD	YOAKUM	YOUNG	ZAPATA	ZAVALA
Native Texans 1980 (%)[T]	77.8	81.8	78.2	79.7	63.5	74.9

Age 1980

	WISE	WOOD	YOAKUM	YOUNG	ZAPATA	ZAVALA
Female (%)	50.6	52.0	49.1	51.9	50.1	51.1
Median Age	32.5	37.5	26.5	34.8	29.6	23.7
Under Age 5 (%)	7.0	6.5	11.0	7.4	10.0	10.5
Age 5-17 (%)	22.3	18.5	24.0	19.1	24.5	29.8
Age 18-64 (%)	56.8	54.8	57.3	54.9	49.7	50.0
Age 65 and Over (%)	13.9	20.2	7.7	18.6	15.8	9.7

	WISE	WOOD	YOAKUM	YOUNG	ZAPATA	ZAVALA
Age 18 and Over (1980)	18,802	18,507	5,397	14,028	4,342	[1]6,958
Registered Voters (11/2/82)	13,187	12,137	4,114	9,563	4,286	[2]7,022

1980 Selected Ancestry Groups

	WISE	WOOD	YOAKUM	YOUNG	ZAPATA	ZAVALA
Black	152	2,564	100	264	1	20
Hispanic	1,316	283	2,306	760	5,042	10,386
American Indian/Eskimo	86	53	57	70	5	9
Asian/Pacific Islander	25	29	7	68	4	3
English[F]	4,867	5,091	1,425	3,719	207	228
French[F]	148	159	18	181	14	19
German[F]	1,156	561	202	874	209	174
Irish[F]	1,708	1,660	443	1,387	113	72
Italian[F]	56	42	5	17	10	
Polish[F]	3	23	17	18		

	WISE	WOOD	YOAKUM	YOUNG	ZAPATA	ZAVALA
Veterans 1980 (%)	17.8	16.1	13.4	17.1	11.8	7.7

1980 Family Characteristics

	WISE	WOOD	YOAKUM	YOUNG	ZAPATA	ZAVALA
Households	9,411	9,242	2,700	7,361	2,059	3,068
Single Persons (Age 15+)	3,291	3,226	1,000	2,105	1,025	2,160
Families	7,577	7,100	2,250	5,595	1,750	2,622
Both Spouses Employed	2,611	1,981	733	1,950	190	607
With Children Under Age 18	3,697	2,946	1,357	2,525	899	1,733
Child. Living w/Two Parents (%)	87.7	82.9	86.0	84.6	80.7	78.1
Employed Mothers/Ages 0-5 (%)[M]	33.9	40.2	34.4	40.9	31.6	43.3
Age 3-4 in Nursery School (%)	15.1	19.7	6.4	16.8	25.2	32.7
Foreign Language in Home (%)[S]	5.4	2.5	27.8	3.7	75.1	89.2
Age 60+ Living Alone	24.0	22.0	22.5	27.4	14.8	18.6

1980

	WISE	WOOD	YOAKUM	YOUNG	ZAPATA	ZAVALA
School Dropouts Age 16-19 (%)	21.1	11.7	20.3	29.2	23.1	30.0
H.S. Graduates Age 25+ (%)	52.1	50.7	51.8	51.9	41.3	25.9
College Graduates Age 25+ (%)	7.5	9.0	8.8	10.3	7.2	7.5

1982

	WISE	WOOD	YOAKUM	YOUNG	ZAPATA	ZAVALA
Birth Rate[R]	17.1	14.5	23.5	19.3	24.1	23.9
Death Rate[R]	8.7	15.1	6.3	14.1	9.1	6.7
Marriage Rate[R]	12.7	13.6	13.6	13.8	13.5	11.6
Divorce Rate[R]	6.1	7.1	4.7	5.7	0.4	2.7

[E]Estimate.   [T]Born in Texas and residing in Texas in 1980.   [R]Per 1,000 population.   [1]Verified by the Bureau of Census   [2]Verified by the Elections Division
[M]Employed female with children ages 0-5   [S]Children ages 5+ who speak a language other than English at home.   [F]Those reporting single ancestry.

FLYING THE COLORS: TEXAS ©JOHN CLEMENTS 1984

COUNTY AGRICULTURE

	STATE TOTALS	ANDERSON	ANDREWS	ANGELINA	ARANSAS	ARCHER	ARMSTRONG	ATASCOSA	AUSTIN	BAILEY
1982 Acres										
Approx. Land Area	167,776,000	686,000	963,000	472,000	176,000	584,000	580,000	772,000	424,000	534,000
Land in Farms/Ranches	138,400,000	356,000	895,000	118,000	58,000	543,000	563,000	717,000	354,000	509,000
Cropland Planted	28,473,000	32,000	65,000	13,000	8,000	98,000	145,000	121,000	59,000	370,000
Land Irrigated	7,800,000	*	12,000	*		2,000	15,000	42,000	6,000	170,000
Pasture/Rangeland	103,300,000	303,000	707,000	105,000	55,000	434,000	393,000	571,000	274,000	174,000
No. of Farms[P]	185,026	1,356	128	723	61	465	241	1,256	1,677	442
Ave. Farm Size[P]	707	236	5,831	164	457	1,170	2,294	601	186	1,021
Foreign Owned Acres (1983)	983,409	1,309				8		19,193	145	
1982 Acres Harvested										
Barley	35,000					*	900	*		*
Corn	1,140,000	*		*	*	*	*	8,100	5,600	41,100
Cotton (Am. Pima Irrig.)	19,500									
Cotton (Upland)	4,300,000		30,200		*	3,100	1,600		1,700	15,800
Cowpeas (Green)	2,000	*		*		*			*	*
Cowpeas (Dry)	21,000							300		
Hay	2,980,000	22,600	1,900	10,100	*	7,000	3,100	21,900	28,700	9,900
Oats	290,000	200		*		1,500	*	500	200	*
Peanuts	225,000	1,200	*					16,100	*	*
Rice (Irrig.)	474,000	*							4,000	
Rye	28,000	*		100			*	*	*	*
Sorghum (Grain)	5,550,000	800	15,000	*	7,000	600	26,500	9,300	11,500	96,500
Sorghum (Hay)	165,000	*	*			*	*	6,300	*	*
Soybeans	920,000								*	13,500
Sugarbeets (Irrig.)	29,400									*
Sugarcane (Irrig.)	36,700									
Sunflowers	245,000						2,800			21,500
Wheat	6,000,000	600	1,700	*		50,600	75,900	12,100	1,000	52,800
Vegetables	211,900	390		*			*	1,960	*	1,315
1982										
Grapefruit (Boxes)	13,900,000									
Oranges (Boxes)	5,940,000									
Peaches (Bushels)	292,000	1,000		*		*		10,000	*	*
Pecans (Pounds)	17,000,000	*		*	*	*	*	70,000	*	*
Livestock										
Cattle (1/1/82)	15,000,000	72,000	21,000	25,000	2,000	82,000	37,000	117,000	99,000	54,000
Hogs (12/1/81)	550,000	4,200	*		*	7,000	1,000	5,500	2,500	*
Sheep (1/1/82)	2,225,000		*			*	*	*	*	21,000
Angora Goats (1/1/82)	1,140,000									
1982										
Milk (Thousand Lbs.)	3,770,000	14,200	*	*	*	101,000	*	21,200	*	13,000
Wool (Lbs.)	18,700,000		*			*	*	*	*	250,000
Mohair (Lbs.)	9,800,000									
1982										
Crop Receipts (Thousands)	$4,248,953	$2,224	$8,979	$2,245	$1,292	$6,910	$9,203	$15,056	$6,377	$34,309
Livestock/Prod. Receipts (Thous.)	$5,430,712	$22,881	$4,884	$10,002	$578	$33,202	$8,849	$36,769	$31,447	$26,026
Total Cash Receipts (Thous.)	$9,679,665	$25,105	$13,863	$12,247	$1,870	$40,112	$18,052	$51,825	$37,824	$60,335
Rank in State		149	201	211	253	83	177	51	100	36
Income										
Farm Population (1980)	268,893	1,513	157	971	50	900	426	1,810	1,570	1,103
Farm Households[F]	60,585	302	33	163	6	200	104	417	493	268
Average Total Income (1979)	$25,864	$25,876	$8,408	$29,053	$37,385	$28,541	$21,245	$26,493	$19,776	$31,793
Average Farm Income (1979)	$7,944	$4,008	-$393	$1,705	$8,915	$13,034	$10,281	$6,506	$4,407	$17,525

Source: Texas Department of Agriculture/U.S. Department of Agriculture/U.S. Department of Commerce, Bureau of Census
*Withheld due to limited production, or to avoid disclosure of individual operations.   [P]Preliminary figures, 1982 Census of Agriculture, Bureau of Census
[F]Households with Farm Self-Employment Income   [E]Estimate

COUNTY AGRICULTURE

	BANDERA	BASTROP	BAYLOR	BEE	BELL	BEXAR	BLANCO	BORDEN	BOSQUE	BOWIE	BRAZORIA
1982 Acres											
Approx. Land Area	488,000	570,000	541,000	539,000	670,000	797,000	460,000	580,000	634,000	570,000	911,000
Land in Farms/Ranches	398,000	448,000	499,000	499,000	537,000	523,000	409,000	553,000	559,000	289,000	655,000
Cropland Planted	17,000	53,000	132,000	86,000	203,000	142,000	15,000	32,000	99,000	85,000	119,000
Land Irrigated	*	1,000	4,000	4,000	2,000	20,000	*	2,000	2,000	3,000	68,000
Pasture/Rangeland	361,000	371,000	297,000	366,000	343,000	371,000	372,000	474,000	459,000	194,000	442,000
No. of Farms[P]	475	1,507	351	688	1,677	2,009	488	135	1,005	1,130	1,316
Ave. Farm Size[P]	714	250	1,144	602	268	249	760	4,268	550	225	478
Foreign Owned Acres (1983)	4,014	905	39		1,453	4,194	3,876		2,012	30,173	5,778
1982 Acres Harvested											
Barley			*		*	*	*	*	*		
Corn	*	2,800	*	28,200	8,500	20,000	*			500	2,200
Cotton (Am. Pima Irrig.)											
Cotton (Upland)		*	12,400	*	6,000			20,900	*		4,500
Cowpeas (Green)		*	*			*	*		*		*
Cowpeas (Dry)											
Hay	6,300	23,400	3,100	14,500	17,400	20,800	6,200	1,400	30,000	29,400	9,100
Oats	500	400	1,100	200	2,800	1,100	700	*	8,700	100	300
Peanuts		1,300	*			2,400		*	*		
Rice (Irrig.)									2,200		48,900
Rye	*	400			300		*	*	*	200	800
Sorghum (Grain)	600	8,400	1,500	33,000	70,000	25,000	400	500	9,500	4,000	13,000
Sorghum (Hay)	*	*	*	*	1,400	3,200	*	*	*	*	
Soybeans						*				13,000	24,100
Sugarbeets (Irrig.)											
Sugarcane (Irrig.)											
Sunflowers											
Wheat	600	6,000	90,800	2,100	70,000	10,300	900	600	23,200	15,600	1,200
Vegetables		*	*	1,525	*	1,460			*	180	230
1982											
Grapefruit (Boxes)											
Oranges (Boxes)											1,000
Peaches (Bushels)	*	*	*	*	1,400	2,100	3,000	*	*	*	1,500
Pecans (Pounds)	*	112,000	*		182,000	509,000	*	*	65,000	*	*
Livestock											
Cattle (1/1/82)	21,000	85,000	35,000	63,000	64,000	63,000	27,000	14,000	92,000	66,000	57,000
Hogs (12/1/81)	*	6,900	*	*	2,700	8,700	1,200		2,400	2,000	4,100
Sheep (1/1/82)	8,000			*	1,900	2,500	11,000	7,000	3,400		
Angora Goats (1/1/82)	6,000				*	*	12,000		5,000		
1982											
Milk (Thousand Lbs.)	*	*	*	*	*	33,100	7,200	*	7,500	44,000	4,900
Wool (Lbs.)	75,000			*	16,000	16,000	65,000	60,000	30,000		
Mohair (Lbs.)	60,000				8,000	*	68,000		42,000		
1982											
Crop Receipts (Thousands)	$324	$3,501	$12,013	$10,213	$18,505	$19,408	$1,589	$6,156	$4,918	$6,140	$29,035
Livestock/Prod. Receipts (Thous.)	$6,415	$24,558	$5,523	$17,246	$22,289	$30,353	$10,703	$3,033	$31,500	$24,351	$20,674
Total Cash Receipts (Thous.)	$6,739	$28,059	$17,536	$27,459	$40,794	$49,761	$12,292	$9,189	$36,418	$30,491	$19,709
Rank in State	238	137	181	139	79	53	210	227	107	127	54
Income											
Farm Population (1980)	606	1,767	359	997	2,547	2,345	693	393	1,231	1,590	1,689
Farm Households[F]	175	392	107	249	649	587	192	75	339	321	235
Average Total Income (1979)	$21,796	$18,083	$19,025	$31,768	$23,782	$20,476	$20,729	$26,348	$19,422	$33,140	$49,946
Average Farm Income (1979)	$3,616	$2,430	$10,134	$5,223	$3,629	$3,312	$4,539	$15,382	$2,928	$3,338	$6,151

Source: Texas Department of Agriculture/U.S. Department of Agriculture/U.S. Department of Commerce, Bureau of Census
*Withheld due to limited production, or to avoid disclosure of individual operations.   [P]Preliminary figures, 1982 Census of Agriculture, Bureau of Census.
[F]Households with Farm Self-Employment Income   [E]Estimate

FLYING THE COLORS: TEXAS ©JOHN CLEMENTS 1984

BRAZOS	BREWSTER	BRISCOE	BROOKS	BROWN	BURLESON	BURNET	CALDWELL	CALHOUN	CALLAHAN	CAMERON	CAMP	CARSON	CASS
375,000	3,971,000	559,000	579,000	600,000	429,000	637,000	348,000	337,000	548,000	573,000	123,000	576,000	602,000
250,000	2,808,000	537,000	549,000	539,000	329,000	558,000	288,000	236,000	498,000	475,000	66,000	561,000	248,000
46,000	6,000	160,000	14,000	71,000	51,000	23,000	57,000	70,000	90,000	238,000	12,000	261,000	25,000
9,000	7,000	54,000	7,000	3,000	14,000	*	*	24,000	4,000	215,000	*	140,000	*
197,000	2,649,000	360,000	474,000	446,000	258,000	505,000	219,000	149,000	410,000	194,000	54,000	289,000	212,000
874	111	251	331	1,181	1,260	827	977	273	800	1,173	413	351	894
294	23,196	1,582	1,463	444	264	641	262	723	673	329	169	1,771	219
8,166	422				8,617	213	9,410	4,333	787	16,109			
*		*		*		*			*	*		*	
*		1,700	*	*	1,600	*	3,300	6,700	*	19,600	*	2,700	*
11,800		19,500		*	9,500	*	5,100		*	93,600		*	
*		*	*	*	1,700		*		*	100	*		*
										200			
14,500	5,600	4,400	4,100	15,500	16,400	9,400	13,500	1,500	9,100	2,700	9,200	4,100	21,200
100		*	*	5,500	500	1,100	300	*	2,600	*	*	*	*
		*		5,300					2,400				*
								12,300					
*		*		400	*		*	*	*		*		*
5,100		19,500	4,400	3,500	8,400	500	18,500	43,000	4,100	89,000	*	95,500	*
2,000		2,100	*	1,200	*	*	*	*	*		*	2,300	
*		7,200			*			2,100		2,000			
										6,500			
										*		*	
1,300		21,900	*	9,500	1,900	2,100	4,000	1,300	38,900	*	*	129,200	800
*		275	3,410		650		325		230	3,810	360		440
										1,800,000			
										326,000			
1,200			*	1,300	*	2,300	*		2,300		8,000		2,000
*	*	*	129,000	*	*	*	*	*	*	*	*		*
92,000	59,000	15,000	45,000	67,000	62,000	55,000	50,000	26,000	62,000	41,000	19,000	52,000	41,000
6,900	*	*	*	8,900	7,000	4,100	15,000	*	2,500	1,300	*	*	*
	10,000	*		10,000	*	15,000	*		1,100			*	
	3,000			8,000		11,000			*				
10,200	*	*	6,700	51,000	*	*	*	*	*	9,400	20,400	*	*
	65,000	8,000		68,000	*	115,000	*		7,000			*	
	40,000			50,000		96,000			*				
$6,738	$743	$10,362	$3,416	$4,316	$6,497	$1,012	$5,109	$12,343	$4,770	$67,041	$1,118	$27,137	$2,831
$26,163	$13,630	$3,724	$13,878	$28,956	$19,918	$15,481	$26,027	$8,119	$13,095	$21,971	$42,993	$11,500	$11,017
$32,901	$14,373	$14,086	$17,294	$33,272	$26,415	$16,493	$31,136	$20,462	$17,865	$89,012	$44,111	$38,637	$13,848
118	195	197	182	117	144	188	125	168	180	19	66	93	202
1,279	48	443	294	1,356	1,374	1,041	1,036	378	1,137	2,393	465	809	1,112
258	*	124	62	301	288	283	307	83	291	374	98	163	199
$29,135	*	$15,453	$19,611	$22,915	$20,889	$21,107	$24,600	$28,862	$29,517	$25,261	$29,221	$32,410	$21,762
$5,511	*	$9,338	$1,648	$4,997	$2,924	$3,965	$3,681	$11,122	$7,080	$10,024	$8,170	$20,204	$1,379

COUNTY AGRICULTURE

	CASTRO	CHAMBERS	CHEROKEE	CHILDRESS	CLAY	COCHRAN	COKE	COLEMAN	COLLIN	COLLINGS-WORTH	COLORADO
1982 Acres											
Approx. Land Area	563,000	394,000	671,000	447,000	705,000	501,000	583,000	819,000	535,000	572,000	607,000
Land in Farms/Ranches	550,000	356,000	334,000	428,000	618,000	465,000	559,000	759,000	420,000	542,000	569,000
Cropland Planted	388,000	107,000	34,000	113,000	111,000	364,000	33,000	149,000	243,000	145,000	114,000
Land Irrigated	323,000	66,000	*	6,000	3,000	101,000	1,000	3,000	4,000	18,000	68,000
Pasture/Rangeland	142,000	223,000	289,000	279,000	505,000	169,000	472,000	567,000	206,000	367,000	435,000
No. of Farms[P]	483	331	1,441	323	813	279	357	837	1,543	388	1,424
Ave. Farm Size[P]	1,136	946	173	1,059	717	1,345	1,402	800	230	1,185	419
Foreign Owned Acres (1983)		1,842	58			1,018		9,453	29,933		2,961
1982 Acres Harvested											
Barley	*		*	*	*		*	*	*	*	
Corn	86,900	*				*		*	4,300		29,800
Cotton (Am. Pima Irrig.)											
Cotton (Upland)	40,900			43,700	3,500	47,400		3,800	10,500	58,800	*
Cowpeas (Green)		*	*	*		*			*		
Cowpeas (Dry)											
Hay	4,400	2,900	28,000	2,700	8,000	*	7,300	14,900	21,000	7,500	21,900
Oats	1,300	*	200	600	1,300	*	500	24,600	4,200	*	200
Peanuts			*								
Rice (Irrig.)			44,000								44,800
Rye	500	*	100	200	*				*	*	*
Sorghum (Grain)	30,500	*	*	2,000	2,100	203,000	1,200	20,000	66,500	9,600	2,200
Sorghum (Hay)	*		*	*	*		*	2,200	3,300	2,300	
Soybeans	27,900	52,400				*			*		7,100
Sugarbeets (Irrig.)	8,500										
Sugarcane (Irrig.)											
Sunflowers	3,500					*					
Wheat	97,600	*	600	47,300	54,700	27,300	2,700	36,200	103,600	26,000	*
Vegetables	5,935	*	300		*	*	*	*	130		
1982											
Grapefruit (Boxes)											
Oranges (Boxes)											
Peaches (Bushels)		*	1,500		6,000		*	*	*		*
Pecans (Pounds)	*	*	*		70,000		*	*	*	*	68,000
Livestock											
Cattle (1/1/82)	145,000	24,000	71,000	20,000	101,000	34,000	26,000	55,000	65,000	37,000	81,000
Hogs (12/1/81)	7,300	*	2,400	*		*	1,200	3,200	1,500	1,700	10,300
Sheep (1/1/82)	39,000				*		60,000	57,000	*	*	
Angora Goats (1/1/82)							4,000	*	*		
1982											
Milk (Thousand Lbs.)	11,400	*	87,000	*	51,000	*	*	9,100	10,100		6,300
Wool (Lbs.)	365,000				*		540,000	370,000	*	*	
Mohair (Lbs.)							36,000	*	*		
1982											
Crop Receipts (Thousands)	$98,749	$28,477	$19,274	$17,068	$9,038	$32,540	$570	$5,623	$21,298	$11,576	$34,450
Livestock/Prod. Receipts (Thous.)	$67,821	$8,138	$34,572	$3,995	$32,662	$10,908	$10,231	$16,598	$22,306	$8,926	$27,541
Total Cash Receipts (Thous.)	$66,570	$36,615	$53,846	$21,063	$41,700	$43,448	$10,801	$22,221	$43,604	$20,502	$61,991
Rank in State	4	104	45	164	76	69	214	159	67	167	35
Income											
Farm Population (1980)	1,967	458	1,713	444	1,405	618	352	1,109	2,293	750	1,495
Farm Households[F]	313	98	445	94	383	120	93	310	432	173	368
Average Total Income (1979)	$25,101	$57,912	$26,625	$21,973	$26,711	$28,688	$30,339	$20,707	$30,737	$19,777	$25,368
Average Farm Income (1979)	$16,773	$16,476	$6,284	$10,034	$11,266	$15,901	$11,394	$9,442	$6,071	$11,694	$7,368

Source: Texas Department of Agriculture/U.S. Department of Agriculture/U.S. Department of Commerce, Bureau of Census.
*Withheld due to limited production, or to avoid disclosure of individual operations.   [P]Preliminary figures, 1982 Census of Agriculture, Bureau of Census.
[F]Households with Farm Self-Employment Income.   [E]Estimate

COMAL	COMANCHE	CONCHO	COOKE	CORYELL	COTTLE	CRANE	CROCKETT	CROSBY	CULBERSON	DALLAM	DALLAS	DAWSON	DEAF SMITH
363,000	604,000	643,000	579,000	668,000	576,000	509,000	1,788,000	583,000	2,465,000	956,000	550,000	577,000	566,000
297,000	529,000	609,000	474,000	589,000	540,000	449,000	1,680,000	555,000	2,098,000	934,000	129,000	550,000	939,000
23,000	136,000	122,000	119,000	120,000	105,000		2,000	307,000	14,000	361,000	72,000	309,000	397,000
*	21,000	8,000	3,000	1,000	6,000		*	125,000	19,000	207,000	*	35,000	260,000
262,000	379,000	455,000	359,000	489,000	328,000	424,000	1,585,000	267,000	1,956,000	544,000	64,000	165,000	392,000
585	1,350	376	1,230	991	235	31	154	430	71	378	1,046	581	653
334	366	1,608	335	627	2,080	10,580	11,363	1,110	26,941	2,226	183	1,006	1,235
1,648	2,810	5,270		1,618		133			72,025	8,957	4,971		4,377
*	*	*	1,400					*	500	*	*	*	1,900
1,400	1,300			1,500				*		49,500	*	*	
	200	19,000	*	*	53,600			114,700	2,900		3,000	251,200	5,800
	*											200	*
									700			300	
7,000	25,800	4,600	23,700	19,000	2,400		*	2,800	3,300	14,000	26,700	1,700	8,200
600	4,600	3,600	8,500	9,000	300			*	*	500	1,800		900
	37,700		*					*					
*	2,200		200	*	600			*	*	*	*	*	*
5,400	6,200	17,000	15,500	20,000	9,700			39,500	2,200	132,000	11,500	23,000	82,000
*	1,800	1,200	1,400	*	*			*	*	1,600	*	*	*
					*				14,500	*		900	*
													11,700
									16,500				4,700
2,300	5,000	55,600	48,500	46,400	13,100		800	12,000	2,300	118,500	16,800	1,400	183,200
*	690		195	*	*			1,395	190		*	*	4,860
*	15,000		*	*	*		*		*		*	*	*
*	652,000	*	*	113,000			*		*		*	*	*
24,000	122,000	19,000	86,000	85,000	25,000	12,000	37,000	17,000	29,000	120,000	21,000	5,000	334,000
2,300	10,000	5,100	2,000	7,200	*		*	*	*	3,800	1,500	6,000	9,400
3,600	5,000	128,000	*	9,000	*	1,300	181,000	*	1,000		*	*	*
2,600	11,000	16,000		16,000			70,000						
*	156,000	*	77,000	*	*	*	*	*	*	*	10,400	*	15,900
19,000	30,000	900,000	*	75,000	*	16,000	1,400,000	*	*		*	*	*
25,000	88,000	100,000	155,000			560,000							
$1,164	$14,124	$12,650	$7,067	$7,753	$10,578		$84	$38,464	$2,952	$47,381	$25,082	$94,204	$65,623
$7,615	$54,965	$9,507	$35,862	$30,362	$6,126	$2,568	$15,895	$4,056	$4,594	$18,106	$9,455	$2,080	$173,298
$8,779	$69,089	$22,157	$42,929	$38,115	$16,704	$2,568	$15,979	$42,520	$7,546	$65,487	$34,537	$96,284	$238,921
228	27	161	72	97	185	251	190	75	237	31	111	17	2
743	2,715	554	2,412	1,212	422	21	156	1,391	69	1,057	402	1,468	1,974
174	702	133	538	340	110	*	46	265	*	169	51	344	420
$28,223	$24,629	$18,156	$23,900	$23,205	$36,738	*	$30,648	$18,906	*	$22,641	$36,199	$27,769	$30,317
$8,889	$9,422	$7,990	$4,364	$5,562	$19,252	*	$22,857	$12,171	*	$17,093	$7,121	$12,161	$15,865

COUNTY AGRICULTURE

	DELTA	DENTON	DE WITT	DICKENS	DIMMIT	DONLEY	DUVAL	EASTLAND	ECTOR	EDWARDS	ELLIS
1982 Acres											
Approx. Land Area	177,000	583,000	582,000	596,000	860,000	579,000	1,161,000	609,000	580,000	1,329,000	602,000
Land in Farms/Ranches	143,000	470,000	539,000	569,000	769,000	561,000	1,008,000	498,000	467,000	1,150,000	485,000
Cropland Planted	73,000	187,000	55,000	102,000	14,000	75,000	38,000	100,000	3,000	6,000	251,000
Land Irrigated	5,000	5,000	*	16,000	14,000	14,000	3,000	17,000	2,000	*	4,000
Pasture/Rangeland	75,000	307,000	452,000	413,000	709,000	403,000	901,000	392,000	444,000	1,079,000	224,000
No. of Farms[P]	446	1,418	1,619	330	223	365	1,074	1,111	215	225	1,608
Ave. Farm Size[P]	337	272	323	1,557	3,301	1,618	904	422	2,621	4,504	277
Foreign Owned Acres (1983)	16,354	8,592	16				3,000	1,100	14		10,419
1982 Acres Harvested											
Barley		*		*		*		*		*	*
Corn	*	*	7,900		*		900	*	*		3,600
Cotton (Am. Pima Irrig.)											
Cotton (Upland)	2,400	5,100		40,600	2,400	27,500		*	*		24,200
Cowpeas (Green)	*	*	*			*		*			*
Cowpeas (Dry)							1,100				
Hay	14,100	22,900	23,300	3,500	1,200	5,200	11,200	25,900		3,200	30,400
Oats		8,100	600	300	400	*	100	2,100		*	4,700
Peanuts		4,000	*				*	26,000	300		
Rice (Irrig.)											
Rye	*	*		*		400		900			*
Sorghum (Grain)	13,400	31,500	5,500	8,900	2,400	12,000	13,500	5,300	*	*	57,500
Sorghum (Hay)		*	*	*	*	1,400	4,500	*	*		2,000
Soybeans	4,700			1,200			*				
Sugarbeets (Irrig.)											
Sugarcane (Irrig.)											
Sunflowers											
Wheat	27,200	89,400	1,900	12,500	1,000	6,500	1,400	6,300	*	*	101,800
Vegetables		*	*		2,580	*	250	620			
1982											
Grapefruit (Boxes)					10,000						
Oranges (Boxes)					5,000		100				
Peaches (Bushels)	*	*	*		*	1,000	9,500	17,000	*	*	*
Pecans (Pounds)	*	*	160,000	*	82,000	*		263,000	*	*	132,000
Livestock											
Cattle (1/1/82)	40,000	89,000	110,000	30,000	57,000	37,000	82,000	62,000	21,000	27,000	61,000
Hogs (12/1/81)		4,000	5,500	*	2,000	*	*	8,000		7,100	4,400
Sheep (1/1/82)	*	1,000	1,100	*		*		1,900		75,000	*
Angora Goats (1/1/82)					*			1,400		155,000	
1982											
Milk (Thousand Lbs.)	12,700	15,600	22,400	*	*	*	18,600	6,400	*	*	19,900
Wool (Lbs.)	*	8,000	8,000	6,000			*	10,000		440,000	*
Mohair (Lbs.)					*			10,000		1,250,000	
1982											
Crop Receipts (Thousands)	$5,023	$17,483	$3,342	$7,694	$8,247	$6,691	$2,154	$9,643	$146	$112	$23,570
Livestock/Prod. Receipts (Thous.)	$13,663	$37,446	$34,571	$13,404	$15,475	$8,641	$26,218	$18,750	$4,551	$13,686	$20,556
Total Cash Receipts (Thous.)	$18,686	$54,929	$37,913	$21,098	$23,722	$15,332	$28,372	$28,393	$4,697	$3,798	$44,126
Rank in State	176	42	99	163	153	192	135	134	245	203	65
Income											
Farm Population (1980)	567	2,196	1,799	653	153	580	379	1,620	246	208	2,437
Farm Households[F]	167	485	508	166	57	156	89	392	50	60	506
Average Total Income (1979)	$21,476	$31,456	$19,346	$15,830	$24,271	$19,925	$29,179	$21,811	$64,322	$35,804	$25,367
Average Farm Income (1979)	$6,744	$6,133	$5,560	$8,249	$2,087	$8,434	$6,415	$12,606	$31,470	$25,585	$5,700

Source: Texas Department of Agriculture/U.S. Department of Agriculture/U.S. Department of Commerce, Bureau of Census

*Withheld due to limited production, or to avoid disclosure of individual operations. [P]Preliminary figures, 1982 Census of Agriculture, Bureau of Census.
[F]Households with Farm Self-Employment Income. [E]Estimate.

EL PASO	ERATH	FALLS	FANNIN	FAYETTE	FISHER	FLOYD	FOARD	FORT BEND	FRANKLIN	FREESTONE	FRIO	GAINES	GALVESTON
676,000	694,000	489,000	579,000	598,000	579,000	636,000	433,000	556,000	188,000	554,000	714,000	953,000	255,000
501,000	609,000	412,000	460,000	503,000	543,000	626,000	410,000	465,000	130,000	394,000	667,000	899,000	96,000
51,000	88,000	200,000	286,000	76,000	145,000	577,000	91,000	162,000	28,000	42,000	111,000	525,000	14,000
61,000	8,000	5,000	15,000	2,000	3,000	260,000	5,000	32,000	*	1,000	75,000	320,000	12,000
391,000	483,000	191,000	211,000	401,000	354,000	159,000	253,000	277,000	100,000	347,000	528,000	291,000	71,000
452	1,563	1,117	1,576	2,610	688	590	250	1,179	478	1,101	525	619	438
663	354	346	274	179	738	1,047	1,370	341	245	346	1,222	1,237	224
	6,412	8,038	8,263	542				6,589	3,894	1,729	2,968	1,319	1,295
*	600	*	*		*	*				*	*	*	
*	*	9,600	1,600	18,600		16,900		21,000		*	3,500	*	*
17,100													
4,500	*	9,700	1,600		76,000	63,900	21,000	35,100			*		295,300
*	*		*		*	*	*	*		*		*	*
											3,600		
8,100	43,200	15,300	32,700	36,600	7,600	2,800	3,000	6,400	21,500	27,600	7,800	6,900	1,800
*	5,000	3,200	1,200	300	200		*	1,000	100	400	1,600	*	*
	8,000	*	6,700	1,100			*		*		16,300	10,800	
								21,500		*			8,600
	200		*	*	*	*	*	*	*	*	*	*	*
4,100	2,100	40,500	30,000	5,300	4,800	50,500	1,300	42,500	1,000	*	16,500	69,500	
*	*	1,600	*	*	1,900		*		*	*	*	*	*
			25,000	*		80,300		28,100				3,300	1,200
						68,500							
6,400	2,700	36,300	130,000	2,000	24,200	119,400	64,000	*	2,400	1,300	14,500	42,100	*
110	130	190	*	*	*	4,865	*	330	*	*	7,570	1,800	*
													1,000
*	7,000	*	*	*	*		*	*	*	*	4,600	*	*
2,550,000	54,000	*	*	127,000	*	*		*	*	*	*	55,000	*
30,000	108,000	112,000	94,000	103,000	32,000	39,000	12,000	50,000	48,000	62,000	72,000	18,000	16,000
2,000	8,600	4,000	1,000	14,200	9,500	1,000	*	2,000	*	1,200	*	1,200	*
*	3,200	*	*	*	*	3,200	*				*	13,000	
	3,000												
85,000	399,000	*	10,800	20,500	7,500	*	*	*	79,000	*	7,500	*	*
*	17,000	*	*	*	*	12,000	*	*				30,000	
	25,000										*		
$24,400	$9,370	$13,942	$16,234	$6,875	$27,028	$65,379	$7,742	$47,856	$1,080	$1,360	$30,541	$121,459	$3,080
$20,924	$89,610	$23,802	$26,992	$45,014	$10,105	$16,672	$2,975	$17,389	$27,556	$19,554	$24,943	$5,480	$4,943
$45,324	$98,980	$37,744	$43,226	$51,889	$37,133	$82,051	$10,717	$65,245	$28,636	$20,914	$55,484	$126,939	$8,023
64	15	101	70	50	102	21	217	32	132	165	40	10	235
570	2,548	1,919	2,079	2,969	1,196	1,677	325	2,454	623	893	730	1,257	180
62	653	465	534	768	321	358	94	457	165	180	145	225	34
$24,575	$37,533	$18,332	$19,733	$19,536	$29,116	$20,840	$26,072	$67,330	$20,543	$22,097	$26,570	$27,485	$39,734
$6,019	$14,392	$5,357	$1,956	$3,762	$13,434	$10,208	$16,182	$6,880	$5,461	$4,271	$6,920	$18,094	$2,564

COUNTY AGRICULTURE

	GARZA	GILLESPIE	GLASSCOCK	GOLIAD	GONZALES	GRAY	GRAYSON	GREGG	GRIMES	GUADALUPE	HALE
1982 Acres											
Approx. Land Area	585,000	675,000	552,000	557,000	676,000	598,000	602,000	180,000	513,000	457,000	627,000
Land in Farms/Ranches	549,000	639,000	525,000	504,000	628,000	579,000	472,000	70,000	356,000	367,000	612,000
Cropland Planted	55,000	66,000	70,000	24,000	73,000	151,000	186,000	8,000	44,000	105,000	578,000
Land Irrigated	8,000	2,000	35,000	2,000	6,000	36,000	6,000	*	*	7,000	441,000
Pasture/Rangeland	461,000	550,000	421,000	442,000	526,000	397,000	324,000	64,000	291,000	235,000	116,000
No. of Farms[P]	240	1,285	200	674	1,632	349	1,765	378	1,196	1,702	832
Ave. Farm Size[P]	2,379	494	2,519	650	383	1,420	230	170	293	203	734
Foreign Owned Acres (1983)		2,769	1,600		481	300	2,433	1,249	670	294	
1982 Acres Harvested											
Barley		700		*	*	*				*	
Corn		*		5,500	4,400	1,000	*		2,800	5,900	67,100
Cotton (Am. Pima Irrig.)											
Cotton (Upland)	40,700		53,200			800	*			*	129,300
Cowpeas (Green)			*	*		*			*		28,800
Cowpeas (Dry)		600									
Hay	2,300	14,300	1,700	7,700	27,200	5,900	25,400	6,500	27,100	18,700	2,800
Oats	*	7,800	*	300	600	600	1,900	*	200	1,700	*
Peanuts	*				1,100		4,300			*	
Rice (Irrig.)											
Rye	*	*			*	*	*	*	400	*	*
Sorghum (Grain)	8,300	6,300	8,600	2,500	8,100	23,000	38,500		1,100	31,000	43,500
Sorghum (Hay)		1,700	2,000	*	*	1,100	*		*	2,200	*
Soybeans	*				*				1,700		141,200
Sugarbeets (Irrig.)											*
Sugarcane (Irrig.)											
Sunflowers				*							6,900
Wheat	1,800	10,700	2,700	600	1,300	96,100	69,300	*	400	9,900	58,100
Vegetables		*	*	2,020	2,425	*	*	*	*	240	2,760
1982											
Grapefruit (Boxes)											
Oranges (Boxes)											
Peaches (Bushels)		28,000		*	*		*		*	8,600	
Pecans (Pounds)		*	*	*	676,000		*		*	687,000	*
Livestock											
Cattle (1/1/82)	16,000	56,000	17,000	66,000	139,000	73,000	74,000	10,000	98,000	53,000	46,000
Hogs (12/1/81)	*	14,900	1,000	*	9,300	6,800	2,700	*	1,700	6,300	13,000
Sheep (1/1/82)		67,000	10,000	*	*		*			*	1,200
Angora Goats (1/1/82)		36,000									
1982											
Milk (Thousand Lbs.)	*	9,000	*	*	*	*	25,600	*	74,000	5,100	6,100
Wool (Lbs.)		570,000	45,000	*	*		*			*	7,000
Mohair (Lbs.)		270,000									
1982											
Crop Receipts (Thousands)	$10,388	$2,438	$27,946	$3,599	$5,927	$10,038	$11,070	$871	$2,703	$7,395	$119,835
Livestock/Prod. Receipts (Thous.)	$9,390	$28,716	$4,083	$19,432	$149,054	$36,310	$24,483	$3,712	$38,680	$18,178	$23,442
Total Cash Receipts (Thous.)	$19,778	$31,154	$32,029	$23,031	$154,981	$46,348	$35,553	$4,583	$41,383	$25,573	$143,277
Rank in State	171	124	121	155	5	61	109	247	78	145	6
Income											
Farm Population (1980)	632	1,924	580	589	2,160	893	2,238	260	1,347	2,494	3,049
Farm Households[F]	153	561	108	178	549	208	567	48	276	638	555
Average Total Income (1979)	$34,056	$18,723	$33,048	$21,096	$22,435	$29,584	$26,669	$27,428	$34,100	$19,748	$23,561
Average Farm Income (1979)	$13,461	$4,403	$19,826	$7,058	$7,114	$17,513	$4,021	$5,978	$5,053	$3,474	$14,994

Source: Texas Department of Agriculture/U.S. Department of Agriculture/U.S. Department of Commerce, Bureau of Census.
*Withheld due to limited production, or to avoid disclosure of individual operations. [P]Preliminary figures, 1982 Census of Agriculture, Bureau of Census.
[F]Households with Farm Self-Employment Income. [E]Estimate.

FLYING THE COLORS: TEXAS ©JOHN CLEMENTS 1984

HALL	HAMILTON	HANSFORD	HARDEMAN	HARDIN	HARRIS	HARRISON	HARTLEY	HASKELL	HAYS	HEMPHILL	HENDERSON	HIDALGO	HILL
566,000	540,000	580,000	440,000	574,000	1,103,000	572,000	952,000	561,000	416,000	579,000	604,000	988,000	646,000
540,000	483,000	569,000	421,000	123,000	465,000	215,000	935,000	519,000	342,000	566,000	336,000	904,000	513,000
119,000	91,000	348,000	168,000	7,000	100,000	31,000	165,000	269,000	33,000	53,000	58,000	466,000	264,000
14,000	2,000	222,000	14,000	2,000	28,000	*	120,000	14,000	*	3,000	2,000	395,000	3,000
347,000	397,000	225,000	210,000	103,000	308,000	183,000	644,000	196,000	288,000	481,000	269,000	289,000	274,000
341	956	315	362	331	1,944	1,031	208	670	643	221	1,509	2,307	1,544
1,346	458	1,857	892	212	200	192	4,230	677	328	2,797	215	361	300
	659			1,000	17,101	913	3,765	23	1,126		6,091	132,106	2,980

HALL	HAMILTON	HANSFORD	HARDEMAN	HARDIN	HARRIS	HARRISON	HARTLEY	HASKELL	HAYS	HEMPHILL	HENDERSON	HIDALGO	HILL
	1,200	1,000	*		*			*	*				*
*	*	3,900			8,200	*	3,100	*	3,300		*	43,800	600
78,700	*		26,600				*	87,700	*		*	46,300	18,900
*				*	*		*		*			100	
											500		1,000
4,200	24,800	3,100	4,400	1,500	15,500	25,100	3,900	4,800	9,200	6,400	37,500	4,000	27,200
*	12,600	*	600	*	*	200	100	500	1,600	*	700	*	2,800
*					1,200		*				*		2,800
				1,600	17,900								
200	*	*	*		*	200	200	*		*	1,300		
5,000	9,300	103,000	1,000		2,200		21,000	35,000	5,400	6,000	2,700	199,000	94,000
1,000	1,800	1,200	*		*		*	2,800	*		*		3,300
	1,800	*		3,000	47,000		*		*			*	
												25,000	
		*					*	*				*	
4,000	16,400	144,800	118,100		1,000	400	106,400	71,000	4,600	26,900	500	1,800	91,400
			*	120	260	140	*	135	*		595	78,250	*

HALL	HAMILTON	HANSFORD	HARDEMAN	HARDIN	HARRIS	HARRISON	HARTLEY	HASKELL	HAYS	HEMPHILL	HENDERSON	HIDALGO	HILL
												11880000	
												5,390,000	
*	2,000		*	*	1,600	4,000		*	*		2,000	*	*
	*		*	*	*	*		*	*		*	*	*

HALL	HAMILTON	HANSFORD	HARDEMAN	HARDIN	HARRIS	HARRISON	HARTLEY	HASKELL	HAYS	HEMPHILL	HENDERSON	HIDALGO	HILL
23,000	76,000	125,000	18,000	3,000	52,000	51,000	103,000	19,000	40,000	70,000	122,000	57,000	68,000
*	4,000	1,200	*		8,000	*	*	*	*	*	1,800	1,000	1,500
*	14,000		*		*				2,900	*		*	*
									2,300				

HALL	HAMILTON	HANSFORD	HARDEMAN	HARDIN	HARRIS	HARRISON	HARTLEY	HASKELL	HAYS	HEMPHILL	HENDERSON	HIDALGO	HILL
*	58,000	*	*	*	16,600	*	*	*	*	*	8,900	18,200	32,900
*	115,000		*		*				14,000	*		*	*
	145,000								15,000				*

HALL	HAMILTON	HANSFORD	HARDEMAN	HARDIN	HARRIS	HARRISON	HARTLEY	HASKELL	HAYS	HEMPHILL	HENDERSON	HIDALGO	HILL
$20,922	$4,488	$36,933	$17,358	$4,394	$34,440	$1,995	$16,349	$28,836	$2,540	$3,159	$8,483	$319,475	$27,785
$6,089	$32,632	$65,964	$4,807	$984	$20,198	$15,015	$66,677	$4,861	$10,438	$27,484	$30,106	$20,525	$30,708
$27,081	$37,120	$102,897	$22,165	$5,378	$54,638	$17,010	$83,026	$33,697	$12,978	$30,643	$38,589	$340,000	$58,493
141	103	13	160	244	44	183	20	115	206	126	94	1	37

HALL	HAMILTON	HANSFORD	HARDEMAN	HARDIN	HARRIS	HARRISON	HARTLEY	HASKELL	HAYS	HEMPHILL	HENDERSON	HIDALGO	HILL
615	1,521	463	666	313	1,129	957	602	1,115	988	653	1,601	3,800	2,410
166	450	110	195	94	206	143	97	287	223	99	287	553	601
$25,331	$16,945	$42,907	$22,893	$25,428	$27,682	$25,111	$26,228	$23,352	$28,717	$43,191	$28,113	$33,600	$26,014
$15,924	$5,506	$19,514	$12,138	$3,896	$5,739	$3,611	$14,675	$14,940	$2,787	$6,736	$2,189	$8,479	$8,346

COUNTY AGRICULTURE

		HOCKLEY	HOOD	HOPKINS	HOUSTON	HOWARD	HUDSPETH	HUNT	HUTCHINSON	IRION	JACK	JACKSON
1982 Acres	Approx. Land Area	581,000	273,000	508,000	798,000	583,000	2,915,000	529,000	560,000	687,000	605,000	544,000
	Land in Farms/Ranches	544,000	229,000	377,000	435,000	533,000	2,518,000	425,000	548,000	650,000	529,000	488,000
	Cropland Planted	380,000ᴱ	68,000	94,000	61,000	111,000	36,000	185,000	76,000	2,000	22,000	147,000
	Land Irrigated	186,000	4,000	*	2,000	10,000	49,000	3,000	60,000	1,000	*	51,000
	Pasture/Rangeland	125,000	148,000	281,000	363,000	394,000	2,342,000	284,000	384,000	611,000	479,000	288,000
	No. of Farmsᴾ	633	594	1,672	1,387	398	140	1,866	157	127	643	801
	Ave. Farm Sizeᴾ	831	401	213	317	1,157	15,367	193	3,003	6,243	771	553
	Foreign Owned Acres (1983)			7,374	7,210		4,677	4,366			888	10,185
1982 Acres Harvested	Barley		*	*			700		*		*	
	Corn	*	*		1,000	*	*	*	700			19,000
	Cotton (Am. Pima Irrig.)						2,400					
	Cotton (Upland)	111,800		*	5,600	92,600	8,800	9,600		*		2,000
	Cowpeas (Green)				*							*
	Cowpeas (Dry)	500				200						
	Hay	1,100	12,100	68,900	29,000	1,800	14,300	31,900	200	*	4,200	3,300
	Oats		700	600	1,600		*	1,600	*	*	1,100	*
	Peanuts	*	4,400	*	3,000							
	Rice (Irrig.)			*								36,800
	Rye	*	*	300	1,000	*		*		*		*
	Sorghum (Grain)	232,000	1,600	2,000	4,400	2,500	3,700	18,500	11,000		*	79,500
	Sorghum (Hay)		*	*	*	1,500	*		*	*		*
	Soybeans	5,800		2,300	*			*		*		1,100
	Sugarbeets (Irrig.)											
	Sugarcane (Irrig.)											
	Sunflowers	6,500				*		*	*			
	Wheat	21,500	1,700	3,300	1,200	2,200	1,500	98,900	33,700	*	7,100	700
	Vegetables	*	*	*	160	*	1,140	*			*	
1982	Grapefruit (Boxes)											
	Oranges (Boxes)											
	Peaches (Bushels)	*	1,500	*	*		*	*			*	*
	Pecans (Pounds)	*	2,556,000	*	*	*	63,000	*		*	*	*
Livestock	Cattle (1/1/82)	9,000	32,000	176,000	115,000	15,000	26,000	80,000	21,000	23,000	51,000	45,000
	Hogs (12/1/81)	3,100	*	1,900	3,500	*	7,800	1,300	2,000		1,500	*
	Sheep (1/1/82)	*	*	*		1,600	4,000	*		56,000		*
	Angora Goats (1/1/82)									4,000		
1982	Milk (Thousand Lbs.)	*	19,400	595,000	11,500	*	*	11,100	*	*	*	*
	Wool (Lbs.)	*	*	*		10,000	25,000	*		440,000	*	*
	Mohair (Lbs.)									25,000	*	
1982	Crop Receipts (Thousands)	$48,720	$4,307	$2,888	$5,468	$38,367	$11,833	$16,448	$7,043	$196	$890	$33,506
	Livestock/Prod. Receipts (Thous.)	$4,683	$12,241	$133,941	$33,470	$4,524	$8,804	$23,476	$6,277	$8,005	$13,174	$14,221
	Total Cash Receipts (Thous.)	$53,403	$16,548	$136,829	$38,938	$42,891	$20,637	$39,924	$13,320	$8,201	$14,064	$47,727
	Rank in State	47	186	7	91	73	166	84	205	234	198	59
Income	Farm Population (1980)	1,686	834	2,675	1,225	804	351	2,041	479	101	542	1,200
	Farm Householdsᶠ	358	206	629	334	169	38	508	116	25	151	282
	Average Total Income (1979)	$18,155	$24,934	$25,569	$23,329	$45,057	$30,053	$19,933	$15,709	$47,511	$20,478	$26,415
	Average Farm Income (1979)	$8,643	$6,910	$11,201	$4,357	$28,443	$20,118	$3,011	$12,584	$21,146	$5,952	$10,624

Source: Texas Department of Agriculture/U.S. Department of Agriculture/U.S. Department of Commerce, Bureau of Census.
*Withheld due to limited production, or to avoid disclosure of individual operations. ᴾPreliminary figures, 1982 Census of Agriculture, Bureau of Census.
ᶠHouseholds with Farm Self-Employment Income. ᴱEstimate.

JASPER	JEFF DAVIS	JEFFERSON	JIM HOGG	JIM WELLS	JOHNSON	JONES	KARNES	KAUFMAN	KENDALL	KENEDY	KENT	KERR	KIMBLE
580,000	1,446,000	609,000	732,000	541,000	474,000	612,000	485,000	522,000	429,000	892,000	563,000	705,000	815,000
116,000	1,249,000	390,000	689,000	468,000	368,000	574,000	419,000	421,000	368,000	659,000	532,000	599,000	759,000
7,000	10,000	80,000	14,000	144,000	90,000	298,000	97,000	124,000	18,000	3,000	41,000	12,000	9,000
*	9,000	65,000	3,000	15,000	4,000	11,000	1,000	1,000	*	*	2,000	*	2,000
105,000	1,170,000	272,000	594,000	293,000	249,000	235,000	303,000	310,000	329,000	614,000	465,000	535,000	709,000
659	78	502	206	785	1,798	950	1,075	1,507	586	25	177	529	423
115	20,794	734	4,122	588	179	564	391	260	593	22,786	3,279	1,114	1,702
	15,078	6,741	1,541	724			132	11,538	1,321		1,920	4,282	70
	900				*	900	*		*			*	*
*	*			11,300	*	*	20,000	*	*	*	*	*	
				5,300	3,700	88,900			5,700		16,100		
*			500		*	*	*		*				
				2,600									
4,900	*	3,200	3,100	16,300	28,200	10,400	25,900	32,900	7,200	1,000	*	4,100	2,300
*			*	100	2,400	500	300	5,300	700	*	300	1,200	100
					1,500	*	*						
		43,000											
*		*			*	*	*	200	*		*		*
*	*	*	7,400	83,500	9,400	31,000	16,000	12,500	800	*	1,700	500	*
	*			1,100	1,900	2,400	1,900		1,000	*	*	*	*
		32,100				2,000							
						1,600							
*	2,800	*	*	7,900	23,600	109,700	13,400	34,200	1,100	*	9,000	500	800
*			1,120	1,680	*	155	100	*		500			
				4,000									
				1,000									
*	*	*		*	1,200	*	2,000	5,000	*			*	*
*	*	*			65,000	*	*	*	*			*	*
15,000	49,000	21,000	49,000	55,000	65,000	35,000	82,000	98,000	24,000	63,000	18,000	25,000	22,000
2,400	*		*	*	1,700	3,400	12,100	2,300	2,500			*	*
		*	*		*	2,100	*	*	17,500		*	27,000	54,000
	12,000								15,000			20,000	57,000
*	*	*	*	23,700	148,000	*	15,400	*	15,100	*	*	*	*
		*				*	10,000	*	140,000		*	260,000	480,000
	85,000								110,000			130,000	480,000
$1,749	$847	$23,766	$2,006	$14,687	$6,074	$42,046	$5,986	$5,894	$635	$506	$4,140	$273	$212
$6,971	$7,749	$7,884	$14,475	$20,585	$41,956	$7,322	$27,470	$30,684	$10,133	$15,993	$5,200	$8,956	$10,680
$8,720	$8,596	$31,650	$16,481	$35,272	$48,030	$49,368	$33,456	$36,578	$10,768	$16,499	$9,340	$9,229	$10,892
229	230	123	189	110	58	56	116	105	216	187	225	226	213
592	137	571	17	1,214	2,451	1,869	1,452	1,985	973	127	284	592	405
76	14	96	*	244	572	430	330	348	204	17	75	144	145
$31,083	$21,019	$33,379	*	$34,284	$27,095	$25,482	$22,140	$41,115	$27,611	$36,187	$21,253	$17,844	$18,335
$197	$10,444	$3,698	*	$12,703	$4,495	$11,395	$6,856	$5,094	$3,713	$9,134	$8,157	$6,239	$7,656

COUNTY AGRICULTURE

	KING	KINNEY	KLEBERG	KNOX	LAMAR	LAMB	LAMPASAS	LA SALLE	LAVACA	LEE	LEON
1982 Acres											
Approx. Land Area	604,000	892,000	545,000	545,000	572,000	654,000	465,000	960,000	624,000	408,000	705,000
Land in Farms/Ranches	580,000	810,000	518,000	514,000	447,000	634,000	428,000	869,000	529,000	318,000	439,000
Cropland Planted	21,000	7,000	85,000	215,000	160,000	532,000	38,000	29,000	51,000	51,000	40,000
Land Irrigated	2,000	7,000	2,000	33,000	7,000	320,000	*	7,000	8,000	1,000	*
Pasture/Rangeland	517,000	758,000	444,000	259,000	271,000	131,000	371,000	790,000	439,000	248,000	367,000
No. of Farms[P]	45	108	255	403	1,432	823	611	256	2,315	1,447	1,227
Ave. Farm Size[P]	9,289	6,523	3,605	1,183	271	678	706	3,157	212	202	361
Foreign Owned Acres (1983)					15,635			3,148	1,544	195	4,100
1982 Acres Harvested											
Barley					*		*		*	*	*
Corn		1,600	4,000	*	*	62,300	*	*	5,700	1,900	*
Cotton (Am. Pima Irrig.)											
Cotton (Upland)	7,600		5,200	43,200	2,300	118,200			*		*
Cowpeas (Green)			*	*		*				*	*
Cowpeas (Dry)								500			
Hay	*	1,200	4,500	4,600	52,000	8,800	13,900	3,800	26,300	17,800	36,900
Oats	*	200	*	2,600	2,600	*	3,900	400	200	400	100
Peanuts	*				1,400		*	*	*	6,700	*
Rice (Irrig.)									4,800		
Rye	400	*	*		*	*	*		*	*	*
Sorghum (Grain)	*	*	67,500	7,000	12,500	73,000	900	7,800	4,500	1,600	*
Sorghum (Hay)		*			*	*					
Soybeans					16,400	48,700					
Sugarbeets (Irrig.)											
Sugarcane (Irrig.)											
Sunflowers					*	28,000					
Wheat	3,400	1,100	*	117,000	55,800	59,100	7,700	3,300	*	3,600	600
Vegetables		240	1,485	1,585	120	1,070	*	2,115	*	*	190
1982											
Grapefruit (Boxes)											
Oranges (Boxes)			1,000								
Peaches (Bushels)			*	*	1,300		*	*	*	*	*
Pecans (Pounds)		*	*	*	*		*	*	88,000	*	*
Livestock											
Cattle (1/1/82)	29,000	23,000	75,000	36,000	93,000	79,000	50,000	80,000	98,000	81,000	118,000
Hogs (12/1/81)	1,300		*	1,200	*	3,600	6,300	*	6,100	7,700	4,000
Sheep (1/1/82)		110,000	*			*	20,000		*	*	
Angora Goats (1/1/82)		41,000					13,000				
1982											
Milk (Thousand Lbs.)	*	*	*	*	31,600	*	*	*	11,300	*	*
Wool (Lbs.)		880,000	*			*	190,000		*	*	
Mohair (Lbs.)		330,000					140,000				
1982											
Crop Receipts (Thousands)	$1,368	$1,189	$12,915	$24,177	$10,443	$78,554	$1,285	$3,183	$4,633	$2,620	$2,952
Livestock/Prod. Receipts (Thous.)	$8,304	$8,530	$26,657	$7,825	$32,123	$39,563	$18,054	$22,010	$35,782	$29,664	$36,478
Total Cash Receipts (Thous.)	$9,672	$9,719	$39,572	$32,002	$42,566	$118,117	$19,339	$25,193	$40,415	$32,284	$39,430
Rank in State	220	219	85	122	74	11	172	148	81	119	87
Income											
Farm Population (1980)	138	265	780	739	1,670	2,348	953	202	3,046	1,477	1,183
Farm Households[F]	23	53	85	209	431	502	292	49	726	364	263
Average Total Income (1979)	$22,006	$27,558	$35,996	$28,325	$24,718	$27,123	$21,138	$39,214	$20,437	$20,989	$22,603
Average Farm Income (1979)	$16,067	$5,209	$14,193	$17,375	$7,655	$8,607	$4,536	$5,962	$4,047	$3,788	$3,384

Source: Texas Department of Agriculture/U.S. Department of Agriculture/U.S. Department of Commerce, Bureau of Census.
*Withheld due to limited production, or to avoid disclosure of individual operations.   [P]Preliminary figures, 1982 Census of Agriculture, Bureau of Census.
[F]Households with Farm Self-Employment Income.   [E]Estimate.

FLYING THE COLORS: TEXAS ©JOHN CLEMENTS 1984

LIBERTY	LIMESTONE	LIPSCOMB	LIVE OAK	LLANO	LOVING	LUBBOCK	LYNN	McCULLOCH	McLENNAN	McMULLEN	MADISON	MARION	MARTIN
755,000	596,000	598,000	675,000	602,000	415,000	572,000	586,000	682,000	640,000	742,000	307,000	243,000	583,000
396,000	504,000	584,000	578,000	559,000	360,000	475,000	555,000	649,000	486,000	649,000	227,000	77,000	560,000
143,000	123,000	144,000	86,000	7,000		474,000	414,000	116,000	238,000	13,000	26,000	9,000	164,000
48,000	3,000	26,000	3,000	520,000	*	230,000	40,000	7,000	4,000	*	*	*	10,000
240,000	339,000	407,000	454,000		340,000	85,000	166,300	526,000	261,000	600,000	190,000	63,000	364,000
858	1,209	294	770	520	14	1,029	556	521	1,951	208	708	207	390
418	381	1,836	677	1,023	23,472	536	933	1,285	240	2,553	277	237	1,448
7,976	3,876			243		987			6,703	7,938			
	*	*	*				*	*				*	*
*	1,000	*	20,300			1,400			9,400	800		*	*
	1,400					170,400	142,400	2,900	4,500				136,200
	*		*			200	100		*		*	*	800
4,800	24,300	14,000	20,500	3,400		2,500	2,100	13,000	30,800	2,200	14,100	6,900	3,700
*	100	1,000	100	200			*	6,200	19,200	100	100		*
	*		*	*			*	*	800				
34,100													
*	*	*		*			*	*	600		*	*	*
1,500	20,500	8,900	17,000	*		86,500	90,000	16,500	72,000	5,200	1,200		4,000
	*	2,100	1,400				*	3,500	3,200	3,300	*	*	1,200
89,300						18,500	3,900						
						31,500	32,300						
5,200	19,500	93,100	10,000	*		10,200	9,100	47,900	63,500	*	400	*	600
220	130		*	*		820	*	110	*	*	*	*	*
*	10,000		*	*			*		1,000		1,600		
*	*		*	*		*	*	*	66,000		132,000	*	*
22,000	118,000	44,000	72,000	47,000	2,000	66,000	10,000	47,000	87,000	31,000	68,000	12,000	10,000
*	*	1,700	2,000	24,500		24,000	1,300	6,200	5,000	*	3,300	*	*
		*	*	4,000		2,400		*	72,000	1,100			
			*	5,000					17,000	1,200			
*	*	*	*	*	*	6,500	*	*	45,000	*	8,400	*	*
	*	*		25,000		10,000	*	*	580,000	9,000			
			*	45,000				115,000	9,000				
$32,873	$6,149	$9,404	$6,289	$683		$62,993	$50,292	$7,398	$29,059	$627	$16,728	$933	$53,448
$7,650	$32,209	$10,468	$21,285	$17,225	$501	$39,557	$2,756	$15,829	$41,292	$8,765	$19,787	$3,598	$3,052
$40,523	$38,358	$19,872	$27,574	$17,908	$501	$102,550	$53,048	$23,227	$70,351	$9,392	$36,515	$4,591	$56,500
80	96	170	138	179	254	14	49	154	26	224	106	246	38
1,160	1,073	558	1,030	683	13	4,086	1,565	766	2,800	247	828	204	1,026
283	288	128	248	181	*	695	333	204	705	56	132	55	206
$30,696	$26,049	$21,071	$21,578	$15,760	*	$26,063	$23,991	$17,440	$23,148	$25,559	$30,561	$17,412	$29,113
$4,371	$3,930	$9,689	$6,526	$5,015	*	$13,905	$13,880	$9,943	$4,488	$8,867	$4,998	$1,819	$20,233

FLYING THE COLORS: TEXAS ©JOHN CLEMENTS 1984

	MASON	MATAGORDA	MAVERICK	MEDINA	MENARD	MIDLAND	MILAM	MILLS	MITCHELL	MONTAGUE	MONT-GOMERY
1982 Acres											
Approx. Land Area	598,000	740,000	825,000	865,000	585,000	601,000	658,000	470,000	589,000	596,000	698,000
Land in Farms/Ranches	559,000	595,000	728,000	728,000	549,000	541,000	536,000	424,000	563,000	499,000	216,000
Cropland Planted	16,000	168,000	17,000	154,000	11,000	47,000	162,000	49,000	89,000	76,000	9,000
Land Irrigated	9,000	67,000	15,000	46,000	3,000	17,000	5,000	3,000	5,000	2,000	*
Pasture/Rangeland	510,000	356,000	665,000	578,000	507,000	428,000	348,000	359,000	437,000	403,000	192,000
No. of Farms[P]	566	702	176	1,480	268	336	1,583	677	406	1,065	797
Ave. Farm Size[P]	970	815	4,081	480	1,731	2,447	326	565	1,669	408	207
Foreign Owned Acres (1983)		4,773	502	412		1,126	3,941				4,025
1982 Acres Harvested											
Barley	*			*	*		*	*	*	*	
Corn	*	1,400	*	29,200	*		8,700		*	*	*
Cotton (Am. Pima Irrig.)											
Cotton (Upland)		3,300		1,100		33,100	11,900		53,900		
Cowpeas (Green)	*			*		*	*		*	*	*
Cowpeas (Dry)											
Hay		4,400	4,700	13,900	2,000	5,300	24,600	9,500	3,400	13,900	6,200
Oats	200		900	6,500	300	800	1,000	7,00	100	1,100	*
Peanuts	4,600		*	1,800			*	*		1,700	
Rice (Irrig.)		48,300									
Rye	*	*		*	*	*	*		*	700	
Sorghum (Grain)	*	69,000	*	48,000	700	1,800	44,000	1,900	3,400	1,800	
Sorghum (Hay)		*		2,600	*	*	2,100	*	1,000	*	*
Soybeans		26,800		*			*				*
Sugarbeets (Irrig.)											
Sugarcane (Irrig.)											
Sunflowers				13,500							
Wheat	*	3,500	1,800		2,600	2,100	37,200	3,200	4,600	31,100	*
Vegetables	130	*	965	1,565	*	*	200	*	*	325	140
1982											
Grapefruit (Boxes)											
Oranges (Boxes)											
Peaches (Bushels)	*	*	*				*	*	1,200	14,000	*
Pecans (Pounds)	*	*	707,000	221,000	*	*	134	1,547,000	*	75,000	*
Livestock											
Cattle (1/1/82)	51,000	72,000	86,000	84,000	18,000	14,000	116,000	47,000	27,000	75,000	23,000
Hogs (12/1/81)	13,900	*	*	1,000	*	1,000	10,000	6,800	*	4,800	*
Sheep (1/1/82)	14,000	*	*	2,500	85,000	10,000	*	51,000	11,000	*	*
Angora Goats (1/1/82)	33,000		*	*	18,000			50,000			
1982											
Milk (Thousand Lbs.)	*	*		9,400	*	10,400	12,900	6,800	*	18,100	5,000
Wool (Lbs.)	110,000	*	*	12,000	850,000	47,000	*	470,000	55,000	*	
Mohair (Lbs.)	260,000		*	*	190,000			480,000			
1982											
Crop Receipts (Thousands)	$4,351	$50,110	$3,904	$18,816	$490	$15,172	$14,929	$3,305	$13,470	$4,790	$14,199
Livestock/Prod. Receipts (Thous.)	$17,398	$24,607	$32,225	$27,649	$13,288	$7,843	$39,749	$20,633	$5,470	$,22,259	$8,181
Total Cash Receipts (Thous.)	$21,749	$74,717	$36;129	$46,465	$13,778	$23,015	$54,678	$23,938	$18,940	$27,049	$22,380
Rank in State	162	23	108	60	204	156	43	151	175	143	158
Income											
Farm Population (1980)	723	934	322	1,930	319	594	2,194	1,037	924	1,381	1,268
Farm Households[F]	188	199	38	526	94	127	463	276	231	319	172
Average Total Income (1979)	$24,588	$27,145	$23,162	$22,792	$18,770	$24,789	$19,524	$13,500	$34,455	$20,736	$27,379
Average Farm Income (1979)	$12,753	$10,444	$2,637	$4,599	$8,217	$8,972	$3,392	$3,798	$20,145	$4,600	$2,426

Source: Texas Department of Agriculture/U.S. Department of Agriculture/U.S. Department of Commerce, Bureau of Census.
*Withheld due to limited production, or to avoid disclosure of individual operations.   [P]Preliminary figures, 1982 Census of Agriculture, Bureau of Census.
[F]Households with Farm Self-Employment Income   [E]Estimate.

MOORE	MORRIS	MOTLEY	NACOG- DOCHES	NAVARRO	NEWTON	NOLAN	NUECES	OCHILTREE	OLDHAM	ORANGE	PALO PINTO	PANOLA	PARKER
582,000	166,000	627,000	577,000	685,000	607,000	590,000	538,000	580,000	946,000	230,000	607,000	556,000	578,000
572,000	84,000	594,000	247,000	588,000	120,000	553,000	455,000	568,000	920,000	63,000	474,000	235,000	428,000
227,000	18,000	77,000	36,000	164,000	5,000	98,000	352,000	344,000	140,000	6,000	34,000	28,000	53,000
195,000	2,000	7,000	*	2,000	*	4,000	2,000	98,000	26,000	2,000	*	*	3,000
284,000	67,000	476,000	205,000	439,000	103,000	408,000	92,000	183,000	765,000	51,000	412,000	207,000	349,000
270	379	233	1,237	1,464	323	452	735	394	149	315	655	934	1,751
1,983	195	2,199	190	342	320	1,046	624	1,555	6,547	189	713	222	214
	253		315	1,888	292	1,990	400	1,130		4			22
1,800		*				*		*	*		*		*
19,300	*	*	*	*	*		10,100	*	*	*		*	*
		45,100		14,700		45,700	53,800				*		*
			*		*	*	*			*		*	
2,500	11,900	3,200	30,500	38,500	2,800	10,700	10,500	3,800	2,300	2,100	7,700	22,000	20,100
700	*	300	400	7,900	*	1,200	*	900	*		1,200	*	3,900
	*	2,000									1,300		4,400
						*				1,400			
83,500	*	200	*	*	*		*	*	*	*	*	200	*
*	1,000	4,700		23,500		14,500	270,000	48,500	46,000	*	*	1,000	1,100
	*	1,100	*		*		740	*	*				*
14,000			*		*					1,200			*
									*				
*		*							*				
85,800	800	3,200	*	38,500	*	85,00	3,300	228,300	58,300	*	8,100	800	2,400
	560	*	145	*	*	*	170		*	*	*	*	310
	*	*	*	1,500	*	*	*			*	9,000	*	22,000
*	*	*	*	*	*	*	*	*		*	82,000	*	123,000
113,000	20,000	36,000	66,000	108,000	5,000	43,000	15,000	61,000	56,000	4,000	41,000	59,000	76,000
10,600		*	1,000	1,000	*	1,300	1,400	5,700	1,100		1,400	1,000	4,100
		*				15,000	*	3,500	*		1,600		*
						1,600					5,000		
*	*	*	58,000	6,400	*	*	6,200	*	*	*	*	28,700	76,000
		*				100,000	*	15,000	*		17,000		*
						11,000					42,000		
$38,938	$1,786	$7,689	$2,362	$10,523	$2,264	$13,656	$57,536	$27,255	$9,420	$7,079	$1,286	$2,185	$10,380
$58,372	$9,009	$9,188	$106,543	$31,107	$1,758	$15,095	$8,592	$26,195	$16,142	$1,458	$11,180	$32,092	$28,968
$97,310	$10,795	$16,877	$108,905	$41,630	$4,022	$28,751	$66,128	$53,450	$25,562	$8,537	$12,466	$34,277	$39,348
16	215	184	12	77	248	131	29	46	146	231	208	112	88
549	530	481	2,227	1,465	230	741	1,302	666	259	438	710	980	3,112
131	109	90	449	384	45	207	285	199	41	49	181	247	717
$40,935	$23,446	$16,482	$24,650	$22,341	$17,675	$30,883	$28,786	$33,329	$13,005	$53,363	$29,157	$24,875	$29,824
$15,508	$3,817	$10,226	$7,420	$3,598	$2,632	$7,095	$6,750	$20,714	$6,591	$2,305	$6,475	$2,280	$5,721

COUNTY AGRICULTURE

	PARMER	PECOS	POLK	POTTER	PRESIDIO	RAINS	RANDALL	REAGAN	REAL	RED RIVER	REEVES
1982 Acres											
Approx. Land Area	550,000	3,034,000	704,000	575,000	2,491,000	134,000	585,000	724,000	398,000	661,000	1,669,000
Land in Farms/Ranches	537,000	2,597,000	193,000	522,000	2,059,000	99,000	562,000	680,000	329,000	460,000	1,447,000
Cropland Planted	449,000	31,000	17,000	52,000	9,000	25,000	255,000	35,000	6,000	155,000	30,000
Land Irrigated	325,000	35,000	*	12,000	11,000	1,000	55,000	35,000	*	2,000	35,000
Pasture/Rangeland	82,000	2,424,000	166,000	431,000	1,937,000	69,000	287,000	603,000	304000	295,000	1,338,000
No. of Farms[P]	661	284	530	178	137	438	575	123	177	1,027	148
Ave. Farm Size[P]	824	9,186	305	2,758	14,463	215	838	5,177	1,759	349	8,307
Foreign Owned Acres (1983)		29,820			80,711		640			32,476	32,065
1982 Acres Harvested											
Barley	3,300	800	*				1,000				1,400
Corn	101,000	*	*	*	*	*	400			1,600	
Cotton (Am. Pima Irrig.)											
Cotton (Upland)	33,900	17,000			*	1,900		20,900	*	1,800	8,700
Cowpeas (Green)			*								
Cowpeas (Dry)											
Hay	3,100	3,700	12,700	1,500	1,300	10,900	5,100	*	3,200	46,000	6,700
Oats	*	*	100	*	*	600	*		*	200	
Peanuts	*									*	
Rice (Irrig.)											
Rye	*				*			*	*	*	
Sorghum (Grain)	56,500	600	*	14,500	700	*	26,500	1,500	1,000	11,500	1,200
Sorghum (Hay)	*	*		*				*	*	*	
Soybeans	31,400		*							16,000	
Sugarbeets (Irrig.)	7,200			*			1,200				
Sugarcane (Irrig.)											
Sunflowers	10,800			*				1,300		1,400	*
Wheat	118,400	1,000	*	25,000	2,100	3,400	162,100	1,500	*	50,000	1,700
Vegetables	870	2,440	100	*	1,910	390		*		620	730
1982											
Grapefruit (Boxes)											
Oranges (Boxes)											
Peaches (Bushels)		*	*		*	*			*	1,400	*
Pecans (Pounds)	*	519,000	*		*	*		*	*	*	*
Livestock											
Cattle (1/1/82)	160,000	44,000	26,000	16,000	51,000	31,000	119,000	9,000	12,000	57,000	73,000
Hogs (12/1/81)	2,000	1,500	*		*	2,500	2,500			1,000	*
Sheep (1/1/82)	3,300	102,000			8,000		*	37,000	18,000	*	
Angora Goats (1/1/82)		21,000			4,000			2,300	20,000		
1982											
Milk (Thousand Lbs.)	7,300	*	*	*	*	35,300	18,300	*	*	*	12,900
Wool (Lbs.)	16,000	660,000			56,000		*	250,000	140,000	*	*
Mohair (Lbs.)		180,000			25,000			14,000	215,000		
1982											
Crop Receipts (Thousands)	$92,250	$12,176	$2,464	$4,050	$6,032	$1,527	$15,167	$5,943	$182	$8,864	$7,613
Livestock/Prod. Receipts (Thous.)	$79,729	$16,156	$8,146	$4,170	$13,009	$13,513	$47,454	$3,648	$5,575	$20,704	$31,651
Total Cash Receipts (Thous.)	$171,979	$28,332	$10,610	$8,220	$19,041	$15,040	$62,621	$9,591	$5,757	$29,568	$39,264
Rank in State	3	136	218	233	174	193	34	222	241	129	90
Income											
Farm Population (1980)	2,218	170	432	406	150	544	970	333	339	1,299	81
Farm Households[F]	333	36	73	49	21	99	240	54	69	253	14
Average Total Income (1979)	$22,960	$40,615	$20,747	$29,350	$11,328	$50,944	$30,699	$31,460	$21,339	$19,492	$25,463
Average Farm Income (1979)	$17,326	$32,261	-$1,012	$5,151	$4,232	$9,779	$12,644	$18,449	$5,266	$1,782	$13,005

Source: Texas Department of Agriculture/U.S. Department of Agriculture/U.S. Department of Commerce, Bureau of Census.
*Withheld due to limited production, or to avoid disclosure of individual operations.   [P]Preliminary figures, 1982 Census of Agriculture, Bureau of Census.
[F]Households with Farm Self-Employment Income   [E]Estimate.

REFUGIO	ROBERTS	ROBERTSON	ROCKWALL	RUNNELS	RUSK	SABINE	SAN AUGUSTINE	SAN JACINTO	SAN PATRICIO	SAN SABA	SCHLEICHER	SCURRY	SHACKELFORD
495,000	575,000	561,000	94,000	677,000	601,000	292,000	303,000	399,000	438,000	717,000	852,000	579,000	568,000
448,000	564,000	395,000	69,000	635,000	300,000	56,000	73,000	98,000	406,000	679,000	799,000	548,000	520,000
79,000	50,000	91,000	33,000	247,000	35,000	4,000	9,000	10,000	248,000	71,000	29,000	104,000	50,000
	9,000	24,000	1,000	8,000	1,000	*	*	*	1,000	6,000	3,000	4,000	1,000
358,000	488,000	290,000	37,000	365,000	257,000	46,000	62,000	88,000	151,000	567,000	709,000	329,000	464,000
262	103	1,100	191	866	1,372	256	355	316	605	643	265	614	258
2,002	5,491	351	265	696	205	145	170	246	632	1,103	3,027	789	2,222
		21,061	2,563	710	194	518	252	2,700	3,905		74		
	*			*			*				*	*	*
10,000	*	2,300	*	*	*	*	*	*	8,700	*			*
4,400		16,000	*	45,500					66,500		5,900	69,200	2,400
		*			*	*	*	*	*			*	
2,800	2,200	28,600	5,600	18,900	29,500	2,600	6,300	6,600	4,100	11,700	2,300	5,800	5,400
*	*	500	200	3,200		*	*	*	*	1,600	300	1,500	900
		*		*						4,200			
		*			*		*			500			
57,500	2,600	5,700	1,900	64,500	*	*	*	*	163,000	2,200	7,100	4,100	2,600
		*	*	1,600	*		*	*			*	2,500	*
	*		*		*	*		*					
2,800	19,200	3,500	22,800	71,300	500	*	*	*	*	10,300	6,200	5,200	26,200
*		670	*	*	810	430	100	*	380	130	*		
		1,400		*	*	*	*	*	*	*		1,100	*
*		*		*	*	*	*	*	*	1,293,000	*	*	*
37,000	33,000	81,000	16,000	48,000	73,000	9,000	11,000	14,000	51,000	79,000	30,000	35,000	45,000
3,700	1,400	8,500		2,900	*	*	*	*	1,200	7,500	3,500	5,800	*
		*		65,000	*					45,000	90,000	3,000	
				2,200						15,000	14,000		
*	*	*	*	12,200	12,900	*	*	*	*	*	*	*	*
		*		820,000					290,000		630,000	11,000	
				34,000					150,000		120,000		
$11,350	$1,865	$11,572	$1,677	$22,455	$2,809	$1,048	$1,217	$1,985	$46,308	$4,258	$2,796	$18,334	$3,389
$13,182	$6,389	$27,243	$4,146	$23,878	$24,438	$8,597	$11,317	$4,647	$22,005	$24,183	11,979	$8,722	$10,702
$24,532	$8,254	$38,815	$5,823	$46,333	$27,247	$9,645	$12,534	$6,632	$68,313	$28,441	$14,775	$27,056	$14,091
150	232	92	240	62	140	221	207	239	28	133	194	142	196
354	262	1,312	380	1,745	1,601	445	469	357	1,033	1,118	441	1,284	239
31	56	284	89	475	373	89	146	58	214	277	104	330	57
$13,773	$31,481	$29,504	$33,130	$19,315	$26,817	$27,659	$19,425	$23,029	$33,940	$21,624	$35,031	$24,761	$22,788
$5,153	$17,612	$2,316	$4,603	$7,727	$6,653	$4,999	$6,472	$1,701	$16,027	$9,210	$11,880	$10,591	$13,416

COUNTY AGRICULTURE

	SHELBY	SHERMAN	SMITH	SOMERVELL	STARR	STEPHENS	STERLING	STONEWALL	SUTTON	SWISHER	TARRANT
1982 Acres											
Approx. Land Area	498,000	586,000	598,000	126,000	775,000	575,000	585,000	593,000	956,000	573,000	551,000
Land in Farms/Ranches	220,000	575,000	308,000	100,000	619,000	519,000	560,000	560,000	890,000	557,000	231,000
Cropland Planted	20,000	259,000	54,000	8,000	105,000	45,000	6,000	99,000	3,000	433,000	86,000
Land Irrigated	*	153,000	*	1,000	2,000	1,000	*	6,000	*	260,000	*
Pasture/Rangeland	179,000	221,000	257,000	87,000	457,000	458,000	525,000	447,000	835,000	126,000	154,000
No. of Farms[P]	1,117	279	1,690	234	830	430	78	337	177	551	1,229
Ave. Farm Size[P]	179	2,036	146	268	670	936	9,318	1,574	5,194	912	165
Foreign Owned Acres (1983)	5,541	2	41		15,591			7,396			14,886
1982 Acres Harvested											
Barley		1,000	*			*	200	*	*		
Corn	*	9,200	600			*				27,100	*
Cotton (Am. Pima Irrig.)											
Cotton (Upland)						*	*	14,300		54,700	
Cowpeas (Green)	*			*							
Cowpeas (Dry)											
Hay	15,600	4,900	44,600	2,200	3,100	5,900	1,100	5,900	*	7,500	17,000
Oats	200	1,400	*	300		1,400	*	300	*	800	3,400
Peanuts				1,500		*		3,100			
Rice (Irrig.)											
Rye	*	*.	100			600		*		600	*
Sorghum (Grain)	*	71,000	*	*	84,500	2,100	*	3,200		38,000	15,000
Sorghum (Hay)		*				*	*	1,800	*		*
Soybeans		6,000								28,000	
Sugarbeets (Irrig.)										*	
Sugarcane (Irrig.)											
Sunflowers										*	
Wheat	1,300	111,700	800	200	*		1,300	31,500	800	136,400	28,900
Vegetables	260		710	*	13,060	*		*			135
1982											
Grapefruit (Boxes)											
Oranges (Boxes)					3,000						
Peaches (Bushels)	1,200		20,000	*		*		*			*
Pecans (Pounds)	*		*	*		*	*		*	*	298,000
Livestock											
Cattle (1/1/82)	41,000	115,000	67,000	8,000	89,000	41,000	12,000	23,000	31,000	153,000	46,000
Hogs (12/1/81)	*	4,100	1,000	*	*	*			*	7,500	3,700
Sheep (1/1/82)	*	*			*	3,700	68,000		69,000	*	
Angora Goats (1/1/82)						2,300	4,100		73,000		
1982											
Milk (Thousand Lbs.)	*	*	17,000	*	*	*	*	*	*	*	43,500
Wool (Lbs.)	*	*			*	25,000	500,000		580,000	11,000	
Mohair (Lbs.)						8,000	29,000		720,000		
1982											
Crop Receipts (Thousands)	$2,710	27,100	50,912	489	$42,622	$1,651	$171	$7,214	$103	$60,980	$6,205
Livestock/Prod. Receipts (Thous.)	$70,829	$51,594	$23,148	$2,549	$23,429	$10,775	$5,382	$6,660	$13,879	$67,664	$23,299
Total Cash Receipts (Thous.)	$73,539	$78,694	$74,060	$3,038	$66,051	$12,426	$5,553	$13,874	$13,982	$128,644	$29,504
Rank in State	25	22	24	249	30	209	242	200	199	9	130
Income											
Farm Population (1980)	1,947	559	1,920	429	464	354	224	500	252	1,456	1,014
Farm Households[F]	426	92	319	101	62	119	21	126	22	351	182
Average Total Income (1979)	$23,641	$40,162	$32,437	$26,789	$30,325	$20,495	$42,731	$21,095	$26,988	$21,453	$27,615
Average Farm Income (1979)	$9,134	$34,039	$792	$3,487	$14,223	$2,749	$24,991	$10,089	$17,630	$13,967	$3,002

Source: Texas Department of Agriculture/U.S. Department of Agriculture/U.S. Department of Commerce, Bureau of Census.

*Withheld due to limited production, or to avoid disclosure of individual operations.   [P]Preliminary figures, 1982 Census of Agriculture, Bureau of Census.

[F]Households with Farm Self-Employment Income.   [E]Estimate.

FLYING THE COLORS: TEXAS ©JOHN CLEMENTS 1984

TAYLOR	TERRELL	TERRY	THROCK-MORTON	TITUS	TOM GREEN	TRAVIS	TRINITY	TYLER	UPSHUR	UPTON	UVALDE	VAL VERDE	VAN ZANDT
584,000	1,530,000	575,000	589,000	268,000	960,000	648,000	452,000	588,000	374,000	840,000	1,016,000	2,074,000	541,000
520,000	1,359,000	551,000	545,000	179,000	907,000	405,000	162,000	126,000	169,000	770,000	860,000	1,969,000	399,000
86,000	1,000	464,000	107,000	28,000	157,000	94,000	19,000	10,000	24,000	15,000	124,000	2,000	86,000
*	*	115,000	3,000	1,000	34,000	2,000	*	*	1,000	13,000	67,000	*	3,000
154,000	1,283,000	110,000	441,000	146,000	717,000	264,000	136,000	113,000	138,000	710,000	714,000	1,860,000	310,000
911	76	533	306	778	806	1,061	520	497	1,022	89	532	253	2,328
478	15,879	960	1,649	245	1,201	342	277	202	153	8,431	1,598	7,210	161
	50			15	96	2,732			171		187	9,666	1,189
*		*	*		500								
*		*		*	*	4,200	*		*		19,400		*
15,400		253,800	4,900		56,000	8,100				10,100	6,200		2,600
		800		*			*	*	*				300
15,900		*	4,100	20,900	6,700	16,100	16,200	6,600	20,400	*	14,400	*	56,700
2,200		*	500	*	1,500	400	*	*			3,900	*	1,600
		*											*
*		*					*	*	*	*	*		300
21,000		131,000	1,200	1,100	51,500	26,500	*	*	*	*	10,500		*
2,600		1,200	*	*	*	*	*			*	*		
				*				1,200			*		
											*		
										*			*
99,300		18,500	67,000	1,600	22,600	13,900	*	*	*	700	23,000	*	7,700
*		370		920	*	*	*	120	960	100	8,270		1,710
*		*	*	2,000	*	*	*	*	4,200		*	*	1,100
*	*	181,000	*	*	*	79,000	*	*	*	*	*	*	*
82,000	36,000	5,000	43,000	59,000	61,000	48,000	29,000	17,000	44,000	5,000	49,000	14,000	119,000
1,000	*	3,500	*	*	5,300	3,000	*	*	*	*	13,500	*	*
6,000	93,000	*	*		127,000	1,400				41,000	52,000	189,000	1,300
1,300	65,000				18,000	*				*	86,000	104,000	
*	*	*	*	12,800	27,600	16,300	*	*	88,000	*	*	*	43,000
30,000	770,000	*	*		960,000	10,000				290,000	400,000	1,500,000	*
9,000	580,000				170,000	*				*	780,000	1,100,000	
$16,288	$1	$88,431	$8,598	$1,708	$24,647	$8,684	$2,038	$3,008	$3,008	$3,085	$29,821	$52	$11,393
$33,106	$9,565	$1,733	$11,841	$28,566	$30,717	$16,662	$9,976	$4,771	$36,484	$2,419	$26,182	$15,508	$40,179
$49,394	$9,566	$90,164	$20,439	$30,274	$55,364	$25,346	$12,014	$7,779	$39,572	$5,504	$56,003	$15,560	$51,572
55	223	18	169	128	41	147	212	236	86	243	39	191	52
1,365	83	1,402	429	1,318	1,415	1,568	477	461	1,502	109	745	257	2,548
345	29	278	105	272	315	343	97	92	295	26	185	50	659
$25,821	$60,977	$19,451	$22,084	$28,469	$43,695	$25,783	$18,267	$21,167	$23,233	$46,331	$22,413	$113,508	$21,378
$7,525	$41,985	$7,918	$8,348	$4,148	$14,839	$3,163	$3,731	$4,478	$5,786	$34,220	$7,630	$79,220	$4,103

COUNTY AGRICULTURE

	VICTORIA	WALKER	WALLER	WARD	WASHINGTON	WEBB	WHARTON	WHEELER	WICHITA	WILBARGER	WILLACY
1982 Acres											
Approx. Land Area	571,000	506,000	326,000	529,000	380,000	2,116,000	689,000	585,000	391,000	609,000	378,000
Land in Farms/Ranches	492,000	255,000	263,000	464,000	329,000	2,007,000	648,000	558,000	342,000	569,000	287,000
Cropland Planted	103,000	25,000	87,000	2,000	46,000	8,000	417,000	143,000	109,000	233,000	164,000
Land Irrigated	8,000	*	20,000	*	*	7,000	144,000	10,000	6,000	20,000	30,000
Pasture/Rangeland	364,000	230,000	169,000	436,000	261,000	1,876,000	259,000	403,000	197,000	307,000	60,000
No. of Farms[P]	1,057	624	809	80	1,839	422	1,259	507	583	557	322
Ave. Farm Size[P]	466	416	295	5,568	166	3,897	512	972	544	1,582	728
Foreign Owned Acres (1983)	3,394		3,859		665	15,221	916				2,212
1982 Acres Harvested											
Barley					*	*		*	*	1,800	
Corn	25,900	*	16,200		2,000	*	39,900		800	*	1,500
Cotton (Am. Pima Irrig.)											
Cotton (Upland)		1,400				*	13,100	10,300	12,700	64,900	68,200
Cowpeas (Green)	*		*				*		*	*	300
Cowpeas (Dry)											400
Hay	5,200	17,200	17,500	*	32,200	2,000	8,300	15,000	8,300	18,200	1,200
Oats	100	200	300		400	*		700	1,200	1,900	*
Peanuts		*	3,400								
Rice (Irrig.)	5,300		13,500				79,900				
Rye	*		*		*		1,000	4,700	7,100	*	
Sorghum (Grain)	60,500	400	1,200	*	200	1,300	218,000	31,000	*	2,100	72,500
Sorghum (Hay)		*		*	*	*	*	1,500		*	*
Soybeans	*		20,400	*			39,000				*
Sugarbeets (Irrig.)											
Sugarcane (Irrig.)											5,200
Sunflowers											
Wheat	700	*	1,300	*	1,500	*	3,700	52,300	66,300	111,900	*
Vegetables	*	*	1,430	*		2,370	365	*	*	330	1,530
1982											
Grapefruit (Boxes)						6,000					200,000
Oranges (Boxes)						1,000					208,000
Peaches (Bushels)	*	*	*		*	*	*	1,500	*	*	
Pecans (Pounds)	*	*	60,000		*	*	*	*	*	*	*
Livestock											
Cattle (1/1/82)	58,000	39,000,000	69,000	8,000	82,000	107,000	73,000	72,000	34,000	49,000	13,000
Hogs (12/1/81)	2,000	3,100	1,500		4,000	*	*	1,800	1,500	4,000	*
Sheep (1/1/82)	*	*	1,400		*				1,200	*	
Angora Goats (1/1/82)		*									
1982											
Milk (Thousand Lbs.)	*	6,400	6,700	*	22,000	*	*	*	3,600	*	*
Wool (Lbs.)	*		*		*				7,000	*	
Mohair (Lbs.)											
1982											
Crop Receipts (Thousands)	$15,008	$5,676	$18,143	$80	$3,387	$6,313	$104,683	$8,713	$13,742	$29,707	$36,641
Livestock/Prod. Receipts (Thous.)	$19,075	$13,538	$20,310	$2,637	$30,465	$31,796	$24,793	$23,354	$10,117	$13,477	$3,644
Total Cash Receipts (Thous.)	$34,083	$19,214	$38,453	$2,717	$33,852	$38,109	$129,476	$32,067	$23,859	$43,184	$40,285
Rank in State	113	173	95	250	114	98	8	120	152	71	82
Income											
Farm Population (1980)	1,701	490	994	46	2,091	200	2,383	835	929	1,163	752
Farm Households[F]	355	105	254	*	501	13	486	201	253	310	164
Average Total Income (1979)	$26,909	$18,211	$27,688	*	$25,481	$41,700	$25,272	$30,772	$25,977	$30,183	$38,991
Average Farm Income (1979)	$5,734	$3,780	$5,967	*	$3,493	$28,313	$12,200	$11,591	$3,930	$17,014	$23,476

Source: Texas Department of Agriculture/U.S. Department of Agriculture/U.S. Department of Commerce, Bureau of Census.

*Withheld due to limited production, or to avoid disclosure of individual operations.   [P]Preliminary figures, 1982 Census of Agriculture, Bureau of Census.

[F]Households with Farm Self-Employment Income.   [E]Estimate.

FLYING THE COLORS: TEXAS ©JOHN CLEMENTS 1984

WILLIAMSON	WILSON	WINKLER	WISE	WOOD	YOAKUM	YOUNG	ZAPATA	ZAVALA
707,000	513,000	568,000	590,000	461,000	531,000	568,000	612,000	826,000
609,000	437,000	499,000	469,000	242,00	494,000	510,000	539,000	779,000
248,000	107,000	1,000	82,000	40,000	219,000	97,000	5,000	73,000
2,000	9,000	*	1,000	2,000	74,000	2,000	3,000	85,000
385,000	307,000	470,000	363,000	195,000	203,000	388,000	475,000	656,000
1,850	1,672	32	1,561	1,277	296	711	313	264
279	265	13,854	260	173	1,166	771	1,227	2,894
1,706	1,866				170		6,195	17,242

WILLIAMSON	WILSON	WINKLER	WISE	WOOD	YOAKUM	YOUNG	ZAPATA	ZAVALA
*	*		*			*		
8,300	7,700		*	*	4,000		*	8,600
46,800					120,700	5,000		10,300
*	100				*			*
	600							
19,500	26,900		32,000	31,000	5,100	4,400	1,500	3,200
2,500	200	*	4,000	300		2,300	*	800
	13,400		3,100		*	*		
300	*	*	*	200	*	*		
82,500	23,000		2,600	*	64,000	3,100		10,500
1,400	1,300		1,200		*		*	*
*					*			*
					1,000			
56,800	6,900	*	12,500	1,300	6,700	49,900	*	17,600
*	2,100		505	1,680	130	*	1,290	7,555

WILLIAMSON	WILSON	WINKLER	WISE	WOOD	YOAKUM	YOUNG	ZAPATA	ZAVALA
							1,000	
*	1,400		*	*	4,200	1,000		*
78,000	*	*	77,000	*	*	*		60,000

WILLIAMSON	WILSON	WINKLER	WISE	WOOD	YOAKUM	YOUNG	ZAPATA	ZAVALA
96,000	86,000	10,000	93,000	61,000	6,000	44,000	55,000	59,000
5,000	16,500	*	3,500	*	2,500	*	*	2,600
10,000	*		*			*	*	3,100
3,300								13,000

WILLIAMSON	WILSON	WINKLER	WISE	WOOD	YOAKUM	YOUNG	ZAPATA	ZAVALA
13,100	46,500	*	170,000	89,000	*	*	*	*
65,000	*		*			*	*	9,000
35,000								80,000

WILLIAMSON	WILSON	WINKLER	WISE	WOOD	YOAKUM	YOUNG	ZAPATA	ZAVALA
32,368	$10,935	$4	$3,536	$4,166	$45,962	$9,892	$2,834	$26,689
$32,070	$32,536	$2,374	$49,606	$35,176	$2,641	$12,529	$15,211	$19,594
$64,438	$43,471	$2,378	$53,142	$39,342	$48,603	$22,421	$18,045	$46,283
33	68	252	48	89	57	157	178	63

WILLIAMSON	WILSON	WINKLER	WISE	WOOD	YOAKUM	YOUNG	ZAPATA	ZAVALA
3,100	2,341	39	2,791	1,363	532	830	81	350
783	661	6	561	289	125	203	19	55
$23,509	$20,285	$37,505	$28,517	$24,658	$31,692	$36,823	$31,048	$27,790
$7,561	$4,863	$37,505	$4,132	$6,520	$25,840	$9,375	$15,847	$11,999

COUNTY EMPLOYMENT

	STATE TOTALS	ANDERSON	ANDREWS	ANGELINA	ARANSAS	ARCHER	ARMSTRONG	ATASCOSA	AUSTIN	BAILEY
1982 Employment										
Civilian Labor Force	7,352,100	16,077	6,065	27,945	4,550	3,082	823	12,141	8,477	3,663
Total Employment	6,846,900	14,778	5,797	25.128	4,215	2,929	762	11,499	8,143	3,487
Agriculture[P]	62,159	91	*	149	368	102	*	118	35	244
Mining[P]	302,781	1,378	2,529	513	349	446		1,068	191	*
Construction[P]	430,934	1,251	912	2,038	836	168	63	455	506	57
Manufacturing[P]	1,045,644	2,250	*	8,758	456	*	*	104	943	42
Transport./Comm./Pub. Util.[P]	357,924	420	357	1,177	306	67	4	362	223	177
Trade[P]	1,551,983	2,968	1,130	5,838	1,433	433	82	1,445	1,498	608
Finance/Insurance/Real Estate[P]	356,093	951	124	892	148	42	22	191	343	70
Service/Other[P]	1,064,378	1,833	905	3,437	395	371	327	712	1,187	464
State Government[P]	209,735	825	20	1,246	74	21	15	78	85	25
Local Government[P]	613,750	1,633	919	2,343	528	308	68	978	727	331
Total Annual Wages (Millions)[P]	$103,638	$208	$135	$398	$77	$29	$12	$74	$74	$25
Average Weekly Wage[P]	$332	$294	$377	$290	$297	$301	$423	$258	$248	$244
Fed. Employment[P]	171,040	129	35	359	13	21	14	60	66	39
Total Annual Fed. Wages (Thous.)[P]	$3,768,631	$2,867	$954	$8,134	$353	$371	$232	$1,057	$1,185	$675
1983										
Unemployment Rate (%)	8.0	9.9	4.6	12.8	10.7	4.5	7.4	5.6	5.2	6.1
Benefit Payments (Thous.)	$1,174,097	2,903	$349	$7,628	$1,310	$143	$72	$723	$850	$217
Ave. No. of Claimants Per Month	206,343	574	58	1,448	202	25	12	130	128	43
Retail Trade										
% Change in Sales (1st Qtr. 1984)	33.1	20.1	9.2	13.9	19.2	22.3	9.9	16.9	5.5	4.8
Est. 1982 Retail Sales (Thous.)	$82,731,512	$180,520	$69,245	$330,745	$68,061	$22,767	$4,518	$78,616	$70,496	$35,830
Retail Establishments (1981)	83,840	226	86	367	92	37	13	135	122	60
Bldg. Materials/Garden Sup.	3,729	11	3	22	6	1	1	9	7	3
General Merchandise	2,667	13	4	15	1	1		8	10	4
Food Stores	12,236	34	15	54	14	9	2	28	19	9
Auto Dealers/Service Stations	14,158	40	18	76	23	9	4	35	23	10
Apparel/Accessories	9,304	27	10	51	3	2	1	6	8	7
Home Furnishings	5,510	15	6	27	9			4	9	3
Eating/Drinking	17,601	31	16	49	19	9	2	26	29	9
Misc. Retail	17,493	55	14	73	17	6	3	19	17	15
Finance										
Commercial Banks (6/30/83)	1,679	6	3	7	2	1	1	6	6	2
Savings & Loan Assoc. (12/31/82)	283		1	3				1		
Credit Unions (12/31/82)	1,306	5	2	11		19				
1981 Income										
Personal Income (Millions)	$158,462	$329	$159	$591	$129	$79	$20	$193	$183	$79
% Change 1980-81	16.3	19.0	27.4	14.7	17.6	25.3	0.9	18.9	19.5	20.7
Per Capita Income	$10,731	$8,319	$11,292	$8,950	$8,579	$10,384	$10,475	$7,602	$9,744	$9,514
Rank in State		186	36	145	170	70	66	211	100	117
1979 Income										
Median Family Income	$19,618	$16,827	$20,571	$18,393	$16,104	$18,533	$18,333	$14,737	$18,811	$14,039
% of Fam. Below Poverty Level	11.1	14.6	8.8	10.3	12.6	6.2	8.0	19.6	11.7	16.9
Households with Pub. Assistance	307,842	1,326	203	1,608	262	139	31	976	407	178
Average Public Assistance	$1,815	$1,620	$2,149	$1,809	$2,663	$1,892	$2,123	$1,865	$1,934	$1,754
Households with Soc. Sec. Income	1,102,371	4,579	807	5,965	1,773	781	264	2,288	2,415	781
Ave. Annual Soc. Sec. Income	$3,731	$3,537	$3,690	$3,858	$4,156	$3,818	$3,905	$3,419	$3,464	$3,558

Source: Texas Employment Commission/Texas Comptroller of Public Accounts/U.S. Department of Commerce, Bureau of Census
*Withheld to avoid disclosure of information concerning individuals, or individual business operations. [P]Preliminary figures.

FLYING THE COLORS: TEXAS ©JOHN CLEMENTS 1984

BANDERA	BASTROP	BAYLOR	BEE	BELL	BEXAR	BLANCO	BORDEN	BOSQUE	BOWIE	BRAZORIA	BRAZOS	BREWSTER	BRISCOE
2,160	9,998	2,752	9,945	51,048	431,181	1,781	528	5,960	29,451	102,848	50,212	3,637	1,339
2,031	9,373	2,672	9,445	47,652	403,347	1,730	512	5,710	26,272	95,867	48,181	3,495	1,294
*	*	*	51	145	1,910	*	*	81	153	507	243	*	40
37	83	223	914	81	2,732	40	173	*	48	2,447	1,526	80	*
136	211	33	437	2,945	25,882	86	*	76	,1,129	6,608	3,045	68	*
126	765	*	190	7,135	44,088	80	*	826	3,900	18,645	3,443	*	20
*	123	183	226	2,359	15,940	*	*	114	1,123	2,480	1,864	140	26
182	1,081	356	1,758	12,668	102,606	258	*	761	7,171	10,384	9,572	574	116
81	233	66	262	2,080	27,117	68	*	115	1,028	1,861	1,737	92	*
365	485	583	1,269	8,964	80,757	404	40	724	4,500	6,989	5,657	555	86
30	78	31	82	438	9,485	41	11	40	379	1,181	13,326	771	17
244	1,105	280	1,246	7,787	44,036	207	64	512	3,028	6,877	2,974	403	74
$14	$48	$21	$85	$581	$5,108	$13	$6	$40	$301	$1,180	$579	$29	$4
$228	$221	$237	$253	$251	$277	$220	$414	$237	$258	$392	$257	$208	$219
18	285	34	593	7,115	36,703	63	6	52	7,018	318	753	126	22
$338	$6,557	$624	$10,069	$115,294	$766,573	$879,309	$91	$916	$140,136	$6,952	$20,673	$1,971	$334
4.4	6.2	3.3	8.2	7.0	6.3	3.2	3.5	3.8	10.0	7.4	4.6	3.8	4.0
$128	$956	$77	$1,526	$5,480	$34,048	$81	$32	$343	$4,377	$14,047	$3,416	$149	$21
23	167	14	258	1,087	6,678	15	5	59	853	2,314	604	29	4
10.0	22.2	7.3	16.7	14.1	19.6	18.1	N/A	22.3	13.1	20.6	9.2	11.6	34.3
$14,812	$71,820	$19,039	$107,263	$783,898	$5114,896	$17,635	$556	$44,188	$395,217	$810,768	$492,656	$44,025	$6,902
31	132	46	160	941	5,272	33	*5	65	488	870	496	66	20
4	9	2	8	34	175	3			36	50	25	3	4
1	8	3	4	33	138			7	14	29	12	2	2
9	26	5	25	132	748	6		14	79	151	71	7	5
4	28	15	28	177	902	5		12	90	135	75	15	3
2	8	6	15	108	517	2		4	59	101	46	6	
1	5	1	12	61	335	2		2	40	55	38	2	
6	22	6	41	178	1,351	10		8	78	173	132	13	3
4	26	8	27	218	1,106	5		18	92	176	97	18	3
2	5	2	3	16	55	2		5	9	23	9	1	2
	2			3	9	1		3	3	3	4		
			2	8	74				12	8	2	1	
$67	$191	$56	$216	$1,400	$9,636	$41	$9	$138	$688	$1,799	$790	$65	$26
16.5	16.2	17.2	17.1	11.0	14.1	16.2	19.4	20.	013.6	9.4	21.8	11.7	35.5
$9,518	$7,351	$11,101	$8,259	$8,767	$9,452	$8,637	$9,904	$10,323	$9,065	$10,127	$8,013	$8,497	$10,524
116	225	43	187	154	121	165	94	74	139	85	197	177	64
$16,198	$15,321	$15,685	$14,738	$15,009	$17,158	$14,427	$15,924	$14,895	$17,240	$25,302	$18,121	$13,147	$12,847
10.2	14.4	11.1	17.7	13.4	14.8	7.2	14.4	11.4	12.4	6.3	10.4	14.8	18.5
190	1,037	129	807	3,029	26,256	98	5	311	2,642	1,961	1,417	168	64
$1,785	$1,961	$2,251	$1,460	$1,653	$1,778	$1,862	$2,898	$1,598	$1,685	$1,899	$1,819	$1,782	$1,211
1,025	3,171	896	2,094	10,257	69,456	749	72	2,547	8,196	8,592	5,437	716	340
$3,724	$3,592	$3,887	$3,483	$3,452	$3,550	$3,408	$3,650	$3,845	$3,567	$3,915	$3,417	$3,628	$3,640

COUNTY EMPLOYMENT

	BROOKS	BROWN	BURLESON	BURNET	CALDWELL	CALHOUN	CALLAHAN	CAMERON	CAMP	CARSON	CASS
1982 Employment											
Civilian Labor Force	3,404	15,889	8,408	8,121	9,407	8,435	5,925	85,987	4,977	2,858	13,119
Total Employment	3,152	14,583	7,927	7,861	8,772	7,479	5,749	75,267	4,456	2,710	11,088
Agriculture[P]	108	47	*	31	117	*	*	2,041	338	*	8
Mining[P]	299	177	941	168	1,019	181	179	152	*	88	174
Construction[P]	35	662	277	495	243	1,793	71	4,010	385	238	294
Manufacturing[P]	*	3,127	365	718	506	*	97	11,141	707	*	1,463
Transport./Comm./Pub. Util.[P]	103	815	224	264	138	415	82	3,485	101	70	268
Trade[P]	529	2,516	948	1,165	1,217	1,431	264	18,591	806	292	1,377
Finance/Insurance/Real Est.[P]	61	469	148	277	197	210	86	3,098	97	66	243
Service/Other[P]	319	2,269	531	630	1,243	3,856	240	10,054	458	2,620	906
State Government[P]	45	530	49	63	58	47	34	1,664	15	35	264
Local Government[P]	543	1,175	496	730	832	1,069	348	9,940	434	293	1,079
Total Annual Wages (Millions)[P]	$26	$155	$60	$57	$73	$192	$18	$786	$36	$76	$87
Average Weekly Wage[P]	$243	$253	$298	$241	$251	$408	$247	$236	$219	$394	$276
Fed. Employment[P]	41	139	44	50	54	42	31	1,006	27	24	73
Total Annual Fed. Wages (Thous.)[P]	$1,058	$2,960	$765	$1,060	$1,071	$876	$554	$24,688	$579	$438	$1,299
1983											
Unemployment Rate (%)	8.0	9.4	6.6	2.6	5.3	13.2	3.9	15.3	13.7	6.8	16.6
Benefit Payments (Thous.)	$490	$2,313	$655	$257	$548	$2,430	$294	$22,027	$1,458	$334	$4,315
Ave. No. of Claimants Per Month	81	455	120	45	110	405	55	4,909	253	58	.769
Retail Trade											
% Change in Sales (1st Qtr. 1984)	–7.8	17.4	8.8	17.9	8.6	6.6	17.0	13.4	9.6	–5.6	15.4
Est. 1982 Retail Sales (Thous.)	$35,747	$174,271	$37,805	$80,719	$82,854	$90,055	$32,046	$901,664	$37,008	$19,574	$115,146
Retail Establishments (1981)	58	243	72	132	129	122	54	1,228	69	31	139
Bldg. Materials/Garden Sup.	3	9	3	10	10	7		51	5	1	10
General Merchandise	2	9	5	9	9	7	4	51	4		8
Food Stores	13	38	20	21	22	24	14	194	8	8	31
Auto Dealers/Service Stations	11	43	13	21	22	26	17	165	14	8	25
Apparel/Accessories	4	28	4	12	13	7	3	185	4	1	13
Home Furnishings	5	21	3	8	5	5		69	6		8
Eating/Drinking	11	41	16	18	22	25	6	263	11	8	19
Misc. Retail	9	54	8	33	26	21	10	250	17	5	25
Finance											
Commercial Banks (6/30/83)	1	5	5	5	4	4	3	20	2	3	6
Savings & Loan Assoc. (12/31/82)	1	1	1	1	2	1		4	1		
Credit Unions (12/31/82)		3				3		15		2	2
1981 Income											
Personal Income (Millions)	$54	$293	$113	$186	$189	$199	$100	$1,341	$95	$80	$223
% Change 1980-81	16.5	17.7	31.4	19.0	19.4	12.1	18.3	15.3	18.6	5.9	12.8
Per Capita Income	$6,325	$8,713	$8,771	$10,139	$7,765	$9,799	$8,985	$6,172	$10,105	$11,611	$7,457
Rank in State	239	160	153	83	206	99	143	242	87	28	218
1979 Income											
Median Family Income	$11,893	$15,652	$16,446	$14,117	$14,600	$20,772	$16,338	$12,931	$17,552	$20,208	$16,848
% of Fam. Below Poverty Level	26.2	9.3	13.7	11.7	18.1	11.7	9.7	26.0	13.7	6.6	14.5
Households with Pub. Assistance	557	858	506	360	782	399	304	8,252	430	75	1,096
Average Public Assistance	$1,869	$1,903	$1,841	$2,127	$1,601	$1,487	$2,038	$1,779	$2,069	$1,887	$1,665
Households with Soc. Sec. Income	836	4,296	1,751	3,115	2,448	1,346	1,627	15,627	1,205	635	3,768
Ave. Annual Soc. Sec. Income	$3,429	$3,824	$3,437	$4,042	$3,398	$3,788	$3,567	$3,518	$3,314	$4,270	$3,527

Source: Texas Employment Commission/Texas Comptroller of Public Accounts/U.S. Department of Commerce, Bureau of Census.
*Withheld to avoid disclosure of information concerning individuals, or individual business operations. [P]Preliminary figures.

FLYING THE COLORS: TEXAS ©JOHN CLEMENTS 1984

CASTRO	CHAMBERS	CHEROKEE	CHILDRESS	CLAY	COCHRAN	COKE	COLEMAN	COLLIN	COLLINGSWORTH	COLORADO	COMAL	COMANCHE	CONCHO
3,880	9,890	16,902	3,530	4,788	2,109	1,791	4,655	80,799	1,982	9,818	15,702	5,731	1,336
3,683	9,401	15,612	3,374	4,606	1,986	1,727	4,377	77,451	1,904	9,452	14,867	5,402	1,279
518	89	354	51	*	131	*	17	358	69	198	36	199	*
*	754	124	*	221	44	295	289	*	*	982	252	*	*
73	*	598	76	*	35	*	143	2,221	*	429	1,036	104	*
*	*	2,885	*	239	*	42	304	6,661	*	883	3,518	501	*
133	241	442	160	73	33	*	99	817	54	239	495	138	8
557	1,199	2,247	542	340	197	113	614	9,796	221	1,766	2,597	897	112
83	103	374	84	59	*	38	122	1,878	43	208	451	109	28
706	4,034	1,820	793	204	403	173	429	6,154	279	836	2,392	1,041	138
28	44	1,611	125	29	18	18	33	146	25	88	96	76	23
483	955	1,095	370	407	321	283	376	5,868	223	610	1,536	555	178
$34	$153	$144	$25	$22	$17	$14	$28	$505	$11	$88	$158	$42	$5
$252	$397	$240	$218	$267	$279	$280	$220	$286	$234	$271	$247	$225	$208
35	41*	82	54	33	28	18	53	298	31	61	73	60	26
$640	$762	$1,683	$1,098	$593	$479	$328	$817	$6,963	$524	$1,246	$1,799	$1,089	$399
5.7	7.0	7.8	4.6	4.1	4.6	4.0	6.6	4.0	5.2	4.8	5.6	6.7	4.6
$211	$1,042	$2,083	$204	$256	$53	$46	$462	$4,181	$92	$737	$1,081	$482	$68
40	169	398	37	48	11	8	86	682	16	123	204	101	12
16.4	16.0	12.9	3.3	4.7	17.6	8.6	24.0	37.8	5.3	17.4	23.3	22.8	9.0
$40,699	$86,597	$129,427	$32,030	$24,219	$14,489	$15,725	$39,548	$548,807	$16,112	$99,766	$190,595	$54,006	$29,385
49	97	182	70	40	19	21	62	655	32	174	230	101	20
4	8	11	4	3	2	1	4	33	2	10	12	6	4
1	3	20	1	1	1	1	3	25	3	8	7	6	2
10	22	25	6	5	4	8	13	82	6	30	47	17	4
8	21	48	12	15	4	4	13	92	5	40	30	27	6
4	6	12	11	3	1	2	6	111	3	10	22	8	
1	4	8	1		1		2	40	1	8	11	5	
5	15	28	15	8	2	2	6	130	5	36	50	10	1
16	18	30	20	5	4	3	15	142	7	32	51	22	3
2	4	6	2	2	1	2	3	22	2	5	4	4	2
		3	1					3		1	2		
		3	2	1				4		1		1	
$67	$191	$368	$62	$100	$34	$30	$90	$1,622	$33	$195	$396	$109	$27
-12.4	24.7	14.8	8.7	20.5	9.3	23.0	13.8	20.2	1.2	16.0	17.4	18.4	53.1
$6,220	$9,707	$9,621	$8,948	$10,251	$7,156	$9,076	$8,057	$10,607	$6,932	$10,119	$10,376	$8,691	$9,182
241	103	107	146	79	229	138	174	57	231	86	71	163	133
$14,530	$22,316	$15,931	$13,788	$17,667	$13,952	$16,422	$13,688	$26,406	$13,765	$17,688	$18,816	$13,497	$14,040
21.0	11.7	13.7	10.9	8.8	20.4	7.7	12.8	4.9	20.7	15.7	7.6	11.8	14.8
151	322	1,345	165	227	104	61	442	1,763	180	607	546	436	117
$2,001	$1,693	$1,708	$1,590	$1,991	$1,869	$1,999	$1,511	$1,951	$1,760	$1,640	$2,049	$1,519	$1,606
561	1,246	4,995	1,192	1,291	428	531	1,983	7,376	694	2,372	4,030	2,135	462
$3,799	$3,652	$3,558	$3,833	$3,732	$3,740	$3,953	$3,514	$3,659	$3,612	$3,420	$4,010	$3,620	$3,705

COUNTY EMPLOYMENT

	COOKE	CORYELL	COTTLE	CRANE	CROCKETT	CROSBY	CULBERSON	DALLAM	DALLAS	DAWSON	DEAF SMITH
1982 Employment											
Civilian Labor Force	14,940	17,891	1,418	2,128	2,676	3,527	1,716	2,737	882,601	7,332	7,861
Total Employment	13,674	17,133	1,345	2,008	2,468	3,330	1,633	2,600	834,359	6,813	7,138
Agriculture[P]	38	71	45	*	20	228	73	144	3,453	323	655
Mining[P]	984	*	23	1,142	541	12	*	*	24,930	460	*
Construction[P]	212	431	24	87	90	19	*	80	57,981	163	321
Manufacturing[P]	3,099	388	*	221	*	201	*	254	184,994	339	841
Transport./Comm./Pub. Util.[P]	501	116	32	165	160	80	64	141	69,138	276	465
Trade[P]	2,528	1,392	251	259	358	375	283	759	268,207	1,115	1,444
Finance/Insurance/Real Est.[P]	249	274	*	*	*	77	*	159	88,326	163	218
Service/Other[P]	947	887	181	95	358	294	828	308	188,996	473	611
State Government[P]	276	845	39	16	36	28	26	36	7,571	37	47
Local Government[P]	1,406	1,335	156	317	352	406	217	235	69,575	804	955
Total Annual Wages (Millions)[P]	$154	$63	$10	$50	$30	$21	$24	$28	$18,448	$57	$73
Average Weekly Wage[P]	$289	$211	$258	$418	$310	$233	$311	$254	$368	$264	$252
Fed. Employment[P]	77	1,063	24	8	18	39	18	43	20,336	78	58
Total Annual Fed. Wages (Thous.)[P]	$1,598	$17,908	$382	$170	$387	$641	$492	$880	$502,902	$1,247	$1,262
1983											
Unemployment Rate (%)	10.8	5.0	5.0	4.2	6.1	7.7	6.1	4.0	5.1	9.9	8.6
Benefit Payments (Thous.)	$2,858	$869	$83	$63	$184	$327	$122	$67	$67,276	$1,103	$841
Ave. No. of Claimants Per Month	500	161	16	11	32	66	22	14	11,751	213	156
Retail Trade											
% Change in Sales (1st Qtr. 1984)	–1.1	28.3	5.9	–15.8	N/A	5.2	35.3	16.7	23.6	–1.8	15.3
Est. 1982 Retail Sales (Thous.)	$163,578	$102,283	$8,383	$16,320	$33,506	$16,464	$18,598	$52,562	$11,234,280	$76,531	$86,052
Retail Establishments (1981)	206	154	24	33	35	43	42	71	9,418	128	127
Bldg. Materials/Garden Sup.	7	5	2	1	3	3	2	6	317	6	3
General Merchandise	7	11	3	2	1	2	1	2	232	4	4
Food Stores	22	27	3	6	6	10	5	7	1,141	16	17
Auto Dealers/Service Stations	43	31	5	6	12	13	17	20	1,462	26	27
Apparel/Accessories	24	9	1	3	3	3	4	4	1,179	18	23
Home Furnishings	15	9	1	1	1	1	1	1	682	11	13
Eating/Drinking	38	28	4	7	5	4	9	15	2,189	19	15
Misc. Retail	50	34	5	7	4	7	3	16	2,216	28	25
Finance											
Commercial Banks (6/30/83)	5	6	1	1	2	3	1	3	140	2	2
Savings & Loan Assoc. (12/31/82)		2						1	20	1	1
Credit Unions (12/31/82)	4			1		1			193	2	1
1981 Income											
Personal Income (Millions)	$290	$367	$28	$57	$52	$89	$29	$74	$21,875	$145	$184
% Change 1980-81	15.9	18.4	17.6	20.5	20.5	39.2	25.9	–16.2	14.1	22.4	–4.6
Per Capita Income	$10,324	$6,378	$9,522	$11,821	$10,542	$10,156	$8,407	$11,059	$13,530	$9,026	$8,716
Rank in State	73	238	114	21	60	81	182	45	7	140	158
1979 Income											
Median Family Income	$18,791	$13,560	$13,933	$19,140	$18,690	$13,071	$12,894	$14,354	$21,870	$16,357	$16,375
% of Fam. Below Poverty Level	9.3	11.9	15.2	9.5	10.7	22.8	17.3	14.9	7.9	14.7	14.3
Households with Pub. Assistance	536	732	108	54	46	257	58	109	25,116	329	399
Average Public Assistance	$1,845	$1,734	$1,330	$1,085	$990	$1,564	$1,170	$1,178	$1,909	$1,957	$2,125
Households with Soc. Sec. Income	3,189	2,525	450	287	342	873	190	633	100,924	1,503	1,349
Ave. Annual Soc. Sec. Income	$3,745	$3,343	$3,831	$3,682	$3,698	$3,734	$3,290	$3,775	$3,929	$3,723	$3,937

Source: Texas Employment Commission/Texas Comptroller of Public Accounts/U.S. Department of Commerce, Bureau of Census
*Withheld to avoid disclosure of information concerning individuals, or individual business operations.   [P]Preliminary figures.

FLYING THE COLORS: TEXAS ©JOHN CLEMENTS 1984

DELTA	DENTON	DE WITT	DICKENS	DIMMIT	DONLEY	DUVAL	EASTLAND	ECTOR	EDWARDS	ELLIS	EL PASO	ERATH	FALLS
1,540	81,099	9,229	1,603	5,154	1,490	6,874	8,084	75,810	846	34,081	190,343	11,984	7,547
1,436	76,720	8,587	1,492	4,557	1,452	6,429	7,688	71,150	806	32,024	169,301	11,469	7,184
*	273	31	69	247	57	*	*	77	*	187	938	45	70
*	63	254	*	547	*	1,130	798	9,253	*	*	339	449	*
*	1,618	153	*	176	14	*	370	5,925	34	740	8,268	237	39
*	7,838	1,391	*	*	70	*	1,009	8,213	*	7,204	38,022	1,158	415
*	1,461	213	84	117	27	93	347	3,147	51	775	9,352	329	132
109	10,378	1,456	128	552	192	397	1,038	17,824	82	3,261	41,432	1,854	855
42	1,377	318	*	62	57	61	215	2,240	*	581	7,180	327	261
193	4,971	872	190	433	71	743	814	7,817	120	2,660	25,248	1,207	775
47	7,209	197	26	60	25	42	72	696	16	134	4,466	813	46
123	5,112	1,024	150	825	295	1,051	897	5,488	130	2,047	20,665	677	616
$5	$559	$71	$8	$39	$9	$54	$72	$1,151	$5	$247	$2,041	$85	$34
$183	$267	$230	$229	$251	$227	$293	$248	$365	$241	$270	$252	$230	$204
32	362	42	28	50	25	26	77	307	14	141	8,263	117	408
$527	$8,569	$828	$425	$1,161	$384	$484	$1,507	$7,298	$241	$2,816	$167,417	$2,525	$8,527

DELTA	DENTON	DE WITT	DICKENS	DIMMIT	DONLEY	DUVAL	EASTLAND	ECTOR	EDWARDS	ELLIS	EL PASO	ERATH	FALLS
7.0	4.7	7.1	9.1	14.7	3.7	8.3	6.8	8.8	5.6	5.5	12.3	4.7	4.1
$146	$5,191	$1,092	$148	$1,246	$86	$867	$1,116	$13,828	*	$2,768	$34,894	$825	$274
28	910	206	39	274	13	151	202	2,219	3	522	7,837	157	57

DELTA	DENTON	DE WITT	DICKENS	DIMMIT	DONLEY	DUVAL	EASTLAND	ECTOR	EDWARDS	ELLIS	EL PASO	ERATH	FALLS
−0.01	34.8	5.0	−15.6	−7.3	6.2	33.4	21.6	−0.6	85.5	52.5	22.9	6.5	22.6
$9,863	$578,471	$76,947	$18,284	$41,356	$23,381	$31,698	$67,572	$940,291	$4,066	$238,217	$2,171,085	$123,624	$59,508
19	715	137	23	45	28	63	133	810	12	315	2,346	170	111
1	40	10	1	2	2	2	6	29	2	15	73	7	6
2	25	8	2	4	1	2	7	19		12	83	10	9
3	111	16	5	11	4	22	20	110	2	67	336	20	21
4	102	26	7	10	7	15	30	135	1	75	345	27	22
	91	18	1	4	1	3	13	115	1	30	289	23	13
1	49	6			1	3	5	66		17	170	10	7
2	138	30	3	8	7	10	24	176	3	47	575	26	15
6	159	23	4	6	5	6	28	160	3	52	475	47	18

DELTA	DENTON	DE WITT	DICKENS	DIMMIT	DONLEY	DUVAL	EASTLAND	ECTOR	EDWARDS	ELLIS	EL PASO	ERATH	FALLS
3	15	8	1	2	3	2	5	9	1	12	26	4	6
	1	2				1		3		2	5	1	1
	6	2				2	1	19		4	38	1	1

DELTA	DENTON	DE WITT	DICKENS	DIMMIT	DONLEY	DUVAL	EASTLAND	ECTOR	EDWARDS	ELLIS	EL PASO	ERATH	FALLS
$38	$1,421	$170	$26	$68	$36	$94	$169	$1,514	$22	$593	$3,659	$209	$145
15.2	15.8	15.6	10.1	25.8	−11.0	15.1	16.7	26.8	13.6	20.0	14.4	18.0	11.2
7,965	9,426	8,753	7,511	6,027	8,847	7,382	8,406	12,268	10,325	9,708	7,360	8,976	8,106
201	123	155	213	247	152	221	183	14	72	102	223	144	193

DELTA	DENTON	DE WITT	DICKENS	DIMMIT	DONLEY	DUVAL	EASTLAND	ECTOR	EDWARDS	ELLIS	EL PASO	ERATH	FALLS
$14,042	$23,999	$14,145	$10,769	$11,301	$14,375	$13,452	$13,645	$21,068	$11,554	$20,096	$15,366	$15,840	$13,007
13.5	4.6	17.6	20.1	32.8	15.2	24.3	12.6	8.5	23.8	9.7	18.0	10.4	19.3
235	1,383	897	121	568	106	693	613	1,639	87	1,323	11,415	619	1,015
$1,487	$1,822	$1,736	$1,586	$1,707	$1,735	$2,117	$1,931	$1,987	$1,934	$1,745	$1,868	$1,471	$1,738
968	7,877	3,002	610	733	650	1,074	3,292	6,959	222	5,888	26,839	3,221	2,918
$3,375	$3,801	$3,286	$3,479	$3,010	$3,580	$3,103	$3,638	$3,834	$3,727	$3,762	$3,657	$3,631	$3,229

COUNTY EMPLOYMENT

	FANNIN	FAYETTE	FISHER	FLOYD	FOARD	FORT BEND	FRANKLIN	FREESTONE	FRIO	GAINES	GALVESTON
1982 Employment											
Civilian Labor Force	9,904	11,277	2,192	4,183	1,151	78,048	2,627	5,783	5,694	6,116	89,417
Total Employment	9,072	10,820	2,082	3,953	1,099	73,966	2,465	5,467	5,309	5,773	79,964
Agriculture[P]	39	33	95	348	*	288	*	33	299	481	153
Mining[P]	10	633	129	*	*	1,960	*	307	266	662	727
Construction[P]	146	410	*	60	16	2,154	15	373	84	231	4,381
Manufacturing[P]	1,257	808	*	201	*	11,756	242	225	67	213	11,355
Transport./Comm./Pub. Util.[P]	213	247	*	115	*	1,344	14	*	124	422	5,445
Trade[P]	1,127	2,143	230	484	76	5,848	213	740	798	889	13,572
Finance/Insurance/Real Estate[P]	369	248	43	60	*	1,265	*	137	86	155	4,314
Service/Other[P]	664	854	449	280	232	3,450	367	1,564	432	277	9,452
State Government[P]	86	85	21	33	3	2,037	25	49	54	21	6,574
Local Government[P]	928	929	245	486	110	4,752	301	661	679	702	9,680
Total Annual Wages (Millions)[P]	$58	$82	$18	$26	$4	$653	$12	$65	$33	$66	$1,190
Average Weekly Wage[P]	$231	$247	$289	$240	$191	$361	$191	$309	$219	$312	$349
Fed. Employment[P]	455	84	35	55	15	239	13	100	34	39	923
Total Annual Fed. Wages (Thous.)[P]	$9,165	$1,599	$594	$877	$257	$5,319	$225	$2,251	$636	$702	$21,594
1983											
Unemployment Rate (%)	8.4	5.2	6.4	6.3	4.2	7.8	7.5	6.1	9.1	5.0	12.2
Benefit Payments (Thous.)	$1,344	$925	$155	$221	$36	$13,266	$334	$570	$742	$314	$21,194
Ave. No. of Claimants Per Month	272	167	30	44	6	2,029	61	104	142	56	3,675
Retail Trade											
% Change in Sales (1st Qtr. 1984)	9.4	2.3	-2.2	3.2	30.0	20.8	19.1	16.9	-4.4	11.5	13.4
Est. 1982 Retail Sales (Thous.)	$108,410	$80,658	$13,748	$31,485	$5,384	$453,695	$17,616	$78,003	$49,502	$39,364	$1,104,255
Retail Establishments (1981)	135	192	30	55	12	446	28	79	61	75	1,136
Bldg. Materials/Garden Sup.	9	8	2	4	1	30	2	3	5	2	53
General Merchandise	4	12	2	4		9	1	6	1	2	33
Food Stores	23	38	6	7	2	88	4	15	12	14	205
Auto Dealers/Service Stations	32	36	6	12	4	93	7	16	11	17	156
Apparel/Accessories	13	14		2	1	45	2	6	7	10	122
Home Furnishings	9	10	1	1		22	2	6	2	4	66
Eating/Drinking	17	45	6	11	2	75	5	12	11	12	258
Misc. Retail	28	29	7	14	2	84	5	15	12	14	243
Finance											
Commercial Banks (6/30/83)	7	8	2	2	1	13	2	5	2	3	20
Savings & Loan Assoc. (12/31/82)	1	1				2					6
Credit Unions (12/31/82)	3	1		1		4		2	1	1	29
1981 Income											
Personal Income (Millions)	$193	$196	$58	$99	$23	$1,414	$56	$129	$83	$138	$2,362
% Change 1980-81	17.7	19.3	34.4	17.8	7.2	20.2	19.3	14.7	18.3	42.0	14.9
Per Capita Income	$8,067	$9,809	$9,897	$10,079	$10,876	$9,897	$8,110	$8,431	5,965	$10,205	$11,592
Rank in State	196	98	96	88	50	95	191	181	248	80	30
1979 Income											
Median Family Income	$15,415	$15,637	$17,149	$14,677	$13,942	$27,179	$16,896	$15,875	$12,211	$16,290	$22,871
% of Fam. Below Poverty Level	12.0	13.2	12.8	20.3	14.7	6.4	10.0	12.7	26.1	16.1	8.0
Households with Pub. Assistance	1,200	726	171	249	77	1,383	199	767	534	232	3,837
Average Public Assistance	$1,720	$1,993	$1,312	$1,868	$1,263	$1,831	$1,811	$1,797	$1,858	$1,791	$1,714
Households with Soc. Sec. Income	3,802	3,234	890	1,042	376	5,414	998	2,172	1,033	930	15,392
Ave. Annual Soc. Sec. Income	$3,419	3,220	3,526	3,744	3,764	3,472	3,821	3,658	3,213	3,941	3,842

Source: Texas Employment Commission/Texas Comptroller of Public Accounts/U.S. Department of Commerce, Bureau of Census
*Withheld to avoid disclosure of information concerning individuals, or individual business operations. PPreliminary figures.

FLYING THE COLORS: TEXAS ©JOHN CLEMENTS 1984

GARZA	GILLESPIE	GLASSCOCK	GOLIAD	GONZALES	GRAY	GRAYSON	GREGG	GRIMES	GUADALUPE	HALE	HALL	HAMILTON	HANSFORD
2,450	6,147	907	2,203	8,904	14,826	39,964	52,566	9,756	20,161	15,938	2,488	3,079	2,940
2,293	5,879	882	2,053	8,405	14,028	36,568	47,109	9,101	19,052	14,934	2,353	2,931	2,818
157	9	*	*	246	80	91	146	152	85	872	89	34	253
595	*	117	*	472	1,777	263	4,480	70	307	*		*	243
13	321		47	188	723	1,417	3,817	937	855	493	46	24	63
*	476	*	*	1,050	1,882	11,592	9,234	1,289	4,088	2,085	*	226	22
58	241	*	*	298	572	1,386	3,094	166	266	597	*	125	226
260	1,316	*	255	1,485	2,768	6,921	14,192	900	3,052	3,719	253	444	420
*	169	*	42	172	394	1,184	2,011	174	447	451	65	77	79
496	984	168	331	718	1,613	5,159	8,203	539	1,541	1,745	372	444	88
25	85	1	58	66	86	212	298	35	107	109	8	28	16
276	462	85	344	838	907	4,150	4,745	491	2,004	1,970	281	263	380
$25	$43	$6	$14	$65	$194	$488	$797	$74	$165	$157	$12	$17	$30
$253	$206	$338	$239	$225	$346	$290	$306	$302	$249	$250	$213	$195	$320
22	70	6	18	87	96	268	375	40	164	151	32	40	24
$434	$1,732	$108	$292	$1,571	$2,107	$5,453	$8,942	$783	$3,540	$3,145	$571	$716	$436
15.4	3.7	2.9	8.2	6.9	8.4	8.0	12.2	9.3	5.0	9.0	8.4	4.8	3.7
$934	$278	*	$339	$906	$2,536	$5,300	$13,426	$1,424	$1,109	$1,893	$317	$205	$107
175	57	2	58	167	473	1,067	2,314	239	213	386	57	42	17
-2.5	12.1	N/A	30.1	-6.1	8.8	21.3	6.5	11.5	20.5	15.0	14.4	7.1	0.9
$20,858	$62,837	$1,835	$15,915	$57,730	$144,097	$422,808	$797,444	$45,116	$180,310	$213,899	$16,955	$28,331	$36,506
42	131	3	26	123	224	546	906	84	247	239	41	65	45
4	5		3	7	14	41	49	6	19	16	3	6	5
1	8		2	7	7	18	27	8	9	13	3	4	3
8	23	1	7	28	33	76	114	12	45	34	8	11	7
10	18		3	21	33	107	153	16	47	40	8	12	7
3	9		1	11	35	69	111	5	14	28	6	6	7
1	12		1	5	15	37	70	2	13	19	2	5	3
7	29	1	6	24	39	96	179	18	58	33	4	9	6
8	27	1	3	20	48	102	203	17	41	56	7	12	7
1	4		1	4	3	15	16	7	6	6	3	3	2
			1	2	1	2	6		1	1			
		1		1	7	12	19			3			
$53	$144	$31	$60	$163	$331	$891	$1,148	$136	$391	$328	$54	$65	$74
21.2	16.4	22.1	17.0	18.5	15.6	12.7	17.5	20.8	16.5	8.3	20.2	16.5	-0.7
$9,741	$10,466	$23,004	$11,294	$9,320	$12,382	$9,558	$11,164	$9,586	$8,143	$8,662	$10,065	$8,151	$12,076
101	67	2	35	129	13	113	41	109	190	164	89	188	17
$16,480	$15,092	$16,419	$15,185	$13,939	$19,482	$18,371	$19,923	$14,462	$17,777	$15,458	$12,944	$12,800	$21,124
13.9	10.0	17.6	16.2	17.4	7.5	7.3	10.0	21.8	12.9	16.5	21.5	14.7	8.4
199	264	11	193	788	404	2,287	2,310	610	1,091	786	267	250	70
$1,616	$1,879	$1,037	$1,819	$1,692	$1,629	$1,680	$1,645	$1,453	$1,655	$1,648	$1,487	$1,909	$1,497
612	2,192	76	584	2,223	3,051	10,934	8,900	1,983	4,290	3,352	861	1,602	448
$3,798	$3,650	$3,502	$3,068	$3,145	$4,122	$3,811	$3,852	$3,467	$3,507	$3,794	$3,553	$3,474	$3,734

COUNTY EMPLOYMENT

	HARDEMAN	HARDIN	HARRIS	HARRISON	HARTLEY	HASKELL	HAYS	HEMPHILL	HENDERSON	HIDALGO	HILL
1982 Employment											
Civilian Labor Force	2,975	19,149	1,457,467	26,635	1,637	3,418	22,256	2,293	14,972	110,266	9,856
Total Employment	2,842	17,625	1,362,100	24,748	1,587	3,321	21,188	2,163	13,464	92,129	9,227
Agriculture[P]	40	*	6,248	41	*	108	26	*	127	9,882	49
Mining[P]	167	681	103,792	783	*	160	*	642	276	1,737	*
Construction[P]	31	413	135,245	1,353	*	43	720	116	570	5,626	609
Manufacturing[P]	*	1,365	211,090	8,180		84	1,540	40	1,725	9,762	1,056
Transport./Comm./Pub. Util.[P]	152	366	99,479	811	12	113	457	152	644	2,661	322
Trade[P]	313	1,995	353,890	3,372	153	426	3,016	413	2,113	25,360	1,143
Finance/Insurance/Real Estate[P]	73	258	91,837	683	*	66	457	93	343	2,973	283
Service/Other[P]	557	1,063	286,023	2,235	57	165	2,361	370	1,085	10,233	1,040
State Government[P]	48	107	27,007	175	13	39	2,662	22	93	3,029	82
Local Government[P]	377	1,384	99,673	1,825	145	319	1,485	274	1,570	14,489	1,034
Total Annual Wages (Millions)[P]	$24	$111	$29,958	$336	$4	$18	$148	$41	$113	$954	$67
Average Weekly Wage[P]	$258	$279	$408	$332	$212	$226	$224	$373	$255	$214	$228
Fed. Employment[P]	32	58	19,646	116	13	42	94	17	83	1,327	95
Total Annual Fed. Wages (Thous.)[P]	$581	$1,098	$532,034	$2,449	$208	$721	$2,112	$348	$1,623	$33,339	$1,706
1983											
Unemployment Rate (%)	4.8	11.1	9.6	9.6	3.5	4.0	4.9	6.6	10.4	19.5	5.6
Benefit Payments (Thous.)	$116	$4,490	$298,459	$4,756	$32	$115	$1,060	$162	$3,116	$30,436	$815
Ave. No. of Claimants Per Month	29	734	46,958	822	5	26	217	29	577	7,378	159
Retail Trade											
% Change in Sales (1st Qtr. 1984)	4.2	8.2	9.5	10.5	-12.4	-3.2	35.0	-0.5	34.0	17.3	13.4
Est. 1982 Retail Sales (Thous.)	$17,082	$184,663	$18,111,229	$208,248	$5,885	$33,747	$160,557	$32,662	$154,988	$1,269,415	96,372
Retail Establishments (1981)	37	211	13,025	241	12	62	237	35	187	1,431	161
Bldg. Materials/Garden Sup.	3	14	522	9	1	4	14	3	13	63	14
General Merchandise	2	13	249	11		4	10		10	68	10
Food Stores	3	47	1,950	32	4	11	33	5	24	244	28
Auto Dealers/Service Stations	9	42	2,057	53	3	12	50	9	41	243	36
Apparel/Accessories	7	13	1,463	28	1	11	19	3	17	189	13
Home Furnishings	1	7	956	18	1	3	12	2	10	106	6
Eating/Drinking	5	29	2,952	42	1	8	65	9	29	252	27
Misc. Retail	7	46	2,876	48	1	9	34	4	43	266	27
Finance											
Commercial Banks (6/30/83)	3	5	216	6		3	7	2	8	23	7
Savings & Loan Assoc. (12/31/82)		2	26	2			1			4	
Credit Unions (12/31/82)		1	231	6		1	3		1	12	
1981 Income											
Personal Income (Millions)	$55	$366	$35,445	$452	$30	$73	$317	$68	$326	$1,648	$209
% Change 1980-81	9.7	13.8	18.4	13.7	-7.8	23.0	17.3	13.9	15.9	18.5	15.8
Per Capita Income	$8,458	$8,714	$13,911	$8,381	$7,352	$9,492	$7,459	$11,901	$7,370	$5,606	$8,400
Rank in State	180	159	6	185	224	119	217	20	222	251	184
1979 Income											
Median Family Income	$17,002	$21,073	$24,322	$17,559	$20,648	$15,194	$17,028	$21,469	$16,056	$12,083	$14,582
% of Fam. Below Poverty Level	12.2	8.8	8.1	13.1	8.7	14.5	13.1	6.0	10.3	29.0	12.5
Households with Pub. Assistance	137	1,001	34,378	1,945	51	287	733	24	1,286	11,350	902
Average Public Assistance	$2,077	$1,601	$1,965	$1,786	$2,673	$1,595	$1,766	$5,217	$1,629	$1,736	$1,836
Households with Soc. Sec. Income	1,051	3,635	125,571	5,813	333	1,240	2,863	307	6,006	19,920	4,086
Ave. Annual Soc. Sec. Income	$3,918	$3,957	$3,856	$3,766	$4,193	$3,832	$3,559	$4,078	$4,097	$3,506	$3,684

Source: Texas Employment Commission/Texas Comptroller of Public Accounts/U.S. Department of Commerce, Bureau of Census
*Withheld to avoid disclosure of information concerning individuals, or individual business operations. [P]Preliminary figures.

HOCKLEY	HOOD	HOPKINS	HOUSTON	HOWARD	HUDSPETH	HUNT	HUTCHINSON	IRION	JACK	JACKSON	JASPER	JEFF DAVIS	JEFFERSON
11,000	9,926	11,287	9,001	17,484	1,011	26,951	16,042	1,132	4,800	5,918	12,572	866	120,078
10,407	9,495	10,699	8,513	16,441	986	25,147	15,381	1,097	4,598	5,547	11,273	836	108,605
329	68	52	49	106	139	46	20		*	106	*	*	270
2,361	65	97	371	1,342	*	*	2,331	110	773	543	166		2,052
321	146	186	586	613	*	745	2,101	*	37	213	537	*	9,429
228	218	2,172	1,284	2,331	*	7,207	2,794		103	90	2,644		25,802
371	162	646	655	605	25	1,008	566	40	326	247	285	*	9,861
1,449	1,183	2,412	2,012	3,149	75	3,790	2,160	113	353	738	1,615	48	27,985
224	188	280	629	447	*	656	292	*	98	135	257	*	4,453
719	838	635	1,234	1,742	97	1,830	949	107	225	287	1,998	133	19,761
33	30	120	582	832	40	2,016	56	12	32	57	139	93	3,248
1,214	668	1,087	835	1,619	149	2,132	1,364	68	344	685	1,192	66	10,380
$125	$50	$105	$145	$199	$6	$282	$269	$7	$37	$44	$125	$4	$2,192
$331	$270	$263	$339	$299	$224	$279	$411	$341	$316	$272	$277	$235	$372
66	51	79	80	613	61	190	88	8	32	39	70	24	1,078
$1,173	$1,004	$1,551	$1,459	$13,426	$1,483	$4,440	$1,583	$147	$601	$737	$1,392	$268	$26,184
5.6	4.4	5.5	7.0	8.3	2.3	6.8	5.9	4.0	4.3	6.8	11.6	4.2	12.5
$737	$616	$960	$987	$2,512	*	$3,009	$1,616	$41	$248	$695	$2,977	$54	$32,158
133	105	166	177	457	2	556	254	6	44	118	497	9	5,471
15.7	22.7	25.3	16.7	-15.5	17.2	20.0	1.9	13.2	6.5	-0.5	14.1	N/A	10.8
$96,031	$96,732	$101,588	$86,015	$284,917	$3,842	$246,197	$112,779	$7,192	$29,169	$49,540	$167,359	$1,746	$1723,257
132	111	149	113	254	14	341	192	6	60	103	193	10	1,483
8	7	10	5	8	1	17	11	1	4	4	15	1	66
5	4	5	7	9	1	10	6		5	5	10		36
19	16	19	18	33	3	49	30	2	6	23	38	2	237
30	19	23	29	48	3	65	29		13	26	40	1	248
12	8	23	11	36		40	29		9	8	17		155
8	1	7	6	19		26	17		2	4	8		109
31	28	33	15	49	4	70	34		10	17	28	4	317
19	28	29	22	52	2	64	36	3	11	16	37	2	315
5	3	4	7	4	1	10	4	1	3	3	4	1	17
1		1		1		3	2			1	2		6
1			2	6		5	7			2	2		46
$210	$178	$209	$191	$365	$30	$517	$353	$15	$78	$132	$273	$13	$3,061
16.5	26.5	13.8	20.2	20.2	39.6	15.9	22.8	28.7	19.5	14.9	11.7	10.4	14.4
$8,920	$9,451	$8,109	$8,552	$10,859	$10,758	$9,015	$12,815	$9,680	$10,144	$9,596	$8,564	$7,996	$12,061
147	122	192	172	52	56	142	8	104	82	108	171	198	18
$17,710	$20,888	$15,407	$12,704	$17,643	$11,204	$17,262	$21,024	$18,068	$16,497	$16,593	$16,796	$11,365	$21,523
15.6	5.8	11.6	20.6	12.4	25.7	11.8	5.4	11.5	9.4	12.9	12.7	19.6	10.3
449	293	768	1,153	644	56	1,502	357	20	169	372	1,062	35	5,780
$1,634	$1,561	$1,539	$1,630	$2,152	$1,614	$1,522	$2,251	$1,914	$1,509	$1,957	$1,618	$2,009	$1,770
2,018	2,072	3,416	3,019	3,528	159	6,551	2,630	151	1,046	1,596	3,547	198	22,768
$3,507	$4,231	$3,613	$3,439	$4,129	$2,957	$3,752	$4,114	$3,758	$3,701	$3,450	$3,934	$3,476	$4,104

COUNTY EMPLOYMENT

	JIM HOGG	JIM WELLS	JOHNSON	JONES	KARNES	KAUFMAN	KENDALL	KENEDY	KENT	KERR	KIMBLE
1982 Employment											
Civilian Labor Force	2,219	18,158	38,456	9,307	7,627	21,770	5,182	591	468	12,005	2,132
Total Employment	1,990	16,800	36,262	9,032	7,249	20,913	4,995	548	450	11,586	2,070
Agriculture[P]	*	273	*	137	35	140	*	*	32	244	*
Mining[P]	300	3,643	31	340	1,006	74	58	*	*	*	
Construction[P]	31	536	754	150	177	397	225	*	*	410	51
Manufacturing[P]	*	399	4,470	589	415	2,334	180			907	*
Transport./Comm./Pub. Util.[P]	27	694	637	229	227	409	31		*	367	54
Trade[P]	334	2,994	4,210	937	1,182	2,356	476	64	32	2,333	384
Finance/Insurance/Real Estate[P]	*	486	676	191	146	386	139		*	479	43
Service/Other[P]	272	2,154	2,582	443	460	1,537	669	231	91	2,501	299
State Government[P]	44	101	115	58	52	1,509	48	3	11	912	45
Local Government[P]	290	1,614	2,585	923	615	1,437	388	20	102	873	165
Total Annual Wages (Millions)[P]	$15	$202	$204	$53	$64	$135	$26	$5	$3	$109	$12
Average Weekly Wage[P]	$222	$301	$245	$253	$288	$246	$213	$289	$229	$231	$216
Fed. Employment[P]	39	104	170	59	46	122	28	3	13	716	23
Total Annual Fed. Wages (Thous.)[P]	$955	$2,356	$3,409	$1,156	$860	$2,402	$547	$29	$208	$14,262	$411
1983											
Unemployment Rate (%)	13.0	10.5	4.7	3.2	5.6	4.2	2.5	9.2	4.7	2.8	3.5
Benefit Payments (Thous.)	$526	$3,426	$2,508	$325	$530	$1,225	$100	$80	*	$446	$58
Ave. No. of Claimants Per Month	98	568	444	64	93	207	18	14	4	84	10
Retail Trade											
% Change in Sales (1st Qtr. 1984)	N/A	9.6	23.9	6.7	26.8	11.9	29.9	N/A	N/A	31.0	1.5
Est. 1982 Retail Sales (Thous.)	$18,037	$194,464	$282,343	$67,702	$53,289	$187,696	$44,666	$1,164	$2,567	$124,494	$27,777
Retail Establishments (1981)	42	236	346	105	107	260	80	2	6	210	39
Bldg. Materials/Garden Sup.	3	14	15	3	6	19	6			7	1
General Merchandise	1	10	13	5	5	14	4	1		10	2
Food Stores	10	39	66	21	23	47	15		1	30	5
Auto Dealers/Service Stations	11	47	70	22	23	52	14	1	4	38	12
Apparel/Accessories	3	19	33	7	7	20	5			23	1
Home Furnishings	2	12	18	4	4	13	3			12	1
Eating/Drinking	7	46	68	14	26	48	17			41	11
Misc. Retail	5	49	63	29	13	47	16		1	49	6
Finance											
Commercial Banks (6/30/83)	1	6	10	4	4	9	3		1	5	2
Savings & Loan Assoc. (12/31/82)		1		1	1	1				1	
Credit Unions (12/31/82)		2	3	13	2	3				4	
1981 Income											
Personal Income (Millions)	$46	$344	$676	$161	$116	$387	$135	$8	$9	$323	$34
% Change 1980-81	17.7	19.5	14.4	17.7	12.7	14.6	18.1	6.7	15.7	16.1	13.4
Per Capita Income	$8,889	$9,286	$9,585	$9,208	$8,464	$9,571	$12,105	$15,680	$7,467	$11,095	$8,148
Rank in State	149	131	110	132	179	112	16	5	216	44	189
1979 Income											
Median Family Income	$12,721	$16,460	$20,669	$15,892	$15,386	$18,742	$19,259	$11,384	$15,160	$16,878	$15,691
% of Fam. Below Poverty Level	21.8	17.7	6.1	12.3	19.0	11.0	10.4	29.5	17.2	8.0	12.5
Households with Pub. Assistance	253	1,584	1,173	436	501	1,075	133	11	32	624	87
Average Public Assistance	$1,771	$1,691	$1,494	$1,716	$1,798	$1,612	$1,095	$596	$2,095	$2,053	$1,417
Households with Soc. Sec. Income	529	3,166	6,364	2,377	1,563	3,957	1,155	51	162	4,565	540
Ave. Annual Soc. Sec. Income	$2,609	$3,314	$4,040	$3,703	$3,184	$3,622	$3,975	$3,212	$3,787	$4,209	$3,547

Source: Texas Employment Commission/Texas Comptroller of Public Accounts/U.S. Department of Commerce, Bureau of Census
*Withheld to avoid disclosure of information concerning individuals, or individual business operations. [P]Preliminary figures.

FLYING THE COLORS: TEXAS ©JOHN CLEMENTS 1984

	KING	KINNEY	KLEBERG	KNOX	LAMAR	LAMB	LAMPASAS	LA SALLE	LAVACA	LEE	LEON	LIBERTY	LIMESTONE	LIPSCOMB
	318	873	13,844	2,726	18,676	8,783	3,947	2,084	9,078	9,494	5,966	28,621	8,516	2,011
	313	841	13,036	2,611	17,202	8,312	3,718	1,840	8,633	8,983	5,668	26,619	8,060	1,944
	*	*	*	64	64	497	19	*	34	27	*	235	28	13
	131	*	1,225	104	*	8	*	30	371	1,787	250	2,304	447	234
	*	*	453	70	500	*	232	18	272	481	132	754	576	184
		*	386	*	4,836	*	333		1,371	292	*	1,991	818	*
		*	293	28	487	411	35	50	101	457	*	495	149	46
	15	45	2,396	294	2,929	1,164	708	238	1,254	1,104	574	3,166	1,058	250
	*	*	266	54	443	168	120	55	158	175	161	485	214	123
	130	218	1,496	174	2,684	1,969	352	283	702	613	962	1,523	727	162
	1	21	1,230	37	347	53	42	61	71	311	51	114	1,742	1
	39	140	1,635	315	1,630	802	384	313	535	449	350	1,917	629	208
	$6	$4	$124	$15	$194	$72	$25	$11	$53	$96	$39	$212	$82	$20
	$375	$196	$255	$246	$268	$274	$213	$215	$211	$323	$305	$313	$254	$334
	9	16	606	48	167	63	36	31	68	38	49	101	65	29
	$134	$416	$11,078	$701	$3,393	$1,055	$757	$723	$1,372	$665	$787	$2,080	$1,243	$501

	KING	KINNEY	KLEBERG	KNOX	LAMAR	LAMB	LAMPASAS	LA SALLE	LAVACA	LEE	LEON	LIBERTY	LIMESTONE	LIPSCOMB
	1.5	3.5	7.9	4.0	7.2	5.2	4.3	13.3	4.5	4.5	6.5	9.3	6.1	4.3
	*	*	$1,685	$69	$1,938	$467	$205	$408	$557	$366	$676	$5,855	$833	$77
	1	3	293	14	425	88	41	79	97	63	114	933	152	12

	KING	KINNEY	KLEBERG	KNOX	LAMAR	LAMB	LAMPASAS	LA SALLE	LAVACA	LEE	LEON	LIBERTY	LIMESTONE	LIPSCOMB
	N/A	14.7	3.4	2.6	10.2	25.6	17.3	33.7	9.4	16.9	25.9	14.7	19.4	0.5
	$2,291	$4,633	$166,212	$18,025	$206,855	$66,167	$47,259	$18,747	$64,919	$37,238	$22,811	$253,188	$82,880	$13,035
	1	14	189	42	247	112	70	37	152	83	63	290	125	32
			8	6	12	11	2	1	15	8	4	18	6	3
		1	7	2	11	4	6	5	8	6	2	11	4	2
		4	32	9	39	17	7	6	27	18	16	56	27	7
	1	4	33	12	41	17	16	11	30	16	17	56	24	5
			14	5	33	17	7	2	7	4	5	30	11	3
				11	19	5	7	1	12	6	1	9	9	1
		2	45	3	45	19	10	4	24	16	10	48	17	8
		3	39	5	47	22	15	7	29	9	8	62	27	3

	KING	KINNEY	KLEBERG	KNOX	LAMAR	LAMB	LAMPASAS	LA SALLE	LAVACA	LEE	LEON	LIBERTY	LIMESTONE	LIPSCOMB
		1	3	2	6	6	3	1	4	5	5	7	7	4
		1				2				1		3	1	
		2			11	1			1			2	3	*

	KING	KINNEY	KLEBERG	KNOX	LAMAR	LAMB	LAMPASAS	LA SALLE	LAVACA	LEE	LEON	LIBERTY	LIMESTONE	LIPSCOMB
	$7	$17	$286	$60	$343	$171	$98	$33	$165	$113	$87	$528	$162	$41
	20.1	13.3	19.3	22.9	10.6	7.0	12.9	16.9	12.4	29.6	23.2	19.3	19.2	-2.2
	$15,978	$7,402	$8,504	$11,238	$8,000	$9,296	$8,486	$5,948	$9,115	$9,023	$8,742	$10,879	$7,922	$9,125
	4	220	175	38	194	130	178	249	135	141	157	49	204	134

	KING	KINNEY	KLEBERG	KNOX	LAMAR	LAMB	LAMPASAS	LA SALLE	LAVACA	LEE	LEON	LIBERTY	LIMESTONE	LIPSCOMB
	$14,375	$11,483	$16,216	$14,595	$14,948	$14,536	$14,409	$10,563	$15,376	$16,361	$14,180	$19,552	$13,807	$18,071
	12.7	29.0	16.7	17.7	15.1	15.9	13.4	35.5	13.0	14.3	20.3	10.7	17.3	10.9
	10	80	953	201	1,941	557	277	369	797	375	542	1,316	909	53
	$2,347	$2,560	$1,780	$1,812	$1,685	$1,908	$1,703	$1,536	$1,619	$1,816	$1,847	$2,001	$1,691	$2,014
	21	264	2,144	864	5,513	2,154	1,508	535	3,054	1,451	1,828	4,613	3,204	387
	$3,592	$3,537	$3,468	$3,453	$3,372	$3,712	$3,446	$2,701	$3,272	$3,427	$3,491	$3,780	$3,534	$3,309

COUNTY EMPLOYMENT

	LIVE OAK	LLANO	LOVING	LUBBOCK	LYNN	McCULLOCH	McLENNAN	McMULLEN	MADISON	MARION	MARTIN
1982 Employment											
Civilian Labor Force	4,397	3,762	69	105,432	3,276	4,145	83,384	544	4,001	3,517	2,531
Total Employment	4,159	3,656	68	100,077	3,124	3,868	78,564	531	3,818	3,060	2,409
Agriculture[P]	*	*		954	153	11	480		*	*	128
Mining[P]	523	*	295	346	*	*	130	101	237	164	135
Construction[P]	448	119	*	3,864	*	132	3,223	*	116	67	30
Manufacturing[P]	*	89		11,407	38	239	15,515		43	316	15
Transport./Comm./Pub. Util.[P]	74	23		4,564	202	101	3,116	*	55	*	149
Trade[P]	591	552	*	26,247	315	616	17,678	46	708	323	207
Finance/Insurance/Real Estate[P]	106	135		4,693	64	95	4,281	23	117	*	35
Service/Other[P]	518	480	*	16,069	102	485	13,053	97	714	560	116
State Government[P]	46	41		9,610	26	37	2,283	17	233	34	34
Local Government[P]	331	356	9	8,560	379	439	6,195	57	478	284	266
Total Annual Wages (Millions)[P]	$42	$19	$10	$1,239	$17	$26	$908	$5	$35	$20	$18
Average Weekly Wage[P]	$308	$208	$405	$276	$255	$227	$265	$330	$252	$231	$313
Fed. Employment[P]	57	34	3	2,014	43	41	2,690	5	24	18	25
Total Annual Fed. Wages (Thous.)[P]	$1,283	$670	*	$41,879	$694	$657	$58,360	$75	$476	$350	$408
1983											
Unemployment Rate (%)	6.6	2.8	1.3	6.6	5.0	7.2	5.7	2.1	5.9	15.2	5.5
Benefit Payments (Thous.)	$480	$184		$10,182	$88	$478	$6,554	*	$1,135	$113	
Ave. No. of Claimants Per Month	79	31		1,892	17	85	1,330	2	75	197	18
Retail Trade											
% Change in Sales (1st Qtr. 1984)	24.0	23.2	N/A	13.1	8.6	12.0	17.6	N/A	7.5	14.9	-4.7
Est. 1982 Retail Sales (Thous.)	$40,169	$39,342	$204	$1,406,415	$19,273	$46,535	$992,933	$654	$55,481	$25,149	$32,367
Retail Establishments (1981)	66	76	*	1,300	38	71	1,078	5	57	40	12
Bldg. Materials/Garden Sup.	2	7		49	2	2	44		2	3	1
General Merchandise	1	4		33	2	4	35		5	2	
Food Stores	9	16		156	7	10	155	2	9	7	1
Auto Dealers/Service Stations	25	12		196	9	13	187	1	16	9	3
Apparel/Accessories	5	7		147	4	11	124		5	1	1
Home Furnishings	2	3		115	1	5	78		3	1	
Eating/Drinking	9	14		287	7	10	237	1	7	7	2
Misc. Retail	13	13		317	6	16	218	1	10	10	4
Finance											
Commercial Banks (6/30/83)	2	4		16	3	2	18	1	2	1	1
Savings & Loan Assoc. (12/31/82)		1		4		1	2				
Credit Unions (12/31/82)	1			17	1	1	27			1	
1981 Income											
Personal Income (Millions)	$87	$108	$2	$2,072	$66	$79	$1,641	$10	$78	$64	$58
% Change 1980-81	23.2	15.2	14.2	10.6	23.9	16.7	13.5	-3.7	8.6	12.2	42.8
Per Capita Income	$8,691	$10,524	$26,042	$9,655	$7,722	$8,911	$9,494	$12,395	$7,028	$6,054	$11,634
Rank in State	162	63	1	105	208	148	118	12	230	245	27
1979 Income											
Median Family Income	$18,125	$14,558	$17,500	$18,744	$12,941	$12,429	$16,983	$17,824	$14,589	$13,227	$19,257
% of Fam. Below Poverty Level	13.2	8.5		9.9	20.8	16.5	11.4	5.6	16.7	21.9	12.4
Households with Pub. Assistance	282	240		3,060	260	319	4,571	9	439	511	88
Average Public Assistance	$1,808	$1,819		$2,011	$1,455	$1,467	$1,808	$684	$1,637	$1,504	$1,896
Households with Soc. Sec. Income	911	2,262	8	13,834	774	1,481	18,163	90	1,271	1,532	397
Ave. Annual Soc. Sec. Income	$3,636	$4,194	$3,336	$3,825	$3,454	$3,605	$3,667	$4,132	$3,492	$3,519	$3,516

Source: Texas Employment Commission/Texas Comptroller of Public Accounts/U.S. Department of Commerce, Bureau of Census
*Withheld to avoid disclosure of information concerning individuals, or individual business operations. [P]Preliminary figures.

FLYING THE COLORS: TEXAS ©JOHN CLEMENTS 1984

MASON	MATAGORDA	MAVERICK	MEDINA	MENARD	MIDLAND	MILAM	MILLS	MITCHELL	MONTAGUE	MONT-GOMERY	MOORE	MORRIS	MOTLEY
1,656	15,969	10,536	9,946	917	64,822	9,033	1,980	4,093	8,103	77,334	8,265	7,305	816
1,596	13,820	7,492	9,421	888	61,224	8,470	1,883	3,860	7,674	72,633	7,865	6,067	786
*	376	283	67	*	177	149	*	123	*	360	292	37	47
	1,017	103	126	*	13,394	141	*	297	751	2,665	412	492	*
54	1,316	304	256	*	4,221	295	*	42	154	2,694	247	607	*
*	795	*	686	*	4,318	*	*	64	1,141	4,293	*	*	*
18	477	245	168	*	2,891	*	204	203	187	1,182	737	377	*
293	2,806	2,284	1,308	112	12,140	1,087	224	534	1,003	7,883	1,334	1,301	59
48	369	254	172	*	3,104	208	40	77	198	1,443	143	133	*
167	1,502	1,620	725	81	8,789	3,030	584	288	595	5,322	2,392	5,604	114
22	112	99	97	10	282	55	19	50	57	216	40	54	16
169	1,844	1,578	1,019	179	4,063	841	177	603	718	5,607	830	518	68
$7	$169	$71	$50	$4	$1,128	$118	$17	$29	$58	$507	$116	$195	$3
$175	$307	$201	$209	$192	$407	$362	$250	$245	$231	$314	$347	$408	$200
16	92	194	59	15	467	74	26	32	78	314	130	38	21
$257	$1,822	$5,118	$1,141	$242	$12,245	$1,346	$439	$629	$1,529	$7,021	$3,382	$742	$325
3.4	12.5	35.5	4.9	4.6	5.8	5.9	3.9	5.4	5.3	9.0	4.7	24.2	4.8
$47	$4,225	$5,253	$445	$33	$6,167	$736	$107	$299	$685	$13,438	$435	$3,699	$28
10	674	1,244	96	6	991	140	22	58	128	2,139	71	630	5
6.0	20.9	14.8	18.9	5.4	2.8	13.4	20.3	15.4	2.0	16.5	13.0	–3.5	–0.1
$9,689	$169,365	$113,573	$79,600	$3,972	$624,748	$65,490	$11,806	$32,641	$75,049	$664,341	$87,435	$55,883	$6,666
30	246	158	118	14	574	122	23	68	128	443	124	91	16
3	16	8	8	3	20	8	4	2	8	41	8	2	3
1	8	9	5		17	11	2	2	5	12	3	2	1
4	43	19	22	5	65	19	2	11	23	85	19	19	3
7	52	29	27	1	87	23	5	17	29	75	24	24	4
2	26	33	10	2	84	14	2	9	15	41	16	12	
1	13	7	2		46	7	2	5	8	22	9	5	
6	45	23	22	2	121	19	3	12	17	75	22	12	2
6	43	30	22	1	134	21	3	10	23	92	23	15	13
2	4	2	6	2	9	6	1	3	5	11	3	4	1
	2		1		2	1		1		2	1		
	3	2	1		14	1		1		3	3	1	
$31	$374	$124	$182	$23	$1,455	$215	$47	$80	$170	$1,561	$176	$174	$16
9.7	14.8	8.2	17.1	5.0	25.2	10.5	13.9	7.9	19.2	232.1	17.4	17.9	5.0
$8,695	$9,472	$3,741	$7,758	$9,947	$16,467	$9,424	$10,129	$8,851	$9,642	$11,342	$10,420	$11,602	$8,543
161	120	254	207	93	3	124	84	151	106	34	68	29	173
$14,792	$21,264	$10,623	$14,895	$11,531	$24,232	$15,747	$12,850	$15,070	$14,974	$24,442	$19,981	$19,486	$11,695
13.0	9.8	34.4	17.6	22.3	6.2	17.0	14.0	16.2	10.4	6.2	7.3	12.1	23.0
85	669	1,288	762	111	970	1,021	132	301	419	2,028	180	508	67
$1,567	$1,969	$1,816	$1,924	$1,426	$2,165	$1,799	$1,575	$1,714	$1,613	$1,947	$2,675	$1,603	$1,544
604	3,267	1,685	2,275	385	5,086	3,229	859	1,283	2,788	8,179	1,048	1,715	365
$3,635	$3,694	$3,008	$3,501	$3,245	$3,878	$3,318	$3,565	$3,635	$3,638	$3,879	$3,924	$3,475	$3,769

COUNTY EMPLOYMENT

	NACOG-DOCHES	NAVARRO	NEWTON	NOLAN	NUECES	OCHILTREE	OLDHAM	ORANGE	PALO PINTO	PANOLA	PARKER
1982 Employment											
Civilian Labor Force	20,022	17,535	3,931	7,896	134,710	6,289	997	42,743	11,428	8,926	24,976
Total Employment	18,774	16,242	3,442	7,475	124,791	5,959	938	36,284	10,435	8,284	23,912
Agriculture[P]	226	44	*	117	501	*	*	145	12	64	232
Mining[P]	126	234	*	424	8,169	1,542	60	178	920	980	394
Construction[P]	728	531	25	200	11,665	191	*	2,289	295	335	423
Manufacturing[P]	3,873	3,291	620	1,393	13,483	157		8,403	2,461	526	1,325
Transport./Comm./Pub. Util.[P]	426	490	126	436	7,084	342	*	1,196	526	280	368
Trade[P]	3,505	2,731	273	1,549	30,091	967	114	4,948	1,734	1,107	2,209
Finance/Insurance/Real Estate[P]	579	464	*	245	5,658	127	*	652	291	161	328
Service/Other[P]	1,975	2,033	281	644	20,247	437	222	2,918	896	500	885
State Government[P]	2,449	231	58	230	2,492	30	18	179	107	58	90
Local Government[P]	1,915	1,407	507	948	14,397	591	180	3,176	1,180	1,163	1,642
Total Annual Wages (Millions)[P]	$191	$156	$23	$85	$1,876	$83	$8	$482	$116	$70	$99
Average Weekly Wage[P]	$233	$262	$236	$265	$317	$362	$251	$385	$265	$261	$241
Fed. Employment[P]	174	140	27	56	5,829	35	18	142	63	59	92
Total Annual Fed. Wages (Thous.)[P]	$3,743	$2,812	$429	$1,106	$133,062	$642	$280	$3,058	$1,328	$1,158	$1,832
1983											
Unemployment Rate (%)	7.3	7.9	12.0	7.0	10.8	3.5	5.8	19.2	10.4	9.1	4.6
Benefit Payments (Thous.)	$2,288	$2,093	$1,088	$814	$28,822	$180	$24	$20,428	$2,222	$1,540	$1,642
Ave. No. of Claimants Per Month	503	418	186	154	4,806	30	5	3,384	414	268	294
Retail Trade											
% Change in Sales (1st Qtr. 1984)	28.6	14.0	−1.4	4.5	7.4	6.3	18.4	12.9	7.6	12.8	25.7
Est. 1982 Retail Sales (Thous.)	$224,299	$228,775	$22,979	$114,592	$1,385,487	$50,748	$5,672	$423,098	$151,639	$78,808	$202,320
Retail Establishments (1981)	288	221	49	137	1,602	67	15	401	177	96	173
Bldg. Materials/Garden Sup.	20	11	2	5	47	3		28	9	4	12
General Merchandise	9	7	2	6	39	2		14	5	7	9
Food Stores	37	30	13	20	249	11	1	77	37	14	29
Auto Dealers/Service Stations	43	49	9	26	264	14	4	73	35	25	39
Apparel/Accessories	30	29	4	15	163	8	1	32	12	9	10
Home Furnishings	15	14	1	9	120	5		23	7	4	5
Eating/Drinking	56	37	7	23	387	7	3	74	40	16	32
Misc. Retail	78	44	11	33	333	17	6	80	32	17	37
Finance											
Commercial Banks (6/30/83)	8	10	1	3	22	2	1	6	6	3	5
Savings & Loan Assoc. (12/31/82)	3			1	3	1		3	1	1	1
Credit Unions (12/31/82)	5	2			31	1		11	4		1
1981 Income											
Personal Income (Millions)	$378	$343	$82	$176	$2,851	$123	$18	$903	$228	$181	$405
% Change 1980-81	17.2	16.5	9.5	13.1	17.1	20.1	12.5	15.3	15.8	16.0	16.8
Per Capita Income	$7,901	$9,406	$6,032	$10,061	$10,400	$11,782	$8,499	$10,307	$9,083	$8,635	$8,614
Rank in State	205	125	246	90	69	22	176	76	137	166	167
1979 Income											
Median Family Income	$15,760	$15,048	$15,541	$16,486	$19,008	$22,281	$15,760	$22,404	$16,000	$17,527	$19,823
% of Fam. Below Poverty Level	12.9	13.5	16.3	11.9	13.4	5.5	5.9	8.2	8.9	11.3	9.0
Households with Pub. Assistance	1,251	1,344	542	516	6,917	52	20	1,642	649	817	819
Average Public Assistance	$1,828	$1,804	$1,840	$1,752	$1,734	$845	$2,494	$1,894	$1,417	$1,933	$1,794
Households with Soc. Sec. Income	4,567	5,403	1,558	2,161	18,701	680	202	5,451	2,966	2,758	4,475
Ave. Annual Soc. Sec. Income	$3,397	$3,544	$3,632	$3,690	$3,635	$3,864	$3,541	$3,981	$3,736	$3,427	$3,862

Source: Texas Employment Commission/Texas Comptroller of Public Accounts/U.S. Department of Commerce, Bureau of Census
*Withheld to avoid disclosure of information concerning individuals, or individual business operations.   [P]Preliminary figures.

FLYING THE COLORS: TEXAS ©JOHN CLEMENTS 1984

PARMER	PECOS	POLK	POTTER	PRESIDIO	RAINS	RANDALL	REAGAN	REAL	RED RIVER	REEVES	REFUGIO	ROBERTS	ROBERTSON
5,411	7,126	7,578	53,107	2,091	2,119	39,214	2,043	936	6,778	6,377	5,330	453	5,763
5,216	6,618	6,925	49,562	1,909	1,989	37,716	1,919	898	6,131	5,777	5,089	435	5,291
303	172	*	416	*	*	304	*	*	27	562	111	*	71
*	1,827	158	2,488	87	*	69	680	*	27	378	646	30	*
41	329	245	2,775	68	64	969	27	10	20	181	82		72
*	245	1,433	8,456	*	254	1,280	*	*	1,287	242	*		473
91	790	251	4,761	50	*	316	208	*	110	451	276	45	133
579	1,249	1,545	17,614	288	176	4,948	232	71	608	984	673	53	799
82	210	275	3,097	54	44	580	41	*	106	153	126	*	92
1,467	496	708	10,910	278	133	2,778	193	82	465	751	281	34	441
22	97	135	1,132	35	26	1,731	4	11	63	102	26	1	69
477	950	1,030	7,434	216	162	706	252	139	667	795	512	77	543
$47	$107	$78	$938	$11	$10	$187	$28	$3	$36	$62	$42	$4	$33
$294	$325	$260	$305	$196	$220	$262	$350	$180	$205	$258	$298	$322	$238
64	59	59	1,668	129	16	38	17	7	55	50	42	15	42
$1,296	$1,349	$1,101	$42,689	$3,382	$283	$826	$299	$121	$1,015	$1,167	$792	$229	$819

PARMER	PECOS	POLK	POTTER	PRESIDIO	RAINS	RANDALL	REAGAN	REAL	RED RIVER	REEVES	REFUGIO	ROBERTS	ROBERTSON
3.4	7.2	12.3	6.9	13.6	5.1	3.6	4.3	5.6	9.2	12.9	4.8	7.4	8.5
$74	$753	$2,118	$6,258	$426	$201	$1,834	$81	$82	$980	$1,398	$334	$33	$741
15	135	350	1,085	83	39	310	13	14	207	259	54	6	132

PARMER	PECOS	POLK	POTTER	PRESIDIO	RAINS	RANDALL	REAGAN	REAL	RED RIVER	REEVES	REFUGIO	ROBERTS	ROBERTSON
15.4	-6.1	31.9	18.1	17.3	-6.3	37.4	17.8	17.8	4.3	-8.8	13.1	88.4	7.1
$39,175	$86,078	$135,989	$902,046	$21,178	$12,947	$496,531	$17,239	$6,201	$52,948	$63,478	$35,353	$1,941	$44,843
48	124	126	879	58	18	331	22	19	80	103	76	5	97
5	9	8	40	6	2	18	1	2	6	4	3	1	7
1	5	8	24	6		9	4		3	7	3		8
9	18	20	109	8	5	41	4	4	19	13	12	1	19
8	30	31	138	12	3	53	7	6	11	25	20		22
3	11	8	83	5	1	45		1	6	8	5		8
1	5	7	71	1	1	26			4	5	2	1	3
15	25	23	227	14	2	73	4	3	10	21	16	1	16
6	21	21	187	6	4	66	2	3	21	20	15	1	14

PARMER	PECOS	POLK	POTTER	PRESIDIO	RAINS	RANDALL	REAGAN	REAL	RED RIVER	REEVES	REFUGIO	ROBERTS	ROBERTSON
3	3	4	8	2	2	3	1	1	3	2	2	1	4
	1	1	1			1					1	1	1
2	1		21		1				2	4	1		1

PARMER	PECOS	POLK	POTTER	PRESIDIO	RAINS	RANDALL	REAGAN	REAL	RED RIVER	REEVES	REFUGIO	ROBERTS	ROBERTSON
$88	$149	$194	$1,127	$44	$39	$792	$52	$17	$108	$120	$101	$12	$117
17.7	26.6	15.4	12.8	27.7	18.9	15.5	27.5	20.1	17.8	8.1	16.5	-9.5	12.1
$7,925	$9,575	$7,676	$11,218	$8,590	$7,954	$10,052	$11,588	$6,509	$6,759	$7,550	$10,313	$10,542	$7,996
203	111	209	40	168	202	91	31	237	233	212	75	61	199

PARMER	PECOS	POLK	POTTER	PRESIDIO	RAINS	RANDALL	REAGAN	REAL	RED RIVER	REEVES	REFUGIO	ROBERTS	ROBERTSON
$14,996	$17,717	$13,387	$17,409	$10,394	$15,066	$24,229	$18,284	$10,674	$11,902	$14,985	$17,593	$20,529	$14,335
17.2	12.1	15.5	9.8	34.6	13.6	3.4	12.4	23.9	20.5	21.0	13.4	8.3	20.1
179	233	795	1,880	216	246	546	69	111	1,079	342	243	7	1,002
$2,409	$1,525	$1,776	$2,012	$1,611	$1,880	$1,967	$1,244	$1,649	$1,914	$1,918	$1,837	$711	$1,938
749	872	3,633	9,329	585	827	4,703	230	357	2,507	1,040	1,024	109	2,351
$3,936	$3,282	$3,985	$3,927	$3,060	$3,477	$4,085	$3,481	$3,468	$3,298	$3,017	$3,973	$3,755	$3,182

COUNTY EMPLOYMENT

	ROCKWALL	RUNNELS	RUSK	SABINE	SAN AUGUSTINE	SAN JACINTO	SAN PATRICIO	SAN SABA	SCHLEICHER	SCURRY	SHACKELFORD
1982 Employment											
Civilian Labor Force	8,054	5,305	25,058	2,399	2,607	3,675	29,146	2,479	1,649	10,160	2,382
Total Employment	7,788	5,099	23,480	2,153	2,253	3,335	26,992	2,381	1,559	9,706	2,272
Agriculture[P]	*	52	20		*	*	586	12	*	123	*
Mining[P]	*	485	1,104	*	*	*	840	*	269	2,079	590
Construction[P]	584	111	1,098	114	43	74	2,045	29	*	292	17
Manufacturing[P]	571	688	1,947	*	174	64	2,037	*	*	320	156
Transport./Comm./Pub. Util.[P]	49	152	*	52	*	23	772	27	118	394	36
Trade[P]	937	689	2,396	326	322	188	3,099	359	150	1,500	168
Finance/Insurance/Real Estate[P]	141	141	489	54	92	138	544	116	28	213	35
Service/Other[P]	360	335	3,347	710	479	156	2,062	447	150	680	100
State Government[P]	41	39	164	24	48	30	129	25	2	54	21
Local Government[P]	505	521	1,459	335	317	350	2,580	223	206	1,157	145
Total Annual Wages (Millions)[P]	$45	$42	$218	$20	$17	$12	$223	$12	$16	$113	$21
Average Weekly Wage[P]	$272	$252	$332	$244	$220	$230	$293	$187	$337	$320	$324
Fed. Employment[P]	42	42	106	52	31	31	80	30	13	56	15
Total Annual Fed. Wages (Thous.)[P]	$831	$882	$2,259	$806	$567	$474	$1,865	$495	$233	$1,109	$259
1983											
Unemployment Rate (%)	3.5	3.8	7.9	13.7	14.3	11.7	11.6	5.2	5.1	4.1	3.4
Benefit Payments (Thous.)	$328	$190	$3,258	$716	$706	$998	$7,369	$138	$99	$378	$86
Ave. No. of Claimants Per Month	52	35	600	123	129	156	1,163	27	16	73	15
Retail Trade											
% Change in Sales (1st Qtr. 1984)	55.6	6.1	10.8	0.6	5.0	13.1	7.6	2.7	-38.1	7.1	-0.01
Est. 1982 Retail Sales (Thous.)	$62,472	$49,792	$143,925	$34,854	$32,584	$15,068	$257,523	$16,958	$5,877	$112,744	$16,465
Retail Establishments (1981)	87	83	210	55	42	32	333	35	14	145	28
Bldg. Materials/Garden Sup.	10	9	16	3	3	2	14	2	1	2	4
General Merchandise	2	5	12	1	3	1	16	2	2	4	2
Food Stores	17	12	31	14	6	14	54	8	4	20	4
Auto Dealers/Service Stations	15	12	49	10	7	8	84	8	3	30	8
Apparel/Accessories	7	8	20	3	6		27	4	1	20	2
Home Furnishings	3	4	13	2	2		10	3		12	1
Eating/Drinking	17	16	26	8	7	3	67	1	2	23	4
Misc. Retail	16	17	43	14	8	4	61	7	1	34	3
Finance											
Commercial Banks (6/30/83)	4	6	6	2	2	2	10	2	1	3	2
Savings & Loan Assoc. (12/31/82)			2		1			1		1	
Credit Unions (12/31/82)	1		3	2			2			1	
1981 Income											
Personal Income (Millions)	$179	$111	$401	$63	$59	$72	$508	$46	$34	$199	$48
% Change 1980-81	20.1	13.3	17.4	10.9	14.4	15.2	14.8	13.4	41.0	20.0	27.5
Per Capita Income	$11,265	$9,375	$9,519	$7,311	$6,624	$6,089	$8,586	$7,662	$11,756	$10,876	$12,158
Rank in State	37	126	115	226	235	244	169	210	24	51	15
1979 Income											
Median Family Income	$25,734	$14,737	$17,335	$12,642	$12,294	$15,462	$18,944	$12,446	$16,772	$18,757	$16,582
% of Fam. Below Poverty Level	6.6	14.0	11.1	17.6	19.1	18.7	14.7	18.0	13.4	9.0	8.1
Households with Pub. Assistance	226	355	1,434	356	578	550	1,637	271	53	366	87
Average Public Assistance	$1,958	$1,717	$1,660	$1,818	$1,718	$1,897	$1,939	$1,817	$1,658	$2,131	$2,056
Households with Soc. Sec. Income	1,042	1,871	5,392	1,445	1,267	1,540	3,974	1,068	287	1,738	567
Ave. Annual Soc. Sec. Income	$3,555	$3,517	$3,802	$3,539	$3,364	$3,795	$3,567	$3,563	$3,333	$3,724	$3,835

Source: Texas Employment Commission/Texas Comptroller of Public Accounts/U.S. Department of Commerce, Bureau of Census
*Withheld to avoid disclosure of information concerning individuals, or individual business operations.   PPreliminary figures.

SHELBY	SHERMAN	SMITH	SOMERVELL	STARR	STEPHENS	STERLING	STONEWALL	SUTTON	SWISHER	TARRANT	TAYLOR	TERRELL	TERRY
8,338	1,460	72,646	8,252	10,904	5,180	743	1,039	3,318	4,212	495,002	61,486	756	6,584
7,568	1,426	67,874	8,012	7,249	4,937	719	1,009	3,154	4,005	461,459	58,020	721	6,166
*	120	940	*	720	*	*	*	31	300	1,573	210	*	373
31	71	4,223	*	279	937	182	128	856	*	4,658	4,722	*	1,074
127	*	2,385	*	72	161	*	64	102	101	21,105	3,004	41	135
1,714	*	12,181	*	17	636			*	182	97,642	6,256	*	270
206	29	2,412	*	118	199	*	30	218	160	19,708	2,706	*	373
1,008	269	14,691	115	941	736	50	99	368	697	109,726	14,165	99	1,115
226	*	2,947	*	93	153	*	*	61	95	20,098	2,735	24	181
787	451	10,403	5,277	632	360	82	110	245	220	72,322	10,383	545	400
72	13	2,040	32	95	45	17	13	53	28	7,506	2,378	16	49
774	180	4,621	162	1,866	417	121	164	266	469	32,270	4,038	106	804
$59	$18	$912	$137	$148	$56	$7	$8	$36	$28	$6,349	$762	$12	$75
$230	$313	$309	$472	$185	$293	$317	$271	$321	$235	$316	$290	$274	$303
101	21	567	15	186	27	6	22	29	48	10,563	1,295	18	50
$1,851	$344	$14,033	$269	$4,554	$619	$120	$310	$819	$813	$259,753	$21,176	$379	$943

SHELBY	SHERMAN	SMITH	SOMERVELL	STARR	STEPHENS	STERLING	STONEWALL	SUTTON	SWISHER	TARRANT	TAYLOR	TERRELL	TERRY
9.8	3.2	6.5	1.6	40.5	7.0	4.7	2.9	5.0	4.9	5.9	5.8	4.6	6.5
$1,413	*	$7,490	$167	$5,281	$646	*	*	$201	$144	$43,726	$4,538	$38	$498
265	3	1,515	26	1,141	108	4	4	33	27	7,769	858	6	88

SHELBY	SHERMAN	SMITH	SOMERVELL	STARR	STEPHENS	STERLING	STONEWALL	SUTTON	SWISHER	TARRANT	TAYLOR	TERRELL	TERRY
14.9	18.5	20.8	18.0	29.6	17.2	22.7	−0.1	−14.2	8.1	21.1	14.3	N/A	29.4
$94,257	$15,880	$833,088	$22,843	$75,911	$45,277	$4,536	$6,278	$43,597	$32,260	$5,619,043	$731,801	$7,048	$99,977
133	24	814	17	108	88	8	14	32	60	5,182	814	11	89
12	1	48	1	8	2		1	1	6	188	26		7
9	1	22	1	7	3			3	4	136	27	1	7
22	3	89	3	25	12	3	3	3	8	691	118		17
27	7	159	3	28	17	3	1	9	11	826	136	7	17
13	3	107		11	10		1	2	4	619	104		12
6	2	66		4	3			2	3	349	64		5
14	4	138	6	18	20		5	9	12	1,223	145	2	12
30	3	185	3	7	21	2	3	3	12	1,150	194	1	12

SHELBY	SHERMAN	SMITH	SOMERVELL	STARR	STEPHENS	STERLING	STONEWALL	SUTTON	SWISHER	TARRANT	TAYLOR	TERRELL	TERRY
5	1	14	1	2	2	1	1	2	4	70	12	1	2
2		5			1				1	5	2		1
		13		2	2				1	73	1		1

SHELBY	SHERMAN	SMITH	SOMERVELL	STARR	STEPHENS	STERLING	STONEWALL	SUTTON	SWISHER	TARRANT	TAYLOR	TERRELL	TERRY
$174	$41	$1,401	$44	$111	$102	$13	$25	$60	$118	$10,239	$1,278	$16	$155
16.3	4.5	16.4	13.6	14.4	20.4	17.4	37.6	14.5	19.1	14.3	17.2	−0.3	34.3
$7,508	$12,779	$10,605	$10,272	$3,884	$9,836	$10,303	$10,534	$10,988	$12,516	$11,219	$11,140	$9,371	$10,843
214	9	58	78	253	97	77	62	47	11	39	42	127	54

SHELBY	SHERMAN	SMITH	SOMERVELL	STARR	STEPHENS	STERLING	STONEWALL	SUTTON	SWISHER	TARRANT	TAYLOR	TERRELL	TERRY
$14,077	$19,036	$19,246	$19,281	$8,627	$16,150	$15,417	$15,371	$19,151	$14,453	$21,577	$17,723	$18,750	$16,662
17.1	8.5	9.5	8.3	45.0	10.7	14.4	12.9	15.8	19.3	6.9	8.6	16.1	17.3
1,227	24	3,125	112	1,437	229	16	73	83	246	13,057	1,832	34	346
$1,666	$2,898	$1,757	$1,818	$1,789	$2,161	$1,021	$1,748	$1,265	$1,689	$1,842	$1,772	$1,317	$1,781
3,422	322	12,182	466	1,710	1,311	99	358	322	999	60,699	9,317	140	1,288
$3,203	$3,658	$3,908	$3,498	$2,607	$3,886	$3,784	$3,328	$3,243	$3,873	$3,918	$3,768	$3,678	$3,600

COUNTY EMPLOYMENT

	THROCK-MORTON	TITUS	TOM GREEN	TRAVIS	TRINITY	TYLER	UPSHUR	UPTON	UVALDE	VAL VERDE	VAN ZANDT
1982 Employment											
Civilian Labor Force	1,175	12,982	47,453	230,023	3,383	5,590	10,669	2,276	7,959	11,597	11,698
Total Employment	1,135	12,001	44,754	218,873	3,185	5,045	9,231	2,153	7,298	10,084	10,994
Agriculture[P]	*	64	251	736	*	*	43	*	432	58	145
Mining[P]	129	401	1,299	435	*	*	79	678	297	*	381
Construction[P]	*	775	2,336	12,853	85	236	167	23	298	339	281
Manufacturing[P]	*	1,473	6,338	27,931	237	599	460	*	450	778	703
Transport./Comm./Pub. Util.[P]	24	1,742	3,794	7,022	57	100	294	202	299	350	159
Trade[P]	67	1,651	9,280	54,244	421	681	989	206	1,954	2,441	1,130
Finance/Insurance/Real Estate[P]	22	309	1,455	14,836	124	158	129	39	347	450	198
Service/Other[P]	104	1,416	6,589	44,544	356	504	737	132	802	1,048	883
State Government[P]	17	94	2,160	44,598	32	62	83	24	203	228	65
Local Government[P]	150	1,197	3,179	19,944	314	687	787	375	1,191	1,868	868
Total Annual Wages (Millions)[P]	$7	$135	$520	$3,518	$18	$39	$45	$32	$75	$81	$57
Average Weekly Wage[P]	$266	$300	$273	$298	$216	$241	$232	$373	$231	$206	$229
Fed. Employment[P]	17	101	836	8,591	52	34	54	10	91	1,117	74
Total Annual Fed. Wages (Thous.)[P]	$242	$2,146	$15,228	$161,431	$823	$656	$920	$197	$2,236	$19,705	$1,380
1983											
Unemployment Rate (%)	3.1	8.8	5.4	4.5	7.3	13.8	16.4	5.1	11.0	15.7	5.9
Benefit Payments (Thous.)	$49	$2,078	$3,317	$11,723	$492	$1,674	$3,898	$106	$1,331	$2,800	$1,004
Ave. No. of Claimants Per Month	9	380	616	2,202	856	274	679	17	267	555	178
Retail Trade											
% Change in Sales (1st Qtr. 1984)	12.0	18.0	-2.3	28.2	10.0	17.9	18.3	-7.6	2.0	3.9	21.9
Est. 1982 Retail Sales (Thous.)	$3,127	$170,316	$579,716	$2,839,899	$46,403	$50,775	$103,017	$11,395	$92,463	$136,146	$117,217
Retail Establishments (1981)	14	170	578	2,745	56	61	107	31	141	230	161
Bldg. Materials/Garden Sup.		9	26	102	6	5	6	2	8	9	15
General Merchandise	1	7	14	58	4	6	3	4	6	10	11
Food Stores	3	22	82	330	10	14	14	6	20	29	18
Auto Dealers/Service Stations	3	25	92	355	12	15	26	8	31	40	46
Apparel/Accessories	1	20	80	323	6	1	11	1	16	38	14
Home Furnishings		16	46	222	1	3	5	1	11	15	4
Eating/Drinking	2	33	115	741	9	10	16	8	28	43	25
Misc. Retail	4	38	123	614	8	7	26	1	21	46	28
Finance											
Commercial Banks (6/30/83)	2	4	7	32	2	3	4	2	4	4	8
Savings & Loan Assoc. (12/31/82)		1	3	7		1	1		2	2	
Credit Unions (12/31/82)			15	42			3		2	4	
1981 Income											
Personal Income (Millions)	$26	$237	$921	$4,771	$70	$120	$220	$59	$166	$244	$260
% Change 1980-81	27.1	16.4	19.0	16.8	15.8	10.5	16.0	33.5	12.6	12.8	16.5
Per Capita Income	$$11,961	$10,857	$10,522	$11,055	$7,286	$7,278	$7,423	$12,651	$7,491	$6,734	$8,075
Rank in State	19	53	65	46	227	228	219	10	215	234	195
1979 Income											
Median Family Income	$13,562	$18,427	$17,596	$20,514	$14,191	$15,314	$17,383	$17,009	$13,234	$12,274	$15,968
% of Fam. Below Poverty Level	14.5	8.8	8.9	8.9	15.2	12.7	10.6	13.6	22.3	24.3	10.5
Households with Pub. Assistance	46	636	1,413	6,451	524	480	979	84	687	1,108	880
Average Public Assistance	$1,066	$1,877	$1,765	$1,870	$1,898	$1,431	$1,618	$2,497	$1,467	$1,768	$1,882
Households with Soc. Sec. Income	370	2,524	7,818	25,847	1,625	2,328	3,264	305	2,046	2,251	4,632
Ave. Annual Soc. Sec. Income	$3,569	$3,579	$3,784	$3,843	$3,535	$3,860	$3,850	$3,577	$3,568	$3,184	$3,791

Source: Texas Employment Commission/Texas Comptroller of Public Accounts/U.S. Department of Commerce, Bureau of Census
*Withheld to avoid disclosure of information concerning individuals, or individual business operations.   [P]Preliminary figures.

FLYING THE COLORS: TEXAS ©JOHN CLEMENTS 1984

VICTORIA	WALKER	WALLER	WARD	WASHINGTON	WEBB	WHARTON	WHEELER	WICHITA	WILBARGER	WILLACY	WILLIAMSON	WILSON	WINKLER
39,524	18,004	11,665	7,649	12,004	40,984	19,348	3,878	62,604	7,879	5,686	41,543	6,486	4,438
36,481	17,300	11,192	7,133	11,443	34,293	18,065	3,718	58,205	7,395	4,988	39,939	6,117	4,204
98	103	191	*	84	438	673	65	139	352	661	160	101	*
3,396	135	*	1,898	313	1,487	1,703	642	4,433	246	20	334	132	860
3,499	380	140	160	639	1,807	409	188	2,145	378	73	1,327	114	204
3,673	1,970	283	218	1,629	2,009	976	*	9,529	829	*	3,455	160	82
1,419	313	58	570	187	3,364	544	121	2,597	164	167	626	32	307
8,207	3,701	1,317	1,033	2,284	12,097	3,381	458	12,481	1,068	665	3,934	741	644
1,417	393	152	137	523	1,415	444	81	2,348	223	90	673	106	93
4,925	1,455	609	338	1,537	4,588	1,722	411	8,288	700	625	2,893	320	313
240	5,095	1,558	216	903	575	115	25	2,143	975	71	115	81	17
3,447	1,220	737	876	1,078	5,618	1,836	502	5,161	904	826	3,303	635	663
$507	$206	$68	$105	$125	$403	$175	$39	$746	$76	$34	$211	$27	$55
$322	$268	$256	$372	$261	$233	$285	$312	$291	$251	$208	$242	$219	$336
234	112	47	29	71	566	111	35	2,972	89	41	179	50	26
$5,403	$2,253	$965	$589	$1,510	$14,636	$2,161	$607	$47,966	$1,904	$769	$3,769	$823	$606
10.0	4.8	5.9	6.5	4.0	25.5	9.0	6.3	7.0	5.1	14.5	3.7	5.2	6.3
$7,344	$1,671	$897	$733	$676	$16,972	$3,309	$418	$7,201	$524	$1,160	$1,806	$379	$408
1,230	284	144	121	119	3,855	552	66	1,286	113	260	307	66	73
8.7	18.7	21.4	-0.1	-1.9	15.9	10.1	-11.4	7.2	9.3	0.9	43.6	7.5	29.3
$518,358	$193,616	$182,472	$66,471	$117,487	$607,334	$205,122	$38,867	$766,884	$74,692	$48,581	$262,775	$43,867	$47,014
483	208	87	90	167	704	278	57	828	98	76	371	74	69
21	11	7	1	11	28	15	7	32	3	5	28	3	3
15	8	4	5	5	36	11	4	23	5	2	14	5	4
68	27	19	15	31	96	54	9	100	12	17	63	17	11
81	40	16	19	27	94	47	14	134	22	19	71	19	11
59	25	3	8	16	145	29	4	103	16	6	30	4	6
30	11	3	5	17	45	17	2	71	7	3	20	1	8
110	45	19	20	27	92	52	8	182	19	11	77	12	15
99	41	16	17	33	168	53	9	183	14	13	68	13	11
5	5	3	2	5	6	7	4	10	3	2	20	4	3
2		1	1	2	3		1	4	1		3		1
4	2	1	3		7	4		2	1		1		2
$808	$291	$166	$160	$258	$634	$384	$79	$1,421	$163	$98	$710	$109	$111
21.9	16.2	21.5	27.1	20.4	17.2	20.3	6.4	16.0	20.9	14.8	18.6	22.2	23.3
$11,359	$6,841	$7,987	$10,905	$11,345	$6,148	$9,365	$10,767	$11,669	$10,013	$5,615	$8,749	$6,524	$10,597
32	232	200	48	33	243	128	55	26	92	250	156	236	59
$20,857	$17,809	$20,063	$18,797	$17,648	$12,181	$18,784	$16,399	$18,047	$15,750	$11,443	$21,797	$15,407	$18,929
9.9	13.1	13.3	11.3	12.0	29.0	13.6	11.3	9.4	14.2	29.6	7.7	15.6	10.0
1,613	975	460	197	783	3,882	1,194	172	1,932	441	807	1,227	555	139
$1,802	$1,580	$1,604	$2,385	$1,742	$1,751	$2,094	$1,652	$1,846	$1,575	$1,842	$1,681	$1,661	$1,972
4,549	3,001	1,577	994	3,060	5,953	3,938	1,029	10,739	2,337	1,341	5,668	1,730	754
$3,643	$3,537	$3,290	$3,880	$3,408	$3,147	$3,374	$3,750	$3,743	$3,740	$3,203	$3,543	$3,157	$4,048

COUNTY EMPLOYMENT

	WISE	WOOD	YOAKUM	YOUNG	ZAPATA	ZAVALA
1982 Employment						
Civilian Labor Force	14,897	9,768	4,315	9,953	3,135	4,883
Total Employment	14,245	9,110	4,123	9,496	2,715	3,875
Agriculture[P]	14	73	126	49	*	437
Mining[P]	1,229	728	1,250	1,808	356	81
Construction[P]	116	250	131	270	*	82
Manufacturing[P]	997	952	130	1,391	*	*
Transport./Comm./Pub. Util.[P]	560	277	273	322	27	32
Trade[P]	1,263	1,362	466	1,585	180	373
Finance/Insurance/Real Estate[P]	194	242	72	313	*	47
Service/Other[P]	668	1,112	171	826	262	799
State Government[P]	70	81	14	48	16	53
Local Government[P]	984	859	539	997	445	620
Total Annual Wages (Millions)[P]	$94	$78	$62	$116	$16	$26
Average Weekly Wage[P]	$298	$252	$374	$294	$245	$207
Fed. Employment[P]	80	69	24	59	27	20
Total Annual Fed. Wages (Thous.)[P]	$1,562	$1,368	$441	$1,210	$537	$443
1983						
Unemployment Rate (%)	3.8	7.4	3.6	4.8	15.1	25.2
Benefit Payments (Thous.)	$759	$1,282	$88	$791	$943	$1,571
Ave. No. of Claimants Per Month	138	229	14	138	168	448
Retail Trade						
% Change in Sales (1st Qtr. 1984)	17.4	11.8	–3.9	5.4	N/A	4.7
Est. 1982 Retail Sales (Thous.)	$88,833	$97,298	$29,497	$92,379	$10,984	$23,186
Retail Establishments (1981)	125	152	55	143	40	51
Bldg. Materials/Garden Sup.	6	10	5	5	2	3
General Merchandise	13	11	4	8	1	1
Food Stores	30	20	9	17	10	8
Auto Dealers/Service Stations	26	36	15	28	8	11
Apparel/Accessories	12	14	5	17	2	6
Home Furnishings	4	10	3	9	1	3
Eating/Drinking	12	24	5	26	9	12
Misc. Retail	22	27	9	33	7	7
Finance						
Commercial Banks (6/30/83)	6	7	3	4	1	2
Savings & Loan Assoc. (12/31/82)		1		2		
Credit Unions (12/31/82)		1	3			
1981 Income						
Personal Income (Millions)	$245	$227	$99	$230	$37	$72
% Change 1980-81	22.8	15.7	32.0	19.6	17.3	19.4
Per Capita Income	$8,883	$9,091	$11,712	$11,775	$5,263	$6,286
Rank in State	150	136	25	23	252	240
1979 Income						
Median Family Income	$18,862	$15,963	$19,193	$17,015	$11,523	$9,728
% of Fam. Below Poverty Level	9.3	10.6	12.7	8.2	23.8	34.7
Households with Pub. Assistance	506	728	106	388	335	788
Average Public Assistance	$2,195	$1,866	$1,863	$1,687	$1,867	$1,428
Households with Soc. Sec. Income	2,904	3,685	549	2,708	777	960
Ave. Annual Soc. Sec. Income	$3,865	$3,951	$3,592	$3,742	$4,171	$3,025

Source: Texas Employment Commission/Texas Comptroller of Public Accounts/U.S. Department of Commerce, Bureau of Census
*Withheld to avoid disclosure of information concerning individuals, or individual business operations.   [P]Preliminary figures.

FLYING THE COLORS: TEXAS ©JOHN CLEMENTS 1984

STANDARD METROPOLITAN STATISTICAL AREA (SMSA) is a standard used by the federal government in compiling and publishing data on metropolitan areas. SMSAs are also used extensively by states, local planning regions and marketing departments of companies. For example the placement of television, radio and newspaper advertisements and direct mail are often determined by the rank and size of an SMSA. As a result SMSAs are commonly referred to as major market areas. In general an SMSA is one or more counties with one or more large population centers plus adjacent communities with a high degree of economic and social ties to the central city(ies). SMSAs are designated and defined by the U.S. Office of Management and Budget (OMB). In 1980 in order for a county(ies) to be designated an SMSA, there had to be an urbanized area with at least 50,000 population, or a total of at least 100,000 residents within the county. The central city is the city with the largest population plus additional cities if they meet a list of requirements. Outlying counties are included in an SMSA if the population density of the county is at least 25 persons per square mile and at least 50 percent of the labor force in the county commute to the central county(ies) of an SMSA for employment. If an outlying county does not meet that requirement, it may still be included if it meets a list of further qualifications. In June, 1981, as a result of the 1980 Census, Victoria was designated a new SMSA, bringing the Texas total to 26. **METROPOLITAN STATISTICAL AREAS** In June, 1983 new definitions were announced by the OMB. The metropolitan concept remains the same—a county(ies) with a large population center together with adjacent communities having a high degree of social and economic ties with the central city(ies)—but the name has been shortened to Metropolitan Statistical Area (MSA) and there are new criteria. Under the new definitions, those counties with at least half their population in the urbanized area now qualify as part of the central core. New criteria require a population of at least 25,000 for central cities with a limit of three city names in the title of an MSA and there are four levels of size: 25,000; 100,000; 250,000 and 1,000,000. **CONSOLIDATED METROPOLITAN STATISTICA AREA** (CMSA) Now metropolitan areas with over 1,000,000 population and having subunits called **PRIMARY METROPOLITAN STATISTICAL AREAS** (PMSA) are called CMSAs. For example Dallas is a PMSA and Fort Worth-Arlington is a PMSA and both are in the Dallas-Fort Worth CMSA. Most major metropolitan areas are now called PMSAs. In Texas there are now two CMSAs with 5 PMSAs. Due to the recent change in definitions the SMSA categories have been used as current data still reflect that definition.

SMSA	1980 POP.
1. Abilene SMSA	139,192
Abilene city 98,315, Callahan Co. 10,992, Jones Co. 17,268, Taylor Co. 110,932	
2. Amarillo SMSA	173,699
Amarillo city 149,230, Potter Co. 98,637, Randall Co. 75,062	
3. Austin SMSA	536,688
Hays Co. 40,594, Travis Co. 419,573, Austin city 345,496, Williamson Co. 76,521	
4. Beaumont-Port Arthur-Orange SMSA	375,497
Beaumont city 118,102, Orange city 23,628, Port Arthur city 61,251, Hardin Co. 40,721, Jefferson Co. 250,938, Orange Co. 83,838	
5. Brownsville-Harlingen-San Benito SMSA	209,727
Brownsville city 84,997, Harlingen city 43,543, San Benito city 17,988, Cameron Co. 209,727	
6. Bryan-College Station SMSA	93,588
Bryan city 44,337, College Station city 37,272, Brazos Co. 93,588	
7. Corpus Christi SMSA	326,228
Corpus Christi city 231,999, Nueces Co. 268,215, San Patricio Co. 58,013	
8. Dallas-Fort Worth SMSA	2,974,805
Dallas city 904,078, Fort Worth city 385,164, Collin Co. 144,576, Dallas Co. 1,556,390, Denton Co. 143,126, Ellis Co. 59,743, Hood Co. 17,714, Johnson Co. 67,649, Kaufman Co. 39,015, Parker Co. 44,609, Rockwall Co. 14,528, Tarrant Co. 860,880, Wise Co. 26,575	
9. El Paso SMSA	479,899
El Paso city 425,259, El Paso Co. 479,899	
10. Galveston-Texas City SMSA	195,940
Galveston city 61,902, Texas City 41,403, Galveston Co. 195,940	
11. Houston SMSA	2,905,353
Houston city 1,595,138, Brazoria Co. 169,587, Fort Bend Co. 130,846, Harris Co. 2,409,547, Liberty Co. 47,088, Montgomery Co. 128,487, Waller Co. 19,798	
12. Killeen-Temple SMSA	214,656
Killeen city 46,296, Temple city 42,483, Bell Co. 157,889, Coryell Co. 56,767	

SMSA	1980 POP.
13. Laredo SMSA	99,258
Laredo city 91,449, Webb Co. 99,258	
14. Longview-Marshall SMSA	151,752
Longview city 62,762, Marshall city 24,921, Gregg Co. 99,487, Harrison Co. 52,265	
15. Lubbock SMSA	211,651
Lubbock city 173,979, Lubbock Co. 211,651	
16. McAllen-Pharr-Edinburg SMSA	283,229
Edinburg city 24,075, McAllen city 66,281, Pharr city 21,381, Hidalgo Co. 283,229	
17. Midland SMSA	82,636
Midland city 70,525, Midland Co. 82,636	
18. Odessa SMSA	115,374
Odessa city 90,027, Ector Co. 115,374	
19. San Angelo SMSA	84,784
San Angelo city 73,240, Tom Green Co. 84,784	
20. San Antonio SMSA	1,071,954
San Antonio city 785,880, Bexar Co. 988,800, Comal Co. 36,446, Guadalupe Co. 46,708	
21. Sherman-Denison SMSA	89,796
Denison city 23,884, Sherman city 30,413, Grayson Co. 89,796	
22. Texarkana SMSA	127,019
Texarkana city, AR 21,459, Texarkana city, TX 31,271, Little River Co., AR 13,952, Miller Co., AR 37,766, Bowie Co., TX 75,301	
23. Tyler SMSA	128,366
Tyler city 70,508, Smith Co. 128,366	
24. Victoria SMSA	68,807
Victoria city 50,695, Victoria Co. 68,807	
25. Waco SMSA	170,755
Waco city 101,261, McLennan Co. 170,755	
26. Wichita Falls SMSA	130,664
Wichita Falls city 94,201, Clay Co. 9,582, Wichita Co. 121,082	

MAJOR MARKET AREAS

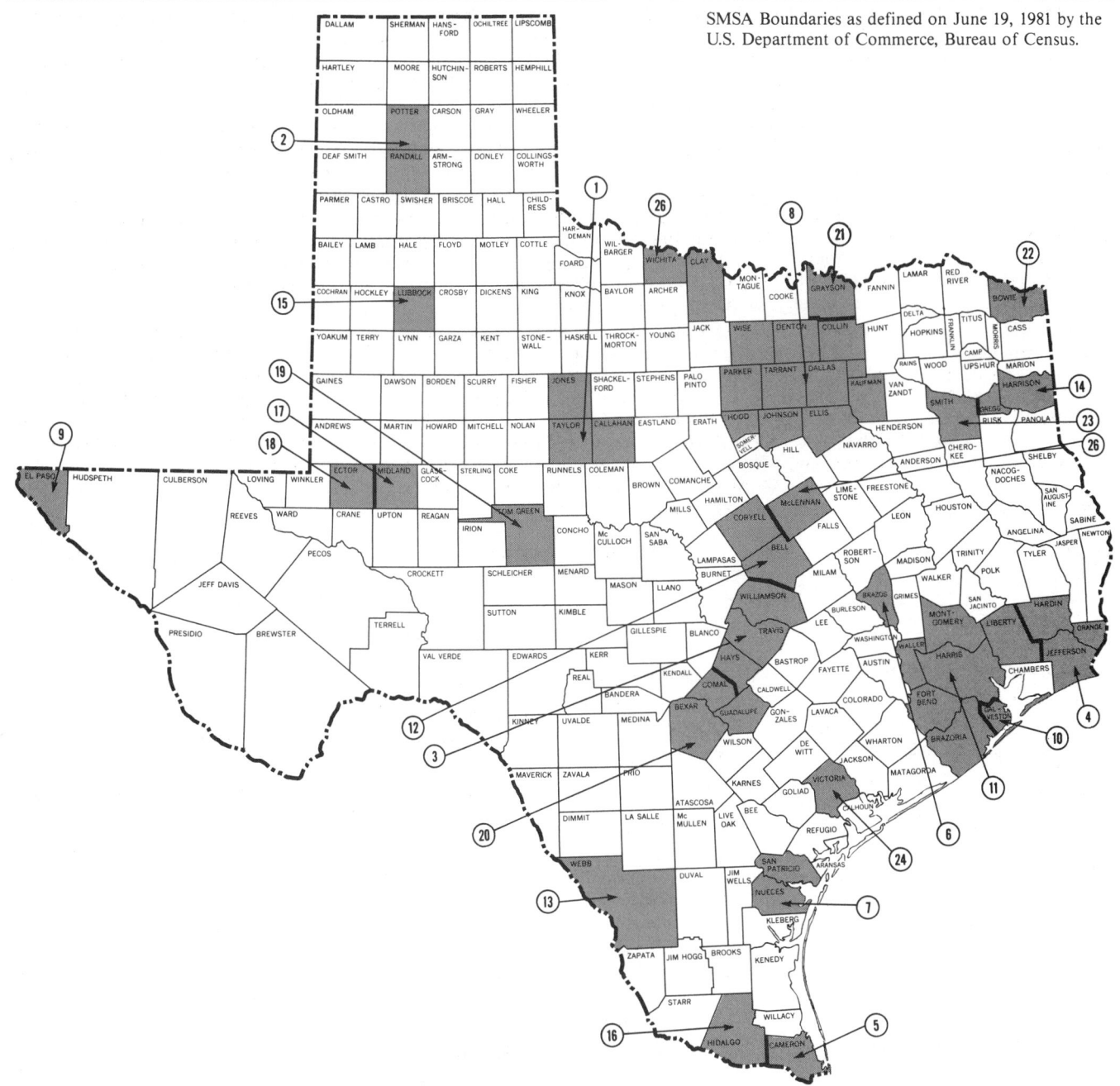

SMSA Boundaries as defined on June 19, 1981 by the
U.S. Department of Commerce, Bureau of Census.

STANDARD METROPOLITAN STATISTICAL AREAS

City	County
1 Abilene	Taylor, Jones, Callahan
2 Amarillo	Potter, Randall
3 Austin	Travis, Hays, Williamson
4 Beaumont/Port Arthur/Orange	Jefferson, Orange, Hardin
5 Brownsville/Harlingen/ San Benito	Cameron
6 Bryan/College Station	Brazos
7 Corpus Christi	Nueces, San Patricio
8 Dallas/Fort Worth	Dallas, Tarrant, Collin, Denton, Ellis, Hood, Johnson, Kaufman, Parker, Rockwall, Wise
9 El Paso	El Paso
10 Galveston/Texas City	Galveston
11 Houston	Harris, Brazoria, Fort Bend, Liberty, Montgomery, Waller

STANDARD METROPOLITAN STATISTICAL AREAS

City	County
12 Killeen/Temple	Bell, Coryell
13 Laredo	Webb
14 Longview/Marshall	Gregg, Harrison
15 Lubbock	Lubbock
16 McAllen/Pharr/Edinburg	Hidalgo
17 Midland	Midland
18 Odessa	Ector
19 San Angelo	Tom Green
20 San Antonio	Bexar, Comal, Guadalupe
21 Sherman/Denison	Grayson
22 Texarkana (TX/AR)	Bowie (Little River/Miller, AR)
23 Tyler	Smith
24 Victoria	Victoria
25 Waco	McLennan
26 Wichita Falls	Wichita, Clay

FLYING THE COLORS: TEXAS ©JOHN CLEMENTS 1984

ABILENE

THE LAND Abilene is the primary city in a major market area that covered Callahan, Jones and Taylor Counties until June, 1983 when both Callahan and Jones counties were deleted from the statistical area. On rolling plains with hills to the south and west, there are few trees other than mesquite. **THE CLIMATE** Rainfall amounts vary; on the average there will be 65 days of measurable precipitation with a total of 23 inches each year. In July the average high temperature is 95 °F with an average low of 73 °F. Summer days are usually characterized by fair skies and low humidity, while the winter is generally mild with brief periods of very cold weather. The average high in January is 55 °F with an average low of 31 °F. Abilene is windy, especially in the spring. The average annual wind speed is 12 mph with southerly winds prevailing. In winter northerly winds are frequent. During the year the wind will be calm only 2% of the time. **THE PEOPLE** The 1980 population of 139,192 was up 14% from 1970 for the Abilene Standard Metropolitan Statistical Area (SMSA). This increase reversed a slight decline in the population between 1960 and 1970. The population density is 51 people per square mile in the SMSA and 1,295 per square mile in Abilene. The population in the SMSA is 23% single, 62% married and 6% divorced. Hispanics make up 12% and Blacks 5% of the population. The median age is 29; over 28% of the population is under 18 and 12% are age 65 and over. Among persons ages 25 and over, 61% are high school graduates and 16% have completed four or more years of college. **THE ECONOMY** In January, 1984 the estimated total civilian labor force in the SMSA was 76,900 down from 77,900 in January, 1983 with 5.3% unemployed in January, 1984 as compared with 5.1% in January, 1983. The greatest change between 1983 and 1984 occurred in the manufacturing sector which dropped from a labor force of 7,500 in January, 1983 to 5,800 in January, 1984. Employment in other areas includes 4,200 in mining, 3,000 in construction, 3,200 in transportation, communication and utilities, 14,900 in trade, 3,200 in finance and real estate, 13,600 in services and 9,600 in government. Average gross weekly earnings rose from $195 in 1980 to $221 in 1981. Corporate charters granted from January through June, 1983 totaled 185. Revenue collected in Abilene city sales tax for January through May, 1984 was $4,650,430, a 15% increase over the $4,030,091 collected in the same 1983 period. During the first three quarters of 1983 the total construction permit volume was $112,582,000, a 1% increase from the same 1982 period. Dollar volume for nonresidential construction was $22,892,000 a 38% decrease. Total value of permits for single family houses issued the first three quarters of 1983 was $57,941,000 a 36% increase from the same 1982 period. Multifamily construction for January through September, 1983 was valued at $18,315,000 for apartments and condominiums, a 24% decrease from the same 1982 period and $4,729,000 for two to four family units, a 140% increase. Residential sales totaled $27,590,000 during the third quarter 1983, an 82% increase from the same 1982 period. The average residential sales price was $65,065 a 20% increase from the third quarter of 1982. Abilene savings and loan activity during the third quarter of 1983 included construction loans totaling $23,200,000. Of that total residential loans were $16,400,000 and nonresidential were $4,300,000. **OVERVIEW** Abilene is located in a major sheep and wool producing area with diversified agribusiness. The city's economy centers around petroleum production and oil related industries. Current government plans for Dyess Air Force Base, which plays a significant role in the area's economy, will add about 2,000 persons to the city's population over the next year. A commercial airline recently inaugurated jet service to Abilene enhancing the city's transportation services. Cultural aspects are influenced by two universities and one college. Recreational activities are abundant through such attractions as the Abilene State Park, Nelson Park Zoo, Fort Phantom Hill, area lakes and various fine arts programs. See the county section for additional information.

AMARILLO

THE LAND Amarillo is the primary city in a major market area that covers Potter and Randall Counties. With wide open vistas, the city is on grassy plains that have few trees. The elevation of the city is 3,604 feet. **THE CLIMATE** Amarillo receives varied amounts of rainfall, however the average annual precipitation is 18 inches with 68 days having measurable precipitation. In July the average high temperature is 91 °F with an average low of 66 °F. Low humidity moderates the high temperatures. During the winter rapid temperature changes occur as cold front smove through the area. About 14 inches of snow falls during winter, but usually melts within a few days. The average high in January is 49 °F with an average low of 22 °F. On the average 109 days will go below freezing during the year. Amarillo is windy especially in the spring. The average annual wind speed is 14 mph with southerly winds prevailing except for winter when northerly winds prevail. Throughout the year it will be calm about 1% of the time. **THE PEOPLE** The 1980 population of 173,699 was up 20% from 1970 for the Amarillo Standard Metropolitan Statistical Area (SMSA). This reversed a slight decline that occurred between 1960 and 1970. The population density is 95 people per square mile for the SMSA, but 1,863 per square mile for the city of Amarillo. In the entire SMSA the population is 21% single, 63% married and 8% divorced. Hispanics make up 9% and Blacks 5% of the population. The median age is 29; over 28% of the population is under age 18 and 10% are age 65 and over. Among persons ages 25 and over, 69% are high school graduates and 16% have completed four or more years of college. **THE ECONOMY** In January, 1984 the estimated total civilian labor force in the SMSA was 98,400, up from 96,600 in January, 1983 with 5.6% unemployed in January, 1984 as compared with 5.9% in January, 1983. The greatest change between 1983 and 1984 occurred in the government sector which rose from a labor force of 13,100 in January, 1983 to 14,100 in January, 1984. Employment in other areas includes 2,000 in mining, 3,600 in construction, 6,500 in transportation, communication and utilities, 23,400 in trade, 4,300 in finance and real estate, 14,500 in services and 9,400 in manufacturing. Average gross weekly earnings rose from $288 in 1980 to $311 in 1981. Corporate charters granted from January through June 1983 totaled 187. Revenue collected in Amarillo city sales tax for January through May 1984 was $6,364,396 a 17% increase over the $5,432,110 collected in the same 1983 period. In 1983 construction activity within the city of Amarillo increased 63%. During the first three quarters of 1983 the total construction permit volume was $178,005,000, a 113% increase from the same 1982 period. Dollar volume for nonresidential construction was $50,739,000 a 76% increase. Total value of permits for single family houses issued the first three quarters of 1983 was $64,638,000 a 139% increase from the same 1982 period. Multifamily construction for January through September 1983 was valued at $29,932,000 for apartments and condominiums, a 155% increase from the same 1982 period and $2,957,000 for two to four family units, a 731% increase. Residential sales totaled $54,930,000 during the third quarter of 1983, an 73% increase from the same 1982 period. The average residential sales price was $59,509, an 8% increase from third quarter of 1982. Residential lending by Amarillo savings and loan associations increased rapidly from $12,500,000 third quarter 1982 to $23,700,000 third quarter 1983. Loans for construction during third quarter 1983 totalled $4,600,000. **OVERVIEW** Amarillo is the commercial, cultural and

AMARILLO (continued)

recreational center for the Texas Panhandle. Its air is rated as one of the cleanest in the nation for a city its size. Since helium exists in vast quantities the area is the world's leading producer of this natural element. The region's economic stability has attracted developers and manufacturers to the area. Economic activity centers around industries related to oil and natural gas, agribusiness, trade and distribution. Amarillo is headquarters for an immense ranch and cattle feed lot area. More than 600,000 cattle are placed at auction each year. One college and a university in nearby Canyon offer educational opportunities. Tourist attractions include the Alibates National Monument, Palo Duro Canyon State Park, Garden Center and Amarillo Art Center. See the county section for additional information.

AUSTIN

THE LAND Austin, the capital of Texas, is the primary city in a major market area that covers Hays, Travis and Williamson counties. On the edge of both the hill country and the gently rolling central prairies, Austin is located on a bend of the Colorado River and has a tree cover of cedar, oak, walnut, mesquite and pecan. The elevation of the city is 621 feet. **THE CLIMATE** In July the average high temperature is 95 °F with an average low of 74 °F. Winters are mild with freezes occurring on the average less than 25 days a year. The average high in January is 59 °F with an average low of 39 °F. Precipitation averages 32 inches a year with the heaviest rainfall in the late spring. On the average 83 days a year will have measurable precipitation. Austin has an average annual wind speed of 9 mph with southerly winds prevailing. During the winter northerly winds are frequent, but spring is the season of the strongest winds. Throughout the year it is calm about 5% of the time. **THE PEOPLE** Austin is the fourth largest Standard Metropolitan Statistical Area (SMSA) in Texas. In 1980 it had a population of 536,674, a 49% increase over 1970 which continued, at an even greater rate, the growth experienced from 1960 to 1970. The population density is 191 people per square mile for the SMSA, but 2,978 per square mile for the city of Austin. For the entire SMSA the population is 33% single, 52% married and 8% divorced. Hispanics make up 18% and Blacks 9% of the population. The median age is 27; over 26% of the population is under age 18 and 8% is age 65 and over. Among persons ages 25 and over, 73% are high school graduates and 28% have completed four or more years of college. With 21% of those people over 18 being college graduates the Austin SMSA ranks 13th among the United States SMSAs. **THE ECONOMY** In March, 1984 the Austin area's unemployment rate of 3.4% was the lowest in the state. In January, 1984 the estimated total civilian labor force in the SMSA was 331,200, up from 319,700 in January, 1983 with 4.0% unemployed in January, 1984 as compared with 4.8% in January, 1983. The greatest change between 1983 and 1984 occurred in the construction sector which rose from a labor force of 15,700 in January, 1983 to 18,600 in January, 1984. Employment in other areas includes 800 in mining, 34,300 in manufacturing, 8,100 in transportation, communication and utilities, 65,900 in trade, 18,300 in finance and real estate, 57,800 in services and 85,700 in government. Average gross weekly earnings rose from $230 in 1980 to $257 in 1981. Corporate charters granted from January through June 1983 totaled 1,334. Revenue collected in Austin city sales tax for January through May 1984 was $19,792,882 a 31% increase over the $15,083,154 collected in the same 1983 period. During the first three quarters of 1983 the total construction permit volume was $1,035,157,000, a 51% increase from the same period in 1982. Dollar volume for nonresidential

construction was $261,645,000. Total value of permits for single family houses issued the first three quarters of 1983 was $390,193,000 a 90% increase from the same 1982 period. Multifamily construction for January through September 1983 was valued at $229,865,000 for apartments and condominiums, a 175% increase from the same 1982 period and $71,180,000 for two to four family units, a 1% decrease. Residential sales totaled $123,380,000 during the third quarter 1983, an 24% increase from the same 1982 period. The average residential sales price was $87,691, an 5% increase from the third quarter of 1982. During the fourth quarter of 1982 through the third quarter of 1983 construction lending by Austin savings and loan associations far exceeded residential lending with construction loans totalling $224,500,000 during third quarter 1983 as compared with $75,200,000 in residential loans. **OVERVIEW** As the hub of Texas and seat of government, Austin is a center for tourism and education. The recent selection of the city as future headquarters of a major computer research company has stimulated land investment and interest among other high technology firms. The presence of four colleges and two universities including the University of Texas at Austin with a student population of over 48,000 enhances the cultural life of the city. The Tourist Information Center in the State Capitol reported 49,359 visitors for January and February of 1984. In addition to the State Capitol Complex visitors enjoy such attractions a the numerous city parks, the Governor's Mansion, Laguna Gloria Art Museum, various historical sites and the Lyndon B. Johnson Presidential Library. See the county section for additional information.

BEAUMONT-PORT ARTHUR-ORANGE

THE LAND Beaumont, Port Arthur and Orange are the primary cities in a major market area that covers Hardin, Jefferson and Orange Counites. The cities are on the level coastal plain in the southeast corner of the state. Port Arthur is located on Sabine Lake that is connected to the Gulf by the Sabine Pass. Beaumont is on the Neches River and Orange is on the Sabine River bordering Louisiana. **THE CLIMATE** The area averages over 50 inches of rainfall a year with an average of 104 days receiving measurable precipitation. In July the average high temperature is 92 °F with an average low of 74 °F. In January the high temperature averages 62 °F with an average low of 42 °. On the average 18 days a year will be below freezing. The cities have an average annual wind speed of 10 mph with the lowest monthly averages during the summer. **THE PEOPLE** The 1980 population of 375,497 was up 8% from 1970 for the Beaumont-Port Arthur-Orange Standard Metropolitan Statistical Area (SMSA) which continued a similar growth from 1960 to 1970. The population density is 171 people per square mile for the SMSA, 1,620 per square mile for the city of Beaumont, 1,390 for the city of Orange and 1,076 for the city of Port Arthur. For the entire SMSA the population is 21% single, 63% married and 7% divorced. Hispanics make up 3% and Blacks 22% of the population. The median age is 29; over 29% of the population is under age 18 and 10% is age 65 and over. Among persons ages 25 and over, 63% are high school graduates and 12% have completed four or more years of college. **THE ECONOMY** In January, 1984 the estimated total civilian labor force in the SMSA was 175,800, down from 185,100 in January, 1983 with 12.8% unemployed in January, 1984 as compared with 15% in January, 1983. The greatest change between 1983 and 1984 occurred in the manufacturing sector which dropped from a labor force of 33,300 in January, 1983 to 31,400 in January, 1984. Employment in other areas includes 2,500 in mining, 9,200 in construction, 11,400 in transportation, communication and utilities, 32,800 in trade, 5,700 in finance and real estate, 25,700 in services and 20,000 in services and 20,000 in government. Average gross weekly earnings rose from $421 in 1980 to $451 in 1981. Corporate charters granted from January through June 1983 totaled 272. Revenue collected in Beaumont, Port Arthur and Orange city sales tax for January through May 1984 was $7,385,757, an 11% increase over the $6,609,443 collected in the same 1983 period. During the first three quarters of 1983, the total construction permit volume was $153,561,000, building permits were issued, a 25% increase from the same 1982 period. Dollar volume for nonresidential construction was $39,411,000 a 12% decrease. Total value of permits for single family houses issued the first three quarters of 1983 was $59,024,000 a 59% increase from the same 1982 period. Multifamily construction for January through September 1983 was valued at $13,565,000 for apartments and condominiums, a 29% increase from the same 1982 period and $1,318,000 for two to four family units, a 72% increase. Residential sales totaled $21,120,000 during the third quarter 1983, a 40% increase from the same 1982 period. The average residential sales price was $68,795, a 10% increase from the third quarter of 1982. During the first three quarters of 1983 residential and nonresidential permanent lending by savings and loan associations in Beaumont, Port Arthur and Orange had a very strong increase. Residential loans totalled $70,200,000 in third quarter 1983 with nonresidential loans reaching $25,700,000. **OVERVIEW** The Beaumont-Port Arthur-Orange SMSA is an industrial hub, major port and agricultural center. The oil discoveries which made Beaumont a boom town overnight created the present day economy which centers around oil-related industries such as refineries, oil field servicing and the manufacture of oil field equipment. Nearly a million barrels of crude oil are refined in Port Arthur daily. More than 25 varieties of fresh and saltwater fish can be taken in this year-round fisherman's paradise. The city of Orange is known as an industrial as well as a recreational port. Recent hotel expansion in Beaumont and Port Arthur have stimulated the area's economy. Educational opportunities are provided by a university in Beaumont with branches in Port Arthur and Orange. Popular regional tourist attractions include Sabine Pass Battleground State Historical Park, Sea Rim State Park, Port of Beaumont and "Rainbow Bridge". See the county section for additional information.

BROWNSVILLE-HARLINGEN-SAN BENITO

THE LAND Brownsville, Harlingen and San Benito are the primary cities in a major market area that covers Cameron County. On alluvial soils in the lush Rio Grande River Valley the area is known for its cotton, citrus fruits and vegetables. **THE CLIMATE** The average yearly rainfall is 29 inches with most occurring in May, June and September. An average of 73 days a year receive measurable precipitation. In July the average high temperature is 94°F with an average low of 74°F. Gulf breezes help moderate the afternoon high temperatures. Winters are mild with an average high in January is 69°F with an average low 51°F. Usually it will not freeze, but on occasion winters will have damaging freezes. The cities are windy especially in the spring with an average annual wind speed of 12 mph. Southeasterly and south southeasterly winds prevail except during winter when southerly winds prevail slightly over north northwesterly winds. Throughout the year it will be calm about 4% of the time. **THE PEOPLE** The 1980 population of 209,727 was up 49% from 1970 for the Brownsville-Harlingen-San Benito Standard Metropolitan Statistical Area (SMSA). This increase reversed the slight decline of population between 1960 and 1970. The population density is 232 people per square mile for the SMSA, but 3,057 per square mile for the city of Brownsville, 1,437 for Harlingen and 1,999 for San Benito. For the entire SMSA the population is 26% single, 60% married and 4% divorced. Hispanics

make up 77% of the people with the city of Brownsville ranking third among cities of 50,000 or more with 84% of its population being Hispanic in 1980. The median age is 25; over 38% of the population is under age 18 and 10% is age 65 and over. Among persons age 25 and over, 44% are high school graduates and 11% have completed four or more years of college. **THE ECONOMY** In January, 1984 the estimated total civilian labor force in the SMSA was 91,600, down from 92,500 in January, 1983 with 15.9% unemployed in January, 1984 as compared with 16.8% in January, 1983. The greatest change between 1983 and 1984 occurred in the government sector which rose from a labor force of 13,600 in January, 1983 to 14,100 in January, 1984. Employment in other areas includes 100 in mining, 3,400 in construction, 3,100 in transportation, communication and utilities, 17,000 in trade, 3,100 in finance and real estate, 11,200 in services and 10,800 in manufacturing. Corporate charters granted from January through June 1983 totaled 194. Revenue collected in Brownsville, Harlingen and San Benito city sales tax for January through May 1984 was $3,986,756 a 15% increase over the $3,451,727 collected in the same 1983 period. During the first three quarters of 1983 the total construction permit volume was $91,189,000, a 43% decrease from the same 1982 period. Dollar volume for nonresidential construction was $26,256,000 a 42% decrease. Total value of permits for single family houses issued the first three quarters of 1983 was $40,931,000 a 15% increase from the same 1982 period. Multifamily construction for January through September 1983 was valued at $10,183,000 for apartments and condominiums, an 84% decrease from the same 1982 period and $3,889,000 for two to four family units, a 64% increase. Lending activity by savings and loan associations in Brownsville, Harlingen and San Benito from the last quarter of 1982 through third quarter of 1983 grew slowly with the greatest increase occurring in residential loans which totalled $7,200,000 during third quarter 1983. **OVERVIEW** The southernmost SMSA in Texas, the Brownsville-Harlingen-San Benito area is a major food-processing region with a subtropical climate which attracts winter tourists throughout the nation. Brownsville is an international seaport, airport and railroad interchange point on the Mexican border. Major industries include electronics, food-processing and petrochemicals. Harlingen is not only a transportation and distribution center for the lower Rio Grande Valley but also an agricultural area with continuous harvests such as oranges and grapefruit in winter or cotton and sugarcane in summer. Despite the recent winter freeze and the effects of the suffering Mexican economy, industrial growth, increased consumer spending and rising tourism provide a positive economic picture. One college in Brownsville and one in Harlingen offer educational opportunities. Visitor attractions include Laguna Atascosa Wildlife Refuge, Brazos Island State Park and South Padre Island. See the county section for additional information.

BRYAN-COLLEGE STATION

THE LAND Bryan and College Station are the primary cities in a major market area that covers Brazos County. Located on level grasslands, the cities are situated between the Brazos and Navasota rivers. **THE CLIMATE** The average yearly rainfall is 39 inches. The average high temperature in July is 95°F with the average low 74°F. In January the average high is 59° with the average low 39°F. **THE PEOPLE** The 1980 population of 93,588 was up 61% from 1970 making Bryan-College Station the fastest growing Standard Metropolitan Statistical Area (SMSA) in Texas. The population density is 159 people per square mile. In the entire SMSA the population is 45% single, 45% married and 4% divorced. Hispanics make up 10% and Blacks 11% of the population. The median age is 23; over 21% of the population is under age 18 and 7% is age 65 and over. Among persons

MAJOR MARKET AREAS

BRYAN-COLLEGE STATION (continued)

ages 25 and over, 69% are high school graduates and 32% have completed four or more years of college. The population density for the city of Bryan is 1,887 people per square mile, for College State it is 1,559. **THE ECONOMY** In January, 1984 the estimated total civilian labor force in the SMSA was 53,700, up from 53,300 in January, 1983 with 4.8% unemployed in January, 1984 as compared with 4.9% in January, 1983. The greatest change between 1983 and 1984 occurred in the manufacturing sector which rose from a labor force of 2,900 in January, 1983 to 3,100 in January, 1984. Employment in other areas includes 1,100 in mining, 3,200 in construction, 1,700 in transportation, communication and utilities, 10,000 in trade, 1,900 in finance and real estate, 6,400 in services and 16,600 in government. Corporate charters granted from January through June 1983 totaled 124. Revenue collected in Bryan-College Station city sales tax for January through May 1984 was $3,430,887 a 9% increase over the $3,134,574 collected in the same 1983 period. During the first three quarters of 1983 the total construction permit volume was $107,481,000, an 11% decrease from the same 1982 period. Dollar volume for nonresidential construction was $36,447,000 a 59% increase. Total value of permits for single family houses issued the first three quarters of 1983 was $42,656,000 a 16% increase from the same 1982 period. Multifamily construction for January through September 1983 was valued at $6,708,000 for apartments and condominiums, a 77% decrease from the same 1982 period and $8,976,000 for two to four family units, a 66% decrease. Residential sales totaled $18,850,000 during the third quarter 1983, a 6% decrease from the same 1982 period. The average residential sales price was $60,236, a 10% decrease from third quarter of 1982. Lending activity by Bryan-College Station savings and loan associations dropped sharply during the third quarter 1983 with construction loans totalling $1,200,000 and residential loans reaching $600,000. **OVERVIEW** The economy of Bryan-College Station is based on diversified agriculture and enhanced by the presence of Texas A & M University. Increasing industrial development in the area includes chemicals, furniture and metal fabrication. The steady expansion of Texas A&M with over 35,000 students and recent hotel construction indicate the continuation of a strong economy. Tourists enjoy events at the Texas World Speedway in addition to hunting, fishing, and camping in nearby streams and woodlands. See the county section for additional information.

CORPUS CHRISTI

THE LAND Corpus Christi is the primary city in a major market area which covers Nueces and San Patricio Counties. Situated on lowlands surrounding Corpus Christi Bay, the city is on the Gulf coast. A bluff rising up to 40 feet in height helps to protect the area from flooding. **THE CLIMATE** The average rainfall is 29 inches per year with May and September the months of heaviest precipitation. On the average 78 days a year receive measurable precipitation. The summer months are generally dry with the chance of tropical storms. Temperatures in the summer rarely rise above 100 °F as the afternoon breeze off the Coast moderates temperatures. In July the average high temperature is 94 °F with the average low 74 °F. During the summer this area receives about 80% of the possible sunshine. The winter is basically mild with the high in January averaging 64 °F and the low averaging 46 °F. Inland areas may drop below 32 °F. a few times each winter. Corpus Christi is windy especially in the spring. The average annual wind speed is 12 mph with south

southeasterly to southeasterly winds prevailing except during winter when northerly winds prevail. Throughout the year it is calm about 2% of the time. **THE PEOPLE** The 1980 population of 326,228 was up 15% from 1970 for the Corpus Christi Standard Metropolitan Statistical Area (SMSA). This continued, at an even greater rate, the growth experienced between 1960 and 1970. The population density is 212 people per square mile for the SMSA, but 2,237 per square mile for the city of Corpus Christi. For the entire SMSA the population is 24% single, 61% married and 7% divorced. Hispanics make up 49% of the people which is sixth highest of all SMSAs in the United States. The median age is 27. Persons under 18 make up 34% of the population which is tenth highest among all SMSAs in the U.S. Over 18% is age 65 and over. Among persons ages 25 and over, 58% are high school graduates and 14% have completed four or more years of college. **THE ECONOMY** In January, 1984 the estimated total civilian labor force in the SMSA was 162,900, down from 168,900 in January, 1983 with 10% unemployed in January, 1984 as compared with 9.5% in January, 1983. The greatest change between 1983 and 1984 occurred in the construction sector which dropped from a labor force of 14,100 in January, 1983 to 9,700 in January, 1984. Employment in other areas includes 7,300 in mining, 14,000 in manufacturing, 7,400 in transportation, communication and utilities, 31,800 in trade, 6,400 in finance and real estate, 23,500 in services and 26,600 in government. Average gross weekly earnings rose from $313 in 1980 to $345 in 1981. Corporate charters granted from January through June 1983 totaled 389. Revenue collected in Corpus Christi city sales tax for January through May 1984 was $8,897,039, a 10% increase over the $8,099,357 collected in the same 1983 period. During the first three quarters of 1983 the total construction permit volume was $300,008,000, a 54% increase from the same 1982 period. Dollar volume for nonresidential construction was $72,505,000 a 5% decrease. Total value of permits for single family houses issued the first three quarters of 1983 was $103,560,000 a 78% increase from the same 1982 period. Multifamily construction for January through September 1983 was valued at $90,731,000 for apartments and condominiums, a 161% increase from the same 1982 period and $6,374,000 for two to four family units, a 6% decrease. Residential sales totaled $28,350,000 during the third quarter 1983, a 14% increase from the same 1982 period. The average residential sales price was $74,412. Lending activity by Corpus Christi savings and loan associations decreased steadily during the first three quarters of 1983 with construction loans totalling $11,400,000 during third quarter 1983 and residential loans reaching $2,900,000. **OVERVIEW** Corpus Christi is a major deepwater port and one of Texas' most popular coastal resort cities. The Port of Corpus Christi is one of the ten busiest in the nation. Among its major cargoes are oil and refined products, grain, cotton and chemicals. The tourist industry, a major economic factor, shows signs of continued growth with convention facilities almost fully booked for 1984 and hotel expansion underway. Tourists enjoy boating, sailing, fishing, swimming and coastal-oriented sporting events. Educational facilities include one college and one university in the city of Corpus Christi. See the county section for additional information.

DALLAS-FORT WORTH

THE LAND Dallas and Fort Worth are the primary cities in a major market area that covers Collin, Dallas, Denton, Ellis, Hood, Johnson, Kaufman, Parker, Rockwall, Tarrant and Wise Counties. Under the new federal government definition for metropolitan areas, Hood and Wise Counties were dropped in forming the Dallas-Fort Worth Consolidated Metropolitan

Statistical Area (CMSA) which includes Dallas Primary Metropolitan Statistical Area (PMSA) and Fort Worth-Arlington PMSA. On prairie land with mesquite, this area is mostly level but has rolling hills in the west. Along streams are oak, elm and pecan trees. The elevation of the area is 576 feet. **THE CLIMATE** Rainfall amounts vary widely from year to year, but the average annual precipitation is 32 inches with 78 days receiving measurable amounts. In July the average high temperature is 98 °F with the average low 75 °F. Summer days are characterized by fair skies, westerly winds and low humidity. Winters are mild with an average high in January of 55 °F and an average low of 33 °F. About three times a month during the winter, cold fronts move through dropping the temperatures to cold extremes. About once a year measurable snow falls, but it usually melts the same day. An average of 41 days a year will be below freezing. Dallas and Fort Worth are windy, especially in the spring. The average annual wind speed is 11 mph with southerly winds prevailing. During winter, northerly winds are frequent. Throughout the year it is calm about 5% of the time. **THE PEOPLE** The 1982 population of 3,143,000 was up 7% from 1980 and made the Dallas-Fort Worth Standard Metropolitan Statistical Area (SMSA) the second fastest growing SMSA in the country. The city of Dallas is the seventh largest city in the U.S. The population density in 1980 was 357 people per square mile for the SMSA, but 2,715 per square mile for the city of Dallas and 1,604 for the city of Fort Worth. For the entire SMSA, the population is 24% single, 60% married and 8% divorced. In 1980 the city of Dallas had the twelfth highest population of Hispanics with 110,511 and the twelfth highest number of Blacks with 265,105. The city of Fort Worth is 33rd in Black population and 28th in Hispanic. The median age is 29; over 29% are under age 18 and 8% are age 65 and over. Among persons ages 25 and over, 70% are high school graduates and 20% have completed four or more years of college. **THE ECONOMY** In March, 1984 the Dallas-Fort Worth area's Dallas/Fort Worth unemployment rate was 3.9%, one of the lowest in the state. In January, 1984 the estimated total civilian labor force in the SMSA was 1,821,600, up from 1,763,200 in January, 1983 with 4.6% unemployed in January, 1984 as compared with 6% in January, 1983. The greatest change between 1983 and 1984 occurred in the services sector which rose from a labor force of 298,200 in January, 1983 to 318,400 in January, 1984. Employment in other areas includes 28,400 in mining, 97,800 in construction, 97,700 in transportation, communication and utilities, 434,900 in trade, 130,900 in finance and real estate, 312,800 in manufacturing and 186,800 in government. Average gross weekly earnings rose from $274 in 1980 to $309 in 1981. Corporate charters granted from January through June 1983 totaled 7,048. Revenue collected in city sales tax in the city of Dallas for January through May 1984 was $55,141,345 a 20% increase over the $45,974,185 collected in the same 1983 period. Revenue collected for the DART program of the Dallas Metropolitan Transity Authority from January through May 1984 totalled $8,500,000. Fort Worth city sales tax for January through May 1984 totalled $16,938,170, a 14% increase over the $14,804,791 collected in the same 1983 period. Revenue collected for the Fort Worth Metropolitan Transit Authority totalled $466,000 from January through May 1984. In 1983 the city of Dallas was second in the nation in construction activity based on total value of building permits. Construction in Arlington rose by about 264% during 1983, one of the biggest increases in the U.S., while Fort Worth construction rose 101%. During the first three quarters of 1983 the total construction permit dollar volume was $4,971,119,000 the Dallas-Fort Worth SMSA, an 80% increase from the same 1982 period. Dollar volume for nonresidential construction was $1,415,844,000 a 32% increase. Total value of permits for single family houses issued the first three quarters of 1983 was $1,718,637,000 a 119% increase from

the same 1982 period. Multifamily construction for January through September 1983 was valued at $1,155,157,000 for apartments and condominiums, a 146% increase from the same 1982 period and $138,016,000 for two to four family units, a 110% increase. Residential sales in the city of Dallas totaled $698,170,000 during the third quarter 1983, a 181% increase from the same 1982 period. The average residential sales price was $109,022, a 10% increase from third quarter of 1982. Residential sales in the city of Fort Worth totaled $96,720,000 during the third quarter 1983, a 35% increase from the same 1982 period. The average residential sales price was $66,020 a 5% increase from third quarter of 1982. Lending activity by Dallas and Fort Worth savings and loan associations increased over the last quarter of 1982 through the first three quarters of 1983 with the construction lending volume exceeding all others. Construction loans closed during third quarter 1983 totalled $707,100,000 with residential loans reaching $445,300,000. **OVERVIEW** The Dallas-Fort Worth SMSA, with its diversified industrial base, was less affected than other Texas areas by the recent recession as reflected by its 1983 growth rate in the areas of employment, business activity, retail sales and construction. Dallas is the Southwest's largest banking center, home of more insurance companies than any other city in the nation and is one of the nation's top three fashion markets. Fort Worth has a wide range of manufacturing industries including two major aviation plants. Several other cities within the region have had significant population growth such as Arlington, a major manufacturing, education and entertainment area and Irving, a thriving commercial, industrial and residential city on the eastern boundary of the Dallas-Fort Worth International Airport. Population and economic growth in Plano and Richardson rapidly increased in recent years as Dallas grew northward. Cultural life within the SMSA is enriched by more than 20 colleges and universities. Tourist attractions include Texas Stadium, Amon Carter Museum of Western Art, Fort Worth Stockyards, Kimbell Art Museum and the new Dallas Museum of Fine Arts. See the county section for additional information.

EL PASO

THE LAND El Paso is the primary city in a major market area that covers the county of El Paso. On a plateau in the mountains of far west Texas the business district sits at 3,700 feet. The Franklin Mountains start within the city and extend north with peaks over 7,000 feet. Desert vegetation is prevalent in the city. **THE CLIMATE** Rainfall is light, averaging eight inches a year. In July the average high temperature is 95 °F with low humidity with the average low 70 °F. In January the average high is 58 °F with the average low 30 °F. Because of the dry, loose soil and sparse vegetation, sandstorms occur with moderately strong winds which are most frequent in March and April. The average annual wind speed is 9 mph with the prevailing winds from the north during the fall and winter, the west in spring, and the south in summer. During spring and summer it is calm about 6% of the time and during fall and winter about 12% of the time. **THE PEOPLE** The 1980 population of 479,899 was up 37% from 1970 for the El Paso Standard Metropolitan Statistical Area (SMSA). The growth was more than double that experienced from 1960 to 1970. The population density is 473 people per square mile for the SMSA, and 1,778 per square mile for the city of El Paso. For the entire SMSA the population is 28% single, 58% married and 6% divorced. Over 62% of the people are Hispanic which ranks the El Paso SMSA sixth highest among SMSAs. El Paso is also sixth among SMSAs in persons under 18 with 35%. Over 6% of the residents are age 65 and over. Among persons age 25 and over, 60% are high school graduates and 14% have completed four or more years of college. **THE**

MAJOR MARKET AREAS

ECONOMY In January, 1984 the estimated total civilian labor force in the SMSA was 195,500, down from 198,100 in January, 1983 with 11% unemployed in January, 1984 as compared with 13.4% in January, 1983. The greatest change between 1983 and 1984 occurred in the manufacturing sector which rose from a labor force of 34,200 in January, 1983 to 35,900 in January, 1984. Employment in other areas includes 8,800 in construction, 9,600 in transportation, communication and utilities, 40,200 in trade, 7,800 in finance and real estate, 28,000 in services and 34,500 in government. Average gross weekly earnings rose from $204 in 1980 to $223 in 1981. Corporate charters granted from January through June 1983 totaled 378. Revenue collected in El Paso city sales tax for January through May 1984 was $10,264,450 a 22% increase over the $8,434,443 collected in the same 1983 period. During the first three quarters of 1983 the total construction permit volume was $224,962,000, a 39% increase from the same 1982 period. Dollar volume for nonresidential construction was $48,588,000 a 3% increase. Total value of permits for single family houses issued the first three quarters of 1983 was $87,216,000 a 75% increase from the same 1982 period. Multifamily construction for January through September 1983 was valued at $50,285,000 for apartments and condominiums, an 84% increase from the same 1982 period and $12,921,000 for two to four family units, an 89% increase. Residential sales totaled $76,690,000 during the third quarter 1983, a 35% increase from the same 1982 period. The average residential sales price was $69,400, a 2% decrease from third quarter of 1982. Approximately two-thirds of the lending by El Paso savings and loan associations during the first three quarters of 1983 were construction loans which totalled $24,600,000 during third quarter 1983 with residential loans reaching $11,000,000. **OVERVIEW** Manufacturing, trade, education and tourism are the sectors of greatest economic activity in the El Paso SMSA, in addition to government installations such as Fort Bliss, a U.S. Army Defense Center for rocket research and combat training. The area's high 1982-83 population growth created a demand for new jobs and contributed to a high unemployment rate in spite of industrial expansion. Ciudad Juarez, Mexico's fourth largest city with a population of 550,000 and linked to El Paso by three bridges over the Rio Grande, creates a large urban area with El Paso. Superb climate, dramatic scenery, historic sites and proximity to Mexico make the region one of Texas' most popular tourist areas. Specific attractions include Chamizal National Memorial and Hueco Tanks State Park. One community college and one university are located in the El Paso area. See the county section for additional information.

GALVESTON-TEXAS CITY

THE LAND Galveston and Texas City are the primary cities in a major market area that covers Galveston County. Under the federal government's new definition for metropolitan areas, Galveston-Texas City has become a Primary Metropolitan Statistical Area (PMSA) within the Houston-Galveston-Brazoria Consolidated Metropolitan Statistical Area (CMSA) which also includes Houston PMSA and Brazoria PMSA. Galveston is located on an island just off the coast and Texas City is across the bay on the low coastal mainland. **THE CLIMATE** Average yearly rainfall is 42 inches with an average of 96 days a year receiving measurable precipitation. Humidity is high all year. In July the average high temperature is 87° with the low 79°F. The winter is mild with an average high in January of 60° and an average low of 49°F. On the average it will be below freezing four times

a year. The cities are windy, with an average wind speed of 11 mph. **THE PEOPLE** The 1980 population of 195,940 was up 15% from 1970 for the Galveston-Texas City Standard Metropolitan Statistical Area (SMSA). This continued the similar growth rate between 1960 and 1970. The population density is 491 people per square mile for the SMSA, with 1,284 per square mile for the city of Galveston and 660 per square mile for Texas City. In the entire SMSA the population is 23% single, 60% married and 8% divorced. Hispanics make up 12% and Blacks 19% of the population. The median age is 29; over 29% of the population is under age 18 and 9% are age 65 and over. Among persons ages 25 and over, 65% are high school graduates and 15% have completed four or more years of college. **THE ECONOMY** In January, 1984 the estimated total civilian labor force in the SMSA was 89,900, down from 91,900 in January, 1983 with 10.7% unemployed in January, 1984 as compared with 13.9% in January, 1983. The greatest change between 1983 and 1984 occurred in the government sector which rose from a labor force of 18,300 in January, 1983 to 19,900 in January, 1984. Employment in other areas includes 800 in mining, 4,100 in construction, 5,800 in transportation, communication and utilities, 12,300 in trade, 4,500 in finance and real estate, 10,200 in services and 10,200 in manufacturing. Average gross weekly earnings rose from $430 in 1980 to $495 in 1981. Corporate charters granted from January through June 1983 totaled 198. Revenue collected in Galveston and Texas City city sales tax for January through May 1984 was $4,444,744 a 9% increase over the $4,067,923 collected in the same 1983 period. During the first three quarters of 1983 the total construction permit volume was $175,562,000, a 50% increase from the same 1982 period. Dollar volume for nonresidential construction was $22,958,000 a 40% increase. Total value of permits for single family houses issued the first three quarters of 1983 was $77,017,000 a 4% increase from the same 1982 period. Multifamily construction for January through September 1983 was valued at $36,376,000 for apartments and condominiums, a 209% increase from the same 1982 period and $4,542,000 for two to four family units, a 9,169% increase. Residential sales totaled $7,280,000 during the third quarter 1983, a 13% decrease from the same 1982 period. The average residential sales price was $68,715, a 7% increase from third quarter of 1982. Residential lending by Galveston and Texas City savings and loan associations had strong growth from fourth quarter 1982 through third quarter 1983 which had significant increases with residential loans totalling $40,300,000 as compared with construction loans which reached $3,600,000. **OVERVIEW** Oil-related industries, shipping and tourism are significant factors in the Galveston-Texas City SMSA economy. The Port of Galveston is the nation's only major port not supported by public funds due largely to the successful coordination of all facilities under one management. Recovering from Hurricane Alicia, August 1983, Galveston tourist facilities are currently expanding with construction underway for new hotels which will provide about 2,000 rooms and resort condominiums totalling 2,500 units. Industries in Texas City include tin smelter, oil refineries, metal fabrication and chemical plants. Tourists are drawn to the Galveston-Texas City area by its scenic beaches, fishing and historic attractions. Two colleges, two universities and one research center provide educational opportunities. See the county section for additional information.

HOUSTON

THE LAND Houston is the primary city of a major market area that covers Brazoria, Fort Bend, Harris, Liberty, Montgomery and Waller Counties. Under the federal government's new definition for metropolitan areas, Brazoria County has been dropped in creating the new Houston Primary Metropolitan Statistical Area (PMSA) to become the Brazoria PMSA which, with Houston PMSA and Galveston-Texas City PMSA, form the Houston-Galveston-Brazoria Consolidated Metropolitan Statistical Area (CMSA). Houston is located on the level coastal plains with many small streams and bayous. **THE CLIMATE** The average yearly rainfall is 48 inches with 107 days receiving measurable precipitation. In July the average high temperature is 94 °F with the average low 72 °F. The winter is mild with an average high in January of 62 °F and an average low of 41 °F. On the average 27 days a year will be below freezing. Fog occurs on the average 78 days a year, but is usually light. Houston has an average annual wind speed of 8 mph with south and southeasterly winds prevailing in the spring and summer and northerly winds prevailing in the fall and winter. The lowest wind speed averages occur during the summer and fall, when it is calm about 10% of the time. During the winter and spring it is calm about 6% of the time. **THE PEOPLE** The 1982 population of 3,458,000 was up almost 12% from 1980 and made Houston the fastest growing Standard Metropolitan Statistical Area (SMSA) in the country. This continued the growth experienced throughout the 1970s. In 1982 the city of Houston became the 4th largest U.S. city and the Houston SMSA became the 8th largest in the U.S. In 1980 the population density of the SMSA was 430 people per square mile but the city of Houston had 2,867 persons per square mile. The SMSA population was 25% single, 59% married and 8% divorced. In 1980 the Houston SMSA was 6th among U.S. SMSAs in largest Hispanic population with 400,944 and 9th in Black population with 513,797. The median age is 28. Persons under 18 make up 31% of the population with people 65 and over making up 6%. Among persons age 25 and over, 70% are high school graduates and 22% have completed four or more years of college. **THE ECONOMY** In January, 1984 the estimated total civilian labor force in the SMSA was 1,743,900, down from 1,779,400 in January, 1983 with 8.0% unemployed in January, 1984 as compared with 9.2% in January, 1983. Unemployment lowered to 7.3% in March, 1984. The greatest change between 1983 and 1984 occurred in the services sector which rose from a labor force of 306,200 in January, 1983 to 318,600 in January, 1984. Employment in other areas includes 98,300 in mining, 131,700 in construction, 102,700 in transportation, communication and utilities, 367,800 in trade, 105,000 in finance and real estate, 195,300 in manufacturing and 182,600 in government. Average gross weekly earnings rose from $374 in 1980 to $420 in 1981. Corporate charters granted from January through June, 1983 totaled 6,868. Revenue collected in Houston city sales tax for January through May, 1984 was $82,175,154 a 8% increase over the $75,841,888 collected in the same 1983 period. Revenue collected for the Houston Metropolitan Transit Authority from January through May, 1984 totalled $11,800,000. During the first three quarters of 1983 the total construction permit volume was $3,722,642,000, a 8% decrease from the same 1982 period. However the city of Houston ranked third in the nation in construction activity in 1983. Dollar volume for nonresidential construction was $1,307,813,000 a 30% decrease. Total value of permits for single family houses issued the first three quarters of 1983 was $1,398,015,000 a 37% increase from the same 1982 period. Multifamily construction for January through September, 1983 was valued at $509,144,000 for apartments and condominiums, a 12% decrease from the same 1982 period and $61,867,000 for two to four family units, a 38% increase. Residential sales totaled $398,910,000 during the third quarter 1983, a 13% increase from the same 1982 period. The average residential sales price was $110,993, a 15% increase from third quarter of 1982. From fourth quarter 1982 through third quarter 1983 the largest lending dollar volume by Houston savings and loan associations was in construction loans which totalled $407,200,000 during third quarter

1983 with residential loans reaching $314,900,000. **OVERVIEW** The Houston SMSA is the industrial and financial center for much of the state, one of the nation's largest seaports and headquarters of the Lyndon B. Johnson Space Center. The Port of Houston, among the top three seaports in the U.S. in total tonnage, is connected to the Gulf of Mexico by a 50-mile-long ship channel. The Texas Medical Center, an immense complex of hospital, medical schools and research institutions, in a typical year will hospitalize more than 150,000 patients, handle more than 1,500,000 outpatient visits and train some 6,000 students in all aspects of medical science. Healthy retail sales and increasing residential construction suggest the beginning of a recovery from the 1983 recession. Due to its rich heritage and broad cultural base, the city has extensive tourist attractions such as Bayou Bend Museum, Hermann Park Zoo and San Jacinto Battleground State Historic Park. Two colleges and five major universities are located in the Houston area, in addition to schools related to the Texas Medical Center. See the county section for additional information.

KILLEEN-TEMPLE

THE LAND Killeen and Temple are the primary cities in a major market area that covers Bell and Coryell counties. They are located on rolling prairies. **THE CLIMATE** The average high temperature in July is 96 ° with the average low 74 °F. The winters are mild with an average high in January of 57 ° and an average low 36 °F. Snow is not common and melts rapidly if it does occur. Rainfall averages 34 inches a year. **THE PEOPLE** The 1980 population of 214,587 was up 34% from 1970 for the the the Killeen-Temple Standard Metropolitan Statistical Area (SMSA) and continues the growth experienced between 1960 and 1970. The SMSA population density is 102 people per square mile with 2,124 people per square mile in the city of Killeen and 1,034 in Temple. The SMSA population is 26% single, 62% married, and 5% divorced. Hispanics make up 10% and Blacks 17%. The median age is 24; over 29% of the population is under age 18 and 7% are over age 64. Of those age 25 and over, 68% are high school graduates and 15% have completed four or more years of college. **THE ECONOMY** In January, 1984 the estimated total civilian labor force in the SMSA was 74,200, up from 71,400 in January, 1983 with 6.2% unemployed in January, 1984 as compared with 7.1% in January, 1983. The greatest change between 1983 and 1984 occurred in the manufacturing sector which rose from a labor force of 7,800 in January, 1983 to 8,600 in January, 1984. Employment in other areas includes 3,700 in construction, 3,000 in transportation, communication and utilities, 14,400 in trade, 2,400 in finance and real estate, 11,000 in services and 18,000 in government. Corporate charters granted from January through June, 1983 totaled 129. Revenue collected in Killeen and Temple city sales tax for January through May 1984 was $3,256,175 a 12% increase over the $2,898,933 collected in the same 1983 period. During the first three quarters of 1983 the construction permit volume was $109,725,000, an 81% increase from the same 1982 period. Dollar volume for nonresidential construction was $1,307,813,000 a 30% decrease. Total value of permits for single family houses issued the first three quarters of 1983 was $61,691,000 a 90% increase from the same 1982 period. Multifamily construction for January through September 1983 was valued at $23,671,000 for apartments and condominiums, a 398% increase from the same 1982 period and $6,747,000 for two to four family units, a 106% increase. There was a quadrupling of construction lending by Killeen and Temple savings and loan associations between the second and third quarters of 1983 with construction loans totaling $216,500,000 during third quarter 1983 as compared with $33,000,000 in residential loans.

MAJOR MARKET AREAS

KILLEEN-TEMPLE (continued)

center, one of the Southwest's leading medical centers and growing industrial producer. The largest single employer in the area is Fort Hood, home of the U.S. Army's 111 Corps 1st Cavalry Division and 2nd Armored Division. The area's economy was strong in 1983 with large increases in construction over the previous year. Current plans for expansion and economic growth include a new shopping mall, additional medical facilities and other major nonresidential projects. Two colleges and two universities are located in the area as well as a school of medicine. Tourists enjoy such attractions as Temple Lake Park and area lakes. See the county section for additional information.

LAREDO

THE LAND Laredo is the primary city in a major market area that covers Webb County. It is located on the lowlands of the Rio Grande River in southwest Texas. **THE CLIMATE** Laredo receives an average of 20 inches of rainfall a year, with hot summers and mild winters. In July the average high temperature is 99 °F with an average low of 76 °F. In January the average high is 68 °F with an average low of 45 °F. The winds in Laredo prevail out of the southeast. During the fall and winter it is calm about 5% of the time, and in spring and summer about 2% of the time. **THE PEOPLE** The 1980 population of 99,258 was up 36% from 1970 for the Laredo Standard Metropolitan Statistical Area (SMSA). The SMSA population density is 30 people per square mile, and the city of Laredo has 4,642 people per square mile. The SMSA population is 30% single, 57% married and 4% divorced. The SMSA ranks 1st among all U.S. SMSA's with 92% of its population Hispanic and 7th in foreign-born residents with 21%. It also ranks 1st in persons under 18 with 40%. People 65 and over make up 8% of the population. The median age is 24; over 42% of those age 25 and over are high school graduates and 10% have completed four or more years of college. **THE ECONOMY** In January, 1984 the estimated total civilian labor force in the SMSA was 40,100, down from 43,400 in January, 1983 with 22.7% unemployed in January, 1984 as compared with 27.2% in January, 1983. The greatest change between 1983 and 1984 occurred in the trade sector which dropped from a labor force of 9,300 in January, 1983 to 8,900 in January, 1984. Employment in other areas include 1,200 in mining, 1,300 in construction, 3,100 in transportation, communication and utilities, 1,900 in manufacturing, 1,400 in finance and real estate, 4,900 in services and 7,300 in government. Corporate charters granted from January through June 1983 totaled 94. Revenue collected in Laredo city sales tax for January through May 1984 was $2,322,056 a 15% increase over the $2,024,393 collected in the same 1983 period. During the first three quarters of 1983 a total of $14,455,000 in building permits was issued, a 65% decrease from the same 1982 period causing the Laredo SMSA to have one of the steepest construction declines in the state. Dollar volume for nonresidential construction was $4,579,000 a 72% decrease. Total value of permits for single family houses issued the first three quarters of 1983 was $4,726,000 a 40% decrease from the same 1982 period. Multifamily construction for January through September 1983 was valued at $80,000 for apartments and condominiums, a 99% decrease from the same 1982 period. Lending for residential and construction loans by Laredo savings and loan associations increased between the second and third quarters of 1983 with third quarter totals reaching $19,400,000 for construction and $3,300,000 for residential. **OVERVIEW** Rich in south-of-the-border flavor the Laredo SMSA is a major international crossing along the U.S.-Mexican border. The declining Mexican economy has adversely affected the area, but unemployment has levelled off. Tourists enjoy the historic sites and shopping in Laredo as well as in Nuevo Laredo, its Mexican sister city of 240,000. One college and one university enrich the cultural life of the area. See the county section for additional information.

LONGVIEW-MARSHALL

THE LAND Longview and Marshall are the primary cities in a major market area that covers Gregg and Harrison counties. They are located on rolling land surrounded by pine and hardwood forests. **THE CLIMATE** The cities receive an average of 46 inches of rain a year. They have warm summers and mild winters; in July the average high temperature is 94 °F with an average low of 72 °F, in January the average high is 55 ° with an average low of 33 °F. Occasional snowfall accumulates, but melts quickly. **THE PEOPLE** The Longview-Marshall Standard Metropolitan Statistical Area (SMSA) ranks 9th in the state in population growth between 1980 and 1982 with a 9% increase following a 26% growth between 1970 and 1980. Among persons age 24 and over, 62% are high school graduates and 14% have completed four or more years of college. Since 12% of its residents are 65 and over, the area has a high median age of 30. Nearly 30% of the population is under 18. The area ranks 33rd among U.S. SMSAs in percent of black residents with 23%. Nearly 20% of the residents are single, 62% married and 7% divorced. The SMSA has a population density of 128 people per square mile, the city of Longview has 1,516 per square mile and Marshall has 1,052 per square mile. **THE ECONOMY** In January, 1984 the estimated total civilian labor force in the SMSA was 79,500, down from 81,300 in January, 1983 with 10.1% unemployed in January, 1984 as compared with 12.4% in January, 1983. The greatest change between 1983 and 1984 occurred in the manufacturing sector which dropped from a labor force of 15,200 in January, 1983 to 14,500 in January, 1984. Employment in other areas includes 4,900 in mining, 4,700 in construction, 3,700 in transportation, communication and utilities, 17,200 in trade, 2,800 in finance and real estate, 11,000 in services and 8,300 in government. Average gross weekly earnings rose from $298 in 1980 to $329 in 1981. Corporate charters granted from January through June 1983 totaled 203. Revenue collected in Longview and Marshall city sales tax for January through May 1984 was $4,490,694 a 7% increase over the $4,171,765 collected in the same 1983 period. During the first three quarters of 1983 the total construction permit volume was $96,717,000, a 4% decrease from the same 1982 period. Dollar volume for nonresidential construction was $25,006,000 a 30% decrease. Total value of permits for single family houses issued the first three quarters of 1983 was $35,937,000 a 13% increase from the same 1982 period. Multifamily construction for January through September 1983 was valued at $12,478,000 for apartments and condominiums, a 121% increase from the same 1982 period and $3,173,000 for two to four family units, a 75% decrease. Residential sales in Longview totaled $22,640,000 during the third quarter 1983, a 8% increase from the same 1982 period. The average residential sales price was $62,725, no change from third quarter of 1982. Lending activity by the savings and loan associations in the city of Longview remained relatively stable from the fourth quarter of 1982 through third quarter of 1983 which had totals of $9,200,000 for construction loans and $15,900,000 for residential loans. **OVERVIEW** Longview-Marshall SMSA is both an agricultural center and a heavily industrialized area. Oil-related industries, a steel plant, food processing plants as well as wholesale and jobbing houses dominate the industrial sector. Longview is the loading end of the "Big Inch" petroleum products pipeline. New construction in 1983 rose significantly and nine new manufacturing firms located in the area.

Tourism is also increasing and attractions include Ginocchio National Historic District, area lakes and the Longview Museum and Arts Center. Two colleges are located in the area. See the county section for additional information.

LUBBOCK

THE LAND Lubbock is the primary city in a major market area that covers Lubbock county. On a high plains plateau the city has an elevation of 3,250 feet. **THE CLIMATE** The average yearly rainfall is 18 inches with an average of 60 days receiving measurable precipitation. July high temperatures average 92 °F with lows averaging 68 °F. Usually summer humidity is low. In January the average high is 53 °F with an average low of 24 °F. At least 10 inches of snowfall is common during winter, but it seldom remains on the ground for more than a few days. On the average, 97 days a year get below freezing. Lubbock is windy, especially in the spring, and the average annual wind speed is 13 mph with southerly winds prevailing except for winter when westerly winds prevail. Throughout the year it is calm about 3% of the time. **THE PEOPLE** The 1980 population of 211,651 in the Lubbock Standard Metropolitan Statistical Area (SMSA) reflects the steady, population growth occurring since 1960 with an 18% increase between 1970 and 1980. The population's median age is 26; nearly 29% of the residents are under 18 and 8% are age 65 and over. Among persons ages 25 and over, 66% are high school graduates and 20% have completed four or more years of college. The population includes 8% Black and 20% Hispanic. Almost 29% of the residents are single, 58% married and 6% divorced. The population per square mile is 235 for the SMSA, and 1,920 per square mile for the city of Lubbock. **THE ECONOMY** In January, 1984 the estimated total civilian labor force in the SMSA was 112,400, up from 111,900 in January, 1983 with 7.3% unemployed in January, 1984 as compared with 6.1% in January, 1983. The greatest employment change between 1983 and 1984 occurred in the manufacturing sector which dropped from a labor force of 13,000 in January, 1983 to 9,400 in January, 1984. Employment in other areas includes 500 in mining, 4,000 in construction, 4,800 in transportation, communication and utilities, 26,700 in trade, 5,300 in finance and real estate, 18,900 in services and 20,500 in government. Average gross weekly earnings rose from $231 in 1980 to $254 in 1981. Corporate charters granted from January through June 1983 totaled 191. Revenue collected in Lubbock city sales tax for January through May 1984 was $7,117,402 a 13% increase over the $6,283,973 collected in the same 1983 period. Construction activity increased 92% in 1983 within the city of Lubbock. During the first three quarters of 1983 the total construction permit volume was $151,155,000, a 67% increase from the same 1982 period. Dollar volume for nonresidential construction was $35,569,000 a 29% increase. Total value of permits for single family houses issued the first three quarters of 1983 was $77,565,000 a 92% increase from the same 1982 period. Multifamily construction for January through September 1983 was valued at $21,314,000 for apartments and condominiums, a 30% increase from the same 1982 period and $8,075,000 for two to four family units, a 657% increase. Residential sales totaled $47,390,000 during the third quarter 1983, a 4% increase from the same 1982 period. The average residential sales price was $60,912, no change from third quarter of 1982. Steady growth has occurred during the past three quarters in lending by Lubbock savings and loan associations. During the first three quarters of 1983 construction lending was more than five times the size of residential lending, with third quarter 1983 construction loans totalling $88,200,000. **OVERVIEW** The Lubbock SMSA is a prosperous area with a diverse economy. Agribusiness, oil-related industries, computer technology and ware-

housing are dominant economic factors. Area farmers anticipate setbacks in 1984 due to the inadequate winter moisture. However, permits in 1983 for nonresidential construction increased over the previous year including plans for hospital expansion and two new shopping centers. Lubbock is the home of Texas Tech University which had a 1982 student population of 22,841. Visitors are drawn to the area by such attractions as Mackenzie State Park. See the county section for additional information.

McALLEN-PHARR-EDINBURG

THE LAND McAllen, Pharr and Edinburg are the primary cities in a major market area that covers Hidalgo County. Under the federal government's new definition for metropolitan areas, McAllen-Pharr-Edinburg SMSA has been renamed McAllen-Edinburg-Mission MSA. In the lush Rio Grande River Valley on alluvial soils the area is known for its citrus fruits, cotton and vegetables. **THE CLIMATE** Hot summers and mild winters prevail with an average high temperature in July of 95 °F and an average low of 74 °F. In January the average high is 70 °F with an average low of 48 °F. The average yearly rainfall is 23 inches. **THE PEOPLE** Among all U.S. Standard Metropolitan Statistical Areas (SMSA), the McAllen-Pharr-Edinburg area ranks second in the highest percent of Hispanics with 81% and second in the highest percent of persons under 18 with 39%. The 1980 population of 283,323 reflects the strong growth rate between 1970 and 1980 of 56%. An 11% increase between 1980 and 1982 caused the area to rank fifth in the state in SMSA growth. Almost 27% of the area residents are single, 61% married and 4% separated. Among persons 25 and older, 41% are high school graduates and 11% completed four or more years of college. Nearly 20% of the area residents are foreign-born, causing the area to rank eighth among all U.S. SMSAs. The population density for the SMSA is 180 people per square mile, with the city of Edinburg having 3,047 per square mile, McAllen 2,350 and Pharr 2,889. **THE ECONOMY** In January, 1984 the estimated total civilian labor force in the SMSA was 117,000, down from 121,200 in January, 1983 with 25.1% unemployed in January, 1984 as compared with 19.9% in January, 1983. In March, 1984, this area had the highest unemployment rate in the state at 24.9%. The greatest employment change between 1983 and 1984 occurred in the trade sector which dropped from a labor force of 25,900 in January, 1983 to 23,400 in January, 1984. Employment in other areas includes 1,500 in mining, 5,200 in construction, 2,700 in transportation, communication and utilities, 9,400 in manufacturing, 3,300 in finance and real estate, 11,200 in services and 20,000 in government. Corporate charters granted from January through June, 1983 totaled 237. Revenue collected in McAllen, Pharr and Edinburg city sales tax for January through May, 1984 was $4,317,637 a 16% increase over the $3,709,803 collected in the same 1983 period. During the first three quarters of 1983 the total construction permit volume was $134,52,000, a 3% decrease from the same 1982 period. Dollar volume for nonresidential construction was $37,793,000 a 37% increase. Total value of permits for single family houses issued the first three quarters of 1983 was $69,139,000 a 3% increase from the same 1982 period. Multifamily construction for January through September, 1983 was valued at $8,292,000 for apartments and condominiums, a 54% decrease from the same 1982 period and $4,205,000 for two to four family units, a 47% decrease. Residential sales in McAllen totaled $9,920,000 during the third quarter 1983, a 27% decrease from the same 1982 period. The average residential sales price was $67,044, a 7% decrease from third quarter of 1982. During the second and third quarters of 1983 construction lending by savings and loan associations in the cities of McAllen, Pharr and Edinburg was three times residential with third quarter

MAJOR MARKET AREAS

McALLEN-PHARR-EDINBURG (continued)

1983 construction loans totalling $24,400,000 as compared with $7,600,000 for residential loans. **OVERVIEW** The McAllen-Pharr-Edinburg area's economy is based on tourism, agribusiness, oil and gas and international trade with Mexico. Mission advertises itself as the "Home of the Grapefruit" and has become a commercial center with more than 30 industrial plants. Edinburg is a major shipping point for the irrigated citrus industry. Recent increases in tourism and commercial real estate activity such as the development of a regional medical center in McAllen have stimulated the economy. Area tourist attractions include area lakes, annual events, Bentsen-Rio Grande Valley State Park and the Santa Ana National Wildlife Refuge. One university in Edinburg with a branch in Brownsville is located in the area. For additional information see the county secion.

MIDLAND

THE LAND Midland is the primary city in a major market area that covers Midland county. It is located on level land with few trees with an elevation of 2,862 feet. **THE CLIMATE** The average yearly rainfall is 14 inches with an average of 52 days of measurable precipitation. Droughts can occur frequently. Summers are hot with an average high temperature in July of 94° and an average low of 69°F. Winters are mild with an average high in January of 58°F and an average low of 30°F. Three inches of measurable snow falls during winter on the average and cold fronts move through, making it very cold for a short period. Duststorms are a problem in late winter and spring since Midland is windy. The average annual wind speed is 11 mph with prevailing southerly to south-southeasterly winds except in spring and fall when west northwesterly winds are frequent. Throughout the year it is calm about 3% of the time. **THE PEOPLE** The Midland area ranks 19th among all U.S. Standard Metropolitan Statistical Areas (SMSA) in the highest percent of college graduates among its adult residents. The area's population grew 26% between 1970 and 1980. An 18% increase between 1980 and 1982 caused the area to rank second in the state in SMSA population growth. The population's median age is 28, over 30% of the residents are under 18 and 7% are age 65 and over. Over 20% of the population is single, 66% married and 7% divorced. The population density of the SMSA is 92 people per square mile, with 2,062 per square mile in the city of Midland. **THE ECONOMY** In January, 1984 the estimated total civilian labor force in the SMSA was 68,200, up from 64,700 in January, 1983 with 5.0%% unemployed in January, 1984 as compared with 5.6% in January, 1983. The greatest employment change between 1983 and 1984 occurred in the trade sector which rose from a labor force of 11,600 in January, 1983 to 13,500 in January, 1984. Employment in other areas includes 12,100 in mining, 3,500 in construction, 2,900 in transportation, communication and utilities, 3,900 in manufacturing, 3,900 in finance and real estate, 9,100 in services and 5,500 in government. Corporate charters granted from January through June, 1983 totaled 225. Revenue collected in Midland city sales tax for January through May, 1984 was $4,487,277 a 15% increase over the $3,895,615 collected in the same 1983 period. During the first three quarters of 1983 the total construction permit volume was $126,336,000, a 43% decrease from the same 1982 period. Dollar volume for nonresidential construction was $50,454 a 28% decrease. Total value of permits for single family houses issued the first three quarters of 1983 was $36,521,000 a 53% decrease from the same 1982 period. Multifamily construction for January through September, 1983 was valued at $18,192,000 for apartments and condominiums, a 56% decrease from the same 1982 period and

$740,000 for two to four family units, a 92% decrease. Residential sales totaled $34,480,000 during the third quarter 1983, a 16% decrease from the same 1982 period. The average residential sales price was $94,465, no change from third quarter of 1982. Nonresidential and refinancing loans by savings and loan associations significantly increased during third quarter 1983 in the city of Midland. Construction and residential lending slumped from fourth quarter 1982 through third quarter 1983 which had construction loans totalling $4,500,000 and residential loans reaching $6,600,000. **OVERVIEW** The Midland area is headquarters for the vast West Texas oil industry with more than 800 petroleum and related businesses. Most of the growth in commercial development in 1983 was in retail construction. The city is located in an agricultural center and provides a variety of services to the area with one college which offers cultural and educational opportunities. Visitor attractions include city parks and the Museum of the Southwest. For additional information see the county section.

ODESSA

THE LAND Odessa is the primary city in a major market area that covers Ector County. It lies on level land with few trees. **THE CLIMATE** The average rainfall for the year is 14 inches. Measurable precipitation is recorded 52 days a year on the average; however, drought conditions can be frequent. The average high temperature in July is 94°F with an average low of 69°F. In January the average high is 58°F with an average low of 30°F. About three inches of snow accumulates each winter, but melts quickly. Odessa is windy and duststorms are frequent during late winter and the spring. The average annual wind speed is 11 mph with prevailing southerly to south-southeasterly winds except in spring and fall when west northwesterly winds are frequent. Throughout the year it is calm about 3% of the time. **THE PEOPLE** The 1980 population of 115,374 for the Odessa Standard Metropolitan Statistical Area (SMSA) reflects the strong growth of the previous 20 years with a 25% increase between 1970 and 1980. A 16% increase between 1980 and 1982 caused the area to rank third in the state in SMSA population growth. Among U.S. SMSAs Odessa ranks 18th in the highest percent of Hispanic residents with 22% and 13th in households containing married couples with 69%. Over 19% is single and 7% divorced. The population has a low median age of 27 with 31% under age 18 and 7% age 65 and over. Among persons ages 25 and over, 61% are high school graduates and 12% have completed four or more years of college. The population density of the SMSA is 128 people per square mile, with 3,062 per square mile in the city of Odessa. **THE ECONOMY** In January, 1984 the estimated total civilian labor force in the SMSA was 74,300, up from 74,200 in January, 1983 with 6.7% unemployed in January, 1984 as compared with 8.1% in January, 1983. The greatest employment change between 1983 and 1984 occurred in the services sector which rose from a labor force of 7,700 in January, 1983 to 8,800 in January, 1984. Employment in other areas includes 8,700 in mining, 4,400 in construction, 3,000 in transportation, communication and utilities, 16,700 in trade, 2,300 in finance and real estate, 6,100 in manufacturing and 7,100 in government. Corporate charters granted from January through June, 1983 totaled 173. Revenue collected in Odessa city sales tax for January through May, 1984 was $4,200,109 a 4% increase over the $4,044,573 collected in the same 1983 period. During the first three quarters of 1983 the total construction permit volume was $50,584,000, a 50% decrease from the same 1982 period causing Odessa SMSA to have one of the steepest construction declines in the state. Dollar volume for nonresidential construction was $29,385,000 a 15% decrease. Total value of permits for single family houses issued the first three quarters of 1983 was $10,264,000 a 59% decrease from the same 1982 period. Multifamily construction for January through September 1983 was valued at $3,535,000 for apartments and condominiums, an 86% decrease from the same 1982 period and $152,000 for two to four family units, an 82% decrease. Residential sales totaled $14,340,000 during the third quarter 1983, a 6% increase from the same 1982 period. The average residential sales price was $69,618, a 3% decrease from third quarter of 1982. Residential and construction loans by savings and loan associations in the city of Odessa continued to slump during third quarter of 1983 with construction loans totalling $1,900,000 and residential reaching $9,800,000. **OVERVIEW** Although petroleum-related industries continue to dominate the economy, manufacturing plays a significant role. In spite of decreased activity in the oilfield equipment industry, retail sales continue to be strong and new plans have been announced for the area's medical facilities. One university and one college are located in the Odessa area. Tourist attractions include Globe of the Great Southwest, special events and area parks. For additional information see the county section.

SAN ANGELO

THE LAND San Angelo is the primary city in a major market area that covers Tom Green County. It lies on a plateau at an elevation of 1,908 feet. **THE CLIMATE** San Angelo has measurable precipitation on the average 58 days a year with a yearly rainfall of 18 inches. Summers are hot with the high temperature in July averaging 97 °F and the low averaging 72 °F. Winters are mild with January high temperatures averaging 59 °F and lows averaging 32 °F. Three inches of snow accumulate during the winter, but melts quickly. San Angelo has an average annual wind speed of 10 mph with southerly winds prevailing. During spring, when the strongest winds occur, and in the winter westerly to south-southwesterly winds are frequent. It is calm about 8% of the time in the fall and winter. **THE PEOPLE** Among U.S. Standard Metropolitan Statistical Areas (SMSA) San Angelo ranks 20th in the highest percentage of Hispanic residents with 21%. In 1980 the population reached 84,784 following a 19% increase from 1970. The median age is 29 with 27% of the residents under age 18 and 12% age 65 and over. The population is 23% single, 60% married and 7% divorced. Among persons 25 and over, 55% are high school graduates and 6% have completed four or more years of college. The population density of the SMSA is 56 people per square mile, with 1,932 per square mile in the city of San Angelo. **THE ECONOMY** In January, 1984 the estimated total civilian labor force in the SMSA was 49,700, down from 50,100 in January, 1983 with 5.0% unemployed in January, 1984 as compared with 5.2% in January, 1983. The greatest employment change between 1983 and 1984 occurred in the manufacturing sector which dropped from a labor force of 5,900 in January, 1983 to 5,600 in January, 1984. Employment in other areas includes 800 in mining, 2,300 in construction, 3,700 in transportation, communication and utilities,8,900 in trade, 1,500 in finance and real estate, 7,400 in services and 6,700 in government. Average gross weekly earnings rose from $206 in 1980 to $222 in 1981. Corporate charters granted from January through June, 1983 totaled 93. Revenue collected in San Angelo city sales tax for January through May, 1984 was $2,806,020, a 3% increase over the $2,716,567 collected in the same 1983 period. During the first three quarters of 1983 the total construction permit volume was $52,026,000, a 12% increase from the same 1982 period. Dollar volume for nonresidential construction was $25,287,000, a 79% increase. Total value of permits for single family houses issued the first three quarters of

1983 was $13,119,000 a 58% increase from the same 1982 period. Multifamily construction for January through September, 1983 was valued at $7,216,000 for apartments and condominiums, a 54% decrease from the same 1982 period and $176,000 for two to four family units, a 69% decrease. Residential sales totaled $11,280,000 during the third quarter 1983, a 12% decrease from the same 1982 period. The average residential sales price was $53,719, a 1% increase from third quarter of 1982. Lending by savings and loan associations in the city of San Angelo increased slightly between the fourth quarter of 1982 and the third quarter of 1983 which had totals of $7,700,000 for construction loans and $8,600,000 for residential loans. **OVERVIEW** The San Angelo area is the largest primary wool market in the U.S. and the home of diversified industries. The current economy has benefited from the presence of Goodfellow Air Force Base which is expanding its operations and San Angelo State University. Excellent fishing on nearby lakes and rivers attract sportsmen. See the county section for additional information.

SAN ANTONIO

THE LAND San Antonio is the primary city in a major market area that covers Bexar, Comal and Guadalupe Counties, at the edge of the hill country. It has an elevation of 794 feet. **THE CLIMATE** During an average year the city receives measurable rainfall on 80 days with an average of 28 inches of precipitation a year. The summers are hot and winters mild with the average high temperature in July 96 °F and the average low 74 °F. In January the average high is 62 °F with the average low 40 °F. During the year it drops below freezing 23 times on the average. The annual average wind speed is 9 mph with south-southeasterly winds prevailing in the spring and summer, and northerly winds prevailing in the winter and fall. Throughout the year it is calm about 3% of the time. **THE PEOPLE** In 1982 San Antonio became the 10th largest U.S. city up from 11th place in 1980 and is the third largest city in Texas with a population of 819,021. It ranks fourth among all U.S. cities in largest Hispanic population with 52%. The Standard Metropolitan Statistical Area (SMSA) has steadily grown since 1960 with a 21% increase between between 1970 and 1980. In 1980 the median age for the SMSA was 27 with 32% of its residents under age 18 and 9% age 65 and over. Among residents age 25 and over, 63% are high school graduates and 16% have completed four or more years of college. Over 25% of the population is single, 58% married and 8% separated. The population density of the SMSA is 426 people per square mile, with 2,992 per square mile in the city of San Antonio. **THE ECONOMY** In January, 1984 the estimated total civilian labor force in the SMSA was 511,200, up from 492,300 in January, 1983 with 6.0% unemployed in January, 1984 as compared with 6.8% in January, 1983. The greatest employment change between 1983 and 1984 occurred in the services sector which rose from a labor force of 90,200 in January, 1983 to 95,500 in January, 1984. Employment in other areas includes 3,500 in mining, 30,600 in construction, 18,500 in transportation, communication and utilities, 113,200 in trade, 32,000 in finance and real estate, 49,400 in manufacturing and 100,100 in government. Average gross weekly earnings rose from $212 in 1980 to $236 in 1981. Corporate charters granted from January through June 1983 totaled 1,173. Revenue collected in San Antonio city sales tax for January through May 1984 was $26,995,853, a 19% increase over the $22,697,077 collected in the same 1983 period. Revenue collected for the VIA program of the San Antonio Metropolitan Transit Authority from January through May, 1984 totalled $1,600,000. During the first three quarters of 1983 a total of $614,928,000 in building permits was issued, a 26% increase from the same 1982 period. Dollar volume

SAN ANTONIO (continued)

for nonresidential construction was $185,041,000, a 10% increase. Total value of permits for single family houses issued the first three quarters of 1983 was $184,618,000 a 71% increase from the same 1982 period. Multifamily construction for January through September 1983 was valued at $132,606,000 for apartments and condominiums, a 5% increase from the same 1982 period and $12,305,000 for two to four family units, a 158% increase. Residential sales totaled $155,880,000 during the third quarter 1983, a 1% increase from the same 1982 period. The average residential sales price was $84,123, a 22% increase from third quarter of 1982. Lending activity by savings and loan associations in the city of San Antonio rose in the first and third quarters of 1983. Totals for the third quarter of 1983 include $192,200,000 for construction loans and $33,600,000 for residential loans. **OVERVIEW** The San Antonio area is indelibly stamped with the flavor of its multicultural heritage. This bilingual region is a major tourist and convention area with three universities and two colleges. The military plays an integral part in the city life of San Antonio with Brooks Air Force Base, the present home of the U.S. Air Force School of Aviation Medicine, and Fort Sam Houston, which headquarters both the Fifth Army and Brooks Army Medical Center. Kelly, Lackland and Randolph Air Force Bases are also located in the area. The economic climate is very positive and a recent breakthrough in transportation was approval for a 10 mile freeway dividing the northwest sector between I-10 and Highway 90 to begin in the late 1980s. Tourists are attracted by the Missions, the River Walk, San Antonio Museum of Art, the Alamo and the Spanish Governor's Palace. For additional information see the county section.

SHERMAN-DENISON

THE LAND Sherman and Denison are the primary cities in a major market area that covers Grayson County. Near Lake Texoma, they are located on level grasslands with wooded, hilly areas. **THE CLIMATE** The cities receive an average of 38 inches of precipitation a year. They have hot summers and mild winters with the average high temperature in July 95 °F and the average low 73 °F. In January the average high is 51 °F with the average low 30 °F. About four inches of snow will accumulate each year. **THE PEOPLE** The Sherman-Denison Standard Metropolitan Statistical Areas (SMSA) ranks 12th among all U.S. SMSA's in the highest percent of residents age 65 and over, 16% of the population falls within that category. The median age is 33 with 25% of the population under age 18. The area's 1980 population of 89,796 reflects the steady growth of the previous 20 years with an 8% increase between 1970 and 1980. Among persons age 25 and over, 61% are high school graduates and 13% have completed four or more years of college. The population density for the SMSA is 96 people per square mile, 1,483 people per square mile in Denison and 1,110 per square mile in Sherman. **THE ECONOMY** In January, 1984 the estimated total civilian labor force in the SMSA was 40,000, down from 40,800 in January, 1983 with 6.8% unemployed in January, 1984 as compared with 9.8% in January, 1983. The greatest employment change between 1983 and 1984 occurred in the manufacturing sector which rose from a labor force of 10,900 in January, 1983 to 11,400 in January, 1984. Employment in other areas includes 200 in mining, 1,300 in construction, 2,100 in transportation, communication and utilities, 6,800 in trade, 1,300 in finance and real estate, 6,300 in services and 4,900 in government. Average gross weekly earnings rose from $257 in 1980 to $285 in 1981. Corporate charters granted from January through June, 1983 totaled 63. Revenue collected in Sherman and Denison city sales tax for January through May, 1984 was $2,315,418 a 26% increase

over the $1,824,035 collected in the same 1983 period. During the first three quarters of 1983 the total construction permit volume was $19,605,000, a 34% increase from the same 1982 period. Dollar volume for nonresidential construction was $10,190,000 a 234% increase. Total value of permits for single family houses issued the first three quarters of 1983 was $6,343,000 a 218% increase from the same 1982 period. Multifamily construction for January through September, 1983 was valued at $469,000 for two to four family units, a 7% increase. Residential sales in Grayson County totaled $7,900,000 during the third quarter 1983, a 39% increase from the same 1982 period. The average residential sales price was $46,755, a 2% decrease from third quarter of 1982. A major jump in construction lending by savings and loan associations in the cities of Sherman and Denison occurred in the fourth quarter of 1982. Total for the third quarter of 1983 include $500,000 in construction loans and $5,200,000 in residential loans. **OVERVIEW** The Sherman-Denison SMSA is an educational, medical, commercial and industrial center. Proximity to Lake Texoma attracts fishermen and tourists to the area. The majority of recent economic expansion projects in the area have been in public facilities including a new justice center and county jail. Ongoing highway improvements and the expansion of the waste-water treatment plant have stimulated economic growth. Two colleges enhance the area's cultural life. See the county section for additional information.

TEXARKANA

THE LAND Texarkana is the primary city in a major market area that covered Bowie County in Texas and Little River and Miller Counties in Arkansas until June, 1983 when Little River County was deleted from the statistical area. It is located on low woodlands near the Red River. **THE CLIMATE** The summers are hot and winters mild with the average high temperature in July 94 ° and the average low 70 °F. In January the average high is 52 ° with the average low 30 °F. The average annual precipitation is 46 inches with some short-lived snow accumulations in the winter. **THE PEOPLE** The Texarkana Standard Metropolitan Statistical Area (SMSA) 1980 population of 127,019 includes 75,301 in Texas and 51,718 residents in Arkansas. The area has had a steady growth in population the last 20 years with a 9% increase in Texas between 1970 and 1980. Over 19% of the population is single, 62% married and 7% divorced. Among persons 25 and older, 58% are high school graduates and 10% have completed four or more years of college. The area ranks 35th among all U.S. SMSA's in highest percent of Black residents with 22%. The median age is 31 with 30% of the population under 18 and 13% age 65 and over. The population density of the SMSA is 63 people per square mile, with 1,503 per square mile in Texarkana, Texas. **THE ECONOMY** In January, 1984 the estimated total civilian labor force in the SMSA was 51,900, down from 52,300 in January, 1983 with 9.6% unemployed in January, 1984 as compared with 10.9% in January, 1983. The greatest employment change between 1983 and 1984 occurred in the services sector which rose from a labor force of 7,800 in January, 1983 to 8,300 in January, 1984. Employment in other areas includes 100 in mining, 1,600 in construction, 2,000 in transportation, communication and utilities, 10,700 in trade, 1,700 in finance and real estate, 8,400 in manufacturing and 12,800 in government. Corporate charters granted from January through June, 1983 totaled 40. Revenue collected in Texarkana city sales tax within Bowie County for January through May, 1984 was $1,603,540 a 15% increase over the $1,397,946 collected in the same 1983 period. During the first three quarters of 1983 the total construction permit volume was $25,568,000, a 195% increase from the same 1982 period. Dollar volume for nonresidential construction was $14,666,000 a 447% increase. Total value of permits for single family houses issued the first three quarters of 1983 was $5,482,000 a 205% increase from the same 1982 period. Multifamily construction for January through September, 1983 was valued at $127,000 for apartments and condominiums, a 76% decrease from the same 1982 period and $2,592,000 for two to four family units, a 70% increase. Residential sales totaled $8,490,000 during the third quarter of 1983, a 117% increase from the same 1982 period. The average residential sales price was $53,709, a 22% increase from third quarter of 1982. Lending activity by savings and loan associations in the city of Texarkana increased steadily between the fourth quarter of 1982 and the third quarter of 1983 which had totals of $40,500,000 for construction loans and $4,700,000 for residential loans. **OVERVIEW** The Texarkana SMSA is a commercial and retail center, and a major economic factor in the area is the Red River Army Depot which receives, warehouses and processes general supplies and ammunition for the Armed Forces, as well as rebuilding ordnance equipment and aircraft components. Expansion of this 50 acre facility is currently underway, plus additions to healthcare facilities and schools. One college and one university are located in the area, and area lakes attract visitors. See the county section for additional information.

TYLER

THE LAND Tyler is the primary city in a major market area that covers Smith County. It is situated on rolling land with an abundance of vegetation throughout the city. **THE CLIMATE** The average high temperature in July is 95° and the average low 72°F. The average high in January is 55° with an average low of 34°F. The average annual rainfall for Tyler is 43 inches. **THE PEOPLE** Since 1960 the Tyler Standard Metropolitan Statistical Area (SMSA) has steadily grown with a 32% increase between 1970 and 1980 raising the population to 128,366. Among persons age 25 and over, 65% are high school graduates and 16% have completed four or more years of college. The median age is 30 with 29% of the residents under age 18 and 13% age 65 and over. Among all U.S. SMSAs Tyler ranks 36th in the highest percentage of Black residents with 22%. Over 20% of the population is single, 63% married and 6% divorced. The population density of the SMSA is 138 people per square mile, with 2,009 per square mile in Tyler. **THE ECONOMY** In January, 1984 the estimated total civilian labor force in the SMSA was 77,900, up from 77,600 in January, 1983 with 5.6% unemployed in January, 1984 as compared with 7.1% in January, 1983. The greatest employment change between 1983 and 1984 occurred in the services sector which rose from a labor force of 11,300 in January, 1983 to 11,700 in January, 1984. Employment in other areas include 3,100 in mining, 2,500 in construction, 2,900 in transportation, communication and utilities, 14,500 in trade, 3,100 in finance and real estate, 11,900 in manufacturing and 8,000 in government. Corporate charters granted from January through June, 1983 totaled 173. Revenue collected in Tyler city sales tax for January through May, 1984 was $4,090,095 a 21% increase over the $3,383,181 collected in the same 1983 period. During the first three quarters of 1983 the total construction permit volume was $138,870,000, a 157% increase from the same 1982 period. Dollar volume for nonresidential construction was $41,975,000 a 47% increase. Total value of permits for single family houses issued the first three quarters of 1983 was $30,922,000 a 109% increase from the same 1982 period. Multifamily construction for January through September, 1983 was valued at $48,475,000 for apartments and condominiums, a 4748% increase from the same 1982 period and $2,206,000 for two to four family units, a 57% increase. Residential sales totaled $17,960,000 during the third quarter 1983, an 8% decrease from the same 1982 period. The average residential sales price was $73,587, a 8% increase from third quarter of 1982. Lending activity by Tyler savings and loan associations decreased steadily from the fourth quarter of 1982 to the third quarter of 1983 in which increases occurred with totals reaching $79,800,000 for construction loans and $33,900,000 for residential loans. **OVERVIEW** The Tyler SMSA has a diversified economy based on tourism, manufacturing and agriculture. The Texas Rose Festival honors Tyler rosebushes and is one of the state's greatest floral pageants. Strong economic growth in 1983 was reflected in increased building permits. Current industrial plans include expansion of radial tire manufacturing, which is a major industry. Tourism is also a major economic contributor with area attractions such as the Tyler State Park, Caldwell Zoo and the Municipal Rose Garden. Two colleges and one university enhance the cultural life. See the county section for additional information.

VICTORIA

THE LAND Victoria is the primary city in a major market area that covers Victoria County. It is located on the coastal plain at an elevation of 117 feet. **THE CLIMATE** In July the average high temperature is 93° with the average low 75°F. High humidity and a diminished sea breeze make for warm summer nights, however by late summer the humidity drops and winds off the Gulf increase. Rainfall is at its peak in May with measurable precipitation occuring on the average of 89 days. An average of 34 inches of rain falls each year. In January the average high temperature is 63° with an average low of 44°F and on the average it will drop below freezing 13 days a year. Rarely will snow accumulate. Victoria has an average annual wind speed of 10 mph with the highest monthly averages in the spring. During the fall and winter, winds prevail out of the north and during spring and summer they prevail out of the south. Throughout the year it is calm about 3% of the time. **THE PEOPLE** The Victoria Standard Metropolitan Statistical Area (SMSA) ranks 14th among U.S. SMSAs in the highest percent of persons under age 18 with 32% of its residents in that age group. The median age is 27 with 9% of the population over age 64. Since 1960 the area has steadily grown with a 28% increase between 1970 and 1980 raising the population to 68,807. Among persons age 25 and over, 58% are high school graduates and 12% have completed four or more years of college. The population is 7% Black and 30% Hispanic. Over 22% of the area residents are single, 64% married and 6% divorced. The population density of the SMSA is 78 people per square mile, with 2,654 per square mile in Victoria. **THE ECONOMY** In January, 1984 the estimated total civilian labor force in the SMSA was 37,200, down from 39,300 in January, 1983 with 8.1% unemployed in January, 1984 as compared with 10.4% in January, 1983. Corporate charters granted from January through June 1983 totaled 76. Revenue collected in Victoria city sales tax for January through May, 1984 was $2,555,852 a 16% increase over the $2,212,496 collected in the same 1983 period. Residential sales totaled $10,130,000 during the third quarter 1983. The average residential sales price was $65,803. Lending activity by savings and loan associations in the city of Victoria the third quarter of 1983 totalled $48,400,000 for construction loans and $5,400,000 for residential loans. **OVERVIEW** The Victoria SMSA is a major industrial and agricultural crossroads of South Texas. The area is having strong growth in the financial sector with extensive bank construction underway. The economy is closely tied to energy-related industry and efforts are being made for greater diversification. One college is located is located in the area. Tourists enjoy such attractions as the Texas Zoo, Riverside Park and area museums. For additional information see the county section.

MAJOR MARKET AREAS

WACO

THE LAND Waco is the primary city in a major market area that covers McLennan County. It is located in the Brazos River Valley on the edge of the rolling prairies at an elevation of 508 feet. **THE CLIMATE** On the average Waco has 76 days of measurable precipitation with a yearly average of 31 inches. April and May are the months with the most rainfall. Summers are hot with an average high temperature in July of 96° and an average low of 75°F. Winters are mild with an average high in January of 63° and average low of 37°F. Winter cold fronts will move through dropping the temperature sharply. On the average 35 days a year will be below freezing. Waco is windy, especially in the spring with an average annual wind speed of 11 mph. Southerly winds prevail. Throughout the year it is calm about 6% of the time. **THE PEOPLE** Following a slight decline the previous decade the Waco Standard Metropolitan Statistical Area (SMSA) had a 16% growth between 1970 and 1980 raising the population to 170,755. The median age is 29 with 27% of the residents under age 18 and 13% age 65 and over. The population is 16% Black and 9% Hispanic. Among persons age 25 and over, 60% are high school graduates and 16% have completed four or more years of college. Over 25% of the population is single, 57% married and 7% divorced. The population density of the SMSA is 166 people per square mile, with 1,367 per square mile in Waco. **THE ECONOMY** In January, 1984 the estimated total civilian labor force in the SMSA was 90,500, up from 87,800 in January, 1983 with 5.3% unemployed in January, 1984 as compared with 6.8% in January, 1983. The greatest employment change between 1983 and 1984 occurred in the manufacturing sector which rose from a labor force of 14,500 in January, 1983 to 15,600 in January, 1984. Employment in other areas include 3,800 in construction, 3,200 in transportation, communication and utilities, 18,800 in trade, 4,500 in finance and real estate, 16,900 in services and 11,600 in government. Average gross weekly earnings rose from $246 in 1980 to $268 in 1981. Corporate charters granted from January through June, 1983 totaled 164. Revenue collected in Waco city sales tax for January through May, 1984 was $4,201,903 a 26% increase over the $3,323,642 collected in the same 1983 period. During the first three quarters of 1983 the total construction permit volume was $111,045,000, a 140% increase from the same 1982 period. Dollar volume for nonresidential construction was $32,357,000 a 75% increase. Total value of permits for single family houses issued the first three quarters of 1983 was $27,199,000 a 161% increase from the same 1982 period. Multifamily construction for January through September 1983 was valued at $28,516,000 for apartments and condominiums, a 430% increase from the same 1982 period and $5,154,000 for two to four family units, a 73% increase. Residential sales totaled $20,730,000 during the third quarter 1983, a 55% increase from the same 1982 period. The average residential sales price was $55,589, a 5% increase from third quarter of 1982. Lending activity by Waco savings and loan associations increased slowly between the fourth quarter of 1982 and the third quarter of 1983 with even distribution between construction and residential lending. The third quarter of 1983 totals were $5,500,000 for construction loans and $6,800,000 for residential loans. **OVERVIEW** The Waco SMSA is an educational, agricultural and recreational center with one university, two colleges and one institute. Baylor University, with 10,473 students, is one of the area's primary employers. The diversified industrial sector of the economy increased last year with the establishment of three new major industries. Increased construction over the previous year also contributed to the positive economic picture. One of the major areas of economic interest has been the development of the Brazos River corridor. Historic homes and area lakes are some of the tourist attractions. For additional information see the county section.

WICHITA FALLS

THE LAND Wichita Falls is the primary city in a major market area that covered Clay and Wichita counties until June 1983 when Clay county was deleted from the statistical area. It is located on gently rolling plains with mesquite trees. The city is just south of the Red River and has an elevation of 1,030 feet. **THE CLIMATE** Characterized by temperature extremes that can occur day to day, long periods of time can lapse between rain showers, though measurable precipitation is recorded on the average 70 days a year. The average yearly rainfall is 27 inches. The average high temperature in July is 99° with the average low 72°F. In January the average high is 54° with the average low 29°F. An average of six inches of snow will accumulate each winter. Wichita Falls is windy, especially in the spring with the average annual wind speed 12 mph. Southerly winds prevail except during winter when northerly winds prevail. Throughout the year it is calm about 2% of the time. **THE PEOPLE** Following a slight decline the previous decade the Wichita Falls Standard Metropolitan Statistical Areas (SMSA) had a 2% growth in population between 1970 and 1980 to 130,664. The median age is 29 with 27% of the residents under age 18 and 12% age 65 and over. The population is 8% Black and 6% Hispanic. Among persons age 25 and over, 64% are high school graduates and 14% have completed four or more years of college. Over 22% of the population is single, 61% married and 7% divorced. The population density of the SMSA is 77 people per square mile with 1,922 per square mile in Wichita Falls. **THE ECONOMY** In January, 1984 the estimated total civilian labor force in the SMSA was 69,000, up from 67,400 in January, 1983 with 7.0% unemployed in January, 1984 as compared with 8.2% in January, 1983. The greatest employment change between 1983 and 1984 occurred in the manufacturing sector which rose from a labor force of 8,300 in January, 1983 to 9,100 in January, 1984. Employment in other areas include 3,300 in mining, 2,100 in construction, 2,800 in transportation, communication and utilities, 13,500 in trade, 2,500 in finance and real estate, 9,300 in services and 10,800 in government. Average gross weekly earnings rose from $264 in 1980 to $295 in 1981. Corporate charters granted from January through June 1983 totaled 102. Revenue collected in Wichita Falls city sales tax for January through May 1984 was $3,597,133 a 11% increase over the $3,559,789 collected in the same 1983 period. During the first three quarters of 1983 the total construction permit volume was $60,167,000, a 66% increase from the same 1982 period. Dollar volume for nonresidential construction was $25,616,000 an 81% increase. Total value of permits for single family houses issued the first three quarters of 1983 was $14,467,000 an 86% increase from the same 1982 period. Multifamily construction for January through September 1983 was valued at $2,364,000 for apartments and condominiums, a 61% decrease from the same 1982 period and $1,534,000 for two to four family units, a 748% increase. Residential sales totaled $19,070,000 during the third quarter 1983, a 35% increase from the same 1982 period. The average residential sales price was $56,915, a 9% increase from third quarter of 1982. Lending activity by Wichita Falls savings and loan associations increased from the fourth quarter of 1982 through the third quarter of 1983, which had totals of $12,000,000 in construction loans and $25,900,000 in residential loans. **OVERVIEW** The Wichita Falls SMSA is a major trade and industrial center with its economy based on oil-processing and manufacturing. Sheppard Air Force Base, the area's largest employer, is a technical training center, including jet pilot training with many military students from foreign countries. Tourists enjoy the water-oriented recreation at the lakes such as Lake Arrowhead State Park. For additional information see the county section.

1500 To the east on land destined to become Texas, the Caddo Indians were living in villages along creeks and rivers in the forest. The Caddoes were traders, weavers of baskets and rugs, farmers of corn and gatherers of the forest products. To the south were the Atakapas and Karankawa, hunters and fishers who were unfriendly toward the explorers to come. In the central and southwest the Tonkawas were accomplished farmers and hunters and the Coahuiltecans were diggers. Many years would pass before the arrival of the Apaches in the west. The Apaches were the first true hunters and fighters in Texas until the arrival of Comanches. After learning about horses from the Spaniards, the Comanches became the most feared of Texas Indians.

UNDER THE FLAG OF SPAIN 1519-1685

1519 Spain was the first of six nations to claim the land of Texas. Alonso Alvarez de Pineda was the first Spaniard to set foot on Texas soil; while his four vessels lay at the mouth of the Rio Grande River for several weeks for repairs, de Pineda mapped and explored the Texas coastlands, naming the land "Amichel". **1520** Garay, the first town in Texas, was established during this year. An expedition under the command of Diego de Camargo brought soldiers and craftsmen to establish the colony. Near the mouth of the River of Palms (Rio Grande), Garay was named for the Jamaican Governor Francisco Garay. The residents of Garay created America's first territorial government and town council, but when Governor Garay arrived by ship in 1523 to visit his town, he found it abandoned. The Coahuiltecans had driven away the settlers. **1528** On November 5 Alonso de Castillo Maldonado's ship was wrecked on the Texas coast and on November 6 Alvar Nunez Cabeza de Vaca and about 80 Spaniards washed ashore on the Texas coast near Galveston, the survivors of the Panifilo de Narvaez expedition from Cuba to Florida. The Indians held the Spaniards captive, but allowed them to move from clan to clan. Thus de Vaca and his men were the first Europeans to penetrate the interior of Texas. After nearly eight years, de Vaca and three companions escaped reaching Culiacan, a northern outpost of New Spain, on May 18, 1536. **MAY, 1539** Hernando de Soto, a conquistador from Peru and Nicaragua, Governor of Cuba and Military Chief of Florida, sailed from Cuba to explore the country north of the Gulf of Mexico. After marching from Florida to Oklahoma then back to the Mississippi River at the mouth of the Arkansas River, de Soto died on May 21, 1542. The remaining explorers under the leadership of Luis Moscoso de Alvarado attempted to reach Mexico by traveling overland across Texas. At the Trinity River they turned back due to inadequate supplies and returned to the Mississippi River where seven brigantines were constructed. On September 10, 1542, the 320 survivors reached a Spanish settlement in Mexico. **FEBRUARY, 1540** Governor Francisco Vasquez Coronado of Nueva Galicia, Mexico set forth with 370 Spaniards and a large number of Indians to explore the country to the north. After they reached the Indian pueblos near the present Arizona/New Mexico border, the Grand Canyon was discovered by one of his captains on a side excursion. In the spring of 1544 Coronado, guided by a Plains Indian known as "The Turk", traveled east into Texas. At the Llano Estacado, Coronado sent his army back to New Mexico and with 30 horsemen headed north until they reached Kansas. Searching for the "seven cities of gold", they found only prairie and returned to Mexico. **1543** Oil was first discovered in Texas when Luis Moscoso de Alvarado found oil near Nacogdoches. **1583** An expedition led by Antonio de Espejo found the Jumano Indians inhabiting the territory of the Conchos and Rio Grande rivers. **1601** Juan de Onate, the founder of Santa Fe, led an expedition of settlers across the Texas Panhandle; de Onate was in search of gold, but he found none. Some settlers did stay, while others quit, leaving their cattle and horses to begin the first of the wild herds in Texas. **1650** Captain Diego del Castillo led an expedition from Santa Fe to explore north central Texas. He reported finding the Escantaque Indians near the upper Colorado River. The settlement of Texas by residents of Coahuila Mexico began about the middle of the seventeenth century and Texas was subject to the Governor of Coahuila until 1720. **1675** The Bosque-Larios Expedition left Mexico for Texas to christianize the many Indian tribes reported in various parts of Texas. The Bosque-Larios Expedition got as far as Edwards County before returning to Mexico. **1680** Silver was first discovered in the El Paso area. **1681** Spanish missionaries built the first mission, Corpus Christi de Isleta, in Texas, near what is now El Paso. **1683** Juan Domingues de Mendoza led an expedition with Father Nicholas Lopez to establish a mission in the San Saba River country. Successive attacks by the Apaches finally drove them back.

UNDER THE FLAG OF FRANCE 1685-1690

1682 Rene-Robert Cavelier, Sieur de La Salle, traveled from Canada to the mouth of the Mississippi River and claimed the entire area drained by it, including Texas, for King Louis XIV of France. He obtained permission from the king to found a colony near the mouth of the Mississippi and on July 24, 1684 set sail from France with 280 persons. **FEBRUARY, 1685** La Salle and company landed on Matagorda Bay, Texas having missed the mouth of the Mississippi River. After exploring to the west, finding the Brazos River and building Fort St. Louis a few miles north of Lavaca Bay, La Salle attempted to reach the Mississippi River by land. On March 20, 1687 he was murdered by one of his men. Six survivors reached Montreal, Canada on July 14, 1688. **1688** The French, under a man named Joutel, launched an expedition from Illinois to locate Fort St. Louis, but were unsuccessful. The Spanish also searched for the fort. After several Spanish expeditions by land and sea to destroy the French settlement, Alonzo de Leon, Governor of Coahuila, found the remains of Fort St. Louis April 22, 1689 on his fourth trip into Texas. De Leon found a few French in the hands of the Karankawa Indians; after an epidemic, the French had decided to make friends of the Indians, but the Indians turned on them, killing many, burning the fort and taking others captive. De Leon marched the remaining French to Mexico in irons.

UNDER THE FLAG OF SPAIN 1690-1821

The banner of Imperial Spain flew over Texas for more than three centuries. The name "Tejas" or Texas came into general use after 1690. **1690** The Spaniards wished to secure their territory from other invaders, so Alonzo de Leon returned to east Texas with Father Damien Massanet to build a mission among the Caddo Indians near the Trinity River. Mission San Francisco de los Tejas, near the present site of San Antonio, was soon joined by a second mission, Santissimo Nombre de Maria, on the Neches River. Within three years, however, the mission priests and soliders were recalled to Mexico. **JULY 18, 1714** Louis Juchereau de St. Denis arrived at San Juan Bautista on the Rio Grande. Commissioned by the Governor of French Louisiana to establish trade across Texas and the northern settlements of Mexico, St. Denis had blazed a trail, later to become a major part of the El Camino Real Trail. Taken to Mexico City under arrest, St. Denis was returned to San Juan Bautista where he married Manuela Sanchez, the niece of Domingo Ramon. **APRIL 27, 1716** An expedition commanded by Domingo Ramon, including St. Denis, set forth to establish six missions and trading posts in east Texas. Alarmed by the westward movement of the French, the Viceroy of Mexico had ordered the reoccupation of Texas. First Ramon and St. Denis rebuilt San Francisco de los Tejas, leaving Father Hidalgo in charge. Other missions were established at Nacogdoches, a Caddo village in eastern Nacogodoches County, near Cushing, at an Indian village near San Augustine and at another

CHRONOLOGICAL HISTORY OF TEXAS

Indian village near Robiline, Louisiana. A presidio, Nuestra Senora de los Dolores de los Tejas on the Neches River, was also established. **1718** Mission San Antonio de Lalero (the Alamo) was established on the site of present-day San Antonio as a supply mission between the Rio Grande and east Texas. A presidio, San Antonio de Bejar, was built across the river from the mission in 1721. The area attracted Spanish settlers and shortly after a settlement, which was to become San Antonio, was developed by Martin de Alarcon, the new Governor of Coahuila. **1718** French Louisiana was determined to establish French trade in Texas so Bernard de la Harpe was commissioned to establish a post on the Red River and to enter into trade with Texas, New Mexico and Nuevo Leon. **1719** The French took possession of Los Adaes, the mission in Louisiana. **MARCH 20, 1721** The renewed French activity ushered in a third Spanish mission founding era. The Marquis de Aguayo, Governor and Captain General of the provinces of Coahuila and Texas, crossed the Rio Grande with over 500 men and 5,000 horses. At six missions and four presidios he left new priests, supplies, troops and at the mission of Los Adaes in Louisiana he left cannons and 100 troops to secure the area. Aguayo had established a new presidio at Los Adaes (which became the colonial capital of Spanish Texas) and a presidio and mission at La Bahia. **1731** Led by Juan Leal Goras, the first group of Canary Islanders settled in San Antonio and the San Juan Capistrano Mission (formerly the San Jose de los Nazonis Mission) moved to San Antonio. **1746** Jose de Escandon received a Spanish commission to start settlements along the Rio Grande to prevent English or French penetration. His new province was called Nuevo Santander and he established 23 towns and 15 missions. **1765** King Charles III of Spain ordered sweeping changes of the entire structure of the Spanish colonial system and the Marquis de Rubi was sent to inspect Texas. On March 18, 1766, accompanied by an engineer and a military escort, de Rubi departed on a two-year, 7,000 mile inspection which took him from California to Louisiana. With respect to Texas he recommended that outlying missions be relocated at San Antonio, that San Antonio should be developed as a political, military and economic center and that trade should be established with all Indians except the Apaches, who should be pursued in active war to keep them away from Spanish settlements. His recommendations became law on September 10, 1772. **1773** The settlers were angered at being forced to move to San Antonio. The Spanish soldiers, to ensure that they would not return, burned down their buildings, trampled their crops and carted off all furniture and livestock. Over 1,000 people were thus forced back to San Antonio. Antonio Gil Y'Barbo, a rancher, persuaded the Mexican government to allow the settlers to return part way to their homes. In 1774 the group was given permission to establish a new community on the Trinity River. **1778** The Spaniards were unable to wage war against the Apaches due to a lack of forces. The Comanches and Apaches raided the Spanish settlements with increasing frequency, with the Apaches staying close to settlements seeking protection from the Comanches. The king created a military jurisdiction on the northern frontier, known as the Interior Provinces, which resulted in a new Indian policy: an alliance with the Comanches and Nortenos (Nations of the North) against the Apaches. The Apaches then sought, and were granted, assistance from France. **1779** Spring floods and Comanche raids forced the settlers led by Y'Barbo to move east to the abandoned mission at Nacogdoches. They established the town of Nacogdoches and Y'Barbo was commissioned its Captain of Militia and Lieutenant-governor. Athanase de Mezieres was named Governor of Texas. Y'Barbo built the Old Stone Fort in Nacogdoches. **DECEMBER 31, 1783** The Spaniards took an annual census of the Texas province: in the Presidio of San Antonio de Bexas, the village of San Fernando and the town of Nuestra Senora del Pilar de los Nacogdoches plus eight missions

there were 935 men, 777 women, 597 boys, 474 girls, 17 male slaves and 19 female slaves. **1793** The last Spanish Texas mission was Nuestra Senora del Refugio. The Spanish missions attempted not only to Christianize and civilize the Indians, but also to hold the frontier against foreigners. The system was a joint venture of both church and state with the state approving the location of the missions, bearing the initial expense of establishment and paying the stipend of the priests. The Texas missionaries were Franciscans and the missions were well developed in three areas: eastern Texas, San Antonio and La Bahia (Goliad). **MARCH, 1801** "Filibusters", North Americans who entered Texas in defiance of Spanish authority and appropriated the Indian trade, became common around the turn of the century. One of the best known filibusters, Philip Nolan, drove horses out of Texas several times until he was killed near Waco in a battle with a Spanish force which had been sent to arrest him. **1806** When Napoleon sold the Louisiana Territory to the United States, no agreement on a boundary between Texas and Louisiana existed. President Thomas Jefferson claimed that Texas was part of the purchase, but Spain sent troops to the border to protect her province. To avoid war, General James Wilkinson, in command of the U.S. forces, agreed to stay east of the Arroyo Hondo (a small stream between the Sabine River and Natchitoches) and General Simon de Herrera, in command of the Spanish forces, agreed to remain west of the Sabine River until a permanent boundary settlement was agreed upon. This area between became known as the "Neutral Ground". Lacking law enforcement, the "Neutral Ground" became a haven for the lawless. At the time there were officially only three towns: San Fernando (San Antonio), La Bahia (Goliad) and Nacogdoches. **1810** The Mexican struggle for independence began in 1810 and quickly spread to Texas. An initial revolt at San Antonio in 1811 was not successful. The revolutionary Father Hidalgo was captured and later executed. Father Hidalgo's agent, Jose Bernardo Gutierrez de Lara, fled to the "Neutral Ground" where he looked to the United States for aid to regain his lands and build an independent government in Texas. **1812** On the west bank of the Sabine River, the Gaines House was constructed to welcome persons coming to Texas from Louisiana. **AUGUST 8, 1812** Jose Bernardo Gutierrez de Lara established his headquarters in the "Neutral Ground" and flooded Texas with propaganda. Together with Augustus W. Magee, an ex-U.S. army officer, they formed the Republican Army of the North in order to liberate Texas. On August 8, the revolutionists advanced to Nacogdoches where the royalist troops deserted to the revolutionary forces. A. Mower, a Philadelphia printer and a member of the Army of the North, published the first newspaper in Texas, *Gaceta de Texas,* at Nacogdoches spreading propaganda for the independence movement. **APRIL 6, 1813** The first proclamation of independence in Texas was made by Guiterrez and Magee at Nacogdoches. Magee and the Army of the North then captured La Bahia (Goliad) and San Antonio. **APRIL 17, 1813** Gutierrez and the junta at San Antonio issued the first constitution of Texas. The constitution provided for the "State of Texas of the Republic of Mexico", disappointing many revolutionaries. Shortly thereafter the Republican forces were defeated by General Joaquin de Arredondo of the Eastern Interior Provinces of Mexico and the first Texas Movement for Independence collapsed. Arredondo killed nearly all of the Americans who remained and threatened to kill all who cooperated with the Republican Army of the North. One of Arredondo's officers was Antonio Lopez de Santa Anna. Many, both Spanish and American, fled to the "Neutral Ground" and Louisiana. **1817** The first Protestant, a Methodist minister William Stevenson, arrived in Texas in the Red River County area. **FEBRUARY 22, 1819** The Adams-Onis Treaty was signed between Spain and the United States, which enabled the United States to purchase Florida and established the boundary between the United States and Spain. The boundary went up the Sabine River to the 32nd parallel, north to the Red River, along the Red River to the 100th meridian, north to the Arkansas River headwaters, north to the 42nd parallel, then west to the Pacific Ocean. The treaty angered Americans who coveted the western lands and protest meetings were held throughout the South.

UNDER THE FLAG OF MEXICO 1821-1836

Mexico's tri-color flew over Texas for less than two decades, yet Hispanic influences remain in both the customs and language of Texas. **JANUARY 17, 1821** Moses Austin was granted permission to bring up to 300 families to settle in Texas. Born in 1765 in Connecticut, Moses married Maria Brown of New Jersey on September 29, 1785. Their son Stephen Fuller Austin was born November 3, 1793 in Virginia. Moses and his brother operated mercantile establishments and later lead mines in Philadelphia, Virginia and the Missouri Territory, where the Austins became Spanish citizens. The Panic of 1819 wiped out the financial resources of the Austins, and Moses traveled to San Antonio with his plan for settlement in Texas. Moses died June 10, 1821 and the project was undertaken by his son Stephen. **FEBRUARY, 1821** The Plan of Iguala, proclaiming Mexico free from Spain, was issued by Augustine de Iturbide, with the support of the upper classes of Mexico, and liberal Guerrero. In August the Spanish Viceroy Juan O'Donoju recognized the independence of Mexico with Iturbide as its leader. Thus the administration of Texas moved to Mexico. Stephen F. Austin had journeyed to San Antonio to confirm the inheritance of his father's land commission and was advised to acquire confirmation of the grant from the new government in Mexico. **APRIL 29, 1822** Stephen Austin arrived in Mexico and found the government divided. **OCTOBER 21, 1822** The first national bank, Banco Nacional de Tejas, was established in San Antonio by order of Governor Jose Felix Trespolacios. **JANUARY 4, 1823** The Mexican Congress passed the General Colonization Law which also authorized Austin's colony, however, Iturbide dismissed the Congress. In March, Iturbide was forced to resign and on April 14, 1823 the new government voided the Colonization Law, but approved Austin's contract. **JULY 26, 1823** The governor established the town of San Felipe de Austin at the Atascosito crossing on the Brazos River in what is now Austin County. The new town was designated the seat of government for the Anglo-American colonies. **AUGUST, 1823** Austin began to issue land titles to his settlers with Baron de Bastrop as the government's land agent. Many of the colonists selected the rich bottomlands along the Brazos and Colorado Rivers. By 1828 the titles to all the land under the contract had been issued and the colonists became known as the "Old Three Hundred". **MAY 7, 1824** The two Mexican provinces of Texas and Coahuila were combined into one Mexican state with the capital at Saltillo. The General Colonization Law of 1824 had turned the administration of land colonization over to the states, thus Saltillo now had charge of land affairs in Texas. The Law stipulated that all persons receiving land become Mexican citizens. **1825-1830** The first sawmill was built in Texas near San Augustine. Approximately 25 land contracts were issued by the state government. Stephen Austin was granted a contract for 500 families on his original lands plus 100 families along the Colorado River and 300 families between the Lavaca and San Jacinto Rivers. **APRIL 15, 1825** Green De Witt contracted to bring 400 "industrious Catholic Families" to Texas in 1825. They settled between the Lavaca and Guadalupe Rivers, the San Antonio-Nacogdoches Road and the Gulf. At the same time Haden Edwards secured a contract to settle 800 families on unoccupied lands around Nacogdoches. Edwards, contrary to the contract, charged a higher fee for the lands than the government price. Problems escalated and resulted in the cancellation of Edwards' contract. **DECEMBER 16, 1826** Haden Edwards

undertook a revolt and declared independence for a Fredonia Republic. On December 21, he signed a treaty with the Cherokees giving them the territory north of Nacogdoches in return for peace. The Fredonia Republic was put down by Mexican authorities with the help of Stephen Austin. **MARCH 11, 1827** The Constitution of Texas and Coahuila was adopted. **1828** Manuel Mier y Teran was commissioned to do a survey of the boundary between Texas and the United States. In his report he noted that a rapid settlement of Anglo-Americans in east Texas had weakened Mexican control over the area. He reported that Anglos outnumbered Mexicans ten to one and that the Anglo population was growing rapidly. An anti-Anglo sentiment was increasing, aided by the actions of President John Quincy Adams, who first attempted to move the boundary west, then offered to purchase Texas for $1 million. President Andrew Jackson later raised the purchase price to $5 million. **1829** The first attempt to produce sugar was made at Stephen Austin's colony. The first Sunday School was established in Sealy, Texas by Thomas J. Pilgrim, a Baptist. **SEPTEMBER 15, 1829** The Guerrero Decree abolished slavery (the only slaves were Africans held by Anglos) in the Republic of Mexico. **APRIL 6, 1830** The Mexican Congress passed a law which prohibited further immigration by Anglos, increased taxes in Texas to erect and strengthen fortifications along the Texas/United States border, relocated Mexican convicts to Texas and prohibited further importations of African slaves. **1831** Haden Edward's lands had been granted to Lorenzo de Zavala, Joseph Vehlein and David G. Burnet, who in defiance of the new law prohibiting immigration from the United States, pooled their extensive land grants in eastern Texas with the Galveston Bay and Texas Land Company, then sold land scrip certificates for millions of acres to prospective settlers from the United States. The scrip only gave permission to settle on the land, but many purchasers believed they held title to the land. The resulting problems significantly increased the tensions between the Anglo-Americans and the Mexicans. **1832** Committees of Safety and Correspondence, similar to the ones during the 1776 American revolution, were set up followed by the Turtle Bayou Resolutions protesting to Mexico the threat to constitutional government. **AUGUST 2, 1832** The battle of Velasco may have been the first instance of bloodshed between Mexicans and Americans (ten Texans and five Mexicans were killed) as Mexican troops were forced out of the area. **APRIL 1-13, 1833** Santa Anna, the leader of a liberal revolution in Mexico, overturned the conservative Mexican government in 1832. Texans hopeful of reforms supported Santa Anna and met in conventions in October, 1832 and April, 1833 to draw up formal petitions. The first convention was ineffective, but the second one in April was attended by a larger number of disillusioned Texans and greater emphasis was placed on separate statehood. William H. Wharton was selected president of the convention with Stephen Austin, David Burnet and Sam Houston in key roles. **JANUARY 3, 1834** Stephen Austin, delegated by the Convention of 1833 to present its petitions to the federal government, journeyed to Mexico City where he obtained Santa Anna's consent to almost every request except for separate statehood. While en route home he was arrested, returned to Mexico City and imprisoned, due to a letter he had written suggesting the organization of a state government. Along with approximately 60 other political prisoners, Austin was held in solitary confinement in a dungeon in the prison of the Inquisition. Friends secured his release on Christmas Day, 1834, but he was kept in Mexico City under house arrest until the next summer. **SEPTEMBER, 1835** Disillusioned after 18 months imprisonment, upon his return to Texas, Austin declared that the rights of Texans must be defended by force of arms. The spark that started the revolution occurred when Colonel Ugartechea, Commander of San Antonio, sent a patrol to Gonzales to retrieve a cannon provided to Green De

Witt for Indian defense. A written request was demanded of the commander, who sent instead 100 troops to confiscate the cannon. On October 2 the Mexican force was greeted by 160 Texans who opened fire on the surprised troops. The Texans pursued the retreating troops to San Antonio. **OCTOBER 17, 1835** Daniel Parker offered a resolution that created the Texas Rangers. **OCTOBER 28, 1835** Colonel James Bowie, Captain D.W. Fannin and a force of about 100 men defeated Mexican troops near Mission Conception. **NOVEMBER 7, 1835** Fifty-five delegates from 12 Texas municipalities met in consultation at San Felipe de Austin as the result of the outbreak of fighting on October 2. Stephen Austin accepted the leadership of the Central Committee of Safety and Correspondence. Opinion was sharply divided as to whether Texas was fighting for independence or for its rights under the Mexican Constitution of 1824. On November 7 the vote went against a declaration of independence. However, on November 13 the Consultation declared that it was the right of Texas to resist the attempt by Santa Anna to overthrow the Federal Government and as a result a temporary government for Texas should be established until the Constitution of 1824 could be restored. On November 13 the Consultation adopted a plan for a provisional state government. Henry Smith was appointed Governor and James Robinson Lieutenant Governor. A governing Council was composed of one delegate from each municipality. **DECEMBER 5, 1835** The Texans began an assault of San Antonio and on December 9 the Mexicans surrendered. The troops left for the Rio Grande shortly thereafter and forfeited all supplies in the city, promising to leave Texas and never return. **DECEMBER 10** The attitude toward independence and the right of revolution was intensifying. The Council passed a resolution calling for an election of delegates for a March 1, 1836 convention. **JANUARY 25, 1836** General Jose Urrea with 1,500 troops was sent by Santa Anna to Matamoros, then into Texas to take Refugio and Goliad. **FEBRUARY 12, 1836** Santa Anna crossed the Rio Grande accompanied by 6,000 troops, arriving in San Antonio on February 23. The old San Antonio de Valero mission, usually called the Alamo, was fortified by about 150 men including Colonel James Bowie with 25 volunteers, William Barrett Travis with 30 men of the provisional government army and David Crockett. Travis was in command of the Alamo when Santa Anna arrived. On February 24 Travis wrote a stirring appeal for men and supplies which has been called the most heroic document in North American history. On March 1, 31 men from Gonzales slipped through the Mexican lines to their aid. On March 6 all within the Alamo had been killed except for seven, including David Crockett, who attempted to surrender and were executed. One hundred eighty-three men perished. **FEBRUARY 23, 1836** Sam Houston and John Forbes concluded a treaty between the Cherokee Indians and the provisional government. Since 1819 Cherokees from the United States had been settling the lands north of the San Antonio Road between the Neches and Sabine Rivers. Mexican government officials respected the Cherokee claims for the most part and the provisional government resolved to recognize those claims and establish a definite boundary with the Indians, thus guaranteeing them the peaceful enjoyment of their lands. **MARCH 2, 1836 TEXAS DECLARATION OF INDEPENDENCE**. A quarrel between Governor Henry Smith and the Council had resulted in an election of delegates to form a new provisional government. The first act of the new President of the Consultation, Richard Ellis, was to appoint a committee chaired by George C. Childress to draft a declaration of independence. It was adopted on March 2. The Consultation reappointed General Sam Houston to lead the army and selected officers for an *ad interim* government: David G. Burnet, President; Lorenzo de Zavala, Vice President; Samuel P. Carson, Secretary of State; Bailey Hardeman, Secretary of the Treasury; Thomas J. Rusk, War Secretary and David Thomas, Attorney

General. **MARCH 14, 1836** James W. Fannin, authorized by the provisional government to lead an expedition against the Mexican forces, learned that General Jose Urrea had an army to invade Texas at Matamoros. On March 14 he received orders to lead the 450 to 500 volunteers assembled at Goliad to Matamoros, blow up the fortress, then fall back to Victoria. Near the crossing on Coleto Creek the Texans were captured by General Urrea's forces and were returned as prisoners to Goliad where on March 27 on orders from Santa Anna about 351 were executed. (Now called the Goliad massacre). **MARCH 17, 1836 THE CONSTITUTION OF THE REPUBLIC OF TEXAS**. The Consultation adopted a republican constitution which followed closely the Constitution of the United States. The delegates at Washington-on-the-Brazos had launched a new government. **APRIL 21, 1836** General Sam Houston and his Texas army defeated Santa Anna near San Jacinto, ending the war. The Texans lost nine men and Houston was severely wounded in the ankle; Santa Anna lost about 600 men and over 700 including Santa Anna were captured. General Vicente Filisola commanding the main Mexican force agreed to return to Mexico. **MAY 14, 1836** The Treaty of Velasco was signed by President David G. Burnet and President Santa Anna. In it Santa Anna ended hostilities, recognized the independence of Texas, promised to work for a commercial treaty between Mexico and Texas and recognized the Rio Grande as the boundary between the two nations.

UNDER THE FLAG OF THE REPUBLIC OF TEXAS
1836-1845

The Lone Star flag waved over the new republic for nearly a decade. **1836** The new nation was destitute. Money did not officially exist as barter had been the traditional method of exchange. The war left crops unplanted, homes plundered and property stolen. Even the population was sparse, with approximately 30,000 Anglo-Americans and 22,000 Mexicans, Indians and African Slaves. **COUNTIES** Prior to 1836 the Mexican *municipio* was the most important unit of local government. The missions were the center of those early municipalities, including the settlements at Austin, Gonzales, Nacogdoches, San Antonio and Victoria. The *municipios* became counties after the establishment of the Republic of Texas. Sparse population caused the early counties to be large and primarily rural. In 1850 the first United States Census in Texas recorded only one of the 72 counties with a population over 10,000. **AUSTIN COUNTY** Named for: Stephen F. Austin, founder of the first permanent American settlement in Texas. Created: 1836. Organized 1837. County Seat: San Felipe de Austin (1837-1848); Bellville (1848-present). Major Events: San Felipe de Austin, established in 1823, was the first permanent Anglo settlement in Texas. The first organized resistance to Mexican rule was expressed here in the Convention of 1832. Austin became one of the original 23 counties of the Republic of Texas. **BASTROP COUNTY** Named for: Baron de Bastrop, first commissioner of Stephen F. Austin's colony. Created: 1836. Organized: 1837. County Seat: Bastrop. Major Events: Families from Stephen F. Austin's colony became the first permanent settlers in 1829. **BEXAR COUNTY** Named for: Second son of the Duke of Bexar. Created: 1836. Organized: 1837. County Seat: San Antonio. Major Events: The villa of San Fernando de Bexar was the first municipality in the Spanish province of Texas in 1731. In 1772 the seat of government of Spanish Texas moved to Bexar. The original county was divided into 128 additional counties **BRAZORIA COUNTY** Named for: the Brazos River. Created: 1836. Organized: 1836. County Seat: Brazoria (1836-1897); Angleton (1897-present). Major Events: First settled by Stephen F. Austin's "Old Three Hundred". In 1836 Velasco was the site of the provisional government of Texas and the site of the signing of the Treaties of Velasco which ended the Texas Revolution. Sugar and cotton plantations made the county the wealthiest in Texas with a Southern Society based on slavery. Oil was discovered in 1902. **COLORADO COUNTY** Named for: the Colorado River (Colorado is a Spanish word which means "colored"). Created: 1836. Organized: 1837. County Seat: Columbus. Major Events: An Indian village known as Montezuma probably occupied the site of present-day Columbus. Permanent Anglo settlement began in 1819, with the arrival of a number of Moses Austin's colonists. Robert Robson's castle, built around 1839, was probably the first building in Texas to have running water. The canned meat factory of Gail Borden, Jr., built shortly after the Civil War, was probably the first in the world. After the Civil War the county became a center for German and subsequently Czech immigration to Texas. **GOLIAD COUNTY** Named for: the municipality of Goliad (the word Goliad is an anagram of *Hidalgo,* a Spanish word meaning "gentleman"). Created: 1836. Organized: 1837. County Seat: Goliad. Major Events: Settlement began in 1749 with the establishment of two Spanish missions. The area was one of three areas of Spanish settlement in Texas when Anglo-American settlers began to arrive. In late 1835 the Mexican garrison at Goliad was expelled and on December 20, 1835 the Goliad Declaration of Independence was signed by 91 residents. On Palm Sunday, March 27, 1836, 342 men of James W. Fannin's command were executed at Goliad after surrendering to Mexican forces. **GONZALES COUNTY** Named for: Rafael Gonzales, Governor of the Mexican province of Coahuila and Texas, Created: 1836. Organized: 1837. County Seat: Gonzales. Major Events: The battle of Gonzales, fought on October 2, 1835 and sometimes referred to as "the Lexington of the Texas Revolution," was the first battle of the Texas Revolution. The town of Gonzales was burned again in 1836 after General Houston's retreat following the fall of the Alamo and was rebuilt in 1837. Some of the first herds of Texas cattle driven overland to market in Kansas originated in Gonzales county. **HARRIS COUNTY** (originally called Harrisburg). Named for: John Richardson Harris, an early Texas pioneer. Created: 1836 (as Harrisburg: renamed Harris in 1839). Organized: 1837 . County Seat: Harrisburg (1836); Houston (1836-present). Major Events: A Spanish presidio was located here from 1756 to 1764. By 1822, 15 to 20 families had settled in the area. John Richardson Harris established Harrisburg in 1826, naming the town in honor of himself and of Harrisburg, Pennsylvania, which had been founded and named by his grandfather. Harrisburg was burned by the Mexican army before the battle of San Jacinto. Although Harrisburg was rebuilt in 1839, Houston (incorporated in 1837) became the county seat and served temporarily as capital of the Republic of Texas. Prospecting activities that ultimately established the city as a center of the oil business began in 1866. **JACKSON COUNTY** Named for: Andrew Jackson, President of the United States. Created: 1836. Organized: 1836. 1837. County Seat: Texana (1836-1883; originally known as Santa Anna); Edna (1883-present). Major Events: The area was included in Mexican land grants to Stephen F. Austin and Martin de Leon. A meeting presided over by James Kerr adopted on July 17, 1835 a resolution urging Texas independence, which was recognized in 1936 by the Texas Centennial Commision as a forerunner of the Texas Declaration of Independence. The first railroad reached the county in 1880. **JASPER COUNTY** Named for: William Jasper, soldier in the American Revolution killed in the 1779 attack on Savannah, Georgia. Created: 1836. Organized: 1836. County Seat: Jasper. Major Events: Settlement began in 1824 when John Bevil established a homestead at the present site of Jasper. Stephen H. Everitt and George W. Smyth, two area residents, were signers of the Texas Declaration of Independence and Everitt was a member of the committee that drafted the Constitution of the Republic of Texas. The lumber industry began when a steam sawmill was established in 1854 at the site where Evadale is presently located. The railroad

reached the county by 1895. **JEFFERSON COUNTY** Named for: Thomas Jefferson, President of the United States. Created: 1836. Organized: 1837. County Seat: Jefferson (1837-1838); Beaumont (1838-present). Major Events: the Cypress Bayou Settlement in the Mexican municipality of Liberty was the nucleus from which the present area of Jefferson County grew. The first permanent settlement within the county's current boundaries was established in 1824 at Tevis Bluff. The Eastern Texas Railroad, probably the first railroad in the state, was completed from Sabine Pass to Beaumont just before the outbreak of the Civil War. On the night of September 7, 1863, Confederate artillary at Fort Sabine turned back a Union fleet attempting to launch an invasion of Texas through Sabine Pass. Spindletop Oil Field, discovered in January, 1901, opened the Gulf Coast to oil production. **LIBERTY COUNTY** Named for: the Spanish municipality of Libertad, from which the county was created. Created: 1836. Organized: 1836. County Seat: Liberty. Major Events: The area was contested by the Spanish and French in the early colonial period. Anglo-American settlers established the unauthorized municipality of Villa de la Santisima Trinidad de la Libertad, subsequently renamed Liberty in 1831, but the land commissioners giving title to the land in the area were arrested in 1832. Area soldiers were active in the Texas Revolution. The Civil War interrupted efforts to bring in the railroad, which first reached the county in 1880. Oil was discovered in 1904. **MATAGORDA COUNTY** Named for: The Spanish words "mata gorda" which means dense cane. Created: 1836. Organized: 1836. County Seat: Matagorda (1836-1894); Bay City (1894-present). Major Events: The first successful settlement, organized by Stephen F. Austin, started in 1822 when land grants were given to 52 families. **MILAM COUNTY** Named for: Benjamin R. Milam, who led a successful attack on San Antonio in 1835. Created: 1836 (out of former municipality of Milam). Organized: 1846 (with present boundaries). County Seat: Cameron. Major Events: in 1836 Milam County constituted one-sixth of the land in the territory in Texas. The population grew rapidly after the coming of the railroad in 1880. **NACOGDOCHES COUNTY** Named for: The town of Nacogdoches, which was named for Indians living in the area. Created: 1836 (out of the Nacogdoches Department). Organized: 1836. County Seat: Nacogdoches. Major Events: Spanish settlers arrived in 1716 and built three missions for the Caddo and Bidai Indians and a presidio for their protection. Following the Revolution the original 23 counties were created from the Nacogdoches Department; subsequently 20 other counties were created from Nacogdoches County. The Old San Antonio Road across the county was the route taken by the 1801 Philip Nolan expedition, the 1812-1813 Gutierrez-Magee expedition, and the Long expedition of 1819. The Fredonia Rebellion took place in 1826-1827, the Battle of Nachogdoches was fought on August 2, 1832, and the Cordova Rebellion occurred in 1838. **RED RIVER COUNTY** Named for: The Red River. Created: 1836. Organized: 1837. County Seat: Clarksville. Major Events: When created the county included all or parts of 39 present day counties. Long occupied by Caddo, Delaware, Kickapoo and Shawnee Indians, the county was first settled by Anglo-Americans in 1814. **REFUGIO COUNTY** Named for: The town of Refugio, built on the site of the Nuestra Senora del Refugio Mission (established 1793). Created: 1836. Organized: 1837. County Seat: Refugio (1836-1839); St. Mary's (1869-1871); Rockport (1871); Refugio (1871-present) Major Events: Explored by the Spanish early in the 16th century. The coastline was charted by Alvaro de Pineda in 1520. Missions to serve the Indians were established in 1722 and 1793. Early Anglo-American settlers were Irish-Catholics. The Battle of Refugio occurred in 1836, just prior to the Goliad Massacre. **SAN AUGUSTINE COUNTY** Named for: The Mexican municipality of San Augustine, created in 1834. Created: 1836. Organized: 1837. County Seat: San Augustine.

CHRONOLOGICAL HISTORY OF TEXAS

Major Events: Visited by Spanish explorers as early as 1542. The mission of Nuestra Senora de los Dolores de los Ais was established to serve the Ais Indians in 1716. Although San Augustine County falls within the twenty border leagues established by the Mexican and Spanish governments to deter Anglo-American settlement, Anglo-Americans arrived by 1818, but they were not considered citizens eligible to vote until after the Fredonia Rebellion. The town of San Augustine, known as Texas' earliest settlement (dating from 1794), was a noted educational center from the early days of the Republic. **SAN PATRICIO COUNTY** Named for: The townsite, San Patricio Hibernia (St. Patrick of Ireland) established in 1830 for 40 families of settlers, most of whom were Irish, under a Mexican colonization contract. Created: 1836. Organized: 1837. County Seat: San Patricio. Major Events: Explored by Cabeza de Vaca as early as 1535. The coastline was charted by Diego Ortiz Parrilla in 1766. James McGloin and John McMullen obtained a Mexican colonization contract in 1828 for the settlement of 191 families. Francis W. Johnson's Command was captured in San Patricio during the Texas Revolution. The colonists sought refuge in Victoria until after the Mexican defeat at the Battle of San Jacinto. **SHELBY COUNTY** Named for: Isaac Shelby, hero of the American Revolution who came from Tennessee. Created: 1836. Organized: 1837. County Seat: Shelbyville (1837-1866); Center (1866-present). Major Events: First permanent settler is believed to be John Latham in 1818. Many settlers moved on to the west. This county was the scene of the Regulator-Moderator War, 1841-1844. **VICTORIA COUNTY** Named for: The first settlement, Nuestra Senora Guadelupe de Jesus Victoria. Created: 1836 (out of the municipality of Victoria). Organized: 1837. County Seat: Victoria. Major Events: The area was inhabited by mound builders centuries before the first explorations by the Spanish early in the 16th century. The first Spanish settlement was at a mission and presidio in 1720. Colonization, mainly by Mexican settlers, started in 1824. Many of these took part in the War for Texan Independence. The Victoria Advocate, the second oldest newspaper in Texas, first appeared in 1856. **WASHINGTON COUNTY** Named for: The first United States President, George Washington. Created: 1836. Organized: 1837. County Seat: Washington-on-the-Brazos (1837-1844); Brenham (1844-present). Major Events: The area was part of the area settled by Stephen F. Austin's "Old Three Hundred". A ferry was established over the Brazos River in 1822 and the town of Washington-on-the-Brazos in 1830. The creation of Brazos, Burleson and Lee counties led to the change of the county seat to Brenham, in 1844. German settlers started to arrive after 1850. Several institutions of higher education were established in Washington County after the Civil War, including Baylor University. **1836** The settled area of the new Republic of Texas included over 30 towns in an area from the Sabine River west to San Antonio and Copano Bay and north to the San Antonio-Nacogdoches Road, including Anahuac, Bastrop, Bell's Landing, Bolivar, Brazoria, Cole's Settlement, Columbia, Cox's Point, Fort Settlement, Galveston, Goliad, Gonzales, Harrisburg, Houston, Liberty, Lynchburg, Matagorda, Nacogdoches, San Antonio de Bexar, San Augustine, San Felipe de Austin, San Patrick, Tenoxticlan, Velasco, Victoria, Washington and Zavala. **SEPTEMBER, 1836** In an election the voters ratified the Constitution, expressed their wish for annexation to the United States and elected the officials of the new Republic. They elected Sam Houston as President (Houston received 5,119 votes, Henry Smith 743 and Stephen Austin 587) and Mirabeau B. Lamar Vice President (uncontested). The public demanded that Houston take office immediately instead of waiting for the second Monday in December. On October 22, 1836 Houston took the oath as the first constitutionally elected President of the Republic of Texas. **NOVEMBER, 1836** President Houston appointed Stephen F. Austin, Secretary of State;

Henry Smith, Secretary of the Treasury; Thomas J. Rusk, Secretary of War; James P. Henderson, Attorney General; S. Rhoads Fisher, Secretary of the Navy and Robert Barr, Postmaster General. The First Congress of the Republic of Texas convened at Columbia. Stephen Austin developed pneumonia working in the drafty, poorly heated capitol building and died December 27, 1836. **DECEMBER 19, 1836** The Mexican Congress declared the Treaty of Velasco invalid and announced plans to subdue Texas. Therefore, the Texas Congress established a statutory boundary for the new nation on December 19. The boundaries established were: "beginning at the mouth of the Sabine River, and running west along the Gulf of Mexico three leagues from land, to the mouth of the Rio Grande, thence up the principal stream of said river to its source, thence due north to the 42nd degree of north latitude, thence along the boundary line as defined in the treaty between the United States and Spain, to the beginning;. . ." **1837** First Cumberland Presbytery was organized in Texas and the first Baptist Church in Texas was established at Washington-on-the-Brazos by Z. N. Morrell. President Houston submitted his treaty with the Cherokees to the Senate for ratification, but the Senate declared the treaty null and void. Houston declared the treaty valid since the Convention of 1836 had confirmed the acts of the provisional government. (In 1838 Houston directed that the boundary be surveyed, however President Mirabeau, who succeeded Houston, enforced the Senate ruling.) **MARCH 3, 1837** President Andrew Jackson formally recognized the Republic of Texas. **DECEMBER 5, 1837** The Philosophical Society of Texas was formed at Houston. **FANNIN COUNTY** Named for: James W. Fannin, Jr., victor at Concepcion but defeated at Goliad. Created: 1837 (out of Red River County). Organized: 1838. County Seat: Bonham. Major Events: The first permanent settlement was at Tulip in 1836. Following Reconstruction the county grew rapidly. The first railroad crossed the county in 1873. **FAYETTE COUNTY** Named for: the Marquis de Lafayette, hero of the American Revolution. Created: 1837 (out of Bastrop and Colorado Counties). Organized: 1838. County Seat: LaGrange. Major Events: First settled by members of Stephen F. Austin's "Old Three Hundred." Monument Hill, burial site of Nicholas M. Dawson's company and the victims of the Mier Expedition, is located near LaGrange. **FORT BEND COUNTY** Named for: Fort Bend, a pioneer blockhouse built by Stephen F. Austin's "Old Three Hundred Colonists" in 1821 in a bend of the Brazos River at the site of present-day Richmond. Created: 1837 (out of Austin County). Organized: 1837. County Seat: Richmond. Major Events: The earliest land titles in the county date from 1824. In 1889 the county was the scene of the "Jaybird-Woodpecker War," which resulted in the return of local government to control by white residents after a period of black control that began with Reconstruction. **HOUSTON COUNTY** Named for: General Sam Houston, United States Representative from and Governor of Tennessee, Commander of the Texas Army during the Texas Revolution, President and Governor of and United States Senator from Texas. Created: 1837 (out of Nacogdoches County). Organized: 1837. County Seat: Crockett. Major Events: French and Spanish explorers visted the area in the seventeenth century. San Francisco de los Tejas, the first Spanish mission in East Texas, was founded in 1690 but abandoned in 1693 due to Indian hostility. Travel and trade were carried on along the Old San Antonio Road for more than a century before settlers began to enter the area in the late 1820s. The town of Randolph raised the first company of men to leave Texas for the Civil War in 1861. Lignite mining and wild-catting for oil began in 1904. **MONTGOMERY COUNTY** Named for: General Richard Montgomery who fought in the American Revolution. Created: 1837. Organized: 1837. County Seat: Montgomery (1837-1874); Willis (1874-1880); Montgomery (1880-1889); Conroe (1889-present). Major Events: The first courthouse was built in 1838. Lumbering was the chief industry. The railroad cut across the county in 1871. **SABINE COUNTY** Named for: The Spanish word "Sabine" meaning "cypress". Created: 1837. Organized: 1837. County Seat: Milam (1837-1858); Hemphill (1858-present). Major Events: Permanent Anglo-American settlement came with the construction of ferries across the Sabine River beginning in 1797. At first organized as the Sabine District of the Department of Nacogdoches, it became the municipality of Sabine in 1835 and Sabine County on December 14, 1837. **ROBERTSON COUNTY** Named for: Sterling C. Robertson, soldier, explorer, colonizer, legislator and signer of the Texas Declaration of Independence. Created: 1837 (out of Milam County). Organized: 1838. County Seat: Old Franklin (1838-1850); Wheelock (1850-1855); Owensville (1855-1860); Calvert (1860-1879); Morgan, later renamed Franklin (1879-present). Major Events: Traversed by Domingo Teran de los Rios in 1690 and occupied by Indians before the white settlement. In 1825 the county was included in the Robertson Colony, a grant second in size only to that made to Stephen F. Austin and containing all or part of 30 present Texas counties. Oil production started in 1920. **OCTOBER, 1838** President Houston could not succeed himself and President Mirabeau Lamar was elected (uncontested) to succeed Houston. Lamar opposed annexation with the United States, he spent money liberally, his policy concerning Mexico was to force recognition and he believed that the Indians should be pushed back, all of which were in opposition to Houston's policies. David G. Burnet was elected Vice President. **OCTOBER 12, 1838** Texas withdrew its annexation request. **GALVESTON COUNTY** Named for: Count Bernardo de Galvez, Spanish Governor of Louisiana. Created: 1838 (out of Brazoria County). Organized: 1838. County Seat: Galveston. Major Events: Spanish and French explorers visited the area in the sixteenth and seventeenth centuries. Galveston was a base for pirates preying on Spanish shipping from 1815 to 1821. Galveston Island was the temporary seat of government of the Republic of Texas during the Texas Revolution. A 14-mile canal to connect Oyster Creek, West Bay and the Brazos River was dug in 1857 and eventually became part of the Gulf Intracoastal Waterway. Oil production began in 1922. **JANUARY 24, 1839** The Congress of the Republic of Texas established the Texas State Library. **JANUARY 25, 1839** The Lone Star Flag was officially determined and accepted. Peter Krag of Austin was the designer (he also drew the official seal of Texas). The flag design cost $10 (the seal cost $8) and depicted bravery (the red stripe), loyalty (the blue stripe) purity and liberty (the white stripe). Prior to this offical acceptance, Texas had as many as 15 flags and many had the five-pointed star as the dominant motif. Most of these early flags were battle standards even though Stephen Austin ordered (unsuccessfully) that no flags be used until an official flag was accepted. Two flags have competed over the years for the honor of being the first Lone Star Flag. One flag was designed by Sarah Dodson of Harrisburg, Texas in September, 1835. This flag was taken in to battle by her husband and is an exact replica of the Texas flag today except that its two rectangles are vertical not horizontal. The other flag was made by Joanna Troutman of Georgia in November, 1835. It had a white background, an azure star and the words "Liberty or Death". The Texas Legislature on February 13, 1913 decided that Joanna Troutman would get the honor of being the "Betsy Ross of Texas", but the dispute continues. **JANUARY 26, 1839** Two homestead laws were passed in an effort to attract permanent settlers. The first provided for liberal land grants and the second protected a household against seizure for debt. This property exemption was unique in that it was the first legislation of its kind passed by any country and was contrary to English common law. **JULY 16, 1839** General Thomas J. Rusk led east Texas Anglos against an Indian rebellion led by Vicente Cordova. At the Battle of Neches the

Cherokees were defeated and pushed from Texas. It was feared that the Cherokees would align with the Mexicans in a war against the Texas Republic. **SEPTEMBER 25, 1839** France was the first nation to formally recognize the independence of Texas when a treaty was signed which was ratified by the Texas Senate on January 14, 1840. **DECEMBER, 1839** In 1838 President Lamar had visited the Austin city area and when he requested in January 1939 a commission to be appointed to select a permanent capital for the republic, he asked them to inspect the Austin area. The commission selected the area (called Waterloo) on both sides of a bend in the Colorado River in central Travis County. Prior to this, Columbia was the temporary capital where Sam Houston was inaugurated president. Then in May, 1837 Congress had moved the capital to Houston until a permanent location could be found. Construction of the new capital began in May, 1839 and in August the capital was moved to a one-story frame capitol building surrounded by an eight-foot stockade for defense against Indian attacks. The city was incorporated in December, 1839 with a population of 856. In 1842 the capital was moved back to Houston as President Houston feared a Mexican attack, then it was moved to Washington-on-the-Brazos by executive order in 1842. In 1845 the capital was returned to Austin and in 1850 a state election designated Austin the permanent capital. The governor's mansion and the state capitol building were built between 1850 and 1860. In 1881 the capitol burned and was replaced with one built of granite from Burnet County. **HARRISON COUNTY** Named for: Jonas Harrison, early Texas pioneer, member of the Convention of 1832, an advocate of Texas independence known as "the Patrick Henry of Texas". Created: 1839 (out of Shelby County). Organized: 1842. County Seat: Marshall. Major Events: The first permanent settlers arrived in the 1830s and were largely cotton planters from Southern states. By 1861 Marshall was connected with Jefferson, Daingerfield, Mount Pleasant, Clarksville, Tyler and Shreveport by ox and freight lines and the county was the third most populous in Texas. **JANUARY 28, 1840** The first Chamber of Commerce in Texas was founded in Houston. **FEBRUARY 1, 1840** The first college in Texas, called Rutersville College, opened its doors in Fayette County with 63 students. A Methodist college, the Texas Congress approved its charter in 1840 as a coeducational and nondenominational land grant college. President Lamar was called "The Father of Texas Education": as he had the Texas Congress set aside three leagues of land in each county for academies and 50 additional leagues of land for two universities. **BOWIE COUNTY** Named for: James Bowie, who invented the Bowie knife and died at the Alamo. Created: 1840 (out of Red River County). Organized: 1841. County Seat: Boston. Major Events: Indians of the Hasinai and Caddo Confederation were farming the area when Ben Milam settled there in 1819. By 1870 there were 23 miles of railroad in operation. The Old Union School opened in 1830 and the first church was organized in 1842 by a Methodist preacher. **LAMAR COUNTY** Named for: Mirabeau B. Lamar, Commander of the Texas Cavalry at the Battle of San Jacinto, Attorney General, Secretary of War, Vice President and President of the Republic of Texas. Created: 1840 (out of Red River County). Organized: 1841. County Seat: Lafayette (1841-1843); Mount Vernon (1843-1844); Paris (1844-present). Major Events: George W. Wright was the first permanent settler in the area, arriving around 1839. He donated 50 acres on which the town of Paris was established. Lamar County's delegates to the Secession Convention cast their votes against the secession ordinance and the voters of the county subsequently voted against leaving the Union by a margin of 663 to 553, making Lamar one of the 14 counties to vote against secession. A great fire of March 21, 1916 destroyed much of Paris. **TRAVIS COUNTY** Named for: William Barret Travis, Commander at the Alamo. Created: 1840 (out of Bastrop County). Organized: 1843. County

CHRONOLOGICAL HISTORY OF TEXAS

Seat: Austin (also capital of the State of Texas). Major Events: The area was explored by the Spanish from 1691 onward. Three missions were established in 1730 around the location of the present Barton Springs. Travis County formed part of Stephen F. Austin's "Third Colony" and Anglo-American settlement began in 1832. In 1839 Waterloo (renamed Austin) was selected as the capital of the Republic, replacing Houston. The original Travis County covered 40,000 square miles and included all or parts of 14 other modern counties. Travis County voted against secession but later provided many volunteers to the Confederate Armies. **1841** President Houston returned as President after defeating David Burnet in the election of 1841. Edward Burleson was elected Vice President. Houston drastically cut expenditures and quietly worked for annexation with the United States. John Neely Bryan became the first settler in Dallas and also near Dallas Johannes Norbdoe was the first known Norwegian to settle in Texas. **JUNE 5, 1841** The Texas Congress in 1836 had included a large area of the Mexican territory of New Mexico as a part of Texas. President Lamar proposed to extend the jurisdiction of Texas to the statutory boundary and sent an expedition to establish a government in the area under the authority of Texas. Lamar sent a letter dated June 5 to the inhabitants of Santa Fe and of the other portions of New Mexico to the east of the Rio Grande asking their cooperation in unification. **BRAZOS COUNTY** Named for: the Brazos River. Created: 1841 as Navasota County (out of Robertson and Washington Counties; renamed Brazos county in 1842). Organized: 1843. County Seat: Boonville (1843-1866); Bryan (1866-present). Major Events: Originally part of Stephen F. Austin's second colony, it was part of the Washington Municipality under the Mexican government. The railroad reached the county in 1860. The Agricultural and Mechanical College of Texas opened in 1876. **TYLER COUNTY** Named for: U.S. President John Tyler. Created: 1841 (as Menard District); 1845. Organized: 1841; 1845. County Seat: Town Bluff (1846-1847); Woodville (1847-present). Major Events: The first Anglo-American permanent settlements were made before 1833 when a ferry was in operation at Town Bluff across the Trinity River. Tyler County was created and organized twice; first as Menard District in 1841 for judicial purposes only-a creation later declared unconstitutional. **JANUARY, 1842** The Texas Supreme Court in the case of *Stockton V. Montgomery* declared that the judicial counties (Waco, Smith, Burleson, La Baca, Guadalupe, De Witt, Hamilton and Madison) were unconstitutional and they had to be abolished. **MARCH 10, 1842** The so-called "Archive War" began between Austin and Houston over the control of the Texas State Archives. **JUNE 28, 1842** After the successful conclusion of a treaty with The Netherlands on September 18, 1840, James Hamilton journeyed to London, however it would be 1842 before a successful treaty was completed with England. The negotiations led to three treaties: one concerning commerce and navigation, one obligating England to mediate disputes between Texas and Mexico and one suppressing the African slave trade. **JUNE, 1843** President Houston agreed to discussions of an armistice with Mexico to prevent war and to get Texans released from Mexican prisons. **RUSK COUNTY** Named for: Thomas J. Rusk, signer of the Texas Declaration of Independence, President of the Convention of 1845 and later U.S. Senator. Created: 1843 (out of Nacogdoches County). Organized: 1843. County Seat: Henderson. Major Events: After the Indians were removed in 1839, a period of prosperity occurred. In 1854 one of the earliest telegraph lines was strung out. Oil was discovered in 1930. On March 18, 1937 a school explosion at New London killed 292 people. **FEBRUARY 5, 1844** The Texas Congress created a commission to construct the Central National Road. **APRIL 12, 1844** President Houston demanded that the United States, as a preliminary condition for annexation, place its armed forces in position to protect Texas in the

event of an attack by Mexico. U.S. Secretary of State John C. Calhoun agreed and signed a treaty of annexation on April 12, but it was rejected by the U.S. Senate in June. **DECEMBER 9, 1844** Dr. Anson Jones became President of the Republic of Texas. He would earn the title "Architect of Annexation."

UNDER THE FLAG OF THE UNITED STATES 1845-1861
1845 The term "maverick", after Samuel A. Maverick, came into use to refer to unbranded cattle. **FEBRUARY 1, 1845** Baylor University was chartered by the Republic of Texas. It opened at Independence, Texas in 1846 and its first degree was granted in 1854. **MARCH 1, 1845** U.S. President Tyler signed a joint resolution of Congress annexing Texas to the United States. The treaty gave Texas the right to divide into new states not to exceed four plus the State of Texas, to retain its public lands and its public debts. **MARCH 6, 1845** Mexico severed diplomatic relations with the United States when the joint resolution annexing Texas was passed. President Polk ordered General Zachary Taylor to take position between the Nueces and Rio Grande. Mexico claimed the Nueces River as the southern boundary of Texas; the United States insisted on the Rio Grande. Skirmishes between Mexican and U.S. troops caused President Polk to request Congress for a war delcaration with Mexico. **MAY 19, 1845** The British and French governments, upon learning of the treaty of annexation with the United States, immediately sent representatives to Washington-on-the-Brazos with an alternate proposal. Both governments pledged their aid in a settlement with Mexico if Texas remained independent. President Jones accepted the offer and the Mexican government consented to the Texas proposal for peace with the reservation that the offer would be void if Texas accepted the offer of the United States. **JUNE 21, 1845** President Jones presented both proposals to the Texas Congress and on June 21 the Mexican treaty was unanimously rejected. On June 23 the Texas Congress voted in favor of annexation with the United States and on July 4 the Annexation Convention passed it by a vote of 55 to 1. **NAVARRO COUNTY** Named for: Jose Antonio Navarro, a Mexican born leader in the struggle for Texan Independence who was a signer of the Declaration of Texas Independence, represented Bexar County in the Republic's Congress and was a delegate to the convention of 1845 which voted for Texas' annexation to the United States. Created: 1845 (out of Robertson County). Organized: 1846. County Seat: Corsicana. Major Events: The first settlement began in 1838 with the foundation of Spring Hill by Dr. George W. Hill. The committee selected to organize the county by the First Texas Legislature was assisted by Jose Antonio Navarro. Oil was discovered in 1894. **OCTOBER 13 - DECEMBER 29, 1845** THE STATE OF TEXAS The task of preparing a new constitution for the state of Texas fell to the Annexation Convention. Modeled after the Louisiana Constitution, it was unanimously adopted by the Convention on August 28. On October 13 Texas voters ratified the Constitution and the annexation with the United States. The U.S. Congress approved the Texas Constitution in December and, when President Polk signed the act on December 29, Texas became the 28th state of the Union. **FEBRUARY, 1846** Thomas J. Rusk and Sam Houston were elected the first U.S. Senators from Texas. **FEBRUARY 19, 1846** A special election was held on December 15, 1845 to elect new state officers. In an emotional public ceremony February 19, as the Lone Star Flag came down ("the Republic of Texas is no more"), President Anson Jones formally relinquished his authority to the new Texas State Governor James Pinckney Henderson, a Democrat. **MARCH 28, 1846** General Zachary Taylor and an army of 2,000 arrived at Matamoras. On April 30 Mexican troops began to cross the Rio Grande River and laid siege to Fort Texas on May 3, but were defeated in the Battle of Palo Alto (the first battle of the war) on May 8 and in the Battle of Resaca de la Palma on May

CHRONOLOGICAL HISTORY OF TEXAS

9. **MAY 13, 1846** The United States declared war on Mexico.
MAY 19, 1846 A.C. Horton, the Lieutenant Governor, served as Governor of Texas until November, 1846 while Governor J. P. Henderson was commanding troops in the Mexican War. **ANDERSON COUNTY** Named for: Kenneth L. Anderson, vice president of Texas from 1844 to annexation. Created: 1846 (out of Houston County). Organized: 1846. County Seat: Palestine. Major Events: The "Old Pilgrim" Church, established north of the present Elkhart in 1833, is believed to be the oldest Protestant church in Texas. **ANGELINA COUNTY** Named for: Angelina River. Created: 1846 (out of Nacogdoches County). Organized: 1846. County Seat: Marion (1846-1854); Jonesville (1854-1858); Homer (1858-1892); Lufkin (1898-present). Major Events: Originally thickly covered by timber, by the turn of the century most of the trees had been timbered and many towns disappeared. In the middle 1900s, considerable attention was given to replanting and scientific timber crop management. **BURLESON COUNTY** Named for: Edward Burleson, who served in the War of 1812 and the Mexican War and was Vice President of the Texas Republic. Created: 1846 (out of Milam and Washington Counties). Organized: 1846. County Seat: Caldwell. Major Events: Between 1850 and 1855 a large number of plantation owners moved to the county. In 1880 the railroad arrived. **CALHOUN COUNTY** Named for: John C. Calhoun, U.S. Senator from South Carolina and U.S. Vice President. Created: 1846 (out of Jackson, Matagorda and Victoria Counties). Organized: 1846. County Seat: Lavaca (1846-1850s); Indianola (1850s-1886); Port Lavaca (1886-present; originally known as Lavaca). Major Events: The first permanent settlement was by Anglo-Americans at Linnville in 1831. The Comanches burned the settlement in 1840. One hundred German families established a tent village called "Karlshaven", later known as Indianola. Oil and gas were discovered in 1935. **CASS COUNTY** Named for: Lewis Cass, U.S. Senator from Michigan who supported the annexation of Texas. Created: 1846 (out of Bowie County). Organized: 1846. County Seat: Jefferson (1846-1860); Linden (1860-present). Major Events: In 1861 the Legislature changed the county's name to Davis after Confederate President Jefferson Davis. In 1871 the county changed its name back to Cass. The railroad arrived in 1872 and oil was discovered in 1935. **CHEROKEE COUNTY** Named for: the expelled Cherokee Indians. Created: 1846 (out of Nacogdoches County). Organized: 1846. County Seat: Rusk. Major Events: The Cherokee Indians entered the area in 1822 receiving permission from the Mexican governor. President Mirabeau B. Lamar ordered the Cherokee to leave in 1839. The railroad came to the county in 1872. **COLLIN COUNTY** Named for: Collin McKinney, signer of the Texas Declaration of Independence, member of the Texas Constitutional Convention, member of the Texas Legislature. Created: 1846 (out of Fannin County). Organized: 1846. County Seat: Buckner (1846-1848); McKinney (1848-present). Major Events: Settlement began in 1842. Immigration was heavy between 1850 and 1860 but few slaves were brought into the area, which may account for the relatively trouble-free passage of Reconstruction in the county. The railroad reached McKinney in 1872. **COMAL COUNTY** Named for: the Comal River (Comal is a Spanish word which means "flat dish" and possibly refers to the valley through which the river flows). Created: 1846 (out of Bexar and Travis Land Districts). Organized: 1846. County Seat: New Braunfels. Major Events: The county was the site of an unofficial Spanish mission, Neustra Senora de Guadalupe, which operated from December, 1756 to March, 1758. Permanent settlement did not begin until the mass immigration from Germany that resulted in the establishment of New Braunfels in 1845. **DALLAS COUNTY** Named for: the statute creating the county does not specify, but the county was probably named for George Mifflin Dallas, then Vice President

of the United States. Created: 1846 (out of Robertson and Nacogdoches Counties). Organized: 1846. County Seat: Dallas. Major Events: Although the area had been open for settlement under Mexican colonization laws, actual settlement did not begin until 1841 when John Neely Bryan built a cabin at the crossing of the Trinity River near the location of the present courthouse. By 1844 the Dallas Post Office was located in the settlement around Neely's cabin; this settlement was referred to as Dallas as early as 1842 and local historians speculate the town, as distinct from the county, may have been named for U.S. Navy Commodore Alexander J. Dallas, older brother of George Mifflin Dallas. The arrival of railroads in the county in 1872 accelerated the county's development. **DENTON COUNTY** Named for: John B. Denton, a pioneer preacher and captain under Colonel Edward H. Tarrant, was killed near Fort Worth in an attack against Indians. Created: 1846 (out of Fannin County). Organized: 1846. County Seat: Denton. Major Events: From the beginning this county's inhabitants have been deeply interested in religion and education. At least eight subscription schools were in operation as early as 1860. Franklin College, established in the early 1870s, was the first institution of higher education in the county. **DE WITT COUNTY** Named for: Green C. De Witt, one of the first Americans to be interested in colonizing Texas. He received a land grant from the Mexican government in 1825. Created: 1846 (out of Goliad, Gonzales and Victoria Counties). Organized: 1846. County Seat: Clinton (1846-1876); Cuero (1876-present). Major Events: In 1840 the first school in the area was opened and in 1841 the Cumberland Presbyterians organized the first church. In 1873 the first railroad arrived in the county. **GRAYSON COUNTY** Named for: Peter William Grayson, early Texas pioneer, first Attorney General of the Republic of Texas and Commissioner of the Republic of Texas to the United States. Created: 1846 (out of Fannin County). Organized: 1846. County Seat: Sherman. Major Events: Anglo-American settlers began to arrive in 1835 and in 1836 the first settlement was established. In 1840 the Republic of Texas created two military posts in the area, Fort Preston and Fort Jackson. The first courthouse, constructed in 1847, was torn down in 1858 to settle a bet as to whether or not a gray goose was nesting beneath it. The courthouse was burned again by a mob on May 9, 1930 in one of the last race riots in Texas. **GRIMES COUNTY** Named for: Jess Grimes, signer of the Texas Declaration of Independence and early settler in the area. Created: 1846 (out of Montgomery County). Organized: 1846. County Seat: Anderson. Major Events: The first permanent settlement in the area was established by members of Stephen F. Austin's colony. Jesse Grimes settled at Grimes' Prairie in 1827 and introduced stock raising. Jared Groce established the first cotton gin in Texas in the area in 1828. By 1833 planters with slaves had settled in the river bottoms. Fanthorp's Inn became the area's first post office in 1835 and was renamed Anderson in 1846. Indian raids ceased by 1841. The railroad reached the county in 1860. Grimes County received numerous German and Polish immigrants after 1900. **GUADALUPE COUNTY** Named for: the Guadalupe River which was named by Captain Alonso de Leon in 1689 in honor of the painting of the Lady of Guadalupe on his standard. Created: 1846 (out of Bexar County and De Witt's Colony). Organized: 1846. County Seat: Sequin. Major Events: From 1827 to 1835, 22 settlers received grants of land from De Witt and 14 through a special grant from the Mexican government. From 1837 to 1839 much of the unclaimed land in the area was granted to veterans of the Texas Revolution. Emigrants from the United States between 1840 and 1860 were primarily from Southern states and they brought slaves, Southern traditions and customs to the area. The last Indian raid into the county occurred in 1885. The first petroleum discovery in the county occurred in 1923. **HENDERSON COUNTY** Named for: James Pinckney

CHRONOLOGICAL HISTORY OF TEXAS

Henderson, Secretary of State for the Republic of Texas, member of the Annexation Convention of 1845, Governor and later United States Senator from Texas. Created: 1846 (out of Houston and Nacogdoches Counties). Organized: 1846. County Seat: Buffalo (1846-1850); Athens (1850-present). Major Events: Caney Creek, Turkey Creek and Buffalo, established in 1837, were the first permanent settlements in the area. The railroad reached the county in 1880. A lignite mining and power generation plant was constructed at Trinidad in the 1920s. Oil was discovered in 1934. **HOPKINS COUNTY** Named for: the David Hopkins family, an early pioneer family. Created: 1846 (out of Lamar and Nacogdoches Counties). Organized: 1846. County Seat: Tarrant (1846-1871); Sulphur Springs (1846-present). Major Events: some settlers followed the Caddo Trace into the area before 1836, but the first permanent settlement was not established until 1842 at Sulphur Bluff. The railroad reached the county in 1876. Lignite mining began at Como in 1901 and oil was discovered at Sulphur Bluff in 1936. **HUNT COUNTY** Named for: Memucan Hunt, Minister of Texas to the United States, Secretary of the Navy of the Republic of Texas, member of the Texas Legislature, United States Commissioner to adjust the southwestern border. Created: 1846 (out of Fannin and Nacogdoches Counties). Organized: 1846. County Seat: Greenville. Major Events: Anglo-American settlement began in 1839. A store was opened at the present site of Greenville in 1844. The railroad reached Greenville in 1876. **LAVACA COUNTY** Named for: the Lavaca River (la vaca is the Spanish word meaning "cow"). Created: 1846 (out of Colorado, Fayette, Gonzales, Jackson and Victoria Counties). Organized: 1846. County Seat: Hallettsville (1852-present). Major Events: Lands in the area of the county were included in grants to both Stephen F. Austin and Green C. De Witt and by 1831 permanent settlements had been established by both Austin's and De Witt's colonists. William Milligan's ginhouse was a center of revolutionary activity by 1835. Lack of transportation delayed development of the county. No stage line crossed the county until 1861 and the first railroad did not reach it until 1887. Large numbers of German and Bohemian immigrants began arriving around 1880 and developed truck farming, poultry and hog raising. **LEON COUNTY** Named for: Statute creating county does not specify; local historians speculate it was named for a yellow wolf of the region called the leon or for Martin de Leon, the Spanish founder of Victoria. Created: 1846 (out of Robertson County). Organized: 1846. County Seat: Leona (1846-1851); Centerville (1856-present). Major Events: The area was a part of the Stephen F. Austin and Samuel W. Williams colonial grant but was not settled until 1840 or 1841 when a blockhouse called Fort Boggy was built in the region later known as Rogers Prairie. The railroad first reached the county in 1872. **LIMESTONE COUNTY** Named for: the area's indigenous limestone rock. Created: 1846 (out of Robertson County). Organized: 1846. County Seat: Springfield (1846-1873); Groesbeck (1873-present). Major Events: The first Anglo-American settlers arrived in 1833. James W. and Silas M. Parker established Fort Parker on the Navasota River in 1834. Caddo and Comanche Indians attacked Fort Parker in May, 1836. Cynthia Ann Parker, mother of Quanah Parker, was captured in this raid. The first school and post office were established in 1846. Three-quarters of the county's voters served in the Confederate Army during the Civil War. The railroad first reached the county in 1869. Gas was discovered in 1912 and Mexia boomed as an oil center in the 1920s. **NEWTON COUNTY** Named for: Corporal John Newton, hero of the American Revolution. Created: 1846 (out of Jasper County). Organized: 1846. County Seat: Newton (1846-1848); Burkeville (1848-1853); Newton (1853-present). Major Events: Considerable unauthorized settlement occurred in the Newton County area before it was included in the land grant made to Lorenzo de Zavala, one of the signers of the Texas Declaration of Independence. The

Mexican government validated the land titles of some Anglo-American settlers in 1834. Oil was first discovered in 1938. **NUECES COUNTY** Named for: Nueces River ("nueces" is the Spanish word for "nuts"). Created: 1846 (out of San Patricio County and Bexar County). Organized: 1846. County Seat: Corpus Christi. Major Events: A short-lived settlement was made by 52 families in the mid-eighteenth century, but otherwise only ranchmen occupied the region until after the Texas Revolution. In 1842 Henry L. Kinney established a settlement that was to become Corpus Christi. Corpus Christi was bombarded by Federal gunboats during the Civil War. Natural gas was discovered in 1922. The port of Corpus Christi was opened in 1926. **PANOLA COUNTY** Named for: The Indian word "ponolo", meaning "cotton". Created: 1846 (out of Shelby and Harrison Counties). Organized: 1846. County Seat: Pulaski (1846-1848); Carthage (1848-present). Major Events: Permanent settlement was delayed by disputed claims to the area from France, Spain, Mexico, the United States and the Republic of Texas between 1690 and 1840. The first settlement was in 1833. Gas was discovered in 1936. **POLK COUNTY** Named for: the President of the United States, James S. Polk (1845-1849). Created: 1846 (out of Liberty County). Organized: 1846. County Seat: Livingston. Major Events: First settlers were the Alabama-Coushatta Indians who still live in the Big Thicket area. **SMITH COUNTY** Named for: General James Smith of the Texas Army during the Revolution. Created: 1846 (out of Nacogdoches County). Organized: 1846. County Seat: Tyler. Major Events: The area was included in land grants given to David G. Burnet in 1826 and Vicente Filisola in 1831. The first settlement was made in 1839. Tyler was a supply point for the Confederate Army and Camp Ford held as many as 6,000 federal prisoners during the Civil War. The rose nursery business commenced in 1880. Oil production started in 1931. **TITUS COUNTY** Named for: Andrew Jackson Titus, who served in the Mexican War and represented his district in the Fourth Legislature of the State of Texas. Created: 1846 (out of Bowie and Red River Counties). Organized: 1846. County Seat: Mount Pleasant. Major Events: In 1873 the present Morris and Franklin Counties were carved out of Titus County. Oil was discovered in 1836. **UPSHUR COUNTY** Named for: Abel Packer Upshur, President John Tyler's Secretary of State (1843-1844). Created: 1846 (out of Harrison and Nacogdoches Counties). Organized: 1846. County Seat: Gilmer. Major Events: The first white settler was John Cotton in 1835. The first trading post was established in 1838. The coming of the Texas and Pacific Railroad in 1871 encouraged the development of the timber industry. Oil was discovered in 1939. **WALKER COUNTY** Named for: Robert J. Walker, a representative from Mississippi to the United States Congress, who introduced the resolution providing for the annexation of Texas. However, during the Civil War, because Robert J. Walker was a Unionist, history was changed to make the honoree Samuel Hamilton Walker, a Texas Ranger, survivor of the "Black Bean Episode", and the man instrumental in modifying the "Texas" revolver, later known as the "Walker Colt". Created: 1846 (out of Montgomery County). Organized: 1846. County Seat: Huntsville. Major Events: First settled by Ephraim and Pleasant Gray in the 1830s at a Bidai Indian post. The state penitentiary was established at Huntsville in 1847. The county was under martial law for a time in 1871 because of the resistance to Reconstruction. **WHARTON COUNTY** Named for: William H. Wharton, who was active in the struggle for Texan Independence. He was the author of the petition to Mexico requesting statehood for Texas in 1832. Following the establishment of the Republic, Wharton was Texas' first Minister to the United States and was at that time an advocate for annexation. Created: 1846 (out of parts of Matagorda and Jackson Counties). Organized: 1846. County Seat: Wharton. Major Events: The area was visited by both

FLYING THE COLORS: TEXAS ©JOHN CLEMENTS 1984

French and Spanish explorers. The first Anglo-American settlers were 25 of Stephen F. Austin's "Old Three Hundred", who arrived in the early 1820s. In 1850 more than two thirds of the population were slaves. A Black, B.H. Davis represented Wharton County at the 1875 Constitutional Convention but by 1880 the White Man's Association was prominent in county politics. Oil was discovered in 1904 and sulphur in 1923. **DECEMBER 21, 1847** George Wood, Democrat, became Governor. He served the constitutionally defined two-year term of office until December 21, 1849. **1848** The earliest recorded instance of imported pure bred cattle occurred as two cows and a bull were brought to Texas from Queen Victoria's herd of Durham cattle. The Texas prison system was established this year. **FEBRUARY 2, 1848** The Treaty of Guadalupe Hidalgo ended the Mexican war and established the Rio Grande River as the boundary between Mexico and Texas. **CALDWELL COUNTY** Named for: Mathew Caldwell, Commander of the Texas Rangers and signer of the Texas Declaration of Independence. Created: 1848 (out of Bastrop and Gonzales Counties). Organized: 1848. County Seat: Lockhart. Major Events: The first settlers received land grants from the Mexican government between 1831 and 1835. Byrd Lockhart made one of the earliest Anglo-American surveys of the area. Oil was discovered in 1922. **CAMERON COUNTY** Named for: Ewen Cameron, a volunteer in the Texas Revolution killed at the order of Santa Anna. Created: 1848 (out of Nueces County). Organized: 1848. County Seat: Brownsville. Major Events: By 1761 Spanish ranches were established. In 1845 Fort Brown was established and Anglo-Americans came to the area. Land disputes arose and in 1852 the Legislature confirmed many of the Spanish and Mexican land grants. Brownsville was an important Confederate shipping port in the Civil War. **COOKE COUNTY** Named for: William G. Cooke, who fought in the Texas Revolution. Created: 1848 (out of Fannin County). Organized: 1848. County Seat: Gainesville. Major Events: Many of the county's early settlers were "Fortyniners" who remained in the area after entering it on the Old California Trail. Cattle raising was the most important occupation in the county until the depression of 1923. Oil was discovered in the 1920s. **GILLESPIE COUNTY** Named for: Captain Richard A. Gillespie, a Texas Ranger killed leading the charge on Bishop's Palace in Monterrey on September 21, 1846 during the Mexican War. Created: 1848 (out of Travis and Bexar Counties). Organized: 1848. County Seat: Fredericksburg. Major Events: The area was colonized by German immigrants led by John O. Meusebach who on May 8, 1846 founded Fredericksburg, named for Prince Frederick of Prussia. A cholera epidemic in 1849 took a heavy toll of the early settlers. **HAYS COUNTY** Named for: Captain John Coffee (Jack) Hays, a Texas Ranger famed as an Indian fighter, signer of the Texas Declaration of Independence, soldier in the Mexican War, "Fortyniner" and Sheriff of San Francisco County, California during the 1850s. Created: 1848 (out of Travis County). Organized: 1848. County Seat: San Marcos. Major Events: There was a Spanish settlement in the area from 1808 to 1812. Mexican land grants in the area date from as early as 1831 but the first Anglo-American settler did not arrive until around 1835. Several of the area's original settlers served in the Texas Ranger company commanded by Captain Jack Hays. The first church was organized in 1847 and the first school in 1849. **KAUFMAN COUNTY** Named for: David Spangler Kaufman, early Jewish pioneer in Texas, member and subsequently Speaker of the House of Representatives of the Republic of Texas, member of the Senate of the Republic of Texas, Charge d'Affaires of the Republic of Texas to the United States, first United States Representative from Texas to be seated in Congress and charter member of the Philosophical Society of Texas. Created: 1848 (out of Henderson County). Organized: 1848. County Seat: Kaufman (originally called Kingsborough). Major Events: The first settlers arrived

around 1841. Although the area was inhabited by Caddo, Cherokee, Delaware and Kickapoo, the county never had any serious Indian problems and only one attack near Kaufman is recorded. **MEDINA COUNTY** Named for: Medina River (possibly named for Spanish engineer Pedro Medina). Created: 1848 (out of Bexar County). Organized: 1848. County Seat: Castroville (1844-1892); Hondo (1892-present). Major Events: Explored by Spanish from 1689 on. Parts of the county were included in a land grant made to Henri Castro, who founded Castroville, then the westernmost settlement in Texas. **STARR COUNTY** Named for: James Harper Starr who served as Secretary of the Treasury for the Texas Republic from 1839-1840 and receiver in the enforcement of the laws for the Confederacy. Created: 1848 (out of Nueces County). Organized: 1848. County Seat: Rio Grande City. Major Events: The first settlement, made in 1753, was part of Jose de Escandion's colony. **VAN ZANDT COUNTY** Named for: Isaac Van Zandt, who served in the Fifth and Sixth Congresses of the Republic of Texas and as Charge d'Affaires to the United States in 1842. He was a delegate to the Convention of 1845 and died while campaigning for the office of governor in 1847. Created: 1848 (out of Henderson County). Organized: 1848. County Seat: Sabine Lake (formerly Jordan's Sabine) (1848-1850); Canton (1850-present). Major Events: The area was occupied by Cherokees under a grant from Mexico from 1822. They were driven out by Anglo-Americans in 1839. The first post office, grist mill and saw mill were set up in 1845. The saw mill is said to have cut the logs used to build the first courthouse in Dallas. During the Civil War the county was popularly known as the "Free State of Van Zandt". The slave population had dropped to 322 (out of 6,494) in 1860. **WEBB COUNTY** Named for: James Webb, Secretary of the State, Secretary of the Treasury and Attorney General for the Republic, who also represented Travis-Bastrop-Fayette-Gonzales District as a Senator in the Sixth, Seventh and Eighth Congresses. He attended the Convention of 1845 and later served as Secretary of State of Texas under Governor Peter H. Bell and as a United States District Judge in Texas. Created: 1848 (out of Bexar County). Organized: 1848. County Seat: Laredo. Major Events: The Webb County area was known to the early Spanish explorers. The first settlement by Spanish and Indian families occurred in 1748. The United States flag was first raised in the area in 1848 by Addison Gillespie and his Texas Rangers. Mirabeau B. Lamar was in command when the United States took over control of the area in 1847. Gas was discovered in 1908 and oil was first produced in 1920. **WILLIAMSON COUNTY** Named for: Major Robert M. Williamson, newspaper editor, soldier, jurist, and legislator for the Republic and the State of Texas. He was crippled at age 15 and used a wooden leg, which accounts for his nickname "Three Legged Willie". Created: 1848 (out of Milam County). Organized: 1848. County Seat: Georgetown. Major Events: The first Anglo-American settlement was in 1835 at a ranger headquarters known as Tumlinson Fort. The "Archive War" ended in 1842 at another settlement called Kenney's Fort. Settlement Proliferated during the 1840s in spite of continuing Indian attacks. Southwestern University was organized at Georgetown in 1877. **DECEMBER 21, 1849** P. Hansborough Bell, Democrat, became Governor of Texas. He resigned near the end of his second term on November 23, 1853. **ELLIS COUNTY** Named for: Richard Ellis, Justice of the Alabama Supreme Court and President of the Convention of 1836. Created: 1849 (out of Robertson and Navarro Counties). Organized: 1850. County Seat: Waxahachie. Major Events: The first settlement was in 1843. The railroad came in 1871. At one time the county led the state in the production of cotton. **TARRANT COUNTY** Named for: General Edward H. Tarrant, who fought in the Texas Revolution, was a Commander of the Texas Rangers on the northwestern frontier and served as a

CHRONOLOGICAL HISTORY OF TEXAS

legislator for the Republic and later for the State of Texas. Created: 1849 (out of Navarro County). Organized: 1850. County Seat: Birdsville (1850-1860); Fort Worth (1860-present). Major Events: The first settlement was made in 1841. The arrival of railroads in 1876 and 1881 and the establishment of meat packing plants in 1902 established Forth Worth's importance as a cattle industry center. **1850** Population: 212,592. Farmers began planting rice in Texas. **FEBRUARY 10, 1850** The Buffalo Bayou, Brazos and Colorado Railway became the first chartered railroad in Texas. **NOVEMBER 25, 1850** The Compromise of 1850 gave Texas $10 million plus interest in return for giving up all claim to the upper Rio Grande (eastern New Mexico). Sante Fe and Worth counties were abolished. The northern boundary of Texas was set at the intersection of the 100th meridian and the 36th parallel west 103rd Meridian then due south to the 32nd parallel to the Rio Bravo del Norte, following the river to the Gulf of Mexico. Texas voters approved this compromise by a two-to-one vote margin and Governor Bell signed the settlement. **BELL COUNTY** Named for: Peter H. Bell, Governor of Texas (1849-1853) and a U.S. Congressman (1853-1857). Created: 1850. Organized: 1850. County Seat: Belton. Major Events: Settled, abandoned and resettled serveral times due to Indian troubles, the last serious Indain raid occurred in 1859. **EL PASO COUNTY** Named for: the historic northern pass (Paso del Norte). Created: 1850 (out of Bexar District). Organized: 1850. County Seat: San Elizario (1850-1866); Ysleta (1866-1868); San Elizario (1868-1873); Ysleta (1873-1883); El Paso (1883-present). Major Events: Zebulon M. Pike arrived in 1807, the first known American to enter the area. The railroads reached El Paso in 1881. The Republican Party dominated the political life of the county until 1886. Apache raids were a problem until the 1890s. **FALLS COUNTY** Named for: the Brazos River falls. Created: 1850 (out of Limestone and Milam Counties). Organized: 1850. County Seat: Old Viesca (1850); Marlin (1850-present). Major Events: The first railroad reached the county in 1869. **FREESTONE COUNTY** Named for: the area's indigenous stone. Created: 1850 (out of Limestone County). Organized: 1851. County Seat: Fairfield. Major Events: Settlement of the area began around 1830. The railroad crossed the county in 1906. **KINNEY COUNTY** Named for: Henry Lawrence Kinney, member of the Senate of the Republic of Texas, member of the Annexation Convention of 1845 and member of the Texas Legislature. Created: 1850 (out of Bexar County). Organized: 1869. County Seat: Brackettville. Major Events: Spanish explorers crossed the area several times in the sixteenth and seventeenth centuries. An Anglo-American settlement established in 1834 was subsequently abandoned and no other Anglo-American settlement was attempted until the establishment of Fort Clark in 1852, when Brackettville (originally called Brackett) was established as a stage stop. Irrigation began in the early 1900s. **McLENNAN COUNTY** Named for: Neil McLennan, early Texas pioneer and early county settler. Created: 1850 (out of Milam County). Organized: 1850. County Seat: Waco. Major Events: The area was originally part of the Robertson Colony but was occupied exclusively by Waco Indians in the 1820s and 1830s. A trading post was established eight miles south of the present site of Waco in 1842 and Neil McLennan established a home in 1845. George B. Erath, who had begun surveying the region in 1840, laid out the town of Waco in 1849. The first railroad reached Waco in 1871. **PRESIDIO COUNTY** Named for: the Spanish words "Presidio del norte" meaning "Fort of the North". Created: 1850 (out of Santa Fe County). Organized: 1875. County Seat: Fort Davis (1875-1885); Marfa (1885-present). Major Events: When first created Presidio County covered 30,380 square miles, more than half of the state that lay west of the Pecos. The county was explored by the Spanish from the early sixteenth century and intermittently settled by Spanish-speaking people. The first Anglo-Americans arrived in the 1880s.

TRINITY COUNTY Named for: the Trinity River. Created: 1850 (out of Houston County). Organized: 1850. County Seat: Sumpter (1850-1873); Trinity (1873-1874); Pennington (1874-1883); Groveton (1883-present). Major Events: The first permanent white settler was Jesse James in 1844. The construction of railroads (1881-1907) and saw mills brought industry and a period of lawlessness that ended in 1905 when law-abiding citizens joined together to establish order and drive out the miscreants. **UVALDE COUNTY** Named for: Captain Juan de Ugalde of the Mexican Army who led a successful expedition against the Comanche Indians in 1790. The name "Ugalde" has been changed to Uvalde. Created: 1850 (out of Bexar County). Organized: 1856. County Seat: Uvalde. Major Events: The area was explored by the Spanish from 1674 onward. Two missions to convert the Apache and Lipan-Apache Indians were established in 1762, but were soon abandoned. The first Anglo-American settlers arrived in 1852. **WOOD COUNTY** Named for: Texas Governor George Tyler Wood, elected in 1847. Created: 1850 (out of Van Zandt County). Organized: 1850. County Seat: Quitman. Major Events: The area was explored by Pedro Vial in 1788 when it was Caddo Indian country. The first Anglo-American settler came in 1824, the first newspaper was published in 1845 and the first school opened in 1852. Oil was discovered in 1940. **FEBRUARY 16, 1852** A joint resolution introduced in the Legislature would have divided Texas into two states—East Texas and West Texas, but it failed to pass. **JANUARY 17, 1853** The Texas Medical Association was formed at Austin. **NOVEMBER 23, 1853** Lieutenant Governor J.W. Henderson, Democrat, became Governor of Texas upon the resignation of P. Hansborough Bell. Henderson served for one month, then Elisha M. Pease, Democrat became Governor on December 21, serving for two terms. **BURNET COUNTY** Named for: David G. Burnet, the first President of the Texas Republic and a district judge. Created: 1852 (out of Bell, Travis and Williamson Counties). Organized: 1854. County Seat: Burnet. Major Events: The county is known as "the Versatile County" because of its varied wealth in farms, ranches, scenic sights for tourism and timber. **HIDALGO COUNTY** Named for: Father Miguel Hidalgo y Costilla, priest and Mexican patriot who led a failed revolution against Spanish rule in 1810 and was executed in 1811. Created: 1852 (out of Cameron and Starr Counties). Organized: 1852. County Seat: Edinburg (1852-1908; now Hidalgo); Edinburg (1908-present). Major Events: Spanish explorers visited the area several times in the seventeenth and eighteenth centuries. Spanish missions and settlements had been established by 1750. Anglo-American settlement did not begin to become significant until around 1883. Citrus fruits and vegetables were produced on a commercial basis around 1907. The railroad reached the county in 1911. **ORANGE COUNTY** Named for: George A. Patillo's orange grove on the east bank of the Nueces River. Created: 1852 (out of Jefferson County). Organized: 1852. County Seat: Orange (formerly known as Madison). Major Events: The area was explored by Joaquin Orobio y Basterra in 1748. Anglo-American settlement came prior to the establishment of the Republic. A saw mill was set up in 1836 but operation was delayed as workmen left to fight the Mexican Army which was under Santa Anna. Shipbuilding commenced before the Civil War. Oil was first discovered in 1913. **HILL COUNTY** Named for: George W. Hill, member of the Congress of the Republic of Texas, Secretary of War and the Navy in the Republic of Texas. Created: 1853 (out of Navarro County). Organized: 1853. County Seat: Hillsborough. Major Events: The area was explored and surveyed in 1835, but Indian resistance delayed settlement until after the establishment of Fort Graham in 1848. The first settlers arrived in 1849. Railroad construction began in 1879. **MADISON COUNTY** Named for: U.S. President James Madison. Created: 1853 (out of Grimes, Leon and Walker Counties). Organized: 1854. County Seat: Madisonville.

Major Events: The area was explored in 1689 by Alonso de Leon, who named the Trinity River. It is crossed by two of the oldest roads in Texas: the old San Antonio and La Bahia Roads. Anglo-American settlement began in the 1820s. A ferry, established at Clapp's Crossing in 1829, was used by settlers retreating in the "Runaway Scrape" after the battle of San Jacinto in 1836. **1854** the Legislature passed an act establishing the public school system, passed the first law regulating alcoholic beverages and passed a law setting aside land for Indian reservations. **FEBRUARY 14, 1854** The first Western Union Telegraph Office opened in Marshall, Texas. **BOSQUE COUNTY** Named for: the Bosque River (Bosque is Spanish for "woods"). Created: 1854. Organized: 1854. County Seat: Meridian. Major Events: Between 1854 and 1875 a large number of Norwegians settled in the western part of the county and between 1870 and 1890 a large number of Germans settled in the eastern part of the county. **CORYELL COUNTY** Named for: James Coryell, a Texas Ranger killed in 1837 by Indians near the Brazos River. Created: 1854 (out of Bell County). Organized: 1854. County Seat: Gatesville. Major Events: Fort Gates, established in 1849 to protect settlers from Indian raids, became the center of the county's early development. **JOHNSON COUNTY** Named for: Middleton Tate Johnson, Commander of the Texas Rangers and member of the Texas Senate. Created: 1854 (out of Navarro and McLennan Counties). Organized: 1854. County Seat: Wardville (1855-1856); Buchanan (1856-1867); Cleburne (1867-present; originally known as Camp Henderson). Major Events: Philip Nolan is believed to have been killed in 1801 in the western part of what became Johnson County. The first Anglo-American settler arrived in the area in 1849. In 1861 the county voted in favor of secession by a margin of approximately ten to one. The railroad crossed the county in 1881. **KARNES COUNTY** Named for: Henry Wax Karnes, soldier of the Army of Texas who fought in the Texas Revolution and in Indian campaigns shortly thereafter. Created: 1854 (out of Bexar and Goliad Counties). Organized: 1854. County Seat: Helena (1854-1894); Karnes City (1894-present). Major Events: The earliest Mexican land grants in the area were made in 1758. Helena, the first Anglo-American settlement, was established in 1852 on the site of an earlier Mexican settlement called Alamita. The railroad was built through the county in 1885. **1855** the American Party was the first organized political opposition to the Democratic Party, capturing many local offices, several places in the Legislature and one seat in Congress. **PARKER COUNTY** Named for: Isaac Parker who fought in the Texas Revolution, served in the Congress of the Republic of Texas and in the Legislature of the State of Texas. He introduced the bill creating Parker County. Created: 1855 (out of Bosque and Navarro Counties). Organized: 1856. County Seat: Weatherford. Major Events: The first permanent settlement occurred after 1849. Oliver Loving, whose cattle were part of the first northward drive from Texas, settled in Parker County in 1855. Indian raids continued until the 1870s. Parker County watermelons received a gold medal at the St. Louis World's Fair in 1904. **1856** U.S. Secretary of War Jefferson Davis, in an attempt to solve the need for transportation across "the Great American Desert" to California, introduced 75 camels into Texas. Headquartered near present day Kerrville, the military conducted several tests into the Big Bend area. The military personnel were recalled at the outbreak of the Civil War, abandoning the camels. **ATASCOSA COUNTY** Named for: derived from the Spanish word meaning "boggy". Created: 1856 (out of Bexar County). Organized: 1856. County Seat: Navatasco (1856-1858); Pleasanton (1858-present). Major Events: Juan Jose Antonio Navarro, signer of the Texas Declaration of Independence and member of the Texas Constitutional Convention, donated the land on which the first county seat was located. **BANDERA COUNTY** Named for: Bandera Mountains in northern part of county

("Bandera" is a Spanish word meaning "banner" or "flag"). Created: 1856 (from Bexar and Uvalde Counties). Organized: 1856. County Seat: Bandera. Major Events: A colony of Mormons settled in the county in 1854 and in 1855 Polish families arrived to work in the saw mill. **BROWN COUNTY** Named for: Captain Henry S. Brown, a trader with the Indians and delegate to the Texas Convention of 1832-1833. Created: 1856 (out of Comanche and Travis Counties). Organized: 1858. County Seat: Brownwood. Major Events: Between 1880 and 1900 farmers clashed with cattle ranchers. Lake Brownwood Dam was built in 1931 and opened up a large area to irrigated truck farming. Oil production began in 1917. **COMANCHE COUNTY** Named for: the Comanche Indians. Created: 1856 (out of Coryell and Bosque Counties). Organized: 1856. County Seat: Cora (1856-1859); Comanche (1859-present). Major Events: Although the area was included in the Mexican government's land grant to Stephen F. Austin, the first settlement was not established until 1854 with the arrival of four families. Growth and development were delayed from 1857 to 1873 due to numerous Indian raids. **ERATH COUNTY** Named for: George B. Erath, a figure in the Texas Revolution and member of the Texas Legislature who later fought in the Civil War. Created: 1856 (out of Bosque and Coryell Counties). Organized: 1856. County Seat: Stephenville. Major Events: Permanent settlers arrived in Stephenville in 1854. Cattle raising was the main occupation until the railroad arrived and land was enclosed in the 1880s. **JACK COUNTY** Named for: William H. and Patrick C. Jack, leaders in the struggle for Texan Independence. William H. Jack served as Secretary of State for the Republic of Texas and was a member of both the House of Representatives and the Senate of the Republic of Texas. Created: 1856 (out of Cooke County). Organized: 1857. County Seat: Jacksboro (originally known as Lost Creek, the town's name was changed to Mesquiteville in 1856, to Jacksborough in 1858 and to Jacksboro in 1899). Major Events: Settlement began in 1854 and by 1860 the county's population had reached 1,688 but declined during the Civil War because of Indian hostilities and absence of military protection. Indian chiefs Satanta and Big Tree were tried in Jacksborough after the Salt Creek Massacre of 1871. The railroad reached the county seat in 1898. **KERR COUNTY** Named for: James Kerr, one of Stephen F. Austin's "Old Three Hundred" colonists, member of the Conventions of 1832 and 1833 and member of the House of Representatives of the Republic of Texas. Created: 1856 (out of Bexar Land District No. 2). Organized: 1856. County Seat: Kerrville (1856-1860), originally known as Brownsborough); Comfort (1860-1862); Kerrville (1862-present). Major Events: The first attempt to settle the area occurred in the early 1840s but Indian hostilities led to a temporary abandonment of the project. Indian hostilities continued to be a problem until the late 1870s. **LAMPASAS COUNTY** Named for: the Lampasas River (Lampasas in Spanish for "lillies"). Created: 1856 (out of Bell and Travis Counties). Organized: 1856. County Seat: Lampasas (formerly known as Burleson). Major Events: One of the earliest settlers was Moses Hughes in 1853. In 1856 Lampasas was a stage stop for trappers, hunters and cattleman. The railroad arrived in 1882 and population increased therafter. **LIVE OAK COUNTY** Named for: the live oak groves in the area. Created: 1856 (out of Nueces and San Patricio Counties). Organized: 1856. County Seat: Oakville (1856-1919); George West (1919-present). Major Events: The area was included in an impresario grant to John McMullen and James McGloin who brought in Irish settlers. Santa Anna crossed the area on his way to the Alamo on the old Mexican oxcart road from Brownsville to San Antonio. The railroad first reached the county in 1919. **LLANO COUNTY** Named for: the surrounding plains (llano is Spanish for "plains"). Created: 1856 (out of Bexar and Gillespie Counties). Organized: 1856. County Seat: Llano. Major Events: In 1845 John O.

CHRONOLOGICAL HISTORY OF TEXAS

Meusebach negotiated a treaty with the Comanches who agreed not to molest settlers in the area in exchange for presents. The first settlement was established in 1847 and others followed in the 1850s. Most settlers were farmers or stock raisers who owned their own land and worked it themselves. There were only 23 slaves in the county before 1860. Indians became troublesome with the coming of the Civil War and raided the area until being defeated in the Packsaddle Mountain Fight in 1873. An iron mining boom brought sudden prosperity in 1886 which lasted until around 1893. **McCULLOCH COUNTY** Named for: Ben McCulloch, soldier in the battle of San Jacinto, member of the Congress of the Republic of Texas, Commander of a Texas Ranger company in the Mexican War and Confederate General during the Civil War killed at the battle of Elk Horn, March 7, 1862. Created: 1856 (out of Bexar County). Organized: 1876. County Seat: Brady (originally Brady City). Major Events: John O. Meusebach made the first attempt to settle the area in 1847 but Indian troubles prevented permanent settlement. By the 1870s the area had been cleared of buffalo and scattered ranches had begun to be established. Railroads and improved roads increased settlement after 1890. **MAVERICK COUNTY** Named for: Samuel A. Maverick, one of the signers of the Texas Declaration of Independence. He represented Bexar County in the Seventh and Eighth Congresses of the Republic and in the Texas State Legislature from 1853-1862. Created: 1856 (out of Kinney County). Organized: 1871. County Seat: Eagle Pass. Major Events: Spanish explorers arrived as early as 1665. The first Mass celebrated on Texas soil was at San Isidro near the present Quemado Valley on May 15, 1675. The last Confederate Flag to fly over the Trans-Mississippi Army was buried by General Joseph Orville Scott while leading his men across the Rio Grande to offer their services to the Mexican Emperor, Maximilian. **PALO PINTO COUNTY** Named for: the Spanish words "palo pinto" mean "painted (or pink) stick". The name was first given to one of the streams in the county. Created: 1856 (out of Bosque and Navarro Counties). Organized: 1857. County Seat: Palo Pinto (formerly known as Golconda). Major Events: The Abner Ashworth Survey in 1840 is believed to be the first Anglo-American survey on this area, where good hunting made it favorite Indian territory. The first settlement was in 1854. The population increased following construction of the Texas and Pacific Railroad across the county in 1880. **SAN SABA COUNTY** Named for: The San Saba River, named by the Spanish. Created: 1856 (out of Bexar County). Organized: 1856. County Seat: Rowe's Land (1856); San Saba (1856-present). Major Events: The first Anglo-American settlement was in 1847. The Fleming San Saba Irrigation Company, chartered in 1875, made farming and ranching profitable. **WISE COUNTY** Named for: Henry A. Wise, a Virginian Senator from 1833 to 1844 and a Brigadier General in the Confederate Army, who supported Texas' annexation to the United States. Created: 1856 (out of Cooke County). Organized: 1856. County Seat: Decatur (formerly called Taylorsville). Major Events: The first white settler arrived in 1854. The first public school opened in 1855. Railroads were constructed through the county in 1882 and 1893. **YOUNG COUNTY** Named for: William C. Young, the first Sheriff in Red River County and delegate from that county to the Convention of 1845. He participated in expeditions against the Indians, fought in the Mexican War and organized and commanded the 11th Texas Regiment of Cavalry, whose operations during the Civil War were mainly against the Indians in what is now Oklahoma. Created: 1856 (out of Bosque and Fannin Counties). Organized: 1856; reorganized in 1874. County Seat: Belknap (1856-1865); Jacksboro (1865-1874); Graham (1874-present). Major Events: The area was explored by the Spanish from 1759 onward. When first organized Young County extended to the New Mexico border. The first school was for 60 students on the Brazos Reservation (then within Young County). The Cattle Raisers Association of Texas was organized at Graham in 1883. Oil production began after the drilling of the Lindy Lou Well in 1917. **DECEMBER 21, 1857** Hardin R. Runnels, Democrat, became Governor of Texas for one term. He defeated Sam Houston who had been away from Texas (in the U.S. Senate). By 1857 hundreds of thousands of new immigrants had arrived in Texas mostly from southern states to the east of Texas. **BEE COUNTY** Named for: General Bernard E. Bee, Texas Secretary of the Treasury, Secretary of State and Secretary of War. Created: 1857 (out of San Patricio, Goliad, Refugio, Live Oak and Karnes Counties). Organized: 1858. County Seat: Beeville (1858-1860); Maryville (1860-present, Maryville was subsequently designated as Beeville on-the-Poesta and is now known as Beeville). Major Events: The railroad reached the county in 1886 and in 1929 oil and gas were discovered. **CLAY COUNTY** Named for: Henry Clay, famous U.S. Orator and statesman from Kentucky. Created: 1857 (out of Cooke County). Organized: 1873. County Seat: Cambridge (1873-1882); Henrietta (1882-present). Major Events: The earliest settlers in the county were ranchers. Oil was discovered in 1902 while a water well was being dug. **MONTAGUE COUNTY** Named for: Daniel Montague, an early Texas Pioneer. Created: 1857 (out of Cooke County). Organized: 1858. County Seat: Montague. Major Events: Visited by French traders and Spanish government officials as early as 1719. A fortified rancheria was successfully defended against a Spanish expedition in 1759 by allied Indians flying a French Flag. The first Anglo-American settlers arrived in 1854. Indian raids continued until 1872. The manufacture of cowboy boots began at Nocona in 1882. **ARCHER COUNTY** Named for: Branch T. Archer, a Revolutionary leader and member of the Texas Congress. Created: 1858 (out of Fannin Land District); Organized: 1880. County Seat: Archer City. Major Events: First railroad arrived in the county in 1890. **BAYLOR COUNTY** Named for: Henry W. Baylor, surgeon for the Texas Rangers. Created: 1858 (out of Fannin County). Organized: 1879. County Seat: Seymour. Major Events: Large ranch companies held most of the land and discouraged the settlement of farmers. In 1906 the discovery of oil brought people to the area. **BLANCO COUNTY** Named for: the Blanco River (Blanco is Spanish for "white"). Created: 1858. Organized: 1858. County Seat: Blanco (1858-1891); Johnson City (1891-present). Major Events: In 1853 Captain James Callahan brought his family and friends to the Blanco Valley. In 1860 large herds of sheep were brought into the area. The county was deeply divided over the Civil War. **CALLAHAN COUNTY** Named for: James H. Callahan, a Texas Ranger. Created: 1858 (out of Bexar, Bosque and Travis Counties). Organized: 1877. County Seat: Belle Plain (1877-1880); Baird (1880-present). Major Events: Hostile Indians delayed settlement although the area had been explored and described by Dr. H.C. Connelly of the Chihuahua Expedition in 1839-1840. The railroad reached the county in 1880. Oil was discovered in 1925. **CHAMBERS COUNTY** Named for: Thomas Jefferson Chambers, who served as Surveyor General of the Mexican state of Coahuila and Texas and as State Attorney helped frame a state judicial code. Created: 1858 (out of Liberty and Jefferson Counties). Organized: 1858. County Seat: Wallisville (1858-1908); Anahuac (1908-present). Major Events: Permanent settlement began in 1821 when the Spanish established a fortress at Anahuac and allowed American colonists to enter. The discovery of oil near Hankamer in 1935 brought new industry and an increase in population. **COLEMAN COUNTY** Named for: Robert M. Coleman, a signer of the Texas Declaration of Independence, Aide de Camp of General Sam Houston at the battle of San Jacinto and a Texas Ranger. Created: 1858 (out of Travis and Brown Counties). Organized: 1876. County Seat: Coleman. Major Events: An extension of the Sante Fe Railroad crossed the county in 1886 and led to an economic boom. The first oil well in the county was drilled in 1904. Federal highways across the county follow the Jingle Bob Cattle Trail and the Van Dorn Miltary Road, which followed old buffalo trails. **CONCHO COUNTY** Named for: the Concho River (Concho is a Spanish word which means "shell" and probably refers to the large number of mussel shells found in the river's bed). Created: 1858 (out of Bexar County). Organized: 1879. County Seat: Paint Rock. Major Events: Spanish explorers visited the area several times in the seventeenth and eighteenth centuries and legends about pearls on the Concho River circulated. A colonization contract which included the area was granted to Henry F. Fisher and Burchard Miller by the Republic of Texas in 1842 but control of the area by Comanche Indians delayed any significant settlement until the 1870s. **DIMMIT COUNTY** Named for: Philip Dimmitt (the statute creating the county misspelled Dimitt's name), captain of the troops at Goliad after its capture. He took poison in 1841 at the siege of Bexar rather than go to a Mexican prison. Created: 1858 (out of Maverick, Webb, Bexar and Uvalde Counties). Organized: 1880. County Seat: Carrizo Springs. Major Events: The first attempted settlement from the United States was made by John Townsend, a Black from Nacogdoches. His colony was driven out by Indians. The first permanent settlement was at Carizzo Springs in 1865. After 1890 farming developed when artesian wells brought irrigation to the county. **DUVAL COUNTY** Named for: B.H., J.C. and T.H. Duval, three brothers who were early Texas settlers. B.H. was killed in the massacre of Goliad, from which J.C. escaped. T.H. was away studying law during the Texas Revolution and subsequently became a District Judge. Created: 1858 (out of Live Oak, Nueces and Starr Counties). Organized: 1876. County Seat: San Diego. Major Events: The earliest settlement was by Mexican ranchers in the early 1800s. In 1879 the railroad reached the county. Oil and gas were discovered in 1903. **EASTLAND COUNTY** Named for: Captain William M. Eastland who fought in the battle of San Jacinto, served in the Texas Rangers and was captured by Mexican troops during the Mier Expedition. He drew the first black bean on March 25, 1843 and was shot the same day. Created: 1858 (out of Bosque, Travis and Coryell Counties). Organized: 1873. County Seat: Merriman (1873-1875); Eastland (1875-present). Major Events: The census of 1860 reported 99 farmers in the county. Oil was discovered near Ranger in 1917. **EDWARDS COUNTY** Named for: Hayden Edwards, founder of a settlement at Nacogdoches. Created: 1858 (out of Bexar District). Organized: 1883. County Seat: Leakey (1883-1891); Rock Springs (1891-present). Major Events: The earliest recorded exploration of the area was in 1675. Indians and the lack of transportation delayed settlement. **FRIO COUNTY** Named for: the Frio River (from the Spanish meaning "cold"). Created: 1858 (out of Atascosa, Bexar and Uvalde Counties). Organized: 1871. County Seat: Frio Town (1871-1883); Pearsal (1883-present). Major Events: The first visitor to the area was probably Rene Robert Cavelier, a member of the La Salle Colony. Santa Anna's army rested at a crossing of the Frio River in the area on its way to the battle of the Alamo. The last Indian raid in the county occurred in 1877. In 1878 the first land was fenced. In 1881 the railroad passed through the county. **HAMILTON COUNTY** Named for: James Hamilton, Governor of South Carolina and diplomatic agent for the Republic of Texas who concluded favorable treaties with the Netherlands and England. Created: 1858 (out of Bosque, Comanche and Lampasas Counties). Organized: 1858. County Seat: Hamilton. Major Events: The Robert Carter family made the first permanent settlement in the area in 1854. The first store opened the following year. Indian attacks continued after the Civil War. The railroad crossed the extreme northeast corner of the county in 1880. **HARDEMAN COUNTY** Named for: Bailey and Thomas J. Hardeman. Bailey

helped draft and signed the Texas Declaration of Independence. Thomas was Chief Justice under the Republic and a State Representative thereafter. Created: 1858 (out of Fannin County; recreated in 1876). Organized: 1884. County Seat: Margaret (1884-1890; originally called Argurita); Quanah (1890-present). Major Events: Indian control of the area and lack of transportation delayed settlement until after the Civil War and Reconstruction. Before 1884 the only inhabitants were buffalo hunters and a few ranchers. The townsite of Quanah was laid out during an 1885 railroad survey. **HARDIN COUNTY** Named for: Augustine Blackburn, Benjamin W., Milton A., Franklin and William Hardin, early Texas pioneers. Created: 1858 (out of Jefferson and Liberty Counties). Organized: 1858. County Seat: Hardin (1858-1887); Kountze (1887-present). Major Events: The area was embraced in Lorenzo de Zavala's colony, which was given grants for settlement in 1835 by the Mexican government, but he made no effort to establish communities. By 1832 an Anglo-American settlement had been established at Providence, eight miles north of present Kountze. **HASKELL COUNTY** Named for: Charles Ready Haskell, soldier in the Texas Army killed in the Goliad Massacre. Created: 1858 (out of Milam and Fannin Counties). Organized: 1885. County Seat: Haskell (known as Rice Springs until 1885, when the Post Office Department changed its name to Haskell). Major Events: Indian hostility delayed settlement until 1876, when ranch headquarters were established in the county. **JONES COUNTY** Named for: Anson Jones, Apothecary General of the Army of Texas, member of the Congress of Texas and last President of the Republic of Texas. Created: 1858 (out of Bexar and Bosque Counties); recreated in 1876. Organized: 1881. County Seat: Anson (originally called Jones City). Major Events: The earliest settlement occurred in 1851 with the establishment of Fort Phantom Hill, which was abandoned in 1854 and re-established in 1872. The first wire fence in the county was erected in 1880. The railroad crossed the county in 1900. **KIMBLE COUNTY** Named for: Lieutenant George C. Kimbell (Kimble or Kimball as variant spellings are recorded), died defending the Alamo. Created: 1858 (out of Bexar Territory). Organized: 1876. County Seat: Kimbleville (1876-1877); Junction (1877-present; originally called Junction City). Major Events: Spanish explorers visited the area several times in the eighteenth century, but it was Apache country and permanent settlement did not begin until the late 1850s. Sheep were introduced in 1862 and racing horses in 1869. The first school was established in 1866 and the first store in 1873. Indian raids and massacres harassed and in some cases destroyed many settements until the early 1870s. The last Indians were expelled in 1874, but the area remained a haven for outlaws until the Texas Rangers rounded them up in 1877 and held court under a live oak tree in Kimbleville. **KNOX COUNTY** Named for: Henry Knox, Secretary of War in George Washington's first cabinet. Created: 1858 (out of Bexar and Young Counties) recreated in 1876 and again in 1879. Organized: 1886. County Seat: Benjamin. Major Events: Captain Robert D. Goree opened up the county to agriculture in the early 1880s by securing the migrations from older states and other Texas counties. The railroads first reached the county in 1905. **LA SALLE COUNTY** Named for: Rene Robert Cavelier, Sieur de la Salle, French explorer who established Fort St. Louis in the Matagorda Bay area of Texas in February, 1685, giving France a claim to Texas, and was murdered by his own men in March, 1687. Created: 1858 (out of Bexar County). Organized: 1880. County Seat: La Salle (1880-1882); Cotulla (1882-present). Major Events: The area was crossed by Alonso de Leon in 1689 and 1690 in his fourth and fifth expeditions to locate Fort St. Louis. The first Anglo-American settlement came with the establishment of Fort Ewell in 1852. Seven persons were killed in the last recorded Indian raid in the county, which occurred in April, 1878. Oil was

CHRONOLOGICAL HISTORY OF TEXAS

discovered in the late 1930s. **McMULLEN COUNTY** Named for: John McMullen, leader with James McGloin of a group of 58 Irish colonists to Texas in 1829, member and subsequently President Protempore of the General Council during the Texas Revolution, San Antonio alderman and merchant murdered by an unknown assassin on January 21, 1853. Created: 1858 (out of Atascosa, Bexar and Live Oak Counties). Organized: 1877. County Seat: Tilden. Major Events: The area was probably crossed by Alonso de Leon in 1689 and 1690 in his fourth and fifth expeditions in search of Fort St. Louis. The inaccessibility of the thicket area delayed settlement and the activities of bandits, combined with the lack of population, led to the abandonment of the county's 1862 organization. By the late 1870s vigilante committees had driven out the outlaws and the fugitives from Mexico. Ranching was the only occupation until around 1900, when there were 91 farms in the county. Natural gas and some oil had been discovered by 1919. **MASON COUNTY** Named for: Fort Mason. Created: 1858 (out of Gillespie County). Organized: 1858. County Seat: Mason (1861-present). Major Events: First settlement was around 1846. German settlers arrived in 1848 led by John O. Meusebach. A dispute over cattle stealing in 1875 is popularly known as the "Mason County War". **MENARD COUNTY** Named for: Michel Menard, a French-Canadian Indian trader who was a signer of the Texas Declaration of Independence. Created: 1858 (out of Bexar County). Organized: 1871. County Seat: Menard. Major Events: Area was explored by Francisco Vasquez de Coronado in 1541. The Presidio of San Luis de las Amarillas, was established in 1757 to protect San Saba de la Santa Cruz mission, was abandoned in 1768. First permanent Anglo-American settlement was at Menard in 1867. **RUNNELS COUNTY** Named for: Hiram George Runnels, a Mississippi legislator who moved to Texas in 1842 and was a delegate to the 1845 Convention. Created: 1858 (out of Bexar and Travis Counties). Organized: 1880. County Seat: Ballinger. Major Events: William Guest was probably the first settler in 1862. Cattlemen arrived in the 1870s and the railroad was built across the county in the 1880s. **SHACKLEFORD COUNTY** Named for: Dr. John Shackleford, who raised a company known as the Red Rovers to fight in the Texas Revolution. Created: 1858 (out of Bosque County). Organized: 1874. County Seat: Fort Griffin (1874-1875); Albany (1875-present). Major Events: The first permanent settler was J.C. Lynch in 1858. Fort Griffin, established in 1867, served as R.S. MacKenzie's base for his Indian campaigns. In 1913 oil was discovered. **STEPHENS COUNTY** Named for: originally named Buchanan County after the U.S. President James Buchanan. Renamed in 1861 in honor of the Vice President of the Confederacy, Alexander H. Stephens. Created: 1858 (out of Bosque County). Organized: 1876. County Seat: Breckenridge. Major Events: John R. Baylor was the first White settler in 1857. Indian raids continued at least until 1871. Coal was first mined in 1878 and oil production began in 1916. **TAYLOR COUNTY** Named for: the Taylor family, who were members of the Robertson Colony. Created: 1858 (out of Bexar and Travis Counties). Organized: 1878. County Seat: Buffalo Gap (1878-1880); Abilene (1880-present). Major Events: Clabe W. Merchant, "the father of Abilene" and other ranchers wintered cattle at the head of Elm Creek near Buffalo Gap in the early 1860s. Abilene was founded in 1880 following the construction of the Texas and Pacific Railroad in northern Taylor County. **THROCKMORTON COUNTY** Named for: Dr. William E. Throckmorton, an early settler of Collin County. Probably as a compliment to his son, James W. Throckmorton, at that time a Texas Senator, later to be a Governor of Texas. Created: 1858 (out of Fannin County). Organized: 1879. County Seat: Throckmorton (1879). Major Events: Throckmorton County was originally part of the Red River Municipality under the Mexican administration. Organization was delayed until the removal

of the Comanche Reservation in 1859 and the Civil War. Lieutenant Gibson's house, built in 1856 was at that time the last house between Texas and settlements in New Mexico. **WILBARGER COUNTY** Named for: Josiah and Mathias Wilbarger, brothers who settled in Stephen F. Austin's colony ten miles from modern Bastrop. Josiah Wilbarger was scalped by Indians while on a surveying trip near Austin. He survived and lived another 12 years. Created: 1858 (out of Bexar Territory). Organized: 1881. County Seat: Vernon. Major Events: Wilbarger was part of Peter's Colony until 1858, but there were no White residents until 1878 when the threat from Indians had diminished. Doan's Crossing and Store, a trading post, was established in 1878. **WICHITA COUNTY** Named for: the Wichita River, which takes its name from the Wichita Indian tribe. The meaning of the word is obscure: suggestions include "big arbor" (Choctaw); "waist deep" or "fond of corn" (Comanche); "people with scattered camps" (Osage); or "men from the north" (Wichita). Created: 1858 (out of Cooke Land District). Organized: 1882. County Seat: Wichita Falls. Major Events: The area was first visited by Pedro Vial and Jose Mares in 1786. Anglo-American expeditions crossed the county from 1841 onward. The first White settler was Mabel Gilbert in 1856, though Indian attacks continued at least until 1874. The county was promoted as early as 1872 as being rich in copper, iron and coal and readily accessible by rail, but the claims were false. However, the existence of oil was discovered in 1905. Oil production led to the "Burk Boom" between 1918 and 1920 followed by the first proration of oil in Texas and a prolonged dispute with Oklahoma over oil rights in the Red River flood plain. **ZAPATA COUNTY** Named for: Colonel Antonio Zapata, a pioneer Mexican rancher in Texas. Created: 1858 (out of Starr and Webb Counties). Organized: 1858. County Seat: Zapata (formerly Carrizo). Major Events: The area, then inhabited by Carrizo, Tepemaca and Borrado Indians, was first explored by a party led by Captain Miguel de la Garza Falcon in 1747. The first Spanish settlers arrived in 1750 and their descendents were active in the struggle for Mexican independence from Spain. The Texan claim to this land was assured under the Treaty of Guadalupe Hidalgo in 1848. **ZAVALA COUNTY** Named for: Lorenzo de Zavala, Mexican empresario and signer of the Texas Declaration of Independence. Created: 1858 (out of Uvalde and Maverick Counties). Organized: 1884. County Seat: Batesville (1884-1924); Crystal City (1928-present). Major Events: Zavala County was explored by the Spanish from 1691 onward. The first permanent settlements occurred in the late 1860s. Indian raids continued until 1878. In the 1880s land was acquired by large ranchers who fenced in the previous open range. Zavala County was attached for judicial purposes to Uvalde, Maverick and Frio Counties before it was separately organized. **1859** Samuel Houston, Democrat, became Governor. The first recorded State Fair of Texas took place in Dallas. **1860** Population: 604,215. There were some 43,000 "foreigners" from Mexico, Germany, Poland, Czechoslovakia and France. San Antonio had about 8,000 people and Galveston 4,000. Blacks held in slavery amounted to 182,000 persons. **MARION COUNTY** Named for: Francis Marion, a General in the American Revolutionary War. Created: 1860 (out of Cass County). Organized: 1860. County Seat: Jefferson. Major Events: The area was traversed by Domingo Teran de los Rios in 1691. Jefferson was founded in 1836 and developed as an important river port, rivalling Shreveport (Louisiana) and Galveston. An iron foundry established in 1848 supplied the Confederate Army during the Civil War. The assassination of A.J. Smith, a carpetbagger administrator led to the imposition of martial law and the opening of a military prison, followed by the formation of the Citizens White Party. Oil was discovered in 1938. **WILSON COUNTY** Named for: James C. Wilson, a member of the Mier Expedition. Created: 1860 (out of Bexar and Karnes Counties).

Organized: 1860. County Seat: Sutherland Springs (1860-1867); Lodi (1867-1871); Sutherland Springs (1871); Lodi (1871-1885); Floresville (1885-present). Major Events: Settlement began sometime before 1830 when Francisco Flores de Abreyo established his hacienda about six miles from modern Floresville. Between 1850 and 1860 the area was settled by German and Polish immigrants and planters from southern states. the county was officially renamed Cibolo in 1869, but the name was never adopted.

UNDER THE CONFEDERATE FLAG 1861-1865

FEBRUARY 1, 1861 Governor Houston attempted to block the secession of Texas from the Union by refusing to call a special session of the Legislature to authorize a convention. Secessionists addressed the people of Texas on December 3, 1860 and requested a January 8 election of delegates for a January 28 convention. Hoping to prevent drastic action, Governor Houston called for a special session on January 21. The Legislature validated the convention but stipulated that any decision had to be submitted to a referendum. On January 29 the Legislature voted 152 to 6 to secede and on February 23 Texas voters approved this secession resolution 46,129 to 14,697 (13 counties voted no to secession). **MARCH 16, 1861** The Secession Convention united Texas with the Confederate States of America on March 5 and modified the Texas state government to conform to the Confederacy. Governor Houston opposed this and refused to take the oath to the Confederacy. The Convention passed an ordinance on March 16 deposing Governor Houston. Lieutenant Governor Edward Clark was then required to take over the state's leadership, serving until November 7, 1861. **NOVEMBER 7, 1861** Francis R. Lubbock, Democrat, became Governor of the Confederate State of Texas. He resigned from office on November 5, 1863. **KENDALL COUNTY** Named for: George Wilkins Kendall, Texas pioneer, journalist and herdsman. Created: 1862 (out of Kerr and Blanco Counties). Organized: 1862. County Seat: Boerne. Major Events: The county's Angora goat industry was established by George Wilkins Kendall. The first school in the county opened in Boerne in 1866. **SEPTEMBER 8, 1863** The Battle of Sabine Pass between the Union forces commanded by Major General W.B. Franklin and the Confederates led by Lieutenant Richard W. Dowling ended with a Union retreat which spared Texas from a military campaign and occupation on Texas soil. **NOVEMBER 5, 1863** Pendleton Murray, Democrat, became Governor of the Confederate State of Texas. He served until the end of the Confederacy. **MAY 13, 1865** The last battle of the Civil War was fought in Texas at Palmito, over a month after General Lee's surrender at Appomattox. **MAY 29, 1865** President Andrew Johnson by proclamation furthered the Reconstruction of the southern states including Texas. On June 17 he issued a proclamation establishing a Provisional Government in Texas. Amnesty was granted to all ex-Confederates who would take the oath of allegiance to the United States, except for certain persons who would have to apply for a presidential pardon. **JUNE 17, 1865** Andrew J. Hamilton became provisional governor of Texas. Serving until August 9, 1866. **JUNE 19, 1865** General Gordon Granger arrived at Galveston with 1,800 men and issued a proclamation that all slaves were free. This day is now known in Texas as "Juneteenth". After hostilities ended in April, Texas had no central government and the Military Division of the Southwest was assigned to command. As Reconstruction progressed there was obvious reluctance on the part of many Texans to comply. John H. Reagan, who had served in the U.S. Congress and in the Confederate Cabinet, urged compliance from his prison cell where he was held as a prisoner of war. He feared that the federal government might impose military rule. **SEPTEMBER 22, 1865** the first national bank was chartered in Texas: the First National Bank of Galveston. **1866** the range cattle industry spread over the plains from the Rio Grande-Nueces River Valleys where abandoned livestock from the days of the Spanish ranchers had formed herds. Those wild Longhorn cattle were spread across the open rangeland by cattlemen and were the source of many legends. Cowboys drove the Longhorns on drives to markets from 1866 to 1880. Jesse Chisholm led the first drive from Texas to Kansas in 1866. Also in 1866 the first producing oil well was dug by Lynis T. Barrett in Melrose. **AUGUST 2, 1866** President Johnson proclaimed the insurrection in Texas over and recognized the new government. Provisional Governor A.J. Hamilton had convened a convention in February which agreed to abolish slavery, adopted limited civil rights for the freed men and revised the state constitution to conform to the United States. At the polls the people of Texas accepted the changes, elected James W. Throckmorton, Democrat, as Governor and elected a new Legislature which took office on August 6. James W. Throckmorton took the oath of office on August 9 and served until August 8, 1867. **OCTOBER 2, 1866** The Legislature refused to ratify the 14th Amendment to the U.S. Constitution, a requirement for readmission into the United States. **HOOD COUNTY** Named for: General John Bell Hood, Confederate officer during the Civil War. Created: 1866 (out of Johnson County). Organized: 1866. County Seat: Granbury. Major Events: Comanche and Kiowa raids delayed settlement until 1853 or 1854 and continued to be a problem as late as 1872, when Long Creek Valley was invaded. **AUGUST 8, 1867** Elisha M. Pease became Provisional Governor, vacating office on September 30, 1869. Texas was without a governor until the following January and Texas and Louisiana were administered jointly as the Fifth U.S. Military District. **FEBRUARY, 1868** For the first time Blacks voted in Texas. **JANUARY 2, 1869** At the Constitutional Convention of 1868-1869 E.J. Davis, President of the Convention, announced that in accordance with the Annexation Treaty, which gave Texas the right to divide into four additional states, a constitution for the state of West Texas had been prepared. Many of the people in West Texas had strongly opposed secession and the Civil War and wanted to be readmitted to the Union as a separate state. A bill introduced in the U.S. Congress for admission of the state of West Texas was stalled in the Committee on Reconstruction and never came to a vote. **FEBRUARY 8, 1869** The Constitutional Convention ended without voting on a new constitution which would conform with the requirements mandated by the U.S. Congress in the Reconstruction Acts. The military commander of the state appointed a committee to complete a draft. **NOVEMBER/DECEMBER, 1869** The people of Texas ratified the new Constitution in hope of ending the military rule. State officials and U.S. Congresssmen were elected following ratification. **SAN JACINTO COUNTY** Named for: The Battle of San Jacinto. Created: 1869 (out of Liberty, Montgomery, Polk and Walker Counties). Organized: 1870. County Seat: Cold Spring. Major Events: The county was best known as the site of Raven Hill, plantation home of Sam Houston. The first post office was established in 1847. The Cold Spring Female College opened in 1853. **1870** Population: 818,579. The five largest counties were Harris, Washington, Fayette, Caldwell and Rusk. **JANUARY 8, 1870** Edmund J. Davis, Republican, became Governor and served until January 15, 1874. **DELTA COUNTY** Named for: Its geographical shape, which resembles the Greek letter delta. Created: 1870 (out of Hopkins and Lamar Counties). Organized: 1870. County Seat: Cooper. Major Events: Settlement began in the early 1840s. The woody section of the county remained a hideout for outlaws until the 1870s. By 1890 the county had 845 farms, with cotton the chief crop. **RAINS COUNTY** Named for: Emory Rains, legislator for the Republic of Texas and the State of Texas. Created: 1870 (out of Hopkins, Hunt and Wood Counties). Organized: 1870. County Seat: Emory. Major Events: The first Anglo-American settler was J. H. Hooker who

CHRONOLOGICAL HISTORY OF TEXAS

established a mill on the Sabine River in the 1840s, serving farmers from as far away as Dallas. Emory is the birthplace of the Farmers' Cooperative and Educational Union of America, organized in 1904. **FEBRUARY, 1870** The Legislature ratified both the 13th and 14th Amendments to the U.S. Constitution as required for readmission into the United States. **MARCH 30, 1870** Texas was granted readmission to the Union and to representation in the U.S. Congress provided that the State Legislature would give indication that it would not amend the State Constitution in the future to deny Blacks the rights to vote, hold public office and have educational privileges.

UNDER THE FLAG OF THE UNITED STATES 1870-1984
First the fabled Longhorn, then black gold started the legendary land of Texas on its climb to greatness. **SEPTEMBER 22-25, 1871** Delegates from 94 counties met in Austin in a taxpayer's convention. Upset with what they considered exorbitant expenditures, enormous taxes and the unconstitutionality of many of the acts of the Davis administration, committee reports were adopted by the convention on January 25, 1872 registering discontent with Reconstruction. **ARANSAS COUNTY** Named for: Rio Nuestra Senora de Aranzazu, a name derived from a Spanish palace. Created: 1871 (out of Refugio County). Organized: 1871. County Seat: Rockport. Major Events: Discovery of oil in 1936. **PECOS COUNTY** Named for: the Pecos River. Origin and meaning of "pecos" is unknown, thought Mexicans referred to it as Puerco (dirty or swinish river). Created: 1871 (out of Presidio County). Organized: 1875. County Seat: Fort Stockton. Major Events: Settlement was late because of the Indian Wars. Fort Stockton, the first permanent settlement, was set up in 1859 to guard the San Antonio to San Diego Mail Route. **JUNE, 1872** The first major labor strike in Texas involved the Houston and Texas Central Railway. **1873** The National Grange was formed in Texas as an effort to combat low farm prices given the oversupply of agricultural products. By 1874 there were 45,000 Grange members in Texas. The Grange achieved railroad regulation, the repeal of the farm produce tax and a deep water port for Texas, but was unable to remove the agricultural depression caused by surpluses. David Boyle invented the ammonia compression refrigeration system at Jefferson, Texas. **GREGG COUNTY** Named for: General John Gregg, Texas Judge, member of Secession Convention and officer in the Confederate Army killed during the Civil War. Created: 1873 (out of Rusk County). Organized: 1873. County Seat: Longview. Major Events: the area was cleared of Indians in 1838 and settlement thereafter was rapid since the area was located on the old military road from the Red River to the interior of Texas. Many wealthy families with slaves entered the area in the 1850s and an aristocratic farming society developed. Further development was stimulated in the 1870s by the arrival of the railroads. The county was the southern terminus of the "Big Inch Oil Line" built to ease oil transportation for World War II. **ROCKWALL COUNTY** Named for: the subterranean dike or "rock wall". Created: 1873 (out of Kaufman County). Organized: 1873. County Seat: Rockwall. Major Events: Settlement by Anglo-Americans commenced in 1846 when the county formed the northwestern portion of Kaufman County. **WALLER COUNTY** Named for: Edwin Waller, who attended the Consultation in 1835 and was a signer of the Texas Declaration of Independence in 1836. He was elected the first Mayor of Austin in 1840 and was later a member of the Secession Convention. Created: 1873 (out of Austin and Grimes Counties). Organized: 1873. County Seat: Hempstead. Major Events: The area was part of Stephen F. Austin's first colony and the first settlement occurred around 1821 under a grant made to Jared E. Gorce. The county was the site of the "Runaway Scrape". Prairie View State Normal and Industrial College for Blacks (later Prairie View University) was

established near Hempstead in 1876. **1874** Richard Coke, Democrat, became Governor. He resigned December 1, 1876. The first municipal library was chartered at Galveston. **CAMP COUNTY** Named for: John L. Camp, a Colonel in the Confederate Army, a Texas Senator and a District Judge. Created: 1874 (out of Upshur County). Organized: 1874. County Seat: Pittsburg. Major Events: Perhaps the first settlement was by Major W.H. Pitts in 1854 at Pittsburgh. Two railroads joined at Pittsburgh in 1876 and 1877. **LEE COUNTY** Named for: General Robert E. Lee, Confederate officer. Created: 1874 (out of Milam Land District). Organized: 1874. County Seat: Giddings. Major Events: The majority of the early Anglo-American settlers came from southern states and brought their slaves with them. About 500 Wends (an ethnic group of Slavic origin) bought a section of land along Rabbs Creek in 1854. There are also sizable German communities in the southern part of the county. **TOM GREEN COUNTY** Named for: General Thomas Green of the Texas Army. Created: 1874 (out of Bexar County). Organized: 1874. County Seat: Ben Ficklin (1874-1882); San Angelo (1882-present). Major Events: The original Tom Green County extended to the Pecos River and covered 12,500 square miles. Twelve other counties have been created from this area. R.F. Tankersley, bringing 700 Longhorn cattle was the first White settler in 1864. Fort Concho was established in 1867 as was J. DeWitt's "Over the River" Trading Post (later San Angelo). Ben Ficklin, the first county seat, was almost completely washed away and 65 people were drowned in 1882. **CROCKETT COUNTY** Named for: David Crockett, who, with his "Tennessee Boys," was killed defending the Alamo. Created: 1875 (out of Bexar County). Organized: 1891. County Seat: Ozona. Major Events: Located in Apache-controlled territory, Crockett County was sparsely settled until U.S. troops were stationed in frontier posts following the Civil War. The Texas Legislature provided three battalions of Texas Rangers for the area's protection in September, 1866. **FRANKLIN COUNTY** Named for: the statute creating the county does not specify for whom the county is named, but it is generally believed to be Benjamin Cromwell Franklin, the first judicial officer of the Republic of Texas, who as Judge of the Second Judicial District held the first court in Fort Bend County and served as a Justice on the first Supreme Court of the Republic. Created: 1875 (out of Titus County). Organized: 1875. County Seat: Mount Vernon. Major Events: The first settlers arrived from Tennessee in 1836. The railroad reached the county in 1876. In 1945 Franklin county led the Counties of Texas in the production of corn and cane syrup. **MORRIS COUNTY** Named for: William Wright Morris, Texas jurist, legislator and railroad promoter. Created: 1875 (out of Titus County). Organized: 1875. County Seat: Daingerfield. Major Events: Believed to have been explored by Luis de Moscoso as early as 1542. The Republic established Daingerfield as the capital of Paschal County and settlement started after 1836. Daingerfield remained the county seat when Morris County was created, shortly before the completion of the East Line and Red River Railroad brought an increase in population. **SOMERVELL COUNTY** Named for: Alexander Somervell who fought in the Battle of San Jacinto, served as David Burnet's Secretary of War in 1836, represented Colorado and Austin Counties in the First and Second Congresses of the Republic and organized the Somervell expedition. Created: 1875 (out of Hood and Johnson Counties). Organized: 1875. County Seat: Glen Rose. Major Events: The first settlement was made by L.B. McClanahan in 1859 at Springton, followed by George Barnard's Barnard's Mill (on the site of the present Glen Rose). **FEBRUARY 15, 1876** The present Constitution of Texas was ratified by the voters of Texas 136,606 to 56,562. Attempts to revise and replace this Constitution in 1919 and 1975 failed. **OCTOBER 4, 1876** Texas A & M University opened its first school year. **DECEMBER 1, 1876** Richard B. Hubbard,

Democrat, was elected Governor for one term. **ANDREWS COUNTY** Named for: Richard Andrews, member of the Texas Revolutionary Army who died at the battle of Concepcion, October 28, 1835. Created: 1876 (out of Bexar County). Organized: 1910. County Seat: Andrews. Major Events: Discovery of petroleum at Deep Rock Pool in 1929 led to the beginning of petroleum production in 1930. **ARMSTRONG COUNTY** Named for: a pioneer family. Created: 1876 (out of Bexar District). Organized: 1890. County Seat: Claude. Major Events: After the Indians were driven out in 1873-74 Charles Goodnight and John G. Adair founded the huge J A Ranch. **BAILEY COUNTY** Named for: Peter J. Bailey, one of the men killed defending the Alamo. Created: 1876 (out of Bexar District). Organized: 1917. County Seat: Muleshoe. Major Events: Discovery of shallow wells suitable for irrigation in the 1930s doubled the amount of cropland in 10 years. **BORDEN COUNTY** Named for: Gail Borden, Jr., a pioneer patriot, inventor and editor. Created: 1876. Organized: 1892. County Seat: Gail. Major Events: Ranchers extended their activities into the county in 1876 and in 1902 a land boom brought in many new inhabitants, but battles with cattlemen prevented farmers from changing this cowman's county. **BRISCOE COUNTY** Named for: Andrew Briscoe, who fought in the Texas Revolution, signed the Texas Declaration of Independence and promoted the railroads. Created: 1876 (out of Bexar County). Organized: 1892. County Seat: Silverton. Major Events: One of the last strongholds of the Indians in Texas, the Land Act of 1887 opened the county to ranchers and farmers. Geologists have found the early remains of a highly civilized, Pre-Columbian people. **CARSON COUNTY** Named for: Samuel P. Carson, Republic of Texas Secretary of State and a signer of the Texas Declaration of Independence. Created: 1876 (out of Bexar County). Organized: 1888. County Seat: Panhandle. Major Events: Coronado explored the area in 1541 and Mexican farmers and ranchers settled there in the early 1800's. The largest natural gas field in the world was discovered in Carson County. **CASTRO COUNTY** Named for: Henri Castro, who established Castro's Colony on the Medina River in 1844 and was the Consul General from Texas to France. Created: 1876 (out of the Bexar District). Organized: 1891. County Seat: Dimmitt. Major Events: William R. Shafter led the expedition in 1875 which ended Indian control in this area. The region was known as "the Great American Desert." **CHILDRESS COUNTY** Named for: George Campbell Childress, author of the Texas Declaration of Independence. Created: 1876 (out of Bexar Territory and Young Land District). Organized: 1887. County Seat: Childress. Major Events: As late as 1886 the county was chiefly occupied by four cattle ranching operations. Farmers began to appear in the fall of 1886 settling in dugouts, in one of which the county's first church was organized. **COCHRAN COUNTY** Named for: Robert Cochran, who was killed defending the Alamo in 1836. Created: 1876 (out of Bexar County). Organized: 1924. County Seat: Morton. Major Events: Settlement was delayed by lack of railroads, Indian hostilities and the distance from building materials and markets. Oil prospectors began to drill in the area around 1924 and a branch line of the Sante Fe Railroad reached Bledsoe in 1925 bringing a rapid increase in population. **COLLINGSWORTH COUNTY** Named for: James Collinsworth, member of the Texas Convention of 1836, Major in the Battle of San Jacinto, Commissioner of Texas to the United States, first Chief Justice of the newly created Supreme Court of Texas (the statute creating the county misspelled Collinsworth's name). Created: 1876 (out of Bexar and Young Territories). Organized: 1890. County Seat: Wellington. Major Events: Cattlemen were the first settlers in the county. Feuds between them and farmers, as well as between those inhabitants who had supported Pearl as the location of the county seat and those who had supported Wellington, led the county

to be nicknamed "Killingsworth" for several years in the 1890s. The county went dry in a 1898 election, one of the first counties in Texas to do so. **COTTLE COUNTY** Named for: George W. Cottle, who was killed defending the Alamo. Created: 1876 (out of Fannin County). Organized: 1892. County Seat: Paducah. Major Events: Although several large ranches had headquarters in Cottle County and grazed cattle on the open range there, settlement was slow to develop and the 1880 census showed only 24 inhabitants. In 1887 Cottle County was attached to Childress County for judicial purposes. An 1889 killing led to a request for a separate county organization so that Cottle County could hold the trial. The organization was completed in January, 1892. **CROSBY COUNTY** Named for: Stephen Crosby, Chief Clerk in the Land Office (1845-1867). Created: 1876 (out of Bexar Land District). Organized: 1886. County Seat: Estacado (1886-1891); Emma (1891-1912); Crosbyton (1912-present). Major Events: The first permanent settler was H.C. Smith, who hauled lumber by ox team from Fort Worth and built a house in 1877. In 1879 a group of Quakers established a colony in the county, becoming the first farmers on the Texas high plains. At the Quaker settlement of Estacado the first school on the Texas high plains was established in 1882. **DALLAM COUNTY** Named for: James Wilmer Dallam, compiler of *A Digest of the Laws of Texas Opinions of the Supreme Court of Texas 1840-44.* Created: 1876 (out of Bexar Land District). Organized: 1891. County Seat: Texline (1891-1893); Dalhart 1893-present). Major Events: In 1882 the Capitol Freehold Land and Investment Company, Ltd., owned two-thirds of the land in the county, which was ultimately included in the XIT Ranch. By 1890 the county's population had reached 112. **DAWSON COUNTY** Named for: Nicholas M. Dawson, a veteran of the battle of San Jacinto. Created: 1876 (out of Bexar Territory). Organized: 1905. County Seat: Lamesa. Major Events: The first bale of cotton in Dawson County was produced in 1903, but cotton did not become a major crop until 1914. Oil development began in 1934. During World War II this county provided more men per capita for the U.S. armed services than any other county in Texas. **DEAF SMITH COUNTY** Named for: Erastus Deaf Smith, scout for General Sam Houston at the battle of Concepcion and captain of a company of raiders in 1837. Created: 1876 (out of Bexar Territory). Organized: 1890. County Seat: Hereford. Major Events: Early settlers were ranchers who built scattered dugouts and moved with the herds. One of the first barbed wire fences in Texas was put up in the county in 1881. The herds of Herefords gave the county seat its name. **DICKENS COUNTY** Named for: J. Dickens, killed defending the Alamo. Created: 1876 (out of Bexar Territory). Organized: 1891. County Seat: Dickens. Major Events: The first visitors were buffalo and mustang hunters. By the mid-1870s cattlemen had herds on the open range. In 1880 the county had three houses and one school. **DONLEY COUNTY** Named for: Stockton P. Donley, District Attorney for the 6th Judicial District and Justice of the Supreme Court of Texas. Created: 1876 (as Wegefarth County out of Bexar Territory). Organized: 1882 (renamed Donley County). County Seat: Clarendon. Major Events: Nomadic Indians came with the movement of buffalo herds and thereafter followed the buffalo hunters, the soldiers, the cattlemen and the farmers. **FISHER COUNTY** Named for: Samuel R. Fisher, signer of the Texas Delcaration of Independence and the Texas Republic Secretary of the Navy. Created: 1876 (out of Bexar County). Organized: 1886. County Seat: Roby. Major Events: The first inhabitants entered the area late in 1876. Oil and gas production began in 1927. Cotton was the chief cash crop by 1945. **FLOYD COUNTY** Named for: Dolphin W. Floyd, who was killed defending the Alamo. Created: 1876 (out of Bexar and Young Territories). Organized: 1890. County Seat: Floyd City; later renamed Floydada. Major Events: The first permanent settlers arrived in 1884. Many settlers left because of

CHRONOLOGICAL HISTORY OF TEXAS

droughts, financial panics and grasshopper plagues. **GAINES COUNTY** Named for: James Gaines, early Texas Pioneer, member of the Convention of 1836, signer of the Texas Declaration of Independence, member of the Senate of the Republic of Texas. Created: 1876 (out of Bexar County). Organized: 1905. County Seat: Seminole. Major Events: Comanche Chief Quanah Parker is believed to have been born around Cedar Lake. Buffalo hunters drifted into the county in the 1880s and many subsequently became cattlemen. The first farm was established around 1904. The first school was organized in Coker Flat in 1904. In 1917 the railroad reached the county. Oil production began in 1935. **GARZA COUNTY** Named for: an early pioneer family. Created: 1876 (out of Bexar County). Organized: 1907. County Seat: Post. Major Events: Buffalo hunters entered the area and were gradually replaced by ranchers. In 1879 the Curry-Comb Ranch of the Llano Cattle Company established a headquarters in a dugout in the northwest quarter of the county. The first wire fence in the county was erected in 1884, the same year the first women established residence in the county. After the drought of 1886 the county's population dropped to 14. The railroad reached Post in 1910. **GRAY COUNTY** Named for: Peter W. Gray, soldier in the Texas Revolution, member of the Legislature of the Republic of Texas and a Justice of the Supreme Court of Texas. Created: 1876 (out of Bexar Territory). Organized: 1902. County Seat: Lefors (1902-1928); Pampa (1928-present). Major Events: Cattle raising was the first industry in Gray County. Farming began in 1903. Exploration for oil began in 1921. Gray County's oil production in 1935 comprised over half of all oil produced in the Texas Panhandle. **HALE COUNTY** Named for: Lieutenant John C. Hale, Soldier in the Texas Revolution killed at the battle of San Jacinto. Created: 1876 (out of Bexar County). Organized: 1888. County Seat: Plainview. Major Events: Methodist minister Horatio Graves, his wife and three daughters were the first settlers in Hale County, arriving in March, 1883. Plainview was established in 1887 in two hackberry groves on the MacKenzie trail beleived to be the only trees on the plains. In 1915 Hale County was awarded the Holt Cup for the best county agricultural display in the world. **HALL COUNTY** Named for: Warren D.C. Hall, early Texas pioneer, member of the Committee of Safety at Columbia in 1835 and Secretary of War in the Republic of Texas. Created: 1876 (out of Bexar and Young Territories). Organized: 1890. County Seat: Memphis. Major Events: The first settler was probably John Fields, who constructed a dugout a mile south of the Red River in 1877. The first ranching operation was established in 1880; at that time the county's population was 36. In 1887 the railroad crossed the county. **HANSFORD COUNTY** Named for: John M. Hansford, member of the Legislature of the Republic of Texas, Speaker of the Republic's Third Congress and Judge under the Republic. Created: 1876 (out of Bexar and Young Territories). Organized: 1889. County Seat: Hansford (1889-1920); Spearman (1920-present). Major Events: The area was known as the "Great American Desert" to early explorers. The first permanent settlement was established around 1874. The first railroad reached the county in 1920. **HARTLEY COUNTY** Named for: Rufus K. and Oliver C. Hartley; early Texas pioneers; Oliver C. Hartley compiled *A Digest of the Laws of Texas* (published in 1850) and served as reporter of the Texas Supreme Court from 1852 to 1876. Created: 1876 (out of Bexar and Young Territories). Organized: 1891. County Seat: Channing. Major Events: The Rita Blanca Lake in northern Hartley County was constructed during World War II at a cost of $500,000. **HEMPHILL COUNTY** Named for: John Hemphill, Justice and later Chief Justice of the Supreme Court of the Republic of Texas, delegate to the Annexation Convention of 1845, United States Senator from Texas (1857-1861) and deputy in the Provisional Government of the Confederacy. Created: 1876 (out of Bexar and Young Territories).

Organized: 1887. County Seat: Canadian. Major Events: The Buffalo Wallow Fight between Indians and William (Billy) Dixon took place in the eastern part of the area in 1874. The railroad crossed the county in 1887. **HOCKLEY COUNTY** Named for: George W. Hockley, Chief of Staff of the Texas Army during the Texas Revolution, Artillery Commander at the Battle of San Jacinto and Secretary of War in the Republic of Texas. Created: 1876 (out of Bexar and Young Territories). Organized: 1921. County Seat: Levelland (originally known as Hockley City). Major Events: Large ranching operations began to be established in the 1870s and dominated the county's development until they were divided and offered for sale in the 1920s. The number of farms increased from 18 in 1920 to 1,344 in 1934. **HOWARD COUNTY** Named for: Volney Erskine Howard, member of the Mississippi House of Representatives, member of the Annexation Convention of 1845 and United States Representative from Texas (1849-1853). Created: 1876 (out of Bexar County). Organized: 1882. County Seat: Big Spring. Major Events: William Travis Roberts, the first known settler in the area, established a home in 1870. The railroad arrived in the county in 1881. The first school opened in 1882. Oil production began in 1926. **HUTCHINSON COUNTY** Named for: Anderson Hutchinson, Judge of the Western District of the Republic of Texas. Created: 1876 (out of Bexar Territory). Organized: 1901. County Seat: Stinnett. Major Events: The area may have been crossed by Coronado in 1540 and was definitely visited by Spanish explorers in 1601. By the 1830s Indian trading posts had been established and one of them, Adobe Walls, served as a hospital site after a battle between Comanche and Kiowa Indians and U.S. troops led by Kit Carson. Another trading post and buffalo hunters' camp, also known as Adobe Walls, was the site of an 1874 battle between Comanches led by Quanah Parker and buffalo hunters and others, including Billy Dixon and Bat Masterson. The railroad reached the county in 1921. **KENT COUNTY** Named for: Andrew Kent, who died defending the Alamo. Created: 1876 (out of Bexar County). Organized: 1892. County Seat: Clairemont (1892-1954); Jayton (1954-present). Major Events: Treasure Butte, a mound southeast of Clairemont, is the legendary hiding place of Mexican treasure and the site of an 1872 battle with Indians. The arrival of fences led to fence-cutting wars between farmers and ranchers in 1891. The first railroad in the county crossed the northeastern corner in 1909. **KING COUNTY** Named for: William P. King, who with his brother John G. King, died defending the Alamo. Created: 1876 (out of Bexar Territory). Organized: 1891. County Seat: Guthrie. Major Events: Ranching has always been the chief occupation, with farming established around 1900. Oil production began in 1943. **LAMB COUNTY** Named for: Lieutenant George A. Lamb, killed in the battle of San Jacinto. Created: 1876 (out of Bexar Territory). Organized: 1908. County Seat: Olton (1908-1946); Littlefield (1946-present). Major Events: The county's location in Indian-controlled territory delayed settlement. Much of the county was patented to the Capitol Syndicate and incorporated in 1885 into XIT Ranch. Lands from the ranch were put on the market in 1907 and 1908 and quickly bought up by small ranchers and farmers. The railroad reached the county in 1913, encouraging further development. **LIPSCOMB COUNTY** Named for: Abner S. Lipscomb, Circuit Judge of Alabama, Chief Justice of the Alabama Supreme Court, member of the Alabama Legislature, Secretary of State for the Republic of Texas, member of the Annexation Convention of 1845 and Associate Justice of the Texas Supreme Court. Created: 1876 (out of Bexar Territory). Organized: 1887. County Seat: Lipscomb. Major Events: The Coronado Expedition probably crossed the area. Juan de Padilla, who has been called "the first Texas Christian martyr," is thought to be buried near the site where Higgins is presently located. Indian raids and the lack of transportation delayed development.

572

The railroad reached the county in 1880. **LUBBOCK COUNTY** Named for: Colonel Thomas S. Lubbock, co-founder of the Texas Rangers. Created: 1876 (out of Bexar Territory). Organized: 1891. County Seat: Lubbock. Major Events: Buffalo hunters crossed the county frequently in the 1870s, but the first permanent settlers did not arrive until 1879 when George W. Singer and his wife established a store about five miles northwest of Lubbock's present location. Cattlemen occupied most of the county through the 1880s. Homesteaders had filed on state land in sufficient numbers by 1900 to make crop production significant. Lubbock led all Texas counties in cotton production in 1944 with 86,924 bales. **LYNN COUNTY** Named for: W. Lynn (or Linn as there are variant spellings), who died defending the Alamo. Created: 1876 (out of Bexar County). Organized: 1903. County Seat: Tahoka. Major Events: In 1880 there were nine persons in the county. By 1900, when the entire county had only five ranches, the population was 17. The railroad first reached the county in 1910-1911, when it crossed the northeast corner. **MARTIN COUNTY** Named for: Wylie Martin, an Indian scout in the U.S. Army. He came to Texas in 1823 as one of Stephen F. Austin's "Old Three Hundred". He was a member of the Conventions of 1832 and 1833, the Consultation and the General Council. He was elected to the Senate of the Sixth Congress. Created: 1876 (out of Bexar Territory). Organized: 1884. County Seat: Stanton (formerly Mariensfield). Major Events: Before its settlement in 1881 by German Catholics, Martin County was traversed by traders en route to Monument Springs, New Mexico. **MITCHELL COUNTY** Named for: Asa and Eli Mitchell. Asa was one of Stephen-Asa F. Austin's "Old Three Hundred" colonists and played a leading role in the drafting of the Texas Declaration of Independence. Created: 1876 (out of Bexar Territory). Organized: 1881. County Seat: Colorado City. Major Events: Explored by the Spanish from 1761 onward. An impresario grant was made to John Cameron in 1827, but settlement did not start until after the expulsion of Indians in 1875. Oil development began in the 1920s. **MOORE COUNTY** Named for: Commodore E. W. Moore of the Republic of Texas Navy. Created: 1876 (out of Bexar County). Organized: 1892. County Seat: Dumas. Major Events: In 1892 the population was 15, nine of which belonged to the Robert Spurlock family. W. J. Morton opened the first bank in 1906. Oil and natural gas were discovered in 1926. **MOTLEY COUNTY** Named for: Dr. Junius William Mottley, a surgeon who served as a delegate from Goliad to the Convention of 1836 and was a signer of the Texas Declaration of Independence. Created: 1876 (out of Bexar Territory). Organized: 1891. County Seat: Matador. Major Events: Harry Campbell established the headquarters for the Matador Ranch in 1878. In 1891 when the county was organized, ranch hands swiftly set up the requisite 20 businesses to constitute a settlement. There were no other settlements in the county at that time. **NOLAN COUNTY** Named for: Philip Nolan, an Irish-born adventurer, who is said to be the first Anglo-American to map Texas. Created: 1876 (out of Young-Bexar Territory). Organized: 1881. County Seat: Sweetwater. Major Events: Occupied by hunters and cattlemen when the county was first created. The first post office was established at Sweetwater in 1879 and the first school opened in 1880. In 1885 a severe blizzard destroyed open-range livestock. **OCHILTREE COUNTY** Named for: William Beck Ochiltree, Texas Jurist, Secretary of the Texas Treasury, Adjutant General in 1845, delegate to the Convention of 1845 and the Secession Convention of 1861. Created: 1876 (out of Bexar Territory). Organized: 1889. County Seat: Ochiltree (1889-1919); Perryton (1919-present). Major Events: Explored by Francisco Vasquez de Coronado in 1541. Ochiltree County was not settled until after 1880. **OLDHAM COUNTY** Named for: Williamson Simpson Oldham, an Arkansan Jurist and Legislator who moved to Texas in 1849, where he was editor of the *State Gazette*. He was a

delegate to the Texas Secessionist Convention and a member of the Provisional Confederate Congress and a Confederate Senator. Created: 1876 (out of Bexar Territory). Organized: 1880. County Seat: Tascosa (1880-1915); Vega (1915-present). Major Events: Traversed by several Spanish explorers from 1541 onward. The first settlers were buffalo hunters and Indian scouts. Don Casimero Romero established a large ranch in Oldham County in the 1870s. By 1882 the Capitol Syndicate's XIT Ranch covered most of the county. Adrian, Vega and Wildorado were founded by 1904 following the construction of the Chicago, Rock Island and Gulf Railroad. **PARMER COUNTY** Named for: Martin Parmer, signer of the Texas Declaration of Independence. Created: 1876 (out of Bexar Territory). Organized: 1907. County Seat: Farwell. Major Events: Traversed by Jose Mares in 1787. Most of the county was included in the XIT Ranch until after the construction of the Pecos and Northern Texas Railroad. In 1904 the Farm Land Development Company started to sell small tracts and run special trains to encourage settlement. **POTTER COUNTY** Named for: Robert Potter, a leader during the Republic of Texas period. Created: 1876 (out of Bexar Territory). Organized: 1887. County Seat: Amarillo. Major Events: Explored by the Spanish from 1541 onward. The first Anglo-American exploration took place in 1849. Ranches were established in the 1870s and settlement started with the completion of the Fort Worth and Denver City Railroad in 1887. Oil was discovered in the Panhandle area in 1921. **RANDALL COUNTY** Named for: Horace Randal, a Confederate soldier killed in 1864 at the battle of Jenkins' Ferry. Created: 1876 (out of Bexar Territory). Organized: 1889. County Seat: Canyon. Major Events: Explored by the Spanish beginning with Francisco Vasquez de Coronado in 1541. Settlement started in 1876 when Charles Goodnight established the Old Home Ranch in Palo Duro Canyon with 1,600 cattle. The railroad arrived in 1898. **ROBERTS COUNTY** Named for: Texas leader John S. Roberts and the Texas Legislator, Governor and Chief Justice, Oran M. Roberts. Created: 1876 (out of Bexar Territory). Organized: 1889. County Seat: Parnell (1889-1898); Miami (1898-present). Major Events: Bill Anderson, the first Anglo-American settler, arrived in 1876. Most of Roberts County was held by W. H. Criswell as a ranch with 45,000 head of cattle until around 1887 when the construction of the Sante Fe Railroad encouraged increased settlement. **SCURRY COUNTY** Named for: Confederate General William R. Scurry, who represented Red River County in the Ninth Congress of the Republic of Texas. Created: 1876 (out of Bexar Territory). Organized: 1884. County Seat: Snyder. Major Events: W. H. Snyder opened a trading post in 1877 on the site of the present county seat to accomodate the buffalo hunters. The Roscoe, Snyder and Pacific Railroad reached Snyder in 1908. **SHERMAN COUNTY** Named for: General Sidney Sherman of the Texas Army, who served at San Jacinto and was a member of the Texas Legislature. Created: 1876 (out of Bexar Territory). Organized: 1889. County Seat: Coldwater (1889-1901); Stratford (1901-present). Major Events: The area became part of the open range after 1880. Settlement increased after the construction of the Chicago, Rock Island and Gulf Railroad in 1900. The first county court held in Stratford in 1901 returned an indictment against William Bonner (Billy the Kid), but he was not arrested and brought to trail at that time. **STONEWALL COUNTY** Named for: Thomas J. "Stonewall" Jackson, the Confederate Army general. Created: 1876 (out of Bexar County). Organized: 1888. County Seat: Rayner (1888-1890); Aspermont (1890-present). Major Events: Buffalo hunters were in the area in the 1870s. The first settlement was in the 1880s by "nesters". Prospecting for oil started in 1922, but none was produced until 1938. **SWISHER COUNTY** Named for: James G. Swisher, one of the four men who met with General Martin Perfecto de Cos to arrange the Mexican surrender on December 11, 1835. He signed the Texas Declaration of Independence. Created: 1876 (out of Bexar and Young Territories). Organized: 1890. County Seat: Tulia. Major Events: General R. S. Mackenzie's victory over the Comanche in Palo Duro Canyon marked the end of Indian warfare in Texas in 1874. Most of the early settlers were English and lived in dugouts or log homes. **TERRY COUNTY** Named for: Benjamin Franklin Terry, delegate to the 1861 Secession Convention. He fought at Manassas and returned to Texas to organize the cavalry troop known as Terry's Texas Rangers. Created: 1876 (out of Bexar Territory). Organized: 1904. County Seat: Brownfield. Major Events: Terry County was a favorite Comanche hunting ground until 1870 when Anglo-American buffalo hunters depleted the herds and opened the area for ranching. The Santa Fe Railroad sent a line through the county in 1917. **WHEELER COUNTY** Named for: Royal T. Wheeler who served as a member of the Supreme Court of The Republic of Texas and later as an Associate then Chief Justice of the State Supreme Court. Created: 1876 (out of Bexar and Young Territories). Organized: 1879. County Seat: Mobeetie (formerly Sweetwater) (1879-1906); Wheeler (1906-present). Major Events: The last battles between Indians, hunters and United States Army scouts took place in the 1870s. A trading post was established at Sweetwater in 1876. Wheeler County was the first to be organized in the Panhandle area and 14 other counties were attached to it for judicial purposes until 1881. Gas and oil production became important in 1926. **YOAKUM COUNTY** Named for: Henderson Yoakum, an early Texas historian. Created: 1876 (out of Bexar Territory). Organized: 1907. County Seat: Plains. Major Events: The area was traversed by Fray Juan de Salas in 1632, but remained Cheyenne, Comanche and Kiowa Indian territory until 1870. By 1880 large ranches covered most of the county. Oil was discovered in 1935 and oil production was the leading industry by 1939. **1878** The extermination of the buffalo, which began in 1870 and ended in 1878, was viewed by many as advantageous. New tanning processes in the east increased the value of the hides, the expansion of the cattle industry was furthered and a solution to the Indian problem was included. The Indians viewed the slaughter of the buffaloes as a threat to their way of life. In 1874 five military forces drove the Indians onto reservations in western Oklahoma so hunters could continue the extermination of the buffalo. **MARCH 18, 1878** The first telephone line was constructed in Galveston and on August 21, 1879 the first telephone exchange was in operation. **JANUARY 21, 1879** When Oran M. Roberts, Democrat, became Governor, the state was heavily in debt. Governor Roberts proposed to the Legislature a plan whereby the balance of the public lands of Texas would be sold at a low price in order to raise much needed revenue. The Legislature enacted a law which allowed several large syndicates, both domestic and foreign, to acquire vast holdings in western Texas. This land policy became a major political issue for many years. **JULY 14, 1879** The Legislature enacted the Fifty Cent Act selling public land at 50 cents an acre to reduce the public debt and establish schools. This act was repealed January 22, 1883. **1880** Population: 1,591,749. **JANUARY 16, 1883** John Ireland, Democrat, became Governor and served two terms. **REEVES COUNTY** Named for: George R. Reeves, farmer, tax collector, Legislator and Colonel in the Confederate Army. Served as Speaker of the Texas House 1881-1882. Created: 1883 (out of Pecos County). Organized: 1884. County Seat: Pecos (formerly Pecos City). Major Events: Traversed by Spanish explorers from 1590 on. First settlers were Mexican farmers. Anglo-American settlement began about 1871. Pecos City became a center for land agents and immigration companies. **FEBRUARY 6, 1884** Governor Ireland called a special session of the Legislature to deal with the frequent range wars. The Legislature made fence-cutting and setting grass fires a felony, made it illegal to fence in the land of another without authority and provided for gates at three-

mile intervals, but they were unable to solve the problem. With the introduction of barbed wire in 1871, the great open-range cattle kingdom began to come to an end. By 1883, almost all of the cattle country in south and central Texas had been fenced. In addition, "nesters" invaded the open range and conflicts developed. The Texas Rangers were kept busy attempting to enforce the 1884 law but in some areas not a fence remained uncut for years. Over half of the 171 organized counties were affected. **MIDLAND COUNTY** Named for: location which was midway between Fort Worth and El Paso on the Texas and Pacific Railroad. Created: 1885 (out of Tom Green County). Organized: 1885. County Seat: Midland. Major Events: Ranchers were riding the ranges by late 1880s with farmers arriving shortly thereafter. Rain-making experiments, sponsored by the U.S. Department of Agriculture, were conducted in 1891. An economic boom came with the discovery of oil in Permian Basin in early 20th century. **VAL VERDE COUNTY** Named for: the Spanish words "Val Verde" which mean "Green Valley". The county was named for the Civil War battle of Val Verde in which Confederate forces were led by H. H. Sibley. Created: 1885 (out of parts of Kinney, Crockett and Pecos Counties). Organized: 1885. County Seat: Del Rio. Major Events: The area was explored by the Spanish, beginning with Cabeza de Vaca in 1535. The first attempt at settlement was a short-lived mission established by a Mexican priest in 1808. An attempt by James Grant and John Charles Beales in 1834 also failed. The United States Government opened a military road west from San Antonio through the county in 1849 and passenger and mail service were inaugurated in 1857. The first colony was established in 1868. **1886** The agricultural depression which began after the Cvil War continued to increase in severity for over 30 years. The Farmer's Alliance was founded to seek reforms through political action and it was successful in gaining control of the Legislature in 1886, placing many of their recommendations on the Democratic Party platform of 1896. The Prohibition Party began its activities in Texas, but in 1887 a prohibition amendment failed. **JANUARY 20, 1887** Lawrence S. Ross, Democrat, became Governor and served for two terms. **BREWSTER COUNTY** Named for: Henry P. Brewster, Secretary of War for the Republic of Texas, an Attorney General for the State of Texas and a soldier in the Confederate Army. Created: 1887 (out of Presidio County). Organized: 1887. County Seat: Murpheyville; renamed Alpine in 1887. Major Events: The addition to Brewster County in 1897 of two proposed new counties made Brewster County the largest in Texas in terms of land area. During World War II large amounts of guayule were extracted and used in the production of synthetic rubber. **CRANE COUNTY** Named for: William Carey Crane, President of Baylor University from 1863 to 1895. Created: 1887 (out of Tom Green County). Organized: 1927. County Seat: Crane. Major Events: As late as 1918 the county had no roads and only 14 persons were known to live there. Oil was discovered in 1925 and the population increased rapidly. **ECTOR COUNTY** Named for: General Mathew D. Ector, a Texas Representative, a Private in the Confederate Army who rose to the rank of Brigadier General and a District Judge. Created: 1887 (out of Tom Green County). Organized: 1891. County Seat: Odessa. Major Events: The railroad came to the county in 1882. Oil and natural gas production became important in 1927 and this county ranks among the highest in oil production. **GLASSCOCK COUNTY** Named for: George Washington Glasscock, an early Texas pioneer who helped to organize Williamson County in 1846, served in the Texas Legislature and was one of the early managers of the Lunatic Asylum (subsequently renamed Austin State Hospital). Created: 1887 (out of Bexar Territory). Organized: 1893. County Seat: Garden City. Major Events: By 1893 there were three small settlments in the county. Acreage for homesteads was opened in 1908 and the resulting land rush lasted until 1922.

Development of the oil industry began in 1917 and in 1926 an oil boom began that increased land values by as much as a thousand fold. **JEFF DAVIS COUNTY** Named for: Jefferson Davis, U.S. Secretary of War and President of the Confederacy. Created: 1887 (out of Presidio County). Organized: 1887. County Seat: Fort Davis (formerly the county seat of Presidio County). Major Events: A Spanish exploration party headed by Antonio de Espejo crossed the area in 1583. There were scattered Mexican ranches in the area when Anglo-American settlement began, following the establishment of Fort Davis in 1854. **LOVING COUNTY** Named for: Oliver Loving, early Texas cattleman who with Charles Goodnight established the Goodnight-Loving Trail. Created: 1887 (out of Tom Green County). Organized: 1893. County Seat: Mentone (1931-present; there was no county government before 1931). Major Events: Although the county was crossed by Spanish explorers in 1590 and again in 1763, settlement was slow to develop. The 1890 census shows only three residents in the county. Oil was discovered in 1925 and the county's population peaked at 285 in 1940. **MILLS COUNTY** Named for: John T. Mills, a pioneer Jurist of Texas. Created: 1887 (out of Brown, Comanche, Hamilton and Lampasas Counties). Organized: 1887. County Seat: Goldthwaite. Major Events: First traversed by Pedro Vial in 1786. Site of many battles between Comanche and Apache. First White settlers were Jese Hanna and his five sons who established Hanna Valley in 1856. **SCHLEICHER COUNTY** Named for: Gustav Schleicher, an engineer and lawyer, who was elected to The Texas House and Senate, served in the Confederate Army, and represented Texas in the U.S. House of Representatives. Created: 1887 (out of Crockett County). Organized: 1901. County Seat: Eldorado. Major Events: In 1876 New Yorker William L. Black purchased 30,000 acres of land at 10 cents an acre. Lack of surface water caused problems until C. C. Doty drilled the first windmill in 1882, opening up the area for grazing. In 1901, the sale of school lands brought increased settlers and cattlemen. **SUTTON COUNTY** Named for: John S. Sutton, Lieutenant Colonel of the 7th Texas Cavalry, who received a mortal wound at the battle of Val Verde on February 21, 1862. Created: 1887 (out of Crockett County). Organized: 1890. County Seat: Sonora. Major Events: The first White settlement in this Apache-occupied territory was at Fort Terrett in 1852. A 100-mile long, 250-feet wide fenced cattle lane was in use from 1919 until 1929 when the Panhandle and Santa Fe Railroad was extended from San Angelo to Sonora. **UPTON COUNTY** Named for: John Cunningham Upton and William Felton Upton, both of whom served in Hood's Texas Brigade during the Civil War. Created: 1887 (out of Tom Green County). Organized: 1910. County Seat: Upland (1910-1921); Rankin (1921-present). Major Events: Dr. George Elliott built the first house in the county in 1880. In June, 1926 George McCamey dug a wildcat oil well which attracted six to seven hundred people within 24 hours. **WARD COUNTY** Named for: Thomas William Ward, fighter, for Texas Independence who died during the Goliad Massacre. Created: 1887 (out of Tom Green County). Organized: 1892. County Seat: Barstow (1887-1939); Monahans (1939-present). Major Events: The area was explored by the Spanish before 1600 and used by Indians until 1876. Anglo-American settlement took place mostly after the construction of the Texas and Pacific Railroad in 1881. Oil production started in the 1930s. **WINKLER COUNTY** Named for: Judge Clinton M. Winkler, member of the Court of Appeals established by the (Texas) Constitution of 1876. He had been a member of the Second Legislature and, after the removal of the "Iron Clad Oath", a member of the Thirteenth Legislature. He rose to the rank of Lieutenant Colonel in the Confederate Army during the Civil War. Created: 1887 (out of Tom Green County). Organized: 1910. County Seat: Kermit. Major Events: Except for a few ranch headquarters, settlement did not start until encouraged by the Homestead Law of 1900. The first post office opened at Hay Flat in 1908. The 1916-1922 drought ruined many ranchers. In 1926, when a wildcat oil well opened a period of alternating boom and depression, there were only six voters in the county and all the county officials lived outside of Winkler County. **1888** In Nacogdoches County the first oil refinery in Texas was constructed by the Lubricating Oil Company. **JANUARY 12, 1888** The famous blizzard of '88 swept from the Dakotoas to Texas and many pioneers and livestock perished. **MARCH 30, 1889** Texas passed a state anti-trust law (there was no national anti-trust law and only one other state had such a law) to control corporations, expecially railroads, that restricted trade and competition and set prices. **COKE COUNTY** Named for: Richard Coke, Governor of Texas (1874-1877), when he resigned to become U.S. Senator, an office he held until 1885. Created: 1889 (out of Tom Green County). Organized: 1889. County Seat: Hayrick (1889-1891); Robert Lee (1891-present). Major Events: The county was settled between 1860 and 1880 by cattlemen who ran herds on the open range. Migration to the area increased with the building of the Texas and Pacific Railroad in the 1880s. **IRION COUNTY** Named for: Robert Anderson Irion, early Texas settler, member of the Committee of Safety and Vigilance for Nacogdoches during the Texas Revolution, member of the Senate of the Republic of Texas, Secretary of State for the Republic of Texas and charter member of the Philosophical Society of Texas. Created: 1889 (out of Tom Green County). Organized: 1889. County Seat: Sherwood (1889-late 1930s); Mertzon (late 1930s-present). Major Events: Spanish explorers visited the area several times in the seventeenth and eighteenth centuries, but Indian hostilities delayed the beginning of settlement until the early 1870s. Population had reached only 870 by 1890, but the county was not really opened for settlement until the railroad arrived in 1910. Oil was discovered in 1928. **1890** Population: 2,235,527. Manufactured products this year were valued at $70 million, the leading industry was timber valued at $14 million and in agriculture the cotton crop was worth over $100 million. **DECEMBER, 1890** The Texas voters adopted a constitutional amendment creating the Railroad Commission. **JANUARY 20, 1891** James S. Hogg, Democrat, became Governor and served two terms. He was the first native-born Governor of Texas. **APRIL 13, 1891** The Legislature passed an Alien Land Law to limit foreign ownership of land. After it was declared unconstitutional on December 11, 1891 (*Gunter v. Texas Land and Mortgage Company*) the Legislature passed a new law on April 12, 1892. **FOARD COUNTY** Named for: Major Robert J. Foard an attorney and Confederate officer during the Civil War. Created: 1891 (out of Cottle, Hardeman, King and Knox Counties). Organized: 1891. County Seat: Crowell. Major Events: In 1860 a company of Texas Rangers recaptured Cynthia Ann Parker, mother of Quanah Parker, the last Chief of the Comanches, in a battle with the Comanches. **STERLING COUNTY** Named for: Captain W. S. Sterling, a buffalo hunter, rancher and Indian fighter who was one of the earliest settlers in the county. Created: 1891 (out of Tom Green County). Organized: 1891. County Seat: Sterling City. Major Events: Anglo-American explorers arrived after 1800. Fort Concho, established in 1874, provided ranches with protection againt Indians. Frank and Jesse James are reputed to have had a base in the area during the 1870s. **1892** The Legislature approved the use of the Australian (secret) ballot in cities with over 10,000 residents. In 1891 a constitutional amendment had passed requiring the registration of voters in cities over 10,000. **1893** The Texas Equal Rights Association was organized to promote the right of women to vote. **JANUARY 15, 1895** Charles A. Culberson, Democrat, became Governor for one term. **FEBRUARY 14, 1895** The heaviest snowstorm in the west Gulf region occurred: the "Big Snow of '95" left 20 inches in Houston, 15.4 inches in Galveston and 6 inches at

CHRONOLOGICAL HISTORY OF TEXAS

Brownsville. **1896** The Adams-Onis Treaty of 1819 had placed the eastern boundary of the Texas Panhandle at the 100th meridian. Maps originally placed the boundary 40 miles east of the confluence of two main forks of the Red River, but surveys in 1859-60 placed the 100th meridian almost 70 miles west of the forks. The Texas Legislature claimed that the surveys of 1859-60 were the correct location and created Greer County out of the territory added to the state. However, the U.S. Commissioner of Indian Affairs claimed the land was part of the Indian Territory. The U.S. Supreme Court ruled that the area north of the Prairie Dog Town (South) Fork of the Red River known as Greer County was not part of the state of Texas, depriving Texas of a large area of fertile land. **JANUARY 17, 1899** Joseph D. Sayers, Democrat, became Governor for two terms. The Texas Legislature passed its first law to regulate the oil industry and another law made labor union membership legal. **FEBRUARY 12, 1899** The coldest Texas morning of modern record occurred in Fort Worth: -8°F. **JANUARY 17-28, 1899** The Brazos Flood caused 284 deaths and over $9 million in damage. **1900** Population: 3,048,710. Texas was the sixth most populous state in the nation with the five largest counties being Dallas, Bexar, Harris, Travis and Tarrant. **SEPTEMBER 8, 1900** The deadliest hurricane ever in the United States, struck Galveston, taking 6,000 to 7,000 victims, destroying 3,000 to 4,000 homes and causing $30 million in property damage. **JANUARY 10, 1901** SPINDLETOP Since the first explorations of Texas it was known that petroleum existed in the area, but techniques for extracting it and demand had not yet developed. In 1867 commercial quantities were found near Nacogdoches and in 1896 near Corsicana, but it was the spectacular gusher known as Spindletop which marks the beginning of the modern oil and gas industry. Anthony F. Lucas drilled into a salt dome structure near Beaumont: in 10 years Spindletop had produced almost 43 million barrels of oil. Other drillers soon found vast reservoirs of oil and boom towns sprang up, creating the first oil boom in the southwest. Guffey Oil Co. of Pennsylvania (Gulf Oil) soon established a refinery and Texas Fuel Co. (Texaco) and Magnolia Oil (Mobil) were established. **1902** The poll tax was established as a voting requirement on January 23, 1964. Texas never ratified the 24th Amendment which made the poll tax unconstitutional as a requirement for voting. **MAY 18, 1902** Goliad was struck by a tornado that killed 114 persons. **1903** In February the Equal Suffrage League was established by women in Houston and in December the Texas Womans Suffrage Association was formed. The Texas Legislature passed a law (13 years before the U.S. Congress) prohibiting the employment of children under 12 in industrial plants and under 16 in mines, distilleries and breweries. In 1911 the ages were raised to 15 and 17 respectively. **JANUARY 20, 1903** Samuel W. T. Lanham, Democrat, became Governor and served for two terms. **REAGAN COUNTY** Named for: John H. Reagan, Texas Legislator, member of the U.S. Congress before and afer the Civil War, Postmaster General and later Secretary of the Treasury for the Confederacy and first Chairman of the Texas Railroad Commission. Created: 1903 (out of Tom Green County). Organized: 1903. County Seat: Stiles (1903-1925); Big Lake (1925-present). Major Events: Explored by the Spanish from 1650 onward. Sheep and cattle ranching by Anglo-Americans started in the 1890s. Following the success of the Santa Rita Oil Well in 1923 the population grew from 377 in 1920 to 3,028 in 1930. **1904** Nearly 10,000 miles of railroad track existed in Texas, leading all other states. The principal lines included the Missouri, Kansas and Texas (Katy), the Texas and Pacific, the Southern Pacific, the Missouri Pacific, the International and Great Northern and the Fort Worth and Denver. **1905** Taylor recorded 2 inches of rain in ten minutes. **MAY 14, 1905** The Terrell Election Law passed, defining the requirements and procedures for voting in Texas. **TERRELL COUNTY** Named for: Alexander Watkins Terrell,

Attorney General for the Republic in 1841, Indian Commissioner and negotiator of treaties with the Indians, and Charge d'Affaires for the Republic in France from 1844-1845. Created: 1905 (out of Pecos County). Organized: 1905. County Seat: Sanderson. Major Events: Terrell County was explored by the Spanish, beginning with Cabeza de Vaca in 1535. Settlement was delayed by the aridity and the rough terrain. **JANUARY 15, 1907** Thomas M. Campbell, Democrat, became Governor for two terms. The Robertson Insurance Law passed the Legislature requiring all insurance companies in Texas to invest 75% of their reserves from paid premiums of Texans in real estate and securities. **1908** Corn production peaked at 124,560,000 bushels. **1909** Sugar cane production peaked at 2,247,000 gallons. **1910** Population: 3,896,542. The first U.S. Army airplane was flown at Fort Sam Houston. **AUGUST 16, 1910** The Legislature ratified the 16th Amendment to the U.S. Constitution, which instituted the federal income tax. **JANUARY 11, 1911** O. B. Colquitt, Democrat, became Governor on an anti-prohibitionist platform. **JULY 22, 1911** A statewide vote on the prohibition of alcohol narrowly failed 237,393 to 231,096. **BROOKS COUNTY** Named for: James A. Brooks, a Texas Ranger, a State Representative and a County Judge. Created: 1911 (out of Starr, Live Oak, Hidalgo and Zapata Counties). Organized: 1912. County Seat: Falfurrias. Major Events: Mexican colonists and vaqueros herding wild cattle were in the area when Edward C. Lasater settled in 1883. The first school opened in 1912. **CULBERSON COUNTY** Named for: David Browning Culberson, member of the Texas Legislature, officer in the Confederate Army, United States Representative from Texas (1875-1897) and Commissioner to codify United States laws (1897-1900). Created: 1911 (out of El Paso County). Organized: 1912. County Seat: Van Horn. Major Events: Apache raids in the area were frequent in the 1870s and 1880s. The first settlers came in 1882 when the Texas and Pacific Railroad reached the area. **JIM WELLS COUNTY** Named for: James B. Wells, Texas Judge. Created: 1911 (out of Nueces County). Organized: 1912. County Seat: Alice. Major Events: Mexican ranchers were the first settlers in the area. Oil was discovered in 1928. **WILLACY COUNTY** Named for: John G. Willacy, who served in the Texas Legislature from 1899 to 1914. He introduced the bill providing for the creation of the new county which was subsequently named in his honor. Created: 1911 (out of Cameron and Hidalgo Counties). Organized: 1911 (reorganized 1921). County Seat: Sarita (1911-1921); Raymondville (1921-present). Major Events: The area was known to the early Spanish explorers and settled by Spanish colonizers towards the end of the 18th century. It was still disputed territory after the Texas Revolution; Texas' attempt to establish the border at the Rio Grande precipitated the Mexican War in 1845. Wild Horse Desert inspired General P.H. Sheridan to remark in 1865: "If I possessed both Texas and Hell I'd rent out Texas and live in Hell". Willacy County forms part of King Ranch. Vast onion crops helped the county survive the Depression. Oil was discovered in the 1940s. **FEBRUARY 7, 1913** The Legislature ratified the 17th Amendment to the U.S. Constitution which provided for the direct election of U.S. Senators. **MARCH 5, 1913** Albert Sidney Burleson was appointed U.S. Postmaster General under President Woodrow Wilson. **DECEMBER, 1913** Major flood damage from Texas rivers amounted to 177 deaths and $147 million in damage. **JIM HOGG COUNTY** Named for: James Stephen Hogg, Governor of Virginia, Attorney General of Texas and Governor of Texas. Created: 1913 (out of Brooks and Duval Counties). Organized: 1913. County Seat: Hebbronville. Major Events: Spanish ranches and haciendas were located in the area as early as 1760, but the Mexican and Texas Revolutions, as well as Indian hostilities, led them to be abandoned. After the Treaty of Guadalupe, Hidalgo Mexican settlers established small ranches and supply posts. **KLEBERG COUNTY** Named for: Robert

Justus Kleburg, lawyer of Richard King (who with Mifflin Kenedy established th King Ranch), subsequently manager of King Ranch, President of the Texas and Southwestern Cattle Raisers Association. Created: 1913 (out of Nueces County). Organized: 1913. County Seat: Kingsville. Major Events: Spanish explorers crossed the area in 1531, but the barrier reef of Padre Island, hostile Indians and the controversy between Texas and Mexico over the territory delayed settlement. Spanish ranches were established in the early 1800's but were abandoned as a result of Indian raids. The King Ranch was established in the area in 1852 and a good part of the county is still comprised of part of the ranch. The railroad crossed the county in 1904, when Kingsville was established on land set aside by Robert Justus Kleberg. **REAL COUNTY** Named for: Julius Real, Texas Legislator. Although a prohibitionist he represented his (wet) district by participating in the "Whiskey Rebellion" of 1911 in which 11 Senators went into hiding to prevent passage of legislation making Texas totally dry. Created: 1913 (out of Bandera, Edwards and Kerr Counties). Organized: 1913. County Seat: Leakey (formerly county seat of Edwards County). Major Events: Archeological remains show existence of prehistoric civilization. Indian (Comanche, Apache and Lipan-Apache) settlements preceded the establishment of the Spanish Mission of San Lorenzo de la Santa Cruz in 1762. Anglo-American settlement began in 1857. Indian raids continued until 1881. **1914** Thomas Watt Gregory appointed U.S. Attorney General under President Woodrow Wilson. **1915** The Legislature passed a law making school attendance compulsory. **JANUARY 19, 1915** James E. Ferguson, Democrat, became Governor, but was impeached in his second term on August 27, 1917 for , among other things, trying to remove faculty members from the University of Texas. Nevertheless for over 30 years James E. Ferguson a banker and merchant from Temple, wielded a powerful influence over the affairs of Texas. On July 21, 1917 he appeared voluntarily before a Travis County Grand Jury and was indicted on nine counts. Perferring impeachment proceedings to court action, both Ferguson and the Speaker of the House called for a special session of the Legislature to consider the charges. On August 24, the House impeached the Governor on 21 counts; on September 24, the Senate found him guilty on 10 of the charges. Removed from office and declared ineligible to hold any public office in Texas, Ferguson nevertheless ran unsuccessfully for Governor in 1918, for U.S. President in 1920, and for the U.S. Senate in 1922. His wife Mrs. Miriam A. (Ma) Ferguson was elected Governor from 1925 to 1927 and from 1933 to 1935. In all Ma Ferguson's campaigns for Governor, including the races in 1926, 1930 and 1940, it was James Ferguson who did most of the campaigning. **1916** The pink bollworm is believed to have entered Texas from Mexico this year and in the following year the Legislature passed the Pink Bollworm Act to control the pest. **MAY 9, 1916** President Woodrow Wilson ordered the militias of Texas, New Mexico and Arizona mobilized along the border with Mexico. Revolutions in Mexico caused many Mexicans to migrate to Texas. **AUGUST 18, 1916** A hurricane struck Corpus Christi killing 20 people and causing $1.5 million in damage. **AUGUST 25, 1917** Lieutenant Governor William P. Hobby became Governor when Governor Ferguson was removed from office. Governor Hobby served untill January 18, 1921. **HUDSPETH COUNTY** Named for: Claude Benton Hudspeth, member of the Texas House of Representatives (1902-1906) and of the Texas Senate (1906-1918) and United States Representative from Texas (1919-1931). Created: 1917 (out of El Paso County). Organized: 1917. County Seat: Sierra Blanca. Major Events: Indian raids continued to be a problem as late as 1881. Pancho Villa's guerrillas raided the area along the Mexican border between 1914 and 1917. **FEBRUARY 28, 1918** Texas ratified 188,982 to 130,907 the 18th Amendment to the Constitution prohibiting the sale or distribution of alcoholic beverages. **1919** The Legislature chose the pecan tree to be the official state tree. Peach production peaked at 221,800,000 pounds. **JUNE 23, 1919** Texas was the first state in the south and the ninth in the nation to ratify the 19th Amendment to the U.S. Constitution which provided women with the right to vote. **JANUARY 18, 1921** Pat M. Neff became Governor of Texas and served for two terms. He was the first Texas Governor to have a college degree. **SEPTEMBER, 1921** Texas rivers flooded causing 215 deaths and $19 million in damage. Thrall, Texas received 38.2 inches of rainfall on September 9 and 10. **KENEDY COUNTY** Named for: Mifflin Kenedy, early Texas sheepman, rancher and railroad developer. Created: 1921 (out of Cameron, Hidalgo and Willacy Counties). Organized: 1921. County Seat: Sarita. Major Events: In 1847 Mifflin Kenedy and his partner Richard King established the King Ranch, part of which is still in operation in Kenedy County. **1922** Sweet potato production peaked at 4,239,000 cwt. **1923** During the 1920s a crime wave produced such well known fugitives as Bonnie Parker and Clyde Barrow. The Knights of the Ku Klux Klan "a patriotic, secret, social and benevolent order" gained strength after World War I when crime became a significant problem. The Klan, an anti-Catholic, anti-Jewish, White-supremicist organization declared war on crime and that was the aspect which appealed to many Texans. The Klan gained its maximum strength during a crime wave in the early 1920s and was the motivating force behind the White Primary Law of 1923. That statute excluded Blacks from participation in the primary elections of the Democratic Party in Texas. In 1927 the U.S. Supreme Court declared the law unconstitutional. **JANUARY 20, 1925** Miriam A. Ferguson became the first woman Governor. She ran on the slogan "A vote for me is a vote for Pa", the former impeached and convicted Governor of Texas. The implication of scandals regarding the rewarding of road contracts and the over 2,000 pardons during Mrs. Ferguson's term limited her to one term in office. **1927** A tornado ravaged Rock Springs, Texas killing 72 persons. **JANUARY 17, 1927** Dan Moody (the former Attorney General of Texas) became Governor of Texas and served for two terms. **1928** Randolph Field at San Antonio opened and all United States military pilots were trained there until the outbreak of World War II. **1930** Population 5,825,000; growth rate 24.9% 1920-30. **1931** The number of farms in Texas peaked at 506,000 in 1931. **JANUARY 20, 1931** Ross S. Sterling defeated Ma Ferguson in a runoff election to become Governor of Texas. The Legislature passed the Cotton Acreage Control Law (New Deal-type legislation) which limited cotton planting to 30 percent of an individuals holdings in an attempt to raise cotton prices for farmers. The Texas Court of Civil Appeals declared the law unconstitutional in March, 1932. **JANUARY 17, 1933** Miriam A. Ferguson was elected Governor again for one term. The 18th Amendment was repealed by the 21st Amendment and liquor sales in Texas were returned to a system of local option. **1934-36** the Dust Bowl covered the plains of Texas. **JANUARY 15, 1935** James V. Allred became Governor of Texas for two terms. During his term the Public Utilities Regulatory Commission, a Pardons Board and a modern police system under the Department of Public Safety came into existence. **AUGUST 12, 1936** The highest recorded temperature in Texas of 120 °F occurred at Seymour. **JANUARY 6-9, 1937** Severe icing with as much as 2 inches forming on wires caused $3 to $4 million in damage. **1938** Nearly 200,000 Texans were on direct relief and about 100,000 worked on federal relief projects during this year of the Great Depression. **JANUARY 17, 1939** W. Lee O'Daniel became Governor of Texas for one term. Lieutenant Governor Stevenson became Governor when O'Daniel resigned to enter the U.S. Senate on August 4, 1941. **1940** Population 6,415,000 (6th most populous state). The number of horses and mules peaked at 1,236,000. **WORLD WAR II** During World War II Texas was the training

CHRONOLOGICAL HISTORY OF TEXAS

center for all branches of the armed services. 23,022 Texans died in World War II; 36 received Congressional Medals of Honor and 10 earned the Navy's Medal of Honor. Both Dwight D. Eisenhower and Audie Murphy were Texas natives. **1941** Cowpea production peaked at 1,680,000 bushels. Milk production peaked at 4,409,000,000 pounds. **AUGUST 8, 1941** Coke R. Stevenson as Lieutenant Governor completed Governor O'Daniel's term of office, then was reelected twice during World War II. **1943** The number of chickens peaked at 53,437,000. **1944** The number of hogs peaked at 3,106,000. Egg production peaked at 3,559,000,000. **1945** Fresh market tomato production peaked at 4,602,000 cwt. The number of milk cows peaked at 1,594,000. **1945-46** Grapefruit production peaked at 24,000,000 boxes. **1946** Tomato production (for processing) peaked at 119,000 tons. Heman Marion Sweatt, a Black, was denied admission to the University of Texas Law School under a law providing for separate educational facilities for Blacks and Whites. In 1954 the U.S. Supreme Court reversed a Texas court ruling which had upheld the right of the University to deny admission. **1947** Beauford H. Jester was elected Governor of Texas but died in office, replaced by Lieutenant Governor Allan Shivers on July 11, 1949. Governor Shivers held the governorship until January 15, 1957—the longest of any previous Texas Governor. **APRIL 9, 1947** The Southern Plains Tri-State Tornado swept through Texas, Oklahoma and Kansas covering a track of 221 miles killing 169, injuring 980 and causing damage estimated at $9.7 million. **1949** Cotton production peaked at 6,040,000 bales, flaxseed production peaked at 2,002,000 bushels, sweetcorn production peaked at 648,000 cwt. and watermelon production peaked at 6,710,000 cwt. The Gilmer-Aikin Acts reorganized the Texas school system from one of primarily local control to a system with more state control. **1950** Population 7,711,194, (fifth most populous state) with a 20% growth rate between 1940-50. Broccoli production peaked at 446,000 cwt. and honey production peaked at 15,850,000 pounds. **JUNE 5, 1950** The U.S. Supreme Court ruled against Texas in the Tidelands Case. The Court ruled that the United States has paramount rights to submerged lands off the coast of Texas. In 1953, however, Congress passed a law restoring to Texas the Tidelands in the Gulf of Mexico. **JANUARY 28 to FEBRUARY 1, 1951** The greatest ice storm in U.S. history spanned from Texas to West Virginia causing $100 million in damages. **MAY 11, 1953** The second most deadly tornado struck Waco, Texas killing 114 persons. **1956** Lettuce production peaked at 2,240,000. The least annual rainfall in Texas was 1.64 inches in Presidio. **1957** Cauliflower production peaked at 455,000 cwt. **JANUARY 15, 1957** Price Daniels, Sr., Democrat became Governor of Texas and served three terms. **1958** Barley production peaked at 11,025,000 bushels. **1960** Population 9,580,000; growth rate 24.2% (1950-60). Snapbean production peaked at 19,800 tons and carrot production peaked at 6,200,000 cwt. **SEPTEMBER 11, 1961** Hurricane Carla battered the Texas coast at Port O'Connor on Lavaca Bay. Torrential rains of 13 to 17 inches in the coastal areas and 4 inches or more over most of Texas caused extensive flooding. Eight tornadoes left 8 dead, 55 injured and about 100 buildings destroyed. The total property and agricultural loss was estimated at $400 million. In all 45 deaths in Texas were attributed to Carla. **JANUARY 15, 1963** John B. Connally became Governor of Texas and was elected for three terms. **SEPTEMBER, 1963** The Houston Manned Spacecraft Center opened. The site was selected in September, 1960 and construction started in April, 1962. The space center was rededicated the Lyndon B. Johnson Space Center on August 27, 1973 (LBJ's birthday). **NOVEMBER 22, 1963** Vice President Lyndon B. Johnson (former U.S. Senator from Texas) succeeded President Kennedy as President of the United States after the tragic assassination in Dallas. **1966** The number of goats peaked at 4,222,000. **SEPTEMBER 20-21, 1967** Hurricane Beulah spawned at least 115 mini-tornadoes in south-

central and coastal Texas. Five persons were killed and 28 injured. **1968** Rice production peaked at 27,164,000 cubic tons, sugar beet production peaked at 824,000 tons and beet production peaked at 26,800 tons. **JANUARY 21, 1969** Preston Smith, Democrat, became Governor for two terms. **1970** Population 11,199,000, (fourth most populous state), growth rate 16.9% 1960-70. Potato production peaked at 4,593,000 cwt. and the number of commercial broilers (chickens) peaked at 185,534,000. **AUGUST 3, 1970** Hurricane Celia struck the Corpus Christi area causing 11 deaths and $454 million in damage. **JANUARY, 1971** Sharpestown Scandal was first exposed by the Securities and Exchange Commission (SEC). In 1969 a banker-real estate developer-insurance broker, Frank C. Sharp, wanted state loans to cover deposits in state-chartered banks. House Speaker Gus Mutscher and Representative Tommy Shannon profited by having such laws passed and were indicted for conspiracy to accept bribes. The "Dirty Thirty", 30 Texas legislators, helped publicize this incident involving the powerful House Speaker. **1972-73** Orange production peaked at 7,800,000 boxes. **1973** Sorghum (grain) production peaked at 233,520,000 cubic tons and the number of turkeys peaked at 8,881,000. Texas achieved first place in mineral production; nearly $8 billion worth of sulfur, salt, helium, asphalt, graphite, bromite, natural gas, cement and clays. **JANUARY 16, 1973** Dolph Briscoe became Governor of Texas and served one two-year term and was reelected to a four-year term after a constitutional amendment in 1974 increased the governor's term of office to four years. **JANUARY, 1974** The legislature led by Speaker of the House Price Daniels, Jr., formed itself into a constitutional convention and spent five months and over $1 million to produce a new, shortened, 11 article constitution. In 1975 eight proposed amendments covering the new constitution were proposed to the electorate and all were defeated. **1975** Guar production peaked at 52,000,000 pounds, rye production peaked at 760,000 bushels, sunflower production peaked at 280,000,000 pounds and the number of cattle peaked at 16,600,000. **1976** Onion production peaked at 6,681,000 cwt. **1978** Cantaloupe production peaked at 1,286,000 cwt. cabbage production peaked at 4,941,000 cwt. and cucumber production peaked at 816,000 cwt. **1979** Hay production peaked at 7,133,000 tons, soybeans production peaked at 20,930,000 bushels, wheat production peaked at 138,000,000 bushels, pecan production peaked at 91,000,000 pounds, honeydew melon production peaked at 800,000 cwt. and green pepper production peaked at 794,000 cwt. **JANUARY 16, 1979** William P. Clements, Jr., Republican, became the first Texas Republican Governor since Reconstruction. **APRIL 10, 1979** Twenty-three tornados tore through the Red River areas of Texas and Oklahoma. Vernon, Texas had 11 deaths and $27 million in damage and Wichita Falls, Texas had 3,095 homes destroyed, 42 deaths and $300 million in damage. **JULY 24-25, 1979** Alvin, Texas received 43.0 inches of rain in 24 hours. **1980** Population 14,229,000, (third most populous state), growth rate 27.1%, 1970-80. Cucumber (for pickles) production peaked at 40,980 tons. Wichita Falls, during a heat wave starting June 23 ending August 3, had 42 days when the temperature was 100 °F or more, with temperatures above 110 °F from June 23 to July 3. **JUNE 15, 1982** The U.S. Supreme Court held that it was a violation of the 14th Amendment for the State of Texas to withhold money for the education of children who were illegal aliens. **AUGUST, 1982** The decline in the value of the Mexican peso hurt Texas businesses along the Mexican border as sales dropped. **JANUARY 18, 1983** Mark White, Democrat, became Governor of Texas. **AUGUST 17,1983** Hurricane Lisa struck the Houston area causing $1.5 to $2 billion in damage and 21 deaths. **JUNE, 1984** The Texas Legislature was called into special session by Governor White to pass an education bill and a tax bill. The $4.6 billion tax bill, the largest tax increase in Texas history, provided revenue for improving education.

PLACE	COUNTY	CHART LOCATION	ZIP CODE
Abbott	Hill	M21	76621
Abell (RRS)	Carson	P13	
Abercrombie (RRS)	Travis	C24	
Aberdeen	Collingsworth	P20	79095
Aberfoyle	Hunt	M8	75496
Abernathy	Hale	P30	79311
	Lubbock	P39	
Abilene	Jones	P62	79601
	Taylor	P70	
Abilene Christian College	Taylor	P70	79601
Abilene Municipal Airport	Taylor	P70	
Ables Springs	Kaufman	M14	75160
Abner	Kaufman	M14	75160
Abram	Hidalgo	B28	78572
Acala	Hudspeth	B2	79839
Ace	Polk	E32	77326
Ackerly	Dawson	P58	79713
	Martin	P66	
Acme (RRS)	Hardeman	P27	
Acton	Hood	M16	76048
Acuff	Lubbock	P39	79401
Acworth	Red River	E2	75426
Adams (RRS)	Bexar	C35	
Adams Gardens	Cameron	B30	78550
Adamsville	Lampasas	C6	76510
Addicks	Harris	G11	77079
Addielou	Red River	E2	75412
Addison	Dallas	M12	75001
Addran	Hopkins	E5	75482
Adell	Parker	M10	76042
Ad Hall	Milam	C18	76520
Adkins (Sayers)	Bexar	C35	78101
Admiral	Callahan	P71	79504
Adrian	Oldham	P11	79001
Adsul	Newton	E35	75956
Ady	Potter	P12	79010
Aero Vista	El Paso	B1	79918
Afton	Dickens	P41	79220
Agnes	Parker	M10	76082
Agua Dulce	Nueces	G32	78330
Agua Nueva	Jim Hogg	B23	78361
Aguilares	Webb	B19	78369
Aiken	Floyd	P31	79221
Aiken	Shelby	E26	75935
Air (Camp Air)	Mason	C13	76856
Air Force Plant No. 4	Tarrant	M11	76108
Airport City	Bexar	C35	78108
Airville	Bell	C17	76501
Alabama-Coushatta Indian Reservation	Polk	E32	77351
Alabama Creek	Trinity	E27	75845
Alamo	Hidalgo	B28	78516
Alamo Alto	El Paso	B1	79853
Alamo Heights	Bexar	C35	78209
Alanreed	Gray	P14	79002
Alazan	Nacogdoches	E25	75961
Alba	Wood	E11	75410
Albany	Shackelford	P63	76430
Albert	Gillespie	C22	78601
Albion	Red River	E2	75426
Aldine (estates, gardens and meadows)	Harris	G11	77039
Aledo	Parker	M10	76008
Aleman	Hamilton	C1	76531
Alexander	Erath	M15	76446
Alexanders Store	Shelby	E26	75973
Aley	Henderson	E19	75143
Alfred	Jim Wells	B21	78332
Algerita	San Saba	C4	76877
Algoa	Galveston	G19	77511
Alibates Flint Quarries National Monument	Potter	P12	
Alice	Jim Wells	B21	78332
Alief	Harris	G11	77411
Allamore (Allamoore)	Hudspeth	B2	79855
Allen	Collin	M7	75002
Allendale (RRS)	Wichita	P36	
Allenfarm	Brazos	C20	77868
Allenhurst	Matagorda	G24	77414
Allens Chapel	Fannin	M4	75492
Allens Point	Fannin	M4	75446
Alley (RRS)	Hale	P30	
Alleyton	Colorado	G15	78935
Allison	Wheeler	P15	79003
Alma	Ellis	M18	75119
Almeda (RRS)	Harris	G11	
Almont	Bowie	E3	75559
Aloe	Victoria	G22	77901
Alpine	Brewster	B6	79830
Alsa	Van Zandt	E15	75169
Alsdorf	Ellis	M18	75119
Altair	Colorado	G15	77412
Alto	Cherokee	E21	75925
Altoga	Collin	M7	75069
Alton	Hidalgo	B28	78572
Alto Springs	Falls	C9	76653
Alum	Wilson	C39	78160
Alum Creek	Bastrop	C25	78602
Alvarado	Johnson	M17	76009
Alvin	Brazoria	G18	77511
Alvord	Wise	M5	76225
Amarillo	Potter	P12	79101
	Randall	P17	
Amarillo International Airport	Potter	P12	79101
Ambia	Lamar	E1	75421
Ambrose	Grayson	M3	75414
Amelbulk (RRS)	Jefferson	G13	
Amelia (RRS)	Jefferson	G13	
Ames	Coryell	C7	76528
Ames	Liberty	G5	77575
Amherst	Lamb	P29	79312
Amistad	Val Verde	B8	78840
Amistad National Recreation Area	Val Verde	B8	78840
Ammansville	Fayette	G8	78945
Amy	Delta	E4	75432
Anadarko	Rusk	E22	75667
Anahuac	Chambers	G12	77514
Anchor	Brazoria	G18	77515
Ander	Goliad	G27	77963
Anderson	Grimes	G2	77830
Andice	Williamson	C16	78626
Andrews	Andrews	P65	79714
Angeles (RRS)	Reeves	P92	
Angelita (RRS)	San Patricio	G30	
Angelo State University	Tom Green	P89	76901
Angleton	Brazoria	G18	77515
Angus	Navarro	M19	75110
Anna	Collin	M7	75003
Annarose	Live Oak	G25	78022
Anneta	Parker	M10	76008
Anneta North	Parker	M10	76086
Anneta South	Parker	M10	76086
Anneville	Wise	M5	76023
Annona	Red River	E2	75550
Anson	Jones	P62	79501
Antelope	Jack	P56	76350
Anthony	El Paso	B1	88021
Antioch	Cass	E9	75551
Antioch	Delta	E4	75432
Antioch	Henderson	E19	75758
Antioch	Houston	E24	75851
Antioch	Madison	C21	75852
Antioch	Rusk	E22	75652
Antioch	Shelby	E26	75935
Anton	Hockley	P38	79313
Apolonia	Grimes	G2	77830

PLACE	COUNTY	CHART LOCATION	ZIP CODE	PLACE	COUNTY	CHART LOCATION	ZIP CODE
Appleby	Nacogdoches	E25	75961	Avalon	Ellis	M18	76623
Apple Springs	Trinity	E27	75926	Avery	Red River	E2	75554
Aquilla	Hill	C3	76622	Avinger	Cass	E9	75630
Aransas Pass	Aransas	G31	78336	Avoca	Jones	P62	79503
	Nueces	G32		Avondale	Tarrant	M11	76106
	San Patricio	G30		Axtell	McLennan	C8	76624
Arbala	Hopkins	E5	75482	Azle	Parker	M10	76020
Arbor	Houston	E24	75847		Tarrant	M11	
Arcade (RRS)	Ector	P75		Bacliff (Bay View)	Galveston	G19	77518
Arcadia	Shelby	E26	75935	Bacon (RRS)	Wichita	P36	
Archer City	Archer	P45	76351	Baden (RRS)	Martin	P66	
Arcola	Fort Bend	G17	77583	Bagby	Fannin	M4	75446
Arden	Irion	P88	76901	Bagwell	Red River	E2	75412
Argenta	Live Oak	G25	78368	Bahia Mar	Cameron	B30	78578
Argo	Titus	E7	75558	Bailey	Fannin	M4	75413
Argyle	Denton	M6	76226	Baileyboro	Bailey	P28	79371
Ariola	Hardin	G6	77625	Baileys Prairie	Brazoria	G18	77515
Arlam	Rusk	E22	75946	Baileyville	Milam	C18	76570
Arlie	Childress	P26	79201	Bainer	Lamb	P29	79339
Arlington	Tarrant	M11	76010	Bainville	Karnes	G20	78119
Armaglas (RRS)	Ellis	M18		Baird	Callahan	P71	79504
Armco (RRS)	Harris	G11		Baker	Parker	M10	76086
Armstrong	Kenedy	B26	78338	Bakersfield	Pecos	P93	79717
Arneckeville	De Witt	G21	77954	Balch Springs	Dallas	M12	75180
Arnett	Coryell	C7	76528	Balcones Heights	Bexar	C35	78201
Arnett	Hockley	P38	79336	Bald Hill	Angelina	E28	75901
Arney	Castro	P22	79042	Bald Prairie	Robertson	C19	77854
Arno (RRS)	Reeves	P92		Baldridge (RRS)	Pecos	P93	
Arp	Smith	E16	75750	Baldwin	Harrison	E18	75661
Arroyo (RRS)	Cameron	B30		Ballinger	Runnels	P80	76821
Art	Mason	C13	76820	Balmorhea	Reeves	P92	79718
Artesia Wells	La Salle	B17	78001	Balsora	Wise	M5	76026
Arthur City	Lamar	E1	75411	Bammel	Harris	G11	77040
Arvana	Dawson	P58	79331	Bancroft	Orange	G7	77630
Asa	McLennan	C8	76707	Bandera	Bandera	C33	78003
Ash	Henderson	E19	75751	Bandera Falls	Bandera	C33	78063
Ash	Houston	E24	75835	Bangs	Brown	P82	76823
Ashby	Matagorda	G24	77465	Bankersmith	Kendall	C29	78624
Asherton	Dimmit	B16	78827	Banquete	Nueces	G32	78339
Ashland	Upshur	E13	75640	Barbarosa	Guadalupe	C36	78130
Ashley (RRS)	El Paso	B1		Barclay	Falls	C9	76656
Ashmore	Gaines	P57	79342	Bardwell	Ellis	M18	75101
Ashtola	Donley	P19	79226	Barker	Harris	G11	77413
Ashwood	Matagorda	G24	77480	Barkman	Bowie	E3	75561
Ashworth (Cedarvale)	Kaufman	M14	75142	Barksdale	Edwards	B9	78828
Asia	Polk	E32	75939	Barnes	Polk	E32	75960
Askew	Hopkins	E5	75431	Barnhart	Irion	P88	76930
Aspermont	Stonewall	P52	79502	Barnum	Polk	E32	75927
Asphalt Belt Junction (A.B. Junction)	Zavala	B14	78829	Barrett	Harris	G11	77532
Astin	Robertson	C19	77859	Barry	Navarro	M19	75102
Atascosa	Bexar	C35	78002	Barstow	Ward	P84	79719
Atco (RRS)	McLennan	C8		Bartlett	Bell	C17	76511
Ater	Coryell	C7	76528		Williamson	C16	
Athens	Henderson	E19	75751	Bartley Woods	Fannin	M4	75492
Atlanta	Cass	E9	75551	Bartons Chapel	Jack	P56	76056
Atlas	Lamar	E1	75460	Bartonville	Denton	M6	76226
Atlee	La Salle	B17	78019	Barwise	Floyd	P31	79235
Atoy	Cherokee	E21	75785	Bascom	Smith	E16	75705
Atreco (RRS)	Jefferson	G13		Basin	Brewster	B6	79834
Attoyac	Nacogdoches	E25	75961	Basin Springs	Grayson	M3	76264
Atwell	Callahan	P71	76437	Bassett	Bowie	E3	75574
Aubrey	Denton	M6	76227	Bastrop	Bastrop	C25	78602
Auburn	Ellis	M18	76050	Bastrop Bayou	Brazoria	G18	77515
Audrey (RRS)	Liberty	G5		Bastrop Beach	Brazoria	G18	77515
Augusta	Houston	E24	75844	Bateman	Bastrop	C25	78662
Augustus (RRS)	Garza	P50		Batesville	Zavala	B14	78829
Aurora	Wise	M5	76078	Batson	Hardin	G6	77519
Austin	Travis	C24	78701	Battle	McLennan	C8	76664
	Williamson	C16		Bautista (RRS)	Moore	P7	
Austonio	Houston	E24	75835	Baxter	Henderson	E19	75751
Austwell	Refugio	G28	77950	Bay City	Matagorda	G24	77414
Authon	Parker	M10	76042	Baylor (RRS)	San Patricio	G30	
				Bayport (RRS)	Harris	G11	

PLACE	COUNTY	CHART LOCATION	ZIP CODE
Bayside	Refugio	G28	78340
Bayside Terrace	Harris	G11	77571
Baytown	Chambers	G12	77520
	Harris	G11	
Bayview	Cameron	B30	78566
Bazette	Navarro	M19	75144
Beach	Montgomery	G4	77301
Beach City	Chambers	G12	77520
Beadle	Matagorda	G24	77424
Beans Creek (RRS)	Cherokee	E21	
Beard (RRS)	Austin	G9	
Bear Grass (Evansville)	Leon	C12	75846
Beasley	Fort Bend	G17	77417
Beattie	Comanche	P83	76442
Beaukiss	Williamson	C16	78621
Beaumont	Jefferson	G13	77701
Beaumont Place	Harris	G11	77049
Beauxart Gardens	Jefferson	G13	77705
Beaver Dam	Bowie	E3	75559
Bebe	Gonzales	C37	78603
Beck	Lamb	P29	79371
Becker	Kaufman	M14	75142
Beckmann (RRS)	Bexar	C35	
Beckville	Panola	E23	75631
Becton	Lubbock	P39	79343
Bedford	Tarrant	M11	76021
Bedias	Grimes	G2	77831
Beecaves	Travis	C24	78746
Beech Grove	Jasper	E34	75951
Bee House	Coryell	C7	76512
Beeville	Bee	G26	78102
Behring Store	Guadalupe	C36	78155
Belcherville	Montague	M1	76255
Belding (RRS)	Pecos	P93	
Belfalls	Bell	C17	76579
Belgrade	Newton	E35	75928
Belk	Lamar	E1	75411
Bellaire	Harris	G11	77401
Bellaire Addition	Smith	E16	75701
Bellaire Junction (RRS)	Harris	G11	
Bellaire West	Harris	G11	77072
Bell Branch	Ellis	M18	76651
Belle Plain	Moore	P7	79029
Bellevue	Clay	P46	76228
Bellmead	McLennan	C8	76705
Bells	Grayson	M3	75414
Bellville	Austin	G9	77418
Belmont	Gonzales	C37	78604
Belott	Houston	E24	75835
Belton	Bell	C17	76513
Ben Arnold	Milam	C18	76517
Benavides	Duval	B20	78341
Ben Bolt	Jim Wells	B21	78342
Benbrook	Tarrant	M11	76126
Benchley	Robertson	C19	77801
Bend	San Saba	C4	76824
Bender (RRS)	Harris	G11	
Bendestsen (RRS)	Liberty	G5	
Ben Franklin	Delta	E4	75415
Ben Hur (Benhur)	Limestone	C10	76664
Benjamin	Knox	P43	79505
Bennett (Lakota)	Parker	M10	76066
Benoit	Runnels	P80	76882
Benonine	Wheeler	P15	79068
Ben Wheeler	Van Zandt	E15	75754
Berclair	Goliad	G27	78107
Berea	Marion	E14	75657
Bergheim	Kendall	C29	78004
Bergs (RRS)	Bexar	C35	
Bergstrom Air Force Base	Travis	C24	78743
Berlin	Washington	G1	77833
Bernardo	Colorado	G15	78933
Bernecker (RRS)	Fisher	P61	
Bernstein (RRS)	Hansford	P3	
Berryville	Henderson	E19	75763
Bertram	Burnet	C15	78605
Bess	Duval	B20	78322
Bessmay	Jasper	E34	77612
Best	Reagan	P87	76931
Bethany	Panola	E23	71007
Bethel	Anderson	E20	75861
Bethel	Ellis	M18	75165
Bethel	Henderson	E19	75751
Bethel	Runnels	P80	76821
Bethlehem	Bowie	E3	75559
Bethlehem	Hill	C3	76692
Bethlehem	Upshur	E13	75644
Bettie	Upshur	E13	75632
Beverly (corporate name Beverly Hills)	McLennan	C8	76711
Beverly Hills	Collin	M7	75069
Beversville (Beyersville)	Williamson	C16	78615
Bevil Oaks	Jefferson	G13	77706
Biardstown	Lamar	E1	75460
Big Bend National Park	Brewster	B6	79834
Bigfoot	Frio	B15	78005
Bighill	Limestone	C10	76687
Big Lake	Reagan	P87	76932
Big Sandy	Upshur	E13	75755
Big Spring	Howard	P67	79720
Big Thicket National Preserve	Hardin	G6	77706
	Jasper	E34	
	Jefferson	G13	
	Liberty	G5	
	Orange	G7	
	Polk	E32	
	Tyler	E33	
Big Wells	Dimmit	B16	78830
Billington	Limestone	C10	76624
Biloxi	Newton	E35	75928
Birch	Burleson	C27	77879
Birds (RRS)	Tarrant	M11	
Birome	Hill	C3	76625
Birthright	Hopkins	E5	75482
Biry	Medina	C34	78016
Bisbee	Tarrant	M11	76063
Bishop	Nueces	G32	78343
Bivins	Cass	E9	75555
Black	Parmer	P21	79004
Blackfoot	Anderson	E20	75853
Black Jack	Cherokee	E21	75789
Blackland	Rockwall	M13	75089
Blackoak	Hopkins	E5	75431
Blackwell	Coke	P79	79506
	Nolan	P69	
Blair	Taylor	P70	79536
Blakeney	Red River	E2	75412
Blanchard	Polk	E32	77351
Blanco	Blanco	C23	78606
Blanconia	Bee	G26	78102
Blandlake (Bland Lake)	San Augustine	E29	75972
Blanket	Brown	P82	76432
Blanks	Caldwell	C32	78644
Blanton	Runnels	P80	76821
Bleakwood	Newton	E35	75956
Bledsoe	Cochran	P37	79314
Bleiblerville	Austin	G9	78931
Blessing	Matagorda	G24	77419
Blevins	Falls	C9	76524
Blewett	Uvalde	B12	78801
Blix (RRS)	Angelina	E28	
Blocker	Harrison	E18	75670
Blodgett	Titus	E7	75686
Bloomburg	Cass	E9	75556
Bloomdale	Collin	M7	75069
Bloomfield	Cooke	M2	76258

PLACE	COUNTY	CHART LOCATION	ZIP CODE
Blooming Grove	Navarro	M19	76626
Bloomington	Victoria	G22	77951
Blossom	Lamar	E1	75416
Blue	Lee	C26	78947
Bluegrove	Clay	P46	76352
Blue Haven Estates	Hunt	M8	75169
Blue Mound (Saginaw Park)	Tarrant	M11	76131
Blue Ridge	Collin	M7	75004
Blue Ridge	Ralls	C9	76680
Blue Roan (RRS)	Colorado	G15	
Bluetown	Cameron	B30	78592
Blue Water Key	Henderson	E19	75758
Bluff Dale (RR name Bluffdale)	Erath	M15	76433
Bluff Springs	Parker	M10	76020
Bluff Springs	Travis	C24	78744
Bluffton	Llano	C14	78607
Blum	Hill	C3	76627
Blumberg Spur (RRS)	Guadalupe	C36	
Blumenthal	Gillespie	C22	78624
Bluntzer	Nueces	G32	78380
Bobsher (RRS)	Orange	G7	
Bobville	Montgomery	G4	77333
Bobwyn (RRS)	Dallas	M12	
Boden (RRS)	Potter	P12	
Bodie (RRS)	Gregg	E17	
Boerne	Kendall	C29	78006
Bogata	Red River	E2	75417
Bogus Springs	Cass	E9	75555
Bois D'Arc	Anderson	E20	75801
Boise (RRS)	Oldham	P11	
Bolin (RRS)	Dallam	P1	
Boling	Wharton	G16	77420
Bolivar	Denton	M6	76266
Bomarton	Baylor	P44	76353
Bon Ami	Jasper	E34	75956
Bonanza	Hill	C3	76692
Bonanza	Hopkins	E5	75420
Bonanza	Montgomery	G4	77356
Bond (RRS)	Morris	E8	
Bonham	Fannin	M4	75418
Bonita	Montague	M1	76255
Bonner (RRS)	Hidalgo	B28	
Bonney	Brazoria	G18	77515
Bonnie View	Refugio	G28	78393
Bono	Johnson	M17	76031
Bon Wier	Newton	E35	75928
Booker	Lipscomb	P5	79005
	Ochiltree	P4	
Boone (RRS)	Hale	P30	
Boonsville	Wise	M5	76026
Booth	Fort Bend	G17	77421
Boothe Spur (RRS)	Floyd	P31	
Boquillas	Brewster	B6	79834
Borden	Colorado	G15	78962
Borderland	El Paso	B1	79940
Borger	Hutchinson	P8	79007
Bovina	Parmer	P21	79009
Bowie	Montague	M1	76230
Bowman (RRS)	Taylor	P70	
Bowser	San Saba	C4	76860
Box Church	Limestone	C10	76642
Boxelder	Red River	E2	75550
Box Quarter	Robertson	C19	77837
Boxwood	Upshur	E13	75683
Boyce	Ellis	M18	75165
Boyd	Fannin	M4	75418
Boyd	Wise	M5	76023
Boydston	Gray	P14	79039
Boy (RRS)	Montgomery	G4	
Boys Ranch	Oldham	P11	79010
Boz	Ellis	M18	75165
Bozar	Mills	C5	76844
Brachfield	Rusk	E22	75681

PLACE	COUNTY	CHART LOCATION	ZIP CODE
Bracken	Comal	C30	78218
Brackettville	Kinney	B11	78832
Brad	Palo Pinto	M9	76475
Bradford	Anderson	E20	75853
Bradshaw	Taylor	P70	79567
Brady	McCulloch	P91	76825
Brady	Shelby	E26	75935
Bragg (RRS)	Hardin	G6	
Branch	Collin	M7	75069
Branchville	Milam	C18	77837
Brand (RRS)	Scurry	P60	
Brandon	Hill	C3	76628
Branton	Eastland	P72	76471
Brashear	Hopkins	E5	75420
Brazlime (RRS)	Hill	C3	
Brazoria	Brazoria	G18	77422
Brazos	Palo Pinto	M9	76472
Brazos Point	Bosque	C2	76652
Breckenridge	Stephens	P64	76024
Bremond	Robertson	C19	76629
Brenham	Washington	G1	77833
Brentwood Manor	Victoria	G22	77901
Breslau	Lavaca	G14	77964
Briar	Parker	M10	76020
	Tarrant	M11	
	Wise	M5	
Briaroaks	Johnson	M17	76028
Briary	Milam	C18	76570
Brice	Hall	P25	79226
Bridge City	Orange	G7	77611
Bridgeport	Wise	M5	76026
Briggs	Burnet	C15	78608
Briggs (RRS)	Dallas	M12	
Bright Star	Rains	E10	75410
Bright Star (Sava)	Van Zandt	E15	75169
Briscoe	Wheeler	P15	79011
Bristol	Ellis	M18	75119
Britton	Ellis	M18	76063
Broaddus	San Augustine	E29	75929
Broadview (RRS)	Lubbock	P39	
Broadway	Crosby	P40	79322
Broadway	Lamar	E1	75460
Broadway Junction	Lamar	E1	75460
Brock	Parker	M10	76086
Brock Junction	Parker	M10	76086
Brogado	Reeves	P92	79718
Bronco	Yoakum	P47	79315
Bronson	Sabine	E30	75930
Bronte	Coke	P79	76933
Brookeland	Sabine	E30	75931
Brookesmith	Brown	P82	76827
Brooks (RRS)	Jefferson	G13	
Brooks Air Force Base	Bexar	C35	78235
Brookshire	Waller	G10	77423
Brookside Village	Brazoria	G18	77581
Brookston	Lamar	E1	75421
Broome	Sterling	P78	76951
Browndell	Jasper	E34	75931
Brownfield	Terry	P48	79316
Browning	Smith	E16	75792
Brownsboro	Caldwell	C32	78644
Brownsboro	Henderson	E19	75756
Brownsville	Cameron	B30	78520
Brownsville International Airport	Cameron	B30	78520
Brownwood	Brown	P82	76801
Broyles	Anderson	E20	75801
Bruceville-Eddy	Falls	C9	76630
	McLennan	C8	
Brumley	Upshur	E13	75686
Brundage	Dimmit	B16	78834
Bruni	Webb	B19	78344
Brunswick	Cherokee	E21	75925
Brushy Creek	Anderson	E20	75801

PLACE	COUNTY	CHART LOCATION	ZIP CODE	PLACE	COUNTY	CHART LOCATION	ZIP CODE
Bryan	Brazos	C20	77801	Caldwell	Burleson	C27	77836
Bryans Mill	Cass	E9	75560	Caledonia	Rusk	E22	75975
Bryson	Jack	P56	76027	Calf Creek	McCulloch	P91	76825
Buck Creek (RRS)	Angelina	E28		Calgary (RRS)	San Augustine	E29	
Buchanan Dam	Llano	C14	78609	Call (Call Junction)	Jasper	E24	75933
Buck	Polk	E32	77351	Call	Newton	E35	75933
Buckeye	Matagorda	G24	77414	Callaghan (RRS)	Webb	B19	
Buckholts	Milam	C18	76518	Calliham (New Calliham)	McMullen	B18	78007
Buckhorn	Austin	G9	77418	Callisburg	Cooke	M2	76240
Buckhorn	Newton	E35	75928	Calvary	Wood	E11	75773
Buckingham	Dallas	M12	75080	Calvert	Robertson	C19	77837
Buckner	Parker	M10	76462	Calvin	Bastrop	C25	78602
Buda	Hays	C31	78610	Camden	Polk	E32	75934
Buena Vista	Bexar	C35	78221	Cameron	Milam	C18	76520
Buenos (RRS)	Garza	P50		Camey	Denton	M6	75034
Buffalo	Leon	C12	75831	Camilla	San Jacinto	E31	77331
Buffalo Gap	Taylor	P70	79508	Camp Alzafar	Kendall	C29	78006
Buffalo Gap	Travis	C24	78746	Campbell	Hunt	M8	75422
Buffalo Springs	Clay	P46	76228	Campbellton	Atascosa	C38	78008
Buford	Mitchell	P68	79512	Camp Bullis	Bexar	C35	78236
Bug Tussle	Fannin	M4	75449	Camp Dallas	Denton	M6	75034
Bula	Bailey	P28	79320	Camp Mabry (Army National Guard)	Travis	C24	
Bulcher	Cooke	M2	76252	Camp Maxey (RRS)	Lamar	E1	
Bullard	Cherokee	E21	75757	Campo Alto	Hidalgo	B28	78516
	Smith	E16		Camp Providence (Providence)	Polk	E32	77351
Bulverde	Comal	C30	78163	Camp Ruby	Polk	E32	77351
Buna	Jasper	E34	77612	Camps (Camp Switch)	Gregg	E17	75601
Bunavista	Hutchinson	P8	79007	Camp San Saba	McCulloch	P91	76829
Buncomb	Panola	E23	75633	Camp Scenic	Kerr	C28	78025
Bunger	Young	P55	76046	Camp Springs	Scurry	P60	79526
Bunker Hill	Lamar	E1	75486	Camp Stewart	Kerr	C28	78024
Bunker Hill Village	Harris	G11	77024	Camp Strake (Boy Scout Camp) (RRS)	Montgomery	G4	
Bunsen (RRS)	El Paso	B1		Campti	Shelby	E26	75935
Bunyan	Erath	M15	76446	Camp Verde	Kerr	C28	78010
Burford (RRS)	Marion	E14		Camp Willow	Guadalupe	C36	78130
Burgess (Reed Lake)	Bell	C17	76569	Camp Wood	Real	B10	78833
Burkburnett	Wichita	P36	76354	Canada Verde	Wilson	C39	78114
Burke	Angelina	E28	75941	Canadian	Hemphill	P10	79014
Burkett	Coleman	P81	76828	Candelaria	Presidio	B5	79843
Burkeville	Newton	E35	75932	Caney	Hopkins	E5	75482
Burleigh	Austin	G9	77418	Caney	Matagorda	G24	77414
Burleson	Johnson	M17	76028	Caney City	Henderson	E19	75148
	Tarrant	M11		Cannon	Grayson	M3	75095
Burlington	Milam	C18	76519	Canton	Van Zandt	E15	75103
Burnell	Karnes	G20	78119	Canutillo	El Paso	B1	79835
Burnet	Burnet	C15	78611	Canyon	Lubbock	P39	79401
Burns	Bowie	E3	75561	Canyon	Randall	P17	79015
Burns	Cooke	M2	76258	Canyon Lake (Canyon City)	Comal	C30	78130
Burr	Wharton	G16	77488	Canyon Valley	Crosby	P40	79356
Burris (RRS)	Lubbock	P39		Caplen	Galveston	G19	77617
Burrow	Hunt	M8	75089	Capps (RRS)	Moore	P7	
Burton	Washington	G1	77835	Capps Corner	Montague	M1	76265
Busby	Fisher	P61	79543	Cap Rock	Crosby	P40	79357
Busco (RRS)	Harris	G11		Caps	Taylor	P70	79605
Bushland	Potter	P12	79012	Caradan	Mills	C5	76844
Bustamante	Zapata	B22	78361	Carancahua	Jackson	G23	77465
Busterville	Hockley	P38	79358	Carbon	Eastland	P72	76435
Butler	Bastrop	C25	78621	Carbondale	Bowie	E3	75567
Butler	Freestone	C11	75855	Cardiff (RRS)	Waller	G10	
Butter Krust (RRS)	Travis	C24		Carey	Childress	P26	79222
Byers	Clay	P46	76357	Cargray (RRS)	Carson	P13	
Bynum	Hill	C3	76631	Carley (RRS)	Robertson	C19	
Byrd	Ellis	M18	75119	Carlisle	Trinity	E27	75862
Byrds	Brown	P82	76847	Carlos	Grimes	G2	77830
Cactus	Moore	P7	79013	Carl Range	Dallas	M12	75062
Caddo	Stephens	P64	76029	Carlsbad	Tom Green	P89	76934
Caddo Mills	Hunt	M8	75005	Carlton	Hamilton	C1	76436
Cadet (RRS)	Bexar	C35		Carmine	Fayette	G8	78923
Cadiz	Bee	G26	78102	Carmona	Polk	E32	75939
Caesar	Bee	G26	78119	Carnes (RRS)	Hardeman	P27	
Cain City	Gillespie	C22	78647	Caro	Nacogdoches	E25	75961
Calallen (RRS)	Nueces	G32					
Calaveras	Wilson	C39	78114				

POPULATED PLACES AND OTHER LOCATIONS

PLACE	COUNTY	CHART LOCATION	ZIP CODE	PLACE	COUNTY	CHART LOCATION	ZIP CODE
Carr (RRS)	Victoria	G22		Centralia	Trinity	E27	75834
Carricitos	Cameron	B30	78586	Cereal (RRS)	Floyd	P31	
Carrizo Springs	Dimmit	B16	78834	Cestohowa (Czestochowa)	Karnes	G20	78113
Carroll	Smith	E16	75701	Chaille (RRS)	Grimes	G2	
Carroll Springs	Anderson	E20	78657	Chaison (RRS)	Jefferson	G13	
Carrollton	Dallas	M12	75006	Chaison Junction (RRS)	Jefferson	G13	
	Denton	M6		Chalk	Cottle	P33	79224
Carson	Fannin	M4	75488	Chalk Bluff	McLennan	C8	76708
Carswell Air Force Base	Tarrant	M11	76127	Chalk Mountain	Erath	M15	76401
Carta Valley	Edwards	B9	78835	Chalybeate (Musgrove)	Wood	E11	75494
Carterville	Cass	E9	75563	Chamberlain (RRS)	Dallam	P1	
Carthage	Panola	E23	75633	Chambersville	Collin	M7	75069
Cartwright	Wood	E11	75494	Chambliss	Collin	M7	75003
Casa Piedra	Presidio	B5	79843	Chamizal National Memorial	El Paso	B1	79905
Casey	El Paso	B1	79836	Chancellor (RRS)	Pecos	P93	
Casey (RRS)	Harris	G11		Chances Store (Chance)	Burleson	C27	77879
Cash	Hunt	M8	75401	Chandler	Henderson	E19	75758
Cason	Morris	E8	75636	Channelview	Harris	G11	77530
Cass	Cass	E9	75556	Channelwood	Harris	G11	77530
Cassin (RRS)	Bexar	C35		Channing	Hartley	P6	79018
Castell	Llano	C14	76831	Chapman	Rusk	E22	75652
Castle Hills	Bexar	C35	78213	Chapman Ranch	Nueces	G32	78347
Castolon	Brewster	B6	79852	Chappel	San Saba	C4	76877
Castroville	Medina	C34	78009	Chappell Hill (Chapel Hill)	Washington	G1	77426
Catarina	Dimmit	B16	78836	Charco	Goliad	G27	77963
Cat Spring	Austin	G9	78933	Charles (RRS)	Travis	C24	
Cavines	Lamar	E1	75460	Charleston	Delta	E4	75424
Cavitt	Coryell	C7	76561	Charlie	Clay	P46	76308
Cawthon	Brazos	C20	77868	Charlotte	Atascosa	C38	78011
Cayote	Bosque	C2	76689	Charter Oak (RRS)	Bell	C17	
Cayuga	Anderson	E20	75832	Chase Field Naval Air Station	Bee	G26	78103
Cedar Creek	Bastrop	C25	78612	Chat	Hill	C3	76645
Cedar Creek	Waller	G10	77445	Chateau Woods	Montgomery	G4	77301
Cedar Grove	Angelina	E28	75901	Chatfield	Navarro	M19	75105
Cedar Hill	Dallas	M12	75104	Chautauqua (RRS)	Callahan	P71	
	Ellis	M18		Cheapside	Gonzales	C37	77952
Cedar Hill	Floyd	P31	79241	Cheek	Jefferson	G13	77705
Cedar Lake	Matagorda	G24	77414	Chemcel (RRS)	Nueces	G32	
Cedar Lane	Matagorda	G24	77415	Cheneyboro	Navarro	M19	75110
Cedar Mills	Grayson	M3	76264	Cherokee	San Saba	C4	76832
Cedar Park	Williamson	C16	78613	Cherry Spring	Gillespie	C22	78624
Cedar Point	Chambers	G12	77520	Chester	Tyler	E33	75936
Cedar Springs	Falls	C9	76570	Chesterville	Colorado	G15	77435
Cedar Springs	Upshur	E13	75683	Chico	Wise	M5	76030
Cedar Valley	Travis	C24	78746	Chicota	Lamar	E1	75425
Cee Vee	Cottle	P33	79223	Chief (Rand)	Kaufman	M14	75142
Cego	Falls	C9	76524	Chihuahua	Hidalgo	B28	78572
Cele	Travis	C24	78653	Childress	Childress	P26	79201
Celeste	Hunt	M8	75423	Chillicothe	Hardeman	P27	79225
Celina	Collin	M7	75009	Chilton	Falls	C9	76632
Cementville (RRS)	Bexar	C35		China	Jefferson	G13	77613
Center	Limestone	C10	76642	China Grove	Bexar	C35	78223
Center	Shelby	E26	75935	China Grove	Scurry	P60	79526
Center City	Mills	C5	76844	China Spring	McLennan	C8	76633
Center Line	Burleson	C27	77879	Chinati	Presidio	B5	79845
Center Mill	Hood	M16	76048	Chipley (RRS)	Victoria	G22	
Center Point	Camp	E12	75686	Chireno	Nacogdoches	E25	75937
Center Point	Ellis	M18	76651	Chita	Trinity	E27	75862
Center Point	Howard	P67	79720	Choate	Karnes	G20	78119
Center Point	Hunt	M8	75401	Chocolate Bayou	Brazoria	G18	77511
Center Point	Kerr	C28	78010	Choice	Shelby	E26	75935
Center Point	Panola	E23	75691	Chriesman	Burleson	C27	77838
Center Point	Parker	M10	76020	Christine	Atascosa	C38	78012
Center Point	Upshur	E13	75755	Christoval	Tom Green	P89	76935
Centerview	Leon	C12	75833	Chuckville	Eastland	P72	76471
Centerville	Leon	C12	75833	Church Hill	Rusk	E22	75652
Centerville	Trinity	E27	75845	Churchill Bridge	Brazoria	G18	77422
Centex (RRS)	Hays	C31		Cibolo	Guadalupe	C36	78108
Central	Angelina	E28	75969	Circle	Cherokee	E21	75785
Central	Cherokee	E21	75925	Circle	Lamb	P29	79064
Central Gardens	Jefferson	G13	77627	Circle Back	Bailey	P28	79371
Central Heights	Jefferson	G13	77627	Circleville	Williamson	C16	76574
Central Heights (Bonita)	Nacogdoches	E25	75961	Cisco	Eastland	P72	76437

PLACE	COUNTY	CHART LOCATION	ZIP CODE
Cistern	Fayette	G8	78941
Citrus City	Hidalgo	B28	78572
Clairmont	Kent	P51	79549
Clairette	Erath	M15	76457
Clara	Wichita	P36	76367
Clardy	Lamar	E1	75468
Clarendon	Donley	P19	79226
Clareville	Bee	G26	78102
Clark	Liberty	G5	77327
Clarks	Calhoun	G29	77979
Clarksville	Red River	E2	75426
Clarksville City	Gregg	E17	75647
Clarkwood (RRS)	Nueces	G32	
Claude	Armstrong	P18	79019
Clauene	Hockley	P38	79336
Clawson	Angelina	E28	75901
Clay	Burleson	C27	77839
Clayton	Jefferson	G13	77627
Clayton	Panola	E23	75637
Claytonville	Fisher	P61	79556
Claytonville	Swisher	P23	79052
Clear Lake	Collin	M7	75069
Clear Lake City	Harris	G11	77058
Clear Lake Shores	Galveston	G19	77565
Clear Spring	Guadalupe	C36	78130
Clearview	Bastrop	C25	78602
Cleburne	Johnson	M17	76031
Clegg	Live Oak	G25	78022
Clemons	Waller	G10	77423
Clemville	Matagorda	G24	77427
Cleta (RRS)	Randall	P17	
Cleveland	Liberty	G5	77327
Clever Creek	Shelby	E26	75935
Cliffside	Potter	P12	79106
Clifton	Bosque	C2	76634
Clifton	Van Zandt	E15	75169
Climax	Collin	M7	75077
Climax (RRS)	Nacogdoches	E25	
Cline	Uvalde	B12	78801
Clint	El Paso	B1	79836
Clinton	De Witt	G21	77954
Clinton	Hunt	M8	75005
Clodine	Fort Bend	G17	77469
Close City (Ragtown)	Garza	P50	79356
Cloudy (RRS)	Dallas	M12	
Cloverleaf	Harris	G11	77015
Clute City (corporate name Clute)	Brazoria	G18	77531
Clyde	Callahan	P71	79510
Coady	Harris	G11	77520
Coahoma	Howard	P67	79511
Cobbs	Kaufman	M14	75160
Coburn (RRS)	Lipscomb	P5	
Cochran	Austin	G9	77418
Cockrell Hill	Dallas	M12	75211
Codman (RRS)	Roberts	P9	
Coffee City	Henderson	E19	75763
Coffeyville	Upshur	E13	75683
Coit	Limestone	C10	76653
Coke	Wood	E11	75431
Colaboz	Cameron	B30	78586
Coldhill	Smith	E16	75701
Coldspring	San Jacinto	E31	77331
Coleman	Coleman	P81	76834
Colfax	Van Zandt	E15	75103
College Hill	Bowie	E3	75559
Collegeport	Matagorda	G24	77428
College Station	Brazos	C20	77840
Colleyville	Tarrant	M11	76034
Collier Spur (RRS)	Reeves	P92	
Collin (RRS)	Collin	M7	
Collins (RRS)	Jasper	E34	
Collinsville	Grayson	M3	76233
Colmesneil	Tyler	E33	75938
Cologne	Goliad	G27	77901
Colony	Fayette	G8	78941
Colorado City	Mitchell	P68	79512
Coltexo	Gray	P14	79054
Colton	Travis	C24	78744
Columbus	Colorado	G15	78934
Comal	Comal	C30	78130
Comanche	Comanche	P83	76442
Combes	Cameron	B30	78535
Combine	Dallas	M12	75159
	Kaufman	M14	
Comfort	Kendall	C29	78013
Commerce	Hunt	M8	75428
Como	Hopkins	E5	75431
Comstock	Val Verde	B8	78837
Comyn	Comanche	P83	76444
Concan	Uvalde	B12	78838
Concepcion	Duval	B20	78349
Concho	Concho	P90	76866
Concord	Cherokee	E21	75789
Concord	Hunt	M8	75401
Concord	Leon	C12	77850
Concord	Rusk	E22	75681
Concrete	De Witt	G21	77954
Cone	Crosby	P40	79321
Conlen	Dallam	P1	79022
Connell (RRS)	Orange	G7	
Connor	Madison	C21	77864
Conroe	Montgomery	G4	77301
Content (Tokeen)	Runnels	P80	79538
Converse	Bexar	C35	78109
Conway	Carson	P13	79068
Cooks Point	Burleson	C27	77836
Cooks Store	Anderson	E20	75861
Cookville	Titus	E7	75558
Cool	Parker	M10	76042
Coolidge	Limestone	C10	76635
Cooper	Delta	E4	75432
Cooper Canyon	Denton	M6	76201
Copano Village	Aransas	G31	78382
Copeville	Collin	M7	75018
Coppell	Dallas	M12	75019
Copperas Cove	Coryell	C7	76522
Copper Canyon	Denton	M6	76226
Corbet	Navarro	M19	75110
Corbyn (RRS)	Comal	C30	
Cordele	Jackson	G23	77957
Corinth	Denton	M6	76201
Corinth	Jones	P62	79553
Corinth	Leon	C12	75831
Corinth	Van Zandt	E15	75140
Corley	Bowie	E3	75567
Cornersville	Hopkins	E5	75494
Cornett	Cass	E9	75568
Cornudas	Hudspeth	B2	79847
Corpus Christi	Nueces	G32	78401
Corpus Christi International Airport	Nueces	G32	78401
Corpus Christi Naval Air Station	Nueces	G32	78419
Corpus Christi Naval Regional Medical Center	Nueces	G32	78419
Corral City	Denton	M6	76226
Corrigan	Polk	E32	75939
Corry	Lamb	P29	79041
Corsicana	Navarro	M19	75110
Corsicana Junction (RRS)	Navarro	M19	
Coryell	Coryell	C7	76689
Cost	Gonzales	C37	78614
Cotton Center (Cotton)	Fannin	M4	75418
Cotton Center	Hale	P30	79021
Cottondale	Wise	M5	76073
Cotton Gin	Freestone	C11	75860
Cotton Mill Spur (RRS)	Grayson	M3	

POPULATED PLACES AND OTHER LOCATIONS

PLACE	COUNTY	CHART LOCATION	ZIP CODE
Cottonwood	Callahan	P71	79504
Cottonwood	Falls	C9	76655
Cottonwood	Madison	C21	77872
Cotulla	La Salle	B17	78014
Coughran	Atascosa	C38	78064
Country Campus	Walker	G3	77340
Country Club Estates	Ector	P75	79760
Country Club Terrace	Victoria	G22	77901
County Line	Camp	E12	75686
County Line	Hale	P30	79363
Coupland	Williamson	C16	78615
Courtney	Grimes	G2	77868
Cove	Chambers	G12	77520
Cove Spring	Cherokee	E21	75766
Covington	Hill	C3	76636
Cow Spur (RRS)	Garza	P50	
Cox	Upshur	E13	75644
Cox Field (Airport)	Lamar	E1	75460
Coyanosa	Pecos	P93	79730
Coy City	Karnes	G20	78110
Crabb	Fort Bend	G17	77469
Crabbs Prairie	Walker	G3	77340
Craft	Cherokee	E21	75766
Crafton	Wise	M3	76030
Craig	Rusk	E22	75652
Crandall	Kaufman	M14	75114
Crane	Crane	P85	79731
Cranell (RRS)	Refugio	G28	
Cranfills Gap	Bosque	C2	76637
Crawford	McLennan	C8	76638
Creagleville	Van Zandt	E15	75140
Crecy	Trinity	E27	75845
Creechville	Ellis	M18	75119
Creedmoor	Travis	C24	78744
Crescent	Wharton	G16	77488
Crescent Heights	Henderson	E19	75751
Cresson	Hood	M16	76035
	Johnson	M17	
Crews	Runnels	P80	79567
Crisp	Ellis	M18	75119
Crockett	Houston	E24	75835
Crosby	Harris	G11	77532
Crosbyton	Crosby	P40	79322
Cross	Grimes	G2	77861
Cross (Franklin Settlement)	McMullen	B18	78026
Cross Cut	Brown	P82	76801
Cross Plains	Callahan	P71	76443
Cross Roads	Comanche	P83	76474
Cross Roads	Delta	E4	75432
Cross Roads	Denton	M6	76227
Crossroads	Harrison	E18	75670
Cross Roads	Henderson	E19	75148
Crossroads	Hopkins	E5	75482
Cross Roads	Milam	C18	76520
Cross Roads	Rusk	E22	75662
Croton	Dickens	P41	79232
Crow	Wood	E11	75765
Crowell	Foard	P34	79227
Crusher (RRS)	Hudspeth	B2	
Crushers (RRS)	Wise	M5	
Cruz Calle (Santa Cruz)	Duval	B20	78349
Cryer Creek	Navarro	M19	75102
Crystal Beach (Patton)	Galveston	G19	77650
Crystal City	Zavala	B14	78839
Crystal Falls	Stephens	P64	76024
Crystal Lake	Anderson	E20	75801
Cuadrilla	El Paso	B1	79836
Cuba (Sand Flat)	Johnson	M17	76031
Cuero	De Witt	G21	77954
Culleoka	Collin	M7	75069
Cumby	Hopkins	E5	75433
Cundiff	Jack	P56	76056
Cuney	Cherokee	E21	75759

PLACE	COUNTY	CHART LOCATION	ZIP CODE
Cunningham	Lamar	E1	75434
Currie	Navarro	M19	76693
Curtis (RRS)	Dallas	M12	
Curtis	Jasper	E34	75951
Curvitas (Cuevitas)	Hidalgo	B28	78565
Cushing	Nacogdoches	E25	75760
Cusseta	Cass	E9	75566
Cut	Houston	E24	75835
Cut and Shoot	Montgomery	G4	77301
Cuthand	Red River	E2	75417
Cuthbert	Mitchell	P68	79512
Cuyler (RRS)	Carson	P13	
Cyclone	Bell	C17	76519
Cypress	Franklin	E6	75494
Cypress	Harris	G11	77429
Cypress Bend	Harris	G11	77040
Cypress Creek Estates	Harris	G11	77429
Cypress Mill	Blanco	C23	78654
Dabney	Uvalde	B12	78801
Da Costa	Victoria	G22	77901
Dacus	Montgomery	G4	77356
Daffan	Travis	C24	78653
Daingerfield	Morris	E8	75638
Daisetta	Liberty	G5	77533
Dalby Springs	Bowie	E3	75559
Dale	Caldwell	C32	78616
Dale Crest	Van Zandt	E15	75140
Dalhart	Dallam	P1	79022
	Hartley	P6	
Dallardsville	Polk	E32	77332
Dallas	Collin	M7	75200
	Dallas	M12	
	Denton	M6	
	Kaufman	M14	
Dallas-Fort Worth Regional Airport	Dallas	M12	
	Tarrant	M11	
Dallas Love Field Airport	Dallas	M12	
Dallas Naval Air Station (Hensley Field)	Dallas	M12	
Dal-Nor (RRS)	Dallas	M12	
Dalton	Cass	E9	75568
Dalworthington Gardens	Tarrant	M11	76010
Dalys	Houston	E24	75844
Damon	Brazoria	G18	77430
Danbury	Brazoria	G18	77534
Danci (RRS)	Johnson	M17	
Danciger	Brazoria	G18	77431
Danevang	Wharton	G16	77432
Daniel	Houston	E24	75835
Daniels	Panola	E23	75633
Daniels	Washington	G1	77880
Danville	Gregg	E17	75662
Daphane (Daphne)	Franklin	E6	75455
Darco (Cave Springs)	Harrison	E18	75670
Darden (RRS)	Bowie	E3	
Darrouzett	Lipscomb	P5	79024
Davenport	Red River	E2	75412
Davilla	Milam	C18	76523
Davis Prairie	Limestone	C10	76687
Davisville	Angelina	E28	75901
Davisville (Pleasant Springs)	Leon	C12	75833
Dawes (RRS)	Harris	G11	
Dawn	Deaf Smith	P16	79025
Dawson	Navarro	M19	76639
Dayton	Liberty	G5	77535
Deadwood	Panola	E23	75633
Dean (Dean Dale)	Clay	P46	76301
Dean	Hockley	P38	79363
Deanwright (RRS)	Anderson	E20	
Deanville	Burleson	C27	77852
Debbie (RRS)	Wood	E11	
De Berry	Panola	E23	75639
Decatur	Wise	M5	76234

PLACE	COUNTY	CHART LOCATION	ZIP CODE
Decker	Nolan	P69	79506
Decker Prairie	Montgomery	G4	77355
Deco (RRS)	Harris	G11	
Deep Water Point Estates	Collin	M7	75018
Deer Creek	Clay	P46	76365
Deer Park	Harris	G11	77536
Defense (RRS)	Bowie	E3	
De Kalb	Bowie	E3	75559
De Leon	Comanche	P83	76444
Delhi	Caldwell	C32	78953
Delia	Limestone	C10	76673)
Dell City	Hudspeth	B2	79837
Del Mar Hills	Webb	B19	78040
Delmita	Starr	B27	78536
Del Monte	Jefferson	G13	77627
Delray	Panola	E23	75633
Del Rio	Val Verde	B8	78840
Delrose	Upshur	E13	75644
Del Valle	Travis	C24	78617
Delwin	Cottle	P33	79248
Demarro (RRS)	Burnet	C15	
Democrat	Comanche	P83	76442
Democrat	Mills	C5	76442
Denhawken	Wilson	C39	78160
Denison	Grayson	M3	75020
Denning	San Augustine	E29	75972
Dennis	Parker	M10	76037
Denny	Falls	C9	76653
Denson Springs	Anderson	E20	75844
Denton	Callahan	P71	79510
Denton	Denton	M6	76201
Denver City	Yoakum	P47	79323
Deport	Lamar	E1	75435
	Red River	E2	
Derby	Frio	B15	78017
Dermott	Scurry	P60	79515
Dernal	Victoria	G22	77901
Desdemona	Eastland	P72	76445
Desert	Collin	M7	75004
DeSoto	Dallas	M12	75115
Dessau	Travis	C24	78751
Detmold	Milam	C18	76577
Detroit	Red River	E2	75436
Devers	Liberty	G5	77538
Devine	Medina	C34	78016
Dew	Freestone	C11	75831
Dewalt	Fort Bend	G17	77433
Dewees	Wilson	C39	78114
Dewey	Montague	M1	76239
Deweyville	Newton	E35	77614
Dewville	Gonzales	C37	78140
Dexter	Cooke	M2	76240
D'Hanis	Medina	C34	78850
Dial	Fannin	M4	75407
Dial	Hutchinson	P8	79026
Dialville	Cherokee	E21	75761
Diana (James)	Upshur	E13	75640
Diboll	Angelina	E28	75941
Dicey	Parker	M10	76086
Dickens	Dickens	P41	79229
Dickinson Village (Dickinson)	Galveston	G19	77539
Dickson Cove	Hunt	M8	75474
Dickworsham (RRS)	Clay	P46	
Dido	Tarrant	M11	76106
Dies (RRS)	Hardin	G6	
Dies	Tyler	E33	75979
Dike	Hopkins	E5	75437
Dilley	Frio	B15	78017
Dilworth	Gonzales	C37	78629
Dime Box	Lee	C26	77853
Dimmitt	Castro	P22	79027
Dimple	Red River	E2	75426
Dinero	Live Oak	G25	78350
Ding Dong	Bell	C17	76544
Dinsmore	Wharton	G16	77488
Direct	Lamar	E1	75486
Dirgin	Rusk	E22	75691
Dittlinger	Comal	C30	78130
Divide	Coke	P79	76945
Divot	Frio	B15	78017
Dixico (RRS)	Harris	G11	
Dixie	Grayson	M3	76273
Dixon	Hunt	M8	75401
Doans Crossing (Doans)	Wilbarger	P35	76384
Dobbin	Montgomery	G4	77333
Dobrowolski	Atascosa	C38	78026
Dodd City (RR name Dodds)	Fannin	M4	75438
Dodge	Walker	G3	77334
Dodson (Dodsonville)	Collingsworth	P20	79230
Dogridge	Bell	C17	76513
Dogwood	Tyler	E33	75979
Dolan (RRS)	Angelina	E28	
Dolen	Liberty	G5	77327
Domino	Cass	E9	75572
Donelton	Hunt	M8	75453
Donie	Freestone	C11	75838
Donna	Hidalgo	B28	78537
Don Tol (RRS)	Wharton	G16	
Doole	McCulloch	P91	76836
Dorchester	Grayson	M3	75030
Doss	Cass	E9	75563
Doss	Gillespie	C22	78618
Dot	Falls	C9	76524
Dothan	Eastland	P72	76437
Dotson	Panola	E23	75669
Double Bayou	Chambers	G12	77514
Double Oak	Denton	M6	76226
Doucette	Tyler	E33	75942
Doud (RRS)	Lubbock	P39	
Dougherty	Floyd	P31	79231
Dougherty	Rains	E10	73440
Douglass	Nacogdoches	E25	75943
Douglassville	Cass	E9	75560
Doule (Doyle)	Limestone	C10	76642
Douro (RRS)	Ector	P75	
Dowling (RRS)	Jefferson	G13	
Downing	Comanche	P83	76442
Downsville	McLennan	C8	76706
Dozier	Collingsworth	P20	79079
Drane	Navarro	M19	75110
Drasco	Runnels	P80	79567
Draughon-Miller Municipal Airport	Bell	C17	76501
Draw	Lynn	P49	79373
Dreka	Shelby	E26	75973
Dresden	Navarro	M19	75102
Dresser (RRS)	Bell	C17	
Dreyer	Gonzales	C37	77984
Dreyfoos	Hemphill	P10	79046
Driftwood	Hays	C31	78619
Dripping Springs	Hays	C31	78620
Driscoll	Nueces	G32	78351
Drop	Denton	M6	76247
Dryden	Terrell	B7	78851
Dubina	Fayette	G8	78956
Dublin	Erath	M15	76446
Dudley	Callahan	P71	79601
Duffau	Erath	M15	76447
Duke	Fort Bend	G17	77583
Dulin	Brown	P82	76827
Dumas	Moore	P7	79029
Dumont	King	P42	79232
Dunagan (RRS)	Angelina	E28	
Dunbar	Rains	E10	75440
Duncans Woods	Orange	G7	77630
Duncanville	Dallas	M12	75116
Dundee	Archer	P45	76358

POPULATED PLACES AND OTHER LOCATIONS

PLACE	COUNTY	CHART LOCATION	ZIP CODE	PLACE	COUNTY	CHART LOCATION	ZIP CODE
Dunlap	Cottle	P33	79248	Eldon (RRS)	Harris	G11	
Dunlay	Medina	C34	78861	Eldorado	Schleicher	P95	76936
Dunn	Scurry	P60	79516	Eldorado Center	Navarro	M19	76639
Dunstan (RRS)	Bastrop	C25		Electra	Wichita	P36	76360
Duplex	Fannin	M4	75447	Electric City	Hutchinson	P8	79006
Durango	Falls	C9	76656	Elevation	Milam	C18	76556
Duster	Comanche	P83	76444	El Gato	Hidalgo	B28	78516
Dye Mound	Montague	M1	76265	Elgin	Bastrop	C25	78621
Dyersdale	Harris	G11	77016	Eli	Hall	P25	79245
Dyess Air Force Base	Taylor	P70	79607	Eliasville	Young	P55	76038
Eagle Flat (RRS)	Husdpeth	B2		El Indio	Maverick	B13	78860
Eagle Ford (RRS)	Dallas	M12		El Jardin	Cameron	B30	78520
Eagle Lake	Colorado	G15	77434	Elk	McLennan	C8	76624
Eagle Mountain	Tarrant	M11	76135	Elkhart	Anderson	E20	75839
Eagle Mountain Acres	Tarrant	M11	76060	Ella (RRS)	Jim Wells	B21	
Eagle Pass	Maverick	B13	78852	El Lago	Harris	G11	77586
Early	Brown	P82	76801	Ellinger	Fayette	G8	78938
Earlywine	Washington	G1	77833	Elliott	Robertson	C19	77856
Earth	Lamb	P29	79031	Elliott	Wilbarger	P35	76364
East Afton	Dickens	P41	79220	Elmaton	Matagorda	G24	77440
East Bernard	Wharton	G16	77435	Elmdale	Taylor	P70	79605
East Columbia	Brazoria	G18	77486	Elmendorf	Bexar	C35	78112
East Direct	Lamar	E1	75486	Elm Grove	Cherokee	E21	75785
Easterly	Robertson	C19	77856	Elm Grove	Fayette	G8	78959
Eastgate	Liberty	G5	77535	Elm Grove	San Saba	C4	76860
East Hamilton	Shelby	E26	75973	Elm Grove	Wharton	G16	77434
Eastland	Eastland	P72	76448	Elm Mott	McLennan	C8	76640
East Liberty	Shelby	E26	75935	Elmo	Kaufman	M14	75118
East Mountain	Upshur	E13	75644	Elmont	Grayson	M3	75095
Easton	Gregg	E17	75641	Elmwood	Anderson	E20	75801
	Rusk	E22		Eloise	Falls	C9	76680
East Point	Wood	E11	75494	El Oso	Karnes	G20	78119
East River	Harris	G11	77327	El Paso	El Paso	B1	79901
East Side	Panola	E23	75639	El Paso International Airport	El Paso	B1	79925
East Stamford	Jones	P62	79553	Elroy	Travis	C24	78617
East Tawakoni	Rains	E10	75453	Elsa	Hidalgo	B28	78543
East Tempe	Polk	E32	77351	El Sauz	Starr	B27	78544
East Texas State Teachers College	Hunt	M8	75429	Elstone	Medina	C34	78861
Eastvale	Denton	M6	75067	El Toro	Jackson	G23	77957
Eaton	Robertson	C19	77856	Elva (RRS)	Ellis	M18	
Ebenezer	Camp	E12	75686	Elwood	Fannin	M4	75439
Ebony	Mills	C5	76864	Elwood	Madison	C21	75852
Echo	Coleman	P81	76834	Ely	Fannin	M4	75439
Echo	Orange	G7	77630	Elysian Fields	Harrison	E18	75642
Echols	Limestone	C10	76635	Emberson	Lamar	E1	75486
Eckert	Gillespie	C22	78675	Emblem	Hopkins	E5	75482
Ecleto	Karnes	G20	78111	Emhouse	Navarro	M19	75110
Ector	Fannin	M4	75439	Emilee	Tyler	E33	75979
Edcouch	Hidalgo	B28	78538	Emmett	Navarro	M19	76641
Eden	Concho	P90	76837	Emory	Rains	E10	75440
Edgar	De Witt	G21	77954	Enchanted Oaks	Henderson	E19	75147
Edge	Brazos	C20	77801	Encinal	La Salle	B17	78019
Edgecliff	Tarrant	M11	76134	Encino	Brooks	B24	78353
Edgewood	Van Zandt	E15	75117	Energy	Comanche	P83	76452
Edgeworth	Bell	C17	76569	Engleman	Hidalgo	B28	78543
Edhube	Fannin	M4	75418	Engle	Fayette	G8	78956
Edinburg	Hidalgo	B28	78539	English	Red River	E2	75426
Edith	Coke	P79	76945	Enloe	Delta	E4	75441
Edmonson	Hale	P30	79032	Ennis	Ellis	M18	75119
Edna	Jackson	G23	77957	Enoch	Upshur	E13	75644
Edna Hill	Erath	M15	76446	Enochs	Bailey	P28	79324
Edom	Van Zandt	E15	75756	Enos	Waller	G10	77423
Edroy	San Patricio	G30	78352	Ensign	Ellis	M18	75119
Egan	Johnson	M17	76031	Enterprise	Cherokee	E21	75766
Egypt	Montgomery	G4	77355	Enterprise	Van Zandt	E15	75169
Egypt	Wharton	G16	77436	Eola	Concho	P90	76937
Eight Mile	Harrison	E18	75670	Eolian	Stephens	P64	76024
Elam (RRS)	Dallas	M12		Era	Cooke	M2	76238
Elbert	Throckmorton	P54	76359	Erin	Jasper	E34	75951
Elberta (RRS)	Smith	E16		Erwin	Grimes	G2	77830
El Campo	Wharton	G16	77437	Esbon	Llano	C14	76885
El Campo South	Wharton	G16	77437	Escobares	Starr	B27	78582
El Centro	Starr	B27	78536	Escobas	Zapata	B22	78361

PLACE	COUNTY	CHART LOCATION	ZIP CODE
Eskota	Fisher	P61	79561
Esperanza	Hudspeth	B2	79841
Esseville	Live Oak	G25	78075
Estacado	Crosby	P40	79343
Estacado	Lubbock	P39	79250
Estelline	Hall	P25	79233
Estes	Aransas	G31	78382
Estes	Harrison	E18	75601
Estes Addition	Wise	M5	76071
Ethel	Grayson	M3	76233
Etoile	Nacogdoches	E25	75944
Etter	Moore	P7	79029
Etter Junction (RRS)	Moore	P7	
Eubank Acres	Travis	C24	78753
Eula	Callahan	P71	79510
Eulalie (Bryce)	Rusk	E22	75975
Euless	Tarrant	M11	76039
Eulogy	Bosque	C2	76652
Eunice (RRS)	Swisher	P23	
Eureka	Navarro	M19	75110
Eustace	Henderson	E19	75124
Evadale	Jasper	E34	77615
Evant	Coryell	C7	76525
	Hamilton	C1	
Everett (RRS)	Oldham	P11	
Evergreen	San Jacinto	E31	77327
Everitt (Magnolia)	San Jacinto	E31	77327
Everman	Tarrant	M11	76140
Ewelder (RRS)	San Patricio	G30	
Ewell	Upshur	E13	75644
Exell	Moore	P7	79058
Exum (RRS)	Hartley	P6	
Eylau	Bowie	E3	75501
Ezzell	Lavaca	G14	77964
Fabens	El Paso	B1	79838
Fairbanks (RRS)	Harris	G11	
Fairchilds	Fort Bend	G17	77461
Fairfield	Freestone	C11	75840
Fairland	Burnet	C15	78654
Fairlie	Hunt	M8	75428
Fairmount	Sabine	E30	75948
Fairoaks	Limestone	C10	75838
Fair Play	Panola	E23	75631
Fairview	Bailey	P28	79371
Fairview	Bosque	C2	76689
Fairview	Collin	M7	75069
Fairview	Hood	M16	76048
Fairview	Howard	P67	79720
Fairview	Rusk	E22	75784
Fairview	Wilson	C39	78114
Fairview	Wise	M5	76078
Fairy (Martin Gap)	Hamilton	C1	76457
Faker	Camp	E12	75686
Falcon	Zapata	B22	78584
Falcon Heights	Starr	B27	78545
Falcon Village	Starr	B27	78545
Falfurrias	Brooks	B24	78355
Fallon	Limestone	C10	76667
Falls City	Karnes	G20	78113
Fannett	Jefferson	G13	77705
Fannin	Goliad	G27	77960
Fargo	Wilbarger	P35	76384
Farmer	Crosby	P40	79357
Farmers Branch	Dallas	M12	75234
Farmers Valley	Wilbarger	P35	76384
Farmersville	Collin	M7	75031
Farmington	Grayson	M3	75058
Farnsworth	Ochiltree	P4	79033
Farrar	Limestone	C10	75838
Farrsville	Newton	E35	75977
Farwell	Parmer	P21	79325
Fashing	Atascosa	C38	78020
Fate	Rockwall	M13	75032
Faught	Lamar	E1	75460
Faulkner (Pin Hook)	Lamar	E1	75416
Fauna (RRS)	Harris	G11	
Fawil	Newton	E35	75928
Fayburg	Collin	M7	75004
Fayetteville	Fayette	G8	78940
Faysville	Hidalgo	B28	78539
Fedor	Lee	C26	78947
Feld (RRS)	Williamson	C16	
Felicia (RRS)	Liberty	G5	
Fentress	Caldwell	C32	78622
Fergus (RRS)	Hunt	M8	
Fern (RRS)	Harris	G11	
Ferris	Ellis	M18	75125
Field Creek	Llano	C14	76869
Fieldton	Lamb	P29	79326
Fife	McCulloch	P91	76839
Figridge	Chambers	G12	77661
Files Valley	Hill	C3	76055
Fincastle	Henderson	E19	75763
Fink	Grayson	M3	75076
Finney	Hale	P30	79072
Finney	King	P42	79248
Fischer	Comal	C30	78623
Fish Branch	San Jacinto	E31	77371
Fisk	Coleman	P81	76834
Fitze	Nacogdoches	E25	75946
Fitzhugh	Hays	C31	78703
Five Points	Ellis	M18	75165
Flagg	Castro	P22	79027
Flanagan	Rusk	E22	75691
Flat	Coryell	C7	76526
Flat Fork	Shelby	E26	75974
Flatonia	Fayette	G8	78941
Flats	Rains	E10	75472
Flatwood	Van Zandt	E15	75754
Flint	Smith	E16	75762
Flint Creek	Young	P55	76046
Flo	Leon	C12	75831
Flomot	Motley	P32	79234
Flora	Hopkins	E5	75437
Florence	Williamson	C16	76527
Floresville	Wilson	C39	78114
Florey	Andrews	P65	79732
Florine (RRS)	Bexar	C35	
Flour Bluff (RRS)	Nueces	G32	
Flour Bluff Junction (RRS)	Nueces	G32	
Flowella	Brooks	B24	78355
Flower Mound	Denton	M6	75067
Floy	Fayette	G8	78941
Floyd	Hunt	M8	75401
Floydada	Floyd	P31	79235
Fluvanna	Scurry	P60	79517
Flynn	Leon	C12	77855
Foard City	Foard	P34	79227
Fodice	Houston	E24	75851
Follett	Lipscomb	P5	79034
Folsom (RRS)	Potter	P12	
Foncine	Collin	M7	75069
Fondren (RRS)	Harris	G11	
Foot	Collin	M7	75069
Ford Oaks	Travis	C24	78704
Fords Corner	San Augustine	E29	75972
Fordtran	Victoria	G22	77995
Forest	Cherokee	E21	75945
Forestburg	Montague	M1	76239
Forest Chapel	Lamar	E1	75411
Forest Glade	Limestone	C10	76667
Forest Grove	Collin	M7	75069
Forest Grove	Henderson	E19	75758
Forest Hill	Lamar	E1	75446
Forest Hill	Tarrant	M11	76119
Forest Hill	Wood	E11	75783

POPULATED PLACES AND OTHER LOCATIONS

PLACE	COUNTY	CHART LOCATION	ZIP CODE
Forney	Kaufman	M14	75126
Forreston	Ellis	M18	76041
Forsan	Howard	P67	79733
Fort Belknap Park	Young	P55	76372
Fort Bliss (U.S. Army)	El Paso	B1	79916
Fort Chadbourne (RRS)	Coke	P79	
Fort Davis	Jeff Davis	B4	79734
Fort Davis National Historic Site	Jeff Davis	B4	79734
Fort Gates	Coryell	C7	76528
Fort Griffin (State Park)	Shackelford	P63	76430
Fort Hancock	Hudspeth	B2	79839
Fort Hood (U.S. Army)	Bell	C17	76544
	Coryell	C7	
Fort McKayett	Menard	P96	76841
Fort Sam Houston (U.S. Army)	Bexar	C35	78234
Fort Spunky	Hood	M16	76031
Fort Stockton	Pecos	P93	79735
Fortune (RRS)	Harris	G11	
Fort Wolters	Palo Pinto	M9	76067
Fort Worth	Tarrant	M11	76101
Foster	Fort Bend	G17	77469
Foster (Forrester)	Terry	P48	79316
Fosters Store	Burleson	C27	77836
Fouke	Wood	E11	75765
Four Corners	Brazoria	G18	77422
Four Corners	Montgomery	G4	77301
Four Way	Moore	P7	79018
Fowlerton	La Salle	B17	78021
Fowlkers (RRS)	Wichita	P36	
Fox	Parker	M10	76086
Frame Switch	Williamson	C16	76574
Francis (RRS)	Orange	G7	
Francitas	Jackson	G23	77961
Frankel City	Andrews	P65	79737
Frankell	Stephens	P64	76470
Franklin	Robertson	C19	77856
Frankston	Anderson	E20	75763
Frankston Lake	Anderson	E20	75763
Fratt (RRS)	Bexar	C35	
Fred	Tyler	E33	77616
Fredericksburg	Gillespie	C22	78624
Fredonia	Gregg	E17	75662
Fredonia	Mason	C13	76842
Freedom (RRS)	McLennan	C8	
Freemound	Cooke	M2	76252
Freeport	Brazoria	G18	77541
Freer	Duval	B20	78357
Freestone	Freestone	C11	75842
Freeway Oaks Estates	Montgomery	G4	77365
Frelsburg	Colorado	G15	78950
Frenstat	Burleson	C27	77836
Fresenius	Hardin	G6	77656
Fresno	Fort Bend	G17	77545
Freyburg	Fayette	G8	78956
Friar	Rusk	E22	75684
Friday	Trinity	E27	75845
Friendship	Jasper	E34	75966
Friendship	Lamb	P29	79371
Friendship	Smith	E16	75647
Friendship	Van Zandt	E15	75140
Friendship	Williamson	C16	76530
Friendswood	Galveston	G19	77546
Friona	Parmer	P21	79035
Frio Town	Frio	B15	78061
Frisco	Collin	M7	75034
	Denton	M6	
Fritch	Hutchinson	P8	79036
	Collin	M7	75004
Fromme (RRS)	Travis	C24	
Front	Panola	E23	75639
Fronton	Starr	B27	78546
Frosa	Limestone	C10	76678
Frost	Navarro	M19	76641
Fruitland	Montague	M1	76230
Fruitvale	Van Zandt	E15	75127
Frydek	Austin	G9	77474
Fulbright	Red River	E2	75436
Fuller (RRS)	Wheeler	P15	
Fuller Springs	Angelina	E28	75901
Fullerville (RRS)	Scurry	P60	
Fulshear	Fort Bend	G17	77441
Fulton	Aransas	G31	78358
Fulton Beach	Aransas	G31	78358
Funston	Jones	P62	79501
Fuqua (RRS)	Liberty	G5	
Furguson (RRS)	Hale	P30	
Furney Richardson	Freestone	C11	75860
Fussel	Rusk	E22	75667
Gail	Borden	P59	79738
Gainesville	Cooke	M2	76240
Galena Park	Harris	G11	77547
Gallatin	Cherokee	E21	75764
Gallaway	Panola	E23	71049
Galle	Guadalupe	C36	78638
Galloway	Cass	E9	75551
Galloway (RRS)	Jefferson	G13	
Galveston	Galveston	G19	77550
Galveston Coast Guard Base	Galveston	G19	
Ganado	Jackson	G23	77962
Gandy (RRS)	Burnet	C15	
Gano	Williamson	C16	76577
Garceno	Starr	B27	78582
Garciasville	Starr	B27	78547
Garden City	Glasscock	P77	79739
Gardendale	Ector	P75	79758
Gardendale	La Salle	B17	78014
Garden Ridge	Comal	C30	78218
Garden Valley	Childress	P26	79238
Garden Valley	Smith	E16	75771
Garden Villas	Victoria	G22	77901
Garfield	De Witt	G21	78164
Garfield	Travis	C24	78617
Garland	Bowie	E3	75559
Garland	Dallas	M12	75040
Garland Air National Guard Station	Dallas	M12	
Garner	Parker	M10	76042
Garrett	Ellis	M18	75119
Garretts Bluff	Lamar	E1	75411
Garrison	Nacogdoches	E25	75946
Garth	Harris	G11	77520
Garvin	Wise	M5	76023
Garwood	Colorado	G15	77442
Gary City	Panola	E23	75643
Gasco (RRS)	Dallas	M12	
Gasoline	Briscoe	P24	79255
Gastonia	Kaufman	M14	75114
Gates (RRS)	Dallas	M12	
Gatesville	Coryell	C7	76528
Gatewood	Harris	G11	77039
Gause	Milam	C18	77857
Gay Hill	Washington	G1	77833
Gaylord (RRS)	Lipscomb	P5	
Gene (RRS)	Colorado	G15	
Geneva	Sabine	E30	75947
Genoa (RRS)	Harris	G11	
Gentry (RRS)	Potter	P12	
George	Madison	C21	77871
Georgetown	Williamson	C16	78626
George West	Live Oak	G25	78022
Georgia	Lamar	E1	75486
Gerald	McLennan	C8	76640
Geronimo	Guadalupe	C36	78115
Gethsemane	Marion	E14	75657
Gholson	McLennan	C8	76705
Gibtown	Jack	P56	76075
Giddings	Lee	C26	78942

PLACE	COUNTY	CHART LOCATION	ZIP CODE
Gilbert	Angelina	E28	75901
Gilchrist	Galveston	G19	77617
Giles	Donley	P19	79237
Gill	Harrison	E18	75670
Gillett	Karnes	G20	78116
Gilliland	Knox	P43	79260
Gillis (RRS)	Morris	E8	
Gilmer	Upshur	E13	75644
Gilpin	Dickens	P41	79370
Ginger	Rains	E10	75410
Girard	Kent	P51	79518
Girvin	Pecos	P93	79740
Gish (RRS)	Harris	G11	
Givens	Lamar	E1	75460
Gladewater	Gregg	E17	75647
	Upshur	E13	
Glad Tidings	Hardin	G6	77625
Gladwater	Titus	E7	75455
Gladys (RRS)	Jefferson	G13	
Glass	Somervell	M20	76690
Glaze City	Gonzales	C37	77984
Glazier	Hemphill	P10	79037
Glecker	Lavaca	G14	78956
Glen Cove	Coleman	P81	76843
Glendale	Trinity	E27	75862
Glenfawn	Rusk	E22	75760
Glen Flora	Wharton	G16	77443
Glenn	Dickens	P41	79220
Glenn Heights	Dallas	M12	75115
	Ellis	M18	
Glenrio	Deaf Smith	P16	88423
Glen Rose	Somervell	M20	76043
Glenwood	Upshur	E13	75644
Glidden	Colorado	G15	78943
Globe	Lamar	E1	75486
Glory	Lamar	E1	75460
Gober	Fannin	M4	75443
Godley	Johnson	M17	76044
Gold	Gillespie	C22	78624
Golden	Wood	E11	75444
Gold Finch (Goldfinch)	Frio	B15	78005
Goldsboro	Coleman	P81	79519
Goldsmith	Ector	P75	79741
Goldthwaite	Mills	C5	76844
Goliad	Goliad	G27	77963
Golinda	Falls	C9	76655
	McLennan	C8	
Gomez	Terry	P48	79316
Gonzales	Gonzales	C37	78629
Goober Hill	Shelby	E26	75973
Goodfellow Air Force Base	Tom Green	P89	76903
Good Hope	Shelby	E26	75935
Goodland	Bailey	P28	79327
Goodlett	Hardeman	P27	79252
Goodlow	Navarro	M19	75144
Goodnight	Armstrong	P18	79226
Goodnight	Navarro	M19	75144
Goodrich	Polk	E32	77335
Goodville (Tomlinson Hill)	Falls	C9	76656
Gordon	Lynn	P49	79356
Gordon	Palo Pinto	M9	76453
Gordonville	Grayson	M3	76245
Goree	Knox	P43	76363
Gorman	Eastland	P72	76454
Goshen	Walker	G3	77340
Gossett	Kaufman	M14	75143
Gould (RRS)	Bell	C17	
Gouldbusk	Coleman	P81	76845
Graceton	Upshur	E13	75644
Graford	Palo Pinto	M9	76045
Graham	Young	P55	76046
Graham Chapel (Graham)	Garza	P50	79356
Granbury	Hood	M16	76048

PLACE	COUNTY	CHART LOCATION	ZIP CODE
Grand Bluff	Panola	E23	75631
Grandfalls	Ward	P84	79742
Grand Lake	Montgomery	G4	77301
Grand Prairie	Dallas	M12	75050
	Ellis	M18	
	Tarrant	M11	
Grand Saline	Van Zandt	E15	75140
Grandview	Dawson	P58	79331
Grandview	Johnson	M17	76050
Grange Hall	Harrison	E18	75670
Granger	Williamson	C16	76530
Grangerland	Montgomery	G4	77302
Granite Mountain (RRS)	Burnet	C15	
Granite Shoals	Burnet	C15	78639
Granite Shoals Lake Estates	Llano	C14	78654
Granjeno	Hidalgo	B28	78572
Granville (RRS)	Angelina	E28	
Grapeland	Houston	E24	75844
Grapevine	Dallas	M12	76051
	Tarrant	M11	
Grassland	Lynn	P49	79356
Gray	Marion	E14	75657
Grayback	Wilbarger	P35	76360
Grayburg	Hardin	G6	77618
Grays Chapel	Anderson	E20	75801
Grays Prairie (Peede's Mill)	Kaufman	M14	75158
Graytown	Wilson	C39	78114
Great Southwest (RRS)	Tarrant	M11	
Green	Karnes	G20	78119
Greenfield Acres	Ector	P75	79760
Green Hill	Titus	E7	75455
Green Lake	Calhoun	G29	77979
Green Valley	Denton	M6	76227
Greenview	Hopkins	E5	75420
Greenview Hills	Dallas	M12	75060
Greenville	Hunt	M8	75401
Greenvine	Washington	G1	77835
Greenwood	Hopkins	E5	75478
Greenwood	Midland	P76	79701
Greenwood	Parker	M10	76086
Greenwood	Red River	E2	75426
Greenwood	Wise	M5	76246
Greer (RRS)	McLennan	C8	
Gregg	Travis	C24	78653
Greggton (RRS)	Gregg	E17	
Gregory	San Patricio	G30	78359
Gresham	Smith	E16	75701
Greta (RRS)	Refugio	G28	
Grey Forest	Bexar	C35	78023
Gribble (RRS)	Dallas	M12	
Grice	Upshur	E13	75644
Griffin	Cherokee	E21	75789
Griffing (RRS)	Jefferson	G13	
Griffing Park	Jefferson	G13	77640
Griffith (Oasis)	Cochran	P37	79346
Griffith	Ellis	M18	76084
Grigsby	Shelby	E26	75935
Grimes (RRS)	Nolan	P69	
Grindstone	Freestone	C11	75840
Grit	Mason	C13	76846
Grit	Rains	E10	75410
Groesbeck	Limestone	C10	76642
Groom	Carson	P13	79039
Grosvenor	Brown	P82	76801
Grove Controls (RRS)	Harrison	E18	
Groves	Jefferson	G13	77619
Groveton	Trinity	E27	75845
Grow	King	P42	79248
Gruenau	De Witt	G21	78164
Gruene	Comal	C30	78130
Gruhlkey (RRS)	Oldham	P11	
Grulla (LaGrulla)	Starr	B27	78548
Gruver	Hansford	P3	79040

POPULATED PLACES AND OTHER LOCATIONS

PLACE	COUNTY	CHART LOCATION	ZIP CODE
Guadalupe	Victoria	G22	77901
Guadalupe Mountains National Park	Cuberson	B3	
	Hudspeth	B2	
Guajillo	Duval	B20	78332
Gude (RRS)	Limestone	C10	
Guerra	Jim Hogg	B23	78360
Guffey (RRS)	Jefferson	G13	
Gulf Camp	Ward	P84	79756
Gum Springs	Harrison	E18	75601
Gun Barrel City	Henderson	E19	75147
Gunsight	Stephens	P64	76437
Gunter	Grayson	M3	75058
Gustine	Comanche	P83	76455
Guthrie	King	P42	79236
Guy	Fort Bend	G17	77444
Guys Store	Leon	C12	75833
Gypsum (RRS)	Hudspeth	B2	
Hackberry (Stewart)	Cottle	P33	79248
Hagansport	Franklin	E6	75487
Haid	Wharton	G16	77453
Hail	Fannin	M4	75492
Hainesville	Wood	E11	75773
Hale Center	Hale	P30	79041
Halesboro	Red River	E2	75417
Halfway	Hale	P30	79072
Hall	San Saba	C4	76871
Hallettsville	Lavaca	G14	77964
Hallsburg	McLennan	C8	76705
Halls Store	Panola	E23	71007
Hallsville	Harrison	E18	75650
Halsted (Halstead)	Fayette	G8	78945
Haltom City	Tarrant	M11	76117
Hamby	Taylor	P70	79601
Hamilton	Hamilton	C1	76531
Hamlin	Jones	P62	79520
Hammond	Robertson	C19	76629
Hamon	Gonzales	C37	78629
Hampton	Tyler	E33	75936
Hamshire	Jefferson	G13	77622
Hancock	Dawson	P58	79331
Handley (RRS)	Tarrant	M11	
Handy	Milam	C18	76567
Haney (RRS)	Randall	P17	
Hanger (RRS)	Grayson	M3	
Hankamer	Chambers	G12	77560
Hannibal	Erath	M15	76401
Hanover	Milam	C18	76520
Hanson	Shelby	E26	75954
Happy	Randall	P17	79042
	Swisher	P23	
Happy Hill	Johnson	M17	76009
Happy Union	Hale	P30	79072
Happy Valley	Taylor	P70	79566
Harbin	Erath	M15	76446
Hardin	Hardin	G6	77625
Hardin	Liberty	G5	77561
Hardin-Simmons University	Taylor	P70	79601
Hardy (RRS)	Harris	G11	
Hardy	Montague	M1	76265
Hare	Williamson	C16	76574
Hargill	Hidalgo	B28	78549
Harker Heights	Bell	C17	76541
Harkeyville	San Saba	C4	76877
Harleton	Harrison	E18	75651
Harlingen	Cameron	B30	78550
Harlingen Industrial Airport	Cameron	B30	78550
Harmon	Lamar	E1	75446
Harmony	Anderson	E20	75801
Harmony	Parker	M10	76086
Harmony	Rusk	E22	75684
Harmony Hill	Rusk	E22	75691
Harper	Gillespie	C22	78631
Harpersville	Stephens	P64	76024
Harriet	Tom Green	P89	76901
Harrisburg (RRS)	Harris	G11	
Harrisburg	Jasper	E34	75951
Harrisdale	Ector	P75	79760
Harrison	McLennan	C8	76682
Harrold	Wilbarger	P35	76364
Harrys (RRS)	Dallas	M12	
Hart	Castro	P22	79043
Hartburg	Newton	E35	77630
Hart Camp	Lamb	P29	79339
Hartley	Hartley	P6	79044
Hart Spur (RRS)	Tarrant	M11	
Hartzo	Marion	E14	75657
Harvard	Camp	E12	75686
Harvey	Brazos	C20	77801
Harwood	Gonzales	C37	78632
Haskell	Haskell	P53	79521
Haslam	Shelby	E26	75954
Haslet	Tarrant	M11	76052
Hasse	Comanche	P83	76456
Hastings (RRS)	Brazoria	G18	
Hatchel	Runnels	P80	79567
Hatchetville	Hopkins	E5	75437
Hauser (RRS)	Hidalgo	B28	
Havana	Hidalgo	B28	78572
Hawkins	Wood	E11	75765
Hawkinsville	Matagorda	G24	77425
Hawley	Jones	P62	79525
Hawthorne	Walker	G3	77358
Hayden	Van Zandt	E15	75169
Haynesville	Wichita	P36	76360
Hays	Hays	C31	78666
Headsville	Robertson	C19	76653
Heaker (RRS)	Harris	G11	
Heald	Wheeler	P15	79057
Hearne	Robertson	C19	77859
Heath	Kaufman	M14	75087
Heath	Rockwall	M13	75087
Heaton (RRS)	Gray	P14	
Hebbronville	Jim Hogg	B23	78561
Hebco (RRS)	Bexar	C35	
Hebron	Denton	M6	75067
Heckville	Lubbock	P39	79329
Hedley	Donley	P19	79237
Hedwigs Hill	Mason	C13	76856
Hedwig Village	Harris	G11	77024
Hefner	Knox	P43	76363
Heidelberg	Hidalgo	B28	78570
Heidenheimer	Bell	C17	76533
Helena	Karnes	G20	78118
Helmic	Trinity	E27	75845
Helotes	Bexar	C35	78023
Helotes Park Estates	Bexar	C35	78023
Helotes Ranch Acres	Bexar	C35	78023
Hemphill	Sabine	E30	75948
Hempstead	Waller	G10	77445
Henderson	Rusk	E22	75652
Henderson Chapel	Concho	P90	76866
Henkhaus	Lavaca	G14	77984
Henly	Hays	C31	78620
Hennessey (RRS)	Harris	G11	
Henning	Nacogdoches	E25	75946
Henrietta	Clay	P46	76365
Henrys Chapel	Cherokee	E21	75789
Hereford	Deaf Smith	P16	79045
Heritage Hills	Travis	C29	78753
Herman (RRS)	Wise	M5	
Hermleigh	Scurry	P60	79526
Hermosa	Reeves	P92	79772
Herring (RRS)	Anderson	E20	
Herty (RRS)	Angelina	E28	
Hester	Navarro	M19	75110

PLACE	COUNTY	CHART LOCATION	ZIP CODE	PLACE	COUNTY	CHART LOCATION	ZIP CODE
Hewitt	McLennan	C8	76643	Holiday Lakes	Brazoria	G18	77515
Hext	Menard	P96	76848	Holland	Bell	C17	76534
Heyser (RRS)	Calhoun	G29		Holland Quarters	Panola	E23	75633
Hickmuntown (Four Points)	Travis	C24	78759	Holliday	Archer	P45	76366
Hickory Creek	Denton	M8	75065	Hollis	Madison	C21	77864
Hickory Creek	Hunt	M6	75423	Holly	Houston	E24	75851
Hickory Grove	Denton	M6	75065	Holly Grove	Polk	E32	77351
Hicks (RRS)	Tarrant	M11		Holly Springs	Jasper	E34	75951
Hickston	Gonzales	C37	78959	Hollywood	Jefferson	G13	77627
Hico	Hamilton	C1	76457	Hollywood Park	Bexar	C35	78232
Hidalgo	Hidalgo	B28	78557	Holman	Fayette	G8	78962
Hidden Valley	Harris	G11	77018	Holt	San Saba	C4	76860
Higginbotham	Gaines	P57	79323	Homer	Angelina	E28	75901
Higgins (RRS)	Jefferson	G13		Hondo	Medina	C34	78861
Higgins	Lipscomb	P5	79046	Honea	Montgomery	G4	77356
High	Lamar	E1	75421	Honey Grove	Fannin	M4	75446
Highbank	Falls	C9	76644	Honey Island	Hardin	G6	77625
High Hill	Fayette	G8	78956	Hood	Cooke	M2	76240
High Island	Galveston	G19	77623	Hooks	Bowie	E3	75561
Highland	Erath	M15	76446	Hooper (RRS)	Travis	C24	
Highland Acres	Grayson	M3	75076	Hoot (RRS)	Bowie	E3	
Highland Acres	Hunt	M8	75453	Hoover	Gray	P14	79065
Highland Addition	Parker	M10	76082	Hoovers Valley	Burnet	C15	78611
Highland Bayou	Galveston	G19	77563	Hope	Lavaca	G14	77995
Highland Estates	Victoria	G22	77901	Hopewell	Franklin	E6	75457
Highland Park	Dallas	M12	75205	Hopewell	Houston	E24	75835
Highlands	Harris	G11	77562	Horizon City	El Paso	B1	77907
Highland Village	Denton	M6	75067	Horn Hill	Limestone	C10	76642
Hightower (RRS)	Liberty	G5		Hornsby Bend	Travis	C24	78702
Hiland Shores	Grayson	M3	75076	Horton	Delta	E4	75428
Hilburn (RRS)	Castro	P22		Horton	Panola	E23	75639
Hilda	Mason	C13	76856	Hoskins Junction (RRS)	Brazoria	G18	
Hill (Hills Prairie)	Bastrop	C25	78602	Hostyn	Fayette	G8	78945
Hill City	Hood	M16	76476	Houmont Park	Harris	G11	77044
Hill Country Village	Bexar	C35	78232	House (RRS)	Fort Bend	G17	
Hillcrest	Brazoria	G18	77511	Houston	Fort Bend	G17	77001
Hillcrest	Colorado	G15	78934		Harris	G11	
Hillebrandt	Jefferson	G13	77705		Montgomery	G4	
Hillister	Tyler	E33	77624	Houston Intercontinental Airport	Harris	G11	77205
Hillje	Wharton	G16	77437	Howard	Ellis	M18	75165
Hills	Lee	C26	78659	Howard (RRS)	Wichita	P36	
Hillsboro	Hill	C3	76645	Howardwick	Donley	P19	79226
Hillsdale Pit (RRS)	Nolan	P69		Howe	Grayson	M3	75059
Hillside Gardens	Harris	G11	77039	Howellville	Harris	G11	77411
Hilltop Lakes	Leon	C12	77871	Howland	Lamar	E1	75460
Hilshire Village	Harris	G11	77055	Howth	Waller	G10	77445
Hinckley	Lamar	E1	75460	Hoxie	Williamson	C16	76574
Hindes	Atascosa	C38	78026	Hoyte	Milam	C18	76520
Hines	Wilbarger	P35	76384	Hub	Parmer	P21	79035
Hinkles Ferry	Brazoria	G18	77422	Hubbard	Hill	C3	76648
Hiram	Kaufman	M14	75169	Hubert	San Patricio	G30	78368
Hitchcock	Galveston	G19	77563	Huckabay	Erath	M15	76401
Hitchland	Hansford	P3	73942	Hudson	Angelina	E28	75901
Hix	Burleson	C27	77857	Hudson (RRS)	Harris	G11	
Hoard	Wood	E11	75773	Hudson Oaks	Parker	M10	79325
Hoban (RRS)	Reeves	P92		Huffines	Cass	E9	75555
Hobbs Spur (RRS)	Bell	C17		Huffman	Harris	G11	77336
Hobbs	Fisher	P61	79526	Hufsmith	Harris	G11	77337
Hobson	Karnes	G20	78117	Hughes Springs	Cass	E9	75656
Hochheim	De Witt	G21	77967	Hulen Park (RRS)	Galveston	G19	
Hockley	Harris	G11	77447	Hull	Liberty	G5	77564
Hockley Mine	Harris	G11	77447	Hulldale (RRS)	Schleicher	P95	
Hodge (RRS)	Tarrant	M11		Humble	Harris	G11	77338
Hodge Junction (RRS)	Tarrant	M11		Humble Government Wells Camp	Duval	B20	78357
Hodges	Jones	P62	79525	Humble Heights	Harris	G11	77338
Hodgson	Bowie	E3	75559	Hume (RRS)	Cherokee	E21	
Hoefer (RRS)	Colorado	B15		Hungerford	Wharton	G16	77448
Hoen	McLennan	C8	76673	Hunt	Kerr	C28	78024
Hogg	Burleson	C27	77836	Hunter	Comal	C30	78130
Holcombs Store	Cherokee	E21	75785	Hunters Creek Village	Harris	G11	77024
Holden (RRS)	Limestone	C10		Huntington	Angelina	E28	75949
Holiday Estates	Hunt	M8	75169	Huntoon (RRS)	Ochiltree	P4	
Holiday Hills	Rains	E10	75453	Huntsville	Walker	G3	77340

POPULATED PLACES AND OTHER LOCATIONS

PLACE	COUNTY	CHART LOCATION	ZIP CODE	PLACE	COUNTY	CHART LOCATION	ZIP CODE
Hurlwood	Lubbock	P39	79328	Jarvis College	Wood	E11	
Hurnville	Clay	P46	76365	Jasper	Jasper	E34	75951
Huron	Hill	C3	76692	Jayray (RRS)	Colorado	G15	
Hurst	Tarrant	M11	76053	Jayton	Kent	P51	79528
Hurstown (Halbert)	Shelby	E26	75973	Jean	Young	P55	76374
Hurst Springs	Coryell	C7	76634	Jeannetta (RRS)	Harris	G11	
Hutchins	Dallas	M12	75141	Jeans	Tyler	E33	75970
Hutto	Williamson	C16	78634	Jeddo	Bastrop	C25	78953
Huxley	Shelby	E26	75973	Jefferson	Marion	E14	75657
Hye	Blanco	C23	78635	Jefferson County Airport	Jefferson	G13	77627
Hylton	Nolan	P69	79506	Jenkins	Morris	E8	75638
Hyman	Mitchell	P68	79720	Jennings	Lamar	E1	75460
Iago	Wharton	G16	77420	Jericho	Donley	P19	79226
Iatan	Mitchell	P68	79565	Jericho	Shelby	E26	75935
Ida	Grayson	M3	75491	Jermyn	Jack	P56	76057
Idalou	Lubbock	P39	79329	Jersey Village	Harris	G11	77040
Ike	Ellis	M18	75165	Jester	Navarro	M19	76679
Ike (RRS)	Live Oak	G25		Jewett	Leon	C12	75846
Illinois Bend	Montague	M1	76265	Jiba	Kaufman	M14	75142
Impact	Taylor	P70	79603	Joaquin	Shelby	E26	75954
Imperial	Pecos	P93	79743	Joe (RRS)	Grayson	M3	
Inadale	Scurry	P60	79545	Joel (RRS)	Deaf Smith	P16	
Independence	Washington	G1	77833	Johnfarris (RRS)	Floyd	P31	
India	Ellis	M18	75125	Johnson	Terry	P48	79316
Indian Creek	Brown	P82	76801	Johnson City	Blanco	C23	78636
Indian Gap	Hamilton	C1	76531	Johnson Mine Spur (RRS)	Palo Pinto	M9	
Indian Hill	Newton	E35	75977	Johnstown	Montgomery	G4	77301
Indian Lake	Cameron	B30	78586	Johnstown	Van Zandt	E15	75169
Indianola	Calhoun	G29	77979	Johnsue (RRS)	Waller	G10	
Indian Rock	Upshur	E13	75644	Johnsville	Erath	M15	76457
Indio	Presidio	B5	79845	Johntown	Red River	E2	75417
Industry	Austin	G9	78944	Joinerville	Rusk	E22	75658
Inez	Victoria	G22	77968	Joliet	Caldwell	C32	78648
Ingleside	San Patricio	G30	78362	Jolly	Clay	P46	76301
Ingleside on the Bay	San Patricio	G30	78362	Jollyville	Williamson	C16	78664
Ingram	Kerr	C28	78025	Jonah	Williamson	C16	78626
Inks Lake Village	Llano	C14	78609	Jones	Van Zandt	B8	75140
Iola	Grimes	G2	77861	Jonesboro	Coryell	C7	76538
Iona (RRS)	Parker	M40			Hamilton	C1	
Iowa Colony	Brazoria	G18	77583	Jones Creek	Brazoria	G18	77541
Iowa Park	Wichita	P36	76367	Jones Creek	Wharton	G16	77437
Ira	Scurry	P60	79527	Jones Prairie	Milam	C18	76520
Iraan	Pecos	P43	79744	Jonestown	Travis	C24	78641
Iredell	Bosque	C2	76649	Jonesville	Harrison	E18	75659
Ireland	Coryell	C7	76528	Joplin	Jack	P56	76056
Irene	Hill	C3	76650	Jordans Store	Shelby	E26	75973
Ironton	Cherokee	E21	75766	Josephine	Collin	M7	75064
Irving	Dallas	M12	75060	Joshua	Johnson	M17	76058
Isla	Sabine	E30	75959	Josserand	Trinity	E27	75845
Island (Hopewell)	Madison	C21	75852	Jot 'Em Down	Delta	E4	75449
Italy	Ellis	M18	76651		Hunt	M8	
Itasca	Hill	C3	76055	Jourdanton	Atascosa	C38	78026
Ivan	Stephens	P64	76024	Joy	Clay	P46	76365
Ivanhoe	Fannin	M4	75447	Joy	Smith	E16	75647
Iverson	Hill	C3	76670	Joyce (RRS)	Harris	G11	
Izoro	Lampasas	C6	76522	Jozye	Madison	C21	77864
Jacinto City	Harris	G11	77029	Jud	Haskell	P53	79544
Jacksboro	Jack	P56	76056	Judkin (RRS)	Ector	P75	
Jackson	Marion	E14	75657	Judson	Gregg	E17	75660
Jackson	Shelby	E26	75954	Juliff	Fort Bend	G17	77583
Jackson	Van Zandt	E15	75401	Julliard (RRS)	Potter	P12	
Jacobia	Hunt	M8	75401	Junction	Kimble	P98	76849
Jacobs	Rusk	E22	75684	Juno	Val Verde	B8	76938
Jamaica Beach	Galveston	G19	77550	Jury (RRS)	Bowie	E3	
James	Houston	E24	75847	Justiceburg	Garza	P50	79330
James	Shelby	E26	75935	Justin	Denton	M6	76247
Jamestown	Newton	E35	75966	Kadane Corner	Wichita	P36	76360
Jamestown (RRS)	Tarrant	M11		Kaffir (RRS)	Swisher	P23	
Janet (RRS)	Wharton	G16		Kalgary	Crosby	P40	79356
Janus (RRS)	Nolan	P69		Kamay	Wichita	P36	76369
Jappa	Burnet	C15	78605	Kamey	Calhoun	G29	77979
Jardin	Hunt	M8	75428	Kanawha	Red River	E2	75436
Jarrell	Williamson	C16	76537	Kane (RRS)	Hidalgo	B28	

PLACE	COUNTY	CHART LOCATION	ZIP CODE
Karen	Montgomery	G4	77355
Karnack	Harrison	E18	75661
Karnes City	Karnes	G20	78118
Katemcy	Mason	C13	76850
Katy	Fort Bend	G17	77450
	Harris	G11	
	Waller	G10	
Kaufman	Kaufman	M14	75142
Kayare (RRS)	Cameron	B30	
Kay Bee Heights	Coryell	C7	76546
Keechi	Leon	C12	75831
Keenan	Montgomery	G4	77356
Keene	Johnson	M17	76059
Keeter	Wise	M5	76023
Keith	Grimes	G2	77861
Keller	Tarrant	M11	76248
Keller Corner	Cameron	B30	78520
Kellerville	Wheeler	P15	79049
Kelly	Collin	M7	75003
Kelly Air Force Base	Bexar	C35	78241
Kellyville	Marion	E14	75657
Kelsay	Jim Hogg	B23	78353
Kelsay (RRS)	Starr	B27	
Kelsey	Upshur	E13	75644
Kelton	Wheeler	P15	79096
Keltys (RRS)	Angelina	E28	
Kemah	Galveston	G19	77565
Kemp	Kaufman	M14	75143
Kempner	Lampasas	C6	76539
Kendalia	Kendall	C29	78027
Kendleton	Fort Bend	G17	77451
Kenedy	Karnes	G20	78119
Kenefick	Liberty	G5	77535
Kennard	Houston	E24	75847
Kennedale	Tarrant	M11	76060
Kennedy Shores	Cameron	B30	78520
Kenney	Austin	G9	77452
Kensing	Delta	E4	75450
Kent	Culberson	B3	79855
Kentuckytown	Grayson	M3	75491
Kenwood Place	Harris	G11	77039
Kerens	Navarro	M19	75144
Kermit	Winkler	P74	79745
Kerr (RRS)	Williamson	C16	
Kerrick	Dallam	P1	79051
Kerrville	Kerr	C28	78028
Kevin (Williams)	Liberty	G5	77327
Key	Dawson	P58	79331
Kickapoo	Anderson	E20	75763
Kildare	Cass	E9	75562
Kildare Junction	Cass	E9	75555
Kilgore	Gregg	E17	75662
	Rusk	E22	
Killeen	Bell	C17	76541
Kilowatt (RRS)	Orange	G7	
Kimball	Bosque	C2	76652
Kimbro	Travis	C24	78653
Kinard Estates	Orange	G7	77630
King	Coryell	C7	76563
King	Red River	E2	75550
King City	Liberty	G5	77327
Kingola	Wilbarger	P35	76373
Kingsbury	Guadalupe	C36	78638
Kingsland	Llano	C14	78639
Kings Mill	Gray	P14	79065
Kingston	Hunt	M8	75401
Kingsville	Kleberg	B25	78363
Kingsville Naval Air Station	Kleberg	B25	78363
Kingwood	Harris	G11	77339
	Montgomery	G4	
Kinkler (New Kinkler)	Lavaca	G14	77964
Kinsloe (RRS)	Gregg	E17	
Kinwood	Harris	G11	77052

PLACE	COUNTY	CHART LOCATION	ZIP CODE
Kiomatia	Red River	E2	75436
Kipfer (RRS)	Cameron	B30	
Kirby	Bexar	C35	78219
Kirby Town	Hardin	G6	77656
Kirbyville	Jasper	E34	75956
Kirk	Limestone	C10	76664
Kirkland	Childress	P26	79238
Kirkpatrick Addition	Smith	E16	75701
Kirtley	Fayette	G8	78957
Kirvin	Freestone	C11	75848
Kitalou (RRS)	Lubbock	P39	
Kittrell	Walker	G3	77862
Klein	Harris	G11	77373
Klondike	Dawson	P58	79331
Klondike	Delta	E4	75448
Klump	Washington	G1	77833
Knapp	Scurry	P60	79527
Knickerbocker	Tom Green	P89	76939
Knight Spur (RRS)	Dallas	M12	
Knippa	Uvalde	B12	78870
Knott	Howard	P67	79748
Knox City	Knox	P43	79529
Knoxville	Kimble	P98	76831
Koch (RRS)	Leon	C12	
Koerth	Lavaca	G14	77964
Kohrville	Harris	G11	77040
Kokomo	Eastland	P72	76454
Koockville	Mason	C13	76856
Kopernik Shores	Cameron	B30	78520
Kopperl	Bosque	C2	76652
Korf (RRS)	Orange	G7	
Kosciusko	Wilson	C39	78160
Kosmos (RRS)	Aransas	G31	
Kosse	Limestone	C10	76653
Kossuth (RRS)	Anderson	C20	
Kountze	Hardin	G6	77625
Kovar	Bastrop	C25	78941
Kress	Swisher	P23	79052
Krugerville	Denton	M6	76227
Krum	Denton	M6	76249
Kurten	Brazos	C20	77862
Kyle	Hays	C31	78640
Kyote	Atascosa	C38	78005
Labatt	Wilson	C39	78114
La Blanca	Hidalgo	B28	78558
La Casita	Starr	B27	78582
Laceola	Madison	C21	77871
Lackland Air Force Base	Bexar	C35	78236
Lacoma (RRS)	Cameron	B30	
La Coste (RR name Lacoste)	Medina	C34	78039
La Cour	Liberty	G5	77575
Lacy	Trinity	E27	75845
Lacy-Lakeview	McLennan	C8	76705
Ladonia	Fannin	M4	75449
LaFayette	Upshur	E13	75686
La Feria	Cameron	B30	78559
La Gloria (RRS)	Jim Wells	B21	
La Gloria	Starr	B27	78591
Lago Vista	Williamson	C16	78641
La Grange	Fayette	G8	78945
Laguna Heights	Cameron	B30	78578
Laguna Park	Bosque	C2	76634
Laguna Vista	Cameron	B30	78578
Laird Hill	Rusk	E22	75666
La Isla	El Paso	B1	79838
Lajitas	Brewster	B6	79852
La Joya	Hidalgo	B28	78560
La Junta	Parker	M10	76020
Lake	Wise	M5	76026
Lake Alaska	Brazoria	G18	77515
Lake Bridgeport	Wise	M5	76026
Lake Brownwood	Brown	P82	76801
Lake Cherokee	Gregg	E17	75652

PLACE	COUNTY	CHART LOCATION	ZIP CODE	PLACE	COUNTY	CHART LOCATION	ZIP CODE
Lake City	San Patricio	G30	78387	Lark	Carson	P13	79039
Lake Creek	Delta	E4	75450	Larue (LaRue)	Henderson	E19	75770
Lake Cypress	Harris	G11	77429	La Salle (Bennview)	Jackson	G23	77969
Lake Dallas	Denton	M6	75065	Lasara (RR name La Sara)	Willacy	B29	78561
Lake Estates	Montgomery	G4	77356	Las Milpas	Hidalgo	B28	78577
Lakehills (North Lake)	Bandera	C33	78063	Las Rusias	Cameron	B30	78586
Lake Jackson	Brazoria	G18	77566	Lassater	Marion	E14	75630
Lake Jackson Farms	Brazoria	G18	77566	Latan (RRS)	Mitchell	P68	
Lake Kiowa	Cooke	M2	76240	Latch	Upshur	E13	75644
Lakeland	Montgomery	G4	77301	Latex (Panola)	Panola	E23	75685
Lakeland Heights	Dallas	M12	75050	Latexo	Houston	E24	75849
Lakeland Hills	Travis	C24	78746	La Tijera (Scissors)	Hidalgo	B28	78537
Lakeland Park	Travis	C24	78759	Latium	Washington	G1	77835
Lake Meredith National Recreational Area	Hutchinson	P8		Laughlin Air Force Base	Val Verde	B8	78840
	Moore	P7		Laureles	Cameron	B30	78586
	Potter	P12		Lautz (RRS)	Sherman	P2	
Lake Placid	Guadalupe	C36	78155	La Vernia (Lavernia)	Wilson	C39	78121
Lakeport	Gregg	E17	75601	La Villa	Hidalgo	B28	78562
Lake Ransom Canyon	Lubbock	P39	79364	Lavon	Collin	M7	75066
Lake Shore	Brown	P82	76801	Lavon Beach Estates	Collin	M7	75031
Lakeside	San Patricio	G30	76108	Lavon Shores Estates	Collin	M7	75069
Lakeside	Tarrant	M11	76108	Law	Brazos	C20	77801
Lakeside City	Archer	P45	76308	La Ward (RR name Laward)	Jackson	G23	77970
Lakeside Heights	Llano	C14	78639	Lawn	Taylor	E33	79530
Lakeside Village	Bosque	C2	76671	Lawrence	Kaufman	M14	75160
Lake Tanglewood	Randall	P17	79105	Lawrence Springs	Van Zandt	E15	75140
Lake Thomas	Scurry	P60	79527	Lawson	Dallas	M12	75149
Laketon	Gray	P14	79065	Lawsonville	Rusk	E22	75681
Lake Victor	Burnet	C15	76550	Lazare	Cottle	P33	79238
Lakeview	Bell	C17	76513		Hardeman	P27	
Lakeview	Floyd	P31	79235	Lazbuddie	Parmer	P21	79053
Lakeview	Hall	P25	79239	Leaday	Coleman	P81	76851
Lakeview	Lynn	P49	79345	League City	Galveston	G19	77573
Lakeview	Orange	G7	7766	Leagueville	Henderson	E19	75778
Lakeview	Swisher	P23	79088	Leakey	Real	B10	78873
Lakeview	Tarrant	M11	76135	Leander	Williamson	C16	78641
Lakeview Estates	Van Zandt	E15	75169	Leary	Bowie	E3	75501
Lakeway	Travis	C24	78703	Lebanon	Collin	M7	75034
Lakewood Village	Denton	M6	76201	Ledbetter	Fayette	G8	78946
Lake Worth (Lake Worth Village)	Tarrant	M11	76135	Ledbetter Hills	Dallas	M12	75211
Laman(RRS)	Morris	E8		Lee (RRS)	Carson	P13	
Lamar	Aransas	G31	78382	Leedale (Gindale)	Bell	C17	76569
La Marque	Galveston	G19	77568	Lees (Lee Store)	Glasscock	P77	79720
Lamar State College of Technology	Jefferson	G13	77705	Leesburg	Camp	E12	75451
Lamasco	Fannin	M4	75488	Leesville	Gonzales	C37	78122
Lamesa	Dawson	P58	79331	Leevan (RRS)	Fayette	G8	
Lamkin	Comanche	P83	76460	Lefors	Gray	P14	79054
Lampasas	Lampasas	C6	76550	Leggett	Polk	E32	77350
Lanark	Cass	E9	75572	Legion (VA Hospital)	Kerr	C28	78028
Lancaster	Dallas	M12	75146	Lehman	Cochran	P37	79346
Landergin (RRS)	Oldham	P11		Lehr (RRS)	Bexar	C35	
Landrum	Cameron	B30	78586	Leigh	Harrison	E18	75661
Lane	Hunt	M8	75423	Lela	Wheeler	P15	79079
Lane City	Wharton	G16	77453	Lelavale (RRS)	Hardin	G6	
Lanely	Freestone	C11	75831	Lelia Lake	Donley	P19	79240
Laneport	Williamson	C16	76574	Leming	Atascosa	C38	78050
Lane Prairie	Johnson	M17	76031	Lemonville (RRS)	Orange	G7	
Laneville	Rusk	E22	75667	Lena	Fayette	G8	78963
Langtry	Val Verde	B8	78871	Lenorah	Martin	P66	79749
Lanham	Hamilton	C1	76538	Lenz	Karnes	G20	78118
Lanier	Cass	E9	75563	Leo	Cooke	M2	76234
Lanius (RRS)	Taylor	P70		Leo	Lee	C26	78947
Lannius	Fannin	M4	75438	Leona	Leon	C12	75850
La Paloma	Cameron	B30	78586	Leonard	Fannin	M4	75452
La Porte	Harris	G11	77571	Leon Junction	Coryell	C7	76552
La Porte Air National Guard Station	Harris	G11	77571	Leon Springs	Bexar	C35	78006
La Pryor	Zavala	B14	78872	Leon Valley	Bexar	C35	78238
Laredo	Webb	B19	78040	Leroy	McLennan	C8	76654
Laredo International Airport	Webb	B19	78041	Lesley	Hall	P25	79239
La Reforma	Starr	B27	78536	Levelland	Hockley	P38	79336
Lariat	Parmer	P21	79335	Leveretts Chapel	Rusk	E22	75684
				Le Verte (RRS)	Jasper	E34	
				Levi	McLennan	C8	76655

PLACE	COUNTY	CHART LOCATION	ZIP CODE
Levita	Coryell	C7	76528
Lewisville	Denton	M6	75067
Lexington	Lee	C26	78947
Libby	Nacogdoches	E25	75961
Liberty	Liberty	G5	77575
Liberty	Lubbock	P39	79401
Liberty	Newton	E35	75966
Liberty	Rusk	E22	75652
Liberty City	Gregg	E17	75647
Liberty Grove	Dallas	M12	75087
Liberty Hill	Hill	C3	76692
Liberty Hill	Milam	C18	76567
Liberty Hill	Williamson	C16	78642
Liggett (RRS)	Dallas	M12	
Lilac	Milam	C18	76577
Lilbert	Nacogdoches	E25	75760
Lillard	Hardin	G6	77656
Lillian	Johnson	M17	76061
Lilly	Collingsworth	P20	79095
Lily Island	Polk	E32	75934
Lincoln	Lee	C26	78948
Lincoln Park	Denton	M6	76227
Lindale	Smith	E16	75771
Linden	Cass	E9	75563
Lindenau	De Witt	G21	77954
Lindsay	Cooke	M2	76250
Lingleville	Erath	M15	76461
Linkwood Estates	Tarrant	M11	76008
Linn (San Manuel)	Hidalgo	B28	78563
Linwood	Cherokee	E21	75925
Lipan	Hood	M16	76462
Lipscomb	Lipscomb	P5	79056
Lissie	Wharton	G16	77454
Littig	Travis	C24	78621
Little Cypress	Orange	G7	77630
Little Elm	Denton	M6	75068
Littlefield	Lamb	P29	79339
Little Hope	Wood	E11	75494
Little Mexico	Pecos	P93	79735
Little River-Academy	Bell	C17	76513
Lively	Kaufman	M14	75143
Live Oak	Bexar	C35	78223
Liveoak	Palo Pinto	M9	76462
Liverpool	Brazoria	G18	77577
Livingston	Polk	E32	77351
Llano	Llano	C14	78643
Lobo	Culberson	B3	79855
Lochridge	Brazoria	G18	77583
Locker Spur (RRS)	Reeves	P92	
Locker	San Saba	C4	76871
Lockett	Wilbarger	P35	76384
Lockettville	Hockley	P38	79358
Lockhart	Caldwell	C32	78644
Lockney	Floyd	P31	79241
Loco	Childress	P26	79201
Locust	Grayson	M3	75076
Lodi	Marion	E14	75564
Lodwick	Marion	E14	75657
Loeb	Hardin	G6	77656
Loebau	Lee	C26	78948
Logan	Panola	E23	71049
Lohn	McCulloch	P91	76852
Loire	Wilson	C39	78064
Lois	Cooke	M2	76272
Lois (RRS)	Harris	G11	
Lolaville	Collin	M7	75034
Lolita	Jackson	G23	77971
Loma	Walker	G3	77876
Loma Alta	Val Verde	B8	78840
Loma Vista	Zavala	B14	78829
Lomax	Harris	G11	77571
Lomax	Howard	P67	79720
Lometa	Lampasas	C6	76853
Lomo Alta	McMullen	B18	78072
London	Kimble	P98	76854
Lone Camp	Palo Pinto	M9	76072
Lone Cedar	Ellis	M18	76641
Lone Elm	Ellis	M18	75165
Lone Elm	Kaufman	M14	75126
Lone Grove	Llano	C14	78646
Lone Mountain	Upshur	E13	75644
Lone Oak	Bexar	C35	78101
Lone Oak	Hunt	M8	75453
Lone Pine	Anderson	E20	75801
Lone Star	Floyd	P31	79241
Lone Star	Morris	E8	75668
Lone Star (Asander)	Titus	E7	75558
Lone Star Spur (RRS)	Wise	M5	
Lone Star Army Ammunition Plant	Bowie	E3	75501
Long Branch	Eastland	P72	76435
Long Branch	Panola	E23	75669
Longfellow	Pecos	P93	79848
Longhorn (RRS)	Bexar	C35	
Longhorn Army Ammunition Plant	Harrison	E18	75670
Long Lake	Anderson	E20	75801
Long Mott	Calhoun	G29	77972
Long Point	Fort Bend	G17	77461
Long Point	Harrison	E18	75661
Longpoint	Washington	G1	77835
Longview	Gregg	E17	75601
	Harrison	E18	
Longview Heights	Harrison	E18	75601
Longworth	Fisher	P61	79543
Lon Hill (RRS)	Nueces	G32	
Looneyville	Nacogdoches	E25	75760
Loop	Gaines	P57	79342
Lopeno	Zapata	B22	78564
Lopezville	Hidalgo	B28	78589
Lora (RRS)	Roberts	P9	
Loraine	Mitchell	P68	79532
Lord (RRS)	Ochiltree	P4	
Lorena	McLennan	C8	76655
Lorenzo	Crosby	P40	79343
Los Angeles	La Salle	B17	78051
Los Coyotes	Willacy	B29	78569
Los Cuates	Cameron	B30	78586
Los Ebanos	Hidalgo	B28	78565
Los Fresnos	Cameron	B30	78566
Los Indios	Cameron	B30	78567
Losoya	Bexar	C35	78221
Lott	Falls	C9	76656
Louetta (RRS)	Harris	G11	
Louise	Wharton	G16	77455
Love Chapel	Cass	E9	75656
Lovelace	Hill	C3	76645
Lovelady	Houston	E24	75851
Lovell Lake	Jefferson	G13	77706
Loving	Young	P55	76062
Lowake	Conco	P90	76855
Lowhill (RRS)	Nueces	G32	
Lowry Crossing	Collin	M7	75069
Loyal Valley	Mason	C13	76856
Loyola Beach	Kleberg	B25	78379
Lozano	Cameron	B30	78568
Lubbock	Lubbock	P39	79401
Lubbock International Airport	Lubbock	P39	79401
Lucas	Collin	M7	75069
Luckenback (Lukenbach)	Gillespie	C22	78624
Lucky Ridge	Wise	M5	76023
Lueders	Jones	P62	79533
Luella	Grayson	M3	75090
Lufkin	Angelina	E28	75901
Luling	Caldwell	C32	78648
Lull	Hidalgo	B28	78539
Lumberton	Hardin	G6	77656
Lums Chapel	Lamb	P29	79339

POPULATED PLACES AND OTHER LOCATIONS

PLACE	COUNTY	CHART LOCATION	ZIP CODE	PLACE	COUNTY	CHART LOCATION	ZIP CODE
Lund	Travis	C24	78621	Magnolia	Montgomery	G4	77355
Lusk	Throckmorton	P54	76091	Magnolia Beach	Calhoun	G29	77979
Luther	Howard	P67	79720	Magnolia Gardens	Harris	G11	77044
Lutie	Collingsworth	P20	79079	Magnolia Springs	Jasper	E34	75957
Lydia	Red River	E2	75554	Magoun (RRS)	Lipscomb	P5	
Lyford	Willacy	B29	78569	Magpetco (RRS)	Jefferson	G13	
Lynchburg (Four Corners)	Harris	G11	77520	Magwalt (RRS)	Winkler	P74	
Lyncrest	Harris	G11	77016	Mahl	Nacogdoches	E25	75961
Lyndon B Johnson National Historic Site	Blano	C23		Mahomet	Burnet	C15	78605
	Gillespie	C22		Mahoney	Hopkins	E5	75482
				Majors	Franklin	E6	75457
Lyndon B Johnson Space Center (NASA)	Harris	G11		Malakoff	Henderson	E19	75148
Lyons	Burleson	C27	77863	Mallard	Montague	M1	76251
Lytle	Atascosa	C38	78052	Mallett (RRS)	Sherman	P2	
	Bexar	C35		Malone	Hill	C3	76660
	Medina	C34		Malta	Bowie	E3	75570
Lytle (RRS)	Tarrant	M11		Malvern	Leon	C12	75854
Lytton Springs	Caldwell	C32	78616	Mambrino	Hood	M16	76048
Mabank	Henderson	E19	75147	Manchaca	Travis	C24	78652
	Kaufman	M14		Manchester	Red River	E2	75412
Mabelle	Baylor	P44	76380	Manda	Travis	C24	78653
Mabry (RRS)	Harris	G11		Mangum	Eastland	P72	76448
Mabry	Red River	E2	75426	Manheim	Lee	C26	78659
McAdoo	Dickens	P41	79243	Mankin	Henderson	E19	75163
McAllen	Hidalgo	B28	78501	Mankins	Archer	P45	76366
McBeth	Brazoria	G18	77515	Mann (RRS)	Reeves	P92	
McBride (RRS)	Carson	P13		Manor	Travis	C24	78653
McCamey	Upton	P86	79752	Mansfield	Johnson	M17	76063
McCaulley	Fisher	P61	79534		Tarrant	M11	
McClanahan	Falls	C9	76661	Manson (RRS)	Jackson	G23	
McColl (RRS)	Hidalgo	B28		Mantu (RRS)	Harris	G11	
McCook	Hidalgo	B28	78539	Manvel	Brazoria	G18	77578
McCoy	Atascosa	C38	78053	Maple	Bailey	P28	79344
McCoy	Floyd	P31	79235	Maple Springs	Titus	E7	75455
McCoy	Kaufman	M14	75160	Mapleton (Stumpville)	Houston	E24	75835
McCoy	Panola	E23	75643	Mara (RRS)	Tarrant	M11	
McDade	Bastrop	C25	78650	Marathon	Brewster	B6	79842
Macdona	Bexar	C35	78054	Marble Falls	Burnet	C15	78654
McDonald (RRS)	Montague	M1		Marfa	Presidio	B5	79843
McDonough (RRS)	Harris	G11		Margaret	Foard	P34	79227
Macedonia	Bowie	E3	75501	Margie (RRS)	Leon	C12	79227
Macedonia	Liberty	G5	77327	Marie	Runnels	P80	76933
McFaddin	Victoria	G22	77973	Marietta	Cass	E9	75566
McGalin	Jasper	E34	77612	Marilee	Collin	M7	75058
McGregor	McLennan	C8	76657		Grayson	M3	
McHattie (RRS)	Fort Bend	G17		Marion	Guadalupe	C36	78124
Machovec (RRS)	Moore	P7		Marjorie (RRS)	Milam	C18	
Mackay	Wharton	G16	77488	Markham	Matagorda	G24	77456
McKee	Moore	P7	79086	Markley	Young	P55	76062
McKibben	Hansford	P3	79081	Marlin	Falls	C9	76661
McKinney	Collin	M7	75069	Marquez	Leon	C12	77865
McKnight	Rusk	E22	75652	Marsh (RRS)	Potter	P12	
McLean	Gray	P14	79057	Marshall	Harrison	E18	75670
McLendon-Chisholm	Rockwall	M13	75087	Marshall Ford (Mansfield Dam)	Travis	C24	78759
McLeod	Cass	E9	75565	Marston	Polk	E32	77351
McMahan	Caldwell	C32	78616	Mart	McLennan	C8	76664
McMillin	San Saba	C4	76877	Martindale	Caldwell	C32	78655
McMurray College	Taylor	P70	79065	Martin Lake Junction (RRS)	Panola	E23	
McNair	Harris	G11	77520	Martins Mills	Van Zandt	E15	75754
McNair Village	Bell	C17	76545	Martin Springs	Hopkins	E5	75482
McNary	Hudspeth	B2	79841	Martinsville	Nacogdoches	E25	75958
McNeil	Caldwell	C32	78648	Marvin	Lamar	E1	75460
McNeil	Travis	C24	78651	Marvin	Robertson	C19	77837
Macon	Franklin	E6	75455	Mary Hardin-Baylor College	Bell	C17	76513
McQueeney	Guadalupe	C36	78123	Maryneal	Nolan	P69	79535
Macune	San Augustine	E29	75972	Marysville	Cooke	M2	76252
Macy	Brazos	C20	77882	Mason	Mason	C13	76856
Madero	Hidalgo	B28	78572	Massey Lake	Anderson	E20	75861
Madisonville	Madison	C21	77864	Masterson	Moore	P7	79058
Magasco	Sabine	E30	75968	Matador	Motley	P32	79244
Maglab (RRS)	Dallas	M12		Matagorda	Matagorda	G24	77457
Magnet	Wharton	G16	77488	Mathis	San Patricio	G30	78368
				Mathis Field (Airport)	Tom Green	P89	76901

PLACE	COUNTY	CHART LOCATION	ZIP CODE
Matinburg	Camp	E12	75686
Mattox	Newton	E35	75977
Maud	Bowie	E3	75567
Mauriceville	Orange	G7	77626
Maurin	Gonzales	C37	78629
Maverick	Runnels	P80	76865
Maxdale	Bell	C17	76544
Maxey	Lamar	E1	75421
Maxwell	Caldwell	C32	78656
May	Brown	P82	76857
Maydelle	Cherokee	E21	75772
Mayfield	Hill	C3	76055
Mayflower	Newton	E35	75977
Mayflower	Rusk	E22	75691
Mayhill	Denton	M6	76201
Maynard	San Jacinto	E31	77358
Maypearl	Ellis	M18	76064
Maysfield	Milam	C18	76555
Meador Grove	Bell	C17	76557
Meadow	Terry	P48	79345
Mecca	Madison	C21	77871
Medicine Mound	Hardeman	P27	79252
Medill	Lamar	E1	75460
Medina	Bandera	C33	78055
Meeker	Jefferson	G13	77706
Meeks	Bell	C17	76519
Megargel	Archer	P45	76370
Meldrum	Shelby	E26	75974
Melendy (RRS)	Harris	G11	
Melissa	Collin	M7	75071
Melody Hills	Tarrant	M11	76111
Melrose	Nacogdoces	E25	75961
Melton	Hunt	M8	75401
Melvin	McCulloch	P91	76858
Memphis	Hall	P25	79245
Menard	Menard	P96	76859
Mendota (RRS)	Hemphill	P10	
Mendoza	Caldwell	C32	78644
Menlow	Hill	C3	76621
Mentone	Loving	P73	79754
Mentz	Colorado	G15	78935
Mercedes	Hidalgo	B28	78570
Mercer's Gap	Comanche	P83	76442
Mercury	McCulloch	P91	76872
Mereta	Tom Green	P89	76940
Meridian	Bosque	C2	76665
Merit	Hunt	M8	75072
Merito (RRS)	Hidalgo	B28	
Merkel	Taylor	P70	79536
Merle	Burleson	C27	75455
Mertens	Hill	C3	76666
Mertzon	Irion	P88	76941
Mesa	El Paso	B1	79838
Mesquite	Borden	P59	79351
Mesquite	Dallas	M12	75149
Metcalf Gap	Palo Pinto	M9	76475
Mexia	Limestone	C10	76667
Mexico	Hunt	M8	75474
Meyersville	De Witt	G21	77974
Miami	Roberts	P9	79059
Mickey	Floyd	P31	79241
Mico	Medina	C34	78056
Middleton	Leon	C12	75833
Middle Water	Hartley	P6	79060
Midfield	Matagorda	G24	77458
Midkiff (Hadacol Corners)	Upton	P86	79755
Midland	Midland	P76	79701
Midland Regional Airport	Midland	P76	79701
Midline	Montgomery	G4	77327
Midlothian	Ellis	M18	76065
Midway	Dawson	P58	79331
Midway	Fannin	M4	75418
Midway	Hill	C3	76645
Midway	Lavaca	G14	77984
Midway (McClung)	Lubbock	P39	79364
Midway	Madison	C21	75852
Midway	Montgomery	G4	77327
Midway	San Patricio	G30	78390
Midway	Scurry	P60	79526
Midway	Smith	E16	79792
Midway	Titus	E7	75455
Midway	Upshur	E13	75686
Midyett	Panola	E23	75639
Miguel	Frio	B15	78005
Milam	Sabine	E30	75959
Milano	Milam	C18	76556
Milburn	McCulloch	P91	76872
Milby (RRS)	Travis	C24	
Mildred	Navarro	M19	75110
Mile High	Hudspeth	B2	79851
Miles	Runnels	P80	76861
Milford	Ellis	M18	76670
Mill Creek	Washington	G1	77833
Miller (RRS)	Dallas	M12	
Miller Grove	Camp	E12	75686
Miller Grove	Hopkins	E5	75433
Miller International Airport	Hidalgo	B28	78501
Miller's Cove	Titus	E7	75445
Millersview	Concho	P90	76862
Millett	La Salle	B18	78014
Millheim	Austin	G9	77474
Millican	Brazos	C20	77866
Milligan	Collin	M7	75069
Millsap	Parker	M10	76066
Millwood	Collin	M7	75089
Milton	Lamar	E1	75435
Milvid (RRS)	Liberty	G5	
Minden	Rusk	E22	75680
Mineola	Wood	E11	75773
Mineral	Bee	G26	78125
Mineral Wells	Palo Pinto	M9	76067
	Parker	M10	
Minerva	Milam	C18	76567
Mings Chapel	Upshur	E13	75644
Mingus	Palo Pinto	M9	76463
Minter	Lamar	E1	75468
Minters Chapel	Tarrant	M11	76051
Mirando City	Webb	B19	78369
Mission	Hidalgo	B28	78572
Mission Valley	Comal	C30	78130
Mission Valley	Victoria	G22	77901
Missouri City	Fort Bend	G17	77459
	Harris	G11	
Mixon	Cherokee	E21	75789
Mobeetie (New Mobeetie)	Wheeler	P15	79061
Moffatt	Bell	C17	76501
Moffett	Angelina	E28	75901
Mohat (RRS)	Colorado	G15	
Monadale (Montadale)	Williamson	C16	78634
Monahans	Ward	P84	79756
	Winkler	P74	
Monaville	Waller	G10	77445
Monkstown	Fannin	M4	75488
Monroe	Rusk	E22	75662
Monroe City	Chambers	G12	77579
Mont	Lavaca	G14	77964
Montague	Montague	M1	76251
Montague Village (West Fort Hood)	Coryell	C7	76544
Montalba	Anderson	E20	75853
Mont Belvieu	Chambers	G12	77580
Monte Alto	Hidalgo	B28	78538
Montell	Uvalde	B12	78801
Monteola	Bee	G26	78119
Montfort	Navarro	M19	75156
Montgomery	Montgomery	G4	77356
Montgomery Gardens	Smith	E16	75701

PLACE	COUNTY	CHART LOCATION	ZIP CODE
Monthalia	Gonzales	C37	78614
Monticello	Titus	E7	75455
Montoya (RRS)	El Paso	B1	
Moody	McLennan	C8	76557
Moonshine Hill	Harris	G11	77338
Moore	Frio	B15	78057
Moore's Chapel	Fannin	M4	75418
Moores Crossing	Travis	C24	78617
Moore Station	Henderson	E19	75770
Mooresville	Falls	C9	76632
Mooring	Brazos	C20	77801
Morales	Jackson	G23	77957
Moran	Shackelford	P63	76464
Moravia	Lavaca	G14	78956
Morey (RRS)	Jefferson	G13	
Morgan	Bosque	C2	76671
Morgan Mill	Erath	M15	76465
Morgan's Point	Harris	G11	77571
Morgan's Point Resort	Bell	C17	76513
Morrill	Cherokee	E21	75925
Morris Ranch	Gillespie	C22	78624
Morse	Hansford	P3	79062
Morton	Cochran	P37	79346
Morton	Harrison	E18	75640
Morton Valley	Eastland	P72	76448
Moscow	Polk	E32	75960
Mosheim	Bosque	C2	76689
Moss Bluff	Liberty	G5	77575
Moss Hill	Liberty	G5	77575
Mostyn	Montgomery	G4	77355
Moulton	Lavaca	G14	77975
Mound	Coryell	C7	76558
Mound City	Anderson	E20	75844
Mountain	Coryell	C7	76528
Mountain Creek (RRS)	Dallas	M12	
Mountain Home	Kerr	C28	78058
Mountain Peak	Ellis	M18	76065
Mountain Springs	Cooke	M2	76258
Mount Airy (RRS)	Erath	M15	
Mount Blanco	Crosby	P40	79322
Mount Calm	Hill	C3	76673
Mount Calvary	Panola	E23	75633
Mount Enterprise	Rusk	E22	75681
Mount Enterprise	Wood	E11	75773
Mount Houston	Harris	G11	77016
Mount Joy	Delta	E4	75432
Mount Lucas	Live Oak	G25	78350
Mount Olive	Lavaca	G14	77984
Mount Pleasant	Titus	E7	75455
Mount Selman	Cherokee	E21	75757
Mount Sharp	Hays	C31	78620
Mount Sylvan	Smith	E16	75777
Mount Union	Jasper	E34	75956
Mount Vernon	Franklin	E6	75457
Mount Zion	Waller	G10	77423
Mozelle	Coleman	P81	76834
Muddig	Hunt	M8	75449
Mudville	Brazos	C20	77801
Muellersville	Washington	G1	77833
Muenster	Cooke	M2	76252
Mulberry	Fannin	M4	75476
Muldoon	Fayette	G8	78949
Muleshoe	Bailey	P28	79347
Mulford (RRS)	Orange	G7	
Mullin	Mills	C5	76864
Mullins Prairie	Fayette	G8	78945
Mumford	Robertson	C19	77867
Muncy	Floyd	P31	79241
Munday	Knox	P43	76371
Mungerville	Dawson	P58	79331
Munson	Rockwall	M13	75089
Murchison	Henderson	E19	75778
Murphy	Collin	M7	75074
Murray	Young	P55	76046
Musgrove	Franklin	E6	75494
	Wood	E11	
Mustang	Denton	M6	76258
Mustang	Limestone	C10	76635
Mustang	Navarro	M19	75110
Mustang (RRS)	Wharton	G16	
Mykawa (RRS)	Harris	G11	
Myra	Cooke	M2	76253
Myrtle Springs	Van Zandt	E15	75169
Nacogdoches	Nacogdoches	E25	75961
Nada	Colorado	G15	77460
Nadeau (RRS)	Galveston	G19	
Naples	Morris	E8	75568
Narcisso (RRS)	Cottle	P33	
Naruna	Burnet	C15	76550
Nash	Bowie	E3	75569
Nash	Ellis	M18	76041
Nassau Bay	Harris	G11	77058
Nat	Nacogdoches	B25	75760
Natalia	Medina	C34	78059
Natural Bridge Caverns	Bexar	C35	78218
Navarro	Navarro	M19	75151
Navarro Mills	Navarro	M19	76679
Navasota	Grimes	G2	77868
Navo	Denton	M6	75034
Nazareth	Castro	P22	79063
Neals Valley	Ellis	M18	75119
Necessity	Stephens	P64	76024
Nechanitz	Fayette	G8	78946
Neches	Anderson	E20	75779
Neches Indian Village	Cherokee	E21	75925
Nederland	Jefferson	G13	77627
Nederland Air National Guard Station	Jefferson	G13	77627
Needmore	Bailey	P28	79371
Needmore	Terry	P48	79345
Needville	Fort Bend	G17	77461
Negley	Red River	E2	75426
Neinda	Jones	P62	79520
Nell	Live Oak	G25	78119
Nelsonville	Austin	G9	77418
Nelta	Hopkins	E5	75437
Nemo	Somervell	M20	76070
Nena (RRS)	Ellis	M18	
Nesbitt	Harrison	E18	75670
Nesbitt	Robertson	C19	76629
Neuville	Shelby	E26	75935
Nevada	Collin	M7	75073
Newark	Wise	M5	76071
New Baden	Robertson	C19	77870
New Berlin	Guadalupe	C36	78155
New Boston	Bowie	E3	75570
New Braunfels	Comal	C30	78130
	Guadalupe	C36	
Newburg	Comanche	P83	76442
Newby	Leon	C12	75846
New Caney	Montgomery	G4	77357
Newcastle	Young	P55	76372
New Chapel Hill	Smith	E16	75701
New Clarkson	Milam	C18	76570
New Colony	Cass	E9	75563
New Corn Hill	Williamson	C16	76537
New Deal (RR name Monroe)	Lubbock	P39	79350
New Fountain	Medina	C34	78861
Newgulf	Wharton	G16	77462
New Harmony	Shelby	E26	75973
New Harmony	Smith	E16	75701
Newharp (New Harp)	Montague	M1	76239
New Hebron	Harrison	E18	75685
New Homes	Lynn	P49	79383
New Hope	Cherokee	E21	75766
New Hope	Collin	M7	75069

PLACE	COUNTY	CHART LOCATION	ZIP CODE
New Hope	Henderson	E19	75756
New Hope	Jones	P62	79553
New Hope	Rusk	E22	75662
New Hope	San Jacinto	E31	77327
New Hope	Smith	E16	75701
New Hope	Wood	E11	75773
Newlin	Hall	P25	79245
New London (RR name Norfolk)	Rusk	E22	75682
New Lynn	Lynn	P49	79373
Newman	El Paso	B1	79924
New Mine	Camp	E12	75686
New Moore	Lynn	P49	79351
New Mountain	Upshur	E13	75644
Newport	Clay	P46	76254
	Jack	P56	
Newport	Harris	G11	77532
New Prospect	Rusk	E22	75652
New Prospect	Shelby	E26	75975
New Salem	Palo Pinto	M9	76472
New Salem	Rusk	E22	75652
Newsome	Camp	E12	75686
New Summerfield (Summerfield)	Cherokee	E21	75780
New Sweden	Travis	C24	78653
New Taiton	Wharton	G16	77437
Newton	Newton	E35	75966
New Ulm	Austin	G9	78950
New Waverly	Walker	G3	77358
New Wehdem	Austin	G9	77833
New Willard	Polk	E32	77350
New York	Henderson	E19	75770
Neylandville	Hunt	M8	75401
Nickel	Gonzales	C37	78629
Nickelberry	Cass	E9	75566
Nickel Creek	Culberson	B3	88220
Niederwald	Caldwell	C32	78640
	Hays	C31	
Nigton	Trinity	E27	75926
Nile	Milam	C18	76577
Nimrod	Eastland	P72	76437
Nineveh	Leon	C12	75831
Nix	Lampasas	C6	76550
Nixon	Gonzales	C37	78140
Noack	Williamson	C16	76574
Nobility	Fannin	M4	75452
Noble	Lamar	E1	75470
Nockenut	Wilson	C39	78160
Nocona	Montague	M1	76255
Noelke (RRS)	Irion	P88	
Nogalus (Nogalus Prairie)	Trinity	E27	75845
Nolan	Nolan	P69	79537
Nolanville	Bell	C17	76559
Nome	Jefferson	G13	77629
Nona	Hardin	G6	77625
Noodle	Jones	P62	79536
Noonday	Smith	E16	75762
Nopal	De Witt	G21	78164
Nordheim	De Witt	G21	78141
Norias	Kenedy	B26	78338
Normandy	Maverick	B13	78875
Normangee	Leon	C12	77871
	Madison	C21	
Normanna	Bee	G26	78142
Norman's Crossing (Norman)	Williamson	C16	76574
Norrick (RRS)	Wheeler	P15	
Norse	Bosque	C2	76634
North Cedar	Trinity	E27	75926
North Cleveland	Liberty	G5	77327
Northcrest	McLennan	C8	76705
Northcrest Estates	Victoria	G22	77901
Northfield	Motley	P32	79246
Northgate	Victoria	G22	77901
North Groesbeck	Hardeman	P27	79252
North Houston	Harris	G11	77018
North Houston Heights	Harris	G11	77016
Northlake	Denton	M6	76247
Northline Terrace	Harris	G11	77022
North Oaks	Travis	C24	78753
North Prairie	Falls	C9	76632
North Richland Hills	Tarrant	M11	76118
North Roby (RRS)	Fisher	P61	
Northrup	Lee	C26	78942
North Rusk (Rusk State Hospital)	Cherokee	E21	75785
North Seadrift (RRS)	Calhoun	G29	
North Texas University	Denton	M6	76203
North Vidor	Orange	G7	77662
North Zulch	Madison	C21	77872
Norton	Runnels	P80	76865
Norwood	San Augustine	E29	75972
Notla	Ochiltree	P4	79070
Notrees	Ector	P75	79759
Novice	Coleman	P81	79538
Novice	Lamar	E1	75460
Novohrad	Lavaca	G14	77975
Noxville (New Knoxville)	Kimble	P98	78631
Nugent	Jones	P62	79601
Nursery	Victoria	G22	77976
Nuway	El Paso	B1	88021
Oakalla	Burnet	C15	76541
Oak Dale	Erath	M15	76401
Oak Flat	Nacogdoches	E25	75760
Oak Flat	Rusk	E22	75681
Oak Forest (Quinton)	Gonzales	C37	78629
Oak Grove	Bowie	E3	75554
Oak Grove	Ellis	M18	75119
Oak Grove	Kaufman	M14	75142
Oak Grove	Tarrant	M11	76028
Oak Grove	Wood	E11	75783
Oak Hill	Johnson	M17	76031
Oak Hill	Rusk	E22	75652
Oak Hill	Travis	C24	78746
Oakhurst	San Jacinto	E31	77359
Oak Island	Chambers	G12	77514
Oak Lake	McLennan	C8	76705
Oakland	Cherokee	E21	75785
Oakland	Colorado	G15	78951
Oakland	Rusk	E22	75652
Oakland	Van Zandt	M15	75103
Oak Point	Denton	M6	75034
Oak Ridge	Bowie	E3	75559
Oak Ridge	Kaufman	M14	75160
Oak Ridge	Nacogdoches	E25	75961
Oak Ridge	Parker	M10	76086
Oak Ridge North	Montgomery	G4	77301
Oaks	Bee	G26	78119
Oaks	Tarrant	M11	76114
Oakville	Live Oak	G25	78060
Oakwood	Leon	C12	75855
Oatmeal	Burnet	C15	78605
O'Brien	Haskell	P53	79539
Ocee	McLennan	C8	76638
Ochoa	Presidio	B5	79845
Odds	Limestone	C10	76687
Odell	Wilbarger	P35	79247
Odem	San Patricio	G30	78370
Odessa	Ector	P75	79760
Odom	Van Zandt	E15	75147
O'Donnell	Dawson	P58	79351
	Lynn	P49	
Oenaville	Bell	C17	76501
O'Farrell	Cass	E9	75551
Ogden (RRS)	Comal	C30	
Ogg	Randall	P17	79042
Oglesby	Coryell	C7	76561
Oildom (RRS)	Wichita	P36	
Oilla	Orange	G7	77630
Oilton	Webb	B19	78371

POPULATED PLACES AND OTHER LOCATIONS

PLACE	COUNTY	CHART LOCATION	ZIP CODE
Ojuelas (Los Ojuelas)	Webb	B19	78369
Oklahoma	Montgomery	G4	77355
Oklahoma Flat	Hockley	P38	79339
Oklahoma Lane	Parmer	P21	79325
Oklaunion	Wilbarger	P35	76373
Okra	Eastland	P72	76435
Ola	Kaufman	M14	75142
Olcott (RRS)	Harris	G11	
Old Boston	Bowie	E3	75570
Old Brazoria	Brazoria	G18	77422
Old Dime Box	Lee	C26	77853
Olden	Eastland	P72	76466
Oldenburg	Fayette	G8	78945
Old Glory	Stonewall	P52	79540
Old Larissa	Cherokee	E21	75757
Old Laurel	Newton	E35	77612
Old London	Rusk	E22	75682
Old Mobeetie	Wheeler	P15	79061
Old Moulton	Lavaca	G14	77975
Old Ocean	Brazoria	G18	77463
Old River Terrace	Harris	G11	77530
Old River-Winfree	Chambers	G12	77514
Old Round Rock	Williamson	C16	78664
Old Salem (Salem)	Newton	E35	75933
Old Union (Poer)	Bowie	E3	75574
Old Union	Limestone	C10	76687
Oletha	Limestone	C10	76687
Olfen	Runnels	P80	76875
Olin	Hamilton	C1	76457
Olivia	Calhoun	G29	77979
Ollie	Polk	E32	77350
Olmito	Cameron	B30	78575
Olmos	Bee	G26	78389
Olmos Park	Bexar	G35	78212
Olney	Young	P55	76374
Olton	Lamb	P29	79064
Omaha	Morris	E8	75571
Omen	Smith	E16	75705
Onalaska	Polk	E32	77360
Onion Creek (RRS)	Ellis	M18	
Opdyke	Hockley	P38	79336
Opelika	Henderson	E19	75778
Oplin	Callahan	P71	79510
O'Quinn	Fayette	G8	78945
Oran	Palo Pinto	M9	76045
Orange	Orange	G7	77630
Orangedale	Bee	G26	78102
Orangefield	Orange	G7	77639
Orange Grove	Jim Wells	B21	78372
Orangeville	Fannin	M4	75491
Orchard	Fort Bend	G17	77464
Ore (RRS)	Morris	E8	
Ore City	Upshur	E13	75683
Orient	Tom Green	P89	76901
Orla	Reeves	P92	79770
Orme (RRS)	Tarrant	M11	
Orr (RRS)	Harris	g11	
Orrs	Marion	E14	75630
Orvil (RRS)	Webb	B19	
Osage	Coryell	C7	76528
Oscar	Bell	C17	76501
Osceola	Hill	C3	76055
Otey (Ramsey State Prison Farm)	Brazoria	G18	77583
Otis Chalk	Howard	P67	79733
Ottine	Gonzales	C37	78658
Otto	Falls	C9	76675
Ovalo	Taylor	P70	79541
Overton	Rusk	E22	75684
	Smith	E16	
Ovilla	Dallas	M12	76065
	Ellis	M18	
Owego (RRS)	Pecos	P93	
Owens	Brown	P82	76857

PLACE	COUNTY	CHART LOCATION	ZIP CODE
Owens	Crosby	P40	79357
Owensville	Robertson	C19	77856
Owentown	Smith	E16	75703
Oxford	Llano	C14	78643
Oyster Creek	Brazoria	G18	77541
Ozarking (RRS)	Ward	P84	
Ozona	Crockett	P94	76943
Pacio	Delta	E4	75450
Packery	Washington	G1	77833
Padgett	Young	P55	76374
Padre Island National Seashore	Kenedy	B26	
	Kleberg	B25	
	Willacy	B29	
Paducah	Cottle	P33	79248
Pagoda	Trinity	E27	75862
Paige	Bastrop	C25	78659
Paint Rock	Concho	P90	76866
Pakan	Wheeler	P15	79079
Palacios	Matagorda	G24	77465
Palava	Fisher	P61	79556
Palestine	Anderson	E20	75801
Palestine (Darden)	Polk	E32	75936
Palito Blanco	Jim Wells	B21	78332
Palmer	Ellis	M18	75152
Palmetal (RRS)	Cameron	B30	
Palmetto	San Jacinto	E31	77359
Palmhurst	Hidalgo	B28	78572
Palm Valley	Cameron	B30	78550
Palmview	Hidalgo	B28	78539
Palo Alto	Nueces	G32	78343
Palo Alto Battlefield National Historic Site	Cameron	B30	
Paloduro	Armstrong	P18	79226
Palo Pinto	Palo Pinto	M9	76072
Paluxy	Hood	M16	76467
Pampa	Gray	P14	79065
Pancake	Coryell	C7	76538
Pandale	Val Verde	B8	76943
Pandora	Wilson	C39	78143
Panhandle	Carson	P13	79068
Panna Maria	Karnes	G20	78144
Panola	Panola	E23	75685
Panorama Estates	Hunt	M8	75169
Panorama Village	Montgomergy	G4	77301
Pantego	Tarrant	M11	76013
Pantex	Carson	P13	79069
Papalote	Bee	G26	78387
Paradise	Wise	M5	76073
Paris	Lamar	E1	75460
Park	Fayette	G8	78945
Parker	Collin	M7	75002
Parker	Johnson	M17	76050
Park Glen	Harris	G11	77072
Park Springs	Wise	M5	76270
Parkview Estates	Guadalupe	C36	78155
Parkwood	Jasper	E34	77612
Parmerton (RRS)	Parmer	P21	
Parnell	Hall	P25	79233
Parvin	Denton	M6	75009
Pasadena	Harris	G11	77501
Patilo (Patillo)	Erath	M15	76462
Patman	Cass	E9	75630
Patrich	Rusk	E22	75681
Patricia	Dawson	P58	79331
Patrick	Dallas	M12	75125
Patroon	Shelby	E26	75973
Pattison	Waller	G10	77466
Patton	McLennan	C8	76689
Patton	Montgomery	G4	77372
Pattonville	Lamar	E1	75468
Pauline	Hardeman	P27	79252
Pauline	Henderson	E19	75124
Pawelekville	Karnes	G20	78113

PLACE	COUNTY	CHART LOCATION	ZIP CODE
Pawnee	Bee	G26	78145
Paxton	Shelby	E26	75954
Payne Springs	Henderson	E19	75124
Peach Creek	Wharton	G16	77488
Peacock	Stonewall	P52	79542
Peadenville	Palo Pinto	M9	76067
Pearl	Coryell	C7	76563
Pearland	Brazoria	G18	77581
	Harris	G11	
Pearl City	De Witt	G21	77995
Pearsall	Frio	B15	78061
Pearson	Medina	C34	78016
Pearsons Chapel (Post Oak)	Houston	E24	75851
Pear Valley	McCulloch	P91	76867
Peaster	Parker	M10	76074
Peavy (RRS)	Angelina	E28	
Pebble Beach-Sunset Acres	Collin	M7	75018
Pecan Gap	Delta	E4	75469
	Fannin	M4	
Pecangrove	Coryell	C7	76561
Pecos	Reeves	P92	79772
Pedeco (RRS)	Liberty	G5	
Peden	Tarrant	M11	76020
Pedigo	Tyler	E33	75979
Peeltown (Liberty)	Kaufman	M14	75158
Peerless	Hopkins	E5	75482
Pegasus (RRS)	Midland	P76	
Peggy	Atascosa	C38	78062
Pelham	Navarro	M19	76648
Pelican Bay	Tarrant	M11	76020
Pendleton	Bell	C17	76564
Penelope	Hill	C3	76676
Penitas	Hidalgo	B28	78576
Penland	Grayson	M3	75414
Pennington	Trinity	E27	75856
Penwell	Ector	P75	79776
Peoria	Hill	C3	76645
Pep	Hockley	P38	79353
Perch Hill (RRS)	Wise	M5	
Percilla	Houston	E24	75844
Perdiz (RRS)	Presidio	B5	
Perezville	Hidalgo	B28	78572
Perico	Dallam	P1	79087
Pernitas Point	Live Oak	G25	78383
Perrin	Jack	P56	76075
Perry	Falls	C9	76677
Perry Landing	Brazoria	G18	77541
Perryton	Ochiltree	P4	79070
Perryville	Wood	E11	75644
Pershing (RRS)	Travis	C24	
Personville	Limestone	C10	76642
Pert	Anderson	E20	75801
Pete (RRS)	Nolan	P69	
Peters	Austin	G9	77474
Petersburg	Hale	P30	79250
Peterson	Jefferson	G13	77627
Peters Prairie	Red River	E2	75426
Petersville	De Witt	G21	77995
Petrolia	Clay	P46	76377
Petronila	Nueces	G32	78380
Petteway	Robertson	C19	76629
Pettibone	Milam	C18	76520
Pettit	Comanche	P83	76455
Pettit	Hockley	P38	79354
Pettus	Bee	G26	78146
Petty	Lamar	E1	75470
Petty	Lynn	P49	79373
Pettys Chapel	Navarro	M19	75110
Peveto (RRS)	Orange	G7	
Pflugerville	Travis	C24	78660
Phalba	Van Zandt	E15	75147
Pharr	Hidalgo	B28	78577
Phelan	Bastrop	C25	78602

PLACE	COUNTY	CHART LOCATION	ZIP CODE
Phelps	Walker	G3	77340
Phillips	Hutchinson	P8	79071
Phillipsburg	Washington	G1	77833
Phillips Camp	Hansford	P3	79040
Philview Camp	Hutchinson	P8	79007
Phoenix (RRS)	Bexar	C35	
Pickens	Henderson	E19	75751
Pickett	Navarro	M19	75110
Pickton	Hopkins	E5	75471
Pickwick	Palo Pinto	M9	76045
Pidcoke	Coryell	G7	76528
Piedmont	Grimes	G2	77830
Pierce	Wharton	G16	77467
Pierce Junction (RRS)	Harris	G11	
Pierces Chapel	Cherokee	E21	75766
Pike	Collin	M7	75004
Pilgrims Rest	Rains	E10	75440
Pillot (RRS)	Fort Bend	G17	
Pilot Grove	Grayson	M3	75491
Pilot Knob	Travis	C24	78744
Pilot Point	Denton	M6	76258
Pine	Camp	E12	75686
Pine Forest	Hopkins	E5	75431
Pine Forest	Orange	G7	77662
Pine Grove	Newton	E35	75966
Pine Hill	Cherokee	E21	75766
Pinehill	Rusk	E22	75652
Pinehurst	Montgomery	G4	77362
Pinehurst	Orange	G7	77630
Pine Island	Jefferson	G4	77356
Pineland	Sabine	E30	75968
Pine Mills	Wood	E11	75733
Pine Ridge	Hardin	P27	77625
Pine Springs	Culberson	B3	88220
Pine Valley	Angelina	E28	75941
Pine Valley	San Jacinto	E21	77358
Pineview	Wood	E11	75494
Pinewood Estates	Hardin	G6	77706
Piney Grove	Montgomery	G4	77355
Piney Grove	Upshur	E13	75686
Piney Point Village (Piney Point)	Harris	G11	77024
Pinnacle	Upshur		75755
Pioneer	Eastland	P72	76471
Pioneer Town	Hays	C37	78676
Pipe Creek (Pipecreek)	Bandera	C33	78063
Pirtle	Rusk	E22	75684
Pitner Junction	Rusk	E22	75684
Pitts (Pittsville)	Montgomery	G4	77338
Pittsburg	Camp	E12	75686
Placedo	Victoria	G22	77977
Placid	McCulloch	P91	76868
Plains	Yoakum	P47	79355
Plainview	Hale	P30	79072
Plainview	Sabine	E30	75968
Planeport (RRS)	El Paso	B1	
Plano	Collin	M7	75074
	Denton	M6	
Plantersville	Grimes	G2	77363
Plaska	Hall	P25	79245
Plata (RRS)	Presidio	B5	
Plateau	Culberson	B3	79855
Pleak	Fort Bend	G17	77469
Pleasant Farms	Ector	P75	79763
Pleasant Green	Gregg	E17	75604
Pleasant Grove	Falls	C9	76570
Pleasant Grove	Rusk	E22	75652
Pleasant Grove	Upshur	E13	75755
Pleasant Grove	Wood	E11	75494
Pleasant Hill	Blanco	C23	78636
Pleasant Hill	Eastland	P72	76437
Pleasant Hill	Polk	E32	75939
Pleasant Hill	Washington	G1	77833
Pleasanton	Atascosa	C28	78064

POPULATED PLACES AND OTHER LOCATIONS

PLACE	COUNTY	CHART LOCATION	ZIP CODE	PLACE	COUNTY	CHART LOCATION	ZIP CODE
Pleasant Point	Johnson	M17	76009	Prairie Point	Cooke	M2	76239
Pleasant Ridge	Leon	C12	75833	Prairie Springs	Johnson	M17	76028
Pleasant Ridge	Panola	E23	75633	Prairie Valley	Montague	M1	76255
Pleasant Valley	Dallas	M12	75040	Prairie View	Waller	G10	77445
Pleasant Valley	Garza	P50	79356	Prairieville	Kaufman	M14	75147
Pleasant Valley	Palo Pinto	M9	76067	Prattville	Delta	E4	75432
Pleasant Valley	Wichita	P36	76301	Premont	Jim Wells	B21	78375
Pledger	Matagorda	G24	77468	Presidio	Presidio	B5	79845
Pluck	Polk	E32	75939	Preston Shores (Preston)	Grayson	M3	75076
Plum	Fayette	G8	78952	Price	Delta	E4	75432
Plum Grove	Liberty	G5	77327	Price	Jefferson	G13	77627
Poe Prairie	Parker	M10	76066	Price (Carlisle)	Rusk	E22	75687
Poesville	Bosque	C2	76671	Priddy	Mills	C5	76870
Poetry	Kaufman	M14	75160	Primera	Cameron	B30	78550
Poindexter (RRS)	Rusk	E22		Primrose	Van Zandt	E15	75754
Point	Rains	E10	75472	Primrose (RRS)	Tarrant	M11	
Point Blank (Pointblank)	San Jacinto	E31	77364	Princeton	Collin	M7	75077
Point Comfort	Calhoun	G29	77978	Pringle	Hutchinson	P8	79083
Point Enterprise	Limestone	C10	76667	Pritchett	Upshur	E13	75755
Polar	Kent	P51	79515	Proctor	Comanche	P83	76468
Pollok	Angelina	E28	75969	Proffit	Young	P55	76372
Pomeroy (RRS)	Carson	P13		Progreso	Hidalgo	B28	78579
Pomona (RRS)	Cherokee	E21		Progreso Lakes	Hidalgo	B28	78579
Ponder	Denton	M6	76259	Progress	Bailey	P28	79347
Pone	Rusk	E22	75667	Progress	Palo Pinto	M9	76067
Ponta	Cherokee	E21	75766	Prospect	Marion	E14	75657
Pontotoc	Mason	C13	76869	Prosper	Collin	M7	75078
Pony	Runnels	P80	76821	Prosser (RRS)	Angelina	E28	
Poolville	Parker	M10	76076	Providence	Angelina	E28	75901
Porfirio	Willacy	B29	78580	Providence	Polk	E32	77351
Port Alto	Calhoun	G29	77979	Providence	Van Zandt	E15	75140
Port Aransas	Nueces	G32	78373	Provident City	Colorado	G15	77455
Port Arthur	Jefferson	G13	77640	Pruett	Cass	E9	75657
Port Bolivar	Galveston	G19	77650	Pruitt	Van Zandt	E15	75140
Porter	Montgomery	G4	77365	Pryor (RRS)	Fort Bend	G17	
Porter Heights	Montgomery	G4	77365	Puente (RRS)	Potter	P12	
Porter Springs	Houston	E24	75835	Puerto Rico	Hidalgo	B28	78563
Portilla (RRS)	Calhoun	G29		Pullman	Potter	P12	79109
Port Isabel	Cameron	B30	78578	Pumphrey	Runnels	P80	79567
Portland	San Patricio	G30	78374	Pumpkin	San Jacinto	E31	77358
Port Lavaca	Calhoun	G29	77979	Pumpkin Center	Dawson	P58	79331
Port Mansfield	Willacy	B29	78580	Pumpkin Center	Eastland	P72	76448
Port Neches	Jefferson	B13	77651	Pumpville	Val Verde	B8	78876
Port O'Connor	Calhoun	G29	77982	Punkin Center	Parker	M10	76086
Porvenir	Presidio	B5	79854	Purdon	Navarro	M19	76679
Posey	Hopkins	E5	75482	Purley	Franklin	E6	75457
Posey	Lubbock	P39	79364	Purmela	Coryell	C7	76566
Possum Kingdom	Palo Pinto	M9	76045	Pursley	Navarro	M19	76679
Post	Garza	P50	79356	Purves	Erath	M15	76446
Postoak	Freestone	C11	75860	Putnam	Callahan	P71	76469
Postoak	Jack	P56	76230	Pyote	Ward	P84	79777
Postoak (Gantt)	Lamar	E1	75436	Pyron	Scurry	P60	79545
Post Oak Bend City	Kaufman	M14	75142	Quail	Collingsworth	P20	79251
Postoak Point	Austin	G9	78950	Quality (RRS)	Harris	G11	
Poteet	Atascosa	C38	78065	Quanah	Hardeman	P27	79252
Poth	Wilson	C39	78147	Quarry	Washington	G1	77833
Potosi	Taylor	P70	79601	Quebec (RRS)	Presidio	B5	
Potters Point	Marion	E14	75657	Queen City	Cass	E9	75572
Pottsboro	Grayson	m3	75076	Quemado	Maverick	B13	78877
Pottsville	Hamilton	C1	76565	Quicksand	Newton	E35	75966
Pounds Field (Airport)	Smith	E16	75710	Quihi	Medina	C34	78018
Powderly	Lamar	E1	75473	Quinif (RRS)	Milam	C18	
Powell	Navarro	M19	75153	Quinlan	Hunt	M8	75474
Powell Point	Fort Bend	G17	77451	Quintana	Brazoria	G18	77541
Poynor	Henderson	E19	75782	Quitaque	Briscoe	P24	79255
Prade Ranch	Real	B10	78058	Quitman	Wood	E11	75783
Praesel	Milam	C18	76567	Rabb	Nueces	G32	78380
Praha	Fayette	G8	78941	Rabbs	Lavaca	G14	77964
Prairie Dell	Bell	C17	76571	Rabbs Prairie	Fayette	G8	78945
Prairie Grove	Limestone	C10	76667	Raccoon Bend	Austin	G9	77418
Prairie Hill	Limestone	C10	76678	Racetrack	Delta	E4	75432
Prairie Hill	Washington	G1	77833	Rachal	Brooks	B24	78353
Prairie Lea	Caldwell	C32	78661	Radium	Jones	P62	79501

PLACE	COUNTY	CHART LOCATION	ZIP CODE
Ragtown	Lamar	E1	75411
Rainbow	Somervell	M20	76077
Raisin	Victoria	G22	77901
Raleigh	Navarro	M19	76641
Ralls	Crosby	P40	79357
Ramah	Shelby	E26	75974
Ramireno	Zapata	B22	78067
Ramirez	Duval	B20	78376
Ramsey	Colorado	G15	78935
Ranchito (Ranchiti)	Cameron	B30	78586
Ranchland (RRS)	Wilbarger	P35	
Rancho Allegre Addition	Jim Wells	B21	78332
Rancho Viejo	Cameron	B30	78361
Rancho Viejo	Jim Hogg	B23	78361
Randolph	Fannin	M4	75475
Randolph Air Force Base	Bexar	C35	78148
Ranger	Eastland	P72	76470
Rangerville	Cameron	B30	78586
Rankin	Ellis	M18	75119
Rankin	Upton	P86	79778
Ratama	Frio	B15	78017
Ratcliff	Houston	E24	75858
Ratcliff	San Augustine	E29	75972
Ratcliff (RRS)	Starr	B27	
Ratibor	Bell	C17	76501
Rattan	Delta	E4	75432
Ravenna	Fannin	M4	75476
Ray (RRS)	Grayson	M3	
Rayburn	Liberty	G5	77327
Rayford	Montgomery	G4	77373
Rayland	Foard	P34	76384
Raymondville	Willacy	B29	78580
Ray Point	Live Oak	G25	78071
Raywood	Liberty	G5	77582
Razor	Lamar	E1	75411
Reagan	Falls	C9	76680
Reagan Wells	Uvalde	B12	78801
Reagor Springs	Ellis	M18	75165
Realitos	Duval	B20	78376
Rebecca (RRS)	San Augustine	E29	
Redbank	Bowie	E3	75561
Red Bluff	Reeves	P92	79770
Reddam (RRS)	Grayson	M3	
Redfield	Nacogdoches	E25	75961
Redfish (RRS)	San Patricio	G30	
Redford	Presidio	B5	79846
Red Gate	Hidalgo	B28	78539
Red Hill	Cass	E9	75563
Red Lake	Freestone	C11	75855
Redland	Angelina	E28	75901
Redland	Leon	C12	75833
Redland	Van Zandt	E15	75754
Redlawn	Cherokee	E21	75925
Redlick	Bowie	E3	75501
Red Oak	Ellis	M18	75154
Red Oak	Kaufman	M14	75142
Red Ranger	Bell	C17	76569
Red River Army Depot	Bowie	E3	75501
Red Rock	Bastrop	C25	78662
Red Springs	Baylor	P44	76378
Red Springs	Bowie	E3	75501
Red Springs	Smith	E16	75771
Red Town	Angelina	E28	75901
Redwater	Bowie	E3	75573
Redwood	Guadalupe	C36	78666
Reedville	Caldwell	C32	78656
Reese	Cherokee	E21	75766
Reese Air Force Base	Lubbock	P39	79489
Reese Village	Lubbock	P39	79401
Refuge	Houston	E24	75844
Refugio	Refugio	G28	78377
Regency	Mills	C5	76864
Rehobeth	Panola	E23	75633

PLACE	COUNTY	CHART LOCATION	ZIP CODE
Reilly Springs	Hopkins	E5	75482
Reinhardt (RRS)	Dallas	M12	
Rek Hill	Fayette	G8	78940
Reklaw	Cherokee	E21	75784
	Rusk	E22	
Relampago	Hidalgo	B28	78750
Reliance	Brazos	C20	77801
Remount (RRS)	Bexar	C35	
Rendon	Tarrant	M11	76028
Reno	Lamar	E1	75460
Reno	Parker	M10	76020
Retreat	Navarro	M19	75110
Retta	Johnson	M17	76028
	Tarrant	M11	
Reynard	Houston	E24	75844
Rhea	Parmer	P21	79035
Rhea Mills	Collin	M7	75069
Rhineland	Knox	P43	76371
Rhome	Wise	M5	76078
Rhonesboro	Upshur	E13	75755
Ricardo	Kleberg	B25	78363
Rice	Ellis	M18	75155
	Navarro	M9	
Rices Crossing	Williamson	C16	76574
Richards	Grimes	G2	77873
Richardson	Collin	M7	75080
	Dallas	M12	
Richland	Navarro	M19	76681
Richland	Rains	E10	75472
Richland Hills	Tarrant	M11	76118
Richland Springs	San Saba	C4	76871
Richmond	Fort Bend	G17	77469
Richwood (Richwood Village)	Brazoria	G18	77531
Rickels (RRS)	Wise	M5	
Riderville	Panila	E23	75633
Ridge	Mills	C5	76864
Ridge	Robertson	C19	77874
Ridgecrest	Jefferson	G13	77627
Ridgecrest	Orange	G7	77630
Ridgeway	Hopkins	E5	75482
Ridings	Fannin	M4	75476
Riesel	McLennan	C8	76682
Rincon	Starr	B27	78582
Ringgold	Montague	M1	76261
Rio Farms	Hidalgo	B28	78538
Rio Frio	Real	B10	78879
Rio Grande City	Starr	B27	78582
Rio Grande Wild and Scenic River	Brewster	B6	79834
	Terrell	B7	
Rio Hondo	Cameron	B30	78583
Riomedina	Medina	C34	78066
Rio Pecos	Crane	P85	79740
Rio Rico	Hidalgo	B28	78570
Rios	Duval	B20	78349
Rio Vista	Johnson	M17	76093
Rising Star	Eastland	P72	76471
Rita	Burleson	C27	77857
Ritchie (RRS)	McLennan	C8	
Rite-Care (RRS)	Shelby	E26	
Riverby	Fannin	M4	75488
River Hill	Panola	E23	75633
River Hills	Travis	C24	78759
River Oaks	Tarrant	M11	76114
Riverside	Walker	G3	77367
River Terrace	Harris	G11	77327
Riverton (RRS)	Reeves	P92	
Riviera	Kleberg	B25	78379
Riviera Beach	Kleberg	B25	78379
Roane	Navarro	M19	75110
Roanoke	Denton	M6	76262
Roans Prairie	Grimes	G2	77875
Roaring Springs	Motley	P32	79256
Robards (RRS)	Bexar	C35	

POPULATED PLACES AND OTHER LOCATIONS

PLACE	COUNTY	CHART LOCATION	ZIP CODE
Robbins	Leon	C12	75846
Robert Lee	Coke	P79	76945
Robert Mueller Municipal Airport	Travis	C24	78723
Robertson	Crosby	P40	79343
Robinson	McLennan	C8	76706
Robstown	Nueces	G32	78380
Roby	Fisher	P61	79543
Rochelle	McCulloch	P91	76872
Rochester	Haskell	P53	79544
Rock Creek	Briscoe	P24	79257
Rock Creek	McLennan	C8	76708
Rockdale	Milam	C18	76567
Rockett	Ellis	M18	75165
Rockhill	Collin	M7	75069
Rock Hill	Wood	E11	75783
Rockhouse	Austin	G9	78950
Rock Island	Colorado	G15	77470
Rock Island	Polk	E32	75939
Rockland	Tyler	E33	75970
Rockne	Bastrop	C25	78602
Rockport	Aransas	G31	78382
Rocksprings	Edwards	B9	78880
Rockwall	Rockwall	M13	75087
Rockwood	Coleman	P81	76873
Rocky Branch	Morris	E8	75568
Rocky Hill	Falls	C9	76661
Rocky Mound	Camp	E12	75686
Roddy	Van Zandt	E15	75147
Rodney	Navarro	M19	76639
Roganville	Jasper	E34	75971
Rogers	Bell	C17	76569
Rogers Hill	McLennan	C8	76691
Rogerslacy	Hidalgo	B28	78593
Rolla	Collingsworth	P20	79095
Rolling Hills	Hunt	M8	75453
Rolling Meadows	Gregg	E17	75601
Rolling Oaks	Van Zandt	E15	75169
Rollingwood	Travis	C24	78746
Roma-Los Saenz (Roma)	Starr	B27	78584
Roman Forest	Montgomery	G4	77357
Romayor	Liberty	G5	77368
Romero	Hartley	P6	79022
Romney	Eastland	P72	76471
Roosevelt	Kimble	P98	76874
Roosevelt	Lubbock	P39	79401
Ropesville (RR name Ropes)	Hockley	P38	79358
Rosalie	Red River	E2	75417
Rosanky	Bastrop	C25	78953
Roscoe	Nolan	P69	79545
Rosebud	Falls	C9	76570
Rose City	Orange	G7	77662
Rosedale	Falls	C9	76680
Rose Hill	Harris	G11	77375
Rose Hill Acres	Hardin	G6	77656
Rosenberg	Fort Bend	G17	77471
Rosenthal	McLennan	C8	76655
Rosevine	Sabine	E30	75930
Rosewood	Upshur	E13	75644
Rosharon	Brazoria	G18	77583
Rosita	Duval	B20	78384
Rosita	Starr	B27	78582
Ross (RRS)	Brazoria	G18	
Ross	McLennan	C8	76684
Ross City	Howard	P67	79720
Rosser	Kaufman	M14	75157
Rosslyn (RRS)	Harris	G11	
Rosston	Cooke	M2	76263
Rossville	Atascosa	C38	78065
Roswell	Bosque	C2	76634
Rotan	Fisher	P61	79546
Round Mountain	Blanco	C23	78663
Round Prairie	Navarro	M19	75144
Round Rock	Williamson	C16	78664
	Baylor	P44	
Round Top	Fayette	G8	78954
Roundup	Hockley	P38	79313
Rowden	Callahan	P71	79504
Rowena	Runnels	P80	76875
Rowlett	Dallas	M12	75088
	Rockwall	M13	
Roxton	Lamar	E1	75477
Roy (RRS)	Castro	P22	
Royalty	Ward	P84	79779
Royse City	Collin	M7	75089
	Rockwall	M13	
Royston	Fisher	P61	79543
Rucker	Comanche	P83	76444
Rudolph	Kenedy	B26	78338
Rugby	Red River	E2	75435
Ruidosa	Presidio	B5	79843
Rule	Haskell	P53	79547
Ruliff (RRS)	Newton	E35	
Rumley	Lampasas	C6	76539
Runaway Bay	Wise	M5	76234
Runge	Karnes	G20	78151
Runnels (RRS)	Matagorda	G24	
Rural Shade	Navarro	M19	75144
Rushing	Navarro	M19	76693
Rush Prairie	Navarro	M19	76641
Rusk	Cherokee	E21	75785
Russelltown (RRS)	Cameron	B30	
Russellville (RRS)	Motley	P32	
Rustler Springs (RRS)	Culberson	B3	
Rutersville	Fayette	G8	78945
Ryan (RRS)	Presidio	B5	
Rye	Brazos	C20	77832
Rye	Liberty	G5	77369
Sabanna	Eastland	P72	76437
Sabathany	Parker	M10	76086
Sabinal	Uvalde	B12	78881
Sachse	Collin	M7	75040
	Dallas	M12	
Sacul	Nacogdoches	E25	75788
Sadler	Grayson	M3	76264
Sagerton	Haskell	P53	79548
Saginaw	Tarrant	M11	76179
St. Clair City	Smith	E16	75789
St. Francis	Potter	P12	79107
St. Francis Village	Tarrant	M11	76036
St. Hedwig	Bexar	C35	78152
St. Jo	Montague	M1	76265
St. Lawrence	Glasscock	P77	79739
St. Louis	Smith	E16	75701
St. Paul	Collin	M7	75098
St. Paul	Falls	C9	76661
St. Paul	San Patricio	G30	78387
St. Paul	Waller	G10	77445
Salado	Bell	C17	76571
Salem	Smith	E16	75789
Salesville	Palo Pinto	M9	76067
Salineno	Starr	B27	78585
Salmon	Anderson	E20	75839
Salona	Montague	M1	76230
Salter (RRS)	Robertson	C19	
Salt Flat (Ables)	Hudspeth	B2	79847
Salt Gap	McCulloch	P91	76876
Saltillo	Hopkins	E5	75478
Salty	Milam	C18	76567
Sam Fordyce (RRS)	Hidalgo	B28	
Sam Houston College	Walker	G3	77340
Samnorwood	Collingsworth	P20	79077
Sam Rayburn	Jasper	E34	75951
San Angelo	Tom Green	P89	76901
San Antonio	Bexar	C35	78201
San Antonio Air Force Station	Bexar	C35	78208
San Antonio International Airport	Bexar	C35	78216

606

PLACE	COUNTY	CHART LOCATION	ZIP CODE
San Antonio Missions Nat'l Historical Park	Bexar	C35	
San Augustine	San Augustine	E29	75972
San Benito	Cameron	B30	78586
San Carlos	Hidalgo	B28	78539
Sanco	Coke	P79	76945
Sanctuary	Parker	M10	76020
Sand	Dawson	P58	79331
Sanderson	Terrell	B7	79848
Sand Flat	Rains	E10	75440
Sandflat	Smith	E16	75701
Sand Flat	Van Zandt	E15	75140
Sand Hill	Floyd	P31	79235
Sand Hill	Upshur	E13	75644
Sandia	Jim Wells	B21	78383
San Diego	Duval	B20	78384
	Jim Wells	B21	
Sand Lake (Sandlake)	Ellis	M18	75119
Sandoval	Williamson	C16	76574
Sandow (RRS)	Milam	C18	
Sand Ridge	Houston	E24	75835
Sand Springs	Howard	P67	79720
Sandune (RRS)	Liberty	G5	
Sandusky	Grayson	M3	76273
Sandy	Blanco	C23	78665
Sandy Corner	Wharton	G16	77437
Sandy Creek	Milam	C18	76556
Sandy Fork	Gonzales	C37	78632
Sandy Harbor	Llano	C14	78654
Sandy Hill	Washington	G1	77833
Sandy Point	Brazoria	G18	77583
San Elizario	El Paso	B1	79849
San Felipe	Austin	G9	77473
Sanford	Hutchinson	P8	79078
San Gabriel	Milam	C18	76577
Sanger	Denton	M6	76266
San Geromino	Bexar	C35	78023
San Isidro	Starr	B27	78588
San Jacinto	Walker	G3	77340
San Jose	Duval	B20	78332
San Juan	Hidalgo	B28	78589
San Juan	Nueces	G32	78401
San Juan Community	Hidalgo	B28	78539
San Leanna	Travis	C24	78767
San Leon	Galveston	G19	77539
San Marcos	Hays	C31	78666
San Patricio	Nueces	G32	78368
	San Patricio	G30	
San Pedro	Nueces	G32	78380
San Perlita	Willacy	B29	78590
San Saba	San Saba	C4	76877
Sansom Park Village	Tarrant	M11	76114
Santa Anna	Coleman	P81	76878
Santa Catarina	Starr	B27	78582
Santa Cruz	Starr	B27	78582
Santa Elena	Starr	B27	78591
Santa Fe	Galveston	G19	77550
Santa Maria	Cameron	B30	78592
Santa Monica	Willacy	B29	78580
Santa Rosa	Cameron	B30	78593
Santo	Palo Pinto	M9	76472
San Ygnacio	Zapata	B22	78067
Saragosa	Reeves	P92	79780
Saratoga	Hardin	G6	77585
Sarco	Goliad	G27	77963
Sardis	Ellis	M18	76065
Sargent (RRS)	Dallas	M12	
Sargent	Matagorda	G24	77414
Sarita	Kenedy	B26	78385
Sash	Fannin	M4	75446
Saspamco	Wilson	C39	78153
Satin	Falls	C9	76685
Satsuma	Harris	G11	77040

PLACE	COUNTY	CHART LOCATION	ZIP CODE
Sattler	Comal	C30	78623
Saturn	Gonzales	C37	78959
Sauney Stand	Washington	G1	77426
Savage	Crosby	P40	79357
Savoy	Fannin	M4	75479
Sayers (Sayersville)	Bastrop	C25	78602
Scallorn	Mills	C5	76853
Schattel	Frio	B15	78005
Schertz	Bexar	C35	78154
	Comal	C30	
	Guadalupe	C36	
Schindler (RRS)	Austin	G9	
Schoenau	Austin	G9	78950
School Land (Schoolland)	Gonzales	C37	78140
Schroeder	Goliad	G27	77963
Schulenburg	Fayette	G8	78956
Schumansville	Guadalupe	C36	78130
Schwab City	Polk	E32	77351
Schwertner	Williamson	C16	76573
Scobee (RRS)	Burnet	C15	
Scotland	Archer	P45	76379
	Clay	P46	
Scott	Van Zandt	E15	75169
Scottdale (RRS)	Dallas	M12	
Scottsville	Harrison	E18	75688
Scranton	Eastland	P72	76473
Scroggins	Franklin	E6	75480
Scurry	Kaufman	M14	75158
Sea Breeze (RRS)	Chambers	G12	
Seabrook	Harris	G11	77586
Seadrift	Calhoun	G29	77983
Seagoville	Dallas	M12	75159
	Kaufman	M14	
Seagraves	Gaines	P57	79359
Seale	Robertson	C19	76687
Sealy	Austin	G9	77474
Seaman (RRS)	Liberty	G5	
Seaton	Bell	C17	76501
Sea Willow	Caldwell	C32	78644
Sebastian	Willacy	B29	78594
Sebastopol	Trinity	E27	75862
Seco Mines (La Gloria)	Maverick	B13	78852
Security	Montgomery	G4	77327
Sedalia	Collin	M7	75095
Seeligson (RRS)	Jim Wells	B21	
Seger (RRS)	Robertson	C19	
Seglar	Bexar	C35	78002
Segno	Polk	E32	77370
Segovia	Kimble	P98	76849
Seguin	Guadalupe	C36	78155
Sejita	Duval	B20	78376
Selden	Erath	M15	76401
Selfs	Fannin	M4	75446
Selma	Bexar	C35	78209
	Comal	C30	
	Guadalupe	C36	
Selman City	Rusk	E22	75689
Seminole	Gaines	P57	79360
Senate (RRS)	Jack	P56	
Senior	Bexar	C35	78073
Serbin	Lee	C26	78942
Service (RRS)	Ellis	M18	
Seth (RRS)	Hardin	G6	
Seth Ward	Hale	P30	79072
Seven Oaks	Polk	E32	77350
Seven Pines	Upshur	E13	75644
Seven Points	Henderson	E19	75143
Seven Sisters	Duval	B20	78357
Sexton	Sabine	E30	75972
Sexton City	Rusk	E22	75684
Seymore	Hopkins	E5	75482
Seymour	Baylor	P44	76380
Stephen F. Austin College	Nacogdoches	E25	75961

POPULATED PLACES AND OTHER LOCATIONS

PLACE	COUNTY	CHART LOCATION	ZIP CODE
Shadow Glen	Harris	B11	77530
Shadowland	Red River	E2	75435
Shady Grove	Angelina	E28	75941
Shady Grove	Cherokee	E21	75785
Shady Grove	Navarro	M19	76679
Shady Grove	Smith	E16	75703
Shady Grove	Upshur	E13	75755
Shady Shores	Denton	M6	76201
Shafter	Presidio	B5	79850
Shallowater	Lubbock	P39	79363
Shamrock	Wheeler	P15	79079
Shamrock Shores	Brown	P82	76801
Shanklerville (Enterprise)	Newton	E35	75932
Shannon	Clay	P46	76365
Sharon	Smith	E16	75701
Sharp	Milam	C18	76518
Sharyland (RRS)	Hidalgo	B28	
Shaufler (RRS)	Nolan	P69	
Shavano Park	Bexar	C35	78213
Shaw Bend	San Saba	C4	76877
Shawnee Shores Estates	Hunt	M8	75474
Shawnee Prairie (Flournoy)	Angelina	E28	75901
Shawville (RRS)	Coke	P79	
Sheerin (RRS)	Moore	P7	
Sheffield	Pecos	P93	79781
Shelby	Austin	G9	78940
Shelbyville	Shelby	E26	75973
Sheldon	Harris	G11	77028
Shenandoah	Montgomery	G4	77301
Shep	Taylor	P70	79566
Shepherd	San Jacinto	E31	77371
Sheppard AFB Wichita Falls Municipal Airport	Wichita	P36	
Sheppard	Newton	E35	77612
Sheridan	Colorado	G15	77475
Sherlock (RRS)	Lipscomb	P5	
Sherman	Grayson	M3	75090
Sherry	Red River	E2	75426
Sherwood	Irion	P88	76941
Sherwood Shores	Burnet	C15	78654
Shields	Coleman	B81	76878
Shiloh	Bastrop	C25	78602
Shiloh	Liberty	G5	77575
Shiloh	Limestone	C10	76667
Shiloh	Williamson	C16	76578
Shiner	Lavaca	G14	77984
Shirley	Hopkins	E5	75482
Shiro	Grimes	G2	77876
Shive	Hamilton	C1	76531
Shoreacres	Harris	G11	77571
Short	Shelby	E26	75935
Sid (RRS)	Hays	C31	
Sidney	Comanche	P83	76474
Sid Richardson (RRS)	Ector	P75	
Sierra Blanca	Hudspeth	B2	79851
Silas	Shelby	E26	75975
Siloam	Bowie	E3	75559
Siloam	Comanche	P83	76455
Siloam	Williamson	C16	78621
Silsbee	Hardin	G6	77656
Silver	Coke	P79	76949
Silver City	Milam	C18	76520
Silver City	Navarro	M19	76679
Silver City	Red River	E2	75426
Silver Lake	Van Zandt	E15	75140
Silverton	Briscoe	P24	79257
Silver Valley	Coleman	P81	76834
Simmons	Live Oak	G25	78071
Simms	Bowie	E3	75574
Simonton	Fort Bend	G17	77476
Simpsonville	Matagorda	G24	77465
Simsboro	Freestone	C11	75860
Sinclair City	Smith	E16	75789

PLACE	COUNTY	CHART LOCATION	ZIP CODE
Singleton	Grimes	G2	77877
Sinton	San Patricio	G30	78387
Sipe Springs	Comanche	P83	76442
Sisterdale	Kendall	C29	78006
Sivells Bend	Cooke	M2	76240
Skeeterville	San Saba	C4	76860
Skellytown	Carson	P13	79080
Skidmore	Bee	G26	78389
Skull Creek (RRS)	Colorado	G15	
Slate Shoals	Lamar	E1	75460
Slaton	Lubbock	P39	79364
Slay	Navarro	M19	76641
Slide	Lubbock	P39	79401
Slidell	Wise	M5	76267
Slocum	Anderson	E20	75839
Slutter	Colorado	G15	78935
Smada (RRS)	Fort Bend	G17	
Small	Hidalgo	B28	75117
Smetana	Brazos	C20	77801
Smiley	Gonzales	C37	78159
Smith (RRS)	Bell	C17	
Smithers Lake (RRS)	Fort Bend	G17	
Smithfield (RRS)	Tarrant	M11	
Smith Grove	Houston	E24	75851
Smith Hill	Bowie	E3	75561
Smithland	Marion	E14	75690
Smith Oaks	Grayson	M3	75090
Smith Point	Chambers	G12	77514
Smiths Bend	Bosque	C2	76634
Smiths Bluff (RRS)	Jefferson	G13	
Smith Springs	Erath	M15	76401
Smithville	Bastrop	C25	78957
Smithwick	Burnet	C15	78654
Smitty (RRS)	Henderson	E19	
Smoot (RRS)	Travis	C24	
Smyer	Hockley	P38	79367
Smyrna	Cass	E9	75551
Smyth (RRS)	Uvalde	B12	
Snap	Panola	E23	75633
Sneed (RRS)	Travis	C24	
Sneedville	Cottle	P33	79248
Snook	Burleson	C27	77878
Snow	Leon	C12	77871
Snow Hill	Collin	M7	75031
Snow Hill	Polk	E32	75939
Snyder	Scurry	P60	79549
Socorro	El Paso	B1	79927
Soda	Polk	E32	77351
Soda Springs	Parker	M10	76066
Sodville	San Patricio	G30	78387
Solms	Comal	C30	78130
Somerset	Bexar	C35	78069
Somerville	Burleson	C27	77879
Soncy	Potter	P12	79106
Sonora	Sutton	P97	76950
Sorrels	Wharton	G16	77488
Sorters	Montgomery	G4	77365
Soules Chapel	Upshur	E13	75644
Soumethun (RRS)	Dallas	M12	
Sour Lake (Sourlake)	Hardin	G6	77659
South Bay City (RRS)	Matagorda	G24	
South Bend	Young	P55	76081
South Bosque	McLennan	C8	76710
South Brice	Hall	P25	79226
South Elm	Milam	C18	76518
Southern Methodist University	Dallas	M12	75275
South Gale	Grayson	M3	75020
South Hanlon	Stephens	P64	76024
South Houston (RR name Dumont)	Harris	G11	77587
Southlake	Denton	M6	76051
	Tarrant	M11	
Southland	Garza	P50	79368
Southland	Wharton	G16	77437

608

PLACE	COUNTY	CHART LOCATION	ZIP CODE
Southland Acres	Tarrant	M11	76010
Southmayd	Grayson	M3	76268
South Padre Island	Cameron	B30	78578
South Plains	Floyd	P31	79258
South Purmela	Coryell	C7	76566
South San Pedro	Nueces	G32	78380
Southside Place	Harris	G11	77005
South Sulphur	Hunt	M8	75496
South Texarkana	Bowie	E3	75501
South Texas Medical Center	Bexar	C35	78229
Southton	Bexar	C35	78221
Sowells Bluff	Fannin	M4	75476
Spade	Lamb	P29	79369
Spanish Camp	Wharton	G16	77488
Spanish Fort	Montague	M1	76255
Sparenberg	Dawson	P58	79331
Sparks	Bell	C17	76534
Spaulding (RRS)	Hidalgo	B28	
Speaks	Lavaca	G14	77985
Spear (RRS)	Brazos	C20	
Spearman	Hansford	P3	79081
Speegleville	McLennan	C8	76710
Spence (RRS)	Harris	G11	
Spicewood	Burnet	C15	78669
Spillers Store	Leon	C12	75850
Spindletop (RRS)	Jefferson	G13	
Splendora	Montgomery	G4	77372
Spofford	Kinney	B11	78882
Spraberry	Midland	P76	79704
Spring	Harris	G11	77379
Spring Branch	Comal	C30	78070
Spring Creek	Gillespie	C22	78624
Spring Creek	San Saba	C4	76871
Spring Creek	Throckmorton	P54	76370
Spring Creek Acres	Victoria	G22	77901
Springdale	Cass	E9	75572
Springfield	Anderson	E20	75853
Springfield	Jim Wells	B21	78332
Springfield	Limestone	C10	76667
Spring Hill	Bowie	E3	75559
Spring Hill	Gregg	E17	75601
Spring Hill	Guadalupe	C36	78155
Springhill	Navarro	M19	76639
Springlake	Lamb	P29	79082
Spring Seat	Leon	C12	75846
Springtown	Parker	M10	76082
Spring Valley	Harris	G11	77024
Spring Valley	McLennan	C8	76557
Sprinkle	Travis	C24	78751
Spur	Dickens	P41	79370
Spurger	Tyler	E33	77660
Stacks (RRS)	Bastrop	C25	
Stacy	McCulloch	P91	76879
Staff	Eastland	P72	76448
Stafford	Fort Bend	G17	77477
	Harris	G11	
Stagecoach	Montgomery	G4	77355
Stairtown	Caldwell	C32	78648
Stallings (RRS)	Colorado	G15	
Stalls (RRS)	Marion	E14	
Stamford	Haskell	P53	79553
	Jones	P62	
Stampede	Bell	C17	76557
Stamps	Upshur	E13	75644
Standard (RRS)	Grayson	M3	
Stanfield	Clay	P46	76365
Stanton	Martin	P66	79782
Staples	Guadalupe	C36	78670
Star	Mills	C5	76880
Star Harbor	Henderson	E19	75148
Starrco (RRS)	Starr	B27	
Starrville	Smith	E16	75792
Startzville	Comal	C30	78130

PLACE	COUNTY	CHART LOCATION	ZIP CODE
Steeltown (RRS)	Jefferson	G13	
Steep Hollow	Brazos	C20	77801
Stegal	Bailey	P28	79327
Stella (RRS)	Harris	G11	
Stellar	Fayette	G8	78949
Stephen Creek	San Jacinto	E31	77331
Stephenville	Erath	M15	76401
Sterley	Floyd	P31	79241
Sterling City	Sterling	P78	76951
Sterrett	Ellis	M18	75165
Stewards Mill	Freestone	C11	75859
Stewart	Rusk	E22	75652
Stieren	Gonzales	C37	78632
Stiles	Reagan	P87	76932
Stilson	Liberty	G5	77535
Stinnett	Hutchinson	P87	79083
Stith	Jones	P62	79536
Stockard	Henderson	E19	75751
Stockdale	Wilson	C39	78160
Stockholm	Hidalgo	B28	78569
Stockman	Shelby	E26	75975
Stolz (RRS)	Llano	C14	
Stoneburg	Montague	M1	76230
Stoneham	Grimes	G2	77868
Stonewall	Gillespie	C22	78761
Stony	Denton	M6	76259
Stormville	Wood	E11	75783
Stout	Wood	E11	75494
Stowell	Chambers	G12	77661
Stranger	Falls	C9	76653
Stratford	Sherman	P2	79084
Stratton	De Witt	G21	77954
Stratton Ridge	Brazoria	G18	77541
Strawn	Palo Pinto	M9	76475
Streeter	Mason	C13	76856
Streetman	Freestone	C11	75859
	Navarro	M19	
Strickland (Strickland Crossing)	Sabine	E30	75968
String Prairie	Bastrop	C25	78953
Structure	Williamson	C16	78621
Stryker Creek (RRS)	Cherokee	E21	
Stuart Place	Cameron	B30	78550
Study Butte	Briscoe	P24	79852
Sturdivant	Palo Pinto	M9	76067
Sturgeon	Cooke	M2	76273
Sturgis Mill	Sabine	E30	75948
Styx	Kaufman	M14	75143
Sublett	Tarrant	M11	76063
Sublime	Lavaca	G14	77986
Sudan	Lamb	P29	79371
Sudduth (RRS)	Burnet	C15	
Suffolk	Upshur	E13	75644
Sugar Land	Fort Bend	G17	77478
Sugarland Junction (RRS)	Fort Bend	G17	
Sugar Valley	Matagorda	G24	77480
Suggs (RRS)	Irion	P88	
Sullivan	Guadalupe	C36	78638
Sullivan City	Hidalgo	B28	78595
Sulphur Bluff	Hopkins	E5	75481
Sulphur Springs	Angelina	E28	75980
Sulphur Springs	Hopkins	E5	75482
Sulphur Springs	Rusk	E22	75760
Sul Ross State University	Brewster	B6	79830
Suman (RRS)	Robertson	C19	
Summerfield	Castro	P22	79085
Summerfield	Potter	P12	79101
Summerfield	Upshur	E13	75644
Summerville	Gonzales	C37	78629
Summit (RRS)	Motley	P32	
Sumner	Lamar	E1	75486
Sun (RRS)	Jefferson	G13	
Sundown	Hockley	P38	79372
Sunniland	Live Oak	G25	78071

POPULATED PLACES AND OTHER LOCATIONS

PLACE	COUNTY	CHART LOCATION	ZIP CODE
Sunnyside	Castro	P22	79027
Sunny Side	Waller	G10	77423
Sunnyvale	Dallas	M12	75149
Sunray	Moore	P7	79086
Sunrise	Falls	C9	76661
Sunrise Beach Village	Llano	C14	78643
Sunset	Montague	M1	76270
Sunset Heights	Ector	P75	79760
Sunset Valley	Travis	C24	78745
Suntide	Nueces	G32	78409
Sun Valley	Lamar	E1	75460
Sunview	Marion	E14	75683
Surfside Beach	Brazoria	G18	77541
Sutherland Springs	Wilson	C39	78161
Swamp City	Gregg	E17	75647
Swan	Smith	E16	75701
Swanson Hill	Anderson	E20	75801
Swearingen	Cottle	P33	79248
Sweeny	Brazoria	G18	77480
Sweeny Switch	Live Oak	G25	78368
Sweet Home	Lavaca	G14	77987
Sweetwater	Comanche	P83	76442
Sweetwater	Nolan	P69	79556
Swenson	Stonewall	P52	79502
Swift	Nacogdoches	E25	75961
Swiss Alp	Fayette	G8	78956
Sycamore	Newton	E35	75932
Sylvan	Lamar	E1	75460
Sylvania (RRS)	Tarrant	M11	
Sylvester	Fisher	P61	79560
Tabor	Brazos	C20	77801
Tacoma	Panola	E23	75633
Tadmor	Houston	E24	75847
Taft	San Patricio	G30	78390
Taft Southwest	San Patricio	G30	78390
Tahoka	Lynn	P49	79373
Taiton	Wharton	G16	77437
Talco	Titus	E7	75487
Talpa	Coleman	P81	76882
Talty	Kaufman	M14	75160
Tamega	Burnet	C15	78605
Tamina	Montgomery	G4	77301
Tampico (RRS)	Hall	P25	
Tanglewood	Lee	C26	78947
Tankersly	Tom Green	P89	76952
Tarkington Prairie	Liberty	G5	77327
Tarleton State University	Erath	M15	76402
Tarpley	Bandera	C33	78883
Tarver	Hill	C3	76692
Tarzan	Martin	P66	79783
Tascosa (RRS)	Oldham	P11	
Tatum	Panola	E23	75691
	Rusk	E22	
Tavener	Fort Bend	G17	77435
Taylor	Williamson	C16	76574
Taylor Lake Village	Harris	G11	77586
Taylorsville	Caldwell	C32	78662
Taylor Town	Lamar	E1	75460
Taylorville	Fannin	M4	75452
Teague	Freestone	C11	75860
Teaselville	Smith	E16	75757
Tecula	Cherokee	E21	75766
Tehuacana	Limestone	C10	76686
Telegraph	Kimble	P98	76883
Telephone	Fannin	M4	75488
Telferner (RR name Telfener)	Victoria	E22	77988
Telico	Ellis	M18	75119
Tell	Childress	P26	79259
Temco (RRS)	Jasper	E34	
Temple	Bell	C17	76501
Tenaha	Shelby	E26	75974
Tennessee Colony	Anderson	E20	75861
Tennyson	Coke	P79	76953

PLACE	COUNTY	CHART LOCATION	ZIP CODE
Terlingua	Brewster	B6	79852
Terrell	Kaufman	M14	75160
Terrell Hills	Bexar	C35	78209
Terrys Chapel	Falls	C9	76570
Terryville	De Witt	G21	77995
Tesco (RRS)	Nolan	P69	
Texarkana	Bowie	E3	75501
Texas Christian University	Tarrant	M11	72008
Texas City	Galveston	G19	77590
Texas City Junction (RRS)	Galveston	G19	
Texas Technological University	Lubbock	P39	79406
Texas Women's University	Denton	M6	76204
Texhoma	Sherman	P2	73949
Texline	Dallam	P1	79087
Texon	Reagan	P87	76954
Texroy	Hutchinson	P8	79080
Thalia	Foard	P34	79227
Thayer	Hidalgo	B28	78570
The Colony	Denton	M6	76056
Thedford	Smith	E16	75771
The Grove	Coryell	C7	76576
The Heights	Brazoria	G18	77511
The Knobbs	Lee	C26	78650
Thelma	Bexar	C35	78221
Thelma	Limestone	C10	76642
The Meadows	Fort Bend	G17	77477
Theon	Williamson	C16	76537
Thermo	Hopkins	E5	75482
The Woodlands	Montgomery	G4	77380
Thicket (Bracken Store)	Hardin	G6	77374
Thomas	Upshur	E13	75686
Thomaston	De Witt	G21	77989
Thompson	Harris	G11	77040
Thompsons	Fort Bend	G17	77481
Thompsonville	Gonzales	C37	78959
Thornberry	Clay	P46	76308
Thorndale	Milam	C18	76577
	Williamson	C16	
Thornton	Limestone	C10	76687
Thorntonville	Ward	P84	79756
Thorp Spring	Hood	M16	76048
Thrall	Williamson	C16	76578
Thrasher (RRS)	Victoria	G22	
Three Leagues	Martin	P66	79713
Three Points	Travis	C24	78664
Three Rivers	Live Oak	G25	78071
Thrifty	Brown	P82	76801
Throckmorton	Throckmorton	P54	76083
Thurber	Erath	M15	76463
Tidwell	Hunt	M8	75401
Tidwell Prairie	Robertson	C19	76629
Tigertown (Cothrans Store)	Lamar	E1	75446
Tiki Island	Galveston	G19	77551
Tigua Indian Reservation	El Paso	B1	79917
Tilden	McMullen	B18	78072
Tilmon	Caldwell	C32	78616
Timberlake	Harris	G11	77429
Timberlake Acres	Montgomery	G4	77365
Timothy	Navarro	M19	75105
Timpson	Shelby	E26	75975
Tinaja (RRS)	Presidio	B5	
Tin Top	Parker	M10	76086
Tioga	Grayson	M3	76271
Tira	Hopkins	E5	75482
Titley (RRS)	Brewster	B6	
Tivoli	Refugio	G28	77990
Tivydale	Gillespie	C22	78624
Tobin (RRS)	El Paso	B1	
Toco	Lamar	E1	75421
Todd City	Anderson	E20	75801
Todd Mission	Grimes	G2	77363
Togo	Bastrop	C25	78957
Tokio	Terry	P48	79376

PLACE	COUNTY	CHART LOCATION	ZIP CODE
Tolar	Hood	M16	76476
Tolbert	Wilbarger	P35	76384
Toledo	Newton	E35	75932
Tolosa	Kaufman	M14	75143
Tomball	Harris	G11	77375
Tom Bean	Grayson	M3	75489
Tool	Henderson	E19	75143
Topsey	Coryell	C7	76522
Tornillo	El Paso	B1	79853
Torpedo (RRS)	Comanche	P83	
Toto	Parker	M10	76076
Tours	McLennan	C8	76691
Tow	Llano	C14	78672
Town Bluff	Tyler	E33	75979
Townley (RRS)	Walker	G3	
Toyah	Reeves	P92	79785
Toyahvale	Reeves	P92	79786
Tracy	Milam	C18	76518
Traprock (RRS)	Uvalde	B12	
Travis	Falls	C9	76656
Travis Peak	Travis	C24	78654
Trawick	Nacogdoches	E25	75961
Trent	Taylor	P70	79561
Trenton	Fannin	M4	75490
Trevat	Trinity	E27	75845
Tri Cities	Henderson	E19	75751
Trickham	Coleman	P81	76878
Trinidad	Henderson	E19	75163
Trinity	Trinity	E27	75862
Trinity Park	Collin	M7	75098
Trophy Club	Denton	M6	
Tropical Acres	Victoria	G22	77901
Troup	Cherokee	E21	75789
	Smith	E16	
Trout Creek	Newton	E35	75933
Troy	Bell	C17	76579
Truby	Jones	P62	79525
Truce (Friendship Church)	Jack	P56	76254
Trumbull	Ellis	M18	75125
Truscott	Knox	P43	79260
Tucker	Anderson	B20	75801
Tuleta	Bee	G26	78162
Tulia	Swisher	P23	79088
Tulip	Fannin	M4	75447
Tulsita	Bee	G26	78119
Tundra	Van Zandt	E15	75103
Tunis	Burleson	C27	77836
Tupelo	Navarro	M19	75155
Turcotte (RRS)	Kenedy	B26	
Turkey	Hall	P25	79261
Turlington	Freestone	C11	75840
Turnersville	Coryell	C7	76580
Turnersville	Travis	C24	78610
Turnertown	Rusk	E22	75689
Turney	Cherokee	E21	75766
Turtle Bayou	Chambers	G12	77514
Tuscola	Taylor	P70	79562
Tuxedo	Jones	P62	79553
Twin Oak (RRS)	Falls	C9	
Twitchell	Ochiltree	P4	79070
Twitty	Wheeler	P15	79090
Tye	Taylor	P70	79563
Tyler	Smith	E16	75701
Tylers Bluff	Cooke	M2	76265
Tynan	Bee	G26	78391
Type	Bastrop	C25	78621
Type	Williamson	C16	78621
Uhland	Caldwell	C32	78640
	Hays	C31	
Umbarger	Randall	P17	79091
Uncertain	Harrison	E18	75661
Underwood (RRS)	Hale	P30	
Union	Lubbock	P39	79364
Union	Scurry	P60	79549
Union	Terry	P48	79316
Union Grove	Upshur	E13	75647
Union High	Navarro	M19	76639
Union Hill	Bosque	C2	76652
Union Hill	Upshur	E13	75644
Union Springs	Nacogdoches	E25	75961
Union Valley	Hunt	M8	75089
Union Valley	Wilson	C39	78140
Unity	Lamar	E1	75486
Universal City	Bexar	C35	78148
University of Texas	Travis	C24	78712
University of Dallas	Dallas	M12	75060
University Park	Dallas	M12	75205
Upper Meyersville	De Witt	G21	78164
Upshaw	Nacogdoches	E25	75943
Upton	Bastrop	C25	78957
Urbana	San Jacinto	E31	77371
Utley	Bastrop	C25	78602
Utopia	Uvalde	B12	78884
Uvalde	Uvalde	B12	78801
Vair (RRS)	Trinity	E27	
Valdasta	Collin	M7	75004
Valentine	Jeff Davis	B4	79854
Valera	Coleman	P81	76884
Valleycreek (Valley Creek)	Fannin	M4	75452
Valley Farm (RRS)	Reeves	P92	
Valley Junction (RRS)	Robertson	C19	
Valley Lodge	Fort Bend	G17	77476
Valley Mills	Bosque	C2	76689
	McLennan	C8	
Valley Spring	Llano	C14	76885
Valley View	Cooke	M2	76272
Valley View	De Witt	G21	77954
Valley View	Midland	P76	79704
Valley View	Mitchell	P68	79512
Valley View	Runnels	P80	76821
Valley View	Upshur	E13	75644
Valley View	Wichita	P36	76367
Valley Wells	Dimmit	B16	78830
Val Verde (RRS)	Hidalgo	B28	
Val Verde	Milam	C18	76518
Van	Van Zandt	E15	75790
Van Alstyne	Grayson	M3	75095
Vance	Real	B10	78828
Vancourt	Tom Green	P89	76955
Vandalia	Red River	E2	75426
Vandenburg	Medina	C34	78861
Vanderbilt	Jackson	G23	77991
Vanderpool	Bandera	C33	78885
Vandyke	Comanche	P83	76442
Vanetia	Leon	C12	77865
Van Horn	Culberson	B3	79855
Van Pelt (RRS)	Brazoria	G18	
Van Raub	Bexar	C35	78006
Van Vleck	Matagorda	G24	77482
Varisco	Brazos	C20	77801
Vasco	Delta	E4	75450
Vashti	Clay	P46	76228
Vattmanville (Vattman)	Kleberg	B25	78379
Vaughan	Hill	C3	76645
Vealmoor	Howard	P67	79720
Veals (RRS)	Morris	E8	
Veal Station	Parker	M10	76082
Vega	Oldham	P11	79092
Venable (RRS)	San Augustine	E29	
Ventura	Montgomery	G4	77355
Venus	Johnson	M17	76084
Vera	Knox	P43	76383
Verdi	Atascosa	C38	78064
Verhalen	Reeves	P92	79772
Verhelle	De Witt	G21	77954
Veribest	Tom Green	P89	76885

POPULATED PLACES AND OTHER LOCATIONS

PLACE	COUNTY	CHART LOCATION	ZIP CODE
Vernon	Wilbarger	P35	76384
Verona	Collin	M7	75004
Veterans Administration Center	Bell	C17	76501
Veterans Administration Hospital	McLennan	C8	
Viboras	Starr	B27	78392
Vick	Concho	P90	76955
Vickery (RRS)	Dallas	M12	
Victoria	Limestone	C10	76664
Victoria	Victoria	G22	77901
Victory City	Bowie	E3	75561
Victory Gardens	Orange	G7	77630
Vidauri	Refugio	G28	77992
Vidor	Orange	G7	77662
Vienna	Lavaca	G14	77964
View	Taylor	P70	79564
Vigo-Park	Swisher	P23	79088
Vilas	Bell	C17	76534
Villa Cavazos	Cameron	B30	78520
Village Mills (Long Station)	Hardin	G6	77663
Villa Nueva	Cameron	B30	78520
Villareales	Starr	B27	78582
Vincent	Howard	P67	79511
Vineyard	Jack	P56	76085
Vinson (RRS)	Travis	C24	
Vinton	El Paso	B1	88021
Viola	Nueces	G32	78409
Violet	Nueces	G32	78380
Virginia Point	Galveston	G19	77550
Vistula	Houston	E24	75851
Viterbo (RRS)	Jefferson	G13	
Voca	McCulloch	P91	76887
Volente	Travis	C24	78641
Von Ormy	Bexar	C35	78073
Voss	Coleman	P81	76888
Votaw	Hardin	G6	77376
Voth (RRS)	Jefferson	G13	
Waco	McLennan	C8	76708
Waco-Madison Cooper Airport	McLennan	C8	76708
Wadsworth	Matagorda	G24	77483
Waelder	Gonzales	C37	78959
Waka	Ochiltree	P4	79093
Wake	Crosby	P40	79243
Wakefield	Polk	E32	75939
Wake Village	Bowie	E3	75501
Walburg	Williamson	C16	78673
Waldeck	Fayette	G8	78946
Walden (RRS)	Jefferson	G13	
Waldrip	McCulloch	P91	76852
Walhalla	Fayette	G8	78954
Walkers Mill	Harrison	E18	75650
Wall	Tom Green	P89	76957
Wallace	Van Zandt	E15	75103
Wallace Chapel	Upshur	E13	75686
Waller	Harris	G11	77484
	Waller	G10	
Wallis	Austin	G9	77485
Wallisville	Chambers	G12	77597
Walnut Forest	Travis	C24	78753
Walnut Grove	Collin	M7	75069
Walnut Grove	Panola	E23	75633
Walnut Grove	Smith	E16	75789
Walnut Springs	Bosque	C2	76690
Walnut Springs	Ellis	M18	75125
Walston Springs	Anderson	E20	75801
Walters (RRS)	San Patricio	G30	
Walton	Cass	E9	71082
Walton	Van Zandt	E15	75751
Wamba	Bowie	E3	75501
Waples	Hood	M16	76048
Ward Spur (RRS)	Ellis	M18	
Warda	Fayette	G8	78960
Wardlaw (RRS)	McLennan	C8	
Ward Prairie	Freestone	C11	75840

PLACE	COUNTY	CHART LOCATION	ZIP CODE
Wards Creek	Bowie	E3	75574
Ware (RRS)	Dallam	P1	
Warfield (RRS)	Midland	P76	
Waring	Kendall	C29	78074
Warlock	Marion	E14	75630
Warren	Tyler	E33	77664
Warren City	Gregg	E17	75647
	Upshur	E13	
Warrenton	Fayette	G8	78961
Warsaw	Kaufman	M14	75142
Washburn	Armstrong	P18	79019
Washington	Washington	G1	77880
Waskom	Harrison	E18	75692
Wasson (RRS)	Hale	P30	
Wastella	Nolan	P69	79545
Watauga	Tarrant	M11	76148
Waterloo	Williamson	C16	76574
Waterman	Shelby	E26	75935
Waters Bluff	Smith	E16	75792
Water Valley	Tom Green	P89	76958
Waterwood	San Jacinto	E31	77359
Watson	Burnet	C15	76550
Watt	Limestone	C10	76664
Waukegan (RRS)	Montgomery	G4	
Waverly	San Jacinto	E31	77358
Waxahachie	Ellis	M18	75165
Wayside	Armstrong	P18	79094
Wayside	Lynn	P49	79381
Wealthy	Leon	C12	77871
Weatherford	Parker	M10	76086
Weaver	Hopkins	E5	75478
Webb	Tarrant	M11	76010
Webberville	Travis	C24	78653
Webbville	Coleman	P81	76828
Webster	Harris	G11	77598
Weches	Houston	E24	75844
Weedhaven	Jackson	G23	77979
Weeping Mary	Cherokee	E21	75925
Weesatche	Goliad	G27	77993
Weimar	Colorado	G15	78962
Weinert	Guadalupe	C36	78638
Weinert	Haskell	P53	76388
Weir	Williamson	C16	78674
Weirville (Weir)	Hopkins	E5	75482
Welch	Dawson	P58	79377
Welcome	Austin	G9	78944
Welcome Valley	Erath	M15	76401
Weldon	Houston	E24	75863
Welfare	Kendall	C29	78006
Wellborn	Brazos	C20	77881
Wellington	Collingsworth	P20	79095
Wellman	Terry	P48	79378
Wells	Cherokee	E21	75976
Wells	Lynn	P49	79351
Wells Creek (RRS)	Anderson	E20	
Welsh (RRS)	Titus	E7	
Wentworth	Van Zandt	E15	75103
Wesco Store Spur (RRS)	Wise	M5	
Weser	Goliad	G27	77963
Weslaco	Hidalgo	B28	78596
Wesley	Washington	G1	77833
Wesley Grove	Walker	G3	77876
West	McLennan	C8	76691
West Bluff	Orange	G7	77630
Westbrook	Mitchell	P68	79565
West Carlisle (Carlisle)	Lubbock	P39	79407
West Cliff	Bell	C17	76513
West Columbia	Brazoria	G18	77486
Westfield	Harris	G11	77090
Westgate	Harris	G11	77429
West Galveston	Galveston	G19	77550
Westhoff	De Witt	G21	77994
West Junction (RRS)	Harris	G11	

PLACE	COUNTY	CHART LOCATION	ZIP CODE	PLACE	COUNTY	CHART LOCATION	ZIP CODE
Westlake	Denton	M6	76248	Wickes Spur (RRS)	Brazoria	G18	
	Tarrant	M11		Wickett	Ward	P84	79788
West Lake Hills	Travis	C24	78746	Wied	Lavaca	G14	77964
Westlawn	Orange	G7	77630	Wieland	Hunt	M8	75401
West Mineola	Wood	E11	75773	Wiergate	Newton	E35	75977
Westminster	Collin	M7	75096	Wiggins	Cass	E9	75555
West Mountain	Upshur	E13	75647	Wiggins	McLennan	C8	76691
West Odessa	Ector	P75	79760	Wigginsville	Montgomery	G4	77301
Weston	Collin	M7	75097	Wilco Spur (RRS)	Hartley	P6	
West Orange	Orange	G7	77630	Wilcox	Burleson	C27	77879
Westover	Baylor	P44	76380	Wilderville	Falls	C4	76570
Westover	Ector	P75	79760	Wild Horse	Culberson	B3	79855
Westover Hills	Tarrant	M11	76106	Wildorado	Oldham	P11	79098
West Park (RRS)	Harris	G11		Wild Peach Village	Brazoria	G18	77422
Westphalia	Falls	C9	76656	Wildwood	Hardin	G6	77663
West Point	Fayette	G8	78963	Wilkins	Upshur	E13	75755
West Point	Lynn	P49	79373	Wilkinson	Titus	E7	75455
West Port Arthur (RRS)	Jefferson	G13		Willamar	Willacy	B29	78580
West Sinton	San Patricio	G30	78370	William Penn	Washington	G1	77833
West Tawakoni	Hunt	M8	75474	Willam P. Hobby Airport	Harris	G11	77061
West Temple	Polk	E32	77351	Willams	Brown	P82	76857
West University Place	Harris	G11	77005	Williams (RRS)	Jefferson	G13	
Westville	Trinity	E27	75862	Williamsburg	Lavaca	G14	77964
Westway	Deaf Smith	P16	79045	Willam Spear Addition	Tyler	E33	75701
Westway	El Paso	B1	79835	Willis	Montgomery	G4	77378
Westworth (Westworth Village)	Tarrant	M11	76114	Willow City	Gillespie	C22	78675
Whaley	Bowie	E3	75570	Willow Grove	Bell	C17	76557
Wharton	Wharton	G16	77488	Willow Grove	McLennan	C8	76710
Wheatland (RRS)	Hardeman	P27		Willow Grove	Shelby	E26	75954
Wheatland	Tarrant	M11	76116	Willow Oak	Upshur	E13	75644
Wheeler	Wheeler	P15	79096	Willow Park	Parker	M10	76086
Wheelock	Robertson	C19	77882	Willow Point	Wise	M5	76026
Whispering Oaks	Rains	E10	75453	Willow Springs	Fayette	G8	78940
Whit (RRS)	Harris	G11		Willow Springs	Rains	E10	75440
White (White Spur) (RRS)	El Paso	B1		Willow Springs	San Jacinto	E31	77331
White (RRS)	Uvalde	B12		Wills Point	Van Zandt	E15	75169
White City	Wise	M5	76231	Wilmer	Dallas	M12	75172
White City	Wilbarger	P35	76384	Wilmeth	Runnels	P80	79567
White Deer	Carson	P13	79097	Wilsey (RRS)	Parmer	P21	
Whiteface	Cochran	P37	79379	Wilson	Lynn	P49	79381
Whiteflat	Motley	P32	79234	Wimberly	Hays	C31	78676
White Hall	Bell	C17	76557	Winchell	Brown	P82	76827
White Hall	Coryell	C7	76528	Winchester	Fayette	G8	78964
White Hall (Wallace Prairie)	Grimes	G2	77868	Windcrest	Bexar	C35	78239
Whitehouse	Smith	E16	75791	Windom	Fannin	M4	75492
Whiteland	McCulloch	P91	76858	Windthorst	Archer	P45	76389
Whiteley (RRS)	Briscoe	P24			Clay	P46	
White Mound	Grayson	M3	75090	Winedale	Fayette	G8	77835
White Oak	Gregg	E17	75693	Winfield	Titus	E7	75493
White Oaks	Montgomery	G4	77365	Winfree	Chambers	G12	77535
White Rock	Grayson	M3	75020	Winfree	Orange	G7	77630
White Rock	Hunt	M8	75423	Wingate	Runnels	P80	79566
White Rock	Red River	E2	75426	Wink	Winkler	P74	79789
White Rock	San Augustine	E29	75972	Winkler	Freestone	C11	75859
Whitesboro	Grayson	M3	76273		Navarro	M19	
White Settlement	Tarrant	M11	76108	Winnie	Chambers	G12	77665
Whitesmine (RRS)	Uvalde	B12		Winnsboro	Franklin	E6	75494
Whites Ranch	Chambers	G12	77661		Wood	E11	
Whitestar	Motley	P32	79234	Winona	Smith	E16	75792
Whitestone	Williamson	C16	78641	Winter Garden (RRS)	Dimmit	B16	
Whiteway (Whitesboro)	Hamilton	C1	76536	Winter Haven	Dimmit	B16	78839
Whitewright	Fannin	M4	75491	Winters	Runnels	P80	79567
	Grayson	M3		Witco (RRS)	Reagan	P87	
Whitharral	Hockley	P38	79380	Witting	Lavaca	G14	77975
Whitman	Washington	G1	77833	Wizard Wells	Jack	P56	76056
Whitney	Hill	C3	76692	Woden	Nacogdoches	E25	75978
Whitsett	Live Oak	G25	78075	Wolfe City	Hunt	M8	75496
Whitson	Coryell	C7	76557	Wolf Flat	Hall	P25	79261
Whitt	Parker	M10	76090	Wolfforth	Lubbock	P39	79382
Whitton	Van Zandt	E15	75103	Womack	Bosque	C2	76634
Whon	Coleman	P81	76889	Woodbine	Cooke	M2	76240
Wichita Falls	Wichita	P36	76301	Woodbranch	Montgomery	G4	77357
Wichita Valley Farms	Wichita	P36	76701	Woodbury	Hill	C3	76645

POPULATED PLACES AND OTHER LOCATIONS

PLACE	COUNTY	CHART LOCATION	ZIP CODE
Woodlake	Trinity	E27	75865
Woodland	Red River	E2	75436
Woodlawn	Angelina	E28	75901
Woodlawn	Harrison	E18	75694
Woodley	Harrison	E18	75670
Woodloch	Montgomery	G4	77301
Woodrow	Lubbock	P39	79401
Woods	Panola	E23	75974
Woodsboro	Refugio	G28	78393
Woodson	Throckmorton	P54	76091
Wood Springs	Smith	E16	75771
Woodville	Tyler	E33	75979
Woodway	McLennan	C8	76710
Woody Acres	Montgomery	G4	77365
Woosley	Rains	E10	75472
Worsham (RRS)	Reeves	P92	
Wortham	Freestone	C11	76693
Worthing	Lavaca	G14	77964
Wright (RRS)	Hale	P30	
Wright City	Rusk	E22	75684
	Smith	E16	
Wrightsboro	Gonzales	C37	78677
Wylie	Collin	M7	75098
Yale	Franklin	E6	75457
Yancey (Kellogg)	Hunt	M8	75401
Yancey	Medina	C34	78886
Yantis	Wood	E11	75497
Yarboro	Grimes	G2	77868
Yard	Anderson	E20	75861
Yarrelton	Milam	C18	76518

PLACE	COUNTY	CHART LOCATION	ZIP CODE
Yates (Yates Crossing)	Kimble	P98	76854
Yellow Mound	Eastland	P72	76448
Yellowpine	Sabine	E30	75948
Yescas (Las Yescas)	Cameron	B30	78586
Yetes	Hill	C3	76692
Yoakum	De Witt	G21	77995
	Lavaca	G14	
Yorktown	De Witt	G21	78164
Youens (RRS)	Montgomery	G4	
Young	Freestone	C11	75840
Youngsport	Bell	C17	76544
Yowell	Delta	E4	75428
	Hunt	M8	
Ysleta (RRS)	El Paso	B1	
Yturria (RRS)	Willacy	B29	
Yucote Acres	Collin	M7	75069
Zabcikville (Marekville)	Bell	C17	76501
Zapata	Zapata	B22	78076
Zavalla	Angelina	E28	75980
Zephyr	Brown	P82	76890
Zionsville (Zion)	Washington	G1	77833
Zipperlenville	Falls	C9	76570
Zippville	Guadalupe	C36	78155
Zita (RRS)	Randall	P17	
Zorn	Guadalupe	C36	78666
Zuehl	Guadalupe	C36	78124
Zummo (RRS)	Jefferson	G13	
Zunkerville	Karnes	G20	78119
Zybach	Hemphill	P10	79011
	Wheeler	P15	